WELCOME to ODYSSEY

J&J's Antiques

ELECTRIC PALACE

To

_____

From

_____

Date

_____

Dedication

_____

_____

Adventures in ODYSSEY BIBLE

NIrV

"Your word is like a lamp that shows me
the way. It is like a light that guides me."
—Psalm 119:105

FOCUS ON THE FAMILY.

Adventures in Odyssey Bible
© 2017 Focus on the Family. All rights reserved.

Illustrations © 2017 Focus on the Family

ISBN: 978-1-58997-928-4

Focus on the Family, Adventures in Odyssey, and The Imagination Station, and any accompanying logos and designs, are federally registered trademarks of Focus on the Family, 8605 Explorer Drive, Colorado Springs, CO 80920.

Cover design by Michael Harrigan. Cover illustration by Sergio Cariello.

Interior design by Hudson Bible. Interior illustrations by Gary Locke.

Bible maps design and illustration by Michael Harrigan.

Imagination Station Adventures illustration by Sergio Cariello, design and lettering by Josh Lewis.

Contributing editors and writers: Dave Arnold, Kathy Buchanan, Stan Campbell, Bob DeMoss, Liz Duckworth, Marianne Hering, Nathan Hoobler, Angie Ralston, Bob Smithouser, Larry Weeden, Marshal Younger.

Library of Congress Cataloging-in-Publication Data for this title can be found at www.loc.gov.

Printed in the U.S.A.

1 2 3 4 5 6 7 / 23 22 21 20 19 18 17

You will be pleased to know that a portion of the purchase price of your new Holy Bible has been provided to Biblica, Inc.® to help spread the gospel of Jesus Christ around the world!

Contents

All of us at Focus on the Family are thrilled that you've decided to make studying the Bible a priority in your life. There really isn't a better way to grow in your faith than to spend time reading this "love letter" from God to us. To help you with your journey into the heart of the Lord, we're pleased to present the *Adventures in Odyssey Bible*.

In addition to the complete New International Reader's Version of the Bible text, you'll discover a wealth of special features hosted by familiar characters from the *Adventures in Odyssey* audio program. Join John Avery Whittaker—better known as Whit—along with his son Jason, Connie Kendall, Eugene Meltsner, and Wooton Bassett as they explore these sacred pages for fresh insights into the Good News of Jesus with you.

Oh, and don't miss the eight illustrated Bible stories where kids from Odyssey find themselves right in the middle of the action . . . with a little help from Whit's invention, of course!

Our prayer is that you'll develop the lifelong habit of reading and turning to the Bible each day for God's wisdom and direction.

If you're ready, let the adventure begin!

Jim Daly
President and CEO
Focus on the Family

Welcome to Odyssey!

Whether you're visiting Odyssey for the first time or you're an old friend, welcome to town! You've arrived on a bright, sunny day. Your first stop is an unusual Victorian mansion with a sign out front that says *Whit's End*. As you walk through the front door, you see that it's an old-fashioned ice cream parlor. But it's so much more than that.

A man behind the counter introduces himself as John Avery Whittaker, but he prefers to simply be called "Whit." He offers to show you around his "discovery emporium." There's a working library, a recording studio for Kids' Radio, and even an auditorium called the Little Theatre.

Upstairs, you discover The Bible Room. It's full of unusual and amazing contraptions that you soon realize were invented and built by Whit himself. In the middle of it all is an incredible machine. It looks like a cross between a telephone booth and helicopter cockpit. A sign above identifies it as the Imagination Station.

"Are you ready for our adventure?" Whit asks. "My friends and I are headed on the greatest journey of all time—through the Bible from Genesis to Revelation. Along the way, you'll see everything from the creation of the universe to the world's destruction at the end of time. You'll see exciting battles, unbelievable miracles, talking donkeys, fierce giants—and even a dragon!

Whit smiles and adds, "But there's so much more. You'll meet brave men and women, read beautiful poetry, visit incredible places, and spend time with the one and only God. And best of all, these stories are all true and *you're* a major character. God has given you the Bible so that you can know who He is and have a relationship with Him!"

With a twinkle in his eye, Whit extends his hand and says, "Want to come along? You never know what'll happen when you have an adventure in Odyssey!"

Features of the Adventures in Odyssey Bible

For your journey through the Bible, Whit invited some of the folks from Odyssey to serve as tour guides along the way. Here's a quick look at what you can expect during this exciting journey into the greatest story ever told.

WHAT ABOUT YOU?

Hey! I'm Matthew Parker. Oops! Sorry about the metal shavings on my fingers. I'm taking this pinball machine apart to see how it works. That's why "What About You?" is my favorite feature of this Bible—we're taking things apart! Together we'll discover new things about the Bible and then see how it applies to kids like me—and you.

CANDID CONVERSATIONS

Sorry, I'm late. Is it time for my feature now? Okay! Hi, I'm Connie. Connie Kendall, I mean, and I'm involved with almost everything that goes on at Whit's End. I have a show on Kids' Radio called "Candid Conversations with Connie" where I talk about whatever's on my mind. Sometimes it's what's going on around Odyssey, and sometimes it's what I'm learning in Scripture. You'll read some clips from my "conversations" in this feature. I hope they show you new ways of looking at the Bible!

WHIT'S WISDOM

Have you ever experienced an event in your life, and wondered why God allowed it? If you've asked God that question, it means you know that God is involved in our everyday lives. In these features, I'll be talking about God's wonderful—and sometimes confusing—work in us.

BIBLE BOOK INTROS

Greetings and salutations! I am Eugene Meltsner, and, might I add in all modesty, I am a recognized genius in nearly all areas of study. I am honored and humbled to be your guide on this epic expedition through the pages of Scripture. To put it succinctly, I'll be providing an introduction with commentary and insight at the beginning of each of the sixty-six books in the Bible. You may notice that the editors of the Bible you currently hold declined to keep my suggested title for this feature—which was Prefaces with Your Most Esteemed Host Eugene Meltsner. Space constraints, they said. Ah, well. You shall nonetheless be enthralled with these fascinating historical tidbits on each book of the Bible!

What's it Mean, Eugene?

In lieu of my previous section's title being edited for time, they offered a quid pro quo by allowing me another feature. I must admit that my wife, Katrina, has had occasion to call me verbose (and so would nearly everyone in Odyssey, if they knew what the word meant). So I do apologize for my plethora of verbiage. However, I do hope that the engaging content of this second feature will prove helpful to you. Each book of the Bible will *also* include a detailed explanation of a particular theological term. Huzzah!

WOOTON'S FUN FACTS

I'm Wooton Bassett, and I'm on my way to deliver the mail, which makes sense since I'm a mailman here in Odyssey. I'm also going to drop off some extra raspberry soda for my dear wife, Penny, because she's working late at the Art Gallery. Anyway, I'm so excited to join you on your trip through the Bible. I'm going to tell you 300 fun trivia facts and random ramblings about anything and everything I can think of—from history to animals to unusual words and their meanings. This is going to be great!

REMEMBER THIS

I'm Penny Bassett. I used to be Penny *Wise,* but then Wooton and I got married so I'm not Wise any more. (I'm not sure I said that correctly.) Anyway, for me, the best way to make Scripture part of your life is to memorize it. These fifty-two verses are some of our favorites. Hey, why not memorize a different verse every week of the year? Over to you, Eva.

Thanks, Penny! I'm Eva Parker, and when I'm not corralling my three kids (Olivia, Matthew, and Camilla), I'm working at a clinic in Odyssey. My job is to keep people's *bodies* healthy. But one of the best ways to keep your *spirit* healthy is to memorize Scripture. As David says in Psalm 119:11, "I have hidden your word in my heart so that I won't sin against you."

Jason's Jargon

Jason Whittaker here. If the last name didn't give it away, I'm Whit's son. For a long time, my life before Odyssey was a mystery to everyone. But then the news leaked out and everyone found my secrets. Yes, it's true: I was a special agent—or spy, if you like—for a government agency. So I know a thing or two about missions. In this feature, the two of us will go on assignment together to find 100 important words in Scripture. Ready? Then let's go!

Imagination Station Adventures

Hi, I'm Beth. My cousin Patrick and I love going on trips in Mr. Whittaker's greatest invention, the Imagination Station. It's sort of like a time machine, and it's full of all sorts of knobs and dials. Right in the middle is the big red button. When you push it, you're sent off on an adventure in the Bible itself! Today, Mr. Whittaker said we should explore some stories in the Bible that many people don't know. Patrick and I will go on some adventures, and then some of the other kids in Odyssey wanted a chance in the machine, too. There's an extra seat. Why don't you join us?

BIBLE ADVENTURES

Hundreds and hundreds of *Adventures in Odyssey* audio drama episodes have been created since the radio show launched in 1987. Many of these adventures bring the Bible stories you're about to read to life! When there's an audio drama on a specific Bible story, you'll see the episode name. The "A" after it shows the album number that contains that episode. The episodes marked "Club" are exclusive to the Adventures in Odyssey Club. Find out how to listen to any episode at WhitsEnd.org.

All *Adventures in Odyssey* audio episodes are based on lessons found in Scripture. Now you can find episodes based on what you're reading in the Bible. While *Bible Adventures* features episodes dramatizing a Bible story (such as David and Goliath or Daniel in the Den of Lions), *Adventures in Odyssey* lists episodes that illustrate a biblical theme (such as honesty, integrity, or faith). Visit WhitsEnd.org to find these episodes.

ADVENTURES IN ODYSSEY

Jesus' Stories and Miracles!

Hey, there. My name is Tori, and my favorite part of the Bible is learning the stories about Jesus. Whether it's His birth, His teaching, His miracles, or His death and resurrection, I love reading about Him over and over again! Sometimes I like to read about stories *from* Jesus also. We call those parables. To help you find some of those stories, I put together a list of Jesus' parables and His miracles. You'll find the list in the back of the Bible on page 1545. You can check them off as you read them. Cool, huh?

A Word about the New International Reader's Version

Have You Ever Heard of the New International Version?

We call it the NIV. Many people read the NIV. In fact, more people read the NIV than any other English Bible. They like it because it's easy to read and understand.

And now we are happy to give you another Bible that's easy to read and understand. It's the New International Reader's Version. We call it the NIrV.

Who Will Enjoy Reading the New International Reader's Version?

People who are just starting to read will understand and enjoy the NIrV. Children will be able to read it and understand it. So will older people who are learning how to read. People who are reading the Bible for the first time will be able to enjoy reading the NIrV. So will people who have a hard time understanding what they read. And so will people who use English as their second language. We hope this Bible will be just right for you.

How Is the NIrV Different From the NIV?

The NIrV is based on the NIV. The NIV Committee on Bible Translation (CBT) didn't produce the NIrV. But a few of us who worked on the NIrV are members of CBT. We worked hard to make the NIrV possible. We used the words of the NIV when we could. When the words of the NIV were too long, we used shorter words. We tried to use words that are easy to understand. We also made the sentences of the NIV much shorter.

Why did we do all these things? Because we wanted to make the NIrV very easy to read and understand.

What Other Helps Does the NIrV Have?

We decided to give you a lot of other help too. For example, sometimes a verse is quoted from another place in the Bible. When it is, we tell you the Bible book, chapter and verse it comes from. We put that information right after the verse that quotes from another place.

We separated each chapter into shorter sections. We gave a title to almost every chapter. Sometimes we even gave a title to a section. We did these things to help you understand what the chapter or section is all about.

Another example of a helpful change has to do with the word "Selah" in the Psalms. What this Hebrew word means is still not clear. So, for now, this word is not helpful for readers. The NIV has moved the word to the bottom of the page. We have followed the NIV and removed this Hebrew word from the NIrV.

Perhaps one day we will learn what this word means. But until then, the Psalms are easier to read and understand without it.

Sometimes the writers of the Bible used more than one name for the same person or place. For example, in the New Testament the Sea of Galilee is also called the Sea of Gennesaret. Sometimes it is also called the Sea of Tiberias. But in the NIrV we decided to call it the Sea of Galilee everywhere it appears. We called it that because that is its most familiar name.

We also wanted to help you learn the names of people and places in the Bible. So sometimes we provided names even in verses where those names don't actually appear. For example, sometimes the Bible says "the River" where it means "the Euphrates River." In those places, we used the full name "the Euphrates River." Sometimes the word "Pharaoh" in the Bible means "Pharaoh Hophra." In those places, we used his full name "Pharaoh Hophra." We did all these things in order to make the NIrV as clear as possible.

Does the NIrV Say What the First Writers of the Bible Said?

We wanted the NIrV to say just what the first writers of the Bible said. So we kept checking the Greek New Testament as we did our work. That's because the New Testament's first writers used Greek. We also kept checking the Hebrew Old Testament as we did our work. That's because the Old Testament's first writers used Hebrew.

We used the best copies of the Greek New Testament. We also used the best copies of the Hebrew Old Testament. Older English Bibles couldn't use those copies because they had not yet been found. The oldest copies are best because they are closer in time to the ones the first Bible writers wrote. That's why we kept checking the older copies instead of the newer ones.

Some newer copies of the Greek New Testament added several verses that the older ones don't have. Sometimes it's several verses in a row. This occurs at Mark 16:9–20 and John 7:53—8:11. We have included these verses in the NIrV. Sometimes the newer copies added only a single verse. An example is Mark 9:44. That verse is not in the oldest Greek New Testaments. So we put the verse number 43-44 right before Mark 9:43. You can look on the list below for Mark 9:44 and locate the verse that was added.

Verses That Were Not Found in Oldest Greek New Testaments

Matthew 17:21   But that kind does not go out except by prayer and fasting.

Matthew 18:11   The Son of Man came to save what was lost.

Matthew 23:14   How terrible for you, teachers of the law and Pharisees! You pretenders! You take over the houses of widows. You say long prayers to show off. So God will punish you much more.

Mark 7:16   Everyone who has ears to hear should listen.

Mark 9:44	In hell, / " 'the worms don't die, / and the fire doesn't go out.'
Mark 9:46	In hell, / " 'the worms don't die, / and the fire doesn't go out.'
Mark 11:26	But if you do not forgive, your Father who is in heaven will not forgive your sins either.
Mark 15:28	Scripture came true. It says, "And he was counted among those who disobey the law."
Luke 17:36	Two men will be in the field. One will be taken and the other left.
Luke 23:17	It was Pilate's duty to let one prisoner go free for them at the Feast.
John 5:4	From time to time an angel of the Lord would come down. The angel would stir up the waters. The first disabled person to go into the pool after it was stirred would be healed.
Acts 8:37	Philip said, "If you believe with all your heart, you can." The official answered, "I believe that Jesus Christ is the Son of God."
Acts 15:34	But Silas decided to remain there.
Acts 24:7	But Lysias, the commander, came. By using a lot of force, he took Paul from our hands.
Acts 28:29	After he said that, the Jews left. They were arguing strongly among themselves.
Romans 16:24	May the grace of our Lord Jesus Christ be with all of you. Amen.

What Is Our Prayer for You?

The Lord has blessed the New International Version in a wonderful way. He has used it to help millions of Bible readers. Many people have put their faith in Jesus after reading it. Many others have become stronger believers because they have read it.

We hope and pray that the New International Reader's Version will help you in the same way. If that happens, we will give God all the glory.

A Word About This Edition

This edition of the New International Reader's Version has been revised to include the changes of the New International Version. Over the years, many helpful changes have been made to the New International Version. Those changes were made because our understanding of the original writings is better. Those changes also include changes that have taken place in the English language. We wanted the New International Reader's Version to include those helpful changes as well. We wanted the New International Reader's Version to be as clear and correct as possible.

We want to thank the people who helped us prepare this new edition. They are Jeannine Brown from Bethel Seminary St. Paul, Yvonne Van Ee from Calvin College, Michael Williams from Calvin Theological Seminary, and Ron Youngblood from Bethel Seminary San Diego. We also want to thank the people at Biblica who encouraged and supported this work.

Following Jesus

Hi. Whit here again. There's one more thing to say before you set off on your adventure. The day you choose to follow Jesus is the day that you begin an exciting new life as a son or daughter adopted into God's family. It's the most important step you will ever make. God loves you. He chose you. And no matter what your life was like before, once you decide to follow Him, He will make you a new creation!

If you've already made a decision to follow Jesus, congratulations—you're ready to head off on your journey through the Bible. If you haven't joined God's family yet, why not do it today? "Say with your mouth, 'Jesus is Lord.' Believe in your heart that God raised him from the dead. Then you will be saved" (Romans 10:9). To follow up, talk to your parent or a pastor or trusted Christian friend, and ask that person how you can come to know Jesus in a life-changing way. If you want to learn more about God's plan for you as a Christian before you talk to someone, the book of John is a good place to start.

And now, hop in the Imagination Station and push the red button.

It's time for our journey together!

The Old Testament

Greetings and salutations! Eugene here. I'm so exhilarated to be your companion for this journey through the Scriptures. What a distinct honor it is. I do hope that you will enjoy reading these introductions as much as I enjoy expounding them!

We start with the Old Testament. Some scholars have argued that it might be more helpful to refer to this hefty section of Scripture as the "First Testament" and the New Testament as the "Second Testament." This would eliminate any confusion over the association of words of the *Old* Testament being stodgy, outdated, or irrelevant to our daily lives. That is simply not the case!

The Old Testament begins with books of history (Genesis—Esther), continues with books of poetry (Job—Song of Songs), and concludes with books of prophecy (Isaiah—Malachi). The Old Testament sets the proverbial stage for God to send a Savior. God makes a number of amazing promises throughout these pages, and each of those promises sees its fulfillment in the New Testament!

And if that weren't enough reason to read these sacred pages, they also contain some of the most exciting stories found anywhere. Among literally hundreds of others, you'll find: a gifted young musician who killed an evil giant, a man who spent days in the belly of a fish, a prophet whose message from God was so frightening that he was bound in chains, a female prophet who went into battle, and a boy who became king at age seven and ruled for forty years!

These stories only scratch the proverbial surface. Without further delay, let's start our journey!

Genesis

Greetings and salutations! I'm so exhilarated to be your companion for this journey through the Scriptures! What a distinct honor it is. I do hope that you will enjoy reading these introductions as much as I enjoy expounding them! Our journey begins here—at the beginning.

The word *genesis* is defined as "origin" or "creation," so it's a fitting title for the opening book of the Bible. Genesis is a book full of beginnings: of life, of nature, of people, of cities, and much more. It also includes the account of how sin originated (chapter 3), a monumental event that resulted in an ongoing defiance of God. The influence of sin is soon seen in Cain's murder of Abel (chapter 4), the wickedness during the days of Noah (chapters 6–9), human pride at the Tower of Babel (11:1–9), and throughout history even to the present day. Yet no sooner had sin begun than God promised to provide a remedy for it (3:15). And you will see in the stories of Abraham, Isaac, Jacob, and Joseph that God calls them to be His people. He makes a covenant to be their God, and through them He will one day bring a Savior into the world to resolve the problem of sin once and for all.

At the end of time, Jesus shall eventually make possible a never-ending life of perfection in the presence of God, which was God's plan for humanity in the beginning. And now, let us delve into the book of Genesis!

WHAT'S IT MEAN, EUGENE?

Complementarity—An intimidating word with a very simple meaning. To complement is to "fill up what's lacking, make complete or whole." The Bible says that God created human beings in two *complementary* halves: *male* and *female* (Genesis 1:27). *Complementarity* refers to the premise that men need women and women need men, especially in the context of *marriage*—a fact that Katrina and I experience daily. It also suggests that both sexes have an important role to play in reflecting the image of God. (See *Image of God* in 1 Chronicles.)

The Beginning

1 In the beginning, God created the heavens and the earth. ²The earth didn't have any shape. And it was empty. There was darkness over the surface of the waves. At that time, the Spirit of God was hovering over the waters.

³God said, "Let there be light." And there was light. ⁴God saw that the light was good. He separated the light from the darkness. ⁵God called the light "day." He called the darkness "night." There was evening, and there was morning. It was day one.

⁶God said, "Let there be a huge space between the waters. Let it separate water from water." ⁷And that's exactly what happened. God made the huge space between the waters. He separated the water under the space from the water above it. ⁸God called the huge space "sky." There was evening, and there was morning. It was day two.

⁹God said, "Let the water under the sky be gathered into one place. Let dry ground appear." And that's exactly what happened. ¹⁰God called the dry ground "land." He called all the water that was gathered together "seas." And God saw that it was good. ¹¹Then God said, "Let the land produce plants. Let them produce their own seeds. And let there be trees on the land that grow fruit with seeds in it. Let each kind of plant or tree have its own kind of seeds." And that's exactly what happened. ¹²So the land produced plants. Each kind of plant had its own kind of seeds. And the land produced trees that grew fruit with seeds in it. Each kind of tree had its own kind of seeds. God saw that it was good. ¹³There was evening, and there was morning. It was day three.

¹⁴God said, "Let there be lights in the huge space of the sky. Let them separate

WOOTON'S FUN FACTS

Gen. 1:18

I used to be afraid of the dark—okay, I still am sometimes. Eugene says that fear of the dark is called "nyctophobia" and I guess it's the most common fear children have.

the day from the night. Let the lights set the times for the holy celebrations and the days and the years. ¹⁵Let them be lights in the huge space of the sky to give light on the earth." And that's exactly what happened. ¹⁶God made two great lights. He made the larger light to rule over the day and the smaller light to rule over the night. He also made the stars. ¹⁷God put the lights in the huge space of the sky to give light on the earth. ¹⁸He put them there to rule over the day and the night. He put them there to separate light from darkness. God saw that it was good. ¹⁹There was evening, and there was morning. It was day four.

²⁰God said, "Let the seas be filled with living things. Let birds fly above the earth across the huge space of the sky." ²¹So God created the great sea creatures. He created every kind of living thing that fills the seas and moves about in them. He created every kind of bird that flies. And God saw that it was good. ²²God blessed them. He said, "Have little ones so that there will be many of you. Fill the water in the seas. Let there be more and more birds on the earth." ²³There was evening, and there was morning. It was day five.

²⁴God said, "Let the land produce every kind of living creature. Let there be

REMEMBER THIS

GENESIS 1:1

"In the beginning, God created the heavens and the earth."

WHIT'S WISDOM
Genesis 1

Even though none of us were alive when God created the world, the Bible clearly says that He created *us*! Where? Read verses 26 to 28. God created the first family and told them to have many children. My wife and I had three. All of us are part of God's Creation.

We also have a job. In Genesis 1:28, God told the first people to bring the earth under control and to rule over the fish, birds, and living creatures. We still have that job today—to be in charge of the earth. We are supposed to use the earth and take care of it.

Do you ever have to mow the lawn at your house? Do you have a garden? Who takes care of pets that belong to your family? When you have one of these chores, remember that you are doing more than obeying Mom or Dad. You are helping to take care of God's world.

---

livestock, and creatures that move along the ground, and wild animals." And that's exactly what happened. ²⁵God made every kind of wild animal. He made every kind of livestock. He made every kind of creature that moves along the ground. And God saw that it was good.

²⁶Then God said, "Let us make human beings so that they are like us. Let them rule over the fish in the seas and the birds in the sky. Let them rule over the livestock and all the wild animals. And let them rule over all the creatures that move along the ground."

²⁷ So God created human beings in his own likeness.
He created them to be like himself.
He created them as male and female.

²⁸God blessed them. He said to them, "Have children so that there will be many of you. Fill the earth and bring it under your control. Rule over the fish in the seas and the birds in the sky. Rule over every living creature that moves along the ground."

²⁹Then God said, "I am giving you every plant on the face of the whole earth that produces its own seeds. I am giving you every tree that has fruit with seeds in it. All of them will be given to you for food. ³⁰I am giving every green plant as food for all the land animals and for all the birds in the sky. I am also giving the plants to all the creatures that move along

the ground. I am giving them to every living thing that breathes." And that's exactly what happened.

³¹God saw everything he had made. And it was very good. There was evening, and there was morning. It was day six.

2 So the heavens and the earth and everything in them were completed.

²By the seventh day God had finished the work he had been doing. So on that day he rested from all his work. ³God blessed the seventh day and made it holy. He blessed it because on that day he rested from all the work he had done.

Adam and Eve

⁴Here is the story of the heavens and the earth when they were created. The LORD God made the earth and the heavens.

⁵At that time, bushes had not yet appeared on the earth. Plants had not started to grow. The LORD God had not sent rain on the earth. And there was no one to farm the land. ⁶But streams came from the earth. They watered the entire surface of the ground. ⁷Then the LORD God formed a man. He made him out of the dust of the ground. God breathed the breath of life into him. And the man became a living person.

⁸The LORD God had planted a garden in the east in Eden. He put in the garden the man he had formed. ⁹The LORD God made every kind of tree grow out of the

ground. The trees were pleasing to look at. Their fruit was good to eat. There were two trees in the middle of the garden. One of them had fruit that let people live forever. The other had fruit that let people tell the difference between good and evil.

¹⁰A river watered the garden. It flowed out of Eden. From there the river separated into four other rivers. ¹¹The name of the first river is the Pishon. It winds through the whole land of Havilah. Gold is found there. ¹²The gold of that land is good. Onyx and sweet-smelling resin are also found there. ¹³The name of the second river is the Gihon. It winds through the whole land of Cush. ¹⁴The name of the third river is the Tigris. It runs along the east side of Ashur. And the fourth river is called the Euphrates.

¹⁵The LORD God put the man in the Garden of Eden. He put him there to farm its land and take care of it. ¹⁶The LORD God gave the man a command. He said, "You may eat fruit from any tree in the garden. ¹⁷But you must not eat the fruit from the tree of the knowledge of good and evil. If you do, you will certainly die."

¹⁸The LORD God said, "It is not good for the man to be alone. I will make a helper who is just right for him."

¹⁹The LORD God had formed all the wild animals and all the birds in the sky. He had made all of them out of the ground. He brought them to the man to see what names he would give them. And the name the man gave each living creature became its name. ²⁰So the man gave names to all the livestock, all the birds in the sky, and all the wild animals.

But Adam didn't find a helper that was just right for him. ²¹So the LORD God caused him to fall into a deep sleep. While the man was sleeping, the LORD God took out one of the man's ribs. Then the LORD God closed the opening in the man's side. ²²Then the LORD God made a woman. He made her from the rib he had taken out of the man. And the LORD God brought her to the man.

²³The man said,

"Her bones have come from my bones.
    Her body has come from my body.
She will be named 'woman,'
    because she was taken out of a
        man."

²⁴That's why a man leaves his father and mother and is joined to his wife. The two of them become one.

²⁵Adam and his wife were both naked. They didn't feel any shame.

Adam and Eve Fall Into Sin

3 The serpent was more clever than any of the wild animals the LORD God had made. The serpent said to the woman, "Did God really say, 'You must not eat fruit from any tree in the garden'?"

²The woman said to the serpent, "We may eat fruit from the trees in the garden. ³But God did say, 'You must not eat the fruit from the tree in the middle of the garden. Do not even touch it. If you do, you will die.'"

⁴"You will certainly not die," the serpent said to the woman. ⁵"God knows that when you eat fruit from that tree, you will know things you have never known before. Like God, you will be able to tell the difference between good and evil."

⁶The woman saw that the tree's fruit was good to eat and pleasing to look at. She also saw that it would make a person wise. So she took some of the fruit and ate it. She also gave some to her husband, who was with her. And he ate it. ⁷Then both of them knew things they had never known before. They realized they were naked. So they sewed together fig leaves and made clothes for themselves.

⁸Then the man and his wife heard the LORD God walking in the garden. It was during the coolest time of the day. They hid from the LORD God among the trees of the garden. ⁹But the LORD God called out to the man. "Where are you?" he asked.

¹⁰"I heard you in the garden," the man answered. "I was afraid, because I was naked. So I hid."

¹¹The LORD God said, "Who told you that you were naked? Have you eaten fruit from the tree I commanded you not to eat from?"

WHIT'S WISDOM

Genesis 3

Most of the story of Jesus is told in the New Testament. But did you know there are many references to Him and the things He would do in the Old Testament, too? Since those words were written hundreds of years before He was born in Bethlehem, we call them *prophecies*.

Here are a few examples:

- In Genesis 3:15, God told Satan that Eve's "son" (Jesus) would one day "crush your head." And God said that Satan would "bite his heel" (injure but not destroy Him).
- In Deuteronomy 18:15, Moses told the people of Israel, "The LORD your God will raise up for you a prophet like me." In John 1:45, Philip said, "We have found the one whom Moses wrote about in the Law . . . He is Jesus of Nazareth."

- In Psalm 22, David, who was both king and prophet, talked about many details of Jesus' eventual death. These included the facts that He would be crucified, that He would be mocked while hanging on the cross, and that men would gamble for His clothing.
- The prophet Isaiah told us the Savior would be born to a virgin and that He would be called "Immanuel" (Isaiah 7:14).
- In chapter 53 of his book, Isaiah wrote about many details of Jesus' suffering and death, including the fact that He would be taking the punishment for *our* sins and that He would die with criminals. Don't forget that two thieves were crucified with Jesus.
- The prophet Micah told us where Jesus would be born—in the little town of Bethlehem (Micah 5:2).
- Another prophet, Zechariah, wrote in chapter 9, verse 9 of his book that Jesus would enter Jerusalem riding on a donkey.

Why not go on an adventure right now and read these prophecies in your Bible?

¹²The man said, "It's the fault of the woman you put here with me. She gave me some fruit from the tree. And I ate it."

¹³Then the LORD God said to the woman, "What have you done?"

The woman said, "The serpent tricked me. That's why I ate the fruit."

¹⁴So the LORD God spoke to the serpent. He said, "Because you have done this,

"You are set apart from all
　　livestock
　　and all wild animals.
　I am putting a curse on you.
You will crawl on your belly.
　You will eat dust
　　all the days of your life.
¹⁵ I will make you and the woman hate
　　each other.

Your children and her children will
　　be enemies.
Her son will crush your head.
　And you will bite his heel."

¹⁶The LORD God said to the woman,

"I will increase your pain when you
　　give birth.
You will be in great pain when you
　　have children.
You will long for your husband.
　And he will rule over you."

¹⁷The LORD God said to Adam, "You listened to your wife's suggestion. You ate fruit from the tree I warned you about. I said, 'You must not eat its fruit.'

"So I am putting a curse on the ground
　　because of what you did.

All the days of your life you will
    have to work hard.
It will be painful for you to get food
    from the ground. [18]You will
    eat plants from the field,
even though the ground produces
    thorns and prickly weeds.
[19] You will have to work hard and sweat
    a lot
    to produce the food you eat.
You were made out of the ground.
    You will return to it when you die.
You are dust,
    and you will return to dust."

[20]Adam named his wife Eve. She would become the mother of every living person.

[21]The LORD God made clothes out of animal skins for Adam and his wife to wear. [22]The LORD God said, "Just like one of us, the man can now tell the difference between good and evil. He must not be allowed to reach out and pick fruit from the tree of life and eat it. If he does, he will live forever." [23]So the LORD God drove the man out of the Garden of Eden. He sent the man to farm the ground he had been made from. [24]The LORD God drove him out and then placed angels on the east side of the garden. He also placed there a flaming sword that flashed back and forth. The angels and the sword guarded the way to the tree of life.

Cain and Abel

4 Adam loved his wife Eve and slept with her. She became pregnant and gave birth to Cain. She said, "With the LORD's help I have had a baby boy." [2]Later she gave birth to his brother Abel.

Abel took care of sheep. Cain farmed the land. [3]After some time, Cain gathered some things he had grown. He brought them as an offering to the LORD. [4]And Abel also brought an offering. He brought the fattest parts of some animals from his flock. They were the first animals born to their mothers. The LORD was pleased

WHAT ABOUT YOU?

When God asked Adam if he ate the forbidden fruit, Adam tried to avoid trouble. He shifted the blame to Eve! "It's the fault of the woman you put here with me," he said. Of course, Eve immediately blamed the serpent.

Maybe you don't think you have much in common with Adam or Eve, but at some point you've probably tried to blame someone else for your mistake. We all have. It takes a brave person to say, "I'm sorry—that was my fault." It's usually easier to make excuses or point a finger. We like to think of ourselves as brave, but true courage includes taking responsibility for our actions.

The good news is, God gives us the courage we need to step up for truth, even if doing the right thing might be humbling or embarrassing. We just have to ask Him. That might mean telling your teacher that you glanced at a neighbor's test. Or maybe it means apologizing to a kid you and your friends made fun of. It may not be easy, but taking a stand for what's right can become a habit if practiced often.

TRY THIS TODAY: Whenever you find yourself starting to blame someone or making an excuse for something you did, stop and hop on one foot for 10 seconds. It'll help you notice how often you shift blame for the things you do, which is the first step (or hop) toward making a positive change.

with Abel and his offering. [5]But he wasn't pleased with Cain and his offering. So Cain became very angry, and his face was sad.

[6]Then the LORD said to Cain, "Why are you angry? Why are you looking so sad? [7]Do what is right and then you will be accepted. If you don't do what is right, sin is waiting at your door to grab you. It desires to control you. But you must rule over it."

[8]Cain said to his brother Abel, "Let's go out to the field." So they went out. There Cain attacked his brother Abel and killed him.

[9]Then the LORD said to Cain, "Where is your brother Abel?"

"I don't know," Cain replied. "Am I supposed to take care of my brother?"

[10]The LORD said, "What have you done? Listen! Your brother's blood is crying out to me from the ground. [11]So I am putting a curse on you. I am driving you away from this ground. It has opened its mouth to receive your brother's blood from your hand. [12]When you farm the land, it will not produce its crops for you anymore. You will be a restless person who wanders around on the earth."

[13]Cain said to the LORD, "You are punishing me more than I can take. [14]Today you are driving me away from the land. I will be hidden from you. I'll be a restless person who wanders around on the earth. Anyone who finds me will kill me."

[15]But the LORD said to him, "No. Anyone who kills you will be paid back seven times." The LORD put a mark on Cain. Then anyone who found him wouldn't kill him. [16]So Cain went away from the LORD. He lived in the land of Nod. It was east of Eden.

[17]Cain loved his wife and slept with her. She became pregnant and gave birth to Enoch. At that time Cain was building a city. He named it after his son Enoch. [18]Enoch had a son named Irad. Irad was the father of Mehujael. Mehujael was the father of Methushael. And Methushael was the father of Lamech.

[19]Lamech married two women. One was named Adah, and the other was named Zillah. [20]Adah gave birth to Jabal. He was the father of people who live in tents and raise livestock. [21]His brother's name was Jubal. He was the father of

everyone who plays stringed instruments and wind instruments. [22]Zillah also had a son. His name was Tubal-Cain. He made all kinds of tools out of bronze and iron. Tubal-Cain's sister was Naamah.

[23]Lamech said to his wives,

"Adah and Zillah, listen to me!
    You wives of Lamech, hear my
        words!
I have killed a man because he
        wounded me.
    I have killed a young man because
        he hurt me.
[24] Anyone who would have killed Cain
        would have been paid back
        seven times.
    But anyone who hurts me will be
        paid back 77 times."

[25]Adam slept with his wife again. She gave birth to a son and named him Seth. She said, "God has given me another child. He will take the place of Abel, because Cain killed him." [26]Seth also had a son and named him Enosh.

Then people began to call on the name of the LORD.

The Family Line of Adam

5 Here is the written story of Adam's family line.

When God created human beings, he made them to be like him. [2]He created them as male and female, and he blessed them. He called them "human beings" when they were created.

[3] When Adam was 130 years old, he
    had a son who was like him. He
    named him Seth. [4]Adam lived
    800 years after Seth was born. He
    also had other sons and daughters. [5]Adam lived a total of 930
    years. And then he died.
[6] Seth lived 105 years. Then he became the father of Enosh. [7]Seth
    lived 807 years after Enosh was
    born. He also had other sons and

daughters. [8]Seth lived a total of 912 years. And then he died.

[9] Enosh lived 90 years. Then he became the father of Kenan. [10]Enosh lived 815 years after Kenan was born. He also had other sons and daughters. [11]Enosh lived a total of 905 years. And then he died.

[12] Kenan lived 70 years. Then he became the father of Mahalalel. [13]Kenan lived 840 years after Mahalalel was born. He also had other sons and daughters. [14]Kenan lived a total of 910 years. And then he died.

[15] Mahalalel lived 65 years. Then he became the father of Jared. [16]Mahalalel lived 830 years after Jared was born. He also had other sons and daughters. [17]Mahalalel lived a total of 895 years. And then he died.

[18] Jared lived 162 years. Then he became the father of Enoch. [19]Jared lived 800 years after Enoch was born. He also had other sons and daughters. [20]Jared lived a total of 962 years. And then he died.

[21] Enoch lived 65 years. Then he became the father of Methuselah. [22]Enoch walked faithfully with God 300 years after Methuselah was born. He also had other sons and daughters. [23]Enoch lived a total of 365 years. [24]Enoch walked faithfully with God. And then he couldn't be found, because God took him from this life.

[25] Methuselah lived 187 years. Then he became the father of Lamech. [26]Methuselah lived 782 years after Lamech was born. He also had other sons and daughters. [27]Methuselah lived a total of 969 years. And then he died.

[28] Lamech lived 182 years. Then he had a son [29]and named him Noah. Lamech said, "He will comfort us when we are working. He'll comfort us when our hands work so hard they hurt. We have to work hard because the LORD put a curse on the ground." [30]Lamech lived 595 years after Noah was born. He also had other sons and daughters. [31]Lamech lived a total of 777 years. And then he died.

[32] After Noah was 500 years old, he became the father of Shem, Ham and Japheth.

The Sins of Everyone on Earth

6 There began to be many human beings on the earth. And daughters were born to them. [2]The sons of God saw that the daughters of human beings were beautiful. So they married any of them they chose. [3]Then the LORD said, "My Spirit will not struggle with human beings forever. They will have only 120 years to live."

[4]The Nephilim were on the earth in those days. That was when the sons of God went to the daughters of human beings. Children were born to them. The Nephilim were famous heroes who lived long ago. Nephilim were also on the earth later on.

[5]The LORD saw how bad the sins of everyone on earth had become. They only thought about evil things. [6]The LORD was very sad that he had made human beings on the earth. His heart was filled with pain. [7]So the LORD said, "I created human beings, but I will wipe them out. I will also destroy the animals, the birds in the sky, and the creatures that move along the ground. I am

Gen. 5:27 If I were 969 years old, I would have witnessed the first Crusade in 1095, the discovery of the New World in 1492, and the comic book's debut in 1837. Whoa!

very sad that I have made human beings."
[8]But the LORD was very pleased with Noah.

Noah and the Flood

[9]Here is the story of Noah's family line.

Noah was a godly man. He was without blame among the people of his time. He walked faithfully with God. [10]Noah had three sons. Their names were Shem, Ham and Japheth.

[11]The earth was very sinful in God's eyes. It was full of people who did mean and harmful things. [12]God saw how sinful the earth had become. All its people were living very sinful lives. [13]So God said to Noah, "I am going to put an end to everyone. They have filled the earth with their harmful acts. I am certainly going to destroy them and the earth. [14]So make yourself an ark out of cypress wood. Make rooms in it. Cover it with tar inside and out. [15]Here is how I want you to build it. The ark has to be 450 feet long. It has to be 75 feet wide and 45 feet high. [16]Make a roof for it. Leave below the roof an opening all the way around that is a foot and a half high. Put a door in one side of the ark. Make lower, middle and upper decks. [17]I am going to bring a flood on the earth. It will destroy all life under the sky. It will destroy every living creature that breathes. Everything on earth will die. [18]But I will make my covenant with you. You will go into the ark. Your sons and your wife and your sons' wives will enter it with you. [19]Bring a male and a female of every living thing into the ark. They will be kept alive with you. [20]Two of every kind of bird will come to you. Two of every kind of animal will also come to you. And so will two of every kind of creature that moves along the ground. All of them will be kept alive with you. [21]Take every kind of food that you will need. Store it away as food for you and them."

[22]Noah did everything just as God commanded him.

7 Then the LORD said to Noah, "Go into the ark with your whole family. I know that you are a godly man among the people of today. [2]Take seven pairs of every kind of 'clean' animal with you. Take a male and a female of each kind. Take one pair of every kind of animal that is not

'clean.' Take a male and a female of each kind. [3]Also take seven pairs of every kind of bird. Take a male and a female of each kind. Then every kind will be kept alive. They can spread out again over the whole earth. [4]Seven days from now I will send rain on the earth. It will rain for 40 days and 40 nights. I will destroy from the face of the earth every living creature I have made."

BIBLE ADVENTURES

Whit told the story of Noah's building the ark and experiencing the flood in "By Faith, Noah" (A#04).

[5]Noah did everything the LORD commanded him to do.

[6]Noah was 600 years old when the flood came on the earth. [7]He and his sons entered the ark. His wife and his sons' wives went with them. They entered the ark to escape the waters of the flood. [8]Male and female pairs of "clean" animals and pairs of animals that were not "clean" came to Noah. So did male and female pairs of birds and of all the creatures that move along the ground. [9]All of them came to Noah and entered the ark. Everything happened just as God had commanded Noah. [10]After seven days the flood came on the earth.

[11]Noah was 600 years old. It was the 17th day of the second month of the year. On that day all of the springs at the bottom of the oceans burst open. God opened the windows of the sky. [12]Rain fell on the earth for 40 days and 40 nights.

[13]On that same day Noah entered the ark together with his sons Shem, Ham and Japheth. Noah's wife and the wives of his three sons also entered it. [14]They had every kind of wild animal with them. They had every kind of livestock, creature that moves along the ground, and bird that flies. [15]Pairs of all living creatures that breathe came to Noah and entered the ark. [16]The animals going in were male and female of every living thing. Everything happened just as God had commanded Noah. Then the LORD shut him in.

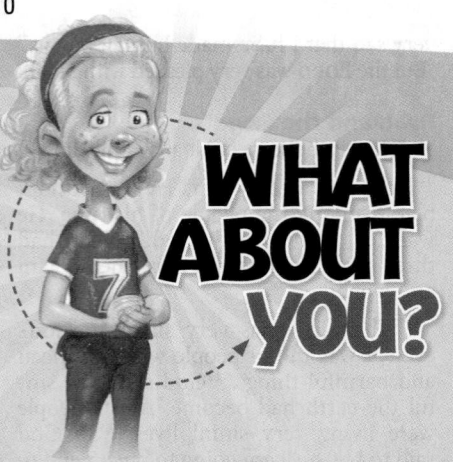

WHAT ABOUT YOU?

The people who lived in Noah's time were wicked and filled with violence. In those dark days, Noah was the only righteous man who obeyed God. Noah stayed true to God in spite of the temptations and evil that surrounded him.

God's Word warns us to keep our feet on firm paths and not veer to the left or right, which can give evil a chance to trip us up (see Proverbs 4:26–27).

That warning comes to life in an Adventures in Odyssey episode called "The Bad Guy." In this episode, Nick Mulligan is surprised by the sudden return of his old buddy, Vince. Nick expects a salty, streetwise dude looking for trouble. But who walks into Whit's End is a new man trying to live for Jesus Christ. Nick is suspicious, so he sets traps to test Vince, convinced that he will slip back into old habits.

Nick should have encouraged Vince to do the right things. But instead of helping his old friend stay on the right path, he tempted him to do wrong. It's a good thing Vince didn't fall for it.

Surround yourself with people who will help you make good choices. And be the kind of person your friends can count on to set a positive example. Who challenges you to make healthy choices? If you haven't thanked that person for being a good role model, let him or her know today. And look for more friends like that.

---

[17]For 40 days the flood kept coming on the earth. As the waters rose higher, they lifted the ark high above the earth. [18]The waters rose higher and higher on the earth. And the ark floated on the water. [19]The waters rose on the earth until all the high mountains under the entire sky were covered. [20]The waters continued to rise until they covered the mountains by more than 20 feet. [21]Every living thing that moved on land died. The birds, the livestock and the wild animals died. All of the creatures that fill the earth also died. And so did every human being. [22]Every breathing thing on dry land died. [23]Every living thing on earth was wiped out. People and animals were destroyed. The creatures that move along the ground and the birds in the sky were wiped out. Everything on earth was destroyed. Only Noah and those with him in the ark were left. [24]The waters flooded the earth for 150 days.

8 But God showed concern for Noah. He also showed concern for all the wild animals and livestock that were with Noah in the ark. So God sent a wind to sweep over the earth. And the waters began to go down. [2]The springs at the bottom of the oceans had been closed. The windows of the sky had also been closed. And the rain had stopped falling from the sky. [3]The water on the earth continued to go down. At the end of the 150 days the water had gone down. [4]On the 17th day of the seventh month, the ark came to rest on the mountains of Ararat. [5]The waters continued to go down until the tenth month. On the first day of that month, the tops of the mountains could be seen.

[6]After 40 days Noah opened a window he had made in the ark. [7]He sent out a raven. It kept flying back and forth until the water on the earth had dried up. [8]Then Noah sent out a dove. He wanted to see if the water on the surface of the ground had gone down. [9]But the dove couldn't find any place to rest. Water still covered the whole surface of the earth. So the dove returned to Noah in the ark.

Noah reached out his hand and took the dove in. He brought it back to himself in the ark. ¹⁰He waited seven more days. Then he sent out the dove again from the ark. ¹¹In the evening the dove returned to him. There in its beak was a freshly picked olive leaf! So Noah knew that the water on the earth had gone down. ¹²He waited seven more days. Then he sent out the dove again. But this time it didn't return to him.

¹³It was the first day of the first month of Noah's 601st year. The water on the earth had dried up. Then Noah removed the covering from the ark. He saw that the surface of the ground was dry. ¹⁴By the 27th day of the second month the earth was completely dry.

¹⁵Then God said to Noah, ¹⁶"Come out of the ark. Bring your wife and your sons and their wives with you. ¹⁷Bring out every kind of living thing that is with you. Bring the birds, the animals, and all the creatures that move along the ground. Then they can multiply on the earth. They can have little ones and the number of them can increase."

¹⁸So Noah came out of the ark. His sons and his wife and his sons' wives were with him. ¹⁹All the animals came out of the ark. The creatures that move along the ground also came out. So did all the birds. Everything that moves on land came out of the ark, one kind after another.

²⁰Then Noah built an altar to honor the Lord. He took some of the "clean" animals and birds. He sacrificed them on the altar as burnt offerings. ²¹The smell of the offerings pleased the Lord. He said to himself, "I will never put a curse on the ground again because of human beings. I will not do it even though their hearts are always directed toward evil. Their thoughts are evil from the time they are young. I will never destroy all living things again, as I have just done.

²² "As long as the earth lasts,
 there will always be a time to plant
 and a time to gather the crops.
As long as the earth lasts,
 there will always be cold and heat.
There will always be summer and
 winter,
 day and night."

God Makes a Covenant With Noah

9 Then God blessed Noah and his sons. He said to them, "Have children so that there are many of you. Fill the earth. ²All the land animals will be afraid of you. All the birds in the sky will be afraid of you. Every creature that moves along the ground will be afraid of you. So will every fish in the seas. Every living thing is put under your control. ³Everything that lives and moves about will be food for you. I have already given you the green plants for food. Now I am giving you everything. ⁴"But you must not eat meat that still has blood in it. ⁵I will certainly hold someone accountable if you are murdered. I will even hold animals accountable if they kill you. I will also hold anyone accountable who murders another person.

⁶ "Anyone who murders a human being
 will be killed by a human being.
That is because I have made human
 beings
 so that they are like me.

⁷Have children so that there will be many of you. Multiply and become many on the earth."

⁸Then God spoke to Noah and to his sons who were with him. He said, ⁹"I am now making my covenant with you and with all your children who will be born after you. ¹⁰I am making it also with every living creature that was with you in the

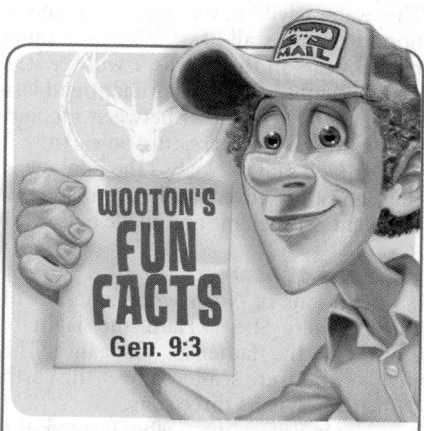

Before the Flood, people were vegetarians. I tried to live on just vegetables for a while, but then I smelled some bacon. It was all over.

ark. I am making my covenant with the birds, the livestock and all the wild animals. I am making it with all the creatures that came out of the ark with you. In fact, I am making it with every living thing on earth. ¹¹Here is my covenant I am making with you. The waters of a flood will never again destroy all life. A flood will never again destroy the earth."

Jason's Jargon

GENESIS 9

Here's our first mission! Ready? Search this chapter for the word *covenant*. A covenant is an agreement made between people where promises are made to one another. Both sides pledge to abide by the words of the agreement. Go!

¹²God continued, "My covenant is between me and you and every living creature with you. It is a covenant for all time to come. Here is the sign of the covenant I am making. ¹³I have put my rainbow in the clouds. It will be the sign of the covenant between me and the earth. ¹⁴Sometimes when I bring clouds over the earth, a rainbow will appear in them. ¹⁵Then I will remember my covenant between me and you and every kind of living creature. The waters will never again become a flood to destroy all life. ¹⁶When the rainbow appears in the clouds, I will see it. I will remember that my covenant will last forever. It is a covenant between me and every kind of living creature on earth."

¹⁷So God said to Noah, "The rainbow is the sign of my covenant. I have made my covenant between me and all life on earth."

The Sons of Noah

¹⁸The sons of Noah who came out of the ark were Shem, Ham and Japheth. Ham was the father of Canaan. ¹⁹The people who were scattered over the earth came from Noah's three sons.

²⁰Noah was a man who farmed the land. He decided to plant a field that produced grapes for making wine. ²¹When he drank some of the wine, it made him

drunk. Then he lay down inside his tent without any clothes on. ²²Ham saw his father naked. Then Ham, the father of Canaan, went outside and told his two brothers. ²³But Shem and Japheth picked up a piece of clothing and laid it across their shoulders. Then they walked backward into the tent. They covered their father's body. They turned their faces away because they didn't want to see their father naked.

²⁴Then Noah woke up from his sleep that was caused by the wine. He found out what his youngest son had done to him. ²⁵He said,

"May a curse be put on Canaan!
   He will be the lowest of slaves to his
      brothers."

²⁶Noah also said,

"May the LORD, the God of Shem, be
      praised.
May Canaan be the slave of Shem.
²⁷ May God add land to Japheth's
      territory.
May Japheth live in the tents of
      Shem.
And may Canaan be the slave of
      Japheth."

²⁸After the flood Noah lived 350 years. ²⁹Noah lived a total of 950 years. And then he died.

A List of Nations

10Here is the story of Shem, Ham and Japheth. They were Noah's sons. After the flood, they also had sons.

The Sons of Japheth

² The sons of Japheth were
   Gomer, Magog, Madai, Javan,
   Tubal, Meshek and Tiras.
³ The sons of Gomer were
   Ashkenaz, Riphath and Togarmah.
⁴ The sons of Javan were
   Elishah, Tarshish, the Kittites and the Rodanites. ⁵From these people came the families who lived near the Mediterranean Sea. Each tribe and nation then spread out into its own territory and had its own language.

The Sons of Ham

6 The sons of Ham were
Cush, Egypt, Put and Canaan.
7 The sons of Cush were
Seba, Havilah, Sabtah, Raamah and Sabteka.
The sons of Raamah were
Sheba and Dedan.
8 Cush was the father of Nimrod. Nimrod became a mighty hero on the earth. 9He was a mighty hunter in the LORD's eyes. That's why people sometimes compare others with Nimrod. They say, "They are like Nimrod, who was a mighty hunter in the LORD's eyes." 10The first capital cities of Nimrod's kingdom were Babylon, Uruk, Akkad and Kalneh. These cities were in the land of Babylon. 11From that land he went to Assyria. There he built Nineveh, Rehoboth Ir and Calah. 12He also built Resen, which is between Nineveh and Calah. Nineveh is the most famous city.
13 Egypt was the father of
the Ludites, Anamites, Lehabites, Naphtuhites, 14Pathrusites, Kasluhites and Caphtorites. The Philistines came from the Kasluhites.
15 Canaan was the father of Sidon.
Sidon was his oldest son. Canaan was also the father of the Hittites, 16Jebusites, Amorites and Girgashites. 17And he was the father of the Hivites, Arkites, Sinites, 18Arvadites, Zemarites and Hamathites.
Later the Canaanite tribes scattered. 19The borders of Canaan reached from Sidon toward Gerar all the way to Gaza. Then they continued toward Sodom, Gomorrah, Admah and Zeboyim all the way to Lasha.
20 These are the sons of Ham. They are listed by their tribes and languages in their territories and nations.

The Sons of Shem

21 Sons were also born to Shem, Japheth's younger brother. All the sons of Eber belonged to Shem's family line.

22 The sons of Shem were
Elam, Ashur, Arphaxad, Lud and Aram.
23 The sons of Aram were
Uz, Hul, Gether and Meshek.
24 Arphaxad was the father of Shelah.
Shelah was the father of Eber.
25 Eber had two sons.
One was named Peleg. That's because the earth was divided up in his time. His brother was named Joktan.
26 Joktan was the father of
Almodad, Sheleph, Hazarmaveth, Jerah, 27Hadoram, Uzal, Diklah, 28Obal, Abimael, Sheba, 29Ophir, Havilah and Jobab. They were all sons of Joktan.
30 The area where they lived stretched from Mesha toward Sephar. It was in the eastern hill country.
31 These are the sons of Shem. They are listed by their tribes and languages in their territories and nations.

32 These are the tribes of Noah's sons. They are listed by their family lines within their nations. From them the nations spread out over the earth after the flood.

The Tower of Babel

11 The whole world had only one language, and everyone spoke it. 2They moved to the east and found a broad valley in Babylon. There they made their home.

3They said to one another, "Come on! Let's make bricks and bake them well." They used bricks instead of stones. They used tar to hold the bricks together. 4Then they said, "Come on! Let's build a city for ourselves. Let's build a tower that reaches to the sky. We'll make a name for ourselves. Then we won't be scattered over the whole earth."

BIBLE ADVENTURES

Nathaniel and Eugene went on an Imagination Station adventure to the Tower of Babel in "The Tower" (A#32).

⁵But the LORD came down to see the city and the tower the people were building. ⁶He said, "All these people are united and speak the same language. That is why they can do all this. Now they will be able to do anything they plan. ⁷Come on! Let us go down and mix up their language. Then they will not be able to understand one another."

⁸So the LORD scattered them from there over the whole earth. And they stopped building the city. ⁹There the LORD mixed up the language of the whole world. That's why the city was called Babel. From there the LORD scattered them over the whole earth.

The Family Line of Shem

¹⁰Here is the story of Shem's family line.

It was two years after the flood. When Shem was 100 years old, he became the father of Arphaxad. ¹¹After Arphaxad was born, Shem lived 500 years and had other sons and daughters. ¹²When Arphaxad had lived 35 years, he became the father of Shelah. ¹³After Shelah was born, Arphaxad lived 403 years and had other sons and daughters.

¹⁴When Shelah had lived 30 years, he became the father of Eber. ¹⁵After Eber was born, Shelah lived 403 years and had other sons and daughters.

¹⁶When Eber had lived 34 years, he became the father of Peleg. ¹⁷After Peleg was born, Eber lived 430 years and had other sons and daughters.

¹⁸When Peleg had lived 30 years, he became the father of Reu. ¹⁹After Reu was born, Peleg lived 209 years and had other sons and daughters.

²⁰When Reu had lived 32 years, he became the father of Serug. ²¹After Serug was born, Reu lived 207 years and had other sons and daughters.

²²When Serug had lived 30 years, he became the father of Nahor. ²³After Nahor was born, Serug lived 200 years and had other sons and daughters.

We've all heard about countries fighting over land or mobs rioting over racial discrimination. Throughout history, people have done terrible things to each other because of their differences. Wouldn't we all get along better if there were only one language and one culture?

Adam and Eve were the first people to disobey the Lord, and ever since, we've all been born with that natural tendency to sin. No matter how hard we try, we'll never be able to achieve a perfect world on Earth—especially when we try to set it up ourselves.

It's impossible to create a perfect world or life. As we look at people's lives—including our own—we can see sin rearing its ugly head. We fight with our brothers and sisters, disobey our parents, or are mean to other people.

What's the solution? The people building the tower thought they could reach the heavens without God. But if we give up our pride and ask God to change our rebellious hearts into obedient hearts, He'll do it. Will we still battle against our human nature? Yes, but with the Holy Spirit on our side, we won't be fighting alone. Only then can we work toward peace in the world.

Because God confused the people at Babel, the different languages spoken in the world today are actually a gift from Him. Choose a foreign language you're interested in and learn to say a few phrases, such as "hello," "thank you," or "I love God."

²⁴ When Nahor had lived 29 years, he became the father of Terah. ²⁵After Terah was born, Nahor lived 119 years and had other sons and daughters.

²⁶ After Terah was 70 years old, he became the father of Abram, Nahor and Haran.

The Family Line of Abram

²⁷Here is the story of Terah's family line.

Terah became the father of Abram, Nahor and Haran. And Haran became the father of Lot. ²⁸Haran died in the city of Ur in Babylonia, the land where he was born. Haran died while his father Terah was still alive. ²⁹Abram and Nahor both got married. The name of Abram's wife was Sarai. The name of Nahor's wife was Milkah, the daughter of Haran. Haran was the father of Milkah and Iscah. ³⁰But Sarai wasn't able to have children.

³¹Terah left Ur in Babylon. He took with him his son Abram and his grandson Lot, the son of Haran. Terah also took his daughter-in-law Sarai, the wife of his son Abram. All of them left together to go to Canaan. But when they came to Harran, they made their home there.

³²Terah lived for 205 years. And then he died in Harran.

God Chooses Abram

12 The LORD had said to Abram, "Go from your country, your people and your father's family. Go to the land I will show you.

² "I will make you into a great nation.
     And I will bless you.
I will make your name great.
     You will be a blessing to others.
³ I will bless those who bless you.
     I will put a curse on anyone who
         puts a curse on you.
All nations on earth
     will be blessed because of you."

⁴So Abram went, just as the LORD had told him. Lot went with him. Abram was 75 years old when he left Harran. ⁵He took his wife Sarai and his nephew Lot. They took all the people and possessions they had acquired in Harran. They started out for the land of Canaan. And they arrived there.

⁶Abram traveled through the land. He went as far as the large tree of Moreh at Shechem. At that time the Canaanites were living in the land. ⁷The LORD appeared to Abram at Shechem. He said, "I will give this land to your family who comes after you." So Abram built an altar there to honor the LORD, who had appeared to him.

⁸From there, Abram went on toward the hills east of Bethel. He set up his tent there. Bethel was to the west, and Ai was to the east. Abram built an altar there and called on the name of the LORD.

⁹Then Abram left and continued south toward the Negev Desert.

Abram Goes to Egypt

¹⁰At that time there was not enough food in the land. So Abram went down to Egypt to live there for a while. ¹¹As he was about to enter Egypt, he spoke to his wife Sarai. He said, "I know what a beautiful woman you are. ¹²The people of Egypt will see you and say, 'This is his wife.' Then they will kill me. But they will let you live. ¹³Tell them you are my sister. Then I'll be treated well and my life will be spared because of you."

¹⁴Abram arrived in Egypt. The Egyptians saw that Sarai was a very beautiful woman. ¹⁵When Pharaoh's officials saw her, they told Pharaoh how beautiful she was. So she was taken into his palace. ¹⁶Pharaoh treated Abram well because of her. So Abram gained more sheep and cattle and male and female donkeys. He also gained more male and female servants and some camels.

¹⁷But the LORD sent terrible sicknesses on Pharaoh and everyone in his palace. The LORD did it because of Abram's wife Sarai. ¹⁸So Pharaoh sent for Abram. "What have you done to me?" he said. "Why didn't you tell me she was your wife? ¹⁹Why did you say she was your sister? That's why I took her to be my wife. Now then, here's your wife. Take her and go!" ²⁰Then Pharaoh gave orders to his men about Abram. They sent him on his way. So he left with his wife and everything he had.

Abram and Lot Separate

13 Abram went up from Egypt to the Negev Desert. He took his wife and everything he had. Lot went with him. ²Abram had become very rich. He had a lot of livestock and silver and gold.

³Abram left the Negev Desert. He went from place to place until he came to Bethel. Then he came to the place between Bethel and Ai where his tent had been earlier. ⁴There he called on the name of the Lord at the altar he had built.

⁵Lot was moving around with Abram. Lot also had flocks and herds and tents. ⁶But the land didn't have enough food for both Abram and Lot. They had large herds and many servants, so they weren't able to stay together. ⁷The people who took care of Abram's herds and those who took care of Lot's herds began to argue. The Canaanites and Perizzites were also living in the land at that time.

⁸So Abram said to Lot, "Let's not argue with each other. The people taking care of your herds and those taking care of mine shouldn't argue with one another either. After all, we're part of the same family. ⁹Isn't the whole land in front of you? Let's separate. If you go to the left, I'll go to the right. If you go to the right, I'll go to the left."

¹⁰Lot looked around. He saw that the whole Jordan River valley toward the town of Zoar had plenty of water. It was like the garden of the Lord, like the land of Egypt. This was before the Lord destroyed Sodom and Gomorrah. ¹¹So Lot chose the whole Jordan River valley for himself. Then he started out toward the east. The two men separated. ¹²Abram lived in the land of Canaan. Lot lived among the cities of the Jordan River valley. He set up his tents near Sodom. ¹³The people of Sodom were evil. They were sinning greatly against the Lord.

¹⁴The Lord spoke to Abram after Lot had left him. He said, "Look around from where you are. Look north and south, east and west. ¹⁵I will give you all the land you see. I will give it forever to you and your family who comes after you. ¹⁶I will make them like the dust of the earth. Can dust be counted? If it can, then your family can be counted. ¹⁷Go! Walk through the land. See how long and wide it is. I am giving it to you."

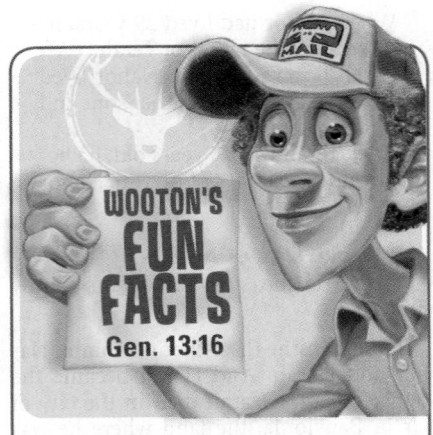

WOOTON'S FUN FACTS
Gen. 13:16

If you're like me and understand the importance of counting dust particles from time to time, don't forget to include cosmic dust! It's found all throughout the galaxy, especially around new stars.

¹⁸So Abram went to live near the large trees of Mamre at Hebron. There he pitched his tents and built an altar to honor the Lord.

Abram Saves Lot

14 Amraphel was the king of Babylon. Arioch was the king of Ellasar. Kedorlaomer was the king of Elam. And Tidal was the king of Goyim. ²They went to war against five other kings. They were Bera king of Sodom, Birsha king of Gomorrah, Shinab king of Admah, Shemeber king of Zeboyim, and the king of Bela. Bela was also called Zoar. ³These five kings all gathered their armies together in the Valley of Siddim. It was also called the valley of the Dead Sea. ⁴For 12 years Kedorlaomer had ruled over them. But in the 13th year they opposed him.

⁵So in the 14th year, Kedorlaomer and the kings who helped him went to war. They won the battle against the Rephaites in Ashteroth Karnaim. They also won the battle against the Zuzites in Ham and the Emites in Shaveh Kiriathaim. ⁶They did the same thing to the Horites in the hill country of Seir. They marched all the way to El Paran near the desert. ⁷Then they turned back and went to En Mishpat. En Mishpat was also called Kadesh. They took over the whole territory of the Amalekites.

They also won the battle against the Amorites who were living in Hazezon Tamar.

[8]Then the kings of Sodom, Gomorrah, Admah, Zeboyim and Bela marched out. Bela was also called Zoar. They lined up their armies for battle in the Valley of Siddim. [9]They got ready to fight against Kedorlaomer king of Elam, Tidal king of Goyim, Amraphel king of Babylonia, and Arioch king of Ellasar. There were four kings against five. [10]The Valley of Siddim was full of tar pits. The kings of Sodom and Gomorrah ran away from the battle. Some of their men fell into the pits, but the rest escaped to the hills. [11]The four kings took all the things that belonged to Sodom and Gomorrah. They also took all their food and then left. [12]They carried away Abram's nephew Lot and the things he owned. Lot was living in Sodom at that time.

[13]A man escaped and came to report everything to Abram. Abram was a Hebrew. He was living near the large trees of Mamre the Amorite. Mamre was a brother of Eshkol and Aner. All of them helped Abram. [14]Abram heard that Lot had been captured. So he called out his 318 trained men. All of them were sons of his servants. Abram and his men chased their enemies as far as Dan. [15]During the night Abram separated his men into groups. They attacked their enemies and drove them away. They chased them north of Damascus as far as Hobah. [16]Abram took back everything the kings had taken. He brought back his nephew Lot and the things Lot owned. He also brought back the women and the other people.

[17]After Abram won the battle over Kedorlaomer and the kings who helped him, he returned home. The king of Sodom came out to meet him in the Valley of Shaveh. It was also called the King's Valley.

[18]Melchizedek was the king of Jerusalem. He brought out bread and wine. He was the priest of the Most High God. [19]He gave a blessing to Abram. He said,

"May the Most High God bless
    Abram.
      May the Creator of heaven and
        earth bless him.
[20] Give praise to the Most High God.
      He gave your enemies into your
        hand."

Then Abram gave Melchizedek a tenth of everything.

[21]The king of Sodom said to Abram, "Give me the people. Keep everything else for yourself."

[22]But Abram said to the king of Sodom, "I have raised my hand to make a promise to the Lord. He is the Most High God. He is the Creator of heaven and earth. [23]I've said I will not accept anything that belongs to you. I will not take even a thread or the strap of a sandal. You will never be able to say, 'I made Abram rich.' [24]I'll accept only what my men have eaten and what belongs to Aner, Eshkol and Mamre. These three men went with me. Let them have their share."

God Makes a Covenant With Abram

15 Some time later, Abram had a vision. The Lord said to him,

"Abram, do not be afraid.
    I am like a shield to you.
    I am your very great reward."

[2]But Abram said, "Lord and King, what can you give me? I still don't have any children. My servant Eliezer comes from Damascus. When I die, he will get everything I own." [3]Abram continued, "You haven't given me any children. So this servant of mine will get everything I own."

[4]Then a message from the Lord came to Abram. The Lord said, "When you die, what you have will not go to this man. You will have a son of your own. He will get everything you have." [5]The Lord took Abram outside and said, "Look up at the sky. Count the stars, if you can." Then he said to him, "That's how many children will be born into your family."

[6]Abram believed the Lord. The Lord was pleased with Abram because he believed. So Abram's faith made him right with the Lord.

⁷He also said to Abram, "I am the Lord. I brought you out of Ur in the land of Babylon. I will give you this land to have as your very own."

⁸But Abram said, "Lord and King, how can I know I will have this land as my own?"

⁹So the Lord said to him, "Bring me a young cow, a goat and a ram. Each must be three years old. Bring a dove and a young pigeon along with them."

¹⁰Abram brought all of them to the Lord. Abram cut them in two and placed the halves opposite each other. But he didn't cut the birds in half. ¹¹Then large birds came down to eat the dead bodies of the animals and birds. But Abram chased the large birds away.

¹²As the sun was going down, Abram fell into a deep sleep. A thick and scary darkness covered him. ¹³Then the Lord said to him, "You can be sure of what I am about to tell you. For 400 years, your family who comes after you will be strangers in another country. They will become slaves there and will be treated badly. ¹⁴But I will punish the nation that makes them slaves. After that, they will leave with many possessions. ¹⁵But you will die in peace. You will join the members of your family who have already died. And you will be buried when you are very old. ¹⁶Your children's grandchildren will come back here. That's because the sin of the Amorites has not yet reached the point where I must punish them."

¹⁷The sun set and it became dark. Then a burning torch and a pot filled with smoking coals appeared. They passed between the pieces of the animals that had been cut in two. ¹⁸On that day the Lord made a covenant with Abram. He said, "I am giving this land to your family who comes after you. It reaches from the River of Egypt to the great Euphrates River. ¹⁹It includes the land of the Kenites, Kenizzites, Kadmonites, ²⁰Hittites, Perizzites and Rephaites. ²¹The Amorites, Canaanites, Girgashites and Jebusites also live there."

Hagar and Ishmael

16 Abram's wife Sarai had never had any children by him. But she had a female slave from Egypt named Hagar. ²So she said to Abram, "The Lord has kept me from having children. Go and

WOOTON'S FUN FACTS

GEN. 16:7

This is the second time an angel appears in the Bible. Hagar says it's a holy place and names it Beer Lahai Roi. The first angel-sighting is in Genesis 3:24.

sleep with my slave. Maybe I can have a family through her."

Abram agreed to what Sarai had said. ³His wife Sarai gave him her slave Hagar to be his wife. That was after he had been living in Canaan for ten years. ⁴Then he slept with Hagar, and she became pregnant.

When Hagar knew she was pregnant, she began to look down on the woman who owned her. ⁵Then Sarai said to Abram, "It's your fault that I'm suffering like this. I put my slave in your arms. Now that she knows she's pregnant, she looks down on me. May the Lord judge between you and me. May he decide which of us is right."

⁶"Your slave belongs to you," Abram said. "Do with her what you think is best." Then Sarai treated Hagar badly. So Hagar ran away from her.

⁷The angel of the Lord found Hagar near a spring of water in the desert. The spring was beside the road to Shur. ⁸The angel said, "Hagar, you are Sarai's slave. Where have you come from? Where are you going?"

"I'm running away from my owner Sarai," she answered.

⁹Then the angel of the Lord told her, "Go back to the woman who owns you. Obey her." ¹⁰The angel continued, "I will

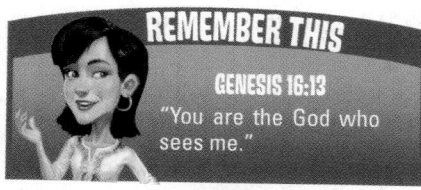

give you and your family many children. There will be more of them than anyone can count."

[11] The angel of the LORD also said to her,

"You are now pregnant
  and will have a son.
You will name him Ishmael,
  because the LORD has heard about
    your suffering.
[12] He will be like a wild donkey.
  He will use his power against
    everyone,
  and everyone will be against him.
  He will not get along with any of
    his family."

[13] She gave a name to the LORD who spoke to her. She called him "You are the God who sees me." That's because she said, "I have now seen the One who sees me." [14] That's why the well was named Beer Lahai Roi. It's still there, between Kadesh and Bered.

[15] So Hagar had a son by Abram and Abram gave him the name Ishmael. [16] Abram was 86 years old when Hagar had Ishmael by him.

The Covenant of Circumcision

17 When Abram was 99 years old, the LORD appeared to him. He said, "I am the Mighty God. Walk faithfully with me. Live in a way that pleases me. [2] I will now act on my covenant between me and you. I will greatly increase the number of your children after you."

[3] Abram fell with his face to the ground. God said to him, [4] "This is my covenant with you. You will be the father of many nations. [5] You will not be called Abram anymore. Your name will be Abraham, because I have made you a father of many nations. [6] I will greatly increase the number of your children after you. Nations and kings will come from you. [7] I will make my covenant with you last forever. It will be between me and you and your

family after you for all time to come. I will be your God. And I will be the God of all your family after you. [8] You are now living in Canaan as an outsider. But I will give you the whole land of Canaan. You will own it forever and so will all your family after you. And I will be their God."

[9] Then God said to Abraham, "You must keep my covenant. You and your family after you must keep it for all time to come. [10] Here is my covenant that you and your family after you must keep. You and every male among you must be circumcised. [11] That will be the sign of the covenant between me and you. [12] It must be done for all time to come. Every male among you who is eight days old must be circumcised. That includes those who are born into your own family or outside it. It also includes those bought with money from a stranger. [13] So any male born into your family or bought with your money must be circumcised. My covenant will last forever. Your body will have the mark of my covenant on it. [14] Any male who has not been circumcised will be separated from his people. He has broken my covenant."

[15] God also said to Abraham, "Do not continue to call your wife by the name Sarai. Her name will be Sarah. [16] I will give her my blessing. You can be sure that I

WOOTON'S FUN FACTS
Gen. 17:5

God changed Abram's name to Abraham when he was 99 years old. (Well, *Abram* was 99; God was way older.) I hope God changes my name someday. Xylophone would be good for a first name. After all, my middle initial is *Z*.

will give you a son by her. I will bless her so that she will be the mother of nations. Kings of nations will come from her."

[17]Abraham fell with his face to the ground. He laughed and said to himself, "Can a 100-year-old man have a son? Can Sarah have a child at the age of 90?" [18]Abraham said to God, "I really wish Ishmael could receive your blessing!"

[19]Then God said, "Yes, I will bless Ishmael. But your wife Sarah will have a son by you. And you will name him Isaac. I will establish my covenant with him. That covenant will last forever. It will be for Isaac and his family after him. [20]I have heard what you said about Ishmael. I will surely bless him. I will make his family very large. He will be the father of 12 rulers. And I will make him into a great nation. [21]But I will establish my covenant with Isaac. By this time next year, Sarah will have a son by you." [22]When God had finished speaking with Abraham, God left him.

[23]On that same day Abraham circumcised his son Ishmael. He also circumcised every male who was born into his family or bought with his money. He did exactly as God had told him. [24]Abraham was 99 years old when he was circumcised. [25]His son Ishmael was 13. [26]Abraham and his son Ishmael were both circumcised on that same day. [27]And every male in Abraham's household was circumcised along with him. That included those born into his family or bought from a stranger.

Three Men Visit Abraham

18 The LORD appeared to Abraham near the large trees of Mamre. Abraham was sitting at the entrance to his tent. It was the hottest time of the day. [2]Abraham looked up and saw three men standing nearby. So he quickly left the entrance to his tent to greet them. He bowed low to the ground.

[3]He said, "My lord, if you are pleased with me, don't pass me by. [4]Let me get you some water. Then all of you can wash your feet and rest under this tree. [5]Let me get you something to eat to give you strength. Then you can go on your way. I want to do this for you now that you have come to me."

"All right," they answered. "Do as you say."

[6]So Abraham hurried into the tent to Sarah. "Quick!" he said. "Get about 36 pounds of the finest flour. Prepare it and bake some bread."

[7]Then he ran over to the herd. He picked out a choice, tender calf. He gave it to a servant, who hurried to prepare it. [8]Then he brought some butter and milk and the calf that had been prepared. He served them to the three men. While they ate, he stood near them under a tree.

[9]"Where is your wife Sarah?" they asked him.

"Over there in the tent," he said.

[10]Then one of them said, "I will surely return to you about this time next year. Your wife Sarah will have a son."

Sarah was listening at the entrance to the tent, which was behind him. [11]Abraham and Sarah were already very old. Sarah was too old to have a baby. [12]So she laughed to herself. She thought, "I'm worn out, and my husband is old. Can I really know the joy of having a baby?"

[13]Then the LORD said to Abraham, "Why did Sarah laugh? Why did she say, 'Will I really have a baby, now that I am old?' [14]Is anything too hard for me? I will return to you at the appointed time next year. Sarah will have a son."

[15]Sarah was afraid. So she lied and said, "I didn't laugh."

But the LORD said, "Yes, you laughed."

Abraham Pleads for Sodom

[16]The men got up to leave. They looked down toward Sodom. Abraham walked along with them to see them on their way. [17]Then the LORD said, "Should I hide from Abraham what I am about to do? [18]He will certainly become a great and powerful nation. All nations on earth will be blessed because of him. [19]I have chosen him. He must direct his children to live in the way that pleases me. And he must direct the members of his family after him to do the same. So he must guide all of them in doing what is right and fair. Then I, the LORD, will do for Abraham what I have promised him."

[20]The LORD also said, "The cries against Sodom and Gomorrah are very great. Their sin is so bad [21]that I will go down

and see for myself. I want to see if what they have done is as bad as the cries that have reached me. If it is not, then I will know."

²²The men turned away and went toward Sodom. But Abraham remained standing in front of the LORD. ²³Then Abraham came up to him. He said, "Will you sweep away godly people along with those who are evil? ²⁴What if there are 50 godly people in the city? Will you really sweep it away? Won't you spare the place because of the 50 godly people in it? ²⁵You would never kill godly people along with those who are evil, would you? Would you treat them all alike? You would never do anything like that! Won't the Judge of the whole earth do what is right?"

²⁶The LORD said, "If I find 50 godly people in the city of Sodom, I will spare it. I will spare the whole place because of them."

²⁷Then Abraham spoke up again. He said, "I have been very bold to speak to the Lord. After all, I'm only dust and ashes. ²⁸What if the number of godly people is five fewer than 50? Will you destroy the whole city because there are five fewer people?"

"If I find 45 there," he said, "I will not destroy it."

²⁹Once again Abraham spoke to him. He asked, "What if only 40 are found there?"

He said, "If there are 40, I will not do it."

³⁰Then Abraham said, "Lord, please don't be angry with me. Let me speak. What if only 30 can be found there?"

He answered, "If I find 30, I will not do it."

³¹Abraham said, "I have been very bold to speak to the Lord. What if only 20 can be found there?"

He said, "If I find 20, I will not destroy it."

³²Then he said, "Lord, please don't be angry with me. Let me speak just one more time. What if only ten can be found there?"

He answered, "If I find ten, I will not destroy it."

³³When the LORD had finished speaking with Abraham, he left. And Abraham returned home.

The LORD Destroys Sodom and Gomorrah

19 The two angels arrived at Sodom in the evening. Lot was sitting near the gate of the city. When Lot saw the angels, he got up to greet them. He bowed down with his face to the ground. ²"My lords," he said, "please come to my house. You can wash your feet and spend the night there. Then you can go on your way early in the morning."

"No," they answered. "We'll spend the night in the town square."

³But Lot wouldn't give up. So they went with him and entered his house. He prepared a meal for them. He baked bread without using yeast. And they ate. ⁴Before Lot and his guests had gone to bed, all the men came from every part of the city of Sodom. Young and old men alike surrounded the house. ⁵They called out to Lot. They said, "Where are the men who came to you tonight? Bring them out to us. We want to have sex with them."

⁶Lot went outside to meet them. He shut the door behind him. ⁷He said, "No, my friends. Don't do such an evil thing. ⁸Look, I have two daughters that no man has ever slept with. I'll bring them out to you now. Then do to them what you want to. But don't do anything to these men. I've brought them inside so they can be safe."

⁹"Get out of our way!" the men of Sodom replied to Lot. "You came here as an outsider. Now you want to act like a judge! We'll treat you worse than them." They kept trying to force Lot to open the door. Then they moved forward to break it down.

¹⁰But the angels inside reached out and pulled Lot back into the house and shut the door. ¹¹Then they made the men who were at the door of the house blind. They blinded both young and old men so that they couldn't find the door.

BIBLE ADVENTURES

O.T. Action News reported on Abram and Lot and the fate of Sodom and Gomorrah in "On Solid Ground" (A#15).

¹²The two angels said to Lot, "Do you have any other family members here? Do you have sons-in-law, sons, daughters or any other relatives in the city? Get them out of here! ¹³We are going to destroy this place. Many have cried out to the LORD against the people of this city. So he has sent us to destroy it."

¹⁴Then Lot went out and spoke to his sons-in-law. They had promised to marry his daughters. He said, "Hurry up! Get out of this place! The LORD is about to destroy the city!" But his sons-in-law thought he was joking.

¹⁵The sun was coming up. So the angels tried to get Lot to leave. They said, "Hurry up! Take your wife and your two daughters who are here. Get out! If you don't, you will be swept away when the city is destroyed."

¹⁶Lot didn't move right away. So the men grabbed him by the hand. They also took hold of the hands of his wife and two daughters. They led all of them safely out of the city. The LORD had mercy on them. ¹⁷As soon as the angels had brought them out, one of them spoke. He said, "Run for your lives! Don't look back! Don't stop anywhere in the valley! Run to the mountains! If you don't, you will be swept away!"

Jason's Jargon

GENESIS 19

Search for the word *sulfur*. Sulfur is an element that is used to make gunpowder and matches. It burns easily and has a terrible odor.

¹⁸But Lot said to them, "No, my lords! Please! ¹⁹You have done me a big favor. You have been very kind to me by sparing my life. But I can't run to the mountains. I won't be able to escape this horrible thing that's going to happen. And then I'll die. ²⁰Look, here's a town near enough to run to. It's small. Let me run to it. It's very small, isn't it? Then my life will be spared."

²¹The LORD said to Lot, "All right. I will also give you what you are asking for.

I will not destroy the town you are talking about. ²²But run there quickly. I can't do anything until you reach it." The town was named Zoar. Zoar means Small.

²³By the time Lot reached Zoar, the sun had risen over the land. ²⁴Then the LORD sent down burning sulfur. It came down like rain on Sodom and Gomorrah. It came from the LORD. It came out of the sky. ²⁵The LORD destroyed these cities and the whole valley. All the people who were living in the cities were wiped out. So were the plants in the land. ²⁶But Lot's wife looked back. When she did, she became a pillar made out of salt.

²⁷Early the next morning Abraham got up. He returned to the place where he had stood in front of the LORD. ²⁸He looked down toward Sodom and Gomorrah and the whole valley. He saw thick smoke rising from the land. It looked like smoke from a furnace.

²⁹So when God destroyed the cities of the valley, he showed concern for Abraham. He brought Lot out safely when he destroyed the cities where Lot had lived.

Lot and His Daughters

³⁰Lot and his two daughters left Zoar. They went to live in the mountains because Lot was afraid to stay in Zoar. So he and his daughters lived in a cave. ³¹One day the older daughter spoke to the younger one. She said, "Our father is old. People all over the earth have men to marry and have children with. We do not. ³²So let's get our father to drink wine. Then we can sleep with him. We can use our father to continue our family line."

³³That night they got their father to drink wine. Then the older daughter went in and slept with him. He wasn't aware when she lay down or when she got up.

³⁴The next day the older daughter spoke to the younger one again. She said, "Last night I slept with my father. Let's get him to drink wine again tonight. Then you go in and sleep with him. We can use our father to continue our family line." ³⁵So they got their father to drink wine that night also. Then the younger daughter slept with him. Again he wasn't aware when she lay down or when she got up.

³⁶So both of Lot's daughters became pregnant by their father. ³⁷The older

daughter had a son. She named him Moab. He's the father of the Moabites of today. ³⁸The younger daughter also had a son. She named him Ben-Ammi. He's the father of the Ammonites of today.

Abraham and Abimelek

20 Abraham moved south into the Negev Desert. He lived between Kadesh and Shur. For a while he stayed in Gerar. ²There Abraham said about his wife Sarah, "She's my sister." Then Abimelek, the king of Gerar, sent for Sarah and took her.

³So God appeared to Abimelek in a dream one night. He said to him, "You are as good as dead because of the woman you have taken. She is already married."

⁴But Abimelek hadn't gone near her. So he said, "Lord, will you destroy a nation that hasn't done anything wrong? ⁵Didn't Abraham say to me, 'She's my sister'? And didn't she also say, 'He's my brother'? I had no idea I was doing anything wrong."

⁶Then God spoke to him in the dream. He said, "Yes, I know you had no idea you were doing anything wrong. So I have kept you from sinning against me. That is why I did not let you touch her. ⁷Now return the man's wife to him. He is a prophet. So he will pray for you, and you will live. But what if you do not return her? Then you can be sure that you and all your people will die."

⁸Early the next morning Abimelek sent for all his officials. When he told them everything that had happened, they were really afraid. ⁹Then Abimelek called Abraham in. Abimelek said, "What have you done to us? Have I done something wrong to you? Why have you brought so much guilt on me and my kingdom? You have done things to me that should never be done." ¹⁰Abimelek also asked Abraham, "Why did you do this?"

¹¹Abraham replied, "I thought, 'There is no respect for God in this place. They will kill me because of my wife.' ¹²Besides, she really is my sister. She's the daughter of my father, but not the daughter of my mother. And she became my wife. ¹³God had me wander away from my father's house. So I said to her, 'Here is how you can show your love to me. Everywhere we go, say about me, "He's my brother." ' "

¹⁴Then Abimelek gave Abraham sheep and cattle and male and female slaves. He also returned his wife Sarah to him. ¹⁵Abimelek said, "Here is my land. Live anywhere you want to."

¹⁶He said to Sarah, "I'm giving your brother 25 pounds of silver. This will show everyone with you that I am sorry for what I did to you. You haven't done anything wrong."

¹⁷Then Abraham prayed to God, and God healed Abimelek. He also healed his wife and his female slaves so they could have children again. ¹⁸The LORD had kept all the women in Abimelek's house from having children. He had done it because of Abraham's wife Sarah.

Isaac Is Born

21 The LORD was gracious to Sarah, just as he had said he would be. The LORD did for Sarah what he had promised to do. ²Sarah became pregnant. She had a son by Abraham when he was old. The child was born at the exact time God had promised. ³Abraham gave the name Isaac to the son Sarah had by him. ⁴When his son Isaac was eight days old, Abraham circumcised him. He did it exactly as God had commanded him. ⁵Abraham was 100 years old when his son Isaac was born to him.

⁶Sarah said, "God has given laughter to me. Everyone who hears about this will laugh with me." ⁷She also said, "Who would have said to Abraham that Sarah would breast-feed children? But I've had a son by him when he is old."

Abraham Sends Hagar and Ishmael Away

⁸Isaac grew. The time came for his mother to stop breast-feeding him. On that day Abraham prepared a big celebration. ⁹But Sarah saw Ishmael making fun of Isaac. Ishmael was the son Hagar had by Abraham. Hagar was Sarah's Egyptian slave. ¹⁰Sarah said to Abraham, "Get rid of that slave woman! Get rid of her son! That woman's son will never have a share of the family's property. All of it belongs to my son Isaac."

¹¹What Sarah said upset Abraham very much. After all, Ishmael was his son. ¹²But God said to Abraham, "Do not be so upset

about the boy and your slave Hagar. Listen to what Sarah tells you, because your family line will continue through Isaac. ¹³I will also make the son of your slave into a nation. I will do it because he is your child."

¹⁴Early the next morning Abraham got some food and a bottle of water. The bottle was made out of animal skin. He gave the food and water to Hagar, placing them on her shoulders. Then he sent her away with the boy. She went on her way and wandered in the Desert of Beersheba.

¹⁵When the water in the bottle was gone, she put the boy under a bush. ¹⁶Then she sat down about as far away as a person can shoot an arrow. She thought, "I can't stand to watch the boy die." As she sat there, she began to sob.

¹⁷God heard the boy crying. Then the angel of God called out to Hagar from heaven. He said to her, "What is the matter, Hagar? Do not be afraid. God has heard the boy crying as he lies there. ¹⁸Lift up the boy and take him by the hand. I will make him into a great nation."

¹⁹Then God opened Hagar's eyes, and she saw a well of water. So she went and filled the bottle with water and gave the boy a drink.

²⁰God was with the boy as he grew up. He lived in the desert and learned to shoot a bow and arrow. ²¹While he was living in the Desert of Paran, his mother got a wife for him from Egypt.

The Agreement at Beersheba

²²At that time Abimelek and his army commander, Phicol, spoke to Abraham. They said to Abraham, "God is with you in everything you do. ²³Now make a promise to me here while God is watching. Give me your word that you will treat me fairly. Promise that you will treat my children and their children the same way. I've been kind to you. Now you be kind to me and the country where you are living as an outsider."

²⁴Abraham said, "I give you my word that I'll do it."

²⁵Then Abraham complained to Abimelek that his servants had taken over a well of water. ²⁶But Abimelek said, "I don't know who has done this. You didn't tell me. And today is the first time I heard about it."

²⁷So Abraham gave Abimelek sheep and cattle. The two men came to an agreement. ²⁸Then Abraham picked out seven female lambs from his flock. ²⁹Abimelek asked Abraham, "What's the meaning of these seven female lambs? Why have you picked them out and set them apart?"

³⁰Abraham replied, "Accept the seven lambs from me. They will be a witness that I dug this well."

³¹So that place was named Beersheba. That's because there the two men came to an agreement.

³²After the agreement had been made at Beersheba, Abimelek went back to the land of the Philistines. His army commander, Phicol, went with him. ³³Abraham planted a tamarisk tree in Beersheba. There he called on the name of the LORD, the God who lives forever. ³⁴Abraham stayed in the land of the Philistines for a long time.

God Tests Abraham

22 Some time later God tested Abraham. He said to him, "Abraham!"

"Here I am," Abraham replied.

²Then God said, "Take your son, your only son. He is the one you love. Take Isaac. Go to the place called Moriah. Give your son to me there as a burnt offering. Sacrifice him on the mountain I will show you."

³Early the next morning Abraham got up and loaded his donkey. He took two of his servants and his son Isaac with him. He cut enough wood for the burnt offering. Then he started out for the place God had shown him. ⁴On the third day Abraham saw the place a long way off. ⁵He said to his servants, "Stay here with the donkey. I and the boy will go over there and worship. Then we'll come back to you."

⁶Abraham had his son Isaac carry the wood for the burnt offering. He himself carried the fire and the knife. And the two of them walked on together. ⁷Then Isaac said to his father Abraham, "Father?"

"Yes, my son?" Abraham replied.

"The fire and wood are here," Isaac said. "But where is the lamb for the burnt offering?"

⁸Abraham answered, "God himself will provide the lamb for the burnt offering, my son." And the two of them walked on together.

⁹They reached the place God had shown Abraham. There Abraham built an altar. He arranged the wood on it. He tied up his son Isaac. Abraham placed him on the altar, on top of the wood. ¹⁰Then he reached out his hand. He picked up the knife to kill his son. ¹¹But the angel of the LORD called out to him from heaven. He said, "Abraham! Abraham!"

"Here I am," Abraham replied.

¹²"Do not lay a hand on the boy," he said. "Do not harm him. Now I know that you would do anything for God. You have not held back from me your son, your only son."

¹³Abraham looked around. There in a bush he saw a ram caught by its horns. He went over and took the ram. He sacrificed it as a burnt offering instead of his son. ¹⁴So Abraham named that place The LORD Will Provide. To this day people say, "It will be provided on the mountain of the LORD."

¹⁵The angel of the LORD called out to Abraham from heaven a second time. ¹⁶He said, "I am giving you my word that I will bless you. I will bless you because of what you have done," announces the LORD. "You have not held back your son, your only son. ¹⁷So I will certainly bless you. I will make the children born into your family as many as the stars in the sky. I will make them as many as the grains of sand on the seashore. They will take over the cities of their enemies. ¹⁸All nations on earth will be blessed because of your children. All these things will happen because you have obeyed me."

¹⁹Then Abraham returned to his servants. They started out together for Beersheba. And Abraham stayed in Beersheba.

Nahor's Sons

²⁰ Some time later Abraham was told,
"Milkah has become a mother. She has had sons by your brother Nahor.
²¹ Uz was born first. Then came his brother Buz.
Kemuel was born next. He became the father of Aram.
²² Milkah's other sons are Kesed, Hazo, Pildash, Jidlaph and Bethuel."
²³ Bethuel became the father of Rebekah.

Milkah had the eight sons by Abraham's brother Nahor.

²⁴ Nahor had a concubine named Reumah. She also had sons.
They were Tebah, Gaham, Tahash and Maakah.

Sarah Dies

23 Sarah lived to be 127 years old. ²She died at Kiriath Arba. Kiriath Arba is also called Hebron. It's in the land of Canaan. Sarah's death made Abraham very sad. He went to the place where her body was lying. There he wept over her.

³Then Abraham got up from beside his wife's body. He said to the Hittites, ⁴"I'm an outsider. I'm a stranger among you. Sell me some property where I can bury those in my family who die. Then I can bury my wife."

⁵The Hittites replied to Abraham, ⁶"Sir, listen to us. You are a mighty prince among us. Bury your wife in the best place we have to bury our dead. None of us will refuse to sell you a place to bury her."

⁷Then Abraham bowed down in front of the Hittites, the people of the land. ⁸He said to them, "If you are willing to let me bury my wife, then listen to me. Speak to Zohar's son Ephron for me. ⁹Ask him to sell me the cave of Machpelah. It belongs to him and is at the end of his field. Ask him to sell it to me for the full price. I want it as a place to bury my dead wife among you."

¹⁰Ephron the Hittite was sitting there among his people. He replied to Abraham. All of the Hittites who had come to the gate of his city heard him. ¹¹"No, sir," Ephron said. "Listen to me. I will give you the field. I'll also give you the cave that's in the field. I will give it to you in front of my people. Bury your wife."

¹²Again Abraham bowed down in front of the people of the land. ¹³He spoke to Ephron so they could hear him. He said, "Please listen to me. I'll pay the price of the field. Accept it from me. Then I can bury my wife there."

¹⁴Ephron answered Abraham, ¹⁵"Sir, listen to me. The land is worth ten pounds of silver. But what's that between the two of us? Bury your wife."

¹⁶Abraham agreed to Ephron's offer. He weighed out for Ephron the price he had

named. The Hittites there had heard the amount. The price was ten pounds of silver. Abraham measured it by the weights that were used by merchants.

¹⁷So Ephron sold his field to Abraham. The field was in Machpelah near Mamre. Abraham bought the field and the cave that was in it. He also bought all the trees that were inside the borders of the field. Everything was sold ¹⁸to Abraham as his property. He bought it in front of all the Hittites who had come to the gate of the city. ¹⁹Then Abraham buried his wife Sarah. He buried her in the cave in the field of Machpelah near Mamre in the land of Canaan. Mamre is at Hebron. ²⁰So the field and the cave that was in it were sold to Abraham by the Hittites. The property became a place to bury those who died in his family.

Abraham's Servant Finds a Wife for Isaac

24 By that time Abraham was very old. The LORD had blessed Abraham in every way. ²The best servant in his house was in charge of everything Abraham had. Abraham said to him, "Put your hand under my thigh. ³The LORD is the God of heaven and the God of earth. I want you to make a promise to me in his name. I'm living among the people of Canaan. But I want you to promise me that you won't get a wife for my son from their daughters. ⁴Instead, promise me that you will go to my country and to my own relatives. Get a wife for my son Isaac from there."

⁵The servant asked Abraham, "What if the woman doesn't want to come back with me to this land? Then should I take your son back to the country you came from?"

⁶"Make sure you don't take my son back there," Abraham said. ⁷"The LORD, the God of heaven, took me away from my father's family. He brought me out of my own land. He made me a promise. He said, 'I will give this land to your family after you.' The LORD will send his angel ahead of you. So you will be able to get a wife for my son from there. ⁸The woman may not want to come back with you. If she doesn't, you will be free from your promise. But don't take my son back there." ⁹So the servant put his hand under Abraham's thigh. He promised to do what his master wanted.

Gen. 23:19-20 We're already twenty-three chapters in and this is the first burial recorded in the Bible. I wonder if that's because people back then sometimes lived to be hundreds of years old. Can you imagine fitting 800 candles on a cake? It would have to be pretty big. Mmm . . . 800 pieces of birthday cake. . . .

¹⁰The servant chose ten of his master's camels and left. He loaded the camels with all kinds of good things from his master. He started out for Aram Naharaim and made his way to the town of Nahor. ¹¹He stopped near the well outside the town. There he made the camels get down on their knees. It was almost evening, the time when women go out to get water.

¹²Then he prayed, "LORD, you are the God of my master Abraham. Make me successful today. Be kind to my master Abraham. ¹³I'm standing beside this spring. The daughters of the people who live in the town are coming out here to get water. ¹⁴I will speak to a young woman. I'll say to her, 'Please lower your jar so I can have a drink.' Suppose she says, 'Have a drink of water, and I'll get some for your camels too.' Then let her be the one you have chosen for your servant Isaac. That's how I'll know you have been kind to my master."

¹⁵Before he had finished praying, Rebekah came out. She was carrying a jar on her shoulder. She was the daughter of Milkah's son Bethuel. Milkah was the wife of Abraham's brother Nahor. ¹⁶The young woman was very beautiful. No man had ever slept with her. She went down to the spring. She filled her jar and came up again.

[17]The servant hurried to meet her. He said, "Please give me a little water from your jar."

[18]"Have a drink, sir," she said. She quickly lowered the jar to her hands and gave him a drink.

[19]After she had given him a drink, she said, "I'll get water for your camels too. I'll keep doing it until they have had enough to drink." [20]So she quickly emptied her jar into the stone tub. Then she ran back to the well to get more water. She got enough for all his camels. [21]The man didn't say a word. He watched her closely. He wanted to learn whether the LORD had given him success on the journey he had made.

[22]The camels finished drinking. Then the man took out a gold nose ring. It weighed about a fifth of an ounce. He also took out two gold bracelets. They weighed about four ounces. [23]Then he asked, "Whose daughter are you? And please tell me something else. Is there room in your father's house for us? Can we spend the night there?"

[24]She answered, "I'm the daughter of Bethuel. He's the son Milkah had by Nahor." [25]She continued, "We have plenty of straw and feed for your camels. We also have room for you to spend the night."

[26]Then the man bowed down and worshiped the LORD. [27]He said, "I praise the LORD, the God of my master Abraham. The LORD hasn't stopped being kind and faithful to my master. The LORD has led me on this journey. He has brought me to the house of my master's relatives."

[28]The young woman ran home. She told her mother's family what had happened. [29]Rebekah had a brother named Laban. He hurried out to the spring to meet the man. [30]Laban had seen the nose ring. He had seen the bracelets on his sister's arms. And he had heard Rebekah tell what the man had said to her. So Laban went out to the man. He found him standing by the camels near the spring. [31]"The LORD has given you his blessing," he said. "So come with me. Why are you standing out here? I've prepared my house for you. I also have a place for the camels."

[32]So the man went to the house. The camels were unloaded. Straw and feed were brought for the camels. And water was brought for him and his men to wash their feet. [33]Then food was placed in front of him. But he said, "I won't eat until I've told you what I have to say."

"Then tell us," Laban said.

[34]So he said, "I am Abraham's servant. [35]The LORD has blessed my master greatly, and he has become rich. The LORD has given him sheep and cattle, silver and gold. He has also given him male and female servants, camels and donkeys. [36]My master's wife Sarah had a son by him when she was old. He has given that son everything he owns. [37]My master made me promise him. He said, 'I'm living in the land of the people of Canaan. But promise me that you won't get a wife for my son from their daughters. [38]Instead, go to my father's family and to my own relatives. Get a wife for my son there.'

[39]"Then I asked my master, 'What if the woman won't come back with me?'

[40]"He replied, 'I have walked faithfully with the LORD. He will send his angel with you. He will give you success on your journey. So you will be able to get a wife for my son. She will be from my own relatives and from my father's family. [41]When you go to my relatives, suppose they refuse to give her to you. Then you will be free from the promise you made to me.'

[42]"Today I came to the spring. I said, 'LORD, you are the God of my master Abraham. Please make me successful on this journey I've made. [43]I'm standing beside this spring. A young woman will come out to get water. I'll say to her, "Please let me drink a little water from your jar." [44]Suppose she says, "Have a drink of water, and I'll get some for your camels too." Then let her be the one the LORD has chosen for my master's son.'

[45]"Before I finished praying in my heart, Rebekah came out. She was carrying a jar on her shoulder. She went down to the spring and got water. I said to her, 'Please give me a drink.'

[46]"She quickly lowered her jar from her shoulder. She said, 'Have a drink, and I'll get water for your camels too.' So I drank. She also got water for the camels.

[47]"I asked her, 'Whose daughter are you?'

"She said, 'The daughter of Bethuel. He's the son Milkah had by Nahor.'

ADVENTURES IN ODYSSEY

God guided Isaac to the person he should marry in Genesis 24. Jack, Joanne, Eugene, Katrina, and Whit all had to seek God's guidance about marriage in "For Whom the Wedding Bells Toll" (A#29).

"Then I put the ring in her nose. I put the bracelets on her arms. ⁴⁸And I bowed down and worshiped the LORD. I praised the LORD, the God of my master Abraham. He had led me on the right road. He had led me to get for my master's son the granddaughter of my master's brother. ⁴⁹Now will you be kind and faithful to my master? If you will, tell me. And if you won't, tell me. Then I'll know which way to turn."

⁵⁰Laban and Bethuel answered, "The LORD has done all of this. We can't say anything to you one way or the other. ⁵¹Here is Rebekah. Take her and go. Let her become the wife of your master's son, just as the LORD has said."

⁵²Abraham's servant heard what they said. So he bowed down to the LORD with his face to the ground. ⁵³He brought out gold and silver jewelry and articles of clothing. He gave all of them to Rebekah. He also gave expensive gifts to her brother and her mother. ⁵⁴Then Abraham's servant and the men who were with him ate and drank. They spent the night there.

When they got up the next morning, Abraham's servant said, "Send me back to my master."

⁵⁵But her brother and her mother replied, "Let the young woman stay with us ten days or so. Then you can go."

⁵⁶But he said to them, "Don't make me wait. The LORD has given me success on my journey. Send me on my way so I can go to my master."

⁵⁷Then they said, "Let's get Rebekah and ask her about it." ⁵⁸So they sent for her and asked, "Will you go with this man?"

"Yes, I'll go," she said.

⁵⁹So they sent their sister Rebekah on her way with Abraham's servant and his men. They also sent Rebekah's servant with her. ⁶⁰And they gave Rebekah their blessing. They said to her,

"Dear sister, may your family grow
     by thousands and thousands.
May they take over
     the cities of their enemies."

⁶¹Then Rebekah and her female servants got ready. They got on their camels to go back with the man. So Abraham's servant took Rebekah and left.

⁶²By that time Isaac had come from Beer Lahai Roi. He was living in the Negev Desert. ⁶³One evening he went out to the field. He wanted to spend some time thinking. When he looked up, he saw camels approaching. ⁶⁴Rebekah also looked up and saw Isaac. She got down from her camel. ⁶⁵She asked the servant, "Who is that man in the field coming to meet us?"

"He's my master," the servant answered. So she covered her face with her veil.

⁶⁶Then the servant told Isaac everything he had done. ⁶⁷Isaac brought Rebekah into the tent that had belonged to his mother Sarah. And he married Rebekah. She became his wife, and he loved her. So Isaac was comforted after his mother died.

Abraham Dies

25 Abraham had married another woman. Her name was Keturah. ²She had Zimran, Jokshan, Medan, Midian, Ishbak and Shuah by Abraham. ³Jokshan was the father of Sheba and Dedan. The children of Dedan were the Ashurites, the Letushites and the Leummites. ⁴The sons of Midian were Ephah, Epher, Hanok, Abida and Eldaah. All of them were members of Keturah's family line.

⁵Abraham left everything he owned to Isaac. ⁶But while he was still living, he gave gifts to the sons of his concubines. Then he sent them away from his son Isaac. He sent them to the land of the east.

[7]Abraham lived a total of 175 years. [8]He took his last breath and died when he was very old. He had lived a very long time. Then he joined the members of his family who had already died. [9]Abraham's sons Isaac and Ishmael. They put his body in the cave of Machpelah near Mamre. It was in the field of Ephron, the son of Zohar the Hittite. [10]Abraham had bought the field from the Hittites. He was buried there with his wife Sarah. [11]After Abraham died, God blessed his son Isaac. At that time Isaac was living near Beer Lahai Roi.

The Sons of Ishmael

[12]Here is the story of the family line of Abraham's son Ishmael. Hagar gave birth to Ishmael by Abraham. Hagar was Sarah's slave from Egypt.

[13]Here are the names of the sons of Ishmael. They are listed in the order they were born.

Nebaioth was Ishmael's oldest son.
Then came Kedar, Adbeel, Mibsam,
[14]Mishma, Dumah, Massa,
[15]Hadad, Tema, Jetur,
Naphish and Kedemah.

[16]All of them were Ishmael's sons. They were rulers of 12 tribes. They all lived in their own settlements and camps.

[17]Ishmael lived a total of 137 years. Then he took his last breath and died. He joined the members of his family who had already died. [18]His children settled in the area between Havilah and Shur. It was near the eastern border of Egypt, as you go toward Ashur. Ishmael's children weren't friendly toward any of the tribes related to them.

Jacob and Esau

[19]Here is the story of the family line of Abraham's son Isaac.

Abraham was the father of Isaac. [20]Isaac was 40 years old when he married Rebekah. She was the daughter of Bethuel, the Aramean from Paddan Aram. She was also the sister of Laban, the Aramean. [21]Rebekah couldn't have children. So Isaac prayed to the LORD for her. And the LORD answered his prayer. His wife Rebekah became pregnant. [22]The babies struggled with each other inside her. She said, "Why is this happening to me?" So she went to ask the LORD what she should do.

[23]The LORD said to her,

"Two nations are in your body.
    Two tribes that are now inside you
        will be separated.
One nation will be stronger than the
        other.
    The older son will serve the
        younger one."

[24]The time came for Rebekah to have her babies. There were twin boys in her body. [25]The first one to come out was red. His whole body was covered with hair. So they named him Esau. [26]Then his brother came out. His hand was holding onto Esau's heel. So he was named Jacob. Isaac was 60 years old when Rebekah had them.

[27]The boys grew up. Esau became a skillful hunter. He liked the open country. But Jacob was content to stay at home among the tents. [28]Isaac liked the meat of wild animals. So Esau was his favorite son. But Rebekah's favorite was Jacob.

[29]One day Jacob was cooking some stew. Esau came in from the open country. He was very hungry. [30]He said to Jacob, "Quick! I'm very hungry! Let me have

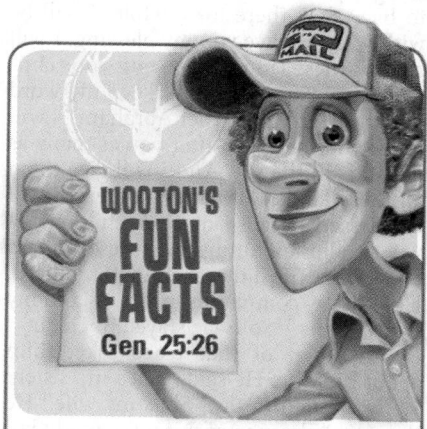

WOOTON'S FUN FACTS
Gen. 25:26

Like Jacob and Esau, my twin brother Wellington and I don't get along very well. However, unlike my brother and me, Jacob and Esau were fraternal twins, so they weren't identical.

BiBLE ADVENTURES

Bernard told the story of Jacob
and Esau in "Two Brothers . . .
and Bernard" (A#20).

some of that red stew!" That's why he was
also named Edom.

³¹Jacob replied, "First sell me the rights
that belong to you as the oldest son in the
family."

³²"Look, I'm dying of hunger," Esau said.
"What good are those rights to me?"

³³But Jacob said, "First promise to sell
me your rights." So Esau promised to do
it. He sold Jacob all the rights that belonged to him as the oldest son.

³⁴Then Jacob gave Esau some bread
and some lentil stew. Esau ate and drank.
Then he got up and left.

So Esau didn't value the rights that belonged to him as the oldest son.

Isaac and Abimelek

26 There was very little food in the
land. The same thing had been true
earlier, in Abraham's time. Isaac went to
Abimelek in Gerar. Abimelek was the
king of the Philistines. ²The LORD appeared to Isaac and said, "Do not go down
to Egypt. Live in the land where I tell you
to live. ³Stay there for a while. I will be
with you and give you my blessing. I will
give all these lands to you and your children after you. And I will keep my word
that I gave to your father Abraham. ⁴I will
make your children after you as many as
the stars in the sky. And I will give them
all these lands. All nations on earth will
be blessed because of your children. ⁵I
will do all these things because Abraham
obeyed me. He did everything I required.
He kept my commands, my rules and my
instructions." ⁶So Isaac stayed in Gerar.

⁷The men of that place asked him
about his wife. He said, "She's my sister."
He was afraid to say, "She's my wife." He
thought, "The men of this place might kill
me because of Rebekah. She's a beautiful
woman."

⁸Isaac had been there a long time. One
day Abimelek, the king of the Philistines,
looked down from a window. He saw Isaac

hugging and kissing his wife Rebekah. ⁹So
Abimelek sent for Isaac. He said, "She's
really your wife, isn't she? Why did you say
she was your sister?"

Isaac answered him, "I thought I might
lose my life because of her."

¹⁰Then Abimelek said, "What have you
done to us? What if one of the men slept
with your wife? Then you would have
made us guilty."

¹¹So Abimelek gave orders to all the
people. He said, "Anyone who harms
this man or his wife will surely be put to
death."

¹²Isaac planted crops in that land. That
same year he gathered 100 times more
than he planted. That was because the
LORD blessed him. ¹³Isaac became rich.
His wealth continued to grow until he became very rich. ¹⁴He had many flocks and
herds and servants. Isaac had so much that
the Philistines became jealous of him. ¹⁵So
they stopped up all the wells the servants
of his father Abraham had dug. They filled
them with dirt.

¹⁶Then Abimelek said to Isaac, "Move
away from us. You have become too powerful for us."

¹⁷So Isaac moved away from there.
He camped in the Valley of Gerar, where
he made his home. ¹⁸Isaac opened up the
wells again. They had been dug in the time
of his father Abraham. The Philistines
had stopped them up after Abraham
died. Isaac gave the wells the same names
his father had given them.

¹⁹Isaac's servants dug wells in the valley. There they discovered fresh water.
²⁰But the people of Gerar who took care
of their own herds argued with the people
who took care of Isaac's herds. "The water
is ours!" the people of Gerar said. So Isaac
named the well Esek. That's because they
argued with him. ²¹Then Isaac's servants
dug another well. They argued about that
one too. So he named it Sitnah. ²²Isaac
moved on from there and dug another
well. But no one argued about that one. So
he named it Rehoboth. He said, "Now the
LORD has given us room. Now we will be
successful in the land."

²³From there Isaac went up to Beersheba. ²⁴That night the LORD appeared
to him. He said, "I am the God of your
father Abraham. Do not be afraid. I am

WOOTON'S FUN FACTS

Gen. 26:16-33 Fighting over water rights in Israel has been going on for a long time. In fact, it's still going on today. That makes me sad.

with you. I will bless you. I will increase the number of your children because of my servant Abraham."

²⁵Isaac built an altar there and worshiped the Lord. There he set up his tent. And there his servants dug a well.

²⁶During that time, Abimelek had come to him from Gerar. His personal adviser, Ahuzzath, had come with him. So had his army commander, Phicol. ²⁷Isaac asked them, "Why have you come to me? You were angry with me and sent me away."

²⁸They answered, "We saw clearly that the Lord was with you. So we said, 'There should be an agreement between us and you.' We want to make a peace treaty with you. ²⁹Give us your word that you won't harm us. We didn't harm us. We always treated you well. We sent you away peacefully. And now the Lord has blessed you."

³⁰Then Isaac had a feast prepared for them. They ate and drank. ³¹Early the next morning the men made a treaty with each other. Then Isaac sent the men of Gerar on their way. And they left peacefully.

³²That day Isaac's servants came to him. They told him about the well they had dug. They said, "We've found water!" ³³So he named it Shibah. To this day the name of the town has been Beersheba.

Jacob Takes Esau's Blessing

³⁴When Esau was 40 years old, he got married to Judith. She was the daughter of Beeri the Hittite. Esau also married Basemath. She was the daughter of Elon the Hittite. ³⁵Isaac and Rebekah became very upset because Esau had married Hittite women.

27 Isaac had become old. His eyes were so weak he couldn't see anymore. One day he called for his older son Esau. He said to him, "My son."

"Here I am," he answered.

²Isaac said, "I'm an old man now. And I don't know when I'll die. ³Now then, get your weapons. Get your bow and arrows. Go out to the open country. Hunt some wild animals for me. ⁴Prepare for me the kind of tasty food I like. Bring it to me to eat. Then I'll give you my blessing before I die."

⁵Rebekah was listening when Isaac spoke to his son Esau. Esau left for the open country. He went to hunt for a wild animal and bring it back. ⁶Then Rebekah said to her son Jacob, "Look, I heard your father speaking to your brother Esau. ⁷He said, 'Bring me a wild animal. Prepare some tasty food for me to eat. Then I'll give you my blessing before I die. The Lord will be my witness.'" ⁸Rebekah continued, "My son, listen carefully. Do what I tell you. ⁹Go out to the flock. Bring me two of the finest young goats. I will prepare tasty food for your father. I'll make it just the way he likes it. ¹⁰I want you to take it to your father to eat. Then he'll give you his blessing before he dies."

¹¹Jacob said to his mother Rebekah, "My brother Esau's body is covered with hair. But my skin is smooth. ¹²What if my father touches me? He would know I was trying to trick him. He would curse me instead of giving me a blessing."

¹³His mother said to him, "My son, let the curse be on me. Just do what I say. Go and get the goats for me."

¹⁴So he went and got the goats. He brought them to his mother. And she prepared some tasty food. She made it just the way his father liked it. ¹⁵The clothes of her older son Esau were in her house. She took Esau's best clothes and put them on her younger son Jacob. ¹⁶She covered his hands with the skins of the goats. She also covered the smooth part of his neck with them. ¹⁷Then she handed to her son

Jacob the tasty food and the bread she had made.

¹⁸He went to his father and said, "My father."

"Yes, my son," Isaac answered. "Who is it?"

¹⁹Jacob said to his father, "I'm your oldest son Esau. I've done as you told me. Please sit up. Eat some of my wild meat. Then give me your blessing."

²⁰Isaac asked his son, "How did you find it so quickly, my son?"

"The LORD your God gave me success," he replied.

²¹Then Isaac said to Jacob, "Come near so I can touch you, my son. I want to know whether you really are my son Esau."

²²Jacob went close to his father. Isaac touched him and said, "The voice is the voice of Jacob. But the hands are the hands of Esau." ²³Isaac didn't recognize Jacob. Jacob's hands were covered with hair like those of his brother Esau. So Isaac blessed him. ²⁴"Are you really my son Esau?" he asked.

"I am," Jacob replied.

²⁵Isaac said, "My son, bring me some of your wild meat to eat. Then I'll give you my blessing."

Jacob brought it to him. So Isaac ate. Jacob also brought some wine. And Isaac drank. ²⁶Then Jacob's father Isaac said to him, "Come here, my son. Kiss me."

²⁷So Jacob went to him and kissed him. When Isaac smelled the clothes, he gave Jacob his blessing. He said,

"It really is the smell of my son.
    It's like the smell of a field
    that the LORD has blessed.
²⁸ May God give you dew from heaven.
    May he give you the richness of the
        earth.
    May he give you plenty of grain and
        fresh wine.
²⁹ May nations serve you.
    May they bow down to you.
    Rule over your brothers.
    May the sons of your mother bow
        down to you.
    May those who curse you be cursed.
    And may those who bless you be
        blessed."

³⁰When Isaac finished blessing him, Jacob left his father. Just then his brother

Wooton's FUN FACTS

Gen. 27:14-19

I used to worry that the stew that Rachel made had moose meat in it. Then I found out that no moose live in Israel.

Esau came in from hunting. ³¹He too prepared some tasty food. He brought it to his father. Then Esau said to him, "My father, please sit up. Eat some of my wild meat. Then give me your blessing."

³²His father Isaac asked him, "Who are you?"

"I'm your son," he answered. "I'm Esau, your oldest son."

³³Isaac began to shake all over. He said, "Then who hunted a wild animal and brought it to me? I ate it just before you came. I gave him my blessing. And he will certainly be blessed!"

³⁴Esau heard his father's words. Then he yelled loudly and bitterly. He said to his father, "Bless me! Bless me too, my father!"

³⁵But Isaac said, "Your brother came and tricked me. He took your blessing."

³⁶Esau said, "Isn't Jacob just the right name for him? This is the second time he has taken advantage of me. First, he took my rights as the oldest son. And now he's taken my blessing!" Then Esau asked, "Haven't you saved any blessing for me?"

³⁷Isaac answered Esau, "I've made him ruler over you. I've made all his relatives serve him. And I've provided him with grain and fresh wine. So what can I possibly do for you, my son?"

[38] Esau said to his father, "Do you have only one blessing, my father? Bless me too, my father!" Then Esau wept loudly.

[39] His father Isaac answered him,

"You will live far away from the fruit
of the earth.
You will live far away from the dew
of heaven above.
[40] You will live by using the sword.
And you will serve your brother.
But you will grow restless.
Then you will throw off the heavy
load
he has caused you to carry."

[41] Esau was angry with Jacob. He was angry because of the blessing his father had given to Jacob. He said to himself, "The days of sorrow over my father's death are near. Then I'll kill my brother Jacob."

[42] Rebekah was told what her older son Esau had said. So she sent for her younger son Jacob. She said to him, "Your brother Esau is planning to get back at you by killing you. [43] Now then, my son, do what I say. Run away at once to my brother Laban in Harran. [44] Stay with him until your brother's anger calms down. [45] When he forgets what you did to him, I'll let you know. Then you can come back from there. Why should I lose both of you in one day?"

[46] Then Rebekah spoke to Isaac. She said, "I'm sick of living because of Esau's Hittite wives. Suppose Jacob also marries a Hittite woman. If he does, my life won't be worth living."

28 So Isaac called for Jacob and blessed him. Then he commanded him, "Don't get married to a Canaanite woman. [2] Go at once to Paddan Aram. Go to the house of your mother's father Bethuel. Find a wife for yourself there. Take her from among the daughters of your mother's brother Laban. [3] May the Mighty God bless you. May he give you children. May he make your family larger until you become a community of nations. [4] May he give you and your children after you the blessing he gave to Abraham. Then you can take over the land where you now live as an outsider. It's the land God gave to Abraham." [5] Isaac sent Jacob on his way.

WHAT ABOUT YOU?

You've probably heard this at home: "Kids, company's coming over, so be on your best behavior. No name-calling, teasing, or fighting!"

It seems like we behave the worst toward people we're closest to. Family is family— so you have to forgive each other, right?

In the Adventures in Odyssey episode "Two Brothers and Bernard," Erica is fed up with the annoying, selfish things her little sister Hayley does. So Bernard Walton tells Erica about Jacob, who tricked his brother Esau out of his most valuable possession. Esau hated Jacob enough to try to kill him. In the end, the brothers' feud kept them apart for more than 20 years.

Erica then realizes she isn't really mad at Hayley. She wants to be friends and is willing to overlook a few offenses to make that happen. Of course, now it's up to Hayley to be more respectful of her big sister. Both Erica and Hayley have some growing up to do.

By the way, the next time Jacob saw Esau, he humbled himself and gave Esau expensive gifts and high praises. He realized that forgiveness was worth any price.

Instead of excusing the way we treat our family members because they are family, what if we treat them even better than we treat strangers? The next time you're ready to tease a sibling or disrespect a parent or grandparent, remember how Jacob's actions affected his family. Seek peace by putting others first.

Jacob went to Paddan Aram. He went to Laban, the son of Bethuel the Aramean. Laban was Rebekah's brother. And Rebekah was the mother of Jacob and Esau.

[6]Esau found out that Isaac had blessed Jacob and had sent him to Paddan Aram. Isaac wanted him to get a wife from there. Esau heard that when Isaac blessed Jacob, he commanded him, "Don't get married to a woman from Canaan." [7]Esau also learned that Jacob had obeyed his father and mother and had gone to Paddan Aram. [8]Then Esau realized how much his father Isaac disliked Canaanite women. [9]So he went to Ishmael and married Mahalath. She was the sister of Nebaioth and the daughter of Abraham's son Ishmael. Esau added her to the wives he already had.

Jacob Has a Dream at Bethel

[10]Jacob left Beersheba and started out for Harran. [11]He reached a certain place and stopped for the night. The sun had already set. He took one of the stones there and placed it under his head. Then he lay down to sleep. [12]In a dream he saw a stairway standing on the earth. Its top reached to heaven. The angels of God were going up and coming down on it. [13]The LORD stood beside the stairway. He said, "I am the LORD. I am the God of your grandfather Abraham and the God of Isaac. I will give you and your children after you the land you are lying on. [14]They will be like the dust of the earth that can't be counted. They will spread out to the west and to the east. They will spread out to the north and to the south. All nations on earth will be blessed because of you and your children after you. [15]I am with you. I will watch over you everywhere you go. And I will bring you back to this land. I will not leave you until I have done what I have promised you."

[16]Jacob woke up from his sleep. Then he thought, "The LORD is surely in this place. And I didn't even know it." [17]Jacob was afraid. He said, "How holy this place is! This must be the house of God. This is the gate of heaven."

[18]Early the next morning Jacob took the stone he had placed under his head. He set it up as a sacred stone. And he poured olive oil on top of it. [19]He named that place Bethel. But the city used to be called Luz.

[20]Then Jacob made a promise. He said, "May God be with me. May he watch over me on this journey I'm taking. May he give me food to eat and clothes to wear. [21]May he do as he has promised so that I can return safely to my father's home. Then you, LORD, will be my God. [22]This stone I've set up as a sacred stone will be God's house. And I'll give you a tenth of everything you give me."

Jacob Arrives in Paddan Aram

29 Then Jacob continued on his journey. He came to the land where the eastern tribes lived. [2]There he saw a well in the open country. Three flocks of sheep were lying near it. The flocks were given water from the well. The stone over the opening of the well was large. [3]All the flocks would gather there. The shepherds would roll the stone away from the well's opening. They would give water to the sheep. Then they would put the stone back in its place over the opening of the well.

[4]Jacob asked the shepherds, "My friends, where are you from?"

"We're from Harran," they replied.

[5]He said to them, "Do you know Nahor's grandson Laban?"

"Yes, we know him," they answered.

[6]Then Jacob asked them, "How is he?"

"He's fine," they said. "Here comes his daughter Rachel with the sheep."

[7]"Look," he said, "the sun is still high in the sky. It's not time for the flocks to be brought together. Give water to the sheep and take them back to the grasslands."

[8]"We can't," they replied. "We have to wait until all the flocks are brought together. The stone has to be rolled away from the opening of the well. Then we'll give water to the sheep."

[9]He was still talking with them when Rachel came with her father's sheep. It was her job to take care of the flock. [10]Rachel was the daughter of Laban, Jacob's uncle. When Jacob saw Rachel with Laban's sheep, he went over to the well. He rolled the stone away from the opening. He gave water to his uncle's sheep. [11]Jacob kissed Rachel. Then he began to cry because he was so happy. [12]He had told Rachel he was a relative of her father. He had also said he was Rebekah's son. Rachel ran and told her father what Jacob had said.

[13]As soon as Laban heard the news about his sister's son Jacob, he hurried to meet him. Laban hugged Jacob and kissed him. Then Laban brought him to his home. There Jacob told him everything. [14]Then Laban said to him, "You are my own flesh and blood."

Jacob Marries Leah and Rachel

Jacob stayed with Laban for a whole month. [15]Then Laban said to him, "You are one of my relatives. But is that any reason for you to work for me for nothing? Tell me what your pay should be."

[16]Laban had two daughters. The name of the older one was Leah. And the name of the younger one was Rachel. [17]Leah was plain, but Rachel was beautiful. She had a nice figure. [18]Jacob was in love with Rachel. He said to Laban, "I'll work for you for seven years so I can marry your younger daughter Rachel."

[19]Laban said, "It's better for me to give her to you than to some other man. Stay here with me." [20]So Jacob worked for seven years so he could marry Rachel. But they seemed like only a few days to him because he loved her so much.

[21]Then Jacob said to Laban, "Give me my wife. I've completed my time. I want to sleep with her."

[22]So Laban brought all the people of the place together and had a feast prepared. [23]But when evening came, he gave his daughter Leah to Jacob. And Jacob slept with her. [24]Laban gave his female servant Zilpah to his daughter as her servant.

[25]When Jacob woke up the next morning, there was Leah next to him! So he said to Laban, "What have you done to me? I worked for you so I could marry Rachel, didn't I? Why did you trick me?"

[26]Laban replied, "It isn't our practice here to give the younger daughter to be married before the older one. [27]Complete this daughter's wedding week. Then we'll give you the younger one also. But you will have to work for another seven years."

[28]So Jacob completed the week with Leah. Then Laban gave him his daughter Rachel to be his wife. [29]Laban gave his female servant Bilhah to his daughter Rachel as her servant. [30]Jacob slept with Rachel also. He loved Rachel more than he loved Leah. And he worked for Laban for another seven years.

Jacob Becomes the Father of Many Children

[31]The LORD saw that Jacob didn't love Leah as much as he loved Rachel. So he let Leah have children. But Rachel wasn't able to have children. [32]Leah became pregnant. She had a son. She named him Reuben. She said, "The LORD has seen me suffer. Surely my husband will love me now."

[33]She became pregnant again. She had a son. Then she said, "The LORD heard that Jacob doesn't love me very much. That's why the LORD gave me this one too." So she named him Simeon.

[34]She became pregnant again. She had a son. Then she said, "Now at last my husband will value me. I have had three sons by him." So the boy was named Levi.

[35]She became pregnant again. She had a son. Then she said, "This time I'll praise the LORD." So she named him Judah. Then she stopped having children.

30 Rachel saw that she wasn't having any children by Jacob. So she became jealous of her sister. She said to Jacob, "Give me children, or I'll die!"

[2]Jacob became angry with her. He said, "Do you think I'm God? He's the one who has kept you from having children."

[3]Then she said, "Here's my servant Bilhah. Sleep with her so that she can have children for me. Then I too can have a family through her."

[4]So Rachel gave Jacob her servant Bilhah as a wife. Jacob slept with her. [5]And Bilhah became pregnant. She had a son by him. [6]Then Rachel said, "God has stood up for my rights. He has listened to my prayer and given me a son." So she named him Dan.

[7]Rachel's servant Bilhah became pregnant again. She had a second son by Jacob. [8]Then Rachel said, "I've had a great struggle with my sister. Now I've won." So she named him Naphtali.

[9]Leah saw that she had stopped having children. So she gave her servant Zilpah to Jacob as a wife. [10]Leah's servant Zilpah had a son by Jacob. [11]Then Leah said, "What good fortune!" So she named him Gad.

[12]Leah's servant Zilpah had a second son by Jacob. [13]Then Leah said, "I'm so

happy! The women will call me happy." So she named him Asher.

[14]While the wheat harvest was being gathered, Reuben went out into the fields. He found some mandrake plants. He brought them to his mother Leah. Rachel said to Leah, "Please give me some of your son's mandrakes."

[15]But Leah said to her, "Isn't it enough that you took my husband away? Are you going to take my son's mandrakes too?"

Rachel said, "All right. Jacob can sleep with you tonight if you give me your son's mandrakes."

[16]Jacob came in from the fields that evening. Leah went out to meet him. "You have to sleep with me tonight," she said. "I've traded my son's mandrakes for that time with you." So he slept with her that night.

[17]God listened to Leah. She became pregnant and had a fifth son by Jacob. [18]Then Leah said, "God has rewarded me because I gave my female servant to my husband." So she named the boy Issachar.

[19]Leah became pregnant again. She had a sixth son by Jacob. [20]Then Leah said, "God has given me a priceless gift. This time my husband will treat me with honor. I've had six sons by him." So she named the boy Zebulun.

[21]Some time later she had a daughter. She named her Dinah.

[22]Then God listened to Rachel. He showed concern for her. He made it possible for her to have children. [23]She became pregnant and had a son. Then she said, "God has taken away my shame." [24]She said, "May the LORD give me another son." So she named him Joseph.

Jacob Becomes the Owner of Large Flocks

[25]After Rachel had Joseph, Jacob spoke to Laban. He said, "Send me on my way. I want to go back to my own home and country. [26]Give me my wives and children. I worked for you to get them. So I'll be on my way. You know how much work I've done for you."

[27]But Laban said to him, "If you are pleased with me, stay here. I've discovered that the LORD has blessed me because of you." [28]He continued, "Name your pay. I'll give it to you."

[29]Jacob said to him, "You know how hard I've worked for you. You know that your livestock has done better under my care. [30]You had only a little before I came. But that little has become a lot. The LORD has blessed you everywhere I've been. But when can I do something for my own family?"

[31]"What should I give you?" Laban asked.

"Don't give me anything," Jacob replied. "Just do one thing for me. Then I'll go on taking care of your flocks and watching over them. [32]Let me go through all your flocks today. Let me remove every speckled or spotted sheep. Let me remove every dark-colored lamb. Let me remove every speckled or spotted goat. They will be my pay. [33]My honesty will be a witness about me in days to come. It will be a witness every time you check on what you have paid me. Suppose I have a goat that doesn't have speckles or spots. Or suppose I have a lamb that isn't dark colored. Then it will be considered stolen."

[34]"I agree," said Laban. "Let's do what you have said." [35]That same day Laban removed all the male goats that had stripes or spots. He removed all the female goats that had speckles or spots. They were the ones that had white on them. He also removed all the dark-colored lambs. He had his sons take care of them. [36]Then he put a journey of three days between himself and Jacob. But Jacob continued to take care of the rest of Laban's flocks.

[37]Jacob took freshly cut branches from poplar, almond and plane trees. He made white stripes on the branches by peeling off their bark. [38]Then he placed the peeled branches in all the stone tubs where the animals drank water. He placed them there so they would be right in front of the flocks when they came to drink. The flocks were ready to mate when they came to drink. [39]So they mated in front of the branches. And the flocks gave birth to striped, speckled or spotted little ones. [40]Jacob put the little ones of the flock to one side by themselves. But he made the older ones face the striped and dark-colored animals that belonged to Laban. In that way, he made separate flocks for himself. He didn't put them with Laban's animals. [41]Every time the stronger females

were ready to mate, Jacob would place the branches in the stone tubs. He would place them in front of the animals so they would mate near the branches. ⁴²But if the animals were weak, he wouldn't place the branches there. So the weak animals went to Laban. And the strong ones went to Jacob. ⁴³That's how Jacob became very rich. He became the owner of large flocks. He also had many male and female servants. And he had many camels and donkeys.

Jacob Runs Away From Laban

31 Jacob heard what Laban's sons were saying. "Jacob has taken everything our father owned," they said. "He has gained all this wealth from what belonged to our father." ²Jacob noticed that Laban's feelings toward him had changed.

³Then the LORD spoke to Jacob. He said, "Go back to your father's land and to your relatives. I will be with you."

⁴So Jacob sent word to Rachel and Leah. He told them to come out to the fields where his flocks were. ⁵He said to them, "I see that your father's feelings toward me have changed. But the God of my father has been with me. ⁶You know that I've worked for your father with all my strength. ⁷But your father has cheated me. He has changed my pay ten times. In spite of everything that's happened, God hasn't let him harm me. ⁸Sometimes Laban would say, 'The speckled ones will be your pay.' Then all the flocks had little ones with speckles. At other times he would say, 'The striped ones will be your pay.' Then all the flocks had little ones with stripes. ⁹So God has taken away your father's livestock and given them to me.

¹⁰"Once during the mating season I had a dream. In my dream I looked and saw male goats mating with the flock. The goats had stripes, speckles or spots. ¹¹The angel of God said to me in the dream, 'Jacob.' I answered, 'Here I am.' ¹²He said, 'Look around you. See the male goats mating with the flock. All of them have stripes, speckles or spots. That's because I have seen everything that Laban has been doing to you. ¹³I am the God of Bethel. That is where you poured olive oil on a sacred stone. There you made a promise to me. Now leave this land. Go back to your own land.' "

¹⁴Rachel and Leah replied, "Do we still have any share of our father's property? ¹⁵Doesn't our father think of us as outsiders? First he sold us. Now he has used up what he was paid for us. ¹⁶All the wealth God took away from our father really belongs to us and our children. So do what God has told you to do."

¹⁷Then Jacob put his children and wives on camels. ¹⁸He drove all his livestock ahead of him. He also took with him everything he had acquired in Paddan Aram. He left to go to his father Isaac in the land of Canaan.

¹⁹Laban had gone to clip the wool from his sheep. While he was gone, Rachel stole the statues of the family gods that belonged to her father. ²⁰And that's not all. Jacob tricked Laban, the Aramean. He didn't tell him he was running away. ²¹So Jacob ran off with everything he had. He crossed the Euphrates River. And he headed for the hill country of Gilead.

Laban Chases Jacob

²²On the third day Laban was told that Jacob had run away. ²³He took his relatives with him and went after Jacob. Seven days later he caught up with him in the hill country of Gilead. ²⁴Then God came to Laban, the Aramean, in a dream at night. He said to him, "Be careful. Do not say anything to Jacob, whether it is good or bad."

²⁵Jacob had set up his tent in the hill country of Gilead. That's where Laban caught up with him. Laban and his relatives camped there too. ²⁶Laban said to Jacob, "What have you done? You have tricked me. You have taken my daughters away like prisoners of war. ²⁷Why did you run away in secret and trick me? Why didn't you tell me? Then I could have sent you away happily. We could have sung to the music of tambourines and harps. ²⁸You didn't even let me kiss my grandchildren and my daughters goodbye. You have done a foolish thing. ²⁹I have the power to harm you. But last night the God of your father spoke to me. He said, 'Be careful. Do not say anything to Jacob, whether it is good or bad.' ³⁰Now you have run away. You longed to go back to your father's home. But why did you have to steal the statues of my gods?"

³¹Jacob answered Laban, "I was afraid. I thought you would take your daughters away from me by force. ³²But if you find anyone who has the statues of your gods, that person will not remain alive. While our relatives are watching, look for yourself. See if there's anything of yours here with me. If you find anything belonging to you, take it." But Jacob didn't know that Rachel had stolen the statues.

³³So Laban went into Jacob's tent and Leah's tent. He went into the tent of their two female servants. But he didn't find anything. After he came out of Leah's tent, he entered Rachel's tent. ³⁴Rachel was the one who had taken the statues of Laban's family gods. She had put them inside her camel's saddle. She was sitting on them. Laban searched the whole tent. But he didn't find anything.

³⁵Rachel said to her father, "I'm sorry, sir. I can't get up for you right now. But don't be angry with me. I'm having my monthly period." So he searched everywhere but couldn't find the statues of his gods.

³⁶Jacob was very angry with Laban. "What is my crime?" he asked. "What have I done to you that you hunt me down like this? ³⁷You have searched through all my things. What have you found that belongs to your family? Put it here in front of your relatives and mine. Let them decide between the two of us.

³⁸"I've been with you for 20 years now. The little ones of your sheep and goats were not dead when they were born. I haven't eaten rams from your flocks. ³⁹I didn't bring you animals torn apart by wild beasts. I made up for the loss myself. Also, you made me pay for anything stolen by day or night. ⁴⁰And what was my life like? The heat burned me in the daytime. And it was so cold at night that I froze. I couldn't sleep. ⁴¹That's what it was like for the 20 years I was living with you. I worked for 14 years to marry your two daughters. I worked for six years to get my share of your flocks. You changed my pay ten times. ⁴²But the God of my father was with me. He is the God of Abraham and the God Isaac worshiped. If he hadn't been with me, you would surely have sent me away without anything to show for all my work. But God has seen my hard times. He has seen all the work my hands have done. So last night he warned you."

⁴³Laban answered Jacob, "The women are my daughters. The children are my children. The flocks are my flocks. Everything you see is mine. But what can I do today about these daughters of mine? What can I do about the children they've had? ⁴⁴Come now. Let's make a formal agreement, you and I. Let it be a witness between us."

⁴⁵So Jacob set up a stone as a way to remember. ⁴⁶He said to his relatives, "Get some stones." So they took stones and put them in a pile. And they ate there by it. ⁴⁷Laban named the pile of stones Jegar Sahadutha. Jacob named it Galeed.

⁴⁸Laban said, "This pile of stones is a witness between you and me today." That's why it was named Galeed. ⁴⁹It was also called Mizpah. That's because Laban said, "May the LORD keep watch between you and me when we are away from each other. ⁵⁰Don't treat my daughters badly. Don't get married to any women besides my daughters. There isn't anyone here to see what we're doing. But remember that God is a witness between you and me."

⁵¹Laban also said to Jacob, "Here is this pile of stones. And here is this stone I've set up. I've set them up between you and me. ⁵²This pile is a witness. And this stone is a witness. They are witnesses that I won't go past this pile to harm you. And they are witnesses that you won't go past this pile and this stone to harm me. ⁵³The God of Abraham and Nahor is also the God of their father. May their God decide which of us is right."

So Jacob made a promise using the name of the God his father Isaac worshiped. ⁵⁴He offered a sacrifice there in the hill country. And he invited his relatives to a meal. After they had eaten, they spent the night there.

⁵⁵Early the next morning Laban kissed his grandchildren and his daughters. He gave them his blessing. Then he left and returned home.

Jacob Gets Ready to Meet Esau

32 Jacob also went on his way. The angels of God met him. ²Jacob saw them. He said, "This is the army of God!" So he named that place Mahanaim.

³Jacob sent messengers ahead of him to his brother Esau. Esau lived in the land of Seir. It was also called the country of Edom. ⁴Jacob told the messengers what to do. He said, "Here's what you must tell my master Esau. 'Your servant Jacob says, "I've been staying with Laban. I've remained there until now. ⁵I have cattle and donkeys and sheep and goats. I also have male and female servants. Now I'm sending this message to you. I hope I can please you." ' "

⁶The messengers came back to Jacob. They said, "We went to your brother Esau. He's coming now to meet you. He has 400 men with him."

⁷Jacob was very worried and afraid. So he separated the people with him into two groups. He also separated the flocks and herds and camels. ⁸He thought, "Esau might come and attack one group. If he does, the group that's left can escape."

⁹Then Jacob prayed, "You are the God of my grandfather Abraham. You are the God of my father Isaac. LORD, you are the one who said to me, 'Go back to your country and your relatives. Then I will give you success.' ¹⁰You have been very kind and faithful to me. But I'm not worthy of any of this. When I crossed this Jordan River, all I had was my walking stick. But now I've become two camps. ¹¹Please save me from the hand of my brother Esau. I'm afraid he'll come and attack me and the mothers with their children. ¹²But you have said, 'I will surely give you success. I will make your children as many as the grains of sand on the seashore. People will not be able to count them.' "

¹³Jacob spent the night there. He chose a gift for his brother Esau from what he had with him. ¹⁴He chose 200 female goats and 20 male goats. He chose 200 female sheep and 20 male sheep. ¹⁵He chose 30 female camels with their little ones. He chose 40 cows and ten bulls. And he chose 20 female donkeys and ten male donkeys. ¹⁶He put each herd by itself. Then he put his servants in charge of them. He said to his servants, "Go on ahead of me. Keep some space between the herds."

¹⁷Jacob spoke to his servant who was leading the way. He said, "My brother Esau will meet you. He'll ask, 'Who is your master? Where are you going? And who owns all these animals in front of you?' ¹⁸Then say to Esau, 'They belong to your servant Jacob. They are a gift to you from him. And Jacob is coming behind us.' "

Jason's Jargon

GENESIS 32

Here's your next quest! Search this chapter for the word *Peniel.* Unusual word, I know. Peniel means to see the face of, or to have a vision of, God.

¹⁹He also spoke to the second and third servants. He told them and all the others who followed the herds what to do. He said, "Say the same thing to Esau when you meet him. ²⁰Make sure you say, 'Your servant Jacob is coming behind us.' " Jacob was thinking, "I'll make peace with him with these gifts I'm sending on ahead. When I see him later, maybe he'll welcome me." ²¹So Jacob's gifts went on ahead of him. But he himself spent the night in the camp.

Jacob Wrestles With God

²²That night Jacob got up. He took his two wives, his two female servants and his 11 sons and sent them across the Jabbok River. ²³After they had crossed the stream, he sent over everything he owned. ²⁴So Jacob was left alone. A man wrestled with him until morning. ²⁵The man saw that he couldn't win. So he touched the inside of Jacob's hip. As Jacob wrestled with the man, Jacob's hip was twisted. ²⁶Then the man said, "Let me go. It is morning."

But Jacob replied, "I won't let you go unless you bless me."

²⁷The man asked him, "What is your name?"

"Jacob," he answered.

²⁸Then the man said, "Your name will not be Jacob anymore. Instead, it will be Israel. You have wrestled with God and with people. And you have won."

²⁹Jacob said, "Please tell me your name."

But he replied, "Why do you want to know my name?" Then he blessed Jacob there.

³⁰So Jacob named the place Peniel. He said, "I saw God face to face. But I'm still alive!"

³¹The sun rose above Jacob as he passed by Peniel. He was limping because of his hip. ³²That's why the Israelites don't eat the meat attached to the inside of an animal's hip. They don't eat it to this day. It's because the inside of Jacob's hip was touched.

Jacob Meets Esau

33 Jacob looked and saw Esau coming with his 400 men! So Jacob separated the children. He put them with Leah, Rachel and the two female servants. ²He put the servants and their children in front. He put Leah and her children next. And he put Rachel and Joseph last. ³He himself went on ahead. As he came near his brother, he bowed down to the ground seven times.

⁴But Esau ran to meet Jacob. He hugged him and threw his arms around his neck. He kissed him, and they cried for joy. ⁵Then Esau looked around and saw the women and children. "Who are these people with you?" he asked.

Jacob answered, "They are the children God has so kindly given to me."

⁶Then the female servants and their children came near and bowed down. ⁷Next, Leah and her children came and bowed down. Last of all came Joseph and Rachel. They bowed down too.

⁸Esau asked, "Why did you send all those herds I saw?"

"I hoped I could do something to please you," Jacob replied.

⁹But Esau said, "I already have plenty, my brother. Keep what you have for yourself."

WHAT ABOUT YOU?

Let's talk about grudges. Pretend for a moment that grudges are menacing little trolls with big ears, bulbous noses, and beady eyes. They jump on your back and force you to carry them around. And they can get really heavy.

Suppose a kid makes fun of you at school. You get mad and refuse to forgive him, even though you know that's what Jesus would want you to do. So you carry a grudge. Now you're walking around with one of those ugly trolls on your back. As the day goes on, it starts to kick and claw, which is terribly distracting. At recess, it whispers in your ear, urging you to tell your friends how rotten that kid was. Meanwhile, the heavy load weighs you down.

How long will you let this go on? Wouldn't it be easier to let go of that nasty grudge and refuse to carry it around?

Conflict happens. Jesus taught us that showing forgiveness is the healthiest way to resolve it. How often should we forgive someone who wrongs us? Seven times? No, "not seven times," Jesus said, "but 77 times"! (See Matthew 18:21–22.) After all, that's the kind of forgiveness God has shown us.

What about you? Are you hurting yourself by carrying a grudge? If so, shake it off your back. It may help to talk with the person who offended you, though often it's better to just pray and ask God to help you forgive with the same love He shows toward us.

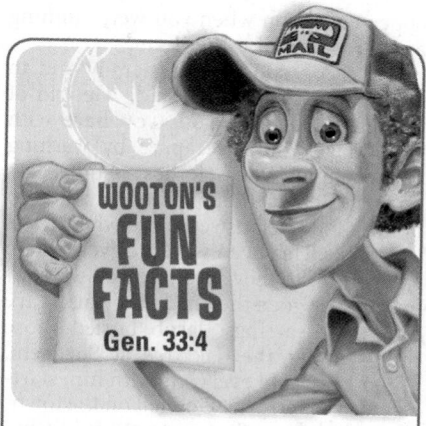

WOOTON'S
FUN
FACTS
Gen. 33:4

This story makes me hope that my brother and I will really get along one day. I'm willing to try.

¹⁰"No, please!" said Jacob. "If I've pleased you, accept this gift from me. Seeing your face is like seeing the face of God. You have welcomed me so kindly. ¹¹Please accept the present that was brought to you. God has given me so much. I have everything I need." Jacob wouldn't give in. So Esau accepted it.

¹²Then Esau said, "Let's be on our way. I'll go with you."

¹³But Jacob said to him, "You know that the children are young. You also know that I have to take care of the cows and female sheep that are feeding their little ones. If the animals are driven hard for just one day, all of them will die. ¹⁴So you go on ahead of me. I'll move along only as fast as the flocks and herds and the children can go. I'll go slowly until I come to you in Seir."

¹⁵Esau said, "Then let me leave some of my men with you."

"Why do that?" Jacob asked. "I just hope I've pleased you."

¹⁶So that day Esau started on his way back to Seir. ¹⁷But Jacob went to Sukkoth. There he built a place for himself. He also made shelters for his livestock. That's why the place is named Sukkoth.

¹⁸After Jacob came from Paddan Aram, he arrived safely at the city of Shechem in Canaan. He camped where he could see the city. ¹⁹For 100 pieces of silver he bought a piece of land. He got it from Hamor's sons. Hamor was the father of Shechem. Jacob set up his tent on that piece of land. ²⁰He also set up an altar there. He named it El Elohe Israel.

Simeon and Levi Kill the Men of Shechem

34 Dinah was the daughter Leah had by Jacob. Dinah went out to visit the women of the land. ²Hamor, the Hivite, was the ruler of that area. When his son Shechem saw Dinah, he took her and raped her. ³Then he longed for Jacob's daughter Dinah. He fell in love with her and spoke tenderly to her. ⁴Shechem said to his father Hamor, "Get me that young woman. I want her to be my wife."

⁵Jacob heard that his daughter Dinah had been raped. His sons were in the fields with his livestock. So he did nothing about it until they came home.

⁶Then Shechem's father Hamor went out to talk with Jacob. ⁷Jacob's sons had come in from the fields. They came as soon as they heard what had happened. They were shocked and very angry. Shechem had done a very terrible thing. He had forced Jacob's daughter to have sex with him. He had done something that should never be done in Israel.

⁸But Hamor said to Jacob and his sons, "My son Shechem wants your daughter. Please give her to him to be his wife. ⁹Let your people and ours get married to each other. Give us your daughters as our wives. You can have our daughters as your wives. ¹⁰You can live among us. Here is the land. Live in it. Trade in it. Buy property in it."

¹¹Then Shechem spoke to Dinah's father and brothers. He said, "I want to please you. I'll give you anything you ask for. ¹²Make the price for the bride as high as you want to. I'll pay you whatever you ask. Just give me the young woman. I want to marry her."

¹³Their sister Dinah had been raped. So Jacob's sons lied to Shechem and his father Hamor. ¹⁴They said to them, "We can't do it. We can't give our sister to a man who isn't circumcised. That would bring shame on us. ¹⁵We'll agree, but only on one condition. You will have to become like us. You will have to circumcise all your males. ¹⁶Then we'll give you our daughters as your wives. And we'll take your daughters as our wives. We'll live among you and become one big family with you. ¹⁷But if you

won't agree to be circumcised, then we'll take our sister and go."

¹⁸Their offer seemed good to Hamor and his son Shechem. ¹⁹The young man was the most honored of all his father's family. He didn't lose any time in doing what Dinah's father and brothers had said, because he was delighted with Jacob's daughter. ²⁰Hamor and his son Shechem went to the city gate. They spoke to the other men there. ²¹"These men are friendly toward us," they said. "Let them live in our land. Let them trade in it. The land has plenty of room for them. We can marry their daughters. And they can marry ours. ²²But they will agree to live with us as one big family only on one condition. All our males must be circumcised, just as they are. ²³Won't their livestock and their property belong to us? Won't all their animals become ours? So let's say yes to them. Then they'll live among us."

²⁴All the men who went out through the city gate agreed with Hamor and his son Shechem. So every male in the city was circumcised.

²⁵Three days later, all of them were still in pain. Then Simeon and Levi took their swords. They were Jacob's sons and Dinah's brothers. They attacked the city when the people didn't expect it. They killed every male. ²⁶They also used their swords to kill Hamor and his son Shechem. Then they took Dinah from Shechem's house and left. ²⁷Jacob's other sons found the dead bodies. They robbed the city where their sister had been raped. ²⁸They took the flocks and herds and donkeys. They took everything in the city and in the fields. ²⁹They carried everything away. And they took all the women and children. They took away everything in the houses.

³⁰Then Jacob said to Simeon and Levi, "You have brought trouble on me. Now I'm like a very bad smell to the Canaanites and Perizzites who live in this land. There aren't many of us. They may join together against me and attack me. Then I and my family will be destroyed."

³¹But they replied, "Should Shechem have treated our sister like a prostitute?"

Jacob Returns to Bethel

35 Then God said to Jacob, "Go up to Bethel and live there. Build an altar there to honor me. That's where I appeared to you when you were running away from your brother Esau."

²So Jacob spoke to his family and to everyone with him. He said, "Get rid of the statues of false gods you have with you. Make yourselves pure by washing and changing your clothes. ³Come, let's go up to Bethel. There I'll build an altar to honor God. He answered me when I was in trouble. He's been with me everywhere I've gone." ⁴So they gave Jacob all the statues of false gods they had. They also gave him their earrings. Jacob buried those things under the oak tree at Shechem. ⁵Then Jacob and everyone with him started out. The terror of God fell on the towns all around them. So no one chased them.

⁶Jacob and all the people with him came to Luz. Luz is also called Bethel. It's in the land of Canaan. ⁷Jacob built an altar at Luz. He named the place El Bethel. There God made himself known to Jacob when he was running away from his brother.

⁸Rebekah's attendant Deborah died. They buried her body under the oak tree outside Bethel. So it was called Allon Bakuth.

⁹After Jacob returned from Paddan Aram, God appeared to him again. And God blessed him. ¹⁰God said to him, "Your name is Jacob. But you will not be called Jacob anymore. Your name will be Israel." So he named him Israel.

¹¹God said to him, "I am the Mighty God. Have children so that there will be many of you. You will become the father of a nation and a community of nations. Your later family will include kings. ¹²I am giving you the land I gave to Abraham and Isaac. I will also give it to your children after you." ¹³Then God left him at the place where he had talked with him.

¹⁴Jacob set up a sacred stone at the place where God had talked with him. He poured out a drink offering on it. He also poured olive oil on it. ¹⁵Jacob named the place Bethel. That's where God had talked with him.

Rachel and Isaac Die

¹⁶They moved on from Bethel. Ephrath wasn't very far away when Rachel began to have a baby. She was having a very hard time of it. ¹⁷The woman who helped her saw that she was having problems. So she

said to Rachel, "Don't be afraid. You have another son." [18]But Rachel was dying. As she took her last breath, she named her son Ben-Oni. But his father named him Benjamin.

[19]So Rachel died. She was buried beside the road to Ephrath. Ephrath was also called Bethlehem. [20]Jacob set up a stone marker over her tomb. To this day, the stone marks the place where Rachel was buried.

[21]Israel moved on again. He set up his tent beyond Migdal Eder. [22]While Israel was living in that area, Reuben went in and slept with Bilhah. She was the concubine of Reuben's father. And Israel heard about it.

Here are the 12 sons Jacob had.

[23] Leah was the mother of
Reuben, Jacob's oldest son.
Her other sons were Simeon, Levi, Judah, Issachar and Zebulun.
[24] The sons of Rachel were
Joseph and Benjamin.
[25] The sons of Rachel's female servant Bilhah were
Dan and Naphtali.
[26] The sons of Leah's female servant Zilpah were
Gad and Asher.

These were Jacob's sons. They were born in Paddan Aram.

[27]Jacob came home to his father Isaac in Mamre. Mamre is near Kiriath Arba, where Abraham and Isaac had stayed. The place is also called Hebron. [28]Isaac lived 180 years. [29]Then he took his last breath and died. He was very old when he joined the members of his family who had already died. His sons Esau and Jacob buried him.

The Family Line of Esau

36 Here is the story of the family line of Esau. Esau was also called Edom.

[2]Esau got his wives from among the women of Canaan. He married Adah, the daughter of Elon the Hittite. He also married Oholibamah, the daughter of Anah and the granddaughter of Zibeon the Hivite. [3]And he married Basemath, the daughter of Ishmael and the sister of Nebaioth.

[4]Adah had Eliphaz by Esau. Basemath had Reuel. [5]Oholibamah had Jeush, Jalam and Korah. All of them were Esau's sons. They were born in Canaan.

[6]Esau moved to a land far away from his brother Jacob. Esau took with him his wives, his sons and daughters, and all the people who lived with him. He also took his livestock and all his other animals. He took everything he had acquired in Canaan. [7]Jacob and Esau owned so much that they couldn't remain together. There wasn't enough land for both of them. They had too much livestock. [8]So Esau made his home in the hill country of Seir. Esau was also called Edom.

[9] Here is the story of the family line of Esau. He's the father of the people of Edom. They live in the hill country of Seir.

[10] Here are the names of Esau's sons. They are Eliphaz, the son of Esau's wife Adah, and Reuel, the son of Esau's wife Basemath.
[11] The sons of Eliphaz were
Teman, Omar, Zepho, Gatam and Kenaz. [12]Esau's son Eliphaz also had a concubine named Timna. She had Amalek by Eliphaz. They were grandsons of Esau's wife Adah.
[13] The sons of Reuel were
Nahath, Zerah, Shammah and Mizzah. They were grandsons of Esau's wife Basemath.
[14] Esau's wife Oholibamah was the daughter of Anah and the granddaughter of Zibeon.
She had Jeush, Jalam and Korah by Esau.
[15] Here are the chiefs among Esau's sons.
Eliphaz was Esau's oldest son. The sons of Eliphaz were
Chiefs Teman, Omar, Zepho, Kenaz, [16]Korah, Gatam and Amalek. They were the chiefs in Edom who were sons of Eliphaz. They were Adah's grandsons.
[17] The sons of Esau's son Reuel were
Chiefs Nahath, Zerah, Shammah and Mizzah. They were the chiefs in Edom who were sons of Reuel.

They were grandsons of Esau's wife Basemath.

[18] The sons of Esau's wife Oholibamah were
Chiefs Jeush, Jalam and Korah. They were the chiefs who were sons of Esau's wife Oholibamah. She was Anah's daughter.

[19] That was the family line of Esau. And these were the chiefs. Esau was also called Edom.

[20] Seir, the Horite, had sons living in the same area.
They were Lotan, Shobal, Zibeon, Anah, [21]Dishon, Ezer and Dishan. These sons of Seir in Edom were Horite chiefs.

[22] The sons of Lotan were
Hori and Homam. Timna was Lotan's sister.

[23] The sons of Shobal were
Alvan, Manahath, Ebal, Shepho and Onam.

[24] The sons of Zibeon were
Aiah and Anah. He was the Anah who discovered the hot springs of water in the desert. He found them while he was taking care of the donkeys that belonged to his father Zibeon.

[25] The children of Anah were
Dishon and Oholibamah. Oholibamah was the daughter of Anah.

[26] The sons of Dishon were
Hemdan, Eshban, Ithran and Keran.

[27] The sons of Ezer were
Bilhan, Zaavan and Akan.

[28] The sons of Dishan were
Uz and Aran.

[29] The Horite chiefs were
Lotan, Shobal, Zibeon, Anah, [30]Dishon, Ezer and Dishan.
They were the Horite chiefs in the land of Seir. They are listed tribe by tribe.

The Rulers of Edom

[31] Before Israel had a king, there were kings who ruled in Edom.

[32] Bela became the king of Edom. Bela was the son of Beor. Bela's city was called Dinhabah.

[33] When Bela died, Jobab became the next king. Jobab was the son of Zerah from Bozrah.

[34] When Jobab died, Husham became the next king. Husham was from the land of the Temanites.

[35] When Husham died, Hadad became the next king. Hadad was the son of Bedad. Hadad had won the battle over Midian in the country of Moab. Hadad's city was called Avith.

[36] When Hadad died, Samlah became the next king. Samlah was from Masrekah.

[37] When Samlah died, Shaul became the next king. Shaul was from Rehoboth on the river.

[38] When Shaul died, Baal-Hanan became the next king. Baal-Hanan was the son of Akbor.

[39] When Baal-Hanan died, Hadad became the next king. Hadad's city was called Pau. His wife's name was Mehetabel. She was Matred's daughter. Matred was the daughter of Me-Zahab.

[40] Here are the chiefs in the family line of Esau. They are listed by name as chiefs in charge of their tribes and territories. They are
Timna, Alvah, Jetheth, [41]Oholibamah, Elah, Pinon, [42]Kenaz, Teman, Mibzar, [43]Magdiel and Iram.
They were the chiefs of Edom. They ruled over their settlements in the land where they lived.

That's the end of the story of the family line of Esau. He was the father of the people of Edom.

Joseph Has Two Dreams

37 Jacob lived in the land of Canaan. It's the land where his father had stayed.

[2]Here is the story of the family line of Jacob.

Joseph was a young man. He was 17 years old. He was taking care of the flocks with some of his brothers. They were the sons of Bilhah and the sons of Zilpah, the wives of his father Jacob. Joseph brought their father a bad report about his brothers.

[3] Israel loved Joseph more than any of his other sons. That's because Joseph had been born to him when he was old. Israel made him a beautiful robe. [4] Joseph's brothers saw that their father loved him more than any of them. So they hated Joseph. They couldn't even speak one kind word to him.

[5] Joseph had a dream. When he told it to his brothers, they hated him even more. [6] He said to them, "Listen to the dream I had. [7] We were tying up bundles of grain out in the field. Suddenly my bundle stood up straight. Your bundles gathered around my bundle and bowed down to it."

[8] His brothers said to him, "Do you plan to be king over us? Will you really rule over us?" So they hated him even more because of his dream. They didn't like what he had said.

[9] Then Joseph had another dream. He told it to his brothers. "Listen," he said. "I had another dream. This time the sun and moon and 11 stars were bowing down to me."

[10] He told his father as well as his brothers. Then his father rebuked him. He said, "What about this dream you had? Will your mother and I and your brothers really do that? Will we really come and bow down to the ground in front of you?" [11] His brothers were jealous of him. But his father kept the dreams in mind.

Joseph Is Sold by His Brothers

[12] Joseph's brothers had gone to take care of their father's flocks near Shechem. [13] Israel said to Joseph, "As you know, your brothers are taking care of the flocks near Shechem. Come. I'm going to send you to them."

"All right," Joseph replied.

[14] So Israel said to him, "Go to your brothers. See how they are doing. Also see how the flocks are doing. Then come back and tell me." So he sent him away from the Hebron Valley.

Joseph arrived at Shechem. [15] A man found him wandering around in the fields. He asked Joseph, "What are you looking for?"

[16] He replied, "I'm looking for my brothers. Can you tell me where they are taking care of their flocks?"

BiBLE ADVENTURES

Bernard told the story of Joseph and his brothers in "Bernard and Joseph" (A#09).

[17] "They've moved on from here," the man answered. "I heard them say, 'Let's go to Dothan.'"

So Joseph went to look for his brothers. He found them near Dothan. [18] But they saw him a long way off. Before he reached them, they made plans to kill him.

[19] "Here comes that dreamer!" they said to one another. [20] "Come. Let's kill him. Let's throw him into one of these empty wells. Let's say that a wild animal ate him up. Then we'll see whether his dreams will come true."

[21] Reuben heard them talking. He tried to save Joseph from them. "Let's not take his life," he said. [22] "Don't spill any of his blood. Throw him into this empty well here in the desert. But don't harm him yourselves." Reuben said that to save Joseph from them. He was hoping he could take him back to his father.

[23] When Joseph came to his brothers, he was wearing his beautiful robe. They took it away from him. [24] And they threw him into the well. The well was empty. There wasn't any water in it.

[25] Then they sat down to eat their meal. As they did, they saw some Ishmaelite traders coming from Gilead. Their camels were loaded with spices, lotion and myrrh. They were on their way to take them down to Egypt.

[26] Judah said to his brothers, "What will we gain if we kill our brother and try to cover up what we've done? [27] Come. Let's sell him to these traders. Let's not harm him ourselves. After all, he's our brother. He's our own flesh and blood." Judah's brothers agreed with him.

[28] The traders from Midian came by. Joseph's brothers pulled him up out of the well. They sold him to the Ishmaelite traders for eight ounces of silver. Then the traders took him to Egypt.

[29] Later, Reuben came back to the empty well. He saw that Joseph wasn't there. He was so upset that he tore his clothes. [30] He went back to his brothers and said,

"The boy isn't there! Now what should I do?"

³¹Then they got Joseph's beautiful robe. They killed a goat and dipped the robe in the blood. ³²They took the robe back to their father. They said, "We found this. Take a look at it. See if it's your son's robe."

³³Jacob recognized it. He said, "It's my son's robe! A wild animal has eaten him up. Joseph must have been torn to pieces."

³⁴Jacob tore his clothes. He put on the rough clothing people wear when they're sad. Then he mourned for his son many days. ³⁵All Jacob's other sons and daughters came to comfort him. But they weren't able to. He said, "I will continue to mourn until I go down into the grave to be with my son." So Joseph's father mourned for him.

³⁶But the traders from Midian sold Joseph to Potiphar in Egypt. Potiphar was one of Pharaoh's officials. He was the captain of the palace guard.

Judah and Tamar

38 At that time, Judah left his brothers. He went down to stay with a man named Hirah from the town of Adullam. ²There Judah met the daughter of a man from Canaan. His name was Shua. Judah married her and slept with her. ³She became pregnant and had a son. They named him Er. ⁴She became pregnant again and had another son. She named him Onan. ⁵She had still another son. She named him Shelah. He was born at Kezib.

⁶Judah got a wife for his oldest son Er. Her name was Tamar. ⁷But Judah's oldest son Er was evil in the LORD's eyes. So the LORD put him to death.

⁸Then Judah said to Onan, "Sleep with your brother's wife. After all, you are her brother-in-law. So carry out your duty to her. Provide children for your brother." ⁹But Onan knew that the children wouldn't belong to him. So every time he slept with his brother's wife, he spilled his semen on the ground. He did it so he wouldn't provide children for his brother. ¹⁰What he did was evil in the LORD's eyes. So the LORD put him to death also.

¹¹Then Judah spoke to his daughter-in-law Tamar. He said, "Live as a widow in your father's home. Wait there until my son Shelah grows up." Judah was thinking, "Shelah might die too, just like his

Joseph and his brothers weren't the only ones who struggled with sibling rivalry. Donna Barclay had it in "Wishful Thinking" (A#09).

brothers." So Tamar went to live in her father's home.

¹²After a long time Judah's wife died. She was the daughter of Shua. When Judah got over his sadness, he went up to Timnah. His friend Hirah from Adullam went with him. Men were clipping the wool from Judah's sheep at Timnah.

¹³Tamar was told, "Your father-in-law is on his way to Timnah to clip the wool from his sheep." ¹⁴So she took off her widow's clothes. She covered her face with a veil so people wouldn't know who she was. Then she sat down at the entrance to Enaim. Enaim is on the road to Timnah. Tamar knew that Shelah had grown up. But she hadn't been given to him as his wife.

¹⁵Judah saw her. He thought she was a prostitute because she had covered her face with a veil. ¹⁶He didn't realize that she was his daughter-in-law. He went over to her by the side of the road. He said, "Come. Let me sleep with you."

"What will you give me to sleep with you?" she asked.

¹⁷"I'll send you a young goat from my flock," he said.

"Will you give me something that belongs to you?" she asked. "I'll keep it until you send the goat."

¹⁸He said, "What should I give you?"

"Give me your official seal and the string that it hangs from," she answered. "And give me your walking stick." So he gave them to her. Then he slept with her. And she became pregnant by him. ¹⁹After she left, she took off her veil. She put on her widow's clothes again.

²⁰Judah sent his friend Hirah with the young goat he had promised. He wanted to get back what he had given to the woman. But his friend Hirah couldn't find her. ²¹He asked the men who lived at Enaim, "Where's the temple prostitute? She used to sit beside the road here."

"There hasn't been any temple prostitute here," they said.

[22] So Hirah went back to Judah. He said, "I couldn't find her. Besides, the men who lived there didn't know anything about her. They said, 'There hasn't been any temple prostitute here.'"

[23] Then Judah said, "Let her keep what she has. I don't want people making fun of us. After all, I did send her this young goat. We can't help it if you couldn't find her."

[24] About three months later people brought word to Judah. They said, "Your daughter-in-law Tamar is guilty of being a prostitute. Now she's pregnant."

Judah said, "Bring her out! Have her burned to death!"

[25] As Tamar was being brought out, she sent a message to her father-in-law. She said, "I am pregnant by the man who owns these." She continued, "Do you recognize this seal and string and walking stick? Do you know who they belong to?"

[26] Judah recognized them. He said, "She's a better person than I am. I should have given her to my son Shelah, but I didn't." Judah never slept with Tamar again.

[27] The time came for Tamar to have her baby. There were twin boys inside her. [28] As the babies were being born, one of them stuck out his hand. So the woman helping Tamar took a bright red thread. The woman tied it on the baby's wrist. She said, "This one came out first." [29] But he pulled his hand back, and his brother came out first instead. She said, "Just look at how you have forced your way out!" So he was called Perez. [30] Then his brother, who had the red thread on his wrist, came out. So he was named Zerah.

Joseph and the Wife of Potiphar

39 Joseph had been taken down to Egypt. An Egyptian named Potiphar had bought him from the Ishmaelite traders who had taken him there. Potiphar was one of Pharaoh's officials. He was the captain of the palace guard.

[2] The LORD was with Joseph. He gave him great success. Joseph lived in Potiphar's house. [3] Joseph's master saw that the LORD was with him. He saw that the LORD made Joseph successful in everything he did. [4] So Potiphar was pleased with Joseph and made him his attendant. He put Joseph in charge of his house. He trusted Joseph to take care of everything he owned. [5] From that time on, the LORD blessed Potiphar's family and servants because of Joseph. He blessed everything Potiphar had in his house and field. [6] So Joseph took good care of everything Potiphar owned. With Joseph in charge, Potiphar didn't have to worry about anything except the food he ate.

Joseph was strong and handsome. [7] After a while, his master's wife noticed Joseph. She said to him, "Come to bed with me!"

[8] But he refused. "My master has put me in charge," he told her. "Now he doesn't have to worry about anything in the house. He trusts me to take care of everything he owns. [9] No one in this house is in a higher position than I am. My master hasn't held anything back from me, except you. You are his wife. So how could I do an evil thing like that? How could I sin against God?" [10] She spoke to Joseph day after day. But he told her he wouldn't go to bed with her. He didn't even want to be with her.

[11] One day Joseph went into the house to take care of his duties. None of the family servants was inside. [12] Potiphar's wife grabbed him by his coat. "Come to bed with me!" she said. But he left his coat in her hand. And he ran out of the house.

[13] She saw that he had left his coat in her hand and had run out of the house. [14] So she called her servants. "Look," she said to them, "this Hebrew slave has been brought here to make fun of us! He came in here to force me to have sex with him. But I screamed for help. [15] He heard my scream. So he left his coat beside me and ran out of the house."

[16] She kept Joseph's coat with her until Potiphar came home. [17] Then she told him her story. She said, "That Hebrew slave you brought us came to me to rape me. [18] But I screamed for help. So he left his coat beside me and ran out of the house."

[19] Potiphar's wife told him, "That's how your slave treated me." When Joseph's master heard her story, he became very angry. [20] So he put Joseph in prison. It was

the place where the king's prisoners were kept.

While Joseph was there in the prison, [21]the LORD was with him. He was kind to him. So the man running the prison was pleased with Joseph. [22]He put Joseph in charge of all the prisoners. He made him responsible for everything done there. [23]The man who ran the prison didn't pay attention to anything in Joseph's care. That's because the LORD was with Joseph. He gave Joseph success in everything he did.

The Wine Taster and the Baker

40 Some time later, the Egyptian king's baker and wine taster did something their master didn't like. [2]So Pharaoh became angry with his two officials, the chief wine taster and the chief baker. [3]He put them in prison in the house of the captain of the palace guard. It was the same prison where Joseph was kept. [4]The captain put Joseph in charge of those men. So Joseph took care of them.

Some time passed while they were in prison. [5]Then each of the two men had a dream. The men were the Egyptian king's baker and wine taster. They were being held in prison. Both of them had dreams the same night. Each of their dreams had its own meaning.

[6]Joseph came to them the next morning. He saw that they were sad. [7]They were Pharaoh's officials, and they were in prison with Joseph in his master's house. So he asked them, "Why do you look so sad today?"

[8]"We both had dreams," they answered. "But no one can tell us what they mean."

Then Joseph said to them, "Only God knows what dreams mean. Tell me your dreams."

[9]So the chief wine taster told Joseph his dream. He said to him, "In my dream I saw a vine in front of me. [10]There were three branches on the vine. As soon as it budded, it flowered. And bunches of ripe grapes grew on it. [11]Pharaoh's cup was in my hand. I took the grapes. I squeezed them into Pharaoh's cup. Then I put the cup in his hand."

[12]"Here's what your dream means," Joseph said to him. "The three branches are three days. [13]In three days Pharaoh will let you out of prison. He'll give your job back to you. And you will put Pharaoh's cup in his hand. That's what you used to do when you were his wine taster. [14]But when everything is going well with you, remember me. Do me a favor. Speak to Pharaoh about me. Get me out of this prison. [15]I was taken away from the land of the Hebrews by force. Even here I haven't done anything to be put in prison for."

[16]The chief baker saw that Joseph had given a positive meaning to the wine taster's dream. So he said to Joseph, "I had a dream too. There were three baskets of bread on my head. [17]All kinds of baked goods for Pharaoh were in the top basket. But the birds were eating them out of the basket on my head."

[18]"Here's what your dream means," Joseph said. "The three baskets are three days. [19]In three days Pharaoh will cut your head off. Then he will stick a pole through your body and set the pole up. The birds will eat your flesh."

[20]The third day was Pharaoh's birthday. He had a feast prepared for all his officials. He brought the chief wine taster and the chief baker out of prison. He did it in front of his officials. [21]He gave the chief wine taster's job back to him. Once again the wine taster put the cup into Pharaoh's hand. [22]But Pharaoh had a pole stuck through the chief baker's body. Then he had the pole set up. Everything happened just as Joseph had told them when he explained their dreams.

[23]But the chief wine taster didn't remember Joseph. In fact, he forgot all about him.

Pharaoh Has Two Dreams

41 When two full years had passed, Pharaoh had a dream. In his dream, he was standing by the Nile River. [2]Seven cows came up out of the river. They looked healthy and fat. They were eating some of the tall grass growing along the river. [3]After them, seven other cows came up out of the Nile. They looked ugly and skinny. They were standing beside the other cows on the riverbank. [4]The ugly, skinny cows ate up the seven cows that looked healthy and fat. Then Pharaoh woke up.

[5]He fell asleep again and had a second dream. In that dream, seven heads

of grain were growing on one stem. They were healthy and good. [6]After them, seven other heads of grain came up. They were thin and dried up by the east wind. [7]The thin heads of grain swallowed up the seven healthy, full heads. Then Pharaoh woke up. It had been a dream.

[8]In the morning he was worried. So he sent for all the magicians and wise men of Egypt. Pharaoh told them his dreams. But no one could tell him what they meant.

[9]Then the chief wine taster spoke up. He said to Pharaoh, "Now I remember that I've done something wrong. [10]Pharaoh was once angry with his servants. He put me and the chief baker in prison. We were in the house of the captain of the palace guard. [11]Each of us had a dream the same night. Each dream had its own meaning. [12]A young Hebrew servant was there with us. He was a servant of the captain of the guard. We told him our dreams. And he explained them to us. He told each of us the meaning of our dreams. [13]Things turned out exactly as he said they would. I was given back my job. The other man had a pole stuck through his body."

[14]So Pharaoh sent for Joseph. He was quickly brought out of the prison. Joseph shaved and changed his clothes. Then he came to Pharaoh.

[15]Pharaoh said to Joseph, "I had a dream. No one can tell me what it means. But I've heard that when you hear a dream you can explain it."

[16]"I can't do it," Joseph replied to Pharaoh. "But God will give Pharaoh the answer he wants."

[17]Then Pharaoh told Joseph what he had dreamed. He said, "I was standing on the bank of the Nile River. [18]Seven cows came up out of the river. They were fat and looked healthy. They were eating the tall grass growing along the river. [19]After them, seven other cows came up. They were bony and very ugly and thin. I had never seen such ugly cows in the whole land of Egypt. [20]The thin, ugly cows ate up the seven fat cows that came up first. [21]But no one could tell that the thin cows had eaten the fat cows. That's because the thin cows looked just as ugly as they had before. Then I woke up.

[22]"In my dream I also saw seven heads of grain. They were full and good. They were all growing on one stem. [23]After them, seven other heads of grain came up. They were weak and thin and dried up by the east wind. [24]The thin heads of grain swallowed up the seven good heads. I told my dream to the magicians. But none of them could explain it to me."

[25]Then Joseph said to Pharaoh, "Both of Pharaoh's dreams have the same meaning. God has shown Pharaoh what he is about to do. [26]The seven good cows are seven years. And the seven good heads of grain are seven years. Both dreams mean the same thing. [27]The seven thin, ugly cows that came up later are seven years. So are the seven worthless heads of grain dried up by the east wind. They are seven years when there won't be enough food.

[28]"It's just as I said to Pharaoh. God has shown Pharaoh what he's about to do. [29]Seven years with plenty of food are coming to the whole land of Egypt. [30]But seven years when there won't be enough food will follow them. Then everyone will forget about all the food Egypt had. Terrible hunger will destroy the land. [31]There won't be anything left to remind people of the years when there was plenty of food in the land. That's how bad the hunger that follows will be. [32]God gave the dream to Pharaoh in two forms. That's because the matter has been firmly decided by God. And it's because God will do it soon.

[33]"So Pharaoh should look for a wise and understanding man. He should put him in charge of the land of Egypt. [34]Pharaoh should appoint officials to be in charge of the land. They should take a fifth of the harvest in Egypt during the seven years when there's plenty of food. [35]They should collect all the extra food of the good years that are coming. Pharaoh should give them authority to store up the grain. They should keep it in the cities for food. [36]The grain should be stored up for the country to use later. It will be needed during the seven years when there isn't enough food in Egypt. Then the country won't be destroyed just because it doesn't have enough food."

[37]The plan seemed good to Pharaoh and all his officials. [38]So Pharaoh said to them, "The spirit of God is in this man.

Gen. 41:31-41,48-49,53-57 Many ancient Egyptian skeletons show teeth that were worn down from eating bread that had sand mixed in it. I think they should have tried licorice instead.

We can't find anyone else like him, can we?"

³⁹Then Pharaoh said to Joseph, "God has made all this known to you. No one is as wise and understanding as you are. ⁴⁰You will be in charge of my palace. All my people must obey your orders. I will be greater than you only because I'm the one who sits on the throne."

Joseph Is Put in Charge of Egypt

⁴¹So Pharaoh said to Joseph, "I'm putting you in charge of the whole land of Egypt." ⁴²Then Pharaoh took from his finger the ring he used to give his official stamp. He put it on Joseph's finger. He dressed him in robes made out of fine linen. He put a gold chain around Joseph's neck. ⁴³He also had him ride in a chariot. Joseph was now next in command after Pharaoh. People went in front of Joseph and shouted, "Get down on your knees!" By doing all these things, Pharaoh put Joseph in charge of the whole land of Egypt.

⁴⁴Then Pharaoh said to Joseph, "I am Pharaoh. But unless you give an order, no one will do anything in the whole land of Egypt." ⁴⁵Pharaoh gave Joseph the name Zaphenath-Paneah. He gave Joseph a wife. She was Asenath, the daughter of Potiphera. Potiphera was the priest of On. Joseph traveled all over the land of Egypt.

⁴⁶Joseph was 30 years old when he began serving Pharaoh, the king of Egypt. He left Pharaoh's palace and traveled all over Egypt. ⁴⁷During the seven years there was plenty of food. The land produced more than the people needed. ⁴⁸Joseph collected all the extra food produced in those seven years in Egypt. He stored it in the cities. In each city he stored up the food grown in the fields around it. ⁴⁹Joseph stored up huge amounts of grain. There was as much of it as sand by the sea. There was so much grain it couldn't be measured. So Joseph stopped keeping records of it.

⁵⁰Before the years when there wasn't enough food, two sons were born to Joseph. He had them by Asenath, the daughter of Potiphera. Potiphera was the priest of On. ⁵¹Joseph named his first son Manasseh. That's because he said, "God has made me forget all my trouble and my father's whole family." ⁵²He named the second son Ephraim. That's because he said, "God has given me children in the land where I've suffered so much."

⁵³The seven years when there was plenty of food in Egypt came to an end. ⁵⁴Then the seven years when there wasn't enough food began. It happened just as Joseph had said it would. There wasn't enough food in any of the other lands. But in the whole land of Egypt there was food. ⁵⁵When all the people of Egypt began to get hungry, they cried out to Pharaoh for food. He told all the Egyptians, "Go to Joseph. Do what he tells you."

⁵⁶There wasn't enough food anywhere in the country. So Joseph opened the storerooms. He sold grain to the Egyptians because people were very hungry all over Egypt. ⁵⁷People from all over the world came to Egypt. They came to buy grain from Joseph. That's because people were very hungry everywhere.

Joseph's Brothers Go Down to Egypt

42 Jacob found out that there was grain in Egypt. So he said to his sons, "Why do you just keep looking at one another?" ²He continued, "I've heard there's grain in Egypt. Go down there. Buy some for us. Then we'll live and not die."

³So ten of Joseph's brothers went down to Egypt to buy grain there. ⁴But Jacob didn't send Joseph's brother Benjamin with them. He was afraid Benjamin might be harmed. ⁵Israel's sons were among

the people who went to buy grain. There wasn't enough food in the land of Canaan.

⁶Joseph was the governor of the land. He was the one who sold grain to all its people. When Joseph's brothers arrived, they bowed down to him with their faces to the ground. ⁷As soon as Joseph saw his brothers, he recognized them. But he pretended to be a stranger. He spoke to them in a mean way. "Where do you come from?" he asked.

"From the land of Canaan," they replied. "We've come to buy food."

⁸Joseph recognized his brothers, but they didn't recognize him. ⁹Then Joseph remembered his dreams about them. So he said to them, "You are spies! You have come to see the places where our land isn't guarded very well."

¹⁰"No, sir," they answered. "We've come to buy food. ¹¹All of us are the sons of one man. We're honest men. We aren't spies."

¹²"No!" he said to them. "You have come to see the places where our land isn't guarded very well."

¹³But they replied, "We were 12 brothers. All of us were the sons of one man. He lives in the land of Canaan. Our youngest brother is now with our father. And one brother is gone."

¹⁴Joseph said to them, "I still say you are spies! ¹⁵So I'm going to test you. And here's the test. You can be sure that you won't leave this place unless your youngest brother comes here. You can be just as sure of this as you are sure that Pharaoh lives. I give you my word that you won't leave here unless your brother comes. ¹⁶Send one of you back to get your brother. The rest of you will be kept in prison. I'll test your words. Then we'll find out whether you are telling the truth. You can be sure that Pharaoh lives. And you can be just as sure that if you aren't telling the truth, we'll know that you are spies!" ¹⁷So Joseph kept all of them under guard for three days.

¹⁸On the third day, Joseph spoke to them again. He said, "Do what I say. Then you will live, because I have respect for God. ¹⁹If you are honest men, let one of your brothers stay here in prison. The rest of you may go and take grain back to your hungry families. ²⁰But you must bring your youngest brother to me. That will prove that your words are true. Then you won't die." So they did what he said.

²¹They said to one another, "God is surely punishing us because of our brother. We saw how upset he was when he begged us to let him live. But we wouldn't listen. That's why all this trouble has come to us."

²²Reuben replied, "Didn't I tell you not to sin against the boy? But you wouldn't listen! Now we're being paid back for killing him." ²³They didn't realize that Joseph could understand what they were saying. He was using someone else to explain their words to him in the Egyptian language.

²⁴Joseph turned away from his brothers and began to weep. Then he came back and spoke to them again. He had Simeon taken and tied up right there in front of them.

²⁵Joseph gave orders to have their bags filled with grain. He had each man's money put back into his sack. He also made sure they were given food for their journey. ²⁶Then the brothers loaded their grain on their donkeys and left.

²⁷When night came, they stopped. One of them opened his sack to get feed for his donkey. He saw his money in the top of his sack. ²⁸"My money has been given back," he said to his brothers. "Here it is in my sack."

They had a sinking feeling in their hearts. They began to tremble. They turned to one another and said, "What has God done to us?"

²⁹They came to their father Jacob in the land of Canaan. They told him everything that had happened to them. They said, ³⁰"The man who is the governor of the land spoke to us in a mean way. He treated us as if we were spying on the land. ³¹But we said to him, 'We're honest men. We aren't spies. ³²We were 12 brothers. All of us were the sons of one father. But now one brother is gone. And our youngest brother is with our father in Canaan.'

³³"Then the man who is the governor of the land spoke to us. He said, 'Here's how I will know whether you are honest men. Leave one of your brothers here with me. Take food for your hungry families and go. ³⁴But bring your youngest brother to me. Then I'll know that you are honest men and not spies. I'll give your brother

back to you. And you will be free to trade in the land.'"

35They began emptying their sacks. There in each man's sack was his bag of money! When they and their father saw the money bags, they were scared to death. 36Their father Jacob said to them, "You have taken my children away from me. Joseph is gone. Simeon is gone. Now you want to take Benjamin. Everything is going against me!"

37Then Reuben spoke to his father. He said, "You can put both of my sons to death if I don't bring Benjamin back to you. Trust me to take care of him. I'll bring him back."

38But Jacob said, "My son will not go down there with you. His brother is dead. He's the only one left here with me. Suppose he's harmed on the journey you are taking. Then I would die as a sad old man."

Joseph's Brothers Go Down to Egypt Again

43 There still wasn't enough food anywhere in the land. 2After a while Jacob's family had eaten all the grain the brothers had brought from Egypt. So their father said to them, "Go back. Buy us a little more food."

3But Judah said to him, "The man gave us a strong warning. He said, 'You won't see my face again unless your brother Benjamin is with you.' 4So send our brother along with us. Then we'll go down and buy food for you. 5If you won't send him, we won't go down. The man said to us, 'You won't see my face again unless your brother is with you.'"

6Israel asked, "Why did you bring this trouble to me? Why did you tell the man you had another brother?"

7They replied, "The man questioned us closely about ourselves and our family. He asked us, 'Is your father still living? Do you have another brother?' We just answered his questions. How could we possibly know he would say, 'Bring your brother down here'?"

8Judah spoke to Israel his father. "Send the boy along with me," he said. "We'll go right away. Then we and you and our children will live and not die. 9I myself promise to keep Benjamin safe. You can blame me if I don't bring him back to you. I'll set him

right here in front of you. If I don't, you can put the blame on me for the rest of my life. 10As it is, we've already waited too long. We could have made the trip to Egypt and back twice by now."

11Then their father Israel spoke to them. He said, "If that's the way it has to be, then do what I tell you. Put some of the best things from our land in your bags. Take them down to the man as a gift. Take some lotion and a little honey. Take some spices and myrrh. Take some pistachio nuts and almonds. 12Take twice the amount of money with you. You have to give back the money that was put in your sacks. Maybe it was a mistake. 13Also take your brother. Go back to the man at once. 14May the Mighty God cause him to show you mercy. May the man let your other brother and Benjamin come back with you. And if I lose my sons, I lose them."

15So the men took the gifts. They took twice the amount of money. They also took Benjamin. They hurried down to Egypt and went to Joseph. 16When Joseph saw Benjamin with them, he spoke to the manager of his house. "Take these men to my house," he said. "Kill an animal and prepare a meal. I want them to eat with me at noon."

17The manager did what Joseph told him to do. He took the men to Joseph's house. 18They were frightened when they were taken to Joseph's house. They thought, "We were brought here because of the money that was put back in our sacks the first time. He wants to attack us and overpower us. Then he can hold us as slaves and take our donkeys."

19So they went up to Joseph's manager. They spoke to him at the entrance to the house. 20"Please, sir," they said. "We came down here the first time to buy food. 21We opened our sacks at the place where we stopped for the night. Each of us found in our sacks the exact amount of the money we had paid. So we've brought it back with us. 22We've also brought more money with us to buy food. We don't know who put our money in our sacks."

23"It's all right," the manager said. "Don't be afraid. Your God, the God of your father, has given you riches in your sacks. I received your money." Then he brought Simeon out to them.

[24] The manager took the men into Joseph's house. He gave them water to wash their feet. He provided feed for their donkeys. [25] The brothers prepared their gifts for Joseph. He was planning to arrive at noon. They had heard that they were going to eat there.

[26] When Joseph came home, they gave him the gifts they had brought into the house. They bowed down low in front of him. [27] He asked them how they were. Then he said, "How is your old father you told me about? Is he still living?"

[28] They replied, "Your servant our father is still alive and well." And they bowed down to show him honor.

[29] Joseph looked around. Then he saw his brother Benjamin, his own mother's son. He asked, "Is this your youngest brother? Is he the one you told me about?" He continued, "May God be gracious to you, my son." [30] It moved him deeply to see his brother. So Joseph hurried out and looked for a place to cry. He went into his own room and cried there.

[31] Then he washed his face and came out. He calmed down and said, "Serve the food."

[32] They served Joseph by himself. They served the brothers by themselves. They also served the Egyptians who ate with Joseph by themselves. Because of their beliefs, Egyptians couldn't eat with Hebrews. [33] The brothers had been given places in front of Joseph. They had been seated in the order of their ages, from the oldest to the youngest. That made them look at each other in great surprise. [34] While they were eating, some food was brought to them from Joseph's table. Benjamin was given five times as much as anyone else. So all Joseph's brothers ate and drank a lot with him.

A Silver Cup in a Sack

44 Joseph told the manager of his house what to do. "Fill the men's sacks with as much food as they can carry," he said. "Put each man's money in his sack. [2] Then put my silver cup in the youngest one's sack. Put it there along with the money he paid for his grain." So the manager did what Joseph told him to do.

[3] When morning came, the men were sent on their way with their donkeys. [4] They hadn't gone very far from the city when Joseph spoke to his manager. "Go after those men right away," he said. "Catch up with them. Say to them, 'My master was good to you. Why have you paid him back by doing evil? [5] Isn't this the cup my master drinks from? Doesn't he also use it to find things out? You have done an evil thing.'"

[6] When the manager caught up with them, he told them what Joseph had said. [7] But they said to him, "Why do you say these things? We would never do anything like that! [8] We even brought back to you from Canaan the money we found in our sacks. So why would we steal silver or gold from your master's house? [9] If you find out that any of us has the cup, he will die. And the rest of us will become your slaves."

[10] "All right, then," he said. "As you wish. The one found to have the cup will become my slave. But the rest of you will not be blamed."

[11] Each of them quickly put his sack down on the ground and opened it. [12] Then the manager started to search. He began with the oldest and ended with the youngest. The cup was found in Benjamin's sack. [13] When that happened, they were so upset they tore their clothes. Then all of them loaded their donkeys and went back to the city.

[14] Joseph was still in the house when Judah and his brothers came in. They threw themselves down on the ground in front of him. [15] Joseph said to them, "What have you done? Don't you know that a man like me has ways to find things out?"

[16] "What can we say to you?" Judah replied. "What can we say? How can we prove we haven't done anything wrong? God has shown you that we are guilty. We are now your slaves. All of us are, including the one found to have the cup."

[17] But Joseph said, "I would never do anything like that! Only the man found to have the cup will become my slave. The rest of you may go back to your father in peace."

[18] Then Judah went up to him. He said, "Please, sir. Let me speak a word to you. Don't be angry with me, even though you are equal to Pharaoh himself. [19] You asked us, 'Do you have a father or a brother?'

²⁰We answered, 'We have an old father. A young son was born to him when he was old. His brother is dead. He's the only one of his mother's sons left. And his father loves him.'

²¹"Then you said to us, 'Bring him down to me. I want to see him for myself.' ²²We said to you, 'The boy can't leave his father. If he does, his father will die.' ²³But you told us, 'Your youngest brother must come down here with you. If he doesn't, you won't see my face again.' ²⁴So we went back to my father. We told him what you had said.

²⁵"Then our father said, 'Go back. Buy a little more food.' ²⁶But we said, 'We can't go down. We'll only go if our youngest brother goes there with us. We can't even see the man's face unless our youngest brother goes with us.'

²⁷"Your servant my father said to us, 'You know that my wife had two sons by me. ²⁸One of them went away from me. And I said, "He must have been torn to pieces." I haven't seen him since. ²⁹What if you take this one from me too and he is harmed? Then you would cause me to die as a sad old man. I would go down into the grave full of pain and suffering.'

³⁰"So now, what will happen if the boy isn't with us when I go back to my father? His life depends on the boy's life. ³¹When he sees that the boy isn't with us, he'll die. Because of us, he'll go down into the grave as a sad old man. ³²I promised my father I would keep the boy safe. I said, 'Father, I'll bring him back to you. If I don't, you can put the blame on me for the rest of my life.'

³³"Now then, please let me stay here. Let me be your slave in place of the boy. Let the boy return with his brothers. ³⁴How can I go back to my father if the boy isn't with me? No! Don't let me see the pain and suffering that would come to my father."

Joseph Tells His Brothers Who He Is

45 Joseph couldn't control himself anymore in front of all his attendants. He cried out, "Have everyone leave me!" So there wasn't anyone with Joseph when he told his brothers who he was. ²He wept so loudly that the Egyptians heard him. Everyone in Pharaoh's house heard about it.

³Joseph said to his brothers, "I am Joseph! Is my father still alive?" But his brothers weren't able to answer him. They were too afraid of him.

⁴Joseph said to his brothers, "Come close to me." So they did. Then he said, "I am your brother Joseph. I'm the one you sold into Egypt. ⁵But don't be upset. And don't be angry with yourselves because you sold me here. God sent me ahead of you to save many lives. ⁶For two years now, there hasn't been enough food in the land. And for the next five years, people won't be plowing or gathering crops. ⁷But God sent me ahead of you to keep some of you alive on earth. He sent me here to save your lives by an act of mighty power.

⁸"So then, it wasn't you who sent me here. It was God. He made me like a father to Pharaoh. He made me master of Pharaoh's entire house. God made me ruler of the whole land of Egypt. ⁹Now hurry back to my father. Say to him, 'Your son Joseph says, "God has made me master of the whole land of Egypt. Come down to me. Don't waste any time. ¹⁰You will live in the area of Goshen. You, your children and grandchildren, your flocks and herds, and everything you have will be near me. ¹¹There I will provide everything you need. There are still five years to come when there won't be enough food. If you don't come down here, you and your family and everyone who belongs to you will lose everything."'

¹²"My brothers, I am Joseph. You can see for yourselves that I am the one speaking to you. My brother Benjamin can see it too. ¹³Tell my father about all the honor given to me in Egypt. Tell him about everything you have seen. And bring my father down here quickly."

¹⁴Then Joseph threw his arms around his brother Benjamin and wept. Benjamin also hugged him and wept. ¹⁵Joseph kissed all his brothers and wept over them. After that, his brothers talked with him.

¹⁶The news reached Pharaoh's palace that Joseph's brothers had come. Pharaoh and all his officials were pleased. ¹⁷Pharaoh said to Joseph, "Here's what I want you to tell your brothers. Say to them, 'Load your animals. Return to the land of Canaan. ¹⁸Bring your father and your families back to me. I'll give you the best

land in Egypt. You can enjoy all the good things in the land.'

[19]"And here's something else I want you to tell them. Say to them, 'Take some carts from Egypt. Your children and your wives can use them. Get your father and come back. [20]Don't worry about the things you have back there. The best of everything in Egypt will belong to you.'"

[21]Then the sons of Israel did so. Joseph gave them carts, as Pharaoh had commanded. He also gave them supplies for their journey. [22]He gave new clothes to each of them. But he gave Benjamin more than seven pounds of silver. He also gave him five sets of clothes. [23]He sent his father ten male donkeys loaded with the best things from Egypt. He also sent ten female donkeys loaded with grain and bread and other supplies for his journey. [24]Then Joseph sent his brothers away. As they were leaving he said to them, "Don't argue on the way!"

[25]So they went up out of Egypt. They came to their father Jacob in the land of Canaan. [26]They told him, "Joseph is still alive! In fact, he is ruler of the whole land of Egypt." Jacob was shocked. He didn't believe them. [27]So they told him everything Joseph had said to them. Jacob saw the carts Joseph had sent to carry him back. That gave new life to their father Jacob. [28]Israel said, "I believe it now! My son Joseph is still alive. I'll go and see him before I die."

Jacob Goes Down to Egypt

46 So Israel started out with everything that belonged to him. When he reached Beersheba, he offered sacrifices to the God of his father Isaac.

[2]God spoke to Israel in a vision at night. "Jacob! Jacob!" he said.

"Here I am," Jacob replied.

[3]"I am God. I am the God of your father," he said. "Do not be afraid to go down to Egypt. There I will make you into a great nation. [4]I will go down to Egypt with you. I will surely bring you back again. And when you die, Joseph will close your eyes with his own hand."

[5]Then Jacob left Beersheba. Israel's sons put their father Jacob and their families in the carts that Pharaoh had sent to carry him. [6]So Jacob and his whole family went to Egypt. They took their livestock with them. And they took everything they had acquired in Canaan. [7]Jacob brought his sons and grandsons with him to Egypt. He also brought his daughters and granddaughters. He brought his whole family with him.

[8]Here are the names of Israel's children and grandchildren who went to Egypt. Jacob and his whole family are included.

Reuben was Jacob's oldest son.
[9]The sons of Reuben were
    Hanok, Pallu, Hezron and Karmi.
[10]The sons of Simeon were
    Jemuel, Jamin, Ohad, Jakin, Zohar and Shaul. Shaul was the son of a woman from Canaan.
[11]The sons of Levi were
    Gershon, Kohath and Merari.
[12]The sons of Judah were
    Er, Onan, Shelah, Perez and Zerah. But Er and Onan had died in the land of Canaan.
    The sons of Perez were
    Hezron and Hamul.
[13]The sons of Issachar were
    Tola, Puah, Jashub and Shimron.
[14]The sons of Zebulun were
    Sered, Elon and Jahleel.
[15]These were the sons and grandsons born to Jacob and Leah in Paddan Aram. Leah also had a daughter by Jacob. Her name was Dinah. The total number of people in the family line of Jacob and Leah was 33.

[16]The sons of Gad were
    Zephon, Haggi, Shuni, Ezbon, Eri, Arodi and Areli.
[17]The sons of Asher were
    Imnah, Ishvah, Ishvi and Beriah. Their sister was Serah.
    The sons of Beriah were
    Heber and Malkiel.
[18]These were the children and grandchildren born to Jacob and Zilpah. Laban had given Zilpah to his daughter Leah. The total number of people in the family line of Jacob and Zilpah was 16.

[19]The sons of Jacob's wife Rachel were
    Joseph and Benjamin.
    [20]In Egypt, Asenath had Manasseh and Ephraim by Joseph.

Asenath was the daughter of Potiphera. Potiphera was the priest of On.

²¹ The sons of Benjamin were Bela, Beker, Ashbel, Gera, Naaman, Ehi, Rosh, Muppim, Huppim and Ard.

²² These were the sons and grandsons born to Jacob and Rachel. The total number of people in the family line of Jacob and Rachel was 14.

²³ The son of Dan was Hushim.

²⁴ The sons of Naphtali were Jahziel, Guni, Jezer and Shillem.

²⁵ These were the sons and grandsons born to Jacob and Bilhah. Laban had given Bilhah to his daughter Rachel. The total number of people in the family line of Jacob and Bilhah was seven.

²⁶ The total number of people who went to Egypt with Jacob was 66. That number includes only his own children and grandchildren. It doesn't include his sons' wives or his grandsons' wives. ²⁷The total number of the members of Jacob's family who went to Egypt was 70. That includes the two sons who had been born to Joseph in Egypt.

²⁸Jacob sent Judah ahead of him to Joseph. He sent him to get directions to Goshen. And so they arrived in the area of Goshen. ²⁹Then Joseph had his servants get his chariot ready. He went to Goshen to meet his father Israel. As soon as he came to his father, Joseph threw his arms around him. Then Joseph wept for a long time.

³⁰Israel said to Joseph, "I have seen for myself that you are still alive. Now I'm ready to die."

³¹Then Joseph spoke to his brothers and to the rest of his father's family. He said, "I will go up and speak to Pharaoh. I'll say to him, 'My brothers and the rest of my father's family have come to me. They were living in the land of Canaan. ³²The men are shepherds. They take care of livestock. They've brought along their flocks and herds and everything they own.' ³³Pharaoh will send for you. He'll ask, 'What do you do for a living?' ³⁴You

should answer, 'We've taken care of livestock from the time we were boys. We've done just as our fathers did.' It's the practice of the people of Egypt not to mix with shepherds. So Pharaoh will let you settle in the area of Goshen."

47 Joseph went to Pharaoh. He told him, "My father and brothers have come from the land of Canaan. They've brought along their flocks and herds and everything they own. They are now in Goshen." ²Joseph had chosen five of his brothers to meet with Pharaoh.

³Pharaoh asked the brothers, "What do you do for a living?"

"We're shepherds," they replied to Pharaoh. "And that's what our fathers were." ⁴They also said to him, "We've come to live in Egypt for a while. There isn't enough food anywhere in Canaan. There isn't any grass for our flocks. So please let us live in Goshen."

⁵Pharaoh said to Joseph, "Your father and your brothers have come to you. ⁶The land of Egypt is open to you. Let your father and brothers live in the best part of the land. Let them live in Goshen. Do any of them have special skills? If they do, put them in charge of my own livestock."

⁷Then Joseph brought his father Jacob in to meet Pharaoh. Jacob gave Pharaoh his blessing. ⁸Then Pharaoh asked him, "How old are you?"

⁹Jacob said to Pharaoh, "The years of my journey through life are 130. My years have been few and hard. They aren't as many as the years of my father and grandfather before me." ¹⁰Jacob gave Pharaoh his blessing. Then he left him.

¹¹So Joseph helped his father and his brothers make their homes in Egypt. He gave them property in the best part of the land, just as Pharaoh had directed him to do. That part was known as the territory of Rameses. ¹²Joseph also provided food for his father and brothers. He provided for them and the rest of his father's family. He gave them enough for all their children.

Joseph Saves Many Lives

¹³But there wasn't any food in the whole area. In fact, there wasn't enough food anywhere. The people of Egypt and Canaan lost their strength because there wasn't enough food to go around. ¹⁴Joseph

collected all the money in Egypt and Canaan. People paid it to him for the grain they were buying. And Joseph brought it to Pharaoh's palace. [15]When the money of the people of Egypt and Canaan was gone, all the Egyptians came to Joseph. They said, "Give us food. What good would it do you to watch us all die? Our money is all gone."

[16]"Then bring your livestock," said Joseph. "You say your money is gone. So I'll trade you food for your livestock." [17]They brought their livestock to Joseph. He traded them food for their animals. They gave him their horses, sheep, goats, cattle and donkeys. He helped the people live through that year by trading them food for all their livestock.

[18]When that year was over, they came to him the next year. They said, "We can't hide the truth from you. Our money is gone. Our livestock belongs to you. We don't have anything left to give you except our bodies and our land. [19]What good would it do you to watch us die? Why should our land be destroyed? Trade us food for ourselves and our land. Then we and our land will belong to Pharaoh. Give us some seeds so we can live and not die. We don't want the land to become a desert."

[20]So Joseph bought all the land in Egypt for Pharaoh. All the people of Egypt sold their fields. They did that because there wasn't enough food anywhere. So the land became Pharaoh's. [21]Joseph made the people slaves from one end of Egypt to the other. [22]But Joseph didn't buy the land that belonged to the priests. They received a regular share of food from Pharaoh. They had enough food from what Pharaoh gave them. That's why they didn't have to sell their land.

[23]Joseph said to the people, "I've bought you and your land today for Pharaoh. So here are some seeds for you to plant in the ground. [24]But when the crop comes in, give a fifth of it to Pharaoh. Keep the other four-fifths for yourselves. They will be seeds for the fields. And they will be food for yourselves, your children, and the other people who live with you."

[25]"You have saved our lives," they said. "If you are pleased with us, we will be Pharaoh's slaves."

[26]So Joseph made a law about land in Egypt. It's still the law today. A fifth of the produce belongs to Pharaoh. Only the land belonging to the priests didn't become Pharaoh's.

[27]The people of Israel lived in Egypt in the area of Goshen. They received property there. They had children and so became many.

[28]Jacob lived 17 years in Egypt. He lived a total of 147 years. [29]The time came near for Israel to die. So he sent for his son Joseph. He said to him, "If you are pleased with me, put your hand under my thigh. Promise me that you will be kind and faithful to me. Don't bury me in Egypt. [30]When I join the members of my family who have already died, carry me out of Egypt. Bury me where they are buried."

"I'll do exactly as you say," Joseph said.

[31]"Give me your word that you will do it," Jacob said. So Joseph gave him his word. And Israel worshiped God as he leaned on the top of his walking stick.

Ephraim and Manasseh

48 Some time later Joseph was told, "Your father is sick." So he took his two sons Manasseh and Ephraim along with him. [2]Jacob was told, "Your son Joseph has come to you." So Israel became stronger and sat up in bed.

[3]Jacob said to Joseph, "The Mighty God appeared to me at Luz in the land of Canaan. He blessed me there. [4]He said to me, 'I am going to give you children. I will make your family very large. I will make you a community of nations. And I will give this land to your children after you. It will belong to them forever.'

[5]"Now then, two sons were born to you in Egypt. It happened before I came to you here. They will be counted as my own sons. Ephraim and Manasseh will belong to me, in the same way that Reuben and Simeon belong to me. [6]Any children born to you after them will belong to you. Any territory they receive will come from the land that will be given to Ephraim and Manasseh. [7]As I was returning from Paddan, Rachel died. It made me very sad. She died in the land of Canaan while we were still on the way. We weren't very far away from Ephrath. So I buried her body

there beside the road to Ephrath." Ephrath was also called Bethlehem.

[8]Israel saw Joseph's sons. He asked, "Who are they?"

[9]"They are the sons God has given me here," Joseph said to his father.

Then Israel said, "Bring them to me. I want to give them my blessing."

[10]Israel's eyes were weak because he was old. He couldn't see very well. So Joseph brought his sons close to him. His father kissed them and hugged them.

[11]Israel said to Joseph, "I never thought I'd see your face again. But now God has let me see your children too."

[12]Then Joseph lifted his sons off Israel's knees. Joseph bowed down with his face to the ground. [13]He placed Ephraim on his right, toward Israel's left hand. He placed Manasseh on his left, toward Israel's right hand. Then he brought them close to Israel. [14]But Israel reached out his right hand and put it on Ephraim's head. He did it even though Ephraim was the younger son. He crossed his arms and put his left hand on Manasseh's head. He did it even though Manasseh was the older son.

[15]Then Israel gave Joseph his blessing. He said,

"May God bless these boys.
   He is the God of my grandfather
      Abraham and my father Isaac.
   They walked faithfully with him.
He is the God who has been my
      shepherd
   all my life right up to this day.
[16] He is the Angel who has saved me
      from all harm.
   May he bless these boys.
May they be called by my name.
   May they also be called by the
      names of my grandfather
      Abraham and my father Isaac.
And may the number of them greatly
      increase
   on the earth."

[17]Joseph saw his father putting his right hand on Ephraim's head. And Joseph didn't like it. So he took hold of his father's hand to move it over to Manasseh's head. [18]Joseph said to him, "No, my father. Here's my older son. Put your right hand on his head."

[19]But his father wouldn't do it. He said, "I know, my son. I know. He too will become a nation. He too will become great. But his younger brother will be greater than he is. His children after him will become a group of nations." [20]On that day, Jacob gave them his blessing. He said,

"The people of Israel will bless others
      in your name.
   They will say, 'May God make you
      like Ephraim and Manasseh.'"

So he put Ephraim ahead of Manasseh.

[21]Then Israel said to Joseph, "I'm about to die. But God will be with all of you. He'll take you back to the land of your fathers. [22]But to you, Joseph, I am giving more land than your brothers. I'm giving you the land I took from the Amorites. I took it with my sword and bow."

Jacob Gives Blessings to His Sons

49 Then Jacob sent for his sons. He said, "Gather around me so I can tell you what will happen to you in days to come.

[2] "Sons of Jacob, come together and
      listen.
   Listen to your father Israel.

[3] "Reuben, you are my oldest son.
   You were my first child. You were
      the first sign of my strength.
   You were first in honor. You were
      first in power.
[4] But you are as unsteady as water. So
      you won't be first anymore.
   You had sex with my concubine on
      my bed.
   You lay on my couch and made it
      'unclean.'

[5] "Simeon and Levi are brothers.
   Their swords have killed a lot of
      people.
[6] I won't share in their plans.
   I won't have anything to do with
      them.
   They became angry and killed people.
   They cut the legs of oxen just for
      the fun of it.
[7] May the LORD put a curse on them
      because of their terrible anger.
   I will scatter them in Jacob's land.
   I will spread them around in Israel.

8 "Judah, your brothers will praise you.
Your enemies will be brought
under your control.
Your father's sons will bow down
to you.
9 Judah, you are like a lion's cub.
You return from hunting, my son.
Like a lion, you lie down and sleep.
You are like a mother lion. Who
dares to wake you up?
10 The right to rule will not leave Judah.
The ruler's scepter will not be taken
from between his feet.
It will be his until the king it belongs
to will come.
The nations will obey that king.
11 He will tie his donkey to a vine.
He will tie his colt to the very best
branch.
He will wash his clothes in wine.
He will wash his robes in the red
juice of grapes.
12 His eyes will be darker than wine.
His teeth will be whiter than milk.

13 "Zebulun will live by the seashore.
He will become a safe harbor for
ships.
His border will go out toward
Sidon.

14 "Issachar is like a wild donkey
lying down among the sheep pens.
15 He sees how good his resting place is.
He sees that his land is pleasant.
So he will carry a heavy load on his
back.
He will obey when he's forced to
work.

16 "Dan will do what is fair for his people.
He will do it as one of the tribes of
Israel.

17 Dan will be a snake by the side of the
road.
He will be a poisonous snake along
the path.
It bites the horse's heels
so that the rider falls off backward.

18 "LORD, I look to you to save me.

19 "Gad will be attacked by a group of
robbers.
But he will attack them as they run
away.

20 "Asher's food will be rich and sweet.
He will provide food that even a
king would enjoy.

21 "Naphtali is a female deer set free
and gives birth to beautiful fawns.

22 "Joseph is a vine that grows a lot of
fruit.
It grows close by a spring.
Its branches climb over a wall.
23 Mean people shot arrows at him.
They shot at him because they were
angry.
24 But his bow remained steady.
His strong arms moved freely.
The hand of the Mighty God of Jacob
was with him.
The Shepherd, the Rock of Israel,
stood by him.
25 Joseph, your father's God helps you.
The Mighty God blesses you.
He gives you blessings from the sky
above.
He gives you blessings from the
deep springs below.
He blesses you with children and
with a mother's milk.
26 Your father's blessings are great.
They are greater than the blessings
from the age-old mountains.
They are greater than the gifts from
the ancient hills.
Let all those blessings rest on the head
of Joseph.
Let them rest on the head of the
one who is prince among his
brothers.

27 "Benjamin is a hungry wolf.
In the morning he eats what he has
killed.
In the evening he shares what he
has stolen."

Jason's Jargon

GENESIS 49

Here we go! Search this chapter for the word *scepter*. A scepter is a long pole that kings would carry that looks like a curtain rod with an impressive ornament on the end.

²⁸All these are the 12 tribes of Israel. That's what their father said to them when he blessed them. He gave each one the blessing that was just right for him.

Jacob Dies

²⁹Then Jacob gave directions to his sons. He said, "I'm about to join the members of my family who have already died. Bury me with them in the cave in the field of Ephron, the Hittite. ³⁰The cave is in the field of Machpelah near Mamre in Canaan. Abraham had bought it as a place where he could bury his wife's body. He had bought the cave and the field from Ephron, the Hittite. ³¹The bodies of Abraham and his wife Sarah were buried there. So were the bodies of Isaac and his wife Rebekah. I also buried Leah's body there. ³²Abraham bought the field and the cave from the Hittites."

³³When Jacob had finished telling his sons what to do, he pulled his feet up into his bed. Then he took his last breath and died. He joined the members of his family who had already died.

50 Joseph threw himself on his father's body. He wept over him and kissed him. ²Then Joseph talked to the doctors who served him. He told them to prepare the body of his father Israel to be buried. So the doctors prepared it. ³They took 40 days to do it. They needed that much time to prepare a body in the right way. The Egyptians mourned for Jacob 70 days.

⁴After the days of sadness had passed, Joseph went to Pharaoh's officials. He said to them, "If you are pleased with me, speak to Pharaoh for me. Tell him, ⁵'My father made me give my word to him. He said, "I'm about to die. Bury me in the tomb I dug for myself in the land of Canaan." So let me go there and bury my father. Then I'll come back.'"

⁶Pharaoh said, "Go there and bury your father. Do what he made you promise to do."

⁷So Joseph went to Canaan to bury his father. All Pharaoh's officials went with him. They were the important people of his court and all the leaders of Egypt. ⁸Joseph's family also went. His brothers and all the rest of his father's family went. Only their children and their flocks and herds were left in Goshen. ⁹Chariots and horsemen also went up with him. It was a very large group.

¹⁰They came to Atad, a place where grain was processed. It was near the Jordan River. There they sobbed loudly and bitterly. Joseph set apart seven days of sadness to honor his father's memory. ¹¹The Canaanites living in that area saw how sad all of them were. They said, "The Egyptians are having a very special service for the dead." That's why that place near the Jordan River is called Abel of the Egyptians.

¹²So Jacob's sons did exactly as he had commanded them. ¹³They carried his body to the land of Canaan. They buried it in the cave in the field of Machpelah near Mamre. Abraham had bought the

CANDiD CONVERSATiONS

Did you read the *entire* story of Joseph? If not, go back and check it out. It's better than any Hollywood movie. Trust me, I know because I've seen a *lot* of movies. It's got a fantastic ending. After Joseph's brothers beg Joseph for his forgiveness for all the awful things they did to him, he says something really cool: "You planned to harm me. But God planned it for good."

God always has a plan even when we don't see it. Think of it this way: If you were given a couple of puzzle pieces for a thousand-piece puzzle, you would have no idea what the whole puzzle looked like. Our lives are like that sometimes. The puzzle pieces don't make sense. But as God starts adding more pieces and fitting them together, we begin to see the bigger picture.

Look back at your life so far and figure out how God used everything to make you who you are today.

cave as a place where he could bury his wife's body. He had bought the cave and the field from Ephron, the Hittite. ¹⁴After Joseph buried his father, he went back to Egypt. His brothers and all the others who had gone to help him bury his father went back with him.

Joseph Calms His Brothers' Fears

¹⁵Now that their father was dead, Joseph's brothers were worried. They said, "Remember all the bad things we did to Joseph? What if he decides to hold those things against us? What if he pays us back for them?" ¹⁶So they sent a message to Joseph. They said, "Your father gave us directions before he died. ¹⁷He said, 'Here's what you must say to Joseph. Tell him, "I'm asking you to forgive your brothers. Forgive the terrible things they did to you. Forgive them for treating you so badly."' Now then, please forgive our sins. We serve the God of your father." When their message came to Joseph, he wept.

¹⁸Then his brothers came and threw themselves down in front of him. "We are your slaves," they said.

¹⁹But Joseph said to them, "Don't be afraid. Do you think I'm God? ²⁰You planned to harm me. But God planned it for good. He planned to do what is now being done. He wanted to save many lives. ²¹So then, don't be afraid. I'll provide for you and your children." He calmed their fears. And he spoke in a kind way to them.

Joseph Dies

²²Joseph stayed in Egypt, along with all his father's family. He lived 110 years.

Just as Joseph forgave his brothers, Renee had to find it in her heart to forgive someone in "A Forgiving Heart" (Club).

²³He lived long enough to see Ephraim's children and grandchildren. When the children of Makir were born, they were placed on Joseph's knees and counted as his own children. Makir was the son of Manasseh.

²⁴Joseph said to his brothers, "I'm about to die. But God will surely come to help you. He'll take you up out of this land. He'll bring you to the land he promised to give to Abraham, Isaac and Jacob." ²⁵Joseph made the Israelites promise him. He said, "God will surely come to help you. Then you must carry my bones up from this place."

²⁶So Joseph died at the age of 110. They prepared his body to be buried. Then he was placed in a casket in Egypt.

Exodus

Our journey continues! The book of Genesis ends with God's people moving to escape a famine, and thanks to Joseph, they live in what might be called today "prime Egyptian real estate" and with the blessing of the Pharaoh, no less! But as Exodus opens, 400 years later, their situation has changed dramatically.

Their numbers have increased to hundreds of thousands! To keep them from becoming a serious threat, the fearful Egyptians have made them slaves. But God is well aware of His people's suffering (2:23–25). Exodus chapters 1–15 describe God's preparing Moses, calling him to "face off" (to borrow the colloquialism) against Pharaoh, and leading the Israelites to freedom.

As the Israelites make their exodus (a word meaning "departure") from Egypt, they have become a nation instead of just a family, so Exodus chapters 18–40 detail how God cares for them through round-the-clock guidance and regular provisions of food and water. He also provides laws to live by and a worship system (priests, tabernacle, sacrifices, and so forth) so they can stay close to Him.

WHAT'S IT MEAN, EUGENE?

Passover/Lamb—As part of His plan to free the Israelites from slavery in Egypt, God told His people to sacrifice a lamb for each family, and brush some of its blood on the doorframes of their houses. Then He said, "That same night I will pass through Egypt. I will strike down all those born first among the people and animals. . . . When I see the blood (on the doorframes), I will *pass over* you" (Exodus 12:12–13). Passover is symbolic of our own salvation as well. John the Baptist called Jesus "the Lamb of God" (John 1:29). Jesus' blood causes God to "pass over" our sins.

The Israelites Become Slaves in Egypt

1 Here are the names of Israel's children who went to Egypt with Jacob. Each one went with his family. ²Jacob's sons were

Reuben, Simeon, Levi, Judah,
³ Issachar, Zebulun, Benjamin,
⁴ Dan, Naphtali,
Gad and Asher.

⁵ The total number of Jacob's children and grandchildren was 70. Joseph was already in Egypt.

⁶Joseph and all his brothers died. So did all their children. ⁷The people of Israel had many children. The number of them greatly increased. There were so many of them that they filled the land.

⁸Then a new king came to power in Egypt. Joseph didn't mean anything to him. ⁹"Look," he said to his people. "The Israelites are far too many for us. ¹⁰Come. We must deal with them carefully. If we don't, there will be even more of them. Then if war breaks out, they'll join our enemies. They'll fight against us and leave the country."

¹¹So the Egyptians put slave drivers over the people of Israel. The slave drivers treated them badly and made them work hard. The Israelites built the cities of Pithom and Rameses so Pharaoh could store things there. ¹²But the worse the slave drivers treated the Israelites, the more Israelites there were. So the Egyptians became afraid of them. ¹³They made them work hard. They didn't show them any pity. ¹⁴The people suffered because of their hard labor. The slave drivers forced them to work with bricks and mud. And they made them do all kinds of work in the fields. The Egyptians didn't show them any pity at all. They made them work very hard.

¹⁵There were two Hebrew women named Shiphrah and Puah. They helped other women having babies. The king of Egypt spoke to them. He said, ¹⁶"You are the ones who help the other Hebrew women. Watch them when they get into a sitting position to have their babies. Kill the boys. Let the girls live." ¹⁷But Shiphrah and Puah had respect for God. They didn't

Exod. 2:5 Yikes! Crocodiles live in the Nile where people take baths! Crocs sometimes attack animals as large as hippos. I'm glad the scariest thing in my bathtub is soap scum.

do what the king of Egypt had told them to do. They let the boys live. ¹⁸Then the king of Egypt sent for the women. He asked them, "Why have you done this? Why have you let the boys live?"

¹⁹The women answered Pharaoh, "Hebrew women are not like the women of Egypt. They are strong. They have their babies before we get there."

²⁰So God was kind to Shiphrah and Puah. And the number of Israelites became even greater. ²¹Shiphrah and Puah had respect for God. So he gave them families of their own.

²²Then Pharaoh gave an order to all his people. He said, "You must throw every Hebrew baby boy into the Nile River. But let every Hebrew baby girl live."

Moses Is Born

2 A man and a woman from the tribe of Levi got married. ²She became pregnant and had a son by her husband. She saw that her baby was a fine child. And she hid him for three months. ³After that, she couldn't hide him any longer. So she got a basket made out of the stems of tall grass. She coated the basket with tar. She placed the child in the basket. Then she put it in the tall grass that grew along the bank of the Nile River. ⁴The child's sister wasn't very far away. She wanted to see what would happen to him.

⁵Pharaoh's daughter went down to the Nile River to take a bath. Her attendants

were walking along the river bank. She saw the basket in the tall grass. So she sent her female slave to get it. ⁶When she opened it, Pharaoh's daughter saw the baby. He was crying. She felt sorry for him. "This is one of the Hebrew babies," she said.

⁷Then his sister spoke to Pharaoh's daughter. She asked, "Do you want me to go and get one of the Hebrew women? She could breast-feed the baby for you."

⁸"Yes. Go," she answered. So the girl went and got the baby's mother. ⁹Pharaoh's daughter said to her, "Take this baby and feed him for me. I'll pay you." So the woman took the baby and fed him. ¹⁰When the child grew older, she took him to Pharaoh's daughter. And he became her son. She named him Moses. She said, "I pulled him out of the water."

Moses Escapes to Midian

¹¹Moses grew up. One day, he went out to where his own people were. He watched them while they were hard at work. He saw an Egyptian hitting a Hebrew man. The man was one of Moses' own people. ¹²Moses looked around and didn't see anyone. So he killed the Egyptian. Then he hid his body in the sand. ¹³The next day Moses went out again. He saw two Hebrew men fighting. He asked the one who had started the fight a question. He said, "Why are you hitting another Hebrew man?"

¹⁴The man said, "Who made you ruler and judge over us? Are you thinking about killing me as you killed the Egyptian?" Then Moses became afraid. He thought, "People must have heard about what I did."

¹⁵When Pharaoh heard about what had happened, he tried to kill Moses. But Moses escaped from Pharaoh and went to live in Midian. There he sat down by a well. ¹⁶A priest of Midian had seven daughters. They came to fill the stone tubs with water. They wanted to give water to their father's flock. ¹⁷Some shepherds came along and chased the girls away. But Moses got up and helped them. Then he gave water to their flock.

¹⁸The girls returned to their father Reuel. He asked them, "Why have you returned so early today?"

BIBLE ADVENTURES

The game show "Who's Got Compassion?" retold the story of baby Moses in the Nile River in "B-TV: Compassion" (A#27).

¹⁹They answered, "An Egyptian saved us from the shepherds. He even got water for us and gave it to the flock."

²⁰"Where is he?" Reuel asked his daughters. "Why did you leave him? Invite him to have something to eat."

²¹Moses agreed to stay with the man. And the man gave his daughter Zipporah to Moses to be his wife. ²²Zipporah had a son by him. Moses named him Gershom. That's because Moses said, "I'm an outsider in a strange land."

²³After a long time, the king of Egypt died. The people of Israel groaned because they were slaves. They also cried out to God. Their cry for help went up to him. ²⁴God heard their groans. He remembered his covenant with Abraham, Isaac and Jacob. ²⁵So God looked on the Israelites with concern for them.

Moses and the Burning Bush

3 Moses was taking care of the flock of his father-in-law Jethro. Jethro was the priest of Midian. Moses led the flock to the western side of the desert. He came to Horeb. It was the mountain of God. ²There the angel of the LORD appeared to him from inside a burning bush. Moses saw that the bush was on fire. But it didn't burn up. ³So Moses thought, "I'll go over and see this strange sight. Why doesn't the bush burn up?"

⁴The LORD saw that Moses had gone over to look. So God spoke to him from inside the bush. He called out, "Moses! Moses!"

"Here I am," Moses said.

⁵"Do not come any closer," God said. "Take off your sandals. The place you are standing on is holy ground." ⁶He continued, "I am the God of your father. I am the God of Abraham. I am the God of Isaac. And I am the God of Jacob." When Moses heard that, he turned his face away. He was afraid to look at God.

[7]The LORD said, "I have seen how my people are suffering in Egypt. I have heard them cry out because of their slave drivers. I am concerned about their suffering. [8]So I have come down to save them from the Egyptians. I will bring them up out of that land. I will bring them into a good land. It has a lot of room. It is a land that has plenty of milk and honey. The Canaanites, Hittites, Amorites, Perizzites, Hivites and Jebusites live there. [9]And now Israel's cry for help has reached me. I have seen how badly the Egyptians are treating them. [10]So now, go. I am sending you to Pharaoh. I want you to bring the Israelites out of Egypt. They are my people."

[11]But Moses spoke to God. "Who am I that I should go to Pharaoh?" he said. "Who am I that I should bring the Israelites out of Egypt?"

[12]God said, "I will be with you. I will give you a sign. It will prove that I have sent you. When you have brought the people out of Egypt, all of you will worship me on this mountain."

[13]Moses said to God, "Suppose I go to the people of Israel. Suppose I say to them, 'The God of your fathers has sent me to you.' And suppose they ask me, 'What is his name?' Then what should I tell them?"

[14]God said to Moses, "I AM WHO I AM. Here is what you must say to the Israelites. Tell them, 'I AM has sent me to you.'"

[15]God also said to Moses, "Say to the Israelites, 'The LORD is the God of your fathers. He has sent me to you. He is the God of Abraham. He is the God of Isaac. And he is the God of Jacob.' My name will always be The LORD. Call me this name for all time to come.

[16]"Go. Gather the elders of Israel together. Say to them, 'The LORD, the God of your fathers, appeared to me. He is the God of Abraham, Isaac and Jacob. God said, "I have watched over you. I have seen what the Egyptians have done to you. [17]I have promised to bring you up out of Egypt where you are suffering. I will bring you into the land of the Canaanites, Hittites, Amorites, Perizzites, Hivites and Jebusites. It is a land that has plenty of milk and honey."'

[18]"The elders of Israel will listen to you. Then you and the elders must go to the king of Egypt. You must say to him, 'The

LORD has met with us. He is the God of the Hebrews. Let us take a journey that lasts about three days. We want to go into the desert to offer sacrifices to the LORD our God.' [19]But I know that the king of Egypt will not let you and your people go. Only a mighty hand could make him do that. [20]So I will reach out my hand. I will strike the Egyptians with all the amazing things I will do. After that, their king will let you go.

[21]"I will cause the Egyptians to treat you in a kind way. Then when you leave, you will not go with your hands empty. [22]Every woman should ask her neighbor and any woman living in her house for things made out of silver and gold. Ask them for clothes too. Put them on your children. In that way, you will take the wealth of Egypt along with you."

Signs for Moses to Do

4 Moses answered, "What if the elders of Israel won't believe me? What if they won't listen to me? Suppose they say, 'The LORD didn't appear to you.' Then what should I do?"

[2]The LORD said to him, "What do you have in your hand?"

"A walking stick," he said.

[3]The LORD said, "Throw it on the ground."

So Moses threw it on the ground. It turned into a snake. He ran away from it. [4]Then the LORD said to Moses, "Reach your hand out. Take the snake by the tail." So he reached out and grabbed the snake. It turned back into a walking stick in his hand. [5]The LORD said, "When they see this sign, they will believe that I appeared to you. I am the LORD, the God of their fathers. I am the God of Abraham. I am the God of Isaac. And I am the God of Jacob."

[6]Then the LORD said, "Put your hand inside your coat." So Moses put his hand inside his coat. When he took it out, the

skin had become as white as snow. His hand was covered with a skin disease.

[7]"Now put it back into your coat," the LORD said. So Moses put his hand back into his coat. When he took it out, the skin was healthy again. His hand was like the rest of his skin.

[8]Then the LORD said, "Suppose they do not believe you or pay attention to the first sign. Then maybe they will believe the second one. [9]But suppose they do not believe either sign. Suppose they will not listen to you. Then get some water from the Nile River. Pour it on the dry ground. The water you take from the river will turn into blood on the ground."

[10]Moses spoke to the LORD. He said, "Lord, I've never been a good speaker. And I haven't gotten any better since you spoke to me. I don't speak very well at all."

[11]The LORD said to him, "Who makes human beings able to talk? Who makes them unable to hear or speak? Who makes them able to see? Who makes them blind? It is I, the LORD. [12]Now go. I will help you speak. I will teach you what to say."

[13]But Moses said, "Lord, please send someone else to do it."

[14]Then the LORD became very angry with Moses. He said, "What about your brother, Aaron the Levite? I know he can speak well. He is already on his way to meet you. He will be glad to see you. [15]Speak to him. Tell him what to say. I will help both of you speak. I will teach you what to do. [16]He will speak to the people for you. He will be like your mouth. And you will be like God to him. [17]But take this walking stick in your hand. You will be able to do signs with it."

Moses Returns to Egypt

[18]Then Moses went back to his father-in-law Jethro. He said to him, "Let me return to my own people in Egypt. I want to see if any of them are still alive."

Jethro said, "Go. I hope everything goes well with you."

[19]The LORD had said to Moses in Midian, "Go back to Egypt. All those who wanted to kill you are dead." [20]So Moses got his wife and sons. He put them on a donkey. Together they started back to Egypt. And he took the walking stick in

CaNDiD CONVERSaTiONS

Have you ever been in class when the teacher asked for volunteers and you *really* didn't want to get picked? What did you do? Crouch down in your chair? Avoid eye contact? Move your head five inches to the left to hide behind Alicia Van de Camp's "lamp shade" haircut? (Okay, that was kind of specific, wasn't it? Yes, I did that.)

When God told Moses to help lead the Israelites out of slavery in Egypt, Moses murmured, "Please, please, please don't pick me." He came up with excuse after excuse about how he wasn't a gifted speaker or a powerful enough person. But God knew He had the right man for the job. God didn't need an articulate leader. He wanted someone who would be obedient.

Just as God helped Moses become a great leader, He can bring out the leader in you too. This week, try volunteering for a leadership position (even if it scares you).

his hand. It was the stick God would use in a powerful way.

[21]The LORD spoke to Moses. He said, "When you return to Egypt, do all the amazing things I have given you the power to do. Do them in the sight of Pharaoh. But I will make him stubborn. He will not let the people go. [22]Then say to Pharaoh, 'The LORD says, "Israel is like an oldest son to me. [23]I told you, 'Let my son go. Then he will be able to worship me.' But you refused to let him go. So I will kill your oldest son."'"

[24]On the way to Egypt, Moses stopped for the night. There the LORD met him and was about to kill him. [25]But Zipporah got a knife made out of flint. She circumcised her son with it. Then she touched Moses'

feet with the skin she had cut off. "Surely, you are a husband who has forced me to spill my son's blood," she said. ²⁶So the Lord didn't kill Moses. When she said "husband who has forced me to spill my son's blood," she was talking about circumcision.

²⁷The Lord said to Aaron, "Go into the desert to see Moses." So Aaron greeted Moses at the mountain of God and kissed him. ²⁸Then Moses told Aaron everything the Lord had sent him to say. Moses also told him about all the signs the Lord had commanded him to do.

²⁹Moses and Aaron gathered all the elders of Israel together. ³⁰Aaron told them everything the Lord had said to Moses. He also performed the signs in the sight of the people. ³¹And they believed. They heard that the Lord was concerned about them. He had seen their suffering. So they bowed down and worshiped him.

5 Later on, Moses and Aaron went to Pharaoh. They said, "The Lord is the God of Israel. He says, 'Let my people go. Then they will be able to hold a feast to honor me in the desert.'"

²Pharaoh said, "Who is the Lord? Why should I obey him? Why should I let Israel go? I don't even know the Lord. And I won't let Israel go."

³Then Moses and Aaron said, "The God of the Hebrews has met with us. Now let us take a journey that lasts about three days. We want to go into the desert to offer sacrifices to the Lord our God. If we don't, he might strike us with plagues. Or he might let us be killed by swords."

⁴But the king of Egypt said, "Moses and Aaron, why are you taking the people away from their work? Get back to work!" ⁵Pharaoh continued, "There are large numbers of your people in the land. But you are stopping them from working."

⁶That same day Pharaoh gave orders to the slave drivers and the overseers in charge of the people. ⁷He said, "Don't give the people any more straw to make bricks. Let them go and get their own straw. ⁸But require them to make the same number of bricks as before. Don't lower the number they have to make. They are lazy. That's why they are crying out, 'Let us go. We want to offer sacrifices to our God.' ⁹Make

WOOTON'S FUN FACTS

Exod. 5:8
The average-sized Egyptian brick was about nine by four by five inches. I always wondered why the Hebrews just didn't make smaller bricks, like Legos. Then they could have made their quota.

them work harder. Then they will be too busy to pay attention to lies."

¹⁰The slave drivers and the overseers left. They said to the people, "Pharaoh says, 'I won't give you any more straw. ¹¹Go and get your own straw anywhere you can find it. But you still have to make the same number of bricks.'" ¹²So the people scattered all over Egypt. They went to gather any pieces of straw left in the fields. ¹³Pharaoh's slave drivers kept making the people work hard. They said, "Finish the work you are required to do each day. Make the same number of bricks you made when you had straw." ¹⁴The slave drivers whipped the Israelite overseers they had appointed. The slave drivers asked, "Why haven't you made the same number of bricks yesterday or today, just as before?"

¹⁵Then the Israelite overseers appealed to Pharaoh. They asked, "Why have you treated us like this? ¹⁶You didn't give us any straw. But you told us, 'Make bricks!' We are being whipped. But it's the fault of your own people."

¹⁷Pharaoh said, "You are lazy! That's why you keep saying, 'Let us go. We want to offer sacrifices to the Lord.' ¹⁸Now get to work. We won't give you any straw. But

you still have to make the same number of bricks."

¹⁹The Israelite overseers realized they were in trouble. They knew it when they were told, "Don't reduce the number of bricks you are required to make each day." ²⁰When they left Pharaoh, they found Moses and Aaron waiting to meet them. ²¹They said to Moses and Aaron, "We want the LORD to look at what you have done! We want him to judge you for it! We are like a very bad smell to Pharaoh and his officials. You have given them an excuse to kill us with their swords."

Jason's Jargon

EXODUS 5

Search this chapter for the word *plague*. A plague is any kind of disaster or disease that causes widespread death. In the 1300s, the Black Plague killed more than 20 million people in Europe!

The LORD Promises to Save the Israelites

²²Moses returned to talk to the LORD. He said to him, "Why, Lord? Why have you brought trouble on these people? Is this why you sent me? ²³I went to Pharaoh to speak to him in your name. Ever since then, he has brought nothing but trouble on these people. And you haven't saved your people at all."

6 Then the LORD said to Moses, "Now you will see what I will do to Pharaoh. Because of my powerful hand, he will let the people of Israel go. Because of my mighty hand, he will drive them out of his country."

²God continued, "I am the LORD. ³I appeared to Abraham, Isaac and Jacob as the Mighty God. But I did not show them the full meaning of my name, The LORD. ⁴I also made my covenant with them. I promised to give them the land of Canaan. That is where they lived as outsiders. ⁵Also, I have heard the groans of the Israelites. The Egyptians are keeping them as slaves. But I have remembered my covenant.

⁶"So tell the people of Israel, 'I am the LORD. I will throw off the heavy load the Egyptians have put on your shoulders. I will set you free from being slaves to them. I will reach out my arm and save you with mighty acts when I judge Egypt. ⁷I will take you to be my own people. I will be your God. I throw off the load the Egyptians have put on your shoulders. Then you will know that I am the LORD your God. ⁸I will bring you to the land I promised to give to Abraham, Isaac and Jacob. I lifted up my hand and promised it to them. The land will belong to you. I am the LORD.' "

⁹Moses reported these things to the Israelites. But they didn't listen to him. That's because they had lost all hope and had to work very hard.

¹⁰Then the LORD said to Moses, ¹¹"Go. Tell Pharaoh, the king of Egypt, to let the people of Israel leave his country."

¹²But Moses said to the LORD, "The people won't listen to me. So why would Pharaoh listen to me? After all, I don't speak very well."

The Family Record of Moses and Aaron

¹³The LORD had spoken to Moses and Aaron. He had talked with them about the Israelites and about Pharaoh, the king of Egypt. He had commanded Moses and Aaron to bring the people of Israel out of Egypt.

¹⁴ Here were the leaders of the family groups of Reuben, Simeon and Levi.

Reuben was the oldest son of Israel.
Reuben's sons were
Hanok, Pallu, Hezron and Karmi.
These were the family groups of Reuben.

¹⁵ The sons of Simeon were
Jemuel, Jamin, Ohad, Jakin, Zohar and Shaul. Shaul was the son of a woman from Canaan.
These were the family groups of Simeon.

¹⁶ Here are the names of the sons of Levi written in their family record. They were
Gershon, Kohath and Merari.
Levi lived for 137 years.

¹⁷ The sons of Gershon, by their
family groups, were
Libni and Shimei.
¹⁸ The sons of Kohath were
Amram, Izhar, Hebron and
Uzziel.
Kohath lived for 133 years.
¹⁹ The sons of Merari were
Mahli and Mushi.
These are the family groups of Levi
written in their family record.

²⁰ Amram married his father's sister
Jochebed. Aaron and Moses were
members of Amram's family line.
Amram lived for 137 years.
²¹ The sons of Izhar were
Korah, Nepheg and Zikri.
²² The sons of Uzziel were
Mishael, Elzaphan and Sithri.
²³ Aaron married Elisheba. She was
the daughter of Amminadab
and the sister of Nahshon. She
had Nadab, Abihu, Eleazar and
Ithamar by Aaron.
²⁴ The sons of Korah were
Assir, Elkanah and Abiasaph.
These were the family groups of
Korah.
²⁵ Eleazar, the son of Aaron, married
one of the daughters of Putiel.
She had Phinehas by Eleazar.

These are the leaders of the families
of Levi. Their names are written in
their family records.

²⁶The LORD had spoken to this same
Aaron and Moses. He had told them,
"Bring the Israelites out of Egypt like an
army on the march." ²⁷They spoke to Pharaoh, the king of Egypt, about bringing the
people of Israel out of Egypt. It was this
same Moses and Aaron.

Aaron Speaks for Moses

²⁸The LORD had spoken to Moses in
Egypt. ²⁹He had told him, "I am the LORD.
Tell Pharaoh, the king of Egypt, everything I tell you."
³⁰But Moses said to the LORD, "I don't
speak very well. So why would Pharaoh
listen to me?"

7 Then the LORD said to Moses, "I have
made you like God to Pharaoh. And

your brother Aaron will be like a prophet
to you. ²You must say everything I command you to say. Then your brother Aaron must tell Pharaoh to let the people of
Israel leave his country. ³But I will make
Pharaoh stubborn. I will multiply the
signs and amazing things I will do in
Egypt. ⁴In spite of that, he will not listen
to you. So I will use my powerful hand
against Egypt. When I judge them with
mighty acts, I will bring my people Israel
out like an army on the march. ⁵Then the
Egyptians will know that I am the LORD.
I will reach out my powerful hand against
them. I will bring the people of Israel out
of Egypt."
⁶Moses and Aaron did exactly as the
LORD had commanded them. ⁷Moses was
80 years old and Aaron was 83 when they
spoke to Pharaoh.

Aaron's Walking Stick Becomes a Snake

⁸The LORD spoke to Moses and Aaron.
⁹He said, "Pharaoh will say to you, 'Do a
miracle.' When he does, speak to Aaron.
Tell him, 'Take your walking stick and
throw it down in front of Pharaoh.' It will
turn into a snake."
¹⁰So Moses and Aaron went to Pharaoh. They did exactly as the LORD had
commanded them. Aaron threw the stick
down in front of Pharaoh and his officials.
It turned into a snake. ¹¹Then Pharaoh
sent for wise men and people who do evil
magic. By doing their magic tricks, the
Egyptian magicians did the same things
Aaron had done. ¹²Each one threw down
his walking stick. Each stick turned into
a snake. But Aaron's walking stick swallowed theirs up. ¹³In spite of that, Pharaoh
became stubborn. He wouldn't listen to
them, just as the LORD had said.

The Plague of Blood

¹⁴Then the LORD said to Moses, "Pharaoh is very stubborn. He refuses to let the
people go. ¹⁵In the morning Pharaoh will
go down to the Nile River. Go and meet
him on the bank of the river. Take in your
hand the walking stick that turned into a
snake. ¹⁶Say to Pharaoh, 'The LORD, the
God of the Hebrews, has sent me to you.
He says, "Let my people go. Then they will
be able to worship me in the desert. But

up to now you have not listened." ¹⁷The LORD says, "Here is how you will know that I am the LORD. I will strike the water of the Nile River with the walking stick that is in my hand. The river will turn into blood. ¹⁸The fish in the river will die. The river will stink. The Egyptians will not be able to drink its water.' " "

¹⁹The LORD said to Moses, "Tell Aaron, 'Get your walking stick. Reach your hand out over the waters of Egypt. The streams, canals, ponds and all the lakes will turn into blood. There will be blood everywhere in Egypt. It will even be in the wooden buckets and stone jars.' "

²⁰Moses and Aaron did exactly as the LORD had commanded them. Aaron held out his staff in front of Pharaoh and his officials. He struck the water of the Nile River. And all the water turned into blood. ²¹The fish in the Nile died. The river smelled so bad the Egyptians couldn't drink its water. There was blood everywhere in Egypt.

²²But the Egyptian magicians did the same things by doing their magic tricks. So Pharaoh became stubborn. He wouldn't listen to Moses and Aaron, just as the LORD had said. ²³Even that miracle didn't change Pharaoh's mind. In fact, he turned around and went into his palace. ²⁴All the Egyptians dug holes near the Nile River to get drinking water. They couldn't drink water from the river.

The Plague of Frogs

²⁵Seven days passed after the LORD struck the Nile River. ¹Then the LORD said to Moses, "Go to Pharaoh. Tell him, 'The LORD says, "Let my people go. Then they will be able to worship me. ²If you refuse to let them go, I will send a plague of frogs on your whole country. ³The Nile River will be full of frogs. They will come up into your palace. You will have frogs in your bedroom and on your bed. They will be in the homes of your officials and your people. They will be in your ovens and in the bowls for kneading your bread. ⁴The frogs will be on you, your people and all your officials." ' "

⁵Then the LORD spoke to Moses. He said, "Tell Aaron, 'Reach out your hand. Hold your walking stick over the streams, canals and ponds. Make frogs come up on the land of Egypt.' "

⁶So Aaron reached out his hand over the waters of Egypt. The frogs came up and covered the land. ⁷But the magicians did the same things by doing their magic tricks. They also made frogs come up on the land of Egypt.

⁸Pharaoh sent for Moses and Aaron. He said to them, "Pray to the LORD to take the frogs away from me and my people. Then I'll let your people go to offer sacrifices to the LORD."

⁹Moses said to Pharaoh, "You can have the honor of setting the time for me to pray. I will pray for you, your officials and your people. I'll pray that the frogs will leave you and your homes. The only frogs left will be the ones in the Nile River."

¹⁰"Tomorrow," Pharaoh said.

Moses replied, "It will happen just as you say. Then you will know that there is no one like the LORD our God. ¹¹The frogs will leave you and your houses. They will leave your officials and your people. The frogs will remain only in the Nile River."

¹²Moses and Aaron left Pharaoh. Then Moses cried out to the LORD about the frogs he had brought on Pharaoh. ¹³And the LORD did what Moses asked. The frogs died in the houses, courtyards and fields. ¹⁴The Egyptians piled them up. The land

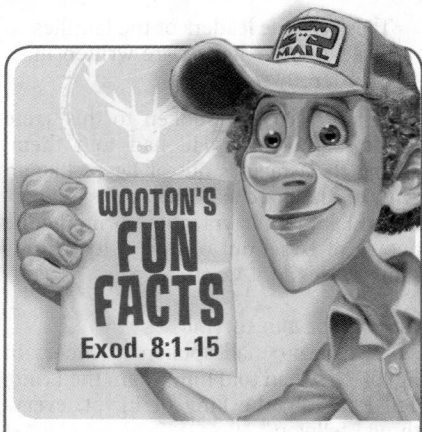

WOOTON'S **FUN FACTS**
Exod. 8:1-15

The Egyptian goddess Heka had a frog's head. I wonder if it looks like that costume I wore last year, but without the kilt. Frogs were so sacred to Egyptians that if a person killed one by accident, that person could be put to death.

smelled very bad because of them. [15]But when Pharaoh saw that the frogs were dead, he became stubborn. He wouldn't listen to Moses and Aaron, just as the LORD had said.

The Plague of Gnats

[16]Then the LORD spoke to Moses. He said, "Tell Aaron, 'Reach out your walking stick. Strike the dust on the ground with it.' Then all over the land of Egypt the dust will turn into gnats." [17]So they did it. Aaron reached out the stick that was in his hand. He struck the dust on the ground with it. The dust all over the land of Egypt turned into gnats. They landed on people and animals alike. [18]The magicians tried to produce gnats by doing their magic tricks. But they couldn't.

The gnats stayed on people and animals everywhere. [19]So the magicians said to Pharaoh, "God's powerful finger has done this." But Pharaoh remained stubborn. He wouldn't listen, just as the LORD had said.

The Plague of Flies

[20]Then the LORD spoke to Moses. He said, "Get up early in the morning. Talk to Pharaoh as he goes down to the Nile River. Say to him, 'The LORD says, "Let my people go. Then they will be able to worship me. [21]If you do not let my people go, I will send large numbers of flies. I will send them on you and your officials. I will send them on your people and into your homes. The houses of the Egyptians will be full of flies. Even the ground will be covered with them.

[22]"'"But on that day I will treat the area of Goshen differently from yours. That is where my people live. There will not be large numbers of flies in Goshen. Then you will know that I, the LORD, am in this land. [23]I will treat my people differently from yours. This sign will take place tomorrow."'"

[24]So the LORD did it. Huge numbers of flies poured into Pharaoh's palace. They came into the homes of his officials. All over Egypt the flies destroyed the land.

[25]Then Pharaoh sent for Moses and Aaron. He said to them, "Go. Offer sacrifices to your God here in the land."

[26]But Moses said, "That wouldn't be right. The sacrifices we offer to the LORD our God wouldn't be accepted by the Egyptians because of their beliefs. For that reason, they would throw stones at us and try to kill us. [27]We have to take a journey that lasts about three days. We want to go into the desert to offer sacrifices to the LORD our God, just as he commands us."

[28]Pharaoh said, "I will let you and your people go to offer sacrifices. You can offer them to the LORD your God in the desert. But you must not go very far. Now pray for me."

[29]Moses replied, "As soon as I leave you, I will pray to the LORD. Tomorrow the flies will leave you. They will also leave your officials and your people. Just be sure you don't try to trick us again. Let the people go to offer sacrifices to the LORD."

[30]Then Moses left Pharaoh and prayed to the LORD. [31]And the LORD did what Moses asked. The flies left Pharaoh, his officials and his people. Not one fly remained. [32]But Pharaoh became stubborn this time also. He wouldn't let the people go.

The Plague on Livestock

9 Then the LORD spoke to Moses. He said, "Go to Pharaoh. Tell him, 'The LORD, the God of the Hebrews, says, "Let my people go. Then they will be able to worship me. [2]Do not refuse to let them go. Do not keep holding them back. [3]If you refuse, my powerful hand will bring a terrible plague on you. I will strike your livestock in the fields. I will strike your horses, donkeys, camels, cattle, sheep and goats. [4]But I will treat Israel's livestock differently from yours. No animal that belongs to the people of Israel will die."'"

[5]The LORD set a time for the plague. He said, "Tomorrow I will send it on the land." [6]So the next day the LORD sent it. All the livestock of the Egyptians died. But not one animal that belonged to the Israelites died. [7]Pharaoh searched and found out what had happened. He discovered that not even one animal that belonged to the Israelites had died. But he was still very stubborn. He wouldn't let the people go.

The Plague of Boils

[8]Then the LORD spoke to Moses and Aaron. He said, "Take handfuls of ashes from a furnace. Have Moses toss them into the air in front of Pharaoh. [9]The ashes will turn into fine dust over the whole land of Egypt. Then painful boils will break out on people and animals all over the land. Their bodies will be covered with them."

[10]So Moses and Aaron took ashes from a furnace and stood in front of Pharaoh. Moses tossed them into the air. Then boils broke out on people and animals alike. [11]The bodies of all the Egyptians were covered with boils. The magicians couldn't stand in front of Moses because of the boils that were all over them. [12]But the LORD made Pharaoh stubborn. Pharaoh wouldn't listen to Moses and Aaron, just as the LORD had said to Moses.

The Plague of Hail

[13]Then the LORD spoke to Moses. He said, "Get up early in the morning. Go to Pharaoh and say to him, 'The LORD, the God of the Hebrews, says, "Let my people go. Then they will be able to worship me. [14]If you do not let them go, I will send the full force of my plagues against you this time. They will strike your officials and your people. Then you will know that there is no one like me in the whole earth. [15]By now I could have reached out my hand. I could have struck you and your people with a plague that would have wiped you off the earth. [16]But I had a special reason for making you king. I decided to show you my power. I wanted my name to become known everywhere on earth. [17]But you are still against my people. You will not let them go. [18]So at this time tomorrow I will send the worst hailstorm ever to fall on Egypt in its entire history. [19]Give an order now to bring your livestock inside to a safe place. Bring in everything that is outside. The hail will fall on all the people and animals that are left outside. They will die."'"

[20]The officials of Pharaoh who had respect for what the LORD had said obeyed him. They hurried to bring their slaves and their livestock inside. [21]But others didn't pay attention to what the LORD had said. They left their slaves and livestock outside.

[22]Then the LORD spoke to Moses. He said, "Reach out your hand toward the sky. Then hail will fall all over Egypt. It will beat down on people and animals alike. It will strike everything growing in the fields of Egypt." [23]Moses reached out his walking stick toward the sky. Then the LORD sent thunder and hail. Lightning flashed down to the ground. The LORD rained hail on the land of Egypt. [24]Hail fell and lightning flashed back and forth. It was the worst storm in Egypt's entire history. [25]Hail struck everything in the fields all over Egypt. It fell on people and animals alike. It beat down everything growing in the fields. It tore all the leaves off the trees. [26]The only place it didn't hail was in the area of Goshen. That's where the people of Israel were.

[27]Then Pharaoh sent for Moses and Aaron. "This time I've sinned," he said to them. "The LORD has done what is right. I and my people have done what is wrong. [28]Pray to the LORD, because we've had enough thunder and hail. I'll let you and your people go. You don't have to stay here any longer."

[29]Moses replied, "When I've left the city, I'll lift up my hands and pray to the LORD. The thunder will stop. There won't be any more hail. Then you will know that the earth belongs to the LORD. [30]But I know that you and your officials still don't have any respect for the LORD God."

[31]The barley was ripe. The flax was in bloom. So they were both destroyed. [32]But the wheat and spelt weren't destroyed. That's because they ripen later.

[33]Then Moses left Pharaoh and went out of the city. Moses lifted up his hands and prayed to the LORD. The thunder and hail stopped. The rain didn't pour down on the land any longer. [34]Pharaoh saw that the rain, hail and thunder had stopped. So he sinned again. He and his officials became stubborn. [35]So Pharaoh was stubborn. He wouldn't let the people of Israel go, just as the LORD had said through Moses.

The Plague of Locusts

10 Then the LORD said to Moses, "Go to Pharaoh. I have made him stubborn. I have also made his officials stubborn so I can perform my signs among them. ²Then you will be able to tell your children and grandchildren how hard I was on the Egyptians. You can tell them I performed my signs among the people of Egypt. And all of you will know that I am the Lord."

³So Moses and Aaron went to Pharaoh. They said to him, "The Lord, the God of the Hebrews, says, 'How long will you refuse to obey me? Let my people go. Then they will be able to worship me. ⁴If you refuse to let them go, I will bring locusts into your country tomorrow. ⁵They will cover the ground so that it can't be seen. They will eat what little you have left after the hail. That includes every tree growing in your fields. ⁶They will fill your houses. They will be in the homes of all your officials and your people. Your parents and your people before them have never seen anything like it as long as they have lived here.'" Then Moses turned around and left Pharaoh.

⁷Pharaoh's officials said to him, "How long will this man be a trap for us? Let the people go. Then they'll be able to worship the Lord their God. After everything that's happened, don't you realize that Egypt is destroyed?"

⁸Moses and Aaron were brought back to Pharaoh. "Go. Worship the Lord your God," he said. "But tell me who will be going."

⁹Moses answered, "We'll go with our young people and old people. We'll go with our sons and daughters. We'll take our flocks and herds. We are supposed to hold a feast to honor the Lord."

¹⁰Pharaoh said, "Suppose I ever let you go, along with your women and children. Then the Lord really will be with all of you! Clearly you are planning to do something bad. ¹¹No! I'll only allow the men to go and worship the Lord. After all, that's what you have been asking for." Then Pharaoh drove Moses and Aaron out of his sight.

¹²The Lord said to Moses, "Reach out your hand over Egypt so that locusts cover the land. They will eat up everything growing in the fields. They will eat up everything left by the hail."

¹³So Moses reached out his walking stick over Egypt. Then the Lord made an east wind blow across the land. It blew all that day and all that night. By morning the wind had brought the locusts. ¹⁴Large numbers of them came down in every part of Egypt. There had never been a plague of locusts like it before. And there will never be one like it again. ¹⁵The locusts covered the ground until it was black. They ate up everything left after the hail. They ate up everything growing in the fields. They ate up the fruit on the trees. There was nothing green left on any tree or plant in the whole land of Egypt.

¹⁶Pharaoh quickly sent for Moses and Aaron. He said, "I have sinned against the Lord your God. I've also sinned against you. ¹⁷Now forgive my sin one more time. Pray to the Lord your God to take this deadly plague away from me."

¹⁸After Moses left Pharaoh, he prayed to the Lord. ¹⁹The Lord changed the wind to a very strong west wind. It picked up the locusts. It blew them into the Red Sea. Not even one locust was left anywhere in Egypt. ²⁰But the Lord made Pharaoh stubborn. So Pharaoh wouldn't let the people of Israel go.

The Plague of Darkness

²¹The Lord spoke to Moses. He said, "Reach out your hand toward the sky so that darkness spreads over Egypt. It will be so dark that people can feel it." ²²So Moses reached out his hand toward the sky. Then complete darkness covered Egypt for three days. ²³No one could see anyone else or go anywhere for three days. But all the people of Israel had light where they lived.

²⁴Then Pharaoh sent for Moses. He said to him, "Go. Worship the Lord. Even your women and children can go with you. Just leave your flocks and herds behind."

²⁵But Moses said, "You must allow us to take our animals. We need to offer them as sacrifices and burnt offerings to the Lord our God. ²⁶Our livestock must also go with us. We have to use some of them to worship the Lord our God. We can't leave even one animal behind. Until we get there, we won't know what we are supposed to use to worship the Lord."

²⁷But the Lord made Pharaoh stubborn. So he wouldn't let the people go. ²⁸Pharaoh said to Moses, "Get out of my

sight! Make sure you don't come to see me again! If you do, you will die."

²⁹"I'll do just as you say," Moses replied. "I will never come to you again."

The Lord Announces the Tenth Plague

11 The Lord had spoken to Moses. He had said, "I will bring one more plague on Pharaoh and on Egypt. After that, he will let you and your people go. When he does, he will drive every one of you away. ²Tell the men and women alike to ask their neighbors for things made out of silver and gold." ³The Lord caused the Egyptians to treat the Israelites in a kind way. Pharaoh's officials and the people had great respect for Moses.

⁴Moses told Pharaoh, "The Lord says, 'About midnight I will go through every part of Egypt. ⁵Every oldest son in Egypt will die. The oldest son of Pharaoh, who sits on the throne, will die. The oldest son of every female slave, who works at her hand mill, will die. All the male animals born first to their mothers among the cattle will also die. ⁶There will be loud crying all over Egypt. It will be worse than it's ever been before. And nothing like it will ever be heard again. ⁷But among the Israelites not even one dog will bark at any person or animal.' Then you will know that the Lord treats Egypt differently from us. ⁸All your officials will come and bow down to me. They will say, 'Go, you and all the people who follow you!' After that, I will leave." Moses was very angry when he left Pharaoh.

⁹The Lord had spoken to Moses. He had said, "Pharaoh will refuse to listen to you. So I will multiply the amazing things I will do in Egypt." ¹⁰Moses and Aaron performed all these amazing things in the sight of Pharaoh. But the Lord made Pharaoh stubborn. He wouldn't let the people of Israel go out of his country.

The First Passover Sacrifice

12 The Lord spoke to Moses and Aaron in Egypt. ²He said, "From now on, this month will be your first month. Each of your years will begin with it. ³Speak to the whole community of Israel. Tell them that on the tenth day of this month each man must get a lamb from

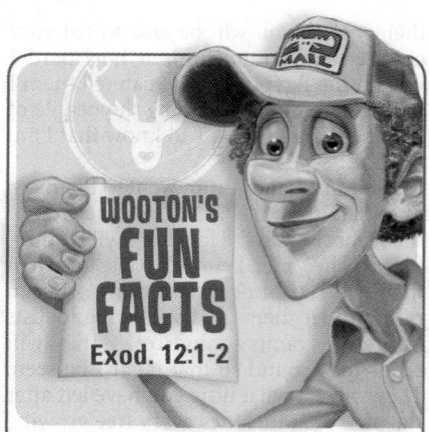

WOOTON'S FUN FACTS
Exod. 12:1-2

On the day of the last plague, God started the calendar year over to mark it. If I could choose any day for New Year's, I would pick Penny's birthday so she would always get the day off. (And I would never forget the date!)

his flock. A lamb should be chosen for each family and home. ⁴Suppose there are not enough people in your family to eat a whole lamb. Then you must share some of it with your nearest neighbor. You must add up the total number of people there are. You must decide how much lamb is needed for each person. ⁵The animals you choose must be males that are a year old. They must not have any flaws. You may choose either sheep or goats. ⁶Take care of them until the 14th day of the month. Then the whole community of Israel must kill them when the sun goes down. ⁷Take some of the blood. Put it on the sides and tops of the doorframes of the houses where you eat the lambs. ⁸That same night eat the meat cooked over a fire. Also eat bitter plants. And eat bread made without yeast. ⁹Do not eat the meat when it is raw. Don't boil it in water. Instead, cook it over a fire. Cook the head, legs and inside parts. ¹⁰Do not leave any of it until morning. If some is left over until morning, burn it up. ¹¹Eat the meat while your coat is tucked into your belt. Put your sandals on your feet. Take your walking stick in your hand. Eat the food quickly. It is the Lord's Passover.

¹²"That same night I will pass through Egypt. I will strike down all those born first among the people and animals. And I will judge all the gods of Egypt. I am the

LORD. [13]The blood on your houses will be a sign for you. When I see the blood, I will pass over you. No deadly plague will touch you when I strike Egypt.

[14]"Always remember this day. You and your children after you must celebrate this day as a feast to honor the LORD. You must do this for all time to come. It is a law that will last forever. [15]For seven days eat bread made without yeast. On the first day remove the yeast from your homes. For the next seven days, anyone who eats anything with yeast in it must be separated from Israel. [16]On the first and seventh days, come together for a sacred assembly. Do not work at all on these days. The only thing you are allowed to do is prepare food for everyone to eat.

[17]"Celebrate the Feast of Unleavened Bread. I brought you out of Egypt on this very day like an army on the march. It is a law that will last for all time to come. [18]In the first month eat bread made without yeast. Eat it from the evening of the 14th day until the evening of the 21st day. [19]For seven days do not let any yeast be found in your homes. Anyone who eats anything with yeast in it must be separated from the community of Israel. That applies to outsiders and Israelites alike. [20]Do not eat anything made with yeast. No matter where you live, eat bread made without yeast."

[21]Then Moses sent for all the elders of Israel. He said to them, "Go at once. Choose the animals for your families. Each family must kill a Passover lamb. [22]Get a branch of a hyssop plant. Dip it into the blood in the bowl. Put some of the blood on the top and on both sides of the doorframe. None of you can go out of the door of your house until morning. [23]The LORD will go through the land to strike down the Egyptians. He'll see the blood on the top and sides of the doorframe. He will pass over that house. He won't let the destroying angel enter your homes to strike you down.

[24]"Obey all these directions. It's a law for you and your children after you for all time to come. [25]The LORD will give you the land, just as he promised. When you enter it, keep this holy day. [26]Your children will ask you, 'What does this holy day mean to you?' [27]Tell them, 'It's the

BiBLe ADVeNTUReS

Through the Imagination Station, Jimmy and George Barclay saw the Passover and the exodus of the Israelites from Egypt in "Moses: The Passover" (A#14).

Passover sacrifice to honor the LORD. He passed over the houses of the Israelites in Egypt. He spared our homes when he struck down the Egyptians.'" Then the Israelites bowed down and worshiped. [28]They did just what the LORD commanded Moses and Aaron.

[29]At midnight the LORD struck down every oldest son in Egypt. He killed the oldest son of Pharaoh, who sat on the throne. He killed all the oldest sons of prisoners. He also killed all the male animals born first to their mothers among the livestock. [30]Pharaoh and all his officials got up during the night. So did all the Egyptians. There was loud crying in Egypt because someone had died in every home.

The Exodus

[31]During the night, Pharaoh sent for Moses and Aaron. He said to them, "Get out of here! You and the Israelites, leave my people! Go. Worship the LORD, just as you have asked. [32]Go. Take your flocks and herds, just as you have said. And also give me your blessing."

[33]The Egyptians begged the people of Israel to hurry up and leave the country. "If you don't," they said, "we'll all die!" [34]So the people took their dough before the yeast was added to it. They carried it on their shoulders in bowls for kneading bread. The bowls were wrapped in clothes. [35]They did just as Moses had directed them. They asked the Egyptians for things made out of silver and gold. They also asked them for clothes. [36]The LORD had caused the Egyptians to treat the Israelites in a kind way. So the Egyptians gave them what they asked for. The Israelites took many expensive things that belonged to the Egyptians.

[37]The Israelites traveled from Rameses to Sukkoth. There were about 600,000 men old enough to go into battle. The women and children went with them.

[38]So did many other people. The Israelites also took large flocks and herds with them. [39]The Israelites brought dough from Egypt. With it they baked loaves of bread without yeast. The dough didn't have any yeast in it. That's because the people had been driven out of Egypt before they had time to prepare their food.

[40]The Israelites lived in Egypt for 430 years. [41]Then all the Lord's people marched out of Egypt like an army. That happened at the end of the 430 years, to the exact day. [42]The Lord kept watch that night to bring them out of Egypt. So on that same night every year all the Israelites must keep watch. They must do it to honor the Lord for all time to come.

Rules for the Passover

[43]The Lord said to Moses and Aaron, "Here are the rules for the Passover meal.

"No one from another country is allowed to eat it. [44]Any slave you have bought is allowed to eat it after you have circumcised him. [45]But a hired worker or someone who lives with you for a short time is not allowed to eat it.

[46]"It must be eaten inside the house. Do not take any of the meat outside. Do not break any of the bones. [47]The whole community of Israel must celebrate the Passover.

[48]"Suppose an outsider living among you wants to celebrate the Lord's Passover. Then all the males in that home must be circumcised. After that, the person can take part, just like an Israelite. Only circumcised males may eat it. [49]The same law applies to Israelites and to outsiders living among you."

[50]All the people of Israel did just what the Lord had commanded Moses and Aaron. [51]On that day the Lord brought the Israelites out of Egypt like an army on the march.

Setting Apart the Oldest Sons

13 The Lord said to Moses, [2]"Set apart for me the first boy born in every family. The oldest son of every Israelite mother belongs to me. Every male animal born first to its mother also belongs to me."

[3]Then Moses said to the people, "Remember this day. It's the day you came out of Egypt. That's the land where you were slaves. The Lord used his mighty hand to bring you out of Egypt. Don't eat anything with yeast in it. [4]You are leaving today. It's the month of Aviv. [5]The Lord will bring you into the land of the Canaanites, Hittites, Amorites, Hivites and Jebusites. He promised your people of long ago that he would give that land to you. It's a land that has plenty of milk and honey. When you get there, celebrate this holy day in this month. [6]For seven days eat bread made without yeast. On the seventh day hold a feast to honor the Lord. [7]Eat bread made without yeast during those seven days. Nothing with yeast in it should be found among you. No yeast should be seen anywhere inside your borders. [8]On that day talk to your child. Say, 'I'm doing this because of what the Lord did for me when I came out of Egypt.' [9]When you celebrate this holy day, it will be like a mark on your hand. It will be like a reminder on your forehead. This law of the Lord must be on your lips. The Lord used his mighty hand to bring you out of Egypt. [10]Obey this law at the appointed time year after year.

[11]"The Lord will bring you into the land of Canaan. He will give it to you, just as he promised he would. He gave his word to you and your people of long ago. [12]After you arrive in the land, give to the Lord the oldest son of every mother. Every male animal born first to its mother among your livestock belongs to the Lord. [13]By sacrificing a lamb, buy back every male donkey born first to its mother. But if you don't buy the donkey back, break its neck. Buy back every oldest son.

[14]"In days to come, your child will ask you, 'What does this mean?' Say to them, 'The Lord used his mighty hand to bring us out of Egypt. That's the land where we were slaves. [15]Pharaoh was stubborn. He refused to let us go. So the Lord killed every oldest son in Egypt. He also killed all those born first among the people and animals. That's why I sacrifice to the Lord every male animal born first. And that's why I buy back each of my oldest sons for the Lord.' [16]This holy day will be like a mark on your hand. It will be like a sign on your forehead. It will remind you that the Lord used his mighty hand to bring us out of Egypt."

Israel Goes Through the Red Sea

[17]Pharaoh let the people go. The shortest road from Goshen to Canaan went through the Philistine country. But God didn't lead them that way. God said, "If they have to go into battle, they might change their minds. They might return to Egypt." [18]So God led the people toward the Red Sea by taking them on a road through the desert. The Israelites were ready for battle when they went up out of Egypt.

[19]Moses took the bones of Joseph along with him. Joseph had made the Israelites give their word to do this. He had said, "God will surely come to help you. When he does, you must carry my bones up from this place with you." (*Genesis 50:25*)

[20]The people left Sukkoth. They camped at Etham on the edge of the desert. [21]By day the LORD went ahead of them in a pillar of cloud. It guided them on their way. At night he led them with a pillar of fire. It gave them light. So they could travel by day or at night. [22]The pillar of cloud didn't leave its place in front of the people during the day. And the pillar of fire didn't leave its place at night.

14 Then the LORD spoke to Moses. [2]He said, "Tell the people of Israel to turn back. Have them camp near Pi Hahiroth between Migdol and the Red Sea. They must camp by the sea, right across from Baal Zephon. [3]Pharaoh will think, 'The Israelites are wandering around the land. They don't know which way to go. The desert is all around them.' [4]I will make Pharaoh stubborn. He will chase them. But I will gain glory for myself because of what will happen to Pharaoh and his whole army. And the Egyptians will know that I am the LORD." So the Israelites camped by the Red Sea.

[5]The king of Egypt was told that the people had escaped. Then Pharaoh and his officials changed their minds about them. They said, "What have we done? We've let the people of Israel go! We've lost our slaves and all the work they used to do for us!" [6]So he had his chariot made ready. He took his army with him. [7]He took 600 of the best chariots in Egypt. He also took along all the other chariots. Officers were in charge of all of them. [8]The LORD made Pharaoh, the king of Egypt, stubborn. So he chased the Israelites as they were marching out boldly. [9]The Egyptians went after the Israelites. All Pharaoh's horses and chariots and horsemen and troops chased them. They caught up with the Israelites as they camped by the sea. The Israelites were near Pi Hahiroth, across from Baal Zephon.

[10]As Pharaoh approached, the Israelites looked back. There were the Egyptians marching after them! The Israelites were terrified. They cried out to the LORD. [11]They said to Moses, "Why did you bring us to the desert to die? Weren't there any graves in Egypt? What have you done to us by bringing us out of Egypt? [12]We told you in Egypt, 'Leave us alone. Let us serve the Egyptians.' It would have been better for us to serve the Egyptians than to die here in the desert!"

[13]Moses answered the people. He said, "Don't be afraid. Stand firm. You will see how the LORD will save you today. Do you see those Egyptians? You will never see them again. [14]The LORD will fight for you. Just be still."

[15]Then the LORD spoke to Moses. He said, "Why are you crying out to me? Tell the people of Israel to move on. [16]Hold out your walking stick. Reach out your hand over the Red Sea to divide the water. Then the people can go through the sea on dry ground. [17]I will make the Egyptians stubborn. They will go in after the Israelites. I will gain glory for myself because of what will happen to Pharaoh, his army, chariots and horsemen. [18]The Egyptians will know that I am the LORD. I will gain glory because of what will happen to Pharaoh, his chariots and his horsemen."

[19]The angel of God had been traveling in front of Israel's army. Now he moved back and went behind them. The pillar of cloud also moved away from in front of them. Now it stood behind them. [20]It came between the armies of Egypt and Israel. All through the night the cloud brought darkness to one side and light to the other. Neither army went near the other all night long.

[21]Then Moses reached out his hand over the Red Sea. All that night the LORD pushed the sea back with a strong east wind. He turned the sea into dry land. The waters were divided. [22]The people of Israel went through the sea on dry ground.

There was a wall of water on their right side and on their left.

²³The Egyptians chased them. All Pharaoh's horses and chariots and horsemen followed them into the sea. ²⁴Near the end of the night the LORD looked down from the pillar of fire and cloud. He saw the Egyptian army and threw it into a panic. ²⁵He jammed the wheels of their chariots. That made the chariots hard to drive. The Egyptians said, "Let's get away from the Israelites! The LORD is fighting for Israel against Egypt."

²⁶Then the LORD spoke to Moses. He said, "Reach out your hand over the sea. The waters will flow back over the Egyptians and their chariots and horsemen." ²⁷So Moses reached out his hand over the sea. At sunrise the sea went back to its place. The Egyptians tried to run away from the sea. But the LORD swept them into it. ²⁸The water flowed back and covered the chariots and horsemen. It covered the entire army of Pharaoh that had followed the people of Israel into the sea. Not one of the Egyptians was left.

²⁹But the Israelites went through the sea on dry ground. There was a wall of water on their right side and on their left. ³⁰That day the LORD saved Israel from the power of Egypt. The Israelites saw the Egyptians lying dead on the shore. ³¹The Israelites saw the amazing power the LORD showed against the Egyptians. So the Israelites had great respect for the LORD and put their trust in him. They also put their trust in his servant Moses.

The Song of Moses and Miriam

15 Here is the song that Moses and the people of Israel sang to the LORD. They said,

"I will sing to the LORD.
   He is greatly honored.
He has thrown Pharaoh's horses and
      chariot drivers
   into the Red Sea.
² The LORD gives me strength and
      protects me.
   He has saved me.
He is my God, I will praise him.
   He is my father's God, and I will
      honor him.
³ The LORD goes into battle.
   The LORD is his name.

WOOTON'S FUN FACTS

Exod. 15
This is the first song recorded in the Bible. The song of Moses is also the last song recorded. Don't believe me? See Revelation 15:3.

⁴ He has thrown Pharaoh's chariots and
      army
   into the Red Sea.
Pharaoh's best officers
   drowned in the sea.
⁵ The deep waters covered them.
   They sank to the bottom like a
      stone.

⁶ "LORD, your right hand
   was majestic and powerful.
LORD, your right hand
   destroyed your enemies.
⁷ Because of your great majesty,
   you threw down those who
      opposed you.
Your burning anger blazed out.
   It burned them up like straw.
⁸ The powerful blast from your nose
   piled up the waters.
The rushing waters stood firm like a
   wall.
   The deep waters stood up in the
      middle of the sea.

⁹ "Your enemies bragged,
   'We will chase Israel and will catch
      them.
We'll divide up what we take from
   them.
   We'll eat them alive.
We'll pull our swords out.

Our powerful hands will destroy
　　them.'
[10] But you blew with your breath.
　　The Red Sea covered your enemies.
They sank like lead
　　in the mighty waters.
[11] "Lord, who among the gods is like
　　you?
　　Who is like you?
You are majestic and holy.
　　Your glory fills me with wonder.
　　You do amazing things.
[12] You reach out your right hand.
　　The earth swallows up your
　　　enemies.
[13] "Because your love is faithful,
　　you will lead the people you have
　　　set free.
Because you are so strong,
　　you will guide them to the holy
　　　place where you live.
[14] The nations will hear about it and
　　tremble.
　　Pain and suffering will take hold of
　　　the Philistines.
[15] The chiefs of Edom will be terrified.
　　The leaders of Moab will tremble
　　　with fear.
The people of Canaan will melt away.
[16] 　Fear and terror will fall on them.
Your powerful arm
　　will make them as still as a stone.
Then your people will pass by, Lord.
　　Then the people you created will
　　　pass by.
[17] You will bring them in.
　　You will plant them on the
　　　mountain you gave them.
Lord, you have made that place your
　　home.
　　Lord, your hands have made your
　　　holy place secure.
[18] "The Lord rules
　　for ever and ever."

[19] Pharaoh's horses, chariots and horsemen went into the Red Sea. The Lord brought the waters of the sea back over them. But the people of Israel walked through the sea on dry ground. [20] Aaron's sister Miriam was a prophet. She took a tambourine in her hand. All the women followed her. They played tambourines and danced. [21] Miriam sang to them,

"Sing to the Lord.
　He is greatly honored.
He has thrown Pharaoh's horses and
　　chariot drivers
　into the Red Sea."

The Waters of Marah and Elim

[22] Then Moses led Israel away from the Red Sea. They went into the Desert of Shur. For three days they traveled in the desert. They didn't find any water there. [23] When they came to Marah, they couldn't drink its water. It was bitter. That's why the place is named Marah. [24] The people told Moses they weren't happy with him. They said, "What are we supposed to drink?"

[25] Then Moses cried out to the Lord. The Lord showed him a stick. Moses threw it into the water. The water became fit to drink.

There the Lord gave a ruling and instruction for the people. And there he tested them. [26] He said, "I am the Lord your God. Listen carefully to me. Do what is right in my eyes. Pay attention to my commands. Obey all my rules. If you do, I will not send on you any of the sicknesses I sent on the Egyptians. I am the Lord who heals you."

[27] The people came to Elim. It had 12 springs and 70 palm trees. They camped there near the water.

The Lord Gives Israel Food Every Day

16 The whole community of Israel started out from Elim. They came to the Desert of Sin. It was between Elim and Sinai. They arrived there on the 15th day of the second month after they had come out of Egypt. [2] In the desert the whole community told Moses and Aaron they weren't happy with them. [3] The Israelites said to them, "We wish the Lord had put us to death in Egypt. There we sat around pots of meat. We ate all the food we wanted. But you have brought us out into this desert. You must want this entire community to die of hunger."

[4] Then the Lord spoke to Moses. He said, "I will rain down bread from heaven for you. The people must go out each day. Have them gather enough bread for that day. Here is how I will test them. I will see if they will follow my directions. [5] On the sixth day they must prepare what they

bring in. On that day they must gather twice as much as on the other days."

[6]So Moses and Aaron spoke to all the people of Israel. They said, "In the evening you will know that the LORD brought you out of Egypt. [7]And in the morning you will see the glory of the LORD. He has heard you say you aren't happy with him. Who are we? Why are you telling us you aren't happy with us?" [8]Moses also said, "You will know that the LORD has heard you speak against him. He will give you meat to eat in the evening. He'll give you all the bread you want in the morning. But who are we? You aren't speaking against us. You are speaking against the LORD."

[9]Then Moses told Aaron, "Talk to the whole community of Israel. Say to them, 'Come to the LORD. He has heard you speak against him.'"

[10]While Aaron was talking to the whole community of Israel, they looked toward the desert. There was the glory of the LORD appearing in the cloud!

[11]The LORD said to Moses, [12]"I have heard the people of Israel talking about how unhappy they are. Tell them, 'When the sun goes down, you will eat meat. In the morning you will be filled with bread. Then you will know that I am the LORD your God.'"

[13]That evening quail came and covered the camp. In the morning the ground around the camp was covered with dew. [14]When the dew was gone, thin flakes appeared on the desert floor. They looked like frost on the ground. [15]The people of Israel saw the flakes. They asked each other, "What's that?" They didn't know what it was.

Moses said to them, "It's the bread the LORD has given you to eat. [16]Here is what the LORD has commanded. He has said, 'Everyone should gather as much as they need. Take three pounds for each person who lives in your tent.'"

[17]The people of Israel did as they were told. Some gathered a lot, and some gathered a little. [18]When they measured it out, the one who gathered a lot didn't have too much. And the one who gathered a little had enough. Everyone gathered only what they needed.

[19]Then Moses said to them, "Don't keep any of it until morning."

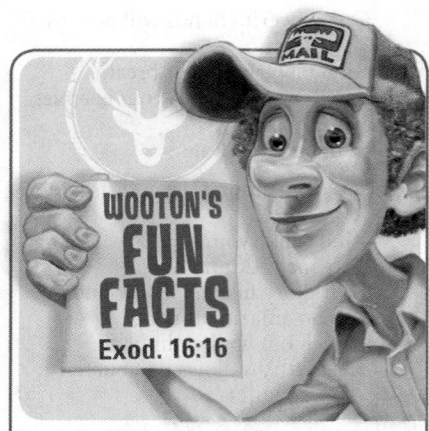

WOOTON'S FUN FACTS
Exod. 16:16

Once I tried to see what it was like to eat three pounds of manna a day. Since we don't have manna these days, I figured the closest I could get was frosted cereal, so I ate two family-sized boxes one morning. It didn't work out so well.

[20]Some of them didn't pay any attention to Moses. They kept part of it until morning. But it was full of maggots and began to stink. So Moses became angry with them.

[21]Each morning everyone gathered as much as they needed. But by the hottest time of the day, the thin flakes had melted away. [22]On the sixth day, the people gathered twice as much. It amounted to six pounds for each person. The leaders of the community came and reported that to Moses. [23]He said to them, "Here is what the LORD commanded. He said, 'Tomorrow will be a day of rest. It will be a holy Sabbath day. It will be set apart for the LORD. So bake what you want to bake. Boil what you want to boil. Save what is left. Keep it until morning.'"

[24]So they saved it until morning, just as Moses commanded. It didn't stink or get maggots in it. [25]"Eat it today," Moses said. "Today is a Sabbath day to honor the LORD. You won't find any flakes on the ground today. [26]Gather them for six days. But on the seventh day there won't be any. It's the Sabbath day."

[27]In spite of what Moses said, some of the people went out on the seventh day to gather the flakes. But they didn't find any. [28]Then the LORD spoke to Moses. He said,

"How long will all of you refuse to obey my commands and my teachings? [29]Keep in mind that I have given you the Sabbath day. That is why on the sixth day I give you bread for two days. Everyone must stay where they are on the seventh day. No one can go out." [30]So the people rested on the seventh day.

[31]The people of Israel called the bread manna. It was white like coriander seeds. It tasted like wafers made with honey. [32]Moses said, "Here is what the LORD has commanded. He has said, 'Get three pounds of manna. Keep it for all time to come. Then those who live after you will see the bread I gave you to eat in the desert. I gave it to you when I brought you out of Egypt.'"

[33]So Moses said to Aaron, "Get a jar. Put three pounds of manna in it. Then place it in front of the LORD. Keep it there for all time to come."

[34]Aaron did exactly as the LORD had commanded Moses. He put the manna with the tablets of the covenant law. He put it there so it would be kept for all time to come. [35]The Israelites ate manna for 40 years. They ate it until they came to a land where people were living. They ate it until they reached the border of Canaan. [36]The jar had three pounds of manna in it.

Water Out of the Rock

17 The whole community of Israel started out from the Desert of Sin. They traveled from place to place, just as the LORD commanded. They camped at Rephidim. But there wasn't any water for the people to drink. [2]So they argued with Moses. They said, "Give us water to drink."

Moses replied, "Why are you arguing with me? Why are you testing the LORD?"

[3]But the people were thirsty for water there. So they told Moses they weren't happy with him. They said, "Why did you bring us up out of Egypt? Did you want us, our children and our livestock to die of thirst?"

WHIT'S WISDOM

Exodus 17

Have you ever gone on a long road trip with your family? I remember a few with my kids. Jason was never the most patient at sitting in the car for long periods. How about you? Have you ever complained about being thirsty or hungry or asked, "Are we there yet?" You're not the first! God's people had to travel from Egypt to their new land by walking through a desert. Along that sandy pathway there weren't any indoor bathrooms, vending machines, or fast-food restaurants. So the Israelites started complaining. They even got angry. Read Exodus 17:1–7 to find out what happened.

Was it wrong for the Israelites to say they were thirsty? No, but there's a big difference between complaining and asking.

Why didn't the Israelites kindly ask God for water instead of immediately complaining? By complaining right away, they showed they didn't trust God to help them.

Sometimes we treat God the same way. We complain before we even ask for His help. And sometimes we do this with our parents too. Try this on your next trip. Decide ahead of time *not* to complain but to ask nicely for help when you need anything. Will your trip be different? There's only one way to find out.

⁴Then Moses cried out to the LORD. He said, "What am I going to do with these people? They are almost ready to kill me by throwing stones at me."

⁵The LORD answered Moses. "Go out in front of the people. Take some of the elders of Israel along with you. Take in your hand the walking stick you used when you struck the Nile River. Go. ⁶I will stand there in front of you by the rock at Mount Horeb. Hit the rock. Then water will come out of it for the people to drink." So Moses hit the rock while the elders of Israel watched. ⁷Moses called the place Massah and Meribah. That's because the people of Israel argued with him there. They also tested the LORD. They asked, "Is the LORD among us or not?"

Joshua Wins the Battle Over the Amalekites

⁸The Amalekites came and attacked the Israelites at Rephidim. ⁹Moses said to Joshua, "Choose some of our men. Then go out and fight against the Amalekites. Tomorrow I will stand on top of the hill. I'll stand there holding the walking stick God gave me."

¹⁰So Joshua fought against the Amalekites, just as Moses had ordered. Moses, Aaron and Hur went to the top of the hill. ¹¹As long as Moses held up his hand, the Israelites were winning. But every time he lowered his hands, the Amalekites began to win. ¹²When Moses' arms got tired, Aaron and Hur got a stone and put it under him. Then he sat on it. Aaron and Hur held up his hands. Aaron was on one side, and Hur was on the other. Moses' hands remained steady until sunset. ¹³So Joshua destroyed the Amalekite army with swords.

¹⁴Then the LORD said to Moses, "This is something to be remembered. So write it on a scroll. Make sure Joshua knows you have done it. I will completely erase the memory of the Amalekites from the earth."

¹⁵Then Moses built an altar. He called it The LORD Is My Banner. ¹⁶He said, "The Amalekites opposed the authority of the LORD. So the LORD will fight against the Amalekites for all time to come."

Jethro Visits Moses

18 Moses' father-in-law Jethro was the priest of Midian. He heard about everything God had done for Moses and for his people Israel. Jethro heard how the LORD had brought Israel out of Egypt.

²Moses had sent his wife Zipporah to his father-in-law. So Jethro welcomed her ³and her two sons. One son was named Gershom. That's because Moses had said, "I'm an outsider in a strange land." ⁴The other was named Eliezer. That's because Moses had said, "My father's God helped me. He saved me from Pharaoh's sword."

⁵Moses' father-in-law Jethro came to Moses in the desert. Moses' sons and wife came with Jethro. Moses was camped near the mountain of God. ⁶Jethro had sent a message to him. It said, "I, your father-in-law Jethro, am coming to you. I'm bringing your wife and her two sons."

⁷So Moses went out to meet his father-in-law. Moses bowed down and kissed him. They greeted each other. Then they went into the tent. ⁸Moses told Jethro everything the LORD had done to Pharaoh and the Egyptians. The LORD did all of this because of how much he loved Israel. Moses told Jethro about all their hard times along the way. He told him about how the LORD had saved them.

⁹Jethro was delighted to hear about all the good things the LORD had done for Israel. He heard about how God had saved them from the power of the Egyptians. ¹⁰He said, "I praise the LORD. He saved you and your people from the power of the Egyptians and of Pharaoh. ¹¹Now I know that the LORD is greater than all other gods. See what he did to those who looked down on Israel." ¹²Then Moses' father-in-law Jethro brought a burnt offering and other sacrifices to God. Aaron came with all the elders of Israel. They ate a meal with Moses' father-in-law in the sight of God.

¹³The next day Moses took his seat to serve the people as their judge. They stood around him from morning until evening. ¹⁴His father-in-law saw everything Moses was doing for the people. So he said, "Aren't you trying to do too much for the people? You are the only judge. And all these people are standing around you from morning until evening."

¹⁵Moses answered, "The people come to me to find out what God wants them to do. ¹⁶Anytime they don't agree with one another, they come to me. I decide between them. I tell them about God's rules and instructions."

¹⁷Moses' father-in-law replied, "What you are doing isn't good. ¹⁸You will just get worn out. And so will these people who come to you. There's too much work for you. You can't possibly handle it by yourself. ¹⁹Listen to me. I'll give you some advice, and may God be with you. You must speak to God for the people. Take their problems to him. ²⁰Teach them his rules and instructions. Show them how to live and what to do. ²¹But choose men of ability from all the people. They must have respect for God. You must be able to trust them. They must not try to get money by cheating others. Appoint them as officials over thousands, hundreds, fifties and tens. ²²Let them serve the people as judges. But have them bring every hard case to you. They can decide the easy ones themselves. That will make your load lighter. They will share it with you. ²³If this is what God wants and if you do it, then you will be able to carry the load. And all these people will go home satisfied."

²⁴Moses listened to his father-in-law. He did everything Jethro said. ²⁵He chose men of ability from the whole community of Israel. He made them leaders of the people. They became officials over thousands, hundreds, fifties and tens. ²⁶They judged the people at all times. They brought the hard cases to Moses. But they decided the easy ones themselves.

²⁷Moses sent his father-in-law on his way. So Jethro returned to his own country.

Israel Comes to Mount Sinai

19 Exactly three months after the people of Israel left Egypt, they came to the Desert of Sinai. ²After they started out from Rephidim, they entered the Desert of Sinai. They camped there in the desert in front of the mountain.

³Then Moses went up to God. The LORD called out to him from the mountain. He said, "Here is what I want you to say to my people, who belong to Jacob's family. Tell the Israelites, ⁴You have seen for yourselves what I did to Egypt. You saw how I carried you on the wings of eagles and brought you to myself. ⁵Now obey me completely. Keep my covenant. If you do, then out of all the nations you will be my special treasure. The whole earth is mine. ⁶But you will be a kingdom of priests to serve me. You will be my holy nation.' That is what you must tell the Israelites."

⁷So Moses went back. He sent for the elders of the people. He explained to them everything the LORD had commanded him to say. ⁸All the people answered together. They said, "We will do everything the LORD has said." So Moses brought their answer back to the LORD.

⁹The LORD spoke to Moses. He said, "I am going to come to you in a thick cloud. The people will hear me speaking with you. They will always put their trust in you." Then Moses told the LORD what the people had said.

¹⁰The LORD said to Moses, "Go to the people. Today and tomorrow set them apart for me. Have them wash their clothes. ¹¹Have the people ready by the third day. On that day the LORD will come down on Mount Sinai. Everyone will see it. ¹²Put limits for the people around the mountain. Tell them, 'Be careful that you do not go near the mountain. Do not even touch the foot of it. Whoever touches the mountain must be put to death. ¹³Do not lay a hand on any of them. Kill them with stones or shoot them with arrows. Whether they are people or animals, do not let them live.' They may go near the mountain only when the ram's horn gives out a long blast."

¹⁴Moses went down the mountain to the people. After he set them apart for the LORD, they washed their clothes. ¹⁵Then he spoke to the people. He said, "Get ready for the third day. Don't have sex."

¹⁶On the morning of the third day there was thunder and lightning. A thick cloud covered the mountain. A trumpet gave out a very loud blast. Everyone in the camp trembled with fear. ¹⁷Then Moses led the people out of the camp to meet with God. They stood at the foot of the mountain. ¹⁸Smoke covered Mount Sinai, because the LORD came down on it in fire. The smoke rose up from it like

smoke from a furnace. The whole mountain trembled and shook. ¹⁹The sound of the trumpet got louder and louder. Then Moses spoke. And the voice of God answered him.

²⁰The LORD came down to the top of Mount Sinai. He told Moses to come to the top of the mountain. So Moses went up. ²¹The LORD said to him, "Go down and warn the people. They must not force their way through to see the LORD. If they do, many of them will die. ²²The priests approach the LORD when they serve him. But even they must set themselves apart for the LORD. If they do not, his anger will break out against them."

²³Moses said to the LORD, "The people can't come up Mount Sinai. You yourself warned us. You said, 'Put limits around the mountain. Set it apart as holy.'"

²⁴The LORD replied, "Go down. Bring Aaron up with you. But the priests and the people must not force their way through. They must not come up to the LORD. If they do, his anger will break out against them."

²⁵So Moses went down to the people and told them.

God Gives His People the Ten Commandments

20 Here are all the words God spoke. He said,

² "I am the LORD your God. I brought you out of Egypt. That is the land where you were slaves.

³ "Do not put any other gods in place of me.

⁴ "Do not make for yourself statues of gods that look like anything in the sky. They may not look like anything on the earth or in the waters either. ⁵Do not bow down to them or worship them. I, the LORD your God, am a jealous God. I cause the sins of the parents to affect their children. I will cause the sins of those who hate me to affect even their grandchildren and great-grandchildren. ⁶But for all time to come I show love to all those who love me and keep my commandments.

⁷ "Do not misuse the name of the LORD your God. The LORD will find guilty anyone who misuses his name.

⁸ "Remember to keep the Sabbath day holy. ⁹Do all your work in six days. ¹⁰But the seventh day is a sabbath to honor the LORD your God. Do not do any work on that day. The same command applies to your sons and daughters, your male and female servants, and your animals. It also applies to any outsiders who live in your towns. ¹¹In six days the LORD made the heavens, the earth, the sea and everything in them. But he rested on the seventh day. So the LORD blessed the Sabbath day and made it holy.

¹² "Honor your father and mother. Then you will live a long time in the land the LORD your God is giving you.

¹³ "Do not murder.

¹⁴ "Do not commit adultery.

¹⁵ "Do not steal.

¹⁶ "Do not be a false witness against your neighbor.

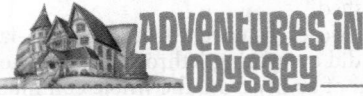

Tamika Washington figured out what it meant to "honor" her parents (even when they are embarrassing) in "Bringing Up Dads" (A#46).

REMEMBER THIS

EXODUS 20:12

"Honor your father and mother. Then you will live a long time in the land the LORD your God is giving you."

¹⁷ "Do not want to have anything your neighbor owns. Do not want to have your neighbor's house, wife, male or female servant, ox or donkey."

¹⁸The people saw the thunder and lightning. They heard the trumpet. They saw the mountain covered with smoke. They trembled with fear and stayed a long way off. ¹⁹They said to Moses, "Speak to us yourself. Then we'll listen. But don't let God speak to us. If he does, we'll die."

²⁰Moses said to the people, "Don't be afraid. God has come to test you. He wants you to have respect for him. That will keep you from sinning."

²¹Moses approached the thick darkness where God was. But the people remained a long way off.

Worship the LORD

²²Then the LORD said to Moses, "Here is what you must tell the people of Israel. Say to them, 'You have seen for yourselves what I said to you from heaven. ²³Do not put any other gods in place of me. Do not make silver or gold statues of them for yourselves.

²⁴"'Make an altar out of dirt for me. Sacrifice your burnt offerings and friendship offerings on it. Sacrifice your sheep, goats and cattle on it. I will come to you and bless you everywhere I cause my name to be honored. ²⁵If you make an altar out of stones to honor me, do not build it with blocks of stone. You will make it "unclean" if you use a tool on it. ²⁶Do not walk up steps to my altar. If you do,

WHAT ABOUT YOU?

Something's different. Usually your dad says, "No sugar before bed." But tonight when you ask him for ice cream he says, "One scoop or two?" The next morning he brings you pancakes in bed. After that, he drives you to the toy store and wheels a shopping cart toward you. "Fill it," he says with a grin. "Whatever you can fit in there, I'll buy."

At first, you're thrilled. You think you have the coolest dad on earth. But after a month of chocolate chip pancakes and tummy aches, you start to reconsider.

Maybe supercool dads are overrated. That's what the Adventures in Odyssey episode "Bringing Up Dads" shows us. Tamika Washington is getting older, and she finds her dad embarrassing. While it might have been "cool" for Tamika to have a father who let her do whatever she wanted, it wouldn't have been God's best for her. Ed Washington knows that he may be a little embarrassing (what dad isn't?), but at least he cares for his daughter.

Exodus 20:12 says, "Honor your father and mother." By talking with her father about the changes in her life, Tamika respectfully shares her feelings while showing him honor. We should do the same.

Are you honoring your parents by obeying them? Do something today to honor your parents. Write them a note, send them a text saying that you love them—or brag about them to your friends. Honoring our parents pleases God. Thank Him for the parents He gave you (even if they embarrass you sometimes).

Jason's Jargon

EXODUS 20

Search this chapter for the words *false witness*. Being a false witness doesn't just mean bad testimony in court, but includes any form of lying or purposefully deceiving another person.

someone might see your naked body under your robes.'

Other Laws

21 "Here are the laws you must explain to the people of Israel.

Set Your Hebrew Servants Free

²"Suppose you buy a Hebrew servant. He must serve you for six years. But in the seventh year, you must set him free. He does not have to pay anything. ³If he does not have a wife when he comes, he must go free alone. But if he has a wife when he comes, she must go with him. ⁴Suppose his master gives him a wife. And suppose she has sons or daughters by him. Then only the man will go free. The woman and her children will belong to her master.

⁵"But suppose the servant says, 'I love my master and my wife and children. I don't want to go free.' ⁶Then his master must take him to the judges. His master must take him to the door or doorpost of his master's house. His master must poke a hole through his servant's earlobe into the door or doorpost. Then he will become his servant for life.

⁷"Suppose a man sells his daughter as a servant. Then she can't go free as male servants do. ⁸But what if the master who has chosen her does not like her? Then he must let the man buy her back. He has no right to sell her to strangers. He has broken his promise to her. ⁹What if he chooses her to marry his son? Then he must grant her the rights of a daughter. ¹⁰What if her master marries another woman? He must still give the first one her food and clothes and sleep with her. ¹¹If he does not provide her with those

three things, she can go free. She does not have to pay anything.

Laws About Harming Others

¹²"Anyone who hits and kills someone else must be put to death. ¹³Suppose they did not do it on purpose. Suppose I let it happen. Then they can escape to a place I will choose. ¹⁴But suppose they kill someone on purpose. Then take them away from my altar and put them to death.

¹⁵"Anyone who attacks their father or mother must be put to death.

¹⁶"Anyone who kidnaps and sells another person must be put to death. If they still have the person with them when they are caught, they must be put to death.

¹⁷"Anyone who asks for something bad to happen to their father or mother must be put to death.

¹⁸"Suppose two people get into a fight and argue with each other. One hits the other with a stone or his fist. And the person who was hit does not die but has to stay in bed. ¹⁹And later that person gets up and walks around outside with a walking stick. Then the person who hit the other person will not be held responsible. But that person must pay the one who was hurt for the time spent in bed. The one who hit the other person must be sure that person is completely healed.

²⁰"Suppose a person beats their male or female slave to death with a club. That person must be punished. ²¹But they will not be punished if the slave gets up after a day or two. After all, the slave is their property.

²²"Suppose some people are fighting and one of them hits a pregnant woman. And suppose she has her baby early but is not badly hurt. Then the one who hurt her must pay a fine. That person must pay what the woman's husband asks for and the court allows. ²³But if someone is badly hurt, a life must be taken for a life. ²⁴An eye must be put out for an eye. A tooth must be knocked out for a tooth. A hand must be cut off for a hand and a foot for a foot. ²⁵A burn must be given for a burn, a wound for a wound, and a bruise for a bruise.

²⁶"Suppose an owner hits a male or female slave in the eye and destroys it. Then the owner must let the slave go free to pay for the eye. ²⁷Suppose an owner knocks out the tooth of a male or female slave.

Then he must let the slave go free to pay for the tooth.

[28]"Suppose a bull kills a man or woman with its horns. Then you must kill the bull by throwing stones at it. Its meat must not be eaten. But the owner of the bull will not be held accountable. [29]But suppose the bull has had the habit of attacking people. And suppose the owner has been warned but has not kept it fenced in. Then if it kills a man or woman, you must kill it with stones. The owner must also be put to death. [30]But suppose payment is required of him instead. Then the owner can save his life by paying what is required. [31]The same law applies if the bull wounds a son or daughter with its horns. [32]Suppose the bull wounds a male or female slave. Then the owner must pay the slave's master about 12 ounces of silver. You must kill the bull with stones.

[33]"Suppose someone uncovers a pit or digs one and does not cover it. And suppose an ox or donkey falls into it. [34]Then the person who opened the pit must pay the animal's owner for the loss. The dead animal will belong to the person who opened the pit.

[35]"Suppose someone's bull wounds a neighbor's bull and it dies. Then the owner and the neighbor must sell the live one. And they must share the money and the dead animal equally. [36]But suppose people knew that the bull had the habit of attacking. And suppose the owner did not keep it fenced in. Then the owner must give another animal to pay for the dead animal. And the dead animal will belong to the owner.

Laws About Keeping Property Safe

22 "Suppose someone steals an ox or a sheep. And suppose that person kills it or sells it. Then the thief must pay back five oxen for the ox. Or the thief must pay back four sheep for the sheep.

[2]"Suppose you catch a thief breaking into your house at night. And suppose you hit the thief and the thief dies. Then you are not guilty of murder. [3]But suppose it happens after the sun has come up. Then you are guilty of murder.

"Anyone who steals must pay for whatever they steal. But suppose the thief does not have anything. Then the thief must be sold to pay for what was stolen. [4]What if the stolen ox, donkey or sheep is found alive with the thief? Then the thief must pay back twice as much.

[5]"Suppose someone lets their livestock eat grass in someone else's field or vineyard. Then they must pay that person back from the best crops of their own field or vineyard.

[6]"Suppose a fire breaks out and spreads into bushes. Suppose it burns cut and stacked grain or grain that is still growing. Or suppose it burns the whole field. Then the one who started the fire must pay for the loss.

[7]"Suppose someone gives a neighbor silver or other things to keep safe. And suppose they are stolen from the neighbor's house. The thief, if caught, must pay back twice as much as was stolen. [8]But suppose the thief is not found. Then the neighbor must go to the judges. They will decide whether the neighbor has stolen the other person's property. [9]Suppose you have an ox, donkey, sheep or clothing that does not belong to you. Or you have other property lost by someone else. And suppose someone says, 'That belongs to me.' Then both people must bring their case to the judges. The one the judges decide is guilty must pay back twice as much to the other person.

[10]"Suppose someone asks their neighbor to take care of a donkey, ox, sheep or any other animal. And suppose the animal dies or gets hurt. Or suppose it is stolen while no one is looking. [11]Then the problem will be settled by promising the LORD to tell the truth. Suppose the neighbor says, 'I didn't steal your property.' Then the owner must accept what the neighbor says. No payment is required. [12]But suppose the animal really was stolen. Then the neighbor must pay the owner back. [13]Or suppose it was torn to pieces by a wild animal. Then the neighbor must bring in what is left as proof. No payment is required.

[14]"Suppose someone borrows an animal from their neighbor. And it gets hurt or dies while the owner is not there. Then the borrower must pay for it. [15]But suppose the owner is with the animal. Then the borrower will not have to pay. If the borrower hired the animal, the money paid to hire it covers the loss.

Laws About Social Problems

[16]"Suppose a man meets a virgin who is not engaged. And he talks her into having sex with him. Then he must pay her father the price for a bride. And he must marry her. [17]But suppose her father absolutely refuses to give her to him. Then he must still pay the price for getting married to a virgin.

[18]"Do not let a woman who does evil magic stay alive. Put her to death.

[19]"Anyone who has sex with an animal must be put to death.

[20]"Anyone who sacrifices to any god other than the LORD must be destroyed.

[21]"Do not treat outsiders badly. Do not give them a hard time. Remember, you were outsiders in Egypt.

[22]"Do not take advantage of widows. Do not take advantage of children whose fathers have died. [23]If you do, they might cry out to me. I will certainly hear them. [24]And I will get angry. I will kill you with a sword. Your wives will become widows. Your children's fathers will die.

[25]"Suppose you lend money to one of my people among you who is in need. Then do not treat it like a business deal. Do not charge any interest at all. [26]Suppose your neighbor owes you money and gives you a coat as a promise to pay it back. Then return it by sunset. [27]That coat is the only thing your neighbor owns to wear or sleep in. When they cry out to me, I will listen, because I am loving and kind.

[28]"Do not speak evil things against God. Do not curse the ruler of your people.

[29]"Do not keep for yourself your grain offerings or wine offerings.

"You must give me the oldest of your sons. [30]Do the same with your cattle and sheep. Let them stay with their mothers for seven days. But give them to me on the eighth day.

[31]"I want you to be my holy people. So do not eat the meat of any animal that has been torn by wild animals. Throw it to the dogs.

Laws About Mercy and Fairness

23 "Do not spread reports that are false. Do not help a guilty person by telling lies in court.

[2]"Do not follow the crowd when they do what is wrong. When you are a witness

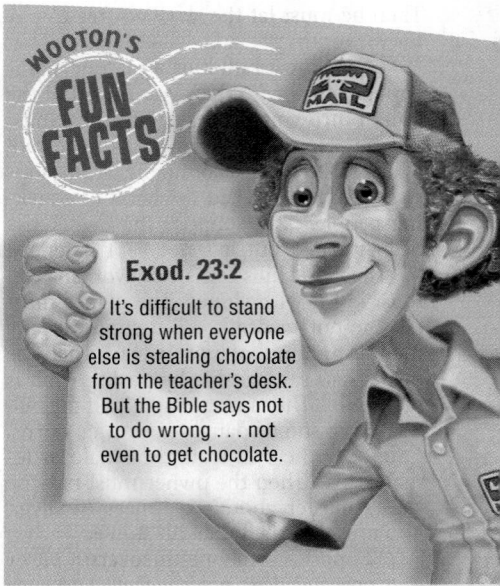

Exod. 23:2

It's difficult to stand strong when everyone else is stealing chocolate from the teacher's desk. But the Bible says not to do wrong . . . not even to get chocolate.

in court, do not turn what is right into what is wrong. Do not go along with the crowd. [3]Do not show favor to a poor person in court.

[4]"Suppose you come across your enemy's ox or donkey wandering away. Then be sure to return it. [5]Suppose you see that the donkey of someone who hates you has fallen down under its load. Then do not leave it there. Be sure you help them with it.

[6]"Be fair to your poor people in their court cases. [7]Do not have anything to do with a false charge. Do not put to death people not guilty of doing anything wrong. I will not let guilty people go free.

[8]"Do not take money from people who want special favors. It makes you blind to the truth. It twists the words of good people.

[9]"Do not treat outsiders badly. You yourselves know how it feels to be outsiders. Remember, you were outsiders in Egypt.

Sabbath Laws

[10]"For six years plant your fields and gather your crops. [11]But during the seventh year do not plow your land or use it. Then the poor people among you can get food from it. The wild animals can eat what is left over. Do the same thing with your vineyards and your groves of olive trees.

[12]"Do all your work in six days. But do not do any work on the seventh day. Then your oxen and donkeys can rest. The slaves born in your house can be renewed. And so can the outsiders who live among you.

[13]"Be careful to do everything I have said to you. Do not speak the names of other gods. Do not even let them be heard on your lips.

Laws About Celebrating the Three Main Feasts

[14]"Three times a year you must celebrate a feast in my honor.

[15]"Celebrate the Feast of Unleavened Bread. For seven days, eat bread made without yeast, just as I commanded you. Do it at the appointed time in the month of Aviv. You came out of Egypt in that month.

"You must not come to worship me with your hands empty.

[16]"Celebrate the Feast of Weeks. Bring the first share of your crops from your fields.

"Celebrate the Feast of Booths. Hold it in the fall when you gather in your crops from your fields.

[17]"Three times a year all your men must come to worship me. I am your LORD and King.

[18]"Do not include anything made with yeast when you offer me the blood of a sacrifice.

"Suppose the fat from sacrifices is left over from my feasts. Then do not keep it until morning.

[19]"Bring the best of the first share of your crops to my house. I am the LORD your God.

"Do not cook a young goat in its mother's milk.

God's Angel Will Prepare the Way

[20]"I am sending an angel ahead of you. He will guard you along the way. He will bring you to the place I have prepared. [21]Pay attention to him. Listen to what he says. Do not refuse to obey him. He will not forgive you if you turn against him. He

WHAT ABOUT YOU?

Some days are peaceful. Everything makes sense. The pacing of life is smooth and easy to manage, and everyone seems to be getting along. You feel content. However, other days are just the *opposite* of that. You struggle with big-time stress. Life doesn't make much sense.

In the midst of these challenges, isn't it wonderful to know that God will calm the storms in our lives? Deuteronomy 31:6 reminds us: "Be strong and brave. Don't be afraid of them. Don't be terrified because of them. The LORD your God will go with you."

God's people were struggling as they wandered in the wilderness before reaching the Promised Land. So God encouraged them by sending an angel to protect them as they traveled and eventually lead them to the place He prepared.

Are you going through challenges right now? Maybe you're struggling with schoolwork, having a hard time making friends, or a coach isn't treating you fairly. It's stressful. But because the Lord walks beside us at all times, we don't have to worry when life is chaotic. Nothing happens that surprises God, and there's nothing He can't handle. So take comfort. If you place your trust in Jesus, He will bring you through those hard times to the peaceful times.

Write Deuteronomy 31:6 on a piece of paper, and put it inside your shoe as you start your day. (That's one way to stand on God's Word!) Later, when you take off your shoes, it will remind you once again that God is always walking with you.

has my full authority. ²²Listen carefully to what he says. Do everything I say. Then I will be an enemy to your enemies. I will fight against those who fight against you. ²³My angel will go ahead of you. He will bring you into the land of the Amorites, Hittites, Perizzites, Canaanites, Hivites and Jebusites. I will wipe them out. ²⁴Do not do what they do. Do not bow down to their gods or worship them. You must destroy the statues of their gods. You must break their sacred stones to pieces. ²⁵Worship the LORD your God. Then he will bless your food and water. I, the LORD, will take away any sickness you may have. ²⁶In your land no woman will give birth to a dead baby. Every woman will be able to have children. I will give you a long life.

²⁷"I will send my terror ahead of you. I will throw every nation you meet into a panic. I will make all your enemies turn their backs and run away. ²⁸I will send hornets ahead of you. They will drive the Hivites, Canaanites and Hittites out of your way. ²⁹But I will not drive them out in just one year. If I did, the land would be deserted. There would be too many wild animals for you. ³⁰I will drive them out ahead of you little by little. I will do that until there are enough of you to take control of the land.

³¹"I will make your borders secure from the Red Sea to the Mediterranean Sea. They will go from the desert to the Euphrates River. I will hand over to you the people who live in the land. You will drive them out to make room for yourselves. ³²Do not make a covenant with them or with their gods. ³³Do not let them live in your land. If you do, they will cause you to sin against me. If you worship their gods, that will certainly be a trap for you."

The Blood of the Covenant

24 The LORD said to Moses, "You and Aaron, Nadab and Abihu, and 70 of the elders of Israel must come to worship the LORD. Do not come close when you worship. ²Only Moses can come close to me. The others must not come near. And the people may not go up with him."

³Moses went and told the people all the LORD's words and laws. They answered with one voice. They said, "We will do everything the LORD has told us to do."

⁴Then Moses wrote down everything the LORD had said.

Moses got up early the next morning. He built an altar at the foot of the mountain. He set up 12 stone pillars. They stood for the 12 tribes of Israel. ⁵Then he sent young Israelite men to sacrifice burnt offerings. They also sacrificed young bulls as friendship offerings to the LORD. ⁶Moses put half of the blood in bowls. He splashed the other half against the altar. ⁷Then he took the Book of the Covenant and read it to the people. They answered, "We will do everything the LORD has told us to do. We will obey him."

⁸Then Moses took the blood and sprinkled it on the people. He said, "This is the blood that puts the covenant into effect. The LORD has made this covenant with you in keeping with all these words."

⁹Moses and Aaron, Nadab and Abihu, and the 70 elders of Israel went up. ¹⁰They saw the God of Israel. Under his feet was something like a street made out of lapis lazuli. It was as bright blue as the sky itself. ¹¹But God didn't destroy those Israelite leaders when they saw him. They ate and drank.

¹²The LORD said to Moses, "Come up to me on the mountain. Stay here. I will give you the stone tablets. They contain the

Exod. 24:10 The Bible has a lot of stories about feet. People are always washing them or sprinkling blood on them or taking their shoes on and off. Even God's feet are mentioned here. Since God is a spirit, it's not clear if He has actual feet or if this is just a metaphor. Other places in the Bible talk about God's hand, palm, arm, and eyes.

law and commandments I have written to teach the people."

[13]Then Moses and Joshua, his helper, started out. Moses went up on the mountain of God. [14]He said to the elders, "Wait for us here until we come back to you. Aaron and Hur are with you. Anyone who has a problem can go to them."

[15]Moses went up on the mountain. Then the cloud covered it. [16]The glory of the LORD settled on Mount Sinai. The cloud covered the mountain for six days. On the seventh day the LORD called out to Moses from inside the cloud. [17]The people of Israel saw the glory of the LORD. It looked like a fire burning on top of the mountain. [18]Moses entered the cloud as he went on up the mountain. He stayed on the mountain for 40 days and 40 nights.

Offerings for the Holy Tent

25 The LORD said to Moses, [2]"Tell the people of Israel to bring me an offering. You must receive the offering for me from everyone whose hearts move them to give.

[3] "Here are the offerings you must receive from them.

"gold, silver and bronze
[4] blue, purple and bright red yarn and fine linen
goat hair
[5] ram skins that are dyed red
another kind of strong leather
acacia wood
[6] olive oil for the lights
spices for the anointing oil and for the sweet-smelling incense
[7] onyx stones and other jewels for the linen apron and chest cloth

[8]"Have them make a sacred tent for me. I will live among them. [9]Make the holy tent and everything that belongs to it. Make them exactly like the pattern I will show you.

The Ark of the Covenant Law

[10]"Have them make an ark out of acacia wood. It must be a chest three feet nine inches long and two feet three inches wide and high. [11]Cover it inside and outside with pure gold. Put a strip of gold around it. [12]Make four gold rings for it. Join them to its four bottom corners. Put two rings on one side and two rings on the other. [13]Then make poles out of acacia wood. Cover them with gold. [14]Put the poles through the rings on the sides of the ark to carry it. [15]The poles must remain in the rings of the ark. Do not remove them. [16]I will give you the tablets of the covenant law. When I do, put them into the ark.

[17]"Make its cover out of pure gold. The cover is the place where sin will be paid for. Make it three feet nine inches long and two feet three inches wide. [18]Make two cherubim out of hammered gold at the ends of the cover. [19]Put one of the cherubim on each end of it. Make the cherubim part of the cover itself. [20]They must have their wings spread up over the cover. The cherubim must face each other and look toward the cover. [21]Place the cover on top of the ark. I will give you the tablets of the covenant law. Put them in the ark. [22]The ark is where the tablets of the covenant law are kept. I will meet with you above the cover between the two cherubim that are over the ark. There I will give you all my commands for the Israelites.

The Table for the Holy Bread

[23]"Make a table out of acacia wood. Make it three feet long, one foot six inches wide and two feet three inches high. [24]Cover it with pure gold. Put a strip of gold around it. [25]Also make a rim around it three inches wide. Put a strip of gold around the rim. [26]Make four gold rings for the table. Join them to the four corners, where the four legs are. [27]The rings must be close to the rim. They must hold the poles that will be used to carry the table. [28]Make the poles out of acacia wood. Cover them with gold. Use them to carry the table. [29]Make its plates and dishes out of pure gold. Also make its pitchers and bowls out of pure gold. Use the pitchers and bowls to pour out drink offerings. [30]Put the holy bread on the table. It must be near my holy throne on the ark of the covenant law at all times.

The Gold Lampstand

[31]"Make a lampstand out of pure gold. Hammer out its base and stem. Its buds, blossoms and cups must branch out from it. They must be part of the lampstand itself. [32]Six branches must come out from

the sides of the lampstand. Make three on one side and three on the other. [33]On one branch make three cups that are shaped like almond flowers with buds and blossoms. Then put three on the next branch. Do the same with all six branches that come out from the lampstand. [34]On the lampstand there must be four cups that are shaped like almond flowers with buds and blossoms. [35]One bud must be under the first pair of branches that come out from the lampstand. Put a second bud under the second pair. And put a third bud under the third pair. Make a total of six branches. [36]The buds and branches must come out from the lampstand. The whole lampstand must be one piece hammered out of pure gold.

[37]"Then make its seven lamps. Set them up on it so that they light the space in front of it. [38]The trays and wick cutters must be made out of pure gold. [39]Use 75 pounds of pure gold to make the lampstand and everything used with it. [40]Be sure to make everything just like the pattern I showed you on the mountain.

The Holy Tent

26 "Make ten curtains out of finely twisted linen for the holy tent. Make them with blue, purple and bright red yarn. Have a skilled worker sew cherubim into the pattern. [2]Make all the curtains the same size. They must be 42 feet long and six feet wide. [3]Join five of the curtains together. Do the same thing with the other five. [4]Make loops out of blue strips of cloth along the edge of the end curtain in one set. Do the same thing with the end curtain in the other set. [5]Make 50 loops on the end curtain of the one set. Do the same thing on the end curtain of the other set. Put the loops across from each other. [6]Make 50 gold hooks. Use them to join the curtains together so that the holy tent is all one piece.

[7]"Make a total of 11 curtains out of goat hair to put over the holy tent. [8]Make all 11 curtains the same size. They must be 45 feet long and six feet wide. [9]Join five of the curtains together into one set. Do the same thing with the other six. Fold the sixth curtain in half at the front of the tent. [10]Make 50 loops along the edge of the end curtain in the one set. Do the same thing

with the other set. [11]Then make 50 bronze hooks. Put them in the loops to join the tent together all in one piece. [12]Let the extra half curtain hang down at the rear of the holy tent. [13]The tent curtains will be 18 inches longer on both sides. What is left over will hang over the sides of the holy tent and cover it. [14]Make a covering for the tent. Make it out of ram skins that are dyed red. Put a covering of the other strong leather over that.

[15]"Make frames out of acacia wood for the holy tent. [16]Make each frame 15 feet long and two feet three inches wide. [17]Add two small wooden pins to each frame. Make the pins stick out so that they are even with each other. Make all the frames for the holy tent in the same way. [18]Make 20 frames for the south side of the holy tent. [19]And make 40 silver bases to go under them. Make two bases for each frame. Put one under each pin that sticks out. [20]For the north side of the holy tent make 20 frames [21]and 40 silver bases. Put two bases under each frame. [22]Make six frames for the west end of the holy tent. [23]Make two frames for the corners at the far end. [24]At those two corners the frames must be double from top to bottom. They must be fitted into a single ring. Make both of them the same. [25]There will be eight frames and 16 silver bases. There will be two bases under each frame.

[26]"Also make crossbars out of acacia wood. Make five for the frames on one side of the holy tent. [27]Make five for the frames on the other side. And make five for the frames on the west, at the far end of the holy tent. [28]The center crossbar must reach from end to end at the middle of the frames. [29]Cover the frames with gold. Make gold rings to hold the crossbars. Also cover the crossbars with gold.

[30]"Set up the holy tent in keeping with the plan I showed you on the mountain.

[31]"Make a curtain out of blue, purple and bright red yarn and finely twisted linen. Have a skilled worker sew cherubim into the pattern. [32]Hang the curtain with gold hooks on four posts that are made out of acacia wood. Cover the posts with gold. Stand them on four silver bases. [33]Hang the curtain from the hooks. Place the ark of the covenant law behind the curtain. The curtain will separate the Holy

Room from the Most Holy Room. [34]Put the cover on the ark of the covenant law in the Most Holy Room. The cover will be the place where sin is paid for. [35]Place the table outside the curtain on the north side of the holy tent. And put the lampstand across from it on the south side.

[36]"Make a curtain for the entrance to the tent. Make it out of blue, purple and bright red yarn and finely twisted linen. Have a person who sews skillfully make it. [37]Make gold hooks for the curtain. Make five posts out of acacia wood. Cover them with gold. And make five bronze bases for them.

The Altar for Burnt Offerings

27 "Build an altar out of acacia wood. It must be four feet six inches high and seven feet six inches square. [2]Make a horn stick out from each of its upper four corners. The horns and the altar must be all one piece. Cover the altar with bronze. [3]Make everything for the altar out of bronze. Make its pots to remove the ashes. Make its shovels, sprinkling bowls, meat forks, and pans for carrying ashes. [4]Make a bronze grate for the altar. Make a bronze ring for each of the four corners of the grate. [5]Put the grate halfway up the altar on the inside. [6]Make poles out of acacia wood for the altar. Cover them with bronze. [7]Put the poles through the rings. They will be on two sides of the altar for carrying it. [8]Make the altar out of boards. Leave it hollow. It must look just like what I showed you on the mountain.

The Courtyard

[9]"Make a courtyard for the holy tent. The south side must be 150 feet long. It must have curtains that are made out of finely twisted linen. [10]The curtains must be hung on 20 posts that have 20 bronze bases. The posts must have silver hooks and bands on them. [11]The north side must also be about 150 feet long. It must have curtains with 20 posts that have 20 bronze bases. The posts must have silver hooks and bands on them.

[12]"The west end of the courtyard must be 75 feet wide. It must have curtains with ten posts that have ten bases. [13]The east end of the courtyard, toward the sunrise, must also be 75 feet wide. [14]On one side

of the entrance you must put curtains that are 22 feet six inches long. Hang them on three posts. Each post must have a base. [15]On the other side you must also put curtains that are 22 feet six inches long. Hang them on three posts. Each post must have a base.

[16]"For the entrance to the courtyard, provide a curtain 30 feet long. Make it out of blue, purple and bright red yarn and finely twisted linen. Have someone who sews skillfully make it. Hang it on four posts. Each post must have a base. [17]All the posts that are around the courtyard must have silver bands and hooks. They must also have bronze bases. [18]The courtyard must be 150 feet long and 75 feet wide. It must have curtains that are made out of finely twisted linen. They must be seven feet six inches high. The posts must have bronze bases. [19]Make out of bronze all the other things used for any purpose in the holy tent. That includes all the tent stakes for the tent and the courtyard.

Oil for the Lampstand

[20]"Command the Israelites to bring you clear oil made from pressed olives. Use it to keep the lamps burning and giving light. [21]Aaron and his sons must keep the lamps burning in the tent of meeting. The lamps will be outside the curtain in front of the tablets of the covenant law. The lamps must be kept burning in front of the LORD from evening until morning. This is a law for the Israelites that will last for all time to come.

The Clothes for the Priests

28 "Have your brother Aaron brought to you from among the Israelites. His sons Nadab, Abihu, Eleazar and Ithamar must also be brought. They will serve me as priests. [2]Make sacred clothes for your brother Aaron. When he is wearing them, people will honor him. They will have respect for him. [3]Speak to all the skilled workers. I have given them the skill to do this kind of work. Tell them to make clothes for Aaron. He will wear them when he is set apart to serve me as priest. [4]The workers must make a chest cloth, a linen apron and an outer robe. They must also make an inner robe, a turban and a belt. They must make sacred clothes for your brother Aaron and his sons. Then they will serve me as priests. [5]Have the workers use thin gold wire, and blue, purple and bright red yarn, and fine linen.

The Linen Apron

[6]"Make the linen apron out of thin gold wire, and out of blue, purple and bright red yarn, and out of finely twisted linen. Have a skilled worker make it. [7]It must have two shoulder straps joined to two of its corners. [8]Its skillfully made waistband must be like the apron. The waistband must be part of the apron itself. Make the waistband out of thin gold wire, and out of blue, purple and bright red yarn, and out of finely twisted linen.

[9]"Get two onyx stones. Carve the names of the sons of Israel on them. [10]Arrange them in the order of their birth. Carve six names on one stone and six on the other. [11]Carve the names of the sons of Israel on the two stones the way a jewel cutter would carve them. Then put the stones in fancy gold settings. [12]Connect them to the shoulder straps of the linen apron. The stones will stand for the sons of Israel. Aaron must carry the names on his shoulders as a constant reminder while he is serving the LORD. [13]Make fancy gold settings. [14]Make two braided chains out of pure gold. Make them like ropes. Join the chains to the settings.

The Chest Cloth

[15]"Make a chest cloth that will be used for making decisions. Have a skilled worker make it. Make it like the linen apron. Use thin gold wire, and blue, purple and bright red yarn, and finely twisted linen. [16]Make it nine inches square. Fold it in half. [17]Put four rows of valuable jewels on it. Put carnelian, chrysolite and beryl in the first row. [18]Put turquoise, lapis lazuli and emerald in the second row. [19]Put jacinth, agate and amethyst in the third row. [20]And put topaz, onyx and jasper in the fourth row. Put them in fancy gold settings. [21]Use a total of 12 stones. Use one for each of the names of the sons of Israel. Each stone must be carved with the name of one of the 12 tribes.

[22]"Make braided chains out of pure gold for the chest cloth. Make them like ropes. [23]Make two gold rings for the chest cloth. Connect them to two corners of it. [24]Join the two gold chains to the rings at the corners of the chest cloth. [25]Join the other ends of the chains to the two settings. Join them to the shoulder straps on the front of the linen apron. [26]Make two gold rings. Connect them to the other two corners of the chest cloth. Put them on the inside edge next to the apron. [27]Make two more gold rings. Connect them to the bottom of the shoulder straps on the front of the apron. Put them close to the seam. Put them right above the waistband of the apron. [28]The rings of the chest cloth must be tied to the rings of the apron. Tie them to the waistband with blue cord. Then the chest cloth will not swing out from the linen apron.

[29]"When Aaron enters the Holy Room, he will carry the names of the sons of Israel over his heart. Their names will be on the chest cloth of decision. They will be a continuing reminder while he is serving the LORD. [30]Also put the Urim and Thummim into the chest cloth. Then they will be over Aaron's heart when he comes to serve the LORD. In that way, Aaron will always have what he needs to make decisions for the people of Israel. He will carry the Urim and Thummim over his heart while he is serving the LORD.

More Clothes for the Priests

[31]"Make the outer robe of the linen apron completely out of blue cloth. [32]In the center of the robe, make an opening for the head of the priest. Make an edge like a collar around the opening. Then it will not tear. [33]Make pomegranates out of blue, purple and bright red yarn. Sew them around the hem of the robe. Sew gold bells between them. [34]Sew a gold bell between every two pomegranates all around the hem of the robe. [35]Aaron must wear the robe when he serves as priest. The bells will jingle when he enters the Holy Room while he is serving the LORD. And they will jingle when he goes out. Then he will not die.

[36]"Make a plate out of pure gold. Carve words on it as if it were an official seal. Carve the words

SET APART FOR THE LORD.

Exod. 28:32, 38 Aaron's priestly robe had bells sewn onto the hem so God could hear him. He also had a gold plate on his forehead. I could trade my postal worker uniform for the robe, but the plate sounds really heavy. I'll stick to a cap.

³⁷Tie the plate to the front of the turban with a blue cord. ³⁸Aaron must wear this plate on his forehead all the time. He will be held responsible for all the sacred gifts the Israelites set apart. Then the LORD will accept the gifts.

³⁹"Make the inner robe out of fine linen. And make the turban out of fine linen. The belt must be made by a person who sews skillfully. ⁴⁰Make inner robes, belts and caps for Aaron's sons. When they are wearing them, people will honor his sons. They will also have respect for them. ⁴¹Put all these clothes on your brother Aaron and his sons. Then pour olive oil on them and prepare them to serve me. Set them apart to serve me as priests.

⁴²"Make linen underwear that reaches from the waist to the thigh. ⁴³Aaron and the priests in his family line must wear it when they enter the tent of meeting. They must also wear it when they approach the altar to serve in the Holy Room. Then they will not be found guilty and die.

"For all time to come, that will be a law for Aaron and the priests in his family line.

Directions for Setting Apart the Priests

29 "Here is what you must do to set apart Aaron and his sons to serve me as priests. Get a young bull and two rams. They must not have any flaws. ²Get

the finest wheat flour. Make round loaves of bread that do not have yeast in them. Make thick loaves of bread that do not have yeast in them. Mix olive oil into the thick loaves of bread. Also make thin loaves of bread that do not have yeast in them. Brush the thin loaves with olive oil. ³Put everything in a basket. Offer them along with the bull and the two rams. ⁴Then bring Aaron and his sons to the entrance to the tent of meeting. Wash them with water. ⁵Take the inner robe, the outer robe of the linen apron, the apron itself and the chest cloth. Dress Aaron in them. Take the skillfully made waistband and tie the apron on him with it. ⁶Put the turban on his head. Connect the sacred plate to the turban. ⁷Take the anointing oil and pour it on his head. ⁸Bring his sons and dress them in their inner robes. ⁹Put caps on their heads. Tie belts on Aaron and his sons. The work of the priests belongs to them. This is my law that will last for all time to come.

"Then you must prepare Aaron and his sons to serve me.

¹⁰"Bring the bull to the front of the tent of meeting. Have Aaron and his sons place their hands on its head. ¹¹Kill it in front of the LORD at the entrance to the tent of meeting. ¹²Dip your finger into some of the bull's blood. Put it on the horns that stick out from the upper four corners of the altar. Pour the rest of it out at the base of the altar. ¹³Then take all the fat on the inside parts. Take the long part of the liver. Get both kidneys with the fat on them. And burn all of it on the altar. ¹⁴But burn the bull's meat, hide and guts outside the camp. It is a sin offering.

¹⁵"Get one of the rams. Have Aaron and his sons place their hands on its head. ¹⁶Kill it. Take the blood and splash it against the sides of the altar. ¹⁷Cut the ram into pieces. Wash the inside parts and the legs. Put them with the head and the other pieces. ¹⁸Then burn the whole ram on the altar. It is a burnt offering to me. It has a pleasant smell. It is a food offering presented to the LORD.

¹⁹"Get the other ram. Have Aaron and his sons place their hands on its head. ²⁰Kill it. Put some of its blood on the right earlobes of Aaron and his sons. Put some on the thumbs of their right hands. Also

put some on the big toes of their right feet. Then splash the blood against the sides of the altar. ²¹Get some of the blood from the altar. Also get some of the anointing oil. Sprinkle both of them on Aaron and his clothes and on his sons and their clothes. Then he and his sons and their clothes will be set apart to serve the LORD.

²²"Here is what you must take from this second ram. Take the fat, the fat tail and the fat around the inside parts. Take the long part of the liver. Also take both kidneys with the fat on them, and the right thigh. It is the ram you must use when you prepare the priests to serve the LORD. ²³Get one round loaf of bread and one thick loaf of bread with olive oil mixed in. Also get one thin loaf of bread. Take them from the basket of bread made without yeast. It is the one in front of the LORD. ²⁴Put all these things in the hands of Aaron and his sons. Tell them to lift them up and wave them in front of the LORD as a wave offering. ²⁵Then take all these things from their hands. Burn them on the altar along with the burnt offering. Its smell pleases the LORD. It is a food offering presented to the LORD. ²⁶Get the breast of the ram used when you prepare Aaron to serve the LORD. Wave it in front of the LORD as a wave offering. It will be your share of the meat.

²⁷"Here are the parts of the second ram that belong to Aaron and his sons. You must set apart the breast that was waved and the thigh that was offered. ²⁸It will be the regular share from the Israelites for Aaron and his sons. The people must give it to the LORD from their friendship offerings.

²⁹"Aaron's sacred clothes will belong to his sons who will come after him. Then they can wear them when you anoint them and prepare them to serve the LORD. ³⁰The son who comes after Aaron as priest must wear them seven days. He will come and serve in the Holy Room in the tent of meeting.

³¹"Get the ram sacrificed when you prepare Aaron and his sons to serve the LORD. Cook the meat in a sacred place. ³²Aaron and his sons must eat the ram's meat. And they must eat the bread in the basket. They must eat all of it at the entrance to the tent of meeting. ³³These are the offerings to pay for their sins. They must eat them. The offerings must be made when Aaron and his sons are set apart and prepared to serve the LORD. No one else can eat them. They are sacred. ³⁴When you prepare Aaron and his sons to serve me, you will sacrifice the ram and the bread. If any parts of the ram or bread are left until morning, burn them up. They must not be eaten. They are sacred.

³⁵"Do everything I have commanded you to do for Aaron and his sons. Take seven days when you prepare them to serve the LORD. ³⁶Sacrifice a bull each day. It is a sin offering to pay for their sins. Make the altar pure. Pour olive oil on it to set it apart. ³⁷Take seven days to make the altar pure. Set it apart. Then the altar will be a very holy place. Anything that touches it will be holy.

³⁸"Every day sacrifice on the altar two lambs that are a year old. ³⁹Sacrifice one in the morning and the other one when the sun goes down. ⁴⁰Along with the first lamb, offer three and a half pounds of fine flour. Mix it with a quart of oil made from pressed olives. Along with that, sacrifice a quart of wine as a drink offering. ⁴¹Sacrifice the other lamb when the sun goes down. Sacrifice it along with the same grain offering and its drink offering as you do in the morning. It has a pleasant smell. It is a food offering presented to the LORD.

⁴²"For all time to come, this burnt offering must be sacrificed regularly. Sacrifice it at the entrance to the tent of meeting in front of the LORD. There I will meet with you and speak to you. ⁴³There I will also meet with the people of Israel. My glory will make the place holy.

⁴⁴"So I will set apart the tent of meeting and the altar. And I will set apart Aaron and his sons to serve me as priests. ⁴⁵Then I will live among the people of Israel. And I will be their God. ⁴⁶They will know that I am the LORD their God. They will know that I brought them out of Egypt so I could live among them. I am the LORD their God.

The Altar for Burning Incense

30 "Make an altar for burning incense. Make it out of acacia wood. ²It must be one and a half feet square and three feet high. Make a horn stick out from each of its upper four corners. ³Cover the top, sides and horns with pure gold. Put a strip of gold around it. ⁴Make two gold rings for the altar below the strip. Put the rings across from each other. They will hold the poles that are used to carry it. ⁵Make the poles out of acacia wood. Cover them with gold. ⁶Put the altar in front of the curtain that hangs in front of the ark. The ark is where the tablets of the covenant law are kept. The ark will have a cover. It will be the place where sin is paid for. There I will meet with you.

⁷"Aaron must burn sweet-smelling incense on the altar. He must do it every morning when he takes care of the lamps. ⁸He must burn incense again when he lights the lamps at sunset. Incense must be burned regularly in front of the LORD. Do it for all time to come. ⁹Do not burn any other incense on the altar. Do not use the altar for burnt offerings or grain offerings. And do not pour drink offerings on it. ¹⁰Once a year Aaron must put the blood of a sin offering on the horns of the altar. He must do this to make the altar pure. He must do this on the day Israel's sin is paid for. Do this for all time to come. The altar is a very holy place to me."

Money to Pay for the People's Lives

¹¹Then the LORD spoke to Moses. He said, ¹²"Make a list of the Israelites and count them. When you do, each one must pay the LORD for his life at the time he is counted. Then a plague will not come on them when you count them. ¹³Each one counted must pay a fifth of an ounce of silver. It must be weighed out in keeping with the standard weights that are used in the sacred tent. The payment is an offering to the LORD. ¹⁴Each one counted must be 20 years old or more. He must give an offering to the LORD. ¹⁵When you make the offering, rich people must not give more than a fifth of an ounce of silver. And poor people must not give less. The offering you give to the LORD will pay for your lives. ¹⁶Receive the money from the people of Israel. Use it for any purpose in the tent of meeting. It will remind the people that they are paying me for their lives."

The Large Bowl for Washing

¹⁷Then the LORD spoke to Moses. He said, ¹⁸"Make a large bronze bowl for washing. Make a bronze stand to put it on. Place the bowl between the tent of meeting and the altar. Put water in it. ¹⁹Aaron and his sons must wash their hands and feet with water from it. ²⁰When they enter the tent of meeting, they must wash with water so that they will not die. They will come to the altar to serve me. They will bring a food offering to the LORD. ²¹When they do, they must wash their hands and feet so that they will not die. For all time to come, that will be a law for Aaron and the priests in his family line."

Anointing Oil

²²Then the LORD said to Moses, ²³"Get some fine spices. Get 12 pounds eight ounces of liquid myrrh. Get six pounds four ounces of sweet-smelling cinnamon and the same amount of sweet-smelling calamus. ²⁴Also get 12 pounds eight ounces of cassia. All the spices must be weighed out in keeping with the standard weights that are used in the sacred tent. And get a gallon of olive oil. ²⁵Have a person who makes perfume mix everything into a sacred anointing oil. It will smell sweet. ²⁶Then use it to anoint the tent of meeting and the ark where the tablets of the covenant law are kept. ²⁷Anoint the table for the holy bread and all its things. Anoint the lampstand and the things that are used with it. Anoint the altar for burning

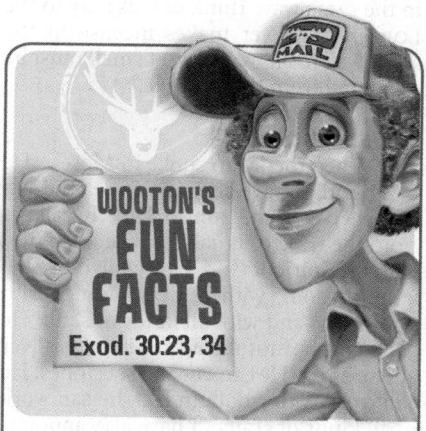

My favorite smell is peppermint lemon. Try it. God has favorite smells too, like the ones used in temple oils. Exodus mentions myrrh and frankincense.

incense. ²⁸Anoint the altar for burnt offerings and all its tools. And anoint the large bowl together with its stand. ²⁹You must set them apart so that they will be very holy. Anything that touches them will be holy.

³⁰"Anoint Aaron and his sons. Set them apart so that they can serve me as priests. ³¹Say to the people of Israel, 'This will be my sacred anointing oil for all time to come. ³²Do not pour it on anyone else's body. Do not make any other oil in the same way. It is sacred. So you must think of it as sacred. ³³Suppose a person makes perfume in the same way. And suppose that person puts it on someone who is not a priest. Then that person must be separated from their people.'"

Incense

³⁴Then the LORD said to Moses, "Get some sweet-smelling spices. Get some gum resin, onycha and galbanum. Also get some pure frankincense. Make sure everything is in equal amounts. ³⁵Have a person who makes perfume mix it all up into a sweet-smelling incense. It must have salt in it. It will be pure and sacred. ³⁶Grind some of it into powder. Place it in front of the ark of the covenant law in the tent of meeting. There I will meet with you. The incense will be very holy to you. ³⁷Do not make any incense for yourselves in the same way. Think of it as holy to the LORD. ³⁸Whoever makes incense in the same way to enjoy its sweet smell must be separated from their people."

Bezalel and Oholiab

31 Then the LORD spoke to Moses. ²He said, "I have chosen Bezalel, the son of Uri. Uri is the son of Hur. Bezalel is from the tribe of Judah. ³I have filled him with the Spirit of God. I have filled Bezalel with wisdom, with understanding, with knowledge and with all kinds of skill. ⁴He can make beautiful patterns in gold, silver and bronze. ⁵He can cut and set stones. He can work with wood. In fact, he can work in all kinds of crafts. ⁶I have also appointed Oholiab, the son of Ahisamak, to help him. Oholiab is from the tribe of Dan.

I have given ability to all the skilled workers. They can make everything I have commanded you to make. Here is the complete list.

⁷ "the tent of meeting
the ark where the tablets of the covenant law are kept
the cover for the ark
⁸ the table for the holy bread and its things
the pure gold lampstand and everything used with it
the altar for burning incense
⁹ the altar for burnt offerings and all its tools
the large bowl with its stand
¹⁰ the sacred clothes for Aaron the priest and the clothes for his sons when they serve as priests
¹¹ the anointing oil
and the sweet-smelling incense for the Holy Room

"The skilled workers must make them just as I commanded you."

The Sabbath Day

¹²Then the LORD spoke to Moses. ¹³He said, "Tell the people of Israel, 'You must always keep my Sabbath days. That will be the sign of the covenant I have made between me and you for all time to come. Then you will know that I am the LORD. I am the one who makes you holy.

¹⁴"'Keep the Sabbath day. It is holy to you. Those who misuse it must be put to death. Those who do any work on that day must be separated from their people. ¹⁵Do your work in six days. But the seventh day is a day of sabbath rest. You must rest on it. It is set apart for the LORD. Those who work on the Sabbath day must be put to death. ¹⁶The Israelites must keep the Sabbath day. They must celebrate it for all time to come. It will be a covenant that lasts forever. ¹⁷It will be the sign of the covenant I have made between me and the Israelites forever. The LORD made the heavens and the earth in six days. But on the seventh day he did not work. He rested.'"

¹⁸The LORD finished speaking to Moses on Mount Sinai. Then he gave him the two tablets of the covenant law. They were made out of stone. The words on them were written by the finger of God.

Israel Worships a Golden Calf

32 The people saw that Moses took a long time to come down from the mountain. So they gathered around Aaron. They said to him, "Come. Make us a god that will lead us. This fellow Moses brought us up out of Egypt. But we don't know what has happened to him."

[2] Aaron answered them, "Take the gold earrings off your wives, your sons and your daughters. Bring the earrings to me." [3] So all the people took off their earrings. They brought them to Aaron. [4] He took what they gave him and made it into a metal statue of a god. It looked like a calf. Aaron shaped it with a tool. Then the people said, "Israel, here is your god who brought you up out of Egypt."

[5] When Aaron saw what they were doing, he built an altar in front of the calf. He said, "Tomorrow will be a feast day to honor the LORD." [6] So the next day the people got up early. They sacrificed burnt offerings and brought friendship offerings. They sat down to eat and drink. Then they got up to dance wildly in front of their god.

[7] The LORD spoke to Moses. He said, "Go down. Your people you brought up out of Egypt have become very sinful. [8] They have quickly turned away from what I commanded them. They have made themselves a metal statue of a god in the shape of a calf. They have bowed down and sacrificed to it. And they have said, 'Israel, here is your god who brought you up out of Egypt.'

[9] "I have seen these people," the LORD said to Moses. "They are stubborn. [10] Now leave me alone. I will destroy them because of my great anger. Then I will make you into a great nation."

[11] But Moses asked the LORD his God to have mercy on the people. "LORD," he said, "why should you destroy your people in anger? You used your great power and mighty hand to bring them out of Egypt. [12] Why should the Egyptians say, 'He brought them out to hurt them. He wanted to kill them in the mountains. He wanted to wipe them off the face of the earth'? Turn away from your great anger. Please take pity on your people. Don't destroy them! [13] Remember your servants Abraham, Isaac and Israel. You made a promise to them in your own name. You said, 'I will make your children after you as many as the stars in the sky. I will give them all this land I promised them. It will belong to them forever.' " [14] Then the LORD took pity on his people. He didn't destroy them as he had said he would.

[15] Moses turned and went down the mountain. He had the two tablets of the covenant law in his hands. Words were written on both sides of the tablets, front and back. [16] The tablets were the work of God. The words had been written by God. They had been carved on the tablets.

[17] Joshua heard the noise of the people shouting. So he said to Moses, "It sounds like war in the camp."

[18] Moses replied,

"It's not the sound of winning.
   It's not the sound of losing.
   It's the sound of singing that I hear."

[19] As Moses approached the camp, he saw the calf. He also saw the people dancing. So he was very angry. He threw the tablets out of his hands. They broke into pieces at the foot of the mountain. [20] He took the calf the people had made. He burned it in the fire. Then he ground it into powder. He scattered it on the water. And he made the Israelites drink it.

[21] He said to Aaron, "What did these people do to you? How did they make you lead them into such terrible sin?"

[22] "Please don't be angry," Aaron answered. "You know how these people like to do what is evil. [23] They said to me, 'Make us a god that will lead us. This fellow Moses brought us up out of Egypt. But we don't know what has happened to him.' [24] So I told them, 'Anyone who has any gold jewelry, take it off.' They gave me the gold. I threw it into the fire. And out came this calf!"

[25] Moses saw that the people were running wild. Aaron had let them get out of control. The people had become a joke to their enemies. [26] Moses stood at the entrance to the camp. He said, "Anyone on the LORD's side, come to me." All the Levites joined him.

[27] Then he spoke to them. He said, "The LORD, the God of Israel, says, 'Each man must put on his sword. Then he must go back and forth through the camp from one

ADVENTURES IN ODYSSEY

Rodney tried to blame other people when he fell through a window at Whit's End in "A Victim of Circumstance" (A#23). Rodney's not the first person to try to pass the blame for his actions. Aaron did the same thing with the golden calf.

end to the other. Each man must kill his brother and friend and neighbor.'" [28]The Levites did as Moses commanded. About 3,000 of the people died that day. [29]Then Moses said to the Levites, "You have been set apart for the LORD today. You fought against your own sons and brothers. And he has blessed you this day."

[30]The next day Moses said to the people, "You have committed a terrible sin. But now I will go up to the LORD. Maybe if I pray to him, he will forgive your sin."

[31]So Moses went back to the LORD. He said, "These people have committed a terrible sin. They have made a god out of gold for themselves. [32]Now please forgive their sin. But if you won't, then erase my name out of the book you have written."

[33]The LORD replied to Moses. The LORD said, "I will erase out of my book only the names of those who have sinned against me. [34]Now go. Lead the people to the place I spoke about. My angel will go ahead of you. But when the time comes for me to punish, I will punish them for their sin."

[35]The LORD struck the people with a plague. That's because of what they did with the calf Aaron had made.

33 Then the LORD said to Moses, "Leave this place. You and the people you brought up out of Egypt must leave it. Go up to the land I promised to give to Abraham, Isaac and Jacob. I said to them, 'I will give it to your children after you.' [2]I will send an angel ahead of you. I will drive out the Canaanites, Amorites, Hittites, Perizzites, Hivites and Jebusites. [3]Go up to the land that has plenty of milk and honey. But I will not go with you. You are stubborn. I might destroy you on the way."

[4]When the people heard these painful words, they began to mourn. No one put on any jewelry. [5]The LORD had said to Moses, "Tell the Israelites, 'You are stubborn. If I went with you even for a moment, I might destroy you. Now take off your jewelry. Then I will decide what to do with you.'" [6]So the people took off their jewelry at Mount Horeb.

The Tent of Meeting

[7]Moses used to take a tent and set it up far outside the camp. He called it the "tent of meeting." Anyone who wanted to ask the LORD a question would go to the tent of meeting outside the camp. [8]When Moses would go out to the tent, everyone would get up and stand at the entrances to their tents. They would watch Moses until he entered the tent. [9]As Moses would go into the tent, the pillar of cloud would come down. It would stay at the entrance while the LORD spoke with Moses. [10]The people would see the pillar of cloud standing at the entrance to the tent. Then all of them would stand and worship at the entrances to their tents. [11]The LORD would speak to Moses face to face like one would speak to a friend. Then Moses would return to the camp. But Joshua, his young helper, didn't leave the tent. Joshua was the son of Nun.

Moses and the Glory of the LORD

[12]Moses said to the LORD, "You have been telling me, 'Lead these people.' But you haven't let me know whom you will send with me. You have said, 'I know your name. I know all about you. And I am pleased with you.' [13]If you are pleased with me, teach me more about yourself. Then I can know you. And I can continue

to please you. Remember that this nation is your people."

[14]The LORD replied, "I will go with you. And I will give you rest."

[15]Then Moses said to him, "If you don't go with us, don't send us up from here. [16]How will anyone know that you are pleased with me and your people? You must go with us. How else will we be different from all the other people on the face of the earth?"

[17]The LORD said to Moses, "I will do exactly what you have asked. I am pleased with you. And I know your name. I know all about you."

[18]Then Moses said, "Now show me your glory."

[19]The LORD said, "I will make all my goodness pass in front of you. And I will announce my name, the LORD, in front of you. I will have mercy on whom I have mercy. And I will show love to those I love. [20]But you can't see my face," he said. "No one can see me and stay alive."

[21]The LORD continued, "There is a place near me where you can stand on a rock. [22]When my glory passes by, I will put you in an opening in the rock. I will cover you with my hand until I have passed by. [23]Then I will remove my hand. You will see my back. But my face must not be seen."

The New Stone Tablets

34 The LORD said to Moses, "Cut out two stone tablets that are just like the first ones. I will write on them the words that were on the first tablets, which you broke. [2]Be ready in the morning. Then come up on Mount Sinai. Meet with me there on top of the mountain. [3]No one must come with you. No one must be seen anywhere on the mountain. Not even the flocks and herds must be allowed to eat grass in front of the mountain."

[4]So Moses carved out two stone tablets just like the first ones. Early in the morning he went up Mount Sinai. He carried the two stone tablets in his hands. He did as the LORD had commanded him to do. [5]Then the LORD came down in the cloud. He stood there with Moses and announced his name, the LORD. [6]As he passed in front of Moses, he called out. He said, "I am the LORD, the LORD. I am

the God who is tender and kind. I am gracious. I am slow to get angry. I am faithful and full of love. [7]I continue to show my love to thousands of people. I forgive those who do evil. I forgive those who refuse to obey me. And I forgive those who sin. But I do not let guilty people go without punishing them. I cause the sins of the parents to affect their children, grandchildren and great-grandchildren."

[8]Moses bowed down to the ground at once and worshiped. [9]"Lord," he said, "if you are pleased with me, then go with us. Even though these people are stubborn, forgive the evil things we have done. Forgive our sin. And accept us as your people."

[10]Then the LORD said, "I am making a covenant with you. I will do wonderful things in front of all your people. I will do amazing things that have never been done before in any nation in the whole world. The people you live among will see the things that I, the LORD, will do for you. And they will see how wonderful those things really are. [11]Obey what I command you today. I will drive out the Amorites, Canaanites, Hittites, Perizzites, Hivites and Jebusites to make room for you. [12]Be careful. Do not make a peace treaty with those who live in the land where you are going. They will be a trap to you. [13]Break down their altars. Smash their sacred stones. Cut down the poles they use to worship the female god named Asherah. [14]Do not worship any other god. The LORD is a jealous God. In fact, his name is Jealous.

[15]"Be careful not to make a peace treaty with the people living in the land. They commit sin by offering sacrifices to their gods. They will invite you to eat their sacrifices, and you will do it. [16]You will choose some of their daughters as wives for your sons. And those daughters will commit sin by worshiping their gods. Then they will lead your sons to do the same thing.

[17]"Do not make any statues of gods.

[18]"Celebrate the Feast of Unleavened Bread. For seven days eat bread made without yeast, just as I commanded you. Do it at the appointed time in the month of Aviv. You came out of Egypt in that month.

[19]"Every male animal born first to its mother belongs to me. That includes your livestock. It includes herds and flocks alike. [20]Sacrifice a lamb to buy back every male donkey born first to its mother. But if you do not buy the donkey back, break its neck. Buy back all your oldest sons.

"You must not come to worship me with your hands empty.

[21]"Do your work in six days. But you must rest on the seventh day. Even when you are plowing your land or gathering your crops, you must rest on the seventh day.

[22]"Celebrate the Feast of Weeks. Bring the first share of your wheat crop. Celebrate the Feast of Booths. Hold it in the fall. [23]Three times a year all your men must come to worship me. I am your LORD and King, the God of Israel. [24]I will drive out nations ahead of you. I will increase your territory. Go up three times a year to worship me. While you are doing that, I will keep others from wanting to take any of your land for themselves. I am the LORD your God.

[25]"Do not include anything made with yeast when you offer me the blood of a sacrifice. You must not keep any of the meat from the sacrifice of the Passover Feast until morning.

[26]"Bring the best of the first share of your crops to the house of the LORD your God.

"Do not cook a young goat in its mother's milk."

[27]Then the LORD said to Moses, "Write down the words I have spoken. I have made a covenant with you and with Israel in keeping with those words." [28]Moses was there with the LORD for 40 days and 40 nights. He didn't eat any food or drink any water. The LORD wrote on the tablets the words of the covenant law. Those words are the Ten Commandments.

The Face of Moses Shines

[29]Moses came down from Mount Sinai. He had the two tablets of the covenant law in his hands. His face was shining because he had spoken with the LORD. But he didn't realize it. [30]Aaron and all the people of Israel saw Moses. His face was shining. So they were afraid to come near him. [31]But Moses called out to them. So Aaron

Exod. 34:29-35 An event when God's presence brings light is called the *Shekinah glory*, which means "to dwell with." Check out these other Bible verses where God's glory is shown: Matthew 17:1–8 and Revelation 1:16.

and all the leaders of the community came to him. And Moses spoke to them. [32]After that, all the Israelites came near him. And he gave them all the commands the LORD had given him on Mount Sinai.

[33]Moses finished speaking to them. Then he covered his face with a veil. [34]But when he would go to speak with the LORD, he would remove the veil. He would keep it off until he came out. Then he would tell the people what the LORD had commanded. [35]They would see that his face was shining. So Moses would cover his face with the veil again. He would keep it on until he went in again to speak with the LORD.

Rules for the Sabbath Day

35 Moses gathered the whole community of Israel together. He said to them, "Here are the things the LORD has commanded you to do. [2]You must do your work in six days. But the seventh day will be your holy day. It will be a day of sabbath rest to honor the LORD. You must rest on it. Anyone who does any work on it must be put to death. [3]Do not even light a fire in any of your homes on the Sabbath day."

Supplies for the Holy Tent

[4]Moses spoke to the whole community of Israel. He said, "Here is what the LORD has commanded. [5]Take an offering for the

LORD from what you have. Those who want to can bring an offering to the LORD. Here is what they can bring.

"gold, silver and bronze
6 blue, purple and bright red yarn and
   fine linen
goat hair
7 ram skins that are dyed red
another kind of strong leather
acacia wood
8 olive oil for the lights
spices for the anointing oil and for
   the sweet-smelling incense
9 onyx stones and other jewels for the
   linen apron and the chest cloth

10"All the skilled workers among you must come. They must make everything the LORD has commanded 11for the holy tent and its covering. Here is what they must make.

"hooks, frames, crossbars, posts and
   bases
12 the ark of the covenant law, the
   poles and cover for the ark, and
   the curtain that hides the ark
13 the table for the holy bread, the
   poles and all the things for the
   table, and the holy bread
14 the lampstand for light and everything used with it, the lamps, and
   the olive oil that gives light
15 the altar for burning incense, the
   poles for the altar, the anointing oil and the sweet-smelling
   incense
the curtain for the entrance to the
   holy tent
16 the altar for burnt offerings with its
   bronze grate, its poles and all its
   tools
the large bronze bowl with its stand
17 the curtains of the courtyard with
   their posts and bases, and the
   curtain for the entrance to the
   courtyard
18 the ropes and tent stakes for the
   holy tent and for the courtyard
19 and the sacred clothes for Aaron the
   priest and the clothes for his sons
   when they serve as priests."

20Then the whole community of Israel left Moses. 21Everyone who wanted to give offerings to the LORD brought them

to him. The offerings were for the work on the tent of meeting. They were also for the sacred clothes and for any other purpose at the tent. 22Every man and woman who wanted to give came. They brought gold jewelry of all kinds. They brought pins, earrings, rings and other jewelry. All of them gave their gold as a wave offering to the LORD. 23People brought what they had. They brought blue, purple or bright red yarn or fine linen. They brought goat hair, ram skins dyed red, or the other kind of strong leather. 24Some brought silver or bronze as an offering to the LORD. Others brought acacia wood for any part of the work. 25All the skilled women spun yarn with their hands. They brought blue, purple or bright red yarn or fine linen. 26All the skilled women who wanted to spin the goat hair did so. 27The leaders brought onyx stones and other jewels for the linen apron and the chest cloth. 28They also brought spices and olive oil. They brought them for the light, for the anointing oil, and for the sweet-smelling incense. 29All the men and women of Israel who wanted to bring offerings to the LORD brought them to him. The offerings were for all the work the LORD had commanded Moses to tell them to do.

Bezalel and Oholiab

30Then Moses spoke to the people of Israel. He said, "The LORD has chosen Bezalel, the son of Uri. Uri is the son of Hur. Bezalel is from the tribe of Judah. 31The LORD has filled him with the Spirit of God. He has filled him with wisdom, with understanding, with knowledge and with all kinds of skill. 32Bezalel can make beautiful patterns in gold, silver and bronze. 33He can cut and set stones. He can work with wood. In fact, he can work in all kinds of arts and crafts. 34And the LORD has given both him and Oholiab the ability to teach others. Oholiab, the son of Ahisamak, is from the tribe of Dan. 35The LORD has filled Bezalel and Oholiab with skill to do all kinds of work. They can carve things and make patterns. They can sew skillfully with blue, purple and bright red yarn and on fine linen. They use thread to make beautiful cloth. Both of them have the skill to

36 work in all kinds of crafts. ¹Bezalel and Oholiab must do the work just as the LORD has commanded. So must every skilled worker to whom the LORD has given skill and ability. They know how to do all the work for every purpose connected with the sacred tent. And that includes setting it up."

²Then Moses sent for Bezalel and Oholiab. He sent for every skilled worker to whom the LORD had given ability and who wanted to come and do the work. ³They received from Moses all the offerings the people of Israel had brought. They had brought the offerings for all the work for every purpose connected with the holy tent. That included setting it up. The people kept bringing the offerings they chose to give. They brought them morning after morning. ⁴So all the skilled workers working on the holy tent stopped what they were doing. ⁵They said to Moses, "The LORD commanded us to do the work. And the people are bringing more than enough for us to do it."

⁶Then Moses gave an order. A message was sent through the whole camp. It said, "No man or woman should make anything else and offer it for the holy tent." And so the people were kept from bringing more offerings. ⁷There was already more than enough to do all the work.

The Holy Tent

⁸All the skilled workers made the holy tent. They made ten curtains out of finely twisted linen. They made them with blue, purple and bright red yarn. A skilled worker sewed cherubim into the pattern. ⁹All the curtains were the same size. They were 42 feet long and six feet wide. ¹⁰The workers joined five of the curtains together. They did the same thing with the other five. ¹¹Then they made loops out of blue strips of cloth along the edge of the end curtain in one set. They did the same thing with the end curtain in the other set. ¹²They also made 50 loops on the end curtain of the one set. They did the same thing on the end curtain of the other set. They put the loops across from each other. ¹³Then they made 50 gold hooks. They used them to join the two sets of curtains together so that the holy tent was all one piece.

Jason's Jargon

EXODUS 36

Your special assignment continues—look for the word *cherubim* in this chapter. Cherubim are angels, represented in art as beautiful winged creatures.

¹⁴The workers made a total of 11 curtains out of goat hair to put over the holy tent. ¹⁵All 11 curtains were the same size. They were 45 feet long and six feet wide. ¹⁶The workers joined five of the curtains together into one set. They did the same thing with the other six. ¹⁷Then they made 50 loops along the edge of the end curtain in the one set. They did the same thing with the other set. ¹⁸They made 50 bronze hooks. They used them to join the tent together all in one piece. ¹⁹They made a covering for the tent. They made it out of ram skins dyed red. Over that, they put a covering of another kind of strong leather.

²⁰The workers made frames out of acacia wood for the holy tent. ²¹Each frame was about 15 feet long and two feet three inches wide. ²²The workers added two small wooden pins to each frame. The pins stuck out so that they were even with each other. The workers made all the frames of the holy tent in the same way. ²³The workers made 20 frames for the south side of the holy tent. ²⁴And they made 40 silver bases to go under them. They made two bases for each frame. They put one under each pin that stuck out. ²⁵For the north side of the holy tent they made 20 frames ²⁶and 40 silver bases. They put two bases under each frame. ²⁷The workers made six frames for the west end of the holy tent. ²⁸They made two frames for the corners of the holy tent at the far end. ²⁹At those two corners the frames were double from top to bottom. They were fitted into a single ring. The workers made both of them the same. ³⁰So there were eight frames and 16 silver bases. There were two bases under each frame.

³¹The workers also made crossbars out of acacia wood. They made five for the

frames on one side of the holy tent. [32]They made five for the frames on the other side. And they made five for the frames on the west, at the far end of the holy tent. [33]The center crossbar reached from end to end at the middle of the frames. [34]The workers covered the frames with gold. They made gold rings to hold the crossbars. They also covered the crossbars with gold.

[35]They made the curtain out of blue, purple and bright red yarn and finely twisted linen. A skilled worker sewed cherubim into the pattern. [36]The workers made four posts out of acacia wood for the curtain. They covered the posts with gold. They made gold hooks and four silver bases for the posts. [37]For the entrance to the tent the workers made a curtain. They made it out of blue, purple and bright red yarn and finely twisted linen. A person who sewed skillfully made it. [38]The workers made five posts with hooks for the curtains. They covered the tops of the posts and their bands with gold. And they made five bronze bases for them.

The Ark of the Covenant Law

37 Bezalel made the ark of the covenant law out of acacia wood. It was three feet nine inches long and two feet three inches wide and high. [2]He covered it inside and outside with pure gold. He put a strip of gold around it. [3]He made four gold rings for it. He joined them to its four bottom corners. He put two rings on one side and two rings on the other. [4]Then he made poles out of acacia wood. He covered them with gold. [5]He put the poles through the rings on the sides of the ark to carry it.

[6]He made its cover out of pure gold. It was three feet nine inches long and two feet three inches wide. The cover is the place where sin is paid for. [7]Then he made two cherubim out of hammered gold at the ends of the cover. [8]He put one of the cherubim on each end of it. [9]He made them as part of the cover itself. Their wings spread up over the cover. The cherubim faced each other and looked toward the cover.

The Table for the Holy Bread

[10]The workers made the table out of acacia wood. It was three feet long, one foot six inches wide and two feet three inches high. [11]Then they covered it with pure gold. They put a strip of gold around it. [12]They also made a rim around it three inches wide. They put a strip of gold around the rim. [13]They made four gold rings for the table. They joined them to the four corners, where the four legs were. [14]The rings were close to the rim. The rings held the poles used to carry the table. [15]The workers made the poles out of acacia wood. They covered them with gold. [16]They made plates, dishes and bowls out of pure gold for the table. They also made pure gold pitchers to pour out drink offerings.

The Gold Lampstand

[17]The workers made the lampstand out of pure gold. They hammered out its base and stem. Its buds, blossoms and cups branched out from it. [18]Six branches came out from the sides of the lampstand. There were three on one side and three on the other. [19]On one branch there were three cups shaped like almond flowers with buds and blossoms. There were three on the next branch. In fact, there were three on each of the six branches that came out from the lampstand. [20]On the lampstand there were four cups shaped like almond flowers with buds and blossoms. [21]One bud was under the first pair of branches that came out from the lampstand. A second bud was under the second pair. And a third bud was under the third pair. There was a total of six branches. [22]The buds and branches came out from the lampstand. The whole lampstand was one piece hammered out of pure gold.

[23]The workers made its seven lamps out of pure gold. They also made its trays and wick cutters out of pure gold. [24]They used 75 pounds of pure gold to make the lampstand and everything used with it.

The Altar for Burning Incense

[25]The workers made the altar for burning incense. They made it out of acacia wood. It was about one foot six inches square and three feet high. A horn stuck out from each of its upper four corners. [26]The workers covered the top, sides and horns with pure gold. They put a strip of gold around it. [27]They made two gold

rings below the strip. They put the rings on the sides across from each other. The rings held the poles used to carry it. [28]The workers made the poles out of acacia wood. They covered them with gold.

[29]They also made the sacred anointing oil and the pure, sweet-smelling incense. A person who makes perfume made them.

The Altar for Burnt Offerings

38 The workers built the altar for burnt offerings out of acacia wood. It was four feet six inches high and seven feet six inches square. [2]They made a horn stick out from each of its four upper corners. They covered the altar with bronze. [3]They made all its tools out of bronze. They made its pots, shovels, sprinkling bowls, meat forks, and pans for carrying ashes. [4]They made a bronze grate for the altar. They put the grate halfway up the altar on the inside. [5]They made a bronze ring for each of the four corners of the grate. [6]They made poles out of acacia wood. They covered them with bronze. [7]They put the poles through the rings. The poles were on two sides of the altar for carrying it. The workers made the altar out of boards. They left it hollow.

The Large Bowl for Washing

[8]The workers made the large bronze bowl and its bronze stand. They made them out of bronze mirrors. The mirrors belonged to the women who served at the entrance to the tent of meeting.

The Courtyard

[9]Next, the workers made the courtyard. The south side was 150 feet long. It had curtains made out of finely twisted linen. [10]The curtains had 20 posts and 20 bronze bases. The posts had silver hooks and bands on them. [11]The north side was also 150 feet long. Its curtains had 20 posts and 20 bronze bases. The posts had silver hooks and bands on them.

[12]The west end was 75 feet wide. It had curtains with ten posts and ten bases. The posts had silver hooks and bands on them. [13]The east end, toward the sunrise, was also 75 feet wide. [14]Curtains 22 feet six inches long were on one side of the entrance to the courtyard. They were

hung on three posts. Each post had a base. [15]Curtains 22 feet six inches long were also on the other side of the entrance. They were hung on three posts. Each post had a base. [16]All the curtains around the courtyard were made out of finely twisted linen. [17]The bases for the posts were made out of bronze. The hooks and bands on the posts were made out of silver. Their tops were covered with silver. So all the posts of the courtyard had silver bands.

[18]The curtain for the courtyard entrance was made out of blue, purple and bright red yarn and finely twisted linen. A person who sewed skillfully made it. It was 30 feet long. Like the curtains of the courtyard, it was seven feet six inches high. [19]It had four posts and four bronze bases. Their hooks and bands were made out of silver. Their tops were covered with silver. [20]All the tent stakes of the holy tent were made out of bronze. So were all the stakes of the courtyard around it.

The Amounts of the Metals Used

[21]Here are the amounts of the metals used for the holy tent, where the tablets of the covenant law were kept. Moses commanded the Levites to record the amounts. The Levites did the work under the direction of Ithamar. Ithamar was the son of Aaron the priest. [22]Bezalel, the son of Uri, made everything the LORD had commanded Moses. Uri was the son of Hur. Bezalel was from the tribe of Judah. [23]Oholiab, the son of Ahisamak, helped Bezalel. Oholiab was from the tribe of Dan. He could carve things and make patterns. And he could sew skillfully with blue, purple and bright red yarn and on fine linen. [24]The total weight of the gold from the wave offering was more than a ton. It was weighed out in keeping with the standard weights used in the sacred tent. The gold was used for all the work done in connection with the sacred tent.

[25]The silver received from the men in the community who were listed and counted weighed almost four tons. It was weighed out in keeping with the weights used in the sacred tent. [26]It amounted to a fifth of an ounce for each person. It was weighed out in keeping with the weights used in the sacred tent. The silver was received from the men who had been listed

and counted. All of them were 20 years old or more. Their total number was 603,550. [27]The four tons of silver were used to make the bases for the holy tent and for the curtain. The 100 bases were made from the four tons. Each base used more than 75 pounds of silver. [28]The workers used 45 pounds to make the hooks for the posts, to cover the tops of the posts, and to make their bands.

[29]The bronze from the wave offering weighed two and a half tons. [30]The workers used some of it to make the bases for the entrance to the tent of meeting. They used some for the bronze altar for burnt offerings and its bronze grate and all its tools. [31]They used some for the bases for the courtyard around the holy tent. They used some for the bases for the courtyard entrance. And they used the rest to make all the tent stakes for the holy tent and the courtyard around it.

The Clothes for the Priests

39 The workers made clothes from the blue, purple and bright red yarn. The clothes were worn by the priests who served in the holy tent. The workers also made sacred clothes for Aaron. They made them just as the LORD had commanded Moses.

The Linen Apron

[2]The workers made the linen apron. They made it out of thin gold wire, and of blue, purple and bright red yarn, and of finely twisted linen. [3]They hammered out thin sheets of gold. They cut it into thin wire. Then they sewed it into the blue, purple and bright red yarn and fine linen. Skilled workers made it. [4]The workers made shoulder straps for the apron. The straps were joined to two of its corners. [5]Its skillfully made waistband was made like the apron. The waistband was part of the apron itself. It was made out of thin gold wire, and out of blue, purple and bright red yarn, and out of finely twisted linen. The workers made it just as the LORD had commanded Moses.

[6]They put the onyx stones in fancy gold settings. They carved the names of the sons of Israel on the stones. They did it the way a jewel cutter would carve them. [7]Then they connected them to the shoulder straps of the linen apron. The stones stood for the sons of Israel and were a constant reminder for them. The workers did those things just as the LORD had commanded Moses.

The Chest Cloth

[8]Skilled workers made the chest cloth. They made it like the linen apron. They used thin gold wire, and blue, purple and bright red yarn, and finely twisted linen. [9]The chest cloth was nine inches square. It was folded in half. [10]The workers put four rows of valuable jewels on it. Carnelian, chrysolite and beryl were in the first row. [11]Turquoise, lapis lazuli and emerald were in the second row. [12]Jacinth, agate and amethyst were in the third row. [13]And topaz, onyx and jasper were in the fourth row. The workers put them in fancy gold settings. [14]They used a total of 12 stones. There was one stone for each of the names of the sons of Israel. Each stone was carved with the name of one of the 12 tribes.

[15]The workers made braided chains out of pure gold for the chest cloth. They made them like ropes. [16]They made two fancy gold settings and two gold rings. They connected them to two corners of the chest cloth. [17]They joined the two gold chains to the rings at the corners of the chest cloth. [18]They joined the other ends of the chains to the two settings. They joined them to the shoulder straps on the front of the linen apron. [19]The workers made two gold rings. They connected them to the other two corners of the chest cloth. They put them on the inside edge next to the apron. [20]Then they made two more gold rings. They connected them to the bottom of the shoulder straps on the front of the apron. They put them close to the seam. They put them right above the waistband of the apron. [21]They tied the rings of the chest cloth to the rings of the apron with blue cord. That connected it to the waistband. Then the chest cloth would not swing out from the linen apron. The workers did those things just as the LORD had commanded Moses.

More Clothes for the Priests

[22]The workers made the outer robe of the linen apron completely out of blue cloth. The cloth was made by a skillful

person. ²³The workers made an opening in the center of the robe. They made an edge like a collar around the opening. Then it couldn't tear. ²⁴They made pomegranates out of blue, purple and bright red yarn and finely twisted linen. They sewed them around the hem of the robe. ²⁵They made bells out of pure gold. They sewed them around the hem between the pomegranates. ²⁶They sewed a bell between every two pomegranates all around the hem of the robe. Aaron had to wear the robe when he served as priest. That's what the LORD commanded Moses.

²⁷The workers made inner robes out of fine linen for Aaron and his sons. The linen cloth was made by a skillful person. ²⁸The workers also made the turban out of fine linen. And they made the caps and the underwear out of finely twisted linen. ²⁹The belt was made out of finely twisted linen and blue, purple and bright red yarn. A person who sewed skillfully made it. The workers did those things just as the LORD had commanded Moses.

³⁰They made the plate out of pure gold. It was a sacred crown. On the plate, they carved the words

SET APART FOR THE LORD.

³¹Then they tied the plate to the turban with a blue cord. They did those things just as the LORD had commanded Moses.

The Holy Tent Is Completed

³²So all the work on the holy tent, the tent of meeting, was completed. The Israelites did everything just as the LORD had commanded Moses. ³³Then they brought the holy tent to Moses along with everything that belonged to it. Here are the things they brought:

hooks, frames, crossbars, posts and bases
³⁴ the covering of ram skins dyed red, the covering of another kind of strong leather and the curtain that hides the ark
³⁵ the ark where the tablets of the covenant law are kept, the poles and the cover for the ark
³⁶ the table for the holy bread with all its things and the holy bread

³⁷ the pure gold lampstand with its row of lamps and everything used with it, and the olive oil that gives light
³⁸ the gold altar for burning incense, the anointing oil and the sweet-smelling incense
the curtain for the entrance to the tent
³⁹ the bronze altar for burnt offerings with its bronze grate, its poles and all its tools
the large bowl with its stand
⁴⁰ the curtains of the courtyard with their posts and bases, and the curtain for the entrance to the courtyard
the ropes and tent stakes for the courtyard
everything that belongs to the holy tent, the tent of meeting
⁴¹ and the sacred clothes for Aaron the priest and the clothes for his sons when they serve as priests

⁴²The Israelites had done all the work just as the LORD had commanded Moses. ⁴³Moses looked over the work carefully. He saw that the workers had done it just as the LORD had commanded. So Moses gave them his blessing.

Moses Sets Up the Holy Tent

40 Then the LORD said to Moses, ²"Set up the holy tent, the tent of meeting. Set it up on the first day of the first month. ³Place in it the ark where the tablets of the covenant law are kept. Hide the ark with the curtain. ⁴Bring in the table for the holy bread. Arrange the loaves of bread on it. Then bring in the lampstand. Set up its lamps. ⁵Place the gold altar for burning incense in front of the ark where the tablets of the covenant law are kept. Put up the curtain at the entrance to the holy tent.

⁶"Place the altar for burnt offerings in front of the entrance to the holy tent, the tent of meeting. ⁷Place the large bowl between the tent of meeting and the altar. Put water in the bowl. ⁸Set up the courtyard around the holy tent. Put the curtain at the entrance to the courtyard.

⁹"Get the anointing oil. Anoint the holy tent and everything in it. Set apart

the holy tent and everything that belongs to it. Then it will be holy. ¹⁰Anoint the altar for burnt offerings and all its tools. Set apart the altar. Then it will be a very holy place. ¹¹Anoint the large bowl and its stand. Set them apart.

¹²"Bring Aaron and his sons to the entrance to the tent of meeting. Wash them with water. ¹³Dress Aaron in the sacred clothes. Anoint him and set him apart. Then he will be able to serve me as priest. ¹⁴Bring his sons and dress them in their inner robes. ¹⁵Anoint them just as you anointed their father. Then they will be able to serve me as priests. They will be anointed to do the work of priests. That work will last for all time to come." ¹⁶Moses did everything just as the LORD had commanded him.

¹⁷So the holy tent was set up. It was the first day of the first month in the second year. ¹⁸Moses set up the holy tent. He put the bases in place. He put the frames in them. He put in the crossbars. He set up the posts. ¹⁹He spread the holy tent over the frames. Then he put the coverings over the tent. Moses did it as the LORD had commanded him.

²⁰He got the tablets of the covenant law. He placed them in the ark. He put the poles through its rings. And he put the cover on it. The cover was the place where sin is paid for. ²¹Moses brought the ark into the holy tent. He hung the curtain to hide the ark where the tablets of the covenant law are kept. Moses did it as the LORD had commanded him.

²²Moses placed the table for the holy bread in the tent of meeting. It was on the north side of the holy tent outside the curtain. ²³He arranged the loaves of bread on it in the sight of the LORD. Moses did it as the LORD had commanded him.

²⁴Moses placed the lampstand in the tent of meeting. It stood across from the table on the south side of the holy tent. ²⁵He set up the lamps in front of the LORD. Moses did it as the LORD had commanded him.

²⁶Moses placed the gold altar for burning incense in the tent of meeting. He placed it in front of the curtain. ²⁷He burned sweet-smelling incense on it. Moses did it as the LORD had commanded him.

²⁸Then Moses put up the curtain at the entrance to the holy tent. ²⁹He set the altar

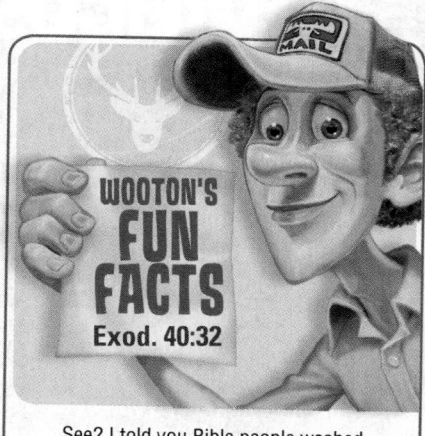

WOOTON'S FUN FACTS
Exod. 40:32

See? I told you Bible people washed their feet a lot. Anyone who approached God's altar had to have clean feet.

for burnt offerings near the entrance to the holy tent, the tent of meeting. He sacrificed burnt offerings and grain offerings on it. Moses did it as the LORD had commanded him.

³⁰Moses placed the large bowl between the tent of meeting and the altar. He put water in the bowl for washing. ³¹Moses and Aaron and his sons used it to wash their hands and feet. ³²They washed whenever they entered the tent of meeting or approached the altar. They did it as the LORD had commanded Moses.

³³Then Moses set up the courtyard around the holy tent and altar. He put up the curtain at the entrance to the courtyard. And so Moses completed the work.

The Glory of the LORD

³⁴Then the cloud covered the tent of meeting. The glory of the LORD filled the holy tent. ³⁵Moses couldn't enter the tent of meeting because the cloud had settled on it. The glory of the LORD filled the holy tent.

³⁶The Israelites continued their travels. Whenever the cloud lifted from above the holy tent, they started out. ³⁷But if the cloud didn't lift, they did not start out. They stayed until the day it lifted. ³⁸So the cloud of the LORD was above the holy tent during the day. Fire was in the cloud at night. All the Israelites could see the cloud during all their travels.

Leviticus

And now we come to the book of Leviticus. The word "Leviticus" is, in fact, a variation of "Levites," the tribe that served as priests and tabernacle workers in ancient Israel. Sometimes when people decide to try to read through the Bible (a noble and honorable endeavor), Leviticus is where they get—how shall we say—bogged down. Not only does this book lack the abundance of exhilarating stories found in Genesis and Exodus, it also contains an abundance of rules—many of which no longer apply to people today. Yet it is still a fascinating book.

You might try this exercise: Read it as if you were a priest and needed to know this information so you could help your people. Note the constant emphasis on being "clean." People who were deemed "unclean" were not allowed to associate with others for a time, and this could happen for any number of reasons: eating the wrong foods, catching certain diseases, or touching dead things, to name but a few.

Reading Leviticus can make you better appreciate that Jesus is our "great high priest" (Heb. 4:14), who takes care of all our unclean thoughts and actions, and who makes it possible for us to talk to God with total confidence!

WHAT'S IT MEAN, EUGENE?

Atonement—The verb *atone* expresses the idea of being "at one" with another person. Atonement, then, is when sinful people are restored into a right relationship with God. Leviticus 17:11 says, "Blood is life. That is why blood pays for your sin." We can only be "at one" with God—that is, *reconciled* to Him—when our sins are blotted out by the blood of our Lord Jesus Christ.

Rules for Burnt Offerings

1 The LORD called out to Moses. He spoke to him from the tent of meeting. He said, ²"Speak to the Israelites. Tell them, 'Suppose anyone among you brings an offering to the LORD. They must bring an animal from their herd or flock.

³" 'If someone brings a burnt offering from the herd, they must offer a male animal. It must not have any flaws. They must bring it to the entrance to the tent of meeting. Then the LORD will accept it. ⁴They must place their hand on the head of the burnt offering. Then the LORD will accept it in place of them. It will pay for their sin. ⁵The young bull must be killed there in the sight of the LORD. Then the priests in Aaron's family line must bring its blood to the altar. They must splash it against the sides of the altar. The altar stands at the entrance to the tent of meeting. ⁶The skin must be removed from the animal brought for the burnt offering. Then the animal must be cut into pieces. ⁷The priests in Aaron's family line must build a fire on the altar. They must place wood on the fire. ⁸Then they must place the pieces of the animal on the burning wood on the altar. The pieces include the head and the fat. ⁹The inside parts of the animal must be washed with water. The legs must also be washed. The priest must burn all of it on the altar. It is a burnt offering. It is a food offering. Its smell pleases the LORD.

¹⁰" 'If someone offers a burnt offering from the flock, it must be a male animal. It can be a sheep or a goat. It must not have any flaws. ¹¹They must kill it at the north side of the altar in the sight of the LORD. The priests in Aaron's family line must splash its blood against the sides of the altar. ¹²They must cut the animal into pieces. The priest must place the pieces on the burning wood on the altar. The pieces include the head and the fat. ¹³They must wash the inside parts with water. The legs must also be washed. The priest must bring all the parts to the altar. He must burn them there. It is a burnt offering. It is a food offering. Its smell pleases the LORD.

¹⁴" 'If someone offers to the LORD a burnt offering of birds, it must be a dove or a young pigeon. ¹⁵The priest must bring it to the altar. He must twist its head off.

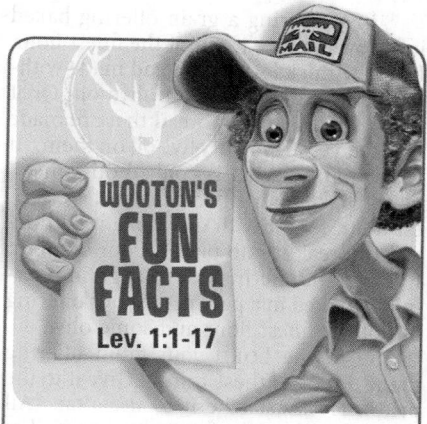

WOOTON'S FUN FACTS
Lev. 1:1-17

Reading about all the blood splashing used to make me sick to my stomach. But Mr. Whittaker told me that I would better understand Jesus' death on the cross if I understood why a sacrifice is important to God.

Then he must burn the rest of the bird on the altar. Its blood must be emptied out on the side of the altar. ¹⁶The priest must remove the small bag inside the bird's throat. He must also remove the feathers. Then he must throw them to the east side of the altar. That is where the ashes are. ¹⁷He must take hold of the wings of the bird and tear it open. But he must not tear it in two. Then the priest will burn it on the wood burning on the altar. It is a burnt offering. It is a food offering. Its smell pleases the LORD.

Rules for Grain Offerings

2 "Suppose anyone brings a grain offering to the LORD. Then their offering must be made out of the finest flour. They must pour olive oil on it. They must also put incense on it. ²They must take it to the priests in Aaron's family line. A priest must take a handful of the flour and oil. He must mix them with all the incense. Then he must burn that part on the altar. It will be a reminder that all good things come from the LORD. It is a food offering. Its smell pleases the LORD. ³The rest of the grain offering belongs to Aaron and to the priests in his family line. It is a very holy part of the food offerings presented to the LORD.

4 " 'If you bring a grain offering baked in an oven, make it out of the finest flour. It can be thick loaves of bread made without yeast. Mix them with olive oil. Or it can be thin loaves of bread that are made without yeast. Spread olive oil on them. 5 If your grain offering is cooked on a metal plate, make your offering out of the finest flour. Mix it with oil. Make it without yeast. 6 Break it into pieces. Pour oil on it. It is a grain offering. 7 If your grain offering is cooked in a pan, make your offering out of the finest flour and some olive oil. 8 Bring to the Lord your grain offering made out of all these things. Give it to the priest. He must take it to the altar. 9 All good things come from the Lord. The priest must take out the part of the grain offering that reminds you of this. He must burn it on the altar. It is a food offering. Its smell pleases the Lord. 10 The rest of the grain offering belongs to Aaron and the priests in his family line. It is a very holy part of the food offerings presented to the Lord.

Jason's Jargon

LEVITICUS 2

Search for the word *yeast* in this chapter. Bread is made of flour, water, and yeast. Yeast causes the bread to rise in the oven. Bread without yeast is flat and looks like a cracker.

11 " 'Every grain offering you bring to the Lord must be made without yeast. You must not add any yeast or honey to a food offering presented to the Lord. 12 You can bring them to the Lord as an offering of the first share of food you gather or produce. But they must not be offered on the altar as a pleasant smell. 13 Put salt on all your grain offerings. Salt stands for the lasting covenant between you and your God. So do not leave it out of your grain offerings. Add salt to all your offerings.

14 " 'Suppose you bring to the Lord a grain offering of the first share of your food. Then offer crushed heads of your first grain that have been cooked in fire.

15 Put olive oil and incense on the grain. It is a grain offering. 16 The priest must burn part of the crushed grain and the oil. It will remind you that all good things come from the Lord. The priest must burn it together with all the incense. It is a food offering presented to the Lord.

Rules for Friendship Offerings

3 " 'Suppose someone brings a friendship offering. If they offer an animal from the herd, it can be either male or female. It must not have any flaws. They must offer it in the sight of the Lord. 2 They must place their hand on the animal's head. It must be killed at the entrance to the tent of meeting. Then the priests in Aaron's family line must splash the blood against the sides of the altar. 3 Part of the friendship offering must be given to the Lord as a food offering. It must include all the fat that is connected to them. 4 It must include both kidneys with the fat on them next to the lower back muscles. It must also include the long part of the liver. All of it must be removed together with the kidneys. 5 Then the priests in Aaron's family line must burn it on the altar. They must burn it on top of the burnt offering that is lying on the burning wood. It is a food offering. Its smell pleases the Lord.

6 " 'Suppose someone brings an animal from the flock as a friendship offering to the Lord. It can be either male or female. It must not have any flaws. 7 If they bring a lamb, they must offer it in the sight of the Lord. 8 They must place their hand on the lamb's head. It must be killed there in front of the tent of meeting. Then the priests in Aaron's family line must splash its blood against the sides of the altar. 9 Part of the offering must be brought as a sacrifice presented to the Lord. It must include the lamb's fat and the entire fat tail cut off close to the backbone. It must include all the fat that is connected to them. 10 It must include both kidneys with the fat on them next to the lower back muscles. The offering must also include the long part of the liver. That must be removed together with the kidneys. 11 Then the priest must burn the offering on the altar as food. It is a food offering presented to the Lord.

12 " 'If someone brings a goat, they must offer it in the sight of the Lord. 13 They

must place their hand on its head. It must be killed there in front of the tent of meeting. Then the priests in Aaron's family line must splash its blood against the sides of the altar. ¹⁴Part of the offering must be brought as a food offering presented to the LORD. It must include all the fat that is connected to them. ¹⁵It must include both kidneys with the fat on them next to the lower back muscles. It must also include the long part of the liver. That must be removed together with the kidneys. ¹⁶Then the priest must burn the offering on the altar as food. It is a food offering. It has a pleasant smell. All the fat belongs to the LORD.

¹⁷" 'You must not eat any fat or any blood. That is a law that will last for all time to come. It applies no matter where you live.' "

Rules for Sin Offerings

4 The LORD spoke to Moses. He said, ²"Speak to the Israelites. Tell them, 'Suppose someone sins without meaning to. And that person does something the LORD commands us not to do.

³" 'Suppose it is the anointed priest who sins. And suppose he brings guilt on the people. Then he must bring a young bull to the LORD. It must not have any flaws. He must bring it as a sin offering for the sin he has committed. ⁴He must bring the bull to the entrance to the tent of meeting in the sight of the LORD. He must place his hand on its head. He must kill it there in the sight of the LORD. ⁵Then the anointed priest must take some of the bull's blood. He must carry it into the tent of meeting. ⁶He must dip his finger into the blood. He must sprinkle some of it seven times in the sight of the LORD. He must do it in front of the curtain of the Most Holy Room. ⁷Then the priest must put some of the blood on the horns of the altar for burning incense. The horns stick out from the upper four corners of the altar. The incense burned on that altar has a sweet smell. The altar stands in front of the LORD in the tent of meeting. The priest must pour out the rest of the bull's blood at the bottom of the altar for burnt offerings. That altar stands at the entrance to the tent. ⁸He must remove all the fat from the bull for the sin offering. It includes the fat that is connected to the inside parts.

⁹It includes both kidneys with the fat on them next to the lower back muscles. It also includes the long part of the liver. He must remove all of it together with the kidneys. ¹⁰He must remove it in the same way the fat is removed from an ox sacrificed as a friendship offering. Then the priest must burn all of it on the altar for burnt offerings. ¹¹But the bull's hide must be taken away. So must all its meat. So must its head and legs. And so must its inside parts and guts. ¹²In other words, all the rest of the bull must be taken away. The priest must take it outside the camp. He must take it to a "clean" place. He must take it to the place where the ashes are thrown. Then he must burn it there in a wood fire on a pile of ashes.

¹³" 'Or suppose the whole community of Israel sins without meaning to. They do something the LORD commands us not to do. Suppose they realize their guilt. ¹⁴And suppose their sin becomes known. Then they must bring a young bull as a sin offering. They must offer it in front of the tent of meeting. ¹⁵The elders of the community must place their hands on the bull's head in the sight of the LORD. The bull must be killed in the sight of the LORD. ¹⁶Then the anointed priest must take some of the bull's blood into the tent of meeting. ¹⁷He must dip his finger into the blood. He must sprinkle it seven times in the sight of the LORD. He must do it in front of the curtain. ¹⁸He must put some of the blood on the horns that stick out from the upper four corners of the altar. The altar stands in front of the LORD in the tent of meeting. The priest must pour out the rest of the blood at the bottom of the altar for burnt offerings. That altar stands at the entrance to the tent. ¹⁹He must remove all the fat from the bull. He must burn it on the altar. ²⁰He must do the same thing with that bull as he did with the bull for the sin offering. When he does, he will pay for the sin of the community. And they will be forgiven. ²¹Then he must take the bull outside the camp. He must burn it just as he burned the first bull. It is the sin offering for the whole community.

²²" 'Or suppose a leader sins without meaning to. He disobeys any of the commands of the LORD his God. ²³And suppose he realizes his guilt and his sin

becomes known. Then he must bring an offering. It must be a male goat. It must not have any flaws. ²⁴He must place his hand on the goat's head. He must kill it. He must do it at the place where the animals for burnt offerings are killed in the sight of the LORD. His offering is a sin offering. ²⁵Then the priest must dip his finger into some of the blood of the sin offering. He must put it on the horns that stick out from the upper four corners of the altar for burnt offerings. He must pour out the rest of the blood at the bottom of the altar. ²⁶He must burn all the fat on the altar. He must burn it in the same way he burned the fat of the friendship offering. When he does, he will pay for the sin of the leader. And the leader will be forgiven.

²⁷"Or suppose someone in the community sins without meaning to. They disobey any of the LORD's commands. ²⁸And suppose they realize their guilt and their sin becomes known. Then they must bring an offering for the sin they have committed. It must be a female goat. It must not have any flaws. ²⁹They must place their hand on the head of the animal for the sin offering. It must be killed at the place where the animals for burnt offerings are killed. ³⁰Then the priest must dip his finger into some of the blood. He must put it on the horns that stick out from the upper four corners of the altar for burnt offerings. He must pour out the rest of the blood at the bottom of the altar. ³¹They must remove all the fat in the same way the fat is removed from the friendship offering. The priest must burn it on the altar. Its smell pleases the LORD. When the priest burns the offering, he will pay for their sin. And they will be forgiven.

³²"Suppose someone brings a lamb as their sin offering. Then they must bring a female animal. It must not have any flaws. ³³They must place their hand on its head. They must kill it as a sin offering. They must do it at the place where the animals for burnt offerings are killed. ³⁴Then the priest must dip his finger into some of the blood of the sin offering. He must put it on the horns that stick out from the upper four corners of the altar for burnt offerings. He must pour out the rest of the blood at the bottom of the altar. ³⁵They must remove all the fat in the same way

the fat is removed from the lamb for the friendship offering. The priest must burn it on the altar on top of the food offerings presented to the LORD. When he does, he will pay for the sin they have committed. And they will be forgiven.

5 "Suppose someone has been called as a witness to something they have seen or learned about. Then if they do not tell what they know, they have sinned. And they will be held responsible for it.

²"Or suppose someone touches something not "clean." It could be the dead bodies of wild animals or of livestock. Or it could be the dead bodies of creatures that move along the ground. Even though those people are not aware that they touched them, they have become "unclean." And they are guilty. ³Or suppose they touch something "unclean" that comes from a human being. It could be anything that would make them "unclean." Suppose they are not aware that they touched it. When they find out about it, they will be guilty. ⁴Or suppose someone makes a promise to do something without thinking it through. It does not matter what they promised. It does not matter whether they made the promise without thinking about it carefully. And suppose they are not aware that they did not think it through. When they find out about it, they will be guilty. ⁵When someone is guilty in any of those

Lev. 5:1 One time, I had to testify against some money counterfeiters. I was scared, but I knew it was the right thing to do. Do you know that for every million $100 bills the US Treasury inspects, it finds that about twenty-five of them are fake?

ways, they must admit they have sinned. [6]They must bring a sin offering to pay for the sin they have committed. They must bring to the LORD a female lamb or goat from the flock. The priest will sacrifice the animal. That will pay for the person's sin.

[7]"Suppose they can't afford a lamb. Then they must get two doves or two young pigeons. They must bring them to the LORD to pay for their sin. One of them is for a sin offering. The other is for a burnt offering. [8]They must bring them to the priest. The priest will offer the one for the sin offering first. He must twist its head. But he must not twist it off completely. [9]Then he must splash some of the blood of the sin offering against the side of the altar. He must empty out the rest of the blood at the bottom of the altar. It is a sin offering. [10]Then the priest will offer the other bird as a burnt offering. He must do it in the way the law requires. That will pay for the sin they have committed. And they will be forgiven.

[11]"But suppose they can't afford two doves or two young pigeons. Then they must bring three and a half pounds of the finest flour as an offering for their sin. It is a sin offering. They must not put olive oil or incense on it. That is because it is a sin offering. [12]They must bring it to the priest. The priest must take a handful of it. He must burn that part on the altar. It will be a reminder that all good things come from the LORD. The priest must burn it on top of the food offerings presented to the LORD. It is a sin offering. [13]In that way the priest will pay for any of the sins they have committed. And they will be forgiven. The rest of the offering will belong to the priest. It is the same as in the case of the grain offering.'"

Rules for Guilt Offerings

[14]The LORD spoke to Moses. He said, [15]"Suppose someone is unfaithful to me and sins. And they do it without meaning to. Here is how they sin against me or my priests. They refuse to give the priests one of the holy things set apart for them. Then they must bring me a ram from the flock. It must not have any flaws. It must be worth the required amount of silver. The silver must be weighed out in keeping with the standard weights that are used in

the sacred tent. The ram is a guilt offering. It will pay for their sin. [16]They must also pay for the holy thing they refused to give. They must add a fifth of its value to it. They must give all of it to the priest. The priest will pay for their sin with the ram. It is a guilt offering. And they will be forgiven.

[17]"Suppose someone sins by doing something I command them not to do. Even though they do not know it, they are guilty. They will be held responsible for it. [18]They must bring to the priest a ram from the flock as a guilt offering. It must not have any flaws. And it must be worth the required amount of money. The priest will sacrifice the animal. That will pay for what they have done wrong without meaning to. And they will be forgiven. [19]It is a guilt offering. They have been guilty of doing wrong against me."

6 The LORD spoke to Moses. He said, [2]"Suppose someone sins by not being faithful to me. They do it by tricking their neighbors. They trick them in connection with something their neighbors have placed in their care. They steal from their neighbors. Or they cheat them. [3]Or they find something their neighbors have lost and then tell a lie about it. Or they go to court. They promise to tell the truth. But instead they tell a lie when they are a witness about it. Or they lie when they are witnesses about any other sin like those sins. [4]When they sin in any of these ways and realize their guilt, they must return what they stole. They must give back what they took by cheating their neighbors. They must return what their neighbors placed in their care. They must return the lost property they found. [5]They must return anything they told a lie about when they were witnesses in court. They must pay back everything in full. They must add a fifth of its value to it. They must give all of it to the owner on the day they bring their guilt offering. [6]He must bring their guilt offering to the priest to pay for their sin. It is an offering to me. They must bring a ram from the flock. It must not have any flaws. It must be worth the required amount of money. [7]The priest will sacrifice the ram to pay for their sin. He will do it in my sight. And they will be forgiven for any of the things they did that made them guilty."

More Rules for Burnt Offerings

[8]The LORD spoke to Moses. He said, [9]"Give Aaron and the priests in his family line a command. Tell them, 'Here are some more rules for burnt offerings. The burnt offering must remain on the altar through the whole night. The fire on the altar must be kept burning until morning. [10]The priest must put on his linen clothes. He must put on linen underwear next to his body. He must remove the ashes of the burnt offering that the fire has burned up on the altar. He must place them beside the altar. [11]Then he must take his clothes off and put others on. He must carry the ashes outside the camp to a "clean" place. [12]The fire on the altar must be kept burning. It must not go out. Every morning the priest must add more wood to the fire. He must place the burnt offering on the fire. He must burn the fat of the friendship offerings on it. [13]The fire must be kept burning on the altar all the time. It must not go out.

More Rules for Grain Offerings

[14]"Here are some more rules for grain offerings. The priests in Aaron's family line must bring the grain offering to the LORD in front of the altar. [15]The priest must take a handful of the finest flour and olive oil. He must add to it all the incense on the grain offering. He must burn that part on the altar. It will remind him that all good things come from the LORD. Its smell pleases the LORD. [16]Aaron and the priests in his family line will eat the rest of it. But they must eat it without yeast in the holy area. They must eat it in the courtyard of the tent of meeting. [17]It must not be baked with yeast added to it. The LORD has given it to the priests as their share of the food offerings presented to him. It is very holy, just like the sin offering and the guilt offering. [18]Any priests in Aaron's family line can eat it. It is their share of the food offerings presented to the LORD. It is their share for all time to come. Anyone who touches these offerings will become holy.'"

[19]The LORD spoke to Moses. He said, [20]"On the day each high priest in Aaron's family line is anointed, he must bring an offering to me. He must bring three and a half pounds of the finest flour as a regular grain offering. He must bring half of it in the morning. He must bring the other half in the evening. [21]Mix it with olive oil. Cook it on a metal plate. Break it in pieces. Bring it as a grain offering. Its smell pleases the LORD. [22]The son of Aaron who will become the next high priest after him will prepare the grain offering. It is the share that must be given to the LORD for all time to come. It must be completely burned up. [23]Every grain offering a high priest offers must be completely burned up. It must not be eaten."

More Rules for Sin Offerings

[24]The LORD spoke to Moses. He said, [25]"Speak to Aaron and the priests in his family line. Tell them, 'Here are some more rules for sin offerings. You must kill the animal for the sin offering in the sight of the LORD. Kill it in the place where the burnt offering is killed. It is very holy. [26]The priest who offers it will eat it. He must eat it in the holy area. He must eat it in the courtyard of the tent of meeting. [27]Anyone who touches any of its meat will become holy. Suppose some of the blood is spilled on someone's clothes. Then you must wash them in the holy area. [28]Break the clay pot the meat is cooked in. But suppose you cook it in a bronze pot. Then you must scrub the pot and rinse it with water. [29]Any male in a priest's family may eat the meat. It is very holy. [30]But suppose some of the blood of a sin offering is brought into the tent of meeting. And that blood is brought into the Holy Room to pay for sin. Then that sin offering must not be eaten. It must be burned up.

More Rules for Guilt Offerings

7 "'Here are some more rules for guilt offerings. The guilt offering is very holy. [2]You must kill the animal for the guilt offering where you kill the animal for the burnt offering. Splash its blood against the sides of the altar. [3]Offer all its fat. It must include the fat tail and the fat that covers the inside parts. [4]It must include both kidneys with the fat on them next to the lower back muscles. It must also include the long part of the liver. Remove all of it together with the kidneys. [5]The priest must burn all of it on the altar. It is a food offering presented to the LORD. It is a guilt offering. [6]Any male in a priest's family can eat it. But he must eat it in the holy area. It is very holy.

[7]"The same law applies to the sin offering and the guilt offering. Both of them belong to the priest who offers them to pay for sin. [8]The priest who offers a burnt offering for anyone can keep its hide for himself. [9]Every grain offering baked in an oven belongs to the priest who offers it. So does every grain offering cooked in a pan or on a metal plate. [10]Every grain offering belongs equally to all the priests in Aaron's family line. That is true whether it is mixed with olive oil or it is dry.

More Rules for Friendship Offerings

[11]"Here are some more rules for friendship offerings anyone may bring to the Lord.

[12]"Suppose they offer a friendship offering to show they are thankful. Then together with the thank offering they must offer thick loaves of bread. They must make them without yeast. They must mix them with olive oil. Or they must offer thin loaves of bread made without yeast. They must spread olive oil on them. Or they must offer thick loaves of bread made out of the finest flour. They must add olive oil to it. They must work the flour and prepare it well. [13]They must bring another friendship offering along with their thank offering. It should be thick loaves of bread made with yeast. [14]They must bring one of each kind of bread as an offering. One kind is made with yeast. The other is not. Both of them are a gift to the Lord. They belong to the priest who splashes the blood of the friendship offering against the altar. [15]The person must eat the meat from their thank offering on the day they offer it. They must not leave any of it until morning.

[16]"But suppose they bring a friendship offering to keep a promise they have made. Or suppose they bring an offering they choose to give. Then they must eat the sacrifice on the day they offer it. But if anything is left over, they may eat it the next day. [17]They must burn up any meat from the sacrifice left over until the third day. [18]Suppose they eat any meat from the friendship offering on the third day. Then the Lord will not accept the offering. He will not accept it as a gift from them. It is not pure. If they eat any of it, they will be held responsible for it.

[19]"They must not eat meat that touches anything "unclean." They must burn it up. Anyone "clean" may eat any other meat. [20]But suppose an "unclean" person eats any meat from the friendship offering that belongs to the Lord. Then they will be separated from their people. [21]Suppose someone touches something "unclean." It does not matter whether it comes from a human being who is not "clean." It does not matter whether it comes from an "unclean" animal. It does not matter whether it comes from something hated and "unclean." And suppose they eat any of the meat from the friendship offering that belongs to the Lord. Then they will be separated from their people.' "

Israel Must Not Eat Fat or Blood

[22]The Lord spoke to Moses. He said, [23]"Speak to the Israelites. Tell them, 'Do not eat any of the fat of cattle, sheep or goats. [24]Do not eat the fat of any animal found dead. Do not eat the fat of an animal that wild animals have torn apart. But you can use the fat for any other purpose. [25]Suppose an animal has been sacrificed as a food offering to the Lord. No one may eat its fat. If they do, they will be separated from their people. [26]No matter where you live, do not eat the blood of any bird or animal. [27]Anyone who eats blood must be separated from their people.' "

The Share That Belongs to the Priests

[28]The Lord spoke to Moses. He said, [29]"Speak to the Israelites. Tell them, 'Suppose someone brings a friendship offering to the Lord. Then they must bring part of it as their special gift to the Lord. [30]They must bring it with their own hands. It is a food offering presented to the Lord. They must bring the fat together with the breast. They must lift the breast up and wave it in front of the Lord as a wave offering. [31]The priest will burn the fat on the altar. But the breast belongs to Aaron and the priests in his family line. [32]Give the right thigh from your friendship offerings to the priest as a gift. [33]The priest who offers the blood and fat from the friendship offering must be given the right thigh. It is his share. [34]I, the Lord, have taken the breast that is waved and the thigh that is given. I have taken them from the friendship offerings of the Israelites. And I have given them to Aaron the priest and the priests in his family line.

The offerings will be their share from the Israelites for all time to come.'"

³⁵That is the part of the food offerings presented to the LORD. It is given to Aaron and the priests in his family line. It was given to Aaron and his sons on the day they were set apart to serve the LORD as priests. ³⁶On the day they were anointed, the LORD commanded the Israelites to give that part to them. For all time to come, it will be the share of Aaron and the priests in his family line.

³⁷These are the rules for burnt offerings, grain offerings, sin offerings, guilt offerings and friendship offerings. They are also the rules for the offerings that are given when priests are being prepared to serve the LORD. ³⁸They are the rules the LORD gave Moses on Mount Sinai. He gave them on the day he commanded the Israelites to bring their offerings to the LORD. That took place in the Sinai Desert.

Preparing the Priests to Serve the LORD

8 The LORD spoke to Moses. He said, ²"Bring Aaron and his sons to the entrance to the tent of meeting. Bring their clothes and the anointing oil. Bring the bull for the sin offering. Also bring two rams. And bring the basket with the bread made without yeast. ³Then gather the whole community at the entrance to the tent of meeting." ⁴Moses did just as the LORD had commanded him. All the people gathered together at the entrance to the tent of meeting.

⁵Moses said to the people, "Here is what the LORD has commanded us to do." ⁶Then Moses brought Aaron and his sons to the people. He washed Aaron and his sons with water. ⁷He put the inner robe on Aaron. He tied the belt around him. He dressed him in the outer robe. He put the linen apron on him. He took the skillfully made waistband and tied the apron on him with it. He wanted to make sure it was securely tied to him. ⁸Moses placed the chest cloth on Aaron. He put the Urim and Thummim in the chest cloth. ⁹Then he placed the turban on Aaron's head. On the front of the turban he put the gold plate. It was a sacred crown. Moses did everything just as the LORD had commanded him.

¹⁰Then Moses took the anointing oil and poured it on the holy tent. He also poured it

WOOTON'S FUN FACTS

Lev. 8
Levites aren't people who wear blue jeans—which is too bad because jeans are so comfortable. *Leviticus* means "about the Levites" because Levi was the Israelite tribe the priests were from, starting with Aaron.

on everything in it. That's how he set apart those things for the LORD. ¹¹He sprinkled some of the oil on the altar seven times. He poured oil on the altar and all its tools. He poured it on the large bowl and its stand. He did it to set them apart. ¹²He poured some of the anointing oil on Aaron's head. He anointed him to set him apart to serve the LORD. ¹³Then Moses brought Aaron's sons to the people. He put the inner robes on them. He tied belts around them. He put caps on their heads. He did everything just as the LORD had commanded him.

¹⁴Then he brought the bull for the sin offering. Aaron and his sons placed their hands on its head. ¹⁵Moses killed the bull. He dipped his finger into some of the blood. He put it on the horns that stick out from the upper four corners of the altar. He did it to make the altar pure. He poured out the rest of the blood at the bottom of the altar. So he set it apart to make it pure. ¹⁶Moses also removed all the fat around the inside parts of the bull. He removed the long part of the liver. He took both kidneys and their fat. Then he burned all of it on the altar. ¹⁷But he burned the rest of the bull outside the camp. He burned up its hide, its meat and its guts. He did it just as the LORD had commanded him.

¹⁸Then Moses brought the ram for the burnt offering. Aaron and his sons placed their hands on its head. ¹⁹Moses killed the ram. He splashed the blood against the sides of the altar. ²⁰He cut the ram into pieces. He burned the head, the other pieces and the fat. ²¹He washed the inside parts and the legs with water. He burned the whole ram on the altar as a burnt offering. It had a pleasant smell. It was a food offering presented to the LORD. Moses did everything just as the LORD had commanded him.

²²Then he brought the other ram. It was sacrificed to prepare the priests for serving the LORD. Aaron and his sons placed their hands on its head. ²³Moses killed the ram. He put some of its blood on Aaron's right earlobe. He put some on the thumb of Aaron's right hand. He also put some on the big toe of Aaron's right foot. ²⁴Then Moses brought Aaron's sons to the people. He put some of the blood on their right earlobes. He put some on the thumbs of their right hands. He also put some on the big toes of their right feet. Then he splashed the rest of the blood against the sides of the altar. ²⁵He removed the fat, the fat tail and all the fat around the inside parts. He removed the long part of the liver. He removed both kidneys and their fat. And he removed the right thigh. ²⁶Then he took a thick loaf of bread from the basket of bread made without yeast. The basket was in front of the LORD. Moses took a thick loaf of bread made with olive oil. He also took a thin loaf of bread. He put all of it on the fat parts of the ram and on its right thigh. ²⁷He put everything in the hands of Aaron and his sons. He told them to lift it up and wave it in front of the LORD as a wave offering. ²⁸Then Moses took it from their hands. He burned it on the altar on top of the burnt offering. It was the offering that was sacrificed to prepare the priests for serving the LORD. It had a pleasant smell. It was a food offering presented to the LORD. ²⁹Moses also lifted up the ram's breast and waved it in front of the LORD as a wave offering. The breast was Moses' share of the ram that was sacrificed to prepare the priests for serving the LORD. Moses did everything just as the LORD had commanded him.

³⁰Then Moses took some of the anointing oil. He also took some of the blood from the altar. He sprinkled some of the oil and blood on Aaron and his clothes. He also sprinkled some on Aaron's sons and their clothes. That's how he set apart Aaron and his clothes. And that's how he set apart Aaron's sons and their clothes.

³¹Then Moses spoke to Aaron and his sons. He said, "Cook the meat at the entrance to the tent of meeting. Eat it there along with the bread from the basket of the offerings that are brought to prepare the priests for serving the LORD. Do it just as I was commanded. I was told, 'Aaron and his sons must eat it.' ³²Then burn up the rest of the meat and the bread. ³³Don't leave the entrance to the tent of meeting for seven days. Don't leave until the days that are required to prepare you for serving the LORD have been completed. Stay here for the full seven days. ³⁴The LORD commanded what has been done here today. It was done to pay for your sin. ³⁵Stay at the entrance to the tent of meeting for seven days. Stay here day and night. Do what the LORD requires. Then you won't die. That's the command the LORD gave me."

³⁶So Aaron and his sons did everything just as the LORD had commanded through Moses.

The Priests Offer Sacrifices

9 On the eighth day Moses sent for Aaron, his sons and the elders of Israel. ²He said to Aaron, "Bring a bull calf for your sin offering. Bring a ram for your burnt offering. They must not have any flaws. Offer them to the LORD. ³Then speak to the Israelites. Tell them, 'Bring a male goat for a sin offering. Bring a calf and a lamb for a burnt offering. Both of them must be a year old. They must not have any flaws. ⁴Bring an ox and a ram for a friendship offering. Sacrifice all of them to the LORD. Also bring a grain offering. Mix it with olive oil. Today the LORD will appear to you.'"

⁵The people got the things Moses commanded them to get. They took them to the front of the tent of meeting. The whole community came up close to the tent. They stood there in front of the LORD. ⁶Then Moses said, "You have done what the LORD has commanded. So the glory of the LORD will appear to you."

⁷Moses said to Aaron, "Come to the altar. Sacrifice your sin offering and your burnt offering. Pay for your sin and the sin of the people. Sacrifice the people's offering. Pay for their sin. Do just as the Lord has commanded."

⁸So Aaron came to the altar. He killed the calf as a sin offering for himself. ⁹His sons brought its blood to him. He dipped his finger into the blood. He put some on the horns that stick out from the upper four corners of the altar. He poured out the rest of the blood at the bottom of the altar. ¹⁰He burned the fat and the kidneys on the altar. He also burned the long part of the liver. All these parts were from the sin offering. Aaron did just as the Lord had commanded Moses. ¹¹He burned up the meat and the hide outside the camp.

¹²Then he killed the animal for the burnt offering. His sons handed him its blood. He splashed it against the sides of the altar. ¹³They handed him the burnt offering piece by piece. It included the animal's head. Aaron burned everything on the altar. ¹⁴He washed the inside parts and the legs. He burned them on top of the burnt offering on the altar.

¹⁵Then Aaron brought the people's offering. He took the goat for their sin offering and killed it. He offered it for a sin offering. He did just as he had done with his own sin offering.

¹⁶He brought the animal for the burnt offering. He offered it in the way the law requires. ¹⁷He also brought the grain offering. He took a handful of it and burned it on the altar. It was in addition to that morning's burnt offering.

¹⁸Aaron killed the ox and the ram as the friendship offering for the people. His sons handed him the blood. He splashed it against the sides of the altar. ¹⁹His sons also brought the fat parts of the ox and the ram. They included the fat tail and the layer of fat. They also included the kidneys and the long part of the liver. ²⁰Aaron's sons placed everything on the breasts of the animals. Aaron burned the fat on the altar. ²¹He lifted up the breasts and the right thigh and waved them in front of the Lord as a wave offering. He did it just as Moses had commanded.

²²Then Aaron lifted up his hands toward the people. He gave them a

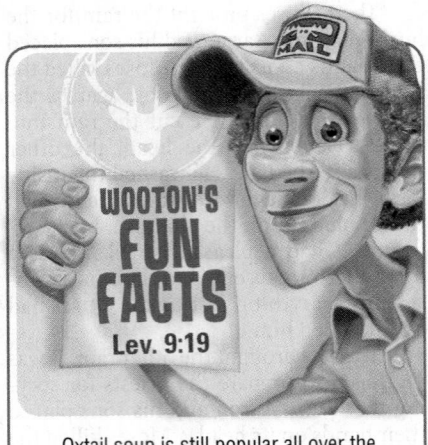

Oxtail soup is still popular all over the world, from Korea to Africa to Jamaica. I think I'll make some tonight.

blessing. He had already sacrificed the sin offering, the burnt offering and the friendship offering. So he stepped down from the altar.

²³Moses and Aaron went into the tent of meeting. When they came out, they gave the people a blessing. The glory of the Lord appeared to all the people. ²⁴The Lord sent fire on the altar. The fire burned up the burnt offering along with the fat parts. All the people saw it. Then they shouted for joy. They fell with their faces to the ground.

The Lord Kills Nadab and Abihu

10 Nadab and Abihu were two of Aaron's sons. They got their shallow cups for burning incense. They put fire in them. They added incense to it. They made an offering to the Lord by using fire that wasn't allowed. They did it against his command. ²So the Lord sent fire on them. It burned them up. They died in front of the Lord. ³Then Moses spoke to Aaron. He said, "That's what the Lord was talking about when he said,

"'Among those who approach me
    I will show that I am holy.
In the sight of all the people
    I will be honored.'"

So Aaron remained silent.

⁴Moses sent for Mishael and Elzaphan. They were sons of Aaron's uncle Uzziel.

NOOTON'S FUN FACTS

Lev. 10:6

I'm glad God understands that we feel sad when people die. I remember when Connie's mom died and how sad all of us felt.

Moses said to them, "Come here. Carry the bodies of your cousins outside the camp. Take them away from in front of the Holy Room." 5So they came and carried them outside the camp. It was just as Moses had ordered. The bodies of Nadab and Abihu still had their inner robes on them.

6Moses spoke to Aaron and to Eleazar and Ithamar. They were Aaron's sons. Moses said, "Don't let your hair hang loose. Don't tear your clothes. If you do, you will die. And the LORD will be angry with the whole community. But all the Israelites are allowed to show they are sad. They are your relatives. They may mourn for those the LORD has destroyed with fire. 7Don't leave the entrance to the tent of meeting. If you do, you will die. That's because the LORD's anointing oil has made you holy." So they did what Moses told them to do.

8Then the LORD spoke to Aaron. He said, 9"You and your sons will go into the tent of meeting. When you do, you must not drink any kind of wine. If you do, you will die. This is a law that will last for all time to come. 10This is so that you can tell the difference between what is holy and what is not. You must be able to tell the difference between what is 'clean' and what is not. 11Then you will be able to teach the Israelites all the rules I have given them through Moses."

12Moses spoke to Aaron and to Eleazar and Ithamar. They were Aaron's two remaining sons. Moses said, "Take the grain offering left over from the food offerings presented to the LORD. It is very holy. Make bread without yeast from it. Eat it beside the altar. 13Eat it in the holy area. It's your share and your sons' share of the food offerings presented to the LORD. These rules are in keeping with the command the LORD gave me. 14But you and your sons and your daughters can eat the breast that was waved. You can also eat the thigh that was offered. Eat them in a 'clean' place. They have been given to you and your children. They are your share of the friendship offerings the Israelites bring. 15The thigh that was offered must be brought together with the fat parts of the food offerings. The breast that was waved must be brought in the same way. All of it must be lifted up and waved in front of the LORD as a wave offering. It will be the share for you and your children for all time to come. That's what the LORD has commanded."

16Moses asked about the goat that was brought as the sin offering. He found out that it had been burned up. So he became angry with Eleazar and Ithamar. They were Aaron's two remaining sons. Moses asked them, 17"Why didn't you eat the sin offering in a place near the Holy Room? The offering is very holy. It was given to you to take the people's guilt away. It paid for their sin in the sight of the LORD. 18The blood of the offering wasn't taken into the Holy Room. So you should have eaten the goat in a place near the Holy Room. That's what I commanded."

19Aaron replied to Moses, "Today the people sacrificed their sin offering to the LORD. They also sacrificed their burnt offerings to him. But a terrible thing has happened to me. Two of my sons have died. Would the LORD have been pleased if I had eaten the sin offering today?" 20When Moses heard that, he was satisfied.

"Clean" and "Unclean" Food

11 The LORD spoke to Moses and Aaron. He said to them, 2"Speak to the Israelites. Tell them, 'Many animals live on land. Here are the only ones you can eat. 3You can eat any animal that has hooves

WOOTON'S FUN FACTS

Lev. 11:1-8 My dog, Sam, chews "crud" but that's not the same as chewing cud. And his paws don't have split hooves, so he's doubly safe. And just looking at him you can tell he's "unclean." Triple safe. Whew!

that are separated completely in two. But it must also chew the cud.

⁴" 'Some animals only chew the cud. Some only have hooves that are separated in two. You must not eat those animals. Camels chew the cud. But their hooves are not separated in two. So they are "unclean" for you. ⁵Rock badgers chew the cud. But their hooves are not separated in two. So they are "unclean" for you. ⁶Rabbits chew the cud. But their hooves are not separated in two. So they are "unclean" for you. ⁷Pigs have hooves that are separated completely in two. But they do not chew the cud. So they are "unclean" for you. ⁸You must not eat the meat of those animals. You must not even touch their dead bodies. They are "unclean" for you.

⁹" 'Many creatures live in the water of the oceans and streams. You can eat all those that have fins and scales. ¹⁰Treat as "unclean" all the creatures in the oceans or streams that do not have fins and scales. That includes all those that move together in groups and all those that do not. ¹¹Treat them as "unclean." Do not eat their meat. Treat their dead bodies as "unclean." ¹²Regard as "unclean" everything that lives in the water that does not have fins and scales.

¹³" 'Here are the birds you must treat as "unclean." Do not eat them because they are "unclean." The birds include eagles, vultures and black vultures. ¹⁴They

include red kites and all kinds of black kites. ¹⁵They include all kinds of ravens. ¹⁶They include horned owls, screech owls, gulls and all kinds of hawks. ¹⁷They include little owls, cormorants and great owls. ¹⁸They include white owls, desert owls and ospreys. ¹⁹They also include storks, hoopoes, bats and all kinds of herons.

²⁰" 'Treat as "unclean" every flying insect that walks on all fours. ²¹But you can eat some flying insects that walk on all fours. Their legs have joints so they can hop on the ground. ²²Here are the insects you can eat. You can eat all kinds of locusts, katydids, crickets and grasshoppers. ²³Treat as "unclean" every other creature with wings and four legs.

²⁴" 'You will make yourselves "unclean" if you eat these things. If you touch their dead bodies, you will be "unclean" until evening. ²⁵If a person picks up one of their dead bodies, that person must wash their clothes. They will be "unclean" until evening.

Jason's Jargon

LEVITICUS 11

Search this chapter for the word *cud.* "Chewing the cud" is how some animals eat— digesting food, bringing it back up into their mouths, and chewing it again. Cows, sheep, and deer do this. (Yuck.)

²⁶" 'Suppose an animal has hooves that are not separated completely in two. Or suppose an animal does not chew the cud. Then these animals are "unclean" for you. If you touch the dead body of any of them, you will be "unclean." ²⁷Many animals walk on all fours. But those that walk on their paws are "unclean" for you. Anyone who touches their dead bodies will be "unclean" until evening. ²⁸If a person picks up their dead bodies, that person must wash their clothes. They will be "unclean" until evening. These animals are "unclean" for you.

²⁹" 'Many animals move along the ground. Here are the ones that are "unclean" for you. They include weasels, rats and all kinds of large lizards. ³⁰They also include geckos, monitor lizards, wall lizards, skinks and chameleons. ³¹These are the animals that move around on the ground that are "unclean" for you. If you touch their dead bodies, you will be "unclean" until evening. ³²Suppose one of them dies and falls on something. Then that thing will be "unclean." It does not matter what it is used for. It does not matter whether it is made out of wood, cloth, hide or rough cloth. Put it in water. It will be "unclean" until evening. After that, it will be "clean." ³³Suppose one of these animals falls into a clay pot. Then everything in the pot will be "unclean." You must break the pot. ³⁴Any food that could be eaten but has water on it that came from that pot is "unclean." And any liquid that could be drunk from it is "unclean." ³⁵Anything that the dead body of one of these animals falls on becomes "unclean." If it is an oven or cooking pot, break it. It is "unclean." And you must consider it "unclean." ³⁶But a spring or a well for collecting water remains "clean." That is true even if the dead body of one of these animals falls into it. But anyone who touches the dead body is not "clean." ³⁷If the dead body falls on any seeds that have not been planted yet, the seeds remain "clean." ³⁸But suppose water has already been put on the seeds. And suppose the dead body falls on them. Then they are "unclean" for you.

³⁹" 'Suppose an animal you are allowed to eat dies. If anyone touches its dead body, they will be "unclean" until evening. ⁴⁰If they eat part of the dead body, they must wash their clothes. They will be "unclean" until evening. If they pick up the dead body, they must wash their clothes. They will be "unclean" until evening.

⁴¹" 'Treat as "unclean" every creature that moves along the ground. Do not eat it. ⁴²Do not eat any of these creatures. It does not matter whether they move on their bellies. It does not matter whether they walk on all fours or on many feet. It is "unclean." ⁴³Do not make yourselves "unclean" by eating any of these animals. Do not make yourselves "unclean"

CANDID CONVERSATIONS

I have a secret to tell you. There have been several times when I have tried to read the entire Bible in a year, and I got bogged down in Leviticus and ended up skipping it. Okay, I admitted it. This is a book filled with laws that are, well, kind of strange on the surface. Whit taught me that we're not bound by all these laws anymore because of Jesus' death on the Cross, but there's actually a lot of wisdom in this book about hygiene, diet, and behavior. This chapter in particular talks about eating habits.

It takes a lot of practice keeping healthy routines for them to become habits. Luckily, it doesn't take too long to retrain ourselves—maybe just a couple of months. Before long, these healthy habits become so much a part of our lives that we hardly have to think about them anymore.

Ask your parents about planning some healthy meals together.

because of them. Do not let them make you "unclean." ⁴⁴I am the LORD your God. Set yourselves apart. Be holy, because I am holy. Do not make yourselves "unclean" by eating any creatures that move around on the ground. ⁴⁵I am the LORD. I brought you up out of Egypt to be your God. So be holy, because I am holy.

⁴⁶" 'These are the rules about animals and birds. These are the rules about every living thing that moves around in the water. And these are the rules about every creature that moves along the ground. ⁴⁷You must be able to tell the difference between what is "clean" and what is not. You must also be able to tell the difference between living creatures that can be eaten and those that can't.' "

Becoming "Clean" After Having a Baby

12 The LORD spoke to Moses. He said, [2] "Speak to the Israelites. Tell them, 'Suppose a woman becomes pregnant and has a baby boy. Then she will be "unclean" for seven days. It is the same as when she is "unclean" during her monthly period. [3] On the eighth day the boy must be circumcised. [4] After that, the woman must wait for 33 days to be made pure from her bleeding. She must not touch anything sacred until the 33 days are over. During that time she must not go to the sacred tent. [5] But suppose she has a baby girl. Then she will be "unclean" for two weeks. It is the same as during her period. After the two weeks, she must wait for 66 days to be made pure from her bleeding.

[6] "'After she has waited the required number of days to be made pure, she must bring two offerings. She must take them to the priest at the entrance to the tent of meeting. She must bring a lamb a year old for a burnt offering. She must also bring a young pigeon or a dove for a sin offering. [7] The priest must offer them to the LORD. They will pay for her sin. Then she will be "clean" from her bleeding.

"'These are the rules for a woman who has a baby boy or girl. [8] But suppose she can't afford a lamb. Then she must bring two doves or two young pigeons. One is for a burnt offering. The other is for a sin offering. The priest will sacrifice those offerings. That will pay for her sin. And she will be "clean."'"

Rules About Skin Diseases

13 The LORD spoke to Moses and Aaron. He told them to say to the people, [2] "Suppose someone's skin has a swelling or a rash or a shiny spot. And suppose it could become a skin disease. Then they must be brought to the priest Aaron. Or they must be brought to a priest in Aaron's family line. [3] The priest must look carefully at the sore on the person's skin. He must see whether the hair in the sore has turned white. He must also see whether the sore seems to be under the skin. If the sore is white and is under the skin, it is a skin disease. When the priest looks that person over carefully, he must announce that the person is 'unclean.' [4] Suppose the shiny spot on the skin is white but does not seem to be under the skin. And suppose the hair in the spot has not turned white. Then the priest must make the person stay away from everyone else for seven days. [5] On the seventh day the priest must look carefully at the sore again. Suppose it has not changed and has not spread in the skin. Then the priest must make the person stay away from everyone else for another seven days. [6] On the seventh day the priest must look carefully at the sore again. If it has faded and has not spread, he must announce that the person is 'clean.' It is only a rash. That person must wash their clothes. They will be 'clean.' [7] But suppose the rash spreads in the skin after they have shown themselves to the priest a second time. Then they must appear in front of the priest again. [8] The priest must look carefully at the sore. If the rash has spread, he must announce that the person is 'unclean.' They have a skin disease.

[9] "When anyone has a skin disease, they must be brought to the priest. [10] The priest must look them over carefully. Suppose there is a white swelling in the skin. Suppose it has turned the hair white. And suppose there are open sores in the swelling. [11] Then the person has a skin disease that will never go away. The priest must announce that they are 'unclean.' The priest must not make them stay away from everyone else. They are already 'unclean.' [12] Suppose the disease breaks out all over their skin. And suppose it covers them from head to foot, as far as the priest can tell. [13] Then the priest must look them over carefully. If the disease has covered their whole body, the priest must announce that they are 'clean.' All their skin has turned white. So they are 'clean.' [14] But when open sores appear on their skin, they will not be 'clean.' [15] When the priest sees the open sores, he must announce that they are 'unclean.' The open sores are not 'clean.' They have a skin disease. [16] But if the open sores change and turn white, they must go to the priest. [17] The priest must look them over carefully. If the sores have turned white, the priest must announce that the person is 'clean.' Then they will be 'clean.'

[18] "Suppose someone has a boil on their skin and it heals. [19] And suppose a white

swelling or shiny pink spot appears where the boil was. Then they must show themselves to the priest. [20]The priest must look at the boil carefully. Suppose it seems to be under the skin. And suppose the hair in it has turned white. Then the priest must announce that the person is 'unclean.' A skin disease has broken out where the boil was. [21]But suppose that when the priest looks at the boil carefully, there is no white hair in it. The boil is not under the skin. And it has faded. Then the priest must make the person stay away from everyone else for seven days. [22]If the boil is spreading in the skin, the priest must announce that the person is 'unclean.' They have a skin disease. [23]But suppose the spot has not changed. And suppose it has not spread. Then it is only a scar from the boil. And the priest must announce that the person is 'clean.'

[24]"Suppose someone has a burn on their skin. And suppose a white or shiny pink spot shows up in the open sores of the burn. [25]Then the priest must look at the spot carefully. Suppose the hair in it has turned white. And suppose the spot seems to be under the skin. Then the person has a skin disease. It has broken out where they were burned. The priest must announce that the person is 'unclean.' They have a skin disease. [26]But suppose the priest looks at the spot carefully. Suppose there is no white hair in it. Suppose the spot is not under the skin. And suppose it has faded. Then the priest must make the person stay away from everyone else for seven days. [27]On the seventh day the priest must look them over carefully. If the spot is spreading in the skin, the priest must announce that the person is 'unclean.' They have a skin disease. [28]But suppose the spot has not changed. It has not spread in the skin. And it has faded. Then the burn has caused it to swell. The priest must announce that the person is 'clean.' It is only a scar from the burn.

[29]"Suppose a man or woman has a sore on their head or chin. [30]Then the priest must look at the sore carefully. Suppose it seems to be under the skin. And suppose the hair in the sore is yellow and thin. Then the priest must announce that the person is 'unclean.' The sore is a skin disease on the head or chin. [31]But suppose the priest looks carefully at the sore. It does not seem to be under the skin. And there is no black hair in it. Then the priest must make the person stay away from everyone else for seven days. [32]On the seventh day the priest must look at the sore carefully. Suppose it has not spread in the skin. It does not have any yellow hair in it. And it does not seem to be under the skin. [33]Then the man or woman must shave their head. But they must not shave the area where the disease is. And the priest must make them stay away from everyone else for another seven days. [34]On the seventh day the priest must look at the sore carefully. Suppose it has not spread in the skin. And suppose it does not seem to be under the skin. Then the priest must announce that the person is 'clean.' They must wash their clothes. They will be 'clean.' [35]But suppose the sore spreads in the skin after the priest announces that the person is 'clean.' [36]Then the priest must look them over carefully. Suppose the sore has spread. Then the priest does not have to look for yellow hair. The person is 'unclean.' [37]But suppose the sore has stopped and black hair has grown there, as far as the priest can tell. Then the person is healed and is 'clean.' The priest must announce that they are 'clean.'

[38]"Suppose a man or woman has white spots on the skin. [39]Then the priest must look at them carefully. Suppose he sees that the spots are dull white. Then a harmless rash has broken out on the skin. That person is 'clean.'

[40]"Suppose a man loses all the hair on his head. Then he is 'clean.' [41]Suppose he loses only the hair on the front of his head. Then he is 'clean.' [42]But suppose he has a shiny pink sore on his head where his hair was. Then he has a skin disease. It is breaking out on his whole head or on the front of his head. [43]The priest must look him over carefully. Suppose the swollen sore on his head or on the front of it is pink and shiny. And suppose it looks like a skin disease. [44]Then he has a skin disease. He is 'unclean.' The priest must announce that the man is 'unclean.' That's because he has a sore on his head.

[45]"Suppose someone has a skin disease that makes them 'unclean.' Then they must wear torn clothes. They must

let their hair hang loose. They must cover the lower part of their face. They must cry out, 'Unclean! Unclean!' [46]As long as they have the disease, they remain 'unclean.' They must live alone. They must live outside the camp.

Rules About Mold

[47]"Suppose some clothes have mold on them. The clothes could be made out of wool or linen. [48]Or there could be cloth woven or knitted out of linen or wool. There could be pieces of leather. Or there could be things that are made out of leather. [49]And suppose the mold on the clothes or on the woven or knitted cloth looks green or red. Or suppose the green or red mold is on the pieces of leather or the leather goods. Then it is mold that spreads. It must be shown to the priest. [50]The priest must look at it carefully. He must keep the thing with the mold on it away from everything else for seven days. [51]On the seventh day he must look at it carefully. Suppose the mold has spread in the clothes or in the woven or knitted cloth. Or suppose it has spread on the pieces of leather or on the leather goods. Then it is mold that destroys. The thing is 'unclean.' [52]The priest must burn everything with the mold in it. He must burn the clothes or the woven or knitted cloth made out of wool or linen. He must burn the leather goods. The mold destroys. So everything must be burned.

[53]"But suppose the priest looks at the thing carefully. The mold has not spread in the clothes. And it has not spread in the woven or knitted cloth or in the leather goods. [54]Then he will order someone to wash the thing with the mold on it. After that, the priest must keep that thing away from everything else for another seven days. [55]After the thing with the mold on it has been washed, the priest must look at it again carefully. Suppose the way the mold looks has not changed. Then even though the mold has not spread, it is 'unclean.' Burn it. It does not matter which side of the thing the mold is on. [56]But suppose the priest looks at it carefully. And suppose the mold has faded after the thing has been washed. Then the priest must tear out the part with mold on it. He must tear it out of the clothes or leather. He must tear it out of the woven or knitted cloth. [57]But suppose it shows up again in the clothes. Or suppose it shows up again in the woven or knitted cloth or in the leather goods. Then it is spreading. Everything with the mold on it must be burned. [58]The clothes that have been washed and do not have any more mold on them must be washed again. So must the woven or knitted cloth or the leather goods. Then they will be 'clean.' "

[59]These are the rules about what to do with anything with mold on it. They apply to clothes that are made out of wool or linen. They apply to woven and knitted cloth and to leather goods. They give a priest directions about when to announce whether something is "clean" or "unclean."

Making People "Clean" From Skin Diseases

14 The LORD spoke to Moses. He told him to say to the people, [2]"Here are the rules for making anyone 'clean' who has had a skin disease. They apply when the person is brought to the priest. [3]The priest must go outside the camp. He must look the person over carefully. Suppose they have been healed of their skin disease. [4]Then the priest will order someone to bring him two live 'clean' birds. He will also order someone to bring him some cedar wood, bright red yarn and branches of a hyssop plant. All these things will be used to make the person 'clean.' [5]The priest will order someone to kill one of the birds. It must be killed over fresh water in a clay pot. [6]Then the priest must take the live bird. He must dip it into the blood of the bird killed over the fresh water. He must dip it into the blood together with the cedar wood, the bright red yarn and the hyssop plant. [7]The priest will sprinkle the blood on the person who had the skin disease. That will make them 'clean.' The priest must sprinkle the blood seven times. Then the priest must announce that they are 'clean.' After that, the priest must let the live bird go free in the open fields.

[8]"The person must also wash their clothes to be made 'clean.' They must shave off all their hair. They must take a bath. Then they will be 'clean.' After that, they may come into the camp. But they must stay outside their tent for seven

days. ⁹On the seventh day they must shave off all their hair. They must shave their head. They must shave off their beard. They must also shave off their eyebrows and the rest of their hair. They must wash their clothes. They must take a bath. Then they will be 'clean.'

¹⁰"On the eighth day they must bring two male lambs and one female lamb as an offering. The female must be a year old. The lambs must not have any flaws. They must also bring 11 pounds of the finest flour as a grain offering. They must mix it with olive oil. They must also bring 11 ounces of oil. ¹¹The priest who announces that the person is 'clean' must bring them and their offerings to me. He must do it at the entrance to the tent of meeting.

¹²"Then the priest must take one of the male lambs. He must offer it as a guilt offering. He must offer it along with 11 ounces of oil. He must lift all of it up and wave it in front of me as a wave offering. ¹³He must kill the lamb in the holy area where sin offerings and burnt offerings are killed. The guilt offering belongs to the priest, just as the sin offering does. The guilt offering is very holy. ¹⁴The priest must take some of the blood from the guilt offering and put it on the person's right earlobe. He must put some on the thumb of their right hand. He must also put some on the big toe of their right foot. ¹⁵Then the priest must take some of the oil and pour it into his own left hand. ¹⁶He must dip his right forefinger into the oil in his hand. He must use his finger to sprinkle some of the oil in front of me seven times. ¹⁷The priest must put some of the oil in his hand on the same places he put the blood of the guilt offering. He must put some on the person's right earlobe. He must put some on the thumb of their right hand. He must put some on the big toe of their right foot. ¹⁸He must put on their head the rest of the oil in his hand. It will pay for the person's sin in my sight.

¹⁹"Then the priest must sacrifice the sin offering. It will pay for the person's sin. They will be made 'clean' after being 'unclean.' After that, the priest will kill the burnt offering. ²⁰He will offer it on the altar. He will offer it together with the grain offering. It will pay for the person's sin. Then they will be 'clean.'

²¹"But suppose they are poor. Suppose they can't afford all these offerings. Then they must bring one male lamb as a guilt offering. It must be lifted up and waved in front of me to pay for their sin. They must also bring three and a half pounds of the finest flour along with the lamb. They must mix the flour with olive oil. It is a grain offering. They must offer it along with 11 ounces of oil. ²²They must also bring two doves or two young pigeons that they can afford. One is for a sin offering. The other is for a burnt offering.

²³"On the eighth day they must bring them to the priest so they can be made 'clean.' They must bring them to the entrance to the tent of meeting. They must do it in my sight. ²⁴The priest must take the lamb for the guilt offering. He must take it together with the 11 ounces of oil. He must lift all of it up and wave it in front of me as a wave offering. ²⁵He must kill the lamb for the guilt offering. He must take some of its blood and put it on the person's right earlobe. He must put some on the thumb of their right hand. He must also put some on the big toe of their right foot. ²⁶The priest must pour some of the oil into his own left hand. ²⁷He must dip his right forefinger into the oil in his hand. He must use his finger to sprinkle some of it seven times in front of me. ²⁸Here is what he must do with some of the oil in his hand. He must put it on the same places where he put the blood of the guilt offering. He must put some on the person's right earlobe. He must put some on the thumb of their right hand. He must also put some on the big toe of their right foot. ²⁹He must put on their head the rest of the oil in his hand. It will pay for the person's sin in my sight. ³⁰The priest will sacrifice the doves or the young pigeons that the person can afford. ³¹One is for a sin offering. The other is for a burnt offering. The priest must offer them together with the grain offering. In that way he will pay for the person's sin in my sight. He will do it to make them 'clean.'"

³²These are the rules for anyone who has a skin disease. They are for people who can't afford the regular offerings that are required to make them "clean."

Making Things "Clean" From Mold

³³The LORD spoke to Moses and Aaron. He told them to say to the people, ³⁴"You will enter the land of Canaan. I am giving it to you as your own. When you enter it, suppose I put mold in one of your houses. And suppose the mold spreads. ³⁵Then the owner of that house must go and speak to the priest. He must say, 'I've seen something that looks like mold in my house.' ³⁶The priest must order everything to be taken out of the house. It must be done before he goes in to look carefully at the mold. If it is not done, the priest must announce that everything in the house is 'unclean.' After the house is empty the priest must go in and check it. ³⁷He must look carefully at the mold on the walls. Suppose it looks as if it has green or red dents in it. And suppose the dents look as if they are behind the surface of the wall. ³⁸Then the priest must go out the door. He must close the house up for seven days. ³⁹On the seventh day the priest will return to check the house. Suppose the mold on the walls has spread. ⁴⁰Then he must order someone to tear out the stones that have mold on them. He must have them thrown into an 'unclean' place outside the town. ⁴¹He must have all the inside walls of the house scraped. Everything scraped off must be dumped into an 'unclean' place outside the town. ⁴²Then other stones must be put in the place of the stones that had mold on them. The inside walls of the house must be coated with new clay.

⁴³"Suppose the stones have been torn out. The house has been scraped. And the walls have been coated with new clay. But the mold appears again. ⁴⁴Then the priest must go and look things over carefully. Suppose the mold has spread in the house. Then it is the kind of mold that destroys things. The house is not 'clean.' ⁴⁵It must be torn down. The stones, the wood and all the clay coating must be torn out. All of it must be taken out of the town to an 'unclean' place.

⁴⁶"Suppose someone goes into the house while it is closed up. Then they will be 'unclean' until evening. ⁴⁷If they sleep or eat in the house, they must wash their clothes.

⁴⁸"But suppose the priest comes to look things over carefully. And suppose the mold has not spread after the walls had been coated with new clay. Then he will announce that the house is 'clean.' The mold is gone. ⁴⁹To make the house pure, the priest must get two birds. He must also get some cedar wood, bright red yarn and branches of a hyssop plant. ⁵⁰He must kill one of the birds over fresh water in a clay pot. ⁵¹Then he must take the cedar wood, the hyssop plant, the bright red yarn and the live bird. He must dip all of them into the blood of the dead bird. He must also dip them into the fresh water. He must sprinkle the house seven times. ⁵²The priest will use the blood and the water to make the house pure. He will use the live bird to make it pure. He will also use the cedar wood, the hyssop plant and the bright red yarn to make it pure. ⁵³Then he must let the live bird go free in the open fields outside the town. In that way he will make the house pure. It will be 'clean.'"

⁵⁴These are the rules for skin diseases. They apply to sores. ⁵⁵They apply to mold in clothes or in houses. ⁵⁶They also apply to swellings, rashes or shiny red spots on the skin. ⁵⁷Use these rules to decide whether something is "clean" or not.

These are the rules for skin diseases and for mold.

WOOTON'S FUN FACTS
Lev. 14:33–53

Household mold causes all kinds of illnesses, so people have to find how to properly kill it. I used to use bleach to clean mold till I learned that it can cause mold to spread! Who knew?

Rules About Liquid Body Wastes

15 The LORD said to Moses and Aaron, [2] "Speak to the Israelites. Tell them, 'Suppose liquid waste is flowing out of a man's body. That liquid is not "clean." [3] It does not matter whether it continues to flow out of his body or is blocked. It will make him "unclean." Here is how his liquid body waste will make him "unclean."

[4] "'Any bed the man who has the flow of liquid body waste lies on will be "unclean." Anything he sits on will be "unclean." [5] Anyone who touches the man's bed must wash their clothes. They must take a bath. They will be "unclean" until evening. [6] Suppose someone sits on something the man sat on. Then they must wash their clothes. They must take a bath. They will be "unclean" until evening.

[7] "'Suppose someone touches the man who has the flow of liquid body waste. Then they must wash their clothes. They must take a bath. They will be "unclean" until evening.

[8] "'Suppose someone is "clean." And suppose the man who has the flow of liquid waste spits on them. Then they must wash their clothes. They must take a bath. They will be "unclean" until evening.

[9] "'Everything the man sits on when he is riding will be "unclean." [10] Suppose someone touches any of the things that were under him. Then they will be "unclean" until evening. Even if they pick up those things, they must wash their clothes. They must take a bath. They will be "unclean" until evening.

[11] "'Suppose the man who has the liquid flow touches someone. And suppose he does it without rinsing his hands with water. Then the person he touched must wash their clothes. They must take a bath. They will be "unclean" until evening.

[12] "'Suppose the man touches a clay pot. Then that pot must be broken. Any wooden thing he touches must be rinsed with water.

[13] "'Suppose the man has been healed from his liquid flow. Then he must wait seven days. He must wash his clothes. He must take a bath in fresh water. After that, he will be "clean." [14] On the eighth day he must get two doves or two young pigeons. He must come to the LORD at the entrance to the tent of meeting. There he must give the birds to the priest. [15] The priest must sacrifice them. One is for a sin offering. The other is for a burnt offering. In that way the priest will pay for the man's sin in the sight of the LORD. He will do it because the man had a liquid flow.

[16] "'Suppose semen flows from a man's body. Then he must wash his whole body with water. He will be "unclean" until evening. [17] Suppose clothes or leather have semen on them. Then they must be washed with water. They will be "unclean" until evening. [18] Suppose a man sleeps with a woman. And suppose semen flows from his body and touches both of them. Then they must take a bath. They will be "unclean" until evening.

[19] "'Suppose a woman is having her regular monthly period. Then for seven days she will be "unclean." Anyone who touches her will be "unclean" until evening.

[20] "'Anything she lies on during her period will be "unclean." Anything she sits on will be "unclean." [21] Anyone who touches her bed must wash their clothes. They must take a bath. They will be "unclean" until evening. [22] Anyone who touches anything she sits on must wash their clothes. They must take a bath. They will be "unclean" until evening. [23] It does not matter whether it was her bed or anything she was sitting on. If anyone touches it, they will be "unclean" until evening.

[24] "'Suppose a man sleeps with that woman. And suppose blood from her monthly period touches him. Then he will be "unclean" for seven days. Any bed he lies on will be "unclean."

[25] "'Suppose blood flows from a woman's body for many days. And it happens at a time other than her monthly period. Or blood keeps flowing after her period is over. Then she will be "unclean" as long as the blood continues to flow. She will be "unclean," just as she is during the days of her period. [26] Any bed she lies on while her blood continues to flow will be "unclean." It is the same as it is when she is having her period. Anything she sits on will be "unclean." [27] If anyone touches those things, they will be "unclean." They must wash their clothes. They must take a bath. They will be "unclean" until evening.

[28] "'Suppose the woman has been healed from her flow of blood. Then she must wait

seven days. After that, she will be "clean." [29]On the eighth day she must get two doves or two young pigeons. She must bring them to the priest at the entrance to the tent of meeting. [30]The priest must sacrifice them. One is for a sin offering. The other is for a burnt offering. In that way he will pay for her sin in the sight of the LORD. He will do it because her flow of blood made her "unclean."

[31]"You must keep the Israelites away from things that make them "unclean." Then they will not die for being "unclean." And they will not die for making the place "unclean" where I, the LORD, live. It is in the middle of the camp.' "

[32]These are the rules for a man who has liquid waste flowing out of his body. They apply to a man made "unclean" by semen that flows from his body. [33]They apply to a woman having her monthly period. They apply to a man or woman who has a liquid flow. And they apply to a man who sleeps with a woman who is "unclean."

The Day When Sin Is Paid For

16 The LORD spoke to Moses after two of Aaron's sons had died. They were the sons who died when they came near the LORD. [2]The LORD said to Moses, "Speak to your brother Aaron. Tell him not to come into the Most Holy Room just anytime he wants to. Tell him not to come behind the curtain in front of the cover of the ark. The cover is the place where sin is paid for. If he comes behind the curtain, he will die. That is because I appear in the cloud over the cover.

[3]"Aaron must not enter the area of the Most Holy Room without bringing a sacrifice. He must bring a young bull for a sin offering. He must also bring a ram for a burnt offering. [4]He must put on the sacred inner robe made out of linen. He must wear linen underwear next to his body. He must tie the linen belt around him. And he must put the linen turban on his head. Those are sacred clothes. So he must take a bath before he puts them on. [5]The community of Israel must give him two male goats and a ram. The goats are for a sin offering. The ram is for a burnt offering.

[6]"Aaron must offer the bull for his own sin offering. It will pay for his own sin and the sin of his whole family. [7]Then he must take the two goats and bring them to me at the entrance to the tent of meeting. [8]He must cast lots for the two goats. One lot is for me. The other is for the goat that carries the people's sins away. [9]Aaron must bring the goat chosen for me by lot. He must sacrifice it for a sin offering. [10]But the goat chosen by the other lot must remain alive. First, it must be brought in to me to pay for the people's sins. Then, it must be sent into the desert as a goat that carries the people's sins away.

[11]"Aaron must bring the bull for his own sin offering. It will pay for his own sin and the sin of his whole family. He must kill the bull for his own sin offering. [12]He must take a shallow cup full of burning coals from the altar in my sight. He must get two handfuls of incense completely ground up. The incense must smell sweet. He must take the cup and the incense behind the curtain. [13]He must put the incense on the fire in my sight. The smoke from the incense will hide the cover of the ark where the tablets of the covenant law are kept. The cover is the place where sin is paid for. Aaron must burn the incense so that he will not die. [14]He must dip his finger in the bull's blood. He must sprinkle it on the front of the cover of the ark. He must sprinkle some in front of the cover. He must do it seven times.

[15]"Then Aaron must kill the goat for the sin offering for the people. He must take its blood behind the curtain. There he must do the same thing with it as he did with the bull's blood. He must sprinkle it on the cover of the ark. He must also sprinkle some in front of it. [16]That is how he will make the Most Holy Room pure. He must do it because the Israelites are not 'clean.' They have not obeyed me. They have also committed other sins. Aaron must do the same for the tent of meeting because it stands in the middle of the camp. And the camp is 'unclean.' [17]Aaron will go into the Most Holy Room to pay for the people's sin. While Aaron is there, no one may be in the tent of meeting. No one may enter the tent until Aaron comes out. He will not come out until he has paid for his own sin and the sin of his whole family. He will not come out until he has also paid for the sin of the whole community of Israel.

[18]"Then he will come out to the altar for burnt offerings. It is in front of the tent where the ark of the LORD is. He will make the altar pure and clean. He will take some of the bull's blood and some of the goat's blood. Then he will put the blood on all the horns that stick out from the upper four corners of the altar. [19]He will sprinkle some of the blood on it with his finger seven times. He will do it to make the altar pure. He will do it to set it apart from the Israelites. They are 'unclean.'

[20]"Aaron will finish making the Most Holy Room pure and 'clean.' He will finish making the tent of meeting and the altar pure. Then he will bring out the live goat. [21]He must place both of his hands on its head. While he does that, he must tell me about all the sins the Israelites have committed. He must tell me about all their evil acts and the times they did not obey me. In that way he puts their sins on the goat's head. Then he will send the goat away into the desert. The goat will be led away by a man appointed to do it. [22]The goat will carry all their sins on itself to a place where there are no people. And the man will set the goat free in the desert.

[23]"Then Aaron must go into the tent of meeting. He must take off the linen clothes he put on before he entered the Most Holy Room. He must leave them there. [24]He must take a bath in the holy area. And he must put on his regular clothes. Then he will come out and sacrifice the burnt offering for himself. He will also sacrifice the burnt offering for the people. That will pay for his own sin and the people's sin. [25]He will also burn the fat of the sin offering on the altar.

[26]"The man who sets free the goat that carries the people's sins away must wash his clothes. He must take a bath. After that, he can come back into the camp. [27]The bull and the goat for the sin offerings must be taken outside the camp. Their blood was brought into the Most Holy Room. It paid for sin. The hides, meat and guts of the animals must be burned up. [28]The man who burns them must wash his clothes. He must take a bath. After that, he can come back into the camp.

[29]"Here is a law for you that will last for all time to come. On the tenth day of the seventh month you must not eat anything. You must not do any work. It does not matter whether you are Israelites or outsiders. [30]On that day your sin will be paid for. You will be made pure and clean. You will be clean from all your sins in my sight. [31]That day is a sabbath for you. You must rest on it. You must not eat anything on that day. This is a law that will last for all time to come. [32]The high priest must pay for sin. He must make everything pure and clean. He has been anointed and prepared to become the next high priest after his father. He must put on the sacred clothes that are made out of linen. [33]He must make the Most Holy Room, the tent of meeting and the altar pure. And he must pay for the sin of the priests and all the members of the community.

[34]"Here is a law for you that will last for all time to come. Once a year you must pay for all the sin of the Israelites.'"

So it was done, just as the LORD commanded Moses.

Do Not Eat Meat With Blood in It

17 The LORD said to Moses, [2]"Speak to Aaron and his sons. Speak to all the Israelites. Tell them, 'Here is what the LORD has commanded. He has said, [3]"Suppose someone sacrifices an ox, a lamb or a goat. They sacrifice it in the camp or outside of it. [4]They do it instead of bringing the animal to the entrance to the tent of meeting. They sacrifice it instead of giving it as an offering to me in front of my holy tent. Then they will be thought of as guilty of spilling blood. Because they have done that, they must be separated from their people. [5]The Israelites are now making sacrifices in the open fields. But they must bring their sacrifices to the priest. They must bring them to me at the entrance to the tent of meeting. There they must sacrifice them as friendship offerings. [6]The priest must splash the blood against my altar. It is the altar at the entrance to the tent of meeting. He must burn the fat. Its smell will please me. [7]The Israelites must stop offering any of their sacrifices to statues of gods that look like goats. When they offer sacrifices to those statues, they are not faithful to me. This is a law for them that will last for all time to come.'"

8"Tell them, 'Suppose someone offers a burnt offering or sacrifice. It does not matter whether they are an Israelite or an outsider. 9And suppose they do not bring it to the entrance to the tent of meeting to sacrifice it to me. Then they must be separated from their people.

10"Suppose someone eats meat that still has blood in it. It does not matter whether they are an Israelite or an outsider. I will turn against them if they eat it. I will separate them from their people. 11The life of each creature is in its blood. So I have given you the blood of animals to pay for your sin on the altar. Blood is life. That is why blood pays for your sin. 12So I say to the Israelites, "You must not eat meat that still has blood in it. And an outsider who lives among you must not eat it either."

13"Suppose any of you hunts any animal or bird that can be eaten. It does not matter whether you are an Israelite or an outsider. You must let the blood flow out of the animal or bird. You must cover the blood with dirt. 14That is because every creature's life is its blood. And that is why I have said to the Israelites, "You must not eat any creature's meat that still has blood in it. Every creature's life is its blood. Anyone who eats that kind of meat must be separated from the community of Israel."

15"Suppose someone eats anything found dead or torn apart by wild animals. It does not matter whether they are an Israelite or an outsider. They must wash their clothes. They must take a bath. They will be "unclean" until evening. After that, they will be "clean." 16But suppose they do not wash their clothes. And suppose they do not take a bath. Then they will be held responsible for what they have done.'"

Do Not Commit Sexual Sins

18 The LORD spoke to Moses. He said, 2"Speak to the Israelites. Tell them, 'I am the LORD your God. 3Do not do what the people of Egypt do. You used to live there. And do not do what the people of Canaan do. I am bringing you into their land. Do not follow their practices. 4Obey my laws. Be careful to follow my rules. I am the LORD your God. 5Keep my rules and laws. The one who obeys them will benefit from living by them. I am the LORD.

6"'Do not have sex with any of your close relatives. I am the LORD.

7"'Do not bring shame on your father by having sex with your mother. Do not have sex with her. She is your mother.

8"'Do not have sex with any other wife of your father. That would bring shame on your father.

9"'Do not have sex with your sister. It does not matter whether she is your father's daughter or your mother's daughter. It does not matter whether she was born in the same home as you were or somewhere else.

10"'Do not have sex with your son's daughter or your daughter's daughter. That would bring shame on you.

11"'Do not have sex with the daughter of your father's wife. She was born to your father. She is your sister.

12"'Do not have sex with your father's sister. She is a close relative on your father's side.

13"'Do not have sex with your mother's sister. She is a close relative on your mother's side.

14"'Do not bring shame on your father's brother by having sex with his wife. She is your aunt.

15"'Do not have sex with your daughter-in-law. She is your son's wife. Do not have sex with her.

16"'Do not have sex with your brother's wife. That would bring shame on your brother.

17"'Do not have sex with both a woman and her daughter. Do not have sex with either her son's daughter or her daughter's daughter. They are close relatives on her side. Having sex with them is an evil thing.

18"'Do not take your wife's sister as another wife and have sex with her. Do not do it while your wife is still living.

19"'Do not have sex with a woman during her monthly period. She is "unclean" at that time.

20"'Do not have sex with your neighbor's wife. That would make you "unclean."

21"'Do not hand over any of your children to be sacrificed to the god Molek. That would be treating my name as if it were not holy. I am the LORD your God.

²²"'Do not have sex with a man as you would have sex with a woman. I hate that.

²³"'Do not have sex with an animal. Do not make yourself "unclean" by doing that. A woman must not offer herself to an animal to have sex with it. That is a wrong use of sex.

²⁴"'Do not make yourselves "unclean" in any of these ways. That is how other nations became "unclean." So I am going to drive those nations out of the land to make room for you. ²⁵Even their land was not "clean." So I punished it because of its sin. The land itself threw out the people who lived there. ²⁶But you must keep my rules and my laws. You must not do any of the things I hate. It does not matter whether you are Israelites or outsiders. ²⁷All these things were done by the people who lived in the land before you. That is how the land became "unclean." ²⁸If you make the land "unclean," it will throw you out. It will get rid of you just as it got rid of the nations there before you.

²⁹"'Suppose you do any of the things I hate. Then you must be separated from your people. ³⁰Do exactly what I require. When you arrive in Canaan, do not follow any of the practices of its people. I hate the things they do. Do not make yourselves "unclean" by doing them. I am the LORD your God.'"

Other Laws

19 The LORD spoke to Moses. He said, ²"Speak to the whole community of Israel. Tell them, 'Be holy, because I am holy. I am the LORD your God.

³"'All of you must have respect for your mother and father. You must always keep my Sabbath days. I am the LORD your God.

⁴"'Do not turn away from me to worship statues of gods. Do not make for yourselves metal statues of gods. I am the LORD your God.

⁵"'Suppose you sacrifice a friendship offering to me. Then do it in the right way. And I will accept it from you. ⁶You must eat it on the same day you sacrifice it or on the next day. Anything left over until the third day must be burned up. ⁷If you eat any of it on the third day, it is not pure. I will not accept it. ⁸Whoever eats it will be held responsible. They have misused what

is holy to me. They will be separated from their people.

⁹"'Suppose you are harvesting your crops. Then do not harvest all the way to the edges of your field. And do not pick up the grain you missed. ¹⁰Do not go over your vineyard a second time. Do not pick up the grapes that have fallen to the ground. Leave them for poor people and outsiders. I am the LORD your God.

¹¹"'Do not steal.

"'Do not tell lies.

"'Do not cheat one another.

¹²"'Do not give your word in my name and then be a false witness. That would be treating the name of your God as if it were not holy. I am the LORD.

¹³"'Do not cheat your neighbor. Do not rob him.

"'Do not hold back the pay of a hired worker until morning.

¹⁴"'Do not ask for bad things to happen to deaf people. Do not put anything in front of blind people that will make them trip. Instead, have respect for me. I am the LORD your God.

¹⁵"'Do not make something wrong appear to be right. Treat poor people and rich people in the same way. Do not favor one person over another. Instead, judge everyone fairly.

¹⁶"'Do not go around spreading lies among your people.

"'Do not do anything that puts your neighbor's life in danger. I am the LORD.

¹⁷"'Do not hate another Israelite in your heart. Correct your neighbor boldly when they do something wrong. Then you will not share their guilt.

¹⁸"'Do not try to get even. Do not hold anything against any of your people. Instead, love your neighbor as you love yourself. I am the LORD.

¹⁹"'Obey my rules.

REMEMBER THIS

LEVITICUS 19:18

"Do not try to get even. Do not hold anything against any of your people. Instead, love your neighbor as you love yourself."

WHAT ABOUT YOU?

Even if you are best friends with your siblings and family members, feelings can get hurt from time to time. Or maybe your personalities are so different that you can't be together in the same room without arguing. Bernard and Eugene fall into that second category. Still, they learn to get along in the Adventures in Odyssey episode "Room Mates."

Both stubbornly cling to their own ideas of what is right. They don't ask what the other person might prefer. Eugene insists he has a better way to wash windows, and Bernard cleans Eugene's computer without considering the consequences. They have forgotten God's instructions in Leviticus 19:18, "Love your neighbor as you love yourself." This means you should treat your neighbors the way you'd want to be treated—with kindness and patience—thinking about things from their point of view.

This lesson applies beyond your immediate family. Like Bernard, maybe you can't get along with your visiting cousin. Or your project partner at school wants to do the opposite of everything you want to do. Or one of your teammates constantly points out your mistakes. The proper response isn't getting angry or insisting that you're right and they're wrong. Rather, it's responding with love and a humble spirit.

Who do you argue with? When you disagree, stop to consider how that person feels. How can you show you value their opinion enough to listen even if you don't see eye to eye? Ask God to help you love that person better.

" 'Do not let different kinds of animals mate with each other.

" 'Do not mix two kinds of seeds and then plant them in your field.

" 'Do not wear clothes that are made out of two kinds of cloth.

²⁰" 'Suppose a man sleeps with a female slave. But she and another man have promised to get married to each other. And her freedom has not yet been paid for or given to her. Then she and the man who slept with her must be punished. But they must not be put to death, because she had not been set free. ²¹The man must bring a ram to the entrance to the tent of meeting. It is for a guilt offering to me. ²²The priest must take the ram for the guilt offering. He must sacrifice it to pay for the man's sin in my sight. Then his sin will be forgiven.

²³" 'When you enter the land, suppose you plant a fruit tree. Then do not eat its fruit for the first three years. The fruit is "unclean." ²⁴In the fourth year all the fruit will be holy. Offer it as a way of showing praise to me. ²⁵But in the fifth year you can eat the fruit. Then you will gather more and more fruit. I am the LORD your God.

²⁶" 'Do not eat any meat that still has blood in it.

" 'Do not practice any kind of evil magic.

²⁷" 'Do not cut the hair on the sides of your head. Do not clip off the edges of your beard.

²⁸" 'Do not make cuts on your bodies when someone dies. Do not put marks on your skin. I am the LORD.

ADVENTURES IN ODYSSEY

Eugene Meltsner and Bernard Walton had to "love their neighbor" when they wound up staying in the same house in "Room Mates" (A#12).

²⁹"'Do not dishonor your daughter's body by making a prostitute out of her. If you do, the Israelites will start going to prostitutes. The land will be filled with evil.

³⁰"'You must always keep my Sabbath days. Have respect for my sacred tent. I am the LORD.

³¹"'Do not look for advice from people who get messages from those who have died. Do not go to people who talk to the spirits of the dead. If you do, they will make you "unclean." I am the LORD your God.

³²"'Stand up in order to show your respect for old people. Also have respect for me. I am the LORD your God.

³³"'Suppose an outsider lives with you in your land. Then do not treat them badly. ³⁴Treat them as if they were one of your own people. Love them as you love yourself. Remember that all of you were outsiders in Egypt. I am the LORD your God.

³⁵"'Be honest when you measure lengths, weights or amounts. ³⁶Use honest scales and honest weights. Use honest dry measures. And use honest liquid measures. I am the LORD your God. I brought you out of Egypt.

³⁷"'Obey all my rules and laws. Follow them. I am the LORD.'"

Israel Will Be Punished for Their Sins

20 The LORD spoke to Moses. He said, ²"Say to the Israelites, 'Suppose a person sacrifices one of his children to the god Molek. It does not matter whether that person is an Israelite or an outsider who lives in Israel. He must be put to death. The members of the community must kill him by throwing stones at him. ³I will turn against that man. I will separate him from his people. That's because he has sacrificed his child to Molek. He has made my sacred tent "unclean." He has treated my name as if it were not holy. ⁴Suppose the members of the community act like they don't know that the man has sacrificed his child to Molek. And suppose they don't put him to death. ⁵Then I will turn against that man and his family. I will separate them from their people. I will also separate all those who follow him by joining themselves to Molek. They are not faithful to me.

⁶"'Suppose someone looks for advice from people who get messages from those who have died. Or they go to people who talk to the spirits of the dead. And they do what those people say. Then they have not been faithful to me. So I will turn against them. I will separate them from their people.

⁷"'Set yourselves apart for me. Be holy, because I am the LORD your God. ⁸Obey my rules. Follow them. I am the LORD. I make you holy.

⁹"'Anyone who asks for bad things to happen to their father or mother must be put to death. They have cursed their father or mother. So anything that happens to them will be their own fault.

¹⁰"'Suppose a man commits adultery with his neighbor's wife. Then the man and the woman must be put to death.

¹¹"'Suppose a man has sex with his father's wife. Then he has brought shame on his father. The man and the woman must be put to death. Anything that happens to them will be their own fault.

¹²"'Suppose a man has sex with his daughter-in-law. Then they must be put to death. They have used sex in the wrong way. Anything that happens to them will be their own fault.

¹³"'Suppose a man has sex with another man as he would have sex with a woman. I hate what they have done. They must be put to death. Anything that happens to them will be their own fault.

¹⁴"'Suppose a man gets married to both a woman and her mother. That is evil. All of them must be burned to death. Then there will not be any evil among you.

¹⁵"'Suppose a man has sex with an animal. Then he must be put to death. You must also kill the animal.

¹⁶"'Suppose a woman has sex with an animal. Then kill the woman and the animal. They must be put to death. Anything that happens to them will be their own fault.

¹⁷"'Suppose a man gets married to his sister and has sex with her. That is a shameful thing to do. It does not matter whether she is the daughter of his father or of his mother. They must be separated from their community in front of everyone. That man has brought shame on his

WHAT ABOUT YOU?

Maybe you've felt like Alex did in the Adventures in Odyssey episode "Relatively Annoying." Forced to spend a week with his grandparents, he's pretty sure he's not going to make it. Grandpa is always grumpy, and Grandma is acting strangely. But once he tries to understand his grandparents and their ways, he begins to enjoy his visit a lot more. He realizes that his grandparents are real people with real feelings.

It's easy to assume that older generations are impossible to relate to. The world is so different from when they were young. Would they even have a clue about the problems we face? You might be surprised. Sure, they may not understand social media, or watch goofy videos online, but they know plenty! They've been around a long time. They've experienced much more than we have.

Even if our relatives are difficult to connect with sometimes, it's important to remember what the Bible says in Leviticus 19:32: "Stand up in order to show your respect for old people. Also have respect for me. I am the LORD your God." When we show respect to our elders, we're also honoring God.

It means a lot to our grandparents when we show interest in their lives and what they have to say. What do your grandparents like to do? Ask them about their work, ministries, or hobbies in an email, letter, phone call, or video chat. With so many ways to connect, there's no excuse *not* to. And it will mean the world to them.

---

sister. He will be responsible for what he has done.

¹⁸"Suppose a man has sex with a woman during her monthly period. He has uncovered the place where her bleeding was coming from. And she has let him do it. So both of them must be separated from their people.

¹⁹"Do not have sex with the sister of either your mother or your father. That would bring shame on a close relative. Both of you would be held responsible for what you have done.

²⁰"Suppose a man has sex with his aunt. Then he has brought shame on his uncle. Both of them will be held accountable for what they have done. They will die without having any children.

²¹"Suppose a man gets married to his brother's wife. That is something that should never be done. He has brought shame on his brother. Neither of them will have any children.

²²"'Obey all my rules and laws. Follow them. Then the land where I am bringing you to live will not throw you out. ²³To make room for you, I am going to drive out the nations that are in the land. You must not follow the practices of those nations. I hated those nations because they did all those things. ²⁴But I said to you, "You will take over their land as your own. I will give it to you. It will belong to you. It is a land that has plenty of milk and honey." I am the LORD your God. I have set you apart from the other nations.

²⁵"'So you must be able to tell the difference between animals that are "clean" and those that are not. You must know which birds are "clean" and which are not. Do not make yourselves "unclean" by eating any "unclean" animal or bird. Do not make yourselves "unclean" by eating anything that moves along the ground. I have set all of them apart as "unclean" for you. ²⁶You must be holy. You must be set apart to me. I am the LORD. I am holy. I have set you

apart from the other nations to be my own people.

²⁷" 'Suppose a man or woman gets messages from those who have died. Or suppose a man or woman talks to the spirits of the dead. Then you must put that man or woman to death. You must kill them by throwing stones at them. Anything that happens to them will be their own fault.' "

Rules for Priests

21 The LORD said to Moses, "Speak to the priests, the sons of Aaron. Tell them, 'A priest must not make himself "unclean" by going near the dead body of any of his people. ²But he can go near the body of a close relative. It could be his mother, father, son, daughter or brother. ³He can also go near a sister who is not married. She would have depended on him because she did not have a husband. The priest can make himself "unclean" by going near her body. ⁴But he must not make himself "unclean" by going near the bodies of people only related to him by marriage. Going near them would make him "unclean."

⁵" 'Priests must not shave any part of their heads. They must not shave off the edges of their beards. They must not make cuts on their bodies when someone dies. ⁶Priests must be holy. They must be set apart for me. I am their God. They must not treat my name as if it were not holy. They must be holy because they bring food offerings to me. That is my food.

⁷" 'They must not get married to women who are "unclean" because they are prostitutes. They must not marry women who are divorced from their husbands. That is because priests are holy. They are set apart for me. I am their God. ⁸Consider them as holy, because they offer up food to me. Consider them as holy, because I am holy. I am the LORD. I make you holy.

⁹" 'Suppose a priest's daughter makes herself "unclean" by becoming a prostitute. Then she brings shame on her father. She must be burned to death.

¹⁰" 'The high priest is the one among his brothers whose head has been anointed with olive oil. He has been appointed to wear the priest's clothes. When someone dies, the high priest must not let his own hair hang loose. He must not tear his clothes to show how sad he is. ¹¹He must not enter a place where there is a dead body. He must not make himself "unclean," even if his father or mother dies. ¹²He must not leave the sacred tent of the LORD to take part in burying a body. That would bring shame on the tent. The anointing oil has set the high priest apart. I am the LORD.

¹³" 'The woman the high priest gets married to must be a virgin. ¹⁴He must not marry a widow or a woman who is divorced. He must not marry a woman who is "unclean" because she is a prostitute. He must only marry a virgin. She must come from his own people. ¹⁵If he doesn't marry a virgin, he makes the children he has by her "unclean." I am the LORD. I make him holy.' "

¹⁶The LORD said to Moses, ¹⁷"Speak to Aaron. Tell him, 'No man in your family line with any flaws may come near to offer food to the LORD. This is true for all time to come. ¹⁸No man who has any flaws can come near. No man who is blind or disabled can come. No man whose body is scarred or twisted can come. ¹⁹No man whose foot or hand is disabled can come. ²⁰No man whose back is bent can come. No man who is too short can come. No man who has anything wrong with his eyes can come. No man who has boils or running sores can come. No man whose sex glands are crushed can come. ²¹No man with any flaws who is in the family line of Aaron the priest may come near me. He can't come to bring the food offerings to the LORD. If he has any flaws, he must not come near to offer food to the LORD. ²²He can eat the holy food. He can also eat my very holy food. ²³But because he has a flaw, he must not go near the curtain or approach the altar. If he does, he will make my sacred tent "unclean." I am the LORD. I make everything holy.' "

²⁴So Moses told all these things to Aaron and his sons. He also told them to all the Israelites.

22 The LORD said to Moses, ²"Here is what I want you to tell Aaron and his sons. Tell them to treat the sacred offerings with respect. They are the offerings the Israelites set apart to honor me. So Aaron and his sons must never treat my name as if it were not holy. I am the LORD.

3"Say to them, 'Suppose a man in your family line is "unclean." And suppose he comes near the sacred offerings. They are the offerings the Israelites set apart to honor me. That man must not be allowed to serve me as a priest. That applies for all time to come. I am the LORD.

4"'Suppose a man in Aaron's family line has a skin disease. Or suppose liquid waste is flowing out of his body. Then he can't eat the sacred offerings until he is made pure and clean. Suppose he touches something made "unclean" by coming near a dead body. Or suppose he touches someone who has semen flowing out of his body. Then he will be "unclean." 5Or suppose he touches any crawling thing that makes him "unclean." Or suppose he touches any person who makes him "unclean." It does not matter what "unclean" thing he touches. It will make him "unclean." 6The one who touches anything of that kind will be "unclean" until evening. He must not eat any of the sacred offerings unless he has taken a bath. 7When the sun goes down, he will be "clean." After that, he can eat the sacred offerings. They are his food. 8He must not eat anything found dead or torn apart by wild animals. If he does, it will make him "unclean." I am the LORD.

9"'The priests must do what I require. But suppose they make fun of what I require. Then they will become guilty and die. I am the LORD. I make them holy.

10"'Only a member of a priest's family can eat the sacred offering. The guest of a priest can't eat it. A priest's hired worker can't eat it either. 11But suppose a priest buys a slave with money. Or suppose slaves are born in his house. Then they can eat the sacred food. 12Suppose a priest's daughter marries someone who is not a priest. Then she can't eat any of the food brought as a sacred gift. 13But suppose the priest's daughter becomes a widow or is divorced. She does not have any children. And she returns to live in her father's house, where she lived when she was young. Then she can eat her father's food. But a person who does not belong to a priest's family can't eat any of it.

14"'Suppose someone eats a sacred offering by mistake. Then they must pay back the priest for the offering. They must also add a fifth of its value to it. 15The priests must not allow the sacred offerings to become "unclean." They are the offerings the Israelites bring to the LORD. 16The priests must not allow the offerings to become "unclean" by letting the people eat them. If they do, they will bring guilt on the people. They will have to pay for what they have done. I am the LORD. I make them holy.'"

Sacrifices the LORD Does Not Accept

17The LORD spoke to Moses. He said, 18"Speak to Aaron and his sons. Speak to all the Israelites. Tell them, 'Suppose any of you brings a gift for a burnt offering to the LORD. It does not matter whether you are an Israelite or an outsider who lives in Israel. It does not matter whether you bring the offering to keep a promise or because you choose to give it. 19You must bring a male animal without any flaws if you want the LORD to accept it from you. It does not matter whether it is from your cattle, sheep or goats. 20Do not bring an animal that has any flaws. If you do, the LORD will not accept it from you. 21Suppose any of you brings an animal for a friendship offering to the LORD. Then it must not have any flaws at all. If it does, the LORD will not accept it. It does not matter whether the animal is from your herd or flock. It does not matter whether you bring it to keep a promise or because you choose to give it. 22Do not offer a blind animal to the LORD. Do not bring a hurt or wounded animal. And do not offer one that has warts or boils or running sores. Do not place any of them on the altar as a food offering presented to the LORD. 23But suppose you bring an offering you choose to give. Then you can bring an ox or a sheep whose body is twisted or too small. But the LORD will not accept it if you offer it to keep a promise. 24You must not offer the LORD a male animal whose sex glands have been hurt. The glands also must not be crushed, torn or cut. You must not offer that kind of animal in your own land. 25And you must not accept that kind of animal from someone who comes from another land. You must not offer it as food for your God. He will not accept it from you. Its body is twisted and has flaws.'"

²⁶The Lord spoke to Moses. He said, ²⁷"When a calf, lamb or goat is born, it must remain with its mother for seven days. From the eighth day on, I will accept it as a food offering presented to me. ²⁸Do not kill a cow and its calf on the same day. Do not kill a female sheep and its lamb on the same day.

²⁹"Sacrifice a thank offering to me in the right way. Then I will accept it from you. ³⁰You must eat it that same day. Do not leave any of it until morning. I am the Lord.

³¹"Obey my commands. Follow them. I am the Lord. ³²Do not treat my name as if it were not holy. The Israelites must recognize me as the holy God. I am the Lord. I made you holy. ³³I brought you out of Egypt to be your God. I am the Lord."

The Appointed Feast Days

23 The Lord said to Moses, ²"Speak to the Israelites. Tell them, 'Here are my appointed feast days. They are the appointed feast days of the Lord. Tell the people that they must come together for these sacred assemblies.

The Sabbath Day

³"There are six days when you can work. But the seventh day is a day of sabbath rest. You must rest on it. Come

Lev. 23:3 It used to be that most stores and restaurants were closed on Sundays. But now most are open. Since I'm a mail carrier, I'm glad the post office closes on Sundays so instead of working, I can worship and rest.

God established feast days so the Israelites would remember moments in their history and what God had done for them. The folks in Odyssey continued this tradition by using holidays to remember what God did for them in the album *Days to Remember* (A#31).

together on that sacred day. You must not do any work on it. No matter where you live, it is a Sabbath day to honor the Lord.

Passover and Unleavened Bread

⁴"Here are the Lord's appointed feasts. Tell the people that they must come together for these sacred gatherings at their appointed times. ⁵The Lord's Passover begins when the sun goes down on the 14th day of the first month. ⁶The Lord's Feast of Unleavened Bread begins on the 15th day of that month. For seven days you must eat bread made without yeast. ⁷On the first day you must come together for a special service. Do not do any regular work on that day. ⁸On each of the seven days bring a food offering to the Lord. On the seventh day come together for a special service. Do not do any regular work on that day.'"

The First Share of Israel's Crops Belongs to the Lord

⁹The Lord said to Moses, ¹⁰"Speak to the Israelites. Tell them, 'When you enter the land I am going to give you, bring an offering to the Lord. Gather your crops. Bring the first bundle of grain to the priest. ¹¹He must lift up the grain and wave it in front of the Lord. Then the Lord will accept it from you. The priest must wave it on the day after the Sabbath. ¹²On the day he waves the grain for you, you must sacrifice

a burnt offering to me. It must be a lamb that does not have any flaws. It must be a year old. [13]You must bring it together with its grain offering. The grain offering must be seven pounds of the finest flour. Mix it with olive oil. It is a food offering presented to the LORD. It has a pleasant smell. You must offer a drink offering along with the burnt offering. It must be a quart of wine. [14]You must not eat any bread until the day you bring your offering to the LORD your God. You must not eat any cooked grain or any of your first grain until that time. This is a law that will last for all time to come. It applies no matter where you live.

The Feast of Weeks

[15]" 'The day you brought the grain for the wave offering was the day after the Sabbath. Count off seven full weeks from that day. [16]Count off 50 days up to the day after the seventh Sabbath. On that day bring to the LORD an offering of your first grain. [17]Bring two loaves of bread that are made with seven pounds of the finest flour. They must be baked with yeast. Bring them to me as a wave offering from the first share of your crops. That applies no matter where you live. [18]Together with the bread, bring seven male lambs. Each lamb must be a year old. It must not have any flaws. Also bring one young bull and two rams. They will be a burnt offering to the LORD. They will be offered together with their grain offerings and drink offerings. They are food offerings. Their smell pleases the LORD. [19]Then sacrifice one male goat for a sin offering. Also sacrifice two lambs for a friendship offering. Each of the lambs must be a year old. [20]The priest must lift up the two lambs and wave them in front of me as a wave offering. He must offer them together with the bread made out of the first share of your crops. They are a sacred offering to the LORD. They will be given to the priest. [21]On that same day tell the people that they must come together for a special worship service. They must not do any regular work. That is a law that will last for all time to come. It applies no matter where you live.

[22]" 'Suppose you are gathering your crops. Then do not harvest all the way to the edges of your field. And do not pick up the grain you missed. Leave some for the poor people and the outsiders who live among you. I am the LORD your God.' "

The Feast of Trumpets

[23]The LORD said to Moses, [24]"Say to the Israelites, 'On the first day of the seventh month you must have a day of sabbath rest. It must be a special service announced with trumpet blasts. [25]Do not do any regular work on that day. Instead, bring a food offering to the LORD.' "

The Day When Sin Is Paid For

[26]The LORD spoke to Moses. He said, [27]"The tenth day of the seventh month is the day when sin is paid for. Come together for a special service. Do not eat any food. Bring a food offering to the LORD. [28]Do not do any work on that day. It is the day when sin is paid for. On that day your sin will be paid for in my sight. I am the LORD your God. [29]Suppose you do eat food on that day. Then you will be separated from your people. [30]I will destroy anyone among your people who does any work on that day. [31]You must not do any work at all. This is a law that will last for all time to come. It applies no matter where you live. [32]That day is a day of sabbath rest for you. You must rest on it. You must not eat anything on that day. You must follow the rules of the sabbath rest. Follow them from the evening of the ninth day of the month until the following evening."

The Feast of Booths

[33]The LORD said to Moses, [34]"Say to the Israelites, 'On the 15th day of the seventh month the LORD's Feast of Booths begins. It lasts for seven days. [35]On the first day you must come together for a special service. Do not do any regular work on that day. [36]On each of the seven days bring a food offering to the LORD. On the eighth day come together for a special service. Bring a food offering to the LORD. That special service is the closing service. Do not do any regular work on that day.

[37]" 'These are the LORD's appointed feasts. Tell the people that they must come together for these sacred assemblies. During those times, the people must bring food offerings to the LORD. They are burnt offerings and grain offerings. They are sacrifices and drink offerings. Each offering

must be brought at its required time. ³⁸The offerings are in addition to those of the days of sabbath rest. The offerings are also in addition to your gifts and anything you have promised. They are also in addition to all the offerings you choose to give to the LORD.

³⁹ "Begin with the 15th day of the seventh month. That is after you have gathered your crops. On that day celebrate the LORD's Feast of Booths for seven days. The first day is a day of rest. The eighth day is also a day of rest. ⁴⁰On the first day you must get branches from palms, willows and other leafy trees. You must be filled with joy in front of the LORD your God for seven days. ⁴¹Celebrate the LORD's Feast of Booths for seven days each year. This is a law that will last for all time to come. Celebrate the feast in the seventh month. ⁴²Live in booths for seven days. All the Israelites must live in booths. ⁴³Then your children after you will know that I made the Israelites live in booths. I made them do it after I brought them out of Egypt. I am the LORD your God.' "

⁴⁴So Moses announced to the Israelites the appointed feasts of the LORD.

Olive Oil, Bread and Incense

24 The LORD said to Moses, ²"Command the Israelites to bring you clear oil made from pressed olives. Use it to keep the lamps burning and giving light all the time. ³Aaron must take care of the lamps in front of the LORD from evening until morning all the time. This is a law that will last for all time to come. The lamps are outside the curtain in front of the tablets of the covenant law in the tent of meeting. ⁴The lamps are on the pure gold lampstand in front of the LORD. They must be taken care of all the time.

⁵"Get the finest flour and bake 12 loaves of bread. Use seven pounds of flour for each loaf. ⁶Arrange them in two stacks. Put six loaves in each stack on the table made out of pure gold. The table stands in front of the LORD. ⁷By each stack put some pure incense. It will remind you that all good things come from the LORD. Burn the incense in place of the bread. The incense is a food offering presented to the LORD. ⁸The bread must be set out in front of the LORD regularly. Do it every Sabbath

day. It will be Israel's duty to provide it for all time to come. ⁹The bread belongs to Aaron and his sons. They must eat it in the holy area. It is a very holy part of their regular share of the food offerings presented to the LORD."

A Person Who Speaks Evil Is Put to Death

¹⁰There was a man who had an Israelite mother. His father was born in Egypt. The man went out among the Israelites. A fight broke out in the camp between him and an Israelite. ¹¹The son of the Israelite woman spoke evil things against the LORD by using a curse. So the people brought him to Moses. The name of the man's mother was Shelomith. She was the daughter of Dibri. Dibri was from the tribe of Dan. ¹²The people kept her son under guard until they could find out what the LORD wanted them to do.

¹³Then the LORD spoke to Moses. He said, ¹⁴"Get the man who spoke evil things against the LORD. Take him outside the camp. All those who heard him say those things must place their hands on his head. Then the whole community must kill him by throwing stones at him. ¹⁵Say to the Israelites, 'Anyone who curses me will be held accountable. ¹⁶Anyone who speaks evil things against my Name must be put to death. The whole community must kill them by throwing stones at them. It does not matter whether they are an outsider or an Israelite. When they speak evil things against my Name, they must be put to death.

¹⁷" 'Anyone who kills another human being must be put to death. ¹⁸Anyone who kills someone's animal must pay its owner. A life must be taken for a life. ¹⁹Suppose someone hurts their neighbor. Then what they have done must be done to them. ²⁰A bone must be broken for a bone. An eye must be put out for an eye. A tooth must be knocked out for a tooth. The one who has hurt his neighbor must be hurt in the same way. ²¹Whoever kills an animal must pay its owner. But if they kill a human being, they must be put to death. ²²The same law applies whether they are an outsider or an Israelite. I am the LORD your God.' "

²³Then Moses spoke to the Israelites. They got the man who had spoken evil

things against the LORD. They took him outside the camp. There they killed him by throwing stones at him. The Israelites did just as the LORD had commanded Moses.

The Sabbath Year

25 The LORD spoke to Moses at Mount Sinai. He said, [2]"Speak to the Israelites. Tell them, 'You will enter the land I am going to give you. When you do, you must honor the LORD every seventh year by not farming the land that year. [3]For six years plant your fields. Trim the branches in your vineyards and gather your crops. [4]But the seventh year must be a year of sabbath rest for the land. The land must rest during it. It is a sabbath year to honor the LORD. Do not plant your fields. Do not trim the branches in your vineyards. [5]Do not gather what grows without being planted. And do not gather the grapes from the vines you have not taken care of. The land must have a year of rest. [6]Anything the land produces during the sabbath year will be food for you. It will be for you and your male and female servants. Your hired workers will eat it. So will people who live with you for a while. [7]And so will your livestock and the wild animals that are in your land. Anything the land produces can be eaten.

The Year of Jubilee

[8]"Count off seven sabbath years. Count off seven times seven years. The seven sabbath years add up to a total of 49 years. [9]The tenth day of the seventh month is the day when sin is paid for. On that day blow the trumpet all through your land. [10]Set the 50th year apart. Announce freedom all over the land to everyone who lives there. The 50th year will be a Year of Jubilee for you. Each of you must return to your own family property. And each of you must return to your own tribe. [11]The 50th year will be a Year of Jubilee for you. Do not plant anything. Do not gather what grows without being planted. And do not gather the grapes from the vines you have not taken care of. [12]It is a Year of Jubilee. It will be holy for you. Eat only what the fields produce.

[13]"In the Year of Jubilee all of you must return to your own property.

Jason's Jargon

LEVITICUS 25

Ready? Find the word *jubilee* in this chapter. Jubilee means joyful, expressed through joyful shouts and the sound of trumpets. The "Year of Jubilee" was a twelve-month celebration of freedom.

[14]"Suppose you sell land to any of your own people. Or you buy land from them. Then do not take advantage of each other. [15]The price you pay must be based on the number of years since the last Year of Jubilee. Here is how the price you charge must be decided. It must be based on the number of years left for gathering crops before the next Year of Jubilee. [16]When there are many years left, you must raise the price. When there are only a few years left, you must lower the price. That is because what is really being sold to you is the number of crops the land will produce. [17]Do not take advantage of each other. Instead, have respect for your God. I am the LORD your God.

[18]"Follow my rules. Be careful to obey my laws. Then you will live safely in the land. [19]The land will produce its fruit. You will eat as much as you want. And you will live there in safety. [20]Suppose you say, "In the seventh year we will not plant anything or gather our crops. So what will we eat?" [21]I will send you a great blessing in the sixth year. The land will produce enough for three years. [22]While you plant during the eighth year, you will eat food from the old crop. You will continue to eat food from it until the crops from the ninth year are gathered.

[23]"The land must not be sold without a way of getting it back. That is because it belongs to me. You are only outsiders and strangers in my land. [24]You must make sure that you can buy the land back. That applies to all the land that belongs to you.

[25]"Suppose one of your own people becomes poor. And suppose they have to sell some of their land. Then their nearest relative must come and buy back what they have sold. [26]But suppose they do

not have anyone to buy it back for them. And suppose things go well for them and they earn enough money to buy it back themselves. [27]Then they must decide how much the crops have become worth since the time they sold the land. They must take that amount off the price the land was sold for. They must give the one selling it back to them the money that is left. Then they can go back to their own property. [28]But suppose they have not earned enough money to pay them back. Then the buyer they sold the land to will keep it until the Year of Jubilee. At that time it will be returned to them. Then they can go back to their property.

[29]"Suppose someone sells a house in a city that has a wall around it. Then for a full year after they sell it they have the right to buy it back. [30]But suppose they do not buy it back before the full year has passed. Then the house in the walled city will continue to belong to the buyer and the buyer's children. It will not be returned to the seller in the Year of Jubilee. [31]But houses in villages that do not have walls around them must be treated like property outside walled cities. Those houses can be bought back at any time. And they must be returned in the Year of Jubilee.

[32]"The Levites always have the right to buy back their houses in the towns that belong to them. [33]So their property among the Israelites can be bought back. That applies to a house sold in any of their towns. Any house that is sold must be returned to its original owner in the Year of Jubilee. That is because the houses of the Levites will always belong to them. [34]But the grasslands around their towns must never be sold. They will belong to them for all time to come.

[35]"Suppose any of your own people become poor. And suppose they can't take care of themselves. Then help them just as you would help an outsider or a stranger. In that way, the poor can continue to live among you. [36]Do not charge them interest of any kind. Instead, have respect for God. Then those who have become poor can continue to live among you. [37]If you lend them money, you must not charge them interest. And you must not sell them food for more than it cost you. [38]I am the LORD your God. I brought you out of Egypt. I

did it to give you the land of Canaan. I wanted to be your God.

[39]"Suppose any of your own people become poor. And suppose they sell themselves to you. Then do not make them work as slaves. [40]You must treat them like hired workers. Or you must treat them like those living among you for a while. They must work for you until the Year of Jubilee. [41]Then they and their children must be set free. They will go back to their own tribes. They will go back to the property their people have always owned. [42]The Israelites are my servants. I brought them out of Egypt. So they must not be sold as slaves. [43]Show them pity when you rule over them. Have respect for God.

[44]"You must get your male and female slaves from the nations that are around you. You can buy slaves from them. [45]You can also buy as slaves some of the people living among you for a while. You can also buy members of their families born among you. They will become your property. [46]You can leave them to your children as their share of your property. You can make them slaves for life. But when you rule over your own people, you must be kind to them.

[47]"Suppose an outsider living among you for a while becomes rich. Then suppose any of your own people become poor. Then they sell themselves to the outsider living among you. Or they sell themselves to a member of the outsider's family. [48]Then they keep the right to buy themselves back after they have sold themselves. One of their relatives can buy them back. [49]An uncle or a cousin can buy them back after they have sold themselves. In fact, any relative in their tribe can do it. Or suppose things go well for them. Then they can buy themselves back. [50]They and their buyer must count the number of years from the time of the sale up to the Year of Jubilee. The price for their freedom must be based on the amount paid to a hired man for that number of years. [51]Suppose there are many years until the Year of Jubilee. Then for their freedom they must pay a larger share of the price paid for them. [52]But suppose there are only a few years left until the Year of Jubilee. Then they must count the number of years that are left. The payment for their freedom must be based on that number.

⁵³They must be treated as workers hired from year to year. You must make sure that those they must work for are kind to them when they rule over them.

⁵⁴"Suppose they are not bought back in any of those ways. Then they and their children must still be set free in the Year of Jubilee. ⁵⁵That's because the Israelites belong to me. They are my servants. I brought them out of Egypt. I am the LORD your God.

Rewards for Obeying the LORD

26 "'Do not make statues of gods for yourselves. Do not set up a likeness of a god or a sacred stone for yourselves. Do not place a carved stone in your land and bow down in front of it. I am the LORD your God.

²"'You must always keep my Sabbath days. Have respect for my sacred tent. I am the LORD.

³"'Follow my rules. Be careful to obey my commands. ⁴Then I will send you rain at the right time. The ground will produce its crops. The trees will bear their fruit. ⁵You will continue to harvest your grain until you gather your grapes. You will continue to gather your grapes until you plant your crops. You will have all you want to eat. And you will live in safety in your land.

⁶"'I will give you peace in the land. You will be able to sleep because no one will make you afraid. I will remove wild animals from the land. There will not be any war in your country. ⁷You will hunt down your enemies. You will kill them with your swords. ⁸Five of you will chase 100. And 100 of you will chase 10,000. You will kill your enemies with your swords.

⁹"'I will bless you. I will give you many children so that there will be many of you. And I will be faithful to the covenant I made with you. ¹⁰You will still be eating last year's crops when you will have to make room for new crops. ¹¹I will live among

you. I will not turn away from you. ¹²I will walk among you. I will be your God. And you will be my people. ¹³I am the LORD your God. I brought you out of Egypt. I did not want you to be slaves in Egypt anymore. I threw off your heavy load. I helped you walk with your heads held high.

Punishment for Not Obeying the LORD

¹⁴"'On the other hand, suppose you do not listen to me. Suppose you do not carry out all my commands. ¹⁵Suppose you say no to my rules and turn away from my laws. And suppose you break my covenant by failing to carry out all my commands. ¹⁶Then here is what I will do to you. All at once I will bring terror on you. I will send sicknesses that will make you weak. I will send fever that will destroy your sight. It will slowly take your strength away. When you plant seeds, it will not do you any good. Instead, your enemies will eat what you have planted. ¹⁷I will turn against you. Then your enemies will win the battle over you. Those who hate you will rule over you. You will run away even when no one is chasing you.

¹⁸"'After all that, suppose you still will not listen to me. Then I will punish you for your sins seven times. ¹⁹I will break down your stubborn pride. I will make the sky above you like iron, and it will not rain. I will make the ground under you like bronze, and you will not be able to farm it. ²⁰You will work with all your strength, but it will not do you any good. That is because your soil will not produce any crops. The trees of your land will not bear any fruit.

²¹"'Suppose you continue to be my enemy. And suppose you still refuse to listen to me. Then I will multiply your troubles many times because of your sins. ²²I will send wild animals against you. They will kill your children. They will destroy your cattle. There will be so few of you left that your roads will be deserted.

²³"'After all those things, suppose you still do not accept my warnings. And suppose you continue to be my enemy. ²⁴Then I myself will be your enemy. I will make you suffer again and again for your sins. ²⁵I will send war against you to punish you for breaking my covenant. When you go back into your cities, I will send a plague among

you. You will be handed over to your enemies. [26]I will cut off your supply of bread. Ten women will need only one oven to bake your bread. They will weigh out the bread piece by piece. Even when you eat all of it, it will not be enough to satisfy you.

[27]"After all that, suppose you still do not listen to me. And suppose you continue to be my enemy. [28]Then I will be angry with you. I will be your enemy. I myself will again punish you for your sins over and over. [29]You will eat the dead bodies of your sons. You will also eat the dead bodies of your daughters. [30]I will destroy the high places where you worship other gods. I will pull down your incense altars. I will pile up your dead bodies on the lifeless statues of your gods. And I will turn away from you. [31]I will completely destroy your cities. I will destroy your places of worship. The pleasant smell of your offerings will not give me any delight. [32]I myself will destroy your land so completely that your enemies who live there will be shocked. [33]I will scatter you among the nations. I will pull out my sword and hunt you down. Your land and your cities will be completely destroyed. [34]Then the deserted land will enjoy its sabbath years. It will rest. It will not be farmed. It will enjoy its sabbaths. But you will become prisoners in the country of your enemies. [35]The land will rest the whole time it is deserted. It was not able to rest during the sabbaths you lived in it.

[36]"Some of you will be left in the lands of your enemies. I will fill your hearts with fear. The sound of a leaf blown by the wind will scare you away. You will run as if you were escaping from swords. You will fall down, even though no one is chasing you. [37]You will trip over one another as if you were running away from the battle. You will run away, even though no one is chasing you. You will not be able to stand and fight against your enemies. [38]While you are still scattered among the nations, you will die. The lands of your enemies will destroy you. [39]You who are left in those lands will become weaker and weaker. You will die because of your sins and the sins of your people who lived before you.

[40]"But suppose you admit that both you and your people who lived before you have sinned. You admit the evil and dishonest things you have done against me. And you admit you have become my enemy. [41]What you did made me become your enemy. I let your enemies take you into their land. But suppose you stop being stubborn. You stop being proud. And you pay for your sin. [42]Then I will remember my covenant with Jacob. I will remember my covenant with Isaac. I will remember my covenant with Abraham. I will remember what I said to them about the land. [43]You will leave the land. It will enjoy its sabbaths while it lies deserted because you are not there. You will pay for your sins because you said no to my laws. You turned away from my rules. [44]But even after all that, I will not say no to you or turn away from you. I will not destroy you completely in the land of your enemies. I will not break my covenant with you. I am the LORD your God. [45]Because of you, I will remember the covenant I made with the people of Israel who lived before you. I brought them out of Egypt to be their God. The nations saw me do it. I am the LORD.'"

[46]These are the orders, the laws and the rules of the covenant the LORD made on Mount Sinai. He made it between himself and the Israelites through Moses.

Keep Your Promises to the LORD

27 The LORD said to Moses, [2]"Speak to the Israelites. Tell them, 'Suppose someone makes a special promise to set a person apart to serve the LORD. Here is how much it will cost to set that person free from the promise to serve. [3]The cost for a male between the ages of twenty and sixty is 20 ounces of silver. It must be weighed out in keeping with the standard weights that are used in the sacred tent. [4]The cost for a female of the same age is 12 ounces of silver. [5]The cost for a male between the ages of five and twenty is 8 ounces of silver. The cost for a female of the same age is 4 ounces of silver. [6]The cost for a male between the ages of one month and five years is 2 ounces of silver. The cost for a female of the same age is 1 ounce of silver. [7]The cost for a male who is sixty years old or more is 6 ounces of silver. The cost for a female of the same age is 4 ounces of silver. [8]But suppose the one who makes the special promise is too poor to pay the required amount. Then they must bring to the priest the person who will be set free. The priest will decide the right value for that person. It will be based on how much the one who makes the promise can afford.

⁹"Suppose what they promised is an animal that the Lord will accept as an offering. Then the animal given to the Lord becomes holy. ¹⁰The one who makes the promise must not trade it. They must not trade a good animal for a bad one. And they must not trade a bad animal for a good one. Suppose they choose one animal instead of another. Then both animals become holy. ¹¹Suppose the animal they promised is not "clean." Suppose the Lord will not accept it as an offering. Then the animal must be brought to the priest. ¹²He will decide whether it is good or bad. Its value will be what he decides it will be. ¹³Suppose the owner wants to buy the animal back. Then a fifth must be added to its cost.

¹⁴"Suppose someone sets apart their house as something holy to the Lord. Then the priest will decide whether it is good or bad. Its value will remain what he decides it will be. ¹⁵Suppose the person sets apart their house. And suppose later they want to buy it back. Then they must add a fifth to its value. The house will belong to them again.

¹⁶"Suppose someone sets apart a piece of their family's land to the Lord. Then here is how its value must be decided. It must be based on the number of seeds that are required to grow a full crop on it. That value will be 20 ounces of silver for every 300 pounds of barley seeds. ¹⁷Suppose they set apart their field during the Year of Jubilee. Then the value that has been decided will not be changed. ¹⁸But suppose they set apart their field after the Year of Jubilee. Then here is how the priest will decide its value. It will be based on the number of years that are left until the next Year of Jubilee. The value decided will be reduced. ¹⁹Suppose the one who set apart their field wants to buy it back. Then they must add a fifth to its value. The field will belong to them again. ²⁰But suppose they do not buy back the field. Instead, suppose they sell it to someone else. Then they can never buy it back. ²¹When the field is set free in the Year of Jubilee, it will become holy. It will be like a field set apart to the Lord. It will become the property of the priests.

²²"Suppose someone sets apart to the Lord a field they have bought. And suppose it is not part of their family's land. ²³Then here is how the priest will decide its value. It will be based on the number of years that are left until the Year of Jubilee. The owner must pay that value on the day it is decided. The money is holy. It is set apart for the Lord. ²⁴In the Year of Jubilee the field will go back to the person it was bought from. That person is the one who had owned the land before. ²⁵Every amount of money must be weighed out in keeping with the standard weights used in the sacred tent.

²⁶"But no one can set apart the first male animal born to its mother. That animal already belongs to the Lord. It does not matter whether it is an ox or a sheep. It belongs to the Lord. ²⁷Suppose it is an "unclean" animal. Then the owner may buy it back at the value that has been decided. And they must add a fifth to its value. But suppose it is not bought back. Then it must be sold at the value that has been decided.

²⁸"But nothing a person owns and sets apart to the Lord can be sold or bought back. It does not matter whether it is a human being or an animal or a family's land. Everything set apart to the Lord is very holy to him.

²⁹"No one set apart in a special way to be destroyed can be bought back. They must be put to death.

³⁰"A tenth of everything the land produces belongs to the Lord. That includes grain from the soil and fruit from the trees. It is holy. It is set apart for him. ³¹Suppose someone wants to buy back some of their tenth. Then they must add a fifth of the cost to it. ³²Every tenth part of herds and flocks will be holy. They will be set apart for the Lord. That includes every tenth animal that its shepherd marks with his wooden staff. ³³No one may pick out the good animals from the bad. They must not choose one animal instead of another. But if anyone does, both animals become holy. They can't be bought back.'"

³⁴The Lord gave Moses all these commands on Mount Sinai for the Israelites.

numbers

A math book in the Bible? Though academics such as myself might greet such a notion with applause, that is not the case. "Numbers" refers to the population of the Israelite tribes as they moved from Egypt to the Promised Land (chapters 1–3; 26). Much of the book of Numbers has to do with priestly duties and additional instructions for the people that God provided through Moses. Other portions (chapters 10–25) are fascinating accounts of the Israelites as they journeyed to the Promised Land. Buried within this book are some of the more exciting stories of Scripture!

- The exploration of the Promised Land and why the people's poor response required them to wander forty extra years in the wilderness (13–14);

- The earthquake, fire, and plague that eliminated a crowd of troublemakers who opposed Moses' and Aaron's authority (16:1–50);

- How God provided water from a rock (20:1–13);

- An attack of deadly snakes remedied by a bronze serpent (21:4–9);

- And Balaam's talking donkey (22:21–38). A conversation between man and beast? I would have loved to have observed that exchange.

And there's so much more.

What's it mean, Eugene?

Orthopraxy—Another rather intimidating word, albeit an important one. Orthopraxy means "correct action." In other words, when we talk about *orthopraxy*, we are really talking about *doing the right thing*—the thing that Jesus Himself would do and wants *us* to do in any given situation. The Good Samaritan in Luke 10:25–37 is one example. Or when my young ward Buck cleans his room, I might say, "Excellent orthopraxy, Buck!" To which he would likely reply, "I don't know what that means." Alas. But now *you* do!

The Men of Israel Are Counted

1 The LORD spoke to Moses in the tent of meeting. It happened in the Desert of Sinai. The LORD spoke to him on the first day of the second month. It was the second year after the Israelites came out of Egypt. The LORD said, ²"Count all the men of Israel. Make a list of them by their tribes and families. List every man by name. List them one by one. ³Count all the men able to serve in the army. They must be 20 years old or more. I want you and Aaron to make a list of them group by group. ⁴One man from each tribe must help you. Those who help must be the heads of their families.

⁵ Here are the names of the men who must help you.

"From the tribe of Reuben will come Elizur, the son of Shedeur.
⁶ From the tribe of Simeon will come Shelumiel, the son of Zurishaddai.
⁷ From the tribe of Judah will come Nahshon, the son of Amminadab.
⁸ From the tribe of Issachar will come Nethanel, the son of Zuar.
⁹ From the tribe of Zebulun will come Eliab, the son of Helon.
¹⁰ From the tribe of Ephraim will come Elishama, the son of Ammihud.
From the tribe of Manasseh will come Gamaliel, the son of Pedahzur.
Ephraim and Manasseh are Joseph's two sons.
¹¹ From the tribe of Benjamin will come Abidan, the son of Gideoni.
¹² From the tribe of Dan will come Ahiezer, the son of Ammishaddai.
¹³ From the tribe of Asher will come Pagiel, the son of Okran.
¹⁴ From the tribe of Gad will come Eliasaph, the son of Deuel.
¹⁵ From the tribe of Naphtali will come Ahira, the son of Enan."

¹⁶ These were the men appointed from the community. They were the leaders of the tribes of their people. They were the heads of the major families in Israel.

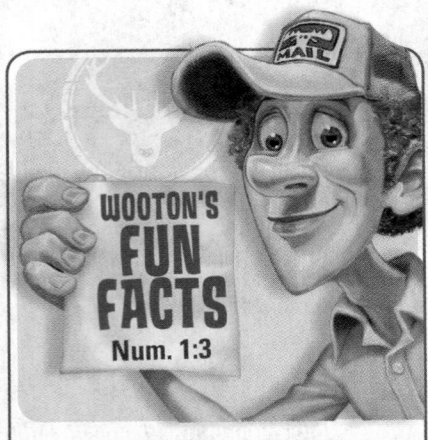

WOOTON'S **FUN FACTS** Num. 1:3

In the United States a person can join the military at age seventeen. The oldest age at which you can join ranges from twenty-seven to thirty-five years old, depending on which branch you want to join.

¹⁷Moses and Aaron went and got the men whose names had been given to them. ¹⁸Then Moses and Aaron gathered all the men of Israel together. It was the first day of the second month. The people wrote down the tribe and family they belonged to. The men 20 years old or more were listed by name. They were listed one by one. ¹⁹Everything was done just as the LORD had commanded Moses. So Moses counted them in the Desert of Sinai.

²⁰ Here is the number of men from the tribe of Reuben. He is Israel's oldest son.
All the men able to serve in the army were counted. They were 20 years old or more. They were listed by name. They were listed one by one. They were listed according to the records of their tribes and families. ²¹The number from the tribe of Reuben was 46,500.

²² Here is the number of men from the tribe of Simeon.
All the men able to serve in the army were counted. They were 20 years old or more. They were listed by name. They were listed one by one. They were listed according to the records of their

tribes and families. [23]The number from the tribe of Simeon was 59,300.

[24] Here is the number of men from the tribe of Gad.

All the men able to serve in the army were counted. They were 20 years old or more. They were listed by name. They were listed according to the records of their tribes and families. [25]The number from the tribe of Gad was 45,650.

[26] Here is the number of men from the tribe of Judah.

All the men able to serve in the army were counted. They were 20 years old or more. They were listed by name. They were listed according to the records of their tribes and families. [27]The number from the tribe of Judah was 74,600.

[28] Here is the number of men from the tribe of Issachar.

All the men able to serve in the army were counted. They were 20 years old or more. They were listed by name. They were listed according to the records of their tribes and families. [29]The number from the tribe of Issachar was 54,400.

[30] Here is the number of men from the tribe of Zebulun.

All the men able to serve in the army were counted. They were 20 years old or more. They were listed by name. They were listed according to the records of their tribes and families. [31]The number from the tribe of Zebulun was 57,400.

[32] Here is the number of men from the tribe of Ephraim. He is the son of Joseph.

All the men able to serve in the army were counted. They were 20 years old or more. They were listed by name. They were listed according to the records of their tribes and families. [33]The number from the tribe of Ephraim was 40,500.

[34] Here is the number of men from the tribe of Manasseh. He is the son of Joseph.

All the men able to serve in the army were counted. They were 20 years old or more. They were listed by name. They were listed according to the records of their tribes and families. [35]The number from the tribe of Manasseh was 32,200.

[36] Here is the number of men from the tribe of Benjamin.

All the men able to serve in the army were counted. They were 20 years old or more. They were listed by name. They were listed according to the records of their tribes and families. [37]The number from the tribe of Benjamin was 35,400.

[38] Here is the number of men from the tribe of Dan.

All the men able to serve in the army were counted. They were 20 years old or more. They were listed by name. They were listed according to the records of their tribes and families. [39]The number from the tribe of Dan was 62,700.

[40] Here is the number of men from the tribe of Asher.

All the men able to serve in the army were counted. They were 20 years old or more. They were listed by name. They were listed according to the records of their tribes and families. [41]The number from the tribe of Asher was 41,500.

[42] Here is the number of men from the tribe of Naphtali.

All the men able to serve in the army were counted. They were 20 years old or more. They were listed by name. They were listed according to the records of their tribes and families. [43]The number from the tribe of Naphtali was 53,400.

[44] These were the men counted by Moses and Aaron. The 12 leaders of Israel helped them. There was one leader from each tribe. [45]The men who were counted were able to serve in Israel's army. All of them were 20 years old or more. They were counted family by family. [46]The total number of men was 603,550.

[47]But the families of the tribe of Levi were not counted along with the others. [48]The LORD had spoken to Moses. He had said, [49]"You must not count the men from the tribe of Levi. Do not include them when you list the other men of Israel. [50]Instead, put the Levites in charge of the holy tent. That is where the tablets of the covenant law are kept. The Levites will be in charge of everything that belongs to the holy tent. They must carry the tent and everything that belongs to it. They must take care of it. They must set up camp around it. [51]When the holy tent must be moved, the Levites must take it down. And when the tent must be set up, the Levites must do it. Anyone else who approaches it must be put to death. [52]The Israelites must set up their tents by military groups. All of them must be in their own camps under their own flags. [53]But the Levites must set up their tents around the holy tent. That's where the tablets of the covenant law are kept. Then I will not be angry with the community of Israel. The Levites will be responsible for taking care of the tent."

[54]The Israelites did everything just as the LORD had commanded Moses.

The Tribes Camp Around the Tent of Meeting

2 The LORD spoke to Moses and Aaron. He said, [2]"The Israelites must camp around the tent of meeting. But they must not camp too close to it. All of them must camp under their flags and under the banners of their families."

[3] The groups of the camp of Judah must be on the east side. They must set up camp toward the sunrise. They must camp under their flag. The leader of the tribe of Judah is Nahshon, the son of Amminadab. [4]There are 74,600 men in Nahshon's group.

[5] The tribe of Issachar will camp next to them. The leader of the tribe of Issachar is Nethanel, the son of Zuar. [6]There are 54,400 men in Nethanel's group.

[7] The tribe of Zebulun will be next. The leader of the tribe of Zebulun is Eliab, the son of Helon. [8]There are 57,400 men in Eliab's group.

[9] So a total of 186,400 men will be set apart for the camp of Judah. They will be arranged group by group. They will start out first.

[10] The groups of the camp of Reuben will be on the south side. They will be under their flag. The leader of the tribe of Reuben is Elizur, the son of Shedeur. [11]There are 46,500 men in Elizur's group.

[12] The tribe of Simeon will camp next to them. The leader of the tribe of Simeon is Shelumiel, the son of Zurishaddai. [13]There are 59,300 men in Shelumiel's group.

[14] The tribe of Gad will be next. The leader of the tribe of Gad is Eliasaph, the son of Deuel. [15]There are 45,650 men in Eliasaph's group.

[16] So a total of 151,450 men will be set apart for the camp of Reuben. They will be arranged group by group. They will start out second.

[17] Then the camp of the Levites will start out. The tent of meeting will go with them. They will march in the middle of the other camps. They will start out in the same order as they do when they set up camp. Each one will be in their own place under their flag.

[18] The groups of the camp of Ephraim will be on the west side. They will be under their flag. The leader of the tribe of Ephraim is Elishama, the son of Ammihud. [19]There are 40,500 men in Elishama's group.

[20] The tribe of Manasseh will be next to them. The leader of the tribe of Manasseh is Gamaliel, the son of Pedahzur. [21]There are 32,200 men in Gamaliel's group.

²² The tribe of Benjamin will be next. The leader of the tribe of Benjamin is Abidan, the son of Gideoni. ²³There are 35,400 men in Abidan's group.

²⁴ So a total of 108,100 men will be set apart for the camp of Ephraim. They will be arranged group by group. They will start out third.

²⁵ The groups of the camp of Dan will be on the north side. They will be under their flag. The leader of the tribe of Dan is Ahiezer, the son of Ammishaddai. ²⁶There are 62,700 men in Ahiezer's group.

²⁷ The tribe of Asher will camp next to them. The leader of the tribe of Asher is Pagiel, the son of Okran. ²⁸There are 41,500 men in Pagiel's group.

²⁹ The tribe of Naphtali will be next. The leader of the tribe of Naphtali is Ahira, the son of Enan. ³⁰There are 53,400 men in Ahira's group.

³¹ So a total of 157,600 men will be set apart for the camp of Dan. They will start out last. They will march under their flags.

³² Those are the men of Israel. They were counted according to their families. The total number of all the men in the camps is 603,550, group by group. ³³But the Levites weren't counted along with the other men of Israel. That's what the LORD had commanded Moses.

³⁴So the Israelites did everything the LORD had commanded Moses. That's the way they set up camp under their flags. And that's the way they started out. Each of them marched out with their own tribe and family.

The Levites

3 Here is the story of the family line of Aaron and Moses. It belongs to the time when the LORD spoke to Moses at Mount Sinai.

²Aaron's oldest son was Nadab. Aaron's other sons were Abihu, Eleazar and Ithamar. ³Those were the names of Aaron's sons. They were the anointed priests.

They were given authority to serve the LORD as priests. ⁴But Nadab and Abihu made an offering to the LORD by using fire that wasn't allowed. So they died in front of him. That happened in the Desert of Sinai. They didn't have any sons. Only Eleazar and Ithamar served as priests while their father Aaron was living.

⁵The LORD spoke to Moses. He said, ⁶"Bring the men of the tribe of Levi to Aaron the priest. They will help him. ⁷They must work at the tent of meeting for Aaron and for the whole community. They must do what needs to be done at the holy tent. ⁸They must take care of everything connected with the tent of meeting. When they do, they are acting for all the Israelites. ⁹Give the Levites to Aaron and his sons. They are the men of Israel who must be given completely to him. ¹⁰Appoint Aaron and his sons to serve as priests. Anyone else who approaches the sacred tent must be put to death."

¹¹The LORD also said to Moses, ¹²"I have taken the Levites from among the Israelites. I have taken them in place of the son born first to each woman in Israel. The Levites belong to me. ¹³That's because every male born first to a mother is mine. In Egypt I struck down all the males born first. I did it when I set apart for myself every male born first to a mother in Israel. That is true for men and animals alike. They belong to me. I am the LORD."

¹⁴The LORD spoke to Moses in the Desert of Sinai. He said, ¹⁵"Count the Levites by their family groups. Count every male a month old or more." ¹⁶So Moses counted them. He did just as the word of the LORD had commanded him.

¹⁷ The sons of Levi were
Gershon, Kohath and Merari.
¹⁸ The major families from Gershon were
Libni and Shimei.
¹⁹ The major families from Kohath were
Amram, Izhar, Hebron and Uzziel.
²⁰ The major families from Merari were
Mahli and Mushi.

These were the major families of the Levites.

²¹ The families of Libni and Shimei belonged to the family of Gershon.

²² All the males a month old or more were counted. There were 7,500 of them.

²³ The families of Gershon had to camp on the west side. They had to camp behind the holy tent.

²⁴ The leader of the families of Gershon was Eliasaph, the son of Lael.

²⁵ Here are the duties of the families of Gershon at the tent of meeting. They were responsible for taking care of the holy tent and its coverings. They took care of the curtain at the entrance to the tent of meeting. ²⁶They took care of the curtains of the courtyard. And they took care of the curtain at the entrance to the courtyard. The courtyard was all around the holy tent and altar. The families of Gershon also took care of the ropes. In fact, they had to take care of everything connected with the use of all those things.

²⁷ The families of Amram, Izhar, Hebron and Uzziel belonged to the family of Kohath.

²⁸ All the males a month old or more were counted. There were 8,600 of them.

The families of Kohath were responsible for taking care of the sacred tent.

²⁹ They had to camp on the south side of the holy tent.

³⁰ The leader of the families of Kohath was Elizaphan, the son of Uzziel.

³¹ They were responsible for taking care of the ark of the covenant law. They took care of the table for the holy bread. They took care of the lampstand and the two altars. They took care of the things used for serving in the sacred tent. They also took care of the inner curtain. In fact, they had to take care of everything connected with the use of all those things.

³² The chief leader of the Levites was Eleazar. He was the son of Aaron the priest. Eleazar was appointed over those responsible for taking care of the sacred tent.

³³ The families of Mahli and Mushi belonged to the family of Merari.

³⁴ All the males a month old or more were counted. There were 6,200 of them.

³⁵ The leader of the families of Merari was Zuriel, the son of Abihail.

The families of Merari had to camp on the north side of the holy tent.

³⁶ They were responsible for taking care of the frames of the tent. They took care of its crossbars, posts and bases. They took care of all its supplies. In fact, they had to take care of everything connected with the use of all those things. ³⁷They also took care of the posts of the courtyard around the holy tent. And they took care of the bases, tent stakes and ropes.

³⁸ Moses, Aaron and Aaron's sons had to camp to the east of the holy tent. They had to camp toward the sunrise in front of the tent of meeting.

They were responsible for taking care of the sacred tent. They had to do it for the Israelites.

Anyone else who approached the tent would be put to death.

39 The total number of the Levite males was 22,000. They were counted family by family. Every male a month old or more was counted. Moses and Aaron counted them, just as the LORD had commanded.

40 The LORD said to Moses, "Count all the Israelite males born first in their families. Count all those a month old or more. Make a list of their names. 41 Take the Levites for me in their place. And take the livestock of the Levites in place of all the male animals in Israel born first to their mothers. I am the LORD."

42 So Moses counted all the oldest sons in Israel. He did just as the LORD had commanded him. 43 There were 22,273 of those sons a month old or more. They were listed by name.

44 The LORD also said to Moses, 45 "Take the Levites in place of all the males born first in Israel. Also take the livestock of the Levites in place of the livestock of Israel. The Levites belong to me. I am the LORD. 46 But there are 273 more males born first in Israel than there are male Levites. 47 Collect two ounces of silver for each of them. Weigh it out according to the standard weights used in the sacred tent. 48 Give the silver to Aaron and his sons. It will buy the freedom of the additional sons in Israel."

49 So Moses collected the silver from the additional sons in Israel to buy their freedom. The Levites took the place of all the others. 50 Moses collected 35 pounds of silver. It was weighed out according to the weights used in the sacred tent. Moses collected it from the oldest sons in Israel. 51 He gave the silver to Aaron and his sons. He did just as the LORD had commanded him.

The Families of Kohath

4 The LORD said to Moses and Aaron, 2 "Count the Levites who belong to the families of Kohath. Make a list of them family by family. 3 Count all the men 30 to 50 years old. Those are the men who must come and serve at the tent of meeting.

4 "Here is the work the men of Kohath must do at the tent of meeting. They must take care of the things that are very holy. 5 When the camp is ready to move, Aaron and his sons must go into the tent. They must take down the curtain that hides the ark where the tablets of the covenant law are kept. They must cover the ark with the curtain. 6 Then they must cover that with strong leather. They must spread a solid blue cloth over the leather. And they must put the poles in place.

7 "They must spread a blue cloth over the table for the holy bread. They must put the plates, dishes and bowls on the cloth. They must also put the jars for drink offerings on it. The bread that is always kept there must remain on it. 8 They must spread a bright red cloth over everything. Then they must cover that with the strong leather. And they must put the poles of the table in place.

9 "They must get a blue cloth. With it they must cover the lampstand that gives light. They must also cover its lamps, trays and wick cutters. And they must cover all its jars. The jars are for the olive oil used in the lampstand. 10 Then Aaron and his sons must wrap the lampstand and all the things used with it. They must cover it with the strong leather. And they must put it on a frame to carry it.

11 "They must spread a blue cloth over the gold altar for burning incense. They must cover that with the strong leather. And they must put the poles of the altar in place.

12 "They must get all the things used for serving in the sacred tent. They must wrap them in a blue cloth. They must cover that with the strong leather. Then they must put those things on a frame to carry them. 13 "They must remove the ashes from the bronze altar for burnt offerings. They must spread a purple cloth over it. 14 Then they must place all the tools on it. The tools are used for serving at the altar. They include the pans for carrying ashes. They also include the meat forks, shovels and sprinkling bowls. Aaron and his sons must cover the altar with the strong leather. And they must put its poles in place.

15 "Aaron and his sons must cover all the holy things that belong to the holy tent. Only then are the men of Kohath to come and carry everything. They must do so only when the camp is ready to move. But they must not touch the holy things. If they do, they will die. The men

of Kohath must carry everything in the tent of meeting.

[16]"Eleazar the priest will be in charge of the olive oil for the light. He is the son of Aaron. Eleazar will be in charge of the sweet-smelling incense. He will be in charge of the regular grain offering and the anointing oil. He will be in charge of the entire holy tent. He will also be in charge of everything in it. That includes all the things that belong to the tent."

[17]The LORD spoke to Moses and Aaron. He said, [18]"Make sure that the Kohath families are not destroyed from among the Levites. [19]I want them to live and not die when they come near the very holy things. So here is what you must do for them. Aaron and his sons must go into the sacred tent and tell each man what to do. They must tell each man what to carry. [20]But the men of Kohath must not go in and look at the holy things. They must not look at them even for a moment. If they do, they will die."

The Families of Gershon

[21]The LORD said to Moses, [22]"Count the families of Gershon. Make a list of them family by family. [23]Count all the men 30 to 50 years old. Those are the men who must come and serve at the tent of meeting.

[24]"Here is how the families of Gershon must serve. They must carry things. [25]They must carry the curtains of the holy tent of meeting. They must carry its covering and the outside covering of strong leather. They must carry the curtains that cover the entrance to the tent of meeting. [26]They must carry the curtains of the courtyard. The courtyard is all around the holy tent and altar. They must carry the curtain for the entrance. They must carry the ropes. They must also carry all the supplies used for any purpose in the tent. The families of Gershon must do everything that needs to be done with those things. [27]All their work must be done under the direction of Aaron and his sons. That includes carrying and everything else they do. Aaron and his sons must tell them what to carry. And that will be their work. [28]It is what the families of Gershon must do at the tent of meeting. They must work under the direction of Ithamar the priest. He is the son of Aaron.

The Families of Merari

[29]"Count the families of Merari. Count them family by family. [30]Count all the men 30 to 50 years old. Those are the men who must come and serve at the tent of meeting. [31]Here is the work they must do at the tent of meeting. They must carry the frames of the holy tent. They must carry its crossbars, posts and bases. [32]They must also carry the posts of the courtyard. The courtyard is all around the holy tent. And they must carry the bases for the posts as well as their tent stakes and ropes. They must also carry all the supplies and everything connected with their use. Tell each man exactly what to carry. [33]That is the work the families of Merari must do at the tent of meeting. They must work under the direction of Ithamar the priest. He is the son of Aaron."

Jason's Jargon

NUMBERS 4

Search this chapter for the word *sacred*. People use the word sacred when referring to something holy. A sacred gift would be anything given to God as an act of worship.

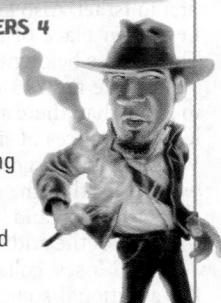

Counting the Families of the Levites

[34] Moses, Aaron and the leaders of the community counted the men of Kohath. They counted them family by family. [35] They counted all the men from 30 to 50 years old. They were the men who came and served at the tent of meeting. [36]There were 2,750 men. They were counted family by family. [37]That was the total of all the men in the families of Kohath who served at the tent of meeting. Moses and Aaron counted them. They did just as the LORD had commanded through Moses.

³⁸ The men of Gershon were counted family by family.

³⁹ All the men from 30 to 50 years old were counted. They were the men who came and served at the tent of meeting. ⁴⁰There were 2,630 men. They were counted family by family. ⁴¹That was the total of the men in the families of Gershon who served at the tent of meeting. Moses and Aaron counted them. They did just as the LORD had commanded.

⁴² The men of Merari were counted family by family.

⁴³ All the men from 30 to 50 years old were counted. They were the men who came and served at the tent of meeting. ⁴⁴There were 3,200 men. They were counted family by family. ⁴⁵That was the total of the men in the families of Merari. Moses and Aaron counted them. They did just as the LORD had commanded through Moses.

⁴⁶ So Moses and Aaron counted all the Levites. The leaders of Israel helped them. They counted the Levites family by family. ⁴⁷All the men from 30 to 50 years old were counted. They were the men who came and served at the tent of meeting. They were also supposed to carry it. ⁴⁸The total number of men was 8,580. ⁴⁹Everything was done as the LORD had commanded through Moses. Each man was given his work. And each one was told what to carry.

So they were counted, just as the LORD had commanded Moses.

Making the Camp Pure

5 The LORD spoke to Moses. He said, ²"Tell the Israelites that certain people must be sent away from the camp. Command them to send away anyone who has a skin disease. They must send away all those who have liquid waste coming from their bodies. And they must send away those who are 'unclean' because they have touched a dead body. ³That applies to men and women alike. Send them out of the camp. They must not make their camp 'unclean.' That is where I live among them." ⁴So the Israelites did what the LORD commanded. They sent out of the camp those who were "unclean." They did just as the LORD had directed Moses.

Sins Against Others Must Be Paid For

⁵The LORD said to Moses, ⁶"Speak to the Israelites. Say to them, 'Suppose a man or woman does something wrong to someone else. Then that person is not being faithful to the LORD. People like that are guilty. ⁷They must admit they have committed a sin. They must pay in full for what they did wrong. And they must add a fifth of the value to it. Then they must give all of it to the person they have sinned against. ⁸But suppose that person has died. And suppose that person does not have a close relative who can be paid for the sin that was committed. Then what is paid belongs to the LORD. It must be given to the priest. A ram must be given along with it. The ram must be sacrificed to the LORD to pay for the sin. ⁹All the sacred gifts the Israelites bring to a priest will belong to him. ¹⁰Sacred gifts belong to their owners. But what they give to the priest will belong to the priest.'"

The Test for an Unfaithful Wife

¹¹Then the LORD spoke to Moses again. He said, ¹²"Speak to the Israelites. Say to them, 'Suppose a man's wife goes astray. And suppose she is not faithful to her husband. ¹³Suppose another man has sex with her. And suppose this is hidden from her husband. No one knows she is not "clean." So there is no witness against her. And she has not been caught in the act. ¹⁴Suppose her husband becomes jealous. He does not trust his wife, and she is really "unclean." Or suppose he does not trust her even though she is "clean." ¹⁵Then he must take his wife to the priest. He must also bring an offering. It must be eight cups of barley flour. The offering is for his wife. He must not pour olive oil on it. And he must not put incense on it. It is a grain offering for being jealous. It calls attention to the wrong thing a person has done.

¹⁶"The priest must have her stand in front of the LORD. ¹⁷He must pour some holy water into a clay jar. He must get

some dust from the floor of the holy tent. And he must put it into the water. [18]The priest must have the woman stand in front of the LORD. Then he must untie her hair. He must place in her hands the offering that calls attention to the wrong thing a person has done. It is the grain offering for being jealous. The priest must keep the bitter water with him. It is the water that brings a curse. [19]Then the priest must have the woman give her word. He must say to her, "Suppose no other man has had sex with you. And suppose you haven't gone astray. You have kept yourself pure while you are married to your husband. Then may the bitter water that brings a curse not harm you. [20]But suppose you have gone astray while you are married to your husband. You have made yourself 'unclean.' You have had sex with a man who isn't your husband." [21]At that point the priest must put the woman under the curse that will come if she breaks her word. He must say, "May the LORD cause you to become a curse among your people. You will become a curse when the LORD makes your body unable to have children. [22]May this water that brings a curse enter your body. May it make your body unable to have children."

"'Then the woman must say, "Amen. Let it happen."

[23]"'The priest must write the curses on a scroll. He must wash them off in the bitter water. [24]It is the water he will make the woman drink. It is bitter water that brings a curse. It will enter her body. And it will cause her to suffer bitterly. [25]The priest must take from her hands the grain offering for being jealous. He must lift it up and wave it in front of the LORD. He must bring it to the altar. [26]Then the priest must take a handful of the grain offering. It is the offering that calls attention to the wrong thing a person has done. The priest must burn it on the altar. After that, he must have the woman drink the water. [27]Suppose she has made herself "unclean." She has not been faithful to her husband. And she has drunk the water that brings a curse. Then it will go into her body. It will cause her to suffer bitterly. It will make her body unable to have children. She will become a curse. [28]Suppose the woman has not made herself "unclean." But suppose

she is "clean." Then she will be free of guilt. And she will be able to have children.

[29]"'This is the law about being jealous. It applies to a woman who has gone astray. She has made herself "unclean" while she is married to her husband. [30]And it applies to a man who becomes jealous. He has doubts about his wife. The priest must have her stand in front of the LORD. He must apply the entire law to her. [31]The husband will not be guilty of doing anything wrong. But the woman will be punished for her sin.'"

Becoming a Nazirite

6 The LORD said to Moses, [2]"Say to the Israelites, 'Suppose a man or woman wants to make a special promise. They want to set themselves apart to the LORD for a certain period of time. They want to be Nazirites. [3]Then they must not drink any kind of wine. They must not drink vinegar made out of wine of any kind. They must not drink grape juice. They must not eat grapes or raisins. [4]As long as they are Nazirites, they must not eat anything grapevines produce. They must not even eat the seeds or skins of grapes.

[5]"'They must not use razors on their heads. They must not cut their hair during the whole time they have set themselves apart to the LORD. They must be holy until that time is over. They must let the hair on their heads grow long.

[6]"'And they must not go near a dead body during that whole time. [7]But what if their father or mother dies? Or what if their brother or sister dies? Then they must not make themselves "unclean" because of them. The hair on their heads shows they are set apart for God. [8]During the whole time they are set apart they are holy to the LORD.

[9]"'Suppose someone dies suddenly in front of them. That makes the hair they have set apart to the LORD "unclean." So they must shave their heads on the day they will be made "clean." That is the seventh day. [10]Then on the eighth day they must bring two doves. Or they can bring two young pigeons. They must bring them to the priest. He will be at the entrance to the tent of meeting. [11]The priest must offer one of the birds as a sin offering. And he must offer the other as a burnt offering.

FUN FACTS

Num. 6:1-5

Samson, Samuel, and John the Baptist were all Nazirites. Like all Nazirites, they promised not to drink wine, eat grapes, or cut their hair.

The sacrifices will pay for the sin of the Nazirite man or woman. They sinned by being near a dead body. That same day they must make their heads holy again. ¹²They must set themselves apart to the LORD again. They must do it for the same period of time they had agreed to at first. And they must bring a male lamb a year old as a guilt offering. The days before that do not count. That is because they became "unclean" during the time they were set apart.

¹³" "The time when the Nazirites are set apart will come to an end. Here is the law that applies to them at that time. They must be brought to the entrance to the tent of meeting. ¹⁴There they must present their offerings to the LORD. They must bring a male lamb a year old. It must not have any flaws. It is for a burnt offering. Then they must bring a female lamb a year old. It must not have any flaws. It is for a sin offering. And they must bring a ram that does not have any flaws. It is for a friendship offering. ¹⁵They must sacrifice the offerings together with their grain offerings and drink offerings. And they must also bring a basket of bread made with the finest flour. The bread must be made without yeast. The offering must include thick loaves with olive oil mixed in. And it must also include thin loaves brushed with olive oil.

¹⁶" "The priest must bring all these things to the LORD. He must sacrifice the sin offering and the burnt offering. ¹⁷He must bring the basket of bread made without yeast. And he must sacrifice the ram. It will be a friendship offering to the LORD. The priest must bring it together with its grain offering and drink offering.

¹⁸" "Then the Nazirites must shave off the hair that shows they have set themselves apart to the LORD. They must do it at the entrance to the tent of meeting. And they must put the hair in the fire that burns the sacrifice of the friendship offering.

¹⁹" "After the Nazirites have shaved off their hair, the priest must take a boiled shoulder of the ram. He must remove one thick loaf and one thin loaf from the basket. They must be made without yeast. And he must place the shoulder and the bread in the hands of the Nazirites. ²⁰Then he must lift up the shoulder and bread and wave them in front of the LORD. They are a wave offering. They are holy and belong to the priest. Other parts of the ram belong to the priest as well. They are the breast that was waved and the thigh that was offered. After the offering is waved, the Nazirites may drink wine.

²¹" "This is the law of the Nazirites. They promise to sacrifice offerings to the LORD. They do it when they set themselves apart. And they should bring anything else they can afford. They must fulfill the promises they have made. They must do so according to the law of the Nazirites.' "

How the Priests Bless the People

²²The LORD spoke to Moses. He said, ²³"Tell Aaron and his sons, 'Here is how I want you to bless the Israelites. Say to them,

²⁴ " ' "May the LORD bless you
and take good care of you.
²⁵ May the LORD smile on you
and be gracious to you.
²⁶ May the LORD look on you with favor
and give you peace." '

²⁷"In that way they will put the blessing of my name on the Israelites. And I will bless them."

Israel's Leaders Bring Offerings for the Holy Tent

7 Moses finished setting up the holy tent. Then he anointed it with olive oil. He set it apart to the LORD. He did the same thing with everything that belonged to it. He also anointed the altar. And he set apart to the LORD the altar and all its tools. ²Then the leaders of Israel brought their offerings. The leaders were the heads of the families. They were the leaders of the tribes. They were in charge of the men who had been counted. ³They brought gifts to the LORD. They brought six covered carts and 12 oxen. Each leader gave an ox. And every two leaders gave a cart. They put their gifts in front of the holy tent.

⁴The LORD said to Moses, ⁵"Accept the gifts from the leaders. I want their gifts to be used in the work at the tent of meeting. Give them to the Levites. They need them to do their work."

⁶So Moses gave the carts and the oxen to the Levites. ⁷He gave two carts and four oxen to the men from the family of Gershon. They needed them to do their work. ⁸He gave four carts and eight oxen to the men from the family of Merari. They needed them to do their work. All these men were under the direction of Ithamar the priest. He was the son of Aaron. ⁹But Moses didn't give any carts or oxen to the men from the family of Kohath. They had to carry the holy things on their shoulders. They were responsible for the holy things.

¹⁰When the altar was anointed, the leaders brought their offerings. They placed them in front of the altar. They brought their offerings in order to set apart the altar. ¹¹The LORD had spoken to Moses. He had said, "Each day one leader must bring his offering. He must bring it in order to set apart the altar."

¹² On the first day Nahshon, the son of Amminadab, brought his offering. Nahshon was from the tribe of Judah.

¹³ He brought:

one silver plate and one silver sprinkling bowl. The plate weighed three pounds four ounces. The sprinkling bowl weighed one pound 12 ounces. Both were weighed according to the standard weights used in the sacred tent. Each plate and bowl was filled with the finest flour mixed with olive oil. It was a grain offering.

¹⁴ He brought one gold dish that weighed four ounces. It was filled with incense.

¹⁵ Nahshon brought one young bull, one ram, and one male lamb a year old. They would be sacrificed as a burnt offering.

Jason's Jargon

NUMBERS 7

Your mission: Find the word *anointed* in this chapter. To anoint means to prepare something for God's service. For example, when God made David king, Samuel anointed his head with oil.

¹⁶ He brought one male goat to be sacrificed as a sin offering.

¹⁷ He brought two oxen, five rams and five male goats. He also brought five male lambs a year old. All of them would be sacrificed as a friendship offering.

That was everything that Nahshon, the son of Amminadab, brought as his offering.

¹⁸ On the second day Nethanel, the son of Zuar, brought his offering. Nethanel was the leader of the tribe of Issachar.

¹⁹ He brought:

one silver plate and one silver sprinkling bowl. The plate weighed three pounds four ounces. The sprinkling bowl weighed one pound 12 ounces. Both were weighed according to the standard weights used in the sacred tent. Each plate and bowl was filled with the finest flour mixed with olive oil. It was a grain offering.

²⁰ He brought one gold dish that weighed four ounces. It was filled with incense.

²¹ Nethanel brought one young bull, one ram, and one male lamb a year old. They would be sacrificed as a burnt offering.

²² He brought one male goat to be sacrificed as a sin offering.

²³ He brought two oxen, five rams and five male goats. He also brought five male lambs a year old. All of them would be sacrificed as a friendship offering.

That was everything that Nethanel, the son of Zuar, brought as his offering.

²⁴ On the third day Eliab, the son of Helon, brought his offering. Eliab was the leader of the people of Zebulun.

²⁵ He brought:

one silver plate and one silver sprinkling bowl. The plate weighed three pounds four ounces. The sprinkling bowl weighed one pound 12 ounces. Both were weighed according to the standard weights used in the sacred tent. Each plate and bowl was filled with the finest flour mixed with olive oil. It was a grain offering.

²⁶ He brought one gold dish that weighed four ounces. It was filled with incense.

²⁷ Eliab brought one young bull, one ram, and one male lamb a year old. They would be sacrificed as a burnt offering.

²⁸ He brought one male goat to be sacrificed as a sin offering.

²⁹ He brought two oxen, five rams and five male goats. He also brought five male lambs a year old. All of them would be sacrificed as a friendship offering.

That was everything that Eliab, the son of Helon, brought as his offering.

³⁰ On the fourth day Elizur, the son of Shedeur, brought his offering. Elizur was the leader of the people of Reuben.

³¹ He brought:

one silver plate and one silver sprinkling bowl. The plate weighed three pounds four ounces. The sprinkling bowl weighed one pound 12 ounces. Both were weighed according to the standard weights used in the sacred tent. Each plate and bowl was filled with the finest flour mixed with olive oil. It was a grain offering.

³² He brought one gold dish that weighed four ounces. It was filled with incense.

³³ Elizur brought one young bull, one ram, and one male lamb a year old. They would be sacrificed as a burnt offering.

³⁴ He brought one male goat to be sacrificed as a sin offering.

³⁵ He brought two oxen, five rams and five male goats. He also brought five male lambs a year old. All of them would be sacrificed as a friendship offering.

That was everything that Elizur, the son of Shedeur, brought as his offering.

³⁶ On the fifth day Shelumiel, the son of Zurishaddai, brought his offering. Shelumiel was the leader of the people of Simeon.

³⁷ He brought:

one silver plate and one silver sprinkling bowl. The plate weighed three pounds four ounces. The sprinkling bowl weighed one pound 12 ounces. Both were weighed according to the standard weights used in the sacred tent. Each plate and bowl was filled with the finest flour mixed with olive oil. It was a grain offering.

³⁸ He brought one gold dish that weighed four ounces. It was filled with incense.

³⁹ Shelumiel brought one young bull, one ram, and one male lamb a year old. They would be sacrificed as a burnt offering.

⁴⁰ He brought one male goat to be sacrificed as a sin offering.

⁴¹ He brought two oxen, five rams and five male goats. He also brought five male lambs a year old. All of them would be sacrificed as a friendship offering.

That was everything that Shelumiel, the son of Zurishaddai, brought as his offering.

⁴² On the sixth day Eliasaph, the son of Deuel, brought his offering. Eliasaph was the leader of the people of Gad.

⁴³ He brought:

one silver plate and one silver sprinkling bowl. The plate weighed three pounds four ounces. The sprinkling bowl weighed one pound 12 ounces. Both were weighed according to the standard weights used in the sacred tent. Each plate and bowl was filled with the finest flour mixed with olive oil. It was a grain offering.

⁴⁴ He brought one gold dish that weighed four ounces. It was filled with incense.

⁴⁵ Eliasaph brought one young bull, one ram, and one male lamb a year old. They would be sacrificed as a burnt offering.

⁴⁶ He brought one male goat to be sacrificed as a sin offering.

⁴⁷ He brought two oxen, five rams and five male goats. He also brought five male lambs a year old. All of them would be sacrificed as a friendship offering.

That was everything that Eliasaph, the son of Deuel, brought as his offering.

⁴⁸ On the seventh day Elishama, the son of Ammihud, brought his offering. Elishama was the leader of the people of Ephraim.

⁴⁹ He brought:

one silver plate and one silver sprinkling bowl. The plate weighed three pounds four ounces. The sprinkling bowl weighed one pound 12 ounces. Both were weighed according to the standard weights used in the sacred tent. Each plate and bowl was

filled with the finest flour mixed with olive oil. It was a grain offering.

⁵⁰ He brought one gold dish that weighed four ounces. It was filled with incense.

⁵¹ Elishama brought one young bull, one ram, and one male lamb a year old. They would be sacrificed as a burnt offering.

⁵² He brought one male goat to be sacrificed as a sin offering.

⁵³ He brought two oxen, five rams and five male goats. He also brought five male lambs a year old. All of them would be sacrificed as a friendship offering.

That was everything that Elishama, the son of Ammihud, brought as his offering.

⁵⁴ On the eighth day Gamaliel, the son of Pedahzur, brought his offering. Gamaliel was the leader of the people of Manasseh.

⁵⁵ He brought:

one silver plate and one silver sprinkling bowl. The plate weighed three pounds four ounces. The sprinkling bowl weighed one pound 12 ounces. Both were weighed according to the standard weights used in the sacred tent. Each plate and bowl was filled with the finest flour mixed with olive oil. It was a grain offering.

⁵⁶ He brought one gold dish that weighed four ounces. It was filled with incense.

⁵⁷ Gamaliel brought one young bull, one ram, and one male lamb a year old. They would be sacrificed as a burnt offering.

⁵⁸ He brought one male goat to be sacrificed as a sin offering.

⁵⁹ He brought two oxen, five rams and five male goats. He also brought five male lambs a year old. All of them would be sacrificed as a friendship offering.

That was everything that Gamaliel, the son of Pedahzur, brought as his offering.

⁶⁰ On the ninth day Abidan, the son of Gideoni, brought his offering. Abidan was the leader of the people of Benjamin.

⁶¹ He brought:

one silver plate and one silver sprinkling bowl. The plate weighed three pounds four ounces. The sprinkling bowl weighed one pound 12 ounces. Both were weighed according to the standard weights used in the sacred tent. Each plate and bowl was filled with the finest flour mixed with olive oil. It was a grain offering.

⁶² He brought one gold dish that weighed four ounces. It was filled with incense.

⁶³ Abidan brought one young bull, one ram, and one male lamb a year old. They would be sacrificed as a burnt offering.

⁶⁴ He brought one male goat to be sacrificed as a sin offering.

⁶⁵ He brought two oxen, five rams and five male goats. He also brought five male lambs a year old. All of them would be sacrificed as a friendship offering.

That was everything that Abidan, the son of Gideoni, brought as his offering.

⁶⁶ On the tenth day Ahiezer, the son of Ammishaddai, brought his offering. Ahiezer was the leader of the people of Dan.

⁶⁷ He brought:

one silver plate and one silver sprinkling bowl. The plate weighed three pounds four ounces. The sprinkling bowl weighed one pound 12 ounces. Both were weighed according to the standard weights used in the sacred tent. Each plate and bowl was filled with the finest flour mixed with olive oil. It was a grain offering.

⁶⁸ He brought one gold dish that weighed four ounces. It was filled with incense.

⁶⁹ Ahiezer brought one young bull, one ram, and one male lamb a year old. They would be sacrificed as a burnt offering.

⁷⁰ He brought one male goat to be sacrificed as a sin offering.

⁷¹ He brought two oxen, five rams and five male goats. He also brought five male lambs a year old. All of them would be sacrificed as a friendship offering.

That was everything that Ahiezer, the son of Ammishaddai, brought as his offering.

⁷² On the eleventh day Pagiel, the son of Okran, brought his offering. Pagiel was the leader of the people of Asher.

⁷³ He brought:

one silver plate and one silver sprinkling bowl. The plate weighed three pounds four ounces. The sprinkling bowl weighed one pound 12 ounces. Both were weighed according to the standard weights used in the sacred tent. Each plate and bowl was filled with the finest flour mixed with olive oil. It was a grain offering.

⁷⁴ He brought one gold dish that weighed four ounces. It was filled with incense.

⁷⁵ Pagiel brought one young bull, one ram, and one male lamb a year old. They would be sacrificed as a burnt offering.

⁷⁶ He brought one male goat to be sacrificed as a sin offering.

⁷⁷ He brought two oxen, five rams and five male goats. He also brought five male lambs a year old. All of them would be sacrificed as a friendship offering.

That was everything that Pagiel, the son of Okran, brought as his offering.

⁷⁸ On the twelfth day Ahira, the son of Enan, brought his offering. Ahira was the leader of the people of Naphtali.

⁷⁹ He brought:

one silver plate and one silver sprinkling bowl. The plate weighed three pounds four ounces. The sprinkling bowl weighed one pound 12 ounces. Both were weighed according to the standard weights used in the sacred tent. Each plate and bowl was filled with the finest flour mixed with olive oil. It was a grain offering.

80 He brought one gold dish that weighed four ounces. It was filled with incense.

81 Ahira brought one young bull, one ram, and one male lamb a year old. They would be sacrificed as a burnt offering.

82 He brought one male goat to be sacrificed as a sin offering.

83 He brought two oxen, five rams and five male goats. He also brought five male lambs a year old. All of them would be sacrificed as a friendship offering.

That was everything that Ahira, the son of Enan, brought as his offering.

84 Those were the offerings the Israelite leaders brought. They gave them to set the altar apart when it was anointed with olive oil.

They gave 12 silver plates, 12 silver sprinkling bowls and 12 gold dishes. 85 Each plate weighed three pounds four ounces. Each sprinkling bowl weighed one pound 12 ounces. The total weight of the silver dishes was 60 pounds. Everything was weighed according to the standard weights used in the sacred tent. 86 Each of the 12 gold dishes weighed four ounces. They were filled with incense. They were weighed according to the weights used in the sacred tent. The total weight of the gold dishes was three pounds.

87 The leaders brought 12 young bulls, 12 rams and 12 male lambs a year old. That was the total number of animals they gave for the burnt offering. They gave them together with the grain offering. They brought 12 male goats for the sin offering.

88 The leaders brought 24 oxen, 60 rams, 60 male goats and 60 male lambs a year old. That was the total number of animals sacrificed as the friendship offering.

Those were the offerings they brought to set apart the altar. The leaders brought them after the altar was anointed with oil.

89 Moses entered the tent of meeting. He wanted to speak with the LORD. There Moses heard the LORD talking to him. The LORD's voice was speaking to him from between the two cherubim. The cherubim were over the place where sin is paid for. It was the cover on the ark where the tablets of the covenant law were kept. In this way the LORD spoke to Moses.

Aaron Sets Up the Lamps

8 The LORD said to Moses, 2 "Say to Aaron, 'Set up the seven lamps. They will light up the area in front of the lampstand.' "

3 So Aaron did it. He set up the lamps so that they faced forward on the lampstand. He did just as the LORD had commanded Moses. 4 The lampstand was made out of hammered gold. From its base to its blooms it was made out of hammered gold. The lampstand was made exactly like the pattern the LORD had shown Moses.

Moses Sets Apart the Levites

5 The LORD spoke to Moses. He said, 6 "Take the Levites from among all the Israelites. Make them 'clean' in the usual way. 7 Here is how to make them pure. Sprinkle the special water on them. Then have them shave their whole bodies. Also have them wash their clothes. That is how they will make themselves pure. 8 Have them get a young bull along with its grain offering. The offering must be made out of the finest flour mixed with olive oil. Then you must get a second young bull. You must sacrifice it as a sin offering. 9 Bring the Levites to the front of the tent of meeting. Gather the whole community of Israel together. 10 You must bring the Levites to me. The Israelites must place their hands on them. 11 Aaron must bring the Levites to me. They are a wave offering from the Israelites. That is how they will be set apart to do my work.

12 "Then I want the Levites to place their hands on the heads of the bulls. They must sacrifice one bull as a sin offering to

me. And they must sacrifice the other as a burnt offering. The blood of the bulls will pay for the sin of the Levites. [13]Have the Levites stand in front of Aaron and his sons. Then give them as a wave offering to me. [14]That is how I want you to set apart the Levites from the other Israelites. The Levites will belong to me.

[15]"Make the Levites pure. Give them to me as a wave offering. Then they must come to do their work at the tent of meeting. [16]They are the Israelites who will be given to me completely. I have taken them to be my own. I have taken them in place of every son born first in his family in Israel. [17]Every male born first in Israel belongs to me. That is true whether it is a human or an animal. In Egypt I struck down all the males born first to their mothers. Then I set apart for myself all the males born first in Israel. [18]And I have taken the Levites in place of all the sons born first in Israel. [19]I have given the Levites as gifts to Aaron and his sons. I have taken them from among all the Israelites. I have appointed them to do the work at the tent of meeting. They will do it in place of the Israelites. That is how they will keep the Israelites from being guilty when they go near the sacred tent. Then no plague will strike the Israelites when they go near the tent."

[20]So Moses and Aaron and all the Israelites did with the Levites just as the Lord had commanded Moses. [21]The Levites made themselves pure. They washed their clothes. Then Aaron gave them to the Lord as a wave offering. That's how he paid for their sin to make them pure. [22]After that, the Levites came to do their work at the tent of meeting. They worked under the direction of Aaron and his sons. And so Moses and Aaron and the whole community of Israel did with the Levites just as the Lord had commanded Moses.

[23]The Lord said to Moses, [24]"Here is what the Levites must do. Men 25 years old or more must come and take part in the work at the tent of meeting. [25]But when they reach the age of 50, they must not work any longer. They must stop doing their regular work. [26]They can help their brothers with their duties at the tent of meeting. But they themselves should not do the work. That is how you must direct the Levites to do their work."

Israel Celebrates the Passover Feast

9 The Lord spoke to Moses in the Desert of Sinai. It was the first month of the second year after the people came out of Egypt. He said, [2]"Tell the Israelites to celebrate the Passover Feast. Have them do it at the appointed time. [3]Celebrate it when the sun goes down on the 14th day of this month. Obey all its rules and laws."

[4]So Moses told the Israelites to celebrate the Passover Feast. [5]They did it in the Desert of Sinai. They celebrated it when the sun went down on the 14th day of the first month. The Israelites did everything just as the Lord had commanded Moses.

[6]But some of them couldn't celebrate the Passover Feast on that day. That's because they weren't "clean." They had gone near a dead body. So they came to Moses and Aaron that same day. [7]They said to Moses, "We went near a dead body. So we aren't 'clean.' But why should we be kept from bringing the Lord's offering at the appointed time? Why shouldn't we bring it along with the other Israelites?"

[8]Moses answered them, "Wait until I find out what the Lord wants you to do."

[9]Then the Lord spoke to Moses. He said, [10]"Tell the Israelites, 'Suppose any of you or your children are "unclean" because they have gone near a dead body. Or suppose they are away on a journey. They must still celebrate the Lord's Passover. [11]They must celebrate it on the 14th day of the second month. They must do so when the sun goes down. They must eat the lamb together with bread made without yeast. They must eat it with bitter plants. [12]They must not leave any of it until morning. They must not break any of its bones. When they celebrate the Passover Feast, they must follow all the rules. [13]But suppose someone is "clean" and not on a journey. And they fail to celebrate the Passover Feast. Then they must be separated from the community of Israel. They did not bring the Lord's offering at the appointed time. They will be punished for their sin.

[14]"What if there is an outsider living among you? And what if they want to celebrate the Lord's Passover? Then they must obey its rules and laws. You must

have the same laws for outsiders as you do for the Israelites.'"

The Cloud Covers the Holy Tent

[15]The holy tent was set up. It was the tent where the tablets of the covenant law were kept. On the day it was set up, the cloud covered it. From evening until morning the cloud above the tent looked like fire. [16]That's what continued to happen. The cloud covered the tent. At night the cloud looked like fire. [17]When the cloud lifted from its place above the tent, the Israelites started out. Where the cloud settled, the Israelites camped. [18]When the LORD gave the command, the Israelites started out. And when he gave the command, they camped. As long as the cloud stayed above the holy tent, they remained in camp. [19]Sometimes the cloud remained above the tent for a long time. Then the Israelites obeyed the LORD's order. They didn't start out. [20]Sometimes the cloud was above the tent for only a few days. When the LORD would give the command, they would camp. And when he would give the command, they would start out. [21]Sometimes the cloud stayed only from evening until morning. When it lifted in the morning, they started out. It didn't matter whether it was day or night. When the cloud lifted, the people started out. [22]It didn't matter whether the cloud stayed above the holy tent for two days or a month or a year. The Israelites would remain in camp. They wouldn't start out. But when the cloud lifted, they would start out. [23]When the LORD gave the command, they camped. And when he gave the command, they started out. They obeyed the LORD's order. They obeyed him, just as he had commanded them through Moses.

The Silver Trumpets

10 The LORD said to Moses, [2]"Make two trumpets out of hammered silver. Blow them when you want the community to gather together. And blow them when you want the camps to start out. [3]When both trumpets are blown, the whole community must gather in front of you. They must come to the entrance to the tent of meeting. [4]Suppose only one trumpet is blown. Then the leaders must gather in front of you. They are the heads of the tribes of Israel. [5]When a trumpet blast is blown, the tribes camped on the east side must start out. [6]When the second blast is blown, the camps on the south side must start out. The blast will tell them when to start. [7]Blow the trumpets to gather the people together. But do not use the same kind of blast.

[8]"The sons of Aaron, the priests, must blow the trumpets. That is a law for you and your children after you for all time to come. [9]Suppose you go into battle in your own land. And suppose it is against an enemy who is treating you badly. Then blow a blast on the trumpets. If you do, I will remember you. I will save you from your enemies. I am the LORD your God. [10]You must also blow the trumpets when you are happy. Blow them at your appointed feasts. Blow them at your New Moon feasts. Blow them when you sacrifice your burnt offerings. Blow them when you sacrifice your friendship offerings. They will remind me of you. I am the LORD your God."

The Israelites Leave the Sinai Desert

[11]It was the 20th day of the second month of the second year. On that day the cloud began to move. It went up from above the holy tent where the tablets of the covenant law were kept. [12]Then the Israelites started out from the Desert of Sinai.

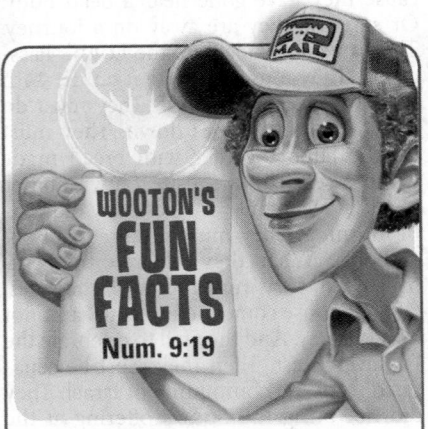

WOOTON'S FUN FACTS
Num. 9:19

I used to get kind of down on cloudy days. But ever since I found out that God traveled with the Israelites in clouds, I now look for God's face in their shapes. It seems like He shows His white beard a lot.

They traveled from place to place. They kept going until the cloud came to rest in the Desert of Paran. [13]The first time they started out, the LORD commanded Moses to tell them to do it. And they did it.

[14]The groups of the camp of Judah went first. They marched out under their flag. Nahshon was their commander. He was the son of Amminadab. [15]Nethanel was over the group of the tribe of Issachar. Nethanel was the son of Zuar. [16]Eliab was over the group of the tribe of Zebulun. Eliab was the son of Helon. [17]The holy tent was taken down. The men of Gershon and Merari started out. They carried the tent.

[18]The groups of the camp of Reuben went next. They marched out under their flag. Elizur was their commander. He was the son of Shedeur. [19]Shelumiel was over the group of the tribe of Simeon. Shelumiel was the son of Zurishaddai. [20]Eliasaph was over the group of the tribe of Gad. Eliasaph was the son of Deuel. [21]The men of Kohath started out. They carried the holy things. The holy tent had to be set up before they arrived.

[22]The groups of the camp of Ephraim went next. They marched out under their flag. Elishama was their commander. He was the son of Ammihud. [23]Gamaliel was over the group of the tribe of Manasseh. Gamaliel was the son of Pedahzur. [24]Abidan was over the group of the tribe of Benjamin. Abidan was the son of Gideoni. [25]Finally, the groups of the camp of Dan started out. They marched out under their flag. They followed behind all the other groups and guarded them. Ahiezer was their commander. He was the son of Ammishaddai. [26]Pagiel was over the group of the tribe of Asher. Pagiel was the son of Okran. [27]Ahira was over the group of the tribe of Naphtali. Ahira was the son of Enan. [28]As the groups of Israel started out, that was the order they marched in.

[29]Moses spoke to Hobab, the son of Reuel. Reuel was Moses' father-in-law. Reuel was from Midian. Moses said to Hobab, "We're starting out for the place the LORD promised to us. He said to us, 'I will give it to you.' So come with us. We'll treat you well. The LORD has promised to give good things to Israel."

WHAT ABOUT YOU?

As the Israelites traveled in the desert, they depended on a guide named Hobab to help them. You can read about him in Numbers 10:29–32.

Have you ever stopped to think about all the people you rely on every day?

There are probably too many to count, including teachers, siblings, coaches, grandparents, friends, and, of course, your parents. All of these people make your life better, not just by helping you reach the cereal box on the top shelf, but by shaping you into the adult you will become. These folks have unique ways of bringing joy, comfort, and learning into your life. And some are sure to take you places you could never go on your own (at least until you get a driver's license).

When we pause to look at how much certain people do for us, we may be astonished. Our gratitude should also make us eager to return the favor and support others.

Like the wilderness guide, Hobab, some people have been a special blessing in our lives, and we need to bless them in return. Who has been extra kind to you? What can you do to say thank you?

Throughout the day, make a note of every time someone does something for you that you couldn't have done for yourself. A ride? A meal? Advice? At the end of the day, reflect on those things, and think of some way to honor those who help you succeed.

³⁰Hobab answered, "No. I can't go. I'm going back to my own land. I'm returning to my own people."

³¹But Moses said, "Please don't leave us. You know where we should camp in the desert. You can be our guide. ³²So come with us. The LORD will give us good things. We'll share them with you."

³³So they started out from the mountain of the LORD. They traveled for three days. The ark of the covenant of the LORD went in front of them during those three days. It went ahead of them to find a place for them to rest. ³⁴They started out from the camp by day. And the cloud of the LORD was above them.

³⁵When the ark started out, Moses said,

"LORD, rise up!
    Let your enemies be scattered.
    Let them run away from you."

³⁶When the ark stopped, Moses said,

"LORD, return.
    Return to the many thousands of
        people in Israel."

The LORD Sends Fire Among the People

11 The people weren't happy about the hard times they were having. The LORD heard what they were saying. It made him very angry. Then the LORD sent fire on them. It blazed out among the people. It burned up some of the outer edges of the camp. ²The people cried out to Moses. Then he prayed to the LORD. And the fire died down. ³So that place was named Taberah. That's because fire from the LORD had blazed out among them there.

The LORD Sends Quail for the People to Eat

⁴Some people with them began to wish for other food. Again the Israelites began to cry out. They said, "We wish we had meat to eat. ⁵We remember the fish we ate in Egypt. It didn't cost us anything. We also remember the cucumbers, melons, leeks, onions and garlic. ⁶But now we've lost all interest in eating. We never see anything but this manna!"

⁷The manna was like coriander seeds. It looked like sap from a tree. ⁸The people went around gathering it. Then they

CANDID CONVERSATIONS

The Israelites must have been pretty hungry. I mean, why else would they be begging Moses for onions, garlic, and leeks? Have you ever begged for onions? Me neither. But the people of Israel had already gotten in the bad habit of whining about lots of things . . . like not being in Egypt anymore. You remember Egypt—the place where they were *slaves*!

Just like the Israelites complained to Moses, we have a tendency to complain to our parents. I'm guessing your parents wouldn't mind so much if you talked to them kindly about things that irritate you. But whining doesn't help anything. Especially because your parents have your best interests at heart. God knew what He was doing with the Israelites, and your parents know what they're doing when they tell you to eat your onions.

If you're feeling angry with your parents, write down your frustrations before trying to talk to them. List the things you love about your parents before you try discussing a disagreement. I'm sure if you stopped for a moment and thought about all your parents have done for you, you might end up saying thank you instead of whining to them. Make it a point to thank your parents once in a while.

ground it up in a small mill they held in their hands. Or they crushed it in a stone bowl. They cooked it in a pot. Or they made loaves out of it. It tasted like something made with olive oil. ⁹When the dew came down on the camp at night, the manna also came down.

¹⁰Moses heard people from every family crying at the entrances to their tents. The LORD became very angry. So Moses

became upset. ¹¹He asked the Lord, "Why have you brought this trouble on me? Why aren't you pleased with me? Why have you loaded me down with the troubles of all these people? ¹²Am I like a mother to them? Are they my children? Why do you tell me to carry them in my arms? Do I have to carry them the way a nurse carries a baby? Do I have to carry them to the land you promised? You promised the land to their people of long ago. ¹³Where can I get meat for all these people? They keep crying out to me. They say, 'Give us meat to eat!' ¹⁴I can't carry all these people by myself. The load is too heavy for me. ¹⁵Is this how you are going to treat me? If you are pleased with me, just put me to death right now. Don't let me live if I have to see myself destroyed anyway."

¹⁶The Lord said to Moses, "Bring me 70 of Israel's elders. Bring men that you know are leaders and officials among the people. Have them come to the tent of meeting. I want them to stand there with you. ¹⁷I will come down and speak with you there. I will take some of the power of the Spirit that is on you. And I will put it on them. They will share the responsibility of these people with you. Then you will not have to carry it alone.

¹⁸"Tell the people, 'Set yourselves apart for tomorrow. At that time you will eat meat. The Lord heard you when you cried out. You said, "We wish we had meat to eat. We were better off in Egypt. Now the Lord will give you meat. And you will eat it. ¹⁹You will not eat it for just one or two days. You will not eat it for just five, ten or 20 days. ²⁰Instead, you will eat it for a whole month. You will eat it until it comes out of your noses. You will eat it until you hate it. The Lord is among you. But you have turned your back on him. You have cried out while he was listening. You have said, "Why did we ever leave Egypt?" ' "

²¹But Moses said to the Lord, "Here I am among 600,000 men on the march. And you say, 'I will give them meat to eat for a whole month'! ²²Would they have enough if flocks and herds were killed for them? Would they have enough even if all the fish in the ocean were caught for them?"

²³The Lord answered Moses, "Am I not strong enough? Now you will see whether what I say will come true for you."

²⁴So Moses went out. He told the people what the Lord had said. He gathered 70 of their elders together. He had them stand around the tent of meeting. ²⁵Then the Lord came down in the cloud. He spoke with Moses. He took some of the power of the Spirit that was on Moses. And he put it on the 70 elders. When the Spirit came on them, they prophesied. But they didn't do it again.

²⁶Two men had remained in the camp. Their names were Eldad and Medad. They were listed among the elders. But they didn't go out to the tent of meeting. In spite of that, the Spirit came on them too. So they prophesied in the camp. ²⁷A young man ran up to Moses. He said, "Eldad and Medad are prophesying in the camp."

²⁸Joshua spoke up. He was the son of Nun. Joshua had been Moses' helper from the time he was young. He said, "Moses! Please stop them!"

²⁹But Moses replied, "Are you jealous for me? I wish that all the Lord's people were prophets. And I wish that the Lord would put his Spirit on them." ³⁰Then Moses and the elders of Israel returned to the camp.

³¹The Lord sent out a wind. It drove quail in from the Red Sea. It scattered them all around the camp. They were about three feet above the ground. They could be seen

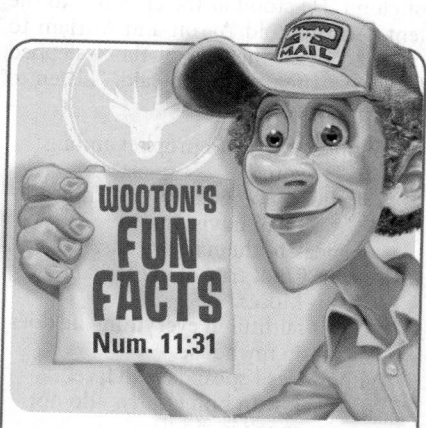

WOOTON'S **FUN FACTS**
Num. 11:31

I had an owl once named Dr. What. He didn't migrate, but quail in Africa migrate north to Egypt in March and April. One ancient historian wrote that a large flock of quail landed on a boat and sank it!

in every direction as far as a person could walk in a day. [32]The people went out all day and gathered quail. They gathered them all night and all the next day. No one gathered less than 60 bushels. Then they spread the quail all around the camp. [33]But while the meat was still in their mouths, the LORD acted. Before the people could swallow it, he became very angry with them. He struck them with a terrible plague. [34]So the place was named Kibroth Hattaavah. That's where the bodies of the people who had wished for other food were buried.

[35]From Kibroth Hattaavah the people traveled to Hazeroth. And they stayed there.

Miriam and Aaron Speak Against Moses

12 Miriam and Aaron began to say bad things about Moses. That's because Moses had married a woman from Cush. [2]"Has the LORD spoken only through Moses?" they asked. "Hasn't he also spoken through us?" The LORD heard what they said.

[3]Moses was a very humble man. In fact, he was more humble than anyone else on the face of the earth.

[4]The LORD spoke to Moses, Aaron and Miriam. He said, "All three of you, come out to the tent of meeting." So they did. [5]Then the LORD came down in a pillar of cloud. He stood at the entrance to the tent. And he told Aaron and Miriam to come to him. The two of them stepped forward. [6]Then the LORD said, "Listen to my words.

"Suppose there is a prophet among
you.
I, the LORD, make myself known to
them in visions.
I speak to them in dreams.
[7] But this is not true of my servant
Moses.
He is faithful in everything he does
in my house.
[8] With Moses I speak face to face.
I speak with him clearly. I do not
speak in riddles.
I let him see something of what I
look like.
So why were you not afraid
to speak against my servant
Moses?"

[9]The LORD was very angry with them. And he left them.

[10]When the cloud went up from above the tent, there stood Miriam. She had a disease that made her skin as white as snow. Aaron turned toward her. He saw that she had a skin disease. [11]So he said to Moses, "We have committed a very foolish sin. Please don't hold it against us. [12]Don't let Miriam be like a baby that was born dead. Don't let her look like a dead baby whose body is half eaten away."

[13]So Moses cried out to the LORD. He said, "Please, God, heal her!"

[14]The LORD answered Moses. He said, "Suppose her father had spit in her face. Then she would have been put to shame for seven days. So keep her outside the camp for seven days. After that, you can bring her back." [15]So Miriam was kept outside the camp for seven days. The people didn't move on until she was brought back.

[16]After that, the people left Hazeroth. They camped in the Desert of Paran.

Twelve Men Check Out the Land of Canaan

13 The LORD said to Moses, [2]"Send some men to check out the land of Canaan. I am giving it to the Israelites. Send one leader from each of Israel's tribes."

[3]So Moses sent them out from the Desert of Paran. He sent them as the LORD had commanded. All of them were leaders of the Israelites.

[4] Here are their names.

There was Shammua from the tribe
of Reuben. Shammua was the
son of Zakkur.
[5] There was Shaphat from the tribe of
Simeon. Shaphat was the son of
Hori.
[6] There was Caleb from the tribe
of Judah. Caleb was the son of
Jephunneh.
[7] There was Igal from the tribe of
Issachar. Igal was the son of
Joseph.
[8] There was Hoshea from the tribe of
Ephraim. Hoshea was the son of
Nun.

ADVENTURES iN ODYSSEY

The Israelites were too afraid to go into the Promised Land. Mandy had to face her own fear about the future in "True Calling" (A#43).

⁹ There was Palti from the tribe of Benjamin. Palti was the son of Raphu.

¹⁰ There was Gaddiel from the tribe of Zebulun. Gaddiel was the son of Sodi.

¹¹ There was Gaddi from the tribe of Manasseh. Gaddi was the son of Susi. Manasseh was a tribe of Joseph.

¹² There was Ammiel from the tribe of Dan. Ammiel was the son of Gemalli.

¹³ There was Sethur from the tribe of Asher. Sethur was the son of Michael.

¹⁴ There was Nahbi from the tribe of Naphtali. Nahbi was the son of Vophsi.

¹⁵ There was Geuel from the tribe of Gad. Geuel was the son of Maki.

¹⁶ Those are the men Moses sent to check out the land. He gave the name Joshua to Hoshea, the son of Nun.

¹⁷Moses sent the 12 men to check out Canaan. He said, "Go up through the Negev Desert. Go on into the central hill country. ¹⁸See what the land is like. See whether the people who live there are strong or weak. See whether they are few or many. ¹⁹What kind of land do they live in? Is it good or bad? What kind of towns do they live in? Do the towns have high walls around them or not? ²⁰How is the soil? Is it rich land or poor land? Are there trees in it or not? Do your best to bring back some of the fruit of the land." It was the season for the first ripe grapes.

²¹So the men went up and checked out the land. They went from the Desert of Zin as far as Rehob. It was in the direction of Lebo Hamath. ²²They went up through the Negev Desert and came to Hebron. That's where Ahiman, Sheshai and Talmai

lived. They belonged to the family line of Anak. Hebron had been built seven years before Zoan. Zoan was a city in Egypt. ²³The men came to the Valley of Eshkol. There they cut off a branch that had a single bunch of grapes on it. Two of them carried it on a pole between them. They carried some pomegranates and figs along with it. ²⁴That place was called the Valley of Eshkol. That's because the men of Israel cut off a bunch of grapes there. ²⁵At the end of 40 days, the men returned from checking out the land.

The Men Report on What They Found

²⁶The men came back to Moses, Aaron and the whole community of Israel. The people were at Kadesh in the Desert of Paran. There the men reported to Moses and Aaron and all the people. They showed them the fruit of the land. ²⁷They gave Moses their report. They said, "We went into the land you sent us to. It really does have plenty of milk and honey! Here's some fruit from the land. ²⁸But the people who live there are powerful. Their cities have high walls around them and are very large. We even saw members of the family line of Anak there. ²⁹The Amalekites live in the Negev Desert. The Hittites, Jebusites and Amorites live in the central hill country. The Canaanites live near the Mediterranean Sea. They also live along the Jordan River."

³⁰Then Caleb interrupted the men speaking to Moses. He said, "We should go up and take the land. We can certainly do it."

³¹But the men who had gone up with him spoke. They said, "We can't attack those people. They are stronger than we are." ³²The men spread a bad report about the land among the Israelites. They said, "The land we checked out destroys those who live in it. All the people we saw there are very big and tall. ³³We saw the Nephilim there. We seemed like grasshoppers in our own eyes. And that's also how we seemed to them." The family line of Anak came from the Nephilim.

The People Refuse to Obey the Lord

14 That night all the members of the community raised their voices. They wept out loud. ²The Israelites spoke against

WHIT'S WISDOM

Numbers 13–14

Siblings Marvin and Tamika Washington came into Whit's End after getting back from their family vacation. Tamika said, "We had a great time! We went to the beach, it was warm, the ocean was so pretty, we made sand castles, and we played volleyball! I loved it!"

I smiled and turned to Marvin. "What did you think?" I asked.

Marvin said, "It was terrible! We went to the beach, it was too hot, the ocean was dirty, sand got in my shorts, and my volleyball team was awful. I hated it!"

Some people like to think about the good things, and some people concentrate on the bad. It was this way when Moses sent spies to scout out Canaan before God's people went into the land. Some said, "It's a land of giants! We'll be stomped on!" while Joshua and Caleb said, "It's a land flowing with milk and honey." God honored Joshua and Caleb because they recognized the good things God was giving to them.

Before you start complaining next time, think about the good things that God has given you.

Moses and Aaron. The whole community said to them, "We wish we had died in Egypt or even in this desert. ³Why is the LORD bringing us to this land? We're going to be killed by swords. Our enemies will capture our wives and children. Wouldn't it be better for us to go back to Egypt?" ⁴They said to one another, "We should choose another leader. We should go back to Egypt."

⁵Then Moses and Aaron fell with their faces to the ground. They did it in front of the whole community of Israel gathered there. ⁶Joshua, the son of Nun, tore his clothes. So did Caleb, the son of Jephunneh. Joshua and Caleb were two of the men who had checked out the land. ⁷They spoke to the whole community of Israel. They said, "We passed through the land and checked it out. It's very good. ⁸If the LORD is pleased with us, he'll lead us into that land. It's a land that has plenty of milk and honey. He'll give it to us. ⁹But don't refuse to obey him. And don't be afraid of the people of the land. We will swallow them up. The LORD is with us. So nothing can save them. Don't be afraid of them."

¹⁰But all the people talked about killing Joshua and Caleb by throwing stones at them. Then the glory of the LORD appeared at the tent of meeting. All the Israelites saw it. ¹¹The LORD said to Moses, "How long will these people not respect me? How long will they refuse to believe in me? They refuse even though I have done many signs among them. ¹²So I will strike them down with a plague. I will destroy them. But I will make you into a greater and stronger nation than they are."

¹³Moses said to the LORD, "Then the Egyptians will hear about it. You used your power to bring these people up from among them. ¹⁴And the Egyptians will tell the people who live in Canaan about it. LORD, they have already heard a lot about you. They've heard that you are with these people. They've heard that you have been seen face to face. They've been told that your cloud stays over them. They've heard that you go in front of them in a pillar of cloud by day. They've been told that you go in front of them in a pillar of fire at night. ¹⁵Suppose you put all these people to death and leave none alive. Then the nations who have heard these things about you will talk. They'll say, ¹⁶'The LORD promised to give these people the land of Canaan. But he wasn't able to bring them into it. So he killed them in the desert.'

¹⁷"Now, Lord, show your strength. You have said, ¹⁸'I am the LORD. I am slow to get angry. I am full of love. I forgive

those who sin. I forgive those who refuse to obey. But I do not let guilty people go without punishing them. I cause the sin of the parents to affect their children, grandchildren and great-grandchildren.' [19]LORD, your love is great. So forgive the sin of these people. Forgive them just as you have done from the time they left Egypt until now."

[20]The LORD replied, "I have forgiven them, just as you asked. [21]You can be sure that I live. You can be just as sure that my glory fills the whole earth. [22]And here is what you can be just as sure of. Not one of these people will see the land I promised to give them. They have seen my glory. They have seen the signs I did in Egypt. And they have seen what I did in the desert. But they did not obey me. And they have tested me ten times. [23]So not even one of them will ever see the land I promised to give to their people of long ago. The person who has not respected me will never see it. [24]But my servant Caleb has a different spirit. He follows me with his whole heart. So I will bring him into the land he went to. And his children after him will receive land there. [25]The Amalekites and the Canaanites are living in the valleys. So turn back tomorrow. Start out toward the desert. Go along the way that leads to the Red Sea."

[26]The LORD said to Moses and Aaron, [27]"How long will this evil community speak against me? I have heard these Israelites talk about how unhappy they are. [28]So tell them, 'Here is what I am announcing. I am the LORD. You can be sure that I live. And here is what you can be just as sure of. I will do to you the very thing that I heard you say. [29]You will die in this desert. Every one of you 20 years old or more will die. Every one of you who was counted in the list of the people will die. Every one of you who has spoken out against me will be wiped out. [30]I lifted up my hand and promised to make this land your home. But now not all of you will enter the land. Caleb, the son of Jephunneh, will enter it. So will Joshua, the son of Nun. They are the only ones who will enter the land. [31]You have said that your enemies would capture your children. But I will bring your children in to enjoy the land you have turned your backs on. [32]As for you, you will die in the desert. [33]Your children will be shepherds here for 40 years. They will suffer because you were not faithful. They will

Sometimes the future can be scary to think about. The Israelites thought so too. Over and over, God told them what He wanted them to do. Often they looked at God's plans and said, "That seems hard" or "We're too scared," and didn't follow His calling. God's plan is always the best, and He promises to be with us to help us succeed.

Isaiah 41:10 reminds us: "Do not be afraid. I am with you. Do not be terrified. I am your God. I will make you strong and help you. I will hold you safe in my hands." God cares just as much for His children today. We can trust that the Lord will help us accomplish whatever He asks us to do.

But what if you're not sure what you're supposed to do with your life? That's okay. We don't always need God to show us what we'll be doing fifteen years from now. Sometimes He just shows us what we should do today. Like asking the new kid to play kickball, or entering the science fair, or learning something new. If we are faithful in the small things, it's great practice for when God calls us to bigger things later in life.

What's something you might like to do when you grow up? Ask your parents if they know anyone who has those jobs. It can be fun to talk to people and ask them questions about what they do and why they enjoy it.

suffer until the last of your bodies lies here in the desert. ³⁴For 40 years you will suffer for your sins. That is one year for each of the 40 days you checked out the land. You will know what it is like to have me against you.' ³⁵I, the LORD, have spoken. I will surely do these things to this entire evil community of Israel. They have joined together against me. They will meet their end in this desert. They will die here."

³⁶So the LORD struck down the men Moses had sent to check out the land. They had returned and had spread a bad report about the land. And that had made the whole community speak out against Moses. ³⁷Those men were to blame for spreading the bad report. So the LORD struck them down. They died of a plague. ³⁸Only two of the men who went to check out the land remained alive. One of them was Joshua, the son of Nun. The other was Caleb, the son of Jephunneh.

³⁹Moses reported to all the Israelites what the LORD had said. And they became very sad. ⁴⁰Early the next morning they set out for the highest point in the hill country. "We have sinned," they said. "Now we are ready to go up to the land the LORD promised to give us."

⁴¹But Moses said, "Why aren't you obeying the LORD's command? You won't succeed. ⁴²So don't go up. The LORD isn't with you. Your enemies will win the battle over you. ⁴³The Amalekites and the Canaanites will meet you on the field of battle. You have turned away from the LORD. So he won't be with you. And you will be killed by swords."

⁴⁴But they wouldn't listen. They still went up toward the highest point in the hill country. They went up even though Moses didn't move from the camp. They went even though the ark of the LORD's covenant didn't move from the camp. ⁴⁵Then the Amalekites and the Canaanites who lived in that hill country came down. They attacked the Israelites. They won the battle over them. They chased the Israelites all the way to Hormah.

Other Offerings

15 Here is what the LORD said to Moses. ²"Say to the Israelites, 'You are going to enter the land I am giving you as a home. ³When you do, you will present

food offerings to the LORD. The animals must come from your herd or flock. The smell of the offerings will please the LORD. They can be either burnt offerings or sacrifices. They can be either for special promises or for feast offerings. Or they can be for offerings you choose to give. ⁴With each of the offerings, the person who brings it must present to the LORD a grain offering. It must be eight cups of the finest flour. It must be mixed with a quart of olive oil. ⁵Also prepare a quart of wine as a drink offering. You must present it with each lamb that you bring for the burnt offering or the sacrifice.

⁶"Prepare a grain offering to present along with a ram. The grain offering must be 16 cups of the finest flour. It must be mixed with two and a half pints of olive oil. ⁷You must bring two and a half pints of wine as a drink offering. Offer everything as a smell that pleases the LORD.

⁸"'Suppose you prepare a young bull as

Jason's Jargon

NUMBERS 15

Find the word *tassels* in this chapter. Tassels are tufts of loose material that hang from curtains or clothes for decorative purposes. In Bible times, each tassel was a reminder of one of God's commandments.

a burnt offering or sacrifice. You prepare it to keep a special promise to the LORD. Or you prepare it to present as a friendship offering. ⁹Then bring a grain offering with the bull. The grain offering must be 24 cups of the finest flour. It must be mixed with two quarts of olive oil. ¹⁰Also bring two quarts of wine as a drink offering. It will be a food offering. Its smell will please the LORD. ¹¹Each bull or ram must be prepared in the same way. Each lamb or young goat must also be prepared in that way. ¹²Do it for each animal. Do it for as many animals as you prepare.

¹³"'Everyone in Israel must do those things in that way. He must do them when he presents a food offering. The smell of

offerings like that pleases the LORD. [14]Everyone must always do what the law requires. It does not matter whether they are an outsider or anyone else living among you. They must do exactly as you do when they present a food offering. The smell of offerings like that pleases the LORD. [15]The community must have the same rules for you and for any outsider living among you. This law will last for all time to come. In the sight of the LORD, the law applies both to you and any outsider. [16]The same laws and rules will apply to you and to any outsider living among you.' "

[17]The LORD said to Moses, [18]"Speak to the Israelites. Say to them, 'You are going to enter the land I am taking you to. [19]You will eat its food. When you do, present part of it as an offering to the LORD. [20]Present a loaf made from the first flour you grind. Present it as an offering from the threshing floor. [21]You must present the offering to the LORD. You must present it from the first grain you grind. You must do it for all time to come.

Offerings for Sins That Aren't Committed on Purpose

[22]"Suppose you as a community fail to keep any of the commands the LORD gave Moses. And suppose you do it without meaning to. [23]That applies to any of the commands the LORD told Moses to give you. And they are in effect from the day the LORD gave them and for all time to come. [24]Suppose the community sins without meaning to. And suppose they do not know they have sinned. Then the whole community must offer a young bull. They must sacrifice it for a burnt offering. Its smell will please the LORD. Along with it, they must offer its required grain offering and drink offering. They must also sacrifice a male goat for a sin offering. [25]With it the priest will pay for the sin of the whole community of Israel. Then they will be forgiven. They did not mean to commit that sin. And they have presented to the LORD a food offering for the wrong thing they did. They have brought a sin offering with it. [26]The LORD will forgive the whole community of Israel and the outsiders living among them. All the people had a part in the sin, even though they did not mean to do it.

[27]"But suppose just one person sins without meaning to. Then that person must bring a female goat for a sin offering. It must be a year old. [28]With it the priest will pay for the person's sin in front of the LORD. The priest will do it for the one who did wrong by sinning without meaning to. When the sin is paid for, that person will be forgiven. [29]The same law applies to everyone who sins without meaning to. It does not matter whether they are an Israelite or an outsider.

[30]"But suppose someone sins on purpose. It does not matter whether they are an Israelite or an outsider. They speak evil things against the LORD. They must be separated from the community of Israel. [31]They have not respected what the LORD has said. They have broken the LORD's commands. They must certainly be separated from the community. They are still guilty.' "

A Man Works on the Sabbath Day

[32]The Israelites were in the desert. One Sabbath day, people saw a man gathering wood. [33]They brought him to Moses and Aaron and the whole community. [34]They kept him under guard. It wasn't clear what should be done to him. [35]Then the LORD said to Moses, "The man must die. The whole community must kill him by throwing stones at him. They must do it outside the camp." [36]So the people took the man outside the camp. There they killed him by throwing stones at him. They did just as the LORD had commanded Moses.

Tassels on Clothes

[37]The LORD said to Moses, [38]"Say to the Israelites, 'You must make tassels on the corners of your clothes. A blue cord must be on each tassel. You must do it for all time to come. [39]You will have the tassels to look at. They will remind you to obey all the LORD's commands. Then you will be faithful to him. You will not chase after what your own hearts and eyes wish for. [40]You will remember to obey all my commands. And you will be set apart for your God. [41]I am the LORD your God. I brought you out of Egypt to be your God. I am the LORD your God.' "

Korah, Dathan and Abiram

16 Korah was the son of Izhar, the son of Kohath. Kohath was the son of Levi. Korah and certain men from the tribe of Reuben turned against Moses. The men from Reuben were Dathan, Abiram and On. Dathan and Abiram were the sons of Eliab. On was the son of Peleth. ²All those men rose up against Moses. And 250 men of Israel joined them. All of them were known as leaders in the community. They had been appointed as members of the ruling body. ³They came as a group to oppose Moses and Aaron. They said to Moses and Aaron, "You have gone too far! The whole community is holy. Every one in it is holy. And the LORD is with them. So why do you put yourselves above the LORD's people?"

⁴When Moses heard what they said, he fell with his face to the ground. ⁵Then he spoke to Korah and all his followers. He said, "In the morning the LORD will show who belongs to him. He will show who is holy. He'll bring that person near him. He'll bring the man he chooses near him. ⁶Korah, here's what you and all your followers must do. Get some shallow cups for burning incense. ⁷Tomorrow put burning coals and incense in them. Offer it to the LORD. The man the LORD chooses will be the one who is holy. You Levites have gone too far!"

⁸Moses also said to Korah, "Listen, you Levites! ⁹The God of Israel has separated you from the rest of the community of Israel. He has brought you near him to work at the LORD's holy tent. He has given you to the people so that you can serve them. Isn't all that enough for you? ¹⁰He has already brought you and all the other Levites near him. But now you want to be priests too. ¹¹You and all your followers have joined together against the LORD. Why are you telling Aaron you aren't happy with him?"

¹²Then Moses sent for Dathan and Abiram, the sons of Eliab. But they said, "We won't come! ¹³You have brought us up out of a land that has plenty of milk and honey. You have brought us here to kill us in this desert. Isn't that enough? Now do you also want to act as if you were ruling over us? ¹⁴Besides, you haven't brought us into a land that has plenty of milk and honey.

You haven't given us fields and vineyards of our own. Do you want to treat these men like slaves? No! We won't come!"

¹⁵Then Moses became very angry. He said to the LORD, "Don't accept their offering. I haven't taken even a donkey from them. In fact, I haven't done anything wrong to any of them."

¹⁶Moses said to Korah, "You and all your followers must stand in front of the LORD tomorrow. You must appear there along with Aaron. ¹⁷Each man must get his shallow cup. He must put incense in it. There will be a total of 250 incense cups. Each man must bring his cup to the LORD. You and Aaron must also bring your cups." ¹⁸So each of them got his cup. He put burning coals and incense in it. All the men came with Moses and Aaron. They stood at the entrance to the tent of meeting. ¹⁹Korah gathered all his followers together at the entrance to the tent. They opposed Moses and Aaron. Then the glory of the LORD appeared to the whole community. ²⁰The LORD said to Moses and Aaron, ²¹"Separate yourselves from these people. Then I can put an end to all of them at once."

²²But Moses and Aaron fell with their faces to the ground. They cried out, "God, you are the God who gives life and breath to all living things. Will you be angry with the whole community when only one man sins?"

²³Then the LORD spoke to Moses. He said, ²⁴"Tell the community, 'Move away from the tents of Korah, Dathan and Abiram.'"

²⁵Moses got up. He went to Dathan and Abiram. The elders of Israel followed him. ²⁶Moses warned the community. He said, "Move away from the tents of these evil men! Don't touch anything that belongs to them. If you do, the LORD will sweep you away because of all their sins." ²⁷So they moved away from the tents of Korah, Dathan and Abiram. Dathan and Abiram had already come out. They were standing at the entrances to their tents. Their wives, children and little ones were standing there with them.

²⁸Then Moses said, "What is about to happen wasn't my idea. The LORD has sent me to do everything I'm doing. Here is how you will know I'm telling you the

truth. [29]These men won't die a natural death. Something will happen to them that doesn't usually happen to people. If what I'm telling you doesn't happen, then you will know that the LORD hasn't sent me. [30]But the LORD will make something totally new happen. The ground will open its mouth and swallow them up. It will swallow up everything that belongs to them. They will be buried alive. When that happens, you will know that these men have disrespected the LORD."

[31]As soon as Moses finished saying all these words, what he had said came true. The ground under them broke open. [32]It opened its mouth. It swallowed up those men. In fact, it swallowed up everyone who lived in their houses. It swallowed all Korah's men. And it swallowed up everything they owned. [33]They went down into the grave alive. Everything they owned went down with them. The ground closed over them and they died. And so they disappeared from the community. [34]All the Israelites around them heard their cries. They ran away from them. They shouted, "The ground is going to swallow us up too!"

[35]Then the LORD sent down fire. It burned up the 250 men offering the incense.

[36]The LORD said to Moses, [37]"Speak to Eleazar the priest. He is the son of Aaron. Remind him that the shallow cups are holy. He must take them out of the ashes. He must scatter the burning coals away from there. [38]The men who sinned used those cups. And it cost them their lives. Hammer the cups into bronze sheets that will cover the altar. The cups were offered to the LORD. They have become holy. Let them serve as a warning to the Israelites."

[39]So the priest Eleazar collected the bronze incense cups. They had been brought by the men who had been burned to death. He had them hammered out to cover the altar. [40]He did just as the LORD had directed Moses to tell him to do. The covering would be a reminder to the Israelites. It would remind them that no one except a son of Aaron should come and burn incense to the LORD. If people other than priests did that, they would become like Korah and his followers.

[41]The next day the whole community of Israel told Moses and Aaron they weren't happy with them. "You have killed the LORD's people," they said.

[42]The community gathered together to oppose Moses and Aaron. The people walked toward the tent of meeting. Suddenly the cloud covered it. The glory of the LORD appeared. [43]Then Moses and Aaron went to the front of the tent of meeting. [44]The LORD said to Moses, [45]"Get away from these people. Then I can put an end to all of them at once." And Moses and Aaron fell with their faces to the ground.

[46]Moses said to Aaron, "Take your incense cup. Put incense in it. And put burning coals from the altar in it. Then hurry to the people and pay for their sin. The LORD has begun to show his anger. The plague has started." [47]So Aaron did as Moses said. He ran in among the people. The plague had already started among them. But Aaron offered the incense and paid for their sin. [48]He stood between those alive and those dead. And the plague stopped. [49]But 14,700 people died from the plague. That doesn't include those who had died because of what Korah did. [50]Then Aaron returned to Moses at the entrance to the tent of meeting. The plague had stopped.

Aaron's Walking Stick Produces Buds

17 The LORD said to Moses, [2]"Speak to the Israelites. Get 12 walking sticks from them. Get one from the leader of each of Israel's tribes. Write the name of each man on his walking stick. [3]Write Aaron's name on Levi's walking stick. There must be one stick for the head of each of Israel's tribes. [4]Put the walking sticks in the tent of meeting. Place them in front of the ark where the tablets of the covenant law are kept. That is where I meet with you. [5]The walking stick that belongs to the man I choose will begin to grow new shoots. The Israelites are never happy with what you do. I will put an end to what they are saying."

[6]So Moses spoke to the Israelites. Their leaders gave him 12 walking sticks. They gave one for the leader of each of Israel's tribes. Aaron's walking stick was among them. [7]Moses put the sticks in front of the

LORD in the tent where the tablets of the covenant law were kept.

[8]The next day Moses entered the tent. He looked at Aaron's walking stick. It stood for the tribe of Levi. Moses saw that it had begun to grow new shoots. It had also produced buds and flowers and almonds. [9]Then Moses brought out all the walking sticks from in front of the LORD. He brought them to all the Israelites. They looked at them. And each man took his own walking stick.

[10]The LORD said to Moses, "Put Aaron's walking stick back in front of the ark where the tablets of the covenant law are kept. The stick will be kept there as a warning to those who refuse to obey. They are never happy with what I do. Aaron's walking stick will put an end to what they are saying. Then they will not die." [11]Moses did just as the LORD commanded him.

[12]The Israelites said to Moses, "We'll die! We are lost! All of us are lost! [13]Anyone who even comes near the LORD's holy tent will die. Are all of us going to die?"

Duties of Priests and Levites

18 The LORD spoke to Aaron. He said, "You, your sons and your family are in charge of the sacred tent. You will be responsible for sins connected with the tent. And you and your sons alone will be responsible for sins connected with the office of priest. [2]Bring the Levites from your tribe to join you. They will help you when you and your sons serve at the tent of meeting. That is where the tablets of the covenant law are kept. [3]The Levites will work for you. They must do everything that needs to be done at the tent. But they must not go near anything that belongs to the sacred tent. And they must not go near the altar. If they do, they and you will die. [4]They will help you take care of the tent of meeting. They will join you in all the work at the tent. No one else can come near you there.

[5]"You will be responsible for taking care of the sacred tent and the altar. Then I will not be angry with the Israelites again. [6]I myself have chosen the Levites. I have chosen them from among the Israelites. They are a gift to you. I have set them apart to do the work at the tent of meeting. [7]But only you and your sons can serve as priests. Only you and your sons can work with everything at the altar and behind the curtain. I am letting you serve as priests. It is a gift from me. Anyone else who comes near the sacred tent must be put to death."

Offerings for Priests and Levites

[8]Then the LORD spoke to Aaron. He said, "I have put you in charge of the offerings brought to me. The Israelites will give me holy offerings. I will give all their offerings to you and your sons. They are the part that belongs to you. They are your share for all time to come. [9]You will have a part of the very holy offerings. It is the part not burned in the fire. That part belongs to you and your sons. You will have a part of all the gifts the people bring me as very holy offerings. It does not matter whether they are grain offerings or sin offerings or guilt offerings. [10]Eat your part as something that is very holy. Every male will eat it. You must consider it holy.

[11]"Part of the gifts the Israelites bring as wave offerings will be set aside. That part will also belong to you. I will give it to you and your sons and daughters. It is your share for all time to come. Everyone in your home who is 'clean' can eat it.

[12]"I will give you all the finest olive oil and grain the people give me. And I will give you all the finest fresh wine they give me. They give all those things as the first share of their harvest. [13]All the first shares of the harvest they bring me will belong to you. Everyone in your home who is 'clean' can eat it.

[14]"Everything in Israel that is set apart to me belongs to you. [15]Offer to me every male born first to its mother. It belongs to you. That includes humans and animals alike. But you must buy back every oldest son. Suppose certain animals are 'unclean.' Then you must buy back every male born first to its mother. [16]When they are a month old, you must buy them back. You must pay the price to buy them back. The price is set at two ounces of silver. It must be weighed out according to the standard weights used in the sacred tent.

[17]"But you must not buy back any male calf, sheep or goat born first. They are holy. Splash their blood against the altar. And burn their fat as a food offering. Its smell pleases me. [18]The meat will belong

to you. It is just like the breast and the right thigh of the wave offering. Those parts belong to you. ¹⁹Part of the holy offerings the Israelites bring to me will be set aside. No matter what it is, I will give it to you and your sons and daughters. It is your share for all time to come. It is a covenant of salt from me. The salt means that the covenant will last for all time to come for you and your children."

²⁰The LORD spoke to Aaron. He said, "You will not receive any part of the land I am giving to Israel. You will not have any share among them. I am your share. I am what you will receive among the Israelites.

²¹"The Israelites will give me a tenth of everything they produce. And I will give it to the Levites. They serve at the tent of meeting. I will give them the tenth for the work they do there. ²²From now on the Israelites must not go near the tent of meeting. If they do, they will be punished for their sin. They will die. ²³The Levites will do the work at the tent of meeting. They will be responsible for any sins connected with the tent. This is a law that will last for all time to come. The Levites will not receive any share among the Israelites. ²⁴Instead, I will give the Levites the tenth as their share. It is the tenth that the Israelites bring me as an offering. That is why I said the Levites would not have any share of land among the Israelites."

²⁵The LORD said to Moses, ²⁶"Speak to the Levites. Say to them, 'You will receive the tenth from the Israelites. I will give it to you as your share. When I do, you must give a tenth of that tenth as an offering to the LORD. ²⁷Your offering will be considered as if you gave grain from a threshing floor. It will be considered as juice from a winepress. ²⁸In that way, you also will bring an offering to the LORD. You will bring it from the tenth you receive from the Israelites. You must give the LORD's part to the priest Aaron. You must bring it from the tenth you receive. ²⁹You must bring to the LORD a part of everything given to you. It must be the best and holiest part.'

³⁰"Say to the Levites, 'You must bring the best part. Then it will be considered as if you gave grain from a threshing floor. It will be considered as juice from a winepress. ³¹You and your families can eat the rest of it anywhere. It is your pay for your work at the tent of meeting. ³²Bring the best part of what you receive. Then you will not be guilty of holding anything back. You will not make the holy offerings of the Israelites "unclean." You will not die.' "

The Special Water That Makes People "Clean"

19 The LORD spoke to Moses and Aaron. He said, ²"Here is what the law I have commanded requires. Tell the Israelites to bring you a young red cow. It must not have any flaws at all. It must never have pulled a load. ³Give it to Eleazar the priest. It must be taken outside the camp and killed in front of him. ⁴Then Eleazar the priest must put some of its blood on his finger. He must sprinkle the blood toward the front of the tent of meeting. He must do it seven times. ⁵While he watches, the young cow must be burned. Its hide, meat, blood and guts must be burned. ⁶The priest must get some cedar wood, branches of a hyssop plant, and bright red wool. He must throw them on the young cow as it burns. ⁷After that, the priest must wash his clothes. He must also take a bath. Then he can come into the camp. But he will be 'unclean' until evening. ⁸The man who burns the young cow must wash his clothes. He must also take a bath. He too will be 'unclean' until evening.

⁹"A man who is 'clean' will gather up the ashes of the young cow. He must put them in a place that is 'clean.' The place must be outside the camp. The ashes must be kept by the community of Israel. They will be added to the special water. The water will be used to make people pure from their sin. ¹⁰The man who gathers up the ashes of the young cow must wash his clothes. He too will be 'unclean' until evening. This law is for the Israelites. It is also for the outsiders living among them. The law will last for all time to come.

¹¹"Anyone who touches a dead person's body will be 'unclean' for seven days. ¹²They must make themselves pure and 'clean' with the special water. They must do it on the third day. They must also do it on the seventh day. Then they will be 'clean.' But suppose they do not make themselves pure and 'clean' on the third and seventh days. Then they will not be 'clean.' ¹³Anyone who touches a dead

person's body and does not make themselves pure and 'clean' makes my holy tent 'unclean.' They must be separated from Israel. The special water has not been sprinkled on them. So they are 'unclean.' And they remain 'unclean.'

¹⁴"Here is the law that applies when a person dies in a tent. Anyone who enters the tent will be 'unclean' for seven days. Anyone in the tent will also be 'unclean' for seven days. ¹⁵And anything in it that is open and has no lid will be 'unclean.'

¹⁶"Suppose someone is out in the country. And suppose they touch someone who has been killed by a sword. Or they touch someone who has died a natural death. Or they touch a human bone or a grave. Then anyone who touches any of those things will be 'unclean' for seven days.

¹⁷"Here is what I want you to do for someone who is 'unclean.' Put some ashes from the burned young cow into a jar. Pour fresh water on the ashes. ¹⁸Then a man who is 'clean' must dip branches of a hyssop plant in the water. He must sprinkle the tent with it. Everything that belongs to the tent must be sprinkled with it. The people in the tent must also be sprinkled. Anyone who has touched a human bone or a grave must be sprinkled. So must anyone who has touched someone who has been killed. And so must anyone who has touched someone who has died a natural death. ¹⁹The man who is 'clean' must sprinkle those who are 'unclean.' That must be done on the third and seventh days. On the seventh day those who are 'unclean' must be made pure and 'clean.' Those being made 'clean' must wash their clothes. They must take a bath. Then that evening they will be 'clean.' ²⁰But what if those who are 'unclean' do not make themselves pure and 'clean?' Then they must be separated from the community. They have made my holy tent 'unclean.' The special water has not been sprinkled on them. They are 'unclean.' ²¹This law will apply to all those people for all time to come.

"The man who sprinkles the special water must also wash his clothes. Anyone who touches the water will be 'unclean' until evening. ²²Anything that an 'unclean' person touches becomes 'unclean.' And anyone who touches it becomes 'unclean' until evening."

The Lord Gives Israel Water Out of the Rock

20 In the first month the whole community of Israel arrived at the Desert of Zin. They stayed at Kadesh. Miriam died and was buried there.

²The people didn't have any water. So they gathered together to oppose Moses and Aaron. ³They argued with Moses. They said, "We wish we had died when our people fell dead in front of the Lord. ⁴Why did you bring the Lord's people into this desert? We and our livestock will die here. ⁵Why did you bring us up out of Egypt? Why did you bring us to this terrible place? It doesn't have any grain or figs. It doesn't have any grapes or pomegranates. There isn't even any water for us to drink!"

⁶Moses and Aaron left the people. They went to the entrance to the tent of meeting. There they fell with their faces to the ground. Then the glory of the Lord appeared to them. ⁷The Lord said to Moses, ⁸"Get your walking stick. You and your brother Aaron gather the people together. Then speak to that rock while everyone is watching. It will pour out its water. You will bring water out of the rock for the community. Then they and their livestock can drink it."

⁹So Moses took the walking stick from the tent. He did just as the Lord had commanded him. ¹⁰He and Aaron gathered the people together in front of the rock. Moses said to them, "Listen, you who refuse to obey! Do we have to bring water out of this rock for you?" ¹¹Then Moses raised his arm. He hit the rock twice with his walking stick. Water poured out. And the people and their livestock drank it.

¹²But the Lord spoke to Moses and Aaron. He said, "You did not trust in me enough to honor me. You did not honor me as the holy God in front of the Israelites. So you will not bring this community into the land I am giving them."

¹³Those were the waters of Meribah. That's where the Israelites argued with the Lord. And that's where he was proven to be holy among them.

Edom Doesn't Let Israel Pass Through Its Territory

¹⁴Moses sent messengers from Kadesh to the king of Edom. The messengers said,

"The nation of Israel is your brother. They say, 'You know about all the hard times we've had. [15]Long ago our people went down into Egypt. We lived there for many years. The Egyptians treated us and our people badly. [16]But we cried out to the LORD. He heard our cry. He sent an angel and brought us out of Egypt.

"'Now here we are at the town of Kadesh. It's on the edge of your territory. [17]Please let us pass through your country. We won't go through any field or vineyard. We won't drink water from any well. We'll travel along the King's Highway. We won't turn to the right or the left. We'll just go straight through your territory.'"

[18]But the people of Edom answered,

"We won't let you pass through here. If you try to, we'll march out against you. We'll attack you with our swords."

[19]The Israelites replied,

"We'll go along the main road. We and our livestock won't drink any of your water. If we do, we'll pay for it. We only want to walk through your country. That's all we ask."

[20]Again the people of Edom answered,

"We won't let you pass through here."

Then the people of Edom marched out against them. They came with a large and powerful army. [21]Edom refused to let Israel go through their territory. So Israel turned away from them.

Aaron Dies

[22]The whole community of Israel started out from Kadesh. They arrived at Mount Hor. [23]It was near the border of Edom. There the LORD spoke to Moses and Aaron. He said, [24]"Aaron will join the members of his family who have already died. He will not enter the land I am giving to the Israelites. Both of you refused to obey my command. You did it at the waters of Meribah. [25]So get Aaron and his son Eleazar. Take them up Mount Hor.

[26]Take Aaron's official robes off of him. Put them on his son Eleazar. Aaron will die on Mount Hor. He will join the members of his family who have already died."

[27]Moses did just as the LORD had commanded. The three men went up Mount Hor while the whole community was watching. [28]Moses took Aaron's official robes off of him. He put them on Aaron's son Eleazar. And Aaron died there on top of the mountain. Then Moses and Eleazar came down from the mountain. [29]The whole community found out that Aaron had died. So all the Israelites mourned for him for 30 days.

Israel Destroys Arad

21 The Canaanite king of the city of Arad lived in the Negev Desert. He heard that Israel was coming along the road to Atharim. So he attacked the Israelites. He captured some of them. [2]Then Israel made a promise to the LORD. They said, "Hand these people over to us. If you do, we will set their cities apart to you in a special way to be destroyed." [3]The LORD gave Israel what they asked for. He handed the Canaanites over to them. Israel completely destroyed them and their towns. So that place was named Hormah.

Moses Makes a Bronze Snake

[4]The Israelites traveled from Mount Hor along the way to the Red Sea. They wanted to go around Edom. But they grew tired on the way. [5]So they spoke against God and against Moses. They said, "Why have you brought us up out of Egypt? Do you want us to die here in the desert? We don't have any bread! We don't have any water! And we hate this awful food!"

[6]Then the LORD sent poisonous snakes among the Israelites. The snakes bit them. Many of the people died. [7]The others came to Moses. They said, "We sinned when we spoke against the LORD and against you. Pray that the LORD will take the snakes away from us." So Moses prayed for the people.

[8]The LORD said to Moses, "Make a snake. Put it up on a pole. Then anyone who is bitten can look at it and remain alive." [9]So Moses made a bronze snake. He put it up on a pole. Then anyone who was

bitten by a snake and looked at the bronze snake remained alive.

The People Continue On to Moab

[10]The Israelites moved on. They camped at Oboth. [11]Then they started out from Oboth. They camped in Iye Abarim. It's in the desert on the eastern border of Moab. [12]From there they moved on. They camped in the Zered Valley. [13]They started out from there and camped by the Arnon River. It's in the desert that spreads out into the territory of the Amorites. The Arnon is the border of Moab. It's between Moab and the Amorites. [14]Here is what the Book of the Wars of the LORD says about it.

"Sing about Zahab in Suphah and the
valleys.
Sing about the Arnon [15]and the
slopes of the valleys.
They lead to the settlement called Ar.
They lie along the border of Moab."

[16]From there the Israelites continued on to Beer. That was the well where the LORD spoke to Moses. He said, "Gather the people together. I will give them water to drink."

[17]Then Israel sang a song. They said,

"Spring up, you well!
Sing about it.
[18] Sing about the well the princes dug.
Sing about the well the nobles of
the people dug.
All their rulers were holding their
scepters and walking sticks."

Then the Israelites went from the desert to Mattanah. [19]They went from Mattanah to Nahaliel. They went from Nahaliel to Bamoth. [20]And they went from Bamoth to a valley in Moab. It's the valley where the highest slopes of Pisgah look out over a dry and empty land.

Israel Wins the Battle Over Sihon and Og

[21]The Israelites sent messengers to speak to Sihon. He was the king of the Amorites. The messengers said to him,

[22]"Let us pass through your country. We won't go off the road into any field or vineyard. We won't drink water from any well. We'll travel along the King's Highway. We'll just go straight through your territory."

[23]But Sihon wouldn't let Israel pass through his territory. He gathered his whole army together. Then he marched out into the desert against Israel. When he reached Jahaz, he fought against Israel. [24]But Israel put him to death with their swords. They took over his land. They took everything from the Arnon River to the Jabbok River. But they didn't take over any of the land of the Ammonites. That's because the Ammonites had built strong forts along their border. [25]The Israelites captured all the cities of the Amorites. Then they settled down in them. They captured the city of Heshbon. They also captured all the settlements around it. [26]Sihon, the king of the Amorites, ruled in Heshbon. He had fought against an earlier king of Moab. Sihon had taken from him all his land all the way to the Arnon River. [27]That's why the poets say,

"Come to Heshbon. Let it be built
again.
Let Sihon's city be made as good as
new.

[28] "Fire went out from Heshbon.
A blaze went out from the city of
Sihon.
It burned up Ar in Moab.
It burned up the citizens who lived
on Arnon's hills.
[29] Moab, how terrible it is for you!
People of Chemosh, you are
destroyed!
Chemosh has deserted his sons and
daughters.
His sons have run away from the
battle.
His daughters have become prisoners.
He has handed all of them over to
Sihon,
the king of the Amorites.

[30] "But we have taken them over.
Heshbon's rule has been destroyed
all the way to Dibon.
We have destroyed them as far as
Nophah.
Nophah goes all the way to
Medeba."

[31]So Israel settled in the land of the Amorites.

[32]Moses sent spies to the city of Jazer. The Israelites captured the settlements around it. They drove out the Amorites who were there. [33]Then they turned and went up along the road toward Bashan. Og was the king of Bashan. He and his whole army marched out. They went to fight against Israel at Edrei.

[34]The Lord said to Moses, "Do not be afraid of Og. I have handed him over to you. I have given you his whole army. I have also given you his land. Do to him what you did to Sihon, the king of the Amorites. He ruled in Heshbon."

[35]So the Israelites struck down Og and his sons. And they wiped out his whole army. They didn't leave anyone alive. They took over his land for themselves.

Balak Sends For Balaam

22 Then the Israelites traveled to the plains of Moab. They camped along the Jordan River across from Jericho.

[2]Balak saw everything that Israel had done to the Amorites. Balak was the son of Zippor. [3]The Moabites were terrified because there were so many Israelites. In fact, the Moabites were filled with panic because of the Israelites.

[4]The Moabites spoke to the elders of Midian. They said, "This huge mob is going to destroy everything around us. They'll lick it up as an ox licks up all the grass in the fields."

Balak, the son of Zippor, was the king of Moab at that time. [5]He sent messengers to get Balaam. Balaam was the son of Beor. Balaam was at the city of Pethor near the Euphrates River. Pethor was in the land where Balaam had been born. Balak told the messengers to say to Balaam,

"A nation has come out of Egypt. They are covering the face of the land. They've set up camp next to me. [6]So come and put a curse on these people. They are too powerful for me. Maybe I'll be able to win the battle over them. Maybe I'll be able to drive them out of the land. I know that whoever you bless is blessed. And I know that whoever you cursed is cursed."

[7]The elders of Moab and Midian left. They took with them the money they knew Balaam would ask for. They wanted him to use evil magic to figure things out for them. They came to where Balaam was. And they told him what Balak had said.

[8]"Spend the night here," Balaam said to them. "I'll report back to you with the answer the Lord gives me." So the Moabite officials stayed with him.

[9]God came to Balaam. He asked, "Who are these men with you?"

[10]Balaam said to God, "Balak king of Moab, the son of Zippor, sent me a message. [11]He said, 'A nation has come out of Egypt. They are covering the whole surface of the land. So come and put a curse on them for me. Maybe I'll be able to fight them. Maybe I'll be able to drive them away.'"

[12]But God said to Balaam, "Do not go with them. You must not put a curse on those people. I have blessed them."

[13]The next morning Balaam got up. He said to Balak's officials, "Go back to your own country. The Lord won't let me go with you."

[14]So the Moabite officials returned to Balak. They said, "Balaam wouldn't come with us."

[15]Then Balak sent other officials. They were more important than the first ones. And there were more of them. [16]They came to Balaam. They said,

"Balak, the son of Zippor, says, 'Don't let anything keep you from coming to me. [17]I'll make you very rich. I'll do anything you say. So come and put a curse on those people for me.'"

[18]But Balaam gave them his answer. He said, "Balak could give me all the silver and gold in his palace. Even then, I still couldn't do anything at all that goes beyond what the Lord my God commands. [19]Now spend the night here so that I can find out what else the Lord will tell me."

[20]That night God came to Balaam. He said, "These men have come to get you. So go with them. But do only what I tell you to do."

Balaam's Donkey

²¹Balaam got up in the morning. He put a saddle on his donkey. Then he went with the Moabite officials. ²²But God was very angry when Balaam went. So the angel of the LORD stood in the road to oppose him. Balaam was riding on his donkey. His two servants were with him. ²³The donkey saw the angel of the LORD standing in the road. The angel was holding a sword. He was ready for battle. So the donkey left the road and went into a field. Balaam hit the donkey. He wanted to get it back on the road.

²⁴Then the angel of the LORD stood in a narrow path. The path went through the vineyards. There were walls on both sides. ²⁵The donkey saw the angel of the LORD. So it moved close to the wall. It crushed Balaam's foot against the wall. So he hit the donkey again.

²⁶Then the angel of the LORD moved on ahead. He stood in a narrow place. There was no room to turn, either right or left. ²⁷The donkey saw the angel of the LORD. So it lay down under Balaam. That made him angry. He hit the donkey with his walking stick. ²⁸Then the LORD opened the donkey's mouth. It said to Balaam, "What have I done to you? Why did you hit me these three times?"

²⁹Balaam answered the donkey. He said, "You have made me look foolish! I wish I had a sword in my hand. If I did, I'd kill you right now."

³⁰The donkey said to Balaam, "I'm your own donkey. I'm the one you have always ridden. Haven't you been riding me to this very day? Have I ever made you look foolish before?"

"No," he said.

³¹Then the LORD opened Balaam's eyes. He saw the angel of the LORD standing in the road. He saw that the angel was holding a sword. The angel was ready for battle. So Balaam bowed down. He fell with his face to the ground.

Num. 22:21-39 You've got to read this amazing story—it's about Jack or . . . Jenny. (A Jack is a boy donkey. A Jenny is a girl donkey.) This is a pretty exciting angel-sighting.

³²The angel of the LORD spoke to him. He asked him, "Why have you hit your donkey three times? I have come here to oppose you. What you are doing is foolish. ³³The donkey saw me. It turned away from me three times. Suppose it had not turned away. Then I would certainly have killed you by now. But I would have spared the donkey."

³⁴Balaam said to the angel of the LORD, "I have sinned. I didn't realize you were standing in the road to oppose me. Tell me whether you are pleased with me. If you aren't, I'll go back."

³⁵The angel of the LORD said to Balaam, "Go with the men. But say only what I tell you to say." So Balaam went with Balak's officials.

³⁶Balak heard that Balaam was coming. So he went out to meet him. They met at a Moabite town near the Arnon River. The town was on the border of Balak's territory. ³⁷Balak said to Balaam, "Didn't I send messengers to you? I wanted you to come quickly. So why didn't you come? I can make you very rich."

³⁸"Well, I've come to you now," Balaam replied. "But I can't say whatever I please. I can only speak the words God puts in my mouth."

³⁹Then Balaam went with Balak to Kiriath Huzoth. ⁴⁰Balak sacrificed cattle and sheep. He gave some to Balaam. He also gave some to the officials with him.

BIBLE ADVENTURES

Olivia saw the story of Balaam and his donkey in the Imagination Station in "Hidden Gems" (Club).

[41]The next morning Balak took Balaam up to Bamoth Baal. From there he could see the outer edges of the Israelite camp.

Balaam's First Message From God

23 Balaam said to Balak, "Build me seven altars here. Prepare seven bulls and seven rams for me to sacrifice." [2]Balak did just as Balaam said. The two of them offered a bull and a ram on each altar.

[3]Then Balaam said to Balak, "Stay here beside your offering. I'll go and try to find out what the LORD wants me to do. Maybe he'll come and meet with me. Then I'll tell you what he says to me." So Balaam went off to a bare hilltop.

[4]God met with him there. Balaam said, "I've prepared seven altars. On each altar I've offered a bull and a ram."

[5]The LORD put a message in Balaam's mouth. The LORD said, "Go back to Balak. Give him my message."

[6]So Balaam went back to him. He found Balak standing beside his offering. All the Moabite officials were with him. [7]Then Balaam spoke the message he had received from God. He said,

"Balak brought me from the land of
      Aram.
   The king of Moab sent for me from
      the mountains in the east.
'Come,' he said. 'Put a curse on Jacob's
      people for me.
   Come. Speak against Israel.'
[8] But how can I put a curse on
      people God hasn't cursed?
   How can I speak against
      people the LORD hasn't spoken
         against?
[9] I see them from the rocky peaks.
   I view them from the hills.
I see a group of people who live by
      themselves.
   They don't consider themselves to
      be one of the nations.
[10] Jacob's people are like the dust of the
      earth.
   Can dust be counted?
   Who can count even a fourth of the
      Israelites?
Let me die as godly people die.
   Let my death be like theirs!"

[11]Balak said to Balaam, "What have you done to me? I brought you here to put a curse on my enemies! But all you have done is give them a blessing!"

[12]He answered, "I have to speak only the words the LORD puts in my mouth."

Balaam's Second Message From God

[13]Then Balak said to Balaam, "Come with me to another place. You can see the Israelites from there. You won't see all of them. You will only see the outer edges of their camp. From there, put a curse on them for me." [14]So Balak took Balaam to the field of Zophim. It was on the highest slopes of Pisgah. There Balak built seven altars. He offered a bull and a ram on each altar.

[15]Balaam said to Balak, "Stay here beside your offering. I'll meet with the LORD over there."

[16]The LORD met with Balaam. He put a message in Balaam's mouth. The LORD said, "Go back to Balak. Give him my message."

[17]So Balaam went to Balak. He found him standing beside his offering. The Moabite officials were with him. Balak asked him, "What did the LORD say?"

[18]Then Balaam spoke the message he had received from God. He said,

"Balak, rise up and listen.
   Son of Zippor, hear me.
[19] God isn't a mere human. He can't lie.
   He isn't a human being. He doesn't
      change his mind.
He speaks, and then he acts.
   He makes a promise, and then he
      keeps it.
[20] He has commanded me to bless Israel.
   He has given them his blessing.
   And I can't change it.

[21] "I don't see any trouble coming on the
      people of Jacob.
   I don't see any suffering in Israel.
The LORD their God is with them.
   The shout of the King is among
      them.
[22] God brought them out of Egypt.
   They are as strong as a wild ox.
[23] There isn't any magic that can hurt the
      people of Jacob.
   No one can use magic words to
      harm Israel.

Here is what will be said about the
   people of Jacob.
Here is what will be said about
   Israel.
People will say, 'See what God has
   done!'
24 The Israelites are going to wake up like
      a female lion.
They are going to get up like a male
   lion.
They are like a lion that won't rest
   until it eats what it has caught.
They are like a lion that won't rest
   until it drinks the blood of what it
   has killed."

25Then Balak said to Balaam, "Don't
put a curse on them at all! And don't give
them a blessing at all!"

26Balaam answered, "Didn't I tell you
that I must do only what the LORD says?"

Balaam's Third Message From God

27Then Balak said to Balaam, "Come.
Let me take you to another place. Perhaps
God will be pleased to let you put a curse
on the Israelites for me from there." 28Ba-
lak took Balaam to the top of Mount Peor.
It looks out over a dry and empty land.

29Balaam said, "Build me seven altars
here. Prepare seven bulls and seven rams
for me to sacrifice." 30Balak did just as Balaam said. He offered a bull and a ram on
each altar.

24 Balaam saw that the LORD was
pleased to give his blessing to Israel.
So he didn't try to use evil magic as he had
done at other times. Instead, he turned
and looked toward the desert. 2He looked
out and saw Israel. They had set up their
camps tribe by tribe. The Spirit of God
came on him. 3Balaam spoke the message
he had received from God. He said,

"Here is the message God gave
   Balaam, the son of Beor.
It's the message God gave to the
   one who sees clearly.
4 It's the message God gave to the one
   who hears the words of God.
He sees a vision from the Mighty
   One.
He falls down flat with his face toward
   the ground.
His eyes have been opened by the
   LORD.

5 "People of Jacob, your tents are very
      beautiful.
Israel, the places where you live are
   very beautiful.
6 "They spread out like valleys.
They are like gardens beside a river.
They are like aloes the LORD has
   planted.
They are like cedar trees beside a
   stream.
7 Their water buckets will run over.
Their seeds will have plenty of
   water.

"Their king will be greater than King
      Agag.
Their kingdom will be honored.
8 "God brought them out of Egypt.
They are as strong as a wild ox.
They destroy nations at war with
      them.
They break their bones in pieces.
They wound them with their
   arrows.
9 Like a male lion they lie down and
      sleep.
They are like a female lion.
Who dares to wake them up?

"May those who bless you be blessed!
   May those who curse you be
      cursed!"

10Then Balak became very angry with
Balaam. He slapped his hands together.
He said to Balaam, "I sent for you to put
a curse on my enemies. But you have
given them a blessing three times. 11Get
out of here right away! Go home! I said
I'd make you very rich. But the LORD has
kept you from getting rich."

12Balaam answered Balak, "Here is
what I told the messengers you sent me.
13I said, 'Balak could give me all the silver
and gold in his palace. Even if I wanted to,
I still couldn't do anything at all that goes
beyond what the LORD commands. I must
say only what the LORD tells me to say.'
14Now I'm going back to my people. But
come. Let me warn you about what these
people will do to your people in days to
come."

Balaam's Fourth Message From God

15Then Balaam spoke the message he
had received from God. He said,

"Here is the message God gave
  Balaam, the son of Beor.
It's the message God gave to the
  one who sees clearly.
[16] It's the message God gave to the one
    who hears the words of God.
The Most High God has given him
  knowledge.
He sees a vision from the Mighty One.
He falls down flat with his face
  toward the ground.
His eyes have been opened by the
  LORD.

[17] "I see him, but I don't see him now.
I view him, but he isn't near.
A star will come from among the
  people of Jacob.
A king will rise up out of Israel.
He'll crush the foreheads of the people
  of Moab.
He'll crush the heads of all the
  people of Sheth.
[18] He'll win the battle over Edom.
He'll win the battle over his enemy
  Seir.
But Israel will grow strong.
[19] A ruler will come from among the
  people of Jacob.
He'll destroy those from the city
  who are still alive."

Balaam's Fifth Message From God

[20] Then Balaam saw the Amalekites. He spoke the message he had received from God. He said,

"Amalek was the first nation to attack
  Israel.
But their end will be total
  destruction."

Balaam's Sixth Message From God

[21] Then Balaam saw the Kenites. He spoke the message he had received from God. He said,

"The place where you live is safe.
Your nest is on a high cliff.
[22] But you Kenites will be destroyed.
Ashur will take you as prisoners."

Balaam's Seventh Message From God

[23] Then Balaam spoke the message he had received from God. He said,

"Who can live when God does this?
[24]   Ships will come from the shores of
      Cyprus.
They will bring Ashur and Eber under
  their control.
But they themselves will also be
  destroyed."

[25] Then Balaam got up and returned home. And Balak went on his way.

Moab Leads Israel Astray

25 Israel was staying in Shittim. The men of Israel began to commit sexual sins with the women of Moab. [2] The women invited the men to feasts and sacrifices to honor their gods. The people ate the sacrifices and bowed down in front of the statues of those gods. [3] So Israel joined in worshiping the god named Baal that was worshiped at Peor. The LORD became very angry with Israel.

[4] The LORD said to Moses, "Take all the leaders of these people. Kill them. Put their dead bodies out in the open. I want to see you do it in the middle of the day. Then I will not be angry with Israel."

[5] So Moses spoke to Israel's judges. He said, "Some of your people have joined in worshiping the god named Baal that is worshiped at Peor. Each of you must kill the people in your tribe who have done that."

[6] Then an Israelite man brought into the camp a Midianite woman. He did it right in front of the eyes of Moses and the whole community of Israel. They were weeping at the entrance to the tent of meeting. [7] Phinehas was a priest. He was the son of Eleazar, the son of Aaron. When Phinehas saw what had happened, he left the people. He took a spear in his hand. [8] He followed the man into the tent. Phinehas stuck the spear through the man and into the woman's stomach. Then the LORD stopped the plague against the Israelites. [9] But the plague had already killed 24,000 of them.

[10] The LORD said to Moses, [11] "Phinehas is a priest. He is the son of Eleazar, the son of Aaron. Phinehas has turned my anger away from the Israelites. I am committed to making sure I am honored among them. And he is as committed as I am. So even though I was angry with them, I did not put an end to them. [12] So tell Phinehas I am making my covenant with him. It is

my promise to give him peace. [13]He and his sons after him will have a covenant to be priests forever. That is because he was committed to making sure that I, his God, was honored. In that way he paid for the sin of the Israelites."

[14]The name of the Israelite man who was killed was Zimri. He was the son of Salu. Zimri was killed along with the Midianite woman. Salu was a family leader in the tribe of Simeon. [15]The name of the Midianite woman who was killed was Kozbi. She was the daughter of Zur. He was the chief of a Midianite family.

[16]The LORD spoke to Moses. He said, [17]"Treat the Midianites just as you would treat enemies. Kill them. [18]After all, they treated you like enemies. They tricked you into worshiping the god named Baal that is worshiped at Peor. They also tricked you because of what Kozbi did. She was the woman killed when the plague came that was connected with Peor. Kozbi was the daughter of a Midianite leader."

The Men of Israel Are Counted a Second Time

26 After the plague, the LORD spoke to Moses and Eleazar the priest. Eleazar was the son of Aaron. The LORD said, [2]"Count all the men of Israel. Make a list of them by their families. Count all the men who are able to serve in Israel's army. They must be 20 years old or more."

[3]At that time the Israelites were on the plains of Moab. They were by the Jordan River across from Jericho. Moses and Eleazar the priest spoke with them. They said, [4]"Count all the men 20 years old or more. Do it just as the LORD commanded Moses."

Here are the men of Israel who came out of Egypt.

[5] Reuben was Israel's oldest son. Here are the names of his sons.
The Hanokite family came from Hanok.
The Palluite family came from Pallu.
[6] The Hezronite family came from Hezron.
The Karmite family came from Karmi.

[7] These were the families of Reuben. The number of men was 43,730.

[8] Eliab was the son of Pallu. [9]Eliab's sons were Nemuel, Dathan and Abiram. Dathan and Abiram were the same community officials who refused to obey Moses and Aaron. They were among the followers of Korah who refused to obey the LORD. [10]The ground opened its mouth. It swallowed them up along with Korah. The followers of Korah died when fire burned up 250 men. Their deaths were a warning to the rest of Israel. [11]But the family line of Korah didn't die out completely.

[12] Here are the names of Simeon's sons. They are listed by their families.
The Nemuelite family came from Nemuel.
The Jaminite family came from Jamin.
The Jakinite family came from Jakin.
[13] The Zerahite family came from Zerah.
The Shaulite family came from Shaul.

[14] These were the families of Simeon. The number of the men counted was 22,200.

[15] Here are the names of Gad's sons. They are listed by their families.
The Zephonite family came from Zephon.
The Haggite family came from Haggi.
The Shunite family came from Shuni.
[16] The Oznite family came from Ozni.
The Erite family came from Eri.
[17] The Arodite family came from Arodi.
The Arelite family came from Areli.

[18] These were the families of Gad. The number of the men counted was 40,500.

[19] Er and Onan were sons of Judah. But they died in Canaan.

20 Here are the names of Judah's sons. They are listed by their families. The Shelanite family came from Shelah. The Perezite family came from Perez. The Zerahite family came from Zerah. 21 Here are the names of the sons of Perez.

The Hezronite family came from Hezron. The Hamulite family came from Hamul. 22 These were the families of Judah. The number of the men counted was 76,500.

23 Here are the names of Issachar's sons. They are listed by their families. The Tolaite family came from Tola. The Puite family came from Puah. 24 The Jashubite family came from Jashub. The Shimronite family came from Shimron. 25 These were the families of Issachar. The number of the men counted was 64,300.

26 Here are the names of Zebulun's sons. They are listed by their families. The Seredite family came from Sered. The Elonite family came from Elon. The Jahleelite family came from Jahleel. 27 These were the families of Zebulun. The number of the men counted was 60,500.

28 Here are the names of Joseph's sons. They are listed by their families. The families came from Manasseh and Ephraim, the sons of Joseph. 29 Here are the names of Manasseh's sons.

The Makirite family came from Makir. Makir was the father of Gilead. The Gileadite family came from Gilead.

30 Here are the names of Gilead's sons. The Iezerite family came from Iezer. The Helekite family came from Helek. 31 The Asrielite family came from Asriel. The Shechemite family came from Shechem. 32 The Shemidaite family came from Shemida. The Hepherite family came from Hepher. 33 Zelophehad was the son of Hepher. Zelophehad didn't have any sons. All he had was daughters. Their names were Mahlah, Noah, Hoglah, Milkah and Tirzah.

34 These were the families of Manasseh. The number of the men counted was 52,700.

35 Here are the names of Ephraim's sons. They are listed by their families. The Shuthelahite family came from Shuthelah. The Bekerite family came from Beker. The Tahanite family came from Tahan. 36 The sons of Shuthelah were the Eranite family. They came from Eran.

37 These were the families of Ephraim. The number of the men counted was 32,500.

These were the sons of Joseph. They are listed by their families.

38 Here are the names of Benjamin's sons. They are listed by their families. The Belaite family came from Bela. The Ashbelite family came from Ashbel. The Ahiramite family came from Ahiram. 39 The Shuphamite family came from Shupham. The Huphamite family came from Hupham. 40 Bela's sons came from Ard and Naaman.

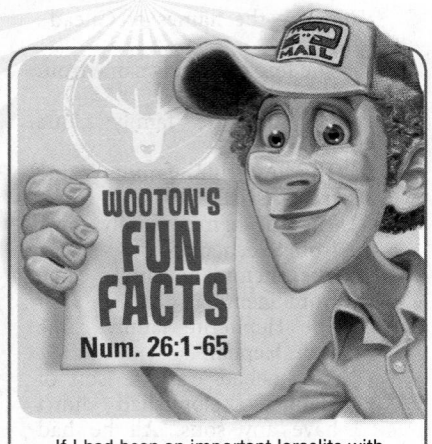

WOOTON'S FUN FACTS

Num. 26:1-65

If I had been an important Israelite with land, my clan would be described like this: "The Wootonite family came from Wooton. Wooton also had a wife named Penny and a dog named Sam."

The Ardite family came from Ard.

The Naamite family came from Naaman.

⁴¹ These were the families of Benjamin. The number of the men counted was 45,600.

⁴² Here is the name of Dan's son. He is listed by his family.

The Shuhamite family came from Shuham.

This was the family of Dan. ⁴³ All the men in Dan's family were Shuhamites. The number of the men counted was 64,400.

⁴⁴ Here are the names of Asher's sons. They are listed by their families.

The Imnite family came from Imnah.

The Ishvite family came from Ishvi.

The Beriite family came from Beriah.

⁴⁵ Here are the names of the families that came from Beriah's sons.

The Heberite family came from Heber.

The Malkielite family came from Malkiel.

⁴⁶ Asher also had a daughter named Serah.

⁴⁷ These were the families of Asher. The number of the men counted was 53,400.

⁴⁸ Here are the names of Naphtali's sons. They are listed by their families.

The Jahzeelite family came from Jahzeel.

The Gunite family came from Guni.

⁴⁹ The Jezerite family came from Jezer.

The Shillemite family came from Shillem.

⁵⁰ These were the families of Naphtali. The number of the men counted was 45,400.

⁵¹ The total number of the men of Israel was 601,730.

⁵² The Lord said to Moses, ⁵³ "I will give the land to them. The amount of land each family receives will be based on the number of its men. ⁵⁴ Give a larger share to a larger family. Give a smaller share to a smaller family. Each family will receive its share based on the number of men listed in it.

⁵⁵ "Be sure that you cast lots when you give out the land. What each family receives will be based on the number of men listed in its tribe. ⁵⁶ Cast lots when you give out each share. Cast lots for the larger and smaller families alike."

⁵⁷ Here are the names of the Levites. They are listed by their families.

The Gershonite family came from Gershon.

The Kohathite family came from Kohath.

The Merarite family came from Merari.

⁵⁸ Here are the names of the other Levite families. They are the Libnite family, the Hebronite family, the Mahlite family, the Mushite family, the Korahite family.

Amram came from the Kohathite family. ⁵⁹ The name of Amram's wife was Jochebed. She was from the family line of Levi. She was born to the Levites in Egypt. Aaron, Moses and their sister Miriam were born in the family line of Amram and Jochebed. ⁶⁰Aaron was the father of Nadab and Abihu. He was also the father of Eleazar and Ithamar. ⁶¹But Nadab and Abihu made an offering to the Lord by using fire that wasn't allowed. So they died.

⁶² The number of male Levites a month old or more was 23,000. They weren't listed along with the other men of Israel. That's because they didn't receive a share among them.

⁶³These are the men counted by Moses and Eleazar the priest. At that time the Israelites were on the plains of Moab. They were by the Jordan River across from Jericho. ⁶⁴The men of Israel had been counted before in the Sinai Desert by Moses and Aaron the priest. But not one of them was among the men counted this time. ⁶⁵The Lord had told the Israelites at Kadesh Barnea that they would certainly die in the desert. Not one of them was left alive except Caleb and Joshua. Caleb was the son of Jephunneh, and Joshua was the son of Nun.

Zelophehad's Daughters

27 The daughters of Zelophehad belonged to the family groups of Manasseh. Zelophehad was the son of Hepher. Hepher was the son of Gilead. Gilead was the son of Makir. Makir was the son of Manasseh. And Manasseh was the son of Joseph. The names of Zelophehad's daughters were Mahlah, Noah, Hoglah, Milkah and Tirzah. They approached ²the entrance to the tent of meeting. There they stood in front of Moses and Eleazar the priest. The leaders and the whole community were there too. Zelophehad's daughters said, ³"Our father died in the Sinai Desert. But he wasn't one of the men who followed Korah. He wasn't one of those who joined together against the Lord. Our father died because of his own sin. He didn't leave any sons. ⁴Why should our father's name disappear from his family just because he didn't have a son? Give us property among our father's relatives."

⁵So Moses brought their case to the Lord. ⁶The Lord said to him, ⁷"What Zelophehad's daughters are saying is right. You must certainly give them property. Give them a share among their father's relatives. Give their father's property to them.

⁸"Say to the Israelites, 'Suppose a man dies who doesn't have a son. Then give his property to his daughter. ⁹Suppose the man doesn't have a daughter. Then give his property to his brothers. ¹⁰Suppose the man doesn't have any brothers. Then give his property to his father's brothers. ¹¹Suppose his father doesn't have any brothers. Then give his property to the nearest male relative in his family group. It will belong to him. That is what the law will require of the Israelites. It is just as the Lord commanded me.'"

Joshua Becomes Israel's New Leader

¹²Then the Lord said to Moses, "Go up this mountain in the Abarim Range. See the land I have given the Israelites. ¹³After you have seen it, you too will join the members of your family who have already died. You will die, just as your brother Aaron did. ¹⁴The community refused to obey me at the waters of Meribah Kadesh in the Desert of Zin. At that time, you and Aaron did not obey my command. You did not honor me in front of them as the holy God."

¹⁵Moses spoke to the Lord. He said, ¹⁶"Lord, you are the God who gives life

and breath to all living things. Please put someone in charge of this community. [17]Have that person lead them and take care of them. Then your people won't be like sheep without a shepherd."

[18]So the LORD said to Moses, "Joshua, the son of Nun, has the ability to be a wise leader. Get him and place your hand on him. [19]Have him stand in front of Eleazar the priest and the whole community. Put him in charge while everyone is watching. [20]Give him some of your authority. Then the whole community of Israel will obey him. [21]Joshua will stand in front of Eleazar the priest. Eleazar will help him make decisions. Eleazar will get help from me by using the Urim. Joshua and the whole community of Israel must not make any move at all unless I command them to."

[22]Moses did just as the LORD commanded him. He got Joshua and had him stand in front of Eleazar the priest and the whole community. [23]Then Moses placed his hands on Joshua. And he put him in charge of the people. He did just as the LORD had directed through Moses.

Offerings That Israel Must Bring Each Day

28 The LORD said to Moses, [2]"Here is a command I want you to give the Israelites. Tell them, 'Make sure to present to me my food offerings. Do it at the appointed time. Their smell will please me.' [3]Tell them, 'Here is the food offering you must present to the LORD. Present to him two lambs a year old. They must not have any flaws. Present them as a regular burnt offering each day. [4]Offer one lamb in the morning. Offer the other when the sun goes down. [5]Present a grain offering along with them. It must have eight cups of the finest flour. Mix it with a quart of oil made from pressed olives. [6]It is the regular burnt offering. The LORD established it at Mount Sinai. It has a pleasant smell. It is a food offering presented to the LORD. [7]Along with that, offer a quart of wine as a drink offering. It must be given along with each lamb. Pour out the drink offering to the LORD at the sacred tent. [8]Offer the second lamb when the sun goes down. Sacrifice it along with the same kind of grain offering and drink offering that you

present in the morning. It is a food offering. Its smell pleases the LORD.

Offerings That Israel Must Bring on the Sabbath Day

[9]"'On the Sabbath day, make an offering of two lambs. They must be a year old. They must not have any flaws. Sacrifice them along with their drink offering. Sacrifice them along with a grain offering of 16 cups of the finest flour. Mix it with olive oil. [10]It is the burnt offering for every Sabbath day. It is in addition to the regular burnt offering and its drink offering.

Offerings That Israel Must Bring Every Month

[11]"'On the first day of every month, bring to the LORD a burnt offering. Bring two young bulls and one ram. Also bring seven male lambs a year old. They must not have any flaws. [12]Present a grain offering along with each bull. It must have 24 cups of the finest flour. Mix it with olive oil. Present a grain offering along with the ram. It must have 16 cups of the finest flour. Mix it with oil. [13]Present a grain offering along with each lamb. It must have eight cups of the finest flour. Mix it with oil. It is for a burnt offering. It has a pleasant smell. It is a food offering presented to the LORD. [14]Present a drink offering along with each bull. It must have two quarts of wine. Offer two and a half pints along with the ram. And offer one quart along with each lamb. It is the burnt offering for each month. It must be made on the day of each New Moon feast during the year. [15]One male goat must be sacrificed to the LORD as a sin offering. It is in addition to the regular burnt offering and its drink offering.

The Passover Feast

[16]"'The LORD's Passover Feast must be held on the 14th day of the first month. [17]On the 15th day of the month there must be a feast. For seven days eat bread made without yeast. [18]On the first day come together for a special service. Do not do any regular work. [19]Present to the LORD a food offering. Present a burnt offering of two young bulls and one ram. Also present seven male lambs a year old. They must not have any flaws. [20]Present a grain

offering along with each bull. The offering must have 24 cups of the finest flour. Mix it with olive oil. Offer 16 cups along with the ram. [21]Offer eight cups along with each of the seven lambs. [22]Include a male goat as a sin offering. It will pay for your sin. [23]Offer everything in addition to the regular morning burnt offering. [24]Present the food offering every day for seven days. The smell of the offering will please the LORD. You must present the offering in addition to the regular burnt offering and its drink offering. [25]On the seventh day come together for a special service. Do not do any regular work.

The Feast of Weeks

[26]"On the day you gather the first share of your crops, present to the LORD an offering of your first grain. Do it during the Feast of Weeks. Come together for a special service. Do not do any regular work. [27]Sacrifice a burnt offering of two young bulls and one ram. Also sacrifice seven male lambs a year old. The smell of the offering will please the LORD. [28]Present a grain offering along with each bull. It must have 24 cups of the finest flour. Mix it with olive oil. Offer 16 cups along with the ram. [29]Offer eight cups along with each of the seven lambs. [30]Include a male goat to pay for your sin. [31]Present everything along with the drink offerings. Do it in addition to the regular burnt offering and its grain offering. Be sure the animals do not have any flaws.

The Feast of Trumpets

29 "On the first day of the seventh month, come together for a special service. Do not do any regular work. Blow the trumpets on that day. [2]Sacrifice a burnt offering. Its smell will please the LORD. Sacrifice one young bull and one ram. Also sacrifice seven male lambs a year old. They must not have any flaws. [3]Present a grain offering along with the bull. It must have 24 cups of the finest flour. Mix it with olive oil. Offer 16 cups along with the ram. [4]Offer eight cups along with each of the seven lambs. [5]Include a male goat as a sin offering. It will pay for your sin. [6]Each month and each day you must sacrifice burnt offerings. Sacrifice them along with their grain offerings and drink offerings

as they are required. The offerings for the Feast of Trumpets are in addition to the monthly and daily burnt offerings. They are food offerings presented to the LORD. They have a pleasant smell.

The Day When Sin Is Paid For

[7]"On the tenth day of the seventh month, come together for a special service. You must not eat anything on that day. You must not do any work on it. [8]Sacrifice a burnt offering. Its smell will please the LORD. Sacrifice one young bull and one ram. Also sacrifice seven male lambs a year old. They must not have any flaws. [9]Present a grain offering along with the bull. The offering must have 24 cups of the finest flour. Mix it with olive oil. Offer 16 cups along with the ram. [10]Offer eight cups along with each of the seven lambs. [11]Include a male goat as a sin offering. It is in addition to the offering that pays for sin. It is in addition to the regular burnt offering along with its grain offering. It is also in addition to their drink offerings.

The Feast of Booths

[12]"On the 15th day of the seventh month, come together for a special service. Do not do any regular work. Celebrate the Feast of Booths for seven days to honor the LORD. [13]Present a food offering. Its smell will please the LORD. Sacrifice a burnt offering of 13 young bulls and two rams. Also sacrifice 14 male lambs a year old. They must not have any flaws. [14]Present a grain offering along with each of the 13 bulls. It must have 24 cups of the finest flour. Mix it with olive oil. Offer 16 cups along with each of the two rams. [15]Offer eight cups along with each of the 14 lambs. [16]Include a male goat as a sin offering. It is in addition to the regular burnt offering. It is also in addition to its grain offering and drink offering.

[17]"On the second day sacrifice 12 young bulls and two rams. Also sacrifice 14 male lambs a year old. They must not have any flaws. [18]Present their grain offerings and drink offerings. Present them along with the bulls, rams and lambs. Present them according to the required number. [19]Include a male goat as a sin offering. It is in addition to the regular burnt

offering along with its grain offering. It is also in addition to their drink offerings.

20 " 'On the third day sacrifice 11 bulls and two rams. Also sacrifice 14 male lambs a year old. They must not have any flaws. 21 Present their grain offerings and drink offerings. Present them along with the bulls, rams and lambs. Present them according to the required number. 22 Include a male goat as a sin offering. It is in addition to the regular burnt offering. It is also in addition to its grain offering and drink offering.

23 " 'On the fourth day sacrifice ten bulls and two rams. Also sacrifice 14 male lambs a year old. They must not have any flaws. 24 Present their grain offerings and drink offerings. Present them along with the bulls, rams and lambs. Present them according to the required number. 25 Include a male goat as a sin offering. It is in addition to the regular burnt offering. It is also in addition to its grain offering and drink offering.

26 " 'On the fifth day sacrifice nine bulls and two rams. Also sacrifice 14 male lambs a year old. They must not have any flaws. 27 Present their grain offerings and drink offerings. Present them along with the bulls, rams and lambs. Present them according to the required number. 28 Include a male goat as a sin offering. It is in addition to the regular burnt offering. It is also in addition to its grain offering and drink offering.

29 " 'On the sixth day sacrifice eight bulls and two rams. Also sacrifice 14 male lambs a year old. They must not have any flaws. 30 Present their grain offerings and drink offerings. Present them along with the bulls, rams and lambs. Present them according to the required number. 31 Include a male goat as a sin offering. It is in addition to the regular burnt offering. It is also in addition to its grain offering and drink offering.

32 " 'On the seventh day sacrifice seven bulls and two rams. Also sacrifice 14 male lambs a year old. They must not have any flaws. 33 Present their grain offerings and drink offerings. Present them along with the bulls, rams and lambs. Present them according to the required number. 34 Include a male goat as a sin offering. It is in addition to the regular burnt offering. It is

also in addition to its grain offering and drink offering.

35 " 'On the eighth day come together for a closing sacred service. Do not do any regular work. 36 Present a food offering. Its smell will please the LORD. Sacrifice a burnt offering of one bull and one ram. Also sacrifice seven male lambs a year old. They must not have any flaws. 37 Present their grain offerings and drink offerings. Present them along with the bull, the ram and the lambs. Present them according to the required number. 38 Include a male goat as a sin offering. It is in addition to the regular burnt offering. It is also in addition to its grain offering and drink offering.

39 " 'Here are the offerings you must present to the LORD at your appointed feasts. They are burnt offerings, grain offerings, drink offerings and friendship offerings. They are in addition to the offerings you bring to keep a special promise you make to the LORD. They are also in addition to the offerings you choose to give.' "

40 Moses told the Israelites everything the LORD had commanded him.

Special Promises

30 Moses spoke to the heads of the tribes of Israel. He said, "Here is what the LORD commands. 2 Suppose a man makes a special promise to the LORD. Or suppose he gives his word to do something. Then he must keep his promise. He must do everything he said he would do.

3 "Suppose a young woman is still living in her father's house. She makes a special promise to the LORD. Or she gives her word to do something. 4 Suppose her father hears about her promise. And he doesn't say anything to her about it. Then she must keep her promise. She must do what she agreed to do. 5 But suppose her father doesn't allow her to keep her promises when he hears about them. Then she doesn't have to do what she promised or agreed to do. The LORD will set her free. He'll do it because her father hasn't allowed her to keep her promises.

6 "Suppose she gets married after she makes a special promise. Or she gets married after agreeing to do something without thinking it through. 7 Suppose her

husband hears about what she did. And he doesn't say anything to her about it. Then she must keep her promise. She must do what she agreed to do. ⁸But suppose her husband doesn't allow her to keep her promises when he hears about them. Then she doesn't have to do what she promised. She doesn't have to do what she agreed to do without thinking it through. The LORD will set her free.

⁹"Suppose a widow makes a special promise. Or suppose she gives her word to do something. Then she must keep her promise. She must do what she agreed to do. The same rules apply to a woman who has been divorced.

¹⁰"Suppose a woman living with her husband makes a special promise. Or she gives her word to do something. ¹¹Suppose her husband hears about what she did. He doesn't say anything to her about it. And he doesn't try to stop her from keeping her promises. Then she must keep all of them. She must do what she agreed to do. ¹²But suppose her husband doesn't allow her to keep her promises when he hears about them. Then she doesn't have to do what she promised. She doesn't have to do what she agreed to do. Her husband has kept her from doing what she said she would do. The LORD will set her free. ¹³Her husband can let her keep any special promise she makes. Or he can refuse to let her keep it. Suppose she gives her word not to eat anything. Then her husband can let her keep her promise. Or he can refuse to let her keep it. ¹⁴But suppose day after day her husband doesn't say anything to her about what she did. Then he lets her keep all her promises. He lets her do everything she agreed to do. That's because he didn't say anything to her when he heard about what she had done. ¹⁵But suppose some time after he hears about her promises he doesn't let her keep them. Then she will be guilty. But he will bear the consequences for her guilt."

¹⁶These are the rules the LORD gave Moses about a man and his wife. And these are the rules the LORD gave about a father and his young daughter still living at home.

The LORD Punishes the Midianites

31 The LORD spoke to Moses. He said, ²"Pay the Midianites back for what they did to the Israelites. After that, you will join the members of your family who have already died."

³So Moses said to the people, "Prepare some of your men for battle. They must go to war against Midian. They will carry out the LORD's plan to punish Midian. ⁴Send 1,000 men from each of the tribes of Israel into battle." ⁵So Moses prepared 12,000 men for battle. There were 1,000 from each tribe. They came from the families of Israel. ⁶Moses sent them into battle. He sent 1,000 from each tribe. Phinehas the priest went along with them. Phinehas was the son of Eleazar. Phinehas took some things from the sacred tent with him. He also took the trumpets. The trumpet blasts would tell the people what to do and when to do it.

⁷They fought against Midian, just as the LORD had commanded Moses. They killed every man. ⁸Evi, Rekem, Zur, Hur and Reba were among the men they killed. Those men were the five kings of Midian. The Israelites also killed Balaam with their swords. Balaam was the son of Beor. ⁹The Israelites captured the Midianite women and children. They took for themselves all the herds, flocks and goods. ¹⁰They burned down all the towns where the Midianites lived. They also burned all their camps. ¹¹They carried off everything they had taken. That included the people and the animals. ¹²They brought back to Israel's camp the prisoners and everything else they had taken. They took them to Moses and to Eleazar the priest. They brought them to the whole community. Israel was camped on the plains of Moab. They were by the Jordan River across from Jericho.

¹³Moses and Eleazar the priest went to meet them outside the camp. So did all the leaders of the community. ¹⁴Moses was angry with the officers of the army who had returned from the battle. Some of them were the commanders of thousands of men. Others were the commanders of hundreds.

¹⁵"Have you let all the women remain alive?" Moses asked them. ¹⁶"The women followed Balaam's advice. They caused the

Israelites to be unfaithful to the LORD. The people worshiped the god named Baal that was worshiped at Peor. So a plague struck them. ¹⁷Kill all the boys. And kill every woman who has slept with a man. ¹⁸But save for yourselves every woman who has never slept with a man.

¹⁹"Anyone who has killed a person must stay outside the camp for seven days. And anyone who has touched a person who was killed must do the same thing. On the third and seventh days you must make yourselves pure. You must also make your prisoners pure. ²⁰Make all your clothes pure and 'clean.' Everything made out of leather, goat hair or wood must be made pure and 'clean.' "

²¹Then Eleazar the priest spoke to the soldiers who had gone into battle. He said, "Here is what the law the LORD gave Moses requires. ²²All your gold, silver, bronze, iron, tin and lead ²³must be put through fire. So must everything else that doesn't burn up. Then those things will be 'clean.' But they must also be made pure with the special water. In fact, everything that won't burn up must be put through that water. ²⁴On the seventh day wash your clothes. And you will be 'clean.' Then you can come into the camp."

The People Divide Up What They Had Taken

²⁵The LORD spoke to Moses. He said, ²⁶"Here is what you and Eleazar the priest and the family leaders of the community must do. You must count all the people and animals you captured. ²⁷Divide up some of what you took with the soldiers who fought in the battle. Divide up the rest with the others in the community. ²⁸Set apart a gift for me. Take something from the soldiers who fought in the battle. Set apart one out of every 500 people, cattle, donkeys or sheep. ²⁹Take my gift from the soldiers' half. Give it to Eleazar the priest. It is my share. ³⁰Also take something from the half that belongs to the Israelites. Choose one out of every 50 people, cattle, donkeys, sheep or other animals. Give them to the Levites. They are responsible for taking care of my holy tent." ³¹So Moses and Eleazar the priest did just as the LORD had commanded Moses.

³²What the soldiers took included 675,000 sheep. ³³There were also 72,000 cattle ³⁴and 61,000 donkeys. ³⁵And there were 32,000 women who had never slept with a man.

³⁶ Here is the half that belonged to those who had fought in the battle.

There were 337,500 sheep. ³⁷From among them, the LORD's gift was 675.
³⁸ There were 36,000 cattle. From among them, the LORD's gift was 72.
³⁹ There were 30,500 donkeys. From among them, the LORD's gift was 61.
⁴⁰ There were 16,000 women. From among them, the LORD's gift was 32.

⁴¹Moses gave the gift to Eleazar the priest. It was the LORD's share. Moses did just as the LORD had commanded him. ⁴²The other half belonged to the Israelites. Moses set it apart from what belonged to the fighting men. ⁴³The community's half was 337,500 sheep, ⁴⁴36,000 cattle, ⁴⁵30,500 donkeys ⁴⁶and 16,000 women. ⁴⁷Moses chose one out of every 50 people and animals. He gave them to the Levites. They were accountable for taking care of the LORD's holy tent. Moses did just as the LORD had commanded him.

⁴⁸Then the army officers went to Moses. Some of them were the commanders of thousands of men. Others were the commanders of hundreds. ⁴⁹All of them said to Moses, "We have counted the soldiers under our command. Not a single one is missing. ⁵⁰So we've brought an offering to the LORD. We've brought the gold each of us took in the battle. That includes armbands, bracelets, rings, earrings and necklaces. We've brought them in front of the LORD to pay for our sin." ⁵¹Moses and Eleazar the priest accepted the beautiful gold things from the army officers. ⁵²The gold received from the commanders of thousands and commanders of hundreds weighed 420 pounds. Moses and Eleazar offered all of it as a gift to the LORD. ⁵³Each soldier had taken things from the battle for himself. ⁵⁴Moses and Eleazar the priest accepted

the gold from all the commanders. They brought it into the tent of meeting. It reminded the Lord of the Israelites.

The Tribes on the East Side of the Jordan River

32 The tribes of Reuben and Gad had very large herds and flocks. They looked at the lands of Jazer and Gilead. They saw that those lands were just right for livestock. ²So they came to Moses and Eleazar the priest. They also came to the leaders of the community. They said, ³"We have seen the cities of Ataroth, Dibon, Jazer, Nimrah and Heshbon. We've seen Elealeh, Sebam, Nebo and Beon. ⁴All of them are in the land the Lord has brought under Israel's control. This land is just right for livestock. And we have livestock. ⁵We hope you are pleased with us," they continued. "If you are, please give us this land. Then it will belong to us. But don't make us go across the Jordan River."

⁶Moses spoke to the people of Gad and Reuben. He said, "Should the rest of us go to war while you stay here? ⁷The Lord has given the land of Canaan to the Israelites.

So why would you want to keep them from going over into it? ⁸That's what your fathers did. I sent them from Kadesh Barnea to check out the land. ⁹They went up to the Valley of Eshkol and looked at the land. Then they talked the Israelites out of entering the land the Lord had given them. ¹⁰The Lord's anger was stirred up that day. So he made a promise. He said, ¹¹'Not one of those who were 20 years old or more when they came up out of Egypt will see the land. They have not followed me with their whole heart. I promised to give the land to Abraham, Isaac and Jacob. ¹²But not one of the people who came up out of Egypt will see the land except Caleb and Joshua. Caleb is the son of Jephunneh, the Kenizzite. And Joshua is the son of Nun. They will see the land. They followed the Lord with their whole heart.' ¹³The Lord became very angry with Israel. He made them wander around in the desert for 40 years. They wandered until all the people who had done evil in his sight had died.

¹⁴"Now here you are, you bunch of sinners! You have taken the place of your

WHAT ABOUT YOU?

Imagine you own a spyglass that lets you see into the future. You could glimpse events that haven't happened yet. Think of all the problems you could solve before they ever happened!

Well, our loving God *does* know the future, and He doesn't need a magic spyglass. He can see everything that will ever happen. To the Lord, it's like it's going on right now. Time is really different for God.

In the first part of the Adventures in Odyssey episode "The Mystery of the Clock Tower," we learn that Alicia made a bad choice that hurt two other people. She couldn't imagine how to fix it, and she felt guilty afterward. But God had a plan to solve the problem—a plan Alicia discovered eventually. Nothing is a surprise to God; He can turn any situation into something good.

As the Israelites wandered for years in the wilderness, they must have wondered where they were headed. Sometimes they complained, yet they traveled on and trusted

God's promises. God knew about those desert years and brought His people through them. He will do the same in our lives. Do you trust Him?

This weekend, set an alarm. When it goes off, do something that will make another person happy. Give somebody a hug. Write a letter or send a message to someone who's lonely or far from home.

BIBLE ADVENTURES

The Israelites wandered in the desert for forty years. B-TV gave a small glimpse into this time in "B-TV: Obedience" (A#39).

fathers. And you are making the LORD even angrier with Israel. [15]What if you turn away from following him? Then he'll leave all these people in the desert again. And it will be your fault when they are destroyed."

[16]Then they came up to Moses. They said, "We would like to build pens here for our livestock. We would also like to build cities for our women and children. [17]But we will prepare ourselves for battle. We're even ready to go ahead of the Israelites. We'll march out with them until we've brought them to their place. While we're gone, our women and children will live in cities that have high walls around them. That will keep them safe from the people living in this land. [18]We won't return to our homes until each of the Israelites has received their share of the land. [19]We won't receive any share with them on the west side of the Jordan River. We've already received our share here on the east side."

[20]Then Moses said to them, "Do what you have promised to do. Get ready to fight for the LORD. [21]Prepare yourselves and go across the Jordan River. Fight for the LORD until he has driven out his enemies in front of him. [22]When the land is under the LORD's control, you can come back here. Your duty to the LORD and Israel will be over. Then the LORD will give you this land as your own.

[23]"But what if you fail to do your duty? Then you will be sinning against the LORD. And you may be sure that your sin will be discovered. It will be brought out into the open. [24]So build up cities for your women and children. Make sheep pens for your flocks. But do what you have promised to do."

[25]The people of Gad and Reuben spoke to Moses. They said, "We will do just as you command. [26]Our children and wives will remain here in the cities of Gilead. So will our flocks and herds. [27]But we will prepare ourselves for battle. We'll go across the Jordan River and fight for the LORD. We will do just as you have said."

[28]Then Moses gave orders about them to Eleazar the priest. He gave the same orders to Joshua, the son of Nun. He also spoke to the family leaders of the Israelite tribes. [29]He said, "The men of Gad and Reuben must get ready for battle. They must go across the Jordan River with you. They must help you fight for the LORD. They must stay with you until the land has been brought under your control. If they do, you must give them the land of Gilead as their own. [30]But what if they don't get ready for battle? What if they don't go across the Jordan with you? Then they must accept a share with you in Canaan."

[31]The people of Gad and Reuben gave their answer. They said, "We will do what the LORD has said. [32]We'll get ready for battle. We'll go across the Jordan into Canaan. We'll fight for the LORD there. But the property we receive will be on this side of the Jordan River."

[33]Then Moses gave their land to them. He gave it to the tribes of Gad and Reuben and half of the tribe of Manasseh. Manasseh was Joseph's son. One part of that land had belonged to the kingdom of Sihon. He was the king of the Amorites. The other part had belonged to the kingdom of Og. He was the king of Bashan. Moses gave that whole land to those two and a half tribes. It included its cities and the territory around them.

[34]The people of Gad built up the cities of Dibon, Ataroth and Aroer. [35]They built up Atroth Shophan, Jazer, Jogbehah, [36]Beth Nimrah and Beth Haran. They built a high wall around each of those cities. They also built sheep pens for their flocks. [37]The people of Reuben built up Heshbon, Elealeh and Kiriathaim. [38]They also built up Nebo, Baal Meon and Sibmah. They

ADVENTURES IN ODYSSEY

Rodney's sin of stealing and cheating "found him out" in "The Case of the Candid Camera" (A#15).

Num. 32:28 A sermon confused me one time. The pastor said that Joshua was the son of "none." I couldn't figure out how that was possible. Everyone has parents, right? Then I found out "Nun" was a man's name. Who would name their son "Nun"?!

gave new names to the cities they had built up. ³⁹The people of Makir, the son of Manasseh, went to the land of Gilead. They captured it. They drove out the Amorites living there. ⁴⁰So Moses gave Gilead to the people of Makir, the son of Manasseh. And they settled there. ⁴¹Jair was from the family line of Manasseh. Jair captured Gilead's settlements. He called them Havvoth Jair. ⁴²Nobah captured Kenath and the settlements around it. He named it after himself.

The Places Where Israel Camped During Their Journey

33 Here are the places where the Israelites camped during their journey. When they came out of Egypt, they marched in groups like an army. Moses and Aaron led them. ²The LORD commanded Moses to record their journey. Here are the places where they camped.

³The Israelites started out from Rameses on the 15th day of the first month. It was the day after the Passover Feast. They marched out boldly in plain sight of all the Egyptians. ⁴The Egyptians were burying all their oldest sons. The LORD had struck them down. He had done it when he punished their gods.

⁵The Israelites left Rameses and camped at Sukkoth.

⁶They left Sukkoth and camped at Etham. Etham was on the edge of the desert.

⁷They left Etham and turned back to Pi Hahiroth. It was east of Baal Zephon. They camped near Migdol.

⁸They left Pi Hahiroth. Then they passed through the Red Sea into the desert. They traveled for three days in the Desert of Etham. Then they camped at Marah.

⁹They left Marah and went to Elim. Twelve springs and 70 palm trees were there. So they camped at Elim.

¹⁰They left Elim and camped by the Red Sea.

¹¹They left the Red Sea and camped in the Desert of Sin.

¹²They left the Desert of Sin and camped at Dophkah.

¹³They left Dophkah and camped at Alush.

¹⁴They left Alush and camped at Rephidim. But there was no water there for the people to drink.

¹⁵They left Rephidim and camped in the Desert of Sinai.

¹⁶They left the Desert of Sinai and camped at Kibroth Hattaavah.

¹⁷They left Kibroth Hattaavah and camped at Hazeroth.

¹⁸They left Hazeroth and camped at Rithmah.

¹⁹They left Rithmah and camped at Rimmon Perez.

²⁰They left Rimmon Perez and camped at Libnah.

²¹They left Libnah and camped at Rissah.

²²They left Rissah and camped at Kehelathah.

²³They left Kehelathah and camped at Mount Shepher.

²⁴They left Mount Shepher and camped at Haradah.

²⁵They left Haradah and camped at Makheloth.

²⁶They left Makheloth and camped at Tahath.

²⁷They left Tahath and camped at Terah.

²⁸They left Terah and camped at Mithkah.

²⁹They left Mithkah and camped at Hashmonah.

³⁰They left Hashmonah and camped at Moseroth.

³¹They left Moseroth and camped at Bene Jaakan.

³²They left Bene Jaakan and camped at Hor Haggidgad.

³³They left Hor Haggidgad and camped at Jotbathah.

³⁴They left Jotbathah and camped at Abronah.

³⁵They left Abronah and camped at Ezion Geber.

³⁶They left Ezion Geber and camped at Kadesh. Kadesh was in the Desert of Zin.

³⁷They left Kadesh and camped at Mount Hor. It was on the border of Edom. ³⁸Aaron the priest went up Mount Hor when the LORD commanded him to. That's where he died. It happened on the first day of the fifth month. It was the 40th year after the Israelites came out of Egypt. ³⁹Aaron was 123 years old when he died on Mount Hor.

⁴⁰The Canaanite king of Arad lived in the Negev Desert in Canaan. He heard that the Israelites were coming.

⁴¹They left Mount Hor and camped at Zalmonah.

⁴²They left Zalmonah and camped at Punon.

⁴³They left Punon and camped at Oboth.

⁴⁴They left Oboth and camped at Iye Abarim. It was on the border of Moab.

⁴⁵They left Iye Abarim and camped at Dibon Gad.

⁴⁶They left Dibon Gad and camped at Almon Diblathaim.

⁴⁷They left Almon Diblathaim and camped in the mountains of Abarim near Nebo.

⁴⁸They left the mountains of Abarim and camped on the plains of Moab. That area was by the Jordan River across from Jericho. ⁴⁹They camped there along the Jordan River from Beth Jeshimoth to Abel Shittim.

Jason's Jargon

NUMBERS 33

Here's your next mission: search this chapter for the words *cast lots*. Casting lots was like flipping a coin. In the Old Testament, God sometimes instructed His people to determine how land was divided by casting lots.

⁵⁰On the plains of Moab the LORD spoke to Moses. He spoke to him by the Jordan River across from Jericho. The LORD said, ⁵¹"Speak to the Israelites. Tell them, 'Go across the Jordan River into Canaan. ⁵²Drive out all those living in the land. The statues of their gods are made out of stone and metal. Destroy all those statues. And destroy all the high places where they are worshiped. ⁵³Take the land as your own. Make your homes in it. I have given it to you. ⁵⁴Cast lots when you divide up the land. Do it based on the number of people in each tribe and family. Give a larger share to a larger group. And give a smaller group a smaller share. The share they receive by casting lots will belong to them. Give out the shares based on the number of people in Israel's tribes.

⁵⁵"'But suppose you do not drive out the people living in the land. Then those you allow to remain there will become like needles in your eyes. They will become like thorns in your sides. They will give you trouble in the land where you will live. ⁵⁶Then I will do to you what I plan to do to them.'"

Israel Arrives at the Borders of Canaan

34 The LORD said to Moses, ²"Give the Israelites a command. Tell them, 'You are going to enter Canaan. The land will be given to you as your own. Here are the borders it must have.

³ "'Your southern border will include part of the Desert of Zin. It will be

along the border of Edom. Your southern border will start in the east from the southern end of the Dead Sea. ⁴It will cross south of Scorpion Pass. It will continue on to Zin. From there it will go south of Kadesh Barnea. Then it will go to Hazar Addar and over to Azmon. ⁵There it will turn and join the Wadi of Egypt. It will come to an end at the Mediterranean Sea.

⁶ "'Your western border will be the coast of the Mediterranean Sea. That will be your border on the west.

⁷ "'For your northern border, run a line from the Mediterranean Sea to Mount Hor. ⁸Continue it from Mount Hor to Lebo Hamath. Then the border will go to Zedad. ⁹It will continue to Ziphron. It will come to an end at Hazar Enan. That will be your border on the north.

¹⁰ "'For your eastern border, run a line from Hazar Enan to Shepham. ¹¹The border will go down from Shepham to Riblah. Riblah is on the east side of Ain. From there the border will continue along the slopes east of the Sea of Galilee. ¹²Then the border will go down along the Jordan River. It will come to an end at the Dead Sea.

"'That will be your land. And those will be its borders on every side.'"

¹³Moses gave the Israelites a command. He said, "Cast lots when you divide up the land. Each tribe will have its own share. The LORD has ordered it to be given to the nine and a half tribes. ¹⁴The families of the tribes of Reuben and Gad have already received their shares. The families of half of the tribe of Manasseh have also received their share. ¹⁵Those two and a half tribes have received their shares east of the Jordan River. It flows near Jericho. Their land is toward the sunrise."

¹⁶The LORD spoke to Moses. He said, ¹⁷"Here are the names of the men who will give out the shares of the land to your people. They are Eleazar the priest and Joshua, the son of Nun. ¹⁸Also appoint one leader from each of the nine and a half tribes. They will help you give out the land.

¹⁹ Here are their names.

"Caleb, the son of Jephunneh, is from the tribe of Judah.
²⁰ Shemuel, the son of Ammihud, is from the tribe of Simeon.
²¹ Elidad, the son of Kislon, is from the tribe of Benjamin.
²² Bukki, the son of Jogli, is the leader from the tribe of Dan.
²³ Hanniel, the son of Ephod, is the leader from the tribe of Manasseh. Manasseh was the son of Joseph.
²⁴ Kemuel, the son of Shiphtan, is the leader from the tribe of Ephraim. Ephraim was the son of Joseph.
²⁵ Elizaphan, the son of Parnak, is the leader from the tribe of Zebulun.
²⁶ Paltiel, the son of Azzan, is the leader from the tribe of Issachar.
²⁷ Ahihud, the son of Shelomi, is the leader from the tribe of Asher.
²⁸ Pedahel, the son of Ammihud, is the leader from the tribe of Naphtali."

²⁹ These are the men the LORD commanded to give out the shares of the land. They were commanded to give them to Israel in the land of Canaan.

The Levites Receive Their Towns

35 On the plains of Moab, the LORD spoke to Moses. It was by the Jordan River across from Jericho. The LORD said, ²"Command the Israelites to give the Levites towns to live in. The towns must come from the shares of land the people will have as their own. Also give the Levites the grasslands around the towns. ³Then the Levites will have towns to live in. They will also have grasslands for their cattle and all their other livestock.

⁴"The grasslands around each town you give them will go out to 1,500 feet from the town wall. ⁵Outside each town, the east side will measure 3,000 feet. So will the south side, the west side and the north side. The town must be in the center. And the Levites will own the grasslands around each town.

Cities to Run to for Safety

⁶"Six of the towns you give the Levites will be cities to go to for safety. A person who has killed someone can run to one of them. Also give the Levites 42 other towns. ⁷You must give the Levites a total of 48 towns. Also give them the grasslands around those towns. ⁸The towns you give the Levites must come from the land the Israelites have as their own. So the number you give from each tribe will depend on the size of that tribe's share. Take many towns from a tribe that has many towns. But take only a few towns from a tribe that has only a few."

⁹Then the LORD said to Moses, ¹⁰"Speak to the Israelites. Tell them, 'You will soon go across the Jordan River. You will enter Canaan. ¹¹When you do, choose the cities to go to for safety. People who have killed someone by accident can run to one of those cities. ¹²They will be places of safety for them. People will be safe there from those who want to kill them. Then anyone charged with murder will not die before their case has been brought to the community court. ¹³Six towns will be the cities you can go to for safety. ¹⁴Three will be east of the Jordan River. The other three will be in Canaan. ¹⁵Those six towns will be places where the Israelites can go for safety. Outsiders living in Israel can also go to them for safety. So anyone who has killed another person by accident can run there.

¹⁶"Suppose a person uses an iron object to hit and kill someone. Then that person is a murderer and must be put to death. ¹⁷Or suppose a person is holding a stone that could kill. And they use it to hit and kill someone. Then that person is a murderer and must be put to death. ¹⁸Or suppose a person is holding a wooden object that could kill. And they use it to hit and kill someone. Then that person is a murderer and must be put to death. ¹⁹The dead person's nearest male relative must kill the murderer. When he meets up with him, he must kill the murderer. ²⁰What if a person makes evil plans against someone else? And what if that person pushes them so that they die? Or what if that person throws something at them so that they die? ²¹Or what if that person hits another person with a fist so that the other

dies? Then the person who does any of those things must be put to death. That person is a murderer. The dead person's nearest male relative must kill the murderer. When he meets up with him, he must kill the murderer.

²²"But what if a person suddenly pushes someone else without being angry? Or what if that person throws something at someone else without meaning to? ²³Or what if that person does not see the other person and drops a stone on them that kills them? He was not the dead person's enemy. He did not mean to harm them. ²⁴Then the court must decide between the person who did the act and the nearest male relative of the one who was killed. Here are the rules the court must follow. ²⁵The court must provide a safe place for the person accused of murder. It must keep the one accused of murder safe from those who want to kill them. The court must send the accused person back to the city they ran to for safety. The accused person must stay there until the high priest dies. That priest has been anointed with holy oil.

²⁶"But suppose the accused person goes outside that city. ²⁷And suppose the dead person's nearest male relative finds them outside the city. Then the relative can kill the accused person. The relative will not be guilty of murder. ²⁸The accused person must stay in that city until the high priest dies. Only then may they return home.

²⁹"This is what the law requires of you for all time to come. It will apply to you no matter where you live.

³⁰"Suppose a person kills someone. Then that person must be put to death as a murderer. But do it only when there are witnesses who can tell what happened. Do not put anyone to death if only one witness tells what happened.

³¹"Do not accept payment for a murderer's life. A murderer deserves to die. They must certainly be put to death.

³²"Do not accept payment for anyone who has run to a city for safety. Do not let them buy their freedom to return home. They must not go back and live on their own land before the high priest dies.

³³"Do not pollute the land where you are. Murder pollutes the land. Only one

thing can pay to remove the pollution in the land where murder has been committed. The blood of the one who spilled another's blood must be spilled. [34]So do not make the land where you live "unclean," because I live there too. I, the LORD, live among the Israelites.'"

The Property Zelophehad's Daughters Will Receive

36 The heads of the families of Gilead came to Moses. Gilead was the son of Makir. The family heads were from the tribe of Manasseh. So they were in the family line of Joseph. They spoke to Moses in front of the leaders of the families of Israel. [2]They said, "The LORD commanded you to give shares of the land to the Israelites. He told you to cast lots when you do it. At that time the LORD ordered you to give our brother Zelophehad's share to his daughters. [3]Suppose they marry men from other tribes in Israel. Then their share will be taken away from our family's land. It will be added to the land of the tribe they marry into. So a part of the share given to us will be taken away. [4]The Year of Jubilee for the Israelites will come. Then their share will be added to the land of the tribe they marry into. Their land will be taken away from the share given to our tribe."

[5]Then the LORD gave a command to Moses. He told Moses to give an order to the Israelites. Moses said, "What the tribe in the family line of Joseph is saying is right. [6]Here is what the LORD commands for Zelophehad's daughters. They can marry anyone they want to. But they have to marry someone in their own family's tribe. [7]Property in Israel must not pass from one tribe to another. Everyone in Israel must keep their family's share of their tribe's land. [8]Suppose a daughter in any tribe of Israel receives land from her parents. Then she must marry someone in her father's family and tribe. In that way, every family's share will remain in its family line in Israel. [9]Property can't pass from one tribe to another. Each tribe of Israel must keep the land it receives."

[10]So Zelophehad's daughters did just as the LORD commanded Moses. [11]The names of the daughters were Mahlah, Tirzah, Hoglah, Milkah and Noah. All of them married their cousins on their father's side. [12]They married men in the family line of Manasseh, the son of Joseph. So the land they received remained in their father's family and tribe.

[13]These are the commands and rules the LORD gave through Moses. He gave them to the Israelites on the plains of Moab. They were by the Jordan River across from Jericho.

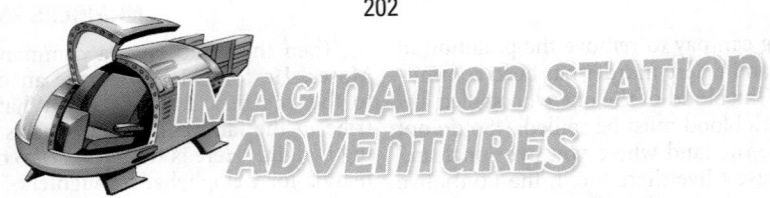

BALAAM'S DONKEY

Read Numbers 22:21-39.

MR. WHITTAKER SENDS COUSINS PATRICK AND BETH TO MOAB IN OLD TESTAMENT TIMES. IN THE HOME OF BALAAM THE SORCERER, THE COUSINS ARE HIS SERVANTS.

THERE ARE VISITORS COMING. PREPARE FOOD AND DRINK FOR THEM.

TWO MESSENGERS FROM MOAB DELIVER THEIR KING'S REQUEST.

KING BALAK WANTS YOU TO **CURSE THE ISRAELITES** SO THEY LEAVE MOAB.

I CANNOT PUT A CURSE ON THEM. THEIR GOD TOLD ME **NOT** TO.

ONLY A FOOL WOULD CURSE GOD'S PEOPLE.

THE ISRAELITES ARE LIKE OXEN THAT WILL EAT ALL THE GRASS. THEY MUST **LEAVE** MOAB.

WHY DOES KING BALAK WANT THEM TO GO?

LET ME SLEEP ON IT. YOU CAN STAY IN MY HOUSE TONIGHT.

IF YOU CURSE THEM, THERE **WILL BE** PLENTY MORE OF THIS!

YOU HAVE OWNED ME FOR MANY YEARS. HAVE I EVER DISOBEYED YOU BEFORE?

NO.

I AM HERE TO STOP YOU FROM CURSING THE ISRAELITES.

I WAS FOOLISH TO COME.

DUH! EVEN I KNEW THAT!

YOU MAY GO TO KING BALAK. BUT SAY ONLY WHAT GOD TELLS YOU TO.

YES!

LATER BALAAM AND THE COUSINS MEET WITH KING BALAK. THEY STAND ON A HILL OVERLOOKING THE ISRAELITE CAMP.

CURSE THE ISRAELITES SO THEY WILL LEAVE. AND **YOU WILL BE RICH!**

I WILL SAY ONLY WHAT **THE GOD OF ISRAEL WANTS** ME TO.

OH?

MAY THE ISRAELITES BE LIKE DUST! **WHO** CAN COUNT THE SPECKS?

WHAT? A BLESSING SO THAT THEY MULTIPLY! **NO!**

BALAAM BLESSES THE ISRAELITES SEVEN TIMES. AND SEVEN TIMES KING BALAK GETS ANGRY.

IF YOU CAN'T SAY ANYTHING MEAN, **DON'T SAY ANYTHING AT ALL!**

I HAVE TO SAY WHAT GOD WANTS ME TO. I'M **NO FOOL** ... ANYMORE.

BACK AT WHIT'S END ...

WHAT DID YOU THINK OF BALAAM?

HIS DONKEY HAD MORE SENSE THAN **HE DID.**

HE HAD A HARD TIME CHOOSING **GOD OVER GOLD.**

Deuteronomy

Now we have arrived at Deuteronomy, a word which means "repetition of the law." This is appropriate because this book is essentially a series of speeches given by Moses to remind the Israelites of all God has done for them. The people have come out of Egypt, have wandered the wilderness for forty years, and are about to enter the Promised Land under Joshua's leadership. In these speeches, Moses emphasizes the essential things they need to know and remember as they move into a new homeland with a new leader.

Deuteronomy covers some of the same material you will find in Exodus, Leviticus, and Numbers, including the Ten Commandments (5:6–21). Even so, Moses comes across as more passionate and personal as he looks back at God's faithfulness. Looking to the New Testament, when Jesus was asked to identify the most important commandment in all of the Law, He immediately quoted Deuteronomy 6:5: "Love the LORD your God with all your heart and with all your soul. Love him with all your strength [mind]" (Matt. 22:37).

What's it mean, Eugene?

Natural Law—Some things are *right* and other things are *wrong*. God reveals which is which in the Bible you're reading right now! Nonetheless, even people who don't have a Bible *still* know right from wrong because as Romans 2:14–15 says, God has written it in their hearts. This natural occurrence is what is meant by "natural law."

The LORD Commands Israel to Leave Mount Horeb

These are the words Moses spoke to all the Israelites. At that time, they were in the desert east of the Jordan River. It's in the Arabah Valley across from Suph. The people were between Paran and Tophel, Laban, Hazeroth and Dizahab. ²It takes 11 days to go from Mount Horeb to Kadesh Barnea if you travel on the Mount Seir road.

³It was the 40th year since the Israelites had left Egypt. On the first day of the 11th month, Moses spoke to them. He told them everything the LORD had commanded him to tell them. ⁴They had already won the battle over Sihon. Sihon was the king of the Amorites. He had ruled in Heshbon. Israel had also won the battle over Og at Edrei. Og was the king of Bashan. He had ruled in Ashtaroth.

⁵The people were east of the Jordan River in the territory of Moab. There Moses began to explain the law. Here is what he said.

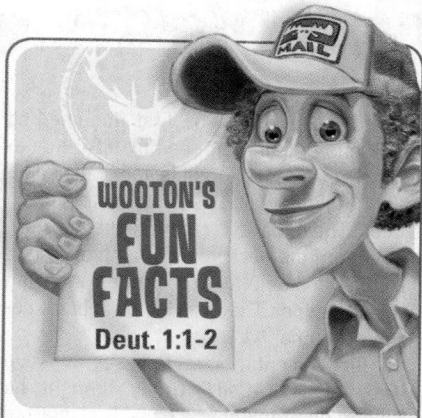

Did you know that Mount Horeb and Mount Sinai might be the same place? Some scholars think Mount Sinai faces the east side and Mount Horeb faces the west, kind of like a two-headed coin.

⁶The LORD our God spoke to us at Mount Horeb. He said, "You have stayed long enough at this mountain. ⁷Take your tents down. Go into the hill country of the Amorites. Go to all the people who are their neighbors. Go to the people who live in the Arabah Valley. Travel to the mountains and the western hills. Go to the people in the Negev Desert and along the coast. Travel to the land of Canaan and to Lebanon. Go as far as the great Euphrates River. ⁸I have given you all this land. Go in and take it as your own. The LORD promised he would give the land to your fathers. He promised it to Abraham, Isaac and Jacob. He also said he would give it to their children after them."

Some Officials Are Chosen to Help Moses

⁹At that time I spoke to you. I said, "You are too heavy a load for me to carry alone. ¹⁰The LORD your God has caused there to be many of you. Today you are as many as the stars in the sky. ¹¹The LORD is the God of your people. May he cause there to be a thousand times more of you. May he bless you, just as he promised he would. ¹²But I can't handle your problems and troubles all by myself. I can't settle your arguments. ¹³So choose some wise men from each of your tribes. They must understand how to give good advice. The people must have respect for them. I will appoint those men to have authority over you."

¹⁴You answered me, "Your suggestion is good."

¹⁵So I chose the leading men of your tribes who were wise and respected. I appointed them to have authority over you. I made them commanders of thousands, hundreds, fifties and tens. I appointed them to be officials over the tribes. ¹⁶Here is what I commanded your judges at that time. I said, "Listen to your people's cases when they argue with one another. Judge them fairly. It doesn't matter whether the case is between two Israelites or between an Israelite and an outsider living among you. ¹⁷When you judge them, treat everyone the same. Listen to those who are important and those who are not. Don't be afraid of anyone. God is the highest judge. Bring me any case that is too hard for you. I'll listen to it." ¹⁸At that time I told you everything you should do.

Twelve Men Check Out the Land of Canaan

¹⁹The LORD our God commanded us to start out from Mount Horeb. So we

WHAT ABOUT YOU?

As far as we know, the first documented prank phone call happened in 1884. Someone in Providence, Rhode Island, called a local funeral home and asked them to pick up a body. The undertaker went to the address, only to find the person very much alive and surprised to see a funeral director standing at his front door. That was history's first telephone "gotcha"!

In the Adventures in Odyssey episode "Three O'clock Call," Grady thought he was getting prank phone calls. It all started during his birthday party. The phone rang, but there was no one on the other end. Was it Grady's dad, who abandoned the family? His sister Samantha thought so. When the calls kept coming at three o'clock every afternoon, Grady became convinced that his father wanted to reconnect. Meanwhile, he struggled to see God as a loving father because of the way his earthly dad had let him down.

Do you know what it's like to have someone you love let you down? When that happens, we might wonder if God has forgotten about us. But Deuteronomy 1:31 tells us that God cares for us and will help us through the most challenging circumstances in life. We can trust the Lord, and He'll never let us down.

Our electronics can be useful tools that connect us with each other. Grab your address list and look through all of your contacts today. Read through the names out loud. Pray that each person on your list would know that God loves him or her.

---

did. We went toward the hill country of the Amorites. We traveled all through the huge and terrible desert you saw. Finally, we reached Kadesh Barnea. [20]Then I said to you, "You have reached the hill country of the Amorites. The LORD our God is giving it to us. [21]The LORD your God has given you the land. Go up and take it. Do what the LORD says. He's the God of your people. Don't be afraid. Don't lose hope."

[22]Then all of you came to me. You said, "Let's send some men ahead of us. They can check out the land for us and bring back a report. They can suggest to us which way to go. They can tell us about the towns we'll come to."

[23]That seemed like a good idea to me. So I chose 12 of you. I picked one man from each tribe. [24]They left and went up into the hill country. There they came to the Valley of Eshkol. They checked it out. [25]They got some of the fruit of that land. Then they brought it down to us and gave us their report. They said, "The LORD our God is giving us a good land."

Israel Refuses to Obey the LORD

[26]But you wouldn't go up. You refused to obey the command of the LORD your God. [27]You spoke against him in your tents. You said, "The LORD hates us. That's why he brought us out of Egypt to hand us over to the Amorites. He wanted to destroy us. [28]Where can we go? The men who checked out the land have made us afraid. They say, 'The people are stronger and taller than we are. The cities are large. They have walls that reach up to the sky. We even saw the Anakites there.'"

[29]Then I said to you, "Don't be terrified. Don't be afraid of them. [30]The LORD your God will go ahead of you. He will fight for you. With your own eyes you saw how he fought for you in Egypt. [31]You also saw how the LORD your God brought you through the desert. He carried you

everywhere you went, just as a father carries his son. And now you have arrived here."

[32] In spite of that, you didn't trust in the LORD your God. [33] He went ahead of you on your journey. He was in the fire at night and in the cloud during the day. He found places for you to camp. He showed you the way you should go.

[34] The LORD heard what you said. So he became angry. He made a promise. He said, [35] "I promised to give this good land to your people of long ago. But no one alive today will see it. [36] Only Caleb will see the land. He is the son of Jephunneh. I will give him and his children after him the land he walked on. He followed me with his whole heart."

[37] Because of you, the LORD became angry with me also. He said, "You will not enter the land either. [38] But Joshua, the son of Nun, is your helper. Joshua will enter the land. Help him to be brave. Give him hope. He will lead Israel to take the land as their own. [39] You said your little ones would be taken prisoner. But they will enter the land. They do not yet know right from wrong. But I will give them the land. They will take it as their own. [40] As for you, turn around. Start out toward the desert. Go along the road that leads to the Red Sea."

[41] Then you replied, "We have sinned against the LORD. We will go up and fight. We'll do just as the LORD our God has commanded us." So all of you got your swords and put them on. You thought it would be easy to go up into the hill country.

[42] But the LORD spoke to me. He said, "Tell them, 'Do not go up and fight. I will not be with you. Your enemies will win the battle over you.'"

[43] So I told you what the LORD said. But you wouldn't listen. You refused to obey his command. You were so filled with pride that you marched up into the hill country. [44] The Amorites who lived in those hills came out and attacked you. Like large numbers of bees they chased you. They beat you down from Seir all the way to Hormah. [45] You came back and wept in front of the LORD. But he didn't pay any attention to your weeping. He wouldn't listen to you. [46] So you stayed in Kadesh for many years. You spent a long time in that area.

Israel Wanders in the Desert

2 We turned back and started out toward the desert. We went along the road that leads to the Red Sea. That's how the LORD had directed me. For a long time we made our way around the hill country of Seir.

[2] Then the LORD spoke to me. He said, [3] "You have made your way around this hill country long enough. So now turn north. [4] Here are the orders I want you to give the people. Tell them, 'You are about to pass through the territory of your relatives. They are from the family line of Esau. They live in Seir. They will be afraid of you. But be very careful. [5] Do not make them angry. If you do, they will go to war against you. I will not give you any of their land. You will not have even enough to put your foot on. I have given Esau's people the hill country of Seir as their own. [6] Pay them with silver for the food you eat and the water you drink.'"

[7] The LORD your God has blessed you in everything your hands have done. He watched over you when you traveled through that huge desert. For these 40 years the LORD your God has been with you. So you have had everything you need.

[8] We went on past our relatives. They are from the family line of Esau. They live in Seir. We turned away from the Arabah Valley road. It comes up from Elath and Ezion Geber. We traveled along the desert road of Moab.

[9] Then the LORD said to me, "Do not attack the Moabites. Do not even make them angry. If you do, they will go to war against you. I will not give you any part of their land. I have given Moab to the people in the family line of Lot. I have given it to them as their own."

[10] The Emites used to live there. They were strong people. There were large numbers of them. They were as tall as the Anakites. [11] Like the Anakites, they too were thought of as Rephaites. But the Moabites called them Emites. [12] The Horites used to live in Seir. But the people of Esau drove them out. They destroyed the Horites to make room for themselves. Then they settled in their territory. They did just as

Israel has done in the land the LORD gave them as their own.

¹³The LORD said, "Now get up. Go across the Zered Valley." So we went across it.

¹⁴Between the time we left Kadesh Barnea and the time we went across the Zered Valley, 38 years had passed. By then, all the fighting men who had been in our camp from the beginning had died. The LORD had warned them that it would happen. ¹⁵He used his power against them until he had gotten rid of all of them. Not one was left in the camp.

¹⁶Finally, the last of the fighting men among the people died. ¹⁷Then the LORD said to me, ¹⁸"Today you must pass near the border of Moab. Moab is also called Ar. ¹⁹When you come to the Ammonites, do not attack them. Do not make them angry. If you do, they will go to war against you. I will not give you any of their land as your own. I have given it to the people in the family line of Lot. I have given it to them as their own."

²⁰That land was also thought of as a land of the Rephaites. They used to live there. But the Ammonites called them Zamzummites. ²¹The Rephaites were strong people. There were large numbers of them. They were as tall as the Anakites. The LORD destroyed the Rephaites to make room for the Ammonites. So the Ammonites drove them out. Then they settled in the territory of the Rephaites. ²²The LORD had done the same thing for the people of Esau. They lived in Seir. The LORD destroyed the Horites to make room for Esau's people. They drove the Horites out. So the people of Esau have lived in Seir in the territory of the Horites to this very day. ²³The Avvites lived in villages as far away as Gaza. But people came from Crete and destroyed the Avvites. Then the people of Crete made their home in the territory of the Avvites.

Israel Wins the Battle Over Sihon

²⁴The LORD said, "Start out and go across the valley of the Arnon River. I have handed Sihon over to you. He is the Amorite king of Heshbon. I have also given you his country. Begin to take it as your own. Go to war against him. ²⁵This very day I will bring fear and terror on all the nations because of you. They will hear about you. They will tremble with fear. Pain and suffering will grip them because of you."

²⁶I sent messengers from the Desert of Kedemoth. I told them to go to Sihon, the king of Heshbon. They offered him peace. They said, ²⁷"Let us pass through your country. We'll stay on the main road. We won't turn off it to one side or the other. ²⁸We'll pay you the right amount of silver for food to eat and water to drink. Just let us walk through your country. ²⁹The people of Esau, who live in Seir, allowed us to do that. The people of Moab, who live in Ar, also allowed us to do it. So let us walk through until we go across the Jordan River. Then we'll be able to go into the land the LORD our God is giving us." ³⁰But Sihon, the king of Heshbon, refused to let us walk through. The LORD your God had made him stubborn in his heart and spirit. The LORD wanted to hand him over to you. And that's exactly what he has done.

³¹The LORD said to me, "I have begun to hand Sihon and his country over to you. So begin the battle to take his land as your own."

³²Sihon and his whole army came out to fight against us at Jahaz. ³³But the LORD our God handed him over to us. We struck him down together with his sons and his whole army. ³⁴At that time we took all his towns. We completely destroyed them. We killed all the men, women and children. We didn't leave any of them alive. ³⁵But we took for ourselves the livestock and everything else from the towns we had captured. ³⁶Not a single town was too strong for us. That includes all the towns from Aroer on the rim of the Arnon River valley all the way to Gilead. It also includes the town in the valley. The LORD our God gave us all of them. ³⁷And you obeyed the LORD's command. You didn't go near any part of the land of the Ammonites. That includes the land along the Jabbok River. It also includes the land around the towns in the hills.

Israel Wins the Battle Over Og

3 Next, we turned and went up along the road toward Bashan. Og marched out with his whole army. They fought against us at Edrei. Og was the king of Bashan.

²The Lord said to me, "Do not be afraid of Og. I have handed him over to you. I have also handed over his whole army and his land. Do to him what you did to Sihon. Sihon was the Amorite king who ruled in Heshbon."

³So the Lord our God also handed Og, the king of Bashan, and his whole army over to us. We struck them down. We didn't leave any of them alive. ⁴At that time we took all his cities. There were 60 of them. We took the whole area of Argob. That was Og's kingdom in Bashan. ⁵All those cities had high walls around them. The city gates were made secure with heavy metal bars. There were also large numbers of villages that didn't have walls. ⁶We completely destroyed them. We did to them just as we had done to Sihon, the king of Heshbon. We destroyed all their cities. We destroyed the men, women and children. ⁷But we kept for ourselves the livestock and everything else we took from their cities.

⁸So at that time we took the territory east of the Jordan River. We captured it from those two Amorite kings. The territory goes all the way from the Arnon River valley to Mount Hermon. ⁹Hermon is called Sirion by the people of Sidon. The Amorites call it Senir. ¹⁰We captured all the towns on the high plains. We took the whole land of Gilead. And we captured the whole land of Bashan as far away as Salekah and Edrei. Those were towns that belonged to Og's kingdom in Bashan. ¹¹Og, the king of Bashan, was the only Rephaite left. His bed was decorated with iron. It was more than 13 feet long and six feet wide. It is still in the Ammonite city of Rabbah.

Moses Divides Up the Land

¹²I divided up the land we took over at that time. I gave the tribes of Reuben and Gad the territory north of Aroer by the Arnon River valley. It includes half of the hill country of Gilead together with its towns. ¹³I gave the rest of Gilead to half of the tribe of Manasseh. I also gave them the whole land of Bashan, the kingdom of Og. The whole area of Argob in Bashan used to be known as a land of the Rephaites. ¹⁴Jair took the whole area of Argob. He was from the family line of Manasseh.

Argob goes all the way to the border of the people of Geshur and Maakah. It was named after Jair. So Bashan is called Havvoth Jair to this very day. ¹⁵I gave Gilead to Makir. ¹⁶But I gave to the tribes of Reuben and Gad the territory that reaches from Gilead down to the Arnon River valley. It goes all the way to the Jabbok River. The Jabbok is the northern border of Ammon. The middle of the Arnon River valley is its southern border. ¹⁷The western border of Reuben and Gad is the Jordan River in the Arabah Valley. It reaches from the Sea of Galilee to the Dead Sea. It runs below the slopes of Pisgah.

¹⁸Here is the command I gave at that time to the tribes of Reuben and Gad and half of the tribe of Manasseh. I said, "The Lord your God has given you this land as your very own. But all your strong men must be prepared for battle. They must cross over ahead of the rest of the Israelites. ¹⁹But your wives and children can stay in the towns I've given you. You can keep your livestock there too. I know you have a lot of livestock. ²⁰The Lord has given you peace and rest. Then let your families and livestock stay in those towns until the Lord gives peace and rest to the other tribes. And let your families stay until the other tribes have taken over the land the Lord your God is giving them. That land is across the Jordan River. After that, each of you may go back to the land I've given you as your very own."

The Lord Will Not Allow Moses to Cross the Jordan River

²¹At that time I gave Joshua a command. I said, "Your own eyes have seen everything the Lord your God has done to Sihon and Og. He will do the same thing to all the kingdoms in the land where you are going. ²²Don't be afraid of them. The Lord your God himself will fight for you."

²³At that time I made my appeal to the Lord. I said, ²⁴"Lord and King, you have begun to show me how great you are. You have shown me how strong your hand is. You do great works and mighty acts. There isn't any god in heaven or on earth who can do what you do. ²⁵Let me go across the Jordan River. Let me see the good land beyond it. I want to see that fine hill country and Lebanon."

²⁶But the LORD was angry with me because of what you did. He wouldn't listen to me. "That is enough!" the LORD said. "Do not speak to me anymore about this matter. ²⁷Go up to the highest slopes of Pisgah. Look west and north and south and east. Look at the land with your own eyes. But you are not going to go across this Jordan River. ²⁸So appoint Joshua as the new leader. Help him to be brave. Give him hope and strength. He will take these people across the Jordan. You will see the land. But he will lead them into it to take it as their own." ²⁹So we stayed in the valley near Beth Peor.

Obey the LORD

4 Now, Israel, listen to the rules and laws I'm going to teach you. Obey them and you will live. You will go in and take over the land. The LORD was the God of your people of long ago. He's giving you the land. ²Don't add to what I'm commanding you. Don't subtract from it either. Instead, obey the commands of the LORD your God that I'm giving you.

³Your own eyes saw what the LORD your God did at Baal Peor. He destroyed every one of your people who worshiped the Baal that was worshiped at Peor. ⁴But all of you who remained true to the LORD your God are still alive today.

⁵I have taught you rules and laws, just as the LORD my God commanded me. Obey them in the land you are entering to take as your very own. ⁶Be careful to keep them. That will show the nations how wise and understanding you are. They will hear about all these rules. They'll say, "That great nation certainly has wise and understanding people." ⁷The LORD our God is near us every time we pray to him. What other nation is great enough to have its gods that close to them? ⁸I'm giving you the laws of the LORD today. What other nation is great enough to have rules and laws as fair as these?

⁹Don't be careless. Instead, be very careful. Don't forget the things your eyes have seen. As long as you live, don't let them slip from your mind. Teach them to your children and their children after them. ¹⁰Remember the day you stood at Mount Horeb. The LORD your God was there. He said to me, "Bring the people to me to hear my words. I want them to learn to have respect for me as long as they live in the land. I want them to teach my words to their children." ¹¹You came near and stood at the foot of the mountain. It blazed with fire that reached as high as the very heavens. There were black clouds and deep darkness. ¹²Then the LORD spoke to you out of the fire. You heard the sound of his words. But you didn't see any shape or form. You only heard a voice. ¹³He announced his covenant to you. That covenant is the Ten Commandments. He commanded you to obey them. Then he wrote them down on two stone tablets. ¹⁴At that time the LORD directed me to teach you his rules and laws. You must obey them in the land you are crossing the Jordan River to take as your own.

Don't Make or Worship Statues of Gods

¹⁵The LORD spoke to you at Mount Horeb out of the fire. But you didn't see any shape or form that day. So be very careful. ¹⁶Make sure you don't commit a horrible sin. Don't make for yourselves a statue of a god. Don't make a god that looks like a man or woman or anything else. ¹⁷Don't make one that looks like any animal on earth or any bird that flies in the sky. ¹⁸Don't make a statue that looks like any creature that moves along the ground or any fish that swims in the water. ¹⁹When you look up at the heavens, you will see the sun and moon. And you will see huge numbers of stars. Don't let anyone tempt you to bow down to the sun, moon or stars. Don't worship things the LORD your God has provided for all the nations on earth. ²⁰Egypt was like a furnace that melts iron down and makes it pure. But the LORD took you and brought you out of Egypt. He wanted you to be his very own people. And that's exactly what you are.

²¹The LORD was angry with me because of what you did. He promised that he would never let me go across the Jordan River. He promised that I would never enter that good land. It's the land the LORD your God is giving you as your own. ²²I'll die here in this land. I won't go across the Jordan. But you are about to cross over it. You will take that good land as your

WOOTON'S FUN FACTS
Deut. 4:16-18

I once made a statue of a sea monkey from chewed gum. I asked Mr. Whittaker if that was okay and he said it was kind of gross, but yes . . . it was okay. A statue is "art" until you worship it. Then it becomes an "idol." Nobody worshiped my gum monkey.

own. ²³Be careful. Don't forget the covenant the LORD your God made with you. Don't make for yourselves a statue of any god at all. He has told you not to. So don't do it. ²⁴The LORD your God is like a fire that burns everything up. He wants you to worship only him.

²⁵So don't make a statue of a god. Don't commit that horrible sin. Don't do it even after you have had children and grandchildren. Don't do it even after you have lived in the land a long time. If you do, that will be an evil thing in the sight of the LORD your God. You will make him angry. ²⁶Today I'm calling out to the heavens and the earth to be witnesses against you. Suppose you do these things. Then you will quickly die in the land you are going across the Jordan River to take over. You won't live there very long. You will certainly be destroyed. ²⁷The LORD will drive you out of your land. He will scatter you among the nations. Only a few of you will remain alive there. ²⁸There you will worship gods that men have made out of wood and stone. Those gods can't see, hear, eat or smell. ²⁹Perhaps while you are there, you will seek the LORD your God. You will find him if you seek him with all your heart and with all your soul. ³⁰All the things I've told you about might happen to you. And you will be in trouble. But later you will return to the LORD your God. You will obey him. ³¹The LORD your God is tender and loving. He won't leave you or destroy you. He won't forget the covenant he made with your people of long ago. He gave his word when he made it.

The LORD Is God

³²Ask now about the days of long ago. Find out what happened long before your time. Ask about what has happened since the time God created human beings on the earth. Ask from one end of the world to the other. Has anything as great as this ever happened? Has anything like it ever been heard of? ³³You heard the voice of God speaking out of fire. And you lived! Has that happened to any other people? ³⁴Has any god ever tried to take one nation out of another to be his own? Has any god done it by testing his people? Has any god done it with signs and amazing deeds or with war? Has any god reached out his mighty hand and powerful arm? Or has any god shown his people his great and wonderful acts? The LORD your God did all those things for you in Egypt. With your very own eyes you saw him do them.

³⁵The LORD showed you those things so that you might know he is God. There is no other God except him. ³⁶From heaven he made you hear his voice. He wanted to teach you. On earth he showed you his great fire. You heard his words coming out of the fire. ³⁷He loved your people of long ago. He chose their children after them. So he brought you out of Egypt. He used his great strength to do it. ³⁸He drove out nations to make room for you. They were greater and stronger than you are. He will bring you into their land. He wants to give it to you as your very own. The whole land is as good as yours right now.

³⁹The LORD is God in heaven above and on the earth below. Today you must agree with that and take it to heart. There is no other God. ⁴⁰I'm giving you his rules and commands today. Obey them. Then things will go well with you and your children after you. You will live a long time in the land. The LORD your God is giving you the land for all time to come.

Cities to Run to for Safety

⁴¹Then Moses set apart three cities east of the Jordan River. ⁴²Suppose someone killed a person they didn't hate and without meaning to do it. That person could run to one of those cities and stay alive. ⁴³Here are the names of the cities. Bezer was for the people of Reuben. It was in the high plains in the desert. Ramoth was for the people of Gad. It was in Gilead. Golan was for the people of Manasseh. It was in Bashan.

Jason's Jargon

DEUTERONOMY 4

Another quest! Find *furnace* in this chapter. Here, a furnace is an enclosed space that is heated to very high temperatures and is used for melting metals and baking pottery.

Moses Gives the Law to Israel

⁴⁴Here is the law Moses gave the Israelites. ⁴⁵Here are its terms, rules and laws. Moses gave them to the people when they came out of Egypt. ⁴⁶They were now east of the Jordan River in the valley near Beth Peor. They were in the land of Sihon, the king of the Amorites. He ruled in Heshbon. But Moses and the Israelites won the battle over him after we came out of Egypt. ⁴⁷They captured his land and made it their own. They also took the land of Og, the king of Bashan. Sihon and Og were the two Amorite kings east of the Jordan River. ⁴⁸Their land reached from Aroer on the rim of the Arnon River valley to Mount Hermon. ⁴⁹It included the whole Arabah Valley east of the Jordan. It included land all the way to the Dead Sea below the slopes of Pisgah.

The Ten Commandments

5 Moses sent for all the Israelites. Here is what he said to them.

Israel, listen to me. Here are the rules and laws I'm announcing to you today. Learn them well. Be sure to obey them. ²The LORD our God made a covenant with us at Mount Horeb. ³He didn't make it only with our people of long ago. He also made it with us. In fact, he made it with all of us who are alive here today. ⁴The LORD spoke to you face to face. His voice came out of the fire on the mountain. ⁵At that time I stood between the LORD and you. I announced to you the LORD's message. I did it because you were afraid of the fire. You didn't go up the mountain.

The LORD said,

⁶ "I am the LORD your God. I brought you out of Egypt. That is the land where you were slaves.

⁷ "Do not put any other gods in place of me.

⁸ "Do not make statues of gods that look like anything in the sky or on the earth or in the waters. ⁹Do not bow down to them or worship them. I am the LORD your God. I want you to worship only me. I cause the sins of the parents to affect their children. I will cause the sins of those who hate me to affect even their grandchildren and great-grandchildren. ¹⁰But for all time to come I show love to all those who love me and keep my commandments.

¹¹ "Do not misuse the name of the LORD your God. The LORD will find guilty anyone who misuses his name.

¹² "Keep the Sabbath day holy. Do this just as the LORD your God has commanded you. ¹³Do all your work in six days. ¹⁴But the seventh day is a sabbath to honor the LORD your God. Do not do any work on that day. The same command applies to your sons and daughters, your male and female servants, your oxen, your donkeys and your other animals. It also applies to any outsiders who live in your towns. I want your male and female servants to rest, just as you do. ¹⁵Remember that you were slaves in Egypt. The LORD your God reached out his mighty hand and powerful arm and brought you out of there. So the LORD your

WHIT'S WISDOM

Deuteronomy 5

Last summer, there was a big thunderstorm in Odyssey and some of the kids hung out at Whit's End until it passed. Suddenly, there was a flash and explosion as lightning struck a tree in McAlister Park! Everybody jumped.

"Maybe God just decided to give us ten more commandments," said Matthew as everyone started to calm down. "You know, the Bible talks about the lightning before He gave us the first ten."

"If you're ready for ten more commandments, do you remember the first ten?" I asked.

Matthew thought for a minute and came up with six of them. No one could name all ten. Even Connie had trouble remembering every one. How many can you name?

God included His commandments *twice* in the Old Testament. Most people know about Exodus 20:1–20, but they are also in Deuteronomy 5:1–22. They're important because they are God's rules for how to live. As the thunderstorm continued, the kids and I started to come up with ways to remember the Ten Commandments. Can you think of any?

And then, after you start remembering the commandments, don't forget to do what they say!

God has commanded you to keep the Sabbath day holy.

[16] "Honor your father and mother, just as the LORD your God has commanded you. Then you will live a long time in the land he is giving you. And things will go well with you there.

[17] "Do not murder.

[18] "Do not commit adultery.

[19] "Do not steal.

[20] "Do not be a false witness against your neighbor.

[21] "Do not want to have your neighbor's wife. Do not desire anything your neighbor owns. Do not desire to have your neighbor's house or land, male or female servant, ox or donkey."

[22] These are the commandments the LORD announced in a loud voice to your whole community. He gave them to you there on the mountain. He spoke out of the fire, cloud and deep darkness. He didn't add anything else. Then he wrote the commandments on two stone tablets. And he gave them to me.

[23] The mountain was blazing with fire. You heard the voice coming out of the darkness. So your elders and all the leaders of your tribes came to me. [24] You said, "The LORD our God has shown us his glory and majesty. We have heard his voice coming out of the fire. Today we have seen that a person can still stay alive even if God speaks with them. [25] But why should we die? This great fire will burn us up. We'll die if we hear the voice of the LORD our God again. [26] We have heard the voice of the living God. We've heard him speaking out of the fire. Has any other human being ever heard him speak like that and stayed alive? [27] Go near and listen to everything the LORD our God says. Then tell us what he tells you. We will listen and obey."

[28] The LORD heard you when you spoke to me. He said to me, "I have heard what these people said to you. Everything they said was good. [29] But I wish they would always have respect for me in their hearts. I wish they would always obey all my commands. Then things would go well with them and their children forever.

[30] "Go and tell them to return to their tents. [31] But you stay here with me. Then I

will give you all my commands, rules and laws. You must teach the people to obey them in the land I am giving them as their very own."

³²So be careful to do what the LORD your God has commanded you. Don't turn away from his commands to the right or the left. ³³Live exactly as the LORD your God has commanded you to live. Then you will enjoy life in the land you will soon own. Things will go well with you there. You will live there for a long time.

Love the LORD Your God

6 The LORD your God has directed me to teach you his commands, rules and laws. Obey them in the land you will take over when you go across the Jordan River. ²Then you, your children and their children after them will honor the LORD your God as long as you live. Obey all his rules and commands I'm giving you. If you do, you will enjoy long life. ³Israel, listen to me. Make sure you obey me. Then things will go well with you. The number of your people will increase greatly in a land that has plenty of milk and honey. That's what the LORD, the God of your parents, promised you.

⁴Israel, listen to me. The LORD is our God. The LORD is the one and only God. ⁵Love the LORD your God with all your heart and with all your soul. Love him with all your strength. ⁶The commandments I give you today must be in your hearts. ⁷Make sure your children learn them. Talk about them when you are at home. Talk about them when you walk along the road. Speak about them when you go to bed. And speak about them when you get up. ⁸Write them down and tie them on your hands as a reminder. Also tie them on your foreheads. ⁹Write them on the doorframes of your houses. Also write them on your gates.

CANDID CONVERSATIONS

Last year I kept all my receipts and figured out how much money I spent on things for the whole year. It was shocking when I found out that I spent almost twice as much on movies, fashion magazines, and music as I did on giving to my church! I don't see *that* many movies, but over time, it all added up!

Loving God with *all* my heart means putting more value on my relationship with Him than I do on things that—well—things that I should love with only *half* of my heart, or maybe even a third. Do you believe that following Jesus is more important than anything else in your life? When you truly believe this, it changes the way you act and think about lots of things. You may not have a lot of money to spend at your age, but you do have a lot of *time*. How do you spend your time?

Today, instead of spending time on unimportant things like television and video games, why not spend some extra time with God?

¹⁰The LORD your God will bring you into the land of Canaan. He gave his word. He promised he would give the land to your fathers, to Abraham, Isaac and Jacob. The land has large, wealthy cities you didn't build. ¹¹It has houses filled with all kinds of good things you didn't provide. The land has wells you didn't dig. And it has vineyards and groves of olive trees you didn't plant. You will have plenty to eat. ¹²But be careful that you don't forget the LORD. Remember that he brought you out of Egypt. That's the land where you were slaves.

¹³Worship the LORD your God. He is the only one you should serve. When you

REMEMBER THIS

DEUTERONOMY 6:5

"Love the LORD your God with all your heart and with all your soul. Love him with all your strength."

make promises, do so in his name. [14]Don't serve the gods of the nations around you. [15]The LORD your God is among you. He wants you to worship only him. If you worship other gods, God will be very angry with you. And he will destroy you from the face of the land. [16]Don't test the LORD your God as you did at Massah. [17]Be sure to obey the LORD's commands. Obey the terms and rules he has given you. [18]Do what is right and good in the LORD's eyes. Then things will go well with you. You will go in and take over the land. It's the good land the LORD promised to your people of long ago. [19]You will drive out all your enemies to make room for you. That's what the LORD said would happen.

[20]Later on, your child might ask you, "What is the meaning of the terms, rules and laws the LORD our God has commanded you to obey?" [21]If they do ask you, tell them, "We were Pharaoh's slaves in Egypt. But the LORD used his mighty hand to bring us out of Egypt. [22]With our own eyes we saw the LORD send amazing signs. They were great and terrible. He sent them on Egypt and Pharaoh and everyone in his house. [23]But the LORD brought us out of Egypt. He planned to bring us into the land of Canaan and give it to us. It's the land he promised to our people of long ago. [24]The LORD our God commanded us to obey all his rules. He commanded us to honor him. If we do, we will always succeed and be kept alive. That's what is happening today. [25]We must make sure we obey the whole law in the sight of the LORD our God. That's what he has commanded us to do. If we obey his law, we'll be doing what he requires of us."

The LORD Will Drive Out Many Nations

7 The LORD your God will bring you into the land. You are going to enter it and take it as your own. He'll drive out many nations to make room for you. He'll drive out the Hittites, Girgashites, Amorites, Canaanites, Perizzites, Hivites and Jebusites. Those seven nations are larger and stronger than you are. [2]The LORD your God will hand them over to you. You will win the battle over them. You must completely destroy them. Don't make a peace treaty with them. Don't show them any mercy. [3]Don't marry any of their people. Don't give your daughters to their sons. And don't take their daughters for your sons. [4]If you do, those people will turn your children away from serving the LORD. Then your children will serve other gods. The LORD will be very angry with you. He will quickly destroy you. [5]So here is what you must do to those people. Break down their altars. Smash their sacred stones. Cut down the poles they use to worship the female god named Asherah. Burn the statues of their gods in the fire. [6]You are a holy nation. The LORD your God has set you apart for himself. He has chosen you to be his special treasure. He chose you out of all the nations on the face of the earth to be his people.

[7]The LORD chose you because he loved you very much. He didn't choose you because you had more people than other nations. In fact, you had the smallest number of all. [8]The LORD chose you because he loved you. He wanted to keep the promise he had made to your people of long ago. That's why he used his mighty hand to bring you out of Egypt. He bought you back from the land where you were slaves. He set you free from the power of Pharaoh, the king of Egypt. [9]So I want you to realize that the LORD your God is God. He is the faithful God. He keeps his covenant for all time to come. He keeps it with those who love him and obey his commandments. He shows them his love. [10]But he will pay back those who hate him. He'll destroy them. He'll quickly pay back

ADVENTURES IN ODYSSEY

Whit and Eugene got to see a firsthand example of the importance of what it means to fear God in "The Cross of Cortes" (A#12).

Deut. 7:8 Okay, so it's not *all* about feet in the Bible. God's mighty hand (or arm) is mentioned more than thirty-five times in the Scriptures.

those who hate him. [11]So be careful to obey the commands, rules and laws I'm giving you today.

[12]Pay attention to the laws of the LORD your God. Be careful to obey them. Then he will keep his covenant of love with you. That's what he promised to your people of long ago. [13]The LORD will love you and bless you. He'll cause there to be many of you. He'll give you many children. He'll bless the crops of your land. He'll give you plenty of grain, olive oil and fresh wine. He'll bless your herds with many calves. He'll give your flocks many lambs. He'll do all these things for you in the land of Canaan. It's the land he promised your people of long ago that he would give you. [14]He will bless you more than any other nation. All your men and women will have children. All your livestock will have little ones. [15]The LORD will keep you from getting sick. He won't send on you any of the horrible sicknesses you saw all around you in Egypt. But he'll send them on everyone who hates you. [16]You must destroy all the nations the LORD your God hands over to you. Don't feel sorry for them. Don't serve their gods. If you do, they will be a trap for you.

[17]You might say to yourselves, "These nations are stronger than we are. How

WHAT ABOUT YOU?

A will is a legal document that tells people what to do with our belongings after we die. Most people leave instructions about who gets their money and property. Some wills even include sentimental items like grandma's homemade quilt or grandpa's pocket watch. This is called an "inheritance." A will is very important for making sure a person's wishes are carried out once he or she is gone.

God's chosen people, a small and powerless nation, were promised the inheritance of a land of their own, free from slavery. In the Old Testament, we learn about how God kept His promise to the nation of Israel. In the New Testament, we read that God's children can look forward to an inheritance as well. But we don't have to worry about who gets more. The inheritance is eternal life. Our hope lies in what Jesus did when He died on the Cross and rose from the dead, and our heavenly inheritance will never perish, spoil, or fade (see 1 Peter 1:3–4).

Suppose you were a mega-gazillionaire with so much money it wouldn't fit inside a ten-story building. Who would you want to have it once you've left this earth? How do you want people to remember you? Today's challenge is to write out a will befitting a mega-gazillionaire so that people know what matters most in your life. Of course, we shouldn't wait until we're gone to show people that we care. What can you do today to live more generously?

can we drive them out?" ¹⁸But don't be afraid of them. Be sure to remember what the LORD your God did to Pharaoh and all the Egyptians. ¹⁹With your own eyes you saw what the LORD did to them. You saw the signs and amazing things he did. He reached out his mighty hand and powerful arm. The LORD your God used all those things to bring you out. You are now afraid of the nations that are in the land the LORD promised you. But the LORD your God will do to them the same things he did to Egypt. ²⁰The LORD your God will also send hornets among those nations. Some of the people left alive will hide from you. But even they will die. ²¹So don't be terrified by them. The LORD your God is with you. He is a great and wonderful God. ²²The LORD your God will drive out those nations to make room for you. But he will do it little by little. You won't be allowed to get rid of them all at once. If you did, wild animals would multiply all around you. ²³But the LORD your God will hand those nations over to you. He will throw them into a panic until they are destroyed. ²⁴He will hand their kings over to you. You will wipe out their names from the earth. No one will be able to stand up against you. You will destroy them. ²⁵Burn the statues of their gods in the fire. Don't wish for the silver and gold on those statues. Don't take it for yourselves. If you do, it will be a trap for you. The LORD your God hates it. ²⁶Don't bring anything he hates into your house. If you do, you will be completely destroyed along with it. So hate it with all your heart. It is set apart to be destroyed.

Remember What the LORD Has Done

8 Make sure you obey every command I'm giving you today. Then you will live, and there will be many of you. You will enter the land and take it as your own. It's the land the LORD promised to your people of long ago. ²Remember how the LORD your God led you all the way. He guided you in the desert for these 40 years. He wanted to take your pride away. He wanted to test you to know what was in your hearts. He wanted to see whether you would obey his commands. ³He took your pride away. He let you go hungry. Then he gave you manna to eat. You and

your parents had never even known anything about manna before. He tested you to teach you that man doesn't live only on bread. He also lives on every word that comes from the mouth of the LORD. ⁴Your clothes didn't wear out during these 40 years. Your feet didn't swell. ⁵Here is what I want you to know in your hearts. The LORD your God guides you, just as parents guide their children.

⁶Obey the commands of the LORD your God. Live as he wants you to live. Have respect for him. ⁷The LORD your God is bringing you into a good land. It has brooks, streams and deep springs of water. Those springs flow in its valleys and hills. ⁸It has wheat, barley, vines, fig trees, pomegranates, olive oil and honey. ⁹There is plenty of food in that land. You will have everything you need. Its rocks have iron in them. And you can dig copper out of its hills.

¹⁰When you have eaten and are satisfied, praise the LORD your God. Praise him for the good land he has given you. ¹¹Make sure you don't forget the LORD your God. Don't fail to obey his commands, laws and rules. I'm giving them to you today. ¹²But suppose you don't obey his commands. And suppose you have plenty to eat. You build fine houses and live in them. ¹³The number of your herds and flocks increases. You also get more and more silver and gold. And everything you have multiplies. ¹⁴Then your hearts will become proud. And you will forget the LORD your God. The LORD brought you out of Egypt. That's the land where you were slaves. ¹⁵He led you through that huge and terrible desert. It was a dry land. It didn't have any water. It had poisonous snakes and scorpions. The LORD gave you water out of solid rock. ¹⁶He gave you manna to eat in the desert. Your people had never even known anything about manna before. The LORD took your pride away. He tested you. He did it so that things would go well with you in the end. ¹⁷You might say to yourself, "My power and my strong hands have made me rich." ¹⁸But remember the LORD your God. He gives you the ability to produce wealth. That shows he stands by the terms of the covenant he made with you. He promised

it to your people of long ago. And he's still faithful to his covenant today.

¹⁹Don't forget the LORD your God. Don't serve other gods. Don't worship them and bow down to them. I am a witness against you today that if you do, you will certainly be destroyed. ²⁰You will be destroyed just like the nations the LORD your God is destroying to make room for you. That's what will happen if you don't obey him.

Why the LORD Gave Canaan to Israel

9 Israel, listen to me. You are now about to go across the Jordan River. You will take over the land of the nations that live there. Those nations are greater and stronger than you are. Their large cities have walls that reach up to the sky. ²The people who live there are Anakites. They are strong and tall. You know all about them. You have heard people say, "Who can stand up against the Anakites?" ³But today you can be sure the LORD your God will go over there ahead of you. He is like a fire that will burn them up. He'll destroy them. He'll bring them under your control. You will drive them out. You will put an end to them quickly, just as the LORD has promised you.

⁴The LORD your God will drive them out to make room for you. When he does, don't say to yourself, "The LORD has done it because I am godly. That's why he brought me here to take over this land." That isn't true. The LORD is going to drive out those nations to make room for you because they are very evil. ⁵You are not going in to take over their land because you have done what is right or honest. It's because those nations are so evil. That's why the LORD your God will drive them out to make room for you. He will do what he said he would do. He made a promise to your fathers, to Abraham, Isaac and Jacob. ⁶The LORD your God is giving you this good land to take as your own. But you must understand that it isn't because you are a godly nation. In fact, you are stubborn.

Israel Worshiped the Golden Calf

⁷Here is something you must remember. Never forget it. You made the LORD your God angry in the desert. You refused to obey him from the day you left Egypt until you arrived here. ⁸At Mount Horeb you made the LORD angry enough to destroy you. ⁹I went up the mountain. I went there to receive the tablets of the covenant law. They were made out of stone. It was the covenant the LORD had made with you. I stayed on the mountain for 40 days and 40 nights. I didn't eat any food or drink any water. ¹⁰The LORD gave me two stone tablets. The words on them were written by the finger of God. All the commandments the LORD gave you were written on the tablets. He announced them to you out of the fire on the mountain. He wrote them on the day you gathered together there.

¹¹The 40 days and 40 nights came to an end. Then the LORD gave me the two stone tablets. They were the tablets of the covenant law. ¹²The LORD told me, "Go down from here right away. The people you brought out of Egypt have become very sinful. They have quickly turned away from what I commanded them. They have made a statue of a god for themselves."

¹³The LORD also said to me, "I have seen these people. They are so stubborn! ¹⁴Do not try to stop me. I am going to destroy them. I will wipe them out from the earth. Then I will make you into a great nation. Your people will be stronger than they were. There will be more of you than there were of them."

¹⁵So I turned and went down the mountain. It was blazing with fire. I was carrying the two tablets of the covenant law. ¹⁶When I looked, I saw that you had sinned against the LORD your God. You had made for yourselves a metal statue of a god. It looked like a calf. You had quickly turned away from the path the LORD had commanded you to follow. ¹⁷So I threw the two tablets out of my hands. You watched them break into pieces.

¹⁸Then once again I fell down flat in front of the LORD with my face toward the ground. I lay there for 40 days and 40 nights. I didn't eat any food or drink any water. You had committed a terrible sin. You had done an evil thing in the LORD's sight. You had made him angry. ¹⁹I was afraid of the LORD's great anger. He was so angry with you he wanted to destroy you. But the LORD listened to me again. ²⁰And

he was so angry with Aaron he wanted to destroy him too. But at that time I prayed for Aaron. ²¹I also got that sinful calf you had made. I burned it in the fire. I crushed it and ground it into fine powder. Then I threw the powder into a stream that was flowing down the mountain.

²²You also made the LORD angry at Taberah, Massah and Kibroth Hattaavah.

²³The LORD sent you out from Kadesh Barnea. He said, "Go up and take over the land I have given you." But you refused to do what the LORD your God had commanded you to do. You didn't trust him or obey him. ²⁴You have been refusing to obey the LORD as long as I've known you.

²⁵I lay down in front of the LORD with my face toward the ground for 40 days and 40 nights. I did it because the LORD had said he would destroy you. ²⁶I prayed to him. "LORD and King," I said, "don't destroy your people. They belong to you. You set them free by your great power. You used your mighty hand to bring them out of Egypt. ²⁷Remember your servants Abraham, Isaac and Jacob. Forgive the Israelites for being so stubborn. Don't judge them for the evil and sinful things they've done. ²⁸If you do, the Egyptians will say, 'The LORD wasn't able to take them into the land he had promised to give them. He hated them. So he brought them out of Egypt to put them to death in the desert.' ²⁹But they are your people. They belong to you. You used your great power to bring them out of Egypt. You reached out your mighty arm and saved them."

The New Stone Tablets

10 At that time the LORD spoke to me. He said, "Carve out two stone tablets, just like the first ones. Then come up to me on the mountain. Also make a wooden ark. ²I will write on the tablets the words that were on the first tablets, which you broke. Then you must put the tablets in the ark."

³So I made the ark out of acacia wood. I carved out two stone tablets that were just like the first ones. I went up the mountain. I carried the two tablets in my hands. ⁴The LORD wrote on the tablets what he had written before. It was the Ten Commandments. He had announced them to you

You've had it. You're tired of friends treating you badly. They need to learn a lesson about how to behave. Starting now, you're going to charge a fifty-cent fine to anyone who borrows something and fails to give it back on time. A quarter if anyone misspells your name. A dollar if they make plans to get together with you, then forget to show up.

That's one way to get a little respect, right? But after a few weeks of doing this, how many friends do you think you'd have left? Punishing people who hurt us isn't the right choice. God cares about how we do things and why we do them. He looks at our hearts as well as our actions. And as He commanded the nation of Israel, He wants us to respect Him and put Him first. He wants us to care for others as well.

Want to know what takes real courage? *Not* insulting the mean kid. *Not* trying to make someone pay for accidentally breaking or forgetting to return your stuff. Admitting when you're wrong. Asking for forgiveness and offering grace to others. Those can be hard things to do, but God has promised to be with us and help us obey Him, even when it's hard.

Think about the things other people do that make you mad. Got a few? Now rely on God's wisdom, pray, and ask Him to show you how to take actions that honor Him, even when you don't feel like it.

out of the fire on the mountain. It was on the day you had gathered together there. So the LORD gave the tablets to me. [5]Then I came back down the mountain. I put the tablets in the ark I had made, just as the LORD had commanded me. And that's where they are now.

[6]Remember how the Israelites traveled from the wells of Bene Jaakan to Moserah. That's where Aaron died. And his body was buried there. His son Eleazar became the next priest after him. [7]From Moserah the people traveled to Gudgodah. Then they went on to Jotbathah. That land has streams of water. [8]At that time the LORD set the tribe of Levi apart. He appointed them to carry the ark of the covenant of the LORD. He wanted them to serve him. He told them to bless the people in his name. And they still do it today. [9]That's why the Levites don't have any part of the land the LORD gave the other tribes in Israel. They don't have any share among them. The LORD himself is their share. That's what the LORD your God told them.

[10]I had stayed on the mountain for 40 days and 40 nights, just as I did the first time. The LORD listened to me that time also. He didn't want to destroy you. [11]"Go," the LORD said to me. "Lead the people on their way. Then they can enter the land and take it over. I have given my word. I promised I would give the land to their fathers, to Abraham, Isaac and Jacob."

Honor the LORD

[12]And now, Israel, what is the LORD your God asking you to do? Honor him. Live exactly as he wants you to live. Love him. Serve him with all your heart and with all your soul. [13]Obey the LORD's commands and rules. I'm giving them to you today for your own good.

[14]The heavens belong to the LORD your God. Even the highest heavens belong to him. He owns the earth and everything in it. [15]But the LORD loved your people of long ago very much. You are their children. And he chose you above all the other nations. His love and his promise remain with you to this very day. [16]So don't be stubborn anymore. Obey the LORD. [17]The LORD your God is the greatest God of all. He is the greatest LORD of all. He is the great God. He is mighty and wonderful.

He treats everyone the same. He doesn't accept any money from those who want special favors. [18]He stands up for widows and for children whose fathers have died. He loves outsiders living among you. He gives them food and clothes. [19]So you also must love outsiders. Remember that you yourselves were outsiders in Egypt. [20]Honor the LORD your God. Serve him. Remain true to him. When you make promises, do so in his name. [21]He is the one you should praise. He's your God. With your own eyes you saw the great and amazing things he did for you. [22]Long ago, your people went down into Egypt. The total number of them was 70. And now the LORD your God has made you as many as the stars in the sky.

Love and Obey the LORD

11 Love the LORD your God. Do what he requires. Always obey his rules, laws and commands. [2]Remember today that your children weren't the ones the LORD your God guided and corrected. They didn't see his majesty. They weren't in Egypt when he reached out his mighty hand and powerful arm. [3]They didn't see the signs and the other things he did in Egypt. They didn't see what he did to Pharaoh, the king of Egypt, and to his whole country. [4]They weren't there when the LORD destroyed the army of Egypt and its horses and chariots. He swept the waters of the Red Sea over the Egyptians while they were chasing you. He wiped them out forever. [5]Your children didn't see what he did for you in the desert before you arrived here. [6]They didn't see what he did to Dathan and Abiram, the sons of Eliab. Eliab was from the tribe of Reuben. The earth opened its mouth right in the middle of the Israelite camp. It swallowed up Dathan and Abiram. It swallowed them up together with their families, tents and every living thing that belonged to them. [7]But with your own eyes you saw all the great things the LORD has done.

[8]So obey all the commands I'm giving you today. Then you will be strong enough to go in and take over the land. You will go across the Jordan River and take the land as your own. [9]You will live there for a long time. It's the land the LORD promised to give to Abraham, Isaac and Jacob

and their children after them. He gave his word when he made that promise. The land has plenty of milk and honey. ¹⁰You will enter it and take it over. It isn't like the land of Egypt. That's where you came from. You planted your seeds there. You had to water them, just as you have to water a vegetable garden. ¹¹But you will soon go across the Jordan River. The land you are going to take over has mountains and valleys in it. It drinks rain from heaven. ¹²It's a land the LORD your God takes care of. His eyes always look on it with favor. He watches over it from the beginning of the year to its end.

¹³So be faithful. Obey the commands the LORD your God is giving you today. Love him. Serve him with all your heart and with all your soul. ¹⁴Then the LORD will send rain on your land at the right time. He'll send rain in the fall and in the spring. You will be able to gather your grain. You will also be able to make olive oil and fresh wine. ¹⁵He'll provide grass in the fields for your cattle. You will have plenty to eat.

Jason's Jargon

DEUTERONOMY 11

Search this chapter for the word *majesty*. Majesty describes the greatness of a person in power, such as a king. When we worship God's majesty, we show our respect for Him.

¹⁶But be careful. Don't let anyone tempt you to do something wrong. Don't turn away and worship other gods. Don't bow down to them. ¹⁷If you do, the LORD will be very angry with you. He'll close up the sky. It won't rain. The ground won't produce its crops. Soon you will die. You won't live to enjoy the good land the LORD is giving you. ¹⁸So keep my words in your hearts and minds. Write them down and tie them on your hands as a reminder. Also tie them on your foreheads. ¹⁹Teach them to

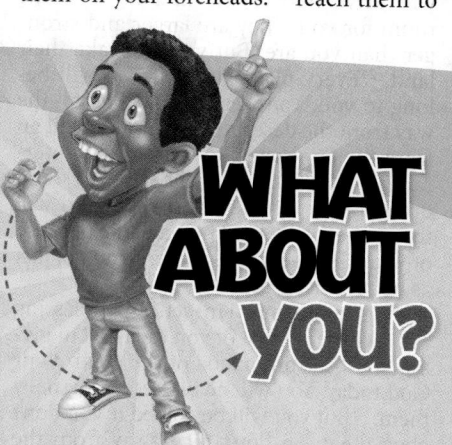

WHAT ABOUT YOU?

Has a storm ever caused the electricity to go out in your house? All of a sudden, you have no lights and no TV or Internet. What if the power stayed off for three days? Would you handle it well or would you complain a lot?

People who expect life to always be comfortable can suffer from a sense of "entitlement." Entitlement is the belief that you deserve to get what you want all the time. It is the opposite of thankfulness.

In the Adventures in Odyssey episode "License to Deprive," the Washington family learned about being thankful. They agreed to live like a frontier family from the 1800s. It was a hard adjustment. They had no electricity or running water. Daily chores included sewing their clothes, working a vegetable garden, and taking care of farm animals.

We often take our blessings for granted. We forget that not everyone has a nice home, plenty of food, or a family who loves them. The Washingtons realized they could live without twenty-first century luxuries and still find things to be grateful for. They

also discovered that working and playing games as a family is rewarding and fun.

Try spending an entire weekend with no TV, Internet, or handheld electronics. Instead, use the time to interact with your family. Work together on a project, play a game, assemble a puzzle, or read a Bible story and discuss it. You might make great new memories and rediscover all you have to be thankful for.

ADVENTURES IN ODYSSEY

The Israelites had to remember what was truly important. Grady McKay learned the same lesson in "Buddy Guard" (A#49).

your children. Talk about them when you are at home. Talk about them when you walk along the road. Speak about them when you go to bed. And speak about them when you get up. ²⁰Write them on the doorframes of your houses. Also write them on your gates. ²¹Then you and your children will live for a long time in the land. The LORD promised to give the land to Abraham, Isaac and Jacob. Your family line will continue as long as the heavens remain above the earth.

²²So be careful. Obey all the commands I'm giving you to follow. Love the LORD your God. Live exactly as he wants you to live. Remain true to him. ²³Then the LORD will drive out all the nations to make room for you. They are larger and stronger than you are. But you will take their land. ²⁴Every place you walk on will belong to you. Your territory will go all the way from the desert to Lebanon. It will go from the Euphrates River to the Mediterranean Sea. ²⁵No one will be able to stand up against you. The LORD your God will throw the whole land into a panic because of you. He'll do it everywhere you go, just as he promised you.

²⁶Listen to me. I'm setting a blessing and a curse in front of you today. ²⁷I'm giving you the commands of the LORD your God today. You will be blessed if you obey them. ²⁸But you will be cursed if you don't obey them. So don't turn away from the path I'm now commanding you to take. Don't turn away by worshiping other gods you didn't know before. ²⁹The LORD your God will bring you into the land to take it over. When he does, you must announce the blessings from Mount Gerizim. You must announce the curses from Mount Ebal. ³⁰As you know, those mountains are across the Jordan River. They are on the west side of the Jordan toward the setting sun. They are near the large trees of Moreh. The mountains are in the territory of the Canaanites, who live in the Arabah Valley near Gilgal. ³¹You are about to go across the Jordan River. You will enter the land and take it over. The LORD your God is giving it to you. You will take it over and live there. ³²When you do, make sure you obey all the rules and laws I'm giving you today.

Worship Only Where the LORD Wants You To

12 Here are the rules and laws you must obey. Be careful to obey them in the land the LORD has given you to take as your own. He's the God of your people who lived long ago. Obey these rules and laws as long as you live in the land. ²You will soon drive the nations out of it. Completely destroy all the places where they worship their gods. Destroy them on the high mountains, on the hills and under every green tree. ³Break down their altars. Smash their sacred stones. Burn up the poles they use to worship the female god named Asherah. Cut down the statues of their gods. Wipe out the names of their gods from those places.

⁴You must not worship the LORD your God the way those nations worship their gods. ⁵Instead, go to the special place he will choose from among all your tribes. He will put his Name there. That's where you must go. ⁶Take your burnt offerings and sacrifices to that place. Bring your special gifts and a tenth of everything you produce. Take with you what you have promised to give. Bring any other offerings you choose to give. And bring the male animals among your livestock that were born first to their mothers. ⁷You and your families will eat at the place the LORD your God will choose. He will be with you there. You will find joy in everything you have done. That's because he has blessed you.

⁸You must not do as we're doing here today. All of us are doing only what we think is right. ⁹That's because you haven't yet reached the place the LORD is giving you. Your God will give you peace and rest there. ¹⁰But first you will go across the Jordan River. You will settle in the land he's giving you. It will belong to you as your share. He will give you peace and rest from all your enemies around you. You will live in safety. ¹¹The LORD your God

will choose a special place. He will put his Name there. That's where you must bring everything I command you to bring. That includes your burnt offerings and sacrifices. It includes your special gifts and a tenth of everything you produce. It also includes all the things of value that you promised to give to the LORD. [12]Be filled with joy there in the sight of the LORD your God. Your children should also be joyful. So should your male and female servants. And so should the Levites from your towns. The Levites won't receive any part of the land as their share. [13]Be careful not to sacrifice your burnt offerings anywhere you want to. [14]Offer them only at the place the LORD will choose in one of your tribes. There you must obey everything I command you.

[15]But you can kill your animals in any of your towns. You can eat as much of the meat as you want to. You can eat it as if it were antelope or deer meat. That is part of the blessing the LORD your God is giving you. Those who are "clean" and those who are not can eat it. [16]But you must not eat meat that still has blood in it. Pour the blood out on the ground like water. [17]Here are the things you must not eat in your own towns. You must not eat the tenth part of your grain, olive oil and fresh wine. It belongs to the LORD. You must not eat the male animals among your livestock that were born first to their mothers. Don't eat anything you have promised to give. Don't eat any offerings you have chosen to give. And you must not eat any of your special gifts. [18]Instead, you must eat all those things in the sight of the LORD your God. Do it at the place he will choose. You, your children, your male and female servants and the Levites from your towns can eat them. Be filled with joy in the sight of the LORD your God. Be joyful in everything you do. [19]Don't forget to take care of the Levites as long as you live in your land.

[20]The LORD your God will increase your territory, just as he has promised you. When he does, you might get hungry for meat. You might say, "I'd really like some meat." Then you can eat as much of it as you want to. [21]The LORD your God will choose a special place. He will put his Name there. But suppose that place is too far away from you.

Then you can kill animals from the herds and flocks the LORD has given you. Do it just as I have commanded you. In your own towns you can eat as much of the meat as you want to. [22]Eat it as you would eat antelope or deer meat. Those who are "clean" and those who are not can eat it. [23]But be sure you don't eat meat that still has blood in it. The blood is the animal's life. So you must not eat the life along with the meat. [24]You must not eat the blood. Pour it out on the ground like water. [25]Don't eat it. Then things will go well with you and your children after you. You will be doing what is right in the eyes of the LORD.

[26]But go to the place the LORD will choose. Take with you the things you have set apart for him. Bring what you have promised to give him. [27]Sacrifice your burnt offerings on the altar of the LORD your God. Offer the meat and the blood there. The blood of your sacrifices must be poured out beside his altar. But you can eat the meat. [28]Make sure you obey all the rules I'm giving you. Then things will always go well with you and your children after you. That's because you will be doing what is good and right in the eyes of the LORD your God.

[29]You are about to attack the land and take it over as your own. When you do, the LORD your God will destroy the nations who live there. He will do it to make

Deut. 12:31 I learned a song that goes, "Jesus loves the little children, all the children of the world." The Israelites loved their children too, and that set them apart from other nations. Many of those other nations killed their infants. Isn't that terrible?

room for you. You will drive them out. You will settle in their land. ³⁰They will be destroyed to make room for you. But when they are destroyed, be careful. Don't be trapped. Don't ask questions about their gods. Don't say, "How do these nations serve their gods? We'll do it in the same way." ³¹You must not worship the LORD your God the way they worship their gods. When they worship, they do all kinds of evil things the LORD hates. They even burn up their children in the fire as sacrifices to their gods.

³²Be sure you do everything I am commanding you to do. Do not add anything to my commands. And do not take anything away from them.

Do Not Worship Other Gods

13 Suppose a prophet appears among you. Or someone comes who uses dreams to tell what's going to happen. He tells you that a sign or something amazing is going to take place. ²The sign or amazing thing he has spoken about might really take place. And then the prophet might say, "Let's serve other gods. Let's worship them." But you haven't known anything about those gods before. ³So you must not listen to what that prophet or dreamer has said. The LORD your God is testing you. He wants to know whether you love him with all your heart and with all your soul. ⁴You must worship him. You must honor him. Keep his commands. Obey him. Serve him. Remain true to him. ⁵That prophet or dreamer must be put to death. He told you not to obey the LORD your God. The LORD brought you out of Egypt. He set you free from the land where you were slaves. He commanded you to live the way he wants you to. But that prophet or dreamer has tried to get you to be unfaithful to the LORD. Get rid of that evil person.

⁶Suppose your very own brother or sister secretly tempts you to do something wrong. Or your child or the wife you love tempts you. Or your closest friend does it. Suppose one of them says, "Let's go and worship other gods." But you and your people of long ago hadn't known anything about those gods before. ⁷They are the gods of the nations around you. Those nations might be near or far away. In fact, they might reach from one end of the land to the other. ⁸Don't give in to those who are tempting you. Don't listen to them. Don't feel sorry for them. Don't spare them or save them. ⁹You must certainly put them to death. You must be the first to throw stones at them. Then all the people must do the same thing. ¹⁰Put them to death by throwing stones at them. They tried to turn you away from the LORD your God. He brought you out of Egypt. That's the land where you were slaves. ¹¹After you kill those who tempted you, all the Israelites will hear about it. And they will be too scared to do an evil thing like that again.

¹²The LORD your God is giving you towns to live in. But suppose you hear something bad about one of those towns. ¹³You hear that people who cause trouble have appeared among you. They've tried to get the people of their town to do something wrong. They've said, "Let's go and worship other gods." But you haven't known anything about those gods before. ¹⁴So you must ask people some questions. You must check out the matter carefully. If it's true, an evil thing has really happened among you. It's something the LORD hates. ¹⁵Then you must certainly kill with your swords everyone who lives in that town. You must destroy it completely. You must wipe out its people and livestock. ¹⁶You must gather all the goods of that town into the middle of the main street. You must burn the town completely. You must burn up everything in it. It's a whole burnt offering to the LORD your God. The town must remain a pile of stones forever. It must never be built again. ¹⁷Don't keep anything that should be destroyed. Then the LORD will turn away from his great anger. He will show you mercy. He'll have deep concern for you. He'll cause there to be many of you. That's what he promised your people of long ago. He gave his word when he made the promise. ¹⁸The LORD your God will do those things if you obey him. I'm giving you his commands today. And you must obey all of them. You must do what is right in his eyes.

"Clean" and "Unclean" Food

14 You are the children of the LORD your God. Don't cut yourselves to honor the dead. Don't shave the front of your heads to honor the dead. ²You are a holy nation. The LORD your God has set you apart for himself. He has chosen you to be his special treasure. He chose you out of all the nations on the face of the earth.

³Don't eat anything the LORD hates. ⁴Here are the only animals you can eat. You can eat oxen, sheep, goats, ⁵deer, gazelles, roe deer, wild goats, ibexes, antelope and mountain sheep. ⁶You can eat any animal that has a divided hoof. But it must also chew the cud. ⁷Some animals only chew the cud. Others only have a divided hoof. The camel, rabbit and rock badger chew the cud, but they don't have a divided hoof. So you can't eat them. They are not "clean" for you. ⁸Pigs aren't "clean" for you either. They have a divided hoof, but they don't chew the cud. So don't eat their meat. And don't touch their dead bodies.

⁹Many creatures live in water. You can eat all the ones that have fins and scales. ¹⁰But don't eat anything that doesn't have fins and scales. It isn't "clean" for you.

¹¹You can eat any "clean" bird. ¹²But there are many birds you can't eat. They include eagles, vultures, and black vultures. ¹³They include red kites, black kites and all kinds of falcons. ¹⁴They include all kinds of ravens. ¹⁵They include horned owls, screech owls, gulls and all kinds of hawks. ¹⁶They include little owls, great owls, white owls ¹⁷and desert owls. They include ospreys and cormorants. ¹⁸They include storks and all kinds of herons. They also include hoopoes and bats.

¹⁹All flying insects are "unclean" for you. So don't eat them. ²⁰But you can eat any creature that has wings and is "clean."

²¹If you find something that's already dead, don't eat it. You can give it to an outsider living in any of your towns. They may eat it. Or you can sell it to someone from another country. But you are a holy nation. The LORD your God has set you apart for himself.

Don't cook a young goat in its mother's milk.

Give a Tenth of What You Produce

²²Be sure to set apart a tenth of everything your fields produce each year. ²³Here are the things you should eat in the sight of the LORD your God. You should eat a tenth part of your grain, olive oil and fresh wine. You should also eat the male animals among your livestock that were born first to their mothers. Eat all these things at the special place the LORD your God will choose. He will put his Name there. You will learn to honor him always. ²⁴But suppose the place the LORD will choose for his Name is too far away from you. And suppose your God has blessed you. And your tenth part is too heavy for you to carry. ²⁵Then sell it for silver. Take the silver with you. Go to the place the LORD your God will choose. ²⁶Use the silver to buy anything you like. It can be cattle or sheep. It can be any kind of wine. In fact, it can be anything else you wish. Then you and your family can eat there in the sight of the LORD your God. You can be filled with joy. ²⁷Don't forget to take care of the Levites who will live in your towns. They won't receive any part of the land as their share.

²⁸At the end of every three years, bring a tenth of everything you produce that year. Store it in your towns. ²⁹Then the Levites can come and eat. That's because they won't receive any part of the land as their share. The outsiders and widows who live in your towns can come. So can the children whose fathers have died. Everyone can have plenty to eat. Then the LORD your God will bless you in everything you do.

The Year for Forgiving People What They Owe

15 At the end of every seven years you must forgive people what they owe you. ²Have you made a loan to one of your own people? Then forgive what is owed to you. You can't require that person to pay you back. The LORD's time to forgive what is owed has been announced. ³You can require someone from another nation to pay you back. But you must forgive what any of your own people owes you. ⁴There shouldn't be any poor people among you. The LORD will greatly bless you in the land he is giving you. You will take it over as your own. ⁵The LORD your God will bless you if you obey him completely. Be careful to follow all the commands I'm giving you today. ⁶The LORD your God will bless you, just as he has promised. You will lend money to many nations. But you won't have to borrow from any of them. You will rule over many nations. But none of them will rule over you.

⁷Suppose someone is poor among you. And suppose they live in one of the towns in the land the Lord your God is giving you. Then don't be mean to them. They are poor. So don't hold back money from them. ⁸Instead, open your hands and lend them what they need. Do it freely. ⁹Be careful not to have an evil thought in your mind. Don't say to yourself, "The seventh year will soon be here. It's the year for forgiving people what they owe." If you think like that, you might treat the needy people among you badly. You might not give them anything. Then they might make their appeal to the Lord against you. And he will find you guilty of sin. ¹⁰So give freely to needy people. Let your heart be tender toward them. Then the Lord your God will bless you in all your work. He will bless you in everything you do. ¹¹There will always be poor people in the land. So I'm commanding you to give freely to those who are poor and needy in your land. Open your hands to them.

Set Your Hebrew Servants Free

¹²Suppose any Hebrew men or women sell themselves to you. If they do, they will serve you for six years. Then in the seventh year you must let them go free. ¹³But when you set them free, don't send them away without anything to show for all their work. ¹⁴Freely give them some animals from your flock. Also give them some of your grain and wine. The Lord your God has blessed you richly. Give to them as he has given to you. ¹⁵Remember that you were slaves in Egypt. The Lord your God set you free. That's why I'm giving you this command today.

¹⁶But suppose your servant says to you, "I don't want to leave you." He loves you and your family. And you are taking good care of him. ¹⁷Then take him to the door of your house. Poke a hole through his earlobe into the doorpost. And he will become your servant for life. Do the same with your female servant.

¹⁸Don't think you are being cheated when you set your servants free. After all, they have served you for six years. The service of each of them has been worth twice as much as the service of a hired

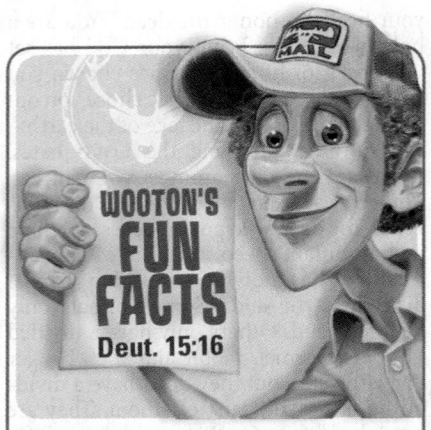

Seventy-seven percent of butlers in the United States are men, and most of them say they are "very satisfied" with their jobs. I don't think my parents' butler, Bradford, would ever leave.

worker. And the Lord your God will bless you in everything you do.

Male Animals Born First to Their Mothers

¹⁹Set apart every male animal among your livestock that was born first to its mother. Set it apart to the Lord your God. Don't put a firstborn cow to work. Don't clip the wool from a firstborn sheep. ²⁰Each year you and your family must eat them. Do it in front of the Lord your God at the place he will choose. ²¹Suppose an animal has something wrong with it. It might not be able to see or walk. Or it might have a bad flaw. Then you must not sacrifice it to the Lord your God. ²²You must eat it in your own towns. Those who are "clean" and those who are "unclean" can eat it. Eat it as if it were antelope or deer meat. ²³But you must not eat meat that still has blood in it. Pour the blood out on the ground like water.

The Passover Feast

16 Celebrate the Passover Feast of the Lord your God in the month of Aviv. In that month he brought you out of Egypt at night. ²Sacrifice an animal from your flock or herd. It is the Passover sacrifice to honor the Lord your God. Sacrifice it at the special place the Lord will choose. He will put his Name there. ³Don't eat the animal along with bread made with yeast. Instead, for seven days eat bread made without yeast. It's the bread that reminds you of how much you suffered. Remember that you left Egypt in a hurry. Remember it all the days of your life. Don't forget the day you left Egypt. ⁴Don't keep any yeast anywhere in your land for seven days. You will sacrifice the Passover animal on the evening of the first day. Do not let any of its meat be left over until the next morning.

⁵You must not sacrifice the Passover animal in just any town the LORD your God is giving you. ⁶Sacrifice it only in the special place he will choose for his Name. Sacrifice it there in the evening when the sun goes down. Do it on the same day every year. Be sure it's the day you left Egypt. ⁷Cook the animal and eat it. Do it at the place the LORD your God will choose. Then in the morning return to your tents. ⁸For six days eat bread made without yeast. On the seventh day come together for a service to honor the LORD your God. Don't do any work on that day.

The Feast of Weeks

⁹Count off seven weeks from the time you begin to cut your grain in the field. ¹⁰Then celebrate the Feast of Weeks to honor the LORD your God. Give to the LORD anything you choose to give as an offering. Give, just as the LORD has given to you. ¹¹Be filled with joy in the sight of the LORD your God. Be joyful at the special place he will choose for his Name. You, your children, and your male and female servants should be joyful. So should the Levites living in your towns. So should the outsiders and widows living among you. And so should the children whose fathers have died. ¹²Remember that you were slaves in Egypt. Be careful to obey the rules I'm giving you.

The Feast of Booths

¹³Gather the grain from your threshing floors. Take the fresh wine from your winepresses. Then celebrate the Feast of Booths for seven days. ¹⁴Be filled with joy at your feast. You, your children, and your male and female servants should be joyful. So should the Levites, the outsiders, and the widows living in your towns. And so should the children whose fathers have

died. ¹⁵For seven days celebrate the feast to honor the LORD your God. Do it at the place he will choose. The LORD will bless you when you gather all your crops. He'll bless you in everything you do. And you will be full of joy. ¹⁶All your men must appear in front of the LORD your God at the holy tent. They must go to the place he will choose. They must do it three times a year. They must go there to celebrate the Feast of Unleavened Bread, the Feast of Weeks and the Feast of Booths. None of your men should appear in front of the LORD without bringing something with him. ¹⁷Each of you must bring a gift. Give to the LORD your God, just as he has given to you.

Appoint Judges and Officials

¹⁸Appoint judges and officials for each of your tribes. Do it in every town the LORD your God is giving you. They must judge the people fairly. ¹⁹Do what is right. Treat everyone the same. Don't take money from people who want special favors. It makes those who are wise close their eyes to the truth. It twists the words of those who have done nothing wrong. ²⁰Do only what is right. Then you will live. You will take over the land the LORD your God is giving you.

Don't Worship Other Gods

²¹Don't set up a wooden pole used to worship the female god named Asherah. Don't set it up beside the altar you build to worship the LORD your God. ²²Don't set up a sacred stone to honor another god. The LORD your God hates Asherah poles and sacred stones.

17 Suppose an ox or sheep has anything at all wrong with it. Then don't sacrifice it to the LORD your God. He hates it.

²Someone living among you might do what is evil in the sight of the LORD your God. It might happen in one of the towns the LORD is giving you. That person is breaking the LORD's covenant. ³The person might have worshiped or bowed down to other gods. That person might have bowed down to the sun or moon or stars in the sky. I have commanded you not to do these things. ⁴When you hear that people have done something like that, check the matter out carefully. If it's true, an evil thing has been done in Israel.

The LORD hates that. ⁵So take the person who has done that evil thing to your city gate. Put that person to death by throwing stones at them. ⁶Two or three witnesses are required to put someone to death. No one can be put to death because of what only one witness says. Two or three witnesses are required. ⁷The witnesses must throw the first stones. Then the rest of the people must also throw stones. Get rid of that evil person.

Law Courts

⁸People will bring their cases to your courts. But some cases will be too hard for you to judge. They might be about murders, attacks or other crimes. Then take those hard cases to the place the LORD your God will choose. ⁹Go to a priest, who is a Levite. And go to the judge who is in office at that time. Ask them for their decision. They will give it to you. ¹⁰They'll hand down their decisions at the place the LORD will choose. You must do what they decide. Be careful to do everything they tell you to do. ¹¹Act according to whatever they teach you. Accept the decisions they give you. Don't turn away from what they tell you. Don't turn to the right or the left. ¹²Someone might show that they don't respect the judge. Or they will show that they don't respect the priest. The priest will serve the LORD your God at the place God will choose. If anyone doesn't show respect for these people, that person must be put to death. Remove that evil person from Israel. ¹³All the Israelites will hear about it. And they will be afraid to disrespect a judge or priest again.

Appoint the King the LORD Chooses

¹⁴You will enter the land the LORD your God is giving you. You will take it as your own. You will make your homes in it. When you do, you will say, "Let's appoint a king over us, just like all the nations around us." ¹⁵When that happens, make sure you appoint over yourselves a king the LORD your God chooses. He must be from among your own people. Don't appoint over yourselves someone from another country. Don't choose anyone who isn't from one of the tribes of Israel. ¹⁶The king must not get large numbers of horses for himself. He must not make the people return to Egypt to get more horses.

The LORD has told you, "You must not go back there again." ¹⁷The king must not have many wives. If he does, they will lead him astray. He must not store up large amounts of silver and gold.

¹⁸When he sits on the throne of his kingdom, he must make for himself a copy of the law. He must write on a scroll the law that I am teaching you. He must copy it from the scroll of a priest, who is a Levite. ¹⁹The king must keep the scroll close to him at all times. He must read it all the days of his life. Then he can learn to have respect for the LORD his God. He can carefully obey all the words of this law and these rules. ²⁰He won't think of himself as being better than his people are. He won't turn away from the law. He won't turn to the right or the left. Then he and his sons after him will rule over his kingdom in Israel for a long time.

Offerings for Priests and Levites

18 The priests, who are Levites, won't receive any part of the land of Israel. That also applies to the whole tribe of Levi. They will eat the food offerings presented to the LORD. That will be their share. ²They won't have any part of the land the LORD gave the other tribes in Israel. The LORD himself is their share, just as he promised them.

³Anyone who sacrifices a bull or a sheep owes a share of it to the priests. Their share is the shoulder, the inside parts and the meat from the head. ⁴You must give the priests the first share of the harvest of your grain, olive oil and fresh wine. You must also give them the first wool you clip from your sheep. ⁵The LORD your God has chosen the Levites and their sons after them to serve him in his name always. He hasn't chosen priests from any of your other tribes.

⁶Sometimes a Levite will move from the town in Israel where he's living. And he will come to the place the LORD will choose. He'll do it because he really wants to. ⁷Then he can serve in the name of the LORD his God. He'll be like all the other Levites who serve the LORD there. ⁸He must have an equal share of the good things they have. That applies even if he has already received money by selling things his family owned.

Jason's Jargon

DEUTERONOMY 18

Your mission: Search this chapter for the word *prophet*. A prophet is a person God uses to speak for Him. Elijah, Ezekiel, Isaiah, and Micah were all Old Testament prophets.

Practices the LORD Hates

⁹You will enter the land the LORD your God is giving you. When you do, don't copy the practices of the nations there. The LORD hates those practices. ¹⁰Here are things you must not do. Don't sacrifice your children in the fire to other gods. Don't practice any kind of evil magic at all. Don't use magic to try to explain the meaning of warnings in the sky or of any other signs. Don't take part in worshiping evil powers. ¹¹Don't put a spell on anyone. Don't get messages from those who have died. Don't talk to the spirits of the dead. Don't get advice from the dead. ¹²The LORD your God hates it when anyone does these things. The nations in the land he's giving you do these things he hates. So he will drive out those nations to make room for you. ¹³You must be without blame in the sight of the LORD your God.

The Prophet of the LORD

¹⁴You will take over the nations that are in the land the LORD is giving you. They listen to those who practice all kinds of evil magic. But you belong to the LORD your God. He says you must not do these things. ¹⁵The LORD your God will raise up for you a prophet like me. He will be one of your own people. You must listen to him. ¹⁶At Mount Horeb you asked the LORD your God for a prophet. You asked him on the day you gathered together. You said, "We don't want to hear the voice of the LORD our God. We don't want to see this great fire anymore. If we do, we'll die." ¹⁷The LORD said to me, "What they are saying is good. ¹⁸I will raise up for them a prophet like you. He will be one of their own people. I will put my words in his mouth. He will tell them everything I command him to say. ¹⁹The prophet will speak in my name. But someone might not listen to what I say through the prophet. I will hold that person responsible for not listening. ²⁰But suppose a prophet dares to speak in my name something I have not commanded. Or he speaks in the name of other gods. Then that prophet must be put to death."

²¹You will say to yourselves, "How can we know when a message hasn't been spoken by the LORD?" ²²Sometimes a prophet will announce something in the name of the LORD. And it won't take place or come true. Then that's a message the LORD hasn't told him to speak. That prophet has dared to speak on his own authority. So don't be afraid of what he says.

Cities to Run to for Safety

19 The LORD your God will destroy the nations whose land he is giving you. You will drive them out. And you will make your homes in their towns and their houses. ²When you do, set apart for yourselves three cities in the land. It's the land the LORD your God is giving you to take as your own. ³Figure out the distances and then separate the land into three parts. Then anyone who kills another person can run to one of these cities for safety. They are in the land the LORD your God is giving you as your own.

⁴Here is the rule about a person who kills someone. That person can run to one of those cities for safety. The rule applies to anyone who kills a neighbor they didn't hate and didn't mean to kill. ⁵For example, suppose a man goes into a forest with his neighbor to cut wood. When he swings his ax to chop down a tree, the head of the ax flies off. And it hits his neighbor and kills him. Then that man can run to one of those cities and save his life. ⁶If he doesn't go to one of those cities, the dead man's nearest male relative might become very angry. He might chase the man. If the city is too far away, he might catch him and kill him. But the man running to the city isn't worthy of death, because he didn't hate his neighbor. ⁷That's why I command you to set apart for yourselves three cities.

⁸The LORD your God will increase the size of your territory. He promised your

people of long ago that he would do it. He will give you the whole land he promised them. ⁹But he'll do it only if you are careful to obey all the laws I'm commanding you today. I command you to love the LORD your God. You must always live as he wants you to live. Suppose you are careful to obey, and the LORD your God gives you more land. Then you must set apart three more cities. ¹⁰Do it to protect those not guilty of murder. Then you won't spill their blood in your land. It's the land the LORD your God is giving you as your own.

¹¹But suppose a man hates his neighbor. So he hides and waits for him. Then he attacks him and kills him. And he runs to one of those cities for safety. ¹²If he does, the elders of his own town must send for him. He must be brought back from the city. He must be handed over to the dead man's nearest male relative. Then the relative will kill him. ¹³Don't feel sorry for him. He has killed someone who hadn't done anything wrong. Crimes like that must be punished in Israel. Then things will go well with you.

¹⁴Don't move your neighbor's boundary stone. It was set up by people who lived there before you. It marks the border of a field in the land you will receive as your own. The LORD your God is giving you that land. You will take it over.

Witnesses

¹⁵Suppose someone is charged with committing a crime of any kind. Then one witness won't be enough to prove that person is guilty. Every matter must be proved by the words of two or three witnesses.

¹⁶Suppose a witness who tells lies goes to court and brings charges against someone. The witness says someone committed a crime. ¹⁷Then the two people in the case must stand in front of the LORD. They must stand in front of the priests and the judges who are in office at that time. ¹⁸The judges must check out the matter carefully. And suppose the witness is proved to be lying. Then he has said something false in court against another Israelite. ¹⁹So do to the lying witness what he tried to do to the other person. Get rid of that evil witness. ²⁰The rest of the people will hear about it. And they will be afraid. They won't allow such an evil thing to be done among them again. ²¹Don't feel sorry for that evil person. A life must be taken for a life. An eye must be put out for an eye. A tooth must be knocked out for a tooth. A hand must be cut off for a hand and a foot for a foot.

Going to War

20 When you go to war against your enemies, you might see that they have horses and chariots. They might even have an army stronger than yours. But don't be afraid of them. The LORD your God will be with you. After all, he brought you up out of Egypt. ²Just before you go into battle, the priest will come forward. He'll speak to the army. ³He'll say, "Men of Israel, listen to me. Today you are going into battle against your enemies. Don't be scared. Don't be afraid. Don't panic or be terrified by them. ⁴The LORD your God is going with you. He'll fight for you. He'll help you win the battle over your enemies."

⁵The officers will speak to the army. They will say, "Has anyone built a new house and not started to live in it? Let him go home. If he doesn't, he might die in battle. Then someone else will live in his house. ⁶Has anyone planted a vineyard and not started to enjoy it? Let him go home. If he doesn't, he might die in battle. Then someone else will enjoy his vineyard. ⁷Has anyone promised to be married to a woman but hasn't done it yet? Let him go home. If he doesn't, he might die in battle. Then someone else will marry her." ⁸The officers will continue, "Is anyone afraid or scared? Let him go home. Then the other soldiers won't lose hope too." ⁹The officers will finish speaking to the army. When they do, they'll appoint commanders over it.

¹⁰Suppose you march up to attack a city. Before you attack it, offer to make peace with its people. ¹¹Suppose they accept your offer and open their gates. Then force all the people in the city to be your slaves. They will have to work for you. ¹²But suppose they refuse your offer of peace and prepare for battle. Then surround that city. Get ready to attack it. ¹³The LORD your God will hand it over to you. When he does, kill all the men with your swords.

¹⁴But you can take the women and children for your families. You can also take the livestock and everything else in the city. What you captured from your enemies you can take for yourselves. The LORD your God will give it to you. ¹⁵That's how you will treat all the cities far away from you. Those cities don't belong to the nations nearby.

But what about the cities the LORD is giving you as your own? Kill everything that breathes in those cities. Completely destroy them. Wipe out the Hittites, Amorites, Canaanites, Perizzites, Hivites and Jebusites. That's what the LORD your God commanded you to do. If you don't destroy them, they'll teach you to do all the things the LORD hates. That's the way they worship their gods. If you do those things, you will sin against the LORD your God.

Suppose you surround a city and get ready to attack it. And suppose you fight against it for a long time in order to capture it. Then don't chop down its trees and destroy them. You can eat their fruit. So don't cut them down. Are the trees people? So why should you attack them? ²⁰But you can cut down trees that you know aren't fruit trees. You can build war machines out of their wood. You can use them until you capture the city you are fighting against.

Deut. 20:19 Eugene had to explain to me that a rhetorical question is one that no one expects an answer to. God's question, "Are trees people?" is rhetorical, though my neighbor Miss Willow's name could be confusing to some people.

What to Do When You Don't Know Who Killed Someone

21 Suppose you find someone who has been killed. The body is lying in a field in the land the LORD your God is giving you as your own. But no one knows who the killer was. ²Then your elders and judges will go out to the field. They will measure the distance from the body to the nearby towns. ³The elders from the town that is nearest to the body will get a young cow. It must never have been used for work. It must never have pulled a load. ⁴The elders must lead it down into a valley. The valley must not have been farmed. There must be a stream flowing through it. There in the valley the elders must break the cow's neck. ⁵The priests, who are sons of Levi, will step forward. The LORD your God has chosen them to serve him. He wants them to bless the people in his name. He wants them to decide all cases that have to do with people arguing and attacking others. ⁶Then all the elders from the town that is nearest to the body will wash their hands. They will wash them over the young cow whose neck they broke in the valley. ⁷They'll say to the LORD, "We didn't kill that person. We didn't see it happen. ⁸Accept this payment for the sin of your people Israel. LORD, you have set your people free. Don't hold them guilty for spilling the blood of someone who hasn't done anything wrong." That will pay for the death of that person. ⁹So you will get rid of the guilt of killing someone who didn't do anything wrong. That's because you have done what is right in the LORD's eyes.

Marrying a Woman Who Is Your Prisoner

¹⁰Suppose you go to war against your enemies. And the LORD your God hands them over to you and you take them as prisoners. ¹¹Then you notice a beautiful woman among them. If you like her, you may marry her. ¹²Bring her home. Have her shave her head and cut her nails. ¹³Have her throw away the clothes she was wearing when she was captured. Let her live in your house and mourn the loss of her parents for a full month. Then you can go to her and be her husband. And she will be your wife. ¹⁴But suppose you

aren't pleased with her. Then let her go where she wants to. You must not sell her. You must not treat her as a slave. You have already brought shame on her.

The Rights of the Oldest Son

[15] Suppose a man has two wives. He loves one but not the other. And both of them have sons by him. But the oldest son is the son of the wife the man doesn't love. [16] Someday he'll leave his property to his sons. When he does, he must not give the rights of the oldest son to the son of the wife he loves. He must give those rights to his oldest son. He must do it even though his oldest son is the son of the wife he doesn't love. [17] He must recognize the full rights of the oldest son. He must do it, even though that son is the son of the wife he doesn't love. He must give that son a double share of everything he has. That son is the first sign of his father's strength. So the rights of the oldest son belong to him.

A Stubborn Son

[18] Suppose someone has a very stubborn son. He doesn't obey his father and mother. And he won't listen to them when they try to correct him. [19] Then his parents will take hold of him and bring him to the elders at the gate of his town. [20] They will say to the elders, "This son of ours is very stubborn. He won't obey us. He eats too much. He's always getting drunk." [21] Then all the people in his town will put him to death by throwing stones at him. Get rid of that evil person. All the Israelites will hear about it. And they will be afraid to disobey their parents.

Several Other Laws

[22] Suppose someone is put to death for a crime worthy of death. And a pole is stuck through their body and set up where people can see it. [23] Then you must not leave the body on the pole all night. Make sure you bury it that same day. Everyone who is hung on a pole is under God's curse. You must not make the land "unclean." The LORD your God is giving it to you as your own.

22 Suppose you see your neighbor's ox or sheep wandering away. Then don't act as if you didn't see it. Instead, make sure you take it back to its owner.

[2] Its owner might not live [...] might not know who own [...] animal home with you. K[...] *So take the* owner comes looking for it *until the* back to them. [3] Do the same *give it* find their donkey, coat or an[...] *you* have lost. Don't act as if you di[...]

[4] Suppose you see your neighb[...] key or ox that has fallen down [...] road. Then don't act as if you didn[...] Help the owner get it up on its feet [...]

[5] A woman must not wear [...] clothes. And a man must not wear w[...] en's clothes. The LORD your God hate[...] when anyone does this.

[6] Suppose you happen to find a bird[...] nest beside the road. It might be in a[...] tree or on the ground. And suppose the[...] mother bird is sitting on her little birds or on the eggs. Then don't act as if you didn't see [...] along with the little ones. [7] You can take the little ones. But make sure you let the mother go. Then things will go well with you. You will live for a long time.

[8] If you build a new house, put a low wall around the edge of your roof. Then you won't be responsible if someone falls off your roof and dies.

[9] Don't plant two kinds of seeds in your vineyard. If you do, the crops you grow there will be impure. Your grapes will also be impure.

[10] Don't let an ox and a donkey pull the same plow together.

[11] Don't wear clothes made out of wool and linen woven together.

[12] Make tassels on the four corners of the coat you wear.

Breaking Marriage Laws

[13] Suppose a man marries a woman and sleeps with her. But then he doesn't like her. [14] So he tells lies about her and says she's a bad woman. He says, "I married this woman. But when I slept with her, I discovered she wasn't a virgin." [15] Then the young woman's parents must bring proof that she was a virgin. They must give the proof to the elders at the gate of the town. [16] Her father will speak to the elders. He'll say, "I gave my daughter to this man to be his wife. But he doesn't like her. [17] So now he has told lies about her. He has said, 'I discovered that your daughter wasn't a virgin.' But here's the proof that

my daughter was a virgin." Then her parents will show the elders of the town the cloth that has her blood on it. [18]The elders will punish the man. [19]They'll make him weigh out two and a half pounds of silver. They'll give it to the young woman's father. That's because the man has said an Israelite virgin is a bad woman. She will continue to be his wife. He must not divorce her as long as he lives.

[20]But suppose the charge is true. And there isn't any proof that the young woman was a virgin. [21]Then she must be brought to the door of her father's house. There the people of her town will put her to death by throwing stones at her. She has done a very terrible thing in Israel. She has slept with a man before she was married. Get rid of that evil person.

[22]Suppose a man is seen sleeping with another man's wife. Then the man and the woman must both die. Get rid of those evil people.

[23]Suppose a man happens to see a virgin in a town. And she has promised to marry another man. But the man who happens to see her sleeps with her. [24]Then you must take both of them to the gate of that town. You must put them to death by throwing stones at them. You must kill the young woman because she was in a town and didn't scream for help. And you must kill the man because he slept with another man's wife. Get rid of those evil people.

[25]But suppose a man happens to see a young woman out in the country. And she has promised to marry another man. But the man who happens to see her rapes her. Then only the man who has done that will die. [26]Don't do anything to the woman. She hasn't committed a sin worthy of death. That case is like the case of someone who attacks and murders a neighbor. [27]The man found the young woman out in the country. And she screamed for help. But there wasn't anyone around who could save her.

[28]Suppose a man happens to see a virgin who hasn't promised to marry another man. And the man who happens to see her rapes her. But someone discovers them. [29]Then the man must weigh out 20 ounces of silver. He must give it to her father. The man must marry the young woman, because he raped her. And he can never divorce her as long as he lives.

[30]A man must not marry his stepmother. He must not bring shame on his father by sleeping with her.

Who Can Join in Worship With the Lord's People?

23 No man whose sex organs have been crushed or cut can join in worship with the Lord's people.

[2]No one born to an unmarried woman can join in worship with the Lord's people. That also applies to the person's children for all time to come.

[3]The people of Ammon and Moab can't join in worship with the Lord's people. That also applies to their children after them for all time to come. [4]The Ammonites and Moabites didn't come to meet you with food and water on your way out of Egypt. They even hired Balaam from Pethor in Aram Naharaim to put a curse on you. Balaam was the son of Beor. [5]The Lord your God wouldn't listen to Balaam. Instead, he turned the curse into a blessing for you. He did it because he loves you. [6]So don't make a peace treaty with the Ammonites and Moabites as long as you live.

[7]Don't hate the people of Edom. They are your relatives. Don't hate the people of Egypt. After all, you lived as outsiders in their country. [8]The great-grandchildren of the Edomites and Egyptians can join in worship with the Lord's people.

Keep the Camp of the Soldiers Pure and "Clean"

[9]There will be times when you are at war with your enemies. And your soldiers will be in camp. Then keep away from anything that isn't pure and "clean." [10]Suppose semen flows from the body of one of your soldiers during the night. Then that will make him "unclean." He must go outside the camp and stay there. [11]But as evening approaches, he must wash himself. When the sun goes down, he can return to the camp.

[12]Choose a place outside the camp where you can go to the toilet. [13]Keep a shovel among your tools. When you go to the toilet, dig a hole. Then cover up your waste. [14]The Lord your God walks around

in your camp. He's there to keep you safe. He's also there to hand your enemies over to you. So your camp must be holy. Then he won't see anything among you that is shameful. He won't turn away from you.

Several Other Laws

¹⁵If a slave comes to you for safety, don't hand them over to their master. ¹⁶Let them live among you anywhere they want to. Let them live in any town they choose. Don't treat them badly.

¹⁷A man or woman in Israel must not become a temple prostitute. ¹⁸The LORD your God hates the money that men and women get for being prostitutes. So don't take that money into the house of the LORD to pay what you promised to give.

¹⁹Don't charge your own people any interest. Don't charge them when they borrow money, food or anything else. ²⁰You can charge interest to people from another country. But don't charge your own people. Then the LORD your God will bless you in everything you do. He will bless you in the land you are entering to take as your own.

²¹Don't put off giving to the LORD your God everything you promise him. He will certainly require it from you. And you will be guilty of committing a sin. ²²But if you don't make a promise, you won't be guilty. ²³Make sure you do what you promised to do. With your own mouth you made the promise to the LORD your God. No one forced you to do it.

²⁴When you enter your neighbor's vineyard, you can eat all the grapes you want. But don't put any of them in your basket. ²⁵When you enter your neighbor's field, you can pick heads of grain. But don't cut down their standing grain.

24 Suppose a man marries a woman. But later he decides he doesn't like her. He finds something shameful about her. So he gives her a letter of divorce and sends her away from his house. ²Then after she leaves his house she becomes another man's wife. ³But her second husband doesn't like her either. So he gives her a letter of divorce and sends her away from his house. Or perhaps he dies. ⁴Then her first husband isn't allowed to marry her again. The LORD would hate that. When her first husband divorced her, she became

"unclean." Don't bring sin on the land the LORD your God is giving you as your own.

⁵Suppose a man has just married his wife. Then don't send him into battle. Don't give him any other duty either. He's free to stay home for one year. He needs time to make his new wife happy.

⁶Someone might borrow money from you and give you two millstones to keep until you are paid back. Don't keep them. Don't even keep the upper one. That person needs both millstones to make a living.

⁷Suppose someone is caught kidnapping another Israelite. And they sell or treat that person as a slave. Then the kidnapper must die. Get rid of that evil person.

⁸What about skin diseases? Be very careful to do exactly what the priests, who are Levites, tell you to do. You must be careful to obey the commands I've given them. ⁹Remember what the LORD your God did to Miriam on your way out of Egypt.

¹⁰Suppose your neighbor borrows something from you. And he offers you something to keep until you get paid back. Then don't go into their house to get it. ¹¹Stay outside. Let the neighbor bring it out to you. ¹²The neighbor might be poor. You might be given their coat to keep until you get paid back. Don't go to sleep while you still have it. ¹³Return it before the sun goes down. They need it to sleep in and will thank you for returning it. The LORD your God will see it and know that you have done the right thing.

¹⁴Don't take advantage of any hired worker who is poor and needy. That applies to your own people. It also applies to outsiders living in one of your towns. ¹⁵Give them their pay every day. They are poor and are counting on it. If you don't pay them, they might cry out to the LORD against you. Then you will be guilty of committing a sin.

¹⁶Parents must not be put to death because of what their children do. And children must not be put to death because of what their parents do. People must die because of their own sins.

¹⁷Do what is right and fair for outsiders and for children whose fathers have died. Suppose a widow borrows something from you. And she offers to give you

her coat until she pays you back. Don't take it. [18]Remember that you were slaves in Egypt. Remember that the LORD your God set you free from there. That's why I'm commanding you to do those things.

[19]When you are gathering crops in your field, you might leave some grain behind by mistake. Don't go back to get it. Leave it behind for outsiders and widows. Leave it for children whose fathers have died. Then the LORD your God will bless you in everything you do. [20]When you knock olives off your trees, don't go back over the branches a second time. Leave what remains for outsiders and widows. Leave it for children whose fathers have died. [21]When you pick grapes in your vineyard, don't go back over the vines a second time. Leave what remains for outsiders and widows. Leave it for children whose fathers have died. [22]Remember that you were slaves in Egypt. That's why I'm commanding you to do these things.

25 Suppose two people don't agree about something. Then they must take their case to court. The judges will decide the case. They will let the one who isn't guilty go free. And they will punish the one who is guilty. [2]The guilty one might have done something that's worthy of a beating. Then the judge will make them lie down and be beaten with a whip right there in court. The number of strokes should fit the crime. [3]But the judge must not give the guilty person more than 40 strokes. If more than that are used, you will have disrespected your Israelite neighbor.

[4]Don't stop an ox from eating while you use it to separate grain from straw.

[5]Suppose two brothers are living near each other. And one of them dies without having a son. Then his widow must not marry anyone outside the family. Her husband's brother should marry her. That's what a brother-in-law is supposed to do. [6]Her first baby boy will be named after her first husband. Then the dead man's name will continue in Israel.

[7]But suppose the man doesn't want to marry his brother's wife. Then she will go to the elders at the gate of the town. She will say, "My husband's brother refuses to keep his brother's name alive in Israel. He won't do for me what a brother-in-law is

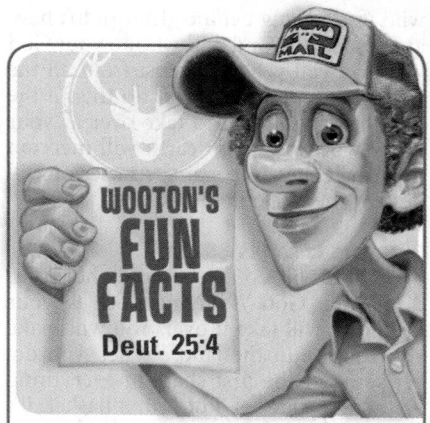

WOOTON'S FUN FACTS
Deut. 25:4

When an ox threshes grain, it walks around in circles on top of cereal grains, like wheat or barley. This loosens the bran or chaff from the grain. I wonder if they made the oxen wash their hoofs before work.

supposed to do." [8]Then the elders in his town will send for him. They will talk to him. But he still might say, "I don't want to marry her." [9]Then his brother's widow will go up to him in front of the elders. She'll pull one of his sandals off his foot. She'll spit in his face. And she'll say, "That's what we do to a man who won't build up his brother's family line." [10]That man's family line will be known in Israel as The Family of the Man Whose Sandal Was Pulled Off.

[11]Suppose two men are fighting. And the wife of one of them comes to save her husband from his attacker. So she reaches out and grabs hold of his attacker's private parts. [12]Then you must cut off her hand. Don't feel sorry for her.

[13]Don't have two different scales. Don't have scales that cause things to seem heavier or lighter than they really are. [14]And don't have two different sets of measures. Don't have measures that cause things to seem larger or smaller than they really are. [15]You must use weights and measures that are honest and exact. Then you will live a long time in the land the LORD your God is giving you. [16]He hates anyone who cheats.

[17]Remember what the Amalekites did to you on your way out of Egypt. [18]You were tired and worn out. They met up with you on your journey. They attacked everyone

who was lagging behind. They didn't have any respect for God. [19]The LORD your God will give you peace and rest from all the enemies around you. He'll do this in the land he's giving you to take over as your very own. No one on earth will mention the Amalekites ever again because you will destroy them. Do not forget!

Give the LORD His Share

26 You will enter the land the LORD your God is giving you as your own. You will take it over. You will make your homes in the land. [2]When you do, get some of the first share of everything your soil produces. Put it in a basket. It's from the land the LORD your God is giving you. Take your gifts and go to the special place he will choose. He will put his Name there. [3]Speak to the priest in office at that time. Tell him, "I announce today to the LORD your God that I have come to this land. It's the land he promised to give us. He promised it to our people of long ago." [4]The priest will receive the basket from you. He'll set it down in front of the altar of the LORD your God. [5]Then you will speak while the LORD is listening. You will say, "My father Jacob was a wanderer from the land of Aram. He went down into Egypt with a few people. He lived there and became the father of a great nation. It had huge numbers of people. [6]But the people of Egypt treated us badly. They made us suffer. They made us work very hard. [7]Then we cried out to the LORD. He is the God of our people who lived long ago. He heard our voice. He saw how much we were suffering. The Egyptians were treating us badly. They were making us work very hard. [8]So the LORD used his mighty hand and powerful arm to bring us out of Egypt. He did great and terrifying things. He did signs and amazing things. [9]He brought us to this place. He gave us this land. It's a land that has plenty of milk and honey. [10]Now, LORD, I'm bringing you the first share of crops from the soil. After all, you have given them to me." Place the basket in front of the LORD your God. Bow down to him. [11]Then you and the Levites and the outsiders among you will be full of joy. You will enjoy all the good things the LORD your God has given to you and your family.

[12]You will set apart a tenth of everything you produce in the third year. That's the year for giving the tenth to people who have greater needs. You will give it to the Levites, outsiders and widows. You will also give it to children whose fathers have died. Then all of them will have plenty to eat in your towns. [13]Speak to the LORD your God. Say to him, "I have taken your sacred share from my house. I have given it to the Levites, outsiders and widows. I have also given it to children whose fathers have died. I've done everything you commanded me to do. I haven't stopped obeying your commands. I haven't forgotten any of them. [14]I haven't eaten any part of your sacred share while I mourned over someone who had died. I haven't taken any of it from my house while I was 'unclean.' And I haven't offered any of it to the dead. LORD my God, I've obeyed you. I've done everything you commanded me to do. [15]Look down from the holy place where you live in heaven. Bless your people Israel. Bless the land you have given us. It's the land you promised to give to our people of long ago. It's a land that has plenty of milk and honey."

Obey the LORD's Commands

[16]This day the LORD your God commands you to obey all these rules and laws. Be careful to obey them with all your heart and with all your soul. [17]Today you have announced that the LORD is your God. You have said you would live exactly as he wants you to live. You have agreed to keep his rules, commands and laws. And you have said you would listen to him. [18]Today the LORD has announced that you are his people. He has said that you are his special treasure. He promised that you would be. He has told you to keep all his commands. [19]He has announced that he will make you famous. He'll give you more praise and honor than all the other nations he has made. And he has said that you will be a holy nation. The LORD your God has set you apart for himself. That's exactly what he promised to do.

The Altar on Mount Ebal

27 Moses and the elders of Israel gave commands to the people. They said, "Obey all the commands we're giving you today. ²You will go across the Jordan River. You will enter the land the Lord your God is giving you. When you do, set up some large stones. Put a coat of plaster on them. ³Write all the words of this law on them. Do it when you have crossed over into the land the Lord your God is giving you. It's a land that has plenty of milk and honey. The Lord is the God of your people of long ago. He promised you that you would enter the land. ⁴After you have gone across the Jordan, set up those stones on Mount Ebal. Put a coat of plaster on them. We're commanding you today to do that. ⁵Build an altar there to honor the Lord your God. Make it out of stones. Don't use any iron tool on them. ⁶Use stones you find in the fields to build his altar. Then offer burnt offerings on it to the Lord your God. ⁷Sacrifice friendship offerings there. Eat them and be filled with joy in the sight of the Lord your God. ⁸You must write all the words of this law on the stones you have set up. Write the words very clearly."

Curses for Not Obeying the Lord

⁹Then Moses and the priests, who are Levites, spoke to all the Israelites. They said, "Israel, be quiet! Listen! You have now become the people of the Lord your God. ¹⁰Obey him. Obey his commands and rules that we're giving you today."

¹¹Here are the commands Moses gave the people that same day.

¹²You will go across the Jordan River. When you do, six tribes will stand on Mount Gerizim to bless the people. Those tribes are Simeon, Levi, Judah, Issachar, Joseph and Benjamin. ¹³The other six tribes will stand on Mount Ebal to announce some curses. Those tribes are Reuben, Gad, Asher, Zebulun, Dan and Naphtali.

¹⁴The Levites will speak to all the Israelites in a loud voice. The Levites will say,

¹⁵"May anyone who makes a statue of a god and sets it up in secret be under the Lord's curse. That statue is made by a skilled worker. And the Lord hates it."

Then all the people will say, "Amen!"

¹⁶"May anyone who brings shame on their father or mother be under the Lord's curse."

Then all the people will say, "Amen!"

¹⁷"May anyone who moves their neighbor's boundary stone be under the Lord's curse."

Then all the people will say, "Amen!"

¹⁸"May anyone who leads blind people down the wrong road be under the Lord's curse."

Then all the people will say, "Amen!"

¹⁹"May anyone who treats unfairly outsiders, widows, and children whose fathers have died be under the Lord's curse."

Then all the people will say, "Amen!"

²⁰"May anyone who sleeps with his stepmother be under the Lord's curse. That man brings shame on his father by doing that."

Then all the people will say, "Amen!"

²¹"May anyone who has sex with animals be under the Lord's curse."

Then all the people will say, "Amen!"

²²"May anyone who sleeps with his sister be under the Lord's curse. It doesn't matter whether she is his full sister or his half sister."

Then all the people will say, "Amen!"

²³"May anyone who sleeps with his mother-in-law be under the Lord's curse."

Then all the people will say, "Amen!"

²⁴"May anyone who kills their neighbor secretly be under the Lord's curse."

Then all the people will say, "Amen!"

²⁵"May anyone who accepts money to kill someone who isn't guilty of doing anything wrong be under the Lord's curse."

Then all the people will say, "Amen!"

²⁶"May anyone who doesn't honor the words of this law by obeying them be under the Lord's curse."

Then all the people will say, "Amen!"

Blessings for Obeying the Lord

28 Make sure you obey the Lord your God completely. Be careful to obey all his commands. I'm giving them to you today. If you do these things, the Lord will honor you more than all the other nations on earth. ²If you obey the Lord your God, here are the blessings that will come to you and remain with you.

³You will be blessed in the cities.
You will be blessed out in the country.
⁴Your children will be blessed.
Your crops will be blessed. The

young animals among your livestock will be blessed. That includes your calves and lambs. ⁵Your baskets and bread pans will be blessed. ⁶You will be blessed no matter where you go.

⁷Enemies will rise up against you. But the LORD will help you win the battle over them. They will come at you from one direction. But they'll run away from you in every direction.

⁸The LORD your God will bless your barns with plenty of grain and other food. He will bless everything you do. He'll bless you in the land he's giving you.

⁹The LORD your God will make you his holy people. He will set you apart for himself. He promised to do this. He promised to do it if you would keep his commands and live exactly as he wants you to live. ¹⁰All the nations on earth will see that you belong to the LORD. And they will be afraid of you. ¹¹The LORD will give you more than you need. You will have many children. Your livestock will have many little ones. Your crops will do very well. All of that will happen in the land he promised to give you. He promised this to your people of long ago.

¹²The LORD will open up the heavens. That's where he stores his riches. He will send rain on your land at just the right time. He'll bless everything you do. You will lend money to many nations. But you won't have to borrow from any of them. ¹³The LORD your God will make you leaders, not followers. Pay attention to his commands that I'm giving you today. Be careful to obey them. Then you will always be on top. You will never be on the bottom. ¹⁴Don't turn away from any of the commands I'm giving you today. Don't turn to the right or the left. Don't follow other gods. Don't worship them.

Curses for Not Obeying the LORD

¹⁵But suppose you don't obey the LORD your God. And you aren't careful to obey all his commands and rules I'm giving you today. Then he will send curses on you. They'll catch up with you. Here are those curses.

¹⁶You will be cursed in the cities. You will be cursed out in the country. ¹⁷Your baskets and bread pans will be cursed. ¹⁸Your children will be cursed. Your crops will be cursed. Your calves and lambs will be cursed. ¹⁹You will be cursed no matter where you go.

²⁰The LORD will send curses on you. You won't know what's going on. In everything you do, he will be angry with you. You will be destroyed suddenly and completely. This will happen because you did an evil thing when you deserted the LORD. ²¹He will send all kinds of sicknesses on you. He'll send them until he has destroyed you. He'll remove you from the land you are entering to take as your own. ²²The LORD will make you sick and very weak. He will strike you with fever and swelling. He'll send burning heat. There won't be any rain. The hot winds will completely dry up your crops. All those things will happen until you die. ²³The sky above you will be like bronze. The ground beneath you will be like iron. ²⁴The LORD will turn the rain of your country into dust and powder. It will come down from the skies until you are destroyed.

²⁵The LORD will help your enemies win the battle over you. You will come at them from one direction. But you will run away from them in every direction. All the kingdoms on earth will be completely shocked when they see you. ²⁶Birds and wild animals will eat up your dead bodies. There won't be anyone left to scare them away. ²⁷The LORD will send boils on you, just like the ones he sent on the Egyptians. You will have growths in your bodies and boils on your skin. You will itch all over. No one will be able to heal you. ²⁸The LORD will make you lose your mind. He will make you blind. You won't know what's going on. ²⁹Even at noon you will have to feel your way around like a blind person in the dark. You won't have success in anything you do. Day after day you will be robbed and treated badly. No one will be able to save you.

³⁰You and a woman will promise to marry each other. But another man will take her and rape her. You will build a

house. But you won't live in it. You will plant a vineyard. But you won't eat a single grape from it. ³¹Your ox will be killed right in front of your eyes. But you won't eat any of it. Your donkey will be taken away from you by force. And you will never get it back. Your sheep will be given to your enemies. No one will be able to save them. ³²Your children will be given to another nation. Day after day you will watch for them to come back. But you will only wear out your eyes. You won't be able to help your children. ³³A nation you don't know anything about will eat what you work to produce on your land. You will only be treated badly as long as you live. ³⁴The things you see will make you lose your mind. ³⁵The LORD will send painful boils on your knees and legs. No one will be able to heal them. They will cover you from head to toe.

³⁶The LORD will drive you out of the land. And he will drive out the king you place over yourselves. All of you will go to another nation. You and your people of long ago didn't know anything about them. There you will worship other gods. They will be made out of wood and stone. ³⁷You will look very bad to all the nations where the LORD sends you. They will be completely shocked when they see you. They will mock you and make fun of you.

³⁸You will plant many seeds in your field. But you will gather very little food. Locusts will eat it up. ³⁹You will plant vineyards and take care of them. But you won't drink the wine. You won't gather the grapes. Worms will eat them up. ⁴⁰You will have olive trees through your whole country. But you won't use the oil. The olives will drop off the trees. ⁴¹You will have children. But you won't be able to keep them. They'll be taken away as prisoners. ⁴²Large numbers of locusts will eat up the leaves on all your trees. They will also eat up the crops on your land.

⁴³Outsiders who live among you will become your leaders. They will rise higher and higher. But you will sink lower and lower. ⁴⁴They will lend money to you. But you won't be able to lend money to them. They will be the leaders. But you will be the followers.

⁴⁵The LORD your God will send all these curses on you. They will follow you everywhere. They'll catch up with you. You will be under the LORD's curse until you are destroyed. That's because you didn't obey him. You didn't keep the commands and rules he gave you. ⁴⁶These curses will remain as signs and awful judgments against you and your children after you forever. ⁴⁷You didn't serve the LORD your God with joy and gladness when times were good. ⁴⁸So he will send enemies against you. You will have to serve them. You will be hungry and thirsty. You will be naked and poor. The LORD will put the iron chains of slavery around your necks until he has destroyed you.

⁴⁹The LORD will bring a nation against you from far away. It will come from the ends of the earth. It will dive down on you like an eagle. You won't understand that nation's language. ⁵⁰Its people will look mean. They won't have any respect for old people. They won't show any kindness to young people. ⁵¹They will eat up the young animals among your livestock. They'll eat up the crops on your land. They'll destroy you. They won't leave you any grain, olive oil or fresh wine. They won't leave you any calves or lambs. They'll destroy you. ⁵²They'll surround all the cities throughout your whole land. They'll attack those cities until the high, strong walls you trust in fall down. That's what will happen to the cities in the land the LORD your God is giving you.

⁵³Your enemies will surround you and attack you. They will make you suffer greatly. So you will eat your own children. You will eat the dead bodies of the sons and daughters the LORD your God has given you. ⁵⁴There may be a gentle and caring man among you. But he will treat his own brother badly. He'll be just as mean to the wife he loves and to any of his children who are still alive. ⁵⁵He won't give to a single one of them any part of the dead bodies of his children that he's eating. It will be all he has left to eat. That's how much your enemies will make you suffer when they surround all your cities and attack them. ⁵⁶There may be a gentle and caring woman among you. She wouldn't even touch the ground with her feet without first putting her sandals on. But she will not share anything with the husband she loves. She won't share with her own children either.

⁵⁷She will eat what comes out of her body after she has a baby. Then she'll even eat her baby. She won't share it with anyone in her family. In her great hunger she'll plan to eat it in secret. There won't be anything else for her to eat because the city she lives in will be surrounded. That's an example of how much your enemies will make you suffer when they are attacking your cities.

⁵⁸Be careful to follow all the words of this law. They are written in this scroll. Have respect for the glorious and wonderful name of the LORD your God. If you don't, ⁵⁹he will send terrible plagues on you and your children after you. He'll send horrible and lasting troubles. He'll make you very sick for a long time. ⁶⁰He'll bring on you all the sicknesses you were afraid of getting when you were in Egypt. You won't be able to get rid of them. ⁶¹The LORD will also bring on you all other kinds of sickness and trouble. I haven't even written those down in this Book of the Law. You will be destroyed. ⁶²At one time you were as many as the stars in the sky. But there will only be a few of you left. That's because you didn't obey the LORD your God. ⁶³It pleased the LORD to give you success and to cause there to be many of you. But it will please him just as much to wipe you out and destroy you. You will be removed from the land you are entering to take as your own.

⁶⁴Then the LORD will scatter you among all the nations. He'll spread you around from one end of the earth to the other. There you will worship statues of gods made out of wood and stone. You and your people of long ago hadn't known anything about those gods. ⁶⁵Among those nations you won't find any peace. There won't be any place where you can make your home and rest your feet. The LORD will give you minds filled with worry. He'll give you eyes worn out from looking for help. You won't have any hope in your hearts. ⁶⁶Your lives will always be in danger. You will be filled with fear night and day. You will never be sure you are safe. ⁶⁷In the morning you will say, "We wish it were evening!" In the evening you will say, "We wish it were morning!" Your hearts will be filled with fear. The things you see will terrify you. ⁶⁸The LORD will send you back to Egypt in ships. He'll send you on a journey I said you should never have to make again. You will offer to sell yourselves to your enemies as slaves in Egypt. But no one will buy you.

Obey the Terms of the Covenant

29 Here are the terms of the covenant the LORD commanded Moses to make with the Israelites in Moab. The terms were added to the covenant he had made with them at Mount Horeb.

²Moses sent for all the Israelites. Here is what he said to them.

With your own eyes you have seen everything the LORD did in Egypt to Pharaoh. You have seen what he did to all Pharaoh's officials and to his whole land. ³With your own eyes you saw how the LORD really made them suffer. You saw the signs and amazing things he did. ⁴But to this day the LORD hasn't given you a mind that understands. He hasn't given you eyes that see. He hasn't given you ears that hear. ⁵Yet the LORD says, "I led you through the desert for 40 years. During that time your clothes didn't wear out. The sandals on your feet didn't wear out either. ⁶You didn't eat any bread. You didn't drink any kind of wine. I did all these things because I wanted you to know that I am the LORD your God."

⁷When you got here, Sihon and Og came out to fight against us. Sihon was the king of Heshbon. And Og was the king of Bashan. But we won the battle over them. ⁸We took their land. We gave it to the tribes of Reuben and Gad and half of the tribe of Manasseh as their share.

⁹Be careful to obey the terms of this covenant. Then you will have success in everything you do. ¹⁰Today all of you are standing here in the sight of the LORD your God. Your leaders and chief men are here. Your elders and officials are here. So are all the other men of Israel. ¹¹Your children and wives are here with you too. So are the outsiders living in your camps. They chop your wood and carry your water. ¹²All of you are standing here in order to enter into a covenant with the LORD your God. He is making the covenant with you today. He's giving you his word. ¹³Today he wants to show you that you are his people and that he is your God. That's what he promised to Abraham, Isaac and

Jacob. ¹⁴I'm making this covenant and the promise that goes along with it. I'm making this covenant with you. ¹⁵You are standing here with us today in front of the Lord our God. And I'm also making this covenant with those who aren't here today.

¹⁶You yourselves know how we lived in Egypt. You also know how we passed through other countries on the way here. ¹⁷You saw the statues of their gods made out of wood, stone, silver and gold. The Lord hates those statues. ¹⁸Make sure there isn't a man or woman among your families or tribes who turns away from the Lord our God. No one must worship the gods of those nations. Make sure that kind of worship doesn't spread like bitter poison through your whole community.

¹⁹Some people who worship those gods will hear the promise that seals the covenant I'm making. They think they can escape trouble by what they're saying. They say, "We'll be safe, even though we're stubborn and go our own way." But they will bring trouble on the whole land. ²⁰The Lord will never be willing to forgive those people. His great anger will blaze out against them. All the curses I've written down in this book will fall on them. And the Lord will erase any mention of them from the earth. ²¹He will find those people in all the tribes of Israel and give them nothing but trouble. That will agree with all the curses of the covenant. They are written down in this Book of the Law.

²²Even your children's children will see the troubles that have fallen on the land. They'll see the sicknesses the Lord has brought on it. People who come from countries far away will also see those things. ²³The whole land will be burned up. Nothing but salt and sulfur will be left. Nothing will be planted there. Nothing will grow there. In fact, nothing will even start to grow there. The land will be like Sodom, Gomorrah, Admah and Zeboyim after they were destroyed. The Lord wiped out those cities because he was very angry. ²⁴All the nations will ask, "Why has the Lord done this to the land? What could have made him so very angry?"

²⁵And they will hear the answer, "It's because the people living there have broken the covenant of the Lord. He's the God of their people of long ago. He made that covenant with them when he brought them out of Egypt. ²⁶They went off and worshiped other gods. They bowed down to them. They hadn't known anything about those gods before. The Lord hadn't given those gods to them. ²⁷So the Lord became very angry with this land. He brought on it all the curses written down in this book. ²⁸The Lord's anger blazed out against his people. So he pulled them up out of their land. He threw them into another land. And that's where they are now."

²⁹The Lord our God keeps certain things hidden. But he makes other things known to us and to our children forever. He does it so we can obey all the words of this law.

The Lord Will Bless His People

30 I have told you about all these blessings and curses. The Lord your God will bring them on you. Then you will think carefully about the blessings and curses. You will think about them everywhere the Lord your God scatters you among the nations. ²You and your children will return to the Lord your God. You will obey him with all your heart and with all your soul. That will be according to everything I'm commanding you today. ³When all that happens, the Lord your God will bless you with great success again. He will be very kind to you. He'll bring you back from all the nations where he scattered you. ⁴Suppose you have been forced to go away to the farthest land on earth. The Lord your God will bring you back even from there. ⁵He will bring you to the land that belonged to your people of long ago. You will take it over. He'll make you better off than your people were. He'll cause there to be more of you than there were of them. ⁶The Lord your God will keep you from being stubborn. He'll do the same thing for your children and their children. Then you will love him with all your heart and with all your soul. And you will live. ⁷The Lord your God will put all these curses on your enemies. They hated you and hunted you down. ⁸You will obey the Lord again. You will obey all his commands that I'm giving you today. ⁹Then the Lord your God will give you great success in everything you do. You will have many children. Your livestock will have many little ones. Your crops will do very well. The LORD will take delight in you again. He'll give you success. That's what he did for your people of long ago. ¹⁰But you must obey the LORD your God. You must keep his commands and rules. They are written in this Book of the Law. You must turn to the LORD your God with all your heart and with all your soul.

Choose Life, not Death

¹¹What I'm commanding you today is not too hard for you. It isn't beyond your reach. ¹²It isn't up in heaven. So you don't have to ask, "Who will go up into heaven to get it? Who will announce it to us so we can obey it?" ¹³And it isn't beyond the ocean. So you don't have to ask, "Who will go across the ocean to get it? Who will announce it to us so we can obey it?" ¹⁴No, the message isn't far away at all. In fact, it's really near you. It's in your mouth and in your heart so that you can obey it.

¹⁵Today I'm giving you a choice. You can have life and success. Or you can have death and harm. ¹⁶I'm commanding you today to love the LORD your God. I'm commanding you to live exactly as he wants you to live. You must obey his commands, rules and laws. Then you will live. There will be many of you. The LORD your God will bless you in the land you are entering to take as your own.

¹⁷Don't let your hearts turn away from the LORD. Instead, obey him. Don't let yourselves be drawn away to other gods. And don't bow down to them and worship them. ¹⁸If you do, I announce to you this day that you will certainly be destroyed. You are about to go across the Jordan River and take over the land. But you won't live there very long.

¹⁹I'm calling for the heavens and the earth to be witnesses against you this very day. I'm offering you the choice of life or death. You can choose either blessings or curses. But I want you to choose life. Then you and your children will live. ²⁰And you will love the LORD your God. You will obey him. You will remain true to him. The LORD is your very life. He will give you many years in the land. He promised

to give that land to your fathers, to Abraham, Isaac and Jacob.

Joshua Becomes the new Leader

31 Here are the words Moses spoke to all the Israelites. ²He said, "I am now 120 years old. I'm not able to lead you anymore. The LORD has said to me, 'You will not go across the Jordan River.' ³The LORD your God himself will go across ahead of you. He'll destroy the nations there in order to make room for you. You will take over their land. Joshua will also go across ahead of you, just as the LORD said he would. ⁴The LORD will do to those nations what he did to Sihon and Og. He destroyed those Amorite kings along with their land. ⁵The LORD will hand those nations over to you. Then you must do to them everything I've commanded you to do. ⁶Be strong and brave. Don't be afraid of them. Don't be terrified because of them. The LORD your God will go with you. He will never leave you. He'll never desert you."

⁷Then Moses sent for Joshua. Moses spoke to him in front of all the Israelites. He said, "Be strong and brave. You must go with these people. They are going into the land the LORD promised to give to their people of long ago. You must divide it up among them. They will each receive their share. ⁸The LORD himself will go ahead of you. He will be with you. He will never leave you. He'll never desert you. So don't be afraid. Don't lose hope."

The Law Must Be Read to the People

⁹Moses wrote down this law. He gave it to the priests, who are sons of Levi. They carried the ark of the covenant of the LORD. He also gave the law to all the elders of Israel. ¹⁰Then Moses commanded them, "You must read this law at the end of every seven years. Do it in the year when

REMEMBER THIS

DEUTERONOMY 31:6

"Be strong and brave. Don't be afraid of them. Don't be terrified because of them. The LORD your God will go with you. He will never leave you. He'll never desert you."

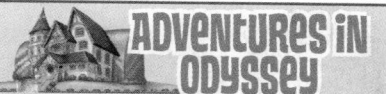

With Whit's help, Jimmy stopped fearing about the future in "Coming of Age" (A#11).

you forgive people what they owe. Read it during the Feast of Booths. [11]That's when all the Israelites come to appear in front of the LORD your God at the holy tent. It will be at the place he will choose. You must read this law to them. [12]Gather the people together. Gather the men, women and children. Also bring together the outsiders living in your towns. Then they can listen and learn to have respect for the LORD your God. And they'll be careful to obey all the words of this law. [13]Their children must hear it read too. They don't know this law yet. They too must learn to have respect for the LORD your God. They must honor him as long as you live in the land. You are about to go across the Jordan River and take that land as your very own."

The Israelites Will Refuse to Obey the LORD

[14]The LORD said to Moses, "The day when you will die is near. Have Joshua go to the tent of meeting. Join him there. That is where I will appoint him as the new leader." So Joshua and Moses went to the tent of meeting.

[15]Then the LORD appeared at the tent in a pillar of cloud. It stood over the entrance to the tent. [16]The LORD spoke to Moses. He said, "You are going to join the members of your family who have already died. The Israelites will not be faithful to me. They will soon join themselves to the false gods that are worshiped in the land they are entering. The people will desert me. They will break the covenant I made with them. [17]In that day I will become angry with them. I will desert them. I will turn my face away from them. And they will be destroyed. Many horrible troubles and hard times will come on them. On that day they will say, 'Trouble has come on us. Our God isn't with us!' [18]I will certainly turn away from them on that day. I will do it because they did a very evil thing when they turned to other gods.

[19]"I want you to write down a song and teach it to the Israelites. Have them sing it. It will be my witness against them. [20]I will bring them into a land that has plenty of milk and honey. I promised the land to their people of long ago. In that land they will eat until they have had enough. They will get fat. When they do, they will turn to other gods and worship them. They will turn their backs on me. They will break my covenant. [21]Many horrible troubles and hard times will come on them. Then the song I am giving you will be a witness against them. That is because the song will not be forgotten by their children and their children's children. I know what they are likely to do. I know it even before I bring them into the land I promised them." [22]So that day Moses wrote the song down. And Moses taught it to the Israelites.

[23]The LORD gave a command to Joshua, the son of Nun. He said, "Be strong and brave. You will bring the Israelites into the land I promised them. I myself will be with you."

[24]Moses finished writing the words of this law in a book. He wrote them down from beginning to end. [25]Then he gave a command to the Levites who carried the ark of the covenant of the LORD. Moses said, [26]"Take this Book of the Law. Place it beside the ark of the covenant of the

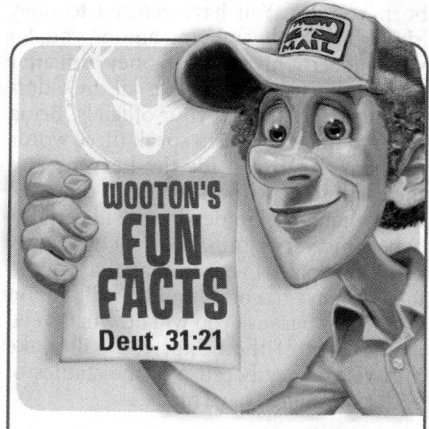

WOOTON'S FUN FACTS
Deut. 31:21

God must know that songs stick in kids' heads. Teachers now call that method of teaching *aural learning style*. I call it fun, especially if it's to the tune of "Camptown Races."

WHAT ABOUT you?

You wave good-bye sadly, tears streaming down your face. You've known this day was coming for months. Now it's finally here. As you stand on the sidewalk, saying good-bye to your best friend who is moving to another state, you're overcome with sadness and grief. Then your mom puts her arm around your shoulders and whispers, "Don't worry . . . good friends will always be with you."

God puts people in our lives to help us become who He wants us to be. He has us meet people who will challenge us, shape us, encourage us, and help us grow in our walk with Him. In the Adventures in Odyssey episode ". . . But Not Forgotten," that's how the people of Odyssey feel about Whit leaving town.

During times of good-byes, it's best to remember Deuteronomy 31:8: "The LORD himself will go ahead of you. He will be with you. He will never leave you. He'll never desert you. So don't be afraid. Don't lose hope." Even though we have to say good-bye to most people in our lives at some point, we never have to say good-bye to God. And even better, because of the influence those individuals have had on your life, part of them will remain with you forever.

Think of the people who have had the greatest impact on your life. How are you different because of things they've said or done? Make a list of five ways you would like to make a difference for other people. Then go for it!

LORD your God. It will remain there as a witness against you. ²⁷I know how you refuse to obey the LORD. I know how stubborn you are. You have refused to obey him while I've been living among you. So you will certainly refuse to obey him after I'm dead! ²⁸Gather together all the elders of your tribes and all your officials. Bring them to me. Then I can speak these words to them. I can call for the heavens and the earth to be witnesses against them. ²⁹I know that after I'm dead you will certainly become very sinful. You will turn away from the path I've commanded you to take. In days to come, trouble will fall on you. That's because you will do what is evil in the sight of the LORD. You will make him very angry because of the statues of gods your hands have made."

The Song of Moses

³⁰Moses spoke the words of this song from beginning to end. The whole community of Israel heard them. Here is what he said.

32 Heavens, listen to me. Then I will speak.
Earth, hear the words of my mouth.
² Let my teaching fall like rain.
Let my words come down like dew.
Let them be like raindrops on new grass.
Let them be like rain on tender plants.

³ I will make known the name of the LORD.
Praise God! How great he is!
⁴ He is the Rock. His works are perfect.
All his ways are right.
He is faithful. He doesn't do anything wrong.
He is honest and fair.

⁵ Israel, you have sinned against him very much.
It's too bad for you that you aren't his children anymore.
You have become a twisted and evil nation.

⁶ Is that how you thank the LORD?
    You aren't wise. You are foolish.
Remember, he's your Father. He's your
    Creator.
    He made you. He formed you.
⁷ Remember the days of long ago.
    Think about what the LORD did
        through those many years.
Ask your father. He will tell you.
    Ask your elders. They'll explain it
        to you.
⁸ The Most High God gave the nations
    their lands.
    He divided up the human race.
He set up borders for the nations.
    He did it based on the number of the
        angels in his heavenly court.
⁹ The LORD's people are his share.
    Jacob is the nation he has received.
¹⁰ The LORD found Israel in a desert.
    He found them in an empty and
        windy land.
    He took care of them and kept them
        safe.
    He guarded them as he would
        guard his own eyes.
¹¹ He was like an eagle that stirs up its
    nest.
    It hovers over its little ones.
It spreads out its wings to catch them.
    It carries them up in the air on its
        feathers.
¹² The LORD was the only one who led
    Israel.
    No other god was with them.
¹³ The LORD made them ride on the
        highest places in the land.
    He fed them what grew in the fields.
He gave them the sweetest honey.
    He fed them olive oil from a rocky
        hillside.
¹⁴ He gave them butter and milk from
        the herds and flocks.
    He fed them the fattest lambs and
        goats.
He gave them the best of Bashan's rams.
    He fed them the finest wheat.
    They drank the bubbling red juice
        of grapes.
¹⁵ When Israel grew fat, they became
    stubborn.
    When they were filled with food,
        they became fat and heavy.

They left the God who made them.
    They turned away from the Rock
        who saved them.
¹⁶ They made him jealous by serving
    false gods.
    They made him angry by
        worshiping statues of gods.
    He hated those gods.
¹⁷ The people sacrificed to those false
        gods, not to God.
    They hadn't known anything about
        those false gods.
Those gods were new to them.
    Their people of long ago didn't
        worship them.
¹⁸ But then they deserted the Rock. He
    was their Father.
    They forgot the God who created
        them.
¹⁹ When the LORD saw this, he turned
    away from them.
    His sons and daughters made him
        angry.
²⁰ "I will turn my face away from them,"
    he said.
    "I will see what will happen to
        them in the end.
They are sinful people.
    They are unfaithful children.
²¹ They made me jealous by serving what
    is not even a god.
    They made me angry by worshiping
        worthless statues of gods.
I will use people who are not a nation
    to make them jealous.
    A nation that has no understanding
        will make them angry.
²² My anger will start a fire.
    It will burn all the way down to the
        kingdom of the dead.
It will eat up the earth and its crops.
    It will set the base of the mountains
        on fire.
²³ "I will pile troubles on my people.
    I will shoot all my arrows at them.
²⁴ I will send them hunger. It will make
        them weak.
    I will send terrible sickness. I will
        send deadly plagues.
I will send wild animals that will tear
    them apart.
    Snakes that glide through the dust
        will bite them.

25 In the streets their children will be
        killed by swords.
    Their homes will be filled with
        terror.
The young men and women will die.
    The babies and old people will die.
26 I said I would scatter them.
    I said I would erase their name
        from human memory.
27 But I was afraid their enemies would
        make fun of that.
    I was afraid their attackers would
        not understand.
I was sure they would say, 'We're the
        ones who've beaten them!
    The LORD isn't the one who did it.'"

28 Israel is a nation that doesn't have any
        sense.
    They can't understand anything.
29 I wish they were wise. Then they
        would understand what's
        coming.
    They'd realize what would happen
        to them in the end.
30 How could one person chase a
        thousand?
    How could two make ten thousand
        run away?
It couldn't happen unless their Rock
        had deserted them.
    It couldn't take place unless the
        LORD had given them up.
31 Their rock is not like our Rock.
    Even our enemies know that.
32 Their vine comes from the vines of
        Sodom.
    It comes from the vineyards of
        Gomorrah.
Their grapes are filled with poison.
    Their bunches of grapes taste bitter.
33 Their wine is like the poison of snakes.
    It's like the deadly poison of cobras.

34 The LORD says, "I have kept all those
        terrible things stored away.
    I have kept them sealed up in my
        strongbox.
35 I punish people. I will pay them back.
    The time will come when their feet
        will slip.
Their day of trouble is near.
    Very soon they will be destroyed."

36 The LORD will come to the aid of his
        people.
He'll show tender love to those who
        serve him.
    He will know when their strength is
        gone.
    He'll see that no one at all is left.
37 He'll say, "Where are their gods now?
    Where is the rock they went to for
        safety?
38 Where are the gods who ate the fat of
        their sacrifices?
    Where are the gods who drank the
        wine of their drink offerings?
Let those gods rise up to help you!
    Let them keep you safe!

39 "Look! I am the One!
    There is no other God except me.
I put some people to death. I bring
        others to life.
    I have wounded, and I will heal.
    No one can save you from my
        power.
40 I raise my hand to heaven. Here is the
        promise I make.
    You can be sure that I live forever.
41 And you can be just as sure
        that I will sharpen my flashing sword.
    My hand will hold it when I judge.
I will get even with my enemies.
    I will pay back those who hate me.
42 I will make my arrows drip with
        blood.
    My sword will destroy people.
It will kill some. It will even kill
        prisoners.
    It will cut off the heads of enemy
        leaders."

43 You nations, be full of joy. Be joyful
        together with God's people.
    The LORD will get even with his
        enemies.
He will pay them back for killing
        those who serve him.
    He will wipe away the sin of his
        land and people.

44 Moses spoke all the words of this song
to the people. Joshua, the son of Nun, was
with him. 45 Moses finished speaking all
these words to all the Israelites. 46 Then he
said to them, "Think carefully about all
the words I have announced to you today.
I want you to command your children to
be careful to obey all the words of this law.
47 They aren't just useless words for you.
They are your very life. If you obey them,

you will live in the land for a long time. It's the land you are going across the Jordan River to take as your own."

Moses Will Die on Mount Nebo

⁴⁸On that same day the LORD said to Moses, ⁴⁹"Go up into the Abarim mountains. Go to Mount Nebo in Moab. It is across from Jericho. From there look out over Canaan. It is the land I am giving the Israelites to take as their own. ⁵⁰You will die there on the mountain you have climbed. You will join the members of your family who have already died. In the same way, your brother Aaron died on Mount Hor. He joined the members of his family who had already died. ⁵¹You and Aaron disobeyed me in front of the Israelites. It happened at the waters of Meribah Kadesh in the Desert of Zin. You did not honor me among the Israelites as the holy God. ⁵²So you will see the land, but only from far away. You will not enter the land I am giving to the Israelites."

Moses Blesses the Tribes

33 Here is the blessing that Moses, the man of God, gave to the Israelites before he died. ²He said,

"The LORD came from Mount Sinai.
    Like the rising sun, he shone on his
        people from Mount Seir.
    He shone on them from Mount
        Paran.
    He came with large numbers of angels.
    He came from his mountain slopes
        in the south.
³ LORD, I'm sure you love your people.
    All the holy ones are in your hands.
    At your feet all of them bow down.
    And you teach them.
⁴ They learn the law Moses gave us.
    It belongs to the community of the
        people of Jacob.
⁵ The LORD was king over Israel
    when the leaders of the people
        came together.
    The tribes of Israel were also there."

⁶Here's what Moses said about Reuben.

"Let Reuben live. Don't let him die.
    And do not let his people be few."

⁷Here's what Moses said about Judah.

"LORD, listen to Judah cry out.
    Bring him to his people.

By his own power he stands up for
    himself.
LORD, help him fight against his
    enemies!"

⁸Here's what Moses said about Levi.

"Your Thummim and Urim belong to
    your faithful servant.
You tested him at Massah.
You argued with him at the waters
    of Meribah.

Jason's Jargon

DEUTERONOMY 33

Search this chapter for the word *Thummim*. It is thought that Urim and Thummim were stones on a priest's breastplate. People used them to pray, especially to ask God important questions.

⁹ Levi didn't show special favor to anyone.
    He did not spare his father and
        mother.
    He didn't excuse his relatives or his
        children.
But he watched over your word.
    He guarded your covenant.
¹⁰ He teaches your rules to the people of
        Jacob.
    He teaches your law to Israel.
He offers incense to you.
    He sacrifices whole burnt offerings
        on your altar.
¹¹ LORD, bless all his skills.
    Be pleased with everything he does.
Destroy those who rise up against him.
    Strike down his enemies until they
        can't get up."

¹²Here's what Moses said about Benjamin.

"Let the one the LORD loves rest safely
    in him.
The LORD guards him all day long.
The one the LORD loves rests in his
    arms."

¹³Here's what Moses said about Joseph.

"May the LORD bless Joseph's land.
    May he bless it with dew from the
        highest heavens.

WHAT ABOUT YOU?

Moses' song and blessing in Deuteronomy 32 and 33 are filled with emotion and power. They help us understand the feelings related to the Israelites' challenges and triumphs. They also describe God's feelings about His people during this time.

"I know how you feel." People say that a lot, but truly understanding what someone else is going through takes work. The ability to put yourself in someone else's shoes is called "empathy." We get better at it with practice, and our life experiences can help us empathize with others.

For example, just about anyone would feel badly for a boy or girl who is tired of moving from one city to the next every time a parent changes jobs. But maybe you have a parent in the military, so you know what it feels like to pack up your room, say goodbye to friends, and learn your way around a new school every few years. That personal experience gives you a unique opportunity to reach out to someone in need because you've lived it.

The Bible tells us that's why Jesus left the comforts of heaven to walk the earth. He wanted to identify with us. Before giving His life as a sacrifice for our sin, the Lord wanted to share the human experience firsthand, feeling our joy and pain, and modeling how we should live.

As you work to show empathy to others today, pray for wisdom from the One who has been there and done that.

May he bless it with water from the
deepest oceans.
¹⁴ May he bless it with the best crops the
sun can produce.
May he bless it with the finest crops
the moon can give.
¹⁵ May he bless it with the best products
of the age-old mountains.
May he bless it with the many crops
of the ancient hills.
¹⁶ May he bless it with the best gifts that
fill the earth.
May he bless it with the favor of
the God who spoke out of the
burning bush.
Let all these blessings rest on the head
of Joseph.
Let them rest on the head of the
one who is prince among his
brothers.
¹⁷ His glory is like the glory of a bull
born first to its mother.
His horns are like the horns of a
wild ox.

He will use them to destroy the
nations.
He'll wipe out the nations that are
very far away.
The ten thousands of men in
Ephraim's army are like the
bull and the ox.
So are the thousands in the army of
Manasseh."

¹⁸Here's what Moses said about Zebulun and Issachar.

"Zebulun, be filled with joy when you
go out.
Issachar, be joyful in your tents.
¹⁹ You will call for other people to go to
the mountain.
There you will offer the sacrifices of
those who do what is right.
You will enjoy the many good things
your ships bring you.
You will enjoy treasures that are
hidden in the sand."

²⁰Here's what Moses said about Gad.

"May the God who gives Gad more
    land be praised!
Gad lives there like a lion
    that tears off arms and heads.
²¹ He chose the best land for his
    livestock.
The leader's share was kept for him.
The leaders of the people came
    together.
Then Gad carried out the LORD's
    holy plan.
He carried out the LORD's decisions
    for Israel."

²²Here's what Moses said about Dan.

"Dan is like a lion's cub
    that charges out of the land of
    Bashan."

²³Here's what Moses said about Naphtali.

"The LORD greatly favors Naphtali.
The LORD fills him with his blessing.
Naphtali's land will reach south to
    the Sea of Galilee."

²⁴Here's what Moses said about Asher.

"Asher is the most blessed of sons.
Let his brothers be kind to him.
Let Asher wash his feet with olive oil.
²⁵ The bars of his gates will be made out
    of iron and bronze.
His strength will last as long as he
    lives.

²⁶ "There is no one like the God of Israel.
He rides across the heavens to help
    you.
He rides on the clouds in his glory.
²⁷ God lives forever! You can run to him
    for safety.
His powerful arms are always there
    to carry you.
He will drive out your enemies to
    make room for you.
He'll say to you, 'Destroy them!'
²⁸ So Israel will live in safety.
Jacob will live secure
in a land that has grain and fresh wine.
There the heavens drop their dew.
²⁹ Israel, how blessed you are!
Who is like you?
The LORD has saved you.
He keeps you safe. He helps you.
He's like a glorious sword to you.

Your enemies will bow down to you
    in fear.
You will walk on the highest places
    of their lands."

Moses Dies

34 Moses climbed Mount Nebo. He
went up from the plains of Moab
to the highest slopes of Pisgah. It's across
from Jericho. At Pisgah the LORD showed
him the whole land from Gilead all the
way to Dan. ²Moses saw the whole land of
Naphtali. He saw the territory of Ephraim
and Manasseh. The LORD showed him
the whole land of Judah all the way to the
Mediterranean Sea. ³Moses saw the Negev
Desert. He saw the whole area from the
Valley of Jericho all the way to Zoar. Jericho was also known as The City of Palm
Trees. ⁴Then the LORD spoke to Moses. He
said, "This is the land I promised to Abraham, Isaac and Jacob. I told them, 'I will
give this land to your children and their
children.' Moses, I have let you see it with
your own eyes. But you will not go across
the Jordan River to enter it."

⁵Moses, the servant of the LORD, died
there in Moab. It happened just as the
LORD had said. ⁶The LORD buried the
body of Moses in Moab. His grave is in
the valley across from Beth Peor. But to
this day no one knows where his grave is.
⁷Moses was 120 years old when he died.
But his eyesight was still good. He was still
very strong. ⁸The Israelites mourned over
Moses on the plains of Moab for 30 days.
They did it until their time for weeping
and crying was over.

⁹Joshua, the son of Nun, was filled with
wisdom. That's because Moses had placed
his hands on him. So the Israelites listened to Joshua. They did what the LORD
had commanded Moses.

¹⁰Since then, Israel has never had a
prophet like Moses. The LORD knew him
face to face. ¹¹Moses did many signs and
amazing things. The LORD had sent him
to do them in Egypt. Moses did them
against Pharaoh, against all his officials
and against his whole land. ¹²No one has
ever had the mighty power Moses had. No
one has ever done the wonderful acts he
did in the sight of all the Israelites.

Joshua

Ah, the book of Joshua! This text details a number of adventures at the end of Israel's long odyssey through the wilderness. Odyssey, you understand, is meant in the original sense of the word meaning *a long journey*. Not the name of our fair town. Anyway, within this book you'll find a story with spies and a narrow escape, thanks to an unlikely heroine (chapter 2). Read about how the nation crossed the Jordan River just as they had the Red Sea—on dry land with the waters parted (chapter 3). Review the famous story of marching around Jericho until God made the walls come down (6). Learn how one person's sin can affect a whole nation (7). And try to imagine a day when the sun refused to set (10:1–15).

Later chapters explain which sections of the new land were assigned to which tribes, and they also contain other down-to-business sorts of matters. But throughout the book of Joshua it is clear that those going into the Promised Land are a new generation with a new leader, and God is giving them all a new start.

Joshua reminded the Israelites (and, by extension, he's also reminding us as readers) that we all must make a choice of whether to serve the idols of the world around us, or to serve the One True God (24:14–15). For Joshua, the choice was clear. After reading of God's faithfulness in this book of the Bible, it should be clear for all of us as well.

WHAT'S IT MEAN, EUGENE?

Canon—No, this term doesn't refer to the archaic weapon from the Civil War era. This canon is another name for *the Bible*: the sixty-six amazing books of the Old and New Testaments, which the church recognizes as having been inspired by God. The Latin word *canon* means "rule or measuring stick." The collection of the *canonical* books found in this Bible, therefore, are trusted as accurate and true for instructing Christians on the journey of faith.

Joshua Becomes Israel's Leader

1 Moses, the servant of the LORD, died. After that, the LORD spoke to Joshua, the son of Nun. Joshua was Moses' helper. The LORD said to Joshua, ²"My servant Moses is dead. Now then, I want you and all these people to get ready to go across the Jordan River. I want all of you to go into the land I am about to give to the Israelites. ³I will give all of you every place you walk on, just as I promised Moses. ⁴Your territory will reach from the Negev Desert all the way to Lebanon. The great Euphrates River will be to the east. The Mediterranean Sea will be to the west. Your territory will include all the Hittite country. ⁵Joshua, no one will be able to oppose you as long as you live. I will be with you, just as I was with Moses. I will never leave you. I will never desert you. ⁶Be strong and brave. You will lead these people. They will take the land as their very own. It is the land I promised to give their people of long ago.

VERSE 1:2 Guess how long the Jordan River is? Take a wild guess! Okay, now a tame guess! (Answer wild or tame: It's 223 miles long.)

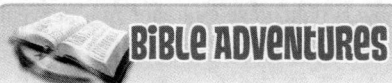

O.T. Action News reported on Joshua and the Israelites and their great battle in "Siege at Jericho" (A#22).

⁷"Be strong and very brave. Make sure you obey the whole law my servant Moses gave you. Do not turn away from it to the right or the left. Then you will have success everywhere you go. ⁸Never stop reading this Book of the Law. Day and night you must think about what it says. Make sure you do everything written in it. Then things will go well with you. And you will have great success. ⁹Here is what I am commanding you to do. Be strong and brave. Do not be afraid. Do not lose hope. I am the LORD your God. I will be with you everywhere you go."

¹⁰So Joshua gave orders to the officers of the people. He said, ¹¹"Go through the camp. Tell the people, 'Get your supplies ready. Three days from now you will go across the Jordan River right here. You will go in and take over the land. The LORD your God is giving it to you as your very own.'"

¹²Joshua also spoke to the tribes of Reuben and Gad and half of the tribe of Manasseh. He said to them, ¹³"Remember what Moses, the servant of the LORD, commanded you. He said, 'The LORD your God is giving you this land. It's a place where you can make your homes and live in peace and rest.' ¹⁴Your wives, children and livestock can stay here east of the Jordan River. Moses gave you this land. But all your fighting men must get ready for battle. They must go across ahead of the other tribes. You must help them ¹⁵until

In the adventure "Cycle of Fear" (A#60), Eva Parker had to be strong and brave when she learned to ride a bike.

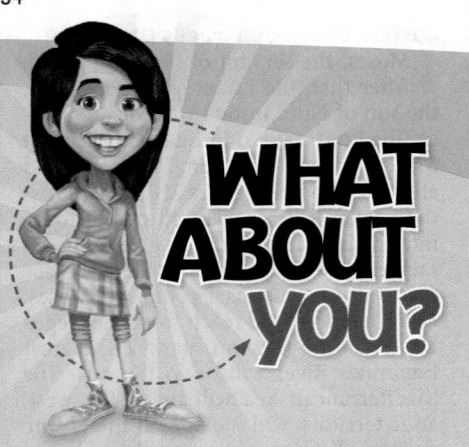

WHAT ABOUT YOU?

Your heart is pounding. Your hands are sweating. And come to think of it, your stomach is doing flip-flops. That doesn't sound very courageous, does it? But sometimes we feel that way when we need courage. Even Joshua, a strong and brave servant of God, must have felt like running away sometimes. But he trusted in God's promises and moved forward with courage.

In the Adventures in Odyssey episode "Isaac the Courageous," Mr. Whittaker has Isaac read verses from the Bible to help him feel brave when he has to go up against Rodney and the Bones of Wrath. For example, Joshua 1:9 says: "Here is what I am commanding you to do. Be strong and brave. Do not be afraid. Do not lose hope. I am the LORD your God. I will be with you everywhere you go." What a great promise!

Sometimes it can be hard to remember that God is always by our side and will never leave us when we're in trouble. But God's Word is filled with comfort that, even though we might be afraid, we should always trust that the Lord is with us.

The next time you're feeling nervous about a test, have courage! God is there. Or when you're giving a speech in front of people, have courage! The Lord is there too. And when you have to stand up for what you know is right, have courage! Your heavenly Father is always at your side.

---

the LORD gives them rest. In the same way, he has already given you rest. You must help them until they also have taken over their land. It's the land the LORD your God is giving them. After that, you can come back here. Then you can live in your own land. It's the land that Moses, the servant of the LORD, gave you east of the Jordan River. It's toward the sunrise."

[16]Then the tribes of Reuben and Gad and half of the tribe of Manasseh answered Joshua. They said, "We'll do what you have commanded us to do. We'll go where you send us. [17]We obeyed Moses completely. And we'll obey you just as completely. But may the LORD your God be with you, just as he was with Moses. [18]Suppose people question your authority. And suppose they refuse to obey anything you command them to do. Then they will be put to death. Just be strong and brave!"

Rahab Helps the Spies

2 Joshua, the son of Nun, sent two spies from Shittim. He sent them in secret. He said to them, "Go and look over the land. Most of all, check out Jericho." So they went to Jericho. They stayed at the house of a prostitute. Her name was Rahab.

[2]The king of Jericho was told, "Look! Some of the Israelites have come here tonight. They've come to check out the land." [3]So the king sent a message to Rahab. It said, "Bring out the men who came into your house. They've come to check out the whole land."

[4]But the woman had hidden the two men. She said, "It's true that the men came here. But I didn't know where they had come from. [5]They left at sunset, when it was time to close the city gate. I don't know which way they went. Go after them quickly. You might catch up with them." [6]But in fact she had taken them up on the roof. There she had hidden them under some flax she had piled up. [7]The king's men left to hunt down the spies. They took the road that leads to where the Jordan River can be crossed. As soon as they had gone out of the city, the gate was shut.

⁸Rahab went up on the roof before the spies settled down for the night. ⁹She said to them, "I know that the LORD has given you this land. We are very much afraid of you. Everyone who lives in this country is weak with fear because of you. ¹⁰We've heard how the LORD dried up the Red Sea for you when you came out of Egypt. We've heard what you did to Sihon and Og, the two Amorite kings. They ruled east of the Jordan River. You completely destroyed them. ¹¹When we heard about it, we were terrified. Because of you, we aren't brave anymore. The LORD your God is the God who rules in heaven above and on the earth below.

¹²"Now then, please give me your word. Promise me in the name of the LORD that you will be kind to my family. I've been kind to you. Promise me ¹³that you will spare the lives of my father and mother. Spare my brothers and sisters. Also spare everyone in their families. Promise that you won't put any of us to death."

¹⁴So the men made a promise to her. "If you save our lives, we'll save yours," they said. "Just don't tell anyone what we're doing. Then we'll be kind and faithful to you when the LORD gives us the land."

¹⁵The house Rahab lived in was part of the city wall. So she let the spies down by a rope through the window. ¹⁶She said to them, "Go up into the hills. The men chasing you won't be able to find you. Hide yourselves there for three days until they return. Then you can go on your way."

¹⁷The spies had said to her, "You made us give our word. But we won't keep our promise ¹⁸unless you do what we say. When we enter the land, you must tie this bright red rope in the window. Tie it in the window you let us down through. Bring your father and mother into your house. Also bring in your brothers and everyone else in your family. ¹⁹None of you must go out into the street. If you do, anything that happens to you will be your own fault. We won't be responsible. But if anyone hurts someone who is inside the house with you, it will be our fault. We will be responsible. ²⁰Don't tell anyone what we're doing. If you do, we won't have to keep the promise you asked us to make."

²¹"I agree," Rahab replied. "I'll do as you say."

So she sent them away, and they left. Then she tied the bright red rope in the window.

²²When the spies left, they went up into the hills. They stayed there for three days. By that time the men chasing them had searched all along the road. They couldn't find them. So they returned. ²³Then the two spies started back. They went down out of the hills. They went across the Jordan River. They came to Joshua, the son of Nun. They told him everything that had happened to them. ²⁴They said, "We're sure the LORD has given the whole land over to us. All the people there are weak with fear because of us."

Israel Goes Across the Jordan River

3 Early one morning Joshua and all the Israelites started out from Shittim. They went down to the Jordan River. They camped there before they went across it. ²After three days the officers went all through the camp. ³They gave orders to the people. They said, "Watch for the ark of the covenant of the LORD your God. The priests, who are Levites, will be carrying it. When you see it, you must move out from where you are and follow it. ⁴Then you will know which way to go. You have never gone this way before. But don't go near the ark. Stay about 1,000 yards away from it."

⁵Joshua said to the people, "Set yourselves apart to the LORD. Tomorrow he'll do amazing things among you."

⁶Joshua said to the priests, "Go and get the ark of the covenant. Walk on ahead of the people." So they went and got it. Then they walked on ahead of them.

⁷The LORD said to Joshua, "Today I will begin to honor you in the eyes of all the Israelites. Then they will know that I am with you, just as I was with Moses. ⁸Speak to the priests who carry the ark of the covenant. Tell them, 'When you reach the edge of the Jordan River, go into the water and stand there.'"

⁹Joshua said to the Israelites, "Come here. Listen to what the LORD your God is saying. ¹⁰You will soon know that the living God is among you. He will certainly drive out the people now living in the land. He'll do it to make room for you. He'll drive out the Canaanites, Hittites,

Hivites, Perizzites, Girgashites, Amorites and Jebusites. [11]The ark will go into the Jordan River ahead of you. It's the ark of the covenant of the Lord of the whole earth. [12]Choose 12 men from the tribes of Israel. Choose one from each tribe. [13]The priests will carry the ark of the LORD. He's the Lord of the whole earth. As soon as the priests step into the Jordan, it will stop flowing. The water that's coming down the river will pile up in one place. That's how you will know that the living God is among you."

[14]So the people took their tents down. They prepared to go across the Jordan River. The priests carrying the ark of the covenant went ahead of them. [15]The water of the Jordan was going over its banks. It always does that at the time the crops are being gathered. The priests came to the river. Their feet touched the water's edge. [16]Right away the water coming down the river stopped flowing. It piled up far away at a town called Adam near Zarethan. The water flowing down to the Dead Sea was completely cut off. So the people went across the Jordan River opposite Jericho. [17]The priests carried the ark of the covenant of the LORD. They stopped in the middle of the river and stood on dry ground. They stayed there until the whole nation of Israel had gone across on dry ground.

4 After the whole nation had gone across the Jordan River, the LORD spoke to Joshua. He said, [2]"Choose 12 men from among the people. Choose one from each tribe. [3]Tell them to get 12 stones from the middle of the river. They must pick them up from right where the priests stood. They must carry the stones over with all of you. And they must put them down at the place where you will stay tonight."

[4]So Joshua called together the 12 men he had appointed from among the Israelites. There was one man from each tribe. [5]He said to them, "Go back to the middle of the Jordan River. Go to where the ark of the LORD your God is. Each one of you must pick up a stone. You must carry it on your shoulder. There will be as many stones as there are tribes in Israel. [6]The stones will serve as a reminder to you. In days to come, your children will ask you, 'What do these stones mean?' [7]Tell them that the LORD cut off the flow of water

WHIT'S WISDOM

Joshua 3–4

children and grandchildren about the time that God parted the Jordan River and gave the land of Canaan to them. It fulfilled a promise God had made to them many years before—a promise that He kept.

Not long ago, I visited Philadelphia, Pennsylvania and saw Independence Hall. The building still looks very much like it did in 1776 when the Declaration of Independence was signed there. It's now a popular place to visit because it reminds us of the incredible moment when America declared its independence and freedom from the British. So many memorials remind us of bad things such as wars, attacks, and death. Those are important too. But Independence Hall reminds us of freedom.

God told the Israelites to create memorials in several places in the Bible. The one in Joshua 4 was to remind the Israelites'

Have you ever thought about making a memorial to remind you of the good things God has done in your life? Try this: draw a picture to commemorate a good thing that God did for you or your family.

heard of the Hindenburg May 6, 1937, a huge German about to land in America when and burned. Thirty-six people accident. As the great ship went orter Herbert Morrison tried to tell eners what he was seeing, but was come at one point that all he could as, "Oh, the humanity!"

ve you ever tried to share a story with someone who wasn't there to experience the event firsthand? It's not easy, is it? In fact, sometimes we end up saying, "Well, I guess you had to be there." News reporters have a difficult job, as we can imagine from the Adventures in Odyssey episode "Siege at Jericho."

This adventure transports us to the scene of another emotionally charged historical event—the Israelites' conquest of Jericho. Lucy, Lawrence, and the gang take us into the first six chapters of the Old Testament book of Joshua. And it all sounds like a live newscast! Told that way, it's hard not to sit up and pay attention when the walls of Jericho crash down.

Have you ever thought of the Bible as an exciting book? As exciting and interesting as breaking news? The "news" may be thousands of years old, but it's as important to us today as back then—especially when these reports remind us that God is looking out for His people.

in the Jordan River. Tell them its water stopped flowing when the ark of the covenant of the LORD went across. The stones will always remind the Israelites of what happened there."

[8]So the Israelites did as Joshua commanded them. They took 12 stones from the middle of the Jordan River. There was one stone for each of the tribes of Israel. It was just as the LORD had told Joshua. The people carried the stones with them to their camp. There they put them down. [9]Joshua also piled up 12 stones in the middle of the river. He piled them up right where the priests who carried the ark of the covenant had stood. And they are still there to this very day.

[10]The priests who carried the ark remained standing in the middle of the Jordan River. They stayed there until the people had done everything the LORD had commanded Joshua. It was just as Moses had directed them. All the people went across quickly. [11]As soon as they did, the ark of the LORD and the priests also went across to the other side. The people were watching them. [12]Among the people who went across the river were men from the tribes of Reuben and Gad and half of the tribe of Manasseh. The men were ready for battle. They went across ahead of the rest of the Israelites. It was just as Moses had directed them. [13]There were about 40,000 of them. All of them were ready for battle. They went across in front of the ark of the LORD. They marched to the plains around Jericho. They were prepared to go to war.

[14]That day the LORD honored Joshua in the eyes of all the Israelites. They had respect for Joshua as long as he lived. They respected him just as much as they had respected Moses.

[15]Then the LORD spoke to Joshua. He said, [16]"Command the priests to come up out of the Jordan River. They are carrying the ark where the tablets of the covenant law are kept."

ADVENTURES IN ODYSSEY

Joshua had the Israelites set up stones as reminders of what God had done for them. In "The Boat People" (Club), young Ricky told how his family kept a ring as a reminder of their history.

¹⁷So Joshua gave a command to the priests. He said, "Come up out of the Jordan River."

¹⁸Then the priests came up out of the river. They were carrying the ark of the covenant of the LORD. As soon as they stepped out on dry ground, the water of the Jordan began to flow again. It went over its banks, just as it had done before.

¹⁹On the tenth day of the first month the people went up out of the Jordan River. They camped at Gilgal on the eastern border of Jericho. ²⁰Joshua set up the 12 stones at Gilgal. They were the ones the people had taken out of the Jordan. ²¹Then he spoke to the Israelites. He said, "In days to come, your children after you will ask their parents, 'What do these stones mean?' ²²Their parents must tell them, 'Israel went across the Jordan River on dry ground.' ²³The LORD your God dried up the Jordan for you until you had gone across it. He did to the Jordan River the same thing he had done to the Red Sea. He dried up the Red Sea ahead of us until we had gone across it. ²⁴He did it so that all the nations on earth would know that he is powerful. He did it so that you would always have respect for the LORD your God."

⁵All the Amorite and C heard how the LORD had Jordan River. They heard the kings dried it up for the Israelites had gone across it. The Amorite lived west of the Jordan. The ki Canaan lived along the Mediterra Sea. When all those kings heard what LORD had done, they were terrified. The weren't brave enough to face the Israelites anymore.

Circumcision and Passover at Gilgal

²At that time the LORD said to Joshua, "Make knives out of flint. Use them to circumcise the men of Israel." ³So Joshua made knives out of flint. Then he used them to circumcise the men of Israel at Gibeath Haaraloth.

⁴Here is why Joshua circumcised them. All the men who came out of Egypt had died. They died while they were wandering through the Sinai Desert. They were the men old enough to serve in the army. ⁵All the men who came out had been circumcised. But all the men born in the desert during the journey from Egypt hadn't been circumcised. ⁶The Israelites had moved around in the desert for 40 years. By the end of that time all the men old enough to serve in the army when they left Egypt had died. That's because they hadn't obeyed the LORD. He had made a promise to them. He had told them they wouldn't see the land. It's the land he had promised to their people to give us. It's a land that has plenty of milk and honey. ⁷Because they hadn't obeyed him, he raised up their sons to take their place. They were the ones Joshua circumcised. They hadn't been circumcised yet. That's because no one had circumcised them during the journey. ⁸So Joshua circumcised all those men. The whole nation remained in the camp until the men were healed.

⁹Then the LORD spoke to Joshua. He said, "Today I have taken away from you the shame of being slaves in Egypt." That's why the place where the men were circumcised has been called Gilgal to this very day.

¹⁰The Israelites celebrated the Passover Feast. They observed it on the evening of the 14th day of the month. They did it

while they were camped at Gilgal on the plains around Jericho. ¹¹The day after the Passover, they ate some of the food grown in the land. On that same day they ate grain that had been cooked. They also ate bread made without yeast. ¹²The manna stopped coming down the day after they ate the food grown in the land. The Israelites didn't have manna anymore. Instead, that year they ate food grown in Canaan.

Jason's Jargon

JOSHUA 5

Find the word *manna* in this chapter. Manna is a small grain—similar to a round cracker—that fell from heaven to feed the Israelites on their journey from Egypt to the Promised Land. Ready? Go!

Israel Captures Jericho

¹³When Joshua was near Jericho, he looked up and saw a man standing in front of him. The man was holding a sword. He was ready for battle. Joshua went up to him. He asked, "Are you on our side? Or are you on the side of our enemies?"

¹⁴"I am not on either side," he replied. "I have come as the commander of the LORD's army." Then Joshua fell with his face to the ground. He asked the man, "What message does my Lord have for me?"

¹⁵The commander of the LORD's army replied, "Take off your sandals. The place you are standing on is holy ground." So Joshua took them off.

6 The gates of Jericho were shut tight and guarded closely because of the Israelites. No one went out. No one came in.

²Then the LORD said to Joshua, "I have handed Jericho over to you. I have also handed over to you its king and its fighting men. ³March around the city once with all your fighting men. In fact, do it for six days. ⁴Have seven priests get trumpets made out of rams' horns. They must carry them in front of the ark. On the seventh day, march around the city seven times. Tell the priests to blow the trumpets as you march. ⁵You will hear them

blow a long blast on the trumpets. When you do, tell the whole army to give a loud shout. The wall of the city will fall down. Then the whole army will march up to the city. Everyone will go straight in."

⁶So Joshua, the son of Nun, called for the priests. He said to them, "Go and get the ark of the covenant of the LORD. I want seven of you to carry trumpets in front of it." ⁷He gave an order to the army. He said, "Move out! March around the city. Some of the fighting men must march in front of the ark of the LORD."

⁸When Joshua had spoken to the men, the seven priests went forward. They were carrying the seven trumpets as they marched in front of the ark of the LORD. They were blowing the trumpets. The ark of the LORD's covenant was carried behind the priests. ⁹Some of the fighting men marched ahead of the priests who were blowing the trumpets. The others followed behind the ark and guarded all the priests. That whole time the priests were blowing the trumpets. ¹⁰But Joshua had given an order to the army. He had said, "Don't give a war cry. Don't raise your voices. Don't say a word until the day I tell you to shout. Then shout!" ¹¹So he had the ark of the LORD carried around the city once. Then the army returned to camp. They spent the night there.

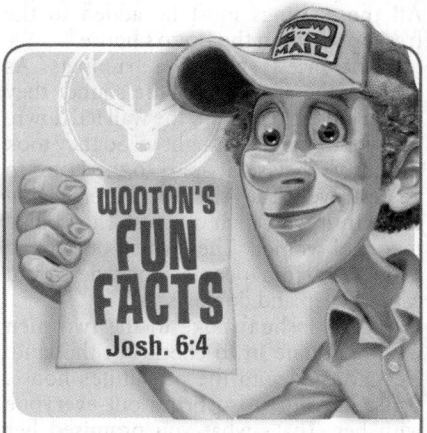

WOOTON'S FUN FACTS
Josh. 6:4

A ram's horn is also known as a *shofar*. The blaster held notes for long and short segments, which meant different things. If I had one, I'd play "Camptown Races," the only song I know.

[12]Joshua got up early the next morning. The priests went and got the ark of the Lord. [13]The seven priests carrying the seven trumpets started out. They marched in front of the ark of the Lord. They blew the trumpets. Some of the fighting men marched ahead of them. The others followed behind the ark and guarded all of them. The priests kept blowing the trumpets. [14]On the second day they marched around the city once. Then the army returned to camp. They did all those things for six days.

[15]On the seventh day, they got up at sunrise. They marched around the city, just as they had done before. But on that day they went around it seven times. [16]On the seventh time around, the priests blew a long blast on the trumpets. Then Joshua gave a command to the army. He said, "Shout! The Lord has given you the city! [17]The city and everything in it must be set apart to the Lord to be destroyed. But the prostitute Rahab and all those with her in her house must be spared. That's because she hid the spies we sent. [18]But keep away from the things that have been set apart to the Lord. If you take any of them, you will be destroyed. And you will bring trouble on the camp of Israel. You will cause it to be destroyed. [19]All the silver and gold is holy. It is set apart to the Lord. So are all the things made out of bronze and iron. All those things must be added to the treasures kept in the Lord's house."

[20]The priests blew the trumpets. As soon as the army heard the sound, they gave a loud shout. Then the wall fell down. Everyone charged straight in. So they took the city. [21]They set it apart to the Lord to be destroyed. They destroyed every living thing in it with their swords. They killed men and women. They wiped out young people and old people. They destroyed cattle, sheep and donkeys.

[22]Then Joshua spoke to the two men who had gone in to check out the land. He said, "Go into the prostitute's house. Bring her out. Also bring out everyone with her. That's what you promised her you would do." [23]So the young men who had checked out the land went into Rahab's house. They brought her out along with her parents and brothers and sisters. They brought out everyone else there with her. They put them in a place outside the camp of Israel.

[24]Then they burned the whole city and everything in it. But they added the silver and gold to the treasures kept in the Lord's house. They also put there the things made out of bronze and iron. [25]But Joshua spared the prostitute Rahab. He spared her family. He also spared everyone else in the house with her. He did it because she hid the spies he had sent to Jericho. Rahab lives among the Israelites to this day.

[26]At that time Joshua made a promise and called down a curse. He said, "May the person who tries to rebuild this city of Jericho be under the Lord's curse.

"If that person lays its foundations,
    it will cost the life of his oldest son.
If he sets up its gates,
    it will cost the life of his youngest
        son."

[27]So the Lord was with Joshua. And Joshua became famous everywhere in the land.

Achan Sins Against the Lord

7 But the Israelites weren't faithful to the Lord. They didn't destroy what had been set apart to him. So they did not do what they had been told to do. Achan had taken some of those things. So the Lord became very angry with Israel. Achan was the son of Karmi. Karmi was the son of Zimri. And Zimri was the son of Zerah. Achan and all his relatives were from the tribe of Judah.

[2]Joshua sent men from Jericho to Ai. Ai is near Beth Aven east of Bethel. Joshua told the men, "Go up and check out the area around Ai." So the men went up and checked it out.

[3]Then they returned to Joshua. They said, "The whole army doesn't have to go up and attack Ai. Send only two or three thousand men. They can take the city. Don't make the whole army go up there. Only a few people live in Ai." [4]So only about 3,000 troops went up. But the men of Ai drove them away. [5]They chased the Israelites from the city gate all the way to Shebarim. They killed about 36 of them on the way down. So the Israelites were terrified.

[6]Joshua and the elders of Israel became sad. Joshua tore his clothes. He fell in front of the ark of the Lord with his face to the ground. He remained there until evening. The elders did the same thing. They also sprinkled dust on their heads. [7]Joshua said, "Lord and King, why did you ever bring these people across the Jordan River? Did you want to hand us over to the Amorites? Did you want them to destroy us? I wish we had been content to stay on the other side of the Jordan! [8]Lord, our enemies have driven us away. What can I say? [9]The Canaanites will hear about it. So will everyone else in the country. They will surround us. They'll erase any mention of our name from the face of the earth. Then what will you do when people don't honor your great name anymore?"

[10]The Lord said to Joshua, "Get up! What are you doing down there on your face? [11]Israel has sinned. I made a covenant with them. I commanded them to keep it. But they have broken it. They have taken some of the things that had been set apart to me in a special way to be destroyed. They have stolen. They have lied. They have taken the things they stole and have put them with their own things. [12]That is why the Israelites can't stand up against their enemies. They turn their backs and run. That's because I have decided to let them be destroyed. You must destroy the things you took that had been set apart to me. If you do not, I will not be with you anymore.

[13]"Go and set the people apart. Tell them, 'Make yourselves pure. Get ready for tomorrow. Here is what the Lord, the God of Israel, wants you to do. He says, "People of Israel, you have kept some of the things that had been set apart to me to be destroyed. You can't stand up against your enemies until you get rid of those things."

[14]"'In the morning, come forward tribe by tribe. The tribe the Lord chooses will come forward group by group. The group the Lord chooses will come forward family by family. And the men in the family the Lord chooses will come forward one by one. [15]Whoever is caught with the things that had been set apart to the Lord will be destroyed by fire. Everything that belongs to that person will also be destroyed. He has broken the Lord's covenant. He has done a very terrible thing in Israel!'"

[16]Early the next morning Joshua had Israel come forward by tribes. The tribe of Judah was chosen. [17]The groups of Judah came forward. The group of Zerah was chosen. Joshua had the group of Zerah come forward by families. The family of Zimri was chosen. [18]He had their men come forward one by one. Achan was chosen. Achan was the son of Karmi. Karmi was the son of Zimri. And Zimri was the son of Zerah. Zerah was from the tribe of Judah.

[19]Joshua said to Achan, "My son, the Lord is the God of Israel. So give him glory and honor him by telling the truth! Tell me what you have done. Don't hide it from me."

[20]Achan replied, "It's true! I've sinned against the Lord, the God of Israel. Here is what I've done. [21]I saw a beautiful robe from Babylonia among the things we had taken. I saw five pounds of silver. And I saw a gold bar that weighed 20 ounces. I wanted them, so I took them. I hid them in the ground inside my tent. The silver is on the bottom."

[22]So Joshua sent some messengers. They ran to Achan's tent. And there was everything, hidden in his tent! The silver was on the bottom. [23]They brought the things out of the tent. They took them to Joshua and all the Israelites. And they spread them out in the sight of the Lord.

[24]Then Joshua and all the people grabbed Achan, the son of Zerah. They took the silver, the robe and the gold bar. They took Achan's sons and daughters. They took his cattle, donkeys and sheep. They also took his tent and everything he had. They carried all of it out to the Valley of Achor. [25]Joshua said to Achan, "Why have you brought this trouble on us? The Lord will bring trouble on you today."

Then all the people killed Achan by throwing stones at him. They also killed the rest of his family with stones. They burned all of them up. [26]They placed a large pile of rocks on top of Achan's body. The place has been called the Valley of Achor ever since. That pile is still there to this day. After the people killed Achan, the Lord was no longer angry with them.

Israel Destroys Ai

8 Then the LORD said to Joshua, "Do not be afraid. Do not lose hope. Go up and attack Ai. Take the whole army with you. I have handed the king of Ai over to you. I have given you his people, his city and his land. ²Remember what you did to Jericho and its king. You will do the same thing to Ai and its king. But this time you can keep for yourselves the livestock and everything else you take from them. Have some of your fighting men hide behind the city and take them by surprise."

³So Joshua and the whole army moved out to attack Ai. He chose 30,000 of his best fighting men. He sent them out at night. ⁴He gave them orders. He said, "Listen carefully to what I'm saying. You must hide behind the city. Don't go very far away from it. All of you must be ready to attack it. ⁵I and all those with me will march up to the city. The men of Ai will come out to fight against us, just as they did before. Then we'll run away from them. ⁶They'll chase us until we've drawn them away from the city. They'll say, 'They are running away from us, just as they did before.' When we run away from them, ⁷come out of your hiding place. Capture the city. The LORD your God will hand it over to you. ⁸When you have taken it, set it on fire. Do what the LORD has commanded. Make sure you obey my orders."

⁹Then Joshua sent them away. They went to the place where they had planned to hide. They hid in a place west of Ai. It was between Bethel and Ai. But Joshua spent that night with his troops.

¹⁰Early the next morning Joshua brought together his army. He and the leaders of Israel marched in front of them to Ai. ¹¹The whole army that was with him marched up to the city. They stopped in front of it. They set up camp north of Ai. There was a valley between them and the city. ¹²Joshua had chosen about 5,000 soldiers. He had ordered them to hide in a place west of Ai. It was between Bethel and Ai. ¹³The men took up their battle positions. All the men in the camp north of the city took up their positions. So did those who were supposed to hide west of the city. That night Joshua went into the valley.

¹⁴The king of Ai saw what the troops with Joshua were doing. So the king and all his men hurried out of the city early in the morning. They marched out to meet Israel in battle. They went to a place that looked out over the Arabah Valley. The king didn't know that some of Israel's fighting men were hiding behind the city. ¹⁵Joshua and all his men let the men of Ai drive them back. The Israelites ran away toward the desert. ¹⁶All the men of Ai were called out to chase them. They chased Joshua. So they were drawn away from the city. ¹⁷Not even one man remained in Ai or Bethel. All of them went out to chase Israel. When they did, they left the city wide open.

¹⁸Then the LORD said to Joshua, "Hold out toward Ai the javelin that is in your hand. I will give the city to you." So Joshua held out toward the city the javelin in his hand. ¹⁹As soon as he did, the men hiding behind the city got up quickly. They came out of their hiding places and rushed forward. They entered the city and captured it. They quickly set it on fire.

²⁰The men of Ai looked back. They saw smoke rising up from the city into the sky. But they couldn't escape in any direction. The Israelites had been running away toward the desert. But now they turned around to face those chasing them. ²¹Joshua and all his men saw that the men who had been hiding behind the city had captured it. They also saw that smoke was going up from it. So they turned around and attacked the men of Ai. ²²The men who had set Ai on fire came out of the city. They also fought against the men of Ai. So the men of Ai were caught in the middle. The army of Israel was on both sides of them. Israel struck them down. They didn't let anyone remain alive or get away. ²³But they captured the king of Ai alive. They brought him to Joshua.

²⁴Israel finished killing all the men of Ai. They destroyed them in the fields and in the desert where they had chased them. They struck down every one of them with their swords. Then all the Israelites returned to Ai. And they killed those who were left in it. ²⁵The total number of men and women they killed that day was 12,000. The Israelites put to death all the people of Ai. ²⁶Joshua continued to hold out his javelin toward Ai. He didn't lower his hand until he and his men had totally

destroyed everyone who lived there. ²⁷But this time Israel kept for themselves the livestock and everything else they had taken from the city. The LORD had directed Joshua to let them do it.

²⁸So Joshua burned down Ai. He tore it down so it could never be built again. It has been deserted to this very day. ²⁹Joshua killed the king of Ai. He stuck a pole through the body. Then he set it up where people could see it. He left it there until evening. At sunset, Joshua ordered his men to remove the body from the pole. He told them to throw the body down at the entrance of the city gate. They put a large pile of rocks over the body. That pile is still there to this day.

Joshua Reads the Book of the Law to the People

³⁰Joshua built an altar to honor the LORD, the God of Israel. He built it on Mount Ebal. ³¹Moses, the servant of the LORD, had commanded the Israelites to do that. Joshua built the altar according to what is written in the Book of the Law of Moses. Joshua built the altar out of stones that iron tools had never touched. Then the people offered on the altar burnt offerings to the LORD. They also sacrificed friendship offerings on it. ³²Joshua copied the law of Moses on stones. He did it while all the Israelites were watching. ³³They were standing on both sides of the ark of the covenant of the LORD. All the Israelites, including outsiders and citizens, were there. Israel's elders, officials and judges were also there. All of them faced the priests, who were Levites. They were carrying the ark. Half of the people stood in front of Mount Gerizim. The other half stood in front of Mount Ebal. Moses, the servant of the LORD, had earlier told them to do it. Moses told them to do it when he had given directions to bless the Israelites.

³⁴Then Joshua read all the words of the law out loud. He read the blessings and the curses. He read them just as they are written in the Book of the Law. ³⁵Joshua read every word Moses had commanded. He read them to the whole community of Israel. That included the women and children. It also included the outsiders living among them.

The People of Gibeon Trick Israel

9 All the kings who ruled west of the Jordan River heard about the battles Israel had won. That included the kings who ruled in the central hill country and the western hills. It also included those who ruled along the entire coast of the Mediterranean Sea all the way to Lebanon. They were the kings of the Hittites, Amorites, Canaanites, Perizzites, Hivites and Jebusites. ²They brought their armies together to fight against Joshua and Israel.

³The people of Gibeon heard about what Joshua had done to Jericho and Ai. ⁴So they decided to trick the Israelites. They packed supplies as if they were going on a long trip. They loaded their donkeys with old sacks and old wineskins. The wineskins were cracked but had been mended. ⁵They put worn-out sandals on their feet. The sandals had been patched. They also wore old clothes. All the bread they took along was dry and moldy. ⁶They went to Joshua in the camp at Gilgal. They spoke to him and the Israelites. They said, "We've come from a country that's far away. Make a peace treaty with us."

⁷The Israelites said to the Hivites, "But suppose you live close to us. If you do, we can't make a peace treaty with you."

⁸"We'll serve you," they said to Joshua.

But Joshua asked, "Who are you? Where do you come from?"

⁹They answered, "We've come from a country that's very far away. We've come because the LORD your God is famous. We've heard reports about him. We've heard about everything he did in Egypt. ¹⁰We've heard about everything he did to Sihon and Og. They were the two kings of the Amorites. They ruled east of the Jordan River. Sihon was the king of Heshbon. Og was the king of Bashan. He ruled in Ashtaroth. ¹¹Our elders and all the people living in our country spoke to us. They said, 'Take supplies for your trip. Go and meet the Israelites. Say to them, "We'll serve you. Make a peace treaty with us."' ¹²Look at our bread. It was warm when we packed it. We packed it at home the day we left to come and see you. But look at how dry and moldy it is now. ¹³When we filled these wineskins, they were new. But look at how cracked they are now. And

our clothes and sandals are worn out because we've traveled so far."

[14]The Israelites looked over the supplies those people had brought. But they didn't ask the LORD what they should do. [15]Joshua made a peace treaty with the people who had come. He agreed to let them live. The leaders of the community gave their word that they agreed with the treaty.

[16]So the Israelites made a peace treaty with the people of Gibeon. But three days later they heard that the people of Gibeon lived close to them. [17]So the Israelites started out to go to the cities of those people. On the third day they came to Gibeon, Kephirah, Beeroth and Kiriath Jearim. [18]But they didn't attack those cities. That's because the leaders of the community had given their word and made a peace treaty with them. They had given their word in the name of the LORD, the God of Israel.

Jason's Jargon

JOSHUA 9

Search this chapter for the word *treaty*. A peace treaty is an agreement between nations that neither will harm the other and a promise that there will be no war between them.

The whole community told the leaders they weren't happy with them. [19]But all the leaders answered, "We've made a peace treaty with them. We've given our word in the name of the LORD, the God of Israel. So we can't touch them now. [20]But here is what we'll do to them. We'll let them live. Then the LORD won't be angry with us because we didn't keep our promise." [21]They continued, "Let them live. But make them cut wood and carry water to serve the whole community." So the leaders kept their promise to them.

[22]Joshua sent for the people of Gibeon. He said to them, "Why did you trick us? You said, 'We live far away from you.' But in fact you live close to us. [23]So now you are under a curse. You will always serve us. You will always cut wood and carry water for the house of my God."

[24]They answered Joshua, "We were clearly told what the LORD your God had commanded his servant Moses to do. He commanded him to give you the whole land. He also ordered him to wipe out all its people to make room for you. So we were afraid you would kill us. That's why we tricked you. [25]We are now under your control. Do to us what you think is good and right."

[26]So Joshua saved the people of Gibeon. He didn't let the Israelites kill them. [27]That day he made them cut wood and carry water. They had to serve the community of Israel. They also had to do work connected with the altar of the LORD. The altar would be at the place the LORD would choose. And they still serve the Israelites to this day.

The Sun Stands Still

10 Adoni-Zedek was the king of Jerusalem. He heard that Joshua had captured Ai. He found out that the city had been set apart to the LORD in a special way to be destroyed. He heard that Joshua had done to Ai and its king the same thing he had done to Jericho and its king. Adoni-Zedek heard that the people of Gibeon had made a peace treaty with Israel. He also found out that they were living among the Israelites. [2]The things he heard alarmed him and his people very much. That's because Gibeon was an important city. It was like one of the royal cities. It was larger than Ai. All its men were good soldiers. [3]So Adoni-Zedek, the king of Jerusalem, made an appeal to Hoham, the king of Hebron. He appealed to Piram, the king of Jarmuth. He appealed to Japhia, the king of Lachish. He also made an appeal to Debir, the king of Eglon. [4]"Come up and help me attack Gibeon," he said. "Its people have made peace with Joshua and the Israelites."

[5]Then the kings of Jerusalem, Hebron, Jarmuth, Lachish and Eglon gathered their armies together. Those five Amorite kings moved all their troops into position to fight against Gibeon. Then they attacked it.

[6]Joshua was in the camp at Gilgal. The people of Gibeon sent a message to him there. They said, "Don't desert us. We serve you. Come up to us quickly! Save us!

Help us! All the Amorite kings from the central hill country have gathered their armies together to fight against us."

⁷So Joshua marched up from Gilgal with his whole army. The army included all his best fighting men. ⁸The Lord said to Joshua, "Do not be afraid of them. I have handed them over to you. Not one of them will be able to fight against you and win."

⁹Joshua marched all night from Gilgal. He took the Amorite armies by surprise. ¹⁰The Lord threw them into a panic as Israel marched toward them. Then Joshua and the Israelites won a complete victory over them at Gibeon. The Israelites chased them along the road that goes up to Beth Horon. They struck them down all the way to Azekah and Makkedah. ¹¹The Amorites tried to escape as Israel marched toward them. They ran down the road from Beth Horon to Azekah. Then the Lord threw large hailstones down on them. The hailstones killed more of them than the swords of the Israelites did.

¹²So the Lord gave the Amorites over to Israel. On that day Joshua spoke to the Lord while the Israelites were listening. He said,

"Sun, stand still over Gibeon.
　　And you, moon, stand still over the
　　　　Valley of Aijalon."
¹³ So the sun stood still.
　　The moon stopped.
　　They didn't move again until the
　　　　nation won the battle over its
　　　　enemies.

You can read about it in the Book of Jashar.

The sun stopped in the middle of the sky. It didn't go down for about a full day. ¹⁴There has never been a day like it before or since. It was a day when the Lord listened to a mere human being. Surely the Lord was fighting for Israel!

¹⁵Joshua and his whole army returned to the camp at Gilgal.

Joshua Kills the Five Amorite Kings

¹⁶The five Amorite kings had run away. They had hidden in the cave at Makkedah. ¹⁷Joshua was told that the five kings had been found. He was also told that they were hiding in the cave at Makkedah.

Josh. 10:12–13 My dog Sam can't stand still for more than a second if a squirrel passes by. Even more unlikely is the sun standing still. But it did. And the moon too. That miracle should stop *you* in your tracks.

¹⁸He said, "Roll some large rocks up to the opening of the cave. Put some men there to guard it. ¹⁹But keep on going! Chase your enemies! Attack them from behind. Don't let them get back to their cities. The Lord your God has handed them over to you."

²⁰So Joshua and the men of Israel had complete victory over them. They killed almost every one of them. But a few escaped. They went back to their cities that had high walls around them. ²¹Then Israel's whole army returned safely to Joshua. He was in the camp at Makkedah. No one in the land dared to say anything against the Israelites.

²²Joshua said, "Open up the cave. Bring those five kings out to me." ²³So Joshua's men brought the kings out of the cave. They were the kings of Jerusalem, Hebron, Jarmuth, Lachish and Eglon. ²⁴The men brought them to Joshua. Then he sent for all the men of Israel. He spoke to the army commanders who had come with him. He said, "Come here. Put your feet on the necks of these kings." So they came forward and placed their feet on the necks of the kings.

²⁵Joshua said to them, "Don't be afraid. Don't lose hope. Be strong and brave. This is what the Lord will do to all the enemies you are going to fight." ²⁶Joshua put the five kings to death. He stuck a pole through each of their bodies.

Then he set the poles up where people could see the bodies. He left them there until evening. ²⁷At sunset Joshua ordered his men to take down the bodies. So they took them down from the poles and threw them into the cave where the kings had been hiding. They placed large rocks at the opening of the cave. And the rocks are still there to this day.

The Campaign Against the Cities in the South

²⁸That day Joshua captured Makkedah. He cut down its people and their king. He totally destroyed everyone in it. He didn't leave anyone alive. He did to the king of Makkedah the same thing he had done to the king of Jericho.

²⁹Joshua moved on from Makkedah to Libnah. Israel's whole army went with him. They attacked Libnah. ³⁰The LORD also handed that city and its king over to Israel. Joshua destroyed the city. He and his men killed everyone in it with their swords. He didn't leave anyone alive there. He did to its king the same thing he had done to the king of Jericho.

³¹Joshua moved on from Libnah to Lachish. Israel's whole army went with him. The men took up their battle positions. Then Joshua attacked Lachish. ³²The LORD handed it over to Israel. Joshua captured the city on the second day of the battle. He destroyed the city. He and his men killed everyone in it with their swords. He had done the same thing to Libnah. ³³While all that was happening, Horam had come up to help Lachish. He was the king of Gezer. But Joshua won the battle over him and his army. No one was left alive.

³⁴Joshua moved on from Lachish to Eglon. Israel's whole army went with him. They took up their battle positions. Then they attacked Eglon. ³⁵They captured it that same day. They totally destroyed everyone in it with their swords. They had done the same thing to Lachish.

³⁶Joshua went up from Eglon to Hebron. Israel's whole army went with him. Then they attacked Hebron. ³⁷They captured the city. They destroyed it and its villages. They killed all its people and their king with their swords. They didn't leave anyone alive. They totally destroyed the city and everyone in it. They had done the same thing at Eglon.

³⁸Joshua turned back and attacked Debir. Israel's whole army went with him. ³⁹They captured the city, its king and its villages. They totally destroyed everyone in Debir with their swords. They didn't leave anyone alive. They did to Debir and its king the same thing they had done to Libnah and its king. They had also done the same thing to Hebron.

⁴⁰So Joshua brought the whole area under his control. That included the central hill country and the Negev Desert. It included the western hills and the mountain slopes. It also included all the kings in that whole area. Joshua didn't leave anyone alive. He totally destroyed everyone who breathed. He did just as the LORD, the God of Israel, had commanded. ⁴¹Joshua brought everyone from Kadesh Barnea to Gaza under his control. He did the same thing to everyone from the whole area of Goshen to Gibeon. ⁴²He won the battle over all those kings and their lands. He did it in one campaign. That's because the LORD, the God of Israel, fought for Israel.

⁴³Then Joshua returned to the camp at Gilgal. Israel's whole army went with him.

The Campaign Against the Cities in the North

11 Jabin was the king of Hazor. He heard about the battles Israel had won. So he sent a message to Jobab. Jobab was the king of Madon. Jabin sent the same message to the kings of Shimron and Akshaph. ²He also sent it to many other kings. Some ruled in the mountains in the north. Some ruled in the Arabah Valley south of Kinnereth. Others ruled in the western hills. Still others ruled in Naphoth Dor in the west. ³Jabin sent the same message to the people of east Canaan and west Canaan. He sent it to the Amorites, Hittites, Perizzites and Jebusites. They lived in the central hill country. He also sent it to the Hivites who lived below Mount Hermon in the area of Mizpah. ⁴Those kings marched out with all their troops. They had a large number of horses and chariots. It was a huge army. The fighting men were as many as the grains of sand on the seashore. ⁵All those kings gathered their armies together to fight against Israel. They set up camp together at the Waters of Merom.

⁶The Lord said to Joshua, "Do not be afraid of them. By this time tomorrow I will hand all of them over to Israel. All of them will be killed. You must cut the legs of their horses. You must burn their chariots."

⁷So Joshua and his whole army attacked them suddenly. They fought against them at the Waters of Merom. ⁸The Lord handed them over to Israel. The Israelites won the battle over them. They hunted them down all the way to Greater Sidon. They chased them to Misrephoth Maim. They chased them to the Valley of Mizpah in the east. Not one of them was left alive. ⁹Joshua did to them what the Lord had ordered him to do. He cut the legs of their horses. He burned up their chariots.

¹⁰At that time Joshua turned back. He captured Hazor. He killed its king with his sword. Hazor was the most important city in all those kingdoms. ¹¹The army of Israel killed everyone in Hazor with their swords. Its people had been set apart to the Lord to be destroyed. Israel's army didn't spare anyone who breathed. Then Joshua burned down the city.

¹²Joshua captured all those royal cities and their kings. He and his men killed everyone in those cities with their swords. He totally destroyed them. He did just as Moses, the servant of the Lord, had commanded. ¹³Many cities were built on top of earlier cities that had been destroyed. Israel didn't burn any of those except Hazor. Joshua burned it down. ¹⁴The army of Israel kept for themselves the livestock and everything else they took from those cities. But they killed all the people with their swords. They completely destroyed them. They didn't spare anyone who breathed. ¹⁵The Lord had commanded his servant Moses to do all these things. Moses had passed that command on to Joshua. And Joshua carried it out. He did everything the Lord had commanded Moses.

¹⁶So Joshua captured the whole land. He took over the central hill country and the whole Negev Desert. He took over the whole area of Goshen. He took over the western hills. He took over the Arabah Valley. He took over the mountains of Israel and the hills around them. ¹⁷He took over the area that begins at Mount Halak, which rises toward Seir. The area ends at Baal Gad in the Valley of Lebanon below Mount Hermon. Joshua captured the kings who ruled over that whole land. He put them to death. ¹⁸He fought battles against all those kings for a long time. ¹⁹Only the Hivites who lived in Gibeon made a peace treaty with the Israelites. No other city made a treaty with them. So Israel captured all those cities in battle. ²⁰The Lord himself made their people stubborn. He made them go to war against Israel so he could totally destroy them. He wanted to wipe them out. He didn't show them any mercy. The Lord had commanded Moses to destroy the Canaanites.

²¹At that time Joshua went and destroyed the Anakites. They lived all through the hill country of Judah and Israel. They lived in Hebron, Debir and Anab. Joshua totally destroyed the Anakites and their towns. ²²There weren't any Anakites left alive in Israel's territory. But a few were left alive in Gaza, Gath and Ashdod.

²³So Joshua captured the whole land, just as the Lord had directed Moses. Joshua gave the land to Israel as their very own. He divided it up and gave each tribe its share. Then the land had peace and rest.

Israel Wins the Battle Over the Kings in the Land

12 The Israelites took over the territory east of the Jordan River. The land they captured reached from the Arnon River valley to Mount Hermon. It included the whole east side of the Arabah Valley. Israel won the battle over the kings of that whole territory. Here are the lands Israel captured from the kings they won the battle over.

² They took over the land of Sihon.
   He was the king of the Amorites.
   He ruled in Heshbon.
   The land he ruled over begins at Aroer. Aroer is on the rim of the Arnon River valley. Sihon ruled from the middle of the valley to the Jabbok River. The Jabbok is

the border of Ammon. Sihon's territory included half of Gilead. ³ He also ruled over the east side of the Arabah Valley. That land begins at the Sea of Galilee. It goes to the Dead Sea and over to Beth Jeshimoth. Then it goes south, below the slopes of Pisgah.

⁴ Israel also took over the territory of Og. He was the king of Bashan. He was one of the last of the Rephaites. He ruled in Ashtaroth and Edrei. ⁵ He ruled over Mount Hermon, Salekah and the whole land of Bashan. Og's kingdom reached all the way to the border of Geshur and Maakah. He ruled over half of Gilead. His land reached the border of Sihon, the king of Heshbon.

⁶ Moses was the servant of the LORD. Moses and the Israelites won the battle over those two kings. He gave their land to the tribes of Reuben and Gad and half of the tribe of Manasseh. He gave it to them as their share.

⁷Joshua and the Israelites won the battle over the kings who ruled west of the Jordan River. The lands of those kings reached from Baal Gad in the Valley of Lebanon to Mount Halak, which rises toward Seir. Joshua gave their lands to the tribes of Israel as their very own. He divided them up and gave each tribe its share. ⁸Those lands included the central hill country, the western hills and the Arabah Valley. They also included the mountain slopes, the Desert of Judah and the Negev Desert. Those lands belonged to the Hittites, Amorites, Canaanites, Perizzites, Hivites and Jebusites.

Here are the kings Israel won the battle over.

⁹ the king of Jericho	one
the king of Ai, which is near Bethel	one
¹⁰ the king of Jerusalem	one
the king of Hebron	one
¹¹ the king of Jarmuth	one
the king of Lachish	one
¹² the king of Eglon	one
the king of Gezer	one
¹³ the king of Debir	one
the king of Geder	one
¹⁴ the king of Hormah	one
the king of Arad	one
¹⁵ the king of Libnah	one
the king of Adullam	one
¹⁶ the king of Makkedah	one
the king of Bethel	one
¹⁷ the king of Tappuah	one
the king of Hepher	one
¹⁸ the king of Aphek	one
the king of Lasharon	one
¹⁹ the king of Madon	one
the king of Hazor	one
²⁰ the king of Shimron Meron	one
the king of Akshaph	one
²¹ the king of Taanach	one
the king of Megiddo	one
²² the king of Kedesh	one
the king of Jokneam in Carmel	one
²³ the king of Dor in Naphoth Dor	one
the king of Goyim in Gilgal	one
²⁴ the king of Tirzah	one

The total number of kings was 31.

The Land That Remained to Be Taken Over

13 Joshua was now very old. The LORD said to him, "You are very old. And there are still very large areas of land that have not yet been taken over.

² "Here is the land that remains to be taken over.

It includes all the areas of Philistia and Geshur. ³Those areas begin at the Shihor River in the eastern part of Egypt. They go to the territory of Ekron in the north. All that land is considered Canaanite even though it is controlled by five Philistine rulers. They rule over Gaza, Ashdod, Ashkelon, Gath and Ekron.

The Avvites ⁴live south of them. The rest of the land of Canaan that remains to be taken over reaches from Arah all the way to Aphek. Arah belongs to the people of Sidon. The land that remains to be taken reaches the border of Amorite territory. ⁵ It includes the area of Byblos.

It also includes all of Lebanon to the east. It reaches from Baal Gad below Mount Hermon all the way to Lebo Hamath.

⁶"I myself will drive out all the people who live in the mountain areas. Those areas reach from Lebanon to Misrephoth Maim. They include the area where all the people of Sidon live. I myself will drive out those people to make room for the Israelites. Make sure you set that land apart for Israel. Give it to them as their share, just as I have directed you. ⁷Divide it up among the nine tribes and half of the tribe of Manasseh. Give each tribe its share."

Land for the Tribes East of the Jordan River

⁸ The other half of Manasseh's tribe had already received the share of land Moses had given them. Their share was east of the Jordan River. The tribes of Reuben and Gad had already received their share too. Moses, the servant of the LORD, had given it to them.

⁹ That land starts at Aroer on the rim of the Arnon River valley. It includes the town in the middle of the valley. It includes the high plains of Medeba all the way to Dibon. ¹⁰It also includes all the towns of Sihon, the king of the Amorites. He had ruled in Heshbon. That area reaches to the border of Ammon.

¹¹ It also includes Gilead. It includes the territory of Geshur and Maakah. It includes Mount Hermon and the whole land of Bashan all the way to Salekah. ¹²So it includes the entire kingdom of Og in Bashan. Og had ruled in Ashtaroth and Edrei. He was the last of the Rephaites. Moses had won the battle over Sihon and Og. He had taken over their land. ¹³But the Israelites didn't drive out the people of Geshur and Maakah. So they continue to live among the Israelites to this day.

¹⁴ Moses hadn't given any share of the land to the tribe of Levi. That's because the food offerings are their share. Those offerings are presented to the LORD, the God of Israel. Moses gave the Levites what he had promised them.

¹⁵ Here is what Moses had given to the tribe of Reuben, according to its family groups.
¹⁶ Their territory starts at Aroer on the rim of the Arnon River valley. It includes the town in the middle of the valley. It includes all of the high plains near Medeba. ¹⁷It includes Heshbon and all its towns on those plains. Those towns include Dibon, Bamoth Baal, Beth Baal Meon, ¹⁸Jahaz, Kedemoth and Mephaath. ¹⁹They include Kiriathaim, Sibmah and Zereth Shahar on the hill in the valley. ²⁰They also include Beth Peor, Beth Jeshimoth and the slopes of Pisgah. ²¹All those towns are on the high plains. The territory includes the whole kingdom of Sihon, the king of the Amorites. He had ruled in Heshbon. Moses had won the battle over him and over the chiefs of Midian. Those chiefs were Evi, Rekem, Zur, Hur and Reba. They were princes who helped Sihon fight against Israel. They lived in that country. ²²The Israelites killed many of them in battle. They also killed Balaam with their swords. He was the son of Beor. Balaam had used evil magic to find out what was going to happen.

²³ The border of the tribe of Reuben was the bank of the Jordan River. All those towns and their villages were given to the tribe of Reuben as their very own. Each family group received its share.

²⁴ Here is what Moses had given to the tribe of Gad, according to its family groups.
²⁵ Their territory includes Jazer and all the towns of Gilead. It includes half of the country of Ammon all the way to Aroer, which was near Rabbah. ²⁶Their territory reaches from Heshbon to Ramath

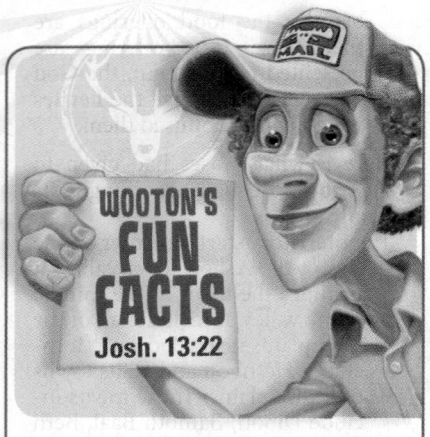

WOOTON'S FUN FACTS

Josh. 13:22

Balaam was a man who used evil magic. There are a bunch of magicians mentioned in the Bible. See Genesis 41:8; 2 Chronicles 33:5–6; Jeremiah 27:9; Daniel 4:9; and Acts 8:9 for just a few.

Mizpah and Betonim. It reaches from Mahanaim to the territory of Debir. ²⁷In the valley their land includes Beth Haram, Beth Nimrah, Sukkoth and Zaphon. It also includes the rest of the kingdom of Sihon. He was the king of Heshbon. His kingdom included the east side of the Jordan River. It reached up to the south end of the Sea of Galilee.

²⁸All those towns and their villages were given to the tribe of Gad as their very own. Each family group received its share.

²⁹Here is what Moses had given to half of the tribe of Manasseh, according to its family groups. It's what Moses had given to half of Manasseh's family line.

³⁰Their territory starts at Mahanaim. It includes the whole land of Bashan. That was the entire kingdom of Og, the king of Bashan. Manasseh's territory includes all the 60 towns of Jair in Bashan. ³¹It includes half of the land of Gilead. It also includes Ashtaroth and Edrei. They were the royal cities of Og in Bashan. That land was given to half of the family line of Makir. He was the son

of Manasseh. Each family group received its share.

³²Those were the shares of land Moses had given the eastern tribes when he was in the plains of Moab. The plains are across the Jordan River east of Jericho. ³³But Moses hadn't given any share to the tribe of Levi. The LORD, the God of Israel, is their share. Moses gave the Levites what he had promised them.

Land for the Tribes West of the Jordan River

14 The rest of the tribes of Israel received their shares of land in Canaan. Eleazar the priest and Joshua, the son of Nun, decided what each of the tribes should receive. The leaders of the tribes helped them make these decisions. ²The shares of nine tribes and half of the tribe of Manasseh were decided by casting lots. That's what the LORD had commanded through Moses. ³Moses had given two tribes and the other half of the tribe of Manasseh their shares east of the Jordan River. But Moses had not given the Levites a share among the other tribes. ⁴Manasseh and Ephraim were the sons of Joseph. They had become two tribes. The Levites didn't receive any share of the land. They only received towns to live in and grasslands for their flocks and herds. ⁵So the Israelites divided up the land, just as the LORD had commanded Moses.

Joshua Gives Hebron to Caleb

⁶The people of Judah approached Joshua at Gilgal. Caleb, the son of Jephunneh the Kenizzite, spoke to Joshua. He said, "You know what the LORD said to Moses, the man of God. He spoke to him at Kadesh Barnea about you and me. ⁷Moses, the servant of the LORD, sent me from Kadesh Barnea to check out the land. I was 40 years old at that time. I brought back an honest report to him. I told him exactly what I had seen. ⁸Several other men of Israel went up with me. What they reported terrified the people. But I followed the LORD my God with my whole heart. ⁹So on that day Moses made a promise to me. He said, 'The land you have walked on will be your share. It will be the share of your children forever. That's because

you have followed the Lord my God with your whole heart.' *(Deuteronomy 1:36)*

¹⁰"The Lord has done just as he promised. He made the promise while Israel was wandering around in the desert. That was 45 years ago. He has kept me alive all this time. So here I am today, 85 years old! ¹¹I'm still as strong today as I was the day Moses sent me out. I'm just as able to go out to battle now as I was then. ¹²So give me this hill country. The Lord promised it to me that day. At that time you yourself heard that the Anakites were living there. You also heard that their cities were large and had high walls around them. But I'll drive them out, just as the Lord said I would. He will help me do it."

¹³Then Joshua blessed Caleb, the son of Jephunneh. He gave him Hebron as his share. ¹⁴So ever since that time Hebron has belonged to Caleb, the son of Jephunneh the Kenizzite. That's because he followed the Lord, the God of Israel, with his whole heart. ¹⁵Hebron used to be called Kiriath Arba. It was named after Arba. He was the greatest man among the Anakites.

So the land had peace and rest.

Land Is Given to Judah

15 Land was given to the tribe of Judah, according to its family groups. It reached down to the territory of Edom. It went as far south as the Desert of Zin.

² Judah's border on the south started from the bay at the south end of the Dead Sea. ³It went across to the south of Scorpion Pass. It continued on to Zin. It went over to the south of Kadesh Barnea. Then it ran past Hezron up to Addar. It curved around to Karka. ⁴It then went along to Azmon. There it joined the Wadi of Egypt and ended at the Mediterranean Sea. That was the southern border of Judah.

⁵ The border on the east was the Dead Sea. It went north all the way to where the Jordan River enters the sea.

The border on the north started at the bay of the Dead Sea. That's where the Jordan River enters the sea. ⁶From there it went up to Beth Hoglah. It continued north of Beth Arabah to the Stone of Bohan, the son of Reuben. ⁷Then it went from the Valley of Achor up to Debir. It turned north to Gilgal. Gilgal faces the Pass of Adummim south of the valley. The border continued along to the springs of En Shemesh. It came to an end at En Rogel. ⁸Then it ran up the Valley of Ben Hinnom. It went along the south slope of Jerusalem. From there it climbed to the top of the hill west of the Hinnom Valley. The hill is also at the north end of the Valley of Rephaim. ⁹From the top of the hill the border headed toward the springs of Nephtoah. It went to the towns near Mount Ephron. It went down toward Kiriath Jearim. ¹⁰Then it curved west from Kiriath Jearim to Mount Seir. It ran along the north slope of Mount Kesalon. It continued down to Beth Shemesh and crossed over to Timnah. ¹¹It went to the north slope of Ekron. Then it turned toward Shikkeron. It passed along to Mount Baalah and reached Jabneel. The border came to an end at the Mediterranean Sea.

¹² The border on the west was the coastline of the Mediterranean Sea.

Those were the borders of the family groups of the tribe of Judah.

¹³Joshua gave a part of Judah's share of land to Caleb, the son of Jephunneh. That was according to the Lord's command to Joshua. The share Caleb received was the city of Hebron. It was also called Kiriath Arba. Anak came from the family line of Arba. ¹⁴Caleb drove three Anakites out of Hebron. Their names were Sheshai, Ahiman and Talmai. They were from the family line of Anak. ¹⁵From Hebron, Caleb marched out against the people living in Debir. It used to be called Kiriath Sepher. ¹⁶Caleb said, "I will give my daughter Aksah to be married. She'll be the wife of the man who attacks and captures Kiriath Sepher." ¹⁷Othniel captured it. So

Caleb gave his daughter Aksah to him to be his wife. Othniel was the son of Kenaz. He was Caleb's brother.

¹⁸One day Aksah came to Othniel. She begged him to ask her father for a field. When she got off her donkey, Caleb spoke to her. He asked, "What can I do for you?"

¹⁹She replied, "Do me a special favor. You have given me some land in the Negev Desert. Give me springs of water also." So Caleb gave her the upper and lower springs.

²⁰ Here is the share of land given to the tribe of Judah, according to its family groups.

²¹ The towns farthest south that were given to Judah were in the Negev Desert. They were near the border of Edom. Here is a list of those towns.

Kabzeel, Eder, Jagur, ²²Kinah, Dimonah, Adadah, ²³Kedesh, Hazor, Ithnan, ²⁴Ziph, Telem, Bealoth, ²⁵Hazor Hadattah, Hazor, ²⁶Amam, Shema, Moladah, ²⁷Hazar Gaddah, Heshmon, Beth Pelet, ²⁸Hazar Shual, Beersheba, Biziothiah, ²⁹Baalah, Iyim, Ezem, ³⁰Eltolad, Kesil, Hormah, ³¹Ziklag, Madmannah, Sansannah, ³²Lebaoth, Shilhim, Ain and Rimmon. The total number of towns was 29. Some of them had villages near them.

³³ Towns were also given to Judah in the western hills. Here is a list of those towns.

Eshtaol, Zorah, Ashnah, ³⁴Zanoah, En Gannim, Tappuah, Enam, ³⁵Jarmuth, Adullam, Sokoh, Azekah, ³⁶Shaaraim, Adithaim and Gederah. Gederah is also called Gederothaim. The total number of towns was 14. Some of them had villages near them.

³⁷ Here's another list of towns given to Judah in the western hills.

Zenan, Hadashah, Migdal Gad, ³⁸Dilean, Mizpah, Joktheel, ³⁹Lachish, Bozkath, Eglon, ⁴⁰Kabbon, Lahmas, Kitlish, ⁴¹Gederoth, Beth Dagon, Naamah and Makkedah. The total number of towns was 16. Some of them had villages near them.

⁴² Here's another list of towns given to Judah in the western hills.

Libnah, Ether, Ashan, ⁴³Iphtah, Ashnah, Nezib, ⁴⁴Keilah, Akzib and Mareshah. The total number of towns was nine. Some of them had villages near them.

⁴⁵ Judah was also given Ekron and the settlements and villages around it. ⁴⁶West of Ekron, Judah was given all the settlements and villages near Ashdod. ⁴⁷Judah was given Ashdod and the settlements and villages around it. And Judah was given Gaza and its settlements and villages. Judah's territory went all the way to the Wadi of Egypt and the coast of the Mediterranean Sea.

⁴⁸ Towns were also given to Judah in the central hill country. Here is a list of those towns.

Shamir, Jattir, Sokoh, ⁴⁹Dannah, Debir, ⁵⁰Anab, Eshtemoh, Anim, ⁵¹Goshen, Holon and Giloh. The total number of towns was 11. Some of them had villages near them.

⁵² Here's another list of towns given to Judah in the central hill country.

Arab, Dumah, Eshan, ⁵³Janim, Beth Tappuah, Aphekah, ⁵⁴Humtah, Hebron and Zior. The total number of towns was nine. Some of them had villages near them.

⁵⁵ Here's another list of towns given to Judah in the central hill country.

Maon, Carmel, Ziph, Juttah, ⁵⁶Jezreel, Jokdeam, Zanoah, ⁵⁷Kain, Gibeah and Timnah. The total number of towns was ten. Some of them had villages near them.

⁵⁸ Here's another list of towns given to Judah in the central hill country.

Halhul, Beth Zur, Gedor, ⁵⁹Maarath, Beth Anoth and Eltekon. The total number of towns was six. Some of them had villages near them.

⁶⁰ Here's another list of towns given to Judah in the central hill country.

Kiriath Jearim and Rabbah. The total number of towns was two. They had villages near them.

⁶¹ Towns were also given to Judah in the desert. Here is a list of those towns.

Beth Arabah, Middin, Sekakah, ⁶²Nibshan, the City of Salt and En Gedi. The total number of towns was six. Some of them had villages near them.

⁶³Judah couldn't drive out the Jebusites who were living in Jerusalem. So they live there with the people of Judah to this day.

Land Is Given to Ephraim and Manasseh

16 The land given to the two tribes in the family line of Joseph began at the Jordan River. Their border started east of the springs of Jericho. It went up from there through the desert into the hill country of Bethel. ²Bethel is also called Luz. From Bethel the border crossed over to Ataroth. That's where the Arkites live. ³Then it went west down to the territory of the Japhletites. It went all the way to the area of Lower Beth Horon. It went on to Gezer. The border came to an end at the Mediterranean Sea.

⁴ The tribes of Manasseh and Ephraim were from the family line of Joseph. So they received that land as their share.

⁵ Here is the territory given to the tribe of Ephraim, according to its family groups.

The border of their share of land started at Ataroth Addar in the east. It went to Upper Beth Horon. ⁶It continued toward the Mediterranean Sea. From Mikmethath on the north, it curved toward the east. It went to Taanath Shiloh. It passed by Taanath Shiloh to Janoah on the east. ⁷Then it went down from Janoah to Ataroth and Naarah. It touched Jericho and came to an end at the Jordan River. ⁸From Tappuah the border went west to the Kanah Valley. It came to an

Jason's Jargon

JOSHUA 16

Your odyssey continues! Find *tribe* in this chapter. A tribe is a collection of families with a common ancestor. The twelve tribes of Israel are named after Jacob's twelve sons.

end at the Mediterranean Sea. That was the land given to the tribe of Ephraim. Each family group received its share.

⁹ The tribe of Ephraim was also given other towns and villages that were set apart for them. Those towns and villages were in the share of land given to the tribe of Manasseh.

¹⁰The people of Ephraim didn't drive out the Canaanites living in Gezer. The Canaanites live among the people of Ephraim to this day. But they are forced to work hard for the people of Ephraim.

17 Land was given to the tribe of Manasseh. It was given to Makir. Manasseh was Joseph's oldest son. Makir was Manasseh's oldest son. The people of Gilead came from the family line of Makir. The people of Gilead had received the lands of Gilead and Bashan. That's because the people of Makir were great soldiers. ²So land was given to the rest of the people of Manasseh. It was given to the family groups of Abiezer, Helek, Asriel, Shechem, Hepher and Shemida. They were the other men in the family line of Manasseh, the son of Joseph. Those were their names by their family groups.

³Makir was the son of Manasseh. Gilead was the son of Makir. Hepher was the son of Gilead. And Zelophehad was the son of Hepher. Zelophehad didn't have any sons. He only had daughters. Their names were Mahlah, Noah, Hoglah, Milkah and Tirzah. ⁴The daughters of Zelophehad went to Eleazar the priest and to Joshua, the son of Nun. They also went to the other leaders. They said, "The LORD commanded Moses to give us our

share of land among our male relatives." So Joshua gave them land along with their male relatives. That was according to what the LORD had commanded. [5]Manasseh's share was made up of ten pieces of land. That land was in addition to Gilead and Bashan east of the Jordan River. [6]So the five granddaughters of Hepher in the family line of Manasseh received land, just as the other five sons of Manasseh did. The land of Gilead belonged to the rest of the family line of Manasseh.

[7] The territory of Manasseh reached from Asher to Mikmethath. Mikmethath was east of Shechem. The border ran south from Mikmethath. The people living at En Tappuah were inside the border. [8]Manasseh had the land around Tappuah. But the town of Tappuah itself was on the border of Manasseh's land. It belonged to the people of Ephraim. [9]The border continued south to the Kanah Valley. Some of the towns that belonged to Ephraim were located among the towns of Manasseh. But the border of Manasseh was the north side of the valley. The border came to an end at the Mediterranean Sea. [10]The land on the south belonged to Ephraim. The land on the north belonged to Manasseh. The territory of Manasseh reached the Mediterranean Sea. The tribe of Asher was the border on the north. The tribe of Issachar was the border on the east.

[11] Inside the land given to Issachar and Asher, the towns of Beth Shan and Ibleam belonged to Manasseh. The towns of Dor, Endor, Taanach and Megiddo and their people also belonged to Manasseh. Manasseh was given all those towns and the settlements around them. The third town in the list was also called Naphoth Dor.

[12]But the people of Manasseh weren't able to take over those towns. That's because the Canaanites had made up their minds to live in that area. [13]The Israelites grew stronger. Then they forced the Canaanites to work hard for them. But they didn't drive them out completely.

[14]The people in the family line of Joseph spoke to Joshua. They said, "Why have you given us only one share of the land to have as our own? There are large numbers of us. The LORD has blessed us greatly."

[15]"That's true," Joshua said. "There are large numbers of you. And the hill country of Ephraim is too small for you. So go up into the forest. Clear out some land for yourselves in the territory of the Perizzites and Rephaites."

[16]The people in Joseph's family line replied, "The hill country isn't big enough for us. And all the Canaanites who live in the plains use chariots that have iron parts. They include the people of Beth Shan and its settlements. They also include the people who live in the Valley of Jezreel."

[17]Joshua spoke again to the people in Joseph's family line. He said to the people of Ephraim and Manasseh, "There are large numbers of you. And you are very powerful. You will have more than one piece of land. [18]You will also have the central hill country. It's covered with trees. Cut them down and clear the land. That whole land from one end to the other will belong to you. The Canaanites use chariots that have iron parts. And those people are strong. But you can drive them out."

Josh. 17:18 Many ancient war chariots were two-wheeled and carried men armed with javelins or bows and arrows. The chariots were drawn by horses, which is strange because most horses I know aren't good artists. Uh, get it?

The Rest of the Land Is Divided Up

18 The whole community of Israel gathered together at Shiloh. They set up the tent of meeting there. The country was brought under their control. ²But there were still seven tribes in Israel who had not yet received their shares of land.

³So Joshua spoke to the Israelites. He said, "The LORD, the God of your people, has given you this land. How long will you wait before you begin to take it over? ⁴Appoint three men from each tribe. I'll send them to map out the land. Then they'll write a report about its features. The report will point out the share of land each tribe will receive. Then the men will return to me. ⁵You must divide the land up into seven shares. Judah must remain in its territory in the south. The people in Joseph's family line must remain in their territory in the north. ⁶Write reports about the features of those seven shares of land. Bring them here to me. Then I'll cast lots for you in the sight of the LORD our God. ⁷But the Levites don't get any share of your land. That's because their share is to serve the LORD as priests. The tribes of Gad and Reuben and half of the tribe of Manasseh have already received their shares. They are on the east side of the Jordan River. Moses, the servant of the LORD, gave their shares to them."

⁸The men started out on their way to map out the land. Joshua directed them, "Go and map out the land. Write a report about its features. Then return to me. I'll cast lots for you here at Shiloh in the sight of the LORD." ⁹So the men left and went through the land. They wrote a report about its features on a scroll. It showed how they divided up the land into seven shares. It listed the towns in each share. The men returned to Joshua in the camp at Shiloh.

¹⁰ Then Joshua cast lots for them in Shiloh in the sight of the LORD. There he gave out a share of land to each of the remaining tribes in Israel.

Land Is Given to Benjamin

¹¹ The first lot drawn out was for the tribe of Benjamin, according to its family groups. The territory they were given was located between the tribes of the people of Judah and the people of Joseph. Here are the borders of Benjamin's territory.

¹² On the north side their border started at the Jordan River. It went past the north slope of Jericho. Then it headed west into the central hill country. It came to an end at the Desert of Beth Aven. ¹³From there the border crossed to the south slope of Bethel. Then it went down to Ataroth Addar on the hill south of Lower Beth Horon.

¹⁴ From the hill that faces Beth Horon on the south the border turned south. Then the border went along the west side of the hill. It came to an end at Kiriath Jearim. That town belongs to the people of Judah. That was the border on the west.

¹⁵ The border on the south side started at the west edge of Kiriath Jearim. It came to an end at the springs of Nephtoah. ¹⁶It went down to the foot of the hill that faces the Valley of Ben Hinnom. The hill is north of the Valley of Rephaim. The border continued down the Hinnom Valley. It went along the south slope of Jerusalem, where the people of Jebus live. It continued on to En Rogel. ¹⁷Then it curved north. It went to En Shemesh. It continued on to Geliloth. Geliloth faces the Pass of Adummim. The border ran down to the Stone of Bohan, the son of Reuben. ¹⁸It continued to the north slope of Beth Arabah. It went on down into the Arabah Valley. ¹⁹From there it went to the north slope of Beth Hoglah. It came to an end at the north bay of the Dead Sea. That's where the Jordan River flows into the Dead Sea. That was the border on the south.

²⁰ The Jordan River formed the border on the east side.

Those were the borders that marked out on all sides the land the family groups of Benjamin received as their share.

²¹ Here is a list of towns given to the tribe of Benjamin, according to its family groups.

Jericho, Beth Hoglah, Emek Keziz, [22]Beth Arabah, Zemaraim, Bethel, [23]Avvim, Parah, Ophrah, [24]Kephar Ammoni, Ophni and Geba. The total number of towns and their villages was 12.

[25] Here is another list of towns given to Benjamin.

Gibeon, Ramah, Beeroth, [26]Mizpah, Kephirah, Mozah, [27]Rekem, Irpeel, Taralah, [28]Zelah, Haeleph, Jerusalem, Gibeah and Kiriath. The total number of towns and their villages was 14.

That was the share of land the family groups of Benjamin received.

Land Is Given to Simeon

19 The second lot drawn out was for the tribe of Simeon, according to its family groups. The share of land they were given was in the territory of Judah.

[2] Here is what Simeon's share included.

Beersheba, Moladah, [3]Hazar Shual, Balah, Ezem, [4]Eltolad, Bethul, Hormah, [5]Ziklag, Beth Markaboth, Hazar Susah, [6]Beth Lebaoth and Sharuhen. The total number of towns was 13. Some of them had villages near them.

[7] Here's another list of towns given to Simeon.

Ain, Rimmon, Ether and Ashan. The total number of towns was four. Some of them had villages near them. [8]The towns and all the villages around them reached all the way to Ramah in the Negev Desert.

That was the share of land the tribe of Simeon received, according to its family groups. [9]Simeon's share of land was taken from Judah's share. That's because Judah had more land than they needed. So the people of Simeon received their share of land inside the territory of Judah.

Land Is Given to Zebulun

[10] The third lot drawn out was for the tribe of Zebulun, according to its family groups. Here are the borders of Zebulun's territory.

The border of their share of land went as far as Sarid. [11]It ran west to Maralah and touched Dabbesheth. It reached to the valley near Jokneam. [12]It turned east from Sarid toward the sunrise. It went to the territory of Kisloth Tabor. It went on to Daberath and up to Japhia. [13]Then it continued east to Gath Hepher and Eth Kazin. It came to an end at Rimmon and turned toward Neah. [14]There the border went around on the north to Hannathon. It came to an end at the Valley of Iphtah El.

[15] Zebulun's territory included Kattath, Nahalal, Shimron, Idalah and Bethlehem.

The total number of towns was 12. Some of them had villages near them.

[16] Those towns and their villages were Zebulun's share, according to its family groups.

Land Is Given to Issachar

[17] The fourth lot drawn out was for the tribe of Issachar, according to its family groups. [18]Here is what Issachar's share included.

Jezreel, Kesulloth, Shunem, [19]Hapharaim, Shion, Anaharath, [20]Rabbith, Kishion, Ebez, [21]Remeth, En Gannim, En Haddah and Beth Pazzez.

[22] The border touched Tabor, Shahazumah and Beth Shemesh. It came to an end at the Jordan River.

The total number of towns was 16. Some of them had villages near them.

[23] Those towns and their villages were the share the tribe of Issachar received, according to its family groups.

Land Is Given to Asher

[24] The fifth lot drawn out was for the tribe of Asher, according to its family groups. [25]Here is what Asher's share included.

Helkath, Hali, Beten, Akshaph, [26]Allammelek, Amad and Mishal. On the west the border touched Carmel and Shihor Libnath. [27]Then it turned east toward Beth Dagon.

It touched Zebulun and the Valley of Iphtah El. It went north to Beth Emek and Neiel. It went past Kabul on the left. [28]It went to Abdon, Rehob, Hammon and Kanah. It reached all the way to Greater Sidon. [29]The border then turned back toward Ramah. It went to Tyre, a city that had high walls around it. It turned toward Hosah. It came to an end at the Mediterranean Sea in the area of Akzib, [30]Ummah, Aphek and Rehob.

The total number of towns was 22. Some of them had villages near them.

[31] Those towns and their villages were the share the tribe of Asher received, according to its family groups.

Land Is Given to Naphtali

[32] The sixth lot drawn out was for Naphtali, according to its family groups.

[33] Their border started at Heleph and the large tree in Zaanannim. It went past Adami Nekeb and Jabneel. It went to Lakkum and came to an end at the Jordan River. [34]The border ran west through Aznoth Tabor. It came to an end at Hukkok. It touched Zebulun on the south. It touched Asher on the west. It touched the Jordan on the east.

[35] The towns that had high walls around them were Ziddim, Zer, Hammath, Rakkath, Kinnereth, [36]Adamah, Ramah, Hazor, [37]Kedesh, Edrei, En Hazor, [38]Iron, Migdal El, Horem, Beth Anath and Beth Shemesh.

The total number of towns was 19. Some of them had villages near them.

[39] Those towns and their villages were the share the tribe of Naphtali received, according to its family groups.

Land Is Given to Dan

[40] The seventh lot drawn out was for the tribe of Dan, according to its family groups. [41]Here is what Dan's share of land included.

Zorah, Eshtaol, Ir Shemesh, [42]Shaalabbin, Aijalon, Ithlah, [43]Elon, Timnah, Ekron, [44]Eltekeh, Gibbethon, Baalath, [45]Jehud, Bene Berak, Gath Rimmon, [46]Me Jarkon and Rakkon. Dan's share included the area that faces Joppa.

[47] The people of Dan lost their territory. So they went up and attacked Leshem. They captured it. They killed its people with their swords. Then they moved into Leshem and made their homes there. They named it Dan. That's because they traced their family line back to him.

[48] All those towns and their villages were the share the tribe of Dan received, according to its family groups.

Land Is Given to Joshua

[49] The Israelites finished dividing up the shares of land the tribes received. Then they gave a share to Joshua, the son of Nun. [50]They did what the LORD had commanded them to do. They gave Joshua the town he asked for. It was Timnath Serah in the hill country of Ephraim. He built up the town and made his home there.

[51] All those territories were given out by casting lots at Shiloh. The lots were drawn out by Eleazar the priest and by Joshua, the son of Nun. The leaders of the tribes of Israel helped them. The lots were drawn out in front of the LORD at the entrance to the tent of meeting. So the work of dividing up the land was finished.

Cities to Run to for Safety

20 Then the LORD spoke to Joshua. He said, [2]"Tell the Israelites to choose the cities to go to for safety, just as I directed you through Moses. [3]Anyone who kills a person by accident can run there for safety. So can anyone who kills a person without meaning to. The one charged with murder will be kept safe from the nearest male relative of the person killed. [4]Suppose those who are charged with murder run for safety to one of these cities. Then they must stand in the entrance of the city gate. They must state their case in front of the elders of that city. The elders must let them come into their city. The elders must provide a place for them to live in their city. ⁵Suppose the nearest male relative of the person killed chases the one charged with murder. Then the elders must not hand them over to that relative. That's because that person didn't mean to kill their neighbor. They didn't make evil plans to do it. ⁶They must stay in that city until their case has been brought to the community court. They must stay there until the high priest serving at that time dies. Then they can go back to their own home. They can return to the town they ran away from."

⁷So the Israelites set apart Kedesh in Galilee. It's in the hill country of Naphtali. They set apart Shechem. It's in the hill country of Ephraim. They set apart Kiriath Arba. It's in the hill country of Judah. Kiriath Arba is also called Hebron. ⁸On the east side of the Jordan River near Jericho they chose Bezer. It's in the desert on the high plains. It's in the territory of the tribe of Reuben. They chose Ramoth in Gilead. It's in the territory of the tribe of Gad. They chose Golan in the land of Bashan. It's in the territory of the tribe of Manasseh. ⁹Suppose you kill someone by accident. Or another Israelite does it. Or an outsider who lives among you does it. Then any of you can run for safety to one of these cities that have been chosen. There you won't be killed by the nearest male relative of the person killed by accident. First your case must be brought to the community court.

Towns Are Given to the Levites

21 The leaders of the Levite family groups approached Eleazar the priest and Joshua, the son of Nun. They also approached the leaders of the family groups of Israel's other tribes. ²They went to all of them at Shiloh in Canaan. They said to them, "Give us towns to live in. Also give us grasslands for our livestock. That's what the LORD commanded through Moses."

³ So the Israelites gave the Levites towns and grasslands out of their own shares of land. They did what the LORD had commanded. Here are the towns the Levites were given.

⁴ The first lot drawn out was for the people of Kohath, according to their family groups. Some of the Levites came from the family line of Aaron the priest. They were given 13 towns from the tribes of Judah, Simeon and Benjamin.

⁵ The rest of Kohath's family groups were given ten towns. Those towns were from the family groups of the tribes of Ephraim and Dan and half of the tribe of Manasseh.

⁶ The family groups of Gershon were given 13 towns. Those towns were from the family groups of the tribes of Issachar, Asher and Naphtali and half of the tribe of Manasseh. That part of Manasseh was in the land of Bashan.

⁷ The family groups of Merari received 12 towns from the tribes of Reuben, Gad and Zebulun. Each family group received its share.

⁸ So the Israelites gave those towns and their grasslands to the Levites. They did what the LORD had commanded through Moses.

⁹ Some towns were given from the territories of the tribes of Judah and Simeon. ¹⁰The Israelites gave them to the members of the family line of Aaron. The towns were given to the family groups of Kohath. They were Levites. The first lot drawn out was for them. Here are the towns the family groups of Kohath were given.

¹¹ The Israelites gave them Kiriath Arba and the grasslands around it. Kiriath Arba is also called Hebron. It's in the hill country of Judah. Anak came from the family line of Arba. ¹²But Israel had already given away the fields and villages around the city. They had given them to Caleb as his share. Caleb was the son of Jephunneh. ¹³So they gave Hebron to the members of the family line of Aaron the priest. Hebron was a city where anyone charged with murder could go for safety. They also gave them Libnah, ¹⁴Jattir,

Eshtemoa, ¹⁵Holon, Debir, ¹⁶Ain, Juttah and Beth Shemesh. They gave those towns and their grasslands to the family groups of Kohath. The total number of towns from the tribes of Judah and Simeon came to nine.

¹⁷ The Israelites gave some towns from the tribe of Benjamin to the family groups of Kohath.

The towns were Gibeon, Geba, ¹⁸Anathoth and Almon. The total number of these towns and their grasslands came to four.

¹⁹ So the total number of towns and their grasslands given to the priests in Aaron's family line came to 13.

²⁰ There were other family groups of Kohath among the Levites. They were given towns from the tribe of Ephraim. Here are the towns those other family groups of Kohath were given.

²¹ In the hill country of Ephraim they were given

Shechem. It was a city where anyone charged with murder could go for safety. They were also given Gezer, ²²Kibzaim and Beth Horon. The total number of these towns and their grasslands came to four.

²³ From the tribe of Dan they received Eltekeh, Gibbethon, ²⁴Aijalon and Gath Rimmon. The total number of these towns and their grasslands came to four.

²⁵ From half of the tribe of Manasseh they received

Taanach and Gath Rimmon. The total number of these towns and their grasslands came to two.

²⁶ So all these ten towns and their grasslands were given to the other family groups of Kohath.

²⁷ Here are the towns given to the family groups of Gershon among the Levites.

From half of the tribe of Manasseh they received

Golan in the land of Bashan. Golan was a city where anyone charged with murder could go for safety. They also received Be

Eshterah. The total number of these towns and their grasslands came to two.

²⁸ From the tribe of Issachar they received

Kishion, Daberath, ²⁹Jarmuth and En Gannim. The total number of these towns and their grasslands came to four.

³⁰ From the tribe of Asher they received

Mishal, Abdon, ³¹Helkath and Rehob. The total number of these towns and their grasslands came to four.

³² From the tribe of Naphtali they received

Kedesh in Galilee. Kedesh was a city where anyone charged with murder could go for safety. They also received Hammoth Dor and Kartan. The total number of these towns and their grasslands came to three.

³³ So the total number of towns and their grasslands given to the family groups of Gershon came to 13.

³⁴ The rest of the Levites were from the family groups of Merari. Here are the towns they were given.

From the tribe of Zebulun they received

Jokneam, Kartah, ³⁵Dimnah and Nahalal. The total number of these towns and their grasslands came to four.

³⁶ From the tribe of Reuben they received

Bezer, Jahaz, ³⁷Kedemoth and Mephaath. The total number of these towns and their grasslands came to four.

³⁸ From the tribe of Gad they received Ramoth in Gilead. Ramoth was a city where anyone charged with murder could go for safety. They also received Mahanaim, ³⁹Heshbon and Jazer. The total number of these towns and their grasslands came to four.

⁴⁰ So the total number of towns given to the family groups of Merari came to 12. That concludes the list of towns the rest of the Levites received.

⁴¹ The total number of Levite towns and their grasslands in the territory given to Israel came to 48. ⁴²Each of those towns had grasslands around it. That was true of all of them.

⁴³So the LORD gave Israel all the land he had promised to give to Abraham, Isaac and Jacob. And Israel took it over. Then they made their homes there. ⁴⁴The LORD gave them peace and rest on every side. He had promised their people of long ago that he would do that. Not one of Israel's enemies was able to fight against them and win. The LORD handed all their enemies over to them. ⁴⁵The LORD kept all the good promises he had made to the Israelites. Every one of them came true.

The Eastern Tribes Return Home

22 Joshua sent for the tribes of Reuben and Gad and half of the tribe of Manasseh. ²He said to them, "You have done everything that Moses, the servant of the LORD, commanded. You have also obeyed everything I commanded. ³For a long time now you haven't deserted the other Israelites. Instead, you have done what the LORD your God sent you to do. You have obeyed him right up to this day. ⁴Now the LORD your God has given the other tribes peace and rest. That's what he promised to do. So return to your homes. They are in the land that Moses, the servant of the LORD, gave you. It's on the east side of the Jordan River. ⁵Be very careful to obey the law that Moses, the servant of the LORD, gave you. He commanded you to love the LORD your God. He told you to live exactly as the LORD wants you to. He told you to obey the LORD's commands. He told you to remain faithful to the LORD. And he told you to serve the LORD with all your heart and with all your soul."

⁶Joshua gave the eastern tribes his blessing. Then he sent them home. So they went. ⁷Moses had given land in Bashan to half of the tribe of Manasseh. Joshua had given land to the other half of the tribe. He had given it to them along with the other tribes on the west side of the Jordan River. When Joshua sent them home, he blessed them. ⁸He said, "Return to your homes. Take your great wealth with you. Return with your large herds of livestock. Take your silver, gold, bronze

CANDID CONVERSATIONS

One time I thought my old boyfriend Mitch had forgotten my birthday. The entire day, he never mentioned it once. By 8:00 that night, I was pretty mad. He dropped me off at my house, and when I went inside, there were about fifty of my closest friends inside screaming, "Happy birthday!" He had set up the whole thing. I forgave him pretty quickly.

A similar thing is happening here in the book of Joshua. One Israelite tribe thought the other was being disloyal to God, but actually, they were building a huge altar for God as a grand gesture to show their love for Him.

What is a grand gesture *you* can make for God? Giving a big offering in church? Spending your entire Saturday serving Him? Hmm . . . those might work, but what about giving Him your heart? That shows Him how much you love Him!

and iron with you. Return with all the extra clothes you acquired. Divide up the things you have taken from your enemies. Share them with your people."

⁹So the tribes of Reuben and Gad and half of the tribe of Manasseh went home. They left the other Israelites at Shiloh in Canaan. They returned to Gilead. That was their own land. They had acquired it according to the LORD's command through Moses.

¹⁰The tribes of Reuben and Gad and half of the tribe of Manasseh came to Geliloth. It was near the Jordan River in the land of Canaan. They built a large altar there by the Jordan. ¹¹The rest of the Israelites heard that the eastern tribes had built the altar. They heard that it had been built on the border of Canaan at Geliloth. It was near the Jordan River on the west side. ¹²So the whole community of Israel

gathered together at Shiloh. They decided to go to war against the eastern tribes.

¹³The Israelites sent Phinehas the priest to the land of Gilead. Phinehas was the son of Eleazar. They sent him to the tribes of Reuben and Gad and half of the tribe of Manasseh. ¹⁴They sent ten of their leaders with him. There was one from each of the tribes of Israel. Each man was the leader of a family group among the larger family groups of Israel.

¹⁵Those leaders went to the tribes of Reuben and Gad and half of the tribe of Manasseh. Those tribes were in the land of Gilead. The leaders said to them, ¹⁶"We're speaking for the LORD's whole community. How could you disobey the God of Israel like this? How could you turn away from the LORD? How could you disobey him by building an altar for yourselves? ¹⁷Don't you remember how we sinned at Peor? The LORD struck us with a plague because of what we did. Up to this day we're still suffering because of that sin. ¹⁸Are you turning away from the LORD now?

"Suppose you disobey the LORD today. If you do, he'll be angry with the whole community of Israel tomorrow. ¹⁹If your own land is 'unclean,' come over to the LORD's land. It's where his holy tent stands. Share our land with us. But don't disobey the LORD. Don't turn against us by building an altar for yourselves. Don't build any altar other than the altar of the LORD our God. ²⁰Remember what happened to Achan, the son of Zerah. Achan wasn't faithful to the LORD. He took the things that had been set apart to the LORD in a special way to be destroyed. Didn't the whole community of Israel experience the LORD's anger? Achan wasn't the only one who died because of his sin."

²¹Then the tribes of Reuben and Gad and half of the tribe of Manasseh replied. They answered the leaders of the family groups of Israel. ²²They said, "The Mighty One, God, the LORD! The Mighty One, God, the LORD! He knows! And we want Israel to know! Have we opposed the LORD? Have we refused to obey him? If we have, don't spare us today. ²³Have we built our own altar so we can turn away from the LORD? Have we built it to offer burnt offerings and grain offerings on it?

Have we built it to sacrifice friendship offerings on it? If we have, may the LORD himself hold us accountable.

²⁴"No! We built it because we were afraid. Someday your children might speak to our children. We were afraid they might say, 'What do you have to do with the LORD? What do you have to do with the God of Israel? ²⁵The LORD has made the Jordan River a border between us and you. You people of Reuben! You people of Gad! You don't have anything to do with the LORD.' If your children say that, they might cause our children to stop worshiping the LORD.

²⁶"That's why we said to ourselves, 'Let's get ready and build an altar. But let's not build it to offer burnt offerings or sacrifices on it.' ²⁷So just the opposite is true. The altar will be a witness between us and you. It will be a witness between our children and yours after us. It will also be a witness that we will worship the LORD at his sacred tent. We'll worship him there with our burnt offerings, sacrifices and friendship offerings. Then in days to come your children won't be able to say to ours, 'You don't have anything to do with the LORD.'

²⁸"So we said to ourselves, 'Suppose they say that to us sometime. Or suppose they say it to our children after us. Then we'll answer, "Look at this altar. It's exactly like the LORD's altar. Our people built it. They didn't build it to offer burnt offerings and sacrifices on it. Instead, they built it to be a witness between us and you."'

²⁹"We would never refuse to obey the LORD. We would never turn away from him now. We wouldn't build an altar to offer burnt offerings, grain offerings and sacrifices on it. We wouldn't use any altar other than the altar of the LORD our God. That altar stands in front of his holy tent."

³⁰Phinehas the priest heard what the tribes of Reuben, Gad and Manasseh had to say. The leaders of the family groups of the community of Israel heard it too. All of them were pleased with what they heard. ³¹Phinehas the priest spoke to the tribes of Reuben, Gad and Manasseh. Phinehas was the son of Eleazar. He said, "Today we know that the LORD is with us. That's because you have been faithful to him in this matter. Now you have saved the Israelites from the LORD's anger against them."

³²Then Phinehas the priest, the son of Eleazar, returned to Canaan. So did the leaders. All of them went back from their meeting with the tribes of Reuben and Gad in Gilead. They brought a report back to the Israelites. ³³The people were glad to hear the report. They praised God. They didn't talk anymore about going to war against the eastern tribes. And they didn't talk anymore about destroying the country where the tribes of Reuben and Gad lived.

³⁴The tribes of Reuben and Gad gave the altar a name. They called it A Witness Between Us that the LORD is God.

Joshua Says Goodbye to the Leaders

23 A long time had passed. The LORD had given Israel peace and rest from all their enemies around them. By that time Joshua was very old. ²So he sent for all the elders, leaders, judges and officials of Israel. He said to them, "I'm very old. ³You yourselves have seen everything the LORD your God has done. You have seen what he's done to all these nations because of you. The LORD your God fought for you. ⁴Remember how I've given you all the land of the nations that remain here. I've given each of your tribes a share of it. It's the land of the nations I conquered. It's between the Jordan River and the Mediterranean Sea in the west. ⁵The LORD your God himself will drive those nations out of your way. He will push them out to make room for you. You will take over their land, just as the LORD your God promised you.

⁶"Be very strong. Be careful to obey everything written in the Book of the Law of Moses. Don't turn away from it to the right or the left. ⁷Don't have anything to do with the nations that remain among you. Don't use the names of their gods for any reason at all. Don't give your word and make promises in their names. You must not serve them. You must not bow down to them. ⁸You must remain true to the LORD your God, just as you have done until now.

⁹"The LORD has driven out great and powerful nations to make room for you. To this day no one has been able to fight against you and win. ¹⁰One of you can

chase a thousand away. That's because the LORD your God fights for you, just as he promised he would. ¹¹So be very careful to love the LORD your God.

¹²"But suppose you turn away from him. You mix with the people who are left alive in the nations that remain among you. Later, you and they get married to each other. And you do other kinds of things with them. ¹³Then you can be sure of what the LORD your God will do. He won't drive out those nations to make room for you anymore. Instead, they will become traps and snares for you. They will be like whips on your backs. They will be like thorns in your eyes. All that will continue until you are destroyed. It will continue until you are removed from this good land. It's the land the LORD your God has given you.

¹⁴"Now I'm about to die, just as everyone else on earth does. The LORD your God has kept all the good promises he gave you. Every one of them has come true. Not one has failed to come true. And you know that with all your heart and soul. ¹⁵Every good thing has come to pass that the LORD your God has promised you. So you know that he can also bring against you all the evil things he has warned you about. He'll do it until he has destroyed you. He'll do it until he has removed you from this good land. It's the land he has given you. ¹⁶Suppose you break the covenant the LORD your God made with you. He commanded you to obey it. But suppose you go and serve other gods. And you bow down to them. Then the LORD will be very angry with you. You will quickly be destroyed. You will be removed from the good land he has given you."

The Covenant Is Renewed at Shechem

24 Joshua gathered all Israel's tribes together at Shechem. He sent for the elders, leaders, judges and officials of Israel. They came and stood there in the sight of God.

²Joshua spoke to all the people. He said, "The LORD is the God of Israel. He says, 'Long ago your people lived east of the Euphrates River. They worshiped other gods there. Your people included Terah. He was the father of Abraham and

Nahor. ³I took your father Abraham from the land east of the Euphrates. I led him all through Canaan. I gave him many children and grandchildren. I gave him Isaac. ⁴To Isaac I gave Jacob and Esau. I gave the hill country of Seir to Esau. But Jacob and his family went down to Egypt.

⁵"Then I sent Moses and Aaron. I made the people of Egypt suffer because of the plagues I sent on them. But I brought you out of Egypt. ⁶When I brought your people out, they came to the Red Sea. The people of Egypt chased them with chariots and with men on horses. They chased them all the way to the sea. ⁷But your people cried out to me for help. So I put darkness between you and the people of Egypt. I swept them into the sea. It completely covered them. Your own eyes saw what I did to them. After that, you lived in the desert for a long time.

⁸"I brought you to the land of the Amorites. They lived east of the Jordan River. They fought against you. But I handed them over to you. I destroyed them to make room for you. Then you took over their land. ⁹Balak, the son of Zippor, prepared to fight against Israel. Balak was the king of Moab. He sent for Balaam, the son of Beor. Balak wanted Balaam to put a curse on you. ¹⁰But I would not listen to Balaam's curses. So he blessed you

again and again. And I saved you from his power.

¹¹"Then you went across the Jordan River. You came to Jericho. Its people fought against you. So did the Amorites, Perizzites, Canaanites, Hittites, Girgashites, Hivites and Jebusites. But I handed them over to you. ¹²I sent hornets ahead of you. They drove your enemies out to make room for you. That included the two Amorite kings. You did not do that with your own swords and bows. ¹³So I gave you a land you had never farmed. I gave you cities you had not built. You are now living in them. And you are eating the fruit of vineyards and olive trees you did not plant.'

¹⁴"So have respect for the LORD. Serve him. Be completely faithful to him. Throw away the gods your people worshiped east of the Euphrates River and in Egypt. Serve the LORD. ¹⁵But suppose you don't want to serve him. Then choose for yourselves right now whom you will serve. You can choose the gods your people served east of the Euphrates River. Or you can serve the gods of the Amorites. After all, you are living in their land. But as for me and my family, we will serve the LORD."

¹⁶Then the people answered Joshua, "We would never desert the LORD! We would never serve other gods! ¹⁷The LORD our God himself brought us and our parents up out of Egypt. He brought us out of that land where we were slaves. With our own eyes, we saw those great signs he did. He kept us safe on our entire journey. He kept us safe as we traveled through all the nations. ¹⁸He drove them out to make room for us. That included the Amorites. They also lived in the land. We too will serve the LORD. That's because he is our God."

¹⁹Joshua said to the people, "You aren't able to serve the LORD. He is a holy God. He is a jealous God. He won't forgive you when you disobey him. He won't forgive you when you sin against him. ²⁰Suppose you desert the LORD. Suppose you serve the gods that people in other lands serve. If you do, he will turn against you. He will bring trouble on you. He will destroy you, even though he has been good to you."

²¹But the people said to Joshua, "No! We will serve the LORD."

In many languages, *amor* means "love." Pretty, huh? But the Amorites have nothing to do with love. They're descendants of Ham. Not the meat ham, which is delicious, but the Ham who is one of Noah's sons. Got it?

[22]Then Joshua said, "You are witnesses against yourselves. You have said that you have chosen to serve the LORD."

"Yes. We are witnesses," they replied.

[23]"Now then," said Joshua, "throw away the statues of the gods that are among you. People from other lands serve those gods. Give yourselves completely to the LORD. He is the God of Israel."

[24]Then the people said to Joshua, "We will serve the LORD our God. We will obey him."

[25]On that day Joshua made a covenant for the people. There at Shechem he reminded them of its rules and laws. [26]He recorded these things in the Book of the Law of God. Then he got a large stone. He set it up in Shechem under the oak tree. It was near the place that had been set apart for the LORD.

[27]"Look!" he said to all the people. "This stone will be a witness against us. It has heard all the words the LORD has spoken to us. Suppose you aren't faithful to your God. Then the stone will be a witness against you."

[28]Joshua sent the people away. He sent all of them to their own shares of land.

Joshua Is Buried in the Promised Land

[29]Then Joshua, the servant of the LORD, died. He was the son of Nun. He was 110 years old when he died. [30]His people buried him at Timnath Serah on his own property. It's north of Mount Gaash in the hill country of Ephraim.

[31]Israel served the LORD as long as Joshua lived. They also served him as long as the elders lived. Those were the elders who lived longer than Joshua did. They had seen for themselves everything the LORD had done for Israel.

[32]The Israelites had brought Joseph's bones up from Egypt. They buried his bones at Shechem in the piece of land Jacob had bought. He had bought it from the sons of Hamor. He had paid 100 pieces of silver for it. Hamor was the father of Shechem. That piece of land became the share that belonged to Joseph's children after him.

[33]Aaron's son Eleazar died. He was buried at Gibeah in the hill country of Ephraim. Gibeah had been given to Eleazar's son Phinehas.

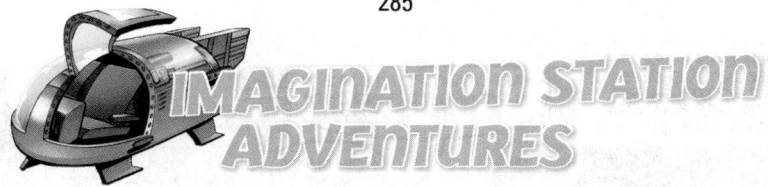

IMAGINATION STATION ADVENTURES

ACHAN'S SIN Read Joshua 7.

MR. WHITTAKER SENDS COUSINS PATRICK AND BETH TO JERICHO IN OLD TESTAMENT TIMES VIA THE IMAGINATION STATION.

WHAT HAPPENS NEXT?

TOO BAD THE WALLS HAVE ALREADY FALLEN.

THE ISRAELITES MUST BURN EVERYTHING IN THE CITY.

GOD TELLS THE ISRAELITES TO GATHER ALL THE GOLD, SILVER, BRONZE, AND IRON IN JERICHO. GOD SAYS THOSE VALUABLES SHOULD BE PUT INTO THE TEMPLE TREASURY. NO ONE MAY KEEP ANY OF IT.

JOSHUA, I FOUND A GOLD IDOL.

TAKE IT TO THE PRIESTS. THEY WILL MELT IT AND PUT IT IN THE TREASURY.

AFTER JERICHO IS BURNED, THE ISRAELITES' LEADER, JOSHUA, PUTS A CURSE ON IT.

WHOEVER REBUILDS THIS CITY WILL LOSE THE LIFE OF HIS OLDEST SON. WHOEVER SETS UP ITS GATES WILL LOSE THE LIFE OF HIS YOUNGEST SON.

A FEW DAYS LATER, THE ISRAELITE LEADERS AND SCOUTS GATHER TO DISCUSS PLANS FOR CAPTURING THE CITY OF AI.

HARDLY ANY PEOPLE LIVE IN AI. WE SHOULD SEND ONLY PART OF THE ARMY.

HOW MANY MEN?

THE CITY SHOULD BE EASILY TAKEN WITH ONLY 3000 MEN.

AT THE BATTLE OF AI...

GET OUT OF HERE, YOU PIGS!

SCRAM, YOU BAAL HATERS.

WE OUTNUMBER THEM! WHAT WENT WRONG?

RUN FOR YOUR LIFE! GOD HAS LEFT US!

THE ISRAELITES LOSE THE BATTLE OF AI. THIRTY-SIX MEN DIE. JOSHUA HEARS THE BAD NEWS. HE TEARS HIS CLOTHES IN GRIEF AND FALLS IN FRONT OF THE ARK OF THE COVENANT.

HOW LONG IS HE GOING TO STAY LIKE THAT?

AS LONG AS IT TAKES.

GET UP, JOSHUA. AN ISRAELITE STOLE TREASURES FROM JERICHO.

SOMEONE IN THE CAMP SINNED THEN. IS THAT WHY WE LOST THE BATTLE?

YES! FIND THE LOOT AND DESTROY IT!

LET'S GET THIS TO JOSHUA.

THIS REALLY IS HEAVY METAL!

THE FAMILY OF ACHAN GATHERS IN FRONT OF JOSHUA'S TENT. THE STOLEN SILVER AND GOLD IS PUT BEFORE ALL OF ISRAEL.

THE FAMILY OF ACHAN HAS DISOBEYED GOD. THEY KEPT GOLD AND SILVER FOR THEMSELVES!

THE LORD WILL BRING TROUBLE TO ACHAN'S FAMILY THIS DAY!

ISRAEL MUST BE PURIFIED, OR I WON'T GO WITH YOU INTO BATTLE.

BACK AT WHIT'S END ...

WHAT KIND OF "TROUBLE" DID ACHAN'S FAMILY GET INTO?

THE WORST KIND.

WHY DID THEY HAVE TO DIE?

ISRAEL WAS GETTING A NEW START. GOD WANTED HIS PEOPLE OBEDIENT AND PURE.

SO GOD DOES TAKE WRONGDOING SERIOUSLY?

VERY.

BUT WHAT ABOUT LOVE?

HERE'S HOW I THINK OF IT. GOD IS JUST. AND GOD IS LOVING. BUT HE'S NOT JUST LOVING.

Judges

Judges. The word itself is wrought with meaning and images. But they can be misleading, thanks to our modern-day notions. When you read about biblical "judges," don't envision men (and a woman!) in long flowing robes, calmly determining justice at the front of a fancy courtroom. Instead of a gavel, these judges were more likely to be holding a sword. Biblical judges were in fact warrior leaders, called by God during times when the people were being cruelly oppressed by their enemies.

Although this book contains some thrilling heroic stories including Gideon, Samson, Deborah, and others, overall it remains a tragic account. Over and over and over again (yes, multiple overs are warranted), God's people go through a downward cycle: God gives them victory over their enemies; they get comfortable and forget about God; God allows their enemies to overcome them; they despair and cry out to God; and God gives them victory over their enemies. This cycle is repeated many times in the book of Judges. You would think the Israelites would learn, but alas that is not the case. As you read the stories of the judges, think of how people today tend to repeat the same cycle . . . and how we can learn to avoid it.

WHAT'S IT MEAN, EUGENE?

Depravity—*Depravity* refers to the damage created through sin. This word comes from a Latin verb that means "to bend, to make crooked or bad." To be *depraved* then, is to be wounded, twisted, hurt, and "messed up" because of our disobedience to God. One might say, "Dr. Regis Blackgaard was a depraved man." But the truth is, we are all depraved until we are saved through faith in Christ.

The Israelites Fight Against the Remaining Canaanites

1 Joshua died. After that, the Israelites spoke to the LORD. They asked him, "Who of us will go up first and fight against the Canaanites?"

²The LORD answered, "The tribe of Judah will go up. I have handed the land over to them."

³Then the men of Judah spoke to their fellow Israelites, the men of Simeon. They said, "Come up with us. Come into the territory Joshua gave us. Help us fight against the Canaanites. Then we'll go with you into your territory." So the men of Simeon went with them.

⁴When the men of Judah attacked, the LORD helped them. He handed the Canaanites and Perizzites over to them. They struck down 10,000 men at Bezek. ⁵The men of Judah found Adoni-Bezek there. They fought against him. They struck down the Canaanites and Perizzites. ⁶But Adoni-Bezek ran away. The men of Judah chased him and caught him. Then they cut off his thumbs and big toes.

⁷Adoni-Bezek said, "I cut off the thumbs and big toes of 70 kings. I made them pick up scraps under my table. Now God has paid me back for what I did to them." The men of Judah brought Adoni-Bezek to Jerusalem. That's where he died.

⁸The men of Judah attacked Jerusalem and captured it. They set the city on fire. They killed its people with their swords.

⁹After that, the men of Judah went down to fight against some Canaanites. Those Canaanites were living in the central hill country. They also fought against those living in the Negev Desert and the western hills. ¹⁰Then the men of Judah marched out against the Canaanites living in Hebron. Hebron used to be called Kiriath Arba. The men of Judah won the battle over Sheshai, Ahiman and Talmai. ¹¹From Hebron they marched out against the people living in Debir. It used to be called Kiriath Sepher.

¹²Caleb said, "I will give my daughter Aksah to be married. I'll give her to the man who attacks and captures Kiriath Sepher." ¹³Othniel captured it. So Caleb gave his daughter Aksah to him to be his wife. Othniel was the son of Kenaz. He was Caleb's younger brother.

WOOTON'S FUN FACTS

Judg. 1:8

Jerusalem is a special city, called the "Holy City" or the "City of God." This is the first time the Israelites take possession of it.

¹⁴One day Aksah came to Othniel. She begged him to ask her father for a field. When she got off her donkey, Caleb asked her, "What can I do for you?"

¹⁵She replied, "Do me a special favor. You have given me some land in the Negev Desert. Give me springs of water also." So Caleb gave her the upper and lower springs.

¹⁶Moses' father-in-law was a Kenite. His family went up from Jericho. Jericho was also known as the City of Palm Trees. His family went up with the people of Judah to the Desert of Judah. They went there to live among its people. Those people were living in the Negev Desert near Arad.

¹⁷The men of Judah marched out with their fellow Israelites, the men of Simeon. They attacked the people of Canaan living in Zephath. They set the city apart to the LORD in a special way to be destroyed. That's why the city was called Hormah. ¹⁸The men of Judah captured Gaza, Ashkelon and Ekron. They also captured the territory around each of those cities.

¹⁹The LORD was with the men of Judah. They took over the central hill country. But they weren't able to drive the people out of the plains. That's because those people used chariots that had some iron parts. ²⁰Moses had promised to give

Hebron to Caleb. So Hebron was given to Caleb. He drove the three sons of Anak out of it. [21] But the people of Benjamin did not drive out the Jebusites living in Jerusalem. So to this day they live there with the people of Benjamin.

[22] The tribes of Joseph attacked Bethel. The LORD was with them. [23] They sent men to Bethel to check it out. It used to be called Luz. [24] Those who were sent saw a man coming out of the city. They said to him, "Show us how to get into the city. If you do, we'll see that you are treated well." [25] So he showed them how to get in. The men of Joseph killed the people in the city with their swords. But they spared the man from Bethel. They also spared his whole family. [26] Then he went to the land of the Hittites. He built a city there. He called it Luz. That's still its name to this day.

[27] But the tribe of Manasseh didn't drive out the people of Beth Shan. They didn't drive out the people of Taanach, Dor, Ibleam and Megiddo. And they didn't drive out the people of the settlements that are around those cities either. That's because the Canaanites had made up their minds to continue living in that land. [28] Later, Israel became stronger. Then they forced the Canaanites to work hard for them. But Israel never drove them out completely. [29] The tribe of Ephraim didn't drive out the Canaanites living in Gezer. So the Canaanites continued to live there among them. [30] The tribe of Zebulun didn't drive out the Canaanites living in Kitron and Nahalol. So these Canaanites lived among them. But the people of Zebulun forced the Canaanites to work hard for them. [31] The tribe of Asher didn't drive out the people living in Akko and Sidon. They didn't drive out the people of Ahlab, Akzib, Helbah, Aphek and Rehob. [32] So the people of Asher lived among the Canaanites who were in the land. [33] The tribe of Naphtali didn't drive out the people living in Beth Shemesh and Beth Anath. So the people of Naphtali lived among the Canaanites who were in the land. The people of Beth Shemesh and Beth Anath were forced to work hard for them. [34] The Amorites made the people of Dan stay in the central hill country. They didn't let them come down into the plain. [35] The Amorites made up their minds to stay in

Mount Heres. They also stayed in Aijalon and Shaalbim. But the power of the tribes of Joseph grew. Then the Amorites were forced to work hard for them. [36] The border of the Amorites started at Scorpion Pass. It went to Sela and even past it.

The Angel of the LORD Warns Israel at Bokim

2 The angel of the LORD went up from Gilgal to Bokim. There he said to the Israelites, "I brought you up out of Egypt. I led you into this land. It is the land I promised to give to Abraham, Isaac and Jacob. At that time I said, 'I will never break the covenant I made with you. [2] So you must not make a covenant with the people of this land. Instead, you must tear down their altars.' But you have disobeyed me. Why did you do it? [3] I have said something else. I said, 'I will not drive out those people to make room for you. They and their gods will become traps for you.' "

[4] The angel of the LORD spoke these things to all the Israelites. Then the people wept out loud. [5] So that place was called Bokim. The people offered sacrifices there to the LORD.

The People Disobey the LORD and Lose Their Battles

[6] Joshua sent the Israelites away. Then they went to take over the land. All of them went to their own shares of land. [7] The people served the LORD as long as Joshua lived. They also served him as long as the elders lived. Those were the elders who lived longer than Joshua did. They had seen all the great things the LORD had done for Israel.

[8] Joshua, the servant of the LORD, died. He was the son of Nun. He was 110 years old when he died. [9] His people buried him on his own property at Timnath Heres. It's north of Mount Gaash in the hill country of Ephraim.

[10] All the people of Joshua's time joined the members of their families who had already died. Then those who were born after them grew up. They didn't know the LORD and what he had done for Israel. [11] The Israelites did what was evil in the sight of the LORD. They served gods that were named Baal. [12] They deserted the LORD, the God of their people.

He had brought them out of Egypt. But now the Israelites served other gods and worshiped them. They served the gods of the nations that were around them. They made the LORD angry [13]because they deserted him. They served Baal. They also served female gods that were named Ashtoreth. [14]The LORD became angry with the Israelites. So he handed them over to robbers. The robbers stole everything from them. The LORD handed the Israelites over to their enemies all around them. Israel wasn't able to fight against them anymore and win. [15]When the Israelites went out to fight, the LORD's power was against them. He let their enemies win the battle over them. The LORD had warned them that it would happen. And now they were suffering terribly.

Jason's Jargon

JUDGES 2

Search this chapter for *Baal*. The false god Baal was an idol worshiped in different forms in and around Canaan. God instructed His people not to worship Baal, but they kept disobeying.

[16]Then the LORD gave them leaders. The leaders saved them from the power of those robbers. [17]But the people wouldn't listen to their leaders. They weren't faithful to the LORD. They served other gods and worshiped them. They didn't obey the LORD's commands as their people before them had done. They quickly turned away from the path their people had taken. [18]When the LORD gave them a leader, he was with that leader. The LORD saved the people from the power of their enemies. He did it as long as the leader lived. The LORD felt very sorry for the people. They groaned because of what their enemies did to them. Their enemies treated them badly. [19]But when the leader died, the people returned to their evil ways. The things they did were even more sinful than the things their people before them had done. They served other gods and worshiped them. They refused to give up their evil practices. They wouldn't change their stubborn ways.

[20]So the LORD became very angry with the Israelites. He said, "This nation has broken my covenant. I made it with their people of long ago. But this nation has not listened to me. [21]Joshua left some nations in the land when he died. I will no longer drive out those nations to make room for Israel. [22]I will use those nations to test Israel. I will see whether Israel will live the way I, the LORD, want them to. I will see whether they will be like their people of long ago. I will see whether they will follow my path." [23]The LORD had let those nations remain in the land. He didn't drive them out right away. He didn't hand them over to Joshua.

3 The LORD left some nations in the land. He left them to test the Israelites who hadn't lived through any of the wars in Canaan. [2]He wanted to teach the men in Israel who had never been in battle before. He wanted them to learn how to fight. [3]So he left the five rulers of the Philistines. He left the people of Canaan and the people of Sidon. He left the Hivites living in the Lebanon mountains. They lived in the area between Mount Baal Hermon and Lebo Hamath. [4]The LORD left those nations where they were to test the Israelites. He wanted to see whether they would obey his commands. He had given those commands through Moses to their people of long ago.

[5]So the Israelites lived among the Canaanites, Hittites, Amorites, Perizzites, Hivites and Jebusites. [6]They married the daughters of those people. They gave their own daughters to the sons of those people. And they served the gods of those people.

Othniel

[7]The Israelites did what was evil in the sight of the LORD. They forgot the LORD their God. They served gods that were named Baal. They also served female gods that were named Asherah. [8]So the LORD was very angry with Israel. He handed them over to the power of Cushan-Rishathaim, the king of Aram Naharaim. For eight years Israel was under his rule. [9]They cried out to the LORD. Then he provided someone to save them. The man's name was Othniel, the son of Kenaz. He was Caleb's younger brother. [10]The

Spirit of the LORD came on Othniel. So he became Israel's leader. He went to war. The LORD handed over to him Cushan-Rishathaim, the king of Aram. Othniel won the battle over him. ¹¹So the land was at peace for 40 years. Then Othniel, the son of Kenaz, died.

Ehud

¹²Again the Israelites did what was evil in the sight of the LORD. So the LORD gave Eglon power over Israel. Eglon was the king of Moab. ¹³He got the Ammonites and Amalekites to join him. All of them came and attacked Israel. They captured Jericho. Jericho was also known as The City of Palm Trees. ¹⁴For 18 years the Israelites were under the rule of Eglon, the king of Moab.

¹⁵Again the Israelites cried out to the LORD. Then he provided someone to save them. The man's name was Ehud, the son of Gera. Ehud was left-handed. He was from the tribe of Benjamin. The Israelites sent Ehud to Eglon, the king of Moab. They sent him to give the king what he required them to bring him. ¹⁶Ehud had made a sword that had two edges. It was about a foot and a half long. He tied it to his right leg under his clothes. ¹⁷Eglon, the king of Moab, was a very fat man. Ehud gave him the gift he had brought. ¹⁸After that, Ehud sent away those who had carried it. ¹⁹When he came to the place where some statues of gods stood near Gilgal, Ehud went back to Eglon. He said, "Your Majesty, I have a secret message for you."

The king said to his attendants, "Leave us!" And all his attendants left him.

²⁰Then Ehud approached him. King Eglon was sitting alone in the upstairs room of his palace. Ehud said, "I have a message from God for you." So the king got up from his seat. ²¹Then Ehud reached out his left hand. He pulled out the sword tied to his right leg. He stuck it into the king's stomach. ²²Even the handle sank in after the blade. Eglon sagged and fell to the floor. Ehud didn't pull out the sword. And the fat closed over it. ²³Ehud went out to the porch. He shut the doors of the upstairs room behind him. Then he locked them.

²⁴After he had gone, the servants came. They found the doors of the upstairs room locked. They said, "Eglon must be going to the toilet in the inside room of the palace." ²⁵They waited for a long time. They waited so long they became worried. But the king still didn't open the doors of the room. So they took a key and unlocked them. There they saw their king. He had fallen to the floor and was dead.

²⁶While Eglon's servants had been waiting, Ehud had gotten away. He passed by the statues of gods and escaped to Seirah. ²⁷There in the hill country of Ephraim he blew a trumpet. Then he led the Israelites down from the hills.

²⁸"Follow me," Ehud ordered. "The LORD has handed your enemy Moab over to you." So they followed him down. They took over the only places where people could go across the Jordan River to get to Moab. They didn't let anyone go across. ²⁹At that time they struck down about 10,000 men of Moab. All those men were strong and powerful. But not even one escaped. ³⁰That day Moab was brought under the rule of Israel. So the land was at peace for 80 years.

Shamgar

³¹After Ehud, Shamgar became the next leader. He was the son of Anath. Shamgar struck down 600 Philistines with a large, pointed stick used to drive oxen. He too saved Israel.

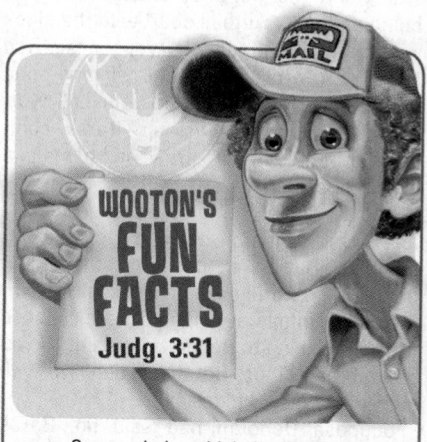

WOOTON'S FUN FACTS
Judg. 3:31

Some scholars think that Shamgar was a farmer turned warrior. His only weapon was a stick. Pretty unusual. Come to think of it, I might just name my next comic superhero Shamgar.

Deborah

4 After Ehud died, the Israelites once again did what was evil in the sight of the LORD. ²So the LORD handed them over to the power of Jabin. He was a king in Canaan. He ruled in Hazor. The commander of his army was Sisera. He lived in Harosheth Haggoyim. ³Jabin used 900 chariots that had some iron parts. He treated the Israelites very badly for 20 years. So they cried out to the LORD for help.

⁴Deborah was a prophet. She was the wife of Lappidoth. She was leading Israel at that time. ⁵Under the Palm Tree of Deborah she served the people as their judge. That place was between Ramah and Bethel in the hill country of Ephraim. The Israelites went up to her there. They came to have her decide cases for them. She settled matters between them. ⁶Deborah sent for Barak. He was the son of Abinoam. Barak was from Kedesh in the land of Naphtali. Deborah said to Barak, "The LORD, the God of Israel, is giving you a command. He says, 'Go! Take 10,000 men from the tribes of Naphtali and Zebulun with you. Then lead them up to Mount Tabor. ⁷I

BIBLE ADVENTURES

O.T. Action News reported on Deborah's and Barak's story in "O.T. Action News: Battle at the Kishon" (A#37).

will lead Sisera into a trap. He is the commander of Jabin's army. I will bring him, his chariots and his troops to the Kishon River. There I will hand him over to you.'"

⁸Barak said to her, "If you go with me, I'll go. But if you don't go with me, I won't go."

⁹"All right," Deborah said. "I'll go with you. But because of the way you are doing this, you won't receive any honor. Instead, the LORD will hand Sisera over to a woman." So Deborah went to Kedesh with Barak. ¹⁰There he sent for men from Zebulun and Naphtali. And 10,000 men followed him into battle. Deborah also went with him.

¹¹Heber, the Kenite, had left the other Kenites. They came from the family line of Hobab. He was the brother-in-law of Moses. Heber set up his tent by the large tree in Zaanannim near Kedesh.

WHAT ABOUT YOU?

Have you ever worried that you might fail? That you're just not good enough? Imagine being on the basketball court with the clock winding down. Suddenly, you sense God telling you to take the game-winning shot. Would you? Or would you pass the ball, worried that you might mess up? Barak, commander of the Israelite army, had to make a similar decision.

God, through the prophetess Deborah, told Barak to march out and face the Canaanites. But Barak hesitated. Instead of trusting God's promise that He would deliver the enemy into Israel's hands, Barak passed the ball. Turning to Deborah, he said, "If you go with me, I'll go. But if you don't go with me, I won't go" (Judges 4:8).

Suppose Deborah had said no. Barak still had a job to do. God wanted Barak to trust in Him and obey, regardless. Likewise, we shouldn't doubt our heavenly Father or question His instructions. God will always be with us when He calls us to do something difficult—even if it feels like we're taking the first step alone.

What has God asked you to do that you've been putting off? Write it down on a sheet of paper. God is bigger than that obstacle. He's bigger than what's on your paper. So wad that thing up and take the shot. If you miss the trash can, shoot again. And again. Just keep on shooting until you hit that game-winner. It may be time to take aim at that challenge you've been avoiding as well.

Judg. 4:13 Technology matters in warfare. The Israelites didn't know how to make iron, so they were worse off with their bronze-only weapons. (Except for Shamgar with his stick—He had God to give him an advantage!)

¹²Sisera was told that Barak, the son of Abinoam, had gone up to Mount Tabor. ¹³So Sisera gathered together his 900 chariots that had some iron parts. He also gathered together all his men. He brought them from Harosheth Haggoyim to the Kishon River.

¹⁴Then Deborah said to Barak, "Go! Today the LORD will hand Sisera over to you. Hasn't the LORD gone ahead of you?" So Barak went down Mount Tabor. His 10,000 men followed him. ¹⁵As Barak's men marched out, the LORD drove Sisera away from the field of battle. The LORD scattered all of Sisera's chariots. Barak's men struck down Sisera's army with their swords. Sisera got down from his chariot. He ran away on foot.

¹⁶Barak chased Sisera's chariots and army. Barak chased them all the way to Harosheth Haggoyim. All of Sisera's troops were killed by swords. Not even one was left. ¹⁷But Sisera ran away on foot. He ran to the tent of Jael. She was the wife of Heber, the Kenite. Sisera ran there because there was a treaty between Heber's family and Jabin, the king of Hazor.

¹⁸Jael went out to meet Sisera. "Come in, sir," she said. "Come right in. Don't be afraid." So he entered her tent. Then she covered him with a blanket.

¹⁹"I'm thirsty," he said. "Please give me some water." So Jael opened a bottle of milk. The bottle was made out of animal skin. She gave him a drink of milk. Then she covered him up again.

²⁰"Stand in the doorway of the tent," he told her. "Someone might come by and ask you, 'Is anyone in there?' If that happens, say 'No.'"

²¹But Heber's wife Jael picked up a tent stake and a hammer. She went quietly over to Sisera. He was lying there, fast asleep. He was very tired. She drove the stake through his head right into the ground. So he died.

²²Just then Barak came by because he was chasing Sisera. Jael went out to meet him. "Come right in," she said. "I'll show you the man you are looking for." So he went in with her. Sisera was lying there with the stake through his head. He was dead.

²³On that day God brought Jabin under Israel's control. He was a king in Canaan. ²⁴Israel's power grew stronger and stronger against King Jabin. The Israelites became so strong that they destroyed him.

The Song of Deborah

5 On that day Deborah and Barak sang a song. Barak was the son of Abinoam. Here is what Deborah and Barak sang.

² "The princes in Israel lead the way.
　　The people follow them just
　　　　　because they want to.
　　When this happens, praise the
　　　　　LORD!

³ "Kings, hear this! Rulers, listen!
　　I will sing to the LORD.
　　I will praise the LORD in song. He is
　　　　　the God of Israel.

⁴ "LORD, you went out from Seir.
　　You marched out from the land of
　　　　　Edom.
　The earth shook. The heavens poured.
　　The clouds poured down their
　　　　　water.
⁵ The mountains shook because of the
　　　　　LORD. He was at Mount Sinai.
　　They shook because of the LORD.
　　　　　He is the God of Israel.

⁶ "The main roads were deserted. So
　　　　　travelers used the winding
　　　　　paths.
　That happened in the days of
　　　　　Shamgar, the son of Anath.
　It happened in the days of Jael.

⁷ Those who lived in the villages of
     Israel would not fight.
   They held back until I, Deborah,
     came.
   I came as a mother in Israel.
⁸   War came to the city gates. Then
     God chose new leaders.
   But no shields or spears were seen
     anywhere.
   There weren't any among 40,000
     men in Israel.
⁹ My heart is with the princes in Israel.
   It's with the people who follow
     them just because they want
     to.
   Praise the LORD!

¹⁰ "Some of you ride on white donkeys.
   Some of you sit on your saddle
     blankets.
   Some of you walk along the road.
   Think about ¹¹the voices of the singers
     at the watering places.
   They sing about the victories of the
     LORD.
   They sing about the victories of
     his people who live in Israel's
     villages.

   "The people of the LORD
     went down to the city gates.
¹² 'Wake up, Deborah! Wake up!' they
     said.
     'Wake up! Wake up! Begin to sing!
   Barak, get up!
     Son of Abinoam, capture your
       prisoners!'

¹³ "The nobles who were left came down.
   The people of the LORD
     came down to me against the
       powerful enemy.
¹⁴ Some came from the part of Ephraim
     where some Amalekites
     lived.
   Some from Benjamin were with
     the people who followed
     Ephraim.
   Captains came down from Makir.
   Those who rule like commanders
     came down from Zebulun.
¹⁵ The princes of Issachar were with
     Deborah.
   The men of Issachar were with Barak.
   They went into the valley under his
     command.

In the territories of Reuben,
   men looked deeply into their
     hearts.
¹⁶ Why did they stay among the sheep
     pens?
   Why did they stay to hear
     shepherds whistling for the
     flocks?
In the territories of Reuben,
   men looked deeply into their
     hearts.
¹⁷ Gilead stayed east of the Jordan River.
   Why did Dan stay near the ships?
The men of Asher remained on the
   coast of the Mediterranean
   Sea.
   They stayed in their safe harbors.
¹⁸ The people of Zebulun put their very
     lives in danger.
   So did Naphtali on the hillside
     fields.

¹⁹ "Kings came and fought.
   The kings of Canaan fought
     at Taanach by the streams of
       Megiddo.
But they didn't carry away any silver.
   They didn't take anything at all.
²⁰ From the heavens the stars fought.
   From the sky they fought against
     Sisera.
²¹ The Kishon River swept them away.
   The Kishon is a very old river.
   My spirit, march on! Be strong!
²² The hooves of the horses pounded like
     thunder.
   The powerful horses of our enemies
     galloped away.
²³ 'Let Meroz be cursed,' said the angel of
     the LORD.
   'Let bitter curses fall on its people.
They did not come to help the LORD.
   They did not come to help him
     against our powerful enemies.'

²⁴ "May Jael be the most blessed woman
     of all.
   May the wife of Heber, the Kenite,
     be blessed.
   May she be the most blessed
     woman of all those who live
     in tents.
²⁵ Sisera asked for water. She gave him
     milk.
   In a bowl fit for nobles she brought
     him buttermilk.

26 Her hand reached out for a tent stake.
  Her right hand reached for a
      hammer.
  She hit Sisera. She crushed his head.
  She drove the stake right through
      his head.
27 He sank down. He fell at her feet.
  He was lying there.
  At her feet he sank down. He fell.
  He fell where he sank down.
  That's where he died.
28 "Sisera's mother looked out through
      the window.
  From behind the wooden screen
      she cried out.
  'Why is his chariot taking so long to
      get here?' she said.
  'Why can't I hear the noise of his
      chariots yet?'
29 Her wisest ladies answer her.
  And here's what she keeps saying to
      herself.
30 She says, 'They must be finding riches
      to bring back.
  They must be dividing them up.
  Each man is getting a woman or two.
  They are giving colorful clothes to
      Sisera.
  The clothes are very beautiful.
  He will bring some for me to wear.
  The men must be finding many
      things to bring home.'
31 "Lord, may all your enemies be
      destroyed.
  But may all who love you be like
      the morning sun.
  May they be like the sun when it
      shines the brightest."

So the land was at peace for 40 years.

Gideon

6 The Israelites did what was evil in the sight of the Lord. So for seven years he handed them over to the people of Midian. 2 The Midianites treated the Israelites very badly. That's why they made hiding places for themselves. They hid in holes in the mountains. They also hid in caves and in other safe places. 3 Each year the people planted their crops. When they did, the Midianites came into the country and attacked it. So did the Amalekites and other tribes from the east. 4 They camped on the land. They destroyed the crops all the way to Gaza. They didn't spare any living thing for Israel. They didn't spare sheep or cattle or donkeys. 5 The Midianites came up with their livestock and tents. They came like huge numbers of locusts. It was impossible to count the men and their camels. They came into the land to destroy it. 6 The Midianites made the Israelites very poor. So they cried out to the Lord for help.

7 They cried out to the Lord because of what the Midianites had done. 8 So he sent a prophet to Israel. The prophet said, "The Lord is the God of Israel. He says, 'I brought you up out of Egypt. That is the land where you were slaves. 9 I saved you from the power of the Egyptians. I saved you from all those who were treating you badly. I drove out the Canaanites to make room for you. I gave you their land. 10 I said to you, "I am the Lord your God. You are now living in the land of the Amorites. Do not worship their gods." But you have not listened to me.' "

11 The angel of the Lord came. He sat down under an oak tree in Ophrah. The tree belonged to Joash. He was from the family line of Abiezer. Gideon was threshing wheat in a winepress at Ophrah. He was the son of Joash. Gideon was threshing in a winepress to hide the wheat from the Midianites. 12 The angel of the Lord appeared to Gideon. He said, "Mighty warrior, the Lord is with you."

13 "Pardon me, sir," Gideon replied, "you say the Lord is with us. Then why has all this happened to us? Where are all the wonderful things he has done? Our people of long ago told us about them. They said, 'Didn't the Lord bring us up out of Egypt?' But now the Lord has deserted us. He has handed us over to Midian."

14 The Lord turned to Gideon. He said to him, "You are strong. Go and save Israel from the power of Midian. I am sending you."

15 "Pardon me, sir," Gideon replied, "but how can I possibly save Israel? My family group is the weakest in the tribe of Manasseh. And I'm the least important member of my family."

16 The Lord answered, "I will be with you. So you will strike down the Midianites. You will leave no one alive."

17 Gideon replied, "If you are pleased with me, give me a special sign. Then I'll

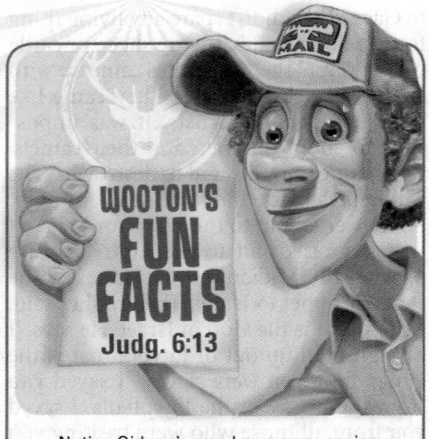

WOOTON'S FUN FACTS
Judg. 6:13

Notice Gideon's good manners, saying
"Pardon me, sir" and other nice things. I
can only hope that when I meet an angel
in disguise I use proper etiquette. (Another
angel-sighting here if you're collecting angels!)

know that it's really you talking to me. ¹⁸Please don't go away until I come back. I'll bring my offering and set it down in front of you."

The LORD said, "I will wait until you return."

¹⁹Gideon went inside and prepared a young goat. From 36 pounds of flour he made bread without using yeast. He put the meat in a basket. In a pot he put soup made from the meat. Then he brought all of it and offered it to the LORD under the oak tree.

²⁰The angel of God said to Gideon, "Take the meat and the bread. Place them on this rock. Then pour out the soup." So Gideon did it. ²¹The angel of the LORD had a walking stick in his hand. With the tip of the stick he touched the meat and the bread. Fire blazed out of the rock. It burned up the meat and the bread. Then the angel of the LORD disappeared. ²²Gideon realized it was the angel of the LORD. He cried out, "Oh no, my LORD and King, I have seen the angel of the LORD face to face!"

²³But the LORD said to him, "May peace be with you! Do not be afraid. You are not going to die."

²⁴So Gideon built an altar there to honor the LORD. He called it The LORD Is Peace. It still stands in Ophrah to this day.

Ophrah is in the territory that belongs to the family line of Abiezer.

²⁵That same night the LORD spoke to Gideon. He said, "Get the second bull from your father's herd. Get the one that is seven years old. Tear down the altar your father built to honor the god named Baal. Cut down the pole beside it. The pole is used to worship the female god named Asherah. ²⁶Then build the right kind of altar. Build it to honor the LORD your God. Build it on top of this hill. Then use the wood from the Asherah pole you cut down. Sacrifice the second bull as a burnt offering."

²⁷So Gideon went and got ten of his servants. He did just as the LORD had told him. But he was afraid of his family. He was also afraid of the people in the town. So he did everything at night instead of during the day.

²⁸In the morning the people in the town got up. They saw that Baal's altar had been torn down. The Asherah pole beside it had been cut down. And the second bull had been sacrificed on the new altar that had been built.

²⁹They asked each other, "Who did this?"

They looked into the matter carefully. Someone told them, "Gideon, the son of Joash, did it."

³⁰The people in the town spoke to Joash. They ordered him, "Bring your son out here. He must die. He has torn down Baal's altar. He has cut down the Asherah pole beside it."

³¹But Joash replied to the angry crowd around him. He asked, "Are you going to stand up for Baal? Are you trying to save him? Those who stand up for him will be put to death by morning! Is Baal really a god? If he is, he can stand up for himself when someone tears down his altar."

³²That's why they gave Gideon the name Jerub-Baal on that day. Gideon had torn down Baal's altar. So they said, "Let Baal take his stand against him."

³³All the Midianites and Amalekites gathered their armies together. Other tribes from the east joined them. All of them went across the Jordan River. They camped in the Valley of Jezreel. ³⁴Then the Spirit of the LORD came on Gideon. So Gideon blew a trumpet to send for the men of Abiezer. He told them to follow him. ³⁵He sent messengers all through

Manasseh's territory. He called for the men of Manasseh to fight. He also sent messengers to the men of Asher, Zebulun and Naphtali. So all those men went up to join the others.

³⁶Gideon said to God, "You promised you would use me to save Israel. ³⁷Please do something for me. I'll put a piece of wool on the threshing floor. Suppose dew is only on the wool tomorrow morning. And suppose the ground all around it is dry. Then I will know that you will use me to save Israel. I'll know that your promise will come true." ³⁸And that's what happened. Gideon got up early the next day. He squeezed the dew out of the wool. The water filled a bowl.

³⁹Then Gideon said to God, "Don't be angry with me. Let me ask you for just one more thing. Let me use the wool for one more test. But this time make the wool dry. And let the ground be covered with dew." ⁴⁰So that night God did it. Only the wool was dry. The ground all around it was covered with dew.

Gideon Wins the Battle Over the Midianites

7 Early in the morning Jerub-Baal and all his men camped at the spring of Harod. Jerub-Baal was another name for Gideon. The camp of Midian was north of Gideon's camp. It was in the valley near the hill of Moreh. ²The LORD said to Gideon, "I want to hand Midian over to you. But you have too many men for me to do that. Then Israel might brag, 'My own strength has saved me.' ³So here is what I want you to announce to the army. Tell them, 'Those who tremble with fear can turn back. They can leave Mount Gilead.' " So 22,000 men left. But 10,000 remained.

⁴The LORD said to Gideon, "There are still too many men. So take them down to the water. There I will reduce the number of them for you. If I say, 'This one will go with you,' he will go. But if I say, 'That one will not go with you,' he will not go."

⁵So Gideon took the men down to the water. There the LORD said to him, "Some men will drink the way dogs do. They will lap up the water with their tongues. Separate them from those who get down on their knees to drink." ⁶Three hundred men brought up the water to their mouths with their hands. And they lapped it up the way dogs do. All the rest got down on their knees to drink.

⁷The LORD spoke to Gideon. He said, "With the help of the 300 men who lapped up the water I will save you. I will hand the Midianites over to you. Let all the other men go home." ⁸So Gideon sent those Israelites home. But he kept the 300 men. They took over the supplies and trumpets the others had left.

The Midianites had set up their camp in the valley below where Gideon was. ⁹During that night the LORD said to Gideon, "Get up. Go down against the camp. I am going to hand it over to you. ¹⁰But what if you are afraid to attack? Then go down to the camp with your servant Purah. ¹¹Listen to what they are saying. After that, you will not be afraid to attack the camp." So Gideon and his servant Purah went down to the edge of the camp. ¹²The Midianites had set up their camp in the valley. So had the Amalekites and all the other tribes from the east. There were so many of them that they looked like huge numbers of locusts. Like the grains of sand on the seashore, their camels couldn't be counted.

¹³Gideon arrived just as a man was telling a friend about his dream. "I had a dream," he was saying. "A round loaf of barley bread came rolling into the camp of Midian. It hit a tent with great force. The tent turned over and fell down flat."

¹⁴His friend replied, "That can only be the sword of Gideon, the son of Joash.

Judg. 7:13 This is the weirdest of all dreams in the Bible, hands down. I'm gonna write a comic about it called *Attack of the Angry Barley Loaf.*

BiBLe ADVeNTUReS

The Ancient World of Sports
covered Gideon's battle in
"B-TV: Obedience" (A#39).

Gideon is from Israel. God has handed the Midianites over to him. He has given him the whole camp."

[15]Gideon heard the man explain what the dream meant. Then Gideon bowed down and worshiped. He returned to the camp of Israel. He called out, "Get up! The LORD has handed the Midianites over to you." [16]Gideon separated the 300 men into three fighting groups. He put a trumpet and an empty jar into the hands of each man. And he put a torch inside each jar.

[17]"Watch me," he told them. "Do what I do. I'll go to the edge of the enemy camp. Then do exactly as I do. [18]I and everyone with me will blow our trumpets. Then blow your trumpets from your positions all around the camp. And shout the battle cry, 'For the LORD and for Gideon!'"

[19]Gideon and the 100 men with him reached the edge of the enemy camp. It was about ten o'clock at night. It was just after the guard had been changed. Gideon and his men blew their trumpets. They broke the jars that were in their hands. [20]The three fighting groups blew their trumpets. They smashed their jars. They held their torches in their left hands. They held in their right hands the trumpets they were going to blow. Then they shouted the battle cry, "A sword for the LORD and for Gideon!" [21]Each man stayed in his position around the camp. But all the Midianites ran away in fear. They were crying out as they ran.

[22]When the 300 trumpets were blown, the LORD caused all the men in the enemy camp to start fighting one another. They attacked one another with their swords. The army ran away to Beth Shittah toward Zererah. They ran all the way to the border of Abel Meholah near Tabbath. [23]Israelites from the tribes of Naphtali, Asher and all of Manasseh were called out. They chased the Midianites. [24]Gideon sent messengers through the entire hill country of Ephraim. They said, "Come on down against the Midianites. Take control of the waters of the Jordan River before they get there. Do it all the way to Beth Barah."

So all the men of Ephraim were called out. They took control of the waters of the Jordan all the way to Beth Barah. [25]They also captured Oreb and Zeeb. Those men were two of the Midianite leaders. The men of Ephraim killed Oreb at the rock of Oreb. They killed Zeeb at the winepress of Zeeb. They chased the Midianites. And they brought the heads of Oreb and Zeeb to Gideon. He was by the Jordan River.

Zebah and Zalmunna

8 The men of Ephraim asked Gideon, "Why have you treated us like this? Why didn't you ask us to help you when you went out to fight against Midian?" In anger they challenged Gideon.

[2]But he answered them, "What I've done isn't anything compared to what you have done. Ephraim's grapes have been gathered. Isn't what is left over better than all the grapes that have been gathered from Abiezer's vines? [3]God handed Oreb and Zeeb over to you. They were Midianite leaders. So what was I able to do compared to what you did?" After Gideon had said that, they didn't feel angry with him anymore.

[4]Gideon and his 300 men were very tired. But they kept on chasing their enemies. They came to the Jordan River and went across it. [5]Gideon said to the men of Sukkoth, "Give my troops some bread. They are worn out. And I'm still chasing Zebah and Zalmunna. They are the kings of Midian."

[6]But the officials of Sukkoth objected. They said, "Have you already killed Zebah and Zalmunna? Have you cut their hands off and brought them back to prove it? If you haven't, why should we give bread to your troops?"

[7]Gideon replied, "The LORD will hand Zebah and Zalmunna over to me. When he does, I'll tear your skin with thorns from desert bushes."

[8]From there Gideon went up to Peniel. He asked its men for the same thing. But they answered as the men of Sukkoth had. [9]So he said to the men of Peniel, "I'll be back after I've won the battle. Then I'll tear down this tower."

[10]Zebah and Zalmunna were in Karkor. They had an army of about 15,000 men.

That's all that were left of the armies of the tribes from the east. About 120,000 men who carried swords had died in battle. ¹¹Gideon went up the trail the people of the desert had made. It ran east of Nobah and Jogbehah. He attacked the army by surprise. ¹²Zebah and Zalmunna ran away. They were the two kings of Midian. Gideon chased them and captured them. He destroyed their whole army.

Jason's Jargon

JUDGES 8

Try to find an *apron* in this chapter. An apron is a piece of clothing made from leather or cloth worn on the front of the body to protect the clothing underneath from dirt.

¹³Then Gideon, the son of Joash, returned from the battle. He came back through the Pass of Heres. ¹⁴He caught a young man from Sukkoth. He asked him about the elders of the town. The young man wrote down for him the names of Sukkoth's 77 officials. ¹⁵Then Gideon came and said to the men of Sukkoth, "Here are Zebah and Zalmunna. You made fun of me because of them. You said, 'Have you already killed Zebah and Zalmunna? Have you cut their hands off and brought them back to prove it? If you haven't, why should we give bread to your tired men?'" ¹⁶Gideon went and got the elders of the town. Then he taught the men of Sukkoth a lesson. He tore their skin with thorns from desert bushes. ¹⁷He also pulled down the tower at Peniel. He killed the men in the town.

¹⁸Then he spoke to Zebah and Zalmunna. He asked, "What were the men like that you killed at Tabor?"

"Men like you," they answered. "Each one walked as if he were a prince."

¹⁹Gideon replied, "Those were my brothers. They were the sons of my own mother. You can be sure that the LORD lives. And you can be just as sure that if you had spared their lives, I wouldn't kill

you." ²⁰Then Gideon turned to his oldest son Jether. He said, "Kill them!" But Jether didn't pull out his sword. He was only a boy. So he was afraid.

²¹Zebah and Zalmunna said, "Come on. Do it yourself. 'The older the man, the stronger he is.'" So Gideon stepped forward and killed them. Then he took the gold chains off the necks of their camels.

Gideon's Linen Apron

²²The Israelites said to Gideon, "Rule over us. We want you, your son and your grandson to be our rulers. You have saved us from the power of Midian."

²³But Gideon told them, "I will not rule over you. My son won't rule over you either. The LORD will rule over you." ²⁴He continued, "I do ask one thing. I want each of you to give me an earring. I'm talking about the earrings you took from your enemies." It was the practice of the people in the family line of Ishmael to wear gold earrings.

²⁵The Israelites said, "We'll be glad to give them to you." So they spread out a piece of clothing. Each of them threw a ring on it from what he had taken. ²⁶The weight of the gold rings Gideon asked for was 43 pounds. That didn't include the moon-shaped necklaces the kings of Midian had worn. It didn't include their other necklaces or their purple clothes. And it didn't include the gold chains that had been on the necks of their camels. ²⁷Gideon made an object out of all the gold. It looked like the linen apron the high priest of Israel wore. Gideon placed it in Ophrah. That was his hometown. All the Israelites worshiped it there. They weren't faithful to the LORD. So the gold object became a trap to Gideon and his family.

Gideon Dies

²⁸Israel brought Midian under their control. Midian wasn't able to attack Israel anymore. So the land was at peace for 40 years. The peace lasted as long as Gideon was living.

²⁹Jerub-Baal, the son of Joash, went back home to live. Jerub-Baal was another name for Gideon. ³⁰He had 70 sons of his own. That's because he had many wives. ³¹And he had a concubine who lived in Shechem. She also had a son by

him. Gideon named that son Abimelek. [32]Gideon, the son of Joash, died when he was very old. He was buried in the tomb of his father Joash in Ophrah. Ophrah was in the territory that belonged to the family line of Abiezer.

[33]As soon as Gideon had died, the Israelites began serving and worshiping gods that were named Baal. Israel wasn't faithful to the LORD. They worshiped Baal-Berith as their god. [34]They forgot what the LORD their God had done for them. He had saved them from the power of their enemies all around them. [35]Jerub-Baal had done many good things for the Israelites. But they weren't faithful to his family. Jerub-Baal was another name for Gideon.

Abimelek

9 Abimelek was the son of Jerub-Baal. He went to his mother's brothers in Shechem. He spoke to them and to all the members of his mother's family group. He said, [2]"Speak to all the citizens of Shechem. Tell them, 'You can have all 70 of Jerub-Baal's sons rule over you. Or you can have just one man rule over you. Which would you rather have?' Remember, I'm your own flesh and blood."

[3]The brothers told all of that to the citizens of Shechem. Then the people decided to follow Abimelek. They said, "He's related to us." [4]They gave him 28 ounces of silver. They had taken it from the temple of the god named Baal-Berith. Abimelek used it to hire some men. They were wild and weren't good for anything. They became his followers. [5]Abimelek went to his father's home in Ophrah. There on a big rock he murdered his 70 brothers. All of them were the sons of Jerub-Baal. But Jotham escaped by hiding. He was Jerub-Baal's youngest son. [6]All the citizens of Shechem and Beth Millo came together. They gathered at the stone pillar that was beside the large tree in Shechem. They wanted to crown Abimelek as their king.

[7]Jotham was told about it. So he climbed up on top of Mount Gerizim. He shouted down to them, "Citizens of Shechem! Listen to me! Then God will listen to you. [8]One day the trees went out to anoint a king for themselves. They said to an olive tree, 'Be our king.'

[9]"But the olive tree answered, 'Should I give up my olive oil? It's used to honor gods and people alike. Should I give that up just to rule over the trees?'

[10]"Next, the trees said to a fig tree, 'Come and be our king.'

[11]"But the fig tree replied, 'Should I give up my fruit? It's so good and sweet. Should I give that up just to rule over the trees?'

[12]"Then the trees said to a vine, 'Come and be our king.'

[13]"But the vine answered, 'Should I give up my wine? It cheers up gods and people alike. Should I give that up just to rule over the trees?'

[14]"Finally, all the trees spoke to a bush that had thorns. They said, 'Come and be our king.'

[15]"The bush asked the trees, 'Do you really want to anoint me as king over you? If you do, come and rest in my shade. But if you don't, I will destroy you! Fire will come out of me and burn up the cedar trees of Lebanon!'

[16]"Did you act in an honest way when you made Abimelek your king? Did you really do the right thing? Have you been fair to Jerub-Baal and his family? Have you given him the honor he's worthy of? [17]Remember that my father fought for you. He put his life in danger for you. He saved you from the power of Midian. [18]But today you have turned against my father's family. You have murdered his 70 sons on a big rock. Abimelek is only the son of my father's female slave. But you have made him king over the citizens of Shechem. You have done that because he's related to you. [19]Have you citizens of Shechem and Beth Millo acted in an honest way toward Jerub-Baal? Have you done the right thing to his family today? If you have, may you be happy with Abimelek! And may he be happy with you! [20]But if you haven't, let fire come out from Abimelek and burn you up! And let fire come out from you and burn Abimelek up!"

[21]Then Jotham ran away. He escaped to a town named Beer. He lived there because he was afraid of his brother Abimelek.

[22]Abimelek ruled over Israel for three years. [23]Then God stirred up trouble between Abimelek and the citizens of Shechem. So they turned against Abimelek. They decided not to follow him

anymore. [24]God made that happen because of what Abimelek had done to Jerub-Baal's 70 sons. He had spilled their blood. God wanted to punish their brother Abimelek for doing that. He also wanted to punish the citizens of Shechem. They had helped Abimelek murder his brothers. [25]The citizens of Shechem didn't want Abimelek to be their ruler anymore. So they hid some men on top of the hills. They wanted them to attack and rob everyone who passed by. Abimelek was told about it.

[26]Gaal and his relatives moved into Shechem. Gaal was the son of Ebed. The citizens of Shechem put their trust in Gaal. [27]The people of Shechem went out into the fields. They gathered the grapes. They pressed the juice out of them by stomping on them. Then they held a feast in the temple of their god. While they were eating and drinking, they cursed Abimelek. [28]Then Gaal, the son of Ebed, said, "Who is Abimelek? And who is Shechem? Why should we citizens of Shechem be under Abimelek's rule? Isn't he Jerub-Baal's son? Isn't Zebul his helper? It would be better to serve the family of Hamor. He was the father of Shechem. So why should we serve Abimelek? [29]I wish these people were under my command. Then I would get rid of Abimelek. I would say to him, 'Call out your whole army!'"

[30]Zebul was the governor of Shechem. He heard about what Gaal, the son of Ebed, had said. So he was very angry. [31]Zebul secretly sent messengers to Abimelek. They said, "Gaal, the son of Ebed, has come to Shechem. His relatives have come with him. They are stirring up the city against you. [32]So come with your men during the night. Hide in the fields and wait. [33]In the morning at sunrise, attack the city. Gaal and his men will come out against you. Then take that opportunity to attack them."

[34]So Abimelek and all his troops started out at night. They went into their hiding places near Shechem. Abimelek had separated them into four fighting groups. [35]Gaal, the son of Ebed, had already gone out. He was standing at the entrance of the city gate. He had arrived there just as Abimelek and his troops came out of their hiding places.

[36]Gaal saw them. He said to Zebul, "Look! People are coming down from the tops of the mountains!"

Zebul replied, "You are wrong. Those aren't people. They are just the shadows of the mountains."

[37]But Gaal spoke up again. He said, "Look! People are coming down from the central hill. Another group is coming from the direction of the fortune tellers' tree."

[38]Then Zebul said to Gaal, "Where is your big talk now? You said, 'Who is Abimelek? Why should we be under his rule?' Aren't these the people you made fun of? Go out and fight against them!"

[39]So Gaal led the citizens out of Shechem. They fought against Abimelek. [40]He chased Gaal from the field of battle. Abimelek chased them all the way to the entrance of the city gate. Many men were killed as they ran away. [41]Abimelek stayed in Arumah. And Zebul drove Gaal and his relatives out of Shechem.

[42]The next day the people of Shechem went out to work in the fields. Abimelek was told about it. [43]So he gathered his men together. He separated them into three fighting groups. Then he hid them in the fields and told them to wait. When he saw the people coming out of the city, he got up to attack them. [44]Abimelek and the men with him ran forward. They placed themselves at the entrance of the city gate. Then the other two groups attacked the people in the fields. There they struck them down. [45]Abimelek kept up his attack against the city all day long. He didn't stop until he had captured it. Then he killed its people. He destroyed the city. He scattered salt on it to make sure that nothing would be able to grow there.

[46]The citizens in the tower of Shechem heard about what was happening. So they went to the safest place in the temple of the god named El-Berith. [47]Abimelek heard that they had gathered together there. [48]He and all his men went up Mount Zalmon. He got an ax and cut off some branches. He carried them on his shoulders. He ordered the men with him to do the same thing. "Quick!" he said. "Do what you have seen me do!" [49]So all the men cut branches and followed Abimelek. They piled them against the place where the people had gone for safety. Then they

set the place on fire with the people still inside. There were about 1,000 men and women in the tower of Shechem. All of them died.

⁵⁰Next, Abimelek went to Thebez. He surrounded it. Then he attacked it and captured it. ⁵¹But inside the city there was a strong tower. All the people in the city had run to it for safety. All the men and women had gone into it. They had locked themselves in. They had climbed up on the roof of the tower. ⁵²Abimelek went to the tower and attacked it. He approached the entrance to the tower to set it on fire. ⁵³But a woman dropped a large millstone on him. It broke his head open.

⁵⁴He quickly called out to the man carrying his armor. He said, "Pull out your sword and kill me. Then people can't say, 'A woman killed him.'" So his servant stuck his sword through him. And Abimelek died. ⁵⁵When the Israelites saw he was dead, they went home.

⁵⁶That's how God punished Abimelek for the evil thing he had done to his father. He had murdered his 70 brothers. ⁵⁷God also made the people of Shechem pay for all the evil things they had done. The curse of Jotham came down on them. He was the son of Jerub-Baal.

Tola

10 Tola rose up to save Israel. That happened after the time of Abimelek. Tola was from the tribe of Issachar. He was the son of Puah, who was the son of Dodo. Tola lived in Shamir. It's in the hill country of Ephraim. ²Tola led Israel for 23 years. After he died, he was buried in Shamir.

Jair

³Jair became the leader after Tola. Jair was from the land of Gilead. He led Israel for 22 years. ⁴He had 30 sons. They rode on 30 donkeys. His sons controlled 30 towns in Gilead. Those towns are called Havvoth Jair to this day. ⁵After Jair died, he was buried in Kamon.

Jephthah

⁶Once again the Israelites did what was evil in the sight of the LORD. They served gods that were named Baal. They served female gods that were named Ashtoreth. They worshiped the gods of Aram and Sidon. They served the gods of Moab and Ammon. They also worshiped the gods of the Philistines. The Israelites deserted the LORD. They didn't serve him anymore. ⁷So the LORD became very angry with them. He handed them over to the Philistines and the Ammonites. ⁸That year they broke Israel's power completely. They treated the Israelites badly for 18 years. The people who did this lived east of the Jordan River. They lived in Gilead. That was the land of the Amorites. ⁹The Ammonites also went across the Jordan. They crossed over to fight against the tribes of Judah, Benjamin and Ephraim. Israel was suffering terribly. ¹⁰Then the Israelites cried out to the LORD. They said, "We have sinned against you. We have deserted our God. We have served gods that are named Baal."

¹¹The LORD replied, "The Egyptians and Amorites treated you badly. So did the Ammonites and Philistines. ¹²And so did the Amalekites and the people of Sidon and Maon. Each time you cried out to me for help. And I saved you from their power. ¹³But you have deserted me. You have served other gods. So I will not save you anymore. ¹⁴Go and cry out to the gods you have chosen. Let them save you when you get into trouble!"

¹⁵But the Israelites replied to the LORD, "We have sinned. Do to us what you think is best. But please save us now." ¹⁶Then they got rid of the false gods that were among them. They served the LORD. And he couldn't stand to see Israel suffer anymore.

¹⁷The Ammonites were called together to fight. They camped in the land of Gilead. Then the Israelites gathered together. They camped at the city of Mizpah. ¹⁸The leaders of Gilead spoke to one another. They said, "Who will lead the attack against the Ammonites? That person will be the ruler of all the people who live in Gilead."

11 Jephthah was a mighty warrior. He was from the land of Gilead. His father's name was Gilead. Jephthah's mother was a prostitute. ²Gilead's wife also had sons by him. When they had grown up, they drove Jephthah away. "You aren't going to get any share of our family's property," they said. "You are the son of another woman." ³So Jephthah ran away from his brothers. He made his home in the land of Tob. A group of men who weren't good

BiBLE ADVENTURES

O.T. Action News reported on Jephthah's battle and his rash promise in "O.T. Action News: Jephthah's Vow" (A#30).

for anything gathered around him there. And they followed him.

⁴Some time later, the Ammonites were fighting against Israel. ⁵So the elders of Gilead went to get Jephthah from the land of Tob. ⁶"Come with us," they said. "Be our commander. Then we can fight against the Ammonites."

⁷Jephthah said to them, "Didn't you hate me? Didn't you drive me away from my father's house? Why are you coming to me only when you are in trouble?"

⁸The elders of Gilead replied to him. "You are right," they said. "That's why we're turning to you now. Come with us and fight against the Ammonites. Then you will rule over all of us who live in Gilead."

⁹Jephthah said, "Suppose you take me back to fight against the Ammonites. And suppose the LORD gives me victory over them. Then will I really be your leader?"

¹⁰The elders of Gilead replied, "The LORD is our witness. We'll certainly do as you say." ¹¹So Jephthah went with the elders of Gilead. And the people made him their leader and commander. He went to Mizpah. There he repeated to the LORD everything he had said.

¹²Then Jephthah sent messengers to the king of Ammon. They asked, "What do you have against me? Why have you attacked my country?"

¹³The king of Ammon answered Jephthah's messengers. He said, "Israel came up out of Egypt. At that time they took my land away. They took all the land between the Arnon River and the Jabbok River. It reached all the way to the Jordan River. Now give it back. Then there will be peace."

¹⁴Jephthah sent messengers back to the king of Ammon. ¹⁵They said,

"Here is what Jephthah says to you. Israel didn't take the land of Moab. They didn't take the land of Ammon. ¹⁶When Israel came up

out of Egypt, they went through the desert to the Red Sea. From there they went on to Kadesh. ¹⁷Then Israel sent messengers to the king of Edom. They said, 'Please let us go through your country.' But the king of Edom wouldn't listen to them. They sent the same message to the king of Moab. But he refused too. So Israel stayed at Kadesh.

¹⁸"Next, they traveled through the desert. They traveled along the borders of the lands of Edom and Moab. They passed along the east side of the country of Moab. They camped on the other side of the Arnon River. They didn't enter the territory of Moab. The Arnon River was Moab's border.

¹⁹"Then Israel sent messengers to Sihon. He was the king of the Amorites. He ruled in Heshbon. They said to him, 'Let us pass through your country to our own land.' ²⁰But Sihon didn't trust Israel to pass through his territory. Instead, he gathered all his troops together. They camped at Jahaz. And they fought against Israel.

²¹"Then the LORD, the God of Israel, handed Sihon and his whole army over to Israel. Israel won the battle over them. Amorites were living in the country at that time. And Israel took over all their land. ²²Israel captured all the land between the Arnon River and the Jabbok River. It reached from the desert all the way to the Jordan River.

²³"The LORD, the God of Israel, has driven the Amorites out to make room for his people. So what right do you have to take it over? ²⁴You will take what your god Chemosh gives you, won't you? In the same way, we will take over what the LORD our God has given us. ²⁵Are you any better than Balak, the son of Zippor? Balak was the king of Moab. Did he ever argue with Israel? Did he ever fight against them? ²⁶For 300 years Israel has been living in Heshbon and Aroer. They have been living in the settlements around those cities. They have also been living in

A lot of Bible stories have happy endings—but not Jephthah's. Stories like his help us learn from the mistakes of others, to avoid similar heartbreak in our own lives.

Jephthah was a godly warrior forced to leave home by his hateful brothers. Yet it was Jephthah the Israelites called on when they needed a key victory against their oppressors. He took the job, perhaps hoping to prove his worth, advance his career, and show the men in his family they were wrong to treat him so poorly.

Jephthah's battle plan included promising God that, in exchange for victory over the Ammonites, he would sacrifice the first thing to come out of his house to greet him when he arrived home. A goat? A sheep? That's probably what he expected. To his shock and horror, it turned out to be his only child, his beloved daughter. It's all right here in Judges 11.

Jephthah became so focused on succeeding at his job that he overlooked something even more important—his child.

WHAT ABOUT YOU?

Fortunately, dads can learn from Jephthah's mistake by realizing that a truly great legacy starts with being a hero at home.

Do something today to make your dad feel like a hero. Ask him for advice—or why he likes a certain movie in his video library. Surprise him with his favorite candy bar. Believe it or not, kids can help their fathers keep work in perspective by making Dad feel as valued and appreciated around the house as he feels on the job.

---

all the towns along the Arnon River. Why didn't you take those places back during that time? ²⁷I haven't done anything wrong to you. But you are doing something wrong to me. You have gone to war against me. The LORD is the Judge. So let him decide our case today. Let him settle matters between the Israelites and the Ammonites."

²⁸But the king of Ammon didn't pay any attention to the message Jephthah sent him.

²⁹Then the Spirit of the LORD came on Jephthah. He went across the territories of Gilead and Manasseh. He passed through Mizpah in the land of Gilead. From there he attacked the people of Ammon. ³⁰Jephthah made a promise to the LORD. Jephthah said, "Hand the Ammonites over to me. ³¹If you do, here's what I'll do when I come back from winning the battle. Anything that comes out the door of my house to meet me will belong to the LORD. I will sacrifice it as a burnt offering."

³²Then Jephthah went over to fight against the Ammonites. The LORD handed them over to him. ³³Jephthah destroyed 20 towns between Aroer and the area of Minnith. He destroyed them all the way to Abel Keramim. So Israel brought Ammon under their control.

³⁴Jephthah returned to his home in Mizpah. And guess who came out to meet him. It was his daughter! She was dancing to the beat of tambourines. She was his only child. He didn't have any other sons or daughters. ³⁵When Jephthah saw her, he was so upset that he tore his clothes. He cried out, "Oh no, my daughter! You have filled me with trouble and sorrow. I've made a promise to the LORD. And I can't break it."

³⁶"My father," she replied, "you have given your word to the LORD. So do to me just what you promised to do. The Ammonites were your enemies. And the LORD has paid them back for what they did to you. ³⁷But please do one thing for me," she continued. "Give me two months

to wander around in the hills. Let me weep there with my friends. I want to do that because I'll never get married."

³⁸"You may go," he said. He let her go for two months. She and her friends went into the hills. They were filled with sadness because she would never get married. ³⁹After the two months were over, she returned to her father. He did to her just what he had promised to do. And she was a virgin.

So that became a practice in Israel. ⁴⁰Each year the young women of Israel go away for four days. They do it in honor of the daughter of Jephthah. He was from the land of Gilead.

Jephthah Wins the Battle Over Ephraim

12 The troops of Ephraim were called out. The troops went across the Jordan River to Zaphon. When they arrived, they said to Jephthah, "You went to fight against the Ammonites. Why didn't you ask us to go with you? We're going to burn down your house over your head."

²Jephthah answered, "I and my people were taking part in a great struggle. We were at war with the Ammonites. I asked you for help. But you didn't come to save me from their power. ³I saw that you wouldn't help. So I put my own life in danger. I went across the Jordan to fight against the Ammonites. The LORD helped me win the battle over them. So why have you come up today to fight against me?"

⁴Then Jephthah called the men of Gilead together. They fought against Ephraim. The men of Gilead struck them down. The people of Ephraim had said, "You people of Gilead are nothing but deserters from Ephraim and Manasseh." ⁵The men of Gilead captured the places where people go across the Jordan River to get to Ephraim. Some men of Ephraim weren't killed in the battle. When they arrived at the river, they would say, "Let us go across." Then the men of Gilead would ask each one, "Are you from Ephraim?" Suppose he replied, "No." ⁶Then they would say, "All right. Say 'Shibboleth.'" If he said "Shibboleth," the way he said the word would give him away. He couldn't say it correctly. So they would grab him. Then they would kill him at one of the places where people

go across the Jordan. At that time, 42,000 men of Ephraim were killed.

⁷Jephthah led Israel for six years. Then he died. He was buried in a town in Gilead. Jephthah was from the land of Gilead.

Ibzan, Elon and Abdon

⁸After Jephthah, Ibzan from Bethlehem led Israel. ⁹He had 30 sons and 30 daughters. He gave his daughters to be married to men who were outside his family group. He brought in 30 young women to be married to his sons. Those women also came from outside his family group. Ibzan led Israel for seven years. ¹⁰Then he died. He was buried in Bethlehem.

¹¹After Ibzan, Elon led Israel. He was from the tribe of Zebulun. Elon led Israel for ten years. ¹²Then he died. He was buried in Aijalon. It was in the land of Zebulun.

¹³After Elon, Abdon led Israel. Abdon was the son of Hillel. Abdon was from Pirathon. ¹⁴He had 40 sons and 30 grandsons. They rode on 70 donkeys. Abdon led Israel for eight years. ¹⁵Then he died. He was buried at Pirathon in Ephraim. Pirathon was in the hill country of the Amalekites. Abdon was the son of Hillel.

Samson Is Born

13 Once again the Israelites did what was evil in the sight of the LORD. So the LORD handed them over to the Philistines for 40 years.

²A certain man from Zorah was named Manoah. He was from the tribe of Dan. Manoah had a wife who wasn't able to have children. ³The angel of the LORD appeared to Manoah's wife. He said, "You are not able to have children. But you are going to become pregnant. You will have a baby boy. ⁴Make sure you do not drink any kind of wine. Also make sure you do not eat anything that is 'unclean.' ⁵You will become pregnant. You will have a son. The hair on his head must never be cut. That is because the boy will be a Nazirite. He will be set apart to God from the day he is born. He will take the lead in saving Israel from the power of the Philistines."

⁶Then the woman went to her husband. She told him, "A man of God came to me. He looked like an angel of God. His appearance was so amazing that it filled me with great wonder. I didn't ask him where

he came from. And he didn't tell me his name. [7]But he said to me, 'You will become pregnant. You will have a son. So do not drink any kind of wine. Do not eat anything that is "unclean." That is because the boy will be a Nazirite. He will belong to God in a special way from the day he is born until the day he dies.'"

[8]Then Manoah prayed to the LORD. He said, "Pardon your servant, Lord. I beg you to let the man of God you sent to us come again. He told us we would have a son. We want the man of God to teach us how to bring up the boy."

[9]God heard Manoah. And the angel of God came again to the woman. He came while she was out in the field. But her husband Manoah wasn't with her. [10]The woman hurried to her husband. She told him, "He's here! The man who appeared to me the other day is here!"

[11]Manoah got up and followed his wife. When he came to the man, he spoke to him. He said, "Are you the man who talked to my wife?"

"I am," he replied.

[12]So Manoah asked him, "What will happen when your words come true? What rules should we follow for the boy's life and work?"

[13]The angel of the LORD answered him. He said, "Your wife must do everything I have told her to do. [14]She must not eat anything that comes from grapevines. She must not drink any kind of wine. She must not eat anything that is 'unclean.' She must do everything I have commanded her to do."

[15]Manoah said to the angel of the LORD, "We would like you to stay and eat. We want to prepare a young goat for you."

[16]The angel of the LORD replied, "Even if I stay, I will not eat any of your food. But if you still want to prepare a burnt offering, you must offer it to the LORD." Manoah didn't realize it was the angel of the LORD.

[17]Then Manoah asked the angel of the LORD a question. "What is your name?" he said. "We want to honor you when your word comes true."

[18]The angel replied, "Why are you asking me what my name is? You would not be able to understand it." [19]Manoah got a young goat. He brought it along with the grain offering. He sacrificed it on a rock to the LORD. Then the LORD did an amazing

thing. It happened while Manoah and his wife were watching. [20]A flame blazed up from the altar toward heaven. The angel of the LORD rose up in the flame. When Manoah and his wife saw it, they fell with their faces to the ground. [21]The angel of the LORD didn't show himself again to Manoah and his wife. Then Manoah realized it was the angel of the LORD.

[22]"We're going to die!" he said to his wife. "We've seen God!"

[23]But his wife answered, "The LORD doesn't want to kill us. If he did, he wouldn't have accepted a burnt offering and a grain offering from us. He wouldn't have shown us all these things. He wouldn't have told us we're going to have a son."

[24]Later, the woman had a baby boy. She named him Samson. As he grew up, the LORD blessed him. [25]The Spirit of the LORD began to work in his life. It happened while he was in Mahaneh Dan. That place is between Zorah and Eshtaol.

Samson Marries a Philistine Woman

14 Samson went down to Timnah. There he saw a young Philistine woman. [2]When he returned, he spoke to his father and mother. He said, "I've seen a Philistine woman in Timnah. Get her for me. I want her to be my wife."

[3]His father and mother replied, "Can't we find a wife for you among your relatives? Isn't there one among any of our people? Do you have to go to the Philistines to get a wife? They aren't God's people. They haven't even been circumcised."

But Samson said to his father, "Get her for me. She's the right one for me." [4]Samson's parents didn't know that the LORD wanted things to happen this way. He was working out his plans against the Philistines. That's because the Philistines were ruling over Israel at that time.

[5]Samson went down to Timnah. His father and mother went with him. They approached the vineyards of Timnah.

Suddenly a young lion came roaring toward Samson. ⁶Then the Spirit of the LORD came powerfully on Samson. So he tore the lion apart with his bare hands. He did it as easily as he might have torn a young goat apart. But he didn't tell his father or mother what he had done. ⁷Then he went down and talked with the woman. He liked her.

⁸Some time later, he was going back to marry her. But he turned off the road to look at the lion's dead body. He saw large numbers of bees and some honey in it. ⁹He dug out the honey with his hands. He ate it as he walked along. Then he joined his parents again. He gave them some honey. They ate it too. But he didn't tell them he had taken it from the lion's dead body.

¹⁰Samson's father went down to see the woman. Samson had a feast prepared there. He was following the practice of young men when they married their wives. ¹¹When the people saw Samson, they gave him 30 men to be his companions.

¹²"Let me tell you a riddle," Samson said to the companions. "The feast will last for seven days. Give me the answer to the riddle before the feast ends. If you do, I'll give you 30 linen shirts. I'll also give you 30 sets of clothes. ¹³But suppose you can't give me the answer. Then you must give me 30 linen shirts. You must also give me 30 sets of clothes."

"Tell us your riddle," they said. "Let's hear it."

¹⁴Samson replied,

"Out of the eater came something to eat.
Out of the strong came something sweet."

For three days they couldn't give him the answer.

¹⁵On the fourth day they spoke to Samson's wife. "Get your husband to explain the riddle for us," they said. "If you don't, we'll burn you to death. We'll burn up everyone in your family. Did you invite us here to steal our property?"

¹⁶Then Samson's wife threw herself on him. She sobbed, "You hate me! You don't really love me. You have given my people a riddle. But you haven't told me the answer."

"I haven't even explained it to my father or mother," he replied. "So why should I explain it to you?" ¹⁷She cried during the whole seven days the feast was going on. So on the seventh day he finally told her the answer to the riddle. That's because she kept on asking him to tell her. Then she explained the riddle to her people.

¹⁸Before sunset on the seventh day of the feast the men of the town spoke to Samson. They said,

"What is sweeter than honey?
What is stronger than a lion?"

Samson said to them,

"You have plowed with my young cow.
If you hadn't, you wouldn't have known the answer to my riddle."

¹⁹Then the Spirit of the LORD came powerfully on Samson. He went down to Ashkelon. He struck down 30 of their men. He took everything they had with them. And he gave their clothes to those who had explained the riddle. Samson was very angry as he returned to his father's home. ²⁰Samson's wife was given to someone else. She was given to a companion of Samson. The companion had helped him at the feast.

Samson Gets Even With the Philistines

15 Later on, Samson went to visit his wife. He took a young goat with him. He went at the time the wheat was being gathered. He said, "I'm going to my wife's room." But her father wouldn't let him go in.

²Her father said, "I was sure you hated her. So I gave her to your companion. Isn't her younger sister more beautiful? Take her instead."

³Samson said to them, "This time I have a right to get even with the Philistines. I'm going to hurt them badly." ⁴So he went out and caught 300 foxes. He tied them in pairs by their tails. Then he tied a torch to each pair of tails. ⁵He lit the torches. He let the foxes loose in the fields of grain that belonged to the Philistines. He burned up the grain that had been cut and stacked. He burned up the grain that was still growing. He also burned up the vineyards and olive trees.

⁶The Philistines asked, "Who did this?" They were told, "Samson did. He's the son-in-law of the man from Timnah. Samson did it because his wife was given to his companion."

So the Philistines went up and burned the woman and her father to death. ⁷Samson said to the Philistines, "Is that how you act? Then I promise I won't stop until I pay you back." ⁸He struck them down with heavy blows. He killed many of them. Then he went down and stayed in a cave. It was in the rock of Etam.

⁹The Philistines went up and camped in Judah. They spread out near Lehi. ¹⁰The people of Judah asked, "Why have you come to fight against us?"

"We've come to take Samson as our prisoner," they answered. "We want to do to him what he did to us."

¹¹Then 3,000 men from Judah went to get Samson. They went down to the cave in the rock of Etam. They said to Samson, "Don't you realize the Philistines are ruling over us? What have you done to us?"

Samson answered, "I only did to them what they did to me."

Jason's Jargon

JUDGES 15

Search this chapter for the word *jawbone*. The jawbone of a donkey contains its complete set of teeth and is as long as the human forearm. It's a weapon when swung like a baseball bat.

¹²The men of Judah said to him, "We've come to tie you up. We're going to hand you over to the Philistines."

Samson said, "Promise me you won't kill me yourselves."

¹³"We agree," they answered. "We'll only tie you up and hand you over to them. We won't kill you." So they tied him up with two new ropes. They led him up from the rock. ¹⁴Samson approached Lehi. The Philistines came toward him shouting. Then the Spirit of the LORD came powerfully on Samson. The ropes on his arms became like burned thread. They dropped off his hands. ¹⁵He found a fresh jawbone of a donkey. He grabbed it and struck down 1,000 men.

¹⁶Then Samson said,

"By using a donkey's jawbone
   I've made them look like donkeys.
By using a donkey's jawbone
   I've struck down 1,000 men."

¹⁷Samson finished speaking. Then he threw the jawbone away. That's why the place was called Ramath Lehi.

¹⁸Samson was very thirsty. So he cried out to the LORD. He said, "You have helped me win this great battle. Do I have to die of thirst now? Must I fall into the power of people who haven't even been circumcised? They aren't your people." ¹⁹Then God opened up the hollow place in Lehi. Water came out of it. When Samson drank the water, his strength returned. He felt as good as new. So the spring was called En Hakkore. It's still there in Lehi.

²⁰Samson led Israel for 20 years. In those days the Philistines were in the land.

Samson and Delilah

16 One day Samson went to Gaza. There he saw a prostitute. He went in to spend the night with her. ²The people of Gaza were told, "Samson is here!" So they surrounded the place. They hid and waited for him at the city gate all night long. They didn't make any move against him during the night. They said, "Let's wait until the sun comes up. Then we'll kill him."

³But Samson stayed there only until the middle of the night. Then he got up. He took hold of the doors of the city gate. He also took hold of the two doorposts. He tore them loose, together with their metal bar. He picked them up and put them on his shoulders. Then he carried them to the top of the hill that faces Hebron.

⁴Some time later, Samson fell in love again. The woman lived in the Valley of Sorek. Her name was Delilah. ⁵The rulers of the Philistines went to her. They said, "See if you can get him to tell you the secret of why he's so strong. Find out how we can overpower him. Then we can tie him up. We can bring him under

our control. Each of us will give you 28 pounds of silver."

⁶So Delilah said to Samson, "Tell me the secret of why you are so strong. Tell me how you can be tied up and controlled."

⁷Samson answered her, "Let someone tie me up with seven new bowstrings. They must be strings that aren't completely dry. Then I'll become as weak as any other man."

⁸So the Philistine rulers brought seven new bowstrings to her. They weren't completely dry. Delilah tied Samson up with them. ⁹Men were hiding in the room. She called out to him, "Samson! The Philistines are attacking you!" But he snapped the bowstrings easily. They were like pieces of string that had come too close to a flame. So the secret of why he was so strong wasn't discovered.

¹⁰Delilah spoke to Samson again. "You have made me look foolish," she said. "You told me a lie. Come on. Tell me how you can be tied up."

¹¹Samson said, "Let someone tie me tightly with new ropes. They must be ropes that have never been used. Then I'll become as weak as any other man."

¹²So Delilah got some new ropes. She tied him up with them. Men were hiding in the room. She called out to him, "Samson! The Philistines are attacking you!" But he snapped the ropes off his arms. They fell off just as if they were threads.

¹³Delilah spoke to Samson again. "All this time you have been making me look foolish," she said. "You have been telling me lies. This time really tell me how you can be tied up."

He replied, "Weave the seven braids of my hair into the cloth on a loom. Then tighten the cloth with a pin. If you do, I'll become as weak as any other man." So while Samson was sleeping, Delilah took hold of the seven braids of his hair. She wove them into the cloth on a loom. ¹⁴Then she tightened the cloth with a pin.

Again she called out to him, "Samson! The Philistines are attacking you!" He woke up from his sleep. He pulled up the pin and the loom, together with the cloth.

¹⁵Then she said to him, "How can you say, 'I love you'? You won't even share your secret with me. This is the third time you have made me look foolish. And you still haven't told me the secret of why you are so strong." ¹⁶She continued to pester him day after day. She nagged him until he was sick and tired of it.

¹⁷So he told her everything. He said, "My hair has never been cut. That's because I've been a Nazirite since the day I was born. A Nazirite is set apart to God. If you shave my head, I won't be strong anymore. I'll become as weak as any other man."

¹⁸Delilah realized he had told her everything. So she sent a message to the Philistine rulers. She said, "Come back one more time. He has told me everything." So the rulers returned. They brought the silver with them. ¹⁹Delilah got Samson to go to sleep on her lap. Then she called for someone to shave off the seven braids of his hair. That's how she began to bring Samson under her control. And he wasn't strong anymore.

²⁰She called out, "Samson! The Philistines are attacking you!"

He woke up from his sleep. He thought, "I'll go out just as I did before. I'll shake myself free." But he didn't know that the LORD had left him.

²¹Then the Philistines grabbed him. They poked his eyes out. They took him down to Gaza. They put bronze chains

WOOTON'S FUN FACTS
Judg. 16:19

Delilah was a bad girl in the Bible. Once you're thinking about dating or getting married, choose more carefully than Samson did. Penny may want to style my hair sometimes, but she would never turn me over to the Philistines to have my eyes gouged out. Yuck!

around him. Then they made him grind grain in the prison. ²²His head had been shaved. But the hair on it began to grow again.

Samson Dies

²³The rulers of the Philistines gathered together. They were going to offer a great sacrifice to their god Dagon. They were going to celebrate. They said, "Our god has handed our enemy Samson over to us."

²⁴When the people saw Samson, they praised their god. They said,

"Our god has handed our enemy over to us.
Our enemy has destroyed our land.
He has killed large numbers of our people."

²⁵After they had drunk a lot of wine, they shouted, "Bring Samson out. Let him put on a show for us." So they called Samson out of the prison. He put on a show for them.

They had him stand near the temple pillars. ²⁶Then he spoke to the servant who was holding his hand. He said, "Put me where I can feel the pillars. I'm talking about the ones that hold up the temple. I want to lean against them." ²⁷The temple was crowded with men and women. All the Philistine rulers were there. About 3,000 men and women were on the roof. They were watching Samson put on a show. ²⁸Then he prayed to the LORD. Samson said, "LORD and King, show me that you still have concern for me. Please, God, make me strong just one more time. Let me pay the Philistines back for what they did to my two eyes. Let me do it with only one blow." ²⁹Then Samson reached toward the two pillars that were in the middle of the temple. They were the ones that held up the temple. He put his right hand on one of them. He put his left hand on the other. He leaned hard against them. ³⁰Samson said, "Let me die together with the Philistines!" Then he pushed with all his might. The temple came down on the rulers. It fell on all the people in it. So Samson killed many more Philistines when he died than he did while he lived.

³¹Then his brothers went down to get him. So did his father's whole family. All of them brought Samson back home. They buried him in the tomb of his father Manoah. It's between Zorah and Eshtaol. Samson had led Israel for 20 years.

Micah's False Gods

17 A man named Micah lived in the hill country of Ephraim. ²He said to his mother, "Someone took 28 pounds of silver from you. I heard you curse the one who took it. I have the silver with me. I'm the one who took it."

Then his mother said, "My son, may the LORD bless you!"

³He gave the 28 pounds of silver back to his mother. She said to him, "I'm making a promise to set apart my silver to the LORD. My son, I want you to use it to cover a statue of a god made out of wood or stone. That's why I'll give the silver back to you."

⁴Micah gave the silver back to his mother. Then she gave five pounds of it to a skilled worker who made things out of silver. He used the silver for the statue. The statue was put in Micah's house.

⁵That same Micah had a small temple. He made a sacred linen apron and some statues of his family gods. He appointed one of his sons to serve as his priest. ⁶In those days Israel didn't have a king. The people did anything they thought was right.

⁷A young Levite had been living in land that belonged to the tribe of Judah. He was from Bethlehem in Judah. ⁸He left that town to look for some other place to stay. On his way he came to Micah's house. It was in the hill country of Ephraim.

⁹Micah asked him, "Where are you from?"

"I'm a Levite," he said. "I'm from Bethlehem in Judah. I'm looking for a place to stay."

¹⁰Then Micah said to him, "Live with me. Be my father and priest. I'll give you four ounces of silver a year. I'll also give you clothes and food." ¹¹So the Levite agreed to live with him. The young man became just like one of Micah's sons to him. ¹²Then Micah appointed the Levite to serve as his priest. He lived in Micah's house. ¹³Micah said, "Now I know that the LORD will be good to me. This Levite has become my priest."

CANDID CONVERSATIONS

Have you ever seen the movie *Pinocchio*? If you have, forget about the song about wishing on a star and think about the part on Pleasure Island for a minute. Remember that? Pinocchio and his friend went to a place where kids ruled the world. There were no adults, and children got to run around doing whatever they wanted. When I was little, I always thought that would be so cool. But as an adult, I would never want to step foot in that place. It would be crazy! And dangerous! If you've seen Pinocchio, you know things don't turn out well. If you haven't seen it, I won't spoil it.

The Israelites sometimes acted like little kids without adults around. In fact, there was one period of time where they decided not to have a leader at all. They just did whatever they wanted and wouldn't even listen to God. Can you imagine that? A world without a leader, a world without law? Without God as our leader, would we ever make the right choices?

Whenever you need to know the right direction to go, don't rely on yourself. Rely on the One who is way smarter than all of us . . . and a way better conscience than Jiminy Cricket! God's rules are there to help us make the right choices.

The People of Dan Make Their Homes in Laish

18 In those days Israel didn't have a king.

And in those days the tribe of Dan was looking for a place where they could make their homes. They hadn't been able to take over their own share of land among the tribes of Israel. ²So the people of Dan sent out five of their leading men from Zorah and Eshtaol. They told the men to look over the land and check it out. Those men did it for all the people of Dan. Those people told the men, "Go. Check out the land."

So they entered the hill country of Ephraim. They went to the house of Micah. That's where they spent the night. ³When they came near Micah's house, they recognized a voice. It was the voice of the young Levite. So they turned off the road and stopped there. They asked him, "Who brought you here? What are you doing in this place? Why are you here?"

⁴The Levite told them what Micah had done for him. He said, "He has hired me. I'm his priest."

⁵Then they said to him, "Please ask God for advice. Try to find out whether we'll have success on our journey."

⁶The priest answered them, "Go in peace. The LORD is pleased with your journey."

⁷So the five men left. They came to Laish. There they saw that the people felt secure. They were living in safety. Like the people in Sidon, they were at peace. Their land had everything they needed. Things were going very well for them. They lived a long way from the people of Sidon. And they didn't think they would ever need help from anyone else.

⁸The men returned to Zorah and Eshtaol. Their people asked them, "What did you find out?"

⁹They answered, "Come on! Let's attack them! We've seen the land, and it is very good. Aren't you going to do something? Don't wait any longer. Go there and take it over. ¹⁰When you get there, you will find people who aren't expecting anything bad to happen to them. Their land has plenty of room. God has handed it over to you. It's a land that has everything you will ever need."

¹¹So 600 men from the tribe of Dan started out from Zorah and Eshtaol. They were prepared for battle. ¹²On their way they set up camp. Their camp was near Kiriath Jearim in Judah. That's why the place is called Mahaneh Dan to this day. It's west of Kiriath Jearim. ¹³From there they went to the hill country of Ephraim. They came to Micah's house.

[14]Then the five men who had looked over the land of Laish spoke to the other members of their tribe. They said, "Don't you know that one of these houses has a sacred linen apron in it? Some statues of family gods are there. That house also has another statue of a god covered with silver. Now you know what to do." [15]So they turned off the road and stopped there. They went to the house of the young Levite. He was at Micah's place. They greeted the young man. [16]The 600 men from Dan stood at the entrance of the gate. They were prepared for battle. [17]The five men who had looked over the land went inside. They took the statue covered with silver. They also took the family gods and the linen apron. During that time, the priest stood at the entrance of the gate. The 600 men stood there with him. They were prepared for battle.

[18]When the five men went into Micah's house and took all those things, the priest spoke to them. He asked, "What are you doing?"

[19]They answered him, "Be quiet! Don't say a word. Come with us. Be our father and priest. You can serve a whole tribe and family group in Israel as our priest. Isn't that better than serving just one man's family?" [20]The priest was very pleased. He took the linen apron and the family gods. He also took the statue of the god that was covered with silver. Then the priest left with the people. [21]They put their little children and their livestock in front of them. They also put everything else they owned in front of them. And they turned and went on their way.

[22]The men who lived near Micah were called together. Then they left and caught up with the people of Dan. That's because Dan's people hadn't gone very far from Micah's house. [23]Those who lived near Micah shouted at them. The people of Dan turned around and asked Micah, "What's the matter with you? Why did you call out your men to fight against us?"

[24]He replied, "You took away the gods I made. And you took away my priest. What do I have left? So how can you ask, 'What's the matter with you?' "

[25]The people of Dan answered, "Don't argue with us. Some of the men may get angry and attack you. Then you and your family will lose your lives." [26]So the people of Dan went on their way. Micah saw that they were too strong for him. So he turned around and went back home.

[27]The people of Dan took what Micah had made. They also took his priest. They continued on their way to Laish. They went there to fight against a people who were at peace and secure. The people of Dan struck them down with their swords. They burned down their city. [28]No one could save those people and their city. They lived a long way from Sidon. And they didn't think they would ever need help from anyone else. Their city was located in a valley near Beth Rehob.

The people of Dan rebuilt the city. Then they made their homes there. [29]They named it Dan. That's because they traced their family line back to Dan. He was a son of Israel. The city used to be called Laish. [30]There the people of Dan set up for themselves the statue of the god that was covered with silver. Jonathan and his sons were priests for the tribe of Dan. Jonathan was the son of Gershom, the son of Moses. Jonathan and his sons were priests until the time when the land was captured. [31]The people of Dan continued to use the statue Micah had made. They used it during the whole time the house of God was in Shiloh.

A Levite and His Concubine

19 In those days Israel didn't have a king.

There was a Levite who lived deep in the hill country of Ephraim. He got a concubine from Bethlehem in Judah. [2]But she wasn't faithful to him. She left him. She went back to her parents' home in Bethlehem in Judah. She stayed there for four months. [3]Then her husband went to see her. He tried to talk her into coming back with him. He had his servant and two donkeys with him. She took her husband into her parents' home. When her father saw him, he gladly welcomed him. [4]His father-in-law, the woman's father, begged him to stay. So the Levite remained with him for three days. He ate, drank and slept there.

[5]On the fourth day they got up early. The Levite prepared to leave. But the woman's father said to his son-in-law,

"Have something to eat. It will give you strength. Then you can go on your way." ⁶So the two of them sat down. They ate and drank together. After that, the woman's father said, "Please stay tonight. Enjoy yourself." ⁷The man got up to go. But his father-in-law talked him into staying. So he stayed there that night. ⁸On the morning of the fifth day, the Levite got up to go. But the woman's father said, "Have something to eat. It will give you strength. Wait until this afternoon!" So the two of them ate together.

⁹Then the man got up to leave. His concubine and his servant got up when he did. But his father-in-law, the woman's father, spoke to him again. "Look," he said. "It's almost evening. The day is nearly over. So spend another night here. Please stay. Enjoy yourself. Early tomorrow morning you can get up and go back home." ¹⁰But the man didn't want to stay another night. So he left. He went toward Jebus. Jebus is also called Jerusalem. The Levite had his two donkeys and his concubine with him. The donkeys had saddles on them.

¹¹By the time the travelers came near Jebus, the day was almost over. So the servant said to his master, "Come. Let's stop at this Jebusite city. Let's spend the night here."

¹²His master replied, "No. We won't go into any city where strangers live. The people there aren't Israelites. We'll continue on to Gibeah." ¹³He added, "Come. Let's try to reach Gibeah or Ramah. We can spend the night in one of those places." ¹⁴So they continued on. As they came near Gibeah in Benjamin, the sun went down. ¹⁵They stopped there to spend the night. They went to the city's main street and sat down. But no one took them home for the night.

¹⁶That evening an old man came into the city. He had been working in the fields. He was from the hill country of Ephraim. But he was living in Gibeah. The people who lived there were from the tribe of Benjamin. ¹⁷The old man saw the traveler in the main street. He asked, "Where are you going? Where did you come from?"

¹⁸The Levite answered, "We've come from Bethlehem in Judah. We're on our way to Ephraim. I live deep in the hill country there. I've been to Bethlehem.

Now I'm going to the house of the LORD. But no one has taken me home for the night. ¹⁹We have straw and feed for our donkeys. We have food and wine for ourselves. We have enough for me, the woman and the young man with us. We don't need anything."

²⁰"You are welcome at my house," the old man said. "I'd be happy to supply anything you might need. But don't spend the night in the street." ²¹So the old man took him into his house and fed his donkeys. After the travelers had washed their feet, they had something to eat and drink.

²²They were inside enjoying themselves. But some of the evil men who lived in the city surrounded the house. They pounded on the door. They shouted to the old man who owned the house. They said, "Bring out the man who came to your house. We want to have sex with him."

²³The owner of the house went outside. He said to them, "No, my friends. Don't do such an evil thing. This man is my guest. So don't do this terrible thing. ²⁴Look, here is my virgin daughter. And here's the Levite's concubine. I'll bring them out to you now. You can have them. Do to them what you want to. But don't do such a terrible thing to this man."

²⁵The men wouldn't listen to him. So the Levite sent his concubine out to them. They forced her to have sex with them. They raped her all night long. As the night was ending, they let her go. ²⁶At sunrise she went back to the house where her master was staying. She fell down at the door. She stayed there until daylight.

²⁷Later that morning her master got up. He opened the door of the house. He stepped out to continue on his way. But his concubine was lying there. She had fallen at the doorway of the house. Her hands were reaching out toward the door. ²⁸He said to her, "Get up. Let's go." But there wasn't any answer. Then he put her dead body on his donkey. And he started out for home.

²⁹When he reached home, he got a knife. He cut up his concubine. He cut her into 12 pieces. He sent them into all the territories of Israel. ³⁰Everyone who saw it spoke to one another. They said, "Nothing like this has ever been seen or done before. Nothing like this has happened

since the day the Israelites came up out of Egypt. Just imagine! We must do something! So let's hear your ideas!"

The Israelites Punish the Tribe of Benjamin

20 Then all the Israelites came out. They came from the whole land between Dan and Beersheba. They also came from the land of Gilead. All of them gathered together in front of the LORD at Mizpah. [2]The leaders of all the tribes of Israel came. They took their places among the people of God gathered together. There were 400,000 men carrying swords. [3]The tribe of Benjamin heard that the Israelites had gone up to Mizpah. The Israelites said, "Tell us how this awful thing happened."

[4]So the Levite spoke. He was the husband of the woman who had been murdered. He said, "I and my concubine went to Gibeah in Benjamin. We spent the night there. [5]During the night the men of Gibeah came after me. They surrounded the house. They were planning to kill me. They raped my concubine, and she died. [6]I took my concubine and cut her into pieces. I sent one piece to each part of Israel's territory. I did it because the men of Gibeah had done a very terrible thing in Israel. [7]All you men of Israel, speak up now. Tell me what you have decided to do."

[8]All the men got up together. They said, "None of us will go home. Not one of us will return to his house. [9]Here is what we'll do to Gibeah. We'll cast lots to tell us how to attack the city. [10]We'll take ten men out of every 100 from all the tribes of Israel. We'll take 100 from every 1,000. We'll take 1,000 from every 10,000. The men we take will get supplies for the army. Then the army will go to Gibeah in Benjamin. They'll give Gibeah exactly what they should get because of the terrible thing they did in Israel." [11]So all the men of Israel came together to fight against the city.

[12]The tribes of Israel sent people to carry a message through the whole tribe of Benjamin. They said, "What about this awful crime that was committed among you? [13]Hand over to us those evil men of Gibeah. We'll put them to death. In that way we'll get rid of those evil people."

But the people of Benjamin wouldn't listen to the other Israelites. [14]They came

WOOTON'S FUN FACTS

Judg. 20

This was another civil war among the twelve tribes of Israel. Eleven tribes took up arms against Benjamin. I'm surprised they didn't take up feet.

together at Gibeah from their towns. They came to fight against the other Israelites. [15]Right away the people of Benjamin gathered together 26,000 men from their towns. They were carrying swords. These men were added to the 700 capable young men from Gibeah. [16]Among all these men there were 700 who were left-handed. Each of them could sling a stone at a hair and not miss.

[17]Israel gathered 400,000 men together. They were carrying swords. All of them were trained for battle. That number didn't include the tribe of Benjamin.

[18]The Israelites went up to Bethel. There they asked God, "Who should go up first and fight against the people of Benjamin?"

The LORD answered, "The tribe of Judah will go first."

[19]The next morning the Israelites got up. They set up camp near Gibeah. [20]The Israelites went out to fight against the men of Benjamin. They took up their battle positions against them at Gibeah. [21]The men of Benjamin came out of Gibeah. They killed 22,000 Israelites on the field of battle that day. [22]But the Israelites cheered one another on. They again took up their positions in the places where they had been the first day. [23]The Israelites went

and wept in front of the LORD until evening. They asked the LORD, "Should we go up again to fight against the men of Benjamin? They are our fellow Israelites."

The LORD answered, "Go up and fight against them." [24]The Israelites came near the men of Benjamin on the second day. [25]The men of Benjamin came out from Gibeah to oppose them. That time they killed 18,000 more Israelites. All the men who died had been carrying swords.

[26]Then all the Israelites, the whole army, went up to Bethel. They sat there and wept in front of the LORD. They didn't eat anything that day until evening. Then they brought burnt offerings and friendship offerings to the LORD. [27]Again the Israelites spoke to the LORD. In those days the ark of the covenant of God was there. [28]Phinehas was serving as priest at the ark. He was the son of Eleazar. Eleazar was the son of Aaron. The Israelites asked, "Should we go up again to fight against the men of Benjamin? They are our fellow Israelites."

The LORD answered, "Go. Tomorrow I will hand them over to you."

[29]Then Israel hid some men and had them wait all around Gibeah. [30]They went up to fight against the men of Benjamin on the third day. They took up their positions against Gibeah, just as they had done before. [31]The men of Benjamin came out to fight against them. They were drawn away from the city. They began to wound and kill the Israelites just as they had done before. About 30 men fell in battle. They fell in the open fields and on the roads. One of the roads led to Bethel. The other led to Gibeah. [32]The men of Benjamin said, "We're winning the battle over them, just as we did before." But the men of Israel said, "Let's pull back. Let's draw them away from the city to the roads."

[33]All the men of Israel moved away from their places. They took up new battle positions at Baal Tamar. The men who had been hiding charged out. They came from west of Gibeah. [34]Then 10,000 of Israel's capable young men attacked Gibeah. The men of Benjamin didn't realize they were about to be destroyed. The fighting was very heavy. [35]The LORD helped Israel win the battle over Benjamin. On that

day the Israelites struck down 25,100 men of Benjamin. All the men who died had been carrying swords. [36]Then the men of Benjamin saw that they had lost the battle.

The men of Israel had moved away from their positions in front of Benjamin. They had depended on the men they had hidden near Gibeah. [37]Suddenly those men who had been hiding rushed into Gibeah. They spread out. Then they killed everyone in the city with their swords. [38]The Israelites had made a plan with those who had been hiding. They had told them to send up a large cloud of smoke from the city. [39]Then the Israelites would turn around and attack.

The men of Benjamin had begun to wound and kill the men of Israel. They had struck down about 30 of them. They had said, "We're winning the battle over them, just as we did the first time." [40]But a large cloud of smoke began to go up from the city. The men of Benjamin turned around. They saw the whole city going up in smoke. [41]Then the Israelites turned around and attacked them. The men of Benjamin were terrified. They realized they were going to be destroyed. [42]So they ran away from the men of Israel. They ran toward the desert. But they couldn't escape the battle. Other Israelites came out of the towns. There they struck down the men of Benjamin. [43]Here's how it happened. The Israelites had surrounded them. They had chased them and easily caught up with them east of Gibeah. [44]So 18,000 men of Benjamin fell in battle. All of them were brave fighters. [45]Some men of Benjamin turned back. They ran toward the desert to the rock of Rimmon. As they did, the Israelites struck down 5,000 of them along the roads. They kept chasing the men of Benjamin all the way to Gidom. Along the way they struck down 2,000 more.

[46]On that day 25,000 men of Benjamin fell in battle. They had been carrying swords. All of them were brave fighters. [47]But 600 of them turned back. They ran into the desert to the rock of Rimmon. They stayed there for four months. [48]The men of Israel went back to Benjamin. In all the towns they killed the people with their swords. They even killed the animals. So they killed everything they

found. They set on fire all the towns they came to.

Wives for the Men of Benjamin

21 The men of Israel had made a promise at Mizpah. They had said, "Not one of us will give his daughter to be married to a man from Benjamin."

[2]The people went to Bethel. They sat there until evening in front of God. They wept loudly and bitterly. [3]"LORD, you are the God of Israel," they cried. "Why has this happened to Israel? Why is one tribe missing from Israel today?"

[4]Early the next day the people built an altar. They brought burnt offerings and friendship offerings.

[5]Then the Israelites asked, "Has anyone failed to come here in front of the LORD? Is anyone missing from all the tribes of Israel?" The people had made a promise. They had said that anyone who failed to come to Mizpah in front of the LORD must be put to death.

[6]The Israelites were very sad because of what had happened to the tribe of Benjamin. After all, they were their fellow Israelites. "Today one tribe has been cut off from Israel," they said. [7]"How can we provide wives for the men who are left? We've made a promise in front of the LORD. We've promised not to give any of our daughters to be married to them." [8]Then they asked, "Has any tribe of Israel failed to come here to Mizpah in front of the LORD?" They discovered that no one from Jabesh Gilead had come. No one from there had gathered together with the others in the camp. [9]They counted the people. They found that none of the people of Jabesh Gilead had come to Mizpah.

[10]So the community sent 12,000 fighting men to Jabesh Gilead. They directed them to take their swords and kill those living there. That included the women and children. [11]"Here is what you must do," they said. "Kill every male. Also kill every woman who is not a virgin." [12]They found 400 young women in Jabesh Gilead who had never slept with a man. So they took them to the camp at Shiloh in Canaan.

[13]Then the whole community sent an offer of peace to the men of Benjamin. The men were at the rock of Rimmon.

[14]So the men of Benjamin returned at that time. They were given the women of Jabesh Gilead who had been spared. But there weren't enough women for all of them.

[15]The people were very sad because of what had happened to the tribe of Benjamin. The LORD had left a gap in the tribes of Israel. They weren't complete without Benjamin. [16]The elders of the community spoke up. They said, "All the women of Benjamin have been wiped out. So how will we find wives for the men who are left? [17]The men of Benjamin who are still alive need to have children," they said. "If they don't, a tribe of Israel will be wiped out. [18]But we can't give them our daughters to be their wives. We Israelites have made a promise. We've said, 'May anyone who gives a wife to a man from Benjamin be under the LORD's curse.' [19]Look, a feast is celebrated every year in Shiloh to honor the LORD. Shiloh is north of Bethel. It's east of the road that goes from Bethel to Shechem. It's south of Lebonah."

[20]So they told the men of Benjamin what to do. They said, "Go. Hide in the vineyards [21]and watch. The young women of Shiloh will come out. They'll join in the dancing. When they do, run out of the vineyards. Each of you grab a young woman from Shiloh to be your wife. Then return to the land of Benjamin. [22]Their fathers or brothers might not be happy with what we're doing. If they aren't, we'll say to them, 'Do us a favor. Help the men of Benjamin. We didn't get wives for them during the battle. You aren't guilty of doing anything wrong. After all, you didn't give your daughters to them. Your daughters were stolen from you.'"

[23]So that's what the men of Benjamin did. While the young women were dancing, each man caught one. He carried her away to be his wife. Then the men returned to their own share of land. They built the towns again. They made their homes in them.

[24]At that time the Israelites also left. They went home to their tribes and family groups. Each one went to his own share of land.

[25]In those days Israel didn't have a king. The people did anything they thought was right.

Ruth

Now we arrive at one of two books in the Bible named after women: the book of Ruth. The integrity demonstrated by the main characters of the story—Naomi, Boaz, and Ruth herself—stands in bold contrast to the mentality of the general population of Israel during this period of judges when, in the words of Judges 21:25, everyone essentially did anything they thought was right. This short account has its share of tragedy, to be sure, but it is a prime example of how God is always with us during our difficulties and sufferings . . . and even brings good from them by providing amazing blessings we never would have otherwise experienced.

All of us can learn from Naomi. Her name meant "pleasant," but after she lost her husband and two sons she wanted to be called *Mara*, which means "bitter." Yet by the end of this story, she is thrilled to be called, indeed, Grandma! God gave her new hope and vitality. As for Ruth, through her marriage to Boaz she will become the great-grandmother of one of the Old Testament's most heroic figures: King David—not to mention the great grandmother of Jesus. According to Luke's genealogy she was His forty-third great grandmother.

But let's not get ahead of ourselves and keep our attention on the book of Ruth.

WHat's it MEaN, EUGENE?

Creed—A creed is a summary statement of Christian beliefs. In fact, the word *creed* comes from the Latin *credo*, which means, "I believe." The *Apostles' Creed*, which begins, "I believe in God the Father Almighty, Maker of heaven and earth," is arguably the most well-known of the creeds passed down to us from the early church. If you wish to study the essentials of the faith, the creeds are a most advantageous place to start!

Naomi Loses Her Husband and Sons

1 There was a time when Israel didn't have kings to rule over them. But they had leaders to help them. This is a story about some things that happened during that time. There wasn't enough food in the land of Judah. So a man went to live for a while in the country of Moab. He was from Bethlehem in Judah. His wife and two sons went with him. ²The man's name was Elimelek. His wife's name was Naomi. The names of his two sons were Mahlon and Kilion. They were from the tribe of Ephraim. Their home had been in Bethlehem in Judah. They went to Moab and lived there.

³Naomi's husband Elimelek died. So she was left with her two sons. ⁴They married women from Moab. One was named Orpah. The other was named Ruth. Naomi's family lived in Moab for about ten years. ⁵Then Mahlon and Kilion also died. So Naomi was left without her two sons and her husband.

Naomi and Ruth Return to Bethlehem

⁶While Naomi was in Moab, she heard that the LORD had helped his people. He had begun to provide food for them again. So Naomi and her two daughters-in-law prepared to go from Moab back to her home. ⁷She left the place where she had been living. Her daughters-in-law went with her. They started out on the road that would take them back to the land of Judah.

⁸Naomi said to her two daughters-in-law, "Both of you go back. Each of you go to your own mother's home. You were kind to your husbands, who have died. You have also been kind to me. So may the LORD be just as kind to you. ⁹May the LORD help each of you find rest in the home of another husband."

Then she kissed them goodbye. They broke down and wept loudly. ¹⁰They said to her, "We'll go back to your people with you."

¹¹But Naomi said, "Go home, my daughters. Why would you want to come with me? Am I going to have any more sons who could become your husbands? ¹²Go home, my daughters. I'm too old to have another husband. Suppose I thought there was still some hope for me. Suppose I

CANDID CONVERSATIONS

Family must have been really important to Ruth! She pledged her devotion to her mother-in-law, Naomi, even though Naomi told her to go without her. After both of their husbands died, Ruth could've gone back to her own country, but she chose to remain loyal to the only family she had left.

It was one of the saddest days of my life when my parents got divorced, because it felt like I had lost my family. But one of the first things Whit said to me after I became a Christian was "Welcome to the family of God." I hadn't really thought about it, but that was really great! Being a part of the family of God made me realize that I could lean on my Christian brothers and sisters—and they could lean on me.

Call a fellow Christian today and tell that person you're praying for him or her, and ask for prayer in return. And then, don't forget to pray! Like Ruth, you're showing your devotion to the other person—and to God!

married a man tonight. And later I had sons by him. ¹³Would you wait until they grew up? Would you stay single until you could marry them? No, my daughters. My life is more bitter than yours. The LORD's power has turned against me!"

¹⁴When they heard that, they broke down and wept again. Then Orpah kissed her mother-in-law goodbye. But Ruth held on to her.

¹⁵"Look," said Naomi. "Your sister-in-law is going back to her people and her gods. Go back with her."

¹⁶But Ruth replied, "Don't try to make me leave you and go back. Where you go I'll go. Where you stay I'll stay. Your people will be my people. Your God will

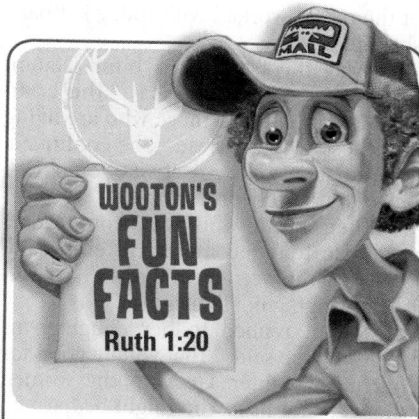

WOOTON'S FUN FACTS
Ruth 1:20

Naomi means "pleasantness." *Mara*, meaning "bitter," is a much better fit for her at this time.

be my God. ¹⁷Where you die I'll die. And there my body will be buried. I won't let even death separate you from me. If I do, may the LORD punish me greatly." ¹⁸Naomi realized that Ruth had made up her mind to go with her. So she stopped trying to make her go back.

¹⁹The two women continued on their way. At last they arrived in Bethlehem. The whole town was stirred up because of them. The women in the town asked, "Can this possibly be Naomi?"

²⁰"Don't call me Naomi," she told them. "Call me Mara. The Mighty One has made my life very bitter. ²¹I was full when I went away. But the LORD has brought me back empty. So why are you calling me Naomi? The LORD has made me suffer. The Mighty One has brought trouble on me."

²²So Naomi returned from Moab. Ruth, her daughter-in-law from Moab, came with her. They arrived in Bethlehem just when people were beginning to harvest the barley.

Ruth Meets Boaz in the Grain Field

2 Naomi had a relative on her husband's side of the family. The relative's name was Boaz. He was a very important man from the family of Elimelek.

²Ruth, who was from Moab, spoke to Naomi. Ruth said, "Let me go out to the fields. I'll pick up the grain that has been left. I'll do it behind anyone who is pleased with me."

Naomi said to her, "My daughter, go ahead." ³So Ruth went out to a field and began to pick up grain. She worked behind those cutting and gathering the grain. As it turned out, she was working in a field that belonged to Boaz. He was from the family of Elimelek.

⁴Just then Boaz arrived from Bethlehem. He greeted those cutting and gathering the grain. He said, "May the LORD be with you!"

"And may the LORD bless you!" they replied.

⁵Boaz spoke to the man in charge of his workers. He asked, "Who does that young woman belong to?"

⁶The man replied, "She's from Moab. She came back from there with Naomi. ⁷The young woman said, 'Please let me walk behind the workers. Let me pick up the grain that is left.' She came into the field. She has kept on working here from morning until now. She took only one short rest in the shade."

⁸So Boaz said to Ruth, "Dear woman, listen to me. Don't pick up grain in any other field. Don't go anywhere else. Stay here with the women who work for me. ⁹Keep your eye on the field where the men are cutting grain. Walk behind the women who are gathering it. Pick up the grain that is left. I've told the men not to bother you. When you are thirsty, go and get a drink. Take water from the jars the men have filled."

¹⁰When Ruth heard that, she bowed down with her face to the ground. She asked him, "Why are you being so kind to me? In fact, why are you even noticing me? I'm from another country."

¹¹Boaz replied, "I've been told all about you. I've heard about everything you have done for your mother-in-law since your husband died. I know that you left your father and mother. I know that you left your country. You came to live with people you didn't know before. ¹²May the LORD reward you for what you have done. May the LORD, the God of Israel, bless you

BIBLE ADVENTURES

Connie told Courtney and Jenny the story of Ruth in "Three Funerals and a Wedding" (A#28).

Ruth 2:11 Spoiler alert! Boaz and Ruth get married. See how Boaz was different from Samson (Judges 16)? Boaz picked a girl with good character, and things go much better for him.

richly. You have come to him to find safety under his care."

¹³"Sir, I hope you will continue to be kind to me," Ruth said. "You have made me feel safe. You have spoken kindly to me. And I'm not even as important as one of your servants!"

¹⁴When it was time to eat, Boaz spoke to Ruth again. "Come over here," he said. "Have some bread. Dip it in the wine vinegar."

She sat down with the workers. Then Boaz offered her some grain that had been cooked. She ate all she wanted. She even had some left over. ¹⁵Ruth got up to pick up more grain. Then Boaz gave orders to his men. He said, "Let her take some stalks from what the women have tied up. Don't tell her she can't. ¹⁶Even pull out some stalks for her. Leave them for her to pick up. Don't tell her she shouldn't do it."

¹⁷So Ruth picked up grain in the field until evening. Then she separated the barley from the straw. The barley weighed 30 pounds. ¹⁸She carried it back to town. Her mother-in-law saw how much she had gathered. Ruth also brought out the food left over from the lunch Boaz had given her. She gave it to Naomi.

¹⁹Her mother-in-law asked her, "Where did you pick up grain today? Where did you work? May the man who noticed you be blessed!"

Then Ruth told her about the man whose field she had worked in. "The name of the man I worked with today is Boaz," she said.

²⁰"May the LORD bless him!" Naomi said to her daughter-in-law. "The LORD is still being kind to those who are living and those who are dead." She continued, "That man is a close relative of ours. He's one of our family protectors."

²¹Then Ruth, who was from Moab, said, "He told me more. He even said, 'Stay with my workers until they have finished bringing in all my grain.'"

²²Naomi replied to her daughter-in-law Ruth. She said, "That will be good for you, my daughter. Go with the women who work for him. You might be harmed if you go to someone else's field."

²³So Ruth stayed close to the women who worked for Boaz as she picked up grain. She worked until the time when all the barley and wheat had been harvested. And she lived with her mother-in-law.

Ruth and Boaz at the Threshing Floor

3 One day Ruth's mother-in-law Naomi spoke to her. She said, "My daughter, I must find a home for you. It should be a place where you will be provided for. ²You have been working with the women who work for Boaz. He's a relative of ours. Tonight he'll be separating the straw from

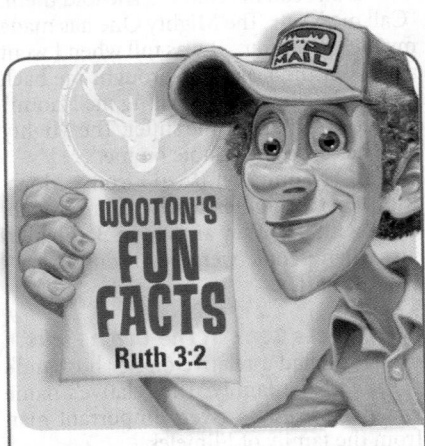

If oxen didn't thresh grain (see Deuteronomy 25:4), then a person had to do it by hand using a tool called a flail. A threshing flail is a long pole with a shorter stick at the end used to beat the grains. Never use them on people.

his barley on the threshing floor. ³So wash yourself. Put on some perfume. And put on your best clothes. Then go down to the threshing floor. But don't let Boaz know you are there. Wait until he has finished eating and drinking. ⁴Notice where he lies down. Then go over and uncover his feet. Lie down there. He'll tell you what to do."

⁵"I'll do everything you say," Ruth answered. ⁶So she went down to the threshing floor. She did everything her mother-in-law had told her to do.

⁷When Boaz had finished eating and drinking, he was in a good mood. He went over to lie down at the far end of the grain pile. Then Ruth approached quietly. She uncovered his feet and lay down there. ⁸In the middle of the night, something surprised Boaz and woke him up. He turned and found a woman lying there at his feet!

⁹"Who are you?" he asked.

"I'm Ruth," she said. "You are my family protector. So take good care of me by making me your wife."

¹⁰"Dear woman, may the LORD bless you," he replied. "You are showing even more kindness now than you did earlier. You didn't run after the younger men, whether they were rich or poor. ¹¹Dear woman, don't be afraid. I'll do for you everything you ask. All the people of my town know that you are an excellent woman. ¹²It's true that I'm a relative of yours. But there's a family protector who is more closely related to you than I am. ¹³So stay here for the night. In the morning if he wants to help you, good. Let him help you. But if he doesn't want to, then I'll do it. You can be sure that the LORD lives. And you can be just as sure that I'll help you. Lie down here until morning."

¹⁴So she stayed at his feet until morning. But she got up before anyone could be recognized. Boaz thought, "No one must know that a woman came to the threshing floor."

¹⁵He said to Ruth, "Bring me the coat you have around you. Hold it out." So she did. He poured more than fifty pounds of barley into it and helped her pick it up. Then he went back to town.

¹⁶Ruth came to her mother-in-law. Naomi asked, "How did it go, my daughter?"

Then Ruth told her everything Boaz had done for her. ¹⁷She said, "He gave me all this barley. He said, 'Don't go back to your mother-in-law with your hands empty.'"

Jason's Jargon

RUTH 3

Ready for your next hunt? Great! Find *threshing floor* in this chapter. Grain was separated from straw on the threshing floor. Often cows and oxen would stomp on the straw to thresh it.

¹⁸Naomi said, "My daughter, sit down until you find out what happens. The man won't rest until he settles the whole matter today."

Boaz Marries Ruth

4 Boaz went up to the town gate and sat down there. Right then, the family protector he had talked about came by. Then Boaz said, "Come over here, my friend. Sit down." So the man went over and sat down.

²Boaz brought ten of the elders of the town together. He said, "Sit down here." So they did. ³Then he spoke to the family protector. He said, "Naomi has come back from Moab. She's selling the piece of land that belonged to our relative Elimelek. ⁴I thought I should bring the matter to your attention. I suggest that you buy the land. Buy it while those sitting here and the elders of my people are looking on as witnesses. If you are willing to buy it back, do it. But if you aren't, tell me. Then I'll know. No one has the right to buy it back except you. And I'm next in line."

"I'll buy it," he said.

⁵Then Boaz said, "When you buy the property from Naomi, you must also marry Ruth. She is from Moab and is the dead man's widow. So you must marry her. That's because his property must continue to belong to his family."

⁶When the family protector heard that, he said, "Then I can't buy the land. If I did,

I might put my own property in danger. So you buy it. I can't do it."

⁷In earlier times in Israel, there was a certain practice. It was used when family land was bought back and changed owners. The practice made the sale final. One person would take his sandal off and give it to the other. That was how people in Israel showed that a business matter had been settled.

⁸So the family protector said to Boaz, "Buy it yourself." And he took his sandal off.

⁹Then Boaz said to the elders and all the people, "Today you are witnesses. You have seen that I have bought land from Naomi. I have bought all the property that had belonged to Elimelek, Kilion and Mahlon. ¹⁰I've also taken Ruth, who is from Moab, to become my wife. She is Mahlon's widow. I've decided to marry her so the dead man's name will stay with his property. Now his name won't disappear from his family line or from his hometown. Today you are witnesses!"

¹¹Then the elders and all the people at the gate said, "We are witnesses. The woman is coming into your home. May the LORD make her like Rachel and Leah. Together they built up the family of Israel. May you be an important person in Ephrathah. May you be famous in Bethlehem. ¹²The LORD will give you children through this young woman. May your family be like the family of Perez. He was the son Tamar had by Judah."

Naomi Gains a Son

¹³So Boaz married Ruth. Then he slept with her. The LORD blessed her so that she became pregnant. And she had a son. ¹⁴The women said to Naomi, "We praise the LORD. Today he has provided a family protector for you. May this child become famous all over Israel! ¹⁵He will make your life new again. He'll take care of you when you are old. He's the son of your very own daughter-in-law. She loves you. She is better to you than seven sons."

¹⁶Then Naomi took the child in her arms and took care of him. ¹⁷The women living there said, "Naomi has a son!" They named him Obed. He was the father of Jesse. Jesse was the father of David.

¹⁸ Here is the family line of Perez.

Perez was the father of Hezron.
¹⁹ Hezron was the father of Ram.
Ram was the father of Amminadab.
²⁰ Amminadab was the father of Nahshon.
Nahshon was the father of Salmon.
²¹ Salmon was the father of Boaz.
Boaz was the father of Obed.
²² Obed was the father of Jesse.
And Jesse was the father of David.

1 Samuel

As we begin the first of two books named after Samuel, the nation of Israel finds itself at a crossroads. The judges of Israel had been "a mixed lot" as leaders. Indeed, God used them to repel Israel's powerful enemies, yet many of them could have used some education on self-esteem, anger management, and other basic life skills. As a result, the people started clamoring for a king. Although they were in the unique position of having God as their king, they wanted to be just like everybody else. (Does such an idea sound familiar?)

God granted their request, along with severe warnings of what they could expect from a human king (chapter 8). And before making that major shift in leadership, God prepared Samuel and called him to provide stability and direction for the nation during the transition. Samuel served God faithfully from childhood throughout his life and was involved with the coronation of both Saul and David—Israel's first two kings.

It isn't common knowledge that the books of 1 Samuel and 2 Samuel are actually parts one and two of what was originally a single lengthy book. First Samuel ends with the death of Saul, and 2 Samuel picks up immediately with David's rise to the throne. Let us begin with Part 1.

WHAT'S IT MEAN, EUGENE?

Anointing—Literally, "Putting oil on someone's head." Not as a prank, mind you. Pouring oil on someone's head has several distinct spiritual purposes. In the Old Testament, oil was a symbol of God's authority. King David was *anointed* as a sign that God had chosen him to rule over His people (1 Samuel 16:13). The New Testament uses the word "anointing" to speak of God's gift of the *Holy Spirit* to all believers (2 Corinthians 1:21–22).

Samuel Is Born

1 A certain man from Ramathaim in the hill country of Ephraim was named Elkanah. He was the son of Jeroham. Jeroham was the son of Elihu. Elihu was the son of Tohu. Tohu was the son of Zuph. Elkanah belonged to the family line of Zuph. Elkanah lived in the territory of Ephraim. ²Elkanah had two wives. One was named Hannah. The other was named Peninnah. Peninnah had children, but Hannah didn't.

³Year after year Elkanah went up from his town to Shiloh. He went there to worship and sacrifice to the LORD who rules over all. Hophni and Phinehas served as priests of the LORD at Shiloh. They were the two sons of Eli. ⁴Every year at Shiloh, the day would come for Elkanah to offer a sacrifice. On that day, he would give a share of the meat to his wife Peninnah. He would also give a share to each of her sons and daughters. ⁵But he would give two shares of meat to Hannah. That's because he loved her. He also gave her two shares because the LORD had kept her from having children. ⁶Peninnah teased Hannah to make her angry. She did it because the LORD had kept Hannah from having children. ⁷Peninnah teased Hannah year after year. Every time Hannah would go up to the house of the LORD, Elkanah's other wife would tease her. She would keep doing it until Hannah cried and wouldn't eat. ⁸Her husband Elkanah would say to her, "Hannah, why are you crying? Why don't you eat? Why are you so unhappy? Don't I mean more to you than ten sons?"

⁹One time when they had finished eating and drinking in Shiloh, Hannah stood up. Eli the priest was sitting on his chair by the doorpost of the LORD's house. ¹⁰Hannah was very sad. She wept and wept. She prayed to the LORD. ¹¹She made a promise to him. She said, "LORD, you rule over all. Please see how I'm suffering! Show concern for me! Don't forget about me! Please give me a son! If you do, I'll give him back to the LORD. Then he will serve the LORD all the days of his life. He'll never use a razor on his head. He'll never cut his hair."

¹²As Hannah kept on praying to the LORD, Eli watched her lips. ¹³She was praying in her heart. Her lips were moving. But she wasn't making a sound. Eli thought Hannah was drunk. ¹⁴He said to her, "How long are you going to stay drunk? Stop drinking your wine."

¹⁵"That's not true, sir," Hannah replied. "I'm a woman who is deeply troubled. I haven't been drinking wine or beer. I was telling the LORD all my troubles. ¹⁶Don't think of me as an evil woman. I've been praying here because I'm very sad. My pain is so great."

¹⁷Eli answered, "Go in peace. May the God of Israel give you what you have asked him for."

¹⁸She said, "May you be pleased with me." Then she left and had something to eat. Her face wasn't sad anymore.

¹⁹Early the next morning Elkanah and his family got up. They worshiped the LORD. Then they went back to their home in Ramah. Elkanah slept with his wife Hannah. And the LORD blessed her. ²⁰So after some time, Hannah became pregnant. She had a baby boy. She said, "I asked the LORD for him." So she named him Samuel.

Hannah Gives Samuel to the LORD

²¹Elkanah went up to Shiloh to offer the yearly sacrifice to the LORD. He also went there to keep a promise he had made. His whole family went with him. ²²But Hannah didn't go. She said to her husband, "When the boy doesn't need me to breast-feed him anymore, I'll take him to the LORD's house. I'll give him to the LORD there. He'll stay there for the rest of his life."

²³Her husband Elkanah told her, "Do what you think is best. Stay here at home until Samuel doesn't need you to breast-feed him anymore. May the LORD make his promise to you come true." So Hannah stayed home. She breast-fed her son until he didn't need her milk anymore.

²⁴When the boy didn't need her to breast-feed him anymore, she took him

with her to Shiloh. She took him there even though he was still very young. She brought him to the LORD's house. She brought along a bull that was three years old. She brought 36 pounds of flour. She also brought a bottle of wine. The bottle was made out of animal skin. ²⁵After the bull was sacrificed, Elkanah and Hannah brought the boy to Eli. ²⁶Hannah said to Eli, "Pardon me, sir. I'm the woman who stood here beside you praying to the LORD. And that's just as sure as you are alive. ²⁷I prayed for this child. The LORD has given me what I asked him for. ²⁸So now I'm giving him to the LORD. As long as he lives he'll be given to the LORD." And there Eli worshiped the LORD.

Hannah's Prayer

2 Then Hannah prayed. She said,

"The LORD has filled my heart with
   joy.
He has made me strong.
I can laugh at my enemies.
I'm so glad he saved me.

² "There isn't anyone holy like the LORD.
There isn't anyone except him.
There isn't any Rock like our God.

³ "Don't keep talking so proudly.
Don't let your mouth say such
   proud things.
The LORD is a God who knows
   everything.
He judges everything people do.

⁴ "The bows of great heroes are broken.
But those who trip and fall are
   made strong.

⁵ Those who used to be full have to
   work for food.
But those who used to be hungry
   aren't hungry anymore.
The woman who couldn't have
   children has seven of them
   now.
But the woman who has had many
   children is sad now because
   hers have died.

⁶ "The LORD causes people to die. He
   also gives people life.
He brings people down to the
   grave. He also brings people
   up from death.

⁷ The LORD makes people poor. He also
   makes people rich.
He brings people down. He also
   lifts people up.

⁸ He raises poor people up from the
   trash pile.
He lifts needy people out of the
   ashes.
He lets them sit with princes.
He gives them places of honor.

"The foundations of the earth belong
   to the LORD.
On them he has set the world.

⁹ He guards the paths of his faithful
   servants.
But evil people will lie silent in
   their dark graves.

"People don't win just because they are
   strong.

¹⁰ Those who oppose the LORD will be
   totally destroyed.
The Most High God will thunder from
   heaven.
The LORD will judge the earth from
   one end to the other.

"He will give power to his king.
He will give honor to his anointed
   one."

¹¹Then Elkanah went home to Ramah. But the boy Samuel served the LORD under the direction of Eli the priest.

Eli's Evil Sons

¹²Eli's sons were good for nothing. They didn't honor the LORD. ¹³When any of the people came to offer a sacrifice, here is what the priests would do. While the meat was being boiled, the servant of the priest would come with a large fork in his hand. ¹⁴He would stick the fork into the pan or pot or small or large kettle. Then the priest would take for himself everything the fork brought up. That's how Eli's sons treated all the Israelites who came to Shiloh. ¹⁵Even before the fat was burned, the priest's servant would come over. He would speak to the person who was offering the sacrifice. He would say, "Give the priest some meat to cook. He won't accept boiled meat from you. He'll only accept raw meat."

¹⁶Sometimes the person would say to him, "Let the fat be burned first. Then take

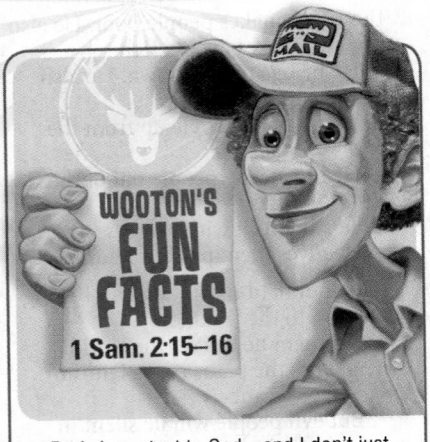

WOOTON'S FUN FACTS
1 Sam. 2:15–16

Fat is important to God—and I don't just mean how good bacon tastes and smells. The sons of Eli were taking the meat with the fat for themselves, but the fat was supposed to be offered to God. (See also Genesis 4:4 and Leviticus 1:8.)

what you want." But the servant would answer, "No. Hand it over right now. If you don't, I'll take it away from you by force."

¹⁷That sin of Eli's sons was very great in the LORD's sight. That's because they were not treating his offering with respect.

¹⁸But the boy Samuel served the LORD. He wore a sacred linen apron. ¹⁹Each year his mother made him a little robe. She took it to him when she went up to Shiloh with her husband. She did it when her husband went to offer the yearly sacrifice. ²⁰Eli would bless Elkanah and his wife. He would say, "May the LORD give you children by this woman. May they take the place of the boy she prayed for and gave to the LORD." Then they would go home. ²¹The LORD was gracious to Hannah. Over a period of years she had three more sons and two daughters. During that whole time the boy Samuel grew up serving the LORD.

²²Eli was very old. He kept hearing about everything his sons were doing to all the Israelites. He also heard how his sons were sleeping with the women who served at the entrance to the tent of meeting. ²³So Eli said to his sons, "Why are you doing these things? All the people are telling me about the evil things you are doing. ²⁴No, my sons. The report I hear isn't good. And it's spreading among the LORD's people. ²⁵If a person sins against someone else, God can help that sinner. But if anyone sins against the LORD, who can help them?" In spite of what their father Eli said, his sons didn't pay any attention to his warning. That's because the LORD had already decided to put them to death.

²⁶The boy Samuel continued to grow stronger. He also became more and more pleasing to the LORD and to people.

Prophecy Against Eli's Family

²⁷A man of God came to Eli. He told him, "The LORD says, 'I made myself clearly known to your relatives who lived long ago. I did it when they were in Egypt under Pharaoh's rule. ²⁸At that time, I chose Aaron from your family line to be my priest. I chose him out of all the tribes of Israel. I told him to go up to my altar. I told him to burn incense. I chose him to wear a linen apron when he served me. I also gave his family all the food offerings presented by the Israelites. ²⁹Why don't you treat my sacrifices and offerings with respect? I require them to be brought to the house where I live. Why do you honor your sons more than me? Why do you fatten yourselves on the best parts of every offering that is made by my people Israel?'

³⁰"The LORD is the God of Israel. He announced, 'I promised that members of your family line would serve me as priests forever.' But now the LORD announces, 'I will not let that happen! I will honor those who honor me. But I will turn away from those who look down on me. ³¹The time is coming when I will cut your life short. I will also cut short the lives of those in your family line of priests. No one in your family line will grow old. ³²You will see nothing but trouble in the house where I live. Good things will still happen to Israel. But no one in your family line will ever grow old. ³³I will prevent the members of your family from serving me at my altar. I will destroy the eyesight of all of you I allow to live. I will also cause you to lose your strength. And everyone in your family line will die while they are still young.

³⁴"'Something is going to happen to your two sons, Hophni and Phinehas. When it does, it will show you that what I am saying is true. They will both die on the same day. ³⁵I will raise up for myself a faithful priest. He will do what my heart

and mind want him to do. I will make his family line of priests very secure. They will always serve as priests to my anointed king. [36]Everyone left in your family line will come and bow down to him. They will beg him for a piece of silver and a loaf of bread. They will say, "Please give me a place to serve among the priests. Then I can have food to eat." ' "

The Lord Calls Out to Samuel

The boy Samuel served the Lord under the direction of Eli. In those days the Lord didn't give many messages to his people. He didn't give them many visions. [2]One night Eli was lying down in his usual place. His eyes were becoming so weak he couldn't see very well. [3]Samuel was lying down in the Lord's house. That's where the ark of God was kept. The lamp of God was still burning. [4]The Lord called out to Samuel.

Samuel answered, "Here I am." [5]He ran over to Eli and said, "Here I am. You called out to me."

But Eli said, "I didn't call you. Go back and lie down." So he went and lay down.

[6]Again the Lord called out, "Samuel!" Samuel got up and went to Eli. He said, "Here I am. You called out to me."

"My son," Eli said, "I didn't call you. Go back and lie down."

[7]Samuel didn't know the Lord yet. That's because the Lord still hadn't given him a message.

[8]The Lord called out for the third time. He said, "Samuel!" Samuel got up and went to Eli. He said, "Here I am. You called out to me."

Then Eli realized that the Lord was calling the boy. [9]So Eli told Samuel, "Go and lie down. If someone calls out to you again, say, 'Speak, Lord. I'm listening.'" So Samuel went and lay down in his place.

[10]The Lord came and stood there. He called out, just as he had done the other times. He said, "Samuel! Samuel!"

Then Samuel replied, "Speak. I'm listening."

[11]The Lord said to Samuel, "Pay attention! I am about to do something terrible in Israel. It will make the ears of everyone who hears about it tingle. [12]At that time I will do everything to Eli and his family that I said I would. I will finish what I have started. [13]I told Eli I would punish his family forever. He knew his sons were sinning. He knew they were saying bad things about me. In spite of that, he did not stop them. [14]So I made a promise to the family of Eli. I said, 'The sins of Eli's family will never be paid for by bringing sacrifices or offerings.' "

[15]Samuel lay down until morning. Then he opened the doors of the Lord's house. He was afraid to tell Eli about the vision he had received. [16]But Eli called out to him. He said, "Samuel, my son."

Samuel answered, "Here I am."

[17]"What did the Lord say to you?" Eli asked. "Don't hide from me anything he told you. If you do, may God punish you greatly." [18]So Samuel told him everything. He didn't hide anything from him. Then Eli said, "He is the Lord. Let him do what he thinks is best."

[19]As Samuel grew up, the Lord was with him. He made everything Samuel said come true. [20]So all the Israelites recognized that Samuel really was a prophet of the Lord. Everyone from Dan all the way to Beersheba knew it. [21]The Lord continued to appear at Shiloh. There he made himself known to Samuel through the messages he gave him.

And Samuel gave those messages to all the Israelites.

The Philistines Capture the Ark

The Israelites went out to fight against the Philistines. The Israelites camped at Ebenezer. The Philistines camped at Aphek. [2]The Philistines brought their forces together to fight against Israel. As the fighting spread, the Israelites lost the battle to the Philistines. The Philistines killed about 4,000 of them on the field of battle. [3]The rest of the Israelite soldiers returned to camp. Then the elders asked them, "Why did the Lord let the Philistines win the battle over us today? Let's bring the ark of the Lord's covenant from Shiloh. Let's take it with us. Then the Lord will save us from the power of our enemies."

[4]So the people sent men to Shiloh. They brought back the ark of the Lord's covenant law. He sits there on his throne between the cherubim. The Lord is the one who rules over all. Eli's two sons, Hophni

WOOTON'S FUN FACTS

1 Sam. 4:1 Aphek uses the letters *ph* to fill in for the letter *f*, sorta like phone or graph or peephole. (Okay, maybe not that last one.) Most Hebrew names in the Bible follow that pattern. Phancy that.

and Phinehas, were with the ark of God's covenant law. The ark was in Shiloh.

⁵The ark of the LORD's covenant law was brought into the camp. Then all the Israelites shouted so loudly that the ground shook. ⁶The Philistines heard the noise. They asked, "What's all that shouting about in the Hebrew camp?"

Then the Philistines found out that the ark of the LORD had come into the camp. ⁷So they were afraid. "A god has come into their camp," they said. "Oh no! Nothing like this has ever happened before. ⁸How terrible it will be for us! Who will save us from the power of these mighty gods? They struck down the people of Egypt in the desert. They sent all kinds of plagues on them. ⁹Philistines, be strong! Fight like men! If you don't, you will come under the control of the Hebrews. You will become their slaves, just as they have been your slaves. Fight like men!"

¹⁰So the Philistines fought. The Israelites lost the battle, and every man ran back to his tent. A large number of them were killed. Israel lost 30,000 soldiers who were on foot. ¹¹The ark of God was captured. And Eli's two sons Hophni and Phinehas died.

Eli Dies

¹²That same day a man from the tribe of Benjamin ran from the front lines of the battle. He went to Shiloh. His clothes were torn. He had dust on his head. ¹³When he arrived, there was Eli sitting on his chair. He was by the side of the road. He was watching because his heart was really concerned about the ark of God. The man entered the town and told everyone what had happened. Then the whole town cried out.

¹⁴Eli heard the people crying out. He asked, "What's the meaning of all this noise?"

The man hurried over to Eli. ¹⁵Eli was 98 years old. His eyes were so bad he couldn't see. ¹⁶The man told Eli, "I've just come from the front lines of the battle. I just ran away from there today."

Eli asked, "What happened, son?"

¹⁷The man who brought the news replied, "Israel ran away from the Philistines. Large numbers of men in the army were wounded or killed. Your two sons Hophni and Phinehas are also dead. And the ark of God has been captured."

¹⁸When the man spoke about the ark of God, Eli fell backward off his chair. He had been sitting by the side of the gate. When he fell, he broke his neck and died. He was old and fat. He had led Israel for 40 years.

¹⁹The wife of Phinehas was pregnant. She was Eli's daughter-in-law. It was near the time for her baby to be born. She heard the news that the ark of God had been captured. She heard that her father-in-law and her husband were dead. So she went into labor and had her baby. Her pain was more than she could bear. ²⁰As she was dying, the women helping her spoke up. They said, "Don't be afraid. You have had a son." But she didn't reply. She didn't pay any attention.

²¹She named the boy Ichabod. She said, "The God of glory has left Israel." She said it because the ark of God had been captured. She also said it because her father-in-law and her husband had died. ²²She said, "The God of glory has left Israel." She said it because the ark of God had been captured.

The Ark in Ashdod and Ekron

5 The Philistines had captured the ark of God. They took it from Ebenezer to Ashdod. ²They carried the ark into the temple of their god Dagon. They set it down beside the statue of Dagon. ³The people of Ashdod got up early the next day. They saw the statue of Dagon. There it was, lying on the ground! It had fallen on its face in front of the ark of the LORD. So they picked up the statue of Dagon. They put it back in its place. ⁴But the following morning when they got up, they saw the statue of Dagon. There it was, lying on the ground again! It had fallen on its face in front of the ark of the LORD. Its head and hands had been broken off. Only the body of the statue was left. Its head and hands were lying in the doorway of the temple. ⁵That's why to this day no one steps on the bottom part of the doorway of Dagon's temple at Ashdod. Not even the priests of Dagon step there.

⁶The LORD's power was against the people of Ashdod and the settlements near it. He destroyed them. He made them suffer with growths in their bodies. ⁷The people of Ashdod saw what was happening. They said, "The ark of the god of Israel must not stay here with us. His power is against us and against our god Dagon." ⁸So they called together all the rulers of the Philistines. They asked them, "What should we do with the ark of the god of Israel?"

The rulers answered, "Have the ark moved to Gath." So they moved it.

⁹But after the people of Ashdod had moved the ark, the LORD's power was against Gath. That threw its people into a great panic. The LORD made them break out with growths in their bodies. It happened to young people and old people alike. ¹⁰So the ark of God was sent to Ekron.

As the ark was entering Ekron, the people of the city cried out. They shouted, "They've brought the ark of the god of Israel to us. They want to kill us and our people." ¹¹So they called together all the rulers of the Philistines. They said, "Send the ark of the god of Israel away. Let it go back to its own place. If you don't, it will kill us and our people." The death of so many people had filled the city with panic. God's power was against the city. ¹²Those who didn't die suffered with growths in their bodies. The people of Ekron cried out to heaven for help.

The Philistines Return the Ark to Israel

6 The ark of the LORD had been in Philistine territory for seven months. ²The Philistines called for the priests and for those who practice evil magic. They wanted their advice. They said to them, "What should we do with the ark of the LORD? Tell us how we should send it back to its place."

³They answered, "If you return the ark of the god of Israel, don't send it back to him without a gift. Be sure you send a guilt offering to their god along with it. Then you will be healed. You will find out why his power has continued to be against you."

⁴The Philistines asked, "What guilt offering should we send to him?"

Their advisers replied, "There are five Philistine rulers. So send five gold rats. Also send five gold models of the growths in your bodies. Do it because the same plague has struck you and your rulers alike. ⁵Make models of the rats and the growths that are destroying the country. Give honor to Israel's god. Then perhaps his power will no longer be against you, your gods and your land. ⁶Why are you stubborn, as Pharaoh and the people of Egypt were? Israel's god was very hard on them. Only then did they send the Israelites out. Only then did they let them go on their way.

⁷"Now then, get a new cart ready. Get two cows that have just had calves. Be sure the cows have never pulled a cart before. Tie the cart to them. But take their calves away and put them in a pen. ⁸Then put the ark of the LORD on the cart. Put the gold models in a chest beside the ark. Send them back to the LORD as a guilt offering. Send the cart on its way. ⁹But keep an eye on the cart. See if it goes up toward Beth Shemesh to its own territory. If it does, then it's the LORD who has brought this horrible trouble on us. But if it doesn't, then we'll know it wasn't his hand that struck us. We'll know it happened to us by chance."

¹⁰So that's what they did. They took the two cows and tied the cart to them. They put the calves in a pen. ¹¹They placed the ark of the LORD on the cart. They put the chest there along with it. The chest held the gold models of the rats and of the growths. ¹²Then the cows went straight up toward Beth Shemesh. They stayed on the road. They were mooing all the way. They didn't turn to the right or the left. The Philistine rulers followed them all the way to the border of Beth Shemesh.

¹³The people of Beth Shemesh were working in the valley. They were gathering their wheat crop. They looked up and saw the ark. When they saw it, they were filled with joy. ¹⁴The cart came to the field of Joshua of Beth Shemesh. It stopped there beside a large rock. The people chopped up the wood the cart was made out of. They sacrificed the cows as a burnt offering to the LORD. ¹⁵Some Levites had taken the ark of the LORD off the cart. They had also taken off the chest that held the gold models. They placed them on the large rock. On that day the people of Beth Shemesh offered burnt offerings to the LORD. They also made sacrifices to him. ¹⁶The five Philistine rulers saw everything that happened. On that same day they returned to Ekron.

Jason's Jargon

1 SAMUEL 6

Your top-secret expedition through the Bible goes on! Search this chapter for the word *magic*. Many ancient religions practiced evil magic, and often magicians gave advice to rulers.

¹⁷The Philistines sent gold models of growths as a guilt offering to the LORD. There was one each for Ashdod, Gaza, Ashkelon, Gath and Ekron. ¹⁸They also sent five gold models of rats. There was one for each of the Philistine towns that belonged to the five rulers. Each of those towns had high walls around it. The towns also had country villages around them. The Levites set the ark of the LORD on the large rock. To this day the rock is a witness to what happened there. It's in the field of Joshua of Beth Shemesh.

¹⁹But some of the people of Beth Shemesh looked into the ark of the LORD. So he struck them down. He put 70 of them to death. The rest of the people were filled with sorrow. That's because the LORD had killed so many of them. ²⁰The people of Beth Shemesh said, "The LORD is a holy God. Who can stand in front of him? Where can the ark go up to from here?"

²¹Then messengers were sent to the people of Kiriath Jearim. The messengers said, "The Philistines have returned the ark of the LORD. Come down and take it up to your town." ¹So the men of Kiriath Jearim came and got the ark of the LORD. They brought it up to Abinadab's house on the hill. They set his son Eleazar apart to guard the ark. ²The ark remained at Kiriath Jearim for a long time. It was there for a full 20 years.

Samuel Brings the Philistines Under Israel's Control

Then all the Israelites turned back to the LORD. ³So Samuel spoke to all the Israelites. He said, "Do you really want to return to the LORD with all your hearts? If you do, get rid of your false gods. Get rid of your statues of female gods that are named Ashtoreth. Commit yourselves to the LORD. Serve him only. Then he will save you from the power of the Philistines." ⁴So the Israelites put away their statues of gods that were named Baal. They put away their statues of female gods that were named Ashtoreth. They served the LORD only.

⁵Then Samuel said, "Gather all the Israelites together at Mizpah. I will pray to the LORD for you." ⁶When the people had come together at Mizpah, they went to the well and got water. They poured it out in front of the LORD. On that day they didn't eat any food. They admitted they had sinned. They said, "We've sinned against the LORD." Samuel was serving as the leader of Israel at Mizpah.

⁷The Philistines heard that Israel had gathered together at Mizpah. So the Philistine rulers came up to attack them. When the Israelites heard about it, they were afraid. ⁸They said to Samuel, "Don't stop crying out to the LORD our God to help us. Keep praying that he'll save us from the power of the Philistines." ⁹Then Samuel got a very young lamb. He sacrificed it as a whole burnt offering to the LORD. He cried out to the LORD to help Israel. And the LORD answered his prayer.

¹⁰The Philistines came near to attack Israel. At that time Samuel was sacrificing the burnt offering. But that day the LORD

thundered loudly against the Philistines. He threw them into such a panic that the Israelites were able to chase them away. ¹¹The men of Israel rushed out of Mizpah. They chased the Philistines all the way to a point below Beth Kar. They killed them all along the way.

¹²Then Samuel got a big stone. He set it up between Mizpah and Shen. He named it Ebenezer. He said, "The LORD has helped us every step of the way."

¹³So the Philistines were brought under Israel's control. The Philistines didn't attack their territory again. The LORD used his power against the Philistines as long as Samuel lived. ¹⁴The Philistines had captured many towns between Ekron and Gath. But they had to give all of them back. Israel took back the territories near those towns from the control of the Philistines. During that time Israel and the Amorites were friendly toward each other.

¹⁵Samuel continued to lead Israel all the days of his life. ¹⁶From year to year he traveled from Bethel to Gilgal to Mizpah. He served Israel as judge in all those places. ¹⁷But he always went back to Ramah. That's where his home was. He served Israel as judge there too. And he built an altar there to honor the LORD.

Israel Asks for a King

8 When Samuel became old, he appointed his sons as Israel's leaders. ²The name of his oldest son was Joel. The name of his second son was Abijah. They served as judges at Beersheba. ³But his sons didn't live as he did. They were only interested in making money. They accepted money from people who wanted special favors. They made things that were wrong appear to be right.

⁴So all the elders of Israel gathered together. They came to Samuel at Ramah. ⁵They said to him, "You are old. Your sons don't live as you do. So appoint a king to lead us. We want a king just like the kings all the other nations have."

⁶Samuel wasn't pleased when they said, "Give us a king to lead us." So he prayed to the LORD. ⁷The LORD told him, "Listen to everything the people are saying to you. You are not the one they have turned their backs on. I am the one they do not want as their king. ⁸They are doing just as they have always done. They have deserted me

and served other gods. They have done that from the time I brought them up out of Egypt until this day. Now they are deserting you too. ⁹Let them have what they want. But give them a strong warning. Let them know what the king who rules over them will expect to be done for him."

¹⁰Samuel told the people who were asking him for a king everything the LORD had said. ¹¹Samuel told them, "Here's what the king who rules over you will expect to be done for him. He will take your sons. He'll make them serve with his chariots and horses. They will run in front of his chariots. ¹²He'll choose some of your sons to be commanders of thousands of men. Some will be commanders of fifties. Others will have to plow his fields and gather his crops. Still others will have to make weapons of war and parts for his chariots. ¹³He'll also take your daughters. Some will have to make perfume. Others will be forced to cook and bake. ¹⁴He will take away your best fields and vineyards and olive groves. He'll give them to his attendants. ¹⁵He will take a tenth of your grain and a tenth of your grapes. He'll give it to his officials and attendants. ¹⁶He will also take your male and female servants. He'll take your best cattle and donkeys. He'll use all of them any way he wants to. ¹⁷He will take a tenth of your sheep and goats. You yourselves will become his slaves. ¹⁸When that time comes, you will cry out for help because of the king you have chosen. But the LORD won't answer you at that time."

¹⁹In spite of what Samuel said, the people refused to listen to him. "No!" they said. "We want a king to rule over us. ²⁰Then we'll be like all the other nations. We'll have a king to lead us. He'll go out at the head of our armies and fight our battles."

²¹Samuel heard everything the people said. He told the LORD about it. ²²The LORD answered, "Listen to them. Give them a king."

Then Samuel said to the Israelites, "Each of you go back to your own town."

Samuel Anoints Saul to Be Israel's King

9 There was a man named Kish from the tribe of Benjamin. Kish was a very important person. He was the son of Abiel,

the son of Zeror. Zeror was the son of Bekorath, the son of Aphiah from the tribe of Benjamin. ²Kish had a son named Saul. Saul was a handsome young man. He was more handsome than anyone in Israel. And he was a head taller than anyone else.

³The donkeys that belonged to Saul's father Kish were lost. So Kish spoke to his son Saul. He said, "Go and look for the donkeys. Take one of the servants with you." ⁴Saul and his servant went through the hill country of Ephraim. They also went through the area around Shalisha. But they didn't find the donkeys. So they went on into the area of Shaalim. But the donkeys weren't there either. Then Saul went through the territory of Benjamin. But they still didn't find the donkeys.

⁵When Saul and the servant with him reached the area of Zuph, Saul spoke to the servant. He said, "Come on. Let's go back. If we don't, my father will stop thinking about the donkeys. Instead, he'll start worrying about us."

⁶But the servant replied, "There's a man of God here in Ramah. People have a lot of respect for him. Everything he says comes true. So let's go and see him now. Perhaps he'll tell us which way to go."

⁷Saul said to his servant, "If we go to see the man, what can we give him? There isn't any food in our sacks. We don't have a gift for the man of God. So what can we give him?"

⁸The servant answered Saul again. "Look," he said. "I've got a tenth of an ounce of silver. I'll give it to the man of God. Then maybe he'll tell us which way to go." ⁹In Israel, prophets used to be called seers. So if someone wanted to ask God for advice, they would say, "Come on. Let's go to the seer."

¹⁰Saul said to his servant, "That's a good idea. Come on. Let's go and ask the seer." So they started out for the town where the man of God lived.

¹¹They were going up the hill toward the town. Along the way they met some young women who were coming out to get water from the well. Saul and his servant asked them, "Is the seer here?"

¹²"Yes, he is," they answered. "In fact, he's just up ahead of you. So hurry along. He has just come to our town today. The people are going to offer a sacrifice at the high place where they worship. ¹³As soon as you enter the town, you will find him. He'll be there until he goes up to the high place to eat. The people won't start eating until he gets there. He must bless the sacrifice first. After that, those who are invited will eat. So go on up. You should find him there just about now."

¹⁴They went up to the town. As they were entering it, they saw Samuel. He was coming toward them. He was on his way up to the high place.

¹⁵The LORD had spoken to Samuel the day before Saul came. He had said, ¹⁶"About this time tomorrow I will send you a man. He is from the land of Benjamin. Anoint him to be the king of my people Israel. He will save them from the power of the Philistines. I have seen how much my people are suffering. Their cry for help has reached me."

¹⁷When Samuel saw a man coming toward him, the LORD spoke to Samuel again. He said, "He is the man I told you about. His name is Saul. He will govern my people."

¹⁸Saul approached Samuel at the gate of the town. He asked Samuel, "Can you please show me the seer's house?"

¹⁹"I'm the seer," Samuel replied. "Go on up to the high place ahead of me. I want you and your servant to eat with me today. Tomorrow morning I'll tell you what's on your mind. Then I'll send you on your way. ²⁰Don't worry about the donkeys you lost three days ago. They've already been found. But who do all the Israelites want? You and your father's whole family!"

²¹Saul answered, "But I'm from the tribe of Benjamin. It's the smallest tribe in Israel. And my family group is the least important in the whole tribe of Benjamin. So why are you saying that to me?"

²²Then Samuel brought Saul and his servant into the room where they would be eating. He seated them at the head table. About 30 people had been invited. ²³Samuel said to the cook, "Bring the piece of meat I gave you. It's the one I told you to put to one side."

²⁴So the cook went and got a choice piece of thigh. He set it in front of Saul. Samuel said, "Here is what has been kept for you. Eat it. It was put to one side for you for this special occasion. We've saved

it for you ever since I invited the guests." And Saul ate with Samuel that day.

[25]They came down from the high place to the town. After that, Samuel talked with Saul on the roof of Samuel's house. [26]The next day they got up at about the time the sun was rising. Samuel called out to Saul on the roof. He said, "Get ready. Then I'll send you on your way." So Saul got ready. And he and Samuel went outside together. [27]As they were on their way down to the edge of town, Samuel spoke to Saul. He said, "Tell the servant to go ahead of us." So the servant went on ahead. Then Samuel continued, "Stay here for a while. I'll give you a message from God."

10 Then Samuel took a bottle of olive oil. He poured it on Saul's head and kissed him. He said, "The LORD has anointed you to be the king of his people. [2]When you leave me today, you will meet two men. They will be near Rachel's tomb at Zelzah on the border of Benjamin. They'll say to you, 'The donkeys you have been looking for have been found. Now your father has stopped thinking about them. Instead, he's worried about you. He's asking, "What can I do to find my son?"'

[3]"You will go on from Zelzah until you come to the large tree at Tabor. Three men will meet you there. They'll be on their way up to Bethel to worship God. One of them will be carrying three young goats. Another will be carrying three loaves of bread. A third will be carrying a bottle of wine. It will be a bottle made out of animal skin. [4]The men will greet you. They'll offer you two loaves of bread. You will accept the loaves from them.

[5]"After that, you will go to Gibeah of God. Some Philistine soldiers are stationed there. As you approach the town, you will meet a group of prophets. They'll be coming down from the high place where they worship. People will be playing lyres, tambourines, flutes and harps at the head of the group. The prophets will be prophesying. [6]The Spirit of the LORD will come powerfully on you. Then you will prophesy along with them. You will become a different person. [7]All these things will happen. Then do what you want to do. God is with you.

[8]"Go down ahead of me to Gilgal. You can be sure that I'll come down to you there. I'll come and sacrifice burnt offerings and friendship offerings. But you must wait there for seven days until I come to you. Then I'll tell you what to do."

Saul Becomes King of Israel

[9]As Saul turned to leave Samuel, God changed Saul's heart. All these things happened that day. [10]When Saul and his servant arrived at Gibeah, a group of prophets met Saul. Then the Spirit of God came powerfully on him. He prophesied along with them. [11]Those who had known Saul before saw him prophesying with the prophets. They asked one another, "What has happened to the son of Kish? Is Saul also one of the prophets?"

[12]A man who lived in Gibeah answered, "Yes, he is. In fact, he's their leader." That's why people say, "Is Saul also one of the prophets?" [13]After Saul stopped prophesying, he went to the high place to worship.

[14]Later, Saul's uncle spoke to him and his servant. He asked, "Where have you been?"

"Looking for the donkeys," Saul said. "But we couldn't find them. So we went to Samuel."

[15]Saul's uncle said, "Tell me what Samuel said to you."

[16]Saul replied, "He told us the donkeys had been found." But Saul didn't tell his uncle that Samuel had said he would become king.

1 Sam. 10:14 Donkeys carry a heavy load in the Bible; they're around for a lot of big important events. Can you think of any more famous donkeys? (We've already seen two in Numbers 22 and Genesis 42.) Spoiler alert! There are a few in Jesus' story.

¹⁷Samuel sent a message to the Israelites. He told them to meet with the LORD at Mizpah. ¹⁸He said to them, "The LORD is the God of Israel. He says, 'Israel, I brought you up out of Egypt. I saved you from their power. I also saved you from the power of all the kingdoms that had treated you badly.' ¹⁹But now you have turned your backs on your God. He saves you out of all your trouble and suffering. In spite of that, you have said, 'We refuse to listen. Place a king over us.' So now gather together to meet with the LORD. Do it tribe by tribe and family group by family group."

²⁰Then Samuel had each tribe of Israel come forward. The tribe of Benjamin was chosen by casting lots. ²¹Next he had the tribe of Benjamin come forward, family group by family group. Matri's group was chosen. Finally Saul, the son of Kish, was chosen. But when people looked for him, they realized he wasn't there. ²²They needed more help from the LORD. So they asked him, "Has the man come here yet?"

The LORD said, "Yes. He has hidden himself among the supplies."

²³So they ran over there and brought him out. When he stood up, the people saw that he was a head taller than any of them. ²⁴Samuel spoke to all the people. He said, "Look at the man the LORD has chosen! There isn't anyone like him among all the people."

Then the people shouted, "May the king live a long time!"

²⁵Samuel explained to the people the rights and duties of the king who ruled over them. He wrote them down in a book. He placed it in front of the LORD in the holy tent. Then he sent the people away. He sent each of them to their own homes.

²⁶Saul also went to his home in Gibeah. Some brave men whose hearts God had touched went with Saul. ²⁷But some people who wanted to stir up trouble said, "How can this fellow save us?" They looked down on him. They didn't bring him any gifts. But Saul kept quiet about it.

Saul Rescues the City of Jabesh Gilead

11 Nahash was the king of Ammon. He and his army went up to Jabesh Gilead. They surrounded it and got ready to attack it. All the men of Jabesh spoke to

> **BIBLE ADVENTURES**
>
> Bernard told the story of Saul, his anointing as king, and his pursuit of King David in "Bernard and Saul" (A#42).

Nahash. They said, "Make a peace treaty with us. Then we'll be under your control."

²Nahash, the king of Ammon, replied, "I will make a peace treaty with you. But I'll do it only on one condition. You must let me put out the right eye of every one of you. I want to bring shame on the whole nation of Israel."

³The elders of Jabesh said to him, "Give us seven days to report back to you. We'll send messengers all through Israel. If no one comes to save us, we'll hand ourselves over to you."

⁴The messengers came to Gibeah of Saul. They reported to the people the terms Nahash had required. Then all the people wept out loud. ⁵Just then Saul was coming in from the fields. He was walking behind his oxen. He asked, "What's wrong with everyone? Why are they weeping?" He was told what the men of Jabesh had said.

⁶When Saul heard their words, the Spirit of God came powerfully on him. He became very angry. ⁷He got a pair of oxen and cut them into pieces. He sent the pieces by messengers all through Israel. They announced, "You must follow Saul and Samuel. If you don't, this is what will happen to your oxen." The terror of the LORD fell on the people. So all of them came together with one purpose in mind. ⁸Saul brought his army together at Bezek. There were 300,000 men from Israel and 30,000 from Judah.

⁹The messengers who had come were told, "Go back and report to the men of Jabesh Gilead. Tell them, 'By the hottest time of the day tomorrow, you will be rescued.'" The messengers went and reported it to the men of Jabesh. It made those men very happy. ¹⁰They said to the people of Ammon, "Tomorrow we'll hand ourselves over to you. Then you can do to us whatever you like."

¹¹The next day Saul separated his men into three groups. While it was still dark, they broke into the camp of the Ammonite army. They kept killing the men of Ammon

until the hottest time of the day. Those who got away were scattered. There weren't two of them left together anywhere.

The People Agree to Have Saul as King

[12] The people said to Samuel, "Who asked, 'Is Saul going to rule over us?' Turn these men over to us. We'll put them to death."

[13] But Saul said, "No one will be put to death today! After all, this is the day the Lord has rescued Israel."

[14] Then Samuel said to the people, "Come on. Let's go to Gilgal. There we'll agree again to have Saul as our king." [15] So all the people went to Gilgal. There, with the Lord as witness, they made Saul their king. There they sacrificed friendship offerings to the Lord. And there Saul and all the Israelites celebrated with great joy.

Samuel's Final Speech to Israel

[12] Samuel spoke to all the Israelites. He said, "I've done everything you asked me to do. I've placed a king over you. [2] Now you have a king as your leader. But I'm old. My hair is gray. My sons are here with you. I've been your leader from the time I was young until this day. [3] Here I stand. Bring charges against me if you can. The Lord is a witness. And so is his anointed king. Whose ox have I taken? Whose donkey have I taken? Have I cheated anyone? Have I treated anyone badly? Have I accepted money from anyone who wanted special favors? If I've done any of these things, I'll make it right."

[4] "You haven't cheated us," they replied. "You haven't treated us badly. You haven't taken anything from anyone."

[5] Samuel said to them, "The Lord is a witness against you this day. And so is his anointed king. They are witnesses that I haven't taken anything from any of you."

"The Lord is a witness," they said.

[6] Then Samuel said to the people, "The Lord appointed Moses and Aaron. He brought out of Egypt your people who lived long ago. [7] Now then, stand here. I'm going to remind you of all the good things the Lord has done for you and your people. He is a witness.

[8] "After Jacob's family entered Egypt, they cried out to the Lord for help.

The Lord sent Moses and Aaron. They brought your people out of Egypt. They had them make their homes in this land.

[9] "But the people forgot the Lord their God. So he put them under the control of Sisera. Sisera was the commander of the army of Hazor. The Lord also put the Israelites under the control of the Philistines and the king of Moab. All those nations fought against Israel. [10] So the people cried out to the Lord. They said, 'We have sinned. We've deserted the Lord. We've served gods that are named Baal. We've served female gods that are named Ashtoreth. But save us now from the power of our enemies. Then we will serve you.' [11] The Lord sent Gideon, Barak, Jephthah and me. He saved you from the power of your enemies who were all around you. So you lived in safety.

[12] "But then you saw that Nahash, the king of Ammon, was about to attack you. So you said to me, 'No! We want a king to rule over us.' You said it even though the Lord your God was your king. [13] Now here is the king you have chosen. He's the one you asked for. The Lord has placed a king over you. [14] But you must have respect for the Lord. You must serve him and obey him. You must not say no to his commands. Both you and the king who rules over you must obey the Lord your God. If you do, that's good. [15] But you must not disobey him. You must not say no to his commands. If you do, his power will be against you. That's what happened to your people who lived before you.

[16] "So stand still. Watch the great thing the Lord is about to do right here in front of you! [17] It's time to gather in the wheat, isn't it? I'll call out to the Lord to send thunder and rain. Then you will realize what an evil thing you did in the sight of the Lord. You shouldn't have asked for a king."

[18] Samuel called out to the Lord. That same day the Lord sent thunder and rain. So all the people had great respect for the Lord and for Samuel.

[19] They said to Samuel, "Pray to the Lord your God for us. Pray that we won't die because we asked for a king. That was an evil thing to do. We added it to all our other sins."

[20] "Don't be afraid," Samuel replied. "It's true that you have done all these

evil things. But don't turn away from the LORD. Serve him with all your heart. [21]Don't turn away and worship statues of gods. They are useless. They can't do you any good. They can't save you either. They are completely useless. [22]But the LORD will be true to his great name. He won't turn his back on his people. That's because he was pleased to make you his own people. [23]I would never sin against the LORD by failing to pray for you. I'll teach you to live in a way that is good and right. [24]But be sure to have respect for the LORD. Serve him faithfully. Do it with all your heart. Think about the great things he has done for you. [25]But don't be stubborn. Don't continue to do what is evil. If you do, both you and your king will be destroyed."

Samuel Judges Saul's Sin

13 Saul was 30 years old when he became king. He ruled over Israel for 42 years.

[2]Saul chose 3,000 of Israel's men. Two thousand of them were with him at Mikmash and in the hill country of Bethel. One thousand were with Jonathan at Gibeah in the land of Benjamin. Saul sent the rest back to their homes.

[3]Some Philistine soldiers were stationed at Geba. Jonathan attacked them. The other Philistines heard about it. Saul announced, "Let the Hebrew people hear about what has happened!" He had trumpets blown all through the land. [4]So all the Israelites heard the news. They were told, "Saul has attacked the Philistine army camp at Geba. Now the Philistines can't stand the Israelites." The Israelites were called out to join Saul at Gilgal.

[5]The Philistines gathered together to fight against Israel. They had 3,000 chariots and 6,000 chariot drivers. Their soldiers were as many as the grains of sand on the seashore. They went up and camped at Mikmash. It was east of Beth Aven. [6]The Israelites saw that their army was in deep trouble. So they hid in caves. They hid among bushes and rocks. They also hid in pits and empty wells. [7]Some of them even went across the Jordan River. They went to the lands of Gad and Gilead.

Saul remained at Gilgal. All the troops with him were shaking with fear. [8]He waited seven days, just as Samuel had told him to. But Samuel didn't come to Gilgal. And Saul's men began to scatter. [9]So he said, "Bring me the burnt offering and the friendship offerings." Then he offered up the burnt offering. [10]Just as Saul finished offering the sacrifice, Samuel arrived. Saul went out to greet him.

[11]"What have you done?" asked Samuel.

Saul replied, "I saw that the men were scattering. I saw that the Philistines were gathering together at Mikmash. You didn't come when you said you would. [12]So I thought, 'Now the Philistines will come down to attack me at Gilgal. And I haven't asked the LORD for his blessing.' So I felt I had to sacrifice the burnt offering."

Jason's Jargon

1 SAMUEL 13

Your next assignment: Find the word *blacksmith* in this chapter. A blacksmith created tools out of iron using a hot oven called a forge. They made horseshoes, weapons, and farming tools.

[13]"You have done a foolish thing," Samuel said. "You haven't obeyed the command the LORD your God gave you. If you had, he would have made your kingdom secure over Israel for all time to come. [14]But now your kingdom won't last. The LORD has already looked for a man who is dear to his heart. He has appointed him king of his people. That's because you haven't obeyed the LORD's command."

[15]Then Samuel left Gilgal and went up to Gibeah in the land of Benjamin. Saul counted the men who were with him. The total number was about 600.

Israel Doesn't Have Weapons

[16]Saul and his son Jonathan were staying in Gibeah in the land of Benjamin. The men who remained in the army were there with them. At the same time, the Philistines camped at Mikmash. [17]Three groups of soldiers went out from

CANDID CONVERSATIONS

"You've got one more chance."

"Three strikes and you're out."

"If I have to tell you again, you're going to be in real trouble."

It seems like everybody has a limit for how many times you can mess up before there are consequences. It also seems like God has more patience than most people do. King Saul messed up over and over and over, and finally, God took away his kingdom and gave it to David.

I'm sure glad it doesn't look like God has to decide to punish me too harshly for my sins so far. I mean, yeah, I feel the consequences for the foolish things I do, but God has shown me patience time and time again. Today, confess your sins to Him out loud and thank Him for His forgiveness. As it says in 1 John 1:9, "God is faithful and fair. If we confess our sins, he will forgive our sins. He will forgive every wrong thing we have done. He will make us pure."

the Philistine camp to attack Israel. One group turned and went toward Ophrah in the area of Shual. [18] Another went toward Beth Horon. The third went toward the border that looked out over the Valley of Zeboim. That valley faces the desert.

[19] There weren't any blacksmiths in the whole land of Israel. That's because the Philistines had said, "The Hebrews might hire them to make swords or spears!" [20] So all the Israelites had to go down to the Philistines. They had to go to them to get their plows, hoes, axes and sickles sharpened. [21] It cost a fourth of an ounce of silver to sharpen a plow or a hoe. It cost an eighth of an ounce to sharpen a pitchfork or an axe. That's also what it cost to put

new tips on the large sticks used to drive oxen.

[22] So the Israelite soldiers went out to battle without swords or spears in their hands. That was true for all of Saul's and Jonathan's soldiers. Only Saul and his son Jonathan had those weapons.

Jonathan Attacks the Philistines

[23] A group of Philistine soldiers had gone out to the pass at Mikmash. **14** [1] One day Jonathan, the son of Saul, spoke to the young man carrying his armor. "Come on," he said. "Let's go over to the Philistine army camp on the other side of the pass." But he didn't tell his father about it.

[2] Saul was staying just outside Gibeah. He was under a pomegranate tree in Migron. He had about 600 men with him. [3] Ahijah was one of them. He was wearing a sacred linen apron. He was a son of Ichabod's brother Ahitub. Ahitub was the son of Eli's son Phinehas. Eli had been the LORD's priest in Shiloh. No one was aware that Jonathan had left.

[4] Jonathan planned to go across the pass to reach the Philistine camp. But there was a cliff on each side of the pass. One cliff was called Bozez. The other was called Seneh. [5] One cliff stood on the north side of the pass toward Mikmash. The other stood on the south side toward Geba.

[6] Jonathan spoke to the young man carrying his armor. He said, "Come on. Let's go over to the camp of those fellows who aren't circumcised. Perhaps the LORD will help us. If he does, it won't matter how many or how few of us there are. That won't keep the LORD from saving us."

[7] "Go ahead," the young man said. "Do everything you have in mind. I'm with you all the way."

[8] Jonathan said, "Come on, then. We'll go across the pass toward the Philistines and let them see us. [9] Suppose they say to us, 'Wait there until we come to you.' Then we'll stay where we are. We won't go up to them. [10] But suppose they say, 'Come up to us.' Then we'll climb up. That will show us that the LORD has handed them over to us."

[11] So Jonathan and the young man let the soldiers in the Philistine camp see them. "Look!" said the Philistines. "Some

of the Hebrews are crawling out of the holes they were hiding in." [12]The men in the Philistine camp shouted to Jonathan and the young man carrying his armor. They said, "Come on up here. We'll teach you a thing or two."

So Jonathan said to the young man, "Climb up after me. The LORD has handed them over to Israel."

[13]Using his hands and feet, Jonathan climbed up. The young man was right behind him. Jonathan struck down the Philistines. The young man followed him and killed those who were still alive. [14]In that first attack, Jonathan and the young man killed about 20 men. They did it in an area of about half an acre.

Israel Chases the Philistines Away

[15]Then panic struck the whole Philistine army. It struck those who were in the camp and those in the field. It struck those who were at the edge of the camp. It also struck those who were in the groups that had been sent out to attack Israel. The ground shook. It was a panic that God had sent.

[16]Saul's lookouts at Gibeah in the land of Benjamin saw what was happening. They saw the Philistine army melting away in all directions. [17]Then Saul spoke to the men with him. He said, "Bring the troops together. See who has left our camp." When they did, they discovered that Jonathan and the young man carrying his armor weren't there.

[18]Saul said to Ahijah the priest, "Bring the ark of God." At that time it was with the Israelites. [19]While Saul was talking to the priest, the noise in the Philistine camp got louder and louder. So Saul said to the priest, "Stop what you are doing."

[20]Then Saul and all his men gathered together. They went to the battle. They saw that the Philistines were in total disorder. They were striking one another with their swords. [21]At an earlier time some of the Hebrews had been on the side of the Philistines. They had gone up with them to their camp. But now they changed sides. They joined the Israelites who were with Saul and Jonathan. [22]Some of the Israelites had hidden in the hill country of Ephraim. They heard that the Philistines were running away. They quickly joined the battle and chased after them. [23]So on that day the LORD saved Israel. And the fighting continued on past Beth Aven.

Jonathan Eats Honey

[24]The Israelites became very hungry that day. That's because Saul had forced the army to make a promise. He had said, "None of you must eat any food before evening comes. You must not eat until I've paid my enemies back for what they did. If you do, may you be under a curse!" So none of the troops ate any food at all.

[25]The whole army entered the woods. There was honey on the ground. [26]When they went into the woods, they saw the honey dripping out of a honeycomb. No one put any of the honey in his mouth. They were afraid of the curse that would come if they broke their promise. [27]But Jonathan hadn't heard that his father had forced the army to make a promise. Jonathan had a long stick in his hand. He reached out and dipped the end of it into the honeycomb. He put some honey in his mouth. It gave him new life. [28]Then one of the soldiers told him, "Your father forced the army to make a promise that everyone must obey. He said, 'None of you must eat any food today. If you do, may you be under a curse!' That's why the men are weak and ready to faint."

[29]Jonathan said, "My father has made trouble for the country. See how I gained new life after I tasted a little of this honey. [30]Our soldiers took food from their enemies today. Suppose they had eaten some of it. How much better off they would have been! Even more Philistines would have been killed."

[31]That day the Israelites struck down the Philistines. They killed them from Mikmash to Aijalon. By that time they were tired and worn out. [32]They grabbed what they had taken from their enemies. They killed some of the sheep, cattle and calves right there on the ground. They ate the meat while the blood was still in it. [33]Then someone said to Saul, "Look! The men are sinning against the LORD. They're eating meat that still has blood in it."

Saul said to them, "You have broken your promise. Roll a large stone over here at once." [34]He continued, "Go out among the men. Tell them, 'Each of you bring me your cattle and sheep. Kill them here and eat them. Don't sin against the LORD by eating meat that still has blood in it.'"

So that night everyone brought the ox he had taken and killed it there. ³⁵Then Saul built an altar to honor the LORD. It was the first time he had done that.

³⁶Saul said, "Let's go down and chase after the Philistines tonight. Let's not leave even one of them alive. Let's take everything they have before morning."

"Do what you think is best," they replied.

But the priest said, "Let's ask God for advice first."

³⁷So Saul asked God, "Should I go down and chase after the Philistines? Will you hand them over to Israel?" But God didn't answer him that day.

³⁸Saul said to the leaders of the army, "Come here. Let's find out what sin has been committed today. ³⁹The LORD is the one who rescues Israel. You can be sure that the LORD lives. And you can be just as sure that the sinner must die. He must die even if he's my son Jonathan." But no one said anything.

⁴⁰Then Saul said to all the Israelites, "You stand over there. I and my son Jonathan will stand over here."

"Do what you think is best," they replied.

⁴¹Then Saul prayed to the LORD, the God of Israel. He said, "Why haven't you answered your servant today? If I or my son Jonathan is to blame, answer with Urim. But if the Israelites are to blame, answer with Thummim." Jonathan and Saul were chosen by casting lots. The other men were cleared of blame. ⁴²Saul said, "Cast the lot to find out whether I or my son Jonathan is to blame." And Jonathan was chosen.

⁴³Then Saul said to Jonathan, "Tell me what you have done."

So Jonathan told him, "I used the end of my stick to get a little honey and taste it. And now do I have to die?"

⁴⁴Saul said, "Jonathan, I must certainly put you to death. If I don't, may God punish me greatly."

⁴⁵But the men said to Saul, "Should Jonathan be put to death? Never! He has saved Israel in a wonderful way. He did it today with God's help. You can be sure

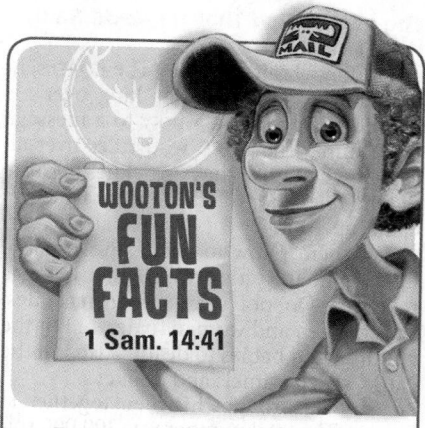

WOOTON'S FUN FACTS
1 Sam. 14:41

The terms *Urim* and *Thummim* appear only in the Old Testament. Scholars think the words represent dark and light colors and that they were special stones or sticks put inside a priest's breastplate.

that the LORD lives. And you can be just as sure that not even one hair on Jonathan's head will fall to the ground." So the men rescued Jonathan. He wasn't put to death.

⁴⁶Then Saul stopped chasing the Philistines. They went back to their own land.

⁴⁷After Saul became the king of Israel, he fought against Israel's enemies who were all around them. He went to war against Moab, Ammon and Edom. He fought against the kings of Zobah and the Philistines. No matter where he went, he punished his enemies. ⁴⁸He fought bravely. He won the battle over the Amalekites. He saved Israel from the power of those who had carried off what belonged to Israel.

Saul's Family

⁴⁹Saul's sons were Jonathan, Ishvi and Malki-Shua. Saul's older daughter was named Merab. His younger daughter was named Michal. ⁵⁰Saul's wife was named Ahinoam. She was the daughter of Ahimaaz. The commander of Saul's army was named Abner. He was the son of Ner. Ner was Saul's uncle. ⁵¹Saul's father Kish and Abner's father Ner were sons of Abiel.

⁵²As long as Saul was king, he had to fight hard against the Philistines. So every time Saul saw a strong or brave man, he took him into his army.

The LORD Is Sad That He Made Saul King

15 Samuel said to Saul, "The LORD sent me to anoint you as king over his people Israel. So listen now to a message from him. ²The LORD who rules over all says, 'I will punish the Amalekites because of what they did to Israel. As the Israelites came up from Egypt, the Amalekites attacked them. ³Now go. Attack the Amalekites. Completely destroy all that belongs to them. Do not spare the Amalekites. Put the men and women to death. Put the children and babies to death. Also kill the cattle, sheep, camels and donkeys.' "

⁴So Saul brought his men together at Telaim. The total number was 200,000 soldiers on foot from Israel and 10,000 from Judah. ⁵Saul went to the city of Amalek. Then Saul had some of his men hide and wait in the valley. ⁶Then Saul said to the Kenites, "You were kind to all the Israelites when they came up out of Egypt. Get away from the Amalekites. Then I won't have to destroy you along with them." So the Kenites moved away from the Amalekites.

⁷Saul attacked the Amalekites. He struck them down all the way from Havilah to Shur. Shur was near the eastern border of Egypt. ⁸Saul captured Agag, the king of the Amalekites. But he and his men totally destroyed with their swords all Agag's people. ⁹So Saul and the army spared Agag. They spared the best of the sheep and cattle. They spared the fat calves and lambs. They spared everything that was valuable. They weren't willing to completely destroy any of those things. But they totally destroyed everything that was worthless and weak.

¹⁰Then the LORD gave Samuel a message. He said, ¹¹"I am very sad I have made Saul king. He has turned away from me. He has not done what I directed him to do." When Samuel heard that, he was angry. He cried out to the LORD during that whole night.

¹²Early the next morning Samuel got up. He went to see Saul. But Samuel was told, "Saul went to Carmel. There he set up a monument in his own honor. Now he has gone on down to Gilgal."

WHAT ABOUT YOU?

After seeing a video about starving children in Africa, you might feel guilty about having access to so much food. So you promise God that you'll give up cookies for a whole month. Completely. No Oreos. No snickerdoodles. No macaroons, ginger snaps, or warm chocolate chip cookies.

The next week, you're over at a friend's house. Your friend's mom just made her famous seven-layer bars. There's cookie dough in them, sure, but they're not technically cookies. That makes them okay to eat—right? Ugh! Painful as it may be, you turn down the seven-layer bars too. You planned to make a sacrifice, and so you do.

Is all of this suffering necessary? Well, there are plenty of good reasons to make sacrifices, from improving our health to putting someone else's needs ahead of our own. On the other hand, some people make sacrifices out of guilt, or because they think that's what God demands of them.

First Samuel 15:22 says: "What pleases the LORD more? Burnt offerings and sacrifices, or obeying the LORD? It is better to obey than to offer a sacrifice." God would rather have you seek Him and do what He says than torture yourself by giving up anything specific. It's putting our focus on Him that's most important.

Is there a sacrifice you could make today that would draw you closer to God? What might that be? Maybe God isn't looking for a sacrifice at all, but simply faithful obedience.

¹³When Samuel got there, Saul said, "May the LORD bless you. I've done what he directed me to do."

¹⁴But Samuel said, "Then why do I hear the baaing of sheep? Why do I hear the mooing of cattle?"

¹⁵Saul answered, "The soldiers brought them from the Amalekites. They spared the best of the sheep and cattle. They did it to sacrifice them to the LORD your God. But we totally destroyed everything else."

¹⁶"That's enough!" Samuel said to Saul. "Let me tell you what the LORD said to me last night."

"Tell me," Saul replied.

¹⁷Samuel said, "There was a time when you didn't think you were important. But you became the leader of the tribes of Israel. The LORD anointed you to be king over Israel. ¹⁸He sent you to do something for him. He said, 'Go and completely destroy the Amalekites. Go and destroy those evil people. Fight against them until you have wiped them out.' ¹⁹Why didn't you obey the LORD? Why did you keep for yourselves what you had taken from your enemies? Why did you do what is evil in the sight of the LORD?"

²⁰"But I did obey the LORD," Saul said. "I went to do what he sent me to do. I completely destroyed the Amalekites. I brought back Agag, their king. ²¹The soldiers took sheep and cattle from what had been taken from our enemies. They took the best of what had been set apart to God. They wanted to sacrifice them to the LORD your God at Gilgal."

²²But Samuel replied,

"What pleases the LORD more?
   Burnt offerings and sacrifices, or
      obeying the LORD?
It is better to obey than to offer a
   sacrifice.
   It is better to do what he says than
      to offer the fat of rams.
²³ Refusing to obey the LORD is as sinful
   as using evil magic.
   Being proud is as evil as worshiping
      statues of gods.
You have refused to do what the LORD
   told you to do.
   So he has refused to have you as king."

²⁴Then Saul said to Samuel, "I have sinned. I've broken the LORD's command.

ADVENTURES IN ODYSSEY

The Barclay family learned the truth of the phrase "obedience is better than sacrifice" in "The Meaning of Sacrifice" (A#11).

I haven't done what you directed me to do. I was afraid of the men. So I did what they said I should do. ²⁵Now I beg you, forgive my sin. Come back into town with me so I can worship the LORD."

²⁶But Samuel said to him, "I won't go back with you. You have refused to do what the LORD told you to do. So he has refused to have you as king over Israel!"

²⁷Samuel turned to leave. But Saul grabbed the hem of his robe, and it tore. ²⁸Samuel said to Saul, "The LORD has torn the kingdom of Israel away from you today. He has given it to one of your neighbors. He has given it to someone better than you. ²⁹The God who is the Glory of Israel does not lie. He doesn't change his mind. That's because he isn't a mere human being. If he were, he might change his mind."

³⁰Saul replied, "I have sinned. But please honor me in front of the elders of my people and in front of Israel. Come back with me so I can worship the LORD your God." ³¹So Samuel went back with Saul. And Saul worshiped the LORD.

³²Then Samuel said, "Bring me Agag, the king of the Amalekites."

Agag was in chains when he came to Samuel. Agag thought, "The time for me to be put to death must have passed by now."

³³But Samuel said,

"Your sword has killed the children of
      other women.
   So the child of your mother will be
      killed."

Samuel put Agag to death at Gilgal in front of the LORD.

³⁴Then Samuel left to go to Ramah. But Saul went up to his home in Gibeah of Saul. ³⁵Until the day Samuel died, he didn't go to see Saul again. Samuel was filled with sorrow because of Saul. And the LORD was very sad he had made Saul king over Israel.

Samuel Anoints David to Be Israel's King

16 The LORD said to Samuel, "How long will you be filled with sorrow because of Saul? I have refused to have him as king over Israel. Fill your animal horn with olive oil and go on your way. I am sending you to Jesse in Bethlehem. I have chosen one of his sons to be king."

²But Samuel said, "How can I go? Suppose Saul hears about it. Then he'll kill me."

The LORD said, "Take a young cow with you. Tell the elders of Bethlehem, 'I've come to offer a sacrifice to the LORD.' ³Invite Jesse to the sacrifice. Then I will show you what to do. You must anoint for me the one I point out to you."

⁴Samuel did what the LORD said. He arrived at Bethlehem. The elders of the town met him. They were trembling with fear. They asked, "Have you come in peace?"

⁵Samuel replied, "Yes, I've come in peace. I've come to offer a sacrifice to the LORD. Set yourselves apart to him and come to the sacrifice with me." Then he set Jesse and his sons apart to the LORD. He invited them to the sacrifice.

⁶When they arrived, Samuel saw Eliab. He thought, "This has to be the one the LORD wants me to anoint for him."

⁷But the LORD said to Samuel, "Do not consider how handsome or tall he is. I have not chosen him. The LORD does not look at the things people look at. People look at the outside of a person. But the LORD looks at what is in the heart."

⁸Then Jesse called for Abinadab. He had him walk in front of Samuel. But Samuel said, "The LORD hasn't chosen him either." ⁹Then Jesse had Shammah walk by. But Samuel said, "The LORD hasn't chosen him either." ¹⁰Jesse had seven of his sons walk in front of Samuel. But Samuel said to him, "The LORD hasn't chosen any of them." ¹¹So he asked Jesse, "Are these the only sons you have?"

"No," Jesse answered. "My youngest son is taking care of the sheep."

Samuel said, "Send for him. We won't sit down to eat until he arrives."

¹²So Jesse sent for his son and had him brought in. He looked very healthy. He had a fine appearance and handsome features.

Then the LORD said, "Get up and anoint him. This is the one."

¹³So Samuel got the animal horn that was filled with olive oil. He anointed David in front of his brothers. From that day on, the Spirit of the LORD came powerfully on David. Samuel went back to Ramah.

David Serves Saul

¹⁴The Spirit of the LORD had left Saul. And an evil spirit sent by the LORD terrified him.

¹⁵Saul's attendants said to him, "An evil spirit sent by God is terrifying you. ¹⁶Give us an order to look for someone who can play the harp. He will play it when the evil spirit sent by God comes on you. Then you will feel better."

¹⁷So Saul said to his attendants, "Find someone who plays the harp well. Bring him to me."

¹⁸One of the servants said, "I've seen someone who knows how to play the harp. He is a son of Jesse from Bethlehem. He's a brave man. He would make a good soldier. He's a good speaker. He's very handsome. And the LORD is with him."

¹⁹Then Saul sent messengers to Jesse. He said, "Send me your son David, the one who takes care of your sheep." ²⁰So Jesse got some bread and a bottle of wine. The bottle was made out of animal skin. He also got a young goat. He loaded everything on the back of a donkey. He sent all of it to Saul with his son David.

ADVENTURES IN ODYSSEY

Whit told Donny McCoy that who he was on the outside wasn't as important as who he was on the inside in "Camp What-a-Nut" (A#02). Shortly after, they both had to use their knowledge to escape from a bear.

²¹David went to Saul and began to serve him. Saul liked him very much. David became one of the men who carried Saul's armor. ²²Saul sent a message to Jesse. Saul said, "Let David stay here. I want him to serve me. I'm pleased with him."

²³When the evil spirit sent by God would come on Saul, David would get his harp and play it. That would help Saul. He would feel better, and the evil spirit would leave him.

David and Goliath

17 The Philistines gathered their army together for war. They came to Sokoh in Judah. They set up camp at Ephes Dammim. It was between Sokoh and Azekah. ²Saul and the army of Israel gathered together. They camped in the Valley of Elah. They lined up their men to fight against the Philistines. ³The Philistine army was camped on one hill. Israel's army was on another. The valley was between them.

⁴A mighty hero named Goliath came out of the Philistine camp. He was from Gath. He was more than nine feet tall. ⁵He had a bronze helmet on his head. He wore bronze armor that weighed 125 pounds. ⁶On his legs he wore bronze guards. He carried a bronze javelin on his back. ⁷His spear was as big as a weaver's rod. Its iron point weighed 15 pounds. The man who carried his shield walked along in front of him.

⁸Goliath stood there and shouted to the soldiers of Israel. He said, "Why do you come out and line up for battle? I'm a Philistine. You are servants of Saul. Choose one of your men. Have him come down and face me. ⁹If he's able to fight and kill me, we'll become your slaves. But if I win and kill him, you will become our slaves and serve us." ¹⁰Goliath continued, "This day I dare the soldiers of Israel to send a man down to fight against me." ¹¹Saul and the whole army of Israel heard what the Philistine said. They were terrified.

¹²David was the son of Jesse, who belonged to the tribe of Ephraim. Jesse was from Bethlehem in Judah. He had eight sons. When Saul was king, Jesse was already very old. ¹³Jesse's three oldest sons had followed Saul into battle. The oldest son was Eliab. The second was Abinadab. The third was Shammah. ¹⁴David was the youngest. The three oldest sons followed

BIBLE ADVENTURES

Connie saw David being anointed as king and witnessed his battle with Goliath through the Environment Enhancer, in "The Shepherd and the Giant" (A#04).

Saul. ¹⁵But David went back and forth from Saul's camp to Bethlehem. He went to Bethlehem to take care of his father's sheep.

¹⁶Every morning and evening Goliath came forward and stood there. He did it for 40 days.

¹⁷Jesse said to his son David, "Get at least half a bushel of grain that has been cooked. Also get ten loaves of bread. Take all of it to your brothers. Hurry to their camp. ¹⁸Take along these ten chunks of cheese to the commander of their military group. Find out how your brothers are doing. Bring me back some word about them. ¹⁹They are with Saul and all the men of Israel. They are in the Valley of Elah. They are fighting against the Philistines."

²⁰Early in the morning David left his father's flock in the care of a shepherd. David loaded up the food and started out, just as Jesse had directed. David reached the camp as the army was going out to its battle positions. The soldiers were shouting the war cry. ²¹The Israelites and the Philistines were lining up their armies for battle. The armies were facing each other. ²²David left what he had brought with the man who took care of the supplies. He ran to the battle lines and asked his brothers how they were. ²³As David was talking with them, Goliath stepped forward from his line. Goliath was a mighty Philistine hero from Gath. He again dared someone to fight him, and David heard it. ²⁴Whenever Israel's army saw Goliath, all of them ran away from him. That's because they were so afraid.

²⁵The Israelites had been saying, "Just look at how this man keeps daring Israel to fight him! The king will make the man who kills Goliath very wealthy. The king will also give his own daughter to be that man's wife. The king won't require anyone in the man's family to pay any taxes in Israel."

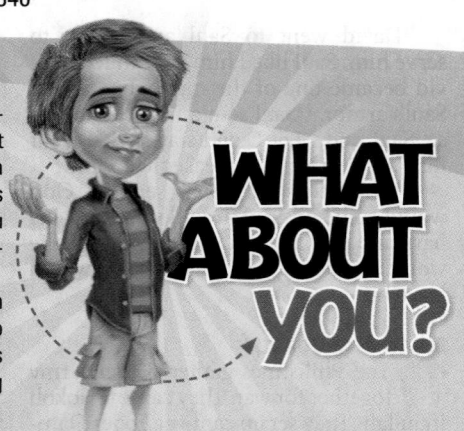

Put yourself in David's place. A huge shadow stretches toward you, confirming what you've heard from the other soldiers: "He's a giant ready to squash anyone who opposes him." Standing on the ridge across from you is Goliath, the Philistine, towering above everyone else at nine feet, six inches tall.

From morning to dusk, Goliath has been cursing the One True God of Israel, yet no one seems willing to fight him. No one has the courage to stand up to this frightening warrior. Well, almost no one.

Have you ever faced a seemingly "insurmountable" challenge? That's a big word that basically means a huge hill that's too high to climb. How did you overcome your huge hill? Did you pray? In our daily routine, gigantic issues can arise. Sometimes we feel like we can't get through them. But when we place our trust in the Lord like David did, we can have faith that He will see us through and His plans will be fulfilled.

Read 1 Samuel 17 and make a list of the giants in your life. Then take time to pray about them and ask God to equip you to have a victory over them.

David often turned to music during times of trouble. Do you have a favorite song that inspires you to trust God? Listen to it and be reminded of God's love and care.

---

²⁶David spoke to the men standing near him. He asked them, "What will be done for the man who kills this Philistine? Goliath is bringing shame on Israel. What will be done for the one who removes it? This Philistine isn't even circumcised. He dares the armies of the living God to fight him. Who does he think he is?"

²⁷The men told David what Israel's soldiers had been saying. The men told him what would be done for the man who killed Goliath.

²⁸David's oldest brother Eliab heard him speaking with the men. So Eliab became very angry with him. Eliab asked David, "Why have you come down here? Who is taking care of those few sheep in the desert for you? I know how proud you are. I know how evil your heart is. The only reason you came down here was to watch the battle."

²⁹"What have I done now?" said David. "Can't I even speak?" ³⁰Then he turned away to speak to some other men. He asked them the same question he had asked before. And they gave him the same answer. ³¹Someone heard what David said and reported it to Saul. So Saul sent for David.

³²David said to Saul, "Don't let anyone lose hope because of that Philistine. I'll go out and fight him."

³³Saul replied, "You aren't able to go out there and fight that Philistine. You are too young. He's been a warrior ever since he was a boy."

³⁴But David said to Saul, "I've been taking care of my father's sheep. Sometimes a lion or a bear would come and carry off a sheep from the flock. ³⁵Then I would go after it and hit it. I would save the sheep it was carrying in its mouth. If it turned around to attack me, I would grab its hair. I would strike it down and kill it. ³⁶In fact, I've killed both a lion and a bear. I'll do the same thing to this Philistine. He isn't even circumcised. He has dared the armies of the living God to fight him. ³⁷The LORD saved me from the paw of the lion. He saved me from the paw of the bear. And

he'll save me from the powerful hand of this Philistine too."

Saul said to David, "Go. And may the LORD be with you."

[38]Then Saul dressed David in his own military clothes. He put a coat of armor on him. He put a bronze helmet on his head. [39]David put on Saul's sword over his clothes. He walked around for a while in all that armor because he wasn't used to it.

"I can't go out there in all this armor," he said to Saul. "I'm not used to it." So he took it off. [40]Then David picked up his wooden staff. He went down to a stream and chose five smooth stones. He put them in the pocket of his shepherd's bag. Then he took his sling in his hand and approached Goliath.

[41]At that same time, the Philistine kept coming closer to David. The man carrying Goliath's shield walked along in front of him. [42]Goliath looked David over. He saw how young he was. He also saw how healthy and handsome he was. And he hated him. [43]He said to David, "Why are you coming at me with sticks? Do you think I'm only a dog?" The Philistine cursed David in the name of his gods.

[44]"Come over here," he said. "I'll feed your body to the birds and wild animals!"

[45]David said to Goliath, "You are coming to fight against me with a sword, a spear and a javelin. But I'm coming against you in the name of the LORD who rules over all. He is the God of the armies of Israel. He's the one you have dared to fight against. [46]This day the LORD will give me the victory over you. I'll strike you down. I'll cut your head off. This day I'll feed the bodies of the Philistine army to the birds and wild animals. Then the whole world will know there is a God in Israel. [47]The LORD doesn't rescue people by using a sword or a spear. And everyone here will know it. The battle belongs to the LORD. He will hand all of you over to us."

[48]As the Philistine moved closer to attack him, David ran quickly to the battle line to meet him. [49]He reached into his bag. He took out a stone. He put it in his sling. He slung it at Goliath. The stone hit him on the forehead and sank into it. He fell to the ground on his face.

[50]So David won the fight against Goliath with a sling and a stone. He struck down the Philistine and killed him. He did it without even using a sword.

WHIT'S WISDOM

1 Samuel 17

A boy named Zach used to come into Whit's End and talk about how kids picked on him and bullied him at school. He always wondered why the kids chose him to tease. Then, a few years later, Zach's family adopted a girl named Eden who had a medical condition that affected her speech. Some of school kids started picking on her too. Zach knew what it felt like to be bullied, so he was more than ready to stick up for Eden. Zach was prepared to help his sister because of his experiences.

David probably had no idea what he was being prepared for when he was watching sheep as a young boy. But as it turns out, his experiences fighting off lions and bears helped prepare him for his battle with Goliath. He was very good with a slingshot long before he had to use it on a giant!

You never know what God is using to prepare you or what He has planned for your life. Today, thank God for tough things you might be going through, and trust that God is using these experiences for your benefit.

1 Sam. 17:4–51 The giant Goliath was more than nine feet tall. His armor weighed about 125 pounds—the same weight as my dog, Sam. Can you lift 125 pounds?

⁵¹David ran and stood over him. He picked up Goliath's sword and cut off his head with it.

The Philistines saw that their hero was dead. So they turned around and ran away. ⁵²Then the men of Israel and Judah shouted and rushed forward. They chased the Philistines to the entrance of Gath. They chased them to the gates of Ekron. Bodies of dead Philistines were scattered all along the road to Gath and Ekron. That's the road that leads to Shaaraim. ⁵³Israel's army returned from chasing the Philistines. They had taken everything from the Philistine camp.

⁵⁴David picked up Goliath's head. He brought it to Jerusalem. He put Goliath's weapons in his own tent.

⁵⁵Saul had been watching David as he went out to meet the Philistine. He spoke to Abner, the commander of the army. Saul said to him, "Abner, whose son is that young man?"

Abner replied, "Your Majesty, I don't know. And that's just as sure as you are alive."

⁵⁶The king said, "Find out whose son that young man is."

⁵⁷After David killed Goliath, he returned to the camp. Then Abner brought him to Saul. David was still carrying Goliath's head.

⁵⁸"Young man, whose son are you?" Saul asked him.

David said, "I'm the son of Jesse from Bethlehem."

Saul's Growing Fear of David

18 David finished talking with Saul. After that, Jonathan and David became close friends. Jonathan loved David just as he loved himself. ²From that time on, Saul kept David with him. He didn't let him return home to his family. ³Jonathan made a covenant with David because he loved him just as he loved himself. ⁴Jonathan took off the robe he was wearing and gave it to David. He also gave him his military clothes. He even gave him his sword, his bow and his belt.

⁵David did everything Saul sent him to do. He did it so well that Saul gave him a high rank in the army. That pleased Saul's whole army, including his officers.

⁶After David had killed Goliath, the men of Israel returned home. The women came out of all the towns of Israel to meet King Saul. They danced and sang joyful songs. They played harps and tambourines. ⁷As they danced, they sang,

"Saul has killed thousands of men.
    David has killed tens of thousands."

⁸That song made Saul very angry. It really upset him. He said to himself, "They are saying David has killed tens of thousands of men. But they are saying I've killed only thousands. The only thing left for him to get is the kingdom itself." ⁹From that time on, Saul watched David closely.

¹⁰The next day an evil spirit sent by God came powerfully on Saul. Saul began to prophesy in his house. At that same time David began to play the harp, just as he usually did. Saul was holding a spear. ¹¹He threw it at David. As he did, he said to himself, "I'll pin David to the wall." But David got away from him twice.

¹²The LORD had left Saul and was with David. So Saul was afraid of David. ¹³He sent David away. He put him in command of 1,000 men. David led the troops in battle. ¹⁴In everything he did, he was very successful. That's because the LORD was with him. ¹⁵When Saul saw how successful David was, he became afraid of him. ¹⁶But all the troops of Israel and Judah loved David. That's because he led them in battle.

¹⁷Saul said to David, "Here is my older daughter Merab. I'll give her to you to be

WHAT ABOUT YOU?

As you sit at the awards ceremony on the last day of school, you watch the same kid claim every single honor for your class and wonder why no one is clapping for you. You got all A's. And you tried really hard to get involved in more after-school activities. You even served in the community. But it wasn't enough. And to make things worse, this kid hardly studies or does any work outside of class. Before you know it, jealousy starts to creep into your heart.

It's easy to let jealousy take hold of us. After David's victory over Goliath, Saul's jealousy grew into a rage. He nearly ended David's life by throwing his spear at the young man, but David escaped—twice.

Feeling jealous of someone never helps the situation. In fact, it can hurt you and the person you're envying. Proverbs 14:30 says: "A peaceful heart gives life to the body. But jealousy rots the bones." Jealousy won't help you be a better friend. Instead it can cause you to cut people down so that you look better by comparison. Let's choose to follow Romans 12:15, which tells us to rejoice with others when they are joyful, not to be envious.

When you feel jealousy coming on, first thank God for the things you have. List the talents and skills God has given you. Next, pray for and congratulate the person you're jealous of. It's hard to be mad at someone when you're giving them a high five!

your wife. Just serve me bravely and fight the LORD's battles." Saul said to himself, "I won't have to lift my hand to strike him down. The Philistines will do that!"

[18] But David said to Saul, "Who am I? Is anyone in my whole family that important in Israel? Am I worthy to become the king's son-in-law?" [19] The time came for Saul to give his daughter Merab to David. Instead, Saul gave her to Adriel from Meholah to be his wife.

[20] Saul's daughter Michal was in love with David. When they told Saul about it, he was pleased. [21] "I'll give her to David to be his wife," Saul said to himself. "Then maybe she'll trap him. And maybe the Philistines will strike him down." So Saul said to David, "Now you have a second chance to become my son-in-law."

[22] Then Saul gave an order to his attendants. He said, "Speak to David in private. Tell him, 'The king likes you. All his attendants love you. So become his son-in-law.'"

[23] Saul's attendants spoke those very words to David. But David said, "Do you think it's a small thing to become the king's son-in-law? I'm only a poor man. I'm not very well known."

[24] Saul's attendants told him what David had said. [25] Saul said, "Tell David, 'Here's the price the king wants for the bride. He wants you to kill 100 Philistines. Then bring back the skins you cut off when you circumcise them. That's how Saul will get even with his enemies.'" Saul hoped that the Philistines would strike David down.

[26] Saul's attendants also told David those things. Then David was pleased to become the king's son-in-law. So before the wedding day, [27] David and his men went out and killed 200 Philistines. They circumcised the Philistines. Then David brought back all the skins. They counted out the full number and gave them to the king. By doing that, David could become the king's son-in-law. So Saul gave David his daughter Michal to be his wife.

Jason's Jargon

1 SAMUEL 18

Search this chapter for the word *tambourine*. A tambourine is a musical instrument in the percussion section of an orchestra. It looks like a small drum with jingles on the side.

[28]Saul realized that the LORD was with David. He also realized that his daughter Michal loved David. [29]So Saul became even more afraid of him. As long as Saul lived, he remained David's enemy.

[30]The Philistine commanders kept on going out to battle. Every time they did, David had more success against them than the rest of Saul's officers. So his name became well known.

Saul Tries to Kill David

19 Saul told his son Jonathan and all the attendants to kill David. But Jonathan liked David very much. [2]So Jonathan warned him, "My father Saul is looking for a chance to kill you. Be very careful tomorrow morning. Find a place to hide and stay there. [3]My father and I will come and stand in the field where you are hiding. I'll speak to him about you. Then I'll tell you what I find out."

[4]Jonathan told his father Saul some good things about David. He said to him, "Please don't do anything to harm David. He hasn't done anything to harm you. And what he's done has helped you a lot. [5]He put his own life in danger when he killed Goliath. The LORD used him to win a great battle for the whole nation of Israel. When you saw it, you were glad. So why would you do anything to harm a man like David? He isn't guilty of doing anything to harm you. Why would you want to kill him without any reason?"

[6]Saul paid attention to Jonathan. Saul made a promise. He said, "You can be sure that the LORD lives. And you can be just as sure that David will not be put to death."

[7]So Jonathan sent for David and told him everything he and Saul had said. Then he brought David to Saul. David served Saul as he had done before.

[8]Once more war broke out. So David went out and fought against the Philistines. He struck them down with so much force that they ran away from him.

[9]But an evil spirit sent by the LORD came on Saul. It happened as he was sitting in his house and holding his spear. While David was playing the harp, [10]Saul tried to pin him to the wall with his spear. But David got away from him just as Saul drove the spear into the wall. That night David escaped.

[11]Saul sent some men to watch David's house. He told them to kill David the next morning. But David's wife Michal warned him. She said, "You must run for your life tonight. If you don't, tomorrow you will be killed." [12]So Michal helped David escape through a window. He ran and got away. [13]Then Michal got a statue of a god. She laid it on David's bed. She covered it with clothes. And she put some goat hair at the place where David's head would have been.

[14]Saul sent the men to capture David. But Michal told them, "He's sick."

[15]Then Saul sent the men back to see David. He told them, "Bring him up here to me in his bed. Then I'll kill him." [16]But when the men entered, the only thing they found in the bed was the statue. Some goat hair was at the place where David's head would have been.

[17]Saul said to Michal, "Why did you trick me like this? Why did you help my enemy escape?"

Michal told him, "He said to me, 'Help me get away. If you don't, I'll kill you.'"

[18]After David had run away and escaped, he went to Samuel at Ramah. He told him everything Saul had done to him. Then David and Samuel went to Naioth and stayed there. [19]Saul was told, "David is in Naioth at Ramah." [20]So Saul sent some men to capture him. When they got there, they saw a group of prophets who were prophesying. Samuel was standing there as their leader. Then the Spirit of God came on Saul's men. So they also began to prophesy. [21]Saul was told about it. So he sent some more men. They began to prophesy too. Saul sent some men a third time. And they also began to

prophesy. ²²Finally, Saul decided to go to Ramah himself. He went to the large well at Seku. He asked some people, "Where are Samuel and David?"

"Over in Naioth at Ramah," they said.

²³So Saul went to Naioth at Ramah. But the Spirit of God even came on him. He walked along and prophesied until he came to Naioth. ²⁴There he took off his clothes. Then he also prophesied in front of Samuel. He lay there without his clothes on all that day and night. That's why people say, "Is Saul also one of the prophets?"

David and Jonathan

20 David was in Naioth at Ramah. He ran away from there to where Jonathan was. He asked him, "What have I done? What crime have I committed? I haven't done anything to harm your father. So why is he trying to kill me?"

²"That will never happen!" Jonathan replied. "You aren't going to die! My father doesn't do anything at all without letting me know. So why would he hide this from me? He isn't going to kill you!"

David and Jonathan modeled true friendship. Whit taught Craig Moorhead about what friendship means in "The Life of the Party" (A#01).

³But David strongly disagreed. He said, "Your father knows very well that you are pleased with me. He has said to himself, 'I don't want Jonathan to know I'm planning to kill David. If he finds out, he'll be very sad.' But I'm very close to being killed. And that's just as sure as the LORD and you are alive."

⁴Jonathan said to David, "I'll do anything you want me to do for you."

⁵So David said, "Tomorrow is the time for the New Moon feast. I'm supposed to eat with the king. But let me go and hide in the field. I'll stay there until the evening of the day after tomorrow. ⁶Your father might miss me. If he does, then tell him, 'David begged me to let him hurry

Do you have a best friend? One who laughs at your worst jokes? Maybe your best friend had to move away, or you haven't experienced this kind of friendship yet.

Find out about true friendship by studying David and Jonathan. One lesson we can learn from their relationship is that Jonathan didn't give it a half-hearted effort, waiting to see if David would return his kindness. Jonathan was all-in from the start. He gave David gifts and his undying support, even though Jonathan knew that David would become king instead of him.

That's no small thing. Think about it: Your dad is king over all the land, which means you are next in line for the throne. All the power. A cool crown. Servants to take care of your every need. Then one day, some other kid slays a giant, moves into the palace, and seems to be taking your place. Would you want to be best buddies with this guy, or might you resent him a little? Jonathan humbly embraced David as a true friend.

WHAT ABOUT YOU?

If you want to be somebody's best friend, remember Jonathan. He was there for David in good times and bad. He rooted for David. He served and defended David. Find a creative way to serve your best friend today. Bake cookies for her. Help him fix his bike. Or just listen and be supportive. If you're still looking for a friend like that, think about what Jonathan did and put others first. You never know whom you might meet!

home to Bethlehem. A yearly sacrifice is being offered there for his whole family group.' ⁷Your father might say, 'That's all right.' If he does, it will mean I'm safe. But he might become very angry. If he does, you can be sure he's made up his mind to harm me. ⁸Please be kind to me. You have made a covenant with me in front of the LORD. If I'm guilty, kill me yourself! Don't hand me over to your father!"

⁹"I would never do that!" Jonathan said. "Suppose I had even the smallest clue that my father had made up his mind to harm you. Then I would tell you."

¹⁰David asked, "Who will tell me if your father answers you in a mean way?"

¹¹"Come on," Jonathan said. "Let's go out to the field." So they went there together.

¹²Then Jonathan spoke to David. He said, "I promise you that I'll find out what my father is planning to do. I'll find out by this time the day after tomorrow. The LORD, the God of Israel, is my witness. Suppose my father has kind feelings toward you. Then I'll send you a message and let you know. ¹³But suppose he wants to harm you. And I don't let you know about it. Suppose I don't help you get away in peace. Then may the LORD punish me greatly. May he be with you, just as he has been with my father. ¹⁴But always be kind to me, just as the LORD is. Be kind to me as long as I live. Then I won't be killed. ¹⁵And never stop being kind to my family. Don't stop even when the LORD has cut off every one of your enemies from the face of the earth."

¹⁶So Jonathan made a covenant of friendship with David and his family. He said, "May the LORD hold David's enemies responsible for what they've done." ¹⁷Jonathan had David promise his friendship again because he loved him. In fact, Jonathan loved David just as he loved himself.

¹⁸Then Jonathan said to David, "Tomorrow is the time for the New Moon feast. You will be missed, because your seat at the table will be empty. ¹⁹Go to the place where you hid when all this trouble

WOOTON'S FUN FACTS

1 Sam. 20:17
Leviticus 19:18 is the famous verse, "Love your neighbor as you love yourself." Jesus quoted this verse too. Jonathan lived it out through his friendship with David.

began. Go there the day after tomorrow, when evening is approaching. There's a stone out there called Ezel. ²⁰Wait by it. I'll shoot three arrows to one side of the stone. I'll pretend I'm practicing my shooting. ²¹Then I'll send a boy out there. I'll tell him, 'Go and find the arrows.' Suppose I say to him, 'The arrows are on this side of you. Bring them here.' Then come. That will mean you are safe. You won't be in any danger. And that's just as sure as the LORD is alive. ²²But suppose I tell the boy, 'The arrows are far beyond you.' Then go. That will mean the LORD is sending you away. ²³And remember what we talked about. Remember that the LORD is a witness between you and me forever."

²⁴So David hid in the field. When the time for the New Moon feast came, the king sat down to eat. ²⁵He sat in his usual place by the wall. Jonathan sat across from him. Abner sat next to Saul. But David's place was empty. ²⁶Saul didn't say anything that day. He said to himself, "Something must have happened to David to make him 'unclean.' That must be why he isn't here." ²⁷But the next day, David's place was empty again. It was the second day of the month. Finally, Saul spoke to his son Jonathan. He said, "Why hasn't the son of Jesse come to the meal? He hasn't been here yesterday or today."

BIBLE ADVENTURES

Isaac got in the Imagination Station to see the story of David and Jonathan in "Isaac the True Friend" (A#LE).

[28]Jonathan replied, "David begged me to let him go to Bethlehem. [29]He said, 'Let me go. Our family is offering a sacrifice in the town. My brother has ordered me to be there. Are you pleased with me? If you are, let me go and see my brothers.' That's why he hasn't come to eat at your table."

[30]Saul became very angry with Jonathan. He said to him, "You are an evil son. You have refused to obey me. I know that you are on the side of Jesse's son. You should be ashamed of that. And your mother should be ashamed of having a son like you. [31]You will never be king as long as Jesse's son lives on this earth. And you will never have a kingdom either. So send someone to bring the son of Jesse to me. He must die!"

[32]"Why do you want to put him to death?" Jonathan asked his father. "What has he done?" [33]But Saul threw his spear at Jonathan to kill him. Then Jonathan knew that his father wanted to kill David.

[34]So Jonathan got up from the table. He was very angry. On that second day of the feast, he refused to eat. He was very sad that his father was treating David so badly.

[35]The next morning Jonathan went out to the field to meet David. He took a young boy with him. [36]He said to the boy, "Run and find the arrows I shoot." As the boy ran, Jonathan shot an arrow far beyond him. [37]The boy came to the place where Jonathan's arrow had fallen. Then Jonathan shouted to him, "The arrow went far beyond you, didn't it?" [38]He continued, "Hurry up! Run fast! Don't stop!" The boy picked up the arrow and returned to his master. [39]The boy didn't know what was going on. Only Jonathan and David knew. [40]Jonathan gave his weapons to the boy. He told him, "Go back to town. Take the weapons with you."

[41]After the boy had gone, David got up from the south side of the stone. He bowed down in front of Jonathan with his face to the ground. He did it three times. Then they kissed each other and cried. But David cried more than Jonathan did.

[42]Jonathan said to David, "Go in peace. In the name of the LORD we've promised to be friends. We have said, 'The LORD is a witness between you and me. He's a witness between your children and my children forever.'" Then David left, and Jonathan went back to the town.

David at Nob

21 David went to Ahimelek the priest at Nob. Ahimelek trembled with fear when he met him. He asked David, "Why are you alone? Why isn't anyone with you?"

[2]David answered Ahimelek the priest, "The king gave me a special job to do. He said to me, 'I don't want anyone to know what I'm sending you to do. So don't say anything about it.' I've told my men to meet me at a certain place. [3]Do you have anything for us to eat? Give me five loaves of bread, or anything else you can find."

[4]But the priest answered David, "I don't have any bread that isn't holy. I only have some holy bread here. But it's for men who haven't slept with women recently."

[5]David replied, "Well, we haven't slept with women recently. That's the way it is every time I lead my men out to battle. We keep ourselves holy even when we do jobs that aren't holy. And that's even more true today." [6]So the priest gave him the holy bread. It was the only bread he had. It had been removed from the table that was in front of the LORD. On the same day, hot bread had been put in its place.

[7]One of Saul's servants was there that day. He had been made to stay at the holy tent for a while. He was Doeg from Edom. Doeg was Saul's chief shepherd.

[8]David asked Ahimelek, "Don't you have a spear or sword here? I haven't brought my sword or any other weapon. That's because the job the king gave me to do had to be done right away."

[9]The priest replied, "The sword of Goliath, the Philistine, is here. You killed him in the Valley of Elah. His sword is wrapped in a cloth. It's behind the sacred linen apron. If you want it, take it. It's the only sword here."

David said, "There isn't any sword like it. Give it to me."

David at Gath

[10]That day David ran away from Saul. He went to Achish, the king of Gath. [11]But the servants of Achish spoke to him. They said, "Isn't this David, the king of the land? Isn't he the one the Israelites sing about when they dance? They sing,

"'Saul has killed thousands of men. David has killed tens of thousands.'"

[12]David paid close attention to what the servants were saying. He became very much afraid of what Achish, the king of Gath, might do. [13]So he pretended to be out of his mind when he was with them. As long as he was in Gath, he acted like a crazy person. He made marks on the doors of the city gate. He let spit run down his beard.

[14]Achish said to his servants, "Just look at the man! He's out of his mind! Why are you bringing him to me? [15]Don't I have enough crazy people around me already? So why do you have to bring this fellow here? Just look at how he's carrying on in front of me! Why do you have to bring this man into my house?"

David at Adullam and Mizpah

22 David left Gath and escaped to the cave of Adullam. His brothers and the other members of his family heard about it. So they went down to join him there. [2]Everyone who was in trouble or owed money or was unhappy gathered around him. He became their commander. About 400 men were with him.

[3]From there David went to Mizpah in Moab. He spoke to the king of Moab. He said, "Please let my father and mother come and stay with you. Let them stay until I learn what God will do for me." [4]So David left his parents with the king of Moab. They stayed with him as long as David was in his usual place of safety.

[5]But the prophet Gad spoke to David. He said, "Don't stay in your usual place of safety. Go into the land of Judah." So David left and went to the forest of Hereth.

Saul Kills the Priests at Nob

[6]Saul heard that the place where David and his men were hiding had been discovered. Saul was sitting under a tamarisk tree on the hill at Gibeah. He was holding his spear. All his officials were standing at his side. [7]Saul said to them, "Men of Benjamin, listen to me! Do you think Jesse's son will give all of you fields and vineyards? Do you think he'll make some of you commanders of thousands of men? Do you think he'll make the rest of you commanders of hundreds? [8]Is that why all of you have joined together against me? No one tells me when my son makes a covenant with Jesse's son. None of you is

concerned about me. No one tells me that my son has stirred up Jesse's son to hide and wait to attack me. But that's exactly what's happening now."

[9]Doeg was standing with Saul's officials. He was from Edom. He said, "I saw Jesse's son David come to Ahimelek at Nob. Ahimelek is the son of Ahitub. [10]Ahimelek asked the LORD a question for David. He also gave him food and the sword of Goliath, the Philistine."

[11]Then the king sent for the priest Ahimelek, the son of Ahitub. The king also sent for all the men in his family. They were the priests at Nob. All of them came to the king. [12]Saul said, "Son of Ahitub, listen to me."

"Yes, master," he answered.

[13]Saul said to him, "Why have you and Jesse's son joined together against me? Why did you give him bread and a sword? Why did you ask God a question for him? Now he has turned against me. He is hiding and waiting to attack me right now."

[14]Ahimelek answered the king, "David is faithful to you. In fact, he's more faithful to you than anyone else who serves you. He's your own son-in-law. He's the captain of your own personal guards. He's highly respected by everyone in your palace. [15]Was that day the first time I asked God a question for him? Of course not! Please don't bring charges against me. Please don't bring charges against anyone in my family. I don't know anything at all about this whole matter."

[16]But the king said, "Ahimelek, you will certainly be put to death. You and your whole family will be put to death."

[17]Then the king gave an order to the guards at his side. He said, "Go and kill the priests of the LORD. They are on David's side too. They knew he was running away from me. And they didn't even tell me."

But the king's officials wouldn't raise a hand to strike down the priests of the LORD.

[18]Then the king ordered Doeg, "You go and strike down the priests." So Doeg, the Edomite, went and struck them down. That day he killed 85 priests who wore linen aprons. [19]He also killed the people of Nob with his sword. Nob was a town where priests lived. Doeg killed its men and women. He killed its children and

babies. He also destroyed its cattle, donkeys and sheep. ²⁰But Abiathar, a son of Ahimelek, escaped. Ahimelek was the son of Ahitub. Abiathar ran away and joined David. ²¹He told David that Saul had killed the priests of the Lord. ²²Then David said to Abiathar, "One day I was at Nob. I saw Doeg, the Edomite, there. I knew he would be sure to tell Saul. Your whole family has been killed. And I'm responsible for it. ²³So stay with me. Don't be afraid. The man who wants to kill you wants to kill me too. You will be safe with me."

David Saves the People of Keilah

23 David was told, "The Philistines are fighting against the town of Keilah. They are stealing grain from the threshing floors." ²So he asked the Lord for advice. He said, "Should I go and attack those Philistines?"

The Lord answered him, "Go and attack them. Save Keilah."

³But David's men said to him, "We're afraid here in Judah. Suppose we go to Keilah and fight against the Philistine army. Then we'll be even more afraid."

⁴Once again David asked the Lord what he should do. The Lord answered him, "Go down to Keilah. I am going to hand the Philistines over to you." ⁵So David and his men went to Keilah. They fought against the Philistines and carried off their livestock. David wounded and killed large numbers of Philistines. And he saved the people of Keilah. ⁶Abiathar, the son of Ahimelek, had brought down the sacred linen apron with him from Nob. He did it when he ran away to David at Keilah.

Saul Chases David

⁷Saul was told that David had gone to Keilah. He said, "God has handed him over to me. David has trapped himself by entering a town that has gates with metal bars." ⁸So Saul brought together all his soldiers to go to battle. He ordered them to go down to Keilah. He told them to surround David and his men. He told them to get ready to attack them.

⁹David learned that Saul was planning to attack him. So he said to Abiathar the priest, "Bring the linen apron." ¹⁰Then David said, "Lord, you are the God of Israel. I know for sure that Saul plans to come to Keilah. He plans to destroy the town because of me. ¹¹Will the citizens of Keilah hand me over to him? Will Saul come down here, as I've heard he would? Lord, you are the God of Israel. Please answer me."

The Lord said, "He will come down."

¹²Again David asked, "Will the citizens of Keilah hand me and my men over to Saul?"

And the Lord said, "They will."

¹³So David and his men left Keilah. The total number of them was about 600. They kept moving from place to place. Saul was told that David had escaped from Keilah. So he didn't go there.

¹⁴Sometimes David stayed in places of safety in the desert. At other times he stayed in the hills of the Desert of Ziph. Day after day Saul looked for him. But God didn't hand David over to him.

¹⁵David was at Horesh in the Desert of Ziph. There he learned that Saul had come out to kill him. ¹⁶Saul's son Jonathan went to David at Horesh. He told David that God would make him strong. ¹⁷"Don't be afraid," he said. "My father Saul won't harm you. You will be king over Israel. And I will be next in command. Even my father Saul knows this." ¹⁸The two of them made a covenant of friendship in front of the Lord. Then Jonathan went home. But David remained at Horesh.

¹⁹The people of Ziph went up to Saul at Gibeah. They said, "David is hiding among us. He's hiding in places of safety at Horesh. Horesh is south of Jeshimon on the hill of Hakilah. ²⁰Your Majesty, come down when it pleases you to come. It will be our duty to hand David over to you."

²¹Saul replied, "May the Lord bless you because you were concerned about me. ²²Make sure you are right. Go and check things out again. Find out where David usually goes. Find out who has seen him there. People tell me he's very tricky. ²³Find out about all the hiding places he uses. Come back to me with all the facts. I'll go with you. Suppose he's in the area. Then I'll track him down among all the family groups of Judah."

²⁴So they started out. They went to Ziph ahead of Saul. David and his men were in the Desert of Maon. Maon is south of Jeshimon in the Arabah Valley.

²⁵Saul and his men started out to look for David. David was told about it. So he went down to a rock in the Desert of Maon to hide. Saul heard he was there. So he went into the Desert of Maon to chase David.

²⁶Saul was going along one side of the mountain. David and his men were on the other side. They were hurrying to get away from Saul. Saul and his army were closing in on David and his men. They were about to capture them. ²⁷Just then a messenger came to Saul. He said, "Come quickly! The Philistines are attacking the land." ²⁸So Saul stopped chasing David. He went to fight against the Philistines. That's why they call that place Sela Hammahlekoth. ²⁹David left that place. He went and lived in places of safety near En Gedi.

David Doesn't Kill Saul When He Has the Chance

24 Saul returned from chasing the Philistines. Then he was told, "David is in the Desert of En Gedi." ²So Saul took 3,000 of the best soldiers from the whole nation of Israel. He started out to look for David and his men. He planned to look near the Rocky Cliffs of the Wild Goats.

³He came to some sheep pens along the way. A cave was there. Saul went in to go to the toilet. David and his men were far back in the cave. ⁴David's men said, "This is the day the LORD told you about. He said to you, 'I will hand your enemy over to you. Then you can deal with him as you want to.'" So David came up close to Saul without being seen. He cut off a corner of Saul's robe.

⁵Later, David felt sorry that he had cut off a corner of Saul's robe. ⁶He said to his men, "May the LORD keep me from doing a thing like that again to my master. He is the LORD's anointed king. So I promise that I will never lay my hand on him. The LORD has anointed him." ⁷David said that to correct his men. He wanted them to know that they should never suggest harming the king. He didn't allow them to attack Saul. So Saul left the cave and went on his way.

⁸Then David went out of the cave. He called out to Saul, "King Saul! My master!" When Saul looked behind him, David bowed down. He lay down flat with his face toward the ground. ⁹He said to

Saul, "Why do you listen when men say, 'David is trying to harm you'? ¹⁰This day you have seen with your own eyes how the LORD handed you over to me in the cave. Some of my men begged me to kill you. But I didn't. I said, 'I will never lay my hand on my master. He is the LORD's anointed king.' ¹¹Look, my father! Look at this piece of your robe in my hand! I cut off the corner of your robe. But I didn't kill you. See, there is nothing in my hand that shows I am guilty of doing anything wrong. I haven't turned against you. I haven't done anything to harm you. But you are hunting me down. You want to kill me. ¹²May the LORD judge between you and me. And may the LORD pay you back because of the wrong things you have done to me. But I won't do anything to hurt you. ¹³People say, 'Evil acts come from those who do evil.' So I won't do anything to hurt you.

¹⁴"King Saul, who are you trying to catch? Who do you think you are chasing? I'm nothing but a dead dog or a flea! ¹⁵May the LORD be our judge. May he decide between us. May he consider my case and stand up for me. May he show that I'm not guilty of doing anything wrong. May he save me from you."

¹⁶When David finished speaking, Saul asked him a question. He said, "My son David, is that your voice?" And Saul wept out loud. ¹⁷"You are a better person than I am," he said. "You have treated me well. But I've treated you badly. ¹⁸You have just now told me about the good things you did to me. The LORD handed me over to you. But you didn't kill me. ¹⁹Suppose a man finds his enemy. He doesn't let him get away without harming him. May the LORD reward you with many good things. May he do it because of the way you treated me today. ²⁰I know for sure that you will be king. I know that the kingdom of Israel will be made secure under your control. ²¹Now make a promise in the name of the LORD. Promise me that you won't kill the children of my family. Also promise me that you won't wipe out my name from my family line."

²²So David made that promise to Saul. Then Saul returned home. But David and his men went up to his usual place of safety.

David, Nabal and Abigail

25 When Samuel died, the whole nation of Israel gathered together. They were filled with sorrow because he was dead. They buried him at his home in Ramah. Then David went down into the Desert of Paran.

²A certain man in Maon was very wealthy. He owned property there at Carmel. He had 1,000 goats and 3,000 sheep. He was clipping the wool off the sheep in Carmel. ³His name was Nabal. His wife's name was Abigail. She was a wise and beautiful woman. But her husband was rude and mean in the way he treated others. He was from the family of Caleb.

⁴David was staying in the Desert of Paran. While he was there, he heard that Nabal was clipping the wool off his sheep. ⁵So he sent for ten young men. He said to them, "Go up to Nabal at Carmel. Greet him for me. ⁶Say to him, 'May you live a long time! May everything go well with you and your family! And may things go well with everything that belongs to you!

⁷"'I hear that you are clipping the wool off your sheep. When your shepherds were with us, we treated them well. The whole time they were at Carmel nothing that belonged to them was stolen. ⁸Ask your own servants. They'll tell you. We've come to you now at a happy time of the year. Please be kind to my men. Please give me and my men anything you can find for us.'"

⁹When David's men arrived, they gave Nabal the message from David. Then they waited.

¹⁰Nabal answered David's servants, "Who is this David? Who is this son of Jesse? Many servants are running away from their masters these days. ¹¹Why should I give away my bread and water? Why should I give away the meat I've prepared for those who clip the wool off my sheep? Why should I give food to men who come from who knows where?"

¹²So David's men turned around and went back. When they arrived, they reported to David every word Nabal had spoken. ¹³David said to his men, "Each of you put on your swords!" So they did. David put his sword on too. About 400 men went up with David. Two hundred men stayed behind with the supplies.

¹⁴One of the servants warned Abigail, Nabal's wife. He said, "David sent some

WHAT ABOUT YOU?

Read the story of Nabal, who was in a position to have serious regrets over the way he treated King David. Unfortunately, he made a mistake that nearly cost the lives of his entire household. Fortunately, he was blessed with a wife, Abigail, who saved the day. Unfortunately, he didn't live long after that. Fortunately, this freed Abigail to marry David, who recognized her wisdom and intelligence.

No doubt, you've made mistakes of your own. Most of us look back on certain things we've done and wish we had acted differently. Can you relate? Have you ever missed an opportunity or regretted a decision? Maybe you didn't encourage someone who was having a bad day. Or you felt too scared to try out for the church play.

We can avoid regrets by taking advantage of the opportunities God wants us to pursue. That may include showing kindness, standing up for a friend, or telling someone about Jesus. We all make mistakes. Everyone has regrets. Thankfully, God is there to forgive us and encourage us to be bolder next time.

What is something you've regretted doing or not doing? Why? How would you change things if given a do-over? Maybe it's not too late to try again with a phone call or apology. Ask God for courage to make the most of your opportunities.

messengers from the desert to give his greetings to our master. But Nabal shouted at them and was rude to them. ¹⁵David's men had been very good to us. They treated us well. The whole time we were near them out in the fields, nothing was stolen. ¹⁶We were taking care of our sheep near them. During that time, they were like a wall around us night and day. They kept us safe. ¹⁷Now think it over. See what you can do. Horrible trouble will soon come to our master and his whole family. He's such an evil man that no one can even talk to him."

¹⁸Abigail didn't waste any time. She got 200 loaves of bread and two bottles of wine. The bottles were made out of animal skins. She got five sheep that were ready to be cooked. She got a bushel of grain that had been cooked. She got 100 raisin cakes. And she got 200 cakes of pressed figs. She loaded all of it on the backs of donkeys. ¹⁹Then she told her servants, "Go on ahead. I'll follow you." But she didn't tell her husband Nabal about it.

²⁰Abigail rode her donkey into a mountain valley. There she saw David and his men. They were coming down toward her. ²¹David had just said, "Everything we've done hasn't been worth a thing! I watched over that fellow's property in the desert. I made sure none of it was stolen. But he has paid me back evil for good. ²²I won't leave even one of his men alive until morning. If I do, may God punish me greatly!"

²³When Abigail saw David, she quickly got off her donkey. She bowed down in front of David with her face toward the ground. ²⁴She fell at his feet. She said, "Pardon your servant, sir. Please let me speak to you. Listen to what I'm saying. Let me take the blame myself. ²⁵Please don't pay any attention to that evil man Nabal. His name means Foolish Person. And that's exactly what he is. He's always doing foolish things. I'm sorry I didn't get a chance to see the men you sent. ²⁶Sir, the LORD has kept you from killing Nabal and his men. He has kept you from using your own hands to get even. So may what's about to happen to Nabal happen to all your enemies. May it happen to everyone who wants to harm you. And may it happen just as surely as the LORD your God

and you are alive. ²⁷I've brought a gift for you. Give it to the men who follow you.

²⁸"Please forgive me if I shouldn't have done that. The LORD your God will certainly give you and your family line a kingdom that will last. That's because you fight the LORD's battles. You won't do anything wrong as long as you live. ²⁹Someone may chase you and try to kill you. But the LORD your God will keep your life safe like a treasure hidden in a bag. And he'll destroy your enemies. Their lives will be thrown away, just as a stone is thrown from a sling. ³⁰The LORD will do for you every good thing he promised to do. He'll appoint you ruler over Israel. ³¹When that happens, you won't have this heavy load on your mind. You won't have to worry about how you killed people without any reason. You won't have to worry about how you got even. The LORD your God will give you success. When that happens, please remember me."

³²David said to Abigail, "Give praise to the LORD. He is the God of Israel. He has sent you today to find me. ³³May the LORD bless you for what you have done. You have shown a lot of good sense. You have kept me from killing Nabal and his men this day. You have kept me from using my own hands to get even. ³⁴It's a good thing you came quickly to meet me. If you hadn't come, not one of Nabal's men

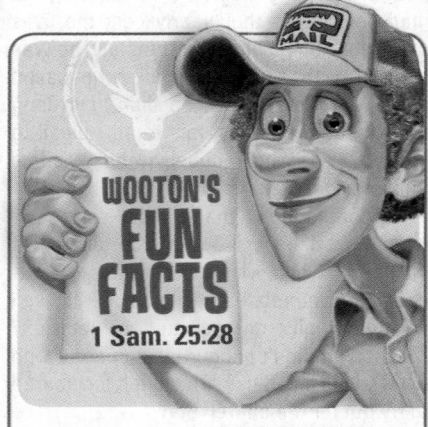

WOOTON'S **FUN FACTS**
1 Sam. 25:28

Abigail had a lot of good things to say. But unfortunately, her prophecy wasn't actually true; David would do something very wrong. Stay tuned for 2 Samuel 11.

would have been left alive by sunrise. And that's just as sure as the LORD, the God of Israel, is alive. He has kept me from harming you."

³⁵Then David accepted from her what she had brought him. He said, "Go home in peace. I've heard your words. I'll do what you have asked."

³⁶Abigail went back to Nabal. He was having a dinner party in the house. It was the kind of dinner a king would have. He had been drinking too much wine. He was very drunk. So she didn't tell him anything at all until sunrise. ³⁷The next morning Nabal wasn't drunk anymore. Then his wife told him everything. When she did, his heart grew weak. He became like a stone. ³⁸About ten days later, the LORD struck Nabal down. And he died.

³⁹David heard that Nabal was dead. So he said, "Give praise to the LORD. Nabal was rude to me. But the LORD stood up for me. He has kept me from doing something wrong. He has paid Nabal back for the wrong things he did."

Then David sent a message to Abigail. He asked her to become his wife. ⁴⁰His servants went to Carmel. They said to Abigail, "David has sent us to you. He wants you to come back with us and become his wife."

⁴¹Abigail bowed down with her face toward the ground. She said, "I am your servant. I'm ready to serve him. I'm ready to wash the feet of his servants." ⁴²Abigail quickly got on a donkey and went with David's messengers. Her five female servants went with her. She became David's wife. ⁴³David had also married Ahinoam from Jezreel. Both of them became his wives. ⁴⁴But Saul had given his daughter Michal, David's first wife, to Paltiel. Paltiel was from Gallim. He was the son of Laish.

Once Again David Doesn't Kill Saul When He Has the Chance

26 Some people from Ziph went to Saul at Gibeah. They said, "David is hiding on the hill of Hakilah. It faces Jeshimon."

²So Saul went down to the Desert of Ziph. He took 3,000 of the best soldiers in Israel with him. They went to the desert to look for David. ³Saul set up his camp beside the road. It was on the hill of Hakilah facing Jeshimon. But David stayed in the desert. He saw that Saul had followed him there. ⁴So he sent out scouts. From them he learned that Saul had arrived.

⁵Then David started out. He went to the place where Saul had camped. He saw where Saul and Abner were lying down. Saul was lying inside the camp. The army was camped all around him. Abner was commander of the army. He was the son of Ner.

⁶Then David spoke to Ahimelek, the Hittite. He also spoke to Joab's brother Abishai, the son of Zeruiah. He asked them, "Who will go down with me into the camp to Saul?"

"I'll go with you," said Abishai.

⁷So that night David and Abishai went into the camp. They found Saul lying asleep inside the camp. His spear was stuck in the ground near his head. Abner and the soldiers were lying asleep around him.

⁸Abishai said to David, "Today God has handed your enemy over to you. So let me pin him to the ground. I can do it with one jab of the spear. I won't even have to strike him twice."

⁹But David said to Abishai, "Don't destroy him! No one can do any harm to the LORD's anointed king and not be guilty. ¹⁰You can be sure that the LORD lives," he said. "And you can be just as sure that the LORD himself will strike Saul down. Perhaps he'll die a natural death. Or perhaps he'll go into battle and be killed. ¹¹May the LORD keep me from doing anything to harm his anointed king. Now get the spear and water jug that are near his head. Then let's leave."

¹²So David took the spear and water jug that were near Saul's head. Then he and Abishai left. No one saw them. No one knew about what they had done. In fact, no one even woke up. Everyone was sleeping. That's because the LORD had put them into a deep sleep.

¹³David went across to the other side of the valley. He stood on top of a hill far away from Saul's camp. There was a wide space between them. ¹⁴He called out to the army and to Abner, the son of Ner. He said, "Abner! Aren't you going to answer me?"

Abner replied, "Who is calling out to the king?"

¹⁵David said, "You are a great soldier, aren't you? There isn't anyone else like you

in Israel. So why didn't you guard the king? He's your master, isn't he? Someone came into the camp to destroy him. ¹⁶You didn't guard him. And that isn't good. You can be sure that the LORD lives. And you can be just as sure that you and your men must die. That's because you didn't guard your master. He's the LORD's anointed king. Look around you. Where are the king's spear and water jug that were near his head?"

¹⁷Saul recognized David's voice. He said, "My son David, is that your voice?"

David replied, "Yes it is, King Saul, my master." ¹⁸He continued, "Why are you chasing me? What evil thing have I done? What am I guilty of? ¹⁹King Saul, please listen to what I'm saying. Was it the LORD who made you angry with me? If it was, may he accept my offering. Was it people who made you angry at me? If it was, may the LORD see them cursed. They have driven me today from my share of the LORD's land. By doing that, they might as well have said, 'Go and serve other gods.' ²⁰Don't spill my blood on the ground far away from where the LORD lives. King Saul, you have come out to look for nothing but a flea. It's as if you were hunting a partridge in the mountains."

²¹Then Saul said, "I have sinned. My son David, come back. Today you thought my life was very special. So I won't try to harm you again. I've really acted like a foolish person. I've made a huge mistake."

²²"Here's your spear," David answered. "Send one of your young men over to get it. ²³The LORD rewards everyone for doing what is right and being faithful. He handed you over to me today. But I wouldn't harm you. You are the LORD's anointed king. ²⁴Today I thought your life had great value. In the same way, may the LORD think of my life as having great value. May he save me from all trouble."

²⁵Then Saul said to David, "May the LORD bless you, David my son. You will do great things. You will also have great success."

So David went on his way. And Saul returned home.

David Among the Philistines

27 David thought, "Some day Saul will destroy me. So the best thing I can do is escape. I'll go to the land of the Philistines. Then Saul will stop looking for me everywhere in Israel. His hand won't be able to reach me."

²So David and his 600 men left Israel. They went to Achish, the king of Gath. He was the son of Maok. ³David and his men made their homes in Gath near Achish. Each of David's men had his family with him. David had his two wives with him. They were Ahinoam from Jezreel and Abigail from Carmel. Abigail was Nabal's widow. ⁴Saul was told that David had run away to Gath. So he didn't look for David anymore.

⁵David said to Achish, "If you are pleased with me, give me a place in one of your country towns. I can live there. I don't really need to live near you in the royal city."

⁶So on that day Achish gave David the town of Ziklag. It has belonged to the kings of Judah ever since that time. ⁷David lived in Philistine territory for a year and four months.

⁸Sometimes David and his men would go up and attack the Geshurites. At other times they would attack the Girzites or the Amalekites. All those people had lived in the land that reached all the way to Shur and Egypt. They had been there for a long time. ⁹When David would attack an area, he wouldn't leave a man or woman alive. But he would take their sheep, cattle, donkeys, camels and clothes. Then he would return to Achish.

¹⁰Achish would ask, "Who did you attack today?" David would answer, "The people who live in the Negev Desert of Judah." Or he would answer, "The people in the Negev Desert of Jerahmeel." Or he would answer, "The people in the Negev Desert of the Kenites." ¹¹David wouldn't leave a man or woman alive to be brought back to Gath. He thought, "They might tell on us. They might tell Achish who we really attacked." That's what David did as long as he lived in Philistine territory. ¹²Achish trusted David. He thought, "David's own people, the Israelites, can't stand him anymore. So he'll be my servant for life."

28 While David was living in Ziklag, the Philistines gathered their army together. They planned to fight against Israel. Achish said to David, "Here is what you must understand. You and your men must march out with me and my army."

²David said, "I understand. You will see for yourself what I can do."

Achish replied, "All right. I'll make you my own personal guard for life."

Saul and the Woman at Endor

³Samuel had died. The whole nation of Israel was filled with sorrow because he was dead. They had buried him in his own town of Ramah. Saul had thrown out of the land people who get messages from those who have died. He had also thrown out people who talk to the spirits of the dead.

⁴The Philistines gathered together and set up camp at Shunem. At the same time, Saul gathered together all the Israelites. They set up camp at Gilboa. ⁵When Saul saw the Philistine army, he was afraid. Terror filled his heart. ⁶He asked the LORD for advice. But the LORD didn't answer him through dreams or prophets. He didn't answer him when Saul had the priest cast lots by using the Urim. ⁷Saul spoke to his attendants. He said, "Find me a woman who gets messages from those who have died. Then I can go and ask her some questions."

"There's a woman like that in Endor," they said.

⁸Saul put on different clothes so people wouldn't know who he was. At night he and two of his men went to see the woman. "I want you to talk to a spirit for me," he said. "Bring up the spirit of the dead person I choose."

⁹But the woman said to him, "By now you must know what Saul has done. He has removed everyone who gets messages from those who have died. He has also removed everyone who talks to the spirits of the dead. He has thrown all of them out of the land. Why are you trying to trap me? Why do you want to have me put to death?"

¹⁰Saul made a promise in the name of the LORD. He said to the woman, "You can be sure that the LORD lives. And you can be just as sure that you won't be punished for helping me."

¹¹Then the woman asked, "Whose spirit should I bring up for you?"

"Bring Samuel up," he said.

¹²When the woman saw Samuel, she let out a loud scream. She said to Saul, "Why have you tricked me? You are King Saul!"

¹³He said to her, "Don't be afraid. Tell me what you see."

The woman said, "I see a ghostly figure. He's coming up out of the earth."

¹⁴"What does he look like?" Saul asked.

"An old man wearing a robe is coming up," she said.

Then Saul knew it was Samuel. He bowed down. He lay down flat with his face toward the ground.

¹⁵Samuel said to Saul, "Why have you troubled me by bringing me up from the dead?"

"I'm having big problems," Saul said. "The Philistines are fighting against me. God has left me. He doesn't answer me anymore. He doesn't speak to me through prophets or dreams. So I've called on you to tell me what to do."

¹⁶Samuel said, "The LORD has left you. He has become your enemy. So why are you asking me what you should do? ¹⁷The LORD has spoken through me and has done what he said he would do. The LORD has torn the kingdom out of your hands. He has given it to one of your neighbors. He has given it to David. ¹⁸You didn't obey the LORD. You didn't show his great anger against the Amalekites by destroying them. So he's punishing you today. ¹⁹He will hand both Israel and you over to the Philistines. Tomorrow you and your sons will be down here with me. The LORD will also hand Israel's army over to the Philistines."

²⁰Immediately Saul fell flat on the ground. What Samuel had said filled Saul with fear. His strength was gone. He hadn't eaten anything all that day and all that night.

²¹The woman went over to Saul because she saw that he was very upset. She said, "Look, I've obeyed you. I put my own life in danger by doing what you told me to do. ²²So please listen to me. Let me give you some food. Eat it. Then you will have the strength to go on your way."

²³But he refused. He said, "I don't w anything to eat."

Then his men joined the w begging him to eat. Finally, h tion to them. He got up f and sat on a couch.

²⁴The woman had a fat calf at her house. She killed it at once. She got some flour. She mixed it and baked some bread that didn't have any yeast in it. ²⁵Then she set the food in front of Saul and his men. They ate it. That same night they got up and left.

Achish Sends David Back to Ziklag

29 The Philistines gathered their whole army together at Aphek. Israel's army camped by the spring of water at Jezreel. ²The Philistine rulers marched out in groups of hundreds and thousands. David and his men were marching with Achish behind the others. ³The commanders of the Philistines asked, "Why are these Hebrews here?"

Achish replied, "That's David, isn't it? Wasn't he an officer of Saul, the king of Israel? He has already been with me for more than a year. I haven't found any fault in him. That's been true from the day he left Saul until now."

⁴But the Philistine commanders were angry with Achish. They said, "Send David back. Let him return to the town you gave him. He must not go with us into battle. If he does, he'll turn against us during the fighting. In fact, he might even cut off the heads of our own men. What better way could he choose to win back his master's favor? ⁵Isn't David the one the Israelites sang about when they danced? They sang,

" 'Saul has killed thousands of men.
    David has killed tens of
        thousands.' "

⁶So Achish called David over to him. He said, "You have been faithful to me. And that's just as sure as the LORD is alive. I would be pleased to have you serve with me in the army. I haven't found any fault in you. That's been true from the day you came to me until today. But the Philistine to have you come ack home in peace. at wouldn't please one?" asked David. d against me from until now? Why nst your enemies? g and master."

⁹Achish answered, "You have been as pleasing to me as an angel of God. But the Philistine commanders have said, 'We don't want David to go up with us into battle.' ¹⁰So get up early in the morning. Take with you the men who used to serve Saul. Leave as soon as the sun begins to come up."

¹¹So David and his men got up early in the morning. They went back to the land of the Philistines. And the Philistines went up to Jezreel.

David Destroys the Amalekites

30 On the third day David and his men arrived in Ziklag. The Amalekites had attacked the people of the Negev Desert. They had also attacked Ziklag and burned it. ²They had captured the women and everyone else in Ziklag. They had taken as prisoners young people and old people alike. But they didn't kill any of them. Instead, they carried them off as they went on their way.

³David and his men reached Ziklag. They saw that it had been destroyed by fire. They found out that their wives and sons and daughters had been captured. ⁴So David and his men began to weep out loud. They wept until they couldn't weep anymore. ⁵David's two wives had been captured. Their names were Ahinoam from Jezreel and Abigail from Carmel. Abigail was Nabal's widow. ⁶David was greatly troubled. His men were even talking about killing him by throwing stones at him. All of them were very bitter because their sons and daughters had been taken away. But David was made strong by the LORD his God.

⁷Then David spoke to Abiathar the priest, the son of Ahimelek. He said, "Bring me the linen apron." Abiathar brought it to him. ⁸David asked the LORD for advice. He said, "Should I chase after the men who attacked Ziklag? If I do, will I catch up with them?"

"Chase after them," the LORD answered. "You will certainly catch up with them. You will succeed in saving those who were captured."

⁹David and his 600 men came to the Besor Valley. Some of them stayed behind there. ¹⁰That's because 200 of them were too tired to go across the valley. But David and the other 400 continued the chase.

[11]David's men found an Egyptian in a field. They brought him to David. They gave him water to drink and food to eat. [12]They gave him part of a cake of pressed figs. They also gave him two raisin cakes. After he ate them, he felt as good as new. That's because he hadn't eaten any food for three days and three nights. He hadn't drunk any water during that time either.

[13]David asked him, "Who do you belong to? Where do you come from?"

The man said, "I'm from Egypt. I'm the slave of an Amalekite. My master deserted me when I became ill three days ago. [14]We attacked the people in the Negev Desert of the Kerethites. We attacked the territory that belongs to Judah. We attacked the people in the Negev Desert of Caleb. And we burned Ziklag."

[15]David asked him, "Can you lead me down to the men who attacked Ziklag?"

He answered, "Make a promise to me in the name of God. Promise that you won't kill me. Promise that you won't hand me over to my master. Then I'll take you down to them."

[16]He led David down to where the men were. They were scattered all over the countryside. They were eating and drinking and dancing wildly. That's because they had taken a large amount of goods from those they had attacked. They had taken it from the land of the Philistines and from the people of Judah. [17]David fought against them from sunset until the evening of the next day. None of them escaped except 400 young men. They rode off on camels and got away. [18]David got everything back that the Amalekites had taken. That included his two wives. [19]Nothing was missing. Not one young person or old person or boy or girl was missing. None of the goods or anything else the Amalekites had taken was missing. David brought everything back. [20]He brought back all the flocks and herds. His men drove them on ahead of the other livestock. They said, "Here's what David has captured."

[21]Then David came to the 200 men who had been too tired to follow him. They had been left behind in the Besor Valley. They came out to welcome David and the men with him. As David and his men approached, he asked them how they were. [22]But some of the men who had gone out with David were evil. They wanted to stir up trouble. They said, "The 200 men didn't go out into battle with us. So we won't share with them the goods we brought back. But each man can take his wife and children and go home."

[23]David replied, "No, my friends. You must not hold back their share of what the Lord has given us. He has kept us safe. He has handed over to us the men who attacked us. [24]So no one will pay any attention to what you are saying. Each man who stayed with the supplies will receive the same share as each man who went down to the battle. Everyone's share will be the same." [25]David made that a law and a rule for Israel. It has been followed from that day until now.

[26]David reached Ziklag. He sent some of the goods to the elders of Judah. They were his friends. He said, "Here's a gift for you. It's part of the things we took from the Lord's enemies."

[27]David sent some goods to the elders in Bethel, Ramoth Negev and Jattir. [28]He sent some to the elders in Aroer, Siphmoth, Eshtemoa [29]and Rakal. He sent some to the elders in the towns of the Jerahmeelites and Kenites. [30]He sent some to the elders in Hormah, Bor Ashan, Athak [31]and Hebron. He also sent some to the elders in all the other places where he and his men had wandered around.

Saul Takes His Own Life

31 The Philistines fought against the Israelites. The Israelites ran away from them. But many Israelites were killed on Mount Gilboa. [2]The Philistines kept chasing Saul and his sons. They killed his sons Jonathan, Abinadab and Malki-Shua. [3]The fighting was heavy around Saul. Men who were armed with bows and arrows caught up with him. They shot their arrows at him and wounded him badly.

[4]Saul spoke to the man carrying his armor. He said, "Pull out your sword. Stick it through me. If you don't, these fellows who aren't circumcised will come. They'll stick their swords through me and hurt me badly."

But the man was terrified. He wouldn't do it. So Saul took his own sword and fell on it. [5]The man saw that Saul was dead.

So he fell on his own sword and died with him. ⁶Saul and his three sons died together that same day. The man who carried his armor also died with them that day. So did all of Saul's men.

⁷The Israelites who lived along the valley saw that their army had run away. So did those who lived across the Jordan River. They saw that Saul and his sons were dead. So they left their towns and ran away. Then the Philistines came and made their homes in them.

⁸The day after the Philistines had won the battle, they came to take what they wanted from the dead bodies. They found Saul and his three sons dead on Mount Gilboa. ⁹So they cut off Saul's head. They took his armor from his body. Then they sent messengers through the whole land of the Philistines. They announced the news in the temple where they had set up statues of their gods. They also announced it among their people. ¹⁰They put Saul's armor in the temple where they had set up statues of female gods that were named Ashtoreth. They hung his body up on the wall of Beth Shan.

¹¹The people of Jabesh Gilead heard about what the Philistines had done to Saul. ¹²So all their brave men marched through the night to Beth Shan. They took down the bodies of Saul and his sons from the wall of Beth Shan. They brought them to Jabesh. There they burned them. ¹³Then they got the bones of Saul and his sons and buried them under a tamarisk tree at Jabesh. They didn't eat anything for seven days.

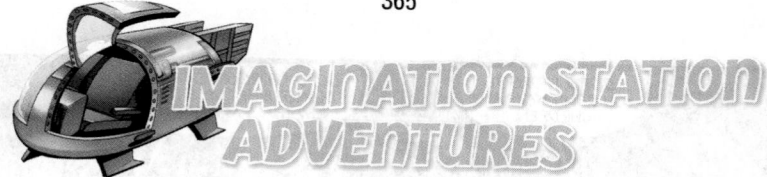

HANNAH'S HOPE
Read 1 Samuel 1—3.

MR. WHITTAKER SENDS COUSINS PATRICK AND BETH TO RAMAH IN OLD TESTAMENT TIMES. THEY JOIN THE FAMILY OF ELKANAH. ELKANAH HAS TWO WIVES. PENINNAH HAS SEVERAL CHILDREN. HANNAH HAS NONE.

HERE, HANNAH, SHARE THESE DATES WITH YOUR CHILDREN.

OOPS! I FORGOT. YOU DON'T HAVE ANY CHILDREN.

IT'S ALL RIGHT, HANNAH. MY LOVE FOR YOU RUNS DEEP. AREN'T I BETTER THAN TEN SONS?

HE'S KIDDING, RIGHT?

I DON'T THINK SO.

THE NEXT DAY THE FAMILY OF ELKANAH VISITS THE TEMPLE AT SHILOH.

DEAR GOD, PLEASE DON'T FORGET ME! GIVE ME A SON. HE WILL SERVE YOU ALL HIS DAYS.

HAVE YOU BEEN DRINKING TOO MUCH WINE? I WILL ASK GOD TO ANSWER YOUR PRAYER ANYWAY.

SHE IS A BIT DRAMATIC.

NOT HAVING A BABY IN THOSE DAYS WAS A BIG DEAL.

HERE, HANNAH, SHARE THESE OLIVES WITH YOUR CHILDREN.

GOD HEARS HANNAH'S PRAYER. SHE BECOMES PREGNANT.

IN DUE TIME HANNAH GIVES BIRTH TO A SON. SHE DEDICATES HIM TO THE LORD AS A NAZARITE.

HERE, HANNAH, SHARE THESE GRAPES WITH YOUR CHILDREN.

OOPS! I FORGOT TO MENTION SAMUEL IS DEDICATED TO THE LORD. HE CAN'T EAT GRAPES.

2 Samuel

Continuing the account of 1 Samuel, the book of 2 Samuel resumes as David hears of the death of King Saul. Samuel had already anointed David to be the next king some time before (1 Sam. 16:13), yet David's succession to the throne was no simple matter. The civil war created by Saul's persistent attempts to kill David had left the nation divided, and the Philistines and other powerful enemies added an additional ongoing threat. In 2 Samuel we soon see how David dealt with all those problems, captured Jerusalem and made it the new capital, and brought order to the land as a more-than-competent king.

However, David's infamous affair with Bathsheba was a major sin and a blot on his up-till-then honorable reputation. David confessed, God forgave him, and David and Bathsheba later became parents of Solomon, the next king. Yet one consequence of David's sin was that trouble would persist in his family (12:11). Most of the last half of 2 Samuel details the family feud that resulted in the deaths of two of David's sons and a rebellion that nearly cost him his kingdom.

WHAT'S IT MEAN, EUGENE?

Son of Man—When I was a wee child, my mother sometimes referred to me as "Little Man." "Son of Man", however, is the title that Jesus most often used for Himself. Before Jesus was born, the most common Jewish title for the coming Messiah was "Son of David," as the Jews were looking for the coming of an *earthly* King who would conquer the Romans and set up His kingdom on earth. In calling himself Son of Man, Jesus conveyed that He was a Divine Person who came to earth from heaven.

David Hears That Saul Has Died

1 After Saul died, David returned to Ziklag. He had won the battle over the Amalekites. He stayed in Ziklag for two days. ²On the third day a man arrived from Saul's camp. His clothes were torn. He had dust on his head. When he came to David, he fell to the ground to show him respect.

³"Where have you come from?" David asked him.

He answered, "I've escaped from Israel's camp."

⁴"What happened?" David asked. "Tell me."

He said, "Israel's men ran away from the battle. Many of them were killed. Saul and his son Jonathan are dead."

⁵David spoke to the young man who brought him the report. He asked him, "How do you know that Saul and his son Jonathan are dead?"

⁶"I just happened to be there on Mount Gilboa," the young man said. "Saul was there too. He was leaning on his spear. The enemy chariots and chariot drivers had almost caught up with him. ⁷Then he turned around and saw me. He called out to me. I said, 'What do you want me to do?'

⁸"He asked me, 'Who are you?'

"'An Amalekite,' I answered.

⁹"Then he said to me, 'Stand here by me and kill me! I'm close to death, but I'm still alive.'

¹⁰"So I stood beside him and killed him. I did it because I knew that after he had lost the battle he would be killed anyway. So I took the crown that was on his head. I also took his armband. I've brought them here to you. You are my master."

¹¹Then David tore his clothes. And all his men tore their clothes. ¹²All of them were filled with sadness. They mourned over the whole nation of Israel. They didn't eat anything until evening. That's because Saul and Jonathan and the LORD's army had been killed by swords.

¹³David spoke to the young man who had brought him the report. He asked, "Where are you from?"

"I'm the son of an outsider, an Amalekite," he answered.

¹⁴David asked him, "Why weren't you afraid to lift your hand to kill the LORD's anointed king?"

¹⁵Then David called for one of his men. He said, "Go! Strike him down!" So he struck the man down, and the man died. ¹⁶That's because David had said to him, "Anything that happens to you will be your own fault. What your own mouth has spoken is a witness against you. You said, 'I killed the LORD's anointed king.'"

David's Song of Sadness About Saul and Jonathan

¹⁷David sang a song of sadness about Saul and his son Jonathan. ¹⁸He ordered that it be taught to the people of Judah. It is a song that is played on a stringed instrument. It is written down in the Book of Jashar. David sang,

¹⁹ "Israel, a gazelle lies dead on your hills.
    Your mighty men have fallen.

²⁰ "Don't announce it in Gath.
    Don't tell it in the streets of
        Ashkelon.
If you do, the daughters of the
        Philistines will be glad.
    The daughters of men who haven't
        been circumcised will be joyful.

²¹ "Mountains of Gilboa,
    may no dew or rain fall on you.
    May no showers fall on your hillside
        fields.
The shield of the mighty king wasn't
        respected there.
    The shield of Saul lies there. It isn't
        rubbed with oil anymore.
²² The bow of Jonathan didn't turn back.
    The sword of Saul didn't return
        without being satisfied.
They spilled the blood of their enemies.
    They killed mighty men.

Jason's Jargon

2 SAMUEL 1

A sad quest: Look for *mourn* in this chapter. To mourn means to express grief or sorrow, usually because of a loved one's death. People mourned by weeping, fasting, and tearing their clothes.

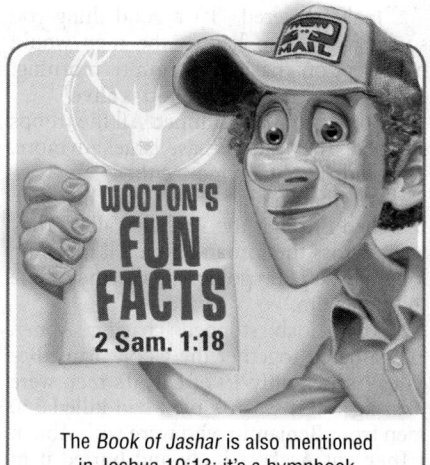

WOOTON'S FUN FACTS

2 Sam. 1:18

The *Book of Jashar* is also mentioned in Joshua 10:13; it's a hymnbook and maybe a manual of prayers and tips for battle. No copies exist today. It's too bad. I'd love to read it!

²³ "When they lived, Saul and Jonathan
were loved and respected.
When they died, they were not parted.
They were faster than eagles.
They were stronger than lions.

²⁴ "Daughters of Israel, mourn over Saul.
He dressed you in the finest clothes.
He decorated your clothes with
ornaments of gold.

²⁵ "Your mighty men have fallen in battle.
Jonathan lies dead on your hills.

²⁶ My brother Jonathan, I'm filled with
sadness because of you.
You were very special to me.
Your love for me was wonderful.
It was more wonderful than the love
of women.

²⁷ "Israel's mighty men have fallen.
Their weapons of war are broken."

David Is Anointed to Be King Over Judah

2 After Saul and Jonathan died, David asked the LORD for advice. "Should I go up to one of the towns of Judah?" he asked. The LORD said, "Go up."

David asked, "Where should I go?"

"To Hebron," the LORD answered.

²So David went up there with his two wives. Their names were Ahinoam from Jezreel and Abigail from Carmel. Abigail was Nabal's widow. ³David also took his men and their families with him. They made their homes in Hebron and its towns. ⁴Then the men of Judah came to Hebron. There they anointed David to be king over the people of Judah.

David was told that the men from Jabesh Gilead had buried Saul's body. ⁵So he sent messengers to them to speak for him. The messengers said, "You were kind to bury the body of your master Saul. May the LORD bless you for that. ⁶And may he now be kind and faithful to you. David will treat you well for being kind to Saul's body. ⁷Now then, be strong and brave. Your master Saul is dead. And the people of Judah have anointed David to be king over them."

The Armies of David and Saul Fight Each Other

⁸Abner, the son of Ner, was commander of Saul's army. Abner had brought Saul's son Ish-Bosheth to Mahanaim. ⁹There Abner made Ish-Bosheth king over Gilead, Ashuri and Jezreel. He also made him king over Ephraim, Benjamin and other areas of Israel. ¹⁰Ish-Bosheth was 40 years old when he became king over Israel. He ruled for two years. But the people of Judah remained faithful to David. ¹¹David was king in Hebron over the people of Judah for seven and a half years.

¹²Abner, the son of Ner, left Mahanaim and went to Gibeon. The men of Ish-Bosheth, the son of Saul, went with him. ¹³Joab, the son of Zeruiah, and David's men also went out. All of them met at the pool in Gibeon. One group sat down on one side of the pool. The other group sat on the other side.

¹⁴Then Abner said to Joab, "Let's have some of the young men get up and fight. Let's tell them to fight hand to hand in front of us."

"All right. Let them do it," Joab said.

¹⁵So the young men stood up and were counted off. There were 12 on the side of Benjamin and Saul's son Ish-Bosheth. And there were 12 on David's side. ¹⁶Each man grabbed one of his enemies by the head. Each one stuck his dagger into the other man's side. And all of them fell down together and died. So that place in Gibeon was named Helkath Hazzurim.

¹⁷The fighting that day was very heavy. Abner and the Israelites lost the battle to David's men.

2 Sam. 2:7 Judah has a separate identity from the other tribes. And the tribe of Benjamin shows some rebellion in Judges 20. Spoiler alert! Eventually the two tribes unite.

¹⁸The three sons of Zeruiah were there. Their names were Joab, Abishai and Asahel. Asahel was as quick on his feet as a wild antelope. ¹⁹He chased Abner. He didn't turn to the right or the left as he chased him. ²⁰Abner looked behind him. He asked, "Asahel, is that you?"

"It is," he answered.

²¹Then Abner said to him, "Turn to the right or the left. Fight one of the young men. Take his weapons away from him." But Asahel wouldn't stop chasing him.

²²Again Abner warned Asahel, "Stop chasing me! If you don't, I'll strike you down. Then how could I look your brother Joab in the face?"

²³But Asahel refused to give up the chase. So Abner drove the dull end of his spear into Asahel's stomach. The spear came out through his back. He fell and died right there on the spot. Every man stopped when he came to the place where Asahel had fallen and died.

²⁴But Joab and Abishai chased Abner. As the sun was going down, they came to the hill of Ammah. It was near Giah on the way to the dry and empty land close to Gibeon. ²⁵The men of Benjamin gathered in a group around Abner. They took their stand on top of a hill.

²⁶Abner called out to Joab, "Do you want our swords to keep on killing us off? Don't you know that all this fighting will end in bitter feelings? How long will it be before you order your men to stop chasing their fellow Israelites?"

²⁷Joab answered, "It's a good thing you spoke up. If you hadn't, the men would have kept on chasing them until morning. And that's just as sure as God is alive."

²⁸So Joab blew a trumpet. All the troops stopped. They didn't chase Israel anymore. They didn't fight anymore either.

²⁹All that night Abner and his men marched through the Arabah Valley. They went across the Jordan River. All morning long they kept on going. Finally, they came to Mahanaim.

³⁰Then Joab stopped chasing Abner. He gathered together the whole army. Besides Asahel, only 19 of David's men were missing. ³¹But David's men had killed 360 men from Benjamin who were with Abner. ³²They got Asahel's body and buried it in his father's tomb at Bethlehem. Then Joab and his men marched all night. They arrived at Hebron at sunrise.

3 The war between Saul's royal house and David's royal house lasted a long time. David grew stronger and stronger. But the royal house of Saul grew weaker and weaker.

² Sons were born to David in Hebron.

His first son was Amnon. Amnon's mother was Ahinoam from Jezreel.
³ His second son was Kileab. Kileab's mother was Abigail. She was Nabal's widow from Carmel.
The third son was Absalom. His mother was Maakah. She was the daughter of Talmai, the king of Geshur.
⁴ The fourth son was Adonijah. His mother was Haggith.
The fifth son was Shephatiah. His mother was Abital.
⁵ The sixth son was Ithream. His mother was David's wife Eglah.

Those sons were born to David in Hebron.

Abner Goes Over to David's Side

⁶The fighting continued between David's royal house and Saul's royal house. Abner gained more and more power in the royal house of Saul. ⁷While Saul was still alive, he had a concubine named Rizpah. She was the daughter of Aiah. Ish-Bosheth said to Abner, "Why did you sleep with my father's concubine?"

[8]Abner was very angry because of what Ish-Bosheth said. So Abner answered, "Do you think I'm only a dog's head? Am I on Judah's side? To this day I've been faithful to the royal house of your father Saul. I've been faithful to his family and friends. I haven't handed you over to David. But now you claim that I've sinned with this woman! [9]I will do for David what the LORD promised him. If I don't, may God punish me greatly. [10]I'll take the kingdom away from Saul's royal house. I'll set up the throne of David's kingdom over Israel and Judah. He will rule from Dan all the way to Beersheba." [11]Ish-Bosheth didn't dare to say another word to Abner. He was much too afraid of him.

[12]Then Abner sent messengers to David to speak for him. They said, "Who will rule over this land? Make a covenant with me. Then I'll help you bring all the Israelites over to your side."

[13]"Good," said David. "I will make a covenant with you. But there's one thing I want you to do. Bring Saul's daughter Michal to me. Don't come to see me unless she's with you." [14]Then David sent messengers to Saul's son Ish-Bosheth. He ordered them to say, "Give me my wife Michal. She was promised to me. I paid for her the price that was demanded. I paid for her with the skins of 100 circumcised Philistines."

[15]So Ish-Bosheth gave the order. He sent men who took Michal away from her husband Paltiel. Paltiel was the son of Laish. [16]But her husband followed her to Bahurim. He was crying all the way. Then Abner said to him, "Go back home!" So he did.

[17]Abner talked with the elders of Israel. He said, "For some time you have wanted to make David your king. [18]Now do it! The LORD made a promise to David. He said, 'I will rescue my people Israel from the power of the Philistines. I will also rescue them from all their enemies. I will rescue them through my servant David.'"

[19]Abner also spoke to the people of Benjamin in person. Then he went to Hebron to tell David everything. He told him what Israel and all the people of Benjamin wanted to do. [20]Abner had 20 men with him. They came to David at Hebron. So David prepared a feast for Abner and his men. [21]Then Abner said to David, "Let me go right now. I'll gather together all the Israelites for you. After all, you are now my king and master. The people can make a covenant with you. Then you can rule over everyone you want to." So David sent Abner away. And he went in peace.

Joab Murders Abner

[22]Just then David's men and Joab came back from attacking their enemies. They brought with them the large amount of goods they had taken. But Abner wasn't with David in Hebron anymore. That's because David had sent him away, and he had gone in peace. [23]Joab and all the soldiers with him arrived. Then he was told that Abner, the son of Ner, had come to see the king. He was told that the king had sent Abner away. He was also told that Abner had gone in peace.

[24]So Joab went to the king. He said, "What have you done? Abner came to you. Why did you let him get away? Now he's gone! [25]You know what Abner, the son of Ner, is like. He came to trick you. He wanted to watch your every move. He came to find out everything you are doing."

[26]Then Joab left David. He sent messengers to get Abner. They brought Abner back from the well of Sirah. But David didn't know about it. [27]When Abner returned to Hebron, Joab took him to one side. He brought him into an inside room. Joab acted as if he wanted to speak to him in private. But he really wanted to get even with him. That's because Abner had spilled the blood of Joab's brother Asahel. So Joab stabbed Abner in the stomach, and he died.

[28]Later on, David heard about it. He said, "I and the people of my kingdom aren't guilty of spilling the blood of Abner, the son of Ner. We are free of blame forever in the sight of the LORD. [29]May Joab and his whole family line be held accountable for spilling Abner's blood! May Joab's family never be without someone who has an open sore or skin disease. May his family never be without someone who has to use a crutch to walk. May his family never be without someone who gets killed by a sword. And may his family never be without someone who doesn't have enough to eat."

[30]Joab and his brother Abishai murdered Abner. They did it because he had killed their brother Asahel in the battle at Gibeon.

[31]David spoke to Joab and all the people with him. He said, "Tear your clothes. Put on the rough clothing people wear when

they're sad. Mourn when you walk in front of Abner's body." King David himself walked behind it. ³²Abner's body was buried in Hebron. The king wept out loud at Abner's tomb. So did the rest of the people. ³³King David sang a song of sadness over Abner. He said,

"Should Abner have died as sinful
        people do?
³⁴   His hands were not tied.
    His feet were not chained.
    He died as if he had been killed by evil
        people."

All the people mourned over Abner again. ³⁵Then all of them came and begged David to eat something. They wanted him to eat while it was still day. But David made a promise. He said, "I won't taste bread or anything else before the sun goes down. If I do, may God punish me greatly!" ³⁶All the people heard his promise and were pleased. In fact, everything the king did pleased them. ³⁷So on that day all the people there and all the Israelites understood. They knew that the king didn't have anything to do with the murder of Abner, the son of Ner. ³⁸The king spoke to his men. He said, "Don't you realize that a great commander has died in Israel today? ³⁹I'm the anointed king. But today I'm weak. These sons of Zeruiah are too powerful for me. May the LORD pay back the one who killed Abner! May he pay him back for the evil thing he has done!"

Ish-Bosheth Is Murdered

4 Ish-Bosheth, the son of Saul, heard that Abner had died in Hebron. Then he wasn't so brave anymore. And all the Israelites became alarmed. ²Two men in Ish-Bosheth's army led small fighting groups that attacked their enemies. The names of the men were Baanah and Rekab. They were sons of Rimmon from the town of Beeroth. Rimmon was from the tribe of Benjamin. Beeroth is considered to be part of Benjamin. ³That's because the people who used to live in Beeroth had run away to Gittaim. They have lived there as outsiders to this day.

⁴Jonathan, the son of Saul, had a son named Mephibosheth. Both of Mephibosheth's feet were hurt. He was five years old when the news that Saul and Jonathan had died came from Jezreel. His nurse picked him up and ran. But as she hurried to get away, he fell down. That's how his feet were hurt.

⁵Rekab and Baanah started out for the house of Ish-Bosheth. They were the sons of Rimmon from Beeroth. They arrived there during the hottest time of the day. Ish-Bosheth was taking his early afternoon nap. ⁶Rekab and his brother Baanah went into the inside part of the house. They acted as if they were going to get some wheat. Instead, they stabbed Ish-Bosheth in the stomach. Then they slipped away.

⁷They had gone into the house while Ish-Bosheth was lying on his bed in his bedroom. They stabbed him and killed him. Then they cut off his head and took it with them. They traveled all night through the Arabah Valley. ⁸They brought the head of Ish-Bosheth to King David at Hebron. They said to him, "Here's the head of Ish-Bosheth, the son of Saul. Saul was your enemy. He often tried to kill you. Today the LORD has paid back Saul and his family. He has let you get even with them. You are our king and master."

⁹David gave an answer to Rekab and his brother Baanah. They were the sons of Rimmon from Beeroth. David said, "The LORD has saved me from every trouble. ¹⁰Someone once told me, 'Saul is dead.' He thought he was bringing me good news. But I grabbed him. I had him put to death in Ziklag. That's the reward I gave him for his news! And that's just as sure as the LORD is alive. ¹¹Now you evil men have killed a man in his own house. He hadn't done anything wrong. You killed him while he was lying on his own bed. You spilled his blood. So shouldn't I spill your blood? Shouldn't I wipe you off the face of the earth?"

¹²Then David gave an order to his men. They killed Rekab and Baanah. They cut off their hands and feet. They hung their bodies by the pool in Hebron. But they buried the head of Ish-Bosheth in Abner's tomb at Hebron.

David Becomes King Over Israel

5 All the tribes of Israel came to see David at Hebron. They said, "We are your own flesh and blood. ²In the past, Saul was our king. But you led Israel on their military campaigns. And the LORD said to you, 'You

will be the shepherd over my people Israel. You will become their ruler.'"

³All the elders of Israel came to see King David at Hebron. There the king made a covenant with them in front of the LORD. They anointed David as king over Israel.

⁴David was 30 years old when he became king. He ruled for 40 years. ⁵In Hebron he ruled over Judah for seven and a half years. In Jerusalem he ruled over all of Israel and Judah for 33 years.

David Captures Jerusalem

⁶The king and his men marched to Jerusalem. They went to attack the Jebusites who lived there. The Jebusites said to David, "You won't get in here. Even people who can't see or walk can keep you from coming in." The Jebusites thought, "David can't get in here." ⁷But David captured the fort of Zion. It became known as the City of David.

⁸On that day David had said, "Someone might win the battle over the Jebusites. But they will have to crawl through the water tunnel to get into the city. That's the only way they can reach those enemies of mine that you say can't see or walk." That's why people say, "Those who 'can't see or walk' won't enter David's palace."

⁹David moved into the fort. He called it the City of David. He built up the area around the fort. He filled in the low places. He started at the bottom and worked his way up. ¹⁰David became more and more powerful. That's because the LORD God who rules over all was with him.

¹¹Hiram was king of Tyre. He sent messengers to David. He sent cedar logs along with them. He also sent skilled workers. They worked with wood and stone. They built a palace for David. ¹²Then David knew that the LORD had made his position as king secure. He knew that he had made him king over the whole nation of Israel. He knew that the LORD had greatly honored his kingdom. The LORD had done it because the Israelites were his people.

¹³After David left Hebron, he got more concubines and wives in Jerusalem. More sons and daughters were born to him there. ¹⁴Here is a list of the children who were born to him in Jerusalem. Their names were Shammua, Shobab, Nathan, Solomon, ¹⁵Ibhar, Elishua, Nepheg, Japhia, ¹⁶Elishama, Eliada and Eliphelet.

David Wins the Battle Over the Philistines

¹⁷The Philistines heard that David had been anointed king over Israel. So their whole army went to look for him. But David heard about it. He went down to his usual place of safety. ¹⁸The Philistines had come and spread out in the Valley of Rephaim. ¹⁹So David asked the LORD for advice. He said, "Should I go and attack the Philistines? Will you hand them over to me?"

The LORD answered him, "Go. I will surely hand over the Philistines to you."

²⁰So David went to Baal Perazim. There he won the battle over the Philistines. He said, "The LORD has broken through against my enemies when I've attacked them. He has broken through just as water breaks through a dam." That's why the place was called Baal Perazim. ²¹The Philistines left the statues of their gods there. So David and his men carried off the statues.

²²Once more the Philistines came up. They spread out in the Valley of Rephaim. ²³So David asked the LORD for advice. The LORD answered, "Do not go straight up. Instead, circle around behind them. Attack them in front of the poplar trees. ²⁴Listen for the sound of marching in the tops of the trees. Then move quickly. The sound will mean that I have gone out in front of you. I will strike down the Philistine army." ²⁵So David did just as the LORD had commanded him. He struck down the Philistines. He struck them down from Gibeon all the way to Gezer.

David Brings the Ark to Jerusalem

6 Again David brought together the best soldiers in Israel. The total number was 30,000. ²He and all his men went to Baalah in Judah. They wanted to bring the ark of God up to Jerusalem from there. The ark is named after the LORD. He is the LORD who rules over all. He sits on his throne between the cherubim that are on the ark. ³The ark of God was placed on a new

BIBLE ADVENTURES

Whit told Connie the story of Uzzah and the ark in "Rights, Wrongs, & Reasons" (A#15).

cart. Then it was brought from Abinadab's house, which was on a hill. Uzzah and Ahio were guiding the cart. They were the sons of Abinadab. ⁴The ark of God was on the cart. Ahio was walking in front of it. ⁵David was celebrating with all his might in front of the LORD. So was the whole community of Israel. All of them were playing castanets, harps, lyres, tambourines, rattles and cymbals.

⁶They came to the threshing floor of Nakon. The oxen nearly fell there. So Uzzah reached out and took hold of the ark of God. ⁷Then the LORD was very angry with Uzzah. That's because what Uzzah did showed that he didn't have any respect for the LORD. So God struck him down. He died there beside the ark of God.

⁸David was angry because the LORD's great anger had broken out against Uzzah. That's why the place is still called Perez Uzzah to this day.

⁹David was afraid of the LORD that day. He asked, "How can the ark of the LORD ever be brought to me?" ¹⁰He didn't want to take the ark of the LORD to be with him in the City of David. Instead, he took it to the house of Obed-Edom. Obed-Edom was from Gath. ¹¹The ark of the LORD remained in Obed-Edom's house for three months. And the LORD blessed him and his whole family.

¹²King David was told, "The LORD has blessed the family of Obed-Edom. He has also blessed everything that belongs to him. That's because the ark of God is in Obed-Edom's house." So David went down there to bring up the ark. With great joy he brought it up from the house of Obed-Edom. He took it to the City of David. ¹³Those carrying the ark of the LORD took six steps forward. Then David sacrificed a bull and a fat calf. ¹⁴David was wearing a sacred linen apron. He danced in front of the LORD with all his might. ¹⁵He did it while he was bringing up the ark of the LORD. The whole community of Israel helped him bring it up. They shouted. They blew trumpets.

BIBLE ADVENTURES

B-TV History News reported on the arrival of the ark in Jerusalem in "B-TV: Thanks" (A#31).

¹⁶The ark of the LORD was brought into the City of David. Saul's daughter Michal was watching from a window. She saw King David leaping and dancing in front of the LORD. That made her hate him in her heart.

¹⁷The ark of the LORD was brought into Jerusalem. It was put in its place in the tent David had set up for it. David sacrificed burnt offerings and friendship offerings to the LORD. ¹⁸After he finished sacrificing those offerings, he blessed the people in the name of the LORD who rules over all. ¹⁹He gave to each Israelite man and woman a loaf of bread. He also gave each one a date cake and a raisin cake. Then all the people went home.

²⁰David returned home to bless his family. Saul's daughter Michal came out to meet him. She said, "You are the king of Israel. You have really brought honor to yourself today, haven't you? You have gone around half-naked right in front of the female slaves of your officials. You acted like a fool!"

²¹David said to Michal, "I did it to honor the LORD. He chose me instead of your father or anyone else in Saul's family. The LORD appointed me ruler over his people Israel. I will celebrate to honor the LORD. ²²And that's not all. I will bring even less honor to myself. I will bring even more shame on myself. But those female slaves you spoke about will honor me." ²³Saul's daughter Michal didn't have any children as long as she lived.

God's Promise to David

7 The king moved into his palace. The LORD had given him peace and rest from all his enemies around him. ²Then the king spoke to Nathan the prophet. He said, "Here I am, living in a house that has beautiful cedar walls. But the ark of God remains in a tent."

³Nathan replied to the king, "Go ahead and do what you want to. The LORD is with you."

⁴But that night the word of the LORD came to Nathan. The LORD said,

⁵"Go and speak to my servant David. Tell him, 'The LORD says, "Are you the one to build me a house to live in? ⁶I brought the Israelites up out of Egypt. But I have not lived in

a house from then until now. I have been moving from place to place. I have been living in a tent. ⁷I have moved from place to place with all the Israelites. I commanded their rulers to be shepherds over them. I never asked any of those rulers, 'Why haven't you built me a house that has beautiful cedar walls?' "'

⁸"So tell my servant David, 'The LORD who rules over all says, "I took you away from the grasslands. That's where you were taking care of your father's sheep and goats. I made you ruler over my people Israel. ⁹I have been with you everywhere you have gone. I have destroyed all your enemies. Now I will make you famous. Your name will be just as respected as the names of the most important people on earth. ¹⁰I will provide a place where my people Israel can live. I will plant them in the land. Then they will have a home of their own. They will not be bothered anymore. Evil people will no longer crush them, as they did at first. ¹¹That is what your enemies have done ever since I appointed leaders over my people Israel. But I will give you peace and rest from all of them.

" "'I tell you that I, the LORD, will set up a royal house for you. ¹²Some day your life will come to an end. You will join the members of your family who have already died. Then I will make one of your own sons the next king after you. And I will make his kingdom secure. ¹³He is the one who will build a house where I will put my Name. I will set up the throne of his kingdom. It will last forever. ¹⁴I will be his father. And he will be my son. When he does what is wrong, I will use other men to beat him with rods and whips. ¹⁵I took my love away from Saul. I removed him from being king. You were there when I did it. But I will never take my love away from your son. ¹⁶Your royal house and your kingdom will last forever in my sight. Your throne will last forever.' " "

¹⁷Nathan reported to David all the words that the LORD had spoken to him.

Jason's Jargon

2 SAMUEL 7

Your mission: Examine this chapter for the word *secure*. Secure means safe. When God promised David that his son would have a secure kingdom, He meant that He would protect it from enemies.

David's Prayer to the LORD

¹⁸Then King David went into the holy tent. He sat down in front of the LORD. He said,

"LORD and King, who am I? My family isn't important. So why have you brought me this far? ¹⁹I would have thought that you had already done more than enough for me. But now, LORD and King, you have also said what will happen to my royal house in days to come. And, my LORD and King, this promise is for a mere human being!

²⁰"What more can I say to you? LORD and King, you know all about me. ²¹You have done a wonderful thing. You have made it known to me. You have done it because that's what you said you would do. It's exactly what you wanted to do for me.

²²"LORD and King, how great you are! There isn't anyone like you. There isn't any God but you. We have heard about it with our own ears. ²³Who is like your people Israel? God, we are the one nation on earth you have saved. You have set us free for yourself. Your name has become famous. You have done great and wonderful things. You have driven out nations and their gods to make room for your people. You saved us when you set us free from Egypt. ²⁴You made Israel your very own people forever. LORD, you have become our God.

²⁵"And now, LORD God, keep forever the promise you have made to me and my royal house. Do exactly as you promised. ²⁶Then your name

will be honored forever. People will say, 'The LORD rules over all. He is God over Israel.' My royal house will be made secure in your sight. ²⁷"LORD who rules over all, you are the God of Israel. Here's what you have shown me. You told me, 'I will build you a royal house.' So I can boldly pray this prayer to you. ²⁸LORD and King, you are God! Your covenant can be trusted. You have promised many good things to me. ²⁹Now please bless my royal house. Then it will continue forever in your sight. LORD and King, you have spoken. Because you have given my royal house your blessing, it will be blessed forever."

David Wins Many Battles

8 While David was king of Israel, he won many battles over the Philistines. He brought them under his control. He took Metheg Ammah away from them.

²David also won the battle over the people of Moab. He made them lie down on the ground. Then he measured them off with a piece of rope. He put two-thirds of them to death. He let the other third remain alive. So the Moabites were brought under David's rule. They gave him the gifts he required them to bring him.

³David fought against Hadadezer, the son of Rehob. Hadadezer was king of Zobah. He had gone to repair his monument at the Euphrates River. ⁴David captured 1,000 of Hadadezer's chariots, 7,000 chariot riders and 20,000 soldiers on foot. He cut the legs of all but 100 of the chariot horses. ⁵The Arameans of Damascus came to help Hadadezer, the king of Zobah. But David struck down 22,000 of them. ⁶He stationed some soldiers in the Aramean kingdom of Damascus. The people of Aram were brought under his rule. They gave him the gifts he required them to bring him. The LORD helped David win his battles everywhere he went.

⁷David took the gold shields that belonged to the officers of Hadadezer. He brought the shields to Jerusalem. ⁸He took a huge amount of bronze from Tebah and Berothai. Those towns belonged to Hadadezer.

⁹Tou was king of Hamath. He heard that David had won the battle over the entire army of Hadadezer. ¹⁰So Tou sent his son Joram to King David. Joram greeted David. He praised David because he had won the battle over Hadadezer. Hadadezer had been at war with Tou. So Joram brought with him gifts made out of silver, of gold and of bronze.

¹¹King David set those gifts apart for the LORD. He had done the same thing with the silver and gold he had taken from the other nations. Those were nations he had brought under his control. ¹²Those nations were Edom, Moab, Ammon, Philistia and Amalek. He also set apart for the LORD what he had taken from Hadadezer, the son of Rehob. Hadadezer was king of Zobah.

¹³David returned after he had struck down 18,000 men of Edom in the Valley of Salt. He became famous for doing it.

¹⁴He stationed some soldiers all through Edom. The whole nation of Edom was brought under David's rule. The LORD helped him win his battles everywhere he went.

David's Officials

¹⁵David ruled over the whole nation of Israel. He did what was fair and right for all his people. ¹⁶Joab, the son of Zeruiah, was commander over the army. Jehoshaphat, the son of Ahilud, kept the records. ¹⁷Zadok, the son of Ahitub, was a priest. Ahimelek, the son of Abiathar, was also a priest. Seraiah was the secretary. ¹⁸Benaiah, the son of Jehoiada, was commander over the Kerethites and Pelethites. And David's sons were priests.

David and Mephibosheth

9 David asked, "Is anyone left from the royal house of Saul? If there is, I want to be kind to him because of Jonathan."

²Ziba was a servant in Saul's family. David sent for him to come and see him. The king said to him, "Are you Ziba?"

"I'm ready to serve you," he replied.

³The king asked, "Isn't there anyone still alive from the royal house of Saul? God has been very kind to me. I would like to be kind to that person in the same way."

BiBLe ADVeNtuReS

The game show "Who's Got Compassion?" retold the story of David and Mephibosheth in "B-TV: Compassion" (A#27).

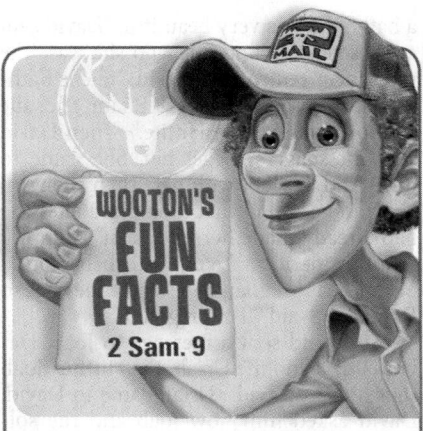

WOOTON'S
FUN
FACTS

2 Sam. 9

David honored his promise to Jonathan (1 Samuel 20:15) by caring for Mephibosheth. Someone as honest as David should work for the post office where we take our promise to deliver the mail very seriously.

Ziba answered the king, "A son of Jonathan is still living. Both of his feet were hurt so that he can't walk."

⁴"Where is he?" the king asked.

Ziba answered, "He's in the town of Lo Debar. He's staying at the house of Makir, the son of Ammiel."

⁵So King David had Mephibosheth brought from Makir's house in Lo Debar. ⁶Mephibosheth came to David. He was the son of Jonathan, the son of Saul. Mephibosheth bowed down to David to show him respect.

David said, "Mephibosheth!"

"I'm ready to serve you," he replied.

⁷"Don't be afraid," David told him. "You can be sure that I will be kind to you because of your father Jonathan. I'll give back to you all the land that belonged to your grandfather Saul. And I'll always provide what you need."

⁸Mephibosheth bowed down to David. He said, "Who am I? Why should you pay attention to me? I'm nothing but a dead dog."

⁹Then the king sent for Saul's servant Ziba. He said to him, "I'm giving your master's grandson everything that belonged to Saul and his family. ¹⁰You and your sons and your servants must farm the land for him. You must bring in the crops. Then he'll be taken care of. I'll always provide what he needs." Ziba had 15 sons and 20 servants.

¹¹Then Ziba said to the king, "I'll do anything you command me to do. You are my king and master." So David provided what Mephibosheth needed. He treated him like one of the king's sons.

¹²Mephibosheth had a young son named Mika. All the members of Ziba's family became servants of Mephibosheth. ¹³Mephibosheth lived in Jerusalem. The king always provided what he needed. Both of his feet were hurt so that he could not walk.

David Wins the Victory Over the Ammonites

10 The king of Ammon died. His son Hanun became the next king after him. ²David thought, "I'm going to be kind to Hanun. His father Nahash was kind to me." So David sent messengers to Hanun. He wanted them to tell Hanun how sad he was that Hanun's father had died.

David's messengers went to the land of Ammon. ³The Ammonite commanders spoke to their master Hanun. They said, "David has sent messengers to tell you he is sad. They say he wants to honor your father. But the real reason they've come is to look the city over. They want to destroy it." ⁴So Hanun grabbed David's messengers. He shaved off half of each man's beard. He cut their clothes off just below the waist and left them half naked. Then he sent them away.

⁵David was told about it. So he sent messengers to his men because they were filled with shame. King David said to them, "Stay at Jericho until your beards grow out again. Then come back here."

⁶The Ammonites realized that what they had done had made David very angry with them. So they hired 20,000 Aramean soldiers who were on foot. The soldiers came from Beth Rehob and Zobah. The Ammonites also hired the king of Maakah and 1,000 men. And they hired 12,000 men from Tob.

⁷David heard about it. So he sent Joab out with the entire army of Israel's fighting men. ⁸The Ammonites marched out. They took up their battle positions at the entrance of their city gate. The Arameans of Zobah and Rehob gathered their troops together in the open country. So did the men of Tob and Maakah.

⁹Joab saw that there were lines of soldiers in front of him and behind him. So

he chose some of the best troops in Israel. He sent them to march out against the Arameans. [10]He put the rest of the men under the command of his brother Abishai. Joab sent them to march out against the Ammonites. [11]He said, "Suppose the Arameans are too strong for me. Then you must come and help me. But suppose the Ammonites are too strong for you. Then I'll come and help you. [12]Be strong. Let's be brave as we fight for our people and the cities of our God. The LORD will do what he thinks is best."

[13]Then Joab and the troops with him marched out to attack the Arameans. They ran away from him. [14]The Ammonites realized that the Arameans were running away. So they ran away from Abishai. They went inside the city. After Joab had fought against the Ammonites, he went back to Jerusalem.

[15]The Arameans saw that they had been driven away by Israel. So they brought their troops together. [16]Hadadezer had some Arameans brought from east of the Euphrates River. They went to Helam under the command of Shobak. He was the commander of Hadadezer's army.

[17]David was told about it. So he gathered the whole army of Israel together. They went across the Jordan River to Helam. The Arameans lined up their soldiers to go to war against David. They began to fight against him. [18]But then they ran away from Israel. David killed 700 of their chariot riders. He killed 40,000 of their soldiers who were on foot. He also struck down Shobak, the commander of their army. Shobak died there. [19]All the kings who were under the rule of Hadadezer saw that Israel had won the battle over them. So they made a peace treaty with the Israelites. They were brought under Israel's rule.

After that, the Arameans were afraid to help the Ammonites anymore.

David and Bathsheba

11 It was spring. It was the time when kings go off to war. So David sent Joab out with the king's special troops and the whole army of Israel. They destroyed the Ammonites. They marched to the city of Rabbah. They surrounded it and got ready to attack it. But David remained in Jerusalem.

[2]One evening David got up from his bed. He walked around on the roof of his palace. From the roof he saw a woman taking a bath. She was very beautiful. [3]David sent a messenger to find out who she was. The messenger returned and said, "She is Bathsheba. She's the daughter of Eliam. She's the wife of Uriah. He's a Hittite." [4]Then David sent messengers to get her. She came to him. And he slept with her. Then she went back home. All of that took place after she had already made herself "clean" from her monthly period. [5]Later, Bathsheba found out she was pregnant. She sent a message to David. She said, "I'm pregnant."

[6]So David sent a message to Joab. David said, "Send me Uriah, the Hittite." Joab sent him to David. [7]Uriah came to David. David asked him how Joab and the soldiers were doing. He also asked him how the war was going. [8]David said to Uriah, "Go home and enjoy some time with your wife." So Uriah left the palace. Then the king sent him a gift. [9]But Uriah didn't go home. Instead, he slept at the entrance to the palace. He stayed there with all his master's servants.

[10]David was told, "Uriah didn't go home." So he sent for Uriah. David said to him, "You have been away for a long time. Why didn't you go home?"

[11]Uriah said to David, "The ark and the army of Israel and Judah are out there in

Whit told Camilla an unusual version of the story of David, Bathsheba, and Uriah in the adventure "In a Kingdom Far Away" (Club).

CANDID CONVERSATIONS

Have you ever felt jealous or envious of another person? It happens to everybody! Maybe it's triggered by that athlete who plays ball better than anybody or by that student who seems to easily grab top grades. Do you know anyone who hasn't been jealous for one reason or another?

When you read the Old Testament, you'll discover jealousy raising its ugly head—even among those we consider heroes of the Bible! Jealousy and envy drive them to do things they never expected to do.

Just ask King David. David had a beautiful palace, power, and the love of his people. Yet he concentrated on one thing he didn't have. A good way to deal with jealousy is to concentrate on the things God has given us instead of the things He *hasn't* given us. Go to God in prayer today with a spirit of gratitude.

where the fighting is the heaviest. Then pull your men back from him. When you do, the Ammonites will strike him down and kill him."

[16]So Joab attacked the city. He put Uriah at a place where he knew the strongest enemy fighters were. [17]The troops came out of the city. They fought against Joab. Some of the men in David's army were killed. Uriah, the Hittite, also died.

[18]Joab sent David a full report of the battle. [19]He told the messenger, "Tell the king everything that happened in the battle. When you are finished, [20]his anger might explode. He might ask you, 'Why did you go so close to the city to fight against it? Didn't you know that the enemy soldiers would shoot arrows down from the wall? [21]Don't you remember how Abimelek, the son of Jerub-Besheth, was killed? A woman dropped a large millstone on him from the wall. That's how he died in Thebez. So why did you go so close to the wall?' If the king asks you that, tell him, 'And your servant Uriah, the Hittite, is also dead.'"

[22]The messenger started out for Jerusalem. When he arrived there, he told David everything Joab had sent him to say. [23]The messenger said to David, "The men in the city were more powerful than we were. They came out to fight against us in the open. But we drove them back to the entrance of the city gate. [24]Then those who were armed with bows shot arrows at us from the wall. Some

tents. My commander Joab and your special troops are camped in the open country. How could I go to my house to eat and drink? How could I go there and sleep with my wife? I could never do a thing like that. And that's just as sure as you are alive!"

[12]Then David said to him, "Stay here one more day. Tomorrow I'll send you back to the battle." So Uriah remained in Jerusalem that day and the next. [13]David invited Uriah to eat and drink with him. David got him drunk. But Uriah still didn't go home. In the evening he went out and slept on his mat. He stayed there among his master's servants.

[14]The next morning David wrote a letter to Joab. He sent it along with Uriah. [15]In it he wrote, "Put Uriah out in front. That's

WOOTON'S FUN FACTS

2 Sam. 11:24 They didn't have the Navy Seals or Army Special Forces in King David's day, but they did have "special troops." Later they were called David's Mighty Men.

of your special troops were killed. Your servant Uriah, the Hittite, is also dead."

²⁵David told the messenger, "Tell Joab, 'Don't get upset over what happened. Swords kill one person as well as another. So keep on attacking the city. Destroy it.' Tell that to Joab. It will cheer him up."

²⁶Uriah's wife heard that her husband was dead. She mourned over him. ²⁷When her time of sadness was over, David had her brought to his house. She became his wife. And she had a son by him. But the LORD wasn't pleased with what David had done.

Nathan Tells David He Has Sinned

12 The LORD sent the prophet Nathan to David. When Nathan came to him, he said, "Two men lived in the same town. One was rich. The other was poor. ²The rich man had a very large number of sheep and cattle. ³But all the poor man had was one little female lamb. He had bought it. He raised it. It grew up with him and his children. It shared his food. It drank from his cup. It even slept in his arms. It was just like a daughter to him.

⁴"One day a traveler came to the rich man. The rich man wanted to prepare a meal for him. But he didn't want to kill one of his own sheep or cattle. Instead, he took the little female lamb that belonged to the poor man. Then the rich man cooked it for the traveler who had come to him."

⁵David was very angry with the rich man. He said to Nathan, "The man who did this must die! And that's just as sure as the LORD is alive. ⁶The man must pay back four times as much as that lamb was worth. How could he do such a thing? And he wasn't even sorry he had done it."

⁷Then Nathan said to David, "You are the man! The LORD, the God of Israel, says, 'I anointed you king over Israel. I saved you from Saul. ⁸I gave you everything that belonged to your master Saul. I even put his wives into your arms. I made you king over all the people of Israel and Judah. And if all of that had not been enough for you, I would have given you even more. ⁹Why did you turn your back on what I told you to do? You did what is evil in my sight. You made sure that Uriah, the Hittite, would be killed in battle. You took his wife to be your own. You let the men of Ammon kill him with their swords. ¹⁰So time after time

members of your own royal house will be killed with swords. That's because you turned your back on me. You took the wife of Uriah, the Hittite, to be your own.'

¹¹"The LORD also says, 'I am going to bring trouble on you. It will come from your own family. I will take your wives away. Your own eyes will see it. I will give your wives to a man who is close to you. He will sleep with them in the middle of the day. ¹²You committed your sins in secret. But I will make sure that the man commits his sin in the middle of the day. Everyone in Israel will see it.' "

¹³Then David said to Nathan, "I have sinned against the LORD."

Nathan replied, "The LORD has taken away your sin. You aren't going to die. ¹⁴But you have dared to show great disrespect for the LORD. So the son who has been born to you will die."

¹⁵Nathan went home. Then the LORD made David's child very sick. That was the child David had by Uriah's wife. ¹⁶David begged God to heal the child. David didn't eat anything. He spent his nights lying on the ground. He put on the rough clothes people wear when they're sad. ¹⁷His most trusted servants stood beside him. They wanted him to get up from the ground. But he refused to do it. And he wouldn't eat any food with them.

¹⁸On the seventh day the child died. David's attendants were afraid to tell him the child was dead. They thought, "While the child was still alive, we spoke to David. But he wouldn't listen to us. So how can we now tell him the child is dead? He might do something terrible to himself."

¹⁹David saw that his attendants were whispering to one another. Then he realized the child was dead. "Has the child died?" he asked.

"Yes," they replied. "He's dead."

²⁰Then David got up from the ground. After he washed himself, he put on lotions. He changed his clothes. He went into the house of the LORD and worshiped him. Then

WHIT'S WISDOM
2 Samuel 12

Have you ever heard of a man named Charles Colson? He was once famous for being a criminal. He broke the law during a scandal called Watergate and went to prison. While he was there, he became a Christian and his life changed. After he got out of prison, he started a ministry called Prison Fellowship where he helped prisoners learn about Jesus.

This story reminds me that God can use anyone. For example, King David defeated Goliath and wrote wonderful psalms. He brought the Ark of the Covenant to Jerusalem and worshiped God with all his heart. But he also stole another man's wife and had the man murdered! David later asked for forgiveness. There were consequences for his sin, but God forgave him. Later, David took a census of his soldiers without asking God first. God was angry and David repented. Again, there were consequences, but God forgave David and continued to use him.

Even though David was called "a man dear to my own heart," (Acts 13:22) he still made some big mistakes. If God can use someone as sinful as David, He can certainly use you for His purposes. He has great plans for all of us.

---

he went to his own house. He asked for some food. They served it to him. And he ate it.

^{21}His attendants asked him, "Why are you acting like this? While the child was still alive, you wouldn't eat anything. You cried a lot. But now that the child is dead, you get up and eat!"

^{22}He answered, "While the child was still alive, I didn't eat anything. And I cried a lot. I thought, 'Who knows? The LORD might have mercy on me. He might let the child live.' ^{23}But now he's dead. So why should I continue to go without food? Can I bring him back to life again? Someday I'll go to him. But he won't return to me."

^{24}Then David comforted his wife Bathsheba. He went to her and slept with her. Some time later she had a son. He was given the name Solomon. The LORD loved him. ^{25}So the LORD sent a message through Nathan the prophet. The LORD said, "Name the boy Jedidiah."

^{26}During that time, Joab fought against Rabbah. It was the royal city of the Ammonites. It had high walls around it. Joab was about to capture it. ^{27}He sent messengers to David. He told them to say, "I have fought against Rabbah. I've taken control of its water supply. ^{28}So bring the rest of the troops together. Surround the city and get ready to attack it. Then capture it. If you don't, I'll capture it myself. Then it will be named after me."

^{29}So David brought together the whole army and went to Rabbah. He attacked it and captured it. ^{30}David took the gold crown off the head of the king of Ammon. Then the crown was placed on David's head. The crown weighed 75 pounds. It had jewels in it. David took a huge amount of goods from the city. ^{31}He brought out the people who were there. He made them work with saws and iron picks and axes. He forced them to make bricks. David did that to all the towns in Ammon. Then he and his entire army returned to Jerusalem.

Amnon and Tamar

13 Some time later, David's son Amnon fell in love with Tamar. She was the beautiful sister of Absalom. He was another one of David's sons.

^{2}Amnon wanted his sister Tamar so much that it made him sick. She was a virgin, and it seemed impossible for him to do what he wanted with her.

^{3}Amnon had an adviser named Jonadab. He was the son of David's brother Shimeah. Jonadab was a very clever man. ^{4}He asked Amnon, "You are the king's son, aren't you?

So why do you look so worn out every morning? Won't you tell me?"

Amnon answered, "I'm in love with Tamar. She's the sister of my brother Absalom."

[5]"Go to bed," Jonadab said. "Pretend to be sick. Your father will come to see you. When he does, tell him, 'I would like my sister Tamar to come and give me something to eat. Let her prepare the food right here in front of me where I can watch her. Then she can feed it to me.'"

[6]So Amnon went to bed. He pretended to be sick. The king came to see him. Amnon said to him, "I would like my sister Tamar to come here. I want to watch her make some special bread. Then she can feed it to me."

[7]David sent a message to Tamar at the palace. He said, "Go to your brother Amnon's house. Prepare some food for him."

[8]So Tamar went to the house of her brother Amnon. He was lying in bed. She got some dough and mixed it. She shaped the bread right there in front of him. And she baked it. [9]Then she took the bread out of the pan and served it to him. But he refused to eat it.

"Send everyone out of here," Amnon said. So everyone left him. [10]Then he said to Tamar, "Bring the food here into my bedroom. Please feed it to me." So Tamar picked up the bread she had prepared. She brought it to her brother Amnon in his bedroom. [11]She took it to him so he could eat it. But he grabbed her. He said, "My sister, come to bed with me."

[12]"No, my brother!" she said to him. "Don't force me! An evil thing like that should never be done in Israel! Don't do it! [13]What about me? How could I ever get rid of my shame? And what about you? You would be as foolish as any evil person in Israel. Please speak to the king. He won't keep me from marrying you." [14]But Amnon refused to listen to her. He was stronger than she was. So he raped her.

[15]Then Amnon hated Tamar very much. In fact, he hated her more than he had loved her before. He said to her, "Get up! Get out!"

[16]"No!" she said to him. "Don't send me away. That would be worse than what you have already done to me."

But he refused to listen to her. [17]He sent for his personal servant. He said, "Get this woman out of my sight. Lock the door behind her." [18]So his servant threw her out. Then he locked the door behind her. Tamar was wearing a beautiful robe. It was the kind of robe the virgin daughters of the king wore. [19]She put ashes on her head. She tore the beautiful robe she was wearing. She put her hands on her head and went away. She was weeping out loud as she went.

[20]When her brother Absalom saw her, he spoke to her. He said, "Has Amnon, that brother of yours, forced you to go to bed with him? My sister, don't let it upset you. Don't let it bother you. He's your brother." After that, Tamar lived in her brother Absalom's house. She was very lonely.

[21]King David heard about everything that had happened. So he became very angry. [22]And Absalom never said a word of any kind to Amnon. He hated Amnon because he had brought shame on his sister Tamar.

Absalom Kills Amnon

[23]Two years later, Absalom invited all the king's sons to come to Baal Hazor. It was near the border of Ephraim. The workers who clipped the wool off Absalom's sheep were there. [24]Absalom went to the king. He said, "I've had my workers come to clip the wool. Will you and your attendants please join me?"

[25]"No, my son," the king replied. "All of us shouldn't go. It would be too much trouble for you." Although Absalom begged him, the king still refused to go. But he gave Absalom his blessing.

[26]Then Absalom said, "If you won't come, please let my brother Amnon come with us."

The king asked him, "Why should he go with you?" [27]But Absalom begged him. So the king sent Amnon with him. He also sent the rest of his sons.

[28]Absalom ordered his men, "Listen! When Amnon has had too much wine to drink, I'll say to you, 'Strike Amnon down.' When I do, kill him. Don't be afraid. I've given you an order, haven't I? Be strong and brave." [29]So Absalom's men killed Amnon, just as Absalom had ordered. Then all the king's sons got on their mules and rode away.

[30]While they were on their way, a report came to David. It said, "Absalom has struck down all your sons. Not one of them is left alive." [31]The king stood up and tore his clothes. Then he lay down on the ground.

All his attendants stood near him. They had also torn their clothes.

³²Jonadab, the son of David's brother Shimeah, spoke up. He said, "You shouldn't think that all the princes have been killed. The only one who is dead is Amnon. Absalom had planned to kill him ever since the day Amnon raped his sister Tamar. ³³You are my king and master. You shouldn't be concerned about this report. It's not true that all your sons are dead. The only one who is dead is Amnon."

³⁴While all of that was taking place, Absalom ran away.

The man on guard duty at Jerusalem looked up. He saw many people coming on the road west of him. They were coming down the side of the hill. He went and spoke to the king. He said, "I see men coming down the road from Horonaim. They are coming down the side of the hill."

³⁵Jonadab said to the king, "See, your sons are coming. It has happened just as I said it would."

³⁶As he finished speaking, the king's sons came in. They were weeping out loud. The king and all his attendants were also weeping very bitterly.

³⁷When Absalom ran away, he went to Talmai, the son of Ammihud. Talmai was king of Geshur. King David mourned many days for his son Amnon.

³⁸So Absalom ran away and went to Geshur. He stayed there for three years. ³⁹After some time the king got over his sorrow because of Amnon's death. Then King David longed to go to Absalom.

Absalom Returns to Jerusalem

14 Joab, the son of Zeruiah, knew that the king longed to see Absalom. ²So Joab sent someone to Tekoa to have a wise woman brought back from there. Joab said to her, "Pretend you are filled with sadness. Put on the rough clothing people wear when they're sad. Don't use any makeup. Act like a woman who has spent many days mourning for someone who has died. ³Then go to the king. Give him the message I'm about to give you." And Joab told her what to say.

⁴The woman from Tekoa went to the king. She bowed down with her face toward the ground. She did it to show him respect. She said, "Your Majesty, please help me!"

⁵The king asked her, "What's bothering you?"

She said, "I'm a widow. My husband is dead. ⁶I had two sons. They got into a fight with each other in a field. No one was there to separate them. One of my sons struck down the other one and killed him. ⁷Now my whole family group has risen up against me. They say, 'Hand over the one who struck down his brother. Then we can put him to death for killing his brother. That will also get rid of the one who will receive the family property.' They want to kill the only living son I have left, just as someone would put out a burning coal. That would leave my husband without any son on the face of the earth to carry on the family name."

⁸The king said to the woman, "Go home. I'll give an order to make sure you are taken care of."

⁹But the woman from Tekoa said to him, "You are my king and master. Please pardon me and my family. You and your royal family won't be guilty of doing anything wrong."

¹⁰The king replied, "If people give you any trouble, bring them to me. They won't bother you again."

¹¹She said, "Please pray to the LORD your God. Pray that he will keep our nearest male relative from killing my other son. Then my son won't be destroyed."

"You can be sure that the LORD lives," the king said. "And you can be just as sure that not one hair of your son's head will fall to the ground."

¹²Then the woman said, "King David, please let me say something else to you."

"Go ahead," he replied.

¹³The woman said, "You are the king. So why have you done something that brings so much harm on God's people? When you do that, you hand down a sentence against yourself. You won't let the son you drove away come back. ¹⁴All of us must die. We are like water spilled on the ground. It can't be put back into the jar. But that is not what God desires. Instead, he finds a way to bring back anyone who was driven away from him.

¹⁵"King David, I've come here to say this to you now. I've done it because people have made me afraid. I thought, 'I'll go and speak to the king. Perhaps he'll do what I'm

asking. [16]A man is trying to separate me and my son from the property God gave us. Perhaps the king will agree to save me from that man.'

[17]"So now I'm saying, 'May what you have told me prevent that man from doing what he wants. You are like an angel of God. You know what is good and what is evil. May the LORD your God be with you.'"

[18]Then the king said to the woman, "I'm going to ask you a question. I want you to tell me the truth."

"Please ask me anything you want to," the woman said.

[19]The king asked, "Joab told you to say all of this, didn't he?"

The woman answered, "What you have told me is exactly right. And that's just as sure as you are alive. It's true that Joab directed me to do this. He told me everything he wanted me to say. [20]He did it to change the way things now are. You are as wise as an angel of God. You know everything that happens in the land."

[21]Later the king said to Joab, "All right. I'll do what you want. Go. Bring back the young man Absalom."

[22]Joab bowed down with his face toward the ground. He did it to honor the king. And he asked God to bless the king. He said, "You are my king and master. Today I know that you are pleased with me. You have given me what I asked for."

[23]Then Joab went to Geshur. He brought Absalom back to Jerusalem. [24]But the king said, "He must go to his own house. I don't want him to come and see me." So Absalom went to his own house. He didn't go to see the king.

[25]In the whole land of Israel there wasn't any man as handsome as Absalom was. That's why everyone praised him. From the top of his head to the bottom of his feet he didn't have any flaws. [26]He used to cut his hair once a year when it became too heavy for him. Then he would weigh it. It weighed five pounds in keeping with the standard weights used in the palace.

[27]Three sons and a daughter were born to Absalom. His daughter's name was Tamar. She became a beautiful woman.

[28]Absalom lived in Jerusalem for two years without going to see the king. [29]Then Absalom sent for Joab. He wanted to send Joab to the king. But Joab refused to come

to Absalom. So Absalom sent for him a second time. But Joab still refused to come. [30]Then Absalom said to his servants, "Joab's field is next to mine. He has barley growing there. Go and set it on fire." So Absalom's servants set the field on fire.

[31]Joab finally went to Absalom's house. He said to Absalom, "Why did your servants set my field on fire?"

[32]Absalom said to Joab, "I sent a message to you. I said, 'Come here. I want to send you to the king. I want to ask him for me, "Why did you bring me back from Geshur? I would be better off if I were still there!"' Now then, I want to go and see the king. If I'm guilty of doing anything wrong, let him put me to death."

[33]So Joab went to the king and told him that. Then the king sent for Absalom. He came in and bowed down to the king with his face toward the ground. And the king kissed Absalom.

Absalom Makes Secret Plans Against David

15 Some time later, Absalom got a chariot and horses for himself. He also got 50 men to run in front of him. [2]He would get up early. He would stand by the side of the road that led to the city gate. Sometimes a person would come with a case for the king to decide. Then Absalom would call out to him, "What town are you from?" He would answer, "I'm from one of the tribes of Israel." [3]Absalom would say, "Look, your claims are based on the law. So you have every right to make them. But the king doesn't have anyone here who can listen to your case." [4]Absalom would continue, "I wish I were appointed judge in the land! Then anyone who has a case or a claim could come to me. I would make sure they are treated fairly."

[5]Sometimes people would approach Absalom and bow down to him. Then he would reach out his hand. He would take hold of them and kiss them. [6]Absalom did that to all the Israelites who came to the king with their cases or claims. That's why the hearts of the people were turned toward him.

[7]After Absalom had lived in Jerusalem for four years, he went and spoke to the king. He said, "Let me go to Hebron. I want to keep a promise I made to the LORD. [8]When I was living at Geshur in Aram, I made a promise. I said, 'If the LORD takes

WHAT ABOUT YOU?

Absalom was envious of his father, King David, for his power and position in Israel. His envy led him to secretly plot to win the hearts of the people and overthrow his father.

Envy isn't an obvious sin, such as lying or murder. It's something that grows quietly in our hearts—maybe without us even realizing it. Envy can start when we admire something a friend has, and we wish we had it too. It can grow to the point where all we think about is how much we want what we don't have. Though you'd probably never go to these extremes, envy can ruin friendships, create distrust, and leave you with big-time regrets.

One solution for envy includes appreciating and taking care of the things we have. But what if you envy someone who really does have cooler stuff than you do? A nicer bike. A bigger birthday party. You may need to practice being content. It's a habit worth forming.

When we're satisfied with our possessions (whether we have a lot or a little) and don't focus on what other people have, we will be grateful for God's blessings in our lives. The key to happiness is deciding that whatever the Lord chooses to give us is enough.

Another way to battle feelings of envy is to give something away. Put aside some of your allowance to donate to your church. Or share things you've outgrown with those who might enjoy them. Ask your parents for more ideas.

---

me back to Jerusalem, I'll go to Hebron and worship him there.'"

⁹The king said to him, "Go in peace." So he went to Hebron.

¹⁰Then Absalom sent messengers secretly to all the tribes of Israel. They said, "Listen for the sound of trumpets. As soon as you hear them, say, 'Absalom has become king in Hebron.'" ¹¹Absalom had taken 200 men from Jerusalem with him to Hebron. He had invited them to be his guests. They went without having any idea what was going to happen. ¹²While Absalom was offering sacrifices, he sent for Ahithophel. Ahithophel was David's adviser. He came to Absalom from Giloh, his hometown. The number of people who followed Absalom kept growing. So he became more and more able to carry out his plans against David.

David Runs Away From Absalom

¹³A messenger came and spoke to David. He told him, "The hearts of the Israelites are turned toward Absalom."

¹⁴Then David spoke to all his officials who were with him in Jerusalem. He said, "Come on! We have to leave right away! If we don't, none of us will escape from Absalom. He'll move quickly to catch up with us. He'll destroy us. His men will kill everyone in the city with their swords."

¹⁵The king's officials answered him, "You are our king and master. We're ready to do anything you want."

¹⁶The king started out. Everyone in his whole family went with him. But he left ten concubines behind to take care of the palace. ¹⁷So the king and all those with him left. They stopped at the edge of the city. ¹⁸All of David's officials marched past him. All the Kerethites and Pelethites marched along with them. And all of the 600 men who had come with him from Gath marched in front of him.

¹⁹The king spoke to Ittai. He was from Gath. The king said to him, "Why do you want to come along with us? Go back. Stay with King Absalom. You are an outsider.

You left your own country. [20]You came to join me only a short time ago. So why should I make you wander around with us now? I don't even know where I'm going. So go on back. Take your people with you. And may the LORD be kind and faithful to you."

[21]But Ittai replied to the king, "You are my king and master. I want to be where you are. It doesn't matter whether I live or die. And that's just as sure as the LORD and you are alive."

[22]David said to Ittai, "Go ahead then. Keep marching with my men." So Ittai, the Gittite, kept marching. All his men and their families marched with him.

[23]All the people in the countryside wept out loud as David and all his followers passed by. The king went across the Kidron Valley. He and all the people with him moved on toward the desert.

[24]Zadok also went with them. Some of the Levites went with him. They were carrying the ark of the covenant of God. They set down the ark. Abiathar offered sacrifices until all the people had left the city.

[25]Then the king said to Zadok, "Take the ark of God back into the city. If the LORD is pleased with me, he'll bring me back. He'll let me see the ark again. He'll also let me see Jerusalem again. That's the place where he lives. [26]But suppose he says, 'I am not pleased with you.' Then I accept that. Let him do to me what he thinks is best."

[27]The king said again to Zadok the priest, "Do you understand? Go back to the city with my blessing. Take your son Ahimaaz with you. Also take Abiathar and his son Jonathan with you. [28]I'll wait at the place in the desert where we can go across the Jordan River. I'll wait there until you send word to let me know what's happening."

[29]So Zadok and Abiathar took the ark of God back to Jerusalem. They stayed there.

[30]But David went on up the Mount of Olives. He was weeping as he went. His head was covered, and he was barefoot. All the people with him covered their heads too. And they were weeping as they went up. [31]David had been told, "Ahithophel, along with Absalom, is one of the people making secret plans against you." So David prayed, "LORD, make Ahithophel's advice look foolish."

[32]David arrived at the top of the Mount of Olives. That's where people used to worship God. Hushai, the Arkite, was there to meet him. His robe was torn. There was dust on his head. [33]David said to him, "If you go with me, you will be too much trouble for me. [34]So return to the city. Say to Absalom, 'Your Majesty, I'll be your servant. In the past, I was your father's servant. But now I'll be your servant.' If you do that, you can help me by making sure Ahithophel's advice fails. [35]Zadok and Abiathar, the priests, will be there with you. Tell them everything you hear in the king's palace. [36]They have their sons Ahimaaz and Jonathan there with them. Send them to tell me everything you hear."

[37]So David's trusted friend Hushai went to Jerusalem. He arrived just as Absalom was entering the city.

David and Ziba

16 David went just beyond the top of the Mount of Olives. Ziba was waiting there to meet him. He was Mephibosheth's manager. He had several donkeys with saddles on them. They were carrying 200 loaves of bread and 100 raisin cakes. They were also carrying 100 fig cakes and a bottle of wine. The bottle was made out of animal skin.

[2]The king asked Ziba, "Why have you brought all these things?"

Ziba answered, "The donkeys are for the king's family to ride on. The bread and fruit are for the people to eat. The wine will make those who get tired in the desert feel like new again."

[3]Then the king asked, "Where is your master's grandson Mephibosheth?"

Ziba said to him, "He's staying in Jerusalem. He thinks, 'Today the Israelites will cause me to rule once again over my grandfather Saul's kingdom.'"

[4]Then the king said to Ziba, "Everything that belonged to Mephibosheth belongs to you now."

"You are my king and master," Ziba said. "I make myself humble in front of you. I bow down to you. May you be pleased with me."

Shimei Curses David

[5]King David approached Bahurim. As he did, a man came out toward him. The man was from the same family group that Saul was from. His name was Shimei. He was the son of Gera. As he came out of the

town, he cursed David. [6]He threw stones at David and all his officials. He did it even though all the troops and the special guard were there. They were to the right and left of David. [7]As Shimei cursed, he said, "Get out! Get out, you murderer! You are a worthless and evil man! [8]You spilled the blood of a lot of people in Saul's family. You took over his kingdom. Now the LORD is paying you back. He has handed the kingdom over to your son Absalom. You have been destroyed because you are a murderer!"

[9]Then Abishai, the son of Zeruiah, spoke to the king. He said, "King David, why should we let this dead dog curse you? Let me go over there. I'll cut off his head."

[10]But the king said, "You and Joab are sons of Zeruiah. What does this have to do with you? Maybe the LORD said to him, 'Curse David.' If he did, who can ask him, 'Why are you doing this?'"

[11]Then David spoke to Abishai and all his officials. He said, "My very own son Absalom is trying to kill me. How much more should this man from Benjamin want to kill me! Leave him alone. Let him curse. The LORD has told him to do it. [12]Maybe the LORD will see how much I'm suffering. Maybe he'll bring back to me his covenant blessing instead of his curse I'm hearing today."

[13]So David and his men kept going along the road. At the same time, Shimei was going along the hillside across from him. He was cursing David as he went. He was throwing stones at David. He was showering him with dirt. [14]The king and all the people with him came to the place they had planned to go to. They were very tired. So David rested there.

Ahithophel and Hushai Give Advice to Absalom

[15]During that time, Absalom and all the men of Israel came to Jerusalem. Ahithophel was with him. [16]Then Hushai, the Arkite, went to Absalom. He said to him, "May the king live a long time! May the king live a long time!" Hushai was David's trusted friend.

[17]Absalom said to Hushai, "So this is the way you show love to your friend? If he's your friend, why didn't you go with him?"

[18]Hushai said to Absalom, "Why should I? You are the one the LORD has chosen. These people and all the men of Israel have also chosen you. I want to be on your side. I want to stay with you. [19]After all, who else should I serve? Shouldn't I serve the king's son? I will serve you, just as I served your father."

[20]Absalom said to Ahithophel, "Give us your advice. What should we do?"

[21]Ahithophel answered, "Your father left some concubines behind to take care of the palace. Go and sleep with them. Then all the Israelites will hear about it. They will hear that you have made your father hate you. Everyone with you will be encouraged to give you more support." [22]So they set up a tent for Absalom on the roof of the palace. He went in and slept with his father's concubines. Everyone in Israel saw it.

[23]In those days the advice Ahithophel gave was as good as advice from someone who asks God for guidance. That's what David and Absalom thought about all of Ahithophel's advice.

17 One day Ahithophel said to Absalom, "Here's what I suggest. Choose 12,000 men. Start out tonight and go after David. [2]Attack him while he's tired and weak. Fill him with terror. Then all the people with him will run away. Don't strike down anyone except the king. [3]Bring all the other people back. After the man you want to kill is dead, everyone else will return to you. And none of the people will be harmed." [4]Ahithophel's plan seemed good to Absalom. It also seemed good to all the elders of Israel.

[5]But Absalom said, "Send for Hushai, the Arkite. Then we can find out what he suggests as well." [6]Hushai came to him. Absalom said, "Ahithophel has given us his advice. Should we do what he says? If we shouldn't, tell us what you would do."

[7]Hushai replied to Absalom, "The advice Ahithophel has given you isn't good this time. [8]You know your father and his men. They are fighters. They are as strong as a wild bear whose cubs have been stolen from her. Besides, your father really knows how to fight. He won't spend the night with his troops. [9]In fact, he's probably hiding in a cave or some other place right now. Suppose he attacks your troops first. When people hear about it, they'll say, 'Many of the troops who followed Absalom have been killed.' [10]Then the hearts of your

soldiers will melt away in fear. Even those as brave as a lion will be terrified. That's because everyone in Israel knows that your father is a fighter. They know that those with him are brave.

¹¹"So here's what I suggest. Bring together all the men of Israel from the town of Dan all the way to Beersheba. They are as many as the grains of sand on the seashore. You yourself should lead them into battle. ¹²Then we'll attack David no matter where we find him. As dew completely covers the ground, we'll completely overpower his entire army. We won't leave him or any of his men alive. ¹³He might try to get away by going into a city. If he does, all of us will bring ropes to that city. We'll drag the whole city down into the valley. Not even a pebble of that city will be left."

¹⁴Absalom and all the men of Israel agreed. They said, "The advice of Hushai, the Arkite, is better than the advice of Ahithophel." The LORD had decided that Ahithophel's good advice would fail. The LORD wanted to bring horrible trouble on Absalom.

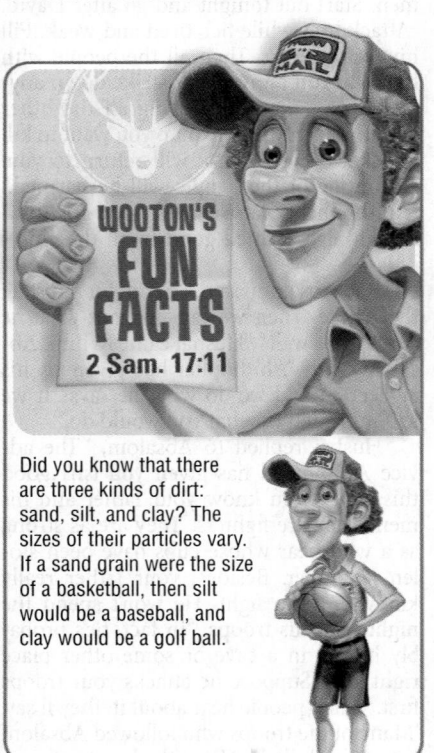

WOOTON'S
FUN
FACTS
2 Sam. 17:11

Did you know that there are three kinds of dirt: sand, silt, and clay? The sizes of their particles vary. If a sand grain were the size of a basketball, then silt would be a baseball, and clay would be a golf ball.

¹⁵Hushai spoke to Zadok and Abiathar, the priests. He said, "Ahithophel has given advice to Absalom and the elders of Israel. He suggested that they should do one thing. But I suggested something else. ¹⁶Send a message right away. Tell David, 'Don't spend the night in the desert at a place where people cross the Jordan River. Make sure you go on across. If you don't, you and all the people with you will be swallowed up.'"

¹⁷Jonathan and Ahimaaz were staying at En Rogel just outside Jerusalem. They knew they would be in danger if anyone saw them entering the city. A female servant was supposed to go and tell them what had happened. Then they were supposed to go and tell King David. ¹⁸But a young man saw Jonathan and Ahimaaz and told Absalom about it. So the two men left right away. They went to the house of a man in Bahurim. He had a well in his courtyard. They climbed down into it. ¹⁹The man's wife got a covering and spread it out over the opening of the well. Then she scattered grain on the covering. So no one knew that the men were hiding in the well.

²⁰Absalom's men came to the house. They asked the woman, "Where are Ahimaaz and Jonathan?"

She answered, "They went across the brook." When the men looked around, they didn't find anyone. So they returned to Jerusalem.

²¹After they had gone, Jonathan and Ahimaaz climbed out of the well. They went to tell King David what they had found out. They said to him, "Go across the river right away. Ahithophel has told Absalom how to come after you and strike you down." ²²So David and all the people with him started out. They went across the Jordan River. By sunrise, everyone had crossed over.

²³Ahithophel saw that his advice wasn't being followed. So he put a saddle on his donkey. He started out for his house in his hometown. When he arrived, he made everything ready for his death. He made out his will. Then he killed himself. And so he died and was buried in his father's tomb.

Absalom Dies

²⁴David went to Mahanaim. Absalom went across the Jordan River with all the men of Israel. ²⁵Absalom had made Amasa commander of the army in place of Joab.

Amasa was the son of Jether. Jether belonged to the family line of Ishmael. He had married Abigail. She was the daughter of Nahash and the sister of Zeruiah. Zeruiah was the mother of Joab. ²⁶Absalom and the Israelites camped in the land of Gilead.

²⁷David came to Mahanaim. Shobi, the son of Nahash, met him there. Shobi was from Rabbah in the land of Ammon. Makir, the son of Ammiel from Lo Debar, met him there too. So did Barzillai from Rogelim in the land of Gilead. ²⁸They brought beds, bowls and clay pots. They brought wheat, barley, flour, and grain that had been cooked. They brought beans and lentils. ²⁹They brought honey, butter, sheep, and cheese that was made from cows' milk. They brought all that food for David and his people to eat. They said, "These people have become tired. They've become hungry and thirsty in the desert."

18 David brought together the men with him. He appointed commanders of thousands over some of them. He appointed commanders of hundreds over the others. ²Then David sent out his troops in military groups. One group was under the command of Joab. Another was under Joab's brother Abishai, the son of Zeruiah. The last was under Ittai, the Gittite. The king told the troops, "You can be sure that I myself will march out with you."

³But the men said, "You must not march out. If we are forced to run away, our enemies won't care about us. Even if half of us die, they won't care. But you are worth 10,000 of us. So it would be better for you to stay here in the city. Then you can send us help if we need it."

⁴The king said, "I'll do what you think is best."

So the king stood beside the city gate. His whole army marched out in groups of hundreds and groups of thousands. ⁵The king gave an order to Joab, Abishai and Ittai. He commanded them, "Be gentle with the young man Absalom. Do it for me." All the troops heard the king give the commanders that order about Absalom.

⁶David's army marched out of the city to fight against Israel. The battle took place in the forest of Ephraim. ⁷There David's men won the battle over Israel's army. A huge number of men were wounded or killed that day. The total number was 20,000. ⁸The fighting spread out over the whole countryside. But more men were killed in the forest that day than out in the open.

⁹Absalom happened to come across some of David's men. He was riding his mule. The mule went under the thick branches of a large oak tree. Absalom's hair got caught in the tree. He was left hanging in the air. The mule he was riding kept on going.

¹⁰One of David's men saw what had happened. He told Joab, "I just saw Absalom hanging in an oak tree."

¹¹Joab said to the man, "What! You saw him? Why didn't you strike him down right there? Then I would have had to give you four ounces of silver and a soldier's belt."

¹²But the man replied, "I wouldn't do anything to hurt the king's son. I wouldn't do it even for 25 pounds of silver. We heard the king's command to you and Abishai and Ittai. He said, 'Be careful not to hurt the young man Absalom. Do it for me.' ¹³Suppose I had put my life in danger by killing him. The king would have found out about it. Nothing is hidden from him. And you wouldn't have stood up for me."

¹⁴Joab said, "I'm not going to waste any more time on you." So he got three javelins. Then he went over and plunged them into Absalom's heart. He did it while Absalom was still hanging there alive in the oak tree. ¹⁵Ten of the men carrying Joab's armor surrounded Absalom. They struck him and killed him.

¹⁶Then Joab blew his trumpet. He ordered his troops to stop chasing Israel's army. ¹⁷Joab's men threw Absalom into a big pit in the forest. They covered him with a large pile of rocks. While all of that was going on, all the Israelites ran back to their homes.

¹⁸Earlier in his life Absalom had set up a pillar in the King's Valley. He had put it up as a monument to himself. He thought, "I don't have a son to carry on the memory of my name." So he named the pillar after himself. It is still called Absalom's Monument to this day.

David Mourns Over Absalom

¹⁹Ahimaaz, the son of Zadok, said to Joab, "Let me run and take the news to the king. Let me tell him that the LORD has shown that

David is in the right. The LORD has done this by saving David from his enemies."

²⁰"I don't want you to take the news to the king today," Joab told him. "You can do it some other time. But you must not do it today, because the king's son is dead."

²¹Then Joab said to a man from Cush, "Go. Tell the king what you have seen." The man bowed down in front of Joab. Then he ran off.

²²Ahimaaz, the son of Zadok, spoke again to Joab. He said, "I don't care what happens to me. Please let me run behind the man from Cush."

But Joab replied, "My son, why do you want to go? You don't have any news that will bring you a reward."

²³He said, "I don't care what happens. I want to run."

So Joab said, "Run!" Then Ahimaaz ran across the plain of the Jordan River. As he ran, he passed the man from Cush.

²⁴David was sitting in the area between the inner and outer gates of the city. The man on guard duty went up to the roof over the entrance of the gate by the wall. As he looked out, he saw someone running alone. ²⁵The guard called out to the king and reported it.

The king said, "If the runner is alone, he must be bringing good news." The runner came closer and closer.

²⁶Then the man on guard duty saw another runner. He called out to the man guarding the gate. He said, "Look! There's another man running alone!"

The king said, "He must be bringing good news too."

²⁷The man on guard duty said, "I can see that the first one runs like Ahimaaz, the son of Zadok."

"He's a good man," the king said. "He's bringing good news."

²⁸Then Ahimaaz called out to the king, "Everything's all right!" He bowed down in front of the king with his face toward the ground. He said, "You are my king and master. Give praise to the LORD your God! He has handed over to you those who lifted their hands to kill you."

²⁹The king asked, "Is the young man Absalom safe?"

Ahimaaz answered, "I saw total disorder. I saw it just as Joab was about to send the king's servant and me to you. But I don't know what it was all about."

³⁰The king said, "Stand over there and wait." So he stepped over to one side and stood there.

³¹Then the man from Cush arrived. He said, "You are my king and master. I'm bringing you some good news. The LORD has shown that you are in the right. He has done this by rescuing you today from all those trying to kill you."

³²The king asked the man from Cush, "Is the young man Absalom safe?"

The man replied, "King David, may your enemies be like that young man. May all those who rise up to harm you be like him."

³³The king was very upset. He went up to the room over the entrance of the gate and wept. As he went, he said, "My son Absalom! My son, my son Absalom! I wish I had died instead of you. Absalom! My son, my son!"

19 Someone told Joab, "The king is weeping and mourning for Absalom. He's filled with sadness because his son has died." ²The army had won a great battle that day. But their joy turned into sadness. That's because someone had told the troops, "The king is filled with sorrow because his son is dead." ³The men came quietly into the city that day. They were like fighting men who are ashamed because they've run away from a battle. ⁴The king covered his face. He cried loudly, "My son Absalom! Absalom, my son, my son!"

⁵Then Joab went into the king's house. He said to him, "Today you have made all your men feel ashamed. They have just saved your life. They have saved the lives of your sons and daughters. And they have saved the lives of your wives and concubines. ⁶You love those who hate you. You hate those who love you. The commanders and their troops don't mean anything to you. You made that very clear today. I can see that you would be pleased if Absalom were alive today and all of us were dead. ⁷Now go out there and cheer up your men. If you don't, you won't have any of them left with you by sunset. That will be worse for you than all the troubles you have ever had in your whole life. That's what I promise you in the LORD's name."

⁸So the king got up and took his seat in the entrance of the city gate. His men were told, "The king is sitting in the entrance of the gate." Then all of them came and stood in front of him.

While all of that was going on, the Israelites had run back to their homes.

David Returns to Jerusalem

[9]People from all the tribes of Israel began to argue among themselves. They were saying, "The king saved us from the power of our enemies. He saved us from the power of the Philistines. But now he has left the country to escape from Absalom. [10]We anointed Absalom to rule over us. But he has died in battle. So why aren't any of you talking about bringing the king back?"

[11]King David sent a message to Zadok and Abiathar, the priests. David said, "Speak to the elders of Judah. Tell them I said, 'News has reached me where I'm staying. People all over Israel are talking about bringing me back to my palace. Why should you be the last to do something about it? [12]You are my relatives. You are my own flesh and blood. So why should you be the last to bring me back?' [13]Say to Amasa, 'Aren't you my own flesh and blood? You will be the commander of my army for life in place of Joab. If that isn't true, may God punish me greatly.'"

[14]So the hearts of all the men of Judah were turned toward David. All of them had the same purpose in mind. They sent a message to the king. They said, "We want you to come back. We want all your men to come back too." [15]Then the king returned. He went as far as the Jordan River.

The men of Judah had come to Gilgal to welcome the king back. They had come to bring him across the Jordan. [16]Shimei, the son of Gera, was among them. Shimei was from Bahurim in the territory of Benjamin. He hurried down to welcome King David back. [17]There were 1,000 people from Benjamin with him. Ziba, the manager of Saul's house, was with him too. And so were Ziba's 15 sons and 20 servants. All of them rushed down to the Jordan River. That's where the king was. [18]They went across at the place where people usually cross it. Then they brought the king's family back over with them. They were ready to do anything he wanted them to do.

Shimei, the son of Gera, had also gone across the Jordan. When he did, he fell down flat with his face toward the ground in front of the king. [19]He said to him, "You are my king and master. Please don't hold me guilty. Please forgive me for the wrong things I did on the day you left Jerusalem.

Please forget all about them. [20]I know I've sinned. But today I've come down here to welcome you. I'm the first member of Joseph's whole family to do it."

[21]Then Abishai, the son of Zeruiah, said, "Shouldn't Shimei be put to death for what he did? He cursed you. And you are the Lord's anointed king."

[22]But David replied, "You and Joab are sons of Zeruiah. What does this have to do with you? What right do you have to interfere? Should anyone be put to death in Israel today? Don't I know that today I am king over Israel again?" [23]So the king made a promise to Shimei. He said to him, "You aren't going to be put to death."

[24]Mephibosheth was Saul's grandson. He had also gone down to welcome the king back. He had not taken care of his feet. He hadn't trimmed his mustache or washed his clothes. He hadn't done any of those things from the day the king left Jerusalem until the day he returned safely. [25]He came from Jerusalem to welcome the king. The king asked him, "Mephibosheth, why didn't you go with me?"

[26]He said, "You are my king and master. I'm not able to walk. So I thought, 'I'll have a saddle put on my donkey. I'll ride on it. Then I can go with the king.' But my servant Ziba turned against me. [27]He has told you lies about me. King David, you are like an angel of God. So do what you wish. [28]You should have put all the members of my grandfather's family to death, including me. Instead, you always provided what I needed. So what right do I have to make any more appeals to you?"

[29]The king said to him, "You don't have to say anything else. I order you and Ziba to divide up Saul's land between you."

[30]Mephibosheth said to the king, "I'm happy that you have returned home safely. So just let Ziba have everything."

[31]Barzillai had also come down to go across the Jordan River with the king. He wanted to send the king on his way from there. Barzillai was from Rogelim in the land of Gilead. [32]He was very old. He was 80 years old. He had given the king everything he needed while the king was staying in Mahanaim. That's because Barzillai was very wealthy. [33]The king said to Barzillai, "Come across the river with me. Stay with me in Jerusalem. I'll take good care of you."

³⁴But Barzillai said to the king, "I won't live for many more years. So why should I go up to Jerusalem with you? ³⁵I'm already 80 years old. I can hardly tell the difference between what is enjoyable and what isn't. I can hardly taste what I eat and drink. I can't even hear the voices of male and female singers anymore. So why should I add my problems to yours? ³⁶I'll go across the Jordan River with you for a little way. Why should you reward me by taking care of me? ³⁷Let me go back home. Then I can die in my own town. I can be buried there in the tomb of my father and mother. But let Kimham take my place. Let him go across the river with you. Do for him whatever you wish."

³⁸The king said, "Kimham will go across with me. I'll do for him whatever you wish. And I'll do for you anything you wish."

³⁹So all the people went across the Jordan River. Then the king crossed over. The king kissed Barzillai and said goodbye to him. And Barzillai went back home.

⁴⁰After the king had gone across the river, he went to Gilgal. Kimham had gone across with him. All the troops of Judah and half of the troops of Israel had taken the king across.

⁴¹Soon all the men of Israel were coming to the king. They were saying to him, "Why did the men of Judah take you away from us? They are our relatives. What right did they have to bring you and your family across the Jordan River? What right did they have to bring all your men over with you?"

⁴²All the men of Judah answered the men of Israel. They said, "We did that because the king is our close relative. So why should you be angry about what happened? Have we eaten any of the king's food? Have we taken anything for ourselves?"

⁴³Then the men of Israel answered the men of Judah. They said, "We have ten of the 12 tribes in the kingdom. So we have a stronger claim on David than you have. Why then are you acting as if you hate us? Weren't we the first ones to talk about bringing back our king?"

But the men of Judah argued their side even more forcefully than the men of Israel.

Sheba Urges Israel not to Follow David

20 An evil man who always stirred up trouble happened to be in Gilgal. His name was Sheba, the son of Bikri. Sheba was from the tribe of Benjamin. He blew his trumpet. Then he shouted,

"We don't have any share in David's kingdom!
Jesse's son is not our king!
Men of Israel, every one of you go back home!"

²So all the men of Israel deserted David. They followed Sheba, the son of Bikri. But the men of Judah stayed with their king. They remained with him from the Jordan River all the way to Jerusalem.

³David returned to his palace in Jerusalem. He had left ten concubines there to take care of the palace. He put them in a house and kept them under guard. He gave them what they needed. But he didn't sleep with them. They were kept under guard until the day they died. They lived as if they were widows.

⁴The king said to Amasa, "Send for the men of Judah. Tell them to come to me within three days. And be here yourself." ⁵So Amasa went to get the men of Judah. But he took longer than the time the king had set for him.

⁶David said to Abishai, "Sheba, the son of Bikri, will do more harm to us than Absalom ever did. Take my men and go after him. If you don't, he'll find cities that have high walls around them. He'll go into one of them and escape from us." ⁷So Joab's men marched out with the Kerethites and Pelethites. They went out with all the mighty soldiers. All of them were under Abishai's command. They marched out from Jerusalem and went after Sheba, the son of Bikri.

⁸They arrived at the great rock in Gibeon. Amasa went there to welcome them. Joab was wearing his military clothes. Over them at his waist he had strapped on a belt that held a dagger. As he stepped forward, he secretly took the dagger out.

⁹Joab said to Amasa, "How are you, my friend?" Then Joab reached out his right hand. He took hold of Amasa's beard to kiss him. ¹⁰Amasa didn't notice the dagger in Joab's left hand. Joab stuck it into his stomach. His insides spilled out on the ground. Joab didn't have to stab him again. Amasa was already dead. Then Joab and his brother Abishai went after Sheba, the son of Bikri.

[11]One of Joab's men stood beside Amasa's body. He said to the other men, "Are you pleased with Joab? Are you on David's side? Then follow Joab!" [12]Amasa's body lay covered with his blood in the middle of the road. The man saw that all the troops stopped there. He realized that everyone was stopping to look at Amasa's body. So he dragged it from the road into a field. Then he threw some clothes on top of it. [13]After that happened, everyone continued on with Joab. They went after Sheba, the son of Bikri.

[14]Sheba passed through all the territory of the tribes of Israel. He arrived at the city of Abel Beth Maakah. He had gone through the entire area of the Bikrites. They had gathered together and followed him. [15]Joab and all his troops came to Abel Beth Maakah. They surrounded it because Sheba was there. They built a ramp up to the city. It stood against the outer wall. They pounded the wall with huge logs to bring it down. [16]While that was going on, a wise woman called out from the city. She shouted, "Listen! Listen! Tell Joab to come here. I want to speak to him." [17]So Joab went toward her. She asked, "Are you Joab?"

"I am," he answered.

She said, "Listen to what I have to say."

"I'm listening," he said.

[18]She continued, "Long ago people used to say, 'Get your answer at Abel.' And that would settle the matter. [19]We are the most peaceful and faithful people in Israel. You are trying to destroy a city that is like a mother in Israel. Why do you want to swallow up what belongs to the LORD?"

[20]"I would never do anything like that!" Joab said. "I would never swallow up or destroy what belongs to the LORD! [21]That isn't what I have in mind at all. There's a man named Sheba, the son of Bikri, in your city. He's from the hill country of Ephraim. He's trying to kill King David. Hand that man over to me. Then I'll pull my men back from your city."

The woman said to Joab, "We'll throw his head down to you from the wall."

[22]Then the woman gave her wise advice to all the people in the city. They cut off the head of Sheba, the son of Bikri. They threw it down to Joab. So he blew his trumpet. Then his men pulled back from the city. Each of them returned to his home. And Joab went back to the king in Jerusalem.

David's Officials

[23]Joab was commander over Israel's entire army.

Benaiah, the son of Jehoiada, was commander over the Kerethites and Pelethites.

[24]Adoniram was in charge of those who were forced to work hard.

Jehoshaphat, the son of Ahilud, kept the records.

[25]Sheva was the secretary.

Zadok and Abiathar were priests.

[26]Ira, the Jairite, was David's priest.

David Makes Things Right for the People of Gibeon

21 For three years in a row there wasn't enough food in the land. That was while David was king. So David asked the LORD why he wasn't blessing his people. The LORD said, "It is because Saul and his family committed murder. He put the people of Gibeon to death."

[2]The people of Gibeon weren't a part of Israel. Instead, they were some of the Amorites who were still left alive. The Israelites had promised to spare them. But Saul had tried to put an end to them. That's because he wanted to make Israel and Judah strong. So now King David sent for the people of Gibeon and spoke to them. [3]He asked them, "What would you like me to do for you? How can I make up for the wrong things that were done to you? I want you to be able to pray that the LORD will once again bless his land."

[4]The people of Gibeon answered him. They said, "No amount of silver or gold can make up for what Saul and his family did to us. And we can't put anyone in Israel to death."

"What do you want me to do for you?" David asked.

[5]They answered the king, "Saul nearly destroyed us. He made plans to wipe us out. We don't have anywhere to live in Israel. [6]So let seven of the males in his family line be given to us. We'll kill them. We'll put their dead bodies out in the open in the sight of the LORD. We'll do it at Gibeah of Saul. Saul was the LORD's chosen king."

So King David said, "I'll give seven males to you."

[7]The king spared Mephibosheth. He was the son of Jonathan and the grandson of

Saul. David had made a promise in front of the LORD. He had promised to be kind to Jonathan and the family line of his father Saul. [8]But the king chose Armoni and another Mephibosheth. They were the two sons of Aiah's daughter Rizpah. Saul was their father. The king also chose the five sons of Saul's daughter Merab. Adriel, the son of Barzillai, was their father. Adriel was from Meholah. [9]King David handed them over to the people of Gibeon. They killed them. They put their dead bodies out in the open on a hill in the sight of the LORD. All seven of them died together. They were put to death during the first days of the harvest. It happened just when people were beginning to harvest the barley.

[10]Aiah's daughter Rizpah took some rough cloth people wear when they're sad. She spread it out for herself on a rock. She stayed there from the beginning of the harvest until it rained. The rain poured down from the sky on the dead bodies of the seven males. She didn't let the birds touch them by day. She didn't let the wild animals touch them at night. [11]Someone told David what Rizpah had done. She was Aiah's daughter and Saul's concubine. [12]David went and got the bones of Saul and his son Jonathan. He got them from the citizens of Jabesh Gilead. They had stolen their bodies from the main street in Beth Shan. That's where the Philistines had hung their bodies up on the city wall. They had done it after they struck Saul down on Mount Gilboa. [13]David brought the bones of Saul and his son Jonathan from Jabesh Gilead. The bones of the seven males who had been killed and put out in the open were also gathered up.

[14]The bones of Saul and his son Jonathan were buried in the tomb of Saul's father Kish. The tomb was at Zela in the territory of Benjamin. Everything the king commanded was done. After that, God answered prayer and blessed the land.

Wars Against the Philistines

[15]Once again there was a battle between the Philistines and Israel. David went down with his men to fight against the Philistines. He became very tired. [16]Ishbi-Benob belonged to the family line of Rapha. The tip of his bronze spear weighed seven and a half pounds. He was also armed with a new sword. He said he would kill David. [17]But Abishai, the son of Zeruiah, came to save David. He struck down the Philistine and killed him. Then David's men made a promise. They said to David, "We never want you to go out with us to battle again. You are the lamp of Israel's kingdom. We want that lamp to keep on burning brightly."

[18]There was another battle against the Philistines. It took place at Gob. At that time Sibbekai killed Saph. Sibbekai was a Hushathite. Saph was from the family line of Rapha.

[19]In another battle against the Philistines at Gob, Elhanan killed Goliath's brother. Elhanan was the son of Jair from Bethlehem. Goliath was from the city of Gath. His spear was as big as a weaver's rod.

[20]There was still another battle. It took place at Gath. A huge man lived there. He had six fingers on each hand and six toes on each foot. So the total number of his toes and fingers was 24. He was also from the family of Rapha. [21]He made fun of Israel. So Jonathan killed him. Jonathan was the son of David's brother Shimeah.

[22]Those four Philistine men lived in Gath. They were from the family line of Rapha. David and his men killed them.

David's Song of Praise

22 David sang the words of this song to the LORD. He sang them when the LORD saved him from the power of all his enemies and of Saul. [2]He said,

"The LORD is my rock and my fort. He
    is the God who saves me.
[3]   My God is my rock. I go to him for
    safety.
He is like a shield to me. He's the
    power that saves me.
He's my place of safety. I go to him for
    help. He's my Savior.
He saves me from those who want to
    hurt me.
[4] I called out to the LORD. He is worthy
    of praise.
He saved me from my enemies.

[5] "The waves of death were all around
    me.
A destroying flood swept over me.
[6] The ropes of the grave were tight
    around me.
Death set its trap in front of me.

⁷ When I was in trouble I called out to
     the LORD.
  I called out to my God.
From his temple he heard my voice.
My cry for help reached his ears.

⁸ "The earth trembled and shook.
  The pillars of the heavens rocked
     back and forth.
  They trembled because the LORD
     was angry.
⁹ Smoke came out of his nose.
  Flames of fire came out of his mouth.
  Burning coals blazed out of it.
¹⁰ He opened the heavens and came
     down.
  Dark clouds were under his feet.
¹¹ He got on the cherubim and flew.
  The wings of the wind lifted him up.
¹² He covered himself with darkness.
  The dark rain clouds of the sky were
     like a tent around him.
¹³ From the brightness all around him
     flashes of lightning blazed out.
¹⁴ The LORD thundered from heaven.
  The voice of the Most High God was
     heard.
¹⁵ He shot his arrows and scattered the
     enemy.
  He sent flashes of lightning and
     chased them away.
¹⁶ The bottom of the sea could be seen.
  The foundations of the earth were
     uncovered.
  It happened when the LORD's anger
     blazed out.
  It came like a blast of breath from
     his nose.

¹⁷ "He reached down from heaven. He
     took hold of me.
  He lifted me out of deep waters.

¹⁸ He saved me from my powerful
     enemies.
  He set me free from those who were
     too strong for me.
¹⁹ They stood up to me when I was in
     trouble.
  But the LORD helped me.
²⁰ He brought me out into a wide and safe
     place.
  He saved me because he was pleased
     with me.

²¹ "The LORD has been good to me
     because I do what is right.
  He has rewarded me because I lead a
     pure life.
²² I have lived the way the LORD wanted
     me to.
  I'm not guilty of turning away from
     my God.
²³ I keep all his laws in mind.
  I haven't turned away from his
     commands.
²⁴ He knows that I am without blame.
  He knows I've kept myself from
     sinning.
²⁵ The LORD has rewarded me for doing
     what is right.
  He has rewarded me because I
     haven't done anything wrong.

²⁶ "LORD, to those who are faithful you
     show that you are faithful.
  To those who are without blame
     you show that you are without
     blame.
²⁷ To those who are pure you show that
     you are pure.
  But to those whose paths are crooked
     you show that you are clever.
²⁸ You save those who aren't proud.
  But you watch the proud to bring
     them down.
²⁹ LORD, you are my lamp.
  You bring light into my darkness.
³⁰ With your help I can attack a troop of
     soldiers.
  With the help of my God I can climb
     over a wall.

³¹ "God's way is perfect.
  The LORD's word doesn't have any
     flaws.
  He protects like a shield
     all who go to him for safety.
³² Who is God except the LORD?

2 Sam. 22 David was a great musician who played the harp and the lyre. A lyre is like a small harp. David wrote a bunch of songs to praise God. Most of the ones we know about are recorded in the book of *Psalms*, which means "songs" or "hymns."

Who is the Rock except our God?
³³ God gives me strength for the battle.
He keeps my way secure.
³⁴ He makes my feet like the feet of a deer.
He causes me to stand on the highest places.
³⁵ He trains my hands to fight every battle.
My arms can bend a bow of bronze.
³⁶ LORD, you shield me with your saving help.
Your help has made me great.
³⁷ You give me a wide path to walk in so that I don't twist my ankles.

³⁸ "I chased my enemies and crushed them.
I didn't turn back until they were destroyed.
³⁹ I crushed them completely so that they couldn't get up.
They fell under my feet.
⁴⁰ LORD, you gave me strength to fight the battle.
You caused my enemies to be humble in front of me.
⁴¹ You made them turn their backs and run away.
So I destroyed my enemies.
⁴² They cried out for help. But there was no one to save them.
They called out to the LORD. But he didn't answer them.
⁴³ I beat them as fine as the dust of the earth.
I pounded them and walked on them like mud in the streets.
⁴⁴ "You saved me when people attacked me.
You have kept me as the ruler over nations.
People I didn't know serve me now.
⁴⁵ People from other lands bow down to me in fear.
As soon as they hear about me, they obey me.
⁴⁶ All of them give up hope.
They come trembling out of their hiding places.

⁴⁷ "The LORD lives! Give praise to my Rock!
Give honor to my God, the Rock! He is my Savior!
⁴⁸ He is the God who pays back my enemies.
He brings the nations under my control.
⁴⁹ He sets me free from my enemies.
You have honored me more than them.
You have saved me from a man who wanted to hurt me.
⁵⁰ LORD, I will praise you among the nations.
I will sing your praise.
⁵¹ He gives his king great victories.
He shows his faithful love to his anointed king.
He shows it to David and his family forever."

David's Last Words

23 Here are David's last words. He said,

"I am David, the son of Jesse. God has given me a message.
The Most High God has greatly honored me.
The God of Jacob anointed me as king.
I am the hero of Israel's songs.

² "The Spirit of the LORD spoke through me.
I spoke his word with my tongue.
³ The God of Israel spoke.
The Rock of Israel said to me,
'A king must rule over people in a way that is right.
He must have respect for God when he rules.
⁴ Then he will be like the light of morning at sunrise
when there aren't any clouds.

He will be like the bright sun after rain that makes grass grow on the earth.'

5 "Suppose my royal family was not right with God.
Then he would not have made a covenant with me that will last forever.
Every part of it was well prepared and made secure.
Then God would not have saved me completely
or given me everything I longed for.
6 But evil people are like thorns that are thrown away.
You can't pick them up with your hands.
7 Even if you touch them,
you must use an iron tool or a spear.
Thorns are burned up right where they are."

David's Mighty Warriors

8Here are the names of David's mighty warriors.

Josheb-Basshebeth was chief of the three mighty warriors. He was a Tahkemonite. He used his spear against 800 men. He killed all of them at one time.

9Next to him was Eleazar. He was one of the three mighty warriors. He was the son of Dodai, the Ahohite. Eleazar was with David at Pas Dammim. That's where Israel's army made fun of the Philistines who were gathered there for battle. Then the Israelites pulled back. 10But Eleazar stayed right where he was. He struck down the Philistines until his hand grew tired. But he still held on to his sword. The LORD helped him win a great battle that day. The troops returned to Eleazar. They came back to him only to take what they wanted from the dead bodies.

11Next to him was Shammah, the son of Agee. Shammah was a Hararite. The Philistines gathered together at a place where there was a field full of lentils. Israel's troops ran away from the Philistines. 12But Shammah took his stand in the middle of the field. He didn't let the Philistines capture it. He struck them down. The LORD helped him win a great battle.

13David was at the cave of Adullam. During harvest time, three of the 30 chief warriors came down to him there. A group of Philistines was camped in the Valley of Rephaim. 14At that time David was in his usual place of safety. Some Philistine troops were stationed at Bethlehem. 15David longed for a drink of water. He said, "I wish someone would get me water from the well near the gate of Bethlehem." 16So the three mighty warriors fought their way past the Philistine guards. They got some water from the well near the gate of Bethlehem. They took the water back to David. But David refused to drink it. Instead, he poured it out as a drink offering to the LORD. 17"LORD, I would never drink that water!" David said. "It stands for the blood of these men. They put their lives in danger by going to Bethlehem to get it." So David wouldn't drink it.

Those were some of the brave things the three mighty warriors did.

18Abishai was chief over the three mighty warriors. He was the brother of Joab, the son of Zeruiah. He used his spear against 300 men. He killed all of them. So he became as famous as the three mighty warriors were. 19In fact, he was even more honored than the three mighty warriors. He became their commander. But he wasn't included among them.

20Benaiah was a great hero from Kabzeel. He was the son of Jehoiada. Benaiah did many brave things. He struck down two of Moab's best warriors. He also went down into a pit on a snowy day. He killed a lion there. 21And he struck down a huge Egyptian. The Egyptian was holding a spear. Benaiah went out to fight against him with a club. He grabbed the spear out of the Egyptian's hand. Then he killed him with it. 22Those were some of the brave things Benaiah, the son of Jehoiada, did. He too was as famous as the three mighty warriors were. 23He was honored more than any of the thirty chief warriors. But he wasn't included among the three mighty warriors. David put him in charge of his own personal guards.

24 Here is a list of David's men who were among the thirty chief warriors.

Asahel, the brother of Joab
Elhanan, the son of Dodo, from Bethlehem
25 Shammah, the Harodite
Elika, the Harodite
26 Helez, the Paltite
Ira, the son of Ikkesh, from Tekoa

²⁷ Abiezer from Anathoth
   Sibbekai, the Hushathite
²⁸ Zalmon, the Ahohite
   Maharai from Netophah
²⁹ Heled, the son of Baanah, from
   Netophah
   Ithai, the son of Ribai, from Gibeah
   in Benjamin
³⁰ Benaiah from Pirathon
   Hiddai from the valleys of Gaash
³¹ Abi-Albon, the Arbathite
   Azmaveth, the Barhumite
³² Eliahba, the Shaalbonite
   the sons of Jashen
   Jonathan, ³³the son of Shammah, the
   Hararite
   Ahiam, the son of Sharar, the Hararite
³⁴ Eliphelet, the son of Ahasbai, the
   Maakathite
   Eliam, the son of Ahithophel, from
   Giloh
³⁵ Hezro from Carmel
   Paarai, the Arbite
³⁶ Igal, the son of Nathan, from Zobah
   the son of Hagri
³⁷ Zelek from Ammon
   Naharai from Beeroth, who carried the
   armor of Joab, the son of Zeruiah
³⁸ Ira, the Ithrite
   Gareb, the Ithrite
³⁹ and Uriah, the Hittite

The total number of men was 37.

David Counts His Fighting Men

24 The Lord was very angry with Israel. He stirred up David against them. He said, "Go! Count the men of Israel and Judah."

²So the king spoke to Joab and the army commanders with him. He said, "Go all through the territories of the tribes of Israel. Go from the town of Dan all the way to Beersheba. Count the fighting men. Then I'll know how many there are."

³Joab replied to the king. He said, "King David, you are my master. May the Lord your God multiply the troops 100 times. And may you live to see it. But why would you want me to count the fighting men?"

⁴The king's word had more authority than the word of Joab and the army commanders. That was true in spite of what Joab had said. So they left the king and went out to count the fighting men of Israel.

⁵They went across the Jordan River. They camped south of the town in the middle of the Arnon River valley near Aroer. Then they went through Gad and continued on to Jazer. ⁶They went to Gilead and the area of Tahtim Hodshi. They continued to Dan Jaan and on around toward Sidon. ⁷Then they went toward the fort of Tyre. They went to all the towns of the Hivites and Canaanites. Finally, they went on to Beersheba. It was in the Negev Desert of Judah. ⁸They finished going through the entire land. Then they came back to Jerusalem. They had been gone for nine months and 20 days.

⁹Joab reported to the king how many fighting men he had counted. In Israel there were 800,000 men who were able to handle a sword. In Judah there were 500,000.

¹⁰David felt sorry that he had counted the fighting men. So he said to the Lord, "I committed a great sin when I counted Judah and Israel's men. Lord, I beg you to take away my guilt. I've done a very foolish thing."

¹¹Before David got up the next morning, a message from the Lord came to Gad the prophet. He was David's seer. The message said, ¹²"Go and tell David, 'The Lord says, "I could punish you in three different ways. Choose one of them for me to use against you."'"

¹³So Gad went to David. He said to him, "Take your choice. Do you want three years when there won't be enough food in your land? Or do you want three months when you will run away from your enemies while they chase you? Or do you want three days when there will be a plague in your land? Think it over. Then take your pick. Tell me how to answer the one who sent me."

¹⁴David said to Gad, "I'm suffering terribly. Let us fall into the hands of the Lord. His mercy is great. But don't let me fall into human hands."

¹⁵So the Lord sent a plague on Israel. It lasted from that morning until he decided to end it. From Dan all the way to Beersheba 70,000 people died. ¹⁶The angel reached his hand out to destroy Jerusalem. But the Lord stopped sending the plague. So he spoke to the angel who was making the people suffer. He said, "That is enough! Do not kill any more people." The angel of

the LORD was at Araunah's threshing floor. Araunah was from the city of Jebus.

[17]David saw the angel who was striking down the people. David said to the LORD, "I'm the one who has sinned. I'm the one who has done what is wrong. I'm like a shepherd for these people. These people are like sheep. What have they done? Let your judgment be on me and my family."

David Builds an Altar

[18]On that day Gad went to David. Gad said to him, "Go up to the threshing floor of Araunah, the Jebusite. Build an altar there to honor the LORD." [19]So David went up and did it. He did what the LORD had commanded through Gad. [20]Araunah looked and saw the king and his officials coming toward him. So he went out to welcome them. He bowed down to the king with his face toward the ground.

[21]Araunah said, "King David, you are my master. Why have you come to see me?"

"To buy your threshing floor," David answered. "I want to build an altar there to honor the LORD. When I do, the plague on the people will be stopped."

[22]Araunah said to David, "Take anything you wish. Offer it up. Here are oxen for the burnt offering. Here are threshing sleds. And here are wooden collars from the necks of the oxen. Use all the wood to burn the offering. [23]Your Majesty, I'll give all of it to you." Araunah continued, "And may the LORD your God accept you."

[24]But the king replied to Araunah, "No. I want to pay you for it. I won't sacrifice to the LORD my God burnt offerings that haven't cost me anything."

So David bought the threshing floor and the oxen. He paid 20 ounces of silver for them. [25]David built an altar there to honor the LORD. He sacrificed burnt offerings and friendship offerings. Then the LORD answered David's prayer and blessed the land. The plague on Israel was stopped.

1 Kings

In our journey together, we have now come to the first of two books titled "Kings." First Kings opens with the transfer of power from David to Solomon, which wasn't without its difficulties. But once Solomon established himself as Israel's new leader, his reign was marked by greater peace, power, and renown than any other time in Israel's history. After Solomon asked God for the ability to lead his people wisely (3:4–15), God answered with an abundance of wisdom like the world had never seen. Yet when Solomon allowed his many wives to turn him away from his faithfulness to God, the nation was divided again.

It was a critical moment in the history of the nation. From that point onward, the ten northern tribes (Israel) had one king and the southern tribes (Judah) had another. As you will see, very few of the kings from either Israel or Judah had any redeeming values. Yet during this time of spiritual weakness among Israel's political leaders, God called upon a number of faithful prophets to proclaim His truth. One of the main prophets in 1 Kings is Elijah. He brought a widow's son back to life (chapter 17), faced down hundreds of false prophets on Mount Carmel (18:16–46), called out King Ahab and Queen Jezebel about their sin (chapter 21), and much more. A servant of the Lord indeed!

WHaT'S iT MeaN, EUGeNe?

Heaven/Hell— First, *heaven* refers to the *unseen world* where God and the angels are actively working behind the scenes of our visible reality (Ephesians 6:12). Second, "the heavenly world" denotes the *present power, rule, and authority of God.* Third, heaven is a place where believers will live *in God's presence for all eternity. Hell* (or *Gehenna* in Aramaic) is the place where those who have rejected Christ will experience separation from Him—forever.

Adonijah Makes Himself King

1 King David was now very old. He couldn't keep warm even when blankets were spread over him. ²So his attendants spoke to him. They said, "You are our king and master. Please let us try to find a young virgin to serve you. She can take care of you. She can lie down beside you to keep you warm."

³So David's attendants looked all over Israel for a beautiful young woman. They found Abishag. She was from the town of Shunem. They brought her to the king. ⁴The woman was very beautiful. She took care of the king and served him. But the king didn't have sex with her.

⁵Adonijah was the son of David and his wife Haggith. He came forward and announced, "I'm going to be the next king." So he got chariots and horses ready. He also got 50 men to run in front of him. ⁶His father had never tried to stop him from doing what he wanted to. His father had never asked him, "Why are you acting the way you do?" Adonijah was also very handsome. Now that Absalom was dead, Adonijah was David's oldest son.

⁷Adonijah talked things over with Joab, the son of Zeruiah. He also talked with Abiathar the priest. They agreed to help him. ⁸But Zadok the priest and Benaiah, the son of Jehoiada, didn't join Adonijah. Nathan the prophet didn't join him. Shimei and Rei didn't join him. And neither did David's special guard.

⁹Adonijah sacrificed sheep, cattle and fat calves. He sacrificed them at the Stone of Zoheleth near En Rogel. He invited all his brothers, the king's sons, and all the royal officials of Judah. ¹⁰But he didn't invite Benaiah or Nathan the prophet. He didn't invite the special guard or his brother Solomon either.

¹¹Nathan asked Solomon's mother Bathsheba, "Haven't you heard? Adonijah, the son of Haggith, has made himself king. And King David doesn't know anything about it. ¹²So let me tell you what to do to save your life. It will also save the life of your son Solomon. ¹³Go in and see King David. Say to him, 'You are my king and master. You promised me, "You can be sure that your son Solomon will be king after me. He will sit on my throne." If that's really true, why has Adonijah become king?' ¹⁴While you are still talking to the king, I'll come in and support what you have said."

¹⁵So Bathsheba went to see the old king in his room. Abishag, the Shunammite, was taking care of him there. ¹⁶Bathsheba bowed low in front of the king.

"What do you want?" the king asked.

¹⁷She said to him, "My master, you made a promise in the name of the LORD your God. You promised me, 'Your son Solomon will be king after me. He will sit on my throne.' ¹⁸But now Adonijah has made himself king. And you don't even know about it. ¹⁹He has sacrificed large numbers of cattle, fat calves and sheep. He has invited all the king's sons. He has also invited Abiathar the priest and Joab, the commander of the army. But he hasn't invited your son Solomon. ²⁰You are my king and master. All the Israelites are watching to see what you will do. They want to find out from you who will sit on the throne after you. ²¹If you don't do something, I and my son Solomon will be treated like people who have committed crimes. That will happen as soon as you join the members of your family who have already died."

²²While she was still speaking with the king, Nathan the prophet arrived. ²³The king was told, "Nathan the prophet is here." So Nathan went to the king. He bowed down with his face toward the ground.

²⁴Nathan said, "You are my king and master. Have you announced that Adonijah will be king after you? Have you said he will sit on your throne? ²⁵Today he has gone down outside the city. He has sacrificed large numbers of cattle, fat calves and sheep. He has invited all the king's sons. He has also invited the commanders of the army and Abiathar the priest. Even now they are eating and drinking with him. They are saying, 'May King Adonijah live a long time!' ²⁶But he didn't invite me. He didn't invite Zadok the priest or Benaiah, the son of Jehoiada. He didn't invite your son Solomon either. ²⁷King David, have you allowed all of that to happen? Did you do it without letting us know about it? Why didn't you tell us who is going to sit on your throne after you?"

David Makes Solomon King

²⁸King David said, "Tell Bathsheba to come in." So she came and stood in front of the king.

²⁹Then the king made a promise. He said, "The LORD has saved me from all

my troubles. You can be sure that he lives. ³⁰And you can be just as sure I will do what I promised. This is the day I will do what I promised in the name of the LORD. He is the God of Israel. I promised you that your son Solomon would be king after me. He will sit on my throne in my place."

³¹Then Bathsheba bowed down in front of the king. Her face was toward the ground. She said, "King David, you are my master. May you live forever!"

³²King David said, "Tell Zadok the priest and Nathan the prophet to come in. Also tell Benaiah, the son of Jehoiada, to come." So they came to the king. ³³He said to them, "Take my officials with you. Have my son Solomon get on my own mule. Take him down to the Gihon spring. ³⁴Have Zadok the priest and Nathan the prophet anoint him as king over Israel there. Blow a trumpet. Shout, 'May King Solomon live a long time!' ³⁵Then come back up to the city with him. Have him sit on my throne. He will rule in my place. I've appointed him ruler over Israel and Judah."

³⁶Benaiah, the son of Jehoiada, answered the king. "Amen!" he said. "May the LORD your God make it come true. ³⁷You are my king and master. The LORD has been with you. May he also be with Solomon. King David, may the LORD make Solomon's kingdom even greater than yours!"

³⁸So Zadok the priest and Nathan the prophet left the palace. Benaiah, the son of Jehoiada, went with them. So did the Kerethites and Pelethites. They had Solomon get on King David's mule. And they brought him down to the Gihon spring. ³⁹Zadok the priest had taken an animal horn from the sacred tent. The horn was filled with olive oil. He anointed Solomon with the oil. A trumpet was blown. All the people shouted, "May King Solomon live a long time!" ⁴⁰Then they went up toward the city. Solomon was leading the way. The people were playing flutes. They were filled with great joy. The ground shook because of all the noise.

⁴¹Adonijah and all his guests heard it. They were just finishing their meal. Joab heard the sound of the trumpet. So he asked, "What does all this noise in the city mean?"

⁴²While Joab was still speaking, Jonathan arrived. Jonathan was the son of Abiathar the priest. Adonijah said, "Come in. I have respect for you. You must be bringing good news."

⁴³"No! I'm not!" Jonathan answered. "Our master King David has made Solomon king. ⁴⁴David sent Zadok the priest and Nathan the prophet along with Solomon. He also sent Benaiah, the son of Jehoiada, with him. He sent the Kerethites and Pelethites with him too. They put him on the king's mule. ⁴⁵They took him down to the Gihon spring. There Zadok the priest and Nathan the prophet anointed him as king. Now they've gone back up to the city. They were cheering all the way. The city is filled with the sound of it. That's the noise you hear. ⁴⁶And that's not all. Solomon has taken his seat on the royal throne. ⁴⁷The royal officials came to give their blessing to our master King David. They said, 'May your God make Solomon's name more famous than yours! May he make Solomon's kingdom greater than yours!' While King David was sitting on his bed, he bowed in worship. ⁴⁸He said, 'I praise the LORD. He is the God of Israel. He has let me live to see my son sitting on my throne today as the next king.'"

⁴⁹When all Adonijah's guests heard that, they were terrified. So they got up and scattered. ⁵⁰Adonijah was afraid of what Solomon might do to him. So he went and grabbed the horns of the altar for burnt offerings. Those horns stuck out from its upper corners. ⁵¹Then Solomon was told, "King Solomon, Adonijah is afraid of you. He's holding onto the horns of the altar. He says, 'I want King Solomon to make a promise today. I want him to promise that he won't kill me with his sword.'"

⁵²Solomon replied, "Let him show that he's a man people can respect. Then not even one hair on his head will fall to the ground. But if I find out he's done something evil, he will die." ⁵³King Solomon got some men to bring Adonijah down from the altar. He came and bowed down to King Solomon. Solomon said, "Go on home."

David Gives Orders to Solomon

2 The time came near for David to die. So he gave orders to his son Solomon. ²He said, "I'm about to die, just as everyone else on earth does. So be strong. Show how brave you are. ³Do everything

the LORD your God requires. Live the way he wants you to. Obey his orders and commands. Keep his laws and rules. Do everything written in the Law of Moses. Then you will have success in everything you do. You will succeed everywhere you go. ⁴The LORD will keep the promise he made to me. He said, 'Your sons must be careful about how they live. They must be faithful to me with all their heart and soul. Then you will always have a son from your family line to sit on the throne of Israel.'

⁵"You yourself know what Joab, the son of Zeruiah, did to me. You know that he killed Abner, the son of Ner, and Amasa, the son of Jether. They were the two commanders of Israel's armies. He killed them in a time of peace. It wasn't a time of war. Joab spilled the blood of Abner and Amasa. With that blood he stained the belt around his waist. He also stained the sandals on his feet. ⁶You are wise. So I leave him in your hands. Just don't let him live to become an old man. Don't let him die peacefully.

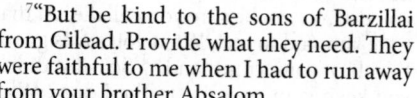

Jason's Jargon

1 KINGS 2

The next quest: Hunt through this chapter for *accountable*. To be held accountable means that someone is responsible. In this case, the king wanted Joab to be accountable for Abner's death.

⁷"But be kind to the sons of Barzillai from Gilead. Provide what they need. They were faithful to me when I had to run away from your brother Absalom.

⁸"Don't forget that Shimei, the son of Gera, is still around. He's from Bahurim in the territory of Benjamin. Shimei cursed me bitterly. He did it on the day I went to Mahanaim. Later, he came down to welcome me at the Jordan River. At that time I made a promise in the name of the LORD. I promised Shimei, 'I won't put you to death with my sword.' ⁹But now I want you to think of him as guilty. You are wise. You will know what to do to him. Don't let him live to become an old man. Put him to death."

¹⁰David joined the members of his family who had already died. He was buried in the City of David. ¹¹He had ruled over Israel for 40 years. He ruled for seven years in Hebron. Then he ruled for 33 years in Jerusalem. ¹²So Solomon sat on the throne of his father David. His position as king was made secure.

Solomon's Kingdom Is Made Secure

¹³Adonijah was the son of David's wife Haggith. He went to Bathsheba. She was Solomon's mother. She asked Adonijah, "Have you come in peace?"

He answered, "Yes. I've come in peace." ¹⁴He continued, "I want to ask you something."

"Go ahead," she replied.

¹⁵He said, "As you know, the kingdom belonged to me. The whole nation of Israel thought of me as their king. But now things have changed. The kingdom belongs to my brother. The LORD has given it to him. ¹⁶But I have a favor to ask of you. Don't say no to me."

"Go ahead," she said.

¹⁷So he continued, "Please ask King Solomon for a favor. He won't say no to you. Ask him to give me Abishag from Shunem to be my wife."

¹⁸"All right," Bathsheba replied. "I'll speak to the king for you."

¹⁹So Bathsheba went to King Solomon. She went to him to speak for Adonijah. The king stood up to greet her. He bowed down to her. Then he sat down on his throne. He had a throne brought for his mother. She sat down at his right side.

²⁰"I have one small favor to ask of you," she said. "Don't say no to me."

The king replied, "Mother, go ahead and ask. I won't say no to you."

²¹She said, "Let your brother Adonijah marry Abishag, the Shunammite."

²²King Solomon answered his mother, "Why are you asking me to give Abishag, the Shunammite, to Adonijah? You might as well ask me to give him the whole kingdom! After all, he's my older brother. And he doesn't want the kingdom only for himself. He also wants it for Abiathar the priest and for Joab, the son of Zeruiah."

²³Then King Solomon made a promise in the name of the LORD. He said, "Adonijah will pay with his life because of what he has

asked for. If he doesn't, may God punish me greatly. ²⁴The LORD has made my position as king secure. I'm sitting on the throne of my father David. The LORD has built a royal house for me, just as he promised. You can be sure that the LORD lives. And you can be just as sure that Adonijah will be put to death today." ²⁵So King Solomon gave the order to Benaiah, the son of Jehoiada. Benaiah struck down Adonijah, and he died.

²⁶The king spoke to Abiathar the priest. He said, "Go back to your fields in Anathoth. You should really be put to death. But I won't have it done now. That's because you carried the ark of the LORD and King. You did it for my father David. You shared all of his hard times." ²⁷So Solomon wouldn't let Abiathar serve as a priest of the LORD anymore. That's how the message the LORD had spoken at Shiloh came true. He had spoken it about the family of Eli.

²⁸News of what Solomon had done reached Joab. Joab had never made evil plans along with Absalom. But he had joined Adonijah. So he ran to the tent of the LORD. He grabbed the horns that stuck out from the upper corners of the altar for burnt offerings. ²⁹King Solomon was told that Joab had run to the tent. He was also told that Joab was by the altar. Then Solomon gave the order to Benaiah, the son of Jehoiada. He told him, "Go! Strike him down!"

³⁰So Benaiah entered the tent of the LORD. He said to Joab, "The king says, 'Come on out!'"

But Joab answered, "No. I'd rather die here."

Benaiah told the king what Joab had said to him. ³¹Then the king commanded Benaiah, "Do what he says. Strike him down and bury him. Then I and my family line won't be held accountable for the blood Joab spilled. He killed people who weren't guilty of doing anything wrong. ³²The LORD will pay him back for the blood he spilled. Joab attacked two men. He killed them with his sword. And my father David didn't even know anything about it. Joab killed Abner, the son of Ner. Abner was the commander of Israel's army. Joab also killed Amasa, the son of Jether. Amasa was the commander of Judah's army. Abner and Amasa were better men than Joab is. They were more honest than he is. ³³May Joab and his children after

him be held forever accountable for spilling the blood of Abner and Amasa. But may David and his children after him enjoy the LORD's peace and rest forever. May the LORD also give his peace to David's royal house and kingdom forever."

³⁴So Benaiah, the son of Jehoiada, went up to the LORD's tent. There he struck down Joab. And he killed him. Joab was buried at his home out in the country. ³⁵The king put Benaiah in charge of the army. Benaiah took Joab's place. The king also put Zadok the priest in Abiathar's place.

³⁶Then the king sent for Shimei. He said to him, "Build yourself a house in Jerusalem. Live there. Don't go anywhere else. ³⁷You must not leave the city and go across the Kidron Valley. If you do, you can be sure you will die. And it will be your own fault."

³⁸Shimei replied to the king, "You are my king and master. What you say is good. I'll do it." Shimei stayed in Jerusalem for a long time.

³⁹Three years after Solomon had talked with Shimei, two of Shimei's slaves ran off. They went to Achish, the king of Gath. He was the son of Maakah. Shimei was told, "Your slaves are in Gath." ⁴⁰When Shimei heard that, he put a saddle on his donkey. Then he went to Achish at Gath to look for his slaves. Shimei found them and brought them back from Gath.

⁴¹Solomon was told that Shimei had left Jerusalem. He was told he had gone to Gath and had returned. ⁴²So the king sent for Shimei. He said to him, "Didn't I force you to make a promise in the name of the LORD? Didn't I warn you? I said, 'You must not leave the city and go somewhere else. If you do, you can be sure you will die.' At that time you said to me, 'What you say is good. I'll obey your command.' ⁴³So why didn't you keep your promise to the LORD? Why didn't you obey the command I gave you?"

⁴⁴The king continued, "You know all the wrong things you did to my father David. In your heart you know them. Now the LORD will pay you back for what you did. ⁴⁵But I will be blessed. The LORD will make David's kingdom secure forever."

⁴⁶Then the king gave the order to Benaiah, the son of Jehoiada. Benaiah left the palace and struck down Shimei. And he died.

So the kingdom was now made secure in Solomon's hands.

Solomon Asks God for Wisdom

3 Solomon and Pharaoh, the king of Egypt, agreed to help each other. So Solomon married Pharaoh's daughter. He brought her to the City of David. She stayed there until he finished building his palace, the LORD's temple, and the wall around Jerusalem. ²But the people continued to offer sacrifices at the high places where they worshiped. That's because a temple hadn't been built yet where the LORD would put his Name. ³Solomon showed his love for the LORD. He did it by obeying the laws his father David had taught him. But Solomon offered sacrifices at the high places. He also burned incense there.

⁴King Solomon went to the city of Gibeon to offer sacrifices. That's where the most important high place was. There he offered 1,000 burnt offerings on the altar. ⁵The LORD appeared to Solomon at Gibeon. He spoke to him in a dream during the night. God said, "Ask for anything you want me to give you."

⁶Solomon answered, "You have been very kind to my father David, your servant. That's because he was faithful to you. He did what was right. His heart was honest. And you have continued to be very kind to him. You have given him a son to sit on his throne this day."

ADVENTURES IN ODYSSEY

Solomon asked God for wisdom in 1 Kings 3. Kids' Radio showed the importance of wisdom through "Pinocchio: The Tale of a Foolish Puppet" (Club).

⁷"LORD my God, you have now made me king. You have put me in the place of my father David. But I'm only a little child. I don't know how to carry out my duties. ⁸I'm here among the people you have chosen. They are a great nation. They are more than anyone can count. ⁹So give me a heart that understands. Then I can rule over your people. I can tell the difference between what is right and what is wrong. Who can possibly rule over this great nation of yours?"

¹⁰The Lord was pleased that Solomon had asked for that. ¹¹So God said to him, "You have not asked to live for a long time. You have not asked to be wealthy. You have not even asked to have your enemies killed. Instead, you have asked for wisdom. You want to do what is right and fair when you judge people. Because that is what you have asked for, ¹²I will give it to you. I will give you a wise and understanding heart. So here is what will be true of you. There has never been anyone like you. And there never will be. ¹³And that is not all. I will give you what you have not asked for. I will give you wealth and honor. As long as you live, no other king will be as great as you are. ¹⁴Live the way I want you to. Obey my laws and commands, just as your father David did. Then I will let you live for a long time."

WOOTON'S FUN FACTS

1 Kgs. 3:1

In 2010, an archaeologist found evidence of this wall. It's one of the first historical finds showing King David and Solomon's building efforts from three thousand years ago. I've built a house, but these guys built whole temples! I doubt my house will last thousands of years, but I can dream, can't I?

¹⁵Solomon woke up. He realized he had been dreaming.

He returned to Jerusalem. He stood in front of the ark of the Lord's covenant. He sacrificed burnt offerings and friendship offerings. Then he gave a feast for all his officials.

A Wise Ruling

¹⁶Two prostitutes came to the king. They stood in front of him. ¹⁷One of them said, "Pardon me, my master, this woman and I live in the same house. I had a baby while she was there with me. ¹⁸Three days after my child was born, this woman also had a baby. We were alone. There wasn't anyone in the house but the two of us.

¹⁹"During the night this woman's baby died. It happened because she was lying on top of him. ²⁰So she got up in the middle of the night. She took my son from my side while I was asleep. She put him by her breast. Then she put her dead son by my breast. ²¹The next morning, I got up to nurse my son. But he was dead! I looked at him closely in the morning light. And I saw that it wasn't my baby."

²²The other woman said, "No! The living baby is my son. The dead one belongs to you."

But the first woman said, "No! The dead baby is yours. The living one belongs to me." So they argued in front of the king.

1 Kgs. 3:16–28 Today the "whose baby?" question could be solved with DNA testing. Good thing the baby didn't have to wait till 1987 when DNA evidence was first used in court. My twin brother tells me that the DNA barely overlaps between us, but I know he's wrong.

²³The king said, "One of you says, 'My son is alive. Your son is dead.' The other one says, 'No! Your son is dead. Mine is alive.'"

²⁴He continued, "Bring me a sword." So a sword was brought to him. ²⁵Then he gave an order. He said, "Cut the living child in two. Give half to one woman and half to the other."

²⁶The woman whose son was alive was filled with deep love for her son. She said to the king, "My master, please give her the living baby! Don't kill him!"

But the other woman said, "Neither one of us will have him. Cut him in two!"

²⁷Then the king made his decision. He said, "Give the living baby to the first woman. Don't kill him. She's his mother."

²⁸All the Israelites heard about the decision the king had given. That gave them great respect for him. They saw that God had given him wisdom. They knew that Solomon would do what was right and fair when he judged people.

Solomon's Officials and Governors

4 So King Solomon ruled over the whole nation of Israel.

² Here are the names of his chief officials.

Azariah was the priest. He was the son of Zadok.
³ Elihoreph and Ahijah were secretaries. They were the sons of Shisha.
Jehoshaphat kept the records. He was the son of Ahilud.
⁴ Benaiah was the commander in chief. He was the son of Jehoiada.
Zadok and Abiathar were priests.
⁵ Azariah was in charge of the local governors. He was the son of Nathan.
Zabud was a priest. He was also the king's adviser. He was the son of Nathan.
⁶ Ahishar was in charge of the palace.
Adoniram was in charge of those who were forced to work for the king. He was the son of Abda.

⁷Solomon had 12 local governors over the whole land of Israel. They provided supplies for the king and the royal family. Each governor had to provide supplies for one month out of each year.

⁸ Here are their names and areas.

Ben-Hur's area was the hill country of Ephraim.

⁹ Ben-Deker's area was Makaz, Shaalbim, Beth Shemesh and Elon Bethhanan.

¹⁰ Ben-Hesed's area was Arubboth. Sokoh and the whole land of Hepher were included in his area.

¹¹ Ben-Abinadab's area was Naphoth Dor. He married Solomon's daughter Taphath.

¹² Baana's area was Taanach, Megiddo and the whole territory of Beth Shan. Beth Shan was next to Zarethan below Jezreel. Baana's area reached from Beth Shan all the way to Abel Meholah. It also went across to Jokmeam. Baana was the son of Ahilud.

¹³ Ben-Geber's area was Ramoth Gilead. The settlements of Jair, the son of Manasseh, were included in his area in Gilead. The area of Argob in Bashan was also included. That area had 60 large cities that had high walls around them. The city gates were made secure with heavy bronze bars.

¹⁴ Ahinadab's area was Mahanaim. He was the son of Iddo.

¹⁵ Ahimaaz's area was Naphtali. He had married Basemath. She was Solomon's daughter.

¹⁶ Baana's area was Asher and Aloth. He was the son of Hushai.

¹⁷ Jehoshaphat's area was Issachar. He was the son of Paruah.

¹⁸ Shimei's area was Benjamin. He was the son of Ela.

¹⁹ Geber's area was Gilead. He was the only governor over the area. He was the son of Uri. Gilead had been the country of Sihon and Og. Sihon had been king of the Amorites. Og had been king of Bashan.

Solomon's Daily Supplies

²⁰There were many people in Judah and Israel. In fact, they were as many as the grains of sand on the seashore. They ate, drank and were happy. ²¹Solomon ruled over all the kingdoms from the Euphrates River to the land of the Philistines. He

BiBLE ADVENTURES

Bernard told King Solomon's life story in "B-TV: Temptation" (A#49).

ruled as far as the border of Egypt. All those countries brought the gifts he required them to bring him. And Solomon ruled over those countries for his whole life.

²² Here are the supplies Solomon required every day.

five and a half tons of the finest flour
11 tons of meal
²³ ten oxen that had been fed by hand
20 oxen that had been fed on grasslands
100 sheep and goats
deer, antelopes and roebucks
the finest birds

²⁴Solomon ruled over all the kingdoms that were west of the Euphrates River. He ruled from Tiphsah all the way to Gaza. And he had peace and rest on every side. ²⁵While Solomon was king, Judah and Israel lived in safety. They were secure from Dan all the way to Beersheba. Everyone had their own vine and their own fig tree. ²⁶Solomon had 4,000 spaces where he kept his chariot horses. He had a total of 12,000 horses. ²⁷The local governors provided supplies for King Solomon. They provided them for all who ate at the king's table. Each governor provided supplies for one month every year. The governors made sure the king had everything he needed. ²⁸They also brought barley and straw for the chariot horses and the other horses. Each of the governors brought the amounts required of them. They brought them to the proper places.

God Makes Solomon Very Wise

²⁹God made Solomon very wise. His understanding couldn't even be measured. It was like the sand on the seashore. People can't measure that either. ³⁰Solomon's wisdom was greater than the wisdom of all the people of the east. It was greater than all the wisdom of Egypt. ³¹Solomon was wiser than anyone else. He was wiser than Ethan, the Ezrahite. He was wiser than

Heman, Kalkol and Darda. They were the sons of Mahol. Solomon became famous in all the nations around him. ³²He spoke 3,000 proverbs. He wrote 1,005 songs. ³³He spoke about plants. He knew everything about them, from the cedar trees in Lebanon to the hyssop plants that grow out of walls. He spoke about animals and birds. He also spoke about reptiles and fish. ³⁴The kings of all the world's nations heard about how wise Solomon was. So they sent their people to listen to him.

Solomon Prepares to Build the Temple

5 Hiram was the king of Tyre. He heard that Solomon had been anointed as king. He heard that Solomon had become the next king after his father David. Hiram had always been David's friend. So Hiram sent his messengers to Solomon. ²Then Solomon sent a message back to Hiram. Solomon said,

³"As you know, my father David had to fight many battles. His enemies attacked him from every side. So he couldn't build a temple where the LORD his God would put his Name. That wouldn't be possible until the LORD had put his enemies under his control. ⁴But now the LORD my God has given me peace and rest on every side. We don't have any enemies. And we don't have any other major problems either. ⁵So I'm planning to build a temple. I want to build it for the Name of the LORD my God. That's what he told my father David he wanted me to do. He said, 'I will put your son on the throne in your place. He will build a temple. I will put my Name there.'

⁶"So give your men orders to cut down cedar trees in Lebanon for me. My men will work with yours. I'll pay you for your men's work. I'll pay any amount you decide on. As you know, we don't have anyone as skilled in cutting down trees as the men of Sidon are."

⁷When Hiram heard Solomon's message, he was very pleased. He said, "May the LORD be praised today. He has given David a wise son to rule over that great nation."

⁸So Hiram sent a message to Solomon. Hiram said,

"I have received the message you sent me. I'll do everything you want me to. I'll provide the cedar and juniper logs. ⁹My men will bring them from Lebanon down to the Mediterranean Sea. I'll make them into rafts. I'll float them to the place you want me to. When the rafts arrive, I'll separate the logs from each other. Then you can take them away. And here's what I want in return. Provide food for all the people in my palace."

¹⁰So Hiram supplied Solomon with all the cedar and juniper logs he wanted. ¹¹Solomon gave Hiram 3,600 tons of wheat as food for the people in his palace. He also gave him 120,000 gallons of oil made from pressed olives. He did that for Hiram year after year. ¹²The LORD made Solomon wise, just as he had promised him. There was peace between Hiram and Solomon. The two of them made a peace treaty.

¹³King Solomon forced men from all over Israel to work hard for him. There were 30,000 of them. ¹⁴He sent them off to Lebanon in groups of 10,000 each month. They spent one month in Lebanon. Then they spent two months at home. Adoniram was in charge of the people who were forced to work. ¹⁵Solomon had 70,000 people who carried things. He had 80,000 who cut stones in the hills. ¹⁶He had 3,300 men in charge of the project. They also directed the workers. ¹⁷The people did what the king commanded. They removed large blocks of the best quality stone from a rock pit. They used them to provide a foundation for the temple. ¹⁸The skilled workers of Solomon and Hiram cut and prepared the logs and stones. They would later be used in building the temple. Workers from Byblos also helped.

Solomon Builds the Temple

6 Solomon began to build the temple of the LORD. It was 480 years after the Israelites came out of Egypt. It was in the fourth year of Solomon's rule over Israel. He started in the second month. That was the month of Ziv.

²The temple King Solomon built for the LORD was 90 feet long. It was 30 feet wide.

And it was 45 feet high. ³The temple had a porch in front of the main hall. The porch was as wide as the temple itself. It was 30 feet wide. It came out 15 feet from the front of the temple. ⁴Solomon made narrow windows high up in the temple walls. ⁵He built side rooms around the temple. They were built against the walls of the main hall and the Most Holy Room. ⁶On the first floor the side rooms were seven and a half feet wide. On the second floor they were nine feet wide. And on the third floor they were ten and a half feet wide. Solomon made the walls of the temple thinner as they went up floor by floor. The result was ledges along the walls. So the floor beams of the side rooms rested on the ledges. The beams didn't go into the temple walls.

⁷All the stones used for building the temple were shaped where they were cut. So hammers, chisels and other iron tools couldn't be heard where the temple was being built.

⁸The entrance to the first floor was on the south side of the temple. A stairway led up to the second floor. From there it went on up to the third floor. ⁹So Solomon built the temple and finished it. He made its roof out of beams and cedar boards. ¹⁰He built side rooms all along the temple. Each room was seven and a half feet high. They were joined to the temple by cedar beams.

¹¹A message came to Solomon from the LORD. The LORD said, ¹²"You are now building this temple. Follow my orders. Keep my rules. Obey all my commands. Then I will make the promise I gave your father David come true. I will do it through you. ¹³I will live among my people Israel. I will not desert them."

¹⁴So Solomon built the temple and finished it. ¹⁵He put cedar boards on its inside walls. He covered them from floor to ceiling. He covered the temple floor with juniper boards. ¹⁶He put up a wall 30 feet from the back of the temple. He made it with cedar boards from floor to ceiling. That formed a room inside the temple. It was the Most Holy Room. ¹⁷The main hall in front of the room was 60 feet long. ¹⁸The inside of the temple was covered with cedar wood. Gourds and open flowers were carved on the wood. Everything was cedar. There wasn't any stone showing anywhere.

¹⁹Solomon prepared the Most Holy Room inside the temple. That's where the ark of the covenant of the LORD would be placed. ²⁰The Most Holy Room was 30 feet long. It was 30 feet wide. And it was 30 feet high. Solomon covered the inside of it with pure gold. He prepared the cedar altar for burning incense. He covered it with gold. ²¹Solomon covered the inside of the main hall with pure gold. He placed gold chains across the front of the Most Holy Room. That room was covered with gold. ²²So Solomon covered the inside of the whole temple with gold. He also covered the altar for burning incense with gold. It was right in front of the Most Holy Room.

²³For the Most Holy Room Solomon made a pair of cherubim. He made them out of olive wood. Each cherub was 15 feet high. ²⁴One wing of the first cherub was seven and a half feet long. The other wing was also seven and a half feet long. So the wings measured 15 feet from tip to tip. ²⁵The second cherub's wings also measured 15 feet from tip to tip. The two cherubim had the same size and shape. ²⁶Each cherub was 15 feet high. ²⁷Solomon placed the cherubim inside the Most Holy Room in the temple. Their wings were spread out. The wing tip of one cherub touched one wall. The wing tip of the other touched the other wall. The tips of their wings touched each other in the middle of the room. ²⁸Solomon covered the cherubim with gold.

²⁹On the walls all around the temple he carved cherubim, palm trees and open flowers. He carved them on the walls of the Most Holy Room and the main hall. ³⁰He also covered the floors of those two rooms with gold.

³¹For the entrance to the Most Holy Room he made two doors out of olive wood. Each door was one-fifth of the width of the Most Holy Room. ³²On the two olive wood doors he carved cherubim, palm trees and open flowers. He covered the cherubim and palm trees with hammered gold. ³³In the same way he made olive wood doorposts for the entrance to the main hall. Each doorpost was one-fourth of the width of the hall. ³⁴He also made two doors out of juniper wood. Each door had two parts. They turned in bases shaped like cups. ³⁵He carved cherubim, palm trees and open flowers on the doors. He covered the doors

CaNDiD CoNVeRSaTiON

A girl came into Whit's End the other day and asked a really good question: "God doesn't care what we wear, does He?" It turned out that she had just had an argument with her mother about something she wanted to wear that was a little, uh . . . immodest.

I said, "God definitely cares more about your character than your clothes, but what you wear *does* say something about who you think you are."

Look at how God wanted His temple decorated: gems, fine linens, elaborate carvings, and floors of gold! When the people looked at this awe-inspiring building, they were reminded it represented their awe-inspiring God—a God who was holy, perfect, glorious, and worthy of worship.

When we dress in clothes that show off the wrong things, we're not giving ourselves credit for how valuable we are. But when we dress modestly and tastefully, it shows that we respect and honor our bodies. It says we value what's inside.

with gold. He hammered the gold evenly over the carvings.

³⁶He used blocks of stone to build a wall around the inside courtyard. The first three layers of the wall were made out of stone. The top layer was made out of beautiful cedar wood.

³⁷The foundation of the LORD's temple was laid in Solomon's fourth year. It was in the month of Ziv. ³⁸The temple was finished in his 11th year. It was in the month of Bul. That was the eighth month. Everything was finished just as the plans required. Solomon had spent seven years building the temple.

Solomon Builds His Palace

7 But it took Solomon 13 years to finish constructing his palace and the other buildings related to it. ²He built the Palace of the Forest of Lebanon. It was 150 feet long. It was 75 feet wide. And it was 45 feet high. It had four rows of cedar columns. They held up beautiful cedar beams. ³Above the beams was a roof made out of cedar boards. It rested on the columns. There were three rows of beams with 15 in each row. The total number of beams was 45. ⁴The windows of the palace were placed high up in the walls. They were in groups of three. And they faced each other. ⁵All the doorways had frames shaped like rectangles. They were in front. They were in groups of three. And they faced each other.

⁶Solomon made a covered area. It was 75 feet long. And it was 45 feet wide. Its roof was held up by columns. In front of it was a porch. In front of that were pillars and a roof that went out beyond them.

⁷Solomon built the throne hall. It was called the Hall of Justice. That's where he would serve as judge. He covered the hall with cedar boards from floor to ceiling. ⁸The palace where he would live was set farther back. Its plan was something like the plan for the hall. Solomon had married Pharaoh's daughter. He made a palace for her. It was like the hall.

⁹All those buildings were made out of blocks of good quality stone. They were cut to the right size. They were made smooth on their back and front sides. Those stones were used for the outside of each building and for the large courtyard. They were also used from the foundations up to the roofs. ¹⁰Large blocks of good quality stone were used for the foundations. Some were 15 feet long. Others were 12 feet long. ¹¹The walls above them were made out of good quality stones. The stones were cut to the right size. On top of them was a layer of cedar beams. ¹²The large courtyard had a wall around it. The first three layers of the wall were made out of blocks of stone. The top layer was made out of beautiful cedar wood. The same thing was done with the inside courtyard of the LORD's temple and its porch.

More Facts About the Temple

¹³King Solomon sent messengers to Tyre. He wanted them to bring Huram

back with them. [14]Huram's mother was a widow. She was from the tribe of Naphtali. Huram's father was from Tyre. He was skilled in working with bronze. Huram also had great skill, knowledge and understanding in working with bronze. He came to King Solomon and did all the work he was asked to do.

[15]Huram made two bronze pillars. Each of them was 27 feet high. And each was 18 feet around. [16]Each pillar had a decorated top made out of bronze. Each top was seven and a half feet high. [17]Chains that were linked together hung down from the tops of the pillars. There were seven chains for each top. [18]Huram made two rows of pomegranates. They circled the chains. The pomegranates decorated the tops of the pillars. Huram did the same thing for each pillar. [19]The tops on the pillars of the porch were shaped like lilies. The lilies were 6 feet high. [20]On the tops of both pillars were 200 pomegranates. They were in rows all around the tops. They were above the part that was shaped like a bowl. And they were next to the chains. [21]Huram set the pillars up at the temple porch. The pillar on the south he named Jakin. The one on the north he named Boaz. [22]The tops of the pillars were shaped like lilies. So the work on the pillars was finished.

[23]Huram made a huge metal bowl for washing. Its shape was round. It measured 15 feet from rim to rim. It was seven and a half feet high. And it was 45 feet around. [24]Below the rim there was a circle of gourds around the bowl. In every 18 inches around the bowl there were ten gourds. The gourds were arranged in two rows. They were made as part of the bowl itself. [25]The huge bowl stood on 12 bulls. Three of them faced north. Three faced west. Three faced south. And three faced east. The bowl rested on top of the bulls. Their rear ends were toward the center. [26]The bowl was three inches thick. Its rim was like the rim of a cup. The rim was shaped like the bloom of a lily. The bowl held 12,000 gallons of water.

[27]Huram also made ten stands out of bronze. They could be moved around. Each stand was six feet long. It was six feet wide. And it was four and a half feet high. [28]Here is how the stands were made. They had sides that were joined to posts. [29]On the sides between the posts were lions, bulls and cherubim. They were also on all of the posts. Above and below the lions and bulls were wreaths made out of hammered metal. [30]Each stand had four bronze wheels with bronze axles. Each stand had a bowl that rested on four supports. The stand had wreaths on each side. [31]There was a round opening on the inside of each stand. The opening had a frame 18 inches deep. The sides were 27 inches high from the top of the opening to the bottom of the base. There was carving around the opening. The sides of the stands were square, not round. [32]The four wheels were under the sides. The axles of the wheels were connected to the stand. Each wheel was 27 inches across. [33]The wheels were made like chariot wheels. All the axles, rims, spokes and hubs were made out of metal.

[34]Each stand had four handles on it. There was one on each corner. They came out from the stand. [35]At the top of the stand there was a round band. It was nine inches deep. The sides and supports were connected to the top of the stand. [36]Huram carved cherubim, lions and palm trees on the sides of the stands. He also carved them on the surfaces of the supports. His carving covered every open space. He had also carved wreaths all around. [37]That's how he made the ten stands. All of them were made in the same molds. And they had the same size and shape.

[38]Then Huram made ten bronze bowls. Each one held 240 gallons. The bowls measured six feet across. There was one bowl for each of the ten stands. [39]He placed five of the stands on the south side of the temple. He placed the other five on the north side. He put the huge bowl on the south side. It was at the southeast corner of the temple. [40]He also made the pots, shovels and sprinkling bowls.

So Huram finished all the work he had started for King Solomon. Here's what he made for the LORD's temple.

[41] He made the two pillars.
He made the two tops for the pillars.
The tops were shaped like bowls.
He made the two sets of chains that were linked together. They decorated the two bowl-shaped tops of the pillars.
[42] He made the 400 pomegranates for the two sets of chains. There were

two rows of pomegranates for each chain. They decorated the bowl-shaped tops of the pillars. ⁴³ He made the ten stands with their ten bowls. ⁴⁴ He made the huge bowl. He made the 12 bulls that were under it. ⁴⁵ He made the pots, shovels and sprinkling bowls.

Huram made all those objects for King Solomon for the LORD's temple. He made them out of bronze. Then he shined them up. ⁴⁶The king had made them in clay molds. It was done on the plain of the Jordan River between Sukkoth and Zarethan. ⁴⁷Solomon didn't weigh any of those things. There were too many of them to weigh. No one even tried to weigh the bronze they were made out of.

⁴⁸Solomon also made everything in the LORD's temple.

He made the golden altar.
He made the golden table for the holy bread.
⁴⁹ He made the pure gold lampstands. There were five on the right and five on the left. They were in front of the Most Holy Room.
He made the gold flowers. He made the gold lamps and tongs.
⁵⁰ He made the bowls, wick cutters, sprinkling bowls, dishes, and shallow cups for burning incense. All of them were made out of pure gold.
He made the gold bases for the doors of the inside room. That's the Most Holy Room. He also made gold bases for the doors of the main hall of the temple.

⁵¹King Solomon finished all the work for the LORD's temple. Then he brought in the things his father David had set apart for the LORD. They included the silver and gold and all the other things for the LORD's temple. Solomon placed them with the other treasures that were there.

The Ark Is Brought to the Temple

8 Then King Solomon sent for the elders of Israel. He told them to come to him in Jerusalem. They included all the leaders of the tribes. They also included the chiefs of the families of Israel. Solomon wanted them to bring up the ark of the LORD's covenant from Zion. Zion was the City of David. ²All the Israelites came together to where King Solomon was. It was at the time of the Feast of Booths. The feast was held in the month of Ethanim. That's the seventh month.

³All the elders of Israel arrived. Then the priests picked up the ark and carried it. ⁴They brought up the ark of the LORD. They also brought up the tent of meeting and all the sacred things in the tent. The priests and Levites carried everything up. ⁵The entire community of Israel had gathered around King Solomon. All of them were in front of the ark. They sacrificed huge numbers of sheep and cattle. There were so many animals that they couldn't be recorded. In fact, they couldn't even be counted.

⁶The priests brought the ark of the LORD's covenant law to its place in the Most Holy Room of the temple. They put it under the wings of the cherubim. ⁷Their wings were spread out over the place where the ark was. They covered the ark. They also covered the poles used to carry it. ⁸The poles were very long. Their ends could be seen from the Holy Room in front of the Most Holy Room. But they couldn't be seen from outside the Holy Room. They are still there to this day. ⁹There wasn't anything in the ark except the two stone tablets. Moses had placed them in it at Mount Horeb. That's where the LORD had made a covenant with the Israelites. He made it after they came out of Egypt.

¹⁰The priests left the Holy Room. Then the cloud filled the temple of the LORD. ¹¹The priests couldn't do their work because of it. That's because the glory of the LORD filled his temple.

¹²Then Solomon said, "LORD, you have said you would live in a dark cloud. ¹³As you can see, I've built a beautiful temple for you. You can live in it forever."

¹⁴The whole community of Israel was standing there. The king turned around and gave them his blessing. ¹⁵Then he said,

"I praise the LORD. He is the God of Israel. With his own mouth he made a promise to my father David. With his own powerful hand he made it come true. He said, ¹⁶'I brought my people Israel out of Egypt. Ever since, I haven't chosen a city in any tribe of Israel where a temple could be built for my Name. But I have chosen David to rule over my people Israel.'

¹⁷"With all his heart my father David wanted to build a temple. He wanted to do it so the LORD could put his Name there. The LORD is the God of Israel. ¹⁸But the LORD spoke to my father David. He said, 'With all your heart you wanted to build a temple for my Name. It is good that you wanted to do that. ¹⁹But you will not build the temple. Instead, your son will build the temple for my Name. He is your own flesh and blood.'

²⁰"The LORD has kept the promise he made. I've become the next king after my father David. Now I'm sitting on the throne of Israel. That's exactly what the LORD promised would happen. I've built the temple where the LORD will put his Name. He is the God of Israel. ²¹I've provided a place for the ark there. The tablets of the LORD's covenant law are inside it. He made that covenant with our people of long ago. He made it when he brought them out of Egypt."

Solomon Prays to Set the Temple Apart to the LORD

²²Then Solomon stood in front of the LORD's altar. He stood in front of the whole community of Israel. He spread out his hands toward heaven. ²³He said,

"LORD, you are the God of Israel. There is no God like you in heaven above or on earth below. You keep the covenant you made with us. You show us your love. You do that when we follow you with all our hearts. ²⁴You have kept your promise to my father David. He was your servant. With your mouth you made a promise. With your powerful hand you have made it come true. And today we can see it.

²⁵"LORD, you are the God of Israel. Keep the promises you made to my father David. Do it for him. He was your servant. Here is what you said to him. 'A son from your family line will sit before me on the throne of Israel. This will always be true if your children after you are careful in everything they do. They must live in

my sight faithfully the way you have lived.' ²⁶God of Israel, let your promise to my father David come true.

²⁷"But will you really live on earth? After all, the heavens can't hold you. In fact, even the highest heavens can't hold you. So this temple I've built certainly can't hold you! ²⁸But please pay attention to my prayer. LORD my God, be ready to help me as I make my appeal to you. Listen to my cry for help. Hear the prayer I'm praying to you today. ²⁹Let your eyes look toward this temple night and day. You said, 'I will put my Name there.' So please listen to the prayer I'm praying toward this place. ³⁰Hear me when I ask you to help us. Listen to your people Israel when they pray toward this place. Listen to us from heaven. It's the place where you live. When you hear us, forgive us.

³¹"Suppose someone does something wrong to their neighbor. And the person who has done something wrong is required to give their word. They must tell the truth about what they have done. They must come and do it in front of your altar in this temple. ³²When they do, listen to them from heaven. Take action. Judge between the person and their neighbor. Punish the guilty one. Do to that person what they have done to their neighbor. Deal with the one who isn't guilty in a way that shows they are free from blame. That will prove they aren't guilty.

³³"Suppose your people Israel have lost the battle against their enemies. And suppose they've sinned against you. But they turn back to you and praise your name. They pray to you in this temple. And they ask you to help them. ³⁴Then listen to them from heaven. Forgive the sin of your people Israel. Bring them back to the land you gave to their people who lived long ago.

³⁵"Suppose your people have sinned against you. And because of that, the sky is closed up and there isn't any rain. But your people pray toward this place. They praise you by admitting they've sinned. And they

turn away from their sin because you have made them suffer. ³⁶Then listen to them from heaven. Forgive the sin of your people Israel. Teach them the right way to live. Send rain on the land you gave them as their share.

³⁷"Suppose there isn't enough food in the land. And a plague strikes the land. The hot winds completely dry up our crops. Or locusts or grasshoppers come and eat them up. Or an enemy surrounds one of our cities and gets ready to attack it. Or trouble or sickness comes. ³⁸But suppose one of your people prays to you. They ask you to help them. They are aware of how much their own heart is suffering. And they spread out their hands toward this temple to pray. ³⁹Then listen to them from heaven. It's the place where you live. Forgive them. Take action. Deal with everyone in keeping with everything they do. You know their hearts. In fact, you are the only one who knows every human heart. ⁴⁰Your people will have respect for you. They will respect you as long as they are in the land you gave our people long ago.

⁴¹"Suppose there are outsiders who don't belong to your people Israel. And they have come from a land far away. They've come because they've heard about your name. ⁴²When they get here, they will find out even more about your great name. They'll hear about how you reached out your mighty hand and powerful arm. So they'll come and pray toward this temple. ⁴³Then listen to them from heaven. It's the place where you live. Do what those outsiders ask you to do. Then all the nations on earth will know you. They will have respect for you. They'll respect you just as your own people Israel do. They'll know that your Name is in this house I've built.

⁴⁴"Suppose your people go to war against their enemies. It doesn't matter where you send them. And suppose they pray to you toward the city you have chosen. They pray toward the temple I've built for your Name. ⁴⁵Then listen to them from heaven.

Listen to their prayer for your help. Stand up for them.

⁴⁶"Suppose your people sin against you. After all, there isn't anyone who doesn't sin. And suppose you get angry with them. You hand them over to their enemies. They take them as prisoners to their own lands. It doesn't matter whether those lands are near or far away. ⁴⁷But suppose your people change their ways in the land where they are held as prisoners. They turn away from their sins. They beg you to help them in the land of those who won the battle over them. They say, 'We have sinned. We've done what is wrong. We've done what is evil.' ⁴⁸And they turn back to you with all their heart and soul. Suppose it happens in the land of their enemies who took them away as prisoners. There they pray to you toward the land you gave their people long ago. They pray toward the city you have chosen. And they pray toward the temple I've built for your Name. ⁴⁹Then listen to them from heaven. It's the place where you live. Listen to their prayer. Listen to them when they ask you to help them. Stand up for them. ⁵⁰Your people have sinned against you. Please forgive them. Forgive them for all the wrong things they've done against you. And make those who won the battle over them

1 Kgs. 8:46–49 The prophet Daniel wound up in exactly this situation. In Babylon, he prayed three times a day facing Jerusalem. Check out the story in Daniel 6:10.

show mercy to them. ⁵¹After all, they are your people. They belong to you. You brought them out of Egypt. You brought them out of that furnace that melts iron down and makes it pure.

⁵²"Let your eyes be open to me when I ask you to help us. Let them be open to your people Israel when they ask you to help them. Pay attention to them every time they cry out to you. ⁵³After all, you chose them out of all the nations in the world. You made them your very own people. You did it just as you had announced through your servant Moses. That's when you brought out of Egypt our people of long ago. You are our LORD and King."

⁵⁴Solomon finished praying. He finished asking the LORD to help his people. Then he got up from in front of the LORD's altar. He had been down on his knees with his hands spread out toward heaven. ⁵⁵He stood in front of the whole community of Israel. He blessed them with a loud voice. He said,

⁵⁶"I praise the LORD. He has given peace and rest to his people Israel. That's exactly what he promised to do. He gave his people good promises through his servant Moses. Every single word of those promises has come true. ⁵⁷May the LORD our God be with us, just as he was with our people who lived long ago. May he never leave us. May he never desert us. ⁵⁸May he turn our hearts to him. Then we will live the way he wants us to. We'll obey the commands, rules and directions he gave our people of long ago. ⁵⁹I've prayed these words to the LORD our God. May he keep them close to him day and night. May he stand up for me. May he also stand up for his people Israel. May he give us what we need every day. ⁶⁰Then all the nations on earth will know that the LORD is God. They'll know that there isn't any other god. ⁶¹And may you commit your lives completely to the LORD our God. May you live by his rules. May you obey his commands. May you always do as you are doing now."

The Temple Is Set Apart to the LORD

⁶²Then the king and the whole community of Israel offered sacrifices to the LORD. ⁶³Solomon sacrificed friendship offerings to the LORD. He sacrificed 22,000 oxen. He also sacrificed 120,000 sheep and goats. So the king and the whole community set the temple of the LORD apart to him.

⁶⁴On that same day the king set the middle area of the courtyard apart to the LORD. It was in front of the LORD's temple. There Solomon sacrificed burnt offerings and grain offerings. He also sacrificed the fat of the friendship offerings there. He did it there because the bronze altar that stood in front of the LORD was too small. It wasn't big enough to hold all the burnt offerings, the grain offerings and the fat of the friendship offerings.

⁶⁵At that time Solomon celebrated the Feast of Booths. The whole community of Israel was with him. It was a huge crowd. People came from as far away as Lebo Hamath and the Wadi of Egypt. For seven days they celebrated in front of the LORD our God. The feast continued for seven more days. That made a total of 14 days. ⁶⁶On the following day Solomon sent the people away. They asked the LORD to bless the king. Then they went home. The people were glad. Their hearts were full of joy. That's because the LORD had done so many good things for his servant David and his people Israel.

The LORD Appears to Solomon

9 Solomon finished building the LORD's temple and the royal palace. He had accomplished everything he had planned to do. ²The LORD appeared to him a second time. He had already appeared to him at Gibeon. ³The LORD said to him,

"I have heard you pray to me. I have heard you ask me to help you. You have built this temple. I have set it apart for myself. My Name will be there forever. My eyes and my heart will always be there.

⁴"But you must walk faithfully with me, just as your father David did. Your heart must be honest. It must be without blame. Do everything I command you to do. Obey my rules and laws. ⁵Then I will set

up your royal throne over Israel forever. I promised your father David I would do that. I said to him, 'You will always have a son from your family line on the throne of Israel.'

[6]"But suppose all of you turn away from me. Or your children turn away from me. You refuse to obey the commands and rules I have given you. And you go off to serve other gods and worship them. [7]Then I will remove Israel from the land. It is the land I gave them. I will turn my back on this temple. I will do it even though I have set it apart for my Name to be there. Then Israel will be hated by all the nations. They will laugh and joke about Israel. [8]This temple will become a pile of stones. All those who pass by it will be shocked. They will make fun of it. And they will say, 'Why has the LORD done a thing like this to this land and temple?' [9]People will answer, 'Because they have deserted the LORD their God. He brought out of Egypt their people of long ago. But they have been holding on to other gods. They've been worshiping them. They've been serving them. That's why the LORD has brought all this horrible trouble on them.'"

Other Things Solomon Did

[10]Solomon built the LORD's temple and the royal palace. It took him 20 years to construct those two buildings. [11]King Solomon gave 20 towns in Galilee to Hiram, the king of Tyre. That's because Hiram had provided him with all the cedar and juniper logs he wanted. He had also provided Solomon with all the gold he wanted. [12]Hiram went from Tyre to see the towns Solomon had given him. But he wasn't pleased with them. [13]"My friend," he asked, "what have you given me? What kind of towns are these?" So he called them the Land of Kabul. And that's what they are still called to this day. [14]Hiram had sent four and a half tons of gold to Solomon.

[15]King Solomon forced people to work hard for him. Here is a record of what they did. They built the LORD's temple and Solomon's palace. They filled in the low places. They rebuilt the wall of Jerusalem. They built up Hazor, Megiddo and Gezer. [16]Pharaoh, the king of Egypt, had attacked Gezer and captured it. He had set it on fire. He had killed the Canaanites who lived there. Then he had given Gezer as a wedding gift to his daughter. She was Solomon's wife. [17]Solomon rebuilt Gezer. He built up Lower Beth Horon [18]and Baalath. He built up Tadmor in the desert. All those towns were in his land. [19]He built up all the cities where he could store things. He also built up the towns for his chariots and horses. He built anything he wanted to build in Jerusalem, Lebanon and all the territory he ruled over.

[20]There were still many people left in the land who weren't Israelites. They included Amorites, Hittites, Perizzites, Hivites and Jebusites. [21]They were children of the people who had lived in the land before the Israelites came. Those people had been set apart to the LORD in a special way to be destroyed. But the Israelites hadn't been able to kill all of them. Solomon forced them to work very hard as his slaves. And they still work for Israel as slaves to this day. [22]But Solomon didn't force any of the Israelites to work as his slaves. Instead, some were his fighting men. Others were his government officials, his officers and his captains. Others were commanders of his chariots and chariot drivers. [23]Still others were the chief officials in charge of Solomon's projects. There were 550 officials in charge of those who did the work.

[24]Pharaoh's daughter moved from the City of David up to the palace Solomon had built for her. After that, he filled in the low places near the palace.

[25]Three times a year Solomon sacrificed burnt offerings and friendship offerings. He sacrificed them on the altar he had built to honor the LORD. Along with the offerings, he burned incense to the LORD. So he carried out his duties for the temple.

[26]King Solomon also built ships at Ezion Geber. It's near Elath in Edom. It's on the shore of the Red Sea. [27]Hiram sent his men to serve on the ships together with Solomon's men. Hiram's sailors knew the sea. [28]All of them sailed to Ophir. They brought back 16 tons of gold. They gave it to King Solomon.

The Queen of Sheba Visits Solomon

10 The queen of Sheba heard about how famous Solomon was. She also heard about how he served and worshiped the

LORD. So she came to test Solomon with hard questions. ²She arrived in Jerusalem with a very large group of attendants. Her camels were carrying spices, huge amounts of gold, and valuable jewels. She came to Solomon and asked him about everything she wanted to know. ³Solomon answered all her questions. There wasn't anything too hard for the king to explain to her. ⁴So the queen of Sheba saw how very wise Solomon was. She saw the palace he had built. ⁵She saw the food on his table. She saw his officials sitting there. She saw the robes of the servants who waited on everyone. She saw his wine tasters. And she saw the burnt offerings Solomon sacrificed at the LORD's temple. She could hardly believe everything she had seen.

⁶She said to the king, "Back in my own country I heard a report about you. I heard about how much you had accomplished. I also heard about how wise you are. Everything I heard is true. ⁷But I didn't believe those things. So I came to see for myself. And now I believe it! You are twice as wise and wealthy as people say you are. The report I heard doesn't even begin to tell the whole story about you. ⁸How happy your people must be! How happy your officials must be! They always get to serve you and hear the wise things you say. ⁹May the LORD your God be praised. He takes great delight in you. He placed you on the throne of Israel. The LORD will love Israel for all time to come. That's why he has made you king. He knows that you will do what is fair and right."

¹⁰She gave the king four and a half tons of gold. She also gave him huge amounts of spices and valuable jewels. No one would ever bring to King Solomon as many spices as the queen of Sheba gave him.

¹¹Hiram's ships brought gold from Ophir. From there they also brought huge amounts of almugwood and valuable jewels. ¹²The king used the almugwood to make supports for the LORD's temple and the royal palace. He also used it to make harps and lyres for those who played the music. That much almugwood has never been brought into Judah or seen there since that day.

¹³King Solomon gave the queen of Sheba everything she wanted and asked for. That was in addition to what he had given her out of his royal riches. Then she left. She returned to her own country with her attendants.

Solomon's Greatness

¹⁴Each year Solomon received 25 tons of gold. ¹⁵That didn't include the money brought in by business and trade. It also didn't include the money from all the kings of Arabia and the governors of the territories.

¹⁶King Solomon made 200 large shields out of hammered gold. Each one weighed 15 pounds. ¹⁷He also made 300 small shields out of hammered gold. Each one weighed seven and a half pounds. The king put all the shields in the Palace of the Forest of Lebanon.

¹⁸Then he made a large throne. It was covered with ivory. And that was covered with fine gold. ¹⁹The throne had six steps. Its back had a rounded top. The throne had armrests on both sides of the seat. A statue of a lion stood on each side of the throne. ²⁰Twelve lions stood on the six steps. There was one at each end of each step. Nothing like that throne had ever been made for any other kingdom. ²¹All of King Solomon's cups were made out of gold. All the things used in the Palace of the Forest of Lebanon were made out of pure gold. Nothing was made out of silver. When Solomon was king, silver wasn't considered to be worth very much. ²²He had many ships that carried goods to be traded. His ships went to sea along with Hiram's ships. Once every three years the ships returned. They brought gold, silver, ivory, apes and peacocks.

²³King Solomon was richer than all the other kings on earth. He was also wiser than they were. ²⁴People from the whole world wanted to meet Solomon in person. They wanted to see for themselves how wise God had made him. ²⁵Year after year, everyone who came to him brought a gift. They brought gifts made out of silver and gold. They brought robes, weapons and spices. They also brought horses and mules.

²⁶Solomon had 1,400 chariots and 12,000 horses. He kept some of his horses and chariots in the chariot cities. He kept the others with him in Jerusalem. ²⁷The king made silver as common in Jerusalem as stones. He made cedar wood as common there as sycamore-fig trees in the western hills.

WOOTON'S FUN FACTS

1 Kgs. 10:21–23

Just as in Bible times, gold is still valuable today. In recent years, it's been valued at more than one hundred dollars for a single ounce. And what's this about apes and peacocks? Some scholars guess that because Solomon pursued knowledge, he was importing animals so he could study them.

[28]Solomon got horses from Egypt and from Kue. The royal traders bought them from Kue at the current price. [29]They weighed out 15 pounds of silver for a chariot from Egypt. And they weighed out almost four pounds of silver for a horse. They also sold horses and chariots to all the kings of the Hittites and the kings of the Arameans.

Solomon's Wives

11 King Solomon loved many women besides Pharaoh's daughter. They were from other lands. They were Moabites, Ammonites, Edomites, Sidonians and Hittites. [2]The LORD had warned Israel about women from other nations. He had said, "You must not marry them. If you do, you can be sure they will turn your hearts toward their gods." But Solomon continued to love them anyway. He wouldn't give them up. [3]He had 700 wives who came from royal families. And he had 300 concubines. His wives led him astray. [4]As Solomon grew older, his wives turned his heart toward other gods. He didn't follow the LORD his God with all his heart. So he wasn't like his father David. [5]Solomon worshiped Ashtoreth. Ashtoreth was the female god of the Sidonians. He also worshiped Molek. Molek was the god of the Ammonites. The LORD hated that god. [6]Solomon did what was evil in the sight of the LORD. He didn't completely obey the LORD. He didn't do what his father David had done.

[7]There is a hill east of Jerusalem. Solomon built a high place for worshiping Chemosh there. He built a high place for worshiping Molek there too. Chemosh was the god of Moab. Molek was the god of Ammon. The LORD hated both of those gods. [8]Solomon also built high places so that all his wives from other nations could worship their gods. Those women burned incense and offered sacrifices to their gods.

[9]The LORD became angry with Solomon. That's because his heart had turned away from the LORD, the God of Israel. He had appeared to Solomon twice. [10]He had commanded Solomon not to worship other gods. But Solomon didn't obey the LORD. [11]So the LORD said to Solomon, "You have chosen not to keep my covenant. You have decided not to obey my rules. I commanded you to do what I told you. But you did not do it. So you can be absolutely sure I will tear the kingdom away from you. I will give it to one of your officials. [12]But I will not do that while you are still living. Because of your father David I will wait. I will tear the kingdom out of your son's hand. [13]But I will not tear the whole kingdom away from him. I will give him one of the tribes because of my servant David. I will also do it because of Jerusalem. That is the city I have chosen."

Solomon's Enemies

[14]Then the LORD brought an enemy against Solomon. The enemy's name was Hadad. He was from Edom. In fact, he belonged to the royal family of Edom. [15]David had fought against Edom. Joab had been the commander of the army. He had gone up to bury the dead bodies of the Israelites who had been killed in battle. At that time he had struck down all the men in Edom. [16]In fact, Joab and all the men of Israel stayed there for six months. During that time they destroyed all the men in Edom. [17]But when Hadad was only a boy, he ran away to Egypt. Some officials from Edom went with him. They had served Hadad's father. [18]They started out from Midian and went to Paran. They took some people from Paran with them. Then they went to Egypt.

They went to Pharaoh, the king of Egypt. He gave Hadad a house and some land. He also supplied him with food. ¹⁹Pharaoh was very pleased with Hadad. Pharaoh's wife was Queen Tahpenes. He gave Hadad her sister to be his wife. ²⁰The sister of Tahpenes had a son by Hadad. The baby was named Genubath. Tahpenes brought him up in the royal palace. Genubath lived there with Pharaoh's own children.

²¹Hadad heard that David had joined the members of his family who had already died. He also heard that Joab, the commander of the army, was dead. Hadad heard those things while he was in Egypt. He said to Pharaoh, "Let me go. I want to return to my own country."

²²"Why do you want to go back to your own country?" Pharaoh asked. "Don't you have everything you need right here?"

"Yes," Hadad replied. "But I want you to let me go anyway!"

²³God brought another enemy against Solomon. The enemy's name was Rezon. He was the son of Eliada. Rezon had run away from his master Hadadezer, the king of Zobah. ²⁴David had destroyed Zobah's army. Then Rezon gathered together some men to follow him. He became their leader. They went to Damascus where they made their homes. They also took control of Damascus. ²⁵Rezon was Israel's enemy as long as Solomon was living. Rezon added to the trouble Hadad had caused. So Rezon ruled in Aram. He was Israel's enemy.

Jeroboam Refuses to Follow Solomon

²⁶Jeroboam refused to follow King Solomon. He was one of Solomon's officials. He was from Zeredah in the territory of Ephraim. His father was Nebat. His mother was a widow named Zeruah.

²⁷Here is the story of how Jeroboam refused to follow the king. Solomon had filled in the low places near the palace. He had also repaired the wall of the city of his father David. ²⁸Jeroboam was a very important young man. Solomon saw how well he did his work. So he put him in charge of all the workers in northern Israel.

²⁹About that time Jeroboam was going out of Jerusalem. Ahijah the prophet met him on the road. Ahijah was from Shiloh. He was wearing a new coat. The two of them were all alone out in the country.

³⁰Ahijah grabbed the new coat he had on. He tore it up into 12 pieces. ³¹Then he said to Jeroboam, "Take ten pieces for yourself. The LORD is the God of Israel. He says, 'I am going to tear the kingdom out of Solomon's hand. I will give you ten of its tribes. ³²Solomon will have one of its tribes. I will let him keep it because of my servant David and because of Jerusalem. I have chosen that city out of all the cities in the tribes of Israel. ³³I will do these things because the tribes have deserted me. They have worshiped Ashtoreth, the female god of the people of Sidon. They have worshiped Chemosh, the god of the people of Moab. And they have worshiped Molek, the god of the people of Ammon. They have not lived the way I wanted them to. They have not done what is right in my eyes. They have not obeyed my rules and laws as Solomon's father David did.

³⁴" 'But I will not take the whole kingdom out of Solomon's hand. I have made him ruler all the days of his life. I have done it because of my servant David. I chose him, and he obeyed my commands and rules. ³⁵I will take the kingdom out of his son's hands. And I will give you ten of the tribes. ³⁶I will give one of the tribes to David's son. Then my servant David will always have a son on his throne in Jerusalem. The lamp of David's kingdom will always burn brightly in my sight. Jerusalem is the city I chose for my Name. ³⁷But I will make you king over Israel. You will rule over everything your heart desires. So you will be the king of Israel. ³⁸Do everything I command you to do. Live the way I want you to. Do what is right in my eyes. Obey my rules and commands. That is what my servant David did. If you do those things, I will be with you. I will build you a kingdom. It will last as long as the one I built for David. I will give Israel to you. ³⁹I will punish David's family because of what Solomon has done. But I will not punish them forever.' "

⁴⁰Solomon tried to kill Jeroboam. But Jeroboam ran away to Egypt. He went to Shishak, the king of Egypt. He stayed there until Solomon died.

Solomon Dies

⁴¹The other events of Solomon's rule are written down. Everything he did and the wisdom he showed are written down.

They are written in the official records of Solomon. ⁴²Solomon ruled in Jerusalem over the whole nation of Israel for 40 years. ⁴³Then he joined the members of his family who had already died. He was buried in the city of his father David. Solomon's son Rehoboam became the next king after him.

Israel Refuses to Follow Rehoboam

12 Rehoboam went to the city of Shechem. All the Israelites had gone there to make him king. ²Jeroboam heard about it. He was the son of Nebat. Jeroboam was still in Egypt at that time. He had gone there for safety. He wanted to get away from King Solomon. But now he returned from Egypt. ³So the people sent for Jeroboam. He and the whole community of Israel went to Rehoboam. They said to him, ⁴"Your father put a heavy load on our shoulders. But now make our hard work easier. Make the heavy load on us lighter. Then we'll serve you."

⁵Rehoboam answered, "Go away for three days. Then come back to me." So the people went away.

⁶King Rehoboam asked the elders for advice. They had served his father Solomon while he was still living. Rehoboam asked them, "What advice can you give me? How should I answer these people?"

⁷They replied, "Serve them today. Give them what they are asking for. Then they'll always serve you."

⁸But Rehoboam didn't accept the advice the elders gave him. Instead, he asked for advice from the young men. They had grown up with him and were now serving him. ⁹He asked them, "What's your advice? How should I answer these people? They say to me, 'Make the load your father put on our shoulders lighter.'"

¹⁰The young men who had grown up with him gave their answer. They replied, "These people have said to you, 'Your father put a heavy load on our shoulders. Make it lighter.' Now tell them, 'My little finger is stronger than my father's legs. ¹¹My father put a heavy load on your shoulders. But I'll make it even heavier. My father beat you with whips. But I'll beat you with bigger whips.'"

¹²Three days later Jeroboam and all the people returned to Rehoboam. That's because the king had said, "Come back to me in three days." ¹³The king answered the people in a mean way. He didn't accept the advice the elders had given him. ¹⁴Instead, he followed the advice of the young men. He said, "My father put a heavy load on your shoulders. But I'll make it even heavier. My father beat you with whips. But I'll beat you with bigger whips." ¹⁵So the king didn't listen to the people. That's because the LORD had planned it that way. What he had said through Ahijah came true. Ahijah had spoken the LORD's message to Jeroboam, the son of Nebat. Ahijah was from Shiloh.

Jason's Jargon

1 KINGS 12

Search this chapter for the word *Booths*. The Feast of Booths was a celebration to remember the Israelites' journey to the Promised Land, when they lived in small shelters called booths.

¹⁶All the Israelites saw that the king refused to listen to them. So they answered the king. They said,

"We don't have any share in David's
    royal family.
We don't have any share in Jesse's
    son.
People of Israel, let's go back to our
    homes.
David's royal family, take care of
    your own kingdom!"

So the Israelites went home. ¹⁷But Rehoboam still ruled over the Israelites living in the towns of Judah.

¹⁸Adoniram was in charge of those who were forced to work hard for King Rehoboam. The king sent him out among all the Israelites. But they killed Adoniram by throwing stones at him. King Rehoboam was able to get away in his chariot. He escaped to Jerusalem. ¹⁹Israel has refused to follow the royal family of David to this day.

²⁰All the Israelites heard that Jeroboam had returned. They sent for him. They wanted him to meet with the whole community. Then they made him king over the

entire nation of Israel. Only the tribe of Judah remained true to David's royal family.

²¹Rehoboam arrived in Jerusalem. He brought together 180,000 capable young men from Judah and the tribe of Benjamin. He had decided to go to war against Israel. Solomon's son Rehoboam wanted his fighting men to get the kingdom of Israel back for him.

²²But a message from God came to Shemaiah. He was a man of God. God said to him, ²³"Speak to Solomon's son Rehoboam, the king of Judah. Speak to all Judah and the tribe of Benjamin. Also speak to the rest of the people. Tell all of them, ²⁴"The LORD says, "Do not go up to fight against the Israelites. They are your relatives. I want every one of you to go back home. Things have happened exactly the way I planned them." " So the fighting men obeyed the LORD's message. They went home again, just as he had ordered.

Golden Calves at Bethel and Dan

²⁵Jeroboam built up the walls of Shechem. It was in the hill country of Ephraim. Jeroboam made Shechem his home. From there he went out and built up Peniel.

²⁶Jeroboam thought, "My kingdom still isn't secure. It could very easily go back to the royal family of David. ²⁷Suppose the Israelites go up to Jerusalem to offer sacrifices at the LORD's temple. If they do, they will again decide to follow Rehoboam as their master. Then they'll kill me. They'll return to King Rehoboam. He is king of Judah."

²⁸So King Jeroboam asked for advice. Then he made two golden statues that looked like calves. He said to the people, "It's too hard for you to go up to Jerusalem. Israel, here are your gods who brought you up out of Egypt." ²⁹He set up one statue in Bethel. He set up the other one in Dan. ³⁰What Jeroboam did was sinful. And it caused Israel to sin. The people came to worship the statue at Bethel. They went all the way to Dan to worship the statue that was there.

³¹Jeroboam built temples for worshiping gods on high places. He appointed all kinds of people as priests. They didn't even have to be Levites. ³²He established a feast. It was on the 15th day of the eighth month. He wanted to make it like the Feast of Booths that was held in Judah. Jeroboam built an altar at Bethel. He offered sacrifices on it. He sacrificed to the calves he had made. He also put priests in Bethel. He did it at the high places he had made. ³³He offered sacrifices on the altar he had built at Bethel. It was on the 15th day of the eighth month. That's the month he had chosen for it. So he established the feast for the Israelites. And he went up to the altar to sacrifice offerings.

A Man of God From Judah

13 A man of God went from Judah to Bethel. He had received a message from the LORD. He arrived in Bethel just as Jeroboam was standing by the altar to offer a sacrifice. ²The man cried out. He shouted a message from the LORD against the altar. He said, "Altar! Altar! The LORD says, 'A son named Josiah will be born into the royal family of David. Altar, listen to me! Josiah will sacrifice the priests of the high places on you. They will be the children of the priests who are offering sacrifices here. So human bones will be burned on you.'" ³That same day the man of God spoke about a miraculous sign. He said, "Here is the sign the LORD has announced. This altar will be broken to pieces. The ashes on it will be spilled out."

⁴The man of God announced that message against the altar at Bethel. When King Jeroboam heard it, he reached out his hand from the altar. He said, "Grab him!" But as he reached out his hand toward the man, it dried up. He couldn't even pull it back. ⁵Also, the altar broke into pieces. Its ashes spilled out. That happened in keeping with the miraculous sign the man of God had announced. He had received a message from the LORD.

⁶King Jeroboam spoke to the man of God. He said, "Pray to the LORD your God for me. Pray that my hand will be as good as new again." So the man of God prayed to the LORD for the king. And the king's hand became as good as new. It was just as healthy as it had been before.

⁷The king said to the man of God, "Come home with me for a meal. I'll give you a gift."

⁸But the man of God replied to the king. He said, "What if you were to give me half of what you own? Even then I wouldn't go with you. I wouldn't eat bread or drink water here. ⁹The LORD gave me a command.

He said, 'Do not eat bread or drink water there. Do not return the same way you came.'" [10]So he took another road. He didn't go back on the same road he had taken when he came to Bethel.

[11]An old prophet was living in Bethel. His sons came and spoke to him. They told him everything the man of God had done there that day. They also told their father what the man had said to the king. [12]Their father asked them, "Which way did he go?" His sons showed him the road the man of God from Judah had taken. [13]So he said to his sons, "Put a saddle on the donkey for me." When they had done it, he got on the donkey. [14]He traveled on the same road the man of God had taken. He found the man sitting under an oak tree. He asked him, "Are you the man of God who came from Judah?"

"I am," he replied.

[15]So the prophet said to him, "Come home with me. I'll give you something to eat."

[16]The man of God said, "I can't go back to Bethel with you. I can't eat bread or drink water with you there. [17]I've received a message from the LORD. He told me, 'Do not eat bread or drink water there. Do not return the same way you came.'"

[18]The old prophet answered, "I'm also a prophet, just like you. An angel gave me a message from the LORD. The message said, 'Bring the man of God back with you to your house. Then he can eat bread and drink water with you.'" But the old prophet was telling him a lie. [19]The man of God returned with him. He ate and drank in his house.

[20]They were sitting at the table. The LORD gave a message to the old prophet who had brought the man of God back. [21]He cried out to the man who had come from Judah. He told him, "The LORD says, 'You have not done what I told you to do. You have not obeyed the command I gave you. I am the LORD your God. [22]You came back here and ate bread and drank water. You did it in the place where I told you not to. So your body will not be buried in your family tomb.'"

[23]The man of God finished eating and drinking. Then the old prophet who had brought him back put a saddle on the man's donkey for him. [24]And the man went on his way. A lion attacked him on the road and killed him. His body was left lying on the road. The donkey and the lion were standing beside it. [25]Some people passed by. They saw the body lying on the road. They saw the lion standing beside the body. Then they went and reported it in the city where the old prophet lived.

[26]The prophet who had brought the man back from his journey heard about what had happened. He said, "It's the man of God. He didn't do what the LORD told him to do. So the LORD has given him over to the lion. The lion has attacked him and killed him. Everything has happened just as the LORD's message had warned him it would."

[27]The old prophet said to his sons, "Put a saddle on the donkey for me." So they did. [28]Then he went out. He found the body of the man of God lying on the road. The donkey and the lion were standing beside it. The lion hadn't eaten the body. It hadn't attacked the donkey either. [29]So the prophet picked up the man's body. He put it on the donkey. He brought it back to his own city. He wanted to mourn for him and bury him. [30]Then he placed the body in his own tomb. People mourned for him. They said, "Oh, no, my friend! My dear friend!"

[31]After the old prophet had buried the man of God, he spoke to his sons. He said, "When I die, bury me in the grave where the man of God is buried. Put my bones next to his bones. [32]I want you to do that because he announced a message from the LORD. He spoke against the altar in Bethel. He also spoke against all the temples that are on the high places. They are in the towns of Samaria. What the man of God said will certainly come true."

[33]Even after all of that happened, Jeroboam still didn't change his evil ways. Once more he appointed priests for the high places. He made priests out of all kinds of people. In fact, he let anyone become a priest who wanted to. He set them apart to serve at the high places. [34]All of that was the great sin the royal family of Jeroboam committed. It led to their fall from power. Because of it, they were destroyed from the face of the earth.

Ahijah's Prophecy Against Jeroboam

14 At that time Abijah became sick. He was the son of Jeroboam. [2]Jeroboam said to his wife, "Go. Put on some different clothes. Then no one will recognize you as my wife. Go to Shiloh. That's where Ahijah the prophet is. He told me I would be king over the Israelites. ³Take ten loaves of bread with you. Take some cakes and a jar of honey. Go to him. He'll tell you what will happen to our son." ⁴So Jeroboam's wife did what he said. She went to Ahijah's house in Shiloh.

Ahijah couldn't see. He was blind because he was so old. ⁵But the LORD had told Ahijah, "Jeroboam's wife is coming. Her son is sick. She'll ask you about him. Give her the answer I give you. When she arrives, she'll pretend to be someone else."

⁶Ahijah heard the sound of her footsteps at the door. He said, "Come in. I know that you are Jeroboam's wife. Why are you pretending to be someone else? I have some bad news for you. ⁷Go. Tell Jeroboam that the LORD has a message for him. The LORD is the God of Israel. He says, 'I chose you from among the people. I appointed you king over my people Israel. ⁸I tore the kingdom away from the royal house of David. I gave it to you. But you have not been like my servant David. He obeyed my commands. He followed me with all his heart. He did only what was right in my eyes. ⁹You have done more evil things than all those who lived before you. You have made other gods for yourself. You have made statues of gods out of metal. You have made me very angry. You have turned your back on me.

¹⁰" 'Because of that, I am going to bring horrible trouble on your royal house. I will cut off from you every male in Israel. It does not matter whether they are slaves or free. I will burn up your royal house, just as someone burns up trash. I will burn it until it is all gone. ¹¹Some of the people who belong to you will die in the city. Dogs will eat them up. Others will die in the country. The birds will eat them. The LORD has spoken!'

¹²"Now go back home. When you enter your city, your son will die. ¹³All the Israelites will mourn for him. Then he will be buried. He is the only one who belongs to Jeroboam who will be buried. That is because he is the only one in Jeroboam's royal house in whom I have found anything good. I am the LORD, the God of Israel.

¹⁴"I will choose for myself a king over Israel. He will destroy the family of Jeroboam. This day your son will die. Even now this is beginning to happen. ¹⁵I, the LORD, will strike down Israel. Israel will be like tall grass swaying in the water. I will pull Israel up from this good land by the roots. I gave it to their people who lived long ago. I will scatter Israel to the east side of the Euphrates River. That is because they made the LORD very angry. They made poles used to worship the female god named Asherah. ¹⁶I will give Israel up because of the sins Jeroboam has committed. He has also caused Israel to commit those same sins."

¹⁷Then Jeroboam's wife got up and left. She went to the city of Tirzah. As soon as she stepped through the doorway of the house, her son died. ¹⁸He was buried and all the Israelites mourned for him. That's what the LORD had said would happen. He had said it through his servant, Ahijah the prophet.

¹⁹The other events of Jeroboam's rule are written down. His wars and how he ruled are written down. They are written in the official records of the kings of Israel. ²⁰Jeroboam ruled for 22 years. Then he joined the members of his family who had already died. Jeroboam's son Nadab became the next king after him.

Rehoboam King of Judah

²¹Rehoboam was king in Judah. He was the son of Solomon. Rehoboam was 41 years old when he became king. He ruled for 17 years in Jerusalem. It was the city the LORD had chosen out of all the cities in the tribes of Israel. He wanted to put his Name there. Rehoboam's mother was Naamah from Ammon.

²²The people of Judah did what was evil in the sight of the LORD. The sins they had committed made the LORD angry. The LORD was angry because they refused to worship only him. They did more to make him angry than their people who lived before them had done. ²³Judah also set up for themselves high places for worship. They set up sacred stones. They set up poles used to worship the female god named Asherah. They did it on every high hill and under every green tree. ²⁴There were even male prostitutes at the temples in the land. The people took part in all the practices of other nations. The LORD hated those practices. He had driven those nations out to make room for the Israelites.

²⁵Shishak attacked Jerusalem. It was in the fifth year that Rehoboam was king.

Shishak was king of Egypt. ²⁶He carried away the treasures of the LORD's temple. He also carried away the treasures of the royal palace. He took everything. That included all the gold shields Solomon had made. ²⁷So King Rehoboam made bronze shields to take their place. He gave them to the commanders of the guards on duty at the entrance to the royal palace. ²⁸Every time the king went to the LORD's temple, the guards carried the shields. Later, they took them back to the room where they were kept.

²⁹The other events of Rehoboam's rule are written down. Everything he did is written in the official records of the kings of Judah. ³⁰Rehoboam and Jeroboam were always at war with each other. ³¹Rehoboam joined the members of his family who had already died. He was buried in his family tomb in the City of David. His mother was Naamah from Ammon. Rehoboam's son Abijah became the next king after him.

Abijah King of Judah

15 Abijah became king of Judah. It was in the 18th year of Jeroboam's rule over Israel. Jeroboam was the son of Nebat. ²Abijah ruled in Jerusalem for three years. His mother's name was Maakah. She was Abishalom's daughter.

³Abijah committed all the sins his father had committed before him. Abijah didn't obey the LORD his God with all his heart. He didn't do what King David had done. ⁴But the LORD still kept the lamp of Abijah's kingdom burning brightly in Jerusalem. He did it by giving him a son to be the next king after him. He also did it by making Jerusalem strong. The LORD did those things because of David. ⁵David had done what was right in the sight of the LORD. He had kept all the LORD's commands. He had obeyed them all the days of his life. But he hadn't obeyed the LORD in the case of Uriah, the Hittite.

⁶There was war between Abijah and Jeroboam all through Abijah's life. ⁷The other events of Abijah's rule are written down. Everything he did is written down. All these things are written in the official records of the kings of Judah. There was war between Abijah and Jeroboam. ⁸Abijah joined the members of his family who had already died. He was buried in the City of David. Abijah's son Asa became the next king after him.

Asa King of Judah

⁹Asa became king of Judah. It was in the 20th year that Jeroboam was king of Israel. ¹⁰Asa ruled in Jerusalem for 41 years. His grandmother's name was Maakah. She was Abishalom's daughter.

¹¹Asa did what was right in the sight of the LORD. That's what King David had done. ¹²Asa threw out of the land the male prostitutes who were at the temples. He got rid of all the statues of gods made by his people of long ago. ¹³He even removed his grandmother Maakah from her position as queen mother. That's because she had made a pole used to worship the female god named Asherah. The LORD hated it. So Asa cut it down. He burned it in the Kidron Valley. ¹⁴Asa didn't remove the high places from Israel. But he committed his whole life completely to the LORD. ¹⁵He and his father had set apart silver, gold and other things to the LORD. Asa brought them into the LORD's temple.

¹⁶There was war between Asa and Baasha, the king of Israel. It lasted the whole time they were kings. ¹⁷Baasha was king of Israel. He marched out against Judah. Baasha built up the walls of Ramah. He did it to keep people from leaving or entering the territory of Asa, the king of Judah.

¹⁸Asa took all the silver and gold left among the treasures of the LORD's temple and his own palace. He put his officials in charge of it. He sent the officials to

1 Kgs 15:13 Maakah—Asa's grandmother—made an Asherah pole. Asherah was a goddess of fertility. The wood pole might have had the goddess's picture carved into it, but no one knows for sure.

Ben-Hadad. Ben-Hadad was king of Aram. He was ruling in Damascus. He was the son of Tabrimmon and the grandson of Hezion. ¹⁹"Let's make a peace treaty between us," Asa said. "My father and your father had made a peace treaty between them. Now I'm sending you a gift of silver and gold. So break your treaty with Baasha, the king of Israel. Then he'll go back home."

²⁰Ben-Hadad agreed with King Asa. He sent his army commanders against the towns of Israel. He captured Ijon, Dan, Abel Beth Maakah and the whole area of Kinnereth in addition to Naphtali. ²¹Baasha heard about it. So he stopped building up Ramah. He went back home to Tirzah. ²²Then King Asa gave an order to all the men of Judah. Everyone was required to help. They carried away from Ramah the stones and wood Baasha had been using there. King Asa used them to build up Geba in the territory of Benjamin. He also used them to build up Mizpah.

²³All the other events of Asa's rule are written down, including the cities he built. Everything he did is written in the official records of the kings of Judah. But when Asa became old, his feet began to give him trouble. ²⁴He joined the members of his family who had already died. He was buried in his family tomb. It was in the city of King David. Asa's son Jehoshaphat became the next king after him.

Nadab King of Israel

²⁵Nadab became king of Israel. It was in the second year that Asa was king of Judah. Nadab ruled over Israel for two years. He was the son of Jeroboam. ²⁶Nadab did what was evil in the sight of the LORD. He lived the way his father had lived. He committed the same sin his father Jeroboam had caused Israel to commit.

²⁷Baasha was from the tribe of Issachar. He was the son of Ahijah. Baasha made plans against Nadab and struck him down at Gibbethon. It was a Philistine town. Baasha struck him down while Nadab and all the men of Israel were getting ready to attack Gibbethon. ²⁸He killed Nadab in the third year that Asa was king of Judah. Baasha became the next king after Nadab.

²⁹As soon as Baasha became king, he killed Jeroboam's whole family. He didn't leave any of them alive. He destroyed every one of them. He did what the LORD had said would happen. The LORD had spoken that message through his servant Ahijah from Shiloh. ³⁰The LORD judged Jeroboam's family because of the sins Jeroboam had committed. He had also caused Israel to commit those same sins. He had made the LORD very angry. The LORD is the God of Israel.

³¹The other events of Nadab's rule are written down. Everything he did is written in the official records of the kings of Israel. ³²There was war between Asa and Baasha, the king of Israel. It lasted the whole time they were kings.

Baasha King of Israel

³³Baasha became king of Israel in Tirzah. It was in the third year that Asa was king of Judah. Baasha ruled for 24 years. He was the son of Ahijah. ³⁴Baasha did what was evil in the sight of the LORD. He lived the way Jeroboam had lived. He committed the same sin Jeroboam had caused Israel to commit.

16 The LORD's message about Baasha came to Jehu, the son of Hanani. Here is what the LORD said about Baasha. ²"I lifted you up from the dust. I appointed you king over my people Israel. But you lived the way Jeroboam had lived. You also caused my people Israel to sin. And their sins made me very angry. ³So I am about to destroy you, Baasha, and your royal house. I will make your house like the royal house of Jeroboam, the son of Nebat. ⁴Some of the people who belong to you will die in the city. Dogs will eat them up. Others will die in the country. The birds will eat them."

⁵The other events of Baasha's rule are written down. What he did and what he accomplished are written in the official records of the kings of Israel. ⁶Baasha joined the members of his family who had already died. He was buried in Tirzah. Baasha's son Elah became the next king after him.

⁷The LORD's message came through the prophet Jehu, the son of Hanani. It was against Baasha and his royal house. Baasha had done all kinds of evil things in the sight of the LORD. Baasha had also destroyed the royal house of Jeroboam. What Baasha did had made the LORD very angry. So Baasha had become as sinful as the royal house of Jeroboam had been.

Elah King of Israel

[8]Elah became king of Israel. It was in the 26th year that Asa was king of Judah. Elah ruled in Tirzah for two years. He was the son of Baasha.

[9]Zimri was one of Elah's officials. He commanded half of Elah's chariot drivers. He made plans against Elah. Elah was in Tirzah at the time. He was getting drunk in the home of Arza. Arza was in charge of the palace at Tirzah. [10]Zimri came in. He struck Elah down and killed him. It was in the 27th year of Asa, the king of Judah. Zimri became the next king after Elah.

[11]As soon as Zimri was seated on the throne as king, he killed off Baasha's whole family. He didn't even spare one male. It didn't matter whether it was a relative or a friend. [12]So Zimri destroyed the whole family of Baasha. That's what the LORD had said would happen. He had spoken against Baasha through Jehu the prophet. [13]Baasha and his son Elah had committed all kinds of sin. They had also caused Israel to commit the same sins. So Israel made the LORD very angry. They did it by worshiping worthless statues of gods. The LORD is the God of Israel.

[14]The other events of Elah's rule are written down. Everything he did is written in the official records of the kings of Israel.

Zimri King of Israel

[15]Zimri ruled in Tirzah for seven days. It was in the 27th year that Asa was king of Judah. The army of Israel had set up camp near Gibbethon. It was a Philistine town. [16]The Israelites in the camp heard that Zimri had made plans against King Elah. They also heard that Zimri had murdered him. So they announced that Omri was king over Israel. He was the commander of the army. They made him king that day in the camp. [17]Then Omri and all his men pulled back from Gibbethon. They marched to Tirzah and surrounded it. They attacked it and captured it. [18]Zimri saw that they had taken over the city. So he went into the safest place in the royal palace. He set the palace on fire all around him. He died there [19]because of the sins he had committed. He had done what was evil in the sight of the LORD. He had lived the way Jeroboam had lived. He had committed the same sin Jeroboam had caused Israel to commit.

[20]The other events of Zimri's rule are written down. The way he turned against King Elah and killed him is written down. All these things are written in the official records of the kings of Israel.

Omri King of Israel

[21]The Israelites divided up into two groups. Half of them wanted Tibni to be king. He was the son of Ginath. The other half wanted Omri. [22]But Omri's followers were stronger than those of Tibni, the son of Ginath. So Tibni died. And Omri began to rule.

[23]Omri became king of Israel. It was in the 31st year that Asa was king of Judah. Omri ruled for 12 years. He ruled in Tirzah for six of those years. [24]He bought the hill of Samaria from Shemer. He weighed out 150 pounds of silver for it. Then he built a city on the hill. He called it Samaria. He named it after Shemer. Shemer had owned the hill before him.

[25]But Omri did what was evil in the sight of the LORD. He sinned more than all the kings who had ruled before him. [26]He lived the way Jeroboam, the son of Nebat, had lived. He committed the same sin Jeroboam had caused Israel to commit. Israel made the LORD very angry. They did it by worshiping worthless statues of gods. The LORD is the God of Israel.

[27]The other events of Omri's rule are written down. Everything he did and the things he accomplished are written in the official records of the kings of Israel. [28]Omri joined the members of his family who had already died. He was buried in Samaria. Omri's son Ahab became the next king after him.

Ahab King of Israel

[29]Ahab became king of Israel. It was in the 38th year that Asa was king of Judah. Ahab ruled over Israel in Samaria for 22 years. He was the son of Omri. [30]Ahab, the son of Omri, did what was evil in the sight of the LORD. He did more evil things than any of the kings who had ruled before him. [31]He thought it was only a small thing to commit the sins Jeroboam, the son of Nebat, had committed. Ahab also married Jezebel. She was Ethbaal's daughter. Ethbaal was king of the people of Sidon. Ahab began to serve the god named Baal and worship him. [32]He set up an altar to honor Baal.

He set it up in the temple of Baal that he built in Samaria. [33]Ahab also made a pole used to worship the female god named Asherah. He made the LORD very angry. Ahab did more to make him angry than all the kings of Israel had done before him. The LORD is the God of Israel.

[34]In Ahab's time, Hiel from Bethel rebuilt Jericho. When he laid its foundations, it cost him the life of his oldest son Abiram. When he set up its gates, it cost him the life of his youngest son Segub. That's what the LORD had said would happen. He had spoken it through Joshua, the son of Nun.

Elijah Announces No Dew or Rain

17 Elijah was from Tishbe in the land of Gilead. He said to Ahab, "I serve the LORD. He is the God of Israel. You can be sure that he lives. And you can be just as sure that there won't be any dew or rain on the whole land. There won't be any during the next few years. It won't come until I say so."

Elijah Is Fed by Ravens

[2]Then a message came to Elijah from the LORD. He said, [3]"Leave this place. Go east and hide in the Kerith Valley. It is east of the Jordan River. [4]You will drink water from the brook. I have directed some ravens to supply you with food there."

[5]So Elijah did what the LORD had told him to do. He went to the Kerith Valley. It was east of the Jordan River. He stayed there. [6]The ravens brought him bread and meat in the morning. They also brought him bread and meat in the evening. He drank water from the brook.

Elijah and the Widow at Zarephath

[7]Some time later the brook dried up. It hadn't rained in the land for quite a while. [8]A message came to Elijah from the LORD. He said, [9]"Go right away to Zarephath in the region of Sidon. Stay there. I have directed a widow there to supply you with food." [10]So Elijah went to Zarephath. He came to the town gate. A widow was there gathering sticks. He called out to her. He asked, "Would you bring me a little water in a jar? I need a drink." [11]She went to get the water. Then he called out to her, "Please bring me a piece of bread too."

[12]"I don't have any bread," she replied. "And that's just as sure as the LORD your God is alive. All I have is a small amount of flour in a jar and a little olive oil in a jug.

WHAT ABOUT YOU?

God sent Elijah to tell King Ahab that no rain or dew would fall in Israel until God said so. It was a consequence for Ahab's evil actions. Elijah delivered the news, after which God had him hide beside a brook where ravens would take him food.

But with no rain, the brook eventually dried up. God then directed Elijah to a town outside of Israel where he found a widow preparing to use the last of her oil and flour for a final meal for herself and her son. God miraculously kept that little bit of food from running out as she prepared meal after meal.

When Elijah had nothing in the wilderness, God fed him. When the widow and her son were down to their last meal, God came through again. Isn't it great to serve a God who knows what we need and promises to provide for us? All Elijah had to do to witness God's power was to follow His instructions and trust that He would do the rest.

Green, yellow, and red—where are you likely to find these three colors? That's right, a traffic light! They tell us to "go," "slow down," and "stop." If you like to highlight verses as you study your Bible, consider using these three colors to color code the instructions that God gives His people. What colors would you need while studying 1 Kings 17?

I'm gathering a few sticks to take home. I'll make one last meal for myself and my son. We'll eat it. After that, we'll die." [13]Elijah said to her, "Don't be afraid. Go home. Do what you have said. But first make a small loaf of bread for me. Make it out of what you have. Bring it to me. Then make some for yourself and your son. [14]The LORD is the God of Israel. He says, 'The jar of flour will not be used up. The jug will always have oil in it. You will have flour and oil until the day the LORD sends rain on the land.' "

[15]She went away and did what Elijah had told her to do. So Elijah had food every day. There was also food for the woman and her family. [16]The jar of flour wasn't used up. The jug always had oil in it. That's what the LORD had said would happen. He had spoken that message through Elijah.

[17]Some time later the son of the woman who owned the house became sick. He got worse and worse. Finally he stopped breathing. [18]The woman said to Elijah, "You are a man of God. What do you have against me? Did you come to bring my sin out into the open? Did you come to kill my son?"

Jason's Jargon

1 KINGS 17

Your task: Find the word *raven* in this chapter. The raven is most commonly a black bird. It is often associated with death, yet God chose ravens to help Elijah stay alive.

[19]"Give me your son," Elijah replied. He took him from her arms. He carried him to the upstairs room where he was staying. He put him down on his bed. [20]Then Elijah cried out to the LORD. He said, "LORD my God, I'm staying with this widow. Have you brought pain and sorrow even to her? Have you caused her son to die?" [21]Then he lay down on the boy three times. He cried out to the LORD. He said, "LORD my God, give this boy's life back to him!"

[22]The LORD answered Elijah's prayer. He gave the boy's life back to him. So the boy

lived. [23]Elijah picked up the boy. He carried him down from the upstairs room into the house. He gave him to his mother. He said, "Look! Your son is alive!"

[24]Then the woman said to Elijah, "Now I know that you are a man of God. I know that the message you have brought from the LORD is true."

BiBLe ADVeNtUReS

Grady saw the story of Elijah and the widow at Zarephath in the Imagination Station in "Run-of-the-Mill Miracle" (A#49).

Elijah and Obadiah

18 It was now three years since it had rained. A message came to Elijah from the LORD. He said, "Go. Speak to Ahab. Then I will send rain on the land." [2]So Elijah went to speak to Ahab.

There wasn't enough food in Samaria. The people there were very hungry. [3]Ahab had sent for Obadiah. He was in charge of Ahab's palace. Obadiah had great respect for the LORD. [4]Ahab's wife Jezebel had been killing off the LORD's prophets. So Obadiah had hidden 100 prophets in two caves. He had put 50 in each cave. He had supplied them with food and water. [5]Ahab had said to Obadiah, "Go through the land. Go to all the valleys and springs of water. Maybe we can find some grass there. It will keep the horses and mules alive. Then we won't have to kill any of our animals." [6]So they decided where each of them would look. Ahab went in one direction. Obadiah went in another.

[7]As Obadiah was walking along, Elijah met him. Obadiah recognized him. He bowed down to the ground. He said, "My master Elijah! Is it really you?"

[8]"Yes," he replied. "Go and tell your master Ahab, 'Elijah is here.' "

[9]"What have I done wrong?" asked Obadiah. "Why are you handing me over to Ahab to be put to death? [10]My master has sent people to look for you everywhere. There isn't a nation or kingdom where he hasn't sent someone to look for you. Suppose a nation or kingdom would claim you weren't there. Then Ahab would make

them give their word that they couldn't find you. And that's just as sure as the LORD your God is alive. [11]But now you are telling me to go to my master. You want me to say, 'Elijah is here.' [12]But the Spirit of the LORD might carry you away when I leave you. Then I won't know where you are. If I go and tell Ahab and he doesn't find you, he'll kill me. But I've worshiped the LORD ever since I was young. [13]My master, haven't you heard what I did? Jezebel was killing the LORD's prophets. But I hid 100 of them in two caves. I put 50 in each cave. I supplied them with food and water. [14]And now you are telling me to go to my master Ahab. You want me to say to him, 'Elijah is here.' Ahab will kill me!"

[15]Elijah said, "I serve the LORD who rules over all. You can be sure that he lives. And you can be just as sure that I will speak to Ahab today."

Elijah on Mount Carmel

[16]Obadiah went back to Ahab. He told Ahab that Elijah wanted to see him. So Ahab went to where Elijah was. [17]When he saw Elijah, he said to him, "Is that you? You are always stirring up trouble in Israel."

[18]"I haven't made trouble for Israel," Elijah replied. "But you and your father's family have. You have turned away from the LORD's commands. You have followed gods that are named Baal. [19]Now send for people from all over Israel. Tell them to meet me on Mount Carmel. And bring the 450 prophets of the god named Baal. Also bring the 400 prophets of the female god named Asherah. All of them eat at Jezebel's table."

[20]So Ahab sent that message all through Israel. He gathered the prophets together on Mount Carmel. [21]Elijah went there and stood in front of the people. He said, "How long will it take you to make up your minds? If the LORD is the one and only God, worship him. But if Baal is the one and only God, worship him."

The people didn't say anything.

[22]Then Elijah said to them, "I'm the only one of the LORD's prophets left. But Baal has 450 prophets. [23]Get two bulls for us. Let Baal's prophets choose one for themselves. Let them cut it into pieces. Then let them put it on the wood. But don't let them set fire to it. I'll prepare the other bull. I'll put

it on the wood. But I won't set fire to it. [24]Then you pray to your god. And I'll pray to the LORD. The god who answers by sending fire down is the one and only God."

Then all the people said, "What you are saying is good."

[25]Elijah said to the prophets of Baal, "Choose one of the bulls. There are many of you. So prepare your bull first. Pray to your god. But don't light the fire." [26]So they prepared the bull they had been given.

They prayed to Baal from morning until noon. "Baal! Answer us!" they shouted. But there wasn't any reply. No one answered. Then they danced around the altar they had made.

[27]At noon Elijah began to tease them. "Shout louder!" he said. "I'm sure Baal is a god! Perhaps he has too much to think about. Or maybe he has gone to the toilet. Or perhaps he's away on a trip. Maybe he's sleeping. You might have to wake him up." [28]So they shouted louder. They cut themselves with swords and spears until their blood flowed. That's what they usually did when things really looked hopeless. [29]It was now past noon. The prophets of Baal continued to prophesy with all their might. They did it until the time came to offer the evening sacrifice. But there wasn't any reply. No one answered. No one paid any attention.

[30]Then Elijah said to all the people, "Come here to me." So they went to him. He rebuilt the altar of the LORD. It had been torn down. [31]Elijah got 12 stones. There was one for each tribe in the family line of Jacob. The LORD's message had come to Jacob. It had said, "Your name will be Israel." [32]Elijah used the stones to build an altar to honor the LORD. He dug a ditch around it. The ditch was large enough to hold 24 pounds of seeds. [33]He arranged the wood for the fire. He cut the bull into pieces. He placed the pieces on the wood. Then he said to some of the people, "Fill four large jars

BIBLE ADVENTURES

Via the Imagination Station, Jack and Robyn saw Elijah challenge the prophets of Baal on Mount Carmel in "Elijah" (A#06).

with water. Pour it on the offering and the wood." So they did.

[34] "Do it again," he said. So they did it again.

"Do it a third time," he ordered. And they did it the third time. [35] The water ran down around the altar. It even filled the ditch.

[36] When it was time to offer the evening sacrifice, the prophet Elijah stepped forward. He prayed, "LORD, you are the God of Abraham, Isaac and Israel. Today let everyone know that you are God in Israel. Let them know I'm your servant. Let them know I've done all these things because you commanded me to. [37] Answer me. LORD, answer me. Then these people will know that you are the one and only God. They'll know that you are turning their hearts back to you again."

[38] The fire of the LORD came down. It burned up the sacrifice. It burned up the wood and the stones and the soil. It even dried up the water in the ditch.

[39] All the people saw it. Then they fell down flat with their faces toward the ground. They cried out, "The LORD is the one and only God! The LORD is the one and only God!"

[40] Then Elijah commanded them, "Grab the prophets of Baal. Don't let a single one of them get away!" So they grabbed them. Elijah had them brought down to the Kishon Valley. There he had them put to death.

[41] Elijah said to Ahab, "Go. Eat and drink. I can hear the sound of a heavy rain."

[42] So Ahab went off to eat and drink. But Elijah climbed to the top of Mount Carmel. He bent down toward the ground. Then he put his face between his knees.

[43] "Go and look toward the sea," he told his servant. So he went up and looked.

"I don't see anything there," he said.

Seven times Elijah said, "Go back."

[44] The seventh time the servant said, "I see a cloud. It's as small as a man's hand. It's coming up over the sea."

Elijah said, "Go to Ahab. Tell him, 'Tie your chariot to your horse. Go down to Jezreel before the rain stops you.'"

[45] Black clouds filled the sky. The wind came up, and a heavy rain began to fall. Ahab rode off to Jezreel. [46] The power of the LORD came on Elijah. He tucked his coat

WOOTON'S FUN FACTS

1 Kgs. 18:16–46

Elijah wasn't the first guy to challenge false prophets. Moses and Aaron dueled with Pharaoh's magicians in Exodus 7.

into his belt. And he ran ahead of Ahab all the way to Jezreel.

Elijah Runs Away to Mount Horeb

19 Ahab told Jezebel everything Elijah had done. He told her how Elijah had killed all the prophets of Baal with his sword. [2] So Jezebel sent a message to Elijah. She said, "You can be sure that I will kill you, just as I killed the other prophets. I'll do it by this time tomorrow. If I don't, may the gods punish me greatly."

[3] Elijah was afraid. So he ran for his life. He came to Beersheba in Judah. He left his servant there. [4] Then he traveled for one day into the desert. He came to a small bush. He sat down under it. He prayed that he would die. "LORD, I've had enough," he said. "Take my life. I'm no better than my people of long ago." [5] Then he lay down under the bush. And he fell asleep.

Suddenly an angel touched him. The angel said, "Get up and eat." [6] Elijah looked around. Near his head he saw some bread. It had been baked over hot coals. A jar of water was also there. So Elijah ate and drank. Then he lay down again.

[7] The angel of the LORD came to him a second time. He touched him and said, "Get up and eat. Your journey will be long and hard." [8] So he got up. He ate and drank. The food gave him new strength.

He traveled for 40 days and 40 nights. He kept going until he arrived at Horeb. It was the mountain of God. ⁹There he went into a cave and spent the night.

The Lord Appears to Elijah

A message came to Elijah from the Lord. He said, "Elijah, what are you doing here?"

¹⁰He replied, "Lord God who rules over all, I've been very committed to you. The Israelites have turned their backs on your covenant. They have torn down your altars. They've put your prophets to death with their swords. I'm the only one left. And they are trying to kill me."

¹¹The Lord said, "Go out. Stand on the mountain in front of me. I am going to pass by."

As the Lord approached, a very powerful wind tore the mountains apart. It broke up the rocks. But the Lord wasn't in the wind. After the wind there was an earthquake. But the Lord wasn't in the earthquake. ¹²After the earthquake a fire came. But the Lord wasn't in the fire. And after the fire there was only a gentle whisper. ¹³When Elijah heard it, he pulled his coat over his face. He went out and stood at the entrance to the cave.

Then a voice said to him, "Elijah, what are you doing here?"

¹⁴He replied, "Lord God who rules over all, I've been very committed to you. The Israelites have turned their backs on your covenant. They have torn down your altars. They've put your prophets to death with their swords. I'm the only one left. And they are trying to kill me."

¹⁵The Lord said to him, "Go back the way you came. Go to the Desert of Damascus. When you get there, anoint Hazael as king over Aram. ¹⁶Also anoint Jehu as king over Israel. He is the son of Nimshi. And anoint Elisha from Abel Meholah as the next prophet after you. He is the son of Shaphat. ¹⁷Jehu will put to death anyone who escapes Hazael's sword. And Elisha will put to death anyone who escapes Jehu's sword. ¹⁸But I will keep 7,000 people in Israel for myself. They have not bowed down to Baal. And they have not kissed him."

The Lord Chooses Elisha

¹⁹Elijah left Mount Horeb. He saw Elisha, the son of Shaphat. Elisha was plowing in a field. He was driving the last of 12 pairs of oxen. Elijah went up to him. He threw his coat around him. ²⁰Then Elisha left his oxen. He ran after Elijah. "Let me kiss my father and mother goodbye," he said. "Then I'll come with you."

"Go back," Elijah replied. "What have I done to you?"

²¹So Elisha left him and went back. He got his two oxen and killed them. He burned the plow to cook the meat. He gave it to the people, and they ate it. Then he started to follow Elijah. He became Elijah's servant.

Ben-Hadad Attacks Samaria

20 Ben-Hadad brought his whole army together. He was king of Aram. He went up to Samaria. He took 32 kings and their horses and chariots with him. All of them surrounded Samaria and attacked it. ²Ben-Hadad sent messengers into the city. They spoke to Ahab, the king of Israel. They told him, "Ben-Hadad says, ³'Your silver and gold belong to me. The best of your wives and children also belong to me.'"

⁴The king of Israel replied, "What you say is true. You are my king and master. I belong to you. And everything I have belongs to you."

⁵The messengers came again. They told Ahab, "Ben-Hadad says, 'I commanded you to give me your silver and gold. I also commanded you to give me your wives and children. ⁶But now I'm going to send my officials to you. They will come about this time tomorrow. They'll search your palace. They'll search the houses of your officials. They'll take everything you value. And they'll carry it all away.'"

⁷The king of Israel sent for all the elders of the land. He said to them, "This man is really looking for trouble! He sent for my wives and children. He sent for my silver and gold. And I agreed to give them to him."

⁸All the elders and people answered, "Don't listen to him. Don't agree to give him what he wants."

⁹So Ahab replied to Ben-Hadad's messengers. He said, "Tell my king and master, 'I will do everything you commanded me to do the first time. But this time, I can't do what you want me to do.'" They took Ahab's answer back to Ben-Hadad.

[10]Then Ben-Hadad sent another message to Ahab. Ben-Hadad said, "There won't be enough dust left in Samaria to give each of my followers even a handful. If there is, may the gods punish me greatly."

[11]The king of Israel replied. He said, "Tell him, 'Someone who puts his armor on shouldn't brag like someone who takes it off.'"

[12]Ben-Hadad and the kings were in their tents drinking. That's when he heard the message. He ordered his men, "Get ready to attack." So they prepared to attack the city.

Ahab Wins the Battle Over Ben-Hadad

[13]During that time a prophet came to Ahab, the king of Israel. He announced, "The LORD says, 'Do you see this huge army? I will hand it over to you today. Then you will know that I am the LORD.'"

[14]"But who will do it?" Ahab asked.

The prophet answered, "The LORD says, 'The junior officers who are under the area commanders will do it.'"

"And who will start the battle?" Ahab asked.

The prophet answered, "You will."

[15]So Ahab sent for the junior officers who were under the area commanders. The total number of officers was 232. Ahab gathered together the rest of the Israelites. The total number of them was 7,000. [16]They started out at noon. At that time Ben-Hadad and the 32 kings helping him were in their tents. They were getting drunk. [17]The junior officers who were under Ahab's area commanders marched out first.

Ben-Hadad had sent out scouts. They came back and reported, "Men are marching against us from Samaria."

[18]Ben-Hadad said, "They might be coming to make peace. If they are, take them alive. Or they might be coming to make war. If they are, take them alive."

[19]The junior officers marched out of the city. The army was right behind them. [20]Each man struck down the one fighting against him. When that happened, the army of Aram ran away. The Israelites chased them. But Ben-Hadad, the king of Aram, escaped on a horse. Some of his horsemen escaped with him. [21]The king of Israel attacked them. He overpowered the horses and chariots. Large numbers of the men of Aram were wounded or killed.

[22]After that, the prophet came to the king of Israel again. The prophet said, "Make your position stronger. Do what needs to be done. Next spring the king of Aram will attack you again."

[23]During that time, the officials of the king of Aram gave him advice. They said, "The gods of Israel are gods of the hills. That's why they were too strong for us. But suppose we fight them on the plains. Then we'll certainly be stronger than they are. [24]Here's what you should do. Don't let any of the kings continue as military leaders. Have other officers take their places. [25]You must also put another army together. It should be just like the one you lost. It should have the same number of horses and chariots. Then we'll be able to fight against Israel on the plains. And we'll certainly be stronger than they are." Ben-Hadad agreed with their advice. He did what they suggested.

[26]The next spring Ben-Hadad brought together the men of Aram. They went up to the city of Aphek to fight against Israel. [27]The Israelites were also brought together. They were given supplies. They marched out to fight against their enemies. Israel's army camped across from Aram's army. The Israelites looked like two small flocks of goats that had become separated from the others. But the men of Aram covered the countryside.

[28]The man of God came up to the king of Israel again. He told him, "The LORD says, 'The men of Aram think the LORD is a god of the hills. They do not think he is a god of the valleys. So I, the LORD, will hand their huge army over to you. Then you will know that I am the LORD.'"

[29]For seven days the two armies camped across from each other. On the seventh day the battle began. The Israelites wounded or killed 100,000 Aramean soldiers who were on foot. That happened in a single day. [30]The rest of the men of Aram escaped to the city of Aphek. Its wall fell down on 27,000 of them. Ben-Hadad ran to the city. He hid in a secret room.

[31]His officials said to him, "Look, we've heard that the kings of Israel often show mercy. So let's go to the king of Israel. Let's wear the rough clothing people wear when they're sad. Let's tie ropes around our heads. Perhaps Ahab will spare your life."

[32]So they wore rough clothing. They tied ropes around their heads. Then they

went to the king of Israel. They told him, "Your servant Ben-Hadad says, 'Please let me live.'"

The king answered, "Is he still alive? He used to be my friend."

[33]The men thought that was good news. So they quickly used the word Ahab had used. "Yes! Your friend Ben-Hadad!" they said.

"Go and get him," the king said. Ben-Hadad came out of the secret room. Then Ahab had him get into his chariot.

[34]"I'll return the cities my father took from your father," Ben-Hadad offered. "You can set up your own market areas in Damascus. That's what my father did in Samaria."

Ahab said, "If we sign a peace treaty, I'll set you free." So Ben-Hadad made a treaty with him. Then Ahab let him go.

A Prophet Accuses Ahab

[35]There was a group of people called the group of the prophets. A message from the LORD came to one of their members. He said to his companion, "Strike me down with your weapon." But he wouldn't do it.

[36]The prophet said, "You haven't obeyed the LORD. So as soon as you leave me, a lion will kill you." The companion went away. And a lion found him and killed him.

[37]The prophet found another man. He said, "Please strike me down." So the man struck him down and wounded him. [38]Then the prophet went and stood by the road. He waited for the king to come by. He pulled his headband down over his eyes so no one would recognize him. [39]The king passed by. Then the prophet called out to him. He said, "I went into the middle of the battle. Someone came to me with a prisoner. He said, 'Guard this man. Don't let him get away. If he does, you will pay for his life with yours. Or you can pay 75 pounds of silver.' [40]While I was busy here and there, the man disappeared."

The king of Israel spoke to him. He told him, "What you've just said is what will happen to you."

[41]Then the prophet quickly removed the headband from his eyes. The king of Israel recognized him as one of the prophets. [42]He told the king, "The LORD says, 'You have set a man free. But I had said he should be set apart to the LORD in a special way to be destroyed. So you must pay for his life with yours. You must pay for his people's lives with the lives of your people.'" [43]The king of Israel was angry. He was in a bad mood. He went back to his palace in Samaria.

Naboth's Vineyard

21 Some time later King Ahab wanted a certain vineyard. It belonged to Naboth from Jezreel. The vineyard was in Jezreel. It was close to the palace of Ahab, the king of Samaria. [2]Ahab said to Naboth, "Let me have your vineyard. It's close to my palace. I want to use it for a vegetable garden. I'll trade you a better vineyard for it. Or, if you prefer, I'll pay you what it's worth."

[3]But Naboth replied, "May the LORD keep me from giving you the land my family handed down to me."

[4]So Ahab went home. He was angry. He was in a bad mood because of what Naboth from Jezreel had said. He had told Ahab, "I won't give you the land my family handed down to me." So Ahab lay on his bed. He was in a very bad mood. He wouldn't even eat anything.

[5]His wife Jezebel came in. She asked him, "Why are you in such a bad mood? Why won't you eat anything?"

[6]He answered her, "Because I spoke to Naboth from Jezreel. I said, 'Sell me your vineyard. Or, if you prefer, I'll give you another vineyard in its place.' But he said, 'I won't sell you my vineyard.'"

[7]His wife Jezebel said, "Is this how the king of Israel acts? Get up! Eat something! Cheer up. I'll get you the vineyard of Naboth from Jezreel."

[8]So she wrote some letters in Ahab's name. She stamped them with his royal seal. Then she sent them to the elders and nobles who lived in the city where Naboth lived. [9]In those letters she wrote,

"Announce a day when people are supposed to go without eating. Have Naboth sit in an important place among the people. [10]But put two worthless and evil men in seats across from him. Have them bring charges that he has cursed God and the king. Then take him out of the city. Kill him by throwing stones at him."

[11]So the elders and nobles who lived in that city did what Jezebel wanted. They did everything she directed in the letters she had written to them. [12]They announced a day of fasting. They had Naboth sit in an important place among the people. [13]Then two worthless and evil men came and sat across from him. They brought charges against Naboth in front of the people. The two men said, "Naboth has cursed God and the king." So they took him outside the city. They killed him by throwing stones at him. [14]Then they sent a message to Jezebel. They said, "Naboth is dead. We killed him by throwing stones at him."

[15]Jezebel heard that Naboth had been killed. As soon as she heard it, she said to Ahab, "Get up. Take over the vineyard of Naboth from Jezreel. It's the one he wouldn't sell to you. He isn't alive anymore. He's dead." [16]Ahab heard that Naboth was dead. So Ahab got up and went down to take over Naboth's vineyard.

[17]Then a message from the LORD came to Elijah, who was from Tishbe. The LORD said, [18]"Go down to see Ahab, the king of Israel. He rules in Samaria. You will find him in Naboth's vineyard. Ahab has gone there to take it over. [19]Tell him, 'The LORD says, "Haven't you murdered a man? Haven't you taken over his property?"' Then tell Ahab, 'The LORD says, "Dogs licked up Naboth's blood. In that same place dogs will lick up your blood. Yes, I said your blood!"'"

[20]Ahab said to Elijah, "My enemy! You have found me!"

"I have found you," he answered. "That's because you gave yourself over to do evil things. You did what was evil in the sight of the LORD. [21]So the LORD says, 'I am going to bring horrible trouble on you. I will destroy your children after you. I will destroy every male in Israel who is related to you. It does not matter whether they are slaves or free. [22]I will make your royal house like the house of Jeroboam, the son of Nebat. I will make it like the house of Baasha, the son of Ahijah. You have made me very angry. You have caused Israel to sin.'

[23]"The LORD also says, 'Dogs will eat up Jezebel near the wall of Jezreel.'

[24]"Some of the people who belong to Ahab will die in the city. Dogs will eat them up. Others will die in the country. The birds will eat them."

BIBLE ADVENTURES

The N.V.P.D. Squad investigated the case of Ahab and his envy of Naboth's vineyard in "B-TV: Envy" (A#24).

[25]There was never anyone like Ahab. He gave himself over to do what was evil in the sight of the LORD. His wife Jezebel talked him into it. [26]He acted in the most evil way. He worshiped statues of gods. He was like the Amorites. The LORD drove them out to make room for Israel.

[27]When Ahab heard what Elijah had said, he tore his clothes. He put on the rough clothing people wear when they're sad. He went without eating. He even slept in his clothes. He went around looking sad.

[28]Then a message from the LORD came to Elijah, who was from Tishbe. The LORD said, [29]"Have you seen how Ahab has made himself humble in my sight? Because he has done that, I will not bring trouble on him while he lives. But I will bring it on his royal house when his son is king."

Micaiah Prophesies Against Ahab

22 For three years there wasn't any war between Aram and Israel. [2]In the third year Jehoshaphat went down to see Ahab, the king of Israel. Jehoshaphat was king of Judah. [3]The king of Israel had spoken to his officials. He had said, "Don't you know that Ramoth Gilead belongs to us? And we aren't even doing anything to take it back from the king of Aram."

[4]So Ahab asked Jehoshaphat, "Will you go with me to fight against Ramoth Gilead?"

Jehoshaphat replied to the king of Israel, "Yes. I'll go with you. My men will go with you. My horses will also go with you." [5]Jehoshaphat continued, "First ask the LORD for advice."

[6]So the king of Israel brought about 400 prophets together. He asked them, "Should I go to war against Ramoth Gilead? Or should I stay here?"

"Go," they answered. "The Lord will hand it over to you."

[7]But Jehoshaphat asked, "Is there no longer a prophet of the LORD here? If there is, ask him what we should do."

[8]The king of Israel answered Jehoshaphat. He said, "There is still one other

man we can go to. We can ask the Lord for advice through him. But I hate him. He never prophesies anything good about me. He only prophesies bad things. His name is Micaiah. He's the son of Imlah."

"You shouldn't say bad things about him," Jehoshaphat replied.

⁹So the king of Israel called for one of his officials. He told him, "Bring Micaiah, the son of Imlah, right away."

¹⁰The king of Israel and Jehoshaphat, the king of Judah, were wearing their royal robes. They were sitting on their thrones at the threshing floor. It was near the entrance of the gate of Samaria. All the prophets were prophesying in front of them. ¹¹Zedekiah was the son of Kenaanah. Zedekiah had made horns out of iron. They looked like animal horns. He announced, "The Lord says, 'With these horns you will drive back the men of Aram until they are destroyed.'"

¹²All the other prophets were prophesying the same thing. "Attack Ramoth Gilead," they said. "Win the battle over it. The Lord will hand it over to you."

¹³A messenger went to get Micaiah. He said to him, "Look. The other prophets agree. All of them are saying the king will have success. So agree with them. Say the same thing they do."

¹⁴But Micaiah said, "You can be sure that the Lord lives. And here is something you can be just as sure of. I can only tell the king what the Lord tells me to say."

¹⁵When Micaiah arrived, the king spoke to him. He asked, "Should we go to war against Ramoth Gilead, or not?"

"Attack," he answered. "You will win. The Lord will hand Ramoth Gilead over to you."

¹⁶The king said to him, "I've made you promise to tell the truth many times before. So don't tell me anything but the truth in the name of the Lord."

¹⁷Then Micaiah answered, "I saw all the Israelites scattered on the hills. They were like sheep that didn't have a shepherd. The Lord said, 'These people do not have a master. Let each of them go home in peace.'"

¹⁸The king of Israel spoke to Jehoshaphat. He said, "Didn't I tell you he never prophesies anything good about me? He only prophesies bad things."

¹⁹Micaiah continued, "Listen to the Lord's message. I saw the Lord sitting on his throne. All the angels of heaven were standing around him. Some were standing at his right side. The others were standing at his left side. ²⁰The Lord said, 'Who will get Ahab to attack Ramoth Gilead? I want him to die there.'

"One angel suggested one thing. Another suggested something else. ²¹Finally, a spirit came forward and stood in front of the Lord. The spirit said, 'I'll get Ahab to do it.'

²²"'How?' the Lord asked.

"The spirit said, 'I'll go out and put lies in the mouths of all his prophets.'

"'You will have success in getting Ahab to attack Ramoth Gilead,' said the Lord. 'Go and do it.'

²³"So the Lord has put lies in the mouths of all your prophets. He has said that great harm will come to you."

²⁴Then Zedekiah, the son of Kenaanah, went up and slapped Micaiah in the face. Zedekiah asked Micaiah, "Do you think the spirit sent by the Lord left me? Do you think that spirit went to speak to you?"

²⁵Micaiah replied, "You will find out on the day you go to hide in an inside room to save your life."

²⁶Then the king of Israel gave an order. He said, "Take Micaiah away. Send him back to Amon. Amon is the ruler of the city of Samaria. And send him back to Joash. Joash is a member of the royal court. ²⁷Tell him, 'The king says, "Put this fellow in prison. Don't give him anything but bread and water until I return safely."'"

²⁸Micaiah announced, "Do you really think you will return safely? If you do, the Lord hasn't spoken through me." He continued, "All of you people, remember what I've said!"

Ahab Is Killed at Ramoth Gilead

²⁹So the king of Israel went up to Ramoth Gilead. Jehoshaphat, the king of Judah, went there too. ³⁰The king of Israel spoke to Jehoshaphat. He said, "I'll go into battle wearing different clothes. Then people won't recognize me. But you wear your royal robes." So the king of Israel put on different clothes. Then he went into battle.

³¹The king of Aram had given an order to his 32 chariot commanders. He had said, "Fight only against the king of Israel. Don't fight against anyone else." ³²The

chariot commanders saw Jehoshaphat. They thought, "That has to be the king of Israel." So they turned to attack him. But Jehoshaphat cried out. ³³Then the commanders saw he wasn't the king of Israel after all. So they stopped chasing him.

³⁴But someone shot an arrow without taking aim. The arrow hit the king of Israel between the parts of his armor. The king told his chariot driver, "Turn the chariot around. Get me out of this battle. I've been wounded." ³⁵All day long the battle continued. The king kept himself standing up by leaning against the inside of his chariot. He kept his face toward the men of Aram. The blood from his wound ran down onto the floor of the chariot. That evening he died. ³⁶As the sun was setting, a cry spread through the army. "Every man must go to his own town!" they said. "Every man must go to his own land!"

³⁷So the king died. He was brought to Samaria. They buried him there. ³⁸They washed the chariot at a pool in Samaria. It was where the prostitutes took baths. The dogs licked up Ahab's blood. It happened exactly as the LORD had said it would.

³⁹The other events of Ahab's rule are written down. Everything he did is written down. That includes the palace he built and decorated with ivory. It also includes the cities he built up and put high walls around. All these things are written in the official records of the kings of Israel. ⁴⁰Ahab joined the members of his family who had already died. Ahab's son Ahaziah became the next king after him.

Jehoshaphat King of Judah

⁴¹Jehoshaphat began to rule over Judah. It was in the fourth year that Ahab was king of Israel. Jehoshaphat was the son of Asa. ⁴²Jehoshaphat was 35 years old when he became king. He ruled in Jerusalem for 25 years. His mother's name was Azubah. She was the daughter of Shilhi. ⁴³Jehoshaphat

followed all the ways of his father Asa. He didn't wander away from them. He did what was right in the sight of the LORD. But the high places weren't removed. The people continued to offer sacrifices and burn incense at them. ⁴⁴Jehoshaphat was also at peace with the king of Israel.

⁴⁵The other events of Jehoshaphat's rule are written down. The brave things he did in battle and everything else he accomplished are written down. All these things are written in the official records of the kings of Judah. ⁴⁶Jehoshaphat got rid of the rest of the male prostitutes who were at the temples. They had remained in the land even after the rule of his father Asa. ⁴⁷At that time Edom didn't have a king. An area governor was in charge.

⁴⁸Jehoshaphat built many ships that he used to carry goods to be traded. The ships were supposed to go to Ophir for gold. But they never had a chance to sail. They were wrecked at Ezion Geber. ⁴⁹At that time Ahaziah, the son of Ahab, spoke to Jehoshaphat. He said, "Let my men sail with yours." But Jehoshaphat refused.

⁵⁰Jehoshaphat joined the members of his family who had already died. He was buried in the family tomb in the city of King David. Jehoshaphat's son Jehoram became the next king after him.

Ahaziah King of Israel

⁵¹Ahaziah became king of Israel in Samaria. It was in the 17th year that Jehoshaphat was king of Judah. Ahaziah ruled over Israel for two years. He was the son of Ahab. ⁵²Ahaziah did what was evil in the sight of the LORD. He lived the way his father and mother had lived. He lived the way Jeroboam, the son of Nebat, had lived. Jeroboam had caused Israel to sin. ⁵³Ahaziah served and worshiped the god named Baal. He made the LORD, the God of Israel, very angry. That's exactly what Ahaziah's father had done.

2 Kings

As was true for 1 and 2 Samuel, the books of 1 and 2 Kings were in their original form a single book, so 2 Kings picks up immediately where 1 Kings leaves off. One of the first major events is the departure of Elijah, who rode into heaven in a whirlwind without having to die (2:1–18). Second Kings focuses more on his student, Elisha. Clearly, Elisha had the same power of God that Elijah had displayed, demonstrated in restoring a young man to life (4:17–37), healing leprosy (5:1–19), causing a lost ax head to float to the surface of the river (6:1–7), and numerous other miraculous events—28 miracles in all because he requested a double portion of Elijah's spirit.

Other notable high points of 2 Kings are King Joash's much-needed repair of the Temple (12:1–16) and a spiritual revival under King Josiah (22:1–23:30). But for the most part, 2 Kings continues to detail the sorrowful downward spiral of weak and unfit kings. When God's people failed to respond to the messages of the prophets and repent of their sinful behavior, the result was their eventual defeat and exile. The people of Israel (the northern kingdom) were carried off to Assyria (chapter 17). About a century and a half later, the people of Judah (the southern kingdom) were overrun by King Nebuchadnezzar and taken into captivity in Babylon (chapter 25).

WHAT'S IT MEAN, EUGENE?

Holiness—A condition toward which we should all aspire. It means *sacred* or *set apart* to serve and glorify God. The apostle Peter said, "God chose you to be his people. You are royal priests. You are a *holy* nation" (1 Peter 2:9). And in 1 Peter 1:15–16 he also urges us to "be holy in all that you do. It is written, 'Be holy, because I [the Lord] am holy.'"

The LORD Judges Ahaziah

1 After King Ahab died, Moab refused to remain under Israel's control. [2]Ahaziah had fallen through the window of his upstairs room in Samaria. He had hurt himself. So he sent messengers to ask the god named Baal-Zebub for advice. Baal-Zebub was the god of the city of Ekron. Ahaziah said to the messengers, "Go and ask Baal-Zebub whether I will get well again."

[3]But the angel of the LORD spoke to Elijah, who was from Tishbe. The angel said, "Go up to see the messengers of Ahaziah, the king of Samaria. Tell them, 'You are on your way to ask Baal-Zebub for advice. He is the god of Ekron. Are you going there to pray to that god? Do you think there is no God in Israel?' [4]The LORD says to Ahaziah, 'You will never leave the bed you are lying on. You can be sure that you will die!'" So Elijah went to see the messengers.

[5]They returned to the king. He asked them, "Why have you come back?"

[6]"A man met us on our way there," they replied. "He said to us, 'Go back to the king who sent you. Tell him, "The LORD says, 'You are sending messengers to ask Baal-Zebub for advice. He is the god of Ekron. Are you going there to pray to that god? Do you think there is no God in Israel? You will never leave the bed you are lying on. You can be sure that you will die!'"'"

[7]The king asked the messengers, "What kind of man came to see you? Who told you these things?"

[8]They replied, "He was wearing clothes made out of hair. He had a leather belt around his waist."

The king said, "That was Elijah from Tishbe."

[9]Then Ahaziah sent a captain to Elijah. The captain had his group of 50 fighting men with him. Elijah was sitting on top of a hill. The captain went up to him. He said to Elijah, "Man of God, the king says, 'Come down!'"

[10]Elijah answered the captain, "If I'm really a man of God, may fire come down from heaven! May it burn up you and your 50 men!" Then fire came down from heaven. It burned up the captain and his men.

[11]After that happened, the king sent another captain to Elijah. The captain had his 50 men with him. He said to Elijah, "Man of God, the king says, 'Come down at once!'"

[12]Elijah replied, "If I'm really a man of God, may fire come down from heaven! May it burn up you and your 50 men!" Then the fire of God came down from heaven. It burned up the captain and his 50 men.

[13]So the king sent a third captain with his 50 men. The captain went up to Elijah. He fell on his knees in front of him. "Man of God," he begged, "please have respect for my life! Please have respect for the lives of these 50 men! [14]Fire has come down from heaven. It has burned up the first two captains and all their men. But please have respect for my life!"

[15]The angel of the LORD said to Elijah, "Go down along with him. Don't be afraid of him." So Elijah got up and went down to the king with the captain.

[16]Elijah told the king, "The LORD says, 'You have sent messengers to ask Baal-Zebub for advice. He is the god of Ekron. Did you go there to pray to that god for advice? Do you think there is no God in Israel? You will never leave the bed you are lying on. You can be sure that you will die!'" [17]So King Ahaziah died. It happened just as the LORD had said it would. He had spoken that message through Elijah.

Ahaziah didn't have any sons. So Joram, his younger brother, became the next king after him. It was the second year of Jehoram, the king of Judah. Jehoram was the son of Jehoshaphat. [18]All the other events of Ahaziah's rule are written down. Everything he did is written in the official records of the kings of Israel.

Elijah Is Taken Up to Heaven

2 Elijah and Elisha were on their way from Gilgal. The LORD was going to use a strong wind to take Elijah up to heaven. [2]Elijah said to Elisha, "Stay here. The LORD has sent me to Bethel."

But Elisha said, "I won't leave you. And that's just as sure as the LORD and you are alive." So they went down to Bethel.

[3]There was a group of prophets at Bethel. They came out to where Elisha was. They asked him, "Do you know what the LORD is going to do? He's going to take your master away from you today."

"Yes, I know," Elisha replied. "So be quiet."

[4]Then Elijah said to him, "Stay here, Elisha. The LORD has sent me to Jericho."

Elisha replied, "I won't leave you. And that's just as sure as the LORD and you are alive." So they went to Jericho.

[5]There was a group of prophets at Jericho. They went up to where Elisha was. They asked him, "Do you know what the LORD is going to do? He's going to take your master away from you today."

"Yes, I know," Elisha replied. "So be quiet."

[6]Then Elijah said to him, "Stay here. The LORD has sent me to the Jordan River."

Elisha replied, "I won't leave you. And that's just as sure as the LORD and you are alive." So the two of them walked on.

[7]Fifty men from the group of prophets followed them. The men stopped and stood not far away from them. They faced the place where Elijah and Elisha had stopped at the Jordan River. [8]Elijah rolled up his coat. Then he struck the water with it. The water parted to the right and to the left. The two of them went across the river on dry ground.

[9]After they had gone across, Elijah said to Elisha, "Tell me. What can I do for you before I'm taken away from you?"

"Please give me a double share of your spirit," Elisha replied.

[10]"You have asked me for something that's very hard to do," Elijah said. "But suppose you see me when I'm taken away from you. Then you will receive what you have asked for. If you don't see me, you won't receive it."

[11]They kept walking along and talking together. Suddenly there appeared a chariot and horses made of fire. The chariot and horses came between the two men. Then Elijah went up to heaven in a strong wind. [12]Elisha saw it and cried out to Elijah, "My father! You are like a father to me! You, Elijah, are the true chariots and horsemen of Israel!" Elisha didn't see Elijah anymore. Then Elisha took hold of his own garment and tore it in two.

[13]He picked up the coat that had fallen from Elijah. He went back and stood on the bank of the Jordan River. [14]Then he struck the water with Elijah's coat. "Where is the power of the LORD?" he asked. "Where is the power of the God of Elijah?" When Elisha struck the water, it parted to the right and to the left. He went across the river.

[15]The group of prophets from Jericho were watching. They said, "The spirit of Elijah has been given to Elisha." They went over to Elisha. They bowed down to him with their faces toward the ground. [16]"Look," they said. "We have 50 capable men. Let them go and look for your master. Perhaps the Spirit of the LORD has lifted him up. Maybe he has put him down on a mountain or in a valley."

"No," Elisha replied. "Don't send them."

[17]But they kept asking until he felt he couldn't say no. So he said, "Send them." And they sent 50 men. They looked for Elijah for three days. But they didn't find him. [18]So they returned to Elisha. He was staying in Jericho. Elisha said to them, "Didn't I tell you not to go?"

Elisha Makes Jericho's Water Pure

[19]The people of Jericho said to Elisha, "Look. This town has a good location. You can see that for yourself. But the spring of water here is bad. So the land doesn't produce anything."

[20]"Bring me a new bowl," Elisha said. "Put some salt in it." So they brought it to him.

[21]Then he went out to the spring. He threw the salt into it. He told the people, "The LORD says, 'I have made this water pure. It will never cause death again. It will never keep the land from producing crops again.'" [22]The water has stayed pure to this day. That's what Elisha had said would happen.

Some Boys Make Fun of Elisha

[23]Elisha left Jericho and went up to Bethel. He was walking along the road. Some boys came out of the town. They made fun of him. "Get out of here, baldy!" they said. "Get out of here! You don't even have any hair on your head!" [24]He turned around and looked at them. And he asked for bad things to happen to them. He did it in the name of the LORD. Then two bears came out of the woods. They attacked 42 of the boys. [25]Elisha went on to Mount Carmel. From there he returned to Samaria.

Moab's King Refuses to Obey Israel's King

[3] Joram became king of Israel in Samaria. It was in the 18th year that Jehoshaphat was king of Judah. Joram ruled for 12 years. He was the son of Ahab. [2]Joram did what

was evil in the sight of the LORD. But he wasn't as bad as his father and mother had been. Joram's father had made a sacred stone used to worship the god named Baal. Joram got rid of it. ³But he kept on committing the sins of Jeroboam, the son of Nebat. Jeroboam had also caused Israel to commit those same sins. Joram didn't turn away from them.

⁴Mesha raised sheep. He was king of Moab. He had to pay the king of Israel 100,000 lambs a year. He also had to pay him with the wool of 100,000 rams a year. ⁵After Ahab died, Moab's king refused to obey the next king of Israel. ⁶So at that time King Joram started out from Samaria. He gathered together all of Israel's troops. ⁷He also sent a message to Jehoshaphat, the king of Judah. Joram said, "The king of Moab is refusing to obey me. Will you go with me to fight against Moab?"

"Yes. I'll go with you," Jehoshaphat replied. "My men will go with you. My horses will also go with you."

⁸"What road should we take to attack Moab?" Joram asked.

"The one that goes through the Desert of Edom," Jehoshaphat answered.

⁹So the king of Israel marched out. The king of Judah and the king of Edom went with him. Their armies marched around the southern end of the Dead Sea. After seven days they ran out of water. There wasn't any water for the men or their animals.

¹⁰"What should we do now?" exclaimed the king of Israel. "The LORD has called us three kings together. Did he do it only to hand us over to Moab?"

¹¹But Jehoshaphat asked, "Isn't there a prophet of the LORD here? Can't we ask the LORD for advice through him?"

An officer of the king of Israel answered, "Elisha is here. He's the son of Shaphat. Elisha used to serve Elijah."

¹²Jehoshaphat said, "The LORD speaks through him." So the king of Israel went down to see Elisha. Jehoshaphat and the king of Edom also went there.

¹³Elisha said to the king of Israel, "Why do you want to come to me? Go to your father's prophets. Go to your mother's prophets."

"No," the king of Israel answered. "The LORD called us three kings together. He did it to hand us over to Moab."

Jason's Jargon

2 KINGS 3

Another expedition! Find a *sling* in this chapter. A sling was a deadly military weapon that allowed a person to heave a round stone farther, faster, and more accurately than throwing it.

¹⁴Elisha said, "I serve the LORD who rules over all. You can be sure that he lives. And you can be just as sure that I have respect for Jehoshaphat, the king of Judah. If I didn't, I wouldn't pay any attention to you. ¹⁵But now bring me someone who plays the harp."

While that person was playing the harp, the LORD's power came on Elisha. ¹⁶Elisha announced, "The LORD says, 'I will fill this valley with pools of water.' ¹⁷This will happen because the LORD says, 'You will not see wind or rain. But this valley will be filled with water. Then you, your cattle and your other animals will have water to drink.' ¹⁸This is an easy thing for the LORD to do. He will also hand Moab over to you. ¹⁹You will destroy every city that has high walls around it. You will destroy every major town. You will cut down every good tree. You will stop up all the springs of water. And you will cover every good field with stones."

²⁰The next day, the time came to offer the morning sacrifice. And then it happened! Water was flowing from the direction of Edom! In fact, the land was filled with water! ²¹Now all the people of Moab had heard that the kings had come to fight against them. So the king of Moab sent for all Moab's fighting men. It didn't matter whether they were young or old. He sent for everyone who could carry a weapon. All of them were stationed at the border. ²²They got up early in the morning. The sun was already shining on the water. Across the way, the water looked red to the men of Moab. It looked like blood. ²³"That's blood!" they said. "Those kings must have fought and killed each other. Let's go, Moab! Let's take everything that has any value."

²⁴So the men of Moab went to the camp of Israel. Just as they arrived there, the men of Israel got ready to fight. They fought against the men of Moab until those men ran away. The men of Israel marched into the land and attacked it. They killed the people of Moab. ²⁵They destroyed the towns. Each man threw a large stone on every good field. They did that until the fields were covered. They stopped up all the springs of water. And they cut down every good tree. The only town left with any stones in place was Kir Hareseth. But some of the Israelites armed with slings surrounded it. Then they attacked it.

²⁶The king of Moab saw that the battle had gone against him. So he took with him 700 men who had swords. They tried to break through the battle lines to the king of Edom. But they couldn't do it. ²⁷Then the king of Moab took his oldest son. He was the son who would become the next king of Moab. But the king offered his son as a sacrifice on the city wall. That shocked and terrified the men of Israel. So they pulled back and returned to their own land.

Elisha Provides Olive Oil for a Widow

4 The wife of a man from the group of the prophets cried out to Elisha. She said, "My husband is dead. You know how much respect he had for the LORD. But he owed money to someone. And now that person is coming to take my two boys away. They will become his slaves."

²Elisha replied to her, "How can I help you? Tell me. What do you have in your house?"

"I don't have anything there at all," she said. "All I have is a small jar of olive oil."

³Elisha said, "Go around to all your neighbors. Ask them for empty jars. Get as many as you can. ⁴Then go inside your house. Shut the door behind you and your sons. Pour oil into all the jars. As each jar is filled, put it over to one side."

⁵The woman left him. Then she shut the door behind her and her sons. They brought the jars to her. And she kept pouring. ⁶When all the jars were full, she spoke to one of her sons. She said, "Bring me another jar."

But he replied, "There aren't any more left." Then the oil stopped flowing.

⁷She went and told the man of God about it. He said, "Go and sell the oil. Pay

2 Kgs. 4:1–7 I love olive oil with breadsticks, garlic, and ice cream. (Yes, really.) High-quality olive oil is still produced in Israel and neighboring countries like Lebanon and Jordan. The olive leaf is now a part of Israel's national symbol.

what you owe. You and your sons can live on what is left."

The Son of a Woman From Shunem Is Brought Back to Life

⁸One day Elisha went to the town of Shunem. A rich woman lived there. She begged him to stay and have a meal. So every time he came by, he stopped there to eat. ⁹The woman said to her husband, "That man often comes by here. I know that he is a holy man of God. ¹⁰Let's make a small room for him on the roof. We'll put a bed and a table in it. We'll also put a chair and a lamp in it. Then he can stay there when he comes to visit us."

¹¹One day Elisha came. He went up to his room and lay down there. ¹²He said to his servant Gehazi, "Go and get the woman from Shunem." So he did. She stood in front of Elisha. ¹³He said to Gehazi, "Tell her, 'You have gone to a lot of trouble for us. Now what can we do for you? Can we speak to the king for you? Or can we speak to the commander of the army for you?' "

She replied, "I live among my own people. I have everything I need here."

¹⁴After she left, Elisha asked Gehazi, "What can we do for her?"

Gehazi said, "She doesn't have a son. And her husband is old."

¹⁵Then Elisha said, "Bring her here again." So he did. She stood in the doorway. ¹⁶"You will hold a son in your arms," Elisha said. "It will be about this time next year."

"No, my master!" she objected. "You are a man of God. So please don't lie to me!"

[17]But the woman became pregnant. She had a baby boy. It happened the next year about that same time. That's exactly what Elisha had told her would happen.

[18]The child grew. One day he went out to get his father. His father was with the people who were gathering the crops. [19]The boy said to his father, "My head hurts! It really hurts!"

His father told a servant, "Carry him to his mother." [20]The servant lifted up the boy. He carried him to his mother. The boy sat on her lap until noon. Then he died. [21]She went up to the room on the roof. There she laid him on the bed of the man of God. Then she shut the door and went out.

[22]She sent for her husband. She said, "Please send me one of the servants and a donkey. Then I can go quickly to the man of God and return."

[23]"Why do you want to go to him today?" he asked. "It isn't the time for the New Moon feast. It isn't the Sabbath day."

"Don't let that bother you," she said.

[24]She put a saddle on her donkey. She said to her servant, "Let's go. Don't slow down for me unless I tell you to." [25]So she started out. She came to Mount Carmel. That's where the man of God was.

When she was still a long way off, he saw her coming. He said to his servant Gehazi, "Look! There's the woman from Shunem! [26]Run out there to meet her. Ask her, 'Are you all right? Is your husband all right? Is your child all right?'"

"Everything is all right," she said.

[27]She came to the man of God at the mountain. Then she took hold of his feet. Gehazi came over to push her away. But the man of God said, "Leave her alone! She is suffering terribly. But the LORD hasn't told me the reason for it. He has hidden it from me."

[28]"My master, did I ask you for a son?" she said. "Didn't I tell you, 'Don't make me hope for something that won't happen'?"

[29]Elisha said to Gehazi, "Tuck your coat into your belt. Take my walking stick and run to Shunem. Don't say hello to anyone you see. If anyone says hello to you, don't answer. Lay my walking stick on the boy's face."

[30]But the child's mother said, "I won't leave you. And that's just as sure as the LORD and you are alive." So Elisha got up and followed her.

[31]Gehazi went on ahead. He laid Elisha's walking stick on the boy's face. But there wasn't any sound. The boy didn't move at all. So Gehazi went back to Elisha. He told him, "The boy hasn't awakened."

[32]Elisha arrived at the house. The boy was dead. He was lying on Elisha's bed. [33]Elisha went into the room. He shut the door. He was alone with the boy. He prayed to the LORD. [34]Then Elisha got on the bed. He lay down on the boy. His mouth touched the boy's mouth. His eyes touched the boy's eyes. And his hands touched the boy's hands. As Elisha lay on the boy, the boy's body grew warm. [35]Elisha turned away. He walked back and forth in the room. Then he got on the bed again. He lay down on the boy once more. The boy sneezed seven times. After that, he opened his eyes.

[36]Elisha sent for Gehazi. He said to him, "Go and get the woman from Shunem." So he did. When she came, Elisha said, "Take your son." [37]She came in and fell at Elisha's feet. She bowed down with her face toward the ground. Then she took her son and went out.

Deadly Food in a Pot

[38]Elisha returned to Gilgal. There wasn't enough food to eat in that area. The group of the prophets was meeting with Elisha. So he said to his servant, "Put the large pot over the fire. Cook some stew for these prophets."

[39]One of them went out into the fields to gather herbs. He found a wild vine and picked some of its gourds. He picked as many as he could fit in his coat. Then he cut them up and put them into the pot of stew. But no one knew what they were. [40]The stew was poured out for the men. They began to eat it. But then they cried out, "Man of God, the food in that pot will kill us!" They couldn't eat it.

[41]Elisha said, "Get some flour." He put it in the pot. He said, "Serve it to the men to eat." Then there wasn't anything in the pot that could harm them.

Elisha Feeds 100 People

[42]A man came from Baal Shalishah. He brought the man of God 20 loaves of barley bread. They had been baked from the

first grain that had ripened. The man also brought some heads of new grain. "Give this food to the people to eat," Elisha said.

[43] "How can I put this in front of 100 men?" his servant asked.

But Elisha answered, "Give it to the people to eat. Do it because the LORD says, 'They will eat and have some left over.'" [44] Then the servant put the food in front of them. They ate it and had some left over. It happened just as the LORD had said it would.

Naaman Is Healed of a Skin Disease

5 Naaman was army commander of the king of Aram. He was very important to his master and was highly respected. That's because the LORD had helped him win the battle over Aram's enemies. He was a brave soldier. But he had a skin disease.

[2] Groups of soldiers from Aram had marched out. They had captured a young girl from Israel. She became a servant of Naaman's wife. [3] The young girl spoke to the woman she was serving. She said, "I wish my master would go and see the prophet who is in Samaria. He would heal my master of his skin disease."

[4] Naaman went to see his own master. He told him what the girl from Israel had said. [5] "I think you should go," the king of Aram replied. "I'll give you a letter to take to the king of Israel." So Naaman left. He took 750 pounds of silver with him. He also took 150 pounds of gold. And he took ten sets of clothes. [6] He carried the letter to the king of Israel. It said, "I'm sending my servant

Naaman to you with this letter. I want you to heal him of his skin disease."

[7] The king of Israel read the letter. As soon as he did, he tore his royal robes. He said, "Am I God? Can I kill people and bring them back to life? Why does this fellow send someone to me to be healed of his skin disease? He must be trying to pick a fight with me!"

[8] Elisha, the man of God, heard that the king of Israel had torn his robes. So he sent the king a message. Elisha said, "Why have you torn your robes? Tell the man to come to me. Then he will know there is a prophet in Israel." [9] So Naaman went to see Elisha. He took his horses and chariots with him. He stopped at the door of Elisha's house. [10] Elisha sent a messenger out to him. The messenger said, "Go! Wash yourself in the Jordan River seven times. Then your skin will be healed. You will be pure and 'clean' again."

[11] But Naaman went away angry. He said, "I was sure Elisha would come out to me. I thought he would stand there and pray to the LORD his God. I thought he would wave his hand over my skin. Then I would

WHIT'S WISDOM

2 Kings 5

You usually hear about children learning from grown-ups and kids getting advice from grown-ups. There are many times that kids stop by Whit's End to ask what I think about a problem or a question. But the Bible records times where it was the other way around: Adults got wisdom from kids!

Second Kings 5 is one of those places. A young girl who was working as a servant knew that Naaman should go to the prophet Elisha to be healed. Naaman took the young girl's advice and he was eventually healed!

It reminds me of a verse much later in the Bible in 1 Timothy 4:12: "Don't let anyone look down on you.... Set an example for the believers in what you say and in how you live."

It's easy to forget that others are looking at you and learning from you even when you're a kid. But God uses kids too! If you need another example, check out 1 Samuel 3. There are plenty of times that the kids in Odyssey give me great advice too.

BiBLe ADVeNTUReS

Whit told the story of Naaman and his quest to be healed of leprosy in "B-TV: Obedience" (A#39).

be healed. [12]And what about the Abana and Pharpar rivers of Damascus? Aren't they better than all the rivers of Israel? Couldn't I wash in the rivers of Damascus and be made pure and 'clean'?" So he turned and went away. He was very angry.

[13]Naaman's servants went over to him. They said, "You are like a father to us. What if Elisha the prophet had told you to do some great thing? Wouldn't you have done it? But he only said, 'Wash yourself. Then you will be pure and "clean." ' You should be even more willing to do that!" [14]So Naaman went down to the Jordan River. He dipped himself in it seven times. He did exactly what the man of God had told him to do. Then his skin was made pure again. It became "clean" like the skin of a young boy.

[15]Naaman and all his attendants went back to the man of God. Naaman stood in front of Elisha. Naaman said, "Now I know that there is no God anywhere in the whole world except in Israel. So please accept a gift from me."

[16]The prophet answered, "I serve the LORD. You can be sure that he lives. And you can be just as sure that I won't accept a gift from you." Even though Naaman begged him to take it, Elisha wouldn't.

[17]"I can see that you won't accept a gift from me," said Naaman. "But please let me have some soil from your land. Give me as much as a pair of mules can carry. Here's why I want it. I won't ever bring burnt offerings and sacrifices to any other god again. I'll bring them only to the LORD. I'll worship him on his own soil. [18]But there is one thing I hope the LORD will forgive me for. From time to time my master will enter the temple to bow down to his god Rimmon. When he does, he'll lean on my arm. Then I'll have to bow down there also. I hope the LORD will forgive me for that."

[19]"Go in peace," Elisha said.

Naaman started out on his way. [20]Gehazi was the servant of Elisha, the man of God. Gehazi said to himself, "My master was too easy on Naaman from Aram. He should have accepted the gift Naaman brought. I'm going to run after him. I'm going to get something from him. And that's just as sure as the LORD is alive."

[21]Gehazi hurried after Naaman. Naaman saw him running toward him. So he got down from the chariot to greet him. "Is everything all right?" he asked.

[22]"Everything is all right," Gehazi answered. "My master sent me to say, 'Two young men from the group of the prophets have just come to me. They've come from the hill country of Ephraim. Please give them 75 pounds of silver and two sets of clothes.' "

[23]"I wish you would take twice as much silver," said Naaman. He begged Gehazi to accept it. Then Naaman tied up 150 pounds of silver in two bags. He also gave Gehazi two sets of clothes. He gave all of it to two of his own servants. They carried it ahead of Gehazi. [24]Gehazi came to the hill where Elisha lived. Then the servants handed the things over to Gehazi. He put them away in Elisha's house. He sent the men away, and they left. [25]Then he went back inside the house. He stood in front of his master Elisha.

"Gehazi, where have you been?" Elisha asked.

"I didn't go anywhere," Gehazi answered.

[26]But Elisha said to him, "Didn't my spirit go with you? I know that the man got down from his chariot to greet you. Is this the time for you to accept money or clothes? Is it the time to take olive groves, vineyards, flocks or herds? Is it the time to accept male and female slaves? [27]You and your children after you will have Naaman's skin disease forever." Then Gehazi left Elisha. And he had Naaman's skin disease. His skin had become as white as snow.

An Ax Blade Floats

6 The group of the prophets said to Elisha, "Look. The place where we meet with you is too small for us. [2]We would like to go to the Jordan River. Each of us can get some wood there. We want to build a place there for us to meet."

Elisha said, "Go."

[3]Then one of them said, "Won't you please come with us?"

"I will," Elisha replied. [4]And he went with them.

They went to the Jordan River. There they began to cut down trees. [5]One of them was cutting down a tree. The iron blade of his ax fell into the water. "Oh no, master!" he cried out. "This ax was borrowed!"

⁶The man of God asked, "Where did the blade fall?" He showed Elisha the place. Then Elisha cut a stick and threw it there. That made the iron blade float. ⁷"Take it out of the water," he said. So the man reached out and took it.

Elisha Makes the Soldiers of Aram Blind

⁸The king of Aram was at war with Israel. He talked things over with his officers. Then he said, "I'm going to set up my camp in a certain place."

⁹Elisha, the man of God, sent a message to the king of Israel. Elisha said, "Try to stay away from that place. Aram's army is going to be down there." ¹⁰The king of Israel checked on the place the man of God had told him about. Time after time Elisha warned the king. So the king was on guard in those places.

¹¹All of that made the king of Aram very angry. He sent for his officers. He said to them, "Tell me! Which of us is on the side of the king of Israel?"

¹²"You are my king and master," said one of his officers. "None of us is on Israel's side. But Elisha is a prophet in Israel. He tells the king of Israel even the words you speak in your own bedroom."

WOOTON'S FUN FACTS
2 Kgs. 6:6

The oldest iron artifacts that have been found were made from meteor deposits. Your body needs iron to survive. You know what has iron in it? Black licorice! So eat some today to stay healthy!

¹³"Go and find out where he is," the king ordered. "Then I can send my men and capture him." The report came back. The officers said, "He's in Dothan." ¹⁴Then the king sent horses and chariots and a strong army there. They went at night and surrounded the city.

¹⁵The servant of the man of God got up the next morning. He went out early. He saw that an army with horses and chariots had surrounded the city. "Oh no, my master!" the servant said. "What can we do?"

¹⁶"Don't be afraid," the prophet answered. "Those who are with us are more than those who are with them."

¹⁷Elisha prayed, "Lord, open my servant's eyes so that he can see." Then the Lord opened his eyes. Elisha's servant looked up and saw the hills. He saw that Elisha was surrounded by horses and chariots made of fire.

¹⁸Aram's army came down toward Elisha. Then he prayed to the Lord, "Make these soldiers blind." So the Lord made them blind, just as Elisha had prayed.

¹⁹Elisha told them, "This isn't the right road. This isn't the right city. Follow me. I'll lead you to the man you are looking for." He led them to Samaria.

²⁰They entered the city. Then Elisha said, "Lord, open the eyes of these men. Help them see again." Then the Lord opened their eyes. They looked around. And there they were, inside Samaria!

²¹The king of Israel saw them. So he asked Elisha, "Should I kill them? I need your advice. You are like a father to me. Should I kill them?"

²²"Don't kill them," he answered. "Would you kill people you have captured with your own sword or bow? Put some food and water in front of them. Then they can eat and drink. They can go back to their master."

²³So the king of Israel prepared a great feast for them. After they had finished eating and drinking, he sent them away. They returned to their master. So the groups of fighting men from Aram stopped attacking Israel's territory.

Aram's Army Attacks Samaria and People Go Hungry

²⁴Some time later, Ben-Hadad gathered his entire army together. Ben-Hadad was the king of Aram. His army marched

In 2 Kings 6, the prophet Elisha kept telling Israel's king where the enemy was going to attack. As you might guess, the enemy wasn't too happy about that, so one night they sent an army to encircle the city where Elisha was. The next morning, Elisha's servant nervously told him that they were completely surrounded.

However, Elisha wasn't worried, saying, "We've got them outnumbered." What? Had the prophet lost his marbles?

Suddenly, Elisha began praying. When the servant looked outside the city again, glowing horses and chariots straight from heaven surrounded the enemy's army, covering every hill as far as the eye could see. God gave Elisha and his servant a peek at what they were hoping for—God's deliverance.

That's what hope is about—confidently trusting that He will come through. It's not like saying, "I hope it isn't going to rain tomorrow," or "I hope Mom made cookies." It's counting on something you know will happen.

Hope doesn't always come easily. God's Word teaches us to praise God even in the hard times because He's using challenges to help us grow in confidence and hope.

Ask your mom if you can help her make a favorite recipe that takes a long time to cook, like a slow-cooker stew or pot roast. Maybe you can have it for dinner. As you smell the food, you can be confident that supper's coming. That assurance will fill you with hope and anticipation as you wait patiently for it.

up and surrounded Samaria. Then they attacked it. ²⁵There wasn't enough food anywhere in the city. It was surrounded for so long that people had to weigh out two pounds of silver for a donkey's head. They had to weigh out two ounces of silver for half a pint of seed pods.

²⁶One day the king of Israel was walking on top of the city wall. A woman cried out to him, "You are my king and master. Please help me!"

²⁷The king replied, "If the LORD doesn't help you, where can I get help for you? From the threshing floor? From the winepress?" ²⁸He continued, "What's wrong?"

She answered, "A woman said to me, 'Give up your son. Then we can eat him today. Tomorrow we'll eat my son.' ²⁹So we cooked my son. Then we ate him. The next day I said to her, 'Give up your son. Then we can eat him.' But she had hidden him."

³⁰When the king heard the woman's words, he tore his royal robes. As he walked along the wall, the people looked up at him.

They saw that under his robes he was wearing the rough clothing people wear when they're sad. ³¹He said, "I'll cut the head of Shaphat's son Elisha off his shoulders today. If I don't, may God punish me greatly!"

³²Elisha was sitting in his house. The elders were sitting there with him. The king went to see Elisha. He sent a messenger on ahead of him. Before the messenger arrived, Elisha spoke to the elders. He said, "That murderer is sending someone here to cut off my head. Can't you see that? When the messenger comes, close the door. Hold it shut against him. Can't you hear his master's footsteps right behind him?" ³³Elisha was still talking to the elders when the messenger came down to him.

The king also arrived. He said, "The LORD has sent this horrible trouble on us. Why should I wait any longer for him to help us?"

7 Elisha replied, "Listen to a message from the LORD. He says, 'About this time tomorrow, flour won't cost very much. Even

12 pounds of the finest flour will cost less than half of an ounce of silver. You will also be able to buy 20 pounds of barley for the same price. That's all you will have to pay for those things at the gate of Samaria.' "

[2]The king was leaning on an officer's arm. The officer spoke to the man of God. The officer said, "Suppose the LORD opens the sky and pours down food on us. Even if he does, could what you are saying really happen?"

"You will see it with your own eyes," answered Elisha. "But you won't eat any of it!"

The Attack on Samaria Ends

[3]There were four men who had a skin disease. They were at the entrance of the gate of Samaria. They said to one another, "Why should we stay here until we die? [4]Suppose we say, 'We'll go into the city.' There isn't any food there, and we'll die. But if we stay here, we'll die anyway. So let's go over to Aram's army camp. Let's give ourselves up. If they spare us, we'll live. If they kill us, we'll die."

[5]At sunset they got up and went to Aram's army camp. They arrived at the edge of it. But no one was there. [6]The Lord had caused the soldiers of Aram to hear a noise. It sounded like chariots and horses and a huge army. So the soldiers said to one another, "Listen! The king of Israel has hired the Hittite and Egyptian kings. He has paid them to attack us!" [7]So the soldiers of Aram had run away at sunset. They had left their tents and horses and donkeys behind. They had left the camp just as it was. And they had run for their lives.

[8]The men who had a skin disease arrived at the edge of the camp. They entered one of the tents. They ate and drank. Then they took silver, gold and clothes. They went off and hid them. They returned and entered another tent. They took some things from it and hid them also.

[9]But then they said to one another, "What we're doing isn't right. This is a day of good news. And we're keeping it to ourselves. If we wait until sunrise, we'll be punished. Let's go at once. Let's report this to the royal palace."

[10]So they went. They called out to the people who were guarding the city gates. They told them, "We went into Aram's army camp. No one was there. We didn't hear anyone. The horses and donkeys were still tied up. The tents were left just as they were." [11]The people who guarded the gates shouted the news. It was reported inside the palace.

[12]The king of Israel got up in the night. He spoke to his officers. He said, "I'll tell you what the men of Aram have done to us. They know we are very hungry. So they have left the camp to hide in the countryside. They are thinking, 'We are sure they'll come out. Then we'll take them alive. And we'll get into the city.' "

[13]One of the king's officers said, "A few horses are still left in the city. Have some men get five of them. Those men won't be any worse off than all the other Israelites who are left here. In fact, all of us will soon be dead anyway. So let's send the men to find out what happened."

[14]The men chose two chariots and their horses. The king sent them out to look for Aram's army. He commanded the drivers, "Go and find out what has happened." [15]They followed the trail of Aram's soldiers all the way to the Jordan River. They found clothes and supplies all along the road. The soldiers had thrown them down when they ran away. So the men who were sent out returned. They reported to the king what they had seen. [16]Then the people went out of the city. They took everything of value from Aram's army camp. So 12 pounds of the finest flour sold for less than half of an ounce of silver. And 20 pounds of barley sold for the same price. That's exactly what the LORD had said would happen.

[17]The king had put an officer in charge of the city gate. He was the officer on whose arm the king leaned. On their way out of the city, the people knocked the officer down. In the entrance of the gate he was crushed as they walked on top of him. And so he died. That's exactly what the man of God had said would happen. He had said it when the king came down to his house. [18]What Elisha, the man of God, had told the king came true. Elisha had said, "About this time tomorrow, flour won't cost very much. Even 12 pounds of the finest flour will cost less than half of an ounce of silver. You will also be able to buy 20 pounds of barley for the same price. That's all you will have to pay for those things at the gate of Samaria."

[19]The officer had spoken to the man of God. The officer had said, "Suppose the LORD opens the sky and pours down food on us. Even if he does, could what you are saying really happen?" The man of God had replied, "You will see it with your own eyes. But you won't eat any of it!" [20]And that's exactly what happened to the officer. On their way out of the city, the people knocked him down. In the entrance of the gate he was crushed as they walked on top of him. And so he died.

The Woman From Shunem Gets Her Land Back

8 Elisha had brought a woman's son back to life. He had said to her, "Go away with your family. Stay for a while anywhere you can. The LORD has decided that there won't be enough food in the land. That will be true for seven years." [2]The woman did just as the man of God told her to. She and her family went away. They stayed in the land of the Philistines for seven years.

[3]The seven years passed. Then she came back from the land of the Philistines. She went to the king of Israel. She wanted to ask him to get her house and land back. [4]The king was talking to Gehazi. Gehazi was the servant of the man of God. The king had said, "Tell me about all the great things Elisha has done." [5]Gehazi was telling the king how Elisha had brought a dead boy back to life. Just then the woman came to ask the king to get her house and land back. She was the woman whose son Elisha had brought back to life.

Gehazi said, "King Joram, this is the woman I've been telling you about. And this is her son. He's the one Elisha brought back to life." [6]The king asked the woman about her house and land. And she told him.

Then he appointed an official to look into her case. The king told him, "Give her back everything that belonged to her. That includes all the money that was earned from her land. It was earned from the day she left the country until now."

Hazael Murders Ben-Hadad

[7]Elisha went to Damascus. Ben-Hadad was sick. He was king of Aram. The king was told, "The man of God has come all the way up here." [8]Then the king said to Hazael,

"Take a gift with you. Go and see the man of God. Ask him for the LORD's advice. Ask him whether I will get well again."

[9]Hazael went to see Elisha. Hazael took 40 camels with him as a gift. The camels were loaded with all the finest goods of Damascus. Hazael went into Elisha's house and stood in front of him. Hazael said, "Ben-Hadad has sent me. He is the king of Aram. He asks, 'Will I get well again?'"

[10]Elisha answered, "Go and tell him, 'Yes. You will get well again.' But the LORD has shown me that he will in fact die." [11]Elisha stared at him without looking away. He did it until Hazael felt uncomfortable. Then the man of God began to weep.

[12]"Why are you weeping?" asked Hazael.

"Because I know how much harm you will do to the people of Israel," Elisha answered. "You will set fire to their cities that have high walls around them. You will kill their young men with your swords. You will smash their little children on the ground. You will rip open their pregnant women."

[13]Hazael said, "How could I possibly do a thing like that? I'm nothing but a dog. I don't have that kind of power."

"You will become king of Aram," Elisha answered. "That's what the LORD has shown me."

[14]Then Hazael left Elisha and returned to his master. Ben-Hadad asked, "What did Elisha say to you?" Hazael replied, "He told me you would get well again." [15]But the next day Hazael got a thick cloth. He soaked it in water. He spread it over the king's face. He held it there until the king died. Then Hazael became the next king after him.

Jehoram King of Judah

[16]Jehoram began to rule as king over Judah. It was in the fifth year that Joram was king of Israel. Joram was the son of Ahab. Jehoram was the son of Jehoshaphat. [17]Jehoram was 32 years old when he became king. He ruled in Jerusalem for eight years. [18]He followed the ways of the kings of Israel, just as the royal family of Ahab had done. In fact, he married a daughter of Ahab. Jehoram did what was evil in the sight of the LORD. [19]But the LORD didn't want to destroy Judah. That's because the LORD had made a covenant with his servant David. The LORD had promised to keep the lamp

of David's kingdom burning brightly. The LORD had promised that for him and his children after him forever.

²⁰When Jehoram was king over Judah, Edom refused to remain under Judah's control. Edom set up their own king. ²¹So Jehoram went to Zair. He took all his chariots with him. The men of Edom surrounded him and his chariot commanders. He got up at night and fought his way out. But his army ran back home. ²²To this day Edom has refused to remain under Judah's control. When Jehoram was Judah's king, Libnah also refused to remain under the control of Judah.

²³The other events of Jehoram's rule are written down. Everything he did is written in the official records of the kings of Judah. ²⁴Jehoram joined the members of his family who had already died. He was buried in the family tomb in the City of David. Jehoram's son Ahaziah became the next king after him.

Ahaziah King of Judah

²⁵Ahaziah began to rule as king over Judah. It was in the 12th year that Joram was king of Israel. Joram was the son of Ahab. Ahaziah was the son of Jehoram. ²⁶Ahaziah was 22 years old when he became king. He ruled in Jerusalem for one year. His mother's name was Athaliah. She was a granddaughter of Omri. Omri had been the king of Israel. ²⁷Ahaziah followed the ways of the royal family of Ahab. Ahaziah did what was evil in the sight of the LORD, just as the family of Ahab had done. That's because he had married into Ahab's family.

²⁸Ahaziah joined forces with Joram. They went to war against Hazael at Ramoth Gilead. Joram was the son of Ahab. Hazael was king of Aram. The soldiers of Aram wounded King Joram. ²⁹So he returned to Jezreel to give his wounds time to heal. The soldiers of Aram had wounded him at Ramoth in his battle against Hazael, the king of Aram.

Ahaziah, the son of Jehoram, went down to Jezreel. He went there to see Joram. That's because Joram had been wounded. Ahaziah was king of Judah. Joram was the son of Ahab.

Jehu Is Anointed as King of Israel

9 Elisha the prophet sent for a man from the group of the prophets. Elisha said to him, "Tuck your coat into your belt. Take

this bottle of olive oil with you. Go to Ramoth Gilead. ²When you get there, look for Jehu. He's the son of Jehoshaphat, the son of Nimshi. Go to Jehu. Get him away from his companions. Take him into an inside room. ³Then get the bottle. Pour the oil on his head. Announce to him, 'The LORD says, "I anoint you as king over Israel."' After that, open the door and run away. Do it quickly!"

⁴So the young prophet went to Ramoth Gilead. ⁵When he arrived, he found the army officers sitting together. "Commander, I have a message for you," he said.

"For which one of us?" asked Jehu.

"For you, commander," he replied.

⁶Jehu got up and went into the house. Then the prophet poured the oil on Jehu's head. He announced, "The LORD is the God of Israel. He says, 'I am anointing you as king over the LORD's people Israel. ⁷You must destroy the royal house of your master Ahab. I will pay them back for spilling the blood of my servants the prophets. I will also pay them back for the blood of all the LORD's servants that Jezebel spilled. ⁸The whole house of Ahab will die out. I will destroy every male in Israel who is related to Ahab. It does not matter whether they are slaves or free. ⁹I will make Ahab's royal house like the house of Jeroboam, the son of Nebat. I will make it like the house of Baasha, the son of Ahijah. ¹⁰Dogs will eat up Jezebel on a piece of land at Jezreel. No one will bury her.'" Then the prophet opened the door and ran away.

¹¹Jehu went out to where the other officers were. One of them asked him, "Is everything all right? Why did that crazy man come to you?"

"You know the man. You know the kinds of things he says," Jehu replied.

¹²"That's not true!" they said. "Tell us."

Jehu said, "Here is what he told me. He announced, 'The LORD says, "I am anointing you as king over Israel."'"

¹³The officers quickly grabbed their coats. They spread them out under Jehu on the bare steps of the house. Then they blew a trumpet. They shouted, "Jehu is king!"

Jehu Kills Joram and Ahaziah

¹⁴Jehu was the son of Jehoshaphat, the son of Nimshi. Jehu made plans against Joram. During that time Joram and Israel's whole army had been guarding Ramoth

Gilead. They had been guarding it against Hazael, the king of Aram. [15]But King Joram had returned to Jezreel. He had gone there to give his wounds time to heal. The soldiers of Aram had wounded him in his battle against Hazael, the king of Aram. Jehu said to his men, "Do you want to make me king? If you do, don't let anyone sneak out of the city. Don't let them go and tell the news in Jezreel." [16]Then Jehu got into his chariot. He rode off to Jezreel. Joram was resting there. And Ahaziah, the king of Judah, had gone down to see him.

[17]A lookout was standing on the roof of the tower in Jezreel. He saw Jehu's troops approaching. So he called out, "I see some troops coming."

"Get a horseman," Joram ordered. "Send him to ride out to them. Have him ask, 'Are you coming in peace?'"

[18]The horseman rode out to where Jehu was. He said, "The king asks, 'Are you coming in peace?'"

"What do you know about peace?" Jehu answered. "Get in line behind me."

The lookout reported, "The messenger has reached them. But he isn't coming back."

[19]So the king sent out a second horseman. When he came to them, he said, "The king asks, 'Are you coming in peace?'"

Jehu replied, "What do you know about peace? Get in line behind me."

[20]The lookout reported, "The second messenger has reached them. But he isn't coming back either. The one driving the chariot drives like Jehu, the son of Nimshi. He's driving like a crazy person."

[21]"Get my chariot ready," King Joram ordered. When it was ready, he rode out. Ahaziah, the king of Judah, rode out with him. Each of them was in his own chariot. They both went to meet Jehu. They met him at the piece of land that had belonged to Naboth from Jezreel. [22]When Joram saw Jehu he asked, "Have you come here in peace, Jehu?"

"Your mother Jezebel worships statues of gods," Jehu replied. "She also worships evil powers. The evil things she does have spread everywhere. As long as all of that goes on, how can there be peace?"

[23]Joram turned around and tried to get away. He called out, "It's treason, Ahaziah!"

[24]Then Jehu shot an arrow at Joram. It hit him between the shoulders. It went

2 Kgs. 9:20 Chariot racing was popular in ancient times and even launched the Olympic games in ancient Greece. Some people still practice it in Wyoming today. Two horses pull a man in a chariot down a straight track a quarter-mile long. They reach speeds of fifty miles per hour.

through his heart. He sank down slowly in his chariot. [25]Jehu spoke to Bidkar, his chariot officer. Jehu said, "Pick Joram up. Throw him on the field that belonged to Naboth from Jezreel. Remember how you and I were riding together in chariots behind Joram's father Ahab? It was when the LORD spoke this prophecy against him. The LORD announced, [26]'Yesterday I saw the blood of Naboth and the blood of his sons. You can be sure that I will make you pay for it on this piece of land.' So pick Joram up. Throw him on that piece of land. That's what the LORD said would happen."

[27]Ahaziah, the king of Judah, saw what had happened. So he tried to get away. He went up the road toward Beth Haggan. Jehu chased him. He shouted, "Kill him too!" Jehu's men wounded Ahaziah in his chariot. It happened on the way up to Gur near Ibleam. But Ahaziah escaped to Megiddo. And that's where he died. [28]Ahaziah's servants took him to Jerusalem in his chariot. They buried him in his family tomb in the City of David. [29]Ahaziah had become king of Judah. It was in the 11th year of Joram, the son of Ahab.

Jehu Kills Jezebel

[30]Jehu went to Jezreel. Jezebel heard about it. So she put makeup on her eyes and fixed her hair. Then she looked out of a window. [31]Jehu entered the gate below.

Jezebel said to him, "You are just like Zimri. You murdered your master. Have you come here in peace?"

³²Jehu looked up at the window. "Who is on my side?" he called out. "Who?" Two or three officials looked down at him. ³³"Throw her down!" Jehu said. So they threw her down. Some of her blood splashed on the wall. Some of it splashed on Jehu's chariot horses as they ran over her.

³⁴Jehu went inside. He ate and drank. "The Lord put a curse on that woman," he said. "Take proper care of her body. Bury her. After all, she was a king's daughter." ³⁵So they went out to bury her. But all they found was her head, feet and hands. ³⁶They went back and reported it to Jehu. He told them, "That's what the Lord said would happen. He announced it through his servant Elijah, who was from Tishbe. He said, 'On a piece of land at Jezreel, dogs will eat up Jezebel's body. ³⁷Her body will end up as garbage on that piece of land. So no one will be able to say, "Here's where Jezebel is buried."'"

Jehu Wipes Out Ahab's Royal House

10 Ahab's royal family in the city of Samaria had a total of 70 sons. Jehu wrote some letters to the officials of the city. He also sent them to the elders there. And he sent them to the people who took care of Ahab's children. Jehu said, ²"Your master's sons are with you. You also have chariots and horses and weapons. And you are living in a city that has high walls around it. As soon as you read this letter, here's what I want you to do. ³Choose the best and most respected son of your master. Place him on his father Joram's throne. Then fight for your master's royal house."

⁴The leaders of Samaria were terrified. They said, "King Joram and King Ahaziah couldn't stand up against Jehu. So how can we?"

⁵The city governor and the person in charge of the palace sent a message to Jehu. The message was also from the elders and the people who took care of Ahab's children. In the message, they said, "We will serve you. We'll do anything you say. We won't appoint anyone to be king. Do what you think is best."

⁶Then Jehu wrote them a second letter. He said, "You say you are on my side. You say you will obey me. If you really mean it, bring me the heads of your master's sons. Meet me in Jezreel by this time tomorrow."

There were 70 royal princes. They were with the most important men of the city. Those men were in charge of raising them. ⁷When Jehu's letter arrived, the men went and got the princes. They killed all 70 of them. They put their heads in baskets. Then they sent them to Jehu in Jezreel. ⁸When the messenger arrived, he spoke to Jehu. He told him, "The heads of the princes have been brought here."

Then Jehu ordered his men, "Put them in two piles. Stack them up at the entrance of the city gate until morning."

⁹The next morning Jehu went out. He stood in front of all the people. He said, "You aren't guilty of doing anything wrong. I'm the one who made plans against my master Joram. I killed him. But who killed all these? ¹⁰I want you to know that the Lord has spoken against Ahab's royal house. Not a word of what he has said will fail. The Lord has done exactly what he announced through his servant Elijah." ¹¹So Jehu killed everyone from Ahab's family who was in Jezreel. He also killed all Ahab's chief men. And he killed Ahab's close friends and his priests. He didn't leave anyone alive in Ahab's family.

¹²Then Jehu started out for Samaria. At Beth Eked of the Shepherds, ¹³he saw some people. They were relatives of Ahaziah, the king of Judah. Jehu asked them, "Who are you?"

They said, "We are Ahaziah's relatives. We've come down to visit the families of the king and of his mother."

¹⁴"Take them alive!" Jehu ordered. So his men took them alive. Then they killed them by the well of Beth Eked. They killed a total of 42 of them. Jehu didn't leave anyone alive.

¹⁵Jehu left there. On the way he met Jehonadab. He was the son of Rekab. Jehonadab was on his way to see Jehu. Jehu greeted him. He asked, "Are you my friend? You know I'm your friend."

"I am," Jehonadab answered.

"If that's true," said Jehu, "hold out your hand." So he did. Then Jehu helped him up into the chariot. ¹⁶Jehu said, "Come along with me. See how committed I am to serve the Lord." Jehu had Jehonadab ride along in his chariot.

[17]Jehu came to Samaria. He killed everyone there who was left from Ahab's family. And so he completely destroyed Ahab's royal house. That's what the LORD had said would happen. He had spoken that message to Elijah.

Jehu Kills the People Who Serve Baal

[18]Then Jehu brought together all the people. He said to them, "Ahab served the god named Baal a little. I will serve him a lot. [19]Send for all of Baal's prophets. Also send for all his priests and the others who serve him. Make sure that not a single one is missing. I'm going to hold a great sacrifice to honor Baal. Anyone who doesn't come will be killed." But Jehu was lying to them. He was planning to destroy everyone who served Baal.

[20]Jehu said, "Call everyone together to honor Baal." So they did. [21]Then he sent a message all through Israel. All those who served Baal came. Not a single one of them stayed away. They crowded into Baal's temple. It was full from one end to the other. [22]Jehu spoke to the one who took care of the sacred robes. He told him, "Bring robes for everyone who serves Baal." So he brought the robes out for them.

[23]Then Jehu went into Baal's temple. Jehonadab, the son of Rekab, went with him. Jehu said to those who served Baal, "Look around. Make sure that no one who serves the LORD is here with you. Make sure only those who serve Baal are here." [24]So they went in to offer sacrifices and burnt offerings. Jehu had stationed 80 men outside. He warned them, "I'm placing some men in your hands. Don't let a single one of them escape. If you do, you will pay for his life with yours."

[25]Jehu finished sacrificing the burnt offering. As soon as he did, he gave an order to the guards and officers. He commanded them, "Go inside and kill everyone. Don't let a single one of them escape." So they cut them down with their swords. The guards and officers threw the bodies outside. Then they entered the most sacred area inside Baal's temple. [26]They brought the sacred stone of Baal outside. They burned it up. [27]So they destroyed Baal's sacred stone. They also tore down Baal's temple. People have used it as a public toilet to this day.

[28]So Jehu destroyed the worship of the god named Baal in Israel. [29]But he didn't turn away from the sins of Jeroboam, the son of Nebat. Jeroboam had caused Israel to commit those same sins. Jehu worshiped the golden calves at Bethel and Dan.

[30]The LORD said to Jehu, "You have done well. You have accomplished what is right in my eyes. You have done to Ahab's royal house everything I wanted you to do. So your sons after you will sit on the throne of Israel. They will rule until the time of your children's grandchildren." [31]But Jehu wasn't careful to obey the law of the LORD. He didn't obey the God of Israel with all his heart. He didn't turn away from the sins of Jeroboam. Jeroboam had caused Israel to commit those same sins.

[32]In those days the LORD began to make the kingdom of Israel smaller. Hazael gained control over many parts of Israel. He gained control over all their territory [33]east of the Jordan River. It included the whole land of Gilead from Aroer by the Arnon River valley all the way to Bashan. That was the territory of Gad, Reuben and Manasseh.

[34]The other events of Jehu's rule are written down. Everything he did and accomplished is written in the official records of the kings of Israel.

[35]Jehu joined the members of his family who had already died. He was buried in Samaria. His son Jehoahaz became the next king after him. [36]Jehu had ruled over Israel in Samaria for 28 years.

Athaliah and Joash

11 Athaliah was Ahaziah's mother. She saw that her son was dead. So she began to destroy the whole royal house of Judah. [2]But Jehosheba went and got Joash, the son of Ahaziah. Jehosheba was the daughter of King Jehoram and the sister of Ahaziah. She stole Joash away from among the royal princes. All of them were about to be murdered. She put Joash and his nurse in a bedroom. That's how she hid him from Athaliah. And that's why Athaliah didn't kill him. [3]The child remained hidden with his nurse at the LORD's temple for six years. Athaliah ruled over the land during that time.

[4]In the seventh year Jehoiada the priest sent for the commanders of military groups of 100 men. They were the commanders over the Carites and the guards. Jehoiada had them brought to him at the temple of the LORD. He made a covenant with them.

At the temple he made them promise to be faithful. Then he showed them the king's son. [5]He gave them a command. He said, "Here's what you must do. There are five groups of you. Some of you are in the three groups that are going on duty on the Sabbath day. A third of you must guard the royal palace. [6]A third of you must guard the Sur Gate. And a third of you must guard the gate that is behind the guard. All of you must take turns guarding the temple. [7]The rest of you are in the other two groups. Normally you are not on duty on the Sabbath day. But you also must guard the temple for the king. [8]Station yourselves around the king. Each of you must have his weapon in his hand. Anyone else who approaches your groups must be put to death. Stay close to the king no matter where he goes."

[9]The commanders of the military groups did just as Jehoiada the priest ordered. Each commander got his men and came to Jehoiada. Some of the men were going on duty on the Sabbath day. Others were going off duty. [10]Then Jehoiada gave weapons to the commanders. He gave them spears and shields. The weapons had belonged to King David. They had been in the LORD's temple. [11]The guards stationed themselves around the new king. Each of them had his weapon in his hand. They were near the altar and the temple. They stood from the south side of the temple to its north side.

[12]Jehoiada brought out Ahaziah's son. He put the crown on him. He gave him a copy of the covenant. And he announced that Joash was king. Jehoiada and his sons anointed him. The people clapped their hands. Then they shouted, "May the king live a long time!"

[13]Athaliah heard the noise the guards and the people were making. So she went to the people at the LORD's temple. [14]She looked, and there was the king! He was standing next to the pillar. That was the usual practice. The officers and trumpet players were standing beside the king. All the people of the land were filled with joy. They were blowing trumpets. Then Athaliah tore her royal robes. She called out, "Treason! It's treason!"

[15]Jehoiada the priest gave an order to the commanders of the military groups of 100 men. The commanders were in charge of the troops. He said to them, "Bring her away from the temple between the line of guards. Use your swords to kill anyone who follows her." The priest had said, "She must not be put to death at the LORD's temple." [16]So they grabbed her as she reached the place where the horses enter the palace grounds. There she was put to death.

[17]Then Jehoiada made a covenant between the LORD and the king and people. He had the king and people promise that they would be the LORD's people. Jehoiada also made a covenant between the king and the people. [18]All the people of the land went to Baal's temple. They tore it down. They smashed to pieces the altars and the statues of gods. They killed Mattan in front of the altars. He was the priest of Baal.

Then Jehoiada the priest stationed guards at the temple of the LORD. [19]Jehoiada took with him the commanders of groups of 100 men. They were the commanders over the Carites and the guards. He also took with him all the people of the land. All of them brought the new king down from the LORD's temple. They went into the palace. They entered it by going through the gate of the guards. Then the king sat down on the royal throne. [20]All the people of the land were filled with joy. And the city was calm. That's because Athaliah had been killed with a sword at the palace.

[21]Joash was seven years old when he became king.

Joash Repairs the Temple

12 Joash became king of Judah. It was in the seventh year of Jehu's rule. Joash ruled in Jerusalem for 40 years. His mother's name was Zibiah. She was from Beersheba. [2]Joash did what was right in the eyes of the LORD. Joash lived that way as long as Jehoiada the priest was teaching him. [3]But the high places weren't removed. The people continued to offer sacrifices and burn incense there.

[4]Joash spoke to the priests. He said, "Collect all the money the people bring as sacred offerings to the LORD's temple. That includes the money collected when the men who are able to serve in the army are counted. It includes the money received from people who make a special promise to the LORD. It also includes the money people bring to the temple just because they want to. [5]Let each priest receive the money from

one of the people in charge of the temple's treasures. Then use all of that money to repair the temple where it needs it."

⁶It was now the 23rd year of the rule of King Joash. And the priests still hadn't repaired the temple. ⁷So the king sent for Jehoiada the priest and the other priests. He asked them, "Why aren't you repairing the temple where it needs it? Don't take any more money from the people in charge of the treasures. Instead, hand it over so the temple can be repaired." ⁸The priests agreed that they wouldn't collect any more money from the people. They also agreed that they wouldn't repair the temple themselves.

Jason's Jargon

2 KINGS 12

Search this chapter for the word *wick*. The wick is the cord in a candle that supplies fuel for a flame. The wick cutter was a sharp blade used to cut the wick to the perfect length.

⁹Jehoiada the priest got a chest. He drilled a hole in its lid. He placed the chest beside the altar for burnt offerings. The chest was on the right side as people enter the LORD's temple. Some priests guarded the entrance. They put into the chest all the money the people brought to the temple. ¹⁰From time to time there was a large amount of money in the chest. When that happened, the royal secretary and the high priest came. They counted the money the people had brought to the temple. Then they put it into bags. ¹¹After they added it all up, they used it to repair the temple. They gave it to the men who had been put in charge of the work. Those men used it to pay the workers. They paid the builders and those who worked with wood. ¹²They paid those who cut stones and those who laid them. They bought lumber and blocks of stone. So they used the money to repair the LORD's temple. They also paid all the other costs to make the temple like new again.

¹³The money the people brought to the LORD's temple wasn't used to make silver bowls. It wasn't used for wick cutters, sprinkling bowls or trumpets. And it wasn't used for any other things made out of gold or silver. ¹⁴Instead, it was paid to the workers. They used it to repair the temple. ¹⁵The royal secretary and the high priest didn't require a report from those who were in charge of the work. That's because they were completely honest. They always paid the workers. ¹⁶Money was received from people who brought guilt offerings and sin offerings. But it wasn't taken to the LORD's temple. It belonged to the priests.

¹⁷About that time Hazael, the king of Aram, went up and attacked Gath. Then he captured it. After that, he turned back to attack Jerusalem. ¹⁸But Joash, the king of Judah, didn't want to go to war. So he took all the sacred objects. They had been set apart to the LORD by the kings who had ruled over Judah before him. Those kings were Jehoshaphat, Jehoram and Ahaziah. Joash took the gifts he himself had set apart. He took all the gold that was among the temple treasures. He also took all the gold from the royal palace. He sent all those things to Hazael, the king of Aram. Then Hazael pulled his army back from Jerusalem.

¹⁹The other events of the rule of Joash are written down. Everything he did is written in the official records of the kings of Judah. ²⁰The officials of Joash made evil plans against him. They killed him at Beth Millo. It happened on the road that goes down to Silla. ²¹The officials who murdered him were Jozabad and Jehozabad. Jozabad was the son of Shimeath. Jehozabad was the son of Shomer. After Joash died, he was buried in the family tomb in the City of David. Joash's son Amaziah became the next king after him.

Jehoahaz King of Israel

13 Jehoahaz became king of Israel in Samaria. It was in the 23rd year of the rule of Joash, the king of Judah. Jehoahaz ruled for 17 years. Joash was the son of Ahaziah. Jehoahaz was the son of Jehu. ²Jehoahaz did what was evil in the eyes of the LORD. He committed the sins Jeroboam, the son of Nebat, had committed. Jeroboam had caused Israel to commit those same sins. Jehoahaz didn't turn away from them. ³So the LORD was very angry with Israel. For a long time he kept them under the power of Hazael, the king of Aram. The

LORD also kept them under the power of his son Ben-Hadad.

⁴Then Jehoahaz asked the LORD for help. The LORD listened to him. The LORD saw how badly the king of Aram was treating Israel. ⁵The LORD provided someone to save Israel. And they escaped from the power of Aram. So the Israelites lived in their own homes, just as they had before. ⁶But the people didn't turn away from the sins of the royal house of Jeroboam. He had caused Israel to commit those same sins. The people continued to commit them. And the pole used to worship the female god named Asherah remained standing in Samaria. ⁷The army of Jehoahaz had almost nothing left. All it had was 50 horsemen, 10 chariots and 10,000 soldiers on foot. The king of Aram had destroyed the rest of them. He had made them like dust at threshing time.

⁸The other events of the rule of Jehoahaz are written down. Everything he did and accomplished is written in the official records of the kings of Israel. ⁹Jehoahaz joined the members of his family who had already died. He was buried in Samaria. Jehoahaz's son Jehoash became the next king after him.

Jehoash King of Israel

¹⁰Jehoash became king of Israel in Samaria. It was in the 37th year that Joash was king of Judah. Jehoash ruled for 16 years. He was the son of Jehoahaz. ¹¹Jehoash did what was evil in the eyes of the LORD. Jehoash didn't turn away from any of the sins of Jeroboam, the son of Nebat. Jeroboam had caused Israel to commit those same sins. And Jehoash continued to commit them. ¹²The other events of the rule of Jehoash are written down. That includes his war against Amaziah, the king of Judah. Everything he did and accomplished is written in the official records of the kings of Israel. ¹³Jehoash joined the members of his family who had already died. He was buried in the royal tombs in Samaria. Jeroboam became the next king on Israel's throne after him.

¹⁴Elisha had been suffering from a sickness. Later he would die from it. Jehoash, the king of Israel, went down to see him. Jehoash wept over him. "My father!" he cried. "You are like a father to me! You, Elisha, are the true chariots and horsemen of Israel!"

¹⁵Elisha said to Jehoash, "Get a bow and some arrows." So he did. ¹⁶"Hold the bow in your hands," Elisha said to the king of Israel. So Jehoash took hold of the bow. Then Elisha put his hands on the king's hands.

¹⁷"Open the east window," Elisha said. So he did. "Shoot!" Elisha said. So he shot. "That's the LORD's arrow!" Elisha announced. "It means you will win the battle over Aram! You will completely destroy the men of Aram at Aphek."

¹⁸Elisha continued, "Get some arrows." So the king did. Elisha told him, "Strike the ground." Jehoash struck it three times. Then he stopped. ¹⁹The man of God was angry with him. He said, "You should have struck the ground five or six times. Then you would have won the war over Aram. You would have completely destroyed them. But now you will win only three battles over them."

²⁰Elisha died and was buried.

Some robbers from Moab used to enter the country of Israel every spring. ²¹One day some Israelites were burying a man. Suddenly they saw a group of robbers. So they threw the man's body into Elisha's tomb. The body touched Elisha's bones. When it did, the man came back to life again. He stood up on his feet.

²²Hazael, the king of Aram, treated Israel badly. He did it the whole time Jehoahaz

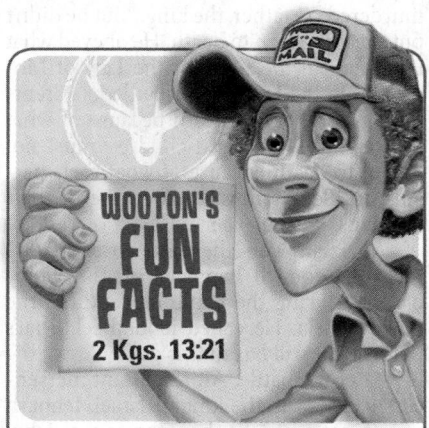

Elijah and Elisha were involved in the first three death-to-life episodes. Check out 1 Kings 17:17–24 and 2 Kings 4:35 to read about them all. These miracles point to the greatest miracle of all—Jesus' resurrection.

was king. ²³But the LORD helped Israel. He was tender and kind to them. He showed concern for them. He did all these things because of the covenant he had made with Abraham, Isaac and Jacob. To this day he hasn't been willing to destroy Israel. And he hasn't driven them out of his land.

²⁴Hazael, the king of Aram, died. His son Ben-Hadad became the next king after him. ²⁵Then Jehoash won back some towns from Ben-Hadad, the son of Hazael. Ben-Hadad had captured them in battle from Jehoahaz, the father of Jehoash. Jehoash won three battles over Ben-Hadad. So Jehoash won back the Israelite towns.

Amaziah King of Judah

14 Amaziah began to rule as king over Judah. It was in the second year that Jehoash was king of Israel. He was the son of Jehoahaz. Amaziah was the son of Joash. ²Amaziah was 25 years old when he became king. He ruled in Jerusalem for 29 years. His mother's name was Jehoaddan. She was from Jerusalem. ³Amaziah did what was right in the eyes of the LORD. But he didn't do what King David had done. He always followed the example of his father Joash. ⁴But the high places weren't removed. The people continued to offer sacrifices and burn incense there.

⁵The kingdom was firmly under his control. So he put to death the officials who had murdered his father, the king. ⁶But he didn't put their children to death. He obeyed what is written in the Book of the Law of Moses. There the LORD commanded, "Parents must not be put to death because of what their children do. And children must not be put to death because of what their parents do. People must die because of their own sins." (Deuteronomy 24:16)

⁷Amaziah won the battle over 10,000 men of Edom. It happened in the Valley of Salt. During the battle he captured the town of Sela. He called it Joktheel. That's the name it still has to this day.

⁸After the battle, Amaziah sent messengers to Jehoash, the king of Israel. Jehoash was the son of Jehoahaz, the son of Jehu. Amaziah said, "Come on. Let us face each other in battle."

⁹But Jehoash, the king of Israel, answered Amaziah, the king of Judah. Jehoash said, "A thorn bush in Lebanon sent a message to a cedar tree there. The thorn bush said, 'Give your daughter to be married to my son.' Then a wild animal in Lebanon came along. It crushed the thorn bush by walking on it. ¹⁰It's true that you have won the battle over Edom. So you are proud. Enjoy your success while you can. But stay home and enjoy it! Why ask for trouble? Why bring yourself crashing down? Why bring Judah down with you?"

¹¹But Amaziah wouldn't listen. So Jehoash, the king of Israel, attacked. He and Amaziah, the king of Judah, faced each other in battle. The battle took place at Beth Shemesh in Judah. ¹²Israel drove Judah away. Every man ran home. ¹³Jehoash king of Israel captured Amaziah king of Judah at Beth Shemesh. Amaziah was the son of Joash. Joash was the son of Ahaziah. Jehoash went to Jerusalem. He broke down part of its wall. It's the part that went from the Ephraim Gate to the Corner Gate. That part of the wall was 600 feet long. ¹⁴Jehoash took all the gold, silver and objects that were in the LORD's temple. He also took all those same kinds of things that were among the treasures of the royal palace. And he took prisoners. Then he returned to Samaria.

¹⁵The other events of the rule of Jehoash are written down. That includes his war against Amaziah, the king of Judah. Everything he did and accomplished is written in the official records of the kings of Israel. ¹⁶Jehoash joined the members of his family who had already died. He was buried in Samaria in the royal tombs of Israel. Jehoash's son Jeroboam became the next king after him.

¹⁷Amaziah king of Judah lived for 15 years after Jehoash king of Israel died. Amaziah was the son of Joash. Jehoash was the son of Jehoahaz. ¹⁸The other events of Amaziah's rule are written down. They are written in the official records of the kings of Judah.

¹⁹Some people made evil plans against Amaziah in Jerusalem. So he ran away to Lachish. But they sent men to Lachish after him. There they killed him. ²⁰His body was brought back on a horse. Then he was buried in the family tomb in Jerusalem, the City of David.

²¹All the people of Judah made Uzziah king. He was 16 years old. They made him king in place of his father Amaziah. ²²Uzziah rebuilt Elath. He brought it under

Judah's control again. He did it after Amaziah joined the members of his family who had already died.

Jeroboam II King of Israel

[23]Jeroboam became king of Israel in Samaria. It was in the 15th year that Amaziah was king of Judah. Jeroboam ruled for 41 years. Amaziah was the son of Joash. Jeroboam was the son of Jehoash. [24]Jeroboam did what was evil in the eyes of the LORD. He didn't turn away from any of the sins the earlier Jeroboam, the son of Nebat, had committed. That Jeroboam had caused Israel to commit those same sins. [25]Jeroboam, the son of Jehoash, made the borders of Israel the same as they were before. They reached from Lebo Hamath all the way to the Dead Sea. That's what the LORD, the God of Israel, had said would happen. He had spoken that message through his servant Jonah. Jonah the prophet was the son of Amittai. Jonah was from the town of Gath Hepher. [26]The LORD had seen how much everyone in Israel was suffering. It didn't matter whether they were slaves or free. They didn't have anyone to help them. [27]The LORD hadn't said he would wipe out Israel's name from the earth. So he saved them by the power of Jeroboam, the son of Jehoash. [28]The other events of the rule of Jeroboam are written down. What he and his army accomplished is written down. That includes how he brought Damascus and Hamath back under Israel's control. Damascus and Hamath had belonged to the territory of Judah. Everything he did is written in the official records of the kings of Israel. [29]Jeroboam joined the members of his family who had already died. He was buried in the royal tombs of Israel. Jeroboam son Zechariah became the next king after him.

Uzziah King of Judah

15 Uzziah began to rule as king over Judah. It was in the 27th year that Jeroboam was king of Israel. Uzziah was the son of Amaziah. [2]Uzziah was 16 years old when he became king. He ruled in Jerusalem for 52 years. His mother's name was Jekoliah. She was from Jerusalem. [3]Uzziah did what was right in the eyes of the LORD, just as his father Amaziah had done. [4]But the high places weren't removed. The

people continued to offer sacrifices and burn incense there.

[5]The LORD caused King Uzziah to suffer from a skin disease until the day he died. He lived in a separate house. His son Jotham was in charge of the palace. Jotham ruled over the people of the land. [6]The other events of the rule of Uzziah are written down. Everything he did is written in the official records of the kings of Judah. [7]Uzziah joined the members of his family who had already died. He was buried near them in the City of David. Uzziah's son Jotham became the next king after him.

Zechariah King of Israel

[8]Zechariah became king of Israel in Samaria. It was in the 38th year that Uzziah was king of Judah. Zechariah ruled for six months. He was the son of Jeroboam, the son of Jehoash. [9]Zechariah did what was evil in the eyes of the LORD. He did what the kings of Israel before him had done. He didn't turn away from the sins Jeroboam, the son of Nebat, had committed. Jeroboam had caused Israel to commit those same sins. [10]Shallum made evil plans against Zechariah. He attacked Zechariah in front of the people and killed him. Then he became the next king after him. Shallum was the son of Jabesh. [11]The other events of the rule of Zechariah are written down. They are written in the official records of the kings of Israel. [12]What happened to Zechariah is what the LORD said would happen. He had spoken that message to Jehu. The LORD had said, "Your sons after you will sit on the throne of Israel. They will rule until the time of your children's grandchildren." *(2 Kings 10:30)*

Shallum King of Israel

[13]Shallum became king of Israel. It was in the 39th year that Uzziah was king of Judah. Shallum ruled in Samaria for one month. He was the son of Jabesh. [14]Menahem went from Tirzah up to Samaria. There he attacked Shallum, the son of Jabesh. Menahem killed him and became the next king after him. Menahem was the son of Gadi.

[15]The other events of Shallum's rule are written down. The evil things he planned are written down. All these things are written in the official records of the kings of Israel.

16At that time Menahem started out from Tirzah and attacked Tiphsah. He attacked everyone in the city and the area around it. That's because they refused to open their gates for him. He destroyed Tiphsah. He ripped open all their pregnant women.

Menahem King of Israel

17Menahem became king of Israel. It was in the 39th year that Uzziah was king of Judah. Menahem ruled in Samaria for ten years. He was the son of Gadi. 18Menahem did what was evil in the eyes of the LORD. During his entire rule he didn't turn away from the sins Jeroboam, the son of Nebat, had committed. Jeroboam had caused Israel to commit those same sins.

19Then Tiglath-Pileser marched into the land of Israel. He was king of Assyria. Menahem gave him 38 tons of silver to get his help. He wanted to make his control over the kingdom stronger. 20Menahem forced Israel to give him that money. Every wealthy person had to give him 20 ounces of silver. All of it went to the king of Assyria. So he pulled his troops back. He didn't stay in the land anymore.

21The other events of the rule of Menahem are written down. Everything he did is written in the official records of the kings of Israel. 22Menahem joined the members of his family who had already died. Menahem's son Pekahiah became the next king after him.

Pekahiah King of Israel

23Pekahiah became king of Israel in Samaria. It was in the 50th year that Uzziah was king of Judah. Pekahiah ruled for two years. He was the son of Menahem. 24Pekahiah did what was evil in the eyes of the LORD. He didn't turn away from the sins Jeroboam, the son of Nebat, had committed. Jeroboam had caused Israel to commit those same sins. 25One of Pekahiah's chief officers was Pekah. He was the son of Remaliah. Pekah made evil plans against Pekahiah. He took 50 men from Gilead with him and killed Pekahiah. Pekah also killed Argob and Arieh. He killed all of them in the safest place in the royal palace at Samaria. So Pekah killed Pekahiah. He became the next king after him.

26The other events of the rule of Pekahiah are written down. Everything he did is written in the official records of the kings of Israel.

Pekah King of Israel

27Pekah became king of Israel in Samaria. It was in the 52nd year that Uzziah was king of Judah. Pekah ruled for 20 years. He was the son of Remaliah. 28Pekah did what was evil in the eyes of the LORD. He didn't turn away from the sins Jeroboam, the son of Nebat, had committed. Jeroboam had caused Israel to commit those same sins.

29During the rule of Pekah, the king of Israel, Tiglath-Pileser marched into the land again. He was king of Assyria. He captured the towns of Ijon, Abel Beth Maakah, Janoah, Kedesh and Hazor. He also captured the lands of Gilead and Galilee. That included the whole territory of Naphtali. He took the people away from their own land. He sent them off to Assyria. 30Then Hoshea made evil plans against Pekah, the son of Remaliah. Hoshea was the son of Elah. Hoshea attacked Pekah and killed him. Then Hoshea became the next king after him. It was in the 20th year of the rule of Jotham, the son of Uzziah.

31The other events of the rule of Pekah are written down. Everything he did is written in the official records of the kings of Israel.

Jotham King of Judah

32Jotham began to rule as king over Judah. It was in the second year that Pekah was king of Israel. He was the son of Remaliah. Jotham was the son of Uzziah. 33Jotham was 25 years old when he became king. He ruled in Jerusalem for 16 years. His mother's name was Jerusha. She was the daughter of Zadok. 34Jotham did what was right in the eyes of the LORD, just as his father Uzziah had done. 35But the high places weren't removed. The people continued to offer sacrifices and burn incense there. Jotham rebuilt the Upper Gate of the LORD's temple.

36The other events of the rule of Jotham are written down. Everything he did is written in the official records of the kings of Judah. 37In those days the LORD began to send Rezin and Pekah against Judah. Rezin was king of Aram. Pekah was the son of Remaliah. 38Jotham joined the members of his family who had already died. He was buried in the family tomb in the city of King David. Jotham's son Ahaz became the next king after him.

Ahaz King of Judah

16 Ahaz began to rule as king over Judah. It was in the 17th year of the rule of Pekah, the son of Remaliah. Ahaz was the son of Jotham. [2]Ahaz was 20 years old when he became king. He ruled in Jerusalem for 16 years. Ahaz didn't do what was right in the eyes of the LORD his God. He didn't do what King David had done. [3]He followed the ways of the kings of Israel. He even sacrificed his son in the fire to another god. He followed the practices of the nations. The LORD hated those practices. He had driven out those nations to make room for the Israelites. [4]Ahaz offered sacrifices and burned incense at the high places. He also did it on the tops of hills and under every green tree.

[5]Rezin and Pekah marched up to Jerusalem and surrounded it. Rezin was king of Aram. Pekah, the son of Remaliah, was king of Israel. They attacked Ahaz. But they couldn't overpower him. [6]At that time Rezin, the king of Aram, won back Elath for Aram. He drove out the people of Judah. Then the people of Edom moved into Elath. And they still live there to this day.

[7]Ahaz sent messengers to Tiglath-Pileser. He was king of Assyria. The message of Ahaz said, "I am your servant. You are my master. Come up and save me from the power of the kings of Aram and Israel. They are attacking me." [8]Ahaz took the silver and gold that were in the LORD's temple. He also took the silver and gold that were among the treasures in the royal palace. He sent all of it as a gift to the king of Assyria. [9]So the king of Assyria did what Ahaz asked him to do. He attacked the city of Damascus and captured it. He sent its people away to Kir. And he put Rezin to death.

[10]Then King Ahaz went to Damascus. He went there to see Tiglath-Pileser, the king of Assyria. Ahaz saw an altar in Damascus. He sent a drawing of it to Uriah the priest. Ahaz also sent him plans for building it. [11]So Uriah the priest built an altar. He followed all the plans King Ahaz had sent from Damascus. He finished it before Ahaz returned. [12]The king came back from Damascus. When he saw the altar, he approached it.

Then he offered sacrifices on it. [13]He offered up his burnt offering and grain offering. He poured out his drink offering. And he splashed the blood from his friendship offerings against the altar. [14]The bronze altar for burnt offerings stood in front of the LORD. It was between the new altar and the LORD's temple. Ahaz took the bronze altar away from the front of the temple. He put it on the north side of the new altar.

[15]Then King Ahaz gave orders to Uriah the priest. He said, "Offer sacrifices on the large new altar. Offer the morning burnt offering and the evening grain offering. Offer my burnt offering and my grain offering. Offer the burnt offering of all the people of the land. Offer their grain offering and their drink offering. Splash against this altar the blood from all the burnt offerings and sacrifices. But I will use the bronze altar to look for advice and direction." [16]Uriah the priest did just as King Ahaz had ordered.

[17]Ahaz cut off the sides of the bronze stands. He removed the bowls from the stands. He removed the huge bowl from the bronze bulls it stood on. He placed the bowl on a stone base. [18]He took away the covered area that had been used on the Sabbath day. It had been built at the LORD's temple. He removed the royal entrance that was outside the temple. Ahaz did all these things to honor the king of Assyria.

[19]The other events of the rule of Ahaz are written down. Everything he did is written in the official records of the kings of Judah. [20]Ahaz joined the members of his family who had already died. He was buried in the family tomb in the City of David. Ahaz's son Hezekiah became the next king after him.

Hoshea the Last King of Israel

17 Hoshea became king of Israel in Samaria. It was in the 12th year that Ahaz was king of Judah. Hoshea ruled for nine years. He was the son of Elah. [2]Hoshea did what was evil in the eyes of the LORD. But he wasn't as evil as the kings of Israel who ruled before him.

[3]Shalmaneser came up to attack Hoshea. Shalmaneser was king of Assyria. He had been Hoshea's master. He had forced Hoshea to bring him gifts. [4]But the king of Assyria found out that Hoshea had turned against him. Hoshea had sent messengers to So, the king of Egypt. Hoshea didn't

send gifts to the king of Assyria anymore. He had been sending them every year. So Shalmaneser grabbed him and put him in prison. [5]The king of Assyria marched into the whole land of Israel. He marched to Samaria and surrounded it for three years. From time to time he attacked it. [6]Finally, the king of Assyria captured Samaria. It was in the ninth year of Hoshea. The king of Assyria took the Israelites away from their own land. He sent them off to Assyria. He made some of them live in Halah. He made others live in Gozan on the Habor River. And he made others live in the towns of the Medes.

Israel Is Forced to Leave the Land Because of Sin

[7]All of this took place because the Israelites had sinned against the LORD their God. He had brought them up out of Egypt. He had brought them out from under the power of Pharaoh, the king of Egypt. But they worshiped other gods. [8]The LORD had driven out other nations to make room for Israel. But they followed the evil practices of those nations. They also followed the practices that the kings of Israel had started. [9]The Israelites did things in secret against the LORD their God. What they did wasn't right. They built high places for worship in all their towns. They built them at lookout towers. They also built them at cities that had high walls around them. [10]They set up sacred stones. And they set up poles used to worship the female god named Asherah. They did that on every high hill and under every green tree. [11]The LORD had driven out nations to make room for Israel. But the Israelites burned incense at every high place, just as those nations had done. The Israelites did evil things that made the LORD very angry. [12]They worshiped statues of gods. They did it even though the LORD had said, "Do not do that." [13]The LORD warned Israel and Judah through all his prophets and seers. He said, "Turn from your evil ways. Keep my commands and rules. Obey every part of my Law. I commanded your people who lived long ago to obey it. And I gave it to you through my servants the prophets."

[14]But the people wouldn't listen. They were as stubborn as their people of long ago had been. Those people didn't trust in the LORD their God. [15]They refused to obey his rules. They broke the covenant he had made with them. They didn't pay any attention to the rules he had warned them to keep. They worshiped worthless statues of gods. Then they themselves became worthless. They followed the example of the nations around them. They did it even though the LORD had ordered them not to. He had said, "Do not do as they do."

[16]They turned away from all the commands of the LORD their God. They made two statues of gods for themselves. The statues were shaped like calves. They made a pole used to worship the female god named Asherah. They bowed down to all the stars. And they worshiped the god named Baal. [17]They sacrificed their sons and daughters in the fire. They practiced all kinds of evil magic. They gave up following God's rules. They did only what was evil in the eyes of the LORD. All these things made him very angry.

[18]So the LORD was very angry with Israel. He removed them from his land. Only the tribe of Judah was left. [19]And even Judah didn't obey the commands of the LORD their God. They followed the practices Israel had started. [20]So the LORD turned his back on all the people of Israel. He made them suffer. He handed them over to people who stole everything they had. And finally he threw them out of his land.

[21]The LORD took control of Israel away from the royal house of David. The Israelites made Jeroboam, the son of Nebat, their king. Jeroboam tried to get Israel to stop following the LORD. He caused them to commit a terrible sin. [22]The Israelites were stubborn. They continued to commit all the sins Jeroboam had committed. They didn't turn away from them. [23]So the LORD removed them from his land. That's what he had warned them he would do. He had given that warning through all his servants the prophets. So the people of Israel were taken away from their country. They were forced to go to Assyria. And that's where they still are.

Assyria Makes Other People Live in Samaria

[24]The king of Assyria brought people from Babylon, Kuthah, Avva, Hamath and Sepharvaim. He made all of them live in the towns of Samaria. They took the place

of the people of Israel. They lived in all the towns of Samaria. ²⁵When they first lived there, they didn't worship the Lord. So he sent lions among them. And the lions killed some of the people. ²⁶A report was given to the king of Assyria. He was told, "You forced people to leave their own homes and live in the towns of Samaria. But they don't know what the god of that country requires. So he has sent lions among them. And the lions are killing the people off. That's because the people don't know what that god requires."

²⁷Then the king of Assyria gave an order. He said, "Get one of the priests you captured from Samaria. Send him back to live there. Have him teach the people what the god of that land requires." ²⁸So a priest went back to live in Bethel. He was one of the priests who had been forced to leave Samaria. He taught the people of Bethel how to worship the Lord.

²⁹In spite of that, the people from each nation made statues of their own gods. They made them in all the towns where they had been forced to live. They set up those statues in small temples. The people of Samaria had built the temples at the high places. ³⁰The people from Babylon made statues of the god named Sukkoth Benoth. Those from Kuthah made statues of the god named Nergal. Those from Hamath made statues of the god named Ashima. ³¹The Avvites made statues of the gods named Nibhaz and Tartak. The Sepharvites sacrificed their children in the fire to the gods named Adrammelek and Anammelek. They were the gods of Sepharvaim. ³²So the people of Samaria worshiped the Lord. But they also appointed all kinds of their own people to be their priests. The priests served in the small temples at the high places. ³³The people worshiped the Lord. But they also served their own gods. They followed the evil practices of the nations they had been taken from.

³⁴The people of Samaria are still stubborn. They continue in their old practices to this day. And now they don't even worship the Lord. They don't follow his directions and rules. They don't obey his laws and commands. The Lord had given all these laws to the family of Jacob. He gave the name Israel to Jacob. ³⁵The Lord made a covenant with the Israelites. At that time he commanded them, "Do not worship any other gods. Do not bow down to them. Do not serve them or sacrifice to them. ³⁶The Lord is the one you must worship. The Lord brought you up out of Egypt by his great power. He saved you by reaching out his mighty arm. You must bow down only to him. You must offer sacrifices only to him. ³⁷You must always be careful to follow his directions and rules. You must obey the laws and commands he wrote for you. Do not worship other gods. ³⁸Do not forget the covenant I made with you. And remember, you must not worship other gods. ³⁹Instead, worship the Lord your God. He will save you from the powerful hand of all your enemies."

⁴⁰But the people wouldn't listen. Instead, they were stubborn. They continued in their old practices. ⁴¹They worshiped the Lord. But at the same time, they served the statues of their gods. And to this day their children and grandchildren continue to do what their people before them did.

Hezekiah King of Judah

18 Hezekiah began to rule as king over Judah. It was in the third year that Hoshea was king of Israel. He was the son of Elah. Hezekiah was the son of Ahaz. ²Hezekiah was 25 years old when he became king. He ruled in Jerusalem for 29 years. His mother's name was Abijah. She was the daughter of Zechariah. ³Hezekiah did what was right in the eyes of the Lord, just as King David had done. ⁴Hezekiah removed the high places. He smashed the sacred stones. He cut down the poles used to worship the female god named Asherah. He broke into pieces the bronze snake Moses had made. Up to that time the Israelites had been burning incense to it. They called it Nehushtan.

⁵Hezekiah trusted in the Lord, the God of Israel. There was no one like Hezekiah among all the kings of Judah. There was no king like him either before him or after him. ⁶Hezekiah remained faithful to the Lord. He didn't stop serving him. He obeyed the commands the Lord had given Moses. ⁷The Lord was with Hezekiah. Because of that, Hezekiah was successful in everything he did. He refused to remain under the control of the king of Assyria. He didn't serve him. ⁸He won the war against the Philistines. He won battles at their lookout towers. He won battles at their cities that had high walls around them. He

won battles against the Philistines all the way to Gaza and its territory.

[9]Shalmaneser marched to Samaria and surrounded it. It was in the fourth year of King Hezekiah. That was the seventh year of Hoshea, the king of Israel. Hoshea was the son of Elah. Shalmaneser was king of Assyria. [10]At the end of three years the army of Assyria captured Samaria. That happened in the sixth year of Hezekiah's rule. It was the ninth year of the rule of Hoshea, the king of Israel. [11]The king of Assyria took the people of Israel away from their own land. He sent them off to Assyria. He made some of them live in Halah. He made others live in Gozan on the Habor River. And he made others live in the towns of the Medes. [12]These things happened because the Israelites hadn't obeyed the LORD their God. They had broken the covenant he had made with them. They had refused to do everything Moses, the servant of the LORD, had commanded. They hadn't paid any attention to those commands. They hadn't obeyed them.

[13]Sennacherib attacked and captured all the cities of Judah that had high walls around them. It was in the 14th year of the rule of Hezekiah. Sennacherib was king of Assyria. [14]Hezekiah, the king of Judah, sent a message to the king of Assyria at Lachish. Hezekiah said, "I have done what is wrong. Pull your troops back from me. Then I'll pay you anything you ask me to." The king of Assyria forced Hezekiah, the king of Judah, to give him 11 tons of silver. Hezekiah also had to give him one ton of gold. [15]So Hezekiah gave him all the silver in the LORD's temple. He also gave him all the silver among the treasures in the royal palace. [16]Hezekiah, the king of Judah, had covered the doors and doorposts of the LORD's temple with gold. But now he had to strip it off. He had to give it to the king of Assyria.

Sennacherib Warns Jerusalem

[17]The king of Assyria sent his highest commander from Lachish to King Hezekiah at Jerusalem. He also sent his chief officer and his field commander along with a large army. All of them came up to Jerusalem. They stopped at the channel that brings water from the Upper Pool. The channel was on the road to the Washerman's Field. [18]The Assyrians called for King Hezekiah.

Eliakim, Shebna and Joah went out to them. Eliakim, the son of Hilkiah, was in charge of the palace. Shebna was the secretary. Joah, the son of Asaph, kept the records.

[19]The field commander said to them, "Give Hezekiah this message. Tell him,

" 'Sennacherib is the great king of Assyria. He says, "Why are you putting your faith in what your king says? [20]You say you have a military plan. You say you have a strong army. But your words don't mean anything. Who are you depending on? Why don't you want to stay under my control? [21]Look, I know you are depending on Egypt. Why are you doing that? Egypt is nothing but a broken papyrus stem. Try leaning on it. It will only cut your hand. Pharaoh, the king of Egypt, is just like that to everyone who depends on him. [22]But suppose you say to me, 'We are depending on the LORD our God.' Didn't Hezekiah remove your god's high places and altars? Didn't Hezekiah say to the people of Judah and Jerusalem, 'You must worship at the altar in Jerusalem'?

[23]" ' "Go ahead and make a deal with my master, the king of Assyria. I'll give you 2,000 horses. But only if you can put riders on them! [24]You are depending on Egypt for chariots and horsemen. You can't drive away even the least important officer among my master's officials. [25]Besides, do you think I've come without receiving a message from the LORD? Have I come to attack and destroy this place without a message from him? The LORD himself told me to march out against your country. He told me to destroy it." ' "

[26]Then Shebna, Joah and Eliakim, the son of Hilkiah, spoke to the field commander. They said, "Please speak to us in the Aramaic language. We understand it. Don't speak to us in Hebrew. If you do, the people sitting on the city wall will be able to understand you."

[27]But the commander replied, "My master sent me to say these things. Are these words only for your master and you to hear? Aren't they also for the people sitting on the wall? They are going to suffer just like you.

They'll have to eat their own waste. They'll have to drink their own urine."

²⁸Then the commander stood up and spoke in the Hebrew language. He called out, "Pay attention to what the great king of Assyria is telling you. ²⁹He says, 'Don't let Hezekiah trick you. He can't save you from my power. ³⁰Don't let Hezekiah talk you into trusting in the Lord. Don't believe him when he says, "You can be sure that the Lord will save us. This city will not be handed over to the king of Assyria."'

³¹"Don't listen to Hezekiah. The king of Assyria says, 'Make a peace treaty with me. Come over to my side. Then each one of you will eat fruit from your own vine and fig tree. Each one of you will drink water from your own well. ³²You will do that until I come back. Then I'll take you to a land just like yours. It's a land that has a lot of grain and fresh wine. It has plenty of bread and vineyards. It has olive trees and honey. So choose life! Don't choose death!'

"Don't pay any attention to Hezekiah. He's telling you a lie when he says, 'The Lord will save us.' ³³Has the god of any nation ever saved his land from the power of the king of Assyria? ³⁴Where are the gods of Hamath and Arpad? Where are the gods of Sepharvaim, Hena and Ivvah? Have they saved Samaria from my power? ³⁵Which one of all the gods of those countries has been able to save his land from me? So how can the Lord save Jerusalem from my power?"

³⁶But the people remained silent. They didn't say anything. That's because King Hezekiah had commanded, "Don't answer him."

³⁷Then Eliakim, the son of Hilkiah, went to Hezekiah. Eliakim was in charge of the palace. Shebna the secretary went with him. So did Joah, the son of Asaph. Joah kept the records. All of them went to Hezekiah with their clothes torn. They told him what the field commander had said.

Isaiah Prophesies That Jerusalem Will Be Saved

19 When King Hezekiah heard what the field commander had said, he tore his clothes. He put on the rough clothing people wear when they're sad. Then he went into the Lord's temple. ²Hezekiah sent Eliakim, who was in charge of the palace, to Isaiah the prophet. Isaiah was the son

2 Kgs. 19:1 The "rough clothing" here is sackcloth, which is a lot like modern-day burlap. People don't usually wear it for clothes now. They use it to make sacks to carry stuff. The Israelites wore it to show repentance or sadness.

of Amoz. Hezekiah also sent to Isaiah the leading priests and Shebna the secretary. All of them were wearing the same rough clothing. ³They told Isaiah, "Hezekiah says, 'Today we're in great trouble. The Lord is warning us. He's bringing shame on us. Sometimes babies come to the moment when they should be born. But their mothers aren't strong enough to allow them to be born. Today we are like those mothers. We aren't strong enough to save ourselves. ⁴Perhaps the Lord your God will hear everything the field commander has said. His master, the king of Assyria, has sent him to make fun of the living God. Maybe the Lord your God will punish him for what he has heard him say. So pray for the remaining people who are still alive here.'"

⁵King Hezekiah's officials came to Isaiah. ⁶Then Isaiah said to them, "Tell your master, 'The Lord says, "Do not be afraid of what you have heard. The officers of the king of Assyria have spoken evil things against me. ⁷Listen! I will send him news from his own country. It will make him want to return home. There I will have him killed by a sword."'"

⁸The field commander heard that the king of Assyria had left Lachish. So the commander pulled his troops back from Jerusalem. He went to join the king. He found out that the king was fighting against Libnah. ⁹During that time Sennacherib received a report. He was told that Tirhakah was

marching out to fight against him. Tirhakah was the king of Cush. Sennacherib sent messengers again to Hezekiah with a letter. Sennacherib said, ¹⁰"Tell Hezekiah, the king of Judah, 'Don't let the god you depend on trick you. He says, "Jerusalem will not be handed over to the king of Assyria." But don't believe him. ¹¹I'm sure you have heard about what the kings of Assyria have done to all the other countries. They have destroyed them completely. So do you think you will be saved? ¹²The kings who ruled before me destroyed many nations. Did the gods of those nations save them? Did the gods of Gozan, Harran or Rezeph save them? What about the gods of the people of Eden who were in Tel Assar? ¹³Where is the king of Hamath? Where is the king of Arpad? Where are the kings of Lair, Sepharvaim, Hena and Ivvah?' "

Hezekiah's Prayer

¹⁴When Hezekiah received the letter from the messengers, he read it. Then he went up to the LORD's temple. There he spread the letter out in front of the LORD. ¹⁵Hezekiah prayed to the LORD. He said, "LORD, you are the God of Israel. You sit on your throne between the cherubim. You alone are God over all the kingdoms on earth. You have made heaven and earth. ¹⁶Listen, LORD. Hear us. Open your eyes, LORD. Look at the trouble we're in. Listen to what Sennacherib is saying. You are the living God. And he dares to make fun of you! ¹⁷"LORD, it's true that the kings of Assyria have completely destroyed many nations and their lands. ¹⁸They have thrown the statues of the gods of those nations into the fire. And they have destroyed them. That's because they weren't really gods at all. They were nothing but statues made out of wood and stone. They were made by human hands. ¹⁹LORD our God, save us from the power of Sennacherib. Then all the kingdoms of the earth will know that you alone are the LORD. You alone are God."

Isaiah Prophesies That Sennacherib Will Fall From Power

²⁰Isaiah sent a message to Hezekiah. Isaiah was the son of Amoz. Isaiah said, "The LORD is the God of Israel. The LORD says, 'I have heard your prayer about Sennacherib, the king of Assyria.' ²¹Here is the message

the LORD has spoken against him. The LORD says,

" 'You will not win the battle over Zion.
    Its people hate you and make fun of you.
The people of Jerusalem lift up their heads proudly
    as you run away.
²² Who have you laughed at?
    Who have you spoken evil things against?
Who have you raised your voice against?
Who have you looked at so proudly?
    You have done it against me.
    I am the Holy One of Israel!
²³ Through your messengers
    you have dared to make fun of the Lord.
And you have said,
    "I have many chariots.
With them I have gone to the tops of the mountains.
I've climbed the highest mountains in Lebanon.
I've cut down its tallest cedar trees.
    I've cut down the best of its juniper trees.
I've reached its farthest parts.
    I've reached its finest forests.
²⁴ I've dug wells in strange lands.
    I've drunk the water from them.
I've walked through all of Egypt's streams.
    I've dried up every one of them."
²⁵ " 'But I, the LORD, say, "Haven't you heard what I have done?
    Long ago I arranged for you to do all of that.
In days of old I planned it.
    Now I have made it happen.
You have turned cities with high walls into piles of stone.
²⁶ Their people do not have any power left.
    They are troubled and put to shame.
They are like plants in the field.
    They are like new green plants.
They are like grass that grows on a roof.
    It dries up before it is completely grown.
²⁷ " ' "But I know where you are.
    I know when you come and go.
I know how very angry you are with me.

²⁸ You roar against me and brag.
And I have heard your bragging.
So I will put my hook in your nose.
I will put my bit in your mouth.
And I will make you go home
by the same way you came." ' "

²⁹The LORD said, "Hezekiah, here is a miraculous sign for you.

"This year you will eat what grows by itself.
In the second year you will eat what grows from that.
But in the third year you will plant your crops and gather them in.
You will plant your grapevines and eat their fruit.
³⁰ Those who remain from the kingdom of Judah will be like plants.
Once more they will put down roots and produce fruit.
³¹ Out of Jerusalem will come those who remain.
Out of Mount Zion will come those who survive.

"The LORD's great love will make sure that happens.
He rules over all.

³²"Here is a message from me about the king of Assyria. The LORD says,

" 'The king of Assyria will not enter this city.
He will not even shoot an arrow at it.
He will not come near it with a shield.
He will not build a ramp in order to climb over its walls.
³³ By the same way he came he will go home.
He will not enter this city,'
announces the LORD.
³⁴ " 'I will guard this city and save it.
I will do it for myself. And I will do it for my servant David.' "

³⁵That night the angel of the LORD went into the camp of the Assyrians. He put to death 185,000 people there. The people of Jerusalem got up the next morning and looked out at the camp. There were all the dead bodies! ³⁶So Sennacherib, the king of Assyria, took the army tents down. Then he left. He returned to Nineveh and stayed there.

³⁷One day Sennacherib was worshiping in the temple of his god Nisrok. His sons Adrammelek and Sharezer killed him with their swords. Then they escaped to the land of Ararat. Esarhaddon became the next king after his father Sennacherib.

Hezekiah Becomes Sick

20 In those days Hezekiah became very sick. He was about to die. Isaiah the prophet, the son of Amoz, went to him. Isaiah told Hezekiah, "The LORD says, 'Put everything in order. Make out your will. You are going to die soon. You will not get well again.' "

²Hezekiah turned his face toward the wall. He prayed to the LORD. He said, ³"LORD, please remember how faithful I've been to you. I've lived the way you wanted me to. I've served you with all my heart. I've done what is good in your sight." And Hezekiah wept bitterly.

⁴Isaiah was leaving the middle courtyard. Before he had left it, a message came to him from the LORD. He said, ⁵"Go back and speak to Hezekiah. He is the ruler of my people. Tell him, 'The LORD, the God of King David, says, "I have heard your prayer. I have seen your tears. And I will heal you. On the third day from now you will go up to my temple. ⁶I will add 15 years to your life. And I will save you and this city from the power of the king of Assyria. I will guard this city. I will do it for myself. And I will do it for my servant David." ' "

⁷Then Isaiah said, "Press some figs together. Spread them on a piece of cloth." So that's what they did. Then they applied it to Hezekiah's boil. And he got well again.

⁸Hezekiah had said to Isaiah, "You say the LORD will heal me. You say that I'll go up to his temple on the third day from now. What will the sign be to prove he'll really do that?"

⁹Isaiah answered, "The LORD will do what he has promised. Here is his sign to you. Do you want the shadow the sun makes to go forward ten steps? Or do you want it to go back ten steps?"

¹⁰"It's easy for the shadow to go forward ten steps," said Hezekiah. "So have it go back ten steps."

¹¹Then Isaiah the prophet called out to the LORD. And the LORD made the shadow go back ten steps. It went back the ten steps it had gone down on the stairway Ahaz had made.

Jason's Jargon

2 KINGS 20

Sorry, it's time for a gross assignment. Examine this chapter for a *boil*. A boil is a swollen and painful skin sore. Hezekiah had such a bad boil that it threatened to kill him!

Messengers Come From Babylon to Hezekiah

[12]At that time Marduk-Baladan, the king of Babylon, sent Hezekiah letters and a gift. He had heard that Hezekiah had been sick. Marduk-Baladan was the son of Baladan. [13]Hezekiah received the messengers. He showed them everything in his storerooms. He showed them the silver and gold. He showed them the spices and the fine olive oil. He showed them where he kept his weapons. And he showed them all his treasures. In fact, he showed them everything in his palace and in his whole kingdom.

[14]Then Isaiah the prophet went to King Hezekiah. He asked him, "What did those men say? Where did they come from?"

"They came from a land far away," Hezekiah said. "They came from Babylon."

[15]The prophet asked, "What did they see in your palace?"

"They saw everything in my palace," Hezekiah said. "I showed them all my treasures."

[16]Then Isaiah said to Hezekiah, "Listen to the LORD's message. He says, [17]"You can be sure the time will come when everything in your palace will be carried off to Babylon. Everything the kings before you have stored up until this day will be taken away. There will not be anything left,' says the LORD. [18]"Some of the members of your family line will be taken away. They will be your own flesh and blood. They will include the children who will be born into your family line in years to come. And they will serve the king of Babylon in his palace.'"

[19]"The message the LORD has spoken through you is good," Hezekiah replied. He thought, "There will be peace and safety while I'm still living."

[20]The other events of the rule of Hezekiah are written down. That includes how he made the pool and the tunnel. He used them to bring water into Jerusalem. Everything he accomplished is written in the official records of the kings of Judah. [21]Hezekiah joined the members of his family who had already died. Hezekiah's son Manasseh became the next king after him.

Manasseh King of Judah

21 Manasseh was 12 years old when he became king. He ruled in Jerusalem for 55 years. His mother's name was Hephzibah. [2]Manasseh did what was evil in the eyes of the LORD. He followed the practices of the nations. The LORD hated those practices. He had driven those nations out to make room for the Israelites. [3]Manasseh rebuilt the high places. His father Hezekiah had destroyed them. Manasseh also set up altars to the god named Baal. He made a pole used to worship the female god named Asherah. Ahab, the king of Israel, had done those same things. Manasseh even bowed down to all the stars. And he worshiped them. [4]He built altars in the LORD's temple. The LORD had said about his temple, "I will put my Name there in Jerusalem." [5]In the two courtyards of the LORD's temple Manasseh built altars to honor all the stars. [6]He sacrificed his own son in the fire to another god. He practiced all kinds of evil magic. He got messages from those who had died. He talked to the spirits of the dead. He did many things that were evil in the eyes of the LORD. Manasseh made the LORD very angry.

[7]Manasseh had carved a pole used to worship the female god named Asherah. He put it in the temple. The LORD had spoken to David and his son Solomon about the temple. He had said, "My Name will be in this temple and in Jerusalem forever. Out of all the cities in the tribes of Israel I have chosen Jerusalem. [8]I gave this land to your people who lived long ago. I will not make the Israelites wander away from it again. But they must be careful to do everything I commanded them. They must obey the whole Law that my servant Moses gave them." [9]But the people didn't pay any attention. Manasseh led them astray. They did more evil things than the nations the LORD had destroyed. He had destroyed them to make room for the Israelites.

¹⁰The LORD spoke through his servants the prophets. He said, ¹¹"Manasseh, the king of Judah, has committed terrible sins. I hate them. Manasseh has done more evil things than the Amorites who were in the land before him. And he has led Judah to commit sin by worshiping his statues of gods. ¹²I am the LORD, the God of Israel. I tell you, 'I am going to bring trouble on Jerusalem and Judah. It will be so horrible that the ears of everyone who hears about it will tingle. ¹³I will measure out punishment against Jerusalem, just as I did against Samaria. I used a plumb line against the royal family of Ahab. I used it to prove that they did not measure up to my standards. I will use the same plumb line against Jerusalem. I will wipe out Jerusalem, just as someone wipes a dish. I will wipe it and turn it upside down. ¹⁴I will desert those who remain among my people. I will hand them over to their enemies. All their enemies will rob them. ¹⁵That's because my people have done what is evil in my sight. They have made me very angry. They have done that from the day their own people came out of Egypt until this day.' "

¹⁶Manasseh also spilled the blood of many people who weren't guilty of doing anything wrong. He spilled so much blood that he filled Jerusalem with it from one end of the city to the other. And he caused Judah to commit sin. So they also did what was evil in the eyes of the LORD.

¹⁷The other events of the rule of Manasseh are written down. That includes the sin he committed. Everything he did is written in the official records of the kings of Judah. ¹⁸Manasseh joined the members of his family who had already died. He was buried in his palace garden. It was called the garden of Uzza. Manasseh's son Amon became the next king after him.

Amon King of Judah

¹⁹Amon was 22 years old when he became king. He ruled in Jerusalem for two years. His mother's name was Meshullemeth. She was the daughter of Haruz. She was from Jotbah. ²⁰Amon did what was evil in the eyes of the LORD, just as his father Manasseh had done. ²¹He lived the way his father had lived. He worshiped the statues of the gods his father had worshiped. He bowed down to them. ²²He deserted the LORD, the God of his people. He didn't obey the LORD.

²³Amon's officials made plans against him. They murdered the king in his palace. ²⁴Then the people of the land killed all those officials who had made plans against King Amon. Then the people of the land made his son Josiah king in his place. ²⁵The other events of the rule of Amon are written down. Everything he did is written in the official records of the kings of Judah. ²⁶Amon was buried in his grave in the garden of Uzza. Amon's son Josiah became the next king after him.

Hilkiah Finds the Book of the Law

22 Josiah was eight years old when he became king. He ruled in Jerusalem for 31 years. His mother's name was Jedidah. She was the daughter of Adaiah. She was from Bozkath. ²Josiah did what was right in the eyes of the LORD. He lived the way King David had lived. He didn't turn away from it to the right or the left.

³King Josiah sent his secretary Shaphan to the LORD's temple. It was in the 18th year of Josiah's rule. Shaphan was the son of Azaliah. Azaliah was the son of Meshullam. Josiah said, ⁴"Go up to Hilkiah the high priest. Have him add up the money that has been brought into the LORD's temple. The men who guard the doors have collected it from the people. ⁵Have them put all the money in the care of certain men. These men have been put in charge of the work on the LORD's temple. Have them pay the workers who repair it. ⁶Have them pay the builders and those who work with wood. Have them pay those who lay the stones. Also have them buy lumber and blocks of stone to repair the temple. ⁷But they don't have to report how they use the money that is given to them. That's because they are completely honest."

⁸Hilkiah the high priest spoke to Shaphan the secretary. Hilkiah said, "I've found the Book of the Law in the LORD's temple." Hilkiah gave it to Shaphan, who read it. ⁹Then Shaphan went to King Josiah. Shaphan told him, "Your officials have paid out the money that was in the LORD's temple. They've put it in the care of the workers and directors there." ¹⁰Shaphan continued, "Hilkiah the priest has given me a book." Shaphan read some of it to the king.

¹¹The king heard the words of the Book of the Law. When he did, he tore his royal robes. ¹²He gave orders to Hilkiah the priest,

King Josiah used the Book of the Law to bring the Israelites back to God. In "The Feud of Mason County" (A#61) Whit brought peace between two clans by sharing Scripture with them.

Ahikam, Akbor, Shaphan the secretary and Asaiah. Ahikam was the son of Shaphan. Akbor was the son of Micaiah. And Asaiah was the king's attendant. Josiah commanded them, [13]"Go. Ask the Lord for advice. Ask him about what is written in this book that has been found. Do it for me. Also do it for the people and the whole nation of Judah. The Lord is very angry with us. That's because our people who have lived before us didn't obey the words of this book. They didn't do everything written there about us."

[14]Hilkiah the priest went to speak to Huldah the prophet. So did Ahikam, Akbor, Shaphan and Asaiah. Huldah was the wife of Shallum. Shallum was the son of Tikvah. Tikvah was the son of Harhas. Shallum took care of the sacred robes. Huldah lived in the New Quarter of Jerusalem.

[15]Huldah said to them, "The Lord is the God of Israel. He says, 'Here is what you must tell the man who sent you to me. [16]Tell him, "The Lord says, 'I am going to bring horrible trouble on this place and its people. Everything written in the book the king of Judah has read will take place. [17]That's because the people have deserted me. They have burned incense to other gods. They have made me very angry because of the statues of gods their hands have made. So my anger will burn like a fire against this place. And the fire of my anger will not be put out.'"' [18]The king of Judah sent you to ask the Lord for advice. Tell him, 'The Lord is the God of Israel. He has a message for you about the things you heard. He says, [19]"Your heart was tender. You made yourself humble in the eyes of the Lord. You heard what I spoke against this place and its people. I said they would be under a curse. I told them they would be destroyed. You tore your royal robes and wept in front of me. And I have heard you," announces the Lord. [20]"You will join the members of your family who have already

died. You will be buried in peace. Your eyes will not see all the trouble I am going to bring on this place." ' "

Huldah's answer was taken back to the king.

Josiah Promises Again to Obey the Covenant

23 Then the king called together all the elders of Judah and Jerusalem. [2]He went up to the Lord's temple. The people of Judah and Jerusalem went with him. So did the priests and prophets. All of them went, from the least important of them to the most important. The king had all the words of Book of the Covenant read to them. The book had been found in the Lord's temple. [3]The king stood next to his pillar. He agreed to the terms of the covenant in front of the Lord. The king promised to serve the Lord and obey his commands, directions and rules. He promised to obey them with all his heart and with all his soul. So he agreed to the terms of the covenant written down in that book. Then all the people committed themselves to the covenant as well.

[4]Certain things in the Lord's temple had been made to honor other gods. They were the god named Baal, the female god named Asherah and all the stars in the sky. The king ordered Hilkiah the high priest to remove those things. The king ordered the priests who were next in rank and the men who guarded the doors to help Hilkiah. Josiah took those things that had been in the Lord's temple and burned them outside Jerusalem. He burned them in the fields in the Kidron Valley. And he took the ashes to Bethel. [5]Josiah got rid of the priests who served other gods. The kings of Judah had appointed those priests to burn incense. They burned the incense on the high places of the towns of Judah. And they burned it on the high places around Jerusalem. They burned incense to honor Baal and the sun and moon. They burned it to honor all the stars. [6]Josiah removed the Asherah pole from the Lord's temple. It had been used to worship the female god named Asherah. He took it to the Kidron Valley outside Jerusalem. There he burned it. He ground it into powder. And he scattered it over the graves of the ordinary people. [7]He also tore down the rooms where the male temple prostitutes stayed. Those rooms were in the

LORD's temple. Women had made cloth for Asherah in them.

⁸Josiah brought all the priests from the towns of Judah and destroyed the high places. He destroyed them from Geba all the way to Beersheba. The priests had burned incense on them. Josiah broke down the gate at the entrance of the Gate of Joshua. It was on the left side of Jerusalem's city gate. Joshua was the city governor. ⁹The priests of the high places didn't serve at the LORD's altar in Jerusalem. In spite of that, they ate with the other priests. All of them ate bread made without yeast.

¹⁰Josiah destroyed the high place at Topheth in the Valley of Ben Hinnom. He didn't want anyone to use the high place to sacrifice his son or daughter in the fire to the god named Molek. ¹¹Josiah removed the statues of horses from the entrance to the LORD's temple. The kings of Judah had set them apart to honor the sun. The statues were in the courtyard. They were near the room of an official named Nathan-Melek. Josiah burned the chariots that had been set apart to honor the sun.

¹²He pulled down the altars the kings of Judah had set up. They had put them on the palace roof near the upstairs room of Ahaz. Josiah also pulled down the altars Manasseh had built. They were in the two courtyards of the LORD's temple. Josiah removed the altars from there. He smashed them to pieces. Then he threw the broken pieces into the Kidron Valley. ¹³The king also destroyed the high places that were east of Jerusalem. They were at the southern end of the Mount of Olives. They were the ones Solomon, the king of Israel, had built. He had built a high place for worshiping Ashtoreth. She was the evil female god of the people of Sidon. Solomon had also built one for worshiping Chemosh. He was the evil god of Moab. And Solomon had built one for worshiping Molek. He was the god of the people of Ammon. The LORD hated that god. ¹⁴Josiah smashed the sacred stones. He cut down the poles used

to worship the female god named Asherah. Then he covered all those places with human bones.

¹⁵There was an altar at Bethel. It was at the high place made by Jeroboam, the son of Nebat. Jeroboam had caused Israel to commit sin. Even that altar and high place were destroyed by Josiah. He burned the high place. He ground it into powder. He also burned the Asherah pole. ¹⁶Then Josiah looked around. He saw the tombs on the side of the hill. He had the bones removed from them. And he burned them on the altar to make it "unclean." That's what the LORD had said would happen. He had spoken that message through a man of God. The man had announced those things long before they took place.

¹⁷The king asked, "What's that stone on the grave over there?"

The people of the city said, "It marks the tomb where the man of God is buried. He came from Judah. He spoke against the altar at Bethel. He announced the very things you have done to it."

¹⁸"Leave it alone," Josiah said. "Don't let anyone touch his bones." So they spared his bones. They also spared the bones of the prophet who had come from the northern kingdom of Israel.

¹⁹Josiah did in the rest of the northern kingdom the same things he had done at Bethel. He removed all the small temples at the high places. He made them "unclean." The kings of Israel had built them in the towns of the northern kingdom. The people in those towns had made the LORD very angry. ²⁰Josiah killed all the priests of those high places on the altars. He burned human bones on the altars. Then he went back to Jerusalem.

²¹The king gave an order to all the people. He said, "Celebrate the Passover Feast to honor the LORD your God. Do what is written in this Book of the Covenant." ²²A Passover Feast like that one had not been held for a long time. There hadn't been any like it in the days of the judges who led Israel. And there hadn't been any like it during the whole time the kings of Israel and Judah were ruling. ²³King Josiah celebrated the Passover Feast in Jerusalem to honor the LORD. It was in the 18th year of his rule.

²⁴And that's not all. Josiah got rid of those who got messages from people who had

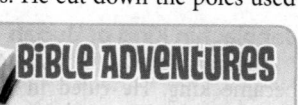

BIBLE ADVENTURES

Olivia saw the story of King Josiah in "Hidden Gems" (Club).

died. He got rid of those who talked to the spirits of people who had died. He got rid of the statues of family gods and the statues of other gods. He got rid of everything else the LORD hates that was in Judah and Jerusalem. He did it to carry out what the law required. That law was written in the book that Hilkiah the priest had found in the LORD's temple. ²⁵There was no king like Josiah either before him or after him. None of them turned to the LORD as he did. He obeyed the LORD with all his heart and all his soul. He obeyed him with all his strength. He did everything the Law of Moses required.

²⁶In spite of that, the LORD didn't turn away from his great anger against Judah. That's because of everything Manasseh had done to make him very angry. ²⁷So the LORD said, "I will remove Judah from my land. I will do to them what I did to Israel. I will turn my back on Jerusalem. It is the city I chose. I will also turn my back on this temple. I spoke about it. I said, 'I will put my Name there.'" *(1 Kings 8:29)*

²⁸The other events of the rule of Josiah are written down. Everything he did is written in the official records of the kings of Judah.

²⁹Pharaoh Necho was king of Egypt. He marched up to the Euphrates River. He went there to help the king of Assyria. It happened while Josiah was king. Josiah marched out to meet Necho in battle. When Necho saw him at Megiddo, he killed him. ³⁰Josiah's servants brought his body in a chariot from Megiddo to Jerusalem. They buried him in his own tomb. Then the people of the land went and got Jehoahaz. They anointed him as king in place of his father Josiah.

Jehoahaz King of Judah

³¹Jehoahaz was 23 years old when he became king. He ruled in Jerusalem for three months. His mother's name was Hamutal. She was the daughter of Jeremiah. She was from Libnah. ³²Jehoahaz did what was evil in the eyes of the LORD. He did just as the kings who had ruled before him had done. ³³Pharaoh Necho put him in chains at Riblah in the land of Hamath. That kept him from ruling in Jerusalem. Necho made the people of Judah pay him a tax of almost four tons of silver and 75 pounds of gold. ³⁴Pharaoh Necho made Eliakim king in place of his father Josiah. Necho changed Eliakim's name to Jehoiakim. But he took Jehoahaz with

him to Egypt. And that's where Jehoahaz died. ³⁵Jehoiakim paid Pharaoh Necho the silver and gold he required. To get the money, Jehoiakim taxed the land. He forced the people to give him the silver and gold. He made each one pay him what he required.

Jehoiakim King of Judah

³⁶Jehoiakim was 25 years old when he became king. He ruled in Jerusalem for 11 years. His mother's name was Zebidah. She was the daughter of Pedaiah. She was from Rumah. ³⁷Jehoiakim did what was evil in the eyes of the LORD. He did just as the kings who had ruled before him had done.

24 During Jehoiakim's rule, Nebuchadnezzar marched into the land and attacked it. He was king of Babylon. He became Jehoiakim's master for three years. But then Jehoiakim decided he didn't want to remain under Nebuchadnezzar's control. ²The LORD sent robbers against Jehoiakim from Babylon, Aram, Moab and Ammon. He sent them to destroy Judah. That's what the LORD had said would happen. He had spoken that message through his servants the prophets. ³These things happened to Judah in keeping with what the LORD had commanded. He brought enemies against his people in order to remove them from his land. He removed them because of all the sins Manasseh had committed. ⁴Manasseh had spilled the blood of many people who weren't guilty of doing anything wrong. In fact, he spilled so much of their blood that he filled Jerusalem with it. So the LORD refused to forgive him.

⁵The other events of the rule of Jehoiakim are written down. Everything he did is written in the official records of the kings of Judah. ⁶Jehoiakim joined the members of his family who had already died. Jehoiakim's son Jehoiachin became the next king after him.

⁷The king of Egypt didn't march out from his own country again. That's because the king of Babylon had taken so much of his territory. It reached from the Wadi of Egypt all the way to the Euphrates River.

Jehoiachin King of Judah

⁸Jehoiachin was 18 years old when he became king. He ruled in Jerusalem for three months. His mother's name was Nehushta. She was the daughter of Elnathan. She was from Jerusalem. ⁹Jehoiachin did

what was evil in the eyes of the LORD. He did just as his father Jehoiakim had done.

[10]At that time the officers of Nebuchadnezzar, the king of Babylon, marched to Jerusalem. They surrounded it and got ready to attack it. [11]Nebuchadnezzar himself came up to the city. He arrived while his officers were attacking it. [12]Jehoiachin, the king of Judah, handed himself over to Nebuchadnezzar. Jehoiachin's mother did the same thing. And so did all his attendants, nobles and officials.

The king of Babylon took Jehoiachin away as his prisoner. It was in the eighth year of Nebuchadnezzar's rule. [13]Nebuchadnezzar removed the treasures from the LORD's temple. He also removed the treasures from the royal palace. He cut up the gold objects that Solomon, the king of Israel, had made for the temple. That's what the LORD had announced would happen. [14]Nebuchadnezzar took all the people of Jerusalem to the land of Babylon as prisoners. That included all the officers and fighting men. It also included all the skilled workers. The total number of prisoners was 10,000. Only the poorest people were left in the land.

[15]Nebuchadnezzar took Jehoiachin to Babylon as his prisoner. He also took the king's mother from Jerusalem to Babylon. And he took Jehoiachin's wives, his officials and the most important people of the land. [16]The king also forced the whole army of 7,000 soldiers to go away to the land of Babylon. Those men were strong and able to go to war. And the king forced 1,000 skilled workers to go to Babylon. [17]Nebuchadnezzar made Jehoiachin's uncle Mattaniah king in his place. And Nebuchadnezzar changed Mattaniah's name to Zedekiah.

Zedekiah King of Judah

[18]Zedekiah was 21 years old when he became king. He ruled in Jerusalem for 11 years. His mother's name was Hamutal. She was the daughter of Jeremiah. She was from Libnah. [19]Zedekiah did what was evil in the eyes of the LORD. He did just as Jehoiakim had done. [20]The enemies of Jerusalem and Judah attacked them because the LORD was angry. In the end the LORD threw them out of his land.

The Fall of Jerusalem

Zedekiah also refused to remain under the control of Nebuchadnezzar.

WOOTON'S FUN FACTS

2 Kgs. 24:12

Jehoiachin had to go to prison. Archaeological digs have uncovered Babylonian tablets that show the expenses of King Jehoiachin's prison rations. Even back in Bible times, someone had to file the paperwork.

25 Nebuchadnezzar was king of Babylon. He marched out against Jerusalem. His whole army went with him. It was in the ninth year of the rule of Zedekiah. It was on the tenth day of the tenth month. Nebuchadnezzar set up camp outside the city. He brought in war machines all around it. [2]It was surrounded until the 11th year of King Zedekiah's rule.

[3]By the ninth day of the fourth month, there wasn't any food left in the city. So the people didn't have anything to eat. [4]Then the Babylonians broke through the city wall. Judah's whole army ran away at night. They went out through the gate between the two walls near the king's garden. They escaped even though the Babylonians surrounded the city. Judah's army ran toward the Arabah Valley. [5]But the Babylonian army chased King Zedekiah. They caught up with him in the plains near Jericho. All his soldiers were separated from him. They had scattered in every direction. [6]The king was captured.

He was taken to the king of Babylon at Riblah. That's where Nebuchadnezzar decided how he would be punished. [7]Nebuchadnezzar's men killed the sons of Zedekiah. They forced him to watch it with his own eyes. Then they poked out his eyes. They put him in bronze chains. And they took him to Babylon.

[8]Nebuzaradan was an official of the king of Babylon. In fact, he was commander of

the royal guard. He came to Jerusalem. It was in the 19th year that Nebuchadnezzar was king of Babylon. It was on the seventh day of the fifth month. [9]Nebuzaradan set the LORD's temple on fire. He also set fire to the royal palace and all the houses in Jerusalem. He burned down every important building. [10]The whole Babylonian army broke down the walls around Jerusalem. That's what the commander told them to do. [11]Some people still remained in the city. But Nebuzaradan the commander took them away as prisoners. He also took the rest of the people of the land. That included those who had joined the king of Babylon. [12]But the commander left behind some of the poorest people of the land. He told them to work in the vineyards and fields.

[13]The Babylonian army destroyed the LORD's temple. They broke the bronze pillars into pieces. They broke up the bronze stands that could be moved around. And they broke up the huge bronze bowl. Then they carried the bronze away to Babylon. [14]They also took away the pots, shovels, wick cutters and dishes. They took away all the bronze objects used for any purpose in the temple. [15]The commander of the royal guard took away the shallow cups for burning incense. He took away the sprinkling bowls. So he took away everything made out of pure gold or silver.

[16]The bronze was more than anyone could weigh. It included the bronze from the two pillars, the huge bowl and the stands. Solomon had made all those things for the LORD's temple. [17]Each pillar was 27 feet high. The bronze top of one pillar was four and a half feet high. It was decorated with a set of bronze chains and pomegranates all around it. The other pillar was just like it. It also had a set of chains.

[18]The commander of the guard took some prisoners. They included Seraiah the chief priest and Zephaniah the priest who was next in rank. They also included the three men who guarded the temple doors. [19]Some people were still left in the city. The commander took as a prisoner the officer who was in charge of the fighting men. He took the five men who gave advice to the king. He also took the secretary. He was the chief officer in charge of getting the people of the land to serve in the army. And he took 60 of those people serving in the army who were still in the city. [20]Nebuzaradan the commander took all of them away. He brought them to the king of Babylon at Riblah. [21]There the king had them put to death. Riblah was in the land of Hamath.

So the people of Judah were taken as prisoners. They were taken far away from their own land.

[22]Nebuchadnezzar, the king of Babylon, had left some people behind in Judah. He appointed Gedaliah to govern them. Gedaliah was the son of Ahikam. Ahikam was the son of Shaphan. [23]All of Judah's army officers and their men heard about what had happened. They heard that the king had appointed Gedaliah as governor. So they came to Gedaliah at Mizpah. Ishmael, the son of Nethaniah, came. So did Johanan, the son of Kareah. Seraiah, the son of Tanhumeth, also came. And so did Jaazaniah, the son of the Maakathite. All their men came too. Seraiah was from Netophah. [24]Gedaliah promised to help them and their men. He spoke in a kind way to them. He said, "Don't be afraid of the Babylonian officials. Make your homes in the land of Judah. Serve the king of Babylon. Then things will go well with you."

[25]But in the seventh month Ishmael, the son of Nethaniah, came with ten men. He killed Gedaliah. He also killed the people of Judah and the Babylonians who were with Gedaliah at Mizpah. Nethaniah was the son of Elishama. Ishmael was a member of the royal family. [26]After he had killed Gedaliah, all the people ran away to Egypt. Everyone from the least important of them to the most important ran away. The army officers went with them. All of them went to Egypt because they were afraid of the Babylonians.

Jehoiachin Is Set Free

[27]Awel-Marduk set Jehoiachin, the king of Judah, free from prison. It was in the 37th year after Jehoiachin had been taken away to Babylon. It was also the year Awel-Marduk became king of Babylon. It was on the 27th day of the 12th month. [28]Awel-Marduk spoke kindly to Jehoiachin. He gave him a place of honor. Other kings were with Jehoiachin in Babylon. But his place was more important than theirs. [29]So Jehoiachin put his prison clothes away. For the rest of Jehoiachin's life the king provided what he needed. [30]The king did that for Jehoiachin day by day as long as he lived.

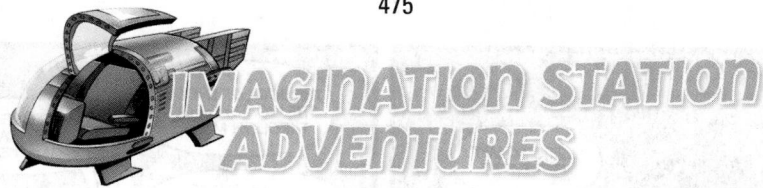

IMAGINATION STATION ADVENTURES

JOSIAH'S FEAST

Read 2 Kings 22—23.

MR. WHITTAKER, "WHIT", HAS SENT FRIENDS TORI AND MATTHEW TO OLD TESTAMENT JERUSALEM IN THE IMAGINATION STATION. WHIT WANTS THEM TO SEE WHAT HAPPENS WHEN LEADERS STOP FOLLOWING GOD'S WAYS.

THE DASHBOARD SAYS IT'S 701 BC. KING SENNACHERIB OF ASSYRIA IS LAYING SIEGE TO JERUSALEM.

I DON'T WANT TO GET OUT HERE—THOSE ASSYRIANS LOOK **MEAN**. LET'S TRY ANOTHER TIME PERIOD.

HA! YOUR GOD CAN'T SAVE YOU! **YOU'RE GOING TO STARVE!**

SIXTY YEARS LATER JERUSALEM EXPERIENCES A PERIOD OF PEACE. MATTHEW AND TORI VISIT SOLOMON'S TEMPLE. THE TEMPLE IS IN DISREPAIR BECAUSE THE KINGS OF JUDAH HAVE CHASED AFTER OTHER GODS.

KING JOSIAH WANTS ME TO TAKE THE TEMPLE TAX AND CLEAN UP THE TEMPLE. HE WANTS ME TO HIRE CARPENTERS AND STONEMASONS TO **RESTORE THE TEMPLES BEAUTY!**

MATTHEW AND TORI DECIDE TO STAY AND HELP THE HIGH PRIEST, HILKIAH, CLEAN UP THE TEMPLE.

SHOULDN'T THERE BE GOLD STUFF ALL OVER, AND THE ARK OF THE COVENANT?

ALAS, MANY OF THE TREASURES HAVE BEEN **SOLD** TO PAY TRIBUTE TO THE ASSYRIAN KINGS— OTHERWISE THEY WOULD DESTROY US. YEARS AGO KING JOSIAH HID THE ARK OF THE COVENANT.

SO THE ARK COULDN'T BE STOLEN BY YOUR ENEMIES. **THAT'S SMART.**

1 Chronicles

A "chronicle" is a historical account of something. It comes from the same root as the word "chronological," thus implying the stories are usually in chronological order. If you were taking on the task of chronicling your family, you would talk to everyone you could—especially the older and wiser members—to collect facts and stories to include. And if you came across a particular story that might be embarrassing to your family, you might choose to leave that information out. That's precisely what the author of Chronicles did.

No one knows for sure who the author of this narrative was (although Ezra is often given credit), but it does seem evident that he used a lot of different sources to gather the material. Approximately half of it comes from 1 and 2 Samuel and 1 and 2 Kings. The author starts his family story with Adam and many early Bible characters (chapters 1–9). The rest of 1 Chronicles is devoted to the life and reign of David. The Chronicler's view of David is overwhelmingly positive, omitting the affair with Bathsheba, the troubles created by David's sons, and other stories of struggle and turmoil. So while much of the material might be the same as in previous books, it is still good to read both accounts to get the full and complete picture.

What's it Mean, Eugene?

Image of God—Genesis 1:27 states that God created human beings "in his own likeness." Older translations use the phrase "in His *image*." We may never grasp the full significance of this statement, but we do know that it at least means that every time we look at someone, we see a reflection (though imperfect) of who God is and what He is like. This is why human life is so sacred and special. We're all image-bearers of God, regardless of our size, skin color, or status.

A List of Names From Adam to Abraham

A List of Names From Adam to the Sons of Noah

1 Adam, Seth, Enosh, ² Kenan, Mahalalel, Jared, ³ Enoch, Methuselah, Lamech, Noah.

⁴ The sons of Noah were Shem, Ham and Japheth.

The Sons of Japheth

⁵ The sons of Japheth were
Gomer, Magog, Madai, Javan, Tubal, Meshek and Tiras.
⁶ The sons of Gomer were
Ashkenaz, Riphath and Togarmah.
⁷ The sons of Javan were
Elishah, Tarshish, the Kittites and the Rodanites.

The Sons of Ham

⁸ The sons of Ham were
Cush, Egypt, Put and Canaan.
⁹ The sons of Cush were
Seba, Havilah, Sabta, Raamah and Sabteka.
The sons of Raamah were
Sheba and Dedan.
¹⁰ Cush was the father of
Nimrod. Nimrod became a mighty hero on the earth.
¹¹ Egypt was the father of
the Ludites, Anamites, Lehabites and Naphtuhites. ¹²He was also the father of the Pathrusites, Kasluhites and Caphtorites. The Philistines came from the family line of the Kasluhites.
¹³ Canaan was the father of Sidon. Sidon was his oldest son.
Canaan was also the father of the Hittites, ¹⁴Jebusites, Amorites and Girgashites. ¹⁵And he was the father of the Hivites, Arkites, Sinites, ¹⁶Arvadites, Zemarites and Hamathites.

The Sons of Shem

¹⁷ The sons of Shem were
Elam, Ashur, Arphaxad, Lud and Aram.
The sons of Aram were
Uz, Hul, Gether and Meshek.
¹⁸ Arphaxad was the father of Shelah.
Shelah was the father of Eber.

¹⁹ Eber was the father of two sons.
One was named Peleg. That's because the earth was divided up in his time. His brother was named Joktan.
²⁰ Joktan was the father of
Almodad, Sheleph, Hazarmaveth and Jerah. ²¹He was also the father of Hadoram, Uzal, Diklah, ²²Obal, Abimael, Sheba, ²³Ophir, Havilah and Jobab. All of them were sons of Joktan.

²⁴ Shem, Arphaxad, Shelah,
²⁵ Eber, Peleg, Reu,
²⁶ Serug, Nahor, Terah,
²⁷ Abram. Abram was also called Abraham.

The Family of Abraham

²⁸ The sons of Abraham were Isaac and Ishmael.

The Family Line of Hagar

²⁹ Here are the members of the family line of Hagar.
Nebaioth was Ishmael's oldest son. Then came Kedar, Adbeel, Mibsam, ³⁰Mishma, Dumah, Massa, Hadad, Tema, ³¹Jetur, Naphish and Kedemah.
All of them were Ishmael's sons.

The Family Line of Keturah

³² Here are the sons born to Abraham's concubine Keturah.
They were Zimran, Jokshan, Medan, Midian, Ishbak and Shuah.
The sons of Jokshan were
Sheba and Dedan.
³³ The sons of Midian were
Ephah, Epher, Hanok, Abida and Eldaah.
All of them were from the family line of Keturah.

The Family Line of Sarah

³⁴ Abraham was the father of Isaac.
The sons of Isaac were
Esau and Israel.

The Sons of Esau

³⁵ The sons of Esau were
Eliphaz, Reuel, Jeush, Jalam and Korah.

36 The sons of Eliphaz were
Teman, Omar, Zepho, Gatam and
Kenaz.
Timna had Amalek by Eliphaz.
37 The sons of Reuel were
Nahath, Zerah, Shammah and
Mizzah.

The People of Seir in Edom
38 The sons of Seir were
Lotan, Shobal, Zibeon, Anah, Dishon, Ezer and Dishan.
39 The sons of Lotan were
Hori and Homam. Timna was
Lotan's sister.
40 The sons of Shobal were
Alvan, Manahath, Ebal, Shepho
and Onam.
The sons of Zibeon were
Aiah and Anah.
41 The son of Anah was
Dishon.
The sons of Dishon were
Hemdan, Eshban, Ithran and
Keran.
42 The sons of Ezer were
Bilhan, Zaavan and Akan.
The sons of Dishan were
Uz and Aran.

The Rulers of Edom
43 Before Israel had a king, there were
kings who ruled in Edom.
Bela was the son of Beor. Bela's city
was called Dinhabah.
44 When Bela died, Jobab became the
next king. Jobab was the son of
Zerah from Bozrah.
45 When Jobab died, Husham became
the next king. Husham was from
the land of the people of Teman.
46 When Husham died, Hadad became
the next king. Hadad was the son
of Bedad. Hadad had won the
battle over Midian in the country
of Moab. Hadad's city was called
Avith.
47 When Hadad died, Samlah became
the next king. Samlah was from
Masrekah.
48 When Samlah died, Shaul became the
next king. Shaul was from the town
of Rehoboth. It was by a river.
49 When Shaul died, Baal-Hanan became the next king. Baal-Hanan
was the son of Akbor.

50 When Baal-Hanan died, Hadad became the next king. Hadad's city
was called Pau. His wife's name
was Mehetabel. She was the
daughter of Matred. Matred was
the daughter of Me-Zahab. 51 Hadad also died.

The chiefs of Edom were
Timna, Alvah, Jetheth, 52 Oholibamah, Elah, Pinon, 53 Kenaz,
Teman, Mibzar, 54 Magdiel and
Iram.
They were the chiefs of Edom.

The Sons of Israel
2 Here are the names of the sons
of Israel. Reuben, Simeon, Levi,
Judah, Issachar, Zebulun, 2 Dan,
Joseph, Benjamin, Naphtali, Gad,
Asher.

The Family of Judah
The Family Line From Judah's Sons to Hezron's Sons
3 The sons of Judah were
Er, Onan and Shelah. A woman
from Canaan had these three sons
by him. She was the daughter of
Shua.
Er was Judah's oldest son. He was
evil in the Lord's sight. So the
Lord put him to death.
4 Tamar was Judah's daughter-in-law. She had Perez and Zerah by
him.
The total number of Judah's sons was
five.

5 The sons of Perez were
Hezron and Hamul.
6 The sons of Zerah were
Zimri, Ethan, Heman, Kalkol and
Darda. The total number of Zerah's sons was five.
7 The son of Karmi was Achar.
He brought trouble on Israel.
Some things that had been set
apart to the Lord in a special way
to be destroyed. He took some of
those things. When he did that, he
disobeyed the Lord's command.
8 The son of Ethan was
Azariah.
9 Hezron was the father of
Jerahmeel, Ram and Caleb.

The Family Line of Ram

¹⁰ Ram was the father of Amminadab. Amminadab was the father of Nahshon. Nahshon was the leader of the people of Judah.
¹¹ Nahshon was the father of Salmon. Salmon was the father of Boaz.
¹² Boaz was the father of Obed. And Obed was the father of Jesse.

¹³ Jesse's first son was
Eliab. His second son was Abinadab.
The third was Shimea. ¹⁴The fourth was Nethanel.
The fifth was Raddai. ¹⁵The sixth was Ozem.
And the seventh was David.
¹⁶ Their sisters were Zeruiah and Abigail.
Zeruiah's three sons were Abishai, Joab and Asahel.
¹⁷ Abigail was the mother of Amasa. Amasa's father was Jether. Jether belonged to the family line of Ishmael.

The Family Line of Caleb

¹⁸ Caleb was the son of Hezron. Caleb's wife Azubah had children by him. Jerioth also had children by him. Azubah's sons were
Jesher, Shobab and Ardon.
¹⁹ When Azubah died, Caleb married Ephrath. She had Hur by him.
²⁰ Hur was the father of Uri. And Uri was the father of Bezalel.

²¹ When he was 60 years old, Hezron married the daughter of Makir. Makir was the father of Gilead. Hezron slept with his wife, and she had Segub by him.
²² Segub was the father of Jair. Jair controlled 23 towns in Gilead.
²³ But Geshur and Aram captured Havvoth Jair. They also captured Kenath and the settlements around it. The total number of towns captured was 60.
Hezron, Segub and Jair belonged to the family line of Makir. Makir was the father of Gilead.
²⁴ Hezron died in Caleb Ephrathah. Abijah was Hezron's wife. She had Ashhur by him. Ashhur was born after Hezron died. Ashhur was the father of Tekoa.

The Family Line of Jerahmeel

²⁵ Here are the sons of Jerahmeel. He was the oldest son of Hezron.
Ram was Jerahmeel's oldest son. Then came Bunah, Oren, Ozem and Ahijah. ²⁶Jerahmeel had another wife. Her name was Atarah. She was the mother of Onam.
²⁷ Here are the sons of Ram. He was the oldest son of Jerahmeel. The sons of Ram were
Maaz, Jamin and Eker.
²⁸ The sons of Onam were
Shammai and Jada.
The sons of Shammai were
Nadab and Abishur. ²⁹Abishur's wife was named Abihail. She had Ahban and Molid by him.
³⁰ The sons of Nadab were
Seled and Appaim. Seled died without having any children.
³¹ The son of Appaim was
Ishi. Ishi was the father of Sheshan. Sheshan was the father of Ahlai.
³² The sons of Jada were
Jether and Jonathan. Jada was Shammai's brother. Jether died without having any children.
³³ The sons of Jonathan were
Peleth and Zaza.
They belonged to the family line of Jerahmeel.

³⁴ Sheshan didn't have any sons. All he had was daughters.
He had a servant from Egypt named Jarha. ³⁵Sheshan gave his daughter to be married to his servant Jarha. She had Attai by Jarha.
³⁶ Attai was the father of Nathan. Nathan was the father of Zabad.
³⁷ Zabad was the father of Ephlal. Ephlal was the father of Obed.
³⁸ Obed was the father of Jehu. Jehu was the father of Azariah.
³⁹ Azariah was the father of Helez. Helez was the father of Eleasah.
⁴⁰ Eleasah was the father of Sismai. Sismai was the father of Shallum.
⁴¹ Shallum was the father of Jekamiah. And Jekamiah was the father of Elishama.

The Family Groups of Caleb

42 Caleb was the brother of Jerahmeel. Caleb's oldest son was Mesha. Mesha was the father of Ziph. Caleb had another son named Mareshah. Mareshah was the father of Hebron.
43 The sons of Hebron were Korah, Tappuah, Rekem and Shema.
44 Shema was the father of Raham. Raham was the father of Jorkeam. Rekem was the father of Shammai.
45 The son of Shammai was Maon. Maon was the father of Beth Zur.
46 Caleb had a concubine named Ephah. She was the mother of Haran, Moza and Gazez. Haran was the father of Gazez.
47 The sons of Jahdai were Regem, Jotham, Geshan, Pelet, Ephah and Shaaph.
48 Caleb had a concubine named Maakah. She was the mother of Sheber and Tirhanah.
49 She was also the mother of Shaaph and Sheva. Shaaph was the father of Madmannah. Sheva was the father of Makbenah and Gibea. Caleb's daughter was Aksah.
50 All of them belonged to the family line of Caleb.

Hur was the oldest son of Ephrathah. Hur was the brother of Shobal. Shobal was the father of Kiriath Jearim. 51 Hur was the father of Salma. Salma was the father of Bethlehem. Hur was also the father of Hareph. Hareph was the father of Beth Gader.
52 Here is the family line of Shobal, the father of Kiriath Jearim. It included Haroeh and half of the people of Manahath. 53 It also included the family groups of Kiriath Jearim. They were the Ithrites, Puthites, Shumathites and Mishraites. The people of Zorah and Eshtaol belonged to these family groups.
54 Here is the family line of Salma. It included Bethlehem, the people of Netophah, Atroth Beth Joab, half of the people of Manahath, and the Zorites. 55 It also included the family groups of secretaries who lived at Jabez. They were the Tirathites, Shimeathites and Sucathites. They were the Kenites who belonged to the family line of Hammath. Hammath was the father of the family line of Rekab.

The Sons of David

3 Here are the sons of David who were born to him in Hebron.

His first son was Amnon. Amnon's mother was Ahinoam from Jezreel.

The second son was Daniel. His mother was Abigail from Carmel. 2 The third son was Absalom. His mother was Maakah. She was the daughter of Talmai, the king of Geshur.

The fourth son was Adonijah. His mother was Haggith. 3 The fifth son was Shephatiah. His mother was Abital.

The sixth son was Ithream. David's wife Eglah had Ithream by him.

4 These six sons were born to David in Hebron. He ruled there for seven and a half years.

After that, he ruled in Jerusalem for 33 years. 5 Children were born to him there.

They included Shammua, Shobab, Nathan and Solomon. The mother of these four sons was Bathsheba. She was the daughter of Ammiel. 6 David's children also included Ibhar, Elishua, Eliphelet, 7 Nogah, Nepheg, Japhia, 8 Elishama, Eliada and Eliphelet. There were nine of them.

9 David was the father of all these sons. His concubines also had sons by him. David's sons had a sister named Tamar.

The Kings of Judah

10 Solomon's son was Rehoboam. Abijah was the son of Rehoboam.

Asa was the son of Abijah.
Jehoshaphat was the son of Asa.
[11] Jehoram was the son of Jehoshaphat.
Ahaziah was the son of Jehoram.
Joash was the son of Ahaziah.
[12] Amaziah was the son of Joash.
Azariah was the son of Amaziah.
Jotham was the son of Azariah.
[13] Ahaz was the son of Jotham.
Hezekiah was the son of Ahaz.
Manasseh was the son of Hezekiah.
[14] Amon was the son of Manasseh.
Josiah was the son of Amon.
[15] Josiah's first son was Johanan.
Jehoiakim was his second son.
Zedekiah was the third son.
Shallum was the fourth son.
[16] The next king after Jehoiakim was his son Jehoiachin.
After that, Josiah's son Zedekiah became king.

The Royal Family Line After Jehoiachin

[17] Here are the members of the family line of Jehoiachin. He was taken as a prisoner to Babylon.
His sons were Shealtiel, [18]Malkiram, Pedaiah, Shenazzar, Jekamiah, Hoshama and Nedabiah.
[19] The sons of Pedaiah were Zerubbabel and Shimei.
The sons of Zerubbabel were Meshullam and Hananiah. Shelomith was their sister. [20]There were also five other sons. They were Hashubah, Ohel, Berekiah, Hasadiah and Jushab-Hesed.
[21] The family line of Hananiah included Pelatiah and Jeshaiah. It also included the sons of Rephaiah, Arnan, Obadiah and Shekaniah.
[22] The family line of Shekaniah included Shemaiah and his sons. They were Hattush, Igal, Bariah, Neariah and Shaphat. The total number of men was six.
[23] The sons of Neariah were Elioenai, Hizkiah and Azrikam. The total number of sons was three.
[24] The sons of Elioenai were Hodaviah, Eliashib, Pelaiah, Akkub, Johanan, Delaiah and Anani. The total number of sons was seven.

Other Family Groups of Judah

4 The family line of Judah included Perez, Hezron, Karmi, Hur and Shobal.
[2] Reaiah was the son of Shobal and the father of Jahath. Jahath was the father of Ahumai and Lahad. These were the family groups of the people of Zorah.
[3] The sons of Etam were Jezreel, Ishma and Idbash. Their sister was named Hazzelelponi. [4]Penuel was the father of Gedor. Ezer was the father of Hushah. These people belonged to the family line of Hur. He was the oldest son of Ephrathah and the father of Bethlehem.
[5] Ashhur was the father of Tekoa. Ashhur had two wives. Their names were Helah and Naarah.
[6] Naarah had Ahuzzam, Hepher, Temeni and Haahashtari by Ashhur. They belonged to the family line of Naarah.
[7] The sons of Helah were Zereth, Zohar, Ethnan [8]and Koz. Koz was the father of Anub and Hazzobebah. He was also the father of the family groups of Aharhel. Aharhel was the son of Harum.

[9]Jabez was more respected than his brothers. His mother had named him Jabez. She had said, "I was in a lot of pain when he was born." [10]Jabez cried out to the God of Israel. He said, "I wish you would bless me. I wish you would give me more territory. Let your power protect me. Keep me from harm. Then I won't have any pain." God gave him what he asked for.

[11] Kelub was the brother of Shuhah and the father of Mehir. Mehir was the father of Eshton. [12]Eshton was the father of Beth Rapha, Paseah and Tehinnah. Tehinnah was the father of Ir Nahash. These were the men of Rekah.

[13] The sons of Kenaz were Othniel and Seraiah.
The sons of Othniel were Hathath and Meonothai. [14]Meonothai was the father of Ophrah.

Seraiah was the father of Joab. Joab was the father of Ge Harashim. Ge Harashim was called by that name because all its people were skilled workers. ¹⁵ The sons of Caleb were

Iru, Elah and Naam. Caleb was the son of Jephunneh.

The son of Elah was

Kenaz. ¹⁶ The sons of Jehallelel were

Ziph, Ziphah, Tiria and Asarel. ¹⁷ The sons of Ezrah were

Jether, Mered, Epher and Jalon.

One of Mered's wives had Miriam, Shammai and Ishbah by him. Ishbah was the father of Eshtemoa. ¹⁸These were the children of Pharaoh's daughter Bithiah. Mered had married her.

His wife from the tribe of Judah had Jered, Heber and Jekuthiel by him. Jered was the father of Gedor. Heber was the father of Soko. Jekuthiel was the father of Zanoah. ¹⁹ Hodiah's wife was the sister of Naham. Her sons were

the father of Keilah the Garmite and Eshtemoa the Maakathite. ²⁰ The sons of Shimon were

Amnon, Rinnah, Ben-Hanan and Tilon.

The family line of Ishi included Zoheth and Ben-Zoheth. ²¹ Shelah was the son of Judah. The sons of Shelah were

Er and Laadah. Er was the father of Lekah. Laadah was the father of Mareshah. He was also the father of the family groups of the linen workers who lived in Beth Ashbea. ²² Other sons of Shelah were Jokim, Joash, Saraph and the men of Kozeba. Moab and Jashubi Lehem were ruled by sons of Shelah. The records of all these matters are very old.²³Some of Shelah's sons were potters who lived in Netaim and Gederah. They stayed there and worked for the king.

The Family Line of Simeon

²⁴ The family line of Simeon included

Nemuel, Jamin, Jarib, Zerah and Shaul. ²⁵Shallum was Shaul's son.

Mibsam was Shallum's son. Mishma was Mibsam's son. ²⁶ The family line of Mishma included

Hammuel. Hammuel was Mishma's son. Zakkur was Hammuel's son. Shimei was Zakkur's son.

²⁷Shimei had 16 sons and six daughters. But his brothers didn't have many children. So their whole family group didn't have as many people as Judah had. ²⁸Shimei's family group lived in Beersheba, Moladah, Hazar Shual, ²⁹Bilhah, Ezem, Tolad, ³⁰Bethuel, Hormah, Ziklag, ³¹Beth Markaboth, Hazar Susim, Beth Biri and Shaaraim. These were their towns until David became king. ³²Five of the villages around these towns were Etam, Ain, Rimmon, Token and Ashan. ³³The territory of all the villages around these towns reached all the way to Baalath. These were their settlements.

The tribe of Simeon kept its own family history.

³⁴ Simeon's family line included Meshobab, Jamlech and Joshah. Joshah was the son of Amaziah. ³⁵ Simeon's family line also included

Joel and Jehu. Jehu was the son of Joshibiah. Joshibiah was the son of Seraiah. Seraiah was the son of Asiel. ³⁶ And the family line included Elioenai, Jaakobah, Jeshohaiah, Asaiah, Adiel, Jesimiel, Benaiah ³⁷ and Ziza. Ziza was the son of Shiphi. Shiphi was the son of Allon. Allon was the son of Jedaiah. Jedaiah was the son of Shimri. And Shimri was the son of Shemaiah.

³⁸ The men whose names are listed above were leaders of their family groups.

Their families greatly increased their numbers. ³⁹They spread out all the way to the edge of Gedor east of the valley. They looked for grasslands for their flocks. ⁴⁰They found grasslands that were rich and good. The land had plenty of room. It was peaceful and quiet. Some of the people of Ham had lived there before.

⁴¹The men whose names are listed lived at the time when Hezekiah was king of Judah. They came and attacked the Hamites in their homes. They also attacked the

Meunites who were there. And they completely destroyed them. What happened to them is clear even to this day. The men of Simeon made their homes where the Meunites had lived. That's because in that place there were enough grasslands for their flocks. ⁴²Five hundred of these men came into the hill country of Seir and attacked it. They were led by Pelatiah, Neariah, Rephaiah and Uzziel. These four men were the sons of Ishi. ⁴³They killed the rest of the Amalekites who had escaped. And they still live there to this day.

The Family Line of Reuben

5 Reuben was the oldest son of Israel. But he slept with his father's concubine. By doing that, he made his father's bed "unclean." That's why his rights as the oldest son were given to the sons of Joseph, the son of Israel. So Reuben isn't listed in the family history as the one who had the rights of the oldest son. ²Judah also did not have the rights of the oldest son. Judah didn't have them even though he was the leader among his brothers. And a ruler came from his family line. But the rights of the oldest son belonged to Joseph. ³Reuben was the oldest son of Israel. Reuben's sons were

Hanok, Pallu, Hezron and Karmi.
⁴ The family line of Joel includes
his son Shemaiah. Gog was the
son of Shemaiah.
Shimei was the son of Gog. ⁵Micah was the son of Shimei.
Reaiah was the son of Micah. Baal
was the son of Reaiah.
⁶ And Beerah was the son of Baal.
Beerah was a leader of the people
of Reuben. Tiglath-Pileser took
Beerah as a prisoner to another
country. Tiglath-Pileser was the
king of Assyria.
⁷ Here are the relatives of the family
groups of Reuben. They are listed
in their family history.
They include Chief Jeiel, Zechariah ⁸and Bela. Bela was the son of
Azaz. Azaz was the son of Shema.
Shema was the son of Joel.

All of them made their homes in the area from Aroer to Nebo and Baal Meon.

⁹To the east they made their homes in the land up to the edge of the desert. That desert reaches all the way to the Euphrates River. They made their homes there because their livestock had increased in Gilead.

¹⁰While Saul was king, the people of Reuben went to war against the Hagrites. They won the battle over them. Then they lived in the houses of the Hagrites. The people of Reuben lived in the entire area east of Gilead.

The Family Line of Gad

¹¹ The people of Gad lived next to the people of Reuben in Bashan. They spread out all the way to Salekah.

¹² Joel was their chief. Shapham was next. Then came Janai and Shaphat in Bashan.

¹³ Here are their relatives family by family. They included
Michael, Meshullam, Sheba, Jorai, Jakan, Zia and Eber. The total number of them was seven.

¹⁴ These were the sons of Abihail. Abihail was the son of Huri. Huri was the son of Jaroah. Jaroah was the son of Gilead. Gilead was the son of Michael. Michael was the son of Jeshishai. Jeshishai was the son of Jahdo. And Jahdo was the son of Buz.

¹⁵ Ahi was the leader of some of the families of Gad. Ahi was the son of Abdiel. Abdiel was the son of Guni.

¹⁶The people of Gad lived in the land of Gilead. They lived in the villages of Bashan. They also lived on all the grasslands of Sharon as far as they reached.

¹⁷All these names were written down in the family history. They were written during the time when Jotham was king of Judah and Jeroboam was king of Israel.

¹⁸The tribes of Reuben, Gad and half the tribe of Manasseh had 44,760 men able to serve in the army. Each one was able to handle a shield and sword. Each was also able to use a bow. Each was trained for battle. ¹⁹They went to war against the Hagrites, Jetur, Naphish and Nodab. ²⁰God helped his people fight against the Hagrites and all who were helping them. He handed over all those enemies to his people. That's

because they cried out to him during the battle. He answered their prayers, because they trusted in him. ²¹They captured the livestock of the Hagrites. They captured 50,000 camels, 250,000 sheep and 2,000 donkeys. They also took 100,000 people as prisoners. ²²Many others were killed, because God won the battle over them. His people lived in the land until they themselves were taken as prisoners to other countries.

The Family Line of Half of the Tribe of Manasseh

²³The people in half of the tribe of Manasseh became a very large group. They made their homes in the land from Bashan to Baal Hermon. Baal Hermon is also called Senir. Another name for it is Mount Hermon. ²⁴Here are the leaders of their families. They included Epher, Ishi, Eliel, Azriel, Jeremiah, Hodaviah and Jahdiel. They were brave fighting men. They were also famous and were leaders of their families. ²⁵But they weren't faithful to the God of their people. They joined themselves to the gods of the nations of the land and worshiped them. God had destroyed those nations to make room for his people. ²⁶So the God of Israel stirred up the spirit of Pul. He was king of Assyria. He was also called Tiglath-Pileser. He took the tribes of Reuben and Gad and half of the tribe of Manasseh to other countries as his prisoners. He took

1 Chr. 5:26 Not all of the Israelite captives were taken to Babylon. These tribe members were taken to cities that don't exist anymore. Some scholars think the captives were taken as far as Russia. That's a long walk.

them to Halah, Habor, Hara and the river of Gozan. And that's where they still are to this day.

The Family Line of Levi

6 The sons of Levi were
Gershon, Kohath and Merari.
² The sons of Kohath were
Amram, Izhar, Hebron and Uzziel.
³ Aaron, Moses and Miriam
were born into the family line of Amram.
The sons of Aaron were
Nadab, Abihu, Eleazar and Ithamar.
⁴ Eleazar was the father of Phinehas.
Phinehas was the father of Abishua.
⁵ Abishua was the father of Bukki.
Bukki was the father of Uzzi.
⁶ Uzzi was the father of Zerahiah.
Zerahiah was the father of Meraioth.
⁷ Meraioth was the father of Amariah.
Amariah was the father of Ahitub.
⁸ Ahitub was the father of Zadok.
Zadok was the father of Ahimaaz.
⁹ Ahimaaz was the father of Azariah.
Azariah was the father of Johanan.
¹⁰ Johanan was the father of Azariah.
Azariah served as priest in the temple Solomon built in Jerusalem.
¹¹ Azariah was the father of Amariah.
Amariah was the father of Ahitub.
¹² Ahitub was the father of Zadok.
Zadok was the father of Shallum.
¹³ Shallum was the father of Hilkiah.
Hilkiah was the father of Azariah.
¹⁴ Azariah was the father of Seraiah.
And Seraiah was the father of Jozadak.
¹⁵ Jozadak was taken away from his own land. The LORD took the people of Judah and Jerusalem to the land of Babylon. He used Nebuchadnezzar to take them there as prisoners.
¹⁶ The sons of Levi were
Gershon, Kohath and Merari.
¹⁷ The names of the sons of Gershon were
Libni and Shimei.

¹⁸ The sons of Kohath were
Amram, Izhar, Hebron and Uzziel.
¹⁹ The sons of Merari were
Mahli and Mushi.

Here are the members of the family groups of the Levites. They are listed under the names of their fathers. ²⁰ Gershon was the father of Libni.
Jahath was Libni's son.
Zimmah was Jahath's son.
²¹ Joah was Zimmah's son.
Iddo was Joah's son.
Zerah was Iddo's son.
And Jeatherai was Zerah's son.
²² The family line of Kohath included his son Amminadab.
Korah was Amminadab's son.
Assir was Korah's son.
²³ Elkanah was Assir's son.
Ebiasaph was Elkanah's son.
Assir was Ebiasaph's son.
²⁴ Tahath was Assir's son.
Uriel was Tahath's son.
Uzziah was Uriel's son.
And Shaul was Uzziah's son.
²⁵ The family line of Elkanah included his son Amasai.
Amasai was the father of Ahimoth.
²⁶ Elkanah was Ahimoth's son.
Zophai was Elkanah's son.
Nahath was Zophai's son.
²⁷ Eliab was Nahath's son.
Jeroham was Eliab's son.
Elkanah was Jeroham's son.
And Samuel was Elkanah's son.
²⁸ The sons of Samuel were
his first son Joel
and his second son Abijah.
²⁹ The family line of Merari included his son Mahli.
Libni was Mahli's son.
Shimei was Libni's son.
Uzzah was Shimei's son.
³⁰ Shimea was Uzzah's son.
Haggiah was Shimea's son.
And Asaiah was Haggiah's son.

The Levites Who Were in Charge of the Music

³¹Here are the Levites David put in charge of the music in the house of the LORD. He did it after the ark was placed there. ³²The men used their music to serve in front of the holy tent, the tent of meeting. They served there until Solomon built

Jason's Jargon

1 CHRONICLES 6

Your next mission: Find the words *Most Holy Room* in this chapter. It was an inner chamber inside the temple and only the high priest could go there. Inside, he prayed and gave offerings to God.

the temple of the LORD in Jerusalem. They did their work according to the rules they had been given.

³³ Here are the men who served. The list also includes their sons.

The family line of Kohath included Heman. He led the music.
He was the son of Joel.
Joel was the son of Samuel.
³⁴ Samuel was the son of Elkanah.
Elkanah was the son of Jeroham.
Jeroham was the son of Eliel.
Eliel was the son of Toah.
³⁵ Toah was the son of Zuph.
Zuph was the son of Elkanah.
Elkanah was the son of Mahath.
Mahath was the son of Amasai.
³⁶ Amasai was the son of Elkanah.
Elkanah was the son of Joel.
Joel was the son of Azariah.
Azariah was the son of Zephaniah.
³⁷ Zephaniah was the son of Tahath.
Tahath was the son of Assir.
Assir was the son of Ebiasaph.
Ebiasaph was the son of Korah.
³⁸ Korah was the son of Izhar.
Izhar was the son of Kohath.
Kohath was the son of Levi.
And Levi was the son of Israel.
³⁹ Heman had a relative named Asaph.
Asaph served as Heman's helper at his right side.
Asaph was the son of Berekiah.
Berekiah was the son of Shimea.
⁴⁰ Shimea was the son of Michael.
Michael was the son of Baaseiah.
Baaseiah was the son of Malkijah.
⁴¹ Malkijah was the son of Ethni.
Ethni was the son of Zerah.

Zerah was the son of Adaiah. ⁴² Adaiah was the son of Ethan. Ethan was the son of Zimmah. Zimmah was the son of Shimei. ⁴³ Shimei was the son of Jahath. Jahath was the son of Gershon. And Gershon was the son of Levi. ⁴⁴ Here are the Levites in the family line of Merari who served as Heman's helpers at his left side. They were relatives of the Kohathites. Ethan was the son of Kishi. Kishi was the son of Abdi. Abdi was the son of Malluk. ⁴⁵ Malluk was the son of Hashabiah. Hashabiah was the son of Amaziah. Amaziah was the son of Hilkiah. ⁴⁶ Hilkiah was the son of Amzi. Amzi was the son of Bani. Bani was the son of Shemer. ⁴⁷ Shemer was the son of Mahli. Mahli was the son of Mushi. Mushi was the son of Merari. And Merari was the son of Levi.

⁴⁸The rest of the Levites were appointed to do all the other work at the holy tent. It was the house of God. ⁴⁹Aaron and his sons after him brought the offerings. They sacrificed them on the altar of burnt offering. They also burned incense on the altar of incense. That was part of what they did in the Most Holy Room. That's how they paid for the sin of Israel. They did everything just as Moses, the servant of God, had commanded.

⁵⁰ Here are the members of the family line of Aaron.
Eleazar was Aaron's son.
Phinehas was Eleazar's son.
Abishua was Phinehas's son.
⁵¹ Bukki was Abishua's son.
Uzzi was Bukki's son.
Zerahiah was Uzzi's son.
⁵² Meraioth was Zerahiah's son.
Amariah was Meraioth's son.
Ahitub was Amariah's son.
⁵³ Zadok was Ahitub's son.
And Ahimaaz was Zadok's son.

⁵⁴ Here were the places where they made their homes. These places were given to them as their territory. Some were given to the children of Aaron who were from the family group of Kohath. They were given out by casting lots. The first lot was for Kohath.

⁵⁵ In Judah the Kohathites were given Hebron. They also received the grasslands around Hebron. ⁵⁶But the fields and villages around the city were given to Caleb, the son of Jephunneh. ⁵⁷So the people in the family line of Aaron received Hebron. It was a city where people could go for safety. Aaron's family line received Libnah, Jattir, Eshtemoa, ⁵⁸Hilen and Debir. ⁵⁹They also received Ashan, Juttah and Beth Shemesh. They were given all these towns together with their grasslands.

⁶⁰ From the tribe of Benjamin they received Gibeon, Geba, Alemeth and Anathoth. They received these towns together with their grasslands.
All these towns were handed out to the family groups of Kohath. The total number of towns was 13.

⁶¹ The rest of the members of the family line of Kohath were given ten towns. The towns were from the family groups of half of the tribe of Manasseh.
⁶² The members of the family line of Gershon were given 13 towns. They received them family group by family group. Most of the towns were from the tribes of Issachar, Asher and Naphtali. The rest were from the other half of the tribe of Manasseh. It's in Bashan.
⁶³ The members of the family line of Merari were given 12 towns. They received them family group by family group. The towns were from the tribes of Reuben, Gad and Zebulun.

⁶⁴ So the Israelites gave the Levites all these towns and their grasslands.
⁶⁵ They gave other towns to them from the tribes of Judah, Simeon and Benjamin.

⁶⁶ Some of the family groups of Kohath were given towns from the tribe of Ephraim as their territory.
⁶⁷ In the hill country of Ephraim they received Shechem. Shechem was a city where people could

go for safety. The Kohathites also received Gezer, ⁶⁸Jokmeam, Beth Horon, ⁶⁹Aijalon and Gath Rimmon. They were given all these towns together with their grasslands.

⁷⁰ From half of the tribe of Manasseh the people of Israel gave the towns of Aner and Bileam. They gave them to the rest of the family groups of Kohath. They gave them together with their grasslands.

⁷¹ Here is what the members of the family line of Gershon were given.

From half of the tribe of Manasseh they received Golan in Bashan and also Ashtaroth. They received them together with their grasslands.

⁷² From the tribe of Issachar they received Kedesh, Daberath, ⁷³Ramoth and Anem. They received them together with their grasslands.

⁷⁴ From the tribe of Asher they received Mashal, Abdon, ⁷⁵Hukok and Rehob. They received them together with their grasslands.

⁷⁶ From the tribe of Naphtali they received Kedesh in Galilee. They also received Hammon and Kiriathaim. They were given all these towns together with their grasslands.

⁷⁷ The members of the family line of Merari make up the rest of the Levites. Here is what they were given.

From the tribe of Zebulun they received Jokneam, Kartah, Rimmono and Tabor. They received them together with their grasslands.

⁷⁸ The tribe of Reuben was across the Jordan River east of Jericho. From that tribe the Merarites received Bezer in the desert, Jahzah, ⁷⁹Kedemoth and Mephaath. They received them together with their grasslands.

⁸⁰ From the tribe of Gad they received Ramoth in Gilead. They also received Mahanaim, ⁸¹Heshbon and Jazer. They received all these towns together with their grasslands.

The Family Line of Issachar

7 The sons of Issachar were
Tola, Puah, Jashub and Shimron.
The total number of sons was four.

² The sons of Tola were
Uzzi, Rephaiah, Jeriel, Jahmai, Ibsam and Samuel. They were the leaders of their families. The total number of fighting men who were listed in the history of the family line of Tola was 22,600. That was when David was king.

³ The son of Uzzi was
Izrahiah.

The sons of Izrahiah were
Michael, Obadiah, Joel and Ishiah. All five of them were chiefs. ⁴According to their family history, 36,000 of their men were ready for battle. That's because they had many wives and children.

⁵ The total number of fighting men who belonged to all the family groups of Issachar was 87,000. The men were listed in their family history.

The Family Line of Benjamin

⁶ The three sons of Benjamin were
Bela, Beker and Jediael.

⁷ The sons of Bela were
Ezbon, Uzzi, Uzziel, Jerimoth and Iri. They were the leaders of their families. The total number of sons was five. Their family history listed 22,034 fighting men.

⁸ The sons of Beker were
Zemirah, Joash, Eliezer, Elioenai, Omri, Jeremoth, Abijah, Anathoth and Alemeth. All of them were the sons of Beker. ⁹Their family history listed the leaders of their families. It also listed 20,200 fighting men.

¹⁰ The son of Jediael was
Bilhan.

The sons of Bilhan were
Jeush, Benjamin, Ehud, Kenaanah, Zethan, Tarshish and Ahishahar. ¹¹All these sons of Jediael were the leaders of their families. There were 17,200 fighting men who were ready to go to war.

¹² The Shuppites and Huppites belonged to the family line of Ir. The Hushites belonged to the family line of Aher.

The Family Line of Naphtali

¹³ The sons of Naphtali were
Jahziel, Guni, Jezer and Shillem.
They belonged to the family line
of Bilhah.

The Family Line of Manasseh

¹⁴ Here is the family line of Manasseh.
He had a concubine who was
from the land of Aram. She had
Asriel and Makir by him. Makir
was the father of Gilead. ¹⁵Makir
married a woman from among the
Huppites and Shuppites. He had
a sister named Maakah. Another
member of Manasseh's family
line was Zelophehad. All he had
was daughters. ¹⁶Makir's wife
Maakah had a son by him. She
named the boy Peresh. He had a
brother named Sheresh. The sons
of Sheresh were Ulam and Rakem.
¹⁷ The son of Ulam was
Bedan.
These were the members of the
family line of Makir, the son of
Manasseh. Gilead was the son of
Makir.
¹⁸ Gilead's sister was Hammoleketh.
She was the mother of Ishhod,
Abiezer and Mahlah.
¹⁹ The sons of Shemida were
Ahian, Shechem, Likhi and Aniam.

The Family Line of Ephraim

²⁰ Here are the members of the family
line of Ephraim.
Shuthelah was Ephraim's son.
Bered was Shuthelah's son.
Tahath was Bered's son.
Eleadah was Tahath's son.
Tahath was Eleadah's son.
²¹ Zabad was Tahath's son.
And Shuthelah was Zabad's son.
Men from Gath killed Ezer and
Elead when they went down to
steal their livestock. ²²Their father Ephraim mourned for them
for many days. His relatives came
to comfort him. ²³Then he slept
with his wife. She became pregnant and had a baby boy. Ephraim
named him Beriah. That's because
something bad had happened
in his family. ²⁴His daughter was

Sheerah. She built Lower and Upper Beth Horon. She also built Uzzen Sheerah.
²⁵ Rephah was Beriah's son.
Resheph was Rephah's son.
Telah was Resheph's son.
Tahan was Telah's son.
²⁶ Ladan was Tahan's son.
Ammihud was Ladan's son.
Elishama was Ammihud's son.
²⁷ Nun was Elishama's son.
And Joshua was the son of Nun.
²⁸ The lands and settlements of the
members of Ephraim's line included Bethel and the villages around it.
Naaran was on the east. Gezer and its
villages were on the west. The lands
and settlements included Shechem.
They also included the villages
around Shechem all the way to Ayyah
and its villages. ²⁹Along the borders of
Manasseh were Beth Shan, Taanach,
Megiddo and Dor, together with their
villages. The members of the family
line of Joseph lived in these towns.
Joseph was the son of Israel.

The Family Line of Asher

³⁰ The sons of Asher were
Imnah, Ishvah, Ishvi and Beriah.
They had a sister named Serah.
³¹ The sons of Beriah were
Heber and Malkiel. Malkiel was
the father of Birzaith.
³² Heber was the father of Japhlet,
Shomer, Hotham and their sister
Shua.
³³ The sons of Japhlet were
Pasak, Bimhal and Ashvath.
They were Japhlet's sons.
³⁴ The sons of Shomer were
Ahi, Rohgah, Hubbah and Aram.
³⁵ The sons of Shomer's brother Helem
were
Zophah, Imna, Shelesh and Amal.
³⁶ The sons of Zophah were
Suah, Harnepher, Shual, Beri,
Imrah, ³⁷Bezer, Hod, Shamma,
Shilshah, Ithran and Beera.
³⁸ The sons of Jether were
Jephunneh, Pispah and Ara.
³⁹ The sons of Ulla were
Arah, Hanniel and Rizia.
⁴⁰ All of them were members of the
family line of Asher. They were the

leaders of their families. They were fine men. They were brave fighting men. They were outstanding leaders. The total number of men who were ready for battle was 26,000. They were listed in their family history.

The Family History of Saul

8 Benjamin was the father of Bela. Bela was his first son.
Ashbel was his second son. Aharah was the third.

2 Nohah was the fourth. And Rapha was the fifth.

3 The sons of Bela were
Addar, Gera, Abihud, 4Abishua, Naaman, Ahoah, 5Gera, Shephuphan and Huram.

6 Here are the members of the family line of Ehud. They were the leaders of the families who were living in Geba. Later, they were taken away from their own land. They were forced to go to Manahath. 7The sons of Ehud were
Naaman, Ahijah and Gera. Gera took them away from their land. He was the father of Uzza and Ahihud.

8 Sons were born to Shaharaim in Moab. That happened after he had divorced his wives Hushim and Baara. 9His wife Hodesh had sons by him. Their names were Jobab, Zibia, Mesha, Malkam, 10Jeuz, Sakia and Mirmah. His sons were the leaders of their families. 11His wife Hushim had Abitub and Elpaal by him.

12 The sons of Elpaal were
Eber, Misham and Shemed. Shemed built Ono and Lod and the villages around it. 13Beriah and Shema were also sons of Elpaal. They were the leaders of the families who were living in Aijalon. Beriah and Shema drove out the people who were living in Gath.

14 Ahio, Shashak, Jeremoth, 15Zebadiah, Arad, Eder, 16Michael, Ishpah and Joha were the sons of Beriah.

17 Zebadiah, Meshullam, Hizki, Heber, 18Ishmerai, Izliah and Jobab were other sons of Elpaal.

19 Jakim, Zikri, Zabdi, 20Elienai, Zillethai, Eliel, 21Adaiah, Beraiah and Shimrath were the sons of Shimei.

22 Ishpan, Eber, Eliel, 23Abdon, Zikri, Hanan, 24Hananiah, Elam, Anthothijah, 25Iphdeiah and Penuel were the sons of Shashak.

26 Shamsherai, Shehariah, Athaliah, 27Jaareshiah, Elijah and Zikri were the sons of Jeroham.

28 All these men were the leaders of their families. They were listed as chiefs in their family history. They lived in Jerusalem.

29 Jeiel lived in the city of Gibeon. He was the father of Gibeon.
Jeiel had a wife named Maakah. 30His oldest son was Abdon. His other sons were Zur, Kish, Baal, Ner, Nadab, 31Gedor, Ahio, Zeker 32and Mikloth. Mikloth was the father of Shimeah. Mikloth and Shimeah also lived in Jerusalem. They lived near their relatives.

33 Ner was the father of Kish. Kish was the father of Saul. Saul was the father of Jonathan, Malki-Shua, Abinadab and Esh-Baal.

34 The son of Jonathan was
Merib-Baal. Merib-Baal was the father of Micah.

35 The sons of Micah were
Pithon, Melek, Tarea and Ahaz. 36Ahaz was the father of Jehoaddah. Jehoaddah was the father of Alemeth, Azmaveth and Zimri. Zimri was the father of Moza. 37Moza was the father of Binea. Raphah was Binea's son. Eleasah was Raphah's son. And Azel was Eleasah's son.

38 Azel had six sons. Their names were Azrikam, Bokeru, Ishmael, Sheariah, Obadiah and Hanan. All of them were the sons of Azel.

39 Here are the sons of Azel's brother Eshek.
Ulam was his first son. Jeush was the second. Eliphelet was the third. 40The sons of Ulam were brave fighting men. They could use a bow. They had many sons and grandsons. The total number of sons and grandsons was 150.

All these men belonged to the family line of Benjamin.

9 The whole community of Israel was listed in their family histories. They were written down in the records of the kings of Israel and Judah. The people of Judah were taken away from their own land. They were taken as prisoners to Babylon. That's because they weren't faithful to the LORD.

The People Who Lived in Jerusalem

2 The first people who came back from Babylon were some Israelites, priests, Levites and temple servants. They made their homes again in their own towns on their own property.

3 Some of them lived in Jerusalem. They included people from Judah, Benjamin, Ephraim and Manasseh.

4 They included Uthai. He was the son of Ammihud. Ammihud was the son of Omri. Omri was the son of Imri. Imri was the son of Bani. Bani belonged to the family line of Perez. Perez was the son of Judah.

5 The family line of Shelah included his oldest son Asaiah. It also included the sons of Asaiah.

6 The family line of Zerah included Jeuel.

The total number of the people of Judah was 690.

7 The family line of Benjamin included Sallu. He was the son of Meshullam. Meshullam was the son of Hodaviah. Hodaviah was the son of Hassenuah.

8 Ibneiah was the son of Jeroham. Elah was the son of Uzzi. Uzzi was the son of Mikri.

Meshullam was the son of Shephatiah. Shephatiah was the son of Reuel. Reuel was the son of Ibnijah.

9 The total number of the people of Benjamin was 956. They were listed in their family history. All these men were the leaders of their families.

10 The family line of the priests included Jedaiah, Jehoiarib and Jakin.

11 It also included Azariah. He was the son of Hilkiah. Hilkiah was the son of Meshullam. Meshullam was the son of Zadok. Zadok was the son of Meraioth. Meraioth was the son of Ahitub. Azariah was the official who was in charge of the house of God.

12 Adaiah was the son of Jeroham. Jeroham was the son of Pashhur. Pashhur was the son of Malkijah. Maasai was the son of Adiel. Adiel was the son of Jahzerah. Jahzerah was the son of Meshullam. Meshullam was the son of Meshillemith. Meshillemith was the son of Immer.

13 The total number of priests was 1,760. They were the leaders of their families. They were able men. It was their duty to serve in the house of God.

14 The family line of the Levites included Shemaiah. He was the son of Hasshub. Hasshub was the son of Azrikam. Azrikam was the son of Hashabiah. Shemaiah belonged to the family line of Merari.

15 The family line of the Levites also included Bakbakkar, Heresh, Galal and Mattaniah. Mattaniah was the son of Mika. Mika was the son of Zikri. Zikri was the son of Asaph.

16 Obadiah was the son of Shemaiah. Shemaiah was the son of Galal. Galal was the son of Jeduthun. Berekiah was the son of Asa. Asa was the son of Elkanah. He lived in the villages of the people of Netophah.

17 The men who guarded the gates were Shallum, Akkub, Talmon, Ahiman and other Levites. Shallum was their chief. 18 He was stationed at the King's Gate on the east side. That duty has continued to this day. These guards belonged to the camp of the Levites.

19 Shallum was the son of Kore. Kore was the son of Ebiasaph. Ebiasaph was the son of Korah. Shallum and the other Levites in his family belonged to the family line of Korah. They had the duty of guarding the entrances to the tent. From long ago, their people had the duty of guarding the entrance to the house of the LORD.

20 Long ago Phinehas, the son of Eleazar, was in charge of those who

WOOTON'S FUN FACTS

1 Chr. 9:15

My middle initial is Z. No, it doesn't stand for Zikri. Nope, not Zechariah. Actually, it's kind of top secret. But there are more than 150 people and place names in the Bible that start with Z, so you have a lot of guesses. No, not Zephaniah either.

guarded the gate. And the LORD was with him.

[21] Zechariah guarded the entrance to the tent of meeting. He was the son of Meshelemiah.

[22] The total number of the men who were chosen to guard the entrances was 212. They were listed in their family history in their villages.

David and Samuel the prophet had appointed them to their positions. They appointed them because they trusted them. [23] These Levites and their children after them were in charge of guarding the gates of the house of the LORD. The house of the LORD was also called the tent of meeting. [24] The men who guarded the gates were on the four sides of the tent. They were on the east, west, north and south sides. [25] From time to time, their relatives in their villages had to come to help them. They had to share their duties for a week at a time. [26] But the four main men who guarded the gates were Levites. They were trusted with the duty of taking care of the storerooms and the other rooms in the house of God. [27] They spent the night in their positions around the house of God. That's because they had to guard it. They were in charge of the key that opened it each morning.

[28] Some Levites were in charge of the objects that were used when they served at the temple. They counted the objects when they were brought in. They also counted them when they were taken out. [29] Other Levites were appointed to take care of all the other things that belonged to the temple. They also took care of the special flour, wine, olive oil, incense and spices. [30] Some of the priests took care of mixing the spices. [31] There was a Levite named Mattithiah. He was the oldest son of Shallum. Shallum belonged to the family line of Korah. Mattithiah was trusted with the duty of baking the offering bread. [32] The bread was placed on the table every Sabbath day. Some Levites in the family line of Kohath were in charge of preparing the bread.

[33] Those who led the music lived in rooms in the temple. They were the leaders of their Levite families. Their only duty was to lead the music. They had to do that work day and night.

[34] All of them were the leaders of their Levite families. They were listed as chiefs in their family history. They lived in Jerusalem.

The Family History of Saul

[35] Jeiel lived in the city of Gibeon. He was the father of Gibeon.
Jeiel had a wife named Maakah. [36] His oldest son was Abdon. His other sons were Zur, Kish, Baal, Ner, Nadab, [37] Gedor, Ahio, Zechariah and Mikloth. [38] Mikloth was the father of Shimeam. Mikloth and Shimeam lived near their relatives in Jerusalem.

[39] Ner was the father of Kish. Kish was the father of Saul. Saul was the father of Jonathan, Malki-Shua, Abinadab and Esh-Baal.

[40] The son of Jonathan was Merib-Baal. Merib-Baal was the father of Micah.

[41] The sons of Micah were Pithon, Melek, Tahrea and Ahaz. [42] Ahaz was the father of Jadah. Jadah was the father of Alemeth, Azmaveth and Zimri. Zimri was the father of Moza. [43] Moza was the father of Binea. Rephaiah was Binea's son. Eleasah was Rephaiah's son. And Azel was Eleasah's son.

[44] Azel had six sons. Their names were

Azrikam, Bokeru, Ishmael, Sheariah, Obadiah and Hanan. They were the sons of Azel.

Saul Takes His Own Life

10 The Philistines fought against Israel. The men of Israel ran away from them. But many Israelites were killed on Mount Gilboa. [2] The Philistines kept chasing Saul and his sons. They killed his sons Jonathan, Abinadab and Malki-Shua. [3] The fighting was heavy around Saul. Men armed with bows and arrows caught up with him. They shot their arrows at him and wounded him badly.

[4] Saul spoke to the man who was carrying his armor. He said, "Pull out your sword and stick it through me. If you don't, these men who aren't circumcised will come and hurt me badly."

But the man was terrified. He wouldn't do it. So Saul took his own sword and fell on it. [5] The man saw that Saul was dead. So he fell on his own sword and died. [6] Saul and his three sons died. All of them died together.

[7] All the Israelites who lived in the valley saw that their army had run away. They saw that Saul and his sons were dead. So the Israelites left their towns and ran away. Then the Philistines came and lived in them.

[8] The day after the Philistines had won the battle, they came to take what they wanted from the dead bodies. They found Saul and his sons dead on Mount Gilboa. [9] So they took what they wanted from Saul's body. They cut off his head and took his armor. Then they sent messengers through the whole land of the Philistines. They announced the news to the statues of their gods. They also announced it among their people. [10] They put Saul's armor in the temple of their gods. They hung up his head in the temple of their god Dagon.

[11] The people of Jabesh Gilead heard what the Philistines had done to Saul. [12] So all the brave men of Jabesh Gilead went and got the bodies of Saul and his sons. They brought them to Jabesh. Then they buried the bones of Saul and his sons under the great tree that was there. They didn't eat anything for seven days.

[13] Saul died because he wasn't faithful to the LORD. He didn't obey the word of the LORD. He even asked for advice from a person who gets messages from people who have died. [14] He didn't ask the LORD for advice. So the LORD put him to death. He turned the kingdom over to David. David was the son of Jesse.

David Becomes King Over Israel

11 The whole community of Israel came together to see David at Hebron. They said, "We are your own flesh and blood. [2] In the past, Saul was our king. But you led the men of Israel in battle. The LORD your God said to you, 'You will be the shepherd over my people Israel. You will become their ruler.'"

[3] All the elders of Israel came to see King David at Hebron. There he made a covenant with them in front of the LORD. They anointed David as king over Israel. It happened just as the LORD had promised through Samuel.

David Captures Jerusalem

[4] David and all the men of Israel marched to Jerusalem. Jerusalem was also called Jebus. The Jebusites who lived there [5] said to David, "You won't get in here." But David captured the fort of Zion. It became known as the City of David.

[6] David had said, "Anyone who leads the attack against the Jebusites will become the commander of Israel's army." Joab went up first. So he became the commander of the army. He was the son of Zeruiah.

[7] David moved into the fort. So it was called the City of David. [8] He built up the city around the fort. He filled in the low places. He built a wall around it. During that time, Joab built up the rest of the city. [9] David became more and more powerful. That's because the LORD who rules over all was with him.

David's Mighty Warriors

[10] The chiefs of David's mighty warriors and the whole community of Israel helped David greatly. They helped him become king over the entire land. That's exactly what the LORD had promised him. [11] Here is a list of David's mighty warriors.

Jashobeam was chief of the officers. He was a Hakmonite. He used his spear against 300 men. He killed all of them at one time.

[12] Next to him was Eleazar. He was one of the three mighty warriors. He was the son of Dodai, the Ahohite. [13] Jashobeam was with David at Pas Dammim. The Philistines

had gathered there for battle. Israel's troops ran away from the Philistines. At the place where that happened, there was a field full of barley. [14]The three mighty warriors took their stand in the middle of the field. They didn't let the Philistines capture it. They struck them down. The LORD helped them win a great battle.

[15]David was near the rock at the cave of Adullam. Three of the 30 chiefs came down to him there. A group of Philistines was camped in the Valley of Rephaim. [16]At that time David was in his usual place of safety. Some Philistine troops were stationed at Bethlehem. [17]David really wanted some water. He said, "I wish someone would get me a drink of water from the well near the gate of Bethlehem!" [18]So the three mighty warriors fought their way past the Philistine guards. They got some water from the well near the gate of Bethlehem. They took the water back to David. But David refused to drink it. Instead, he poured it out as a drink offering to the LORD. [19]"I would never drink that water!" David said. "It would be like drinking the blood of these men. They put their lives in danger by going to Bethlehem." The men had put their lives in danger by bringing the water back. So David wouldn't drink it.

Those were some of the brave things the three mighty warriors did.

[20]Abishai was chief over the three mighty warriors. He was the brother of Joab. Abishai used his spear against 300 men. He killed all of them. So he became as famous as the three mighty warriors. [21]He was honored twice as much as the three mighty warriors. He became their commander. But he wasn't included among them.

[22]Benaiah was a great hero from Kabzeel. He was the son of Jehoiada. Benaiah did many brave things. He struck down two of Moab's best fighting men. He also went down into a pit on a snowy day. He killed a lion there. [23]And Benaiah struck down an Egyptian who was seven and a half feet tall. The Egyptian was holding a spear as big as a weaver's rod. Benaiah went out to fight against him with a club. He grabbed the spear out of the Egyptian's hand. Then he killed him with it. [24]Those were some of the brave things Benaiah, the son of Jehoiada, did. He too was as famous as the three mighty warriors. [25]He was honored more than any of the 30 chiefs. But he wasn't included among the three mighty warriors. And David put him in charge of his own personal guards.

[26]Here is a list of David's mighty warriors.

Asahel, the brother of Joab
Elhanan, the son of Dodo, from Bethlehem
[27]Shammoth, the Harorite
Helez, the Pelonite
[28]Ira, the son of Ikkesh, from Tekoa
Abiezer from Anathoth
[29]Sibbekai, the Hushathite
Ilai, the Ahohite
[30]Maharai from Netophah
Heled, the son of Baanah, from Netophah
[31]Ithai, the son of Ribai, from Gibeah in Benjamin
Benaiah from Pirathon
[32]Hurai from the valleys of Gaash
Abiel, the Arbathite
[33]Azmaveth, the Baharumite
Eliahba, the Shaalbonite
[34]the sons of Hashem, the Gizonite
Jonathan, the son of Shagee, the Hararite
[35]Ahiam, the son of Sakar, the Hararite
Eliphal, the son of Ur
[36]Hepher, the Mekerathite
Ahijah, the Pelonite
[37]Hezro from Carmel
Naarai, the son of Ezbai
[38]Joel, the brother of Nathan
Mibhar, the son of Hagri
[39]Zelek from Ammon
Naharai, from Beeroth, who carried the armor of Joab, the son of Zeruiah
[40]Ira, the Ithrite
Gareb, the Ithrite
[41]Uriah, the Hittite
Zabad, the son of Ahlai
[42]Adina, the son of Shiza, the Reubenite, who was chief of the Reubenites and the 30 men with him
[43]Hanan, the son of Maakah
Joshaphat, the Mithnite
[44]Uzzia, the Ashterathite
Shama and Jeiel, the sons of Hotham from Aroer
[45]Jediael, the son of Shimri
his brother Joha, the Tizite

⁴⁶ Eliel, the Mahavite
Jeribai and Joshaviah, the sons of Elnaam
Ithmah from Moab
⁴⁷ Eliel
Obed
Jaasiel, the Mezobaite

Fighting Men Join David

12 Some fighting men came to David at Ziklag. They were among those who helped him in battle. David had been forced to hide from Saul, the son of Kish. ²The men were armed with bows. They were able to shoot arrows or throw stones from a sling with either hand. They were relatives of Saul from the tribe of Benjamin. Here is a list of them.

³ Their chief Ahiezer and Joash, the sons of Shemaah the Gibeathite
Jeziel and Pelet, the sons of Azmaveth
Berakah
Jehu from Anathoth
⁴ Ishmaiah, the Gibeonite, who was a mighty warrior among the 30 chiefs and a leader of the 30 chiefs
Jeremiah
Jahaziel
Johanan
Jozabad from Gederah
⁵ Eluzai
Jerimoth
Bealiah
Shemariah
Shephatiah, the Haruphite
⁶ the Korahites Elkanah, Ishiah, Azarel, Joezer and Jashobeam
⁷ Joelah and Zebadiah, the sons of Jeroham from Gedor

⁸Some men of Gad went over to David's side at his usual place of safety in the desert. They were brave fighting men. They were ready for battle. They were able to use shields and spears. Their faces were like the faces of lions. They could run as fast as antelopes in the mountains.

⁹ Ezer was their chief.
Obadiah was next in command. Eliab was third.
¹⁰ Mishmannah was fourth. Jeremiah was fifth.
¹¹ Attai was sixth. Eliel was seventh.

1 Chr. 12:8 Penny once told me that I had a face like a lion. Maybe it's because I forgot to shave that week . . . or, um, that month. In the Bible, lions are known as being strong, frightening, and protective. Figures of lions stood next to Solomon's throne (see 1 Kings 10:19).

¹² Johanan was eighth. Elzabad was ninth.
¹³ Jeremiah was tenth. And Makbannai was eleventh.

¹⁴All these men of Gad were army commanders. The least important of them was equal to 100 men. The most important was equal to 1,000. ¹⁵They went across the Jordan River when it was flowing over its banks. That happened in the first month of spring. They chased away everyone who lived in the valleys. They chased them away from the east and west sides of the river.

¹⁶Some men from the territories of Benjamin and Judah also came to David at his usual place of safety. ¹⁷David went out to meet them. He said to them, "Have you come to me in peace? Have you come to help me? If you have, I'm ready for you to join me. But suppose you have come to hand me over to my enemies when I haven't even harmed anyone. Then may the God of our people see it and judge you."

¹⁸The Spirit of God came on Amasai. He was leader of the 30 chiefs. He said,

"David, we belong to you!
  Son of Jesse, we're on your side!
May you have great success.
  May those who help you also have success.
Your God will help you."

So David welcomed them. He made them leaders in his army.

[19] Some people from the tribe of Manasseh went over to David's side. They did this when he marched out with the Philistines to fight against Saul. But David and his men didn't help the Philistines. That's because after all the Philistine rulers had discussed the matter, they sent him away. They said, "Suppose he deserts to his master Saul. Then our heads will be cut off!" [20] So David went to Ziklag. Here are the men of Manasseh who went over to his side. They were Adnah, Jozabad, Jediael, Michael, Jozabad, Elihu and Zillethai. They were leaders of groups of 1,000 men in Manasseh. [21] They helped David fight against enemy armies. All the men of Manasseh were brave fighting men. They were commanders in David's army. [22] Day after day men came to help David. Soon he had a large army. It was like the army of God.

Jason's Jargon

1 CHRONICLES 12

Search this chapter for the word *antelope*. An antelope can run up to 55 miles per hour. Calling David's army as fast as antelopes was probably an overstatement.

Other Fighting Men Join David at Hebron

[23] Large numbers of men came to David at Hebron. They were prepared for battle. They came to hand Saul's kingdom over to him, just as the LORD had said. Here are the numbers of the men who came.

[24] The men from Judah carried shields and spears. They were prepared for battle. The total number of them was 6,800.

[25] The fighting men from Simeon were ready for battle. The total number of them was 7,100.

[26] The total number of men from Levi was 4,600. [27] They included Jehoiada. He was the leader of the family of Aaron. He came with 3,700 men. [28] The men from Levi also included Zadok. He was a brave young fighter. He came with 22 officers from his family.

[29] The men from Benjamin were from Saul's tribe. Most of them had remained faithful to Saul's family until that time. The total number of them was 3,000.

[30] The men from Ephraim were brave fighting men. They were famous in their own family groups. The total number of them was 20,800.

[31] The men from half of the tribe of Manasseh had been chosen by name to come and make David king. The total number of them was 18,000.

[32] The men from Issachar understood what was going on at that time. They knew what Israel should do. The total number of their chiefs was 200. They came with all their relatives who were under their command.

[33] The men from Zebulun knew how to fight well. That's because they had done it many times before. They were prepared for battle. They had every kind of weapon. They came to help David with their whole heart. The total number of them was 50,000.

[34] The total number of officers from Naphtali was 1,000. They came with 37,000 men who carried shields and spears.

[35] The men from Dan were ready for battle. The total number of them was 28,600.

[36] The men from Asher knew how to fight well. That's because they had done it many times before. They were prepared for battle. The total number of them was 40,000.

[37] The men from the tribes of Reuben, Gad and half the tribe of Manasseh were armed with every kind of weapon. The men came from the east side of the Jordan River. The total number of them was 120,000.

WOOTON'S FUN FACTS

1 Chr. 12:40

Just like the people of Israel, I eat cake when I'm happy. And when I'm sad. And when I'm stressed. And when I'm not. The Old Testament specifically mentions that people ate fig, date, raisin, and honey cakes. Okay, excuse me. I'm headed to the kitchen.

³⁸ All these fighting men offered to serve in the army.

Before they came to Hebron, they had agreed completely to make David king over all the Israelites. All the rest of the people also agreed to make David king. ³⁹The men spent three days there with David. They ate and drank what their families had given them. ⁴⁰Their neighbors also brought food. They brought it on donkeys, camels, mules and oxen. They came from as far away as the territories of Issachar, Zebulun and Naphtali. There was plenty of flour, fig cakes, raisin cakes, wine, olive oil, cattle and sheep. The Israelites brought all these things because they were so happy.

David Brings Back the Ark

13 David talked with each of his officers. He wanted to get their advice. Some of them were commanders of thousands of men. Others were commanders of hundreds. ²David spoke to the whole community of Israel. He said, "Let's send word to the rest of our people no matter how far away they live. They live in all the territories of Israel. Let's also send word to the priests and Levites who are with them in their towns and on their grasslands. Let's invite everyone to come and join us. Let's do it if it seems good to you and if that's

what the LORD our God wants. ³Let's bring the ark of our God back here to us. We didn't use it to ask God for advice during the whole time Saul was king." ⁴So that's what the whole community agreed to do. It seemed right to them.

⁵David gathered together all the Israelites. They came from the area between the Shihor River in Egypt and Lebo Hamath. They came to bring the ark of God from Kiriath Jearim to Jerusalem. ⁶David went to Baalah of Judah. The whole community of Israel went with him. Baalah is also called Kiriath Jearim. All the people went there to get the ark of God the LORD. He sits on his throne between the cherubim. The ark is named after the LORD.

⁷The ark of God was placed on a new cart. Then it was moved from Abinadab's house. Uzzah and Ahio were guiding it. ⁸David was celebrating with all his might in front of God. So was the whole community of Israel. All of them were singing songs. They were also playing harps, lyres, tambourines, cymbals and trumpets.

⁹They came to the threshing floor of Kidon. The oxen nearly fell there. So Uzzah reached out his hand to hold the ark steady. ¹⁰Then the LORD became very angry with Uzzah. The LORD struck him down because he had put his hand on the ark. So Uzzah died there in front of God.

¹¹David was angry because the LORD's great anger had broken out against Uzzah. That's why the place is still called Perez Uzzah to this day.

¹²David was afraid of God that day. David asked, "How can I ever bring the ark of God back here to me?" ¹³So he didn't take the ark to be with him in the City of David. Instead, he took it to the house of Obed-Edom. Obed-Edom was from Gath. ¹⁴The ark of God remained with the family of Obed-Edom. It stayed in his house for three months. And the LORD blessed his family. He also blessed everything that belonged to him.

David's Palace and Family

14 Hiram was king of Tyre. He sent messengers to David. He sent cedar logs along with them. He also sent skilled workers to build a palace for David. They worked with stone and wood. ²David knew that the LORD had made his position as king secure. He knew that the LORD had made him king over the whole nation of Israel. He knew that the LORD had greatly honored his kingdom. The LORD had done it because the Israelites were his people.

³In Jerusalem David married more women. He also became the father of more sons and daughters. ⁴Here is a list of the children born to him in Jerusalem. Their names were Shammua, Shobab, Nathan, Solomon, ⁵Ibhar, Elishua, Elpelet, ⁶Nogah, Nepheg, Japhia, ⁷Elishama, Beeliada and Eliphelet.

David Wins the Battle Over the Philistines

⁸The Philistines heard that David had been anointed king over the entire nation of Israel. So the whole Philistine army went to look for him. But David heard about it. He went out to where they were. ⁹The Philistines had come and attacked the people in the Valley of Rephaim. ¹⁰So David asked God for advice. David asked, "Should I go and attack the Philistines? Will you hand them over to me?"

The LORD answered him, "Go. I will hand them over to you."

¹¹So David and his men went up to Baal Perazim. There David won the battle over the Philistines. He said, "God has broken through against my enemies, just as water breaks through a dam." That's why the place was called Baal Perazim. ¹²The Philistines had left statues of their gods there. So David gave orders to burn them up.

¹³Once more the Philistines attacked the people in the valley. ¹⁴So David asked God for advice again. God answered him, "Do not go straight after them. Instead, circle around them. Attack them in front of the poplar trees. ¹⁵Listen for the sound of marching in the tops of the trees. Then move out to fight. The sound will mean that I have gone out in front of you. I will strike down the Philistine army." ¹⁶So David did just as God had commanded him. He and his men struck down the Philistine army. They struck them down from Gibeon all the way to Gezer.

¹⁷So David became famous in every land. The LORD made all the nations afraid of him.

David Brings the Ark to Jerusalem

15 David constructed buildings for himself in the City of David. Then he prepared a place for the ark of God. He set up a tent for it. ²He said, "Only Levites can carry the ark of God. That's because the LORD chose them to carry his ark. He chose them to serve him forever in front of the place where his throne is."

³David gathered the whole community of Israel together in Jerusalem. He wanted to carry up the ark of the LORD to the place he had prepared for it.

⁴ He called together the members of the family line of Aaron. He also called the Levites together. Here are the men who came from the families of the Levites.

⁵ From the families of Kohath came the leader Uriel and 120 relatives.
⁶ From the families of Merari came the leader Asaiah and 220 relatives.
⁷ From the families of Gershon came the leader Joel and 130 relatives.
⁸ From the families of Elizaphan came the leader Shemaiah and 200 relatives.
⁹ From the families of Hebron came the leader Eliel and 80 relatives.
¹⁰ From the families of Uzziel came the leader Amminadab and 112 relatives.

¹¹David sent for Zadok and Abiathar, the priests. He also sent for Uriel, Asaiah, Joel, Shemaiah, Eliel and Amminadab. They were Levites. ¹²He said to them, "You are the leaders of the families of Levi. You and the other Levites must set yourselves apart to serve the LORD and his people. You must carry up the ark of the LORD. He is the God of Israel. Put the ark in the place I've prepared for it. ¹³Remember when the anger of the LORD our God broke out against us? That's because it wasn't you Levites who tried to carry up the ark the first time. We didn't ask the LORD how to do it in the way the law requires." ¹⁴So the priests and Levites set themselves apart. Then they carried up the ark of the LORD. He is the God of Israel. ¹⁵This time the Levites used the poles to carry on their shoulders the ark of God. That's what Moses had commanded in keeping with the word of the LORD.

[16]David told the Levite leaders to appoint other Levites as musicians. He wanted them to make a joyful sound with lyres, harps and cymbals.

[17]So the Levites appointed Heman, the son of Joel. From his relatives they chose Asaph, the son of Berekiah. Other relatives were from the family of Merari. From them they chose Ethan, the son of Kushaiah. [18]Along with them they chose their relatives who were next in rank. Their names were Zechariah, Jaaziel, Shemiramoth, Jehiel, Unni, Eliab, Benaiah, Maaseiah, Mattithiah, Eliphelehu, Mikneiah, Obed-Edom and Jeiel. They guarded the gates.

[19]Heman, Asaph and Ethan played the bronze cymbals. [20]Zechariah, Jaaziel, Shemiramoth, Jehiel, Unni, Eliab, Maaseiah and Benaiah played the lyres according to *alamoth*. [21]Mattithiah, Eliphelehu, Mikneiah, Obed-Edom, Jeiel and Azaziah played the harps according to *sheminith*. [22]Kenaniah was the leader of the Levites. He was in charge of the singing because he was good at it.

[23]Berekiah and Elkanah guarded the ark. [24]Some of the priests blew trumpets in front of the ark of God. Their names were Shebaniah, Joshaphat, Nethanel, Amasai, Zechariah, Benaiah and Eliezer. Obed-Edom and Jehiah also helped guard the ark.

[25]David and the elders of Israel went to carry up the ark of the covenant of the LORD. So did the commanders of military groups of 1,000 men. With great joy they carried up the ark from the house of Obed-Edom. [26]God had helped the Levites who were carrying the ark of the covenant of the LORD. So seven bulls and seven rams were sacrificed. [27]David was wearing a robe made out of fine linen. So were all the Levites who were carrying the ark. And so were the musicians and the choir director Kenaniah. David was also wearing a sacred linen apron. [28]So the whole community of Israel brought up the ark of the covenant of the LORD. They shouted. They blew rams' horns and trumpets. They played cymbals, lyres and harps.

[29]The ark of the covenant of the LORD was brought into the City of David. Saul's daughter Michal was watching from a window. She saw King David dancing and celebrating. That made her hate him in her heart.

Serving God in Front of the Ark

16 The ark of God was carried into Jerusalem. It was put in the tent David had set up for it. The priests brought burnt offerings and friendship offerings to God. [2]After David finished sacrificing those offerings, he blessed the people in the name of the LORD. [3]He gave to each Israelite man and woman a loaf of bread. He also gave each one a date cake and a raisin cake.

[4]He appointed some of the Levites to serve in front of the ark of the LORD. David wanted them to give honor, thanks and praise to the LORD. He is the God of Israel. [5]Asaph was the leader of those Levites. Zechariah was next in rank. Then came Jaaziel, Shemiramoth, Jehiel, Mattithiah, Eliab, Benaiah, Obed-Edom and Jeiel. They played the lyres and harps. Asaph played the cymbals. [6]Benaiah and Jahaziel, the priests, blew the trumpets. They blew them at regular times in front of the ark of the covenant of God.

[7]That day was the first time David appointed Asaph and his helpers. He appointed them to give praise to the LORD with these words.

[8] Give praise to the LORD. Make his name
    known.
  Tell the nations what he has done.
[9] Sing to him. Sing praise to him.
  Tell about all the wonderful things
    he has done.
[10] Honor him, because his name is holy.
  Let the hearts of those who trust in
    the LORD be glad.
[11] Look to the LORD and to his strength.
  Always look to him.
[12] Remember the wonderful things he has
    done.
  Remember his miracles and how he
    judged our enemies.
[13] Remember, you his servants, the
    children of Israel.

WHAT ABOUT YOU?

In 1 Chronicles 16 we can read David's beautiful song of thanksgiving to God. It is a passage that is filled with joy, expressed in phrases like this: "Let the heavens be filled with joy. Let the earth be glad."

Today we have our own traditions of giving thanks, especially on Thanksgiving Day in the United States, including parades, turkey, family, and gratitude. In the Adventures in Odyssey episode "Thanksgiving at Home," Jimmy and Donna learn to be thankful for their parents. They wake up expecting that Mom and Dad will take care of everything for the special day. When they realize their Thanksgiving is in jeopardy, the kids think they can just throw together the traditions their family is used to sharing. That doesn't work out so well, and they soon realize what Thanksgiving is really about.

These days, a lot of people miss the point. They think this holiday is about football games, pumpkin pie, and bargain shopping. It's actually a chance to gather with friends and family to reflect on how God has provided for us.

It might not be Thanksgiving season, but take a moment to list ten things you are thankful for. Then find a quiet place in your house or outside and sit and thank God for what He has provided. You may want to challenge your family to do the same. Discuss ways you can follow the commands of Psalm 105:1–2 and "tell about all the wonderful things he has done."

Remember, you people of Jacob.
  Remember, you who are
    chosen by God.
^{14} He is the LORD our God.
  He judges the whole earth.
^{15} He will keep his covenant forever.
  He will keep his promise for all time
    to come.
^{16} He will keep the covenant he made with
    Abraham.
  He will keep the promise he made
    to Isaac.
^{17} He made it stand as a law for Jacob.
  He made it stand as a covenant for
    Israel. It will last forever.
^{18} He said, "I will give you the land of
    Canaan.
  It will belong to you."

^{19} At first there weren't very many of
    God's people.
  There were only a few. And they
    were strangers in the land.
^{20} They wandered from nation to nation.
  They wandered from one kingdom
    to another.

^{21} But God didn't allow anyone to treat
    them badly.
  To keep them safe, he gave a
    command to kings.
^{22} He said to them, "Do not touch my
    anointed ones.
  Do not harm my prophets."

^{23} All you people of the earth, sing to the
    LORD.
  Day after day tell about how he saves
    us.
^{24} Tell the nations about his glory.
  Tell all people about the wonderful
    things he has done.
^{25} The LORD is great. He is really worthy
    of praise.
  People should have respect for him
    as the greatest God of all.
^{26} All the gods of the nations are like their
    statues.
  They can't do anything.
  But the LORD made the heavens.
^{27} Glory and majesty are all around him.
  Strength and joy are in the place
    where he lives.

28 Praise the LORD, all you nations.
    Praise the LORD for his glory and
    strength.
29   Praise the LORD for the glory that
    belongs to him.
Bring an offering and come to him.
    Worship the LORD because of his
    beauty and holiness.
30 All you people of the earth, tremble
    when you are with him.
The world is firmly set in place. It
    can't be moved.
31 Let the heavens be filled with joy. Let
    the earth be glad.
Let them say among the nations,
    "The LORD rules!"
32 Let the ocean and everything in it roar.
    Let the fields and everything in them
    be glad.
33 Let the trees in the forest sing with joy.
    They will sing before the LORD.
He will judge the people of the
    world.
34 Give thanks to the LORD, because he is
    good.
    His faithful love continues forever.
35 Cry out, "Save us, God our Savior.
    Save us. Bring us back from among
    the nations.
Then we will give thanks to you,
    because your name is holy.
    We will celebrate by praising you."
36 Give praise to the LORD, the God of
    Israel,
    for ever and ever.

Then all the people said, "Amen!" They also said, "Praise the LORD."

37David left Asaph and his helpers to serve in front of the ark of the covenant of the LORD. They served there at regular times. They did it as they were required to do each day. 38David also left Obed-Edom and his 68 helpers to serve with them. Obed-Edom and Hosah guarded the gates. Obed-Edom was the son of Jeduthun. 39David left Zadok the priest and some other priests in front of the holy tent of the LORD. It was at the high place in Gibeon. 40David left them there to sacrifice burnt offerings to the LORD on the altar every morning and evening. They did it according to everything written in the Law of the LORD. That's the Law he had given to Israel. 41Heman and Jeduthun were with

the priests. So were the rest of those who had been chosen by name and appointed to serve. They had been chosen to give thanks to the LORD, "because his faithful love continues forever." 42It was the duty of Heman and Jeduthun to blow the trumpets. They also had the duty of playing the cymbals and other instruments for the sacred songs. The sons of Jeduthun were stationed at one of the gates. 43All the people left. Everyone went home. And David returned home to bless his family.

God Makes a Promise to David

17 David moved into his palace. Then he spoke to Nathan the prophet. He said, "Here I am, living in a house that has beautiful cedar walls. But the ark of the covenant of the LORD is under a tent."

2Nathan replied to David, "Do what you want to. God is with you."

3But that night a message came to Nathan from God. He said,

4"Go and speak to my servant David. Tell him, 'The LORD says, "You are not the one who will build me a house to live in. 5I have not lived in a house from the day I brought Israel up out of Egypt until now. I have moved my tent from one place to another. I have moved my home from one place to another. 6I have moved from place to place with all the Israelites. I commanded their leaders to be shepherds over my people. I never asked any of those leaders, 'Why haven't you built me a house that has beautiful cedar walls?' " '

7"So tell my servant David, 'The LORD who rules over all says, "I took you away from the grasslands. That is where you were taking care of your father's sheep and goats. I appointed you ruler over my people Israel. 8I have been with you everywhere you have gone. I destroyed all your enemies when you were attacking them. Now I will make you famous. Your name will be just as respected as the names of the most important people on earth. 9I will provide a place where my people Israel can live. I will plant them in the land. Then they will have a home of their own. They will not be bothered anymore. Sinful people will no longer crush them, as they did at first. [10]That is what your enemies have done ever since I appointed leaders over my people Israel. But I will bring all your enemies under your control.

" " 'I tell you that I, the LORD, will build a royal house for your family. [11]Some day your life will come to an end. You will join the members of your family who have already died. Then I will give you one of your own sons to become the next king after you. I will make his kingdom secure. [12]He is the one who will build me a house. I will set up his throne. It will last forever. [13]I will be his father. And he will be my son. I took my love away from the man who ruled before you. But I will never take my love away from your son. [14]I will place him over my house and my kingdom forever. His throne will last forever.' ' "

[15]Nathan reported to David all the words that the LORD had spoken to him.

David's Prayer

[16]Then King David went into the holy tent. He sat down in front of the LORD. He said,

"LORD God, who am I? My family isn't important. So why have you brought me this far? [17]I would have thought that you had already done more than enough for me. But now, my God, you have spoken about my royal house. You have said what will happen to it in days to come. LORD God, you have treated me as if I were the most honored man of all.

[18]"What more can I say to you for honoring me? You know all about me. [19]LORD, you have done a wonderful thing. You have given me many great promises. All of them are for my good. They are exactly what you wanted to give me.

[20]"LORD, there isn't anyone like you. There isn't any God but you. We have heard about it with our own ears. [21]Who is like your people Israel? God, we are the one nation on earth you have saved. You have set us free for yourself. Your name has become famous. You have done great and wonderful things. You have driven out nations to make room for your people. You saved us when you set us free from Egypt. [22]You made Israel your very own people forever. LORD, you have become our God.

[23]"And now, LORD, let the promise you have made to me and my royal house stand forever. Do exactly as you promised. [24]When your promise comes true, your name will be honored forever. People will say, 'The LORD rules over all. He is the God over Israel. He is Israel's God!' My royal house will be made secure in your sight.

[25]"My God, you have shown me that you will build me a royal house. So I can pray to you boldly. [26]You, LORD, are God! You have promised many good things to me. [27]You have been pleased to bless my royal house. Now it will continue forever in your sight. LORD, you have blessed it. And it will be blessed forever."

David Wins Many Battles

18 While David was king of Israel, he won many battles over the Philistines. He brought them under his control. He took Gath away from the Philistines. He also captured the villages around Gath.

[2]David also won the battle over the people of Moab. They were brought under his rule. They gave him the gifts he required them to bring him.

[3]David fought against Hadadezer in the area of Hamath. Hadadezer was king of Zobah. He had gone to set up his monument at the Euphrates River. [4]David captured 1,000 of Hadadezer's chariots, 7,000 chariot riders and 20,000 soldiers on foot. He cut the legs of all but 100 of the chariot horses.

[5]The Arameans of Damascus came to help Hadadezer, the king of Zobah. But David struck down 22,000 of them. [6]David stationed some soldiers in the Aramean kingdom of Damascus. The people of Aram were brought under his rule. They gave him the gifts he required them to bring him. The LORD helped David win his battles wherever he went.

[7]David took the gold shields carried by the officers of Hadadezer. He brought the shields to Jerusalem. [8]He took a huge

amount of bronze from Tebah and Kun. Those towns belonged to Hadadezer. Later, Solomon used the bronze to make the huge bronze bowl for washing. He also used it to make the pillars and many other bronze objects for the temple.

⁹Tou was king of Hamath. He heard that David had won the battle over the entire army of Hadadezer, the king of Zobah. ¹⁰So Tou sent his son Hadoram to King David. Hadoram greeted David. He praised him because David had won the battle over Hadadezer. Hadadezer had been at war with Tou. So Hadoram brought David all kinds of things made out of gold, of silver and of bronze.

¹¹King David set those things apart for the LORD. He had done the same thing with the silver and gold he had taken from other nations. The nations were Edom, Moab, Ammon, Philistia and Amalek.

¹²Abishai struck down 18,000 men of Edom in the Valley of Salt. Abishai was the son of Zeruiah. ¹³Abishai stationed some soldiers in Edom. The whole nation of Edom was brought under his rule. The LORD helped David win his battles wherever he went.

David's Officials

¹⁴David ruled over the whole nation of Israel. He did what was fair and right for all his people.

¹⁵ Joab, the son of Zeruiah, was commander over the army.

Jehoshaphat, the son of Ahilud, kept the records.

¹⁶ Zadok, the son of Ahitub, was a priest. Ahimelek, the son of Abiathar, was also a priest.

Shavsha was the secretary.

¹⁷ Benaiah, the son of Jehoiada, was commander over the Kerethites and Pelethites.

And King David's sons were the chief officials who served at his side.

David Wins the Battle Over the Ammonites

19 Nahash was king of Ammon. After he died, his son became the next king after him. ²David thought, "I'm going to be kind to Hanun. His father Nahash was kind to me." So David sent messengers to Hanun.

He wanted them to tell Hanun how sad he was that Hanun's father had died. David's messengers went to the land of Ammon. They told Hanun how sad David was.

³The Ammonite commanders spoke to Hanun. They said, "David has sent messengers to tell you he is sad. They say he wants to honor your father. But the real reason they've come is to look the land over. They want to destroy it." ⁴So Hanun grabbed David's messengers. He shaved them. He cut off their clothes just below the waist and left them half naked. Then he sent them away.

⁵Someone came and told David what had happened to his men. So David sent messengers to them because they were filled with shame. King David said to them, "Stay at Jericho until your beards grow out again. Then come back here."

⁶The Ammonites realized that what they had done had made David very angry with them. So Hanun and the Ammonites got 38 tons of silver. They used it to hire chariots and chariot riders from Aram Naharaim, Aram Maakah and Zobah. ⁷They hired 32,000 chariots and riders. They also hired the king of Maakah and his troops. All of them came out and camped near Medeba. At the same time the Ammonites brought their troops together from their towns. Then they marched out to fight.

⁸David heard about it. So he sent Joab out with the entire army of Israel's fighting men. ⁹The Ammonites marched out. They took up their battle positions at the entrance to their city. The kings who came to help them gathered their troops together in the open country.

¹⁰Joab saw that there were lines of soldiers in front of him and behind him. So he chose some of the best troops in Israel. He sent them to march out against the Arameans. ¹¹He put the rest of the men under the command of his brother Abishai. They were sent to march out against the Ammonites. ¹²Joab said, "Suppose the Arameans are too strong for me. Then you must come and help me. But suppose the Ammonites are too strong for you. Then I'll come and help you. ¹³Be strong. Let's be brave as we fight for our people and the cities of our God. The LORD will do what he thinks is best."

¹⁴Then Joab and the troops with him marched out to attack the Arameans. They ran away from him. ¹⁵The Ammonites

realized that the Arameans were running away. So they also ran away from Joab's brother Abishai. They went inside the city. Then Joab went back to Jerusalem.

[16]The Arameans saw that they had been driven away by Israel. So they sent messengers to get some Arameans from east of the Euphrates River. The Arameans were under the command of Shophak. He was the commander of Hadadezer's army.

[17]David was told about it. So he gathered together the whole army of Israel. They went across the Jordan River. David marched out against the Arameans. He lined up his soldiers opposite them. He lined them up to meet the Arameans in battle. The Arameans began to fight against him. [18]But then they ran away from Israel. David killed 7,000 of their chariot riders. He killed 40,000 of their soldiers who were on foot. He also killed Shophak, the commander of their army.

[19]The people who were under the rule of Hadadezer saw that Israel had won the battle over them. So they made a peace treaty with David. They were brought under his rule.

After that, the Arameans wouldn't help the Ammonites anymore.

Joab Captures the City of Rabbah

20 In the spring, Joab led Israel's army out. It was the time when kings march out to war. Joab destroyed the land of Ammon. He went to the city of Rabbah. He surrounded it and got ready to attack it. But David remained in Jerusalem. Later, Joab attacked Rabbah and completely destroyed it. [2]David took the gold crown off the head of the king of Ammon. The crown weighed 75 pounds. It had jewels in it. It was placed on David's head. He took a huge amount of goods from the city. [3]He brought out the people who were there. He made them work with saws and iron picks and axes. David did that to all the towns in Ammon. Then he and his entire army returned to Jerusalem.

Israel Goes to War Against the Philistines

[4]War broke out at Gezer against the Philistines. At that time Sibbekai killed Sippai. So the Philistines were brought under Israel's control. Sibbekai was a Hushathite. Sippai was from the family line of Rapha.

1 Chr. 20:2 King David must have had really strong neck muscles to wear that seventy-five-pound crown. Penny tells me that a swan-neck-roll exercise would help with that. It's no wonder that kings are often painted sitting in high-backed thrones. They needed help with that crown!

[5]In another battle against the Philistines, Elhanan killed Lahmi. Elhanan was the son of Jair. Lahmi was the brother of Goliath. Goliath was from the city of Gath. Lahmi's spear was as big as a weaver's rod.

[6]There was still another battle. It took place at Gath. A huge man lived there. He had six fingers on each hand and six toes on each foot. So the total number of his toes and fingers was 24. He was also from the family line of Rapha. [7]He made fun of Israel. So Jonathan killed him. Jonathan was the son of David's brother Shimea.

[8]Those Philistine men lived in Gath. They were from the family line of Rapha. David and his men killed them.

David Counts His Fighting Men

21 Satan rose up against Israel. He stirred up David to count the men of Israel. [2]So David said to Joab and the commanders of the troops, "Go! Count the men of Israel from Beersheba all the way to Dan. Report back to me. Then I'll know how many there are."

[3]Joab replied, "May the LORD multiply his troops 100 times. King David, you are my master. Aren't all the men under your control? Why would you want to count them? Do you want to make Israel guilty?"

[4]In spite of what Joab said, the king's order had more authority than Joab's reply did. So Joab left and went all through Israel.

CANDID CONVERSATIONS

Have your parents ever asked you to "pick your punishment"? My mom used to do that every now and then. If I disobeyed, she would say, "All right, you can either go to your room for the rest of the day, or you can clean the downstairs bathroom."

As much as I hated both of those options, that was nothing compared with the choice God gave to David for disobedience. Look at it in verses 11 and 12. Are you kidding me?

It might seem harsh, but it's obvious God wanted David (and us!) to know that there are consequences for sin. We will pay for the things we do wrong in one way or another. Personally, I'm glad there are consequences so I'm more motivated to stay away from evil when I see it in the future. As hard as it is for me to say this, I thank God (and my mom) for punishment.

Then he came back to Jerusalem. ⁵Joab reported to David how many fighting men he had counted. In the whole land of Israel there were 1,100,000 men who could use their swords well. That included 470,000 men in Judah.

⁶But Joab didn't include the tribes of Levi and Benjamin in the total number. The king's command was sickening to Joab. ⁷It was also evil in the sight of God. So he punished Israel.

⁸Then David said to God, "I committed a great sin when I counted Israel's men. I beg you to take away my guilt. I've done a very foolish thing."

⁹The LORD spoke to Gad, David's prophet. The LORD said, ¹⁰"Go and tell David, 'The LORD says, "I could punish you in three different ways. Choose one of them for me to punish you with." '"

¹¹So Gad went to David. Gad said to him, "The LORD says, 'Take your choice. ¹²You can have three years when there will not be enough food in the land. You can have three months when your enemies will sweep you away. They will catch up with you. They will destroy you with their swords. Or you can have three days when the sword of the LORD will punish you. That means there would be three days of plague in the land. My angel would strike down people in every part of Israel.' So take your pick. Tell me how to answer the one who sent me."

¹³David said to Gad, "I'm suffering terribly. Let me fall into the hands of the LORD. His mercy is very great. But don't let me fall into human hands."

¹⁴So the LORD sent a plague on Israel. And 70,000 Israelites died. ¹⁵God sent an angel to destroy Jerusalem. But as the angel was doing it, the LORD saw it. The LORD decided to end the plague he had sent. So he spoke to the angel who was destroying the people. He said, "That is enough! Do not kill any more people!" The angel of the LORD was standing at Araunah's threshing floor. Araunah was from the city of Jebus.

¹⁶David looked up. He saw the angel of the LORD standing between heaven and earth. The angel was holding out a sword over Jerusalem. David and the elders fell with their faces to the ground. They were wearing the rough clothing people wear when they're sad.

¹⁷David said to God, "I ordered the fighting men to be counted. I'm the one who has sinned. I am the shepherd of these people. I'm the one who has done what is wrong. These people are like sheep. What have they done? LORD my God, punish me and my family. But don't let this plague continue to strike your people."

David Builds an Altar

¹⁸Then the angel of the LORD ordered Gad to tell David to go up to the threshing floor of Araunah, the Jebusite. He wanted David to build an altar there to honor the LORD. ¹⁹So David went up and did it. He obeyed the message that Gad had spoken in the LORD's name.

²⁰Araunah was threshing wheat. He turned and saw the angel. Araunah's four children were with him. They hid

themselves. [21]David approached the threshing floor. Araunah looked up and saw him. So Araunah left the threshing floor. He bowed down to David with his face toward the ground.

[22]David said to him, "Let me have the property your threshing floor is on. I want to build an altar there to honor the Lord. When I do, the plague on the people will be stopped. Sell the threshing floor to me for the full price."

[23]Araunah said to David, "Take it! King David, you are my master. Do what you please. I'll even provide the oxen for the burnt offerings. Use boards from the threshing sleds for the wood. Use the wheat for the grain offering. I'll give it all to you."

[24]But King David replied to Araunah, "No! I want to pay the full price. I won't take what belongs to you and give it to the Lord. I won't sacrifice a burnt offering that hasn't cost me anything."

[25]So David paid Araunah 15 pounds of gold for the property. [26]David built an altar there to honor the Lord. He sacrificed burnt offerings and friendship offerings. He called out to the Lord. The Lord answered him by sending fire from heaven on the altar for burnt offerings.

[27]Then the Lord spoke to the angel. And the angel put his sword away. [28]When the angel did that, David was still at the threshing floor of Araunah, the Jebusite. David saw that the Lord had answered him. So he offered sacrifices there. [29]At that time, the Lord's holy tent was at the high place in Gibeon. The altar for burnt offerings was there too. Moses had made the holy tent in the desert. [30]David couldn't go to the tent to pray to God. That's because he was afraid of the sword of the angel of the Lord.

22 David announced, "The house of the Lord God will be built here. Israel's altar for burnt offerings will also be here."

David Makes Plans for Building the Temple

[2]David gave orders to bring together the outsiders who were living in Israel. He appointed some of them to cut stones. He wanted them to prepare blocks of stone for building the house of God. [3]David provided a large amount of iron to make nails. They were for the doors of the gateways and for the fittings. He provided more bronze than

anyone could weigh. [4]He also provided more cedar logs than anyone could count. The people of Sidon and Tyre brought large numbers of logs to David.

[5]David said, "My son Solomon is young. He's never done anything like this before. The house that will be built for the Lord should be very grand and wonderful. All the nations should consider it to be famous and beautiful. I'll get things ready for it." So David got many things ready before he died.

[6]Then he sent for his son Solomon. He told him to build a house for the Lord, the God of Israel. [7]David said to Solomon, "My son, with all my heart I wanted to build a house for the Lord my God. That's where his Name will be. [8]But a message from the Lord came to me. It said, 'You have spilled the blood of many people. You have fought many wars. You are not the one who will build a house for my Name. That is because I have seen you spill the blood of many people on the earth. [9]But you are going to have a son. He will be a man of peace. And I will give him peace and rest from all his enemies on every side. His name will be Solomon. I will give Israel peace and quiet while he is king. [10]He will build a house for my Name. He will be my son. And I will be his father. I will make his kingdom secure over Israel. It will last forever.'

[11]"My son, may the Lord be with you. May you have success. May you build the house of the Lord your God, just as he said you would. [12]May the Lord give you good sense. May he give you understanding when he makes you king over Israel. Then you will keep the law of the Lord your God. [13]Be careful to obey the rules and laws the Lord gave Moses for Israel. Then you will have success. Be strong and brave. Don't be afraid. Don't lose hope.

[14]"I've tried very hard to provide for the Lord's temple. I've provided 3,750 tons of gold and 37,500 tons of silver. I've provided more bronze and iron than anyone can weigh. I've also given plenty of wood and stone. You can add to it. [15]You have a lot of workers. You have people who can cut stones and people who can lay the stones. You have people who can work with wood. You also have people who are skilled in every other kind of work. [16]Some of them can work with gold and silver. Others can work with bronze and iron. There are more

workers than anyone can count. So begin the work. May the LORD be with you." [17]Then David ordered all Israel's leaders to help his son Solomon. [18]He said to them, "The LORD your God is with you. He's given you peace and rest on every side. He's handed over to me the people who are living in the land. The land has been brought under the control of the LORD and his people. [19]So be committed to the LORD your God with all your heart and soul. Start building the temple of the LORD God. Then bring the ark of the covenant of the LORD into it. Also bring in the sacred objects that belong to God. The temple will be built for the Name of the LORD."

The Family Line of Levi

23 David had become very old. So he made his son Solomon king over Israel.

[2]He gathered together all the leaders of Israel. He also gathered the priests and the Levites together. [3]The Levites who were 30 years old or more were counted. The total number of men was 38,000. [4]David said, "From them, 24,000 will be in charge of the work of the LORD's temple. And 6,000 will be officials and judges. [5]Another 4,000 will guard the gates. And 4,000 will praise the LORD with the instruments of music I've provided for that purpose."

[6] David separated the Levites into groups. He did it according to the sons of Levi. The sons were Gershon, Kohath and Merari.

The Family of Gershon

[7] Ladan and Shimei belonged to the family of Gershon.
[8] The sons of Ladan were
    Jehiel, Zetham and Joel. Jehiel was the oldest son. The total number of sons was three.
[9] The sons of Shimei were
    Shelomoth, Haziel and Haran. The total number of sons was three. They were the leaders of the families of Ladan.
[10] The sons of Shimei were
    Jahath, Ziza, Jeush and Beriah. The total number of the sons of Shimei was four.
[11] Jahath was the first son. Ziza was the second son. But Jeush and

Beriah didn't have many sons. So they were counted as one family. They had only one task.

The Family of Kohath

[12] The sons of Kohath were
    Amram, Izhar, Hebron and Uzziel. The total number of sons was four.
[13] The sons of Amram were
    Aaron and Moses.
Aaron and his family line were set apart forever as the LORD's priests. They had the duty of setting the most holy things apart to the LORD. They offered sacrifices to the LORD. They served him. They gave blessings in his name forever.
[14]The sons of Moses, the man of God, were counted as part of the tribe of Levi.
[15] The sons of Moses were
    Gershom and Eliezer.
[16] Shubael was the oldest son in the family line of Gershom.
[17] Rehabiah was the oldest son in the family line of Eliezer.
Eliezer didn't have any other sons. But Rehabiah had a great many sons.
[18] Shelomith was the oldest son of Izhar.
[19] Jeriah was the first son of Hebron.
    Amariah was his second son. Jahaziel was the third. Jekameam was the fourth.
[20] Micah was the first son of Uzziel. Ishiah was his second son.

The Family of Merari

[21] The sons of Merari were
    Mahli and Mushi.
    The sons of Mahli were
    Eleazar and Kish.
[22] Eleazar died without having any sons. All he had was daughters. They married their cousins. The cousins were the sons of Kish.
[23] The sons of Mushi were
    Mahli, Eder and Jerimoth. The total number of sons was three.

[24] Those were the family lines of Levi. They were recorded under the names of the family leaders. Each worker who was 20 years old or more was counted. They served in the LORD's

temple. ²⁵David had said, "The LORD is the God of Israel. He has given peace and rest to his people. He has come to Jerusalem to live there forever. ²⁶So the Levites don't need to carry the holy tent anymore. They don't need to carry any of its objects anymore. Those were the things that were used to serve there." ²⁷The Levites who were 20 years old or more were counted. That was in keeping with David's final directions.

²⁸The Levites had the duty of helping the members of Aaron's family line. They helped them serve in the LORD's temple. They were in charge of the courtyards and the side rooms. They made all the sacred things pure and "clean." They also had other duties at the house of God. ²⁹They were in charge of setting the holy bread out on the table. They prepared the special flour for the grain offerings. They made the thin loaves without using any yeast. They did the baking and the mixing. They measured the amount and size of everything. ³⁰They stood every morning to thank and praise the LORD. They did the same thing every evening. ³¹They also did it every time burnt offerings were brought to the LORD. Those offerings were brought every Sabbath day. They were also brought at every New Moon feast and during the appointed yearly feasts. The Levites served in front of the LORD at regular times. The proper number of Levites was always used when they served. They served in the way the law required.

³²So the Levites carried out their duties for the tent of meeting and for the Holy Room. They worked under their relatives who were in the family line of Aaron. They helped them serve at the LORD's temple.

The Groups of Priests

24 The priests in the family line of Aaron were separated into groups. The groups were separated according to the sons of Aaron.

The sons of Aaron were Nadab, Abihu, Eleazar and Ithamar. ²But Nadab and Abihu died before their father did. They didn't have any sons. So Eleazar and Ithamar served as the priests. ³With the help of Zadok and Ahimelek, David separated the priests into groups. Each group served in its appointed order and time. Zadok belonged to the family line of Eleazar. Ahimelek belonged to the family line of Ithamar. ⁴More leaders were found among Eleazar's family line than among Ithamar's. So the priests were separated into their groups based on that fact. There were 16 family leaders from Eleazar's line. There were eight family leaders from Ithamar's line. ⁵The priests were separated into their groups by casting lots. That was the fair way to do it. The priests were officials of the temple and officials of God. They came from the family lines of Eleazar and Ithamar.

⁶Shemaiah was a Levite. He was the son of Nethanel. Shemaiah was the writer who recorded the names of the priests. He wrote them down in front of the king and the officials. The officials included Zadok the priest and Ahimelek. Ahimelek was the son of Abiathar. The officials also included the leaders of the families of the priests and the Levites. One family was chosen by lot from Eleazar's group. Then one was chosen from Ithamar's group.

⁷ The 1st lot chosen was for Jehoiarib.
The 2nd was for Jedaiah.
⁸ The 3rd was for Harim.
The 4th was for Seorim.
⁹ The 5th was for Malkijah.
The 6th was for Mijamin.
¹⁰ The 7th was for Hakkoz.
The 8th was for Abijah.
¹¹ The 9th was for Jeshua.
The 10th was for Shekaniah.
¹² The 11th was for Eliashib.
The 12th was for Jakim.
¹³ The 13th was for Huppah.
The 14th was for Jeshebeab.
¹⁴ The 15th was for Bilgah.
The 16th was for Immer.
¹⁵ The 17th was for Hezir.
The 18th was for Happizzez.
¹⁶ The 19th was for Pethahiah.
The 20th was for Jehezkel.
¹⁷ The 21st was for Jakin.
The 22nd was for Gamul.
¹⁸ The 23rd was for Delaiah.
The 24th was for Maaziah.

¹⁹That was their appointed order for serving when they entered the LORD's temple. That order was based on the rules Aaron had given them long ago. Everything was

done exactly as the LORD had commanded Aaron. The LORD is the God of Israel.

The Rest of the Levites

²⁰ Here are the other members of the family line of Levi.

From the sons of Amram came Shubael.
From the sons of Shubael came Jehdeiah.
²¹ From the sons of Rehabiah came Ishiah. Ishiah was the oldest.
²² From the people of Izhar came Shelomoth.
From the sons of Shelomoth came Jahath.
²³ Jeriah was the first son of Hebron. Amariah was his second son. Jahaziel was the third. Jekameam was the fourth.
²⁴ The son of Uzziel was Micah.
From the sons of Micah came Shamir.
²⁵ The brother of Micah was Ishiah.
From the sons of Ishiah came Zechariah.
²⁶ The sons of Merari were Mahli and Mushi.
The son of Jaaziah was Beno.
²⁷ The sons of Merari
from Jaaziah were Beno, Shoham, Zakkur and Ibri.
²⁸ From Mahli came Eleazar. Eleazar didn't have any sons.
²⁹ From Kish came Jerahmeel. Jerahmeel was the son of Kish.
³⁰ The sons of Mushi were Mahli, Eder and Jerimoth.

Those were the Levites, family by family.

³¹They cast lots just as their relatives had done. Their relatives were in the family line of Aaron. They cast lots in front of King David, Zadok and Ahimelek. They did it in front of the family leaders of the priests. They also did it in front of the family leaders of the Levites. The families of the oldest brother were treated in the same way as the families of the youngest.

The Musicians

25 David and the commanders of the army set apart some of the sons of Asaph, Heman and Jeduthun. They set them apart to serve the LORD by prophesying while harps, lyres and cymbals were being played. Here is the list of the men who served in that way.

² From the sons of Asaph came Zakkur, Joseph, Nethaniah and Asarelah. The sons of Asaph were under the direction of Asaph. He prophesied under the king's direction.
³ From the sons of Jeduthun came Gedaliah, Zeri, Jeshaiah, Shimei, Hashabiah and Mattithiah. The total number was six. They were under the direction of their father Jeduthun. He prophesied while playing the harp. He used it to thank and praise the LORD.
⁴ From the sons of Heman came Bukkiah, Mattaniah, Uzziel, Shubael, Jerimoth, Hananiah, Hanani, Eliathah, Giddalti, Romamti-Ezer, Joshbekashah, Mallothi, Hothir and Mahazioth. ⁵All of them were sons of the king's prophet Heman. They were given to Heman to bring him honor. That's what God had promised. God gave him 14 sons and three daughters.

⁶All of them were under the direction of their father. They played music for the LORD's temple. They served at the house of God by playing cymbals, lyres and harps. Asaph, Jeduthun and Heman were under the king's direction.
⁷All of them were trained and skilled in playing music for the LORD. Their total number was 288. That included their relatives. ⁸Young and old alike cast lots for their duties. That was true for students as well as teachers.

⁹ The 1st lot chosen was for Asaph. It was for Joseph and his sons and relatives. The total number was 12.
The 2nd lot was for Gedaliah and his relatives and sons. The total number was 12.
¹⁰ The 3rd was for Zakkur and his sons and relatives. The total number was 12.
¹¹ The 4th was for Izri and his sons and relatives. The total number was 12.
¹² The 5th was for Nethaniah and his sons and relatives. The total number was 12.

¹³ The 6th was for Bukkiah and his sons and relatives. The total number was 12.

¹⁴ The 7th was for Jesarelah and his sons and relatives. The total number was 12.

¹⁵ The 8th was for Jeshaiah and his sons and relatives. The total number was 12.

¹⁶ The 9th was for Mattaniah and his sons and relatives. The total number was 12.

¹⁷ The 10th was for Shimei and his sons and relatives. The total number was 12.

¹⁸ The 11th was for Azarel and his sons and relatives. The total number was 12.

¹⁹ The 12th was for Hashabiah and his sons and relatives. The total number was 12.

²⁰ The 13th was for Shubael and his sons and relatives. The total number was 12.

²¹ The 14th was for Mattithiah and his sons and relatives. The total number was 12.

²² The 15th was for Jerimoth and his sons and relatives. The total number was 12.

²³ The 16th was for Hananiah and his sons and relatives. The total number was 12.

²⁴ The 17th was for Joshbekashah and his sons and relatives. The total number was 12.

²⁵ The 18th was for Hanani and his sons and relatives. The total number was 12.

²⁶ The 19th was for Mallothi and his sons and relatives. The total number was 12.

²⁷ The 20th was for Eliathah and his sons and relatives. The total number was 12.

²⁸ The 21st was for Hothir and his sons and relatives. The total number was 12.

²⁹ The 22nd was for Giddalti and his sons and relatives. The total number was 12.

³⁰ The 23rd was for Mahazioth and his sons and relatives. The total number was 12.

³¹ The 24th was for Romamti-Ezer and his sons and relatives. The total number was 12.

The Men Who Guarded the Gates

26 Here are the groups of men who guarded the gates.

From the family of Korah came Meshelemiah, the son of Kore. Kore was one of the sons of Asaph. ²Meshelemiah had sons.
Zechariah was his first son.
Jediael was his second son.
Zebadiah was the third.
Jathniel was the fourth.
³ Elam was the fifth.
Jehohanan was the sixth.
And Eliehoenai was the seventh.
⁴ Obed-Edom also had sons.
Shemaiah was his first son.
Jehozabad was his second son.
Joah was the third.
Sakar was the fourth.
Nethanel was the fifth.
⁵ Ammiel was the sixth.
Issachar was the seventh.
And Peullethai was the eighth.
God had blessed Obed-Edom.

⁶ Obed-Edom's son Shemaiah also had sons. They were leaders in their family. That's because they were men of great ability. ⁷The sons of Shemaiah were Othni, Rephael, Obed and Elzabad. Elzabad's relatives Elihu and Semakiah were also capable men.

⁸ All of them belonged to the family line of Obed-Edom. They and their sons and relatives were capable men. They were strong enough to do their work. The total number of men in the family line of Obed-Edom was 62.

⁹ Meshelemiah's sons and relatives were capable men. Their total number was 18.

¹⁰ Hosah belonged to the family line of Merari. Hosah's first son was Shimri. But Shimri wasn't the oldest son. His father had made him the first.

¹¹ Hilkiah was Hosah's second son. Tabaliah was the third. Zechariah was the fourth.

The total number of Hosah's sons and relatives was 13.

¹² Those groups of men guarded the gates. They worked under their leaders. They served at the LORD's temple,

just as their relatives had served. ¹³Lots were cast for each gate, family by family. Young and old alike were chosen.

¹⁴ The lot chosen for the East Gate was for Shelemiah.

Then lots were cast for his son Zechariah, who gave wise advice. The lot chosen for the North Gate was for Zechariah.

¹⁵ The lot chosen for the South Gate was for Obed-Edom. The lot chosen for the storeroom was for his sons.

¹⁶ Lots were chosen for the West Gate and the Shalleketh Gate on the upper road. Those lots were chosen for Shuppim and Hosah.

One guard stood next to another.

¹⁷ There were six Levites a day on the east.

There were four a day on the north. There were four a day on the south. And there were two at a time at the storeroom.

¹⁸ Two Levite guards were at the courtyard to the west. And four were at the road.

¹⁹ Those were the groups of the men who guarded the gates. They belonged to the family lines of Korah and Merari.

Other Officials

²⁰Men were in charge of the treasures in the house of God. They were the Levite relatives of the men who guarded the gates. These men were also in charge of other treasures that had been set apart for God.

²¹Ladan was from the family line of Gershon. Some leaders of families belonged to Ladan's family line. One of them was Jehieli. ²²The sons of Jehieli were Zetham and his brother Joel. They were in charge of the treasures in the LORD's temple.

²³ Here are the officials who were from the family lines of Amram, Izhar, Hebron and Uzziel.

²⁴ Shubael was from the family line of Moses' son Gershom. Shubael was the official in charge of the treasures. ²⁵His relatives through Eliezer included his son Rehabiah. Jeshaiah was Rehabiah's son.

Joram was Jeshaiah's son. Zikri was Joram's son. And Shelomith was Zikri's son.

²⁶ Shelomith and his relatives were in charge of all the treasures that had been set apart for God. King David had set those treasures apart. Some family leaders had also set them apart. They were the commanders of thousands of men and commanders of hundreds. The treasures had also been set apart by other army commanders. ²⁷Some of the goods that had been taken in battle were set apart to repair the LORD's temple. ²⁸Samuel the prophet had set apart some things for God. Saul, the son of Kish, had set apart other things. So had Abner, the son of Ner. And so had Joab, the son of Zeruiah. All these things and everything else that had been set apart were taken care of by Shelomith and his relatives.

²⁹ From the family line of Izhar came Kenaniah and his sons. They were given duties that were away from the temple. They were officials and judges over Israel.

³⁰ From the family line of Hebron came Hashabiah and his relatives. They were capable men. The total number was 1,700. It was their duty to serve the king in Israel west of the Jordan River. It was also their duty to do all the LORD's work there. ³¹Jeriah was the chief of the family line of Hebron. That's based on their family history.

In the 40th year of David's rule, a search was made in the records. That's how capable men were found in the family line of Hebron at Jazer in Gilead. ³²Jeriah had 2,700 relatives. They were capable men and family leaders. King David had put them in charge of the tribes of Reuben and Gad and half of the tribe of Manasseh. They were in charge of matters having to do with God and the king.

The Groups of Fighting Men in the Army

27 Here is the list of the Israelites who served in the king's army.

They included leaders of families. They included commanders of thousands of men and commanders of hundreds. They also included other officers. All of them served the king in everything concerning the army's fighting groups. These groups were on duty month by month all through the year. The total number of men in each group was 24,000.

2 Jashobeam was in charge of the first fighting group for the first month. He was the son of Zabdiel. The total number of men in Jashobeam's group was 24,000. 3 He belonged to the family line of Perez. He was chief of all the army officers for the first month.

4 Dodai was in charge of the second fighting group for the second month. He belonged to the family line of Ahoah. Mikloth was the leader of Dodai's group. The total number of men in Dodai's group was 24,000.

5 The third army commander for the third month was Benaiah the priest, the son of Jehoiada. Benaiah was the chief. The total number of men in Benaiah's fighting group was 24,000. 6 That same Benaiah was a mighty warrior among the 30 chiefs. In fact, he was leader over the 30 chiefs. His son Ammizabad was in charge of Benaiah's group.

7 The fourth commander for the fourth month was Joab's brother Asahel. Asahel's son Zebadiah was the next commander after him. The total number of men in Asahel's fighting group was 24,000.

8 The fifth commander for the fifth month was Shamhuth. He was an Izrahite. The total number of men in Shamhuth's fighting group was 24,000.

9 The sixth commander for the sixth month was Ira. He was the son of Ikkesh from Tekoa. The total number of men in Ira's fighting group was 24,000.

10 The seventh commander for the seventh month was Helez. He was a Pelonite from Ephraim. The total number of men in Helez's fighting group was 24,000.

11 The eighth commander for the eighth month was Sibbekai. He was a Hushathite from Zerah. The total number of men in Sibbekai's fighting group was 24,000.

12 The ninth commander for the ninth month was Abiezer. He was from Anathoth in Benjamin. The total number of men in Abiezer's fighting group was 24,000.

13 The tenth commander for the tenth month was Maharai. He was a Netophathite from Zerah. The total number of men in Maharai's fighting group was 24,000.

14 The 11th commander for the 11th month was Benaiah. He was from Pirathon in Ephraim. The total number of men in Benaiah's fighting group was 24,000.

15 The 12th commander for the 12th month was Heldai. He was a Netophathite from the family line of Othniel. The total number of men in Heldai's fighting group was 24,000.

The Leaders of the Tribes

16 Here are the leaders of the tribes of Israel.

Over the tribe of Reuben was Eliezer, the son of Zikri.

Over Simeon was Shephatiah, the son of Maakah.

17 Over Levi was Hashabiah, the son of Kemuel.

Over Aaron was Zadok.

18 Over Judah was Elihu. He was David's brother.

Over Issachar was Omri, the son of Michael.

19 Over Zebulun was Ishmaiah, the son of Obadiah.

Over Naphtali was Jerimoth, the son of Azriel.

20 Over Ephraim was Hoshea, the son of Azaziah.

Over half of the tribe of Manasseh was Joel, the son of Pedaiah.

21 Over the half of the tribe of Manasseh in Gilead was Iddo, the son of Zechariah.

Over Benjamin was Jaasiel, the son of Abner. [22] Over Dan was Azarel, the son of Jeroham.

These were the leaders of the tribes of Israel.

[23]David didn't count the men who were 20 years old or less. That's because the LORD had promised to make the people of Israel as many as the stars in the sky. [24]Joab, the son of Zeruiah, began to count the men. But he didn't finish. The LORD was angry with Israel because David had begun to count the men. So the number wasn't written down in the official records of King David.

Other Officials of the King

[25] Azmaveth was in charge of the royal storerooms. He was the son of Adiel.

Jonathan was in charge of the storerooms in the fields, towns, villages and lookout towers. He was the son of Uzziah. [26] Ezri was in charge of the workers who farmed the land. He was the son of Kelub. [27] Shimei was in charge of the vineyards. He was from Ramah.

Zabdi was in charge of the grapes from the vineyards. He was also in charge of storing the wine. He was a Shiphmite. [28] Baal-Hanan was in charge of the olive trees and sycamore-fig trees in the western hills. He was from Geder.

Joash was in charge of storing the olive oil. [29] Shitrai was in charge of the herds that ate grass in Sharon. He was from Sharon.

Shaphat was in charge of the herds in the valleys. He was the son of Adlai. [30] Obil was in charge of the camels. He was from the family line of Ishmael.

Jehdeiah was in charge of the donkeys. He was from Meronoth. [31] Jaziz was in charge of the flocks. He was a Hagrite.

All these men were the officials in charge of King David's property.

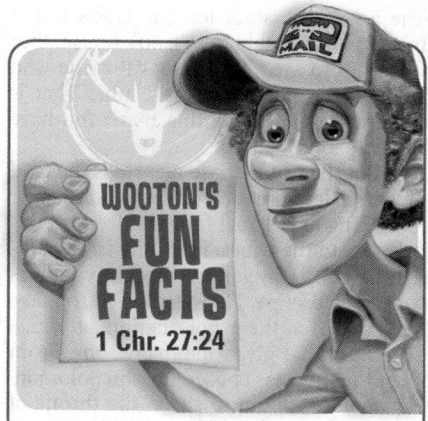

This was a sin because David was thinking of the military men as his own, not God's. His heart was prideful. God already knew how many men there were. He's God after all! David didn't need to count them.

[32] Jonathan was David's uncle. He gave good advice. He was a man of understanding. He was also a secretary.

Jehiel took care of the king's sons. He was the son of Hakmoni. [33] Ahithophel was the king's adviser.

Hushai was the king's trusted friend. He was an Arkite. [34] Jehoiada and Abiathar became the next advisers after Ahithophel. Jehoiada was the son of Benaiah.

Joab was the commander of the royal army.

David's Plans for the Temple

28 David asked all the officials of Israel to come together at Jerusalem. He sent for the officers who were over the tribes. He sent for the commanders of the military groups who served the king. He sent for the commanders of thousands of men and commanders of hundreds. He sent for the officials who were in charge of all the royal property and livestock. They belonged to the king and his sons. He sent for the palace officials and the warriors. He also sent for all the brave fighting men.

[2]King David stood up. He said, "All of you Israelites, listen to me. With all my heart I wanted to build a house for the LORD. I wanted it to be a place of peace and rest for the ark of the covenant of the LORD.

The ark is the stool for our God's feet. I made plans to build the LORD's house. ³But God said to me, 'You are not the one who will build a house for my Name. That is because you are a fighting man. You have spilled people's blood.'

⁴"But the LORD chose me. He is the God of Israel. He chose me from my whole family to be king over Israel forever. He chose Judah to lead the tribes. From the tribe of Judah he chose my family. From my father's sons he chose me. He was pleased to make me king over the whole nation of Israel. ⁵The LORD has given me many sons. From all of them he has chosen my son Solomon. He wants Solomon to sit on the throne of the LORD's kingdom. He wants him to rule over Israel. ⁶The LORD said to me, 'Your son Solomon is the one who will build my house and my courtyards. I have chosen him to be my son. And I will be his father. ⁷I will make his kingdom secure. It will last forever. That will happen if he continues to obey my commands and laws. He must continue to obey them, just as he is doing now.'

⁸"So I'm giving you a command in the sight of all the people of Israel. The LORD's community is watching. And our God is listening. I command you to be careful to follow all the commands of the LORD your God. Then you will own this good land. You will pass it on to your children after you as their share forever.

⁹"My son Solomon, always remember the God of your father. Serve him with all your heart. Do it with a mind that wants to obey him. The LORD looks deep down inside every heart. He understands every desire and every thought. If you look to him, you will find him. But if you desert him, he will turn his back on you forever. ¹⁰Think about it. The LORD has chosen you to build a house as a holy place where he can live. So be strong. Get to work."

¹¹Then David gave his son Solomon the plans for the porch of the temple. He gave him the plans for its buildings and its storerooms. He gave him the plans for its upper parts and its inside rooms. He gave him the plans for the place where sin is paid for and forgiven. ¹²He gave him the plans for everything the Spirit of the LORD had put in his mind. There were plans for the courtyards of the LORD's temple. There were plans for all the rooms around it. There were plans for the places where the treasure of God's temple would be kept. There were plans for the places where the things set apart for God would be kept. ¹³David told Solomon how to separate the priests and Levites into groups. He gave him directions for all the work they should do when they served in the LORD's temple. David also showed Solomon how all the objects should be used at the temple. ¹⁴Different things were used for different purposes. David told Solomon how much gold should be used for each gold object. He also told him how much silver should be used for each silver object. ¹⁵He told him how much gold should be used to make each gold lampstand and its lamps. He told him how much silver should be used to make each silver lampstand and its lamps. The amount depended on how each lampstand would be used. ¹⁶David told Solomon how much gold should be used to make each table for holy bread. He told him how much silver should be used to make the silver tables. ¹⁷He told him how much pure gold should be used to make the forks, sprinkling bowls and pitchers. He told him how much gold should be used to make each gold dish. He told him how much silver should be used to make each silver dish. ¹⁸And David told Solomon how much pure gold should be used to make the altar for burning incense. He also gave Solomon the plan for the chariot of the gold cherubim. The cherubim spread their wings over the ark of the covenant of the LORD.

¹⁹David said, "I have written everything down. I wrote it all down as the LORD guided me. He helped me understand every part of the plan."

²⁰David also said to his son Solomon, "Be strong and brave. Get to work. Don't be

---

Jason's Jargon

1 CHRONICLES 28

Ready for your next quest? Find *desert* in this chapter. To desert someone means you abandon them or forget about them. It's spelled the same as the word that means a barren sandy area.

afraid. Don't lose hope. The Lord God is my God. He is with you. He won't fail you. He won't desert you until all the work for serving in the Lord's temple is finished. [21]The groups of the priests and Levites are ready to do all the work on God's temple. Every person who is willing and skilled can help you do all the work. The officials and all the people will obey every command you give them."

Gifts Are Brought for Building the Temple

29 Then King David spoke to the whole community. He said, "God has chosen my son Solomon. But Solomon is young. He's never done anything like this before. The task is huge. This grand and wonderful temple won't be built for human beings. It will be built for the Lord God. [2]With all my riches I've done everything I could for the temple of my God. I've provided gold for the gold work and silver for the silver work. I've provided bronze for the bronze work and iron for the iron work. I've given wood for the things that will be made out of wood. I've given onyx and turquoise for the settings. I've given stones of different colors and all kinds of fine stone and marble. I've provided everything in huge amounts. [3]With all my heart I want the temple of my God to be built. So I'm giving my personal treasures of gold and silver for it. I'm adding them to everything else I've provided for the holy temple. [4]I'm giving 110 tons of gold and 260 tons of pure silver. Cover the walls of the buildings with it. [5]Use it for the gold work and the silver work. Use it for everything the skilled workers will do. How many of you are willing to set yourselves apart to the Lord today?"

[6]Many people were willing to give. They included the leaders of families and the officers of the tribes of Israel. They included the commanders of thousands of men and commanders of hundreds. They also included the officials who were in charge of the king's work. [7]All of them gave to the work on God's temple. They gave more than 190 tons of gold and 380 tons of silver. They also gave 675 tons of bronze and 3,800 tons of iron. [8]Anyone who had valuable jewels added them to the treasure for the Lord's temple. Jehiel was in charge of the temple treasure. He was from the family line of Gershon. [9]The people were happy when they saw what their leaders had been willing to give. The leaders had given freely. With their whole heart they had given everything to the Lord. King David was filled with joy.

David's Prayer

[10]David praised the Lord in front of the whole community. He said,

"Lord, we give you praise.
     You are the God of our father Israel.
     We give you praise for ever and ever.
[11] Lord, you are great and powerful.
     Glory, majesty and beauty belong
         to you.
     Everything in heaven and on earth
         belongs to you.
     Lord, the kingdom belongs to you.
     You are honored as the one who
         rules over all.
[12] Wealth and honor come from you.
     You are the ruler of all things.
     In your hands are strength and power.
     You can give honor and strength to
         everyone.
[13] Our God, we give you thanks.
     We praise your glorious name.

[14]"But who am I? And who are my people? Without your help we wouldn't be able to give this much. Everything comes from you. We've given back to you only what comes from you. [15]We are outsiders and strangers in your sight. So were all of our people who lived long ago. Our days on this earth are like a shadow. We don't have any hope. [16]Lord our God, we've given more than enough. We've provided it to build you a temple where you will put your holy Name. But all of it comes from you. All of it belongs to you. [17]My God, I know that you tested our hearts. And you are pleased when we are honest. I've given all these things just because I wanted to. When I did it, I was completely honest with you. Your people here have also been willing to give to you. And I've been happy to see this. [18]Lord, you are the God of our fathers Abraham, Isaac and Israel. Keep these desires and thoughts in the hearts of your people forever. Keep their hearts faithful to you. [19]Help my son Solomon serve you with all his heart. Then he will keep your commands and rules. He will do what you require. He'll

do everything to build the grand and wonderful temple I've provided for."

²⁰Then David said to the whole community, "Praise the LORD your God." So all of them praised the LORD. He's the God of their people who lived long ago. The whole community bowed low. They fell down flat with their faces toward the ground. They did it in front of the LORD and the king.

Solomon Becomes the next King

²¹The next day they offered sacrifices to the LORD. They brought burnt offerings to him. They sacrificed 1,000 bulls, 1,000 rams and 1,000 male lambs. They also brought the required drink offerings. And they offered many other sacrifices for the whole community of Israel. ²²They ate and drank with great joy that day. They did it in front of the LORD. Then they announced a second time that Solomon was king. He was the son of David. They anointed Solomon in front of the LORD. They anointed him to be ruler. They also anointed Zadok to be priest.

²³So Solomon sat on the throne of the LORD. He ruled as king in place of his father David. Things went well with him. All the people of Israel obeyed him. ²⁴All the officers and warriors promised to be completely faithful to King Solomon. So did all of King David's sons.

²⁵The LORD greatly honored Solomon in the sight of all the people. He gave him royal majesty. Solomon was given more glory than any king over Israel ever had before.

David Dies

²⁶David was king over the whole nation of Israel. He was the son of Jesse. ²⁷He ruled over Israel for 40 years. He ruled for seven years in Hebron and for 33 years in Jerusalem. ²⁸He died when he was very old. He had enjoyed a long life. He had enjoyed wealth and honor. David's son Solomon became the next king after him.

²⁹The events of King David's rule from beginning to end are written down. They are written in the records of Samuel, Nathan and Gad, the prophets. ³⁰The records tell all about David's rule and power. They tell about what happened concerning him and Israel and the kingdoms of all the other lands.

2 Chronicles

We see another "Part 2" in our journey! In this book the Chronicler continues the history he began in 1 Chronicles, picking up with the story of Solomon (chapters 1–9). As he did with David, he excludes most all the critical accounts of Solomon and portrays him in a much more positive light. According to the account in 1 Kings 1–2, we see that Solomon underwent some competition for the throne and was forced to deal with a number of problems that the Chronicler never mentions. Nor does the author bring up the late-in-life falling away from God that came as a result of Solomon's many wives (1 Kings 11:1–13).

But as he moves beyond Solomon into the series of kings, both of Israel and Judah (chapters 10–36), there is then no way to remain upbeat. Far too many of the nations' leaders were corrupt, self-serving, and spiritually bankrupt, and the era of the kings ended with the destruction of their homelands and domination by powerful enemies. As we saw previously, the Chronicler got his information from a number of places, including not only several of the psalms and prophetic books, but also a number of sources unknown or unfamiliar to us (16:11; 20:34; 24:27).

WHAT'S IT MEAN, EUGENE?

Immutability—If a thing cannot change or be changed we could call it "immutable." When theologians and Bible scholars talk about the *immutability* of God, they mean that He is constant, consistent, and never subject to shifting moods or changing opinions. Hebrews 13:8 assures us that "Jesus Christ is the same yesterday and today and forever." Likewise, though we as humans change in looks, thoughts, and perhaps even our tastes as the years go by, we should always hold fast to the truth of the Bible in what we believe. While I am changeable, the truth of God is immutable.

Solomon Asks God for Wisdom

1 Solomon was the son of David. Solomon made his position secure over his kingdom. The LORD his God was with him. He made Solomon very great.

²Solomon spoke to the whole community of Israel. He spoke to the commanders of thousands of men and commanders of hundreds. He spoke to the judges and all the leaders in Israel. He spoke to the leaders of Israel's families. ³Solomon and the whole community went to the high place at Gibeon. That's because God's tent of meeting was there. The LORD's servant Moses had made the tent in the desert. ⁴David had carried up the ark of God from Kiriath Jearim. He had it brought to the place he had prepared for it. He had set up a tent for it in Jerusalem. ⁵But the bronze altar that Bezalel had made was in Gibeon. Bezalel was the son of Uri. Uri was the son of Hur. The altar was in front of the LORD's holy tent. So Solomon and the whole community asked the LORD for advice in Gibeon. ⁶Solomon went up to the bronze altar in front of the LORD at the tent of meeting. Solomon sacrificed 1,000 burnt offerings on the altar.

⁷That night God appeared to Solomon. He said to him, "Ask for anything you want me to give you."

⁸Solomon answered God, "You were very kind to my father David. Now you

1 Chr. 1 I wonder what Solomon was thinking when God said, "Ask for anything you want." Solomon could have asked for a new houseboat in the Dead Sea. Or the whole Dead Sea. Or all the seas in the world! But instead, he asked God for wisdom. THAT is pretty wise!

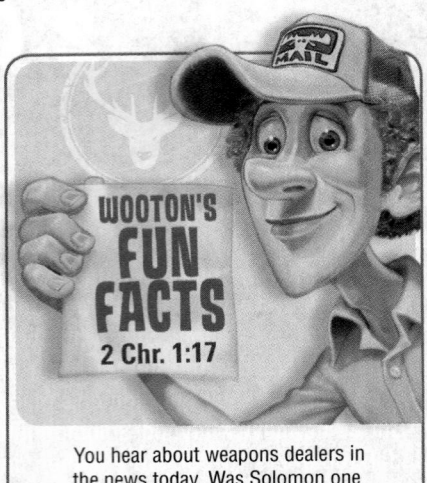

WOOTON'S FUN FACTS
2 Chr. 1:17

You hear about weapons dealers in the news today. Was Solomon one of those? Not exactly, but he did sell military supplies to his neighbors. It was Solomon's way of building an army that one day might come to help Israel.

have made me king in his place. ⁹LORD God, let the promise you gave to my father David come true. You have made me king. My people are as many as the dust of the earth. They can't be counted. ¹⁰Give me wisdom and knowledge. Then I'll be able to lead these people. Without your help, who would be able to rule this great nation of yours?"

¹¹God said to Solomon, "I am glad that those are the things you really want. You have not asked for wealth, possessions or honor. You have not even asked to have your enemies killed. You have not asked to live for a long time. Instead, you have asked for wisdom and knowledge. You want to be able to rule my people wisely. I have made you king over them. ¹²So wisdom and knowledge will be given to you. I will also give you wealth, possessions and honor. You will have more than any king before you ever had. And no king after you will have as much."

¹³Then Solomon left the high place at Gibeon. He went from the tent of meeting there to Jerusalem. And he ruled over Israel.

¹⁴Solomon had 1,400 chariots and 12,000 horses. He kept some of them in the chariot cities. He kept others with him in Jerusalem. ¹⁵The king made silver and gold as common in Jerusalem as stones. He made

cedar wood as common there as sycamore-fig trees in the western hills. ¹⁶Solomon got horses from Egypt and Kue. The king's buyers purchased them from Kue at the current price. ¹⁷They could get a chariot from Egypt for 15 pounds of silver. They could get a horse for less than four pounds of silver. They sold horses and chariots to all the Hittite and Aramean kings.

Solomon Prepares to Build the Temple

Solomon gave orders to build a temple. That's where the LORD would put his Name. Solomon also gave orders to build a royal palace for himself. ²He chose 70,000 men to carry things. He chose 80,000 to cut stones in the hills. He put 3,600 men in charge of them.

³Solomon sent a message to Hiram. Hiram was king of Tyre. Solomon said,

"Send me cedar logs, just as you did for my father David. You sent him cedar to build a palace to live in. ⁴Now I'm about to build a temple. The Name of the LORD my God will be there. I'll set the temple apart for him. Sweet-smelling incense will be burned in front of him there. The holy bread will be set out at regular times. Burnt offerings will be sacrificed there every morning and evening. They will be sacrificed every Sabbath day. They will be sacrificed at every New Moon feast. And they will be sacrificed at every yearly appointed feast of the LORD our God. That's a law for Israel that will last for all time to come.

⁵"The temple I'm going to build will be beautiful. That's because our God is greater than all other gods. ⁶So who is able to build a temple for him? After all, the heavens can't hold him. In fact, not even the highest heavens can hold him. So who am I to build a temple for him? It will only be a place to burn sacrifices in front of him.

⁷"Send me a man skilled at working with gold, silver, bronze and iron. He must also be able to work with purple, blue and bright red yarn. He must be skilled in the art of carving. Send him to work in Judah and

Jerusalem with my skilled workers. My father David provided them to help me.

⁸"Also send me cedar, juniper and algum logs from Lebanon. I know that your servants are skilled in cutting wood there. My servants will work with yours. ⁹They'll provide me with plenty of lumber. That's because the temple I'm building must be large and beautiful. ¹⁰I'll pay your servants. They will cut the wood. I'll pay them 3,600 tons of wheat that has been ground up. I'll pay them 3,000 tons of barley. I'll also pay them 120,000 gallons of wine and 120,000 gallons of olive oil."

Jason's Jargon

2 CHRONICLES 2

Find the word *skilled* in this chapter. A skilled worker might be anyone talented in the art of carpentry, carving, embroidery, glass-making, spinning and weaving, painting, and more.

¹¹King Hiram of Tyre replied to Solomon. He wrote a letter to him. In it Hiram said,

"The LORD loves his people. That's why he has made you their king."

¹²Hiram continued,

"I praise the LORD. He is the God of Israel. He made heaven and earth. He has given King David a wise son. You have good sense. You understand what is right. You will build a temple for the LORD. You will also build a palace for yourself.

¹³"I'm sending Huram-Abi to you. He is very skillful. ¹⁴His mother was from Dan. His father was from Tyre. He is trained to work with gold, silver, bronze and iron. He knows how to work with stone and wood. He can also work with purple, blue and bright red yarn and fine linen. He's skilled in all kinds of carving. He can

follow any pattern you give him. He'll work with your skilled workers. He'll also work with those of your father David. David was my master.

¹⁵"Now please send us what you promised. Send us the wheat, barley, olive oil and wine. ¹⁶And we'll cut all the logs from Lebanon that you need. We'll make rafts out of them. We'll float them by sea down to Joppa. Then you can take them up to Jerusalem."

¹⁷Solomon counted all the outsiders who were living in Israel. He did it after his father David had counted them. There were 153,600 of them. ¹⁸He chose 70,000 to carry things. He chose 80,000 to cut stones in the hills. He put 3,600 men in charge of the people to keep them working.

Solomon Builds the Temple

3 Then Solomon began to build the temple of the LORD. He built it on Mount Moriah in Jerusalem. That's where the LORD had appeared to Solomon's father David. The LORD had appeared at the threshing floor of Araunah. Araunah was from Jebus. David had provided the threshing floor. ²Solomon began building the temple on the second day of the second month. It was in the fourth year of his rule.

³Solomon laid the foundation for God's temple. It was 90 feet long and 30 feet wide. Solomon's men followed the standard measure used at that time. ⁴The porch in front of the temple was 30 feet across and 30 feet high.

Solomon covered the inside of the temple with pure gold. ⁵He covered the inside of the main hall with juniper boards. Then he covered the boards with fine gold. He decorated the hall with palm tree patterns and chain patterns. ⁶He decorated the temple with valuable jewels. The gold he used came from Parvaim. ⁷He covered the ceiling beams, doorframes, walls and doors of the temple with gold. He carved cherubim on the walls.

⁸He built the Most Holy Room. It was as long as the temple was wide. It was 30 feet long and 30 feet wide. He covered the inside of the Most Holy Room with 23 tons of fine gold. ⁹He also covered the upper parts with gold. The gold on the nails weighed 20 ounces.

¹⁰For the Most Holy Room, Solomon made a pair of carved cherubim. He covered them with gold. ¹¹The total length of the cherubim's wings from tip to tip was 30 feet. One wing of the first cherub was seven and a half feet long. Its tip touched the temple wall. The other wing was also seven and a half feet long. Its tip touched the wing tip of the other cherub. ¹²In the same way one wing of the second cherub was seven and a half feet long. Its tip touched the other temple wall. The other wing was also seven and a half feet long. Its tip touched the wing tip of the first cherub. ¹³So the total length of the wings of the two cherubim was 30 feet from tip to tip. The cherubim stood facing the main hall.

¹⁴Solomon made the curtain out of blue, purple and bright red yarn and fine linen. A skilled worker sewed cherubim into its pattern.

¹⁵For the front of the temple, Solomon made two pillars. Each pillar was 26 feet tall. Each had a decorated top seven and a half feet high. ¹⁶Solomon made chains that were linked together. He put them on top of the pillars. He also made 100 pomegranates. He fastened them to the chains. ¹⁷Solomon set the pillars up in front of the temple. One was on the south. The other was on the north. He named the one on the south Jakin. The one on the north he named Boaz.

More Facts About the Temple

4 Solomon made a bronze altar 30 feet long, 30 feet wide and 15 feet high. ²He made a huge metal bowl for washing. Its shape was round. It measured 15 feet from rim to rim. It was seven and a half feet high. And it was 45 feet around. ³Below the rim there was a circle of bull figures around the bowl. In every 18 inches around the bowl there were ten bulls. The bulls were arranged in two rows. They were made as part of the bowl itself.

⁴The bowl stood on 12 bulls. Three of them faced north. Three faced west. Three faced south. And three faced east. The bowl rested on top of them. Their rear ends were toward the center. ⁵The bowl was three inches thick. Its rim was like the rim of a cup. The rim was shaped like the bloom of a lily. The bowl held 18,000 gallons of water.

⁶Solomon made ten smaller bowls for washing. He placed five of them on the

2 Chr. 4:5 A big bathtub holds fifty gallons of water. This bowl is way, way, *way* bigger than that. It would have held the equivalent of 360 bathtubs or a twenty-eight-foot around swimming pool filled four feet deep. Too bad cannonballs weren't allowed.

¹³ He made the 400 pomegranates for the two sets of chains. There were two rows of pomegranates for each chain. They decorated the bowl-shaped tops of the pillars.
¹⁴ He made the stands and their bowls.
¹⁵ He made the huge bowl. He made the 12 bulls that were under it.
¹⁶ He made the pots, shovels and meat forks. He also made all the things used with them.

Huram-Abi made all these objects for King Solomon for the LORD's temple. He made them out of bronze. Then he shined them up. ¹⁷The king had them made in clay molds. It was done on the plains of the Jordan River between Sukkoth and Zarethan. ¹⁸Solomon made huge numbers of these things. There were too many of them to weigh. In fact, it was impossible to add up the weight of all the bronze.

¹⁹Solomon also made all the objects that were in God's temple.

He made the golden altar.
He made the tables for the holy bread.
²⁰ He made the pure gold lampstands and their lamps. The lamps burned in front of the Most Holy Room, just as the law required.
²¹ He made the gold flowers. He made the gold lamps and tongs. They were made out of solid gold.
²² He made the wick cutters, sprinkling bowls, dishes, and shallow cups for burning incense. All of them were made out of pure gold. He made the gold doors of the temple. They were the inner doors to the Most Holy Room and the doors of the main hall.

5 Solomon finished all the work for the LORD's temple. Then he brought in the things his father David had set apart for the LORD. They included the silver and gold and all the objects for God's temple. Solomon placed them there with the other treasures.

The Ark Is Brought to the Temple

²Then Solomon sent for the elders of Israel. He told them to come to Jerusalem. They included all the leaders of the tribes. They also included the chiefs of the families

south side of the huge bowl. He placed the other five on the north side. The things used for the burnt offerings were rinsed in the smaller bowls. But the priests used the huge bowl for washing.

⁷Solomon made ten gold lampstands. He followed the pattern the LORD had given him. He placed the lampstands in the temple. He put five of them on the south side. He put the other five on the north side.

⁸He made ten tables. He placed them in the temple. He put five of them on the south side. He put the other five on the north side. He also made 100 gold sprinkling bowls.

⁹He made the courtyard of the priests. He also made the large courtyard. He made doors for it. He covered the doors with bronze. ¹⁰He placed the huge bowl on the south side of the courtyard. He put it at the southeast corner.

¹¹And Huram also made the pots, shovels and sprinkling bowls.

So Huram finished the work he had started for King Solomon. Here's what he made for God's temple.

¹² He made the two pillars.
He made the two tops for the pillars. The tops were shaped like bowls.
He made the two sets of chains that were linked together. They decorated the two bowl-shaped tops of the pillars.

of Israel. Solomon wanted them to bring up the ark of the LORD's covenant from Zion. Zion was the City of David. ³All the Israelites came together to where the king was. It was at the time of the Feast of Booths. The feast was held in the seventh month.

⁴All the elders of Israel arrived. Then the Levites picked up the ark and carried it. ⁵They brought up the ark. They also brought up the tent of meeting and all the sacred things in the tent. The priests, who were Levites, carried up everything. ⁶The entire community of Israel had gathered around King Solomon. All of them were in front of the ark. They sacrificed huge numbers of sheep and cattle. There were so many animals that they couldn't be recorded. In fact, they couldn't even be counted.

⁷The priests brought the ark of the LORD's covenant to its place in the Most Holy Room of the temple. They put it under the wings of the cherubim. ⁸The cherubim's wings were spread out over the place where the ark was. They covered the ark. They also covered the poles used to carry it. ⁹The poles reached out from the ark. They were so long that their ends could be seen from in front of the Most Holy Room. But they couldn't be seen from outside the Holy Room. They are still there to this day. ¹⁰There wasn't anything in the ark except the two tablets. Moses had placed them in it at Mount Horeb. That's where the LORD had made a covenant with the Israelites. He made it after they came out of Egypt.

¹¹The priests left the Holy Room. All the priests who were there had set themselves apart to the LORD. It didn't matter what group they were in. ¹²All the Levites who played music stood near the east side of the altar. They included Asaph, Heman, Jeduthun and their sons and relatives. They were dressed in fine linen. They were playing cymbals, harps and lyres. They were joined by 120 priests who were blowing trumpets. ¹³The trumpet players and other musicians played their instruments together. They praised the LORD and gave thanks to him. The singers sang to the music of the trumpets, cymbals and other instruments. They sang in praise to the LORD,

"The LORD is good.
His faithful love continues forever."

Then a cloud filled the temple of the LORD. ¹⁴The priests couldn't do their work. That's because the cloud of the LORD's glory filled God's temple.

6 Then Solomon said, "LORD, you have said you would live in a dark cloud. ²I've built a beautiful temple for you. You can live in it forever."

³The whole community of Israel was standing there. The king turned around and gave them his blessing. ⁴Then he said,

"I praise the LORD. He is the God of Israel. With his mouth he made a promise to my father David. With his powerful hands he made it come true. He said, ⁵'I brought my people out of Egypt. Since then, a temple for my Name has not been built. I have not chosen a city in any tribe of Israel for that purpose. And I have not chosen anyone to be ruler over my people Israel. ⁶But now I have chosen Jerusalem. I will put my Name there. And I have chosen David to rule over my people Israel.'

⁷"With all his heart my father David wanted to build a temple. He wanted to do it so the Name of the LORD could be there. The LORD is the God of Israel. ⁸But the LORD spoke to my father David. He said, 'With all your heart you wanted to build a temple for my Name. It is good that you wanted to do that. ⁹But you will not build the temple. Instead, your son will build the temple for my Name. He is your own flesh and blood.'

¹⁰"The LORD has kept the promise he made. I've become the next king after my father David. Now I'm sitting on the throne of Israel. That's exactly what the LORD promised would happen. I've built the temple for the Name of the LORD. He is the God of Israel. ¹¹I've placed the ark there. The tablets of the LORD's covenant are inside it. He made that covenant with the people of Israel."

Solomon Prays to Set the Temple Apart to the LORD

¹²Then Solomon stood in front of the LORD's altar. He stood in front of the whole community of Israel. He spread out his hands to pray. ¹³He had made a bronze

CANDID CONVERSATIONS

God created each of us with the knowledge in our heart that good will win in the end. That's why we like stories with happy endings. We want evil to be stopped and the good guys to succeed. We want the princess to be rescued, the underdog to win, and the weeping mother to find her missing child.

The history of the Israelites has many low points. They had their share of terrible kings, terrible wars, and terrible deeds. But this day—the day Solomon dedicated the Temple in front of all of Israel—brought the fulfillment of a promise God made to His people. It was a day of rejoicing that reminded the people that God was still in control and that good eventually wins out over evil.

Sometimes we need to stop focusing on all the bad things that are happening in the world and remember the good things that God has given us . . . and all the good things that He's promised ahead!

stage. It was seven and a half feet long and seven and a half feet wide. It was four and a half feet high. He had placed it in the center of the outer courtyard. He stood on the stage. Then he got down on his knees in front of the whole community of Israel. He spread out his hands toward heaven. ¹⁴He said,

"Lord, you are the God of Israel. There is no God like you in heaven or on earth. You keep the covenant you made with us. You show us your love. You do that when we follow you with all our hearts. ¹⁵You have kept your promise to my father David. He was your servant. With your mouth you made a promise. With your powerful hand you have made it come true. And today we can see it.

¹⁶"Lord, you are the God of Israel. Keep the promises you made to my father David. Do it for him. He was your servant. You said to him, 'You will always have a son from your family line to sit on Israel's throne. He will sit in front of the Most Holy Room, where my own throne is. That will be true only if your children after you are careful in everything they do. They must live the way my law tells them to. That is the way you have lived.' ¹⁷Lord, you are the God of Israel. So let your promise to your servant David come true.

¹⁸"But will God really live on earth with human beings? After all, the heavens can't hold you. In fact, even the highest heavens can't hold you. So this temple I've built certainly can't hold you! ¹⁹But please pay attention to my prayer. Lord my God, be ready to help me as I make my appeal to you. Listen to my cry for help. Hear the prayer I'm praying to you. ²⁰Let your eyes look toward this temple day and night. You said you would put your Name here. Listen to the prayer I'm praying toward this place. ²¹Hear me when I ask you to help us. Listen to your people Israel when they pray toward this place. Listen to us from heaven. It's the place where you live. When you hear us, forgive us.

²²"Suppose someone does something wrong to their neighbor. And the person who has done something wrong is required to give their word. They must tell the truth about what they have done. They must come and do it in front of your altar in this temple. ²³When they do, listen to them from heaven. Take action. Judge between the person and their neighbor. Pay back the guilty one. Do to them what they have done to their neighbor. Deal with the one who isn't guilty in a way that shows they are free from blame. That will prove they aren't guilty.

²⁴"Suppose your people Israel have lost the battle against their enemies.

And suppose they've sinned against you. But they turn back to you and praise your name. They pray to you in this temple. And they ask you to help them. ²⁵Then listen to them from heaven. Forgive the sin of your people Israel. Bring them back to the land you gave to them and their people who lived long ago.

²⁶"Suppose your people have sinned against you. And because of that, the sky is closed up and there isn't any rain. But your people pray toward this place. They praise you by admitting they've sinned. And they turn away from their sin because you have made them suffer. ²⁷Then listen to them from heaven. Forgive the sin of your people Israel. Teach them the right way to live. Send rain on the land you gave them as their share.

²⁸"Suppose there isn't enough food in the land. And a plague strikes the land. The hot winds completely dry up our crops. Or locusts or grasshoppers come and eat them up. Or enemies surround one of our cities and get ready to attack it. Or trouble or sickness comes. ²⁹But suppose one of your people prays to you. They ask you to help them. They are aware of how much they are suffering. And they spread out their hands toward this temple to pray. ³⁰Then listen to them from heaven. It's the place where you live. Forgive them. Deal with everyone in keeping with everything they do. You know their hearts. In fact, you are the only one who knows every human heart. ³¹Your people will have respect for you. They will live the way you want them to. They'll live that way as long as they are in the land you gave our people long ago.

³²"Suppose an outsider who doesn't belong to your people Israel has come from a land far away. They have come because they've heard about your great name. They have heard that you reached out your mighty hand and powerful arm. So they come and pray toward this temple. ³³Then listen to them from heaven. It's the place where you live. Do what that outsider asks you to do. Then all the nations on earth will know you. They will have respect for you. They'll respect you just as your own people Israel do. They'll know that your Name is in this house I've built.

³⁴"Suppose your people go to war against their enemies. It doesn't matter where you send them. And suppose they pray to you toward this city you have chosen. They pray toward the temple I've built for your Name. ³⁵Then listen to them from heaven. Listen to their prayer. Listen to them when they ask you to help them. Stand up for them.

³⁶"Suppose they sin against you. After all, there isn't anyone who doesn't sin. And suppose you get angry with them. You hand them over to their enemies. They take them as prisoners to another land. It doesn't matter whether that land is near or far away. ³⁷But suppose your people change their ways in the land where they are held as prisoners. They turn away from their sins. They beg you to help them in the land where they are prisoners. They say, 'We have sinned. We've done what is wrong. We've done what is evil.' ³⁸And they turn back to you with all their heart and soul. Suppose it happens in the land where they were taken as prisoners. There they pray toward the land you gave their people long ago. They pray toward the city you have chosen. And they pray toward the temple I've built for your Name. ³⁹Then listen to them from heaven. It's the place where you live. Listen to their prayer. Listen to them when they ask you to help them. Stand up for them. Your people have sinned against you. Please forgive them.

⁴⁰"My God, let your eyes see us. Let your ears pay attention to the prayers offered in this place.

⁴¹ "Lord God, rise up and come to
          your resting place.
     Come in together with the ark.
     It's the sign of your power.
     Lord God, may your priests put
          on salvation as if it were
          their clothes.

May your faithful people be
    glad because you are so
    good.
[42] LORD God, don't turn your back
    on your anointed king.
    Remember the great love
    you promised to your
    servant David."

The Temple Is Set Apart to the LORD

7 Solomon finished praying. Then fire
came down from heaven. It burned up
the burnt offering and the sacrifices. The
glory of the LORD filled the temple. [2]The
priests couldn't enter the temple of the LORD
because his glory filled it. [3]All the Israelites
saw the fire coming down. They saw the
glory of the LORD above the temple. So they
got down on their knees in the courtyard
with their faces toward the ground. They
worshiped the LORD. They gave thanks to
him and said,

"The LORD is good.
    His faithful love continues forever."

[4]Then the king and all the people offered
sacrifices to the LORD. [5]King Solomon sacrificed 22,000 oxen and 120,000 sheep and
goats. So the king and all the people set the
temple of God apart. [6]The priests and Levites took their positions. The Levites played
the LORD's musical instruments. King David had made them for praising the LORD.
They were used when he gave thanks to the
LORD. He said, "His faithful love continues
forever." Across from where the Levites
were, the priests blew their trumpets. All
the people of Israel were standing.
[7]Solomon set the middle area of the
courtyard apart to the LORD. It was in front
of the LORD's temple. There Solomon sacrificed burnt offerings. He also sacrificed
the fat of the friendship offerings there. He
did it there because the bronze altar he had
made couldn't hold it all. It couldn't hold
the burnt offerings, the grain offerings and
the fat parts.
[8]At that time Solomon celebrated the
Feast of Booths for seven days. The whole
community of Israel was with him. It was a
huge crowd. People came from as far away
as Lebo Hamath and the Wadi of Egypt. [9]On
the eighth day they held a special service.
For seven days they had celebrated by setting the altar apart to honor God. The feast

continued for seven more days. [10]Then Solomon sent the people home. It was the 23rd
day of the seventh month. The people were
glad. Their hearts were full of joy. That's because the LORD had done good things for
David and Solomon and his people Israel.

The LORD Appears to Solomon

[11]Solomon finished the LORD's temple
and the royal palace. He had done everything he had planned to do in the LORD's
temple and his own palace. [12]The LORD appeared to him at night. The LORD said,

"I have heard your prayer. I have
chosen this place for myself. It is a
temple where sacrifices will be offered.
[13]"Suppose I close up the sky and
there isn't any rain. Suppose I command locusts to eat up the crops.
And I send a plague among my
people. [14]But they make themselves
humble in my sight. They pray and
look to me. And they turn from their
evil ways. Then I will listen to them
from heaven. I will forgive their sin.
And I will heal their land. After all,
they are my people. [15]Now my eyes
will see them. My ears will pay attention to the prayers they offer in this
place. [16]I have chosen this temple. I
have set it apart for myself. My Name
will be there forever. My eyes and my
heart will always be there.
[17]"But you must walk faithfully with me, just as your father David did. Do everything I command
you to do. Obey my rules and laws.
[18]Then I will set up your royal throne.
I made a covenant with your father
David to do that. I said to him, 'You
will always have a son from your
family line to rule over Israel.'
[19]"But suppose all of you turn
away from me. You refuse to obey
the rules and commands I have giv-
en you. And you go off to serve other
gods and worship them. [20]Then I
will remove Israel from my land. It
is the land I gave them. I will turn
my back on this temple. I will do it
even though I have set it apart for my
Name to be there. I will make all the
nations hate it. They will laugh and
joke about it. [21]This temple will become a pile of stones. All those who

pass by it will be shocked. They will say, 'Why has the LORD done a thing like this to this land and temple?' [22]People will answer, 'Because they have deserted the LORD. He is the God of their people who lived long ago. He brought them out of Egypt. But they have been holding on to other gods. They've been worshiping them. They've been serving them. That's why the LORD has brought all this horrible trouble on them.'"

Other Things Solomon Did

8 Solomon built the LORD's temple and his own palace. It took him 20 years to build them. After that, [2]Solomon rebuilt the villages Hiram had given him. Solomon had Israelites make their homes in them. [3]Then Solomon went to Hamath Zobah. He captured it. [4]He also built up Tadmor in the desert. He built up all the cities in Hamath where he could store things. [5]He rebuilt Upper Beth Horon and Lower Beth Horon. He put up high walls around them. He made their city gates secure with heavy metal bars. [6]He rebuilt Baalath and all the cities where he could store things. He also rebuilt all the cities for his chariots and horses. Solomon built anything he wanted in Jerusalem, Lebanon and all the territory he ruled.

[7]There were still many people left in the land who weren't Israelites. They included Hittites, Amorites, Perizzites, Hivites and Jebusites. [8]They were children of the people who had lived in the land before the Israelites came. The people of Israel hadn't destroyed them. Solomon forced them to work very hard as his slaves. And they still work for Israel to this day. [9]But Solomon didn't force the Israelites to work as his slaves. Instead, some were his fighting men. Others were commanders of his captains, chariots and chariot drivers. [10]Still others were King Solomon's chief officials. There were 250 officials in charge of the other men.

[11]Solomon brought Pharaoh's daughter up from the City of David to the palace he had built for her. Solomon said, "My wife must not live in the palace of David, who was the king of Israel. It's one of the places the ark of the LORD has entered. That makes it holy."

[12]Solomon had built the LORD's altar. It stood in front of the temple porch. On that altar Solomon sacrificed burnt offerings to the LORD. [13]Each day he sacrificed what the Law of Moses required. He sacrificed the required offerings every Sabbath day. He also sacrificed them at each New Moon feast and during the three yearly feasts. Those three were the Feast of Unleavened Bread, the Feast of Weeks and the Feast of Booths. [14]Solomon followed the orders his father David had given him. He appointed the groups of priests for their duties. He appointed the Levites to lead the people in praising the LORD. They also helped the priests do their required tasks each day. Solomon appointed the groups of men who guarded all the gates. That's what David, the man of God, had ordered. [15]The king's commands were followed completely. They applied to the priests and Levites. They also applied to the temple treasure.

[16]All of Solomon's work was carried out. It started the day the foundation of the LORD's temple was laid. It ended when the LORD's temple was finished.

[17]Solomon went to Ezion Geber and Elath on the coast of Edom. [18]Hiram sent him ships that his own officers commanded. They were sailors who knew the sea. Together with Solomon's men they sailed to Ophir. They brought back 17 tons of gold. They gave it to King Solomon.

The Queen of Sheba Visits Solomon

9 The queen of Sheba heard about how famous Solomon was. So she came to Jerusalem to test him with hard questions. She arrived with a very large group of attendants. Her camels were carrying spices, huge amounts of gold, and valuable jewels. She came to Solomon and asked him about everything she wanted to know. [2]He answered all her questions. There wasn't anything too hard for him to explain to her. [3]So the queen of Sheba saw how wise Solomon was. She saw the palace he had built. [4]She saw the food on his table. She saw his officials sitting there. She saw the robes of the servants who waited on everyone. She saw the robes the wine tasters were wearing. And she saw the burnt offerings Solomon sacrificed at the LORD's temple. She could hardly believe everything she had seen.

[5]She said to the king, "Back in my own country I heard a report about you. I heard

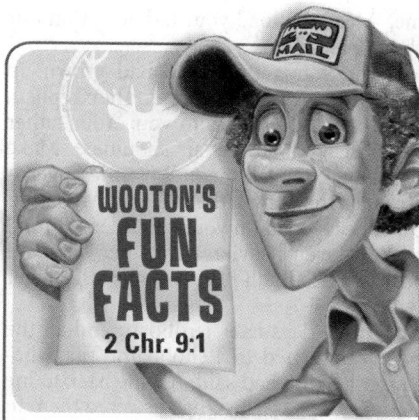

WOOTON'S FUN FACTS
2 Chr. 9:1

Scholars believe Sheba (or Saba) was probably a city in the modern-day country of Yemen. In Bible times, that region was known for its varied and fine spices. I wonder if they had saffron. That's my wife's favorite spice (and favorite color!).

¹²King Solomon gave the queen of Sheba everything she wanted and asked for. In fact, he gave her more than she had brought to him. Then she left. She returned to her own country with her attendants.

Solomon's Greatness

¹³Each year Solomon received 25 tons of gold. ¹⁴That didn't include the money brought in by business and trade. All the kings of Arabia also brought gold and silver to Solomon. So did the governors of the territories.

¹⁵King Solomon made 200 large shields out of hammered gold. Each one weighed 15 pounds. ¹⁶He also made 300 small shields out of hammered gold. Each one weighed almost eight pounds. The king put all the shields in the Palace of the Forest of Lebanon.

¹⁷Then he made a large throne. It was covered with ivory. And that was covered with pure gold. ¹⁸The throne had six steps. A gold stool for the king's feet was connected to it. The throne had armrests on both sides of the seat. A statue of a lion stood on each side of the throne. ¹⁹Twelve lions stood on the six steps. There was one at each end of each step. Nothing like that throne had ever been made for any other kingdom. ²⁰All of King Solomon's cups were made out of gold. All the things used in the Palace of the Forest of Lebanon were made out of pure gold. Nothing was made out of silver. When Solomon was king, silver wasn't considered to be worth very much. ²¹He had many ships that carried goods to be traded. The crews of those ships were made up of Hiram's servants. Once every three years the ships returned. They brought gold, silver, ivory, apes and peacocks.

²²King Solomon was richer than all the other kings on earth. He was also wiser than they were. ²³All these kings wanted to meet Solomon in person. They wanted to see for themselves how wise God had made him. ²⁴Year after year, everyone who came to him brought a gift. They brought gifts made out of silver and gold. They brought robes, weapons and spices. They also brought horses and mules.

²⁵Solomon had 4,000 spaces where he kept his horses and chariots. He had 12,000 horses. He kept some of his horses and chariots in the chariot cities. He kept the others with him in Jerusalem. ²⁶Solomon

about how much you had accomplished. I also heard about how wise you are. Everything I heard is true. ⁶But I didn't believe what people were saying. So I came to see for myself. And now I believe it! You are twice as wise as people say you are. The report I heard doesn't even begin to tell the whole story about you. ⁷How happy your people must be! How happy your officials must be! They always get to serve you and hear the wise things you say. ⁸May the LORD your God be praised. He takes great delight in you. He placed you on his throne as king. He put you there to rule for him. Your God loves Israel very much. He longs to take good care of them forever. That's why he has made you king over them. He knows that you will do what is fair and right."

⁹She gave the king four and a half tons of gold. She also gave him huge amounts of spices and valuable jewels. There had never been as many spices as the queen of Sheba gave to King Solomon.

¹⁰The servants of Hiram and the servants of Solomon brought gold from Ophir. They also brought algumwood and valuable jewels. ¹¹The king used the algumwood to make steps for the LORD's temple and the royal palace. He also used it to make harps and lyres for those who played the music. No one had ever seen anything like those instruments in Judah before.

ruled over all the kings from the Euphrates River to the land of the Philistines. He ruled all the way to the border of Egypt. ²⁷The king made silver as common in Jerusalem as stones. He made cedar wood as common there as sycamore-fig trees in the western hills. ²⁸Solomon got horses from Egypt. He also got them from many other countries.

Solomon Dies

²⁹The other events of Solomon's rule from beginning to end are written down. They are written in the records of Nathan the prophet. They are written in the prophecy of Ahijah. He was from Shiloh. They are also written in the records of the visions of Iddo the prophet about Jeroboam. Jeroboam was the son of Nebat. ³⁰Solomon ruled in Jerusalem over the whole nation of Israel for 40 years. ³¹Then he joined the members of his family who had already died. He was buried in the city of his father David. Solomon's son Rehoboam became the next king after him.

Israel Refuses to Follow Rehoboam

10 Rehoboam went to the city of Shechem. All the Israelites had gone there to make him king. ²Jeroboam heard about it. He was the son of Nebat. Jeroboam was in Egypt at that time. He had gone there for safety. He wanted to get away from King Solomon. But now he returned from Egypt. ³So the people sent for Jeroboam. He and all the people went to Rehoboam. They said to him, ⁴"Your father put a heavy load on our shoulders. But now make our hard work easier. Make the heavy load on us lighter. Then we'll serve you."

⁵Rehoboam answered, "Come back to me in three days." So the people went away.

⁶Then King Rehoboam asked the elders for advice. They had served his father Solomon while he was still living. Rehoboam asked them, "What advice can you give me? How should I answer these people?"

⁷They replied, "Be kind to them. Please them. Give them what they are asking for. Then they'll always serve you."

⁸But Rehoboam didn't accept the advice the elders gave him. He asked for advice from the young men who had grown up with him and were now serving him. ⁹He asked them, "What's your advice? How should I answer these people? They said to

me, 'Make the load your father put on our shoulders lighter.'"

¹⁰The young men who had grown up with him gave their answer. They replied, "The people have said to you, 'Your father put a heavy load on our shoulders. Make it lighter.' Now tell them, 'My little finger is stronger than my father's legs. ¹¹My father put a heavy load on your shoulders. But I'll make it even heavier. My father beat you with whips. But I'll beat you with bigger whips.'"

¹²Three days later Jeroboam and all the people returned to Rehoboam. That's because the king had said, "Come back to me in three days." ¹³The king answered them in a mean way. He didn't accept the advice of the elders. ¹⁴Instead, he followed the advice of the young men. He said, "My father put a heavy load on your shoulders. But I'll make it even heavier. My father beat you with whips. But I'll beat you with bigger whips." ¹⁵So the king didn't listen to the people. That's because God had planned it that way. What the Lord had said through Ahijah came true. Ahijah had spoken the Lord's message to Jeroboam, the son of Nebat. Ahijah was from Shiloh.

¹⁶All the Israelites saw that the king refused to listen to them. So they answered the king. They said,

"We don't have any share in David's
    royal family.
  We don't have any share in Jesse's
    son.
  People of Israel, let's go back to our
    homes.
  David's royal family, take care of
    your own kingdom!"

So all the Israelites went home. ¹⁷But Rehoboam still ruled over the Israelites who were living in the towns of Judah.

¹⁸Adoniram was in charge of those who were forced to work hard for King Rehoboam. The king sent him out among the Israelites. But they killed Adoniram by throwing stones at him. Rehoboam was able to get away in his chariot. He escaped to Jerusalem. ¹⁹Israel has refused to follow the royal family of David to this day.

11 Rehoboam arrived in Jerusalem. He brought together 180,000 capable young men from the tribes of Judah and Benjamin. He had decided to go to war against Israel. He wanted his fighting men to get the kingdom of Israel back for him. [2]But a message came to Shemaiah from the LORD. Shemaiah was a man of God. The LORD said to him, [3]"Speak to Solomon's son Rehoboam, the king of Judah. Speak to all the people of Israel in Judah and Benjamin. Tell them, [4]'The LORD says, "Do not go up to fight against your relatives. I want every one of you to go back home. Things have happened exactly the way I planned them."'" So the young men obeyed the LORD's message. They turned back. They didn't march out against Jeroboam.

Rehoboam Builds Up Judah's Towns

[5]Rehoboam lived in Jerusalem. He made Judah more secure by building up its towns. [6]He built up Bethlehem, Etam, Tekoa, [7]Beth Zur, Soko and Adullam. [8]He also built up Gath, Mareshah, Ziph, [9]Adoraim, Lachish, Azekah, [10]Zorah, Aijalon and Hebron. All of them were cities in Judah and Benjamin that had high walls around them. [11]Rehoboam made those cities even more secure. He put commanders in them. He gave the cities plenty of food, olive oil and wine. [12]He put shields and spears in all those cities. He made them very strong. So he ruled over Judah and Benjamin.

[13]The priests and Levites were on Rehoboam's side. They came from their territories all over Israel. [14]The Levites even left their grasslands and other property behind. They came to Judah and Jerusalem. That's because Jeroboam and his sons had refused to accept them as priests of the LORD. [15]Jeroboam had appointed his own priests to serve at the high places. He had made statues of gods that looked like goats and calves. His priests served those gods. [16]Some people from every tribe in Israel followed the Levites to Jerusalem. With all their hearts they wanted to worship the LORD. He is the God of Israel. They came to Jerusalem to offer sacrifices to him. He was the God of their people of long ago. [17]All those who came to Jerusalem made the kingdom of Judah strong. They helped Solomon's son Rehoboam for three years. During that time they lived the way David and Solomon had lived.

Rehoboam's Family

[18]Rehoboam married Mahalath. She was the daughter of David's son Jerimoth.

Her mother was Abihail. Abihail was the daughter of Jesse's son Eliab. [19]Mahalath had sons by Rehoboam. Their names were Jeush, Shemariah and Zaham. [20]Then Rehoboam married Maakah. She was the daughter of Absalom. She had sons by Rehoboam. Their names were Abijah, Attai, Ziza and Shelomith. [21]Rehoboam loved Absalom's daughter Maakah. In fact, he loved her more than any of his other wives and concubines. He had a total of 18 wives and 60 concubines. And he had a total of 28 sons and 60 daughters.

[22]Rehoboam appointed Maakah's son Abijah to be the chief prince among his brothers. He did it because he wanted to make him king. [23]Rehoboam acted wisely. He scattered some of his sons through all the territories of Judah and Benjamin. He put them in all the cities that had high walls around them. He gave them plenty of food and everything else they needed. He also gave them many wives.

Shishak Attacks Jerusalem

12Rehoboam had made his position as king secure. He had become very strong. Then he turned away from the law of the LORD. So did all the people of Judah. [2]They hadn't been faithful to the LORD. So Shishak attacked Jerusalem. It was in the fifth year that Rehoboam was king. Shishak was king of Egypt. [3]He came with 1,200 chariots and 60,000 horsemen. Troops of Libyans, Sukkites and Cushites came with him from Egypt. There were so many of them they couldn't be counted. [4]Shishak captured the cities of Judah that had high walls around them. He came all the way to Jerusalem.

[5]Then Shemaiah the prophet came to Rehoboam and the leaders of Judah. They had gathered together in Jerusalem. They were afraid of Shishak. Shemaiah said to them, "The LORD says, 'You have left me. So now I am leaving you to Shishak.'"

[6]The king and the leaders of Israel made themselves humble in the LORD's sight. They said, "The LORD does what is right and fair."

[7]The LORD saw they had made themselves humble. So he gave a message to Shemaiah. The LORD said, "They have made themselves humble in my sight. So I will not destroy them. Instead, I will soon save

them. Even though I am very angry with Jerusalem, I will not use Shishak to destroy them. ⁸But the people of Jerusalem will be brought under his control. Then they will learn the difference between serving me and serving the kings of other lands."

⁹Shishak, the king of Egypt, attacked Jerusalem. He carried away the treasures of the LORD's temple. He also carried the treasures of the royal palace away. He took everything. That included the gold shields Solomon had made. ¹⁰So King Rehoboam made bronze shields to take their place. He gave them to the commanders of the guards who were on duty at the entrance to the royal palace. ¹¹Every time the king went to the LORD's temple, the guards went with him. They carried the shields. Later, they took them back to the room where they were kept.

¹²Rehoboam had made himself humble in the LORD's sight. So the LORD turned his anger away from him. Rehoboam wasn't totally destroyed. In fact, some good things happened in Judah.

¹³King Rehoboam had made his position secure in Jerusalem. He continued as king. He was 41 years old when he became king. He ruled for 17 years in Jerusalem. It was the city the LORD had chosen out of all the cities in the tribes of Israel. He wanted to put his Name there. The name of Rehoboam's mother was Naamah from Ammon. ¹⁴Rehoboam did what was evil. That's because he hadn't worshiped the LORD with all his heart.

¹⁵The events of Rehoboam's rule from beginning to end are written down. They are written in the records of Shemaiah and Iddo, the prophets. The records deal with family histories. Rehoboam and Jeroboam were always at war with each other. ¹⁶Rehoboam joined the members of his family who had already died. He was buried in the City of David. Rehoboam's son Abijah became the next king after him.

Abijah King of Judah

13 Abijah became king of Judah. It was in the 18th year of Jeroboam's rule over Israel. ²Abijah ruled in Jerusalem for three years. His mother's name was Maakah. She was a daughter of Uriel. Uriel was from Gibeah.

There was war between Abijah and Jeroboam. ³Abijah went into battle with an army of 400,000 capable fighting men. Jeroboam lined up his soldiers against them. He had 800,000 able troops.

⁴Abijah stood on Mount Zemaraim. It's in the hill country of Ephraim. Abijah said, "Jeroboam and all you Israelites, listen to me! ⁵The LORD is the God of Israel. Don't you know that he has placed David and his sons after him on Israel's throne forever? The LORD made a covenant of salt with David. The salt means the covenant will last for all time to come. ⁶Jeroboam, the son of Nebat, was an official of David's son Solomon. But he refused to obey his master. ⁷Some worthless and evil men gathered around him. They opposed Solomon's son Rehoboam. At that time Rehoboam was young. He couldn't make up his mind. He wasn't strong enough to stand up against those men.

⁸"Now you plan to stand up against the kingdom of the LORD. His kingdom is in the hands of men in David's family line. It's true that you have a huge army. You have the statues of the golden calves that Jeroboam made to be your gods. ⁹But you drove out the priests of the LORD, the sons of Aaron. You also drove out the Levites. You appointed your own priests. That's what the people of other nations do. Anyone can come and set himself apart. All he has to do is sacrifice a young bull and seven rams. Then he becomes a priest of gods that aren't really gods at all!

¹⁰"But the LORD is our God. We haven't deserted him. The priests who serve the LORD belong to the family line of Aaron. The Levites help them. ¹¹Every morning and evening the priests bring burnt offerings and sweet-smelling incense to the LORD. They set out the holy bread on the table. That table is 'clean.' They light the lamps on the gold lampstand every evening. We always do what the LORD our God requires in his law. But you have deserted him. ¹²God is with us. He's our leader. His priests will blow their trumpets. They will sound the battle cry against you. People of Israel, don't fight against the LORD. He's the God of your people who lived long ago. You can't possibly succeed."

¹³Jeroboam had sent some troops behind Judah's battle lines. He told them to hide and wait there. He and his men stayed in front of Judah's lines. ¹⁴Judah turned and

saw that they were being attacked from the front and from the back. Then they cried out to the LORD. The priests blew their trumpets. ¹⁵The men of Judah shouted the battle cry. When they did, God drove Jeroboam and all the Israelites away from Abijah and Judah. ¹⁶The Israelites ran away from them. God handed Israel over to Judah. ¹⁷Abijah and his troops wounded and killed large numbers of them. In fact, 500,000 of Israel's capable men lay dead or wounded. ¹⁸So at that time the Israelites were brought under Judah's control. The people of Judah won the battle over them. That's because they trusted in the LORD, the God of their people.

¹⁹Abijah chased Jeroboam. He captured from him the towns of Bethel, Jeshanah and Ephron. He also captured the villages around them. ²⁰Jeroboam didn't get his power back during the time of Abijah. In fact, the LORD struck Jeroboam down, and he died.

²¹But Abijah grew stronger. He married 14 wives. He had 22 sons and 16 daughters.

²²The other events of Abijah's rule are written down. The things he did and said are written in the notes of Iddo the prophet.

14 Abijah joined the members of his family who had already died. He was buried in the City of David. Abijah's son Asa became the next king after him. While Asa was king, the country had peace and rest for ten years.

Asa Becomes King of Judah

²Asa did what was good and right in the eyes of the LORD his God. ³Asa removed the altars where false gods were worshiped. He took away the high places. He smashed the sacred stones. He cut down the poles used to worship the female god named Asherah. ⁴He commanded Judah to worship the LORD, the God of their people. He commanded them to obey the LORD's laws and commands. ⁵Asa removed the high places and incense altars from every town in Judah. The kingdom had peace and rest under his rule. ⁶He built up the cities of Judah that had high walls around them. The land was at peace. No one was at war with Asa during those years. That's because the LORD gave him peace and rest.

⁷"Let's build up our towns," Asa said to the people of Judah. "Let's put walls around

2 Chr. 14:5 "High places" were hilltops and ridges where lots of people could see a long distance. Only two kings sent troops to take down *all* the altars to false gods in high places: Hezekiah (2 Kings 18:4–5) and Josiah (2 Kings 23:8).

them. Let's provide them with towers. Let's make them secure with gates that have heavy metal bars. The land still belongs to us. That's because we've trusted in the LORD our God. We trusted in him, and he has given us peace and rest on every side." So they built. And things went well for them.

⁸Asa had an army of 300,000 men from Judah. They carried spears and large shields. There were 280,000 men from Benjamin. They were armed with bows and small shields. All these men were brave soldiers.

⁹Zerah marched out against them. He was from Cush. He had a huge army of thousands. He also had 300 chariots. They came all the way to Mareshah. ¹⁰Asa went out to meet Zerah in battle. They took up their positions in the Valley of Zephathah. It's near Mareshah.

¹¹Then Asa called out to the LORD his God. He said, "LORD, there isn't anyone like you. You help the weak against the strong. LORD our God, help us. We trust in you. In your name we have come out to fight against this huge army. LORD, you are our God. Don't let mere human beings win the battle over you."

¹²The LORD struck down the men of Cush for Asa and Judah. The Cushites ran away. ¹³Asa and his army chased them all the way to Gerar. A large number of Cushites fell down wounded or dead. So they couldn't fight back. The LORD and his army crushed them. The men of Judah carried

off a large amount of goods. [14]They destroyed all the villages around Gerar. The LORD had made the people in those villages afraid of him. The men of Judah took everything from all the villages. [15]They also attacked the camps of those who took care of the herds. They carried off large numbers of sheep, goats and camels. Then they returned to Jerusalem.

Asa Makes Judah a Better Nation

15 The Spirit of God came on Azariah. He was the son of Oded. [2]Azariah went out to meet Asa. He said to him, "Asa and all you people of Judah and Benjamin, listen to me. The LORD is with you when you are with him. If you really look for him, you will find him. But if you desert him, he will desert you. [3]For a long time Israel didn't worship the true God. They didn't have a priest who taught them. So they didn't know God's law. [4]But when they were in trouble, they turned to the LORD, the God of Israel. When they did, they found him. [5]In those days it wasn't safe to travel around. The people who lived in all the areas of the land were having a lot of

trouble. [6]One nation was crushing another. One city was crushing another. That's because God was causing them to suffer terribly. [7]But be strong. Don't give up. God will reward you for your work."

[8]Asa heard that prophecy. He paid attention to the words of Azariah the prophet, the son of Oded. So Asa became bolder than ever. He removed the statues of gods from the whole land of Judah and Benjamin. He also removed them from the towns he had captured in the hills of Ephraim. He did it because the LORD hated those gods. Asa repaired the altar of the LORD. It was in front of the porch of the LORD's temple.

[9]Then Asa gathered together all the people of Judah and Benjamin. He also gathered together the people from Ephraim, Manasseh and Simeon who were living among them. Large numbers of people had come over to him from Israel. They came because they saw that the LORD his God was with him.

[10]They gathered in Jerusalem. It was the third month of the 15th year of Asa's rule. [11]At that time they sacrificed to the LORD 700 oxen and 7,000 sheep and goats. The

We still use many things that Thomas Edison invented in the late 1800s and early 1900s. But he wasn't the only famous inventor of his time. In fact, the next time you switch on a light or plug in the toaster, you can thank Edison's rival, Nikola Tesla. Tesla came up with the idea behind alternating current (also known as AC), the electrical power that runs into your house.

Because both men worked to power homes and cities with electricity, they often clashed. Each wanted his idea to win. Their rivalry was so intense that some people think Edison may have taken credit for a few of Tesla's inventions.

Sometimes things like that happen today. People work long and hard on an idea, only to have someone else swoop in to take credit and recognition for that work. Has that ever happened to you?

What would you do if someone tried to take credit for your work? Read 2 Chronicles 15:7, keeping in mind that God knows the

work we've done, and He is the One who will reward us.

Do you know someone who is working on a big project like a school play or a class presentation? Or how about the people who cook your meals, clean your clothes, and drive you to church? Take a minute to give them credit and thank them for their hard work. They'll appreciate it.

animals were among the things they had taken after the battle. [12] They made a covenant to obey the LORD, the God of their people. They would obey him with all their heart and soul. [13] All those who wouldn't obey the LORD, the God of Israel, would be killed. It wouldn't matter how important they were. It wouldn't matter whether they were men or women. [14] They made a promise to the LORD. They praised him out loud. They shouted. They blew trumpets and horns. [15] All the people of Judah were happy about the promise they had made. They turned to God with all their heart. When they did, they found him. So the LORD gave them peace and rest on every side.

[16] King Asa also removed his grandmother Maakah from her position as queen mother. That's because she had made a pole used to worship the female god named Asherah. The LORD hated it. So Asa cut it down. He broke it up. He burned it in the Kidron Valley. [17] Asa didn't remove the high places from Israel. But he committed his whole life completely to the LORD. [18] He and his father had set apart silver, gold and other things to the LORD. Asa brought them into God's temple. [19] There weren't any more wars until the 35th year of Asa's rule.

Asa's Last Years

16 Baasha was king of Israel. He marched out against Judah. It was in the 36th year of Asa's rule over Judah. Baasha built up the walls of Ramah. He did it to keep people from leaving or entering the territory of Asa, the king of Judah.

[2] Asa took the silver and gold from among the treasures of the LORD's temple and his own palace. He sent it to Ben-Hadad. Ben-Hadad was king of Aram. He was ruling in Damascus. [3] "Let's make a peace treaty between us," Asa said. "My father and your father had made a peace treaty between them. Now I'm sending you silver and gold. So break your treaty with Baasha, the king of Israel. Then he'll go back home."

[4] Ben-Hadad agreed with King Asa. He sent his army commanders against the towns of Israel. His army captured Ijon, Dan, Abel Maim and all the cities in Naphtali where Baasha stored things. [5] Baasha heard about it. So he stopped building up Ramah and left that place. [6] Then King Asa brought all the men of Judah to Ramah. They carried away the stones and wood Baasha had been using. Asa used them to build up Geba and Mizpah.

[7] At that time Hanani the prophet came to Asa, the king of Judah. He said to him, "You trusted the king of Aram. You didn't trust in the LORD your God. So the army of the king of Aram has escaped from you. [8] The people of Cush and Libya had a strong army. They had large numbers of chariots and horsemen. But you trusted in the LORD. So he handed them over to you. [9] The LORD looks out over the whole earth. He gives strength to those who commit their lives completely to him. You have done a foolish thing. From now on you will be at war."

[10] Asa was angry with the prophet because of what he had said. In fact, he was so angry he put him in prison. At the same time, Asa treated some of his own people very badly.

[11] The events of Asa's rule from beginning to end are written down. They are written in the records of the kings of Judah and Israel. [12] In the 39th year of Asa's rule his feet began to hurt. The pain was terrible. But even though he was suffering, he didn't look to the LORD for help. All he did was go to the doctors. [13] In the 41st year of Asa's rule he joined the members of his family who had already died. [14] He was buried in a tomb. He had cut it out for himself in the City of David. His body was laid on a wooden frame. It was covered with spices and different mixes of perfume. A huge fire was made to honor him.

Jehoshaphat King of Judah

17 Jehoshaphat was the son of Asa. Jehoshaphat became the next king after him. He made his kingdom strong in case Israel would attack him. [2] He placed troops in all the cities of Judah that had high walls around them. He stationed some soldiers in Judah. He also put some in the towns of Ephraim that his father Asa had captured.

[3] The LORD was with Jehoshaphat. That's because he lived the way King David had lived. He didn't ask for advice from the gods that were named Baal. [4] Instead, Jehoshaphat obeyed the God of his father. He obeyed the LORD's commands instead of

the practices of Israel. ⁵The LORD made the kingdom secure under Jehoshaphat's control. All the people of Judah brought gifts to Jehoshaphat. So he had great wealth and honor. ⁶His heart was committed to living the way the LORD wanted him to. He removed the high places from Judah. He also removed the poles used to worship the female god named Asherah.

⁷In the third year of his rule, he sent his officials to teach in the towns of Judah. The officials were Ben-Hail, Obadiah, Zechariah, Nethanel and Micaiah. ⁸Some Levites were with them. Their names were Shemaiah, Nethaniah, Zebadiah, Asahel, Shemiramoth, Jehonathan, Adonijah, Tobijah and Tob-Adonijah. Elishama and Jehoram, the priests, were also with them. ⁹They taught people all through Judah. They took the Book of the Law of the LORD with them. They went around to all the towns of Judah. And they taught the people.

¹⁰All the kingdoms of the lands around Judah became afraid of the LORD. So they didn't go to war against Jehoshaphat. ¹¹Some Philistines brought to Jehoshaphat the gifts and silver he required of them. The Arabs brought him their flocks. They brought him 7,700 rams and 7,700 goats.

¹²Jehoshaphat became more and more powerful. He built forts in Judah. He also built cities in Judah where he could store things. ¹³He had large supplies in the towns of Judah. In Jerusalem he kept men who knew how to fight well. ¹⁴Here is a list of them, family by family.

From Judah there were commanders of groups of 1,000.
One of them was Adnah. He commanded 300,000 fighting men.
¹⁵ Another was Jehohanan. He commanded 280,000.
¹⁶ Another was Amasiah, the son of Zikri. Amasiah commanded 200,000. He had offered to serve the LORD.
¹⁷ From Benjamin there were also commanders.
One of them was Eliada. He was a brave soldier. He commanded 200,000 men. They were armed with bows and shields.
¹⁸ Another was Jehozabad. He commanded 180,000 men. They were prepared for battle.

¹⁹These were the men who served the king. He stationed some other men in the cities all through Judah. The cities had high walls around them.

Micaiah Prophesies Against Ahab

18 Jehoshaphat had great wealth and honor. He joined forces with Ahab by marrying Ahab's daughter. ²Some years later he went down to see Ahab in Samaria. Ahab killed a lot of sheep and cattle for Jehoshaphat and the people with him. Ahab tried to get Jehoshaphat to attack Ramoth Gilead. ³Ahab was the king of Israel. He spoke to Jehoshaphat, the king of Judah. He asked, "Will you go with me to fight against Ramoth Gilead?"

Jehoshaphat replied, "Yes. I'll go with you. My men will also go with your men. We'll join you in the war." ⁴He continued, "First ask the LORD for advice."

⁵So the king of Israel brought 400 prophets together. He asked them, "Should we go to war against Ramoth Gilead, or not?"

"Go," they answered. "God will hand it over to you."

⁶But Jehoshaphat asked, "Is there no longer a prophet of the LORD here? If there is, ask him what we should do."

⁷The king of Israel answered Jehoshaphat. He said, "There is still one prophet we can go to. We can ask the LORD for advice through him. But I hate him. He never prophesies anything good about me. He only prophesies bad things. His name is Micaiah. He's the son of Imlah."

"You shouldn't say bad things about him," Jehoshaphat replied.

⁸So the king of Israel called for one of his officials. He told him, "Bring Micaiah, the son of Imlah, right away."

⁹The king of Israel and Jehoshaphat, the king of Judah, were wearing their royal robes. They were sitting on their thrones at the threshing floor. It was near the entrance of the gate of Samaria. All the prophets were prophesying in front of them. ¹⁰Zedekiah was the son of Kenaanah. Zedekiah had made horns out of iron. They looked like animal horns. He announced, "The LORD says, 'With these horns you will drive back the men of Aram until they are destroyed.'"

¹¹All the other prophets were prophesying the same thing. "Attack Ramoth

Jason's Jargon

2 CHRONICLES 18

Sift through this chapter for the word *shepherd*. A shepherd's job is to protect the sheep from predators. Sheep without a shepherd often wander and get into trouble.

Gilead," they said. "Win the battle over it. The LORD will hand it over to you."

¹²A messenger went to get Micaiah. He said to him, "Look. The other prophets agree. All of them are saying the king will have success. So agree with them. Say the same thing they do."

¹³But Micaiah said, "You can be sure that the LORD lives. And you can be just as sure that I can only tell the king what my God says."

¹⁴When Micaiah arrived, the king spoke to him. He asked, "Should we go to war against Ramoth Gilead, or not?"

"Attack," he answered. "You will win. The people of Ramoth Gilead will be handed over to you."

¹⁵The king said to him, "I've made you promise to tell the truth many times before. So don't tell me anything but the truth in the name of the LORD."

¹⁶Then Micaiah answered, "I saw all the Israelites scattered on the hills. They were like sheep that didn't have a shepherd. The LORD said, 'These people do not have a master. Let each of them go home in peace.'"

¹⁷The king of Israel spoke to Jehoshaphat. He said, "Didn't I tell you he never prophesies anything good about me? He only prophesies bad things."

¹⁸Micaiah continued, "Listen to the LORD's message. I saw the LORD sitting on his throne. Some of the angels of heaven were standing at his right side. The others were standing at his left side. ¹⁹The LORD said, 'Who will get Ahab, the king of Israel, to attack Ramoth Gilead? I want him to die there.'

"One angel suggested one thing. Another suggested something else. ²⁰Finally, a spirit came forward and stood in front of the LORD. The spirit said, 'I'll get Ahab to do it.'

"'How?' the LORD asked.

²¹"The spirit said, 'I'll go and put lies in the mouths of all his prophets.'

"'You will have success in getting Ahab to attack Ramoth Gilead,' said the LORD. 'Go and do it.'

²²"So the LORD has put lies in the mouths of your prophets. He has said that great harm will come to you."

²³Then Zedekiah, the son of Kenaanah, went up and slapped Micaiah in the face. Zedekiah asked Micaiah, "Do you think the spirit sent by the LORD left me? Do you think that spirit went to speak to you?"

²⁴Micaiah replied, "You will find out on the day you go to hide in an inside room to save your life."

²⁵Then the king of Israel gave an order. He said, "Take Micaiah away. Send him back to Amon. Amon is the ruler of the city of Samaria. And send Micaiah back to Joash. Joash is a member of the royal court. ²⁶Tell them, 'The king says, "Put this fellow in prison. Don't give him anything but bread and water until I return safely."'"

²⁷Micaiah announced, "Do you really think you will return safely? If you do, the LORD hasn't spoken through me." He continued, "All you people, remember what I've said!"

Ahab Is Killed at Ramoth Gilead

²⁸So the king of Israel went up to Ramoth Gilead. Jehoshaphat, the king of Judah, went there too. ²⁹The king of Israel spoke to Jehoshaphat. He said, "I'll go into battle wearing different clothes. Then people won't recognize me. But you wear your royal robes." So the king of Israel put on different clothes. Then he went into battle.

³⁰The king of Aram had given an order to his chariot commanders. He had said, "Fight only against the king of Israel. Don't fight against anyone else." ³¹The chariot commanders saw Jehoshaphat. They thought, "That's the king of Israel." So they turned to attack him. But Jehoshaphat cried out. And the LORD helped him. God drew the commanders away from him. ³²They saw he wasn't the king of Israel after all. So they stopped chasing him.

³³But someone shot an arrow without taking aim. The arrow hit the king of Israel

between the parts of his armor. The king told the chariot driver, "Turn the chariot around. Get me out of this battle. I've been wounded." ³⁴All day long the battle continued. The king of Israel kept himself standing up by leaning against the inside of his chariot. He kept his face toward the men of Aram until evening. At sunset he died.

19 Jehoshaphat, the king of Judah, returned safely to his palace in Jerusalem. ²Jehu the prophet went out to meet him. He was the son of Hanani. Jehu said to the king, "You shouldn't help evil people. You shouldn't love those who hate the LORD. The LORD is angry with you. ³But there's some good in you. You have removed all the poles in the land used to worship the female god named Asherah. And you have worshiped God with all your heart."

Jehoshaphat Appoints Judges

⁴Jehoshaphat lived in Jerusalem. He went out again among the people. He went from Beersheba to the hill country of Ephraim. He turned the people back to the LORD, the God of Israel. ⁵Jehoshaphat appointed judges in the land. He put them in all the cities of Judah that had high walls around them. ⁶He told the judges, "Think carefully about what you do. After all, you aren't judging for human beings. You are judging for the LORD. He's with you every time you make a decision. ⁷Have respect for the LORD. Judge carefully. He is always right. He treats everyone the same. Our God doesn't want his judges to take money from people who want special favors."

⁸In Jerusalem, Jehoshaphat chose some Levites and priests. He also chose some leaders of Israelite families. He appointed all of them to apply the law of the LORD fairly. He wanted them to decide cases. He wanted them to settle matters between people. All those judges lived in Jerusalem. ⁹Here are the orders Jehoshaphat gave them. He said, "Have respect for the LORD. Serve him faithfully. Do it with all your heart. ¹⁰Cases will come to you from your people who live in the other cities. The cases might be about murder or other matters dealt with by the law, commands, directions and rules. Warn the people not to sin against the LORD. If you don't warn them, he will be angry with you and your people. Do what I say. Then you won't sin.

¹¹"Amariah the chief priest will be over you in any matter that concerns the LORD. Zebadiah is the leader of the tribe of Judah. He is the son of Ishmael. Zebadiah will be over you in any matter that concerns the king. The Levites will serve as your officials. Be brave. And may the LORD be with those of you who do well."

Jehoshaphat Wins the Battle Over Moab and Ammon

20 After that, the Moabites, Ammonites and some Meunites went to war against Jehoshaphat.

²Some people came and told him, "A huge army is coming from Edom to fight against you. They have come across the Dead Sea. They are already in Hazezon Tamar." Hazezon Tamar is also called En Gedi. ³Jehoshaphat was alarmed. So he decided to ask the LORD for advice. He told all the people of Judah to go without eating. ⁴The people came together to ask the LORD for help. In fact, they came from every town in Judah to pray to him.

⁵Then Jehoshaphat stood up among the people of Judah and Jerusalem. He was in front of the new courtyard at the LORD's temple. ⁶He said,

"LORD, you are the God of our people who lived long ago. You are the God who is in heaven. You rule over all the kingdoms of the nations. You are strong and powerful. No one can fight against you and win. ⁷Our God, you drove out the people who lived in this land. You drove them out to make room for your people Israel. You gave this land forever to those who belong to the family line of your friend Abraham. ⁸They have lived in this land. They've built a temple here for your Name. They have said, ⁹'Suppose trouble comes on us. It doesn't matter whether it's a punishing sword, or plague or hunger. We'll serve you. We'll stand in front of this temple where your Name is. We'll cry out to you when we're in trouble. Then you will hear us. You will save us.'

¹⁰"But here are men from Ammon, Moab and Mount Seir. You wouldn't allow Israel to march in and attack their territory when the

WHAT ABOUT you?

The book of 2 Chronicles is filled with accounts of fierce battles that the Lord helped His people to fight and win.

In the Adventures in Odyssey episode "Shining Armor," Jason Whittaker finds himself in the middle of two conflicts. One is physical: a country ravaged by civil war. The other is spiritual: a church deceived by false teaching. When Jason presents the truth to his friends, he is horrified to discover that they actually prefer the lies they are being taught.

That's the nature of false teaching. It's enticing. Once the seed of deception takes root in our lives, it flourishes. It produces tempting fruit. Actors, musicians, cartoon characters, even people close to us may tell us we need to follow our hearts. They say our hearts will guide us to truth. But God's Word says, "A human heart is more dishonest than anything else. It can't be healed. Who can understand it?" (Jeremiah 17:9). The heart can lie, so God wants us to follow Him.

Much like Jason, you and I are at war against evil. But don't panic. Don't be afraid. Instead, prepare for this unseen battle by putting on "all of God's armor. Then you can remain strong against the devil's evil plans" (Ephesians 6:11).

Read Ephesians 6:10–18. Take a sheet of paper and draw a soldier wearing each piece of armor listed. Label them. Then tape that picture to your bathroom mirror as a reminder to dress for battle daily.

Israelites came from Egypt. So Israel turned away from them. They didn't destroy them. [11]See how they are paying us back. They are coming to drive us out. They want to take over the land you gave us as our share. [12]Our God, won't you please judge them? We don't have the power to face this huge army that's attacking us. We don't know what to do. But we're looking to you to help us."

[13]All the men of Judah stood there in front of the LORD. Their wives, children and little ones were with them.

[14]Then the Spirit of the LORD came on Jahaziel. He was standing among the people of Israel. He was the son of Zechariah. Zechariah was the son of Benaiah. Benaiah was the son of Jeiel. Jeiel was the son of Mattaniah. Jahaziel was a Levite. He was from the family line of Asaph.

[15]Jahaziel said, "King Jehoshaphat, listen! All you who live in Judah and Jerusalem, listen! The LORD says to you, 'Do not be afraid. Do not lose hope because of this huge army. The battle is not yours. It is God's. [16]Tomorrow march down against them. They will be climbing up by the Pass of Ziz. You will find them at the end of the valley in the Desert of Jeruel. [17]You will not have to fight this battle. Take your positions. Stand firm. You will see how the LORD will save you. Judah and Jerusalem, do not be afraid. Do not lose hope. Go out and face them tomorrow. The LORD will be with you.' "

[18]Jehoshaphat bowed down with his face toward the ground. All the people of Judah and Jerusalem also bowed down. They worshiped the LORD. [19]Then some Levites from the families of Kohath and Korah stood up. They praised the LORD, the God of Israel. They praised him with very loud voices.

[20]Early in the morning all the people left for the Desert of Tekoa. As they started out, Jehoshaphat stood up. He said, "Judah, listen to me! People of Jerusalem, listen to me! Have faith in the LORD your God.

ADVENTURES iN ODYSSEY

Just like Jehoshaphat, Isaac Morton needed to be reminded that God is the One who is truly in control in "The Power" (A#17).

He'll take good care of you. Have faith in his prophets. Then you will have success." ²¹Jehoshaphat asked the people for advice. Then he appointed men to sing to the LORD. He wanted them to praise the LORD because of his glory and holiness. They marched out in front of the army. They said,

"Give thanks to the LORD.
His faithful love continues forever."

²²They began to sing and praise him. Then the LORD hid some men and told them to wait. He wanted them to attack the people of Ammon, Moab and Mount Seir. They had gone into Judah and attacked it. But they lost the battle. ²³The Ammonites and Moabites rose up against the men from Mount Seir. They destroyed them. They put an end to them. When they finished killing the men from Seir, they destroyed one another.

²⁴The men of Judah came to the place that looks out over the desert. They turned to look down at the huge army. But all they saw was dead bodies lying there on the ground. No one had escaped. ²⁵So Jehoshaphat and his men went down there to carry off anything of value. Among the dead bodies they found a large amount of supplies, clothes and other things of value. There was more than they could take away. There was so much it took three days to collect all of it. ²⁶On the fourth day they gathered together in the Valley of Berakah. There they praised the LORD. That's why it's called the Valley of Berakah to this day.

²⁷Then all the men of Judah and Jerusalem returned to Jerusalem. They were filled with joy. Jehoshaphat led them. The LORD had made them happy because all their enemies were dead. ²⁸They entered Jerusalem and went to the LORD's temple. They were playing harps, lyres and trumpets. ²⁹All the surrounding kingdoms began to have respect for God. They had heard how the LORD had fought against Israel's enemies. ³⁰The kingdom of Jehoshaphat

was at peace. His God had given him peace and rest on every side.

Jehoshaphat's Rule Comes to an End

³¹So Jehoshaphat ruled over Judah. He was 35 years old when he became Judah's king. He ruled in Jerusalem for 25 years. His mother's name was Azubah. She was the daughter of Shilhi. ³²Jehoshaphat followed the ways of his father Asa. He didn't wander away from them. He did what was right in the eyes of the LORD. ³³But the high places weren't removed. The people still hadn't worshiped the God of Israel with all their hearts.

³⁴The other events of Jehoshaphat's rule from beginning to end are written down. They are written in the official records of Jehu, the son of Hanani. They are written in the records of the kings of Israel.

³⁵Jehoshaphat king of Judah and Ahaziah king of Israel agreed to be friends. Ahaziah did what was evil. ³⁶Jehoshaphat agreed with him to build a lot of ships. They were built at Ezion Geber. They carried goods that were traded for other goods. ³⁷Eliezer was the son of Dodavahu from Mareshah. Eliezer prophesied against Jehoshaphat. He said, "You have joined forces with Ahaziah. So the LORD will destroy what you have made." The ships were wrecked. They were never able to sail or trade goods.

21 Jehoshaphat joined the members of his family who had already died. He was buried in the family tomb in the City of David. Jehoshaphat's son Jehoram became the next king after him. ²Jehoram's brothers, the sons of Jehoshaphat, were Azariah, Jehiel, Zechariah, Azariahu, Michael and Shephatiah. All of them were sons of Jehoshaphat, the king of Israel. ³Their father had given them many gifts. He had given them silver, gold and other things of value. He had also given them cities in Judah that had high walls around them. But he had made Jehoram king. That's because Jehoram was his oldest son.

Jehoram King of Judah

⁴Jehoram made his position secure over his father's kingdom. Then he killed all his brothers with his sword. He also killed some of the officials of Israel. ⁵Jehoram was 32 years old when he became king. He ruled in Jerusalem for eight years. ⁶He followed

the ways of the kings of Israel, just as the royal family of Ahab had done. In fact, he married a daughter of Ahab. Jehoram did what was evil in the eyes of the LORD. ⁷But the LORD didn't want to destroy the royal family of David. That's because the LORD had made a covenant with him. The LORD had promised to keep the lamp of David's kingdom burning brightly. The LORD had promised that for David and his children after him forever.

⁸When Jehoram was king over Judah, Edom refused to remain under Judah's control. They set up their own king. ⁹So Jehoram went to Edom. He took his officers and all his chariots with him. The men of Edom surrounded him and his chariot commanders. But he got up at night and fought his way out. ¹⁰To this day Edom has refused to remain under Judah's control.

At that same time, Libnah also refused to remain under the control of Judah. That's because Jehoram had deserted the LORD, the God of his people. ¹¹Jehoram had also built high places on the hills of Judah. He had caused the people of Jerusalem to worship other gods. They weren't faithful to the LORD. Jehoram had led Judah down the wrong path.

¹²Jehoram received a letter from Elijah the prophet. In it, Elijah said,

"The LORD is the God of your father David. The LORD says, 'You have not followed the ways of your own father Jehoshaphat or of Asa, the king of Judah. ¹³Instead, you have followed the ways of the kings of Israel. You have led Judah and the people of Jerusalem to worship other gods, just as the royal family of Ahab did. Also, you have murdered your own brothers. They were members of your own family. They were better men than you are. ¹⁴So now the LORD is about to strike down your people with a heavy blow. He will strike down your sons, your wives and everything that belongs to you. ¹⁵And you yourself will be very sick for a long time. The sickness will finally cause your insides to come out.'"

¹⁶The LORD stirred up the anger of the Philistines against Jehoram. He also stirred up the anger of the Arabs. They lived near the people of Cush. ¹⁷The Philistines and Arabs attacked Judah. They went in and carried off all the goods they found in the king's palace. They also took his sons and wives. The only son he had left was Ahaziah. He was the youngest son.

¹⁸After all of that, the LORD made Jehoram very sick. He couldn't be healed. ¹⁹After he had been sick for two years, the sickness caused his insides to come out. He died in great pain. His people didn't make a funeral fire to honor him. They had made funeral fires to honor the kings who ruled before him.

²⁰Jehoram was 32 years old when he became king. He ruled in Jerusalem for eight years. No one was sorry when he passed away. He was buried in the City of David. But he wasn't placed in the tombs of the kings.

Ahaziah King of Judah

22 The people of Jerusalem made Ahaziah king in place of Jehoram. Ahaziah was Jehoram's youngest son. Robbers had come with the Arabs into Jehoram's camp. The robbers had killed all his older sons. So Ahaziah, the king of Judah, began to rule. He was the son of Jehoram.

²Ahaziah was 22 years old when he became king. He ruled in Jerusalem for one year. His mother's name was Athaliah. She was a granddaughter of Omri.

³Ahaziah also followed the ways of the royal family of Ahab. That's because Ahaziah's mother gave him bad advice. She told him to do what was wrong. ⁴So he did what was evil in the eyes of the LORD. He did what the family of Ahab had done. After Ahaziah's father died, the members of Ahab's family became his advisers. That's what destroyed him. ⁵He also followed their advice when he joined forces with Joram, the king of Israel. They went to war against Hazael at Ramoth Gilead. Joram was the son of Ahab. Hazael was king of Aram. The soldiers of Aram wounded Joram. ⁶So he returned to Jezreel to give his wounds time to heal. His enemies had wounded him at Ramoth in his battle against Hazael, the king of Aram.

Ahaziah, the son of Jehoram, went down to Jezreel. He went there to see Joram. That's because Joram had been wounded. Ahaziah was king of Judah. Joram was the son of Ahab.

⁷Through Ahaziah's visit to Joram, God caused Ahaziah to fall from power. When Ahaziah arrived, he rode out with Joram to meet Jehu, the son of Nimshi. The LORD had anointed Jehu to destroy the royal family of Ahab. ⁸So Jehu punished Ahab's family, just as the LORD had told him to. While he was doing it, he found the officials of Judah and the sons of Ahaziah's relatives. They had been serving Ahaziah. So Jehu killed them. ⁹Then he went to look for Ahaziah. Jehu's men captured him while he was hiding in Samaria. Ahaziah was brought to Jehu and put to death. People buried him, because they said, "He was a grandson of Jehoshaphat, who followed the LORD with all his heart." So no one in the royal family of Ahaziah was powerful enough to keep the kingdom.

Athaliah and Joash

¹⁰Athaliah was Ahaziah's mother. She saw that her son was dead. So she began to wipe out the whole royal family of Judah. ¹¹But Jehosheba went and got Joash, the son of Ahaziah. Jehosheba was the daughter of King Jehoram. She stole Joash away from among the royal princes. All of them were about to be murdered. She put Joash and his nurse in a bedroom. Jehosheba, the daughter of King Jehoram, was the wife of Jehoiada the priest. She was also Ahaziah's sister. So Jehosheba hid the child from Athaliah. That's why Athaliah couldn't kill him. ¹²The child remained hidden with the priest and his wife at God's temple for six years. Athaliah ruled over the land during that time.

23 When Joash was seven years old, Jehoiada showed how strong he was. He made a covenant with the commanders of groups of 100 men. The commanders were Azariah son of Jeroham, Ishmael son of Jehohanan, Azariah son of Obed, Maaseiah son of Adaiah, and Elishaphat son of Zikri. ²They went all through Judah. They gathered together the Levites and the leaders of Israelite families from all the towns. They came to Jerusalem. ³The whole community made a covenant with the new king at God's temple.

Jehoiada said to them, "Ahaziah's son will rule over Judah. That's what the LORD promised concerning the family line of David. ⁴Here's what I want you to do. A third

of you priests and Levites who are going on duty on the Sabbath day must guard the doors. ⁵A third of you must guard the royal palace. And a third of you must guard the Foundation Gate. All the other men must guard the courtyards of the LORD's temple. ⁶Don't let anyone enter the temple except the priests and Levites who are on duty. They can enter because they are set apart to the LORD. But all the other men must obey the LORD's command not to enter. ⁷The Levites must station themselves around the new king. Each man must have his weapon in his hand. Anyone else who enters the temple must be put to death. Stay close to the king no matter where he goes."

⁸The Levites did just as Jehoiada the priest ordered. So did all the men of Judah. Each commander got his men. Some of the men were going on duty on the Sabbath day. Others were going off duty. Jehoiada didn't let any of the groups go. ⁹Then he gave weapons to the commanders of the groups. He gave them spears, large shields and small shields. The weapons had belonged to King David. They had been in God's temple. ¹⁰Jehoiada stationed all the men around the new king. Each man had his weapon in his hand. They were standing near the altar and the temple. They stood from the south side of the temple to its north side.

¹¹Jehoiada and his sons brought Ahaziah's son out. They put the crown on him. They gave him a copy of the covenant. And they announced that he was king. They anointed him. Then they shouted, "May the king live a long time!"

¹²Athaliah heard the noise of the people running and cheering the new king. So she went to them at the LORD's temple. ¹³She looked, and there was the king! He was standing next to his pillar at the entrance. The officers and trumpet players were standing beside the king. All the people of the land were filled with joy. They were blowing trumpets. Musicians with their musical instruments were leading the songs of praise. Then Athaliah tore her royal robes. She shouted, "Treason! It's treason!"

¹⁴Jehoiada the priest sent out the commanders of the groups of 100 men. They were in charge of the troops. He said to them, "Bring her away from the temple

between the line of guards. Use your swords to kill anyone who follows her." The priest had said, "Don't put her to death at the LORD's temple." ¹⁵So they grabbed her as she reached the entrance of the Horse Gate on the palace grounds. There they put her to death.

¹⁶Then Jehoiada made a covenant. He promised that he, the people and the king would be the LORD's people. ¹⁷All the people went to Baal's temple. They tore it down. They smashed the altars and the statues of gods. They killed Mattan in front of the altars. He was the priest of Baal.

Jason's Jargon

2 CHRONICLES 23

Carefully examine this chapter for *treason*. Treason is betraying your country, especially by attempting to kill your leader or overthrow the government. A good agent could never consider it.

¹⁸Then Jehoiada put the priests, who were Levites, in charge of the LORD's temple. David had given them their duties in the temple. He had appointed them to sacrifice burnt offerings to the LORD. He wanted them to do it in keeping with what was written in the Law of Moses. David wanted them to sing and be full of joy. ¹⁹Jehoiada stationed guards at the gates of the LORD's temple. No one who was "unclean" in any way could enter. ²⁰Jehoiada took with him the commanders of hundreds, the nobles, the rulers of the people, and all the people of the land. He brought the new king down from the LORD's temple. They went into the palace through the Upper Gate. Then they seated the king on the royal throne. ²¹All the people of the land were filled with joy. And the city was calm. That's because Athaliah had been killed by a sword.

Joash Repairs the Temple

24 Joash was seven years old when he became king. He ruled in Jerusalem for 40 years. His mother's name was Zibiah. She was from Beersheba. ²Joash did what was right in the eyes of the LORD. Joash lived that way as long as Jehoiada the priest was alive. ³Jehoiada chose two wives for Joash. They had sons and daughters by Joash.

⁴Some time later Joash decided to make the LORD's temple look like new again. ⁵He called together the priests and Levites. He said to them, "Go to the towns of Judah. Collect the money that the nation of Israel owes every year. Use it to repair the temple of your God. Do it now." But the Levites didn't do it right away.

⁶So the king sent for Jehoiada the chief priest. He said to him, "Why haven't you required the Levites to bring in the tax from Judah and Jerusalem? It was set up by the LORD's servant Moses and the whole community of Israel. It was used for the tent where the tablets of the covenant law were kept."

⁷The children of that evil woman Athaliah had broken into God's temple. They had used even its sacred objects for the gods that were named Baal.

⁸King Joash commanded that a wooden chest be made. It was placed outside near the gate of the LORD's temple. ⁹Then a message went out in Judah and Jerusalem. It said that the people should bring the tax to the LORD. God's servant Moses had required Israel to pay that tax when they were in the desert. ¹⁰All the officials and people gladly brought their money. They dropped it into the chest until it was full. ¹¹The chest was brought in by the Levites to the king's officials. Every time the officials saw there was a large amount of money in the chest, it was emptied out. The royal secretary and the officer of the chief priest came and emptied it. Then they carried it back to its place. They did it regularly. They collected a great amount of money. ¹²The king and Jehoiada gave it to the people who were doing the work on the LORD's temple. They hired people who could lay the stones and people who could work with wood. They also hired people who could work with iron and bronze. They hired all of them to repair the temple.

¹³The men in charge of the work did their best. The repairs went very well under them. They rebuilt God's temple. They did it in keeping with its original plans. They

made the temple even stronger. [14]So they finished the work. Then they brought the rest of the money to the king and Jehoiada. It was used to pay for the objects that were made for the LORD's temple. The objects were used for serving at the temple. They were also used for the burnt offerings. The objects included dishes and other things made out of gold and silver. As long as Jehoiada lived, burnt offerings were sacrificed continually at the LORD's temple.

[15]Jehoiada had become very old. He died at the age of 130. [16]He was buried with the kings in the City of David. That's because he had done so many good things in Israel for God and his temple.

The Evil Things Joash Did

[17]After Jehoiada died, the officials of Judah came to King Joash. They bowed down to him. He listened to them. [18]They turned their backs on the temple of the LORD, the God of their people. They worshiped poles made to honor the female god named Asherah. They also worshiped statues of other gods. Because Judah and Jerusalem were guilty of sin, God became angry with them. [19]The LORD sent prophets to the people to bring them back to him. The prophets told the people what they were doing wrong. But the people wouldn't listen.

[20]Then the Spirit of God came on Zechariah the priest. He was the son of Jehoiada. Zechariah stood in front of the people. He told them, "God says, 'Why do you refuse to obey my commands? You will not have success. You have deserted me. So I have deserted you.'"

[21]But the people made evil plans against Zechariah. The king ordered them to kill Zechariah by throwing stones at him. They did it in the courtyard of the LORD's temple. [22]King Joash didn't remember how kind Zechariah's father Jehoiada had been to him. So he killed Jehoiada's son. As Zechariah was dying he said, "May the LORD see this. May he hold you responsible."

[23]In the spring, the army of Aram marched into Judah and Jerusalem against Joash. They killed all the leaders of the people. They took a large amount of goods from Judah. They sent it to their king in Damascus. [24]The army of Aram had come with only a few men. But the LORD allowed them to win the battle over a much larger army.

Judah had deserted the LORD, the God of their people. That's why the LORD punished Joash. [25]The army of Aram pulled back. They left Joash badly wounded. His officials planned to do evil things to him. That's because he murdered the son of Jehoiada the priest. They killed Joash in his bed. So he died. He was buried in the City of David. But he wasn't placed in the tombs of the kings.

[26]Those who made the plans against Joash were Zabad and Jehozabad. Zabad was the son of Shimeath. She was from Ammon. Jehozabad was the son of Shimrith. She was from Moab. [27]The story of the sons of Joash is written in the notes on the records of the kings. The many prophecies about him are written there too. So is the record of how he made God's temple look like new again. Joash's son Amaziah became the next king after him.

Amaziah King of Judah

25 Amaziah was 25 years old when he became king. He ruled in Jerusalem for 29 years. His mother's name was Jehoaddan. She was from Jerusalem. [2]Amaziah did what was right in the eyes of the LORD. But he didn't do it with all his heart. [3]The kingdom was firmly under his control. So he put to death the officials who had murdered his father, the king. [4]But he didn't put their children to death. He obeyed what is written in the Law, the Book of Moses. There the LORD commanded, "Parents must not be put to death because of what their children do. And children must not be put to death because of what their parents do. People must die because of their own sins." *(Deuteronomy 24:16)*

[5]Amaziah called the people of Judah together. He arranged them by families under commanders of thousands and commanders of hundreds. He did it for all the people of Judah and Benjamin. Then he brought together the men who were 20 years old or more. He found out there were 300,000 men who were able to serve in the army. They could handle spears and shields. [6]He also hired 100,000 fighting men from Israel. He had to pay them almost four tons of silver.

[7]But a man of God came to him. He said, "Your Majesty, these troops from Israel must not march out with you. The LORD is not with Israel. He isn't with any of the

people of Ephraim. [8]Go and fight bravely in battle if you want to. But God will destroy you right in front of your enemies. God has the power to help you or destroy you."

[9]Amaziah asked the man of God, "But what about all that silver I paid for these Israelite troops?"

The man of God replied, "The LORD can give you much more than that."

[10]So Amaziah let the troops go who had come to him from Ephraim. He sent them home. They were very angry with Judah. They were still very angry when they went home.

[11]Then Amaziah showed how strong he was. He led his army to the Valley of Salt. There he killed 10,000 men of Seir. [12]The army of Judah also captured 10,000 men alive. The army of Judah took them to the top of a cliff. Then they threw them down. All of them were smashed to pieces.

[13]The troops Amaziah had sent back attacked some towns that belonged to Judah. Amaziah hadn't allowed the troops to take part in the war. They attacked towns from Samaria to Beth Horon. They killed 3,000 people. They carried off huge amounts of goods.

[14]Amaziah returned from killing the men of Edom. He brought back the statues of the gods of Seir. He set them up as his own gods. He bowed down to them. He burned sacrifices to them. [15]The LORD was very angry with Amaziah. He sent a prophet to him. The prophet said, "Why do you ask the gods of those people for advice? They couldn't even save their own people from your power!"

[16]While the prophet was still speaking, the king spoke to him. He said, "Did I ask you for advice? Stop! If you don't, you will be struck down."

So the prophet stopped. But then he said, "I know that God has decided to destroy you. That's because you have worshiped other gods. You haven't listened to my advice."

[17]Amaziah, the king of Judah, spoke to his advisers. Then he sent a message to Jehoash, the king of Israel. Jehoash was the son of Jehoahaz. Jehoahaz was the son of Jehu. Amaziah dared Jehoash, "Come on! Let us face each other in battle!"

[18]But Jehoash, the king of Israel, answered Amaziah, the king of Judah. Jehoash said, "A thorn bush in Lebanon sent a message to a cedar tree there. The thorn bush said, 'Give your daughter to be married to my son.' Then a wild animal in Lebanon came along. It crushed the thorn bush by walking on it. [19]You brag that you have won the battle over Edom. You are very proud. But stay home! Why ask for trouble? Why bring yourself crashing down? Why bring Judah down with you?"

[20]But Amaziah wouldn't listen. That's because God had planned to hand Judah over to Jehoash. After all, they had asked the gods of Edom for advice. [21]So Jehoash, the king of Israel, attacked. He and Amaziah, the king of Judah, faced each other in battle. The battle took place at Beth Shemesh in Judah. [22]Israel drove Judah away. Every man ran home. [23]Jehoash king of Israel captured Amaziah king of Judah at Beth Shemesh. Amaziah was the son of Joash. Joash was the son of Ahaziah. Jehoash brought Amaziah to Jerusalem. Jehoash broke down part of its wall. It's the part that went from the Ephraim Gate to the Corner Gate. That part of the wall was 600 feet long. [24]Jehoash took all the gold and silver. He took all the objects he found in God's temple. Obed-Edom had been in charge of them. Jehoash also took the palace treasures and the prisoners. Then he returned to Samaria.

[25]Amaziah king of Judah lived for 15 years after Jehoash king of Israel died. Amaziah was the son of Joash. Jehoash was the son of Jehoahaz. [26]The other events of Amaziah's rule from beginning to end are written down. They are written in the records of the kings of Judah and Israel. [27]Amaziah turned away from obeying the LORD. From that time on, some people made evil plans against him in Jerusalem. So he ran away to Lachish. But they sent men after him to Lachish. There they killed him. [28]His body was brought back on a horse to Jerusalem, the City of Judah. There he was buried in the family tomb.

Uzziah King of Judah

26 All the people of Judah made Uzziah king. He was 16 years old. They made him king in place of his father Amaziah. [2]Uzziah rebuilt Elath. He brought it under Judah's control again. He did it after Amaziah joined the members of his family who had already died.

³Uzziah was 16 years old when he became king. He ruled in Jerusalem for 52 years. His mother's name was Jekoliah. She was from Jerusalem. ⁴Uzziah did what was right in the eyes of the LORD, just as his father Amaziah had done. ⁵He tried to obey God during the days of Zechariah. Zechariah taught him to have respect for God. As long as Uzziah obeyed the LORD, God gave him success.

⁶Uzziah went to war against the Philistines. He broke down the walls of Gath, Jabneh and Ashdod. Then he rebuilt some towns that were near Ashdod. He also rebuilt some other towns where Philistines lived. ⁷God helped him fight against the Philistines. He also helped him fight against the Meunites and against the Arabs who lived in Gur Baal. ⁸The Ammonites brought to Uzziah the gifts he required of them. He became famous all the way to the border of Egypt. That's because he had become very powerful.

⁹Uzziah built towers in Jerusalem. They were at the Corner Gate, the Valley Gate and the angle of the wall. He made the towers very strong. ¹⁰He also built towers in the desert. He dug many wells, because he had a lot of livestock. The livestock were in the western hills and on the plains. Uzziah had people working in his fields and vineyards in the hills and in the rich lands. That's because he loved the soil.

¹¹Uzziah's army was well trained. It was ready to march out by military groups according to their numbers. Jeiel and Maaseiah brought them together. Jeiel was the secretary. Maaseiah was the officer. They were under the direction of Hananiah. He was one of the royal officials. ¹²The total number of family leaders who were over the fighting men was 2,600. ¹³An army of 307,500 men was under their command. The men were trained for war. They were a powerful force. They helped the king against his enemies. ¹⁴Uzziah provided the entire army with shields, spears, helmets, coats of armor, bows, and stones for their slings. ¹⁵In Jerusalem he invented machines to be used on the towers and on the corners of city walls. These machines were used by men who shot arrows from the walls. The machines were also used by men to throw large stones from the walls. Uzziah became famous everywhere. God greatly helped him until he became powerful.

¹⁶But after Uzziah became powerful, his pride brought him down. He wasn't faithful to the LORD his God. He entered the LORD's temple to burn incense on the altar for burning incense. ¹⁷Azariah the priest followed him in. So did 80 other brave priests of the LORD. ¹⁸They stood up to Uzziah. They said, "Uzziah, it isn't right for you to burn incense to the LORD. Only the priests are supposed to do that. They are members of the family line of Aaron. They have been set apart to burn incense. So get out of here. Leave the temple. You haven't been faithful. The LORD God won't honor you."

¹⁹Uzziah was holding a shallow cup. He was ready to burn incense in it. He became angry. He shouted at the priests in the LORD's temple. He did it near the altar for burning incense. While he was shouting, a skin disease suddenly broke out on his forehead. ²⁰Azariah the chief priest and all the other priests looked at him. They saw that Uzziah had a skin disease on his forehead. So they hurried him out of the temple. Actually, he himself really wanted to leave. He knew that the LORD was making him suffer.

²¹King Uzziah had the skin disease until the day he died. He lived in a separate house because he had the disease. And he wasn't allowed to enter the LORD's temple. Uzziah's son Jotham was in charge of the palace. Jotham ruled over the people of the land.

²²The other events of Uzziah's rule from beginning to end were written down by Isaiah the prophet. Isaiah was the son of Amoz. ²³Uzziah joined the members of his family who had already died. He was buried near them in a royal burial ground. People said, "He had a skin disease." Uzziah's son Jotham became the next king after him.

Jotham King of Judah

27 Jotham was 25 years old when he became king. He ruled in Jerusalem for 16 years. His mother's name was Jerusha. She was the daughter of Zadok. ²Jotham did what was right in the eyes of the LORD, just as his father Uzziah had done. But Jotham didn't enter the LORD's temple as Uzziah had done. The people, however, continued to do very sinful things. ³Jotham rebuilt the Upper Gate of the LORD's temple. He did a lot of work on the wall at the hill of Ophel. ⁴He built towns in the hill country of Judah.

He also built forts and towers in areas that had a lot of trees in them.

⁵Jotham went to war against the king of Ammon. He won the battle over the Ammonites. That year they paid Jotham almost four tons of silver. They paid him 1,800 tons of wheat and 1,500 tons of barley. They also brought him the same amount in the second and third years.

⁶Jotham became powerful. That's because he had worshiped the LORD his God with all his heart.

⁷The other events of Jotham's rule are written down. That includes all his wars and the other things he did. All these things are written in the records of the kings of Israel and Judah. ⁸Jotham was 25 years old when he became king. He ruled in Jerusalem for 16 years. ⁹Jotham joined the members of his family who had already died. He was buried in the City of David. Jotham's son Ahaz became the next king after him.

Ahaz King of Judah

28 Ahaz was 20 years old when he became king. He ruled in Jerusalem for 16 years. He didn't do what was right in the eyes of the LORD. He didn't do what King David had done. ²He followed the ways of the kings of Israel. He also made statues of gods that were named Baal. ³He burned sacrifices in the Valley of Ben Hinnom. He sacrificed his children in the fire to other gods. He followed the practices of the nations. The LORD hates these practices. The LORD had driven out those nations to make room for the people of Israel. ⁴Ahaz offered sacrifices and burned incense at the high places. He also did it on the tops of hills and under every green tree.

⁵So the LORD his God handed him over to the king of Aram. The men of Aram won the battle over him. They took many of his people as prisoners. They brought them to Damascus.

God also handed Ahaz over to Pekah. Pekah was king of Israel. His army wounded or killed many of the troops of Ahaz. ⁶In one day Pekah, the son of Remaliah, killed 120,000 soldiers in Judah. That's because Judah had deserted the LORD, the God of their people. ⁷Zikri was a fighting man from Ephraim. He killed Maaseiah, Azrikam and Elkanah. Maaseiah was the king's son. Azrikam was the officer who was in charge of the palace. And Elkanah was next in command after the king. ⁸The men of Israel captured 200,000 wives, sons and daughters from their relatives in Judah. They also took a large amount of goods. They carried all of it back to Samaria.

⁹But a prophet of the LORD was there. His name was Oded. When the army returned to Samaria, he went out to meet them. He said to them, "The LORD is the God of your people. He was very angry with Judah. So he handed them over to you. But you have killed them. Your anger reached all the way to heaven. ¹⁰Now you are planning to make the men and women of Judah and Jerusalem your slaves. But aren't you also guilty of sins against the LORD your God? ¹¹Listen to me! You have taken your relatives from Judah as prisoners. The LORD is very angry with you. So send your relatives back."

¹²Then some of the leaders in Ephraim stood up to those who were returning from the war. The leaders were Azariah, Berekiah, Jehizkiah and Amasa. Azariah was the son of Jehohanan. Berekiah was the son of Meshillemoth. Jehizkiah was the son of Shallum. And Amasa was the son of Hadlai. ¹³"Don't bring those prisoners here," they said. "If you do, we'll be guilty in the sight of the LORD. Do you really want to add to our sin and guilt? We're already very guilty. The LORD is very angry with Israel."

¹⁴So the soldiers gave up the prisoners and the goods they had taken. They did it in front of the officials and the whole community. ¹⁵Azariah, Berekiah, Jehizkiah and Amasa received the prisoners. From the goods that had been taken, they gave clothes to everyone who was naked. They gave them clothes, sandals, food, drink and healing lotion. They put all the weak people on donkeys. They took them back to their relatives at Jericho. Then they returned to Samaria. Jericho was also known as the City of Palm Trees.

¹⁶At that time King Ahaz sent men to the king of Assyria to get help. ¹⁷The men of Edom had come and attacked Judah again. They had carried away prisoners. ¹⁸At the same time the Philistines had attacked towns in the western hills and in the Negev Desert of Judah. They had captured Beth Shemesh, Aijalon and Gederoth. They had also captured Soko, Timnah and Gimzo

and the villages around them. They had settled down in all of them. [19]The LORD had made Judah less powerful because of Ahaz, their king. Ahaz had stirred up the people of Judah to do evil things. He hadn't been faithful to the LORD at all. [20]Tiglath-Pileser came to Ahaz. But he gave Ahaz trouble instead of help. Tiglath-Pileser was king of Assyria. [21]Ahaz took some things from the LORD's temple. He also took some from the royal palace and from the officials. He gave all of them to the king of Assyria. But that didn't help Ahaz.

[22]When King Ahaz was in trouble, he became even more unfaithful to the LORD. [23]Ahaz offered sacrifices to the gods of Damascus. They had won the battle over him. Ahaz thought, "The gods of the kings of Aram have helped them. So I'll sacrifice to those gods. Then they'll help me." But those gods only caused his ruin. In fact, those gods caused the ruin of the whole nation of Israel.

[24]Ahaz gathered together everything that belonged to God's temple. He cut all of it in pieces. Ahaz shut the doors of the LORD's temple. He set up altars at every street corner in Jerusalem. [25]In every town in Judah he built high places. Sacrifices were burned there to other gods. That made the LORD, the God of his people, very angry.

[26]The other events of the rule of Ahaz and all his evil practices from beginning to end are written down. They are written in the records of the kings of Judah and Israel. [27]Ahaz joined the members of his family who had already died. He was buried in the city of Jerusalem. But he wasn't placed in the tombs of the kings of Israel. Ahaz's son Hezekiah became the next king after him.

Hezekiah Purifies the Temple

29 Hezekiah was 25 years old when he became king. He ruled in Jerusalem for 29 years. His mother's name was Abijah. She was the daughter of Zechariah. [2]Hezekiah did what was right in the eyes of the LORD, just as King David had done.

[3]In the first month of Hezekiah's first year as king, he opened the doors of the LORD's temple. He repaired them. [4]He brought the priests and Levites in. He gathered them together in the open area on the east side of the temple. [5]He said, "Levites, listen to me! Set yourselves apart to the LORD. Set apart the temple of the LORD. He's the God of your people who lived long ago. Remove anything 'unclean' from the temple. [6]Our people weren't faithful. They did what was evil in the eyes of the LORD our God. They deserted him. They turned their faces away from the place where he lives. They turned their backs on him. [7]They also shut the doors of the temple porch. They put the lamps out. They didn't burn incense at the temple. They didn't sacrifice burnt offerings there to the God of Israel. [8]So the LORD has become angry with Judah and Jerusalem. He has made them look so bad that everyone is shocked when they see them. They laugh at them. You can see it with your own eyes. [9]That's why our fathers have been killed by swords. That's why our sons and daughters and wives have become prisoners. [10]So I'm planning to make a covenant with the LORD, the God of Israel. Then he'll stop being angry with us. [11]My sons, don't fail to obey the LORD. He has chosen you to stand in front of him and work for him. He wants you to serve him and burn incense to him."

[12] Here are the Levites who went to work.

Mahath and Joel were from the family line of Kohath.
Mahath was the son of Amasai.
Joel was the son of Azariah.
Kish and Azariah were from the family line of Merari.
Kish was the son of Abdi. Azariah was the son of Jehallelel.
Joah and Eden were from the family line of Gershon.
Joah was the son of Zimmah.
Eden was the son of Joah.

[13] Shimri and Jeiel were from the family line of Elizaphan.
Zechariah and Mattaniah were from the family line of Asaph.

[14] Jehiel and Shimei were from the family line of Heman.
Shemaiah and Uzziel were from the family line of Jeduthun.

[15]All these Levites gathered the other Levites together. They set themselves apart to the LORD. Then they went in to purify the LORD's temple. That's what the king had ordered them to do. They did what the LORD told them to. [16]The priests went into the LORD's temple to make it pure. They brought out to the temple courtyard everything that

was "unclean." They had found "unclean" things in the LORD's temple. The Levites took them and carried them out to the Kidron Valley. [17]On the first day of the first month they began to set everything in the temple apart to the LORD. By the eighth day of the month they reached the LORD's porch. For eight more days they set the LORD's temple itself apart to him. They finished on the 16th day of the first month.

[18]Then they went to King Hezekiah. They reported, "We've purified the whole temple of the LORD. That includes the altar for burnt offerings and all its tools. It also includes the table for the holy bread and all its objects. [19]We've prepared all the things King Ahaz had removed. We've set them apart to the LORD. Ahaz had removed them while he was king. He wasn't faithful to the LORD. Those things are now in front of the LORD's altar."

[20]Early the next morning King Hezekiah gathered together the city officials. They all went up to the LORD's temple. [21]They brought seven bulls, seven rams, seven male lambs and seven male goats with them. They sacrificed the animals as a sin offering for the kingdom, for the temple and for Judah. The king commanded the priests to offer them on the LORD's altar. The priests were from the family line of Aaron. [22]They killed the bulls. Then they splashed the blood against the altar. Next they killed the rams and splashed the blood against the altar. Then they killed the lambs and splashed the blood against the altar. [23]The goats for the sin offering were brought to the king and the whole community. They placed their hands on them. [24]Then the priests killed the goats. They put the blood on the altar as a sin offering. It paid for the sin of the whole nation of Israel. The king had ordered the burnt offering and the sin offering for the whole nation.

[25]Hezekiah stationed the Levites in the LORD's temple. They had cymbals, harps and lyres. They did everything in the way King David, his prophet Gad, and Nathan the prophet had required. The LORD had given commands about all these things through his prophets. [26]So the Levites stood ready with David's musical instruments. And the priests had their trumpets ready. [27]Hezekiah gave the order to sacrifice the burnt offering on the altar. The offering

began. Singing to the LORD also began. The singing was accompanied by the trumpets and by the instruments of David. He had been king of Israel. [28]The whole community bowed down. They worshiped the LORD. At the same time the musicians played their musical instruments. The priests blew their trumpets. All of that continued until the burnt offering had been sacrificed.

[29]So the offerings were finished. King Hezekiah got down on his knees. He worshiped the LORD. So did everyone who was with him. [30]The king and his officials ordered the Levites to praise the LORD. They used the words of David and Asaph the prophet. They sang praises with joy. They bowed down and worshiped the LORD.

[31]Then Hezekiah said, "You have set yourselves apart to the LORD. Come and bring sacrifices and thank offerings to his temple." So the whole community brought sacrifices and thank offerings. Everyone who wanted to brought burnt offerings.

[32]The whole community brought 70 bulls, 100 rams and 200 male lambs. They brought all of them as burnt offerings to the LORD. [33]The total number of animals set apart as sacrifices to the LORD was 600 bulls and 3,000 sheep and goats. [34]But there weren't enough priests to skin all the burnt offerings. So their relatives, the Levites, helped them. They worked until the task was finished. By that time other priests had been set apart to the LORD. The Levites had been more careful than the priests when they set themselves apart. [35]There were large numbers of burnt offerings, along with the drink offerings and the fat from the friendship offerings. They were offered along with the burnt offerings.

So the service of the LORD's temple was started up again. [36]Hezekiah and all the people were filled with joy. That's because everything had been done so quickly. God had provided for his people in a wonderful way.

Hezekiah Celebrates the Passover Feast

30 Hezekiah sent a message to all the people of Israel and Judah. He also wrote letters to the tribes of Ephraim and Manasseh. He invited everyone to come to the LORD's temple in Jerusalem. He wanted them to celebrate the Passover Feast to honor the LORD. He is the God of Israel. ²The king, his officials and the whole community in Jerusalem decided to celebrate the Passover Feast in the second month. ³They hadn't been able to celebrate it at the regular time. That's because there weren't enough priests who had set themselves apart to the LORD. Also, the people hadn't gathered together in Jerusalem. ⁴The plan seemed good to the king and the whole community. ⁵They decided to send a message all through Israel. It was sent out from Beersheba all the way to Dan. The message invited the people to come to Jerusalem. It invited them to celebrate the Passover Feast to honor the LORD, the God of Israel. The Passover Feast hadn't been celebrated by large numbers of people for a long time. It hadn't been done in keeping with what was written in the law.

⁶Messengers went all through Israel and Judah. They carried letters from the king and his officials. The king had ordered them to do that. The letters said,

"People of Israel, return to the LORD. He is the God of Abraham, Isaac and Israel. Return to him. Then he will return to you who are left in the land. You have escaped from the power of the kings of Assyria. ⁷Don't be like your parents and the rest of your people. They weren't faithful to the LORD, the God of their people. That's why he punished them. He made them look so bad that everyone was shocked when they saw them. You can see it for yourselves. ⁸Don't be stubborn. Don't be as your people were. Obey the LORD. Come to his temple. He has set it apart to himself forever. Serve the LORD your God. Then he'll stop being angry with you. ⁹Suppose you return to the LORD. Then those who captured your relatives and children will be kind to them. In fact, your relatives and children will come back to this land. The LORD your God is kind and tender. He won't turn away from you if you return to him."

¹⁰The messengers went from town to town in Ephraim and Manasseh. They went all the way to Zebulun. But people laughed and made fun of them. ¹¹In spite of that, some people from Asher, Manasseh and Zebulun made themselves humble. They went to Jerusalem. ¹²God helped the people of Judah. He helped them agree with one another. So they did what the king and his officials had ordered. They did what the LORD told them to do.

¹³A very large crowd of people gathered together in Jerusalem. They went there to celebrate the Feast of Unleavened Bread. It took place in the second month. ¹⁴They removed the altars in Jerusalem. They cleared away the altars for burning incense. They threw all the altars into the Kidron Valley. ¹⁵They killed the Passover lamb on the 14th day of the second month. The priests and Levites were ashamed of how they had lived. They set themselves apart to the LORD. They brought burnt offerings to his temple. ¹⁶Then they did their regular tasks just as the Law of Moses, the man of God, required. The Levites gave the blood of the animals to the priests. The priests splashed it against the altar. ¹⁷Many people in the crowd hadn't set themselves apart to the LORD. They weren't "clean." They couldn't set apart their lambs to him. So the Levites had to kill the Passover lambs for all of them. ¹⁸Many people came from Ephraim, Manasseh, Issachar and Zebulun. Most of them hadn't made themselves pure and "clean." But they still ate the Passover meal. That was against what was written in the law. But Hezekiah prayed for them. He said, "The LORD is good. May he forgive everyone ¹⁹who wants to worship God with all their heart. God is the LORD, the God of their people. May God forgive them even if they aren't 'clean' in keeping with the rules of the temple." ²⁰The LORD answered Hezekiah's prayer. He healed the people.

²¹The people of Israel who were in Jerusalem celebrated the Feast of Unleavened Bread. They celebrated for seven days with great joy. The Levites and priests praised the LORD every day. They praised the LORD with loud musical instruments. The instruments had been set apart to the LORD.

²²Hezekiah spoke words that gave hope to all the Levites. They understood how to serve the LORD well. For the seven days of the feast they ate the share given to them. They also sacrificed friendship offerings. They praised the LORD, the God of their people.

²³Then the whole community agreed to celebrate the feast for seven more days. So

for another seven days they celebrated with joy. ²⁴Hezekiah, the king of Judah, provided 1,000 bulls and 7,000 sheep and goats for the community. The officials provided 1,000 bulls and 10,000 sheep and goats for them. A large number of priests set themselves apart to the LORD. ²⁵The entire community of Judah was filled with joy. So were the priests and Levites. And so were all the people who had gathered together from Israel. That included the outsiders who had come from Israel. It also included those who lived in Judah. ²⁶There was great joy in Jerusalem. There hadn't been anything like it in Israel since the days of Solomon, the son of David. Solomon had been king of Israel. ²⁷The priests and Levites gave their blessing to the people. God heard them. Their prayer reached all the way to heaven. It's the holy place where God lives.

31 The Passover Feast came to an end. The people of Israel who were in Jerusalem went out to the towns of Judah. They smashed the sacred stones. They cut down the poles used to worship the female god named Asherah. They destroyed the high places and the altars. They did those things all through Judah and Benjamin. They also did them in Ephraim and Manasseh. They destroyed all the objects used to worship other gods. Then the Israelites returned to their own towns and property.

The People Bring Gifts to the LORD

²Hezekiah put the priests and Levites in groups based on their duties. The priests sacrificed burnt offerings and friendship offerings. The Levites served the LORD by giving thanks and singing praises at the gates of his house. ³The king gave some of his own possessions to the temple. He gave them for the morning and evening burnt offerings. He gave them for the burnt offerings for every Sabbath day. He gave them for the burnt offerings for every New Moon feast. And he gave them for the burnt offerings for every yearly appointed feast. He did it in keeping with what is written in the Law of the LORD. ⁴Hezekiah gave an order to the people who were living in Jerusalem. He commanded them to give to the priests and Levites the share they owed them. Then the priests and Levites could give their full attention to the Law of the LORD. ⁵The order went out. Right away the people of Israel began to

give freely. They gave the first share of the harvest of their grain, fresh wine, olive oil and honey. They also gave the first share of everything else their fields produced. They brought a large amount. It was a tenth of everything. ⁶Here is what the people of Israel and Judah who lived in the towns of Judah brought. They brought a tenth of their herds and flocks. They also brought a tenth of the holy things they had set apart to the LORD their God. They put them in piles. ⁷They began doing it in the third month. They finished in the seventh month. ⁸Hezekiah and his officials came and saw the piles. When they did, they praised the LORD. And they blessed his people Israel.

⁹Hezekiah asked the priests and Levites about the piles. ¹⁰Azariah the chief priest answered him. He said, "The people have been bringing their gifts to the LORD's temple. Ever since they began to bring them, we've had enough to eat. We have even had plenty to spare. That's because the LORD has blessed his people. So we have a large amount left over." Azariah was from the family line of Zadok.

¹¹Hezekiah gave orders to prepare storerooms in the LORD's temple. And it was done. ¹²The people were faithful. They brought in their offerings and a tenth of everything they produced. They also brought the gifts they had set apart to the LORD. Konaniah the Levite was in charge of everything they brought. His brother Shimei was next in command after him. ¹³Konaniah and his brother Shimei had helpers who worked with them. Their names were Jehiel, Azaziah, Nahath, Asahel, Jerimoth, Jozabad, Eliel, Ismakiah, Mahath and Benaiah. King Hezekiah and Azariah had appointed them. Azariah was the official in charge of God's temple.

¹⁴Kore the Levite guarded the East Gate. He was in charge of the offerings people chose to give to God. He handed out the offerings made to the LORD. He also handed out the gifts that had been set apart to the LORD. Kore was the son of Imnah. ¹⁵Eden, Miniamin, Jeshua, Shemaiah, Amariah and Shekaniah helped Kore. They were faithful in helping him in the towns of the priests. They handed out gifts to their brother priests, group by group. They gave the gifts to old men and young men alike.

¹⁶In addition to that, they handed out gifts to the males who were three years old

or more. The names of those males were listed in their family history. All of them would enter the LORD's temple. They would carry out their duties each day. Each group did all the different things it was supposed to do. ¹⁷Kore and his Levite companions also handed out gifts to the priests. The priests were listed by their families in their family history. Those Levites also handed out gifts to the Levites who were 20 years old or more. Each group did all the different things it was supposed to do. ¹⁸Those groups included all the little ones, the wives, and the sons and daughters of the whole community. All of them were listed in their family history. They were faithful in setting themselves apart to serve the LORD.

¹⁹Some of the priests lived in other towns or on farms around their towns. They were from the family line of Aaron. Men were chosen by name to hand out shares to those priests. They gave a share to every male among them. They also gave a share to everyone whose name was written down in the family history of the Levites.

²⁰That's what Hezekiah did all through Judah. He did what was good and right. He was faithful to the LORD his God. ²¹He tried to obey his God. He worked for him with all his heart. That's the way he worked in everything he did to serve God's temple. He obeyed the law. He followed the LORD's commands. So he had success.

Sennacherib Warns Jerusalem

32 Hezekiah had been completely faithful to the LORD. However, Sennacherib king of Assyria came and marched into Judah. Sennacherib surrounded the cities that had high walls around them. He got ready to attack them. He thought he could win the battle over them. He thought he could take them for himself. ²Hezekiah saw that Sennacherib had come to Jerusalem to fight against it. ³So he asked his officials and military leaders for advice. He asked them about blocking off the water from the springs outside the city. They gave him the advice he asked for. ⁴They gathered together a large group of people. They blocked all the springs. They also blocked the stream that flowed through the land. "Why should the kings of Assyria come and find plenty of water?" they asked. ⁵Then Hezekiah worked hard repairing all the broken parts of the wall. He built towers on it. He built another wall outside that one. He built up the areas that had been filled in around the City of David. He also made large numbers of weapons and shields.

⁶He appointed military officers over the people. He gathered the officers together in front of him in the open area at the city gate. He gave them words of hope. He said, ⁷"Be strong. Be brave. Don't be afraid. Don't lose hope. The king of Assyria has a huge army with him. But there's a greater power with us than there is with him. ⁸The only thing he has is human strength. But the LORD our God is with us. He will help us. He'll fight our battles." The people had great faith in what Hezekiah, the king of Judah, said.

⁹Later Sennacherib, the king of Assyria, and all his forces surrounded Lachish. They prepared to attack it. At that time, Sennacherib sent his officers to Jerusalem. They went there with a message for Hezekiah, the king of Judah. The message was also for all the people of Judah who were there. The message said,

¹⁰"Sennacherib, the king of Assyria, says, 'Why are you putting your faith in what your king says? Why do you remain in Jerusalem when you are surrounded? ¹¹Hezekiah says, "The LORD our God will save us from the power of the king of Assyria." But he isn't telling you the truth. If you listen to him, you will die of hunger and thirst. ¹²Didn't Hezekiah himself remove your god's high places and altars? Didn't Hezekiah say to the people of Judah and Jerusalem, "You must worship at one altar. You must burn sacrifices on it"?

¹³"'Don't you know what I and the kings who ruled before me have done? Don't you know what we've done to all the peoples of the other lands? Were the gods of those nations ever able to save their lands from my power? ¹⁴The kings who ruled before me destroyed many nations. Which one of the gods of those nations has been able to save his people from me? So how can your god save you from my power? ¹⁵Don't let Hezekiah trick you. He's telling you lies. Don't believe him. No god of any nation or kingdom has been able to save his people from my power. No

There are lots of ways to show courage. We usually think of brave acts, such as soldiers helping each other on the battlefield, or firefighters running into burning buildings to rescue people. Or maybe it's simply being that first kid to sample today's mystery meat in the school cafeteria ("I think it's some kind of beef"). They're all heroes. But courage can also be the quiet, personal decision to do the right thing even when it's not popular.

In the Adventures in Odyssey episode "The Courage to Stand," Robyn Jacobs wanted to be accepted by the cool girls on the cheerleading squad. But eventually she had to choose between impressing their leader, Shannon, or respecting her parents' rules. Robyn did the right thing, even though it made her an outcast with Shannon.

If we're not careful, looking cool or being accepted can become so important that we forget who we are and what we believe. Before we know it, we're trapped—compromising and feeling miserable. It's

definitely better to stand tall at the start, as Robyn did. That takes courage.

In 2 Chronicles 32:7–8, King Hezekiah urged his people to "Be strong. Be brave," trusting God to fight their battles when things looked grim. We may not face enemies with swords and spears, but sometimes people can jab us with sharp words and harsh looks. Can you think of a time when that happened to you? How has the Lord protected you when you decided to do the right thing?

god has been able to save his people from the power of the kings who ruled before me. So your god won't save you from my power either!' "

[16]Sennacherib's officers spoke even more things against the Lord God and his servant Hezekiah. [17]The king also wrote letters against the Lord. His letters made fun of the God of Israel. They said, "The peoples of other lands have their gods. But those gods didn't save their people from my power. So the god of Hezekiah won't save his people from my power either." [18]Then the officers called out in the Hebrew language to the people of Jerusalem who were on the wall. They were trying to scare them and make them afraid. That's because they wanted to capture the city. [19]They were comparing the God of Jerusalem to the gods of the other nations of the world. But those gods were only statues. They had been made by human hands.

[20]King Hezekiah cried out in prayer to God in heaven. He prayed about the

problem Jerusalem was facing. So did Isaiah the prophet. He was the son of Amoz. [21]The Lord sent an angel. The angel wiped out all the enemy's fighting men, commanders and officers. He put an end to them right there in the camp of the Assyrian king. So Sennacherib went back to his own land in shame. He went into the temple of his god. There some of his own sons, the people closest to him, killed him with their swords. [22]So the Lord saved Hezekiah and the people of Jerusalem. He saved them from the power of Sennacherib, the king of Assyria. He also saved them from all their other enemies. He took care of them on every side. [23]Many people brought offerings to Jerusalem for the Lord. They brought expensive gifts for Hezekiah, the king of Judah. From then on, all the nations thought well of him.

Hezekiah's Pride, Success and Death

[24]In those days Hezekiah became sick. He knew he was about to die. So he prayed to the Lord. And the Lord answered him.

He gave him a miraculous sign. ²⁵But Hezekiah's heart was proud. He didn't give thanks for the many kind things the LORD had done for him. So the LORD became angry with him. He also became angry with Judah and Jerusalem. ²⁶Then Hezekiah had a change of heart. He was sorry he had been proud. The people of Jerusalem were also sorry they had sinned. So the LORD wasn't angry with them as long as Hezekiah was king.

²⁷Hezekiah was very rich. He received great honor. He made storerooms for his silver and gold. He also made them for his jewels, spices, shields and all kinds of expensive things. ²⁸He made buildings to store the harvest of grain, fresh wine and olive oil. He made barns for all kinds of cattle. He made sheep pens for his flocks. ²⁹He built villages. He gained large numbers of flocks and herds. God had made him very rich.

³⁰Hezekiah blocked up the upper opening of the Gihon spring. He directed the water to flow down to the west side of the City of David. He had success in everything he did. ³¹The rulers of Babylon sent messengers to him. They asked him about the miraculous sign that had taken place in the land. Then God left Hezekiah to test him. God wanted to know everything in Hezekiah's heart.

³²Hezekiah did many things that showed he was faithful to the LORD. Those things and the other events of his rule are written down.

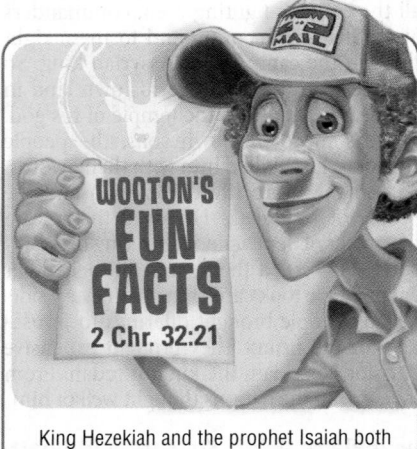

WOOTON'S FUN FACTS
2 Chr. 32:21

King Hezekiah and the prophet Isaiah both cried out for God to save them from King Sennacherib of Assyria. The result? Oh yeah: an angel-sighting—and an angel-smiting!

They are written in the record of the vision of the prophet Isaiah, the son of Amoz. That record is part of the records of the kings of Judah and Israel. ³³Hezekiah joined the members of his family who had already died. He was buried on the hill where the tombs of David's family are. The whole nation of Judah honored him when he died. So did the people of Jerusalem. Hezekiah's son Manasseh became the next king after him.

Manasseh King of Judah

33 Manasseh was 12 years old when he became king. He ruled in Jerusalem for 55 years. ²Manasseh did what was evil in the eyes of the LORD. He followed the practices of the nations. The LORD hated those practices. The LORD had driven out those nations to make room for the Israelites. ³Manasseh rebuilt the high places. His father Hezekiah had destroyed them. Manasseh also set up altars to the gods that were named Baal. He made poles used to worship the female god named Asherah. He even bowed down to all the stars and worshiped them. ⁴He built altars in the LORD's temple. The LORD had said about his temple, "My Name will remain in Jerusalem forever." ⁵In the two courtyards of the LORD's temple Manasseh built altars to honor all the stars in the sky. ⁶He sacrificed his children in the fire to other gods. He did it in the Valley of Ben Hinnom. He practiced all kinds of evil magic. He took part in worshiping evil powers. He got messages from people who had died. He talked to the spirits of people who have died. He did many things that were evil in the eyes of the LORD. Manasseh made the LORD very angry.

⁷Manasseh had carved a statue of a god. He put it in God's temple. God had spoken to David and his son Solomon about the temple. He had said, "My Name will be in this temple and in Jerusalem forever. Out of all the cities in the tribes of Israel I have chosen Jerusalem. ⁸I gave this land to your people who lived long ago. I will not make the Israelites leave it again. But they must be careful to do everything I commanded them. They must follow all the laws, directions, and rules I gave them through Moses." ⁹But Manasseh led Judah and the people of Jerusalem astray. They did more evil things than the nations the LORD had destroyed to make room for the Israelites.

[10]The LORD spoke to Manasseh and his people. But they didn't pay any attention to him. [11]So the LORD brought the army commanders of the king of Assyria against them. They took Manasseh as a prisoner. They put a hook in his nose. They put him in bronze chains. And they took him to Babylon. [12]When Manasseh was in trouble, he asked the LORD his God to help him. He made himself very humble in the sight of the God of his people. [13]Manasseh prayed to him. When he did, the LORD felt sorry for him. He answered his prayer. The LORD brought Manasseh back to Jerusalem and his kingdom. Then Manasseh knew that the LORD is God.

[14]After that, Manasseh rebuilt the outer wall of the City of David. It was west of the Gihon spring in the valley. It reached all the way to the entrance of the Fish Gate. It went around the entire hill of Ophel. Manasseh also made the wall much higher. He stationed military commanders in all the cities in Judah that had high walls around them.

[15]Manasseh got rid of the false gods. He removed the statue of one of those gods from the LORD's temple. He also removed all the altars he had built on the temple hill and in Jerusalem. He threw them out of the city. [16]Then he made the LORD's altar look like new again. He sacrificed friendship offerings and thank offerings on it. He told the people of Judah to serve the LORD, the God of Israel. [17]The people continued to offer sacrifices at the high places. But they offered them only to the LORD their God.

[18]The other events of Manasseh's rule are written down in the official records of the kings of Judah. These records include his prayer to his God. They also include the words the prophets spoke to him in the name of the LORD, the God of Israel. [19]Everything about Manasseh is written in the records of the prophets. That includes his prayer and the fact that God felt sorry for him. It includes everything he did before he made himself humble in the LORD's sight. It includes all his sins and the fact that he wasn't faithful to the LORD. It includes the locations where he built high places. It includes the places where he set up poles used to worship the female god named Asherah. And it includes the places where he set up statues of other gods. [20]Manasseh joined the members of his family who had already died.

He was buried in his palace. Manasseh's son Amon became the next king after him.

Amon King of Judah

[21]Amon was 22 years old when he became king. He ruled in Jerusalem for two years. [22]Amon did what was evil in the eyes of the LORD, just as his father Manasseh had done. Amon worshiped and offered sacrifices to all the statues of gods that Manasseh had made. [23]He didn't make himself humble in the LORD's sight as his father Manasseh had done. So Amon became even more guilty.

[24]Amon's officials made plans against him. They murdered him in his palace. [25]Then the people of the land killed all those who had made plans against King Amon. They made his son Josiah king in his place.

Josiah Makes Judah a Better Nation

34 Josiah was eight years old when he became king. He ruled in Jerusalem for 31 years. [2]He did what was right in the eyes of the LORD. He lived the way King David had lived. He didn't turn away from it to the right or the left.

[3]While he was still young, he began to worship the God of King David. It was the eighth year of Josiah's rule. In his 12th year Josiah began to get rid of the high places in Judah and Jerusalem. He removed the poles used to worship the female god named Asherah. He also removed the statues of other false gods. [4]He ordered the altars of the gods that were named Baal to be torn down. Josiah cut to pieces the altars above them that were used for burning incense. He smashed the Asherah poles. He also smashed the statues of other false gods. Josiah broke all of them to pieces. He scattered the pieces over the graves of those who had offered sacrifices to those gods. [5]He burned the bones of the priests on their altars. That's the way he made Judah and Jerusalem pure and "clean." [6]Josiah went to the towns of Manasseh, Ephraim and Simeon. He went all the way to Naphtali. He also went to the destroyed places around all those towns. [7]Everywhere Josiah went he tore down the altars and the Asherah poles. He crushed the statues of gods to powder. He cut to pieces all the altars for burning incense. He destroyed all those things everywhere in Israel. Then he went back to Jerusalem.

⁸In the 18th year of Josiah's rule, he decided to make the land and temple pure and "clean." So he sent Shaphan, Maaseiah and Joah to repair the temple of the LORD his God. Shaphan was the son of Azaliah. Maaseiah was ruler of the city. And Joah, the son of Joahaz, kept the records.

⁹These men went to Hilkiah the high priest. They gave him the money that had been brought into God's temple. The Levites who guarded the gates had collected it. They had received some of the money from the people of Manasseh and Ephraim. They had also received some from the other people who remained in Israel. The rest of the money came from other people. It came from all the people of Judah and Benjamin and the people living in Jerusalem. ¹⁰Men were appointed to direct the work on the LORD's temple. All the money collected was given to them. These men paid the workers who repaired the temple. They made it look like new again. ¹¹They also gave money to the builders and those who worked with wood. The workers used it to buy lumber and blocks of stone. The lumber was used for the supports and beams for the buildings. The kings of Judah had let the buildings fall down.

¹²The workers were faithful in doing the work. Jahath and Obadiah directed them. They were Levites from the family line of Merari. Zechariah and Meshullam also directed them. They were from the family line of Kohath. The Levites were skilled in playing musical instruments. ¹³They were in charge of the laborers. They directed all the workers from job to job. Some of the Levites were secretaries and writers. Other Levites guarded the gates.

Hilkiah Finds the Book of the Law

¹⁴The money that had been taken into the LORD's temple was being brought out. At that time Hilkiah the priest found the Book of the Law of the LORD. It had been given through Moses. ¹⁵Hilkiah spoke to Shaphan the secretary. Hilkiah said, "I've found the Book of the Law in the LORD's temple." Hilkiah gave the book to Shaphan. ¹⁶Then Shaphan took the book to King Josiah. He told him, "Your officials are doing everything they've been asked to do. ¹⁷They have paid out the money that was in the LORD's temple. They've put it in the care of the directors and workers." ¹⁸Shaphan continued, "Hilkiah the priest has given me a book." Shaphan read some of it to the king.

¹⁹The king heard the words of the Law. When he did, he tore his royal robes. ²⁰He gave orders to Hilkiah, Ahikam, Abdon, Shaphan the secretary and Asaiah. Ahikam was the son of Shaphan. Abdon was the son of Micah. And Asaiah was the king's attendant. Josiah commanded them, ²¹"Go. Ask the LORD for advice. Ask him about what is written in this book that has been found. Do it for me. Also do it for the people who remain in Israel and Judah. The LORD has been very angry with us. That's because our people before us didn't obey what the LORD had said. They didn't do everything written in this book."

²²Hilkiah and the people the king had sent with him went to speak to Huldah the prophet. She was the wife of Shallum. Shallum was the son of Tokhath. Tokhath was the son of Hasrah. Shallum took care of the sacred robes. Huldah lived in the New Quarter of Jerusalem.

²³Huldah said to them, "The LORD is the God of Israel. He says, 'Here is what you should tell the man who sent you to me. ²⁴"The LORD says, 'I am going to bring horrible trouble on this place and its people. There are curses written down in the book that has been read to the king of Judah. All those curses will take place. ²⁵That's because the people have deserted me. They have burned incense to other gods. They have made me very angry because of everything their hands have made. So my anger will burn like a fire against this place. And the fire of my anger will not be put out.' " ' ²⁶The king of Judah sent you to ask for advice. Tell him, 'The LORD is the God of Israel. He has a message for you about the things you heard. ²⁷The LORD says, "Your heart was tender. You made yourself humble in my sight. You heard what I spoke against this place and its people. So you made yourself humble. You tore your royal robes and wept. And I have heard you," announces the LORD. ²⁸You will join the members of your family who have already died. You will be buried in peace. You will not see all the trouble I am going to bring. I am going to bring trouble on this place and the people who live here.' "

Huldah's answer was taken back to the king.

²⁹Then the king called together all the elders of Judah and Jerusalem. ³⁰He went up to the LORD's temple. The people of Judah and Jerusalem went with him. So did the priests and Levites. All of them went, from the least important of them to the most important. The king had all the words of the Book of the Covenant read to them. The book had been found in the LORD's temple. ³¹The king stood next to his pillar. He agreed to the terms of the covenant in front of the LORD. The king promised to serve the LORD and obey his commands, directions and rules. He promised to obey them with all his heart and with all his soul. So the king promised to obey the terms of the covenant that were written in that book.

³²Then he had everyone in Jerusalem and in Benjamin commit themselves to the covenant. The people of Jerusalem did it in keeping with the covenant of the God of Israel.

³³Josiah removed all the statues of false gods from the whole territory that belonged to the Israelites. The LORD hated those statues. Josiah had everyone in Israel serve the LORD their God. As long as he lived, they didn't fail to follow the LORD, the God of their people.

Josiah Celebrates the Passover Feast

35 Josiah celebrated the Passover Feast in Jerusalem to honor the LORD. The Passover lamb was killed on the 14th day of the first month. ²Josiah appointed the priests to their duties. He cheered them up as they served the LORD at his temple. ³The Levites taught all the people of Israel. The Levites had been set apart to the LORD. Josiah said to them, "Put the sacred ark of the covenant in the temple Solomon built. He was the son of David and king of Israel. The ark must not be carried around on your shoulders. Serve the LORD your God. Serve his people Israel. ⁴Prepare yourselves by families in your groups. Do it based on the directions written by David, the king of Israel, and by his son Solomon.

⁵"Stand at the temple. Stand there with a group of Levites for each group of families among your people. ⁶Kill the Passover lambs. Set yourselves apart to the LORD. Prepare the lambs for your people. Do what the LORD commanded through Moses."

⁷Josiah provided animals for the Passover offerings. He gave them for all the people who were there. He gave a total of 30,000 lambs and goats and 3,000 oxen. He gave all of them from his own possessions.

⁸His officials also gave freely. They gave to the people and the priests and Levites. Hilkiah, Zechariah and Jehiel were in charge of God's temple. They gave the priests 2,600 Passover lambs and 300 oxen. ⁹Konaniah and his brothers Shemaiah and Nethanel also gave offerings. So did Hashabiah, Jeiel and Jozabad. All of them were the leaders of the Levites. They gave 5,000 Passover lambs and 500 oxen for the Levites.

¹⁰The Passover service was arranged. The priests stood in their places. The Levites were in their groups. That's what the king had ordered. ¹¹The Passover lambs were killed. The priests splashed against the altar the blood handed to them. The Levites skinned the animals. ¹²They set the burnt offerings to one side. These offerings were for the smaller family groups to offer to the LORD. That's what was written in the Book of Moses. The Levites did the same thing with the oxen. ¹³They cooked the Passover animals over the fire, just as the law required. They boiled the holy offerings in pots, large kettles and pans. They served the offerings quickly to all the people. ¹⁴After that, they got things ready for themselves and the priests. That's because the priests, who were from the family line of Aaron, were busy until dark. They were sacrificing the burnt offerings and the fat parts. The Levites got things ready for themselves and for the priests, who belonged to Aaron's family line.

¹⁵Those who played music were from the family line of Asaph. They were in the places that had been set up by David, Asaph, Heman and Jeduthun. Jeduthun had been the king's prophet. The guards at each gate didn't have to leave their places. That's because their brother Levites got things ready for them.

¹⁶So at that time the entire service to honor the LORD was carried out. The Passover Feast was celebrated. The burnt offerings were sacrificed on the LORD's altar. That's what King Josiah had ordered. ¹⁷The Israelites who were there celebrated the Passover Feast at that time. They observed the Feast of Unleavened Bread for seven days. ¹⁸The Passover Feast hadn't been

observed like that in Israel since the days of Samuel the prophet. None of the kings of Israel had ever celebrated a Passover Feast like Josiah's. He celebrated it with the priests and Levites. All the people of Judah and Israel were there along with the people of Jerusalem. He celebrated it with them too. ¹⁹That Passover Feast was celebrated in the 18th year of Josiah's rule.

Josiah Dies

²⁰Josiah had put the temple in order. After all of that, Necho went up to fight at Carchemish. He was king of Egypt. Carchemish was on the Euphrates River. Josiah marched out to meet Necho in battle. ²¹But Necho sent messengers to him. They said, "Josiah king of Judah, there isn't any trouble between you and me. I'm not attacking you at this time. I'm at war with another country. God told me to hurry. He's with me. So stop opposing him. If you don't, he'll destroy you."

²²But Josiah wouldn't turn away from Necho. Josiah wore different clothes so people wouldn't recognize him. He wanted to go to war against Necho. He wouldn't listen to what God had commanded Necho to say. Instead, Josiah went out to fight him on the plains of Megiddo.

²³Men who had bows shot arrows at King Josiah. After he was hit, he told his officers, "Take me away. I'm badly wounded." ²⁴So they took him out of his chariot. They put him in his other chariot. They brought him to Jerusalem. There he died. He was buried in the tombs of his family. All the people of Judah and Jerusalem mourned for him.

²⁵Jeremiah wrote songs of sadness about Josiah. To this day all the male and female singers remember Josiah by singing those songs. That became a practice in Israel. The songs are written down in the Book of the Songs of Sadness.

²⁶Josiah did many things that showed he was faithful to the LORD. Those things and the other events of Josiah's rule were in keeping with what is written in the Law of the LORD. ²⁷All the events from beginning to end are written down. They are written in the records of the kings of Israel and Judah. ¹The people of the land went and got Jehoahaz. He was the son of Josiah. The people made Jehoahaz king in Jerusalem in place of his father.

36

2 Chr. 35:25 This "Book of the Songs of Sadness" is known as a *lament*. No copies of this collection of songs exist today. But it sounds like some of the songs Penny writes when she thinks about eating salmon (she's allergic).

Jehoahaz King of Judah

²Jehoahaz was 23 years old when he became king. He ruled in Jerusalem for three months. ³The king of Egypt removed him from his throne in Jerusalem. The king of Egypt made the people of Judah pay him a huge tax. The tax was almost four tons of silver and 75 pounds of gold. ⁴Necho, the king of Egypt, made Eliakim king over Judah and Jerusalem. Eliakim was a brother of Jehoahaz. Necho changed Eliakim's name to Jehoiakim. But Necho took Eliakim's brother Jehoahaz with him to Egypt.

Jehoiakim King of Judah

⁵Jehoiakim was 25 years old when he became king. He ruled in Jerusalem for 11 years. He did what was evil in the eyes of the LORD his God. ⁶Nebuchadnezzar attacked him. Nebuchadnezzar was king of Babylon. He put Jehoiakim in bronze chains. And he took him to Babylon. ⁷Nebuchadnezzar also took to Babylon objects from the LORD's temple. He put them in his own temple there.

⁸The other events of Jehoiakim's rule are written in the records of the kings of Israel and Judah. He did things the LORD hated. Those things and everything that happened to him are also written in those records. Jehoiakim's son Jehoiachin became the next king after him.

Jehoiachin King of Judah

[9] Jehoiachin was 18 years old when he became king. He ruled in Jerusalem for three months and ten days. He did what was evil in the eyes of the LORD. [10] In the spring, King Nebuchadnezzar sent for him. He brought him to Babylon. He also brought things of value from the LORD's temple. He made Zedekiah king over Judah and Jerusalem. Zedekiah was Jehoiachin's uncle.

Zedekiah King of Judah

[11] Zedekiah was 21 years old when he became king. He ruled in Jerusalem for 11 years. [12] He did what was evil in the eyes of the LORD his God. He didn't pay any attention to the message the LORD spoke through Jeremiah the prophet. [13] Zedekiah also refused to remain under the control of King Nebuchadnezzar. The king had forced Zedekiah to make a promise in God's name. But Zedekiah's heart became very stubborn. He wouldn't turn to the LORD, the God of Israel. [14] And that's not all. The people and all the leaders of the priests became more and more unfaithful. They followed all the practices of the nations. The LORD hated those practices. The people and leaders made the LORD's temple "unclean." The LORD had set the temple in Jerusalem apart in a special way for himself.

The Fall of Jerusalem

[15] The LORD, the God of Israel, sent word to his people through his messengers. He sent it to them again and again. He took pity on his people. He also took pity on the temple where he lived. [16] But God's people made fun of his messengers. They hated his words. They laughed at his prophets. Finally the LORD's great anger was stirred up against his people. Nothing could save them. [17] The LORD brought the king of the Babylonians against them. The Babylonian army killed their young people with their swords at the temple. They didn't spare young men or young women. They didn't spare the old people or weak people either. God handed all of them over to Nebuchadnezzar. [18] Nebuchadnezzar carried off to Babylon all the objects from God's temple. Some of those things were large. Others were small. He carried off the treasures of the temple. He also carried off the treasures

that belonged to the king and his officials. [19] The Babylonians set God's temple on fire. They broke down the wall of Jerusalem. They burned all the palaces. They destroyed everything of value there.

[20] Nebuchadnezzar took the rest of the people to Babylon as prisoners. They had escaped from being killed by swords. They served him and those who ruled after him. That lasted until the kingdom of Persia came to power. [21] The land of Israel enjoyed its sabbath years. It rested. That deserted land wasn't farmed for a full 70 years. What the LORD had spoken through Jeremiah came true.

[22] It was the first year of the rule of Cyrus. He was king of Persia. The LORD inspired him to send a message all through his kingdom. It happened so that what the LORD had spoken through Jeremiah would come true. The message was written down. It said,

[23] "Cyrus, the king of Persia, says,

"'The LORD is the God of heaven. He has given me all the kingdoms on earth. He has appointed me to build a temple for him at Jerusalem in Judah. Any of his people among you may go up to Jerusalem. And may the LORD their God be with them.'"

WOOTON'S FUN FACTS
2 Chr. 36:10

Even though it shows up in a movie, no one really knows what happened to the Ark of the Covenant. It's a big mystery. King Nebuchadnezzar took *all* the temple objects and burned the rest, according to verse 19. The Ark isn't listed in the items from Jeremiah 52:12–23. Do you think it's still out there?

Ezra

Our adventure through the Scriptures has brought us to the end of the era of the kings. The nations of Israel and Judah were defeated by their enemies, and many of the people were carried off into captivity (Israel to Assyria in the 730s BC and Judah to Babylon about 150 years later). The books of Ezra, Nehemiah, and Esther describe events *after* those devastating exiles.

When the Babylonians were in turn defeated by the Persians, King Cyrus didn't mind if God's people wanted to return to their homeland. He gave back the sacred items that the Babylonians had confiscated from the Temple, and he even took up a collection to help pay for their return journey (chapter 1). Still, the scene upon their return was distressing. Jerusalem stood in ruins, its walls and even the Temple itself destroyed. Rebuilding the Temple was a top priority.

Yet all was not well (to borrow the colloquialism). Many of the priests had intermarried with unbelieving neighbors, were neglecting sacrifices and worship services, and were generally leading lives in clear defiance of God's laws. By the time Ezra arrived in Jerusalem, he had to make some difficult and unpleasant decisions to get his people to return to obedience to God.

WHat's it MeaN, EUGeNE?

Inerrancy—The quality of being *without error*. While I might tease Ms. Kendall that I am never wrong, the only thing that can truly lay claim to being "without error" is the Bible—the inspired Word of God. Because God has "breathed life into all Scripture," as 2 Timothy 3:16 says, we believe it is entirely reliable, trustworthy, and free of mistakes and contradictions of any kind. Jesus Himself said as much in John 17:17 when He prayed for His disciples: "Use the truth to make them holy. Your word is truth."

Cyrus Helps the Jews to Return to Jerusalem

1 It was the first year of the rule of Cyrus. He was king of Persia. The LORD inspired him to send a message all through his kingdom. It happened so that what the LORD had spoken through Jeremiah would come true. The message was written down. It said,

²"Cyrus, the king of Persia, says,

"'The LORD is the God of heaven. He has given me all the kingdoms on earth. He has appointed me to build a temple for him at Jerusalem in Judah. ³Any of his people among you may go up to Jerusalem and build the LORD's temple. He is the God of Israel. He is the God who is in Jerusalem. And may their God be with them. ⁴The people still left alive in every place must bring gifts to the people going. They must provide silver and gold to the people going up to Jerusalem. The people must bring goods and livestock. They should also bring any offerings they choose to. All those gifts will be for God's temple in Jerusalem.'"

⁵Then everyone God had inspired prepared to go. They wanted to go up to Jerusalem and build the LORD's temple there. They included the family leaders of Judah and Benjamin. They also included the priests and Levites. ⁶All their neighbors helped them. They gave them silver and gold objects. They gave them goods and livestock. And they gave them gifts of great value. All those things were added to the other offerings the people chose to give.

⁷King Cyrus also brought out the objects that belonged to the LORD's temple. Nebuchadnezzar had carried them off from Jerusalem. He had put them in the temple of his own god. ⁸Cyrus, the king of Persia, told Mithredath to bring them out. Mithredath was in charge of the temple treasures. He counted those objects. Then he gave them to Sheshbazzar, the prince of Judah.

⁹ Here is a list of the objects.

There were 30 gold dishes.
There were 1,000 silver dishes.
There were 29 silver pans.

Ezra 1:2 The journey from Babylon to Jerusalem is 900 miles. The average person takes about two thousand steps per mile, so this journey would be 1.8 million steps. It's too bad they didn't have gel shoe inserts back then. They save my feet when I have to do all the steps on my mail route.

¹⁰ There were 30 gold bowls.
There were 410 matching silver bowls.
There were 1,000 other objects.

¹¹ The total number of gold and silver objects was 5,400.

Sheshbazzar brought all of these back with him to Jerusalem. So Sheshbazzar and the Jews who had been forced to leave Judah came up from Babylon to Jerusalem.

The List of the Jews Who Returned to Judah

2 Nebuchadnezzar had taken many Jews away from the land of Judah. He had forced them to go to Babylon as prisoners. Now they returned to Jerusalem and Judah. All of them went back to their own towns. Nebuchadnezzar was king of Babylon. ²The leaders of the Jews included Zerubbabel, Joshua, Nehemiah, Seraiah and Reelaiah. They also included Mordecai, Bilshan, Mispar, Bigvai, Rehum and Baanah.

Here is a list of the men of Israel who returned home.

³ There were 2,172 from the family line of Parosh.
⁴ There were 372 from Shephatiah.
⁵ There were 775 from Arah.

⁶ There were 2,812 from Pahath-Moab through the family line of Jeshua and Joab.

⁷ There were 1,254 from Elam.

⁸ There were 945 from Zattu.

⁹ There were 760 from Zakkai.

¹⁰ There were 642 from Bani.

¹¹ There were 623 from Bebai.

¹² There were 1,222 from Azgad.

¹³ There were 666 from Adonikam.

¹⁴ There were 2,056 from Bigvai.

¹⁵ There were 454 from Adin.

¹⁶ There were 98 from Ater through the family line of Hezekiah.

¹⁷ There were 323 from Bezai.

¹⁸ There were 112 from Jorah.

¹⁹ There were 223 from Hashum.

²⁰ There were 95 from Gibbar.

²¹ There were 123 from the men of Bethlehem.

²² There were 56 from Netophah.

²³ There were 128 from Anathoth.

²⁴ There were 42 from Azmaveth.

²⁵ There were 743 from Kiriath Jearim, Kephirah and Beeroth.

²⁶ There were 621 from Ramah and Geba.

²⁷ There were 122 from Mikmash.

²⁸ There were 223 from Bethel and Ai.

²⁹ There were 52 from Nebo.

³⁰ There were 156 from Magbish.

³¹ There were 1,254 from the other Elam.

³² There were 320 from Harim.

³³ There were 725 from Lod, Hadid and Ono.

³⁴ There were 345 from Jericho.

³⁵ There were 3,630 from Senaah.

³⁶ Here is a list of the priests. There were 973 from the family line of Jedaiah through the line of Jeshua.

³⁷ There were 1,052 from Immer.

³⁸ There were 1,247 from Pashhur.

³⁹ There were 1,017 from Harim.

⁴⁰ Here is a list of the Levites. There were 74 from the family lines of Jeshua and Kadmiel. Kadmiel was from the line of Hodaviah.

⁴¹ Here is a list of the musicians. There were 128 from the family line of Asaph.

⁴² Here is a list of the men who guarded the gates. There were 139 from the family lines of Shallum, Ater, Talmon, Akkub, Hatita and Shobai.

⁴³ Here is a list of the members of the family lines of the temple servants. Ziha, Hasupha, Tabbaoth,

⁴⁴ Keros, Siaha, Padon,

⁴⁵ Lebanah, Hagabah, Akkub,

⁴⁶ Hagab, Shalmai, Hanan,

⁴⁷ Giddel, Gahar, Reaiah,

⁴⁸ Rezin, Nekoda, Gazzam,

⁴⁹ Uzza, Paseah, Besai,

⁵⁰ Asnah, Meunim, Nephusim,

⁵¹ Bakbuk, Hakupha, Harhur,

⁵² Bazluth, Mehida, Harsha,

⁵³ Barkos, Sisera, Temah,

⁵⁴ Neziah, Hatipha

⁵⁵ Here is a list of the members of the family lines of the servants of Solomon. Sotai, Hassophereth, Peruda,

⁵⁶ Jaala, Darkon, Giddel,

⁵⁷ Shephatiah, Hattil, Pokereth-Hazzebaim, Ami

⁵⁸ The total number of the members of the family lines of the temple servants and the servants of Solomon was 392.

⁵⁹ Many people came up to Judah from the towns of Tel Melah, Tel Harsha, Kerub, Addon and Immer. But they weren't able to prove that their families belonged to the people of Israel.

⁶⁰ There were 652 of them from the family lines of Delaiah, Tobiah and Nekoda.

⁶¹ Here is a list of the members of the family lines of the priests. They were Hobaiah, Hakkoz and Barzillai. Barzillai had married a daughter of Barzillai from Gilead. So he was also called Barzillai.

⁶² The priests looked for their family records. But they couldn't find them. So they weren't able to serve as priests. They were "unclean." ⁶³The governor gave them an order. He told them not to eat any of the most sacred food. They had to wait until there was a priest who could use the Urim and Thummim. The priest would use them to find out what the LORD wanted the people to do.

⁶⁴ The total number of the entire group that returned was 42,360. ⁶⁵That didn't include their 7,337 male and female slaves. There were also 200 male and female singers. ⁶⁶And there were 736 horses, 245 mules, ⁶⁷435 camels and 6,720 donkeys.

⁶⁸All the people arrived at the place in Jerusalem where the LORD's temple would be rebuilt. Then some of the leaders of the families brought offerings they chose to give. They would be used for rebuilding the house of God. It would stand in the same place it had been before. ⁶⁹The people gave money for the work. It was based on how much they had. They gave 1,100 pounds of gold. They also gave three tons of silver. And they gave 100 sets of clothes for the priests. All of that was added to the temple treasure.

⁷⁰The priests and Levites made their homes in their own towns. So did the musicians, the men who guarded the gates, and the temple servants. The rest of the Israelites also made their homes in their own towns.

The People Rebuild the Altar

3 The Israelites had made their homes in their towns. In the seventh month all of them gathered together in Jerusalem. ²Then Joshua began to build the altar for burnt offerings to honor the God of Israel. Joshua was the son of Jozadak. The other priests helped Joshua. So did Zerubbabel and his men. They built the altar according to what is written in the Law of Moses. Moses was a man of God. Zerubbabel was the son of Shealtiel. ³The people who built the altar were afraid of the nations around them. But they built it anyway. They set it up where it had stood before. They sacrificed burnt offerings on it to the LORD. They offered the morning and evening sacrifices on it. ⁴Then they celebrated the Feast of Booths. They did it according to what is written in the Law. They sacrificed the number of burnt offerings required for each day. ⁵After they celebrated the Feast of Booths, they sacrificed the regular burnt offerings. They offered the New Moon sacrifices. They also offered the sacrifices for all the appointed sacred feasts of the LORD. And they sacrificed the offerings the people chose to give him. ⁶On the first day of the seventh month they began to offer burnt offerings to the LORD. They did

it even though the foundation of the LORD's temple hadn't been laid yet.

The People Begin to Rebuild the Temple

⁷The people gave money to those who worked with stone and those who worked with wood. They gave food and drink and olive oil to the people of Sidon and Tyre. Then those people brought cedar logs down from Lebanon to the Mediterranean Sea. They floated them down to Joppa. Cyrus, the king of Persia, authorized them to do it.

⁸It was the second month of the second year after they had arrived at the house of God in Jerusalem. Zerubbabel, the son of Shealtiel, began the work. Joshua, the son of Jozadak, helped him. So did everyone else. That included the priests and Levites. It also included the rest of those who had returned to Jerusalem. They had been prisoners in the land of Babylon. Levites who were 20 years old or more were appointed to be in charge of building the LORD's house. ⁹Those who joined together to direct the work included Joshua and his sons and brothers. They also included Kadmiel and his sons. And they included the sons of Henadad and their sons and brothers. All those men were Levites. Kadmiel and his sons were members of the family line of Hodaviah.

Jason's Jargon

EZRA 3

Your next mission is to hunt through this chapter for the word *foundation*. A foundation is the lowest and sturdiest part of a building, on top of which everything in the building rests.

¹⁰The builders laid the foundation of the LORD's temple. Then the priests came. They were wearing their special clothes. They brought their trumpets with them. The Levites who belonged to the family line of Asaph also came. They brought their cymbals with them. The priests and Levites took their places to praise the LORD. They did everything just as King David had required them

to. [11]They sang to the LORD. They praised him. They gave thanks to him. They said,

"The LORD is good.
His faithful love to Israel continues forever."

All the people gave a loud shout. They praised the LORD. They were glad because the foundation of the LORD's temple had been laid. [12]But many of the older priests and Levites and family leaders wept out loud. They had seen the first temple. So when they saw the foundation of the second temple being laid, they wept. Others shouted with joy. [13]No one could tell the difference between the shouts of joy and the sounds of weeping. That's because the people made so much noise. The sound was heard far away.

Enemies Oppose the Rebuilding of the Temple

4 The people who had returned from Babylon were building a temple to honor the LORD. He is the God of Israel. The enemies of Judah and Benjamin heard about it. [2]Then those enemies came to Zerubbabel. The family leaders of Israel were with him. The enemies said, "We want to help you build. We're just like you. We worship your God. We offer sacrifices to him. We've been doing that ever since the time of Esarhaddon. He was king of Assyria. He brought our people here."

[3]Zerubbabel and Joshua answered them. So did the rest of the family leaders of Israel. They said, "You can't help us build a temple to honor our God. You aren't part of us. We'll build it ourselves. We'll do it to honor the LORD, the God of Israel. Cyrus, the king of Persia, commanded us to build it."

[4]Then the nations around Judah tried to make its people lose hope. They wanted to make them afraid to go on building. [5]So those nations paid some of the Jewish officials to work against the people of Judah. They wanted their plans to fail. They did it during the whole time Cyrus was king of Persia. They kept doing it until Darius became king.

Later Enemies Also Oppose the Jews

[6]The enemies of the Jews brought charges against the people of Judah and Jerusalem. It happened when Xerxes began to rule over Persia.

WOOTON'S FUN FACTS

Ezra 4:7

Verses 4:8 to 6:18 and 7:12–26 were written in a language called Aramaic and not in Hebrew like most of the Bible. The book of Daniel also has some Aramaic writing.

[7]Then Artaxerxes became king of Persia. During his rule, Bishlam, Mithredath, Tabeel and their friends wrote a letter to Artaxerxes. It was written in the Aramaic language. And it used the Aramaic alphabet.

[8]Rehum and Shimshai also wrote a letter to King Artaxerxes. Rehum was the commanding officer. Shimshai was the secretary. Their letter was against the people of Jerusalem. It said,

[9]We, Rehum and Shimshai, are writing this letter. Rehum is the commanding officer. Shimshai is the secretary. Our friends join us in writing. They include the judges, officials and managers in charge of the people from Persia, Uruk and Babylon. They are also over the Elamites from Susa. [10]And they are over those who were forced to leave their countries. The great King Ashurbanipal, who is worthy of honor, forced them to leave. He moved them to the city of Samaria. He also moved them to other places west of the Euphrates River.

[11]Here is a copy of the letter sent to Artaxerxes.

We are sending this letter to you, King Artaxerxes.

It is from your servants who live west of the Euphrates River.

[12]We want you to know about the people who left you and have come up to us. They have gone to Jerusalem and are rebuilding that evil city. It has caused trouble for a long time. Those people are making its walls like new again. They are repairing the foundations.

[13]Here is something else we want you to know. Suppose this city is rebuilt. And suppose its walls are made like new again. Then no more taxes, gifts or fees will be collected. And sooner or later there will be less money for you. [14]We owe a lot to you. We don't want to see dishonor brought on you. So we're sending this letter to tell you what is going on. [15]Then you can have a search made in the official records. Have someone check the records of the kings who ruled before you. If you do, you will find out that Jerusalem is an evil city. It causes trouble for kings and countries. For a long time the city has refused to let anyone rule over it. That's why it was destroyed. [16]We want you to know that this city shouldn't be rebuilt. Its walls shouldn't be made like new again. If

that happens, you won't have anything left west of the Euphrates River.

[17]The king replied,

I am writing this letter to Rehum, the commanding officer. I am also writing it to Shimshai the secretary. And I am writing it to your friends living in Samaria and in other places west of the Euphrates River.

I give you my greetings.

[18]The letter you sent us has been read to me. It has been explained to me in my language. [19]I gave an order. I had a search made. Here is what we found out. Jerusalem has a long history of turning against the kings of the countries that have ruled over it. It has refused to remain under their control. It is always stirring up trouble. [20]Jerusalem has had powerful kings. Some of them ruled over everything west of the Euphrates. Taxes, gifts and fees were paid to them. [21]So give an order to those men. Make them stop their work. Then the city won't be rebuilt until I give the order. [22]Pay careful attention to this matter. Why should we let this danger grow? That would not be in our best interests.

[23]The copy of the letter of King Artaxerxes was read to Rehum and Shimshai the secretary. It was also read to their friends. Right away they went to the Jews in Jerusalem. They forced them to stop their work.

[24]And so the work on the house of God in Jerusalem came to a stop. No more work was done on it until the second year that Darius was king of Persia.

Tattenai's Letter to King Darius

5 Haggai and Zechariah, the prophets, prophesied to the Jews in Judah and Jerusalem. They spoke to them in the name of the God of Israel. God had spoken to those prophets. Zechariah belonged to the family line of Iddo. [2]Zerubbabel, the son of Shealtiel, began to work. So did Joshua, the son of Jozadak. They began to rebuild the house of God in Jerusalem. The prophets of God were right there with them. They were helping them.

WOOTON'S FUN FACTS

Ezra 4:11

Artaxerxes was a magician. And not the good kind who pulled rabbits out of hats, did card tricks, and made doves appear. He pretended to be the son of Cyrus so he could take the throne. I bet he couldn't even get out of handcuffs.

[3]At that time Tattenai was governor of the land west of the Euphrates River. He and Shethar-Bozenai and their friends went to the Jews. They asked them, "Who authorized you to rebuild this temple? Who told you that you could finish it?" [4]They also asked, "What are the names of the people who are putting up this building?" [5]But the God of the Jews was watching over their elders. So they didn't have to stop their work. First a report would have to be sent to Darius. Then they would have to receive his answer in writing.

[6]Here is a copy of the letter sent to King Darius. It was from Tattenai, the governor of the land west of the Euphrates. Shethar-Bozenai joined him in writing it. So did their friends. They were officials of that land. [7]The report they sent to the king said,

We are sending this letter to you, King Darius.

We give you our most friendly greetings.

[8]We want you to know that we went to the land of Judah. We went to the temple of the great God. The people are building it with large stones. They are putting wooden beams in the walls. The people are working hard. The work is moving ahead very quickly under the direction of the people.

[9]We asked the elders some questions. We said to them, "Who authorized you to rebuild this temple? Who told you that you could finish it?" [10]We also asked them what their names were. We wanted to write down the names of their leaders for your information.

[11]Here is the answer they gave us. They said,

"We serve the God of heaven and earth. We are rebuilding the temple that was built many years ago. The great King Solomon built it and finished it. [12]But our people made the God of heaven angry. So he handed them over to Nebuchadnezzar from Chaldea. He was king of Babylon. He destroyed this temple. He forced the Jews to leave their own country. He took them away to Babylon.

[13]"But King Cyrus gave an order to rebuild this house of God. He gave it in the first year he was king of Babylon. [14]He even removed some gold and silver objects from the temple of Babylon. Nebuchadnezzar had brought them there from the house of God in Jerusalem. He had taken them to the temple in Babylon. Then King Cyrus brought the objects out. He gave them to a man named Sheshbazzar. Cyrus had appointed him as governor. [15]Cyrus told him, 'Take these objects with you. Go and put them in the temple in Jerusalem. Rebuild the house of God in the same place where it stood before.'

[16]"So Sheshbazzar made the trip to Jerusalem. He laid the foundations of the house of God there. From that day until now the people have been working on it. But they haven't finished it yet."

[17]If it pleases you, King Darius, let a search be made in the royal records. Search the official records of the kings of Babylon. Find out whether King Cyrus really did give an order to rebuild this house of God in Jerusalem. Then tell us what you decide to do.

King Darius's Reply to Tattenai

6 King Darius gave an order. He had a search made in the official records stored among the treasures at Babylon. [2]A book was found in a safe storeroom at Ecbatana in the land of Media. Here is what was written on it.

This is my official reply to your letter.

[3]In the first year that Cyrus was king, he gave an order. It concerned God's temple in Jerusalem. King Cyrus said,

Rebuild the temple. Then the Jews can offer sacrifices there. Lay its foundations. The temple must be 90 feet high and 90 feet wide. [4]Its walls must have three layers of large stones. They must also have a layer of beautiful wood. Use money from the royal treasures to pay for everything. [5]The gold and silver objects from the house of God must be returned. Nebuchadnezzar had taken them from the first temple in Jerusalem. And he had brought them to Babylon. Now they must be returned to their places in the temple at Jerusalem. They must be put in the house of God there.

[6]Tattenai, you are governor of the land west of the Euphrates River. I want you to stay away from the temple in Jerusalem. I also want you, Shethar-Bozenai, and you other officials of that area to stay away from it. [7]Don't try to stop the work on the temple of God. Let the governor of the Jews and their elders rebuild the house of their God. Let them build it in the same place where it stood before.

[8]Here is what I want you to do for the elders of the Jews. Here is how you must help them to build the house of their God.

Pay all their expenses from the royal treasures. Use the money you collect from the people who live west of the Euphrates. Don't let the work on the temple stop. [9]Don't fail to give the priests in Jerusalem what they ask for each day. Give them what they need. Give them young bulls, rams and male lambs. The priests can use them to sacrifice burnt offerings to the God of heaven. Also give them wheat, salt, wine and olive oil. [10]Give them those things so they can offer sacrifices that please the God of heaven. And I want them to pray that things will go well for me and my sons.

[11]Don't change this order. If anyone tries to change it, they must be put to death. A pole must be pulled from their house. The pole must be stuck through their body. Because that person tried to change my royal order, their house must be broken to pieces. [12]God has chosen to put his Name in the temple at Jerusalem. May he wipe out any king or nation that lifts a hand to change this order. May he also wipe out anyone who tries to destroy the temple in Jerusalem.

That's what I have ordered. I am King Darius. Make sure you carry out my order.

The Temple Is Completed and Set Apart to God

[13]The governor Tattenai and Shethar-Bozenai carried out King Darius's order. And so did their friends. [14]The elders of the Jews continued to build the temple. They enjoyed great success because of the preaching of Haggai and Zechariah, the prophets. Zechariah belonged to the family line of Iddo. The people finished building the temple. That's what the God of Israel had commanded them to do. Cyrus and Darius had given orders allowing them to do it. Later, Artaxerxes supplied many things that were needed in the temple. Those three men were kings of Persia. [15]So the temple was completed on the third day of the month of Adar. It was in the sixth year that Darius was king.

[16]When the house of God was set apart, the people of Israel celebrated with joy. The priests and Levites joined them. So did the rest of those who had returned from the land of Babylon. [17]When the house of God was set apart to him, the people sacrificed 100 bulls. They also sacrificed 200 rams and 400 male lambs. As a sin offering for the whole nation of Israel, the people sacrificed 12 male goats. One goat was sacrificed for each tribe in Israel. [18]The priests were appointed to their groups. And the Levites were appointed to their groups. All of them served God at Jerusalem. They served him in keeping with what is written in the Book of Moses.

The People Celebrate the Passover Feast

[19]The people who had returned from the land of Babylon celebrated the Passover Feast. It was on the 14th day of the first month. [20]The priests and Levites had made themselves pure and "clean." The Levites killed Passover lambs for the people who had returned from Babylon. They also did it for themselves and their relatives, the priests. [21]So the Israelites who had returned ate the Passover lamb. They ate it together with all those who had separated themselves from the practices of their Gentile neighbors. Those practices were "unclean." The people worshiped the LORD. He is the God of Israel. [22]For seven days they celebrated the Feast of Unleavened Bread with joy. That's because the LORD had filled them with joy. They were glad because he had

changed the mind of the king of Persia. So the king had helped them with the work on the house of the God of Israel.

Ezra Comes to Jerusalem

7 After all these things had happened, Ezra came up to Jerusalem from Babylon. It was during the rule of Artaxerxes. He was king of Persia. Ezra was the son of Seraiah. Seraiah was the son of Azariah. Azariah was the son of Hilkiah. [2]Hilkiah was the son of Shallum. Shallum was the son of Zadok. Zadok was the son of Ahitub. [3]Ahitub was the son of Amariah. Amariah was the son of Azariah. Azariah was the son of Meraioth. [4]Meraioth was the son of Zerahiah. Zerahiah was the son of Uzzi. Uzzi was the son of Bukki. [5]Bukki was the son of Abishua. Abishua was the son of Phinehas. Phinehas was the son of Eleazar. And Eleazar was the son of Aaron the chief priest. [6]So Ezra came up from Babylon. He was a teacher who knew the Law of Moses very well. The LORD, the God of Israel, had given Israel that law. The king had given Ezra everything he asked for. That's because the LORD his God helped him. [7]Some of the Israelites came up to Jerusalem too. They included priests, Levites and musicians. They also included the temple servants and those who guarded the temple gates. It was in the seventh year that Artaxerxes was king.

[8]Ezra arrived in Jerusalem in the fifth month of the seventh year of the king's rule. [9]Ezra had begun his journey from Babylon on the first day of the first month. He arrived in Jerusalem on the first day of the fifth month. That's because God was gracious to him and helped him. [10]Ezra had committed himself to study and obey the Law of the LORD. He also wanted to teach the LORD's rules and laws in Israel.

King Artaxerxes's Letter to Ezra

[11]Ezra was a priest and teacher of the Law. He was an educated man. He knew the LORD's commands and rules for Israel very well. Here is a copy of a letter King Artaxerxes had given to Ezra. It said,

[12]I, Artaxerxes, am writing this letter. I am the greatest king of all.

I have given it to Ezra the priest. He is the teacher of the Law of the God of heaven.

I give you my greetings.

[13]Ezra, I am giving an order about the Israelites in my kingdom. Any of them who want to go to Jerusalem with you may go. The order also allows priests and Levites to go with you. [14]I and my seven advisers are sending you to see how things are going in Judah and Jerusalem. Find out whether the people there are obeying the Law of your God. You have a copy of that law with you. [15]I and my advisers have freely given some silver and gold to the God of Israel. He is the God who lives in Jerusalem. Take that silver and gold with you. [16]Also take any other silver and gold you can get from the land of Babylon. And take the offerings the people and priests choose to give for the temple of their God in Jerusalem. [17]Make sure you use the money to buy bulls, rams and male lambs. Also buy their grain offerings and drink offerings. Then sacrifice them on the altar of the temple of your God in Jerusalem. [18]You and the other Jews can do what you think is best with the rest of the silver and gold. Do what your God wants you to do. [19]Give to the God of Jerusalem all the things you are responsible for. Use them for

Ezra 7:12 When I think of important government jobs, I think of the president, the secretary of agriculture, and the postmaster general. So Ezra being the "scribe" doesn't sound all that impressive. But he had a big job. Think of Ezra as the secretary of state for Jewish affairs.

worshiping your God in his temple.
²⁰You might need to supply some
other things for the temple of your
God. If you do, take them from
among the royal treasures.

²¹I, King Artaxerxes, also give this
order. It applies to all those who are
in charge of the treasures west of the
Euphrates River. Make sure you provide anything Ezra the priest might
ask you to give. He is the teacher of
the Law of the God of heaven. ²²Give
Ezra up to three and three-fourths
tons of silver. Give him up to 18 tons
of wheat. Give him up to 600 gallons
of wine and up to 600 gallons of olive oil. And give him as much salt as
he needs. ²³Work hard for the temple
of the God of heaven. Do everything
he has required. I don't want him
to be angry with my kingdom and
the kingdom of my sons. ²⁴Here is
something else I want you to know.
You have no authority to collect taxes, gifts or fees from these people.
You may not collect them from the
priests, Levites or musicians. You
may not collect them from those
who guard the temple gates. You may
not collect them from the temple servants. And you may not collect them
from other workers at the house of
God in Jerusalem.

²⁵Ezra, appoint judges and other
court officials. When you do it, use
the wisdom your God gives you.
Those you appoint should do what
is right and fair when they judge
people. They should do it for everyone who lives west of the Euphrates
River. They should do it for everyone
who knows the laws of your God.
And I want you to teach the people
who don't know those laws. ²⁶Anyone
who doesn't obey the law of your God
must be punished. The same thing
applies to anyone who doesn't obey
my law. The people must be punished
in keeping with the laws they have
broken. Some of them must be put to
death. Others must be forced to leave
the places where they live. Others
must have their property taken away
from them. Still others must be put
in prison.

²⁷So here is what I, Ezra, say to you
people of Israel. "Give praise to the Lord.
He is the God of our people who lived long
ago. He has put it in the king's heart to
bring honor to the Lord's temple in Jerusalem. The king has honored the Lord in his
letter. ²⁸The Lord has been kind to me. He
has caused the king and his advisers to be
kind to me. In fact, all the king's powerful
officials have been kind to me. The strong
hand of the Lord my God helped me. That
gave me new strength. So I gathered together leaders from Israel to go up to Jerusalem with me."

The Family Leaders Who Returned to Jerusalem With Ezra

8 Many family leaders came up to
Jerusalem with me from Babylon.
So did others who were listed with
them. It was during the time when
Artaxerxes was king. Here is a list of
those who came.

² Gershom came from the family line
of Phinehas.
Daniel came from the family line of
Ithamar.
Hattush came from the family line of
David. ³Hattush also belonged to
the family of Shekaniah.
Zechariah came from the family
line of Parosh. The total number
of men who were listed with him
was 150.
⁴ Eliehoenai came from the family
line of Pahath-Moab. Eliehoenai
was the son of Zerahiah. The total
number of men with him was 200.
⁵ Shekaniah came from the family line
of Zattu. Shekaniah was the son of
Jahaziel. The total number of men
with him was 300.
⁶ Ebed came from the family line of
Adin. Ebed was the son of Jonathan. The total number of men
with him was 50.
⁷ Jeshaiah came from the family line
of Elam. Jeshaiah was the son of
Athaliah. The total number of
men with him was 70.
⁸ Zebadiah came from the family line
of Shephatiah. Zebadiah was the
son of Michael. The total number
of men with him was 80.

⁹ Obadiah came from the family line of Joab. Obadiah was the son of Jehiel. The total number of men with him was 218.

¹⁰ Shelomith came from the family line of Bani. Shelomith was the son of Josiphiah. The total number of men with him was 160.

¹¹ Zechariah came from the family line of Bebai. Zechariah was the son of Bebai. The total number of men with him was 28.

¹² Johanan came from the family line of Azgad. Johanan was the son of Hakkatan. The total number of men with him was 110.

¹³ Eliphelet, Jeuel and Shemaiah came from the family line of Adonikam. Some members of their family had gone up to Jerusalem before them. The total number of men with them was 60.

¹⁴ Uthai and Zakkur came from the family line of Bigvai. The total number of men with them was 70.

Ezra Leads Many Jews Back to Jerusalem

¹⁵ I gathered the people together at the canal that flows toward Ahava. We camped there for three days. I looked for Levites among the people and priests. But I didn't find any. ¹⁶ So I sent for Eliezer, Ariel, Shemaiah, Elnathan and Jarib. I also sent for Elnathan, Nathan, Zechariah and Meshullam. All of them were leaders. And I sent for Joiarib and Elnathan. They were very well educated. ¹⁷ I ordered all those men to go to Iddo. He was the leader in Kasiphia. He and his Levite relatives were temple servants there. I told my men what to say to them. I wanted Iddo and his Levite relatives to bring some attendants to us for the house of our God. ¹⁸ God was gracious to us and helped us. So they brought us Sherebiah, a very capable man. He came from the family line of Mahli. Mahli was the son of Levi. Levi was a son of Israel. They also brought us Sherebiah's sons and brothers. The total number of men was 18. ¹⁹ And they brought Hashabiah and his brothers and nephews. They brought them together with Jeshaiah. He came from the family line of Merari. The total number of men was 20. ²⁰ They also brought 220 of the temple servants. That was a special group David and his officials had established. They were supposed to help the Levites. All of them were listed by name.

²¹ By the canal that flows toward Ahava, I announced a fast. I told the people not to eat any food. In that way, we made ourselves humble in God's sight. We prayed that he would give us and our children a safe journey. We asked him to keep safe everything we owned. ²² I was ashamed to ask King Artaxerxes for soldiers and horsemen. They could have kept us safe from enemies on the road. But we had told the king that our God would keep us safe. We had said, "Our God is gracious and helps everyone who looks to him. But he becomes very angry with anyone who deserts him." ²³ So we didn't eat anything. We prayed to our God about all these matters. And he answered our prayers.

²⁴ Then I set apart 12 of the leading priests. They were Sherebiah, Hashabiah and ten of their relatives. ²⁵ I weighed out to them the offering of silver and gold and other things. They had been given for the house of our God. The king, his advisers and officials, and all the Israelites who were there had given them. ²⁶ I weighed out 24 tons of silver and gave it to those men. I weighed out almost four tons of silver things. I weighed out almost four tons of gold. ²⁷ I weighed out 20 gold bowls. They weighed 19 pounds. I also weighed out two fine objects. The bronze they were made out of was highly polished. They were as priceless as gold.

²⁸ I said to those men, "You are set apart to the LORD. So are these things. The silver and gold were offered to the LORD by those who chose to give them. He is the God of your people. ²⁹ Guard all these things carefully until you weigh them out. Weigh them in the special rooms of the LORD's temple in Jerusalem. Do this in front of the leading priests and the Levites. Make sure the family leaders of Israel are watching." ³⁰ Then the priests and Levites received the silver and gold and sacred objects. All of them had been weighed out. They were going to be taken to the house of our God in Jerusalem.

³¹ On the 12th day of the first month we started out. We left the canal that flows toward Ahava. And we headed for Jerusalem. Our God helped us. He kept us safe from enemies and robbers along the way. ³² So we arrived in Jerusalem. There we rested for three days.

[33]On the fourth day we weighed out the silver and gold. We also weighed out the sacred objects. We weighed everything in the house of our God. We handed all of it over to Meremoth the priest. He was the son of Uriah. Eleazar, Jozabad and Noadiah were with him. Eleazar was the son of Phinehas. Jozabad was the son of Jeshua. Noadiah was the son of Binnui. Jozabad and Noadiah were Levites. [34]Everything was listed by number and weight. And the total weight was recorded at that time.

[35]Then the people sacrificed burnt offerings to the God of Israel. They had returned from Babylon. They offered 12 bulls for the whole nation of Israel. They offered 96 rams and 77 male lambs. All of that was a burnt offering to the LORD. They sacrificed 12 male goats as a sin offering. [36]They also handed over the king's orders. They gave them to the royal officials and governors who ruled over the land west of the Euphrates River. Then those men helped the people. They also did many things for the house of God.

Ezra Prays for the People

9 After all these things had been done, the leaders came to me. They said, "The people of Israel have committed sins. Even the priests and Levites have sinned. They haven't kept themselves separate from the nations around them. The LORD hates the practices of those nations. He hates what the Canaanites, Hittites, Perizzites and Jebusites do. He also hates what the Ammonites, Moabites, Egyptians and Amorites do. [2]The men of Israel have married the daughters of some of those people. They've also taken some of those women for their sons to marry. So they've mixed our holy nation with the nations around us. We leaders and officials have also married women who don't worship the LORD. By doing this, we have led the way in breaking our covenant with the LORD."

[3]When I heard that, I tore my inner robe and my coat. I pulled hair from my head and beard. I was so shocked I sat down. [4]Then everyone who trembled with fear at God's words gathered around me. That's because the people who had returned from Babylon had not been faithful. So I was very upset. I just sat there until the time of the evening sacrifice.

[5]Then I got up. I had been very sad for quite a while. My inner robe and my coat were torn. I fell down on my knees. I spread my hands out to the LORD my God. [6]I prayed,

"I'm filled with shame and dishonor, my God. I can hardly look to you and pray. That's because our sins are piled up above our heads. Our guilt reaches all the way to the heavens. [7]We are filled with it. It has been like that ever since the days of our people who lived long ago. Kings of other countries have killed many of us and our kings and priests with their swords. They've forced others to leave their own land. They've taken them away as prisoners. They've robbed others. They've made still others feel ashamed and dishonored. All these things have happened to us because we've committed so many sins. And that's how things still are to this day.

[8]"But you are the LORD our God. Now you have shown us your kindness for a short time. That's because you have allowed a few of us to remain here. Your temple has given us new hope. So you have made things easier for us. You have given us a little rest from our slavery. [9]We are still slaves. But you are our God. You haven't turned away from us. You haven't left us in our slavery. You have been kind to us. The kings of Persia have seen it. You have given us new life to repair your temple and rebuild it. You have given us a place of safety in Judah and Jerusalem.

[10]"You are our God. What can we say after the way you have blessed us? We have turned away from your commands. [11]You gave us your commands through your servants the prophets. You said, 'You are entering the land to take it as your own. The sinful practices of its people have made the land impure. They have filled it with their "unclean" acts from one end to the other. The LORD hates all their practices. [12]So don't let your daughters marry their sons. And don't let their daughters marry your sons. Don't make a peace treaty with them at any time. Then you will be strong. You will eat the good

Jason's Jargon

EZRA 9

Search this chapter for the word *dishonor*. When Ezra says he is filled with dishonor, he means he is no longer respectable in the eyes of God. The people had lost their integrity.

things the land produces. And you will leave all of it to your children as their share. They and their children after them will enjoy it forever.'

¹³"Our evil acts and our terrible sins have brought about the things that have happened to us. You are our God. Because we sinned so much, you should have punished us even more than you have. But you have left many of your people alive. ¹⁴Suppose we don't obey your commands again. And suppose we continue to marry people who commit sins that you hate. If we do, you will be so angry with us that you will destroy us. You won't leave us even a few people. You won't leave anyone alive. ¹⁵LORD, you are the God of Israel. You are holy. You always do what is right. Today you have left many of your people alive. Here we are with all our guilt. You see the guilt of our sin. Because we have sinned, not one of us can stand in front of you."

The People Admit They Have Sinned

10 Ezra was praying and admitting to God that his people had sinned. He was weeping and throwing himself down in front of the house of God. Then a large crowd of Israelites gathered around him. Men, women and children were there. They too wept bitterly. ²Shekaniah spoke to Ezra. Shekaniah was the son of Jehiel. He belonged to the family line of Elam. Shekaniah said, "We haven't been faithful to our God. We've married women from the nations around us. In spite of that, there is still hope for Israel. ³So let's make a covenant in front of our God. Let's promise to

send away all these women and their children. That's what you have advised us to do. Those who respect our God's commands have given us the same advice. We want to do what the Law says. ⁴Get up, Ezra. This matter is in your hands. Do what you need to. We will be behind you all the way. Be brave and do it."

⁵So Ezra got up. He made the leading priests and Levites and all the Israelites make a promise. He made them promise they would do what Shekaniah had suggested. And they made that promise. ⁶Then Ezra left the house of God. He went to Jehohanan's room. Jehohanan was the son of Eliashib. While Ezra was there, he didn't eat any food. He didn't drink any water. That's because he was filled with sadness. He mourned because the people weren't faithful to the LORD's commands. Those people were the ones who had returned from the land of Babylon.

⁷Then an announcement was sent all through Judah and Jerusalem. All the people who had returned were told to gather together in Jerusalem. ⁸They were supposed to come there before three days had passed. If they didn't, they would lose all their property. They would also be removed from the community of those who had returned. That's what the officials and elders had decided.

⁹Before the three days were over, all the men of Judah and Benjamin had gathered together in Jerusalem. It was the 20th day of the ninth month. They were sitting in the open area in front of the house of God. They were very upset by what they knew would happen. And they were upset because it was raining. ¹⁰Then Ezra the priest stood up. He said, "You haven't been faithful to the LORD. You have married women from other lands. So you have added to Israel's guilt. ¹¹Now honor the LORD, the God of your people. Then do what he wants you to do. Separate yourselves from the nations around you. Send away your wives from other lands."

¹²The whole community answered with a loud voice. They said, "You are right! We must do as you say. ¹³But there are a lot of people here. And it's the rainy season. So we can't stand outside. Besides, this matter can't be taken care of in just a day or two. That's because we have sinned terribly by what we've done. ¹⁴Our officials can act

for the whole community. Have everyone in our towns who has married a woman from another land come at a certain time. Tell them to come together with the elders and judges of each town. Then our God will no longer be angry with us concerning this whole matter." ¹⁵Only a few men opposed that. They included Jonathan and Jahzeiah. Meshullam and Shabbethai the Levite joined them. Jonathan was the son of Asahel. Jahzeiah was the son of Tikvah.

¹⁶So those who had returned did what had been suggested. Ezra the priest chose some family leaders. There was one from each family group. All of them were chosen by name. They sat down to check out each case. They started on the first day of the tenth month. ¹⁷By the first day of the first month they were finished. They had handled all the cases of the men who had married women from other lands.

A List of Those Who Had Married Women From Other Lands

¹⁸ Among the family lines of the priests, here are the men who had married women from other lands.

Maaseiah, Eliezer, Jarib and Gedaliah came from the family line of Joshua and his brothers. Joshua was the son of Jozadak. ¹⁹All of them made a firm promise to send their wives away. Each of these men brought a ram from his flock as a guilt offering.

²⁰ Hanani and Zebadiah
came from the family line of Immer.

²¹ Maaseiah and Elijah
came from the family line of Harim. So did Shemaiah, Jehiel and Uzziah.

²² Elioenai, Maaseiah and Ishmael
came from the family line of Pashhur. So did Nethanel, Jozabad and Elasah.

²³ Among the Levites, here are the men who had married women from other lands.
There were Jozabad, Shimei and Kelaiah. There were also Pethahiah, Judah and Eliezer. Kelaiah's other name was Kelita.

²⁴ Eliashib
came from the musicians.

Shallum, Telem and Uri
came from the men who guarded the temple gates.

²⁵ Among the other Israelites, here are the men who had married women from other lands.
Ramiah, Izziah, Malkijah and Mijamin came from the family line of Parosh. So did Eleazar, Malkijah and Benaiah.

²⁶ Mattaniah, Zechariah and Jehiel
came from the family line of Elam. So did Abdi, Jeremoth and Elijah.

²⁷ Elioenai, Eliashib and Mattaniah
came from the family line of Zattu. So did Jeremoth, Zabad and Aziza.

²⁸ Jehohanan, Hananiah, Zabbai and Athlai
came from the family line of Bebai.

²⁹ Meshullam, Malluk and Adaiah
came from the family line of Bani. So did Jashub, Sheal and Jeremoth.

³⁰ Adna, Kelal, Benaiah and Maaseiah
came from the family line of Pahath-Moab. So did Mattaniah, Bezalel, Binnui and Manasseh.

³¹ Eliezer, Ishijah, Malkijah, Shemaiah and Shimeon
came from the family line of Harim. ³²So did Benjamin, Malluk and Shemariah.

³³ Mattenai, Mattattah, Zabad and Eliphelet
came from the family line of Hashum. So did Jeremai, Manasseh and Shimei.

³⁴ Maadai, Amram and Uel
came from the family line of Bani. ³⁵So did Benaiah, Bedeiah, Keluhi, ³⁶Vaniah, Meremoth, Eliashib, ³⁷Mattaniah, Mattenai and Jaasu.

³⁸ Shimei
came from the family line of Binnui. ³⁹So did Shelemiah, Nathan, Adaiah, ⁴⁰Maknadebai, Shashai, Sharai, ⁴¹Azarel, Shelemiah, Shemariah, ⁴²Shallum, Amariah and Joseph.

⁴³ Jeiel, Mattithiah, Zabad and Zebina
came from the family line of Nebo. So did Jaddai, Joel and Benaiah.

⁴⁴ All these men had married women from other lands. Some of them had even had children by those wives.

nehemiah

Picture this, if you will: You're attempting to finish an important chore or science experiment, but you continue to be bothered by someone who doesn't want you to succeed. Can you imagine such a scenario? If so, you aren't far from the frustration that Nehemiah experienced.

Like Ezra, Nehemiah had been in Babylon when he heard that Jerusalem had not been repaired and the city lay exposed to attack. Because he had the prominent position of wine taster for King Artaxerxes, he got permission to return to Judah to oversee the rebuilding. The king even went so far as to provide letters to ensure Nehemiah's safe transport and ability to secure anything he needed for his mission.

Upon arrival, however, Nehemiah and his crew of builders faced direct opposition from a number of troublemakers. When nothing these agitators did could stop Nehemiah, they even planned his assassination. But when he finished the project in just fifty-two days in spite of all their sinister efforts, the surrounding nations realized that God was the source of the success (6:15–16).

Ezra had restored order to the Temple worship, while Nehemiah had seen to rebuilding the walls around Jerusalem, so the two of them celebrated together by leading a worship service and holding a day of celebration. The joy that day was greater than anything the people had experienced in hundreds of years (8:17).

WHAT'S IT MEAN, EUGENE?

Mercy—Mr. Whittaker says that grace is *getting* what we *don't* deserve (the blessing of God's favor), and mercy is *not* getting what we *do deserve* (punishment for our sins). *Mercy* extends kindness, even to those who haven't earned it. I forgot to pick up some groceries that Katrina asked me to procure, but instead of being upset, she simply cooked a different—and delicious I might add—dinner that night. Though everyone deserves punishment (see why in Romans 3:23; 6:23), God shows us His *mercy* by forgiving our sins through Jesus Christ. "God loves us deeply. He is full of mercy . . . He gave us life even when we were dead in sin" (Ephesians 2:4–5).

Nehemiah Prays to the Lord

These are the words of Nehemiah. He was the son of Hakaliah.

I was in the fort of Susa. I was there in the 20th year that Artaxerxes was king. It was in the month of Kislev. ²At that time Hanani came from Judah with some other men. He was one of my brothers. I asked him and the other men about the Jews who were left alive in Judah. They had returned from Babylon. I also asked him about Jerusalem. ³He and the men with him said to me, "Some of the people who returned are still alive. They are back in the land of Judah. But they are having a hard time. They are ashamed. The wall of Jerusalem is broken down. Its gates have been burned with fire." ⁴When I heard about these things, I sat down and wept. For several days I was very sad. I didn't eat any food. And I prayed to the God of heaven. ⁵I said,

"Lord, you are the God of heaven. You are a great and wonderful God. You keep the covenant you made with those who love you and obey your commandments. You show them your love. ⁶Please pay careful attention to my prayer. See how your people are suffering. Please listen to me. I'm praying to you day and night. I'm praying for the people of Israel. We Israelites have committed sins against you. All of us admit it. I and my family have also sinned against you. ⁷We've done some very evil things. We haven't obeyed the commands, rules and laws you gave your servant Moses.

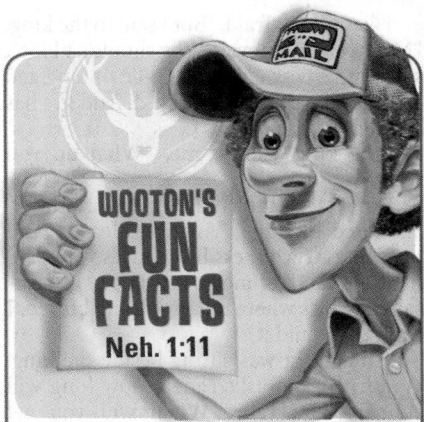

WOOTON'S FUN FACTS
Neh. 1:11

Nehemiah's job was to serve drinks at the royal table and to make sure the king didn't get poisoned. I guess a lot of people tried to get rid of the king by slipping something into his food. Ezra had to guard the liquids and possibly even taste them. As long as the drinks include raspberry soda, you could count me in.

⁸"Remember what you told him. You said, 'If you people are not faithful, I will scatter you among the nations. ⁹But if you return to me, I will bring you back. If you obey my commands, I will gather you together again. I will bring you back from the farthest places on earth. I will bring you to the special place where I have chosen to put my Name.'

¹⁰"Lord, they are your people. They serve you. You used your great strength and mighty hand to set them free from Egypt. ¹¹Lord, please pay careful attention to my prayer. Listen to the prayers of all of us. We take delight in bringing honor to your name. Give me success today when I bring my request to King Artaxerxes."

I was the king's wine taster.

Artaxerxes Sends Nehemiah to Jerusalem

Wine was brought in for King Artaxerxes. It was the month of Nisan in the 20th year of his rule. I got the wine and gave it to him. I hadn't been sad in front of him before. But now I was. ²So the king asked me, "Why are you looking so sad? You aren't sick. You must be feeling very sad."

Jason's Jargon

NEHEMIAH 1

Your task: Find *Kislev* in this chapter.
Kislev was a month in the Jewish calendar. It usually coincided with parts of what we now call November and December.

I was really afraid. [3]But I said to the king, "May you live forever! Why shouldn't I look sad? The city where my people of long ago are buried has been destroyed. And fire has burned up its gates."

[4]The king said to me, "What do you want?"

I prayed to the God of heaven. [5]Then I answered the king, "Are you pleased with me, King Artaxerxes? If it pleases you, send me to Judah. Let me go to the city of Jerusalem. That's where my people are buried. I want to rebuild it."

[6]The queen was sitting beside the king. He turned and asked me, "How long will your journey take? When will you get back?" It pleased the king to send me. So I chose a certain time.

[7]I also said to him, "If it pleases you, may I take some letters with me? I want to give them to the governors of the land west of the Euphrates River. Then they'll help me travel safely through their territory until I arrive in Judah. [8]May I also have a letter to Asaph? He takes care of the royal park. I want him to give me some logs so I can make beams out of them. I want to use them for the gates of the fort that is by the temple. Some of the logs will also be used in the city wall. And I'll need some for the house I'm going to live in." God was kind to me and helped me. So the king gave me what I asked for. [9]Then I went to the governors of the land west of the Euphrates River. I gave them the king's letters. He had also sent army officers and horsemen along with me.

[10]Sanballat and Tobiah heard about what was happening. Sanballat was a Horonite. Tobiah was an official from Ammon. They were very upset that someone had come to help the Israelites.

Nehemiah Checks Out the Walls of Jerusalem

[11]I went to Jerusalem and stayed there for three days. [12]Then at night I took a few other people with me to check out the walls. I hadn't told anyone what my God wanted me to do for Jerusalem. There weren't any donkeys with me except the one I was riding on.

[13]That night I went out through the Valley Gate. I went toward the Jackal Well and the Dung Gate. I checked out the walls of Jerusalem. They had been broken down. I also checked the city gates. Fire had burned them up. [14]I moved on toward the Fountain Gate and the King's Pool. But there wasn't enough room for my donkey to get through. [15]It was still night. I went up the Kidron Valley. I kept checking the wall. Finally, I turned back. I went back in through the Valley Gate. [16]The officials didn't know where I had gone or what I had done. That's because I hadn't said anything to anyone yet. I hadn't told the priests or nobles or officials. And I hadn't spoken to any other Jews who would be rebuilding the wall.

[17]I said to them, "You can see the trouble we're in. Jerusalem has been destroyed. Fire has burned up its gates. Come on. Let's rebuild the wall of Jerusalem. Then people won't be ashamed anymore." [18]I also told them how my gracious God was helping me. And I told them what the king had said to me.

They replied, "Let's start rebuilding." So they began that good work.

[19]But Sanballat, the Horonite, heard about it. So did Tobiah, the official from Ammon. Geshem, the Arab, heard about it too. All of them laughed at us. They made fun of us. "What do you think you are doing?" they asked. "Are you turning against the king?"

[20]I answered, "The God of heaven will give us success. We serve him. So we'll start rebuilding the walls. But you don't have any share in Jerusalem. You don't have any claim to it. You don't have any right to worship here."

A List of the People Who Repaired the Wall

3 Eliashib the high priest and the other priests went to work. They rebuilt the Sheep Gate. They set it apart to God. They put its doors in place. They continued to rebuild the wall up to the Tower of the Hundred. They set the tower apart to God. Then they continued to rebuild the wall all the way to the Tower of Hananel. [2]Some men from Jericho rebuilt the next part of the wall. And Zakkur rebuilt the next part. He was the son of Imri.

[3]The sons of Hassenaah rebuilt the Fish Gate. They laid its beams. They put in place its doors with their metal bolts and bars. [4]Meremoth repaired the next part of the

Neh. 3 The ten gates' names tell what they are for. The Horse Gate was near the stables and horses came in there. The Fish Gate was where fishermen would bring their catch to be sold. And the Dung Gate? Uh, I'll let you guess!

wall. He was the son of Uriah. Uriah was the son of Hakkoz. Next to Meremoth, Meshullam made some repairs. He was the son of Berekiah. Berekiah was the son of Meshezabel. Next to Meshullam, Zadok also made some repairs. He was the son of Baana. ⁵Some men from Tekoa repaired the next part of the wall. But their nobles refused to do any work at all. They didn't pay any attention to the people who were in charge of the work.

⁶Joiada and Meshullam repaired the Jeshanah Gate. Joiada was the son of Paseah. Meshullam was the son of Besodeiah. Joiada and Meshullam laid the beams of the gate. They put in place its doors with their metal bolts and bars. ⁷Next to them, some men from Gibeon and Mizpah made repairs. They included Melatiah from Gibeon and Jadon from Meronoth. Those places were under the authority of the governor of the land west of the Euphrates River. ⁸Uzziel repaired the next part of the wall. He made his living by working with gold. He was the son of Harhaiah. Hananiah made repairs on the next part. He made his living by making perfume. So the wall of Jerusalem was made like new again all the way to the Broad Wall. ⁹Rephaiah repaired the next part. He was the son of Hur. Rephaiah ruled over half of the territory where Jerusalem was located. ¹⁰Jedaiah repaired the part of the wall that was across from his

house. He was the son of Harumaph. Hattush made repairs next to Jedaiah. Hattush was the son of Hashabneiah. ¹¹Malkijah and Hasshub repaired another part of the wall. They also repaired the Tower of the Ovens. Malkijah was the son of Harim. Hasshub was the son of Pahath-Moab. ¹²Shallum repaired the next part. His daughters helped him. He was the son of Hallohesh. Shallum ruled over the other half of the territory where Jerusalem was located.

¹³Hanun repaired the Valley Gate. Some people who lived in Zanoah helped him. They rebuilt it. They put in place its doors with their metal bolts and bars. They also repaired 1,500 feet of the wall. They repaired it all the way to the Dung Gate.

¹⁴Malkijah repaired the Dung Gate. He was the son of Rekab. Malkijah ruled over the territory where Beth Hakkerem was located. He rebuilt the gate. He put in place its doors with their metal bolts and bars.

¹⁵Shallun repaired the Fountain Gate. He was the son of Kol-Hozeh. Shallun ruled over the territory where Mizpah was located. He rebuilt the gate. He put a roof over it. And he put in place the doors of the gate with their metal bolts and bars. He also repaired the wall by the Pool of Siloam. It was near the King's Garden. Shallun repaired the wall as far as the steps that go down from the City of David. ¹⁶Next to Shallun, Nehemiah made some repairs. He was the son of Azbuk. Nehemiah ruled over half of the territory where Beth Zur was located. He repaired the wall up to the part that was across from the tombs of David. He repaired it all the way to the man-made pool and the House of the Heroes.

¹⁷Next to Nehemiah, some Levites made repairs. They worked under the direction of Rehum. He was the son of Bani. Next to Rehum, Hashabiah made repairs for his territory. He ruled over half of the territory where Keilah was located. ¹⁸Next to him, other Levites made some repairs. They worked under the direction of Binnui. He was the son of Henadad. Binnui ruled over the other half of the territory where Keilah was located. ¹⁹Next to Binnui, Ezer repaired another part of the wall. He was the son of Jeshua. Ezer ruled over Mizpah. He repaired the part across from the place that went up to the storeroom where the

weapons were kept. He repaired the wall up to the angle of the wall. [20]Next to Ezer, Baruch worked hard to repair another part of the wall. He was the son of Zabbai. He repaired the part from the angle of the wall to the entrance to Eliashib's house. Eliashib was the high priest. [21]Next to Baruch, Meremoth repaired another part. He was the son of Uriah. Uriah was the son of Hakkoz. Meremoth repaired the part from the entrance to Eliashib's house to the end of the house.

[22]Next to Meremoth, some priests from the surrounding area made repairs. [23]Next to them, Benjamin and Hasshub repaired the part of the wall that was in front of their house. Next to them, Azariah repaired the part that was beside his house. He was the son of Maaseiah. Maaseiah was the son of Ananiah. [24]Next to Azariah, Binnui made repairs on another part. Binnui was the son of Henadad. Binnui repaired the wall from Azariah's house to the angle and the corner. [25]Palal worked across from the angle. He was the son of Uzai. Palal also worked across from the tower that was part of the upper palace. It was near the courtyard of the guard. Next to him, Pedaiah made some repairs. He was the son of Parosh. [26]The temple servants who lived on the hill of Ophel helped Pedaiah. They repaired the wall up to the part that was across from the Water Gate. It was toward the east and the palace tower. [27]Next to the temple servants, the men from Tekoa repaired another part. They made repairs from the large palace tower to the wall of Ophel.

[28]The priests made repairs above the Horse Gate. Each priest repaired the part of the wall that was in front of his own house. [29]Next to them, Zadok made repairs across from his house. He was the son of Immer. Next to Zadok, Shemaiah made some repairs. He was the son of Shekaniah. Shemaiah guarded the East Gate. [30]Next to him, Hananiah and Hanun repaired another part of the wall. Hananiah was the son of Shelemiah. Hanun was the sixth son of Zalaph. Next to Hananiah and Hanun, Meshullam made some repairs. He was the son of Berekiah. Meshullam repaired the part that was across from where he lived. [31]Next to him, Malkijah made some repairs. He made his living by working with gold. He repaired the wall up to the house

of the temple servants and the traders. It was across from the Inspection Gate. He also repaired the wall as far as the room above the corner. [32]The traders and those who made their living by working with gold made some repairs. They repaired the wall from the room above the corner to the Sheep Gate.

Nehemiah's Enemies Oppose the Rebuilding

4 Sanballat heard that we were rebuilding the wall. So he became very angry and upset. He made fun of the Jews. [2]He spoke to his friends and the army of Samaria. He said, "What are those Jews trying to do? Can they make their city wall like new again? Will they offer sacrifices? Can they finish everything in a single day? The stones from their city wall and buildings are piled up like trash. And everything has been badly burned. Can they use those stones to rebuild everything again?"

[3]Tobiah from Ammon was at Sanballat's side. He said, "What are they building? They're putting up a stone wall. But suppose a fox climbs on top of it. Even that will break it down!"

[4]I prayed to God. I said, "Our God, please listen to our prayer. Some people hate us. They're saying bad things about us. So let others say bad things about them. Let them be carried off like stolen goods. Let them be taken to another country as prisoners. [5]Don't hide your eyes from their guilt. Don't forgive their sins. They have said bad things about the builders."

[6]So we rebuilt the wall. We repaired it until all of it was half as high as we wanted it to be. The people worked with all their heart.

[7]But Sanballat and Tobiah heard that Jerusalem's walls continued to be repaired. The Arabs, the Ammonites and the people of Ashdod heard about it too. They heard that the gaps in the wall were being filled in. So they were very angry. [8]All of them made evil plans to come and fight against Jerusalem. They wanted to stir up trouble against it. [9]But we prayed to our God. We put guards on duty day and night to watch out for danger.

[10]During that time, the people in Judah spoke up. They said, "The workers are

getting weaker and weaker all the time. Broken stones are piled up everywhere. They are in our way. So we can't rebuild the wall."

[11]And our enemies said, "We will be right there among them. We'll kill them. We'll put an end to their work. We'll do it before they even know it or see us."

[12]Then the Jews who lived near our enemies came to us. They told us ten times, "No matter where you are, they'll attack us."

[13]So I stationed some people behind the lowest parts of the wall. That's where our enemies could easily attack us. I stationed the people family by family. They had their swords, spears and bows with them. [14]I looked things over. Then I stood up and spoke to the nobles, the officials and the rest of the people. I said, "Don't be afraid of your enemies. Remember the Lord. He is great and powerful. So fight for your families. Fight for your sons and daughters. Fight for your wives and homes."

[15]Our enemies heard that we knew what they were trying to do. They heard that God had blocked their evil plans. So all of us returned to the wall. Each of us did our own work.

[16]From that day on, half of my men did the work. The other half were given spears, shields, bows and armor. The officers stationed themselves behind all the people of Judah. [17]The people continued to build the wall. The people who carried supplies did their work with one hand. They held a weapon in the other hand. [18]Each of the builders wore his sword at his side as he worked. But the man who blew the trumpet stayed with me.

[19]Then I spoke to the nobles, the officials and the rest of the people. I said, "This is a big job. It covers a lot of territory. We're separated too far from one another along the wall. [20]When you hear the sound of the trumpet, join us at that location. Our God will fight for us!"

[21]So we continued the work. Half of the men held spears. We worked from the first light of sunrise until the stars came out at night. [22]At that time I also spoke to the people. I told them, "Have every man and his helper stay inside Jerusalem at night. Then they can guard us at night. And they can work during the day." [23]My relatives and I didn't take off our clothes. My men and the guards didn't take theirs off either. Each

man kept his weapon with him, even when he went to get water.

Nehemiah Helps Some Poor People

5 Some men and their wives cried out against their Jewish brothers and sisters. [2]Some of them were saying, "There are now many of us. We have many sons and daughters. We have to get some grain so we can eat and stay alive."

[3]Others were saying, "We're being forced to sell our fields, vineyards and homes. We have to do it to buy grain. There isn't enough food for everyone."

[4]Still others were saying, "We've had to borrow money. We needed it to pay the king's tax on our fields and vineyards. [5]We belong to the same family lines as the rest of our people. Our children are as good as theirs. But we've had to sell them off as slaves. Some of our daughters have already been made slaves. But we can't do anything about it. That's because our fields and vineyards now belong to others."

[6]I heard them when they cried out. And I was very angry when I heard what they were saying. [7]I thought it over for a while. Then I accused the nobles and officials of breaking the law. I told them, "You are charging your own people interest!" So I called together a large group of people to handle the matter. [8]I said, "Our Jewish brothers and sisters were sold to other nations. We've done everything we could to buy them back and bring them home. But look at what you are doing! You are actually selling your own people! Now we'll have to buy them back too!" The people kept quiet. They couldn't think of anything to say.

[9]So I continued, "What you are doing isn't right. Shouldn't you show respect for our God? Shouldn't you live in a way that will keep our enemies from saying bad things about us? [10]I'm lending the people money and grain. So are my relatives and my men. But we must stop charging interest! [11]Give the people's fields back to them. Give them back their vineyards, olive groves and houses. Do it right away. Give everything back to them. Also give them back the one percent on the money, grain, fresh wine and olive oil you have charged them."

[12]"We'll give it back," they said. "And we won't require anything more from them. We'll do exactly as you say."

Then I sent for the priests. I made the nobles and officials promise to do what they had said. ¹³I also shook out my pockets and emptied them. I said, "Someone might decide not to keep this promise they have made. If that happens, may God shake them out of their house! May he empty them of everything they own!"

The whole community said, "Amen." They praised the LORD. And the leaders did what they had promised to do.

¹⁴And that's not all. I was appointed as governor of Judah in the 20th year that Artaxerxes was king of Persia. I remained in that position until his 32nd year. During those 12 years, I and my relatives didn't eat the food that was provided for my table. ¹⁵But there had been governors before me. They had put a heavy load on the people. They had taken a pound of silver from each of them. They had also taken food and wine from them. Their officials had acted like high and mighty rulers over them. But because of my great respect for God, I didn't act like that. ¹⁶Instead, I spent all my time working on this wall. All my men were gathered there to work on it too. We didn't receive any land for ourselves.

¹⁷Many people ate at my table. They included 150 Jews and officials. They also included leaders who came to us from the nations that were around us. ¹⁸Each day one ox, six of the best sheep and some birds were prepared for me. Every ten days plenty of wine of all kinds was brought in as well. In spite of all that, I never asked for the food that was provided for my table. That's because the people were already paying too many taxes.

¹⁹You are my God. Please remember me and help me. Keep in mind everything I've done for these people.

Nehemiah's Enemies Continue to Oppose the Rebuilding

6 Sanballat, Tobiah and Geshem, the Arab, heard about what I had done. So did the rest of our enemies. All of them heard I had rebuilt the wall. In fact, they heard there weren't any gaps left in it. But up to that time I hadn't put up the gates at the main entrances to the city. ²Sanballat and Geshem sent me a message. They said, "Come. Let's talk with one another. Let's meet in one of the villages on the plain of Ono."

Jason's Jargon

NEHEMIAH 6

Another mission! Seek out the word *nobles* in this chapter. Nobles were high-ranking officials in the king's court known to be honorable people of good character. A noble's words were respected.

But they were planning to harm me. ³So I sent messengers to them with my answer. I replied, "I'm working on a huge project. So I can't get away. Why should the work stop while I leave it? Why should I go down and talk with you?" ⁴They sent me the same message four times. And I gave them the same answer each time.

⁵Sanballat sent his helper to me a fifth time. He brought the same message. He was carrying a letter that wasn't sealed. ⁶It said,

"A report is going around among the nations. Geshem says it's true. We hear that you and the other Jews are planning to turn against the Persian rulers. And that's why you are building the wall. It's also reported that you are about to become their king. ⁷People say that you have even appointed prophets to make an announcement about you. In Jerusalem they are going to say, 'Judah has a king!' That report will get back to the king of Persia. So come. Let's meet together."

⁸I sent a reply to Sanballat. I said, "What you are saying isn't really happening. You are just making it up."

⁹All of them were trying to frighten us. They thought, "Their hands will get too weak to do the work. So it won't be completed."

But I prayed to God. I said, "Make my hands stronger."

¹⁰One day I went to Shemaiah's house. He was the son of Delaiah. Delaiah was the son of Mehetabel. Shemaiah had shut himself up in his home. He said, "Let's go to God's house. Let's meet inside the temple

and close the doors. Some men are coming at night to kill you."

[11]But I said, "Should a man like me run away? Should someone like me go into the temple just to save his life? No! I won't go!" [12]I realized that God hadn't sent Shemaiah. Tobiah and Sanballat had hired him. That's why he had prophesied lies about me. [13]They had hired him to scare me. They wanted me to commit a sin by doing what he said. That would give me a bad name in the community. People would find fault with me and my work.

[14]You are my God. Remember what Tobiah and Sanballat have done. Also remember the prophet Noadiah. She and the rest of the prophets have been trying to scare me. [15]So the city wall was completed on the 25th day of the month of Elul. It was finished in 52 days.

Nehemiah's Enemies Oppose the Completed Wall

[16]All our enemies heard about it. All the nations around us became afraid. They weren't sure of themselves anymore. They realized that our God had helped us finish the work. [17]In those days the nobles of Judah sent many letters to Tobiah. And replies from Tobiah came back to them. [18]Many people in Judah had promised that they would be faithful to him. That's because he was Shekaniah's son-in-law. Shekaniah was the son of Arah. Tobiah's son Jehohanan had married Meshullam's daughter. Meshullam was the son of Berekiah. [19]Tobiah's friends kept reporting to me the good things he did. They also kept telling him what I said. And Tobiah himself sent letters to scare me.

7 The wall had been rebuilt. I had put up the gates at the main entrances to the city. The people who guarded the gates were appointed to their positions. So were the musicians and the Levites. [2]I put my brother Hanani in charge of Jerusalem. Hananiah helped him. Hananiah was commander of the fort that was by the temple. Hanani was an honest man. He had more respect for God than most people do. [3]I said to Hanani and Hananiah, "Don't open the gates of Jerusalem until the hottest time of the day. Tell the men who guard the gates to shut them before they go off duty. Make sure they lock them up tight. Also appoint as guards some people who live in Jerusalem. Station some of them at their appointed places. Station others near their own homes."

A List of People Who Returned to Judah

[4]Jerusalem was large. It had a lot of room. But only a few people lived there. The houses hadn't been rebuilt yet. [5]So my God gave me the idea and encouraged me to gather the people together. He also encouraged me to gather the nobles and officials together with them. He wanted me to list them by families. I found the family history of those who had been the first to return. Here is what I found written in it.

[6]Nebuchadnezzar had taken many Jews away from the land of Judah. He had forced them to go to Babylon as prisoners. Now they returned to Jerusalem and Judah. All of them went back to their own towns. Nebuchadnezzar was king of Babylon. [7]The leaders of the Jews included Zerubbabel, Joshua, Nehemiah, Azariah, Raamiah and Nahamani. They also included Mordecai, Bilshan, Mispereth, Bigvai, Nehum and Baanah.

Here is a list of the men of Israel who returned home.

[8]There were 2,172 from the family line of Parosh.

[9]There were 372 from Shephatiah.

[10]There were 652 from Arah.

[11]There were 2,818 from Pahath-Moab through the family line of Jeshua and Joab.

[12]There were 1,254 from Elam.

[13]There were 845 from Zattu.

[14]There were 760 from Zakkai.

[15]There were 648 from Binnui.

[16]There were 628 from Bebai.

[17]There were 2,322 from Azgad.

[18]There were 667 from Adonikam.

[19]There were 2,067 from Bigvai.

[20]There were 655 from Adin.

[21]There were 98 from Ater through the family line of Hezekiah.

[22]There were 328 from Hashum.

[23]There were 324 from Bezai.

[24]There were 112 from Hariph.

[25]There were 95 from Gibeon.

[26]There were 188 from the men of Bethlehem and Netophah.

27 There were 128 from Anathoth.
28 There were 42 from Beth Azmaveth.
29 There were 743 from Kiriath Jearim, Kephirah and Beeroth.
30 There were 621 from Ramah and Geba.
31 There were 122 from Mikmash.
32 There were 123 from Bethel and Ai.
33 There were 52 from the other Nebo.
34 There were 1,254 from the other Elam.
35 There were 320 from Harim.
36 There were 345 from Jericho.
37 There were 721 from Lod, Hadid and Ono.
38 There were 3,930 from Senaah.

39 Here is a list of the priests.
There were 973 from the family line of Jedaiah through the line of Jeshua.
40 There were 1,052 from Immer.
41 There were 1,247 from Pashhur.
42 There were 1,017 from Harim.

43 The Levites belonged to
the family line of Jeshua through Kadmiel through the line of Hodaviah. The total number of men was 74.

44 The musicians belonged to
the family line of Asaph. The total number of men was 148.

45 The men who guarded the temple gates belonged to
the family lines of Shallum, Ater, Talmon, Akkub, Hatita and Shobai. The total number of men was 138.

46 Here is a list of the members of the family lines of the temple servants.
Ziha, Hasupha, Tabbaoth,
47 Keros, Sia, Padon,
48 Lebana, Hagaba, Shalmai,
49 Hanan, Giddel, Gahar,
50 Reaiah, Rezin, Nekoda,
51 Gazzam, Uzza, Paseah,
52 Besai, Meunim, Nephusim,
53 Bakbuk, Hakupha, Harhur,
54 Bazluth, Mehida, Harsha,
55 Barkos, Sisera, Temah,
56 Neziah, Hatipha
57 Here is a list of the members of the family lines of the servants of Solomon.
Sotai, Sophereth, Perida,

58 Jaala, Darkon, Giddel,
59 Shephatiah, Hattil, Pokereth-Hazzebaim, Amon
60 The total number of the members of the family lines of the temple servants and the servants of Solomon was 392.

61 Many people came up to Judah from the towns of Tel Melah, Tel Harsha, Kerub, Addon and Immer. But they weren't able to prove that their families belonged to the people of Israel.
62 There were 642 of them from the family lines of
Delaiah, Tobiah and Nekoda.

63 Here is a list of the members of the family lines of the priests.
They were
Hobaiah, Hakkoz and Barzillai. Barzillai had married a daughter of Barzillai from Gilead. So he was also called Barzillai.
64 The priests looked for their family records. But they couldn't find them. So they weren't able to serve as priests. They weren't "clean." 65The governor gave them an order. He told them not to eat any of the most sacred food. They had to wait until there was a priest who could use the Urim and Thummim. The priest would use them to get decisions from the LORD.

66 The total number of the entire group that returned was 42,360. 67That didn't include their 7,337 male and female slaves. There were also 245 male and female singers. 68And there were 736 horses, 245 mules, 69435 camels and 6,720 donkeys.

70Some of the family leaders helped pay for the work. The governor gave 19 pounds of gold to be added to the temple treasure. He also gave 50 bowls and 530 sets of clothes for the priests. 71Some of the family leaders gave 375 pounds of gold for the work. They also gave one and a third tons of silver. All of that was added to the temple treasure. 72The rest of the people gave a total of 375 pounds of gold and one and a fourth tons of silver. They also gave 67 sets of clothes for the priests.
73The priests and Levites made their homes in their own towns. So did the

musicians, the temple servants and the men who guarded the gates. The rest of the Israelites also made their homes in their own towns.

Ezra Reads the Law to the People

8 The Israelites had made their homes in their towns. In the seventh month, ¹all of them gathered together. They went to the open area in front of the Water Gate. They told Ezra to bring out the Book of the Law of Moses. The Lord had given Israel that Law so they would obey him. Ezra was the teacher of the Law.

²Ezra the priest brought the Law out to the whole community. It was the first day of the seventh month. The group was made up of men, women, and children old enough to understand what Ezra was going to read. ³He read the Law to them from sunrise until noon. He did it as he faced the open area in front of the Water Gate. He read it to the men, the women, and the children old enough to understand. And all the people paid careful attention as Ezra was reading the Book of the Law.

⁴Ezra, the teacher of the Law, stood on a high wooden stage. It had been built for the occasion. Mattithiah, Shema and Anaiah stood at his right side. So did Uriah, Hilkiah and Maaseiah. Pedaiah, Mishael and Malkijah stood at his left side. So did Hashum, Hashbaddanah, Zechariah and Meshullam.

⁵Ezra opened the book. All the people could see him. That's because he was standing above them. As he opened the book, the people stood up. ⁶Ezra praised the Lord. He is the great God. All the people lifted up their hands and said, "Amen! Amen!" Then they bowed down. They turned their faces toward the ground and worshiped the Lord.

⁷The Levites taught the Law to the people. They remained standing while the Levites taught them. The Levites who were there included Jeshua, Bani, Sherebiah, Jamin, Akkub, Shabbethai and Hodiah. They also included Maaseiah, Kelita, Azariah, Jozabad, Hanan and Pelaiah. ⁸All these Levites read to the people parts of the Book of the Law of God. They made it clear to them. They told them what it meant. So the people understood what was being read.

⁹Nehemiah was the governor. Ezra was a priest and the teacher of the Law. They

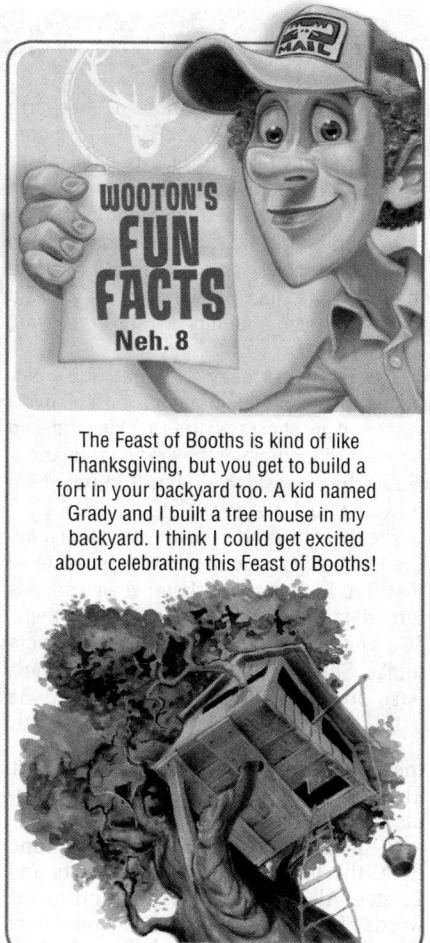

WOOTON'S FUN FACTS
Neh. 8

The Feast of Booths is kind of like Thanksgiving, but you get to build a fort in your backyard too. A kid named Grady and I built a tree house in my backyard. I think I could get excited about celebrating this Feast of Booths!

spoke up. So did the Levites who were teaching the people. All these men said to the people, "This day is set apart to honor the Lord your God. So don't weep. Don't be sad." All the people had been weeping as they listened to the words of the Law.

¹⁰Nehemiah said, "Go and enjoy some good food and sweet drinks. Send some of it to people who don't have any. This day is holy to our Lord. So don't be sad. The joy of the Lord makes you strong."

¹¹The Levites calmed all the people down. They said, "Be quiet. This is a holy day. So don't be sad."

¹²Then all the people went away to eat and drink. They shared their food with others. They celebrated with great joy. Now

Have you ever seen pictures of the earth taken from outer space? From the moon, Earth is about the size of a beach ball or even a baseball. And from Saturn, Earth would be little more than a point of light, not much bigger than a star. Feeling small yet? Don't worry. God's got the whole world in His hands, just as the song says. And He has amazing things in store for you, His child.

Sometimes it's easy to forget God's big-picture plans. If you often find yourself overwhelmed by the pressures of life and bad news, or caught up in the drama of relationships, then consider all that God has done for you. Count it all joy.

The people of Nehemiah's time discovered that it was a good thing to celebrate all that God had done for them. Their sadness turned to smiles as Nehemiah told them, "Go and enjoy some good food and sweet drinks. Send some of it to people who don't have any. This day is holy to our Lord. So don't be sad. The joy of the Lord makes you strong" (Neh. 8:10).

Joy comes from remembering our problems are only a tiny piece of a bigger picture. Grab a sheet of paper and write down some tough things that have happened to you in the past week or problems you might face next week. Then think about the big picture and how God can use each trial to bring you closer to Him.

---

they understood the words they had heard. That's because everything had been explained to them.

¹³All the family leaders gathered around Ezra, the teacher. So did the priests and Levites. All of them paid attention to the words of the Law. It was the second day of the month. ¹⁴The Lord had given the Law through Moses. He wanted the Israelites to obey it. It is written there that they were supposed to live in booths during the Feast of Booths. That feast was celebrated in the seventh month. ¹⁵They were also supposed to spread the message all through their towns and in Jerusalem. They were supposed to announce, "Go out into the central hill country. Bring back some branches from olive and wild olive trees. Also bring some from myrtle, palm and shade trees. Use the branches to make booths."

¹⁶So the people went out and brought back some branches. They built themselves booths on their own roofs. They made them in their courtyards. They put them up in the courtyards of the house of God. They built them in the open area in front of the Water Gate. And they built them in the open area in front of the Gate of Ephraim. ¹⁷All the people who had returned from the land of Babylon made booths. They lived in them during the Feast of Booths. They hadn't celebrated the feast with so much joy for a long time. In fact, they had never celebrated it like that from the days of Joshua, the son of Nun, until that day. So their joy was very great.

¹⁸Day after day, Ezra read parts of the Book of the Law of God to them. He read it out loud from the first day to the last. They celebrated the Feast of Booths for seven days. On the eighth day they gathered together. They followed the required rules for celebrating the feast.

The Israelites Admit They Have Sinned

9 It was the 24th day of the seventh month. The Israelites gathered together again. They didn't eat any food. They wore the rough clothing people wear when they're sad. They put dust on their heads. ²The Israelites separated themselves from

everyone else. They stood and admitted they had sinned. They also admitted that their people before them had sinned. ³They stood where they were. They listened while the Levites read parts of the Book of the Law of the LORD their God. They listened for a fourth of the day. They spent another fourth of the day admitting their sins. They also worshiped the LORD their God. ⁴Some people were standing on the stairs of the Levites. They included Jeshua, Bani, Kadmiel, Shebaniah, Bunni, Sherebiah, Bani and Kenani. With loud voices they called out to the LORD their God. ⁵Then some Levites spoke up. They included Jeshua, Kadmiel, Bani, Hashabneiah, Sherebiah, Hodiah, Shebaniah and Pethahiah. They said to the people, "Stand up. Praise the LORD your God. He lives for ever and ever!"

So the people said, "LORD, may your glorious name be praised. May it be lifted high above every other name that is blessed and praised. ⁶You are the one and only LORD. You made the heavens. You made even the highest heavens. You created all the stars in the sky. You created the earth and everything on it. And you made the oceans and everything in them. You give life to everything. Every living being in heaven worships you.

⁷"You are the LORD God. You chose Abram. You brought him out of Ur in the land of Babylon. You named him Abraham. ⁸You knew that his heart was faithful to you. And you made a covenant with him. You promised to give to his children after him a land of their own. It was the land of the Canaanites, Hittites and Amorites. The Perizzites, Jebusites and Girgashites also lived there. You have kept your promise. That's because you always do what is right and fair.

⁹"You saw how our people of long ago suffered in Egypt. You heard them cry out to you at the Red Sea. ¹⁰You sent signs and wonders against Pharaoh. You sent plagues on all his officials. In fact, you sent them on all the people of Egypt. You knew how they treated our people. They looked

CANDID CONVERSATIONS

How many times do we start our prayers by immediately diving into the list of things we want from God?

I used to do that all the time, but now I've learned to do what the Israelites did here. They started off their prayer by *praising* God. They didn't just say something like, "God, you're great." Instead they praised Him for all of His creation, for giving life to everything, for His deliverance from Egypt and for His promise to Abraham. They praised His name higher than any other!

The key thing for the Israelites, I think, is that they focused first on the One they were talking to. We should do that too. Don't forget that when we're praying, we're talking to the almighty God, wonderful Creator of the universe! Then, later, we can shift to asking for things we need from Him.

If you're like me, it changes your entire day to focus on how grateful you are to be alive and in the presence of our great God.

down on them. But you made a name for yourself. That name remains to this very day. ¹¹You parted the waters of the Red Sea for the Israelites. They passed through it on dry ground. But you threw into the sea those who chased them. They sank down like a stone into the mighty waters. ¹²By day you led the Israelites with a pillar of cloud. At night you led them with a pillar of fire. It gave them light to show them the way you wanted them to go.

¹³"You came down on Mount Sinai. From heaven you spoke to our people. You gave them rules and laws. Those laws are right and fair. You gave

them orders and commands that are good. [14]You taught them about your holy Sabbath day. You gave them commands, orders and laws. You did it through your servant Moses. [15]When the people were hungry, you gave them bread from heaven. When they were thirsty, you brought them water out of a rock. You told them to go into the land of Canaan. You told them to take it as their own. It was the land you had promised to give them.

[16]"But our people before us became proud and stubborn. They didn't obey your commands. [17]They refused to listen to you. They forgot the miracles you had done among them. So they became stubborn. When they refused to obey you, they appointed a leader for themselves. They wanted to go back to being slaves in Egypt. But you are a God who forgives. You are gracious. You are tender and kind. You are slow to get angry. You are full of love. So you didn't desert them. [18]They made for themselves a metal statue of a god that looked like a calf. They said to one another, 'Here is your god. He brought you up out of Egypt.' And they did evil things that dishonored you. But you still didn't desert them.

[19]"Because you loved them so much, you didn't leave them in the desert. During the day the pillar of cloud didn't stop guiding them on their path. At night the pillar of fire didn't stop shining on the way you wanted them to go. [20]You gave them your good Spirit to teach them. You didn't hold back your manna from their mouths. And you gave them water when they were thirsty. [21]For 40 years you took good care of them in the desert. They had everything they needed. Their clothes didn't wear out. And their feet didn't swell up.

[22]"You gave them kingdoms and nations. You even gave them lands far away. They took over the country of Sihon. He was the king of Heshbon. They also took over the country of Og. He was the king of Bashan. [23]You gave them as many children

as there are stars in the sky. You told their parents to enter the land. You told them to take it over. And you brought their children into it. [24]Their children went into the land. They took it as their own. You brought the Canaanites under Israel's control. The Canaanites lived in the land. But you handed them over to Israel. You also handed over their kings and the other nations in the land to Israel. You allowed Israel to deal with them just as they wanted to. [25]Your people captured cities that had high walls around them. They also took over the rich land in Canaan. They took houses filled with all kinds of good things. They took over wells that had already been dug. They took many vineyards, olive groves and fruit trees. They ate until they were very full and satisfied. They were filled with joy because you were so good to them.

[26]"But they didn't obey you. Instead, they turned against you. They turned their backs on your law. They killed your prophets. The prophets had warned them to return to you. But they did very evil things that dishonored you. [27]So you handed them over to their enemies, who treated them badly. Then they cried out to you. From heaven you heard them. You loved them very much. So you sent leaders to help them. The leaders saved them from the power of their enemies.

[28]"Then the people were enjoying peace and rest again. That's when they did what you did not want them to do. Then you handed them over to their enemies. So their enemies ruled over them. When they cried out to you again, you heard them from heaven. You loved them very much. So you saved them time after time.

[29]"You warned them so that they would obey your law again. But they became proud. They didn't obey your commands. They sinned against your rules. You said, 'Anyone who obeys my rules will live by them.' But the people didn't care about that. They turned their backs on you. They became very stubborn. They refused to

listen to you. ³⁰For many years you put up with them. By your Spirit you warned them through your prophets. In spite of that, they didn't pay any attention. So you handed them over to the nations that were around them. ³¹But you loved them very much. So you didn't put an end to them. You didn't desert them. That's because you are a gracious God. You are tender and kind.

³²"Our God, you are the great God. You are mighty and wonderful. You keep the covenant you made with us. You show us your love. So don't let all our suffering seem like a small thing to you. We've suffered greatly. So have our kings and leaders. So have our priests and prophets. Our people who lived long ago also suffered. And all your people are suffering right now. In fact, we've been suffering from the time of the kings of Assyria until today. ³³In spite of everything that has happened to us, you have been fair. You have been faithful in what you have done. But we did what was evil. ³⁴Our kings and leaders didn't follow your law. Our priests and our people before us didn't follow it either. They didn't pay any attention to your commands or rules that you warned them to keep. ³⁵They didn't serve you. They didn't turn from their evil ways. They didn't obey you even when they had a kingdom. You were very good to them. And they enjoyed it. You gave them a rich land. It had plenty of room in it. But they still didn't serve you. ³⁶"Now look at us. We are slaves today. We're slaves in the land you gave our people of long ago. You gave it to them so they could eat its fruit and the other good things it produces. ³⁷But we have sinned against you. So its great harvest goes to the kings of Persia. You have placed them over us. They rule over our bodies and cattle just as they please. And we are suffering terribly.

The People Agree to Obey God's Law

³⁸"So we are making a firm agreement. We're writing it down. Our leaders are putting their official marks on it. And so are our Levites and priests."

10 Here are the names of those who put their official marks on the agreement.

Nehemiah, the son of Hakaliah
He was the governor.
    Zedekiah,   ²Seraiah,   Azariah,
    Jeremiah,
³ Pashhur, Amariah, Malkijah,
⁴ Hattush, Shebaniah, Malluk,
⁵ Harim, Meremoth, Obadiah,
⁶ Daniel, Ginnethon, Baruch,
⁷ Meshullam, Abijah, Mijamin,
⁸ Maaziah, Bilgai, Shemaiah
    They were the priests.
⁹ Here are the names of the Levites.
    Jeshua, the son of Azaniah,
    Binnui, one of the sons of Henadad,
    Kadmiel
¹⁰ Here are the names of those who helped them.
    Shebaniah, Hodiah, Kelita, Pelaiah, Hanan,
¹¹ Mika, Rehob, Hashabiah,
¹² Zakkur, Sherebiah, Shebaniah,
¹³ Hodiah, Bani, Beninu

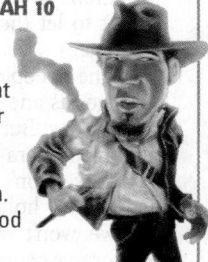

Jason's Jargon

NEHEMIAH 10

Study this chapter for the words *first share*. People brought the first share of their crops to the temple at the beginning of every harvest season. Giving them first to God showed gratitude.

¹⁴ Here are the names of the leaders of the people.
    Parosh, Pahath-Moab, Elam, Zattu, Bani,
¹⁵ Bunni, Azgad, Bebai,
¹⁶ Adonijah, Bigvai, Adin,
¹⁷ Ater, Hezekiah, Azzur,
¹⁸ Hodiah, Hashum, Bezai,
¹⁹ Hariph, Anathoth, Nebai,
²⁰ Magpiash, Meshullam, Hezir,
²¹ Meshezabel, Zadok, Jaddua,

²² Pelatiah, Hanan, Anaiah,
²³ Hoshea, Hananiah, Hasshub,
²⁴ Hallohesh, Pilha, Shobek,
²⁵ Rehum, Hashabnah, Maaseiah,
²⁶ Ahiah, Hanan, Anan,
²⁷ Malluk, Harim, Baanah

²⁸The rest of the people gathered together. They included the priests, the Levites and the men who guarded the gates. They included the musicians and temple servants. They also included all the people who separated themselves from the surrounding nations to obey the Law of God. All these men brought their wives with them. And they brought all their sons and daughters who were old enough to understand what was being agreed to. ²⁹All the men joined the nobles of their people. They made a firm agreement. They made a promise and said they would be cursed if they didn't keep it. They promised to follow the Law of God. It had been given through Moses, the servant of God. They promised to obey carefully all the commands, rules and laws of the LORD our Lord.

³⁰Here is what the priests, Levites and people said. "We promise not to let our daughters marry men from the nations around us. And we promise not to let their daughters marry our sons.

³¹"The people around us will bring goods and grain to sell on the Sabbath day. But we won't buy anything from them on the Sabbath day. In fact, we won't buy anything from them on any holy day. Every seventh year we won't farm the land. And we'll forgive people what they owe us.

³²"We will be accountable for carrying out the commands for serving in the house of our God. Each of us will give an eighth of an ounce of silver every year. ³³It will pay for the holy bread that is placed on the table in the temple. It will pay for the regular grain offerings and burnt offerings. It will pay for the offerings on the Sabbath days. It will pay for the offerings at the New Moon feasts and at the appointed feasts. It will pay for the holy offerings. It will be used for sin offerings to pay for the sins of Israel. It will also pay for everything else that needs to be done at the house of our God.

³⁴"We are the priests, Levites and people. Each of our families should bring a gift of wood to the house of our God. We have cast lots to decide when they will do that. They will bring it at certain appointed times every year. The wood will be burned on the altar of the LORD our God. That's what the Law requires.

³⁵"We will also be accountable for bringing the first share of our crops each year. And we'll bring the first share of every fruit tree. We'll bring them to the LORD's house.

³⁶"Each of us will bring our oldest son to the priests who serve there. We'll also bring the male animals that were born first to their mothers among our cattle, herds and flocks. We'll bring them to the house of our God. That's what the Law requires.

³⁷"We will also bring the first part of the meal we grind. We'll bring the first of our grain offerings. We'll bring the first share of fruit from all our trees. And we'll bring the first share of our olive oil and fresh wine. We'll give all those things to the priests. They'll put them in the storerooms of the house of our God. And we'll give a tenth of our crops to the Levites. They collect the tenth shares. They do it in all the towns where we work. ³⁸A priest from Aaron's family line must go with the Levites when they receive the tenth shares. And the Levites must bring a tenth of those shares up to the house of our God. They must put it in the rooms where the treasures are stored. ³⁹The people of Israel, including the Levites, must bring their gifts. They must bring grain, olive oil and fresh wine. They must put them in the storerooms where the objects for the temple are kept. That's also where the objects are kept for the priests serving at the temple, the musicians and the men who guard the gates.

"We won't forget to take care of the house of our God."

People Are Chosen to Live in Jerusalem

11 The leaders of the people made their homes in Jerusalem. The rest of the people cast lots. They did it to choose one person out of every ten of them. That person was chosen to live in the holy city of Jerusalem. The other nine had to stay in their own towns. ²The people thanked everyone who agreed to live in Jerusalem.

³ Here are the leaders from different parts of the country who made their homes in Jerusalem. Some Israelites, priests and Levites lived in the towns of Judah. So did some temple servants and some members of the family lines of Solomon's servants. All of them lived on their own property in the towns of Judah. ⁴At the same time, other people from the tribes of Judah and Benjamin lived in Jerusalem.

Here are the leaders from the family line of Judah.

There was Athaiah. He was the son of Uzziah. Uzziah was the son of Zechariah. Zechariah was the son of Amariah. Amariah was the son of Shephatiah. Shephatiah was the son of Mahalalel. Mahalalel belonged to the family line of Perez.

⁵ There was also Maaseiah. He was the son of Baruch. Baruch was the son of Kol-Hozeh. Kol-Hozeh was the son of Hazaiah. Hazaiah was the son of Adaiah. Adaiah was the son of Joiarib. Joiarib was the son of Zechariah. Zechariah belonged to the family line of Shelah.

⁶ Many important men who belonged to the family line of Perez lived in Jerusalem. The total number of them was 468.

⁷ Here are the leaders from the family line of Benjamin.

There was Sallu. He was the son of Meshullam. Meshullam was the son of Joed. Joed was the son of Pedaiah. Pedaiah was the son of Kolaiah. Kolaiah was the son of Maaseiah. Maaseiah was the son of Ithiel. Ithiel was the son of Jeshaiah. ⁸There were also Gabbai and Sallai.

They were Sallu's followers. The total number of men was 928.

⁹ Joel was their chief officer. He was the son of Zikri. A man named Judah was in charge of the New Quarter of Jerusalem. He was the son of Hassenuah.

¹⁰ Here are the leaders from among the priests.

There were Jedaiah, Jakin and the son of Joiarib.

¹¹ There was also Seraiah. He was the son of Hilkiah. Hilkiah was the son of Meshullam. Meshullam was the son of Zadok. Zadok was the son of Meraioth. Meraioth was the son of Ahitub. Ahitub was the official in charge of God's house. ¹²There were also people who helped them. They carried out the work for the temple. The total number of men was 822.

There was also Adaiah. He was the son of Jeroham. Jeroham was the son of Pelaliah. Pelaliah was the son of Amzi. Amzi was the son of Zechariah. Zechariah was the son of Pashhur. Pashhur was the son of Malkijah. ¹³There were also people who helped Adaiah. They were family leaders. The total number of men was 242.

There was also Amashsai. He was the son of Azarel. Azarel was the son of Ahzai. Ahzai was the son of Meshillemoth. Meshillemoth was the son of Immer. ¹⁴There were also people who helped Amashsai. They were important men. The total number of them was 128. Their chief officer was Zabdiel. He was the son of Haggedolim.

¹⁵ Here are the leaders from among the Levites.

There was Shemaiah. He was the son of Hasshub. Hasshub was the son of Azrikam. Azrikam was the son of Hashabiah. Hashabiah was the son of Bunni.

¹⁶ There were also Shabbethai and Jozabad. They were two of the leaders of the Levites. They were in charge of the work that was done outside God's house.

¹⁷ There was also Mattaniah. He led in prayer and in giving thanks. He was the son of Mika. Mika was the son of Zabdi. Zabdi was the son of Asaph.

There was also Bakbukiah. He was second among those who helped Mattaniah.

And there was Abda. He was the son of Shammua. Shammua was the son of Galal. Galal was the son of Jeduthun.

¹⁸ The total number of Levites in the holy city was 284.

¹⁹ Here are the leaders from among the men who guarded the gates.

There were Akkub, Talmon and those who helped them. They stood guard at the gates. The total number of men was 172.

²⁰The rest of the Israelites were in all the towns of Judah. The priests and Levites were with them. All of them lived on their own family property.

²¹The temple servants lived on the hill of Ophel. Ziha and Gishpa were in charge of them.

²²Uzzi was the chief officer of the Levites in Jerusalem. He was the son of Bani. Bani was the son of Hashabiah. Hashabiah was the son of Mattaniah. Mattaniah was the son of Mika. Uzzi was one of the members of Asaph's family line. They were musicians in charge of the worship services at the house of God. ²³The musicians received their orders from the Persian king. He told them what they should do every day.

²⁴Pethahiah worked for the king in all matters that were connected with the people. He was the son of Meshezabel. Meshezabel belonged to the family line of Zerah. Zerah was the son of Judah.

²⁵Many of the people of Judah lived in villages that had fields around them. Some of them lived in Kiriath Arba and the settlements that were around it. Others lived in Dibon and its settlements. Others lived in Jekabzeel and its villages. ²⁶Others lived in Jeshua, Moladah and Beth Pelet. ²⁷Others lived in Hazar Shual and in Beersheba and its settlements. ²⁸Others lived in Ziklag and in Mekonah and its settlements. ²⁹Others lived in En Rimmon and Zorah. Others lived in Jarmuth, ³⁰Zanoah and Adullam and their villages. Others

lived in Lachish and its fields. Still others lived in Azekah and its settlements. So the people of Judah were living all the way from Beersheba to the Valley of Hinnom.

³¹Some of the members of the family line of Benjamin who were from Geba lived in Mikmash. Others lived in Aija and in Bethel and its settlements. ³²Others lived in Anathoth, Nob and Ananiah. ³³Others lived in Hazor, Ramah and Gittaim. ³⁴Others lived in Hadid, Zeboim and Neballat. ³⁵Others lived in Lod and Ono. Still others lived in Ge Harashim.

³⁶Some of the groups of the Levites from Judah made their homes in the territory of Benjamin.

The Priests and Levites Who Returned to Judah

12 Some priests and Levites returned to Judah with Zerubbabel and Joshua. Zerubbabel was the son of Shealtiel. Here are the names of those priests and Levites.

Seraiah, Jeremiah, Ezra,
² Amariah, Malluk, Hattush,
³ Shekaniah, Rehum, Meremoth,
⁴ Iddo, Ginnethon, Abijah,
⁵ Mijamin, Moadiah, Bilgah,
⁶ Shemaiah, Joiarib, Jedaiah,
⁷ Sallu, Amok, Hilkiah, Jedaiah

All of them were the leaders of the priests and those who helped them. They lived in the days of Joshua.

⁸The Levites were Jeshua, Binnui, Kadmiel, Sherebiah and Judah. There were also Mattaniah and those who helped him. They were in charge of the songs for giving thanks. ⁹Bakbukiah and Unni helped them. They stood and sang across from them during the services.

¹⁰ Joshua was the father of Joiakim. Joiakim was the father of Eliashib. Eliashib was the father of Joiada.
¹¹ Joiada was the father of Jonathan. And Jonathan was the father of Jaddua.

¹² Here are the names of the family leaders of the priests. They were the leaders in the days of Joiakim.

Meraiah was from Seraiah's family.
Hananiah was from Jeremiah's family.

¹³ Meshullam was from Ezra's family. Jehohanan was from Amariah's family. ¹⁴ Jonathan was from Malluk's family. Joseph was from Shekaniah's family. ¹⁵ Adna was from Harim's family. Helkai was from Meremoth's family. ¹⁶ Zechariah was from Iddo's family. Meshullam was from Ginnethon's family. ¹⁷ Zikri was from Abijah's family. Piltai was from Miniamin's and Moadiah's family. ¹⁸ Shammua was from Bilgah's family. Jehonathan was from Shemaiah's family. ¹⁹ Mattenai was from Joiarib's family. Uzzi was from Jedaiah's family. ²⁰ Kallai was from Sallu's family. Eber was from Amok's family. ²¹ Hashabiah was from Hilkiah's family. And Nethanel was from Jedaiah's family.

²²The names of the family leaders of the Levites in the days of Eliashib, Joiada, Johanan and Jaddua were written down. So were the names of the family leaders of the priests. That happened while Darius ruled over Persia. ²³The names of the leaders in Levi's family line up to the time of Johanan were written down. They were written in the official records. Johanan was the son of Eliashib. ²⁴The leaders of the Levites were Hashabiah, Sherebiah and Jeshua. Jeshua was the son of Kadmiel. Those who helped them stood across from them to sing praises and give thanks. One group would sing back to the other. That's what David, the man of God, had ordered.

²⁵Mattaniah, Bakbukiah, Obadiah, Meshullam, Talmon and Akkub stood at the gates of the temple. They guarded the storerooms at the gates. ²⁶They served in the days of Joiakim. He was the son of Joshua. Joshua was the son of Jozadak. They also served in the days of Nehemiah and Ezra. Nehemiah was the governor. Ezra was a priest and the teacher of the Law.

The Wall of Jerusalem Is Set Apart to God

²⁷The wall of Jerusalem was set apart to God. For that occasion, the Levites were gathered together from where they lived. They were brought to Jerusalem to celebrate that happy occasion. They celebrated the fact that the wall was being set apart to God. They did it by singing and giving their thanks to him. They celebrated by playing music on cymbals, harps and lyres. ²⁸The musicians were also brought together. Some of them came in from the area around Jerusalem. Others came from the villages where the people of Netophah lived. ²⁹Others came from Beth Gilgal. Still others came from the area of Geba and Azmaveth. The musicians had built villages for themselves around Jerusalem. ³⁰The priests and Levites made themselves pure. Then they made the people, the gates and the wall pure and "clean."

³¹I, Nehemiah, had the leaders of Judah go up on top of the wall. I also appointed two large choirs to sing and give thanks. I told one of them to walk south on top of the wall. That was toward the Dung Gate. ³²Hoshaiah and half of the leaders of Judah followed them. ³³Azariah, Ezra, Meshullam, ³⁴Judah, Benjamin, Shemaiah and Jeremiah also followed them. ³⁵Some priests who had trumpets followed them. So did Zechariah. He was the son of Jonathan. Jonathan was the son of Shemaiah. Shemaiah was the son of Mattaniah. Mattaniah was the son of Micaiah. Micaiah was the son of Zakkur. Zakkur was the son of Asaph. ³⁶Those who helped Zechariah also marched along. They were Shemaiah, Azarel, Milalai, Gilalai, Maai, Nethanel, Judah and Hanani. They brought musical instruments with them. That's what David, the man of God, had ordered. Ezra led the group that was marching south. He was the teacher of the Law. ³⁷At the Fountain Gate they continued straight up the steps of the City of David. The steps went up to the wall. Then the group passed above the place where David's palace had been. They continued on to the Water Gate on the east.

³⁸The second choir went north. I followed them on top of the wall. Half of the people went with me. They went past the Tower of the Ovens. They went to the Broad Wall. ³⁹They marched over the Gate of Ephraim. They went over the Jeshanah Gate and the Fish Gate. They went past the Tower of Hananel and the Tower of the Hundred. They continued on to the Sheep Gate. At the Gate of the Guard they stopped.

⁴⁰Then the two choirs that sang and gave thanks took their places in God's house. So

did I. So did half of the officials. ⁴¹And so did the priests. They were Eliakim, Maaseiah, Miniamin, Micaiah, Elioenai, Zechariah and Hananiah. They had their trumpets with them. ⁴²Maaseiah, Shemaiah, Eleazar, Uzzi, Jehohanan, Malkijah, Elam and Ezer were also there. The choirs sang under the direction of Jezrahiah. ⁴³On that day large numbers of sacrifices were offered. The people were glad because God had given them great joy. The women and children were also very happy. The joyful sound in Jerusalem could be heard far away.

Nehemiah Makes Some Final Changes

⁴⁴At that time some men were put in charge of the storerooms. That's where all the gifts the people brought were placed. Those gifts included the first shares of their crops. They also included a tenth of everything the Law required. Crops were harvested from the fields around the towns. The people had to bring the shares of those crops that were required by the Law. They gave them to the priests and Levites. That's because the people of Judah were pleased with the priests and Levites who were serving God. ⁴⁵The priests and Levites did everything their God wanted them to do. They made things pure and "clean." The musicians and the men who guarded the temple gates also served God. Everything was done just as David and his son Solomon had commanded. ⁴⁶A long time ago there had been directors for the musicians. There had also been directors for the songs for giving thanks and praise to God. It was in the time of David and Asaph. ⁴⁷So now in the days of Zerubbabel and Nehemiah, all the people of Israel brought their gifts. They gave the musicians and the men who guarded the gates what they were supposed to give them every day. They also set apart the shares for the other Levites. And the Levites set apart the shares for the priests in the family line of Aaron.

13 At that time the Book of Moses was read out loud. All the people heard it. It was written there that no Ammonite or Moabite could ever become a member of God's community. ²That's because they hadn't given the people of Israel food and water. Instead, they had hired Balaam to put a curse on them. But our God turned the curse into a blessing. ³When that law

was read, the people of Judah obeyed it. They sent out of Israel everyone who was from another nation.

⁴Eliashib the priest had been put in charge of the storerooms in the house of our God. He had worked closely with Tobiah. ⁵He had also provided a large room for Tobiah. It had been used to store the grain offerings. The incense and the objects for the temple had been put there. And a tenth of the grain, olive oil and fresh wine had been kept there. That's what the Law required for the Levites. That's also what it required for the musicians and the men who guarded the temple gates. The gifts for the priests had been kept there too.

⁶But I wasn't in Jerusalem while all of that was going on. I had returned to the Persian King Artaxerxes, the king of Babylon. I went to him in the 32nd year of his rule. Some time later I asked him to let me return to Jerusalem. ⁷When I got back, I learned about the evil thing Eliashib had done. He had provided a room for Tobiah. It was in the courtyards of God's house. ⁸So I was very unhappy. I threw all of Tobiah's things out of the room. ⁹I gave orders to make the rooms pure and "clean" again. Then I put the supplies from God's house back into them. That included the grain offerings and the incense.

¹⁰I also learned that the shares the Levites were supposed to receive hadn't been given to them. So all the Levites and musicians had to leave their regular temple duties. They had to go back and farm their own fields. ¹¹I gave a warning to the officials. I asked them, "Why aren't you taking care of God's house?" Then I brought the Levites and musicians together. I stationed them in their proper places. I put them back to work.

¹²All the people of Judah brought a tenth of the grain, olive oil and fresh wine. They took it to the storerooms. ¹³I put some men in charge of the storerooms. They were Shelemiah, Zadok and Pedaiah. Shelemiah was a priest. Zadok was a teacher of the law. And Pedaiah was a Levite. I made Hanan their assistant. He was the son of Zakkur. Zakkur was the son of Mattaniah. I knew that these men could be trusted. They were put in charge of handing out the supplies to the other Levites.

¹⁴You are my God. Remember me because of what I've done. I've worked

faithfully for your temple and its services. So please don't forget the good things I've done.

[15]In those days I saw some people of Judah stomping on grapes in winepresses. They were doing it on the Sabbath day. Other people were bringing in grain. They were loading it on donkeys. Still other people were loading up wine, grapes, figs and other kinds of things. They were bringing all of it into Jerusalem on the Sabbath day. So I warned them not to sell food on that day. [16]People from Tyre who lived in Jerusalem were bringing in fish. In fact, they were bringing in all kinds of goods. They were selling them in Jerusalem on the Sabbath day. The people of Judah were buying them. [17]I gave a warning to the nobles of Judah. I said, "Why are you doing such an evil thing? You are misusing the Sabbath day! [18]Your people of long ago did the very same things. That's why our God has brought all this trouble on us. That's why he's making this city suffer so much. Now you are making him even angrier against Israel. You are misusing the Sabbath day."

[19]Evening shadows fell on the gates of Jerusalem before the Sabbath day started. So I ordered the gates to be shut. They had to remain closed until the Sabbath day was over. I stationed some of my own men at the gates. I told them not to let anything be brought in on the Sabbath day. [20]Once or twice some traders and sellers spent the night outside Jerusalem. They were hoping to sell all kinds of goods. [21]But I gave them a warning. I said, "Why are you spending the night by the wall? If you do this again, I'll arrest you." So from that time on they didn't come on the Sabbath day anymore. [22]I commanded the Levites to make themselves pure. Then I told them to go and guard the gates. I wanted the Sabbath day to be kept holy.

You are my God. Remember me because of the good things I've done. Be kind to me according to your great love.

[23]In those days I also saw that some men of Judah had married women from Ashdod. Others had married women from Ammon or Moab. [24]Half of their children spoke the language of Ashdod. Or they spoke the language of one of the other nations. They didn't even know how to speak the language of Judah. [25]So I gave them a warning. I cursed them. I beat up some of them. I pulled their hair out. I had them make a promise in God's name. I said, "You must promise not to give your daughters to be married to their sons. You must promise not to let their daughters marry your sons. And you must not marry their daughters either. [26]That's how Solomon, the king of Israel, sinned. He married women from other nations. There wasn't a king like him anywhere. His God loved him. In fact, God made him king over the whole nation of Israel. But even he was led into sin by women from other lands. [27]Now I hear that you too are doing all of the same terrible and evil things. You aren't being faithful to our God. You are marrying women from other lands."

[28]One of the sons of Joiada was the son-in-law of Sanballat the Horonite. Joiada, the son of Eliashib, was the high priest. I drove Joiada's son away from me.

[29]You are my God. Remember what those priests have done. They have brought shame to their own work. They have also brought shame to the covenant that God made with the priests and Levites long ago.

[30]So I made the priests and Levites pure. I made them pure from every practice that had come from other countries and had made them impure. I gave them their duties. Each one had his own job to do. [31]I also made plans for gifts of wood to be brought at certain appointed times. And I made plans for the first share of the crops to be brought.

You are my God. Please remember me with kindness.

Esther

And now we've come to a book that reads like a best-selling thriller: Esther. This page-turner truly contains something for everyone: beauty contests, close calls, surprise twists, devious and power-hungry schemers, and the ultimate triumph of good over evil. But surprisingly, one thing it doesn't contain is any mention of God. It is, in fact, the single book of the Bible that doesn't once use the name of "God." However, it is clear that the Lord protects His people through the heroic efforts of Esther and her cousin Mordecai.

The setting is Susa, a Persian city where some of the Jews had settled after being carried away from Jerusalem. While Ezra and Nehemiah (the title characters of the two previous Bible books) had faithfully returned to Jerusalem to repair and rebuild the city's Temple and walls, Esther was faithful in her immediate vicinity—far away in Persia. Yet you will see that because of her steadfast courage and great faithfulness, she was responsible for saving the Hebrew people from extinction. Her action was so significant that it instituted an annual holiday, Purim, which Jewish people still celebrate today.

What's it mean, Eugene?

Miracles—Events or occurrences that have no *natural* explanation and which would not occur without God's supernatural power. Of course the parting of the Red Sea, the raising of Lazarus from the dead, and acts of healing noted throughout the Bible are the most referenced miracles. In truth though, life itself is a *great* miracle. We exist merely because God created us to do so.

Vashti Is Removed From Her Position as Queen

1 King Xerxes ruled over the 127 territories in his kingdom. They reached from India all the way to Cush. Here is what happened during the time Xerxes ruled over the whole Persian kingdom. ²He was ruling from his royal throne in the fort of Susa. ³In the third year of his rule King Xerxes gave a feast. It was for all his nobles and officials. The military leaders of Persia and Media were there. So were the princes and the nobles of the territories he ruled over.

⁴Every day for 180 days he showed his guests the great wealth of his kingdom. He also showed them how glorious his kingdom was. ⁵When those days were over, the king gave another feast. It lasted for seven days. It was held in the garden of the king's courtyard. It was for all the people who lived in the fort of Susa. Everyone from the least important person to the most important was invited. ⁶The garden was decorated with white and blue linen banners. They hung from ropes that were made out of white linen and purple cloth. The ropes were connected to silver rings on marble pillars. There were gold and silver couches in the garden. They were placed on a floor that was made out of small stones. The floor had purple crystal, marble, mother-of-pearl and other stones of great value. ⁷Royal wine was served in gold cups. Each cup

Esth. 1:2 The city of Susa was so rich that when Alexander the Great plundered it in the fourth century BC, it took ten thousand pairs of mules and five thousand camels to carry away all the wealth. That would have been an amazing parade!

BIBLE ADVENTURES

Bernard told the story of Esther to Robyn and Melanie Jacobs in "Bernard and Esther" (A#11).

was different from all the others. There was plenty of wine. The king always provided as much as his guests wanted. ⁸He commanded that they should be allowed to drink as much or as little as they wished. He directed all his servants to give his guests what they asked for.

⁹Queen Vashti also gave a feast. Only women were invited. It was held in the royal palace of King Xerxes.

¹⁰On the seventh day Xerxes was in a good mood because he had drunk a lot of wine. So he gave a command to the seven officials who served him. They were Mehuman, Biztha, Harbona, Bigtha, Abagtha, Zethar and Karkas. ¹¹King Xerxes told them to bring Queen Vashti to him. He wanted her to come wearing her royal crown. He wanted to show off her beauty to the people and nobles. She was lovely to look at. ¹²The attendants told Queen Vashti what the king had ordered her to do. But she refused to come. So the king became very angry.

¹³It was the king's practice to ask for advice about matters of law and fairness. So he spoke with the wise men who understood what was going on at that time. ¹⁴They were the men closest to the king. Their names were Karshena, Shethar, Admatha, Tarshish, Meres, Marsena and Memukan. They were the seven nobles of Persia and Media. They were the king's special advisers and the most important men in the kingdom.

¹⁵"You know the law," the king said. "What should I do to Queen Vashti? She hasn't obeyed my command. The officials told her what I ordered her to do, didn't they?"

¹⁶Then Memukan gave a reply to the king and the nobles. He said, "Queen Vashti has done what is wrong. But she didn't do it only against you, King Xerxes. She did it also against all the nobles. And she did it against the people in all the territories you rule over. ¹⁷All the women will hear about what the queen has done. Then they won't respect their husbands. They'll say, 'King Xerxes commanded Queen Vashti to be brought to him. But she wouldn't come.'

WHAT ABOUT YOU?

Have you ever been in exactly the right place at exactly the right time? Maybe you caught a home-run ball at a baseball game, or you grabbed a big bowl of food just as it fell off the dinner table. Sometimes, being in the right place at the right time can even save a life!

Some people would call this luck. But as Christians, we know that God often plays a role in situations like this. It's referred to as His "providence." God's providence and care can be seen clearly in the biblical story of Queen Esther.

Esther came from humble beginnings, but she grew up to become queen of one of the largest empires the world has ever seen. God had a plan for her life, and she was obedient to Him. Because of Esther's willingness to follow God's plan (and trust that He had placed her in the right place at the right time), she could boldly go before the throne of King Xerxes and save her people. While lovely, she was still a fairly ordinary girl who became a hero because of her faith in God.

If you've never read the book of Esther, read it today. Then make a list of talents or qualities God has given you. How do you think you can use them for the Lord? If you're not sure, pray for wisdom and guidance, and that He will put you in the right place at just the right time.

---

[18]Here is what will start today. The leading women in Persia and Media who have heard about the queen's actions will act in the same way. They'll disobey all your nobles, just as she disobeyed you. They won't have any respect for their husbands. They won't honor them.

[19]"So if it pleases you, send out a royal order. Let it be written down in the laws of Persia and Media. Those laws can never be changed. Let the royal order say that Vashti can never see you again. Also let her position as queen be given to someone who is better than she is. [20]And let your order be announced all through your entire kingdom. Then all women will have respect for their husbands, from the least important to the most important."

[21]The king and his nobles were pleased with that advice. So he did what Memukan had suggested. [22]The king sent messages out to every territory in the kingdom. He sent them to each territory in its own writing. He sent them to every nation in its own language. The messages announced that every man should rule over his own family, using his own language.

Esther Becomes Queen of Persia

2 Later, the great anger of King Xerxes calmed down. Then he remembered Vashti and what she had done. He also remembered the royal order he had sent out concerning her. [2]At that time the king's personal attendants made a suggestion. They said, "King Xerxes, let a search be made for some beautiful young virgins for you. [3]Appoint some officials in every territory in your kingdom. Have them bring all these beautiful young women into the fort of Susa. Put them in the special place where the virgins stay. Then put Hegai in charge of them. He's the official who serves you. He's in charge of the women. Let beauty care be given to the new group of women. [4]Then let the young woman who pleases you the most become queen in Vashti's place." The king liked that advice. So he followed it.

[5]There was a Jew living in the fort of Susa. He was from the tribe of Benjamin. His name was Mordecai. He was the son of Jair. Jair was the son of Shimei. Shimei was the son of Kish. [6]Nebuchadnezzar had forced Mordecai to leave Jerusalem. He was among the prisoners who were carried off

along with Jehoiachin. Jehoiachin had been king of Judah. Nebuchadnezzar was king of Babylon. ⁷Mordecai had a cousin named Hadassah. He had raised her because she didn't have a father or mother. Hadassah was also called Esther. She had a lovely figure and was very beautiful. Mordecai had adopted her as his own daughter. He had done it when her father and mother died.

⁸After the king's order and law were announced, many young women were brought to the fort of Susa. Hegai was put in charge of them. Esther was also taken to the king's palace. She was put under the control of Hegai. He was in charge of the place where the virgins stayed. ⁹Esther pleased him. He showed her how happy he was with her. Right away he provided her with her beauty care and special food. He appointed seven female attendants to help her. They were chosen from the king's palace. He moved her and her attendants into the best part of the place where the virgins stayed.

¹⁰Esther hadn't told anyone who her people were. She hadn't talked about her family. That's because Mordecai had told her not to. ¹¹Mordecai tried to find out how Esther was getting along. He wanted to know what was happening to her. So he walked back and forth near the courtyard by the place where the virgins stayed. He did it every day.

¹²Each young woman had to complete 12 months of beauty care. They used oil of myrrh for six months. And they used perfume and makeup for the other six months. A virgin's turn to go in to King Xerxes could come only after a full 12 months had passed. ¹³And here is how she would go to the king. She would be given anything she wanted from the place where the virgins stayed. She could take it with her to the king's palace. ¹⁴In the evening she would go there. In the morning she would leave. Then she would go to the special place where the king's concubines stayed. She would be put under the control of Shaashgaz. He was the king's official who was in charge of the concubines. She would never return to the king unless he was pleased with her. He had to send for her by name before she could go to him again.

¹⁵Mordecai had adopted Esther. She had been the daughter of his uncle Abihail.

Her turn came to go in to the king. She only asked for what Hegai suggested. He was the king's official who was in charge of the place where the virgins stayed. Everyone who saw Esther was pleased with her. ¹⁶She was taken to King Xerxes in the royal house. It was now the tenth month. That was the month of Tebeth. It was the seventh year of the rule of Xerxes.

¹⁷The king liked Esther more than he liked any of the other women. She pleased him more than any of the other virgins. So he put a royal crown on her head. He made her queen in Vashti's place. ¹⁸Then the king gave a feast to honor Esther. All his nobles and officials were invited. He announced a holiday all through the territories he ruled over. He freely gave many gifts in keeping with his royal wealth.

Mordecai Uncovers a Plan to Kill the King

¹⁹The virgins were gathered together a second time. At that time Mordecai was sitting at the palace gate. ²⁰Esther had kept her family history a secret. She hadn't told anyone who her people were. Mordecai had told her not to. She continued to follow his directions. That's what she had always done when he was bringing her up.

²¹Bigthana and Teresh were two of the king's officers. They guarded the door of the royal palace. They became angry with King Xerxes. So they decided to kill him. They made their evil plans while Mordecai was sitting at the palace gate. ²²So Mordecai found out about it and told Queen Esther. Then she reported it to the king. She told him that Mordecai had uncovered the plans against him. ²³Some people checked Esther's report. And they found out it was true. So the two officials were put to death. Then poles were stuck through them. They were set up where people could see them. All of that was written in the official records. It was written down while the king was watching.

Haman Plans to Destroy the Jews

3 After those events, King Xerxes honored Haman. Haman was the son of Hammedatha. He was from the family line of Agag. The king gave Haman a higher position than he had before. He gave him a seat of honor. It was higher than the positions any

Jason's Jargon

ESTHER 3

Ready? Find *official mark* in this chapter. When a king sent out an order that could never be disobeyed or changed, he would place his official mark, also known as his royal seal, on it.

of the other nobles had. ²All the royal officials at the palace gate got down on their knees. They gave honor to Haman. That's because the king had commanded them to do it. But Mordecai refused to get down on his knees. He wouldn't give Haman any honor at all.

³The royal officials at the palace gate asked Mordecai a question. They said, "Why don't you obey the king's command?" ⁴Day after day they spoke to him. But he still refused to obey. So they told Haman about it. They wanted to see whether he would let Mordecai get away with what he was doing. Mordecai had told them he was a Jew.

⁵Haman noticed that Mordecai wouldn't get down on his knees. He wouldn't give Haman any honor. So Haman was very angry. ⁶But he had found out who Mordecai's people were. So he didn't want to kill only Mordecai. He also looked for a way to destroy all Mordecai's people. They were Jews. He wanted to kill all of them everywhere in the kingdom of Xerxes.

⁷The lot was cast in front of Haman. The lot was called Pur. It was cast in the first month of the 12th year that Xerxes was king. That month was called Nisan. The lot was cast to choose a day and a month. The month chosen was the 12th month. That month was called Adar.

⁸Then Haman said to King Xerxes, "Certain people are scattered among the nations. They live in all the territories in your kingdom. They keep themselves separate from everyone else. Their practices are different from the practices of all other people. They don't obey your laws. It really isn't good for you to put up with them. ⁹If it pleases you, give the order to destroy them.

I'll even add 375 tons of silver to the king's officials for the royal treasures."

¹⁰So the king took his ring off his finger. The ring had his royal seal on it. He gave the ring to Haman. Haman was the son of Hammedatha, the Agagite. Haman was the enemy of the Jews. ¹¹"Keep the money," the king said to Haman. "Do what you want to with those people."

¹²The king sent for the royal secretaries. It was the 13th day of the first month. The secretaries wrote down all Haman's orders. They wrote them down in the writing of each territory in the kingdom. They also wrote them in the language of each nation. The orders were sent to the royal officials and to the governors of the territories. And the orders were also sent to the nobles of the nations. The orders were written in the name of King Xerxes himself. And they were stamped with his own official mark. ¹³They were carried by messengers. They were sent to all the king's territories. The orders commanded people to destroy, kill and wipe out all the Jews. That included young people and old people alike. It included women and children. All the Jews were supposed to be killed on a single day. That day was the 13th day of the 12th month. It was the month of Adar. The orders also commanded people to take everything that belonged to the Jews. ¹⁴A copy of the order had to be sent out as law. It had to be sent to every territory in the kingdom. It had to be announced to the people of every nation. Then they would be ready for that day.

¹⁵The king commanded the messengers to go out. So they did. The order was sent out from the fort of Susa. Then the king and Haman sat down to drink wine. But the people in the city were bewildered.

Mordecai Talks Esther Into Helping the Jews

4 Mordecai found out about everything that had been done. So he tore his clothes. He put on the rough clothing people wear when they're sad. He sat down in ashes. Then he went out into the city. He wept out loud. He cried bitter tears. ²But he only went as far as the palace gate. That's because no one dressed in that rough clothing was allowed to go through it. ³All the Jews were very sad. They didn't

CANDID CONVERSATIONS

I have to admit something. There are times when I don't want to hear from God. Okay, there I said it. When don't I? Usually it's when He asks me to do something I don't want to do. Last week, I felt like God was telling me to talk to a stranger in front of the post office—a homeless woman sitting on a bench with her young daughter. I quickly asked Him if I could just hand them a dollar, but no. I really felt like God wanted me to talk to her. So I did. And we had a good talk! I invited them to church the next day.

Can you imagine how Esther felt when she knew she needed to talk to the king on behalf of the Jews? She could've been killed for approaching the king! I look up to Esther and admire her courage. After what Jesus did on the Cross for me, I need to be able to get out of my comfort zone and do something for Him. You should try it too. What is God asking you to do?

eat anything. They wept and cried. Many of them put on the rough clothing people wear when they're sad. They were lying down in ashes. They did all these things in every territory where the king's order and law had been sent.

⁴Esther's male and female attendants came to her. They told her about Mordecai. So she became very troubled. She wanted him to take off his rough clothing. So she sent him other clothes to wear. But he wouldn't accept them. ⁵Then Esther sent for Hathak. He was one of the king's officials. He had been appointed to take care of her. She ordered him to find out what was troubling Mordecai. She wanted to know why he was so upset.

⁶So Hathak went out to see Mordecai. He was in the open area in front of the palace gate. ⁷Mordecai told him everything that had happened to him. He told him about the exact amount of money Haman had promised to add to the royal treasures. He said Haman wanted it to be used to pay some men to destroy the Jews. ⁸Mordecai also gave Hathak a copy of the order. It commanded people to wipe out the Jews. The order had been sent from Susa. Mordecai told Hathak to show the order to Esther. He wanted Hathak to explain it to her. Mordecai told him to tell her to go and beg the king for mercy. Mordecai wanted her to make an appeal to the king for her people.

⁹Hathak went back and reported to Esther what Mordecai had said. ¹⁰Then Esther directed him to give an answer to Mordecai. She told him to say, ¹¹"There is a certain law that everyone knows about. All the king's officials know about it. The people in the royal territories know about it. It applies to any man or woman who approaches the king in the inner courtyard without being sent for. It says they must be put to death. But there is a way out. Suppose the king reaches out his gold scepter toward them. Then their lives will be spared. But 30 days have gone by since the king sent for me."

ADVENTURES IN ODYSSEY

Esther's uncle told her that she became queen for "a time just like this." In the adventure "The Mystery of the Clock Tower" (A#52), Eugene, Connie, and Whit uncovered a story from history that showed that none of us know which moment in our lives could be "a time just like this."

¹²Esther's words were reported to Mordecai. ¹³Then he sent back an answer. He said, "You live in the king's palace. But don't think that just because you are there you will be the only Jew who will escape. ¹⁴What if you don't say anything at this time? Then help for the Jews will come from another place. But you and your family will die. Who knows? It's possible that you became queen for a time just like this."

¹⁵Then Esther sent a reply to Mordecai. She said, ¹⁶"Go. Gather together all the Jews who are in Susa. And fast for my benefit. Don't eat or drink anything for three days. Don't do it night or day. I and my attendants will fast just as you do. Then I'll go to the king. I'll do it even though it's against the law. And if I have to die, I'll die."

¹⁷So Mordecai went away. He carried out all Esther's directions.

Esther Asks the King for a Favor

5 On the third day Esther put on her royal robes. She stood in the inner courtyard of the palace. It was in front of the king's hall. The king was sitting on his royal throne in the hall. He was facing the entrance. ²He saw Queen Esther standing in the courtyard. He was pleased with her. So he reached out toward her the gold scepter that was in his hand. Then Esther approached him. She touched the tip of the scepter.

³The king asked, "What is it, Queen Esther? What do you want? I'll give it to you. I'll even give you up to half of my kingdom."

⁴Esther replied, "King Xerxes, if it pleases you, come to a feast today. I've prepared it for you. Please have Haman come with you."

⁵"Bring Haman at once," the king said to his servants. "Then we'll do what Esther asks."

So the king and Haman went to the feast Esther had prepared. ⁶As they were drinking wine, the king asked Esther the same question again. He said, "What do you want? I'll give it to you. What do you want me to do for you? I'll even give you up to half of my kingdom."

⁷Esther replied, "Here is what I want. Here is my appeal to you. ⁸I hope you will be pleased to give me what I want. And I hope you will be pleased to listen to my appeal. If you are, I'd like you and Haman to come tomorrow to the feast I'll prepare for you. Then I'll answer your question."

Haman Is Very Angry With Mordecai

⁹That day Haman was happy. So he left the palace in a good mood. But then he saw Mordecai at the palace gate. He noticed that Mordecai didn't stand up when he walked by. In fact, Mordecai didn't have any respect for him at all. So he was very angry with him. ¹⁰But Haman was able to control himself. He went on home.

Haman called together his friends and his wife Zeresh. ¹¹He bragged to them about how rich he was. He talked about how many sons he had. He spoke about all the ways the king had honored him. He bragged about how the king had given him a high position. It was higher than the position of any of the other nobles and officials. ¹²"And that's not all," Haman added. "I'm the only person Queen Esther invited to come with the king to the feast she gave. Now she has invited me along with the king tomorrow. ¹³But even all of that doesn't satisfy me. I won't be satisfied as long as I see that Jew Mordecai sitting at the palace gate."

¹⁴Haman's wife Zeresh and all his friends said to him, "Get a pole. In the morning, ask the king to have Mordecai put to death. Have the pole stuck through his body. Set it up at a place where it will be 75 feet above the ground. Everyone will be able to see it there. Then go to the feast with the king. Have a good time." Haman was delighted with that suggestion. So he got the pole ready.

The King Honors Mordecai

6 That night the king couldn't sleep. So he ordered the official records of his rule to be brought in. He ordered someone to read them to him. ²What Mordecai had done was written there. He had uncovered the plans of Bigthana and Teresh. They were two of the king's officers who guarded the door of the royal palace. They had decided to kill King Xerxes.

³"What great honor has Mordecai received for doing that?" the king asked.

"Nothing has been done for him," his attendants answered.

⁴The king asked, "Who is in the courtyard?" Haman had just entered the outer courtyard of the palace. He had come to speak to the king about putting Mordecai to death. He wanted to talk about putting

Mordecai's body on the pole he had prepared for him.

[5]The king's attendants said to him, "Haman is standing in the courtyard."

"Bring him in," the king ordered.

[6]Haman entered. Then the king asked him, "What should be done for the man I want to honor?"

Haman said to himself, "Is there anyone the king would rather honor than me?" [7]So he answered the king. He said, "Here is what you should do for the man you want to honor. [8]Have your servants get a royal robe you have worn. Have them bring a horse you have ridden on. Have a royal mark placed on its head. [9]Then give the robe and horse to one of your most noble princes. Let the robe be put on the man you want to honor. Let him be led on the horse through the city streets. Let people announce in front of him, 'This is what is done for the man the king wants to honor!'"

[10]"Go right away," the king commanded Haman. "Get the robe. Bring the horse. Do exactly what you have suggested. Do it for Mordecai the Jew. He's sitting out there at the palace gate. Make sure you do everything you have suggested."

[11]So Haman got the robe and the horse. He put the robe on Mordecai. And he led him on horseback through the city streets. He walked along in front of him and announced, "This is what is done for the man the king wants to honor!"

[12]After that, Mordecai returned to the palace gate. But Haman rushed home. He covered his head because he was very sad. [13]He told his wife Zeresh everything that had happened to him. He also told all his friends.

His advisers and his wife Zeresh spoke to him. They said, "Your fall from power started with Mordecai. He's a Jew. So now you can't stand up against him. You are going to be destroyed!" [14]They were still talking with him when the king's officials arrived. They hurried Haman away to the feast Esther had prepared.

Haman Is Put to Death

7 So the king and Haman went to Queen Esther's feast. [2]They were drinking wine on the second day. The king again asked, "What do you want, Queen Esther? I'll give it to you. What do you want me to do

WOOTON'S FUN FACTS
Esth. 7

Have you ever used the common phrase to "hang as high as Haman"? Me either. It means that you'll be publically ridiculed and defeated. In 1832, President Andrew Jackson used the phrase to blast his political enemies.

for you? I'll even give you up to half of my kingdom."

[3]Then Queen Esther answered, "Your Majesty, I hope you will be pleased to let me live. That's what I want. Please spare my people. That's my appeal to you. [4]My people and I have been sold to be destroyed. We've been sold to be killed and wiped out. Suppose we had only been sold as male and female slaves. Then I wouldn't have said anything. That kind of suffering wouldn't be a good enough reason to bother you."

[5]King Xerxes asked Queen Esther, "Who is the man who has dared to do such a thing? And where is he?"

[6]Esther said, "The man hates us! He's our enemy! He's this evil Haman!"

Then Haman was terrified in front of the king and queen. [7]The king got up. He was very angry. He left his wine and went out into the palace garden. But Haman realized that the king had already decided what he was going to do to him. So he stayed behind to beg Queen Esther for his life.

[8]The king returned from the palace garden to the dinner hall. Just then he saw Haman falling on the couch where Esther was lying.

The king shouted, "Will he even treat the queen like this? Will he harm her while she's right here with me in the palace?"

As soon as the king finished speaking, his men covered Haman's face. [9]Then

Harbona said, "There's a pole standing near Haman's house. He has prepared it for Mordecai. Mordecai is the one who spoke up to help you. Haman had planned to have him put to death. He was going to have the pole stuck through his body. Then he was going to set it up at a place where it would be 75 feet above the ground." Harbona was one of the officials who attended the king.

The king said to his men, "Put Haman to death! Stick the pole through his body! Set it up where everyone can see it!" ¹⁰So they did. And they used the pole Haman had prepared for Mordecai. Then the king's anger calmed down.

The King Allows the Jews to Fight for Their Lives

8 That same day King Xerxes gave Queen Esther everything Haman had owned. Haman had been the enemy of the Jews. Esther had told the king that Mordecai was her cousin. So Mordecai came to see the king. ²The king took his ring off. It had his royal mark on it. He had taken it back from Haman. Now he gave it to Mordecai. And Esther put Mordecai in charge of everything Haman had owned.

³Esther made another appeal to the king. She fell at his feet and wept. She begged him to put an end to the evil plan of Haman, the Agagite. He had decided to kill the Jews. ⁴The king reached out his gold scepter toward Esther. She got up and stood in front of him.

⁵She said, "King Xerxes, I hope you will think what I'm asking is the right thing to do. I hope you are pleased with me. If you are, and if it pleases you, let an order be written. Let it take the place of the messages Haman wrote. Haman was the son of Hammedatha, the Agagite. He planned to kill the Jews. He wrote orders to destroy us in all your territories. ⁶I couldn't stand by and see the horrible trouble that would fall on my people! I couldn't stand to see my family destroyed!"

⁷King Xerxes gave a reply to Queen Esther and Mordecai the Jew. He said, "Haman attacked the Jews. So I've given Esther

WHAT ABOUT YOU?

What's the bravest thing you've ever done? Have you ever stood up to a bully? Or maybe you decided to do the right thing, even though you knew it would cost you. Well, Queen Esther was challenged to do both.

Even though she was married to King Xerxes, Esther knew she could be killed for entering his inner court without an invitation. But she also knew that a bully named Haman was ready to wipe out the Jews if she didn't step in and earn the king's favor. So Esther, a Jew herself, had a decision to make. Would she be brave?

Esther's cousin Mordecai knew that God wouldn't let the Jews disappear completely. There was a nation to protect and prophecies to fulfill. Yet many of God's chosen people—including Esther's closest friends and family—were still in serious danger. So Esther blessed them by doing the right thing, standing up to Haman's schemes, and approaching the king with a plan to save many lives.

Esther acted with true bravery. When it comes to heroes of the faith, she was the real thing.

Ask your friends and family to share the bravest act they've ever heard or read about. See what they say. Then read Luke 22:39–44. In this passage, we see how stressed Jesus was just before dying for the sins of the world. But He trusted God and bravely did the right thing—the loving thing—by going to the Cross. Take a moment to thank Him for that.

everything he owned. My men have stuck a pole through his dead body. And they've set it up where everyone can see it. [8]Now write another order in my name. Do it for the benefit of the Jews. Do what seems best to you. Stamp the order with my royal mark. Nothing that is written in my name and stamped with my mark can ever be changed."

[9]Right away the king sent for the royal secretaries. It was the 23rd day of the third month. That was the month of Sivan. They wrote down all Mordecai's orders to the Jews. They also wrote them to the royal officials, the governors and the nobles of the 127 territories in his kingdom. The territories reached from India all the way to Cush. The orders were written down in the writing of each territory. They were written in the language of each nation. They were also written to the Jews in their own writing and language. [10]Mordecai wrote the orders in the name of King Xerxes. He stamped them with the king's royal mark. He sent them by messengers on horseback. They rode fast horses that were raised just for the king.

[11]The Jews in every city could now gather together and fight for their lives. The king's order gave them that right. But suppose soldiers from any nation or territory attacked them, their women or children. Then the Jews could destroy, kill and wipe out those soldiers. They could also take the goods that belonged to their enemies. [12]A day was appointed for the Jews to do that in all the king's territories. It was the 13th day of the 12th month. That was the month of Adar. [13]A copy of the order was sent out as law in every territory. It was announced to the people of every nation. So the Jews would be ready on that day. They could pay back their enemies.

[14]The messengers rode on the royal horses. They raced along. That's what the king commanded them to do. The order was also sent out in the fort of Susa.

The Jews Win the Battle Over Their Enemies

[15]Mordecai left the king and went on his way. Mordecai was wearing royal clothes when he went. They were blue and white. He was also wearing a large gold crown. And he was wearing a purple coat. It was made out of fine linen. The city of Susa

Esth. 8:14 The Persian royal horses were Nisean, a rare breed developed in what is now Iran. They were beautiful and multicolored. I went to a stable to try to find some so I could go on a horseback-riding date with Penny. Unfortunately, I found out they are now extinct.

celebrated with great joy. [16]The Jews were filled with joy and happiness. They were very glad because now they were being honored. [17]They celebrated and enjoyed good food. They were glad and full of joy. That was true everywhere the king's order came. It was true in every territory and every city. Many people from other nations announced that they had become Jews. That's because they were so afraid of the Jews.

9 The king's order had to be carried out on the 13th day of the 12th month. That was the month of Adar. On that day the enemies of the Jews had hoped to win the battle over them. But now everything had changed. The Jews had gained the advantage over those who hated them. [2]The Jews gathered together in their cities. They gathered in all the territories King Xerxes ruled over. They came together to attack those who were trying to destroy them. No one could stand up against them. The people from all the other nations were afraid of them. [3]All the nobles in the territories helped the Jews. So did the royal officials, the governors and the king's officers. That's because they were so afraid of Mordecai. [4]He was well known in the palace. His fame spread all through the territories. So he became more and more important.

[5]The Jews struck down with swords all their enemies. They killed them and

destroyed them. They did what they pleased to those who hated them. ⁶The Jews killed 500 men. They destroyed them in the fort of Susa. ⁷They also killed Parshandatha, Dalphon, Aspatha, ⁸Poratha, Adalia, Aridatha, ⁹Parmashta, Arisai, Aridai and Vaizatha. ¹⁰They were the ten sons of Haman. He was the son of Hammedatha. Haman had been the enemy of the Jews. They didn't take anything that belonged to their enemies.

Jason's Jargon

ESTHER 9

Search this chapter for the word *Purim*. Purim is a two-day celebration to remember when Esther saved the Jews. Today, Purim is celebrated with a public reading of the book of Esther.

¹¹A report was brought to the king that same day. He was told how many men had been killed in the fort of Susa. ¹²He said to Queen Esther, "The Jews have killed 500 men. They destroyed them in the fort of Susa. They also killed the ten sons of Haman there. What have they done in the rest of my territories? Now what do you want? I'll give it to you. What do you want me to do for you? I'll do that too."

¹³"If it pleases you," Esther answered, "let the Jews in Susa carry out today's order tomorrow also. Stick poles through the dead bodies of Haman's ten sons. Set them up where everyone can see them."

¹⁴So the king commanded that it be done. An order was sent out in Susa. And the king's men did to the bodies of Haman's sons everything they were told to do. ¹⁵The Jews in Susa came together on the 14th day of the month of Adar. They put 300 men to death in Susa. But they didn't take anything that belonged to those men.

¹⁶During that time, the rest of the Jews also gathered together. They lived in the king's territories. They came together to fight for their lives. They didn't want their enemies to bother them anymore. They wanted to get some peace and rest. So they killed 75,000 of their enemies. But they didn't take anything that belonged to them. ¹⁷It happened on the 13th of Adar. On the 14th day they rested. They made it a day to celebrate with great joy. And they enjoyed good food.

¹⁸But the Jews in Susa had gathered together on the 13th and 14th. Then on the 15th they rested. They made it a day to celebrate with great joy. And they enjoyed good food.

¹⁹That's why Jews who live out in the villages celebrate on the 14th of Adar. They celebrate that day with great joy. And they enjoy good food. They also give presents to each other on that day.

Purim Is Celebrated

²⁰Mordecai wrote down these events. He sent letters to all the Jews all through the territories of King Xerxes. It didn't matter whether the Jews lived nearby or far away. ²¹Mordecai told them to celebrate the 14th and 15th days of the month of Adar. He wanted them to do it every year. ²²Mordecai told the Jews to celebrate the time when they got rest from their enemies. That was the month when their sadness was turned into joy. It was when their weeping turned into a day for celebrating. He wrote the letters to celebrate those days as times of joy. He wanted the people to enjoy good food. He told them to give presents of food to one another. He also wanted them to give gifts to people who were poor.

²³So the Jews agreed to continue the celebrating they had started. They kept doing what Mordecai had written to them. ²⁴Haman was the son of Hammedatha, the Agagite. He had been the enemy of all the Jews. He had planned to destroy them. He had cast the lot to destroy them completely. The lot was called Pur. ²⁵But the king had found out about Haman's evil plan. So the king had sent out written orders. He had ordered that Haman's evil plan against the Jews should happen to him instead. The king also commanded that poles be stuck through the dead bodies of Haman and his sons. Then they should be set up where everyone could see them. ²⁶The days the Jews were celebrating were called Purim. Purim comes from the word Pur. Pur means Lot. Now the Jews celebrate these two days every year. They do it because of everything that

was written in Mordecai's letter. They also do it because of what they had seen and what had happened to them. [27]So they established it as a regular practice. They decided they would always observe these two days of the year. They would celebrate in the required way. And they would celebrate at the appointed time. They and their children after them would always observe these days. And so would all who join them. [28]The days should be remembered and celebrated. They should be remembered by every family for all time to come. They should be celebrated in every territory and in every city. The Jews should never stop celebrating the days of Purim. Their children after them should always remember these days.

[29]So Queen Esther, the daughter of Abihail, wrote a second letter. She wrote it together with Mordecai the Jew. They wanted to give their full authority to this second letter about Purim. [30]Mordecai sent letters to all the Jews in the 127 territories of the kingdom of Xerxes. The letters had messages of kindness and hope in them. [31]The letters established the days of Purim at their appointed times. They spoke about what Mordecai the Jew and Queen Esther had ordered the people to do. Everything should be done in keeping with the directions the Jews had set up for themselves and their children after them. The directions applied to their times of fasting and sadness. [32]Esther's order established the rules about Purim. It was written down in the records.

The Greatness of Mordecai

10 King Xerxes required people all through his kingdom to bring gifts. King Xerxes required gifts from its farthest shores. [2]All the king's powerful and mighty acts are written down. That includes the whole story of how important Mordecai was. The king had given him a position of great honor. All these things are written in the official records of the kings of Media and Persia. [3]The position of Mordecai the Jew was second only to the position of King Xerxes. Mordecai was the most important Jew. All the other Jews had the highest respect for him. That's because he worked for the good of his people. And he spoke up for the benefit of all the Jews.

Job

Even in the course of my scholarly pursuits, I face the oft-asked question, "Why do bad things happen to good people?" It's a matter that has confounded and troubled many people throughout the ages. Perhaps no one was more confused than Job. He was a good and faithful man, yet in the first two chapters of this book he loses essentially everything he has: wealth, health, and even his children. Only his wife is left, and her best advice is to speak evil against God and then die! (2:9) Hardly the soul of wit and sage council.

But Job refused to be so petty. He struggled to find the truth. His friends felt obliged to offer their opinions, though they didn't have the facts or even a reasonable degree of sensitivity. I pray that you don't get too mired in their arguments back and forth (chapters 3–37), but persevere to the grand finale when God Himself appears (chapters 38–41). He quizzes Job with question after question, quickly showing that our human understanding of God is vastly incomplete.

Ultimately, God makes it clear that Job's know-it-all friends were wrong. (Know-it-alls often are too proud in their knowledge. Take it from me.) God restored Job's health and wealth and gave him a new family as well. This book demonstrates the importance of perseverance during troublesome times and shows us how to avoid making things worse whenever we want to help friends who are having a rough time.

WHat's it MEAN, EUGENE?

Satan/the Devil—The veritable enemy of God and tempter of mankind. The word *devil* comes from *diabolos,* from which our word *diabolical* stems. Isaiah 14:12 identifies him as a powerful angel who was cast out of heaven for rebelling against God. Revelation 12:7–11 describes his fall and names him "the dragon" and "that old serpent" who "leads the whole world astray" and "brings charges against our brothers and sisters."

The Story Begins

1 There was a man who lived in the land of Uz. His name was Job. He was honest. He did what was right. He had respect for God and avoided evil. ²Job had seven sons and three daughters. ³He owned 7,000 sheep and 3,000 camels. He owned 500 pairs of oxen and 500 donkeys. He also had a large number of servants. He was the most important man among all the people in the east.

⁴His sons used to give feasts in their homes on their birthdays. They would invite their three sisters to eat and drink with them. ⁵The time for enjoying good food would end. Then Job would make plans for his children to be made pure and "clean." He would sacrifice a burnt offering for each of them. He would do it early in the morning. He would think, "Perhaps my children have sinned. Maybe they have spoken evil things against God in their hearts." That's what Job always did for his children when he felt they had sinned.

⁶One day angels came to the LORD. Satan also came with them. ⁷The LORD said to Satan, "Where have you come from?"

Satan answered, "From traveling all around the earth. I've been going from one end of it to the other."

⁸Then the LORD said to Satan, "Have you thought about my servant Job? There isn't

Job 1:4 Birthday parties are some of my favorite times. Especially when they involve lots of dairy products. Job 1 is the second mention of a birthday party in the Bible. The first was Pharaoh's birthday (Genesis 40:20).

anyone on earth like him. He is honest. He does what is right. He has respect for God and avoids evil."

⁹"You always give Job everything he needs," Satan replied. "That's why he has respect for you. ¹⁰Haven't you guarded him and his family? Haven't you taken care of everything he has? You have blessed everything he does. His flocks and herds are spread all through the land. ¹¹But now reach out your hand and strike down everything he has. Then I'm sure he will speak evil things against you. In fact, he'll do it right in front of you."

¹²The LORD said to Satan, "All right. I am handing everything he has over to you. But do not touch the man himself."

Then Satan left the LORD and went on his way.

¹³One day Job's sons and daughters were at their oldest brother's house. They were enjoying good food and drinking wine. ¹⁴During that time a messenger came to Job. He said, "The oxen were plowing. The donkeys were eating grass near them. ¹⁵Then the Sabeans attacked us and carried off the animals. They killed some of the servants with their swords. I'm the only one who has escaped to tell you!"

¹⁶While he was still speaking, a second messenger came. He said, "God sent lightning from the sky. It struck the sheep and killed them. It burned up some of the

WOOTON'S FUN FACTS

Job 1:1

That's Uz, not Oz. No wonderful wizard involved. It's in southern Syria and it's a very short name for a place. Other places in the Bible with two letters include Ai, Ar, No, and Ur. At least twenty-four cities have only three letters, among them are Gob, Gog, Put, Pul, Zin, and Ziz. Sounds like a song.

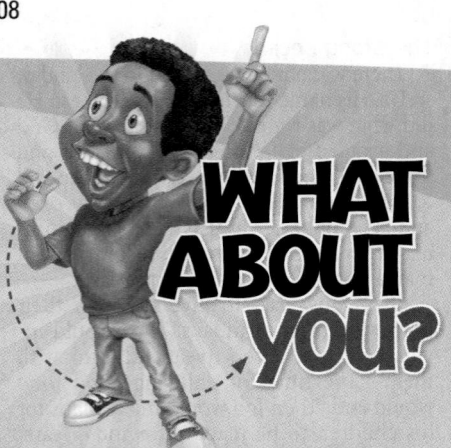

WHAT ABOUT YOU?

Imagine a world as flat as a sheet of paper. All the creatures living in it are two-dimensional shapes and lines. They can move around next to each other, but not above or below. Author Edwin Abbott explored this idea in his novel *Flatland*, in which a round ball visits a flat shape and helps the flat shape understand the 3-D world.

Have you ever felt like there's another dimension—a spiritual dimension—that you're not quite able to grasp? We all feel that way sometimes. Let's face it. How are people in our world supposed to wrap our minds around an invisible, eternal God who knows everything and is all-powerful? That's a human limitation that Job faced.

At the beginning of the book, Job can't understand why so many bad things are happening to him. After all, he's a righteous man. But after a lot of wrong answers and complaining, God steps in to straighten Job out. God describes His incredible creations, reminding Job that His power and will are beyond knowing.

Even if we can't understand why certain things happen, God has a plan. Like two-dimensional creatures trying to figure out a round ball, we are limited in our understanding. But we know God loves us and is powerful enough to create and manage the whole universe. So we can trust Him.

Among God's creations described in Job 38:31–33 are constellations of stars. On a clear night, go stargazing with your family. When you see those groups of stars in the sky, thank God for what He has made, and for loving you even in the hard times.

---

servants. I'm the only one who has escaped to tell you!"

¹⁷While he was still speaking, a third messenger came. He said, "The Chaldeans separated themselves into three groups. They attacked your camels and carried them off. They killed the rest of the servants with their swords. I'm the only one who has escaped to tell you!"

¹⁸While he was still speaking, a fourth messenger came. He said, "Your sons and daughters were at their oldest brother's house. They were enjoying good food and drinking wine. ¹⁹Suddenly a strong wind blew in from the desert. It struck the four corners of the house. The house fell down on your children. Now all of them are dead. I'm the only one who has escaped to tell you!"

²⁰After Job heard all these reports, he got up and tore his robe. He shaved his head. Then he fell to the ground and worshiped the LORD. ²¹He said,

"I was born naked.
    And I'll leave here naked.
The LORD has given, and the LORD has
        taken away.
    May the name of the LORD be praised."

²²In spite of everything, Job didn't sin by blaming God for doing anything wrong.

2 On another day angels came to the LORD. Satan also came to him along with them. ²The LORD said to Satan, "Where have you come from?"

Satan answered, "From traveling all around the earth. I've been going from one end of it to the other."

³Then the LORD said to Satan, "Have you thought about my servant Job? There isn't anyone on earth like him. He is honest. He does what is right. He has respect for God and avoids evil. You tried to turn me against him. You wanted me to destroy him without any reason. But he still continues to be faithful."

⁴Satan replied, "A man will give everything he has to save himself. So Job is willing to give up the lives of his family to save his own life. ⁵But now reach out your hand and strike his flesh and bones. Then I'm sure he will speak evil things against you. In fact, he'll do it right in front of you."

⁶The LORD said to Satan, "All right. I am handing him over to you. But you must spare his life."

⁷Then Satan left the LORD and went on his way. He sent painful sores on Job. They covered him from the bottom of his feet to the top of his head. ⁸He got part of a broken pot. He used it to scrape his skin. He did it while he was sitting in ashes.

⁹His wife said to him, "Are you still continuing to be faithful to the LORD? Speak evil things against him and die!"

¹⁰Job replied, "You are talking like a foolish woman. We accept good things from God. So we should also accept trouble when he sends it."

In spite of everything, Job didn't say anything that was sinful.

Mandy Straussberg had a day that felt like Job's in "Worst Day Ever" (A#35).

¹¹Job had three friends named Eliphaz the Temanite, Bildad the Shuhite, and Zophar the Naamathite. They heard about all the troubles that had come to Job. So they started out from their homes. They had agreed to meet together. They wanted to go and show their concern for Job. They wanted to comfort him. ¹²When they got closer to where he lived, they could see him. But they could hardly recognize him. They began to weep out loud. They tore their robes and sprinkled dust on their heads. ¹³Then they sat down on the ground with him for seven days and seven nights. No one said a word to him. That's because they saw how much he was suffering.

Job Wishes He Had Never Been Born

3 After a while, Job opened his mouth to speak. He cursed the day he had been born. ²He said,

³ "May the day I was born be wiped out.
    May the night be wiped away when
        people said, 'A boy is born!'
⁴ May that day turn into darkness.
    May God in heaven not care about it.
    May no light shine on it.
⁵ May gloom and total darkness take it
        back.
    May a cloud settle over it.
    May blackness cover it up.
⁶ May deep darkness take over the night I
        was born.
    May it not be included among the
        days of the year.
    May it never appear in any of the
        months.
⁷ May no children ever have been born
        on that night.
    May no shout of joy be heard in it.
⁸ May people say evil things about that
        day.
    May people ready to wake the sea
        monster Leviathan say evil
        things about that day.
⁹ May its morning stars become dark.
    May it lose all hope of ever seeing
        daylight.
    May it not see the first light of the
        morning sun.
¹⁰ It didn't keep my mother from letting
        me be born.
    It didn't keep my eyes from seeing
        trouble.
¹¹ "Why didn't I die when I was born?
    Why didn't I die as I came out of my
        mother's body?
¹² Why was I placed on her knees?
    Why did her breasts give me milk?
¹³ If all of that hadn't happened,
    I would be lying down in peace.
    I'd be asleep and at rest in the grave.

Jason's Jargon

JOB 3

Ready? Find *sigh* in this chapter! A sigh is a long, loud breath that usually expresses sadness or relief. In Job's case, his sighs meant he was unhappy with his life.

¹⁴ I'd be with the earth's kings and rulers.
They had built for themselves places
that are now destroyed.
¹⁵ I'd be with princes who used to have
gold.
They had filled their houses with
silver.
¹⁶ Why wasn't I buried like a baby who
was born dead?
Why wasn't I buried like a child who
never saw the light of day?
¹⁷ In the grave, sinful people don't cause
trouble anymore.
And there tired people find rest.
¹⁸ Prisoners also enjoy peace there.
They don't hear a slave driver
shouting at them anymore.
¹⁹ The least important and most
important people are there.
And there the slaves are set free
from their owners.

²⁰ "Why should those who suffer ever be
born?
Why should life be given to those
whose spirits are bitter?
²¹ Why is life given to those who long for
death that doesn't come?

Why is it given to those who would
rather search for death
than for hidden treasure?
²² Why is life given to those who are
actually happy and glad
when they reach the grave?
²³ Why is life given to a man like me?
God hasn't told me what will happen
to me.
He has surrounded me with nothing
but trouble.
²⁴ Sighs have become my food every day.
Groans pour out of me like water.
²⁵ What I was afraid of has come on me.
What I worried about has happened
to me.
²⁶ I don't have any peace and quiet.
I can't find any rest. All I have is
trouble."

The First Speech of Eliphaz

4 Then Eliphaz the Temanite replied,

² "Job, suppose someone tries to talk to
you.
Will that make you uneasy?
I can't keep from speaking up.

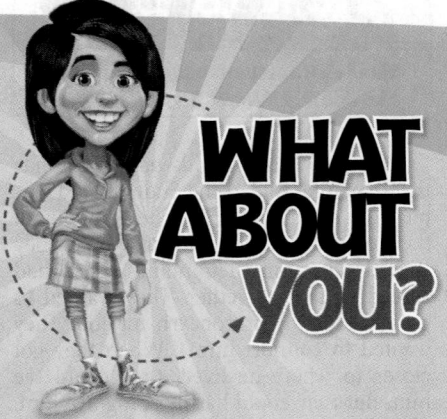

WHAT ABOUT YOU?

My life is over. Have you ever felt that way? Mandy surely did. After being late to class one morning, Mandy got slapped with an hour of detention. And that was just the start of her "Worst Day Ever." In this Adventures in Odyssey episode, Mandy lost her book report, broke an ice machine, injured her lip, fell in a toilet, crashed her bike, ruined her sweater, and had to chase down a dog that stole her backpack. It's no surprise that Mandy later complained.

There are a lot of ways to respond when you find yourself in a sticky mess. Sure, you can sing a hymn like Paul and Silas did when they were in prison. But did you know we can complain to God in a way that honors Him and gives us some relief?

Job poured out his complaints to the Lord. David did it too—and so did Jesus. The night He was betrayed, Jesus prayed to His Father, asking to be spared from suffering if that was God's will. That's the key. To truly honor God in our complaints, we should also pray that His will be done. And be willing to roll with that plan.

Think of a time when you complained to someone. Why not complain to the One who can do immeasurably more than we could ask or imagine? Today, when you think about that impossible math test, the mean bully, or that nasty stomach bug, tell God about it. He wants to help.

³ Look, you taught many people.
  You made weak hands strong.
⁴ Your words helped those who had
    fallen down.
  You made shaky knees strong.
⁵ Now trouble comes to you. And you are
    unhappy about it.
  It strikes you down. And you are
    afraid.
⁶ Shouldn't you worship God and trust in
    him?
  Shouldn't your honest life give you
    hope?

⁷ "Here's something to think about.
  Have people who aren't guilty ever
    been wiped out?
  Have honest people ever been
    completely destroyed?
⁸ Here's what I've observed.
  People gather a crop from what they
    plant.
  If they plant evil and trouble, that's
    what they will harvest.
⁹ The breath of God destroys them.
  The blast of his anger wipes them
    out.
¹⁰ Powerful lions might roar and growl.
  But their teeth are broken.
¹¹ Lions die because they don't have any
    food.
  Then their cubs are scattered.

¹² "A message came to me in secret.
  It was as quiet as a whisper.
¹³ I had a scary dream one night.
  I was sound asleep.
¹⁴ Fear and trembling seized me.
  That made every bone in my body
    shake.
¹⁵ A spirit glided past my face.
  The hair on my body stood on end.
¹⁶ Then the spirit stopped.
  But I couldn't tell what it was.
  Something stood there in front of me.
  I heard a soft voice.
¹⁷ It said, 'Can a human being be more
    right than God?
  Can even a strong man be more pure
    than the God who made him?
¹⁸ God doesn't trust those who serve him.
  He even brings charges against his
    angels.
¹⁹ So he'll certainly find fault with human
    beings.
  After all, they are made out of dust.

They can be crushed more easily
    than a moth.
²⁰ Between sunrise and sunset they are
    broken to pieces.
  Nobody even notices. They
    disappear forever.
²¹ Like a tent that falls down, they get
    weak.
  They die because they didn't follow
    God's wisdom.'"

5 Eliphaz continued,

"Call out if you want to, Job.
  But who will answer you?
  Which one of the holy angels will
    you turn to?
² Anger kills foolish people.
  Jealousy destroys those who are
    childish.
³ I saw that foolish people were having
    success.
  But suddenly harm came to their
    homes.
⁴ Their children aren't safe at all.
  They lose their case in court.
  No one speaks up for them.
⁵ Hungry people eat up the crops of the
    foolish.
  They even take the food that grows
    among thorns.
  Thirsty people long for the wealth of
    the foolish.
⁶ Hard times don't just grow out of the
    soil.
  Trouble doesn't jump out of the
    ground.
⁷ People are born to have trouble.
  And that's just as sure as sparks fly up.

⁸ "If I were you, I'd make my appeal to
    God.
  I'd bring my case to be judged by
    him.
⁹ He does wonderful things that can't be
    understood.
  He does miracles that can't even be
    counted.
¹⁰ He sends rain on the earth.
  He sends water on the countryside.
¹¹ He lifts up people who are lowly in
    spirit.
  He lifts up those who are sad.
  He keeps them safe.
¹² He stops the evil plans of those who are
    clever.

The work of their hands doesn't
　　succeed.
¹³ Some people think they are so wise.
　　But God catches them in their own
　　　tricks.
　　He sweeps away the evil plans of
　　　sinful people.
¹⁴ Darkness covers them in the daytime.
　　At noon they feel their way around
　　　as if it were night.
¹⁵ God saves needy people from the
　　cutting words of their enemies.
　　He saves them from their power.
¹⁶ So poor people have hope.
　　And God shuts the mouths of those
　　　who don't treat others fairly.

¹⁷ "Blessed is the person God corrects.
　　So don't hate the Mighty One's
　　　training.
¹⁸ He wounds. But he also bandages up
　　those he wounds.
　　He harms. But his hands also heal
　　　those he harms.
¹⁹ From six troubles he will save you.
　　Even if you are in trouble seven times,
　　　no harm will come to you.
²⁰ When there isn't enough food, God will
　　keep you from dying.
　　When you go into battle, he won't let
　　　a sword strike you down.
²¹ He will keep you safe from words that
　　can hurt you.
　　You won't need to be afraid
　　when everything is being destroyed.
²² You will laugh when things are being
　　destroyed.
　　You will enjoy life even when there
　　　isn't enough food.
　　You won't be afraid of wild animals.
²³ You will make a covenant with the
　　stones in the fields.
　　They won't keep your crops from
　　　growing.
　　Even wild animals will be at peace
　　　with you.
²⁴ You will know that the tent you live in
　　is secure.
　　You will check out your property.
　　You will see that nothing is missing.
²⁵ You can be sure you will have a lot of
　　children.
　　They will be as many as the blades of
　　　grass on the earth.
²⁶ You will go down to the grave
　　while you are still very strong.

You will be like a crop that is
　　gathered at the right time.
²⁷ "We have carefully studied all these
　　things.
　　And they are true.
　　So pay attention to them.
　　Apply them to yourself."

Job's Reply

6 Job replied,

² "I wish my great pain could be
　　weighed!
　　I wish all my suffering could be
　　　weighed on scales!
³ I'm sure it would weigh more than the
　　grains of sand on the seashore.
　　No wonder I've been so quick to
　　　speak!
⁴ The Mighty One has shot me with his
　　arrows.
　　I have to drink their poison.
　　God's terrors are aimed at me.
⁵ Does a wild donkey cry out when it has
　　enough grass?
　　Does an ox call out when it has
　　　plenty of food?
⁶ Is food that doesn't have any taste eaten
　　without salt?
　　Is there any flavor in the sap of a
　　　mallow plant?
⁷ I refuse to touch that kind of food.
　　It makes me sick.

⁸ "I wish I could have what I'm asking for!
　　I wish God would give me what I'm
　　　hoping for!
⁹ I wish he would crush me!
　　I wish he would just cut off my life!
¹⁰ Then I'd still have one thing to comfort
　　me.
　　It would be that I haven't said no to
　　　the Holy One's commands.
　　That would give me joy in spite of
　　　my pain that never ends.

¹¹ "I'm so weak that I no longer have any
　　hope.
　　Things have gotten so bad that I can't
　　　wait for help anymore.
¹² Am I as strong as stone?
　　Is my body made out of bronze?
¹³ I don't have the power to help myself.
　　All hope of success has been taken
　　　away from me.

¹⁴ "A person shouldn't stop being kind to a
friend.
Anyone who does that stops
showing respect for the
Mighty One.
¹⁵ But my friends have stopped being kind
to me.
They are like streams that only flow
for part of the year.
They are like rivers that flow over
their banks
¹⁶ when the ice begins to break up.
The streams rise when the snow
starts to melt.
¹⁷ But they stop flowing when the dry
season comes.
They disappear from their stream
beds when the weather warms
up.
¹⁸ Groups of traders turn away from their
usual paths.
They go off into the dry and empty
land.
And they die there.
¹⁹ Traders from Tema look for water.
Traveling merchants from Sheba also
hope to find it.
²⁰ They become troubled because they
had expected to find some.
But when they arrive at the stream
beds,
they don't find any water at all.
²¹ And now, my friends, you haven't
helped me either.
You see the horrible condition I'm in.
And that makes you afraid.
²² I've never said, 'Give me something to
help me.
Use your wealth to set me free.
²³ Save me from the power of my enemy.
Rescue me from the power of mean
people.'
²⁴ "Teach me. Then I'll be quiet.
Show me what I've done wrong.
²⁵ Honest words are so painful!
But your reasoning doesn't prove
anything.
²⁶ Are you trying to correct what I'm
saying?
Are you treating my hopeless words
like nothing but wind?
²⁷ You would even cast lots for those
whose fathers have died.
You would even trade away your
closest friend.

Job 6–7 If you opened your Bible to
find something encouraging, skip to the
Psalms. Job isn't going to get happy until
the end. (Whoops, I missed a spoiler
alert!) Time for my blue bunny slippers.

²⁸ "But now please look at me.
Would I tell you a lie right here in
front of you?
²⁹ Stop what you are saying. Don't be so
unfair.
Think it over again.
You are trying to take my honesty
away from me.
³⁰ Has my mouth spoken anything that is
evil?
Do my lips say things that are
hateful?"

7 Job continued,

"Don't all human beings have to work
hard on this earth?
Aren't their days like the days of
hired workers?
² I've been like a slave
who longs for the evening shadows
to come.
I've been like a hired worker
who is waiting to be paid.
³ I've been given several months that
were useless to me.
My nights have been filled with
suffering.
⁴ When I lie down I think,
'How long will it be before I can get
up?'
The night drags on.
I toss and turn until sunrise.
⁵ My body is covered with worms and
sores.

My skin is broken. It has boils all
    over it.

⁶ "My days pass by faster than a weaver
    can work.
They come to an end. I don't have
    any hope.
⁷ God, remember that my life is only a
    breath.
I'll never be happy again.
⁸ The eyes that see me now won't see me
    anymore.
You will look for me. But I'll be
    gone.
⁹ When a cloud disappears, it's gone
    forever.
And anyone who goes down to the
    grave never returns.
¹⁰ He never comes home again.
Even his own family doesn't
    remember him.

¹¹ "So I won't keep quiet.
When I'm suffering greatly, I'll speak
    out.
When my spirit is bitter, I'll tell you
    how unhappy I am.
¹² Am I the ocean? Am I the sea monster?
If I'm not, why do you guard me so
    closely?
¹³ Sometimes I think my bed will comfort
    me.
I think my couch will keep me from
    being unhappy.
¹⁴ But even then you send me dreams that
    frighten me.
You send me visions that terrify me.
¹⁵ So I would rather choke to death.
That would be better than living in
    this body of mine.
¹⁶ I hate my life. I don't want to live
    forever.
Leave me alone. My days don't mean
    anything to me.

¹⁷ "What are human beings that you think
    so much of them?
What are they that you pay so much
    attention to them?
¹⁸ You check up on them every morning.
You test them every moment.
¹⁹ Won't you ever look away from me?
Won't you leave me alone even for
    one second?
²⁰ If I've really sinned, tell me what I've
    done to you.
You see everything we do.

Why do you shoot your arrows at me?
Have I become a problem to you?
²¹ Why don't you forgive the wrong things
    I've done?
Why don't you forgive me for my
    sins?
I'll soon lie down in the dust of my
    grave.
You will search for me. But I'll be
    gone."

The First Speech of Bildad

8 Then Bildad the Shuhite replied,

² "Job, how long will you talk like that?
Your words don't have any
    meaning.
³ Does God ever treat people unfairly?
Does the Mighty One make what is
    wrong
appear to be right?
⁴ Your children sinned against him.
So he punished them for their sin.
⁵ But seek God with all your heart.
Make your appeal to the Mighty
    One.
⁶ Be pure and honest.
And he will rise up and help you
    now.
He'll give you everything you had
    before.
⁷ In the past, things went well with you.
But in days to come, things will get
    even better.

⁸ "Find out what our parents taught.
Discover what those who lived
    before them learned.
⁹ After all, we were born only yesterday.
So we don't know anything.
Our days on this earth are like a
    shadow that disappears.
¹⁰ Won't your people of long ago teach
    you and tell you?
Won't the things they said help you
    understand?
¹¹ Can grass grow tall where there isn't
    any swamp?
Can plants grow well where there
    isn't any water?
¹² While they are still growing and haven't
    been cut,
they dry up faster than grass does.
¹³ The same thing happens to everyone
    who forgets God.

The hope of ungodly people dies out.
¹⁴ What they trust in is very weak.
What they depend on is like a spider's web.
¹⁵ They lean on it, but it falls apart.
They hold on to it, but it gives way.
¹⁶ They are like a plant in the sunshine that receives plenty of water.
It spreads its new growth all over the garden.
¹⁷ It wraps its roots around a pile of rocks.
It tries to find places to grow among the stones.
¹⁸ But when the plant is pulled up from its spot,
that place says, 'I never saw you.'
¹⁹ The life of that plant is sure to dry up.
But from the same soil other plants will grow.

²⁰ "I'm sure God doesn't turn his back on anyone who is honest.
And he doesn't help those who do what is evil.
²¹ He will fill your mouth with laughter.
Shouts of joy will come from your lips.
²² Your enemies will put on shame as if it were clothes.
The tents of sinful people will be gone."

Job's Reply

9 Job replied,

² "I'm sure that what you have said is true.
But how can human beings prove to God they are not guilty?
³ They might wish to argue with him.
But they couldn't answer him even once in a thousand times.
⁴ His wisdom is deep. His power is great.
No one opposes him and comes away unharmed.
⁵ He moves mountains, and they don't even know it.
When he is angry, he turns them upside down.
⁶ He shakes the earth loose from its place.
He makes its pillars tremble.
⁷ When he tells the sun not to shine, it doesn't.

He turns off the light of the stars.
⁸ He's the only one who can spread out the heavens.
He alone can walk on the waves of the ocean.
⁹ He made the Big Dipper and Orion.
He created the Pleiades and the southern stars.
¹⁰ He does wonderful things that can't be understood.
He does miracles that can't even be counted.
¹¹ When he passes by me, I can't see him.
When he goes past me, I can't recognize him.
¹² If he takes something, who can stop him?
Who would dare to ask him, 'What are you doing?'
¹³ God doesn't hold back his anger.
Even the helpers of the sea monster Rahab
bowed in fear at his feet.

¹⁴ "So how can I disagree with God?
How can I possibly argue with him?
¹⁵ Even if I hadn't done anything wrong, I couldn't answer him.
I could only beg my Judge to have mercy on me.
¹⁶ Suppose I called out to him and he answered.
I don't believe he'd listen to me.

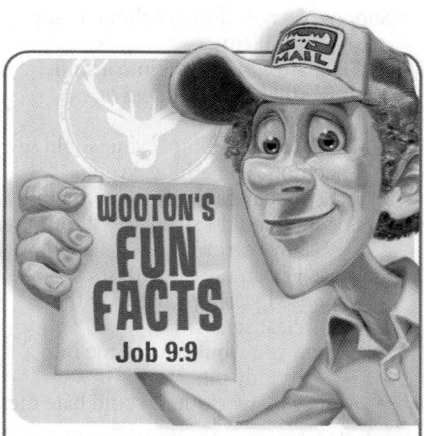

WOOTON'S FUN FACTS
Job 9:9

The constellation Orion (called "The Hunter") contains two of the brightest stars in the sky: Rigel (Beta Orionis) and Betelgeuse (Alpha Orionis).

¹⁷ He would send a storm to crush me.
　　He'd increase my wounds without
　　　　any reason.
¹⁸ He wouldn't let me catch my breath.
　　He'd make my life very bitter.
¹⁹ If it's a matter of strength, he is mighty!
　　And if it's a matter of being fair,
　　who would dare to bring charges
　　　　against him?
²⁰ Even if I hadn't sinned, what I said
　　　　would prove me guilty.
　　Even if I were honest, my words
　　　　would show that I'm wrong.

²¹ "Even though I'm honest,
　　I'm not concerned about myself.
　　I hate my own life.
²² It all amounts to the same thing. That's
　　　　why I say,
　　'God destroys honest people and
　　　　sinful people alike.'
²³ Suppose a plague brings sudden death.
　　Then he laughs when those who
　　　　haven't sinned lose hope.
²⁴ Suppose a nation falls into the power of
　　　　sinful people.
　　Then God makes its judges blind to
　　　　the truth.
　　If he isn't the one doing it, who is?

²⁵ "God, my days race by like a runner.
　　They fly away without seeing any joy.
²⁶ They speed along like papyrus boats.
　　They are like eagles swooping down
　　　　on their food.
²⁷ Suppose I say, 'I'll forget about all my
　　　　problems.
　　I'll change my frown into a smile.'
²⁸ Then I'd still be afraid I'd go on
　　　　suffering.
　　That's because I know you would say
　　　　I had done something wrong.
²⁹ In fact, you have already said I'm guilty.
　　So why should I struggle without
　　　　any reason?
³⁰ Suppose I clean myself with soap.
　　Suppose I wash my hands with
　　　　cleanser.
³¹ Even then you would throw me into a
　　　　muddy pit.
　　And even my clothes would hate me.

³² "God isn't a mere human being like me.
　　I can't answer him.
　　We can't take each other to court.
³³ I wish someone would settle matters
　　　　between us.

I wish someone would bring us
　　　　together.
³⁴ I wish someone would keep God from
　　　　punishing me.
　　Then his terror wouldn't frighten me
　　　　anymore.
³⁵ I would speak up without being afraid
　　　　of him.
　　But as things stand now, I can't do
　　　　that.

10 "I'm sick of living.
　　So I'll talk openly about my
　　　　problems.
　　I'll speak out because my spirit is
　　　　bitter.
² I say to God, 'Don't find me guilty.
　　Instead, tell me what charges
　　　　you are bringing against me.
³ Does it make you happy when you
　　　　crush me?
　　Does it please you to turn your back
　　　　on what you have made?
　　While you do those things,
　　　　you smile on the plans of sinful
　　　　　　people!
⁴ You don't have human eyes.
　　You don't see as people see.
⁵ Your days aren't like the days of a mere
　　　　human being.
　　Your years aren't even like the years
　　　　of a strong man.
⁶ So you search for my mistakes.
　　You look for my sin.
⁷ You already know I'm not guilty.
　　No one can save me from your
　　　　power.

⁸ "'Your hands shaped me and made me.
　　So are you going to destroy me now?
⁹ Remember, you molded me like clay.
　　So are you going to turn me back
　　　　into dust?
¹⁰ Didn't you pour me out like milk?
　　Didn't you form me like cheese?
¹¹ Didn't you put skin and flesh on me?
　　Didn't you sew me together with
　　　　bones and muscles?
¹² You gave me life. You were kind to me.
　　You took good care of me. You
　　　　watched over me.

¹³ "'But here's what you hid in your heart.
　　Here's what you had on your mind.
¹⁴ If I sinned, you would be watching me.
　　You wouldn't let me go without
　　　　punishing me.

¹⁵ If I were guilty, how terrible that would
be for me!
Even if I haven't sinned,
I can't be proud of what I've done.
That's because I'm so full of shame.
I'm drowning in my suffering.
¹⁶ If I become proud, you hunt me down
like a lion.
You show your mighty power
against me.
¹⁷ You bring new witnesses against me.
You become more and more angry
with me.
You use your power against me
again and again.
¹⁸ "'Why did you bring me out of my
mother's body?
I wish I had died before anyone saw
me.
¹⁹ I wish I'd never been born!
I wish I'd been carried straight from
my mother's body to the
grave!
²⁰ Aren't my few days almost over?
Leave me so I can have a moment
of joy.
²¹ Turn away before I go to the place I
can't return from.
It's the land of gloom and total
darkness.
²² It's the land of darkest night
and total darkness and disorder.
There even the light is like
darkness.'"

The First Speech of Zophar

11 Then Zophar the Naamathite replied,

² "Don't all your words require an
answer?
I'm sure that what you are saying
can't be right.
³ Your useless talk won't keep us quiet.
Someone has to correct you when
you make fun of truth.
⁴ You say to God, 'My beliefs are perfect.
I'm pure in your sight.'
⁵ I wish God would speak.
I wish he'd answer you.
⁶ I wish he'd show you the secrets of
wisdom.
After all, true wisdom has two sides.
Here's what I want you to know.
God has forgotten some of your sins.

⁷ "Do you know how deep the mysteries
of God are?
Can you discover the limits of the
Mighty One's knowledge?
⁸ They are higher than the heavens above.
What can you do?
They are deeper than the deepest parts
of the earth below.
What can you know?
⁹ They are longer than the earth.
They are wider than the ocean.

¹⁰ "Suppose God comes along and puts
you in prison.
Suppose he takes you to court.
Then who can oppose him?
¹¹ He certainly knows when people tell
lies.
When he sees evil, he pays careful
attention to it.
¹² A wild donkey's colt can't be born a
human being.
And it's just as impossible that a
person without sense can
become wise.

¹³ "So commit yourself to God completely.
Reach out your hands to him for
help.
¹⁴ Get rid of all the sin you have.
Don't let anything that is evil stay in
your tent.
¹⁵ Then, free of those things, you can face
others.
You can stand firm without being
afraid.
¹⁶ You can be sure you will forget your
troubles.
They will be like water that has
flowed on by.
¹⁷ Life will be brighter than the sun at
noon.
And darkness will become like
morning.
¹⁸ You will be secure, because there is
hope.
You will look around you and find a
safe place to rest.
¹⁹ You will lie down, and no one will make
you afraid.
Many people will want you to help
them.
²⁰ But sinful people won't find what they
are looking for.
They won't be able to escape.
All they can hope for is to die."

Job's Reply

12 Job replied,

2 "You people think you are the only ones
who matter!
You are sure that wisdom will die
with you!
3 But I have a brain, just like you.
I'm as clever as you are.
In fact, everyone knows as much as
you do.

4 "My friends laugh at me all the time,
even though I called out to God and
he answered.
My friends laugh at me,
even though I'm honest and right.
5 People who have an easy life look
down on those who have
problems.
They think trouble comes only to
those whose feet are slipping.
6 Why doesn't anyone bother the tents of
robbers?
Why do those who make God angry
remain secure?
They are in God's hands!

7 "But ask the animals what God does.
They will teach you.
Or ask the birds in the sky.
They will tell you.
8 Or speak to the earth. It will teach you.
Or let the fish in the ocean educate
you.
9 Are there any of these creatures that
don't know
what the powerful hand of the LORD
has done?
10 He holds the life of every creature in his
hand.
He controls the breath of every
human being.
11 Our tongues tell us what tastes good
and what doesn't.
And our ears tell us what's true and
what isn't.
12 Old people are wise.

Those who live a long time have
understanding.
13 "Wisdom and power belong to God.
Advice and understanding also
belong to him.
14 What he tears down can't be rebuilt.
The people he puts in prison can't be
set free.
15 If he holds back the water, everything
dries up.
If he lets the water loose, it floods
the land.
16 Strength and understanding belong to
him.
Those who tell lies and those who
believe them also belong to
him.
17 He removes the wisdom of rulers and
leads them away.
He makes judges look foolish.
18 He sets people free from the chains that
kings put on them.
Then he dresses the kings in the
clothes of slaves.
19 He removes the authority of priests and
leads them away.
He removes from their positions
officials who have been in control for
a long time.
20 He shuts the mouths of trusted advisers.
He takes away the understanding of
elders.
21 He looks down on proud leaders.
He takes away the strength of those
who are mighty.
22 He tells people the secrets of darkness.
He brings total darkness out into the
light.
23 He makes nations great, and then he
destroys them.
He makes nations grow, and then he
scatters them.
24 He takes away the understanding of the
leaders of the earth.
He makes them wander in a desert
where no one lives.
25 Without any light, they feel their way
along in darkness.
God makes them unsteady like those
who get drunk.

13 "My eyes have seen everything God
has done.
My ears have heard it and
understood it.

² What you know, I also know.
  I'm as clever as you are.
³ In fact, I long to speak to the Mighty
    One.
  I want to argue my case with God.
⁴ But you spread lies about me and take
    away my good name.
  If you are trying to heal me,
  you aren't very good doctors!
⁵ I wish you would keep your mouths
    shut!
  Then people would think you were
    wise.
⁶ Listen to my case.
  Listen as I make my appeal.
⁷ Will you say evil things in order to help
    God?
  Will you tell lies for him?
⁸ Do you want to be on God's side?
  Will you argue his case for him?
⁹ Would it turn out well if he looked you
    over carefully?
  Could you fool him as you might
    fool human beings?
¹⁰ He would certainly hold you
    responsible
  if you took his side in secret.
¹¹ Wouldn't his glory terrify you?
  Wouldn't the fear of him fall on you?
¹² Your sayings are as useless as ashes.
  The answers you give are as weak
    as clay.

¹³ "So be quiet and let me speak.
  Then I won't care what happens to
    me.
¹⁴ Why do I put myself in danger?
  Why do I take my life in my hands?
¹⁵ Even if God kills me, I'll still put my
    hope in him.
  I'll argue my case in front of him.
¹⁶ No matter how things turn out,
  I'm sure I'll still be saved.
  After all, no ungodly person
    would dare to come into his court.
¹⁷ Listen carefully to what I'm saying.
  Pay close attention to my words.
¹⁸ I've prepared my case.
  And I know I'll be proved right.
¹⁹ Can others bring charges against me?
  If they can, I'll keep quiet and die.

²⁰ "God, I won't hide from you.
  Here are the only two things I want.
²¹ Stop treating me this way.
  And stop making me so afraid.

²² Then send for me, and I'll answer.
  Or let me speak, and you reply.
²³ How many things have I done wrong?
  How many sins have I committed?
  Show me my crime. Show me my
    sin.
²⁴ Why do you turn your face away from
    me?
  Why do you think of me as your
    enemy?
²⁵ I'm already like a leaf that is blown by
    the wind.
  Are you going to terrify me even
    more?
  I'm already like dry straw.
  Are you going to keep on chasing
    me?
²⁶ You write down bitter things against me.
  You make me suffer for the sins
  I committed when I was young.
²⁷ You put my feet in chains.
  You watch every step I take.
  You do it by putting marks on the
    bottom of my feet.

²⁸ "People waste away like something that
    is rotten.
  They are like clothes that are eaten
    by moths.

14 ¹ Human beings have only a few days
    to live.
  Their lives are full of trouble.
² They grow like flowers, and then they
    dry up.
  They are like shadows that quickly
    disappear.

³ "God, do you even notice them?
  Will you let them appear in your
    court?
⁴ Who can bring what is pure from
    something that isn't pure?
  No one!
⁵ You decide how long anyone will live.
  You have established the number of
    his months.
  You have set a limit to the number of
    his days.
⁶ So look away from him. Leave him
    alone.
  Let him put in his time like a hired
    worker.

⁷ "At least there is hope for a tree.
  If it's cut down, it will begin to grow
    again.
  New branches will appear on it.

8 Its roots may grow old in the ground.
    Its stump may die in the soil.
9 But when it smells water, it will begin to
        grow.
    It will send out new growth like a
        plant.
10 No man is like that. When he dies, he is
        buried in a grave.
    He takes his last breath. Then he is
        gone.
11 Water dries up from lakes.
    Riverbeds become empty and dry.
12 In the same way, people lie down and
        never get up.
    People won't wake or rise from their
        sleep
    until the heavens are gone.

13 "I wish you would hide me in a grave!
    I wish you would cover me up until
        your anger passes by!
    I wish you would set the time for me to
        spend in the grave
    and then bring me back up!
14 If someone dies, will they live again?
    All the days of my hard work
    I will wait for the time when you
        give me new life.
15 You will call out to me, and I will
        answer you.
    You will long for the person your
        hands have made.
16 Then you will count every step I take.
    But you won't keep track of my sin.
17 The wrong things I've done will be
        sealed up in a bag.
    You will wipe out my sins by
        forgiving them.

18 "A mountain wears away and
        crumbles.
    A rock is moved from its place.
19 Water wears away stones.
    Storms wash away soil.
    In the same way, you destroy a
        person's hope.
20 You overpower them completely, and
        then they're gone.
    You change the way they look and
        send them to their graves.
21 If their children are honored, they don't
        even know it.
    If their children are dishonored, they
        don't even see it.
22 All they feel is the pain of their own
        bodies.

They are full of sadness only for
    themselves."

The Second Speech of Eliphaz

15 Then Eliphaz the Temanite replied,

2 "Job, would a wise person answer with
        a lot of meaningless talk?
    Would they fill their stomach with
        the hot east wind?
3 Would they argue with useless words?
    Would they give worthless speeches?
4 But you even cause others to lose their
        respect for God.
    You make it hard for them to be
        faithful to him.
5 Your sin makes you say evil things.
    You talk like people who twist the
        truth.
6 Your own mouth judges you, not mine.
    Your own lips witness against you.

7 "Are you the first man who was ever
        born?
    Were you created before the hills?
8 Do you listen in when God speaks with
        his angels?
    Do you think you are the only wise
        person?
9 What do you know that we don't know?
    What understanding do you have
        that we don't have?
10 People who are old and gray are on our
        side.
    And they are even older than your
        parents!
11 Aren't God's words of comfort enough
        for you?
    He speaks them to you gently.
12 Why have you let your wild ideas carry
        you away?
    Why do your eyes flash with anger?
13 Why do you get so angry with God?
    Why do words like those pour out of
        your mouth?

14 "Can human beings really be pure?
    Can those who are born really be
        right with God?
15 God doesn't trust his holy angels.
    Even the heavens aren't pure in his
        sight.
16 So he'll certainly find fault with human
        beings.
    After all, they are evil and sinful.
    They drink up evil as if it were water.

¹⁷ "Listen to me. I'll explain things to you.
　　Let me tell you what I've seen.
¹⁸ I'll tell you what those who are wise
　　　have said.
　　They don't hide anything they've
　　　received
　　from their people of long ago.
¹⁹ The land was given only to those people.
　　Their wisdom didn't come from
　　　outsiders.
　　And here's what those who are wise
　　　have said.
²⁰ Sinful people always suffer pain.
　　Mean people suffer all their lives.
²¹ Terrifying sounds fill their ears.
　　When everything seems to be going
　　　well,
　　robbers attack them.
²² They lose all hope of escaping the
　　　darkness of death.
　　They will certainly be killed by
　　　swords.
²³ Like vultures, they look around for food.
　　They know that the day they will die
　　　is near.
²⁴ Suffering and pain terrify them.
　　Their troubles overpower them,
　　like a king ready to attack his
　　　enemies.
²⁵ They shake their fists at God.
　　They brag about themselves and
　　　oppose the Mighty One.
²⁶ They boldly charge against him
　　with their thick, strong shields.

²⁷ "Their faces are very fat.
　　Their stomachs hang out.
²⁸ They'll live in towns that have been
　　　destroyed.
　　They'll live in houses where no one
　　　else lives.
　　The houses will crumble to pieces.
²⁹ They won't be rich anymore. Their
　　　wealth won't last.
　　Their property will no longer spread
　　　out over the land.
³⁰ They won't escape the darkness of
　　　death.
　　A flame will dry up everything they
　　　have.
　　The breath of God will blow them
　　　away.
³¹ Don't let them fool themselves
　　by trusting in what is worthless.
　　They won't get anything out of it.

³² Even before they die, they will dry up.
　　No matter what they do, it won't
　　　succeed.
³³ They'll be like vines
　　that are stripped of their unripe
　　　grapes.
　　They'll be like olive trees
　　that drop their flowers.
³⁴ People who are ungodly won't have any
　　　children.
　　Fire will burn up the tents of people
　　　who accept money
　　from those who want special favors.
³⁵ Instead of having children,
　　ungodly people create suffering.
　　All they produce is evil.
　　They are full of lies."

Job's Reply

16 Job replied,

² "I've heard many of these things before.
　　All of you are terrible at comforting
　　　me!
³ Your speeches go on forever.
　　Won't they ever end?
　　What's wrong with you?
　　Why do you keep on arguing?
⁴ If you and I changed places,
　　I could say the same things you are
　　　saying.
　　I could make fine speeches against you.
　　I could shake my head at you.
⁵ But what I might say would give you
　　　hope.
　　My words of comfort would help
　　　you.

⁶ "If I speak, it doesn't help me.
　　And if I keep quiet, my pain doesn't
　　　go away.
⁷ God has worn me out completely.
　　He has destroyed my whole family.
⁸ People can see the condition he has put
　　　me in.
　　My thin body stands as a witness
　　　against me.
⁹ God is angry with me.
　　He attacks me and tears me up.
　　He grinds his teeth at me.
　　He stares at me as if he were my
　　　enemy.
¹⁰ People make fun of me.
　　They slap my face and laugh at me.
　　All of them join together against
　　　me.

¹¹ God has turned me over to sinful people.
He has handed me over to them.
¹² Everything was going well with me.
But he broke me into pieces like a
clay pot.
He grabbed me by the neck and
crushed me.
He has taken aim at me.
¹³ He shoots his arrows at me from all
sides.
Without pity, he stabs me in the kidneys.
He spills my insides on the ground.
¹⁴ He smashes through me as if I were a
wall.
He rushes at me like a fighting man.

¹⁵ "I've sewed rough clothing over my skin.
All I can do is sit here in the dust.
¹⁶ My face is red from crying.
I have dark circles under my eyes.
¹⁷ But I haven't harmed anyone.
My prayers to God are pure.

¹⁸ "Earth, please don't cover up my blood!
May God always hear my cry for
help!
¹⁹ Even now my witness is in heaven.
The one who speaks up for me is
there.
²⁰ My go-between is my friend
as I pour out my tears to God.
²¹ He makes his appeal to God to help me
as a person pleads for a friend.

²² "Only a few years will pass by.
Then I'll take the path of no return.

17 ¹ My strength is almost gone.
I won't live much longer.
A grave is waiting for me.
² People who make fun of me are all
around me.
I'm forced to watch as they attack
me with their words.

³ "God, please pay the price to have me
set free.
Who else would put up money for
me?
⁴ You have closed the minds of those who
are trying to comfort me.
They don't understand that I haven't
done anything wrong.
So don't let them win the argument.
⁵ Suppose someone tells lies about their
friends to get a reward.
Then their own children will suffer
for it.

⁶ "God has made an example of me.
People spit in my face.
⁷ My eyes have grown weak because I'm
so sad.
My body is so thin it hardly casts a
shadow.
⁸ People who claim to be honest
are shocked when they see me.
Those who think they haven't sinned
are stirred up against me.
They think I'm ungodly.
⁹ But godly people will keep doing what
is right.
Those who have clean hands will
grow stronger.

¹⁰ "Come on, all of you! Try again!
I can't find a wise person among you.
¹¹ My life is almost over. My plans are
destroyed.
Yet the desires of my heart
¹² turn night into day.
Even though it's dark,
'Light is nearby.'
¹³ Suppose the only home I can hope for
is a grave.
And suppose I make my bed in the
darkness of death.
¹⁴ Suppose I say to the grave,
'You are like a father to me.'
And suppose I say to its worms,
'You are like a mother or sister to
me.'
¹⁵ Then what hope do I have?
Who can give me any hope?
¹⁶ Will hope go down to the gates of death
with me?
Will we go down together into the
dust of the grave?"

The Second Speech of Bildad

18 Then Bildad the Shuhite replied,

² "Job, when will you stop these speeches
of yours?
Be reasonable! Then we can talk.
³ Why do you look at us as if we were
cattle?
Why do you think of us as being
stupid?
⁴ Your anger is tearing you to pieces.
Does the earth have to be deserted
just to prove you are right?
Must all the rocks be moved from
their places?

⁵ "The lamps of sinful people are blown
     out.
   Their flames will never burn again.
⁶ The lights in their tents become dark.
   The lamps beside those who are evil
     go out.
⁷ They walk more slowly than they used to.
   Their own evil plans make them fall.
⁸ Their feet take them into a net.
   They wander right into it.
⁹ A trap grabs hold of their heels.
   It refuses to let them go.
¹⁰ A trap lies in their path.
   A rope to catch them is hidden on
     the ground.
¹¹ Terrors alarm them on every side.
   They follow them every step of the
     way.
¹² Trouble would like to eat them up.
   Danger waits for them when they fall.
¹³ It eats away parts of their skin.
   Death itself feeds on their arms and
     legs.
¹⁴ They are torn away from the safety of
     their tents.
   They are marched off to the one who
     rules over death.
¹⁵ Fire races through their tents.
   Burning sulfur is scattered over their
     homes.
¹⁶ Their roots dry up under them.
   Their branches dry up above them.
¹⁷ No one on earth remembers them.
   Their names are forgotten in the land.
¹⁸ They are driven from light into the
     place of darkness.
   They are thrown out of the world.
¹⁹ Their family dies out among their
     people.
   No one is left where they used to live.
²⁰ What has happened to them shocks the
     people in the west.
   It terrifies the people in the east.
²¹ Now you know what the homes of
     sinners are like.
   Those who don't know God live in
     places like that."

Job's Reply

19 Job replied,

² "How long will you people make me
     suffer?
   How long will you crush me with
     your words?

³ You have already accused me many
     times.
   You have attacked me without
     feeling any shame.
⁴ Suppose it's true that I've gone down
     the wrong path.
   Then it's my concern, not yours.
⁵ Suppose you want to place yourselves
     above me.
   Suppose you want to use my shame
     to prove I'm wrong.
⁶ Then I want you to know that God
     hasn't treated me right.
   In fact, he has captured me in his
     net.

Jason's Jargon

JOB 19

Search this
chapter for the
word *redeemer*. An
unworthy person who
becomes worthy is
redeemed. God is our
redeemer in that, even
in our sins, He made
us worthy through His
grace.

⁷ "I cry out, 'Someone harmed me!'
   But I don't get any reply.
   I call out for help.
   But I'm not treated fairly.
⁸ God has blocked my way, and I can't get
     through.
   He has made my paths so dark I
     can't see where I'm going.
⁹ He has taken my wealth away from me.
   He has stripped me of my honor.
¹⁰ He tears me down on every side until
     I'm gone.
   He pulls up the roots of my hope as
     if I were a tree.
¹¹ His anger burns against me.
   He thinks I'm one of his enemies.
¹² His troops march toward me in force.
   They come at me from every
     direction.
   They camp around my tent.

¹³ "God has caused my family to desert
     me.
   The people I used to know are now
     strangers to me.

¹⁴ My relatives have gone away.
　My closest friends have forgotten
　　me.
¹⁵ My guests and my female servants
　　think of me as a stranger.
　They look at me as if I were an
　　outsider.
¹⁶ I send for my servant, but he doesn't
　　answer.
　He doesn't come, even though I beg
　　him to.
¹⁷ My wife can't stand the way my breath
　　smells.
　My own family won't have anything
　　to do with me.
¹⁸ Even little children mock me.
　When I appear, they make fun of
　　me.
¹⁹ All my close friends hate me.
　Those I love have turned against me.
²⁰ I'm nothing but skin and bones.
　I've barely escaped death.

²¹ "Have pity on me, my friends! Please
　　have pity!
　God has struck me down with his
　　powerful hand.
²² Why do you chase after me as he does?
　Aren't you satisfied with what you
　　have done to me already?

²³ "I wish my words were written down!
　I wish they were written in a book!

Job 19:17 Eugene tells me that bad
breath is called *halitosis*. I just know it's
gross. People in Bible times didn't have
multicolored superhero toothpaste like
we have today. So they probably cleaned
their mouths by chewing on the seeds of
clove, cardamom, or fennel. Or they might
have chewed on plants such as mint.

²⁴ I wish they were cut into lead with an
　　iron tool!
　I wish they were carved in rock
　　forever!
²⁵ I know that my redeemer lives.
　In the end he will stand on the earth.
²⁶ Though my skin will be destroyed,
　in my body I'll see God.
²⁷ I myself will see him with my own eyes.
　I'll see him, and he won't be a
　　stranger to me.
　How my heart longs for that day!

²⁸ "You might say, 'Let's keep bothering Job.
　After all, he's the cause of all his
　　suffering.'
²⁹ But you should be afraid when God
　　comes to judge you.
　He'll be angry. He'll punish you with
　　his sword.
　Then you will know that he is the
　　Judge."

The Second Speech of Zophar

20 Then Zophar the Naamathite replied,

² "My troubled thoughts force me to
　　answer you.
　That's because I'm very upset.
³ What you have just said dishonors me.
　So I really have to reply to you.

⁴ "I'm sure you must know how things
　　have always been.
　They've been that way
　ever since human beings were placed
　　on this earth.
⁵ Those who are evil are happy for only a
　　short time.
　The joy of ungodly people lasts only
　　for a moment.
⁶ Their pride might reach all the way up
　　to the heavens.
　Their heads might touch the clouds.
⁷ But they will disappear forever,
　like the waste from their own bodies.
　Anyone who has seen them will say,
　'Where did they go?'
⁸ Like a dream they will fly away.
　They will never be seen again.
　They will be driven away like visions
　　in the night.
⁹ The eyes that saw them won't see them
　　anymore.
　Even their own families won't
　　remember them.

¹⁰ Their children must pay back what they
took from poor people.
    Their own hands must give back the
wealth they stole.
¹¹ They might feel young and very strong.
    But they will soon lie down in the
dust of their graves.

¹² "Anything that is evil tastes sweet to
them.
    They keep it under their tongues for
a while.
¹³ They can't stand to let it go.
    So they hold it in their mouths.
¹⁴ But their food will turn sour in their
stomachs.
    It will become like the poison of a
serpent inside them.
¹⁵ They will spit out the rich food they
swallowed.
    God will make their stomachs throw
it up.
¹⁶ They will suck the poison of a serpent.
    The fangs of an adder will kill them.
¹⁷ They won't enjoy streams that flow with
honey.
    They won't enjoy rivers that flow
with cream.
¹⁸ What they worked for they must give
back
before they can eat it.
    They won't enjoy what they have
earned.
¹⁹ They've crushed poor people and left
them with nothing.
    They've taken over houses they
didn't even build.

²⁰ "No matter how much they have,
they always long for more.
    But their treasure can't save them.
²¹ There isn't anything left for them to eat
up.
    Their success won't last.
²² While they are enjoying the good life,
trouble will catch up with them.
    Terrible suffering will come on them.
²³ When they've filled their stomachs,
    God will pour out his great anger on
them.
    He'll strike them down with blow
after blow.
²⁴ They might run away from iron
weapons.
    But arrows that have bronze tips will
wound them.

²⁵ They will pull the arrows out of their
backs.
    They will remove the shining tips
from their livers.
    They will be filled with terror.
²⁶ Total darkness hides and waits for
their treasures.
    God will send a fire that will destroy
them.
    It will burn up everything that's left
in their tents.
²⁷ Heaven will show their guilt to everyone.
    The earth will be a witness against
them.
²⁸ A flood will carry their houses away.
    Rushing water will wash them away
on the day when God judges.
²⁹ Now you know what God will do to
sinful people.
    Now you know what he has planned
for them."

Job's Reply

21 Job replied,

² "Listen carefully to what I'm saying.
    Let that be the comfort you people
give me.
³ Put up with me while I speak.
    After I've spoken, you can make fun
of me!

⁴ "I'm not arguing with mere human
beings.
    So why shouldn't I be angry and
uneasy?
⁵ Look at me and be shocked.
    Put your hand over your mouth and
stop talking!
⁶ When I think about these things, I'm
terrified.
    My whole body trembles.
⁷ Why do sinful people keep on living?
    The older they grow, the richer they
get.
⁸ They see their children grow up around
them.
    They watch their family grow larger.
⁹ Their homes are safe.
    They don't have to be afraid.
    God isn't punishing them.
¹⁰ Every time their bulls mate, their cows
become pregnant.
    And the calves don't die before they
are born.

¹¹ Sinful people send their children out
      like a flock of lambs.
   Their little ones dance around.
¹² They sing to the music of tambourines
      and lyres.
   They have a good time while flutes
      are being played.
¹³ Those who are evil spend their years
      living well.
   They go down to their graves in
      peace.
¹⁴ But they say to God, 'Leave us alone!
   We don't want to know how you
      want us to live.
¹⁵ Who is the Mighty One? Why should
      we serve him?
   What would we get if we prayed to
      him?'
¹⁶ But they aren't in control of their own
      success.
   So I don't pay any attention to their
      plans.

¹⁷ "How often are their lamps blown out?
   How often does trouble come on
      them?
   How often does God punish them
      when he's angry?
¹⁸ How often are they like straw blowing
      in the wind?
   How often are they like tumbleweeds
      swept away by a storm?
¹⁹ People say, 'God stores up the
      punishment of evil people for
      their children.'
   But let God punish the evil people
      themselves.
   Then they'll learn a lesson from it.
²⁰ Let their own eyes see how they are
      destroyed.
   Let them drink the wine of the
      Mighty One's anger.
²¹ What do they care about the families
      they leave behind?
   What do they care about them
      when their lives come to an end?

²² "Can anyone teach God anything?
   After all, he judges even the angels
      in heaven.
²³ Some people die while they are still
      very strong.
   They are completely secure. They
      have an easy life.
²⁴ They are well fed.
   Their bodies are healthy.

²⁵ Others die while their spirits are bitter.
   They've never enjoyed anything
      good.
²⁶ Side by side they lie in the dust of death.
   The worms in their graves cover all
      of them.

²⁷ "I know exactly what you people are
      thinking.
   I know you are planning to do bad
      things to me.
²⁸ You are saying to yourselves,
   'Where is the great man's house now?
   Where are the tents where his evil
      family lived?'
²⁹ Haven't you ever asked questions of
      those who travel?
   Haven't you paid any attention to
      their stories?
³⁰ They'll tell you that sinful people
      are spared from the day of trouble.
   They'll say that those people
      are saved from the day when God
      will judge.
³¹ Who speaks against them for the way
      they act?
   Who pays them back for what
      they've done?
³² Their bodies will be carried to their
      graves.
   Guards will watch over their tombs.
³³ The soil in the valley will be pleasant
      to those who have died.
   Many people will walk along behind
      their bodies.
   Many others will walk in front of
      them.

³⁴ "So how can you comfort me with your
      speeches?
   They don't make any sense at all.
   Your answers are nothing but lies!"

The Third Speech of Eliphaz

22 Then Eliphaz the Temanite replied,

² "Can any person be of benefit to God?
   Can even a wise person be of any
      help to him?
³ Job, what pleasure would it give the
      Mighty One if you were right?
   What would he get if you were
      completely honest?

⁴ "You say you have respect for him.
   Is that why he corrects you?

Is that why he brings charges against
you?
⁵ Haven't you done many evil things?
Don't you sin again and again?
⁶ You took clothes away from your
relatives
just because they owed you some
money.
You left them naked for no reason
at all.
⁷ You didn't give any water to people who
were tired.
You held food back from those who
were hungry.
⁸ You did it even though you were
honored and powerful.
You owned land and lived on it.
⁹ But you sent widows away without
anything.
You mistreated children whose
fathers had died.
¹⁰ That's why traps have been set all
around you.
That's why sudden danger terrifies
you.
¹¹ That's why it's so dark you can't even
see.
That's why a flood covers you up.
¹² "Isn't God in the highest parts of
heaven?
See how high the highest stars are!
¹³ But you still say, 'What does God know?
Can he see through the darkest
clouds to judge us?
¹⁴ He goes around in the highest heavens.
Thick clouds keep him from seeing
us.'
¹⁵ Will you stay on the old path
that sinful people have walked on?
¹⁶ They were carried off even before they
died.
Their foundations were washed away
by a flood.
¹⁷ They said to God, 'Leave us alone!
What can you do to us, you Mighty
One?'
¹⁸ But he was the one who filled their
houses with good things.
So I don't pay any attention to the
plans of evil people.

¹⁹ Those who do what is right are joyful
when they see sinners destroyed.
Those who haven't done anything
wrong make fun of them.

²⁰ They say, 'Our enemies are completely
destroyed.
Fire has burned up their wealth.'

²¹ "Job, obey God and be at peace with
him.
Then he will help you succeed.
²² Do what he teaches you to do.
Keep his words in your heart.
²³ If you return to the Mighty One,
you will have what you had before.
But first you must remove
everything that is evil far from your
tent.
²⁴ You must throw your gold nuggets
away.
You must toss your gold from Ophir
into a valley.
²⁵ Then the Mighty One himself will be
your gold.
He'll be like the finest silver to you.
²⁶ You will find delight in the Mighty One.
You will honor God and trust in
him.
²⁷ You will pray to him, and he will hear
you.
You will keep the promises you
made to him.
²⁸ What you decide to do will be done.
Light will shine on the path you take.
²⁹ When people are brought low you will
say, 'Lift them up!'
Then God will help them.
³⁰ He'll even save those who are guilty.
He'll save them because your hands
are clean."

Job's Reply

23 Job replied,

² "Even today my problems are more
than I can handle.
In spite of my groans, God's hand is
heavy on me.
³ I wish I knew where I could find him!
I wish I could go to the place where
he lives!
⁴ I would state my case to him.
I'd give him all my arguments.
⁵ I'd find out what his answers would be.
I'd think about what he would say
to me.
⁶ Would he strongly oppose me?
No. He wouldn't bring charges
against me.

7 There honest people can prove to him
    they're not guilty.
There my Judge would tell me once
    and for all that I'm not guilty.

8 "But if I go to the east, God isn't there.
    If I go to the west, I don't find him.
9 When he's working in the north, I don't
    see him there.
When he turns to the south, I don't
    see him there either.
10 But he knows every step I take.
    When he has tested me,
    I'll come out as pure as gold.
11 My feet have closely followed his steps.
    I've stayed on his path without
    turning away.
12 I haven't disobeyed his commands.
    I've treasured his words more than
    my daily bread.

13 "But he's the only God. Who can
    oppose him?
He does anything he wants to do.
14 He carries out his plans against me.
    And he still has many other plans
    just like them.
15 That's why I'm so terrified.
    When I think about all of this, I'm
    afraid of him.
16 God has made my heart weak.
    The Mighty One has filled me with
    terror.
17 But even the darkness of death won't
    make me silent.
When the darkness of the grave
    covers my face, I won't be
    quiet.

24 "Why doesn't the Mighty One set a
    time for judging sinful people?
Why do those who know him have
    to keep waiting for that day?
2 People move their neighbor's boundary
    stones.
They steal their neighbor's flocks.
3 They take away the donkeys
    that belong to children whose
    fathers have died.
They take a widow's ox until she has
    paid what she owes.
4 They push those who are needy out of
    their way.
They force all the poor people in the
    land to go into hiding.
5 The poor are like wild donkeys in the
    desert.

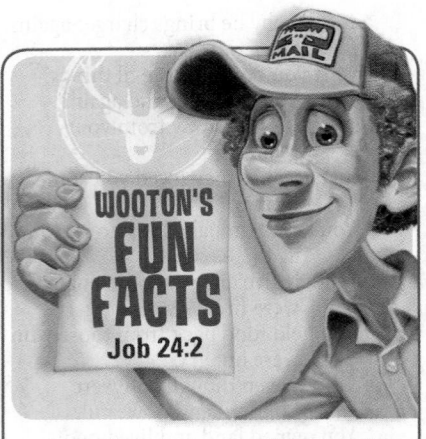

WOOTON'S FUN FACTS
Job 24:2

A boundary stone marks where property
begins and ends. It's against the law to
move them because it's the same as stealing
someone else's property. Like that time
my cousin tried to steal my artwork.

They have to go around looking for
    food.
The dry and empty land provides the
    only food for their children.
6 The poor go to the fields and get a little
    grain.
They gather up what is left in the
    vineyards of sinners.
7 The poor don't have any clothes. So
    they spend the night naked.
They don't have anything to cover
    themselves in the cold.
8 They are soaked by mountain rains.
    They hug the rocks because they
    don't have anything to keep
    them warm.
9 Children whose fathers have died
    are torn away from their mothers.
A poor person's baby is taken away
    to pay back what is owed.
10 The poor don't have any clothes. They
    go around naked.
They carry bundles of grain, but they
    still go hungry.
11 They work very hard as they crush olives.
    They stomp on grapes in winepresses,
    but they are still thirsty.
12 The groans of those who are dying are
    heard from the city.
Those who are wounded cry out for
    help.
But God doesn't charge anyone with
    doing what is wrong.

13 "Some people hate it when daylight comes.
  In the daytime they never walk outside.
14 When daylight is gone, murderers get up.
  They kill poor people and those who are in need.
  In the night they sneak around like robbers.
15 Those who commit adultery wait until the sun goes down.
  They think, 'No one will see us.'
  They keep their faces hidden.
16 In the dark, thieves break into houses.
  But by day they shut themselves in.
  They don't want anything to do with the light.
17 Midnight is like morning to them.
  The terrors of darkness are their friends.

18 "But sinners are like bubbles on the surface of water.
  Their share of the land is under God's curse.
  So no one goes to their vineyards.
19 Melted snow disappears when the air is hot and dry.
  And sinners disappear when they go down into their graves.
20 Even their mothers forget them.
  The worms in their graves eat them up.
  No one remembers sinful people anymore.
  They are cut down like trees.
21 They mistreat women who aren't able to have children.
  They aren't kind to widows.
22 But God is powerful.
  He even drags away people who are strong.
  When he rises up against them,
    they can never be sure they are safe.
23 God might let them rest and feel secure.
  But his eyes see how they live.
24 For a little while they are honored.
  Then they are gone.
  They are brought low.
  And they die like everyone else.
  They are cut off like heads of grain.

25 "Who can prove that what I'm saying is wrong?
  Who can prove that my words aren't true?"

The Third Speech of Bildad

25 Then Bildad the Shuhite replied,

2 "God is King. He should be feared.
  He establishes peace in the highest parts of heaven.
3 Can anyone count his troops?
  Is there anyone his light doesn't shine on?
4 How can human beings be right with God?
  How can mere people really be pure?
5 Even the moon isn't bright
    and the stars aren't pure in God's eyes.
6 So how about human beings? They are like maggots.
  How about mere people? They are like worms."

Job's Reply

26 Job replied,

2 "Bildad, you haven't helped people who aren't strong!
  You haven't saved people who are weak!
3 You haven't offered advice to those who aren't wise!
  In fact, you haven't understood anything at all!
4 Who helped you say these things?
  Whose spirit was speaking through you?

5 "The spirits of the dead are suffering greatly.
  So are those that are under the waters.
  And so are all those that live in them.
6 The place of the dead is naked in the sight of God.
  The grave lies open in front of him.
7 He spreads out the northern skies over empty space.
  He hangs the earth over nothing.
8 He wraps up water in his clouds.
  They are heavy, but they don't burst.
9 He covers the face of the full moon.
  He spreads his clouds over it.
10 He marks out the place where the sky meets the sea.

Adventures in Odyssey

Whit and Wooton used a vacuum cleaner to demonstrate that we don't understand how powerful God truly is in "A Glass Darkly" (A#43).

He marks out the boundary between light and darkness.
11 The pillars of the heavens shake.
　　They are terrified when his anger blazes out.
12 With his power he stirred up the oceans.
　　In his wisdom he cut the sea monster Rahab to pieces.
13 His breath made the skies bright and clear.
　　His hand wounded the serpent that glides through the sea.
14 Those are only on the edges of what he does.
　　They are only the soft whispers that we hear from him.
　　So who can understand how very powerful he is?"

Job's Final Reply to His Friends

27 Job continued to speak. He said,
2 "God hasn't treated me fairly.
　　The Mighty One has made my life bitter.

You can be sure that God lives.
　　And here's something else you can be sure of.
3 As long as I have life
　　and God gives me breath,
4 my mouth won't say evil things.
　　My lips won't tell lies.
5 I'll never admit you people are right.
　　Until I die, I'll say I'm telling the truth.
6 I'll continue to say I'm right.
　　I'll never let go of that.
　　I won't blame myself as long as I live.

7 "May my enemies suffer like sinful people!
　　May my attackers be punished like those who aren't fair!
8 What hope do ungodly people have when their lives are cut short?
　　What hope do they have when God takes away their lives?
9 God won't listen to their cry
　　when trouble comes on them.
10 They won't take delight in the Mighty One.
　　They'll never call out to God.

11 "I'll teach all of you about God's power.
　　I won't hide the things the Mighty One does.
12 You have seen those things yourselves.
　　So why do you continue your useless talk?

13 "Here's what God does to sinful people.
　　Here's what those who are mean receive from the Mighty One.
14 All their children will be killed by swords.
　　They'll never have enough to eat.
15 A plague will kill those who are left alive.
　　The widows of sinful men won't even weep over their own children.
16 Sinners might store up silver like dust and clothes like piles of clay.
17 But people who do what is right will wear those clothes.
　　People who haven't done anything wrong
　　will divide up that silver.
18 The house an evil person builds is like a moth's cocoon.

It's like a hut that's made by someone
on guard duty.

[19] Sinful people lie down wealthy, but
their wealth is taken away.
When they open their eyes,
everything is gone.

[20] Terrors sweep over them like a flood.
A storm takes them away during the
night.

[21] The east wind carries them off, and they
are gone.
It sweeps them out of their houses.

[22] It blows against them without mercy.
They try to escape from its power.

[23] It claps its hands and makes fun of
them.
It hisses them out of their houses."

The Place Where Wisdom Is Found Is Explained

28 There are mines where silver is
found.
There are places where gold is
purified.

[2] Iron is taken out of the earth.
Copper is melted down from ore.

[3] Human beings light up the darkness.
They search for ore in the deepest pits.
They look for it in the blackest
darkness.

[4] Far from where people live they cut a
tunnel.
They do it in places where other
people don't go.
Far away from people they swing
back and forth on ropes.

[5] Food grows on the surface of the earth.
But far below, the earth is changed
as if by fire.

[6] Lapis lazuli is taken from the rocky
earth.
Its dust contains nuggets of gold.

[7] No bird knows that hidden path.
No falcon's eye has seen it.

[8] Proud animals don't walk on it.
Lions don't prowl there.

[9] Human hands attack the hardest rock.
Their strong hands uncover the base
of the mountains.

[10] They tunnel through the rock.
Their eyes see all its treasures.

[11] They search the places where the rivers
begin.
They bring hidden things out into
the light.

[12] But where can wisdom be found?
Where does understanding live?

[13] No human being understands how
much it's worth.
It can't be found anywhere in the
world.

[14] The ocean says, "It's not in me."
The sea says, "It's not here either."

[15] It can't be bought with the finest gold.
Its price can't be weighed out in
silver.

[16] It can't be bought with gold from
Ophir.
It can't be bought with priceless onyx
or lapis lazuli.

[17] Gold or crystal can't compare with it.
It can't be bought with jewels made
of gold.

[18] Don't bother to talk about coral and
jasper.
Wisdom is worth far more than
rubies.

[19] A topaz from Cush can't compare
with it.
It can't be bought with the purest
gold.

[20] So where does wisdom come from?
Where does understanding live?

[21] It's hidden from the eyes of every living
thing.
Even the birds in the sky can't
find it.

[22] Death and the Grave say,
"Only reports about it have reached
our ears."

[23] But God understands the way to it.
He is the only one who knows where
it lives.

[24] He sees from one end of the earth to
the other.
He views everything in the world.

[25] He made the mighty wind.
He measured out the waters.

[26] He gave orders for the rain to fall.
He made paths for the
thunderstorms.

[27] Then he looked at wisdom and set its
price.
He established it and tested it.

[28] He said to human beings,
"Have respect for the Lord. That will
prove you are wise.
Avoid evil. That will show you have
understanding."

CANDID CONVERSATIONS

Since my parents' divorce years ago, I don't see my dad very often. And it sometimes hurts to know that he's not around to teach me how to fix a flat tire, laugh at my corny jokes, or just pat me on the shoulder and tell me he's proud of me.

I'm grateful that Whit has been like a father to me, but I've also learned to lean on God more when I miss having a dad around. Bible passages like this one show me that God knows and understands me better than any-one (even Whit!). God is in complete control over the world. If He can tell the rain when to fall, surely He can help me with any problem I might have.

Think of a difficult problem you have right now. Got it? Okay, now hand it over to the God who can see from one end of the earth to the other.

Job's Final Speech

29 Job continued to speak. He said,

2 "How I long for the times when things
    were better!
  That's when God watched over me.
3 The light of his lamp shone on me.
  I walked through darkness by his
    light.
4 Those were the best days of my life.
  That's when God's friendship blessed
    my house.
5 The Mighty One was still with me.
  My children were all around me.
6 The path in front of me was like sweet
    cream.
  It was as if the rock poured out olive
    oil for me.

7 "In those days I went to the city gate.

I took my seat as a member of the
    council.
8 Young people who saw me stepped to
    one side.
  Old people stood up as I
    approached.
9 The leaders stopped speaking.
  They covered their mouths with
    their hands.
10 The voices of the nobles became quiet.
  Their tongues stuck to the roofs of
    their mouths.
11 Everyone who heard me said good
    things about me.
  Those who saw me honored me.
12 That's because I saved poor people who
    cried out for help.
  I saved helpless children whose
    fathers had died.
13 Those who were dying gave me their
    blessing.
  I made the hearts of widows sing.
14 I put on a godly life as if it were my
    clothes.
  Fairness was my robe and my
    turban.
15 I was like eyes for those who were
    blind.
  I was like feet for those who couldn't
    walk.
16 I was like a father to needy people.
  I stood up for strangers in court.
17 Sinners are like animals that have
    powerful teeth.
  But I took from their mouths the
    people they had caught.

18 "I thought, 'I'll die in my own house.
  The days of my life will be as many
    as the grains of sand.
19 My roots will reach down to the water.
  The dew will lie all night on my
    branches.
20 I will remain healthy and strong.
  My bow will stay as good as new in
    my hand.'

21 "People wanted to hear what I had to
    say.
  They waited silently for the advice I
    gave them.
22 After I had spoken, they didn't speak
    anymore.
  My words fell gently on their ears.
23 They waited for me just as they would
    wait for rain showers.

They drank my words just as they
would drink the spring rain.
²⁴ When I smiled at them, they could
hardly believe it.
The light of my face lifted their
spirits.
²⁵ I chose the way they should go. I sat as
their chief.
I lived as a king lives among his
troops.
I was like someone who comforts
those who are sad.

30 "But now those who are younger
than I am make fun of me.
I wouldn't even put their parents
with my sheep dogs!
² Their strong hands couldn't give me any
help.
That's because their strength was
gone.
³ They were weak because they were
needy and hungry.
They wandered through dry and
empty deserts at night.
⁴ Among the bushes they gathered salty
plants.
They ate the roots of desert bushes.
⁵ They were driven away from human
society.
They were shouted at as if they were
robbers.
⁶ They were forced to live in dry stream
beds.
They had to stay among rocks
and in holes in the ground.
⁷ Like donkeys they cried out among the
bushes.
There they crowded together and hid.
⁸ They were so foolish that no one
respected them.
They were driven out of the land.

⁹ "Now their children laugh at me.
They make fun of me with their
songs.
¹⁰ They hate me. They stay away from me.
They even dare to spit in my face.
¹¹ God has made my body weak.
It's like a tent that has fallen down.
So those children do what they want
to in front of me.
¹² Many people attack me on my right side.
They lay traps for my feet.
They come at me from every
direction.

¹³ They tear up the road I walk on.
They succeed in destroying me.
They say, 'No one can help him.'
¹⁴ They attack me like troops smashing
through a wall.
Among the destroyed buildings they
come rolling in.
¹⁵ Terrors sweep over me.
My honor is driven away as if by the
wind.
My safety vanishes like a cloud.

¹⁶ "Now my life is slipping away.
Days of suffering grab hold of me.
¹⁷ At night my bones hurt.
My aches and pains never stop.
¹⁸ God's great power becomes like clothes
to me.
He chokes me like the neck of my
shirt.
¹⁹ He throws me down into the mud.
I'm nothing but dust and ashes.

²⁰ "God, I cry out to you. But you don't
answer me.
I stand up. But all you do is look at
me.
²¹ You do mean things to me.
You attack me with your mighty
power.
²² You pick me up and blow me away with
the wind.
You toss me around in the storm.
²³ I know that you will bring me down to
death.
That's what you have appointed for
everyone.

²⁴ "No one would crush people
when they cry out for help in their
trouble.
²⁵ Haven't I wept for those who are in
trouble?
Haven't I felt sorry for poor people?
²⁶ I hoped good things would happen, but
something evil came.
I looked for light, but all I saw was
darkness.
²⁷ My insides are always churning.
Nothing but days of suffering are
ahead of me.
²⁸ My skin has become dark, but the sun
didn't do it.
I stand up in the community and cry
out for help.
²⁹ I've become a brother to wild dogs.
Owls are my companions.

³⁰ My skin grows black and peels.
  My body burns with fever.
³¹ My lyre is tuned to sadness.
  My flute makes a sound like
    weeping.

31 "I made an agreement with my eyes.
  I promised not to look at a young
    woman with impure
    thoughts.
² What do we receive from God above?
  What do we get from the Mighty
    One in heaven?
³ Sinful people are destroyed.
  Trouble comes to those who do what
    is wrong.
⁴ Doesn't God see how I live?
  Doesn't he count every step I take?

⁵ "I haven't told any lies.
  My feet haven't hurried to cheat
    others.
⁶ So let God weigh me in honest scales.
  Then he'll know I haven't done
    anything wrong.
⁷ Suppose my steps have turned away
    from the right path.
  Suppose my heart has wanted what
    my eyes have seen.
  Or suppose my hands have become
    'unclean.'
⁸ Then may others eat what I've planted.
  May my crops be pulled up by the
    roots.

⁹ "Suppose my heart has been tempted by
    a woman.
  Or suppose I've prowled around my
    neighbor's home.
¹⁰ Then may my wife grind another man's
    grain.
  May other men sleep with her.
¹¹ Wanting another woman would have
    been an evil thing.
  It would have been a sin that should
    be judged.
¹² It's like a fire that burns down to the
    grave.
  It would have caused my crops to be
    pulled up by the roots.

¹³ "Suppose I haven't treated any of my
    male and female servants fairly
  when they've brought charges
    against me.
¹⁴ Then what will I do when God opposes
    me?

What answer will I give him
  when he asks me to explain myself?
¹⁵ Didn't he who made me make my
    servants also?
  Didn't the same God form us inside
    our mothers?

¹⁶ "I haven't said no to what poor people
    have wanted.
  I haven't let widows lose their hope.
¹⁷ I haven't kept my bread to myself.
  I've shared it with children whose
    fathers had died.
¹⁸ From the time I was young, I've helped
    those widows.
  I've raised those children as a father
    would.
¹⁹ Suppose I've seen people dying
    because they didn't have enough
    clothes.
  I've seen needy people
    who didn't have enough to keep
    warm.
²⁰ And they didn't give me their blessing
    when I warmed them with wool
    from my sheep.
²¹ Suppose I've raised my hand
    against children whose fathers have
    died.
  And I did it because I knew
    I had power in the courts.
²² Then let my arm fall from my shoulder.
  Let it be broken off at the joint.
²³ I was afraid God would destroy me.
  His glory terrifies me.
  So I'd never do things like that.

²⁴ "Suppose I've put my trust in gold.
  I've said to pure gold, 'You make me
    feel secure.'
²⁵ And I'm happy because I'm so wealthy.
  I'm glad because my hands have
    earned so much.
²⁶ Suppose I've worshiped the sun in all its
    glory.
  I've bowed down to the moon in all
    its beauty.
²⁷ My heart has been secretly tempted.
  My hand has thrown kisses to the
    sun and moon.
²⁸ Then these things would have been sins
    that should be judged.
  And I wouldn't have been faithful to
    God in heaven.

²⁹ "I wasn't happy when hard times came
    to my enemies.

I didn't enjoy seeing the trouble they
had.
³⁰ I didn't allow my mouth to sin
by asking for bad things to happen
to them.
³¹ The workers in my house always said,
'Job always gives plenty of food to
everyone.'
³² No stranger ever had to spend the night
in the street.
My door was always open to travelers.
³³ I didn't hide my sin as other people do.
I didn't hide my guilt in my heart.
³⁴ I was never afraid of the crowd.
I never worried that my relatives
might hate me.
I didn't have to keep quiet or stay
inside.

³⁵ "I wish someone would listen to me!
I'm signing my name to everything
I've said.
I hope the Mighty One will give me his
answer.
I hope the one who brings charges
against me will write them
down.
³⁶ I'll wear them on my shoulder.
I'll put them on my head like a
crown.
³⁷ I'll give that person a report of every
step I take.
I'll present it to him like I would to
a ruler.

³⁸ "Suppose my land cries out against me.
And all its soil is wet with tears.
³⁹ Suppose I've used up its crops without
paying for them.
Or I've broken the spirit of its
renters.
⁴⁰ Then let thorns grow instead of wheat.
Let stinkweed come up instead of
barley."

The words of Job end here.

The Speech of Elihu

32 So the three men stopped answering Job, because he thought he was right. ²But Elihu the Buzite was very angry with Job. That's because Job said he himself was right instead of God. Elihu was the son of Barakel. He was from the family of Ram. ³Elihu was also very angry with Job's three friends. They hadn't found any way to prove that Job was wrong. But they still said he was guilty. ⁴Elihu had waited before he spoke to Job. That's because the others were older than he was. ⁵But he saw that the three men didn't have anything more to say. So he was very angry.

⁶Elihu the Buzite, the son of Barakel, said,

"I'm young, and you are old.
So I was afraid to tell you what I
know.
⁷ I thought, 'Those who are older should
speak first.
Those who have lived for many years
should teach people how to be wise.'
⁸ But the spirit in people gives them
understanding.
The breath of the Mighty One gives
them wisdom.
⁹ Older people aren't the only ones who
are wise.
They aren't the only ones who
understand what is right.

¹⁰ "So I'm saying you should listen to me.
I'll tell you what I know.
¹¹ I waited while you men spoke.
I listened to your reasoning.
While you were searching for words,
¹² I paid careful attention to you.
But not one of you has proved that Job
is wrong.
None of you has answered his
arguments.
¹³ Don't claim, 'We have enough wisdom
to answer Job.'
Let God, not a mere man, prove that
he's wrong.
¹⁴ Job hasn't directed his words against me.
I won't answer him with your
arguments.

¹⁵ "Job, these men are afraid.
They don't have anything else to say.
They've run out of words.
¹⁶ Do I have to keep on waiting, now that
they are silent?
They are just standing there with
nothing to say.
¹⁷ I too have something to say.
I too will tell what I know.
¹⁸ I'm full of words.
My spirit inside me forces me to
speak.
¹⁹ Inside I'm like wine that is bottled up.
I'm like new wineskins ready to
burst.

²⁰ I must speak so I can feel better.
    I must open my mouth and reply.
²¹ I'll treat everyone the same.
    I won't praise anyone without
       meaning it.
²² If I weren't honest when I praised
       people,
    my Maker would soon take me from
       this life.

33

"Job, listen now to my words.
Pay attention to everything I say.
² I'm about to open my mouth.
    My words are on the tip of my
       tongue.
³ What I say comes from an honest heart.
    My lips speak only what I know is
       true.
⁴ The Spirit of God has made me.
    The breath of the Mighty One gives
       me life.
⁵ So answer me if you can.
    Stand up and argue your case in
       front of me.
⁶ To God I'm just the same as you.
    I too am a piece of clay.
⁷ You don't have to be afraid of me.
    My hand won't be too heavy on you.

⁸ "But I heard what you said.
    And here are the exact words I heard.
⁹ You said, 'I'm pure. I have done no
       wrong.
    I'm clean. I'm free from sin.
¹⁰ But God has found fault with me.
    He thinks I'm his enemy.
¹¹ He puts my feet in chains.
    He watches every step I take.'

¹² "But I'm telling you that you aren't right
       when you talk like that.
    After all, God is greater than any
       human being.
¹³ Why do you claim that God
    never answers anybody's questions?
¹⁴ He speaks in one way and then another.
    But we do not even realize it.
¹⁵ He might speak in a dream or in a
       vision at night.
    That's when people are sound asleep
       in their beds.
¹⁶ He might speak in their ears.
    His warnings might terrify them.
¹⁷ He warns them in order to turn them
       away from sinning.
    He wants to keep them from being
       proud.

¹⁸ He wants to stop them from going
       down into the grave.
    He doesn't want them to be killed by
       swords.
¹⁹ Someone might be punished by
       suffering in bed.
    The pain in their bones might never
       go away.
²⁰ They might feel so bad they can't eat
       anything.
    They might even hate the finest food.
²¹ Their body might waste away to nothing.
    Their bones might have been hidden.
    But now they stick out.
²² They might approach the very edge of
       the grave.
    The messengers of death might come
       for them.

²³ But suppose there is an angel who will
       speak up for him.
    The angel is very special. He's one
       out of a thousand.
    He will tell that person how to do
       what is right.
²⁴ That angel will be gracious to them.
    He'll say to God,
    'Spare them from going down into
       the grave.
    I know a way that can set them free.'
²⁵ Then their body is made like new again.
    They become as strong and healthy
       as when they were young.
²⁶ Then that person can pray to God and
       be blessed by him.
    They will see God's face and shout
       for joy.
    God will make them well and happy
       again.
²⁷ Then that person will come to others
       and say,
    'I sinned. I made what is wrong
       appear to be right.
    But I wasn't punished as I should
       have been.
²⁸ God has set me free. He has kept me
       from going down into the
       darkness of the grave.
    So I'll live to enjoy the light of life.'

²⁹ "God does all these things to people.
    In fact, he does them again and
       again.
³⁰ He wants to stop people from going
       down into the darkness of the
       grave.

Then the light of life will shine on
them.

³¹ "Pay attention, Job! Listen to me!
Be quiet so I can speak.
³² If you have anything to say, answer me.
Speak up. I want to help you be
cleared of all charges.
³³ But if you don't have anything to say,
listen to me.
Be quiet so I can teach you how to
be wise."

34 Elihu continued,

² "Hear what I'm saying, you wise men.
Listen to me, you who have learned
so much.
³ Our tongues tell us what tastes good
and what doesn't.
And our ears tell us what's true and
what isn't.
⁴ So let's choose for ourselves what is
right.
Let's learn together what is good.

⁵ "Job says, 'I'm not guilty of doing
anything wrong.
But God doesn't treat me fairly.
⁶ Even though I'm right,
he thinks I'm a liar.
Even though I'm not guilty,
his arrows give me wounds that can't
be healed.'
⁷ Is there anyone like Job?
He accuses God as easily as he
drinks water.
⁸ He's a companion of those who do evil.
He spends his time with sinful
people.
⁹ He asks, 'What good is it
to try to please God?'

¹⁰ "So listen to me, you men who have
understanding.
God would never do what is evil.
The Mighty One would never do
what is wrong.
¹¹ He pays back everyone for what they've
done.
He gives them exactly what they
should get.
¹² It isn't possible for God to do wrong.
The Mighty One would never treat
people unfairly.
¹³ Who appointed him to rule over the
earth?

Who put him in charge of the whole
world?
¹⁴ If he really wanted to,
he could hold back his spirit and
breath.
¹⁵ Then everyone would die together.
They would return to the dust.

¹⁶ "Job, if you have understanding, listen
to me.
Pay attention to what I'm saying.
¹⁷ Can someone who hates to be fair
govern?
Will you bring charges against the
holy and mighty God?
¹⁸ He says to kings, 'You are worthless.'
He says to nobles, 'You are evil.'
¹⁹ He doesn't favor princes.
He treats rich people and poor
people the same.
His hands created all of them.
²⁰ They die suddenly in the middle of the
night.
God strikes them down, and they
pass away.
Even people who are mighty are
removed, but not by human
hands.

²¹ "His eyes see how people live.
He watches every step they take.
²² There is no deep shadow or total
darkness
where those who do what is evil can
hide.
²³ God doesn't need to bring charges
against anyone.
He knows they are guilty.
So he doesn't need to have them
appear in his court to be
judged.
²⁴ He destroys the mighty without asking
them questions in court.
Then he sets others up in their places.
²⁵ He knows what they do.
So he crushes them during the night.
²⁶ He punishes them for the sins they
commit.
He does it where everyone can see
them.
²⁷ That's because they turned away from
following him.
They didn't have respect for anything
he does.
²⁸ They caused poor people to cry out to
him.

He heard the cries of those who were
in need.

²⁹ But if he remains silent, who can judge
him?

If he turns his face away, who can
see him?

He rules over individual people and
nations alike.

³⁰ He keeps those who are ungodly
from ruling.

He keeps them from laying traps for
others.

³¹ "Someone might say to God,
'I'm guilty of sinning,
but I won't do it anymore.

³² Show me my sins that I'm not aware of.
If I've done what is wrong,
I won't do it again.'

³³ But you refuse to turn away from your
sins.

So God won't treat you the way you
want to be treated.

You must decide, Job. I can't do it for
you.

So tell me what you know.

³⁴ "You men who have understanding
have spoken.

You wise men who hear me have
said to me,

³⁵ 'Job doesn't know what he's talking
about.

The things he has said don't make
any sense.'

³⁶ I wish Job would be given the hardest
test possible!

He answered like someone who is
evil.

³⁷ To his sin he adds even more sin.
He claps his hands and makes fun
of us.

He multiplies his words against God."

35 Elihu continued,

² "Job, do you think it's fair for you to say,
'I am the one who is right, not God'?

³ You ask him, 'What good is it for me
not to sin?

What do I get by not sinning?'

⁴ "I'd like to reply to you
and to your friends who are with you.

⁵ Look up at the heavens.
Observe the clouds that are high
above you.

⁶ If you sin, what does that mean to
God?

If you sin many times, what does
that do to him?

⁷ If you do what is right, how does that
help him?

What does he get from you?

⁸ The evil things you do only hurt people
like yourself.

The right things you do only help
other human beings.

⁹ "People cry out when they are treated
badly.

They beg to be set free from the
power of those who are over
them.

¹⁰ But no one says, 'Where is the God who
made me?

He gives us songs even during the
night.

¹¹ He teaches us more than he teaches the
wild animals.

He makes us wiser than the birds in
the sky.'

¹² He doesn't answer sinful people when
they cry out to him.

That's because they are so proud.

¹³ In fact, God doesn't listen to their
empty cries.

The Mighty One doesn't pay any
attention to them.

¹⁴ So he certainly won't listen to you.
When you say you don't see him, he
won't hear you.

He won't listen when you state your
case to him.

He won't pay attention even if you
wait for him.

¹⁵ When you say his anger never punishes
sin, he won't hear you.

He won't listen when you say he
doesn't pay any attention to
evil.

¹⁶ So you say things that don't mean
anything.

You use a lot of words,
but you don't know what you are
talking about."

36 Elihu continued,

² "Put up with me a little longer.
I'll show you I can speak up for God
even more.

³ I get my knowledge from far away.

I'll announce that the God who
      made me is fair.
⁴ You can be sure that my words are true.
      One who has perfect knowledge is
         talking to you.

⁵ "God is mighty, but he doesn't hate
         people.
      He's mighty, and he knows exactly
         what he's going to do.
⁶ He doesn't keep alive those who are evil.
      Instead, he gives suffering people
         their rights.
⁷ He watches over those who do what is
         right.
      He puts them on thrones as if they
         were kings.
      He honors them forever.
⁸ But some people are held by chains.
      Their pain ties them up like ropes.
⁹ God tells them what they've done.
      He tells them they've become proud
         and sinned against him.
¹⁰ He makes them listen when he corrects
         them.
      He commands them to turn away
         from the evil things they've done.
¹¹ If they obey him and serve him,
      they'll enjoy a long and happy life.
      Things will go well with them.
¹² But if they don't listen to him,
      they'll be killed by swords.
      They'll die because they didn't want
         to know anything about him.

¹³ "Those whose hearts are ungodly are
         always angry.
      Even when God puts them in chains,
         they don't cry out for help.
¹⁴ They die while they are still young.
      They die among the male prostitutes
         at the temples.
¹⁵ But God saves suffering people while
         they suffer.
      He speaks to them while they are
         hurting.

¹⁶ "Job, he wants to take you out of the
         jaws of trouble.
      He wants to bring you to a wide and
         safe place.
      He'd like to seat you at a table that is
         loaded with the best food.
¹⁷ But now you are loaded down
      with the punishment sinners will
         receive.
      You have been judged fairly.

¹⁸ Be careful that no one tempts you with
         riches.
      Don't take money from people who
         want special favors,
      no matter how much it is.
¹⁹ Can your wealth keep you out of trouble?
      Can all your mighty efforts keep you
         going?
²⁰ Don't wish for the night to come
      so you can drag people away from
         their homes.
²¹ Be careful not to do what is evil.
      You seem to like evil better than
         suffering!

²² "God is honored because he is so
         powerful.
      There is no teacher equal to him.
²³ Who has told him what he can do?
      Who has said to him, 'You have
         done what is wrong'?
²⁴ Remember to thank him for what he's
         done.
      People have praised him with their
         songs.
²⁵ Every human being has seen his work.
      People can see it from far away.
²⁶ How great God is! We'll never
         completely understand him.
      We'll never find out how long he has
         lived.

²⁷ "He makes mist rise from the water.
      Then it falls as rain into the streams.
²⁸ The clouds pour down their moisture.
      Rain showers fall on people
         everywhere.
²⁹ Who can understand how God spreads
         out the clouds?
      Who can explain how he thunders
         from his home in heaven?
³⁰ See how he scatters his lightning
         around him!
      He lights up the deepest parts of the
         ocean.
³¹ The rain he sends makes things grow
         for the nations.
      He provides them with plenty of
         food.
³² He holds lightning bolts in his hands.
      He commands them to strike their
         marks.
³³ His thunder announces that a storm is
         coming.
      Even the cattle let us know it's
         approaching.

37 "When I hear the thunder, my heart pounds.
It beats faster inside me.
² Listen! Listen to the roar of his voice!
Listen to the thunder that comes from him!
³ He sends his lightning across the sky.
It reaches from one end of the earth to the other.
⁴ Next comes the sound of his roaring thunder.
He thunders with his majestic voice.
When his voice fills the air,
he doesn't hold anything back.
⁵ God's voice thunders in wonderful ways.
We'll never understand the great things he does.
⁶ He says to the snow, 'Fall on the earth.'
He tells the rain, 'Pour down your mighty waters.'
⁷ He stops everyone from working.
He wants them to see his work.
⁸ The animals go inside.
They remain in their dens.
⁹ The storm comes out of its storeroom in the heavens.
The cold comes from the driving winds.
¹⁰ The breath of God produces ice.
The shallow water freezes over.
¹¹ He loads the clouds with moisture.
He scatters his lightning through them.
¹² He directs the clouds to circle above the surface of the whole earth.
They do everything he commands them to do.
¹³ He tells the clouds to punish people.
Or he brings them to water his earth and show his love.

¹⁴ "Job, listen to me.
Stop and think about the wonderful things God does.
¹⁵ Do you know how he controls the clouds?
Do you understand how he makes his lightning flash?
¹⁶ Do you know how the clouds stay up in the sky?
Do you understand the wonders of the God who has perfect knowledge?
¹⁷ Even your clothes are too hot for you when the land lies quiet under the south wind.

¹⁸ Can you help God spread out the skies?
They are as hard as a mirror that's made out of bronze.

¹⁹ "Job, tell us what we should say to God.
We can't prepare our case because our minds are dark.
²⁰ Should he be told that I want to speak?
Would anyone ask to be destroyed by him?
²¹ No one can look at the sun.
It's too bright after the wind has swept the skies clean.
²² Out of the north, God comes in his shining glory.
He comes in all his wonderful majesty.
²³ We can't reach up to the Mighty One.
He is lifted high because of his power.
Everything he does is fair and right.
So he doesn't crush people.
²⁴ That's why they have respect for him.
He cares about all those who are wise."

The Lord Speaks

38 The Lord spoke to Job out of a storm. He said,

² "Who do you think you are to disagree with my plans?
You do not know what you are talking about.
³ Get ready to stand up for yourself.
I will ask you some questions.
Then I want you to answer me.

⁴ "Where were you when I laid the earth's foundation?
Tell me, if you know.
⁵ Who measured it? I am sure you know!
Who stretched a measuring line across it?
⁶ What was it built on?
Who laid its most important stone?
⁷ When it happened, the morning stars sang together.
All the angels shouted with joy.

⁸ "Who created the ocean?
Who caused it to be born?
⁹ I put clouds over it as if they were its clothes.
I wrapped it in thick darkness.

WHIT'S WISDOM

Job 38–41

Job can be a difficult story to read and understand. He was a man who already trusted God, but he had to learn to trust God even more. God allowed Satan to take everything away from Job. His children died, he lost his possessions, and he even got a terrible skin disease!

In his suffering, Job asked God to explain. Though God did speak to Job, He never explained what happened. He didn't tell Job *why* his children died. He didn't tell him the reasons behind all the bad things.

I think of this story when I'm wondering about my own life. I certainly did some pondering after my wife passed away unexpectedly. Why would God let that happen? God doesn't explain everything that happens to us. God's ways are higher than our own ways. We still have to trust Him even when we don't understand. Or as a young friend of mine put it: "My arms are too short to box with God."

Read what God said to Job in Job 38:1–41:34. What has happened in your life that you don't understand? Be sure to read the very last chapter of Job to see what happened next.

---

¹⁰ I set limits for it.
     I put its doors and metal bars in
         place.
¹¹ I said, 'You can come this far.
     But you can't come any farther.
     Here is where your proud waves
         have to stop.'
¹² "Job, have you ever commanded the
         morning to come?
     Have you ever shown the sun where
         to rise?
¹³ The daylight takes the earth by its
         edges
     as if it were a blanket.
     Then it shakes sinful people out of it.
¹⁴ The earth takes shape like clay stamped
         with an official's mark.
     Its features stand out
     like the different parts of your
         clothes.
¹⁵ Sinners would rather have darkness
         than light.
     When the light comes, their power
         is broken.
¹⁶ "Have you traveled to the springs at the
         bottom of the ocean?
     Have you walked in its deepest
         parts?
¹⁷ Have the gates of death been shown to
         you?

Have you seen the gates of the
         deepest darkness?
¹⁸ Do you understand how big the earth
         is?
     Tell me, if you know all these things.
¹⁹ "Where does light come from?
     And where does darkness live?
²⁰ Can you take them to their places?
     Do you know the paths to their
         houses?
²¹ I am sure you know! After all, you were
         already born!
     You have lived so many years!
²² "Have you entered the places where the
         snow is kept?
     Have you seen the storerooms for
         the hail?
²³ I store up snow and hail for times of
         trouble.
     I keep them for days of war and
         battle.
²⁴ Where does lightning come from?
     Where do the east winds live that
         blow across the earth?
²⁵ Who tells the rain where it should
         fall?
     Who makes paths for the
         thunderstorms?
²⁶ They bring water to places where no
         one lives.

Job 38:2–41:34 Have you ever played the game Twenty Questions? Well, in this section God asks Job eighty-eight questions in a row. Can you find at least five that are rhetorical? If you're like me and you need a reminder of what *rhetorical* means once in a while, see Deuteronomy 20:19.

They water deserts that do not have anyone in them.
27 They satisfy the needs of dry and empty lands.
They make grass start growing there.
28 Does the rain have a father?
Who is the father of the drops of dew?
29 Does the ice have a mother?
Who is the mother of the frost from the heavens?
30 The waters become as hard as stone.
The surface of the ocean freezes over.

31 "Can you tie up the cords of the Pleiades?
Can you untie the belt that Orion wears?
32 Can you bring out all the stars in their seasons?
Can you lead out the Big Dipper and the Little Dipper?
33 Do you know the laws that govern the heavens?
Can you rule over the earth the way I do?

34 "Can you give orders to the clouds?
Can you make them pour rain down on you?
35 Do you send the lightning bolts on their way?
Do they report to you, 'Here we are'?

36 Who gives the ibis wisdom?
Who gives the rooster understanding?
37 Who is wise enough to count the clouds?
Who can tip over the water jars of the heavens?
38 I tip them over when the ground becomes hard.
I do it when the dirt sticks together.

39 "Do you hunt for food for mother lions?
Do you satisfy the hunger of their cubs?
40 Some of them lie low in their dens.
Others lie waiting in the bushes.
41 Who provides food for ravens when their babies cry out to me?
They wander around because they do not have anything to eat.

39 "Job, do you know when mountain goats have their babies?
Do you watch when female deer give birth?
2 Do you count the months until the animals have their babies?
Do you know the time when they give birth?
3 They bend their back legs and have their babies.
Then their labor pains stop.
4 Their little ones grow strong and healthy in the wild.
They leave and do not come home again.

5 "Who let the wild donkeys go free?
Who untied their ropes?
6 I gave them the dry and empty land as their home.
I gave them salt flats to live in.
7 They laugh at all the noise in town.
They do not hear the shouts of the donkey drivers.
8 They wander over the hills to look for grass.
They search for anything green to eat.

9 "Job, will wild oxen agree to serve you?
Will they stay by your feed box at night?
10 Can you keep them in straight rows with harnesses?

Will they plow the valleys behind
you?

[11] Will you depend on them for their
great strength?
Will you let them do your heavy
work?

[12] Can you trust them to haul in your
grain?
Will they bring it to your threshing
floor?

[13] "The wings of ostriches flap with joy.
But they can't compare with the
wings and feathers of storks.

[14] Ostriches lay their eggs on the ground.
They let them get warm in the sand.

[15] They do not know that something
might step on them.
A wild animal might walk all over
them.

[16] Ostriches are mean to their little ones.
They treat them as if they did not
belong to them.
They do not care that their work was
useless.

[17] I did not provide ostriches with
wisdom.
I did not give them good sense.

[18] But when they spread their feathers to
run,
they laugh at a horse and its rider.

[19] "Job, do you give horses their strength?

Do you put flowing manes on their
necks?

[20] Do you make them jump like locusts?
They terrify others with their proud
snorting.

[21] They paw the ground wildly.
They are filled with joy.
They charge at their enemies.

[22] They laugh at fear. They are not afraid
of anything.
They do not run away from swords.

[23] Many arrows rattle at their sides.
Flashing spears and javelins are also
there.

[24] They are so excited that they race over
the ground.
They can't stand still when trumpets
are blown.

[25] When they hear the trumpets they
snort, 'Aha!'
They catch the smells of battle far
away.
They hear the shouts of commanders
and the battle cries.

[26] "Job, are you wise enough to teach
hawks where to fly?
They spread their wings and fly
toward the south.

[27] Do you command eagles to fly so
high?
They build their nests as high as they
can.

[28] They live on cliffs and stay there at
night.
High up on the rocks they think
they are safe.

[29] From there they look for their food.
They can see it from far away.

[30] Their little ones like to eat blood.
Eagles gather where they see dead
bodies."

40 The LORD continued,

[2] "I am the Mighty One.
Will the man who argues with me
correct me?
Let him who brings charges against
me answer me!"

[3] Job replied to the LORD,

[4] "I'm not worthy. How can I reply to
you?
I'm putting my hand over my
mouth. I'll stop talking.

WOOTON'S FUN FACTS
Job 39:9-12

The King James version of the Bible translates
the word *oxen* here as "unicorn." However,
the animal most likely was an Arabian ox,
which was next to impossible to tame.
Kind of like the time I tried to keep a pet
moose named Dexter. It didn't end well.

⁵ I spoke once. But I really don't have any
answer.
I spoke twice. But I won't say
anything else."

⁶ Then the LORD spoke to Job out of the
storm. He said,

⁷ "Get ready to stand up for yourself.
I will ask you some more questions.
Then I want you to answer me.

⁸ "Would you dare to claim that I am not
being fair?
Would you judge me in order to
make yourself seem right?
⁹ Is your arm as powerful as mine is?
Can your voice thunder as mine
does?
¹⁰ Then put on glory and beauty as if they
were your clothes.
Also put on honor and majesty.
¹¹ Let loose your great anger.
Look at those who are proud and
bring them low.
¹² Look at proud people and make them
humble.
Crush evil people right where they
are.
¹³ Bury their bodies together in the dust.
Cover their faces in the grave.
¹⁴ Then I myself will admit to you
that your own right hand can save
you.

¹⁵ "Look at Behemoth. It is a huge animal.
I made both of you.
It eats grass like an ox.
¹⁶ Look at the strength it has in its hips!
What power it has in the muscles of
its stomach!
¹⁷ Its tail sways back and forth like a cedar
tree.
The tendons of its thighs are close
together.
¹⁸ Its bones are like tubes made out of
bronze.
Its legs are like rods made out of
iron.
¹⁹ It ranks first among my works.
I made it. I can approach it with my
sword.
²⁰ The hills produce food for it.
All the other wild animals play
near it.
²¹ It lies under lotus plants.
It hides in tall grass in the swamps.

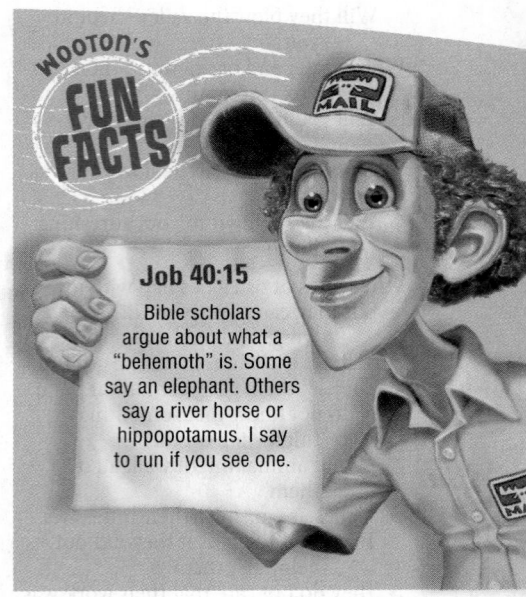

WOOTON'S FUN FACTS

Job 40:15

Bible scholars
argue about what a
"behemoth" is. Some
say an elephant. Others
say a river horse or
hippopotamus. I say
to run if you see one.

²² The lotus plants hide it in their shade.
Poplar trees near streams surround
it.
²³ It is not afraid when the river roars.
It is secure even when the Jordan
River rushes against its mouth.
²⁴ Can anyone capture it by its eyes?
Can anyone trap it and poke a hole
through its nose?

41 "Job, can you pull Leviathan out of
the sea with a fishhook?
Can you tie down its tongue with a
rope?
² Can you put a rope through its nose?
Can you stick a hook through its jaw?
³ Will it keep begging you for mercy?
Will it speak gently to you?
⁴ Will it make an agreement with you?
Can you make it your slave for life?
⁵ Can you make a pet out of it like a bird?
Can you put it on a leash for the
young women in your house?
⁶ Will traders offer you something for it?
Will they divide it up among the
merchants?
⁷ Can you fill its body with harpoons?
Can you throw fishing spears into
its head?
⁸ If you touch it, it will fight you.
Then you will remember never to
touch it again!

Jason's Jargon

JOB 41

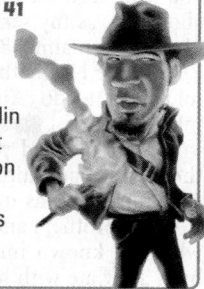

Ready for another quest? Find *javelin* in this chapter. At this time in history, a javelin was a light spear that was used as a weapon in warfare. Now, throwing the javelin is an event at track and field competitions.

⁹ No one can possibly control Leviathan.
　　Just looking at it will terrify you.
¹⁰ No one dares to wake it up.
　　So who can possibly stand up to me?
¹¹ Who has a claim against me that I must pay?
　　Everything on earth belongs to me.

¹² "Now I will speak about the Leviathan's legs.
　　I will talk about its strength and its graceful body.
¹³ Who can strip off its outer coat?
　　Who would try to pierce its double coat of armor?
¹⁴ Who dares to open its jaws?
　　Its mouth is filled with terrifying teeth.
¹⁵ Its back has rows of shields
　　that are close together.
¹⁶ Each one is so close to the next one
　　that not even air can pass between them.
¹⁷ They are joined tightly to one another.
　　They stick together and can't be forced apart.
¹⁸ Leviathan's snorting throws out flashes of light.
　　Its eyes shine like the first light of day.
¹⁹ Flames spray out of its mouth.
　　Sparks of fire shoot out.
²⁰ Smoke pours out of its nose.
　　It is like smoke from a boiling pot over burning grass.
²¹ Its breath sets coals on fire.
　　Flames fly out of its mouth.
²² Its neck is very strong.
　　People run to get out of its way.
²³ Its rolls of fat are close together.
　　They are firm and can't be moved.

²⁴ Its chest is as hard as rock.
　　It is as hard as a lower millstone.
²⁵ When Leviathan rises up,
　　even mighty people are terrified.
　　They run away when it moves around wildly.
²⁶ A sword that strikes it has no effect.
　　Neither does a spear or dart or javelin.
²⁷ It treats iron as if it were straw.
　　It crushes bronze as if it were rotten wood.
²⁸ Arrows do not make it run away.
　　Stones that are thrown from slings are like straw hitting it.
²⁹ A club seems like a piece of straw to it.
　　It laughs when it hears a javelin rattling.
³⁰ Its undersides are like broken pieces of pottery.
　　It leaves a trail in the mud like a threshing sled.
³¹ It makes the ocean churn like a boiling pot.
　　It stirs up the sea like perfume someone is making.
³² It leaves a shiny trail behind it.
　　You would think the ocean had white hair.
³³ Nothing on earth is equal to Leviathan.
　　That creature is not afraid of anything.
³⁴ It looks down on proud people.
　　It rules over all those who are proud."

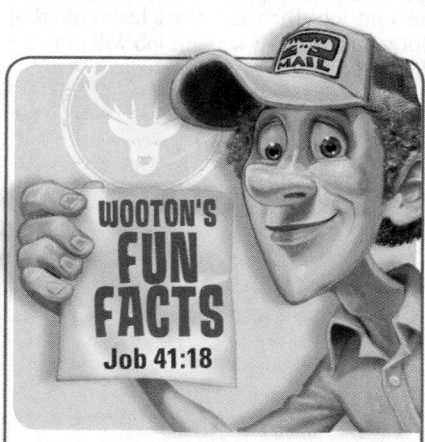

WOOTON'S FUN FACTS
Job 41:18

The Egyptian hieroglyph for "morning" is a crocodile eye because it glows at dawn. Creepy. Some Bible scholars think a leviathan is a large crocodile. But others think it's a whale. What do you think?

Job's Reply

42 Job replied to the Lord,

2 "I know that you can do anything.
No one can keep you from doing
what you plan to do.
3 You asked me, 'Who do you think you
are to disagree with my plans?
You do not know what you are
talking about.'
I spoke about things I didn't completely
understand.
I talked about things that were too
wonderful for me to know.
4 "You said, 'Listen now, and I will speak.
I will ask you some questions.
Then I want you to answer me.'
5 My ears had heard about you.
But now my own eyes have seen you.
6 So I hate myself.
I'm really sorry for what I said about
you.
That's why I'm sitting in dust and
ashes."

The Story Ends

7 After the Lord finished speaking to
Job, he spoke to Eliphaz the Temanite. He
said, "I am angry with you and your two
friends. You have not said what is true
about me, as my servant Job has. 8 So now
get seven bulls and seven rams. Go to my
servant Job. Then sacrifice a burnt offering
for yourselves. My servant Job will pray for
you. And I will accept his prayer. I will not
punish you for saying the foolish things
you said. You have not said what is true
about me, as my servant Job has." 9 So Eliphaz the Temanite, Bildad the Shuhite, and
Zophar the Naamathite did what the Lord
told them to do. And the Lord accepted
Job's prayer.

10 After Job had prayed for his friends,
the Lord made him successful again. He
gave him twice as much as he had before.
11 All his brothers and sisters and everyone
who had known him before came to see
him. They ate with him in his house. They
showed their concern for him. They comforted him because of all the troubles the
Lord had brought on him. Each one gave
him a piece of silver and a gold ring.

12 The Lord blessed the last part of Job's
life even more than the first part. He gave
Job 14,000 sheep and 6,000 camels. He gave
him 1,000 pairs of oxen and 1,000 donkeys. 13 Job also had seven sons and three
daughters. 14 He named the first daughter
Jemimah. He named the second Keziah.
And he named the third Keren-Happuch.
15 Job's daughters were more beautiful than
any other women in the whole land. Their
father gave them a share of property along
with their brothers.

16 After all of that happened, Job lived for
140 years. He saw his children, his grandchildren and his great-grandchildren.
17 And so Job died. He had lived for a very
long time.

Psalms

Our journey reaches the longest—and arguably, most beautiful—book in the Bible: Psalms.

Has anyone ever attempted to bully you? Or have people ever teamed up to threaten you and make you feel like you have no escape? Or have you ever felt so guilty about something that you just wanted to come clean and tell the truth, regardless of what it cost you? Or, perchance, do you ever get out into the natural world and become so overwhelmed that you can hardly put your feelings into words? The book of Psalms describes each of these experiences and more.

The original word for "psalms" referred to instruments with strings, which at the time would be lyres and harps and the like. In fact, the very last psalm in the massive collection (chapter 150) encourages you to pick up the nearest instrument and praise God with it. I personally suggest the ukulele, the most noble of instruments—with the added benefit of continuing in the tradition of strings. In time, the word "psalms" shifted from a reference to the instrument to meaning the song itself.

The Psalms are a wonderful collection to explore whenever you feel like reading the Bible but don't have any particular passage in mind. Peruse them and see for yourself!

What's it Mean, Eugene?

Revelation—When watching movies or reading novels, you will eventually experience "reveals." Reveals are those hidden pieces of information that give away important plot details. Similarly, God shows us His greatness and glory through the wonders of His creation (Psalm 19:1). We call this *general revelation*. He has also *revealed* important truths to us through His written Word, the Bible. This is known as *special revelation*. Of course, God has also allowed us to see Him as He is by coming to us in the flesh in Christ Jesus (John 1:18). And finally, God explains the future of mankind in the book of Revelation, which is the last book in the Bible.

BOOK 1
PSALMS 1–41

Psalm 1

¹ Blessed is the person who obeys the law
of the LORD.
They don't follow the advice of evil
people.
They don't make a habit of doing what
sinners do.
They don't join those who make fun
of the LORD and his law.
² Instead, the law of the LORD gives them
joy.
They think about his law day and
night.
³ That kind of person is like a tree that is
planted near a stream of water.
It always bears its fruit at the right
time.
Its leaves don't dry up.
Everything godly people do turns
out well.

⁴ Sinful people are not like that at all.
They are like straw

ADVENTURES IN ODYSSEY

Sam Johnson wondered if he should
be bad (or "sinful" in the phrasing
of Psalm 1) to get attention in
"When Bad Isn't So Good" (A#20).

that the wind blows away.
⁵ When the LORD judges them, their life
will come to an end.
Sinners won't have any place among
those who are godly.

⁶ The LORD watches over the lives of
godly people.
But the lives of sinful people will
lead to their death.

Psalm 2

¹ Why do the nations plan evil
together?
Why do they make useless plans?
² The kings of the earth rise up against
the LORD.

WHAT ABOUT YOU?

Who was Anna Anderson? Was she really
the daughter of Czar Nicholas, Russia's final
czar? Or an imposter? For decades, Anna
claimed to be Anastasia, Grand Duchess of
Russia. But after her death in 1984, scientists
used DNA testing to discover the truth: Anna
was just Anna, a girl pretending to be royalty.

Why do people lie and pretend to be
someone they're not? It comes down to their
motivation. For Anna, it was a thirst for money and fame.

The Bible gives us good advice about
having proper motives and being careful
about the people we allow to influence us.
As we see in Psalm 1:1–2: "Blessed is the
person who obeys the law of the LORD. They
don't follow the advice of evil people. They
don't make a habit of doing what sinners
do. They don't join those who make fun of
the LORD and his law. Instead, the law of
the LORD gives them joy. They think about his
law day and night."

Would you say that you and your friends
love the Lord's teachings? Remember to

choose your friends carefully. Make sure
they're honest with you, and are willing to
let you be yourself.

Write your name on a piece of paper. Then
write, "God loves me, and I don't have to
pretend." When you're tempted to act like
someone different so that people will like
you, remember to be who God created you to
be. You don't need to pretend to be royalty—
you *are* royalty—the person He loves and
sent His only Son to save.

Wooton's FUN FACTS

Ps. 2:1

The New Testament quotes verses from the Psalms written by King David at least nine times. The first one is Psalm 2:1, which is quoted in Acts 4:25–26. I love it when people quote me!

The rulers of the earth join together
    against his anointed king.
³ "Let us break free from their chains,"
    they say.
    "Let us throw off their ropes."

⁴ The God who sits on his throne in
    heaven laughs.
    The Lord makes fun of those rulers
    and their plans.
⁵ When he is angry, he warns them.
    When his anger blazes out, he
    terrifies them.
⁶ He says to them,
    "I have placed my king on my holy
    mountain of Zion."

⁷ I will announce what the LORD has promised.

He said to me, "You are my son.
    Today I have become your father.
⁸ Ask me, and I will give the nations to
    you.
    All nations on earth will belong to
    you.
⁹ You will break them with an iron scepter.
    You will smash them to pieces like
    clay pots."

¹⁰ Kings, be wise!
    Rulers of the earth, be warned!
¹¹ Serve the LORD and have respect for
    him.
    Celebrate his rule with trembling.
¹² Obey the son completely, or he will be
    angry.
    Your way of life will lead to your
    death.
His anger can blaze out at any
    moment.
    Blessed are all those who go to him
    for safety.

Psalm 3

A psalm of David when he ran
    away from his son Absalom.

¹ LORD, I have so many enemies!
    So many people are rising up against
    me!
² Many are saying about me,
    "God will not save him."

³ LORD, you are like a shield that keeps
    me safe.
    You bring me honor. You help me
    win the battle.
⁴ I call out to the LORD.
    He answers me from his holy
    mountain.

⁵ I lie down and sleep.
    I wake up again, because the LORD
    takes care of me.
⁶ I won't be afraid even though tens of
    thousands
    attack me on every side.

⁷ LORD, rise up!
    My God, save me!
Strike all my enemies in the face.
    Break the teeth of sinful people.

⁸ LORD, you are the one who saves.
    May your blessing be on your
    people.

Psalm 4

For the director of music. A psalm of David
    to be played on stringed instruments.

¹ My faithful God,
    answer me when I call out to you.
Give me rest from my trouble.
    Have mercy on me. Hear my prayer.

² How long will you people turn my
    glory into shame?
How long will you love what will
    certainly fail you?
How long will you pray to statues of
    gods?

WHIT'S WISDOM

Psalm 3:3

Can you think of your worst day ever? What happened on that day? For Eugene, it was the day that Bernard Walton beat him in chess. For King David, it may have been the day that he wrote Psalm 3. He was on the run from someone who was trying to kill him and take his throne. And who was that someone? His own son Absalom.

David desperately needed comfort in this difficult time. He looked to God and wrote this psalm as a song of praise to Him. He described God as our shield that keeps us safe in battle.

There have been times when I needed God's comfort as well. A few years ago, a huge thunderstorm hit Odyssey. The wind was so strong that it blew in the window at Whit's End, and shards of glass hit my leg. While Connie tried to get help, I said the Psalms aloud—both as a prayer to God and as a reminder that even in the midst of scary situations, God is still in control. Next time you are scared, sad, or worried about something, ask God for comfort. Only He can truly calm our hearts. And remember, He is right there beside us!

³ Remember that the LORD has set apart his faithful servant for himself.
The LORD hears me when I call out to him.

⁴ Tremble and do not sin.
When you are in bed,
look deep down inside yourself and be silent.

⁵ Offer to the LORD the sacrifices that godly people offer.
Trust in him.

⁶ LORD, many are asking, "Who will make us successful?"
LORD, may you do good things for us.

⁷ Fill my heart with joy
when the people have lots of grain and fresh wine.

⁸ In peace I will lie down and sleep.
LORD, you alone keep me safe.

REMEMBER THIS

PSALM 4:8

"In peace I will lie down and sleep. LORD, you alone keep me safe."

Psalm 5

For the director of music. A psalm of David to be played on flutes.

¹ LORD, listen to my words.
Pay attention when I mourn.

² My King and my God,
hear me when I cry for help.
I pray to you.

³ LORD, in the morning you hear my voice.
In the morning I pray to you.
I wait for you in hope.

⁴ For you, God, aren't happy with anything that is evil.
Those who do what is wrong can't live where you are.

⁵ Those who are proud can't stand in front of you.
You hate everyone who does what is evil.

⁶ You destroy those who tell lies.
LORD, you hate murderers and those who cheat others.

⁷ Because of your great love
I can come into your house.
With deep respect I bow down toward your holy temple.

⁸ LORD, I have many enemies.
Lead me in your right path.

WOOTON'S FUN FACTS
Ps. 5:12

This shield is not like a normal-sized shield, which would cover only part of your body. It's a shield for a giant! It would easily cover the body of even a full-grown man. I'm so glad God's protection is complete.

Make your way smooth and straight for me.

⁹ Not a word from their mouths can be trusted.
　Their hearts are filled with a desire to hurt others.
　Their throats are like open graves.
　With their tongues they tell lies.
¹⁰ God, show that they are guilty.
　Let their evil plans bring them down.
Send them away because of their many sins.
　They have refused to obey you.

¹¹ But let all those who go to you for safety be glad.
　Let them always sing for joy.
Spread your cover over them and keep them safe.
　Then those who love you will be glad because of you.
¹² Surely, Lord, you bless those who do what is right.
　Like a shield, your loving care keeps them safe.

Psalm 6

For the director of music. According to *sheminith*. A psalm of David to be played on stringed instruments.

¹ Lord, don't correct me when you are angry.

Don't punish me when you are very angry.
² Lord, have mercy on me. I'm so weak.
　Lord, heal me. My body is full of pain.
³ My soul is very troubled.
　Lord, how long will it be until you save me?

⁴ Lord, turn to me and help me.
　Save me. Your love never fails.
⁵ Dead people can't call out your name.
　How can they praise you when they are in the grave?

⁶ My groaning has worn me out.
　All night long my tears flood my bed.
　My bed is wet because of my crying.
⁷ I'm so sad I can't see very well.
　My eyesight gets worse because of all my enemies.

⁸ Get away from me, all you who do evil.
　The Lord has heard my weeping.
⁹ The Lord has heard my cry for his mercy.
　The Lord accepts my prayer.
¹⁰ All my enemies will be covered with shame and trouble.
　They will turn back in shame. It will happen suddenly.

Jason's Jargon

PSALM 6

Your task: Hunt for the word *mercy* in this chapter. Mercy is compassion shown to someone even when that person doesn't deserve it. We show humility when we ask God to have mercy on us.

Psalm 7

A *shiggaion* of David. He sang it to the Lord about Cush, who was from the tribe of Benjamin.

¹ Lord my God, I go to you for safety.
　Help me. Save me from all those who are chasing me.
² If you don't, they will tear me apart as if they were lions.

They will rip me to pieces so that no
one can save me.

3 LORD my God, suppose I have done
something wrong.
Suppose I am guilty.
4 Or I have done evil to my friend.
Or I have robbed my enemy without
any reason.
5 Then let my enemy chase me and catch
me.
Let him stomp me into the ground.
Let him bury me in the dust.

6 LORD, rise up in your anger.
Rise up against the great anger of my
enemies.
My God, wake up. Command that
the right thing be done.
7 Let all the people of the earth gather
around you.
Rule over them from your throne in
heaven.
8   LORD, judge all people.
LORD, show that I have done what is
right.
Most High God, remember that I am
honest.
9 God, you always do what is right.
You look deep down inside the
hearts and minds of people.
Bring to an end the terrible things
sinful people do.
Make godly people safe.

10 The Most High God is like a shield that
keeps me safe.
He saves those whose hearts are
honest.
11 God judges fairly.
He shows his anger every day.
12 If evil people don't change their ways,
God will sharpen his sword.
He will get his bow ready to use.
13 He has prepared his deadly weapons.
He has made his flaming arrows
ready.

14 Whoever is full of evil
plans trouble and ends up telling
lies.
15 Whoever digs a hole and shovels it out
falls into the pit they have made.
16 The trouble they cause comes back on
them.
The terrible things they do will
happen to them.

17 I will give thanks to the LORD because
he does what is right.
I will sing the praises of the name of
the LORD Most High.

Psalm 8

For the director of music. According
to *gittith*. A psalm of David.

1 LORD, our Lord,
how majestic is your name in the
whole earth!

You have set your glory
in the heavens.
2 You have made sure that children
and infants praise you.
Their praise is a wall
that stops the talk of your enemies.

3 I think about the heavens.
I think about what your fingers have
created.
I think about the moon and stars
that you have set in place.
4 What are human beings that you think
about them?
What is a son of man that you take
care of him?
5 You have made them a little lower than
the angels.
You placed on them a crown of glory
and honor.

Ps. 8:3 Some scientists—including
Eugene—think that without the moon,
life on Earth couldn't survive. The tides,
temperature, seasons, and rotation of
the earth would be very, very different
without the moon. Plus, moonlight walks
wouldn't exist. Penny would hate that.

⁶ You made human beings rule over
  everything your hands created.
  You put everything under their
  control.
⁷ They rule over all flocks and herds
  and over the wild animals.
⁸ They rule over the birds in the sky
  and over the fish in the ocean.
  They rule over everything that
  swims in the oceans.
⁹ Lᴏʀᴅ, our Lord,
  how majestic is your name in the
  whole earth!

Psalm 9

For the director of music. A
psalm of David to the tune of
"The Death of the Son."

¹ Lᴏʀᴅ, I will give thanks to you with all
  my heart.
  I will tell about all the wonderful
  things you have done.
² I will be glad and full of joy because of
  you.

Most High God, I will sing the
  praises of your name.
³ My enemies turn back.
  They fall down and die right in front
  of you.
⁴ You have proved that I haven't done
  anything wrong.
  You have sat on your throne and
  judged fairly.
⁵ You have punished the nations. You
  have destroyed evil people.
  You have erased their names from
  your book for ever and ever.
⁶ My enemies have been destroyed
  forever.
  You have leveled their cities to the
  ground.
  Even the memory of them is gone.
⁷ The Lᴏʀᴅ rules forever.
  He has set up his throne so that he
  can judge people.
⁸ He rules the world in keeping with
  what is right.
  He judges all its people fairly.

WHAT ABOUT YOU?

You and your brother have been told over and over not to shoot your giant slingshot in the house. Do you listen? No.

One day when your parents are out, you unleash an awesome shot—right through the living room wall. You panic. Then your brother remembers the roll of wallpaper left over from remodeling. After you do an impressive patch job, your parents arrive home and don't notice a thing. That is until your dad leans against the wall and puts his hand right through it.

Covering over a problem is different from fixing it, isn't it? Our sins have a way of revealing themselves, even if we think we've "made up" for them. Psalm 9:16 says, "Evil people are trapped by what they have done." That means bad deeds naturally get people into trouble. They may get caught and face punishment. Or they might not get caught, yet live with guilt for a long time until they confess and ask for forgiveness.

God knows when we've only patched over a sin, and that's not good enough for Him. We need to come clean in order to experience the peace that God wants us to have.

Here's a great way to learn about some real-life truths. Visit an elderly friend or relative, or meet someone new at church or a local nursing home. Give them a hug. Talk to them. Invite them to share stories about growing up, their family, or where they've lived. Prepare to hear about an interesting life!

⁹ The Lord is a place of safety for those
who have been treated badly.
He keeps them safe in times of
trouble.
¹⁰ Lord, those who know you will trust in
you.
You have never deserted those who
look to you.

¹¹ Sing the praises of the Lord. He rules
from his throne in Zion.
Tell among the nations what he has
done.
¹² The God who pays back murderers
remembers.
He doesn't forget the cries of those
who are hurting.

¹³ Lord, see how badly my enemies treat
me!
Help me! Don't let me go down to
the gates of death!
¹⁴ Then I can give praise to you
at the gates of the city of Zion.
There I will be full of joy
because you have saved me.
¹⁵ The nations have fallen into the pit they
have dug.
Their feet are caught in the net they
have hidden.
¹⁶ The Lord is known to be fair by the
things he does.
Evil people are trapped by what they
have done.
¹⁷ Sinful people go down to the place of
the dead.
So do all the nations that forget God.
¹⁸ But God will never forget needy people.
The hope of those who are hurting
will never die.

¹⁹ Lord, rise up. Don't let people win the
battle.
Let the nations come to you and be
judged.
²⁰ Lord, strike them with terror.
Let the nations know they are only
human beings.

Psalm 10

¹ Lord, why are you so far away?
Why do you hide yourself in times
of trouble?

² An evil person is proud and hunts
down those who are weak.

He catches weak people by making
clever plans.
³ He brags about what his heart desires.
He speaks well of those who always
want more.
He attacks the Lord with his words.
⁴ Because he is proud, that evil person
doesn't turn to the Lord.
There is no room for God in any of
his thoughts.
⁵ Everything always goes well for him.
So he is proud.
He doesn't want to have anything to do
with God's laws.
He makes fun of all his enemies.
⁶ He says to himself, "I will always be
secure."
He promises himself, "No one will
ever harm me."
⁷ His mouth is full of lies and warnings.
With his tongue he speaks evil and
makes trouble.

⁸ Sinful people hide and wait near the
villages.
From their hiding places they
murder people who aren't
guilty.
They watch in secret for those they
want to attack.
⁹ They hide and wait like a lion in the
bushes.
From their hiding places they
wait to catch those who are
helpless.
They catch them and drag them off
in their nets.
¹⁰ Those they have attacked are beaten up.
They fall to the ground.
They fall because their attackers are
too strong for them.
¹¹ Sinful people say to themselves, "God
will never notice.
He covers his face. He never sees
us."

¹² Lord, rise up! God, show your power!
Don't forget those who are helpless.
¹³ Why do sinful people attack you with
their words?
Why do they say to themselves,
"He won't hold us accountable"?
¹⁴ God, you see the problems of people in
trouble.
You take note of their pain. You do
something about it.

So those who are attacked place
     themselves in your care.
  You help children whose fathers
     have died.
¹⁵ Take away the power of sinful people.
  Hold them accountable for the evil
     things they do.
  Uncover all the evil they have done.

¹⁶ The LORD is King for ever and ever.
  The nations will disappear from his
     land.
¹⁷ LORD, you hear the desires of those who
     are hurting.
  You cheer them up and give them
     hope.
  You listen to their cries.
¹⁸ You stand up for those whose fathers
     have died
  and for those who have been treated
     badly.
  You do it so that mere human beings
     made of dust
  may not terrify others anymore.

Psalm 11

For the director of music.
A psalm of David.

¹ I run to the LORD for safety.
  So how can you say to me,
  "Fly away like a bird to your
     mountain.

WOOTON'S FUN FACTS
Ps. 11:1

This verse refers to little birds trying to
hide, and not an eagle that would roost
high on a cliff like the one in Jeremiah
49:16. This verse might be talking about a
finch. They can live off seeds found in the
mountains. Definitely not my owl, Dr. What.

² Look! Evil people are bending their
     bows.
  They are placing their arrows against
     the strings.
  They are planning to shoot from the
     shadows
  at those who have honest hearts.
³ When law and order are being
     destroyed,
  what can godly people do?"

⁴ The LORD is in his holy temple.
  The LORD is on his throne in heaven.
  He watches everyone on earth.
  His eyes study them.
⁵ The LORD watches over those who do
     what is right.
  But he really hates sinful people and
     those who love to hurt others.
⁶ He will pour out flaming coals and
     burning sulfur
  on those who do what is wrong.
  A hot and dry wind will destroy
     them.

⁷ The LORD always does what is right.
  So he loves it when people do what
     is fair.
  Those who are honest will enjoy his
     blessing.

Psalm 12

For the director of music. According
to *sheminith*. A psalm of David.

¹ Help, LORD! No one does what is right
     anymore.
  Those who are faithful have
     disappeared from the human
     race.
² Everyone tells lies to their neighbors.
  With their lips they praise others,
     but they don't really mean it.

³ May the LORD close all lips that don't
     mean what they say.
  May he stop every tongue that
     brags.
⁴ They say, "What we speak with our
     tongues will win the battle.
  What we say with our lips will keep
     us safe. No one will have
     victory over us."

⁵ The LORD says, "The poor are being
     robbed.
  Those who are in need groan.

So I will stand up to help them.
I will keep them safe from those
who tell lies about them."
⁶ The words of the LORD are perfect.
They are like silver made pure in a
clay furnace.
They are like gold made pure seven
times over.

⁷ LORD, you will keep needy people
safe.
You will always keep sinners from
hurting us.
⁸ Proud and sinful people walk around
openly
when the evil they do is praised by
the human race.

Psalm 13

For the director of music.
A psalm of David.

¹ LORD, how long must I wait? Will you
forget me forever?
How long will you turn your face
away from me?
² How long must I struggle with my
thoughts?
How long must my heart be sad day
after day?

ADVENTURES IN ODYSSEY

In Psalm 13, David chose to trust in
God despite the difficult times he
was going through. In the adventure
"Take It on Trust" (Club), Olivia
learned to trust her friend despite
everything that was going on.

How long will my enemies keep
winning the battle over me?
³ LORD my God, look at me and answer
me.
Give me new life, or I will die.
⁴ Then my enemies will say, "We have
beaten him."
They will be filled with joy when I
die.

⁵ But I trust in your faithful love.
My heart is filled with joy because
you will save me.
⁶ I will sing praise to the LORD.
He has been so good to me.

Psalm 14

For the director of music.
A psalm of David.

¹ Foolish people say in their hearts,
"There is no God."
They do all kinds of horrible and evil
things.
No one does anything good.

² The LORD looks down from heaven
on all people.
He wants to see if there are any who
understand.
He wants to see if there are any who
trust in God.
³ All of them have turned away.
They have all become evil.
No one does anything good,
no one at all.

⁴ Do all these people who do evil know
nothing?
They eat up my people as if they
were eating bread.
They never call out to the LORD.
⁵ But just look at them! They are filled
with terror
because God is among those who
do right.
⁶ You who do evil keep poor people from
succeeding.
But the LORD is their place of
safety.

⁷ How I pray that the God who saves
Israel will come out of Zion!
Then the LORD will bless his people
with great success again.
So let the people of Jacob be filled
with joy! Let Israel be glad!

Psalm 15
A psalm of David.

¹ Lord, who can live in your sacred tent?
Who can stay on your holy
mountain?

² Anyone who lives without blame
and does what is right.
They speak the truth from their heart.
³   They don't tell lies about other
people.
They don't do wrong to their neighbors.
They don't say anything bad about
them.

Ps. 15:3 A survey showed that 60
percent of adults can't tell the truth
for ten minutes straight. Many people
lie so people will like them better. I've
heard my brother do it to make business
deals. What tempts you to lie?

⁴ They hate evil people.
But they honor those who have
respect for the Lord.
They keep their promises even when it
hurts.
They do not change their mind.
⁵ They lend their money to poor people
without charging interest.
They don't accept money to harm
those who aren't guilty.

Anyone who lives like that
will always be secure.

Psalm 16
A *miktam* of David.

¹ My God, keep me safe.
I go to you for safety.

² I say to the Lord, "You are my Lord.
Without you, I don't have anything
that is good."
³ I say about God's people who live in our
land, "They are the noble ones.
I take great delight in them."
⁴ Those who run after other gods
will suffer more and more.
I will not pour out offerings of blood to
those gods.
My lips will not speak their names.

⁵ Lord, you alone are everything I need.
You make my life secure.
⁶ I am very pleased with what you have
given me.
I am very happy with what I've
received from you.

⁷ I will praise the Lord. He gives me
good advice.
Even at night my heart teaches me.
⁸ I keep my eyes always on the Lord.
He is at my right hand.
So I will always be secure.

⁹ So my heart is glad. Joy is on my
tongue.
My body also will be secure.
¹⁰ You will not leave me in the place of the
dead.
You will not let your faithful one rot
away.
¹¹ You always show me the path of life.
You will fill me with joy when I am
with you.
You will make me happy forever at
your right hand.

Psalm 17
A prayer of David.

¹ Lord, hear me, because I ask for what
is right.
Listen to my cry for help.
Hear my prayer.
It doesn't come from lips that tell
lies.
² When you hand down your sentence,
may it be in my favor.
May your eyes see what is right.

³ Look deep down into my heart.
Study me carefully at night and test
me.
You won't find anything wrong.
I have planned nothing evil.
My mouth has not said sinful things.

⁴ Though evil people tried to pay me to
  do wrong,
  I have not done what they wanted.
Instead I have done what you
  commanded.
⁵ My steps have stayed on your paths.
  My feet have not slipped.

⁶ My God, I call out to you because you
  will answer me.
  Listen to me. Hear my prayer.
⁷ Show me the wonders of your great
  love.
  By using your great power,
  you save those who go to you for
    safety from their enemies.
⁸ Take good care of me, just as you
  would take care of your own
    eyes.
  Hide me in the shadow of your
    wings.
⁹ Save me from the sinful people who
  want to destroy me.
  Save me from my deadly enemies
    who are all around me.

¹⁰ They make their hearts hard and
   stubborn.
   Their mouths speak with pride.
¹¹ They have tracked me down. They are
   all around me.
   Their eyes watch for a chance to
     throw me to the ground.
¹² They are like a hungry lion, waiting to
   attack.
   They are like a powerful lion, hiding
     in the bushes.

¹³ Lord, rise up. Oppose them and bring
   them down.
   With your sword, save me from
     those evil people.
¹⁴ Lord, by your power save me from
   people like that.
   They belong to this world. They get
     their reward in this life.

May what you have stored up for evil
  people fill their bellies.
May their children's stomachs be
  filled with it.
And may there even be leftovers for
  their little ones.
¹⁵ You will show that I am right; I will
   enjoy your blessing.
   When I wake up, I will be satisfied
     because I will see you.

Psalm 18

For the director of music. A psalm
of David, the servant of the Lord.
He sang the words of this song to
  the Lord. He sang them when
the Lord saved him. He saved him
  from the power of all his enemies
  and of Saul. David said,

¹ I love you, Lord.
  You give me strength.

² The Lord is my rock and my place
    of safety. He is the God who
    saves me.
  My God is my rock. I go to him for
    safety.
  He is like a shield to me. He's the
    power that saves me. He's my
    place of safety.
³ I called out to the Lord. He is worthy
    of praise.
  He saved me from my enemies.

⁴ The ropes of death were almost
    wrapped around me.
  A destroying flood swept over me.
⁵ The ropes of the grave were tight
    around me.
  Death set its trap in front of me.
⁶ When I was in trouble, I called out to
    the Lord.
  I cried to my God for help.
From his temple he heard my voice.
  My cry for help reached his ears.

⁷ The earth trembled and shook.
  The base of the mountains rocked
    back and forth.

Eugene told his father about how God
was his fortress, rock, and refuge
in "Cover of Darkness" (A#47).

One hundred people gone. Vanished. Not only that, even their buildings had been dismantled. Did everyone in Virginia's Roanoke Colony leave their settlement and seek help from local Indian tribes? Or did something else happen?

The Lost Colony of Virginia is one of the oldest mysteries in America. In 1587, Governor John White helped about 100 people move from England to Virginia. Shortly after their arrival, the colonists asked White to return to England for supplies. A round trip from England to America and back usually took three or four months. But White was gone for three *years* because of a war between England and Spain. When he returned, everyone was gone. He never found out what happened. To this day, archaeologists are still trying to solve the mystery of Roanoke Colony.

How do you feel when the answers just aren't coming? When you're dealing with tough questions without clear answers, turn to the Lord. Psalm 18:2 tells us that God is a safe place—a refuge—and we can ask Him

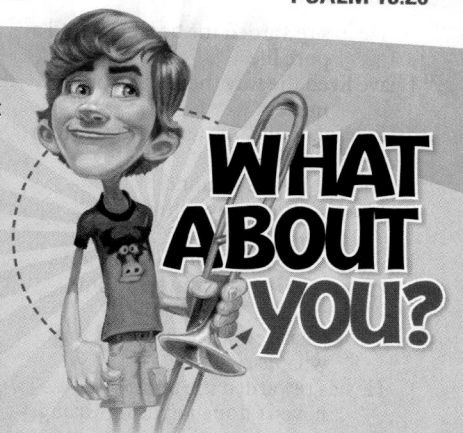

WHAT ABOUT you?

to protect us and stand with us when life gets hard. He's always ready to help.

With all this talk of mysteries, you can host a fun mystery of your own by playing Three Clues. It's like hide and seek, but with an object instead of a person. Hide your favorite action figure or stuffed bear. Then give your family three clues, one at a time, and challenge them to find the hidden object. The person who finds the item gets to hide his or her favorite object for *you* to find!

It trembled because the Lord was
    angry.
8 Smoke came out of his nose.
    Flames of fire came out of his mouth.
    Burning coals blazed out of it.
9 He opened the heavens and came down.
    Dark clouds were under his feet.
10 He stood on the cherubim and flew.
    The wings of the wind lifted him up.
11 He covered himself with darkness.
    The dark rain clouds of the sky were
      like a tent around him.
12 Clouds came out of the brightness that
    was all around him.
    They came with hailstones and
      flashes of lightning.
13 The Lord thundered from heaven.
    The voice of the Most High God was
      heard.
14 He shot his arrows and scattered our
    enemies.
    He sent great flashes of lightning and
      chased the enemies away.

15 The bottom of the sea could be seen.
    The foundations of the earth were
      uncovered.
    Lord, it happened when your anger
      blazed out.
    It came like a blast of breath from
      your nose.
16 He reached down from heaven. He took
    hold of me.
    He lifted me out of deep waters.
17 He saved me from my powerful enemies.
    He set me free from those who were
      too strong for me.
18 They opposed me when I was in
    trouble.
    But the Lord helped me.
19 He brought me out into a wide and safe
    place.
    He saved me because he was pleased
      with me.
20 The Lord has been good to me because
    I do what is right.

He has rewarded me because I lead a
pure life.
²¹ I have lived the way the Lord wanted
me to.
I am not guilty of turning away from
my God.
²² I keep all his laws in mind.
I haven't turned away from his
commands.
²³ He knows that I am without blame.
He knows I've kept myself from
sinning.
²⁴ The Lord has rewarded me for doing
what is right.
He has rewarded me because I
haven't done anything wrong.
²⁵ Lord, to those who are faithful you
show that you are faithful.
To those who are without blame
you show that you are without
blame.
²⁶ To those who are pure you show that
you are pure.
But to those whose paths are crooked
you show that you are clever.
²⁷ You save those who aren't proud.
But you bring down those whose
eyes are proud.
²⁸ Lord, you keep the lamp of my life
burning brightly.
You are my God. You bring light into
my darkness.
²⁹ With your help I can attack a troop of
soldiers.
With the help of my God I can climb
over a wall.

³⁰ God's way is perfect.
The Lord's word doesn't have any
flaws.
He is like a shield
to all who go to him for safety.
³¹ Who is God except the Lord?
Who is the Rock except our God?
³² God gives me strength for the battle.
He keeps my way secure.
³³ He makes my feet like the feet of a deer.
He causes me to stand on the highest
places.
³⁴ He trains my hands to fight every battle.
My arms can bend a bow of bronze.
³⁵ Lord, you are like a shield that keeps
me safe.
Your strong right hand keeps me
going.
Your help has made me great.

³⁶ You give me a wide path to walk on
so that I don't twist my ankles.
³⁷ I chased my enemies and caught them.
I didn't turn back until they were
destroyed.
³⁸ I crushed them so that they couldn't get
up.
They fell under my feet.
³⁹ Lord, you gave me strength to fight the
battle.
You made my enemies humble in
front of me.
⁴⁰ You made them turn their backs and
run away.
So I destroyed my enemies.
⁴¹ They cried out for help. But there was
no one to save them.
They called out to the Lord. But he
didn't answer them.
⁴² I beat them as fine as dust blown by the
wind.
I stomped on them like mud in the
streets.
⁴³ You saved me when my own people
attacked me.
You made me the ruler over
nations.
People I didn't know serve me now.
⁴⁴ People from other lands bow down to
me in fear.
As soon as they hear me, they obey
me.

WOOTON'S FUN FACTS
Ps. 18:43

Turn over to 2 Samuel 3:1. Psalm 18:43
talks about when Israel was in a civil
war with David's people fighting Saul's
people. Amazing how a dark time
could produce such good poetry!

⁴⁵ All of them give up hope.
    They come trembling out of their
       hiding places.
⁴⁶ The Lord lives! Give praise to my Rock!
    Give honor to God my Savior!
⁴⁷ He is the God who pays back my
      enemies.
    He brings the nations under my
      control.
⁴⁸   He saves me from my enemies.
  You have honored me more than them.
  You have saved me from a man who
     wanted to hurt me.
⁴⁹ Lord, I will praise you among the
     nations.
    I will sing the praises of your name.
⁵⁰ The Lord helps his king win great
     battles.
    He shows his faithful love to his
      anointed king.
    He shows it to David and to his
      family forever.

Psalm 19

For the director of music.
A psalm of David.

¹ The heavens tell about the glory of God.
    The skies show that his hands
      created them.
² Day after day they speak about it.
    Night after night they make it known.
³ But they don't speak or use words.
    No sound is heard from them.
⁴ Yet their voice goes out into the whole
     earth.
    Their words go out from one end of
     the world to the other.

God has set up a tent in the heavens for
    the sun.
⁵   The sun is like a groom leaving the
     room of his wedding night.
  The sun is like a great runner who
     takes delight in running a race.
⁶ It rises at one end of the heavens.
    Then it moves across to the other end.
    Everything enjoys its warmth.

Ps. 19:7 You can actually increase your brain function by eating oily fish, bananas, and avocados. Once I tried making a dish with all of them together. We refer to that as the dinner we will never talk about again. Your brain function may help you become more *intelligent*. However, *intelligence* is different from *wisdom*. Reading your Bible is the best way to become wise.

⁷ The law of the Lord is perfect.
    It gives us new strength.
  The laws of the Lord can be trusted.
    They make childish people wise.
⁸ The rules of the Lord are right.
    They give joy to our hearts.
  The commands of the Lord shine
     brightly.
    They give light to our minds.
⁹ The law that brings respect for the
     Lord is pure.
    It lasts forever.
  The commands the Lord gives are true.
    All of them are completely right.
¹⁰ They are more priceless than gold.
    They have greater value than huge
     amounts of pure gold.
  They are sweeter than honey
    that is taken from the honeycomb.
¹¹ Your servant is warned by them.
    When people obey them, they are
     greatly rewarded.

REMEMBER THIS

PSALM 19:1

"The heavens tell about the glory of God. The skies show that his hands created them."

ADVENTURES IN ODYSSEY

Leslie learned that there's not a lot of difference between lying and exaggerating in "It Sure Seems Like It to Me" (A#LE).

¹² But who can know their own mistakes?
Forgive my hidden faults.
¹³ Also keep me from the sins I want to commit.
May they not be my master.
Then I will be without blame.
I will not be guilty of any great sin against your law.
¹⁴ Lord, may these words of my mouth please you.
And may these thoughts of my heart please you also.
You are my Rock and my Redeemer.

Psalm 20

For the director of music.
A psalm of David.

¹ May the Lord answer you when you are in trouble.
May the God of Jacob keep you safe.
² May he send you help from the sacred tent.
May he give you aid from Zion.
³ May he remember all your sacrifices.
May he accept your burnt offerings.
⁴ May he give you what your heart wishes for.
May he make all your plans succeed.
⁵ May we shout for joy over your victory.
May we lift up our flags in the name of our God.
May the Lord give you everything you ask for.

⁶ Now I know that the Lord gives victory to his anointed king.
He answers him from his sacred home in heaven.
The power of God's right hand gives victory to the king.
⁷ Some trust in chariots. Some trust in horses.
But we trust in the Lord our God.
⁸ They are brought to their knees and fall down.
But we get up and stand firm.
⁹ Lord, give victory to the king!
Answer us when we call out to you!

WHAT ABOUT YOU?

One minute you're babysitting your baby sister while your mom runs to the store. The next thing you know, your sister is crying (probably because she needs her diaper changed), the dog knocks over your glass of juice, and the washing machine overflows. How did things get so bad so fast?

Who or what do you trust when things get crazy?

Psalm 20:7 says: "Some trust in chariots. Some trust in horses. But we trust in the Lord our God." When David wrote this, chariots and horses were the most powerful weapons people had. They were virtually unstoppable in battle. But God showed many times that He could win a battle that looked unwinnable.

The next time you feel overwhelmed by your problems, look to God first and trust that He will get you through.

Get out the biggest sheet of paper you can find (a white board or driveway works too). Start by drawing the biggest objects you can think of. Then draw a circle around all of them and write "God" outside the circle. Repeat the activity, but this time write your biggest problems inside a circle to remind you that God is bigger than everything.

Psalm 21

For the director of music.
A psalm of David.

[1] LORD, the king is filled with joy because
you are strong.
How great is his joy because you
help him win his battles!
[2] You have given him what his heart
wished for.
You haven't kept back from him
what his lips asked for.
[3] You came to greet him with rich
blessings.
You placed a crown of pure gold on
his head.
[4] He asked you for life, and you gave it to
him.
You promised him days that would
never end.
[5] His glory is great because you helped
him win his battles.
You have honored him with glory
and majesty.
[6] You have given him blessings that will
never end.
You have made him glad and joyful
because you are with him.
[7] The king trusts in the LORD.
The faithful love of the Most High
God
will keep the king secure.
[8] You, the king, will capture all your
enemies.
Your right hand will take hold of
them.
[9] When you appear for battle,
you will burn them up like they were
in a flaming furnace.
The LORD will swallow them up in his
great anger.
His fire will burn them up.
[10] You will wipe their children from the
face of the earth.
You will remove them from the
human race.
[11] Your enemies make evil plans against
you.
They think up evil things to do. But
they can't succeed.
[12] You will make them turn their backs
and run away
when you aim your arrows at them.
[13] LORD, may you be honored because you
are strong.
We will sing and praise your might.

Psalm 22

For the director of music. A
psalm of David to the tune of
"The Doe of the Morning."

[1] My God, my God, why have you
deserted me?
Why do you seem so far away when
I need you to save me?
Why do you seem so far away that
you can't hear my groans?
[2] My God, I cry out in the daytime. But
you don't answer.
I cry out at night. But you don't let
me sleep.
[3] But you rule from your throne as the
Holy One.
You are the God Israel praises.
[4] Our people of long ago put their trust
in you.
They trusted in you, and you saved
them.
[5] They cried out to you and were saved.
They trusted in you, and you didn't
let them down.
[6] Everyone treats me like a worm and not
a man.
They hate me and look down on me.
[7] All those who see me laugh at me.
They shout at me and make fun of me.
They shake their heads at me.
[8] They say, "He trusts in the LORD.
Let the LORD help him.
If the LORD is pleased with him,
let him save him."
[9] But you brought me out of my mother's
body.
You made me trust in you
even when I was at my mother's
breast.
[10] From the time I was born, you took
good care of me.
Ever since I came out of my mother's
body, you have been my God.
[11] Don't be far away from me.
Trouble is near,
and there is no one to help me.
[12] Many enemies are all around me.
They are like strong bulls from the
land of Bashan.
[13] They are like roaring lions that tear to
pieces what they kill.

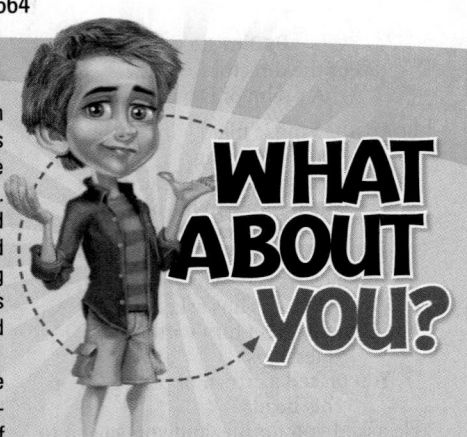

Do you know why Queen Isabella of Spain was so eager to fund Christopher Columbus's journey to the New World? She wanted the gospel of Jesus Christ spread to a new land. Even though Europeans sometimes treated the natives and resources in the New World poorly, settlers accomplished something great by sharing the good news of Christ's death and resurrection with people who had never heard about Jesus before.

David wrote in Psalm 22:27–28: "People from one end of the earth to the other will remember and turn to the LORD. The people of all the nations will bow down in front of him. The LORD is King. He rules over the nations."

Columbus's journey was a significant step toward fulfilling David's vision. But David's prediction hasn't happened yet. There are still people who haven't heard what Jesus has done for them. God wants people from every nation to believe in Him, and it's our job to send missionaries and resources to every corner of the world . . . and to go there ourselves if that's what God calls us to do.

We can be explorers and spiritual trailblazers too. Find a mission organization that reaches people who haven't heard about Jesus yet. Learn about what tribes the group is serving, and pray that the people they're trying to reach will be open to the gospel.

They open their mouths wide to
    attack me.
14 My strength is like water that is poured
    out on the ground.
I feel as if my bones aren't
    connected.
My heart has turned to wax.
    It has melted away inside me.
15 My mouth is dried up like a piece of
    broken pottery.
My tongue sticks to the roof of my
    mouth.
You bring me down to the edge of
    the grave.
16 A group of sinful people has closed in
    on me.
They are all around me like a pack
    of dogs.
They have pierced my hands and
    my feet.
17 Everyone can see all my bones right
    through my skin.
People stare at me. They laugh when
    I suffer.
18 They divide up my clothes among them.
    They cast lots for what I am wearing.
19 LORD, don't be so far away from me.

You give me strength. Come quickly
    to help me.
20 Save me from being killed by the sword.
Save the only life I have. Save me
    from the power of those dogs.
21 Save me from the mouths of those lions.
Save me from the horns of those
    wild oxen.

22 I will announce your name to my people.
I will praise you among those who
    are gathered to worship you.
23 You who have respect for the LORD,
    praise him!
All you people of Jacob, honor him!
All you people of Israel, worship him!
24 He has not forgotten the one who is
    hurting.
He has not turned away from his
    suffering.
He has not turned his face away from
    him.
He has listened to his cry for help.

25 Because of what you have done,
I will praise you in the whole
    community of those who
    worship you.

ADVENTURES IN ODYSSEY

Lawrence saw how the Lord rules over all nations, everywhere in the world, in "Columbus: The Grand Voyage" (A#16).

In front of those who respect you,
    I will keep my promises.
²⁶ Those who are poor will eat and be
        satisfied.
    Those who seek the LORD will praise
        him.
    May their hearts be filled with new
        hope!
²⁷ People from one end of the earth to the
        other
    will remember and turn to the LORD.
    The people of all the nations
        will bow down in front of him.
²⁸ The LORD is King.
    He rules over the nations.

²⁹ All rich people of the earth will feast
        and worship God.
    All who go down to the grave will
        kneel in front of him.
    Those who cannot keep themselves
        alive will kneel.
³⁰ Those who are not yet born will serve
        him.
    Those who are born later will be told
        about the Lord.
³¹ And they will tell people who have not
        yet been born,
    "The Lord has done what is right!"

Psalm 23
A psalm of David.

¹ The LORD is my shepherd. He gives me
        everything I need.
²   He lets me lie down in fields of
        green grass.

He leads me beside quiet waters.
³   He gives me new strength.
    He guides me in the right paths
        for the honor of his name.
⁴ Even though I walk
        through the darkest valley,
    I will not be afraid.
    You are with me.
    Your shepherd's rod and staff
        comfort me.

ADVENTURES IN ODYSSEY

Donna Barclay learned how God should be our shepherd when her friend was in the hospital in "Karen" (A#03).

⁵ You prepare a feast for me
        right in front of my enemies.
    You pour oil on my head.
    My cup runs over.
⁶ I am sure that your goodness and love
            will follow me
    all the days of my life.
    And I will live in the house of the LORD
        forever.

WOOTON'S FUN FACTS
Ps. 23:4

This is one of my favorite parts of Scripture. Did you know that the shepherd's *rod* is a club or stick used as a weapon? You know, to beat up lions or wolves. The *staff* is something the shepherd leans on or uses to gather the sheep—it's also called a *crook* and it's shaped like the letter *J*.

Jason's Jargon

PSALM 23

Search this chapter for the word *oil*. In Bible times, people might anoint their guests with a fragrant perfume or oil to show love and respect. The prophet Samuel anointed David's head with oil to show that he would be the next king.

Psalm 24
A psalm of David.

¹ The earth belongs to the LORD. And so
    does everything in it.
    The world belongs to him. And so
        do all those who live in it.
² He set it firmly on the oceans.
    He made it secure on the waters.

³ Who can go up to the temple on the
    mountain of the LORD?
    Who can stand in his holy place?
⁴ Anyone who has clean hands and a
    pure heart.
    Anyone who does not trust in the
        statue of a god.
    Anyone who doesn't use the name
        of that god when he makes a
        promise.
⁵ People like that will receive the LORD's
    blessing.
    When God their Savior hands down
        his sentence, it will be in their
        favor.
⁶ The people who look to God are like
    that.
    God of Jacob, they look to you.

⁷ Open wide, you gates.
    Open up, you ancient doors.
    Then the King of glory will come in.
⁸ Who is the King of glory?
    The LORD, who is strong and
        mighty.
    The LORD, who is mighty in battle.
⁹ Open wide, you gates.
    Open wide, you ancient doors.
    Then the King of glory will come in.
¹⁰ Who is he, this King of glory?
    The LORD who rules over all.
    He is the King of glory.

Psalm 25
A psalm of David.

¹ In you, LORD my God, I put my trust.
²   I trust in you.
    Don't let me be put to shame.
    Don't let my enemies win the battle
        over me.
³ Those who put their hope in you
    will never be put to shame.
    But those who lie to other people for no
        reason
    will be put to shame.

⁴ LORD, show me your ways.
    Teach me how to follow you.
⁵ Guide me in your truth. Teach me.
    You are God my Savior.
    I put my hope in you all day long.
⁶ LORD, remember your great mercy and
    love.
    You have shown them to your
        people for a long time.
⁷ Don't remember the sins I committed
    when I was young.
    Don't remember how often I refused
        to obey you.
    Remember me because you love me.
    LORD, you are good.

⁸ The LORD is honest and good.
    He teaches sinners to walk in his
        ways.
⁹ He shows those who aren't proud how
    to do what is right.
    He teaches them his ways.
¹⁰ All the LORD's ways are loving and
    faithful
    toward those who obey what his
        covenant commands.
¹¹ LORD, be true to your name.
    Forgive my sin, even though it is
        great.
¹² Who are the people who have respect
    for the LORD?
    God will teach them the ways they
        should choose.
¹³ Things will always go well for them.
    Their children will be given the
        land.
¹⁴ The LORD shares his plans with those
    who have respect for him.
    He makes his covenant known to
        them.
¹⁵ My eyes always look to the LORD.
    He alone can set my feet free from
        the trap.

¹⁶ Turn to me and help me.
 I am lonely and hurting.
¹⁷ Take away the troubles of my heart.
 Set me free from my great pain.
¹⁸ Look at how I'm hurting! See how
  much I suffer!
 Take away all my sins.
¹⁹ Look at how many enemies I have!
 See how terrible their hatred is for me!
²⁰ Guard my life. Save me.
 Don't let me be put to shame.
 I go to you for safety.
²¹ May my honest and good life keep me
  safe.
 Lord, I have put my hope in you.

²² God, set Israel free
 from all their troubles!

Psalm 26
A psalm of David.

¹ Lord, when you hand down your
  sentence, let it be in my favor.
 I have lived without blame.
 I have trusted in the Lord.
 I have never doubted him.
² Lord, test me. Try me out.
 Look deep down into my heart and
  mind.
³ I have always remembered your love
  that never fails.
 I have always depended on the fact
  that you are faithful.
⁴ I don't spend time with people who tell
  lies.
 I don't keep company with
  pretenders.
⁵ I hate to be with a group of sinful people.
 I refuse to spend time with those
  who are evil.
⁶ I wash my hands to show that I'm not
  guilty.
 Lord, I come near your altar.
⁷ I shout my praise to you.
 I tell about all the wonderful things
  you have done.
⁸ Lord, I love the house where you live.
 I love the place where your glory is.

⁹ Don't destroy me together with sinners.
 Don't take away my life along with
  murderers.
¹⁰ Their hands are always planning to do
  evil.
 Their right hands are full of money
  that has bought their help.

¹¹ But I live without blame.
 Save me from harm and treat me
  with kindness.

¹² My feet stand on level ground.
 In the whole community I will praise
  the Lord.

Psalm 27
A psalm of David.

¹ The Lord is my light, and he saves me.
 Why should I fear anyone?
 The Lord is my place of safety.
 Why should I be afraid?
² My enemies are evil.
 They will trip and fall
when they attack me
 and try to swallow me up.
³ Even if an army attacks me,
 my heart will not be afraid.
Even if war breaks out against me,
 I will still trust in God.

⁴ I'm asking the Lord for only one thing.
 Here is what I want.
I want to live in the house of the Lord
 all the days of my life.
I want to look at the beauty of the Lord.
 I want to worship him in his temple.
⁵ When I'm in trouble,
 he will keep me safe in his house.
He will hide me in the safety of his holy
  tent.
 He will put me on a rock that is very
  high.
⁶ Then I will win the battle
 over my enemies who are all around
  me.
At his holy tent I will offer my sacrifice
  with shouts of joy.
 I will sing and make music to the
  Lord.

⁷ Lord, hear my voice when I call out to
  you.
 Treat me with kindness and answer
  me.

If someone offered you a dangerous mission, would you take it? What if you could take one other person with you—someone to watch your back? This person would rescue you if anything went wrong and help you know where to go and whom to trust. Would that make your decision any easier?

If you were going to be a secret agent, whom would you want on your team . . . to have your back? Someone strong? Or brave? Maybe even a superhero?

Believe it or not, there's something even better than having Captain America or Batman at your side: trusting the God of the universe to protect you. No, Jesus didn't get a cool cape or a car that could change into a submarine. But He's always with us. He understands what we need. And He will never, ever double-cross us. That's why His promises in the Bible are so great. We know beyond a doubt that what God says, He will do.

If you were a spy, what three gadgets would you want to have handy? What power or knowledge would they give you? Did you know that God is "omnipotent," which means all-powerful? He's also "omniscient," a fancy word that means He knows everything. That's an awesome combination to have on your side—and our heavenly Father does it all without gadgets!

⁸ My heart says, "Seek him!"
    LORD, I will seek you.
⁹ Don't turn your face away from me.
    Don't turn me away because you are angry.

Ps. 27:10 One of the reasons I came to believe in God was because my parents and I didn't get along very well. I needed love and God offered it to me; He accepted me—goofy jokes, funny diet, and all.

You have helped me.
God my Savior, don't say no to me.
    Don't desert me.
¹⁰ My father and mother may desert me,
    but the LORD will accept me.
¹¹ LORD, teach me your ways.
    Lead me along a straight path.
    There are many people who treat me badly.
¹² My enemies want to harm me. So don't turn me over to them.
    Witnesses who tell lies are rising up against me.
    They say all sorts of evil things about me.
¹³ Here is something I am still sure of.
    I will see the LORD's goodness
    while I'm still alive.
¹⁴ Wait for the LORD.
    Be strong and don't lose hope.
    Wait for the LORD.

Psalm 28
A psalm of David.

¹ LORD, my Rock, I call out to you.
    Pay attention to me.

If you remain silent, I will die.
   I will be like those who go down into
     the grave.
² Hear my cry for your favor
   when I call out to you for help.
Hear me when I lift up my hands in
     prayer
   toward your Most Holy Room.

³ Don't drag me away with sinners.
   Don't drag me away with those who
     do evil.
They speak in a friendly way to their
     neighbors.
   But their hearts are full of hate.
⁴ Pay them back for their evil actions.
   Pay them back for what their hands
     have done.
   Give them exactly what they should
     get.
⁵ They don't care about the LORD's
     mighty acts.
   They don't care about what his hands
     have done.
So he will tear them down.
   He will never build them up again.

⁶ Give praise to the LORD.
   He has heard my cry for his favor.
⁷ The LORD gives me strength. He is like
     a shield that keeps me safe.
My heart trusts in him, and he helps
     me.
My heart jumps for joy.
   With my song I praise him.

⁸ The LORD gives strength to his people.
   He guards and saves his anointed
     king.
⁹ Save your people. Bless those who
     belong to you.
   Be their shepherd. Take care of them
     forever.

Psalm 29

A psalm of David.

¹ Praise the LORD, you angels in heaven.
   Praise the LORD for his glory and
     strength.
² Praise the LORD for the glory that
     belongs to him.
   Worship the LORD because of his
     beauty and holiness.

³ The voice of the LORD is heard over the
     waters.
   The God of glory thunders.

The LORD thunders over the mighty
     waters.
⁴ The voice of the LORD is powerful.
   The voice of the LORD is majestic.
⁵ The voice of the LORD breaks the cedar
     trees.
The LORD breaks the cedars of
     Lebanon into pieces.
⁶ He makes the mountains of Lebanon
     leap like a calf.
He makes Mount Hermon jump like
     a young wild ox.
⁷ The voice of the LORD strikes
   with flashes of lightning.
⁸ The voice of the LORD shakes the desert.
   The LORD shakes the Desert of
     Kadesh.
⁹ The voice of the LORD twists the oak
     trees.
   It strips the forests bare.
   And in his temple everyone cries
     out, "Glory!"

¹⁰ The LORD on his throne rules over the
     flood.
   The LORD rules from his throne as
     King forever.
¹¹ The LORD gives strength to his people.
   The LORD blesses his people with
     peace.

Psalm 30

A psalm of David. A song for setting
apart the completed temple to God.

¹ LORD, I will give you honor.
   You brought me out of deep trouble.
   You didn't give my enemies the joy
     of seeing me die.
² LORD my God, I called out to you for
     help.
   And you healed me.
³ LORD, you brought me up from the
     place of the dead.
   You kept me from going down into
     the pit.

⁴ Sing the praises of the LORD, you who
     are faithful to him.
   Praise him, because his name is holy.
⁵ His anger lasts for only a moment.
   But his favor lasts for a person's
     whole life.
Weeping can stay for the night.
   But joy comes in the morning.

⁶ When I felt safe, I said,
   "I will always be secure."

WOOTON'S FUN FACTS
Ps. 30:5

Studies show that morning people—the ones who get up early—are happier than those who stay up late. I have to get up early because that's when my mail route starts.

⁷ LORD, when you gave me your help,
  you made Mount Zion stand firm.
But when you took away your help,
  I was terrified.

⁸ LORD, I called out to you.
  I cried to you for mercy.
⁹ I said, "What good will come if I
    become silent in death?
What good will come if I go down
    into the grave?
Can the dust of my dead body praise
    you?
  Can it tell how faithful you are?
¹⁰ LORD, hear me. Have mercy on me.
  LORD, help me."

¹¹ You turned my loud crying into dancing.
  You removed my clothes of sadness
    and dressed me with joy.
¹² So my heart will sing your praises. I
    can't keep silent.
  LORD, my God, I will praise you
    forever.

Psalm 31
For the director of music.
A psalm of David.

¹ LORD, I have come to you for safety.
  Don't let me ever be put to shame.
  Save me, because you do what is right.
² Pay attention to me.
  Come quickly to help me.
  Be the rock I go to for safety.

Be the strong fort that saves me.
³ You are my rock and my fort.
  Lead me and guide me for the honor
    of your name.
⁴ Keep me free from the trap that is set
    for me.
  You are my place of safety.
⁵ Into your hands I commit my very life.
  LORD, set me free. You are my
    faithful God.

⁶ I hate those who worship worthless
    statues of gods.
  But I trust in the LORD.
⁷ I will be glad and full of joy because
    you love me.
  You saw that I was hurting.
  You took note of my great pain.
⁸ You have not handed me over to the
    enemy.
  You have put me in a wide and safe
    place.

⁹ LORD, have mercy on me. I'm in deep
    trouble.
  I'm so sad I can hardly see.
  My whole body grows weak with
    sadness.
¹⁰ Pain has taken over my life.
  My years are spent in groaning.
I have no strength because I'm hurting
    so much.
  My body is getting weaker and
    weaker.
¹¹ My neighbors make fun of me
    because I have so many enemies.
My closest friends are afraid of me.
  People who see me on the street run
    away from me.
¹² No one remembers me. I might as well
    be dead.
  I have become like broken pottery.
¹³ I hear many people whispering,
    "There is terror all around him!"
Many have joined together against me.
  They plan to kill me.

¹⁴ But I trust in you, LORD.
  I say, "You are my God."
¹⁵ My whole life is in your hands.
  Save me from the hands of my
    enemies.
  Save me from those who are chasing
    me.
¹⁶ May you look on me with favor.
  Save me because your love is faithful.
¹⁷ LORD, I have cried out to you.

Don't let me be put to shame.
But let sinners be put to shame.
Let them lie silent in the place of the
dead.
¹⁸ Their lips tell lies. Let them be silenced.
They speak with pride against those
who do right.
They make fun of them.

¹⁹ You have stored up so many good
things.
You have stored them up for those
who have respect for you.
You give those things while everyone
watches.
You give them to people who run to
you for safety.
²⁰ They are safe because you are with
them.
You hide them from the evil plans of
their enemies.
In your house you keep them safe
from those who bring charges
against them.

²¹ Give praise to the Lord.
He showed me his wonderful love
when my enemies attacked the city
I was in.
²² I was afraid and said,
"I've been cut off from you!"
But you heard my cry for your favor.
You heard me when I called out to
you for help.

²³ Love the Lord, all you who are faithful
to him!
The Lord keeps safe those who are
faithful to him.
But he completely pays back those
who are proud.
²⁴ Be strong, all you who put your hope in
the Lord.
Never give up.

Psalm 32
A *maskil* of David.

¹ Blessed is the person whose lawless acts
are forgiven.
Their sins have been taken away.
² Blessed is the person whose sin the Lord
never counts against them.
That person doesn't want to cheat
anyone.

³ When I kept silent about my sin,
my body became weak

because I groaned all day long.
⁴ Day and night
you punished me.
I became weaker and weaker
as I do in the heat of summer.
⁵ Then I admitted my sin to you.
I didn't cover up the wrong I had
done.
I said, "I will admit my lawless acts to
the Lord."
And you forgave the guilt of my sin.

⁶ Let everyone who is faithful pray to you
while they can still look to you.
When troubles come like a flood,
they certainly won't reach those who
are faithful.
⁷ You are my hiding place.
You will keep me safe from trouble.
You will surround me with songs sung
by those who praise you
because you save your people.

⁸ I will guide you and teach you the way
you should go.
I will give you good advice and
watch over you with love.
⁹ Don't be like a horse or a mule.
They can't understand anything.
They have to be controlled by bits and
bridles.
If they aren't, they won't come to you.
¹⁰ Sinful people have all kinds of trouble.
But the Lord's faithful love
is all around those who trust in him.

Ps. 32:8 Did you know that sheep
sometimes can't find their way home even
if their pen is within sight? Sheep have very
poor depth perception. A good shepherd
always watches his wandering sheep.

¹¹ Be glad because of what the LORD has
   done for you.
   Be joyful, you who do what is right!
   Sing, all you whose hearts are honest!

Psalm 33

¹ You who are godly, sing with joy to the
   LORD.
   It is right for honest people to praise
   him.
² With the harp, praise the LORD.
   With the lyre that has ten strings,
   make music to him.
³ Sing a new song to him.
   Play with skill, and shout with joy.

⁴ What the LORD says is right and true.
   He is faithful in everything he does.
⁵ The LORD loves what is right and fair.
   The earth is full of his faithful love.

⁶ The heavens were made when the LORD
   commanded it to happen.
   All the stars were created by the
   breath of his mouth.
⁷ He gathers together the waters of the sea.
   He puts the oceans in their places.

⁸ Let the whole earth have respect for the
   LORD.
   Let all the people in the world honor
   him.
⁹ He spoke, and the world came into
   being.
   He commanded, and it stood firm.
¹⁰ The LORD blocks the sinful plans of the
   nations.
   He keeps them from doing what
   they want to do.
¹¹ But the plans of the LORD stand firm
   forever.
   What he wants to do will last for all
   time.

¹² Blessed is the nation whose God is the
   LORD.
   Blessed are the people he chose to be
   his own.
¹³ From heaven the LORD looks down
   and sees everyone.
¹⁴ From his throne he watches
   all those who live on the earth.
¹⁵ He creates the hearts of all people.
   He is aware of everything they do.

WHAT ABOUT YOU?

Paul Revere's story is filled with courage and patriotism. We can learn a lot from Revere's actions, starting with his urgent journey on April 18, 1775, at the beginning of the Revolutionary War. For one thing, he never questioned why leaders behind the revolution needed him so often in the days surrounding his famous ride. He never said, "Why can't someone else make this trip?" He was always ready and willing to serve the colonists fighting for freedom.

Revere was also very brave, putting his life at risk for a noble cause. Although this patriot was unusually courageous, we can all be brave when we stand for the values Paul Revere believed in: freedom, justice, and a trustworthy God.

Psalm 33:12 says, "Blessed is the nation whose God is the LORD." Many of the Founding Fathers believed this promise. No nation, family or individual can be all God intends if they trust in their own strength. But when we trust in God to save and protect us, we will be rewarded.

The soldiers in the Revolutionary War fought to form a nation that could worship freely. Ask your parents to help you learn about countries in our world that don't enjoy religious freedom. What penalties await those who claim Jesus as Lord? If you find a specific missionary trying to make a difference in a hostile culture, pray for that person. Then thank God that you live in a country where you can talk about Christ, own a Bible, and worship openly.

Tom and Whit saw how God's eyes are on those who fear Him in "Timmy's Cabin" (A#14).

¹⁶ A king isn't saved just because his army
    is big.
    A soldier doesn't escape just because
    he is very strong.
¹⁷ People can't trust a horse to save them
    either.
    Though it is very strong, it can't save
    them.
¹⁸ But the LORD looks with favor on those
    who respect him.
    He watches over those who put their
    hope in his faithful love.
¹⁹ He watches over them to save them
    from death.
    He wants to keep them alive when
    there is no food in the land.

²⁰ We wait in hope for the LORD.
    He helps us. He is like a shield that
    keeps us safe.
²¹ Our hearts are full of joy because of him.
    We trust in him, because he is holy.
²² LORD, may your faithful love be with us.
    We put our hope in you.

Psalm 34

A psalm of David when he was
with Abimelek and pretended to be
out of his mind. Abimelek drove
him away, and David left.

¹ I will thank the LORD at all times.
    My lips will always praise him.
² I will find my glory in knowing the LORD.
    Let those who are hurting hear me
    and be joyful.
³ Join me in giving glory to the LORD.
    Let us honor him together.

⁴ I looked to the LORD, and he answered
    me.
    He saved me from everything I was
    afraid of.
⁵ Those who look to him have joyful
    faces.
    They are never covered with shame.
⁶ This poor man called out, and the LORD
    heard him.
    He saved him out of all his troubles.

⁷ The angel of the LORD stands guard
    around those who have respect for
    him.
    And he saves them.

⁸ Taste and see that the LORD is good.
    Blessed is the person who goes to
    him for safety.
⁹ You holy people of God, have respect
    for the LORD.
    Those who respect him have
    everything they need.
¹⁰ The lions may grow weak and hungry.
    But those who look to the LORD have
    every good thing they need.

¹¹ My children, come. Listen to me.
    I will teach you to have respect for
    the LORD.
¹² Do you love life
    and want to see many good days?
¹³ Then keep your tongues from speaking
    evil.
    Keep your lips from telling lies.
¹⁴ Turn away from evil, and do good.
    Look for peace, and go after it.

¹⁵ The LORD looks with favor on those
    who are godly.
    His ears are open to their cry.
¹⁶ But the LORD doesn't look with favor on
    those who do evil.
    He removes all memory of them
    from the earth.

¹⁷ Godly people cry out, and the LORD
    hears them.
    He saves them from all their
    troubles.
¹⁸ The LORD is close to those whose hearts
    have been broken.
    He saves those whose spirits have
    been crushed.

¹⁹ The person who does what is right may
    have many troubles.
    But the LORD saves him from all of
    them.
²⁰ The LORD watches over all his bones.
    Not one of them will be broken.

²¹ Sinners will be killed by their own evil.
    The enemies of godly people will be
    judged.
²² The LORD will save those who serve
    him.
    No one who goes to him for safety
    will be found guilty.

Psalm 35

A psalm of David.

[1] LORD, stand up against those who stand
    up against me.
  Fight against those who fight against
    me.
[2] Pick up your shield and your armor.
  Rise up and help me.
[3] Get your spear and javelin ready to fight
  against those who are chasing me.
  Say to me, "I will save you."

[4] Let those who are trying to kill me
  be brought down in dishonor.
  Let those who plan to destroy me
  be turned back in terror.
[5] Let them be like straw blowing in the
    wind,
    while the angel of the LORD drives
      them away.
[6] Let their path be dark and slippery,
    while the angel of the LORD chases
      them.
[7] They set a trap for me without any
    reason.
  Without any reason they dug a pit to
    catch me.
[8] So let them be destroyed without
    warning.
  Let the trap they set for me catch
    them.
  Let them fall into the pit and be
    destroyed.
[9] Then I will be full of joy because of
    what the LORD has done.
  I will be glad because he has saved
    me.
[10] My whole being will cry out,
  "Who is like you, LORD?
  You save poor people from those who
    are too strong for them.
  You save poor and needy people
    from those who rob them."

[11] Mean people come forward to speak
    against me.
  They ask me things I don't know
    anything about.
[12] They pay me back with evil, even
    though I was good to them.
  They leave me like someone who has
    lost a family member.
[13] But when they were sick, I put on the
    clothing of sadness.
  I made myself humble by going
    without food.

My prayers for them weren't always
    answered.
[14] So I went around crying
    as if I were mourning over my friend
    or relative.
  I bowed my head in sadness
    as if I were weeping over my mother.
[15] But when I tripped and fell, they were
    all very happy.
  Attackers gathered against me when
    I didn't even know it.
  They kept on telling lies about me.
[16] Like ungodly people, they were mean
    and made fun of me.
  They ground their teeth at me in hate.
[17] Lord, how much longer will you just
    look on?
  Save me from their deadly attacks.
  Save the only life I have.
  Save me from these lions.
[18] I will give you thanks in the whole
    community.
  Among all your people I will praise
    you.

[19] Don't let those who are my enemies
    without any reason
    laugh at me and make fun of me.
  Don't let those who hate me without
    any reason
    wink at me with an evil purpose.
[20] They don't speak words of peace.
  They make up false charges
    against those who live quietly in the
    land.
[21] They make fun of me.
  They say, "With our own eyes we
    have seen what you did."

[22] LORD, you have seen this. Don't be
    silent.
  Lord, don't be far away from me.
[23] Wake up! Rise up to help me!
  My God and Lord, stand up for me.
[24] LORD my God, when you hand down
    your sentence, let it be in my
    favor.
  You always do what is right.
  Don't let my enemies have the joy of
    seeing me fall.
[25] Don't let them think, "That's exactly
    what we wanted!"
  Don't let them say, "We have
    swallowed him up."

[26] Let all those who laugh at me because
    I'm in trouble

be ashamed and bewildered.
Let all who think they are better than
    I am
put on shame and dishonor as if they
    were clothes.
²⁷ Let those who are happy when my
    name is cleared
shout with joy and gladness.
Let them always say, "May the LORD be
    honored.
He is pleased when everything goes
    well with the one who serves
    him."
²⁸ You always do what is right. My tongue
    will speak about it
and praise you all day long.

Psalm 36

For the director of music. A psalm of
David, the servant of the LORD.

¹ I have a message from God in my heart.
    It is about the evil ways of anyone
    who sins.
They don't have any respect for God.
² They praise themselves so much
    that they can't see their sin or hate it.
³ Their mouths speak words that are evil
    and false.
They do not act wisely or do what is
    good.
⁴ Even as they lie in bed they make evil
    plans.
They commit themselves to a sinful
    way of life.
They never say no to what is wrong.
⁵ LORD, your love is as high as the heavens.
    Your faithful love reaches up to the
    skies.
⁶ Your holiness is as great as the height of
    the highest mountains.
You are as honest as the oceans are
    deep.
LORD, you keep people and animals
    safe.
⁷   How priceless your faithful love is!
People find safety in the shadow of
    your wings.
⁸ They eat well because there is more
    than enough in your house.
You let them drink from your river
    that flows with good things.
⁹ You have the fountain of life.
    We are filled with light because you
    give us light.
¹⁰ Keep on loving those who know you.

Ps. 36:6 Did you know that the deepest spot in the ocean is the Mariana Trench? It's 36,070 feet below sea level. Foot-long shrimplike creatures live there along with large sea cucumbers and jellyfish. I wish it were the Marinara Trench. Then we could have pasta.

Keep on doing right to those whose
    hearts are honest.
¹¹ Don't let the feet of those who are
    proud step on me.
Don't let the hands of those who are
    evil drive me away.
¹² See how those who do evil have fallen!
    They are thrown down and can't get
    up.

Psalm 37

A psalm of David.

¹ Don't be upset because of sinful people.
    Don't be jealous of those who do
    wrong.
² Like grass, they will soon dry up.
    Like green plants, they will soon die.

³ Trust in the LORD and do good.
    Then you will live in the land and
    enjoy its food.
⁴ Find your delight in the LORD.
    Then he will give you everything
    your heart really wants.
⁵ Commit your life to the LORD.
    Here is what he will do if you trust
    in him.
⁶ He will make the reward for your godly
    life shine like the dawn.
He will make the proof of your
    honest life shine like the sun
    at noon.

⁷ Be still and wait patiently for the LORD
    to act.

ADVENTURES IN ODYSSEY

Whit waited patiently on God in "The W.E." (A#36).

Don't be upset when other people succeed.
Don't be upset when they carry out their evil plans.

8 Turn away from anger and don't give in to wrath.
Don't be upset, because that only leads to evil.
9 Sinful people will be destroyed.
But those who put their hope in the LORD will receive the land.

10 In a little while, there won't be any more sinners.
Even if you look for them, you won't be able to find them.
11 But those who are free of pride will be given the land.
They will enjoy peace and success.

12 Sinful people make plans to harm those who do what is right.
They grind their teeth at them.
13 But the Lord laughs at those who do evil.
He knows the day is coming when he will judge them.

14 Sinners pull out their swords.
They bend their bows.
They want to kill poor and needy people.
They plan to murder those who lead honest lives.
15 But they will be killed by their own swords.
Their own bows will be broken.

16 Those who do what is right may have very little.
But it's better than the wealth of many sinners.
17 The power of those who are evil will be broken.
But the LORD takes good care of those who do what is right.

18 Those who are without blame spend their days in the LORD's care.

WHAT ABOUT YOU?

If you've ever been stranded alone on a rainy day, you know it's not much fun. Drawing gets boring with no one to show your pictures to. A Nerf gun battle against an invisible enemy isn't very exciting. You win—and lose—every single game of Battleship, Clue, and tic-tac-toe that you play against yourself. Some things are just better with other people.

The same thing is true with our faith. Sharing our spiritual journey with other Christians is important. This includes prayer. Sometimes praying with our family helps remind us of what's important. If we pray with other Christians, we can thank God together when He answers prayers. And we can pray that God will help us love each other more.

In Matthew 18:20, Jesus says, "Where two or three people gather in my name, I am there with them." Jesus isn't saying He isn't there when you're alone—sometimes that's the time we need God the most. He's saying we aren't meant to live life alone. God wants us to have other believers around us, praying for and with us. There's a lot of power when that happens!

As you read Psalm 37, you'll see David comparing the company of godly people (those free of pride and without blame) and the company of sinners. Next time you're alone on a rainy day, make two lists: one of what David says about evil people and one of what he says about "those who do right."

What he has given them will last
forever.
¹⁹ When trouble comes to them, they will
have what they need.
When there is little food in the land,
they will still have plenty.

²⁰ But sinful people will die.
The LORD's enemies may be like
flowers in the field.
But they will be swallowed up.
They will disappear like smoke.

²¹ Sinful people borrow and don't pay back.
But those who are godly give freely
to others.
²² The LORD will give the land to those he
blesses.
But he will destroy those he curses.

²³ The LORD makes secure the footsteps
of the person who delights in him,
²⁴ Even if that person trips, he won't fall.
The LORD's hand takes good care of
him.

²⁵ I once was young, and now I'm old.
But I've never seen godly people
deserted.
I've never seen their children
begging for bread.
²⁶ The godly are always giving and lending
freely.
Their children will be a blessing.

²⁷ Turn away from evil and do good.
Then you will live in the land forever.
²⁸ The LORD loves those who are honest.
He will not desert those who are
faithful to him.

Those who do wrong will be completely
destroyed.
The children of sinners will die.
²⁹ Those who do what is right will be
given the land.
They will live in it forever.

³⁰ The mouths of those who do what is
right speak words of wisdom.
They say what is honest.
³¹ God's law is in their hearts.
Their feet do not slip.

³² Those who are evil hide and wait for
godly people.
They want to kill them.
³³ But the LORD will not leave the godly in
their power.

He will not let them be found guilty
when they are brought into
court.

³⁴ Put your hope in the LORD.
Live as he wants you to.
He will honor you by giving you the
land.
When sinners are destroyed, you
will see it.

³⁵ I saw a mean and sinful person.
He was doing well, like a green tree
in its own land.
³⁶ But he soon passed away and was gone.
Even though I looked for him, I
couldn't find him.

³⁷ Consider honest people who are
without blame.
People who seek peace will have a
tomorrow.
³⁸ But all sinners will be destroyed.
Those who are evil won't have a
tomorrow.

³⁹ The LORD saves those who do what is
right.
He is their place of safety when
trouble comes.
⁴⁰ The LORD helps them and saves them.
He saves them from sinful people
because they go to him for safety.

Psalm 38
A psalm of David. A prayer.

¹ LORD, don't correct me when you are
angry.
Don't punish me when you are
burning with anger.
² You have wounded me with your arrows.
You have struck me with your hand.
³ Because of your anger, my whole body
is sick.
Because of my sin, I'm not healthy.
⁴ My guilt has become too much for me.
It is a load too heavy to carry.

⁵ My wounds are ugly. They stink.
I've been foolish. I have sinned.
⁶ I am bent over. I've been brought very
low.
All day long I go around weeping.
⁷ My back is filled with burning pain.
My whole body is sick.
⁸ I am weak and feel as if I've been
broken in pieces.

I groan because of the great pain in
my heart.

9 Lord, everything I really want is clearly
known to you.
You always hear me when I sigh.
10 My heart pounds, and my strength is
gone.
My eyes can hardly see.
11 My friends and companions avoid me
because of my wounds.
My neighbors stay far away from me.
12 Those who are trying to kill me set their
traps.
Those who want to harm me talk
about destroying me.
All day long they make their plans
and tell their lies.

13 Like a deaf person, I can't hear.
Like someone who can't speak, I
can't say a word.
14 I'm like someone who doesn't hear.
I'm like someone whose mouth can't
make any reply.
15 LORD, I wait for you to help me.
Lord my God, I know you will
answer.
16 I said, "Don't let my enemies have the
joy of seeing me fall.
Don't let them brag when my feet
slip."

17 I am about to fall.
My pain never leaves me.
18 I admit that I have done wrong.
I am troubled by my sin.
19 Though I have done nothing to cause it,
many people have become my
enemies.
They hate me without any reason.
20 They pay me back with evil, even
though I was good to them.
They bring charges against me,
though I try only to do what
is good.

21 LORD, don't desert me.
My God, don't be far away from me.
22 Lord my Savior,
come quickly to help me.

Psalm 39

For the director of music. For
Jeduthun. A psalm of David.

1 I said, "I will be careful about how I live.
I will not sin by what I say.

I will keep my mouth closed
when I am near sinful people."
2 So I was completely silent.
I didn't even say anything good.
But the pain inside me grew worse.
3 My heart was deeply troubled.
As I thought about what was
happening to me,
I became even more troubled.
Then I spoke out.
4 I said, "LORD, show me when my life
will end.
Show me how many days I have left.
Tell me how short my life will be.
5 You have given me only a few days to
live.
My whole life doesn't seem like
anything to you.
No one lasts any longer than a breath.
This is true even for those who feel
secure.
6 People are only shadows as they go here
and there.
They rush around, but it doesn't
mean anything.
They pile up wealth, but they don't
know who will finally get it.

7 "Lord, what can I look forward to now?
You are the only hope I have.
8 Save me from all the wrong things I've
done.
Don't let foolish people make fun
of me.
9 I keep silent. I don't open my mouth.
You are the one who has caused all
this to happen.
10 Please stop beating me.
I'm about to die from the blows of
your hand.
11 You correct and punish people for their
sin.
Then, just as a moth eats cloth, you
destroy their wealth.
No one lasts any longer than a breath.

12 "LORD, hear my prayer.
Listen to my cry for help.

Pay attention to my weeping.
I'm like an outsider in your home.
I'm just a stranger, like all my family
    who lived before me.
¹³ Leave me alone.
Let me enjoy life again before I die."

Psalm 40
For the director of music.
A psalm of David.

¹ I was patient while I waited for the
    LORD.
He turned to me and heard my cry
    for help.
² I was sliding down into the pit of death,
    and he pulled me out.
He brought me up out of the mud
    and dirt.
He set my feet on a rock.
He gave me a firm place to stand on.
³ He gave me a new song to sing.
It is a hymn of praise to our God.
Many people will see and have respect
    for the LORD.
They will put their trust in him.

⁴ Blessed is the person
    who trusts in the LORD.
They don't trust in proud people.
Those proud people worship statues
    of gods.
⁵ LORD my God,
    no one can compare with you.
You have done many wonderful things.
You have planned to do these things
    for us.
There are too many of them
    for me to talk about.

⁶ You didn't want sacrifices and offerings.
You didn't require burnt offerings
    and sin offerings.
You opened my ears so that I could
    hear you and obey you.
⁷ Then I said, "Here I am.
It is written about me in the book.
⁸ My God, I have come to do what you
    want.
Your law is in my heart."

⁹ I have told the whole community of
    those who worship you.
I have told them what you have done
    to save me.
LORD, you know
    that I haven't kept quiet.

¹⁰ I haven't kept to myself that what you
    did for me was right.
I have spoken about how faithful
    you were when you saved me.
I haven't hidden your love and your
    faithfulness
from the whole community.

¹¹ LORD, don't hold back your mercy from
    me.
May your love and faithfulness
    always keep me safe.
¹² There are more troubles all around me
    than I can count.
My sins have caught up with me,
    and I can't see any longer.
My sins are more than the hairs of my
    head.
I have lost all hope.

¹³ LORD, please save me.
    LORD, come quickly to help me.
¹⁴ Let all those who are trying to kill me
    be put to shame.
Let them lose their way.
Let all those who want to destroy me
    be turned back in shame.
¹⁵ Some people make fun of me.
Let them be shocked when their
    plans fail.
¹⁶ But let all those who seek you
    be joyful and glad because of what
    you have done.
Let those who count on you to save
    them always say,
"The LORD is great!"

¹⁷ But I am poor and needy.
May the Lord be concerned about
    me.
You are the God who helps me and
    saves me.
You are my God, so don't wait any
    longer.

Psalm 41
For the director of music.
A psalm of David.

¹ Blessed are those who care about weak
    people.
When they are in trouble, the LORD
    saves them.
² The LORD guards them and keeps them
    alive.
They are counted among those who
    are blessed in the land.

The LORD won't hand them over to
the wishes of their enemies.
³ The LORD will take care of them when
they are lying sick in bed.
He will make them well again.

⁴ I said, "LORD, have mercy on me.
Heal me, because I have sinned
against you."
⁵ My enemies are saying bad things about
me.
They say, "When will he die and his
name be forgotten?"
⁶ When one of them comes to see me,
he says things that aren't true.
At the same time, he thinks up lies to
tell against me.
Then he goes out and spreads those
lies around.

⁷ All my enemies whisper to each other
about me.
They want something terrible to
happen to me.
⁸ They say, "He is sick and will die very
soon.
He will never get up from his bed
again."
⁹ Even my close friend, someone I
trusted, has failed me.
I even shared my bread with him.

¹⁰ But LORD, may you have mercy on me.
Make me well, so I can pay them
back.
¹¹ Then I will know that you are pleased
with me,
because my enemies haven't won the
battle over me.
¹² You will take good care of me because
I've been honest.
You will let me be with you forever.

¹³ Give praise to the LORD, the God of
Israel,
for ever and ever.
Amen and Amen.

BOOK II
PSALMS 42–72

Psalm 42
For the director of music. A
maskil of the Sons of Korah.

¹ A deer longs for streams of water.
God, I long for you in the same way.

WOOTON'S FUN FACTS

Ps. 42:1

Did you know that about 6,800 gallons of water are required to grow a day's food for a family of four? And that doesn't count the water for a warm bath after dinner!

² I am thirsty for God. I am thirsty for
the living God.
When can I go and meet with him?
³ My tears have been my food
day and night.
All day long people say to me,
"Where is your God?"
⁴ When I remember what has happened,
I tell God all my troubles.
I remember how I used to walk to the
house of God.
The Mighty One guarded my steps.
We shouted with joy and praised God
as we went along with the joyful
crowd.

⁵ My spirit, why are you so sad?
Why are you so upset deep down
inside me?
Put your hope in God.
Once again I will have reason to
praise him.
He is my Savior and my God.

⁶ My spirit is very sad deep down inside
me.
So I will remember you here where
the Jordan River begins.
I will remember you here on the
Hermon mountains
and on Mount Mizar.
⁷ You have sent wave upon wave of
trouble over me.

It roars down on me like a
   waterfall.
All your waves and breakers have rolled
   over me.

[8] During the day the Lord sends his love
   to me.
   During the night I sing about him.
   I say a prayer to the God who gives
    me life.

[9] I say to God my Rock,
   "Why have you forgotten me?
Why must I go around in sorrow?
   Why am I treated so badly by my
    enemies?"

[10] My body suffers deadly pain
   as my enemies make fun of me.
All day long they say to me,
   "Where is your God?"

[11] My spirit, why are you so sad?
   Why are you so upset deep down
    inside me?
Put your hope in God.
   Once again I will have reason to
    praise him.
   He is my Savior and my God.

Psalm 43

[1] My God, when you hand down your
    decision, let it be in my favor.
   Stand up for me against an
    unfaithful nation.
   Save me from those lying and sinful
    people.

[2] You are God, my place of safety.
   Why have you turned your back on
    me?
Why must I go around in sorrow?
   Why am I beaten down by my
    enemies?

[3] Send me your light and your faithful
    care.
   Let them lead me.
Let them bring me back to your holy
    mountain,
   to the place where you live.

[4] Then I will go to the altar of God.
   I will go to God. He is my joy and
    my delight.
God, you are my God.
   I will praise you by playing the lyre.

[5] My spirit, why are you so sad?
   Why are you so upset deep down
    inside me?

Put your hope in God.
   Once again I will have reason to
    praise him.
   He is my Savior and my God.

Psalm 44

For the director of music. A
maskil of the Sons of Korah.

[1] God, we have heard what you did.
   Those who came before us have told
    us
what you did in their days,
   in days long ago.

[2] By your power you drove out the
    nations.
   You gave our people homes in the
    land.
You crushed the people who were
    there.
   And you made our people do well.

[3] They didn't win the land with their
    swords.
   They didn't gain success by their
    own power.
Your powerful right hand and your
    mighty arm gave them
    victory.
   You gave them success because you
    loved them.

[4] You are my King and my God.
   You give victories to the people of
    Jacob.

[5] With your help we push back our
    enemies.
   By your power we walk all over
    them.

[6] I put no trust in my bow.
   My sword doesn't bring me victory.

[7] But you give us victory over our
    enemies.
   You put them to shame.

[8] All day long we talk about how great
    God is.
   We will praise your name forever.

[9] But now you have turned your back on
    us and made us humble.
   You don't march out with our armies
    anymore.

[10] You made us turn and run from our
    enemies.
   They have taken what belongs to
    us.

[11] You handed us over to be eaten up like
    sheep.

You have scattered us among the
nations.
¹² You sold your people for very little.
You didn't gain anything when you
sold them.

¹³ You have made us something that our
neighbors laugh at.
Those who live around us make fun
of us and tease us.
¹⁴ The nations make jokes about us.
They shake their heads at us.
¹⁵ All day long I have to live with my
shame.
My face is covered with it.
¹⁶ That's because they laugh at me and
attack me with their words.
They want to get even with me.

¹⁷ All of this happened to us,
even though we had not forgotten
you.
We had not broken the covenant you
made with us.
¹⁸ Our hearts had not turned away from
you.
Our feet had not wandered from
your path.
¹⁹ But you crushed us and left us to the
wild dogs.
You covered us over with deep
darkness.

²⁰ We didn't forget our God.
We didn't spread out our hands in
prayer to a false god.
²¹ If we had, God would have discovered
it.
He knows the secrets of our hearts.
²² But because of you, we face death all
day long.
We are considered as sheep to be
killed.

²³ Lord, wake up! Why are you
sleeping?
Get up! Don't say no to us forever.
²⁴ Why do you turn your face away from
us?
Why do you forget our pain and
troubles?

²⁵ We are brought down to the dust.
Our bodies lie flat on the ground.
²⁶ Rise up and help us.
Save us because of your faithful
love.

CANDID CONVERSATIONS

One night, Penny and I were making dinner when we heard the doorbell ring. Someone had left a vase full of beautiful red roses on our doorstep. The card sticking out of the bouquet was addressed to "Connie." My hand shook as I tore open the envelope. I read the card aloud. "You make my heart soar. From your secret admirer."

"A secret admirer!" Penny exclaimed. "This is so exciting. Look, footprints! They could lead us back to your secret admirer!"

I carried the bouquet inside and set it on the kitchen table, knowing Penny was chasing after her own footprints from five minutes ago. I hated to tell her that I recognized Jay Smouse's handwriting on the card. I knew it was another one of his schemes.

Penny's obsession with my secret admirer reminded me of a verse: "He knows the secrets of our hearts" (Psalm 44:21). God knows what we really feel, no matter how hard we try to hide it. He loves us unconditionally and wants us to love Him back. And that's no secret.

Psalm 45

For the director of music. A *maskil* of the Sons of Korah. A wedding song to the tune of "Lilies."

¹ My heart is full of beautiful words
 as I say my poem for the king.
 My tongue is like the pen of a skillful writer.

² You are the most excellent of men.
 Your lips have been given the ability to speak gracious words.
 God has blessed you forever.

³ Mighty one, put your sword at your side.
 Put on glory and majesty as if they were your clothes.

⁴ In your majesty ride out with power
 to fight for what is true, humble and fair.
 Let your right hand do wonderful things.

⁵ Shoot your sharp arrows into the hearts of your enemies.
 Let the nations come under your control.

⁶ Your throne is the very throne of God.
 Your kingdom will last for ever and ever.
 You will rule by treating everyone fairly.

⁷ You love what is right and hate what is evil.
 So your God has placed you above your companions.
 He has filled you with joy by pouring the sacred oil on your head.

⁸ Myrrh and aloes and cassia make all your robes smell good.
 In palaces decorated with ivory the music played on stringed instruments makes you glad.

⁹ Daughters of kings are among the women you honor.
 At your right hand is the royal bride dressed in gold from Ophir.

¹⁰ Royal bride, listen and pay careful attention.
 Forget about your people and the home you came from.

¹¹ Let the king be charmed by your beauty.
 Honor him. He is now your master.

¹² The people of Tyre will come with gifts.
 Wealthy people will try to gain your favor.

¹³ In her room, the princess looks glorious.
 Her gown has gold threads running through it.

¹⁴ Dressed in beautiful clothes, she is led to the king.
 Her virgin companions follow her.
 They have been brought to be with her.

¹⁵ They are led in with joy and gladness.
 They enter the palace of the king.

¹⁶ Your sons will rule just as your father and grandfather did.
 You will make them princes through the whole land.

¹⁷ I will make sure that people will always remember you.
 The nations will praise you for ever and ever.

Psalm 46

For the director of music. A song of the Sons of Korah. According to *alamoth*.

¹ God is our place of safety. He gives us strength.
 He is always there to help us in times of trouble.

² The earth may fall apart.
 The mountains may fall into the middle of the sea.

Ps. 46:1 Studies show that Psalm 46:1 is the second-most read verse in the book of Psalms. The first? Psalm 23:4.

ADVENTURES iN ODYSSEY

Whit had to rely on God as his refuge and strength during difficult times in "The Nemesis" (A#05).

But we will not be afraid.
³ The waters of the sea may roar and foam.
The mountains may shake when the waters rise.
But we will not be afraid.

⁴ God's blessings are like a river. They fill the city of God with joy.
That city is the holy place where the Most High God lives.
⁵ Because God is there, the city will not fall.
God will help it at the beginning of the day.
⁶ Nations are in disorder. Kingdoms fall.
God speaks, and the people of the earth melt in fear.

⁷ The LORD who rules over all is with us.
The God of Jacob is like a fort to us.

⁸ Come and see what the LORD has done.
See the places he has destroyed on the earth.
⁹ He makes wars stop from one end of the earth to the other.
He breaks every bow. He snaps every spear.
He burns every shield with fire.
¹⁰ He says, "Be still, and know that I am God.
I will be honored among the nations.
I will be honored in the earth."

¹¹ The LORD who rules over all is with us.
The God of Jacob is like a fort to us.

Psalm 47

For the director of music. A psalm of the Sons of Korah.

¹ Clap your hands, all you nations.
Shout to God with cries of joy.
² Do this because the LORD Most High is wonderful.
He is the great King over the whole earth.
³ He brought nations under our control.
He made them fall under us.
⁴ He chose our land for us.
The people of Jacob are proud of their land,
and God loves them.

⁵ God went up to his throne while his people were shouting with joy.
The LORD went up while trumpets were playing.
⁶ Sing praises to God. Sing praises.
Sing praises to our King. Sing praises.
⁷ God is the King of the whole earth.
Sing a psalm of praise to him.
⁸ God rules over the nations.
He is seated on his holy throne.
⁹ The nobles of the nations come together.
They are now part of the people of the God of Abraham.
The kings of the earth belong to God.
He is greatly honored.

Psalm 48

A song. A psalm of the Sons of Korah.

¹ The LORD is great. He is really worthy of praise.
Praise him in the city of our God, his holy mountain.
² Mount Zion is high and beautiful.
It brings joy to everyone on earth.
Mount Zion is like the highest parts of Mount Zaphon.
It is the city of the Great King.
³ God is there to keep it safe.
He has shown himself to be like a fort to the city.

⁴ Many kings joined forces.
They entered Israel together.
⁵ But when they saw Mount Zion, they were amazed.
They ran away in terror.

⁶ Trembling took hold of them.
    They felt pain like a woman giving
      birth.
⁷ Lord, you destroyed them like ships of
    Tarshish
    that were torn apart by an east wind.

⁸ What we heard we have also seen.
    We have seen it
in the city of the Lord who rules over
    all.
    We have seen it in the city of our
      God.
    We have heard and seen that God
      makes it secure forever.

⁹ God, inside your temple
    we think about your faithful love.
¹⁰ God, your fame reaches from one end
    of the earth to the other.
    So people praise you from one end
      of the earth to the other.
    You use your power to do what is
      right.
¹¹ Mount Zion is filled with joy.
    The villages of Judah are glad.
    That's because you judge fairly.

¹² Walk all around Zion.
    Count its towers.
¹³ Think carefully about its outer walls.
    Just look at how safe it is!
    Then you can tell its people that God
      keeps them safe.
¹⁴ This God is our God for ever and ever.
    He will be our guide to the very end.

Psalm 49

For the director of music. A
psalm of the Sons of Korah.

¹ Hear this, all you nations.
    Listen, all you who live in this world.
² Listen, people, whether you are
      ordinary or important.
    Listen, people, whether you are rich
      or poor.
³ My mouth will speak wise words.
    What I think about in my heart will
      give you understanding.
⁴ I will pay attention to a proverb.
    I will explain my riddle as I play the
      harp.
⁵ Why should I be afraid when trouble
      comes?
    Why should I fear when sinners are
      all around me?

    They are the kind of people who
      want to take advantage of me.
⁶ They trust in their wealth.
    They brag about how rich they are.
⁷ No one can pay for the life of anyone
      else.
    No one can give God what that
      would cost.
⁸ The price for a life is very high.
    No payment is ever enough.
⁹ No one can pay enough to live forever
    and not rot in the grave.

¹⁰ Everyone can see that even wise people
      die.
    People who are foolish and who have
      no sense also pass away.
    All of them leave their wealth to
      others.
¹¹ Their tombs will remain their houses
      forever.
    Their graves will be their homes for
      all time to come.
    Naming lands after themselves won't
      help either.

¹² Even though people may be very rich,
      they don't live on and on.
    They are like the animals. They die.
¹³ That's what happens to those who trust
      in themselves.
    It also happens to their followers,
      who agree with what they say.
¹⁴ They are like sheep and will end up in
      the grave.
    Death will be their shepherd.
But when honest people come to power,
    a new day will dawn.
    The bodies of sinners will waste
      away in the grave.
    They will end up far away from their
      princely houses.
¹⁵ But God will save me from the place of
      the dead.
    He will certainly take me to himself.

¹⁶ Don't get too upset when other people
      become rich.
    Don't be troubled when they become
      more and more wealthy.
¹⁷ They won't take anything with them
      when they die.
    Their riches won't go down to the
      grave with them.
¹⁸ While they lived, they believed they
      were blessed.

People praised them when things
were going well for them.
¹⁹ But they will die, like their people of
long ago.
They will never again see the light
of life.

²⁰ People who have riches but don't
understand
are like the animals. They die.

Psalm 50
A psalm of Asaph.

¹ The Mighty One, God, the LORD, speaks.
He calls out to the earth
from the sunrise in the east
to the sunset in the west.
² From Zion, perfect and beautiful,
God's glory shines out.
³ Our God comes, and he won't be silent.
A burning fire goes ahead of him.
A terrible storm is all around him.
⁴ He calls out to heaven and earth to be
his witnesses.
Then he judges his people.

⁵ He says, "Gather this holy people
around me.
They made a covenant with me by
offering a sacrifice."
⁶ The heavens announce that what God
decides is right.
That's because he is a God of justice.

⁷ God says, "Listen, my people, and I will
speak.
I will be a witness against you, Israel.
I am God, your God.
⁸ I don't bring charges against you
because of your sacrifices.
I don't bring charges because of the
burnt offerings you always
bring me.
⁹ I don't need a bull from your barn.
I don't need goats from your pens.
¹⁰ Every animal in the forest already
belongs to me.
And so do the cattle on a thousand
hills.
¹¹ I own every bird in the mountains.
The insects in the fields belong to me.

WHAT ABOUT YOU?

Sprinting through the house, you trip and knock over your mom's favorite vase. Although you survived the fall, Mom's vase is a goner. You collect the broken pieces and take them to your mother, apologizing profusely. She forgives you, but you can't shake the feeling of guilt. Have you ever felt something like that?

There are two types of guilt: unnecessary guilt and helpful guilt. When we've done something wrong and asked for forgiveness, any guilt we might feel from that point on is unnecessary. We all make mistakes. And we've already done what God wanted us to do by apologizing. Forgive yourself and try to do better next time.

Of course, if we've done something wrong but haven't asked for forgiveness, we still have work to do. Guilt pokes at us to confess and seek forgiveness. And God is always ready to forgive us, just as it says in 1 John 1:9: "God is faithful and fair. If we confess our sins, he will forgive our sins. He will forgive every wrong thing we have done. He will make us pure."

Draw a heart on a piece of construction paper and cut it out. Next, cut the heart into several pieces. This step symbolizes our brokenness and the guilt we feel when we've blown it. Now reassemble your heart, much like God mends our hearts when we confess our sin. He forgives us. No guilt necessary. Tape your heart together and keep it as a reminder of God's forgiveness, which may help you be more forgiving of those who have hurt you.

¹² If I were hungry, I wouldn't tell you.
> The world belongs to me. And so
> > does everything in it.
¹³ Do I eat the meat of bulls?
> Do I drink the blood of goats?
¹⁴ Bring me thank offerings, because I am
> > your God.
> Carry out the promises you made
> > to me, because I am the Most
> > High God.
¹⁵ Call out to me when trouble comes.
> I will save you. And you will honor
> > me."

¹⁶But here is what God says to a sinful person.

"What right do you have to speak the
> > words of my laws?
> How dare you speak the words of my
> > covenant!
¹⁷ You hate my teaching.
> You turn your back on what I say.
¹⁸ When you see a thief, you join him.
> You make friends with those who
> > commit adultery.
¹⁹ You use your mouth to speak evil.
> You use your tongue to spread lies.
²⁰ You are a witness against your brother.
> You always tell lies about your own
> > mother's son.
²¹ When you did these things, I kept
> > silent.
> So you thought I was just like you.
> But now I'm going to bring you to court.
> I will bring charges against you.
²² "You who forget God, think about this.
> If you don't, I will tear you to pieces.
> No one will be able to save you.
²³ People who sacrifice thank offerings to
> > me honor me.
> To those who are without blame I
> > will show my power to save."

Psalm 51

For the director of music. A psalm of David when the prophet Nathan came to him. Nathan came to him after David had committed adultery with Bathsheba.

¹ God, have mercy on me
> according to your faithful love.
> Because your love is so tender and kind,
> > wipe out my lawless acts.
² Wash away all the evil things I've done.
> Make me pure from my sin.

Robyn Jacobs was sad because she cheated in "A Test for Robyn" (A#13). She saw how God would accept her broken heart.

³ I know the lawless acts I've committed.
> I can't forget my sin.
⁴ You are the one I've really sinned against.
> I've done what is evil in your sight.
> So you are right when you sentence me.
> You are fair when you judge me.
⁵ I know I've been a sinner ever since I
> > was born.
> I've been a sinner ever since my
> > mother became pregnant with
> > me.
⁶ I know that you wanted faithfulness
> > even when I was in my
> > mother's body.
> You taught me wisdom in that secret
> > place.
⁷ Sprinkle me with hyssop, then I will be
> > clean.
> Wash me, then I will be whiter than
> > snow.
⁸ Let me hear you say, "Your sins are
> > forgiven."
> That will bring me joy and gladness.
> Let the body you have broken be
> > glad.
⁹ Take away all my sins.
> Wipe away all the evil things I've
> > done.
¹⁰ God, create a pure heart in me.
> Give me a new spirit that is faithful
> > to you.
¹¹ Don't send me away from you.
> Don't take your Holy Spirit away
> > from me.
¹² Give me back the joy that comes from
> > being saved by you.
> Give me a spirit that obeys you so
> > that I will keep going.
¹³ Then I will teach your ways to those
> > who commit lawless acts.
> And sinners will turn back to you.
¹⁴ You are the God who saves me.
> I have committed murder.
> God, take away my guilt.

Then my tongue will sing about how
    right you are
        no matter what you do.
¹⁵ Lord, open my lips so that I can speak.
        Then my mouth will praise you.
¹⁶ You don't take delight in sacrifice.
        If you did, I would bring it.
        You don't take pleasure in burnt
            offerings.
¹⁷ The greatest sacrifice you want is a
        broken spirit.
        God, you will gladly accept a heart
        that is broken because of sadness
            over sin.

¹⁸ May you be pleased to give Zion
        success.
        May it please you to build up the
            walls of Jerusalem.
¹⁹ Then you will delight in the sacrifices of
        those who do what is right.
        Whole burnt offerings will bring
            delight to you.
        And bulls will be offered on your altar.

Psalm 52

For the director of music. A *maskil* of
David when Doeg, who was from Edom,
had gone to Saul. Doeg had told Saul,
"David has gone to the house of Ahimelek."

¹ You think you are such a big, strong
        man!
        Why do you brag about the evil
            things you've done?
        You are a dishonor to God all the
            time.
² You plan ways to destroy others.
        Your tongue is like a blade that has a
            sharp edge.
        You are always telling lies.
³ You love evil instead of good.
        You would rather lie than tell the
            truth.
⁴   You love to harm others with your
            words, you liar!

⁵ So God will destroy you forever.
        He will grab you and pluck you from
            your tent.
        He will remove you from this life.
⁶ Those who do what is right will see it
            and learn a lesson from it.
        They will laugh at you and say,
⁷ "Just look at this fellow!
        He didn't depend on God for his
            safety.

He put his trust in all his wealth.
        He grew strong by destroying
            others!"

⁸ But I am like a healthy olive tree.
        My roots are deep in the house of
            God.
    I trust in your faithful love
        for ever and ever.
⁹ I will praise you forever for what you
            have done.
        I will praise you when I'm with your
            faithful people.
        I will put my hope in you because
            you are good.

Psalm 53

For the director of music. According
to *mahalath*. A *maskil* of David.

¹ Foolish people say in their hearts,
        "There is no God."
    They do all kinds of horrible and evil
            things.
        No one does anything good.

² God looks down from heaven
        on all people.
    He wants to see if there are any who
            understand.
        He wants to see if there are any who
            trust in God.
³ All of them have turned away.
        They have all become evil.
    No one does anything good,
        no one at all.

⁴ Don't these people who do evil know
            anything?
        They eat up my people as if they
            were eating bread.
        They never call out to God for help.
⁵ Just look at them! They are filled with
            terror
        even when there is nothing to be
            afraid of!
    People of Israel, God scattered the
            bones of those who attacked
            you.
        You put them to shame, because
            God hated them.

⁶ How I pray that the God who saves
            Israel will come out of Zion!
        God will bless his people with great
            success again.
        Then let the people of Jacob be filled
            with joy! Let Israel be glad!

Psalm 54

For the director of music. To be played on stringed instruments. A *maskil* of David when the men from Ziph had gone to Saul. They had said, "Isn't David hiding among us?"

[1] God, save me by your power.
Set me free by your might.
[2] God, hear my prayer.
Listen to what I'm saying.

[3] Enemies who are proud are attacking me.
Mean people are trying to kill me.
They don't care about God.

[4] But I know that God helps me.
The Lord is the one who keeps me going.

[5] My enemies tell lies about me.
Do to them the evil things they planned against me.
God, be faithful and destroy them.

[6] I will sacrifice an offering to you just because I choose to.
LORD, I will praise your name because it is good.
[7] You have saved me from all my troubles.
With my own eyes I have seen you win the battle over my enemies.

Psalm 55

For the director of music. A *maskil* of David to be played on stringed instruments.

[1] God, listen to my prayer.
Pay attention to my cry for help.
[2] Hear me and answer me.
My thoughts upset me. I'm very troubled.
[3] I'm troubled by what my enemies say about me.
I'm upset because they say they will harm me.
They cause me all kinds of suffering.
When they are angry, they attack me with their words.

[4] I feel great pain deep down inside me.
The terrors of death have fallen on me.
[5] Fear and trembling have taken hold of me.
Panic has overpowered me.
[6] I said, "I wish I had wings like a dove!
Then I would fly away and be at rest.

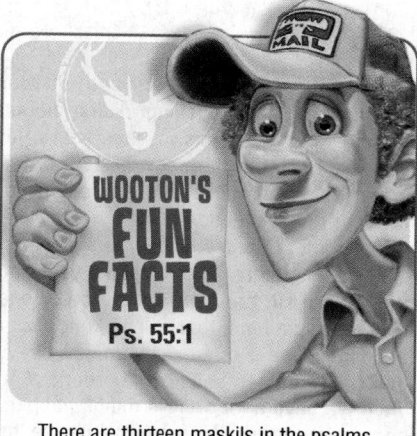

WOOTON'S FUN FACTS
Ps. 55:1

There are thirteen maskils in the psalms. Eugene said that a *maskil* is "a poem or psalm that teaches you something." I need more maskils in my life. What does this psalm teach you?

[7] I would escape to a place far away.
I would stay out in the desert.
[8] I would hurry to my place of safety.
It would be far away from the winds and storms I'm facing."

[9] Lord, confuse the sinners and keep them from understanding one another.
I see people destroying things and fighting in the city.
[10] Day and night they prowl around on top of its walls.
The city is full of crime and trouble.
[11] Forces that destroy are at work inside it.
Its streets are full of people who cheat others and take advantage of them.

[12] If an enemy were making fun of me,
I could stand it.
If he were getting ready to oppose me,
I could hide.
[13] But it's you, someone like myself.
It's my companion, my close friend.
[14] We used to enjoy good friendship at the house of God.
We used to walk together among those who came to worship.

[15] Let death take my enemies by surprise.
Let them be buried alive,
because their hearts and homes are full of evil.

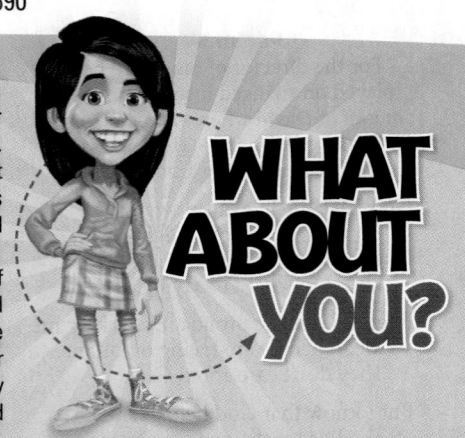

WHAT ABOUT YOU?

Time for a camping trip! You get out your backpack and start packing. A first-aid kit. Binoculars. Extra socks in case yours get wet. Five DVDs for the car ride. Two boxes of granola bars. Your favorite stuffed animal and your rock collection.

That's a lot to carry all by yourself. But if you give your mom the binoculars, your dad the first-aid kit, and your little brother one box of granola bars, that will make it easier (and maybe leave the rocks home). A heavy load is sometimes called a "burden." And when we have a lot of hard things happening to us, it can weigh us down. Just like the camping trip, we may need someone to help us carry that load too.

It's also important to talk to other people when we need help. But the first person you should go to when you feel scared or lonely is God. He's a friend standing beside you all the time!

To remember what it means to share a burden, do a backpack relay! Set an empty backpack at one end of your yard. At the other end, pile things that will fit into the backpack. Get a few friends and start a relay, passing books or toys down the line to the backpack, one at a time. See how fast you can fill it up! When you're done, pick up the full pack. Remember how easy it was to carry one object at a time? Compare that with carrying the whole burden yourself!

---

16 But I call out to God.
　　And the LORD saves me.
17 Evening, morning and noon
　　I groan and cry out.
　　And he hears my voice.
18 Even though many enemies are fighting
　　　against me,
　　he brings me safely back from the
　　　battle.
19 God has been on his throne since
　　　ancient times and does not
　　　change.
　　He will hear my enemies and make
　　　them humble.
　　That's because they have no respect
　　　for God.

20 My companion attacks his friends.
　　He breaks his promise.
21 His talk is as smooth as butter.
　　But he has war in his heart.
　　His words flow like olive oil.
　　But they are like swords ready for
　　　battle.

22 Turn your worries over to the LORD.
　　He will keep you going.

He will never let godly people be
　　shaken.
23 God, you will bring sinners
　　down to the grave.
　　Murderers and liars
　　won't live out even half of their lives.

But I trust in you.

Psalm 56

For the director of music. A *miktam*
of David after the Philistines had
captured him in Gath. To the tune of
"A Dove on Distant Oak Trees."

1 Help me, God. Men are chasing me.
　　All day long they keep attacking
　　　me.
2 My enemies chase me all day long.
　　Many proud people are attacking
　　　me.
3 When I'm afraid,
　　I put my trust in you.
4 I trust in God. I praise his word.
　　I trust in God. I am not afraid.
　　What can mere people do to me?

ADVENTURES IN ODYSSEY

Facing their worst fears made the folks in Odyssey remember to trust in God in "Blood, Sweat, and Fears" (A#47).

5 All day long they twist my words.
　They are always making plans to
　　destroy me.
6 They get together and hide.
　They watch my steps.
　They hope to kill me.

7 Because they are so evil, make sure you
　　don't let them escape.
　God, bring down the nations in your
　　anger.
8 Make a record of my sadness.
　List my tears in your book.
　Aren't you making a record of
　　them?

9 My enemies will turn back
　when I call out to you for help.
　Then I will know that God is on my
　　side.
10 I trust in God. I praise his word.
　I trust in the LORD. I praise his word.
11 I trust in God. I am not afraid.
　What can mere people do to me?

12 God, I have made promises to you.
　I will bring my thank offerings to
　　you.
13 You have saved me from the darkness
　　of death.
　You have kept me from tripping and
　　falling.
　Now I can live with you
　　in the light of life.

Psalm 57

For the director of music. A *miktam*
of David when he had run away
from Saul into the cave. To the
tune of "Do Not Destroy."

1 Have mercy on me, God. Have mercy
　　on me.
　I go to you for safety.
　I will find safety in the shadow of your
　　wings.
　There I will stay until the danger is
　　gone.

2 I cry out to God Most High.
　I cry out to God, and he shows that I
　　am right.
3 He answers from heaven and saves me.
　He puts to shame those who chase
　　me.
　He shows his love and that he is
　　faithful.

4 Men who are like lions are all around
　　me.
　I am forced to lie down among
　　people who are like hungry
　　animals.
　Their teeth are like spears and arrows.
　Their tongues are like sharp swords.

5 God, may you be honored above the
　　heavens.
　Let your glory be over the whole
　　earth.

6 My enemies spread a net to catch me by
　　the feet.
　I felt helpless.
　They dug a pit in my path.
　But they fell into it themselves.

7 God, my heart feels secure.
　My heart feels secure.
　I will sing and make music to you.
8 My spirit, wake up!
　Harp and lyre, wake up!
　I want to sing and make music
　　before the sun rises.

9 Lord, I will praise you among the
　　nations.
　I will sing about you among the
　　people of the earth.
10 Great is your love. It reaches to the
　　heavens.
　Your truth reaches to the skies.

11 God, may you be honored above the
　　heavens.
　Let your glory be over the whole
　　earth.

Psalm 58

For the director of music. A *miktam* of
David to the tune of "Do Not Destroy."

1 Are you rulers really fair when you
　　speak?
　Do you judge people honestly?
2 No, in your hearts you plan to be unfair.
　With your hands you do terrible
　　things on the earth.

³ Even from birth those who are evil go
down the wrong path.
From the day they are born they go
the wrong way and spread lies.
⁴ Their words are like the poison of a
snake.
They are like the poison of a cobra
that has covered up its ears.
⁵ It won't listen to a snake charmer's
tune,
even if the charmer plays very well.

⁶ God, break the teeth in the mouths of
those sinners!
LORD, tear out the sharp teeth of
those lions!
⁷ Let those people disappear like water
that flows away.
When they draw their bows, let their
arrows fall short of the target.
⁸ Let them be like a slug that melts away
as it moves along.
Let them be like a baby that is born
dead and never sees the sun.

⁹ Evil people will be swept away before
burning thorns can heat a pot.
And it doesn't matter if the thorns
are green or dry.
¹⁰ Godly people will be glad when those
who have hurt them are paid
back.
They will dip their feet in the blood
of those who do evil.
¹¹ Then people will say,
"The godly will get their reward.
There really is a God who judges the
earth."

Psalm 59

For the director of music. A *miktam* of
David when Saul had sent men to watch
David's house. Saul sent the men to kill
David. To the tune of "Do Not Destroy."

¹ God, save me from my enemies.
Keep me safe from people who are
attacking me.
² Save me from those who do evil.
Save me from people who want to
kill me.
³ See how they hide and wait for me!
LORD, angry people plan to harm me,
even though I haven't hurt them
in any way or sinned against
them.

⁴ I haven't done anything wrong to them.
But they are ready to attack
me.
Rise up and help me! Look at what
I'm up against!
⁵ LORD God who rules over all, rise up.
God of Israel,
punish all the nations.
Don't show any mercy to those sinful
people
who have turned against me.

⁶ My enemies are like a pack of barking
dogs
that come back to the city in the
evening.
They prowl around the city.
⁷ Listen to what pours out of their
mouths.
The words from their lips are like
swords.
They think, "Who can hear us?"
⁸ But you laugh at them, LORD.
You make fun of all those nations.

⁹ You give me strength. I look to you.
God, you are like a fort to me. ¹⁰You
are my God, and I can depend
on you.

God will march out in front of me.
He will let me look down on those
who tell lies about me.
¹¹ Lord, you are like a shield that keeps us
safe.
Don't kill my enemies all at once.
If you do, my people will forget
about it.
Use your power to pull my enemies up
by the roots like weeds.
Destroy them.
¹² They have sinned with their mouths.
Their lips have spoken evil words.
They have cursed me and lied.
Let them be caught in their pride.
¹³ Burn them up in your anger.
Burn them up until there isn't
anything left of them.
Then everyone from one end of the
earth to the other will know
that God rules over the people of
Jacob.

¹⁴ My enemies are like a pack of barking
dogs
that come back into the city in the
evening.

They prowl around the city.
15 They wander around looking for food.
　They groan if they don't find
　　something that will satisfy
　　them.
16 But I will sing about your strength.
　In the morning I will sing about
　　your love.
　You are like a fort to me.
　You keep me safe in times of trouble.
17 You give me strength. I sing praise to
　　you.
　God, you are like a fort to me. You
　　are my God, and I can depend
　　on you.

Psalm 60

For the director of music. For teaching.
A *miktam* of David when he fought
against Aram Naharaim and Aram
Zobah. That was when Joab returned
and struck down 12,000 people from
Edom in the Valley of Salt. To the
tune of "The Lily of the Covenant."

1 God, you have turned away from us.
　You have attacked us.
　You have been angry. Now turn back
　　to us!
2 You have shaken the land and torn it
　　open.
　Fix its cracks, because it is falling
　　apart.
3 You have shown your people hard times.
　You have made us drink the wine of
　　your anger.
　Now we can't even walk straight.

4 But you lead into battle those who have
　　respect for you.
　You give them a flag to wave against
　　the enemy's weapons.

5 Save us and help us by your power.
　Do this so that those you love may
　　be saved.
6 God has spoken from his temple.
　He has said, "I will win the battle.
　Then I will divide up the land around
　　Shechem.
　I will divide up the Valley of
　　Sukkoth.
7 Gilead belongs to me.
　So does the land of Manasseh.
　Ephraim is the strongest tribe.
　It is like a helmet for my head.

Judah is the royal tribe.
　It is like a ruler's scepter.
8 Moab serves me like one who washes
　　my feet.
　I toss my sandal on Edom to show
　　that I own it.
　I shout to Philistia that I have won
　　the battle."

9 Who will bring me to the city that has
　　high walls around it?
　Who will lead me to the land of
　　Edom?
10 God, isn't it you, even though you have
　　now turned away from us?
　Isn't it you, even though you don't
　　lead our armies into battle
　　anymore?
11 Help us against our enemies.
　The help people give doesn't amount
　　to anything.
12 With your help we will win the battle.
　You will walk all over our enemies.

Psalm 61

For the director of music.
A psalm of David to be played
on stringed instruments.

1 God, hear my cry for help.
　Listen to my prayer.

2 From a place far away I call out to you.
　I call out as my heart gets weaker.
　Lead me to the safety of a rock that
　　is high above me.
3 You have always kept me safe from my
　　enemies.
　You are like a strong tower to me.
4 I long to live in your holy tent forever.
　There I find safety in the shadow of
　　your wings.
5 God, you have heard my promises.
　You have given me what belongs to
　　those who worship you.

6 Add many days to the king's life.
　Let him live on and on for many
　　years.
7 May he always enjoy your blessing as he
　　rules.
　Let your love and truth keep him
　　safe.

8 Then I will always sing praise to you.
　I will keep my promises day after
　　day.

Psalm 62

For the director of music. For
Jeduthun. A psalm of David.

[1] It is surely true that I find my rest in
God.
He is the God who saves me.
[2] It is surely true that he is my rock. He is
the God who saves me.
He is like a fort to me. I will always
be secure.

[3] How long will you enemies attack me?
Will all of you throw me down?
I'm like a leaning wall.
I'm like a fence about to fall.
[4] Surely my enemies only want to pull me
down
from my place of honor.
They take delight in telling lies.
They bless me with what they say.
But in their hearts they ask for bad
things to happen to me.

[5] Yes, I must find my rest in God.
He is the God who gives me hope.
[6] It is surely true that he is my rock and
the God who saves me.
He is like a fort to me, so I will
always be secure.
[7] I depend on God to save me and to
honor me.
He is my mighty rock and my place
of safety.
[8] Trust in him at all times, you people.
Tell him all your troubles.
God is our place of safety.

[9] Surely ordinary people are only a breath.
Important people are not what they
seem to be.
If they were weighed on a scale, they
wouldn't amount to anything.
Together they are only a breath.
[10] Don't trust in money you have taken
from others.
Don't put false hope in things you
have stolen.
Even if your riches grow,
don't put your trust in them.

[11] God, I have heard you say two things.
One is that power belongs to you,
God.
[12] The other is that your love, Lord,
never ends.
You will reward everyone
in keeping with what they have done.

Psalm 63

A psalm of David when he was
in the Desert of Judah.

[1] God, you are my God.
I seek you with all my heart.
With all my strength I thirst for you
in this dry desert
where there isn't any water.

[2] I have seen you in the sacred tent.
There I have seen your power and
your glory.
[3] Your love is better than life.
So I will bring glory to you with my
lips.
[4] I will praise you as long as I live.
I will call on your name when I lift
up my hands in prayer.
[5] I will be as satisfied as if I had eaten the
best food there is.
I will sing praise to you with my
mouth.

[6] As I lie on my bed I remember you.
I think of you all night long.
[7] Because you have helped me,
I sing in the shadow of your wings.
[8] I hold on to you tightly.
Your powerful right hand takes good
care of me.

[9] Those who want to kill me will be
destroyed.
They will go down into the grave.
[10] They will be killed by swords.
They will become food for wild dogs.

[11] But the king will be filled with joy
because of what God has done.
All those who make promises in
God's name will be able to brag.
But the mouths of liars will be shut.

Psalm 64

For the director of music.
A psalm of David.

[1] God, hear me as I tell you my problem.
Don't let my enemies kill me.
[2] Hide me from evil people who talk
about how to harm me.
Hide me from those people who are
planning to do evil.
[3] They make their tongues like sharp
swords.
They aim their mean words like
deadly arrows.

⁴ They shoot from their hiding places at
  people who aren't guilty.
They shoot quickly and aren't afraid
  of being caught.
⁵ They help one another make evil plans.
They talk about hiding their traps.
They say, "Who can see what we are
  doing?"
⁶ They make plans to do what is evil.
They say, "We have thought up a
  perfect plan!"
The hearts and minds of people are
  so clever!

⁷ But God will shoot my enemies with his
  arrows.
He will suddenly strike them down.
⁸ He will turn their own words against
  them.
He will destroy them.
All those who see them will shake their
  heads
and look down on them.

⁹ All people will respect God.
They will tell about his works.
They will think about what he has
  done.
¹⁰ Godly people will be full of joy because
  of what the LORD has done.
They will go to him for safety.
All those whose hearts are honest
  will be proud of what he has
  done.

Psalm 65

For the director of music.
A psalm of David. A song.

¹ Our God, we look forward to praising
  you in Zion.
We will keep our promises to you.
² All people will come to you,
  because you hear and answer
  prayer.
³ When our sins became too much for
  us,
  you forgave our lawless acts.
⁴ Blessed are those you choose
  and bring near to worship you.
You bring us into the courtyards of
  your holy temple.
There in your house we are filled
  with all kinds of good things.

⁵ God our Savior, you answer us with
  right and wonderful deeds.
People all over the world and beyond
  the farthest oceans
  put their hope in you.
⁶ You formed the mountains by your
  power.
You showed how strong you are.
⁷ You calmed the oceans and their
  roaring waves.
You calmed the angry words and
  actions of the nations.
⁸ Everyone on earth is amazed at the
  wonderful things you have
  done.
What you do makes people from one
  end of the earth to the other
  sing for joy.

⁹ You take care of the land and water it.
You make it able to grow many
  crops.
You fill your streams with water.
You do that to provide the people
  with grain.
That's what you have decided to do
  for the land.
¹⁰ You water its rows.
You smooth out its bumps.
You soften it with showers.
And you bless its crops.
¹¹ You bring the year to a close with huge
  crops.
You provide more than enough
  food.
¹² The grass grows thick even in the
  desert.
The hills are dressed with gladness.
¹³ The meadows are covered with flocks
  and herds.
The valleys are dressed with grain.
They sing and shout for joy.

Psalm 66

For the director of music.
A song. A psalm.

¹ Shout to God for joy, everyone on
  earth!
²   Sing about the glory of his name!
Give him glorious praise!
³ Say to God, "What wonderful things
  you do!
Your power is so great
  that your enemies bow down to you
  in fear.
⁴ Everyone on earth bows down to you.
They sing praise to you.

They sing the praises of your name."

5 Come and see what God has done.
  See what wonderful things he has
    done for people!
6 He turned the Red Sea into dry land.
  The people of Israel passed through
    the waters on foot.
  Come, let us be full of joy because of
    what he did.
7 He rules by his power forever.
  His eyes watch the nations.
  Let no one who refuses to obey him
    rise up against him.

8 Praise our God, all you nations.
  Let the sound of the praise you give
    him be heard.
9 He has kept us alive.
  He has kept our feet from slipping.
10 God, you have tested us.
  You put us through fire to make us
    like silver.
11 You put us in prison.
  You placed heavy loads on our
    backs.
12 You let our enemies ride their chariots
    over our heads.
  We went through fire and water.
  But you brought us to a place
    where we have everything we need.

13 I will come to your temple with burnt
    offerings.
  I will keep my promises to you.
14 I made them with my lips.
  My mouth spoke them when I was
    in trouble.
15 I will sacrifice fat animals to you as
    burnt offerings.
  I will offer rams, bulls and goats to
    you.

16 Come and hear, all you who have
    respect for God.
  Let me tell you what he has done
    for me.
17 I cried out to him with my mouth.
  I praised him with my tongue.
18 If I had enjoyed having sin in my heart,
    the Lord would not have listened.
19 But God has surely listened.
  He has heard my prayer.
20 Give praise to God.
  He has accepted my prayer.
  He has not held back his love from
    me.

Psalm 67

For the director of music.
A psalm. A song to be played
on stringed instruments.

1 God, have mercy on us and bless us.
  May you be pleased with us.
2 Then your ways will be known on
    earth.
  All nations will see that you have the
    power to save.

3 God, may the nations praise you.
  May all the people on earth praise
    you.
4 May the nations be glad and sing for
    joy.
  You rule the people of the earth
    fairly.
  You guide the nations of the earth.
5 God, may the nations praise you.
  May all the people on earth praise
    you.

6 The land produces its crops.
  God, our God, blesses us.
7 May God continue to bless us.
  Then people from one end of the
    earth to the other
  will have respect for him.

Psalm 68

For the director of music. A
psalm of David. A song.

1 May God rise up and scatter his
    enemies.
  May they turn and run away from
    him.
2   May you, God, blow them away like
    smoke.
  As fire melts wax,
    so may God destroy sinful people.
3 But may those who do what is right be
    glad
  and filled with joy when they are
    with him.
  May they be happy and joyful.

4 Sing to God, sing praise to his name.
  Lift up a song to the God who rides
    on the clouds.
  Be glad when you are with him.
  His name is the LORD.
5 God is in his holy temple.
  He is a father to children whose
    fathers have died.

ADVENTURES IN ODYSSEY

Even in the midst of crazy accidents and wild adventures, the Barclays and Rathbones understood the value of spending time as a family in "Aloha, Oy!" (A#19).

He takes care of women whose
        husbands have died.
⁶ God gives lonely people a family.
        He sets prisoners free, and they go
        out singing.
But those who refuse to obey him
        live in a land that is baked by the
        sun.

⁷ God, you led your people out.
        You marched through the desert.
⁸ The ground shook
        when you, the God of Sinai,
        appeared.
The heavens poured down rain
        when you, the God of Israel,
        appeared.
⁹ God, you gave us plenty of rain.
        You renewed your worn-out land.
¹⁰ God, your people made their homes
        in it.
        From all your riches, you provided
        for those who were poor.

¹¹ The Lord gives the message.
        The women who make it known are
        a huge group.
¹² They said, "Kings and armies are
        running away.
        The women at home are dividing up
        the things the army took from their
        enemies.
¹³ Even while the soldiers sleep near the
        sheep pens,

God wins the battle for them.
        He gives the enemy's silver and gold
        to Israel, his dove."
¹⁴ The Mighty One has scattered the kings
        around the land.
        It was like snow falling on Mount
        Zalmon.

¹⁵ Mount Bashan is a majestic mountain.
        Mount Bashan is a very rocky
        mountain.
¹⁶ Why are you jealous of Mount Zion,
        you rocky mountain?
        That's where God chooses to rule.
        That's where the LORD himself will
        live forever.
¹⁷ God has come with tens of thousands
        of his chariots.
        He has come with thousands and
        thousands of them.
The Lord has come from Mount Sinai.
        He has entered his holy place.
¹⁸ When he went up to his place on high,
        he took many prisoners.
He received gifts from people,
        even from those who refused to
        obey him.
        The LORD God went up to live on
        Mount Zion.

¹⁹ Give praise to the Lord. Give praise to
        God our Savior.
        He carries our heavy loads day after
        day.
²⁰ Our God is a God who saves.
        He is the King and the LORD. He
        saves us from death.

²¹ God will certainly smash the heads of
        his enemies.
        He will break the hairy heads of
        those who keep on sinning.
²² The Lord says, "I will bring your
        enemies from Bashan.
        I will bring them up from the
        bottom of the sea.
²³ Then your feet can wade in their blood.
        The tongues of your dogs can lick up
        all the blood they want."

²⁴ God, those who worship you come
        marching into view.
        My God and King, those who follow
        you have entered the sacred
        tent.
²⁵ The singers are walking in front.
        Next come the musicians.

Young women playing tambourines
are with them.
²⁶ The leaders sing, "Praise God among all
those who worship him.
Praise the Lᴏʀᴅ in the community
of Israel."
²⁷ The little tribe of Benjamin leads the
worshipers.
Next comes the great crowd of
Judah's princes.
Then come the princes of Zebulun
and the princes of Naphtali.

²⁸ God, show us your power.
Show us your strength.
God, do as you have done before.
²⁹ Do it from your temple at Jerusalem,
where kings will bring you gifts.
³⁰ Give a strong warning to Egypt, that
beast among the tall grass.
It is like a herd of bulls among the
calves.
May that beast bow down before you
with gifts of silver.
Scatter the nations who like to make
war.
³¹ Messengers will come from Egypt.
The people of Cush will be quick to
bring gifts to you.

³² Sing to God, you kingdoms of the earth.
Sing praise to the Lord.
³³ He rides across the highest places in
heaven.
He rides across the ancient skies above.
He thunders with his mighty voice.
³⁴ Tell how powerful God is.
He rules as king over Israel.
The skies show how powerful he is.
³⁵ How wonderful is God in his holy
place!
The God of Israel gives power and
strength to his people.

Give praise to God!

Psalm 69

For the director of music. A psalm
of David to the tune of "Lilies."

¹ God, save me.
My troubles are like a flood.
I'm up to my neck in them.
² I'm sinking in deep mud.
I have no firm place to stand.
I am out in deep water.
The waves roll over me.

Ps. 69:1–2 Quicksand looks solid, but it's
being held up only by water and friction.
Unlike in the movies, people don't get
swallowed by the sand, but it can be
exhausting to wade through. It's like
slogging through Jell-O.

³ I'm worn out from calling for help.
My throat is very dry.
My eyes grow tired
looking for my God.
⁴ Those who hate me without any reason
are more than the hairs on my head.
Many people who don't have any reason
to be my enemies
are trying to destroy me.
They force me to give back
what I didn't steal.

⁵ God, you know how foolish I've been.
My guilt is not hidden from you.

⁶ Lord, you are the Lᴏʀᴅ who rules over
all.
May those who put their hope in
you not be dishonored because
of me.
You are the God of Israel.
May those who worship you not be
put to shame because of me.
⁷ Because of you, people laugh at me.
My face is covered with shame.
⁸ I'm an outsider to my own family.
I'm a stranger to my own mother's
children.
⁹ My great love for your house destroys
me.
Those who make fun of you make
fun of me also.
¹⁰ When I weep and go without eating,
they laugh at me.

¹¹ When I put on rough clothing to show
how sad I am,
people make jokes about me.
¹² Those who gather in public places make
fun of me.
Those who get drunk make up songs
about me.

¹³ But Lord, I pray to you.
May this be the time you help me.
God, answer me because you love me
so much.
Save me, as you always do.
¹⁴ Save me from the trouble I'm in.
It's like slippery mud, so don't let me
sink in it.
Save me from those who hate me.
Save me from the deep water I'm in.
¹⁵ Don't let the floods cover me.
Don't let the deep water swallow
me up.
Don't let the grave close its mouth
over me.
¹⁶ Lord, answer me because your love is
so good.
Turn to me because you are so
kind.
¹⁷ Don't turn your face away from me.
Answer me quickly. I'm in trouble.
¹⁸ Come near and save me.
Set me free from my enemies.

¹⁹ You know how they make fun of me.
They dishonor me and put me to
shame.
You know all about my enemies.
²⁰ They have broken my heart by saying
evil things about me.
It has left me helpless.
I looked for pity, but I didn't find any.
I looked for someone to comfort me,
but I didn't find anyone.
²¹ They put bitter spices in my food.
They gave me vinegar when I was
thirsty.

²² Let their feast be a trap and a snare.
Let my enemies get what's coming
to them.
²³ Let their eyes grow weak so they can't
see.
Let their backs be bent forever.
²⁴ Pour out your anger on them.
Let them feel what it is like.
²⁵ May their homes be deserted.
May no one live in their tents.

²⁶ They attack those you have wounded.
They talk about the pain of those
you have hurt.
²⁷ Charge them with one crime after
another.
Don't save them.
²⁸ May their names be erased from the
book of life.
Don't include them in the list of
those who do right.

²⁹ I'm in pain. I'm in deep trouble.
God, save me and keep me safe.
³⁰ I will praise God's name by singing to
him.
I will bring him glory by giving him
thanks.
³¹ That will please the Lord more than
offering him an ox.
It will please him more than offering
him a bull with its horns and
hooves.
³² Poor people will see it and be glad.
The hearts of those who worship
God will be strengthened.
³³ The Lord hears those who are in need.
He doesn't forget his people in prison.

³⁴ Let heaven and earth praise him.
Let the oceans and everything that
moves in them praise him.
³⁵ God will save Zion.
He will build the cities of Judah
again.
Then people will live in them and own
the land.
³⁶ The children of those who serve God
will receive it.
Those who love him will live there.

Psalm 70

For the director of music.
A prayer of David.

¹ God, hurry and save me.
Lord, come quickly and help me.
² Let those who are trying to kill me be
put to shame.
Let them not be honored.
Let all those who want to destroy me
be turned back in shame.
³ Some people make fun of me.
Let them be turned back when their
plans fail.
⁴ But let all those who seek you
be joyful and glad because of what
you have done.

Let those who want you to save them
always say,
"The LORD is great!"

5 But I am poor and needy.
God, come quickly to me.
You are the God who helps me and
saves me.
LORD, please don't wait any longer.

Psalm 71

1 LORD, I have gone to you for safety.
Let me never be put to shame.
2 You do what is right, so save me and
help me.
Pay attention to me and save me.
3 Be my rock of safety
that I can always go to.
Give the command to save me.
You are my rock and my fort.
4 My God, save me from the power of
sinners.
Save me from the hands of those
who are mean and evil.

5 You are the King and the LORD. You
have always been my hope.
I have trusted in you ever since I was
young.
6 From the time I was born I have
depended on you.
You brought me out of my mother's
body.
I will praise you forever.
7 To many people I am an example of
how much you care.
You are my strong place of safety.
8 My mouth is filled with praise for you.
All day long I will talk about your
glory.

9 Don't push me away when I'm old.
Don't desert me when my strength
is gone.
10 My enemies speak against me.
Those who want to kill me get
together and make evil plans.
11 They say, "God has deserted him.
Go after him and grab him.
No one will save him."
12 God, don't be far away from me.
My God, come quickly and help me.
13 May those who bring charges against
me die in shame.
May those who want to harm me
be covered with shame and
dishonor.

14 But I will always have hope.
I will praise you more and more.
15 I will tell other people about all the
good things you have done.
All day long I will talk about how
you have saved your people.
But there's no way I could say how
many times you've done this.
16 LORD and King, I will come and
announce your mighty acts.
I will announce all the good things
that you alone do.
17 God, ever since I was young you have
taught me.
To this very day I tell about your
wonderful acts.
18 God, don't leave me
even when I'm old and have gray
hair.
Let me live to tell my children about
your power.
Let me tell all of them about your
mighty acts.

19 God, your saving acts reach to the skies.
You have done great things.
God, who is like you?
20 You have sent many bitter troubles my
way.
But you will give me new life.
Even if I'm almost in the grave,
you will bring me back.
21 You will honor me more and more.
You will comfort me once again.

22 My God, I will use the harp to praise
you
because you are always faithful.
Holy One of Israel,
I will use the lyre to sing praise to
you.
23 My lips will shout with joy
when I sing praise to you.
You have saved me.
24 All day long my tongue will say
that you have done what is right.
Those who wanted to harm me have
been put to shame.
They have not been honored.

Psalm 72
A psalm of Solomon.

1 God, give the king the ability to judge
fairly.
He is your royal son. Help him to do
what is right.

² May he rule your people in the right
        way.
    May he be fair to those among your
        people who are hurting.
³ May the mountains and the hills
        produce rich crops,
    because the people will do what is
        right.
⁴ May the king stand up for those who
        are hurting.
    May he save the children of those
        who are in need.
    May he crush those who treat others
        badly.
⁵ May the king rule as long as the sun
        shines
    and the moon gives its light.
    May he rule for all time to come.
⁶ May he be like rain falling on the fields.
    May he be like showers watering the
        earth.
⁷ May godly people do well as long as he
        rules.
    May they have more than they need
        as long as the moon lasts.

⁸ May the king rule from sea to sea.
    May his kingdom reach from the
        Euphrates River to the ends of
        the earth.
⁹ May the desert tribes bow down to him.
    May his enemies lick the dust.
¹⁰ May the kings of Tarshish and of places
        far away
    bring him gifts.
    May the kings of Sheba and Seba
        give him presents.
¹¹ May all kings bow down to him.
    May all nations serve him.

¹² The king will save needy people who
        cry out to him.
    He will save those who are hurting
        and have no one else to help.
¹³ He will take pity on those who are weak
        and in need.
    He will save them from death.
¹⁴ He will save them from people who
        treat others badly.
    He will save them from people who
        do mean things to them.
    Their lives are very special to him.

¹⁵ May the king live a long time!
    May gold from Sheba be given to him.
    May people always pray for him.
    May they ask the LORD to bless him
        all day long.
¹⁶ May there be plenty of grain
        everywhere in the land.
    May it sway in the wind on the tops
        of the hills.
    May the crops grow well, like those in
        Lebanon.
    May they grow like the grass of the
        field.
¹⁷ May the king's name be remembered
        forever.
    May his fame last as long as the sun
        shines.

    Then all nations will be blessed because
        of him.
    They will call him blessed.

¹⁸ Give praise to the LORD God, the God
        of Israel.
    Only he can do wonderful things.
¹⁹ Give praise to his glorious name
        forever.
    May his glory fill the whole earth.
    Amen and Amen.

²⁰ The prayers of David, the son of Jesse,
        end here.

BOOK III
PSALMS 73–89

Psalm 73
A psalm of Asaph.

¹ God is truly good to Israel.
    He is good to those who have pure
        hearts.
² But my feet had almost slipped.
    I had almost tripped and fallen.
³ I saw that proud and sinful people were
        doing well.
    And I began to long for what they
        had.
⁴ They don't have any troubles.
    Their bodies are healthy and strong.
⁵ They don't have the problems most
        people have.
    They don't suffer as other people do.
⁶ Their pride is like a necklace.
    They put on meanness as if it were
        their clothes.
⁷ Many sins come out of their hard and
        stubborn hearts.

There is no limit to the evil things
they can think up.
8 They laugh at others and speak words
of hatred.
They are proud. They warn others
about the harm they can do
to them.
9 They brag as if they owned heaven itself.
They talk as if they controlled the
earth.
10 So people listen to them.
They lap up their words like water.
11 They say, "How would God know what
we're doing?
Does the Most High God know
anything?"

12 Here is what sinful people are like.
They don't have a care in the world.
They keep getting richer and richer.

13 It seems as if I have kept my heart pure
for no reason.
It didn't do me any good to wash my
hands
to show that I wasn't guilty of doing
anything wrong.

14 Day after day I've been in pain.
God has punished me in a new way
every morning.

15 What if I had talked like that?
Then I wouldn't have been faithful to
God's children.
16 I tried to understand it all.
But it was more than I could handle.
17 It troubled me until I entered God's
temple.
Then I understood what will finally
happen to bad people.

18 God, I'm sure you will make them slip
and fall.
You will throw them down and
destroy them.
19 It will happen very suddenly.
A terrible death will take them away
completely.
20 A dream goes away when a person
wakes up.
Lord, it will be like that when you
rise up.
It will be as if those people were only
a dream.

WHAT ABOUT YOU?

In some countries, citizens are told what they can say, where they can live, what they can do with their lives, and what religion they must follow. The reason you can chase dreams, speak freely, and publicly worship the true Savior, Jesus Christ, is that people have fought for your freedom.

In the Adventures in Odyssey episode "Memories of Jerry," Jason tells Connie stories of his brother Jerry, who was killed as a soldier in the Vietnam War. He was fighting for the freedom of people across the world.

First John 3:16 says: "We know what love is because Jesus Christ gave his life for us. So we should give our lives for our brothers and sisters." We should be thankful for men and women like Jerry who fought so that future generations could live in freedom. Some even laid down their lives, as the verse says, so we don't need to live in fear or become slaves to someone else's idea of who we should be.

Take a moment to thank God for the people defending your country now, as well as those who have made the ultimate sacrifice so that you could be everything you were created to be.

Ask your parents if they know someone who has fought for your country. Talk to that person and be sure to express thanks for his or her service. If you're curious, ask your parents to help you research the Vietnam War online, including photos of the Vietnam Veterans Memorial in Washington, D.C.

21 At one time my heart was sad
  and my spirit was bitter.
22 I didn't have any sense. I didn't know
  anything.
  I acted like a wild animal toward
  you.
23 But I am always with you.
  You hold me by my right hand.
24 You give me wise advice to guide me.
  And when I die, you will take me
  away
  into the glory of heaven.
25 I don't have anyone in heaven but you.
  I don't want anything on earth
  besides you.
26 My body and my heart may grow
  weak.
  God, you give strength to my
  heart.
  You are everything I will ever need.
27 Those who don't want anything to do
  with you will die.
  You destroy all those who aren't
  faithful to you.
28 But I am close to you. And that's good.
  Lord and King, I have made you my
  place of safety.
  I will talk about everything you have
  done.

Psalm 74

A *maskil* of Asaph.

1 God, why have you turned your back
  on us for so long?
  Why are you so angry with us? We
  are your very own sheep.
2 Remember the nation that you chose as
  your own so long ago.
  Remember that you set us free from
  slavery to be your very own
  people.
  Remember Mount Zion, where you
  lived.
3 Walk through this place that has been
  torn down beyond repair.
  See how completely your enemies
  have destroyed the temple!
4 In the place where you used to meet
  with us,
  your enemies have shouted, "We've
  won the battle!"
  They have set up their flags to show
  they have beaten us.

5 They acted like people cutting down a
  forest with axes.
6 They smashed all the beautiful
  wooden walls
  with their axes and hatchets.
7 They burned your temple to the
  ground.
  They polluted the place where your
  Name is.
8 They had said in their hearts, "We will
  crush them completely!"
  They burned every place where you
  were worshiped in the land.
9 We don't get signs from God anymore.
  There aren't any prophets left.
  None of us knows how long that will
  last.
10 God, how long will your enemies make
  fun of you?
  Will they attack you with their
  words forever?
11 Why don't you help us? Why do you
  hold back your power?
  Use your strong power to destroy
  your enemies!
12 God, you have been my king for a long
  time.
  You are the only God who can save
  anyone on earth.
13 You parted the waters of the Red Sea by
  your power.
  You broke the heads of that sea
  monster in Egypt.
14 You crushed the heads of the sea
  monster Leviathan.
  You fed it to the creatures of the
  desert.
15 You opened up streams and springs.
  You dried up rivers that flow all year
  long.
16 You rule over the day and the night.
  You created the sun and the moon.
17 You decided where the borders of the
  earth would be.
  You made both summer and winter.
18 Lord, remember how your enemies
  have made fun of you.
  Remember how foolish people
  have attacked you with their
  words.
19 Don't hand over Israel, your dove, to
  those wild animals.
  Don't forget your suffering people
  forever.

20 Honor the covenant you made with us.
    Horrible things are happening in
        every dark corner of the land.
21 Don't let your suffering people be put to
        shame.
    May those who are poor and needy
        praise you.
22 God, rise up. Stand up for your cause.
    Remember how foolish people make
        fun of you all day long.
23 Pay close attention to the shouts of your
        enemies.
    The trouble they cause never stops.

Psalm 75

For the director of music.
A psalm of Asaph. A song to the
tune of "Do Not Destroy."

1 God, we praise you.
    We praise you because you are near
        to us.
    People talk about the wonderful
        things you have done.

2 You say, "I choose the appointed time
        to judge people.
    And I judge them fairly.
3 When the earth and all its people
        tremble,
    I keep everything from falling to
        pieces.
4 To the proud I say, 'Don't brag
        anymore.'
    To sinners I say, 'Don't show off your
        power.
5 Don't show it off against me.
    Don't talk back to me.'"

6 No one from east or west or north or
        south
    can judge themselves.
7 God is the one who judges.
    He says to one person, "You are
        guilty."
    To another he says, "You are not
        guilty."
8 In the hand of the LORD is a cup.
    It is full of wine mixed with spices.
    It is the wine of his anger.
    He pours it out. All the evil people on
        earth
    drink it down to the very last drop.

9 I will speak about this forever.
    I will sing praise to the God of Jacob.

10 God says, "I will destroy the power of
        all sinful people.
    But I will make godly people more
        powerful."

Psalm 76

For the director of music. A psalm
of Asaph. A song to be played
on stringed instruments.

1 In the land of Judah, God is well
        known.
    In Israel, his name is great.
2 His tent is in Jerusalem.
    The place where he lives is on Mount
        Zion.
3 There he broke the deadly arrows of his
        enemies.
    He broke their shields and swords.
    He broke their weapons of war.

4 God, you shine like a very bright light.
    You are more majestic than
        mountains full of wild animals.
5 Brave soldiers have been robbed of
        everything they had.
    Now they lie there, sleeping in death.
    Not one of them can even lift his
        hands.
6 God of Jacob, at your command
    both horse and chariot lie still.
7 People should have respect for you
        alone.
    Who can stand in front of you when
        you are angry?
8 From heaven you handed down your
        sentence.
    The land was afraid and became
        quiet.
9 God, that happened when you rose up
        to judge.
    It happened when you came to save
        all your suffering people in the
        land.
10 Your anger against sinners brings you
        praise.
    Those who live through your anger
        gather to worship you.

11 Make promises to the LORD your God
        and keep them.
    Let all the neighboring nations
        bring gifts to the God who should be
        respected.
12 He breaks the proud spirit of rulers.
    The kings of the earth have respect
        for him.

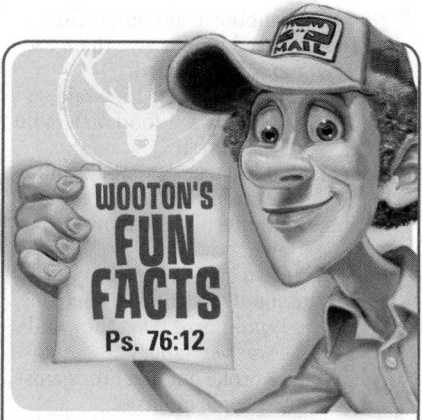

WOOTON'S
FUN
FACTS
Ps. 76:12

Good leaders must develop a vision
and get the job done. Or they wouldn't
be leaders! Danger comes when leaders
think they are above God's law or treat
their followers with disrespect. I think
Mr. Whittaker is a good leader.

Psalm 77

For the director of music. For
Jeduthun. A psalm of Asaph.

¹ I cried out to God for help.
　I cried out to God to hear me.
² When I was in trouble, I looked to the
　　Lord for help.
　During the night I lifted up my
　　hands in prayer.
　But I refused to be comforted.

³ God, I remembered you, and I groaned.
　I thought about you, and I became
　　weak.
⁴ You kept me from going to sleep.
　I was so troubled I couldn't speak.
⁵ I thought about days gone by.
　I thought about the years of long ago.
⁶ I remembered how I used to sing praise
　　to you in the night.
　I thought about it, and here is what I
　　asked myself.

⁷ "Will the Lord turn away from us
　　forever?
　Won't he ever show us his kindness
　　again?
⁸ Has his faithful love disappeared forever?
　Has his promise failed for all time?
⁹ Has God forgotten to help us?
　Has he held back his tender love
　　because he was angry?"

¹⁰ Then I thought, "Here is what gives me
　　hope.
　For many years the Most High God
　　showed how powerful he is.
¹¹ LORD, I will remember what you did.
　Yes, I will remember your miracles
　　of long ago.
¹² I will spend time thinking about
　　everything you have done.
　I will consider all your mighty acts."

¹³ God, everything you do is holy.
　What god is as great as our God?
¹⁴ You are the God who does miracles.
　You show your power among the
　　nations.
¹⁵ With your mighty arm you set your
　　people free.
　You set the children of Jacob and
　　Joseph free.

¹⁶ God, the water of the Red Sea saw you.
　It saw you and boiled up.
　The deepest waters were stirred up.
¹⁷ The clouds poured down rain.
　The skies rumbled with thunder.
　Lightning flashed back and forth like
　　arrows.
¹⁸ Your thunder was heard in the
　　windstorm.
　Your lightning lit up the world.
　The earth trembled and shook.
¹⁹ Your path led through the Red Sea.
　You walked through the mighty
　　waters.
　But your footprints were not seen.

²⁰ You led your people like a flock.
　You led them by the hands of Moses
　　and Aaron.

Psalm 78

A *maskil* of Asaph.

¹ My people, listen to my teaching.
　Pay attention to what I say.
² I will open my mouth and tell a story.
　I will speak about things that were
　　hidden.
　They happened a long time ago.
³ We have heard about them and we
　　know them.
　Our people who lived before us have
　　told us about them.
⁴ We won't hide them from our children.
　We will tell them to those who live
　　after us.

We will tell them what the Lord has
  done that is worthy of praise.
We will talk about his power and the
  wonderful things he has done.
5 He gave laws to the people of Jacob.
  He gave Israel their law.
He commanded our people who lived
  before us
to teach his laws to their children.
6 Then those born later would know his
  laws.
  Even their children yet to come
    would know them.
  And they in turn would tell their
    children.
7 Then they would put their trust in God.
  They would not forget what he had
    done.
  They would obey his commands.
8 They would not be like their people
    who lived long ago.
  Those people were stubborn. They
    refused to obey God.
They turned away from him.
  Their spirits were not faithful to him.

9 The soldiers of Ephraim were armed
    with bows.
  But they ran away on the day of battle.
10 They didn't keep the covenant God had
    made with them.
  They refused to live by his law.
11 They forgot what he had done.
  They didn't remember the wonders
    he had shown them.
12 He did miracles right in front of their
    people who lived long ago.
  At that time they were living in
    Egypt, in the area of Zoan.
13 God parted the Red Sea and led them
    through it.
  He made the water stand up like a
    wall.
14 He guided them with the cloud during
    the day.
  He led them with the light of a fire
    all night long.
15 He broke the rocks open in the desert.
  He gave them as much water as there
    is in the oceans.
16 He brought streams out of a rocky cliff.
  He made water flow down like rivers.

17 But they continued to sin against him.
  In the desert they refused to obey
    the Most High God.

18 They were stubborn and tested God.
  They ordered him to give them the
    food they wanted.
19 They spoke against God. They said,
  "Can God really put food on a table
    in the desert?
20 It is true that he struck the rock, and
    streams of water poured out.
  Huge amounts of water flowed
    down.
  But can he also give us bread?
  Can he supply meat for his people?"
21 When the Lord heard what they said,
    he was very angry.
  His anger broke out like fire against
    the people of Jacob.
  He became very angry with Israel.
22 That was because they didn't believe in
    God.
  They didn't trust in his power to save
    them.
23 But he gave a command to the skies
    above.
  He opened the doors of the heavens.
24 He rained down manna for the people
    to eat.
  He gave them the grain of heaven.
25 Mere human beings ate the bread of
    angels.
  He sent them all the food they could
    eat.
26 He made the east wind blow from the
    heavens.
  By his power he caused the south
    wind to blow.
27 He rained down meat on them like
    dust.
  He sent them birds like sand on the
    seashore.
28 He made the birds come down inside
    their camp.
  The birds fell all around their tents.
29 People ate until they couldn't eat any
    more.
  He gave them what they had wanted.
30 But even before they had finished
    eating, God acted.
  He did it while the food was still in
    their mouths.
31 His anger rose up against them.
  He put to death the strongest among
    them.
  He struck down Israel's young men.
32 But even after all that, they kept on
    sinning.

Even after the wonderful things
he had done, they still didn't
believe.
³³ So he brought their days to an end like
a puff of smoke.
He ended their years with terror.
³⁴ Every time God killed some of them,
the others would seek him.
They gladly turned back to him
again.
³⁵ They remembered that God was their
Rock.
They remembered that God Most
High had set them free.
³⁶ But they didn't mean it when they
praised him.
They lied to him when they spoke.
³⁷ They turned away from him.
They weren't faithful to the covenant
he had made with them.
³⁸ But he was full of tender love.
He forgave their sins
and didn't destroy his people.
Time after time he held back his anger.
He didn't let all his burning anger
blaze out.
³⁹ He remembered that they were only
human.
He remembered they were only a
breath of air
that drifts by and doesn't return.
⁴⁰ How often they refused to obey him in
the desert!
How often they caused him sorrow
in that dry and empty land!
⁴¹ Again and again they tested God.
They made the Holy One of Israel
sad and angry.
⁴² They didn't remember his power.
They forgot the day he set them free
from those who had treated them so
badly.
⁴³ They forgot how he had shown them
his signs in Egypt.
They forgot his miracles in the area
of Zoan.
⁴⁴ He turned the river of Egypt into blood.
The people of Egypt couldn't drink
water from their streams.
⁴⁵ He sent large numbers of flies that bit
them.
He sent frogs that destroyed their
land.
⁴⁶ He gave their crops to the grasshoppers.
He gave their food to the locusts.

⁴⁷ He destroyed their vines with hail.
He destroyed their fig trees with
sleet.
⁴⁸ He killed their cattle with hail.
Their livestock were struck by
lightning.
⁴⁹ Because he was so angry with Egypt,
he caused them to have great
trouble.
In his great anger he sent destroying
angels against them.
⁵⁰ God prepared a path for his anger.
He didn't spare their lives.
He gave them over to the plague.
⁵¹ He killed the oldest son of each family
in Egypt.
He struck down the oldest son in
every house in the land of
Ham.
⁵² But he brought his people out like a
flock.
He led them like sheep through the
desert.
⁵³ He guided them safely, and they weren't
afraid.
But the Red Sea swallowed up their
enemies.
⁵⁴ And so he brought his people to the
border of his holy land.
He led them to the central hill
country he had taken by his
power.
⁵⁵ He drove out the nations to make room
for his people.
He gave to each family a piece
of land to pass on to their
children.
He gave the tribes of Israel a place to
make their homes.
⁵⁶ But they tested God.
They refused to obey the Most High
God.
They didn't keep his laws.
⁵⁷ They were like their people who lived
long ago.
They turned away from him and
were not faithful.
They were like a bow that doesn't shoot
straight.
They couldn't be trusted.
⁵⁸ They made God angry by going to their
high places.
They made him jealous by
worshiping the statues of their
gods.

⁵⁹ When God saw what the people were
      doing, he was very angry.
   He turned away from them
      completely.
⁶⁰ He deserted the holy tent at Shiloh.
   He left the tent he had set up among
      his people.
⁶¹ He allowed the ark to be captured.
   Into the hands of his enemies he sent
      the ark where his glory rested.
⁶² He let his people be killed by swords.
   He was very angry with them.
⁶³ Fire destroyed their young men.
   Their young women had no one to
      marry.
⁶⁴ Their priests were killed by swords.
   Their widows weren't able to weep.

⁶⁵ Then the Lord woke up as if he had
      been sleeping.
   He was like a warrior waking up from
      the deep sleep caused by wine.
⁶⁶ He drove back his enemies.
   He put them to shame that will last
      forever.
⁶⁷ He turned his back on the tents of the
      people of Joseph.
   He didn't choose to live in the tribe
      of Ephraim.
⁶⁸ Instead, he chose to live in the tribe of
      Judah.
   He chose Mount Zion, which he
      loved.
⁶⁹ There he built his holy place as secure
      as the heavens.
   He built it to last forever, like the
      earth.
⁷⁰ He chose his servant David.
   He took him from the sheep pens.
⁷¹ He brought him from tending sheep
      to be the shepherd of his people
      Jacob.
   He made him the shepherd of Israel,
      his special people.
⁷² David cared for them with a faithful
      and honest heart.
   With skilled hands he led them.

Psalm 79

A psalm of Asaph.

¹ God, an army from the nations has
      attacked your land.
   They have polluted your holy temple.
   They have completely destroyed
      Jerusalem.

² They have left the dead bodies of your
      people.
   They have left them as food for the
      birds in the sky.
   They have left the bodies of your
      faithful people.
   They have left them for the wild
      animals.
³ They have poured out the blood of your
      people like water.
   It is all around Jerusalem.
   No one is left to bury the dead.
⁴ We are something our neighbors joke
      about.
   The nations around us laugh at us
      and make fun of us.

⁵ Lord, how long will you be angry with
      us? Will it be forever?
   How long will your jealousy burn
      like fire?
⁶ Bring your great anger against the
      nations
      that don't pay any attention to you.
   Bring it against the kingdoms
      that don't worship you.
⁷ They have swallowed up the people of
      Jacob.
   They have destroyed Israel's
      homeland.
⁸ Don't hold against us the sins of our
      people who lived before us.
   May you be quick to show us your
      tender love.
   We are in great need.

⁹ God our Savior, help us.
   Then glory will come to you.
   Save us and forgive our sins.
   Then people will honor your name.
¹⁰ Why should the nations say,
      "Where is their God?"
   Show the nations that you punish those
      who kill your people.
   We want to see it happen.
¹¹ Listen to the groans of the prisoners.
   Use your strong arm
      to save people sentenced to death.

¹² Lord, our neighbors have laughed at you.
   Pay them back seven times for what
      they have done.
¹³ We are your people, your very own
      sheep.
   We will praise you forever.
   For all time to come
      we will keep on praising you.

Psalm 80

For the director of music.
A psalm of Asaph to the tune of
"The Lilies of the Covenant."

¹ Shepherd of Israel, hear us.
You lead the people of Joseph like a
flock.
You sit on your throne between the
cherubim.
Show your glory
² to the people of Ephraim, Benjamin
and Manasseh.
Call your strength into action.
Come and save us.

³ God, make us new again.
May you be pleased with us.
Then we will be saved.

⁴ Lord God, you rule over all.
How long will you be angry?
Will you be angry with your people
even when they pray to you?
⁵ You have given us tears as our food.
You have made us drink tears by the
bowlful.
⁶ You have let our neighbors mock us.
Our enemies laugh at us.

⁷ God who rules over all, make us new
again.
May you be pleased with us.
Then we will be saved.

⁸ You brought Israel out of Egypt.

Ps. 80 Asaph was probably a leader
in David's choir and a songwriter
(1 Chronicles 6:39). He may also have
been a seer who could predict the
future (2 Chronicles 29:30; Nehemiah
12:46). His psalms are 50 and 73–83.

Israel was like a vine.
After you drove the nations out of
Canaan,
you planted the vine in their land.
⁹ You prepared the ground for it.
It took root and spread out over the
whole land.
¹⁰ The mountains were covered with its
shade.
The shade of its branches covered
the mighty cedar trees.
¹¹ Your vine sent its branches out all the
way to the Mediterranean Sea.
They reached as far as the Euphrates
River.

¹² Why have you broken down the walls
around your vine?
Now all who pass by it can pick its
grapes.
¹³ Wild pigs from the forest destroy it.
Insects from the fields feed on it.
¹⁴ God who rules over all, return to us!
Look down from heaven and see us!
Watch over your vine.
¹⁵ Guard the root you have planted
with your powerful right hand.
Take care of the branch you have
raised up for yourself.

¹⁶ Your vine has been cut down and
burned in the fire.
You have been angry with us, and we
are dying.
¹⁷ May you honor the people at your right
hand.
May you honor the nation you have
raised up for yourself.
¹⁸ Then we won't turn away from you.
Give us new life. We will worship you.

¹⁹ Lord God who rules over all, make us
new again.
May you be pleased with us.
Then we will be saved.

Psalm 81

For the director of music. According
to *gittith*. A psalm of Asaph.

¹ Sing joyfully to God! He gives us
strength.
Give a loud shout to the God of
Jacob!
² Let the music begin. Play the
tambourines.
Play sweet music on harps and lyres.

³ Blow the ram's horn on the day of the
    New Moon feast.
    Blow it again when the moon is
      full and the Feast of Booths
      begins.
⁴ This is an order given to Israel.
    It is a law of the God of Jacob.
⁵ He gave it as a covenant law for the
    people of Joseph.
    It was given when God went out to
      punish Egypt.
    There I heard a voice I didn't
      recognize.

Jason's Jargon

PSALM 81

And now a musical quest: Find a *lyre* in this chapter. A lyre is a stringed instrument that is usually shaped like a "U" and can be held in the musician's lap.

⁶ The voice said, "I removed the load
    from your shoulders.
    I set your hands free from carrying
      heavy baskets.
⁷ You called out when you were in
    trouble, and I saved you.
    I answered you out of a
      thundercloud.
    I tested you at the waters of
      Meribah.
⁸ "My people, listen and I will warn you.
    Israel, I wish you would listen to
      me!
⁹ Don't have anything to do with the gods
    of other nations.
    Don't bow down and worship any
      god other than me.
¹⁰ I am the LORD your God.
    I brought you up out of Egypt.
    Open your mouth wide, and I will
      fill it with good things.
¹¹ "But my people wouldn't listen to me.
    Israel wouldn't obey me.
¹² So I let them go their own stubborn
    way.
    I let them follow their own sinful
      plans.

¹³ "I wish my people would listen to me!
    I wish Israel would live as I want
      them to live!
¹⁴ Then I would quickly bring their
    enemies under control.
    I would use my power against their
      attackers.
¹⁵ Those who hate me would bow down to
    me in fear.
    They would be punished forever.
¹⁶ But you would be fed with the finest
    wheat.
    I would satisfy you with the sweetest
      honey."

Psalm 82
A psalm of Asaph.

¹ God takes his place at the head of a
    large gathering of leaders.
    He announces his decisions among
      them.

² He says, "How long will you stand up
    for those who aren't fair to
      others?
    How long will you show mercy to
      sinful people?
³ Stand up for the weak and for children
    whose fathers have died.
    Protect the rights of people who are
      poor or treated badly.

ADVENTURES IN ODYSSEY

Jack Allen learned a story from American history when a pastor had to stand up for the weak and protect the rights of slaves who were treated badly in "The Underground Railroad" (A#24).

⁴ Save those who are weak and needy.
    Save them from the power of sinful
        people.
⁵ "You leaders don't know anything.
    You don't understand anything.
    You are in the dark about what is right.
    Law and order have been destroyed
        all over the world.
⁶ "I said, 'You leaders are like gods.
    You are all children of the Most
        High God.'
⁷ But you will die, like mere human
        beings.
    You will die like every other leader."
⁸ God, rise up. Judge the earth.
    All the nations belong to you.

Psalm 83

A song. A psalm of Asaph.

¹ God, don't remain silent.
    Don't refuse to listen.
    Do something, God.
² See how your enemies are growling like
        dogs.
    See how they are rising up against
        you.
³ They make clever plans against your
        people.
    They make evil plans against those
        you love.
⁴ "Come," they say. "Let's destroy that
        whole nation.
    Then the name of Israel won't be
        remembered anymore."
⁵ All of them agree on the evil plans they
        have made.
    They join forces against you.
⁶ Their forces include the people of
        Edom,
    Ishmael, Moab and Hagar.
⁷ They also include the people of Byblos,
        Ammon, Amalek,
    Philistia and Tyre.
⁸ Even Assyria has joined them
    to give strength to the people of
        Moab and Ammon.
⁹ Do to them what you did to the people
        of Midian.
    Do to them what you did to Sisera
        and Jabin at the Kishon River.
¹⁰ Sisera and Jabin died near the town of
        Endor.

Their bodies were left on the ground
    like human waste.
¹¹ Do to the nobles of your enemies what
        you did to Oreb and Zeeb.
    Do to all their princes what you did
        to Zebah and Zalmunna.
¹² They said, "Let's take over
    the grasslands that belong to God."
¹³ My God, make them like straw that the
        wind blows away.
    Make them like tumbleweed.
¹⁴ Destroy them as fire burns up a forest.
    Destroy them as a flame sets
        mountains on fire.
¹⁵ Chase them with your mighty winds.
    Terrify them with your storm.
¹⁶ Lord, put them to shame
    so that they will seek you.
¹⁷ May they always be filled with terror
        and shame.
    May they die in dishonor.
¹⁸ May you, the Lord, let your enemies
        know who you are.
    You alone are the Most High God
        over the whole earth.

Psalm 84

For the director of music. According to
gittith. A psalm of the Sons of Korah.

¹ Lord who rules over all,
    how lovely is the place where you
        live!
² I can't wait to be in the courtyards of
        the Lord's temple.
    I really want to be there.
    My whole being cries out
        for the living God.
³ Lord who rules over all,
    even the sparrow has found a home
        near your altar.
    My King and my God,
        the swallow also has a nest there,
        where she may have her young.
⁴ Blessed are those who live in your house.
    They are always praising you.
⁵ Blessed are those whose strength comes
        from you.
    They have firmly decided to travel to
        your temple.
⁶ As they pass through the dry Valley of
        Baka,
    they make it a place where water
        flows.

The rain in the fall covers it with
pools.
⁷ Those people get stronger as they go
along,
until each of them appears in Zion,
where God lives.

⁸ LORD God who rules over all, hear my
prayer.
God of the people of Jacob, listen
to me.
⁹ God, may you be pleased with your
anointed king.
You appointed him to be like a
shield that keeps us safe.

¹⁰ A single day in your courtyards is better
than a thousand anywhere else.
I would rather guard the door of the
house of my God
than live in the tents of sinful people.
¹¹ The LORD God is like the sun that gives
us light.
He is like a shield that keeps us safe.
The LORD blesses us with favor and
honor.
He doesn't hold back anything good
from those whose lives are without
blame.

¹² LORD who rules over all,
blessed is the person who trusts in
you.

Psalm 85

For the director of music.
A psalm of the Sons of Korah.

¹ LORD, you were good to your land.
You blessed the people of Jacob with
great success again.
² You forgave the evil things your people
did.
You took away all their sins.
³ You stopped being angry with them.
You turned your great anger away
from them.

⁴ God our Savior, make us new again.
Stop being unhappy with us.
⁵ Will you be angry with us forever?
Will you be angry for all time to
come?
⁶ Won't you give us new life again?
Then we'll be joyful because of what
you have done.
⁷ LORD, show us your faithful love.
Save us.

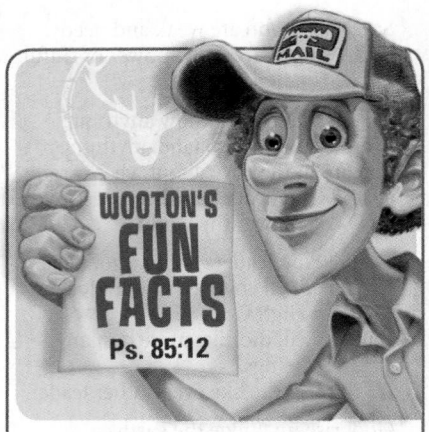

Crops could mean the seven main foods of Israel: wheat, barley, figs, grapes, olives, pomegranates, and dates. Mmmm. Sounds like dinner! But in a spiritual sense, crops would be "good works" or "righteousness."

⁸ I will listen to what God the LORD says.
He promises peace to his faithful
people.
But they must not turn to foolish
ways.
⁹ I know he's ready to save those who
have respect for him.
Then his glory can be seen in our
land.

¹⁰ God's truth and faithful love join
together.
His peace and holiness kiss each
other.
¹¹ His truth springs up from the earth.
His holiness looks down from
heaven.
¹² The LORD will certainly give what is
good.
Our land will produce its crops.
¹³ God's holiness leads the way in front of
him.
It prepares the way for his coming.

Psalm 86

A prayer of David.

¹ LORD, hear me and answer me.
I am poor and needy.
² Keep my life safe, because I am faithful
to you.
Save me, because I trust in you.
You are my God.

³ Lord, have mercy on me.
    I call out to you all day long.
⁴ Bring joy to me.
    Lord, I put my trust in you.

⁵ Lord, you are forgiving and good.
    You are full of love for all who call
      out to you.
⁶ Lord, hear my prayer.
    Listen to my cry for mercy.
⁷ When I'm in trouble, I will call out to
      you.
    And you will answer me.

⁸ Lord, there's no one like you among the
      gods.
    No one can do what you do.
⁹ Lord, all the nations you have made
    will come and worship you.
    They will bring glory to you.
¹⁰ You are great. You do wonderful
      things.
    You alone are God.

¹¹ Lord, teach me how you want me to
      live.
    Do this so that I will depend on you,
      my faithful God.
    Give me a heart that doesn't want
      anything
    more than to worship you.
¹² Lord my God, I will praise you with all
      my heart.
    I will bring glory to you forever.
¹³ Great is your love for me.
    You have kept me from going down
      into the place of the dead.

¹⁴ God, proud people are attacking me.
    A gang of mean people is trying to
      kill me.
    They don't care about you.
¹⁵ But Lord, you are a God who is tender
      and kind.
    You are gracious.
    You are slow to get angry.
    You are faithful and full of love.
¹⁶ Come to my aid and have mercy on
      me.
    Show your strength by helping me.
    Save me because I serve you just as
      my mother did.
¹⁷ Prove your goodness to me.
    Then my enemies will see it and be
      put to shame.
    Lord, you have helped me and given
      me comfort.

Psalm 87

A psalm of the Sons of Korah. A song.

¹ The Lord has built his city
    on the holy mountain.
² He loves the city of Zion
    more than all the other places
    where the people of Jacob live.
³ City of God,
    the Lord says glorious things about
      you.
⁴ He says, "I will include Egypt and
      Babylon
    in a list of nations who recognize me
      as king.
I will also include Philistia and Tyre,
    along with Cush.
    I will say about them, 'They were
      born in Zion.'"

⁵ Certainly it will be said about Zion,
    "This nation and that nation were
      born in it.
    The Most High God himself will
      make it secure."
⁶ Here is what the Lord will write in his
      list of the nations.
    "Each of them was born in Zion."
⁷ As they make music they will sing,
    "Zion, all our blessings come from
      you."

Psalm 88

For the director of music. According
    to *mahalath leannoth.* A song.
    A psalm of the Sons of Korah. A
    maskil of Heman the Ezrahite.

¹ Lord, you are the God who saves me.
    Day and night I cry out to you.
² Please hear my prayer.
    Pay attention to my cry for help.

³ I have so many troubles
    I'm about to die.
⁴ People think my life is over.
    I'm like someone who doesn't have
      any strength.
⁵ People treat me as if I were dead.
    I'm like those who have been killed
      and are now in the grave.
    You don't even remember them
      anymore.
    They are cut off from your care.

⁶ It's as if you have put me deep down in
      the grave.

It's as if you have put me in that
    deep, dark place.
[7] Your great anger lies heavy on me.
    All the waves of your anger have
        crashed over me.
[8] You have taken my closest friends away
        from me.
    You have made me sickening to
        them.
    I feel trapped and can't escape.
[9]   I'm crying so much I can't see very
        well.

Lord, I call out to you every day.
    I lift up my hands to you in prayer.
[10] Do you do wonderful things for those
        who are dead?
    Do their spirits rise up and praise
        you?
[11] Do those who are dead speak about
        your love?
    Do those who are in the grave tell
        how faithful you are?
[12] Are your wonderful deeds known in
        that dark place?
    Are your holy acts known in that
        land where the dead are
        forgotten?

[13] Lord, I cry out to you for help.
    In the morning I pray to you.
[14] Lord, why do you say no to me?
    Why do you turn your face away
        from me?

[15] I've been in pain ever since I was
        young.
    I've been close to death.
    You have made me suffer terrible
        things.
    I have lost all hope.
[16] Your great anger has swept over me.
    Your terrors have destroyed me.
[17] All day long they surround me like a
        flood.
    They have closed in all around me.
[18] You have taken my friends and
        neighbors away from me.
    Darkness is my closest friend.

Psalm 89
A *maskil* of Ethan the Ezrahite.

[1] Lord, I will sing about your great love
        forever.
    For all time to come, I will tell how
        faithful you are.

[2] I will tell everyone that your love stands
        firm forever.
    I will tell them that you are always
        faithful, even in heaven itself.

[3] You said, "Here is the covenant I have
        made with my chosen one.
    Here is the promise I have made to
        my servant David.
[4] 'I will make your family line continue
        forever.
    I will make your kingdom secure for
        all time to come.'"

[5] Lord, the heavens praise you for your
        wonderful deeds.
    When your holy angels gather
        together,
    they praise you for how faithful you
        are.
[6] Who in the skies above can compare
        with the Lord?
    Who among the angels is like the
        Lord?
[7] God is highly respected among his holy
        angels.
    He's more wonderful than all those
        who are around him.
[8] Lord God who rules over all, who is
        like you?
    Lord, you are mighty. You are
        faithful in everything you do.

[9] You rule over the stormy sea.
    When its waves rise up, you calm
        them down.
[10] You crushed Egypt and killed her people.
    With your powerful arm you
        scattered your enemies.
[11] The heavens belong to you. The earth is
        yours also.
    You made the world and everything
        that is in it.
[12] You created everything from north to
        south.
    Mount Tabor and Mount Hermon
        sing to you with joy.
[13] Your arm is powerful.
    Your hand is strong.
    Your right hand is mighty.

[14] Your kingdom is built on what is right
        and fair.
    Your faithful love leads the way in
        front of you.
[15] Blessed are those who have learned to
        shout praise to you.

ADVENTURES iN ODYSSEY

A courtroom drama at Whit's End showed how justice ultimately prevailed in "The Scales of Justice" (A#13).

You are pleased to honor our king.
¹⁸ Our king is like a shield that keeps us
    safe.
He belongs to the LORD.
He belongs to the Holy One of
    Israel.

¹⁹ You once spoke to your faithful people
    in a vision.
You said, "I have given strength to a
    soldier.
I have raised up a young man from
    among the people.
²⁰ I have found my servant David.
I have poured my sacred oil on his
    head.
²¹ My powerful hand will keep him going.
My mighty arm will give him
    strength.
²² No enemy will have the victory over
    him.
No evil person will treat him badly.
²³ I will crush the king's enemies.
I will completely destroy them.
²⁴ I will love him and be faithful to him.
Because of me his power will
    increase.
²⁵ I will give him a great kingdom.

LORD, they live in the light of your
    kindness.
¹⁶ All day long they are full of joy because
    of who you are.
They celebrate the fact that you do
    what is right.
¹⁷ You bring them glory and give them
    strength.

WHAT ABOUT YOU?

"Order in the court!" When you see those words, what kind of court do you picture? If you guessed a legal court for a trial, you're right.

Imagine facing God as your judge someday. Psalm 89:14 describes Him as fair and loving: "Your kingdom is built on what is right and fair. Your faithful love leads the way in front of you."

Remember, as our judge, God can see everything. He knows the full story for each of us. And unlike any of us, He can see into our hearts and know why we do what we do. That's why His rulings are always just, and we can trust that justice will be done.

Do you know that our enemy, Satan, wants to put us on trial? It's true. Like a determined prosecutor, the devil likes to remind us of our mistakes and present evidence proving our sin. And let's be honest—there's plenty of evidence against us all. So isn't it good to know that we have the best lawyer in the universe defending us? It's Jesus! First John 2:1 calls Jesus our "friend who speaks to the Father for us."

Are we guilty? Yes. However, because our Savior is standing in the gap for us, "Order in the court!" soon turns into "Case dismissed!"

Read Psalm 145 and write down all the words used to describe the perfect judge, God. Underline the word if it's used more than once—that means it's especially important!

It will reach from the Mediterranean
   Sea to the Euphrates River.
²⁶ He will call out to me, 'You are my
   Father.
You are my God. You are my Rock
   and Savior.'
²⁷ I will also make him my oldest son.
   Among all the kings of the earth, he
      will be the most important one.
²⁸ I will continue to love him forever.
   I will never break my covenant with
      him.
²⁹ I will make his family line continue
   forever.
His kingdom will last as long as the
   heavens.

³⁰ "What if his sons turn away from my
   laws
and do not follow them?
³¹ What if they disobey my orders
   and fail to keep my commands?
³² Then I will punish them for their sins.
   I will strike them with a rod.
I will whip them for their evil acts.
³³ But I will not stop loving David.
   I will always be faithful to him.
³⁴ I will not break my covenant.
   I will not go back on my word.
³⁵ Once and for all, I have made a promise.
   It is based on my holiness.
And I will not lie to David.
³⁶ His family line will continue forever.
   His kingdom will last as long as the
      sun.
³⁷ It will last forever like the moon,
   that faithful witness in the sky."

³⁸ But you have turned your back on your
   anointed king.
You have been very angry with him.
³⁹ You have broken the covenant you
   made with him.
You have thrown your servant's
   crown into the dirt.
⁴⁰ You have broken through the walls
   around his city.
You have completely destroyed his
   secure places.
⁴¹ All those who pass by have carried off
   what belonged to him.
His neighbors make fun of him.
⁴² You have made his enemies strong.
   You have made all of them happy.
⁴³ You have made his sword useless.
   You have not helped him in battle.

⁴⁴ You have put an end to his glory.
   You have knocked his throne to the
      ground.
⁴⁵ You have cut short the days of his life.
   You have covered him with shame.

⁴⁶ Lord, how long will you hide yourself?
   Will it be forever?
How long will your anger burn like
   fire?
⁴⁷ Remember how short my life is.
   You have created all people for such
      a useless purpose!
⁴⁸ Who can live and not die?
   Who can escape the power of the
      grave?
⁴⁹ Lord, where is the great love you used
   to have?
You faithfully promised it to David.
⁵⁰ Lord, remember how my enemies have
   made fun of me.
I've had to put up with mean words
   from all the nations.
⁵¹ Lord, your enemies have said mean
   things.
They have laughed at everything
   your anointed king has done.

⁵² Give praise to the Lord forever!
   Amen and Amen.

BOOK IV
PSALMS 90–106

Psalm 90
A prayer of Moses, the man of God.

¹ Lord, from the very beginning
   you have been like a home to us.
² Before you created the whole world and
   the mountains were made,
from the beginning to the end you
   are God.

³ You turn human beings back to dust.
   You say to them, "Return to dust."
⁴ To you a thousand years
   are like a day that has just gone by.
They are like a few hours of the night.
⁵ Yet you sweep people away, and they die.
   They are like new grass that grows in
      the morning.
⁶ In the morning it springs up new,
   but by evening it's all dried up.

⁷ Your anger destroys us.
   Your burning anger terrifies us.

NOOTON'S FUN FACTS

Ps. 90:10

The average age of death in the United States rose steadily for decades, but lately it seems like it has stalled at age 79. A child born today can expect to live, on average, 78 years and 10 months.

¹⁵ Make us glad for as many days as you
have made us suffer.
Give us joy for as many years as
we've had trouble.
¹⁶ Show us your mighty acts.
Let our children see your glorious
power.

¹⁷ May the Lord our God always be
pleased with us.
Lord, make what we do succeed.
Please make what we do succeed.

Psalm 91

¹ Whoever rests in the shadow of the
Most High God
will be kept safe by the Mighty
One.
² I will say about the LORD,
"He is my place of safety.
He is like a fort to me.
He is my God. I trust in him."

³ He will certainly save you from hidden
traps
and from deadly sickness.
⁴ He will cover you with his wings.
Under the feathers of his wings you
will find safety.
He is faithful. He will keep you safe
like a shield or a tower.
⁵ You won't have to be afraid of the
terrors that come during the
night.
You won't have to fear the arrows
that come at you during the
day.
⁶ You won't have to be afraid of the
sickness that attacks in the
darkness.
You won't have to fear the plague
that destroys at noon.
⁷ A thousand may fall dead at your side.
Ten thousand may fall near your
right hand.
But no harm will come to you.
⁸ You will see with your own eyes
how God punishes sinful people.

⁸ You have put our sins right in front of
you.
You have placed our secret sins
where you can see them
clearly.
⁹ You have been angry with us all of our
days.
We groan as we come to the end of
our lives.
¹⁰ We live to be about 70.
Or we may live to be 80, if we stay
healthy.
But even our best days are filled with
trouble and sorrow.
The years quickly pass, and we are
gone.

¹¹ If only we knew the power of your
anger!
It's as great as the respect we should
have for you.
¹² Teach us to realize how short our lives
are.
Then our hearts will become wise.

¹³ LORD, please stop punishing us!
How long will you keep it up?
Be kind to us.
¹⁴ Satisfy us with your faithful love every
morning.
Then we can sing for joy and be glad
all our days.

⁹ Suppose you say, "The LORD is the one
who keeps me safe."
Suppose you let the Most High God
be like a home to you.
¹⁰ Then no harm will come to you.
No terrible plague will come near
your tent.

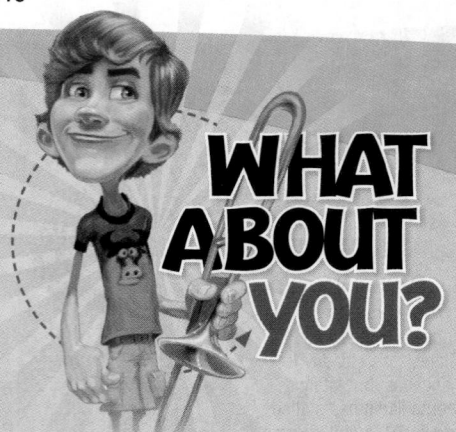

WHAT ABOUT YOU?

Leaping from a World War II bomber. Fighting pirates on the high seas. Evading secret agents and zipping through outer space. Jimmy Barclay did it all in the Odyssey adventure "Someone to Watch over Me." Though Jimmy went through a lot in this episode, he wasn't alone.

Psalm 91:11–12 says, "The LORD will command his angels to take good care of you. They will lift you up in their hands. Then you won't trip over a stone." Sure enough, Jimmy's guardian angel was fighting right beside him. At each corner, he faced grim circumstances, but heaven-sent guidance and protection allowed him to overcome.

Our God truly is mighty. He cares for each one of us. He's always watching, and is never taken by surprise. That includes times when we're sick or hurting. Trials will challenge us. It can be hard to understand why our loving, all-powerful God doesn't always fix things the way we think He should. That's where faith comes in.

The better we know God's heart, the easier it is to trust Him when life takes a hard turn. Even though we may travel some bumpy roads here on Earth, trusting Jesus and inviting Him into our hearts guarantees we'll be with Him forever in heaven.

Do you have friends who haven't received Jesus into their hearts yet? Take a moment to pray for them now. The greatest act of kindness we can show another person is to introduce him or her to Jesus Christ.

---

¹¹ The LORD will command his angels
    to take good care of you.
¹² They will lift you up in their hands.
    Then you won't trip over a stone.
¹³ You will walk on lions and cobras.
    You will crush mighty lions and
      poisonous snakes.

¹⁴ The LORD says, "I will save the one who
    loves me.
    I will keep him safe, because he
      trusts in me.
¹⁵ He will call out to me, and I will answer
    him.
    I will be with him in times of trouble.
    I will save him and honor him.
¹⁶ I will give him a long and full life.
    I will save him."

Psalm 92
A psalm. A song for the Sabbath day.

¹ LORD, it is good to praise you.
    Most High God, it is good to make
      music to honor you.

² It is good to sing every morning about
    your love.
    It is good to sing every night about
      how faithful you are.
³ I sing about it to the music of the lyre
    that has ten strings.
    I sing about it to the music of the
      harp.

⁴ LORD, you make me glad by your
    deeds.
    I sing for joy about what you have
      done.
⁵ LORD, how great are the things you do!
    How wise your thoughts are!
⁶ Here is something that people without
    sense don't know.
    Here is what foolish people don't
      understand.
⁷ Those who are evil spring up like
    grass.
    Those who do wrong succeed.
    But they will be destroyed forever.

⁸ But LORD, you are honored forever.

⁹ Lord, your enemies will certainly die.
    All those who do evil will be
        scattered.
¹⁰ You have made me as strong as a wild
        ox.
    You have poured the finest olive oil
        on me.
¹¹ I've seen my evil enemies destroyed.
    I've heard that they have lost the
        battle.

¹² Those who do what is right will grow
        like a palm tree.
    They will grow strong like a cedar
        tree in Lebanon.
¹³ Their roots will be firm in the house of
        the Lord.
    They will grow strong and healthy in
        the courtyards of our God.
¹⁴ When they get old, they will still bear
        fruit.
    Like young trees they will stay fresh
        and strong.
¹⁵ They will say to everyone, "The Lord is
        honest.
    He is my Rock, and there is no evil
        in him."

Psalm 93

¹ The Lord rules.
    He puts on majesty as if it were
        clothes.
    The Lord puts on majesty and
        strength.
    Indeed, the world has been set in place.
    It is firm and secure.
² Lord, you began to rule a long time ago.
    You have always existed.

³ Lord, the seas have lifted up their voice.
    They have lifted up their pounding
        waves.
⁴ But Lord, you are more powerful than
        the roar of the ocean.
    You are stronger than the waves of
        the sea.
    Lord, you are powerful in heaven.

⁵ Your laws do not change, Lord.
    Your temple will be holy
    for all time to come.

Psalm 94

¹ The Lord is a God who punishes.
    Since you are the one who punishes,
        come and show your anger.
² Judge of the earth, rise up.

Pay back proud people for what they
        have done.
³ Lord, how long will those who are evil
        be glad?
    How long will they be full of joy?

⁴ Proud words pour out of their mouths.
    All those who do evil are always
        bragging.
⁵ Lord, they crush your people.
    They treat badly those who belong
        to you.
⁶ They kill outsiders. They kill widows.
    They murder children whose fathers
        have died.
⁷ They say, "The Lord doesn't see what's
        happening.
    The God of Jacob doesn't pay any
        attention to it."

⁸ You who aren't wise, pay attention.
    You foolish people, when will you
        become wise?
⁹ Does he who made the ear not hear?
    Does he who formed the eye not see?
¹⁰ Does he who corrects nations not
        punish?
    Does he who teaches human beings
        not know anything?
¹¹ The Lord knows what people think.
    He knows that their thoughts don't
        amount to anything.

¹² Lord, blessed is the person you
        correct.
    Blessed is the person you teach from
        your law.
¹³ You give them rest from times of trouble,
    until a pit is dug to trap sinners.
¹⁴ The Lord won't say no to his people.
    He will never desert those who
        belong to him.
¹⁵ He will again judge people in keeping
        with what is right.
    All those who have honest hearts
        will follow the right way.

¹⁶ Who will rise up for me against sinful
        people?
    Who will stand up for me against
        those who do evil?
¹⁷ Suppose the Lord had not helped me.
    Then I would soon have been lying
        quietly in the grave.
¹⁸ I said, "My foot is slipping."
    But Lord, your faithful love kept me
        from falling.

ADVENTURES IN ODYSSEY

Whit showed a man named Lester how to overcome his worry and fear in "No Way Out" (A#42).

He will destroy them for their evil acts.
The LORD our God will destroy them.

Psalm 95

¹ Come, let us sing for joy to the LORD.
    Let us give a loud shout to the Rock who saves us.
² Let us come to him and give him thanks.
    Let us praise him with music and song.

³ The LORD is the great God.
    He is the greatest King.
    He rules over all the gods.
⁴ He owns the deepest parts of the earth.
    The mountain peaks belong to him.
⁵ The ocean is his, because he made it.
    He formed the dry land with his hands.

⁶ Come, let us bow down and worship him.
    Let us fall on our knees in front of the LORD our Maker.
⁷ He is our God.
    We are the sheep belonging to his flock.
    We are the people he takes good care of.

¹⁹ I was very worried.
    But your comfort brought me joy.

²⁰ Can you have anything to do with rulers who aren't fair?
    Can those who make laws that cause suffering be friends of yours?
²¹ Evil people join together against those who do what is right.
    They sentence to death those who aren't guilty of doing anything wrong.
²² But the LORD has become like a fort to me.
    My God is my rock. I go to him for safety.
²³ He will pay them back for their sins.

WOOTON'S FUN FACTS
Ps. 95:4

I always thought that the Grand Canyon was the biggest in the world. But the *Guinness Book of World Records* says El Canon de Colca in Peru, at 10,574 feet, is the deepest canyon. King's Canyon in California is 8,200 feet deep. The Grand Canyon is only 5,300 feet deep. I guess that's still pretty grand.

If only you would listen to his voice
   today.
8 He says, "Don't be stubborn as you
   were at Meribah.
Don't be stubborn as you were that
   day at Massah in the desert.
9 There your people of long ago really
   tested me.
They did it even though they had
   seen what I had done for
   them.
10 For 40 years I was angry with them.
I said, 'Their hearts are always going
   astray.
They do not know how I want them
   to live.'
11 So when I was angry, I made a
   promise.
I said, 'They will never enjoy the rest
   I planned for them.' "

Psalm 96

1 Sing a new song to the LORD.
All you people of the earth, sing to
   the LORD.
2 Sing to the LORD. Praise him.
Day after day tell about how he saves
   us.

3 Tell the nations about his glory.
Tell all people about the wonderful
   things he has done.

4 The LORD is great. He is really worthy
   of praise.
People should have respect for him
   as the greatest God of all.
5 All the gods of the nations are like their
   statues.
They can't do anything.
But the LORD made the heavens.
6 Glory and majesty are all around him.
Strength and glory can be seen in his
   temple.

7 Praise the LORD, all you nations.
Praise the LORD for his glory and
   strength.
8 Praise the LORD for the glory that
   belongs to him.
Bring an offering and come into the
   courtyards of his temple.
9 Worship the LORD because of his
   beauty and holiness.
All you people of the earth, tremble
   when you are with him.

10 Say to the nations, "The LORD rules."

Do you know any old songs? Can you name one written fifty years ago? How about 100? Do you know any songs that are 1,000 years old? Seriously, does anybody still know melodies that were sung that long ago? Actually, yes. In fact, we know of some that are even older.

Speaking of old songs, do you know that we're still singing Christian hymns written hundreds of years ago? For example, the hymn "A Mighty Fortress is Our God" was written by Martin Luther in the year 1529. It's almost 500 years old and is still sung in many churches today!

Music is an important part of worship. Psalm 96:1–2 encourages us to praise God with our songs. Some tunes remind us of who God is, while others help us say "thank you" to our heavenly Father for loving us enough to send His Son to die for our sins. Christians have many, many songs to sing. Some are ancient. Some are new.

But anything that honors the Lord is music to His ears.

Sing your favorite song! Then do some research and get to know the person or people who wrote it. If you can, find out what was happening in the artist's life when he or she got creative. You might just find out that their stories will encourage you!

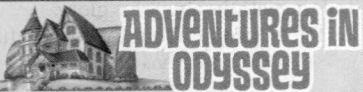

The world is firmly set in place. It
    can't be moved.
The LORD will judge the people of
    the world fairly.
11 Let the heavens be full of joy. Let the
    earth be glad.
    Let the ocean and everything in it
    roar.
12   Let the fields and everything in them
    be glad.
    Let all the trees in the forest sing for joy.
13   Let all creation be full of joy in front
    of the LORD,
    because he is coming to judge the
    earth.
He will faithfully judge the people of
    the world
    in keeping with what is right.

Psalm 97

1 The LORD rules. Let the earth be glad.
    Let countries that are far away be
    full of joy.
2 Clouds and thick darkness surround
    him.
    His rule is built on what is right and
    fair.
3 The LORD sends fire ahead of him.
    It burns up his enemies all around
    him.
4 His lightning lights up the world.
    The earth sees it and trembles.
5 The mountains melt like wax when the
    LORD is near.
    He is the Lord of the whole earth.
6 The heavens announce that what he
    does is right.
    All people everywhere see his glory.
7 All who worship statues of gods or brag
    about them are put to shame.
    All you gods, worship the LORD!
8 Zion hears about it and is filled with joy.
    LORD, the villages of Judah are glad
    because of how you judge.

9 LORD, you are the Most High God.
    You rule over the whole earth.
    You are honored much more than
    all gods.
10 Let those who love the LORD hate evil.
    He guards the lives of those who are
    faithful to him.
    He saves them from the power of
    sinful people.
11 Good things come to those who do
    what is right.
    Joy comes to those whose hearts are
    honest.
12 You who are godly, be glad because of
    what the LORD has done.
    Praise him, because his name is
    holy.

Psalm 98
A psalm.

1 Sing a new song to the LORD.
    He has done wonderful things.
    By the power of his right hand and his
    holy arm
    he has saved his people.
2 The LORD has made known his power
    to save.
    He has shown the nations that he
    does what is right.
3 He has shown his faithful love
    to the people of Israel.
People from one end of the earth to the
    other
    have seen that our God has saved us.
4 Shout for joy to the LORD, everyone on
    earth.
    Burst into joyful songs and make
    music.
5 Make music to the LORD with the harp.
    Sing and make music with the harp.
6 Blow the trumpets. Give a blast on the
    ram's horn.
    Shout for joy to the LORD. He is the
    King.
7 Let the ocean and everything in it roar.
    Let the world and all who live in it
    shout.
8 Let the rivers clap their hands.
    Let the mountains sing together with
    joy.
9 Let them sing to the LORD,
    because he is coming to judge the
    earth.

WOOTON'S FUN FACTS

Ps. 98:5 The verb *harp* can mean two things: (1) "to play on the harp" or (2) "to harp on," which means to talk about something on and on and on. Some people say I harp on about licorice. But I don't mention it that often . . . uh . . . do I?

He will judge the nations of the world
in keeping with what is right and
fair.

Psalm 99

[1] The LORD rules.
Let the nations tremble.
He sits on his throne between the
cherubim.
Let the earth shake.
[2] Great is the LORD in Zion.
He is honored over all the nations.
[3] Let them praise his great and wonderful
name.
He is holy.

[4] The King is mighty and loves justice.
He has set up the rules for fairness.
He has done what is right and fair
for the people of Jacob.
[5] Honor the LORD our God.
Worship at his feet.
He is holy.

[6] Moses and Aaron were two of his
priests.
Samuel was one of those who
worshiped him.
They called out to the LORD.
And he answered them.
[7] He spoke to them from the pillar of
cloud.
They obeyed his laws and the orders
he gave them.

[8] LORD our God, you answered them.
You showed Israel that you are a
God who forgives.
But when they did wrong, you
punished them.
[9] Honor the LORD our God.
Worship at his holy mountain.
The LORD our God is holy.

Psalm 100

A psalm for giving grateful praise.

[1] Shout for joy to the LORD, everyone on
earth.
[2] Worship the LORD with gladness.
Come to him with songs of joy.
[3] Know that the LORD is God.
He made us, and we belong to him.
We are his people.
We are the sheep belonging to his
flock.

[4] Give thanks as you enter the gates of his
temple.
Give praise as you enter its
courtyards.
Give thanks to him and praise his
name.
[5] The LORD is good. His faithful love
continues forever.
It will last for all time to come.

Psalm 101

A psalm of David.

[1] I will sing about your love and fairness.
LORD, I will sing praise to you.
[2] I will be careful to lead a life
that is without blame.
When will you come and help me?

In my own home I will lead a life
that is without blame.
[3] I won't look at anything that is evil
and call it good.

I hate the acts of people who aren't
faithful to you.
I won't have anything to do with
those things.
[4] I will stay away from those whose
hearts are twisted.
I won't have anything to do with
what is evil.

[5] I will get rid of anyone
who tells lies about their neighbor
in secret.

I won't put up with anyone
>> whose eyes and heart are proud.
6 I will look with favor on the faithful
>> people in the land.
>> They will live with me.
>> Those whose lives are without blame
>> will serve me.
7 No one who lies and cheats
>> will live in my house.
No one who tells lies
>> will serve me.
8 Every morning I will get rid of
>> all the sinful people in the land.
I will remove from the city of the LORD
>> everyone who does what is evil.

Psalm 102

A prayer of a suffering person who
has become weak. They pour out
their problems to the LORD.

1 LORD, hear my prayer.
>> Listen to my cry for help.
2 Don't turn your face away from me
>> when I'm in trouble.
Pay attention to me.
>> When I call out for help, answer me
>> quickly.
3 My days are disappearing like smoke.
>> My body burns like glowing coals.
4 My strength has dried up like grass.
>> I even forget to eat my food.
5 I groan out loud because of my suffering.
>> I'm nothing but skin and bones.
6 I'm like a desert owl.
>> I'm like an owl among destroyed
>> buildings.
7 I can't sleep. I've become
>> like a bird alone on a roof.
8 All day long my enemies laugh at me.
>> Those who make fun of me use my
>> name as a curse.
9 I eat ashes as my food.
>> My tears fall into what I'm drinking.
10 You were very angry with me.
>> So you picked me up and threw me
>> away.
11 The days of my life are like an evening
>> shadow.
>> I dry up like grass.
12 But LORD, you are seated on your
>> throne forever.
>> Your fame will continue for all time
>> to come.

13 You will rise up and show deep concern
>> for Zion.
The time has come for you to help
>> Zion.
14 The stones of your destroyed city are
>> priceless to us.
Even its dust brings deep concern
>> to us.
15 The nations will worship the LORD.
>> All the kings on earth will respect
>> his glorious power.
16 The LORD will build Zion again.
>> He will appear in his glory.
17 He will answer the prayer of those who
>> don't have anything.
He won't say no to their cry for help.
18 Let this be written down for those born
>> after us.
Then people who are not yet born
>> can praise the LORD.
19 Here is what should be written.
>> "The LORD looked down from his
>> temple in heaven.
From heaven he viewed the earth.
20 He heard the groans of the prisoners.
>> He set free those who were
>> sentenced to death."
21 So people will talk about him in Zion.
>> They will praise him in Jerusalem.
22 Nations and kingdoms
>> will gather there to worship the
>> LORD.
23 When I was still young, he took away
>> my strength.
He wasn't going to let me live much
>> longer.
24 So I said, "My God, don't let me die in
>> the middle of my life.
You will live for all time to come.
25 In the beginning you made the earth
>> secure.
You placed it on its foundations.
Your hands created the heavens.
26 They will pass away. But you will
>> remain.
They will all wear out like a piece of
>> clothing.
You will make them like clothes
>> that are taken off and thrown away.
27 But you remain the same.
>> Your years will never end.
28 Our children will live with you.
>> Their sons and daughters will be safe
>> in your care."

Psalm 103

A psalm of David.

¹ I will praise the LORD.
  Deep down inside me, I will praise him.
  I will praise him, because his name is holy.
² I will praise the LORD.
  I won't forget anything he does for me.
³ He forgives all my sins.
  He heals all my sicknesses.
⁴ He saves my life from going down into the grave.
  His faithful and tender love makes me feel like a king.
⁵ He satisfies me with the good things I desire.
  Then I feel young and strong again, just like an eagle.

⁶ The LORD does what is right and fair for all who are treated badly.

⁷ He told Moses all about his plans.
  He let the people of Israel see his mighty acts.
⁸ The LORD is tender and kind. He is gracious.
  He is slow to get angry. He is full of love.
⁹ He won't keep bringing charges against us.
  He won't stay angry with us forever.
¹⁰ He doesn't punish us for our sins as much as we should be punished.
  He doesn't pay us back in keeping with the evil things we've done.
¹¹ He loves those who have respect for him.
  His love is as high as the heavens are above the earth.
¹² He has removed our sins from us.
  He has removed them as far as the east is from the west.
¹³ A father is tender and kind to his children.
  In the same way, the LORD is tender and kind
  to those who have respect for him.
¹⁴ He knows what we are made of.
  He remembers that we are dust.
¹⁵ The life of human beings is like grass.
  People grow like the flowers in the field.

ADVENTURES IN ODYSSEY

Whit recited verses from Psalm 103 when he was in trouble in "Stormy Weather" (A#02). He said it reminded him that no matter what happens, God loves us and will do what's best for us.

¹⁶ When the wind blows on them, they are gone.
  No one can tell that they had ever been there.
¹⁷ But the LORD's love
  for those who have respect for him lasts for ever and ever.
  Their children's children will know that he always does what is right.
¹⁸ He always loves those who keep his covenant.
  He always does what is right for those who remember to obey his commands.

¹⁹ The LORD has set up his throne in heaven.
  His kingdom rules over all.

²⁰ Praise the LORD, you angels of his.
  Praise him, you mighty ones who carry out his orders and obey his word.
²¹ Praise the LORD, all you angels in heaven.
  Praise him, all you who serve him and do what he wants.
²² Let everything the LORD has made praise him
  everywhere in his kingdom.

I will praise the LORD.

Psalm 104

¹ I will praise the LORD.

LORD my God, you are very great.
  You are dressed in glory and majesty.
² The LORD wraps himself in light as if it were a robe.
  He spreads out the heavens like a tent.
³ He builds his palace high in the heavens.
  He makes the clouds serve as his chariot.
  He rides on the wings of the wind.

WHIT'S WISDOM

Psalm 104

Eugene enjoys reading Psalm 104 because it's like an encyclopedia of praise. The psalmist praises God for His power, His majesty, His protection, His care, and His provision. He thanks God for all of His creation: the oceans, mountains, grass, trees, cows, birds, food, the sun, the moon, and even sea monsters! The psalmist was certainly serious about worshiping God.

What is worship, anyway? It's praising God for who He is and what He has done. Who do we worship? God and God alone. Nothing else is truly worthy of our worship except God. Why do we worship? We worship God because of His power, His wisdom, and His love for all of us. How can we worship? In many ways: through prayer, song, reading His Word, and by giving, listening, and serving.

Where can we worship? Anywhere! And when? At any time.

Say a little prayer to God. Sing a song in your head. Think of something that God has created or something He has done for you. It certainly won't be hard!

⁴ He makes the winds serve as his
    messengers.
  He makes flashes of lightning serve
    him.
⁵ He placed the earth on its foundations.
  It can never be moved.
⁶ You, LORD, covered it with the oceans
    like a blanket.
  The waters covered the mountains.
⁷ But you commanded the waters, and
    they ran away.
  At the sound of your thunder they
    rushed off.
⁸ They flowed down the mountains.
  They went into the valleys.
  They went to the place you
    appointed for them.
⁹ You drew a line they can't cross.
  They will never cover the earth again.
¹⁰ The LORD makes springs pour water
    into the valleys.
  It flows between the mountains.
¹¹ The springs give water to all the wild
    animals.
  The wild donkeys satisfy their thirst.
¹² The birds in the sky build nests by the
    waters.
  They sing among the branches.
¹³ The LORD waters the mountains from
    his palace high in the clouds.
  The earth is filled with the things he
    has made.

¹⁴ He makes grass grow for the cattle
    and plants for people to take care of.
  That's how they get food from the
    earth.
¹⁵ There is wine to make people glad.
  There is olive oil to make their skin
    glow.
  And there is bread to make them
    strong.
¹⁶ The cedar trees of Lebanon belong to
    the LORD.
  He planted them and gave them
    plenty of water.
¹⁷ There the birds make their nests.
  The stork has its home in the juniper
    trees.
¹⁸ The high mountains belong to the wild
    goats.
  The cliffs are a safe place for the rock
    badgers.
¹⁹ The LORD made the moon to mark off
    the seasons.
  The sun knows when to go down.
²⁰ You, LORD, bring darkness, and it
    becomes night.
  Then all the animals of the forest
    prowl around.
²¹ The lions roar while they hunt.
  All their food comes from God.
²² The sun rises, and they slip away.
  They return to their dens and lie
    down.

²³ Then people get up and go to work.
　They keep working until evening.

²⁴ Lord, you have made so many things!
　How wise you were when you made
　　all of them!
　The earth is full of your creatures.
²⁵ Look at the ocean, so big and wide!
　It is filled with more creatures than
　　people can count.
　It is filled with living things, from
　　the largest to the smallest.
²⁶ Ships sail back and forth on it.
　Leviathan, the sea monster you
　　made, plays in it.

²⁷ All creatures depend on you
　to give them their food when they
　　need it.
²⁸ When you give it to them,
　they eat it.
　When you open your hand,
　　they are satisfied with good things.
²⁹ When you turn your face away from
　　them,
　they are terrified.
　When you take away their breath,
　　they die and turn back into dust.
³⁰ When you send your Spirit,
　you create them.
　You give new life to the ground.

³¹ May the glory of the Lord continue
　forever.

Lawrence taught Jimmy about using
his imagination in "Wonderworld"
(A#15). The writer of Psalm
104 shows the power of God's
imagination in creating the world.

May the Lord be happy with what
　he has made.
³² When he looks at the earth, it trembles.
　When he touches the mountains,
　　they pour out smoke.
³³ I will sing to the Lord all my life.
　I will sing praise to my God as long
　　as I live.
³⁴ May these thoughts of mine please him.
　I find my joy in the Lord.
³⁵ But may sinners be gone from the
　　earth.
　May evil people disappear.

I will praise the Lord.

Praise the Lord.

Psalm 105

¹ Give praise to the Lord and announce
　who he is.
　Tell the nations what he has done.
² Sing to him, sing praise to him.
　Tell about all the wonderful things
　　he has done.
³ Praise him, because his name is holy.
　Let the hearts of those who trust in
　　the Lord be glad.
⁴ Seek the Lord and the strength he gives.
　Always seek him.

⁵ Remember the wonderful things he has
　　done.
　Remember his miracles and how he
　　judged our enemies.
⁶ Remember what he has done, you
　　children of his servant
　　Abraham.
　Remember it, you people of Jacob,
　　God's chosen ones.
⁷ He is the Lord our God.
　He judges the whole earth.

⁸ He will keep his covenant forever.
　He will keep his promise for all time
　　to come.
⁹ He will keep the covenant he made with
　　Abraham.
　He will keep the promise he made
　　to Isaac.
¹⁰ He made it stand as a law for Jacob.
　He made it stand as a covenant for
　　Israel that will last forever.
¹¹ He said, "I will give you the land of
　　Canaan.
　It will belong to you."

¹² At first there weren't very many of
God's people.
There were only a few, and they were
strangers in the land.
¹³ They wandered from nation to nation.
They wandered from one kingdom
to another.
¹⁴ But God didn't allow anyone to treat
them badly.
To keep them safe, he gave a
command to kings.
¹⁵ He said to them, "Do not touch my
anointed ones.
Do not harm my prophets."

¹⁶ He made the people in the land go
hungry.
He destroyed all their food supplies.
¹⁷ He sent a man ahead of them into
Egypt.
That man was Joseph. He had been
sold as a slave.
¹⁸ The Egyptians put his feet in chains.
They put an iron collar around his
neck.
¹⁹ He was in prison until what he said
would happen came true.
The word of the LORD proved that he
was right.
²⁰ The king of Egypt sent for Joseph and
let him out of prison.
The ruler of many nations set him
free.
²¹ He put Joseph in charge of his palace.
He made him ruler over everything
he owned.
²² Joseph was in charge of teaching the
princes.
He taught the elders how to think
and live wisely.

²³ Then the rest of Jacob's family went to
Egypt.
The people of Israel lived as
outsiders in the land of Ham.
²⁴ The LORD gave his people so many
children
that there were too many of them for
their enemies.
²⁵ He made the Egyptians hate his people.
The Egyptians made evil plans
against them.
²⁶ The LORD sent his servant Moses to the
king of Egypt.
He sent Aaron, his chosen one,
along with him.

²⁷ The LORD gave them the power to do
signs among the Egyptians.
They did his wonders in the land of
Ham.
²⁸ The LORD sent darkness over the land.
He did it because the Egyptians had
refused to obey his words.
²⁹ He turned their rivers and streams into
blood.
He caused the fish in them to die.
³⁰ Their land was covered with frogs.
Frogs even went into the bedrooms
of the rulers.
³¹ The LORD spoke, and large numbers of
flies came.
Gnats filled the whole country.
³² He turned their rain into hail.
Lightning flashed all through their
land.
³³ He destroyed their vines and fig trees.
He broke down the trees in Egypt.
³⁴ He spoke, and the locusts came.
There were so many of them they
couldn't be counted.
³⁵ They ate up every green thing in the land.
They ate up what the land produced.
³⁶ Then he killed the oldest son of every
family in Egypt.
He struck down the oldest of all
their sons.

³⁷ He brought the people of Israel out of
Egypt.
The Egyptians loaded them down
with silver and gold.
From among the tribes of Israel no
one got tired or fell down.
³⁸ The Egyptians were glad when the
people of Israel left.
They were terrified because of Israel.
³⁹ The LORD spread out a cloud to cover
his people.
He gave them a fire to light up the
night.
⁴⁰ They asked for meat, and he brought
them quail.
He fed them well with manna, the
bread of heaven.
⁴¹ He broke open a rock, and streams of
water poured out.
They flowed like a river in the desert.
⁴² He remembered the holy promise
he had made to his servant Abraham.
⁴³ His chosen people shouted for joy
as he brought them out of Egypt.

⁴⁴ He gave them the lands of other
>   nations.
>   He let them take over what others
>   had worked for.
⁴⁵ He did it so they might obey his rules
>   and follow his laws.

Praise the LORD.

Psalm 106

¹ Praise the LORD.

Give thanks to the LORD, because he is
>   good.
>   His faithful love continues forever.
² Who can speak enough about the
>   mighty acts of the LORD?
>   Who can praise him as much as he
>   should be praised?
³ Blessed are those who always do what is
>   fair.
>   Blessed are those who keep doing
>   what is right.
⁴ LORD, remember me when you bless
>   your people.
>   Help me when you save them.

⁵ Then I will enjoy the good things you
>   give your chosen ones.
>   I will be joyful together with your
>   people.
>   I will join them when they praise
>   you.

⁶ We have sinned, just as our people of
>   long ago did.
>   We too have done what is evil and
>   wrong.
⁷ When our people were in Egypt,
>   they forgot about the LORD's
>   miracles.
>   They didn't remember his many kind
>   acts.
>   At the Red Sea they refused to obey
>   him.
⁸ But he saved them for the honor of his
>   name.
>   He did it to make his mighty power
>   known.
⁹ He ordered the Red Sea to dry up, and
>   it did.
>   He led his people through it as if it
>   were a desert.

WHAT ABOUT YOU?

Imagine that you're a sculptor. You've been working on a fantastic piece for years. When you finally show it to people, most applaud. But there's one guy who wants to make a small change. So you hand him your tool, and he starts chipping away. Then a woman from the crowd notices a minor imperfection. She starts chipping at your sculpture as well. More people join in. Before long, the sculpture you spent years perfecting is practically unrecognizable.

The same thing can happen to our hearts and minds when we compromise our beliefs. Someone encourages us to change how we think or act. It may seem like a small thing at first. But as we let more and more people chip away at what we believe, they slowly reshape us.

Psalm 106:3 says, "Blessed are those who always do what is fair. Blessed are those who keep doing what is right." The world wants to chip, mold, and shape us a certain way—and it's not God's way. But if we keep doing what is fair and right, we can stand firm when others go soft.

Have you ever heard of Shrinky Dinks? This classic craft starts with a special sheet of flexible plastic that shrinks to one-third the original size—and becomes nine times thicker and stronger! Likewise, when the heat is on, our beliefs will get stronger when we refuse to compromise. See if a local craft store has a Shrinky Dink–like craft your family can do together.

¹⁰ He saved them from the power of their
enemies.
He set them free from their control.
¹¹ The waters covered their enemies.
Not one of them escaped alive.
¹² Then his people believed his promises
and sang praise to him.

¹³ But they soon forgot what he had
done.
They didn't wait for what he had
planned to happen.
¹⁴ In the desert they longed for food.
In that dry and empty land they
tested God.
¹⁵ So he gave them what they asked for.
But he also sent a sickness that killed
many of them.

¹⁶ In their camp some of them became
jealous of Moses and Aaron.
Aaron had been set apart to serve
the Lord.
¹⁷ The ground opened up and swallowed
Dathan.
It buried Abiram and his followers.
¹⁸ Fire blazed among all of them.
Flames destroyed those evil people.

¹⁹ At Mount Horeb they made a metal
statue of a bull calf.
They worshiped that statue of a
god.
²⁰ They traded their glorious God
for a statue of a bull that eats grass.
²¹ They forgot the God who saved them.
They forgot the God who had done
great things in Egypt.
²² They forgot the miracles he did in the
land of Ham.
They forgot the wonderful things he
did by the Red Sea.
²³ So he said he would destroy them.
But Moses, his chosen one,
stood up for them.
He kept God's anger from destroying
them.

²⁴ Later on, they refused to enter the
pleasant land of Canaan.
They didn't believe God's promise.
²⁵ In their tents they told the Lord how
unhappy they were.
They didn't obey him.
²⁶ So he lifted up his hand and promised
that he would make them die in the
desert.

²⁷ He promised he would scatter their
children's children among the
nations.
He would make them die in other
lands.
²⁸ They joined in worshiping the Baal that
was worshiped at Peor.
They ate food that had been offered
to gods that aren't even alive.
²⁹ Their evil ways made the Lord angry.
So a plague broke out among them.
³⁰ But Phinehas stood up and took action.
Then the plague stopped.
³¹ What Phinehas did made him right
with the Lord.
It will be remembered for all time to
come.

³² By the waters of Meribah the Lord's
people made him angry.
Moses got in trouble because of
them.
³³ They refused to obey the Spirit of God.
So Moses spoke without thinking.

³⁴ They didn't destroy the nations in
Canaan
as the Lord had commanded them.
³⁵ Instead, they mixed with those nations
and adopted their ways.
³⁶ They worshiped statues of their gods.
That became a trap for them.
³⁷ They sacrificed their sons and
daughters
as offerings to false gods.
³⁸ They killed those who weren't guilty of
doing anything wrong.
They killed their own sons and
daughters.
They sacrificed them as offerings to
statues of the gods of Canaan.
The land became "unclean" because
of the blood of their children.
³⁹ The people made themselves impure by
what they had done.
They weren't faithful to the Lord.

⁴⁰ So the Lord became angry with his
people.
He turned away from his own
children.
⁴¹ He handed them over to the nations.
Their enemies ruled over them.
⁴² Their enemies treated them badly
and kept them under their power.
⁴³ Many times the Lord saved them.

But they refused to obey him.
So he destroyed them because of
their sins.

[44] Yet he heard them when they cried out.
He paid special attention to their
suffering.
[45] Because they were his people, he
remembered his covenant.
Because of his great love, he felt
sorry for them.
[46] He made all those who held them as
prisoners
have mercy on them.

[47] Lord our God, save us.
Bring us back from among the
nations.
Then we will give thanks to you,
because your name is holy.
We will celebrate by praising you.

[48] Give praise to the Lord, the God of
Israel,
for ever and ever.
Let all the people say, "Amen!"

Praise the Lord.

BOOK V
PSALMS 107–150

Psalm 107

[1] Give thanks to the Lord, because he is
good.
His faithful love continues forever.
[2] Let those who have been set free by the
Lord tell their story.
He set them free from the power of
the enemy.
[3] He brought them back from other lands.
He brought them back from east and
west, from north and south.

[4] Some of them wandered in deserts that
were dry and empty.
They couldn't find a city where they
could make their homes.
[5] They were hungry and thirsty.
Their lives were slipping away.
[6] Then they cried out to the Lord
because of their problems.
And he saved them from their
troubles.
[7] He led them straight
to a city where they could make
their homes.

WOOTON'S FUN FACTS
Ps. 107:1

This is really neat! The psalms are divided into five sections that present roughly two patterns: oldest first but also by topic or author. For example, Psalm 90 is the oldest praise psalm! And Moses wrote it.

[8] Let them give thanks to the Lord for
his faithful love.
Let them give thanks for the
wonderful things he does for
people.
[9] He gives those who are thirsty all the
water they want.
He gives those who are hungry all
the good food they can eat.

[10] Others lived in the deepest darkness.
They suffered as prisoners in iron
chains.
[11] That's because they hadn't obeyed the
commands of God.
They had refused to follow the plans
of the Most High God.
[12] So he made them do work that was
hard and bitter.
They tripped and fell, and there was
no one to help them.
[13] Then they cried out to the Lord
because of their problems.
And he saved them from their
troubles.
[14] He brought them out of the deepest
darkness.
He broke their chains off.
[15] Let them give thanks to the Lord for
his faithful love.
Let them give thanks for the
wonderful things he does for
people.

16 He breaks down gates that are made of
        bronze.
    He cuts through bars that are made
        of iron.
17 Others were foolish. They suffered
        because of their sins.
    They suffered because they wouldn't
        obey the LORD.
18 They refused to eat anything.
    They came close to passing through
        the gates of death.
19 Then they cried out to the LORD
        because of their problems.
    And he saved them from their
        troubles.
20 He gave his command and healed them.
    He saved them from the grave.
21 Let them give thanks to the LORD for
        his faithful love.
    Let them give thanks for the
        wonderful things he does for
        people.
22 Let them sacrifice thank offerings.
    Let them talk about what he has
        done as they sing with joy.
23 Some people sailed out on the ocean in
        ships.
    They traded goods on the mighty
        waters.
24 They saw the works of the LORD.
    They saw the wonderful deeds he
        did on the ocean.
25 He spoke and stirred up a storm.
    It lifted the waves high.
26 They rose up to the heavens. Then they
        went down deep into the ocean.
    In that kind of danger the people's
        boldness melted away.
27 They were unsteady like people who
        have become drunk.
    They didn't know what to do.
28 Then they cried out to the LORD
        because of their problems.
    And he brought them out of their
        troubles.
29 He made the storm as quiet as a whisper.
    The waves of the ocean calmed
        down.
30 The people were glad when the ocean
        became calm.
    Then he guided them to the harbor
        they were looking for.
31 Let them give thanks to the LORD for
        his faithful love.

Let them give thanks for the
        wonderful things he does for
        people.
32 Let them honor him among his people
        who gather for worship.
    Let them praise him in the meeting
        of the elders.
33 He turned rivers into a desert.
    He turned flowing springs into
        thirsty ground.
34 He turned land that produced crops
        into a salty land where nothing
        could grow.
    He did it because the people who
        lived there were evil.
35 He turned the desert into pools of water.
    He turned the dry and cracked
        ground into flowing springs.
36 He brought hungry people there to live.
    They built a city where they could
        make their homes.
37 They planted fields and vineyards
        that produced large crops.
38 He blessed the people, and they greatly
        increased their numbers.
    He kept their herds from getting
        smaller.
39 Then the number of God's people got
        smaller.
    They were made humble by trouble,
        suffering and sorrow.
40 The God who looks down on proud
        nobles
    made them wander in a desert
        where no one lives.
41 But he lifted needy people out of their
        suffering.
    He made their families increase like
        flocks of sheep.
42 Honest people see it and are filled with
        joy.
    But no one who is evil has anything
        to say.
43 Let those who are wise pay attention to
        these things.
    Let them think about the loving
        deeds of the LORD.

Psalm 108
A song. A psalm of David.

1 God, my heart feels secure.
    I will sing and make music to you
        with all my heart.

2 Harp and lyre, wake up!
I want to sing and make music
before the sun rises.
3 LORD, I will praise you among the
nations.
I will sing about you among the
people of the earth.
4 Great is your love. It is higher than the
heavens.
Your truth reaches to the skies.
5 God, may you be honored above the
heavens.
Let your glory be over the whole
earth.

6 Save us. Help us with your powerful
right hand,
so that those you love may be saved.
7 God has spoken from his temple.
He has said, "I will win the battle.
Then I will divide up the land around
Shechem.
I will divide up the Valley of Sukkoth.
8 Gilead belongs to me, and so does the
land of Manasseh.
Ephraim is the strongest tribe. It is
like a helmet for my head.
Judah is the royal tribe. It is like a
ruler's scepter.
9 Moab serves me like one who washes
my feet.
I toss my sandal on Edom to show
that I own it.
I shout to Philistia that I have won
the battle."

10 Who will bring me to the city that has
high walls around it?
Who will lead me to the land of
Edom?
11 God, isn't it you, even though you have
now turned away from us?
Isn't it you, even though you don't
lead our armies into battle
anymore?
12 Help us against our enemies.
The help people give doesn't amount
to anything.
13 With your help we will win the battle.
You will walk all over our enemies.

Psalm 109
For the director of music.
A psalm of David.

1 God, I praise you.
Don't remain silent.

2 Sinful people who lie and cheat have
spoken against me.
They have used their tongues to tell
lies about me.
3 They gather all around me with their
words of hatred.
They attack me without any reason.
4 They bring charges against me,
even though I love them
and pray for them.
5 They pay me back with evil for the
good things I do.
They pay back my love with hatred.

6 Appoint an evil person to take my
enemies to court.
Let him stand at their right hand
and bring charges against
them.
7 When they are tried, let them be found
guilty.
May even their prayers judge them.
8 May their days be few.
Let others take their places as
leaders.
9 May their children's fathers die.
May their wives become widows.
10 May their children be driven from their
destroyed homes.
May they wander around like
beggars.
11 May everything those people own be
taken away to pay for what
they owe.
May strangers rob them of
everything they've worked for.
12 May no one be kind to them
or take pity on the children they
leave behind.
13 May their family line come to an end.
May their names be forgotten by
those who live after them.
14 May the LORD remember the evil things
their fathers have done.
May he never erase the sins of their
mothers.
15 May the LORD never forget their sins.
Then he won't let people remember
the names of my enemies
anymore.

16 They never thought about doing
anything kind.
Instead, they drove those who
were poor and needy to their
deaths.

They did the same thing to those
whose hearts were broken.
¹⁷ They loved to curse others.
May their curses come back on them.
They didn't find any pleasure in giving
anyone their blessing.
May no blessing ever come to them.
¹⁸ They cursed others as easily as they put
on clothes.
Cursing was as natural to them as
getting a drink of water
or putting olive oil on their bodies.
¹⁹ May their curses cover them like coats.
May their curses be wrapped around
them like a belt forever.
²⁰ May that be the Lord's way of paying
back
those who bring charges against me.
May it happen to those who say
evil things about me.

²¹ But Lord and King,
help me so that you bring honor to
yourself.
Because your love is so good, save
me.
²² I am poor and needy.
My heart is wounded deep down
inside me.
²³ I fade away like an evening shadow.
I'm like a locust that someone
brushes off.
²⁴ My knees are weak because I've gone
without food.
My body is very thin.
²⁵ Those who bring charges against me
laugh at me.
When they see me, they shake their
heads at me.
²⁶ Lord my God, help me.
Save me because of your faithful
love.
²⁷ Lord, let my enemies know that you
yourself have saved me.
You have done it with your own
hand.
²⁸ They may curse me.
But may you bless me.
May those who attack me be put to
shame.
But may I be filled with joy.
²⁹ May those who bring charges against
me be clothed with dishonor.
May they be wrapped in shame as if
it were a coat.

³⁰ With my mouth I will continually
praise the Lord.
I will praise him when all his people
gather for worship.
³¹ He stands ready to help those who
need it.
He saves them from those who are
ready to sentence them to
death.

Psalm 110

A psalm of David.

¹ The Lord says to my lord,
"Sit at my right hand
until I put your enemies
under your control."

² The Lord will make your royal
authority spread out from
Zion to other lands.
He says, "Rule over your enemies
who are all around you."
³ Your troops will be willing to fight for
you
on the day of battle.
Your young men will be wrapped in
holy majesty.
They will come to you like the fresh
dew that falls early in the
morning.

⁴ The Lord has made a promise.
He will not change his mind.
He has said, "You are a priest forever,
just like Melchizedek."

⁵ The Lord is at your right hand.
He will crush kings on the day when
he is angry.
⁶ He will judge the nations. He will pile
up dead bodies on the field of
battle.
He will crush the rulers of the whole
earth.
⁷ He will drink from a brook along the
way and receive new strength.
And so he will win the battle.

Psalm 111

¹ Praise the Lord.

I will praise the Lord with all my heart.
I will praise him where honest
people gather for worship.

² The Lord has done great things.
All who take delight in those things
think deeply about them.

³ What he does shows his glory and
majesty.
     He will always do what is right.
⁴ The Lord causes his wonders to be
remembered.
     He is kind and tender.
⁵ He provides food for those who have
respect for him.
     He remembers his covenant forever.
⁶ He has shown his people what his
power can do.
     He has given them the lands of other
nations.
⁷ He is faithful and right in everything he
does.
     All his rules can be trusted.
⁸ They will stand firm for ever and ever.
     They were given by the Lord.
     He is faithful and honest.
⁹ He set his people free.
     He made a covenant with them that
will last forever.
     His name is holy and wonderful.

¹⁰ If you really want to become wise,
you must begin by having respect
for the Lord.
     All those who follow his rules have
good understanding.
     People should praise him forever.

Psalm 112

¹ Praise the Lord.

Blessed are those who have respect for
the Lord.
     They find great delight when they
obey God's commands.

² Their children will be powerful in the
land.
     Because they are honest, their
children will be blessed.

Jason's Jargon

PSALM 112

Your assignment: Locate *grind* in this chapter. To grind your teeth means to rub them together, usually in anger. If something is out of your control, you may grind your teeth in frustration.

Ps. 112:4 In 1988, President-elect George H. W. Bush asked Americans to be a "kinder, gentler nation." Do you think he had this verse in mind? I used to ask my English teacher to be "kinder and gentler" before reading my essays.

³ Their family will have wealth and
riches.
     They will always be blessed for doing
what is right.
⁴ Even in the darkness light shines on
honest people.
     It shines on those who are kind and
tender and godly.
⁵ Good things will come to those who are
willing to lend freely.
     Good things will come to those
who are fair in everything
they do.
⁶ Those who do what is right will always
be secure.
     They will be remembered forever.
⁷ They aren't afraid when bad news
comes.
     They stand firm because they trust
in the Lord.
⁸ Their hearts are secure. They aren't
afraid.
     In the end they will see their
enemies destroyed.
⁹ They have spread their gifts around to
poor people.
     Their good works continue forever.
     They will be powerful and honored.

¹⁰ Evil people will see it and be upset.
     They will grind their teeth and
become weaker and weaker.
     What evil people long to do can't
succeed.

Psalm 113

¹ Praise the LORD.

Praise him, you who serve the LORD.
   Praise the name of the LORD.
² Let us praise the name of the LORD,
   both now and forever.
³ From the sunrise in the east to the
     sunset in the west,
   may the name of the LORD be praised.

⁴ The LORD is honored over all the nations.
   His glory reaches to the highest
     heavens.
⁵ Who is like the LORD our God?
   He sits on his throne in heaven.
⁶ He bends down to look
   at the heavens and the earth.

⁷ He raises poor people up from the trash
     pile.
   He lifts needy people out of the ashes.
⁸ He causes them to sit with princes.
   He causes them to sit with the
     princes of his people.
⁹ He gives children to the woman who
     doesn't have any children.
   He makes her a happy mother in her
     own home.

Praise the LORD.

Psalm 114

¹ The people of Israel came out of Egypt.
   The people of Jacob left a land
     where a different language was
     spoken.
² Then Judah became the holy place
     where God lived.
   Israel became the land he ruled over.

³ The Red Sea saw him and parted.
   The Jordan River stopped flowing.
⁴ The mountains leaped like rams.
   The hills skipped like lambs.

⁵ Red Sea, why did you part?
   Jordan River, why did you stop
     flowing?
⁶ Why did you mountains leap like rams?
   Why did you hills skip like lambs?

⁷ Earth, tremble with fear when the Lord
     comes.
   Tremble when the God of Jacob is
     near.
⁸ He turned the rock into a pool.
   He turned the hard rock into springs
     of water.

Psalm 115

¹ LORD, may glory be given to you, not to
     us.
   You are loving and faithful.

² Why do the nations ask,
   "Where is their God?"
³ Our God is in heaven.
   He does anything he wants to do.
⁴ But the statues of their gods are made
     out of silver and gold.
   They are made by human hands.
⁵ They have mouths but can't speak.
   They have eyes but can't see.
⁶ They have ears but can't hear.
   They have noses but can't smell.
⁷ They have hands but can't feel.
   They have feet but can't walk.
   They have throats but can't say
     anything.
⁸ Those who make statues of gods will be
     like them.
   So will all those who trust in them.

⁹ All you Israelites, trust in the LORD.
   He helps you like a shield that keeps
     you safe.
¹⁰ Priests of Aaron, trust in the LORD.
   He helps you like a shield that keeps
     you safe.
¹¹ You who have respect for the LORD,
     trust in him.
   He helps you like a shield that keeps
     you safe.

¹² The LORD remembers us and will bless
     us.
   He will bless Israel, his people.
   He will bless the priests of Aaron.
¹³ The LORD will bless those who have
     respect for him.
   He will bless important and
     unimportant people alike.

¹⁴ May the LORD give you many children.
   May he give them to you and to your
     children after you.
¹⁵ May the LORD bless you.
   He is the Maker of heaven and
     earth.

¹⁶ The highest heavens belong to the
     LORD.
   But he has given the earth to human
     beings.
¹⁷ Dead people don't praise the LORD.
   Those who lie quietly in the grave
     don't praise him.

¹⁸ But we who are alive praise the LORD,
both now and forever.

Praise the LORD.

Psalm 116

¹ I love the LORD, because he heard my
voice.
He heard my cry for his help.
² Because he paid attention to me,
I will call out to him as long as I live.

³ The ropes of death were wrapped
around me.
The horrors of the grave came over
me.
I was overcome by sadness and
sorrow.
⁴ Then I called out to the LORD.
I cried out, "LORD, save me!"

⁵ The LORD is holy and kind.
Our God is full of tender love.
⁶ The LORD takes care of those who are
not aware of danger.
When I was in great need, he saved
me.

⁷ I said to myself, "Be calm.
The LORD has been good to me."

⁸ LORD, you have saved me from death.
You have dried the tears from my
eyes.
You have kept me from tripping and
falling.
⁹ So now I can enjoy life here with you
while I'm still living.
¹⁰ I trusted in the LORD even when I said
to myself,
"I am in great pain."
¹¹ When I was terrified, I said to myself,
"No one tells the truth."

¹² The LORD has been so good to me!
How can I ever pay him back?
¹³ I will bring an offering of wine to the
LORD
and thank him for saving me.
I will worship him.
¹⁴ In front of all the LORD's people,
I will do what I promised him.

¹⁵ The LORD pays special attention
when his faithful people die.
¹⁶ LORD, I serve you.
I serve you just as my mother did.
You have set me free from the chains
of my suffering.

¹⁷ LORD, I will sacrifice a thank offering to
you.
I will worship you.
¹⁸ In front of all the LORD's people,
I will do what I promised him.
¹⁹ I will keep my promise in the
courtyards of the LORD's
temple.
I will keep my promise in Jerusalem
itself.

Praise the LORD.

Psalm 117

¹ All you nations, praise the LORD.
All you people on earth, praise him.
² Great is his love for us.
The LORD is faithful forever.

Praise the LORD.

Psalm 118

¹ Give thanks to the LORD, because he is
good.
His faithful love continues forever.

² Let the people of Israel say,
"His faithful love continues forever."
³ Let the priests of Aaron say,
"His faithful love continues forever."
⁴ Let those who have respect for the
LORD say,
"His faithful love continues forever."

⁵ When I was in great trouble, I cried out
to the LORD.

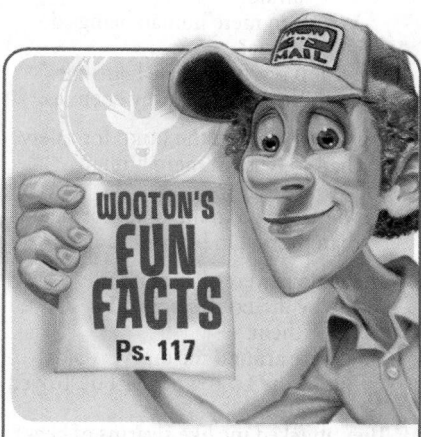

WOOTON'S FUN FACTS
Ps. 117

Memorize Psalm 117 and you can say "I know
a chapter of the Bible by heart." It's only two
verses. But if you memorize Psalm 119, you
can say, "I know the *longest* chapter by heart."

WHAT ABOUT YOU?

Who is shaping the way you think? As much as we'd like to believe that our thoughts are not being shaped by other people, they are. Our friends. Our parents. Even the shows we watch on TV can influence the person we're becoming.

In the Adventures in Odyssey episode "The One about Trust," Connie has a lot of different messages coming her way. Of course, Mr. Whittaker has had a huge impact on her life, including her beliefs, but when she starts working with Margaret Faye, Connie's opinions are challenged. She doesn't know who or what to believe.

We all face decisions like Connie's. Whom we trust for advice is very important, whether it involves personal decisions, how we view other people, or what we think of the Bible. If we trust the wrong people, we might be led astray from God's Word or believe things about ourselves that aren't true.

People may disappoint us, but we'll never go wrong if we rely on God to shape our thinking and lead us in the right direction. As it says in Psalm 118:8, "It is better to go to the LORD for safety than to trust in mere human beings."

Who has been shaping your beliefs lately? Are those friends, teachers, authors, or entertainers trustworthy? Today, make a list of the voices that try to influence your behavior, including commercials and advertisements. What are they saying to you, and why? How do those messages compare with what God says in the Bible?

He answered me and set me free
    from my trouble.
⁶ The LORD is with me. I will not be
    afraid.
    What can mere human beings do
    to me?
⁷ The LORD is with me. He helps me.
    I win the battle over my enemies.

⁸ It is better to go to the LORD for safety
    than to trust in mere human
    beings.
⁹ It is better to go to the LORD for safety
    than to trust in human leaders.

¹⁰ The nations were all around me.
    But by the LORD's power I destroyed
    them.
¹¹ They were around me on every side.
    But by the LORD's power I destroyed
    them.
¹² They attacked me like swarms of bees.
    But they were burned up as quickly
    as thorns in a fire.
    By the LORD's power I destroyed
    them.

¹³ I was pushed back and about to be
    killed.
    But the LORD helped me.
¹⁴ The LORD gives me strength and makes
    me secure.
    He has saved me.

¹⁵ Shouts of joy ring out in the tents of
    godly people.
    They praise him for his help in
    battle.
    They shout, "The LORD's powerful right
    hand has done mighty things!
¹⁶   The LORD's powerful right hand has
    won the battle!
    The LORD's powerful right hand has
    done mighty things!"

¹⁷ I will not die but live.
    I will talk about what the LORD has
    done.
¹⁸ The LORD has really punished me.
    But he didn't let me die.
¹⁹ Open for me the gates where the godly
    can go in.

As Kids' Radio reported about a "typical day" at Whit's End, Whit talked about enjoying what God can do each and every day in our lives in "It's a Wrap!" (A#28).

I will enter and give thanks to the LORD.

²⁰ This is the gate of the LORD.
Only those who do what is right can go through it.

²¹ LORD, I will give thanks to you, because you answered me.
You have saved me.

²² The stone the builders didn't accept has become the most important stone of all.

²³ The LORD has done it.
It is wonderful in our eyes.

²⁴ The LORD has done it on this day.
Let us be joyful today and be glad.

²⁵ LORD, save us.
LORD, give us success.

²⁶ Blessed is the one who comes in the name of the LORD.
From the temple of the LORD we bless you.

²⁷ The LORD is God.
He has been good to us.
Take branches in your hands. Join in the march on the day of the feast.
March up to the corners of the altar.

²⁸ You are my God, and I will praise you.
You are my God, and I will honor you.

²⁹ Give thanks to the LORD, because he is good.
His faithful love continues forever.

Psalm 119

א Aleph

¹ Blessed are those who live without blame.
They live in keeping with the law of the LORD.

² Blessed are those who obey his covenant laws.
They trust in him with all their hearts.

³ They don't do anything wrong.
They live as he wants them to live.

⁴ You have given me rules
that I must obey completely.

⁵ I hope I will always stand firm
in following your orders.

⁶ Then I won't be put to shame
when I think about all your commands.

⁷ I will praise you with an honest heart
as I learn about how fair your decisions are.

⁸ I will obey your orders.
Please don't leave me all alone.

ב Beth

⁹ How can a young person keep their life pure?
By living according to your word.

¹⁰ I trust in you with all my heart.
Don't let me wander away from your commands.

¹¹ I have hidden your word in my heart
so that I won't sin against you.

¹² LORD, I give praise to you.
Teach me your orders.

¹³ With my lips I talk about
all the decisions you have made.

¹⁴ Following your covenant laws gives me joy
just as great riches give joy to others.

¹⁵ I spend time thinking about your rules.
I consider how you want me to live.

¹⁶ I take delight in your orders.
I won't fail to obey your word.

ג Gimel

¹⁷ Be good to me while I am alive.
Do this so that I may obey your word.

¹⁸ Open my eyes so that I can see
the wonderful truths in your law.

¹⁹ I'm a stranger on earth.
Don't hide your commands from me.

REMEMBER THIS

PSALM 119:9

"How can a young person keep their life pure? By living according to your word."

Kids' Radio showed the value of learning and memorizing Scripture through Rescue 119, Laffy the Wonder Dog, as well as a journey to a mysterious planet, in "Hidden in My Heart" (A#26).

20 My heart is filled with longing
  for your laws at all times.
21 You correct proud people. They are
      under your curse.
  They wander away from your
      commands.
22 I obey your covenant laws.
  So don't let evil people laugh at me
      or hate me.
23 Even if rulers sit together and tell lies
      about me,
  I will spend time thinking about
      your orders.
24 Your covenant laws are my delight.
  They give me wise advice.

ד Daleth

25 I lie in the dust. I'm about to die.
  Keep me alive as you have promised.
26 I told you how I've lived, and you gave
      me your answer.
  Teach me your orders.
27 Help me understand how your rules
      direct me to live.

Then I may think deeply about the
      wonderful things you have
      done.
28 My sadness has worn me out.
  Give me strength as you have
      promised.
29 Keep me from cheating and telling lies.
  Be kind to me and teach me your law.
30 I have chosen to be faithful to you.
  I put my trust in your laws.
31 LORD, I'm careful to obey your
      covenant laws.
  Don't let me be put to shame.
32 I am quick to follow your commands,
  because you have added to my
      understanding.

ה He

33 LORD, teach me how your orders direct
      me to live.
  Then I will live that way to the very
      end.
34 Help me understand your law so that I
      may follow it.
  I will obey it with all my heart.
35 Teach me to live as you command,
  because that makes me very happy.
36 Make me want to follow your covenant
      laws
  instead of wanting to gain things
      only for myself.
37 Turn my eyes away from things that are
      worthless.
  Keep me alive as you have promised.
38 Keep your promise to me.
  Then other people will have respect
      for you.
39 Please don't let me be put to shame.
  Your laws are good.
40 I really want to follow your rules.
  Keep me alive, because you do what
      is right.

ו Waw

41 LORD, show me your faithful love.
  Save me as you have promised.
42 Then I can answer anyone who makes
      fun of me,
  because I trust in your word.
43 Help me always to tell the truth about
      how faithful you are.
  I have put my hope in your laws.
44 I will always obey your law,
  for ever and ever.

REMEMBER THIS

PSALM 119:11

"I have hidden your word in my heart so that I won't sin against you."

WOOTON'S FUN FACTS

Ps. 119:51

Does anyone ever make fun of you for doing the right thing? I know that my brother, Wellington, does. Read this psalm and I'm guessing you'll stand a little taller.

⁴⁵ I will lead a full and happy life,
  because I've tried to obey your
  rules.
⁴⁶ I will talk about your covenant laws to
  kings.
  I will not be put to shame.
⁴⁷ I take delight in obeying your
  commands
  because I love them.
⁴⁸ I reach out for your commands that I
  love.
  I do this so that I may think deeply
  about your orders.

ז Zayin

⁴⁹ Remember what you have said to me.
  You have given me hope.
⁵⁰ Even when I suffer, I am comforted
  because you promised to keep me
  alive.
⁵¹ Proud people make fun of me without
  mercy.
  But I don't turn away from your law.
⁵² Lord, I remember the laws you gave
  long ago.
  I find comfort in them.
⁵³ I am very angry
  because evil people have turned
  away from your law.
⁵⁴ No matter where I live,
  I sing about your orders.

⁵⁵ Lord, during the night I remember
  who you are.
  That's why I keep your law.
⁵⁶ I have really done my best
  to obey your rules.

ח Heth

⁵⁷ Lord, you are everything I need.
  I have promised to obey your words.
⁵⁸ I have looked to you with all my heart.
  Be kind to me as you have
  promised.
⁵⁹ I have thought about the way I live.
  And I have decided to follow your
  covenant laws.
⁶⁰ I won't waste any time.
  I will be quick to obey your
  commands.
⁶¹ Evil people may tie me up with ropes.
  But I won't forget to obey your law.
⁶² At midnight I get up to give you
  thanks
  because your decisions are very fair.
⁶³ I'm a friend to everyone who has
  respect for you.
  I'm a friend to everyone who follows
  your rules.
⁶⁴ Lord, the earth is filled with your love.
  Teach me your orders.

ט Teth

⁶⁵ Lord, be good to me
  as you have promised.
⁶⁶ Increase my knowledge and give me
  good sense,
  because I trust your commands.
⁶⁷ Before I went through suffering, I went
  down the wrong path.
  But now I obey your word.
⁶⁸ You are good, and what you do is good.
  Teach me your orders.
⁶⁹ The lies of proud people have taken
  away my good name.
  But I follow your rules with all my
  heart.
⁷⁰ Their unfeeling hearts are hard and
  stubborn.
  But I take delight in your law.
⁷¹ It was good for me to suffer.
  That's what helped me to understand
  your orders.
⁷² The law you gave is worth more to me
  than thousands of pieces of silver
  and gold.

י Yodh

⁷³ You made me and formed me with your own hands.
     Give me understanding so that I can learn your commands.
⁷⁴ May those who have respect for you be filled with joy when they see me.
     I have put my hope in your word.
⁷⁵ LORD, I know that your laws are right.
     You were faithful to your promise when you made me suffer.
⁷⁶ May your faithful love comfort me as you have promised me.
⁷⁷ Show me your tender love so that I can live.
     I take delight in your law.
⁷⁸ May proud people be put to shame for treating me badly for no reason.
     I will think deeply about your rules.
⁷⁹ May those who have respect for you come to me.
     Then I can teach them your covenant laws.
⁸⁰ May I follow your orders with all my heart.
     Then I won't be put to shame.

כ Kaph

⁸¹ I deeply long for you to save me.
     I have put my hope in your word.
⁸² My eyes grow tired looking for what you have promised.
     I say, "When will you comfort me?"
⁸³ I'm as useless as a wineskin that smoke has dried up.
     But I don't forget to follow your orders.
⁸⁴ How long do I have to wait?
     When will you punish those who attack me?
⁸⁵ Proud people do what is against your law.
     They dig pits for me to fall into.
⁸⁶ All your commands can be trusted.
     Help me, because people attack me without any reason.
⁸⁷ They almost wiped me off the face of the earth.
     But I have not turned away from your rules.
⁸⁸ Keep me alive, because of your faithful love.

     Do this so that I may obey the covenant laws you have given.

ל Lamedh

⁸⁹ LORD, your word lasts forever.
     It stands firm in the heavens.
⁹⁰ You will be faithful for all time to come.
     You made the earth, and it continues to exist.
⁹¹ Your laws continue to this very day, because all things serve you.
⁹² If I had not taken delight in your law, I would have died because of my suffering.
⁹³ I will never forget your rules.
     You have kept me alive, because I obey them.
⁹⁴ Save me, because I belong to you.
     I've tried to obey your rules.
⁹⁵ Sinful people are waiting to destroy me.
     But I will spend time thinking about your covenant laws.
⁹⁶ I've learned that everything has its limits.
     But your commands are perfect.
     They are always there when I need them.

מ Mem

⁹⁷ LORD, I really love your law!
     All day long I spend time thinking about it.

Ps. 119 The breaks in this chapter are the English names of the letters in the ancient Hebrew alphabet. In the original language, the first word of each section began with that letter. Sort of like "Wooton wore wonderful wigs." Actually, I guess that would be the first letter of every *word*. But you get the idea, don't you?

Why do we need to memorize things anyway? State capitals. Computer passwords. Bible verses. In the Adventures In Odyssey episode "Hidden in My Heart," the gang puts together a series of TV show parodies to remind us that God's Word is more powerful than a phaser gun, more helpful than an emergency services phone operator, and more dependable than a spiritual Wonder Dog. To have God's Word when we need it, we can commit verses to memory—even in a world where Bible passages are just a few clicks away online.

In his book *How to Be Born Again*, Rev. Billy Graham tells of a woman who was imprisoned in a Chinese concentration camp. The Bible was forbidden there, but this missionary managed to memorize the entire Gospel of John before disposing of it, one page at a time. When the prisoners were finally released, most had lost hope. But the missionary lady survived surprisingly well.

Psalm 119:11 tells us to carry God's Word in our heart, because when we take time to memorize Bible verses, God's Word helps us see the world His way—and make right decisions in tough times. God is faithful to remind us of those verses just when we need them most.

Hide God's Word in your heart. Start by memorizing Psalm 119:11. Read it out loud three times. Then see how many words you can remember without looking at the verse. Keep trying until you've got all the words safely tucked away.

---

[98] Your commands make me wiser than
     my enemies,
  because your commands are always
     in my heart.
[99] I know more than all my teachers do,
  because I spend time thinking about
     your covenant laws.
[100] I understand more than the elders do,
  because I obey your rules.
[101] I've kept my feet from every path that
     sinners take
  so that I might obey your word.
[102] I haven't turned away from your laws,
  because you yourself have taught me.
[103] Your words are very sweet to my taste!
  They are sweeter than honey to me.
[104] I gain understanding from your rules.
  So I hate every path that sinners take.

נ Nun

[105] Your word is like a lamp that shows me
     the way.
  It is like a light that guides me.

[106] I have made a promise
  to follow your laws, because they are
     right.
[107] I have suffered very much.
  LORD, keep me alive as you have
     promised.
[108] LORD, accept the praise I freely give you.
  Teach me your laws.
[109] I keep putting my life in danger.
  But I won't forget to obey your law.
[110] Evil people have set a trap for me.
  But I haven't wandered away from
     your rules.
[111] Your covenant laws are your gift to me
     forever.
  They fill my heart with joy.
[112] I have decided to obey your orders
  to the very end.

ס Samekh

[113] I hate people who can't make up their
     minds.
  But I love your law.

REMEMBER THIS

PSALM 119:105

"Your word is like a lamp that shows me the way. It is like a light that guides me."

114 You are my place of safety.
    You are like a shield that keeps me safe.
    I have put my hope in your word.
115 Get away from me, you who do evil!
    Then I can do what my God commands me to do.
116 My God, keep me going as you have promised. Then I will live.
    Don't let me lose all hope.
117 Take good care of me, and I will be saved.
    I will always honor your orders.
118 You turn your back on all those who wander away from your orders.
    Their wrong thoughts will be proved to be wrong.
119 You throw away all the sinners on earth as if they were trash.
    So I love your covenant laws.
120 My body trembles because I have respect for you.
    I have great respect for your laws.

ע Ayin

121 I have done what is right and fair.
    So don't leave me to those who treat me badly.
122 Make sure that everything goes well with me.
    Don't let proud people treat me badly.
123 My eyes grow tired as I look to you to save me.
    Please save me as you have promised.
124 Be good to me, because you love me.
    Teach me your orders.
125 I serve you, so help me to understand what is right.
    Then I will understand your covenant laws.
126 LORD, it's time for you to act.
    People are breaking your law.
127 I love your commands more than gold.
    I love them more than pure gold.

128 I consider all your rules to be right.
    So I hate every path that sinners take.

פ Pe

129 Your covenant laws are wonderful.
    So I obey them.
130 When your words are made clear, they bring light.
    They bring understanding to childish people.
131 I open my mouth and pant like a dog, because I long to know your commands.
132 Turn to me and have mercy on me.
    That's what you've always done for those who love you.
133 Teach me how to live as you have promised.
    Don't let any sin be my master.
134 Set me free from people who treat me badly.
    Then I will obey your rules.
135 Have mercy on me.
    Teach me your orders.
136 Streams of tears flow from my eyes, because people don't obey your law.

צ Tsadhe

137 LORD, you do what is fair.
    And your laws are right.
138 The laws you have made are fair.
    They can be completely trusted.
139 My anger is wearing me out, because my enemies don't pay any attention to your words.
140 Your promises have proved to be true.
    I love them.
141 I'm not important. People look down on me.
    But I don't forget to obey your rules.
142 You always do what is right.
    And your law is true.
143 I've had my share of trouble and suffering.
    But your commands give me delight.
144 Your covenant laws are always right.
    Help me to understand them. Then I will live.

ק Qoph

145 LORD, I call out to you with all my heart.
    Answer me, and I will obey your orders.

¹⁴⁶ I call out to you.
Save me, and I will keep your
covenant laws.
¹⁴⁷ I get up before the sun rises. I cry out
for help.
I've put my hope in your word.
¹⁴⁸ My eyes stay open all night long.
I spend my time thinking about your
promises.
¹⁴⁹ Listen to me, because you love me.
LORD, keep me alive as you have
promised.
¹⁵⁰ Those who think up evil plans are near.
They have wandered far away from
your law.
¹⁵¹ But LORD, you are near.
All your commands are true.
¹⁵² Long ago I learned from your covenant
laws
that you made them to last forever.

ר Resh

¹⁵³ Look at how I'm suffering!
Save me, because I haven't forgotten
to obey your law.
¹⁵⁴ Stand up for me and set me free.
Keep me alive as you have promised.
¹⁵⁵ Those who are evil are far from being
saved.
They don't want to obey your
orders.
¹⁵⁶ LORD, you have deep concern for me.
Keep me alive as you have promised.
¹⁵⁷ Many enemies attack me.
But I haven't turned away from your
covenant laws.
¹⁵⁸ I get very angry when I see people who
aren't faithful to you.
They don't obey your word.
¹⁵⁹ See how I love your rules!
LORD, keep me alive, because you
love me.
¹⁶⁰ All your words are true.
All your laws are right. They last
forever.

ש Sin and Shin

¹⁶¹ Rulers attack me for no reason.
But I tremble because of your word.
¹⁶² I'm filled with joy because of your
promise.
It's like finding a great fortune.
¹⁶³ I hate lies with a deep hatred.
But I love your law.

¹⁶⁴ Seven times a day I praise you
for your laws, because they are right.
¹⁶⁵ Those who love your law enjoy great
peace.
Nothing can make them trip and fall.
¹⁶⁶ LORD, I wait for you to save me.
I follow your commands.
¹⁶⁷ I obey your covenant laws,
because I love them greatly.
¹⁶⁸ I obey your rules and your covenant
laws,
because you know all about how I
live.

ת Taw

¹⁶⁹ LORD, may you hear my cry.
Give me understanding, just as you
said you would.
¹⁷⁰ May you hear my prayer.
Save me, just as you promised.
¹⁷¹ May my lips pour out praise to you,
because you teach me your orders.
¹⁷² May my tongue sing about your word,
because all your commands are right.
¹⁷³ May your hand be ready to help me,
because I have chosen to obey your
rules.
¹⁷⁴ LORD, I long for you to save me.
Your law gives me delight.
¹⁷⁵ Let me live so that I can praise you.
May your laws keep me going.
¹⁷⁶ Like a lost sheep, I've gone down the
wrong path.
Come and look for me,
because I haven't forgotten to obey
your commands.

Psalm 120

A song for those who go up to
Jerusalem to worship the LORD.

¹ I call out to the LORD when I'm in
trouble,
and he answers me.
² LORD, save me from people whose lips
tell lies.
Save me from people whose tongues
don't tell the truth.

³ What will the LORD do to you, you
lying tongue?
And what more will he do?
⁴ He will punish you with the sharp
arrows of a soldier.
He will punish you with burning
coals from a desert bush.

⁵ How terrible it is for me to live in the
     tents of the people of Meshek!
     How terrible to live in the tents of
     the people of Kedar!
⁶ I have lived too long
     among those who hate peace.
⁷ I want peace.
     But when I speak, they want war.

Psalm 121

A song for those who go up to
Jerusalem to worship the LORD.

¹ I look up to the mountains.
     Where does my help come from?
² My help comes from the LORD.
     He is the Maker of heaven and
     earth.

³ He won't let your foot slip.
     He who watches over you won't get
     tired.
⁴ In fact, he who watches over Israel
     won't get tired or go to sleep.

⁵ The LORD watches over you.
     The LORD is like a shade tree at your
     right hand.
⁶ The sun won't harm you during the day.
     The moon won't harm you during
     the night.

⁷ The LORD will keep you from every
     kind of harm.
     He will watch over your life.
⁸ The LORD will watch over your life no
     matter where you go,
     both now and forever.

Psalm 122

A song for those who go up to Jerusalem
to worship the LORD. A psalm of David.

¹ I was very glad when they said to me,
     "Let us go up to the house of the
     LORD."
² Jerusalem, our feet are standing
     inside your gates.

³ Jerusalem is built like a city
     where everything is close together.
⁴ The tribes of the LORD go there to
     praise his name.
     They do it in keeping with the law he
     gave to Israel.
⁵ The thrones of the family line of David
     are there.
     That's where the people are judged.

⁶ Pray for the peace of Jerusalem. Say,
     "May those who love you be secure.
⁷ May there be peace inside your walls.
     May your people be kept safe."
⁸ I'm concerned for my family and
     friends.
     So I say to Jerusalem, "May you
     enjoy peace."
⁹ I'm concerned about the house of the
     LORD our God.
     So I pray that things will go well
     with Jerusalem.

Psalm 123

A song for those who go up to
Jerusalem to worship the LORD.

¹ I look up and pray to you.
     Your throne is in heaven.
² Slaves depend on their masters.
     A female slave depends on the
     woman she works for.
In the same way, we depend on the
     LORD our God.
     We wait for him to have mercy on
     us.

³ LORD, have mercy on us. Have mercy
     on us,
     because people haven't stopped
     making fun of us.
⁴ We have had to put up with a lot from
     those who are proud.
     They were always laughing at us.

Psalm 124

A song for those who go up
to Jerusalem to worship the
LORD. A psalm of David.

¹ Here is what Israel should say.
     Suppose the LORD had not been on
     our side.
² Suppose the LORD had not been on our
     side
     when our enemies attacked us.
³ Suppose he had not been on our side
     when their burning anger blazed out
     against us.
     Then they would have swallowed us
     alive.
⁴ They would have been like a flood that
     drowned us.
     They would have swept over us like a
     rushing river.
⁵ They would have washed us away
     like a swollen stream.

⁶ Give praise to the LORD.
 He has not let our enemies chew us
 up.
⁷ We have escaped like a bird
 from a hunter's trap.
 The trap has been broken,
 and we have escaped.
⁸ Our help comes from the LORD.
 He is the Maker of heaven and
 earth.

Psalm 125

A song for those who go up to
Jerusalem to worship the LORD.

¹ Those who trust in the LORD are like
 Mount Zion.
 They will always be secure. They will
 last forever.
² Like the mountains around Jerusalem,
 the LORD is all around his people
 both now and forever.

³ Evil people will not always rule
 the land the LORD gave to those who
 do right.
 If they did, those who do right
 might do what is evil.

⁴ LORD, do good to those who are good.
 Do good to those whose hearts are
 honest.
⁵ But the LORD will drive out those who
 have taken crooked paths.
 He will drive them out with those
 who do evil things.

May Israel enjoy peace.

Psalm 126

A song for those who go up to
Jerusalem to worship the LORD.

¹ Our enemies took us away from Zion.
 But when the LORD brought us
 home,
 it seemed like a dream to us.
² Our mouths were filled with laughter.
 Our tongues sang with joy.
 Then the people of other nations said,
 "The LORD has done great things for
 them."
³ The LORD has done great things for us.
 And we are filled with joy.

⁴ LORD, bless us with great success again,
 as rain makes streams flow in the
 Negev Desert.

⁵ Those who cry as they plant their
 crops
 will sing with joy when they gather
 them in.
⁶ Those who go out weeping
 as they carry seeds to plant
 will come back singing with joy.
 They will bring the new crop back
 with them.

Psalm 127

A song for those who go up to Jerusalem to
worship the LORD. A psalm of Solomon.

¹ If the LORD doesn't build a house,
 the work of the builders is useless.
 If the LORD doesn't watch over a city,
 it's useless for those on guard duty to
 stand watch over it.
² It's useless for you to work from early
 morning
 until late at night
just to get food to eat.
 God provides for those he loves even
 while they sleep.

³ Children are a gift from the LORD.
 They are a reward from him.
⁴ Children who are born to people when
 they are young
 are like arrows in the hands of a
 soldier.

WOOTON'S
FUN
FACTS
Ps. 127:3

Almost half of Americans say two children
per family is the perfect number. Twenty-five
percent say three. Thirteen percent say four
or more. Three percent say one is just right.
There were only two kids in my family, but it
felt like more when I counted the pet moose,
the pet owl, and the seven porcupines.

5 Blessed are those
who have many children.
They won't be put to shame
when they go up against their
enemies in court.

Psalm 128
A song for those who go up to
Jerusalem to worship the LORD.

1 Blessed are all those who have respect
for the LORD.
They live as he wants them to live.
2 Your work will give you what you need.
Blessings and good things will come
to you.
3 As a vine bears a lot of fruit,
so may your wife have many
children by you.
May they sit around your table
like young olive trees.
4 Only a man who has respect for the
LORD
will be blessed like that.

5 May the LORD bless you from Zion.
May you enjoy the good things that
come to Jerusalem
all the days of your life.
6 May you live to see your
grandchildren.

May Israel enjoy peace.

Psalm 129
A song for those who go up to
Jerusalem to worship the LORD.

1 Here is what Israel should say.
"My enemies have treated me badly
ever since I was a young nation.
2 My enemies have treated me badly ever
since I was a young nation.
But they haven't won the battle.
3 They have made deep wounds in my
back.
It looks like a field a farmer has
plowed.
4 The LORD does what is right.
Sinners had tied me up with ropes.
But the LORD has set me free."

5 May all those who hate Zion
be driven back in shame.
6 May they be like grass that grows on
the roof of a house.
It dries up before it can grow.

7 There isn't enough of it to fill a person's
hand.
There isn't enough to tie up and
carry away.
8 May no one who passes by say to those
who hate Zion,
"May the blessing of the LORD be
on you.
We bless you in the name of the
LORD."

Psalm 130
A song for those who go up to
Jerusalem to worship the LORD.

1 LORD, I cry out to you
because I'm suffering so deeply.
2 Lord, listen to me.
Pay attention to my cry for your
mercy.

3 LORD, suppose you kept a close watch
on sins.
Lord, who then wouldn't be found
guilty?
4 But you forgive.
So we can serve you with respect.

5 With all my heart I wait for the LORD to
help me.

ADVENTURES IN ODYSSEY

Psalm 130 reminded the Israelites that
God set them free. Eugene and Katrina
worked to set a group of people free
from lies in "Prisoners of Fear" (A#45).

WHAT ABOUT YOU?

What's your idea of extreme adventure?

Do you know that a missionary's life can be an exciting adventure? Eugene and Katrina didn't understand that until the Adventures in Odyssey episode "Prisoners of Fear." In this story, Eugene and Katrina volunteer to set up a radio transmitter for a remote tribe in Africa. Sounds like a simple job, right? Neither one expected to battle an old "curse," learn about a mysterious man named Marati, or stumble upon a discovery that might change Eugene's life forever.

As the Meltsners continued to face unexpected challenges, they learned the truth of Psalm 130:7, which encourages people to put their hope in the Lord. He knows all about our past and our mistakes. He knows why we hurt. And He invites us to hope in Him and watch as He takes that pain and creates something beautiful out of it. Will you dare to hope and trust in Him, no matter what struggles you are facing?

For a challenge, learn about some real-life missionaries. Ask your mom or dad to help you do some research. Start with Dr. David Livingstone. Print out stories about his life and put them in a notebook where you can go back and read them. But don't stop there. Add more stories and keep learning what God can do when we put our hope in Him.

I put my hope in his word.
⁶ I wait for the Lord to help me.
I want his help more than night
    watchmen want the morning
    to come.
I'll say it again.
I want his help more than night
    watchmen want the morning
    to come.
⁷ Israel, put your hope in the Lord,
    because the Lord's love never fails.
    He sets his people completely free.
⁸ He himself will set Israel
    free from all their sins.

Psalm 131

A song for those who go up to Jerusalem to worship the Lord. A psalm of David.

¹ Lord, my heart isn't proud.
    My eyes aren't proud either.
I don't concern myself with important
    matters.
I don't concern myself with things
    that are too wonderful for me.
² I have made myself calm and content
    like a young child in its mother's arms.

Deep down inside me, I am as
    content as a young child.
³ Israel, put your hope in the Lord
    both now and forever.

Psalm 132

A song for those who go up to Jerusalem to worship the Lord.

¹ Lord, remember David
    and all the times he didn't do what
    he wanted.

² Lord, he made a promise.
    Mighty One of Jacob, he made a
    promise to you.
³ He said, "I won't enter my house
    or go to bed.
⁴ I won't let my eyes sleep.
    I won't close my eyelids
⁵ until I find a place for the Lord.
    I want to build a house for the
    Mighty One of Jacob."

⁶ Here are the words we heard in
    Ephrathah.
    We heard them again in the fields of
    Kiriath Jearim.

⁷ "Let us go to the LORD's house.
Let us worship at his feet. Let us say,
⁸ 'LORD, rise up and come to your resting
place.
Come in together with the ark. It's
the sign of your power.
⁹ May your priests put on godliness as if
it were their clothes.
May your faithful people sing for joy.'"

¹⁰ In honor of your servant David,
don't turn your back on your
anointed king.

¹¹ The LORD made a promise to David.
It is a firm promise that he will never
break.
He said, "After you die,
I will place one of your own sons on
your throne.
¹² If your sons keep my covenant
and the laws I teach them,
then their sons will sit
on your throne for ever and ever."

¹³ The LORD has chosen Zion.
That's the place where he wants to live.
¹⁴ He has said, "This will be my resting
place for ever and ever.
Here I will sit on my throne, because
that's what I want.
¹⁵ I will greatly bless Zion with everything
it needs.
I will give plenty of food to the poor
people living there.
¹⁶ I will put salvation on its priests as if it
were their clothes.
God's faithful people will always sing
for joy.

¹⁷ "Here in Jerusalem I will raise up a
mighty king from the family of
David.
I will set up the lamp of David's
kingdom for my anointed king.
Its flame will burn brightly forever.
¹⁸ I will put shame on his enemies as if it
were their clothes.
But he will wear on his head a
shining crown."

Psalm 133

A song for those who go up to Jerusalem
to worship the LORD. A psalm of David.

¹ How good and pleasant it is
when God's people live together in
peace!

ADVENTURES IN ODYSSEY

Connie, Bernard, and their
TV crew learned how to live and
work together peacefully in
"B-TV: Behind the Scenes" (A#40).

² It's like the special olive oil
that was poured on Aaron's head.
It ran down on his beard
and on the collar of his robe.
³ It's as if the dew of Mount Hermon
were falling on Mount Zion.
There the LORD gives his blessing.
He gives life that never ends.

Psalm 134

A song for those who go up to
Jerusalem to worship the LORD.

¹ All you who serve the LORD, praise the
LORD.
All you who serve at night in the
house of the LORD, praise him.
² Lift up your hands in the temple
and praise the LORD.

³ May the LORD bless you from Zion.
He is the Maker of heaven and earth.

Psalm 135

¹ Praise the LORD.

Praise the name of the LORD.
You who serve the LORD, praise him.
² You who serve in the house of the
LORD, praise him.
You who serve in the courtyards of
the temple of our God, praise
him.

³ Praise the LORD, because he is good.
Sing praise to his name, because that
is pleasant.
⁴ The LORD has chosen the people of
Jacob to be his own.
He has chosen Israel to be his special
treasure.

⁵ I know that the LORD is great.
I know that our Lord is greater than
all gods.
⁶ The LORD does anything he wants to do
in the heavens and on the earth.
He does it even in the deepest parts
of the oceans.

¹⁶ They have mouths but can't speak.
　　They have eyes but can't see.
¹⁷ They have ears but can't hear.
　　They have mouths but can't breathe.
¹⁸ Those who make statues of gods will be
　　like them.
　　So will all those who trust in them.

¹⁹ People of Israel, praise the Lord.
　　Priests of Aaron, praise the Lord.
²⁰ Tribe of Levi, praise the Lord.
　　You who have respect for the Lord,
　　praise him.
²¹ Give praise to the Lord in Zion.
　　Give praise to the God who lives in
　　Jerusalem.

Praise the Lord.

Psalm 136

¹ Give thanks to the Lord, because he is
　　good.
　　His faithful love continues forever.
² Give thanks to the greatest God of all.
　　His faithful love continues forever.
³ Give thanks to the most powerful Lord
　　of all.
　　His faithful love continues forever.
⁴ Give thanks to the only one who can do
　　great miracles.
　　His faithful love continues forever.
⁵ By his understanding he made the
　　heavens.
　　His faithful love continues forever.
⁶ He spread out the earth on the waters.
　　His faithful love continues forever.
⁷ He made the great lights in the sky.
　　His faithful love continues forever.
⁸ He made the sun to rule over the day.
　　His faithful love continues forever.
⁹ He made the moon and stars to rule
　　over the night.
　　His faithful love continues forever.
¹⁰ Give thanks to the God who killed the
　　oldest son of each family in
　　Egypt.
　　His faithful love continues forever.
¹¹ He brought the people of Israel out of
　　Egypt.
　　His faithful love continues forever.
¹² He did it by reaching out his mighty
　　hand and powerful arm.
　　His faithful love continues forever.
¹³ Give thanks to the God who parted the
　　waters of the Red Sea.

WOOTON'S FUN FACTS

Ps. 135:7
Did you know that even dry lightning comes with rain? But the water evaporates before it hits the ground. Lightning is nothing to mess around with.

⁷ He makes clouds rise from one end of
　　the earth to the other.
He sends lightning with the rain.
He brings the wind out of his
　　storerooms.
⁸ He killed the oldest son of each family
　　in Egypt.
He struck down the oldest males
　　that were born to people and
　　animals.
⁹ He did miraculous signs in Egypt.
He did wonders against Pharaoh and
　　everyone who served him.
¹⁰ He destroyed many nations.
He killed mighty kings.
¹¹ He killed Sihon, the king of the Amorites,
　　and Og, the king of Bashan.
He killed all the kings of Canaan.
¹² He gave their land as a gift
　　to his people Israel.

¹³ Lord, your name continues forever.
Lord, your fame will last for all time
　　to come.
¹⁴ When the Lord hands down his
　　sentence, it will be in his
　　people's favor.
He will show deep concern for those
　　who serve him.
¹⁵ The statues of the nations' gods are
　　made out of silver and gold.
They are made by human hands.

His faithful love continues forever.

14 He brought Israel through the middle
     of it.
     His faithful love continues forever.

15 But he swept Pharaoh and his army into
     the Red Sea.
     His faithful love continues forever.

16 Give thanks to the God who led his
     people through the desert.
     His faithful love continues forever.

17 He killed great kings.
     His faithful love continues forever.

18 He struck down mighty kings.
     His faithful love continues forever.

19 He killed Sihon, the king of the
     Amorites.
     His faithful love continues forever.

20 He killed Og, the king of Bashan.
     His faithful love continues forever.

21 He gave their land as a gift.
     His faithful love continues forever.

22 He gave it as a gift to his servant Israel.
     His faithful love continues forever.

23 Give thanks to the God who
     remembered us when things
     were going badly.
     His faithful love continues forever.

24 He set us free from our enemies.
     His faithful love continues forever.

25 He gives food to every creature.
     His faithful love continues forever.

26 Give thanks to the God of heaven.
     His faithful love continues forever.

Ps. 136:20 King Og had a short name but a tall body. His coffin was thirteen feet long (Deuteronomy 3:11). I wonder what else they buried with him!

Psalm 137

1 We were sitting by the rivers of
     Babylon.
     We wept when we remembered what
     had happened to Zion.

2 On the nearby poplar trees
     we hung up our harps.

3 Those who held us as prisoners asked
     us to sing.
     Those who enjoyed hurting us
     ordered us to sing joyful songs.
     They said, "Sing one of the songs of
     Zion to us!"

4 How can we sing the songs of the LORD
     while we are in another land?

5 Jerusalem, if I forget you,
     may my right hand never be able to
     play the harp again.

6 If I don't remember you,
     may my tongue stick to the roof of
     my mouth so I can't sing.
     May it happen if I don't consider
     Jerusalem
     to be my greatest joy.

7 LORD, remember what the people of
     Edom did
     on the day Jerusalem fell.
     "Tear it down!" they cried.
     "Tear it down to the ground!"

8 People of Babylon, you are sentenced to
     be destroyed.
     Happy is the person who pays you
     back
     according to what you have done
     to us.

9 Happy is the person who grabs your
     babies
     and smashes them against the rocks.

Psalm 138

A psalm of David.

1 LORD, I will praise you with all my
     heart.
     In front of those who think they are
     gods
     I will sing praise to you.

2 I will bow down facing your holy
     temple.
     I will praise your name,
     because you are always loving and
     faithful.
     You have honored your holy word
     even more than your own fame.

³ When I called out to you, you answered
me.
  You made me strong and brave.

⁴ LORD, may all the kings on earth praise
you
  when they hear about what you have
  decided.
⁵ LORD, may they sing about what you
have done,
  because your glory is great.

⁶ Though the LORD is high above all, he
cares for the lowly.
  Though he is in heaven above, he
  sees them on earth below.
⁷ Trouble is all around me,
  but you keep me alive.
You reach out your hand to put a stop
  to the anger of my enemies.
  With your powerful right hand you
  save me.
⁸ LORD, you will show that I was right to
trust you.
  LORD, your faithful love continues
  forever.
  You have done so much for us, so
  don't stop now.

Psalm 139
For the director of music.
A psalm of David.

¹ LORD, you have seen what is in my heart.
  You know all about me.
² You know when I sit down and when I
get up.
  You know what I'm thinking even
  though you are far away.
³ You know when I go out to work and
when I come back home.
  You know exactly how I live.
⁴ LORD, even before I speak a word,
  you know all about it.

⁵ You are all around me, behind me and
in front of me.
  You hold me safe in your hand.
⁶ I'm amazed at how well you know me.
  It's more than I can understand.

⁷ How can I get away from your Spirit?
  Where can I go to escape from you?
⁸ If I go up to the heavens, you are there.
  If I lie down in the deepest parts of
  the earth, you are also there.
⁹ Suppose I were to rise with the sun in
the east.

REMEMBER THIS

PSALM 139:14

"How you made me is
amazing and wonderful. I
praise you for that. What
you have done is wonder-
ful. I know that very well."

Suppose I travel to the west where it
  sinks into the ocean.
¹⁰ Your hand would always be there to
guide me.
  Your right hand would still be
  holding me close.

¹¹ Suppose I were to say, "I'm sure the
darkness will hide me.
  The light around me will become as
  dark as night."
¹² Even that darkness would not be dark
to you.
  The night would shine like the day,
  because darkness is like light to
  you.

¹³ You created the deepest parts of my
being.
  You put me together inside my
  mother's body.
¹⁴ How you made me is amazing and
wonderful.
  I praise you for that.

ADVENTURES IN ODYSSEY

Monty learned about how amazing and
wonderful God made him during a cold
winter trip in "Ice Fishing" (A#07).

CANDID CONVERSATIONS

I have a friend named Pamela. I knew her when I lived in California, and our moms were friends when we were babies. We still check in with each other every now and then. We've lived in different places and we know different people, but I still like talking to her because we have the connection that she's known me longer than just about anyone in the world.

But as long as I've known Pamela, it's still not as long as God has known me. God put all of us together inside our mothers! Before we were born, God was busy tinkering with everything we are to make us into the people He wants us to be. And since creating you mattered so much to Him, we know your every day matters to Him. He sees every tear and hears every laugh. No one, even your oldest friend, knows you like God knows you.

Try something: Write a letter to God like you would write to your best friend. Because He is!

What you have done is wonderful.
I know that very well.
¹⁵ None of my bones was hidden from you
when you made me inside my mother's body.
That place was as dark as the deepest parts of the earth.
When you were putting me together there,
¹⁶ your eyes saw my body even before it was formed.
You planned how many days I would live.
You wrote down the number of them in your book
before I had lived through even one of them.

¹⁷ God, your thoughts about me are priceless.
No one can possibly add them all up.
¹⁸ If I could count them,
they would be more than the grains of sand.
If I were to fall asleep counting and then wake up,
you would still be there with me.

¹⁹ God, I wish you would kill the people who are evil!
I wish those murderers would get away from me!
²⁰ They are your enemies. They misuse your name.
They misuse it for their own evil purposes.
²¹ LORD, I really hate those who hate you!
I really hate those who rise up against you!
²² I have nothing but hatred for them.
I consider them to be my enemies.

²³ God, see what is in my heart.
Know what is there.
Test me.
Know what I'm thinking.
²⁴ See if there's anything in my life you don't like.
Help me live in the way that is always right.

Psalm 140
For the director of music.
A psalm of David.

¹ LORD, save me from sinful people.
Keep me safe from those who want to hurt me.
² They make evil plans in their hearts.
They are always starting fights.
³ Their tongues are as deadly as the tongue of a serpent.
The words from their lips are like the poison of a snake.

⁴ LORD, keep me safe from the hands of sinful people.
Protect me from those who want to hurt me.
They plan ways to trip me up and make me fall.
⁵ Proud people have hidden their traps to catch me.

WOOTON'S FUN FACTS
Ps. 140:3

I love reptiles, but I don't ever want anything in my house that could poison me in my sleep. The Inland Taipan is the deadliest snake in the world. One bite has enough venom to kill one hundred men or 250,000 mice or I don't know how many porcupines. The Eastern Diamondback rattlesnake is the most poisonous snake in the US. I've never seen one near Odyssey.

They have spread out their nets.
They have set traps for me along my
path.
⁶ I say to the LORD, "You are my God."
LORD, hear my cry for mercy.
⁷ LORD and King, you save me because
you are strong.
You are like a shield that keeps me
safe in the day of battle.
⁸ LORD, don't give sinners what they
want.
Don't let their plans succeed.

⁹ Those who are all around me proudly
raise their heads.
May the trouble they planned for me
happen to them.
¹⁰ May burning coals fall on people like
that.
May they be thrown into the fire.
May they be thrown into muddy pits
and never get out.
¹¹ Don't let people who lie about me be
secure in the land.
May trouble hunt down those who
want to hurt me.
¹² I know that the LORD makes sure that
poor people are treated fairly.

He stands up for those who are in
need.
¹³ I'm sure that those who do right will
praise your name.
Those who are honest will live with
you.

Psalm 141
A psalm of David.

¹ I call out to you, LORD. Come quickly
to help me.
Listen to me when I call out to you.
² May my prayer come to you like the
sweet smell of incense.
When I lift up my hands in prayer,
may it be like the evening
sacrifice.

³ LORD, guard my mouth.
Keep watch over the door of my
lips.
⁴ Don't let my heart be drawn to what is
evil.
Don't let me join with people who
do evil.
Don't let me eat their fancy food.

⁵ If a godly person hit me, it would be an
act of kindness.
If they would correct me, it would
be like pouring olive oil on my
head.
I wouldn't say no to it.

I will always pray against the things that
sinful people do.
⁶   When their rulers are thrown down
from the rocky cliffs,
those evil people will realize that my
words were true.
⁷ They will say, "As clumps of dirt are
left from plowing up the
ground,
so our bones will be scattered near
an open grave."

⁸ But LORD and King, I keep looking to
you for help.
I go to you for safety. Don't let me
die.
⁹ Keep me from the traps of those who
do evil.
Save me from the traps they have set
for me.
¹⁰ Let evil people fall into their own nets.
But let me go safely on my way.

Psalm 142

A prayer of David when he
was in the cave. A *maskil.*

[1] I call out to the LORD.
  I pray to him for mercy.
[2] I pour out my problem to him.
  I tell him about my trouble.

[3] When I grow weak,
    you are watching over my life.
  In the path where I walk,
    people have hidden a trap to catch
      me.
[4] Look and see that no one is on my right
      side to help me.
  No one is concerned about me.
  I have no place of safety.
    No one cares whether I live or die.

[5] LORD, I cry out to you.
    I say, "You are my place of safety.
    You are everything I need in this
      life."
[6] Listen to my cry.
    I am in great need.
  Save me from those who are chasing
      me.
    They are too strong for me.
[7] My troubles are like a prison.
    Set me free so I can praise your
      name.

  Then those who do what is right will
      gather around me
  because you have been good to me.

Ps. 142:4 To be on the "right side" of God
is to have blessing and strength. In the
Bible, the right side is a symbol of power
and friendship. Funny, my wife Penny
always stands on my right side. Huh!

Psalm 143

A psalm of David.

[1] LORD, hear my prayer.
    Listen to my cry for mercy.
  You are faithful and right.
    Come and help me.
[2] Don't take me to court and judge me,
    because in your eyes no living
      person does what is right.

[3] My enemies chase me.
    They crush me down to the ground.
  They make me live in the darkness
    like those who died long ago.
[4] So I grow weak.
    Deep down inside me, I'm afraid.

[5] I remember what happened long ago.
    I spend time thinking about all your
      acts.
    I consider what your hands have
      done.
[6] I spread out my hands to you in prayer.
    I'm thirsty for you, just as dry
      ground is thirsty for rain.

[7] LORD, answer me quickly.
    I'm growing weak.
  Don't turn your face away from me,
    or I will be like those who go down
      into the grave.
[8] In the morning let me hear about your
      faithful love,
    because I've put my trust in you.
  Show me the way I should live,
    because I trust you with my life.
[9] LORD, save me from my enemies,
    because I go to you for safety.
[10] Teach me to do what you want,
    because you are my God.
  May your good Spirit
    lead me on a level path.

[11] LORD, bring yourself honor by keeping
      me alive.
    Because you do what is right, get me
      out of trouble.
[12] Because your love is faithful, put an end
      to my enemies.
    Destroy all of them, because I serve
      you.

Psalm 144

A psalm of David.

[1] Give praise to the LORD, my Rock.
    He trains my hands for war.
    He trains my fingers for battle.

2 He is my loving God and is like a fort to
me.
He is my place of safety and the God
who saves me.
He is like a shield that keeps me safe.
He brings nations under my control.

3 LORD, what are human beings that you
take care of them?
What are mere people that you think
about them?
4 Their lives don't last any longer than a
breath.
Their days are like a shadow that
quickly disappears.

5 LORD, open up your heavens and come
down.
Touch the mountains, and they will
pour out smoke.
6 Send flashes of lightning and scatter my
enemies.
Shoot your arrows and chase them
away.
7 My enemies are like a mighty flood.
Reach down from heaven and save
me.
Save me from outsiders who attack
me.
8 They tell all kinds of lies with their
mouths.
Even when they make a promise by
raising their right hands, they
don't mean it.

9 My God, I will sing a new song to you.
I will make music to you on a lyre
that has ten strings.
10 You are the God who helps kings win
battles.
You save your servant David.

From death by the sword 11save me.

Set me free from outsiders who
attack me.
They tell all kinds of lies with their
mouths.
Even when they make a promise by
raising their right hands, they
don't mean it.

12 While our sons are young,
they will be like healthy plants.
Our daughters will be like pillars
that have been made to decorate a
palace.
13 Our storerooms will be filled
with every kind of food.
The sheep in our fields will increase by
thousands.
They will increase by tens of
thousands.
14   Our oxen will pull heavy loads.
None of our city walls will be broken
down.
No one will be carried off as a
prisoner.
No cries of pain will be heard in our
streets.

15 Blessed is the nation about whom all
these things are true.
Blessed is the nation whose God is
the LORD.

Psalm 145

A psalm of praise. A psalm of David.

1 I will honor you, my God the King.
I will praise your name for ever and
ever.
2 Every day I will praise you.
I will praise your name for ever and
ever.

3 LORD, you are great. You are really
worthy of praise.
No one can completely understand
how great you are.
4 Parents praise your works to their
children.
They tell about your mighty acts.
5 They speak about your glorious majesty.
I will spend time thinking about
your wonderful deeds.
6 They speak about the powerful and
wonderful things you do.
I will talk about the great things you
have done.
7 They celebrate your great goodness.
They sing for joy about your holy acts.

Jason's Jargon

PSALM 144

A military operation:
Inspect this chapter
for the word *scatter*.
To scatter an army means
to send them running
away in different
directions, making
them easier to defeat.

8 The LORD is gracious, kind and tender.
   He is slow to get angry and full of
      love.
9 The LORD is good to all.
   He shows deep concern for
      everything he has made.
10 LORD, all your works praise you.
   Your faithful people praise you.
11 They tell about your glorious kingdom.
   They speak about your power.
12 Then all people will know about the
      mighty things you have done.
   They will know about the glorious
      majesty of your kingdom.
13 Your kingdom is a kingdom that will
      last forever.
   Your rule will continue for all time
      to come.

The LORD will keep all his promises.
   He is faithful in everything he does.
14 The LORD takes good care of all those
      who fall.
   He lifts up all those who feel helpless.
15 Every living thing looks to you for
      food.
   You give it to them exactly when
      they need it.
16 You open your hand
   and satisfy the needs of every living
      creature.

17 The LORD is right in everything he does.
   He is faithful in everything he does.
18 The LORD is ready to help all those who
      call out to him.
   He helps those who really mean it
      when they call out to him.
19 He satisfies the needs of those who have
      respect for him.
   He hears their cry and saves them.
20 The LORD watches over all those who
      love him.
   But he will destroy all sinful people.

21 I will praise the LORD with my mouth.
   Let every creature praise his holy
      name
   for ever and ever.

Psalm 146

1 Praise the LORD.

I will praise the LORD.
2   I will praise the LORD all my life.
   I will sing praise to my God as long
      as I live.

ADVENTURES IN ODYSSEY

Melanie Jacobs got a reminder that
God was the maker of everything in
heaven and earth in "Pen Pal" (A#15).

3 Don't put your trust in human leaders.
   Don't trust in people who can't save
      you.
4 When they die, they return to the
      ground.
   On that day their plans come to
      nothing.
5 Blessed are those who depend on the
      God of Jacob for help.
   Blessed are those who put their hope
      in the LORD their God.
6 He is the Maker of heaven and earth
      and the ocean.
   He made everything in them.
   He remains faithful forever.
7 He stands up for those who are treated
      badly.
   He gives food to hungry people.
The LORD sets prisoners free.
8   The LORD gives sight to those who
      are blind.
The LORD lifts up those who feel
      helpless.
   The LORD loves those who do what
      is right.
9 The LORD watches over the outsiders
      who live in our land.
   He takes good care of children
      whose fathers have died.
   He also takes good care of widows.
But he causes evil people to fail
   in everything they do.

10 The LORD rules forever.
   The God of Zion will rule for all
      time to come.

Praise the LORD.

Psalm 147

1 Praise the LORD.

How good it is to sing praises to our God!
   How pleasant and right it is to praise
      him!
2 The LORD builds up Jerusalem.
   He gathers the scattered people of
      Israel.

WHAT ABOUT YOU?

Have you ever been hurt by changes? The writer of Psalm 147:3 says: "[The Lord] heals those who have broken hearts. He takes care of their wounds."

God can comfort our hurting hearts in many ways. He may send someone to listen or share a hug. He might also point us to an encouraging Bible verse, or give us peace through the Holy Spirit.

In the meantime, life keeps changing. People move. We graduate from one school grade to the next. Friends enter and exit our world. And we wonder what will happen tomorrow. But to be honest, wouldn't life be boring without some of those changes? Also, if everything stayed the same, we'd never grow—and we'd stop appreciating the blessings God has given us.

If a friend of yours is stinging from change or loss, be there for him or her. Let your concern and kindness be counted on when everything else seems uncertain. That's how you can model God's love, which is one thing that will never, ever change.

If you have a family photo album, page through it and identify everyone in the pictures. Ask for help with the faces you don't recognize. Ask your parents or other relatives to share a story about someone who has passed away.

---

3 He heals those who have broken hearts.
    He takes care of their wounds.

4 He decides how many stars there
        should be.
    He gives each one of them a name.
5 Great is our Lord. His power is mighty.
    There is no limit to his
        understanding.
6 The LORD gives strength to those who
        aren't proud.
    But he throws evil people down to
        the ground.

7 Sing to the LORD and give him grateful
        praise.
    Make music to our God on the harp.
8 He covers the sky with clouds.
    He supplies the earth with rain.
    He makes grass grow on the hills.
9 He provides food for the cattle.
    He provides for the young ravens
        when they cry out.

10 He doesn't take pleasure in the strength
        of horses.
    He doesn't take delight in the strong
        legs of warriors.

11 The LORD takes delight in those who
        have respect for him.
    They put their hope in his faithful
        love.

12 Jerusalem, praise the LORD.
    Zion, praise your God.
13 He makes the metal bars of your gates
        stronger.
    He blesses the people who live inside
        you.
14 He keeps your borders safe and secure.
    He satisfies you with the finest wheat.

15 He sends his command to the earth.
    His word arrives there quickly.
16 He spreads the snow like wool.
    He scatters the frost like ashes.
17 He throws down his hail like pebbles.
    No one can stand his icy blast.
18 He gives his command, and the ice melts.
    He stirs up his winds, and the waters
        flow.

19 He has made his word known to the
        people of Jacob.
    He has made his laws and rules
        known to Israel.

Speaking of wool and snow, wool is an excellent insulator even in bad weather. It can absorb water and still retain heat. That's why I always tell people on camping trips, "Cotton is rotten, but wool is cool." I'm still working on the rhyme.

²⁰ He hasn't done that for any other nation.
　　They don't know his laws.

Praise the LORD.

Psalm 148

¹ Praise the LORD.

Praise the LORD from the heavens.
　　Praise him in the heavens above.
² Praise him, all his angels.
　　Praise him, all his angels in heaven.

Ps. 148:10 Did you know which animal lives the longest? It's the quahog clam. Some live four hundred years. To be able to live that long *and* have a name that starts with a *Q*? Some animals get all the breaks!

³ Praise him, sun and moon.
　　Praise him, all you shining stars.
⁴ Praise him, you highest heavens.
　　Praise him, you waters above the
　　　　skies.
⁵ Let all of them praise the name of the
　　LORD,
　　because at his command they were
　　　　created.
⁶ He established them for ever and ever.
　　He gave them laws they will always
　　　　have to obey.

⁷ Praise the LORD from the earth,
　　you great sea creatures and all the
　　　　deepest parts of the ocean.
⁸ Praise him, lightning and hail, snow
　　　　and clouds.
　　Praise him, you stormy winds that
　　　　obey him.
⁹ Praise him, all you mountains and hills.
　　Praise him, all you fruit trees and
　　　　cedar trees.
¹⁰ Praise him, all you wild animals and
　　　　cattle.
　　Praise him, you small creatures and
　　　　flying birds.
¹¹ Praise him, you kings of the earth and
　　　　all nations.
　　Praise him, all you princes and
　　　　rulers on earth.
¹² Praise him, young men and women.
　　Praise him, old men and children.

¹³ Let them praise the name of the LORD.
　　His name alone is honored.
　　His glory is higher than the earth
　　　　and the heavens.
¹⁴ He has given his people a strong king.
　　All his faithful people praise him for
　　　　that gift.
　　All the people of Israel are close to
　　　　his heart.

Praise the LORD.

Psalm 149

¹ Praise the LORD.

Sing a new song to the LORD.
　　Sing praise to him in the assembly of
　　　　his faithful people.

² Let Israel be filled with joy because God
　　　　is their Maker.
　　Let the people of Zion be glad
　　　　because he is their King.

³ Let them praise his name with
　　dancing.
　Let them make music to him with
　　harps and tambourines.
⁴ The LORD takes delight in his people.
　He awards with victory those who
　　are humble.
⁵ Let his faithful people be filled with joy
　　because of that honor.
　Let them sing for joy even when
　　they are lying in bed.

⁶ May they praise God with their
　　mouths.
　May they hold in their hands a
　　sword that has two edges.
⁷ Let them pay the nations back.
　Let them punish the people of the
　　earth.
⁸ Let them put the kings of those nations
　　in chains.
　Let them put their nobles in iron
　　chains.
⁹ Let them carry out God's sentence
　　against those nations.

This will bring glory to all his
　　faithful people.

Praise the LORD.

Psalm 150

¹ Praise the LORD.

Praise God in his holy temple.
　Praise him in his mighty heavens.
² Praise him for his powerful acts.
　Praise him because he is greater than
　　anything else.
³ Praise him by blowing trumpets.
　Praise him with harps and lyres.
⁴ Praise him with tambourines and
　　dancing.
　Praise him with stringed
　　instruments and flutes.
⁵ Praise him with clashing cymbals.
　Praise him with clanging cymbals.

⁶ Let everything that has breath praise
　　the LORD.

Praise the LORD.

Proverbs

Having passed through Psalms, we arrive at a companion book: Proverbs. According to 1 Kings 4:32, King Solomon spoke a veritable 3,000 proverbs! As you will see in this book, the proverbs of Solomon are still relevant for our lives today.

One goal of Proverbs was to hand down the wisdom that God had given Solomon (and a number of other writers) to the next generations. Frequent references are made to "my son." Older and wiser people can look back and see many dangers of life that younger and more ambitious people do not yet detect. The book of Proverbs attempts to steer us away from common pitfalls: foolishness, temptation, self-centeredness, and others. Young people who heed this advice can prevent a lot of unnecessary trouble throughout their lives.

The first nine chapters contain passages that commend the value of wisdom, warn against foolish behavior, and provide examples of both. Most of the rest of the book is a series of proverb after proverb—essentially every verse is a separate saying. It can be enjoyable to skim through and pick out some favorites to remember, or even to memorize. The book concludes with a passage about "the excellent woman." I love to read this passage and reflect on how my wife Katrina matches these attributes so well.

WHaT'S IT MEaN, EuGENE?

Orthodoxy—It may be a stuffy sounding word, but *orthodoxy* is about the beauty of correct beliefs and teachings. Breaking the word down a bit, *orthos* in Greek means "straight" or "upright" while *doxa* can mean a number of things—including "glory"— but in this case it points toward "belief." Oh, that we had the heart of the psalmist who writes, "Lord, I really love your law! All day long I spend time thinking about it" (Psalm 119:97).

PURPOSE

1 These are the proverbs of Solomon. He was the son of David and the king of Israel.

2 Proverbs teach you wisdom and instruct you.
    They help you understand wise sayings.
3 They provide you with instruction and help you live wisely.
    They lead to what is right and honest and fair.
4 They give understanding to childish people.
    They give knowledge and good sense to those who are young.
5 Let wise people listen and add to what they have learned.
    Let those who understand what is right get guidance.
6 What I'm teaching also helps you understand proverbs and stories.
    It helps you understand the sayings and riddles of those who are wise.

7 If you really want to gain knowledge, you must begin by having respect for the LORD.
    But foolish people hate wisdom and instruction.

THINK AND LIVE WISELY

A Warning Against Sinful Men

8 My son, listen to your father's advice.
    Don't turn away from your mother's teaching.
9 What they teach you will be like a beautiful crown on your head.
    It will be like a chain to decorate your neck.

10 My son, if sinful men tempt you, don't give in to them.
11 They might say, "Come along with us.
    Let's hide and wait to kill someone who hasn't done anything wrong.
    Let's catch some harmless person in our trap.
12 Let's swallow them alive, as the grave does.

WOOTON'S **FUN FACTS** Prov. 1

The "son" here is most likely Rehoboam, who didn't listen very well to his father, King Solomon. Check out the story in 1 Kings 12:1–16. Did you know that King Solomon compiled or wrote chapters 1 through 24 of the book of Proverbs? He's a good guy to write a book on wisdom because he was the wisest man who ever lived.

    Let's swallow them whole, like those who go down into the pit.
13 We'll get all kinds of valuable things.
    We'll fill our houses with what we steal.
14 Cast lots with us for what they own.
    We'll share everything we take from them."
15 My son, don't go along with them.
    Don't even set your feet on their paths.
16 They are always in a hurry to sin.
    They are quick to spill someone's blood.
17 How useless it is to spread a net where every bird can see it!
18 Those who hide and wait will spill their own blood.
    They will be caught in their own trap.

ADVENTURES IN ODYSSEY

Eugene and Bernard saw the dangerous effects of the greed for money in "It Happened at Four Corners" (A#21).

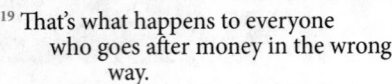

Jason's Jargon

PROVERBS 1

Find the word *guidance* in this chapter. Guidance is counseling we receive from another person. A good way to grow in our faith is to find someone who can give us wise guidance.

¹⁹ That's what happens to everyone
who goes after money in the wrong
way.
That kind of money takes away
the life of those who get it.

Wisdom's Warning

²⁰ Out in the open wisdom calls out.
She raises her voice in a public place.
²¹ On top of the city wall she cries out.
Here is what she says near the gate
of the city.
²² "How long will you childish people love
your childish ways?
How long will you rude people enjoy
making fun of God and others?
How long will you foolish people
hate knowledge?
²³ Pay attention to my warning!
Then I will pour out my thoughts
to you.
I will make known to you my
teachings.
²⁴ But you refuse to listen when I call out
to you.
No one pays attention when I reach
out my hand.
²⁵ You turn away from all my advice.
And you do not accept my warning.
²⁶ So I will laugh at you when you are in
danger.
I will make fun of you when hard
times come.
²⁷ I will laugh when hard times hit you
like a storm.
I will laugh when danger comes
your way like a windstorm.
I will make fun of you when
suffering and trouble come.
²⁸ "Then you will call to me. But I won't
answer.

You will look for me. But you won't
find me.
²⁹ You hated knowledge.
You didn't choose to have respect for
the LORD.
³⁰ You wouldn't accept my advice.
You turned your backs on my
warnings.
³¹ So you will eat the fruit of the way you
have lived.
You will choke on the fruit of what
you have planned.
³² "The wrong path that childish people
take will kill them.
Foolish people will be destroyed by
being satisfied with the way
they live.
³³ But those who listen to me will live in
safety.
They will be at ease and have no fear
of being harmed."

Good Things Come From Wisdom

2 My son, accept my words.
Store up my commands inside you.
² Let your ears listen to wisdom.
Apply your heart to understanding.
³ Call out for the ability to be wise.
Cry out for understanding.
⁴ Look for it as you would look for silver.
Search for it as you would search for
hidden treasure.
⁵ Then you will understand how to have
respect for the LORD.
You will find out how to know God.
⁶ The LORD gives wisdom.
Knowledge and understanding come
from his mouth.
⁷ He stores up success for honest people.
He is like a shield to those who live
without blame.
⁸ He guards the path of those who are
honest.
He watches over the way of his
faithful ones.
⁹ You will understand what is right and
honest and fair.

WHIT'S WISDOM
Proverbs 2

Yesterday, Camilla came into Whit's End asking about the difference between wisdom and knowledge. I explained that knowledge is knowing *about* something. It's information. Wisdom is knowing what to do *with* that knowledge. It's knowing what's right and true.

I showed her Proverbs 2:1–8. These verses give a few answers about wisdom. Who gives us wisdom? Check out verse 6. How are we supposed to look for wisdom? See verse 4.

"This makes it sound like a wisdom treasure hunt," said Camilla. "Where do I start?"

I showed her Proverbs 9:10, which says: "To know the Holy One is to gain understanding."

"Gaining wisdom is a lot like putting on a special pair of sunglasses," I said. "When you look through colored lenses, they change everything you see. The more wisdom you have, the more you'll see life differently. And the more wisdom you have, the easier it is to spot more wisdom! God wants you to see everything the way He sees it! That's why gaining wisdom is so important and so exciting!"

You will understand the right way
    to live.
10 Your heart will become wise.
    Your mind will delight in knowledge.
11 Good sense will keep you safe.
    Understanding will guard you.

12 Wisdom will save you from the ways of
    evil men.
    It will save you from men who twist
        their words.
13 Men like that have left the straight paths
    to walk in dark ways.
14 They take delight in doing what is wrong.
    They take joy in twisting everything
        around.
15 Their paths are crooked.
    Their ways are not straight.

16 Wisdom will save you from a woman
    who commits adultery.
    It will save you from a sinful woman
        and her tempting words.
17 She has left the man she married when
    she was young.
    She has broken the promise she
        made in front of God.
18 Surely her house leads down to death.
    Her paths lead to the spirits of the
        dead.
19 No one who goes to her comes back
    or reaches the paths of life.

20 You will walk in the ways of good people.
You will follow the paths of those
    who do right.
21 Honest people will live in the land.
    Those who are without blame will
        remain in it.
22 But sinners will be cut off from the land.
    Those who aren't faithful will be torn
        away from it.

More Good Things Come From Wisdom

3 My son, do not forget my teaching.
    Keep my commands in your heart.
2 They will help you live for many years.
    They will bring you peace and success.

3 Don't let love and truth ever leave you.
    Tie them around your neck.
    Write them on the tablet of your
        heart.
4 Then you will find favor and a good
    name
    in the eyes of God and people.

5 Trust in the LORD with all your heart.

ADVENTURES IN ODYSSEY

Connie tried to have a positive attitude, but instead saw the need to trust God and not rely on herself, in "A . . . Is for Attitude" (A#08).

Do not depend on your own
understanding.
⁶ In all your ways obey him.
Then he will make your paths
smooth and straight.

⁷ Don't be wise in your own eyes.
Have respect for the LORD and avoid
evil.
⁸ That will bring health to your body.
It will make your bones strong.

⁹ Honor the LORD with your wealth.
Give him the first share of all your
crops.
¹⁰ Then your storerooms will be so full
they can't hold everything.
Your huge jars will spill over with
fresh wine.

¹¹ My son, do not hate the LORD's
training.
Do not object when he corrects you.
¹² The LORD trains those he loves.
He is like a father who trains the son
he is pleased with.

¹³ Blessed is the one who finds wisdom.
Blessed is the one who gains
understanding.
¹⁴ Wisdom pays better than silver does.
She earns more than gold does.
¹⁵ She is worth more than rubies.
Nothing you want can compare with
her.
¹⁶ Long life is in her right hand.
In her left hand are riches and honor.
¹⁷ Her ways are pleasant ways.
All her paths lead to peace.
¹⁸ She is a tree of life to those who take
hold of her.
Those who hold her close will be
blessed.

¹⁹ By wisdom the LORD laid the earth's
foundations.

Through understanding he set the
heavens in place.
²⁰ By his knowledge the seas were
separated,
and the clouds dropped their dew.

²¹ My son, do not let wisdom and
understanding out of your
sight.
Hold on to good sense and the
understanding of what is right.
²² They will be life for you.
They will be like a gracious necklace
around your neck.
²³ Then you will go on your way in safety.
You will not trip and fall.
²⁴ When you lie down, you won't be afraid.
When you lie down, you will sleep
soundly.
²⁵ Don't be terrified by sudden trouble.
Don't be afraid when sinners are
destroyed.
²⁶ The LORD will be at your side.
He will keep your feet from being
caught in a trap.

²⁷ Don't hold back good from those who
are worthy of it.

Prov. 3:19 Eugene told me that in 2016, scientists discovered our galaxy is expanding at 45.5 miles per second per megaparsec. That's a lot of big words isn't it? Well, a megaparsec is the same as 3.26 million light-years. And a light-year is the distance that light can travel in a year. That's a long way because light can travel 186,000 miles in a single second. Whoa! That's a lot of expanding universe! By reading Proverbs, maybe my understanding will expand just as quickly!

Don't hold it back when you can help.
²⁸ Suppose you already have something to
give.
Don't say to your neighbor,
"Come back tomorrow.
I'll give it to you then."

²⁹ Don't plan to harm your neighbor.
He lives near you and trusts you.
³⁰ Don't bring charges against anyone for
no reason.
They have not harmed you.

³¹ Don't be jealous of a person who hurts
others.
Don't choose any of their ways.
³² The LORD really hates sinful people.
But he makes honest people his
closest friends.

³³ The LORD puts a curse on the houses of
sinners.
But he blesses the homes of those
who do what is right.
³⁴ He makes fun of proud people who
make fun of others.
But he gives grace to those who are
humble and treated badly.
³⁵ Wise people receive honor.
But foolish people get only shame.

Get Wisdom at Any Cost

4 My sons, listen to a father's teaching.
Pay attention and gain
understanding.
² I give you good advice.
So don't turn away from what I teach
you.
³ I, too, was once a young boy in my
father's house.
And my mother loved me deeply.
⁴ Then my father taught me.
He said to me, "Take hold of my
words with all your heart.
Keep my commands, and you will
live.
⁵ Get wisdom, and get understanding.
Don't forget my words or turn away
from them.
⁶ Stay close to wisdom, and she will keep
you safe.
Love her, and she will watch over
you.
⁷ To start being wise you must first get
wisdom.
No matter what it costs, get
understanding.

ADVENTURES IN ODYSSEY

On a trip in the Imagination Station
in "Blackgaard's Revenge" (A#33),
Aubrey learned the value of
wisdom and understanding.

⁸ Value wisdom highly, and she will lift
you up.
Hold her close, and she will honor
you.
⁹ She will set a beautiful crown on your
head.
She will give you a glorious crown."

¹⁰ My son, listen. Accept what I say.
Then you will live for many years.
¹¹ I instruct you in the way of wisdom.
I lead you along straight paths.
¹² When you walk, nothing will slow you
down.
When you run, you won't trip and
fall.
¹³ Hold on to my teaching and don't let it
go.
Guard it well, because it is your
life.
¹⁴ Don't take the path of evil people.
Don't live the way sinners do.
¹⁵ Stay away from their path and don't
travel on it.
Turn away from it and go on your
way.
¹⁶ Sinners can't rest until they do what is
evil.
They can't sleep until they make
someone sin.
¹⁷ They do evil just as easily as they eat
food.
They hurt others as easily as they
drink wine.
¹⁸ The path of those who do right is like
the sun in the morning.

It shines brighter and brighter until
the full light of day.
[19] But the way of those who do what is
wrong is like deep darkness.
They don't know what makes them
trip and fall.

[20] My son, pay attention to what I say.
Listen closely to my words.
[21] Don't let them out of your sight.
Keep them in your heart.
[22] They are life to those who find them.
They are health to a person's whole
body.
[23] Above everything else, guard your heart.
Everything you do comes from it.
[24] Don't speak with twisted words.
Keep evil talk away from your lips.
[25] Let your eyes look straight ahead.
Keep looking right in front of you.
[26] Think carefully about the paths that
your feet walk on.
Always choose the right ways.
[27] Don't turn to the right or left.
Keep your feet from the path of evil.

A Warning Against Committing Adultery

5 My son, pay attention to my wisdom.
Listen carefully to my wise sayings.
[2] Then you will continue to have good
sense.
Your lips will keep on speaking
words of knowledge.
[3] A woman who commits adultery has
lips that drip honey.
What she says is smoother than olive
oil.
[4] But in the end she is like bitter poison.
She cuts like a sword that has two
edges.
[5] Her feet go down to death.
Her steps lead straight to the grave.
[6] She doesn't give any thought to her way
of life.
Her paths have no direction, but she
doesn't realize it.
[7] My sons, listen to me.
Don't turn away from what I say.
[8] Stay on a path far away from that evil
woman.
Don't even go near the door of her
house.
[9] If you do, you will lose your honor to
other people.

You will give your self-respect to
someone who is mean.
[10] Strangers will use up all your wealth.
Your hard work will make someone
else rich.
[11] At the end of your life you will groan.
Your skin and your body will be
worn out.
[12] You will say, "How I hated to take
advice!
How my heart refused to be
corrected!
[13] I would not obey my teachers.
I wouldn't listen to those who taught
me.
[14] I was soon in deep trouble.
It happened right in front of the whole
assembly of God's people."

[15] Drink water from your own well.
Drink running water from your own
spring.
[16] Should your springs pour out into the
streets?
Should your streams of water pour
out in public places?
[17] No! Let them belong to you alone.
Never share them with strangers.
[18] May your fountain be blessed.
May the wife you married when you
were young make you happy.
[19] She is like a loving doe, a graceful deer.
May her breasts always satisfy you.
May you always be captured by her
love.
[20] My son, why be captured by another
man's wife?
Why hug a woman who has gone
astray?

[21] The LORD watches your ways.
He studies all your paths.
[22] Sinners are trapped by their own evil
acts.
They are held tight by the ropes of
their sins.

ADVENTURES IN ODYSSEY

Proverbs 5:22 says that sinners will
be trapped by their own evil acts.
In "The Case of the Ball Cap Hero"
(A#60), Emily and Matthew helped
catch the people behind a scam.

23 They will die because they refused to be
   corrected.
   Their sins will capture them because
   they were very foolish.

Warnings Against Foolish Acts

6 My son, don't promise to pay for what
   your neighbor owes.
   Don't agree to pay a stranger's bill.
2 Don't be trapped by what you have said.
   Don't be caught by the words of your
   mouth.
3 Instead, my son, do something to free
   yourself.
   Don't fall into your neighbor's hands.
   Go until you can't go anymore.
   Don't let your neighbor rest.
4 Don't let your eyes go to sleep.
   Don't let your eyelids close.
5 As a deer frees itself from a hunter, free
   yourself.
   As a bird frees itself from a trapper,
   free yourself.

6 You people who don't want to work,
   think about the ant!
   Consider its ways and be wise!
7 It has no commander.
   It has no leader or ruler.

WOOTON'S FUN FACTS
Prov. 6:6

You know ants are strong, right? They can lift 5,000 times their body weight! But they can make *you* strong if you eat them. Red ants are loaded with iron, calcium, and protein. Care for an ant sandwich? No? Good. Your parents probably don't want you eating ants!

8 But it stores up its food in summer.
   It gathers its food at harvest time.

9 You lazy people, how long will you lie
   there?

WHAT ABOUT YOU?

You've been playing a video game for two hours. The Crystal Isle is nearly within reach, though the Orb of Light will not be easy to acquire. Suddenly your mother walks into the room. "Laundry," she says, not smiling. She adds, "I asked you to do it an hour ago." So do you (a) get mad, (b) play dumb, or (c) do the chore without complaining?

In the Adventures in Odyssey episode "Game for a Mystery," Barrett went with the equivalent of "option b." When his dad told him to trim the hedges, he wasn't mad or disrespectful. But he didn't do his work, either. Barrett took the easy way out; he hid behind a tree and played his video game. It didn't end well for him!

Proverbs 6:6–8 says, "Think about the ant! Consider its ways and be wise! . . . It stores up its food in summer. It gathers its food at harvest time." The Bible teaches that laziness ends in poverty. If you work like an ant, you'll have food for the winter. When tough times come, you'll be prepared. But if you're a "lazybones," you'll end up in trouble. So let's remember the ant as we carry out the tasks God has for us.

Go outside, find an anthill, and spend a few minutes watching the worker ants. Place a minor obstacle in their path and watch how they handle it. Do you tackle your chores like that? If not, today would be a great day to start!

The word *muckrake* means "to search out and publicly expose real or apparent misconduct of a prominent individual or business." Let's say that someone said Mr. Whittaker sold spoiled ice cream, and Bart Rathbone peddled faulty gadgets to kids at the Electric Palace. Should we believe those statements without proof?

We can conclude the first statement is false because we know that Mr. Whittaker is honest. But we might be tempted to believe the other based on stories of Rathbone's electronics breaking or shorting out.

Muckraking isn't bad when used to expose the truth for the public's benefit. Reporters do it all the time. But making false accusations without having all the facts or understanding the full story could damage someone's reputation.

Proverbs 6:19 says, "He hates any witness who pours out lies and anyone who stirs up conflict in the community." These are strong words from the Bible about those who misrepresent the truth. It's important to be sure of your facts—and the source you

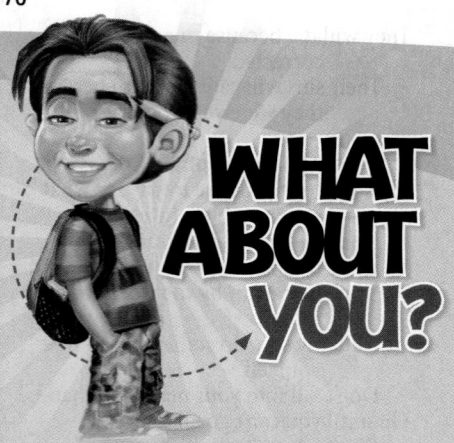

WHAT ABOUT you?

get them from—before speaking about a situation.

It's tempting to read something on the Internet and assume that it's true, but people can post rumors and lies online with no one there to stop them. Have you ever encountered this? Talk to your parents about healthy boundaries and fruitful fact-finding. Ask them which sources they trust and how to be a savvy researcher. Then pray that the God of Truth will guide everything you say and do.

When will you get up from your
    sleep?
¹⁰ You might sleep a little or take a little
    nap.
    You might even fold your hands and
    rest.
¹¹ Then you would be poor, as if someone
    had robbed you.
    You would have little, as if someone
    had stolen from you.

¹² An evil troublemaker
    goes around saying twisted things
    with his mouth.
¹³   He winks with his eyes.
    He makes signals with his feet.
    He motions with his fingers.
¹⁴   His plans are evil, and he has lies in
    his heart.
    He is always stirring up fights.
¹⁵ Trouble will catch up with him in an
    instant.
    He will suddenly be destroyed, and
    nothing can save him.

¹⁶ There are six things the LORD hates.
    In fact, he hates seven things.
¹⁷ The LORD hates proud eyes,
    a lying tongue,
    and hands that kill those who
    aren't guilty.
¹⁸ He also hates hearts that make
    evil plans
    and feet that are quick to do
    evil.
¹⁹ He hates any witness who
    pours out lies
    and anyone who stirs up con-
    flict in the community.

A Warning Against Committing Adultery

²⁰ My son, keep your father's command.
    Don't turn away from your mother's
    teaching.
²¹ Always tie them on your heart.
    Put them around your neck.
²² When you walk, they will guide you.

When you sleep, they will watch
over you.
When you wake up, they will speak
to you.
²³ Your father's command is like a lamp.
Your mother's teaching is like a light.
And whatever instructs and corrects
you
leads to life.
²⁴ It keeps you from your neighbor's wife.
It keeps you from the smooth talk
of a woman who commits
adultery.
²⁵ Don't hunger in your heart after her
beauty.
Don't let her eyes capture you.
²⁶ A prostitute can be bought for only a
loaf of bread.
But another man's wife hunts your
very life.
²⁷ You can't shovel fire into your lap
without burning your clothes.
²⁸ You can't walk on hot coals
without burning your feet.
²⁹ It's the same for anyone who has sex
with another man's wife.
Anyone who touches her will be
punished.
³⁰ People don't hate a thief who steals
to fill his empty stomach.
³¹ But when he is caught, he must pay
seven times as much as he stole.
It may even cost him everything he
has.
³² A man who commits adultery has no
sense.
Anyone who does it destroys
himself.
³³ He will be beaten up and dishonored.
His shame will never be wiped away.
³⁴ Jealousy stirs up a husband's anger.
He will show no mercy when he gets
even.
³⁵ He won't accept any payment.
He won't take any money, no matter
how much he is offered.

A Warning Against a Woman Who Commits Adultery

7 My son, obey my words.
Store up my commands inside you.
² Obey my commands and you will live.
Guard my teachings as you would
guard your own eyes.
³ Tie them on your fingers.
Write them on the tablet of your
heart.
⁴ Say to wisdom, "You are my sister."
Say to understanding, "You are a
member of my family."
⁵ They will keep you from a woman who
commits adultery.
They will keep you from the smooth
talk of a sinful wife.
⁶ I stood at the window of my house.
I looked down through it.
⁷ Among those who were childish
I saw a young man who had no
sense.
⁸ He went down the street near that
sinful woman's corner.
He walked toward her house.
⁹ The sun had gone down, and the day
was fading.
The darkness of night was falling.
¹⁰ A woman came out to meet him.
She was dressed like a prostitute and
had a clever plan.
¹¹ She was wild and pushy.
She never stayed at home.
¹² Sometimes she's in the streets.
Sometimes she's at other places.
At every corner she waits.
¹³ She took hold of the young man and
kissed him.
With a bold face she spoke to him.
She said,
¹⁴ "Today I offered what I promised I
would.
At home I have meat left over from
my fellowship offering.
¹⁵ So I came out to meet you.
I looked for you and have found you!
¹⁶ I have covered my bed
with colored sheets from Egypt.
¹⁷ I've perfumed my bed with spices.
I used myrrh, aloes and cinnamon.
¹⁸ Come, let's drink our fill of love until
morning.
Let's enjoy ourselves by sleeping
together!

¹⁹ My husband isn't home.
     He's gone on a long journey.
²⁰ He took his bag full of money.
     He won't be home for several days."

²¹ She led him astray with her clever
     words.
     She charmed him with her smooth
     talk.
²² All at once he followed her.
     He was like an ox going to be killed.
     He was like a deer stepping into a trap
²³ until an arrow struck its liver.
     He was like a bird rushing into a trap.
     Little did he know it would cost him
     his life!

²⁴ My sons, listen to me.
     Pay attention to what I say.
²⁵ Don't let your hearts turn to her ways.
     Don't step onto her paths.
²⁶ She has brought down a lot of men.
     She has killed a huge crowd.
²⁷ Her house is a road to the grave.
     It leads down to the place of the
     dead.

Wisdom Calls Out

8 Doesn't wisdom call out?
     Doesn't understanding raise her
     voice?
² At the highest point along the way,
     she takes her place where the paths
     meet.
³ Beside the gate leading into the city,
     she cries out at the entrance. She says,
⁴ "People, I call out to you.
     I raise my voice to all human beings.
⁵ You who are childish, get some good
     sense.
     You who are foolish, set your hearts
     on getting it.
⁶ Listen! I have things to say that you can
     depend on.
     I open my lips to speak what is right.
⁷ My mouth speaks what is true.
     My lips hate evil.
⁸ All the words of my mouth are honest.
     None of them is twisted or sinful.
⁹ To those who have understanding, all
     my words are right.
     To those who have found
     knowledge, they are true.
¹⁰ Choose my teaching instead of silver.
     Choose knowledge rather than fine
     gold.

WOOTON'S FUN FACTS

Prov. 8:1

Throughout Proverbs, wisdom is called a person. And not just any person, but a "she"—a woman! We are supposed to love wisdom and pursue "her."

¹¹ Wisdom is worth more than rubies.
     Nothing you want can compare with
     her.
¹² "I, wisdom, live together with
     understanding.
     I have knowledge and good sense.
¹³ To have respect for the LORD is to hate
     evil.
     I hate pride and bragging.
     I hate evil ways and twisted words.
¹⁴ I have good sense and give good
     advice.
     I have understanding and power.
¹⁵ By me kings rule.
     Leaders make laws that are fair.
¹⁶ By me princes and nobles govern.
     It is by me that anyone rules on
     earth.
¹⁷ I love those who love me.
     Those who look for me find me.
¹⁸ With me are riches and honor.
     With me are lasting wealth and
     success.
¹⁹ My fruit is better than fine gold.
     My gifts are better than the finest
     silver.
²⁰ I walk in ways that are honest.
     I take paths that are right.
²¹ I leave riches to those who love me.
     I give them more than they have
     room for.

22 "The LORD created me as the first of his works,
before his acts of long ago.
23 I was formed a long, long time ago.
I was formed at the very beginning,
when the world was created.
24 Before there were any oceans, I was born.
It was before there were springs flowing with water.
25 Before the mountains were settled in place, I was born.
Before there were any hills, I was born.
26 It happened before the LORD made the world and its fields.
It was before he made the dust of the earth.
27 I was there when he set the heavens in place.
When he marked out the place where the sky meets the sea, I was there.
28 That was when he put the clouds above.
It was when he fixed the ocean springs in place.
29 It was when he set limits for the sea so that the waters had to obey his command.
When the LORD marked out the foundations of the earth, I was there.
30 I was constantly at his side.
I was filled with delight day after day.
I was always happy to be with him.
31 His whole world filled me with joy.
I took delight in all human beings.

32 "My children, listen to me.
Blessed are those who keep my ways.
33 Listen to my teaching and be wise.
Don't turn away from it.
34 Blessed are those who listen to me.
They watch every day at my doors.
They wait beside my doorway.
35 Those who find me find life.
They receive blessing from the LORD.
36 But those who don't find me harm only themselves.
Everyone who hates me loves death."

Wisdom and Foolishness Call Out

9 Wisdom has built her house.
She has set up its seven pillars.
2 She has prepared her meat and mixed her wine.
She has also set her table.
3 She has sent out her servants.
She calls out from the highest point of the city.
4 She says, "Let all who are childish come to my house!"
She speaks to those who have no sense. She says,
5 "Come and eat my food.
Drink the wine I have mixed.
6 Leave your childish ways and you will live.
Walk in the way of understanding."

7 When you correct someone who makes fun of others, you might be laughed at.
When you warn a sinner, you might get hurt.
8 Don't warn those who make fun of others, or they will hate you.
Warn those who are wise, and they will love you.
9 Teach a wise person, and they will become even wiser.
Teach a person who does right, and they will learn even more.

10 If you want to become wise, you must begin by respecting the LORD.
To know the Holy One is to gain understanding.
11 Through wisdom, you will live a long time.
Years will be added to your life.
12 If you are wise, your wisdom will reward you.
If you make fun of others, you alone will suffer.

13 The woman called Foolishness is wild.
She is childish and knows nothing.
14 She sits at the door of her house.
She sits at the highest point of the city.
15 She calls out to those who pass by.
She calls out to those who go straight on their way. She says,
16 "Let all who are childish come to my house!"
She speaks to those who have no sense.
17 She says, "Stolen water is sweet.
Food eaten in secret tastes good!"
18 But they don't know that dead people are there.

They don't know that her guests are deep in the place of the dead.

THE PROVERBS OF SOLOMON

10 These are the proverbs of Solomon.

A wise son makes his father glad.
But a foolish son brings sorrow to his mother.

² Riches that are gained by sinning aren't worth anything.
But doing what is right saves you from death.

³ The LORD gives those who do right the food they need.
But he lets those who do wrong go hungry.

⁴ Hands that don't want to work make you poor.
But hands that work hard bring wealth to you.

⁵ A child who gathers crops in summer is wise.
But a child who sleeps at harvest time brings shame.

⁶ Blessings are like crowns on the heads of those who do right.
But the trouble caused by what sinners say destroys them.

⁷ The names of those who do right are used in blessings.
But the names of those who do wrong will rot.

⁸ A wise heart accepts commands.

ADVENTURES IN ODYSSEY

Hard work and diligence were the words of the day when Connie taught Eugene to drive in "A License to Drive" (A#14).

But foolish chattering destroys you.

⁹ Anyone who lives without blame walks safely.
But anyone who takes a crooked path will get caught.

¹⁰ An evil wink gets you into trouble.
And foolish chattering destroys you.

¹¹ The mouths of those who do right pour out life like a fountain.
But the mouths of sinners hide their evil plans.

Jason's Jargon

PROVERBS 10

Seek out *chattering* in this chapter. Chattering is talking quickly and foolishly. Chatter is often associated with gossip, which is also unwise talk.

¹² Hate stirs up fights.
But love erases all sins by forgiving them.

¹³ Wisdom is found on the lips of those who understand what is right.
But those who have no sense are punished.

¹⁴ Wise people store up knowledge.
But the mouths of foolish people destroy them.

¹⁵ The wealth of rich people is like a city that makes them feel safe.
But having nothing destroys those who are poor.

¹⁶ People who do what is right earn life.
But sinners earn sin and death.

¹⁷ Anyone who pays attention to correction
shows the path to life.
But anyone who refuses to be corrected leads others down the wrong path.

¹⁸ Anyone who hides hatred with lying lips and spreads lies is foolish.

¹⁹ Sin is not ended by using many words.

You're spending the night at a new friend's house, and you're a little nervous that your friend will discover your secret: Even though you're too old for it, you still sometimes suck your thumb at night. Your friend notices and asks you about it the next morning, but then admits an affection for a certain blanket he or she has had since infancy. You're relieved—until Monday, when you find out your new "friend" blabbed your secret all over school.

The easy thing to do, and what some people might tell you to do, would be to expose your friend's secret in revenge. Instead, you remain silent, own up to the whole thumb-sucking thing, and everyone forgets about it in a few days. That takes integrity. Integrity means living honestly and responsibly, and in this case not trying to get even with someone who has hurt you.

For example, in the Adventures in Odyssey episode "It Takes Integrity," Lucy faces a similar problem. She knows an awful secret about Curt, and even though he has told the whole school about things about her that she didn't want anyone to know, she always treats him (and his secret) with respect.

Proverbs 10:29 says: "The way of the LORD is a safe place for those without blame. But that way destroys those who do evil." Remember, it's always better to follow God's plan and obey His law than to try to get justice for yourself. Memorize this verse, take it to heart, and find freedom in following God.

But those who are wise control their tongues.

²⁰ The tongues of those who do right are like fine silver.
But the hearts of those who do wrong aren't worth very much.

²¹ The words of those who do right benefit many people.
But those who are foolish die because they have no sense.

²² The blessing of the LORD brings wealth.
And it comes without painful work.

²³ A foolish person finds pleasure in evil plans.
But a person who has understanding takes delight in wisdom.

²⁴ What sinners are afraid of will catch up with them.
But those who do right will get what they want.

²⁵ When the storm is over, sinners are gone.
But those who do right stand firm forever.

²⁶ Those who don't want to work hurt those who send them.
They are like vinegar on the teeth or smoke in the eyes.

²⁷ Having respect for the LORD leads to a longer life.
But the years of evil people are cut short.

²⁸ Those who do right can expect joy.
But the hopes of sinners are bound to fail.

²⁹ The way of the LORD is a safe place for those without blame.
But that way destroys those who do evil.

³⁰ Those who do right will never be removed from the land.
But those who do wrong will not remain in it.

³¹ The mouths of those who do right
    produce wisdom.
But tongues that speak twisted
    words will be made silent.

³² Those who do right know the proper
    thing to say.
But those who do wrong speak only
    twisted words.

11 The LORD hates it when people use
    scales to cheat others.
But he is delighted when people use
    honest weights.

² When pride comes, shame follows.
But wisdom comes to those who are
    not proud.

³ Those who do what is right are guided
    by their honest lives.
But those who aren't faithful are
    destroyed by their lies.

⁴ Wealth isn't worth anything when God
    judges you.
But doing what is right saves you
    from death.

⁵ The ways of honest people are made
    straight because they do what
    is right.
But those who do what is wrong are
    brought down by their own
    sins.

⁶ Godly people are saved by doing what
    is right.
But those who aren't faithful are
    trapped by evil longings.

⁷ Hopes placed in human beings will die
    with them.
Everything their power promised
    comes to nothing.

⁸ Those who do right are saved from
    trouble.
But trouble comes on those who do
    wrong.

⁹ With their words ungodly people
    destroy their neighbors.
But those who do what is right
    escape because of their
    knowledge.

It's a real mystery: There's a broken window in Whit's End and three prime suspects. Who's guilty? Was it Sarah with the juggling ball? Alex with the baseball bat? Rodney Rathbone with, well, Rodney Rathbone?

Here are the facts from the Adventures in Odyssey episode "Broken Window": All three suspects were seen at Whit's End around the time the window was broken. Alex was practicing baseball and admits that he hit—but did not break—the window. So why did Sarah find him hiding behind Whit's End? That raises another question: Why was Sarah taking the back way to the soda shop? Does she usually wander around in the woods? Then there's Rodney. He might have had a motive for breaking the window and framing Alex, who threw a french fry into his milkshake. Could this have been an act of revenge?

There were no witnesses, so it's one person's word against another. Thankfully, "Judge" Connie shows good sense by listening to each person's explanation, then visiting the scene of the crime for further investigation. Connie's quest for an answer demonstrates the importance of searching for truth, even when it's hidden by conflicting stories.

Proverbs 11 deals with controlling our words and treating others with fairness and respect. Take a few minutes to memorize Proverbs 11:12. It's short and simple, so it should be easy to remember. But don't stop there. Ask God to remind you of this verse today if you're tempted to use your words carelessly.

[10] When those who do right succeed, their
city is glad.
When those who do wrong die,
people shout for joy.

[11] The blessing of honest people builds up
a city.
But the words of sinners destroy it.

[12] Whoever makes fun of their neighbor
has no sense.
But the one who has understanding
controls their tongue.

[13] Those who talk about others will tell
secrets.
But those who can be trusted keep
the secrets of others.

[14] Without guidance a nation falls.
But many good advisers can bring
victory to a nation.

[15] Whoever promises to pay for what
someone else owes will
certainly suffer.
But a person who doesn't agree to
pay someone else's bill is safe.

[16] A woman who has a kind heart gains
honor.
But men who are not kind gain only
wealth.

[17] Those who are kind benefit themselves.
But mean people bring ruin on
themselves.

[18] An evil person really earns nothing.
But the one who plants what is right
will certainly be rewarded.

[19] Surely right living leads to life.
But whoever runs after evil finds
death.

[20] The LORD hates those whose hearts are
twisted.
But he is pleased with those who live
without blame.

[21] You can be sure that sinners will be
punished.
And you can also be sure that godly
people will go free.

[22] A beautiful woman who has no sense
is like a gold ring in a pig's nose.

[23] What godly people long for ends only
in what is good.

But what sinners hope for ends only
in God's anger.

[24] One person gives freely but gets even
richer.
Another person doesn't give what
they should but gets even
poorer.

[25] Anyone who gives a lot will succeed.
Anyone who renews others will be
renewed.

[26] People ask for bad things to happen to
those who store up grain for
themselves.
But people ask for God's blessing on
those who are willing to sell.

[27] Anyone who looks for what is good will
be blessed.
But bad things will happen to a
person who plans to do evil.

[28] Those who trust in their riches will fall.
But those who do right will be as
healthy as a green leaf.

[29] Those who bring ruin on their families
will receive nothing but wind.
And foolish people will serve wise
people.

[30] The fruit that godly people bear is like a
tree of life.
And those who are wise save lives.

[31] Godly people get what they should get
on earth.
So ungodly people and sinners will
certainly get what they should
get!

12 Anyone who loves correction loves
knowledge.
Anyone who hates to be corrected is
stupid.

[2] The LORD blesses anyone who does
good.
But he judges anyone who plans to
do evil.

[3] No one can become strong and steady
by doing evil.
But if people do what is right, they
can't be removed from the
land.

[4] An excellent woman is her husband's
crown.

But a wife who brings shame is like
   sickness in his bones.

5 The plans of godly people are right.
   But the advice of sinners will lead
      you the wrong way.

6 The words of those who are evil hide
      and wait to spill people's blood.
   But the speech of those who are
      honest saves them from traps
      like that.

7 Sinners are destroyed and taken away.
   But the houses of godly people stand
      firm.

8 A person is praised for how wise they
      are.
   But people hate anyone who has a
      twisted mind.

9 Being nobody and having a servant
      is better than pretending to be
      somebody and having no food.

10 Those who do what is right take good
      care of their animals.

ADVENTURES IN ODYSSEY

Connie and Eugene had to listen
to advice—from each other!—in
"Connie the Counselor" (A#62).

But the kindest acts of those who do
   wrong are mean.

11 Those who farm their land will have
      plenty of food.
   But those who chase dreams have
      no sense.

12 Those who do what is wrong are safe
      for just a while.
   But those who do what is right last
      forever.

13 Those who do evil are trapped by their
      sinful talk.
   But those who have done no wrong
      escape trouble.

14 Many good things come from what
      people say.

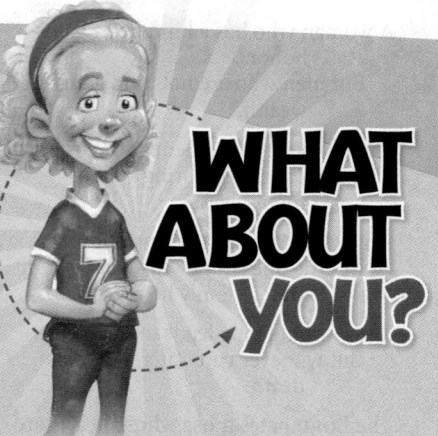

WHAT ABOUT YOU?

How would you respond if someone tried to sell you seeds for a spaghetti tree? "Grow pasta right in your own backyard," the salesperson might say. Are you buying? Believe it or not, hundreds of people who watched a documentary in 1957 did!

One April Fool's Day, the British Broadcasting Company aired a short program about farmers in Switzerland harvesting noodles from trees. People called in afterward to ask how they could grow their own spaghetti tree, not realizing that it was one big hoax. Jokes like that can be funny for a little while, but if you try to keep a deception going, you'll find yourself living a lie.

Proverbs 12:22 tells us that God takes honesty very seriously: "The LORD hates those whose lips tell lies. But he is pleased with people who tell the truth."

Sometimes we lie for reasons that may seem noble at the time. But that doesn't make it right. When we lie, it can take a long time to regain people's trust. Even when it's hard, we need to tell the truth and be the kind of person others can count on.

Close your eyes so you can't see anything. What can you tell about what's around you just by listening or touching? Try to determine the reality of the world around you with your eyes closed. It's hard, isn't it? When you open your eyes, you can see what you were missing because it's in the light. The truth is like our eyesight, helping us to know what is real in our world.

WHIT'S WISDOM

Proverbs 12:22

One day, Connie read a book that I had written called *The Tangled Web*. It's about a boy named Jeremy who lost his money. Instead of telling his mother what had actually happened, he made up a lie about how it had been stolen. The lie got bigger and bigger, eventually involving the police and the whole town. The mayor himself decided to give Jeremy a citation for bravery! When the time came to receive his award, Jeremy nervously stepped to the podium . . . and accepted the award. No one ever found out what he had really done.

Connie was shocked that Jeremy seemed to get away with it. But I pointed out that he didn't get away with it. That's the way a lie works. It sticks in your mind and eats at you until it's just about all you can think of. Then either you make it right, or you spend the rest of your life as Jeremy did, afraid that somebody will find out. Even if no one does, the lie is also just as damaging because at least one person will always know about it, and that's you.

That's why Proverbs 12:22 says God is pleased with those who tell the truth.

And the work of their hands rewards
　　them.
15 The way of foolish people seems right
　　to them.
　But those who are wise listen to
　　advice.
16 Foolish people are easily upset.
　But wise people pay no attention to
　　hurtful words.
17 An honest witness tells the truth.
　But a dishonest witness tells lies.
18 The words of thoughtless people cut
　　like swords.
　But the tongue of wise people brings
　　healing.
19 Truthful words last forever.
　But lies last for only a moment.
20 There are lies in the hearts of those who
　　plan evil.
　But there is joy for those who work
　　to bring peace.
21 No harm comes to godly people.
　But sinners have all the trouble they
　　can handle.
22 The LORD hates those whose lips tell
　　lies.

But he is pleased with people who
　　tell the truth.
23 Wise people keep their knowledge to
　　themselves.
　But the hearts of foolish people
　　shout foolish things.
24 Hands that work hard will rule.
　But people who are lazy will be
　　forced to work.
25 Worry makes the heart heavy.
　But a kind word cheers it up.
26 Godly people are careful about the
　　friends they choose.
　But the way of sinners leads them
　　down the wrong path.
27 Lazy people do not even cook what
　　they catch.
　But those who work hard eat their
　　fill of what is hunted.
28 There is life in doing what is right.
　Along that path you will never die.

13 A wise son pays attention to what his
　　father teaches him.
　But anyone who makes fun of
　　others doesn't listen to
　　warnings.

2 The good things people say benefit them.
But liars love to hurt others.

3 Those who guard what they say guard their lives.
But those who speak without thinking will be destroyed.

4 People who refuse to work want things and get nothing.
But the desires of people who work hard are completely satisfied.

5 Those who do right hate what is false.
But those who do wrong stink and bring shame on themselves.

6 Doing right guards those who are honest.
But evil destroys those who are sinful.

7 Some people pretend to be rich but have nothing.
Others pretend to be poor but have great wealth.

8 A person's riches might save their life.
But a poor person is not able to do anything about danger.

9 The lights of godly people shine brightly.
But the lamps of sinners are blown out.

10 Where there is arguing, there is pride.
But those who take advice are wise.

11 Money gained in the wrong way disappears.
But money gathered little by little grows.

12 Hope that is put off makes one sick at heart.
But a desire that is met is like a tree of life.

13 Anyone who hates what they are taught will pay for it later.
But a person who respects a command will be rewarded.

14 The teaching of wise people is like a fountain that gives life.
It turns those who listen to it away from the jaws of death.

15 Good judgment wins favor.
But the way of liars leads to their ruin.

WHAT ABOUT YOU?

You can't believe it. Your friend got picked for the soccer team ahead of you. Not only can you shoot better, you're a whole lot faster. Now anytime you pass in the hallway, you give your "friend" the cold shoulder.

Proverbs 13:10 says: "Where there is arguing, there is pride. But those who take advice are wise." When we let pride control our lives, it can destroy our relationships with others. Paired with jealousy, it causes us to think bad thoughts and do things we wouldn't normally do. Pride can make us extremely competitive and turn best friends into enemies overnight. We need to let our pride go and be humble, just as Christ tells us to.

Try this activity: With your parent's permission, gather some supplies from around the house—a paper towel, food dye, scissors, and a glass of water. First, put a few drops of food dye into your glass of water and stir gently. Second, take your paper towel and cut one strip from it, approximately two inches wide and five inches long. Third, carefully dip the bottom edge of your paper towel strip into the water. Hold it there for ten seconds or so. Take the strip out and watch the colorful water creep up. Remember that just as the food coloring takes over the paper towel, pride can take over our lives. We need to pray that God will help us control our pride so we can honor Him more each day.

16 Wise people act with knowledge.
But foolish people show how foolish
they are.

17 An evil messenger gets into trouble.
But a trusted messenger brings
healing.

18 Those who turn away from their training
become poor and ashamed.
But those who accept warnings are
honored.

19 A desire that is met is like something
that tastes sweet.
But foolish people hate to turn away
from evil.

20 Walk with wise people and become
wise.
A companion of foolish people
suffers harm.

21 Hard times chase those who are sinful.
But those who do right are rewarded
with good things.

22 A good person leaves what they
own to their children and
grandchildren.
But a sinner's wealth is stored up for
those who do right.

23 An unplowed field produces food for
poor people.
But those who treat them badly
destroy it all.

24 Those who don't correct their children
hate them.
But those who love them are careful
to correct them.

25 Those who do right eat until they are
full.
But the stomachs of those who do
wrong go hungry.

14 A wise woman builds her house.
But a foolish woman tears hers down
with her own hands.

2 Whoever has respect for the LORD lives
a good life.
But those who hate him walk down
an evil path.

3 The proud words of a foolish person
sting like a whip.
But the things wise people say keep
them safe.

4 Where there are no oxen, the feed box
is empty.
But a strong ox brings in huge
harvests.

5 An honest witness does not lie.
But a dishonest witness pours out
lies.

6 Those who make fun of others look for
wisdom and don't find it.
But knowledge comes easily to those
who understand what is right.

7 Stay away from a foolish person.
You won't find knowledge in what
they say.

8 People are wise and understanding
when they think about the way
they live.
But people are foolish when their
foolish ways trick them.

9 Foolish people laugh at making things
right when they sin.
But honest people try to do the right
thing.

10 Each heart knows its own sadness.
And no one else can share its joy.

11 The houses of sinners will be destroyed.
But the tents of honest people will
stand firm.

12 There is a way that appears to be right.
But in the end it leads to death.

13 Even when you laugh, your heart can
be hurting.
And your joy can end in sadness.

14 Those who aren't faithful will be paid
back
for what they've done.
And good people will receive rewards
for how they've lived.

15 A childish person believes anything.
But a wise person thinks about how
they live.

16 A wise person has respect for the LORD
and avoids evil.
But a foolish person has a bad
temper and yet feels secure.

17 Anyone who gets angry quickly does
foolish things.
And a person who is tricky is hated.

WHAT ABOUT YOU?

It's growing hot outside as you hike through the woods. You're getting hungry, so you head back toward the campsite for lunch. You come to a fork in the road where a sign says "Nature Center." The arrow points to a paved path. It is shady and slopes gently downhill. Another arrow on the sign points toward your campsite. But that trail is rocky, steep, and exposed to the scorching sun. Which one do you take?

It wouldn't make sense to take the first path. It might be an easier, more pleasant walk, but it doesn't lead where you want to go. In the same way, we sometimes wonder if it's worth it to do the right thing. Things can still go wrong even when we're being honest and trying to live as Jesus wants us to. Remember, though, Proverbs 14:14 warns, "Those who aren't faithful will be paid back for what they've done." The Bible says our sin will catch up to us, so it's always better to make good choices, regardless of the outcome.

Have you heard of the game Chutes and Ladders? Play your own "live" version with friends. Form a line in the center of a room. Take turns rolling a die. If you get an even number, think of a "right choice statement" ("I studied for my test") and step forward. If you roll an odd number, think of a "wrong choice statement" ("I pushed all the buttons on the elevator before getting off") and take a step backward. Whoever reaches the "right choice" wall first wins!

---

¹⁸ Childish people act in keeping with
    their foolish ways.
  But knowledge makes wise people
    feel like kings.

¹⁹ Evil people will bow down in front of
    good people.
  And those who do wrong will bow
    down at the gates of those who
    do right.

²⁰ Poor people are avoided even by their
    neighbors.
  But rich people have many friends.

²¹ It is a sin to hate your neighbor.
  But blessed is the person who is kind
    to those in need.

²² Those who plan evil go down the wrong
    path.
  But those who plan good find love
    and truth.

²³ All hard work pays off.
  But if all you do is talk, you will be
    poor.

²⁴ The wealth of wise people is their crown.
  But the foolish ways of foolish
    people lead to what is foolish.

²⁵ An honest witness saves lives.
  But a dishonest witness tells lies.

²⁶ Anyone who shows respect for the
    Lord has a strong tower.
  It will be a safe place for their
    children.

²⁷ Respect for the Lord is like a fountain
    that gives life.
  It turns you away from the jaws of
    death.

²⁸ A large population is a king's glory.
  But a prince without followers is
    destroyed.

²⁹ Anyone who is patient has great
    understanding.
  But anyone who gets angry quickly
    shows how foolish they are.

³⁰ A peaceful heart gives life to the body.
  But jealousy rots the bones.

³¹ Anyone who crushes poor people
　　makes fun of their Maker.
　But anyone who is kind to those in
　　need honors God.

³² When trouble comes, sinners are
　　brought down.
　But godly people seek safety in God
　　even as they die.

³³ Wisdom rests in the hearts of those
　　who understand what is right.
　And even among foolish people she
　　makes herself known.

³⁴ Doing what is right lifts people up.
　But sin brings judgment to any
　　nation.

³⁵ A king is pleased with a wise servant.
　But a servant who is full of shame
　　stirs up the king's anger.

15 A gentle answer turns anger away.
　But mean words stir up anger.

² The tongues of wise people use
　　knowledge well.
　But the mouths of foolish people
　　pour out foolish words.

³ The eyes of the LORD are everywhere.
　They watch those who are evil and
　　those who are good.

⁴ A tongue that calms is like a tree of life.
　But a tongue that tells lies produces
　　a broken spirit.

⁵ A foolish person turns their back on
　　their parent's correction.
　But anyone who accepts correction
　　shows understanding.

⁶ The houses of those who do what is
　　right hold great wealth.
　But those who do what is wrong
　　earn only ruin.

⁷ The lips of wise people spread
　　knowledge.
　But the hearts of foolish people are
　　not honest.

⁸ The LORD hates the sacrifice of sinful
　　people.
　But the prayers of honest people
　　please him.

⁹ The LORD hates how sinners live.
　But he loves those who run after
　　what is right.

¹⁰ Hard training is in store for anyone
　　who leaves the right path.
　A person who hates to be corrected
　　will die.

¹¹ Death and the Grave lie open in front
　　of the LORD.
　So human hearts certainly lie open
　　to him!

¹² People who make fun of others don't
　　like to be corrected.
　So they stay away from wise people.

¹³ A happy heart makes a face look
　　cheerful.
　But a sad heart produces a broken
　　spirit.

¹⁴ A heart that understands what is right
　　looks for knowledge.
　But the mouths of foolish people
　　feed on what is foolish.

¹⁵ All the days of those who are crushed
　　are filled with pain and
　　suffering.
　But a cheerful heart enjoys a good
　　time that never ends.

¹⁶ It is better to have respect for the LORD
　　and have little
　than to be rich and have trouble.

¹⁷ A few vegetables where there is love
　　are better than the finest meat where
　　there is hatred.

¹⁸ A person with a bad temper stirs up
　　conflict.
　But a person who is patient calms
　　things down.

¹⁹ The way of people who don't want to
　　work is blocked with thorns.
　But the path of honest people is a
　　wide road.

²⁰ A wise son makes his father glad.
　But a foolish son hates his mother.

²¹ A person who has no sense enjoys
　　doing foolish things.
　But a person who has
　　understanding walks straight
　　ahead.

²² Plans fail without good advice.
　But they succeed when there are
　　many advisers.

ADVENTURES IN ODYSSEY

Mandy and David had to have understanding when they sorted out a crazy story that Bernard told in "I Slap Floor" (A#34).

²³ Joy is found in giving the right answer.
And how good is a word spoken at the right time!

²⁴ The path of life leads up for those who are wise.
It keeps them from going down to the place of the dead.

²⁵ The LORD tears down the proud person's house.
But he keeps the widow's property safe.

²⁶ The LORD hates the thoughts of sinful people.
But he considers kind words to be pure.

²⁷ Those who always want more bring ruin to their households.
But a person who refuses to be paid to lie will live.

²⁸ The hearts of those who do right think about how they will answer.
But the mouths of those who do wrong pour out evil.

²⁹ The LORD is far away from those who do wrong.
But he hears the prayers of those who do right.

³⁰ The cheerful look of a messenger brings joy to your heart.
And good news gives health to your body.

³¹ Whoever listens to a warning that gives life
will be at home among those who are wise.

³² Those who turn away from correction hate themselves.
But anyone who accepts correction gains understanding.

³³ Wisdom teaches you to have respect for the LORD.
So don't be proud if you want to be honored.

16 People make plans in their hearts.
But the LORD puts the correct answer on their tongues.

² Everything a person does might seem pure to them.
But the LORD knows why they do what they do.

³ Commit to the LORD everything you do.
Then he will make your plans succeed.

⁴ The LORD works everything out to the proper end.
Even those who do wrong were made for a day of trouble.

⁵ The LORD hates all those who have proud hearts.
You can be sure that they will be punished.

⁶ Through love and truth sin is paid for.

ADVENTURES IN ODYSSEY

Whit planned new inventions in "The Grand Design" (A#56). Proverbs 16 says that while we plan our lives, God decides where our steps will take us.

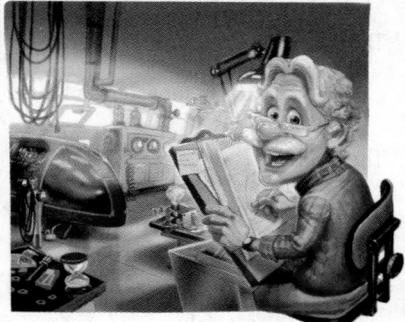

People avoid evil when they have respect for the LORD.

⁷ When the way you live pleases the LORD,
  he makes even your enemies live at peace with you.

⁸ It is better to have a little and do right than to have a lot and be unfair.

⁹ In their hearts human beings plan their lives.
  But the LORD decides where their steps will take them.

¹⁰ A king speaks as if his words come from God.
  And what he says does not turn right into wrong.

¹¹ Honest scales and balances belong to the LORD.
  He made all the weights in the bag.

¹² A king hates it when his people do what is wrong.
  A ruler is made secure when they do what is right.

¹³ Kings are pleased when what you say is honest.
  They value people who speak what is right.

¹⁴ An angry king can order your death.
  But a wise person will try to calm him down.

¹⁵ When a king's face is happy, it means life.
  His favor is like rain in the spring.

¹⁶ It is much better to get wisdom than gold.
  It is much better to choose understanding than silver.

¹⁷ The path of honest people takes them away from evil.
  Those who guard their ways guard their lives.

¹⁸ If you are proud, you will be destroyed.
  If you are proud, you will fall.

¹⁹ Suppose you are lowly in spirit along with those who are treated badly.

WHAT ABOUT YOU?

Have you ever been so involved with one thing that you completely forgot about another?

Maybe you're really into soccer and playing the guitar. That's great. But if you spend all your free time on one, you won't be quite as sharp at the other. Or maybe you've decided that it's really important to get good grades and serve God. Good for you! Both are awesome. But if you invest every waking hour on schoolwork, your walk with God is bound to suffer. How can we get better at multiple things?

The key word to remember is balance. When we get wrapped up in an exciting new project, it's easy to lose track of what's most important. We can unintentionally abandon our first commitment and focus on the fun new thing. No matter what or who else is competing for our attention, God needs to be number one. Proverbs 16:9 reminds us that God is the One who directs our steps. So remember what Jesus said in Matthew 6:33: "Put God's kingdom first. Do what he wants you to do. Then all those things will also be given to you."

Today, set aside a half hour to give completely to God. Pray. Sing. Read Scripture. Write in a journal. See if that time allows you to focus more on the Lord throughout the day ahead. Strive to honor Christ in everything you do, knowing that once you make Him your top priority, everything else will fall into place.

WHIT'S WISDOM

Proverbs 16:18

Mike Caldwell came into Whit's End one day after a fight at school. You see, Mike had started out being a hero and defending other kids from a bully. But when he actually won a fight, he let it go to his head. Then he was punched by a new kid and wasn't the hero anymore. I tried to explain that for every tough guy who comes along, there's always somebody tougher. Like we see with David and Goliath.

Goliath was big, mean and mighty and everyone was afraid of him. Then along came a small boy with a slingshot and . . . boom, Goliath wasn't so tough anymore. But the difference is that David wasn't trying to be tough. David fought Goliath because Goliath was laughing at God. David was just doing what God told him to do. There's a big difference between fighting because you're trying to help a friend and don't have a choice, and fighting because it makes you look cool in front of your friends. That's why Proverbs 16:18 says, "If you are proud, you will fall." In other words, you may think you're hot stuff now, but you won't be for long.

That's better than sharing stolen
goods with those who are
proud.

20 If anyone pays attention to what they're
taught, they will succeed.
Blessed is the person who trusts in
the LORD.

21 Wise hearts are known for
understanding what is right.
Kind words make people want to
learn more.

22 Understanding is like a fountain of life
to those who have it.
But foolish people are punished for
the foolish things they do.

23 The hearts of wise people guide their
mouths.
Their words make people want to
learn more.

24 Kind words are like honey.
They are sweet to the spirit and
bring healing to the body.

25 There is a way that appears to be right.
But in the end it leads to death.

26 The hunger of workers makes them
work.
Their hunger drives them on.

27 A worthless person plans to do evil
things.
Their words are like a burning fire.

28 A twisted person stirs up conflict.
Anyone who talks about others
separates close friends.

29 A person who wants to hurt others tries
to get them to sin.
That person leads them down a path
that isn't good.

30 Whoever winks with their eye is
planning to do wrong.
Whoever closes their lips tightly is
up to no good.

31 Gray hair is a glorious crown.
You get it by living the right way.

32 It is better to be patient than to fight.
It is better to control your temper
than to take a city.

33 Lots are cast into the lap to make
decisions.
But everything they decide comes
from the LORD.

17 It is better to eat a dry crust of bread
in peace and quiet
than to eat a big dinner in a house
full of fighting.

² A wise servant will rule over a shameful
    child.
    He will be given part of the property
        as if he were a family member.

³ Fire tests silver, and heat tests gold.
    But the Lord tests our hearts.

⁴ Evil people listen to lies.
    Lying people listen to evil.

⁵ Anyone who laughs at those who
        are poor makes fun of their
        Maker.
    Anyone who is happy when others
        suffer will be punished.

⁶ Grandchildren are like a crown to older
        people.
    And children are proud of their
        parents.

⁷ Fancy words don't belong in the
        mouths of ungodly fools.
    And lies certainly don't belong in the
        mouths of rulers!

⁸ Those who give money think it will buy
        them favors.
    They think that no matter where
        they turn, they will succeed.

⁹ Whoever wants to show love forgives a
        wrong.
    But those who talk about it separate
        close friends.

¹⁰ A person who understands what is
        right learns more from just a
        warning
    than a foolish person learns from
        100 strokes with a whip.

¹¹ An evil person tries to keep others from
        obeying God.
    The messenger of death will be sent
        against them.

¹² It is better to meet a bear whose cubs
        have been stolen
    than to meet a foolish person who is
        acting foolishly.

¹³ Evil will never leave the house
    of anyone who pays back evil for
        good.

¹⁴ Starting to argue is like making a crack
        in a dam.
    So drop the matter before a fight
        breaks out.

Prov. 17:12 Did you know that grizzly bear mothers are more ferocious than black bear mothers? This isn't the only angry-bear story in the Bible. Check out 2 Kings 2:23–25.

¹⁵ The Lord hates two things.
    He hates it when the guilty are set
        free.
    He also hates it when those who
        aren't guilty are punished.

¹⁶ Why should a foolish person try to buy
        wisdom?
    They are not even able to understand
        it.

¹⁷ A friend loves at all times.
    They are there to help when trouble
        comes.

¹⁸ A person who has no sense agrees to
        pay what other people owe.
    It isn't wise to promise to pay other
        people's bills.

¹⁹ The one who loves to argue loves to sin.
    The one who builds a high gate is
        just asking to be destroyed.

²⁰ If your heart is twisted, you won't
        succeed.
    If your tongue tells lies, you will get
        into trouble.

ADVENTURES IN ODYSSEY

Whit and Jack saw the truth of the verse "A friend loves at all times" in "Clara" (A#28).

"What an awful start to the new year!" I said to Whit one snowy January morning. "It's so cold and gray and dreary outside. I just want to go back to bed and hibernate until spring."

"That would be a shame," Whit said, handing me a cup of hot chocolate. "You'd miss all the surprises." He nodded out the window. "Like the morning snow glistening in the sunrise. Or the kids sledding at McAlister Park." I looked out the window and heard the kids laughing. Their purple scarves and red snow boots danced against the white slopes.

Suddenly, I grabbed a pencil and listed my favorite things I had seen that day: yellow sweaters, peppermint tea, hugs, and red-eyed tree frogs. (Eugene was reading a book on jungle biology. Those frogs are so cute!) I don't need any of the things on my list to survive, but God surprises me with them anyway. He fills the world with beauty because He wants us to enjoy creation, even when it's gray and dreary outside.

"The next time you feel as gloomy as the weather," Whit said with a smile, "remember Proverbs 17:22: 'A cheerful heart makes you healthy.' "

21 It is sad to have a foolish child.
  The parents of a godless fool have no joy.

22 A cheerful heart makes you healthy.
  But a broken spirit dries you up.

23 Anyone who does wrong accepts favors in secret.
  Then they turn what is right into what is wrong.

24 Anyone who understands what is right keeps wisdom in view.
  But the eyes of a foolish person look everywhere else.

25 A foolish child makes his father sad and his mother sorry.

26 It isn't good to fine those who aren't guilty.
  So it certainly isn't good to whip officials just because they are honest.

27 Anyone who has knowledge controls their words.
  Anyone who has understanding is not easily upset.

28 We think even foolish people are wise if they keep silent.
  We think they understand what is right if they control their tongues.

18 A person who isn't friendly looks out only for themselves.
  They oppose all good sense by starting fights.

2 Foolish people don't want to understand.
  They take delight in saying only what they think.

3 People hate it when evil comes.
  And they refuse to honor those who bring shame.

4 The words of a person's mouth are like deep water.
  But the fountain of wisdom is like a flowing stream.

5 It isn't good to favor those who do wrong.
  That would keep justice from those who aren't guilty.

6 What foolish people say leads to arguing.
  They are just asking for a beating.

7 The words of foolish people drag them down.
  They are trapped by what they say.

8 The words of anyone who talks about others are like tasty bites of food.
  They go deep down inside you.

⁹ Anyone who doesn't want to work
is like someone who destroys.

¹⁰ The name of the Lord is like a strong
tower.
Godly people run to it and are safe.

¹¹ The wealth of rich people is like a city
that makes them feel safe.
They think of it as a city with walls
that can't be climbed.

¹² If a person's heart is proud, they will be
destroyed.
So don't be proud if you want to be
honored.

¹³ To answer before listening
is foolish and shameful.

¹⁴ A cheerful spirit gives strength even
during sickness.
But you can't keep going if you have
a broken spirit.

¹⁵ Those whose hearts understand what is
right get knowledge.
That's because the ears of those who
are wise listen for it.

¹⁶ A gift opens the door
and helps the giver meet important
people.

¹⁷ In court, the first one to speak seems
right.
Then someone else comes forward
and questions him.

¹⁸ Casting lots will put a stop to arguing.
It will keep the strongest enemies
apart.

¹⁹ A broken friendship is harder to handle
than a city with high walls
around it.
And arguing is like the locked gates
of a mighty city.

²⁰ Because of what they say a person can
fill their stomach.
What their words produce can
satisfy them.

²¹ Your tongue has the power of life and
death.
Those who love to talk will eat the
fruit of their words.

²² The one who finds a wife finds what is
good.
He receives favor from the Lord.

²³ Poor people beg for mercy.
But rich people answer in a mean
way.

WHAT ABOUT YOU?

Has a close friend ever turned against you?

In the Adventures in Odyssey episode "A Question of Loyalty," Lucy Cunningham Schultz had to deal with a difficult situation. She took time to help a shy girl named Emily discover her skills as a writer. But Emily's work became so popular that she forgot where her help came from, and she turned against Lucy. The friendship was never the same. Lucy felt betrayed.

If you've been hurt the way Lucy was, you understand Proverbs 18:19. It can be hard to once again trust someone who has hurt you. And without trust, true friendship is impossible. So what should you do when you feel betrayed? First, forgive that person. Then ask God for wisdom to know whether you should invest in repairing the relationship or move on and pray the Lord will change that person's heart. It's hard to do, but the alternative is holding a grudge . . . and living a life of sadness.

Make a list of your five closest friends. Then pray for them, asking God to help you be loyal and trustworthy even when you go through tough times together. If you've hurt someone the way Emily hurt Lucy, maybe it's time to apologize and see if you can regain that person's trust.

²⁴ A person with unfaithful friends soon
     comes to ruin.
   But there is a friend who sticks
     closer than a brother.

19 It is better to be poor and to live
     without blame
   than to be foolish and to twist words
     around.

² Getting excited about something
     without knowledge isn't good.
   It's even worse to be in a hurry and
     miss the way.

³ A person's own foolish acts destroy
     their life.
   But their heart is angry with the
     LORD.

⁴ Wealth brings many friends.
   But even the closest friend of a poor
     person abandons them.

⁵ A dishonest witness will be punished.
   And whoever pours out lies will not
     go free.

⁶ Many try to win the favor of rulers.
   And everyone is the friend of a
     person who gives gifts.

⁷ Poor people are avoided by their whole
     family.
   Their friends avoid them even more.
   The poor person runs after his friends
     to beg for help.
   But they can't be found.

⁸ Anyone who gets wisdom loves life.
   Anyone who values understanding
     will soon succeed.

⁹ A dishonest witness will be punished.
   And those who pour out lies will die.

¹⁰ It isn't proper for a foolish person to
     live in great comfort.
   And it is much worse when a slave
     rules over princes!

¹¹ A person's wisdom makes them patient.
   They will be honored if they forgive
     someone who sins against
     them.

¹² A king's anger is like a lion's roar.
   But his favor is like dew on the
     grass.

¹³ A foolish child is a father's ruin.
   A nagging wife is like dripping that
     never stops.

WHAT ABOUT YOU?

"Nothing but the Half Truth" is a funny Adventures in Odyssey episode with a serious message: If you're trying to deceive someone, it doesn't matter how much truth may be sprinkled in—it's still a lie.

Wellington Bassett put his twin brother in a sticky situation by asking Wooton to complete a business deal for him. It would have been fine if Wooton had been allowed to be himself, but to arrive at the meeting and discover that the client thought Wooton was Wellington—oh boy! Wooton realized he should have set things straight sooner, but it's never too late to do the right thing.

If you're ever tempted to tell a half-truth, stop and consider how you would feel if someone tried to deceive you. It might make you mad. You'd probably have less respect for that person. Maybe that's why Proverbs 24:28 asks, "Would you use your lips to tell lies?" Lies includes statements that may be technically true, but fail to reveal all the facts.

When was the last time you played miniature golf? If the weather is nice this week, ask your parents if you and a friend can putt around a little. Just remember, it's only a hole in one if you don't touch your ball a second time while it's rolling. (Sure, that's technically not another full stroke, but like a half-truth, it still counts as deception.)

¹⁴ You will receive houses and wealth
    from your parents.
    But a wise wife is given by the LORD.

¹⁵ Anyone who doesn't want to work
    sleeps his life away.
    And a person who refuses to work
    goes hungry.

¹⁶ Those who keep commandments keep
    their lives.
    But those who don't care how they
    live will die.

¹⁷ Anyone who is kind to poor people
    lends to the LORD.
    God will reward them for what they
    have done.

¹⁸ Train your children, because then there
    is hope.
    Don't do anything to bring about
    their deaths.

¹⁹ A person with a bad temper must pay
    for it.
    If you save them, you will have to do
    it again.

²⁰ Listen to advice and accept correction.
    In the end you will be counted
    among those who are wise.

²¹ A person may have many plans in their
    heart.
    But the LORD's purpose wins out in
    the end.

²² Everyone longs for love that never fails.
    It is better to be poor than to be a
    liar.

²³ Having respect for the LORD leads to
    life.
    Then you will be content and free
    from trouble.

²⁴ A person who doesn't want to work
    leaves his hand in the dish.
    He won't even bring it back up to his
    mouth!

²⁵ If you whip a person who makes fun of
    others,
    childish people will learn to be wise.
    If you warn those who already
    understand what is right,
    they will gain even more knowledge.

²⁶ Anyone who robs their father and
    drives out their mother

is a child who brings shame and
    dishonor.

²⁷ My son, if you stop listening to what I
    teach you,
    you will wander away from the
    words of knowledge.

²⁸ A dishonest witness makes fun of what
    is right.
    The mouths of those who do wrong
    gulp down evil.

²⁹ Those who make fun of others will be
    judged.
    Foolish people will be punished.

20 Wine causes you to make fun of
    others, and beer causes you to
    start fights.
    Anyone who is led astray by them is
    not wise.

² A king's anger brings terror like a lion's
    roar.
    Anyone who makes him angry may
    lose their life.

³ Avoiding a fight brings honor to a
    person.
    But every foolish person is quick to
    argue.

⁴ Anyone who refuses to work doesn't
    plow in the right season.
    When they look for a crop at harvest
    time, they don't find it.

⁵ The purposes of a person's heart are like
    deep water.
    But one who has understanding
    brings them out.

⁶ Many claim to have love that never
    fails.
    But who can find a faithful person?

⁷ Those who do what is right live without
    blame.
    Blessed are their children after them.

⁸ A king sits on his throne to judge.
    He gets rid of all evil when he sees it.

⁹ No one can say, "I have kept my heart
    pure.
    I'm 'clean,' and I haven't sinned."

¹⁰ The LORD hates two things.
    He hates weights that weigh things
    heavier or lighter than they
    really are.

He also hates measures that measure
things larger or smaller than
they really are.

¹¹ Even small children are known by their
actions.
So is their conduct really pure and
right?

¹² The Lord has made two things.
He has made ears that hear.
He has also made eyes that see.

¹³ Don't love sleep, or you will become
poor.
Stay awake, and you will have more
food than you need.

¹⁴ "It's no good. It's no good!" says a buyer.
Then off they go and brag about
what they bought.

¹⁵ There is gold, and there are plenty of
rubies.
But lips that speak knowledge are a
priceless jewel.

¹⁶ Take the coat of one who puts up money
for what a stranger owes.

Hold it until you get paid back if it is
done for an outsider.

¹⁷ Food gained by cheating tastes sweet.
But you will end up with a mouth
full of gravel.

¹⁸ Plans are made by asking for guidance.
So if you go to war, get good advice.

¹⁹ A person who talks about others tells
secrets.
So avoid anyone who talks too much.

²⁰ If anyone asks for bad things to happen
to their father or mother,
that person's lamp will be blown out
in total darkness.

²¹ Property that you claim too soon
will not be blessed in the end.

²² Don't say, "I'll get even with you for the
wrong you did to me!"
Wait for the Lord, and he will make
things right for you.

²³ The Lord hates weights that weigh
things heavier or lighter than
they really are.

WHAT ABOUT YOU?

Have you ever faced the natural result of a bad choice? That has happened in the lives of most of us, often starting at a very young age.

For example, in the Adventures in Odyssey episode "Groundhog Jay," Jay Smouse learns an unforgettable lesson about right and wrong when he's forced to repeat the same series of events over and over in the Room of Consequence. With Priscilla's help, Jay starts to understand why a rough kid named Harry is looking for him—a discovery that could make a lasting change in Jay's heart.

The Bible tells us in Proverbs 20:11 that our choices have consequences. We develop a reputation because of those choices. What kind of reputation are you developing? Will you be known as a person who does what's right, is kind to others, and loves God with all your heart? If that's the person you want to be, the Holy Spirit wants to help you grow in that direction. It doesn't happen overnight, but every time we choose well,

it gets easier next time. Before we know it, we're acting more and more like Jesus . . . without having to relive the same mistakes over and over again.

At first, it seemed to Jay that Harry was just being a bully. However, the more he learned, the easier it was to understand why Harry was upset. Can you recall a time when you needed more information to see an emotional situation more clearly? What did you learn?

Scales that are not honest don't
please him.

24 The Lord directs a person's steps.
So how can anyone understand their
own way?

25 A person is trapped if they make a
hasty promise to God
and only later thinks about what
they said.

26 A wise king gets rid of evil people.
He runs the threshing wheel over
them.

27 The spirit of a person is the lamp of the
Lord.
It lights up what is deep down inside
them.

28 Love and truth keep a king safe.
Faithful love makes his throne secure.

29 Young men are proud of their strength.
Gray hair brings honor to old men.

30 Blows and wounds scrub evil away.
And beatings make you pure deep
down inside.

21 In the Lord's hand the king's heart is
like a stream of water.
The Lord directs it toward all those
who please him.

2 A person might think their own ways
are right.
But the Lord knows what they are
thinking.

3 Do what is right and fair.
The Lord accepts that more than
sacrifices.

4 The proud eyes and hearts of sinful
people are like a field not
plowed.
Those things produce nothing good.

5 The plans of people who work hard
succeed.
You can be just as sure that those in
a hurry will become poor.

6 A fortune made by people who tell lies
amounts to nothing and leads to
death.

7 The harmful things that evil people do
will drag them away.
They refuse to do what is right.

8 The path of those who are guilty is
crooked.
But the conduct of those who are not
guilty is honest.

9 It is better to live on a corner of a roof
than to share a house with a nagging
wife.

10 Sinful people long to do evil.
They don't show their neighbors any
mercy.

11 When you punish someone who makes
fun of others, childish people
get wise.
By paying attention to wise people,
the childish get knowledge.

12 The Blameless One knows where
sinners live.
And he destroys them.

13 Whoever refuses to listen to the cries of
poor people
will also cry out and not be
answered.

14 A secret gift calms down anger.
A hidden favor softens great anger.

15 When you do what is fair, you make
godly people glad.
But you terrify those who do what
is evil.

16 Whoever leaves the path of
understanding
ends up with those who are dead.

17 Anyone who loves pleasure will become
poor.
Anyone who loves wine and olive oil
will never be rich.

18 Evil people become the payment for
setting godly people free.
Those who aren't faithful are the
payment for honest people.

19 It is better to live in a desert
than to live with a nagging wife who
loves to argue.

20 Wise people store up the best food and
olive oil.
But foolish people eat up everything
they have.

21 Anyone who wants to be godly and
loving
finds life, success and honor.

ADVENTURES IN ODYSSEY

When the new word "milajoit" started making the rounds at Whit's End, the kids saw the importance of being careful about what they say in "War of the Words" (A#20).

²² A wise person can attack a strong city.
They can pull down the place of
safety its people trust in.

²³ Those who are careful about what they
say
keep themselves out of trouble.

²⁴ A proud person is called a mocker.
He thinks much too highly of
himself.

²⁵ Some people will die while they are still
hungry.
That's because their hands refuse to
work.

²⁶ All day long they hunger for more.
But godly people give without
holding back.

²⁷ God hates sacrifices that are brought by
evil people.
He hates it even more when they
bring them for the wrong
reason.

²⁸ Witnesses who aren't honest will die.
But anyone who listens carefully will
be a successful witness.

²⁹ Sinful people try to look as if they were
bold.
But honest people think about how
they live.

³⁰ No wisdom, wise saying or plan
can succeed against the LORD.

³¹ You can prepare a horse for the day of
battle.
But the power to win comes from
the LORD.

22 You should want a good name more
than you want great riches.
To be highly respected is better than
having silver or gold.

² The LORD made rich people and poor
people.

That's what they have in common.

³ Wise people see danger and go to a safe
place.
But childish people keep going and
suffer for it.

⁴ Being humble comes from having
respect for the LORD.
This will bring you wealth and honor
and life.

⁵ Thorns and traps lie in the paths of evil
people.
But those who value their lives stay
far away from them.

⁶ Start children off on the right path.
And even when they are old, they
will not turn away from it.

Jason's Jargon

PROVERBS 22

Search this chapter for the word *boundary*. A boundary is a line that, if crossed, can have consequences. A boundary set between people is an understanding that certain behavior between them is unacceptable.

⁷ Rich people rule over those who are
poor.
Borrowers are slaves to lenders.

⁸ Anyone who plants evil gathers a
harvest of trouble.
Their power to treat others badly
will be destroyed.

⁹ Those who give freely will be blessed.
That's because they share their food
with those who are poor.

ADVENTURES IN ODYSSEY

Dale Jacobs remembered the importance of training his child while his daughter Melanie started to make wise media choices in "You Gotta Be Wise" (A#13).

WOOTON'S FUN FACTS
Prov. 22:13

Aesop's fable "The Boy Who Cried Wolf" is one illustration of this parable. Do you ever make excuses to get out of work or chores? See verse 15 and make plans to "drive that foolishness far away!"

¹⁰ If you drive away those who make fun of others, fighting also goes away.
Arguing and unkind words will stop.

¹¹ A person who has a pure and loving heart and speaks kindly
will be a friend of the king.

¹² The eyes of the Lord keep watch over knowledge.
But he does away with the words of those who aren't faithful.

¹³ People who don't want to work say, "There's a lion outside!"
Or they say, "I'll be murdered if I go out into the streets!"

¹⁴ The mouth of a woman who commits adultery is like a deep pit.
Any man the Lord is angry with falls into it.

¹⁵ Children are going to do foolish things.
But correcting them will drive that foolishness far away.

¹⁶ You might treat poor people badly or give gifts to rich people.
Trying to get rich in these ways will instead make you poor.

30 SAYINGS OF WISE PEOPLE

Saying 1

¹⁷ Pay attention and listen to the sayings of wise people.

Apply your heart to the sayings I teach.
¹⁸ It is pleasing when you keep them in your heart.
Have all of them ready on your lips.
¹⁹ You are the one I am teaching today.
That's because I want you to trust in the Lord.
²⁰ I have written 30 sayings for you.
They will give you knowledge and good advice.
²¹ I am teaching you to be honest and to speak the truth.
Then you can give honest reports to those you serve.

Saying 2

²² Don't take advantage of poor people just because they are poor.
Don't treat badly those who are in need by taking them to court.
²³ The Lord will stand up for them in court.
He will require the lives of people who have taken the lives of those in need.

Saying 3

²⁴ Don't be a friend of a person who has a bad temper.
Don't go around with a person who gets angry easily.
²⁵ You might learn their habits.
And then you will be trapped by them.

Saying 4

²⁶ Don't agree to pay for what someone else owes.
And don't agree to pay their bills for them.
²⁷ If you don't have the money to pay, your bed will be taken right out from under you!

Saying 5

²⁸ Don't move old boundary stones set up by your people of long ago.

Saying 6

²⁹ Do you see someone who does good work?
That person will serve kings.
That person won't serve officials of lower rank.

Saying 7

23 When you sit down to eat with a
          ruler,
    look carefully at what's in front of you.
² Put a knife to your throat
    if you like to eat too much.
³ Don't long for his fancy food.
    It can fool you.

Saying 8

⁴ Don't wear yourself out to get rich.
    Don't trust how wise you think you
        are.
⁵ When you take even a quick look at
        riches, they are gone.
    They grow wings and fly away into
        the sky like an eagle.

Saying 9

⁶ Don't eat the food of anyone who
        doesn't want to share it.
    Don't long for his fancy food.
⁷ He is the kind of person
    who is always thinking about how
        much it costs.
    "Eat and drink," he says to you.
    But he doesn't mean it.
⁸ You will throw up what little you have
        eaten.
    You will have wasted your words of
        praise.

Saying 10

⁹ Don't speak to foolish people.
    They will laugh at your wise words.

Saying 11

¹⁰ Don't move old boundary stones.
    Don't try to take over the fields of
        children whose fathers have
        died.
¹¹ That's because the God who guards
        them is strong.
    He will stand up for them in court
        against you.

Saying 12

¹² Apply your heart to what you are
        taught.
    Listen carefully to words of
        knowledge.

Saying 13

¹³ Don't hold back correction from a child.
    If you correct them, they won't die.

¹⁴ So correct them.
    Then you will save them from death.

Saying 14

¹⁵ My son, if your heart is wise,
    my heart will be very glad.
¹⁶ Deep down inside, I will be happy
    when you say what is right.

Saying 15

¹⁷ Do not long for what sinners have.
    But always show great respect for the
        Lord.
¹⁸ There really is hope for you in days to
        come.
    So your hope will not be cut off.

Saying 16

¹⁹ My son, listen and be wise.
    Set your heart on the right path.
²⁰ Don't join those who drink too much
        wine.
    Don't join those who stuff
        themselves with meat.
²¹ Those who drink or eat too much will
        become poor.
    If they sleep too much, they'll have
        to wear rags.

Saying 17

²² Listen to your father, who gave you life.
    Don't hate your mother when she
        is old.
²³ Buy the truth and don't sell it.
    Get wisdom, instruction and
        understanding as well.
²⁴ The father of a godly child is very
        happy.
    A man who has a wise son is glad.
²⁵ May your father and mother be glad.
    May the woman who gave birth to
        you be joyful.

Saying 18

²⁶ My son, give me your heart.
    May you be happy living the way
        you see me live.
²⁷ An unfaithful wife is like a deep pit.
    A wife who commits adultery is like
        a narrow well.
²⁸ She hides and waits like a thief.
    She causes many men to sin.

Saying 19

²⁹ Who has trouble? Who has sorrow?
    Who argues? Who has problems?

Who has wounds for no reason?
Who has red eyes?

[30] Those who spend too much time with
wine.
Or those who like to taste wine
mixed with spices.

[31] Don't look at wine when it is red.
Don't look at it when it bubbles in
the cup.
And don't look at it when it goes
down smoothly.

[32] In the end it bites like a snake.
It bites like a poisonous serpent.

[33] Your eyes will see strange sights.
Your mind will imagine weird
things.

[34] You will feel like someone sleeping on
the ocean.
You will think you are lying among
the ropes in a boat.

[35] "They hit me," you will say. "But I'm not
hurt!
They beat me. But I don't feel it!
When will I wake up
so I can find another drink?"

Saying 20

24 Do not want what evil people have.
Don't long to be with them.

[2] In their hearts they plan to hurt others.
With their lips they talk about
making trouble.

Saying 21

[3] By wisdom a house is built.
Through understanding it is made
secure.

[4] Through knowledge its rooms are filled
with priceless and beautiful things.

Saying 22

[5] Wise people have success by means of
great power.
Those who have knowledge gather
strength.

[6] If you go to war, you surely need
guidance.
If you want to win, you need many
good advisers.

Saying 23

[7] Wisdom is too high for foolish people.
They shouldn't speak when people
meet at the city gate to
conduct business.

Saying 24

[8] Anyone who thinks up sinful things to
do
will be known as one who plans evil.

[9] Foolish plans are sinful.
People hate those who make fun of
others.

Saying 25

[10] If you grow weak when trouble comes,
your strength is very small!

[11] Save those who are being led away to
death.
Hold back those who are about to
be killed.

[12] Don't say, "But we didn't know anything
about this."
Doesn't the God who knows what
you are thinking see it?
Doesn't the God who guards your life
know it?
He will pay back everyone for what
they have done.

Saying 26

[13] Eat honey, my son, because it is good.
Honey from a honeycomb has a
sweet taste.

[14] I want you to know that wisdom is like
honey for you.
If you find it, there is hope for you
tomorrow.
So your hope will not be cut off.

Saying 27

[15] Don't hide and wait like a burglar near
a godly person's house.
Don't rob their home.

[16] Even if godly people fall down seven
times, they always get up.
But those who are evil trip and fall
when trouble comes.

Saying 28

[17] Don't be happy when your enemy falls.
When he trips, don't let your heart
be glad.

[18] The LORD will see it, but he won't be
pleased.
He might turn his anger away from
your enemy.

Saying 29

[19] Don't be upset because of evil people.
Don't long for what sinners have.

²⁰ Tomorrow evil people won't have any
     hope.
     The lamps of sinners will be blown
          out.

Saying 30

²¹ My son, have respect for the LORD and
     the king.
     Don't join with officials who disobey
          them.
²² The LORD and the king will suddenly
     destroy them.
     Who knows what trouble those two
          can bring?

MORE SAYINGS OF WISE PEOPLE

²³Here are more sayings of wise people.

Taking sides in court is not good.
²⁴   A curse will fall on those who say
          the guilty are not guilty.
Nations will ask for bad things to
     happen to them.
     People will speak against them.
²⁵ But it will go well with those who
     sentence guilty people.
     Rich blessings will come to them.

²⁶ An honest answer
     is like a kiss on the lips.

²⁷ Put your outdoor work in order.
     Get your fields ready.
     After that, build your house.

²⁸ Don't be a witness against your
     neighbor for no reason.
     Would you use your lips to tell lies?
²⁹ Don't say, "I'll do to them what they
     have done to me.
     I'll get even with them for what they
          did."

³⁰ I went past the field of someone who
     didn't want to work.
     I went past the vineyard of someone
          who didn't have any sense.
³¹ Thorns had grown up everywhere.
     The ground was covered with weeds.
     The stone wall had fallen down.
³² I applied my heart to what I observed.
     I learned a lesson from what I saw.
³³ You might sleep a little or take a little nap.
     You might even fold your hands and
          rest.
³⁴ Then you would be poor, as if someone
     had robbed you.

You would have little, as if someone
     had stolen from you.

MORE PROVERBS OF SOLOMON

25 These are more proverbs of Solomon.
     They were gathered together by the
men of Hezekiah, the king of Judah.

² When God hides a matter, he gets
     glory.
     When kings figure out a matter, they
          get glory.

³ The heavens are high and the earth is
     deep.
     In the same way, the minds of kings
          are impossible to figure out.

⁴ Remove the scum from the silver.
     Then the master worker can make
          something out of it.
⁵ Remove ungodly officials from where
     the king is.
     Then the king can make his throne
          secure because of the godliness
          around him.

⁶ Don't brag in front of the king.
     Don't claim a place among his great
          men.
⁷ Let the king say to you, "Come up here."
     That's better than for him to shame
          you in front of his nobles.

What you have seen with your own eyes
⁸   don't bring too quickly to court.
What will you do in the end
     if your neighbor puts you to shame?

⁹ If you take your neighbor to court,
     don't tell others any secrets you
          promised to keep.
¹⁰ If you do, someone might hear it and
     put you to shame.
     And the charge against you will
          stand.

¹¹ The right ruling at the right time
     is like golden apples in silver jewelry.

¹² A wise judge's warning to a listening ear
     is like a gold earring or jewelry made
          of fine gold.

¹³ A messenger trusted by the one who
     sends him
     is like a drink cooled by snow at
          harvest time.
     He renews the spirit of his master.

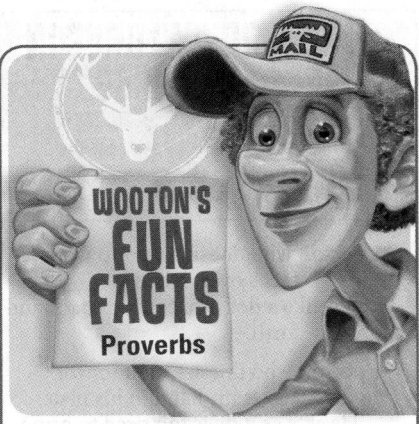

WOOTON'S FUN FACTS
Proverbs

One Bible scholar wrote, "A proverb is a short sentence drawn from long experience. It is a proper mixture of horse sense and holy sense." If you're like me, you might have trouble making sense of the sentence. It helps to know that horse sense is common sense. Does that make sense?

¹⁴ A person who brags about gifts never given
is like wind and clouds that don't produce rain.

¹⁵ If you are patient, you can win an official over to your side.
And gentle words can break a bone.

¹⁶ If you find honey, eat just enough.
If you eat too much of it, you will throw up.

¹⁷ Don't go to your neighbor's home very often.
If they see too much of you, they will hate you.

¹⁸ A person who is a false witness against a neighbor
is like a club, a sword or a sharp arrow.

¹⁹ Trusting someone who is not faithful when trouble comes
is like a broken tooth or a disabled foot.

²⁰ You may sing songs to a troubled heart.
But that's like taking a coat away on a cold day.
It's like pouring vinegar on a wound.

²¹ If your enemy is hungry, give him food to eat.
If he is thirsty, give him water to drink.

²² By doing these things, you will pile up burning coals on his head.
And the LORD will reward you.

²³ Like a north wind that brings rain you didn't expect
is a crafty tongue that brings looks of shock.

²⁴ It is better to live on a corner of a roof
than to share a house with a nagging wife.

²⁵ Hearing good news from a land far away
is like drinking cold water when you are tired.

²⁶ Sometimes godly people give in to those who are evil.
Then they become like a muddy spring of water or a polluted well.

²⁷ It isn't good for you to eat too much honey.
And you shouldn't try to search out matters too deep for you.

²⁸ A person without self-control
is like a city whose walls are broken through.

26 It isn't proper to honor a foolish person.
That's like having snow in summer or rain at harvest time.

² A curse given for no reason is like a wandering bird or a flying sparrow.
It doesn't go anywhere.

³ A whip is for a horse, and a harness is for a donkey.
And a beating is for the backs of foolish people.

⁴ Don't answer a foolish person in keeping with their foolish acts.
If you do, you yourself will be just like them.

⁵ Answer a foolish person in keeping with their foolish acts.
If you do not, they will be wise in their own eyes.

⁶ Sending a message in the hand of a foolish person

is like cutting off your feet or
drinking poison.

7 A proverb in the mouth of a foolish
person
is like disabled legs that are useless.

8 Giving honor to a foolish person
is like tying a stone in a slingshot.

9 A proverb in the mouth of a foolish
person
is like a thorn in the hand of
someone who is drunk.

10 Anyone who hires a foolish person or
someone who is passing by
is like a person who shoots arrows at
just anybody.

11 Foolish people who do the same foolish
things again
are like a dog that returns to where it
has thrown up.

12 Do you see a person who is wise in
their own eyes?
There is more hope for a foolish
person than for them.

13 A person who doesn't want to work
says, "There's a lion in the
road!
There's an angry lion wandering in
the streets!"

ADVENTURES IN ODYSSEY

Whit quoted Proverbs 26:27 to
Bart Rathbone to show him the
folly of taking shortcuts in "A
Rathbone of Contention" (A#11).

14 A person who doesn't want to work
turns over in bed
just like a door that swings back and
forth.

15 A person who doesn't want to work
leaves his hand in his plate.
He acts as if he is too tired to bring
his hand back up to his
mouth.

16 A person who doesn't want to work is
wiser in his own eyes
than seven people who give careful
answers.

17 Don't be quick to get mixed up in
someone else's fight.
That's like grabbing a stray dog by
its ears.

18 Suppose a crazy person shoots
flaming arrows that can kill.

19 Someone who lies to their neighbor
and says, "I was only joking!" is just
like that crazy person.

20 If you don't have wood, your fire goes
out.
If you don't talk about others,
arguing dies down.

21 Coal glows, and wood burns.
And a person who argues stirs up
conflict.

22 The words of anyone who talks about
others are like tasty bites of
food.
They go deep down inside you.

23 Warm words that come from an evil
heart
are like a shiny coating on a clay pot.

24 Enemies use their words as a mask.
They hide their evil plans in their
hearts.

25 Even though what they say can be
charming, don't believe them.

WOOTON'S FUN FACTS

Prov. 26:17 I just learned that a dog's ear
has eighteen muscles that tilt, lift, and turn
it. They can hear sounds from different
directions. Dogs' hearing is so good they
can hear termites in walls! So that's why my
dog Sam always catches me when I sneak
into the kitchen for a midnight snack!

That's because seven things God
    hates fill that person's heart.
26 Their hatred can be hidden by lies.
    But their evil plans will be shown to
    everyone.

27 Whoever digs a pit will fall into it.
    If someone rolls a big stone, it will
    roll back on them.

28 A tongue that tells lies hates the people
    it hurts.
    And words that seem to praise you
    destroy you.

27 Don't brag about tomorrow.
    You don't know what a day will
    bring.

2 Let another person praise you, and not
    your own mouth.
    Let an outsider praise you, and not
    your own lips.

3 Stones are heavy, and sand weighs a lot.
    But letting a foolish person make
    you angry is a heavier load
    than both of them.

4 Anger is mean, and great anger
    overpowers you.
    But who can face jealousy?

5 Being warned openly is better
    than being loved in secret.

6 Wounds from a friend can be trusted.
    But an enemy kisses you many
    times.

7 When you are full, you even hate honey.
    When you are hungry, even what is
    bitter tastes sweet.

8 Anyone who runs away from home
    is like a bird that flies away from its
    nest.

9 Perfume and incense bring joy to your
    heart.
    And the sweetness of a friend comes
    from their honest advice.

10 Don't desert your friend or a friend of
    your family.
    And don't go to your relative's house
    when trouble strikes you.

WHAT ABOUT you?

What's the craziest day you've ever had? Was it your first day at a new school? The day your bike got a flat tire miles from home—and you didn't have your cell phone? That day you were in the talent show and forgot the words to your song? Whatever happened, you discovered that life doesn't always go as planned. There's nothing wrong with making a schedule or plan. But we should be flexible enough to take the detours that arise.

Proverbs 27:1 says: "Don't brag about tomorrow. You don't know what a day will bring." When we make plans without seeking God's wisdom, or brag about things we haven't done yet, we're setting ourselves up for disappointment. Instead, we can just be thankful for every new day God gives us.

When an unexpected development comes your way, how do you respond? Do you complain that your plans are being ruined? Do you hate being interrupted or unable to get certain things done? Or do you see it as an unexpected adventure? Maybe this detour is from God. He might want to get your attention, give you the chance to help someone, or teach you a lesson. Remembering that can make even the craziest days a little easier to take.

If you read the book of James, you'll learn more about how not to boast about tomorrow. Read chapter 4, verses 13 to 16. Then pray about your plans for the future, adding, "If it's Your will, God, this is what I want to do."

A neighbor nearby is better than a
relative far away.

¹¹ My son, be wise and bring joy to my
heart.
Then I can answer anyone who
makes fun of me.

¹² Wise people see danger and go to a safe
place.
But childish people keep on going
and suffer for it.

¹³ Take the coat of one who puts up
money for what a stranger
owes.
Hold it until you get paid back if it is
done for an outsider.

¹⁴ Suppose you loudly bless your
neighbor early in the
morning.
Then you might as well be cursing
him.

¹⁵ A nagging wife is like the dripping
of a leaky roof in a rainstorm.
¹⁶ Stopping her is like trying to stop the
wind.
It's like trying to grab olive oil with
your hand.

¹⁷ As iron sharpens iron,
so one person sharpens another.

¹⁸ A person who guards a fig tree will eat
its fruit.
And a person who protects their
master will be honored.

¹⁹ When you look into water, you see a
likeness of your face.
When you look into your heart, you
see what you are really like.

²⁰ Death and the Grave are never satisfied.
People's eyes are never satisfied
either.

²¹ Fire tests silver, and heat tests gold.
But people are tested by the praise
they receive.

²² Suppose you could grind a foolish
person in a mill.
Suppose you could grind them as
you would grind grain with
a tool.
Even then you could not remove
their foolishness from them.

ADVENTURES IN ODYSSEY

Eugene and Bernard were reminded of
the importance of "iron sharpening iron"
when they traveled across the country
together in "Third Degree" (A#21).

²³ Be sure you know how your flocks are
doing.
Pay careful attention to your herds.
²⁴ Riches don't last forever.
And a crown is not secure for all
time to come.
²⁵ The hay is removed, and new growth
appears.
The grass from the hills is gathered
in.
²⁶ Then your lambs will provide you with
clothes.
And the money from selling your
goats will buy you a field.
²⁷ You will have plenty of goats' milk to
feed your family.
It will also feed your female servants.

28 Sinners run away even when no one
is chasing them.
But those who do what is right are as
bold as lions.

² A country has many rulers when its
people don't obey.
But an understanding ruler knows
how to keep order.

³ A ruler who treats poor people badly
is like a pounding rain that leaves no
crops.

⁴ Those who turn away from instruction
praise sinners.
But those who learn from it oppose
them.

⁵ Sinful people don't understand what is
    right.
  But those who worship the LORD
    understand it completely.

⁶ It is better to be poor and live without
    blame
  than to be rich and follow a crooked
    path.

⁷ A child who understands what is right
    learns from instruction.
  But a child who likes to eat too
    much brings shame on his
    father.

⁸ Someone might get rich by taking
    interest or profit from poor
    people.
  But that person only piles up wealth
    for someone who will be kind
    to poor people.

⁹ If you don't pay attention to my
    instruction,
  even your prayers are hated.

¹⁰ Those who lead honest people down an
    evil path
  will fall into their own trap.
  But those who are without blame
  will receive good things.

¹¹ Rich people may think they are wise.
  But a poor person with
    understanding knows that rich
    people are fooling themselves.

¹² When godly people win, everyone is
    very happy.
  But when sinners take charge,
    everyone hides.

¹³ Anyone who hides their sins doesn't
    succeed.
  But anyone who admits their sins
    and gives them up finds mercy.

¹⁴ Blessed is the one who always trembles
    in front of God.
  But anyone who makes their heart
    stubborn will get into trouble.

¹⁵ An evil person who rules over helpless
    people
  is like a roaring lion or an angry
    bear.

¹⁶ A ruler who is mean to his people takes
    money from them by force.

But one who hates money gained in
    the wrong way will rule a long
    time.

¹⁷ Anyone troubled by the guilt of murder
    will seek to escape their guilt by
    death.
  No one should keep them from it.

¹⁸ Anyone who lives without blame is kept
    safe.
  But anyone whose path is crooked
    will fall into the pit.

¹⁹ Those who work their land will have
    plenty of food.
  But those who chase dreams will be
    very poor.

²⁰ A faithful person will be richly blessed.
  But anyone who wants to get rich
    will be punished.

²¹ Favoring one person over another is not
    good.
  But a person will do wrong for a
    piece of bread.

²² Those who won't share what they have
    want to get rich.
  They don't know they are going to
    be poor.

²³ It is better to warn a person than to
    pretend to praise them.

ADVENTURES IN ODYSSEY

Whit, Connie, and Robyn saw the
effects of greed while following
the clues of a mystery in "The
Treasure of LeMonde!" (A#06).

In the end that person will be more pleased with you.

²⁴ Anyone who steals from their parents
    and says, "It's not wrong,"
is just like someone who destroys.

²⁵ People who always want more stir up conflict.
    But those who trust in the Lord will succeed.

²⁶ Those who trust in themselves are foolish.
    But those who live wisely are kept safe.

²⁷ Those who give to poor people will have all they need.
    But those who close their eyes to the poor will receive many curses.

²⁸ When those who are evil take charge, other people hide.
    But when those who are evil die, godly people grow stronger.

29 Whoever still won't obey after being warned many times
will suddenly be destroyed. Nothing can save them.

² When those who do right grow stronger, the people are glad.
    But when those who do wrong become rulers, the people groan.

³ A man who loves wisdom makes his father glad.
    But a man who spends time with prostitutes wastes his father's wealth.

⁴ By doing what is fair, a king makes a country secure.
    But those who only want money tear it down.

⁵ Those who only pretend to praise their neighbors
    are spreading a net to catch them by the feet.

⁶ Sinful people are trapped by their own sin.
    But godly people shout for joy and are glad.

⁷ Those who do what is right want to treat poor people fairly.

CANDID CONVERSATIONS

Sometimes Penny gets carried away, like that time she used my brand-new, favorite pink shirt to dress a scarecrow for "our" harvest party she forgot to tell me about. "I modeled it after you! Can you recognize the shape of your face?" she chirped.

I wanted to scream, but I didn't—somehow. I swallowed my anger long enough to drive to Whit's End. *Good job, Connie,* I thought. *I handled that pretty well.* Like it says in Proverbs 29:11, "Foolish people let their anger run wild. But wise people keep themselves under control."

I told Whit all about it. "I was really upset," I admitted. "Good thing I left before I hurt Penny's feelings!"

"Are you sure?" Whit asked. "You know, you can't just run away. You need to talk with Penny."

Just then Penny entered with tears in her eyes. "I'm so sorry, Connie. I realized that I should've asked you before I planned a big party. What was I thinking? Can you forgive me?" I gave her a hug and asked her to forgive me too.

But those who do what is wrong don't care about the poor.

⁸ Those who make fun of others stir up a city.
    But wise people turn anger away.

⁹ Suppose a wise person goes to court with a foolish person.
    Then the foolish person gets mad and pokes fun, and there is no peace.

¹⁰ Murderers hate honest people.
    They try to kill those who do what is right.

[11] Foolish people let their anger run wild.
  But wise people keep themselves
    under control.

[12] If rulers listen to lies,
  all their officials become evil.

[13] The LORD gives sight to the eyes of poor
    people and those who treat
    others badly.
  That's what they both have in
    common.

[14] If a king judges poor people fairly,
  his throne will always be secure.

[15] If a child is corrected, they become wise.
  But a child who is not corrected
    brings shame to their mother.

[16] When those who do wrong grow
    stronger, so does sin.
  But those who do right will see them
    destroyed.

[17] If you correct your children, they will
    give you peace.
  They will bring you the delights you
    desire.

[18] Where there is no message from
    God, people don't control
    themselves.
  But blessed is the one who obeys
    wisdom's instruction.

[19] Servants can't be corrected only by
    words.
  Even if they understand, they won't
    obey.

[20] Have you seen someone who speaks
    without thinking?
  There is more hope for foolish
    people than for that person.

[21] A servant who has been spoiled from
    youth
  will have no respect for you later on.

[22] An angry person stirs up fights.
  And a person with a bad temper
    commits many sins.

[23] Pride brings a person low.
  But those whose spirits are low will
    be honored.

[24] To help a thief is to become your own
    enemy.
  When you go to court, you won't
    dare to say anything.

ADVENTURES IN ODYSSEY

Whit and Connie had to trust in the
Lord for safety when they ran into
the evil Dr. Blackgaard in "Waylaid
in the Windy City" (A#10).

[25] If you are afraid of people, it will trap
    you.
  But if you trust in the LORD, he will
    keep you safe.

[26] Many people want to meet a ruler.
  But only the LORD sees that people
    are treated fairly.

[27] Those who do what is right hate
    dishonest people.
  Those who do what is wrong hate
    honest people.

THE SAYINGS OF AGUR

30 These sayings are the words of Agur,
    son of Jakeh. These sayings came
from God.

This man said to Ithiel:

"I am weary, God.
  But I can still have success.
[2] Surely I am only a dumb animal and
    not a man.
  I don't understand as other men do.
[3] I haven't learned wisdom.
  And I don't know the things the
    Holy One knows.
[4] Who has gone up to heaven and come
    down?
  Whose hands have gathered up the
    wind?
Who has wrapped up the waters in a
    coat?
  Who has set in place all the
    boundaries of the earth?
What is his name? What is his son's
    name?
  Surely you know!

[5] "Every word of God is perfect.
  He is like a shield to those who trust
    in him.
  He keeps them safe.
[6] Don't add to his words.
  If you do, he will correct you.
  He will prove that you are a liar.

Jason's Jargon

PROVERBS 30

Let's go bird watching. Catch sight of a *vulture* in this chapter. A vulture is a bird known for circling animals that are about to die, then eating them when they do.

⁷ "LORD, I ask you for two things.
  Don't refuse me before I die.
⁸ Keep lies far away from me.
  Don't make me either poor or rich,
  but give me only the bread I need
  each day.
⁹ If you don't, I might have too much.
  Then I might say I don't know you.
  I might say, 'Who is the LORD?'
  Or I might become poor and steal.
  Then I would bring shame to the
  name of my God.

¹⁰ "Don't tell lies about a servant when
  you talk to their master.
  If you do, they will curse you, and
  you will pay for your lies.

¹¹ "Some people curse their fathers.
  Others don't bless their mothers.
¹² Some are pure in their own eyes.
  But their dirty sins haven't been
  washed away.
¹³ Some have eyes that are very proud.
  They look down on others.
¹⁴ Some people have teeth like swords.
  The teeth in their jaws are as sharp
  as knives.
They are ready to eat up the poor
  people of the earth.
  They are ready to eat up those who
  are the most needy.

¹⁵ "A leech has two daughters.
  They cry out, 'Give! Give!'

"Three things are never satisfied.
  Four things never say, 'Enough!'
  ¹⁶ The first is the grave.
    The second is a woman who
    can't have a baby.
    The third is land, which never
    gets enough water.

And the fourth is fire, which
  never says, 'Enough!'

¹⁷ "One person makes fun of their father.
  Another doesn't honor their mother
    when she is old.
The ravens of the valley will peck out
    their eyes.
  Then the vultures will eat them.

¹⁸ "Three things are too amazing for
  me.
  There are four things I don't
  understand.
  ¹⁹ The first is the way of an eagle
    in the sky.
    The second is the way of a
    snake on a rock.
    The third is the way of a ship
    on the ocean.
    And the fourth is the way of a
    man with a young woman.

²⁰ "This is the way of a woman who
    commits adultery.
  She eats and wipes her mouth.
  Then she says, 'I haven't done
    anything wrong.'

²¹ "Under three things the earth shakes.
  Under four things it can't stand
  up.
    ²² The first is a servant who be-
    comes a king.
    The second is a foolish and un-
    godly person who gets plenty
    to eat.
  ²³ The third is a mean woman
    who gets married.
    And the fourth is a servant
    who takes the place of the
    woman she works for.

²⁴ "Four things on earth are small.
  But they are very wise.
    ²⁵ The first are ants, which aren't
    very strong.
    But they store up their food in
    the summer.
  ²⁶ The second are hyraxes, which
    aren't very powerful.
    But they make their home
    among the rocks.
  ²⁷ The third are locusts, which
    don't have a king.
    But they all march forward in
    ranks.

Prov. 30:26 Hyraxes look like a cross between a fat rat and a rabbit. As soon as Penny saw a picture, she wanted one as a pet! They're so cute! But they're actually more closely related to elephants and manatees. So Penny changed her mind.

28 And the fourth are lizards,
which your hand can catch.
But you will find them in kings'
palaces.
29 "Three things walk as if they were
kings.
Four things move as kings do.
30 The first is a lion, which is mighty
among the animals. It doesn't
back away from anything.
31 The second is a rooster, which
walks proudly.
The third is a billy goat.
And the fourth is a king, who is
secure against any who might
oppose him.
32 "Do you do foolish things?
Do you think you are better than
others?
Do you plan evil?
If you do, put your hand over your
mouth and stop talking!
33 If you churn cream, you will produce
butter.
If you twist a nose, you will produce
blood.
And if you stir up anger, you will
produce a fight."

THE SAYINGS OF KING LEMUEL

31 These are the sayings of King Lemuel. His mother taught them to him.
These sayings came from God.

2 Listen, my son! Listen, my very own
son!
Listen, you who are the answer to
my prayers!
3 Don't waste your strength on women.
Don't waste it on those who destroy
kings.
4 Lemuel, it isn't good for kings to drink
wine.
It isn't good for rulers to long for
beer.
5 If they do, they might drink and forget
what has been commanded.
They might take away the rights of
all those who are treated badly.
6 Let beer be for those who are dying.
Let wine be for those who are sad
and troubled.
7 Let them drink and forget how poor
they are.
Let them forget their suffering.
8 Speak up for those who can't speak for
themselves.
Speak up for the rights of all those
who are poor.
9 Speak up and judge fairly.
Speak up for the rights of those who
are poor and needy.

THE EXCELLENT WOMAN

10 Who can find an excellent woman?
She is worth far more than rubies.
11 Her husband trusts her completely.
She gives him all the important
things he needs.
12 She brings him good, not harm,
all the days of her life.
13 She chooses wool and flax.
She loves to work with her hands.
14 She is like the ships of traders.
She brings her food from far away.
15 She gets up while it is still night.
She provides food for her family.
She also gives some to her female
servants.
16 She considers a field and buys it.
She uses some of the money she
earns to plant a vineyard.
17 She gets ready to work hard.
Her arms are strong.
18 She sees that her trading earns a lot of
money.
Her lamp doesn't go out at night.

¹⁹ With one hand she holds the wool.
   With the other she spins the thread.
²⁰ She opens her arms to those who are
      poor.
   She reaches out her hands to those
      who are needy.
²¹ When it snows, she's not afraid for her
      family.
   All of them are dressed in the finest
      clothes.
²² She makes her own bed coverings.
   She is dressed in fine linen and
      purple clothes.
²³ Her husband is respected at the city
      gate.
   There he takes his seat among the
      elders of the land.
²⁴ She makes linen clothes and sells them.
   She supplies belts to the traders.
²⁵ She puts on strength and honor as if
      they were her clothes.

   She can laugh at the days that are
      coming.
²⁶ She speaks wisely.
   She teaches faithfully.
²⁷ She watches over family matters.
   She is busy all the time.
²⁸ Her children stand up and call her
      blessed.
   Her husband also rises up, and he
      praises her.
²⁹ He says, "Many women do excellent
      things.
   But you are better than all the
      others."
³⁰ Charm can fool you. Beauty fades.
   But a woman who has respect for the
      LORD should be praised.
³¹ Give her honor for all that her hands
      have done.
   Let everything she has done bring
      praise to her at the city gate.

Ecclesiastes

Every journey has difficult passages. Ours is no exception. Upon first reading, the book of Ecclesiastes might seem a bit depressing or even bleak. Like many people today, the writer (some scholars speculate it is Solomon himself or possibly another authority figure) is searching for the meaning of life. However, *unlike* a lot of people today, he was in a position of wealth and power and able to provide the best possible opportunities for himself.

While the writer was devoted to learning and education (a worthy pursuit), he turned to many other activities for meaning—including work and pleasure. But his conclusion after every new attempt was that life is "meaningless." He saw that, ultimately, death was the great equalizer. Everything he achieved in life would be handed down to someone else at his death . . . so why concern oneself with any of it?

Yet by the end of this book, the author realized that the best thing he could do was to "have respect for God and obey his commandments" (12:13). A life lived for God may not result in great wealth or prestige, but it will be anything but meaningless!

As you dive into this book—figuratively speaking, of course—be sure not to miss the famous "a time for everything" passage (3:1–8). It is one of the more familiar passages of Scripture and a personal favorite of mine.

WHAT'S IT MEAN, EUGENE?

Original Sin—Every person born has been morally tarnished by the fall of Adam. Our tendency to sin is inherited because of Adam's "original" sin. The good news, however, is that we can all be saved from our sin through the sacrifice of Jesus Christ. As the apostle Paul put it, "So one man's sin brought guilt to all people. In the same way, one right act made people right with God" (Romans 5:18).

Everything Is Meaningless

1 These are the words of the Teacher. He was the son of David. He was also the king in Jerusalem.

² "Meaningless! Everything is
        meaningless!"
    says the Teacher.
    "Everything is completely meaningless!
        Nothing has any meaning."

³ What do people get for all their work?
    Why do they work so hard on this
        earth?
⁴ People come and people go.
    But the earth remains forever.
⁵ The sun rises. Then it sets.
    And then it hurries back to where
        it rises.
⁶ The wind blows to the south.
    Then it turns to the north.
Around and around it goes.
    It always returns to where it started.
⁷ Every stream flows into the ocean.
    But the ocean never gets full.
The streams return
    to the place they came from.
⁸ All things are tiresome.
    They are more tiresome than anyone
        can say.
But our eyes never see enough of
        anything.
    Our ears never hear enough.
⁹ Everything that has ever been will come
        back again.
    Everything that has ever been done
        will be done again.
    Nothing is new on earth.
¹⁰ There isn't anything about which
        someone can say,
    "Look! Here's something new."
It was already here long ago.
    It was here before we were.
¹¹ No one remembers the people of long
        ago.
    Even those who haven't been born
        yet
won't be remembered
    by those who will be born after
        them.

Wisdom Is Meaningless

¹²I, the Teacher, was king over Israel in Jerusalem. ¹³I decided to study things carefully. I used my wisdom to check everything out. I looked into everything that is done on earth. What a heavy load God has put on human beings! ¹⁴I've seen what is done on this earth. All of it is meaningless. It's like chasing the wind.

¹⁵ People can't straighten things that are
        crooked.
    They can't count things that don't
        even exist.

¹⁶I said to myself, "Look, I've now grown wiser than anyone who ruled over Jerusalem in the past. I have a lot of wisdom and knowledge." ¹⁷Then I used my mind to understand what it really means to be wise. And I wanted to know what foolish pleasure is all about. But I found out that it's also like chasing the wind.

¹⁸ A lot of human wisdom leads to a lot of
        sorrow.
    More knowledge only brings more
        sadness.

Pleasure Is Meaningless

2 I said to myself, "Come on. I'll try out pleasure. I want to find out if it is good." But it also proved to be meaningless. ²"Laughter doesn't make any sense," I said. "And what can pleasure do for me?" ³I tried cheering myself up by drinking wine. I even tried living in a foolish way. But wisdom was still guiding my mind. I wanted to see what was good for people to do on earth during their short lives.

Jason's Jargon

ECCLESIASTES 2

Search this chapter for the word *satisfied*. To be satisfied is to be happy with what you've done or where you are in life. God wants us to be satisfied with what He's given us.

⁴So I started some large projects. I built houses for myself. I planted vineyards. ⁵I made gardens and parks. I planted all kinds of fruit trees in them. ⁶I made lakes to water groves of healthy trees. ⁷I bought male and female slaves. And I had other slaves who were born in my house. I also owned more

herds and flocks than anyone in Jerusalem ever had before. ⁸I stored up silver and gold for myself. I gathered up the treasures of kings and their kingdoms. I got some male and female singers. I also got many women for myself. Women delight the hearts of men. ⁹I became far more important than anyone in Jerusalem had ever been before. And in spite of everything, I didn't lose my wisdom.

¹⁰ I gave myself everything my eyes
    wanted.
        There wasn't any pleasure that I
            refused to give myself.
    I took delight in everything I did.
        And that was what I got for all my
            work.
¹¹ But then I looked over everything my
    hands had done.
        I saw what I had worked so hard to
            get.
    And nothing had any meaning.
        It was like chasing the wind.
        Nothing was gained on this earth.

Wisdom and Foolish Pleasure Are Meaningless
¹² I decided to think about wisdom.
        I also thought about foolish pleasure.
    What more can a new king do?
        Can he do anything more than
            others have already done?
¹³ I saw that wisdom is better than
    foolishness,
        just as light is better than darkness.
¹⁴ The eyes of a wise person see things
    clearly.
        A person who is foolish lives in
            darkness.
    But I finally realized that death catches
        up
        with both of them.

¹⁵Then I said to myself,

"What happens to a foolish person will
    catch up with me too.
        So what do I gain by being wise?"
    I said to myself,
        "That doesn't have any meaning
            either."
¹⁶ Like a foolish person, a wise person won't
        be remembered very long.
    The days have already come when
        both of them have been
            forgotten.

CaNDiD CoNVeRSaTioNS

I was very proud to be valedictorian for Odyssey High School my senior year, but I'm not sure I deserved it as much as Sonya Tarrant. When we did presentations on the Civil War, she dressed up as Abraham Lincoln and recited the entire Gettysburg Address—and she didn't even have to! Today, I admire how hard she worked. But at the time, I used to say stuff like, "Hard work isn't everything you know."

As it turns out, I was right. At least kind of right. In this passage, the writer talks about how there's more to life than hard work. Now I have to admit that hard work is great. Really, it is! But resting in worship is so important to God that He included it in His Ten Commandments.

God wants us to take one day out of every week to stop our busyness and concentrate on worshiping the God who gave us all of our days.

Like a person who is foolish,
    a wise person must die too!

Work Is Meaningless
¹⁷So I hated life. That's because the work done on this earth made me sad. None of it has any meaning. It's like chasing the wind. ¹⁸I hated everything I had worked for on earth. I'll have to leave all of it to someone who lives after me. ¹⁹And who knows whether that person will be wise or foolish? Either way, they'll take over everything on earth I've worked so hard for. That doesn't have any meaning either. ²⁰So I began to lose hope because of all my hard work on this earth. ²¹A person might use wisdom, knowledge and skill to do their work. But then they have to leave everything they

own to someone who hasn't worked for it. That doesn't have any meaning either. In fact, it isn't fair. ²²What do people get for all their hard work on earth? What do they get for all their worries? ²³As long as they live, their work is nothing but pain and sorrow. Even at night their minds can't rest. That doesn't have any meaning either.

²⁴A person can't do anything better than eat, drink and be satisfied with their work. I'm finally seeing that those things also come from the hand of God. ²⁵Without his help, who can eat or find pleasure? ²⁶God gives wisdom, knowledge and happiness to the person who pleases him. But to a sinner he gives the task of gathering and storing up wealth. Then the sinner must hand it over to the one who pleases God. That doesn't have any meaning either. It's like chasing the wind.

There Is a Time for Everything

3 There is a time for everything.
    There's a time for everything that is
        done on earth.

² There is a time to be born.
    And there's a time to die.

ADVENTURES IN ODYSSEY

Ecclesiastes 3 talks about the importance of balance in life. Connie learned this (and how to avoid being overcommitted) in "The 'No' Factor" (A#15).

There is a time to plant.
    And there's a time to pull up what is
        planted.
³ There is a time to kill.
    And there's a time to heal.
There is a time to tear down.
    And there's a time to build up.
⁴ There is a time to weep.
    And there's a time to laugh.
There is a time to be sad.
    And there's a time to dance.
⁵ There is a time to scatter stones.
    And there's a time to gather them.
There is a time to embrace someone.
    And there's a time not to embrace.
⁶ There is a time to search.
    And there's a time to stop searching.

WHAT ABOUT YOU?

It's easy to lose track of time when playing video games or getting lost in your favorite hobbies. Just ask Jared DeWhite and Dwayne Oswald. In the Adventures in Odyssey episode "Gloobers!," the boys learn a lesson in the Room of Consequence about the importance of using time wisely. After entering a game and playing it from the *inside*, they encounter an old man named Gregory who wasted his life playing video games. Could the same happen to them if they don't make a change?

Playing video games isn't necessarily harmful. But when we spend too much time on one thing, our life tips out of balance. Ecclesiastes 3:1–8 refers to the importance of achieving balance in all aspects of life. It can be hard to glorify the Lord when we would rather play a video game or browse social media instead of do homework or help with family chores. But if we work hard and ask God to help us live a complete life for Him, we will get closer to the kind of balance that pleases Him.

Take a whole day to track the time you spend on various activities. Write those totals down and see how many minutes—or hours—you've invested in them. Would you say it was a fairly typical day? Depending on your totals, you may want to develop a plan to spend more time on activities that will make a positive impact on people's lives, including yours.

Eccl. 3:1-8 Ooh, ooh, ooh! Famous verses alert! On December 4, 1965 a song by the Byrds—"Turn! Turn! Turn!"—made the top of Billboard's Hot 100 song list. The song is nearly word-for-word from Ecclesiastes, chapter 3.

There is a time to keep.
　　And there's a time to throw away.
[7] There is a time to tear.
　　And there's a time to mend.
There is a time to be silent.
　　And there's a time to speak.
[8] There is a time to love.
　　And there's a time to hate.
There is a time for war.
　　And there's a time for peace.

[9] What do workers get for their hard work? [10] I've seen the heavy load God has put on human beings. [11] He has made everything beautiful in its time. He has also given people a sense of who he is. But they can't completely understand what God has done from beginning to end. [12] People should be happy and do good while they live. I know there's nothing better for them to do than that. [13] Each of them should eat and drink. People should be satisfied with all their hard work. That is God's gift to them. [14] I know that everything God does will last forever. Nothing can be added to it. And nothing can be taken from it. God does that so people will have respect for him.

[15] Everything that now exists has already been.
　　And what is coming has existed before.
　　God will judge those who treat others badly.

[16] Here's something else I saw on earth.

Where people should be treated right,
　　they are treated wrong.
Where people should be treated fairly,
　　they are treated unfairly.

[17] I said to myself,

"God will judge
　　godly and sinful people alike.
He has a time for every act.
　　He has a time to judge everything
　　　　that is done."

[18] I also said to myself, "God tests human beings. He does this so they can see that in certain ways they are like animals. [19] Surely what happens to animals happens to people too. Death waits for people and animals alike. People die, just as animals do. All of them have the same breath. People don't have any advantage over animals. Nothing has any meaning. [20] People and animals go to the same place. All of them come from dust. And all of them return to dust. [21] Who can know whether the spirit of a person goes up? Who can tell whether the spirit of an animal goes down into the earth?"

[22] So a person should enjoy their work. That's what God made them for. I saw that there's nothing better for them to do than that. After all, who can show them what will happen after they are gone?

Many people have wondered what happens to the souls of animals after they die. The Bible doesn't say, but we do know that God cares for the animals. Look at Matthew 10:29 and Psalm 50:10–11.

Suffering, Hard Work and No Friends

4 I looked and saw how much people were suffering on this earth.

I saw the tears of those who are suffering.
They don't have anyone to comfort them.
Power is on the side of those who treat them badly.
Those who are suffering don't have anyone to comfort them.

² Then I announced that those
who have already died
are happier than those
who are still alive.
³ But someone who hasn't been born yet
is better off than the dead or the living.
That's because that person hasn't seen the evil things
that are done on earth.

⁴I also saw that a person works hard and accomplishes a lot. But they do it only because they want what another person has. That doesn't have any meaning either. It's like chasing the wind.

⁵ Foolish people fold their hands and don't work.
And that destroys them.
⁶ One handful with peace and quiet
is better than two handfuls with hard work.
Working too hard is like chasing the wind.

⁷Again I saw something on earth that didn't mean anything.

⁸ A man lived all by himself.
He didn't have any sons or brothers.
His hard work never ended.
But he wasn't happy with what he had.
"Who am I working so hard for?" he asked.
"Why don't I get the things I enjoy?"
That doesn't have any meaning either.
In fact, it's a very bad deal!

⁹ Two people are better than one.
They can help each other in everything they do.
¹⁰ Suppose either of them falls down.
Then the one can help the other one up.
But suppose a person falls down and doesn't have anyone to help them up.

ADVENTURES IN ODYSSEY

Nick and Xavier had to overcome their differences and work as a team in "The Taming of the Two" (A#41).

Then feel sorry for that person!
¹¹ Or suppose two people lie down together.
Then they'll keep warm.
But how can one person keep warm alone?
¹² One person could be overpowered.
But two people can stand up for themselves.
And a rope made out of three cords isn't easily broken.

Getting Ahead Is Meaningless

¹³A poor but wise young man is better off than an old but foolish king. That king doesn't pay attention to a warning anymore. ¹⁴The young man might have come from prison to become king. Or he might have been born poor within the kingdom but still became king. ¹⁵I saw that everyone was following the young man who had become the new king. ¹⁶At first, all the people served him when he became king. But those who came later weren't pleased with the way he was ruling. That doesn't have any meaning either. It's like chasing the wind.

Keep Your Promise to God

5 Be careful what you say when you go to God's house. Go there to listen. Don't be like foolish people when you offer your sacrifice. They do what is wrong and don't even know it.

² Don't be too quick to speak.
Don't be in a hurry to say anything to God.
God is in heaven. You are on earth.
So use only a few words when you speak.
³ Many worries result in dreams.
Many words result in foolish talk.

⁴When you make a promise to God, don't wait too long to carry it out. He isn't pleased with foolish people. So do what you have promised. ⁵It is not good to make a promise and not keep it. It is better to make

NOOTON'S FUN FACTS

Eccl. 5:15

Ever heard the phrase, "You can't take it with you"? It means that you can't take your money and possessions when you die. Well, this is the verse that sparked that old saying.

no promise at all. ⁶Don't let your mouth cause you to sin. Don't say to the temple messenger, "My promise was a mistake." Why should God be angry with what you say? Why should he destroy what you have done? ⁷Dreaming too much and talking too much are meaningless. So have respect for God.

Riches Are Meaningless

⁸Suppose you see poor people being mistreated somewhere. And what is being done to them isn't right or fair. Don't be surprised by that. One official is watched by a higher one. Officials who are even higher are watching both of them. ⁹All of them take what the land produces. And the king himself takes his share from the fields.

¹⁰ Anyone who loves money never has
        enough.
    Anyone who loves wealth is never
        satisfied with what they get.
    That doesn't have any meaning
        either.

¹¹ As more and more goods are made,
        more and more people use them up.
    So how can those goods benefit their
        owners?
    All they can do is look at them with
        desire.

¹² The sleep of a worker is sweet.
        It doesn't matter whether they eat a
            little or a lot.
    But the wealth of rich people
        keeps them awake at night.

¹³I've seen something very evil on earth.

    It's when wealth is stored up
        and then brings harm to its owners.
¹⁴ It's also when wealth is lost
        because of an unwise business deal.
    Then there won't be anything left
        for the owners' children.
¹⁵ Everyone is born naked.
        They come into the world with
            nothing.
    And they go out of it with nothing.
    They don't get anything from their work
        that they can take with them.

¹⁶Here's something else that is very evil.

    Everyone is born, and everyone dies.
        And what do they get for their work?
    Nothing. It's like working for the
        wind.
¹⁷ All their lives they eat in darkness.
        Their lives are full of trouble,
            suffering and anger.

¹⁸I have seen what is good. It is good for a person to eat and drink. It's good for them to be satisfied with their hard work on this earth. That's what they should do during the short life God has given them. That's what God made them for. ¹⁹Sometimes God gives a person wealth and possessions. God makes it possible for that person to enjoy them. God helps them accept the life he has given them. God helps them to be happy in their work. All these things are gifts from God. ²⁰A person like that doesn't have to think about how their life is going. That's because God fills their heart with joy.

6 I've seen another evil thing on this earth. And it's a heavy load on human beings. ²God gives some people wealth, possessions and honor. They have everything their hearts desire. But God doesn't let them enjoy those things. Instead, strangers enjoy them. This doesn't have any meaning. It's a very evil thing.

³A man might have a hundred children. He might live a long time. But suppose he can't enjoy his wealth. And suppose he isn't buried in the proper way. Then it doesn't matter how long he lives. I'm telling you

that a baby that is born dead is better off than that man is. ⁴That kind of birth doesn't have any meaning. The baby dies in darkness and leaves this world. And in darkness it is forgotten. ⁵It didn't even see the sun. It didn't know anything at all. But it has more rest than that man does. ⁶And that's true even if he lives for 2,000 years but doesn't get to enjoy his wealth. All people die and go to the grave, don't they?

⁷ People eat up everything they work to
    get.
    But they are never satisfied.
⁸ What advantage do wise people have
    over those who are foolish?
    What do poor people gain
    by knowing how to act toward others?
⁹ Being satisfied with what you have
    is better than always wanting more.
    That doesn't have any meaning either.
    It's like chasing the wind.

¹⁰ God has already planned what now
    exists.
    He has already decided what a
    human being is.
    No one can argue with someone
    who is stronger.
¹¹ The more words people use,
    the less meaning there is.
    And that doesn't help anyone.

¹²Who knows what's good for a person? They live for only a few meaningless days. They pass through life like a shadow. Who can tell them what will happen on earth after they are gone?

Good Advice About How to Live

7 A good name is better than fine
    perfume.
    People can learn more from
    mourning when someone dies
    than from being happy when
    someone is born.
² So it's better to go where people are
    mourning
    than to go where people are having a
    good time.
    Everyone will die someday.
    Those who are still living
    should really think about that.
³ Not being able to figure things out is
    better than laughter.
    That's because sorrow is good for the
    heart.

⁴ Those who are wise are found where
    there is sorrow.
    But foolish people are found where
    there is pleasure.
⁵ Pay attention to a wise person's
    warning.
    That's better than listening to the
    songs of those who are foolish.
⁶ A foolish person's laughter
    is like the crackling of thorns
    burning under a pot.
    That doesn't have any meaning
    either.

⁷ When a wise person takes wealth by
    force, they become foolish.
    It is sinful to take money from people
    who want special favors.
⁸ The end of a matter is better than its
    beginning.
    So it's better to be patient than
    proud.
⁹ Don't become angry quickly.
    Anger lives in the hearts of foolish
    people.
¹⁰ Don't say, "Why were things better in
    the good old days?"
    It isn't wise to ask that kind of
    question.

¹¹ Wisdom is a good thing.
    It's like getting a share of the family
    wealth.
    It benefits those who live on this
    earth.
¹² Wisdom provides safety,
    just as money provides safety.
    But here's the advantage of wisdom.
    It guards those who have it.

¹³Think about what God has done.

Who can make straight
    what he has made crooked?
¹⁴ When times are good, be happy.
    But when times are bad, here's
    something to think about.
    God has made bad times.
    He has also made good times.
    So no one can find out anything
    about what's ahead for them.

¹⁵In my meaningless life here's what I've seen.

I've seen godly people dying
    even though they are godly.

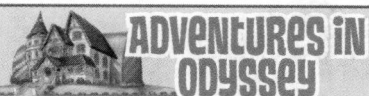

Connie, Eugene, and an armed robber talked about whether people are basically good or evil in "Hold Up!" (A#12). (Find the answer in Ecclesiastes 7:20.)

And I've seen sinful people living a long time
even though they are sinful.
[16] Don't claim to be better than you are.
And don't claim to be wiser than you are.
Why destroy yourself?
[17] Don't be too sinful.
And don't be foolish.
Why die before your time comes?
[18] It's good to hold on to both of those things.
Don't let go of either one.
Whoever has respect for God will avoid going too far in either direction.

[19] Wisdom makes one wise person more powerful
than ten rulers in a city.

[20] It is true that there isn't anyone on earth who does only what is right and never sins.

[21] Don't pay attention to everything people say.
If you do, you might hear your servant cursing you.
[22] Many times you yourself have cursed others.
Deep down inside, you know that's true.

[23] I used wisdom to test all these things. I said,

"I've made up my mind to be wise."
But it was more than I could accomplish.
[24] Whatever exists is far away and very deep.
Who can find it?
[25] So I tried to understand wisdom more completely.
I wanted to study it and figure it out.
I tried to find out everything I could about it.

I tried to understand why it's foolish to be evil.
I wanted to see why choosing foolishness is so unwise.
[26] A woman who hunts a man down is more painful than death.
Her heart is like a trap.
Her hands are like chains.
A man who pleases God will try to get away from her.
But she will trap a sinner.

[27] "Look," says the Teacher. "Here's what I've discovered.

"I added one thing to another to find out everything I could about wisdom.
[28] I searched and searched but found very little.
I did find one honest man among a thousand.
But I didn't find one honest woman among a thousand.
[29] Here's the only other thing I found.
God created human beings as honest.
But they've made many evil plans."

8 Who is like a wise person?
Who knows how to explain things?
A person's wisdom makes their face bright.
It softens the look on their face.

Obey the King

[2] I'm telling you to obey the king's command. You promised to serve him. You made a promise to God. [3] Don't be in a hurry to quit your job in the palace. Don't stand up for something the king doesn't like. He'll do anything he wants to. [4] The king has the final word. So who can ask him, "What are you doing?"

[5] No one who obeys his command will be harmed.
Those who are wise will know the proper time and way to approach him.
[6] There's a proper time and way for people to do everything.
That's true even though a person might be suffering greatly.

[7] No one knows what lies ahead.
So who can tell someone else what's going to happen?

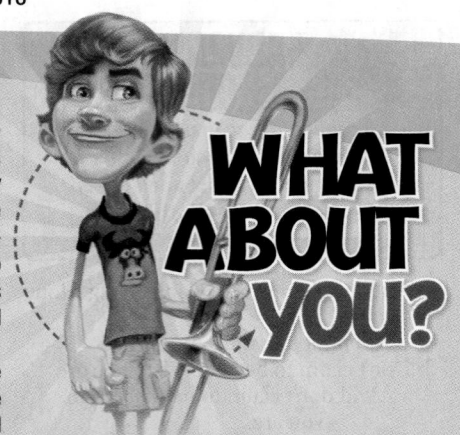

Pete Lemon was an American soldier in Vietnam. One night his platoon was attacked. Despite being wounded, he single-handedly fought off three waves of enemy fighters. He received the Congressional Medal of Honor, then stuck it in a shoebox and refused to wear or talk about it. You see, three of his men died during that battle. It was a painful memory.

Years later, a friend finally convinced Pete to take his medal out of the shoebox in the closet. By displaying the medal, he could use it to tell others about his friends, honoring their sacrifice and keeping their memory alive. Today he tells everyone about Casey Waller, Nathan Mann, and Brent Street, who showed amazing courage and gave their lives for their country.

Those brave soldiers' stories sound like what happens in the Adventures in Odyssey episode "The Price of Freedom." Kirk McGinty never met his dad, but grew up thinking of him as a hero. When his teacher says that Kirk's dad's sacrifice was in vain, he doesn't know what to believe. Fortunately, Whit and Mrs. McGinty help Kirk find the truth—and remember his father as a man who gave his life for others.

Has anyone in your family served in the military? Ask them why they joined the armed forces in the first place. Think of a creative way to record their story for future generations, including places they've visited, people they've served alongside, and acts of bravery they've witnessed.

8 No one can stop the wind from blowing.
And no one has the power to decide when they will die.
No one is let out of the army in times of war.
And evil won't let go of those who practice it.

9I understood all these things. I used my mind to study everything that's done on earth. A man sometimes makes life hard for others. But he ends up hurting himself. 10I also saw sinful people being buried. They used to come and go from the place of worship. And others praised them in the city where they worshiped. That doesn't have any meaning either.

11Sometimes the sentence for a crime isn't carried out quickly. So people make plans to commit even more crimes. 12An evil person may be guilty of a hundred crimes. Yet they may still live a long time. But I know that things will go better with those who have great respect for God. 13Sinful people don't respect God. So things won't go well with them. Like a shadow, they won't be around very long.

14Here's something else on this earth that doesn't have any meaning. Sometimes godly people get what sinful people should receive. And sinful people get what godly people should receive. Here's what I'm telling you. That doesn't have any meaning either. 15So I advise everyone to enjoy life. A person on this earth can't do anything better than eat and drink and be glad. Then they will enjoy their work. They'll be happy all the days of the life God has given them on earth.

16I used my mind to understand what it really means to be wise. I wanted to observe the hard work people do on earth. They don't close their eyes and go to sleep day or night. 17I saw everything God has done. No one can understand what happens on earth. People might try very hard to figure it out. But they still can't discover what it all means. Wise people might claim they know. But they can't really understand it either.

Everyone Dies

9 I thought about all these things. I realized that those who are wise and do what is right are under God's control. What they do is also under his control. But no one knows whether they will be loved or hated. [2]Everyone will die someday. Death comes to godly and sinful people alike. It comes to good and bad people alike. It comes to "clean" and "unclean" people alike. Those who offer sacrifices and those who don't offer them also die.

A good person dies,
      and so does a sinner.
Those who make promises die.
      So do those who are afraid to make
            them.

[3]Here's what is so bad about everything that happens on this earth. Death catches up with all of us. Also, the hearts of people are full of evil. They live in foolish pleasure. After that, they join those who have already died. [4]Anyone who is still living has hope. Even a live dog is better off than a dead lion!

[5] People who are still alive know they'll
            die.
      But those who have died don't know
            anything.
      They don't receive any more rewards.
      And even their name is forgotten.
[6] Their love, hate and jealousy disappear.
      They will never share again
      in anything that happens on earth.

[7]Go and enjoy your food. Be joyful as you drink your wine. God has already approved what you do. [8]Always wear white clothes to show you are happy. Anoint your head with olive oil. [9]You love your wife. So enjoy life with her. Do it all the days of this meaningless life God has given you on earth. That's what he made you for. That's what you get for all your hard work on earth. [10]No matter what you do, work at it with all your might. Remember, you are going to the place of the dead. And there isn't any work or planning or knowledge or wisdom there. [11]Here's something else I've seen on this earth.

Races aren't always won by those who
            run fast.
      Battles aren't always won by those
            who are strong.
Wise people don't always have plenty
            of food.
      Clever people aren't always wealthy.
      Those who have learned a lot aren't
            always successful.
God controls the timing of every event.
      He also controls how things turn
            out.

[12]No one knows when trouble will come to them.

Fish are caught in nets.
      Birds are taken in traps.
And people are trapped by hard times
      that come when they don't expect
            them.

Being Wise Is Better Than Being Foolish

[13]Here's something else I saw on this earth. I saw an example of wisdom that touched me deeply. [14]There was once a small city. Only a few people lived there. A powerful king attacked it. He brought in war machines all around it. [15]A certain man lived in that city. He was poor but wise. He used his wisdom to save the city. But no one remembered that poor man. [16]So I said, "It's better to be wise than to be powerful." But people look down on the poor man's wisdom. No one pays any attention to what he says.

[17] People should listen to the quiet words
            of those who are wise.
      That's better than paying attention to
            the shouts
      of a ruler of foolish people.
[18] Wisdom is better than weapons of war.
      But one sinner destroys a lot of
            good.

10 Dead flies give perfume a bad smell.
      And a little foolishness can make a
            lot of wisdom useless.
[2] The hearts of wise people lead them on
            the right path.
      But the hearts of foolish people take
            them down the wrong path.
[3] Foolish people don't have any sense at
            all.
      They show everyone they are foolish.
      They do it even when they are
            walking along the road.
[4] Suppose a ruler gets very angry with
            you.

Jason's Jargon

ECCLESIASTES 10

Your next assignment: Find *gracious* in this chapter. To be gracious in your speech is to be kind, courteous, and encouraging. Gracious talk is more uplifting than arguing.

If he does, don't quit your job in the palace.
Being calm can overcome what you have done against him.

⁵ Here's something evil I've seen on this earth.
And it's the kind of mistake that rulers make.
⁶ Foolish people are given many important jobs.
Rich people are given unimportant ones.
⁷ I've seen slaves on horseback.
I've also seen princes who were forced to walk as if they were slaves.

⁸ Anyone who digs a pit might fall into it.
Anyone who breaks through a wall might be bitten by a snake.
⁹ Anyone who removes stones from rock pits might get hurt.
Anyone who cuts logs might get wounded.

¹⁰ Suppose the blade of an ax is dull.
And its edge hasn't been sharpened.
Then more effort is needed to use it.
But skill will bring success.

¹¹ Suppose a snake bites before it is charmed.
Then the snake charmer receives no payment.

¹² Wise people say gracious things.
But foolish people are destroyed by what their own lips speak.
¹³ At first what they say is foolish.
In the end their words are very evil.
¹⁴ They talk too much.

No one knows what lies ahead.

Who can tell someone else what will happen after they are gone?
¹⁵ The work foolish people do makes them tired.
They don't even know the way to town.

¹⁶ How terrible it is for a land whose king used to be a servant!
How terrible if its princes get drunk in the morning!
¹⁷ How blessed is the land whose king was born into the royal family!
How blessed if its princes eat and drink at the proper time!
How blessed if they eat and drink to become strong and not to get drunk!

¹⁸ When a person won't work, the roof falls down.
Because of hands that aren't busy, the house leaks.

¹⁹ People laugh at a dinner party.
And wine makes life happy.
People think money can buy everything.

²⁰ Don't say bad things about the king.
Don't even think about those things.
Don't curse rich people.
Don't even curse them in your bedroom.
A bird might fly away and carry your words.
It might report what you said.

Do Many Things to Succeed

11 Sell your grain in the market overseas.
After a while you might earn something from it.
² Try to succeed by doing many things.
After all, you don't know what great trouble might come on the land.

³ Clouds that are full of water pour rain down on the earth.
A tree might fall to the south or the north.
It will stay in the place where it falls.
⁴ Anyone who keeps on watching the wind won't plant seeds.
Anyone who keeps looking at the clouds won't gather crops.

⁵ You don't know the path the wind
takes.
You don't know how a baby is made
inside its mother.
So you can't understand how God
works either.
He made everything.

⁶ In the morning plant your seeds.
In the evening keep your hands busy.
You don't know what will succeed.
It may be one or the other.
Or both might do equally well.

Remember Your Creator While You Are Young

⁷ Light is sweet.
People enjoy being out in the sun.
⁸ No matter how many years anyone
might live,
let them enjoy all of them.
But let them remember the dark days.
There will be many of those.
Nothing that's going to happen will
have any meaning.

⁹ You young people, be happy while you
are still young.
Let your heart be joyful while you
are still strong.
Do what your heart tells you to do.
Go after what your eyes look at.
But I want you to know
that God will judge you for
everything you do.
¹⁰ So drive worry out of your heart.
Get rid of all your troubles.
Being young and strong doesn't have
any meaning.

12 Remember your Creator.
Remember him while you are still
young.
Think about him before your times of
trouble come.
The years will come when you will
say,
"I don't find any pleasure in them."
² That's when the sunlight will become
dark.
The moon and the stars will also
grow dark.
And the clouds will return after it
rains.
³ Remember your Creator before those
who guard the house tremble
with old age.

That's when strong men will be bent
over.
The women who grind grain will stop
because there are so few of
them left.
Those who look through the
windows won't be able to see
very well.
⁴ Remember your Creator before the
front doors are closed.
That's when the sound of grinding
will fade away.
Old people will rise up when they hear
birds singing.
But they will barely hear any of their
songs.
⁵ Remember your Creator before you
become afraid of places that
are too high.
You will also be terrified because of
danger in the streets.
Remember your Creator before the
almond trees have buds on
them.
That's when grasshoppers will drag
themselves along.
Old people will lose their desire.
That's when people will go to their dark
homes in the grave.
And those who mourn for the dead
will walk around in the streets.

⁶ Remember your Creator before the
silver cord is cut.
Remember him before the golden
bowl is broken.
The wheel will be broken at the well.
The pitcher will be smashed at the
spring.
⁷ Remember your Creator before you
return to the dust you came
from.
Remember him before your spirit
goes back to God who gave it.

⁸ "Meaningless! Everything is
meaningless!"
says the Teacher.
"Nothing has any meaning."

Have Respect for God and Obey His Commandments

⁹The Teacher was wise. He gave knowledge to people. He tried out many proverbs. He thought about them carefully. Then he wrote them down in order. ¹⁰He did his best

to find just the right words. And what he wrote was honest and true.

¹¹The sayings of those who are wise move people to take action. Their collected sayings are like nails pounded in firm and deep. These sayings are given to us by one shepherd. ¹²My son, be careful not to pay attention to anything added to them.

Books will never stop being written. Too much studying makes people tired.

¹³ Everything has now been heard.
      And here's the final thing I want to say.
Have respect for God and obey his commandments.
      This is what he expects of all human beings.

¹⁴ God will judge everything people do.
      That includes everything they try to hide.
He'll judge everything, whether it's good or evil.

REMEMBER THIS

ECCLESIASTES 12:13

"Everything has now been heard. And here's the final thing I want to say. Have respect for God and obey his commandments. This is what he expects of all human beings."

Song of Songs

If a boy in your class told a girl that her eyes looked like birds, her hair looked like goats, and her teeth looked like sheep, she might not respond in a positive fashion. But at the right time in history, in the right location, and with the right poetic expression, it was meant to be quite a compliment (4:1–2).

The definition of the title of our next book, "Song of Songs," is given at the very opening: "The greatest song Solomon ever wrote." It is a love story—a conversation between a young bride and her new husband, with occasional comments from observers thrown in. You mustn't miss the powerful description of genuine love toward the end (8:6–7).

Even if you aren't old enough to enjoy all the "mushy talk" (to use youthful vernacular) between two people deeply in love, you can also think of this book as an example of the relationship Jesus has with the church. In other places God's people are referred to as His "bride" (Isa. 62:5; Rev. 19:7–8). Beyond a doubt, God wants to have a closer and more personal relationship with each one of us.

WHAT'S IT MEAN, EUGENE?

Righteousness—*Righteousness* most often refers to doing what is right and good in God's eyes. But it's also about being in a *right relationship* with God. Interestingly, in the New Testament, the words *righteousness*, *justice*, and *justification* are all different forms of the same root word. Fascinating! In Romans 4:3, the apostle Paul writes, "God accepted Abraham's faith, and so his faith made him right with God."

1 This is the greatest song Solomon ever wrote.

A Shulammite woman says to King Solomon

2 "I long for your lips to kiss me!
Your love makes me happier than wine does.
3 The lotion you have on pleases me.
Your name is like perfume that is poured out.
No wonder the young women love you!
4 Take me away with you. Let us hurry!
King Solomon, bring me into your palace."

Jason's Jargon

SONG OF SONGS 1

A romantic mission? Of course! Seek out the word *charming* in this chapter. This love-struck woman thinks her true love is charming. To be charming means to be polite, winsome, and attractive.

The other women say

"King Solomon, you fill us with joy. You make us happy.
We praise your love more than we praise wine."

The woman says to the king

"It is right for them to love you!

5 "Women of Jerusalem,
my skin is dark but lovely.
It is dark like the tents in Kedar.
It's like the curtains of Solomon's tent.
6 Don't stare at me because I'm dark.
The sun has made my skin look like this.
My brothers were angry with me.
They made me take care of the vineyards.
I haven't even taken care of my own vineyard.
7 "King Solomon, I love you.
So tell me where you take care of your flock.

Tell me where you rest your sheep at noon.
Why should I have to act like a prostitute
near the flocks of your friends?"

The other women say

8 "You are the most beautiful woman of all.
Don't you know where to find the king?
Follow the tracks the sheep make.
Take care of your young goats near the tents of the shepherds."

King Solomon says to the Shulammite woman

9 "You are my love.
You are like a mare among Pharaoh's chariot horses.
10 Your earrings make your cheeks even more beautiful.
Your strings of jewels make your neck even more lovely.
11 We will make gold earrings for you.
We'll decorate them with silver."

The woman says

12 "The king was at his table.
My perfume gave off a sweet smell.
13 The one who loves me is like a small bag of myrrh
resting between my breasts.
14 He is like henna flowers from the vineyards of En Gedi."

The king says

15 "You are so beautiful, my love!
So beautiful!
Your eyes are like doves."

The woman says

16 "You are so handsome, my love!
So charming!
The green field is our bed."

The king says

17 "Cedar trees above us are the beams of our house.
Fir trees overhead are its rafters."

The woman says

2 "I am like a rose on the coast of Sharon.
I'm like a lily in the valleys."

The king says

2 "My love, among the young women
you are like a lily among thorns."

The woman says

3 "My love, among the young men
you are like an apple tree among the
trees of the forest.
I'm happy to sit in your shade.
Your fruit tastes so sweet to me.
4 Lead me to the dinner hall.
Let your banner of love be lifted
high above me.
5 Give me some raisins to make me
strong.
Give me some apples to make me
feel like new again.
Our love has made me weak.
6 Your left arm is under my head.
Your right arm is around me.
7 Women of Jerusalem, make me a
promise.
Let the antelopes and the does serve
as witnesses.
Don't stir up love.
Don't wake it up until it's ready.

8 "Listen! I hear my love!
Look! Here he comes!
He's leaping across the mountains.
He's coming over the hills.
9 The one who loves me is like an
antelope or a young deer.
Look! There he stands behind our
wall.
He's gazing through the window.
He's peering through the screen.
10 He said to me, 'Rise up, my love.
Come with me, my beautiful one.
11 Look! The winter is past.
The rains are over and gone.
12 Flowers are appearing on the earth.
The season for singing has come.
The cooing of doves
is heard in our land.
13 The fig trees are producing their early
fruit.
The flowers on the vines are giving
off their sweet smell.
Rise up and come, my love.
Come with me, my beautiful one.' "

The king says

14 "You are like a dove in an opening in
the rocks.
You are like a dove in a hiding place
on a mountainside.
Show me your face.
Let me hear your voice.
Your voice is so sweet.
Your face is so lovely.
15 Catch the foxes for us.
Catch the little foxes.
They destroy our vineyards.
The vineyards are in bloom."

The woman says

16 "My love belongs to me, and I belong to
him.
Like an antelope, he eats among the
lilies.
17 Until the day begins
and the shadows fade away,
turn to me, my love.
Be like an antelope
or like a young deer
on the rocky hills.

3 "All night long on my bed
I searched for the one my heart loves.
I looked for him but didn't find him.
2 I will get up and go around in the city.
I'll look through all of its streets.
I'll search for the one my heart loves.
So I looked for him but didn't find
him.
3 Those on guard duty found me
as they were walking around in the
city.
'Have you seen the one my heart
loves?' I asked.
4 As soon as I had passed by them
I found the one my heart loves.
I threw my arms around him and didn't
let him go
until I had brought him to my
mother's house.
I took him to my mother's room.
5 Women of Jerusalem, make me a
promise.
Let the antelopes and the does serve
as witnesses.
Don't stir up love.
Don't wake it up until it's ready.

6 "Who is this man coming up from the
desert
like a column of smoke?
He smells like myrrh and incense
made from all the spices of the
trader.

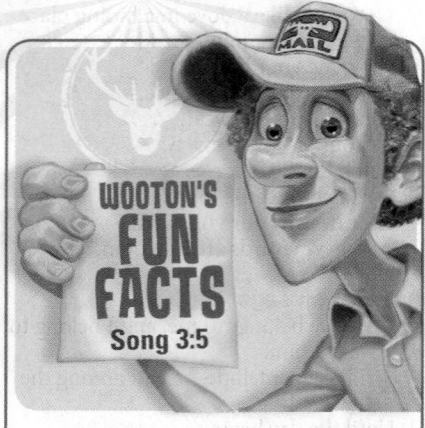

WOOTON'S FUN FACTS

Song 3:5

Song of Songs was written for married couples. In ancient Israel, kids were not allowed to read it because there were things it describes that they weren't ready for. In fact, verse 5 advises: "Don't stir up love. Don't wake it up until it's ready."

⁷ Look! There's Solomon's movable throne.
  Sixty soldiers accompany it.
  They have been chosen from the best
      warriors in Israel.
⁸ All of them are wearing swords.
  They have fought many battles.
  Each one has his sword at his side.
      Each is prepared for the terrors of
      the night.
⁹ King Solomon made the movable
      throne for himself.
  He made it out of wood from
      Lebanon.
¹⁰ He formed its posts out of silver.
  He made its base out of gold.
  Its seat was covered with purple cloth.
  It was decorated inside with love.
  Women of Jerusalem, ¹¹come out.

  "Look, you women of Zion.
  Look at King Solomon wearing his
      crown.
  His mother placed it on him.
  She did it on his wedding day.
  His heart was full of joy."

The king says to the Shulammite woman

4 "You are so beautiful, my love!
  So beautiful!
  Your eyes behind your veil are like
      doves.

Your hair flows like a flock of black
      goats
  coming down from the hills of
      Gilead.
² Your teeth are as clean as a flock of
      sheep.
  Their wool has just been clipped.
  They have just come up from being
      washed.
  Each of your teeth has its twin.
  Not one of them is alone.
³ Your lips are like a bright red ribbon.
  Your mouth is so lovely.
  Your cheeks behind your veil
  are like the halves of a
      pomegranate.
⁴ Your neck is strong and beautiful like
      the tower of David.
  That tower is built with rows of
      stones.
  A thousand shields are hanging on it.
  All of them belong to mighty
      soldiers.
⁵ Your breasts are lovely.
  They are like two young antelopes
      that eat among the lilies.
⁶ I will go to the mountain of myrrh.
  I'll go to the hill of incense.
  I'll stay there until the day begins
  and the shadows fade away.
⁷ Every part of you is so beautiful, my
      love.
  There is no flaw in you.

⁸ "Come with me from Lebanon, my
      bride.
  Come with me from Lebanon.
  Come down from the top of Mount
      Amana.
  Come down from the top of Senir.
  Come to me from the peak of Mount
      Hermon.
  Leave the dens where the lions live.
  Leave the places in the mountains
      where the leopards stay.
⁹ My bride, you have stolen my heart
  with one glance of your eyes.
  My sister, you have stolen my heart
  with one jewel in your necklace.
¹⁰ My bride, your love is so delightful.
  My sister, your love makes me
      happier than wine does.
  Your perfume smells better than any
      spice.
¹¹ Your lips are as sweet as honey, my
      bride.

Song 4:7 Romantic love *is* blind. Scientists now know that couples in love have a hard time seeing flaws in each other because of brain chemicals that promote closeness over common sense. I know that Penny had a hard time seeing that I can sometimes be indecisive before we were married.

Milk and honey are under your
    tongue.
Your clothes smell like the cedar
    trees in Lebanon.
¹² My bride, you are like a garden that is
    locked up.
My sister, you are like a spring of
    water that has a fence around
    it.
You are like a fountain that is sealed
    up.
¹³ You are like trees whose branches are
    loaded
    with pomegranates, fine fruits,
    henna and nard,
¹⁴   with nard and saffron, cane and
    cinnamon.
You are like every kind of incense tree.
You have myrrh, aloes
    and all the finest spices.
¹⁵ You are like a fountain in a garden.
You are like a well of flowing water
    streaming down from Lebanon."

The woman says
¹⁶ "Wake up, north wind!
    Come, south wind!
Blow on my garden.
    Then its sweet smell will spread
    everywhere.
Let my love come into his garden.
Let him taste its fine fruits."

The king says
5 "My bride, I have come into my garden.
    My sister, I've gathered my myrrh
    and my spice.
I've eaten my honeycomb and my honey.
    I've drunk my wine and my milk."

**The other women say to the
Shulammite woman and to Solomon**
"Friends, eat and drink.
    Drink up all the love you want."

The woman says
² "I slept, but my heart was awake.
    Listen! The one who loves me is
    knocking.
He says, 'My sister, I love you.
    Open up so I can come in.
You are my dove.
    You are perfect in every way.
My head is soaked with dew.
    The night air has made my hair wet.'
³ "But I've taken off my robe.
    Must I put it on again?
I've washed my feet.
    Must I get them dirty again?
⁴ My love put his hand through the
    opening.
My heart began to pound for him.
⁵ I got up to open the door for my love.
    My hands dripped with myrrh.
It flowed from my fingers
    onto the handles of the lock.
⁶ I opened the door for my love.
    But he had left and was gone.
    My heart sank because he had left.
I looked for him but didn't find him.
    I called out to him, but he didn't
    answer.
⁷ Those on guard duty found me
    as they were walking around in the
    city.
They beat me. They hurt me.
    Those on guard duty at the walls
    took my coat away from me.
⁸ Women of Jerusalem, make me a
    promise.
If you find the one who loves me,
    tell him our love has made me weak."

The other women say
⁹ "You are the most beautiful woman of
    all.
How is the one you love better than
    others?

How is he better than anyone else?
Why do you ask us to make you this
promise?"

The woman says

10 "The one who loves me is tanned and
handsome.
He's the finest man among 10,000.
11 His head is like the purest gold.
His hair is wavy and as black as a
raven.
12 His eyes are like doves
by streams of water.
They look as if they've been washed in
milk.
They are set like jewels in his head.
13 His cheeks are like beds of spice
giving off perfume.
His lips are like lilies
dripping with myrrh.
14 His arms are like rods of gold
set with topaz.
His body is like polished ivory
decorated with lapis lazuli.
15 His legs are like pillars of marble
set on bases of pure gold.
He looks like the finest cedar tree
in the mountains of Lebanon.
16 His mouth is very sweet.
Everything about him is delightful.
That's what the one who loves me is
like.
That's what my friend is like, women
of Jerusalem."

The other women say

6 "You are the most beautiful woman of
all.
Where has the one who loves you
gone?
Which way did he turn?
We'll help you look for him."

The woman says

2 "My love has gone down to his garden.
He's gone to the beds of spices.
He's eating in the gardens.
He's gathering lilies.
3 I belong to my love, and he belongs to
me.
He's eating among the lilies."

The king says

4 "My love, you are as beautiful as the city
of Tirzah.

You are as lovely as Jerusalem.
You are as majestic as troops
carrying their banners.
5 Turn your eyes away from me.
They overpower me.
Your hair flows like a flock of black
goats
coming down from the hills of
Gilead.
6 Your teeth are as clean as a flock of
sheep
coming up from being washed.
Each of your teeth has its twin.
Not one of them is missing.
7 Your cheeks behind your veil
are like the halves of a pomegranate.
8 There might be 60 queens and 80
concubines.
There might be more virgins than
anyone can count.
9 But you are my perfect dove.
There isn't anyone like you.
You are your mother's favorite
daughter.
The young women see you and call you
blessed.
The queens and concubines praise
you."

The other women say

10 "Who is this woman?
She is like the sunrise in all its glory.
She is as beautiful as the moon.
She is as bright as the sun.
She is as majestic as the stars
traveling across the sky."

The king says

11 "I went down to a grove of nut trees.
I wanted to look at the new plants
growing in the valley.

Jason's Jargon

SONG OF SONGS 6

Food quest! Check
this chapter for a
pomegranate. A
pomegranate looks like a
purple tomato. It is filled
with seeds. Why this
woman's cheeks remind
the king of a pomegranate
is a mystery.

I wanted to find out whether the vines
    had budded.
I wanted to see if the pomegranate
    trees had bloomed.
¹² Before I realized it,
    I was among the royal chariots of my
    people."

The other women say
¹³ "Come back to us.
    Come back, Shulammite woman.
Come back to us.
    Come back. Then we can look at
    you."

The king says to the women
"Why do you want to look at the
    Shulammite woman
    as you would watch a dancer at
    Mahanaim?"

**The king says to the Shulammite
woman**
7 "You are like a prince's daughter.
    Your feet in sandals are so beautiful.
Your graceful legs are like jewels.
    The hands of an artist must have
    shaped them.
² Your navel is like a round bowl
    that always has mixed wine in it.
Your waist is like a mound of wheat
    surrounded by lilies.
³ Your two breasts are lovely.
    They are like two young antelopes.
⁴ Your neck is smooth and beautiful like
    an ivory tower.
Your eyes are like the pools of
    Heshbon
    by the gate of Bath Rabbim.
Your nose is like the towering
    mountains of Lebanon
    that face the city of Damascus.
⁵ Your head is like a crown on you.
    It is as beautiful as Mount Carmel.
Your hair is as smooth as purple silk.
    I am captured by your flowing curls.
⁶ You are so beautiful! You please me so
    much!
You are so delightful, my love!
⁷ You are as graceful as a palm tree.
    Your breasts are as sweet as the
    freshest fruit.
⁸ I said, 'I will climb the palm tree.
    I'll take hold of its fruit.'

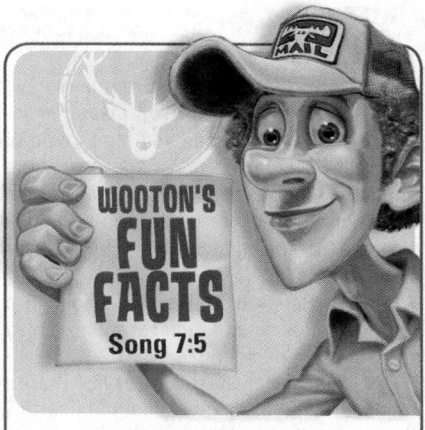

WOOTON'S FUN FACTS
Song 7:5

Okay, Solomon is not colorblind. In verse
4:1 he says his love's hair is black. The
reference to purple means royal. Her hair
is smoother than just any old silk—it feels
like *royal* silk. Talk about silky smooth!

May your breasts be as sweet as grapes
    on the vine.
May your breath smell like the
    tastiest apples.
⁹ May your lips be like the finest
    wine."

The woman says
"May my wine go straight to you, my
    love.
May it flow gently over our lips as
    we sleep.

¹⁰ "I belong to you, my love.
    And you long for me.
¹¹ Come, my love. Let's go to the country.
    Let's spend the night in the villages.
¹² Let's go out to the vineyards early.
    Let's go and see if the vines have
    budded.
Let's find out whether their flowers have
    opened.
Let's see if the pomegranate trees are
    blooming.
There I will give you my love.
¹³ The mandrake flowers give off their
    strong smell.
All the best things are waiting for
    us,
new and old alike.
    I've stored them up for you, my
    love.

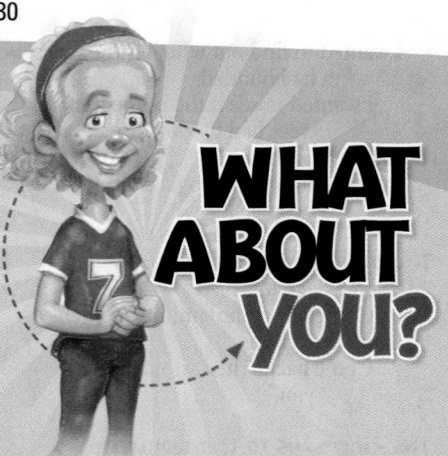

WHAT ABOUT YOU?

Do you know that people in Greenland have different words for good-bye? *Takuss'* is the more common "Bye, see you later" type of farewell. But *inuulluarina* is spoken only to someone you never expect to see again. That's kind of a sad thought. We don't like the idea of saying good-bye, do we? It's tough to do.

Song of Songs 8:6 talks about holding a loved one closely and never wanting to say good-bye, even in death.

Then again, Ecclesiastes 3:1 says, "There's a time for everything that is done on earth." That means the world is experiencing a constant flow of beginnings and endings, hellos and good-byes. It's part of life.

And yet for Christians, there's no such thing as a permanent inuulluarina. Not even in death. That's because one day everyone who loves Jesus will be together in the new heaven and new earth that God will create for us. They will probably look a lot different from anything we can imagine today. But there will be lots of wonderful people, and it will feel like home.

Here's a fun challenge: Learn the words for *hello* and *good-bye* in two languages besides English. You can look them up in a dictionary or online, or ask family members or friends if they know those words in other languages. The rest of today, use your new greetings and farewells instead of the English words. (Remember, a smile is a great way to say hello in any language.)

---

8 "I wish you were like a brother to me.
　　I wish my mother's breasts had
　　　　nursed you.
　Then if I found you outside,
　　I could kiss you.
　　No one would look down on me.
² I'd bring you to my mother's house.
　　She taught me everything I know.
　I'd give you spiced wine to drink.
　　It's the juice of my pomegranates.
³ Your left arm is under my head.
　　Your right arm is around me.
⁴ Women of Jerusalem, make me a
　　　　promise.
　　Don't stir up love.
　　Don't wake it up until it's ready."

The other women say

⁵ "Who is this woman coming up from
　　　　the desert?
　　She's leaning on the one who loves
　　　　her."

The woman says to the king

　"Under the apple tree I woke you up.
　　That's where your mother became
　　　　pregnant with you.
　　She went into labor, and you were
　　　　born there.
⁶ Hold me close to your heart where your
　　　　royal seal is worn.
　　Keep me as close to yourself as the
　　　　bracelet on your arm.
　My love for you is so strong it won't let
　　　　you go.
　　Love is as powerful as death.
　　Love's jealousy is as strong as the grave.

ADVENTURES IN ODYSSEY

Aubrey and Bethany Shepard loved each other as sisters and saw how strong that love was—and how Godly love couldn't be washed away—in "Always" (A#45).

Love is like a blazing fire.
Love burns like a mighty flame.
[7] No amount of water can put it out.
Rivers can't sweep it away.
Suppose someone offers
all their wealth to buy love.
That won't even come close to being
enough."

The woman's brothers say

[8] "We have a little sister.
Her breasts are still small.
What should we do for our sister
when she gets engaged?
[9] If she were a wall,
we'd build silver towers on her.
If she were a door,
we'd cover her with cedar boards."

The woman says to the king

[10] "I am a wall.
My breasts are like well-built
towers.
So in your eyes I've become
like someone who makes you
happy.
[11] Solomon, you had a vineyard in Baal
Hamon.
You rented your vineyard to others.
They had to pay 25 pounds
of silver for its fruit.
[12] But I can give my own vineyard to
anyone I want to.
So I give my 25 pounds of silver to
you, Solomon.
Give 5 pounds to those who take
care of its fruit."

The king says

[13] "My love, you live in the gardens.
My friends listen for your voice.
But let me hear it now."

The woman says

[14] "Come away with me, my love.
Be like an antelope
or like a young deer
on mountains that are full of spices."

Isaiah

We have reached a major milestone in our trip through the Old Testament! All of the remaining books (from Isaiah to Malachi) are called "the writing prophets." Take a moment to find the end of Malachi and hold the pages for all those books between your fingers. You'll notice that this is a rather hefty portion of Scripture. The Bible identifies many other prophets throughout history, but the writing prophets wrote to God's people specifically regarding the fall and captivity of the nations of Israel and Judah. In the case of our current prophet, Isaiah, he warned of terrible things that were soon to happen to Jerusalem and Judah, but he also promised God's eventual comfort and deliverance.

Isaiah is a thorough and powerful writer. In point of fact, he is quoted more by New Testament writers than all of the other writing prophets combined! Jesus began His public ministry by reading from Isaiah and explaining that He was the person Isaiah had written about (Luke 4:14–30).

Isaiah was married to a prophetess and had two children (7:3; 8:3). He also had a fascinating experience when he was called to speak for God (chapter 6).

You're likely to hear from Isaiah at both Christmas *and* Easter (7:14; 9:6–7; 53:3–10). What he has to say about the faithfulness of God is just as relevant to us today as it was for the people to whom it was first written.

What's it Mean, Eugene?

Fall (the)—As a young boy, I was known as a male bovine animal in a vitrified ceramic material retail establishment (a bull in a china shop). In laymen's terms, I was a klutz. I tripped with regularity and fell almost as often. The biblical "fall," however, is an idiom that represents the breaking of mankind's relationship with God, originating with Adam and Eve in the Garden of Eden when the serpent (Satan) enticed them to disobey God's commandment by eating the forbidden fruit.

1 Here is the vision about Judah and Jerusalem that Isaiah saw. It came to him when Uzziah, Jotham, Ahaz and Hezekiah were ruling. They were kings of Judah. Isaiah was the son of Amoz.

The Nation Refuses to Obey the LORD

² Listen to me, you heavens! Pay
        attention to me, earth!
    The LORD has said,
    "I raised children. I brought them up.
    But they have refused to obey me.
³ The ox knows its master.
    The donkey knows where its owner
        feeds it.
    But Israel does not know me.
    My people do not understand me."

⁴ How terrible it will be for this sinful
        nation!
    They are loaded down with guilt.
    They are people who do nothing but
        evil.
    They are children who are always
        sinning.
    They have deserted the LORD.
    They have turned against the Holy
        One of Israel.
    They have turned their backs on
        him.

⁵ Israel, why do you want to be beaten all
        the time?
    Why do you always refuse to obey
        the LORD?
    Your head is covered with wounds.
    Your whole heart is weak.
⁶ There isn't a healthy spot on your body.
    You are not healthy from the bottom
        of your feet to the top of your
        head.
    You have nothing but wounds, cuts
        and open sores.
    They haven't been cleaned up or
        bandaged
    or treated with olive oil.

⁷ Your country has been deserted.
    Your cities have been burned down.
    The food from your fields is being eaten
        up by outsiders.
    They are doing it right in front of
        you.
    Your land has been completely
        destroyed.
    It looks as if strangers have taken it
        over.

⁸ The city of Zion is left like a shed
        where someone stands guard in a
        vineyard.
    It is left like a hut in a cucumber field.
    It's like a city being attacked.
⁹ The LORD who rules over all
    has let some people live through that
        time of trouble.
    If he hadn't, we would have become like
        Sodom.
    We would have been like Gomorrah.

¹⁰ Rulers of Sodom,
        hear the LORD's message.
    People of Gomorrah,
        listen to the instruction of our God.
¹¹ "Do you think I need any more of your
            sacrifices?"
        asks the LORD.
    "I have more than enough of your
            burnt offerings.
    I have more than enough of rams
        and the fat of your fattest animals.
    I do not find any pleasure
        in the blood of your bulls, lambs and
            goats.
¹² Who asked you to bring all these
            animals
        when you come to worship me?
    Who asked you and your animals
        to walk all over my courtyards?
¹³ Stop bringing offerings that do not
            mean anything to me!
    I hate your incense.
    I can't stand your worthless
            gatherings.
    I can't stand the way you celebrate
            your New Moon feasts,
    Sabbath days and special services.
¹⁴ Your New Moon feasts and your other
            appointed feasts
    I hate with my whole being.
    They have become a heavy load to me.
    I am tired of carrying it.
¹⁵ You might spread out your hands
            toward me when you pray.
    But I do not look at you.
    You might even offer many prayers.
    But I am not listening to them.
    Your hands are covered with the
            blood of the people you have
            murdered.
¹⁶   So wash and make yourselves clean.
    Get your evil actions out of my sight!
        Stop doing what is wrong!
¹⁷   Learn to do what is right!

Treat people fairly.
Help those who are treated badly.
Stand up in court for children whose
fathers have died.
And do the same thing for widows.

18 "Come. Let us settle this matter,"
says the LORD.
"Even though your sins are bright red,
they will be as white as snow.
Even though they are deep red,
they will be white like wool.
19 But you have to be willing to change
and obey me.
If you are, you will eat the good
things that grow on the land.
20 But if you are not willing to obey me,
you will be killed by swords."
The LORD has spoken.

21 See how the faithful city of Jerusalem
has become like a prostitute!
Once it was full of people who treated
others fairly.
Those who did what was right used
to live in it.
But now murderers live there!
22 Jerusalem, your silver isn't pure
anymore.
Your best wine has been made weak
with water.
23 Your rulers refuse to obey the LORD.
They join forces with robbers.
All of them love to accept money from
those who want special favors.
They are always looking for gifts
from other people.
They don't stand up in court for
children whose fathers have
died.
They don't do it for widows either.
24 The Lord is the Mighty One of Israel.
The LORD who rules over all
announces,
"Israel, you have become my enemies.
I will act against you in my anger.
I will pay you back for what you
have done.
25 I will turn my power against you.
I will make you completely 'clean.'
I will remove everything that is not
pure.
26 I will give you leaders like the ones you
had long ago.
I will give you rulers like those you
had at the beginning.

Then you will be called
the City That Does What Is Right.
You will also be called the Faithful
City."

27 Zion will be saved when justice is
done.
Those who are sorry for their sins
will be saved
when what is right is done.
28 But sinners and those who refuse
to obey the LORD will be
destroyed.
And those who desert the LORD will
die.

29 "Israel, you take delight in worshiping
among the sacred oak trees.
You will be full of shame for doing
that.
You have chosen to worship in the
sacred gardens.
You will be dishonored for doing
that.
30 You will be like an oak tree whose
leaves are dying.
You will be like a garden that doesn't
have any water.
31 Your strongest men will become like
dry pieces of wood.
Their worship of other gods will be
the spark that lights the fire.
Everything will be burned up.
No one will be there to put the fire
out."

People From Many Nations Will Worship at Mount Zion

2 Here is a vision that Isaiah, the son of
Amoz, saw about Judah and Jerusalem.

2 In the last days

the mountain where the LORD's temple
is located will be famous.
It will be the highest mountain of all.
It will be raised above the hills.
All the nations will go to it.

3 People from many nations will go there.
They will say,

"Come. Let us go up to the LORD's
mountain.
Let's go to the temple of Jacob's God.
He will teach us how we should live.
Then we will live the way he wants
us to."

The law of the LORD will be taught at
    Zion.
  His message will go out from
    Jerusalem.
⁴ He will judge between the nations.
  He'll settle problems among many
    of them.
  They will hammer their swords into
    plows.
  They'll hammer their spears into
    pruning tools.
  Nations will not go to war against one
    another.
  They won't even train to fight
    anymore.
⁵ People of Jacob, come.
  Let us live the way the LORD has
    taught us to.

The Day of the LORD Is Coming

⁶ LORD, you have deserted the people of
    Jacob.
  They are your people.
  The land is full of false beliefs from the
    east.
  The people practice evil magic, just
    as the Philistines do.
  They do what ungodly people do.
⁷ Their land is full of silver and gold.
  There is no end to their treasures.
  Their land is full of horses.
  There is no end to their chariots.
⁸ Their land is full of statues of gods.
  Their people bow down to what
    their own hands have made.
  They bow down to what their fingers
    have shaped.
⁹ So people will be brought low.
  Everyone will be made humble.
  Do not forgive them.
¹⁰ Go and hide in caves in the rocks, you
    people!
  Hide in holes in the ground.
  Hide from the terrifying presence of the
    LORD!
  Hide when he comes in glory and
    majesty!
¹¹ Anyone who brags will be brought low.
  Anyone who is proud will be made
    humble.
  The LORD alone will be honored at
    that time.
¹² The LORD who rules over all has set
    apart a day when he will judge.

He has set it apart for all those who
    are proud and think they are
    important.
He has set it apart for all those who
    brag about themselves.
  All of them will be brought low.
¹³ The LORD has set that day apart for all
    the cedar trees in Lebanon.
  They are very tall.
  He has set that day apart for all the
    oak trees in Bashan.
¹⁴ He has set it apart for all the towering
    mountains.
  He has set it apart for all the high
    hills.
¹⁵ He has set it apart for every high
    tower
  and every strong wall.
¹⁶ He has set it apart for every trading
    ship
  and every beautiful boat.
¹⁷ Anyone who brags will be brought
    low.
  Anyone who is proud will be made
    humble.
  The LORD alone will be honored at that
    time.
¹⁸   And the statues of gods will totally
    disappear.
¹⁹ People will run and hide in caves in the
    rocks.
  They will go into holes in the
    ground.
  They will run away from the terrifying
    presence of the LORD.
  They will run when he comes in
    glory and majesty.
  When he comes, he will shake the
    earth.
²⁰ People had made some statues of gods
    out of silver.
  They had made others out of gold.
  Then they worshiped them.
  But when the LORD comes,
    they will throw the statues away to
    the moles and bats.
²¹ Those people will run and hide in caves
    in the rocks.
  They will go into holes in the cliffs.
  They will run away from the terrifying
    presence of the LORD.
  They will run when he comes in
    glory and majesty.
  When he comes, he will shake the
    earth.

WOOTON'S FUN FACTS
Isa. 2:20

Bats and moles both live in dark places. Bats have poor vision but use a form of radar called echolocation to "see." Moles have small eyes that see only black and white. I'm glad I don't have to live where they do. My eyes just wouldn't cut it!

²² Stop trusting in mere human beings,
　　who can't help you.
　　They only live for a little while.
　　What good are they?

The Lord Will Judge Jerusalem and Judah

3 Here is what
　　the Lord who rules over all is about
　　　to do.
　The Lord will take away from Jerusalem
　　and Judah
　supplies and help alike.
　He will take away all the supplies of
　　food and water.
² 　He'll take away heroes and soldiers.
　He'll take away judges and prophets.
　　He'll take away fortune tellers and
　　　elders.
³ He'll take away captains of groups of 50
　　men.
　　He'll take away government leaders.
　He'll take away advisers, skilled
　　workers
　　and those who are clever at doing
　　　evil magic.
⁴ The Lord will make mere youths their
　　leaders.
　　Children will rule over them.
⁵ People will treat one another badly.
　　They will fight against one another.

They will fight against their
　　neighbors.
Young people will attack old people.
　　Ordinary people will attack those
　　　who are more important.
⁶ A man will grab one of his brothers
　　in his father's house. He will say,
　"You have a coat. So you be our leader.
　　Take charge of all these broken-
　　　down buildings!"
⁷ But at that time the brother will cry out,
　　"I can't help you.
　I don't have any food or clothing in my
　　house.
　　Don't make me the leader of these
　　　people."

⁸ Jerusalem is about to fall.
　　And so is Judah.
　They say and do things against the
　　Lord.
　　They dare to disobey him to his very
　　　face.
⁹ The look on their faces is a witness
　　against them.
　　They show off their sin, just as the
　　　people of Sodom did.
　They don't even try to hide it.
How terrible it will be for them!
　　They have brought trouble on
　　　themselves.

¹⁰ Tell those who do what is right that
　　things will go well with them.
　　They will enjoy the results of the
　　　good things they've done.
¹¹ But how terrible it will be for those who
　　do what is evil!
　　Trouble is about to fall on them.
　　They will be paid back for the evil
　　　things they've done.

¹² Those who are young treat my people
　　badly.
　　Women rule over them.
　My people, your leaders have taken you
　　down the wrong path.
　　They have turned you away from the
　　　right path.

¹³ The Lord takes his place in court.
　　He stands up to judge the people.
¹⁴ He judges the elders and leaders of his
　　people.
　　He says to them,
　"My people are like a vineyard.
　　You have destroyed them.

The things you have taken from
   poor people are in your
   houses.
¹⁵ What do you mean by crushing my
   people?
   Why are you grinding the faces of
     the poor into the dirt?"
   announces the Lord. He is the Lord
     who rules over all.

¹⁶ The Lord continues,
   "The women in Zion are very proud.
   They walk along with their noses in
     the air.
   They tease men with their eyes.
   They sway their hips as they walk
     along.
   Little chains jingle on their ankles.
¹⁷ So I will put sores on the heads of
   Zion's women.
   And I will remove the hair from
     their heads."

¹⁸At that time the Lord will take away the beautiful things they wear. He will take away their decorations, headbands and moon-shaped necklaces. ¹⁹He'll take away their earrings, bracelets and veils. ²⁰He'll remove their headdresses, anklets and belts. He'll take away their perfume bottles and charms. ²¹He'll remove the rings they wear on their fingers and in their noses. ²²He'll take away their fine robes and their capes and coats. He'll take away their purses ²³and mirrors. And he'll take away their linen clothes, turbans and shawls.

²⁴ Instead of smelling sweet,
   the women will smell bad.
   Instead of wearing belts,
   they will wear ropes.
   Instead of having beautiful hair,
   they won't have any hair at all.
   Instead of wearing fine clothes,
   they'll wear rough clothes to show
     how sad they are.
   Instead of being beautiful,
   on their bodies they'll have the
     marks of their owners.
²⁵ Jerusalem, your men will be killed by
   swords.
   Your soldiers will die in battle.
²⁶ The city of Zion will be very sad.
   Like a widow, she will lose
     everything.
   She will sit on the ground and
     mourn.

4 ¹At that time seven women
   will grab hold of one man.
   They'll say to him, "We will eat our own
     food.
   We'll provide our own clothes.
   Just let us become your wives.
   Take away our shame!"

The Branch of the Lord

²At that time Israel's king will be beautiful and glorious. He will be called The Branch of the Lord. The fruit of the land will be the pride and glory of those who are still left alive in Israel. ³Those who are left in Zion will be called holy. They will be recorded among those who are alive in Jerusalem. ⁴The Lord will wash away the sin of the women in Zion. He will clean up the blood that was spilled there. He will judge those who spilled that blood. His burning anger will blaze out at them. ⁵Then the Lord will create over Jerusalem a cloud of smoke by day. He will also create a glow of flaming fire at night. The cloud and fire will appear over all of Mount Zion. They will also appear over the people who gather together there. The Lord's glory will be like a tent over everything. ⁶It will cover the people and give them shade from the hot sun all day long. It will be a safe place where they can hide from storms and rain.

The Song of the Vineyard

5 I will sing a song for the Lord.
   He is the one I love.
   It's a song about his vineyard Israel.
   The one I love had a vineyard.
   It was on a hillside that had rich soil.
² He dug up the soil and removed its
     stones.
   He planted the very best vines in it.
   He built a lookout tower there.
   He also cut out a winepress for it.
   Then he kept looking for a crop of good
     grapes.
   But the vineyard produced only bad
     fruit.

³ So the Lord said, "People of Jerusalem
     and Judah,
   you be the judge between me and
     my vineyard.
⁴ What more could I have done for my
     vineyard?
   I did everything I could.

I kept looking for a crop of good
grapes.
So why did it produce only bad
ones?
5 Now I will tell you
what I am going to do to my
vineyard.
I will take away its fence.
And the vineyard will be destroyed.
I will break down its wall.
And people will walk all over my
vineyard.
6 I will turn my vineyard into a dry and
empty desert.
It will not be pruned or taken care of.
Thorns and bushes will grow there.
I will command the clouds
not to rain on it."

7 The vineyard of the LORD who rules
over all
is the nation of Israel.
The people of Judah
are the vines he took delight in.
He kept looking for them to do what
is fair.
But all he saw was blood being
spilled.
He kept looking for them to do what is
right.
But all he heard were cries of
suffering.

The LORD Judges His Vineyard

8 How terrible it will be for you who get
too many houses!
How terrible for you who get too
many fields!
Finally there won't be any space left in
the land.
Then you will live all alone.

9 I heard the LORD who rules over all announce a message. He said,

"You can be sure that the great houses
will become empty.
The fine homes will be left with no
one living in them.
10 A ten-acre vineyard will produce only
six gallons of wine.
360 pounds of seeds will produce
only 36 pounds of grain."

11 How terrible it will be for those who get
up early in the morning
to start drinking!

How terrible for those who stay up late
at night
until they are drunk with wine!
12 They have harps and lyres at their
banquets.
They have tambourines, flutes and
wine.
But they don't have any concern for the
mighty acts of the LORD.
They don't have any respect for what
his power has done.
13 So my people will be taken away as
prisoners.
That's because they don't understand
what the LORD has done.
Their nobles will die of hunger.
The rest of the people won't have any
water to drink.
14 So Death opens its jaws to receive them.
Its mouth is open wide to swallow
them up.
Their nobles and the rest of the people
will go down into it.
They will go there together with all
those who have wild parties.
15 So people will be brought low.
Everyone will be made humble.
Those who brag will be brought
down.
16 But the LORD who rules all will be
honored
because he judges fairly.
The holy God will prove that he is holy
by doing what is right.
17 Then sheep will graze as if they were in
their own grasslands.
Lambs will eat grass among the
destroyed buildings
where rich people used to live.

18 How terrible it will be for those who
continue to sin
and lie about it!
How terrible for those who keep on
doing what is evil
as if they were tied to it!
19 How terrible for those who say,
"Let God hurry up and do what he
says he will.
We want to see it happen.
Let us see the plan of the Holy One of
Israel.
We want to know what it is."

20 How terrible it will be for those who say
that what is evil is good!

How terrible for those who say
  that what is good is evil!
How terrible for those who say
  that darkness is light
  and light is darkness!
How terrible for those who say
  that what is bitter is sweet
  and what is sweet is bitter!

21 How terrible it will be for those who
  think they are wise!
How terrible for those who think
  they are really clever!

22 How terrible it will be for those
  who are heroes at drinking wine!
How terrible for those
  who are heroes at mixing drinks!
23 How terrible for those
  who take money to set guilty people
    free!
How terrible for those
  who don't treat good people fairly!
24 Flames of fire burn up straw.
  Dry grass sinks down into those
    flames.
Evil people will be like plants whose
    roots rot away.
  They will be like flowers that are
    blown away like dust.
That's because they have said no to the
    law of the LORD who rules
    over all.
  They have turned against the
    message of the Holy One of
    Israel.
25 So the LORD is angry with his people.
  He raises his hand against them and
    strikes them down.
The mountains shake.
  The bodies of dead people lie in the
    streets like trash.

Even then, the LORD is still angry.
  His hand is still raised against
    them.

26 He lifts up a banner to gather the
    nations that are far away.
  He whistles for them to come
    from the farthest places on earth.
Here they come.
  They are moving very quickly.
27 None of them grows tired.
  None of them falls down.
  None of them sleeps or even takes
    a nap.

All of them are ready for battle.
  Every belt is pulled tight.
  Not a single sandal strap is broken.
28 The enemies' arrows are sharp.
  All their bows are ready.
The hooves of their horses are as hard
    as rock.
  Their chariot wheels turn like a
    twister.
29 The sound of their army is like the roar
    of lions.
  It's like the roar of young lions.
They growl as they capture what they
    were chasing.
  They carry it off.
  No one can take it away from them.
30 At that time the enemy army will roar
    over Israel.
  It will sound like the roaring of the
    ocean.
If someone looks at the land of Israel,
  there is only darkness and trouble.
  The clouds will make even the sun
    become dark.

The Lord Appoints Isaiah to Speak for Him

6 In the year that King Uzziah died, I saw the Lord. He was seated on his throne. His long robe filled the temple. He was highly honored. 2 Above him were seraphs. Each of them had six wings. With two wings they covered their faces. With two wings they covered their feet. And with two wings they were flying. 3 They were calling out to one another. They were saying,

"Holy, holy, holy is the LORD who rules
    over all.
  The whole earth is full of his glory."

4 The sound of their voices caused the stone doorframe to shake. The temple was filled with smoke.

5 "How terrible it is for me!" I cried out. "I'm about to be destroyed! My mouth speaks sinful words. And I live among people who speak sinful words. Now I have seen the King with my own eyes. He is the LORD who rules over all."

BIBLE ADVENTURES

Connie had a dream about Isaiah's commission in "Here Am I" (A#TC).

Isa. 6:1–2 Seraphs have six wings and fly *above* God's throne. In Ezekiel, cherubim are described with four wings and four faces. They fly *around* God's throne. Can you picture it? Maybe it's time for me to do a painting.

⁶A seraph flew over to me. He was holding a hot coal. He had used tongs to take it from the altar. ⁷He touched my mouth with the coal. He said, "This has touched your lips. Your guilt has been taken away. Your sin has been paid for."

⁸Then I heard the voice of the Lord. He said, "Who will I send? Who will go for us?"

I said, "Here I am. Send me!"

⁹So he said, "Go and speak to these people. Tell them,

"'You will hear but never understand.
    You will see but never know what
        you are seeing.'
¹⁰ Make the hearts of these people
        stubborn.
    Plug up their ears.
    Close their eyes.
    Otherwise they might see with their
        eyes.
    They might hear with their ears.
    They might understand with their
        hearts.
    And they might turn to me and be
        healed."

¹¹Then I said, "Lord, how long will it be like that?"

He answered,

"It will last until the cities of Israel are
        destroyed.
    It will last until no one is living in
        them.
It will last until the houses are deserted.
    The fields will be completely
        destroyed.
¹² It will last until the LORD has sent
        everyone far away.
    The land will be totally deserted.
¹³ Suppose only a tenth of the people
        remain there.
    Even then the land will be
        completely destroyed again.
    But when oak trees and terebinth trees
        are cut down, stumps are left.
    And my holy people will be like stumps
        that begin to grow again."

The Sign of Immanuel

7 Ahaz was king of Judah. Rezin was king of Aram. And Pekah was king of Israel. Rezin and Pekah marched up to fight against Jerusalem. But they couldn't overpower it. Ahaz was the son of Jotham and the grandson of Uzziah. Pekah was the son of Remaliah.

²The royal family of Ahaz was told, "The army of Aram has joined forces with Ephraim's army." So the hearts of Ahaz and his people trembled with fear. They shook just as trees in the forest shake when the wind blows through them.

³The LORD said to Isaiah, "Go out and see Ahaz. Take your son Shear-Jashub with you. Meet Ahaz at the end of the channel that brings water from the Upper Pool. It is on the road to the Washerman's Field. ⁴Tell Ahaz, 'Be careful. Stay calm. Do not be afraid. Do not lose hope because of the great anger of Rezin, Aram and the son of Remaliah. After all, they are nothing but two pieces of smoking firewood. ⁵Aram, Ephraim and Remaliah's son have planned to destroy you. They said, ⁶"Let's march into Judah and attack it. Let's tear everything down. Then we can share the land among ourselves. And we can make Tabeel's son king over it." ⁷But I am the LORD and King. I say,

"'"That will not happen.
    It will not take place.
⁸ The capital of Aram is Damascus.
    And the ruler of Damascus is only
        Rezin.
Do not worry about the people of
        Ephraim.
    They will be too crushed to be
        considered a people.

That will happen before 65 years are over.
⁹ The capital of Ephraim is Samaria.
And the ruler of Samaria is only Remaliah's son.
If you do not stand firm in your faith, you will not stand at all.' ' "

¹⁰The Lord spoke to Ahaz through Isaiah again. He said, ¹¹"I am the Lord your God. Ask me to give you a sign. It can be anything in the deepest grave or in the highest heaven."

¹²But Ahaz said, "I won't ask. I won't test the Lord."

¹³Then Isaiah said, "Listen, you members of the royal family of David! Isn't it enough for you to test the patience of human beings? Are you also going to test the patience of my God? ¹⁴The Lord himself will give you a sign. The virgin is going to have a baby. She will give birth to a son. And he will be called Immanuel. ¹⁵He will still be very young when he can decide between right and wrong. ¹⁶Even before then, the lands of the two kings you fear will be ruined. ¹⁷The Lord will also bring the king of Assyria against you. And he will bring him against your people and the whole royal family. That will be a time of trouble. It will be unlike any since the people of Ephraim broke away from Judah."

The Lord Uses Assyria to Judge Judah

¹⁸At that time the Lord will whistle for the Egyptians. They will come like flies from the Nile River in Egypt. He will also whistle for the Assyrians. They will come from their country like bees. ¹⁹All of them will come and camp in the deep valleys. They will camp in caves in the rocks. And they'll camp near bushes and water holes. ²⁰At that time the Lord will use the Assyrians to punish you. Ahaz had hired them earlier from east of the Euphrates River. Now their king will be like a razor in the Lord's hand. He will shave the hair from your head and private parts. He will also shave off your beards. ²¹At that time a person may only be able to keep alive one young cow and two goats. ²²But they will give plenty of milk to live on. In fact, everyone left in the land will only have milk curds and honey to eat. ²³The land used to have vineyards with 1,000 vines worth 25 pounds of silver. But

soon the whole land will be covered with thorns and bushes. ²⁴Hunters will go there with bows and arrows. That's because it will be covered with bushes and thorns. ²⁵All the hills used to be plowed with hoes. But you won't go there anymore. That's because you will be afraid of the thorns and bushes. Cattle will be turned loose on those hills. Sheep will also run there.

Isaiah and His Children Are Signs

8 The Lord said to me, "Get a large sheet of paper. Write 'Maher-Shalal-Hash-Baz' on it with a pen." ²So I sent for Zechariah and Uriah the priest. Zechariah is the son of Jeberekiah. Zechariah and Uriah were witnesses for me whom I could trust. ³Then I went and slept with my wife, who was a prophet. She became pregnant and had a baby boy. The Lord said to me, "Name him Maher-Shalal-Hash-Baz. ⁴The king of Assyria will carry off the wealth of Damascus. He will also carry away the goods that were taken from Samaria. That will happen before the boy knows how to say 'My father' or 'My mother.' "

⁵The Lord continued,

⁶ "I am like the gently flowing stream of Siloam.
But the people of Judah have turned their backs on me.

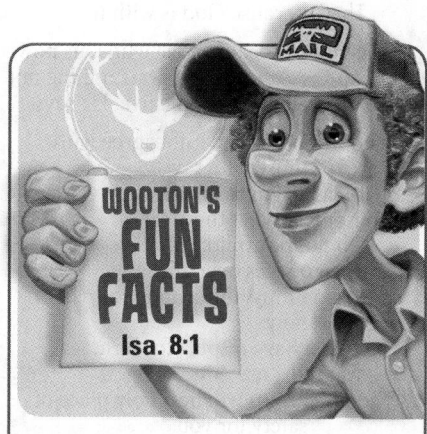

Maher-Shalal-Hash-Baz, with 18 letters, is the longest name in the Bible. In second place is Cushan-Rishathaim, with 17 (Judges 3:8). I'd say their names are supercali-fantastic! Maybe I'll change my middle name to one of those names.

They are filled with joy because of the
    fall of Rezin
    and the son of Remaliah.
⁷ So I am about to bring against these
    people
    the king of Assyria and his whole
      army.
The Assyrians will be like the mighty
    Euphrates River
    when it is flooding.
They will run over everything in
    their path.
⁸ They will sweep on into Judah like a
    flood.
They will pass through Judah
    and reach all the way to
    Jerusalem.
Immanuel, they will attack your land
    like an eagle.
Their wings will spread out and
    cover it."

⁹ Sound the battle cry, you nations!
    But you will be torn apart.
    Listen, all you lands far away!
Prepare for battle! But you will be torn
    apart.
    Prepare for battle! But you will be
      torn apart.
¹⁰ Make your battle plans! But you won't
    succeed.
    Give your orders! But they won't be
      carried out.
    That's because God is with us.

¹¹The LORD speaks to me while his powerful hand is on me. He is warning me not to live the way these people live. He says,

¹² "People of Judah, do not agree with
    those who say
    Isaiah is guilty of treason.
Do not fear what they fear.
    Do not be afraid.
¹³ The LORD rules over all.
    So you must think about him as
      holy.
You must have respect for him.
    You must fear him.
¹⁴ Then the LORD will be a holy place of
    safety for you.
But that's not true for many people
    in Israel and Judah.
He will be a stone that causes them
    to trip.
He will be a rock that makes them
    fall.

And for the people of Jerusalem
    he will be a trap and a snare.
¹⁵ Many of them will trip.
    They will fall and be broken.
    They will be trapped and captured."

¹⁶ Tie up and seal this warning that the
    LORD said to you through me.
Preserve among my followers what
    he taught you through me.
¹⁷ I will wait for the LORD.
    He is turning his face away from
      Jacob's people.
    I will put my trust in him.

¹⁸Here I am. Here are the children the LORD has given me. We are signs and reminders to Israel from the LORD who rules over all. He lives on Mount Zion.

The Darkness Turns to Light

¹⁹There are people who get messages from those who have died. But these people only whisper words that are barely heard. Suppose someone tells you to ask for advice from these people. Shouldn't you ask for advice from your God instead? Why should you get advice from dead people to help those who are alive? ²⁰Follow what the LORD taught you and said to you through me. People who don't speak in keeping with these words will have no hope in the morning. ²¹They will suffer and be hungry. They'll wander through the land. When they are very hungry, they will become angry. They'll look up toward heaven. They'll ask for bad things to happen to their king and their God. ²²Then they will look at the earth. They'll see nothing but suffering and darkness. They'll see terrible sadness. They'll be driven into total darkness.

9 But there won't be any more sadness for those who were suffering. In the past the LORD brought shame on the land of Zebulun. He also brought shame on the land of Naphtali. But in days to come he will honor Galilee, where people from other nations live. He will honor the land along the Mediterranean Sea. And he will honor the territory east of the Jordan River.

² The people who are now living in
    darkness
    will see a great light.
They are now living in a very dark land.
    But a light will shine on them.

³ Lord, you will make our nation larger.
   You will increase their joy.
They will show you how glad they are.
   They will be as glad as people are at
      harvest time.
They will be as glad as warriors are
   when they share the things they've
      taken after a battle.
⁴ You set Israel free from Midian long
   ago.
   In the same way, you will break
the heavy yoke that weighs Israel down.
   You will break the wooden beams
      that are on their shoulders.
   You will break the rods of those who
      strike them down.
⁵ Every fighting man's boot that he wore
      in battle will be burned up.
   So will every piece of clothing
      covered with blood.
   All of them will be thrown into the
      fire.
⁶ A child will be born to us.
   A son will be given to us.
   He will rule over us.

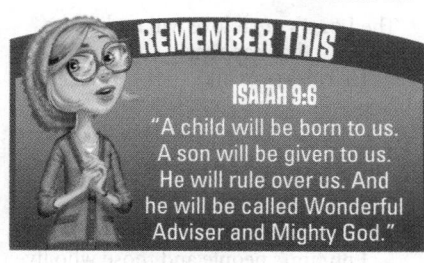

REMEMBER THIS

ISAIAH 9:6

"A child will be born to us. A son will be given to us. He will rule over us. And he will be called Wonderful Adviser and Mighty God."

And he will be called
   Wonderful Adviser and Mighty God.
He will also be called Father Who Lives
      Forever
   and Prince Who Brings Peace.
⁷ There will be no limit to how great his
      authority is.
   The peace he brings will never end.
He will rule on David's throne
   and over his kingdom.
   He will make the kingdom strong
      and secure.
His rule will be based on what is fair
      and right.
   It will last forever.

WHAT ABOUT YOU?

Have you ever done something just for the praise? We all have at some point.

For instance, in the Adventures in Odyssey episode "Fifteen Minutes," Alex and Greg had to deal with different aspects of praise and glory. When Alex scored an all-time best on the miniature golf course, he was very excited to get his name on the board. But soon after, Mandy beat his record. Alex was upset to see his name and score moved into the shadows.

Similarly, Connie's friend Greg had been a hotshot movie star. Before long, his career ended. When Greg came back to Odyssey, the kids still remembered him as an incredible hero, which Greg didn't hear too often anymore. Like Alex, Greg experienced the excitement of fame, as well as its fleeting glory. Both realized that fame doesn't last and isn't what a Christian should desire. If we're living for applause—in little successes or big ones—we have our sights set on the wrong target.

In Isaiah 9:8–10, we can see the example of Israel's pride. Instead of praise, they receive the promise of punishment for their pride and rebellion.

While we want to take pride in our good works, God discourages us from being noticed when giving to the needy (see Matthew 6:1–4). In such situations, He wants us to be secret agents of kindness. Practice today by doing three good deeds under cover. Quietly do someone else's chore. Stealthily help a neighbor. Whatever you come up with, try not to get caught.

The LORD's great love will make sure
that happens.
He rules over all.

The LORD Is Angry With Israel

⁸ The Lord has sent a message against
Jacob's people.
He will punish Israel.
⁹ All the people will know about it.
Ephraim's people and those who live
in Samaria will know about it.
Their hearts are very proud.
They say,
¹⁰ "The brick buildings have fallen down.
But we will rebuild them with blocks
of stone.
The fig trees have been chopped down.
But we'll plant cedar trees in place
of them."
¹¹ In spite of that, the LORD has made
Rezin's enemies stronger.
He has stirred up Assyria to fight
against Israel.
¹² Arameans from the east
have opened their mouths and
swallowed up Israel.
So have Philistines from the west.

Even then, the LORD is still angry.
His hand is still raised against them.

Jason's Jargon

ISAIAH 9

Ready? Seek out
the word *yoke* in
this chapter. A yoke
is a wooden and
metal device used to
fasten an animal to a
plow. A yoke is very
heavy. It's also a
metaphor for bonding
two things together.

¹³ But his people have not returned
to the God who struck them down.
They haven't turned for help
to the LORD who rules over all.
¹⁴ So he will cut off from Israel heads and
tails alike.
In a single day he will cut off palm
branches and tall grass alike.
The palm branches are the people who
rule over others.

The tall grass is the people who bow
down to them.
¹⁵ The elders and important leaders are
the heads.
The prophets who teach lies are the
tails.
¹⁶ Those who guide the people of Israel
are leading them down the
wrong path.
So those who follow them aren't on
the right road.
¹⁷ The Lord will not be pleased with the
young men.
He won't take pity on widows and on
children whose fathers have
died.
All of them are ungodly and evil.
They say foolish things with their
mouths.

Even then, the LORD is still angry.
His hand is still raised against them.

¹⁸ What is evil burns like a fire.
It burns up bushes and thorns.
It sets the forest on fire.
It sends up a huge column of smoke.
¹⁹ The LORD rules over all.
When he gets angry, he will burn up
the land.
The people will burn in the fire.
They will not spare one another.
²⁰ People will eat up everything they can
find on their right.
But they'll still be hungry.
They will eat everything they can find
on their left.
But they won't be satisfied.
So they will eat the dead bodies of their
children.
²¹ That's what Manasseh's people will
do to Ephraim.
And that's what Ephraim's people will
do to Manasseh.
Together they will turn against Judah.

Even then, the LORD is still angry.
His hand is still raised against them.

10 How terrible it will be for you
who make laws that aren't fair!
How terrible for you
who write laws that make life hard
for others!
² You take away the rights of poor people.
You hold back what is fair from my
people who are suffering.

You take for yourselves what belongs to
  widows.
  You rob children whose fathers have
    died.
³ What will you do on the day when the
    LORD punishes you?
  On that day trouble will come from
    far away.
Who will you run to for help?
  Who will you trust your riches with?
⁴ All you can do is bow down in fear
    among the prisoners.
  All you can do is fall among those
    who have died in battle.

Even then, the LORD is still angry.
  His hand is still raised against them.

The LORD Will Judge Assyria

⁵ The LORD says, "How terrible it will be
    for the people of Assyria!
  They are the war club that carries
    out my anger.
⁶ I will send them against the ungodly
    nation of Judah.
  I will order them to fight against my
    own people.
  My people make me angry.
  I will order Assyria to take their goods
    and carry them away.
  I will order Assyria to walk on my
    people
  as if they were walking on mud.
⁷ But that is not what the king of Assyria
    plans.
  It is not what he has in mind.
  His purpose is to destroy many nations.
  His purpose is to put an end to
    them.
⁸ 'Aren't all my commanders kings?' he
    says.
⁹   'I took over Kalno just as I took
    Carchemish.
  I took over Hamath just as I did Arpad.
  I took Samaria just as I did
    Damascus.
¹⁰ My powerful hand grabbed hold of
    kingdoms
  whose people worship statues of
    gods.
  They had more gods than Jerusalem
    and Samaria did.
¹¹ I took over Samaria and its statues of
    gods.
  In the same way, I will take
    Jerusalem and its gods.' "

¹²The Lord will finish everything he has
planned to do against Mount Zion and Jerusalem. Then he'll say, "Now I will punish
the king of Assyria. I will punish him because his heart and his eyes are so proud.
¹³The king of Assyria says,

  " 'By my power
    I have taken over all these nations.
  I am very wise.
    I have great understanding.
  I have wiped out the borders between
    nations.
  I've taken their treasures.
  Like a great hero I've brought their
    kings under my control.
¹⁴ I've taken the wealth of the nations.
  It was as easy as reaching into a
    bird's nest.
  I've gathered the riches of all these
    countries.
  It was as easy as gathering eggs
    that have been left in a nest.
  Not a single baby bird flapped its wings.
  Not one of them opened its mouth
    to chirp.' "

¹⁵ Does an ax claim to be more important
    than the person who swings it?
  Does a saw brag that it is better
    than the one who uses it?
  That would be like a stick
    swinging the person who picks it up!
  It would be like a war club
    waving the one who carries it!
¹⁶ So the LORD who rules over all will
    send a sickness.
  The Lord will send it on the king of
    Assyria's strong fighting men.
  It will make them weaker and weaker.
  The army he was so proud of will be
    completely destroyed.
  It will be as if it had been burned up
    in a fire.
¹⁷ The LORD is the Light of Israel.
  He will become a fire.
  Israel's Holy One will become a
    flame.
  In a single day he will burn up all
    Assyria's bushes.
  He will destroy all their thorns.
¹⁸ He will completely destroy the beauty
    of their forests and rich farm lands.
  The Assyrian army will be like a sick
    person
  who becomes weaker and weaker.

¹⁹ It will be like the trees of their forests.
So few of them will be left standing
that even a child could count them.

The Israelites Who Are Left Alive

²⁰ In days to come, some people will still
be left alive in Israel.
They will be from Jacob's family line.
But they won't depend any longer on
the nation that struck them down.
Instead, they will truly depend on the
LORD.
He is the Holy One of Israel.
²¹ The people of Jacob who are still alive
will return to the Mighty God.
²² Israel, your people might be as many as
the grains of sand by the sea.
But only a few of them will return.
The LORD has handed down a death
sentence.
He will destroy his people.
What he does is right.
²³ The LORD who rules over all will carry
out his sentence.
The Lord will destroy the whole land.

²⁴The LORD rules over all. The Lord says,

"My people who live in Zion,
do not be afraid of the Assyrian
army.
They beat you with rods.
They lift up war clubs against you,
just as the Egyptians did.
²⁵ Very soon I will not be angry with you
anymore.
I will turn my anger against the
Assyrians.
I will destroy them."

²⁶ The LORD who rules over all will beat
them with a whip.
He will strike them down as he
struck down Midian at the
rock of Oreb.
And he will stretch out his walking
stick over the waters.
That's what he did in Egypt.
²⁷ People of Zion, in days to come he will
help you.
He will lift the heavy load of
the Assyrians from your
shoulders.
He will remove their yokes from
your necks.
Their yokes will be broken
because you have become so strong.

²⁸ The Assyrian army has entered the
town of Aiath.
They have passed through Migron.
They have stored up supplies at
Mikmash.
²⁹ They have marched through the pass
there. They said,
"Let's camp for the night at Geba."
The people of Ramah tremble with fear.
Those who live in Gibeah of Saul
run away.
³⁰ Town of Gallim, cry out!
Laishah, listen!
Poor Anathoth!
³¹ The people of Madmenah are running
away.
Those who live in Gebim are hiding.
³² Today the Assyrians have stopped at
Nob.
They are shaking their fists
at Mount Zion in the city of
Jerusalem.

³³ The Assyrian soldiers are like trees in a
forest.
The LORD who rules over all
will chop them down.
The Lord will cut off their branches
with his great power.
He will chop the tall trees down.
He will cut down even the highest
ones.
³⁴ The Mighty One will chop down the
forest with his ax.
He will cut down the cedar trees in
Lebanon.

A Branch Will Come From Jesse's Family Line

11 Jesse's family is like a tree that has
been cut down.
A new little tree will grow from its
stump.
From its roots a Branch will grow
and produce fruit.
² The Spirit of the LORD will rest on that
Branch.
The Spirit will help him to be wise
and understanding.
The Spirit will help him make wise
plans and carry them out.
The Spirit will help him know the
LORD and have respect for
him.
³ The Branch will take delight
in respecting the LORD.

He will not judge things only by the
way they look.
He won't make decisions based
simply on what people say.
⁴ He will always do what is right
when he judges those who are in
need.
He'll be completely fair
when he makes decisions about poor
people.
When he commands that people be
punished,
it will happen.
When he orders that evil people be put
to death,
it will take place.
⁵ He will put on godliness as if it were his
belt.
He'll wear faithfulness around his
waist.

⁶ Wolves will live with lambs.
Leopards will lie down with goats.
Calves and lions will eat together.
And little children will lead them
around.
⁷ Cows will eat with bears.
Their little ones will lie down
together.
And lions will eat straw like oxen.
⁸ A baby will play near a hole where
cobras live.
A young child will put its hand into
a nest
where poisonous snakes live.
⁹ None of those animals will harm or
destroy anything or anyone
on my holy mountain of Zion.
The oceans are full of water.
In the same way, the earth will be
filled
with the knowledge of the LORD.

¹⁰At that time, here is what the man who
is called the Root of Jesse will do. He will
be like a banner that brings nations together. They will come to him. And the place
where he rules will be glorious. ¹¹At that
time the Lord will reach out his hand. He
will gather his people a second time. He
will bring back those who are left alive.
He'll bring them back from Assyria, Lower
Egypt, Upper Egypt and Cush. He'll bring
them from Elam, Babylon and Hamath. He
will also bring them from the islands of the
Mediterranean Sea.

¹² He will lift up a banner.
It will show the nations that he is
gathering the people of Israel.
He'll bring back those who had been
taken away as prisoners.
He'll gather together the scattered
people of Judah.
He'll bring them back from all four
directions.
¹³ Ephraim's people won't be jealous
anymore.
Judah's attackers will be destroyed.
Ephraim won't be jealous of Judah.
And Judah won't attack Ephraim.
¹⁴ Together they will rush down the slopes
of Philistia to the west.
They'll take what belongs to the
people of the east.
They'll take over Edom and Moab.
The people of Ammon will be under
their control.
¹⁵ The LORD will dry up
the Red Sea in Egypt.
By his power he'll send a burning
wind
to sweep over the Euphrates River.
He will break it up into many streams.
Then people will be able to go across
it wearing sandals.
¹⁶ There was a road the people of Israel
used
when they came up from Egypt.
In the same way, there will be a wide
road coming out of Assyria.
It will be used by the LORD's people
who are left alive there.

Two Songs of Praise

12 In days to come, the people of Israel
will sing,

"LORD, we will praise you.
You were angry with us.
But now your anger has turned away
from us.
And you have brought us comfort.
² God, you are the one who saves us.
We will trust in you.
Then we won't be afraid.
LORD, you are the one who gives us
strength.
You are the one who keeps us safe.
LORD, you have saved us."
³ People of Israel, he will save you.
That will bring you joy like water
brought up from wells.

[4]In days to come, the people of Israel will sing,

"Give praise to the LORD. Make his
 name known.
  Tell the nations what he has done.
  Announce how honored he is.
[5] Sing to the LORD. He has done glorious
 things.
  Let it be known all over the world.
[6] People of Zion, give a loud shout!
  Sing for joy!
  The Holy One of Israel is among you.
  And he is great."

A Prophecy Against Babylon

13 Here is the prophecy against Babylon
 that Isaiah, the son of Amoz, saw.

[2] Lift up a banner on the top of a bare
 hill.
  Shout to the enemy soldiers.
  Wave for them to enter the gates
  that are used by the nobles of
  Babylon.
[3] The LORD has commanded the soldiers
  he prepared for battle.
  He has sent for them to carry out his
  anger against Babylon.
  They will be happy when he wins the
  battle for them.
[4] Listen! I hear a noise in the mountains.
  It sounds like a huge crowd.
  Listen! I hear a loud noise among the
  kingdoms.
  It sounds like nations gathering
  together.
  The LORD who rules over all is bringing
  an army together for war.
[5] They come from lands far away.
  They come from the farthest places
  on earth.
  The LORD and those weapons of his
  anger
  are coming to destroy the whole
  country of Babylon.
[6] Cry out! The day of the LORD is near.
  The Mighty One is coming to
  destroy the Babylonians.
[7] Their hands won't be able to help them.
  Everyone's heart will melt away in
  fear.
[8] The people will be filled with terror.
  Pain and suffering will grab hold of
  them.

They will groan with pain like a
 woman having a baby.
  They'll look at one another in terror.
  Their faces will burn with shame.
[9] The day of the LORD is coming.
  It will be a terrible day.
  The LORD's burning anger will blaze
  out.
  He will make the land dry and empty.
  He'll destroy the sinners in it.
[10] All the stars in the sky
  will stop giving their light.
  The sun will be darkened as soon as it
  rises.
  The moon will not shine.
[11] The LORD will punish the world
  because it is so evil.
  He will punish evil people for their
  sins.
  He'll put an end to the bragging of
  those who are proud.
  He'll bring down the pride of those
  who don't show any pity.
[12] He'll make people harder to find than
  pure gold.
  They will be harder to find than gold
  from Ophir.
[13] He will make the heavens tremble.
  He'll shake the earth out of its place.
  The LORD who rules over all will show
  how angry he is.
  At that time his burning anger will
  blaze out.
[14] Outsiders who live in Babylon will scatter
  like antelope that are chased by a
  hunter.
  They are like sheep that don't have a
  shepherd.
  All of them will return to their own
  people.
  They will run back to their own
  countries.
[15] Those who are captured will have
  spears stuck through them.
  Those who are caught will be killed
  by swords.
[16] Their babies will be smashed to pieces
  right in front of their eyes.
  Their houses will be robbed.
  Their wives will be raped.
[17] The LORD will stir up the Medes to
  attack the Babylonians.
  They aren't interested in getting silver.
  They don't want gold.

¹⁸ Instead, they will use their bows and
     arrows
     to strike down the young men.
They won't even show any mercy to
     babies.
     They won't take pity on children.
¹⁹ The city of Babylon is the jewel of
     kingdoms.
     It is the pride and glory of the
     Babylonians.
But God will destroy it
     just as he did Sodom and Gomorrah.
²⁰ No one will ever live in Babylon again.
     No one will live there for all time to
     come.
Those who wander in the desert will
     never set up their tents there.
     Shepherds will never rest their flocks
     there.
²¹ But desert creatures will lie down there.
     Wild dogs will fill its houses.
Owls will live there.
     Wild goats will jump around in it.
²² Hyenas will live in its forts.
     Wild dogs will live in its beautiful
     palaces.
The time for Babylon to be punished
     is near.
     Its days are numbered.

14 The LORD will show tender love
     toward Jacob's people.
     Once again he will choose Israel.
He'll give them homes in their own
     land.
Outsiders will join them.
     They and the people of Jacob will
     become one people.
² Nations will help Israel
     return to their own land.
Israel will possess other nations.
     They will serve Israel as male and
     female servants in the LORD's
     land.
The Israelites will make prisoners of
     those who had held them as
     prisoners.
Israel will rule over those who had
     crushed them.

³ The LORD will put an end to Israel's suffering and trouble. They will no longer be
forced to do hard labor. At that time, ⁴they
will make fun of the king of Babylon. They
will say,

"See how the one who crushed others
     has fallen!
     See how his anger has come to an
     end!
⁵ The LORD has taken away the authority
     of evil people.
     He has broken the power of rulers.
⁶ When they became angry, they struck
     down nations.
     Their blows never stopped.
In their anger they brought nations
     under their control.
     They attacked them again and again.
⁷ All the lands now enjoy peace and rest.
     They break out into singing.
⁸ Even the juniper trees show how happy
     they are.
     The cedar trees of Lebanon celebrate
     too.
They say, 'Babylon, you have fallen.
     Now no one comes and cuts us down.'

⁹ "King of Babylon, many people in the
     place of the dead are really
     excited.
     They're excited about meeting you
     when you go down there.
The spirits of the dead get up to
     welcome you.
     At one time all of them were leaders
     in the world.
They were kings over the nations.
     They get up from their thrones.
¹⁰ All of them call out to you.
     They say,
'You have become weak, just as we are.
     You have become like us.'
¹¹ Your grand show of power has been
     brought down to the grave.
     The noise of your harps has come
     down here along with your
     power.
Maggots are spread out under you.
     Worms cover you.

¹² "King of Babylon, you thought you
     were the bright morning star.
     But now you have fallen from
     heaven!
You once brought down nations.
     But now you have been thrown
     down to the earth!
¹³ You said in your heart,
     'I will go up to the heavens.
I'll raise my throne
     above the stars of God.

I'll sit as king on the mountain where
the gods meet.
I'll set up my throne on the highest
slopes of Mount Zaphon.
[14] I will rise above the tops of the clouds.
I'll make myself like the Most High
God.'
[15] But now you have been brought down
to the place of the dead.
You have been thrown into the
deepest part of the pit.

[16] "Those who see you stare at you.
They think about what has happened
to you.
They say to themselves,
'Is this the man who shook the earth?
Is he the one who made kingdoms
tremble with fear?
[17] Did he turn the world into a desert?
Did he destroy its cities?
Did he refuse to let his prisoners go
home?'

[18] "All the kings of the nations are buried
with honor.
Each of them lies in his own tomb.
[19] But you have been thrown out of your
tomb.
You are like a branch that is cut off
and thrown away.
You are covered with the bodies
of those who have been killed by
swords.
You have been tossed into a stony pit
along with them.
You are like a dead body that people
have walked on.
[20]   You won't be buried like other
kings.
That's because you have destroyed your
land.
You have killed your people.

"Let the children of that evil man be
killed.
Let none of them be left to carry on
the family name.
[21] So prepare a place to kill his children.
Kill them because of the sins of the
rulers
who lived before them.
They must not rise to power.
They must not rule over the world.
They must not cover the earth with
their cities."

[22] "I will rise up against them,"
announces the LORD who rules over
all.
"I will destroy Babylon.
It will not be remembered anymore.
No one will be left alive there.
I will destroy its people and their
children after them,"
announces the LORD.
[23] "I will turn it into a place where
nothing but owls can live.
I will turn it into a swamp.
I will sweep through it like a broom and
destroy everything,"
announces the LORD who rules over
all.

[24]The LORD who rules over all has made
a promise. He has said,

"You can be sure that what I have
planned will happen.
What I have decided will take place.
[25] I will crush the Assyrians in my land.
On my mountains I will walk all
over them.
The yokes they put on my people will
be removed.
The heavy load they put on their
shoulders will be taken away."

[26] That's how the LORD carries out his
plan all over the world.
That's how he reaches out his
powerful hand to punish all
the nations.
[27] The LORD who rules over all has
planned it.
Who can stop him?
He has reached out his powerful hand.
Who can keep him from using it?

A Prophecy Against the Philistines

[28]This prophecy came to me from the
LORD in the year King Ahaz died. The
LORD said,

[29] "The rod of Assyria has struck all of
you Philistines.
But do not be glad that it is broken.
That rod is like a snake that will
produce an even more
poisonous snake.
It will produce a darting, poisonous
serpent.
[30] Even the poorest people in Israel will
have plenty to eat.

Those who are in need will lie down
in safety.
But I will destroy your families.
They will die of hunger.
I will kill any of them who are still
left alive.

31 "Cities of Philistia, cry out for help!
Scream in pain!
All you Philistines, melt away in fear!
An army is coming from the north in a
cloud of dust.
No one in its ranks is falling behind.
32 What answer should be given
to the messengers from that nation?
Tell them, 'The Lord has made Zion
secure.
His suffering people will find safety
there.'"

A Prophecy Against Moab

15 Here is a prophecy against Moab that
the Lord gave me.

The city of Ar in Moab is destroyed.
It happened in a single night.
Kir in Moab is also destroyed.
It happened in a single night.
2 The people of Dibon go up to their
temple to worship.
They go to their high places to weep.
The people of Moab cry over the
cities of Nebo and Medeba.
All their heads are shaved.
All their beards have been cut off.
3 In the streets they wear the rough
clothing people wear when
they're sad.
On their roofs and in the market
places
all of them are crying.
They fall down flat with their faces
toward the ground.
And they weep.
4 The people of Heshbon and Elealeh cry
out.
Their voices are heard all the way to
Jahaz.
So the fighting men of Moab cry out.
Their hearts are weak.

5 My heart cries out over Moab.
Some who run away get as far as Zoar.
Others run all the way to Eglath
Shelishiyah.
Others go up the hill to Luhith.
They are weeping as they go.

Still others travel the road to Horonaim.
They sing a song of sadness because
their town is being destroyed.
6 The waters at Nimrim are dried up.
And so is the grass.
The plants have died.
Nothing green is left.
7 The people are trying to escape
through the Valley of the Poplar
Trees.
They are carrying with them the wealth
they have collected and stored up.
8 Their loud cries echo along the border
of Moab.
They reach as far as Eglaim.
Their songs of sadness reach all the
way to Beer Elim.
9 The waters of the city of Dimon are full
of blood.
But the Lord will bring even more
trouble on Dimon.
He will bring lions against those who
run away from Moab.
They will also attack those who
remain in the land.

16 People of Moab, send lambs as a gift
to the ruler of Judah.
Send them from Sela.
Send them across the desert.
Send them to Mount Zion in the city
of Jerusalem.
2 The women of Moab are at the places
where people go across the Arnon
River.
They are like birds that flap their wings
when they are pushed from their nest.

3 The Moabites say to the rulers of Judah,
"Make up your mind. Make a
decision.
Cover us with your shadow.
Make it like night even at noon.
Hide those of us who are running away.
Don't turn them over to their
enemies.
4 Let those who have run away from
Moab stay with you.
Keep them safe from those who are
trying to destroy them."

Those who crush others will be
destroyed.
The killing will stop.
The attackers will disappear from
the earth.

⁵ A man from the royal house of David
     will sit on Judah's throne.
     He will rule with faithful love.
When he judges he will do what is fair.
     He will be quick to do what is right.

⁶ We have heard all about Moab's pride.
     We have heard how very proud they
     are.
They think they are so much better
     than others.
They brag about themselves.
     But all their bragging is nothing but
     empty words.

⁷ So the people of Moab cry out.
     All of them cry over their country.
Sing a song of sadness.
     Weep that you can no longer enjoy
     the raisin cakes of Kir Hareseth.

⁸ The fields of Heshbon dry up.
     So do the vines of Sibmah.
The rulers of the nations
     have walked all over its finest vines.
Those vines once reached as far as Jazer.
     They spread out toward the desert.
Their new growth went
     all the way to the Dead Sea.

⁹ Jazer weeps for the vines of Sibmah.
     And so do I.
Heshbon and Elealeh,
     I soak you with my tears!
There isn't any ripe fruit for people to
     shout about.
There isn't any harvest to make them
     happy.

¹⁰ Joy and gladness are taken away from
     the orchards.
     No one sings or shouts in the
     vineyards.
No one stomps on grapes at the
     winepresses.
     That's because the LORD has put an
     end to the shouting.

¹¹ My heart mourns over Moab like a song
     of sadness played on a harp.
     Deep down inside me I mourn over
     Kir Hareseth.

¹² Moab's people go to their high place to
     pray.
     But all they do is wear themselves out.
Their god Chemosh can't help them
     at all.

¹³That's the message the LORD has already
spoken against Moab. ¹⁴But now he says, "In
exactly three years, people will look down on

Moab's glory. Now Moab has many people.
But by that time only a few of them will be
left alive. And even they will be weak."

Prophecies Against Damascus and Israel

17 Here is a prophecy against Damascus
that the LORD gave me. He said,

"Damascus will not be a city anymore.
     Instead, all its buildings will be
     knocked down.

² The cities of Aroer will be deserted.
     They will be left to the flocks that lie
     down there.
     No one will make them afraid.

³ Ephraim's people will no longer have
     cities with high walls around
     them.
Royal power will disappear from
     Damascus.
Those who are left alive in Aram
     will be like the glory of the people of
     Israel,"
announces the LORD who rules over
     all.

⁴ "In days to come, the glory of Jacob's
     people will fade.
     Their strength will get weaker and
     weaker.

⁵ It will be as when workers cut and
     gather grain
     in the Valley of Rephaim.
They gather up stalks in their arms.
     Only a few heads of grain are left.

⁶ In the same way, only a few people will
     be left alive.
It will be as when workers knock
     olives off the trees.
Only two or three olives are left on the
     highest branches.
Four or five at most are left on the
     limbs that produce fruit,"
announces the LORD, the God of
     Israel.

⁷ In days to come, people will look to
     their Maker for help.
     They will turn their eyes to the Holy
     One of Israel.

⁸ They won't trust in the altars
     they made with their own hands.
They won't pay any attention to the
     poles they used
     to worship the female god named
     Asherah.

And they won't depend on the incense
altars
they made with their own fingers.

⁹At that time the strong cities in Israel
will be deserted. They will be as they were
when the Israelites drove the Canaanites
away. They will be like places that are taken
over by bushes and weeds. The whole land
will become dry and empty.

¹⁰ Israel, you have forgotten God, who
saves you.
You have not remembered the Rock,
who keeps you safe.
You might set out the finest plants.
You might plant vines from other
lands.
¹¹ The plants might start to grow on the
day you set them out.
The vines might begin to bud on the
morning you plant them.
But even if they do, there won't be any
harvest.
Instead, there will be sickness and
pain that won't go away.

¹² How terrible it will be for the nations
that attack us!
The noise of their armies is like the
sound of the ocean.
How terrible it will be for the nations
who fight against us!
They are as loud as huge waves
crashing on the shore.
¹³ They sound like the roar of rushing
waters.
But when the LORD speaks out
against them, they run far
away.
The wind blows them away like straw
on the hills.
A strong wind drives them along
like tumbleweeds.
¹⁴ In the evening, the nations terrify us.
But before morning comes, they are
gone.
That's what happens to those who steal
our goods.
That's what happens to those who
take what belongs to us.

A Prophecy Against Cush

18 How terrible it will be for the land
whose armies are like large numbers
of flying insects!
That land is along the rivers of Cush.

² Its people send messengers on the Nile
River.
They travel over the water in
papyrus boats.

Messengers, hurry back home!
Go back to your people,
who are tall and have smooth skin.
Everyone is afraid of them.
They are warriors whose language is
different from ours.
Their land is divided up by rivers.

³ Pay attention, all you people of the
world!
Listen, all you who live on earth!
Banners will be lifted up on the
mountains.
And you will see them.
Trumpets will be blown.
And you will hear them.
⁴ The LORD says to me,
"I will look down from heaven,
where I live.
I will be as quiet as summer heat in the
sunshine.
I will be as quiet as a cloud of dew in
the heat of harvest."
⁵ A farmer cuts off new growth with
pruning knives.
He cuts down spreading branches
and takes them away.
He does it before the grapes are
harvested.
That's when the blooms are gone and
the grapes are ripe.
In the same way, the LORD will cut off
the nations
that are gathered against his people.
⁶ Their dead bodies will be left for the
birds of the mountains to eat.
They will be left for the wild
animals.
The birds will eat the dead bodies all
summer long.
The wild animals will eat them all
through the winter.

⁷At that time gifts will be brought to the
LORD who rules over all.

The people who are tall and have
smooth skin will bring them.
Everyone is afraid of those people.
They are warriors whose language is
different from ours.
Their land is divided up by rivers.

They will bring their gifts to Mount Zion. That's where the LORD who rules over all has put his Name.

A Prophecy Against Egypt

19 Here is a prophecy against Egypt that the LORD gave me.

The LORD is coming to Egypt.
   He's riding on a cloud that moves
      very fast.
The statues of the gods in Egypt tremble
   with fear because of him.
   The hearts of the people there melt
      with fear.

2 The LORD says, "I will stir up one
   Egyptian against another.
Relatives will fight against relatives.
   Neighbors will fight against one
      another.
Cities will fight against cities.
   Kingdoms will fight against one
      another.
3 The people of Egypt will lose hope.
   I will keep them from doing what
      they plan to do.
They will ask their gods for advice.
   They will turn to the spirits of dead
      people for help.
They will go to people who get
      messages from those who have
      died.
   They will ask for advice from people
      who talk to the spirits of the
      dead.
4 I will hand the Egyptians over
   to a mean and unkind master.
A powerful king will rule over them,"
      announces the LORD.
   He is the LORD who rules over all.

5 The waters of the Nile River will dry up.
   The bottom of it will be cracked and
      dry.
6 Its canals will stink.
   And the streams of Egypt will get
      smaller and smaller
until they dry up.
The tall grass that grows along the river
   will dry up.
7   So will the plants along the banks of
      the Nile.
Even the planted fields along the Nile
   will dry up.
   Everything that grows there will
      blow away and disappear.

8 The fishermen will moan.
   All those who drop hooks into the
      Nile will weep.
Those who throw their nets on the water
   will become very sad.
9 Those who make clothes out of flax will
      lose hope.
   So will those who weave fine linen.
10 Those who work with cloth will be
      unhappy.
   And all those who work for money
      will be sick at heart.

11 The officials of the city of Zoan are very
      foolish.
   Pharaoh's wise men give advice that
      doesn't make any sense.
How can they dare to say to Pharaoh,
   "We're among the wise men"?
How can they say to him,
   "We're like the advisers to the kings
      of long ago"?

12 Pharaoh, where are your wise men now?
   Let them tell you
what the LORD who rules over all
   has planned against Egypt.
13 The officials of Zoan have become
      foolish.
   The leaders of Memphis have been
      lied to.
The most important leaders in Egypt
   have led its people astray.
14 The LORD has given them
   a spirit that makes them feel dizzy.
They make Egypt unsteady in
      everything it does.
   Egypt is like a person who drinks
      too much.
   He throws up and then walks
      around in the mess he's made.
15 No one in Egypt can do anything to
      help them.
   Its elders and important leaders can't
      help them.
Its prophets and priests can't do
      anything.
   Those who rule over others can't
      help.
   And those who bow down to them
      can't help either.

16 In days to come, the people of Egypt will become weak. The LORD who rules over all will raise his hand against them. Then they will tremble with fear. 17 The people of Judah will bring terror to the

Egyptians. Everyone in Egypt who hears the name of Judah will be terrified. That's because of what the LORD who rules over all is planning to do to them.

¹⁸At that time the people of five cities in Egypt will worship the LORD. He is the LORD who rules over all. They will use the Hebrew language when they worship him. They will promise to be faithful to him. One of those cities will be called the City of the Sun.

¹⁹At that time there will be an altar to the LORD in the middle of Egypt. There will be a monument to him at its border. ²⁰They will remind people that the LORD who rules over all is worshiped in Egypt. The people there will cry out to the LORD. They will cry out because of those who treat them badly. He will send someone to stand up for them and save them. And he will set them free. ²¹So the LORD will make himself known to the people of Egypt. At that time they will recognize that he is the LORD. They will worship him by bringing sacrifices and grain offerings to him. They will make promises to the LORD. And they will keep them. ²²The LORD will strike Egypt with a plague. But then he will heal them. They will turn to the LORD. And he will answer their prayers and heal them.

²³At that time there will be a wide road from Egypt to Assyria. The people of Assyria will go to Egypt. And the people of Egypt will go to Assyria. The people of Egypt and Assyria will worship the LORD together. ²⁴At that time Egypt, Assyria and Israel will be a blessing to the whole earth. ²⁵The LORD who rules over all will bless those three nations. He will say, "Let the Egyptians be blessed. They are my people. Let the Assyrians be blessed. My hands created them. And let the Israelites be blessed. They are my very own people."

A Prophecy Against Egypt and Cush

20 Sargon, the king of Assyria, sent his highest commander to the city of Ashdod. He attacked it and captured it. ²Three years earlier the LORD had spoken to Isaiah, the son of Amoz. The LORD had said, "Take off the rough clothing you are wearing. And take off your sandals." So Isaiah did. He went around barefoot and naked.

³After Ashdod was captured, the LORD said, "My servant Isaiah has gone around barefoot and naked for three years. He is a sign and reminder to Egypt and Cush about what will happen to them. ⁴The king of Assyria will lead prisoners away from Egypt and Cush. Young people and old people alike will be taken away. Like Isaiah, they will be barefoot and naked. Their backsides will be bare. So the Egyptians will be put to shame. ⁵People trusted in Cush to help them. They bragged about what Egypt could do for them. But they will lose heart and be put to shame. ⁶At that time the people who live on the coast of Philistia will speak up. They will say, 'See what has happened to those we depended on! We ran to them for help. We wanted them to save us from the king of Assyria. Now how can we escape?'"

A Prophecy Against Babylon

21 Here is a prophecy against Babylon that the LORD gave me. Babylon is known as the Desert by the Sea.

An attack is coming through the desert.
    It is coming from a land of terror.
    It's sweeping along like a windstorm
        blowing across the Negev
        Desert.

² I have seen a vision about something
        terrible that will happen.
    People are turning against Babylon.
    Robbers are taking its goods.
Elamites, attack the city! Medes,
        surround it!
    The LORD will put an end to all the
        suffering Babylon has caused.

³ The vision fills my body with pain.
    Pains take hold of me.
    They are like the pains of a woman
        having a baby.
I am shaken by what I hear.
    I'm terrified by what I see.
⁴ My heart grows weak.
    Fear makes me tremble.
I longed for evening to come.
    But it brought me horror instead of
        rest.

⁵ In my vision the Babylonians set the
        tables.
    They spread out the rugs.
    They eat and drink.
Get up, you officers!
    Rub your shields with oil!

⁶The Lord said to me,

"Go. Put a guard on duty on Jerusalem's
    walls.
Have him report what he sees.
⁷ Tell him to watch for chariots
    that are pulled by teams of horses.
Tell him to watch for men riding on
    donkeys or camels.
Make sure he stays awake.
Make sure he stays wide awake."

⁸"My master!" the guard shouts back.

"Day after day I stand here on the
    lookout tower.
Every night I stay here on duty.
⁹ Look! Here comes a man in a chariot!
    It's being pulled by a team of horses.
He's calling out the news,
    'Babylon has fallen! It has fallen!
All the statues of its gods
    lie broken in pieces on the ground!' "

¹⁰ My people, you have been crushed
    like grain on a threshing floor.
But now I'm telling you the good news
    I've heard.
It comes from the LORD who rules
    over all.
He is the God of Israel.

A Prophecy Against Edom

¹¹Here is a prophecy against Edom that
the LORD gave me.

Someone is calling out to me from the
    land of Seir. He says,
"Guard, when will the night be over?
Guard, how soon will it end?"
¹² The guard answers,
    "Morning is coming, but the night
    will return.
If you want to ask again,
    come back and ask."

A Prophecy Against Arabia

¹³Here is a prophecy against Arabia that
the LORD gave me.

He told me to give orders to traders
    from Dedan.
    They were camping in the bushes of
    Arabia.
¹⁴   I told them to bring water for those
    who are thirsty.
I also gave orders to those who live in
    Tema.

I told them to bring food for those
    who are running away.
¹⁵ They are running away from where the
    fighting is heaviest.
That's where the swords are ready to
    strike.
That's where the bows are ready to
    shoot.

¹⁶The Lord spoke to me. He said, "In exactly one year, Kedar's splendor will come to an end. ¹⁷Only a few of Kedar's soldiers who shoot arrows will be left alive." The LORD has spoken. He is the God of Israel.

A Prophecy Against Jerusalem

22 Here is a prophecy against Jerusalem that the LORD gave me. Jerusalem is also known as the Valley of Vision.

People of Jerusalem, what's the matter
    with you?
Why have all of you gone up on the
    roofs of your houses?
² Why is your town so full of noise?
Why is your city so full of the sound
    of wild parties?
Those among you who died weren't
    killed by swords.
They didn't die in battle.
³ All your leaders have run away.
    They've been captured without a
    single arrow being shot.
All you who were caught were taken
    away as prisoners.
You ran off while your enemies were
    still far away.
⁴ So I said, "Leave me alone.
Let me weep bitter tears.
Don't try to comfort me.
My people have been destroyed."

⁵ The LORD who rules over all sent the
    noise of battle against you.
The Lord brought disorder and
    terror
to the Valley of Vision.
The walls of the city were knocked
    down.
Cries for help were heard in the
    mountains.
⁶ Soldiers from Elam came armed with
    bows and arrows.
They came with their chariots and
    horses.
Soldiers from Kir got their shields
    ready.

7 Your rich valleys filled up with chariots.
  Horsemen took up their battle
    positions at your city gates.
8   The Lord made Judah a place where
    it wasn't safe to live anymore.

At that time, you depended
  on the weapons in the Palace of the
    Forest of Lebanon.
9 You saw that the walls of the City of
    David
  were broken through in many
    places.
You stored up water
  in the Lower Pool.
10 You picked out the weaker buildings in
    Jerusalem.
  You tore them down and used their
    stones
  to strengthen the city walls against
    attack.
11 You built a pool between the two walls.
  You used it to save the water
    that was running down from the Old
      Pool.
But you didn't look to the God who
    made it all possible.
  You didn't pay any attention to the
    God
  who planned everything long ago.

12 The Lord who rules over all
    called out to you at that time.
  The Lord told you to weep and cry.
    He told you to tear your hair out.
    And he told you to put on the rough
      clothing people wear when
      they're sad.
13 Instead, you are enjoying yourselves at
    wild parties!
  You are killing cattle and sheep.
  You are eating their meat and
    drinking wine.
You are saying, "Let's eat and drink,
    because tomorrow we'll die."

14 I heard the Lord who rules over all
speaking. "Your sin can never be paid for as
long as you live," says the Lord.

15 The Lord who rules over all speaks.
The Lord says,

"Go and speak to Shebna, the head
    servant.
  He is in charge of the palace. Tell him,
16 'What are you doing here outside the
    city?

Isa. 22:13 This phrase, when you add the "glad" from Ecclesiastes 8:15, makes the popular saying, "Eat, drink, and be glad, for tomorrow we die!" Have you ever heard anyone say that?

Who allowed you to cut out a tomb
    for yourself here?
Who said you could carve out your
    grave on the hillside?
Who allowed you to cut out your
    resting place in the rock?

17 " 'Watch out, you mighty man!
  The Lord is about to grab you.
  He is about to throw you away.
18 He will roll you up tightly like a ball.
  He will throw you into a very large
    country.
There you will die.
  And that's where the chariots you
    were so proud of will be.
  Those chariots will then bring
    nothing but shame on your
    master's family!
19 The Lord will remove you from your
    job.
  You will be brought down from your
    high position.

20 " 'At that time he will send for his
servant Eliakim. He is the son of Hilkiah.
21 The Lord will put your robe on Eliakim.
He will tie your belt around him. He will
hand your authority over to him. Eliakim
will be like a father to the people of Jerusalem and Judah. 22 The Lord will give
Eliakim the key of authority in David's royal house. No one can shut what he opens.
And no one can open what he shuts. 23 The
Lord will set him firmly in place like a peg

driven into a wall. He will hold a position of honor in his family. ²⁴The good name of his whole family will depend on him. They will be like bowls and jars hanging on a peg.

²⁵ "But a new day is coming,'" announces the LORD who rules over all. "'At that time the peg that was driven into the wall will give way. It will break off and fall down. And the heavy load hanging on it will also fall.'" The LORD has spoken.

A Prophecy Against Tyre

23 Here is a prophecy against Tyre that the LORD gave me.

Men in the ships of Tarshish, cry out!
    The city of Tyre is destroyed.
Its houses and harbor are gone.
That's the message you have received
    from the island of Cyprus.

² People on the island of Tyre, be silent.
    Traders from the city of Sidon, be
      quiet.
Those who sail on the Mediterranean
    Sea have made you rich.
³ Grain from Egypt
    came across the mighty waters.
The harvest of the Nile River brought
    wealth to Tyre.

WOOTON'S FUN FACTS
Isa. 23:1

Scholars don't agree on where Tarshish is located. Some say Spain. Some say Sardinia, an Italian island. And others say it was on the coast of Africa. Wherever it was, it was mentioned in Genesis, 1 Kings, Psalms, Jeremiah, Ezekiel, and Jonah. It must have been a busy place!

It became the market place of the
    nations.

⁴ Sidon, be ashamed. Mighty Tyre out in
    the sea, be ashamed.
The sea has spoken. It has said,
"It's as if I had never felt labor pains or
    had children.
    It's as if I had never brought up sons
      or daughters.
    It's as if the city of Tyre had never
      existed."
⁵ The Egyptians will hear about what has
    happened to Tyre.
    They'll be very sad and troubled.

⁶ People of the island of Tyre, cry out!
    Go across the sea to Tarshish.
⁷ Just look at Tyre.
    It's no longer the old, old city that
      was known for its wild parties.
It no longer sends its people out
    to make their homes in lands far
      away.
⁸ Tyre was a city that produced kings.
    Its traders were princes.
They were honored all over the earth.
    So who planned to destroy such a
      city?
⁹ The LORD who rules over all planned to
    do it.
    He wanted to bring down all its
      pride and glory.
    He wanted to shame those who were
      honored all over the earth.

¹⁰ People of Tarshish, farm your land
    as they do along the Nile River.
    That's because you don't have a
      harbor anymore.
¹¹ The LORD has reached his powerful
    hand out over the sea.
    He has made its kingdoms tremble
      with fear.
He has given a command concerning
    Phoenicia.
    He has ordered that its forts be
      destroyed.
¹² He said, "No more wild parties for you!
    People of Sidon, you are now
      destroyed!

"Leave your city. Go across the sea to
    Cyprus.
    Even there you will not find any rest."
¹³ Look at the land of the Babylonians.
    No one lives there anymore.

The Assyrians have turned it
into a place for desert creatures.
They built their towers in order to
attack it.
They took everything out of its forts.
They knocked down all its buildings.

[14] Men in the ships of Tarshish, cry out!
Mighty Tyre is destroyed!

[15] A time is coming when people will forget about Tyre for 70 years. That's the length of a king's life. But at the end of those 70 years, Tyre will be like the prostitute that people sing about. They say,

[16] "Forgotten prostitute, pick up a harp.
Walk through the city.
Play the harp well. Sing many songs.
Then you will be remembered."

[17] At the end of the 70 years, the LORD will punish Tyre. He will let it return to its way of life as a prostitute. It will earn its living with all the kingdoms on the face of the earth. [18] But the money it earns will be set apart for the LORD. The money won't be stored up or kept for Tyre. Instead, it will go to those who live the way the LORD wants them to. It will pay for plenty of food and fine clothes for them.

The LORD Will Destroy the Earth

24 The LORD is going to completely
destroy everything on earth.
He will twist its surface.
He'll scatter those who live on it.
[2] Priests and people alike will suffer.
So will masters and their servants.
And so will women and their female
servants.
Sellers and buyers alike will suffer.
So will those who borrow and those
who lend.
And so will those who owe money
and those who lend it.
[3] The earth will be completely destroyed.
Everything of value will be taken
out of it.
That's what the LORD has said.

[4] The earth will dry up completely.
The world will dry up and waste away.
The heavens will fade away along
with the earth.
[5] The earth is polluted by its people.
They haven't obeyed the laws of the
LORD.

They haven't done what he told them
to do.
They've broken the covenant that
will last forever.
[6] So the LORD will send a curse on the
earth.
Its people will pay for what they've
done.
They will be burned up.
Very few of them will be left.
[7] The vines and fresh wine will dry up
completely.
Those who used to have a good time
will groan.
[8] The happy sounds of tambourines will
be gone.
The noise of those who enjoy wild
parties will stop.
The joyful music of harps will
become silent.
[9] People will no longer sing as they drink
wine.
Beer will taste bitter to those who
drink it.
[10] Destroyed cities will lie empty.
People will lock themselves inside
their houses.
[11] In the streets people will cry out for
wine.
All joy will turn into sadness.
All joyful sounds will be driven out
of the earth.
[12] All the buildings will be knocked down.
Every city gate will be smashed to
pieces.
[13] That's how it will be on the earth.
And that's how it will be among the
nations.
It will be as when workers knock all but
a few olives off the trees.
It will be like a vine that has only a
few grapes left after the harvest.

[14] Those who are left alive will shout for
joy.
People from the west will praise the
LORD because he is the King.
[15] So give glory to him, you who live in
the east.
Honor the name of the LORD, you
who are in the islands of the
sea.
He is the God of Israel.
[16] From one end of the earth to the other
we hear singing.
People are saying,

"Give glory to the God who always
    does what is right."

But I said, "I feel very bad.
    I'm getting weaker and weaker.
    How terrible it is for me!
People turn against one another.
    They can't be trusted.
    So they turn against one another."
17 Listen, you people of the earth.
    Terror, a pit and a trap are waiting
        for you.
18 Anyone who runs away from the terror
    will fall into the pit.
Anyone who climbs out of the pit
    will be caught in the trap.

The LORD will open the windows of the
    skies.
    He will flood the land.
The foundations of the earth will
    shake.
19 The earth will be broken up.
    It will split open.
    It will be shaken to pieces.
20 The earth will be unsteady like someone
    who is drunk.
It will sway like a tent in the wind.
Its sin will weigh so heavily on it that it
    will fall.
It will never get up again.

21 At that time the LORD will punish
    the spiritual forces of evil in the
        heavens above.
He will also punish the kings on the
    earth below.
22 They will be brought together
    like prisoners in chains.
They'll be locked up in prison.
After many days the LORD will
    punish them.
23 The LORD who rules over all will rule
    on Mount Zion in Jerusalem.
The elders of the city will be there.
    They will see his great glory.
His rule will be so glorious that the sun
    and moon
    will be too ashamed to shine.

A Song of Praise to the LORD

25 LORD, you are my God.
    I will honor you.
    I will praise your name.
You have been perfectly faithful.
    You have done wonderful things.
    You had planned them long ago.

2 You have turned cities into piles of
    trash.
You have pulled down the high walls
    that were around them.
You have destroyed our enemies' forts.
    They will never be rebuilt.
3 Powerful nations will honor you.
    Even sinful people from their cities
        will have respect for you.
4 Poor people have come to you for
    safety.
You have kept needy people safe
    when they were in trouble.
You have been a place to hide when
    storms came.
You have been a shade from the heat
    of the sun.
Evil people attack us.
    They are like a storm beating against
    a wall.
5   They are like the heat of the desert.
You stopped the noisy shouts of our
    enemies.
You kept them from winning the
    battle over us and singing
    about it.
You are like the shadow of a cloud
    that cools the earth.

6 On Mount Zion the LORD who rules
    over all will prepare
    a feast for all the nations.
The best and richest foods
    and the finest aged wines will be
    served.
7 On that mountain the LORD will
    destroy
    the veil of sadness that covers all the
    nations.
He will destroy the gloom that is spread
    over everyone.
8   He will swallow up death forever.
The LORD and King will wipe away the
    tears
    from everyone's face.
He will remove the shame of his
    people
    from the whole earth.
The LORD has spoken.

9 At that time they will say,

"He is our God.
    We trusted in him, and he saved us.
He is the LORD. We trusted in him.
    Let us be filled with joy because he
    saved us."

¹⁰ The Lᴏʀᴅ's power will keep Mount
        Zion safe.
But the people of Moab will be
        crushed in their land.
They will be crushed just as straw is
        crushed in animal waste.
¹¹ They will try to swim their way out of it.
    They will spread out their hands
        in it,
    just as swimmers spread out their
        hands to swim.
But God will bring down Moab's pride.
None of their skill will help them.
¹² He will pull down their high, strong
        walls.
    He will bring them down to the
        ground.
    He'll bring them right down to the
        dust.

Another Song of Praise

26 At that time a song will be sung in the
    land of Judah. It will say,

"We have a strong city.
    God's saving power surrounds it
        like walls and towers.
² Open its gates
    so that those who do what is right
        can enter.
    They are the people who remain
        faithful to God.
³ Lᴏʀᴅ, you will give perfect peace
    to those who commit themselves to
        be faithful to you.
    That's because they trust in you.

⁴ "Trust in the Lᴏʀᴅ forever.
    The Lᴏʀᴅ himself is the Rock.
    The Lᴏʀᴅ will keep us safe forever.
⁵ He brings down those who are proud.
    He pulls down cities that have high
        walls.
They fall down flat on the ground.
    He throws them down to the dust.
⁶ The feet of those who were treated
        badly stomp on them.
    Those who were poor walk all over
        them."

⁷ The path of godly people is level.
    You are the God who does what is
        right.
    You make their way smooth.
⁸ Lᴏʀᴅ, we are living the way your laws
        command us to live.
    We are waiting for you to act.

We want your honor and fame to be
        known.
⁹ My heart longs for you at night.
    My spirit longs for you in the
        morning.
You will come and judge the earth.
    Then the people of the world will
        learn to do what is right.
¹⁰ Sometimes grace is shown to sinful
        people.
    But they still don't learn to do what
        is right.
They keep on doing evil even in a land
        where others are honest and
        fair.
    They don't have any respect for the
        majesty of the Lᴏʀᴅ.
¹¹ Lᴏʀᴅ, you have raised your hand high
        to punish them.
    But they don't even see it.
Let them see how much you love your
        people.
    Then they will be put to shame.
    Let the fire you are saving for your
        enemies burn them up.

¹² Lᴏʀᴅ, you give us peace.
    You are the one who has done
        everything we've accomplished.
¹³ Lᴏʀᴅ, you are our God.
    Other masters besides you have
        ruled over us.
    But your name is the only one we
        honor.
¹⁴ Those other masters are now dead.
    They will never live again.
    Their spirits won't rise from the
        dead.
You punished them and destroyed them.
    You wiped out all memory of them.
¹⁵ Lᴏʀᴅ, you have made our nation grow.
    You have made it larger.
You have gained glory for yourself.
    You have increased the size of our
        land.

¹⁶ Lᴏʀᴅ, when your people were suffering,
        they came to you.
    When you punished them,
        they could barely whisper a prayer.
¹⁷ Lᴏʀᴅ, you made us like a woman who
        is about to have a baby.
    She groans and cries out in pain.
¹⁸ We were pregnant and groaned with
        pain.
    But nothing was born.

We didn't bring your saving power to
     the earth.
    And the people of the world have
       not come to life.

¹⁹ LORD, your people who have died will
     live again.
    Their bodies will rise from the dead.
Let those who lie in the grave
    wake up and shout for joy.
You give life, LORD, like the dew of the
     morning.
    So the earth will give up its dead
     people.

²⁰ My people, go into your houses.
    Shut the doors behind you.
Hide yourselves for a little while.
    Do it until the LORD's anger is over.
²¹ He is coming from the place where he
     lives.
    He will punish the people of the
      earth for their sins.
The blood spilled on the earth will be
     brought out into the open.
The ground will no longer hide
     those who have been killed.

Israel Will Be Saved

27 At that time

the LORD will punish Leviathan with
    his sword.
    His great, powerful and deadly
     sword will punish
the serpent that glides through the sea.
    He will kill that twisting sea monster.

²At that time the LORD will sing about
his fruitful vineyard. He will say,

³ "I am the LORD. I watch over my
     vineyard.
    I water it all the time.
I guard it day and night.
    I do it so no one can harm it.
⁴ I am not angry with my vineyard.
    I wish thorns and bushes would
     come up in it.
Then I would march out against them
     in battle.
    I would set all of them on fire.
⁵ So the enemies of my people should
     come to me for safety.
    They should make peace with me.
I will say it again.
    They should make peace with me."

⁶ In days to come, Jacob's people will put
     down roots like a vine.
    Israel will bud and bloom.
    They will fill the whole world with
     fruit.

⁷ The LORD struck down those who
     struck down Israel.
    But he hasn't punished Israel as
     much.
The LORD killed those who killed many
     of his people.
    But he hasn't punished his people as
     much.
⁸ The LORD will use war to punish Israel.
    He will make them leave their land.
With a strong blast of his anger he will
     drive them out.
    It will be as if the east wind were
     blowing.
⁹ The people of Jacob will have to pay for
     their sin.
    Here is how they will show that their
     sin has been removed.
They will make all the altar stones like
     limestone.
    They will crush them to pieces.
No poles used to worship the female
     god named Asherah will be
     left standing.
    No incense altars will be left either.
¹⁰ Cities that have high walls around them
     will become empty.
    They will be settlements with no one
     in them.
    They will be like a desert.
Calves will eat and lie down in them.
    They will strip bare the branches of
     their trees.
¹¹ When their twigs are dry, they will be
     broken off.
    Then women will come and make
     fires with them.
The people of Jacob don't understand
     the LORD.
    So the God who made them won't be
     concerned about them.
    Their Creator won't be kind to them.

¹²At that time the LORD will separate
Israel from other people. He will gather
the Israelites together one by one. He will
gather them from the Euphrates River to
the Wadi of Egypt. ¹³At that time a loud
trumpet will be blown. Those who were dying in Assyria will come and worship the

LORD. So will those who were taken away to Egypt. All of them will worship the LORD on his holy mountain in Jerusalem.

The LORD Will Judge the Leaders of Ephraim and Judah

28 How terrible it will be for the city of Samaria!
It sits on a hill like a wreath of flowers.
The leaders of Ephraim are drunk.
They take pride in their city.
It sits above a valley that has rich soil.
How terrible it will be for the glorious beauty of that fading flower!

[2] The Lord will bring the strong and powerful king of Assyria against Samaria.
The Lord will throw that city down to the ground with great force.
It will be like a hailstorm.
It will be like a wind that destroys everything.
It will be like a driving rain and a flooding storm.

[3] That city is like a wreath.
The leaders of Ephraim are drunk.
They take pride in their city.
But its enemies will walk all over it.

[4] It sits on a hill above a rich valley.
The city is like a wreath of flowers whose glorious beauty is fading away.
But it will become like figs that are ripe before harvest.
As soon as people see them, they pick them and swallow them.

[5] At that time the LORD who rules over all will be like a glorious crown.
He will be like a beautiful wreath for those of his people who will be left alive.

[6] He will help those who are fair when they judge.
He will give strength to those who turn back their enemies at the city gate.

[7] Israel's leaders are drunk from wine.
They can't walk straight.
They are drunk from beer.
They are unsteady on their feet.
Priests and prophets drink beer.
They can't walk straight.
They are mixed up from drinking too much wine.

They drink too much beer.
They are unsteady on their feet.
The prophets see visions but don't really understand them.
The priests aren't able to make good decisions.

[8] They throw up. All the tables are covered with the mess they've made.
There isn't one spot on the tables that isn't smelly and dirty.

[9] The LORD's people are making fun of him. They say,
"Who does he think he's trying to teach?
Who does he think he's explaining his message to?
Is it to children who do not need their mother's milk anymore?
Is it to those who have just been taken from her breast?

[10] Here is how he teaches.
Do this and do that.
There is a rule for this and a rule for that.
Learn a little here and learn a little there."

[11] All right then, these people won't listen to me.
So God will speak to them.
He will speak by using people who speak unfamiliar languages.
He will speak by using the mouths of strangers.

[12] He said to his people,
"I am offering you a resting place.
Let those who are tired rest."
He continued, "I am offering you a place of peace and quiet."
But they wouldn't listen.

[13] So then, here is what the LORD's message will become to them.
Do this and do that.
There is a rule for this and a rule for that.
Learn a little here and learn a little there.
So when they try to go forward, they'll fall back and be wounded.
They'll be trapped and captured.

[14] Listen to the LORD's message, you who make fun of the truth.
Listen, you who rule over these people in Jerusalem.

15 You brag, "We have entered into a
     covenant with the place of the
     dead.
  We have made an agreement with
     the grave.
When a terrible plague comes to punish
     us,
  it can't touch us.
That's because we depend on lies to
     keep us safe.
  We hide behind what isn't true."

16So the LORD and King speaks. He says,

"Look! I am laying a stone in Zion.
  It is a stone that has been tested.
It is the most important stone for a firm
     foundation.
  The one who depends on that stone
     will never be shaken.
17 I will use a measuring line to prove that
     you have not been fair.
  I will use a plumb line to prove that
     you have not done what is
     right.
Hail will sweep away the lies you
     depend on to keep you safe.
  Water will flood your hiding place.
18 Your covenant with death will be called
     off.
  The agreement you made with the
     place of the dead will not
     stand.
When the terrible plague comes to
     punish you,
  you will be struck down by it.
19 As often as it comes, it will carry you
     away.
  Morning after morning, day and
     night,
  it will come to punish you."

If you understand this message,
  it will bring you absolute terror.
20 You will be like someone whose bed is
     too short to lie down on.
  You will be like those whose
     blankets are too small to wrap
     themselves in.
21 The LORD will rise up to judge, just as
     he did at Mount Perazim.
  He will get up to act, just as he did in
     the Valley of Gibeon.
He'll do his work, but it will be strange
     work.
  He'll carry out his task, but it will be
     an unexpected one.

22 Now stop making fun of me.
  If you don't, your chains will become
     heavier.
The LORD who rules over all has spoken
     to me.
  The Lord has told me he has ordered
     that the whole land be
     destroyed.

23 Listen and hear my voice.
  Pay attention to what I'm saying.
24 When a farmer plows in order to plant,
     does he plow without stopping?
  Does he keep on breaking up the soil
     and making the field level?
25 When he's made the surface even,
     doesn't he plant caraway seeds?
  Doesn't he scatter cumin seeds?
Doesn't he plant wheat in its proper
     place?
  Doesn't he plant barley where it
     belongs?
  Doesn't he plant spelt along the edge
     of the field?
26 His God directs him.
  He teaches him the right way to do
     his work.

27 Caraway seeds are beaten out with a rod.
  They aren't separated out under a
     threshing sled.
Cumin seeds are beaten out with a
     stick.
  The wheel of a cart isn't rolled over
     them.
28 Grain must be ground up to make
     bread.
  A farmer separates it out.
  But he doesn't go on doing it forever.
He drives the wheels of a threshing cart
     over it.
  But he doesn't use horses to grind
     the grain.
29 All these insights come from the LORD
     who rules over all.
  His advice is wonderful. His wisdom
     is glorious.

The LORD Will Judge Jerusalem

29 Jerusalem, how terrible it will be for
     you!
  Ariel, you are the city where David
     made his home.
The years will come and go.
  Keep on celebrating your regular
     feasts.

² The Lᴏʀᴅ says, "Ariel, I will surround
you.
Jerusalem, I will get ready to attack
you.
Your people will mourn.
They will sing songs of sadness.
I will make you like the front of an altar
covered with blood.
³ I will be like an army camped against
you on all sides.
I will surround you with towers in
order to attack you.
I will build my ramps all around you
and set up my ladders.
⁴ You will be brought down to the grave.
You will speak from deep down
inside the ground.
Your words will be barely heard out
of the dust.
Your voice will sound like the voice of
a ghost
coming from under the ground.
Your words will sound like a whisper
out of the dust."

⁵ Jerusalem, all your enemies will
become like fine dust.
Their terrifying armies will become
like straw
that the wind blows away.
All of a sudden, in an instant,
⁶   the Lᴏʀᴅ who rules over all will
come.
He will come with thunder, earthquakes
and a lot of noise.
He'll bring windstorms and
rainstorms with him.
He'll send a blazing fire that will
burn up everything.

⁷ Armies from all the nations will fight
against Ariel.
They will attack it and its fort.
They'll surround it completely.
But suddenly those armies will
disappear like a dream.
They will vanish like a vision in the
night.
⁸ It will be as when a hungry person
dreams of eating,
but wakes up still hungry.
It will be as when a thirsty person
dreams of drinking,
but wakes up weak and still thirsty.
In the same way, the armies from all the
nations

that fight against Mount Zion will
disappear.

⁹ People of Jerusalem, be shocked and
amazed.
Make yourselves blind so you can't
see anything.
Get drunk, but not from wine.
Be unsteady on your feet, but not
because of beer.
¹⁰ The Lᴏʀᴅ has made you fall into a deep
sleep.
He has closed the eyes of your
prophets.
He has covered the heads of your
seers so they can't see.

¹¹For you, this whole vision is like words
that are sealed up in a scroll. Suppose you
give it to someone who can read. And
suppose you say, "Please read this for us."
Then they'll answer, "I can't. It's sealed up."
¹²Or suppose you give the scroll to someone who can't read. And suppose you say,
"Please read this for us." Then they'll answer, "I don't know how to read."

¹³The Lord says,

"These people worship me only with
their words.
They honor me by what they say.
But their hearts are far away from
me.
Their worship doesn't mean anything
to me.

Isa. 29:10 A seer is a prophet of God who
also sees visions. A few seers include Iddo,
Gad, Samuel, Isaiah, Ezekiel, and Jeremiah.
See Numbers 12:6. I have dreams, but
I've never had a prophetic vision.

They teach nothing but human rules
that they have been taught.
¹⁴ So once more I will shock these people
with many wonderful acts.
I will destroy the wisdom of those who
think they are so wise.
I will do away with the cleverness of
those who think they are so
smart."
¹⁵ How terrible it will be for people who
try hard
to hide their plans from the LORD!
They do their work in darkness.
They think, "Who sees us? Who will
know?"
¹⁶ They turn everything upside down.
How silly they are to think that
potters are like the clay they
work with!
Can what is made say to the one who
made it,
"You didn't make me"?
Can the pot say to the potter,
"You don't know anything"?

¹⁷ In a very short time, Lebanon will be
turned into rich farm lands.
The rich farm lands will seem like a
forest.
¹⁸ At that time those who can't hear will
hear what is read from the
scroll.
Those who are blind will come out
of gloom and darkness.
They will be able to see.
¹⁹ Those who aren't proud will once again
find their joy in the LORD.
And those who are in need will find
their joy in the Holy One of
Israel.
²⁰ Those who don't show any pity will
vanish.
Those who make fun of others will
disappear.
All those who look for ways to do
what is evil will be cut off.
²¹ Without any proof, they claim that a
person is guilty.
In court they try to trap
the one who speaks up for others.
By using dishonest witnesses they keep
people who aren't guilty
from being treated fairly.

²²Long ago the LORD saved Abraham
from trouble. Now he says to Jacob's people,

"You will not be ashamed anymore.
Your faces will no longer grow pale
with fear.
²³ You will see your children living among
you.
I myself will give you those
children.
Then you will honor my name.
You will recognize how holy I am.
I am the Holy One of Jacob.
You will have great respect for me.
I am the God of Israel.
²⁴ I will give understanding to you
who find yourselves going astray.
You who are always speaking against
others
will accept what I teach you."

The LORD Will Judge His Stubborn People

30 "How terrible it will be for these
stubborn children of mine!"
announces the LORD.
"How terrible for those who carry out
plans that did not come from
me!
Their agreement with Egypt did not
come from my Spirit.
So they pile up one sin on top of
another.
² They go down to Egypt
without asking me for advice.
They look to Pharaoh to help them.
They ask Egypt to keep them safe.
³ But looking to Pharaoh will only bring
them shame.
Asking Egypt for help will bring
them dishonor.
⁴ Their officials have gone to the city of
Zoan.
Their messengers have arrived in
Hanes.
⁵ But the people of Judah will be put to
shame.
That's because they are trusting in a
nation that is useless to them.
Egypt will not bring them any help or
advantage.
Instead, it will bring them shame
and dishonor."

⁶Here is a prophecy the LORD gave me
about the animals in the Negev Desert.

Judah's messengers carry their riches on
the backs of donkeys.

They carry their treasures on the
humps of camels.
They travel through a land of danger
and suffering.
It's a land filled with lions.
Poisonous snakes are also there.
The messengers travel to a nation
that can't do them any good.
⁷ They travel to Egypt, whose help is
totally useless.
That's why I call it Rahab the
Do-Nothing.

⁸ The Lord said to me, "Go now.
Write on a tablet for the people of
Judah
what I am about to say.
Also write it on a scroll.
In days to come
it will be a witness that lasts forever.
⁹ That's because these people of Judah
refuse to obey me.
They are children who tell lies.
They will not listen to what I want to
teach them.
¹⁰ They say to the seers,
'Don't see any more visions!'
They say to the prophets,
'Don't give us any more visions of
what is right!
Tell us pleasant things.
Prophesy things we want to hear
even if they aren't true.
¹¹ Get out of our way!
Get off our path!
Keep the Holy One of Israel away
from us!'"

¹²So the Holy One of Israel speaks. He
says,

"You have turned your backs on what I
have said.
You have depended on telling people
lies.
You have crushed others.
¹³ Those sins are like cracks in a high wall.
They get bigger and bigger.
Suddenly the wall breaks apart.
Then it quickly falls down.
¹⁴ It breaks into small pieces like a clay
pot.
It breaks up completely.
Not one piece is left big enough
for taking coals from a fireplace.
Not one piece is left for dipping
water out of a well."

A tablet was made out of clay and was
the preferred Assyrian type of "paper."
Ancient Israelite scrolls were made out
of animal skins. I'm so glad we have the
stuff that's made from trees. It'd be a
shame to dig up some dirt or kill an animal
every time we needed to write a letter!

¹⁵The Lord and King is the Holy One of
Israel. He says,

"You will find peace and rest
when you turn away from your sins
and depend on me.
You will receive the strength you need
when you stay calm and trust in me.
But you do not want to do what I tell
you to.
¹⁶ You said, 'No. We'll escape on horses.'
So you will have to escape!
You said, 'We'll ride off on fast horses.'
So those who chase you will use
faster horses!
¹⁷ When one of them dares you to fight,
a thousand of you will run away.
When five of them dare you,
all of you will run away.
So few of you will be left that you will
be
like a flagpole on top of a mountain.
You will be like only one banner on
a hill."

¹⁸ But the Lord wants to have mercy on
you.
So he will rise up to give you his
tender love.
The Lord is a God who is always fair.
Blessed are all those who wait for
him to act!

ADVENTURES IN ODYSSEY

Eugene and Connie should have stayed calm and trusted God instead of using their own schemes to catch a cash register thief in "Suspicious Minds" (A#08).

¹⁹People of Zion, who live in Jerusalem, you won't weep anymore. When you cry out to the LORD for help, he will have mercy on you. As soon as he hears you, he'll answer you. ²⁰He might treat you like prisoners. You might eat the bread of trouble. You might drink the water of suffering. But he will be your Teacher. He won't hide himself anymore. You will see him with your own eyes. ²¹You will hear your Teacher's voice behind you. You will hear it whether you turn to the right or the left. It will say, "Here is the path I want you to take. So walk on it." ²²Then you will get rid of the silver statues of your gods. You won't have anything to do with the gold statues either. All of them are "unclean." So you will throw them away like dirty rags. You will say to them, "Get away from us!"

²³The LORD will send rain on the seeds you plant in the ground. The crops that grow will be rich and plentiful. At that time your cattle will eat grass in rolling meadows. ²⁴The oxen and donkeys that work the soil will eat the finest feed and crushed grain. The farmers will use pitchforks and shovels to separate it from the straw. ²⁵At that time the towers of your enemies will fall down. Their soldiers will die. Streams of water will flow on every high mountain and hill. ²⁶The moon will shine like the sun. And the sunlight will be seven times brighter than usual. It will be like the light of seven full days. That will happen when the LORD bandages and heals the wounds and bruises he has brought on his people.

²⁷ The LORD will come from far away
  in all his power and glory.
He will show his burning anger.
  Thick clouds of smoke will be all
    around him.
His mouth will speak angry words.
  The words from his tongue will be
    like a destroying fire.
²⁸ His breath will be like a rushing flood
  that rises up to the neck.

WHAT ABOUT YOU?

Your phone rings and the caller ID says, "God's will." When you answer, a deep, booming voice tells you, "You're going to be a doctor." Then the caller hangs up. Smiling, you set off to fulfill God's will for your life.

That would be way too easy, wouldn't it? The truth is, most people wrestle as they try to understand what God wants for them. Yet God has remarkable plans for people, even if they think the task is impossible. It was true of Moses, who tried to talk God out of using him as a public speaker. It was true of Esther, who found favor in the eyes of a king. You'll find many examples in God's Word.

As you search for God's will in your life, pray and listen for God's voice as you read the Bible. As it says in Isaiah 30:21: "You will hear your Teacher's voice behind you. You will hear it whether you turn to the right or the left. It will say, 'Here is the path I want you to take. So walk on it.'" If you get in the habit of listening and obeying God in little ways, day to day, life's bigger decisions will fall right into place.

Make a time capsule. Write down details about your current life for your future self to read. Include your likes and dislikes, hobbies, and what you think God has planned for your life. When you eventually open it, you'll see how God has been working over time.

He'll separate out the nations he is
  going to destroy.
  He'll place a bit in their jaws.
  It will lead them down the road to
    death.
²⁹ You will sing
    as you do on the night you celebrate
      a holy feast.
  Your hearts will be filled with joy.
    You will be as joyful as people
      playing their flutes
  as they go up to the mountain of the
    LORD.
  He is the Rock of Israel.
³⁰ The LORD will cause people to hear his
    powerful voice.
  He will make them see his arm
    coming down to punish them.
  It will come down with burning anger
    and destroying fire.
  It will come down with rain,
    thunderstorms and hail.

³¹ The voice of the LORD will tear the
    Assyrians apart.
  He will strike them down with his
    scepter.
³² He will strike them
    with his club to punish them.
  Each time he does, his people will
    celebrate
    with the music of harps and
      tambourines.
  He will use his powerful arm
    to strike down the Assyrians in battle.
³³ In the Valley of Ben Hinnom, Topheth
    has been prepared for a long
      time.
  It has been made ready for the king
    of Assyria.
  Its fire pit has been made deep and wide.
    It has plenty of wood for the fire.
  The breath of the LORD
    will be like a stream of burning sulfur.
  It will set the wood on fire.

The LORD Will Judge Those Who Depend on Egypt

31 How terrible it will be for those who
    go down to Egypt for help!
  How terrible for those who depend
    on horses!
  They trust in how many chariots they
    have.
    They trust in how strong their
      horsemen are.
  But they don't look to the Holy One of
    Israel.
    They don't ask the LORD for his help.
² He too is wise. He can bring horrible
    trouble.
  He does what he says he'll do.
  He'll rise up against that evil nation.
    He'll fight against those who help
      them.
³ The men of Egypt are only human
    beings.
    They aren't God.
  Their horses are only flesh and blood.
    They aren't spirits.
  The LORD will reach out his powerful
    hand
    to punish everyone.
  The Egyptians provide help.
    But they will be tripped up.
  The people of Judah receive the help.
    But they will fall down.
  All of them will be destroyed.

WOOTON'S **FUN FACTS**
Isa. 30:26

Sunlight brings happiness by helping
you sleep better and lifting your mood. It
also helps your body maintain vitamin D,
an essential element for health. As a mail
carrier, I spend lots of time in the sun.
Huh—maybe that's why I'm so happy!

Jason's Jargon

ISAIAH 31

Your next task: Sift through this chapter for *panic*! Panic is extreme fear or terror. In this case, God's enemies will panic when they see His army coming toward them.

⁴The LORD says to me,

"A powerful lion stands over its food
   and growls.
A lot of shepherds can be brought
   together to drive it away.
But the lion is not frightened by their
   shouts.
   It is not upset by the noise they make.
In the same way, I will come down
   from heaven.
I will fight on Mount Zion and on
   its hills.
Nothing will drive me away.
   I am the LORD who rules over all.
⁵ Like a bird hovering over its nest, I will
   guard Jerusalem.
   I will keep it safe.
I will 'pass over' it and save it.
   I am the LORD who rules over all."

⁶People of Israel, return to the LORD. He's the God you have so strongly opposed. ⁷You sinned when you made your gods out of silver and gold. The time will come when all of you will turn away from them.

⁸ The LORD says, "The Assyrians will be
   killed by swords.
   But the swords that kill them will
      not be used by human beings.
The Assyrians will run away from those
   swords.
   But their young men will be caught
      and forced to work hard.
⁹ Their hiding places will be destroyed
   when terror strikes them.
Their commanders will see their
   enemy's battle flags.
   Then they will be filled with panic,"
announces the LORD.
His fire blazes out from Mount Zion.
   His furnace burns in Jerusalem.

The King Who Will Do What Is Right

32 A king will come who will do what
   is right.
   His officials will govern fairly.
² Each official will be like a place to get
   out of the wind.
   He will be like a place to hide from
      storms.
He'll be like streams of water flowing in
   the desert.
   He'll be like the shadow of a huge
      rock in a dry and thirsty land.

³ Then the eyes of those who see won't be
   closed anymore.
   The ears of those who hear will listen
      to the truth.
⁴ People who are afraid will know and
   understand.
   Tongues that stutter will speak
      clearly.
⁵ Foolish people won't be considered
   noble anymore.
   Those who are worthless won't be
      highly respected.
⁶ Foolish people say foolish things.
   Their minds are set on doing evil
      things.
They don't do what is right.
   They tell lies about the LORD.
They don't give hungry people any
   food.
   They don't let thirsty people have
      any water.
⁷ Those who are worthless use sinful
   methods.
   They make evil plans against poor
      people.
They destroy them with their lies.
   They do it even when those people
      are right.
⁸ But those who are noble make noble
   plans.
   And by doing noble things they
      succeed.

The Sinful Women in Jerusalem

⁹ You women who are so contented,
   pay attention to me.
You who feel so secure,
   listen to what I have to say.
¹⁰ You feel secure now.
   But in a little over a year you will
      tremble with fear.
The grape harvest will fail.
   There won't be any fruit.

¹¹ So tremble, you contented women.
>> Tremble with fear, you who feel so
>> secure.
> Take off your fine clothes.
>> Wrap yourselves in rags.
¹² Beat your chests to show how sad you
>> are.
>> The pleasant fields have been
>> destroyed.
> The fruitful vines have dried up.
¹³ My people's land is overgrown with
>> thorns and bushes.
>> Mourn for all the houses that were
>> once filled with joy.
>> Cry over this city that used to be full
>> of wild parties.
¹⁴ The royal palace will be left empty.
>> The noisy city will be deserted.
> The fort and lookout tower will become
>> a dry and empty desert forever.
> Donkeys will enjoy being there.
>> Flocks will eat there.
¹⁵ That will continue until the Holy Spirit
>> is poured out on us from heaven.
> Then the desert will be turned into rich
>> farm lands.
>> The rich farm lands will seem like a
>> forest.
¹⁶ In the desert, the LORD will make sure
>> people do what is right.
>> In the rich farm lands he will make
>> sure they treat one another
>> fairly.
¹⁷ Doing what is right will bring peace
>> and rest.
>> When my people do that, they will
>> stay calm
> and trust in the LORD forever.
¹⁸ They will live in a peaceful land.
>> Their homes will be secure.
>> They will enjoy peace and quiet.
¹⁹ Hail might strip the forests bare.
>> Cities might be completely destroyed.
²⁰ But how blessed you people will be!
>> You will plant your seeds by every
>> stream.
> You will let your cattle and donkeys
>> wander anywhere they want to.

Trouble for Assyria and Help for God's People

33 How terrible it will be for you, you
>> who destroy others!
>> Assyria, you haven't been destroyed
>> yet.

> How terrible for you, you who turn
>> against others!
>> Others haven't turned against you
>> yet.
> When you stop destroying,
>> you will be destroyed.
> When you stop turning against others,
>> others will turn against you.

² LORD, have mercy on us.
>> We long for you to help us.
> Make us strong every morning.
>> Save us when we're in trouble.
³ At the roar of your army, the nations
>> run away.
>> When you rise up against them, they
>> scatter.
⁴ Nations, what you have taken in battle
>> is destroyed.
>> It's as if young locusts had eaten it up.
> Like large numbers of locusts,
>> people rush to get it.

⁵ The LORD is honored. He lives in
>> heaven.
>> He will make sure Zion's people only
>> do what is fair and right.
⁶ He will be the firm foundation for their
>> entire lives.
>> He will give them all the wisdom,
>> knowledge and saving power
>> they will ever need.
>> Respect for the LORD is the key to
>> that treasure.

⁷ Look! Judah's brave men cry out loud in
>> the streets.
>> The messengers who were sent to
>> bring peace weep bitter tears.
⁸ The wide roads are deserted.
>> No one travels on them.
> Our peace treaty with Assyria is
>> broken.
>> Those who witnessed it are looked
>> down on.
>> No one is respected.
⁹ The land dries up and wastes away.
>> Lebanon is full of shame and dries
>> up.
> The rich land of Sharon is like the
>> Arabah Desert.
>> The trees of Bashan and Carmel
>> drop their leaves.

¹⁰ "Now I will take action," says the LORD.
>> "Now I will be honored.
>> Now I will be respected.

¹¹ Assyria, your plans and actions are like
straw.
Your anger is a fire that will destroy
you.
¹² The nations will be burned to ashes.
They will be like bushes that are cut
down and set on fire.

¹³ "You nations far away, listen to what I
have done!
My people who are near, recognize
how powerful I am!
¹⁴ The sinners in Zion are terrified.
They tremble with fear.
They say, 'Who of us can live through
the LORD's destroying fire?
Who of us can live through the fire
that burns forever?'
¹⁵ People must do what is right.
They must be honest and tell the
truth.
They must not get rich by cheating
others.
Their hands must not receive money
from those who want special
favors.
They must not let their ears listen to
plans to commit murder.
They must close their eyes to even
thinking about doing what is
evil.
¹⁶ People like that will be kept safe.
It will be as if they were living on
high mountains.
It will be as if they were living in a
mountain fort.
They will have all the food they need.
And they will never run out of
water."

¹⁷ People of Judah, you will see the king in
all his glory and majesty.
You will view his kingdom spreading
far and wide.
¹⁸ You will think about what used to
terrify you.
You will say to yourself,
"Where is that chief officer of Assyria?
Where is the one who forced us to send
gifts to his king?
Where is the officer in charge of the
towers
that were used when we were
attacked?"
¹⁹ You won't see those proud people
anymore.

They spoke a strange language.
None of us could understand it.

²⁰ Just look at Zion! It's the city
where we celebrate our regular
feasts.
Turn your eyes toward Jerusalem.
It will be a peaceful place to live in.
It will be like a tent that will never be
moved.
Its stakes will never be pulled up.
None of its ropes will be broken.
²¹ There the LORD will be our Mighty One.
It will be like a place of wide rivers
and streams.
No boat with oars will travel on them.
No mighty ship will sail on them.
²² That's because the LORD is our judge.
The LORD gives us our law.
The LORD is our king.
He will save us.

²³ The ropes on your ship hang loose.
The mast isn't very secure.
The sail isn't spread out.
But the LORD will strike down the
Assyrians.
Then a large amount of goods will be
taken from them and divided
up.
Even people who are disabled will
carry off some of it.
²⁴ No one living in Zion will ever say
again, "I'm sick."
And the sins of those who live there
will be forgiven.

The LORD Will Judge the Nations

34 Nations, come near and listen to me!
Pay attention to what I'm about to
say.
Let the earth and everything in it listen.
Let the world and everything that
comes out of it pay attention.
² The LORD is angry with all the nations.
His anger is against all their armies.
He will totally destroy them.
He will have them killed.
³ Those who are killed won't be buried.
Their dead bodies will be thrown on
the ground.
They will stink.
Their blood will cover the mountains.
⁴ All the stars in the sky will vanish.
The heavens will be rolled up like a
scroll.

All the stars in the sky will fall like
   dried-up leaves from a vine.
They will drop like wrinkled figs
   from a fig tree.
5 The sword of the LORD will finish its
   deadly work in the sky.
Then it will come down to strike
   Edom.
He will totally destroy that nation.
6 His sword will be red with blood.
   It will be covered with fat.
The blood will flow like the blood
   of lambs and goats being sacrificed.
The fat will be like the fat
   taken from the kidneys of rams.
That's because the LORD will offer a
   sacrifice
   in the city of Bozrah.
He will kill many people in the land
   of Edom.
7 The people and their leaders will be
   killed
   like wild oxen and young bulls.
Their land will be wet with their blood.
The dust will be covered with their
   fat.

8 That's because the LORD has set aside a
   day to pay Edom back.
He has set aside a year to pay them
   back. He will pay them back
   for what they did to Zion.
9 The streams of Edom will be turned
   into tar.
Its dust will be turned into blazing
   sulfur.
Its land will become burning tar.
10 The fire will keep burning night and
   day.
It can't be put out.
Its smoke will go up forever.
Edom will lie empty for all time to
   come.
No one will ever travel through it
   again.
11 The desert owl and screech owl will
   make it their home.
The great owl and the raven will
   build their nests there.
God will use his measuring line
   to show how completely Edom will
   be destroyed.
He will use his plumb line
   to show how empty Edom will
   become.

12 Edom's nobles won't have anything left
   there
   that can be called a kingdom.
All its princes will vanish.
13 Thorns will cover its forts.
   Bushes and weeds will cover its
   safest places.
It will become a home for wild dogs.
It will become a place where owls
   live.
14 Desert creatures will meet with hyenas.
   Wild goats will call out to each
   other.
Night creatures will also lie down
   there.
They will find places where they can
   rest.
15 Owls will make their nests and lay their
   eggs there.
And they will hatch them.
They will take care of their little ones
   under the shadow of their wings.
Male and female falcons will also
   gather there.

16 Look in the book of the LORD. Here is
what you will read there.

None of those animals will be missing.
   Male and female alike will be there.
The LORD himself has commanded it.
   And his Spirit will gather them
   together.
17 The LORD will decide what part of the
   land goes to each animal.
Then he will give each one its share.
It will belong to them forever.
   And they will live there for all time
   to come.

The Joy of the LORD's People

35 The desert and the dry ground will
   be glad.
The dry places will be full of joy.
Flowers will grow there.
Like the first crocus in the spring,
2   the desert will bloom with flowers.
It will be very glad and shout for
   joy.
The glorious beauty of Lebanon will be
   given to it.
It will be as beautiful as the rich
   lands
   of Carmel and Sharon.
Everyone will see the glory of the LORD.
   They will see the beauty of our God.

³ Strengthen the hands of those who are
    weak.
    Help those whose knees give way.
⁴ Say to those whose hearts are afraid,
    "Be strong and do not fear.
Your God will come.
    He will pay your enemies back.
    He will come to save you."

⁵ Then the eyes of those who are blind
    will be opened.
    The ears of those who can't hear will
        be unplugged.
⁶ Those who can't walk will leap like a
    deer.
    And those who can't speak will
        shout for joy.
Water will pour out in dry places.
    Streams will flow in the desert.
⁷ The burning sand will become a pool of
    water.

The thirsty ground will become
    bubbling springs.
In the places where wild dogs once lay
    down,
    tall grass and papyrus will grow.

⁸ A wide road will go through the land.
    It will be called the Way of Holiness.
    Only those who lead a holy life can
        use it.
    "Unclean" and foolish people can't
        walk on it.
⁹ No lions will use it.
    No hungry wild animals will be
        on it.
    None of them will be there.
Only people who have been set free will
    walk on it.
¹⁰   Those the LORD has saved will
        return to their land.
They will sing as they enter the city of
    Zion.
    Joy that lasts forever will be
    like beautiful crowns on their heads.
They will be filled with gladness and
    joy.
    Sorrow and sighing will be gone.

Sennacherib Warns Jerusalem

36 Sennacherib attacked and captured all the cities of Judah that had high walls around them. It was in the 14th year of the rule of Hezekiah. Sennacherib was king of Assyria. ²He sent his field commander from Lachish to King Hezekiah at Jerusalem. He sent him along with a large army. The commander stopped at the channel that brings water from the Upper Pool. It was on the road to the Washerman's Field. ³Eliakim, Shebna and Joah went out to him. Eliakim, the son of Hilkiah, was in charge of the palace. Shebna was the secretary. Joah, the son of Asaph, kept the records.

⁴The field commander said to them, "Give Hezekiah this message. Tell him,

"'Sennacherib is the great king of Assyria. He says, "Why are you putting your faith in what your king says? ⁵You say you have a military plan. You say you have a strong army. But your words don't mean anything. Who are you depending on? Why don't you want to stay under my control? ⁶Look, I know you are depending on Egypt. Why are you doing that? Egypt is nothing but a broken papyrus stem. Try leaning on it. It will only cut your hand. Pharaoh, the king of Egypt, is just like that to everyone who depends on him. [7]But suppose you say to me, 'We are depending on the LORD our God.' Didn't Hezekiah remove your god's high places and altars? Didn't Hezekiah say to the people of Judah and Jerusalem, 'You must worship at the altar in Jerusalem'?

[8]"'Come on. Make a deal with my master, the king of Assyria. I'll give you 2,000 horses. But only if you can put riders on them! [9]You are depending on Egypt for chariots and horsemen. You can't drive away even the least important officer among my master's officials. [10]Besides, do you think I've come without being sent by the LORD? Have I come to attack and destroy this land without receiving a message from him? The LORD himself told me to march out against your country. He told me to destroy it.'"'"

[11]Then Eliakim, Shebna and Joah spoke to the field commander. They said, "Please speak to us in the Aramaic language. We understand it. Don't speak to us in Hebrew. If you do, the people on the wall will be able to understand you."

[12]But the commander replied, "My master sent me to say these things. Are these words only for your master and you to hear? Aren't they also for the people sitting on the wall? They are going to suffer just like you. They'll have to eat their own waste. They'll have to drink their own urine."

[13]Then the commander stood up and spoke in the Hebrew language. He called out, "Pay attention to what the great king of Assyria is telling you. [14]He says, 'Don't let Hezekiah trick you. He can't save you! [15]Don't let Hezekiah talk you into trusting in the LORD. Don't believe him when he says, "You can be sure that the LORD will save us. This city will not be handed over to the king of Assyria."'

[16]"Don't listen to Hezekiah. The king of Assyria says, 'Make a peace treaty with me. Come over to my side. Then each one of you will eat fruit from your own vine and fig tree. Each one of you will drink water from your own well. [17]You will do that until

I come back. Then I'll take you to a land just like yours. It's a land that has a lot of grain and fresh wine. It has plenty of bread and vineyards.

[18]"Don't let Hezekiah fool you. He's telling you a lie when he says, "The LORD will save us." Have the gods of any nations ever saved their lands from the power of the king of Assyria? [19]Where are the gods of Hamath and Arpad? Where are the gods of Sepharvaim? Have they saved Samaria from my power? [20]Which one of all the gods of those countries has been able to save their lands from me? So how can the LORD save Jerusalem from my power?'"

[21]But the people remained silent. They didn't say anything. That's because King Hezekiah had commanded, "Don't answer him."

[22]Then Eliakim, the son of Hilkiah, went to Hezekiah. Eliakim was in charge of the palace. Shebna the secretary went with him. So did Joah, the son of Asaph. Joah kept the records. All of them went to Hezekiah with their clothes torn. They told him what the field commander had said.

Isaiah Prophesies That Jerusalem Will Be Saved

37 When King Hezekiah heard what the field commander had said, he tore his clothes. He put on the rough clothing people wear when they're sad. Then he went into the LORD's temple. [2]Hezekiah sent Eliakim, who was in charge of the palace, to Isaiah the prophet, the son of Amoz. He also sent the leading priests and Shebna the secretary to him. All of them were wearing rough clothing. [3]They told Isaiah, "Hezekiah says, 'Today we're in great trouble. The LORD is warning us. He's bringing shame on us. Sometimes babies come to the moment when they should be born. But their mothers aren't strong enough to give birth to them. Today we are like those mothers. We aren't strong enough to save ourselves. [4]Perhaps the LORD your God will hear everything the field commander has said. His master, the king of Assyria, has sent him to make fun of the living God. Maybe the LORD your God will punish him for what he has heard him say. So pray for the remaining people who are still alive here.'"

[5]King Hezekiah's officials came to Isaiah. [6]Then he said to them, "Tell your master,

'The LORD says, "Do not be afraid of what you have heard. The officers who are under the king of Assyria have spoken evil things against me. ⁷Listen! I will send him news from his own country. It will make him want to return home. There I will have him cut down by a sword."'"

⁸The field commander heard that the king of Assyria had left Lachish. So the commander pulled his troops back from Jerusalem. He went to join the king. He found out that the king was fighting against Libnah.

⁹During that time Sennacherib received a report. He was told that Tirhakah was marching out to fight against him. Tirhakah was the king of Cush. When Sennacherib heard the report, he sent messengers again to Hezekiah with a letter. It said, ¹⁰"Tell Hezekiah, the king of Judah, 'Don't let the god you depend on trick you. He says, "Jerusalem will not be handed over to the king of Assyria." But don't believe him. ¹¹I'm sure you have heard about what the kings of Assyria have done to all the other countries. They have destroyed them completely. So do you think you will be saved? ¹²The kings who ruled before me destroyed many nations. Did the gods of those nations save them? Did the gods of Gozan, Harran or Rezeph save them? What about the gods of the people of Eden who were in Tel Assar? ¹³Where is the king of Hamath? Where is the king of Arpad? Where are the kings of Lair, Sepharvaim, Hena and Ivvah?'"

Hezekiah Prays to the LORD

¹⁴When Hezekiah received the letter from the messengers, he read it. Then he went up to the LORD's temple. There he spread the letter out in front of the LORD. ¹⁵Hezekiah prayed to the LORD. He said, ¹⁶"LORD who rules over all, you are the God of Israel. You sit on your throne between the cherubim. You alone are God over all the kingdoms on earth. You have made heaven and earth. ¹⁷Listen, LORD. Hear us. Open your eyes, LORD. Look at the trouble we're in. Listen to what Sennacherib is saying. You are the living God. And he dares to make fun of you!

¹⁸"LORD, it's true that the kings of Assyria have completely destroyed many nations and their lands. ¹⁹They have thrown the statues of the gods of those nations into the fire. And they have destroyed them. That's

because they weren't really gods at all. They were nothing but statues made out of wood and stone. They were made by human hands. ²⁰LORD our God, save us from the power of Sennacherib. Then all the kingdoms of the earth will know that you are the only God."

Sennacherib Falls From Power

²¹Isaiah sent a message to Hezekiah. Isaiah said, "The LORD is the God of Israel. He says, 'You have prayed to me about Sennacherib, the king of Assyria. ²²So here is the message the LORD has spoken against him. The LORD is telling him,

"'"You will not win the battle over
        Zion.
    Its people hate you and make fun
        of you.
The people of Jerusalem lift up their
        heads proudly
    as you run away.
²³ Who have you laughed at?
    Who have you spoken evil things
        against?
    Who have you raised your voice
        against?
Who have you looked at so proudly?
    You have done it against me.
    I am the Holy One of Israel!
²⁴ Through your messengers
    you have laughed at me again and
        again.
And you have said,
    'I have many chariots.
With them I have climbed to the tops of
        the mountains.
    I've climbed the highest mountains
        in Lebanon.
I've cut down its tallest cedar trees.
    I've cut down the best of its juniper
        trees.
I've reached its farthest mountains.
    I've reached its finest forests.
²⁵ I've dug wells in other lands.
    I've drunk the water from them.
I've walked through all the streams of
        Egypt.
    I've dried up every one of them.'
²⁶ "'"But I, the LORD, say, 'Haven't you
        heard what I have done?
    Long ago I arranged for you to do
        this.
In days of old I planned it.
    Now I have made it happen.

You have turned cities with high walls
  into piles of stone.
²⁷ Their people do not have any power
    left.
  They are troubled and put to shame.
  They are like plants in the field.
  They are like new green plants.
  They are like grass that grows on a roof.
  It dries up before it is completely
    grown.
²⁸ " " " "But I know where you are.
  I know when you come and go.
  I know how very angry you are with
    me.
²⁹ You roar against me and brag.
  And I have heard your bragging.
  So I will put my hook in your nose.
  I will put my bit in your mouth.
  And I will make you go home
    by the same way you came.' " ' "

³⁰The Lord said, "Hezekiah, here is a
sign for you.

  "This year you will eat what grows by
    itself.
  Next year you will eat what grows
    from that.
  But in the third year you will plant your
    crops and gather them in.
  You will plant your grapevines and
    eat their fruit.
³¹ The people of the kingdom of Judah
    who are still alive will be like
    plants.
  Once more they will put down roots
    and produce fruit.
³² Out of Jerusalem will come the people
    who remain.
  Out of Mount Zion will come those
    who are still left alive.
  My great love will make sure that
    happens.
  I rule over all.

³³"Here is a message from me about the
king of Assyria. I say,

  " 'He will not enter this city.
  He will not even shoot an arrow at it.
  He will not come near it with a shield.
  He will not build a ramp in order to
    climb over its walls.
³⁴ By the way that he came he will go
    home.
  He will not enter this city,'
    announces the Lord.

³⁵ 'I will guard this city and save it.
  I will do it for myself.
  And I will do it for my servant
    David.' "

³⁶Then the angel of the Lord went into
the camp of the Assyrians. He put to death
185,000 soldiers there. The people of Jerusalem got up the next morning. They
looked out and saw all the dead bodies. ³⁷So
Sennacherib, the king of Assyria, took the
army tents down. Then he left. He returned
to Nineveh and stayed there.

³⁸One day Sennacherib was worshiping
in the temple of his god Nisrok. His sons
Adrammelek and Sharezer killed him with
their swords. Then they escaped to the land
of Ararat. Esarhaddon became the next
king after his father Sennacherib.

Hezekiah Becomes Sick and Is Healed

38 In those days Hezekiah became very
sick. He knew he was about to die.
Isaiah went to see him. Isaiah was the son
of Amoz. Isaiah told Hezekiah, "The Lord
says, 'Put everything in order. Make out
your will. You are going to die soon. You
will not get well again.' "

²Hezekiah turned his face toward the
wall. He prayed to the Lord. He said,
³"Lord, please remember how faithful I've
been to you. I've lived the way you wanted
me to. I've served you with all my heart.
I've done what is good in your sight." And
Hezekiah wept bitterly.

⁴A message from the Lord came to
Isaiah. The Lord said, ⁵"Go and speak to
Hezekiah. Tell him, 'The Lord, the God of
King David, says, "I have heard your prayer.
I have seen your tears. I will add 15 years to
your life. ⁶And I will save you and this city
from the power of the king of Assyria. I will
guard this city.

⁷" ' "Here is a sign from me. It will show
you that I will heal you, just as I promised
I would. ⁸The shadow that was made by the
sun has gone down ten steps on the stairway of Ahaz. I will make it go back up those
ten steps." ' " So the shadow went back up
the ten steps it had gone down.

⁹Here is a song of praise that was written by Hezekiah, the king of Judah. He
wrote it after he was sick and had gotten
well again.

¹⁰ I said, "I'm enjoying the best years of
my life.
Must I now go through the gates of
death?
Will the rest of my years be taken
away from me?"
¹¹ I said, "Lᴏʀᴅ, I'll never see you again
while I'm still alive.
I'll never see people anymore.
I'll never again be with those who
live in this world.
¹² My body is like a shepherd's tent.
It has been pulled down and carried
off.
My life is like a piece of cloth that I've
rolled up.
You have cut it off from the loom.
In a short period of time you have
brought my life to an end.
¹³ I waited patiently until sunrise.
But like a lion you broke all my
bones.
In a short period of time you have
brought my life to an end.
¹⁴ I cried softly like a weak little bird.
I sounded like a dove as I mourned.
My eyes grew tired as I looked up
toward heaven.
Lord, my life is in danger. Please
come and help me!
¹⁵ "But what can I say?
You have promised to heal me.
And you yourself have done it.
Once I was proud and bitter.
But now I will live the rest of my life
free of pride.
¹⁶ Lord, people find the will to live
because you keep your
promises.
And my spirit also finds life in your
promises.
You brought me back to health.
You let me live.
¹⁷ I'm sure it was for my benefit
that I suffered such great pain.
You love me. You kept me
from going down into the pit of
death.
You have put all my sins
behind your back.
¹⁸ People in the grave can't praise you.
Dead people can't sing praise to you.
Those who go down to the grave
can't hope for you to be faithful to
them.

Isa. 38:21 Move over, nurses! Dr. Isaiah
is in the house! But what a good
prescription Isaiah gave! Today figs are
known for their healthy minerals including
potassium, calcium, magnesium, iron,
and copper. I think I'll eat some now!

¹⁹ It is those who are alive who praise
you.
And that's what I'm doing today.
Parents tell their children
about how faithful you are.

²⁰ "The Lᴏʀᴅ will save me.
So we will sing and play music on
stringed instruments.
We will sing all the days of our lives
in the Lᴏʀᴅ's temple."

²¹When Hezekiah was sick, Isaiah had
said, "Press some figs together. Spread
them on a piece of cloth. Apply them to
Hezekiah's boil. Then he'll get well again."
²²At that time Hezekiah had asked,
"What will the sign be to prove I'll go up to
the Lᴏʀᴅ's temple?" That's when the Lᴏʀᴅ
had made the shadow go back ten steps.

Messengers Come From Babylon to Hezekiah

39 At that time Marduk-Baladan, the
king of Babylon, sent Hezekiah letters and a gift. He had heard that Hezekiah
had been sick but had gotten well again.
Marduk-Baladan was the son of Baladan.
²Hezekiah gladly received the messengers.
He showed them what was in his storerooms. He showed them the silver and
gold. He took them to where the spices
and the fine olive oil were kept. He showed
them where he kept all his weapons. And
he showed them all his treasures. In fact,

he showed them everything that was in his palace and in his whole kingdom. ³Then Isaiah the prophet went to King Hezekiah. Isaiah asked him, "What did those men say? Where did they come from?"

"They came from a land far away," Hezekiah said. "They came to me from Babylon."

⁴Isaiah asked, "What did they see in your palace?"

"They saw everything in my palace," Hezekiah said. "I showed them all my treasures."

⁵Then Isaiah said to Hezekiah, "Listen to the message of the LORD who rules over all. He says, ⁶'You can be sure the time will come when everything in your palace will be carried off to Babylon. Everything the kings before you have stored up until this day will be taken away. There will not be anything left,' says the LORD. ⁷'Some of the members of your family line will be taken away. They will be your own flesh and blood. They will include the children who will be born into your family line. And they will serve the king of Babylon in his palace.'"

⁸"The message the LORD has spoken through you is good," Hezekiah replied. He thought, "There will be peace and safety while I'm still living."

God Comforts His People

40 "Comfort my people," says your God. "Comfort them.
² Speak tenderly to the people of
Jerusalem.
Announce to them
that their hard labor has been
completed.
Tell them that their sin has been
paid for.
Tell them the LORD has punished them
enough
for all their sins."

³ A messenger is calling out,
"In the desert prepare
the way for the LORD.
Make a straight road through it
for our God.
⁴ Every valley will be filled in.
Every mountain and hill will be
made level.
The rough ground will be smoothed
out.
The rocky places will be made flat.

⁵ Then the glory of the LORD will appear.
And everyone will see it together.
The LORD has spoken."

⁶ Another messenger says, "Cry out."
And I said, "What should I cry?"

"Cry out, 'All people are like grass.
They don't stay faithful to me any
longer than wildflowers last.
⁷ The grass dries up. The flowers fall to
the ground.
That happens when the LORD makes
his wind blow on them.
So people are just like grass.
⁸ The grass dries up. The flowers fall to
the ground.
But what our God says will stand
forever.'"

⁹ Zion, you are bringing good news to
your people.
Go up on a high mountain and
announce it.
Jerusalem, you are bringing good news
to them.
Shout the message loudly.
Shout it out loud. Don't be afraid.
Say to the towns of Judah,
"Your God is coming!"
¹⁰ The LORD and King is coming with
power.
He rules with a powerful arm.
He has set his people free.
He is bringing them back as his
reward.
He has won the battle over their
enemies.
¹¹ He takes care of his flock like a shepherd.
He gathers the lambs in his arms.
He carries them close to his heart.
He gently leads those that have little
ones.

¹² Who has measured the oceans by using
the palm of his hand?
Who has used the width of his hand
to mark off the sky?
Who has measured out the dust of the
earth in a basket?
Who has weighed the mountains on
scales?
Who has weighed the hills in a
balance?
¹³ Who can ever understand the Spirit of
the LORD?
Who can ever give him advice?

¹⁴ Did the LORD have to ask anyone to
    help him understand?
    Did he have to ask someone to teach
    him the right way?
Who taught him what he knows?
    Who showed him how to
    understand?

¹⁵ The nations are only a drop in a bucket
    to him.
    He considers them as nothing but
    dust on the scales.
    He weighs the islands as if they were
    only fine dust.
¹⁶ Lebanon doesn't have enough trees to
    keep his altar fires burning.
    It doesn't have enough animals to
    sacrifice as burnt offerings to
    him.
¹⁷ To him, all the nations don't amount to
    anything.
    He considers them to be worthless.
    In fact, they are less than nothing in
    his sight.

¹⁸ So who will you compare God with?
    Is there any other god like him?
¹⁹ Will you compare him with a statue of a
    god?
    Anyone who works with metal can
    make a statue.
    Then another worker covers it with gold

and makes silver chains for it.
²⁰ But someone who is too poor to bring
    that kind of offering
    will choose some wood that won't
    rot.
Then they look for a skilled worker.
    They pay the worker to make a
    statue of a god that won't fall
    over.

²¹ Don't you know who made everything?
    Haven't you heard about him?
    Hasn't it been told to you from the
    beginning?
    Haven't you understood it ever since
    the earth was made?
²² God sits on his throne high above the
    earth.
    Its people look like grasshoppers to
    him.
    He spreads out the heavens like a cover.
    He sets it up like a tent to live in.
²³ He takes the power of princes away
    from them.
    He reduces the rulers of this world
    to nothing.
²⁴ They are planted.
    They are scattered like seeds.
    They put down roots in the ground.
But as soon as that happens, God blows
    on them and they dry up.
    Then a windstorm sweeps them
    away like straw.

²⁵ "So who will you compare me with?
    Who is equal to me?" says the Holy
    One.
²⁶ Look up toward the sky.
    Who created everything you see?
The LORD causes the stars to come out
    at night one by one.
    He calls out each one of them by
    name.
His power and strength are great.
    So none of the stars is missing.

WOOTON'S FUN FACTS
Isa. 40:26

Even though you might have heard
people say otherwise, the International
Astronomical Union says that no one can
buy a star and name it after him- or herself.
Scientists call the stars by numbers,
but only God knows their names.

²⁷ Family of Jacob, why do you complain,
  "The LORD doesn't notice our
    condition"?
People of Israel, why do you say,
  "Our God doesn't pay any attention
    to our rightful claims"?
²⁸ Don't you know who made everything?
  Haven't you heard about him?
The LORD is the God who lives forever.
  He created everything on earth.
He won't become worn out or get tired.
  No one will ever know how great his
    understanding is.
²⁹ He gives strength to those who are
    tired.
  He gives power to those who are
    weak.
³⁰ Even young people become worn out
    and get tired.
  Even the best of them trip and fall.
³¹ But those who trust in the LORD
    will receive new strength.
They will fly as high as eagles.
  They will run and not get tired.
  They will walk and not grow weak.

REMEMBER THIS

ISAIAH 40:31

"Those who trust in the LORD
will receive new strength.
They will fly as high as
eagles. They will run and not
get tired. They will walk and
not grow weak."

The LORD Helps Israel

41 The LORD says, "People who live on
    the islands,
  come and stand quietly in front of
    me.
Let the nations gain new strength
  in order to state their case.
Let them come forward and speak.
  Let us go to court and find out who
    is right.

² "Who has stirred up a king from the
    east?
  Who has helped him win his battles?
I hand nations over to him.
  I bring kings under his control.
He turns them into dust with his sword.
  With his bow he turns them into
    straw blowing in the wind.
³ He hunts them down. Then he moves
    on unharmed.
  He travels so fast that his feet
    don't seem to touch the ground.
⁴ Who has made that happen? Who has
    carried it out?
  Who has created all the people who
    have ever lived?
I, the LORD, have done it.
  I was with the first of them.
  And I will be with the last of them."

⁵ The people on the islands have seen
    that king coming.
  And it has made them afraid.
People tremble with fear from one
    end of the earth to the other.
They come and gather together.
⁶   They help one another.
  They say to one another, "Be
    strong!"
⁷ One skilled worker makes a statue of a
    god.
  Another covers it with gold.
The first worker says to the second,
  "You have done a good job."
Another worker smooths out the metal
    with a hammer.
  Still another gives the statue its final
    shape.
The one who hammers says to the one
    who shapes,
  "You have done a good job."
Then they nail the statue down so it
    won't fall over.

⁸ The LORD says, "People of Israel, you
    are my servants.
  Family of Jacob, I have chosen you.
  You are the children of my friend
    Abraham.
⁹ I gathered you from one end of the
    earth to the other.
  From the farthest places on earth I
    brought you together.
I said, 'You are my servants.'
  I have chosen you.
  I have not turned my back on you.

10 So do not be afraid. I am with you.
    Do not be terrified. I am your God.
I will make you strong and help you.
    I will hold you safe in my hands.
    I always do what is right.

11 "All those who are angry with you will
        be put to shame.
    And they will be dishonored.
Those who oppose you will be
        destroyed.
    And they will vanish.
12 You might search for your enemies.
    But you will not find them.
Those who go to war against you
will completely disappear.
13 I am the LORD your God.
    I take hold of your right hand.
I say to you, 'Do not be afraid.
    I will help you.'
14 Family of Jacob, you are as weak as a
        worm.
    But do not be afraid.
People of Israel, there are only a few of
        you.
    But do not be afraid.
I myself will help you," announces the
        LORD.
He is the one who sets his people
        free.
He is the Holy One of Israel.
15 He says, "I will make you into a
        threshing sled.
    It will be new and sharp.
    It will have many teeth.
You will grind the mountains down and
        crush them.
    You will turn the hills into nothing
        but straw.
16 You will toss them in the air.
    A strong wind will catch them and
        blow them away.

WHAT ABOUT YOU?

Don't move a muscle. Don't even breathe. If you're very, very still, it might not know that you're lying there alone in the dark. Remember how, when you were a little kid, you'd worry about what might lurk in the closet or hide under your bed? Now that you're older, you realize how silly those fears were.

But as we grow, our fears shift from make-believe concerns to daily, real-life problems. Suddenly, it's not the monster under the bed that scares us. It's flunking a test, striking out, or dealing with bullies.

What should you do if you wind up facing a bully? Talk to someone about it. Your parents and teachers care and are willing to help. God cares too. And He promises in Isaiah 41:10: "So do not be afraid. I am with you. Do not be terrified. I am your God. I will make you strong and help you. I will hold you safe in my hands." Knowing that God is on our side makes even the scariest situations less stressful.

That's the key to conquering fear. As for the monster under your bed, he just called and asked if you could please pick up your stinky socks. They're really freaking him out.

Memorize Isaiah 41:10 and say it out loud whenever you feel afraid. Remind yourself that God is there to help. In the meantime, ask your parents what they were afraid of as children, what scares them now, and how they deal with fear.

Isa. 41:14 This verse talks about being weak. Some people in ancient times considered women to be weak. But in 2016 April Mathis bench-pressed 451 pounds, a new world record. Boy oh boy, I wish I were that "weak!" Sometimes I have trouble lifting my mailbag!

You will be glad because I will make
    that happen.
    You will praise me.
    I am the Holy One of Israel.

¹⁷ "Those who are poor and needy search
    for water.
    But there isn't any.
    Their tongues are dry because they
    are thirsty.
But I will help them. I am the LORD.
    I will not desert them.
    I am Israel's God.
¹⁸ I will make streams flow on the bare
    hilltops.
    I will make springs come up in the
    valleys.
I will turn the desert into pools of water.
    I will turn the dry and cracked
    ground into flowing springs.
¹⁹ I will make trees grow in the desert.
    I will plant cedar and acacia trees
    there.
    I will plant myrtle and olive trees
    there.
I will make juniper trees grow in the
    dry and empty desert.
    I will plant fir and cypress trees there.
²⁰ Then people will see and know
    that my powerful hand has done it.
They will consider and understand
    that I have created it.
    I am the Holy One of Israel."

²¹ The LORD says to the nations and their
    gods,
    "State your case."
Jacob's King says to them,
    "Prove your case to me.
²² Tell us, you false gods,
    what is going to happen.
Tell us what happened in the past.
    Then we can check it out
    and see if it is really true.
Or announce to us the things that will
    take place.
²³   Tell us what will happen in the days
    ahead.
    Then we will know that you are gods.
Do something. It does not matter
    whether it is good or bad.
    Then we will be terrified and filled
    with fear.
²⁴ But you false gods are less than
    nothing.
    Your actions are completely
    worthless.
    I hate it when people worship you.

²⁵ "I have stirred up a king
    who will come from the north.
He lives in the east.
    He will bring honor to me.
He walks all over rulers as if they were
    mud.
    He steps on them just as a potter
    stomps on clay.
²⁶ Which one of you false gods said those
    things
    would happen before they did?
Who told us about them
    so we could know them?
Who told us ahead of time?
    Who told us so we could say,
    'You are right'?
None of you false gods told us about
    them.
    None of you told us ahead of time.
    In fact, no one heard you say
    anything at all.
²⁷ I was the first to tell Zion.
    I said, 'Look! The people of Israel are
    coming back!'
    I sent a messenger to Jerusalem with
    the good news.
²⁸ I look, but there is no one
    among the gods that can give me
    advice.
None of them can answer

when I ask them the simplest
question.

²⁹ So they are not really gods at all.
What they do does not amount to
anything.
They are as useless as wind.

The LORD's Chosen Servant

42 "Here is my servant. I take good care
of him.
I have chosen him. I am very pleased
with him.
I will put my Spirit on him.
He will bring justice to the nations.

² He will not shout or cry out.
He will not raise his voice in the
streets.

³ He will not break a bent twig.
He will not put out a dimly burning
flame.
He will be faithful and make everything
right.

⁴ He will not grow weak or lose hope.
He will not give up until he brings
justice to the earth.
The islands will put their hope in his
teaching."

⁵ God created the heavens and stretches
them out.
The LORD spreads out the earth with
everything that grows on it.
He gives breath to its people.
He gives life to those who walk on it.
He says to his servant,

⁶ "I, the LORD, have chosen you to do
what is right.
I will take hold of your hand.
I will keep you safe.
You will put into effect my covenant
with the people of Israel.
And you will be a light for the
Gentiles.

⁷ You will open eyes that can't see.
You will set prisoners free.
Those who sit in darkness will come
out of their cells.

⁸ "I am the LORD. That is my name!
I will not let any other god share my
glory.
I will not let statues of gods share my
praise.

⁹ What I said would happen has taken
place.
Now I announce new things to you.

Before they even begin to happen,
I announce them to you."

A Song of Praise to the LORD

¹⁰ Sing a new song to the LORD.
Sing praise to him from one end of
the earth to the other.
Sing, you who sail out on the ocean.
Sing, all you creatures in it.
Sing, you islands.
Sing, all you who live there.

¹¹ Let the desert and its towns raise their
voices.
Let those who live in the settlements
of Kedar be glad.
Let the people of Sela sing for joy.
Let them shout from the tops of the
mountains.

¹² Let them give glory to the LORD.
Let them praise him in the islands.

¹³ The LORD will march out like a mighty
warrior.
He will stir up his anger like a
soldier getting ready to fight.
He will shout the battle cry.
And he will win the battle over his
enemies.

¹⁴ The LORD says, "For a long time I have
kept silent.
I have been calm and quiet.
But now, like a woman having a baby,

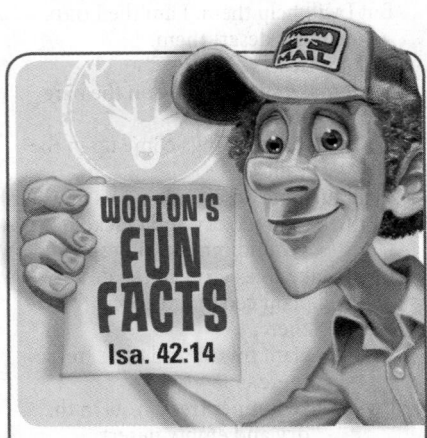

WOOTON'S FUN FACTS
Isa. 42:14

When a woman gives birth to a baby,
the process is called labor. The average
labor time is about eight hours and it's
often very painful. Ask your mom about
your birth story sometime! I know your
mom is very happy that you were born!

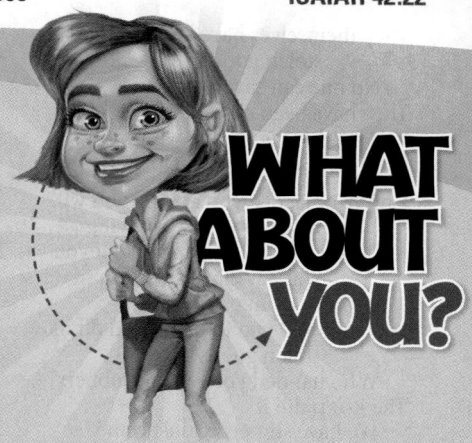

WHAT ABOUT YOU?

What kind of job do you want to have in ten years? What skills will you need to learn before you get there? Those are heavy questions, aren't they? They happen to be the ones Connie is struggling with in the Adventures in Odyssey episode "What Are You Gonna Do with Your Life?"

Connie's high school friends are beginning to think about the jobs they want, and she realizes she doesn't have a clue. Connie wonders if she'll ever know what she's supposed to do with her life.

Deciding on a future career takes time. You'll need to attempt more than just a few jobs to understand what you're good at, what you enjoy, and what type of work fits your personality. You don't have to choose your career path alone. Like Connie, you can talk through those decisions with friends.

When we ask God for wisdom, He'll show us what kinds of opportunities He has in store.

Don't worry! You have many years to learn new skills and try new jobs. For now, work hard in school and think of your classes as little tests to see what interests you. Isaiah 42:16 says that God will guide you on your road and make the rough places smooth.

Does your mom or dad work somewhere that has a "Bring Your Child to Work Day"? If so, see if you can go. Learn what your parents are passionate about. Ask a lot of questions. You never know; it might be something you're also interested in!

I cry out. I gasp and pant.
¹⁵ I will completely destroy the mountains
    and hills.
I will dry up everything that grows
    there.
I will turn rivers into dry land.
I will dry up the pools.
¹⁶ Israel is blind.
    So I will lead them along paths
    they had not known before.
I will guide them on roads they are not
    familiar with.
I will turn the darkness into light as
    they travel.
I will make the rough places smooth.
Those are the things I will do.
I will not desert my people.
¹⁷ Some people trust in statues of gods.
    They say to them, 'You are our gods.'
But they will be dishonored.
    They will be put to shame.

Israel Can't See or Hear

¹⁸ "Israel, listen to me! You can hear,
    but you do not understand.

Look to me! You can see,
    but you do not know what you are
    seeing.
¹⁹ The people of Israel serve me. But who
    is more blind than they are?
Who is more deaf than the
    messengers I send?
Who is more blind than the one who has
    promised to be faithful to me?
Who is more blind than the servant
    of the LORD?
²⁰ Israel, you have seen many things.
    But you do not pay any attention to
    me.
Your ears are open.
    But you do not listen to anything I
    say."
²¹ The LORD wanted his people to see
    how great and glorious his law is.
He wanted to show them
    that he always does what is right.
²² Enemies have carried off everything
    they own.
All my people are trapped in pits
    or hidden away in prisons.

They themselves have become like
　　stolen goods.
No one can save them.
They have been carried off.
　　And there is no one who will say,
　　　"Send them back."

²³ Family of Jacob, who among you will
　　listen to what I'm saying?
People of Israel, which one of you
　　will pay close attention in days
　　to come?
²⁴ Who allowed you to be carried off like
　　stolen goods?
　　Who handed you over to robbers?
The Lord did it!
　　We have sinned against him.
Israel, you wouldn't follow his ways.
　　You didn't obey his law.
²⁵ So he poured out his great anger on
　　you.
　　He had many of you killed in battle.
You were surrounded by flames.
　　But you didn't realize what was
　　　happening.
Many of you were destroyed.
　　But you didn't learn anything
　　　from it.

The Lord Saves Israel

43 Family of Jacob, the Lord created
　　you.
People of Israel, he formed you.
He says, "Do not be afraid.
　　I will set you free.
I will send for you by name.
　　You belong to me.
² You will pass through deep waters.
　　But I will be with you.
You will pass through the rivers.
　　But their waters will not sweep over
　　　you.
You will walk through fire.
　　But you will not be burned.
　　The flames will not harm you.
³ I am the Lord your God.
　　I am the Holy One of Israel.
　　I am the one who saves you.
I will give up Egypt to set you free.
　　I will give up Cush and Seba for you.
⁴ You are priceless to me.
　　I love you and honor you.
So I will trade other people for you.
　　I will give up other nations to save
　　　your lives.
⁵ Do not be afraid. I am with you.

I will bring your people back from
　　the east.
I will gather you from the west.
⁶ I will say to the north, 'Let them go!'
　　And I will say to the south, 'Do not
　　　hold them back.'
Bring my sons from far away.
　　Bring my daughters from the
　　　farthest places on earth.

Jason's Jargon

ISAIAH 43

A problematic trek:
Find the word *lawless*
in this chapter. A
lawless act goes against
the rules. God gave the
Israelites very clear
laws, and they ignored
them.

⁷ Bring back everyone who belongs to me.
　　I created them to bring glory to me.
　　I formed them and made them."

⁸ Lead my people into court.
　　They have eyes but can't see.
　　Bring those who have ears but can't
　　　hear.
⁹ All the nations are gathering together.
　　All of them are coming.
Which one of their gods said ahead of
　　time
　　that the people of Israel would
　　　return?
　　Which of them told us anything at
　　　all about the past?
Let them bring in their witnesses to
　　prove they were right.
　　Then others will hear them. And
　　　they will say,
　　　"What they said is true."
¹⁰ "People of Israel, you are my witnesses,"
　　announces the Lord.
　　"I have chosen you to be my servant.
I wanted you to know me and believe
　　in me.
　　I wanted you to understand that I
　　　am the one and only God.
Before me, there was no other god at
　　all.
　　And there will not be any god after
　　　me.

WHAT ABOUT YOU?

Have you ever dropped a dish or slipped and smashed an egg on the kitchen floor? We need to be careful with breakable things, don't we? And what about broken hearts? How should we treat someone who has been hurt?

While it's important to put an arm around someone who is hurting, some hurts only God can heal as He helps us grow through trials. Isaiah 43:4–5 reminds us He cares for us in the same way He loves the nation of Israel: "You are priceless to me. I love you and honor you.... Do not be afraid. I am with you." Our heavenly Father loves us, and is especially close when we're sad or lonely.

Of course, if a friend is going through a hard time, there are helpful things you can do. First, pray for your friend. Then be there to listen and talk if needed. God will do the rest. There are no magic words to fix the problem. We don't have to have all the answers. We just need to be the best friend we can be.

Being sensitive about how someone else is feeling is a skill called "empathy." One way to practice empathy is to write a short scene between two characters—one struggling with a problem and the other trying to help. By playing both parts as you write, you'll be more sensitive to how each person is feeling as he or she communicates.

11 I am the one and only Lord.
I am the only one who can save you.
12 I have made known what would
happen.
I saved you. I have told you about it.
I did this. It was not some other god
you worship.
You are my witnesses that I am
God," announces the Lord.
13 "And that is not all! I have always been
God,
and I always will be.
No one can save people from my power.
When I do something, who can
undo it?"

The Lord Is Full of Mercy but Israel Is Unfaithful

14 The Lord sets his people free.
He is the Holy One of Israel. He says,
"People of Israel, I will send an army to
Babylon to save you.
I will cause all the Babylonians to
run away.
They will try to escape in the ships
they were so proud of.
15 I am your Lord and King.

I am your Holy One.
I created you."

16 Long ago the Lord opened
a way for his people to go through
the Red Sea.
He made a path through the mighty
waters.
17 He caused Egypt to send out its chariots
and horses.
He sent its entire army to its death.
Its soldiers lay down there.
They never got up again.
They were destroyed.
They were blown out like a dimly
burning flame.
But the Lord says,
18 "Forget the things that happened in the
past.
Do not keep on thinking about them.
19 I am about to do something new.
It is beginning to happen even now.
Don't you see it coming?
I am going to make a way for you to go
through the desert.
I will make streams of water in the
dry and empty land.

20 Even wild dogs and owls honor me.
　　That is because I provide water in
　　　　the desert
　　for my people to drink.
I cause streams to flow in the dry and
　　　　empty land
　　for my chosen ones.
21 I do it for the people I made for myself.
　　I want them to sing praise to me.

22 "Family of Jacob, you have not prayed
　　　　to me as you should.
　　People of Israel, you have not worn
　　　　yourselves out for me.
23 You have not brought me sheep for
　　　　burnt offerings.
　　You have not honored me with your
　　　　sacrifices.
I have not loaded you down
　　by requiring grain offerings.
I have not made you tired
　　by requiring you to burn incense.
24 But you have not bought any sweet-
　　　　smelling cane for me.
　　You have not given me the fattest
　　　　parts
　　of your animal sacrifices.
Instead, you have loaded me down with
　　　　your sins.
　　You have made me tired with the
　　　　wrong things you have done.

25 "I am the one who wipes out your
　　　　lawless acts.
　　I do it because of who I am.
　　I will not remember your sins
　　　　anymore.
26 But let us go to court together.
　　Remind me of what you have done.
　　State your case.
　　Prove to me that you are not guilty.
27 Your father Jacob sinned.
　　The people I sent to teach you
　　　　refused to obey me.
28 So I put the high officials of your
　　　　temple to shame.
　　I let Jacob's family be totally
　　　　destroyed.
　　And I let people make fun of Israel.

The Lord Chooses Israel

44 "Family of Jacob, listen to me. You
　　　　are my servant.
　　People of Israel, I have chosen you.
2 I made you. I formed you when you
　　　　were born as a nation.

I will help you.
　　So listen to what I am saying.
Family of Jacob, do not be afraid. You
　　　　are my servant.
　　People of Israel, I have chosen you.
3 I will pour out water on the thirsty
　　　　land.
　　I will make streams flow on the dry
　　　　ground.
I will pour out my Spirit on your
　　　　children.
　　I will pour out my blessing on their
　　　　children after them.
4 They will spring up like grass in a
　　　　meadow.
　　They will grow like poplar trees near
　　　　flowing streams.
5 Some will say, 'We belong to the LORD.'
　　Others will call themselves by Jacob's
　　　　name.
Still others will write on their hands,
　　'We belong to the LORD.'
　　And they will be called by the name
　　　　of Israel.

Worship the Lord, Not False Gods

6 "I am Israel's King. I set them free.
　　I am the LORD who rules over all.
　　So listen to what I am saying.
I am the first and the last.
　　I am the one and only God.
7 Who is like me? Let him come forward
　　　　and speak boldly.
　　Let him tell me everything that has
　　　　happened
　　since I created my people long ago.
And let him tell me what has not
　　　　happened yet.
　　Let him announce ahead of time
　　　　what is going to take place.
8 Do not tremble with fear. Do not be
　　　　afraid.
　　Didn't I announce everything that
　　　　has happened?
　　Didn't I tell you about it long ago?
You are my witnesses. Is there any other
　　　　God but me?
　　No! There is no other Rock. I do not
　　　　know even one."

9 Those who make statues of gods don't
　　　　amount to anything.
　　And the statues they think so much
　　　　of are worthless.
Those who would speak up for them
　　　　are blind.

They don't know anything.
  So they will be put to shame.
¹⁰ People make statues of gods.
  But those gods can't do any good.
¹¹ People who do that will be put to shame.
  Those who make statues of gods are
    mere human beings.
Let all of them come together and state
    their case.
  They will be terrified and put to
    shame.

¹² A blacksmith gets his tool.
  He uses it to shape metal over the
    burning coals.
He uses his hammers to make a statue
    of a god.
  He forms it with his powerful arm.
He gets hungry and loses his strength.
  He doesn't drink any water.
  He gets weaker and weaker.
¹³ A carpenter measures a piece of wood
    with a line.
  He draws a pattern on it with a
    marker.
He cuts out a statue with sharp tools.
  He marks it with compasses.
He shapes it into the form of a beautiful
    human being.
  He does this so he can put it in a
    temple.
¹⁴ He cuts down a cedar tree.
  Or perhaps he takes a cypress or an
    oak tree.
It might be a tree that grew in the
    forest.
  Or it might be a pine tree he planted.
  And the rain made it grow.
¹⁵ A man gets wood from trees to burn.
  He uses some of it to warm himself.
  He starts a fire and bakes bread.
But he also uses some of it to make a
    god and worship it.
  He makes a statue of a god and bows
    down to it.
¹⁶ He burns half of the wood in the fire.
  He prepares a meal over it.
He cooks meat over it.
  He eats until he is full.
He also warms himself. He says,
  "Good! I'm getting warm.
  The fire is nice and hot."
¹⁷ From the rest of the wood he makes a
    statue.
  It becomes his god.
  He bows down and worships it.

He prays to it. He says,
  "Save me! You are my god!"
¹⁸ People like that don't even know what
    they are doing.
  Their eyes are shut so that they can't
    see the truth.
  Their minds are closed so that they
    can't understand it.
¹⁹ No one even stops to think about this.
  No one has any sense or
    understanding.
  If anyone did, they would say,
"I used half of the wood for fuel.
  I even baked bread over the fire.
  I cooked meat. Then I ate it.
Should I now make a statue of a god
    out of the wood that's left over?
Should I bow down to a block of wood?
  The Lord would hate that."
²⁰ That's as foolish as eating ashes!
  The mind of someone like that
    has led him astray.
He can't save himself.
  He can't bring himself to say,
"This thing I'm holding in my right hand
    isn't really a god at all."

²¹ The Lord says, "Family of Jacob,
    remember these things.
  People of Israel, you are my servant.
I have made you. You are my servant.
  Israel, I will not forget you.
²² I will sweep your sins away as if they
    were a cloud.
  I will blow them away as if they were
    the morning mist.
Return to me.
  Then I will set you free."

²³ Sing for joy, you heavens!
  The Lord does wonderful things.
Shout out loud, you earth!
  Burst into song, you mountains!
  Sing, you forests and all your trees!
The Lord sets the family of Jacob free.
  He shows his glory in Israel.

People Will Live in Jerusalem Again

²⁴ The Lord says,
  "People of Israel, I set you free.
  I formed you when you were born as
    a nation.

"I am the Lord. I am the Maker of
    everything.
  I alone stretch out the heavens.
  I spread out the earth by myself.

25 "Some prophets are not really prophets
at all.
I show that their signs are fake.
I make those who practice evil
magic look foolish.
I destroy the learning of those who
think they are wise.
Their knowledge does not make any
sense at all.
26 I make the words of my servants the
prophets come true.
I carry out what my messengers say
will happen.

"I say about Jerusalem,
'My people will live there again.'
I say about the towns of Judah,
'They will be rebuilt.'
I say about their broken-down
buildings,
'I will make them like new again.'
27 I say to the deep waters,
'Dry up. Let your streams become dry.'
28 I say about Cyrus,
'He is my shepherd.
He will accomplish everything I
want him to.
He will say about Jerusalem,
"Let it be rebuilt."
And he will say about the temple,
"Let its foundations be laid."'

45 "Cyrus is my anointed king.
I take hold of his right hand.
I give him the power
to bring nations under his control.
I help him strip kings of their power
to go to war against him.
I break city gates open so he can go
through them.
I say to him,
2 'I will march out ahead of you.
I will make the mountains level.
I will break down bronze gates.
I will cut through their heavy iron
bars.
3 I will give you treasures that are hidden
away.
I will give you riches that are stored
up in secret places.
Then you will know that I am the LORD.
I am the God of Israel.
I am sending for you by name.
4 Cyrus, I am sending for you by name.
I am doing it for the good of the
family of Jacob.

They are my servant.
I am doing it for Israel.
They are my chosen people.
You do not know anything about me.
But I am giving you a title of honor.
5 I am the LORD. There is no other
LORD.
I am the one and only God.
You do not know anything about me.
But I will make you strong.
6 Then people will know there is no God
but me.
Everyone from where the sun rises
in the east
to where it sets in the west will
know it.
I am the LORD.
There is no other LORD.
7 I cause light to shine. I also create
darkness.
I bring good times. I also create hard
times.
I do all these things. I am the LORD.

8 "'Rain down my godliness, you heavens
above.
Let the clouds shower it down.
Let the earth open wide to receive it.
Let freedom spring to life.
Let godliness grow richly along with it.
I have created all these things.
I am the LORD.'"

9 How terrible it will be for anyone who
argues with their Maker!
They are like a broken piece of
pottery lying on the ground.
Does clay say to a potter,
"What are you making?"
Does a pot say,
"The potter doesn't have any skill"?
10 How terrible it will be for anyone who
says to a father,
"Why did you give me life?"
How terrible for anyone who says to a
mother,
"Why have you brought me into the
world?"

11 The LORD is the Holy One of Israel.
He made them.
He says to them,
"Are you asking me about what will
happen to my children?
Are you telling me what I should
do with what my hands have
made?

¹² I made the earth.
  I created human beings to live there.
My own hands spread out the heavens.
  I put all the stars in their places.
¹³ I will stir up Cyrus and help him win
      his battles.
  I will make all his roads straight.
He will rebuild Jerusalem.
  My people have been taken away
      from their country.
  But he will set them free.
I will not pay him to do it.
  He will not receive a reward for it,"
  says the LORD who rules over all.

¹⁴The LORD says to the people of Jerusalem,

  "You will get everything Egypt
      produces.
  You will receive everything the
      people of Cush
and the tall Sabeans get in trade.
  All of it will belong to you.
And all these people will walk behind
      you as slaves.
  They will be put in chains and come
      over to you.
They will bow down to you.
  They will admit,
'God is with you.
  There is no other God.'"

¹⁵ You are a God who has been hiding
      yourself.
  You are the God of Israel. You save
      us.
¹⁶ All those who make statues of gods will
      be put to shame.
  They will be dishonored.
They will be led away in shame
      together.
¹⁷ But the LORD will save Israel.
  He will save them forever.
They will never be put to shame or
      dishonored.
  That will be true for all time to come.

¹⁸ The LORD created the heavens.
  He is God.
He formed the earth and made it.
  He set it firmly in place.
He didn't create it to be empty.
  Instead, he formed it for people to
      live on.
He says, "I am the LORD.
  There is no other LORD.

¹⁹ I have not spoken in secret.
  I have not spoken from a dark place.
I have not said to Jacob's people,
  'It is useless to look for me.'
I am the LORD. I always speak the truth.
  I always say what is right.

²⁰ "Come together, you people of the
      nations
  who escaped from Babylon.
  Gather together and come into court.
Only people who do not know anything
  would carry around gods that are
      made out of wood.
  They pray to false gods that can't
      save them.
²¹ Tell me what will happen. State your
      case.
  Talk it over together.
Who spoke long ago about what would
      happen?
  Who said it a long time ago?
I did. I am the LORD.
  I am the one and only God.
I always do what is right.
  I am the one who saves.
  There is no God but me.

²² "All you who live anywhere on earth,
  turn to me and be saved.
  I am God. There is no other God.
²³ I have made a promise in my own
      name.
  I have spoken with complete
      honesty.
  I will not take back a single word. I
      said,
'Everyone will kneel down to me.
  Everyone's mouth will make
      promises in my name.'
²⁴ They will say, 'The LORD is the only one
      who can save us.
  Only he can make us strong.'"
All those who have been angry with the
      LORD will come to him.
  And they will be put to shame.
²⁵ But the LORD will save all the people of
      Israel.
  And so they will boast about the
      LORD.

The False Gods of Babylon

46 The gods named Bel and Nebo are
      brought down in shame.
  The statues of them are being carried
      away on the backs of animals.

They used to be carried around by the
    people who worshiped them.
But now they've become a heavy
    load for tired animals.
² The gods named Bel and Nebo are
    brought down in shame
    together.
They aren't able to save their own
    statues.
They themselves are carried off as
    prisoners.

³ The Lord says, "Family of Jacob, listen
    to me.
Pay attention, you people of Israel
    who are left alive.
I have taken good care of you since
    your life began.
I have carried you since you were
    born as a nation.
⁴ I will continue to carry you even when
    you are old.
I will take good care of you even
    when your hair is gray.
I have made you, and I will carry you.
I will take care of you, and I will save
    you.
I am the Lord.

⁵ "Who will you compare me with?
    Who is equal to me?
What am I like?
    Who can you compare me with?
⁶ Some people pour out gold from their
    bags.
They weigh out silver on the scales.
They hire someone who works with
    gold to make it into a god.
They bow down to it and worship it.
⁷ They lift it up on their shoulders and
    carry it.
They set it up in its place, and there
    it stands.
It can't move from that spot.
Someone might cry out to it.
    But it does not answer.
It can't save them from their
    troubles.
⁸ So remember this, you who refuse to
    obey me.
Keep it in your minds and hearts.

⁹ "Remember what happened in the past.
    Think about what took place long
    ago.
I am God. There is no other God.
I am God. There is no one like me.

¹⁰ Before something even happens, I
    announce how it will end.
In fact, from times long ago I
    announced what was still to
    come.
I say, 'My plan will succeed.
    I will do anything I want to do.'
¹¹ I will send for a man from the east to
    carry out my plan.
From a land far away, he will come
    like a bird that kills its food.
I will bring about what I have said.
    I will do what I have planned.
¹² Listen to me, you stubborn people.
Pay attention, you who now refuse
    to do what I have said is right.
¹³ The time is almost here for me to make
    everything right.
It is not far away.
The time for me to save you will not
    be put off.
I will save the city of Zion.
    I will bring honor to Israel.

Babylon Will Fall

47 "City of Babylon,
    go down and sit in the dust.
Leave your throne and sit on the
    ground.
Queen city of the Babylonians,
    your life will not be comfortable
    and easy anymore.
² Get millstones and grind some flour
    like a female slave.
Take off your veil.
Lift up your skirts. Make your legs bare.
Wade through the streams.
³ Everyone will see your naked body.
    Everyone will see your shame.
I will pay you back for what you did.
    I will not spare any of your people."

⁴ The one who sets us free is the Holy
    One of Israel.
His name is the Lord Who Rules
    Over All.

⁵ The Lord says, "Queen city of the
    Babylonians,
go into a dark prison. Sit there
    quietly.
You will not be called
    the queen of kingdoms anymore.
⁶ I was angry with my people.
I treated them as if they did not
    belong to me.

I handed them over to you.
　　And you did not show them any pity.
You even placed heavy loads on their
　　old people.
7　　You said, 'I am queen forever!'
But you did not think about what you
　　were doing.
　　You did not consider how things
　　might turn out.

8 "So listen, you who love pleasure.
　　You think you are safe and secure.
You say to yourself,
　　'I am like a god.
　　No one is greater than I am.
I'll never be a widow.
　　And my children will never be taken
　　away from me.'
9 But both of these things will happen to
　　you in a moment.
　　They will take place on a single day.
You will lose your children.
　　And you will become a widow.
That is what will happen to you.
　　All your evil magic
　　and powerful spells will not save you.
10 You have felt secure in your evil ways.
　　You have said, 'No one sees what I'm
　　doing.'
Your wisdom and knowledge lead you
　　astray.
　　You say to yourself,
　　'I am like a god. No one is greater
　　than I am.'
11 So horrible trouble will come on you.
　　You will not know how to use your
　　evil magic to make it go away.
Great trouble will fall on you.
　　No amount of money can keep it
　　away.
Something terrible will happen to you
　　all at once.
　　You will not see it coming ahead of
　　time.

12 "So keep on casting your magic spells.
　　Keep on practicing your evil magic.
You have been doing those things
　　ever since you were a child.
Perhaps they will help you.
　　Maybe they will scare your enemies
　　away.
13 All the advice you have received
　　has only worn you out!
　　Let those who study the heavens
　　come forward.

They claim to know what is going to
　　happen
　　by watching the stars every month.
So let them save you from the trouble
　　that is coming on you.
14 They are just like straw.
　　Fire will burn them up.
They can't even save themselves
　　from the powerful flames.
These are not like coals that can warm
　　anyone.
　　This is not like a fire to sit by.
15 They can't do you any good.
　　You have done business with them
　　ever since you were a child.
You have always asked them for
　　advice.
All of them are bewildered and
　　continue in their own ways.
　　None of them can save you."

Israel Is Stubborn

48 People of Jacob, listen to me.
　　You are called by the name of Israel.
　　You come from the family line of
　　Judah.
You make promises in the name of the
　　Lord.
　　You pray to Israel's God.
But you aren't honest.
　　You don't mean what you say.
2 You call yourselves citizens of the holy
　　city of Jerusalem.
　　You say you depend on Israel's God.
His name is the Lord Who Rules
　　Over All. He says,
3 "Long ago I told you ahead of time
　　what would happen.
　　I announced it and made it known.
Then all of a sudden I acted.
　　And those things took place.
4 I knew how stubborn you were.
　　Your neck muscles were as
　　unbending as iron.
　　Your forehead was as hard as bronze.
5 So I told you those things long ago.
　　Before they happened I announced
　　them to you.
I did it so you would not be able to say,
　　'My statues of gods did them.
　　My wooden and metal gods made
　　them happen.'
6 You have heard me tell you these
　　things.
　　Think about all of them.

Won't you admit they have taken
    place?

"From now on I will tell you about new
    things that will happen.
I have not made them known to you
    before.
7 These things are taking place right now.
    They did not happen long ago.
You have not heard of them before
    today.
So you can't say,
    'Oh, yes. I already knew about
      them.'
8 You have not heard or understood what
    I said.
Your ears have been plugged up for a
    long time.
I knew very well that you would turn
    against me.
From the day you were born, you
    have refused to obey me.
9 For the honor of my own name I wait
    to show my anger.
I hold it back from you so people
    will continue to praise me.
I do not want to destroy you
    completely.
10 I have tested you in the furnace of
    suffering.
I have tried to make you pure.
But I did not use as much heat as it
    takes to make silver pure.
11 I tried to purify you for my own
    honor.
I did it for the honor of my name.
How can I let myself be dishonored?
I will not give up my glory to any
    other god.

Israel Is Set Free

12 "Family of Jacob, listen to me.
    People of Israel, pay attention.
I have chosen you.
I am the first and the last.
    I am the LORD.
13 With my own hand I laid the
    foundations of the earth.
With my right hand I spread out the
    heavens.
When I send for them,
    they come and stand ready to obey
    me.
14 "People of Israel, come together and
    listen to me.

What other god has said ahead of
    time that certain things would
    happen?
I have chosen Cyrus.
He will carry out my plans against
    Babylon.
He will use his power against the
    Babylonians.
15 I myself have spoken.
I have chosen him to carry out my
    purpose.
I will bring him to Babylon.
He will succeed in what I tell him
    to do.

16 "Come close and listen to me.

"From the first time I said Cyrus was
    coming,
I did not do it in secret.
When he comes, I will be there."

The LORD and King has filled me with
    his Spirit.
People of Israel, he has sent me to
    you.

17 The LORD is the Holy One of Israel.
He sets his people free. He says to
    them,
"I am the LORD your God.
I teach you what is best for you.
I direct you in the way you should
    go.
18 I wish you would pay attention to my
    commands.
If you did, peace would flow over
    you like a river.
Godliness would sweep over you like
    the waves of the ocean.
19 Your family would be like the sand.
Your children after you would be as
    many as the grains of sand by
    the sea.
It would be impossible to count
    them.
I would always accept the members of
    your family line.
They would never disappear or be
    destroyed."

20 People of Israel, leave Babylon!
Hurry up and get away from the
    Babylonians!
Here is what I want you to announce.
Make it known with shouts of joy.
Send the news out from one end of the
    earth to the other.

Say, "The LORD has set free his
    servant Jacob."
21 They didn't get thirsty when he led
    them through the deserts.
    He made water flow out of the rock
        for them.
    He broke the rock open,
        and water came out of it.

22 "There is no peace for those who are
    evil," says the LORD.

The Servant of the LORD

49 People who live on the islands, listen
    to me.
    Pay attention, you nations far away.
    Before I was born the LORD chose me
        to serve him.
    Before I was born the LORD spoke
        my name.
2 He made my words like a sharp sword.
    He hid me in the palm of his hand.
    He made me into a sharpened arrow.
    He took good care of me and kept
        me safe.
3 He said to me, "You are my true servant
    Israel.
    I will show my glory through you."
4 But I said, "In spite of my hard work,
    I feel as if I haven't accomplished
        anything.
    I've used up all my strength.
    It seems as if everything I've done is
        worthless.
    But the LORD will give me what I
        should receive.
    My God will reward me."

5 The LORD formed me in my mother's
    body to be his servant.
    He wanted me to bring the family of
        Jacob back to him.
    He wanted me to gather the people of
        Israel to himself.
    The LORD will honor me.
    My God will give me strength.

6 Here is what the LORD says to me.

"It is not enough for you as my servant
    to bring the tribes of Jacob back to
        their land.
It is not enough for you to bring back
    the people of Israel I have kept
        alive.
I will also make you a light for the
    Gentiles.

Then you will make it possible for
    the whole world to be saved."

7 The LORD sets his people free.
    He is the Holy One of Israel.
    He speaks to his servant, who is looked
        down on and hated by the
        nations.
    He speaks to the servant of rulers.
    He says to him,
    "Kings will see you and stand up to
        honor you.
    Princes will see you and bow down
        to show you their respect.
    I am the LORD. I am faithful.
    I am the Holy One of Israel.
    I have chosen you."

Israel Is Brought Back to Their Land

8 The LORD says to his servant,

"When it is time to have mercy on you,
    I will answer your prayers.
    When it is time to save you, I will
        help you.
    I will keep you safe.
    You will put into effect my covenant
        with the people of Israel.
    Then their land will be made like new
        again.
    Each tribe will be sent back to its
        territory that was left empty.
9 I want you to say to the prisoners,
    'Come out.'
    Tell those who are in their dark cells,
        'You are free!'

"On their way home they will eat beside
    the roads.
    They will find plenty to eat on every
        bare hill.
10 They will not get hungry or thirsty.
    The heat from the desert sun will not
        beat down on them.
    The God who has tender love for them
        will guide them.
    Like a shepherd, he will lead them
        beside springs of water.
11 I will make roads across the mountains.
    I will build wide roads for my
        people.
12 They will come from far away.
    Some of them will come from the
        north.
    Others will come from the west.
    Still others will come from Aswan in
        the south."

Isa. 49:15 My mom left me at the barber once, but I wasn't scared because the barber was our butler, Bradford, who used to cut my hair in our living room. God knows all, even more than moms know!

¹³ Shout for joy, you heavens!
　　Be glad, you earth!
　　Burst into song, you mountains!
　　The LORD will comfort his people.
　　He will show his tender love to those
　　　　who are suffering.

¹⁴ But the city of Zion said, "The LORD
　　　　has deserted me.
　　The Lord has forgotten me."

¹⁵ The LORD answers, "Can a mother
　　　　forget the baby
　　who is nursing at her breast?
　　Can she stop having tender love
　　　　for the child who was born to her?
　　She might forget her child.
　　But I will not forget you.
¹⁶ I have written your name on the palms
　　　　of my hands.
　　Your walls are never out of my sight.
¹⁷ Your people will hurry back.
　　Those who destroyed you so
　　　　completely will leave you.
¹⁸ Look up. Look all around you.
　　All your people are getting together
　　　　to come back to you.
　　You can be sure that I live,"
　　　　announces the LORD.
　　"And you can be just as sure that your
　　　　people
　　will be like decorations you will
　　　　wear.
　　Like a bride, you will wear them
　　　　proudly.

¹⁹ "Zion, you were destroyed. Your land
　　　　was left empty.
　　It was turned into a dry and empty
　　　　desert.
　　But now you will be too small to hold
　　　　all your people.
　　And those who destroyed you will
　　　　be far away.
²⁰ The children born during your time of
　　　　sorrow
　　will speak to you. They will say,
　　'This city is too small for us.
　　Give us more space to live in.'
²¹ Then you will say to yourself,
　　　　'Whose children are these?
　　I lost my children.
　　And I couldn't have any more.
　　My children were taken far away from
　　　　me.
　　And no one wanted them.
　　Who brought these children up?
　　I was left all alone.
　　So where have these children come
　　　　from?'"

²²The LORD and King continues,

"I will call out to the nations.
　　I will give a signal to them.
　　They will bring back your sons in their
　　　　arms.
　　They will carry your daughters on
　　　　their hips.
²³ Their kings will become like fathers to
　　　　you.
　　Their queens will be like mothers
　　　　who nurse you.
　　They will bow down to you with their
　　　　faces toward the ground.
　　They will kiss the dust at your feet to
　　　　show you their respect.
　　Then you will know that I am the LORD.
　　Those who put their hope in me will
　　　　not be ashamed."

²⁴ Can goods that were stolen by soldiers
　　　　be taken away from them?
　　Can prisoners be set free from the
　　　　powerful Babylonians?

²⁵"Yes, they can," the LORD answers.

"Prisoners will be taken away from
　　　　soldiers.
　　Stolen goods will be taken back from
　　　　the powerful Babylonians.
　　Zion, I will fight against those who fight
　　　　against you.

And I will save your people.
26 I will make those who treat you badly
    eat the flesh of others.
They will drink blood and get drunk
    on it as if it were wine.
Then everyone on earth will know
    that I am the one who saves you.
I am the Lord. I set you free.
    I am the Mighty One of Jacob."

Israel Sins but the Lord's Servant Obeys

50 The Lord says to the people in Jerusalem,

"Do you think I divorced your people
    who lived before you?
Is that why I sent them away?
If it is, show me the letter of divorce.
    I did not sell you into slavery to pay
    someone I owe.
You were sold because you sinned
    against me.
Your people were sent away because
    of their lawless acts.
2 When I came to save you, why didn't
    anyone welcome me?
    When I called out to you, why didn't
    anyone answer me?
Wasn't I powerful enough to set you free?
Wasn't I strong enough to save you?
I dry up the sea with a single command.
I turn rivers into a desert.
Then fish rot because they do not have
    any water.
    They die because they are thirsty.
3 I make the sky turn dark.
    It looks as if it's dressed in clothing
    sad people wear."

4 The Lord and King has taught me what
    to say.
He has taught me how to help those
    who are tired.
He wakes me up every morning.
He makes me want to listen like a
    good student.
5 The Lord and King has unplugged my
    ears.
I've always obeyed him.
I haven't turned away from him.
6 I let my enemies beat me on my bare
    back.
I let them pull the hair out of my
    beard.
I didn't turn my face away

when they made fun of me and spit
    on me.
7 The Lord and King helps me.
He won't let me be dishonored.
So I've made up my mind to keep on
    serving him.
I know he won't let me be put to
    shame.
8 He is near. He will prove I haven't done
    anything wrong.
So who will bring charges against
    me?
Let's face each other in court!
Who can bring charges against me?
    Let him come and face me!
9 The Lord and King helps me.
    So who will judge me?
My enemies will be like clothes that
    moths have eaten up.
My enemies will disappear.

10 Does anyone among you have respect
    for the Lord?
Does anyone obey the message of
    the Lord's servant?
Let the person who walks in the dark
    trust in the Lord.
Let the one who doesn't have any light
    to guide them
    depend on their God.
11 But all you sinners who light fires
    should go ahead and walk in their
    light.
You who carry flaming torches
    should walk in their light.
Here's what I'm going to do to you.
    I'll make you lie down in great pain.

The Lord's Saving Power for Zion Lasts Forever

51 The Lord says, "Listen to me, you
    who want to do what is right.
Pay attention, you who look to me.
Consider the rock you were cut out of.
    Think about the rock pit you were
    dug from.
2 Consider Abraham. He is the father of
    your people.
Think about Sarah. She is your
    mother.
When I chose Abraham, he did not
    have any children.
But I blessed him and gave him
    many of them.
3 You can be sure that I will comfort
    Zion's people.

I will look with loving concern on all
their destroyed buildings.
I will make their deserts like Eden.
I will make their dry and empty land
like the garden of the LORD.
Joy and gladness will be there.
People will sing and give thanks to
me.

4 "Listen to me, my people.
Pay attention, my nation.
My instruction will go out to the
nations.
I make everything right.
That will be a guiding light for them.
5 The time for me to set you free is near.
I will soon save you.
My powerful arm will make
everything right among the
nations.
The islands will put their hope in me.
They will wait for my powerful arm
to act.
6 Look up toward the heavens.
Then look at the earth.
The heavens will vanish like smoke.
The earth will wear out like clothes.
Those who live there will die like
flies.
But I will save you forever.
My saving power will never end.

7 "Listen to me, you who know what is
right.
Pay attention, you who have taken
my instruction to heart.
Do not be afraid when mere human
beings make fun of you.
Do not be terrified when they laugh
at you.
8 They will be like clothes that moths
have eaten up.
They will be like wool that worms
have chewed up.
But my saving power will last forever.
I will save you for all time to come."

9 Wake up, arm of the LORD! Wake up!
Dress yourself with strength as if it
were your clothes!
Wake up, just as you did in the past.
Wake up, as you did long ago.
Didn't you cut Rahab to pieces?
Didn't you stab that sea monster to
death?
10 Didn't you dry up the Red Sea?
Didn't you dry up those deep waters?

You made a road on the bottom of that
sea.
Then those who were set free went
across.
11 Those the LORD has saved will return to
their land.
They will sing as they enter the city
of Zion.
Joy that lasts forever will be like
beautiful crowns on their
heads.
They will be filled with gladness and
joy.
Sorrow and sighing will be gone.

12 The LORD says to his people,
"I comfort you because of who I
am.
Why are you afraid of mere human
beings?
They are like grass that dries up.
13 How can you forget me? I made you.
I stretch out the heavens.
I lay the foundations of the earth.
Why are you terrified every day?
Is it because those who are angry
with you are crushing you?
Is it because they are trying to
destroy you?
Their anger can't harm you anymore.
14   You prisoners who are so afraid will
soon be set free.
You will not die in your prison cells.
You will not go without food.
15 I am the LORD your God.
I stir up the ocean. I make its waves
roar.
My name is the LORD Who Rules
Over All.
16 I have put my words in your mouth.
I have kept you safe in the palm of
my hand.
I set the heavens in place.
I laid the foundations of the earth.
I say to Zion, 'You are my people.'"

The Cup of the LORD's Great Anger
17 Wake up, Jerusalem!
Wake up! Get up!
The LORD has handed you the cup of
his great anger.
And you have drunk from it.
That cup makes people unsteady on
their feet.
And you have drunk from it to the
very last drop.

¹⁸ Among all the children who were born
to you
there was none to guide you.
Among all the children you brought up
there was none to lead you by the
hand.
¹⁹ Nothing but trouble has come to you.
You have been wiped out and
destroyed.
And you have suffered hunger and
war.
No one feels sorry for you.
No one can comfort you.
²⁰ Your children have fainted.
They lie helpless at every street
corner.
They are like antelope that have been
caught in a net.
They have felt the full force of the
Lord's great anger.
Jerusalem, your God had to warn
them strongly.

²¹ So listen to me, you suffering people of
Jerusalem.
You have been made drunk, but not
by drinking wine.
²² Your Lord and King speaks.
He is your God.
He stands up for his people. He says,
"I have taken from you the cup of
my great anger.
It made you unsteady on your feet.
But you will never drink
from that cup again.
²³ Instead, I will give it to those who made
you suffer.
They said to you,
'Fall down flat on the ground.
Then we can walk all over you.'
And that is exactly what you did.
You made your back like a street to
be walked on."

52 Wake up! Zion, wake up!
Dress yourself with strength as if it
were your clothes.
Holy city of Jerusalem,
put on your clothes of glory.
Those who haven't been circumcised
will never enter you again.
Neither will those who are "unclean."
² Get up, Jerusalem! Shake off your dust.
Take your place on your throne.
Captured people of Zion,
remove the chains from your neck.

³ The Lord says,
"When you were sold as slaves, no one
paid anything for you.
Now no one will pay any money to
set you free."

⁴ The Lord and King continues,
"Long ago my people went down to
Egypt.
They lived there for a while.
Later, Assyria crushed them without
any reason.

⁵ "Now look at what has happened to
them," announces the Lord.

"Once again my people have been taken
away.
And no one paid anything for them.
Those who rule over them brag about
it,"
announces the Lord.
"All day long without stopping,
people speak evil things against my
name.
⁶ So the day will come when my people
will really know the meaning
of my name.
They will know what kind of God
I am.
They will know that I told them ahead
of time they would return to
their land.
They will know that it was I."

⁷ What a beautiful sight it is
to see messengers coming with good
news!
How beautiful to see them coming
down from the mountains
with a message about peace!
How wonderful it is when they bring
the good news
that we are saved!
How wonderful when they say to Zion,
"Your God rules!"
⁸ Listen! Those on guard duty are
shouting out the message.
With their own eyes
they see the Lord returning to Zion.
So they shout for joy.
⁹ Burst into songs of joy together,
you broken-down buildings in
Jerusalem.
The Lord has comforted his people.
He has set Jerusalem free.

¹⁰ The LORD will use the power of his holy
    arm to save his people.
    All the nations will see him do it.
    Everyone from one end of the earth
    to the other will see it.

¹¹ You who carry the objects that belong
    to the LORD's temple, leave
    Babylon!
    Leave it! Get out of there!
Don't touch anything that isn't pure and
    "clean."
    Come out of Babylon and be pure.
¹² But this time you won't have to leave in
    a hurry.
    You won't have to rush away.
The LORD will go ahead of you and lead
    you.
    The God of Israel will follow behind
    you and guard you.

The Suffering and Glory of the LORD's Servant

¹³ The LORD says, "My servant will act
    wisely and accomplish his
    task.
    He will be highly honored. He will
    be greatly respected.
¹⁴ Many people were shocked when they
    saw him.
    He was so scarred that he no longer
    looked like a person.
    His body was so twisted that he did
    not look like a human being
    anymore.
¹⁵ But many nations will be surprised
    when they see what he has
    done.
    Kings will be so amazed that
    they will not be able to say
    anything.
They will understand things they were
    never told.
    They will know the meaning of
    things they never heard."

53 Who has believed what we've been
    saying?
    Who has seen the LORD's saving
    power?
² His servant grew up like a tender young
    plant.
    He grew like a root coming up out of
    dry ground.
He didn't have any beauty or majesty
    that made us notice him.

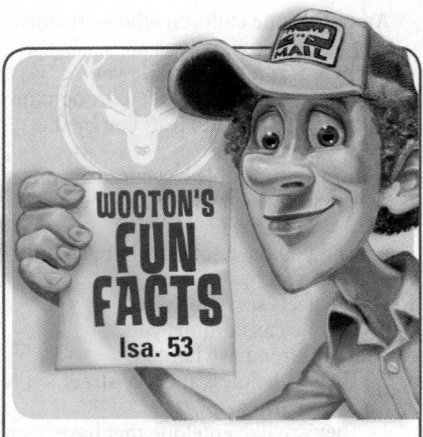

WOOTON'S FUN FACTS
Isa. 53

This chapter is a long prophecy about Jesus.
(Check out verses 7:14 and 9:6 too.) A phrase
in verse 6—from the King James Bible—
is part of a chorus for Handel's *Messiah*,
the most performed musical work of all
time. That phrase is "all we like sheep."

There wasn't anything special about
    the way he looked that drew
    us to him.
³ People looked down on him. They
    didn't accept him.
    He knew all about pain and suffering.
He was like someone people turn their
    faces away from.
    We looked down on him. We didn't
    have any respect for him.

⁴ He suffered the things we should have
    suffered.
    He took on himself the pain that
    should have been ours.
But we thought God was punishing
    him.
    We thought God was wounding him
    and making him suffer.
⁵ But the servant was pierced because we
    had sinned.
    He was crushed because we had
    done what was evil.
He was punished to make us whole
    again.
    His wounds have healed us.
⁶ All of us are like sheep. We have
    wandered away from God.
    All of us have turned to our own
    way.
And the LORD has placed on his servant
    the sins of all of us.

[7] He was treated badly and made to suffer.
  But he didn't open his mouth.
He was led away like a lamb to be killed.
  Sheep are silent while their wool is
    being cut off.
  In the same way, he didn't open his
    mouth.
[8] He was arrested and sentenced to death.
  Then he was taken away.
  He was cut off from this life.
He was punished for the sins of my
    people.
  Who among those who were living
    at that time
  tried to stop what was happening?
[9] He was given a grave with those who
    were evil.
  But his body was buried in the tomb
    of a rich man.
  He was killed even though he hadn't
    harmed anyone.
  And he had never lied to anyone.

[10] The LORD says, "It was my plan to crush
    him
  and cause him to suffer.
  I made his life an offering to pay for
    sin.
But he will see all his children after him.
  In fact, he will continue to live.
  My plan will be brought about
    through him.
[11] After he has suffered, he will see the
    light of life.
  And he will be satisfied.
My godly servant will make many
    people godly
  because of what he will accomplish.
  He will be punished for their sins.
[12] So I will give him a place of honor
    among those who are great.
  He will be rewarded just like others
    who win the battle.
That's because he was willing to give his
    life as a sacrifice.
  He was counted among those who
    had committed crimes.
He took the sins of many people on
    himself.
  And he gave his life for those who
    had done what is wrong."

Jerusalem Will Be Glorious

54 "Jerusalem, sing!
  You are now like a woman who
    never had a child.

Burst into song! Shout for joy!
  You who have never had labor pains,
you are now all alone.
  But you will have more children
    than a woman who still has a
    husband,"
says the LORD.
[2] "Make a large area for your tent.
  Spread out its curtains.
  Go ahead and make your tent wider.
Make its ropes longer.
  Drive the stakes down deeper.
[3] You will spread out to the right and the
    left.
  Your children after you will drive out
    the nations that are now living
    in your land.
  They will make their homes in the
    deserted cities of those nations.

[4] "Do not be afraid. You will not be put
    to shame anymore.
  Do not be afraid of being
    dishonored.
  People will no longer make fun of
    you.
You will forget the time when you
    suffered as slaves in Egypt.
You will no longer remember the
    shame
  of being a widow in Babylon.
[5] I made you. I am now your husband.
  My name is the LORD Who Rules
    Over All.
I am the Holy One of Israel.
  I have set you free.
  I am the God of the whole earth.
[6] You were like a wife who was deserted.
  And her heart was broken.
You were like a wife who married
    young.
  And her husband sent her away.
  But now I am calling you to come
    back," says your God.
[7] "For a brief moment I left you.
  But because I love you so much, I
    will bring you back.
[8] For a moment I turned my face away
    from you.
  I was very angry with you.
But I will show you my loving concern.
  My faithful love will continue
    forever,"
says the LORD. He is the one who set
    you free.

9 "During Noah's time I made a promise.
I said I would never cover the earth
with water again.
In the same way, I have promised not to
be angry with you.
I will never punish you again.
10 The mountains might shake.
The hills might be removed.
But my faithful love for you will never
be shaken.
And my covenant that promises
peace to you will never be
removed,"
says the LORD. He shows you his
loving concern.

11 "Suffering city, you have been beaten by
storms.
You have not been comforted.
I will rebuild you with turquoise stones.
I will rebuild your foundations with
lapis lazuli.
12 I will line the top of your city wall with
rubies.
I will make your gates out of
gleaming jewels.
And I will make all your walls out of
precious stones.
13 I will teach all your children.
And they will enjoy great peace.
14 When you do what is right,
you will be made secure.
Your leaders will not be mean to you.
You will not have anything to be
afraid of.
You will not be terrified anymore.
Terror will not come near you.
15 People might attack you. But I will not
be the cause of it.
Those who attack you will give
themselves up to you.

16 "I created blacksmiths.
They fan the coals into flames of fire.
They make weapons that are fit for their
work.
I also created those who destroy
others.
17 But no weapon used against you will
succeed.
People might bring charges against you.
But you will prove that they are
wrong.
Those are the things I do for my servants.
I make everything right for them,"
announces the LORD.

The LORD Invites Thirsty People to Come to Him

55 "Come, all you who are thirsty.
Come and drink the water I offer to
you.
You who do not have any money, come.
Buy and eat the grain I give you.
Come and buy wine and milk.
You will not have to pay anything
for it.
2 Why spend money on what is not food?
Why work for what does not satisfy
you?
Listen carefully to me.
Then you will eat what is good.
You will enjoy the richest food
there is.
3 Listen and come to me.
Pay attention to me.
Then you will live.
I will make a covenant with you that
will last forever.
I will give you my faithful love.
I promised it to David.
4 I made him a witness to the nations.
He became a ruler and commander
over them.
5 You too will send for nations you do
not know.
Even though you do not know them,
they will come running to you.
That is what I will do. I am the LORD
your God.
I am the Holy One of Israel.
I have honored you."

6 Turn to the LORD before it's too late.
Call out to him while he's still ready
to help you.
7 Let those who are evil stop doing evil
things.
And let them quit thinking evil
thoughts.
Let them turn to the LORD.
The LORD will show them his tender
love.
Let them turn to our God.
He is always ready to forgive.

8 "My thoughts are not like your
thoughts.
And your ways are not like my ways,"
announces the LORD.
9 "The heavens are higher than the earth.
And my ways are higher than your
ways.

WHAT ABOUT YOU?

Maybe you've stepped off the side of a swimming pool, hoping to walk on water . . . and sank like a rock. Or you had poison ivy and prayed that God would take it away . . . but you just kept itching. Have you ever gotten one sad little slice of pizza from the school cafeteria and prayed that God would multiply it as He did with the loaves and fishes . . . and nothing happened?

Sometimes it can seem as though God did impressive miracles only way back in Bible times. But think about the little miracles we so often take for granted.

Perhaps you didn't walk across your swimming pool. But God did create refreshing water for us to drink and swim in. He might not have healed your poison ivy immediately, but He gave us doctors and helped people invent lotions that make poison ivy more bearable as it heals. And even though God didn't turn that wimpy cheese slice into a whole pizza, He provides the food we need every day. Read Isaiah 55:10 and be reminded that God is working behind the scenes in ways we don't realize.

Does God ever do anything "big" anymore? He does. Look for those events. But don't lose sight of the run-of-the-mill miracles happening all around you.

Ask a few adults you know if they can tell you of a time God answered their prayers. It's great to be reminded of all that God is doing in our very midst.

My thoughts are higher than your
thoughts.
¹⁰ The rain and the snow
come down from the sky.
They do not return to it
without watering the earth.
They make plants come up and grow.
The plants produce seeds for
farmers.
They also produce food for people
to eat.
¹¹ The words I speak are like that.
They will not return to me without
producing results.
They will accomplish what I want them
to.
They will do exactly what I sent
them to do.
¹² "My people, you will go out of Babylon
with joy.
You will be led out of it in peace.
The mountains and hills
will burst into song as you go.
And all the trees in the fields
will clap their hands.

¹³ Juniper trees will grow where there
used to be bushes that had
thorns on them.
And myrtle trees will grow where
there used to be thorns.
That will bring me great fame.
It will be a lasting reminder of what
I can do.
It will stand forever."

The Lord Will Save Those Who Come to Him

56 The Lord says,

"Do what is fair and right.
I will soon come and save you.
Soon everyone will know that what I
do is right.
² Blessed is the person who does what I
want them to.
They are faithful in keeping the
Sabbath day.
They do not misuse it.
They do not do what is evil on that
day."

³ Suppose an outsider wants to follow the
LORD.
Then that person shouldn't say,
"The LORD won't accept me as one of
his people."
And a eunuch shouldn't say,
"I'm like a dry tree
that doesn't bear any fruit."

⁴ The LORD says,

"Suppose some eunuchs keep my
Sabbath days.
They choose to do what pleases me.
And they are faithful in keeping my
covenant.
⁵ Then I will set up a monument in the
area of my temple.
Their names will be written on it.
That will be better for them than
having sons and daughters.
The names of the eunuchs will be
remembered forever.
They will never be forgotten.

⁶ "Suppose outsiders want to follow me
and serve me.
They want to love me
and worship me.
They keep the Sabbath day and do not
misuse it.
And they are faithful in keeping my
covenant.
⁷ Then I will bring them to my holy
mountain of Zion.
I will give them joy in my house.
They can pray there.
I will accept their burnt offerings
and sacrifices on my altar.
My house will be called
a house where people from all
nations can pray."
⁸ The LORD and King will gather
those who were taken away from
their homes in Israel.
He announces, "I will gather them to
myself.
And I will gather others to join
them."

The LORD Judges Israel's Evil Leaders

⁹ Come, all you enemy nations! Come
like wild animals.
Come and destroy like animals in
the forest.
¹⁰ Israel's prophets are blind.
They don't know the LORD.

All of them are like watchdogs that can't
even bark.
They just lie around and dream.
They love to sleep.
¹¹ They are like dogs that love to eat.
They never get enough.
They are like shepherds who don't have
any understanding.
All of them do as they please.
They only look for what they can get
for themselves.
¹² "Come!" they shout. "Let's get some
wine!
Let's drink all the beer we can!
Tomorrow we'll do the same thing.
And that will be even better than
today."

57 Those who are right with God die.
And no one really cares about it.
People who are faithful to the LORD are
swept away by trouble.
And no one understands why that
happens
to those who do what is right.
² Those who lead honest lives
will enjoy peace and rest when they
die.

³ The LORD says, "Come here,
you children of women who practice
evil magic!
You are children of prostitutes and
those who commit adultery.
⁴ Who are you making fun of?
Who are you laughing at?
Who are you sticking your tongue
out at?
You are people who refuse to obey me.
You are just a bunch of liars!
⁵ You burn with sinful desire among the
oak trees.
You worship your gods under every
green tree.
You sacrifice your children in the
valleys.
You also do it under the cliffs.
⁶ You have chosen some of the smooth
stones in the valleys to be your
gods.
You have joined yourselves to them.
You have even poured out drink
offerings to them.
You have given grain offerings to
them.
So why should I take pity on you?

⁷ You have made your bed on a very high
     hill.
    You went up there to offer your
       sacrifices.
⁸ You have set up statues to remind you
     of your gods.
    You have put them behind your
       doors and doorposts.
You deserted me. You invited other
     lovers into your bed.
    You climbed into it and welcomed
       them.
You made a deal with them.
    And you looked with desire at their
       naked bodies.
⁹ You took olive oil to the god named
     Molek.
    You took a lot of perfume along with
       you.
You sent your messengers to places far
     away.
    You even sent them down to the
       place of the dead.
¹⁰ You wore yourself out with all your
     efforts.
    But you would not say, 'It's hopeless.'

You received new strength.
    So you did not give up.
¹¹ "Who are you so afraid of
    that you have not been faithful to
       me?
You have not remembered me.
    What you do doesn't even bother
       you.
I have not punished you for a long time.
    That is why you are not afraid of me.
¹² You have not done what is right or
     good.
    I will let everyone know about it.
    And that will not be of any benefit
       to you.
¹³ Go ahead and cry out for help to all the
     statues of your gods.
    See if they can save you!
The wind will carry them off.
    Just a puff of air will blow them
       away.
But anyone who comes to me for safety
    will receive the land.
    They will possess my holy mountain
       of Zion."

WHAT ABOUT YOU?

Have you ever seen a two-way mirror? One side is a normal mirror; all you see is your own face looking back at you. On the other side, though, it's more like a window. You can see everything happening in the other room though no one inside can see you watching.

Aren't you glad that God sees the whole picture on both sides of the mirror? First Corinthians 13:12 puts it like this: "Now we see only a dim likeness of things. It is as if we were seeing them in a foggy mirror. But someday we will see clearly. We will see face to face."

We're still on the mirror side of the glass right now. One day, when we're in heaven with God, we'll get to see things as He does, and everything will finally make sense. We read His promise in Isaiah 57:15: "I live with anyone who turns away from their sins. I live with anyone who is not proud. I give new life to them. I give it to anyone who turns away from their sins."

Play "mirror charades" with friends. Pick a category like "Bible stories" or "song titles."

Have your friends sit down, and stand facing them. Ask a volunteer to step behind the group so only you can see him. He must pick something in the category to act out for you. You will copy all of his actions without knowing the answer. Your friends will watch you as they attempt to guess the original word or phrase. Explain that this is an illustration of how we can struggle to make sense of life, but God already knows the outcome.

The LORD Comforts People Who Are Sorry for Their Sins

[14] A messenger says,

"Build up the road! Build it up! Get it
ready!
Remove anything that would keep
my people from coming back."

[15] The God who is highly honored lives
forever.
His name is holy. He says,
"I live in a high and holy place.
But I also live with anyone who
turns away from their sins.
I live with anyone who is not proud.
I give new life to them.
I give it to anyone who turns away
from their sins.
[16] I will not find fault with my people
forever.
I will not always be angry with them.
If I were, I would cause their spirits to
grow weak.
The people I created would faint
away.
[17] I was very angry with them.
They always longed for more and
more of everything.
So I punished them for that sin.
I turned my face away from them
because I was angry.
But they kept on wanting their own
way.
[18] I have seen what they have done.
But I will heal them.
I will guide them.
I will give those who mourn in Israel
the comfort they had before.
[19] Then they will praise me.
I will give perfect peace to those who
are far away and those who
are near.
And I will heal them," says the LORD.
[20] But those who are evil are like the
rolling sea.
It never rests.
Its waves toss up mud and sand.

[21] "There is no peace for those who are
evil," says my God.

What True Worship Is All About

58 The LORD told me,

"Shout out loud. Do not hold back.
Raise your voice like a trumpet.
Tell my people that they have refused to
obey me.
Tell the family of Jacob how much
they have sinned.
[2] Day after day they worship me.
They seem ready and willing to
know how I want them to live.
They act as if they were a nation that
does what is right.
They act as if they have not turned
away from my commands.
They claim to want me to give them fair
decisions.
They seem ready and willing to
come near and worship me.
[3] 'We have gone without food,' they say.
'Why haven't you noticed it?
We have made ourselves suffer.
Why haven't you paid any attention
to us?'

"On the day when you fast, you do as
you please.
You take advantage of all your
workers.
[4] When you fast, it ends in arguing and
fighting.
You hit one another with your fists.
That is an evil thing to do.
The way you are now fasting
keeps your prayers from being heard
in heaven.
[5] Do you think that is the way I want you
to fast?
Is it only a time for people to make
themselves suffer?
Is it only for people to bow their heads
like tall grass bent by the
wind?
Is it only for people to lie down
in ashes and clothes of
mourning?
Is that what you call a fast?
Do you think I can accept that?

[6] "Here is the way I want you to fast.

"Set free those who are held by chains
without any reason.
Untie the ropes that hold people as
slaves.
Set free those who are crushed.
Break every evil chain.
[7] Share your food with hungry people.
Provide homeless people with a
place to stay.
Give naked people clothes to wear.

Provide for the needs of your own
    family.
8 Then the light of my blessing will shine
    on you like the rising sun.
I will heal you quickly.
I will march out ahead of you.
    And my glory will follow behind you
        and guard you.
    That's because I always do what is
        right.
9 You will call out to me for help.
    And I will answer you.
You will cry out.
    And I will say, 'Here I am.'

"Get rid of the chains you use to hold
    others down.
    Stop pointing your finger at others
        as if they had done something
        wrong.
    Stop saying harmful things about
        them.
10 Work hard to feed hungry people.
    Satisfy the needs of those who are
        crushed.
Then my blessing will light up your
    darkness.
    And the night of your suffering
        will become as bright as the
        noonday sun.
11 I will always guide you.
    I will satisfy your needs in a land
        baked by the sun.
    I will make you stronger.
You will be like a garden that has plenty
    of water.
    You will be like a spring whose water
        never runs dry.
12 Your people will rebuild the cities that
    were destroyed long ago.
    And you will build again on the old
        foundations.
You will be called One Who Repairs
    Broken Walls.
    You will be called One Who Makes
        City Streets Like New Again.

13 "Do not work on the Sabbath day.
    Do not do just anything you want to
        on my holy day.
Make the Sabbath a day you can enjoy.
    Honor the LORD's holy day.
Do not work on it.
    Do not do just anything you want to.
    Do not talk about things that are
        worthless.

14 Then you will find your joy in me.
    I will give you control over the most
        important places in the land.
And you will enjoy all the good things
    in the land I gave your father Jacob."
The LORD has spoken.

The LORD Sets His People Free

59 People of Israel, the LORD's arm is
    not too weak to save you.
    His ears aren't too deaf to hear your
        cry for help.
2 But your sins have separated you from
    your God.
    They have caused him to turn his
        face away from you.
    So he won't listen to you.
3 Your hands and fingers are stained with
    blood.
    You are guilty of committing
        murder.
Your mouth has told lies.
    Your tongue says evil things.
4 People aren't fair when they present
    cases in court.
    They aren't honest when they state
        their case.
They depend on weak arguments. They
    tell lies.
    They plan to make trouble.
    Then they carry it out.
5 The plans they make are like the eggs of
    poisonous snakes.
    Anyone who eats those eggs will die.
    When one of them is broken, a
        snake comes out.
6 Those people weave their evil plans
    together like a spider's web.
    But the webs they make can't be
        used as clothes.
    They can't cover themselves with
        what they make.
Their acts are evil.
    They do things to harm others.
7 They are always in a hurry to sin.
    They run quickly to murder those
        who aren't guilty.
They love to think up evil plans.
    They leave a trail of harmful actions.
8 They don't know how to live at peace
    with others.
    What they do isn't fair.
They lead twisted lives.
    No one who lives like that will enjoy
        peace and rest.

WHIT'S WISDOM

Isaiah 59:2

One day, Camilla came into Whit's End and asked me this question: "Why did Jesus have to die?" It's a very good question. So I answered her by sending her on a trip in the Imagination Station.

In the program, Camilla was excited to be having dinner with Jesus Himself! They had a nice conversation until suddenly, bricks began to fall from the sky and landed on the table between Camilla and Jesus. She screamed in surprise, but soon noticed that the bricks had words on them such as "lying," "greed," and "selfishness." After a minute, the bricks formed a huge wall between Camilla and Jesus, so she couldn't even see Him. Camilla tried to push through the wall, but she couldn't. Suddenly, a cross broke through the bricks like a wrecking ball. And Camilla could see Jesus again.

When she finished the adventure, I asked what she thought. "Pretty strange," Camilla said.

Fair enough. It was an unusual program. But Camilla got the point: Sin separates us from God. Jesus' death on the Cross made a way for us to have a relationship with Him again.

⁹ We aren't being treated fairly.
    We haven't been set free yet.
The God who always does what is right
    hasn't come to help us.
We look for light, but we see nothing
    but darkness.
We look for brightness, but we walk
    in deep shadows.
¹⁰ Like blind people we feel our way along
    the wall.
We are like those who can't see.
At noon we trip and fall as if the sun
    had already set.
Compared to those who are healthy,
    we are like dead people.
¹¹ All of us growl like hungry bears.
    We sound like doves as we mourn.
We want the LORD to do what is fair
    and save us.
But he doesn't do it.
We long for him to set us free.
    But the time for that seems far away.

¹² That's because we've done so many
    things he considers wrong.
Our sins prove that we are guilty.
The wrong things we've done are always
    troubling us.
We admit that we have sinned.
¹³ We've refused to obey the LORD.
We've made evil plans against him.
We've turned our backs on our God.

We've stirred up conflict and refused to
    follow him.
We've told lies that came from our
    own minds.
¹⁴ So people stop others from doing what
    is fair.
They keep them from doing what is
    right.
No one tells the truth in court anymore.
    No one is honest there.
¹⁵ In fact, truth can't be found anywhere.
Those who refuse to do evil are
    attacked.

The LORD sees that people aren't
    treating others fairly.
That makes him unhappy.
¹⁶ He sees that there is no one who helps
    his people.
He is shocked that no one stands up
    for them.

ADVENTURES IN ODYSSEY

Eugene, Bernard, and other members on their jury showed the importance of justice and standing up for the truth in "Blind Justice" (A#27).

So he will use his own powerful arm to
　　save them.
　　He has the strength to do it because
　　　　he is holy.
[17] He will put the armor of holiness on his
　　chest.
　　He'll put the helmet of salvation on
　　　　his head.
　　He'll pay people back for the wrong
　　　　things they do.
　　He'll wrap himself in anger as if it
　　　　were a coat.
[18] He will pay his enemies back for what
　　they have done.
　　He'll pour his anger out on them.
　　He'll punish those who attack him.
　　He'll give the people in the islands
　　　　what they have coming to
　　　　them.
[19] People in the west will show respect for
　　the LORD's name.
　　People in the east will worship him
　　　　because of his glory.
　　The LORD will come like a rushing river
　　　　that was held back.
　　His breath will drive it along.

[20] "I set my people free. I will come to
　　Mount Zion.
　　I will come to those in Jacob's family
　　　　who turn away from their
　　　　sins,"
　　announces the LORD.

[21] "Here is the covenant I will make with
them," says the LORD. "My Spirit is on
you and will not leave you. I have put my
words in your mouth. They will never leave
your mouth. And they will never leave the
mouths of your children or their children
after them. That will be true for all time to
come," says the LORD.

Zion Will Be Glorious

60 "People of Jerusalem, get up.
　　Shine, because your light has come.
　　The glory of the LORD will shine on
　　　　you.
[2] Darkness covers the earth.
　　Thick darkness spreads over the
　　　　nations.
　　But I will rise and shine on you.
　　My glory will appear over you.
[3] Nations will come to your light.
　　Kings will come to the brightness of
　　　　your new day.

[4] "Look up. Look all around you.
　　All your people are getting together
　　　　to come back to you.
　　Your sons will come from far away.
　　Your daughters will be carried on
　　　　the hip like little children.
[5] Then your face will glow with joy.
　　Your heart will beat fast because you
　　　　are so happy.
　　Wealth from across the ocean will be
　　　　brought to you.
　　The riches of the nations will come
　　　　to you.
[6] Herds of young camels will cover your
　　land.
　　They will come from Midian and
　　　　Ephah.
　　They will also come from Sheba.
　　They'll carry gold and incense.
　　And people will shout praises to me.
[7] All of Kedar's flocks will be gathered to
　　you.
　　The rams of Nebaioth will serve as
　　　　your sacrifices.
　　I will accept them as offerings on my
　　　　altar.
　　That is how I will bring honor to my
　　　　glorious temple.

[8] "Whose ships are these that sail along
　　like clouds?
　　They fly like doves to their nests.
[9] People from the islands are coming to
　　me.
　　The ships of Tarshish are out in
　　　　front.
　　They are bringing your children back
　　　　from far away.
　　Your children are bringing their
　　　　silver and gold with them.
　　They are coming to honor me.
　　I am the LORD your God.
　　I am the Holy One of Israel.
　　I have honored you.

[10] "People from other lands will rebuild
　　your walls.
　　Their kings will serve you.
　　When I was angry with you, I struck
　　　　you.
　　But now I will show you my tender
　　　　love.
[11] Your gates will always stand open.
　　They will never be shut, day or night.
　　Then people can bring you the wealth
　　　　of the nations.

ADVENTURES IN ODYSSEY

Israel prepared for a reunion in Isaiah 60. Whit finally had a reunion with his friends in "Home Sweet Home" (A#28).

Their kings will come along with
them.

¹² The nation or kingdom that will not
serve you will be destroyed.
It will be completely wiped out.

¹³ "Lebanon's glorious trees will be
brought to you.
Its junipers, firs and cypress trees
will be brought.
They will be used to make my temple
beautiful.
And I will bring glory to the place
where my throne is.

¹⁴ The children of those who crush you
will come and bow down to
you.
All those who hate you will kneel
down at your feet.
Jerusalem, they will call you the City of
the LORD.
They will name you Zion, the City of
the Holy One of Israel.

¹⁵ "You have been deserted and hated.
No one even travels through you.
But I will make you into something to
be proud of forever.
You will be a place of joy for all time
to come.

¹⁶ You will get everything you need from
kings and nations.
You will be like children who are
nursing
at their mother's breasts.
Then you will know that I am the one
who saves you.
I am the LORD. I set you free.

I am the Mighty One of Jacob.

¹⁷ Instead of bronze I will bring you gold.
In place of iron I will give you silver.
Instead of wood I will bring you bronze.
In place of stones I will give you iron.
I will make peace govern you.
I will make godliness rule over you.

¹⁸ People will no longer harm one another
in your land.
They will not wipe out or destroy
anything inside your borders.
You will call your walls Salvation.
And you will name your gates Praise.

¹⁹ You will not need the light of the sun by
day anymore.
The bright light of the moon will no
longer have to shine on you.
I will be your light forever.
My glory will shine on you.
I am the LORD your God.

²⁰ Your sun will never set again.
Your moon will never lose its light.
I will be your light forever.
Your days of sorrow will come to an
end.

²¹ Then all your people will do what is
right.
The land will belong to them forever.
They will be like a young tree I have
planted.
My hands have created them.
They will show how glorious I am.

²² The smallest family among you will
become a tribe.
The smallest tribe will become a
mighty nation.
I am the LORD.
When it is the right time, I will act
quickly."

The Year When the LORD Sets His People Free

61 The Spirit of the LORD and King is
on me.
The LORD has anointed me
to announce good news to poor
people.
He has sent me to comfort
those whose hearts have been broken.
He has sent me to announce freedom
for those who have been captured.
He wants me to set prisoners free
from their dark cells.

² He has sent me to announce the year
when he will set his people free.

He wants me to announce the day
  when he will pay his enemies back.
Our God has sent me to comfort all
  those who are sad.
³   He wants me to help those in Zion
  who are filled with sorrow.
I will put beautiful crowns on their heads
  in place of ashes.
I will anoint them with olive oil to give
  them joy
  instead of sorrow.
I will give them a spirit of praise
  in place of a spirit of sadness.
They will be like oak trees that are
  strong and straight.
  The LORD himself will plant them in
  the land.
  That will show how glorious he is.

⁴ They will rebuild the places that were
  destroyed long ago.
  They will repair the buildings that
  have been broken down for
  many years.
They will make the destroyed cities like
  new again.
  They have been broken down for a
  very long time.
⁵ Outsiders will serve you by taking care
  of your flocks.
  People from other lands will work in
  your fields and vineyards.
⁶ You will be called priests of the LORD.
  You will be named workers for our
  God.
You will enjoy the wealth of nations.
  You will brag about getting their
  riches.

⁷ Instead of being put to shame
  you will receive a double share of
  wealth.
Instead of being dishonored
  you will be glad to be in your land.
You will receive a double share of riches
  there.
  And you'll be filled with joy that will
  last forever.

⁸ The LORD says, "I love those who do
  what is right.
  I hate it when people steal and do
  other sinful things.
So I will be faithful to my people.
  And I will bless them.
I will make a covenant with them
  that will last forever.

⁹ Their children after them will be
  famous among the nations.
  Their families will be praised by
  people everywhere.
All those who see them will agree
  that I have blessed them."

¹⁰ The people of Jerusalem will say,
  "We take great delight in the LORD.
  We are joyful because we belong to
  our God.
He has dressed us with salvation as if it
  were our clothes.
  He has put robes of godliness on us.
We are like a groom who is dressed up
  for his wedding.
  We are like a bride who decorates
  herself with her jewels.
¹¹ The soil makes the young plant come up.
  A garden causes seeds to grow.
In the same way, the LORD and King
  will make godliness grow.
  And all the nations will praise him."

The LORD Gives Zion a New Name

62 The LORD says, "For the good of
  Zion I will not keep silent.
  For Jerusalem's benefit I will not
  remain quiet.
I will not keep silent until what I will do
  for them
  shines like the sunrise.
I will not remain quiet until they are
  saved
  and shine like a blazing torch.
² Jerusalem, the nations will see
  that I have made everything right
  for you.
  All their kings will see your glory.
You will be called by a new name.
  I myself will give it to you.
³ You will be like a glorious crown in my
  strong hand.
  You will be like a royal crown in my
  powerful hand.
⁴ People will not call you Deserted
  anymore.
  They will no longer name your land
  Empty.
Instead, you will be called One the
  LORD Delights In.
  Your land will be named Married
  One.
That's because the LORD will take
  delight in you.
  And your land will be married.

Isa. 62:1–5 Revelation 21:2 says the new Jerusalem will come as a bride. Marriage is very important to God. Now that I'm married to Penny, I can see why God is all about marriage.

⁵ As a young man marries a young woman,
  so your Builder will marry you.
As a groom is happy with his bride,
  so your God will be full of joy over you."

⁶ Jerusalem, I have stationed guards on your walls.
  They must never be silent day or night.
You who call out to the LORD
  must not give yourselves any rest.
⁷ And don't give him any rest
  until he makes Jerusalem secure.
Don't give him any peace
  until people all over the earth praise that city.

⁸ The LORD has made a promise.
  He has lifted up his right hand and mighty arm.
He has promised, "I will never give your grain
  to your enemies for food again.
Outsiders will never again drink the fresh wine
  you have worked so hard for.
⁹ Instead, those who gather the grain will eat it themselves.
  And they will praise me.
Those who gather grapes to make the wine will enjoy it.
  They will drink it in the courtyards of my temple."

¹⁰ Go out through your gates, people of Jerusalem! Go out!
  Prepare the way for the rest of your people to return.
Build up the road! Build it up!
  Remove the stones.
Raise a banner over the city
  for the nations to see.

¹¹ The LORD has announced a message from one end of the earth to the other.
He has said, "Tell the people of Zion,
  'Look! Your Savior is coming!
He is bringing his people back as his reward.
  He has won the battle over their enemies.'"
¹² They will be called the Holy People.
  They will be called the People the LORD Set Free.
And Jerusalem will be named the City the LORD Cares About.
  It will be named the City No Longer Deserted.

God Will Save His People and Punish Their Enemies

63 Who is this man coming from the city of Bozrah in Edom?
  His clothes are stained bright red.
Who is he? He is dressed up in all his glory.
  He is marching toward us with great strength.

The LORD answers, "It is I.
  I have won the battle.
I am mighty.
  I have saved my people."

² Why are your clothes red?

Jason's Jargon

ISAIAH 63

Search this chapter for the word *possess*. To possess something means to own it. The Israelites had years when they possessed the land God gave them, as well as years when they lost it.

They look as if you have been
stomping
on grapes in a winepress.

³ The LORD answers, "I have been
stomping on the nations
as if they were grapes.
No one was there to help me.
I walked all over the nations because I
was angry.
That is why I stomped on them.
Their blood splashed all over my clothes.
So my clothes were stained bright red.
⁴ I decided it was time to pay back Israel's
enemies.
The year for me to set my people free
had come.
⁵ I looked around, but no one was there
to help me.
I was shocked that no one gave me
any help.
So I used my own power to save my
people.
I had the strength to do it because I
was angry.
⁶ I walked all over the nations because I
was angry with them.
I made them drink from the cup of
my great anger.
I poured out their blood on the
ground."

Isaiah Praises the LORD and Prays to Him

⁷ I will talk about the kind things the
LORD has done.
I'll praise him for everything he's
done for us.
He has done many good things
for the nation of Israel.
That's because he loves us and is very
kind to us.
⁸ In the past he said, "They are my people.
They are children who will be
faithful to me."
So he saved them.
⁹ When they suffered, he suffered with
them.
He sent his angel to save them.
He set them free because he is loving
and kind.
He lifted them up and carried them.
He did it again and again in days
long ago.
¹⁰ But they refused to obey him.
They made his Holy Spirit sad.

So he turned against them and became
their enemy.
He himself fought against them.

¹¹ Then his people remembered what he
did long ago.
They recalled the days of Moses and
his people.
They asked, "Where is the God who
brought
Israel through the Red Sea?
Moses led them as the shepherd of
his flock.
Where is the God who put
his Holy Spirit among them?
¹² He used his glorious and powerful arm
to help Moses.
He parted the waters of the sea in front
of them.
That mighty act made him famous
forever.
¹³   He led them through that deep sea.
Like a horse in open country,
they didn't trip and fall.
¹⁴ They were like cattle that are taken
down to the plains.
They were given rest by the Spirit of
the LORD."
That's how he guided his people.
So he made a glorious name for
himself.

¹⁵ LORD, look down from heaven.
Look down from your holy and
glorious throne.
Where is your great love for us?
Where is your power?
Why don't you show us
your tender love and concern?
¹⁶ You are our Father.
Abraham might not accept us as his
children.
Jacob might not recognize us as his
family.
But you are our Father, LORD.
Your name is One Who Always Sets
Us Free.
¹⁷ LORD, why do you let us wander away
from you?
Why do you let us become so
stubborn
that we don't respect you?
Come back and help us.
We are the tribes that belong to you.
¹⁸ For a little while your holy people
possessed the land.

But now our enemies have torn your
temple down.
¹⁹ We are like people you never ruled over.
We are like those who don't belong
to you.

64 I wish you would open up your
heavens
and come down to us!
I wish the mountains would tremble
when you show your power!
² Be like a fire that causes twigs to burn.
It also makes water boil.
So come down and make yourself
known to your enemies.
Cause the nations to shake with fear
when they see your power!
³ Long ago you did some wonderful
things we didn't expect.
You came down, and the mountains
trembled
when you showed your power.
⁴ No one's ears have ever heard of a God
like you.
No one's eyes have ever seen a God
who is greater than you.
No God but you acts for the good
of those who trust in him.
⁵ You come to help those who enjoy
doing what is right.
You help those who thank you for
teaching them how to live.
But when we continued to disobey you,
you became angry with us.
So how can we be saved?
⁶ All of us have become like someone
who is "unclean."
All the good things we do are like
dirty rags to you.
All of us are like leaves that have dried
up.
Our sins sweep us away like the
wind.
⁷ No one prays to you.
No one asks you for help.
You have turned your face away from us.
You have let us feel the effects of our
sins.
⁸ Lord, you are our Father.
We are the clay. You are the potter.
Your hands made all of us.
⁹ Don't be so angry with us, Lord.
Don't remember our sins anymore.
Please have mercy on us.
All of us belong to you.

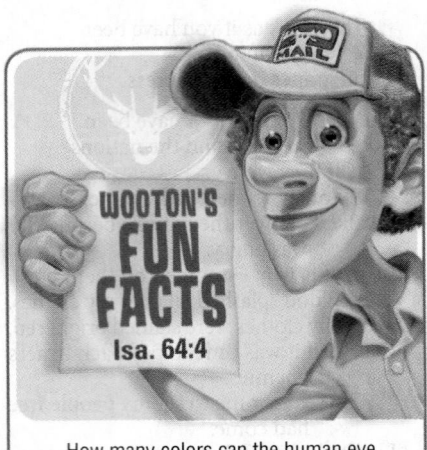

How many colors can the human eye
distinguish? Glad you asked. Eugene
says the answer is as many as 10
million distinct color variations. Wow!
Then again, if you're colorblind, you're
lucky because *all* your socks match.

¹⁰ Your sacred cities have become a desert.
Even Zion is a desert.
Jerusalem is a dry and empty place.
¹¹ Our people of long ago used to praise
you in our holy and glorious
temple.
But now it has been burned down.
Everything we treasured has been
destroyed.
¹² Lord, won't you help us even after
everything that's happened?
Will you keep silent and punish us
more than we can stand?

The Lord Judges and Saves

65 The Lord says, "I made myself
known to those who were not
asking for me.
I was found by those who were not
trying to find me.
I spoke to a nation that did not pray
to me.
'Here I am,' I said. 'Here I am.'
² All day long I have held out my hands
to welcome a stubborn nation.
They lead sinful lives.
They go where their evil thoughts
take them.
³ They are always making me very angry.
They do it right in front of me.
They offer sacrifices in the gardens of
other gods.

They burn incense on altars that are
  made out of bricks.
[4] They sit among the graves.
They spend their nights talking to
    the spirits of the dead.
They eat the meat of pigs.
  Their cooking pots hold soup that
    has 'unclean' meat in it.
[5] They say, 'Keep away! Don't come near
    us!
We are too sacred for you!'
Those people are like smoke in my nose.
  They are like a fire that keeps
    burning all day.

[6] "I will judge them. I have even written
    it down.
  I will not keep silent.
  Instead, I will pay them back for all
    their sins.
[7] I will punish them for their sins.
  I will also punish them for the sins
    of their people before them."
  This is what the LORD says.
"They burned sacrifices on the
    mountains.
  They disobeyed me by worshiping
    other gods on the hills.
So I will make sure they are fully
    punished
  for all the sins they have committed."

[8] The LORD says,

"Sometimes juice is still left in grapes
    that have been crushed.
  So people say, 'Don't destroy them.
  They are still of some benefit.'
That is what I will do for the good of
    those who serve me.
  I will not destroy all my people.
[9] I will give children
  to the families of Jacob and Judah.
  They will possess my entire land.
My chosen people will be given all of it.
  Those who serve me will live there.
[10] Their flocks will eat in the rich
    grasslands of Sharon.
  Their herds will rest in the Valley of
    Achor.
  That is what I will do for my people
    who follow me.
[11] "But some of you have deserted me.
  You no longer worship on my holy
    mountain of Zion.
You spread a table for the god called
  Good Fortune.

You offer bowls of mixed wine to the
    god named Fate.
[12] So I will make it your fate to be killed
    by swords.
  All of you will die in the battle.
That's because I called out to you, but
    you did not answer me.
  I spoke to you, but you did not
    listen.
You did what is evil in my sight.
  You chose to do what does not
    please me."

[13] So the LORD and King says,

"Those who serve me will have food
    to eat.
  But you will be hungry.
My servants will have plenty to drink.
  But you will be thirsty.
Those who serve me will be full of joy.
  But you will be put to shame.
[14] My servants will sing
  with joy in their hearts.
But you will cry out
  because of the great pain in your
    hearts.
  You will cry because your spirits are
    sad.
[15] My chosen ones will use your names
  when they curse others.
I am your LORD and King.
  I will put you to death.
  But I will give new names to those
    who serve me.
[16] They will ask me to bless their land.
  They will do it in my name.
  I am the one true God.
They will make promises in their land.
  They will do it in my name.
  I am the one true God.
The troubles of the past will be forgotten.
  They will be hidden from my eyes.

The LORD Will Create New Heavens and a New Earth

[17] "I will create new heavens and a new
    earth.
  The things that have happened
    before will not be remembered.
  They will not even enter your minds.
[18] So be glad and full of joy forever
  because of what I will create.
I will cause others to take delight in
    Jerusalem.
  They will be filled with joy

when they see its people.
¹⁹ And I will be full of joy because of
Jerusalem.
I will take delight in my people.
Weeping and crying
will not be heard there anymore.

²⁰ "Babies in Jerusalem will no longer
live only a few days.
Old people will not fail
to live for a very long time.
Those who live to the age of 100
will be thought of as mere children
when they die.
Those who die before they are 100
will be considered as having been
under God's curse.
²¹ My people will build houses and live in
them.
They will plant vineyards and eat
their fruit.
²² They will no longer build houses
only to have others live in them.
They will no longer plant crops
only to have others eat them.
My people will live to be as old as trees.
My chosen ones will enjoy for a long
time
the things they have worked for.
²³ Their work will not be worthless
anymore.
They will not have children who are
sure to face sudden terror.
Instead, I will bless them.
I will also bless their children after
them.
²⁴ Even before they call out to me, I will
answer them.
While they are still speaking, I will
hear them.
²⁵ Wolves and lambs will eat together.
Lions will eat straw like oxen.
Serpents will eat nothing but dust.
None of those animals will harm or
destroy
anything or anyone on my holy
mountain of Zion,"
says the LORD.

The LORD Judges Some People and Blesses Others

66 The LORD says,

"Heaven is my throne.
The earth is under my control.
So how could you ever build a house
for me?
Where would my resting place be?
² Didn't I make everything by my power?
That is how all things were created,"
announces the LORD.

"The people I value are not proud.
They are sorry for the wrong things
they have done.
They have great respect for what I
say.
³ But others are not like that.
They sacrifice bulls to me,
but at the same time they kill people.
They offer lambs to me,
but they also sacrifice dogs to other
gods.
They bring grain offerings to me,
but they also offer pig's blood to
other gods.
They burn incense to me,
but they also worship statues of gods.
They have chosen to go their own way.
They take delight in things I hate.
⁴ So I have also made a choice.
I will make them suffer greatly.
I will bring on them what they are
afraid of.
When I called out to them, no one
answered me.
When I spoke to them, no one
listened.
They did what is evil in my sight.
They chose to do what displeases me."

⁵ Listen to the word of the LORD.
Listen, you who tremble with fear
when he speaks. He says,
"Some of your own people hate you.
They turn their backs on you
because you are faithful to me.
They make fun of you and say,
'Let the LORD show his glory by saving
you.
Then we can see how happy you are.'
But they will be put to shame.
⁶ Hear the loud sounds coming from the
city!
Listen to the noise coming from the
temple!
I am the one causing it.
I am paying back my enemies for
everything they have done.

⁷ "Zion is like a woman who has a baby
before she goes into labor.

She has a son
>even before her labor pains begin.
8 Who has ever heard of anything like
>that?
>Who has ever seen such a thing?
Can a country be born in a day?
>Can a nation be created in a
>moment?
But as soon as Zion goes into labor,
>there are many more of her people.
9 Zion, would I bring you to the moment
>of birth
>and not let it happen?"
>says the LORD.
"Would I close up a mother's body
>when it is time for her baby to be
>born?"
>says your God.
10 "Be glad along with Jerusalem, all you
>who love her.
>Be filled with joy because of her.
Take great delight in her,
>all you who mourn over her.
11 You will nurse at her comforting breasts.
>And you will be satisfied.
You will drink until you are full.
>And you will delight in her rich and
>plentiful supply."

12 The LORD continues,

"I will cause peace to flow over her like
>a river.
I will make the wealth of nations
>sweep over her like a flooding
>stream.
You will nurse and be carried in her
>arms.
>You will play on her lap.
13 As a mother comforts her child,
>I will comfort you.
>You will find comfort in Jerusalem."

14 When you see that happen, your hearts
>will be filled with joy.
>Just as grass grows quickly, you will
>succeed.
The LORD will show his power to those
>who serve him.
>But he will pour out his anger on his
>enemies.
15 The LORD will judge them with fire.
>His chariots are coming like a
>windstorm.
He will pour out his burning anger on
>his enemies.

It will blaze out like flames of fire.
16 The LORD will judge with fire and with
>his sword.
>He will judge all people.
>He will put many people to death.

17 "Some people set themselves apart and make themselves pure. They do it so they can go into the gardens to worship other gods. They follow what the worship leader tells them to do. They are among those who eat the meat of pigs and rats. They also eat other 'unclean' things. Those people and the one they follow will come to a horrible end," announces the LORD.

18 "They have planned to do many evil things. And they have carried out their plans. So I will come and gather the people of every nation and language. They will see my glory when I act. 19 "I will give them a sign. I will send to the nations some of those who are left alive. I will send some of them to the people of Tarshish, Libya and Lydia, who are famous for using bows. I will send others to Tubal and Greece. And I will send still others to islands far away. The people who live there have not heard about my fame. They have not seen my glory. But when I act, those I send will tell the nations about my glory. 20 And they will bring back all the people of Israel from all those nations. They will bring them to my holy mountain in Jerusalem. My people will ride on horses, mules and camels. They will come in chariots and wagons," says the LORD. "Those messengers will bring my people as an offering to me. They will bring them to my temple, just as the Israelites bring their grain offerings in bowls that are 'clean.' 21 And I will choose some of them to be priests and Levites," says the LORD.

22 "I will make new heavens and a new earth. And they will last forever," announces the LORD. "In the same way, your name and your children after you will last forever. 23 Everyone will come and bow down to me. They will do it at every New Moon feast and on every Sabbath day," says the LORD. 24 "When they go out of Jerusalem, they will see the dead bodies of those who refused to obey me. The worms that eat their bodies will not die. The fire that burns them will not be put out. It will make everyone sick just to look at them."

Jeremiah

Jeremiah is often referred to as "the weeping prophet." He often showed considerable grief over the things God told him would happen to the people of Judah (4:19; 9:1–2; 23:9–10). Yet in spite of his sad demeanor, he was remarkably persistent and faithful. On one occasion, when the king didn't like Jeremiah's message, he burned all the prophet's writing, a little at a time (36:1–26). Other times Jeremiah was falsely accused of treason and put in prison (chapter 37) and later thrown into a muddy well and left to die, but was eventually rescued (38:1–13). Is it little wonder that he had occasion to weep?

Even though the king and others didn't like Jeremiah's message, what he foretold came to pass. Jerusalem fell to the Babylonians, just as Jeremiah had said. The Temple was burned and the people were carried away into captivity (chapter 52).

Yet Jeremiah was confident that captivity wasn't the end of God's people. In fact, even while the Babylonians were storming the city, God told Jeremiah to purchase a field and put the deed in a safe place. God promised that one day, the people would be back in Judah (32:1–15). The exile would only last seventy years (25:11–14).

In the midst of all the weeping and tragedy, Jeremiah provides one of the Bible's great promises: "Call out to me. I will answer you. I will tell you great things you do not know" (33:3). What great assurance from our Creator!

WHAT'S IT MEAN, EUGENE?

Covenant—A special agreement, usually based on mutual promises, which creates a binding relationship between two parties. Marriage is one example of a *covenant*. God also entered into a *covenant* with the people of Israel when He gave them His law saying, "You will be my people. And I will be your God" (Jeremiah 30:22). Hebrews 8 calls Jesus Christ the mediator of a new and better *covenant*, in which we are brought back into a magnificent relationship with God.

These are the words Jeremiah received from the LORD. Jeremiah was the son of Hilkiah. Jeremiah was one of the priests at Anathoth. That's a town in the territory of Benjamin. ²A message from the LORD came to Jeremiah. It came in the 13th year that Josiah was king over Judah. Josiah was the son of Amon. ³After Josiah, his son Jehoiakim was king over Judah. The LORD's message also came to Jeremiah during the whole time Jehoiakim ruled. The LORD continued to speak to Jeremiah while Zedekiah was king over Judah. He did this until the fifth month of the 11th year of Zedekiah's rule. That's when the people of Jerusalem were forced to leave their country. Zedekiah was the son of Josiah. Here is what Jeremiah said.

The LORD Appoints Jeremiah to Speak for Him

⁴A message from the LORD came to me. The LORD said,

⁵ "Before I formed you in your mother's
    body I chose you.
  Before you were born I set you apart
    to serve me.
  I appointed you to be a prophet to
    the nations."

⁶"You are my LORD and King," I said. "I don't know how to speak. I'm too young."

⁷But the LORD said to me, "Do not say, 'I'm too young.' You must go to everyone I send you to. You must say everything I command you to say. ⁸Do not be afraid of the people I send you to. I am with you. I will save you," announces the LORD.

⁹Then the LORD reached out his hand. He touched my mouth and spoke to me. He said, "I have put my words in your mouth. ¹⁰Today I am appointing you to speak to nations and kingdoms. I give you authority to pull them up by the roots and tear them down. I give you authority to destroy them and crush them. I give you authority to build them up and plant them."

¹¹A message from the LORD came to me. The LORD asked me, "What do you see, Jeremiah?"

"The branch of an almond tree," I replied.

¹²The LORD said to me, "You have seen correctly. I am watching to see that my word comes true."

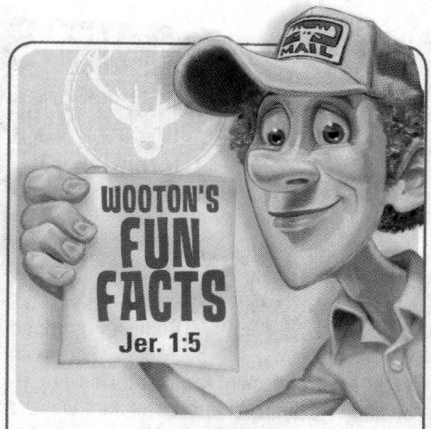

God had a plan for Jeremiah. And He has one for you and for me and for everyone! Check out the popular verse Jeremiah 29:11 too.

¹³Another message from the LORD came to me. The LORD asked me, "What do you see?"

"A pot that has boiling water in it," I answered. "It's leaning toward us from the north."

¹⁴The LORD said to me, "Something very bad will be poured out on everyone who lives in this land. It will come from the north. ¹⁵I am about to send for all the armies in the northern kingdoms," announces the LORD.

"Their kings will come to Jerusalem.
  They will set up their thrones at the
    very gates of the city.
They will attack all the walls that
    surround the city.
  They will go to war against all the
    towns of Judah.
¹⁶ I will judge my people.
  They have done many evil things.
  They have deserted me.
They have burned incense to other
    gods.
  They have worshiped the gods
    their own hands have made.

¹⁷"So get ready! Stand up! Tell them everything I command you to. Do not let them terrify you. If you do, I will terrify you in front of them. ¹⁸Today I have made you like a city that has a high wall around it. I have made you like an iron pillar and a bronze wall. Now you can stand up against the whole land. You can stand against the

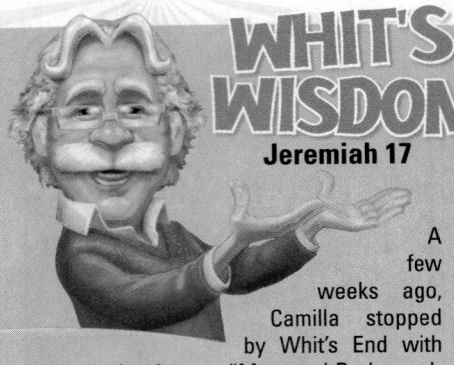

WHIT'S WISDOM
Jeremiah 17

A few weeks ago, Camilla stopped by Whit's End with this question for me: "Mom and Dad are always telling me to be more responsible and that I have responsibilities. What's a responsibility anyway?"

I explained, "Responsibilities are jobs we do even when we don't *feel* like doing them. I think it's good for your parents to teach you responsibility now."

"But why?" Camilla said. "I'm just a kid."

"That's true," I said. "But you won't always be a kid. God wants you to learn responsibility when you're young so you'll be ready for what He has for you to do later."

I reminded her of a prophet in the Bible who wasn't ready for responsibility either.

Check out Jeremiah 1:4–8. Jeremiah told God that he wasn't ready for a job because he was too young. But God didn't agree. He had an important job for Jeremiah and wasn't worried about his age.

You can't handle every responsibility when you're a kid, but you can start practicing to be responsible with jobs your parents give you. Just like Jeremiah (and Camilla), God has special jobs and even *responsibilities* prepared for you!

---

kings and officials of Judah. You can stand against its priests and its people. ¹⁹They will fight against you. But they will not win the battle over you. I am with you. I will save you," announces the LORD.

Israel Deserts the LORD

2 A message from the LORD came to me. The LORD said, ²"Go. Announce my message to the people in Jerusalem. I want everyone to hear it. Tell them,

"Here is what the LORD says.

"'I remember how faithful you were to
    me when you were young.
  You loved me as if you were my bride.
  You followed me through the desert.
    Nothing had been planted there.
³ Your people were holy to me.
  They were the first share of my
    harvest.
  All those who destroyed them were
    held guilty.

And trouble came to their enemies,'"
  announces the LORD.

⁴ People of Jacob, hear the LORD's message.
  Listen, all you tribes of Israel.

⁵The LORD says,

"What did your people of long ago find
    wrong with me?
  Why did they wander so far away
    from me?
They worshiped worthless statues of
    gods.
  Then they themselves became
    worthless.
⁶ They did not ask, 'Where is the LORD?
  He brought us up out of Egypt.
He led us through a dry and empty
    land.
  He guided us through deserts and
    deep valleys.
It was a land of total darkness where
    there wasn't any rain.
  No one lived or traveled there.'

⁷ But I brought you into a land that has
rich soil.
I gave you its fruit and its finest
food.
In spite of that, you made my land
impure.
You turned it into something I hate.
⁸ The priests did not ask,
'Where is the LORD?'
Those who taught my law did not know
me.
The leaders refused to obey me.
The prophets prophesied in the name
of Baal.
They worshiped worthless statues
of gods.

⁹ "So I am bringing charges against you
again,"
announces the LORD.
"And I will bring charges against
your children's children.
¹⁰ Go over to the coasts of Cyprus and
look.
Send people to the land of Kedar
and have them look closely.
See if there has ever been anything
like this.
¹¹ Has a nation ever changed its gods?
Actually, they are not even gods at
all.
But my people have traded away their
glorious God.
They have traded me for worthless
statues of gods.
¹² Sky above, be shocked over this.
Tremble with horror,"
announces the LORD.
¹³ "My people have sinned twice.
They have deserted me,
even though I am the spring of water
that gives life.
And they have dug their own wells.
But those wells are broken.
They can't hold any water.
¹⁴ Are you people of Israel servants?
You were not born as slaves, were
you?
Then why have you been carried off
like stolen goods?
¹⁵ Lions have roared.
They have growled at you.
They have destroyed your land.
Your towns are burned and deserted.
¹⁶ The men of Memphis and Tahpanhes
have cracked your skulls.

¹⁷ Haven't you brought this on yourselves?
I am the LORD your God, but you
deserted me.
You left me even while I was leading
you.
¹⁸ Why do you go to Egypt
to drink water from the Nile River?
Why do you go to Assyria
to drink from the Euphrates River?
¹⁹ You will be punished because you have
sinned.
You will be corrected for turning
away from me.
I am the LORD your God.
If you desert me, bad things will
happen to you.
If you do not respect me, you will suffer
bitterly.
I want you to understand that,"
announces the LORD who rules over
all.

²⁰ "Long ago you broke off the yoke I put
on you.
You tore off the ropes I tied you up
with.
You said, 'I won't serve you!'
In fact, on every high hill
you lay down like a prostitute.
You worshiped other gods under
every green tree.
²¹ You were like a good vine when I
planted you.
You were a healthy plant.
Then how did you turn against me?
How did you become a bad, wild
vine?
²² You might wash yourself with soap.
You might use plenty of strong soap.
But I can still see the stains your
guilt covers you with,"
announces the LORD and King.
²³ "You say, 'I am "clean."
I haven't followed the gods that are
named Baal.'
How can you say that?
Remember how you acted in the
valley.
Consider what you have done.
You are like a female camel running
quickly here and there.
²⁴ You are like a wild donkey that lives in
the desert.
She smells the wind when she longs
for a mate.
Who can hold her back?

The males that run after her do not
need to wear themselves out.
At mating time they will easily find
her.

²⁵ Do not run after other gods
until your sandals are worn out and
your throat is dry.
But you said, 'It's no use!
I love those gods.
I must go after them.'

²⁶ "A thief is dishonored when he is
caught.
And you people of Israel are filled
with shame.
Your kings and officials are
dishonored.
So are your priests and your
prophets.

²⁷ You say to a piece of wood, 'You are my
father.'
You say to a stone, 'You are my
mother.'
You have turned your backs to me.
You refuse to look at me.
But when you are in trouble, you say,
'Come and save us!'

²⁸ Then where are the gods you made for
yourselves?
Let them come when you are in
trouble!
Let them save you if they can!
Judah, you have as many gods
as you have towns.

²⁹ "Why do you bring charges against
me?
All of you have refused to obey me,"
announces the LORD.

³⁰ "I punished your people. But it did not
do them any good.
They did not pay attention when
they were corrected.
You have killed your prophets by
swords.
You have swallowed them up like a
hungry lion.

³¹"You who are now living, consider my
message. I am saying,

"Have I been like a desert to Israel?
Have I been like a land of deep
darkness?
Why do my people say, 'We are free to
wander.
We won't come to you anymore'?

³² Does a young woman forget all about
her jewelry?
Does a bride forget her wedding
jewels?
But my people have forgotten me
more days than anyone can count.

³³ You are very skilled at chasing after love!
Even the worst of women can learn
from how you act.

³⁴ The blood of those you have killed is on
your clothes.
You have destroyed poor people who
were not guilty.
You did not catch them in the act of
breaking in.
In spite of all this,

³⁵ you say, 'I'm not guilty of doing
anything wrong.
The LORD isn't angry with me.'
But I will judge you.
That's because you say, 'I haven't
sinned.'

³⁶ Why do you keep on
changing your ways so much?
Assyria did not help you.
And Egypt will not help you either.

³⁷ So you will also leave Egypt
with your hands tied together above
your heads.
I have turned my back on those you
trust.
They will not help you.

Jer. 2:34 Do you know what forensic
scientists do? They can use a speck of
blood or a fleck of skin to help solve a
crime with DNA evidence. This verse makes
it sound like God was the first forensic
scientist. Scientists can gather *physical*
data, but only God truly knows your heart.

3 "Suppose a man divorces his wife.
      What if she then marries another
         man?
Should her first husband return to her
         again?
If he does, won't the land become
         completely 'unclean'?
People of Israel, you have lived like a
         prostitute.
      You have loved many other gods.
      So do you think you can return to
         me now?"
      announces the Lord.
[2] "Look up at the bare hilltops.
      Is there any place where you have
         not worshiped other gods?
You have been unfaithful to me like
         a wife committing adultery.
By the side of the road you sat waiting
         for lovers.
You sat there like someone who
         wanders in the desert.
You have made the land impure.
      You are like a sinful prostitute.
[3] So I have held back the showers.
      I have kept the spring rains from
         falling.
But you still have the bold face of a
         prostitute.
      You refuse to blush with shame.
[4] You have just now called out to me.
      You said,
'My Father, you have been my friend
         ever since I was young.
[5] Will you always be angry with me?
      Will your anger continue forever?'
This is how you talk.
      But you do all the evil things you
         can."

Israel Is Not Faithful to the Lord

[6] During the time Josiah was king, the
Lord spoke to me. He said, "Have you seen
what the people of Israel have done? They
have not been faithful to me. They have
committed adultery with other gods. They
worshiped them on every high hill and under every green tree. [7] I thought that after
they had done all this, they would return
to me. But they did not. Their sister nation
Judah saw them doing this. And they were
not faithful to me either. [8] I gave Israel their
letter of divorce. I sent them away because
they were unfaithful to me so many times.
But I saw that their sister nation Judah did

not have any respect for me. They were not
faithful to me either. They also went out
and committed adultery with other gods.
[9] Israel was not faithful to me, but that did
not bother them at all. They made the land
'unclean.' They worshiped gods that were
made out of stone and wood. [10] In spite of
all this, their sister nation Judah did not
come back to me. They were not faithful to
me either. They did not return with all their
heart. They only pretended to," announces
the Lord.

[11] The Lord said to me, "Israel and Judah
have not been faithful to me. But Israel was
not as bad as Judah was. [12] Go. Announce
this message to the people in the north. Tell
them,

"'Israel, you have not been faithful,'
         announces the Lord.
      'Return to me. Then I will do good
         things for you again.
That's because I am faithful,' announces
         the Lord.
      'I will not be angry with you forever.
[13] Admit that you are guilty of doing what
         is wrong.
      You have refused to obey me.
      I am the Lord your God.
You have committed adultery with
         other gods.
      You worshiped them under every green
         tree.
      And you have not obeyed me,'"
      announces the Lord.

[14] "You people have not been faithful,"
announces the Lord. "Return to me. I am
your husband. I will choose one of you from
each town. I will choose two from each territory. And I will bring you to the city of
Zion. [15] Then I will give you shepherds who
are dear to my heart. Their knowledge and
understanding will help them lead you.
[16] In those days there will be many more
of you in the land," announces the Lord.
"Then people will not talk about the ark of
the covenant of the Lord anymore. It will
never enter their minds. They will not remember it. The ark will not be missed. And
another one will not be made. [17] At that time
they will call Jerusalem The Throne of the
Lord. All the nations will gather together
there. They will go there to honor me. They
will no longer do what their stubborn and
evil hearts want them to do. [18] In those days

the people of Judah will join the people of Israel. Together they will come from a land in the north. They will come to the land I gave to your people of long ago. I wanted them to have it as their very own.

¹⁹"I myself said,

" 'I would gladly treat you like my
        children.
    I would give you a pleasant land.
    It is the most beautiful land any
        nation could have.'
I thought you would call me 'Father.'
    I hoped you would always obey me.
²⁰ But you people are like a woman who is
        not faithful to her husband.
    Israel, you have not been faithful to
        me,"
    announces the LORD.

²¹ A cry is heard on the bare hilltops.
    The people of Israel are weeping and
        begging for help.
That's because their lives are so twisted.
    They've forgotten the LORD their
        God.

²² "You have not been faithful,"
        says the LORD.
"Return to me. I will heal you.
    Then you will not turn away from
        me anymore."

"Yes," the people say. "We will come to
        you.
    You are the LORD our God.
²³ The gods we worship on the hills
        and mountains are useless.
You are the LORD our God.
    You are the only one who can save us.
²⁴ From our earliest years shameful gods
        have harmed us.
    They have eaten up everything our
        people of long ago worked for.
They have eaten up our flocks and
        herds.
    They've destroyed our sons and
        daughters.
²⁵ Let us lie down in our shame.
    Let our dishonor cover us.
You are the LORD our God. But we have
        sinned against you.
    We and our people of long ago have
        sinned.
We haven't obeyed you
    from our earliest years until now."

⁴ "If you, Israel, will return," announces
        the LORD,
    "then return to me.
Put the statues of your gods out of my
        sight.
    I hate them.
    Stop going astray.
² Make all your promises in my name.
    When you promise say, 'You can be
        sure that the LORD is alive.'
    Be truthful, fair and honest when
        you make these promises.
Then the nations will ask for blessings
        from me.
    And they will boast about me."

³Here is what the LORD is telling the people of Judah and Jerusalem. He says,

"Your hearts are as hard as a field
        that has not been plowed.
So change your ways and produce good
        crops.
    Do not plant seeds among thorns.
⁴ People of Judah and you who live in
        Jerusalem, obey me.
    Do not let your hearts be stubborn.
If you do, my anger will blaze out
        against you.
    It will burn like fire because of the
        evil things you have done.
    No one will be able to put it out.

Trouble Will Come From the North

⁵ "Announce my message in Judah.
    Tell it in Jerusalem.
    Say, 'Blow trumpets all through the
        land!'
Give a loud shout and say,
    'Gather together!
    Let's run to cities that have high
        walls around them!'
⁶ Warn everyone to go to Zion!
    Run for safety! Do not wait!
I am bringing trouble from the north.
    Everything will be totally destroyed."

⁷ Lions have come out of their dens.
    Those who destroy nations have
        begun to march out.
They have left their place
    to destroy your land completely.
Your towns will be broken to pieces.
    No one will live in them.
⁸ So put on the clothes of sadness.
    Mourn and weep over what has
        happened.

The LORD hasn't turned
his great anger away from us.

⁹ "A dark day is coming," announces the
LORD.
"The king and his officials will lose
hope.
The priests will be shocked.
And the prophets will be terrified."

¹⁰Then I said, "You are my LORD and
King. You have completely tricked the
people of Judah and Jerusalem! You have
told them, 'You will have peace and rest.'
But swords are pointed at our throats!"

¹¹At that time the people of Judah and
Jerusalem will be warned. They will be told,
"A hot and dry wind is coming, my people.
It is blowing toward you from the bare hilltops in the desert. But it does not separate
straw from grain. ¹²It is much too strong
for that. The wind is coming from me. I am
making my decision against you."

Jason's Jargon

JEREMIAH 4

Find the word *Zion*
in this chapter.
There are different
interpretations of where
Zion is—it could be
Jerusalem or heaven.
Either way, the people
of Zion are in the
presence of God.

¹³ Look! Our enemies are approaching
like the clouds.
Their chariots are coming like a
strong wind.
Their horses are faster than eagles.
How terrible it will be for us!
We'll be destroyed!
¹⁴ People of Jerusalem, wash your sins
from your hearts and be
saved.
How long will you hold on to your
evil thoughts?
¹⁵ A voice is speaking all the way from the
city of Dan.
From the hills of Ephraim it
announces
that trouble is coming.
¹⁶ "Tell the nations.

Make an announcement concerning
Jerusalem.
Say, 'An army will attack Judah.
It is coming from a land far away.
It will shout a war cry
against the cities of Judah.
¹⁷ It will surround them like people who
guard a field.
Judah has refused to obey me,'"
announces the LORD.
¹⁸ "The army will attack you
because of your conduct and actions.
This is how you will be punished.
It will be so bitter!
It will cut deep down into your
hearts!"

¹⁹ I'm suffering! I'm really suffering!
I'm hurting badly.
My heart is suffering so much!
It's pounding inside me.
I can't keep silent.
I've heard the sound of trumpets.
I've heard the battle cry.
²⁰ One trouble follows another.
The whole land is destroyed.
In an instant my tents are gone.
My home disappears in a moment.
²¹ How long must I look at our enemy's
battle flag?
How long must I hear the sound of
the trumpets?

²² The LORD says, "My people are foolish.
They do not know me.
They are children who do not have any
sense.
They have no understanding at all.
They are skilled in doing what is evil.
They do not know how to do what
is good."

²³ I looked at the earth.
It didn't have any shape. And it was
empty.
I looked at the sky.
Its light was gone.
²⁴ I looked at the mountains.
They were shaking.
All the hills were swaying.
²⁵ I looked. And there weren't any people.
Every bird in the sky had flown away.
²⁶ I looked. And the fruitful land had
become a desert.
All its towns were destroyed.
The LORD had done all this because
of his great anger.

[27] The LORD says,

"The whole land will be destroyed.
But I will not destroy it completely.
[28] So the earth will be filled with sadness.
The sky above will grow dark.
I have spoken, and I will not take pity
on them.
I have made my decision, and I will
not change my mind."

[29] People can hear the sound of horsemen.
Men armed with bows are coming.
The people in every town run away.
Some of them go into the bushes.
Others climb up among the rocks.
All the towns are deserted.
No one is living in them.

[30] What are you doing, you who are
destroyed?
Why do you dress yourself in bright
red clothes?
Why do you put on jewels of gold?
Why do you put makeup on your eyes?
You make yourself beautiful for no
reason at all.
Your lovers hate you.
They want to kill you.

[31] I hear a cry like the cry of a woman
having a baby.
I hear a groan like someone having
her first child.
It's the cry of the people of Zion
struggling to breathe.
They reach out their hands and say,
"Help us! We're fainting!
Murderers are about to kill us!"

No One Is Honest

5 The LORD says, "Go up and down the
streets of Jerusalem.
Look around.
Think about what you see.
Search through the market.
See if you can find one honest person
who tries to be truthful.
If you can, I will forgive this city.
[2] They make their promises in my name.
They say, 'You can be sure that the
LORD is alive.'
But their promises can't be trusted."

[3] LORD, don't your eyes look for truth?
You struck down your people.
But they didn't feel any pain.

You crushed them.
But they refused to be corrected.
They made their faces harder than stone.
They refused to turn away from their
sins.
[4] I thought, "The people of
Jerusalem are foolish.
They don't know how the LORD wants
them to live.
They don't know what their God
requires of them.
[5] So I will go to the leaders.
I'll speak to them.
They should know how the LORD wants
them to live.
They must know what their God
requires of them."
But all of them had broken off the yoke
the LORD had put on them.
They had torn off the ropes he had
tied them up with.
[6] So a lion from the forest will attack them.
A wolf from the desert will destroy
them.
A leopard will hide and wait near their
towns.
It will tear to pieces anyone who
dares to go out.
Again and again they have refused to
obey the LORD.
They have turned away from him
many times.

[7] The LORD says, "Jerusalem, why should
I forgive you?
Your people have deserted me.
They have made their promises in the
names of gods
that are not really gods at all.
I supplied everything they needed.
But they committed adultery.
Large crowds went to the houses of
prostitutes.
[8] Your people are like stallions that have
plenty to eat.
Their sinful desires are out of control.
Each of them goes after another
man's wife.
[9] Shouldn't I punish them for this?"
announces the LORD.
"Shouldn't I pay back the nation
that does these things?

[10] "Armies of Babylon, go through their
vineyards and destroy them.
But do not destroy them completely.

Strip off their branches.
These people do not belong to me.
¹¹ The people of Israel and the people of
Judah
have not been faithful to me at all,"
announces the Lord.

¹² They have told lies about the Lord.
They said, "He won't do anything!
No harm will come to us.
We will never see war or be hungry.
¹³ The prophets are nothing but wind.
Their message doesn't come from
the Lord.
So let what they say will happen be
done to them."

¹⁴The Lord God rules over all. He says
to me,

"The people have spoken these words.
So my words will be like fire in your
mouth.
I will make the people like wood.
And the fire will burn them up."

¹⁵ "People of Israel, listen to me,"
announces the Lord.
"I am bringing against you
a nation from far away.
It is an old nation. And it will last for a
long time.
Its people speak a language you do
not know.
You can't understand what they are
saying.
¹⁶ The bags they carry their arrows in are
like an open grave.
All their soldiers are mighty.
¹⁷ They will eat up your crops and your
food.
They will strike down your sons and
daughters.
They will kill your sheep and cattle.
They will destroy your vines and fig
trees.
You trust in your cities that have high
walls around them.
But the people in them will be killed
by swords.

¹⁸"In spite of that, even in those days I
will not destroy you completely," announces the Lord. ¹⁹'Jeremiah,' the people will
ask, 'Why has the Lord our God done all
this to us?' Then you will tell them, 'You
have deserted the Lord. You have served
other gods in your own land. So now you
will serve another nation in a land that is
not your own.'

²⁰ "Here is what I want you to announce
to the people of Jacob.
Tell it in Judah.
Tell them I say,
²¹ 'Listen to this, you foolish people,
who do not have any sense.
You have eyes, but you do not see.
You have ears, but you do not hear.
²² Shouldn't you have respect for me?'
announces the Lord.
'Shouldn't you tremble with fear in
front of me?
I made the sand to hold the ocean back.
It will do that forever.
The ocean can't go past it.
The waves might roll, but they can't
sweep over it.
They might roar, but they can't go
across it.
²³ But you people have stubborn hearts.
You refuse to obey me.
You have turned away from me.
You have gone astray.
²⁴ You do not say to yourselves,
"Let us have respect for the Lord
our God.
He sends rain in the fall and the spring.
He promises us that the harvest will
come
at the same time each year."
²⁵ But the things you have done wrong
have robbed you of these gifts.
Your sins have kept these good things
far away from you.'

²⁶ "Jeremiah, some of my people are evil.
They hide and wait just as people
hide to catch birds.
They set traps for people.
²⁷ A hunter uses tricks to fill his cage with
birds.
And my people have filled their
houses with a lot of goods.
They have become rich and powerful.
²⁸ They have grown fat and heavy.
There is no limit to the evil things
they do.
In court they do not seek justice.
They don't protect the rights of
children whose fathers have
died.
They do not stand up for poor
people.

²⁹ Shouldn't I punish them for this?"
    announces the LORD.
"Shouldn't I pay back the
    nation that does these things?

³⁰ "Something horrible and shocking
    has happened in the land.
³¹ The prophets prophesy lies.
    The priests rule by their own
       authority.
And my people love it this way.
    But what will you do in the end?"

The Babylonians Will Attack Jerusalem

6 The LORD says, "People of Benjamin,
       run for safety!
    Run away from Jerusalem!
Blow trumpets in the city of Tekoa!
    Warn everyone in Beth Hakkerem!
Horrible trouble is coming from the
       north.
    The Babylonians will destroy
       everything with awful power.
² I will destroy the city of Zion,
    even though it is very beautiful.
³ Shepherds will come against it with
       their flocks.
    They will set up their tents around it.
    All of them will take care of their
       own sheep."

⁴ The Babylonians say, "Prepare for battle
       against Judah!
    Get up! Let's attack them at noon!
But the daylight is fading.
    The shadows of evening are getting
       longer.
⁵ So get up! Let's attack them at night!
    Let's destroy their strongest forts!"

⁶ The LORD who rules over all speaks to
the Babylonians. He says,

"Cut down some trees.
    Use the wood to build ramps against
       Jerusalem's walls.
I must punish that city.
    It is filled with people who treat
       others badly.
⁷ Wells keep giving fresh water.
    And Jerusalem keeps on sinning.
Its people are always fighting and
       causing trouble.
    When I look at them,
    I see nothing but sickness and
       wounds.

⁸ Jerusalem, listen to my warning.
    If you do not, I will turn away from
       you.
Your land will become a desert.
    No one will be able to live there."

⁹ The LORD rules over all. He says to me,

"People gather the few grapes left on a
       vine.
    So let Israel's enemies gather the few
       people left alive in the land
Look carefully at the branches again.
    Do this like someone who gathers
       the last few grapes."

¹⁰ Who can I speak to? Who can I warn?
    Who will even listen to me?
Their ears are closed
    so they can't hear.
The LORD's message displeases them.
    They don't take any delight in it.
¹¹ But the LORD's anger burns inside me.
    I can no longer hold it in.

The LORD says to me, "Pour out my
       anger on the children in the
       street.
Pour it out on the young men who
       are gathered together.
Husband and wife alike will be caught
       in it.
    So will those who are very old.
¹² I will reach out my hand
    against those who live in the land,"
    announces the LORD.
"Then their houses will be turned over
       to others.
    So will their fields and their wives.
¹³ Everyone wants to get richer and richer,
    from the least important of them to
       the most important.
Prophets and priests alike
    try to fool everyone they can.
¹⁴ They bandage the wounds of my people
    as if they were not very deep.
'Peace, peace,' they say.
    But there isn't any peace.
¹⁵ Are they ashamed of their hateful
       actions?
    No. They do not feel any shame at all.
    They do not even know how to blush.
So they will fall like others who have
       already fallen.
    They will be brought down when I
       punish them,"
    says the LORD.

[16] The LORD tells the people of Judah,

"Stand where the roads cross, and look
     around.
   Ask where the old paths are.
Ask for the good path, and walk on it.
   Then your hearts will find rest in
       me.
   But you said, 'We won't walk on it.'
[17] I appointed prophets to warn you. I
     said,
   'Listen to the sound of the trumpets!'
   But you said, 'We won't listen.'
[18] So pay attention, you nations.
   You are witnesses for me.
   Watch what will happen to my
       people.
[19] Earth, pay attention.
   I am going to bring trouble on them.
   I will punish them because of the
       evil things they have done.
They have not listened to my words.
   They have said no to my law.
[20] What do I care about incense from the
     land of Sheba?
   Why should I bother with sweet-
       smelling cane from a land far
       away?
I do not accept your burnt offerings.
   Your sacrifices do not please me."

[21] So the LORD says,

"I will bring an army against the people
     of Judah.
   Parents and children alike will trip
       and fall.
   Neighbors and friends will die."

[22] The LORD says to Jerusalem,

"Look! An army is coming
   from the land of the north.
I am stirring up a great nation.
   Its army is coming from a land that
       is very far away.
[23] Its soldiers are armed with bows and
     spears.
   They are mean. They do not show
       any mercy at all.
They come riding in on their horses.
   They sound like the roaring ocean.
They are lined up for battle.
   They are marching out
       to attack you, city of Zion."

[24] We have heard reports about them.
   And our hands can't help us.

BIBLE ADVENTURES

Bernard and Marvin took an
Imagination Station adventure
to see the story of Jeremiah in
"Bernard and Jeremiah" (A#47).

We are suffering greatly.
   It's like the pain of a woman having
       a baby.
[25] Don't go out to the fields.
   Don't walk on the roads.
Our enemies have swords.
   And there is terror on every side.
[26] My people, put on the clothes of sadness.
   Roll among the ashes.
Mourn with bitter weeping
   just as you would mourn for an only
       son.
The one who is going to destroy us
   will come suddenly.

[27] The LORD says to me, "I have made you
       like one who tests metals.
   My people are the ore.
I want you to watch them
   and test the way they live.
[28] All of them are used to disobeying me.
   They go around telling lies about
       others.
They are like bronze mixed with iron.
   All of them do very sinful things.
[29] The fire is made very hot
   so the lead will burn away.
But it is impossible to make these
       people pure.
   Those who are evil are not removed.
[30] They are like silver that is thrown away.
   That is because I have not accepted
       them."

Worshiping Other Gods Is Worthless

7 A message from the LORD came to Jeremiah. The LORD said, [2] "Stand at the gate
of my house. Announce my message to the
people there. Say,

"'Listen to the LORD's message, all you
people of Judah. You always come through
these gates to worship the LORD. [3] The God
of Israel is speaking to you. He is the LORD
who rules over all. He says, "Change the
way you live and act. Then I will let you live
in this place. [4] Do not trust in lies. Do not
say, 'This is the temple of the LORD! This

is the temple of the LORD! This is the temple of the LORD!' ⁵You must really change the way you live and act. Treat one another fairly. ⁶Do not treat outsiders or widows badly in this place. Do not take advantage of children whose fathers have died. Do not kill those who are not guilty of doing anything wrong. Do not worship other gods. That will only bring harm to you. ⁷If you obey me, I will let you live in this place. It is the land I gave your people of long ago. It was promised to them for ever and ever. ⁸But look! You are trusting in worthless lies.

⁹" "You continue to steal and commit murder. You commit adultery. You tell lies in court. You burn incense to Baal. You worship other gods you didn't know before. ¹⁰Then you come and stand in front of me. You keep coming to this house where I have put my Name. You say, 'We are safe.' You think you are safe when you do so many things I hate. ¹¹My Name is in this house. But you have made it a den for robbers! I have been watching you!" announces the LORD.

¹²" "Go now to the town of Shiloh. Go to the place where I first made a home for my Name. See what I did to it because of the evil things my people Israel were doing. ¹³I spoke to you again and again," announces the LORD. "I warned you while you were doing all these things. But you did not listen. I called out to you. But you did not answer. ¹⁴So what I did to Shiloh I will now do to the house where my Name is. It is the temple you trust in. It is the place I gave to you and your people of long ago. ¹⁵But I will throw you out of my land. That is exactly what I did to the people of Ephraim. And they are your relatives.' "

¹⁶"Jeremiah, do not pray for these people. Do not make any appeal or request for them. Do not beg me. I will not listen to you. ¹⁷Don't you see what they are doing? They are worshiping other gods in the towns of Judah. They are offering sacrifices to them in the streets of Jerusalem. ¹⁸The children go out and gather wood. The fathers light the fire. The women mix the dough. They make flat cakes of bread to offer to the female god called the Queen of Heaven. They pour out drink offerings to other gods. That makes me very angry. ¹⁹But am I the one they are hurting?" announces the LORD. "Aren't they only harming themselves? They should be ashamed of it."

²⁰So the LORD and King says, "I will pour out my burning anger on this place. It will strike people and animals alike. It will destroy the trees in the fields and the crops in your land. It will burn, and no one will be able to put it out."

²¹The LORD who rules over all is the God of Israel. He says, "Go ahead! Add your burnt offerings to your other sacrifices. Eat the meat yourselves! ²²When I brought your people out of Egypt, I spoke to them. But I did not just give them commands about burnt offerings and sacrifices. ²³I also gave them another command. I said, 'Obey me. Then I will be your God. And you will be my people. Live the way I command you to live. Then things will go well with you.' ²⁴But they did not listen. They refused to pay any attention to me. Instead, they did what their stubborn and evil hearts wanted them to do. They went backward and not forward. ²⁵Again and again I sent my servants the prophets to you. They came to you day after day. They prophesied from the time your people left Egypt until now. ²⁶But your people of long ago did not listen. They refused to pay any attention to me. They were stubborn. They did more evil things than their people who lived before them.

²⁷"Jeremiah, when you tell them all this, they will not listen to you. When you call out to them, they will not answer. ²⁸So say to them, 'You are a nation that has not obeyed the LORD your God. You did not pay attention when you were corrected. Truth has died out. You do not tell the truth anymore.' "

²⁹The LORD says to the people of Jerusalem, "Cut off your hair. Throw it away. Sing a song of sadness on the bare hilltops. I am very angry with you. I have turned my back on you. I have deserted you.

The Valley of Death

³⁰"The people of Judah have done what is evil in my eyes," announces the LORD. "They have set up statues of their gods. They have worshiped them in the house where my Name is. They have made my house 'unclean.' I hate those statues. ³¹The people have built the high places of Topheth in the Valley of Ben Hinnom. There they worship other gods. And there they sacrifice their children in the fire. That is something I

did not command. It did not even enter my mind. ³²So watch out!" announces the LORD. "The days are coming when people will not call it Topheth anymore. And they will not call it the Valley of Ben Hinnom either. Instead, they will call it the Valley of Death. They will bury the dead bodies of some people in Topheth. But they will run out of room. ³³Then they will not be able to bury the bodies of other people there. So the bodies will become food for birds and wild animals. And no one will scare them away. ³⁴I will put an end to the sounds of joy and gladness. The voices of brides and grooms will not be heard anymore. There will be no sounds of joy in the towns of Judah. And there will be no joy in the streets of Jerusalem. The land will become a desert.

8 "At that time the tombs will be opened," announces the LORD. "The bones of the kings and officials of Judah will be brought out. The bones of the priests and prophets will be removed. So will the bones of the people of Jerusalem. ²They will lie outside under the sun, moon and all the stars. All these people had loved and served these things. They had followed them and worshiped them. They had asked them for advice. So the bones of these people will not be gathered up or buried again. Instead, they will be like human waste lying there on the ground. ³Everyone left alive in this evil nation will want to die rather than live. That is what they will long for in the lands where I force them to go." The LORD who rules over all announces this.

The LORD Punishes His Sinful People

⁴"Jeremiah, tell them, 'The LORD says,

"'"When people fall down, don't they
 get up again?
When someone turns away, don't
 they come back?
⁵ Then why have the people of Jerusalem
 turned away from me?
Why do they always turn away?
They keep on telling lies.
 They refuse to come back to me.
⁶ I have listened carefully.
 But they do not say what is right.
They refuse to turn away from their
 sins.
 None of them says, 'What have I
  done?'

Each of them goes their own way.
 They are like horses charging into
  battle.
⁷ Storks know when to fly south.
 So do doves, swifts and thrushes.
But my people do not know
 what I require them to do.

⁸ "'"How can you people say, 'We are
  wise.
We have the law of the LORD'?
Actually, the teachers of the law have
 told lies about it.
 Their pens have not written what is
  true.
⁹ Those who think they are wise will be
 put to shame.
They will become terrified. They will
 be trapped.
They have not accepted my message.
 So what kind of wisdom do they
  have?
¹⁰ I will give their wives to other men.
 I will give their fields to new
  owners.
Everyone wants to get richer and
 richer.
 Everyone is greedy, from the
  least important to the most
  important.
Prophets and priests alike
 try to fool everyone they can.
¹¹ They bandage the wounds of my people
 as if they were not very deep.
'Peace, peace,' they say.
 But there isn't any peace.
¹² Are they ashamed of their hateful
  actions?
No. They do not feel any shame at
  all.
They do not even know how to
  blush.
So they will fall like others who have
 already fallen.
They will be brought down when I
 punish them,"
says the LORD.

¹³ "'"I will take away their harvest,"
 announces the LORD.
"There will not be any grapes on the
 vines.
The trees will not bear any figs.
 The leaves on the trees will dry up.
What I have given my people
 will be taken away from them."'"

¹⁴ Why are we sitting here?
  Let's gather together!
Let's run to the cities that have high
    walls around them!
  Let's die there!
The LORD our God has sentenced us to
    death.
  He has given us poisoned water to
    drink.
  That's because we've sinned against
    him.
¹⁵ We hoped peace would come.
  But nothing good has happened to
    us.
We hoped we would finally be healed.
  But there is only terror.
¹⁶ When our enemy's horses snort,
  the noise is heard all the way from
    the city of Dan.
When their stallions neigh,
  the whole land trembles with fear.
They have come to destroy
  the land and everything in it.
The city and everyone who lives
    there will be destroyed.

¹⁷ "People of Judah, I will send poisonous
    snakes among you.
  No one will be able to charm them.
  And they will bite you,"
    announces the LORD.

¹⁸ LORD, my heart is weak inside me.
  You comfort me when I'm sad.
¹⁹ Listen to the cries of my people
  from a land far away.
They cry out, "Isn't the LORD in Zion?
  Isn't its King there anymore?"

The LORD says, "Why have they made
    me so angry
  by worshiping their wooden gods?
Why have they made me angry
  with their worthless statues
  of gods from other lands?"

²⁰ The people say, "The harvest is over.
  The summer has ended.
  And we still haven't been saved."

²¹ My people are crushed, so I am crushed.
  I mourn, and I am filled with
    horror.
²² Isn't there any healing lotion in Gilead?
  Isn't there a doctor there?
Then why doesn't someone heal
  the wounds of my people?

9 ¹I wish my head were a spring of water!
  I wish my eyes were a fountain of
    tears!
I would weep day and night
  for my people who have been killed.
² I wish I had somewhere to go in the
    desert
  where a traveler could stay!
Then I could leave my people.
  I could get away from them.
All of them commit adultery by
    worshiping other gods.
  They aren't faithful to the LORD.

³ "They get ready to use
  their tongues like bows,"
  announces the LORD.
"Their mouths shoot out lies like
    arrows.
  They tell lies to gain power in the
    land.
They go from one sin to another.
  They do not pay any attention to
    me.
⁴ Be on guard against your friends.
  Do not trust the members of your
    own family.
Every one of them cheats.
  Every friend tells lies.
⁵ One friend cheats another.
  No one tells the truth.
They have taught their tongues how
    to lie.
  They wear themselves out sinning.
⁶ Jeremiah, you live among people who
    tell lies.
  When they lie, they refuse to pay any
    attention to me,"
  announces the LORD.

⁷So the LORD who rules over all says,

"I will put them through the fire to test
    them.
  What else can I do?
  My people are so sinful!
⁸ Their tongues are like deadly arrows.
  They tell lies.
With their mouths all of them speak
    kindly to their neighbors.
  But in their hearts they set traps for
    them.
⁹ Shouldn't I punish them for this?"
  announces the LORD.
"Shouldn't I pay back the nation
  that does these things?"

Do you like to win? How much? In the Adventures in Odyssey episode "Top This!" Courtney's competitive drive gets the better of her as she works to raise more funds than her cousin Hannah. She and Hannah have always competed, so Courtney sees winning as her only option. That's why Mr. Allen's question catches her by surprise: What would happen if she just let Hannah win? By giving up, Courtney could stop the endless rivalry, and the cousins might have a chance of being friends.

When we focus too much on competing, not only do we stop caring about others, but we also forget the One who gives our gifts and talents in the first place.

Read Jeremiah 9:23–24: "Do not let wise people brag about how wise they are. Do not let strong people boast about how strong they are. Do not let rich people brag about how rich they are. But here is what the one who brags should boast about. They should brag that they have the understanding to know me. I want them to know that I am the LORD." When competition no longer honors God, it's time to rethink just how important winning is.

Put a twist on your next family game night. Pick a few board games everyone enjoys, and instead of trying your hardest to win, have everyone play to lose! If that's fun, play on. But if people get too competitive trying to be the first to lose, you might want to go back to normal rules.

---

¹⁰ I will cry and mourn over the
     mountains.
     I will sing a song of sadness about
        the desert grasslands.
They are dry and empty. No one travels
     through them.
     The mooing of cattle isn't heard there.
The birds have flown away.
     All the animals are gone.

¹¹ The LORD says, "I will knock down all
     of Jerusalem's buildings.
     I will make it a home for wild dogs.
The towns of Judah will be completely
     destroyed.
     No one will be able to live in them."

¹²Who is wise enough to understand these things? Who has been taught by the LORD? Who can explain them? Why has the land been destroyed so completely? Why has it become like a desert that no one can go across?

¹³The LORD answered me, "Because my people have turned away from my law. I gave it to them. But they have not kept it.

They have not obeyed me. ¹⁴Instead, they have done what their stubborn hearts wanted them to do. They have worshiped the gods that are named Baal. They have done what their people have taught them to do through the years." ¹⁵So now the LORD who rules over all speaks. He is the God of Israel. He says, "I will make these people eat bitter food. I will make them drink poisoned water. ¹⁶I will scatter them among the nations. They and their people before them didn't know about these nations. With swords I will chase these people. I will hunt them down until I have destroyed them."

¹⁷The LORD rules over all. He says,

"Here is something I want you to think
     about.
     Send for the women who mourn for
        the dead.
     Send for the most skilled among
        them."

¹⁸ Let them come quickly
     and weep for us.

Let them cry until tears flow from our
      eyes.
   Let them weep until water pours out
      of our eyes.
19 People are heard weeping in Zion.
   They are saying, "We are destroyed!
   We are filled with shame!
   We must leave our land.
   Our houses have been torn down."

20 You women, hear the LORD's message.
   Listen to what he's saying.
Teach your daughters how to mourn for
      the dead.
   Teach one another a song of sadness.
21 Death has climbed in through our
      windows.
   It has entered our forts.
Death has removed the children from
      the streets.
   It has taken the young men out of
      the market.

22 Say, "The LORD announces,

" 'Dead bodies will be like human waste
   lying in the open fields.
They will lie there like grain
   that is cut down at harvest time.
   No one will gather them up.' "

23 The LORD says,

"Do not let wise people brag about how
      wise they are.
   Do not let strong people boast about
      how strong they are.
   Do not let rich people brag about
      how rich they are.
24 But here is what the one who brags
      should boast about.
   They should brag that they have the
      understanding to know me.
I want them to know that I am the
      LORD.
   No matter what I do on earth, I am
      always kind, fair and right.
   And I take delight in this,"
announces the LORD.

25 "The days are coming when I will judge
people," announces the LORD. "I will punish all those who are circumcised only in
their bodies. 26 That includes the people of
Egypt, Judah, Edom, Ammon and Moab. It
also includes all those who live in the desert in places far away. None of the people in
these nations is really circumcised. And not
even the people of Israel are circumcised in
their hearts."

The LORD Is the Only True God

10 People of Israel, listen to what the
LORD is telling you. 2 He says,

"Do not follow the practices of other
      nations.
   Do not be terrified by warnings in
      the sky.
   Do not be afraid, even though the
      nations are terrified by them.
3 The practices of these nations are
      worthless.
   People cut a tree out of the forest.
   A skilled worker shapes the wood
      with a sharp tool.
4 Others decorate it with silver and gold.
   They use a hammer to nail it to the
      floor.
   They want to keep it from falling
      down.
5 The statues of their gods can't speak.
   They are like scarecrows in a field of
      cucumbers.
Their statues have to be carried around
      because they can't walk.
So do not be afraid of their gods.
   They can't do you any harm.
   And they can't do you any good
      either."

6 LORD, no one is like you.
   You are great.
   You are mighty and powerful.
7 King of the nations,
   everyone should have respect for you.
   That's what people should give you.
Among all the wise leaders of the
      nations
   there is no one like you.
   No one can compare with you in all
      their kingdoms.
8 All of them are foolish. They don't have
      any sense.
   They think they are taught by
      worthless wooden gods.

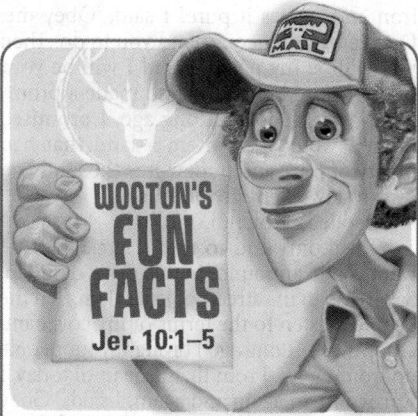

WOOTON'S FUN FACTS
Jer. 10:1–5

I heard someone say that Christmas trees were like idols because they were made of wood and decorated. They used Jeremiah 10:1–5 as evidence. I asked Mr. Whittaker and he said that those verses are referring to idolatry and worshiping things that God made instead of worshiping God.

⁹ Hammered silver is brought from
    Tarshish.
    Gold is brought from Uphaz.
    People skilled in working with wood
        and gold make a statue.
    Then they put blue and purple
        clothes on it.
    The whole thing is made by skilled
        workers.
¹⁰ But you are the only true God.
    You are the only living God.
    You are the King who rules forever.
    When you are angry, the earth trembles
        with fear.
    The nations can't stand up under
        your anger.

¹¹The Lord speaks to the Jews living in Babylon. He says, "Here is what you must tell the people of the nations. Tell them, 'Your gods did not make the heavens and the earth. In fact, these gods will disappear from the earth. They will vanish from under the heavens.'"

¹² But God used his power to make the
    earth.
    His wisdom set the world in place.
    His understanding spread out the
        heavens.
¹³ When he thunders, the waters in the
        heavens roar.
    He makes clouds rise from one end
        of the earth to the other.
    He sends lightning along with the rain.
    He brings the wind out from his
        storerooms.
¹⁴ No one has any sense or knows
        anything at all.
    Everyone who works with gold is
        put to shame by his gods.
    The metal gods he has made are fakes.
    They can't even breathe.
¹⁵ They are worthless things that people
        make fun of.
    When the Lord judges them, they
        will be destroyed.
¹⁶ The God of Jacob is not like them.
    He gives his people everything they
        need.
    He made everything that exists.
    And that includes Israel.
    They are the people who belong to him.
    His name is the Lord Who Rules
        Over All.

The Land Will Be Destroyed

¹⁷ People of Jerusalem, your enemies have
        surrounded you.
    They are attacking you.
    So gather up what belongs to you.
    Then leave the land.
¹⁸ The Lord says,
    "I am about to throw out of this land
        everyone who lives in it.
    I will bring trouble on them.
    They will be captured."
¹⁹ How terrible it will be for me!
    I've been wounded!
    And my wound can't be healed!
    In spite of that, I said to myself,

"I'm sick. But I'll have to put up with
    it."
²⁰ Jerusalem is like a tent that has been
    destroyed.
All its ropes have snapped.
My people have gone away from me.
    Now no one is left to set up my tent.
    I have no one to set up my shelter.
²¹ The leaders of my people are like
    shepherds
    who don't have any sense.
    They don't ask the LORD for advice.
That's why they don't succeed.
    And that's why their whole flock
    is scattered like sheep.
²² Listen! A message is coming!
    I hear the sound of a great army
    marching down from the north!
It will turn Judah's towns into a desert.
    They will become a home for wild
    dogs.

Jeremiah Prays to the LORD

²³ LORD, I know that a person doesn't
    control their own life.
    They don't direct their own steps.
²⁴ Correct me, LORD, but please be fair.
    Don't correct me when you are
    angry.
    If you do, nothing will be left of me.
²⁵ Pour out your great anger on the
    nations.
    They don't pay any attention to you.
    They refuse to worship you.
They have destroyed the people of Jacob.
    They've wiped them out completely.
    They've also destroyed the land they
    lived in.

The LORD's People Have Broken His Covenant

11 A message from the LORD came to
Jeremiah. The LORD said, ²"Listen to
the terms of the covenant I made with my
people of long ago. Tell Judah the terms
still apply to them. Tell those who live in
Jerusalem that they must obey them too. ³I
am the LORD, the God of Israel. So let the
people know what I want them to do. Here
is what I want you to tell them. 'May the
person who does not obey the terms of the
covenant be under my curse. ⁴I gave those
terms to your people of long ago. That was
when I brought them out of Egypt. I saved
them out of that furnace that melts down

iron and makes it pure.' I said, 'Obey me.
Do everything I command you to do. Then
you will be my people. And I will be your
God. ⁵I raised my hand and made a promise to your people of long ago. I promised
them I would give them a land that had
plenty of milk and honey.' It is the land you
own today. I kept my promise."

I replied, "Amen, LORD."

⁶The LORD said to me, "Here is what I
want you to announce in the towns of Judah.
Say it also in the streets of Jerusalem. Tell the
people, 'Listen to the terms of my covenant.
Obey them. ⁷Long ago I brought your people
up from Egypt. From that time until today, I
warned them again and again. I said, "Obey
me." ⁸But they did not listen. They did not
pay any attention to me. Instead, they did
what their stubborn and evil hearts wanted
them to do. So I brought down on them all
the curses of the covenant. I commanded
them to obey it. But they refused.' "

⁹The LORD continued, "The people of
Judah have made some evil plans. So have
those who live in Jerusalem. ¹⁰All of them
have returned to the sins their people of
long ago committed. Those people refused
to listen to what I told them. And now the
people of Israel and Judah alike have worshiped other gods and served them. They
have broken the covenant I made with their
people who lived before them. ¹¹So I say, 'I
will bring trouble on them. They will not be
able to escape it. They will cry out to me. But
I will not listen to them. ¹²The people of Jerusalem and of the towns of Judah will cry
out. They will cry out to the gods they burn
incense to. But those gods will not help them
at all when trouble strikes them. ¹³Judah, you
have as many gods as you have towns. And
in Jerusalem you have set up as many altars
as there are streets. You are burning incense
to that shameful god named Baal.'

¹⁴"Jeremiah, do not pray for these people.
Do not make any appeal or request for
them. They will call out to me when they
are in trouble. But I will not listen to them.

¹⁵ "I love the people of Judah.
    But they are working out their evil
        plans along with many others.
    So what are they doing in my temple?
Can meat that is offered to me keep me
        from punishing you?
    When you do evil things, you get a
        lot of pleasure from them."

¹⁶ People of Judah, the LORD once called
you a healthy olive tree.
He thought its fruit was beautiful.
But now he will come with the roar of a
mighty storm.
He will set the tree on fire.
And its branches will be broken.

¹⁷The LORD who rules over all planted you.
But now he has ordered your enemies to
destroy you. The people of Israel and Judah have both done what is evil. They have
made the LORD very angry by burning incense to Baal.

Jeremiah's Enemies Make Evil Plans Against Him

¹⁸The LORD told me about the evil plans
of my enemies. That's how I knew about
them. He showed me what they were doing.
¹⁹I had been like a gentle lamb led off to be
killed. I didn't realize they had made plans
against me. They had said,

"Let's destroy the tree and its fruit.
Let's take away his life.
Then his name won't be remembered
anymore."
²⁰ But LORD, you rule over all.
You always judge fairly.
You test people's hearts and minds.
So pay them back for what they've
done.
I've committed my cause to you.

²¹The LORD says, "Jeremiah, here is what
I am telling you about the people of Anathoth. They say they're going to kill you.
They are saying, 'Don't prophesy in the
LORD's name. If you do, we will kill you
with our own hands.'" ²²So the LORD who
rules over all says, "I will punish them.
Their young men will be killed by swords.
Their sons and daughters will die of hun-
ger. ²³Only a few people will be left alive.
I will judge the people of Anathoth. I will
destroy them when the time comes to punish them."

Jeremiah Complains to the LORD

12 LORD, when I bring a matter to you,
you always do what is right.
But now I would like to speak with you
about whether you are being fair.
Why are sinful people successful?
Why do those who can't be trusted
have an easy life?

² You have planted them.
Their roots are deep in the ground.
They grow and produce fruit.
They honor you by what they say.
But their hearts are far away from
you.
³ LORD, you know me and see me.
You test my thoughts about you.
Drag those people off like sheep to be
killed!
Set them apart for the day of their
death!
⁴ How long will the land be thirsty for
water?
How long will the grass in every field
be dry?
The people who live in the land are evil.
So the animals and birds have died.
And that's not all. The people are
saying,
"The LORD won't see what happens
to us."

The LORD Answers Jeremiah

⁵ The LORD says, "Suppose you have
raced against people.
And suppose they have worn you
out.
Then how would you be able to race
against horses?
Suppose you feel safe only in open
country.
Then how would you get along in
the bushes near the Jordan
River?
⁶ Even your relatives have turned against
you.
They are members of your own
family.
They have shouted loudly at you.
They might say nice things about you.
But do not trust them.

⁷ "I will turn my back on my people.
I will desert my land.
I love the people of Judah.
In spite of that, I will hand them
over to their enemies.
⁸ My land has become to me
like a lion in the forest.
It roars at me.
So I hate it.
⁹ My own land has become like a spotted
hawk.
And other hawks surround it and
attack it.

Come, all you wild animals!
    Gather together!
    Come together to eat up my land.
[10] Many shepherds will destroy my
        vineyard.
    They will walk all over it.
    They will turn my pleasant vineyard
        into a dry and empty land.
[11] My vineyard will become a desert.
    It will be dry and empty in my sight.
    The whole land will be completely
        destroyed.
    And no one even cares.
[12] Many will come to destroy it.
    They will gather on the bare hilltops
        in the desert.
    I will use them as my sword to destroy
        my people.
    They will kill them from one end of
        the land to the other.
    No one will be safe.
[13] People will plant wheat. But all they will
        gather is thorns.
    They will wear themselves out. But
        they will not have anything to
        show for it.
    I am very angry with them.
    So they will be ashamed of the crop
        they gather."

[14] Here is what the LORD says. "All my
evil neighbors have taken over the land I
gave my people Israel. So I will pull them
up by their roots from the lands they live in.
And I will pull up the roots of the people of
Judah from among them. [15] But after I pull
up those nations, I will give my tender love
to them again. I will bring all of them back
to their own lands. I will take all of them
back to their own countries. [16] Suppose
those nations learn to follow the practices
of my people. And they make their promises in my name. When they promise, they
say, 'You can be sure that the LORD is alive.'
They do this just as they once taught my
people to make promises in Baal's name.
Then I will give them a place among my
people. [17] But what if one of those nations
does not listen? Then you can be sure of
this. I will pull it up by the roots and destroy it," announces the LORD.

A Linen Belt

13 The LORD said to me, "Go and buy a
linen belt. Put it around your waist.
But do not let it get wet." [2] So I bought a belt,

just as the LORD had told me to do. And I
put it around my waist.

[3] Then another message from the LORD
came to me. The LORD said, [4] "Take off the
belt you bought and are wearing around
your waist. Go to Perath. Hide the belt
there in a crack in the rocks." [5] So I went and
hid it at Perath. I did just as the LORD had
told me to do.

[6] Many days later the LORD said to me,
"Go to Perath. Get the belt I told you to
hide there." [7] So I went to Perath. I dug up
the belt. I took it from the place where I
had hidden it. But it had rotted. It was completely useless.

[8] Then another message from the LORD
came to me. The LORD said, [9] "In the same
way, I will destroy Judah's pride. And I will
destroy the great pride of Jerusalem. [10] These
people are evil. They refuse to listen to what I
say. They do what their stubborn hearts want
them to do. They chase after other gods.
They serve them and worship them. So they
will be like this belt. They will be completely useless. [11] A belt is tied around a person's
waist. In the same way, I tied all the people
of Israel to me. I also tied all the people of Judah to me like a belt. I wanted them to be my
people. They should have brought me fame
and praise and honor. But they have not listened to me," announces the LORD.

Wineskins

[12] "Tell them, 'The LORD is the God of
Israel. He says, "Every wineskin should be
filled with wine."' Here is what the people
might say to you. 'Don't we know that every
wineskin should be filled with wine?' [13] If
they do, here is what you must tell them.
'The LORD says, "I am going to fill with
wine everyone who lives in this land. I will
make the kings who sit on David's throne
drunk. And I will fill with wine the priests,
the prophets and everyone who lives in Jerusalem. [14] I will smash them against one
another. I will punish parents and children
alike," announces the LORD. "I will not feel
sorry for them. I will not show them any
kindness. My tender love for them will not
keep me from destroying them."'"

Judah Will Be Taken Away From Their Land

[15] People of Judah, listen to me.
    Pay attention and don't be proud.

The LORD has spoken.

16 Give glory to the LORD your God.
  Honor him before he sends
    darkness to cover the land.
Do this before you trip and fall
  on the darkened hills.
You hope that light will come.
  But he will turn it into thick
    darkness.
  He will change it to deep shadows.

17 If you don't listen,
  I will weep in secret.
  Because you are so proud,
I will weep bitterly.
  Tears will flow from my eyes.
  The LORD's flock will be taken away
    as prisoners.

18 Speak to the king and his mother. Tell
    them,
  "Come down from your thrones.
Your glorious crowns
  are about to fall from your heads."

19 The gates of the cities in the Negev
    Desert will be shut tight.
  There won't be anyone to open them.
Everyone in Judah will be carried away
    as prisoners.
  You will be completely taken away.

20 Jerusalem, look up!
  Your enemies are coming from the
    north.
Where is the flock you were supposed
    to take care of?
  Where are the sheep you were so
    proud of?

21 You have worked hard to make special
    friends.
  But the LORD will let them rule over
    you.
Then what will you say?
Suffering will take hold of you.
  It will be like the pain of a woman
    having a baby.

22 Suppose you ask yourself,
  "Why has this happened to me?"
It's because you have committed so
    many sins.
  That's the reason your skirt has been
    torn off.
  That's why your body has been
    treated so badly.

23 Can people from Ethiopia change their
    skin?
  Can leopards change their spots?

It's the same with you.
  You have always done what is evil.
  So how can you do what is good?

24 The LORD says, "I will scatter you like
    straw
  that the desert wind blows away.

25 This is what will happen to you.
  I have appointed it for you,"
    announces the LORD.
"You have forgotten me.
  You have trusted in other gods.

26 So I will pull your skirt up over your
    face.
  Then people will see the shame of
    your naked body.

27 They will see that you have not been
    faithful to me.
  You have committed adultery with
    other gods.
And you have acted like a prostitute
  who does not have any shame.
I have seen what you did
  on the hills and in the fields.
  And I hate it.
How terrible it will be for you,
    Jerusalem!
  How long will you choose to be
    'unclean'?"

War and Hunger

14 A message from the LORD came to
Jeremiah. He told Jeremiah there
wouldn't be any rain in the land. The LORD
said,

2 "Judah is filled with sadness.
  Its cities are wasting away.
The people weep for the land.
  Crying is heard in Jerusalem.

3 The nobles send their servants to get
    water.
  They go to the wells.
  But they do not find any water.
They return with empty jars.
  They are terrified. They do not have
    any hope.
  They cover their heads.

4 The ground is dry and cracked.
  There isn't any rain in the land.
The farmers are terrified.
  They cover their heads.

5 Even the female deer in the fields
  desert their newborn fawns.
  There isn't any grass to eat.

⁶ Wild donkeys stand on the bare
    hilltops.
        They long for water as wild dogs do.
    Their eyesight fails
        because they do not have any food
            to eat."

⁷ Lᴏʀᴅ, our sins are a witness against us.
    But do something for the honor of
        your name.
    We have often turned away from you.
        We've sinned against you.
⁸ You are Israel's only hope.
    You save us when we're in trouble.
    Why are you like a stranger to us?
        Why are you like a traveler who
            stays for only one night?
⁹ Why are you like a man taken by
        surprise?
    Why are you like a soldier who can't
        save anyone?
    Lᴏʀᴅ, you are among us.
        And we are your people.
        Please don't desert us!

¹⁰The Lᴏʀᴅ gave Jeremiah a message about these people. The Lᴏʀᴅ said,

"They really love to wander away from
    me.
    Their feet go down the wrong path.
I do not accept these people.
    I will remember the evil things they
        have done.
    I will punish them for their sins."

¹¹The Lᴏʀᴅ continued, "Do not pray that things will go well with them. ¹²Even if they go without food, I will not listen to their cry for help. They might sacrifice burnt offerings and grain offerings. But I will not accept them. Instead, I will destroy them with war, hunger and plague."

¹³But I said, "Lᴏʀᴅ and King, the prophets keep telling them something else. They say, 'You won't have to suffer from war or hunger. Instead, the Lᴏʀᴅ will give you peace and rest in this place.'"

¹⁴Then the Lᴏʀᴅ said to me, "The prophets are prophesying lies in my name. I have not sent them or appointed them. I have not even spoken to them. Everything they tell you about their visions or secret knowledge is a lie. They pretend to bring you messages from other gods. They try to get you to believe their own mistaken ideas. ¹⁵So here is what I am saying about the prophets who are prophesying in my name. I did not send them. But they are saying, 'No war or hunger will come to this land.' Those same prophets will die because of war and hunger. ¹⁶And the people they are prophesying to will be thrown out into the streets of Jerusalem. They will die because of hunger and war. No one will bury them. No one will bury their wives and children. I will pour out trouble on them. That is exactly what they should get.

¹⁷"Jeremiah, give them this message. Tell them,

"'Let tears flow from my eyes.
    Let them pour out night and day.
    Never let them stop.
The people of my own nation
    have suffered a terrible wound.
    They have been crushed.
¹⁸ Suppose I go into the country.
    Then I see people who have been
        killed by swords.
Or suppose I go into the city.
    Then I see people who have died of
        hunger.
Prophet and priest alike have gone to
    a land
    they hadn't known about before.'"

¹⁹ Lᴏʀᴅ, have you completely turned your
        back on Judah?
    Do you hate the city of Zion?
    Why have you made us suffer?

Jer. 14:17 A nickname for Jeremiah is "The Weeping Prophet" because of verses like Jeremiah 9:1 and this passage. There's nothing wrong with crying on the right occasions!

We can't be healed.
We hoped peace would come.
But nothing good has happened to
us.
We hoped we would finally be healed.
But all we got was terror.
²⁰ LORD, we admit we've done evil things.
We also admit that our people of
long ago were guilty.
It's true that we've sinned against
you.
²¹ For the honor of your name, don't turn
your back on us.
Don't bring shame on your glorious
throne in the temple.
Remember the covenant you made
with us.
Please don't break it.
²² Do any of the worthless gods of the
nations bring rain?
Do the skies send down showers all
by themselves?
No. LORD our God, you send the rain.
So we put our hope in you.
You are the one who does all these
things.

15 Then the LORD said to me, "Suppose Moses and Samuel were standing in front of me. Even then my heart would not feel sorry for these people. Send them away from me! Let them go! ²Suppose these people ask you, 'Where should we go?' Then tell them, 'The LORD says,

" " "Those I have appointed to die will die.
Those I have appointed to be killed by
swords
will be killed by swords.
Those I have appointed to die of hunger
will die of hunger.
Those I have appointed to be taken
away as prisoners
will be taken away." ' '

³"I will send four kinds of destroyers against them," announces the LORD. "Swords will kill them. Dogs will drag them away. Birds will eat them up. And wild animals will destroy them. ⁴I will make all the kingdoms on earth hate them. That will happen because of what Manasseh did in Jerusalem. He was king of Judah and the son of Hezekiah.

⁵ "Jerusalem, who will have pity on you?
Who will mourn for you?

Who will stop to ask how you are
doing?
⁶ You have said no to me,"
announces the LORD.
"You keep on turning away from
me.
So I will reach out and destroy you.
I am tired of showing you pity.
⁷ I will stand at the city gates of the land.
I will separate the straw from the
grain.
I will destroy my people. I will bring
great sorrow on them.
They have not changed their ways.
⁸ I will increase the number of their
widows.
There will be more of them than the
grains of sand on the seashore.
At noon I will bring a destroyer
against the mothers of the young
men among my people.
All at once I will bring down on them
great suffering and terror.
⁹ Mothers who have many children will
grow weak.
They will take their last breath.
The sun will set on them while it is still
day.
They will be dishonored and put to
shame.
All those who are left alive I will kill by
swords.
I will have their enemies do this,"
announces the LORD.

¹⁰ My mother, I wish I had never been
born!
The whole land opposes me.
They fight against me.
I haven't made loans to anyone.
And I haven't borrowed anything.
But everyone curses me anyway.

¹¹The LORD said,

"Jeremiah, I will keep you safe for a
good purpose.
I will make your enemies ask you to
pray for them.
They will make their appeal to you
when they are in great trouble.

¹² "People of Judah, the armies of Babylon
will come from the north.
They are as strong as iron and bronze.
Can anyone break their power?

¹³ I will give away your wealth and your
treasures.
Your enemies will carry off
everything.
And they will not pay anything for it.
That will happen because you have
sinned so much.
You have done it throughout your
country.
¹⁴ I will make you slaves to your enemies.
You will serve them in a land
you have not known about before.
My anger will start a fire
that will burn you up."

¹⁵ LORD, you understand how much I'm
suffering.
Show concern for me. Take care of
me.
Pay back those who are trying to
harm me.
You are patient. Don't take my life away
from me.
Think about how much shame I
suffer because of you.
¹⁶ When I received your words, I ate them.
They filled me with joy.
My heart took delight in them.
LORD God who rules over all,
I belong to you.
¹⁷ I never sat around with those who go to
wild parties.
I never had a good time with them.
I sat alone because you had put your
powerful hand on me.
Your anger against sin was burning
inside me.
¹⁸ Why does my pain never end?
Why is my wound so deep?
Why can't I ever get well?
To me you are like a stream that runs dry.
You are like a spring that doesn't
have any water.

¹⁹ So the LORD says to Jeremiah,

"If you turn away from your sins, I will
heal you.
And then you will be able to serve me.
Speak words that are worthy, not
worthless.
Then you will be speaking for me.
Let these people turn to you.
But you must not turn to them.
²⁰ I will make you like a wall to them.

I will make you like a strong bronze
wall.
The people will fight against you.
But they will not overcome you.
I am with you.
I will save you,"
announces the LORD.
²¹ "I will save you from the hands of evil
people.
I will set you free from those who
treat you badly."

Times of Trouble Are Coming

16 A message from the LORD came to
me. He said, ²"Jeremiah, you must
not get married. You must not have any
sons or daughters in this land." ³Here is the
LORD's message about the children born in
this place. He says about them and their
parents, ⁴"Some of them will die of deadly sicknesses. No one will mourn for them.
Their bodies will not be buried. Instead,
they will be like human waste lying there
on the ground. Others will die because of
war and hunger. Their bodies will not be
buried. Instead, they will become food for
the birds and the wild animals."

⁵The LORD says, "Jeremiah, suppose a
meal is being served because someone has
died. Do not enter any house where that is
happening. Do not go there to mourn or
to comfort the family. I will not bless these
people anymore. I have taken my love and
pity away from them," announces the LORD.
⁶"Important and unimportant people alike
will die in this land. Their bodies will not
be buried. No one will mourn for them. No
one will cut themselves or shave their head
for the dead. ⁷No one will offer food or
drink to comfort those who mourn for the
dead. No one will do this even if someone's
father or mother has died.

⁸"Do not enter a house where a feast is
being held. Do not sit down there to eat and
drink. ⁹I am the LORD who rules over all. I
am the God of Israel. I am telling you, 'In
your days I will judge your people. You will
see it with your own eyes. I will put an end
to the sounds of joy and gladness here in
Jerusalem. The voices of brides and grooms
will not be heard anymore.'

¹⁰"Tell these people all these things. They
will ask you, 'Why has the LORD decided to
send so much trouble on us? We haven't done
anything wrong. We haven't committed any

sins against the Lord our God.' [11]When they say this, here is what you should tell them. 'I did it because your people of long ago deserted me,' announces the Lord. 'They followed other gods. They served them and worshiped them. They deserted me. They did not obey my law. [12]But you have done more evil things than they did. All of you are doing what your stubborn and evil hearts want you to do. You are not obeying me. [13]So I will throw you out of this land. I will send you away to another land. Neither you nor your people of long ago have known about it. There you will serve other gods day and night. And I will not give you any help.'

[14]"But a new day is coming," announces the Lord. "At that time here is what people will no longer say. 'As sure as he is alive, the Lord brought the Israelites up out of Egypt.' [15]Instead, they will say, 'The Lord brought the Israelites up out of the land of the north. He gathered them out of all the countries where he had forced them to go. And that's just as sure as he is alive.' I will bring them back to the land I gave their people of long ago.

[16]"But now I will send for many fishermen," announces the Lord. "They will catch some of these people. After that, I will send for many hunters. They will hunt down the others on every mountain and hill. They will bring them out of the cracks in the rocks. [17]My eyes see everything these people do. What they do is not hidden from me. I always see their sin. [18]I will pay them back double for their sin and the evil things they have done. They have made my land 'unclean.' They have set up lifeless statues of their evil gods. They have filled my land with them. I hate those gods."

[19] Lord, you give me strength.
    You are like a fort to me.
When I'm in trouble,
    I go to you for safety.
The nations will come to you
    from one end of the earth to the other.
    They will gather together and say,
"Our people of long ago didn't own
    anything
    except statues of gods.
The statues were worthless.
    They didn't do them any good.
[20] Do human beings really make their
    own gods?
    Yes. But they aren't really gods at all!"

[21] The Lord says, "So I will teach them
    about myself.
This time I will show them
    how powerful and mighty I am.
Then they will know
    that I am the Lord.

17

"Judah's sin is carved with an iron tool.
    It is written with the flint point of
    the tool.
It is carved on the tablets of their hearts.
    It is written on the horns that stick
    out
    from the corners of their altars.
[2] Even their children offer sacrifices
    to other gods on those altars.
They use the poles that were made
    to worship the female god named
    Asherah.
They worship strange gods beside the
    green trees
    and on the high hills.
[3] I will give away my holy Mount Zion to
    the Babylonians.
Your enemies will carry off your
    wealth
    and all your treasures.
I will give away your high places.
    That will happen because you have
    sinned.
    You have done it throughout your
    country.
[4] You will lose the land I gave you.
    And it will be your own fault.
I will make you slaves to your enemies.
    You will serve them in a land you
    didn't know about before.
You have set my anger on fire.
    It will burn forever."

[5]The Lord says,

"Those who trust in human beings are
    under my curse.
    They depend on human strength.
    Their hearts turn away from me.
[6] They will be like a bush in a dry and
    empty land.
    They will not enjoy success when it
    comes.
They will live in dry places in the desert.
    It is a land of salt where no one else
    lives.

[7] "But I will bless anyone who trusts in me.
    I will do good things for the person
    who depends on me.

WHAT ABOUT YOU?

It seems our natural response when we get into trouble is to pass the blame on to someone or something else. It wasn't my fault! I was pressured into it. I had no choice or—well, you can fill in the blank.

We all make mistakes. Still, we need to take responsibility for our actions. Think about the last time you got into trouble. It's very likely that you knew exactly what you were doing.

Jeremiah 17:9 says, "A human heart is more dishonest than anything else. It can't be healed. Who can understand it?"

But there's good news. If you've asked God to forgive your sins, He's given you the cure for your sinful heart: He sent the Holy Spirit. The Spirit convicts us when we've done wrong, and helps us resist temptation. He's ready to change your heart from a sinful one to a holy one.

Do you find yourself making the wrong choices, but feel like you can't change? There's hope! Ask the Holy Spirit to convict you and guide you to live God's way. It might be a good idea to talk with your parents or another trusted adult. They can encourage you as you try to stay on the right path.

---

8 They will be like a tree planted near
        water.
    It sends out its roots beside a
        stream.
  It is not afraid when heat comes.
    Its leaves are always green.
  It does not worry when there is no rain.
    It always bears fruit."

9 A human heart is more dishonest than
        anything else.
    It can't be healed.
    Who can understand it?

10 The LORD says, "I look deep down
        inside human hearts.
    I see what is in people's minds.
  I reward each person in keeping with
        their conduct.
    I bless them based on what they
        have done."

11 Some people get rich by doing sinful
        things.
    They are like a partridge that hatches
        eggs it didn't lay.
  When their lives are half over, their
        riches will desert them.
    In the end they will prove how
        foolish they have been.

12 Our temple is where the LORD's
        glorious throne is.
    From the beginning it has been high
        and lifted up.

13 LORD, you are Israel's only hope.
    Everyone who deserts you will be
        put to shame.
  The names of those who turn away
        from you will be listed among
        the dead.
    LORD, they have deserted you.
    You are the spring of water that gives
        life.

14 LORD, heal me. Then I will be healed.
    Save me from my enemies. Then I
        will be saved.
    You are the one I praise.

15 They keep saying to me,
    "What has happened to the message
        the LORD gave you?
    Let it come true right now!"

16 I haven't run away from being the
        shepherd of your people.
    You know I haven't wanted the day
        of Jerusalem's fall to come.
    You are aware of every word that
        comes from my lips.

17 Don't be a terror to me.

When I'm in trouble, I go to you for
   safety.
[18] Let those who attack me be put to shame.
   But keep me from shame.
Let them be terrified.
   But keep me from terror.
Bring the day of trouble on them.
   Destroy them once and for all.

Keep the Sabbath Day Holy

[19]The LORD said to me, "Go. Stand at the city gate called the Gate of the People. That is where the kings of Judah go in and out. Then stand at all the other gates of Jerusalem. [20]Say, 'Listen to the LORD's message, you kings of Judah and all you people of Judah and Jerusalem. You always come through these gates. [21]The LORD says, "Make sure you do not carry a load on the Sabbath day. Do not bring it through the gates of Jerusalem. [22]Do not bring a load out of your houses on the Sabbath day. Do not do any work on that day. Instead, keep the Sabbath day holy. Do as I commanded your people of long ago. [23]But they did not listen. They did not pay any attention to me. They were stubborn. They would not listen or pay attention when I corrected them. [24]Be careful to obey me," announces the LORD. "Do not bring a load through the gates of this city on the Sabbath day. Instead, keep the Sabbath day holy. Do not do any work on it. [25]Then kings who sit on David's throne will come through the gates of this city. They and their officials will come riding in chariots and on horses. The people of Judah and Jerusalem will come along with them. And this city will always have people living in it. [26]Some will come from the towns of Judah. And some will come in from the villages around Jerusalem. Others will come from the territory of Benjamin. And others will come in from the western hills. Still others will come from the central hill country and the Negev Desert. All of them will bring burnt offerings and sacrifices. They will come bringing grain offerings, incense and thank offerings. They will take all these offerings to my house. [27]But what if you do not obey me? Suppose you do not keep the Sabbath day holy. And suppose you carry a load through the gates of Jerusalem on the Sabbath day. Then I will start a fire that can't be put out. It will begin at the gates of Jerusalem. It will destroy its mighty towers.'"'"

The LORD Sends Jeremiah to the Potter's House

18 A message from the LORD came to me. He said, [2]"Jeremiah, go down to the potter's house. I will give you my message there." [3]So I went down to the potter's house. I saw him working at his wheel. [4]His hands were shaping a pot out of clay. But he saw that something was wrong with it. So he formed it into another pot. He shaped it in the way that seemed best to him.

[5]Then the LORD's message came to me. [6]"People of Israel, I can do with you just as this potter does," announces the LORD. "The clay is in the potter's hand. And you are in my hand, people of Israel. [7]Suppose I announce that something will happen to a nation or kingdom. Suppose I announce that it will be pulled up by the roots. And I announce that it will be torn down and destroyed. [8]But suppose the nation I warned turns away from its sins. Then I will not do what I said I would. I will not bring trouble on it as I had planned. [9]But suppose I announce that a nation or kingdom is going to be built up and planted. [10]And then it does what is evil in my eyes. It does not obey me. Then I will think again about the good things I had wanted to do for it.

[11]"So speak to the people of Judah and Jerusalem. Tell them, 'The LORD says, "Look! I am making plans against you. I am going to bring trouble on you. So each one of you must turn from your evil ways. Change the way you live and act."' [12]But they will reply, 'It's no use. We will continue to do what we've already planned. All of us will do what our stubborn and evil hearts want us to do.'"

[13]So the LORD says,

"Ask the nations a question. Say to them,
   'Who has ever heard anything like
      this?
The people of Israel have done
   a very horrible thing.
[14] Does the snow ever disappear
   from Lebanon's rocky slopes?
Do its cool waters ever stop
   flowing from places far away?
[15] But my people have forgotten me.
   They burn incense to worthless
      gods.
Their gods made them trip and fall
   as they walked on the old paths.

They made them use side roads
  instead of roads that were built up.
¹⁶ So their land will become a horrible
    thing.
  People will make fun of it again and
    again.
All those who pass by it will be
    shocked.
  They will shake their heads.
¹⁷ I will sweep over my people like a wind
    from the east.
  I will use the Babylonians to scatter
    them.
  I will show them my back and not my
    face.
  I will desert them when their day of
    trouble comes.' "

¹⁸ They said, "Come on. Let's make plans
against Jeremiah. We'll still have priests to
teach us the law. We'll always have wise
people to give us advice. We'll have prophets to bring us messages from the LORD. So
come on. Let's speak out against Jeremiah.
We shouldn't pay any attention to what he
says."

¹⁹ LORD, please listen to me!
  Hear what my enemies are saying
    about me!
²⁰ Should the good things I've done be
    paid back with evil?
  But my enemies have dug a pit for me.
Remember that I stood in front of you
    and spoke up for them.
  I tried to turn your anger away from
    them.
²¹ So let their children die of hunger.
  Let my enemies be killed in war.
Let their wives lose their children and
    husbands.
  Let their men be put to death.
  Let their young men be killed in
    battle.
²² Bring their enemies against them
    without warning.
  Let cries be heard from their houses.
They have dug a pit to capture me.
  They have hidden traps for my feet.
²³ But LORD, you know
  all about their plans to kill me.
Don't forgive their crimes.
  Don't erase their sins from your sight.
Destroy my enemies.
  Punish them when the time to show
    your anger comes.

19 The LORD said to Jeremiah, "Go and
buy a clay jar from a potter. Take
along some of the elders of the people. Also
tell some of the priests to go with you. ²Go
out to the Valley of Ben Hinnom. Stand
near the entrance of the gate where broken
pieces of pottery are thrown away. There
announce the message I give you. ³Tell the
people, 'Listen to the LORD's message, you
kings of Judah and people of Jerusalem.
The LORD who rules over all is the God of
Israel. He says, "Listen! I am going to bring
trouble on Jerusalem. It will be so horrible
that it will make the ears of everyone who
hears about it ring. ⁴My people have deserted me. They have made this city a place
where other gods are worshiped. They have
burned incense to them here. They, their
people of long ago and the kings of Judah
had never known these gods. My people
have also filled this place with the blood of
those who aren't guilty. ⁵They have built the
high places where they worship Baal. There
they sacrifice their children in the fire as
offerings to Baal. That is something I did
not command or talk about. It did not even
enter my mind. ⁶So watch out!" announces the LORD. "The days are coming when
people will not call this place Topheth anymore. And they will not call it the Valley of
Ben Hinnom either. Instead, they will call it
the Valley of Death.

⁷ " 'In this place I will make the plans
of Judah and Jerusalem as useless as a broken jar. I will use their enemies to kill my
people by swords. They will die at the hands
of those who want to take their lives. I will
give their dead bodies as food to the birds
and the wild animals. ⁸I will completely
destroy this city. I will make it a horrible
thing. People will make fun of it. All those
who pass by it will be shocked. They will
laugh at its people because of all their
wounds. ⁹I will make the people of this city
eat their sons and daughters. And they will
eat one another. They will do this because
things will be so bad during the attack. The
enemies who want to take their lives will
bring all this trouble on them.' '

¹⁰ "Jeremiah, break the jar while those
who go with you are watching. ¹¹Tell them,
'Here is what the LORD who rules over all
says. "This potter's jar is smashed and can't
be repaired. And I will smash this nation
and this city. People will bury their dead

in Topheth. But they will run out of room. [12]Here is what I will do to Jerusalem and those who live here," ' announces the LORD. ' "I will make this city like Topheth. [13]The houses in Jerusalem will be made 'unclean' like Topheth. So will the houses of the kings of Judah. All these people burned incense on their roofs to all the stars. They poured out drink offerings to other gods." ' "

[14]Then Jeremiah returned from Topheth. That's where the LORD had sent him to prophesy. Jeremiah stood in the courtyard of the LORD's temple. He spoke to all the people. He said, [15]"The LORD who rules over all is the God of Israel. He says, 'Listen! I am going to punish this city and all the villages around it. I am going to bring against them all the trouble I have announced. That's because my people were stubborn. They would not listen to what I said.' "

Jeremiah and Pashhur

20 Pashhur the priest was the official in charge of the LORD's temple. He was the son of Immer. Pashhur heard Jeremiah prophesying that Jerusalem would be destroyed. [2]So he had Jeremiah the prophet beaten. Then Pashhur put him in prison at the Upper Gate of Benjamin at the LORD's temple. [3]The next day Pashhur set him free. Jeremiah said to him, "The LORD's name for you isn't Pashhur. The LORD's name for you is Terror on Every Side. [4]The LORD says to you, 'I will make you a terror to yourself. You will also be a terror to all your friends. With your own eyes you will see them die. Their enemies will kill them with swords. I will hand over all the people of Judah to the king of Babylon. He will carry them away to Babylon or kill them with swords. [5]I will hand over all the wealth of this city to Judah's enemies. I will give them all its products and everything of value. I will turn over to them all the treasures that belonged to the kings of Judah. They will take these things and carry them off to Babylon. [6]Pashhur, you and everyone who lives in your house will also be forced to go there. You have prophesied lies to all your friends. So all of you will die and be buried in Babylon.' "

Jeremiah Complains to the LORD

[7] You tricked me, LORD, and I was tricked.
　　You overpowered me and won.
People make fun of me all day long.
　　Everyone laughs at me.
[8] Every time I speak, I cry out.
　　All you ever tell me to talk about
　　　is fighting and trouble.
Your message has brought me nothing
　　　but dishonor.
　　It has made me suffer shame all day
　　　long.
[9] Sometimes I think, "I won't talk about
　　　his message anymore.
　　I'll never speak in his name again."
But then your message burns in my
　　　heart.
　　It's like a fire deep inside my bones.
I'm tired of holding it in.
　　In fact, I can't.
[10] I hear many people whispering,
　　"There is terror on every side!
　　Bring charges against Jeremiah! Let's
　　　bring charges against him!"
All my friends
　　are waiting for me to slip.
They are saying, "Perhaps he will be
　　　tricked
　　into making a mistake.
Then we'll win out over him.
　　We'll get even with him."

[11] But you are with me like a mighty
　　　warrior.
　　So those who are trying to harm me
　　　will trip and fall.
　　They won't win out over me.
They will fail. They'll be totally put to
　　　shame.
　　Their dishonor will never be
　　　forgotten.

[12] LORD, you rule over all.
　　You test those who do what is right.
　　You see what is in people's hearts
　　　and minds.
So pay them back for what they've
　　　done.
　　I've committed my cause to you.

[13] Sing to the LORD, you people!
　　Give praise to him!
He saves the lives of people in need.
　　He saves them from the power of
　　　sinful people.

[14] May the day I was born be cursed!
　　May the day I was born to my
　　　mother not be blessed!

¹⁵ May the man who brought my father
    the news be cursed!
   He's the one who made my father
    very glad.
   He said, "You have had a baby! It's
    a boy!"
¹⁶ May that man be like the towns
    the LORD destroyed without pity.
   May that man hear loud weeping in the
    morning.
   May he hear a battle cry at noon.
¹⁷ He should have killed me in my
    mother's body.
   He should have made my mother
    my grave.
   He should have let her body stay
    large forever.
¹⁸ Why did I ever come out of my
    mother's body?
   I've seen nothing but trouble and
    sorrow.
   My days will end in shame.

The LORD Refuses Zedekiah's Appeal

21 A message from the LORD came to Jeremiah. It came when King Zedekiah sent Pashhur to Jeremiah. Pashhur was the son of Malkijah. Zedekiah sent Zephaniah the priest along with him. Zephaniah was the son of Maaseiah. They said to Jeremiah, ²"Ask the LORD to help us. Nebuchadnezzar king of Babylon is attacking us. In the past the LORD did wonderful things for us. Maybe he'll do them again. Then Nebuchadnezzar will pull his armies back from us."

³But Jeremiah answered them, "Tell Zedekiah and his people, ⁴'The LORD is the God of Israel. He says, "The king of Babylon and his armies are all around this city. They are getting ready to attack you. You have weapons of war in your hands to fight against them. But I am about to turn your weapons against you. And I will bring your enemies inside this city. ⁵I myself will fight against you. I will reach out my powerful hand and mighty arm. I will come against you with all my great anger. ⁶I will strike down those who live in this city. I will kill people and animals alike. They will die of a terrible plague. ⁷After that, I will hand you over to your enemies. They want to kill you," announces the LORD. "I will hand over Zedekiah, the king of Judah, and his officials. I will also hand over the people in this city who live through the plague, war

and hunger. All of them will be handed over to Nebuchadnezzar, the king of Babylon. He will kill them with swords. He will show them no mercy. He will not feel sorry for them. In fact, he will not have any concern for them at all." '

⁸"Tell the people, 'The LORD says, "I am offering you a choice. You can choose the way that leads to life. Or you can choose the way that leads to death. ⁹Those who stay in this city will die of war, hunger or plague. But suppose some go out and give themselves up to the Babylonians attacking you. They will live. They will escape with their lives. ¹⁰I have decided to do this city harm and not good," announces the LORD. "It will be handed over to the king of Babylon. And he will destroy it with fire." '

¹¹"Also speak to Judah's royal family. Tell them, 'Listen to the LORD's message. ¹²Here is what the LORD says to you who belong to David's royal house.

   " ' "Every morning do what is right and
    fair.
   Save those who have been robbed.
   Set them free from the people who
    have treated them badly.
   If you do not, my anger will blaze out
    against you.
   It will burn like fire because of the
    evil things you have done.
   No one will be able to put it out.
¹³ Jerusalem, I am against you,"
   announces the LORD.
   "You live above this valley.
   You are on a high, rocky plain.
   And you say, 'Who can come against us?
   Who can enter our place of safety?'
¹⁴ But I will punish you in keeping with
    what you have done,"
   announces the LORD.
   "I will start a fire in your forests.
   It will burn down everything around
    you." ' "

The LORD Judges Evil Kings

22 The LORD said to Jeremiah, "Go down to the palace of the king of Judah. Announce my message there. Tell him, ²'King of Judah, listen to the LORD's message. You are sitting on David's throne. You and your officials and your people come through these gates. ³The LORD says, "Do what is fair and right. Save those who have been robbed. Set them free from the people who

Jer. 22:3

More than twenty Bible verses refer to widows and orphans and their care. Psalm 68:5 says that God is the father of the fatherless. He is also the husband of widows (Isaiah 54:5).

has the Lord done such a thing to this great city?' ⁹And the answer will be, 'This happened because of what its people have done. They have turned away from the covenant the Lord their God made with them. They have worshiped other gods. And they have served them.' "

¹⁰ Don't weep over dead King Josiah.
    Don't be sad because he's gone.
Instead, weep bitterly over King
      Jehoahaz.
    He was forced to leave his country.
    He'll never return.
    He'll never see his own land again.

¹¹Jehoahaz became king of Judah after his father Josiah. But he has gone away from this place. That's because the Lord says about him, "He will never return. ¹²He will die in Egypt. That is where he was taken as a prisoner. He will not see this land again."

¹³ The Lord says, "How terrible it will be
      for King Jehoiakim!
    He builds his palace
    by mistreating his people.
He builds its upstairs rooms
    with money gained by sinning.
He makes his own people work for
      nothing.
    He does not pay them for what they
      do.
¹⁴ He says, 'I will build myself a great
      palace.
    It will have large rooms upstairs.'
So he makes big windows in it.
    He covers its walls with cedar boards.
    He decorates it with red paint.

¹⁵ "Jehoiakim, does having more and
      more cedar boards
    make you a king?
Your father Josiah had enough to eat
      and drink.
    He did what was right and fair.
    So everything went well with him.
¹⁶ He stood up for those who were poor
      or needy.
    So everything went well with him.
That is what it means to know me,"
    announces the Lord.
¹⁷ "Jehoiakim, the only thing on your mind
    is to get rich by cheating others.
You would even kill people who are not
      guilty
    of doing anything wrong.

have treated them badly. Do not do anything wrong to outsiders or widows in this place. Do not harm children whose fathers have died. Do not kill those who are not guilty of doing anything wrong. ⁴Be careful to obey these commands. Then kings who sit on David's throne will come through the gates of this palace. They will come riding in chariots and on horses. Their officials and their people will come along with them. ⁵But suppose you do not obey these commands," announces the Lord. "Then I promise you that this palace will be destroyed. You can be as sure of this promise as you are sure that I live." ' "

⁶The Lord speaks about the palace of the king of Judah. He says,

"You are like the land of Gilead to me.
    You are like the highest mountain in
      Lebanon.
But I will make you like a desert.
    You will become like towns that no
      one lives in.
⁷ I will send destroyers against you.
    All of them will come with their
      weapons.
They will cut up your fine cedar beams.
    They will throw them into the fire.

⁸"People from many nations will pass by this city. They will ask one another, 'Why

You would mistreat them.
  You would take everything they own."

¹⁸So the LORD speaks about King Jehoiakim, the son of Josiah. He says,

"His people will not mourn for him.
  They will not say,
  'My poor brother! My poor sister!'
They will not mourn for him.
  They will not say,
  'My poor master! How sad that his
    glory is gone!'
¹⁹ In fact, he will be buried like a donkey.
  His body will be dragged away and
    thrown
  outside the gates of Jerusalem."

²⁰ The LORD says, "People of Jerusalem, go
    up to Lebanon.
  Cry out for help.
  Let your voice be heard in the land
    of Bashan.
  Cry out from the mountains of Abarim.
  All those who were going to help
    you are crushed.
²¹ When you felt secure, I warned you.
  But you said, 'I won't listen!'
You have acted like that ever since you
    were young.
  You have not obeyed me.
²² The wind will drive away all your
    shepherds.
  All those who were going to help you
    will be carried off as prisoners.
Then you will be dishonored and put to
    shame.
  That will happen because you have
    been so sinful.
²³ Some of you live in Jerusalem in the
    Palace of the Forest of Lebanon.
  You are comfortable in your cedar
    buildings.
But you will groan when pain comes
    on you.
  It will be like the pain of a woman
    having a baby.

²⁴"King Jehoiachin, you are the son of Jehoiakim," announces the LORD. "Suppose you were a ring on my right hand. And suppose the ring even had my royal mark on it. Then I would still pull you off my finger. And that is just as sure as I am alive. ²⁵I will hand you over to those who want to kill you. I will hand you over to people you are afraid of. I will give you to Nebuchadnezzar, the king of Babylon. I will hand you over to his armies. ²⁶I will throw you out into another country. I will throw your mother out. Neither of you was born in that country. But both of you will die there. ²⁷You will never come back to the land you long to return to."

²⁸ This man Jehoiachin is like a broken pot.
  Everyone hates him. No one wants
    him.
  Why will he and his children be thrown
    out of this land?
  Why will they be sent to a land
    they don't know about?
²⁹ Land, land, land,
  listen to the LORD's message!
³⁰ The LORD says,
"Let the record say that this man did
    not have any children.
  Let it report that he did not have any
    success in life.
None of his children will have success
    either.
  None of them will sit on David's
    throne.
  None of them will ever rule over
    Judah.

The Godly Branch

23 "How terrible it will be for the shepherds who lead my people astray!" announces the LORD. "They are destroying and scattering the sheep that belong to my flock." ²So the LORD, the God of Israel, speaks to the shepherds who take care of my people. He tells them, "You have scattered my sheep. You have driven them away. You have not taken good care of them. So I will punish you for the evil things you have done," announces the LORD. ³"I myself will gather together those who are left alive in my flock. I will gather them out of all the countries where I have driven them. And I will bring them back to their own land. There my sheep will have many lambs. There will be many more of them. ⁴I will place shepherds over them who will take good care of them. My sheep will not be afraid or terrified anymore. And none of them will be missing," announces the LORD.

⁵ "A new day is coming," announces the
    LORD.
  "At that time I will raise up for
    David's royal line
  a godly Branch.

He will be a King who will rule wisely.
  He will do what is fair and right in
    the land.
⁶ In his days Judah will be saved.
  Israel will live in safety.
  And the Branch will be called
    The LORD Who Makes Us Right
      With Himself.

⁷Other days are also coming," announces the LORD. "At that time people will no
longer say, 'The LORD brought the Israelites
up out of Egypt. And that's just as sure as he
is alive.' ⁸Instead, they will say, 'The LORD
brought the Israelites up out of the land of
the north. He gathered them out of all the
countries where he had forced them to go.
And that's just as sure as he is alive.' Then
they will live in their own land."

Prophets Who Tell Lies

⁹Here is my message about the prophets.

My heart is broken inside me.
  All my bones tremble with fear.
I am like a man who is drunk.
  I am like a strong man who has had
    too much wine.
That's what the LORD's holy words
  have done to me.
¹⁰ The land is full of people
  who aren't faithful to the LORD.
Now the land is under his curse.
  And that's why it is thirsty for water.
  That's why the desert grasslands are
    dry.
The prophets are leading sinful lives.
  They don't use their power in the
    right way.

¹¹ "Prophets and priests alike are ungodly,"
  announces the LORD.
  "Even in my temple I find them
    sinning.
¹² So their path will become slippery.
  They will be thrown out into
    darkness.
  There they will fall.
I will bring trouble on them
  when the time to punish them
    comes,"
  announces the LORD.

¹³ "Among the prophets of Samaria
  I saw something I can't stand.
They were prophesying in the name of
  Baal.

They were leading my people Israel
  astray.
¹⁴ I have also seen something horrible
    among Jerusalem's prophets.
  They are not faithful to me.
  They are not living by the truth.
  They strengthen the hands of those who
    do evil.
  So not one of them turns from their
    sinful ways.
All of them are like the people of
  Sodom to me.
  They are just like the people of
    Gomorrah."

¹⁵So the LORD who rules over all speaks
about the prophets. He says,

"I will make them eat bitter food.
  I will make them drink poisoned
    water.
The prophets of Jerusalem have spread
  their ungodly ways all through the
    land."

¹⁶The LORD who rules over all says to the
people of Judah,

"Do not listen to what the prophets are
  saying to you.
  They fill you with false hopes.
They talk about visions that come from
  their own minds.
What they say does not come from
  my mouth.
¹⁷ They keep speaking to those who hate
  me. They say,
  'The LORD says you will have peace.'
They speak to all those who do
  what their stubborn hearts want
    them to do.
  They tell them, 'No harm will come
    to you.'
¹⁸ But which of them has ever stood in my
    courts?
  Have they been there to see a vision
    or hear my message?
  Who has listened and heard my
    message there?
¹⁹ A storm will burst out
  because of my great anger.
A windstorm will sweep down
  on the heads of sinful people.
²⁰ My anger will not turn back.
  I will accomplish everything
  I plan to do.
In days to come

you will understand it clearly.
²¹ I did not send these prophets.
But they have run to tell you their
message anyway.
I did not speak to them.
But they have still prophesied.
²² Suppose they had stood in my courts.
Then they would have announced
my message to my people.
They would have turned my people
from their evil ways.
They would have turned them away
from their sins.

²³ "Am I only a God who is nearby?"
announces the LORD.
"Am I not a God who is also far
away?
²⁴ Who can hide in secret places
so that I can't see them?"
announces the LORD.
"Don't I fill heaven and earth?"
announces the LORD.

²⁵"I have heard what the prophets are saying. They prophesy lies in my name. They say, 'I had a dream! The LORD has given me a dream!' ²⁶How long will that continue in the hearts of these prophets who tell lies? They try to get others to believe their own mistaken ideas. ²⁷They tell one another their dreams. They think that will make my people forget my name. In the same way, their people of long ago forgot my name when they worshiped Baal. ²⁸Let the prophet who has a dream describe the dream. But let the one who has my message speak it faithfully. Your prophets have given you straw to eat instead of grain," announces the LORD. ²⁹"My message is like fire," announces the LORD. "It is like a hammer that breaks a rock in pieces.

³⁰"So I am against these prophets," announces the LORD. "I am against those who steal messages from one another. They claim that the messages come from me. ³¹Yes," announces the LORD. "I am against the prophets who speak their own words. But they still say, 'Here is what the LORD says.' ³²I am against prophets who talk about dreams that did not come from me," announces the LORD. "They tell foolish lies. Their lies lead my people astray. But I did not send these prophets. I did not appoint them. They do not help my people in the least," announces the LORD.

Prophets Who Give Messages That Are Not From the LORD

³³"Jeremiah, these people might ask you a question. Or a prophet or priest might do this. They might ask, 'What message have you received from the LORD?' Then tell them, 'You ask, "What message?" Here it is. "I will desert you," announces the LORD.' ³⁴A prophet or priest might make a claim. Or someone else might do this. He might claim, 'This is a message from the LORD.' Then I will punish them and their family. ³⁵Here is what each of you people keeps on saying to your friends and other Israelites. You ask, 'What is the LORD's answer?' Or you ask, 'What has the LORD spoken?' ³⁶But you must not talk about 'a message from the LORD' again. That's because each person's own words become their message. And so you twist the LORD's words. He is the living God. He is the LORD who rules over all. And he is our God. ³⁷Here is what you keep saying to a prophet. You ask, 'What is the LORD's answer to you?' Or you ask, 'What has the LORD spoken?' ³⁸You claim, 'This is a message from the LORD.' But here is what the LORD says. 'You used the words, "This is a message from the LORD." But I told you that you must not claim, "This is a message from the LORD." ' ³⁹So you can be sure I will forget you. I will throw you out of my sight. I will also destroy the city I gave you and your people of long ago. ⁴⁰I will bring on you shame that will last forever. It will never be forgotten."

Judah Is Like Two Baskets of Figs

24 King Jehoiachin was forced to leave Jerusalem. He was the son of Jehoiakim. Jehoiachin was taken to Babylon by Nebuchadnezzar, the king of Babylon. The officials and all the skilled workers were forced to leave with him. After they left, the LORD showed me two baskets of figs. They were in front of his temple. ²One basket had very good figs in it. They were like figs that ripen early. The other basket had very bad figs in it. In fact, they were so bad they couldn't even be eaten.

³Then the LORD asked me, "What do you see, Jeremiah?"

"Figs," I answered. "The good ones are very good. But the others are so bad they can't be eaten."

⁴Then a message from the LORD came to me. The LORD said, ⁵"I am the LORD, the

God of Israel. I say, 'I consider the people who were forced to leave Judah to be like these good figs. I sent them away from this place. I forced them to go to Babylon. ⁶My eyes will watch over them. I will be good to them. And I will bring them back to this land. I will build them up. I will not tear them down. I will plant them. I will not pull them up by the roots. ⁷I will change their hearts. Then they will know that I am the LORD. They will be my people. And I will be their God. They will return to me with all their heart.

⁸"But there are also bad figs. In fact, they are so bad they can't be eaten,' says the LORD. 'Zedekiah, the king of Judah, is like these bad figs. So are his officials and the people of Jerusalem who are still left alive. I will punish them whether they remain in this land or live in Egypt. ⁹I will make all the kingdoms on earth displeased with them. In fact, they will hate them a great deal. They will shake their heads at them. They will curse them and make fun of them. All this will happen no matter where I force them to go. ¹⁰I will send war, hunger and plague against them. They will be destroyed from the land I gave them and their people of long ago.'"

Seventy Years in Babylon

25 A message from the LORD about all the people of Judah came to Jeremiah. It came in the fourth year that Jehoiakim was the king of Judah. It was the first year that Nebuchadnezzar was the king of Babylon. Jehoiakim was the son of Josiah. ²Jeremiah, the LORD's prophet, spoke to all the people of Judah and Jerusalem. He said, ³"For 23 years the LORD's messages have been coming to me. They began to come in the 13th year that Josiah was king of Judah. He was the son of Amon. The LORD's messages still come to me today. I've spoken to you people again and again. But you haven't listened to me.

⁴"The LORD has sent all his servants the prophets to you. They've come to you again and again. But you haven't listened. You haven't paid any attention to them. ⁵They said, 'Each of you must turn from your evil ways and practices. Then you can stay in the land forever. It's the land the LORD gave you and your people of long ago. ⁶Don't follow other gods. Don't serve them or worship them. Don't make the LORD angry with the gods your own hands have made. Then he won't harm you.'

⁷"But you did not listen to me,' announces the LORD. 'You have made me very angry with the gods your hands have made. And you have brought harm on yourselves.'

⁸"The LORD who rules over all says, 'You have not listened to my words. ⁹So I will send for all the nations in the north. And I will send for my servant Nebuchadnezzar, the king of Babylon,' announces the LORD. 'I will bring all of them against this land and against you who live here. They will march out against all the nations that are around this land. I will set apart Judah and the nations around it in a special way to be destroyed. People will be shocked because of them. And they will make fun of them. Those nations will be destroyed forever. ¹⁰I will put an end to the sounds of joy and gladness. I will put an end to the voices of brides and grooms. The sound of grinding millstones will not be heard anymore. And lamps will not be lit anymore. ¹¹This whole country will become dry and empty. And these nations will serve the king of Babylon for 70 years.

¹²"But I will punish that king and his nation because they are guilty. I will do this when the 70 years are over,' announces the LORD. 'I will make that land a desert forever. ¹³I have spoken against that land. And I will make all these things happen to it. Everything will happen that is written in this book. And I will make everything Jeremiah prophesied against all the nations come true. ¹⁴The people of Babylon will become slaves of many other nations and great kings. I will pay them back for what they have done.'"

The Cup of God's Great Anger

¹⁵The LORD is the God of Israel. He said to me, "Take this cup from my hand. It is filled with the wine of my great anger. Make all the nations to which I send you drink it. ¹⁶When they drink it, they will not even be able to walk straight. It will drive them out of their minds. I am going to send war against them." ¹⁷So I took the cup from the LORD's hand. I made all the nations to which he sent me drink from it.

¹⁸He sent me to Judah's kings and officials. He told me to go to

Jerusalem and the towns of Judah. He wanted me to tell them they would be destroyed. Then people would be shocked because of them. They would make fun of them. They would use their name in a curse. And that's how things still are today.

¹⁹ Here is a list of the other kings and nations he sent me to.

Pharaoh, the king of Egypt
his attendants, his officials, all his people

²⁰ all the people from other lands who lived there
all the kings of Uz
the Philistine kings of Ashkelon, Gaza and Ekron
the Philistines still living in Ashdod

²¹ Edom, Moab, Ammon

²² all the kings of Tyre and Sidon
the kings of the islands and other lands along the Mediterranean Sea

²³ Dedan, Teman, Buz
all the other places far away in the east

²⁴ all the kings of Arabia
all the other kings of people who live in the desert

²⁵ all the kings of Zimri, Elam and Media

²⁶ all the kings in the north, near and far

So he sent me to all the kingdoms on the face of the earth, one after the other. They will all drink from the cup of the LORD's anger. After they drink, the king of Babylon will drink from it too.

²⁷ The LORD says, "Tell them, 'The LORD who rules over all is the God of Israel. He says, "Drink from this cup. Get drunk and throw up. Fall down and do not get up again. I am going to send war against you."' ²⁸ But they might refuse to take the cup from your hand. They might not want to drink from it. Then tell them, 'The LORD who rules over all says, "You must drink from it! ²⁹ I am beginning to bring trouble on the city where I have put my Name. You might think you will not be punished. But you will certainly be punished. I am sending war against everyone who lives on earth," announces the LORD who rules over all.'

³⁰ "Jeremiah, prophesy against them. Tell them,

" 'The LORD will roar from heaven like a lion.
His voice will sound like thunder from his holy temple there.
He will roar loudly against his land.
He will shout like those who stomp on grapes in winepresses.
He will shout against everyone who lives on earth.'

³¹ The noise of battle will be heard from one end of the earth to the other.
That's because the LORD will bring charges against the nations.
He will judge every human being.
He will kill sinful people with his sword,' "
announces the LORD.

³² The LORD who rules over all says,

"Look! Horrible trouble is spreading from one nation to another.
A mighty storm is rising.
It is coming from a place that is very far away."

³³ At that time those the LORD kills will be lying around everywhere. They will be found from one end of the earth to the other. No one will mourn for them. Their dead bodies will not be gathered up or buried. Instead, they will be like human waste lying there on the ground.

Jason's Jargon

JEREMIAH 25

Inspect this chapter for the word *millstones*. Millstones were two stones that, when pounded together, ground up grain to make it better to eat. Leave no stone unturned in your quest!

³⁴ Weep and cry, you shepherds.
Roll in the dust, you leaders of the flock.
Your time to be killed has come.

You will fall like the best of the
  rams.
³⁵ The shepherds won't have any place to
  run to.
The leaders of the flock won't be able
  to escape.
³⁶ Listen to the cries of the shepherds.
Hear the weeping of the leaders of
  the flock.
The Lord is destroying their
  grasslands.
³⁷ Their peaceful meadows will be
  completely destroyed
because of the Lord's great anger.
³⁸ Like a lion he will leave his den.
The land of those leaders will
  become a desert.
That's because the sword of the Lord
  brings great harm.
His anger will burn against them.

Jeremiah's Enemies Try to Have Him Killed

26 A message from the Lord came to Jeremiah. It was shortly after Jehoiakim became king of Judah. He was the son of Josiah. ²The Lord said to Jeremiah, "Stand in the courtyard of my house. Speak to the people of the towns in Judah. Speak to all those who come to worship in my house. Tell them everything I command you. Do not leave out a single word. ³Perhaps they will listen. Maybe they will turn from their evil ways. Then I will not do what I said I would. I will not bring trouble on them. I had planned to punish them because of the evil things they had done. ⁴Tell them, 'The Lord says, "Listen to me. Obey my law that I gave you. ⁵And listen to the words my servants the prophets are speaking. I have sent them to you again and again. But you have not listened to them. ⁶So I will make this house like Shiloh. All the nations on earth will use the name of this city in a curse."'"

⁷Jeremiah spoke these words in the Lord's house. The priests, the prophets and all the people heard him. ⁸Jeremiah finished telling all the people everything the Lord had commanded him to say. But as soon as he did, the priests, the prophets and all the people grabbed him. They said, "You must die! ⁹Why do you prophesy these things in the Lord's name? Why do you say that this house will become like Shiloh? Why do you say that this city will be empty and deserted?" And all the people crowded around Jeremiah in the Lord's house.

¹⁰The officials of Judah heard what had happened. So they went up from the royal palace to the Lord's house. There they took their places at the entrance of the New Gate. ¹¹Then the priests and prophets spoke to the officials and all the people. They said, "This man should be sentenced to death. He has prophesied against this city. You have heard it with your own ears!"

¹²Then Jeremiah spoke to all the officials and people. He said, "The Lord sent me to prophesy against this house and this city. He told me to say everything you have heard. ¹³So change the way you live and act. Obey the Lord your God. Then he won't do what he said he would. He won't bring on you the trouble he said he would bring. ¹⁴As for me, I'm in your hands. Do to me what you think is good and right. ¹⁵But you can be sure of one thing. If you put me to death, you will be held responsible for spilling my blood. And I haven't even done anything wrong. You will bring guilt on yourselves and this city and those who live in it. The Lord has sent me to you. He wanted me to say all these things so you could hear them. And that's the truth."

¹⁶Then the officials and all the people spoke to the priests and prophets. They said, "This man shouldn't be sentenced to death! He has spoken to us in the name of the Lord our God."

¹⁷Some of the elders of the land stepped forward. They spoke to the whole community gathered there. They said, ¹⁸"Micah from Moresheth prophesied. It was during the time Hezekiah was king over Judah. Micah spoke to all the people of Judah. He told them, 'The Lord who rules over all says,

"'"Zion will be plowed up like a field.
Jerusalem will be turned into a pile
  of trash.
The temple hill will be covered with
  bushes and weeds."' *(Micah 3:12)*

¹⁹Did King Hezekiah or anyone else in Judah put Micah to death? Hezekiah had respect for the Lord and tried to please him. And the Lord didn't judge Jerusalem as he said he would. He didn't bring on it the trouble he said he would bring. But we are about to bring horrible trouble on ourselves!"

²⁰Uriah was another man who prophesied in the name of the Lord. He was from Kiriath Jearim. He was the son of Shemaiah. Uriah prophesied against this city and this land. He said the same things Jeremiah did. ²¹King Jehoiakim and all his officers and officials heard Uriah's words. So the king decided to put him to death. But Uriah heard about it. He was afraid. And he ran away to Egypt. ²²So King Jehoiakim sent Elnathan to Egypt. He also sent some other men along with him. Elnathan was the son of Akbor. ²³Those men brought Uriah out of Egypt. They took him to King Jehoiakim. Then the king had Uriah struck down with a sword. He had Uriah's body thrown into one of the graves of the ordinary people.

²⁴In spite of that, Ahikam stood up for Jeremiah. Ahikam was the son of Shaphan. Because of Ahikam, Jeremiah wasn't handed over to the people to be put to death.

Jer. 27:1–11 The yoke's on you—I mean Jeremiah. Ha ha! Get it? Because yoke and joke . . . never mind. Anyway, a yoke is a wood collar that keeps two plowing oxen together. In the Bible a yoke is used as a word picture to show that people are working with God or one another.

Judah Will Serve Nebuchadnezzar

27 A message from the Lord came to Jeremiah. It was shortly after Zedekiah became king of Judah. He was the son of Josiah. ²The Lord said, "Make a yoke out of ropes and wooden boards. Put it on your neck. ³Then write down a message for the kings of Edom, Moab, Ammon, Tyre and Sidon. Give it to their messengers who have come to Jerusalem. They have come to see Zedekiah, the king of Judah. ⁴Give them a message for the kings who sent them. It should say, 'The Lord who rules over all is the God of Israel. He says, "Here is what I want you to tell your masters. ⁵I reached out my great and powerful arm. I made the earth. I made its people and animals. And I can give the earth to anyone I please. ⁶Now I will hand over all your countries to my servant Nebuchadnezzar. He is the king of Babylon. I will put even the wild animals under his control. ⁷All the nations will serve him and his son and grandson. After that, I will judge his land. Then many nations and great kings will make him serve them.

⁸" "But suppose any nation or kingdom will not serve Nebuchadnezzar, the king of Babylon. And suppose it refuses to put its neck under his yoke. Then I will punish that nation with war, hunger and plague," announces the Lord. "I will punish it until his powerful hand destroys it. ⁹So do not listen to your prophets. Do not listen to those who claim to have secret knowledge. Do not listen to those who try to explain your dreams. Do not listen to those who get messages from people who have died. Do not listen to those who practice evil magic. All of them will tell you, 'You won't serve the king of Babylon.' ¹⁰But they prophesy lies to you. If you listen to them, you will be removed far away from your lands. I will drive you away from them. And you will die. ¹¹But suppose any nation will put its neck under the yoke of the king of Babylon. And suppose it serves him. Then I will let that nation remain in its own land. I will let its people plow the land and live there," " announces the Lord.

¹²I gave the same message to Zedekiah, the king of Judah. I said, "Put your neck under the yoke of the king of Babylon. Obey him. Serve his people. Then you will live. ¹³Why should you and your people die? Why should you die of war, hunger and plague? That's what the Lord said would happen to any nation that won't serve the king of Babylon. ¹⁴Don't listen to the words of the prophets who say to you, 'You won't serve the king of Babylon.' They are prophesying lies to you. ¹⁵'I have not sent them,' announces the Lord. 'They are prophesying lies in my name. So I will drive you away from your land. And you will die. So will the prophets who prophesy to you.' "

¹⁶Then I spoke to the priests and all these people. I said, "The LORD says, 'Do not listen to the prophets who speak to you. They say, "Very soon the objects from the LORD's house will be brought back from Babylon." Those prophets are prophesying lies to you. ¹⁷Do not listen to them. Serve the king of Babylon. Then you will live. Why should this city be destroyed? ¹⁸If they are prophets and have received a message from me, let them pray to me. I am the LORD who rules over all. Those prophets should pray that what is still in Jerusalem will remain here. They should pray that the objects in my house and the king's palace will not be taken to Babylon. ¹⁹I am the LORD who rules over all. Do you know what these objects are? They include the two pillars in front of the temple. They include the huge bronze bowl. They include the bronze stands that can be moved around. And they include the other things left in this city. ²⁰Nebuchadnezzar, the king of Babylon, did not take these things away at first. That was when he took King Jehoiachin from Jerusalem to Babylon. Jehoiachin is the son of Jehoiakim. Nebuchadnezzar also took all the nobles of Judah and Jerusalem along with Jehoiachin. ²¹I am the LORD who rules over all. I am the God of Israel. Here is what will happen to the things that are left in my house, the king's palace and Jerusalem. ²²They will be taken to Babylon. They will remain there until the day I come for them,' announces the LORD. 'Then I will bring them back. I will return them to this place.' "

The False Prophet Hananiah Opposes Jeremiah

28 The false prophet Hananiah spoke to me, Jeremiah, in the LORD's house. Hananiah was from Gibeon. He was the son of Azzur. It was shortly after Zedekiah became king of Judah. It was in the fifth month of his fourth year. In front of the priests and all the people Hananiah spoke to me. He said, ²"The LORD who rules over all is the God of Israel. He says, 'I will break the yoke of the king of Babylon. ³Nebuchadnezzar, the king of Babylon, removed all the objects that belong to my house. He took them to Babylon. Before two years are over, I will bring them back to this place. ⁴I will also bring King Jehoiachin back. He is the son of Jehoiakim. And I will bring back

all the others who were taken from Judah to Babylon,' announces the LORD. 'I will break the yoke of the king of Babylon.' "

⁵Then Jeremiah the prophet replied to the false prophet Hananiah. Jeremiah spoke to him in front of the priests and all the people. They were standing in the LORD's house. ⁶Jeremiah said, "Amen, Hananiah! May the LORD do those things! May he make the words you have prophesied come true. May he bring back from Babylon the objects that belong to the LORD's house. May he bring back to this place all the people who were taken away. ⁷But listen to what I have to say. I want you and all the people to hear it. ⁸There have been prophets long before you and I were ever born. They have prophesied against many countries and great kingdoms. They have spoken about war, trouble and plague. ⁹But what if a prophet says peace will come? And suppose peace really does come? Only then will he be recognized as a prophet truly sent by the LORD."

¹⁰The false prophet Hananiah took the yoke off the neck of Jeremiah the prophet. Then Hananiah broke the yoke. ¹¹In front of all the people he said, "The LORD says, 'In the same way, I will break the yoke of Nebuchadnezzar, the king of Babylon. Before two years are over, I will remove it from the necks of all the nations.' " When Jeremiah the prophet heard this, he went on his way.

¹²A message from the LORD came to Jeremiah. It was after the false prophet Hananiah had broken the yoke off Jeremiah's neck. The message said, ¹³"Go. Tell Hananiah, 'The LORD says, "You have broken a wooden yoke. But in its place you will get an iron yoke." ¹⁴The LORD who rules over all is the God of Israel. He says, "I will put an iron yoke on the necks of all these nations. I will make them serve Nebuchadnezzar, the king of Babylon. So they will serve him. I will even give him control over the wild animals." ' "

¹⁵Then Jeremiah the prophet spoke to the false prophet Hananiah. Jeremiah said, "Listen, Hananiah! The LORD hasn't sent you. But you have tricked these people. Now they trust in lies. ¹⁶So the LORD says, 'I am about to remove you from the face of the earth. Before this year is over, you will die. You have taught the people to turn against me.' "

¹⁷In the seventh month of that very year, the false prophet Hananiah died.

Jeremiah's Letter to the Jews in Babylon

29 Jeremiah the prophet sent a letter from Jerusalem to Babylon. It was for the Jewish elders still alive there. It was also for the priests and prophets in Babylon. And it was for all the other people Nebuchadnezzar had taken from Jerusalem to Babylon. ²It was sent to them after King Jehoiachin had been forced to leave Jerusalem. His mother and the court officials were taken with him. The leaders of Judah and Jerusalem had been forced to go to Babylon. All the skilled workers had also been forced to go. ³Jeremiah gave the letter to Elasah and Gemariah. Elasah was the son of Shaphan. Gemariah was the son of Hilkiah. Zedekiah, the king of Judah, had sent Elasah and Gemariah to King Nebuchadnezzar in Babylon. Here is what the letter said.

⁴The LORD who rules over all is the God of Israel. He speaks to all those he forced to go from Jerusalem to Babylon. He says, ⁵"Build houses and make your homes there. Plant gardens and eat what they produce. ⁶Get married. Have sons and daughters. Find wives for your sons. Give your daughters to be married. Then they too can have sons and daughters. Let there be many more of you and not fewer. ⁷Also work for the success of the city I have sent you to. Pray to the LORD for that city. If it succeeds, you too will enjoy success." ⁸The LORD who rules over all is the God of Israel. He says, "Do not let the prophets trick you. Do not be fooled by those who claim to have secret knowledge. Do not listen to people who try to explain their dreams to you. ⁹All of them are prophesying lies to you in my name. I have not sent them," announces the LORD. ¹⁰The LORD says, "You will be forced to live in Babylon for 70 years. After they are over, I will come to you. My good promise to you will come true. I will bring you back home. ¹¹I know the plans I have for

ADVENTURES IN ODYSSEY

Wooton traveled to Alaska to spread a message of hope and how God's plans for us are good in "The Cure" (Club).

you," announces the LORD. "I want you to enjoy success. I do not plan to harm you. I will give you hope for the years to come. ¹²Then you will call out to me. You will come and pray to me. And I will listen to you. ¹³When you look for me with all your heart, you will find me. ¹⁴I will be found by you," announces the LORD. "And I will bring you back from where you were taken as prisoners. I will gather you from all the nations. I will gather you from the places where I have forced you to go," announces the LORD. "I will bring you back to the place I sent you away from."

¹⁵You might say, "The LORD has given us prophets in Babylon." ¹⁶But here is what the LORD says about the king who now sits on David's throne. He also says it about all the people who remain in this city. And he says it about all those who did not go with you to Babylon. ¹⁷The LORD who rules over all says, "I will send war, hunger and plague against them. I will make them like bad figs. They are so bad they can't be eaten. ¹⁸I will hunt them down with war, hunger and plague. I will make all the kingdoms on earth displeased with them. They will use their name in a curse. All the nations where I drive them will be shocked at them. They will make fun of them. And they will

bring shame on them. ¹⁹That's because they have not listened to my words," announces the LORD. "I sent messages to them again and again. I sent them through my servants the prophets. And you who were taken to Babylon have not listened either," announces the LORD.

²⁰So listen to the LORD's message. Listen, all you whom he has sent away from Jerusalem to Babylon. ²¹The LORD who rules over all is the God of Israel. He speaks about Ahab and Zedekiah. Ahab is the son of Kolaiah. Zedekiah is the son of Maaseiah. They are prophesying lies to you in my name. The LORD says about Ahab and Zedekiah, "I will hand them over to Nebuchadnezzar, the king of Babylon. He will put them to death. You will see it with your own eyes. ²²Because of what happens to them, people will use their names when they curse someone. All those who have been taken from Judah to Babylon will use their names in that way.

REMEMBER THIS

JEREMIAH 29:11

"I know the plans I have for you," announces the LORD. "I want you to enjoy success. I do not plan to harm you. I will give you hope for the years to come."

They will say, 'May the LORD treat you like Zedekiah and Ahab. The king of Babylon burned them in the fire.' ²³That will happen because they have done awful things in Israel. They have committed adultery with their neighbors' wives. They have spoken lies in my name. I did not give them the authority to speak those things. I know what they have done. And I am a witness to it," announces the LORD.

Shemaiah Opposes Jeremiah

²⁴Tell Shemaiah, the Nehelamite, ²⁵"The LORD who rules over all is the God of Israel.

WHAT ABOUT YOU?

Most people didn't think Thomas was very smart. He didn't learn to talk until he was four years old. He never paid attention in class. But there was one person who knew Thomas was very bright: his mother. She took him out of school and taught him at home. Here's how her hard work paid off: Thomas Edison became one of America's best-known inventors. By the time he died at age 84, Edison had filed for 1,093 US patents on the things he developed.

The secret to Edison's success is that he didn't give up. He once said he'd tried a thousand ways to invent the lightbulb. That's about 999 failures and one success. But that's all it took.

The prophet Jeremiah could have given up. He had preached God's message for 40 years, but people didn't listen. In fact, members of the tribe of Judah threw Jeremiah in prison and tried to kill him. Why did he stay faithful to God's calling? God had given him a job, and even though he didn't always understand it, he chose to obey.

Do you work hard and stick with projects no matter how tough things get? Make a game of it. Create a tic-tac-toe board and write a current or upcoming task in each of the nine boxes. As you complete one, put an *X* in that space. Mark the next one you finish with an *O*. Try to score three in a row without blocking your own progress, just like in tic-tac-toe.

CANDID CONVERSATIONS

What if, when I was, like, ten years old, God would've said to me, "I'm tired of figuring out your life, Connie. I'll let you decide what's going to happen." I probably would've been so excited! My parents never would've gotten a divorce. I would have been far more popular. But I also probably never would've moved away from California to go to Odyssey. Whew! It's a good thing God didn't give me that option. God is still writing the story of my life.

Whit told me about this old proverb that says, "We plan, God laughs." It reminds me of all the times I thought I was in charge of my own life, when it was really God working behind the scenes for my best interests. And that's such a good thing! God is much smarter than me. He knows all of our futures, and wants us to have lives filled with joy and hope.

Today, thank God for being in control and for planning a wonderful future for us.

He says, 'You sent letters in your own name to all the people in Jerusalem. You also sent them to Zephaniah the priest. He is the son of Maaseiah. And you sent them to all the other priests. You said to Zephaniah, ²⁶"The LORD has appointed you priest in place of Jehoiada. He has put you in charge of the LORD's house. You are supposed to arrest any crazy person who claims to be a prophet. You should put him in prison. You should put iron bands around his neck. ²⁷So why haven't you punished Jeremiah from Anathoth? He claims to be a prophet among you. ²⁸He has sent a message to us in Babylon. It says, 'You will be there a long time. So build houses and make your

homes there. Plant gardens and eat what they produce.'"'"

²⁹But Zephaniah the priest read the letter to me. ³⁰Then a message from the LORD came to me. The LORD said, ³¹"Send a message to all the people who were taken away. Tell them, 'The LORD speaks about Shemaiah, the Nehelamite. He says, "Shemaiah has prophesied to you. But I did not send him. He has made you trust in lies. ³²So I say, 'I will certainly punish Shemaiah, the Nehelamite. I will also punish his children after him. He will not have any children left among these people. I will do good things for my people. But he will not see them,'"'" announces the LORD. "'"'That's because he has taught people to turn against me.'"'"

Israel Will Return to the LORD

30 A message from the LORD came to Jeremiah. The LORD said, ²"I am the LORD. I am the God of Israel. I say, 'Write in a book all the words I have spoken to you. ³A new day is coming,'" announces the LORD. "'At that time I will bring my people Israel and Judah back from where they have been taken as prisoners. I will bring them back to this land. I gave it to their people of long ago to have as their own,'" says the LORD.

⁴Here are the words the LORD spoke about Israel and Judah. He said, ⁵"I am the LORD. I say,

"'Cries of fear are heard.
  There is terror. There isn't any peace.
⁶ Ask and see.
  Can a man give birth to children?
Then why do I see every strong man
  with his hands on his stomach?
Each of them is acting like a woman
  having a baby.
  Every face is as pale as death.
⁷ How awful that day will be!
  No other day will be like it.
It will be a time of trouble for the
  people of Jacob.
  But they will be saved out of it.

⁸ "'At that time I will break the yoke off
  their necks,'
  announces the LORD who rules over
    all.
'I will tear off the ropes that hold them.
  People from other lands will not
    make them slaves anymore.

⁹ Instead, they will serve me.
  And they will serve David their king.
I will raise him up for them.
I am the LORD their God.

¹⁰ " 'People of Jacob, do not be afraid.
  You are my servant.
Israel, do not be terrified,' "
  announces the LORD.
" 'You can be sure that I will save you.
  I will bring you out of a place far
    away.
I will bring your children back
  from the land where they were
    taken.
Your people will have peace and
    security again.
  And no one will make them afraid.
¹¹ I am with you. I will save you,' "
  announces the LORD.
" 'I will completely destroy all the
    nations
  among which I scatter you.
But I will not completely destroy
    you.
I will correct you. But I will be fair.
  I will not let you go without any
    punishment.' "

¹²The LORD says,

"Your wound can't be cured.
  Your pain can't be healed.
¹³ No one will stand up for you.
  There isn't any medicine for your
    sore.
  There isn't any healing for you.
¹⁴ All those who were going to help you
    have forgotten you.
  They do not care about you.
I have struck you as if I were your
    enemy.
  I have punished you as if I were very
    mean.
That is because your guilt is so great.
  You have sinned so much.
¹⁵ Why do you cry out about your wound?
  Your pain can't be healed.
Your guilt is very great.
  And you have committed many sins.
  That is why I have done all these
    things to you.

¹⁶ "But everyone who destroys you will be
    destroyed.
  All your enemies will be forced
    to leave their countries.

Those who steal from you will be stolen
    from.
  I will take the belongings
    of those who take things from you.
¹⁷ But I will make you healthy again.
  I will heal your wounds," announces
    the LORD.
"That's because you have been thrown
    out.
  You are called Zion, the one no one
    cares about."

¹⁸The LORD says,

"I will bless Jacob's people with great
    success again.
  I will show tender love to Israel.
Jerusalem will be rebuilt where it was
    destroyed.
  The palace will stand in its proper
    place.
¹⁹ From those places the songs of people
    giving thanks will be heard.
  The sound of great joy will come
    from there.
I will cause there to be more of my
    people.
  There will not be fewer of them.
I will bring them honor.
  People will have respect for them.
²⁰ Things will be as they used to be for
    Jacob's people.
  I will make their community firm
    and secure.
  I will punish everyone who treats
    them badly.
²¹ Their leader will be one of their own
    people.
  Their ruler will rise up from among
    them.
I will bring him near.
  And he will come close to me.
  He will commit himself to serve me,"
    announces the LORD.
²² "So you will be my people.
  And I will be your God."

²³ A storm will burst out
    because of the LORD's great anger.
A strong wind will sweep down
    on the heads of evil people.
²⁴ The LORD's great anger won't turn
    back.
  He will accomplish everything
    his heart plans to do.
In days to come
  you will understand this.

31 "At that time I will be the God of all the families of Israel," announces the LORD. "And they will be my people."

²The LORD says,

"Some of my people will live through
everything their enemies do to
them.
They will find help in the desert.
I will come to give peace and rest to
Israel."

³The LORD appeared to us in the past.
He said,

"I have loved you with a love that lasts
forever.
I have kept on loving you with a
kindness that never fails.
⁴ I will build you up again.
Nation of Israel, you will be rebuilt.
Once again you will use your
tambourines to celebrate.
You will go out and dance with joy.
⁵ Once again you will plant vineyards
on the hills of Samaria.
Farmers will plant them.
They will enjoy their fruit.
⁶ There will be a day when those on
guard duty will cry out.
They will stand on the hills of
Ephraim.
And they will shout,

ADVENTURES IN ODYSSEY

God told of His everlasting love in
Jeremiah 31. The Parker family passed
on that love during their journey to Africa
in "Mission: Unaccomplished" (Club).

'Come! Let's go up to Zion.
Let's go up to where the LORD our
God is.'"

⁷The LORD says,

"Sing for joy because the people of
Jacob are blessed.
Shout because the LORD has made
them the greatest nation.
Make your praises heard.
Say, 'LORD, save your people.
Save the people who are left alive in
Israel.'
⁸ I will bring them from the land of the
north.
I will gather them from one end of
the earth to the other.
Even those who are blind and those
who can't walk
will be among them.
Pregnant women and women having
their babies
will be among them also.
Many of them will return.
⁹ Their eyes will be filled with tears as
they come.
They will pray as I bring them back.
I will lead them beside streams of
water.
I will lead them on a level path
where they will not trip or fall.
I am Israel's father.
And Ephraim is my oldest son.

¹⁰ "Listen to my message, you nations.
Announce it on shores far away.
Say, 'He who scattered Israel will gather
them.
He will watch over his flock like a
shepherd.'
¹¹ I will set the people of Jacob free.
I will save them from those who are
stronger than they are.
¹² They will come and shout for joy on
Mount Zion.
They will be joyful because of
everything I give them.
I give them grain, olive oil and fresh
wine.
I give them the young animals in
their flocks and herds.
Israel will be like a garden that has
plenty of water.
And they will not be sad anymore.
¹³ Then young women will dance and be
glad.

And so will the men, young and old
alike.
I will turn their mourning into gladness.
I will comfort them.
And I will give them joy instead of
sorrow.
[14] I will satisfy the priests. I will give them
more than enough.
And my people will be filled with the
good things I give them,"
announces the LORD.

[15] The LORD says,

"A voice is heard in Ramah.
It is the sound of weeping and deep
sadness.
Rachel is weeping for her children.
She refuses to be comforted,
because they are gone."

[16] The LORD says,

"Do not weep anymore.
Do not let tears fall from your eyes.
I will reward you for your work,"
announces the LORD.
"Your children will return from the
land of the enemy.
[17] So there is hope for your children,"
announces the LORD.
"Your children will return to their
own land.

[18] "I have heard the groans of Ephraim's
people. They say,
'You corrected us like a calf you were
training.
And we have been trained.
Bring us back to you, and we will come
back.
You are the LORD our God.
[19] After we wandered away from you,
we turned away from our sins.
After we learned our lesson,
we beat our chests in sorrow.
We were full of shame.
What we did when we were young
brought dishonor on us.'
[20] Aren't the people of Ephraim my dear
children?
Aren't they the children I take
delight in?
I often speak against them.
But I still remember them.
So my heart longs for them.
I love them with a tender love,"
announces the LORD.

[21] The LORD says, "Put up road signs.
Set up stones to show the way.
Look carefully for the highway.
Look for the road you will take.
Return, people of Israel.
Return to your towns.
[22] How long will you wander,
my people Israel, who are not
faithful to me?
I will create a new thing on earth.
The woman will return to the man."

[23] The LORD who rules over all is the God
of Israel. He says, "I will bring them back
from the place where they were taken. Here
is what the people in Judah and its towns
will say once again. 'May the LORD bless
you, you successful city. Sacred mountain,
may he bless you.' [24] People will live together in Judah and all its towns. Farmers and
shepherds will live there. [25] I will give rest to
those who are tired. I will satisfy those who
are weak."

[26] When I heard this, I woke up and
looked around. My sleep had been pleasant
to me.

[27] Here is what the LORD announces.
"The days are coming when I will plant
the kingdoms of Israel and Judah again. I
will plant them with children and young
animals. [28] I watched over Israel and Judah
to pull them up by the roots. I tore them
down. I crushed them. I destroyed them.
I brought horrible trouble on them. But
now I will watch over them to build them
up and plant them," announces the LORD.
[29] "In those days people will no longer say,

"'The parents have eaten sour grapes.
But the children have a bitter taste in
their mouths.'

[30] Instead, everyone will die for their own
sin. The one who eats sour grapes will taste
how bitter they are.

[31] "The days are coming," announces the
LORD.
"I will make a new covenant
with the people of Israel.
I will also make it with the people of
Judah.
[32] It will not be like the covenant
I made with their people of long ago.
That was when I took them by the
hand.
I led them out of Egypt.

But they broke my covenant.
> They did it even though I was like a
> husband to them,"
announces the LORD.
33 "This is the covenant I will make with
Israel
> after that time," announces the
> LORD.
"I will put my law in their minds.
> I will write it on their hearts.
I will be their God.
> And they will be my people.
34 They will not need to teach their
> neighbor anymore.
> And they will not need to teach one
> another anymore.
They will not need to say, 'Know the
> LORD.'
That's because everyone will know me.
> From the least important of them to
> the most important,
> all of them will know me,"
announces the LORD.
"I will forgive their evil ways.
> I will not remember their sins
> anymore."

35 The LORD speaks.

He makes the sun
> shine by day.
He orders the moon and stars
> to shine at night.
He stirs up the ocean.
> He makes its waves roar.
> His name is the LORD Who Rules
> Over All.
36 "Suppose my orders for creation
> disappear from my sight,"
> announces the LORD.
"Only then will the people of Israel stop
> being
> a nation in my sight."

37 The LORD says,

"Suppose the sky above could be
> measured.
> Suppose the foundations of the earth
> below could be completely
> discovered.
Only then would I turn away the people
> of Israel.
> Even though they have committed
> many sins,
> I will still accept them,"
> announces the LORD.

38 "The days are coming," announces
the LORD. "At that time Jerusalem will be
rebuilt for me. It will be rebuilt from the
Tower of Hananel to the Corner Gate. 39 The
measuring line will reach out from there. It
will go straight to the hill of Gareb. Then it
will turn and reach as far as Goah. 40 There
is a valley where dead bodies and ashes are
thrown. That whole valley will be holy to
me. The side of the Kidron Valley east of
the city will be holy to me. It will be holy
all the way to the corner of the Horse Gate.
The city will never again be pulled up by
the roots. It will never be destroyed."

Jeremiah Buys a Field

32 A message from the LORD came to
Jeremiah. It came in the 10th year
that Zedekiah was king of Judah. It was in
the 18th year of the rule of Nebuchadnezzar. 2 The armies of the king of Babylon were
getting ready to attack Jerusalem. Jeremiah
the prophet was being held as a prisoner.
He was kept in the courtyard of the guard.
It was part of Judah's royal palace.

3 Zedekiah, the king of Judah, had made
Jeremiah a prisoner there. Zedekiah had
said to him, "Why do you prophesy as you
do? You say, 'The LORD says, "I am about
to hand over this city to the king of Babylon. He will capture it. 4 Zedekiah, the king
of Judah, will not escape from the powerful hands of the armies of Babylon. He
will certainly be handed over to the king
of Babylon. Zedekiah will speak with him
face to face. He will see him with his own
eyes. 5 Nebuchadnezzar will take Zedekiah
to Babylon. Zedekiah will remain there until I deal with him," announces the LORD.
"Suppose you fight against the armies of
Babylon. If you do, you will not succeed." ' "

6 Jeremiah said, "A message from the
LORD came to me. The LORD said, 7 'Hanamel is going to come to you. He is the son
of your uncle Shallum. Hanamel will say,
"Buy my field at Anathoth. You are my
closest relative. So it's your right and duty
to buy it." '

8 "Then my cousin Hanamel came to me.
I was in the courtyard of the guard. It happened just as the LORD had said it would.
Hanamel said, 'Buy my field at Anathoth.
It is in the territory of Benjamin. It is your
right to buy it and own it. So buy it for
yourself.'

"I knew that this was the Lord's message. ⁹So I bought the field at Anathoth from my cousin Hanamel. I weighed out seven ounces of silver for him. ¹⁰I signed and sealed the deed of purchase. I had some people witness everything. And I weighed out the silver on the scales. ¹¹There were two copies of the deed. One was sealed and the other wasn't. The deed included the terms and conditions of the sale. ¹²I gave Baruch the copies of the deed. My cousin Hanamel saw me do this. The witnesses who had signed the deed were there too. So were all the Jews who were sitting in the courtyard of the guard. Baruch was the son of Neriah. Neriah was the son of Mahseiah.

¹³"I gave Baruch directions in front of all of them. I said, ¹⁴'The Lord who rules over all is the God of Israel. He says, "Take this deed of purchase. Take the sealed and unsealed copies. Put them in a clay jar. Then they will last a long time." ¹⁵The Lord who rules over all is the God of Israel. He says, "Houses, fields and vineyards will again be bought in this land." '

¹⁶"I gave the deed of purchase to Baruch, the son of Neriah. Then I prayed to the Lord. I said,

¹⁷" 'Lord and King, you have reached out your great and powerful arm. You have made the heavens and the earth. Nothing is too hard for you. ¹⁸You show your love to thousands of people. But you cause the sins of parents to affect even their children. Great and powerful God, your name is the Lord Who Rules Over All. ¹⁹Your purposes are great. Your acts are mighty. Your eyes see everything people do. You reward each one of them in keeping with their conduct. You do this based on what they have done. ²⁰You performed signs and wonders in Egypt. And you have continued to do them to this day. You have done them in Israel and among all people. You are still known for doing them. ²¹You brought your people Israel out of Egypt. You did it with signs and wonders. You reached out your mighty hand and powerful arm. You did great and wonderful things. ²²You gave Israel this land that you promised to their people of long ago. It is a land that has plenty of milk and honey. ²³Israel came in and took it over. But they did not obey you. They didn't follow your law. They didn't do what you commanded them to do. So you brought all this trouble on them.

²⁴" 'See how ramps are built up against Jerusalem's walls to attack it. The city will be handed over to the armies of Babylon. They are attacking it. It will fall because of war, hunger and plague. What you said would happen is now happening, as you can see. ²⁵Lord and King, the city will be handed over to the armies of Babylon. In spite of that, you tell me to buy a field. You say, "Pay for it with silver. And have the sale witnessed." ' "

²⁶Then a message from the Lord came to Jeremiah. The Lord said, ²⁷"I am the Lord. I am the God of all people. Is anything too hard for me? ²⁸So the Lord says, "I am about to hand this city over to the armies of Babylon. I will give it to Nebuchadnezzar, the king of Babylon. He will capture it. ²⁹The armies of Babylon are now attacking this city. They will come in and set it on fire. They will burn it down. They will burn down the houses where the people made me very angry. They burned incense on their roofs to the god named Baal. And they poured out drink offerings to other gods.

³⁰"The people of Israel and Judah have done nothing but evil in my eyes. They have done it since the nation was young. In fact, they have done nothing but make me very angry. They have worshiped statues of gods their own hands have made," announces the Lord. ³¹"This city has always stirred up my great anger. It has done it since the day it was built. Now I must remove it from my sight. ³²The people of Israel and Judah have made me very angry. They have done many evil things. They, their kings and officials have sinned. So have their priests and prophets. And the people of Judah and Jerusalem have also sinned. ³³They turned their backs to me. They would not face me. I taught them again and again. But they would not listen or pay attention when they were corrected. ³⁴They set up the hateful statues of their gods. They did it in the house where I have put my Name. They made my house 'unclean.' ³⁵The people built high places for Baal in the Valley of

Ben Hinnom. That is where they sacrifice their children to Molek in the fire. That is something I did not command. It did not even enter my mind. They did something I hate. They made Judah sin."

³⁶Here is what you people of Judah are saying about this city. "By war, hunger and plague it will be handed over to the king of Babylon." But here is what the LORD, the God of Israel, says. ³⁷"You can be sure that I will gather my people again. I will send them away when my burning anger blazes out against them. But I will bring them back to this place. And I will let them live in safety. ³⁸They will be my people. And I will be their God. ³⁹I will give them a single purpose in life. Then, they will always have respect for me. Then all will go well for them. And it will also go well for their children after them. ⁴⁰I will make a covenant with them that will last forever. I promise that I will never stop doing good to them. I will cause them to respect me. Then they will never turn away from me again. ⁴¹I will take pleasure in doing good things for them. I will certainly plant them in this land. I will do these things with all my heart and soul."

⁴²The LORD says, "I have brought all this horrible trouble on these people. But now I will give them all the good things I have promised them. ⁴³Once more fields will be bought in this land. It is the land about which you now say, 'It is a dry and empty desert. It doesn't have any people or animals in it. It has been handed over to the armies of Babylon.' ⁴⁴Fields will be bought with silver. Deeds will be signed, sealed and witnessed. That will be done in the territory of Benjamin. It will be done in the villages around Jerusalem and in the towns of Judah. It will also be done in the towns of the central hill country. And it will be done in the towns of the western hills and the Negev Desert. I will bless their people with great success again," announces the LORD.

The LORD Promises to Heal His People

33 Jeremiah was still being held as a prisoner. He was kept in the courtyard of the guard. Then another message from the LORD came to him. The LORD said, ²"I made the earth. I formed it. And I set it in place. The LORD is my name. ³Call out to me. I will answer you. I will tell you great things you do not know. And unless I

do, you wouldn't be able to find out about them." ⁴The LORD is the God of Israel. He speaks about the houses in Jerusalem. He talks about the royal palaces of Judah. The people had torn down many of them. They had used their stones to strengthen the city walls against attack. ⁵That was during their fight with the armies of Babylon. The LORD says, "The houses will be filled with dead bodies. They will be the bodies of the people I will kill. I will kill them when I am very angry with them. I will hide my face from this city. That's because its people have committed so many sins.

⁶"But now I will bring health and healing to Jerusalem. I will heal my people. I will let them enjoy great peace and security. ⁷I will bring Judah and Israel back from the places where they have been taken. I will build up the nation again. It will be just as it was before. ⁸I will wash from its people all the sins they have committed against me. And I will forgive all the sins they committed when they turned away from me. ⁹Then this city will bring me fame, joy, praise and honor. All the nations on earth will hear about the good things I do for this city. They will see the great success and peace I give it. Then they will be filled with wonder. And they will tremble with fear."

¹⁰The LORD says, "You say about this place, 'It's a dry and empty desert. It doesn't have any people or animals in it.' The towns of Judah and the streets of Jerusalem are now deserted. So they do not have any people or animals living in them. But happy sounds will be heard there once more. ¹¹They will be the sounds of joy and gladness. The voices of brides and grooms will fill the streets. And the voices of those who bring thank offerings to my house will be heard there. They will say,

"'Give thanks to the LORD who rules
          over all,
    because he is good.
    His faithful love continues forever.'

That's because I will bless this land with great success again. It will be as it was before," says the LORD.

¹²The LORD who rules over all says, "This place is a desert. It does not have any people or animals in it. But there will again be grasslands near all its towns. Shepherds will rest their flocks there. ¹³Flocks will

again pass under the hands of shepherds as they count their sheep," says the LORD. "That will be done in the towns of the central hill country. It will be done in the western hills and the Negev Desert. It will be done in the territory of Benjamin. And it will be done in the villages around Jerusalem and in the towns of Judah.

[14]"The days are coming," announces the LORD. "At that time I will fulfill my good promise to my people. I made it to the people of Israel and Judah.

[15] "Here is what I will do in those days
    and at that time.
I will make a godly Branch grow
    from David's royal line.
He will do what is fair and right in
    the land.
[16] In those days Judah will be saved.
Jerusalem will live in safety.
And it will be called
    The LORD Who Makes Us Right
    With Himself."

[17]The LORD says, "David will always have a son to sit on the throne of Israel. [18]The priests, who are Levites, will always have a man to serve me. He will sacrifice burnt offerings. He will burn grain offerings. And he will offer sacrifices."

[19]A message from the LORD came to Jeremiah. [20]The LORD said, "Could you ever break my covenant with the day? Could you ever break my covenant with the night? Could you ever stop day and night from coming at their appointed times? [21]Only then could my covenant with my servant David be broken. Only then could my covenant with the Levites who serve me as priests be broken. Only then would David no longer have someone from his family line to rule on his throne. [22]Here is what I will do for my servant David. And here is what I will do for the Levites who serve me. I will make their children after them as many as the stars in the sky. And I will make them as many as the grains of sand on the seashore. It will be impossible to count them."

[23]A message from the LORD came to Jeremiah. The LORD said, [24]"Haven't you noticed what these people are saying? They say, 'The LORD once chose the two kingdoms of Israel and Judah. But now he has turned his back on them.' So they hate my people. They do not think of them as a nation anymore. [25]I say, 'What if I had not made my covenant with day and night? What if I had not established the laws of heaven and earth? [26]Only then would I turn my back on the children of Jacob and my servant David. Only then would I not choose one of David's sons to rule over the children of Abraham, Isaac and Jacob. But I will bless my people with great success again. I will love them with tender love.'"

Zedekiah Is Warned

34 Nebuchadnezzar, the king of Babylon, and all his armies were fighting against Jerusalem. They were also fighting against all the towns around it. All the kingdoms and nations Nebuchadnezzar ruled over were helping him. At that time a message from the LORD came to Jeremiah. The LORD said, [2]"I am the LORD, the God of Israel. Go to Zedekiah, the king of Judah. Tell him, 'The LORD says, "I am about to hand this city over to the king of Babylon. He will burn it down. [3]You will not escape from his power. You will certainly be captured. You will be handed over to him. You will see the king of Babylon with your own eyes. He will speak with you face to face. And you will go to Babylon.

[4]" 'But listen to the LORD's promise to you, Zedekiah king of Judah. I say that you will not be killed by a sword. [5]You will die in a peaceful way. People made fires to honor the kings who died before you. In the same way, they will make a fire in your honor. They will mourn for you. They will say, 'My poor master!' I myself make this promise," announces the LORD.'"

[6]Then Jeremiah the prophet told all this to King Zedekiah in Jerusalem. [7]At that time Nebuchadnezzar's armies were fighting against Jerusalem. They were also fighting against Lachish and Azekah. These two cities were still holding out. They were the only cities left in Judah that had high walls around them.

The People Set Their Slaves Free

[8]A message from the LORD came to Jeremiah. King Zedekiah had made a covenant with all the people in Jerusalem. He had told them to set their Hebrew slaves free. [9]All of them had to do this. That applied to male and female slaves alike. No one was allowed to hold another Hebrew as a slave.

¹⁰So all the officials and people entered into this covenant. They agreed to set their male and female slaves free. They agreed not to hold them as slaves anymore. Instead, they set them free. ¹¹But later they changed their minds. They took back the people they had set free. They made them slaves again.

¹²Then a message from the LORD came to Jeremiah. ¹³The LORD is the God of Israel. He says, "I made a covenant with your people of long ago. I brought them out of Egypt. That is the land where they were slaves. I said, ¹⁴'Every seventh year you must set your people free. Each of you must set free all the Hebrews who have sold themselves to you. Let them serve you for six years. Then you must let them go free.' (Deuteronomy 15:12) But your people of long ago did not listen to me. They did not pay any attention to me. ¹⁵Recently you turned away from your sins. You did what is right in my eyes. Each of you set your Hebrew slaves free. You even made a covenant in front of me. You did it in the house where I have put my Name. ¹⁶But now you have turned around. You have treated my name as if it were not holy. Each of you has taken back your male and female slaves. You had set them free to go where they wished. But now you have forced them to become your slaves again."

¹⁷So the LORD says, "You have not obeyed me. You have not set your Hebrew slaves free. So now I will set you free," announces the LORD. "I will set you free to be destroyed by war, plague and hunger. I will make all the kingdoms on earth displeased with you. ¹⁸Those people who have broken my covenant will be punished. They have not lived up to the terms of the covenant they made in front of me. When you made that covenant, you cut a calf in two. Then you walked between its pieces. Now I will cut you to pieces. ¹⁹That includes all of you who walked between the pieces of the calf. It includes the leaders of Judah and Jerusalem, the court officials and the priests. It also includes some of the people of the land. ²⁰So I will hand over all those people to their enemies who want to kill them. Their dead bodies will become food for the birds and the wild animals.

²¹"I will hand over King Zedekiah and his officials to their enemies. I will hand them over to those who want to kill them. I will hand them over to the armies of the king of Babylon. They have now pulled back from you. ²²But I am going to give an order," announces the LORD. "I will bring them back to this city. They will fight against it. They will capture it and burn it down. And I will completely destroy the towns of Judah. No one will be able to live there."

The Family Line of Rekab

35 A message from the LORD came to Jeremiah. It came during the time Jehoiakim was king over Judah. Jehoiakim was the son of Josiah. The message said, ²"Go to the members of the family line of Rekab. Invite them to come to one of the side rooms in my house. Then give them wine to drink."

³So I went to get Jaazaniah. He was the son of Jeremiah. Jeremiah was the son of Habazziniah. I also went to get Jaazaniah's brothers and all his sons. That included all the members of the family line of Rekab. ⁴I brought them into the LORD's house. I took them into the room of the sons of Hanan. He was the son of Igdaliah. He was also a man of God. His room was next to the room of the officials. Their room was above the room of Maaseiah. He was the son of Shallum. He also was one of those who guarded the temple doors. ⁵Then I got bowls full of wine and some cups. I set them down in front of the men from the family line of Rekab. I said to them, "Drink some wine."

⁶But they replied, "We don't drink wine. That's because Jehonadab gave us a command. He was the son of Rekab. He was also one of our own people from long ago. He commanded, 'You and your children after you must never drink wine. ⁷Also you must never build houses. You must never plant crops or vineyards. You must never have any of these things. Instead, you must always live in tents. Then you will live a long time in the land where you are wandering around.' ⁸We have done everything Jehonadab, the son of Rekab, commanded us to do. So we and our wives and our children have never drunk wine. ⁹We have never built houses to live in. We've never had vineyards, fields or crops. ¹⁰We've always lived in tents. We've completely obeyed everything Jehonadab commanded our people of long ago. ¹¹But Nebuchadnezzar,

the king of Babylon, marched into this land. Then we said, 'Come. We must go to Jerusalem. There we can escape the armies of Babylon and Aram.' So we have remained in Jerusalem."

¹²Then a message from the LORD came to Jeremiah. It said, ¹³"The LORD who rules over all is the God of Israel. He says, 'Go. Speak to the people of Judah and Jerusalem. Tell them, "Won't you ever learn a lesson? Won't you ever obey my words?"' announces the LORD. ¹⁴"Jehonadab, the son of Rekab, ordered his children not to drink wine. And they have kept his command. To this day they do not drink wine. They obey the command Jehonadab gave their people long ago. But I have spoken to you again and again. In spite of that, you have not obeyed me. ¹⁵Again and again I sent all my servants the prophets to you. They said, 'Each of you must turn from your evil ways. You must change the way you act. Do not worship other gods. Do not serve them. Then you will live in the land. I gave it to you and your people of long ago.' But you have not paid any attention. You have not listened to me. ¹⁶The children of Jehonadab, the son of Rekab, have obeyed the command Jehonadab gave them long ago. But the people of Judah have not obeyed me."'"

¹⁷So the LORD God who rules over all speaks. The God of Israel says, "Listen! I am going to bring horrible trouble on Judah. I will also bring it on everyone who lives in Jerusalem. I will bring on them every trouble I said I would. I spoke to them. But they did not listen. I called out to them. But they did not answer."

¹⁸Then Jeremiah spoke to the members of the family line of Rekab. Jeremiah said, "The LORD who rules over all is the God of Israel. He says, 'You have obeyed the command Jehonadab gave your people of long ago. You have followed all his directions. You have done everything he ordered.' ¹⁹So the LORD who rules over all speaks. The God of Israel says, 'Jehonadab, the son of Rekab, will always have someone from his family line to serve me.'"

Jehoiakim Burns Up Jeremiah's Scroll

36 A message from the LORD came to Jeremiah. It came in the fourth year that Jehoiakim was king of Judah. He was

the son of Josiah. The message said, ²"Get a scroll. Write on it all the words I have spoken to you. Write down what I have said about Israel, Judah and all the other nations. Write what I have said to you from the time of King Josiah until now. ³The people of Judah will hear about all the trouble I plan to bring on them. Maybe then each of them will turn from their evil ways. If they do, I will forgive their sins and the evil things they have done."

⁴So Jeremiah sent for Baruch, the son of Neriah. Jeremiah told him to write down all the words the LORD had spoken to him. And Baruch wrote them on the scroll. ⁵Then Jeremiah said to him, "I'm not allowed to go to the LORD's temple. ⁶So you go there. Go on a day when the people are fasting. Read to them from the scroll. Read the words of the LORD you wrote down as I gave them to you. Read them to all the people of Judah who come in from their towns. ⁷They will hear what the LORD will do to them when his burning anger blazes out against them. Then perhaps they will pray to him. And maybe each of them will turn from their evil ways."

⁸Baruch, the son of Neriah, did everything Jeremiah the prophet told him to do. He went to the LORD's temple. There he read the words of the LORD from the scroll. ⁹It was in the fifth year that Jehoiakim, the son of Josiah, was king of Judah. It was the ninth month of that year. A time of fasting at the LORD's temple had been ordered. All the people in Jerusalem were told to take part in it. So were those who had come in from the towns of Judah. ¹⁰Baruch read to all the people who were at the LORD's temple. He read Jeremiah's words from the scroll. He was in the room of Gemariah the secretary. It was located in the upper courtyard at the entrance of the New Gate of the temple. Gemariah was the son of Shaphan.

¹¹Micaiah was the son of Gemariah, the son of Shaphan. Micaiah heard Baruch reading all the LORD's words that were written on the scroll. ¹²Then he went down to the secretary's room in the royal palace. All the officials were sitting there. They included the secretary Elishama and Delaiah, the son of Shemaiah. Elnathan, the son of Akbor, was also there. So was Gemariah, the son of Shaphan. Zedekiah, the son of Hananiah, was there too. And so were all

the other officials. [13]Micaiah told all of them what he had heard. He told them everything Baruch had read to the people from the scroll. [14]All the officials sent Jehudi to speak to Baruch, the son of Neriah. Jehudi was the son of Nethaniah. Nethaniah was the son of Shelemiah. Shelemiah was the son of Cushi. Jehudi said to Baruch, "Come. Bring the scroll you have read to the people." So Baruch went to them. He carried the scroll with him. [15]The officials said to him, "Please sit down. Read the scroll to us."

So Baruch read it to them. [16]They heard all its words. Then they looked at one another in fear. They said to Baruch, "We must report all these words to the king." [17]They said to Baruch, "Tell us. How did you happen to write all these things? Did Jeremiah tell you to do this?"

[18]"Yes," Baruch replied. "He told me to write down all these words. So I wrote them in ink on the scroll."

[19]Then the officials spoke to Baruch. They said, "You and Jeremiah must go and hide. Don't let anyone know where you are."

[20]The officials put the scroll in the room of Elishama the secretary. Then they went to the king in the courtyard. They reported everything to him. [21]The king sent Jehudi to get the scroll. Jehudi brought it from the room of Elishama the secretary. Jehudi read it to the king. All the officials were standing beside the king. So they heard it too. [22]It was the ninth month. The king was sitting in his winter apartment. A fire was burning in the fire pot in front of him. [23]Jehudi read three or four sections from the scroll. Then the king cut them off with a secretary's knife. He threw them into the fire pot. He did that until the entire scroll was burned up in the fire. [24]The king and some of his attendants heard all these words. But they weren't afraid. They didn't tear their clothes. [25]Elnathan, Delaiah and Gemariah begged the king not to burn the scroll. But he wouldn't listen to them. [26]Instead, the king commanded three men to arrest Baruch the secretary and Jeremiah the prophet. But the LORD had hidden them. The three men were Jerahmeel, Seraiah and Shelemiah. Jerahmeel was a member of the royal court. Seraiah was the son of Azriel. And Shelemiah was the son of Abdeel.

[27]A message from the LORD came to Jeremiah. It came after the king burned the scroll. On the scroll were the words Baruch had written down. Jeremiah had told him to write them. The message said, [28]"Get another scroll. Write on it all the words that were on the first one. King Jehoiakim burned that one up. [29]Also tell King Jehoiakim, 'The LORD says, "You burned that scroll. You said to Baruch, 'Why did you write that the king of Babylon would certainly come? Why did you write that he would destroy this land? And why did you write that he would remove from it people and animals alike?' " [30]So now the LORD has something to say about Jehoiakim, the king of Judah. He says, "No one from Jehoiakim's family line will sit on David's throne. Jehoiakim's body will be thrown out. It will lie outside in the heat by day and in the frost at night. [31]I will punish him and his children and his attendants. I will punish them for their sinful ways. I will bring on them all the trouble I said I would. And I will bring it on the people of Jerusalem and Judah. They have not listened to me." ' "

[32]So Jeremiah got another scroll. He gave it to Baruch the secretary. He was the son of Neriah. Jeremiah told Baruch what to write on it. Baruch wrote down all the words that were on the scroll King Jehoiakim had burned up in the fire. And many more words were written on it. They were similar to those that had already been written.

Jeremiah Is Put in Prison

37 Nebuchadnezzar, the king of Babylon, appointed Zedekiah to be king of Judah. He was the son of Josiah. Zedekiah ruled in place of Jehoiachin, the son of Jehoiakim. [2]Zedekiah and his attendants didn't pay any attention to what the LORD had said through Jeremiah the prophet. And the people of the land didn't pay any attention either.

[3]But King Zedekiah sent Jehukal to Jeremiah the prophet. Zedekiah sent Zephaniah the priest along with him. Jehukal was the son of Shelemiah. Zephaniah was the son of Maaseiah. Jehukal and Zephaniah brought the king's message to Jeremiah. It said, "Please pray to the LORD our God for us."

[4]At that time Jeremiah was free to come and go among the people. Jeremiah had not yet been put in prison. [5]The armies of

Babylon were attacking Jerusalem. They received a report that Pharaoh's army had marched out of Egypt to help Zedekiah. So armies of Babylon pulled back from Jerusalem.

⁶A message from the Lord came to Jeremiah. ⁷The Lord is the God of Israel. He says, "The king of Judah has sent you to ask me for advice. Tell him, 'Pharaoh's army has marched out to help you. But it will go back to its own land. It will return to Egypt. ⁸Then the armies of Babylon will come back here. They will attack this city. They will capture it. Then they will burn it down.'

⁹"The Lord says, 'Do not fool yourselves. You think, "The Babylonians will leave us alone." But they will not! ¹⁰Suppose you destroy all the armies of Babylon that are attacking you. Suppose only wounded men are left in their tents. Even then they will come out and burn down this city.'"

¹¹The armies of Babylon had pulled back from Jerusalem because of Pharaoh's army. ¹²So Jeremiah started to leave the city. He was planning to go to the territory of Benjamin. Jeremiah wanted to get his share of the property among the people there. ¹³He got as far as the Benjamin Gate. But the captain of the guard arrested him. He said, "You are going over to the side of the Babylonians!" The captain's name was Irijah, the son of Shelemiah. Shelemiah was the son of Hananiah.

¹⁴Jeremiah said to Irijah, "That isn't true! I'm not going to the side of the Babylonians." But Irijah wouldn't listen to him. Instead, he arrested Jeremiah. He brought Jeremiah to the officials. ¹⁵They were angry with him. So they had him beaten. Then they took him to the house of Jonathan the secretary. It had been made into a prison. That's where they put Jeremiah.

¹⁶Jeremiah was put into a prison cell below ground level. He remained there a long time. ¹⁷Then King Zedekiah sent for him. King Zedekiah had Jeremiah brought to the palace. There the king spoke to him in private. The king asked, "Do you have a message from the Lord for me?"

"Yes," Jeremiah replied. "You will be handed over to the king of Babylon."

¹⁸Then Jeremiah continued, "Why have you put me in prison? What crime have I committed against you? What have I done to your attendants or these people? ¹⁹Where are your prophets who prophesied to you? They said, 'The king of Babylon won't attack you. He won't march into this land.' ²⁰But now please listen, my king and master. Let me make my appeal to you. Please don't send me back to the house of Jonathan the secretary. If you do, I'll die there."

²¹Then King Zedekiah gave the order. His men put Jeremiah in the courtyard of the guard. They gave him a loaf of bread from the street of the bakers. They did it every day until all the bread in the city was gone. So Jeremiah remained in the courtyard of the guard.

Jeremiah Is Thrown Into an Empty Well

38 Shephatiah, Gedaliah, Jehukal and Pashhur heard what Jeremiah was telling all the people. Shephatiah was the son of Mattan. Gedaliah was the son of Pashhur. Jehukal was the son of Shelemiah. And Pashhur was the son of Malkijah. These four men heard Jeremiah say, ²"The Lord says, 'Those who stay in this city will die of war, hunger or plague. But those who go over to the side of the Babylonians will live. They will escape with their lives. They will remain alive.' ³The Lord also says, 'This city will certainly be handed over to the armies of the king of Babylon. They will capture it.'"

⁴Then these officials said to the king, "This man should be put to death. What

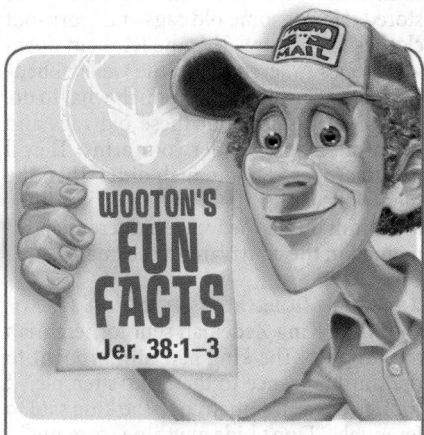

WOOTON'S FUN FACTS

Jer. 38:1–3

Archeological Alert! (I've always wanted to say that!) In recent years archaeologists in Israel have found clay tablets with these Bible names on them—Shephatiah and Gedaliah.

he says is making the soldiers who are left in this city lose hope. It's making all the people lose hope too. He isn't interested in what is best for the people. In fact, he's trying to destroy them."

[5]"He's in his hands," King Zedekiah answered. "I can't do anything to oppose you."

[6]So they took Jeremiah and put him into an empty well. It belonged to Malkijah. He was a member of the royal court. His well was in the courtyard of the guard. Zedekiah's men lowered Jeremiah by ropes into the well. It didn't have any water in it. All it had was mud. And Jeremiah sank down into the mud.

[7]Ebed-Melek was an official in the royal palace. He was from the land of Cush. He heard that Jeremiah had been put into the well. The king was sitting by the Benjamin Gate at that time. [8]Ebed-Melek went out of the palace. He said to the king, [9]"My king and master, everything these men have done to Jeremiah the prophet is evil. They have thrown him into an empty well. Soon there won't be any more bread in the city. Then he'll starve to death."

[10]So the king gave an order to Ebed-Melek the Cushite. He said, "Take with you 30 men from here. Lift Jeremiah the prophet out of the well before he dies."

[11]Then Ebed-Melek took the men with him. He went to a room in the palace. It was under the place where the treasures were stored. He got some old rags and worn-out clothes from there. Then he let them down with ropes to Jeremiah in the well. [12]Ebed-Melek the Cushite told Jeremiah what to do. Ebed-Melek said, "Put these old rags and worn-out clothes under your arms. They'll pad the ropes." So Jeremiah did. [13]Then the men pulled him up with the ropes. They lifted him out of the well. And Jeremiah remained in the courtyard of the guard.

Zedekiah Questions Jeremiah Again

[14]Then King Zedekiah sent for Jeremiah the prophet. The king had him brought to the third entrance to the LORD's temple. "I want to ask you something," the king said to Jeremiah. "Don't hide anything from me."

[15]Jeremiah said to Zedekiah, "Suppose I give you an answer. You will kill me, won't you? Suppose I give you good advice. You won't listen to me, will you?"

Jer. 38:6–13 The name *Jeremiah* means "God throws." And we know that God has strong arms like it says in Psalm 136:12. But it wasn't God who threw Jeremiah into a pit—it was four false prophets. Check out Jeremiah 14:14–15.

[16]But King Zedekiah promised Jeremiah secretly, "I won't kill you. And I won't hand you over to those who want to kill you. That's just as sure as the LORD is alive. He's the one who has given us breath."

[17]So Jeremiah said to Zedekiah, "The LORD God who rules over all is the God of Israel. He says, 'Give yourself up to the officers of the king of Babylon. Then your life will be spared. And this city will not be burned down. You and your family will remain alive. [18]But what if you do not give yourself up to them? Then this city will be handed over to the Babylonians. They will burn it down. And you yourself will not escape from them.'"

[19]King Zedekiah said to Jeremiah, "I'm afraid of some of the Jews. They are the ones who have gone over to the side of the Babylonians. The Babylonians might hand me over to them. And those Jews will treat me badly."

[20]"They won't hand you over to them," Jeremiah replied. "Obey the LORD. Do what I tell you to do. Then things will go well with you. Your life will be spared. [21]Don't refuse to give yourself up. The LORD has shown me what will happen if you do. [22]All the women who are left in your palace will be brought out. They'll be given to the officials of the king of Babylon. Those women will say to you,

" 'Your trusted friends have tricked you.
    They have gotten the best of you.

Your feet are sunk down in the mud.
Your friends have deserted you.'

²³"All your wives and children will be brought out to the Babylonians. You yourself won't escape from them. You will be captured by the king of Babylon. And this city will be burned down."

²⁴Then Zedekiah said to Jeremiah, "Don't let anyone know about the talk we've had. If you do, you might die. ²⁵Suppose the officials find out that I've talked with you. And suppose they come to you and say, 'Tell us what you said to the king. Tell us what the king said to you. Don't hide it from us. If you do, we'll kill you.' ²⁶Then tell them, 'I was begging the king not to send me back to Jonathan's house. I don't want to die there.'"

²⁷All the officials came to Jeremiah. And they questioned him. He told them everything the king had ordered him to say. None of them had heard what he told the king. So they didn't say anything else to him.

²⁸Jeremiah remained in the courtyard of the guard. He stayed there until the day Jerusalem was captured.

Jerusalem Is Destroyed

39 Here is how Jerusalem was captured. ¹Nebuchadnezzar, the king of Babylon, marched out against Jerusalem. He came with all his armies and attacked it. It was in the ninth year that Zedekiah was king of Judah. It was in the tenth month. ²The city wall was broken through. It happened on the ninth day of the fourth month. It was in the 11th year of Zedekiah's rule. ³All the officials of the king of Babylon came. They took seats near the Middle Gate. Nergal-Sharezer from Samgar was there. Nebo-Sarsekim, a chief officer, was also there. So was Nergal-Sharezer, a high official. And all the other officials of the king of Babylon were there too. ⁴King Zedekiah and all the soldiers saw them. Then they ran away. They left the city at night. They went by way of the king's garden. They went out through the gate between the two walls. And they headed toward the Arabah Valley.

⁵But the armies of Babylon chased them. They caught up with Zedekiah in the plains near Jericho. They captured him there. And they took him to Nebuchadnezzar, the king of Babylon. He was at Riblah in the land of Hamath. That's where Nebuchadnezzar decided how Zedekiah would be punished.

⁶The king of Babylon killed the sons of Zedekiah at Riblah. He forced Zedekiah to watch it with his own eyes. He also killed all the nobles of Judah. ⁷Then he poked out Zedekiah's eyes. He put him in bronze chains. And he took him to Babylon.

⁸The Babylonians set the royal palace on fire. They also set fire to the houses of the people. And they broke down the walls of Jerusalem. ⁹Nebuzaradan was commander of the royal guard. Some people still remained in the city. But he took them away to Babylon as prisoners. He also took along those who had gone over to his side. And he took the rest of the people. ¹⁰Nebuzaradan, the commander of the guard, left some of the poor people of Judah behind. They didn't own anything. So at that time he gave them vineyards and fields.

¹¹Nebuchadnezzar, the king of Babylon, had given orders about Jeremiah. He had given them to Nebuzaradan, the commander of the royal guard. Nebuchadnezzar had said, ¹²"Take him. Look after him. Don't harm him. Do for him anything he asks." ¹³So that's what Nebuzaradan, the commander of the guard, did. Nebushazban and Nergal-Sharezer were with him. So were all the other officers of the king of Babylon. Nebushazban was a chief officer. Nergal-Sharezer was a high official. All these men ¹⁴sent for Jeremiah. They had him taken out of the courtyard of the guard. They turned him over to Gedaliah. Gedaliah was the son of Ahikam, the son of Shaphan. They told Gedaliah to take Jeremiah back to his home. So Jeremiah remained among his own people.

¹⁵A message from the LORD came to Jeremiah. It came while he was being kept in the courtyard of the guard. The LORD said, ¹⁶"Go. Speak to Ebed-Melek the Cushite. Tell him, 'The LORD who rules over all is the God of Israel. He says, "I am about to make the words I spoke against this city come true. I will not give success to it. Instead, I will bring horrible trouble on it. At that time my words will come true. You will see it with your own eyes. ¹⁷But I will save you on that day," announces the LORD. "You will not be handed over to those you are afraid of. ¹⁸I will save you. You will not be killed by a sword. Instead, you will escape with your life. That's because you trust in me," announces the LORD.'"

Jeremiah Is Set Free From His Chains

40 A message from the LORD came to Jeremiah. It came after Nebuzaradan, the commander of the royal guard, had set him free at Ramah. Jeremiah was being held by chains when Nebuzaradan found him. Jeremiah was among all the prisoners from Jerusalem and Judah. They were being taken to Babylon. ²But the commander of the guard found Jeremiah. The commander said to him, "The LORD your God ordered that this place be destroyed. ³And now he has brought it about. He has done exactly what he said he would do. All these things have happened because you people sinned against the LORD. You didn't obey him. ⁴But today I'm setting you free from the chains on your wrists. Come with me to Babylon if you want to. I'll take good care of you there. But if you don't want to come, then don't. The whole country lies in front of you. Go anywhere you want to."

⁵But before Jeremiah turned to go, Nebuzaradan continued, "Go back to Gedaliah, the son of Ahikam. The king of Babylon has appointed Gedaliah to be over the towns of Judah. Go and live with him among your people. Or go anywhere else you want to." Ahikam was the son of Shaphan.

The commander gave Jeremiah food and water. He also gave him a gift. Then he let Jeremiah go. ⁶So Jeremiah went to Mizpah to see Gedaliah, the son of Ahikam. Jeremiah stayed with him. Jeremiah lived among the people who were left behind in the land.

Gedaliah Is Murdered

⁷Some of Judah's army officers and their men were still in the open country. They heard that the king of Babylon had appointed Gedaliah as governor over Judah. Gedaliah was the son of Ahikam. The king had put Gedaliah in charge of the men, women and children who were still there. They were the poorest people in the land. They hadn't been taken to Babylon. ⁸When the army officers and their men heard these things, they came to Gedaliah at Mizpah. Ishmael, the son of Nethaniah, came. So did Johanan and Jonathan, the sons of Kareah. Seraiah, the son of Tanhumeth, also came. The sons of Ephai from Netophah came too. And so did Jaazaniah, the son of the Maakathite. All their men came

with them. ⁹Gedaliah, the son of Ahikam, the son of Shaphan, made a promise. He made the promise to give hope to all these men. He spoke in a kind way to them. He said, "Don't be afraid to serve the Babylonians. Make your homes in the land of Judah. Serve the king of Babylon. Then things will go well with you. ¹⁰I myself will stay at Mizpah. I'll speak for you to the officials of Babylon who come to us. But you must harvest the wine, summer fruit and olive oil. Put them in your jars. Store them up. And live in the towns you have taken over."

¹¹All the Jews in Moab, Ammon and Edom heard what had happened. So did the Jews in all the other countries. They heard that the king of Babylon had left some people behind in Judah. They also heard that he had appointed Gedaliah, the son of Ahikam, as governor over them. Ahikam was the son of Shaphan. ¹²When they heard these things, all of them came back to the land of Judah. They went to Gedaliah at Mizpah. They came from all the countries where they had been scattered. And they harvested a large amount of wine and summer fruit.

¹³Johanan and all the other army officers still in the open country came to Gedaliah at Mizpah. Johanan was the son of Kareah. ¹⁴The officers spoke to Gedaliah. They said, "Don't you know that Baalis has sent someone to take your life? Baalis is the king of Ammon. He has sent Ishmael, the son of Nethaniah." But Gedaliah, the son of Ahikam, didn't believe them.

¹⁵Then Johanan, the son of Kareah, spoke in private to Gedaliah in Mizpah. He said, "Let me go and kill Ishmael, the son of Nethaniah. No one will know about it. Why should he take your life? Why should he cause all the Jews gathered around you to be scattered? Why should he cause the people who remain in Judah to die?"

¹⁶But Gedaliah, the son of Ahikam, spoke to Johanan, the son of Kareah. He said, "Don't do an awful thing like that! What you are saying about Ishmael isn't true."

41 In the seventh month Ishmael came with ten men to Gedaliah, the son of Ahikam, at Mizpah. Ishmael was the son of Nethaniah. Nethaniah was the son of Elishama. Ishmael was a member of the royal family. He had been one of the king's officers. Ishmael and his ten men were eating together at Mizpah. [2]They got up and struck down Gedaliah, the son of Ahikam, with their swords. They killed him even though the king of Babylon had appointed him as governor over Judah. Ahikam was the son of Shaphan. [3]Ishmael also killed all the men of Judah who were with Gedaliah at Mizpah. And he killed the Babylonian soldiers who were there.

[4]On the next day, people still hadn't found out that Gedaliah had been murdered. [5]On that day 80 men came from Shechem, Shiloh and Samaria. They had shaved off their beards. They had torn their clothes. And they had cut themselves. They brought grain offerings and incense with them. They took them to the LORD's house. [6]Ishmael, the son of Nethaniah, went out from Mizpah to meet them. He was weeping as he went. When he met them, he said, "Come to Gedaliah, the son of Ahikam." [7]They went with him into the city. Then Ishmael, the son of Nethaniah, and the men who were with him killed them. And they threw them into an empty well. [8]But ten of the men had spoken to Ishmael. They had said, "Don't kill us! We have some wheat and barley. We also have olive oil and honey. We've hidden all of it in a field." So he didn't kill them along with the others. [9]But he had thrown into the empty well all the bodies of the men he had killed. That included Gedaliah's body. The well was the one King Asa had made. He had made it when he strengthened Mizpah against attack by Baasha, the king of Israel. Ishmael, the son of Nethaniah, filled it with the bodies of those he had killed.

[10]Nebuzaradan was the commander of the royal guard. He had appointed Gedaliah son of Ahikam over all the people at Mizpah. But Ishmael made prisoners of the people left at Mizpah. These prisoners included women who were members of the royal court. The prisoners also included everyone else left at Mizpah. Then Ishmael started out to go across the Jordan River to the land of Ammon.

[11]Johanan, the son of Kareah, was told what had happened. And so were all the other army officers with him. They heard about all the crimes Ishmael, the son of Nethaniah, had committed. [12]So they brought all their men together. Then they went to fight against Ishmael, the son of Nethaniah. They caught up with him near the large pool in Gibeon. [13]Ishmael had many people with him. They saw Johanan, the son of Kareah. And they saw the other army officers who were with him. So the people who had been forced to go with Ishmael were glad. [14]Ishmael had taken those people from Mizpah as prisoners. But now they turned and went over to the side of Johanan, the son of Kareah. [15]But Ishmael, the son of Nethaniah, and eight of his men escaped from Johanan. They ran away to the land of Ammon.

Some Jews Take Jeremiah to Egypt

[16]Then Johanan, the son of Kareah, led away all the people of Mizpah who were still alive. All the other army officers with Johanan helped him do this. He had taken them away from Ishmael, the son of Nethaniah. That happened after Ishmael had murdered Gedaliah, the son of Ahikam. The people Johanan had taken away included soldiers, women, children and court officials. He had brought them from Gibeon. [17]They went on their way. They stopped at Geruth Kimham near Bethlehem. They were going to Egypt. [18]They wanted to get away from the Babylonians. They were afraid of them. That's because Ishmael, the son of Nethaniah, had killed Gedaliah, the son of Ahikam. The king of Babylon had appointed Gedaliah as governor over Judah.

42 Then all the army officers approached Jeremiah. They included Johanan, the son of Kareah, and Jezaniah, the son of Hoshaiah. All the people from the least important of them to the most important also came. [2]All of them said to Jeremiah the prophet, "Please listen to our appeal. Pray to the LORD your God. Pray for all of us who are left here. Once there were many of us. But as you can see, only a few of us are left now. [3]So pray to the LORD your God. Pray that he'll tell us where we should go. Pray that he'll tell us what we should do."

[4]"I've heard you," Jeremiah the prophet replied. "I'll certainly pray to the LORD your God. I'll do what you have asked me to do. In fact, I'll tell you everything the LORD says. I won't keep anything back from you."

[5]Then they said to Jeremiah, "We'll do everything the LORD your God sends you to tell us to do. If we don't, may he be a true

and faithful witness against us. ⁶It doesn't matter whether what you say is in our favor or not. We're asking you to pray to the LORD our God. And we'll obey him. Things will go well with us. That's because we will obey the LORD our God."

⁷Ten days later a message came to Jeremiah from the LORD. ⁸So Jeremiah sent for Johanan, the son of Kareah, and all the other army officers with him. Jeremiah also gathered together all the people from the least important of them to the most important. ⁹He said to all of them, "The LORD is the God of Israel. You asked me to present your appeal to him. He told me, ¹⁰'Stay in this land. Then I will build you up. I will not tear you down. I will plant you. I will not pull you up by the roots. I have decided to stop bringing trouble on you. ¹¹Do not be afraid of the king of Babylon. You are afraid of him now. Do not be,' announces the LORD. 'I am with you. I will keep you safe. I will save you from his power. ¹²I will show you my loving concern. Then he will have concern for you. And he will let you return to your land.'

¹³"But suppose you say, 'We won't stay in this land.' If you do, you will be disobeying the LORD your God. ¹⁴And suppose you say, 'No! We'll go and live in Egypt. There we won't have to face war anymore. We won't hear the trumpets of war. And we won't

get hungry.' ¹⁵Then listen to what the LORD says to you who are left in Judah. He is the LORD who rules over all. He is the God of Israel. He says, 'Have you already made up your minds to go to Egypt? Are you going to make your homes there? ¹⁶Then the war you fear will catch up with you there. The hunger you are afraid of will follow you into Egypt. And you will die there. ¹⁷In fact, that will happen to all those who go and make their homes in Egypt. All of them will die of war, hunger and plague. Not one of them will live. None of them will escape the trouble I will bring on them.' ¹⁸He is the LORD who rules over all. He is the God of Israel. He says, 'My great anger has been poured out on those who used to live in Jerusalem. In the same way, it will be poured out on you when you go to Egypt. People will use your name in a curse. They will be shocked at you. They will say bad things about you. And they will say you are shameful. You will never see this place again.'

¹⁹"The LORD has spoken to you who are left in Judah. He has said, 'Do not go to Egypt.' Here is something you can be sure of. I am warning you about it today. ²⁰You made a big mistake when you asked me to pray to the LORD your God. You said, 'Pray to the LORD our God for us. Tell us everything he says. We'll do it.' ²¹I have told you today what the LORD your God wants you to do. But you still haven't obeyed him. You haven't done anything he sent me to tell you to do. ²²So here is something else you can be sure of. You will die of war, hunger and plague. You want to go and make your homes in Egypt. But you will die there."

43 Jeremiah finished telling the people everything the LORD their God had said. Jeremiah told them everything the LORD had sent him to tell them. ²After that, Azariah, the son of Hoshaiah, and Johanan, the son of Kareah, spoke to Jeremiah. And all the proud men joined them. They said, "You are lying! The LORD our God hasn't sent you to speak to us. He hasn't told you to say, 'You must not go to Egypt and make your homes there.' ³But Baruch, the son of Neriah, is turning you against us. He wants us to be handed over to the Babylonians. Then they can kill us. Or they can take us away to Babylon."

⁴So Johanan, the son of Kareah, disobeyed the LORD's command. So did all the

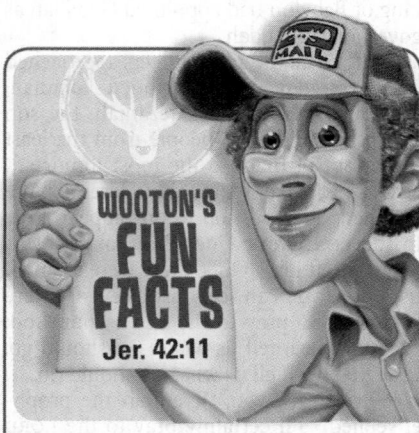

WOOTON'S
FUN
FACTS
Jer. 42:11

Jeremiah was alive when Daniel, Shadrach, Meshach, and Abednego were taken to Babylon. Maybe they knew this prophecy and gained strength from it. (Read Daniel chapters 1, 3, and 6 for more about these four guys with funny names.)

other army officers and all the people. They didn't stay in the land of Judah. ⁵Instead Johanan, the son of Kareah, and all the other army officers led away all the people who were left in Judah. Those people had returned to Judah from all the nations where they had been scattered. ⁶Johanan and the other officers also led away many people Nebuzaradan had left at Mizpah. They included men, women and children. They also included the king's daughters. Nebuzaradan had left them with Gedaliah, the son of Ahikam. They also took Jeremiah the prophet and Baruch son of Neriah along with them. Nebuzaradan was commander of the royal guard. Ahikam was the son of Shaphan. ⁷So the Jewish leaders disobeyed the LORD. They took everyone to Egypt. They went all the way to Tahpanhes.

⁸In Tahpanhes a message from the LORD came to Jeremiah. The LORD said, ⁹"Make sure the Jews are watching you. Then get some large stones. Go to the entrance to Pharaoh's house in Tahpanhes. Bury the stones in the clay under the brick walkway there. ¹⁰Then tell the Jews, 'The LORD who rules over all is the God of Israel. He says, "I will send for my servant Nebuchadnezzar, the king of Babylon. And I will set his throne over these stones that are buried here. He will set up his royal tent over them. ¹¹He will come and attack Egypt. He will bring death to those I have appointed to die. He will take away as prisoners those I have appointed to be taken away. And he will kill with swords those I have appointed to be killed. ¹²He will set the temples of the gods of Egypt on fire. He will burn down their temples. He will take away the statues of their gods. Nebuchadnezzar will be like a shepherd who picks his coat clean of lice. Nebuchadnezzar will pick Egypt clean and then depart. ¹³At Heliopolis in Egypt he will smash the sacred pillars to pieces. And he will burn down the temples of the gods of Egypt."' "

Worshiping Other Gods Brings Horrible Trouble

44 A message from the LORD came to Jeremiah. It was about all the Jews living in Lower Egypt. They were living in Migdol, Tahpanhes and Memphis. It was also about all the Jews living in Upper Egypt. ²The LORD who rules over all is the God of Israel. He said, "You saw all the trouble I brought on Jerusalem. I also brought it on all the towns in Judah. Today they lie there deserted and destroyed. ³That's because of the evil things their people did. They made me very angry. They burned incense to other gods. And they worshiped them. They and you and your people of long ago never knew those gods. ⁴Again and again I sent my servants the prophets. They said, 'Don't worship other gods! The LORD hates it!' ⁵But the people didn't listen. They didn't pay any attention. They didn't turn from their sinful ways. They didn't stop burning incense to other gods. ⁶So my burning anger was poured out. It blazed out against the towns of Judah and the streets of Jerusalem. It made them the dry and empty places they are today."

⁷The LORD God who rules over all is the God of Israel. He says, "Why do you want to bring all this trouble on yourselves? You are removing from Judah its men and women, its children and babies. Not one of you will be left. ⁸Why do you want to make me angry with the gods your hands have made? Why do you burn incense to the gods of Egypt, where you now live? You will destroy yourselves. All the nations on earth will use your name as a curse. They will say you are shameful. ⁹Have you forgotten the evil things done by your people of long ago? The kings and queens of Judah did those same things. So did you and your wives. They were done in the land of Judah and the streets of Jerusalem. ¹⁰To this day the people of Judah have not made themselves humble in my sight. They have not shown any respect for me. They have not obeyed my law. They have not followed the rules I gave you and your people of long ago."

¹¹The LORD who rules over all is the God of Israel. He says, "I have decided to bring horrible trouble on you. I will destroy the whole land of Judah. ¹²I will destroy the people of Judah who are left. They had decided to go to Egypt and make their homes there. But all of them will die in Egypt. They will die of war or hunger. All of them will die, from the least important of them to the most important. They will die of war or hunger. People will use their name as a curse. They will be shocked at them. They will say bad things about them. And they will say they are shameful. ¹³I will use war,

hunger and plague to punish the Jews who live in Egypt. I punished Jerusalem in the same way. [14]None of the people of Judah who have gone to live in Egypt will escape. Not one of them will live to return to Judah. They long to return and live there. But only a few will escape from Egypt and go back."

[15]All the Jews who were living in Lower and Upper Egypt gathered to give Jeremiah their answer. A large crowd had come together. It included men who knew that their wives were burning incense to other gods. Their wives were there with them. All of them said to Jeremiah, [16]"We won't listen to the message you have spoken to us in the LORD's name! [17]We will certainly do everything we said we would. We'll burn incense to the female god called the Queen of Heaven. We'll pour out drink offerings to her. We'll do just as we and our people of long ago have done. Our kings and our officials also did it. All of us did it in the towns of Judah and the streets of Jerusalem. At that time we had plenty of food. We were well off. We didn't suffer any harm. [18]But then we stopped burning incense to the Queen of Heaven. We stopped pouring out drink offerings to her. And ever since that time we haven't had anything. Instead, we've been dying of war and hunger."

[19]The women added, "We burned incense to the Queen of Heaven. We poured out drink offerings to her. And our husbands knew we were making cakes that looked like her. They knew we were pouring out drink offerings to her."

[20]Then Jeremiah spoke to all the people who were answering him. He spoke to men and women alike. He said, [21]"Didn't the LORD know you were burning incense in the towns of Judah? Didn't he care that you were also doing it in the streets of Jerusalem? You and your people of long ago were doing it. Your kings and officials were doing it too. So were the rest of the people in the land. [22]The LORD couldn't put up any longer with the evil things you were doing. He hated the things you did. So your land became a curse. It became a dry and empty desert. No one lived there. And that's the way it still is today. [23]You have burned incense to other gods. You have sinned against the LORD. You haven't obeyed him or his law. You haven't followed his rules. You haven't lived up to the terms of the

covenant he made with you. That's why all this trouble has come on you. You have seen it with your own eyes."

[24]Then Jeremiah spoke to all the people. That included the women. He said, "All you people of Judah in Egypt, listen to the LORD's message. [25]The LORD who rules over all is the God of Israel. He says, 'You and your wives have done what you promised you would do. You said, "We will certainly keep the promises we made to the Queen of Heaven. We'll burn incense to her. We'll pour out drink offerings to her." '

"Go ahead then. Do what you said you would! Keep your promises! [26]But listen to the LORD's message. Listen, all you Jews living in Egypt. 'I make a promise by my own great name,' says the LORD. 'Here is what I promise. "No one from Judah who lives anywhere in Egypt will ever again pray in my name. None of them will ever make this promise. They will never say, 'You can be sure that the LORD and King is alive.' " [27]I am watching over them to do them harm and not good. The Jews in Egypt will die of war and hunger until all of them are destroyed. [28]Some will not be killed. They will return to Judah from Egypt. But they will be very few. Then all the people of Judah who came to live in Egypt will know the truth. They will know whether what I say or what they say will come true.

[29]" 'I will give you a sign that I will punish you in this place,' announces the LORD. 'Then you can be sure that my warnings of harm against you will come true.' [30]The LORD says, 'I am going to hand over Pharaoh Hophra king of Egypt. I will hand him over to his enemies who want to kill him. In the same way, I handed over King Zedekiah to Nebuchadnezzar, the king of Babylon. He was the enemy who wanted to kill Zedekiah.' "

The LORD Speaks to Baruch

45 Jeremiah talked to Baruch, the son of Neriah. It was in the fourth year that Jehoiakim, the son of Josiah, was king of Judah. It was when Baruch had written down on a scroll the words Jeremiah the prophet told him to write. Jeremiah had said, [2]"The LORD is the God of Israel. Baruch, he says to you, [3]'You have said, "How terrible it is for me! The LORD has added sorrow to my pain. I'm worn out from all my groaning. I can't find any rest."' ⁴But here is what the LORD has told me to say to you, Baruch. 'The LORD says, "I will destroy what I have built up. I will pull up by the roots what I have planted. I will do this throughout the earth. ⁵So should you seek great things for yourself? Do not seek them. I will bring trouble on everyone," announces the LORD. "But no matter where you go, I will let you escape with your life."'"

A Message About Egypt

46 A message from the LORD came to Jeremiah the prophet. It was about the nations.

²Here is what the LORD says about Egypt.

Here is his message against the army of Pharaoh Necho. He was king of Egypt. Nebuchadnezzar, the king of Babylon, won the battle over Necho's army. That happened at Carchemish on the Euphrates River. It was in the fourth year that Jehoiakim was king of Judah. He was the son of Josiah. The message says,

Jason's Jargon

JEREMIAH 46

Hunt for the word *locusts* in this chapter. Locusts are similar to grasshoppers. They travel in swarms, where millions of them cover the sky and destroy crops.

³ "Egyptians, prepare your shields!
   Prepare large and small shields alike!
   March out for battle!
⁴ Get the horses and chariots ready to ride!
   Take up your battle positions!
   Put on your helmets!
   Shine up your spears!
   Put on your armor!
⁵ What do I see?
   The Egyptians are terrified.
They are pulling back.
   Their soldiers are losing.
They run away as fast as they can.

They do not look back.
   There is terror on every side,"
      announces the LORD.
⁶ "Those who run fast can't get away.
   Those who are strong can't escape.
In the north by the Euphrates River
   they trip and fall.

⁷ "Who is this that rises like the Nile River?
   Who rises like rivers of rushing waters?
⁸ Egypt rises like the Nile River.
   It rises like rivers of rushing waters.
Egypt says, 'I will rise and cover the earth.
   I'll destroy cities and their people.'
⁹ Charge, you horses!
   Drive fast, you chariot drivers!
March on, you soldiers!
   March on, you men of Cush and Put who carry shields.
   March on, you men of Lydia who shoot arrows.
¹⁰ But that day belongs to me.
   I am the LORD who rules over all.
   It is a day for me to pay back my enemies.
My sword will eat until it is satisfied.
   It will drink until it is not thirsty for blood anymore.
I am the Lord. I am the LORD who rules over all.
   I will offer a sacrifice.
I will offer it in the land of the north
   by the Euphrates River.

¹¹ "People of Egypt,
   go up to Gilead and get some healing lotion.
You may try many medicines, but you will not be healed.
   There isn't any healing for you.
¹² The nations will hear about your shame.
   Your cries of pain will fill the earth.
One soldier will trip over another.
   Both of them will fall down together."

¹³Nebuchadnezzar, the king of Babylon, was coming to attack Egypt. Here is the message the LORD spoke to Jeremiah the prophet about it. He said,

¹⁴ "Egyptians, here is what I want you to announce in your land.
   Announce it in the city of Migdol.

Also announce it in Memphis and
Tahpanhes.
Say, 'Take up your battle positions! Get
ready!
The sword eats up those around
you.'
¹⁵ Why are your soldiers lying on the
ground?
They can't stand, because I bring
them down.
¹⁶ They will trip again and again.
They will fall over one another.
They will say, 'Get up. Let's go back
home.
Let's return to our own people and
our own lands.
Let's get away from the swords
that will bring us great harm.'
¹⁷ The Egyptian soldiers will cry out,
'Pharaoh, our king, is only a loud
noise.
He has missed his chance to win the
battle.'
¹⁸ "I am the King.
My name is the LORD Who Rules
Over All.
Someone will come who is like Mount
Tabor among the mountains.
He is like Mount Carmel by the
Mediterranean Sea.
And that is just as sure as I am alive,"
announces the King.
¹⁹ "So pack your belongings, you who live
in Egypt.
You will be taken away from your
land.
Memphis will be completely destroyed.
Its buildings will be broken down.
No one will live there.
²⁰ "Egypt is like a beautiful young cow.
But Nebuchadnezzar is coming
against her from the north.
He will bite her like a fly.
²¹ Hired soldiers are in Egypt's army.
They are like fat calves.
All of them will turn and run away.
They will not hold their positions.
The day of trouble is coming on them.
The time for them to be punished
is near.
²² The Egyptians will hiss like a snake that
is trying to get away.
A powerful army will advance
against them.

Their enemies will come against them
with axes.
They will be like those who cut
down trees.
²³ Egypt is like a thick forest.
But they will chop it down,"
announces the LORD.
"There are more of their enemies than
there are locusts.
In fact, they can't even be counted.
²⁴ The nation of Egypt will be put to
shame.
It will be handed over to the people
of the north."

²⁵The LORD who rules over all is the God
of Israel. He says, "I am about to punish
Amon, the god of Thebes. I will also punish
Pharaoh. I will punish Egypt and its gods
and kings. And I will punish those who
depend on Pharaoh. ²⁶I will hand them
over to those who want to kill them. I will
give them to Nebuchadnezzar, the king of
Babylon, and his officers. But later, many
people will live in Egypt again as in times
past," announces the LORD.

²⁷ "People of Jacob, do not be afraid.
You are my servant.
Israel, do not be terrified.
I will bring you safely out of a place far
away.
I will bring your children back
from the land where they were
taken.
Your people will have peace and
security again.
And no one will make them afraid.
²⁸ People of Jacob, do not be afraid.
You are my servant.
I am with you,"
announces the LORD.
"I will completely destroy all the
nations
among which I scatter you.
But I will not completely destroy
you.
I will correct you. But I will be fair.
I will not let you go without any
punishment."

A Message About the Philistines

47 A message from the LORD came to
Jeremiah the prophet. It was about
the Philistines before Pharaoh attacked the
city of Gaza.

² The LORD said,

"The armies of Babylon are like waters
rising in the north.
They will become a great flood.
They will flow over the land and
everything in it.
They will flow over the towns and
those who live in them.
The people will cry out.
All those who live in the land will
weep.
³ They will weep when they hear
galloping horses.
They will weep at the noise of enemy
chariots.
They will weep at the rumble of their
wheels.
Parents will not even try to help their
children.
Their hands will not be able to help
them.
⁴ The day has come
to destroy all the Philistines.
The time has come to remove all those
who could help Tyre and Sidon.
I am about to destroy the Philistines.
I will not leave anyone alive
who came from the coasts of Crete.
⁵ The people of Gaza will be so sad
they will shave their heads.
And Ashkelon's people will be silent.
You who remain on the plain,
how long will you cut yourselves?

⁶ "'Sword of the LORD!' you cry out.
'How long will it be until you rest?
Return to the place you came from.
Stop killing us! Be still!'
⁷ But how can his sword rest
when the LORD has given it a
command?
He has ordered it
to attack Ashkelon and the Philistine
coast."

A Message About Moab

48 Here is what the LORD says about
Moab.

The LORD who rules over all is the God
of Israel. He says,

"How terrible it will be for the city of
Nebo!
It will be destroyed.
Kiriathaim will be captured.

It will be put to shame.
Its fort will be broken down.
It will be put to shame.
² Moab will not be praised anymore.
In Heshbon people will plan its fall
from power.
They will say, 'Come. Let's put an
end to that nation.'
City of Madmen, you too will be silent.
My sword will hunt you down.
³ Cries of sorrow come from Horonaim.
The town is being completely
destroyed.
⁴ Moab will be broken.
Her little ones will cry out.
⁵ The people go up the hill to Luhith.
They are weeping bitterly as they go.
Loud cries are heard on the road down
to Horonaim.
People cry out because the town is
being destroyed.
⁶ People of Moab, run away! Run for
your lives!
Become like a lonely bush in the
desert.
⁷ You trust in the things you can do.
You trust in your riches.
So you too will be taken away as
prisoners.
Your god named Chemosh will be
carried away.
So will its priests and officials.
⁸ The one who is going to destroy you
will come against every town.
Not even one of them will escape.
The valley and the high plain
will be destroyed.
The LORD has spoken.
⁹ Sprinkle salt all over Moab.
It will be completely destroyed.
Its towns will be a dry and empty desert.
No one will live in them.

¹⁰ "May anyone who is lazy when they do
the LORD's work
be under my curse!
May anyone who keeps their sword
from killing
be under my curse!

¹¹ "Moab has been at peace and rest from
its earliest days.
It is like wine that has not been
shaken up.
It has not been poured from one jar to
another.

Moab's people have not been taken
away from their land.
They are like wine that tastes as it
always did.
Its smell has not changed at all.
¹² But other days are coming," announces
the LORD.
"At that time I will send people who
pour wine from pitchers.
They will pour Moab out like wine.
They will empty its pitchers.
They will smash its jars.
¹³ Then Moab's people will be ashamed of
their god named Chemosh.
They will be ashamed just as the
people of Israel were
when they trusted in their false god
at Bethel.

¹⁴ "How can you say, 'We are soldiers.
We are men who are brave in battle'?
¹⁵ Moab will be destroyed.
Its enemies will march into its towns.
Its finest young men will die in battle,"
announces the King.
His name is the LORD Who Rules
Over All.
¹⁶ "The fall of Moab is near.
Its time of trouble will come quickly.
¹⁷ All you who live around it, mourn for
its people.
Be sad, you who know how famous
Moab is.
Say, 'Its powerful ruler's scepter is
broken!
His glorious scepter is smashed.'

¹⁸ "Come down from your glorious city,
you who live in Dibon.
Come and sit on the thirsty ground.
The one who destroys Moab
will come up and attack you.
Your enemies will destroy your cities
that have high walls around them.
¹⁹ Stand by the road and watch,
you who live in Aroer.
Ask the men who are running away.
Ask the women who are escaping.
Ask them, 'What has happened?'
²⁰ Moab has been put to shame.
It has been destroyed.
Weep and cry out!
Tell everyone Moab has been destroyed.
Announce it by the Arnon River.
²¹ The high plain has been judged.
So have Holon, Jahzah and Mephaath.

²² Dibon, Nebo and Beth Diblathaim have
been judged.
²³ So have Kiriathaim, Beth Gamul and
Beth Meon.
²⁴ Kerioth and Bozrah have also been
judged.
And so have all the towns of Moab,
far and near alike.
²⁵ Moab's power is gone.
Its strength is broken,"
announces the LORD.

²⁶ "Moab's people think they are better
than I am.
So let their enemies make them
drunk.
Let the people get sick and throw up.
Let them roll around in the mess they
have made.
Let people laugh at them.
²⁷ Moab, you laughed at Israel, didn't you?
Were Israel's people caught among
robbers?
Is that why you shake your head at
them?
Is that why you make fun of them
every time you talk about them?
²⁸ Leave your towns,
you who live in Moab.
Go and live among the rocks.
Be like a dove that makes its nest
at the entrance of a cave.

²⁹ "We have heard all about Moab's pride.
We have heard how very proud they
are.
They think they are so much better
than others.
Their pride reaches deep down
inside their hearts.
³⁰ I know how rude they are.
But it will not get them anywhere,"
announces the LORD.
"Their bragging does not accomplish
anything.
³¹ So I weep over Moab.
I cry for all Moab's people.
I groan for the people of Kir
Hareseth.
³² I weep for you as Jazer weeps,
you vines of Sibmah.
Your branches used to spread out.
They went all the way down to the
Dead Sea.
They reached as far as the sea of
Jazer.

The one who destroys your country
    has taken away your grapes and ripe
        fruit.
[33] Joy has left your orchards.
    Gladness is gone from your fields.
I have stopped the flow of juice from
    your winepresses.
    No one stomps on your grapes with
        shouts of joy.
There are shouts.
    But they are not shouts of joy.

[34] "The sound of their cry rises from
    Heshbon.
    It rises as far as Elealeh and Jahaz.
    It rises from Zoar.
It goes all the way to Horonaim and
    Eglath Shelishiyah.
    Even the waters at Nimrim are dried
        up.
[35] In Moab people sacrifice offerings on
    the high places.
    They burn incense to their gods.
But I will put an end to those people,"
    announces the LORD.
[36] "Like a flute my heart sings a song of
    sadness for Moab.
    It sings like a flute for the people of
        Kir Hareseth.
    The wealth they had acquired is
        gone.
[37] Every head is shaved.
    Every beard is cut off.
Every hand is cut.
    And every waist is covered with the
        clothes of sadness.
[38] Weeping is the only sound in Moab.
    It is heard on all its roofs.
    It is heard in the market.
I have broken Moab
    like a jar that no one wants,"
    announces the LORD.
[39] "How broken Moab is! How the people
    weep!
    They turn away from others
    because they are so ashamed.
All those around them laugh at them.
    They are shocked at them."

[40] The LORD says,

"Look! Nebuchadnezzar is like an eagle
    diving down.
    He is spreading his wings over
        Moab.
[41] Kerioth will be captured.
    Its forts will be taken.

At that time the hearts of Moab's
    soldiers will tremble in fear.
    They will be like the heart of a
        woman having a baby.
[42] Moab will be destroyed as a nation.
    That is because its people thought
    they were better than the LORD.
[43] You people of Moab,"
    announces the LORD,
    "terror, a pit and a trap are waiting
        for you.
[44] Anyone who runs away from the terror
    will fall into the pit.
Anyone who climbs out of the pit
    will be caught in the trap.
The time is coming
    when I will punish Moab,"
    announces the LORD.

[45] "In the shadow of Heshbon
    those who are trying to escape stand
        helpless.
A fire has blazed out from Heshbon.
    Flames have come out from Sihon's
        city.
It burns the foreheads of Moab's
    people.
    It burns the skulls of those who brag
        loudly.
[46] How terrible it will be for you, Moab!
    Those who worship Chemosh are
        destroyed.
Your sons are being taken to another
    country.
    Your daughters are taken away as
        prisoners.
[47] "But in days to come
    I will bless Moab with great success
        again,"
    announces the LORD.

This ends the report about how the
LORD would judge Moab.

A Message About Ammon

49 Here is what the LORD says about the
people of Ammon.

He says,

"Doesn't Israel have any sons?
    Doesn't Israel have anyone
    to take over the family property?
Then why has the god named Molek
    taken over Gad?
    Why do those who worship him live
        in its towns?

² But a new day is coming,"
announces the LORD.
"At that time I will sound the battle cry.
I will sound it against Rabbah in the
land of Ammon.
It will become a pile of broken-down
buildings.
The villages around it will be set on
fire.
Then Israel will drive out
those who drove her out,"
says the LORD.
³ "Heshbon, weep for Ai! It is destroyed!
Cry out, you who live in Rabbah!
Put on the clothes of sadness and
mourn.
Run here and there inside the walls.
Your god named Molek will be carried
away.
So will its priests and officials.
⁴ Why do you brag about your valleys?
You brag that they produce so many
crops.
Ammon, you are an unfaithful country.
You trust in your riches. You say,
'Who will attack me?'
⁵ I will bring terror on you.
It will come from all those around
you,"
announces the Lord. He is the LORD
who rules over all.
"Every one of you will be driven away.
No one will bring back those who
escape.
⁶ "But after that, I will bless the people of
Ammon
with great success again,"
announces the LORD.

A Message About Edom

⁷ Here is what the LORD says about
Edom.

The LORD who rules over all says,

"Isn't there wisdom in the town of
Teman anymore?
Can't those who are wise give advice?
Has their wisdom disappeared
completely?
⁸ Turn around and run away, you who
live in Dedan.
Hide in deep caves.
I will bring trouble on Esau's family line.
I will do this at the time I punish
them.

⁹ Edom, suppose grape pickers came to
harvest your vines.
They would still leave a few grapes.
Suppose robbers came at night.
They would steal only as much as
they wanted.
¹⁰ But I will strip everything away from
Esau's people.
I will uncover their hiding places.
They will not be able to hide
anywhere.
Their army is destroyed.
Their friends and neighbors are
destroyed.
So there is no one to say,
¹¹ 'Leave your children whose fathers have
died.
I will keep them alive.
Your widows can also depend on
me.'"

¹² The LORD says, "What if those who
do not have to drink the cup must drink it
anyway? Then shouldn't you be punished?
You will certainly be punished. You must
drink the cup. ¹³ I make a promise in my
own name. Bozrah will be destroyed," announces the LORD. "People will be shocked
at it. They will say Bozrah is a shameful
place. They will use its name as a curse.
And all its towns will be destroyed forever."

¹⁴ I've heard a message from the LORD.
A messenger was sent to the nations.
The LORD told him to say,
"Gather yourselves together to attack
Edom!
Prepare for battle!"

¹⁵ The LORD says to Edom, "I will make
you weak among the nations.
They will hate you.
¹⁶ You live in the safety of the rocks.
You live on top of the hills.
But the terror you stir up has now
turned against you.
Your proud heart has tricked you.
You build your nest as high as an eagle
does.
But I will bring you down from
there,"
announces the LORD.
¹⁷ "People of Edom,
all those who pass by you will be
shocked.
They will make fun of you
because of all your wounds.

¹⁸ Sodom and Gomorrah were destroyed.
　　So were the towns that were near
　　　them,"
　　says the Lord.
　"You will be just like them.
　　No one will live in your land.
　　No human beings will stay there.

¹⁹ "I will be like a lion coming up
　　from the bushes by the Jordan River.
　I will hunt in rich grasslands.
　I will chase you from your land in an
　　　instant.
　　What nation will I choose to do this?
　　Which one will I appoint?
　Is anyone like me?
　　Who would dare to argue with me?
　　What leader can stand against me?"

²⁰ So listen to what the Lord has planned
　　against the people of Edom.
　　Hear what he has planned against
　　　those who live in Teman.
　Edom's young people will be dragged
　　away.
　Their grasslands will be shocked at
　　their fate.

²¹ When the earth hears Edom fall, it will
　　shake.
　The people's cries will be heard all
　　the way to the Red Sea.

²² Look! An enemy is coming.
　　It's like an eagle diving down.
　It will spread its wings over Bozrah.
　At that time the hearts of Edom's soldiers
　　will tremble in fear.
　　They'll be like the heart of a woman
　　　having a baby.

A Message About Damascus

²³Here is what the Lord says about Damascus. He says,

　"The people of Hamath and Arpad are
　　terrified.
　　They have heard bad news.
　They have lost all hope.
　　They are troubled like the rolling
　　　sea.

²⁴ The people of Damascus have become
　　weak.
　　They have turned to run away.
　　Panic has taken hold of them.
　Suffering and pain have taken hold of
　　them.
　　Their pain is like the pain of a
　　　woman having a baby.

²⁵ Why hasn't the famous city been
　　deserted?
　　It is the town I take delight in.

²⁶ You can be sure its young men will fall
　　dead in the streets.
　All its soldiers will be put to death at
　　that time,"
　　announces the Lord who rules over
　　　all.

²⁷ "I will set the walls of Damascus on fire.
　　It will burn down the strong towers
　　　of King Ben-Hadad."

A Message About Kedar and Hazor

²⁸Here is what the Lord says about the people of Kedar and the kingdoms of Hazor. Nebuchadnezzar, the king of Babylon, was planning to attack them.

The Lord says to the armies of Babylon,

　"Prepare for battle. Attack Kedar.
　　Destroy the people of the east.

²⁹ Their tents and flocks will be taken
　　away from them.
　　Their tents will be carried off.
　All their goods and camels will be
　　stolen.
　People will shout to them,
　　'There is terror on every side!'

³⁰ "Run away quickly!
　　You who live in Hazor, stay in deep
　　　caves,"
　　announces the Lord.
　"Nebuchadnezzar, the king of Babylon,
　　has made plans against you.
　　He has decided to attack you.

³¹ "Armies of Babylon, prepare for battle.
　　Attack a nation that feels secure.
　Its people do not have any worries,"
　　announces the Lord.
　"That nation does not have gates or bars
　　that lock them.
　Its people live far from danger.

³² Their camels will be stolen.
　　Their large herds will be taken away.
　I will scatter to the winds those who are
　　in places far away.
　I will bring trouble on them from
　　every side,"
　　announces the Lord.

³³ "Hazor will become a home for wild
　　dogs.
　It will be a dry and empty desert
　　forever.

No one will live in that land.
No human beings will stay there."

A Message About Elam

[34] A message from the LORD came to Jeremiah the prophet. It was about Elam. It came shortly after Zedekiah became king of Judah.

[35] The LORD who rules over all said,

"Elam's bow is the secret of its strength.
But I will break it.
[36] I will bring the four winds against
Elam.
I will bring them from all four
directions.
I will scatter Elam's people to the four
winds.
They will be taken away
to every nation on earth.
[37] I will use Elam's enemies to smash
them.
Those who want to kill them will kill
them.
I will bring trouble on Elam's people.
My anger will be great against them,"
announces the LORD.
"I will chase them with swords.
I will hunt them down
until I have destroyed them.
[38] I will set up my throne in Elam.
I will destroy its king and officials,"
announces the LORD.

[39] "But in days to come I will bless Elam
with great success again,"
announces the LORD.

A Message About Babylon

50 Here is the message the LORD spoke through Jeremiah the prophet. It was about the city of Babylon and the land of Babylon. He said,

[2] "Announce this message among the
nations.
Lift up a banner.
Let the nations hear the message.
Do not keep anything back.
Say, 'Babylon will be captured.
The god named Bel will be put to
shame.
The god named Marduk will be filled
with terror.
Babylon's gods will be put to shame.
The gods its people made will be
filled with terror.'

[3] A nation from the north will attack it.
That nation will destroy Babylon.
No one will live there.
People and animals alike will run
away.

[4] "The days are coming,"
announces the LORD.
"At that time the people of Israel and
Judah will gather together.
They will come in tears to me.
I am the LORD their God.
[5] They will ask how to get to Zion.
Then they will turn their faces
toward it.
They will come and join themselves to
me.
They will enter into the covenant I
make with them.
It will last forever.
It will never be forgotten.

[6] "My people have been like lost sheep.
Their shepherds have led them astray.
They have caused them to wander in
the mountains.
They have wandered over mountains
and hills.
They have forgotten that I am their
true resting place.
[7] Everyone who found them destroyed
them.
Their enemies said, 'We aren't guilty.
They sinned against the LORD.
He gave them everything they
needed.
He has always been Israel's hope.'

[8] "People of Judah, run away from
Babylon.
Leave the land of Babylon.
Be like the goats that lead the flock.
[9] I will stir up great nations
that will join forces against Babylon.
I will bring them from the land of
the north.
They will take up their battle positions
against Babylon.
They will come from the north and
capture it.
Their arrows will be like skilled soldiers.
They will not miss their mark.
[10] So the riches of Babylon will be taken
away.
All those who steal from it will have
more than enough,"
announces the LORD.

¹¹ "People of Babylon, you have stolen
       what belongs to me.
    That has made you glad and full of
       joy.
    You dance around like a young cow on
       a threshing floor.
    You neigh like stallions.
¹² Because of that, you will bring great
       shame on your land.
    Your whole nation will be
       dishonored.
    It will become the least important of
       the nations.
    It will become a dry and empty
       desert.
¹³ Because I am angry with it, no one will
       live there.
    It will be completely deserted.
    All those who pass by Babylon will be
       shocked.
    They will make fun of it because of
       all its wounds.

¹⁴ "All you who shoot arrows,
       take up your battle positions around
       Babylon.
    Shoot at it! Do not spare any arrows!
       Its people have sinned against me.
¹⁵ Shout against them on every side!
       They are giving up.
    The towers of the city are falling.
       Its walls are being pulled down.
    The LORD is paying back its people.
       So pay them back yourselves.
    Do to them what they have done to
       others.
¹⁶ Do not leave anyone in Babylon to
       plant the fields.
    Do not leave anyone to harvest the
       grain.
    Let each of them return to their own
       people.
    Let them run away to their own
       land.
    If they don't, their enemy's sword
       will bring them great harm.

¹⁷ "Israel is like a scattered flock
       that lions have chased away.
    The first lion that ate them up
       was the king of Assyria.
    The last one that broke their bones
       was Nebuchadnezzar, the king of
       Babylon."

¹⁸ The LORD who rules over all is the God
of Israel. He says,

    "I punished the king of Assyria.
    In the same way, I will punish
       the king of Babylon and his land.
¹⁹ But I will bring Israel back to their own
       grasslands.
    I will feed them on Mount Carmel
       and in Bashan.
    I will satisfy their hunger
       on the hills of Ephraim and Gilead.
²⁰ The days are coming,"
       announces the LORD.
    "At that time people will search for
       Israel's guilt.
    But they will not find any.
    They will search for Judah's sins.
    But they will not find any.
    That is because I will forgive the
       people I have spared.

²¹ "Enemies of Babylon, attack their land
       of Merathaim.
    Make war against those who live in
       Pekod.
    Chase them and kill them. Destroy
       them completely,"
       announces the LORD.
    "Do everything I have commanded
       you to do.
²² The noise of battle is heard in the land.
    It is the noise of a great city being
       destroyed!
²³ It has been broken to pieces.
    It was the hammer that broke the
       whole earth.
    How empty Babylon is among the
       nations!
²⁴ Babylon, I set a trap for you.
    And you were caught before you
       knew it.
    You were found and captured.
    That is because you opposed me.
²⁵ I have opened up my storeroom.
    I have brought out the weapons I use
       when I am angry.
    I am the LORD and King who rules over
       all.
    I have work to do in the land of the
       Babylonians.
²⁶ So come against it from far away.
    Open up its storerooms.
    Stack everything up like piles of
       grain.
    Completely destroy that country.
    Do not leave anyone alive there.
²⁷ Kill all Babylon's strongest warriors.
    Let them die in battle.

How terrible it will be for them!
　　Their time to be judged has come.
　　Now they will be punished.
28 Listen to those who have escaped.
　　Listen to those who have returned
　　　from Babylon.
They are announcing in Zion
　　how I have paid Babylon back.
I have paid it back for destroying my
　　temple.

29 "Send for men armed with bows and
　　arrows.
　　Send them against Babylon.
Set up camp all around it.
　　Do not let anyone escape.
Pay it back for what its people have
　　done.
　　Do to them what they have done to
　　　others.
They have dared to disobey me.
　　I am the Holy One of Israel.
30 You can be sure its young men will fall
　　dead in the streets.
　　All its soldiers will be put to death at
　　　that time,"
　　announces the LORD.
31 "Proud Babylonians, I am against you,"
　　announces the Lord.
The LORD who rules over all says,
　　"Your day to be judged has come.
　　It is time for you to be punished.
32 You proud people will trip and fall.
　　No one will help you up.
I will start a fire in your towns.
　　It will burn up everyone around you."

33 The LORD who rules over all says,

"The people of Israel are being treated
　　badly.
　　So are the people of Judah.
Those who have captured them are
　　holding them.
　　They refuse to let them go.
34 But I am strong and will save them.
　　My name is the LORD Who Rules
　　　Over All.
I will stand up for them.
　　I will bring peace and rest to their
　　　land.
　　But I will bring trouble to those who
　　　live in Babylon.

35 "A sword is coming against the
　　Babylonians!"
　　announces the LORD.

"It is coming against those who live in
　　Babylon.
　　It is coming against their officials
　　　and wise men.
36 A sword is coming against their
　　prophets.
　　But they are not really prophets at
　　　all!
　　So they will look foolish.
A sword is coming against their
　　soldiers!
　　They will be filled with terror.
37 A sword is coming against their horses
　　and chariots!
　　It is coming against all the hired
　　　soldiers in their armies.
　　They will become weak.
A sword is coming against their
　　treasures!
　　They will be stolen.
38 There will not be any rain for their
　　rivers.
　　So they will dry up.
Those things will happen because their
　　land is full of statues of gods.
　　Those gods will go crazy with terror.

39 "Desert creatures and hyenas will live in
　　Babylon.
　　And so will owls.
People will never live there again.
　　It will not be lived in for all time to
　　　come.
40 I destroyed Sodom and Gomorrah.
　　I also destroyed the towns that were
　　　near them,"
　　announces the LORD.
"Babylon will be just like them.
　　No one will live there.
　　No human beings will stay there.

41 "Look! An army is coming from the
　　north.
　　I am stirring up a great nation and
　　　many kings.
　　They are coming from a land that is
　　　very far away.
42 Their soldiers are armed with bows and
　　spears.
　　They are mean.
　　They do not show any mercy at all.
They come riding in on their horses.
　　They sound like the roaring ocean.
They are lined up for battle.
　　They are coming to attack you, city
　　　of Babylon.

⁴³ The king of Babylon has heard reports
about them.
His hands can't help him.
He is in great pain.
It is like the pain of a woman having
a baby.
⁴⁴ I will be like a lion coming up from the
bushes by the Jordan River.
I will hunt in rich grasslands.
I will chase the people of Babylon from
their land in an instant.
What nation will I choose to do this?
Which one will I appoint?
Is anyone like me? Who would dare to
argue with me?
What leader can stand against me?"
⁴⁵ So listen to what the LORD has planned
against Babylon.
Hear what he has planned against
the land of the Babylonians.
Their young people will be dragged
away.
Their grasslands will be shocked at
their fate.
⁴⁶ At the news of Babylon's capture,
the earth will shake.
The people's cries will be heard
among the nations.

51 The LORD says,

"I will stir up the spirits of destroyers.
They will march out against Babylon
and its people.
² I will send other nations against it
to separate the straw from the grain.
I will send them to destroy Babylon
completely.
They will oppose it on every side.
At that time it will be destroyed.
³ Do not let its soldiers get their bows
ready to use.
Do not let them put on their armor.
Do not spare their young men.
Destroy their armies completely.
⁴ They will fall down dead in Babylon.
They will receive deadly wounds in
its streets.
⁵ The land of Israel and Judah is full of
guilt.
Its people have sinned against me.
But I have not deserted them. I am
their God.
I am the LORD who rules over all.
I am the Holy One of Israel.

⁶ "People of Judah, run away from
Babylon!
Run for your lives!
Do not be destroyed because of the
sins of its people.
It is time for me to pay them back.
I will punish them for what they
have done.
⁷ Babylon was like a gold cup in my
hand.
That city made the whole earth
drunk.
The nations drank its wine.
So now they have gone crazy.
⁸ Babylon will suddenly fall and be
broken.
Weep for it!
Get healing lotion for its pain.
Perhaps it can be healed.

⁹ "The nations say, 'We would have
healed Babylon.
But it can't be healed.
So let's leave it. Let's each go to our own
land.
Babylon's sins reach all the way to
the skies.
They rise up as high as the heavens.'

¹⁰ "The people of Judah say,
'The LORD has made things right for
us again.
So come. Let's tell in Zion
what the LORD our God has done.'

¹¹ "I have stirred up you kings of the
Medes.
So sharpen your arrows!
Get your shields!
I plan to destroy Babylon.
I will pay the Babylonians back.
They have destroyed my temple.
¹² Lift up a banner! Attack Babylon's walls!
Put more guards on duty!
Station more of them to watch over
you!
Hide and wait to attack them!
I will do what I have planned.
I will do what I have decided to do
against the people of Babylon.
¹³ You who live by the rivers of Babylon,
your end has come.
You who are rich in treasures,
it is time for you to be destroyed.
¹⁴ I am the LORD who rules over all.
I have made a promise in my own
name.

I have said, 'I will certainly fill your
   land with soldiers.
They will be as many as a huge
   number of locusts.
They will win the battle over you.
   They will shout for joy.'

¹⁵ "I used my power to make the earth.
   I used my wisdom to set the world
     in place.
   I used my understanding to spread
     out the heavens.
¹⁶ When I thunder, the waters in the
   heavens roar.
   I make clouds rise from one end of
     the earth to the other.
I send lightning with the rain.
   I bring out the wind from my
     storerooms.

¹⁷ "No one has any sense.
   No one knows anything.
Everyone who works with gold is put
   to shame
   by his wooden gods.
His metal gods are fakes.
   They can't even breathe.
¹⁸ They are worthless, and people make
   fun of them.
   When I judge them, they will be
     destroyed.
¹⁹ But I, the God of Jacob, am not like
   them.
   I give my people everything they
     need.
   I can do this because I made
     everything, including Israel.
They are the people who belong to me.
   My name is the Lord Who Rules
     Over All.

²⁰ "Babylon, you are my war club.
   You are my weapon for battle.
I use you to destroy nations.
   I use you to wipe out kingdoms.
²¹ I use you to destroy horses and their
   riders.
   I use you to destroy chariots and
     their drivers.
²² I use you to destroy men and women.
   I use you to destroy old people and
     young people.
   I use you to destroy young men and
     young women.
²³ I use you to destroy shepherds and their
   flocks.

I use you to destroy farmers and
   their oxen.
I use you to destroy governors and
   officials.

²⁴ "Judah, I will pay Babylon back. You
will see it with your own eyes. I will pay
back all those who live in Babylon. I will
pay them back for all the wrong things they
have done in Zion," announces the Lord.

²⁵ "Babylon, I am against you.
   Your kingdom is like a destroying
     mountain.
   You have destroyed the whole earth,"
     announces the Lord.
"I will reach out my hand against you.
   I will roll you off the cliffs.
   I will make you like a mountain that
     has been burned up.
²⁶ No rock will be taken from you to be
   used
   as the most important stone for a
     building.
No stones will be taken from you
   to be used for a foundation.
Your land will be empty forever,"
   announces the Lord.

²⁷ "Nations, lift up a banner in the land of
   Babylon!
   Blow a trumpet among yourselves!
Prepare yourselves for battle against
   Babylon.
   Send the kingdoms
   of Ararat, Minni and Ashkenaz
     against it.
Appoint a commander against it.
   Send many horses against it.
   Let them be as many as a huge
     number of locusts.
²⁸ Prepare yourselves for battle against
   Babylon.
   Prepare the kings of the Medes.
Prepare their governors and all their
   officials.
   Prepare all the countries they rule
     over.
²⁹ The Babylonians tremble and shake
   with fear.
   My plans against them stand firm.
I plan to destroy their land completely.
   Then no one will live there.
³⁰ Babylon's soldiers have stopped fighting.
   They remain in their forts.
Their strength is all gone.
   They have become weak.

Their buildings are set on fire.
　　The metal bars that lock their gates
　　　are broken.
³¹ One messenger after another
　　comes to the king of Babylon.
All of them announce that
　　his entire city is captured.
³² The places where people go across the
　　　Euphrates River have been
　　　captured.
　　The swamps have been set on fire.
　　And the soldiers are terrified."

³³The LORD who rules over all is the God
of Israel. He says,

"The city of Babylon is like a threshing
　　　floor
　　when cattle are walking on it.
　　The time to destroy it will soon come."

³⁴ The people of Jerusalem say,
"Nebuchadnezzar, the king of Babylon,
　　　has destroyed us.
　　He has thrown us into a panic.
　　He has emptied us out like a jar.
　　Like a snake he has swallowed us up.
　　He has filled his stomach with our
　　　rich food.
　　Then he has spit us out of his mouth."
³⁵ The people continue, "May the people
　　　of Babylon
　　pay for the harmful things they have
　　　done to us.
May those who live in Babylon
　　pay for spilling the blood of our
　　　people."
　　That's what the people who live in
　　　Zion say.

³⁶So the LORD says,

"I will stand up for you.
　　I will pay the Babylonians back for
　　　what they did to you.
I will dry up their water supply.
　　I will make their springs run dry.
³⁷ Babylon will have all its buildings
　　　knocked down.
　　It will be a home for wild dogs.
No one will live there.
　　People will be shocked at it.
　　They will make fun of it.
³⁸ All its people roar like young lions.
　　They growl like lion cubs.
³⁹ They are stirred up.
　　So I will set a feast in front of them.
　　I will make them drunk.

And they will shout and laugh.
　　But then they will lie down and die.
　　They will never wake up,"
　　announces the LORD.
⁴⁰ "I will lead them down like lambs to be
　　　put to death.
　　They will be like rams and goats that
　　　have been killed.
⁴¹ "Babylon will be captured!
　　The whole earth was very proud of it.
But it will be taken over by others!
　　It will be a deserted place among the
　　　nations.
⁴² Babylon's enemies will sweep over it
　　　like an ocean.
　　Like roaring waves they will cover it.
⁴³ The towns of Babylon will be empty.
　　It will become a dry and desert land.
No one will live there.
　　No one will even travel through it.
⁴⁴ I will punish the god named Bel in
　　　Babylon.
　　I will make Bel spit out what he has
　　　swallowed.
The nations will not come and worship
　　　him anymore.
　　And Babylon's walls will fall down.

⁴⁵ "Come out of there, my people!
　　Run for your lives!
　　Run away from my great anger.
⁴⁶ You will hear about terrible things
　　　that are happening in Babylon.
　　But do not lose hope. Do not be
　　　afraid.
You will hear one thing this year.
　　And you will hear something else
　　　next year.
You will hear about awful things in the
　　　land.
　　You will hear about one ruler
　　　fighting against another.
⁴⁷ I will punish the gods of Babylon.
　　That time will certainly come.
Then the whole land will be full of
　　　shame.
　　Its people will lie down and die
　　　there.
⁴⁸ So heaven and earth and everything in
　　　them will shout for joy.
　　They will be glad because of what
　　　will happen to Babylon.
Armies will attack it from the north.
　　And they will destroy it,"
　　announces the LORD.

⁴⁹ "Babylon's people have killed my people
        Israel.
    They have also killed people all over
        the earth.
    So now Babylon itself must fall.
⁵⁰ You who have not been killed in the
        war against Babylon,
    leave! Do not wait!
    In a land far away remember me.
    And think about Jerusalem."

⁵¹ The people of Judah reply, "No one
        honors us anymore.
    People make fun of us.
    Our faces are covered with shame.
    People from other lands have entered
        the holy places of the LORD's house."

⁵² "But the days are coming," announces
        the LORD.
    "At that time I will punish the gods
        of Babylon.
    And all through its land
        wounded people will groan.
⁵³ What if Babylon reached all the way to
        the heavens?
    What if it made its high walls even
        stronger?
    I would still send destroyers against
        it,"
    announces the LORD.

⁵⁴ "The noise of people screaming comes
        from Babylon.
    A terrible sound comes from its
        land.
    It is the sound of a mighty city being
        destroyed.
⁵⁵ I will destroy Babylon.
    I will put an end to all its noise.
    Waves of enemies will sweep through it
        like great waters.
    The roar of their voices will fill the
        air.
⁵⁶ A destroying army will come against
        Babylon.
    The soldiers in the city will be
        captured.
    Their bows will be broken.
    I am the LORD God who pays people
        back.
    I will pay them back in full.
⁵⁷ I will make Babylon's officials and wise
        men drunk.
    I will do the same thing to its
        governors, officers and
        soldiers.

They will lie down and die. They will
        never wake up,"
    announces the King. His name is the
        LORD Who Rules Over All.

⁵⁸ The LORD who rules over all says,

"Babylon's thick walls will fall down flat.
    Its high gates will be set on fire.
    The nations wear themselves out for no
        reason at all.
    Their hard work will only be burned
        up in the flames."

⁵⁹ Jeremiah the prophet gave a message
to the staff officer Seraiah, the son of Neriah. Neriah was the son of Mahseiah. Jeremiah told Seraiah to take the message with
him to Babylon. Seraiah went there with
Zedekiah, the king of Judah. He left in the
fourth year of Zedekiah's rule. ⁶⁰Jeremiah
had written about all the trouble that would
come on Babylon. He had written it down
on a scroll. It included everything that had
been recorded about Babylon. ⁶¹Jeremiah
said to Seraiah, "When you get to Babylon,
here's what I want you to do. Make sure that
you read all these words out loud. ⁶²Then
say, 'LORD, you have said you will destroy
this place. You have said that no people or
animals will live here. It will be empty forever.' ⁶³Finish reading the scroll. Tie a stone
to it. Throw it into the Euphrates River.
⁶⁴Then say, 'In the same way, Babylon will
sink down. It will never rise again. That is
because I will bring such horrible trouble
on it. And its people will fall along with it.' "

The words of Jeremiah end here.

Nebuchadnezzar Destroys Jerusalem

52 Zedekiah was 21 years old when he
became king. He ruled in Jerusalem
for 11 years. His mother's name was Hamutal. She was the daughter of Jeremiah. She
was from Libnah. ²Zedekiah did what was
evil in the eyes of the LORD. He did just as
Jehoiakim had done. ³The enemies of Jerusalem and Judah attacked them because the
LORD was angry. In the end he threw them
out of his land.

Zedekiah refused to obey the king of
Babylon.

⁴Nebuchadnezzar was the king of Babylon. He marched out against Jerusalem.
All his armies went with him. It was in the

ninth year of the rule of Zedekiah. It was on the tenth day of the tenth month. The armies set up camp outside the city. They set up ladders and built ramps and towers all around it. ⁵It was surrounded until the 11th year of King Zedekiah's rule.

⁶By the ninth day of the fourth month, there wasn't any food left in the city. So the people didn't have anything to eat. ⁷Then the Babylonians broke through the city wall. Judah's whole army ran away. They left the city at night. They went out through the gate between the two walls that were near the king's garden. They escaped even though the Babylonians surrounded the city. Judah's army ran toward the Arabah Valley. ⁸But the armies of Babylon chased King Zedekiah. They caught up with him in the plains near Jericho. All his soldiers were separated from him. They had scattered in every direction. ⁹The king was captured.

He was taken to the king of Babylon at Riblah. Riblah was in the land of Hamath. That's where Nebuchadnezzar decided how Zedekiah would be punished. ¹⁰At Riblah the king of Babylon killed the sons of Zedekiah. He forced him to watch it with his own eyes. Nebuchadnezzar also killed all the officials of Judah. ¹¹Then he poked out Zedekiah's eyes. He put him in bronze chains. And he took him to Babylon. There he put Zedekiah in prison until the day he died.

¹²Nebuzaradan served the king of Babylon. In fact, he was commander of the royal guard. He came to Jerusalem. It was in the 19th year that Nebuchadnezzar was king of Babylon. It was on the tenth day of the fifth month. ¹³Nebuzaradan set the LORD's temple on fire. He also set fire to the royal palace and all the houses in Jerusalem. He burned down every important building. ¹⁴The armies of Babylon broke down all the walls around Jerusalem. That's what the commander told them to do. ¹⁵Some of the poorest people still remained in the city along with the others. But the commander Nebuzaradan took them away as prisoners. He also took the rest of the skilled workers. That included the people who had joined the king of Babylon. ¹⁶But Nebuzaradan left the rest of the poorest people of the land behind. He told them to work in the vineyards and fields.

¹⁷The armies of Babylon destroyed the LORD's temple. They broke the bronze

Jer. 52:12–24 The Ark of the Covenant isn't listed in all the stuff taken or destroyed here. Jewish scholars say maybe King Josiah hid it. Read 2 Chronicles 24:7; 35:3; Jeremiah 3:16; and Daniel 1:2. What's your guess? Is the ark still out there?

pillars into pieces. They broke up the bronze stands that could be moved around. And they broke up the huge bronze bowl. Then they carried away all the bronze to Babylon. ¹⁸They also took away the pots, shovels, wick cutters, sprinkling bowls and dishes. They took away all the bronze objects that were used for any purpose in the temple. ¹⁹The commander of the royal guard took away the bowls and the shallow cups for burning incense. He took away the sprinkling bowls, the pots, the lampstands and the dishes. He took away the bowls used for drink offerings. So he took away everything made out of pure gold or silver.

²⁰The bronze was more than anyone could weigh. It included the bronze from the two pillars. It included the bronze from the huge bowl and the 12 bronze bulls under it. It also included the stands. King Solomon had made all those things for the LORD's temple. ²¹Each pillar was 27 feet high and 18 feet around. The pillars were hollow. The metal in each of them was three inches thick. ²²The bronze top of one pillar was seven and a half feet high. It was decorated with a set of bronze chains and pomegranates all around it. The other pillar was just like it. It also had pomegranates. ²³There were 96 pomegranates on the sides of each of the two tops. The total number of pomegranates above the bronze chains around each top was 100.

²⁴The commander of the guard took many prisoners. They included Seraiah the chief priest and Zephaniah the priest who reported to him. They also included the three men who guarded the temple doors. ²⁵Some people were still left in the city. The commander took as a prisoner the officer in charge of the fighting men. He took the seven men who gave advice to the king. He also took the secretary who was the chief officer in charge of getting the people of the land to serve in the army. There were 60 people of the land still in the city. ²⁶The commander Nebuzaradan took all of them away. He brought them to the king of Babylon at Riblah. ²⁷There the king had them put to death. Riblah was in the land of Hamath.

So the people of Judah were taken as prisoners. They were taken far away from their own land.

²⁸ Here is the number of the people Nebuchadnezzar took to Babylon as prisoners.

In the seventh year of his rule, he took 3,023 Jews.

²⁹ In his 18th year, he took 832 people from Jerusalem.

³⁰ In Nebuchadnezzar's 23rd year, Nebuzaradan, the commander of the royal guard, took 745 Jews to Babylon.

The total number of people taken to Babylon was 4,600.

Jehoiachin Is Set Free

³¹Awel-Marduk set Jehoiachin, the king of Judah, free from prison. It was in the 37th year after Jehoiachin had been taken away to Babylon. It was also the year Awel-Marduk became king of Babylon. It was on the 25th day of the 12th month. ³²Awel-Marduk spoke kindly to Jehoiachin. He gave him a place of honor. Other kings were with Jehoiachin in Babylon. But his place was more important than theirs. ³³So Jehoiachin put away his prison clothes. For the rest of Jehoiachin's life the king of Babylon provided what he needed. ³⁴The king did that for Jehoiachin day by day as long as he lived. He did it until the day Jehoiachin died.

Lamentations

You can put aside any notions that our journey has brought us to the town of Lament and its citizens the Lamentations. Instead, a lament is defined as a declaration of grief or mourning and it's often expressed through poetry or song. Today we might say Lamentations is like singing the blues.

Lamentations is a series of five laments concerning the fall of Jerusalem at the hands of the Babylonians. The author is not identified, but the book has always been associated with Jeremiah, the previously mentioned weeping prophet.

The destruction of Jerusalem wasn't a swift event. In the ancient world, it usually took a lot of time to conquer a walled city—many months or perhaps even years. The attackers would surround the city and cut off the food supply, creating more and more panic as famine grew increasingly severe. And in the case of Jerusalem, the situation was even more intense because the people were realizing, too late, that their circumstances were a result of ignoring God and following idols instead. The once-great nation was now helpless and without excuse.

Yet, in the midst of the depressing and sorrowful laments, is one bright ray of hope. The author realizes that God is still in control and will not ultimately forsake His people. He writes, "The LORD loves us very much. So we haven't been completely destroyed. His loving concern never fails. His great love is new every morning. LORD, how faithful you are!" (3:22–23) Another excellent promise!

WHaT's iT MeaN, EUGeNe?

Sacrament—A ceremony or act that serves as a visible sign or symbol of an experience of God's grace. The two sacraments observed in most Protestant churches are *Baptism*, which is an outward sign of our death, resurrection, and rebirth in Jesus Christ and *Communion* or *The Lord's Supper*, which is symbolic of our ongoing and eternal fellowship with God.

1 The city of Jerusalem is so empty!
    She used to be full of people.
But now she's like a woman whose
        husband has died.
    She used to be great among the
        nations.
    She was like a queen among the
        kingdoms.
    But now she is a slave.

2 Jerusalem weeps bitterly at night.
    Tears run down her cheeks.
    None of her friends comforts her.
All those who were going to help her
    have turned against her.
    They have become her enemies.

3 After Judah's people had suffered
        greatly,
    they were taken away as prisoners.
Now they live among the nations.
    They can't find any place to rest.
All those who were chasing them have
    caught up with them.
    And they can't get away.

Jason's Jargon

LAMENTATIONS 1

Search this chapter
for the word
winepress. One type
of winepress looked like
a swimming pool filled
with grapes. People
stomped on the grapes,
and the juice filtered
down a channel.

4 The roads to Zion are empty.
    No one travels to her appointed feasts.
All the public places near her gates are
        deserted.
    Her priests groan.
Her young women are sad.
    And Zion herself weeps bitterly.

5 Her enemies have become her masters.
    They have an easy life.
The Lord has brought suffering to
        Jerusalem
    because her people have committed
        so many sins.
Her children have been taken away as
    prisoners.

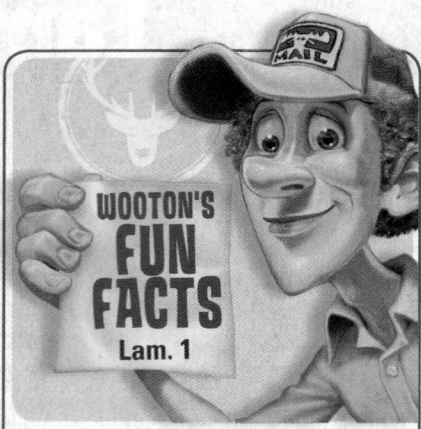

Are you ready for this? This poem is a dirge /
about Jerusalem's purge / due to a Babylonian
scourge / resulting in Jeremiah's tear surge.
Okay, okay, it's not my best work, but there
wasn't room here for a whole comic book!

    Her enemies have forced her people
        to leave their homes.

6 The city of Zion used to be full of glory.
    But now her glory has faded away.
Her princes are like deer.
    They can't find anything to eat.
    They are almost too weak to get away
        from those who hunt them down.

7 Jerusalem's people are suffering and
        wandering.
    They remember all the treasures
    they used to have.
But they fell into the hands of their
        enemies.
    And no one was there to help them.
Their enemies looked at them.
    They laughed because Jerusalem had
        been destroyed.

8 Her people have committed many sins.
    They have become impure.
All those who honored Jerusalem now
        look down on her.
    They all look at her as if she were a
        naked woman.
    The city groans and turns away in
        shame.

9 Her skirts are dirty.
    She didn't think about how things
        might turn out.
Her fall from power amazed everyone.
    And no one was there to comfort her.

She said, "Lord, please pay attention to
how much I'm suffering.
My enemies have won the battle over
me."

10 Jerusalem's enemies took away
all her treasures.
Her people saw outsiders
enter her temple.
The Lord had commanded them
not to do that.

11 All Jerusalem's people groan
as they search for bread.
They trade their treasures for food
just to stay alive.
Jerusalem says, "Lord, look at me.
Think about my condition.
Everyone looks down on me."

12 Jerusalem also says, "All you who are
passing by,
don't you care about what has
happened to me?
Just look at my condition.
Has anyone suffered the way I have?
The Lord has brought all this on me.
He has made me suffer.
His anger has burned against me.

13 "He sent down fire from heaven.
It went deep down into my bones.
He spread a net to catch me by the feet.
He stopped me right where I was.
He made me empty.
I am sick all the time.

14 "My sins have been made into a heavy
yoke.
They were woven together by his
hands.
They have been placed on my neck.
The Lord has taken away my
strength.
He has handed me over to my enemies.
I can't win the battle over them.

15 "The Lord has refused to accept
any of my soldiers.
He has sent for an army
to crush my young men.
I am like grapes in the Lord's winepress.
He has stomped on me,
even though I am his very own.

16 "That's why I am weeping.
Tears are flowing from my eyes.
No one is near to comfort me.
No one can heal my spirit.

My children don't have anything.
My enemies are much too strong
for me."

17 Zion reaches out her hands.
But no one is there to comfort her
people.
The Lord has ordered that
the neighbors of Jacob's people
would become their enemies.
Jerusalem has become impure
among them.

18 Jerusalem says, "The Lord always does
what is right.
But I refused to obey his
commands.
Listen, all you nations.
Pay attention to how much I'm
suffering.
My young men and women
have been taken away as prisoners.

19 "I called out to those who were going to
help me.
But they turned against me.
My priests and elders
died in the city.
They were searching for food
just to stay alive.

20 "Lord, see how upset I am!
I am suffering deep down inside.
My heart is troubled.
Again and again I have refused to
obey you.
Outside the city, people are being killed
by swords.
Inside, there is nothing but death.

21 "People have heard me groan.
But no one is here to comfort me.
My enemies have heard about all my
troubles.
What you have done makes them
happy.
So please judge them, just as you said
you would.
Let them become like me.

22 "Please pay attention to all their sinful
ways.
Punish them as you have punished
me.
You judged me because I had
committed so many sins.
I groan all the time.
And my heart is weak."

2 See how the Lord covered the city of
    Zion
    with the cloud of his anger!
He threw Israel's glory down
    from heaven to earth.
When he was angry, he turned his
    back
    on his own city.

² Without pity the Lord swallowed up
    all the homes of Jacob's people.
When he was angry, he tore down
    the forts of the people of Judah.
He brought down their kingdom and
    princes
    to the ground in dishonor.

³ When he was very angry,
    he took away Israel's power.
He pulled back his powerful right hand
    as the enemy approached.
His burning anger blazed out in Jacob's
    land.
    It burned up everything near it.

⁴ Like an enemy the Lord got his bow
    ready to use.
    He had a sword in his right hand.
Like an enemy he destroyed
    everything that used to be pleasing
    to him.
His anger blazed out like fire.
    It burned up the homes in the city
    of Zion.

⁵ The Lord was like an enemy.
    He swallowed up Israel.
He swallowed up all of its palaces.
    He destroyed its forts.
He filled the people of Judah
    with sorrow and sadness.

⁶ The LORD's temple was like a garden.
    But he completely destroyed it.
He destroyed the place
    where he used to meet with his
    people.
He made Zion's people forget
    their appointed feasts and Sabbath
    days.
When he was very angry, he turned his
    back on
    king and priest alike.

⁷ The Lord deserted his altar.
    He left his temple.
He gave the walls of Jerusalem's palaces
    into the hands of her enemies.

They shouted loudly in the house of the
    LORD.
You would have thought it was the
    day
    of an appointed feast.

⁸ The LORD decided to tear down
    the walls around the city of Zion.
He measured out what he wanted to
    destroy.
    Then he destroyed Jerusalem by his
    power.
He made even her towers and walls sing
    songs of sadness.
    All of them fell down.

⁹ Her gates sank down into the ground.
    He broke the metal bars that locked
    her gates, and he destroyed
    them.
Her king and princes were taken away
    to other nations.
    There is no law anymore.
Jerusalem's prophets no longer receive
    visions from the LORD.

¹⁰ The elders of the city of Zion
    sit silently on the ground.
They have sprinkled dust on their
    heads.
    They've put on the clothes of
    sadness.
The young women of Jerusalem
    have bowed their heads toward the
    ground.

¹¹ I've cried so much I can't see very well.
    I'm suffering deep down inside.
My heart is broken
    because my people are destroyed.
Children and babies are fainting
    in the streets of the city.

¹² They say to their mothers,
    "Where can we find something to
    eat and drink?"
They faint like wounded soldiers
    in the streets of the city.
Their lives are slipping away
    in their mothers' arms.

¹³ City of Jerusalem, what can I say about
    you?
    What can I compare you to?
People of Zion, what are you like?
    I want to comfort you.
Your wound is as deep as the ocean.
    Who can heal you?

¹⁴ The visions of your prophets were lies.
　　They weren't worth anything.
They didn't show you the sins you had
　　committed.
　　So that's why you were captured.
The messages they gave you were lies.
　　They led you astray.

¹⁵ All those who pass by
　　clap their hands and make fun of
　　　you.
They laugh at you and shake their heads
　　at the city of Jerusalem.
They say, "Could that be the city
　　that was called perfect and beautiful?
　　Is that the city that brought joy to
　　　everyone on earth?"

¹⁶ All your enemies open their mouths
　　wide against you.
They laugh at you and grind their teeth.
　　They say, "We have swallowed up
　　　Jerusalem's people.
This is the day we've waited for.
　　And we've lived to see it."

¹⁷ The LORD has done what he planned to
　　do.
　　He has made what he said come
　　　true.
He gave the command long ago.
He has destroyed you without pity.
　　He has let your enemies laugh at you.
　　He has made them stronger than
　　　you are.

¹⁸ People in the city of Zion,
　　cry out from your heart to the Lord.
Let your tears flow like a river
　　day and night.
Don't stop at all.
　　Don't give your eyes any rest.

¹⁹ Get up. Cry out as the night begins.
　　Tell the Lord all your troubles.
Lift up your hands to him.
　　Pray that the lives of your children
　　　will be spared.
At every street corner they faint
　　because they are so hungry.

²⁰ Jerusalem says, "LORD, look at me.
　　Think about my condition.
Have you ever treated anyone else
　　like this?
Should women have to eat their babies?
　　Should they eat the children they've
　　　taken care of?

Should priests and prophets be killed
　　in your own temple?

²¹ "Young people and old people alike
　　lie dead in the dust of my streets.
My young men and women
　　have been killed by swords.
You killed them when you were angry.
　　You put them to death without pity.

²² "You sent for terrors to come against
　　me on every side.
　　It was as if you were inviting people
　　　to enjoy a feast day.
Because you were angry, no one
　　escaped.
　　No one was left alive.
I took good care of my children and
　　brought them up.
　　But my enemies have destroyed
　　　them."

3 I am a man who has suffered greatly.
　　The LORD has used the Babylonians
　　　to punish my people.
² He has driven me away. He has made
　　me walk
　　in darkness instead of light.
³ He has turned his powerful hand
　　against me.
　　He has done it again and again, all
　　　day long.

⁴ He has worn out my body.
　　He has broken my bones.
⁵ He has surrounded me and attacked me.
　　He has made me suffer bitterly.
　　He has made things hard for me.
⁶ He has made me live in darkness
　　like those who are dead and gone.

⁷ He has built walls around me, so I can't
　　escape.
　　He has put heavy chains on me.
⁸ I call out and cry for help.
　　But he won't listen to me when I
　　　pray.
⁹ He has put up a stone wall to block my
　　way.
　　He has made my paths crooked.

¹⁰ He has been like a bear waiting to
　　attack me.
　　He has been like a lion hiding in the
　　　bushes.
¹¹ He has dragged me off the path.
　　He has torn me to pieces.
　　And he has left me helpless.

¹² He has gotten his bow ready to use.
    He has shot his arrows at me.

¹³ The arrows from his bag
    have gone through my heart.
¹⁴ My people laugh at me all the time.
    They sing and make fun of me all
      day long.
¹⁵ The LORD has made my life bitter.
    He has made me suffer bitterly.

¹⁶ He made me chew stones that broke my
      teeth.
    He has walked all over me in the dust.
¹⁷ I have lost all hope of ever having any
      peace.
    I've forgotten what good times are
      like.
¹⁸ So I say, "My glory has faded away.
    My hope in the LORD is gone."

¹⁹ I remember how I suffered and
      wandered.
    I remember how bitter my life was.
²⁰ I remember it very well.
    My spirit is very sad deep down
      inside me.
²¹ But here is something else I remember.
    And it gives me hope.

²² The LORD loves us very much.
    So we haven't been completely
      destroyed.
    His loving concern never fails.
²³ His great love is new every morning.
    LORD, how faithful you are!
²⁴ I say to myself, "The LORD is everything
      I will ever need.
    So I will put my hope in him."

²⁵ The LORD is good to those who put
      their hope in him.
    He is good to those who look to
      him.
²⁶ It is good when people wait quietly
    for the LORD to save them.
²⁷ It is good for a man to carry a heavy
      load of suffering
    while he is young.

²⁸ Let him sit alone and not say anything.
    The LORD has placed that load on
      him.
²⁹ Let him bury his face in the dust.
    There might still be hope for him.
³⁰ Let him turn his cheek toward those
      who would slap him.
    Let him be filled with shame.

CANDID CONVERSATIONS

The person who wrote Lamentations sounds a little like the guy at a party who'd say things like "I don't eat birthday cake because my cat died from eating birthday cake." So depressing! The entire book of Lamentations is about how sad life is, and how it seems like God has abandoned us.

But every now and then, if you read carefully, the writer says something like this: "The LORD is everything I will ever need. So I will put my hope in him" (3:24). Yes, life can be sad sometimes (and cats do die sometimes), but put your hope in God. His concern for us never fails. When something terrible happens, it's hard to believe that, but it's true.

Today put the sad things behind you and thank God that He is there with you when you have times of sorrow.

³¹ The Lord doesn't turn his back
    on people forever.
³² He might bring suffering.
    But he will also show loving
      concern.
    How great his faithful love is!
³³ He doesn't want to bring pain
    or suffering to anyone.

³⁴ Every time people crush prisoners
      under their feet,
    the Lord knows all about it.
³⁵ When people refuse to give someone
      what they should,
    the Most High God knows it.
³⁶ When people don't treat someone fairly,
    the Lord knows it.
³⁷ Suppose people order something to
      happen.
    It won't happen unless the Lord has
      planned it.

38 Troubles and good things alike come to
people
because the Most High God has
commanded them to come.
39 A person who is still alive shouldn't
blame God
when God punishes them for their
sins.

40 Let's take a good look at the way we're
living.
Let's return to the Lord.
41 Let's lift up our hands to God in
heaven.
Let's pray to him with all our hearts.
42 Let's say, "We have sinned.
We've refused to obey you.
And you haven't forgiven us.

43 "You have covered yourself with the
cloud of your anger.
You have chased us.
You have killed us without pity.
44 You have covered yourself with the
cloud of your anger.
Our prayers can't get through to
you.
45 You have made us become like trash
and garbage
among the nations.

46 "All our enemies have opened their
mouths wide
to swallow us up.
47 We are terrified and trapped.
We are broken and destroyed."
48 Streams of tears flow from my eyes.
That's because my people are
destroyed.

49 Tears will never stop flowing from my
eyes.
My eyes can't get any rest.
50 I'll weep until the Lord looks down
from heaven.
I'll cry until he notices my tears.
51 What I see brings pain to my spirit.
All the women of my city are
mourning.
52 Those who were my enemies for no
reason at all
hunted me down as if I were a bird.
53 They tried to end my life
by throwing me into a deep pit.
They threw stones down at me.
54 The water rose and covered my head.
I thought I was going to die.

55 Lord, I called out to you.
I called out from the bottom of the
pit.
56 I prayed, "Please don't close your ears
to my cry for help."
And you heard my appeal.
57 You came near when I called out to you.
You said, "Do not be afraid."

58 Lord, you stood up for me in court.
You saved my life and set me free.
59 Lord, you have seen the wrong things
people have done to me.
Stand up for me again!
60 You have seen how my enemies
have tried to get even with me.
You know all about their plans
against me.

61 Lord, you have heard them laugh at me.
You know all about their plans
against me.
62 You have heard my enemies
whispering among themselves.
They speak against me all day long.
63 Just look at them sitting and standing
there!
They sing and make fun of me.

64 Lord, pay them back.
Punish them for what their hands
have done.
65 Cover their minds with a veil.
Put a curse on them!
66 Lord, get angry with them and hunt
them down.
Wipe them off the face of the earth.

4 Look at how the gold has lost its
brightness!
See how dull the fine gold has
become!
The sacred jewels are scattered
at every street corner.

2 The priceless children of Zion
were worth their weight in gold.
But now they are thought of as clay pots
made by the hands of a potter.

3 Even wild dogs
nurse their young pups.
But my people are as mean
as ostriches in the desert.

4 When the babies get thirsty,
their tongues stick to the roofs of
their mouths.

When the children beg for bread,
no one gives them any.

⁵ Those who once ate fine food
are dying in the streets.
Those who wore royal clothes
are now lying on piles of trash.

⁶ My people have been punished
more than Sodom was.
It was destroyed in a moment.
No one offered it a helping hand.

⁷ Jerusalem's princes were brighter than
snow.
They were whiter than milk.
Their bodies were redder than rubies.
They looked like lapis lazuli.

⁸ But now they are blacker than coal.
No one even recognizes them in the
streets.
Their skin is wrinkled on their bones.
It has become as dry as a stick.

⁹ Those killed by swords are better off
than those who die of hunger.
Those who are hungry waste away to
nothing.
They don't have any food from the
fields.

¹⁰ With their own hands, loving mothers
have had to cook even their own
children.
They ate their children
when my people were destroyed.

¹¹ The LORD has become very angry.
He has poured out his burning anger.
He started a fire in Zion.
It burned its foundations.

¹² The kings of the earth couldn't believe
what was happening.
Neither could any of the peoples of
the world.
Enemies actually attacked and entered
the gates of Jerusalem.

¹³ It happened because Jerusalem's
prophets had sinned.
Her priests had done evil things.
All of them spilled the blood
of those who did what was right.

¹⁴ Now those prophets and priests
have to feel their way along the
streets
as if they were blind.

Lam. 4:7 Have you ever heard of "lapis lazuli" before? It's actually a bright blue rock that's usually used for jewelry and decoration. There was a famous gate in Babylon that was covered in lapis lazuli.

The blood of those they killed has made
them "unclean."
So no one dares to touch their
clothes.

¹⁵ "Go away! You are 'unclean'!"
people cry out to them.
"Go away! Get out of here!
Don't touch us!"
So they run away and wander around.
Then people among the nations say,
"They can't stay here anymore."

¹⁶ The LORD himself has scattered them.
He doesn't watch over them
anymore.
No one shows the priests any respect.
No one honors the elders.

¹⁷ And that's not all. Our eyes grew tired.
We looked for help that never
came.
We watched from our towers.
We kept looking for a nation that
couldn't save us.

¹⁸ People hunted us down no matter
where we went.
We couldn't even walk in our
streets.
Our end was near, so we only had a few
days to live.
Our end had come.

¹⁹ Those who were hunting us down were
faster
than eagles in the sky.

They chased us over the mountains.
>They hid and waited for us in the
>>desert.

20 Zedekiah, the LORD's anointed king,
>was our last hope.
>But he was caught in their traps.
>We thought he would keep us safe.
>>We expected to continue living
>>among the nations.

21 People of Edom, be joyful.
>You who live in the land of Uz, be
>>glad.
>But the cup of the LORD's anger will
>>also be passed to you.
>Then you will become drunk.
>Your clothes will be stripped off.

22 People of Zion, the time for you to be
>>punished
>will come to an end.
>The LORD won't keep you away from
>>your land any longer.
>But he will punish your sin, people of
>>Edom.
>He will show everyone the evil
>>things you have done.

5 LORD, think about what has happened
>>to us.
>Look at the shame our enemies have
>>brought on us.

2 The land you gave us has been turned
>>over to outsiders.
>Our homes have been given to
>>strangers.

3 Our fathers have been killed.
>Our mothers don't have husbands.

4 We have to buy the water we drink.
>We have to pay for the wood we use.

5 Those who chase us are right behind us.
>We're tired and can't get any rest.

6 We put ourselves under the control of
>>Egypt and Assyria
>just to get enough bread.

7 Our people of long ago sinned.
>And they are now dead.
>We are being punished because of
>>their sins.

8 Slaves rule over us.
>No one can set us free
>>from their power.

9 We put our lives in danger just to get
>>some bread to eat.
>Robbers in the desert might kill us
>>with their swords.

10 Our skin is as hot as an oven.
>We are so hungry we're burning up
>>with fever.

11 Our women have been treated badly in
>>Zion.
>Our virgins have been treated badly
>>in the towns of Judah.

12 Our princes have been hung up by their
>>hands.
>No one shows our elders any respect.

13 Our young men are forced to grind
>>grain at the mill.
>Our boys almost fall down
>as they carry heavy loads of wood.

14 Our elders don't go to the city gate
>>anymore.
>Our young men have stopped
>>playing their music.

15 There isn't any joy in our hearts.
>Our dancing has turned into
>>mourning.

16 All of our honor is gone.
>How terrible it is for us because we
>>have sinned!

17 So our hearts are weak.
>Our eyes can't see very clearly.

18 Mount Zion has been deserted.
>Wild dogs are prowling all around
>>on it.

19 LORD, you rule forever.
>Your throne will last for all time to
>>come.

20 Why do you always forget us?
>Why have you deserted us for so
>>long?

21 LORD, please bring us back to you.
>Then we can return.
>Make our lives like new again.

22 Or have you completely turned away
>>from us?
>Are you really that angry with us?

Ezekiel

In our travels, we have met a plethora of interesting people. Here is another! Ezekiel was one of the people of Judah carried away to Babylon. Indeed, he had been in Babylon for five years before God called him to be a prophet (1:1–2). But even after numerous people had been taken to Babylon, it was still many more years before the city of Jerusalem itself was finally overthrown. Therefore, Ezekiel's early prophecies were severe judgments about why the city was being destroyed.

Ezekiel did a lot more than just talk to his people. On several occasions God had Ezekiel perform a variety of specific actions that symbolized what He was doing to Judah (chapters 4–5). For example, Ezekiel wasn't permitted to publicly mourn the death of his wife because God didn't want the people to mourn the destruction of their beloved Temple (24:15–27).

Other times Ezekiel had some fascinating visions and conversations with God. In his first vision, he saw magnificent winged creatures and a heavenly throne of deep blue (chapter 1). Later he was shown a valley filled with decrepit dried-out bones. He watched as God rejoined the skeletons, grew muscles and skin on them again, and breathed life into them (37:1–14). The point was that if God could make those bones live again, He could certainly restore His people who were far away from their homeland for a little while.

WHaT'S iT MeaN, EUGeNe?

Salvation—The apostle Paul wrote, "Say with your mouth, 'Jesus is Lord.' Believe in your heart that God raised him from the dead. Then you will be *saved*" (Romans 10:9). Being *saved* means having a relationship with God right now and living with Him forever in heaven after you die. I shall never forget the day of my salvation. It was the most significant day of my life. I trust the time has come for you to make that life-altering decision as well. If you haven't trusted Jesus as your Savior yet—today can be the day!

The LORD Gives Ezekiel Visions of His Glory

1 I was 30 years old. I was with my people. We had been taken away from our country. We were by the Kebar River in the land of Babylon. On the fifth day of the fourth month, the heavens were opened. I saw visions of God.

²It was the fifth day of the month. Jehoiachin had been king of Judah. It was the fifth year since he had been brought to Babylon as a prisoner. ³A message from the LORD came to me. I was by the Kebar River in Babylon. The power of the LORD came on me there. I am Ezekiel the priest, the son of Buzi.

⁴I looked up and saw a windstorm coming from the north. I saw a huge cloud. The fire of lightning was flashing out of it. Bright light surrounded it. The center of the fire looked like glowing metal. ⁵I saw in the fire something that looked like four living creatures. They appeared to have the shape of a human being. ⁶But each of them had four faces and four wings. ⁷Their legs were straight. Their feet looked like the feet of a calf. They were as bright as polished bronze. ⁸The creatures had human hands under their wings on their four sides. All four of them had faces and wings. ⁹The wings of one touched the wings of another. Each of the creatures went straight ahead. They didn't change their direction as they moved.

Ezek. 1:2 King Jehoiachin and Ezekiel were taken to Babylon in the second round of forced deportations. At the beginning of this book, the city of Jerusalem wasn't destroyed yet.

¹⁰Here's what their faces looked like. Each of the four creatures had the face of a human being. On the right side each had the face of a lion. On the left each had the face of an ox. Each one also had an eagle's face. ¹¹That's what their faces looked like. They each had two wings that spread out and lifted up. Each wing touched the wing of another creature on either side. They each had two other wings that covered their bodies. ¹²All the creatures went straight ahead. Anywhere their spirits would lead them to go, they would go. They didn't change their direction as they went. ¹³The living creatures looked like burning coals of fire or like torches. Fire moved back and forth among the creatures. It was bright. Lightning flashed out of it. ¹⁴The creatures raced back and forth like flashes of lightning.

¹⁵As I looked at the living creatures, I saw wheels on the ground beside them. Each creature had four faces. ¹⁶Here's how the wheels looked and worked. They gleamed like topaz. All four of them looked alike. Each one seemed to be made like a wheel inside another wheel at right angles. ¹⁷The wheels could go in any one of the four directions the creatures faced. The wheels didn't change their direction as the creatures moved. ¹⁸Their rims were high and terrifying. All four rims were full of eyes all the way around them.

¹⁹When the living creatures moved, the wheels beside them moved. When the creatures rose from the ground, the wheels also

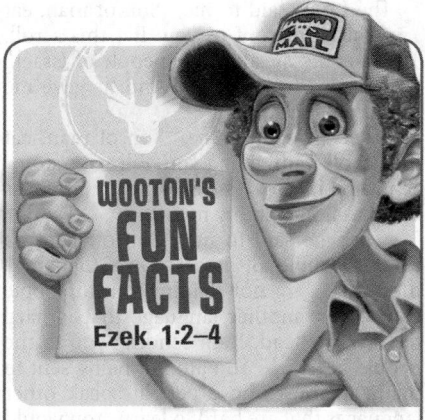

The Kebar River mentioned here is thought by some scholars to have connected the Tigris and Euphrates rivers. It's here that Ezekiel has a vision of a windstorm.

rose. ²⁰Anywhere their spirits would lead them to go, they would go. And the wheels would rise along with them. That's because the spirits of the living creatures were in the wheels. ²¹When the living creatures moved, the wheels also moved. When the creatures stood still, they also stood still. When the creatures rose from the ground, the wheels rose along with them. That's because the spirits of the living creatures were in the wheels.

²²Something that looked like a huge space was spread out above the heads of the living creatures. It gleamed like crystal. It was terrifying. ²³The wings of the creatures were spread out under the space. They reached out toward one another. Each creature had two wings covering its body. ²⁴When the living creatures moved, I heard the sound of their wings. It was like the roar of rushing waters. It sounded like the thundering voice of the Mighty God. It was like the loud noise an army makes. When the creatures stood still, they lowered their wings.

Jason's Jargon

EZEKIEL 1

Dig for *topaz* in this chapter. Topaz is a precious yellow jewel that shines brightly. It is a gem used as a decoration in royal armor, so its presence suggests importance.

²⁵Then a voice came from above the huge space over their heads. They stood with their wings lowered. ²⁶Above the space over their heads was something that looked like a throne made out of lapis lazuli. On the throne high above was a figure that appeared to be a man. ²⁷From his waist up he looked like glowing metal that was full of fire. From his waist down he looked like fire. Bright light surrounded him. ²⁸The glow around him looked like a rainbow in the clouds on a rainy day.

That's what the glory of the Lord looked like. When I saw it, I fell with my face toward the ground. Then I heard the voice of someone speaking.

The Lord Appoints Ezekiel to Speak for Him

2 He said to me, "Son of man, stand up on your feet. I will speak to you." ²As he spoke, the Spirit of the Lord came into me. He raised me to my feet. I heard him speaking to me.

³He said, "Son of man, I am sending you to the people of Israel. That nation has refused to obey me. They have turned against me. They and their people of long ago have been against me to this day. ⁴The people I am sending you to are very stubborn. Tell them, 'Here is what the Lord and King says.' ⁵They might listen, or they might not. After all, they refuse to obey me. But whether they listen or not, they will know that a prophet was among them. ⁶Son of man, do not be afraid of them or of what they say. Do not be afraid, even if thorns and bushes are all around you. Do not be afraid, even if you live among scorpions. Do not be afraid of what they say. Do not be terrified by them. They always refuse to obey me. ⁷You must give them my message. They might listen, or they might not. After all, they refuse to obey me. ⁸Son of man, listen to what I tell you. Do not be like those who refuse to obey me. Open your mouth. Eat what I give you."

⁹Then I looked up. I saw a hand reach out to me. A scroll was in it. ¹⁰He unrolled it in front of me. Both sides had words written on them. They spoke about sadness, sorrow and trouble.

3 The Lord said to me, "Son of man, eat what is in front of you. Eat this scroll. Then go and speak to the people of Israel." ²So I opened my mouth. And he gave me the scroll to eat.

³Then he said to me, "Son of man, eat this scroll I am giving you. Fill your stomach with it." So I ate it. And it tasted as sweet as honey in my mouth.

⁴Then he said to me, "Son of man, go to the people of Israel. Give them my message. ⁵I am not sending you to people who speak another language that is hard to learn. Instead, I am sending you to the people of Israel. ⁶You are not being sent to many nations whose people speak other languages that are hard to learn. You would not be able to understand them. Suppose I had sent you to them. Then they certainly would have listened to you. ⁷But the people of Israel do not want to listen to you. That

ADVENTURES IN ODYSSEY

Ezekiel 3 talks about an encounter with an angel. An angel visited Odyssey and gave direction to Whit and Tom and their friends in "Malachi's Message" (A#32).

is because they do not want to listen to me. All the Israelites are very stubborn. ⁸But I will make you just as stubborn as they are. ⁹I will make you very brave. So do not be afraid of them. Do not let them terrify you, even though they refuse to obey me."

¹⁰He continued, "Son of man, listen carefully. Take to heart everything I tell you. ¹¹Go now to your own people who were brought here as prisoners. Speak to them. Tell them, 'Here is what the Lord and King says.' Speak to them whether they listen or not."

¹²Then the Spirit of the Lord lifted me up. I heard a loud rumbling sound behind

me. The sound was made when the glory of the Lord rose up. It rose up from the place it had been standing. ¹³The sound was made by the wings of the living creatures. They were brushing against one another. The sound was also made by the wheels beside them. It was a loud rumbling sound. ¹⁴Then the Spirit lifted me up and took me away. My spirit was bitter. I was very angry. The power of the Lord was on me. ¹⁵I came to my people who had been brought as prisoners to Tel Aviv. It was near the Kebar River. I went to where they were living. There I sat among them for seven days. I was very sad and scared about everything that had happened.

The Lord Has Appointed Ezekiel to Warn Israel

¹⁶After seven days, a message from the Lord came to me. ¹⁷The Lord said, "Son of man, I have appointed you as a prophet to warn the people of Israel. So listen to my message. Give them a warning from me. ¹⁸Suppose I say to a sinful person, 'You can be sure you will die.' And you do not warn them. You do not try to get them to change their evil ways in order to save their life. Then that sinful person will die because they have sinned. And I will hold you responsible for their death. ¹⁹But suppose you do warn that sinful person. And they do not turn away from their sin or their evil ways. Then they will die because they have sinned. But you will have saved yourself.

WHIT'S WISDOM
Ezekiel 3:1–11

Have you ever eaten anything you thought was disgusting? Don't tell Wooton, but I can't stand black licorice. And don't tell Connie, but I don't think I could ever eat sushi. But at least those things are actually food. How about this: Have you ever eaten something like *paper*?

Normally eating paper is a bad idea. But Ezekiel did. In fact, God told him to swallow an entire scroll! And it wasn't just any scroll. It had the Word of God written on it.

As strange as it may seem to swallow a scroll, it's a good picture of how important the Bible should be to us. We should devour the Word of God as if we're starving and need its food to keep us alive. Because, really, that's how it is! The Word of God gives us energy for life and it allows us to know God better. It's time to eat as much of it as we can!

Are you hungry now? Don't start looking at these pages to satisfy your physical hunger. Grab a sandwich and keep eating your Bible in another way: by *reading* it!

²⁰"Or suppose a godly person turns away from their godliness and does what is evil. And suppose I put something in their way that will trip them up. Then they will die. Since you did not warn them, they will die for their sin. The godly things that person did will not be remembered. And I will hold you responsible for their death. ²¹But suppose you do warn a godly person not to sin. And they do not sin. Then you can be sure that they will live because they listened to your warning. And you will have saved yourself."

²²The power of the LORD was on me. He said, "Get up. Go out to the plain. I will speak to you there." ²³So I got up and went out to the plain. The glory of the LORD was standing there. It was just like the glory I had seen by the Kebar River. So I fell with my face toward the ground.

²⁴Then the Spirit of the LORD came into me. He raised me to my feet. He said to me, "Go, son of man. Shut yourself inside your house. ²⁵Some people will tie you up with ropes. So you will not be able to go out among your people. ²⁶I will make your tongue stick to the roof of your mouth. Then you will be silent. You will not be able to correct them. That's because they always refuse to obey me. ²⁷But later I will speak to you. I will open your mouth. Then you will tell them, 'Here is what the LORD and King says.' Those who listen will listen. And those who refuse to listen will refuse. They always refuse to obey me.

An Attack on Jerusalem Is Pictured

4 "Son of man, get a block of clay. Put it in front of you. Draw the city of Jerusalem on it. ²Then pretend to surround it and attack it. Make some little models of war machines. Build a ramp up to it. Set camps up around it. Surround it with models of logs to be used for knocking down its gates. ³Then get an iron pan. Put it between you and the city. Pretend it is an iron wall. Turn your face toward the city. It will be under attack when you begin to attack it. That will show the people of Israel what is going to happen to Jerusalem.

⁴"Next, lie down on your left side. Pretend that you are putting Israel's sin on yourself. Keep their sin on you for the number of days you lie on your side. ⁵Let each day you lie there stand for one year of

their sin. So you will keep Israel's sin on you for 390 days.

⁶"After you have finished this, lie down again. This time lie on your right side. Pretend that you are putting Judah's sin on yourself. Lie there for 40 days. That is one day for each year of their sin. ⁷Next, turn your face toward the model of Jerusalem under attack. Uncover your arm as if you were a soldier ready to fight. Prophesy against the city. ⁸I will tie you up with ropes. Then you will not be able to turn from one side to the other. You will stay that way until you have finished attacking Jerusalem.

⁹"Get some wheat and barley. Also get some beans and lentils. And get some millet and spelt. Put everything in a storage jar. Use it to make some bread for yourself. Eat it during the 390 days you are lying down on your side. ¹⁰Weigh out eight ounces of food to eat each day. Eat it at your regular mealtimes. ¹¹Also measure out two-thirds of a quart of water. Drink it at your regular mealtimes. ¹²Eat your food as you would eat a loaf of barley bread. Bake it over human waste in front of the people." ¹³The LORD said, "That is how the people of Israel will eat 'unclean' food. They will eat it in the nations where I will drive them."

¹⁴Then I said, "No, LORD and King! I won't do this! I've never eaten anything 'unclean.' From the time I was young until now, I've never eaten anything that was found dead. And I've never eaten anything torn apart by wild animals. 'Unclean' meat has never entered my mouth."

¹⁵"All right," he said. "I will let you bake your bread over waste from cows. You can use that instead of human waste."

¹⁶He continued, "Son of man, I am about to cut off the food supply in Jerusalem. The people will be worried as they eat their tiny share of food. They will not have any hope as they drink their tiny share of water. ¹⁷There will be very little food and water. The people will be shocked as they look at one another. They will become weaker and weaker because of their sin.

God's Judgment Will Be Like a Barber's Razor

5 "Son of man, get a sharp sword. Use it as a barber's razor. Shave your head and beard with it. Then get a set of scales and weigh the hair. Separate it into three piles. ²Burn up a

third of the hair inside the city. Do this when you stop attacking the model of Jerusalem. Next, get another third of the hair. Strike it with a sword all around the city. Then scatter the last third to the winds. That is because I will chase the people with a sword that is ready to strike them down. ³But save a few hairs. Tuck them away in the clothes you are wearing. ⁴Next, get a few more hairs. Throw them into the fire. Burn them up. The fire will spread to all the people of Israel."

⁵The LORD and King says, "What you do with the hair stands for what I will do with Jerusalem's people. I have placed that city in the center of the nations. Countries are all around it. ⁶But its people are sinful. They have refused to obey my laws and rules. They have turned their backs on my laws. They have not followed my rules. These people are worse than the nations and countries around them."

⁷The LORD and King continues, "You people have been worse than the nations around you. You have not lived by my rules or kept my laws. You have not even lived up to the standards of the nations around you."

⁸The LORD and King continues, "Jerusalem, I myself am against you. I will punish you in the sight of the nations. ⁹I will do to you what I have never done before and will never do again. That is because you worship statues of gods. I hate them. ¹⁰So parents will eat their own children inside the city. And children will eat their parents. I will punish you. And I will scatter to the winds anyone who is left alive. ¹¹You have made my temple 'unclean.' You have set up statues of all your evil gods. You have done other things I hate. So I will cut you off just like Ezekiel cut off his hair. I will not spare you or feel sorry for you. And that is just as sure as I am alive," announces the LORD and King. ¹²A third of your people will die of the plague inside your walls. Or they will die of hunger there. Another third will be killed by swords outside your walls. And I will scatter the last third of your people to the winds. I will chase them with a sword that is ready to strike them down.

¹³"Then I will not be angry anymore. My great anger against them will die down. And I will be satisfied. Then they will know that I have spoken with strong feelings. And my great anger toward them will come to an end. I am the LORD.

¹⁴"I will destroy you. I will bring shame on you in the sight of the nations around you. All those who pass by will see it. ¹⁵You will be put to shame. The nations will make fun of you. You will serve as a warning to others. They will be shocked when they see you. So I will punish you because I am very angry with you. You will feel the sting of my warning. I have spoken. I am the LORD. ¹⁶I will shoot at you with my deadly, destroying arrows of hunger. I will shoot to kill. I will bring more and more hunger on you. I will cut off your food supply. ¹⁷I will send hunger and wild animals against you. They will destroy all your children. Plague and murder will sweep over you. And I will send swords to kill you. I have spoken. I am the LORD."

Ezekiel Prophesies Against the Mountains of Israel

6 A message from the LORD came to me. The LORD said, ²"Son of man, turn your attention to the mountains of Israel. Prophesy against them. ³Say, 'Mountains of Israel, listen to the message of the LORD and King. Here is what he says to the mountains and hills. And here is what he says to the canyons and valleys. He tells them, "I will send swords to kill your people. I will destroy the high places where you worship other gods. ⁴Your altars will be torn down. Your incense altars will be smashed. And I will kill your people in front of the statues of your gods. ⁵I will put the dead bodies of Israelites in front of those statues. I will scatter your bones around your altars. ⁶No matter where you live, the towns will be destroyed. The high places will be torn down. So your altars will be completely destroyed. The statues of your gods will be smashed to pieces. Your incense altars will be broken down. And everything you have made will be wiped out. ⁷Your people will fall down dead among you. Then you will know that I am the LORD.

⁸"'"But I will spare some of you. Some will escape from being killed by swords. You will be scattered among other lands and nations. ⁹You will be taken away to those nations as prisoners. Those of you who escape will remember me. You will recall how much pain your unfaithful hearts gave me. You turned away from me. Your eyes longed to see the statues of your gods. You will hate yourselves because of all the evil things you have done. I hate those

things too. [10]You will know that I am the LORD. I said I would bring trouble on you. And my warning came true." '"

[11]The LORD and King said to me, "Clap your hands. Stamp your feet. Cry out, 'How sad!' Do this because the people of Israel have done so many evil things. I hate those things. Israel will be destroyed by war, hunger and plague. [12]The one who is far away will die of the plague. The one who is near will be killed by swords. Anyone who is left alive and is spared will die of hunger. And in this way I will pour out my great anger on them. [13]Then they will know that I am the LORD. Their people will lie dead among the statues of their gods around their altars. Their bodies will lie on every high hill and every mountaintop. They will lie under every green tree and leafy oak tree. They used to offer sweet-smelling incense to all their gods at those places. [14]I will reach out my powerful hand against them. The land will become dry and empty. Those people will live from the desert all the way to Diblah. They will know that I am the LORD."

The End Has Come

7 A message from the LORD came to me. The LORD said, [2]"Son of man, I am the LORD and King. I say to the land of Israel, 'The end has come! It has come on the four corners of the land. [3]The end has now come for you. I will pour out my anger on you. I will judge you based on how you have lived. I will pay you back for all your evil practices. I hate them.

[4]" 'I will not feel sorry for you. I will not spare you. You can be sure that I will pay you back for how you have lived. I will judge you for your evil practices. I hate them. You will know that I am the LORD.'

[5]"I am the LORD and King. I say, 'Horrible trouble is coming! No one has ever heard of anything like it. It is here!

[6]" 'The end has come! The end has come! It has stirred itself up against you. It is here! [7]Death has come on you who live in the land. The time for you to be destroyed has come. The day when it will happen is near. There is no joy on your mountains. There is nothing but panic.'

[8]" 'I am about to pour out all my great anger on you. I will judge you based on how you have lived. I will pay you back for all your evil practices. I hate them.

[9]" 'I will not feel sorry for you. I will not spare you. I will pay you back for how you have lived. I will judge you for your evil practices. I hate them. You will know that I am the one who strikes you down. I am the LORD.

[10]" 'The day for me to punish you is here! It is here! Death has arrived. The time is ripe for you to be judged. Your pride has grown so much that you will be destroyed. [11]Your mean and harmful acts have become like a rod. I will use it to punish those who do evil. None of them will be left. None of their wealth or anything of value will remain.

[12]" 'The time has come! The day has arrived! I will soon pour out my great anger on the whole crowd of you. Do not let the buyer be happy. Do not let the seller be sad. [13]The seller will not get back the land that was sold. That will be true as long as both the buyer and seller are alive.

" 'Ezekiel, the vision I gave you about that whole crowd will come true. They have committed many sins. So not one of them will be able to save their life. [14]They have blown trumpets. They have made everything ready. But no one will go into battle. I will soon pour out my great anger on the whole crowd.

[15]" 'There is trouble everywhere. War is outside the city. Plague and hunger are inside it. Those out in the country will die in battle. Those in the city will be destroyed by hunger and plague. [16]All those who escape and are left alive will run to the mountains. They will sound like doves of the valley when they cry over their sins.

[17]" 'Their hands will be powerless to help them. They will wet themselves. [18]They will put on the rough clothing people wear when they're sad. They will put on terror as if it were their clothes. Every face will be covered with shame. Every head will be shaved.

[19]" 'They will throw their silver into the streets. They will treat their gold like an "unclean" thing. Their silver and gold won't be able to save them on the day I pour out my anger. It will not be able to satisfy their hunger. Their stomachs can't be filled with it. Their silver and gold have tripped them up. It has made them fall into sin. [20]My people were so proud of their beautiful jewelry. They used it to make statues of their evil gods. I hate those gods. So I will turn their jewelry into an "unclean" thing for them.

²¹ "'I will hand over their wealth to outsiders. I will turn it over to sinful people in other countries. They will make it "unclean."
²²I will turn my face away from my people. Robbers will make "unclean" the temple I love. They will enter it and make it "unclean."
²³ "'Ezekiel, get ready to put my people in chains. The land is full of murderers. They are harming one another all over Jerusalem. ²⁴I will bring the most evil nations against them. They will take over the houses in the city. I will put an end to the pride of those who are mighty. Their holy places will be made "unclean."
²⁵ "'When terror comes, they will look for peace. But there will not be any. ²⁶Trouble after trouble will come. One report will follow another. But they will not be true. The people will go searching for a vision from the prophets. But there will not be any. The teaching of the law by the priests will be gone. Advice from the elders will come to an end.
²⁷ "'The king will be filled with sadness. The princes will lose all hope. The hands of the people of the land will tremble. I will punish them based on how they have lived. I will judge them by their own standards. Then they will know that I am the LORD.'"

The People Worship Other Gods in the Temple

8 It was the sixth year since King Jehoiachin had been brought to Babylon as a prisoner. On the fifth day of the sixth month, I was sitting in my house. The elders of Judah were sitting there with me. The power of the LORD and King came on me there. ²I looked up and saw a figure that appeared to be human. From his waist down he looked like fire. From his waist up he looked as bright as glowing metal. ³He reached out what appeared to be a hand. He took hold of me by the hair of my head. The Spirit of the LORD lifted me up between earth and heaven. In visions God gave me, the Spirit took me to Jerusalem. He brought me to the entrance of the north gate of the inner courtyard. The statue of a god was standing there. It made God very angry. ⁴There in front of me was the glory of the God of Israel. It looked just as it did in the vision I had seen on the plain.
⁵Then the LORD said to me, "Son of man, look toward the north." So I did. I saw a statue that made God angry. It was in the entrance of the gate north of the altar.
⁶He said to me, "Son of man, do you see what the Israelites are doing here? They are doing things I hate very much. Those things will cause me to go far away from my temple. But you will see things I hate even more."
⁷Then he brought me to the entrance to the courtyard. I looked up and saw a hole in the wall. ⁸He said to me, "Son of man, dig into the wall." So I did. And I saw a door there.
⁹He continued, "Go through it. Look at the evil things they are doing here. I hate those things." ¹⁰So I went in and looked. All over the walls were pictures of all kinds of crawling things and "unclean" animals. The LORD hates it when people worship those things. There were also carvings of the gods of the people of Israel. ¹¹In front of them stood 70 elders of Israel. Jaazaniah was standing there among them. He is the son of Shaphan. Each elder was holding a shallow cup. A sweet-smelling cloud of incense was rising from the cups.
¹²The LORD spoke to me. He said, "Son of man, do you see what the elders of Israel are doing in the dark? Each of them is in his own room worshiping his own god. They say, 'The LORD doesn't see us. He has deserted the land.'" ¹³He continued, "You will see them doing things I hate even more."
¹⁴Then he brought me to the entrance of the north gate of the LORD's house. I saw women sitting there. They were mourning for the god named Tammuz. ¹⁵The LORD said to me, "Son of man, do you see what they are doing? You will see things I hate even more."
¹⁶Then he brought me into the inner courtyard of the LORD's house. About 25 men were there. They were at the entrance to the LORD's temple between the porch and the altar. Their backs were turned toward the temple. Their faces were turned toward the east. And they were bowing down to the sun.
¹⁷He said to me, "Son of man, have you seen all of this? The people of Judah are doing things here that I hate. This is a very serious matter. They are harming one another all through the land. They continue to make me very angry. Just look at them making fun of me! ¹⁸So I am angry with them. I will punish them. I will not spare

them or feel sorry for them. They might even shout in my ears. But I will not listen to them."

The Lord Judges Those Who Worship Other Gods

9 Then I heard the Lord call out in a loud voice. He said, "Bring here those who are appointed to bring my judgment on the city. Make sure each of them has a weapon in his hand." ²I saw six men coming from the direction of the upper gate. It faces north. Each of them had a deadly weapon in his hand. A man wearing linen clothes came along with them. He was carrying a writing kit at his side. They came in and stood beside the bronze altar.

³The glory of the God of Israel had been above the cherubim. It moved from there to the doorway of the temple. Then the Lord called to the man who was dressed in linen clothes. He had the writing kit. ⁴The Lord said to him, "Go all through Jerusalem. Look for those who are sad and sorry about all the things being done there. I hate those things. Put a mark on the foreheads of those people."

⁵I heard him speak to the six men. He said, "Follow him through the city. Do not show any pity or concern. ⁶Kill the old men and women, the young men and women, and the children. But do not touch anyone who has the mark. Start at my temple." So they began with the old men who were in front of the temple.

⁷Then he said to the men, "Make the temple 'unclean.' Fill the courtyards with dead bodies. Go!" So they went out and started killing people all through the city. ⁸While they were doing it, I was left alone. I fell with my face toward the ground. I cried out, "Lord and King, are you going to destroy all the Israelites who are still left alive? Will you pour out your great anger on all those who remain in Jerusalem?"

⁹He answered me, "The sin of Israel and Judah is very great. The land is full of murderers. Its people are not being fair to one another anywhere in Jerusalem. They say, 'The Lord has deserted the land. He doesn't see us.' ¹⁰So I will not spare them or feel sorry for them. Anything that happens to them will be their own fault."

¹¹Then the man wearing linen clothes returned. He had the writing kit. He reported, "I've done what you commanded."

The Glory of the Lord Moves Out of the Temple

10 I looked up and saw something that appeared to be a throne made out of lapis lazuli. It was above the huge space that was spread out over the heads of the cherubim. ²The Lord spoke to the man who was wearing linen clothes. He said, "Go in among the wheels beneath the cherubim. Fill your hands with burning coals from the fire that is among the cherubim. Scatter the coals over the city." As I watched, he went in.

³The cherubim were standing on the south side of the temple when the man went in. A cloud filled the inner courtyard. ⁴Then the glory of the Lord rose from above the cherubim. It moved to the doorway of the temple. The cloud filled the temple. And the courtyard was full of the brightness of the glory of the Lord. ⁵The sound the wings of the cherubim made could be heard as far away as the outer courtyard. It was like the voice of the Mighty God when he speaks.

⁶The Lord gave a command to the man who was dressed in linen clothes. He said, "Get some coals of fire from among the wheels. Take them from among the cherubim." So the man went in and stood beside a wheel. ⁷Then one of the cherubim reached out his hand. He picked up some of the burning coals that were among the wheels. He handed them to the man who was wearing linen clothes. The man took them and left. ⁸I saw what looked like human hands. They were under the wings of the cherubim.

⁹I looked up and saw four wheels beside the cherubim. One wheel was beside each of them. The wheels gleamed like topaz. ¹⁰All four of them looked alike. Each wheel appeared to be inside another wheel at right angles. ¹¹The wheels could go in any one of the four directions the cherubim faced. The wheels didn't change their direction as the cherubim moved. The cherubim went in the direction their heads faced. They didn't change their direction as they moved. ¹²Their whole bodies were completely covered with eyes. That included their backs, hands and wings. Their four wheels were covered with eyes too. ¹³I heard someone tell the wheels to start spinning around. ¹⁴Each of the cherubim had four faces. One face was the face of a cherub. The second was the face of a human being. The third

WOOTON'S FUN FACTS
Ezek. 10:20

Cherubim are not cherubs. They are very different. Cherubs look like chubby toddlers with wings. Cherubim are mighty angels with four wings and four faces. Cherubs make you think, "May I pinch your cute cheek?" Cherubim make you think, "Please don't hurt me!"

was the face of a lion. And the fourth was an eagle's face.

¹⁵The cherubim rose from the ground. They were the same living creatures I had seen by the Kebar River. ¹⁶When the cherubim moved, the wheels beside them moved. The cherubim spread their wings to rise from the ground. As they did, the wheels didn't leave their side. ¹⁷When the cherubim stood still, the wheels also stood still. When the cherubim rose, the wheels rose along with them. That's because the spirits of the living creatures were in the wheels.

¹⁸Then the glory of the LORD moved away from the doorway of the temple. It stopped above the cherubim. ¹⁹While I watched, they spread their wings. They rose from the ground. As they went, the wheels went along with them. They stopped at the entrance of the east gate of the LORD's house. And the glory of the God of Israel was above them.

²⁰These were the same living creatures I had seen by the Kebar River. I had seen them beneath the God of Israel. I realized that they were cherubim. ²¹Each one had four faces and four wings. Under their wings was what looked like human hands. ²²Their faces looked the same as the ones I had seen by the Kebar River. Each of the cherubim went straight ahead.

The Lord's Judgment of Jerusalem Is Certain

11 Then the Spirit of the LORD lifted me up. He brought me to the east gate of the LORD's house. There were 25 men at the entrance of the gate. I saw Jaazaniah and Pelatiah among them. They were leaders of the people. Jaazaniah is the son of Azzur. Pelatiah is the son of Benaiah. ²The LORD said to me, "Son of man, these men are making evil plans. They are giving bad advice to the city. ³They say, 'Haven't our houses just been built again? The city is like a pot used for cooking. And we are the meat in it.' ⁴So prophesy against them. Prophesy, son of man."

⁵Then the Spirit of the LORD came on me. He told me to tell them, "The LORD says, 'You leaders in Israel, that is what you are saying. But I know what you are thinking. ⁶You have killed many people in this city. In fact, you have filled its streets with dead bodies.'

⁷"So the LORD and King says, 'The bodies you have thrown there are the meat. And the city is the cooking pot. But I will drive you out of it. ⁸You are afraid of the swords of war. But I will bring them against you,' announces the LORD and King. ⁹'I will drive you out of the city. I will hand you over to outsiders. And I will punish you. ¹⁰You will be killed by swords. I will judge you at the borders of Israel. Then you will know that I am the LORD. ¹¹This city will not be a pot for you. And you will not be the meat in it. I will judge you at the borders of Israel. ¹²Then you will know that I am the LORD. You have not obeyed my rules. You have not kept my laws. Instead, you have lived by the standards of the nations around you.'"

¹³Pelatiah, the son of Benaiah, died as I was prophesying. Then I fell with my face toward the ground. I cried out in a loud voice. I said, "LORD and King, will you destroy all the Israelites who are still left alive?"

The Lord Will Bring His People Back Home

¹⁴A message from the LORD came to me. The LORD said, ¹⁵"Son of man, the people of Jerusalem have spoken about you. They have spoken about the others the Babylonians have taken away. They have also spoken about all the other people of Israel.

The people of Jerusalem have said, 'Those people are far away from the LORD. This land was given to us. And it belongs to us.'

¹⁶"So tell them, 'The LORD and King says, "I sent some of my people far away among the nations. I scattered them among the countries. But for a little while I have been their temple in the countries where they have gone."'

¹⁷"Tell them, 'The LORD and King says, "I will gather you from the nations. I will bring you back from the countries where you have been scattered. I will give you back the land of Israel."'

¹⁸"They will return to it. They will remove all its statues of evil gods. I hate those gods. ¹⁹I will give my people hearts that are completely committed to me. I will give them a new spirit that is faithful to me. I will remove their stubborn hearts from them. And I will give them hearts that obey me. ²⁰Then they will follow my rules. They will be careful to keep my laws. They will be my people. And I will be their God. ²¹But some people have hearts that are committed to worshiping the statues of their evil gods. I hate those gods. Anything that happens to those people will be their own fault," announces the LORD and King.

²²Then the cherubim spread their wings. The wheels were beside them. The glory of the God of Israel was above them. ²³The glory of the LORD went up from the city. It stopped above the Mount of Olives east of the city. ²⁴The Spirit of God lifted me up. He took me to those who had been brought to Babylon as prisoners. These are the things that happened in the visions the Spirit gave me.

Then the visions I had seen were gone. ²⁵I told my people everything the LORD had shown me.

Ezekiel Gives a Picture of What Will Happen

12 A message from the LORD came to me. The LORD said, ²"Son of man, you are living among people who refuse to obey me. They have eyes that can see. But they do not really see. They have ears that can hear. But they do not really hear. They refuse to obey me.

³"Son of man, pack your belongings as if you were going on a long trip. Leave in the daytime. Let the people see you. Start out from where you are. Go to another place. Perhaps they will understand the meaning of what you are doing. But they will still refuse to obey me. ⁴Bring out your belongings packed for a long trip. Do this during the daytime. Let the people see you. Then in the evening, pretend you are being forced to leave home. Let the people see you. ⁵While the people are watching, dig through the mud bricks of your house. Then take your belongings out through the hole in the wall. ⁶Put them on your shoulder. Carry them out at sunset. Let the people see you. Cover your face so you can't see the land. All of that will show the Israelites what is going to happen to them."

⁷So I did just as he commanded me. During the day I brought out my things as if I were going on a long trip. In the evening I dug through the wall of my house with my hands. At sunset I took my belongings out. I put them on my shoulders. The people watched what I was doing.

⁸In the morning a message from the LORD came to me. The LORD said, ⁹"Son of man, didn't the Israelites ask you, 'What are you doing?' They always refuse to obey me. ¹⁰"Tell them, 'The LORD and King says, "This prophecy is about Zedekiah, the prince in Jerusalem. It is also about all the Israelites who still live there."' ¹¹Tell them, 'The things I've done are a picture of what's going to happen to you.

" 'So what I've done will happen to you. You will be forced to leave home. You will be taken to Babylon as prisoners.'

¹²"The prince among them will put his things on his shoulder and leave. He will do this at sunset. Someone will dig a hole in the city wall for him to go through. He will cover his face so he can't see the land. ¹³I will spread out my net to catch him. He will be caught in my trap. I will bring him to Babylon. It is the land where the Chaldeans live. But he will not see it. He will die there. ¹⁴I will scatter to the winds all those around him. I will scatter his officials and all his troops. And I will chase them with a sword that is ready to strike them down.

¹⁵"They will know that I am the LORD when I scatter them among the nations. I will send them to other countries. ¹⁶But I will spare a few of them. I will save them from war, hunger and plague. In those countries they will admit they have done

all kinds of evil things. I hate those things. They will know that I am the LORD."

¹⁷A message from the LORD came to me. The LORD said, ¹⁸"Son of man, tremble with fear as you eat your food. Tremble as you drink your water. ¹⁹Speak to the people of the land. Say to them, 'Here is what the LORD and King says. He says this about those who live in Jerusalem and Israel. "They will be worried as they eat their food. They will not have any hope as they drink their water. Their land will be stripped of everything in it because all those who live there are harming one another. ²⁰The towns where people live will be completely destroyed. The land will become a dry and empty desert. Then you will know that I am the LORD." ' "

The LORD's Judgment Will Come Soon

²¹A message from the LORD came to me. The LORD said, ²²"Son of man, you have a proverb in the land of Israel. It says, 'The days go by, and not even one vision comes true.' ²³Tell them, 'The LORD and King says, "I am going to put an end to this proverb. They will not use that saying in Israel anymore." ' Tell them, 'The days are coming soon when every vision will come true. ²⁴There will be no more false visions. People will no longer use magic to find out whether good things are going to happen in Israel. ²⁵I am the LORD. So I will say what I want to. And it will come true when I want it to. In your days I will do everything I say I will. But you people always refuse to obey me,' announces the LORD and King."

²⁶A message from the LORD came to me. The LORD said, ²⁷"Son of man, the Israelites are saying, 'The vision Ezekiel sees won't come true for many years. He is prophesying about a time that is a long way off.'

²⁸"So tell them, 'The LORD and King says, "Everything I say will come true. It will happen when I want it to," announces the LORD and King.' "

The LORD Punishes Those Who Pretend to Be True Prophets

13 A message from the LORD came to me. The LORD said, ²"Son of man, prophesy against those who are now prophesying in Israel. What they prophesy comes out of their own minds. Tell them, 'Listen to the LORD's message! ³The LORD

and King says, "How terrible it will be for you foolish prophets! You say what your own minds tell you to. Your visions do not come from me. ⁴Israel, your prophets are like wild dogs that live among broken-down buildings. ⁵You have not repaired the cracks in the city wall for the people of Israel. So it will not stand firm in the battle on the day I judge you. ⁶The visions of those prophets are false. They use magic to try to find out what is going to happen. But their magic tricks are lies. They say, 'The LORD announces.' But I have not sent them. In spite of that, they expect him to make their words come true. ⁷You prophets have seen false visions. You have used magic to try to find out what is going to happen. But your magic tricks are lies. So you lied when you said, 'The LORD announces.' I did not even speak to you at all."

⁸" 'The LORD and King says, "I am against you prophets. Your messages are false. Your visions do not come true," announces the LORD and King. ⁹"Israel, my power will be against the prophets who see false visions. Their magic tricks are lies. They will not be among the leaders of my people. They will not be listed in the records of Israel. In fact, they will not even enter the land. Then you will know that I am the LORD and King.

¹⁰" ' "They lead my people away from me. They say, 'Peace.' But there isn't any peace. They are like people who build a weak wall. They try to cover up the weakness by painting the wall white. ¹¹Tell those who do this that their wall is going to fall. Heavy rains will come. I will send hailstones crashing down. Powerful winds will blow. ¹²The wall will fall down. Then people will ask them, 'Now where is the paint you covered it with?' "

¹³" 'So the LORD and King speaks. He says, "When I am very angry, I will send a powerful wind. Hailstones and heavy rains will come. They will fall with great force. ¹⁴I will tear down the wall you prophets painted over. I will knock it down. The only thing left will be its foundation. When it falls, you will be destroyed along with it. Then you will know that I am the LORD. ¹⁵So I will pour out all my great anger on the wall. I will also send it against you prophets who painted it. I will say to you, 'The wall is gone. You who painted it will be gone too. ¹⁶You prophets of Israel

prophesied to Jerusalem. You saw visions of peace for its people. But there wasn't any peace,' announces the LORD and King." '

¹⁷"Son of man, turn your attention to the daughters of your people. What they prophesy comes out of their own minds. So prophesy against them. ¹⁸Tell them, 'Here is what the LORD and King says. "How terrible it will be for you women who sew magic charms to put around your wrists! You make veils of different lengths to put on your heads. You do these things to trap people. You trap my people. But you will also be trapped. ¹⁹You have treated me as if I were not holy. You did it among my very own people. You did it for a few handfuls of barley and scraps of bread. You told lies to my people. They like to listen to lies. You killed those who should have lived. And you spared those who should have died."

²⁰"So the LORD and King says, "I am against your magic charms. You use them to trap people as if they were birds. I will tear them off your arms. I will set free the people you trap like birds. ²¹I will tear your veils off your heads. I will save my people from your power. They will no longer be under your control. Then you will know that I am the LORD. ²²I had not made godly people sad. But when you told them lies, you made them lose all hope. You advised sinful people not to turn from their evil ways. You did not want them to save their lives. ²³So you will never see false visions again. You will not use your magic tricks anymore. I will save my people from your power. Then you will know that I am the LORD." ' "

The LORD Judges Those Who Worship Other Gods

14 Some of the elders of Israel came to see me. They sat down with me. ²Then a message from the LORD came to me. The LORD said, ³"Son of man, these men have thought about nothing but other gods. They have fallen into the evil trap of worshiping them. Should I let these men ask me for any advice? ⁴Speak to them. Tell them, 'The LORD and King says, "Suppose any of the Israelites think about other gods. And they fall into the evil trap of worshiping them. Then they go to a prophet to ask for advice. If they do, I myself will tell the prophet to answer them in keeping with their worship of many gods. ⁵I will win back the hearts of

the people of Israel. All of them have deserted me for their other gods." '

⁶"So speak to the people of Israel. Tell them, 'The LORD and King says, "Turn away from your sins! Also turn away from your gods. Give up all the evil things you have done. I hate them.

⁷" ' "Suppose any of the Israelites or any outsiders who live in Israel separate themselves from me. And they think about other gods. They fall into the evil trap of worshiping them. Then they go to a prophet to ask me for advice. If they do, I myself will tell the prophet to answer them. ⁸I will turn against them. I will make an example out of them. People will talk about the bad things that happen to them. I will remove them from you. Then you will know that I am the LORD.

⁹" ' "Suppose that prophet is stirred up to give a prophecy. Then I am the one who has stirred him up. And I will reach out my powerful hand against him. I will destroy him from among my people Israel. ¹⁰The prophet will be as much to blame as the one who asks him for advice. Both of them will be guilty. ¹¹Then the people of Israel will no longer wander away from me. And they will not make themselves 'unclean' anymore with their many sins. They will be my people. And I will be their God," ' announces the LORD and King."

Jerusalem Can't Escape the LORD's Judgment

¹²A message from the LORD came to me. The LORD said, ¹³"Son of man, suppose the people in a certain country sin against me. And they are not faithful to me. So I reach out my powerful hand against them. I cut off their food supply. I make them very hungry. I kill them and their animals. ¹⁴And suppose Noah, Daniel and Job were in that country. Then these three men could save only themselves by doing what is right," announces the LORD and King.

¹⁵"Or suppose I send wild animals through that country. And they kill all its children. It becomes a dry and empty desert. No one can pass through it because of the animals. ¹⁶And suppose these three men were in that country. Then they could not save their own sons or daughters. They alone would be saved. But the land would become a dry and empty desert. And that

is just as sure as I am alive," announces the LORD and King.

[17]"Or suppose I send swords to kill the people in that country. And I say, 'Let swords sweep all through the land.' And I kill its people and their animals. [18]And suppose these three men were in that country. Then they could not save their own sons or daughters. They alone would be saved. And that is just as sure as I am alive," announces the LORD and King.

[19]"Or suppose I send a plague into that land. And I pour out my great anger on it by spilling blood. I kill its people and their animals. [20]And suppose Noah, Daniel and Job were in that land. Then they could not save their own sons or daughters. They could save only themselves by doing what is right. And that is just as sure as I am alive," announces the LORD and King.

[21]The LORD and King says, "It will get much worse. I will punish Jerusalem in four horrible ways. There will be war, hunger, wild animals and plague. They will destroy the people and their animals. [22]But some people will be left alive. Some children will be brought out of the city. They will come to you. You will see how they act and the way they live. And you will be comforted in spite of all the trouble I brought on Jerusalem. [23]You will be comforted when you see how they act and the way they live. Then you will know that I did not do anything there without a reason," announces the LORD and King.

Jerusalem Is Like a Useless Vine

15 A message from the LORD came to me. Here is what the LORD said. [2]"Son of man, how is the wood of a vine different from the wood of any tree in the forest? [3]Can its wood ever be made into anything useful? Can pegs be made from it to hang things on? [4]Suppose it is thrown in the fire to be burned. And the fire burns both ends and blackens the middle. Then is the wood useful for anything? [5]It was not useful when it was whole. So how can it be made into something useful now? The fire has burned it and blackened it."

[6]Here is what the LORD and King says. "Instead of the wood of any tree in the forest, I have given the vine to burn in the fire. I will treat the people who live in Jerusalem the same way. [7]I will turn against

them. They might have come out of the fire. But the fire will destroy them anyway. I will turn against them. Then you will know that I am the LORD. [8]I will make the land a dry and empty desert. My people have not been faithful to me," announces the LORD and King.

Jerusalem Is Like an Unfaithful Wife

16 A message from the LORD came to me. The LORD said, [2]"Son of man, tell the people of Jerusalem the evil things they have done. I hate those things. [3]Tell them, 'The LORD and King speaks to Jerusalem. He says, "Your history in the land of Canaan goes back a long way. Your father was an Amorite. Your mother was a Hittite. [4]On the day you were born your cord was not cut. You were not washed with water to clean you up. You were not rubbed with salt. And you were not wrapped in large strips of cloth. [5]No one took pity on you. No one was concerned enough to do any of these things for you. Instead, you were thrown out into an open field. You were hated on the day you were born.

[6]"'"I was passing by. I saw you kicking around in your blood. As you were lying there, I said to you, 'Live!' [7]I made you grow like a plant in a field. Soon you had grown up. You became a young adult. Your breasts had formed. Your hair had grown. But you were completely naked.

[8]"'"Later, I was passing by again. I looked at you. I saw that you were old enough for love. So I married you and took good care of you. I covered your naked body. I made a firm promise to you. I entered into a covenant with you. And you became mine," announces the LORD and King.

[9]"'"I bathed you with water. I washed the blood off you. And I put lotions on you. [10]I put a beautiful dress on you. I gave you sandals made out of fine leather. I dressed you in fine linen. I covered you with expensive clothes. [11]I decorated you with jewelry. I put bracelets on your arms. I gave you a necklace for your neck. [12]I put rings on your nose and ears. And I gave you a beautiful crown for your head. [13]So you were decorated with gold and silver. Your clothes were made out of fine linen. They were made out of expensive and beautiful cloth. Your food was made out of honey, olive oil and the finest flour. You became

very beautiful. You became a queen. ¹⁴You were so beautiful that your fame spread among the nations. The glory I had given you made your beauty perfect," announces the LORD and King.

¹⁵" "But you trusted in your beauty. You used your fame to become a prostitute. You offered your body freely to anyone who passed by. In fact, you gave yourself to anyone who wanted you. ¹⁶You used some of your clothes to make high places colorful. That is where people worshiped other gods. You were a prostitute there. You went to your lover and he took your beauty. ¹⁷I had given you fine jewelry. It was made out of gold and silver. You used it to make for yourself statues of male gods. You worshiped those gods. You were not faithful to me. ¹⁸You put your beautiful clothes on them. You offered my oil and incense to them. ¹⁹You also offered them food. It was made out of olive oil, honey and the finest flour. I had given it to you to eat. You offered it as sweet-smelling incense to them. That is what you did," announces the LORD and King.

²⁰" "Then you took your sons and daughters who belonged to me. And you sacrificed them as food to other gods. Wasn't it enough for you to be a prostitute? ²¹You killed my children. You sacrificed them to other gods. ²²You did not remember the days when you were young. At that time you were completely naked. You were kicking around in your blood. But now you have done evil things. I hate them. You have worshiped other gods. You have not been faithful to me.

²³" "How terrible it will be for you!" announces the LORD and King. "How terrible for you! You continued to sin against me. ²⁴Your people built up mounds for themselves in every market. They put little places of worship on them. ²⁵They set them up at every street corner. Jerusalem, you misused your beauty. You offered your body to anyone who passed by. You did it again and again. ²⁶You committed shameful acts with the people of Egypt. They were your neighbors who were ready to have sex with you. You offered yourself to them again and again. That made me very angry. ²⁷So I reached out my powerful hand against you. I made your territory smaller. I handed you over to your Philistine enemies. The

people in their towns were shocked by your impure conduct. ²⁸You also committed shameful acts with the people of Assyria. Nothing ever seemed to satisfy you. You could never get enough. ²⁹Then you offered yourself to the people of Babylon. But that did not satisfy you either. There are many traders in the land of Babylon.

Jason's Jargon

EZEKIEL 16

Ready? Find the word *cord* in this chapter. An umbilical cord connects a baby to its mother when he or she is inside the womb. The cord is cut after birth.

³⁰" "I am filled with great anger against you," announces the LORD and King. "Just look at all the things you are doing! You are acting like a prostitute who has no shame at all. ³¹Your people built up mounds at every street corner. You put little places of worship on them in every market. But you did not really act like a prostitute. That's because you refused to let your lovers pay you anything.

³²" "You unfaithful wife! You would rather be with strangers than with your own husband! ³³Every prostitute receives gifts. Instead, you give gifts to all your lovers. You offer them money to come to you from everywhere. You want them to sleep with you. You are not faithful to me. ³⁴As a prostitute, you are the opposite of others. No one runs after you to sleep with you. You are exactly the opposite. You pay them. They do not pay you." "

³⁵You prostitute, listen to the LORD's message. ³⁶The LORD and King says, "You poured out your desire on your lovers. You took off your clothing and slept with them. You did it again and again. You worshiped other gods. I hate them. You even sacrificed your children to them. ³⁷So I am going to gather together all the lovers you found pleasure with. They include those you loved and those you hated. I will gather them against you from everywhere. I

will take your clothes off right in front of them. Then they will see you completely naked. [38]I will hand down my sentence against you. You will be punished like women who commit adultery and sacrifice their children to other gods. I am so angry with you. So I will sentence you to death for everything you have done. [39]Then I will hand you over to your lovers. They will tear down those mounds you built. They will destroy the little places of worship you put on them. They will take your clothes off. They will remove your fine jewelry. And they will leave you completely naked. [40]They will bring a crowd against you. The crowd will put you to death by throwing stones at you. And they will chop you to pieces with their swords. [41]They will burn down your houses and punish you. Many women will see it. I will not let you be a prostitute anymore. You will no longer pay your lovers. [42]Then my great anger against you will die down. My jealous anger will turn away from you. I will be calm. I will not be angry anymore.

[43]"You did not remember the days when you were young. The things you did made me very angry. So anything that happens to you will be your own fault," announces the Lord and King. "You added impure conduct to all the other evil things you did. I hate all those things.

[44]"All those who use proverbs will use this one about you. They will say, 'Like mother, like daughter.' [45]You are a true daughter of your mother. She hated her husband and children. And you are a true sister of your sisters. They hated their husbands and children. Your mother was a Hittite. Your father was an Amorite. [46]Your older sister was Samaria. She lived north of you with her daughters. Your younger sister was Sodom. She lived south of you with her daughters. [47]You lived exactly the way they did. You copied their evil practices. I hate those practices. Everything you did was so sinful that you soon became even worse than they were. [48]Your sister Sodom and her daughters never did what you and your daughters have done. And that is just as sure as I am alive," announces the Lord and King.

[49]"Here is the sin your sister Sodom committed. She and her daughters were proud. They ate too much. They were not concerned about others. They did not help those who were poor and in need. [50]They were very proud. They did many things that were evil in my eyes. I hated those things. So I got rid of Sodom and her daughters, just as you have seen. [51]Samaria did not commit half the sins you did. You sinned even more than they did. I hate those sins. Compared to what you did, you made your sisters seem godly. [52]So you will be dishonored. You have given your sisters an excuse for what they did. Your sins were far worse than theirs. In fact, your sisters appear to be more godly than you. So then, be ashamed. You will be dishonored. You have made them appear to be godly.

[53]"I will not only give you back what you had before. I will also do the same thing for Sodom and her daughters. And I will do the same for Samaria and her daughters. [54]That will make you feel dishonored. You will be ashamed of everything you have done. You have made them feel better because you sinned more and were punished more than they were. [55]Your sisters Sodom and Samaria and their daughters will return to what they were before. And you and your daughters will return to what you were before. [56]In the past you would not even mention your sister Sodom. You were proud at that time. [57]That was before your sin was uncovered. Now the daughters of Edom make fun of you. So do all her neighbors and the daughters of the Philistines. Everyone who lives around you hates you. [58]You will be punished for your impure conduct. I will also punish you for the other evil things you have done. I hate all those things," announces the Lord.

[59]The Lord and King says, "I will punish you in keeping with what you have done. I sealed with a promise the covenant I made with you. You hated that promise. And you broke my covenant. [60]But I will remember my covenant with you. I made it with you when you were young. Now I will make a new covenant with you. It will last forever. [61]Then you will remember how you have lived. You will be ashamed when I give you Samaria and Sodom. Samaria is your older sister. Sodom is your younger one. I will give them and their daughters to you as daughters. That can't happen based on my old covenant with you. [62]So I will make my new covenant with you. Then you will

know that I am the LORD. ⁶³I will pay for all the sins you have committed. Then you will remember what you have done. You will be ashamed of it. Because of your shame, you will never speak against me again," announces the LORD and King.

Two Eagles and a Vine

17 A message from the LORD came to me. The LORD said, ²"Son of man, tell the people of Israel a story about their kings. Let them know what will happen to them. ³Tell them, 'The LORD and King says, "A great eagle came to the city of 'Lebanon.' It had powerful wings and a lot of long feathers. The feathers were colorful and beautiful. The eagle landed in the top of a cedar tree. ⁴It broke off the highest twig. The eagle carried it away to the land of Babylon. There are many traders in that land. The eagle planted the twig in the city of Babylon.

⁵" ' "Then it took from the land a seed that had just sprouted. It put it in rich soil near plenty of water. It planted the seed like a willow tree. ⁶The seed grew into a low, spreading vine. Its branches turned toward the eagle. And its roots remained under the eagle. So the seed became a vine. It produced branches and put out leaves.

⁷" ' "But there was another great eagle. It also had powerful wings and a lot of feathers. The vine now sent out its roots toward that eagle. It sent them out from the place where it was planted. And it reached out its branches to the eagle for water. ⁸The seed had been planted in good soil near plenty of water. Then it could produce branches and bear fruit. It could become a beautiful vine." '

⁹"Ezekiel, tell the Israelites, 'The LORD and King asks, "Will the vine grow? Won't it be pulled up by its roots? Won't all its fruit be stripped off? Won't it dry up? All its new growth will dry up. It will not take a strong arm or many people to pull it up. ¹⁰It has been planted, but will it grow? No. It will dry up completely when the east wind strikes it. It will dry up in the place where it grew." ' "

¹¹A message from the LORD came to me. The LORD said, ¹²"These people refuse to obey me. Ask them, 'Don't you know what these things mean?' Tell them, 'Nebuchadnezzar went to Jerusalem. He was the king of Babylon. He carried off King Jehoiachin and

the nobles. He brought them back with him to the city of Babylon. ¹³Then Nebuchadnezzar made a peace treaty with Zedekiah. He was a member of Jerusalem's royal family. Nebuchadnezzar made him promise he would keep the treaty. He also took away the leading men of the land as prisoners. ¹⁴He did it to bring down their kingdom. It would not rise again. In fact, it would be able to last only by keeping his treaty. ¹⁵But Zedekiah turned against him. He sent messengers to Egypt. They went there to get horses and a large army. Will he succeed? Will he who does things like that escape? Can he break the peace treaty and still escape?

¹⁶" 'Zedekiah will die in Babylon,' announces the LORD and King. 'And that is just as sure as I am alive. He will die in the land of King Nebuchadnezzar, who put him on the throne. Zedekiah didn't keep his promise to Nebuchadnezzar and broke his treaty. ¹⁷So Nebuchadnezzar will build ramps against the walls of Jerusalem. He will set up war machines to destroy many lives. Pharaoh will not be able to help Zedekiah during the war. The huge and mighty army of Egypt will not be of any help. ¹⁸Zedekiah didn't keep his promise to Nebuchadnezzar and broke his treaty. Zedekiah had made a firm promise to keep it. But he broke it anyway. So he will not escape.

¹⁹" 'The LORD and King says, "Zedekiah didn't keep the promise he made in my name. He broke the treaty. So I will pay him back. And that is just as sure as I am alive. ²⁰I will spread out my net to catch him. He will be caught in my trap. I will bring him to Babylon. I will judge him there because he was not faithful to me. ²¹All Zedekiah's best troops will be killed by swords. Those who are left alive will be scattered to the winds. Then you will know that I have spoken. I am the LORD."

²²" 'The LORD and King says, "I myself will get a twig from the very top of a cedar tree and plant it. I will break off the highest twig. I will plant it on a very high mountain. ²³I will plant it on the high mountains of Israel. It will produce branches and bear fruit. It will become a beautiful cedar tree. All kinds of birds will make their nests in it. They will live in the shade of its branches. ²⁴All the trees in the forest will know that I bring down tall trees. I make short trees

grow tall. I dry up green trees. And I make dry trees green."

" 'I have spoken. I will do this. I am the Lord.' "

People Will Die Because of Their Own Sins

18 A message from the Lord came to me. The Lord said, [2]"You people have a proverb about the land of Israel. What do you mean by it? It says,

" 'The parents eat sour grapes.
　　But the children have a bitter taste in
　　　their mouths.'

[3]"You will not use that proverb in Israel anymore," announces the Lord and King. "And that is just as sure as I am alive. [4]Everyone belongs to me. Parents and children alike belong to me. A person will die because of their own sins.

[5] "Suppose there is a godly man
　　who does what is fair and right.
[6] And he does not eat at the mountain
　　　temples.
　　He does not worship the statues of
　　　Israel's gods.
　He does not sleep with another man's
　　　wife.
　　He does not have sex with his own
　　　wife
　　during her monthly period.

[7] He does not treat anyone badly.
　　Instead, he always returns things he
　　　takes
　　to make sure loans are paid back.
　He does not steal.
　　Instead, he gives his food to hungry
　　　people.
　He provides clothes for those who
　　　are naked.
[8] He does not charge interest when he
　　　lends money to them.
　　He does not make money from
　　　them.
　He keeps himself from doing what
　　　is wrong.
　　He judges cases fairly.
[9] He obeys my rules.
　He is faithful in keeping my laws.
　He always does what is right.
　　You can be sure he will live,"
　　announces the Lord and King.

[10]"But suppose he has a mean son who harms other people. The son commits murder. Or he does some other things that are wrong. [11]Suppose he does these things even though his father never did.

"Suppose the son eats at the mountain
　　temples.
　　And he sleeps with another man's
　　　wife.
[12] He treats poor and needy people
　　　badly.
　He steals.
　He does not pay back what he owes.
　He worships statues of gods.
　He does other things I hate.
[13] 　He charges interest when he lends
　　　money to poor people. He
　　　makes money from them.

Will a man like that live? He will not! He must be put to death. And what happens to him will be his own fault. He did many things I hate.

[14]"But suppose this son has a son of his own. And the son sees all the sins his father commits. He sees them, but he does not do them.

[15] "Suppose he does not eat at the
　　　mountain temples.
　　And he does not worship the statues
　　　of Israel's gods.
　He does not sleep with another
　　　man's wife.

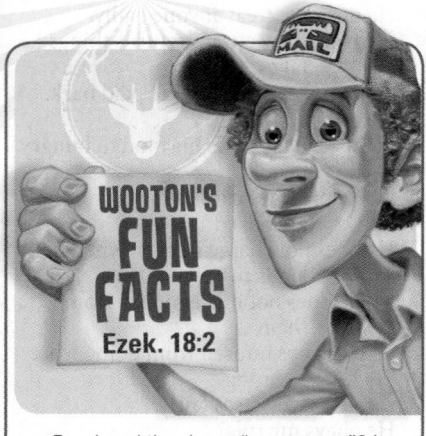

WOOTON'S FUN FACTS

Ezek. 18:2

Ever heard the phrase "sour grapes"? It means pretending you don't want something because you can't have it. The fable-maker Aesop made this phrase popular with the story "The Fox and the Grapes," but the phrase is here in the Bible too. Aesop lived about the same time Ezekiel did.

¹⁶ He does not treat anyone badly.
He does not make people give him something
to prove they will pay back what they owe him.
He does not steal.
Instead, he gives his food to hungry people.
He provides clothes for those who are naked.
¹⁷ He keeps himself from committing sins.
He does not charge interest when he lends money to poor people.
He does not make money from them.
He keeps my laws and obeys my rules.

He will not die because of his father's sin. You can be sure he will live. ¹⁸But his father will die because of his own sin. He got rich by cheating others. He robbed his relatives. He also did what was wrong among his people.

¹⁹"But you still ask, 'Is the son guilty along with his father?' No! The son did what was fair and right. He was careful to obey all my rules. So you can be sure he will live. ²⁰A person will die because of their own sins. A child will not be guilty because of what their parent did. And a parent will

not be guilty because of what their child did. The right things a godly person does will be added to their account. The wrong things a sinful person does will be charged against them.

²¹"But suppose a sinful person turns away from all the sins they have committed. And they obey all my rules. They do what is fair and right. Then you can be sure they will live. They will not die. ²²None of the sins they have committed will be held against them. Because of the godly things they have done, they will live. ²³When sinful people die, it does not give me any joy," announces the LORD and King. "But when they turn away from their sins and live, that makes me very happy.

²⁴"Suppose a godly person stops doing what is right. And they sin. They do the same evil things a sinful person does. They do things I hate. Then they will not live. I will not remember any of the right things they have done. They have not been faithful to me. They have also committed many other sins. So they are guilty. They will die.

²⁵"But you say, 'What the Lord does isn't fair.' Listen to me, you Israelites. What I do is always fair. What you do is not. ²⁶Suppose a godly person stops doing what is right. And they sin. Then they will die because of it. They will die because of the sin they have committed. ²⁷But suppose a sinful person turns away from the evil things they have done. And they do what is fair and right. Then they will save their life. ²⁸They think about all the evil things they have done. And they turn away from them. So you can be sure they will live. They will not die. ²⁹But the Israelites still say, 'What the Lord does isn't fair.' People of Israel, what I do is always fair. What you do is not.

³⁰"So I will judge you Israelites. I will judge each of you in keeping with what you have done," announces the LORD and King. "Turn away from your sins! Turn away from all the evil things you have done. Then sin will not bring you down. ³¹Get rid of all the evil things you have done. Let me give you a new heart and a new spirit. Then you will be faithful to me. Why should you die, people of Israel? ³²When anyone dies, it does not give me any joy," announces the LORD and King. "So turn away from your sins. Then you will live!

A Song of Sadness About Israel's Princes

19 "Sing a song of sadness about Israel's princes. ²Say to Israel,

" 'You were like a mother lion to your
    princes.
  She lay down among the lions.
  She brought up her cubs.
³ One of them was Jehoahaz.
  He became a strong lion.
  He learned to tear apart what he caught.
  And he became a man-eater.
⁴ The nations heard about him.
  They trapped him in their pit.
  They put hooks in his face.
  And they led him away to Egypt.

⁵ " 'The mother lion looked and waited.
  But all her hope was gone.
  So she got another one of her cubs.
  She made him into a strong lion.
⁶ He prowled with the lions.
  He became very strong.
  He learned to tear apart what he caught.
  And he became a man-eater.
⁷ He broke down their forts.
  He completely destroyed their towns.
  The land and all those who were in it
    were terrified when he roared.
⁸ Then nations came against him.
  They came from all around him.
  They spread out their net to catch him.
  He was trapped in their pit.
⁹ They used hooks to pull him into a
    cage.
  They brought him to the king of
    Babylon.
  They put him in prison.
  So his roar was not heard anymore
    on the mountains of Israel.

¹⁰ " 'Israel, you were like a vine in a
    vineyard.
  It was planted near water.
  It had a lot of fruit and many branches.
  There was plenty of water.
¹¹ Its branches were strong.
  Each was good enough to be made
    into a ruler's scepter.
  The vine grew high
    above all the leaves.
  It stood out because it was so tall
    and had so many branches.
¹² But Nebuchadnezzar became angry.
  He pulled it up by its roots.
  He threw it to the ground.

  The east wind dried it up.
  Its fruit was stripped off.
  Its strong branches dried up.
  And fire destroyed them.
¹³ Now it is planted in the Babylonian
    desert.
  It is in a dry and thirsty land.
¹⁴ One of its main branches was Zedekiah.
  Fire spread from it and burned up
    its fruit.
  None of its branches is good enough
    to be made into a ruler's scepter.'

This is a song of sadness. And that is how it should be used."

The LORD Judges Sinful Israel

20 It was the seventh year since King Jehoiachin had been brought to Babylon as a prisoner. On the tenth day of the fifth month, some of the elders of Israel came to ask the LORD for advice. They sat down with me.

²Then a message from the LORD came to me. The LORD said, ³"Son of man, speak to the elders of Israel. Tell them, 'The LORD and King says, "Have you come to ask me for advice? I will not let you do that," announces the LORD and King. "And that is just as sure as I am alive." '

⁴"Are you going to judge them, son of man? Will you judge them? Tell them the evil things done by their people of long ago. I hate those things. ⁵Tell them, 'The LORD and King says, "I chose Israel. On that day I raised my hand and made a promise. I made a promise to the members of Jacob's family line. I made myself known to them in Egypt. I raised my hand and told them, 'I am the LORD your God.' ⁶On that day I promised I would bring them out of Egypt. I told them I would take them to a land I had found for them. It had plenty of milk and honey. It was the most beautiful land of all. ⁷I said to them, 'Each of you must get rid of the statues of the evil gods you worship. Do not make yourselves "unclean" by worshiping the gods of Egypt. I am the LORD your God.'

⁸" ' "But they refused to obey me. They would not listen to me. They did not get rid of the evil gods they worshiped. And they did not turn away from Egypt's gods. So I said I would pour out all my great anger on them in Egypt. ⁹I wanted my name to be honored. So I brought my people out of

Egypt. I did it to keep my name from being treated as if it were not holy. I didn't want this to happen in front of the nations around my people. I had made myself known to Israel in the sight of those nations. [10]So I led them out of Egypt. I brought them into the Desert of Sinai. [11]I gave them my rules. I made my laws known to them. The person who obeys them will live by them. [12]I also told them to observe my Sabbath days. That is the sign of the covenant I made with them. I wanted them to know that I made them holy. I am the Lord.

[13]"'But in the desert the people of Israel refused to obey me. They did not follow my rules. They turned their backs on my laws. The person who obeys them will live by them. They totally misused my Sabbath days. So I said I would pour out my great anger on them. I would destroy them in the desert. [14]But I wanted my name to be honored. I kept it from being treated as if it were not holy. I did not want that to happen in front of the nations. They had seen me bring Israel out of Egypt. [15]I also raised my hand and made a promise in the desert. I told my people I would not bring them into the land I had given them. It had plenty of milk and honey. It was the most beautiful land of all. [16]But they turned their backs on my laws. They did not obey my rules. They misused my Sabbath days. Their hearts were committed to worshiping the statues of their gods. [17]Then I felt sorry for them. So I did not destroy them. I did not put an end to them in the desert. [18]I spoke to their children there. I said, 'Do not follow the rules your parents gave you. Do not obey their laws. Do not make yourselves "unclean" by worshiping their gods. [19]I am the Lord your God. So follow my rules. Be careful to obey my laws. [20]Keep my Sabbath days holy. That is the sign of the covenant I made with you. You will know that I am the Lord your God.'

[21]"'But their children refused to obey me. They did not follow my rules. They were not careful to keep my laws. The person who obeys them will live by them. They misused my Sabbath days. So I said I would pour out all my great anger on them in the desert. [22]But I kept myself from punishing them at that time. I wanted my name to be honored. So I kept it from being treated as if it were not holy. I did not want that to happen in front of the nations. They had seen me bring Israel out of Egypt. [23]I also raised my hand and made a promise in the desert. I told my people I would scatter them among the nations. I would send them to other countries. [24]They had not obeyed my laws. They had turned their backs on my rules. They had misused my Sabbath days. They only wanted to worship the statues of their parents' gods. [25]So I let them follow other rules. Those other rules were not good. I let them have laws they could not live by. [26]I let them become 'unclean' by offering sacrifices to other gods. They even sacrificed the first male child born in each family. I wanted to fill them with horror. Then they would know that I am the Lord.'

[27]"Son of man, speak to the people of Israel. Tell them, 'The Lord and King says, "Your people spoke evil things against me long ago. They were unfaithful to me. [28]But I brought them into the land. I had promised to give the land to them. Then they offered sacrifices that made me very angry. They did it on every high hill and under every green tree. There they brought their sweet-smelling incense. And there they poured out their drink offerings. [29]Then I said to them, 'What is this high place you go to?'"'" That high place is called Bamah to this day.

The Lord Makes Israel New Again

[30]The Lord said to me, "Speak to the Israelites. Tell them, 'Here is what the Lord and King says. "Are you going to make yourselves 'unclean' the way your people of long ago did? Are you also going to want to worship the statues of their evil gods? [31]You make yourselves 'unclean' by offering sacrifices to other gods. You even sacrifice your children in the fire. You continue to do these things to this day. People of Israel, should I let you ask me for advice? I will not let you do that," announces the Lord and King. "And that is just as sure as I am alive.

[32]"'You say, 'We want to be like the other nations. We want to be like all the other people in the world. They serve gods made out of wood and stone.' But what you have in mind will never happen. [33]I will rule over you by reaching out my mighty hand and powerful arm. I will pour my

great anger out on you," announces the Lord and King. "And that is just as sure as I am alive. ³⁴I will bring you back from the nations. I will gather you together from the countries where you have been scattered. I will reach out my mighty hand and powerful arm. I will pour my great anger out on you. ³⁵I will send you among the nations. There I will judge you face to face. It will be as if I were judging you in the desert again. ³⁶Long ago, I judged your people in the desert of Egypt. In the same way, I will judge you," announces the Lord and King. ³⁷"I will take note of you as you pass under my shepherd's stick. I will separate those who obey me from those who do not. And I will give the blessings of the covenant to those of you who obey me. ³⁸I will get rid of those among you who turn against me. They refuse to obey me. I will bring them out of the land where they are living. But they will not enter the land of Israel. Then you will know that I am the Lord.

³⁹" ' "People of Israel, the Lord and King says, 'Go, every one of you! Serve your gods. But later you will listen to me. You will no longer treat my name as if it were not holy. You will not offer sacrifices to other gods anymore. ⁴⁰People of Israel, you will all serve me,' announces the Lord and King. 'You will serve me on my high and holy mountain in Jerusalem. There I will accept you. I will require your offerings and your finest gifts. I want you to bring them along with all your other holy sacrifices. ⁴¹I will bring you back from the nations. I will gather you together from the countries where you have been scattered. Then I will accept you as if you were sweet-smelling incense. I will show that I am holy among you. The nations will see it. ⁴²I will bring you into the land of Israel. Then you will know that I am the Lord. Long ago I raised my hand and made a promise. I promised to give that land to your people of long ago. ⁴³There you will remember your conduct. You will think about everything you did that made you "unclean." And you will hate yourselves because of all the evil things you have done. ⁴⁴People of Israel, I will deal with you for the honor of my name. I will not deal with you based on your evil conduct and sinful practices. Then you will know that I am the Lord,' announces the Lord and King." ' "

Ezekiel Prophesies Against the South

⁴⁵A message from the Lord came to me. The Lord said, ⁴⁶"Son of man, turn your attention to Judah in the south. Preach against it. Prophesy against its forests. ⁴⁷Tell them, 'Listen to the Lord's message. The Lord and King says, "I am about to set you on fire. The fire will destroy all your trees. It will burn down green trees and dry trees alike. The blazing flame will not be put out. The faces of everyone from south to north will be burned by it. ⁴⁸Everyone will see that I started the fire. It will not be put out. I am the Lord." ' "

⁴⁹Then I said, "Lord and King, people are talking about me. They are saying, 'Isn't he just telling stories?' "

God Uses the Babylonians to Judge Israel

21 A message from the Lord came to me. The Lord said, ²"Son of man, turn your attention to Jerusalem. Preach against the temple. Prophesy against the land of Israel. ³Tell them, 'The Lord says, "I am against you. I will pull out my sword. I will remove from you godly people and sinful people alike. ⁴Because I am going to remove them, my sword will be ready to use. I will strike down everyone from south to north. ⁵Then all people will know that I have pulled out my sword. I will not put it back. I am the Lord." '

⁶"Groan, son of man! Groan in front of your people. Groan with a broken heart and bitter sorrow. ⁷They will ask you, 'Why are you groaning?' Then you will say, 'Because of the news that is coming. The hearts of all the people will melt away in fear. Their hands will not be able to help them. Their spirits will grow weak. And they will be so afraid they'll wet themselves.' The news is coming! You can be sure those things will happen," announces the Lord and King.

⁸A message from the Lord came to me. The Lord said, ⁹"Son of man, prophesy. Say, 'The Lord says,

" ' "A sword! A sword!
     A sharp and shiny sword is coming
         from Babylon!
¹⁰ It is sharpened to kill people.
     It flashes like lightning." ' "

The people say, "Should we take delight in the scepter of the Lord's royal son? The sword looks down on every scepter like this." [11]The LORD says,

"I have told Nebuchadnezzar to shine
        his sword.
    It is in his hand.
It has been sharpened and shined.
    It is ready for the killer's hand.
[12] Son of man, cry out and weep.
    The sword is against my people.
It is against all the princes of Israel.
It will kill them
    along with the rest of my people.
    So beat your chest in sorrow.

[13]"You can be sure that testing will come. Why does the sword look down on the scepter? Because even the scepter will not continue to rule," announces the LORD and King.

[14] "Son of man, prophesy.
    Clap your hands.
Let the sword strike twice.
    Let it strike even three times.
It is a sword to kill people.
    It is a sword to kill many people.
    It is closing in on them from every
        side.
[15] People's hearts will melt away in fear.
    Many will be wounded or killed.
I have prepared the sword to kill people
    at all their city gates.
Look! It strikes like lightning.
    It is in the killer's hand.
[16] Sword, cut to the right.
    Then cut to the left.
    Strike down people everywhere your
        blade is turned.
[17] I too will clap my hands.
    I won't be so angry anymore.
    I have spoken. I am the LORD."

[18]A message from the LORD came to me. The LORD said, [19]"Son of man, mark out on a map two roads for the sword to take. The sword belongs to the king of Babylon. Both roads start from the same country. Put up a sign where the road turns off to the city of Rabbah. [20]Mark out one road for the sword to take against Rabbah in Ammon. Mark out another against Judah and the walls of Jerusalem. [21]The king of Babylon will stop at the place where the two roads meet. He will look for a special sign. He will cast lots by pulling arrows out of a bag. He will ask his gods for advice. And he will look

Ezek. 21:19 I am a son of a man: Winston Bassett. But that's not all that different from everyone else. All boys are "sons of men," right? But Jesus uses the phrase "Son of Man" to refer to Himself. Matthew 16:13–20 shows that it's a special name for Jesus the Messiah.

carefully at the liver of a sheep. [22]His right hand will pull out the arrow for Jerusalem. There he will get huge logs ready to knock down its gates. He will give the command to kill its people. He will sound the battle cry. He will build a ramp up to the city wall. He will bring in his war machines. [23]The decision to attack Jerusalem will seem like the wrong advice to those who made a treaty with Nebuchadnezzar. But he will remind them that they are guilty. And he will take them away as prisoners."

[24]So the LORD and King says, "You people have reminded everyone of how guilty you are. You have done it by refusing to obey me or any other authority. Everything you do clearly shows how sinful you are. So you will be taken away as prisoners."

[25]King Zedekiah, your day has come. You are an unholy and evil prince in Israel. The day for you to be punished is here. [26]The LORD and King says, "Take off your turban. Remove your crown. Things will not be as they were in the past. Those who are considered not important will be honored. And those who are honored will be considered not important. [27]Jerusalem will fall. I will destroy it. It will not be rebuilt until the true king comes. After all, the kingdom belongs to him. I will give it to him.

[28]"Son of man, prophesy. Say, 'The LORD and King speaks about the Ammonites. He

also talks about the way they laugh because of Jerusalem's fall. He says,

"'"A sword! A sword!
   Nebuchadnezzar's sword is ready to kill you.
It is shined to destroy you.
It flashes like lightning.
²⁹ The visions of your prophets are false.
   They use magic to try to find out what is going to happen to you.
But their magic tricks are lies.
The sword will strike the necks of you sinful people.
You will be killed.
The day for you to be punished has finally come.
   Your time is up.
³⁰ Ammon, return your sword to its place.
   In the land where you were created, I will judge you.
That is where you came from.
³¹ I will pour out my anger on you.
   I will breathe out my burning anger against you.
I will hand you over to mean people.
   They are skilled at destroying others.
³² You will be burned in the fire.
   Your blood will be spilled in your land.
You will not be remembered anymore.
I have spoken. I am the LORD."'"

The LORD Judges Jerusalem for Its Sins

22 A message from the LORD came to me. The LORD said,

²"Son of man, are you going to judge Jerusalem? Will you judge this city that has so many murderers in it? Then tell its people they have done many evil things. I hate those things. ³Tell them, 'The LORD and King says, "Your city brings death on itself. You spill blood inside its walls. You make yourselves 'unclean' by making statues of gods. ⁴You are guilty of spilling blood. Your statues have made you 'unclean.' You have brought your days to a close. The end of your years has come. So the nations will make fun of you. All the countries will laugh at you. ⁵Those who are near you will tell jokes about you. So will those who are far away. Trouble fills the streets of your sinful city.

⁶"'"The princes of Israel are in your city. All of them use their power to spill blood.

⁷They have made fun of fathers and mothers alike. They have crushed outsiders. They have treated badly the children whose fathers have died. They have done the same thing to widows. ⁸You have looked down on the holy things that were set apart to me. You have misused my Sabbath days. ⁹You have spread lies about others so you can spill someone's blood. You eat at the mountain temples. You commit impure acts. ¹⁰You bring shame on your fathers by having sex with their wives. You have sex with women during their monthly period. That is when they are 'unclean.' ¹¹One of you has sex with another man's wife. I hate that sin. Another brings shame on his daughter-in-law by having sex with her. Still another has sex with his sister, even though she is his own father's daughter. ¹²You accept money from people who want special favors. You do this to spill someone's blood. You charge interest to poor people when you lend them money. You make money from them. You get rich by cheating your neighbors. And you have forgotten me," announces the LORD and King.

¹³"'"I will clap my hands because I am so angry. You got rich by cheating others. You spilled blood inside the walls of your city. ¹⁴Will you be brave on the day I deal with you? Will you be strong at that time? I have spoken. I will do this. I am the LORD. ¹⁵I will scatter you among the nations. I will send you to other countries. I will put an end to your 'uncleanness.' ¹⁶You will be 'unclean' in the sight of the nations. Then you will know that I am the LORD."'"

¹⁷A message from the LORD came to me. The LORD said, ¹⁸"Son of man, the people of Israel have become like scum to me. All of them are like the copper, tin, iron and lead left inside a furnace. They are only the scum that is removed from silver." ¹⁹So the LORD and King says, "People of Israel, all of you have become like scum. So I will gather you together in Jerusalem. ²⁰People put silver, copper, iron, lead and tin into a furnace. They melt it with a blazing fire. In the same way, I will gather you. I will pour out my burning anger on you. I will put you inside the city and melt you. ²¹I will gather you together. My burning anger will blaze out at you. And you will be melted inside Jerusalem. ²²Silver is melted in a furnace. And you will be melted inside the city.

Then you will know that I have poured out my burning anger on you. I am the LORD."

²³Another message from the LORD came to me. The LORD said, ²⁴"Son of man, speak to the land. Tell it, 'You have not been washed clean with rain. That's because I am angry with you.' ²⁵Ezekiel, the princes of the land are like a roaring lion that tears its food apart. They eat people up. They take treasures and other valuable things. They cause many women in the land to become widows. ²⁶Its priests break my law. They treat things set apart to me as if they were not holy. They treat holy and common things as if they were the same. They teach that there is no difference between things that are 'clean' and things that are not. They refuse to keep my Sabbath days. So they treat me as if I were not holy. ²⁷The officials in the land are like wolves that tear their food apart. They spill blood and kill people to get rich. ²⁸The prophets cover up these acts for them. The visions of these prophets are false. They use magic to try to find out what is going to happen. But their magic tricks are lies. They say, 'The LORD and King says.' But I have not spoken to them. ²⁹The people of the land get rich by cheating others. They steal. They crush those who are poor and in need. They treat outsiders badly. They refuse to be fair to them.

³⁰"I looked for someone among them who would stand up for Jerusalem. I tried to find someone who would pray to me for the land. Then I would not have to destroy it. But I could not find anyone who would pray for it. ³¹So I will pour out my anger on its people. I will destroy them because of my great anger against them. And anything that happens to them will be their own fault," announces the LORD and King.

Samaria and Jerusalem Are Like Two Impure Sisters

23 A message from the LORD came to me. The LORD said, ²"Son of man, once there were two women. They had the same mother. ³They became prostitutes in Egypt. They have been unfaithful to me since they were young. In that land they allowed their breasts to be touched. They permitted their virgin breasts to be kissed. ⁴The older sister was named Oholah. The younger one was Oholibah. They belonged to me. Sons and daughters were born to

them. Oholah stands for Samaria. And Oholibah stands for Jerusalem.

⁵"Oholah was unfaithful to me even while she still belonged to me. She longed for her Assyrian lovers. They included soldiers ⁶who wore blue uniforms. They also included governors and commanders. All of them were young and handsome. They rode horses. ⁷She gave herself as a prostitute to all Assyria's finest warriors. She made herself impure with the statues of the gods of everyone she longed for. ⁸She started being a prostitute in Egypt. And she never stopped. When she was young, men had sex with her. They kissed her virgin breasts. They used up all their sinful desires on her.

⁹"So I handed her over to her Assyrian lovers. She longed for them. ¹⁰They stripped her naked. They took away her sons and daughters. And they killed her with their swords. Other women laughed when that happened. I was the one who had punished her.

¹¹"Her sister Oholibah saw it. But her evil desire for sexual sin was worse than her sister's. ¹²She too longed for the men of Assyria. They included governors and commanders. They included soldiers who wore fancy uniforms. They also included men who rode horses. All of them were young and handsome. ¹³I saw that she too made herself impure. So both sisters did the same evil things.

¹⁴"But Oholibah went even further with her sexual sins. She saw pictures of men drawn on a wall. They were figures of Babylonians drawn in red. ¹⁵They had belts around their waists. They wore flowing turbans on their heads. All of them looked like Babylonian chariot officers. They were from the land of the Chaldeans. ¹⁶As soon as she saw the pictures, she longed for the men. So she sent messengers to them in Babylon. ¹⁷Then the Babylonians came to her. They went to bed with her. They had sex with her. They made her impure when they had sex with her. After they did it, she became sick of them. So she turned away from them. ¹⁸She acted like a prostitute who had no shame at all. She openly showed her naked body. I became sick of what she was doing. So I turned away from her. I had also turned away from her sister. ¹⁹But Oholibah offered her body to her lovers again and again. She remembered the days when she was a young prostitute

in Egypt. ²⁰There she had longed for her lovers. Their private parts seemed as big as those of donkeys. And their flow of semen appeared to be as much as that of horses. ²¹So you wanted to return to the days when you were young. You longed for the time when you first became impure in Egypt. That was when you allowed your breasts to be kissed. And you permitted your young breasts to be touched."

²²So the Lord and King says, "Oholibah, I will stir up your lovers against you. You became sick of them. You turned away from them. But I will bring them against you from every side. ²³They include the Babylonians and all the Chaldeans. They include the men from Pekod, Shoa and Koa. They also include all the Assyrians. They are young and handsome. Some of them are governors and commanders. Others are chariot officers. Still others are very high officials. All of them ride horses. ²⁴So a huge army will come against you with weapons, chariots and wagons. They will take up positions against you on every side. They will carry large and small shields. They will wear helmets. I will turn you over to them to be punished. They will punish you in their own way. ²⁵I will pour out my jealous anger on you. And the army's anger will burn against you. They will cut off your noses and ears. Some of you who are left will be killed by swords. They will take away your sons and daughters. Others of you who are left will be burned up. ²⁶The army will also strip off your clothes. They will take your fine jewelry away from you. ²⁷You became an impure prostitute in Egypt. But I will put a stop to all of that. You will no longer want to do any of it. You will not remember Egypt anymore."

²⁸The Lord and King says, "I am about to hand you over to people you hate. You became sick of them. You turned away from them. ²⁹They will punish you because they hate you so much. They will take away from you everything you have worked for. They will leave you completely naked. Then everyone will see that you are a prostitute who has no shame at all. You were impure. You offered your body to your lovers again and again. ³⁰That is why you will be punished. You longed for lovers in other nations. You made yourself impure by worshiping their gods. ³¹You did the same

things your sister Oholah did. So I will put her cup in your hand. It is filled with the wine of my anger."

³²The Lord and King says to Oholibah,

"You will drink from your sister's cup.
    It is large and deep.
    It is filled with the wine of my anger.
So others will laugh at you.
    They will make fun of you.
³³ You will become drunk and sad.
    The cup of my anger will completely
        destroy you.
    It is the same cup your sister
        Samaria drank from.
³⁴ You will drink from it until it is empty.
    Then you will chew on its pieces.
    And you will claw at your breasts.

I have spoken," announces the Lord and King.

³⁵So the Lord and King says, "You have forgotten me. You have turned your back on me. You have been impure. You have acted like a prostitute. So I will punish you."

³⁶The Lord said to me, "Son of man, are you going to judge Oholah and Oholibah? Then tell them they have done many evil things. I hate those things. ³⁷They have committed adultery. Their hands are covered with the blood of the people they have murdered. They have worshiped other gods. They have not been faithful to me. They have even sacrificed their children as food to other gods. Those children belonged to me. ³⁸Here are some other things the sisters have done to me. They have made my temple 'unclean.' They have misused my Sabbath days. ³⁹They have sacrificed their children to their gods. On that same day they entered my temple and made it 'unclean.' That is what they have done in my house.

⁴⁰"They even sent messengers to bring men from far away. When the men arrived, Oholibah took a bath. She put makeup on her eyes. She put her jewelry on. ⁴¹She sat down on a beautiful couch. A table was in front of it. There she put the incense and olive oil that belonged to me.

⁴²"The noise of a carefree crowd was all around her. Men who drink too much were brought from the desert. Other men were brought along with them. They put bracelets on the wrists of the two sisters. They put beautiful crowns on their heads. ⁴³Then I spoke about Oholibah. She was worn out

by adultery. I said, 'Let them use her as a prostitute. After all, that is what she is.' ⁴⁴So they slept with her. In fact, they slept with both of these impure women, Oholah and Oholibah. They slept with them just as men sleep with prostitutes. ⁴⁵But judges who are right with God will sentence the sisters to be punished. They will be punished in the same way as women who commit adultery and murder. After all, they have committed adultery. And their hands are covered with the blood of the people they have murdered."

⁴⁶The Lord and King says, "Bring an angry crowd against the sisters. Hand them over to those who will terrify them and steal everything they have. ⁴⁷The crowd will kill them by throwing stones at them. They will use swords to cut them down. They will kill their sons and daughters. And they will burn down their houses.

⁴⁸"So I will put an end to impurity in the land. Then all its women will be warned. They will not want to be like the sisters. ⁴⁹Those sisters will be punished because of the impure things they have done. They will be judged because they have worshiped other gods. Then they will know that I am the Lord and King."

Jerusalem Is Like a Cooking Pot

24 It was the ninth year since King Jehoiachin had been brought to Babylon as a prisoner. On the tenth day of the tenth month, a message from the Lord came to me. The Lord said, ²"Son of man, write down today's date. The king of Babylon has surrounded Jerusalem and attacked it today. ³Your people refuse to obey me. So tell them a story. Say to them, 'The Lord and King told me,

" ' "Put a cooking pot on the fire.
　　Pour water into it.
⁴ Put pieces of meat in it.
　　Use all the best pieces.
Use the leg and shoulder.
　　Fill it with the best bones.
⁵ Pick the finest animal in the flock.
　　Pile wood under the pot to cook the
　　　bones.
Bring the water to a boil.
　　Cook the bones in it." ' "

⁶The Lord and King says,

"How terrible it will be for this city!
　　It has so many murderers in it.

How terrible for the pot that is coated
　　with scum!
The scum on it will not go away.
Take the meat out of the pot piece by
　　piece.
Take it out in whatever order it
　　comes.

⁷ "The blood Jerusalem's people spilled is
　　inside its walls.
They poured it out on a bare rock.
They did not pour it on the ground.
If they had, dust would have covered
　　it up.
⁸ So I put their blood on the bare rock.
I did not want it to be covered up.
I poured out my great anger on them.
　　I paid them back."

⁹So the Lord and King said to me,

"How terrible it will be for this city!
　　It has so many murderers in it.
　　I too will pile the wood high.
¹⁰ So pile on the wood.
　　Light the fire.
Cook the meat well.
　　Mix in the spices.
　　Let the bones be blackened.
¹¹ Then set the empty pot on the coals.
　　Let it get hot. Let its copper glow.

WOOTON'S FUN FACTS
Ezek. 24:1–14

The Bible often *personifies* cities as women. Here God compares Jerusalem to a cooking pot, almost like the U.S. is sometimes compared to a melting pot. You might think that's *potification*, but sadly for those of us who would use that word every day, it's not a real word. But *metaphor* is a real word, and that's what's going on here.

Then what is not pure in it will melt.
Its scum will be burned away.
[12] But it can't be cleaned up.
Its thick scum has not been
removed.
Even fire can't burn it off.

[13]"Jerusalem, you are really impure. I tried to clean you up. But you would not let me make you pure. So you will not be clean again until I am no longer so angry with you.

[14]"I have spoken. The time has come for me to act. I will not hold back. I will not feel sorry for you. I will do what I said I would do. You will be judged for your conduct and actions. I am the LORD," announces the LORD and King.

Ezekiel's Wife Dies

[15]A message from the LORD came to me. The LORD said, [16]"Son of man, I will take away from you the wife you delight in. It will happen very soon. But do not sing songs of sadness. Do not let any tears flow from your eyes. [17]Groan quietly. Do not mourn for your wife when she dies. Keep your turban on your head. Keep your sandals on your feet. Do not cover your mustache and beard. Do not eat the food people eat to comfort them when someone dies."

[18]So I spoke to my people in the morning. And in the evening my wife died. The next morning I did what I had been commanded to do.

[19]Then the people said to me, "Tell us what these things have to do with us. Why are you acting like this?"

[20]So I told them. I said, "A message from the LORD came to me. The LORD said, [21]'Speak to the people of Israel. Tell them, "The LORD and King says, 'I am about to make my temple "unclean." I will let the Babylonians burn it down. It is the beautiful building you are so proud of. You take delight in it. You love it. The sons and daughters you left behind will be killed by swords. [22]So do what Ezekiel did. Do not cover your mustache and beard. Do not eat the food people eat to comfort them when someone dies. [23]Keep your turbans on your heads. Keep your sandals on your feet. Do not mourn or weep. You will waste away because you have sinned so much. You will groan among yourselves. [24]What Ezekiel

Ezek. 24:15–18 Here Ezekiel finds out that his wife is going to die. In Matthew 8:20–22, Jesus told a would-be follower that he couldn't "bury his father." Tough stuff, huh? Following God is sometimes like being a letter carrier. I deliver mail even when my mood is rainy.

has done will show you what is going to happen to you. You will do just as he has done. Then you will know that I am the LORD and King.'"'

[25]"Son of man, I will take away their beautiful temple. It is their joy and glory. They take delight in it. Their hearts long for it. I will also take away their sons and daughters. [26]On the day I destroy everything, a man will escape. He will come and tell you the news. [27]At that time I will open your mouth. Then you will no longer be silent. You will speak with the man. That will show them what will happen to them. And they will know that I am the LORD."

A Prophecy Against Ammon

25 A message from the LORD came to me. The LORD said, [2]"Son of man, turn your attention to the Ammonites. Prophesy against them. [3]Tell them, 'Listen to the message of the LORD and King. He says, "You laughed when my temple was made 'unclean.' You also laughed when the land of Israel was completely destroyed. You mocked the people of Judah when they were taken away as prisoners. [4]So I am going to hand you over to the people of the east. They will set up their tents in your land. They will camp among you. They will eat your fruit. They will drink your milk. [5]I will turn the city of Rabbah into grasslands for camels. Ammon will become a resting place for sheep. Then you will know that I am the LORD.' " ⁶The LORD and King says, "You clapped your hands. You stamped your feet. Deep down inside, you hated the land of Israel. You were glad because of what happened to it. ⁷So I will reach out my powerful hand against you. I will give you and everything you have to the nations. I will bring you to an end among the nations. I will destroy you. Then you will know that I am the LORD."

A Prophecy Against Moab

⁸The LORD and King says, "Moab and Edom said, 'Look! Judah has become like all the other nations.' ⁹So I will let Moab's enemies attack its lower hills. They will begin at the border towns. Those towns include Beth Jeshimoth, Baal Meon and Kiriathaim. They are the glory of that land. ¹⁰I will hand Moab over to the people of the east. I will also give the Ammonites to them. And the Ammonites will no longer be remembered among the nations. ¹¹I will punish Moab. Then they will know that I am the LORD."

A Prophecy Against Edom

¹²The LORD and King says, "Edom got even with Judah. That made Edom very guilty." ¹³The LORD continues, "I will reach out my hand against Edom. I will kill its people and their animals. I will completely destroy it. They will be killed by swords from Teman all the way to Dedan. ¹⁴I will use my people Israel to pay Edom back. They will punish Edom because my anger against it is great. They will know how I pay back my enemies," announces the LORD and King.

A Prophecy Against the Philistines

¹⁵The LORD and King says, "Deep down inside them, the Philistines hated Judah. So the Philistines tried to get even with them. They had been Judah's enemies for many years. So they tried to destroy them." ¹⁶The LORD continues, "I am about to reach out my hand against the Philistines. I will wipe out the Kerethites. I will destroy those who remain along the coast. ¹⁷You can be sure that I will pay them back. I will punish them because my anger against them is great. When I pay them back, they will know that I am the LORD."

A Prophecy Against Tyre

26 It was the first day of the 11th month. It was the 12th year since King Jehoiachin had been brought to Babylon as a prisoner. A message from the LORD came to me. The LORD said, ²"Son of man, Tyre laughed because of what happened to Jerusalem. The people of Tyre said, 'Jerusalem is the gateway to the nations. But the gate is broken. Its doors have swung open to us. Jerusalem has been destroyed. So now we will succeed.' " ³The LORD and King says, "But I am against you, Tyre. I will bring many nations against you. They will come in like the waves of the sea. ⁴They will destroy your walls. They will pull down your towers. I will clear away the stones of your broken-down buildings. I will turn you into nothing but a bare rock. ⁵Out in the Mediterranean Sea your island city will become a place to spread fishnets. I have spoken," announces the LORD and King. "The nations will take you and everything you have. ⁶Your settlements on the coast will be destroyed by war. Then you will know that I am the LORD."

⁷The LORD and King says, "From the north I am going to bring Nebuchadnezzar against Tyre. He is the king of Babylon. He is the greatest king of all. He will come with horses and chariots. Horsemen and a great army will be brought along with him. ⁸He will go to war against you. He will destroy your settlements on the coast. He will bring in war machines to attack you. A ramp will be built up to your walls. He will raise his shields against you. ⁹He will use huge logs to knock down your walls. He will destroy your towers with his weapons. ¹⁰He will have so many horses that they will cover you with dust. Your walls will shake because of the noise of his war horses, wagons and chariots. He will enter your gates, just as men enter a city whose walls have been broken through. ¹¹The hooves of his horses will pound in your streets. His swords will kill your people. Your strong pillars will fall to the ground. ¹²His men will take away from you your wealth and anything else you have. They will pull down your walls. They will completely destroy your fine houses. They will throw the stones and lumber of your broken-down buildings into the sea. ¹³I will put an end to your noisy songs. No one will hear the music of

your harps anymore. [14]I will turn you into nothing but a bare rock. You will become a place to spread fishnets. You will never be rebuilt. I have spoken. I am the LORD," announces the LORD and King.

[15]The LORD and King speaks to Tyre. He says, "The lands along the coast will shake because of the sound of your fall. Wounded people will groan because so many are dying there. [16]Then all the princes along the coast will step down from their thrones. They will put their robes away. They will take off their beautiful clothes. They will sit on the ground. They will put on terror as if it were their clothes. They will tremble with fear all the time. They will be shocked because of what has happened to you. [17]Then they will sing a song of sadness about you. They will say to you,

" 'Famous city, you have been
    completely destroyed!
  You were filled with sea traders.
You and your citizens
    were a mighty power on the seas.
You terrified everyone
    who lived in you.
[18] The lands along the coast trembled with
    fear
    when you fell.
The islands in the sea
    were terrified when you were
    destroyed.' "

[19]The LORD and King says to Tyre, "I will turn you into an empty city. You will be like cities where no one lives anymore. I will cause the ocean to sweep over you. Its mighty waters will cover you. [20]So I will bring you down together with those who go down into the grave. The people there lived long ago. You will have to live in the earth below. It will be like living in buildings that were destroyed many years ago. You will go down into the grave along with others. And you will never come back. You will not take your place in this world again. [21]I will bring you to a horrible end. You will be gone forever. People will look for you. But they will never find you," announces the LORD and King.

A Song of Sadness About Tyre

27 A message from the LORD came to me. The LORD said, [2]"Son of man, sing a song of sadness about Tyre. [3]It is located at the gateway to the Mediterranean Sea. It does business with nations on many coasts. Say to it, 'The LORD and King says,

" ' "Tyre, you say,
    'I am perfect and beautiful.'
[4] You were like a ship that ruled over the
    high seas.
  Your builders made you perfect and
    beautiful.
[5] They cut all your lumber
    from juniper trees on Mount
    Hermon.
They used a cedar tree from Lebanon
    to make a mast for you.
[6] They made your oars
    out of oak trees from Bashan.
They made your deck out of cypress
    wood
    from the coasts of Cyprus.
  They decorated it with ivory.
[7] Your sail was made out of beautiful
    Egyptian linen.
  It served as your banner.
Your shades were made out of blue and
    purple cloth.
  They were from the coasts of
    Elishah.
[8] Men from Sidon and Arvad manned
    your oars.
  Tyre, your sailors were skillful.
[9] Very skilled workers from Byblos were
    on board.
  They kept you waterproof.
All the ships on the sea and their sailors
    came up beside you.
  They brought their goods to trade
    for yours.

[10] " ' "Men from Persia, Lydia and Put
    served as soldiers in your army, city
    of Tyre.
They hung their shields and helmets on
    your walls.
  That brought glory to you.
[11] Men from Arvad and Helek
    guarded your walls on every side.
Men from Gammad
    were in your towers.
They hung their shields around your
    walls.
  They made you perfect and
    beautiful.

[12] " ' "Tarshish did business with you because you had so much wealth. They traded silver, iron, tin and lead for your goods.

13 " " "Greece, Tubal and Meshek did business with you. They traded human beings and bronze objects for your products.

14 " " "Men from Beth Togarmah traded chariot horses, war horses and mules for your goods.

15 " " "Men from Rhodes did business with you. Many lands along the coast bought goods from you. They paid you with ivory tusks and ebony wood.

16 " " "Aram did business with you because you had so many products for sale. They traded turquoise, purple cloth and needlework for your goods. They also traded fine linen, coral and rubies for them.

17 " " "Judah and Israel did business with you. They traded wheat from Minnith, sweets, honey, olive oil and lotion for your products.

18 " " "Damascus did business with you. That's because you had so many products and so much wealth. They traded to you wine from Helbon and wool from Zahar. 19 They also traded to you casks of wine from Izal. You traded to them wrought iron, cassia and calamus.

20 " " "Dedan traded saddle blankets to you.

21 " " "Arabia and all the princes of Kedar bought goods from you. They traded you lambs, rams and goats for them.

22 " " "Traders from Sheba and Raamah did business with you. They traded the finest spices, jewels and gold for your goods.

23 " " "Harran, Kanneh and Eden did business with you. So did traders from Sheba, Ashur and Kilmad. 24 In your market they traded beautiful clothes, blue cloth, and needlework to you. They also traded colorful rugs that had twisted cords and tight knots.

25 " " "The ships of Tarshish
   carry your products.
You are like a ship filled with a heavy load
   as you sail the sea.
26 The sailors who man your oars take you
   out to the high seas.
But the east wind will break you in pieces
   far out at sea.
27 You will be wrecked on that day.
   Your wealth, goods and products
   will sink deep into the sea.
So will your sailors, officers, carpenters,
   traders and all your soldiers.
   Anyone else on board will sink too.

28 The lands along the coast will shake
   when your sailors cry out.
29 All those who man the oars
   will desert their ships.
The sailors and all the officers
   will stand on the shore.
30 They will raise their voices.
   They will cry bitterly over you.
They will sprinkle dust on their heads.
   They will roll in ashes.
31 They will shave their heads because of
      you.
   And they will put on the clothes of
      sadness.
They will weep over you.
   Their spirits will be greatly troubled.
   They will be very sad.
32 As they weep and mourn over you,
   they will sing a song of sadness
      about you.
They will say, 'Who was ever like Tyre?
   It was destroyed in the sea.'
33 Your goods went out on the seas.
   You supplied many nations with
      what they needed.
You had so much wealth and so many
      products.
   You made the kings of the earth
      rich.
34 Now the sea has torn you apart.
   You have sunk deep down into it.
Your products and all your people
   have gone down with you.
35 All those who live in the lands along
      the coast
   are shocked because of what has
      happened to you.
Their kings tremble with fear.
   Their faces are twisted in horror.
36 The traders among the nations laugh at
      you.
   You have come to a horrible end.
   And you will be gone forever."'"

A Prophecy Against the King of Tyre

28 A message from the LORD came to me. The LORD said, 2 "Son of man, speak to Ethbaal. He is the ruler of Tyre. Tell him, 'The LORD and King says,

" " "In your proud heart
   you say, 'I am a god.
I sit on the throne of a god
   in the Mediterranean Sea.'
But you are only a human being. You
      are not a god.

In spite of that, you think you are as
    wise as a god.
3 Are you wiser than Daniel?
    Isn't even one secret hidden from
        you?
4 You are wise and understanding.
    So you have become very wealthy.
You have piled up gold and silver
    among your treasures.
5 You have used your great skill in
        trading
    to increase your wealth.
You are very rich.
    So your heart has become proud." ' "

6 The LORD and King says,

"You think you are wise.
    In fact, you claim to be as wise as a
        god.
7 So I am going to bring outsiders against
        you.
    They will not show you any pity at all.
They will use their swords against your
        beauty and wisdom.
    They will strike down your shining
        glory.
8 They will bring you down to the grave.
    You will die a horrible death
        in the middle of the sea.
9 Then will you say, 'I am a god'?
    Will you say that to those who kill
        you?
You will be only a human being to
        those who kill you.
    You will not be a god to them.
10 You will die just like those who have
        not been circumcised.
    Outsiders will kill you.

I have spoken," announces the LORD and
King.

11 A message from the LORD came to me.
The LORD said, 12 "Son of man, sing a song
of sadness about the king of Tyre. Tell him,
'The LORD and King says,

" ' "You were the model of perfection.
    You were full of wisdom.
    You were perfect and beautiful.
13 You were in Eden.
    It was my garden.
All kinds of jewels decorated you.
Here is a list of them.
    carnelian, chrysolite and emerald
    topaz, onyx and jasper
    lapis lazuli, turquoise and beryl

Your settings and mountings were
    made out of gold.
On the day you were created,
    they were prepared.
14 I appointed you to be like a guardian
        angel.
    I anointed you for that purpose.
You were on my holy mountain.
    You walked among the gleaming
        jewels.
15 Your conduct was without blame
    from the day you were created.
    But soon you began to sin.
16 You traded with many nations.
    You harmed people everywhere.
    And you sinned.
So I sent you away from my mountain
        in shame.
    Guardian angel, I drove you away
    from among the gleaming jewels.
17 You thought you were so handsome
    that it made your heart proud.
You thought you were so glorious
    that it spoiled your wisdom.
So I threw you down to the earth.
    I made an example out of you in
        front of kings.
18 Your many sins and dishonest trade
    made your holy places impure.
So I made you go up in flames.
    I turned you into nothing but ashes
        on the ground.
    I let everyone see it.
19 All the nations that knew you
    are shocked because of what
        happened to you.
You have come to a horrible end.
    And you will be gone forever." ' "

A Prophecy Against Sidon

20 A message from the LORD came to me.
The LORD said, 21 "Son of man, turn your
attention to the city of Sidon. Prophesy
against it. 22 Say, 'The LORD and King says,

" ' "Sidon, I am against your people.
    Among you I will display my glory.
I will punish your people.
    Among you I will prove that I am
        holy.
    Then you will know that I am the
        LORD.
23 I will send a plague on you.
    I will make blood flow in your
        streets.
Those who are killed will fall inside you.

Swords will strike your people on
    every side.
Then they will know that I am the
    LORD.

²⁴"'"The people of Israel will no longer
have neighbors who hate them. Those
neighbors will not be like sharp and painful
thorns anymore. Then Israel will know that
I am the LORD and King."'"

²⁵The LORD and King says, "I will gather
the people of Israel together from the nations
where they have been scattered. That will
prove that I am holy. I will let the nations see
it. Then Israel will live in their own land. I
gave it to my servant Jacob. ²⁶My people will
live there in safety. They will build houses.
They will plant vineyards. They will live in
safety. I will punish all their neighbors who
told lies about them. Then Israel will know
that I am the LORD their God."

A Prophecy Against Egypt

29 It was the tenth year since King Jehoiachin had been brought to Babylon as a prisoner. On the 12th day of the
tenth month, a message from the LORD
came to me. The LORD said, ²"Son of man,
turn your attention to Pharaoh Hophra. He
is king of Egypt. Prophesy against him and
the whole land of Egypt. ³Tell him, 'The
LORD and King says,

"'"Pharaoh Hophra, I am against you.
    King of Egypt, you are like a huge
        monster
    lying among your streams.
You say, 'The Nile River belongs to me.
    I made it for myself.'
⁴ But I will put hooks in your jaws.
    I will make the fish in your streams
        stick to your scales.
I will pull you out from among your
        streams.
    All the fish will stick to your scales.
⁵ I will leave you out in the desert.
    All the fish in your streams
    will be there with you.
You will fall down in an open field.
    You will not be picked up.
I will feed you to the wild animals
    and to the birds in the sky.

⁶Then everyone who lives in Egypt will
know that I am the LORD.

"'"You have been like a walking stick
made out of a papyrus stem. The people of

Israel tried to lean on you. ⁷They took hold
of you. But you broke under their weight.
You tore open their shoulders. The people
of Israel leaned on you. But you snapped in
two. And their backs were broken."'"

⁸So the LORD and King says, "I will send
Nebuchadnezzar's sword against you. He
will kill people and animals alike. ⁹Egypt
will become a dry and empty desert. Then
your people will know that I am the LORD.

"You said, 'The Nile River belongs to me.
I made it for myself.' ¹⁰So I am against you
and your streams. I will destroy the land of
Egypt. I will turn it into a dry and empty
desert from Migdol all the way to Aswan. I
will destroy everything as far as the border
of Cush. ¹¹No people or animals will travel
through Egypt. No one will even live there
for 40 years. ¹²Egypt will be more empty
than any other land. Its destroyed cities
will lie empty for 40 years. I will scatter the
people of Egypt among the nations. I will
send them to other countries."

¹³But here is what the LORD and King
says. "At the end of 40 years I will gather the
Egyptians together. I will bring them back
from the nations where they were scat-
tered. ¹⁴I will bring them back from where
they were taken as prisoners. I will return
them to Upper Egypt. That is where their
families came from. There they will be an
unimportant kingdom. ¹⁵Egypt will be the
least important kingdom of all. It will never
place itself above the other nations again. I
will make it very weak. Then it will never
again rule over the nations. ¹⁶The people of
Israel will no longer trust in Egypt. Instead,
Egypt will remind them of how they sinned
when they turned to it for help. Then they
will know that I am the LORD and King."

¹⁷It was the 27th year since King Jehoia-
chin had been brought to Babylon as a prisoner. On the first day of the first month, a
message from the LORD came to me. Here
is what the LORD said. ¹⁸"Son of man, King
Nebuchadnezzar drove his army in a hard
military campaign. The campaign was
against Tyre. Their helmets rubbed their
heads bare. The heavy loads they carried
made their shoulders raw. But he and his
army did not gain anything from the cam-
paign he led against Tyre. ¹⁹So I am going to
give Egypt to Nebuchadnezzar, the king of
Babylon. He will carry off its wealth. He will
take away anything else they have. He will

give it to his army. ²⁰I have given Egypt to him as a reward for his efforts. After all, he and his army attacked Egypt because I told them to," announces the LORD and King.

²¹"When Nebuchadnezzar wins the battle over Egypt, I will make the Israelites strong again. Ezekiel, I will open your mouth. And you will be able to speak to them. Then they will know that I am the LORD."

30 A message from the LORD came to me. The LORD said, ²"Son of man, prophesy. Say, 'The LORD and King says,

"'"Cry out,
'A terrible day is coming!'
³ The day is near.
    The day of the LORD is coming.
It will be a cloudy day.
    The nations have been sentenced
      to die.
⁴ I will send Nebuchadnezzar's sword
      against Egypt.
Cush will suffer terribly.
Many will die in Egypt.
    Then its wealth will be carried away.
    Its foundations will be torn down.

⁵The people of Cush, Libya, Lydia, Kub and the whole land of Arabia will be killed by swords. So will the Jews who live in Egypt. They went there from the covenant land of Israel. And the Egyptians will die too."'"

⁶The LORD says,

"Those who were going to help Egypt
    will die.
The strength Egypt was so proud of
    will fail.
Its people will be killed by swords
    from Migdol all the way to Aswan,"
announces the LORD and King.
⁷ "Egypt will be more empty than any
    other land.
Its cities will be completely
    destroyed.
⁸ I will set Egypt on fire.
All those who came to help it will be
    crushed.
Then they will know that I am the
    LORD.

⁹"At that time I will send messengers out in ships. They will terrify the people of Cush who are so contented. Cush will suffer greatly when Egypt falls. And you can be sure it will fall."

¹⁰The LORD and King says,

"I will put an end to the huge armies of
    Egypt.
I will use Nebuchadnezzar, the king
    of Babylon, to do this.
¹¹ He and his armies will attack the land
    and destroy it.
They will not show its people any
    pity at all.
They will use their swords against Egypt.
    They will fill the land with dead
    bodies.
¹² I will dry up the waters of the Nile
    River.
I will sell the land to an evil nation.
I will use the power of outsiders
    to destroy the land and everything
    in it.

I have spoken. I am the LORD."

¹³The LORD and King says,

"I will destroy the statues of Egypt's
    gods.
I will put an end to the gods
    the people in Memphis worship.
Egypt will not have princes anymore.
I will spread fear all through the
    land.
¹⁴ I will completely destroy Upper Egypt.
I will set Zoan on fire.
I will punish Thebes.
¹⁵ I will pour out my burning anger on
    Pelusium.
It is a fort in eastern Egypt.
I will wipe out the huge army of
    Thebes.
¹⁶ I will set Egypt on fire.
Pelusium will groan with terrible
    pain.
Thebes will be ripped apart.
Memphis will suffer greatly
    because of everything that happens.
¹⁷ The young men of Heliopolis and
    Bubastis
    will be killed by swords.
Their people will be taken away as
    prisoners.
¹⁸ I will break Egypt's power over other
    lands.
That will be a dark day for
    Tahpanhes.
There the strength Egypt was so
    proud of
will come to an end.

Egypt will be covered with clouds.
The people in its villages
will be taken away as prisoners.
¹⁹ So I will punish Egypt.
Then they will know that I am the
LORD.”

²⁰It was the 11th year since King Jehoiachin had been brought to Babylon as a prisoner. On the seventh day of the first month,
a message from the LORD came to me. The
LORD said, ²¹“Son of man, I have broken the
powerful arm of Pharaoh Hophra, the king
of Egypt. No bandages have been put on his
arm to heal it. It has not been put in a cast.
So his arm will not be strong enough to use
a sword. ²²I am against Pharaoh, the king
of Egypt. I will break both his arms. I will
break his healthy arm and his broken one.
His sword will fall from his hand. ²³I will
scatter the people of Egypt among the nations. I will send them to other countries. ²⁴I
will make the arms of the king of Babylon
stronger. I will put my sword in his hand.
But I will break the arms of Pharaoh. And
he will groan in front of Nebuchadnezzar.
He will cry out like someone dying from his
wounds. ²⁵I will make the arms of the king
of Babylon stronger. But the arms of Pharaoh will not be able to help Egypt. I will put
my sword in Nebuchadnezzar's hand. He
will get ready to use it against Egypt. Then
they will know that I am the LORD. ²⁶I will
scatter the Egyptians among the nations.
I will send them to other countries. Then
they will know that I am the LORD.”

31 It was the 11th year since King Jehoiachin had been brought to Babylon
as a prisoner. On the first day of the third
month, a message from the LORD came to
me. The LORD said, ²“Son of man, speak to
Pharaoh Hophra, the king of Egypt. Also
speak to his huge army. Tell him,

“‘Who can be compared with your
        majesty?
³   Think about what happened to
        Assyria.
    Once it was like a cedar tree in
        Lebanon.
    It had beautiful branches
        that provided shade for the forest.
    It grew very high.
        Its top was above all the leaves.
⁴ The waters fed it.
    Deep springs made it grow tall.

Their streams flowed
    all around its base.
They made their way
    to all the trees in the fields.
⁵ So it grew higher
    than any other tree in the fields.
It grew more limbs.
    Its branches grew long.
    They spread because they had plenty
        of water.
⁶ All the birds in the sky
    made their nests in its limbs.
All the wild animals
    had their babies under its branches.
All the great nations
    lived in its shade.
⁷ Its spreading branches
    made it majestic and beautiful.
Its roots went down deep
    to where there was plenty of water.
⁸ The cedar trees in my garden
    were no match for it.
The juniper trees
    could not equal its limbs.
The plane trees
    could not compare with its branches.
No tree in my garden
    could match its beauty.
⁹ I gave it many branches.
    They made it beautiful.
All the trees in my Garden of Eden
    were jealous of it.’”

¹⁰So the LORD and King says, “The great
cedar tree grew very high. Its top was above
all the leaves. It was proud of how tall it was.
¹¹So I handed it over to the Babylonian ruler of the nations. I wanted him to punish it
because it was so evil. I decided to get rid of
it. ¹²The Babylonians cut it down and left it
there. They did not show it any pity at all.
Some of its branches fell on the mountains.
Others fell in all the valleys. The branches
lay broken in all the stream beds in the land.
All the nations on earth came out from under its shade. And they went on their way.
¹³All the birds settled on the fallen tree. All
the wild animals lived among its branches.
¹⁴So trees that receive plenty of water must
never grow so high that it makes them
proud. Their tops must never be above the
rest of the leaves. No other trees that receive
a lot of water must ever grow that high.
They are appointed to die and go down into
the earth below. They will join human beings, who go down to the place of the dead.”

¹⁵The Lord and King says, "Assyria was like a cedar tree. But I brought it down to the place of the dead. On that day I dried up the deep springs of water and covered them. I held its streams back. I shut off its rich supply of water. Because of that, Lebanon was dressed in gloom as if it were clothes. All the trees in the fields dried up. ¹⁶I brought the cedar tree down to the place of the dead. It joined the other nations that go down there. I made the nations on earth shake because of the sound of its fall. Then all the trees of Eden were comforted in the earth below. That included the finest and best trees in Lebanon. And it included all the trees that received plenty of water. ¹⁷Others also went down along with the cedar tree into the place of the dead. They included those who had been killed by swords. They also included the armed men among the nations who lived in its shade.

¹⁸"Which one of the trees of Eden can be compared with you? What tree is as glorious and majestic as you are? But you too will be brought down to the earth below. There you will join the trees of Eden. You will lie down with those who have not been circumcised. You will be among those who were killed by swords.

"That is what will happen to Pharaoh and his huge armies," announces the Lord and King.

32 It was the 12th year since King Jehoiachin had been brought to Babylon as a prisoner. On the first day of the 12th month, a message from the Lord came to me. The Lord said, ²"Son of man, sing a song of sadness about Pharaoh Hophra, the king of Egypt. Tell him,

" 'You are like a lion among the nations.
    You are like a monster in the sea.
You move around wildly in your rivers.
    You churn the water with your feet.
    You make the streams muddy.' "

³The Lord and King says,

"I will use a large crowd of people
    to throw my net over you.
    They will pull you up in it.
⁴ Then I will throw you on the land.
    I will toss you into an open field.
I will let all the birds in the sky settle
    on you.
    I will let all the wild animals eat you
    up.

⁵ I will scatter the parts of your body all
    over the mountains.
    I will fill the valleys with your
    remains.
⁶ I will soak the land with your blood.
    It will flow all the way to the
    mountains.
    The valleys will be filled with the
    parts of your body.
⁷ When I wipe you out,
    I will put a cover over the heavens.
    I will darken the stars.
I will cover the sun with a cloud.
    The moon will stop shining.
⁸ I will darken all the bright lights
    in the sky above you.
I will bring darkness over your land,"
    announces the Lord and King.
⁹ "The hearts of many people will be
    troubled.
    That is because I will destroy you
    among the nations.
    You had never known anything
    about those lands before.
¹⁰ Many nations will be shocked
    when they see what has happened
    to you.
Their kings will tremble with fear
    when they find out about it.
I will get ready to use Nebuchadnezzar
    as my sword against them.
On the day you fall from power,
    each of the kings will tremble with
    fear.
    Each will be afraid he is the next to
    die."

¹¹The Lord and King says,

"I will send against you
    the sword of the king of Babylon.
¹² I will destroy your huge army.
    They will be killed by the swords
    of Babylon's mighty soldiers.
The soldiers will not show them any
    pity.
    They will bring Egypt down in all its
    pride.
    Its huge armies will be thrown down.
¹³ I will destroy all its cattle
    from the places where they have
    plenty of water.
Human feet will never stir up the water
    again.
    The hooves of cattle will not make it
    muddy anymore.

¹⁴ I will let the waters of Egypt settle.
  I will make its streams flow like olive
    oil,"
  announces the LORD and King.
¹⁵ "I will turn Egypt into an empty land.
  I will strip away everything in it.
  I will strike down everyone who lives
    there.
  Then they will know that I am the
    LORD.

¹⁶"That is the song of sadness people will sing about Egypt. Women from other nations will sing it. They will weep over Egypt and its huge armies," announces the LORD and King.

¹⁷A message from the LORD came to me. King Jehoiachin had been brought to Babylon as a prisoner. On the 15th day of a month 12 years after that, the message came. The LORD said, ¹⁸"Son of man, weep over the huge army of Egypt. Tell the Egyptians they will go down into the earth below. The women singers from the other mighty nations will go down into the grave along with them and others. ¹⁹Tell them, 'Are you any better than others? Since you are not, go down there. Lie down with those who have not been circumcised.' ²⁰They will fall dead among those who were killed by swords. Nebuchadnezzar is ready to use his sword against them. Let Egypt be dragged off together with its huge armies. ²¹The mighty leaders who are already in the place of the dead will talk about Egypt. They will also speak about the nations that were going to help it. They will say, 'They have come down here. They are lying down with those who had not been circumcised. They are here with those who were killed by swords.'

²²"Assyria is there with its whole army. Its king is surrounded by the graves of all its people who were killed by swords. ²³Their graves are deep down in the pit. Assyria's army lies around the grave of its king. All those who spread terror while they were alive are now dead. They were killed by swords.

²⁴"Elam is also there. Its huge armies lie around the grave of its king. All those who spread terror while they were alive are now dead. They were killed by swords. They had not been circumcised. They went down into the earth below. Their shame is like the shame of others who go down into the grave. ²⁵A bed is made for Elam's

king among the dead. His huge armies lie around his grave. They had not been circumcised. They were killed by swords. They had spread terror while they were alive. So now their shame is like the shame of others who go down into the grave. They lie down among the dead.

²⁶"Meshek and Tubal are also there. Their huge armies lie around the graves of their kings. None of them had been circumcised. They had spread their terror while they were alive. So they were killed by swords. ²⁷But they do not lie down with the other dead soldiers of long ago. Those soldiers and their weapons had gone down into the place of the dead. Their swords had been placed under their heads. Their shields rest on their bones. The soldiers of Meshek and Tubal do not lie down with them. This is true even though they had also spread terror while they were alive.

²⁸"Pharaoh Hophra, you too will be broken. You will lie down among those who had not been circumcised. You will be there with those who were killed by swords.

²⁹"Edom is also there. So are its kings and all its princes. In spite of their power, they lie down with those who were killed by swords. They lie down with those who had not been circumcised. They are there with others who went down into the grave.

³⁰"All the princes of the north are there too. So are all the people of Sidon. They went down into the grave in dishonor. While they were alive, they used their power to spread terror. They had never been circumcised. But now they lie down there with those who were killed by swords. Their shame is like the shame of others who go down into the grave.

³¹"Pharaoh and his whole army will see all of them. That will comfort him even though his huge armies were killed by swords." This is what the LORD and King announces. ³²"I let Pharaoh spread terror while he was alive. But now he and his huge armies will be buried with those who had not been circumcised. They will lie down there with those who were killed by swords," announces the LORD and King.

The LORD Again Appoints Ezekiel to Warn Israel

33 A message from the LORD came to me. The LORD said, ²"Son of man, speak to your people. Tell them, 'Suppose I send enemies against a land. And its people choose one of their men to stand guard. ³He sees the enemies coming against the land. He blows a trumpet to warn the people. ⁴Someone hears the trumpet. But they do not pay any attention to the warning. The enemies come and kill them. Then what happens to them will be their own fault. ⁵They heard the sound of the trumpet. But they did not pay any attention to the warning. So what happened to them was their own fault. If they had paid attention, they would have saved themselves. ⁶But suppose the guard sees the enemies coming. And he does not blow the trumpet to warn the people. The enemies come and kill one of them. Then their life has been taken away from them because they sinned. But I will hold the guard responsible for their death.'

⁷"Son of man, I have appointed you as a prophet to warn the people of Israel. So listen to my message. Give them a warning from me. ⁸Suppose I say to a sinful person, 'You can be sure that you will die.' And suppose you do not try to get them to change their ways. Then they will die because they have sinned. And I will hold you responsible for their death. ⁹But suppose you do warn that sinful person. You tell them to change their ways. But they do not change. Then they will die because they have sinned. But you will have saved yourself.

¹⁰"Son of man, speak to the Israelites. Tell them, 'You are saying, "Our sins and the wrong things we have done weigh us down. We are wasting away because we have sinned so much. So how can we live?"' ¹¹Tell them, 'When sinful people die, it does not give me any joy. But when they turn away from their sins and live, that makes me very happy. And that is just as sure as I am alive,' announces the Lord and King. 'So turn away from your sins! Change your evil ways! Why should you die, people of Israel?'

¹²"Son of man, speak to your people. Tell them, 'Suppose a godly person does not obey the Lord. Then the right things that person has done in the past count for nothing. Suppose a sinful person turns away from doing wrong things. Then the wrong things that person has done in the past won't bring them judgment. A godly person who sins won't be allowed to live.

That's true even though they used to do right things.' ¹³Suppose I tell a godly person that they will live. And they trust in the fact that they used to do what is right. But now they do what is evil. Then I will not remember any of the right things they have done. They will die because they have done so many evil things. ¹⁴Suppose I say to a sinful person, 'You can be sure you will die.' And then they turn away from their sin. They do what is fair and right. ¹⁵They return things they take to make sure loans are repaid. They give back what they have stolen. They obey my rules that give life. They do not do what is evil. Then you can be sure they will live. They will not die. ¹⁶None of the sins they have committed will be held against them. They have done what is fair and right. So you can be sure they will live.

¹⁷"In spite of that, your people say, 'What the Lord does isn't fair.' But it is what you do that is not fair. ¹⁸Suppose a godly person stops doing what is right. And they do what is evil. Then they will die because of it. ¹⁹But suppose a sinful person turns away from the evil things they have done. And they do what is fair and right. Then they will live by doing that. ²⁰In spite of that, you Israelites say, 'What the Lord does isn't fair.' But I will judge each of you based on how you have lived."

The Lord Explains Why Jerusalem Fell

²¹It was the 12th year since we had been brought to Babylon as prisoners. On the fifth day of the tenth month, a man who had escaped from Jerusalem came to bring me a report. He said, "The city has fallen!" ²²The evening before the man arrived, the power of the Lord came on me. He opened my mouth before the man came to me in the morning. So my mouth was opened. I was no longer silent.

²³Then a message from the Lord came to me. The Lord said, ²⁴"Son of man, here is what the people living in Israel's broken-down buildings are saying. 'Abraham was only one man. But he owned the land. We are many people. The land must certainly belong to us.' ²⁵So tell them, 'The Lord and King says, "You eat meat that still has blood in it. You worship your statues of gods. You commit murder. So should you still possess the land? ²⁶You depend on your swords. You do things I hate. Each one of you sleeps

with your neighbor's wife. So should you still possess the land?"'

²⁷"Tell them, 'Here is what the LORD and King says. "The people who are left in those broken-down buildings will be killed by swords. Wild animals will eat up those who are out in the country. Those who are in caves and other safe places will die of a plague. And that is just as sure as I am alive. ²⁸I will turn the land into a dry and empty desert. The strength Jerusalem is so proud of will come to an end. The mountains of Israel will be deserted. No one will travel across them. ²⁹So I will turn the land into a dry and empty desert. I will punish my people because of all the evil things they have done. I hate those things. Then they will know that I am the LORD."'

³⁰"Son of man, your people are talking about you. They are getting together by the walls of their houses and at their doors. They are saying to one another, 'Come. Listen to the LORD's message.' ³¹My people come to you, just as they usually do. They sit in front of you. They hear what you say. But they do not put it into practice. With their mouths they say they love me. But in their hearts they want what belongs to others. They try to get rich by cheating them. ³²You are nothing more to them than someone who sings love songs. They say you have a beautiful voice. They think you play an instrument well. They hear what you say. But they do not put it into practice.

³³"Everything I have told you will come true. You can be sure of it. Then the people will know that a prophet has been among them."

The Lord Will Be the Shepherd of His People

34 A message from the LORD came to me. The LORD said, ²"Son of man, prophesy against the shepherds of Israel. Tell them, 'The LORD and King says, "How terrible it will be for you shepherds of Israel! You only take care of yourselves. You should take good care of your flocks. ³Instead, you eat the butter. You dress yourselves with the wool. You kill the finest animals. But you do not take care of your flocks. ⁴You have not made the weak ones in the flock stronger. You have not healed the sick. You have not bandaged those who are hurt. You have not brought back those who have wandered away. You have not searched for the lost. When you ruled over them, you were mean to them. You treated them badly. ⁵So they were scattered because they did not have a shepherd. They became food for all of the wild animals. ⁶My sheep wandered all over the mountains and high hills. They were scattered over the whole earth. No one searched for them. No one looked for them."

⁷"'Shepherds, listen to the LORD's message. He says, ⁸"My flock does not have a shepherd. Many of my sheep have been stolen. They have become food for all the wild animals. My shepherds did not care for my sheep. They did not even search for them. Instead, they only took care of themselves. And that is just as sure as I am alive," announces the LORD and King. ⁹Shepherds, listen to the LORD's message. ¹⁰The LORD and King says, "I am against the shepherds. I will hold them responsible for my flock. I will stop them from taking care of the flock. Then they will not be able to feed themselves anymore. I will save my flock from their mouths. My sheep will no longer be food for them."'"

¹¹The LORD and King says, "I myself will search for my sheep. I will look after them. ¹²A shepherd looks after his scattered flock when he is with them. And I will look after my sheep. I will save them from all the places where they were scattered on a dark and cloudy day. ¹³I will bring them out from among the nations. I will gather them together from other countries. I will bring them into their own land. There they will eat grass on the mountains and in the valleys. And they will eat in all the fields of Israel. ¹⁴I will take care of them in the best grasslands. They will eat grass on the highest mountains of Israel. There they will lie down in the finest grasslands. They will eat grass in the best places on Israel's mountains. ¹⁵I myself will take care of my sheep. I will let them lie down in safety," announces the LORD and King. ¹⁶"I will search for the lost. I will bring back those who have wandered away. I will bandage the ones who are hurt. I will make the weak ones stronger. But I will destroy those who are fat and strong. I will take good care of my sheep. I will treat them fairly."

¹⁷The LORD and King says, "You are my flock. I will judge between one sheep and another. I will judge between rams and

goats. ¹⁸You already eat in the best grasslands. Must you also stomp all over the other fields? You already drink clear water. Must you also make the rest of the water muddy with your feet? ¹⁹Must my flock have to eat the grass you have stomped on? Must they drink the water you have made muddy?"

²⁰So the Lord and King speaks to them. He says, "I myself will judge between the fat sheep and the skinny sheep. ²¹You push the other sheep around with your hips and shoulders. You use your horns to butt all the weak sheep. Finally, you drive them away. ²²But I will save my sheep. They will not be carried off anymore. I will judge between one sheep and another. ²³I will place one shepherd over them. He will belong to the family line of my servant David. He will take good care of them. He will look after them. He will be their shepherd. ²⁴I am the Lord. I will be their God. And my servant from David's family line will be the prince among them. I have spoken. I am the Lord.

²⁵"I will make a covenant with them. It promises to give them peace. I will get rid of the wild animals in the land. Then my sheep can live safely in the desert. They can sleep in the forests. ²⁶I will make them and the places surrounding my holy mountain of Zion a blessing. I will send down rain at the right time. There will be showers of blessing. ²⁷The trees will bear their fruit. And the ground will produce its crops. The people will be secure in their land. I will break the chains that hold them. I will save them from the power of those who made them slaves. Then they will know that I am the Lord. ²⁸The nations will not carry them off anymore. Wild animals will no longer eat them up. They will live in safety. And no one will make them afraid. ²⁹I will give them a land that is famous for its crops. They will never again be hungry there. The nations will not make fun of them anymore. ³⁰Then they will know that I am with them. I am the Lord their God. And the Israelites will know that they are my people," announces the Lord and King. ³¹"You are my sheep. You belong to my flock. And I am your God," announces the Lord and King.

A Prophecy Against Edom

35 A message from the Lord came to me. The Lord said, ²"Son of man, turn your attention to Mount Seir. Prophesy against it.

³Tell it, 'The Lord and King says, "Mount Seir, I am against you. I will reach out my powerful hand against you. I will turn you into a dry and empty desert. ⁴I will destroy your towns. Your land will become empty. Then you will know that I am the Lord.

⁵"'"People of Edom, you have been Israel's enemies for a long time. You let many Israelites be killed by swords when they were in great trouble. At that time I used Nebuchadnezzar to punish them and destroy them completely. ⁶Now I will hand you over to murderers. They will hunt you down. You murdered others. So murderers will chase you. And that is just as sure as I am alive," announces the Lord and King. ⁷"I will turn Mount Seir into a dry and empty desert. No one will be able to go anywhere or do anything there. ⁸I will fill your mountains with dead bodies. Some of those who are killed by swords will fall down dead on your hills. Others will die in your valleys and in all your canyons. ⁹I will make your land empty forever. No one will live in your towns. Then you will know that I am the Lord.

¹⁰"'"You said, 'The nations of Israel and Judah will belong to us. We will take them over.' You said that, even though I was there. I am the Lord. ¹¹You were full of anger, jealousy and hatred toward my people. So I will punish you. When I judge you, they will know that I am the Lord. And that is just as sure as I am alive," announces the Lord and King. ¹²"You will know that I have heard all the terrible things you said. You said them about those who live in the mountains of Israel. You made fun of them. You said, 'They have been destroyed. They've been handed over to us. Let's wipe them out.' ¹³You bragged that you were better than I am. You spoke against me. You did not hold anything back. But I heard it."'" ¹⁴The Lord and King says, "The whole earth will be glad. But I will make your land empty. ¹⁵You were happy when the land of Israel became empty. So I will treat you in the same way. Mount Seir, you will be empty. So will the whole land of Edom. Then you will know that I am the Lord."

A Prophecy of Hope for the Mountains of Israel

36 "Son of man, prophesy to the mountains of Israel. Tell them, 'Mountains of Israel, listen to the Lord's message. ²The

LORD and King says, "Your enemies made fun of you. They bragged, 'The hills you lived in for a long time belong to us now.'"'

³Ezekiel, prophesy. Say, 'The LORD and King says, "Your enemies destroyed you. They crushed you from every side. So the rest of the nations took over your land. People talked about you. They told lies about you."'" ⁴Mountains of Israel, listen to the message of the LORD and King. He speaks to you mountains, hills, canyons and valleys. He speaks to you destroyed cities and deserted towns. The rest of the nations around you took away from you everything of value. They made fun of you. ⁵So the LORD and King says, "I am very angry with those nations. I have spoken against them and the whole land of Edom. They were very happy when they took over my land. Deep down inside them, they hated Israel. They wanted to take its grasslands. ⁶Ezekiel, prophesy about the land of Israel. Speak to the mountains, hills, canyons and valleys. Tell them, 'The LORD and King says, "I have a jealous anger against the nations. They have laughed at you." ⁷So the LORD and King says, "I raise my hand and make a promise. I promise that the nations around you will also be laughed at.

⁸"'"Mountains of Israel, you will produce branches and bear fruit for my people Israel. They will come home soon. ⁹I am concerned about you. I will do good things for you. Farmers will plow your ground. They will plant seeds in it. ¹⁰I will cause many people to live in Israel. The towns will no longer be empty. Their broken-down houses will be rebuilt. ¹¹I will cause many people and animals to live in you, Israel. They will have many babies. I will cause people to make their homes in your towns, just as I did in the past. I will help you succeed more than ever before. Then you will know that I am the LORD. ¹²I will let my people Israel live there again. They will possess you. They will receive you as their own. You will never take their children away from them again."'"

¹³The LORD and King says, "People say to you mountains, 'You destroy people. You let your nation's children be taken away.' ¹⁴But I will not let you destroy people anymore. I will no longer let your nation's children be taken away," announces the LORD and King. ¹⁵"You will not have to listen to the nations laughing at you anymore. People will no longer make fun of you. You will not let your nation fall," announces the LORD and King.

Israel Will Surely Be Rebuilt

¹⁶Another message from the LORD came to me. The LORD said, ¹⁷"Son of man, the people of Israel used to live in their own land. But they made it 'unclean' because of how they acted and the way they lived. To me they were 'unclean' like a woman having her monthly period. ¹⁸They spilled people's blood in the land. They made the land 'unclean' by worshiping other gods. So I poured out my great anger on them. ¹⁹I scattered them among the nations. I sent them to other countries. I judged them based on how they acted and on how they lived. ²⁰They treated my name as if it were not holy. They did it everywhere they went among the nations. People said about them, 'They are the LORD's people. But they were forced to leave his land.' ²¹I was concerned about my holy name. The people of Israel treated it as if it were not holy. They did it everywhere they went among the nations.

²²"So tell the Israelites, 'The LORD and King speaks. He says, "People of Israel, I will not take action for your benefit. Instead, I will act for the honor of my holy name. You have treated it as if it were not holy. You did it everywhere you went among the nations. ²³But I will show everyone how holy my great name is. You have treated it as if it were not holy. So I will use you to prove to the nations how holy I am. Then they will know that I am the LORD," announces the LORD and King.

²⁴"'"I will take you out of the nations. I will gather you together from all the countries. I will bring you back into your own land. ²⁵I will sprinkle pure water on you. Then you will be 'clean.' I will make you completely pure and 'clean.' I will take all the statues of your gods away from you. ²⁶I will give you new hearts. I will give you a new spirit that is faithful to me. I will remove your stubborn hearts from you. I will give you hearts that obey me. ²⁷I will put my Spirit in you. I will make you want to obey my rules. I want you to be careful to keep my laws. ²⁸Then you will live in the land I gave your people of long ago. You will be my people. And I will be your God. ²⁹I will

save you from all your 'uncleanness.' I will give you plenty of grain. You will have more than enough. So you will never be hungry again. ³⁰I will multiply the fruit on your trees. I will increase the crops in your fields. Then the nations will no longer make fun of you because you are hungry. ³¹You will remember your evil ways and the sinful things you have done. You will hate yourselves because you have sinned so much. I also hate your evil practices. ³²I want you to know that I am not doing those things for your benefit," announces the LORD and King. "People of Israel, you should be ashamed of yourselves! Your conduct has brought dishonor to you."'"

³³The LORD and King says, "I will make you pure from all your sins. On that day I will give you homes in your towns again. Your broken-down houses will be rebuilt. ³⁴The dry and empty land will be farmed again. Everyone who passes through it will see that it is no longer empty. ³⁵They will say, 'This land was completely destroyed. But now it's like the Garden of Eden. The cities were full of broken-down buildings. They were destroyed and empty. But now they have high walls around them. And people live in them.' ³⁶Then the nations that remain around you will know that I have rebuilt what was once destroyed. I have planted again the fields that were once empty. I have spoken. And I will do this. I am the LORD."

³⁷The LORD and King says, "Once again I will answer Israel's prayer. Here is what I will do for them. I will multiply them as if they were sheep. ³⁸Large flocks of animals are sacrificed at Jerusalem during the appointed feasts there. In the same way, the destroyed cities will be filled with flocks of people. Then they will know that I am the LORD."

The Valley of Dry Bones

37 The power of the LORD came on me. His Spirit brought me away from my home. He put me down in the middle of a valley. It was full of bones. ²He led me back and forth among them. I saw a huge number of bones in the valley. The bones were very dry. ³The LORD asked me, "Son of man, can these bones live?"

I said, "LORD and King, you are the only one who knows."

Ezek. 37:1–14 A newborn baby has 300 bones. But as a child grows, the bones fuse which is why an adult has only 206. Okay, okay, I have to tell a joke. Ready? What does a skeleton order at a restaurant? Any guesses? The answer is "Spare ribs!" Get it?!

⁴Then he said to me, "Prophesy to these bones. Tell them, 'Dry bones, listen to the LORD's message. ⁵The LORD and King speaks to you. He says, "I will put breath in you. Then you will come to life again. ⁶I will attach tendons to you. I will put flesh on you. I will cover you with skin. So I will put breath in you. And you will come to life again. Then you will know that I am the LORD."'"

⁷So I prophesied just as the LORD commanded me to. As I was prophesying, I heard a noise. It was a rattling sound. The bones came together. One bone connected itself to another. ⁸I saw tendons and flesh appear on them. Skin covered them. But there was no breath in them.

⁹Then the LORD said to me, "Prophesy to the breath. Prophesy, son of man. Tell it, 'The LORD and King says, "Breath, come from all four directions. Go into these people who have been killed. Then they can live."'" ¹⁰So I prophesied just as he commanded me to. And breath entered them. Then they came to life again. They stood up on their feet. They were like a huge army.

¹¹Then the LORD said to me, "Son of man, these bones stand for all the people of Israel. The people say, 'Our bones are dried up. We've lost all hope. We are destroyed.' ¹²So prophesy. Tell them, 'The LORD and King says, "My people, I am going to open up your graves. I am going to bring you out

of them. I will take you back to the land of Israel. [13]So I will open up your graves and bring you out of them. Then you will know that I am the LORD. You are my people. [14]I will put my Spirit in you. And you will live again. I will settle you in your own land. Then you will know that I have spoken. I have done it," announces the LORD.'"

Israel Will Be One Nation Under One King

[15]A message from the LORD came to me. The LORD said, [16]"Son of man, get a stick of wood. Write on it, 'Belonging to the tribe of Judah and the Israelites who are connected with it.' Then get another stick. Write on it, 'Ephraim's stick. Belonging to the tribes of Joseph and all the Israelites connected with them.' [17]Join them together into one stick in your hand.

[18]"Your people will ask you, 'What do you mean by this?' [19]Tell them, 'The LORD and King says, "I am going to get the stick of Joseph and the Israelites connected with it. That stick is in Ephraim's hand. I am going to join it to Judah's stick. I will make them a single stick of wood in my hand."' [20]Show them the sticks you wrote on. [21]Tell them, 'The LORD and King says, "I will take the Israelites out of the nations where they have gone. I will gather them together from all around. I will bring them back to their own land. [22]There I will make them one nation. They will live on the mountains of Israel. All of them will have one king. They will never be two nations again. They will never again be separated into two kingdoms. [23]They will no longer make themselves 'unclean' by worshiping any of their evil gods. They will not do wrong things anymore. They always turn away from me. But I will save them from that sin. I will make them pure and 'clean.' They will be my people. And I will be their God.

[24]"'A man who belongs to the family line of my servant David will be their king. All of them will have one shepherd. They will obey my laws. And they will be careful to keep my rules. [25]They will live in the land I gave to my servant Jacob. That is where your people of long ago lived. They, their children, their children's children, and their children after them will live there forever. And my servant from David's family line will be their prince forever. [26]I will make

a covenant with them. It promises to give them peace. The covenant will last forever. I will make them my people. And I will cause there to be many of them. I will put my temple among them forever. [27]I will live with them. I will be their God. And they will be my people. [28]My temple will be among them forever. Then the nations will know that I make Israel holy. I am the LORD."'"

The LORD Will Have Great Victory Over the Nations

38 A message from the LORD came to me. The LORD said, [2]"Son of man, turn your attention to Gog. He is from the land of Magog. He is the chief prince of Meshek and Tubal. Prophesy against him. [3]Tell him, 'The LORD and King says, "Gog, I am against you. You are the chief prince of Meshek and Tubal. [4]But I will turn you around. I will put hooks in your jaws. I will bring you out of your land along with your whole army. Your horses will come with you. Your horsemen will be completely armed. Your huge army will carry large and small shields. All of them will be ready to use their swords. [5]The men of Persia, Cush and Put will march out with them. All of them will have shields and helmets. [6]Gomer and all its troops will be there too. Beth Togarmah from the far north will also come with all its troops. Many nations will help you.

[7]"'Get ready. Be prepared. Take command of the huge armies gathered around you. [8]After many years you will be called together to fight. Later, you will march into a land that has not had war for a while. Its people were gathered together from many nations. They came to the mountains of Israel. No one had lived in those mountains for a long time. So the people had been brought back from other nations. Now all the people live in safety. [9]You, all your troops and the many nations with you will march up to attack them. All of you will advance like a storm. You will be like a cloud covering their land."

[10]"'The LORD and King says, "At that time some ideas will come to you. You will make evil plans. [11]You will say, 'I will march out against a land whose villages don't have walls around them. I'll attack those peaceful people. I'll do this when they aren't

expecting it. None of their villages has walls or gates with metal bars on them. [12]I will rob those people. I'll steal everything they have. Then I'll turn my attention to the destroyed houses where people are living again. They have returned there from other nations. Now they are rich. They have plenty of livestock and all kinds of goods. They are living in Israel. It is the center of the earth.' [13]The people of Sheba and Dedan will speak to you. So will the traders of Tarshish and all its villages. They will say, 'Have you come to rob us? Have you gathered your huge army together to steal our silver and gold? Are you going to take away from us our livestock and goods? Do you plan to carry off everything we have?' "'

[14]"Son of man, prophesy. Tell Gog, 'The Lord and King says, "A time is coming when my people Israel will be living in safety. You will see that it is a good time to attack them. [15]So you will come from your place in the far north. Many nations will join you. All their men will be riding on horses. You will have a huge and mighty army. [16]They will advance against my people Israel. They will be like a cloud covering their land. Gog, in days to come I will bring you against my land. Then the nations will know me. I will use you to prove to them how holy I am."

[17]"'Here is what the Lord and King says to Gog. "In the past I spoke about you through my servants, the prophets of Israel. At that time they prophesied for years that I would bring you against them. [18]Here is what will happen in days to come. You will attack the land of Israel. That will stir up my burning anger," announces the Lord and King. [19]"At that time my burning anger will blaze out at you. There will be a great earthquake in the land of Israel. [20]The fish in the sea, the birds in the sky and the wild animals will tremble with fear. They will tremble with fear because of what I will do. So will every creature that moves along the ground. And so will all the people on earth. The mountains will come crashing down. The cliffs will break into pieces. Every wall will fall to the ground. [21]I will punish you on all my mountains," announces the Lord and King. "Your men will use their swords against one another. [22]I will judge you. I will send a plague against you. A lot of blood will be spilled. I will send heavy

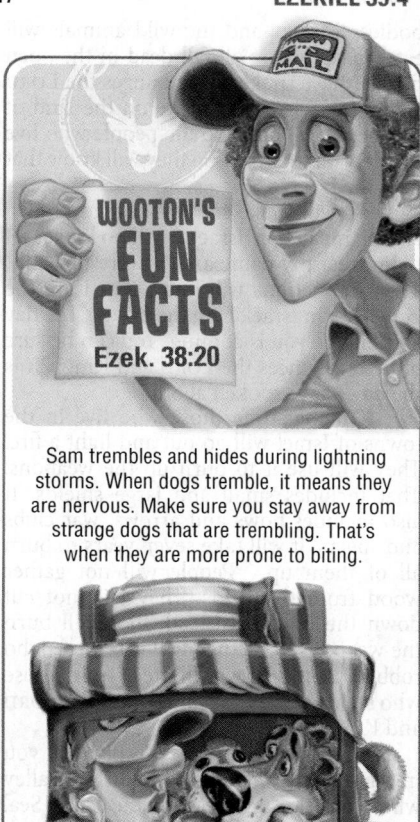

WOOTON'S FUN FACTS
Ezek. 38:20

Sam trembles and hides during lightning storms. When dogs tremble, it means they are nervous. Make sure you stay away from strange dogs that are trembling. That's when they are more prone to biting.

rain, hailstones and burning sulfur down to the earth. They will fall on you and your troops. They will also come down on the many nations that are helping you. [23]That will show how great and holy I am. I will make myself known to many nations. Then they will know that I am the Lord."'

39 "Son of man, prophesy against Gog. Tell him, 'The Lord and King says, "Gog, I am against you. You are the chief prince of Meshek and Tubal. [2]But I will turn you around. I will drag you along. I will bring you from the far north. I will send you against the mountains of Israel. [3]Then I will knock your bow out of your left hand. I will make your arrows drop from your right hand. [4]You will fall dead on the mountains of Israel. You and all your troops will die there. So will the nations that join you. I will feed you to all kinds of birds that eat dead bodies. So they and the wild animals will eat you up. ⁵You will fall dead in the open fields. I have spoken," announces the LORD and King. ⁶"I will send fire on the land of Magog. It will burn up the people who live in safety on the coast. So they will know that I am the LORD.

⁷" 'I will make my holy name known among my people Israel. I will no longer let them treat my name as if it were not holy. Then the nations will know that I am the Holy One in Israel. I am the LORD. ⁸The day I will judge you is coming. You can be sure of it," announces the LORD and King. "It is the day I have spoken about.

⁹" ' "At that time those who live in the towns of Israel will go out and light a fire. They will use it to burn up the weapons. That includes small and large shields. It also includes bows and arrows, war clubs and spears. It will take seven years to burn all of them up. ¹⁰People will not gather wood from the fields. They will not cut down the forests. Instead, they will burn the weapons. And they will rob those who robbed them. They will steal from those who stole from them," announces the LORD and King.

¹¹" ' "Gog, at that time I will bury you in a grave in Israel. It will be in the valley where people travel east of the Dead Sea. It will block the path of travelers. That's because you and your huge armies will be buried there. So it will be called the Valley of Gog's Armies.

¹²" ' "It will take seven months for the Israelites to bury the bodies. They will do this to make the land 'clean' again. ¹³All the people in the land will bury them. The day that I show how glorious I am will be a time to remember." This is what the LORD and King announces. ¹⁴"People will keep being hired to make the land 'clean' again. They will go all through it. They and others will bury any bodies lying on the ground.

" ' "After the seven months they will search even more carefully. ¹⁵As they go through the land here is what they'll do. When anyone sees a bone, they will put a marker beside it. Then those who dig the graves will take the bone to the Valley of Gog's Armies. There they will bury it. ¹⁶That is how they will make the land 'clean' again." ' " Also a town called Gog's Armies is near there.

¹⁷The LORD and King said to me, "Son of man, speak to every kind of bird. Call out to all the wild animals. Tell them, 'Gather together. Come from everywhere. Gather around the sacrifice I am preparing for you. It is the great sacrifice on the mountains of Israel. There you will eat human bodies and drink human blood. ¹⁸You will eat the bodies of mighty men. You will drink the blood of the princes of the earth. You will eat their bodies and drink their blood. You will do this as if they were rams and lambs, goats and bulls. You will enjoy it as if you were eating the fattest animals from Bashan. ¹⁹So I am preparing a sacrifice for you. You will eat fat until you are completely full. You will drink blood until you are drunk. ²⁰At my table you will eat horses, riders, mighty men and soldiers until you are full,' announces the LORD and King.

²¹" 'I will show all the nations my glory. They will see how I punish them when I use my power against them. ²²From that time on, the people of Israel will know that I am the LORD their God. ²³The nations will know that the people of Israel were taken away as prisoners because they sinned against me. They were not faithful to me. So I turned my face away from them. I handed them over to their enemies. All of them were killed by swords. ²⁴I punished them because they were "unclean." They did many things that were wrong. So I turned my face away from them.' "

²⁵The LORD and King says, "I will now cause the people of Jacob to recover from my judgment. I will show my tender love for all the people of Israel. I will make sure that my name is kept holy. ²⁶My people will forget the shameful things they have done. They will not remember all the ways they were unfaithful to me. They used to live in safety in their land. At that time no one made them afraid. ²⁷So I will bring them back from the nations. I will gather them from the countries of their enemies. And I will use them to prove to many nations how holy I am. ²⁸Then they will know that I am the LORD their God. I let the nations take my people away as prisoners. But now I will bring them back to their own land. I will not leave anyone behind. ²⁹I will no longer turn my face away from the people of Israel. I will pour out my Spirit on them," announces the LORD and King.

The New Temple Area

40 It was the 14th year after Jerusalem had been captured. We had been brought to Babylon as prisoners. It was the tenth day of a month near the beginning of the 25th year after that. On that day the power of the LORD came on me. He took me back to my land. [2]In visions God gave me, he brought me to the land of Israel. He set me on a very high mountain. Some buildings were on the south side of it. They looked like a city. [3]He took me there. I saw a man who appeared to be made out of bronze. He was standing at the gate of the outer courtyard. He was holding a linen measuring tape and a measuring rod. [4]The man said to me, "Son of man, look carefully and listen closely. Pay attention to everything I show you. That is why the LORD brought you here. Tell the people of Israel everything you see."

The East Gate to the Outer Courtyard

[5]I saw a wall that completely surrounded the temple area. The measuring rod in the man's hand was 11 feet long. He measured the wall with it. The wall was as thick and as high as one measuring rod.

[6]Then the man went to the east gate. He climbed its steps. He measured the gateway. It was one rod wide. [7]The rooms where the guards stood were one rod long and one rod wide. The walls between the rooms were almost nine feet thick. The gateway next to the porch was one rod wide. The porch faced the front of the temple.

[8]Then the man measured the porch of the gateway. [9]It was 14 feet wide. Each of its doorposts was three and a half feet thick. The porch of the gateway faced the front of the temple.

[10]Inside the east gate were three rooms on each side. All the rooms were the same size. The walls on each side of the rooms had the same thickness. [11]Then the man measured the entrance of the gateway. It was 18 feet wide and 23 feet long. [12]In front of each room was a wall. It was 21 inches high. The rooms measured 11 feet on each side. [13]Then he measured the gateway from the back wall of one room to the back wall of the room across from it. It was 44 feet from the top of one wall to the top of the other. [14]He measured along the front of the side walls all around the inside of the gateway. The total was 105 feet. That didn't include the porch that faced the courtyard. [15]It was 88 feet from the entrance of the gateway to the far end of its porch. [16]The rooms and their side walls inside the gateway had narrow openings on top of them. So did the porch. All the openings faced the inside. The front of each side wall was decorated with a palm tree.

The Outer Courtyard

[17]Then the man brought me into the outer courtyard. There I saw some rooms and a sidewalk. They had been built all around the courtyard. Along the sidewalk were 30 rooms. [18]The sidewalk went all the way up to the sides of the gateways. It was as wide as they were long. This was the lower sidewalk. [19]Then he measured from the inside of the lower gateway to the outside of the inner courtyard. The east side measured 175 feet. So did the north side.

The North Gate

[20]Then the man measured the north gate. He wanted to show me how long and wide it was. The gate led into the outer courtyard. [21]It had three rooms on each side. Their side walls and porch measured the same as the ones at the first gateway. They measured 88 feet long and 44 feet wide. [22]Its openings, porch and palm tree decorations measured the same as the ones at the east gate. Seven steps led up to the north gate. Its porch was across from them. [23]The inner courtyard had a gate. It faced the gate on the north. It was just like the east gate. He measured from one gate to the one across from it. The total was 175 feet.

The South Gate

[24]Then the man led me to the south side of the courtyard. There I saw the south gate. He measured its doorposts and porch. They measured the same as the others. [25]The gateway and its porch had narrow openings all around. The openings were the same as the others had. The side walls and porch measured 88 feet long and 44 feet wide. [26]Seven steps led up to it. Its porch was across from them. The front of each side wall was decorated with a palm tree. [27]The inner courtyard also had a gate that faced south. The man measured from this gate to the outer gate on the south side. The total was 175 feet.

The Gates to the Inner Courtyard

²⁸Then the man brought me into the inner courtyard. We went through the south gate. He measured it. It was the same size as the others. ²⁹Its rooms, side walls and porch measured the same as the ones at the other gateways. The gateway and its porch had openings all around. The side walls and porch measured 88 feet long and 44 feet wide. ³⁰The porches of the gateways around the inner courtyard were 44 feet wide and nine feet long. ³¹Its porch faced the outer courtyard. Palm trees decorated its doorposts. Eight steps led up to it.

³²Then the man brought me to the east side of the inner courtyard. There he measured the gateway. It was the same size as the others. ³³Its rooms, side walls and porch measured the same as the ones at the other gateways. The gateway and its porch had openings all around. The side walls and porch measured 88 feet long and 44 feet wide. ³⁴Its porch faced the outer courtyard. Each doorpost was decorated with a palm tree. Eight steps led up to the porch.

³⁵Then the man brought me to the north gate. He measured it. It was the same size as the others. ³⁶Its rooms, side walls and porch measured the same as the ones at the other gateways. It had openings all around. The side walls and the porch measured 88 feet long and 44 feet wide. ³⁷The porch faced the outer courtyard. Each doorpost was decorated with a palm tree. Eight steps led up to the porch.

The Rooms for Preparing Sacrifices

³⁸A room with a doorway was by the porch of each inner gateway. The burnt offerings were washed there. ³⁹On each side of the porch of the gateway were two tables. The burnt offerings were killed on them. So were the sin offerings and guilt offerings. ⁴⁰Two more tables were by the outer wall of the gateway porch. They were near the steps at the entrance of the north gateway. Two more tables were on the other side of the steps. ⁴¹So there were four tables on each side of the gateway. The total number of tables was eight. Animals for sacrifice were killed on all of them. ⁴²There were also four other tables for the burnt offerings. They were made out of blocks of stone. Each table was two and a half feet long and two and a half feet wide. And each was almost two feet

high. The tools for killing the burnt offerings and other sacrifices were placed on them. ⁴³Large hooks hung on the walls all around. Each was three inches long. The meat of the offerings was placed on the tables.

The Rooms for the Priests

⁴⁴Near the inner gates were two rooms. They were in the inner courtyard. One room was next to the north gate. It faced south. The other one was next to the south gate. It faced north. ⁴⁵The man said to me, "The room that faces south is for the priests who guard the temple. ⁴⁶The one that faces north is for the priests who guard the altar. All these priests are the sons of Zadok. They are the only Levites who can approach the LORD to serve him."

⁴⁷Then the man measured the courtyard. It was square. It measured 175 feet long and 175 feet wide. And the altar was in front of the temple.

The New Temple

⁴⁸The man brought me to the porch of the temple. He measured the doorposts of the porch. Each of them was almost nine feet wide. The entrance was 24 and a half feet wide. Each of the side walls was a little over five feet wide. ⁴⁹The porch was 35 feet wide. It was 21 feet from front to back. It was reached by some stairs. Pillars were on each side of the doorposts.

41 Then the man brought me to the main hall. There he measured the doorposts. Each of them was 11 feet wide. ²The entrance was 18 feet wide. Each of its side walls was almost nine feet wide. He also measured the main hall. It was 70 feet long and 35 feet wide.

³Then he went into the Most Holy Room. There he measured the doorposts at the entrance. Each one of them was three and a half feet wide. The entrance itself was 11 feet wide. Each of its side walls was a little over 12 feet wide. ⁴He also measured the Most Holy Room. It was 35 feet long and 35 feet wide. He said to me, "This is the Most Holy Room." It was beyond the back wall of the main hall.

⁵Then the man measured the wall of the temple. It was 11 feet thick. Each side room around the temple was seven feet wide. ⁶The side rooms were on three floors. There were 30 rooms on each floor. Ledges had

been built all around the wall of the temple. So the floor beams of the side rooms rested on the ledges. The beams didn't go into the temple wall. [7]The side rooms of the temple were wider as we went up floor by floor. A stairway went from the lowest floor all the way up to the top floor. It passed through the middle floor.

[8]I saw that the temple had a raised base all around it. The base formed the foundation of the side rooms. It was as long as one measuring rod. So it was 11 feet long. [9]The outer wall of each side room was almost nine feet thick. The open area between the side rooms of the temple [10]and the priests' rooms was 35 feet wide. It went all around the temple. [11]The side rooms had entrances from the open area. One was on the north side. Another was on the south. The base next to the open area was almost nine feet wide all around.

[12]There was a large building right behind the temple. It was on the west side of the outer courtyard. It was 123 feet wide. Its wall was almost nine feet thick all around. And it was 158 feet long.

[13]Then the man measured the temple. It was 175 feet long. The open area and the large building behind the temple also measured 175 feet. [14]The east side of the inner courtyard was 175 feet wide. That included the front of the temple.

[15]Then the man measured the building that was on the west side of the outer courtyard. It was behind the temple. It was 175 feet long. That included the walkways of the building on each side.

The main hall and the Most Holy Room were covered with wood. [16]And the porch that faced the inner courtyard was covered with wood. So were the gateways, narrow openings and walkways around these three places. The gateways and everything beyond them were covered with wood. The floor, the wall up to the openings, and the openings themselves were also covered. [17]The area above the outside of the entrance to the Most Holy Room was decorated. There were also decorations all around the walls of the Most Holy Room. [18]Carved cherubim and palm trees were used in the decorations. Each cherub had a palm tree next to it. And each palm tree had a cherub next to it. Each cherub had two faces. [19]One was the face of a human being. It looked toward the palm tree on one side. The other was the face of a lion. It looked toward the palm tree on the other side. The decorations were carved all around the whole temple. [20]Cherubim and palm trees decorated the wall of the main hall. They were carved from the floor all the way up to the area above the entrance.

[21]The main hall had a doorframe shaped like a rectangle. So did the Most Holy Room. [22]A wooden altar stood in the main hall. It was a little over five feet high. It was three and a half feet long and three and a half feet wide. Its corners, base and sides were made out of wood. The man said to me, "This is the table that stands in front of the LORD." [23]The main hall had double doors. So did the Most Holy Room. [24]Each door had two parts that could swing back and forth. [25]Cherubim and palm trees were carved on the doors of the main hall. The decorations were like the ones on the walls. A wooden roof went out beyond the front of the porch. [26]The side walls of the porch had narrow openings on top of them. Palm trees were carved on each side. A wooden roof went out beyond the entrance to each side room of the temple.

The Rooms for the Priests

42 Then the man led me north into the outer courtyard of the temple. He brought me to the rooms that were across from the inner courtyard. They were across from the outer wall of the temple on the north side. [2]The rooms were in a building north of the temple. The building had a door that faced north. It was 175 feet long. It was 88 feet wide. [3]One row of rooms was next to the inner courtyard. The other row was across from the sidewalk of the outer courtyard. Each room was 35 feet long. Walkways in front of each row faced each other on all three floors. [4]Between the two rows was an inner sidewalk. It was 18 feet wide and 175 feet long. Each of the rooms had a door on the north side. [5]The rooms on the top floor were narrower than the others. The walkways took up more space from these rooms. The walkways took up less space from the rooms on the other two floors. [6]The courtyards had pillars. But the rooms on the top floor didn't. So their floor space was smaller than the space in the rooms on the other floors. [7]The building

had an outer wall. It was even with the outer row of rooms and with the outer courtyard. The wall continued east of the outer row for 88 feet. [8]So there were two rows of rooms. The row next to the outer courtyard was 88 feet long. The one closest to the temple was 175 feet long. [9]The first floor of the building had an entrance on the east side. It led to the outer courtyard.

[10]There were also two rows of rooms in a building next to the south side of the inner courtyard. The building was across from the south wall of the outer courtyard. [11]Between the two rows was an inner sidewalk. The rooms were like the ones in the north building. They were as long and wide as the rooms on the north. The doorways of the rooms on the south were like the ones on the north. [12]People entered the south rooms through the doorway at the east end of the inner sidewalk. The south wall continued east of the outer row of rooms.

[13]The man said to me, "The north and south rooms face the inner courtyard. They are the priests' rooms. That is where the priests who approach the LORD will eat the very holy offerings. They will also store them there. That includes the grain offerings, sin offerings and guilt offerings. This place is holy. [14]The priests who enter these holy rooms must leave behind the clothes they served in. Then they can go into the outer courtyard. The clothes they served in are holy. So the priests must put other clothes on. They have to do that before they go near the places where other people go."

[15]The man finished measuring what was inside the temple area. Then he led me out through the east gate. He measured all around the area. [16]He measured the east side with his measuring rod. It was 875 feet long. [17]He measured the north side. It was 875 feet long. [18]He measured the south side. It was 875 feet long. [19]Finally, he turned and measured the west side. It was 875 feet long. [20]So he measured the area on all four sides. It had a wall around it. The wall was 875 feet long and 875 feet wide. It separated what was holy from what was not.

The Glory of God Returns to the Temple

43 Then the man brought me to the east gate. [2]There I saw the glory of the God of Israel. He was coming from the east. His voice was like the roar of rushing waters. His glory made the land shine brightly. [3]The vision I saw was like the one I had when he came to destroy the city. It was also like the visions I had seen by the Kebar River. I fell with my face toward the ground. [4]The glory of the LORD entered the temple through the east gate. [5]Then the Spirit lifted me up. He brought me into the inner courtyard. The glory of the LORD filled the temple.

[6]The man was standing beside me. I heard someone speaking to me from inside the temple. [7]He said, "Son of man, this is the place where my throne is. The stool for my feet is also here. I will live here among the people of Israel forever. They will never again treat my name as if it were not holy. They and their kings will not serve other gods anymore. The people will no longer make funeral offerings for their kings. [8]The people of Israel placed their own doorway next to my holy doorway. They put their doorposts right beside mine. Nothing but a thin wall separated us. They treated my name as if it were not holy. I hated it when they did that. So I became angry with them and destroyed them. [9]Now let them stop serving other gods. Let them stop making funeral offerings for their kings. If they obey me, I will live among them forever.

[10]"Son of man, tell the people of Israel about the temple. Then they will be ashamed of their sins. Let them think carefully about how perfect it is. [11]What if they are ashamed of everything they have done? Then show them all the plans of the temple. Explain to them how it is laid out. Tell them about its exits and entrances. Show them exactly what it will look like. Give them all its rules and laws. Write everything down so they can see it. Then they will be faithful to its plan. And they will obey all its rules. [12]"Here is the law of the temple. The whole area on top of Mount Zion will be very holy. That is the law of the temple."

The Great Altar Is Rebuilt

[13]The man said, "Here is the size of the altar. The standard measurement I am using is 21 inches. The altar has a drain on the ground. The drain is 21 inches deep and 21 inches wide. It has a rim that is nine inches wide around the edge. Here is how high the altar is. [14]From the drain to the lower ledge is three and a half feet. The lower ledge goes

around the altar and is 21 inches wide. From the lower ledge to the upper ledge is seven feet. The upper ledge also goes around the altar and is 21 inches wide. [15]The top part of the altar is where the sacrifices are burned. It is seven feet high. A horn sticks out from each of its four corners. [16]The top part of the altar is square. It is 21 feet long and 21 feet wide. [17]The upper ledge is also square. It is 25 feet long and 25 feet wide. The drain goes all the way around the altar. The rim of the drain is 11 inches wide. The steps leading up to the top of the altar face east."

[18]Then the man said to me, "Son of man, the LORD and King speaks. He says, 'Here are the rules for the altar when it is built. Follow them when you sacrifice burnt offerings and splash blood against it. [19]Give a young bull to the priests as a sin offering. They are Levites from the family of Zadok. They approach me to serve me,' announces the LORD and King. [20]'Get some of the bull's blood. Put it on the four horns of the altar. Also put it on the four corners of the upper ledge of the altar and all around the rim. That will make the altar pure and "clean." [21]Use the bull for the sin offering. Burn it in the proper place outside the temple.

[22]" 'On the second day offer a male goat. It must not have any flaws. It is a sin offering to make the altar pure and "clean." So do the same thing with the goat that you did with the bull. [23]When you finish making the altar pure, offer a young bull and a ram from the flock. They must not have any flaws. [24]Offer them to me. The priests must sprinkle salt on them. Then they must sacrifice them as a burnt offering to me.

[25]" 'Provide a male goat each day for seven days. It is a sin offering. Also provide a young bull and a ram from the flock. They must not have any flaws. [26]For seven days the priests must make the altar pure and "clean." That is how they will set it apart to me. [27]From the eighth day on, the priests must bring your burnt offerings and friendship offerings. They must sacrifice them on the altar. Then I will accept you,' announces the LORD and King."

The Priesthood Will Be Established Again

44 Then the man brought me back to the outer gate of the temple. It was the one that faced east. It was shut. [2]The LORD said to me, "This gate must remain shut. It must not be opened. No one can enter through it. It must remain shut because I have entered through it. I am the God of Israel. [3]The prince is the only one who can sit in the gateway. There he can eat in front of me. He must enter through the porch of the gateway. And he must go out the same way."

[4]Then the man brought me through the north gate. He took me to the front of the temple. I looked up and saw the glory of the LORD. It filled his temple. I fell with my face toward the ground.

[5]The LORD said to me, "Son of man, pay attention. Look carefully. Listen closely to everything I tell you. I'm telling you about all the rules and instructions concerning my temple. Pay attention to the entrance to the temple and to all its exits. [6]Speak to the people of Israel. They refuse to obey me. Tell them, 'Here is what the LORD and King says. "People of Israel, I have had enough of your evil practices. I hate them. [7]You brought outsiders into my temple. They were not circumcised. Their hearts were stubborn. You made my temple 'unclean.' But you offered me food, fat and blood anyway. When you did all these things, you broke the covenant I made with you. I hated all the evil things you did. [8]You did not do what I told you to. You did not take care of my holy things. Instead, you put other people in charge of my temple." ' " [9]The LORD and King says, "No outsider whose heart is stubborn can enter my temple. They have not been circumcised. Even if they live among the people of Israel they can't enter my temple.

[10]"Some Levites wandered far away from me when Israel went astray. They worshiped the statues of their gods. So they will be punished because they have sinned. [11]They might serve in my temple. They might be in charge of its gates. They might kill the burnt offerings and sacrifices for the people. And they might stand in front of the people and serve them in other ways. [12]But these Levites served the people of Israel. They served while the Israelites were worshiping the statues of their gods. They made the people fall into sin. So I raised my hand and made a promise. I warned them that I would punish them because of their sin," announces the LORD and King. [13]"They must not approach me to serve me

as priests. They must not come near any of my holy things. They must stay away from my very holy offerings. They did many things they should have been ashamed of. I hated those things. ¹⁴But I will still appoint them to guard the temple. They will guard it for all the work that has to be done there.

¹⁵"But the priests must approach me to serve me. They are Levites from Zadok's family line. They guarded my temple when the people of Israel turned away from me. These priests must serve me by offering sacrifices of fat and blood," announces the Lord and King. ¹⁶"They are the only ones who can enter my temple. Only they can come near to serve me as guards.

¹⁷"They will enter the gates of the inner courtyard. When they do, they must wear linen clothes. They will serve at the gates of the inner courtyard or inside the temple. When they do, they must not wear any clothes made out of wool. ¹⁸They must have linen turbans on their heads. They must wear linen underwear around their waists. They must not wear anything that makes them sweat. ¹⁹They will go into the outer courtyard where the people are. When they do, they must take off the clothes they have been serving in. They must leave them in the sacred rooms. And they must put other clothes on. Then the people will not be made holy if they happen to touch the priests' clothes.

²⁰"The priests must not shave their heads. They must not let their hair grow long. They must keep it cut short. ²¹No priest may drink wine when he enters the inner courtyard. ²²They must not get married to widows or divorced women. They may only marry Israelite virgins or the widows of priests. ²³The priests must teach my people the difference between what is holy and what is not. They must show them how to tell the difference between what is 'clean' and what is not.

²⁴"When people do not agree, the priests must serve as judges between them. They must make their decisions based on my laws. They must obey my laws and rules for all my appointed feasts. And they must keep my Sabbath days holy.

²⁵"A priest must not make himself 'unclean' by going near a dead person. But suppose the dead person was his father or mother. Or suppose it was his son or daughter or brother or unmarried sister. Then the priest may make himself 'unclean.' ²⁶After he is pure and 'clean' again, he must wait seven days. ²⁷Then he may go to the inner courtyard to serve in the temple. But when he does, he must sacrifice a sin offering for himself," announces the Lord and King.

²⁸"The priests will not receive any part of the land of Israel. I myself will be their only share. ²⁹They will eat the grain offerings, sin offerings and guilt offerings. Everything in Israel that is set apart to me in a special way will belong to them. ³⁰The best of every first share of the people's crops will belong to the priests. So will all their special gifts. The people must give the priests the first share of their ground meal. Then I will bless my people's families. ³¹The priests must not eat any bird or animal that is found dead. They must not eat anything that wild animals have torn apart.

The Lord Establishes Israel Again

45 "People of Israel, you will divide up the land you will receive. When you do, give me my share of it. It will be a sacred area. It will be eight miles long and six and a half miles wide. The entire area will be holy. ²The temple area in it will be 875 feet long and 875 feet wide. An 88-foot strip around it will be open land. ³In the sacred area, measure off a large strip of land. It will be eight miles long and three and a third miles wide. The temple will be in it. It will be the most holy place of all. ⁴The large strip will be the sacred share of land for the priests. There they will serve in the temple. And they will approach me to serve me there. Their houses will be built on that land. The holy temple will also be located there. ⁵So the Levites will serve in the temple. They will have an area eight miles long and three and a third miles wide. The towns they live in will be located there.

⁶"Give the city an area one and two-thirds miles wide and eight miles long. It will be right next to the sacred area. It will belong to all the people of Israel.

⁷"The prince will have land on both sides of the sacred area and the city. Its border will run east and west along the land of one of the tribes. ⁸The prince will own this land in Israel. And my princes will not crush my people anymore. Instead, they

will allow the people of Israel to receive their own share of land. It will be divided up based on their tribes."

⁹The LORD and King says, "Princes of Israel, you have gone far enough! Stop hurting others. Do not crush them. Do what is fair and right. Stop taking my people's land away from them," announces the LORD and King. ¹⁰"Use weights and measures that are honest and exact. ¹¹Use the same standard to measure dry and liquid products. Use a 6-bushel measure for dry products. And use a 60-gallon measure for liquids. ¹²Every amount of money must be weighed out in keeping with the standard weights.

¹³"You must offer a special gift. It must be six pounds out of every six bushels of grain. ¹⁴Give two and a half quarts out of every 60 gallons of olive oil. ¹⁵Also give one sheep from every flock of 200 sheep. Get them from the grasslands of Israel that receive plenty of water. Use them for grain offerings, burnt offerings and friendship offerings. They will be used to pay for the sin of the people," announces the LORD and King. ¹⁶"All the people in the land will be required to give this special gift. They must give it to the prince in Israel. ¹⁷He must provide the burnt offerings, grain offerings and drink offerings. They will be for the yearly feasts, New Moon feasts and Sabbath days. So they will be for all the appointed feasts of the people of Israel. The prince will provide the sin offerings, grain offerings, burnt offerings and friendship offerings. They will be used to pay for the sin of the Israelites."

¹⁸The LORD and King says, "Get a young bull. It must not have any flaws. Use it to make the temple pure and 'clean.' Do this on the first day of the first month. ¹⁹The priest must get some of the blood from the sin offering. He must put some on the doorposts of the temple. He must apply some to the four corners of the upper ledge of the altar. He must put the rest on the gateposts of the inner courtyard. ²⁰Do the same thing on the seventh day of the month. Do this for those who sin without meaning to. And do this for those who sin without realizing what they are doing. So you will make the temple pure and 'clean.'

²¹"Keep the Passover Feast on the 14th day of the first month. It will last for seven days. During that time you must eat bread made without yeast. ²²The prince must provide a bull as a sin offering. It will be for him and all the people of the land. ²³For each of the seven days of the feast he must provide seven bulls and seven rams. They must not have any flaws. They will be a burnt offering to me. The prince must also provide a male goat for a sin offering. ²⁴He must bring 35 pounds for each bull or ram. He must also provide four quarts of olive oil for each of them.

²⁵"The seven days of the feast begin on the 15th day of the seventh month. During those days the prince must provide the same sin offerings, burnt offerings, grain offerings and olive oil."

46 The LORD and King says, "On the six working days of each week you must keep the east gate of the inner courtyard of the temple shut. But open it on Sabbath days and during New Moon feasts. ²The prince must enter the temple area through the porch of the gateway. He must stand by the gatepost. The priests must sacrifice his burnt offering and friendship offerings. He must bow down in worship at the entrance of the gateway. Then he must leave. But the gate will not be shut until evening. ³On Sabbath days and during New Moon feasts the people of the land must gather together. They must gather at the entrance of the temple gateway. That is where they must worship me. ⁴The prince must bring a burnt offering to me on the Sabbath day. It will be six male lambs and a ram. They must not have any flaws. ⁵He must offer 35 pounds of grain along with the ram. The grain he offers along with the lambs can be as much as he wants to give. He must also offer four quarts of olive oil for every 35 pounds of grain. ⁶On the day of the New Moon feast the prince must make another offering. He must offer a young bull, six lambs and a ram. They must not have any flaws. ⁷He must offer 35 pounds of grain along with the bull or ram. The grain he offers along with the lambs can be as much as he wants to give. He must also offer four quarts of olive oil for every 35 pounds of grain. ⁸Here is how the prince must enter the temple area. He must go in through the porch of the gateway. And he must leave the same way.

⁹"The people of the land must worship me at the appointed feasts. Those who enter through the north gate must leave through

the south gate. Those who enter through the south gate must leave through the north gate. They must not leave through the same gate they entered. Each one must go out the opposite gate. ¹⁰The prince must be among them. He must go in when they go in. And he must leave when they leave. ¹¹At the yearly feasts and other appointed feasts there must be grain offerings. The prince must offer 35 pounds of grain along with a bull or ram. The grain he offers along with the lambs can be as much as he wants to give. He must also offer four quarts of olive oil for every 35 pounds of grain.

¹²"He may also bring another offering to me because he chooses to. It might be a burnt offering or friendship offering. When he brings it, the east gate must be opened for him. He will bring his offering just as he does on the Sabbath day. Then he will leave. After he has gone out, the gate must be shut.

Jason's Jargon

EZEKIEL 46

Seek out the words *Inner Courtyard* in this chapter. The Inner Courtyard of the temple was only open to priests and only on the Sabbath. The priests would make sacrifices there.

¹³"Every day you must provide a lamb that is a year old. It must not have any flaws. It is a burnt offering to me. You must provide it every morning. ¹⁴You must also offer grain along with it every morning. Bring six pounds of grain. Also bring one and a half quarts of olive oil to make the flour a little wet. So you will give the grain offering to me. That will be a law that will last for all time to come. ¹⁵Provide the lamb, grain offering and oil every morning. They will be used for a regular burnt offering."

¹⁶The LORD and King says, "Suppose the prince makes a gift from his share of land. And he gives it to one of his sons. Then the property will also belong to his sons after him. It will be handed down to them. ¹⁷But suppose he makes a gift from his share of land to one of his servants. Then the servant may keep it until the Year of Jubilee. After that, it will be returned to the prince. His property may be handed down only to his sons. It belongs to them. ¹⁸The prince must not take any share of land that belongs to the people. He must not drive them off their property. He must give his sons their share out of his own property. Then not one of my people will be separated from their property."

¹⁹The man brought me through the entrance at the side of the north building. That's where the priests' sacred rooms were located. He showed me a place west of the building. ²⁰He said to me, "This is where the priests must cook the guilt offerings and sin offerings. They must also bake the grain offerings here. Then they will not have to bring the offerings into the outer courtyard. That will keep the people from touching the offerings and becoming holy."

²¹Then the man brought me to the outer courtyard. He led me around to its four corners. In each corner I saw another smaller courtyard. ²²So in the four corners of the outer courtyard were walled courtyards. Each one was 70 feet long and 53 feet wide. All of them were the same size. ²³Around the inside of each of the four courtyards was a stone ledge. Places for fire were built all around under each ledge. ²⁴The man said to me, "These are the kitchens. Those who serve at the temple must cook the people's sacrifices here."

A River Will Flow From the Temple

47 The man brought me back to the entrance to the temple. I saw water flowing east from under a temple gateway. The temple faced east. The water was coming down from under the south side of the temple. It was flowing south of the altar. ²Then he brought me out through the north gate of the outer courtyard. He led me around the outside to the outer gate that faced east. The water was flowing from the south side of the east gate.

³Then the man went toward the east. He had a measuring line in his hand. He measured off 1,700 feet. He led me through water that was up to my ankles. ⁴Then he measured off another 1,700 feet. He led me through water that was up to

my knees. Then he measured off another 1,700 feet. He led me through water that was up to my waist. [5]Then he measured off another 1,700 feet. But now it was a river that I could not go across. The water had risen so high that it was deep enough to swim in. [6]He asked me, "Son of man, do you see this?"

Then he led me back to the bank of the river. [7]When I arrived there, I saw many trees. They were on both sides of the river. [8]The man said to me, "This water flows toward the eastern territory. It goes down into the Arabah Valley. There it enters the Dead Sea. When it empties into it, the salt water there becomes fresh. [9]Many creatures will live where the river flows. It will have many schools of fish. This water flows there and makes the salt water fresh. So where the river flows everything will live. [10]People will stand along the shore to fish. From En Gedi all the way to En Eglaim there will be places for spreading fishnets. The Dead Sea will have many kinds of fish. They will be like the fish in the Mediterranean Sea. [11]But none of the swamps will have fresh water in them. They will stay salty. [12]Fruit trees of all kinds will grow on both banks of the river. Their leaves will not dry up. The trees will always have fruit on them. Every month they will bear fruit. The water from the temple will flow to them. Their fruit will be used for food. And their leaves will be used for healing."

The Borders of the Land

[13]Here is what the LORD and King says. "People of Israel, here are the borders of the land that you will divide up. You will divide up the land among the 12 tribes of Israel. Each tribe will receive a share. But the family of Joseph will have two shares. [14]Divide the land into equal parts. Long ago I raised my hand and made a promise. I promised to give the land to your people of long ago. So all of it will belong to you.

[15] "Here are the borders of the land.

"On the north side the border will start at the Mediterranean Sea. It will go by the Hethlon road past Lebo Hamath. Then it will continue on to Zedad, [16]Berothah and Sibraim. Sibraim is between Damascus and Hamath. The border will reach all the way to Hazer Hattikon. It is right next to Hauran. [17]The border will go from the sea to Hazar Enan. It will run north of Damascus and south of Hamath. This will be the northern border.

[18] "On the east side the border will run between Hauran and Damascus. It will continue along the Jordan River between Gilead and the land of Israel. It will reach to the Dead Sea and all the way to Tamar. This will be the eastern border.

[19] "On the south side the border will start at Tamar. It will reach all the way to the waters of Meribah Kadesh. Then it will run along the Wadi of Egypt. It will end at the Mediterranean Sea. This will be the southern border.

[20] "On the west side, the Mediterranean Sea will be the border. It will go to a point across from Lebo Hamath. This will be the western border.

[21]"You must divide up this land among yourselves. Do this based on the number of men in your tribes. [22]Each of the tribes must receive a share of the land. You must also give some land to the outsiders who live among you and who have children. Treat them as if they had been born in Israel. Let them have some land among your tribes. [23]Outsiders can live in the land of any tribe. There you must give them their share," announces the LORD and King.

The Land Will Be Divided Up

48 "Here are the tribes. They are listed by their names.

"Dan will receive one share of land. It will be at the northern border of Israel. The border will follow the Hethlon road to Lebo Hamath. Hazar Enan will be part of the border. So will the northern border of Damascus next to Hamath. Dan's northern border will run from east to west.

[2] "Asher will receive one share. It will border the territory of Dan from east to west.

[3] "Naphtali will receive one share. It will border the territory of Asher from east to west.

4 "Manasseh will receive one share. It will border the territory of Naphtali from east to west.

5 "Ephraim will receive one share. It will border the territory of Manasseh from east to west.

6 "Reuben will receive one share. It will border the territory of Ephraim from east to west.

7 "Judah will receive one share. It will border the territory of Reuben from east to west.

8 "You must give one share as a special gift to me. It will border the territory of Judah from east to west. It will be eight miles wide. It will be as long as the border of each of the territories of the tribes. Its border will run from east to west. The temple will be in the center of that strip of land.

9 "Give that special share of land to me. It will be eight miles long and three and a third miles wide. 10 It will be the sacred share of land for the priests. It will be eight miles long on the north side. It will be three and a third miles wide on the west side. It will be three and a third miles wide on the east side. And it will be eight miles long on the south side. My temple will be in the center of it. 11 This share of land will be for the priests who are set apart to me. They will come from the family line of Zadok. The members of that family served me faithfully. They did not go astray as the Levites and other Israelites did. 12 Their share of land will be a special gift to them. It will be part of the sacred share of the land. It will be very holy. Its border will run along the territory of the Levites.

13 "The Levites will receive a share. It will be next to the territory of the priests. The Levites' share will be eight miles long and three and a third miles wide. 14 They must not sell or trade any of it. It is the best part of the land. It must not be handed over to anyone else. It is set apart to me.

15 "The area that remains is one and two-thirds miles wide. It is eight miles long. It will not be holy. The people in Jerusalem can build houses there. They can use some of it as grasslands. The city will be in the center of it. 16 Each of the four sides of the city will be one and a half miles long. 17 Each of the four sides of the city's grasslands will be 440 feet long. 18 What remains of the area will be three and a third miles long on the east and west sides. Its border will run along the border of the sacred share. Its crops will supply food for the city workers. 19 They will farm the area. They will come from all the tribes of Israel. 20 The entire area will be a square. Each of its four sides will be eight miles long. Set the sacred share apart as a special gift to me. Do the same thing with the property of the city.

21 "The area that remains on both sides will belong to the prince. So his land does not include the sacred share and the property of the city. The eastern part of his land will reach from the sacred share all the way to the eastern border. The western part will reach from the sacred share to the western border. The sacred share itself is eight miles long on its east and west sides. Both of those areas will be right next to the borders of the two tribes on the north and south sides. They will belong to the prince. The sacred share will be in the center of them. It will have the temple in it. 22 The property of the Levites will lie in the center of the prince's share. So will the property of the city. The prince's land will lie between the borders of the tribes of Judah and Benjamin.

23 "Here is the land for the rest of the tribes.

"Benjamin will receive one share. It will reach from the eastern border to the western border.

24 "Simeon will receive one share. It will border the territory of Benjamin from east to west.

25 "Issachar will receive one share. It will border the territory of Simeon from east to west.

26 "Zebulun will receive one share. It will border the territory of Issachar from east to west.

27 "Gad will receive one share. It will border the territory of Zebulun from east to west.

28 "The southern border of Gad will run south from Tamar to the waters of Meribah Kadesh. It will continue along the Wadi of Egypt. It will end at the Mediterranean Sea.

29 "This is the land you must divide among the tribes of Israel. And these

will be the shares they will receive," announces the LORD and King.

The Gates of the New City

³⁰ "Here is a list of the gates of the city.

Start with its north side. It will be a mile and a half long. ³¹The city gates will be named after the tribes of Israel. The north side will have three gates. They will be the gates of Reuben, Judah and Levi.

³² "The east side will be a mile and a half long. It will have three gates. They will be the gates of Joseph, Benjamin and Dan.

³³ "The south side will be a mile and a half long. It will have three gates. They will be the gates of Simeon, Issachar and Zebulun.

³⁴ "The west side will be a mile and a half long. It will have three gates. They will be the gates of Gad, Asher and Naphtali.

³⁵ "The city will be six miles around.

"From that time on, its name will be 'The LORD Is There.'"

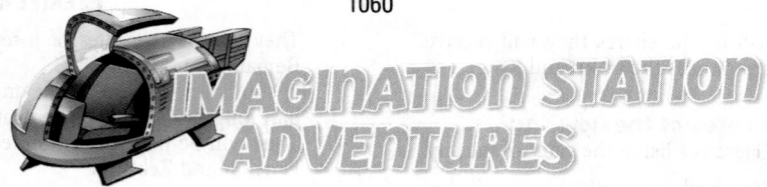

IMAGINATION STATION ADVENTURES

EZEKIEL'S VISIONS

Read Ezekiel 1, 12, 37.

WHIT SENDS MARVIN AND HIS SISTER TAMIKA ON A NEW ADVENTURE IN THE IMAGINATION STATION.

WHY ARE THE OLD TESTAMENT PROPHETS SO **GRUMPY?**

GET IN AND FIND OUT...

WAIT! I WANT TO MEET SOME BIBLE HEROES, BUT YOU'RE SENDING US TO MEET A MR. GLOOM-AND-DOOM.

I THINK YOU'LL FIND THAT BEING A PROPHET HAD SOME **UNUSUAL** BENEFITS.

THEY ARRIVE NEAR BABYLON AT THE RIVER CHEBAR IN 593 B.C. THE PROPHET EZEKIEL IS HAVING A VISION THAT REPRESENTS GOD'S RULE OVER CREATION: MAN, ANIMALS, AND THE WEATHER.

GO TO THE EXILES IN BABYLON AND PREACH TO THEM. IT DOESN'T MATTER IF THEY LISTEN OR NOT.

THIS SCROLL REPRESENTS WHAT I WANT YOU, EZEKIEL, TO SAY TO THE PEOPLE OF ISRAEL.

LET'S GET OUT OF THIS LIGHTNING.

A YEAR LATER...

WHY DO YOU CARRY BAGGAGE **EVERY** NIGHT AND WALK AROUND THE CITY?

TO SHOW THAT SOON ALL THE PEOPLE OF **ISRAEL WILL GO INTO EXILE.** THEY WILL KEEP ONLY WHAT THEY CAN CARRY.

THAT'S NOT GOING TO HAPPEN. GOD WON'T LET JERUSALEM FALL.

GOD TOLD ME IT WILL HAPPEN **SOON.** EVEN THE TEMPLE WILL FALL.

MARVIN PROGRAMS THE IMAGINATION STATION TO 586 BC. THEY WATCH KING NEBUCHADNEZZAR'S ARMY DESTROY JERUSALEM. ALL REMAINING JEWS ARE MARCHED TO BABYLON.

IT HAPPENED *JUST* AS EZEKIEL SAID IT WOULD.

DAD, *HOW LONG* IS THE WALK TO BABYLON?

FIVE HUNDRED MILES.

TAMIKA AND MARVIN DECIDE TO GO BACK TO TALK TO EZEKIEL.

WHO IS IN THE GRAVE?

MY WIFE. SHE DIED ON THE SAME DAY JERUSALEM FELL.

I'M *SO* SORRY.

SO AM I. *BUT GOD HAS GIVEN ME ANOTHER MESSAGE FOR THE ISRAELITES.* I DON'T HAVE TIME TO MOURN.

GOD WILL BRING THE FOUR WINDS AND *BREATHE LIFE INTO THEM.*

GOD WILL BRING HIS PEOPLE *BACK* TO THE LAND OF ISRAEL.

SEEING GOD'S POWER GIVES ME *HOPE.*

THAT'S AMAZING.

SO NO MATTER HOW BAD THINGS GET, *REMEMBER* GOD ALWAYS HAS A PLAN FOR MAKING THINGS TURN OUT RIGHT IN THE END.

EVEN WHEN ALL SEEMS GLOOMY?

ESPECIALLY THEN.

STILL WANT TO SEE *A BIBLE HERO?*

I THINK WE JUST MET *ONE* OF THE BEST.

Daniel

When one lists the Major Prophets, the name Daniel probably stands out from the others. Not only was he taken as a young man from Judah to Babylon, but he also lived to see Babylon fall to the Persian Empire.

It wouldn't be hyperbole to say that nearly everyone knows about his escapade in the lions' den (chapter 6). But before that, he had already negotiated a special vegetarian diet that propelled him and his friends to the top of their proverbial class (chapter 1). He had made a name for himself as a dream interpreter (chapter 2). He had interpreted the mysterious words written on the wall by a "body-less" hand (chapter 5). And his three friends—Shadrach, Meshach, and Abednego—had likewise taken a bold stand for God. They were rewarded by remaining unharmed even after being thrown into a blazing fiery furnace (chapter 3).

However, the last half of the book of Daniel is not as well-known to most readers. Daniel peers into the future, beyond Babylon and Persia to the coming empires of Greece and Rome. And even beyond that, he prepares his readers for the end times. There's much more to the book of Daniel than the familiar story about the lions. Now is the time to read it for yourself.

WHAT'S IT MEAN, EUGENE?

Sanctification—Being sanctified simply means we are "being made holy." Indeed, we are *justified* (or made right) with God the moment we believe in Jesus, but that's just the beginning of our adventure in Christ! The rest of the journey comes with our *sanctification*, when we grow in our faith as we become more and more like Jesus. This is what the Apostle Paul had in mind when he wrote, "Live by the Holy Spirit's power. Then you will not do what your desires controlled by sin want you to do" (Galatians 5:16).

Daniel Is Trained in Babylon

1 It was the third year that Jehoiakim was king of Judah. Nebuchadnezzar, king of Babylon, came to Jerusalem. His armies surrounded the city and attacked it. ²The Lord handed Jehoiakim, the king of Judah, over to him. Nebuchadnezzar also took some of the objects from God's temple. He carried them off to the temple of his god in Babylon. He put them among the treasures of his god.

³The king gave Ashpenaz an order. Ashpenaz was the chief of Nebuchadnezzar's court officials. The king told him to bring him some of the Israelites. The king wanted them to serve him in his court. He wanted nobles and men from the royal family. ⁴He was looking for young men who were healthy and handsome. They had to be able to learn anything. They had to be well educated. They had to have the ability to understand new things quickly and easily. The king wanted men who could serve in his palace. Ashpenaz was supposed to teach them the Babylonian language and writings. ⁵The king had his servants give them food and wine from his own table. They received a certain amount every day. The young men had to be trained for three years. After that, they could begin to serve the king.

⁶Some of the men chosen were from Judah. Their names were Daniel, Hananiah, Mishael and Azariah. ⁷The chief official gave them new names. He gave Daniel the name Belteshazzar. He gave Hananiah the name Shadrach. He gave Mishael the name Meshach. And he gave Azariah the name Abednego.

⁸Daniel decided not to make himself "unclean" by eating the king's food and drinking his wine. So he asked the chief official for a favor. He wanted permission not to make himself "unclean" with the king's food and wine. ⁹God had caused the official to be kind and friendly to Daniel. ¹⁰But the official refused to do what Daniel asked for. He said, "I'm afraid of the king. He is my master. He has decided what you and your three friends must eat and drink. Other young men are the same age as you. Why should he see you looking worse than them? When he sees how you look, he might kill me."

¹¹So Daniel spoke to one of the guards. The chief official had appointed him over Daniel, Hananiah, Mishael and Azariah. ¹²Daniel said to him, "Please test us for ten days. Give us nothing but vegetables to eat. And give us only water to drink. ¹³Then compare us with the young men who eat the king's food. See how we look. After that, do what you want to." ¹⁴So the guard agreed. He tested them for ten days.

¹⁵After the ten days Daniel and his friends looked healthy and well fed. In fact,

WHIT'S WISDOM

Daniel 1:8–17

Imagine Connie is hosting a game show on Kids' Radio and you are a contestant. She says, "You have two choices! You can either choose door number one—which is the evil door—or door number two—which is God's door!" Would you have to phone a friend? Have time to think about it? It's a pretty easy decision, isn't it?

Not all decisions about right and wrong are that simple. Daniel faced a tough choice in the first chapter of his book. He could choose door number one, which meant eating meat that was sacrificed to idols and going along with the crowd. Or he could choose door number two, which meant defying the king and refusing to eat the food. He knew which door was right, but he knew there could be consequences. Daniel made the right choice, and God rewarded him for it.

You are going to be faced with difficult choices in your life. People around you will encourage you to go along with the crowd and choose door number one. Decide now, before you are even in that situation, that you are going to choose door number two and what is right.

they looked better than any of the young men who ate the king's food. [16]So the guard didn't require them to eat the king's special food. He didn't require them to drink the king's wine either. He gave them vegetables instead.

[17]God gave knowledge and understanding to these four young men. So they understood all kinds of writings and subjects. And Daniel could understand all kinds of visions and dreams.

[18]The three years the king had set for their training ended. So the chief official brought them to Nebuchadnezzar. [19]The king talked with them. He didn't find anyone equal to Daniel, Hananiah, Mishael and Azariah. So they began to serve the king. [20]He asked them for advice in matters that required wisdom and understanding. The king always found their answers to be the best. Other men in his kingdom claimed to get knowledge by using magic. But the answers of Daniel and his friends were ten times better than theirs.

[21]Daniel served in Babylon until the first year Cyrus ruled over the land of Babylon. Cyrus was king of Persia.

Nebuchadnezzar Dreams About a Large Statue

2 In the second year of Nebuchadnezzar's rule, he had a dream. His mind was troubled. He couldn't sleep. [2]So the king sent for those who claimed to get knowledge by using magic. He also sent for those who practiced evil magic and those who studied the heavens. He wanted them to tell him what he had dreamed. They came in and stood in front of the king. [3]He said to them, "I had a dream. It troubles me. So I want to know what it means."

[4]Then those who studied the heavens answered the king. They spoke in Aramaic. They said, "King Nebuchadnezzar, may you live forever! Tell us what you dreamed. Then we'll explain what it means."

[5]The king replied to them, "I have made up my mind. You must tell me what I dreamed. And you must tell me what it means. If you don't, I'll have you cut to pieces. And I'll have your houses turned into piles of trash. [6]So tell me what I dreamed. Explain it to me. Then I'll give you gifts. I'll reward you. I'll give you great honor. So tell me the dream. And tell me what it means."

[7]Once more they replied, "King Nebuchadnezzar, tell us what you dreamed. Then we'll tell you what it means."

[8]The king answered, "I know what you are doing. You are trying to gain more time. You realize that I've made up my mind. [9]You must tell me the dream. If you don't, you will pay for it. You have gotten together and made evil plans. You hope things will change. So you are telling me lies. But I want you to tell me what I dreamed. Then I'll know that you can tell me what it means."

[10]They answered the king, "There is no one on earth who can do what you are asking! No king has ever asked for anything like that. Not even a king as great and mighty as you has asked for it. Those who get knowledge by using magic have never been asked to do what you are asking. And those who study the heavens haven't been asked to do it either. [11]What you are asking is much too hard. No one can tell you what you dreamed except the gods. And they don't live among human beings."

[12]That made the king very angry. He ordered that all the wise men in Babylon be put to death. [13]So the order was given to kill them. Men were sent out to look for Daniel and his friends. They were also supposed to be put to death.

Jason's Jargon

DANIEL 2

Here's a quest for every worker. Find *authority* in this chapter. To have authority means to have power or control. For instance, God gives our parents, police, and teachers authority over us.

[14]Arioch was the commander of the king's guard. He went out to put the wise men of Babylon to death. So Daniel spoke to him wisely and carefully. [15]He asked the king's officer, "Why did Nebuchadnezzar give a terrible order like that?" Then Arioch explained to Daniel what was going on. [16]When Daniel heard that, he went to

the king. He told him he would explain the dream to him. But he needed more time.

[17]Then Daniel returned to his house. He explained everything to his friends Hananiah, Mishael and Azariah. [18]He asked them to pray that the God of heaven would give him mercy. He wanted God to help him understand the mystery of the king's dream. Then he and his friends wouldn't be killed along with Babylon's other wise men. [19]During that night, God gave Daniel a vision. He showed him what the mystery was all about. Then Daniel praised the God of heaven. [20]He said,

"May God be praised for ever and ever!
　　He is wise and powerful.
[21] He changes times and seasons.
　　He removes some kings from power.
　　He causes other kings to rule.
　The wisdom of those who are wise
　　　comes from him.
　　He gives knowledge to those who
　　　have understanding.
[22] He explains deep and hidden things.
　　He knows what happens in the
　　　darkest places.
　　And where he is, everything is light.
[23] God of my people of long ago, I thank
　　　and praise you.
　　You have given me wisdom and
　　　power.
　　You have made known to me what we
　　　asked you for.
　　You have shown us the king's
　　　dream."

Daniel Tells the King What His Dream Means

[24]Then Daniel went to Arioch. The king had appointed him to put the wise men of Babylon to death. Daniel said to him, "Don't kill the wise men of Babylon. Take me to the king. I'll tell him what his dream means."

[25]So Arioch took Daniel to the king at once. Arioch said, "I have found a man among those you brought here from Judah. He can tell you what your dream means."

[26]Nebuchadnezzar spoke to Daniel, who was also called Belteshazzar. The king asked him, "Are you able to tell me what I saw in my dream? And can you tell me what it means?"

[27]Daniel replied, "You have asked us to explain a mystery to you. But no wise man

BiBLe ADVeNTuReS

Bernard and Eugene told the story of Daniel's training in Babylon and Nebuchadnezzar's dream in "Deliver Us from Evil" (A#17).

can do that. And those who try to figure things out by using magic can't do it either. [28]But there is a God in heaven who can explain mysteries. King Nebuchadnezzar, he has shown you what is going to happen. Here is what you dreamed while lying in bed. And here are the visions that passed through your mind.

[29]"Your Majesty, while you were still in bed your mind was troubled. You were thinking about things that haven't happened yet. The God who explains mysteries showed these things to you. [30]Now the mystery has been explained to me. But it isn't because I have greater wisdom than anyone else alive. It's because God wants you to know what the mystery means, Your Majesty. He wants you to understand what went through your mind.

[31]"King Nebuchadnezzar, you looked up and saw a large statue standing in front of you. It was huge. It shone brightly. And it terrified you. [32]The head of the statue was made out of pure gold. Its chest and arms were made out of silver. Its stomach and thighs were made out of bronze. [33]Its legs were made out of iron. And its feet were partly iron and partly baked clay. [34]While you were watching, a rock was cut out. But human hands didn't do it. It struck the statue on its feet of iron and clay. It smashed them. [35]Then the iron and clay were broken to pieces. So were the bronze, silver and gold. All of them were broken to pieces. They became like straw on a threshing floor at harvest time. The wind blew them away without leaving a trace. But the rock that struck the statue became a huge mountain. It filled the whole earth.

[36]"This was your dream. Now I will tell you what it means. [37]King Nebuchadnezzar, you are the greatest king of all. The God of heaven has given you authority and power. He has given you might and glory. [38]He has put everyone under your control. He has also given you authority over the wild animals and the birds in the sky.

It doesn't matter where they live. He has made you ruler over all of them. You are that head of gold.

³⁹"After you, another kingdom will take over. It won't be as powerful as yours. Next, a third kingdom will rule over the whole earth. The bronze part of the statue stands for that kingdom. ⁴⁰Finally, there will be a fourth kingdom. It will be as strong as iron. Iron breaks and smashes everything to pieces. And the fourth kingdom will crush and break all the others. ⁴¹You saw that the feet and toes were made out of iron and baked clay. And the fourth kingdom will be divided up. But it will still have some of the strength of iron. That's why you saw iron mixed with clay. ⁴²The toes were partly iron and partly clay. And the fourth kingdom will be partly strong and partly weak. ⁴³You saw the iron mixed with baked clay. And the fourth kingdom will be made up of all kinds of people. They won't hold together any more than iron mixes with clay.

⁴⁴"In the time of those kings, the God of heaven will set up a kingdom. It will never be destroyed. And no other nation will ever take it over. It will crush all those other kingdoms. It will bring them to an end. But it will last forever. ⁴⁵That's what the vision of the rock cut out of a mountain means. Human hands didn't cut out the rock. It broke the statue to pieces. It smashed the iron, bronze, clay, silver and gold.

"The great God has shown you what will take place in days to come. The dream is true. And you can trust the meaning of it that I have explained to you."

⁴⁶Then King Nebuchadnezzar bowed low in front of Daniel. He wanted to honor him. So he ordered that an offering and incense be offered to him. ⁴⁷The king said to Daniel, "I'm sure your God is the greatest God of all. He is the Lord of kings. He explains mysteries. That's why you were able to explain the mystery of my dream."

⁴⁸Then the king put Daniel in a position of authority. He gave him many gifts. He made him ruler over the city of Babylon and the towns around it. He put him in charge of all its other wise men. ⁴⁹The king also did what Daniel asked him to. He appointed Shadrach, Meshach and Abednego to help Daniel govern Babylon and the towns around it. Daniel himself remained at the royal court.

A Gold Statue and a Blazing Furnace

3 King Nebuchadnezzar made a gold statue. It was 90 feet tall and 9 feet wide. He set it up on the plain of Dura near the city of Babylon. ²Then the king sent for the royal rulers, high officials and governors. He sent for the advisers, treasurers, judges and court officers. And he sent for all the other officials of Babylon. He asked them to come to a special gathering to honor the statue he had set up. ³So the royal rulers, high officials and governors came together. So did the advisers, treasurers, judges and court officers. All the other officials joined them. They came to honor the statue that King Nebuchadnezzar had set up. They stood in front of it.

⁴Then a messenger called out loudly, "Listen, you people who come from every nation! Pay attention, you who speak other languages! Here is what the king commands you to do. ⁵You will soon hear the sound of horns and flutes. You will hear zithers, lyres, harps and pipes. In fact, you will hear all kinds of music. When you do, you must fall down and worship the gold statue. That is the statue that King Nebuchadnezzar has set up. ⁶If you don't, you will be thrown into a blazing furnace right away."

⁷All the people heard the sound of the horns and flutes. They heard the zithers, lyres, harps and other musical instruments. As soon as they did, they fell down and worshiped Nebuchadnezzar's gold statue. They were people from all nations no matter what language they spoke.

⁸At this time some people who studied the heavens came forward. They spoke against the Jews. ⁹They said, "King Nebuchadnezzar, may you live forever! ¹⁰Your Majesty has commanded everyone to fall down and worship the gold statue. You told them to do it when they heard the horns, flutes, zithers, lyres, harps, pipes and other musical instruments. ¹¹If they didn't, they would be thrown into a blazing furnace. ¹²But you have appointed some Jews to help Daniel govern Babylon and the towns around it. Their names are Shadrach,

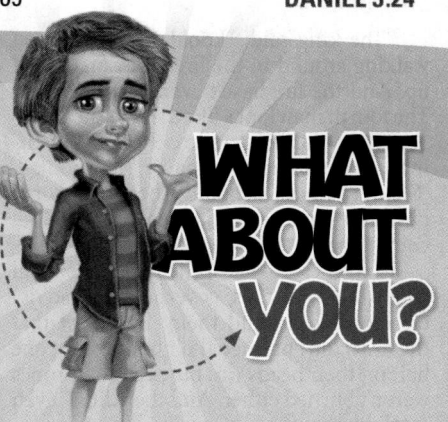

WHAT ABOUT YOU?

Sometimes our plans don't work out. That's okay, because God can take our plans and make something even better out of them.

For example, in the Adventures in Odyssey episode "V.B.S. Blues," Ned may be a drama director, but he feels more like a babysitter. Ned wants to teach the Daniel 3 story of the fiery furnace, but Mugsy and his gang create chaos and refuse to learn their lines. The play seems doomed, and Ned wonders if his directing days are over. But Mugsy and his friends put on a wonderful performance that engages the whole audience, teaching them about the faithfulness of God.

Though the play didn't happen the way Ned thought it would, God still used it to spread His message. And people loved it!

Hebrews 4:12 says, "The word of God is alive and active. It is sharper than any sword that has two edges. It cuts deep enough to separate soul from spirit. It can separate bones from joints. It judges the thoughts and purposes of the heart." That means God's Word will speak to people and bring truth because it is truth. And since God is faithful, we can be sure that His plans for us are better than anything we could have engineered by ourselves.

Read the biblical account of Shadrach, Meshach and Abednego in Daniel chapter 3. It's the Old Testament trio's hottest adventure!

Meshach and Abednego. They don't pay any attention to you, King Nebuchadnezzar. They don't serve your gods. And they refuse to worship the gold statue you have set up."

¹³Nebuchadnezzar was very angry. He sent for Shadrach, Meshach and Abednego. So they were brought to him. ¹⁴The king said to them, "Shadrach, Meshach and Abednego, is what I heard about you true? Don't you serve my gods? Don't you worship the gold statue I set up? ¹⁵You will hear the horns, flutes, zithers, lyres, harps, pipes and other musical instruments. When you do, fall down and worship the statue I made. If you will, that's very good. But if you won't, you will be thrown at once into a blazing furnace. Then what god will be able to save you from my power?"

¹⁶Shadrach, Meshach and Abednego replied to him. They said, "King Nebuchadnezzar, we don't need to talk about this anymore. ¹⁷We might be thrown into the blazing furnace. But the God we serve is able to bring us out of it alive. He will save us from your power. ¹⁸But we want you to know this, Your Majesty. Even if we knew that our God wouldn't save us, we still wouldn't serve your gods. We wouldn't worship the gold statue you set up."

¹⁹Then Nebuchadnezzar was very angry with Shadrach, Meshach and Abednego. The look on his face changed. And he ordered that the furnace be heated seven times hotter than usual. ²⁰He also gave some of the strongest soldiers in his army a command. He ordered them to tie up Shadrach, Meshach and Abednego. Then he told his men to throw them into the blazing furnace. ²¹So they were tied up. Then they were thrown into the furnace. They were wearing their robes, pants, turbans and other clothes. ²²The king's command was carried out quickly. The furnace was so hot that its flames killed the soldiers who threw Shadrach, Meshach and Abednego into it. ²³So the three men were firmly tied up. And they fell into the blazing furnace.

²⁴Then King Nebuchadnezzar leaped to his feet. He was so amazed he asked his advisers, "Didn't we tie up three men? Didn't we throw three men into the fire?"

They replied, "Yes, we did, Your Majesty."

²⁵The king said, "Look! I see four men walking around in the fire. They aren't tied up. And the fire hasn't even harmed them. The fourth man looks like a son of the gods."

²⁶Then the king approached the opening of the blazing furnace. He shouted, "Shadrach, Meshach and Abednego, come out! You who serve the Most High God, come here!"

So they came out of the fire. ²⁷The royal rulers, high officials, governors and advisers crowded around them. They saw that the fire hadn't harmed their bodies. Not one hair on their heads was burned. Their robes weren't burned either. And they didn't even smell like smoke.

²⁸Then Nebuchadnezzar said, "May the God of Shadrach, Meshach and Abednego be praised! He has sent his angel and saved his servants. They trusted in him. They refused to obey my command. They were willing to give up their lives. They would rather die than serve or worship any god except their own God. ²⁹No other god can save people this way. So I'm giving an order about the God of Shadrach, Meshach and Abednego. No one may say anything against him. That's true no matter what language they speak. If they say anything against him, they'll be cut to pieces. And their houses will be turned into piles of trash."

Dan. 3:25 Here's an angel-singeing and an angel-sighting. Get it? Because he's in the fire, he would be singed? Actually, I guess he wouldn't be singed because the Bible says the fire didn't harm them. And maybe he wasn't an angel either. Some Bible scholars think the fourth man is no mere angel (verse 28) but actually Jesus Himself!

³⁰Then the king honored Shadrach, Meshach and Abednego. He gave them higher positions in the city of Babylon and the towns around it.

Nebuchadnezzar Dreams About a Tree

4 I, King Nebuchadnezzar, am writing this letter.

I am sending it to people who live all over the world. I'm sending it to people of every nation no matter what language they speak.

May you have great success!

²I am pleased to tell you what has happened. The Most High God has done miraculous signs and wonders for me.

³ His signs are great.
    His wonders are mighty.
    His kingdom will last forever.
    His rule will never end.

⁴I was at home in my palace. I was content and very successful. ⁵But I had a dream that made me afraid. I was lying in bed. Then dreams and visions passed through my mind. They terrified me. ⁶So I commanded that all the wise men in Babylon be brought to me. I wanted them to tell me what my dream meant. ⁷Those who try to figure things out by using magic came. So did those who study the heavens. I told all of them what I had dreamed. But they couldn't tell me what it meant. ⁸Finally, Daniel came to me. He is called Belteshazzar, after the name of my god. The spirit of the holy gods is in him. I told him my dream.

⁹I said, "Belteshazzar, you are chief of the magicians. I know that the spirit of the holy gods is in you. No mystery is too hard for you to figure out. Here is my dream. Tell me what it means. ¹⁰Here are the visions I saw while I was lying in bed. I looked up and saw a tree standing in the middle of the land. It was very tall. ¹¹It had grown to be large and strong. Its top touched the sky. It could be seen anywhere on earth. ¹²Its leaves were beautiful. It had a lot of fruit on it. It provided enough food for people and animals. Under

WOOTON'S FUN FACTS

Dan. 4:7

Sometimes there are two words that sound the same but mean very different things. Like broth and bath. I always get those mixed up. *Astronomy* is math, physics, and science—no guessing. *Astrology* is fortune-telling and predictions—guessing. The two were actually the same thing until the fourteenth century when science took over.

the tree, the wild animals found safety. The birds lived in its branches. Every creature was fed from that tree.

[13]"While I was still lying in bed, I looked up. In my visions, I saw a holy one. He was a messenger. He was coming down from heaven. [14]He called out in a loud voice. He said, 'Cut down the tree. Break off its branches. Strip off its leaves. Scatter its fruit. Let the animals under it run away. Let the birds in its branches fly off. [15]But leave the stump with its roots in the ground. Let it stay in the field. Put a band of iron and bronze around it.

"'Let King Nebuchadnezzar become wet with the dew of heaven. Let him live with the animals among the plants of the earth. [16]Let him no longer have the mind of a man. Instead, let him be given the mind of an animal. Let him stay that way until seven periods of time pass by.

[17]"'The decision is announced by holy messengers. So all who are alive will know that the Most High God is King. He rules over all kingdoms on earth. He gives them to anyone he wants. Sometimes he puts the least important people in charge of them.'

[18]"This is the dream I, King Nebuchadnezzar, had. Now tell me what it means, Belteshazzar. None of the wise men in my kingdom can explain it to me. But you can. After all, the spirit of the holy gods is in you."

Daniel Explains Nebuchadnezzar's Dream

[19]Daniel, who was also called Belteshazzar, was very bewildered for a while. His thoughts terrified him. So the king said, "Belteshazzar, don't let the dream or its meaning make you afraid."

Belteshazzar answered, "My master, I wish the dream were about your enemies! I wish its meaning had to do with them! [20]You saw a tree. It grew to be large and strong. Its top touched the sky. It could be seen from anywhere on earth. [21]Its leaves were beautiful. It had a lot of fruit on it. It provided enough food for people and animals. Under the tree, the wild animals found safety. The birds lived in its branches. [22]Your Majesty, you are that tree! You have become great and strong. Your greatness has grown until it reaches the sky. Your rule has spread to all parts of the earth.

[23]"Your Majesty, you saw a holy one. He was a messenger. He came down from heaven. He said, 'Cut down the tree. Destroy it. But leave the stump with its roots in the ground. Let it stay in the field. Put an iron and bronze band around it. Let King Nebuchadnezzar become wet with the dew of heaven. Let him live with the wild animals. Let him stay that way until seven periods of time pass by.'

[24]"Your Majesty, here is what your dream means. The Most High God has given an order against you. [25]You will be driven away from people. You will live with the wild animals. You will eat grass just as an ox does. You will become wet with the dew of heaven. Seven periods of time will pass by for you. Then you will recognize that the Most High God rules over all kingdoms on earth. He gives them to anyone he wants. [26]But he gave a command to leave the stump of the tree along with

its roots. That means your kingdom will be given back to you. It will happen when you recognize that the God of heaven rules. ²⁷So, Your Majesty, I hope you will accept my advice. Stop being sinful. Do what is right. Give up your evil practices. Show kindness to those who are being treated badly. Then perhaps things will continue to go well with you."

nebuchadnezzar's Dream Comes True

²⁸All this happened to King Nebuchadnezzar. ²⁹It took place twelve months later. He was walking on the roof of his palace in Babylon. ³⁰He said, "Isn't this the great Babylon I have built as a place for my royal palace? I used my mighty power to build it. It shows how glorious my majesty is."

³¹He was still speaking when he heard a voice from heaven. It said, "King Nebuchadnezzar, here is what has been ordered concerning you. Your royal authority has been taken from you. ³²You will be driven away from people. You will live with the wild animals. You will eat grass just as an ox does. Seven periods of time will pass by for you. Then you will recognize that the Most High God rules over all kingdoms on earth. He gives them to anyone he wants."

³³What had been said about King Nebuchadnezzar came true at once. He was driven away from people. He ate grass just as an ox does. His body became wet with the dew of heaven. He stayed that way until his hair grew like the feathers of an eagle. His nails became like the claws of a bird.

³⁴At the end of that time I, Nebuchadnezzar, looked up toward heaven. My mind became clear again. Then I praised the Most High God. I gave honor and glory to the God who lives forever.

His rule will last forever.
     His kingdom will never end.
³⁵ He considers all the nations on earth
     to be nothing.

WHAT ABOUT YOU?

Have you ever ridden on a train? Years ago, train travel was the way most people traveled long distances in the United States. Now train trips are rare for most people as airlines and interstate highways move us across the country.

Do you know that a train ticket once helped authorities solve a fifty-five-year-old missing person case? The kidnapping took place way back in 1957. In 2012, police finally arrested a man for the crime. The suspect had claimed that he bought a train ticket and traveled to another town. The first part of his story was true; he had purchased the ticket. But police discovered that he had never used it. This final piece of evidence put the man in jail for the rest of his life.

When you're looking for answers (or trying to crack a case), a little thing like a train ticket could make a big difference. Turning to God should be part of that process. As Daniel 4:35 tells us, God is in control of all things. Big stuff. Tiny details. That's encouraging, because when we make mistakes or need solutions, it's good to remember that God wants us to turn to Him.

Have you ever seen an old railway ticket? Some are very artfully designed. Ask your parents to help you find examples online, then design your own ticket and be sure to include the words of Daniel 4:35 to remind you that God is powerful enough to help you, no matter what you face.

In facing dead ends when searching
for his father, Eugene discovered
how God's ways are higher than our
own in "A Time for Action" (A#46).

He does as he pleases
  with the powers of heaven.
He does what he wants
  with the nations of the earth.
No one can hold back his hand.
  No one can say to him,
  "What have you done?"

36My honor and glory were returned to me when my mind became clear again. The glory of my kingdom was given back to me. My advisers and nobles came to me. And I was put back on my throne. I became even greater than I had been before. 37Now I, Nebuchadnezzar, give praise and honor and glory to the King of heaven. Everything he does is right. All his ways are fair. He is able to bring down those who live proudly.

A Hand Writes on the Palace Wall

5 King Belshazzar gave a huge banquet. He invited a thousand of his nobles to it. He drank wine with them. 2While Belshazzar was drinking his wine, he gave orders to his servants. He commanded them to bring in some gold and silver cups. They were the cups his father Nebuchadnezzar had taken from the temple in Jerusalem. Belshazzar had them brought in so everyone could drink from them. That included the king himself, his nobles, his wives and his concubines. 3So the servants brought in the gold cups. The cups had been taken from God's temple in Jerusalem. The king and his nobles drank from them. So did his wives and concubines. 4As they drank the wine, they praised their gods. The statues of those gods were made out of gold, silver, bronze, iron, wood or stone.

5Suddenly the fingers of a human hand appeared. They wrote something on the plaster of the palace wall. It happened near the lampstand. The king watched the hand as it wrote. 6His face turned pale. He was so

afraid that his legs became weak. And his knees were knocking together.

7The king sent for those who try to figure things out by using magic. He also sent for those who study the heavens. All of them were wise men in Babylon. Then the king spoke to them. He said, "I want one of you to read this writing. I want you to tell me what it means. Whoever does this will be dressed in purple clothes. A gold chain will be put around his neck. And he will be made the third highest ruler in the kingdom."

8Then all the king's wise men came in. But they couldn't read the writing. They couldn't tell him what it meant. 9So King Belshazzar became even more terrified. His face grew more pale. And his nobles were bewildered.

10The queen heard the king and his nobles talking. So she came into the dining hall. "King Belshazzar, may you live forever!" she said. "Don't be afraid! Don't look so pale! 11I know a man in your kingdom who has the spirit of the holy gods in him. He has understanding and wisdom and good sense just like the gods. He was chief of those who tried to figure things out by using magic. And he was in charge of those who studied the heavens. Your father, King Nebuchadnezzar, appointed him to that position. 12King Nebuchadnezzar did this because he saw what the man could do. This man's name is Daniel. Your father called him Belteshazzar. He has a clever mind and knowledge and understanding. He is also able to tell what dreams mean. He can explain riddles and solve hard problems. Send for him. He'll tell you what the writing means."

13So Daniel was brought to the king. The king said to him, "Are you Daniel? Are you one of the prisoners my father the king brought here from Judah? 14I have heard that the spirit of the gods is in you. I've also heard that you have understanding and good sense and special wisdom. 15The wise men and those who practice magic were brought to me. They were asked to read this writing and tell me what it means. But they couldn't. 16I have heard that you are able to explain things and solve hard problems. I hope you can read this writing and tell me what it means. If you can, you will be dressed in purple clothes. A gold chain will be put around your neck. And you will be made the third highest ruler in the kingdom."

¹⁷Then Daniel answered the king. He said, "You can keep your gifts for yourself. You can give your rewards to someone else. But I will read the writing for you. I'll tell you what it means.

¹⁸"Your Majesty, the Most High God was good to your father Nebuchadnezzar. He gave him authority and greatness and glory and honor. ¹⁹God gave him a high position. Then people from every nation became afraid of the king. That was true no matter what language they spoke. The king put to death anyone he wanted to. He spared anyone he wanted to spare. He gave high positions to anyone he wanted to. And he brought down anyone he wanted to bring down. ²⁰But his heart became very stubborn and proud. So he was removed from his royal throne. His glory was stripped away from him. ²¹He was driven away from people. He was given the mind of an animal. He lived with the wild donkeys. He ate grass just as an ox does. His body became wet with the dew of heaven. He stayed that way until he recognized that the Most High God rules over all kingdoms on earth. He puts anyone he wants to in charge of them.

²²"But you knew all that, Belshazzar. After all, you are Nebuchadnezzar's son. In spite of that, you are still proud. ²³You have taken your stand against the Lord of heaven. You had your servants bring cups from his temple to you. You and your nobles drank wine from them. So did your wives and concubines. You praised your gods. The statues of those gods are made out of silver, gold, bronze, iron, wood or stone. They can't see or hear or understand anything. But you didn't honor God. He holds in his hand your very life and everything you do. ²⁴So he sent the hand that wrote on the wall.

²⁵"Here is what was written.

MENE, MENE, TEKEL, PARSIN

²⁶"And here is what these words mean.
The word Mene means that God has limited the time of your rule. He has brought it to an end.

²⁷The word Tekel means that you have been weighed on scales. And you haven't measured up to God's standard.

²⁸The word Peres means that your authority over your kingdom will be taken away from you. It will be given to the Medes and Persians."

²⁹Then Belshazzar commanded his servants to dress Daniel in purple clothes. So they did. They put a gold chain around his neck. And he was made the third highest ruler in the kingdom.

³⁰That very night Belshazzar, the king of Babylon, was killed. ³¹His kingdom was given to Darius the Mede. Darius was 62 years old.

Daniel Is Thrown Into a Den of Lions

6 It pleased Darius to appoint 120 royal rulers over his entire kingdom. ²He placed three leaders over them. One of the leaders was Daniel. The royal rulers were made accountable to the three leaders. Then the king wouldn't lose any of his wealth. ³Daniel did a better job than the other two leaders or any of the royal rulers. He was an unusually good and able man. So the king planned to put him in charge of the whole kingdom. ⁴But the other two leaders and the royal rulers heard about it. So they looked for a reason to bring charges against Daniel. They tried to find something wrong with the way he ran the government. But they weren't able to. They couldn't find any fault with his work. He could always be trusted. He never did anything wrong. And he always did what he was supposed to. ⁵Finally these men said, "We want to bring charges against this man Daniel. But it's almost impossible for us to come up with a reason to do it. If we find a reason, it will have to be in connection with the law of his God."

⁶So the two leaders and the royal rulers went as a group to the king. They said, "King Darius, may you live forever! ⁷All the royal leaders, high officials, royal rulers, advisers and governors want to make a suggestion. We've agreed that you should give an order. And you should make sure it's obeyed. Your Majesty, here is the command you should make your people obey for the next 30 days. Don't let any of your people pray to any god or human being except to you. If they do, throw them into the lions' den. ⁸Now give the order. Write it down in the law of the Medes and Persians. Then it can't be changed." ⁹So King Darius put the order in writing.

¹⁰Daniel found out that the king had signed the order. In spite of that, he did just as he had always done before. He went home to his upstairs room. Its windows opened toward Jerusalem. He went to his room three times a day to pray. He got down on his knees and gave thanks to his God. ¹¹Some of the other royal officials went to where Daniel was staying. They saw him praying and asking God for help. ¹²So they went to the king. They spoke to him about his royal order. They said, "Your Majesty, didn't you sign an official order? It said that for the next 30 days your people could pray only to you. They could not pray to anyone else, whether god or human being. If they did, they would be thrown into the lions' den."

The king answered, "The order must still be obeyed. It's what the law of the Medes and Persians requires. So it can't be changed."

¹³Then they spoke to the king again. They said, "Daniel is one of the prisoners from Judah. He doesn't pay any attention to you, Your Majesty. He doesn't obey the order you put in writing. He still prays to his God three times a day." ¹⁴When the king heard this, he was very upset. He didn't want Daniel to be harmed in any way. Until sunset, he did everything he could to save him.

¹⁵Then the men went as a group to King Darius. They said to him, "Your Majesty, remember that no order or command you give can be changed. That's what the law of the Medes and Persians requires."

¹⁶So the king gave the order. Daniel was brought out and thrown into the lions' den. The king said to him, "You always serve your God faithfully. So may he save you!"

¹⁷A stone was brought and placed over the opening of the den. The king sealed it with his own special ring. He also sealed it with the rings of his nobles. Then nothing could be done to help Daniel. ¹⁸The king returned to his palace. He didn't eat anything that night. He didn't ask for anything to be brought to him for his enjoyment. And he couldn't sleep.

¹⁹As soon as the sun began to rise, the king got up. He hurried to the lions' den. ²⁰When he got near it, he called out to Daniel. His voice was filled with great concern. He said, "Daniel! You serve the living God. You always serve him faithfully. So has he been able to save you from the lions?"

BiBLE ADVENTURES

Connie told the story of Daniel in the lions' den in "B-TV: Thanks" (A#31).

²¹Daniel answered, "Your Majesty, may you live forever! ²²My God sent his angel. And his angel shut the mouths of the lions. They haven't hurt me at all. That's because I haven't done anything wrong in God's sight. I've never done anything wrong to you either, Your Majesty."

²³The king was filled with joy. He ordered his servants to lift Daniel out of the den. So they did. They didn't see any wounds on him. That's because he had trusted in his God.

²⁴Then the king gave another order. The men who had said bad things about Daniel were brought in. They were thrown into the lions' den. So were their wives and children. Before they hit the bottom of the den, the lions attacked them. And the lions crushed all their bones.

²⁵Then King Darius wrote to people of all nations, no matter what language they spoke. He said,

"May you have great success!

²⁶"I order people in every part of my kingdom to respect and honor Daniel's God.

"He is the living God.
He will live forever.
His kingdom will not be destroyed.
His rule will never end.
²⁷ He sets people free and saves them.
He does miraculous signs and
wonders.
He does them in the heavens
and on the earth.
He has saved Daniel
from the power of the lions."

²⁸So Daniel had success while Darius was king. Things went well with Daniel during the rule of Cyrus, the Persian.

Daniel Has a Dream About Four Animals

7 It was the first year that Belshazzar was king of Babylon. Daniel had a dream. He was lying in bed. In his dream, visions passed through his mind. He wrote down what he saw.

²Daniel said, "I had a vision at night. I looked up and saw the four winds of heaven. They were stirring up the Mediterranean Sea. ³Four large animals came up out of the sea. Each one was different from the others.

⁴"The first animal was like a lion. It had the wings of an eagle. I watched until its wings were torn off. Then it was lifted up from the ground. It stood on two feet like a human being. And the mind of a human being was given to it.

⁵"I saw a second animal. It looked like a bear. It was raised up on one of its sides. And it had three ribs between its teeth. It was told, 'Get up! Eat meat until you are full!'

⁶"After that, I saw another animal. It looked like a leopard. On its back were four wings like the wings of a bird. The animal I saw had four heads. And it was given authority to rule.

⁷"After that, in my vision I looked up and saw a fourth animal. It was terrifying and very powerful. It had large iron teeth. It crushed those it attacked and ate them up. It stomped on anything that was left. It was different from the other animals. And it had ten horns.

⁸"I thought about the horns. Then I saw another horn. It was a little one. It grew up among the other horns. Three of the first horns were pulled up by their roots to make room for it. The little horn had eyes like the eyes of a human being. Its mouth was always bragging.

⁹"As I watched,

"thrones were set in place.
    The Eternal God took his seat.
His clothes were as white as snow.
    The hair on his head was white like
        wool.
His throne was blazing with fire.
    And flames were all around its
        wheels.
¹⁰ A river of fire was flowing.
    It was coming out from in front of
        God.
Thousands and thousands of angels
        served him.
    Millions of them stood in front of
        him.
The court was seated.
    And the books were opened.

¹¹"Then I continued to watch because of the way the horn was bragging. I kept looking until the fourth animal was killed. I watched until its body was destroyed. It was thrown into the blazing fire. ¹²The authority of the other animals had been stripped away from them. But they were allowed to live for a period of time.

¹³"In my vision I saw one who looked like a son of man. He was coming with the clouds of heaven. He approached the Eternal God. He was led right up to him. ¹⁴And he was given authority, glory and a kingdom. People of all nations, no matter what language they spoke, worshiped him. His authority will last forever. It will not pass away. His kingdom will never be destroyed.

An Angel Tells Daniel What His Dream Means

¹⁵"My spirit was troubled. The visions that passed through my mind upset me. ¹⁶I approached an angel who was standing there. I asked him what all these things really meant.

"So he explained to me what everything meant. ¹⁷He said, 'The four large animals stand for four kings. The kings will appear on the earth. ¹⁸But the holy people of the Most High God will receive the kingdom. They will possess it forever. It will belong to them for ever and ever.'

¹⁹"Then I wanted to know what the fourth animal stood for. It was different from the others. It was the most terrifying of all. It had iron teeth and bronze claws. It crushed everyone it attacked and ate them up. It stomped on anything that was left. ²⁰I also wanted to know about the ten horns on its head. And I wanted to know about the other horn that grew up later. It caused three of the ten horns to fall out. It appeared to be stronger than the others. It had eyes. And its mouth was always bragging. ²¹I saw that the horn was at war with God's holy people. It was winning the battle over them. ²²But then the Eternal God came. He decided in favor of his holy people. So the time came when the kingdom was given to them.

²³"Here's how the angel explained it to me. He said, 'The fourth animal stands for a fourth kingdom. It will appear on earth. It will be different from the other kingdoms. It will eat up the whole earth. It will stomp

on it and crush it. ²⁴The ten horns stand for ten kings. They will come from the fourth kingdom. After them another king will appear. He will be different from the earlier ones. He'll bring three kings under his control. ²⁵He'll speak against the Most High God. He'll treat God's holy people badly. He will try to change the times and laws that were given by God. God's holy people will be placed under his power for three and a half years.

²⁶" 'But the court will be seated. And the power of that king will be taken away from him. It will be completely destroyed forever. ²⁷Then the authority, power and greatness of all the kingdoms on earth will be taken from them. And all they had will be given to the holy people of the Most High God. His kingdom will last forever. Every ruler will worship and obey him.'

²⁸"That's all I saw. My thoughts deeply troubled me. My face turned pale. But I kept those things to myself."

Daniel Has a Vision About a Ram and a Goat

8 It was the third year of King Belshazzar's rule. After the vision that had already appeared to me, I had another one. ²In my vision I saw myself in the city of Susa. It has high walls around it. It is in the land of Elam. In the vision I was beside the Ulai Canal. ³I looked up and saw a ram that had two horns. It was standing beside the canal. Its horns were long. One of them was longer than the other. But that horn grew up later. ⁴I watched the ram as it charged toward the west. It also charged toward the north and the south. No animal could stand up against it. Not one of them could save anyone from its power. It did as it pleased. And it became great.

⁵I was thinking about all of this. Then a goat suddenly came from the west. It had a large horn between its eyes. The goat raced across the whole earth without even touching the ground. ⁶It came toward the ram that had the two horns. It was the ram I had seen standing beside the canal. The goat was very angry. It charged at the ram. ⁷I saw it attack the ram with mighty force. It struck the ram and broke the ram's two horns. The ram didn't have the power to stand up against it. The goat knocked the ram to the ground and stomped on it. No one could save the ram from the goat's power. ⁸The goat became very great. But when its power was at its greatest, the goat's large horn was broken off. In its place four large horns grew up toward the four winds of heaven.

⁹Out of one of the four horns came another horn. It was small at first but became more and more powerful. It grew to the south and to the east and toward the beautiful land of Israel. ¹⁰It grew until it reached the stars in the sky. It threw some of them down to the earth. And it stomped on them. ¹¹It set itself up to be as great as the commander of the Lord's army. It took away the daily sacrifices from the Lord. And his temple in Jerusalem was thrown down. ¹²Because many of the Lord's people refused to obey him, they were handed over to the horn. The daily sacrifices were also given over to it. The horn was successful no matter what it did. And true worship of God was thrown down to the ground.

¹³Then I heard a holy angel speaking. Another holy angel spoke to him. He asked, "How long will it take for the vision to come true? When will the daily sacrifices be stopped? When will those who refuse to obey God be destroyed? When will the temple be handed over to an enemy? And when will some of the Lord's people be stomped on?"

¹⁴One of the holy angels said to me, "It will take 2,300 evenings and mornings. Then the temple will be made holy again."

Jason's Jargon

DANIEL 8

Examine this chapter for the word *bewildered*. To be bewildered is to be puzzled. Daniel just had a very strange vision from God, and it confused him.

Gabriel Tells Daniel What His Vision Means

¹⁵I was having the vision. And I was trying to understand it. Then I saw someone who looked like a man. ¹⁶I heard a voice

WOOTON'S FUN FACTS

Dan. 8:1–27 Have you got your goat? No? Then read this chapter. You'll know what I mean when you finish it. This is probably the least-told story in Daniel because the fiery furnace and the den of lions steal the show. And—spoiler alert! It has the first sighting of the archangel Gabriel!

from the Ulai Canal. It called out, "Gabriel, tell Daniel what his vision means."

[17]Gabriel came close to where I was standing. I was terrified and fell down flat with my face toward the ground. Here is what he said to me. "Son of man, I want you to understand the vision. It's about the time of the end."

[18]While he was speaking to me, I was sound asleep. I lay with my face on the ground. Then he touched me. He raised me to my feet.

[19]He said, "I am going to tell you what will happen later. It will take place when God is angry. The vision is about the appointed time of the end. [20]You saw a ram that had two horns. It stands for the kings of Media and Persia. [21]The goat stands for the king of Greece. The large horn between its eyes is the first king. [22]Four horns took the horn's place when it was broken off. They stand for four kingdoms that will come from his nation. But those kingdoms will not be as powerful as his.

[23]"Toward the end of their rule, those who refuse to obey God will become completely evil. Then another king will appear. He will have a scary-looking face. He will be a master at making clever plans. [24]He will become very strong. But he will not get that way by his own power. People will be amazed at the way he destroys everything. He will be successful no matter what he does. He will destroy mighty people. Those mighty people are God's holy people. [25]He will tell lies in order to succeed. He will think he is more important than anyone else. When people feel safe, he will destroy many of them. He will stand up against the greatest Prince of all. Then he will be destroyed. But he will not be killed by human beings.

[26]"The vision of the evenings and mornings that has been given to you is true. But seal up the vision. It is about a time far off."

[27]I, Daniel, was worn out. I was too tired to get up for several days. Then I got up and returned to my work for the king. The vision bewildered me. I couldn't understand it.

Daniel Prays to the LORD

9 It was the first year that Darius was king of Babylon. He was from Media and was the son of Xerxes. [2]In that year I learned from the Scriptures that Jerusalem would remain destroyed for 70 years. That was what the LORD had told Jeremiah the prophet. [3]So I prayed to the Lord God. I begged him. I made many appeals to him. I didn't eat anything. I put on the rough clothing people wear when they're sad. And I sat down in ashes.

[4]I prayed to the LORD my God. I admitted that we had sinned. I said,

"Lord, you are a great and wonderful God. You keep the covenant you made with all those who love you and obey your commandments. You show them your love. [5]We have sinned and done what is wrong. We have been evil. We have refused to obey you. We have turned away from your commands and laws. [6]We haven't listened to your servants the prophets. They spoke in your name to our kings, our princes and our people of long ago. They also brought your message to all our people in the land.

[7]"Lord, you always do what is right. But we are covered with shame today. We are the people of Judah and Jerusalem. All of us are Israelites, no matter where we live. We are now living in many countries. You scattered us among the nations because we weren't faithful to you. [8]LORD, we are covered with shame. So are our kings and princes, and our people

of long ago. We have sinned against you. [9]You are the Lord our God. You show us your tender love. You forgive us. But we have turned against you. [10]You are the LORD our God. But we haven't obeyed you. We haven't kept the laws you gave us through your servants the prophets. [11]All the people of Israel have broken your law and turned away from it. They have refused to obey you.

"Curses and warnings are written down in the Law of Moses. He was your servant. Those curses have been poured out on us. That's because we have sinned against you. [12]The warnings you gave us and our rulers have come true. You have brought great trouble on us. Nothing like what has been done to Jerusalem has ever happened anywhere else on earth. [13]The curses that are written in the Law of Moses have fallen on us. We have received nothing but trouble. You are the LORD our God. But we haven't asked for your favor. We haven't turned away from our sins. We've refused to pay attention to the laws you gave us. [14]LORD, you didn't hold back from bringing this trouble on us. You always do what is right. But we haven't obeyed you.

[15]"Lord our God, you used your mighty hand to bring your people out of Egypt. You made a name for yourself. It is still great to this day. But we have sinned. We've done what is wrong. [16]Lord, you saved your people before. So turn your great anger away from Jerusalem again. After all, it is your city. It's your holy mountain. You have made those who live around us think little of Jerusalem and your people. That's because we have sinned. Our people before us did evil things too.

[17]"Our God, hear my prayers. Pay attention to the appeals I make to you. Lord, have mercy on your temple that has been destroyed. Do it for your own honor. [18]Our God, please listen to us. The city that belongs to you has been destroyed. Open your eyes and see it. We aren't asking you to answer our prayers because we are godly. Instead, we're asking you to do it because you love us so much. [19]Lord, please listen! Lord, please forgive us! Lord, hear our prayers! Take action for your own honor. Our God, please don't wait. Your city and your people belong to you."

Gabriel Tells Daniel About Seventy "Weeks"

[20]I was speaking and praying. I was admitting that I and my people Israel had sinned. I was making my appeal to the LORD my God. My appeal was about his holy mountain of Zion. [21]While I was still praying, Gabriel came to me. I had seen him in my earlier vision. He flew over to me very quickly. It was about the time when the evening sacrifice is offered. [22]He helped me understand. He said, "Daniel, I have come now to help you know and understand these things. [23]You are highly respected. So as soon as you began to pray, the LORD gave you a message. I have come to tell you what it is. Here is how you must understand the vision.

[24]"The LORD has appointed 70 'weeks' for your people and your holy city. During that time, acts against God's law will be stopped. Sin will come to an end. And the evil things people do will be paid for. Then everyone will always do what is right. Everything that has been made known in visions and prophecies will come true. And the Most Holy Room in the temple will be anointed.

[25]"Here is what I want you to know and understand. There will be seven 'weeks.' Then there will be 62 'weeks.' The seven 'weeks' will begin when an order is given to rebuild Jerusalem and make it like new again. At the end of the 62 'weeks,' the Anointed King will come. Jerusalem will have streets and a water system when it is rebuilt. But that will be done in times of trouble. [26]After the 62 'weeks,' the Anointed King will be put to death. His followers will desert him. And everything he has will be taken away from him. The army of the ruler who will come will destroy the city and the temple. The end will come like a flood. War will continue until the end. The LORD has ordered that many places be destroyed. [27]A covenant will be put into effect with many people for one 'week.' In the middle of the 'week' sacrifices and offerings will come to

an end. And at the temple a hated thing that destroys will be set up. It will remain until that ruler who will come is destroyed. Then he will experience what the LORD has ordered."

Daniel Has a Vision About What Will Happen to Israel

10 It was the third year that Cyrus, the king of Persia, ruled over Babylon. At that time I was living in Babylon. There the people called me Belteshazzar. A message from God came to me. It was true. It was about a great war. I had a vision that showed me what it meant.

²At that time I was very sad for three weeks. ³I didn't eat any rich food. No meat or wine touched my lips. I didn't use any lotions at all until the three weeks were over.

⁴I was standing on the bank of the great Tigris River. It was the 24th day of the first month. ⁵I looked up and saw a man dressed in linen clothes. He had a belt around his waist. It was made out of fine gold from Uphaz. ⁶His body gleamed like topaz. His face shone like lightning. His eyes were like flaming torches. His arms and legs were as bright as polished bronze. And his voice was like the sound of a large crowd.

⁷I was the only one who saw the vision. The people who were there with me didn't see it. But they were so terrified that they ran and hid. ⁸So I was left alone as I was watching this great vision. I felt very weak. My face turned as pale as death. And I was helpless. ⁹Then I heard the man speak. As I listened to him, I fell sound asleep. My face was toward the ground.

¹⁰A hand touched me. It pulled me up on my hands and knees. I began to tremble with fear. ¹¹The man said, "Daniel, you are highly respected. Think carefully about what I am going to say to you. And stand up. God has sent me to you." When he said that, I trembled as I stood up.

¹²He continued, "Do not be afraid, Daniel. You decided to get more understanding. You made yourself humble as you worshiped your God. Since the first day you did those things, your words were heard. I have come to give you an answer. ¹³But the prince of Persia opposed me for 21 days. Then Michael came to help me. He is one of the leaders of the angels. He helped me win the battle over the king of Persia.

¹⁴Now I have come to explain the vision to you. I will tell you what will happen to your people. The vision shows what will take place in days to come."

¹⁵While he was telling me these things, I bowed with my face toward the ground. I wasn't able to speak. ¹⁶Then someone who looked like a man touched my lips. I opened my mouth. I began to speak to the one who was standing in front of me. I said, "My master, I'm greatly troubled because of the vision I've seen. And I feel very weak. ¹⁷How can I talk with you? My strength is gone. In fact, I can hardly breathe."

¹⁸The one who looked like a man touched me again. He gave me strength. ¹⁹"Do not be afraid," he said. "You are highly respected. May peace be with you! Be strong now. Be strong."

When he spoke to me, I became stronger. I said, "Speak, my master. You have given en me strength."

²⁰So he said, "Do you know why I have come to you? Soon I will return to fight against the prince of Persia. When I go, the prince of Greece will come. ²¹But first I will tell you what is written in the Book of Truth. No one gives me any help against those princes except Michael. He is your

11 leader. ¹I stepped forward to help him and keep him safe. It was the first year that Darius, the Mede, was king.

The Kings of Egypt and Syria

²"Now then, what I'm about to tell you is true. Three more kings will come to power in Persia. Then a fourth one will rule. He will be much richer than all the others. He will use his wealth to gain power. And he will stir up everyone against the kingdom of Greece. ³After him, a mighty king will come to power. He will rule with great power and do as he pleases. ⁴Not long after his rule ends, his kingdom will be broken up. It will be divided up into four parts. His children will not receive it when he dies. And it will not be as strong as his kingdom. It will be pulled up by the roots. And it will be given to others.

⁵"The king of Egypt will become strong. But one of his commanders will become even stronger. He will rule over his own kingdom with great power. ⁶After many years, the two kingdoms will join forces. The daughter of the next king of Egypt will

go to the king of Syria. She will join forces with him. But she will not hold on to her power. And he and his power will not last either. In those days she and her attendants will die. They will die when the people she trusts lie to her. The same thing will happen to her father and the one who helped her.

7"Someone from her family line will take her place. He will attack the army of the next king of Syria. Then he will enter his fort. He will fight against that army and win. 8He will take the metal statues of their gods. He will also take away their priceless objects of silver and gold. He will carry everything off to Egypt. For many years he will leave the king of Syria alone. 9Then the king of Syria will march into territory that was controlled by Egypt. After that, he will return to his own country. 10His sons will prepare for war. They will gather a huge army. It will sweep along like a mighty flood. The army will fight its way as far as one of the Egyptian forts.

11"Another king of Egypt will march out with mighty force. He will be very angry. By then, another person will have become king in Syria. The king of Egypt will come to fight against him. The king of Syria will gather a huge army. But that army will lose the battle. 12His soldiers will be carried off. Then the king of Egypt will be filled with pride. He will kill many thousands of soldiers. But his success will not last. 13The king of Syria will bring another army together. It will be larger than the first one. After several years, he will march out with a huge army. It will have everything it needs for battle.

14"In those times many people will rise up against the next king of Egypt. Lawless people in your own nation will refuse to obey him. That is what you saw in your vision. But they will not succeed. 15Then the king of Syria will go to a certain city that has high walls around it. He will build ramps against them. And he will capture that city. The forces of Egypt will not have the power to stop him. Even their best troops will not be strong enough to stand up against him. 16He will do anything he wants to. No one will be able to stand up against him. He will take over the beautiful land of Israel. And he will have the power to destroy it. 17The king of Syria will decide to come with the might of his entire kingdom. He will join forces with the king of Egypt. And the king of Syria will give his daughter to him to become his wife. The king of Syria will do this in order to take control of Egypt. But his plans will not succeed or help him. 18Then he will turn his attention to the lands along the Mediterranean coast. He will take over many of them. But a commander will put an end to his proud actions. He will turn his pride back on him. 19After this, the king of Syria will return to the forts in his own country. But he will trip and fall. And he will never be seen again.

20"The next king after him will send someone out to collect taxes. The taxes will help maintain the glory of his kingdom. But in a few years the king will be destroyed. It will not happen because someone becomes angry with him or kills him in battle.

21"After him, another king will take his place. Many people will hate him. He will not be honored as a king should be. He will lead an army into the kingdom when its people feel secure. He will make clever plans to capture it. 22Then he will sweep away a huge army. The army and a prince of the covenant will be destroyed. 23The king of Syria will make an agreement with that prince. But then the king of Syria will not keep his word. He will rise to even greater power with the help of only a few people. 24When the people in the richest areas feel secure, he will attack them. He will do what the kings before him could not do. And he will reward his followers with the goods and wealth he takes. He will make clever plans to take over the forts. But that will last for only a short time.

25"He will become stronger and more confident. He will do that by gathering a large army. Then he will go to war against the next king of Egypt. That king will fight against him with a huge and very powerful army. But the king of Egypt will not be able to stand up against him. So the plans of the king of Syria will succeed. 26The trusted advisers of the king of Egypt will try to destroy him. His army will be swept away. Many of his soldiers will be wounded or killed. 27The kings of Syria and Egypt will sit at the same table. But in their hearts they will plan to do what is evil. And they will tell lies to each other. But it will not do them any good. God will put an end to their plans at his appointed time. 28The king of Syria will return to his own country. He will go back there with great wealth. But he will make evil plans against the holy temple in Jerusalem. He will do a lot of harm to the temple and the people who worship there. Then he will return to his own country.

²⁹"At God's appointed time, the king of Syria will march south again. But this time things will turn out differently. ³⁰Roman ships will oppose him. He will lose hope. Then he will turn back. He will take out his anger against the holy temple. And he will do good to the Jews who desert it.

³¹"His army will come and make the temple area 'unclean.' They will put a stop to the daily sacrifices. Then they will set up a hated thing that destroys. ³²He will pretend to praise those who have broken the covenant. He will lead them to do what is evil. But the people who know their God will firmly oppose him.

³³"Those who are wise will teach many others. But for a while, some of the wise will be killed by swords. Others will be burned to death. Still others will be made prisoners. Or they will be robbed of everything they have. ³⁴When that happens, they will receive a little help. Many who are not honest will join them. ³⁵So some of the wise people will suffer. They will be made pure in the fire. They will be made spotless until the time of the end. It will still come at God's appointed time.

The King Who Honors Himself

³⁶"A certain king will do as he pleases. He will honor himself. He will put himself above every god. He will say things against the greatest God of all. Those things have never been heard before. He will have success until God is not angry anymore. What God has decided to do must take place. ³⁷The king will not show any respect for the gods his people have always worshiped. There is a god desired by women. He will not respect that god either. He will not have respect for any god. Instead, he will put himself above all of them. ³⁸In place of them, he will worship a god of war. He will honor a god his people have not known before. He will give gold and silver to that god. He will bring jewels and expensive gifts to it. ³⁹He will attack the strongest forts. A new god will help him do it. He will greatly honor those who recognize him as

their leader. He will make them rulers over many people. And he will give them land as a reward.

⁴⁰"A king in the south will go to war against him. It will happen at the time of the end. The king who will honor himself will rush out against him. He will come with chariots and horsemen. He will attack with a lot of ships. He will lead his army into many countries. He will sweep through them like a flood. ⁴¹He will also march into the beautiful land of Israel. Many countries will fall. But Edom, Moab and the leaders of Ammon will be saved from his mighty hand. ⁴²His power will reach out into many countries. Even Egypt will not escape. ⁴³He will gain control of all Egypt's riches. He will take their gold and silver treasures. The people of Libya and Cush will be under his control. ⁴⁴But reports from the east and the north will terrify him. He will march out with great anger to destroy many people and wipe them out. ⁴⁵He will set up his royal tents. He will put them between the Mediterranean Sea and the beautiful holy mountain of Zion. But his end will come. And no one will help him.

The Time of the End

12 "At that time Michael will appear. He is the great prince of the angels. He guards your people. There will be a time of terrible suffering. Things will be worse than at any time since nations began. But at that time of suffering your people will be saved. Their names are written in the book of life. ²Many people who lie dead in their graves will wake up. Some will rise up to life that will never end. Others will rise up to shame that will never end. ³Those who are wise will shine like the brightness of the sky.

Jason's Jargon

DANIEL 12

Time for another quest! Find *spotless* in this chapter. Spotless means pure or perfectly clean. When placed in fire, gold is made pure, just as our faith is made pure by the tests of life.

Those who lead many others to do what is right will be like the stars for ever and ever. ⁴But I want you to roll up this scroll, Daniel. Seal it until the time of the end. Many people will go here and there to increase their knowledge."

⁵Then I looked up and saw two other angels. One was on this side of the Tigris River. And one was on the other side. ⁶The man who was dressed in linen was above the waters of the river. One of the angels spoke to him. He asked, "How long will it be before these amazing things come true?"

⁷The man raised both hands toward heaven. I heard him make a promise in the name of the God who lives forever. He answered me, "Three and a half years. Then the power of the holy people will finally be broken. And all these things will come true."

⁸I heard what he said. But I didn't understand it. So I asked, "My master, what will come of all this?"

⁹He answered, "Go on your way, Daniel. The scroll is rolled up. It is sealed until the time of the end. ¹⁰Many people will be made pure in the fire. They will be made spotless. But sinful people will continue to be evil. Not one sinful person will understand. But those who are wise will.

¹¹"The daily sacrifices will be stopped. And the hated thing that destroys will be set up. After that, there will be 1,290 days. ¹²Blessed are those who wait for the 1,335 days and reach the end of them.

¹³"Daniel, go on your way until the end. Your body will rest in the grave. Then at the end of the days you will rise from the dead. And you will receive what God has appointed for you."

Hosea

Though I might be accused of using the word *milestone* too frequently in our journey through Scripture, it is nevertheless appropriate once again. We've reached the sequence often referred to as the "Minor Prophets." Though these twelve books carry the unfortunate title of "minor," the messages contained within are just as important as those in any other book. In point of fact, they are called "minor" only because they are markedly shorter than the preceding books of prophecy.

Though the Major Prophets all spoke concerning the state of Judah (the southern nation), some of the Minor Prophets will address Israel, the northern tribes that eventually fell to the Assyrians. Such is the case with our first "minor" prophet: Hosea. He warned that Israel's idolatry was about to result in God's judgment.

God instructed Hosea to demonstrate Israel's disloyalty in a most unusual way. The prophet was told to marry a woman whom he knew, ahead of time, would be unfaithful to him (1:2–3). It was most assuredly painful for Hosea to watch his wife's behavior and realize that other people also saw what was going on. Yet after she had several children and deserted Hosea, God instructed the prophet to take her back (3:1–3). This bold and humbling action demonstrated God's great love for His people even when we wander away from Him. The Israelites had deserted God to follow idols, but God never stopped loving them. If they were willing to repent, He would eagerly take them back.

What's it Mean, Eugene?

Sin—The Greek word for sin, *hamartia*, was originally a term employed in the sport of archery. It literally means "missing the mark" as an arrow might miss hitting the target—which would certainly be the case if I attempted to shoot it! The Bible describes *sin* as "disobedience" toward God, "unrighteousness," "guilt," and "falling short" (see Romans 3:23). To be "in sin" means to have broken our relationship with God. Thankfully, Jesus is the Lamb of God who takes away the sin of the world (John 1:29).

A message from the LORD came to Hosea, the son of Beeri. The message came while Uzziah, Jotham, Ahaz and Hezekiah were kings of Judah. It also came while Jeroboam was king of Israel. He was the son of Jehoash. Here is what the LORD said to him.

Hosea's Wife and Children

²The LORD began to speak through Hosea. He said to him, "Go. Marry a woman who has sex with anyone she wants. Have children with her. Do this because the people of the land are like that kind of wife. They have not been faithful to me." ³So Hosea married Gomer. She was the daughter of Diblaim. Gomer became pregnant and had a son by Hosea.

⁴Then the LORD said to Hosea, "Name him Jezreel. That's because I will soon punish Jehu's royal family. He killed many people at the city of Jezreel. So I will put an end to the kingdom of Israel. ⁵At that time I will break their military power. It will happen in the Valley of Jezreel."

⁶Gomer became pregnant again. She had a daughter. Then the LORD said to Hosea, "Name her Lo-Ruhamah." Lo-Ruhamah means Not Loved. "That's because I will no longer show love to the people of Israel. I will not forgive them anymore. ⁷But I will show love to the people of Judah. And I will save them. I will not use bows or swords or other weapons of war to do it. I will not save them by using horses and horsemen either. Instead, I will use my own power to save them. I am the LORD their God. And I will save them."

⁸Later, Gomer stopped nursing Lo-Ruhamah. After that, she had another son. ⁹Then the LORD said, "Name him Lo-Ammi." Lo-Ammi means Not My People. "That's because Israel is no longer my people. And I am no longer their God.

¹⁰"But the time will come when the people of Israel will be like the sand on the seashore. It can't be measured or counted. Now it is said about them, 'You are not my people.' But at that time they will be called 'children of the living God.' ¹¹The people of Judah and Israel will come together again. They will appoint one leader and come up out of the land. And Jezreel's day will be great.

2 "People of Israel, call your brothers 'My people.' And call your sisters 'My loved ones.'

Have you heard the phrase "naked as the day he was born"? It comes from this verse in Hosea and it makes me blush when I read it!

Israel Is Punished and Brought Back to the LORD

² "Tell your mother she is wrong.
   Tell her she is wrong.
She isn't acting like a wife to me
      anymore.
   She no longer treats me as her
      husband.
Tell her to stop looking and acting like
      a prostitute.
   Tell her not to let her lovers
   lie on her breasts anymore.
³ If she doesn't stop it, I will strip her
      naked.
   I'll make her as bare as she was on
      the day she was born.
I'll make her like a desert.
   She will become like dry land.
   And I'll let her die of thirst.

⁴ "I won't show my love to her children.
   They are the children of other men.
⁵ Their mother hasn't been faithful to
      me.
   She who became pregnant with
      them
   has brought shame on herself.
She said, 'I will chase after my lovers.
   They give me my food and water.
They provide me with wool and linen.
   They give me olive oil and wine.'
⁶ So I will block her path with bushes
      that have thorns.
   I'll build a wall around her.
   Then she can't go to her lovers.

Hos. 2:5 In 2016 Ivan Scott sheared 867 sheep in nine hours to set a new world record. One sheep can provide up to thirty pounds of wool per year. That's a lot of socks!

⁷ She will still chase after her lovers.
    But she won't catch them.
She'll look for them.
    But she won't find them.
Then she'll say,
    'I'll go back to my husband.
That's where I was at first.
    I was better off then than I am now.'
⁸ She wouldn't admit that I was the one
    who gave her everything she had.
    I provided her with grain, olive oil
        and fresh wine.
I gave her plenty of silver and gold.
    But she used it to make statues of
        Baal.
⁹ "So I will take away my grain when it
        gets ripe.
    I'll take my fresh wine when it's
        ready.
I'll take back my wool and my linen.
    I gave them to her to cover her
        naked body.
¹⁰ So now I'll uncover her body.
    All her lovers will see it.
    No one can stop me from punishing
        her.
¹¹ I will put a stop to the special times she
        celebrates.
    I'll bring an end to the feasts she
        celebrates each year.
I'll stop her New Moon feasts and her
        Sabbath days.
I'll bring all her appointed feasts to
        an end.

¹² I will destroy her vines and her fig
        trees.
    She said they were her pay from her
        lovers.
I'll make them like clumps of bushes
        and weeds.
    Wild animals will eat them up.
¹³ Israel burned incense to the gods
    that were named Baal.
I will punish her
    for all the times she did that.
She decorated herself with rings and
        jewelry.
Then she went after her lovers.
    But she forgot all about me,"
declares the Lord.

¹⁴ "So now I am going to draw her back to
        me.
    I will lead her into the desert.
    There I will speak tenderly to her.
¹⁵ I will give her back her vineyards.
    I will make the Valley of Achor a
        door of hope for her.
Then she will love me, as she did when
        she was young.
    She will love me just as she did
        when she came up out of Egypt.

¹⁶ "A new day is coming," announces the
    Lord.
    "Israel will call me 'my husband.'
    She will no longer call me 'my
        master.'
¹⁷ She will no longer speak about the gods
    that are named Baal.
    She will not pray to them for help
        anymore.
¹⁸ At that time I will make a covenant
    for the good of my people.
I will make it with the wild animals
    and the birds in the sky.
It will also be made with the creatures
    that move along the ground.
I will remove bows and swords
    and other weapons of war from the
        land.
    Then my people can lie down in
        safety.
¹⁹ I will make Israel my own.
    She will belong to me forever.
I will do to her what is right and fair.
    I will love her tenderly.
²⁰ I will be faithful to her.
    And she will recognize me as the
    Lord.

²¹ "So at that time I will answer her,"
    announces the LORD.
"I will command the skies
    to send rain on the earth.
²² Then the earth will produce grain, olive
    oil and fresh wine.
    And Israel will be called Jezreel.
    That's because I will answer her
        prayers.
²³ I will plant her in the land for myself.
    I will show my love to the one I
        called Not My Loved One.
I will say, 'You are my people'
    to those who were called Not My
        People.
    And they will say, 'You are my God.'"

Hosea Brings His Wife Back to Himself

3 The LORD said to me, "Go. Show your love to your wife again. She is loved by another man. And she has committed adultery. But I want you to love her just as I love the people of Israel. They turn to other gods. And they love to offer raisin cakes to Baal and eat them. In spite of that, I love my people."

²So I bought Gomer for six ounces of silver and 430 pounds of barley. ³Then I told her, "You must wait for me for a long time. You must not be a prostitute. You must not have sex with any man. And I will be faithful to you too."

⁴So the people of Israel will live for a long time without a king or prince. They won't have sacrifices or sacred stones. They won't have sacred linen aprons or statues of family gods. ⁵After that, the people of Israel will return to the LORD their God. They will look to him and to a king from the family line of David. In the last days, they will tremble with fear as they come to the LORD. And they will receive his full blessing.

The LORD Brings Charges Against Israel

4 People of Israel, listen to the LORD's
        message.
    He is bringing charges
    against you who live in Israel.
He says, "There is no faithfulness
    or love in the land.
    No one recognizes me as God.
² People curse one another.
    They tell lies and commit murder.
    They steal and commit adultery.

They break all my laws.
    They keep spilling the blood of other
        people.
³ That is why the land is drying up.
    All those who live in it
    are getting weaker and weaker.
The wild animals and the birds in the
        sky are dying.
    So are the fish in the ocean.

⁴ "But you priests should not blame the
        people.
    You should not find fault with one
        another.
After all, your people
    could also bring charges against you.
⁵ You trip and fall day and night.
    And the prophets fall down along
        with you.
So I will destroy your nation.
    She is the one who gave birth to you.
⁶ My people are destroyed
    because they do not know me.

"You priests have refused to obey me.
    So I will refuse to accept you as my
        priests.
You have not paid any attention to my
        law.
    So I will not let your children be my
        priests.
⁷ The more priests there were,
    the more they sinned against me.
    They have traded their glorious God
        for that shameful god named
        Baal.
⁸ They live off the sins of my people.
    And they want them to keep on
        sinning.
⁹ So here is what I will do.
    I will punish people and priests
        alike.
I will judge them because of their sinful
        lives.
I will pay them back
    for the evil things they have done.

¹⁰ "My people will eat.
    But they will not have enough.
They will have sex with prostitutes.
    But they will not have any children.
    That's because they have deserted
        me.
They have sex ¹¹with prostitutes.
    They drink old wine and fresh wine.
    Their drinking has destroyed their
        ability to understand.

¹² My people ask a wooden statue of a god
     for advice.
     They get answers from a stick of
       wood.
     They are as unfaithful as prostitutes.
     They are not faithful to their God.
¹³ They offer sacrifices on the
       mountaintops.
     They burn offerings on the hills.
     They worship under oak, poplar and
       terebinth trees.
     The trees provide plenty of shade.
So your daughters become prostitutes.
     And your daughters-in-law commit
       adultery.

Jason's Jargon

HOSEA 4

Search this chapter for the word *charges*. When charges are brought against you, someone believes you are guilty of a crime. When God brings charges against Israel, consequences follow.

¹⁴ "I will not punish your daughters
     when they become prostitutes.
I will not judge your daughters-in-law
     when they commit adultery.
After all, the men themselves have sex
       with sinful women.
     They offer sacrifices where temple
       prostitutes earn their living.
     People who can't understand will be
       destroyed!

¹⁵ "Israel, you are not faithful to me.
     But I do not want Judah to become
       guilty too.

"My people, do not go to Gilgal to offer
     sacrifices.
     Do not go up to Bethel to worship
       other gods.
When you make a promise, do not say,
     'You can be sure that the LORD is
       alive.'
¹⁶ The people of Israel are stubborn.
     They are as stubborn as a young
       cow.

So how can I take care of them
     like lambs in a meadow?
¹⁷ The people of Ephraim have joined
       themselves to other gods.
     And nothing can be done to help
       them.
¹⁸ They continue to be unfaithful to me
     even when their drinks are gone.
     And their rulers love to do shameful
       things.
¹⁹ A windstorm will blow all of them away.
     And their sacrifices will bring shame
       on them.

The LORD Judges Israel

5 "Listen to me, you priests!
     Pay attention, people of Israel!
Listen, you members of the royal family!
     Here is my decision against you.
You have been like a trap at Mizpah.
     You have been like a net spread out
       on Mount Tabor.
² You refuse to obey me.
     You are knee-deep in killing.
     So I will punish all of you.
³ I know all about the people of Ephraim.
     What Israel is doing is not hidden
       from me.
Now they have joined themselves to
     other gods.
     They have made themselves 'unclean.'

⁴ "They can't return to me
     because they have done so many evil
       things.
In their hearts they long to act like
     prostitutes.
     They do not recognize me as the
       LORD.
⁵ Israel's pride proves that they are guilty.
     The people of Ephraim trip and fall
       because they have sinned.
     Judah falls down along with them.
⁶ Israel will come to worship the LORD.
     They will bring their animals to offer
       as sacrifices.
But they will not find him.
     He has turned away from them.
⁷ They are not faithful to the LORD.
     Their children are not his.
When they celebrate their New Moon
     feasts,
     he will destroy their fields.

⁸ "My people, blow trumpets in Gibeah!
     Blow horns in Ramah!

Shout the battle cry in Bethel!
   Say to the people of Benjamin, 'Lead
     on into battle!'
⁹ The people of Ephraim will be
   completely destroyed
   when it is time for me to punish them.
They can be sure it will happen.
   I am announcing it among their
     tribes.
¹⁰ Judah's leaders have stolen some land.
   They have moved their borders
     farther north.
So I will pour out my anger on them
   like a flood of water.
¹¹ Ephraim will soon be crushed.
   The Assyrians will stomp all over
     them.
It will happen because they have made
   up their minds
to chase after other gods.
¹² I will be like a moth to Ephraim.
   I will cause Judah to rot away.

¹³ "The people of Ephraim saw how sick
   they were.
The people of Judah saw that they
   were wounded.
Then Ephraim turned to Assyria for
   help.
They sent gifts to the great King
   Tiglath-Pileser.
But he is not able to make you well.
   He can't heal your wounds.
¹⁴ I will be like a lion to Ephraim.
   I will attack Judah like a powerful
     lion.
I will tear them to pieces.
   I will drag them off.
Then I will leave them.
   No one will be able to save them.
¹⁵ I will go back to my lion's den.
   I will stay there until they pay the
     price for their sin.
Then they will turn to me.
   They will suffer so much
   that they will really want me to help
     them."

Israel Refuses to Turn Away From Their Sins

6 The people say, "Come.
   Let us return to the LORD.
He has torn us to pieces.
   But he will heal us.
He has wounded us.
   But he'll bandage our wounds.
² After two days he will give us new life.
   On the third day he'll make us like
     new again.
Then we will enjoy his blessing.
³ Let's recognize him as the LORD.
   Let's keep trying to know him.
You can be sure the sun will rise.
   And you can be just as sure the
     LORD will appear.
He will come to renew us like the
   winter rains.
   He will be like the spring rains that
     water the earth."

⁴ The LORD says, "Ephraim, what can I
   do with you?
   And what can I do with you, Judah?
Your love for me vanishes like the
   morning mist.
   It soon disappears like the early dew.
⁵ So I used the words of my prophets to
   cut you in pieces.
I used my words to put you to
   death.
   Then my judgments blazed out like
     the sun.
⁶ I want mercy and not sacrifice.
   I want you to recognize me as God
     instead of bringing me burnt
     offerings.
⁷ Just as at the city of Adam, they
   disobeyed me,
   they have broken the covenant I
     made with them.
   They were not faithful to me there.
⁸ Ramoth Gilead is a city where sinful
   people live.
   It is stained with footprints of blood.
⁹ On the road to Shechem, groups of
   priests act like robbers.
They hide and wait to attack people.
   They murder them.
   So they carry out their evil plans.
¹⁰ I have seen a horrible thing in Israel.
   The people of Ephraim are unfaithful to
     their own God.
   The people of Israel are 'unclean.'

¹¹ "People of Judah, I have also appointed
   a time
   for you to be destroyed.

"I would like to bless my people
   with great success again.
7 ¹ I would like to heal Israel.
   But when I try to, Ephraim's sins
     are brought out into the open.

The crimes of Samaria
　　are made known to everyone.
The people tell lies.
　　They break into houses and steal.
　　They rob others in the streets.
[2] But they do not realize
　　that I remember all the evil things
　　　　they do.
　　Their sins pile up and cover them.
　　I am always aware of their sins.

[3] "Their evil conduct even makes the
　　　　king glad.
　　Their lies make the princes happy.
[4] But all the people are unfaithful to the
　　　　king.
　　Their anger against him burns
　　　　like the coals in an oven.
　　The baker does not even need to stir up
　　　　the fire
　　until the dough is ready."

[5] On special days to honor our king,
　　the princes get drunk with wine.
And the king enjoys the party.
　　He joins hands with those
　　who pretend to be faithful to him.
[6] Their hearts are as hot as an oven.
　　They make evil plans to get rid of
　　　　him.
Their anger burns like a slow fire all
　　　　night.
　　In the morning it blazes out like a
　　　　flaming fire.
[7] All of them are as hot as an oven.
　　They destroy their rulers.
All their kings fall from power.
　　But none of them calls on the LORD
　　　　for help.

[8] The people of Ephraim mix with the
　　　　nations.
　　They are like a thin loaf of bread
　　　　that is baked on only one side.
[9] People from other lands make them
　　　　weaker and weaker.
　　But they don't realize it.
Their hair is becoming gray.
　　But they don't even notice it.
[10] The pride of Israel proves that they are
　　　　guilty.
　　But in spite of everything,
they don't return to the LORD their
　　　　God.
　　They don't go to him for help.

[11] The LORD says,

"The people of Ephraim are like a dove.
　　They are easily tricked.
　　They do not have any sense at all.
First they call out to Egypt for help.
　　Then they turn to Assyria.
[12] When they send for help,
　　I will throw my net over them.
I will capture them like the birds in the
　　　　sky.
　　When I hear them gathering like
　　　　birds,
　　I will catch them.
[13] How terrible it will be for them!
　　They have wandered away from me.
So they will be destroyed.
　　That's because they have refused to
　　　　obey me.
I long to save them.
　　But they tell lies about me.
[14] They do not cry out to me from their
　　　　hearts.
　　Instead, they just lie on their beds
　　　　and sob.
They cut themselves when they pray to
　　　　their gods
　　for grain and fresh wine.
　　But they turn away from me.
[15] I brought them up and made them
　　　　strong.
　　But they make evil plans against
　　　　me.
[16] I am the Most High God. But they do
　　　　not turn to me.
　　They are like a bow that does not
　　　　shoot straight.
Their leaders will be killed by swords.
　　They will die because they have
　　　　spoken too proudly.
The people of Egypt
　　will make fun of them."

Israel Will Harvest a Windstorm

8 The LORD said to me,

"Put a trumpet to your lips!
　　Give a warning to my people!
Assyria is like an eagle.
　　It is ready to attack my land.
My people have broken the covenant I
　　　　made with them.
　　They have refused to obey my law.
[2] Israel shouts to me,
　　'We recognize you as our God!'
[3] But they have turned away from what is
　　　　good.
　　So an enemy will chase them.

4 My people appoint kings I do not want.
    They choose princes without my
        permission.
They use their silver and gold
    to make statues of gods.
    That is how they destroy themselves."
5 The LORD says, "People of Samaria,
    throw out your god that looks like
        a calf!
I am very angry with them.
How long will it be until they are able
    to remain faithful to me?
6 Their calf is not God.
    A skilled worker from Israel made it.
But that calf of Samaria will be
    broken to pieces."

7 The LORD says,

"Worshiping other gods is like
    worshiping the wind.
It is like planting worthless seeds.
Assyria is like a windstorm.
    That is all my people will harvest.
There are no heads of grain
    on the stems that will come up.
    So they will not produce any flour.
Even if they did produce grain,
    the Assyrians would eat all of it up.
8 So the people of Israel are swallowed up.
    Now they are among the nations
    like something no one wants.
9 They have gone up to Assyria for help.
    They are like a wild donkey
    that wanders around by itself.
Ephraim's people have sold themselves
    to their Assyrian lovers.
10 They have sold themselves to the
        nations
    to get their help.
But now I will gather them together.
They will get weaker and weaker.
    The mighty kings of Assyria will
        crush them.
11 "Ephraim built many altars where they
        sacrificed
    sin offerings to other gods.
So their altars have become
    places where they commit sin.
12 In my law I wrote down many things
    for their good.
    But they considered those things as
        something strange.
13 They offer sacrifices as gifts to me.
    They eat the meat of the animals
        they bring.

But the LORD is not pleased with any
    of this.
He will remember the evil things they
    have done.
He will punish them for their sins.
And they will return to Egypt.
14 Israel has forgotten the God who made
    them.
    They have built palaces for
        themselves.
    Judah has built forts in many towns.
But I will send down fire on their cities.
    It will burn up their forts."

Israel Will Be Punished

9 Israel, don't be joyful.
    Don't be glad as the other nations
        are.
You haven't been faithful to your God.
    You love to get paid for being a
        prostitute.
    Your pay is the grain at every
        threshing floor.
2 But soon there won't be any grain or
    wine to feed you.
    There won't even be any fresh wine.
3 You won't remain in the LORD's land.
    Ephraim, you will return to Egypt.
    You will eat "unclean" food in
        Assyria.
4 You won't pour out wine offerings to
    the LORD.
    Your sacrifices won't please him.
They'll be like the bread people eat
    when someone dies.
    Everyone who eats those sacrifices
        will be "unclean."
They themselves will have to eat that
    kind of food.
    They can't bring it into the LORD's
        temple.

5 What will you do when your appointed
        feasts come?
    What will you do on the LORD's
        special days?
6 Some of you will escape without being
        destroyed.
    But you will die in Egypt.
    Your bodies will be buried at
        Memphis.
Weeds will cover your treasures of
    silver.
    Thorns will grow up in your tents.
7 The time when God will punish you is
    coming.

The day when he will judge you is
near.
I want Israel to know this.
You have committed many sins.
And you hate me very much.
That's why you think the prophet is
foolish.
You think the person the LORD
speaks through is crazy.
[8] People of Ephraim, the prophet, along
with my God,
is warning you of danger.
But you set traps for him everywhere
he goes.
You hate him so much
you even wait for him in God's
house.
[9] You have sunk very deep into sin,
just as your people did at Gibeah
long ago.
God will remember the evil things they
have done.
He will punish them for their sins.

[10]The LORD says,

"When I first found Israel,
it was like finding grapes in the
desert.
When I saw your people of long ago,
it was like seeing the early fruit on a
fig tree.
But then they went to Baal Peor.
There they gave themselves to that
shameful god named Baal.
They became as evil as the god they
loved.
[11] Ephraim's greatness and glory will be
gone.
It will fly away like a bird.
Women will no longer have children.
They will not be able to get pregnant.
[12] But suppose they do have children.
Then I will kill every one of them.
How terrible it will be for them
when I turn away from them!
[13] Tyre is planted in a pleasant place.
And so is Ephraim.
But the Assyrians will kill
Ephraim's children."

[14] LORD, what should you do to Ephraim's
people?
Give them women whose babies die
before they are born.
Give them women whose breasts
have no milk.

WOOTON'S FUN FACTS

Hos. 9:10

The term *Baal* can
mean "lord" or refer
to many false gods.
You can find it all over
the Old Testament.
Baal-Peor was a
false god of Moab.

[15]The LORD says,

"My people did many evil things in
Gilgal.
That is why I hated them there.
They committed many sins.
So I will drive them out of my land.
I will not love them anymore.
All their leaders refuse to obey me.
[16] Ephraim is like a worthless plant.
Its roots are dried up.
It does not produce any fruit.
Suppose Ephraim's people have
children.
Then I will kill the children they love
so much."

[17] My God will turn his back on his
people.
They have not obeyed him.
So they will wander among other
nations.

10 [1]Israel was like a spreading vine.
They produced fruit for themselves.
As they grew more fruit,
they built more altars.
As their land became richer,
they made more beautiful the sacred
stones they worshiped.
[2] Their hearts are dishonest.
So now they must pay for their sins.
The LORD will tear down their altars.
He'll destroy their sacred stones.

³ Then they'll say, "We don't have a king.
    That's because we didn't have
    any respect for the LORD.
But suppose we did have a king.
    What could he do for us?"
⁴ They make a lot of promises.
    They make agreements among
        themselves.
    They make promises they don't
        mean to keep.
So court cases spring up
    like poisonous weeds in a plowed
        field.

Jason's Jargon

HOSEA 10

Your latest mission:
Inspect this chapter
for the word *conduct*.
Conduct is behavior.
"Harvesting the fruit
of your evil conduct"
means that your bad
behavior will come back
to trouble you.

⁵ The people who live in Samaria are
        filled with fear.
    They are afraid for their god that
        looks like a calf.
    They're afraid it will be carried off
        from Beth Aven, that evil town.
They will mourn over it.
    So will the priests who led them to
        worship it.
The priests were full of joy
    because their statue was so glorious.
But it will be captured
    and taken far away from them.
⁶ It will be carried off to Assyria.
    The people of Ephraim will be forced
        to give it to the great king.
They will be dishonored.
    Israel will be ashamed
    of its agreements with other nations.
⁷ Samaria's king will be destroyed.
    He will be like a twig swept away by
        a river.
⁸ The high places where Israel worshiped
        other gods
    will be destroyed.
    That's where they sinned against the
        LORD.

Thorns and weeds will grow up there.
    They will cover the altars.
Then the people will say to the
        mountains, "Cover us!"
    They'll say to the hills, "Fall on us!"

⁹ The LORD says,

"Israel, you have done evil things
    ever since your people sinned at
        Gibeah long ago.
    And you are still doing what is evil.
War will come again
    to those who sinned at Gibeah.
¹⁰ I will punish them when I want to.
    Nations will gather together to fight
        against them.
They will put them in chains
    because they have committed so
        many sins.
¹¹ Ephraim was like a well-trained young
        cow.
    It loved to thresh grain.
So I will put a yoke
    on its pretty neck.
I will make Ephraim do hard work.
    Judah also must plow.
So all the people of Jacob
    must break up the ground.
¹² Your hearts are as hard as a field
        that has not been plowed.
If you change your ways,
    you will produce good crops.
So plant the seeds of doing what is right.
    Then you will harvest the fruit of
        your faithful love.
It is time to seek the LORD.
    When you do, he will come
    and shower his blessings on you.
¹³ But you have planted the seeds of doing
        what is wrong.
    So you have harvested the fruit of
        your evil conduct.
    You have had to eat the fruit of your
        lies.
You have trusted in your own strength.
    You have depended on your many
        soldiers.
¹⁴ But the roar of battle will come against
        you.
    All your forts will be completely
        destroyed.
It will happen just as Shalman
    destroyed Beth Arbel in a battle.
Mothers and their children
    were smashed on the ground.

15 People of Bethel, that will happen to
    you.
    You have committed far too many
        sins.
When the time comes for me to punish
    you,
    the king of Israel will be completely
        destroyed."

God Loves Israel

11 The LORD continues,

"When Israel was a young nation, I
    loved them.
    I chose to bring my son out of Egypt.
2 But the more I called out to Israel,
    the more they went away from me.
They brought sacrifices to the statues of
    the gods
    that were named Baal.
    And they burned incense to them.
3 I taught Ephraim to walk.
    I took them up in my arms.
But they did not realize
    I was the one who took care of them.
4 I led them with kindness and love.
I was to them like a person who lifts
    a little child to their cheek.
    I bent down and fed them.

5 "But they refuse to turn away from
    their sins.
    So they will return to Egypt.
    And Assyria will rule over them.
6 A sword will flash in their cities.
    It will destroy the prophets who
        teach lies.
    It will bring an end to their plans.
7 My people have made up their minds
    to turn away from me.
Even if they call me the Most High God,
    I will certainly not honor them."

8 The LORD continues,

"People of Ephraim, how can I give you
    up?
    Israel, how can I hand you over to
        your enemies?
Can I destroy you as I did the town of
    Admah?
    Can I treat you like Zeboyim?
My heart is stirred inside me.
    It is filled with pity for you.
9 I will not be so angry with you
    anymore.

I will not completely destroy you
    again.
After all, I am God.
    I am not a mere man.
I am the Holy One among you.
    I will not direct my anger against
        their cities.
10 I will roar like a lion against my enemies.
    Then the LORD's people will follow
        him.
When he roars, his children will come
    home trembling with fear.
    They will return from the west.
11 They will come from Egypt, trembling
    like sparrows.
    They will return from Assyria, flying
        in like doves.
I will settle you again in your homes,"
    announces the LORD.

Israel Has Sinned

12 The people of Ephraim tell me nothing
    but lies.
    Israel has not been honest with me.
And Judah continues to wander away
    from God.
    They have deserted the faithful Holy
        One.

12 1 The people of Ephraim look to
    others for help.
    It's like chasing the wind.
The wind they keep chasing
    is hot and dry.
They tell more and more lies.
    They are always hurting others.
They make a peace treaty with Assyria.
    They send olive oil to Egypt to get
        help.
2 The LORD is bringing charges against
    Judah.
    He will punish Jacob's people
    because of how they act.
He'll pay them back
    for the evil things they've done.
3 Even before Jacob was born,
    he was holding on to his brother's
        heel.
When he became a man,
    he struggled with God.
4 At Peniel he struggled with the angel
    and won.
    Jacob wept and begged for his
        blessing.
God also met with him at Bethel.
    He talked with him there.

⁵ He is the LORD God who rules over all.
    His name is the LORD.
⁶ People of Jacob, you must return to
        your God.
    You must hold on to love and do
        what is fair.
    You must trust in your God always.

⁷ You are like a trader who uses dishonest
        scales.
    You love to cheat others.
⁸ People of Ephraim, you brag,
    "We are very rich.
    We've become wealthy.
And no one can prove we sinned
    to gain all this wealth."

⁹ The LORD says,

"I have been the LORD your God
    ever since you came out of Egypt.
But I will make you live in tents again.
    That is what you did when you
        celebrated
    the Feast of Booths in the desert.
¹⁰ I spoke to the prophets.
    They saw many visions.
    I gave you warnings through them."

¹¹ The people of Gilead are evil!
    They aren't worth anything!
Gilgal's people sacrifice bulls to other
        gods.
    Their altars will become like piles of
        stones
    on a plowed field.
¹² Jacob ran away to the country of Aram.
    There Israel served Laban to get a
        wife.
    He took care of sheep to pay for her.
¹³ The prophet Moses brought Israel up
        from Egypt.
    The LORD used him to take care of
        them.
¹⁴ But Ephraim's people have made the
        LORD very angry.
    Their Lord will hold them
        accountable for the blood
        they've spilled.
    He'll pay them back for the shameful
        things they've done.

The LORD Is Angry With Israel

13 When the tribe of Ephraim spoke,
    the other tribes trembled with fear.
    Ephraim was honored in Israel.
But its people sinned by worshiping Baal.
    So they were as good as dead.

² Now they sin more and more.
    They use their silver
    to make statues of gods for
        themselves.
The statues come from their own clever
        ideas.
    Skilled workers make all of them.
The people pray to these gods.
    They offer human sacrifices to them.
    They kiss the gods that look like
        calves.
³ So these people will vanish like the
        morning mist.
    They will soon disappear like the
        early dew.
They will be like straw
    that the wind blows around on a
        threshing floor.
They will be like smoke
    that escapes through a window.

⁴ The LORD says,

"People of Israel, I have been the LORD
        your God
    ever since you came out of Egypt.
You must not worship any god but me.
    You must not have any savior except
        me.
⁵ I took care of you in the desert.
    It was a land of burning heat.
⁶ I fed them until they were satisfied.
    Then they became proud.
    They forgot all about me.
⁷ So I will leap on them like a lion.
    I will hide and wait
    beside the road like a leopard.
⁸ I will attack them like a bear
    that is robbed of her cubs.
    I will rip them wide open.
Like a lion I will eat them up.
    Like a wild animal I will tear them
        apart.

⁹ "Israel, you will be destroyed.
    I helped you. But you turned against
        me.
¹⁰ Where is your king?
    Wasn't he supposed to save you?
Where are the rulers in all your towns?
    You said, 'Give us a king and
        princes.'
¹¹ So I became angry and gave you a king.
    Then I took him away from you.
¹² Ephraim's guilt is piling up.
    I am keeping a record of all their
        sins.

¹³ They will suffer pain like a woman
     having a baby.
They are like foolish children.
It is time for them to be born.
     But they don't have the sense to
        come out of their mother's
        body.

¹⁴ "I will set these people free from the
     power of the grave.
I will save them from death.
Death, where are your plagues?
     Grave, where is your power to
        destroy?

"I will no longer pity Ephraim.
¹⁵   Even though they are doing well
     among the other tribes,
trouble will come to them.
I will send a hot and dry wind from the
     east.
It will blow in from the desert.
Their springs will not have any water.
Their wells will dry up.
All their treasures
     will be taken out of their storerooms.

¹⁶ The people of Samaria must pay for
     their sins.
They have refused to obey me.
They will be killed by swords.
     Their little children will be smashed
        on the ground.
Their pregnant women will be
     ripped wide open."

The Lord Blesses Those Who Turn Away From Sin

14 Israel, return to the Lord your God.
     Your sins have destroyed you!
² Tell the Lord you are turning away
     from your sins.
     Return to him.
Say to him,
     "Forgive us for all our sins.
Please be kind to us.
     Welcome us back to you.
     Then our lips will offer you our praise.
³ Assyria can't save us.
     We won't trust in our war horses.
Our own hands have made statues of
     gods.

WHAT ABOUT YOU?

When have you been afraid of failing at something? Did you train hard to win a race or practice for months for a recital? When the time came, did you get nervous that you would make mistakes?

When we want to achieve something, it's natural to look for ways to increase our confidence. In the Adventures in Odyssey episode "The Owlnapping," the Odyssey Owls basketball team would pat a stuffed owl before every game. They thought it gave them good luck. When the owl was stolen, they began losing. Most of the team was convinced that their losses were due to the missing mascot. But after the owl was recovered and they still lost, the players realized the owl had nothing to do with their abilities.

Putting our confidence in anything but God creates problems. We see His promise to Israel in Hosea 14:8: "I will answer the prayers of my people. I will take good care of them. I will be like a healthy juniper tree to them. All the fruit they bear will come from me." God doesn't promise to help us win every game or impress people. He does, however, promise to be with us, support us, and love us. No failure can change that.

Do you have something that you believe will give you luck or keep you safe? Talk to your parents and ask them to pray with you. Then write down a Bible verse about God's power. Look at it whenever you're worried. Soon you'll be remembering the truth when you need it most.

But we will never call them our gods
again.
We are like children whose fathers have
died.
But you show us your tender love."

[4] Then the LORD will answer,

"My people always wander away from
me.
But I will put an end to that.
My anger has turned away from them.
Now I will love them freely.
[5] I will be like the dew to Israel.
They will bloom like a lily.
They will send their roots down deep
like a cedar tree in Lebanon.
[6] They will spread out like new branches.
They will be as beautiful as an olive
tree.
They will smell as sweet as the cedar
trees in Lebanon.
[7] Once again my people will live
in the safety of my shade.

They will grow like grain.
They will bloom like vines.
And Israel will be as famous
as wine from Lebanon.
[8] Ephraim will have nothing more to do
with other gods.
I will answer the prayers of my
people.
I will take good care of them.
I will be like a healthy juniper tree to
them.
All the fruit they bear will come
from me."

[9] If someone is wise, they will realize
that what I've said is true.
If they have understanding,
they will know what it means.
The ways of the LORD are right.
People who are right with God live
the way he wants them to.
But those who refuse to obey him
trip and fall.

Joel

Trivia point: My father once disguised himself using the name Joel. That's not the only reason this book of the Bible is significant, however. It's also one of the few that talks extensively about agriculture. During a time when much of a nation's basic needs depended on farming, anything that threatened the food supply was a major concern. You might recall that one of the ten plagues God used to get Pharaoh's attention in Exodus was a terrible swarm of locusts that ate every plant in all the land of Egypt (Ex. 10:1–20).

The prophet Joel predicts another destructive plague of locusts, but this time they are sent to God's own people to convince them to repent (2:2–3). Wave after wave of locusts are coming (1:4). They are likened to an army arriving with horses and chariots (2:1–5).

Joel then shifts his focus from the present to the future. He describes a time to come when "everyone who calls out to [God] will be saved" (2:32). Centuries later, when the Holy Spirit came down on the church shortly after Jesus ascended back to heaven, Peter remembered these words of Joel (Acts 2:14–21). That was a day when 3,000 people put their faith in Jesus, and the church has been growing ever since.

WHAT'S IT MEAN, EUGENE?

Theology—As a student of knowledge, I love the "*logys*." The suffix *logy* denotes a field of study; as, for example, in *biology*, "the study of living things," *geology*, "the study of the earth," or *zoology*, "the study of animals." The study of God and everything pertaining to God and godly living is "theology." *Theos* is the Greek word for "God." What better subject to study than the knowledge of God?

1 A message from the LORD came to Joel, the son of Pethuel. Here is what Joel said.

Locusts Attack the Land

² Elders, listen to me.
  Pay attention, all you who live in the
    land.
Has anything like this ever happened in
    your whole life?
  Did it ever happen to your people
    who lived long ago?
³ Tell your children about it.
  Let them tell their children.
And let their children tell it
  to those who live after them.
⁴ The giant locusts have eaten
    what the common locusts have left.
The young locusts have eaten
    what the giant locusts have left.
And other locusts have eaten
    what the young locusts have left.

⁵ Get up and weep, you people who drink
    too much!
  Cry, all you who drink wine!
Cry because the fresh wine
  has been taken away from you.
⁶ The locusts are like a mighty army
    that has marched into our land.
There are so many of them
  they can't even be counted.
Their teeth are as sharp as a lion's
    teeth.
  They are like the fangs of a female
    lion.
⁷ The locusts have completely destroyed
    our vines.
  They have wiped out our fig trees.
They've stripped off the bark and
    thrown it away.
  They've left the branches bare.

⁸ My people, mourn like a virgin
  who is dressed in the clothes of
    sadness.
She is sad because she has lost
  the young man she was going to
    marry.
⁹ No one brings grain offerings and drink
    offerings
  to the LORD's house anymore.
So the priests who serve the LORD
  are filled with sorrow.
¹⁰ Our fields are wiped out.
  The ground is dried up.
  The grain is destroyed.

The fresh wine is gone.
  And there isn't any more olive oil.
¹¹ Farmers, be sad.
  Cry, you who grow vines.
Mourn because the wheat and barley
    are gone.
  The crops in the fields are destroyed.
¹² The vines and fig trees are dried up.
  The pomegranate, palm and apple
    trees
  don't have any fruit on them.
In fact, all the trees in the fields are
    dried up.
  And my people's joy has faded away.

A Call to Mourn

¹³ Priests, put on the clothing of sadness
    and mourn.
  Cry, you who serve at the altar.
Come, you who serve my God in the
    temple.
  Spend the night dressed in the
    clothes of sadness.
Weep because no one brings grain
    offerings and drink offerings
  to the house of your God anymore.
¹⁴ Announce a holy fast.
  Tell the people not to eat anything.
  Gather them together for a special
    service.
Send for the elders
  and all who live in the land.
Have them come to the house of the
    LORD your God.
  And pray to him.

¹⁵ The day of the LORD is near.
  How sad it will be on that day!
  The Mighty One is coming to
    destroy you.

¹⁶ Our food has been taken away
    right in front of our eyes.
There isn't any joy or gladness
  in the house of our God.
¹⁷ The seeds have dried up in the ground.
  The grain is also gone.
The storerooms have been destroyed.
  The barns are broken down.
¹⁸ Listen to the cattle groan!
  The herds wander around.
They don't have any grass to eat.
  The flocks of sheep are also suffering.

¹⁹ LORD, I call out to you.
  Fire has burned up the desert
    grasslands.

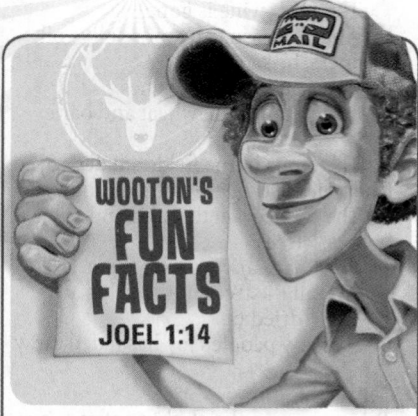

WOOTON'S FUN FACTS

JOEL 1:14

No, "fast and pray" doesn't mean driving fast and praying not to get a ticket. *Fasting means to stop eating for a while to focus on God.* You don't have to give up all food to fast. I once fasted from junk food (that was tough) while Connie gave up primping in the mirror, and Eugene gave up words more than two syllables long. Actually, I think Eugene had it the toughest!

> Flames have destroyed all the trees
>   in the fields.
> ²⁰ Even the wild animals cry out to you
>   for help.
>   The streams of water have dried up.
>   Fire has burned up the desert
>   grasslands.

The LORD Sends an Army of Locusts

2 Priests, blow the trumpets in Zion.
>   Give a warning on my holy
>   mountain.
> Let everyone who lives in the land
>   tremble with fear.
>   The day of the LORD is coming.
>   It is very near.
> ² That day will be dark and sad.
>   It will be black and cloudy.
> A huge army of locusts is coming.
>   They will spread across the mountains
>   like the sun when it rises.
> There has never been an army like it.
>   And there will never be another
>   for all time to come.

> ³ Like fire they eat up everything in their
>   path.
>   Behind them it looks as if flames
>   have burned the land.

> In front of them the land is like the
>   Garden of Eden.
>   Behind them it is a dry and empty
>   desert.
>   Nothing escapes them.
> ⁴ They look like horses.
>   Like war horses they charge ahead.
> ⁵ They sound like chariots as they leap
>   over the mountaintops.
>   They crackle like fire burning up dry
>   weeds.
> They are like a mighty army
>   that is ready for battle.

> ⁶ When people see them, they tremble
>   with fear.
>   All their faces turn pale.
> ⁷ The locusts charge ahead like warriors.
>   They climb over walls like soldiers.
> All of them march in line.
>   They don't turn to the right or the left.
> ⁸ They don't bump into one another.
>   Each of them marches straight
>   ahead.
> They charge through everything that
>   tries to stop them.
>   But they still stay in line.
> ⁹ They attack a city.
>   They run along its wall.
> They climb into houses.
>   They enter through windows like
>   robbers.

> ¹⁰ As they march forward, the earth
>   shakes.
>   The heavens tremble as they
>   approach.
> The sun and moon grow dark.
>   And the stars stop shining.
> ¹¹ The LORD thunders with his mighty
>   voice
>   as he leads his army.

Jason's Jargon

JOEL 2

Find *concerned* in this chapter. To be concerned about people can have two meanings: to be worried about them or to think a lot about them.

He has so many forces they can't even
    be counted.
The army that obeys his commands
    is mighty.
The day of the LORD is great and
    terrifying.
    Who can live through it?

Let Your Hearts Be Broken

¹²The LORD announces to his people,

"Return to me with all your heart.
    There is still time.
Do not eat any food.
    Weep and mourn."

¹³ Don't just tear your clothes to show
    how sad you are.
    Let your hearts be broken.
Return to the LORD your God.
    He is gracious.
    He is tender and kind.
    He is slow to get angry.
    He is full of love.
    He won't bring his judgment.
    He won't destroy you.
¹⁴ Who knows? He might turn toward
    you
    and not bring his judgment.
    He might even give you his blessing.
Then you can bring grain offerings and
    drink offerings
    to the LORD your God.

¹⁵ Priests, blow the trumpets in Zion.
    Announce a holy fast.
Tell the people not to eat anything.
    Gather them together for a special
    service.
¹⁶ Bring them together.
    Set all of them apart to me.
Bring together the elders.
    Gather the children and the babies
    who are still nursing.
Let the groom leave his bedroom.
    Let the bride leave their marriage
    bed.
¹⁷ Let the priests who serve the LORD
    weep.
    Let them cry between the temple
    porch and the altar.
Let them say, "LORD, spare your people.
    Don't let others make fun of them.
    Don't let the nations laugh at them.
Don't let them tease your people and
    say,
    'Where is their God?'"

The LORD Answers the Prayer of His People

¹⁸ Then the LORD was concerned for his
    land.
    He took pity on his people.

¹⁹He replied,

"I am sending you grain, olive oil and
    fresh wine.
    It will be enough to satisfy you
    completely.
I will never allow other nations
    to make fun of you again.

²⁰ "I will drive far away from you
    the army that comes from the north.
I will send some of its forces
    into a dry and empty land.
Its eastern troops will drown in the
    Dead Sea.
    Its western troops will drown in the
    Mediterranean Sea.
    Their dead bodies will stink."

The LORD has done great things.
²¹   Land of Judah, don't be afraid.
Be glad and full of joy.
    The LORD has done great things.
²² Wild animals, don't be afraid.
    The desert grasslands are turning
    green again.
The trees are bearing their fruit.
    The vines and fig trees are producing
    rich crops.
²³ People of Zion, be glad.
    Be joyful because of what the LORD
    your God has done.
He has given you the right amount of
    rain in the fall.
That's because he is faithful.
    He has sent you plenty of showers.
He has sent fall and spring rains alike,
    just as he did before.
²⁴ Your threshing floors will be covered
    with grain.
    Olive oil and fresh wine will spill
    over
    from the places where they are
    stored.

²⁵The LORD says,

"I sent a great army of locusts to attack
    you.
    They included common locusts,
    giant locusts,
    young locusts and other locusts.

I will make up for the years
　　they ate your crops.
²⁶ You will have plenty to eat.
　　It will satisfy you completely.
Then you will praise me.
　　I am the LORD your God.
I have done wonderful things for you.
　　My people will never again be put to
　　　　shame.
²⁷ You will know that I am with you in
　　　　Israel.
　　I am the LORD your God.
There is no other God.
　　So my people will never again be put
　　　　to shame.

The Day of the LORD Is Coming

²⁸ "After that, I will pour out my Spirit on
　　　　all people.
　　Your sons and daughters will
　　　　prophesy.
Your old men will have dreams.
　　Your young men will have visions.
²⁹ In those days I will pour out my Spirit
　　　　on those who serve me, men and
　　　　women alike.
³⁰ I will show wonders in the heavens and
　　　　on the earth.
　　There will be blood and fire and
　　　　clouds of smoke.
³¹ The sun will become dark.
　　The moon will turn red like blood.
　　It will happen before the great and
　　　　terrible day of the LORD comes.
³² Everyone who calls out to me will be
　　　　saved.
　　On Mount Zion and in Jerusalem
　　　　some of my people will be left alive.
I have chosen them.
　　That is what I have promised.

The LORD Judges the Nations

3 "At that time I will bless Judah and
　　　　Jerusalem
　　with great success again.
² I will gather together all the nations.
　　I will bring them down to the Valley
　　　　of Jehoshaphat.
There I will put them on trial.
　　I will judge them for what they have
　　　　done
　　to my people Israel.
They scattered them among the nations.
　　They divided up my land among
　　　　themselves.

Jason's Jargon

JOEL 3

Time for a gardening and military operation! Find *pruning tools* in this chapter. Pruning tools are used to cut back branches on plants. God wanted them to turn these tools into weapons for battle.

³ They cast lots for my people.
　　They sold boys into slavery to get
　　　　prostitutes.
　　They sold girls to buy some wine to
　　　　drink.

⁴"Tyre and Sidon, why are you doing things like that to me? And why are you doing them, all you people in Philistia? Are you trying to get even with me for something I have done? If you are, I will pay you back for it in a quick and speedy way. ⁵You took my silver and gold. You carried off my finest treasures to your temples. ⁶You sold the people of Judah and Jerusalem to the Greeks. You wanted to send them far away from their own country.

⁷"But now I will stir them up into action. I will bring them back from the places you sold them to. And I will do to you what you did to them. ⁸I will sell your sons and daughters to the people of Judah. And they will sell them to the Sabeans. The Sabeans are a nation that is far away." The LORD has spoken.

⁹ Announce this among the nations.
　　Tell them to prepare for battle.
　　Nations, get your soldiers ready!
　　Bring all your fighting men
　　　　together
　　and march out to attack.
¹⁰ Hammer your plows into swords.
　　Hammer your pruning tools into
　　　　spears.
　　Let anyone who is weak say,
　　　　"I am strong!"
¹¹ Come quickly, all you surrounding
　　　　nations.
　　Gather together in the Valley of
　　　　Jehoshaphat.

Lord, send down your soldiers from
    heaven!

The Lord Blesses His People

¹⁷The Lord says,

¹²The Lord says,

"Stir up the nations into action!
    Let them march into the valley
    where I will judge them.
I will take my seat in court.
    I will judge all the surrounding
        nations.
¹³ My soldiers, swing your blades.
    The nations are ripe for harvest.
Come and stomp on them as if they
        were grapes.
    Crush them until the winepress of
        my anger is full.
Do it until the wine spills over
    from the places where it is stored.
    The nations have committed far too
        many sins!"

¹⁴ Huge numbers of soldiers are gathered
        in the valley
    where the Lord will hand down his
        sentence.
    The day of the Lord is near in that
        valley.
¹⁵ The sun and moon will become dark.
    The stars won't shine anymore.
¹⁶ The Lord will roar like a lion from
        Jerusalem.
    His voice will sound like thunder
        from Zion.
    The earth and the heavens will
        tremble.
But the Lord will keep the people of
        Israel safe.
    He will be a place of safety for them.

"You will know that I am the Lord
        your God.
    I live in Zion.
    It is my holy mountain.
Jerusalem will be my holy city.
    People from other lands
    will never again attack it.

¹⁸ "At that time fresh wine will drip from
        the mountains.
    Milk will flow down from the hills.
    Water will run through all Judah's
        valleys.
A fountain will flow out of my temple.
    It will water the places where acacia
        trees grow.
¹⁹ But Egypt will be deserted.
    Edom will become a dry and empty
        desert.
They did terrible harm to the people of
        Judah.
    My people were not guilty of doing
        anything wrong.
    But Egypt and Edom spilled their
        blood anyway.
²⁰ My people will live in Judah and
        Jerusalem forever.
    The land will be their home for all
        time to come.
²¹ Egypt and Edom have spilled my
        people's blood.
    Should I let them escape my
        judgment?
    No, I will not."

    The Lord lives in Zion!

Amos

Many prophets spoke boldly for God during times of great national crisis. However, Amos was called when Israel and Judah were both experiencing a time of peace and prosperity. You might think following God when things were going well would be a piece of cake. But unfortunately, that was not the case.

Rather than utilizing this opportunity to help the less fortunate, the wealthy people regularly took advantage of the poor. Yet they kept going to the Temple and making offerings to God as if everything were just fine. It had gotten to the point where God declared, "I hate your holy feasts. I can't stand them" (5:21).

Amos made it clear that God saw what the surrounding nations were doing wrong and was going to take action against them (1:3–2:3). But then he was much more specific about the numerous sins of Israel (2:4–16) and the self-centered lifestyle of the people.

One other item worthy of attention: Amos was a shepherd (1:1). Other prophets were priests, or associated with kings, or at the minimum got reimbursed for what they did. Amos shows that God can call anyone—great or small—who is willing to speak for Him as He directs.

WHAT'S IT MEAN, EUGENE?

Trinity—Though this word does not appear anywhere in the Bible, the reality of the "trinity" is expressed throughout the totality of the Scriptures. It concerns the concept that there are three individual Persons—Father, Son, and Holy Spirit—within the One Divine Nature or Godhead. *Trinitas* means "three-in-oneness."

1 These are the words of Amos. He was a shepherd from the town of Tekoa. Here is the vision he saw concerning Israel. It came to him two years before the earthquake. At that time Uzziah was king of Judah. Jeroboam, the son of Jehoash, was king of Israel. Here are the words of Amos.

²He said,

"The LORD roars like a lion from
      Jerusalem.
   His voice sounds like thunder from
      Zion.
   The grasslands of the shepherds turn
      brown.
   The top of Mount Carmel dries up."

The LORD Judges Israel's Neighbors

³The LORD says,

"The people of Damascus have sinned
      again and again.
   So I will judge them.
They used threshing sleds with iron
      teeth
   to crush Gilead's people.
⁴ So I will send fire to destroy the palace
      of King Hazael.
   It will burn up the forts of his son
      Ben-Hadad.
⁵ I will break down the city gate of
      Damascus.
   I will kill the king
   who lives in the Valley of Aven, that
      evil place.
He holds the ruler's scepter in Beth Eden.
   The people of Aram will be taken
      away to Kir as prisoners,"
   says the LORD.

⁶The LORD says,

"The people of Gaza have sinned again
      and again.
   So I will judge them.
They captured whole communities.
   They sold them to Edom.
⁷ So I will send fire to destroy the walls of
      Gaza.
   It will burn up its forts.
⁸ I will kill the king of Ashdod.
   He holds the ruler's scepter in
      Ashkelon.
I will use my power against Ekron.
   Every single Philistine will die,"
   says the LORD and King.

Amos 1:1 Like King David, Amos was a shepherd when he was young and carried a sling. Shepherds would fling rocks near sheep that were wandering away in order to "scare" the animals toward the flock.

⁹The LORD says,

"The people of Tyre have sinned again
      and again.
   So I will judge them.
They captured whole communities.
   They sold them to Edom.
They did not honor the treaty
   of friendship they had made.
¹⁰ So I will send fire to destroy the walls of
      Tyre.
   It will burn up its forts."

¹¹The LORD says,

"The people of Edom have sinned again
      and again.
   So I will judge them.
They chased Israel with swords
   that were ready to strike them
      down.
   They killed the women of the land.
They were angry all the time.
   Their anger was like a fire that
      blazed out.
   It could not be stopped.
¹² So I will send fire to destroy the city of
      Teman.
   It will burn up Bozrah's forts."

¹³The LORD says,

"The people of Ammon have sinned
      again and again.
   So I will judge them.
They ripped open the pregnant women
      in Gilead.

They wanted to add land to their
territory.
¹⁴ So I will set fire to destroy the walls of
Rabbah.
It will burn up its forts.
War cries will be heard on that day of
battle.
Strong winds will blow on that
stormy day.
¹⁵ Ammon's king will be carried away.
So will his officials,"
says the LORD.

2 The LORD says,

"The people of Moab have sinned again
and again.
So I will judge them.
They burned the bones
of Edom's king to ashes.
² So I will send fire to destroy Moab.
It will burn up Kerioth's forts.
Moab will come crashing down with a
loud noise.
War cries will be heard.
So will the blast of trumpets.
³ I will kill Moab's ruler.
I will also kill all its officials,"
says the LORD.

⁴ The LORD says,

"The people of Judah have sinned again
and again.
So I will judge them.
They have refused to obey my law.
They have not kept my rules.
Other gods have led them astray.
Their people of long ago
worshiped those gods.
⁵ So I will send fire to destroy Judah.
It will burn up Jerusalem's forts."

The LORD Judges Israel

⁶ The LORD says,

"The people of Israel have sinned again
and again.
So I will judge them.
They sell into slavery those who have
done no wrong.
They trade needy people
for a mere pair of sandals.
⁷ They grind the heads of the poor
into the dust of the ground.
They refuse to be fair to those who
are crushed.
A father and his son have sex with the
same girl.
They treat my name as if it were not
holy.
⁸ They lie down beside every altar on
clothes they have taken.
They lie on those clothes
until the owner pays back what is
owed.
In the house of their God
they drink wine that was paid as
fines.

⁹ "Yet I destroyed the Amorites
to make room in the land for my
people.
The Amorites were as tall as cedar trees.
They were as strong as oak trees.
But I cut off their fruit above the ground
and their roots below it.

¹⁰ "People of Israel, I brought you up out
of Egypt.
I led you in the desert for 40 years.
I gave you the land of the Amorites.
¹¹ I raised up prophets from among your
children.
I also set apart for myself some
of your young people to be
Nazirites.
Isn't that true, people of Israel?"
announces the LORD.
¹² "But you made the Nazirites drink wine.
You commanded the prophets not to
prophesy.

¹³ "A cart that is loaded with grain
crushes anything it runs over.
In the same way, I will crush you.
¹⁴ Your fastest runners will not escape.
The strongest people will not get away.
Even soldiers will not be able
to save their own lives.

Jason's Jargon

AMOS 2

Find *Nazirites* in this
chapter. Nazirites
were Israelites who
were dedicated to God,
taking a vow to serve
Him. Nazirites didn't
cut their hair or drink
wine out of respect for
God.

15 Men who are armed with bows will lose
    the battle.
        Soldiers who are quick on their feet
            will not escape.
    Horsemen will not be able
        to save their own lives.
16 Even your bravest soldiers
        will run away naked on that day,"
    announces the LORD.

The LORD Calls for Witnesses Against Israel

3 People of Israel, listen to the LORD's message. He has spoken his message against you. He has spoken it against the whole family he brought up out of Egypt. He says,

2 "Out of all the families on earth
        I have chosen only you.
    So I will punish you
        because you have committed so
            many sins."

3 Do two people walk together
        unless they've agreed to do so?
4 Does a lion roar in the bushes
        when it doesn't have any food?
    Does it growl in its den
        when it hasn't caught anything?
5 Does a bird fly down to a trap on the
            ground
        when no bait is there?
    Does a net spring up from the ground
        when it has not caught anything?
6 When someone blows a trumpet in a
            city,
        don't the people tremble with fear?
    When trouble comes to a city,
        hasn't the LORD caused it?

7 The LORD and King never does
            anything
    without telling his servants the
            prophets about it.

8 A lion has roared.
        Who isn't afraid?
    The LORD and King has spoken.
        Who can do anything but prophesy?

9 Speak to the people in the forts of
            Ashdod and Egypt.
    Tell them, "Gather together
        on the mountains of Samaria.
    Look at the great trouble in that city.
        Its people are committing many
            crimes."

10 "They do not know how to do what is
            right,"
    announces the LORD.
    "They store up stolen goods in their
            forts."

11 So the LORD and King says,

"Enemies will take over your land.
    They will pull down your places of
            safety.
    They will rob your forts."

12 The LORD says,

"Suppose a shepherd saves only two leg
            bones
        from a lion's mouth.
    Or he might save only a piece of an ear.
        That is how the Israelites living in
            Samaria will be saved.
    They will only have a board
        from a bed
    and a piece of cloth
        from a couch."

13 "Listen to me," announces the Lord.
"Be a witness against the people of Jacob,"
says the LORD God who rules over all.

14 "I will punish Israel for their sins.
        When I do, I will destroy their altars
            at Bethel.
    The horns that stick out from the upper
            corners
        of their main altar will be cut off.
    They will fall to the ground.
15 I will tear down their winter houses.
        I will also pull down their summer
            houses.
    The houses they have decorated with
            ivory will be destroyed.
    And their princely houses will be
            torn down,"
    announces the LORD.

Israel Has Not Returned to the LORD

4 Listen to the LORD's message,
        you women who live on the hill of
            Samaria.
    You treat poor people badly.
        You crush those who are in need.
    You say to your husbands,
        "Bring us some drinks!"
    But you are already as fat
        as the cows in Bashan.
2 The LORD and King has made a promise
        by his own holy name.

He says, "You can be sure
    that the time will come
when your enemies will put hooks in
      your faces.
    They will lead every one of you away
      with fishhooks.
³ Each of you will go straight out
      through gaps made in the wall.
You will be thrown out toward Harmon,"
    announces the LORD.
⁴ "People of Samaria, go to Bethel and sin!
    Go to Gilgal! Sin there even more!
Bring your sacrifices every morning.
    Every third year, bring a tenth
    of everything you produce.
⁵ Bake some bread with yeast.
    Burn it as a thank offering.
Brag about the offerings you freely give.
    This is what you Israelites love to do,"
    announces the LORD and King.

⁶ "I made sure your stomachs were empty
      in every city.
    You did not have enough bread in
      any of your towns.
In spite of that, you still have not
      returned to me,"
    announces the LORD.

⁷ "I also held back rain from you.
    The time to harvest crops
    was still three months away.
I sent rain on one town.
    But I held it back from another.
One field had rain.
    But another had no rain and dried up.
⁸ People wandered from town to town to
      look for water.
    But they did not get enough to drink.
In spite of that, you still have not
      returned to me,"
    announces the LORD.

⁹ "Many times I kept your gardens and
      vineyards from growing.
    I sent hot winds to dry them up
      completely.
Locusts ate up your fig and olive trees.
    In spite of that, you still have not
      returned to me,"
    announces the LORD.

¹⁰ "I sent plagues on you,
    just as I did on Egypt.
I killed your young men by swords.
    I also let the horses you had
      captured be killed.

I filled your noses with the stink of your
      camps.
    In spite of that, you still have not
      returned to me,"
    announces the LORD.

¹¹ "I destroyed some of you,
    just as I did Sodom and Gomorrah.
You were like a burning stick that was
      pulled out of the fire.
    In spite of that, you still have not
      returned to me,"
    announces the LORD.

¹² "So, people of Israel, I will judge you.
    Because I will do that to you, Israel,
    prepare to meet your God!"

¹³ The LORD forms the mountains.
    He creates the wind.
    He makes his thoughts known to
      human beings.
    He turns sunrise into darkness.
    He rules over even the highest places
      on earth.
    His name is the LORD God Who
      Rules Over All.

Mourn and Turn Back to the LORD

5 People of Israel, listen to the LORD's message. Hear my song of sadness about you. I say,

² "The people of Israel have fallen.
    They will never get up again.
    They are deserted in their own land.
    No one can lift them up."

³Here is what the LORD and King says to Israel.

"A thousand soldiers will march out
      from a city.
    But only a hundred will return.
A hundred soldiers will march out from
      a town.
    But only ten will come back."

⁴The LORD speaks to the people of Israel. He says,

"Look to me and live.
⁵   Do not look to Bethel.
Do not go to Gilgal.
    Do not travel to Beersheba.
The people of Gilgal will be taken away
      as prisoners.
    Nothing will be left of Bethel."

⁶ Israel, look to the LORD and live.

If you don't, he will sweep through
the tribes of Joseph like a fire.
It will burn everything up.
And Bethel won't have anyone to put
it out.

[7] There are people among you who turn
what is fair into something
bitter.
They throw down to the ground
what is right.
[8] The LORD made the Pleiades and Orion.
He turns midnight into sunrise.
He makes the day fade into night.
He sends for the waters in the clouds.
Then he pours them out on the
surface of the land.
His name is the LORD.
[9] With a flash of light he destroys places
of safety.
He tears down cities
that have high walls around them.
[10] There are people among you who hate
anyone who stands for justice
in court.
They hate those who tell the truth.

[11] You make poor people pay tax on their
straw.
You also tax their grain.
So, even though you have built stone
houses,
you won't live in them.
You have planted fruitful vineyards.
But you won't drink the wine they
produce.
[12] I know how many crimes you have
committed.
You have sinned far too much.

Among you are people who crush those
who have done no wrong.
They accept money from people who
want special favors.
They take away the rights of poor
people in the courts.
[13] So those who are wise keep quiet in
times like these.
That's because the times are evil.

[14] Look to what is good, not to what is evil.
Then you will live.
And the LORD God who rules over all
will be with you,
just as you say he is.
[15] Hate evil and love good.
Do what is fair in the courts.

Perhaps the LORD God who rules over all
will have mercy on you.
After all, you are the only ones left
in the family line of Joseph.

[16] The LORD God rules over all. The Lord
says,

"People will weep in all the streets.
They will be very sad in every
market place.
Even farmers will be told to cry loudly.
People will mourn for the dead.
[17] Workers will cry in all the vineyards.
That's because I will punish you,"
says the LORD.

The Day of the LORD Is Coming

[18] How terrible it will be for you
who long for the day of the LORD!
Why do you want it to come?
That day will be dark, not light.
[19] It will be like a man running away from
a lion
only to meet a bear.
He enters his house and rests his hand
on a wall
only to be bitten by a snake.
[20] The day of the LORD will be dark, not
light.
It will be very black.
There won't be a ray of sunlight
anywhere.

[21] The LORD says,

"I hate your holy feasts.
I can't stand them.
Your gatherings stink.
[22] You bring me burnt offerings and grain
offerings.
But I will not accept them.
You bring your best friendship
offerings.
But I will not even look at them.
[23] Take the noise of your songs away!
I will not listen to the music of your
harps.
[24] I want you to treat others fairly.
So let fair treatment roll on
just as a river does!
Always do what is right.
Let right living flow along
like a stream that never runs dry!

[25] "People of Israel, did you bring me
sacrifices and offerings
for 40 years in the desert?

ADVENTURES IN ODYSSEY

While using the Room of Consequence in the adventure "Where Your Treasure Is" (Club), Camilla and Asmita recited Amos 5:24 to use the power of God's Word to put out a fire.

²⁶ Yes. But you have honored the place
    where your king worshiped other
    gods.
You have carried the stands
    the statues of your gods were on.
You have lifted up the banners
    of the stars you worship as gods.
    You made all those things for
        yourselves.
²⁷ So I will send you away
    as prisoners beyond Damascus,"
says the LORD.
    His name is God Who Rules Over All.

How Terrible for Those Who Feel Secure When They Shouldn't

6 How terrible it will be for you men
    who are so contented on Mount Zion!
How terrible for you who feel secure
    on the hill of Samaria!
You are famous men from the greatest
    nation.
The people of Israel come to you
    for help and advice.
² Go and look at the city of Kalneh.
    Go from there to the great city of
        Hamath.
Then go down to Gath in Philistia.
Are those places better off than your
    two kingdoms?

Is their land larger than yours?
³ You are trying to avoid the time
    when trouble will come.
But you are only bringing closer
    the Assyrian rule of terror.
⁴ You lie down on beds
    that are decorated with ivory.
You rest on your couches.
You eat the best lambs
    and the fattest calves.
⁵ You pluck away on your harps as David
    did.
    You play new songs on musical
        instruments.
⁶ You drink wine by the bowlful.
    You use the finest lotions.
But Joseph's people will soon be
    destroyed.
    And you aren't even sad about it.
⁷ So you will be among the first
    to be taken away as prisoners.
You won't be able to enjoy good food.
    You won't lie around on couches
        anymore.

The LORD Hates the Pride of Israel

⁸The LORD and King has made a promise in his own name. He is the LORD God who rules over all. He announces,

"I hate the pride of Jacob's people.
    I can't stand their forts.
I will hand the city of Samaria
    and everything in it over to their
        enemies."

⁹Ten people might be left in one house. If they are, they will die there. ¹⁰Relatives might come to burn the dead bodies. If they do, they'll have to carry them out of the house first. They might ask someone still hiding there, "Is anyone else here with you?" If the answer is no, the relatives will go on to say, "Be quiet! We must not pray in the LORD's name."

¹¹ That's because the LORD has already
        given an order.
    He will smash large houses to
        pieces.
    He will crush small houses to bits.

¹² Horses don't run on rocky ground.
    People don't plow the sea with oxen.
But you have turned fair treatment into
    poison.
    You have turned the fruit of right
        living into bitterness.

See the word "ivory" in Amos 6:4? Ivory comes from elephant tusks. Poachers kill thirty thousand elephants worldwide every year for their ivory. In 2016 the U.S. banned almost all ivory sales in order to protect elephants.

¹³ You are happy because you captured the town of Lo Debar.
You say, "We were strong enough to take Karnaim too."

¹⁴ But the LORD God rules over all. He announces, "People of Israel,
I will stir up a nation against you.
They will crush you from Lebo Hamath all the way down to the Arabah Valley."

Amos Has Visions of Locusts, Fire and a Plumb Line

7 The LORD and King gave me a vision. He was bringing large numbers of locusts on the land. The king's share had already been harvested. Now the later crops were coming up. ²The locusts stripped the land clean. Then I cried out, "LORD and King, forgive Israel! How can Jacob's people continue? They are such a weak nation!"

³So the LORD had pity on them.
"I will let them continue for now," he said.

⁴The LORD and King gave me a second vision. He was using fire to punish his people. It dried up the deep waters. It burned the land up. ⁵Then I cried out, "LORD and King, please stop! How can Jacob's people continue? They are such a weak nation!"

⁶So the LORD had pity on them.

"I will let them continue for now," the LORD and King said.

⁷Then the Lord gave me a third vision. He was standing by a wall. It had been built very straight, all the way up and down. He was holding a plumb line. ⁸The LORD asked me, "What do you see, Amos?"

"A plumb line," I replied.

Then the Lord said, "Look at what I am doing. I am hanging a plumb line next to my people Israel. It will show how crooked they are. I will no longer spare them.

⁹ "The high places where Isaac's people worship other gods will be destroyed.
The other places of worship in Israel will also be torn down.
I will use my sword to attack Jeroboam's royal family."

Amaziah Tells Amos to Stop Prophesying

¹⁰Amaziah was priest of Bethel. He sent a message to Jeroboam, the king of Israel. He said, "Amos is making evil plans against you right here in Israel. The people in the land can't stand to listen to what he's saying. ¹¹Amos is telling them,

" 'Jeroboam will be killed by a sword.
The people of Israel will be taken away as prisoners.
They will be carried off from their own land.' "

Jason's Jargon

AMOS 7

Search this chapter for the words *plumb line*. A plumb line is a string with a weight tied to the end. It is hung in the air for comparison to make sure walls are built perfectly straight.

¹²Then Amaziah said to Amos, "Get out of Israel, you prophet! Go back to the land of Judah. Earn your living there. Do your prophesying there. ¹³Don't prophesy here at Bethel anymore. This is where the king

Amos 7:4 If you've ever heard someone say they burn water, it's not true. Water doesn't burn because it evaporates first. A house fire burns at around 1,100 degrees Fahrenheit; this temperature would burn or melt everything in an Old Testament home except some rocks and iron.

worships. The main temple in the kingdom is located here."

[14] Amos answered Amaziah, "I was not a prophet. I wasn't even the son of a prophet. I was a shepherd. I also took care of sycamore-fig trees. [15] But the LORD took me away from taking care of the flock. He said to me, 'Go. Prophesy to my people Israel.' [16] Now then, listen to the LORD's message. You say,

"'Don't prophesy against Israel.
    Stop preaching against the people of
        Isaac.'

[17] "But the LORD says,

"'Your wife will become a prostitute
    in the city of Bethel.
Your sons and daughters will be
    killed by swords.
Your land will be measured and divided
    up.
    And you yourself will die in another
        country.
The people of Israel will surely be taken
    away as prisoners.
    They will be carried off from their
        own land.'"

Amos Has a Vision of a Basket of Ripe Fruit

8 The LORD and King gave me a vision. He showed me a basket of ripe fruit. [2] "What do you see, Amos?" he asked.

"A basket of ripe fruit," I replied.

Then the LORD said to me, "The time is ripe for my people Israel. I will no longer spare them.

[3] "The time is coming when the songs in the temple will turn to weeping," announces the LORD and King. "Many, many bodies will be thrown everywhere! So be quiet!"

[4] Listen to me, you who walk all over
        needy people.
    You crush those who are poor in the
        land.

[5] You say,

"When will the New Moon feast be
        over?
    Then we can sell our grain.
When will the Sabbath day come to an
        end?
    Then people can buy our wheat."
But you measure out less than the right
        amount.
    You raise your prices.
    You cheat others by using dishonest
        scales.
[6] You buy poor people to make slaves out
        of them.
    You buy those who are in need for a
        mere pair of sandals.
    You even sell the worthless parts of
        your wheat.

[7] People of Jacob, you are proud that the LORD is your God. But he has made a promise in his own name. He says, "I will never forget anything Israel has done.

[8] "The land will tremble because of what
        will happen.
    Everyone who lives in it will
        mourn.
So the whole land will rise like the Nile
        River.
    It will be stirred up.
Then it will settle back down again
    like that river in Egypt."

[9] The LORD and King announces,

"At that time I will make the sun go
        down at noon.
    The earth will become dark in the
        middle of the day.
[10] I will turn your holy feasts into times
        for mourning.
    I will turn all your songs into
        weeping.

You will have to wear the clothing of
   sadness.
You will shave your heads.
I will make you mourn as if your only
   son had died.
The end of that time will be like a
   bitter day."

[11] The LORD and King announces,

"The days are coming
   when I will send hunger through the
   land.
But people will not be hungry for food.
   They will not be thirsty for water.
Instead, they will be hungry
   to hear a message from me.
[12] People will wander from the Dead Sea
   to the Mediterranean.
They will travel from north to east.
They will look for a message from me.
   But they will not find it.

[13] "At that time

"the lovely young women and strong
   young men
will faint because they are so thirsty.
[14] Some people make promises in the
   name of Samaria's god.
That god has led them astray.
Others say, 'People of Dan, you can be
   sure
that your god is alive.'
Still others say, 'You can be sure
   that Beersheba's god is alive.'
But all these people will fall dead.
They will never get up again."

Israel Will Be Destroyed

9 I saw the Lord standing next to the altar
in the temple. He said to me,

"Strike the tops of the temple pillars.
   Then the heavy stones at the base of
   the entrance will shake.
Bring everything down on the heads of
   everyone there.
I will kill with my swords
   those who are left alive.
None of the Israelites will escape.
   None will get away.
[2] They might dig down deep.
   But my powerful hand will take
   them out of there.
They might climb up to the heavens.
   But I will bring them down from
   there.

[3] They might hide on top of Mount
   Carmel.
But I will hunt them down
   and grab them.
They might hide from me at the bottom
   of the ocean.
But even there I will command the
   serpent to bite them.
[4] Their enemies might take them away
   as prisoners to another country.
But there I will command Israel's
   enemies
   to cut them down with swords.
I will keep my eye on Israel to harm
   them.
   I will not help them."

[5] The LORD rules over all.
   The Lord touches the earth, and it
   melts.
   Everyone who lives in it mourns.
The whole land rises like the Nile River.
   Then it settles back down again
   like that river in Egypt.
[6] The LORD builds his palace high in the
   heavens.
He lays its foundation on the earth.
He sends for the waters in the clouds.
   Then he pours them out on the
   surface of the land.
   His name is the LORD.

[7] "You Israelites are just like
   the people of Cush to me,"
   announces the LORD.
"I brought Israel up from Egypt.
   I also brought the Philistines from
   Crete
   and the Arameans from Kir.

[8] "I am the LORD and King.
   My eyes are watching the sinful
   kingdom of Israel.
I will wipe it off the face of the earth.
   But I will not totally destroy the
   people of Jacob,"
   announces the LORD.
[9] "I will give an order.
   I will shake the people of Israel
   among all the nations.
They will be like grain that is shaken
   through a screen.
   Not a pebble will fall to the ground.
[10] All the sinners among my people
   will be killed by swords.
   They say, 'Nothing bad will ever
   happen to us.'

Israel Will Be Made Like New Again

11 "The time will come when I will set up
  David's fallen shelter.
I will repair its broken walls.
  I will rebuild what was destroyed.
  I will make it what it used to be.
12 Then my people will take control of
      those
  who are left alive in Edom.
They will also possess all the nations
  that belong to me,"
  announces the LORD.
  He will do all these things.

13 "The days are coming," announces the
LORD.

"At that time those who plow the land
  will catch up with those who harvest
    the crops.

Those who stomp on grapes
  will catch up with those who plant
    the vines.
Fresh wine will drip from the
  mountains.
  It will flow down from all the hills.
14 I will bring my people Israel back home.
  I will bless them with great success
      again.
  They will rebuild the destroyed cities
    and live in them.
They will plant vineyards and drink the
    wine they produce.
  They will make gardens and eat their
    fruit.
15 I will plant Israel in their own land.
  They will never again be removed
    from the land I have given them,"

says the LORD your God.

Obadiah

It would be easy to skip over the book of Obadiah because it is, in fact, the shortest book of the Old Testament. It is also the only book in this Testament with only one chapter. To use traveling vernacular, "blink and you'll miss it." To compound this seeming triviality, a rapid reading of the book could leave one with the impression that Obadiah's message doesn't have application for people today. It was a concise proclamation that God was about to bring judgment on the people of Edom. However, like all parts of the Bible, this book has meaning for us today.

First, some background. The Edomites were descendants of Esau (Gen. 25:30; 36:9). In time, the family had grown into a nation with its own line of kings. Many times throughout their history, they opposed and even fought against the Israelites. Edom caused problems for Moses (Num. 20:14–21), Saul (1 Sam. 14:47), and David (2 Sam. 8:13–14). Throughout its history, Edom had rejoiced whenever other nations triumphed over Israel. God was not pleased with either their hostility or their attitude, and He was about to humble Edom. The Israelites might stumble and suffer at times, but He would restore them. Edom, on the other hand, would be left with no survivors (1:17–18).

So what precisely can we learn from Obadiah? God sees when His people are mistreated. He might not take *immediate* action to punish the offenders, but in due time, He will bring perfect justice.

What's It Mean, Eugene?

Works—Not to be confused with a vocation, such as my work at Whit's End, or as a teacher at Campbell County Community College, our *works* are simply our "deeds" or the "things we do." The apostle Paul tells us that we are not saved by doing "good works," but rather by putting our faith in Jesus Christ: "God's grace has saved you because of your faith in Christ. Your salvation doesn't come from anything you do" (Ephesians 2:8). This doesn't mean, however, that our actions don't matter! James 2:17 says, "If [faith] doesn't cause us to do something, it's dead."

Obadiah's Vision

¹This is the vision about Edom that Obadiah had.

Here is what the LORD and King says about Edom.

We've heard a message from the LORD.
A messenger was sent to the nations.
The LORD told him to say,
"Get up! Let us go and make war
against Edom."

²The LORD says to Edom,

"I will make you weak among the
nations.
They will look down on you.
³ You live in the safety of the rocks.
You make your home high up in the
mountains.
But your proud heart has tricked
you.
So you say to yourself,
'No one can bring me down to the
ground.'
⁴ You have built your home as high as an
eagle does.
You have made your nest among the
stars.
But I will bring you down from
there,"
announces the LORD.
⁵ "Edom, suppose robbers came to you at
night.
They would steal only as much as
they wanted.
Suppose grape pickers came to harvest
your vines.
They would still leave a few grapes.
But you are facing horrible trouble!
⁶ People of Esau, everything will be taken
away from you.
Your hidden treasures will be stolen.
⁷ All those who are helping you
will force you to leave your country.
Your friends will trick you and
overpower you.
Those who eat bread with you
will set a trap for you.
But you will not see it."

⁸ Here is what the LORD announces. "At
that time
I will destroy the wise men of Edom.
I will wipe out the men of understanding
in the mountains of Esau.

⁹ People of Teman, your soldiers will be
terrified.
Everyone in Esau's mountains
will be cut down by swords.
¹⁰ You did harmful things to the people of
Jacob.
They are your relatives.
So you will be covered with shame.
You will be destroyed forever.
¹¹ Outsiders entered the gates of Jerusalem.
They cast lots to see what each one
would get.
Strangers carried off its wealth.
When that happened, you just stood
there and did nothing.
You were like one of them.
¹² That was a time of trouble for your
relatives.
So you shouldn't have been happy
about what happened to them.
The people of Judah were destroyed.
So you should not have been happy
about it.
You should not have laughed at them
so much
when they were in trouble.
¹³ You should not have marched
through the gates of my people's city
when they were in trouble.
You shouldn't have been happy about
what happened to them.
You should not have stolen their
wealth
when they were in trouble.
¹⁴ You waited where the roads cross.
You wanted to cut down those who
were running away.
You should not have done that.
You handed over to their enemies
those who were still left alive.
You should not have done that.
They were in trouble.

¹⁵ "The day of the LORD is near
for all the nations.
Others will do to you
what you have done to them.
You will be paid back
for what you have done.
¹⁶ You Edomites made my holy mountain
of Zion impure
by drinking and celebrating there.
So all the nations will drink
from the cup of my anger.
And they will keep on drinking
from it.

They will vanish.
It will be as if they had never existed.
[17] But on Mount Zion some of my people
will be left alive.
I will save them.
Zion will be my holy mountain once
again.
And the people of Jacob
will again receive the land as their
own.

Jason's Jargon

OBADIAH 1

Examine this chapter
for the word *vision*.
A vision is like a
dream, seen while awake
or asleep. God gave
prophets visions to
show the future and to
give instructions.

[18] They will be like a fire.
Joseph's people will be like a flame.
The nation of Edom will be like straw.

Jacob's people will set Edom on fire
and burn it up.
No one will be left alive
among Esau's people."
The LORD has spoken.

[19] Israelites from the Negev Desert
will take over Esau's mountains.
Israelites from the western hills
will possess the land of the
Philistines.
They'll take over the territories
of Ephraim and Samaria.
Israelites from the tribe of Benjamin
will possess the land of Gilead.
[20] Some Israelites were forced to leave
their homes.
They'll come back to Canaan and
possess
it all the way to the town of
Zarephath.
Some people from Jerusalem were taken
to the city of Sepharad.
They'll return and possess
the towns of the Negev Desert.
[21] Leaders from Mount Zion will go
and rule over the mountains of Esau.
And the kingdom will belong to the
LORD.

Jonah

As we proceed through the Minor Prophets, we now arrive at the only one who is familiar to nearly everyone, whether they have read the Bible or not: Jonah!

His story has been told and retold . . . or to put it more accurately, *half* of it has. Most people have heard the familiar narrative about Jonah's reluctance to go to Nineveh as God instructed him. Instead he took a ship in the opposite direction. You probably know that God first sent a storm (1:4) and then sent a great fish (1:17) that became Jonah's literal "home" for three days.

Less commonly discussed, however, is what happened to Jonah after he finally preached to the people of Nineveh. Did you know that God sent a leafy plant (4:6) . . . and a worm (4:7)? That's a portion of the story that many people have missed. So be sure to read this book in its entirety! As you do, notice God's persistence in trying to get Jonah's attention. He could have given up on Jonah and chosen another messenger, but He wanted Jonah to learn about important concepts like repentance, forgiveness, and mercy.

As you read about God's patience with Jonah, don't neglect to think about your own life as well. In what ways is God patient with you as you try to become more completely the person He created you to be?

WHAT'S IT MEAN, EUGENE?

Sovereignty—When we say that God is *sovereign*, we mean that there is no one above Him. He possesses all power, rules over all things, and makes all the final decisions concerning our world and our lives. The book of Revelation describes it thusly: "Our Lord God is the King who rules over all" (Revelation 19:6) and calls God: "the Greatest King of all and the most powerful Lord of all" (Revelation 19:16).

Jonah Runs Away From the Lord

1 A message from the Lord came to Jonah, the son of Amittai. The Lord said, ²"Go to the great city of Nineveh. Preach against it. The sins of its people have come to my attention."

³But Jonah ran away from the Lord. He headed for Tarshish. So he went down to the port of Joppa. There he found a ship that was going to Tarshish. He paid the fare and went on board. Then he sailed for Tarshish. He was running away from the Lord.

⁴But the Lord sent a strong wind over the Mediterranean Sea. A wild storm came up. It was so wild that the ship was in danger of breaking apart. ⁵All the sailors were afraid. Each one cried out to his own god for help. They threw the ship's contents into the sea. They were trying to make the ship lighter.

But Jonah had gone below deck. There he lay down and fell into a deep sleep. ⁶The captain went down to him and said, "How can you sleep? Get up and call out to your god for help! Maybe he'll pay attention to what's happening to us. Then we won't die."

⁷Here is what the sailors said to one another. "Someone is to blame for getting us into all this trouble. Come. Let's cast lots to find out who it is." So they did. And Jonah was picked. ⁸They asked him, "What terrible thing have you done to bring all this trouble on us? Tell us. What do you do for a living? Where do you come from? What is your country? What people do you belong to?"

⁹He answered, "I'm a Hebrew. I worship the Lord. He is the God of heaven. He made the sea and the dry land."

¹⁰They found out he was running away from the Lord. That's because he had told them. Then they became terrified. So they asked him, "How could you do a thing like that?"

¹¹The sea was getting rougher and rougher. So they asked him, "What should we do to you to make the sea calm down?"

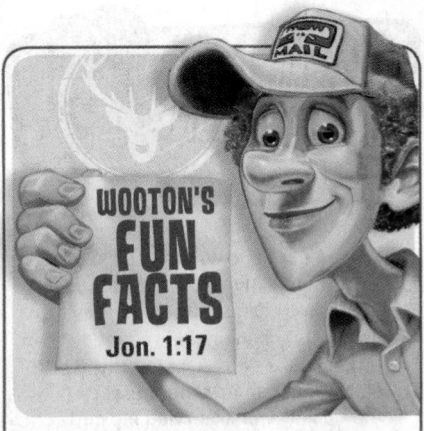

WOOTON'S FUN FACTS
Jon. 1:17

People in Bible days thought of animals as they were described in Genesis 1:20–26. Creatures lived one of three places: in the sea, in the sky, or on land. They thought of a "bat" as a bird (see Leviticus 11:13–19). The word "fish" could refer to a whale because it lives in the sea.

¹²"Pick me up and throw me into the sea," he replied. "Then it will become calm. I know it's my fault that this terrible storm has come on you."

¹³But the men didn't do what he said. Instead, they did their best to row back to land. But they couldn't. The sea got even rougher than before. ¹⁴Then they cried out to the Lord. They prayed, "Please, Lord, don't let us die for taking this man's life. After all, he might not be guilty of doing anything wrong. So don't hold us responsible for killing him. Lord, you always do what you want to." ¹⁵Then they took Jonah and threw him overboard. And the stormy sea became calm. ¹⁶The men saw what had happened. Then they began to have great respect for the Lord. They offered a sacrifice to him. And they made promises to him.

Jonah Prays to the Lord

¹⁷Now the Lord sent a huge fish to swallow Jonah. And Jonah was in the belly of the fish for three days and three nights. **2** ¹From inside the fish Jonah prayed to the Lord his God. ²He said,

"When I was in trouble, I called out to the Lord.
And he answered me.

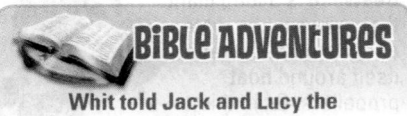

BIBLE ADVENTURES

Whit told Jack and Lucy the story of Jonah in "Return to the Bible Room" (A#02).

A few years ago, when I still lived in an apartment, I invited all my friends over for Thanksgiving. After a morning of heavy-duty cooking, I brought out the turkey and asked Whit to pray. As he started, a rush of water burst through the ceiling and drenched my perfect Thanksgiving dinner! Turns out, my upstairs neighbor owns a water bed . . . or she used to, before it broke and water flooded everywhere. Katrina and Penny mopped up while Wooton and Eugene patched the ceiling.

"Good news," Penny called from the kitchen. "We still have pie!"

"I have lots of macaroni and cheese at my house," Wooton added.

An hour later, we all gathered at Whit's End for a feast of macaroni—molded into a turkey shape—pickles, licorice, tuna sandwiches, and pumpkin pie. During dessert, Whit asked, "What are you thankful for this year, Connie?"

"Leftovers," I said. "They help me remember how great our holiday was. They remind me that I'm thankful for my friends and the memories we've made together." Like Jonah, a wild (and wet) experience reminded me to be thankful.

When I was deep in the place of the
dead,
I called out for help.
And you listened to my cry.
³ You threw me deep into the
Mediterranean Sea.
I was deep down in its waters.
They were all around me.
All your rolling waves
were sweeping over me.
⁴ I said, 'I have been driven away from
you.
But I will look again
toward your holy temple in
Jerusalem.'
⁵ I had almost drowned in the waves.
The deep waters were all around
me.
Seaweed was wrapped around my
head.
⁶ I sank down to the bottom of the
mountains.
I thought I had died
and gone down into the grave
forever.
But you are the Lord my God.
You brought my life up
from the very edge of the pit of
death.

⁷ "When my life was nearly over,
I remembered you, Lord.
My prayer rose up to you.
It reached you in your holy temple
in heaven.

⁸ "Some people worship the worthless
statues of their gods.
They turn away from God's love for
them.
⁹ But I will sacrifice a thank offering to
you.

Jason's Jargon

JONAH 2

An underwater quest! Find some *seaweed* in this chapter. Seaweed is a long plant that grows in the water and sometimes wraps itself around boat propellers. Or, in this case, Jonah's head!

And I will shout with thankful
        praise.
I will do what I have promised.
    I will say, 'LORD, you are the one
        who saves.'"

¹⁰The LORD gave the fish a command. And it spit Jonah up onto dry land.

Jonah Goes to Nineveh

3 A message from the LORD came to Jonah a second time. The LORD said, ²"Go to the great city of Nineveh. Announce to its people the message I give you."

³Jonah obeyed the LORD. He went to Nineveh. It was a very large city. In fact, it took about three days to go through it. ⁴Jonah began by going one whole day into the city. As he went, he announced, "In 40 days Nineveh will be destroyed." ⁵The people of Nineveh believed God's warning. So they decided not to eat any food for a while. And all of them put on the rough clothing people wear when they're sad. That's what everyone did, from the least important of them to the most important.

⁶Jonah's warning reached the king of Nineveh. He got up from his throne. He took off his royal robes. He also dressed himself in the clothing of sadness. And then he sat down in the dust. ⁷Here is the message he sent out to the people of Nineveh.

Jon. 3:8 The people of Nineveh were so sincere about repenting that *even the animals* wore sackcloth, the sign of being sorry for sin. I asked Sam if he wanted to wear some, and he crawled into a potato sack. That's dedication, I'll tell you!

"I and my nobles give this order.

Don't let people or animals taste anything. That includes your herds and flocks. People and animals must not eat or drink anything. ⁸Let people and animals alike be covered with the clothing of sadness. All of you must call out to God with all your hearts. Stop doing what is evil. Don't harm others. ⁹Who knows? God might take pity on us. He might not be angry with us anymore. Then we won't die."

¹⁰God saw what they did. He saw that they stopped doing what was evil. So he took pity on them. He didn't destroy them as he had said he would.

Jonah Is Angry That the LORD Spares Nineveh

4 But to Jonah this seemed very wrong. He became angry. ²He prayed to the LORD. Here is what Jonah said to him. "LORD, isn't this exactly what I thought would happen when I was still at home? That is what I tried to prevent by running away to Tarshish. I knew that you are gracious. You are tender and kind. You are slow to get angry. You are full of love. You are a God who takes pity on people. You don't want to destroy them. ³LORD, take away my life. I'd rather die than live."

⁴But the LORD replied, "Is it right for you to be angry?"

⁵Jonah had left the city. He had sat down at a place east of it. There he put some branches over his head. He sat in their shade. He waited to see what would happen to the city. ⁶Then the LORD God sent a leafy plant and made it grow up over Jonah. It gave him more shade for his head. It made him more comfortable. Jonah was very happy he had the leafy plant. ⁷But before sunrise the next day, God sent a worm. It chewed the plant so much that it dried up. ⁸When the sun rose, God sent a burning east wind. The sun beat down on Jonah's head. It made him very weak. He wanted to die. So he said, "I'd rather die than live."

⁹But God spoke to Jonah. God said, "Is it right for you to be angry about the plant?"

"It is," Jonah said. "In fact, I'm so angry I wish I were dead."

¹⁰But the LORD said, "You have been concerned about this plant. But you did not take care of it. You did not make it grow. It grew up in one night and died the next. ¹¹And shouldn't I show concern for the great city of Nineveh? It has more than 120,000 people. They can't tell right from wrong. Nineveh also has a lot of animals."

ADVENTURES IN ODYSSEY

Jonah was angry when God didn't send destruction on the people of Nineveh. Wilson told Connie a story of someone else who didn't want others to receive grace in "No Friend Like an Old Friend" (A#62).

Micah

Some prophets were called by God to address either the northern kingdom (Israel) or the southern kingdom (Judah). The prophet Micah proved to be an exception because he spoke to both. When early sections of his book refer to a vision concerning Samaria and Jerusalem, bear in mind that Samaria was the capital city of Israel and Jerusalem was the capital of Judah.

The news was worse for Samaria. Their ongoing idolatry and rejection of God was about to result in an invasion by the Assyrians that would leave the city as Micah so colorfully described it: "a pile of trash" (1:6). It wouldn't be long before this prophecy came true for Israel.

Judah and Jerusalem would likewise be severely threatened by the Assyrians. But Hezekiah (1:1), one of the few good kings of this era, had made a number of spiritual reforms. As a result, Jerusalem was spared for another long period of time before eventually falling to Babylon.

Between Micah's messages of judgment he also included a veritable bounty of hope. He was the one who foretold that the Messiah would be born in Bethlehem (5:2). When the wise men were looking for the baby Jesus, they followed the star to Jerusalem, but it was Micah's prophecy that pointed them from there to Bethlehem (Matt. 2:1–12).

WHAT'S IT MEAN, EUGENE?

Justice—If you've ever said to your parent or someone in authority, "That's not fair!" then you were in search of *justice*. Justice simply refers to that which is right, equitable, and fair for everyone concerned. We trust the judge to bring *justice* in a court case, for example. Micah 6:8 says, "The LORD has shown you what is good. He has told you what he requires of you. You must act with justice. You must love to show mercy. And you must be humble as you live in the sight of your God."

1 A message from the LORD came to Micah. He was from the town of Moresheth. The message came while Jotham, Ahaz and Hezekiah were kings of Judah. This is the vision Micah saw concerning Samaria and Jerusalem. Here is what he said.

² Listen to me, all you nations!
> Earth and everyone who lives in it,
> pay attention!
The LORD and King will be a witness
> against you.
The Lord will speak from his holy
> temple in heaven.

The LORD Will Judge Samaria and Jerusalem

³ The LORD is about to come down
> from his home in heaven.
> He rules over even the highest places
> on earth.
⁴ The mountains will melt under him
> like wax near a fire.
The valleys will be broken apart
> by water rushing down a slope.
⁵ All this will happen because
> Jacob's people have done what is
> wrong.
The people of Israel
> have committed many sins.
Who is to blame
> for the wrong things Jacob has done?
> Samaria!
Who is to blame for the high places
> where Judah's people worship other
> gods?
> Jerusalem!

⁶ So the LORD says,

"I will turn Samaria into a pile of trash.
> It will become a place for planting
> vineyards.
I will dump its stones down into the
> valley.
> And I will destroy it
> down to its very foundations.
⁷ All the statues of Samaria's gods
> will be broken to pieces.
All the gifts its people gave to temple
> prostitutes
> will be burned with fire.
I will destroy all the statues of its gods.
Samaria collected gifts that were paid to
> temple prostitutes.
> So the Assyrians will use the gifts
> to pay their own temple prostitutes."

WOOTON'S FUN FACTS
Mic. 1:8

Was Micah playing charades? No. He meant he would make the sad, loud noises of the night animals (wild dogs are *jackals*) to show how upset he was. What sounds do you make to show you're upset?

Micah Weeps Over His People

⁸ I will weep and mourn because Samaria
> will be destroyed.
> I'll walk around barefoot and
> naked.
I'll bark like a wild dog.
> I'll hoot like an owl.
⁹ Samaria's plague can't be healed.
> The plague has spread to Judah.
It has spread right up to the gate of my
> people.
> It has spread to Jerusalem itself.
¹⁰ Don't tell the people of Gath about it.
> Don't let them see you weep.
> People in Beth Ophrah, roll in the
> dust.
¹¹ You who live in the town of Shaphir,
> leave naked and in shame.
Those who live in Zaanan
> won't come out to help you.
The people in Beth Ezel will mourn.
> They won't be able to help keep you
> safe any longer.
¹² Those who live in Maroth will groan
> with pain
> as they wait for help.
That's because the LORD will bring
> trouble on them.
> It will reach the very gate of
> Jerusalem.
¹³ You who live in Lachish,
> get your fast horses ready to pull
> their chariots.

You trust in military power.
  Lachish was where sin began
  for the people of Zion.
The wrong things Israel did
  were also done by you.
¹⁴ People of Judah, you might as well say
    goodbye
  to Moresheth near Gath.
The town of Akzib won't give any help
  to the kings of Israel.
¹⁵ An enemy will attack
  you who live in Mareshah.
Israel's nobles will have to run away
  and hide in the cave of Adullam.
¹⁶ The children you enjoy so much
  will be taken away as prisoners.
So shave your heads and mourn.
  Make them as bare as the head of a
    vulture.

People's Plans and God's Plans

2 How terrible it will be for those
    who plan to harm others!
How terrible for those who make evil
    plans
  before they even get out of bed!
As soon as daylight comes,
  they carry out their plans.
That's because they have the power
  to do it.
² If they want fields or houses,
  they take them.
They cheat people out of their homes.
  They rob them of their property.

³So the LORD says to them,

"I am planning to send trouble on you.
  You will not be able to save
    yourselves from it.
You will not live so proudly anymore.
  It will be a time of trouble.
⁴ At that time people will make fun of
    you.
  They will tease you by singing a song
    of sadness.
They will pretend to be you and say,
'We are totally destroyed.
  Our enemies have divided up our
    land.
The LORD has taken it away from us!
  He has given our fields to those
  who turned against us.'"

⁵ So you won't even have anyone left
  in the LORD's community
  who can divide up the land for you.

Some Prophets Aren't Really Prophets at All

⁶ "Don't prophesy," the people's prophets
    say.
  "Don't prophesy about bad things.
  Nothing shameful is going to
    happen to us."
⁷ People of Jacob, should anyone say,
  "The LORD is patient,
  so he wouldn't do things like that"?

The LORD replies, "What I promise
    brings good things
  to those who lead honest lives.
⁸ But lately my people have attacked one
    another
  as if they were enemies.
You strip off the rich robes
  from those who happen to pass by.
They thought they were as safe as men
  returning from a battle they had
    won.
⁹ You drive the women among my
    people
  out of their pleasant homes.
You take away my blessing
  from their children forever.
¹⁰ Get up! Leave this land!
  It is no longer your resting place.
You have made it 'unclean.'
  You have completely destroyed it.
¹¹ Suppose a prophet goes around telling
    lies.
  And he prophesies that you will have
  plenty of wine and beer.
Then that kind of prophet would be
  just right for this nation!

The LORD Promises to Save His People

¹² "People of Jacob, I will gather all of you.
  I will bring together
  you who are still left alive in Israel.
I will gather you together like sheep in
    a pen.
  You will be like a flock in its
    grasslands.
  Your country will be filled with
    people.
¹³ I will open the way for you to return.
  I will march in front of you.
  You will break through the city gates
    and go free.
I am your King. I will pass through the
    gates
  in front of you.
  I, the LORD, will lead the way."

The LORD Warns Israel's Leaders and Prophets

3 Then I said,

"Listen, you leaders of Jacob's people!
    Pay attention, you rulers of Israel!
You should want to judge others fairly.
² But you hate what is good.
    And you love what is evil.
You are like someone
    who tears the skin off my people.
    You pull the meat off their bones.
³ You eat my people's bodies.
    You strip off their skin.
    You break their bones in pieces.
You chop them up like meat.
    You put them in a cooking pot."

⁴ The time will come when Israel
    will cry out to the LORD.
    But he won't answer them.
In fact, he'll turn his face away from
        them.
    They have done what is evil.

Jason's Jargon

MICAH 3

Time to seek out some *fortune* in this chapter. Did you find the word? Telling someone's fortune means predicting the future for his or her life. God calls fortune-telling a sin.

⁵ The LORD says,

"The prophets are those
    who lead my people astray.
If my people feed them,
    the prophets promise them peace.
If my people do not feed them,
    the prophets prepare to go to war
        against them.
⁶ So night will come on the prophets.
    But they will not have any visions.
Darkness will cover them.
    But they will not be able
    to figure out what is going to happen.
The sun will set on the prophets.

The day will become dark for them.
⁷ Those who see visions will be put to
        shame.
    Those who try to figure out what is
        going to happen
    will be dishonored.
All of them will cover their faces.
    I will not answer them."

⁸ The Spirit of the LORD
    has filled me with power.
He helps me do what is fair.
    He makes me brave.
Now I'm prepared to tell Jacob's people
    what they've done wrong.
    I'm ready to tell Israel they've
        sinned.
⁹ Listen to me, you leaders of Jacob's
        people!
    Pay attention, you rulers of Israel!
You hate to do what is fair.
    You twist everything that is right.
¹⁰ You build up Zion by spilling the blood
        of others.
    You build Jerusalem by doing what
        is evil.
¹¹ Your judges take money from people
        who want special favors.
    Your priests teach only if they get
        paid for it.
Your prophets won't tell fortunes
    unless they receive money.
    But you still look for the LORD's
        help.
You say, "The LORD is with us.
    No trouble will come on us."
¹² So because of what you have done,
    Zion will be plowed up like a field.
Jerusalem will be turned into a pile of
        trash.
    The temple hill will be covered with
        bushes and weeds.

People From Many Nations Will Worship at the LORD's Mountain

4 In the last days

the mountain where the LORD's temple
        is located will be famous.
    It will be the highest mountain of all.
It will be lifted up above the hills.
    And nations will go to it.

² People from many nations will go there.
They will say,

"Come, let us go up to the LORD's
    mountain.
    Let's go to the temple of Jacob's God.
He will teach us how we should live.
    Then we will live the way he wants
    us to."
The law of the LORD will be taught at
    Zion.
    His message will go out from
    Jerusalem.
3 He will judge between people from
    many nations.
    He'll settle problems among strong
    nations everywhere.
They will hammer their swords into
    plows.
    They'll hammer their spears into
    pruning tools.
Nations will not go to war against one
    another.
    They won't even train to fight
    anymore.
4 Everyone will have
    their own vine and fig tree.
And no one will make them afraid.
    That's what the LORD who rules over
    all has promised.
5 Other nations worship and trust in
    their gods.
    But we will worship and obey the
    LORD.
He will be our God for ever and ever.

The LORD's Plan

6 "The time is coming
    when I will gather those who are
    disabled,"
announces the LORD.
"I will bring together those
    who were taken away as prisoners.
I will gather those I have allowed to
    suffer.
7 I will make the disabled my faithful
    people.
I will make into a strong nation
    those driven away from their
    homes.
I will rule over them on Mount Zion.
    I will be their King from that time
    on and forever.
8 Jerusalem, you used to be
    like a guard tower for my flock.
City of Zion, you used to be
    a place of safety for my people.
The glorious kingdom you had before
    will be given back to you.
    Once again a king will rule over
    your people."

9 Why are you crying out so loudly now?
    Don't you have a king?
Has your ruler died?
    Is that why pain comes on you
    like the pain of a woman having a
    baby?
10 People of Zion, groan with pain.
    Cry out like a woman having a baby.
Soon you must leave your city.
    You must camp in the open fields.
You will have to go to the land of
    Babylon.
    But that's where the LORD will save
    you.
There he will set you free
    from the power of your enemies.

11 But now many nations
    have gathered together to attack you.
They say, "Let Jerusalem be made
    'unclean.'
    We want to laugh when Zion
    suffers!"
12 But those nations don't know
    what the LORD has in mind.
They don't understand his plan.
    He has planned to gather them up
    like bundles of grain.
    He has planned to take them to his
    threshing floor.

[13]The LORD says,

"People of Zion, get up
  and crush your enemies.
I will make you like a threshing ox.
I will give you iron horns and bronze
    hooves.
  So you will crush many nations."

They got their money in the wrong way.
  But you will set it apart to the LORD.
You will give their wealth
  to the Lord of the whole earth.

A Promised Ruler Will Come From Bethlehem

5 Jerusalem, you are being attacked.
  So bring your troops together.
Our enemies have surrounded us.
  They want to slap the face of Israel's
    ruler.

[2]The LORD says,

"Bethlehem Ephrathah, you might not
    be
  an important town in the nation of
    Judah.
But out of you will come for me
  a ruler over Israel.
His family line goes back
  to the early years of your nation.
It goes all the way back
  to days of long ago."

[3] The LORD will hand over his people to
    their enemies.
  That will last until the pregnant
    woman bears her promised
    son.
Then the rest of his relatives in Judah
  will return to their land.

[4] That promised son will stand firm
  and be a shepherd for his flock.
The LORD will give him the strength to
    do it.
  The LORD his God will give him
    the authority to rule.
His people will live safely.
  His greatness will reach
  from one end of the earth to the
    other.
[5] And he will be our peace
  when the Assyrians attack our land.
  They will march through our forts.
But we will raise up against them many
    shepherds.
  We'll send out against them
  as many commanders as we need to.
[6] They will use their swords to rule over
    Assyria.
  They'll rule the land of Nimrod
  with swords that are ready to strike.
The Assyrians will march across our
    borders
  and attack our land.

WHIT'S WISDOM

Micah 5:2

Lots of people get paid to predict things. Financial analysts predict the stock market. Meteorologists predict the weather. Sports commentators predict the Super Bowl. Connie predicts the exact second when the kids will get bored with Eugene's lengthy academic discussions. If any of these people get more than 60 percent of their predictions correct, they are considered experts. But what if there was a person who got predictions right 100 percent of the time? That person would be more than just an expert. He or she would be . . . miraculous!

There are many prophecies in the Old Testament about the coming of Jesus, and every single one of them came true! The prophet Micah made an incredibly unlikely prediction—that Jesus would be born in a little town called Bethlehem. Of all places for the Son of God: Bethlehem! When you read the books of Matthew or Luke in the New Testament, you'll see that Micah's prediction turned out to be right.

Seeing how predictions in the Old Testament line up with the New Testament makes me appreciate that God knows what He's talking about. And it reminds me to have faith that God knows what's best for us because He knows the future: what's going to happen in my country, my world, and even my own life.

But the promised ruler will save us
from them.

7 Jacob's people who are still left alive
will be scattered among many
nations.
They will be like dew the LORD has
sent.
Dew doesn't depend on any human
being.
They will be like rain that falls on the
grass.
Rain doesn't wait for someone to
give it orders.
8 So Jacob's people will be scattered
among many nations.
They will be like a lion
among the animals in the forest.
They'll be like a young lion
among flocks of sheep.
Lions attack and tear apart their prey as
they move along.
No one can keep them
from killing what they want.
9 LORD, your power will win the battle
over your enemies.
All of them will be destroyed.

10 "At that time I will destroy
your war horses," announces the
LORD.
"I will smash your chariots.
11 I will destroy the cities in your land.
I will tear down all your forts.
12 I will destroy your worship of evil
powers.
You will no longer be able
to put a spell on anyone.
13 I will destroy the statues of your gods.
I will take your sacred stones away
from you.
You will no longer bow down
to the gods your hands have made.
14 I will pull down the poles you used
to worship the female god named
Asherah.
That will happen when I completely
destroy your cities.
15 I will pay back the nations
that have not obeyed me.
I will direct my anger against them."

The LORD Brings Charges Against Israel

6 Israel, listen to the LORD's message. He
says to me,

"Stand up in court.
Let the mountains serve as
witnesses.
Let the hills hear what you have to
say."

2 Hear the LORD's case, you mountains.
Listen, you age-old foundations of
the earth.
The LORD has a case against his people
Israel.
He is bringing charges against
them.

3 The LORD says,

"My people, what have I done to you?
Have I made things too hard for
you? Answer me.
4 I brought your people up out of Egypt.
I set them free from the land
where they were slaves.
I sent Moses to lead them.
Aaron and Miriam helped him.
5 Remember how Balak, the king of
Moab,
planned to put a curse on your
people.
But Balaam, the son of Beor,
gave them a blessing instead.
Remember their journey from Shittim
to Gilgal.
I want you to know
that I always do what is right."

6 The people of Israel say,

"What should we bring with us
when we go to worship the LORD?
What should we offer the God of
heaven
when we bow down to him?
Should we take burnt offerings to him?
Should we sacrifice calves
that are a year old?

REMEMBER THIS

MICAH 6:8

"The LORD has shown you
what is good. He has told you
what he requires of you. You
must act with justice. You
must love to show mercy. And
you must be humble as you
live in the sight of your God."

WOOTON'S FUN FACTS
Mic. 6:8

If you ever don't know what to do in life, read this verse. It's my favorite verse in the whole Bible because it talks about a godly path. When Penny and I were writing a motto for our family, we used this verse as a basis. We also included things like writing comics, making paintings, and delivering mail no matter the weather. Yeah, our motto is pretty long.

⁷ Will the LORD be pleased with
　　thousands of rams?
　Will he take delight in 10,000 rivers
　　of olive oil?
Should we offer our oldest sons
　for the wrong things we've done?
Should we sacrifice our own children
　to pay for our sins?"

⁸ The LORD has shown you what is good.
　He has told you what he requires of
　　you.
You must act with justice.
　You must love to show mercy.
And you must be humble as you live in
　　the sight of your God.

The LORD Will Punish His Guilty People

⁹ The LORD is calling out to Jerusalem.
　And it would be wise to pay
　　attention to him.
He says, "Listen, tribe of Judah
　and you people who are gathered in
　　the city.
¹⁰ You sinful people, should I forget

What's the biggest decision you've ever had to make? Was someone's future at stake? Have you ever known anyone who served on a jury? Jury duty is an opportunity for most people in our society to have an important say in the direction of another person's life.

For example, in the Adventures in Odyssey episode "Blind Justice," Eugene and Bernard wind up on a jury and must determine whether a young man is guilty of breaking into a safe and stealing a diamond bracelet. It seems like an open-and-shut case. That is, until Eugene looks into the facts. Unfortunately, it seems he's the only person interested in discovering the truth. Thankfully, his persistence makes a difference.

Sometimes when we decide to stand up for something, we may have to stand alone. Especially when it's unpopular or difficult. So how do you know you're doing the right thing? God tells us in Micah 6:8 that we are to seek justice and be merciful and humble before God. People notice when we treat

WHAT ABOUT YOU?

others fairly and try to do what's right. More importantly, so does the Lord.

Are you prepared to stand up for justice? If so, remember that God values every person equally and expects us to treat others fairly, no matter who they are or where they're from. Do you know someone being treated unfairly? Ask God to give you the courage to stand up for them.

that you got your treasures by
   stealing them?
You use dishonest measures to cheat
   others.
I have placed a curse on that
   practice.
[11] Should I forgive anyone who uses
   dishonest scales?
They use weights that weigh things
   heavier
or lighter than they really are.
[12] The rich people among you harm
   others.
You are always telling lies.
You try to fool others by what you
   say.
[13] So I have begun to strike you down.
I have begun to destroy you
   because you have sinned so much.
[14] You will eat. But you will not be
   satisfied.
Your stomachs will still be empty.
You will try to save what you can.
   But you will not be able to.
If you do save something,
   it will be destroyed in battle.
[15] You will plant seeds.
   But you will not harvest any crops.
You will press olives.
   But you will not use the oil.
You will crush grapes.
   But you will not drink the wine
   that is made from them.
[16] You have followed the evil practices
   of King Omri of Israel.
You have done what the family
   of King Ahab did.
You have followed their bad example.
   So I will let you be destroyed.
Others will make fun of you.
   The nations will laugh at you."

Israel's Sin Brings Suffering

7 I'm suffering very much!
   I'm like someone who gathers
      summer fruit in a vineyard
   after the good fruit has already been
      picked.
No grapes are left to eat.
   None of the early figs I long for
      remain.
[2] Faithful people have disappeared from
   the land.
Those who are honest are gone.
Everyone hides and waits

to spill the blood of others.
   They use nets to try and trap one
      another.
[3] They are very good at doing what is
   evil.
Rulers require gifts.
Judges accept money from people
   who want special favors.
Those who are powerful
   always get what they want.
All of them make evil plans together.
[4] The best of these people are as harmful
   as thorns.
The most honest of them are even
   worse.
God has come to punish you.
The time your prophets warned you
   about has come.
Panic has taken hold of you.
[5] Don't trust your neighbors.
   Don't put your faith in your friends.
Be careful what you say
   even to your own wife.
[6] Sons don't honor their fathers.
   Daughters refuse to obey their
      mothers.
Daughters-in-law are against their
      mothers-in-law.
A man's enemies are the members of
      his own family.

[7] But I will look to the Lord.
   I'll put my trust in God my Savior.
   He will hear me.

Jerusalem Will Be Rebuilt

[8] The people of Jerusalem say,

"Don't laugh when we suffer,
   you enemies of ours!
We have fallen.
   But we'll get up.
Even though we sit in the dark,
   the Lord will give us light.
[9] We've sinned against the Lord.
   So he is angry with us.

His anger will continue until he takes
up our case.
Then he'll do what is right for us.
He'll bring us out into the light.
Then we'll see him save us.
¹⁰ Our enemies will see it too.
And they will be put to shame.
After all, they said to us,
'Where is the LORD your God?'
But we will see them destroyed.
Soon they will be stomped on
like mud in the streets.'

¹¹ People of Jerusalem, the time will come
when your walls will be rebuilt.
Land will be added to your territory.
¹² At that time your people will come
back to you.
They'll return from Assyria
and the cities of Egypt.
They'll come from the countries
between Egypt and the Euphrates
River.
They'll return from the lands
between the seas.
They'll come back from the countries
between the mountains.
¹³ But the rest of the earth will be
deserted.
The people who live in it
have done many evil things.

Jason's Jargon

MICAH 7

Ready to find *favor*?
Look through this
chapter for the word.
A special favor means
giving someone a
gift he or she doesn't
deserve. Here, judges
let criminals go free in
exchange for money.

Prayer and Praise
¹⁴ LORD, be like a shepherd to your
people.
Take good care of them.

They are your flock.
They live by themselves
in the safety of a forest.
Rich grasslands are all around them.
Let them eat grass in Bashan and
Gilead
just as they did long ago.

¹⁵ The LORD says to his people,

"I showed you my wonders
when you came out of Egypt long
ago.
In the same way, I will show them to
you again."

¹⁶ When the nations see those wonders,
they will be put to shame.
All their power will be taken away
from them.
They will be so amazed
that they won't be able to speak or
hear.
¹⁷ They'll be forced to eat dust like a
snake.
They'll be like creatures
that have to crawl on the ground.
They'll come out of their dens
trembling with fear.
They'll show respect for the LORD our
God.
They will also have respect for his
people.
¹⁸ LORD, who is a God like you?
You forgive sin.
You forgive your people
when they do what is wrong.
You don't stay angry forever.
Instead, you take delight in
showing
your faithful love to them.
¹⁹ Once again you will show loving
concern for us.
You will completely wipe out
the evil things we've done.
You will throw all our sins
into the bottom of the sea.
²⁰ You will be faithful to Jacob's people.
You will show your love
to Abraham's children.
You will do what you promised to do
for our people.
You made that promise long ago.

Nahum

We tend to associate Nineveh with a different stop in our biblical journey: the book of Jonah. You'll recall that the people of Nineveh displayed an amazing example of repentance upon hearing Jonah's message of coming destruction (Jon. 3:1–9). And in response, God had mercy and spared the city (Jon. 3:10).

But tragically, the humble attitude of the Ninevites wasn't long lasting. Nineveh was the capital city of Assyria, and Assyria was a wicked and vicious empire. The people soon went back to their cruelty and disregard for others. The prophet Nahum was sent with a new message that Nineveh was going to fall. (As a side point, even this is not the last stop on our trip where Nineveh will be mentioned. You'll find a similar message to Nineveh from the prophet Zephaniah.) God had given these people a marvelous opportunity to avoid destruction, but their pride had returned and they forfeited their chance for salvation.

Instead of remaining a shining example of God's great grace and mercy, Nineveh became a tragic tale of heartbreak and sorrow. Nahum reminds us that God is both good (1:7) and patient, but He is also just (1:3). We must never forget the importance of repentance and confession when we see that we have sinned against God.

WHAT'S IT MEAN, EUGENE?

Wrath—An old English word for "anger." Romans 1:18 states, "God shows his anger from heaven. It is against all the godless and evil things people do." The use of the word *anger* in that verse is very important as it proves that God considers sin to be a serious problem. That's why we should confess our sins, for when we do, God "will forgive our sins. He will forgive every wrong thing we have done. He will make us pure" (1 John 1:9).

1 Here is a prophecy the LORD gave Nahum, who was from the town of Elkosh. The prophecy came in a vision and is written in a book. The prophecy is about Nineveh.

The Lord Is Angry With Nineveh

² The LORD is a jealous God who
     punishes people.
He pays them back for the evil
     things they do.
He directs his anger against them.
The LORD punishes his enemies.
     He holds his anger back
     until the right time to use it.
³ The LORD is slow to get angry.
     But he is very powerful.
The LORD will not let guilty people go
     without punishing them.
When he marches out, he stirs up
     winds and storms.
     Clouds are the dust kicked up by
     his feet.
⁴ He controls the seas. He dries them up.
     He makes all the rivers run dry.
Bashan and Mount Carmel dry up.
     The flowers in Lebanon fade.
⁵ He causes the mountains to shake.
     The hills melt away.
The earth trembles because he is there.
     The world and all those who live in
     it also tremble.
⁶ Who can stand firm when his anger
     burns?
     Who can live when he is angry?
His anger blazes out like fire.
     He smashes the rocks to pieces.

⁷ The LORD is good.
     When people are in trouble,
     they can go to him for safety.

Nah. 1:1

Nahum is from the town of Elkosh. The town doesn't exist anymore, but the place is only a few miles from the modern-day city of Mosel, Iraq.

He takes good care of those
     who trust in him.
⁸ But he will destroy Nineveh
     with a powerful flood.
He will chase his enemies
     into the place of darkness.
⁹ The LORD will put an end
     to anything they plan against him.
He won't allow Assyria to win the
     battle
     over his people a second time.
¹⁰ His enemies will be tangled up among
     thorns.
     Their wine will make them drunk.
     They'll be burned up like dry straw.
¹¹ Nineveh, a king has marched out from
     you.
     He makes evil plans against the
     LORD.
     He thinks about how he can do what
     is wrong.

¹²The LORD says,

"His army has many soldiers.
     Other nations are helping them.
     But they will be destroyed and pass
     away.
Judah, I punished you.
     But I will not do it anymore.
¹³ Now I will break Assyria's yoke off your
     neck.

Jason's Jargon

NAHUM 1

Your assignment: Find the word *jealous* in this chapter. "A jealous God" isn't envious. It means God wants to be the only one we worship. Idols are not worthy of our worship. God is.

I will tear off the ropes that hold
you."

14 Nineveh, the LORD has given an order
concerning you.
He has said, "You will not have any
children
to carry on your name.
I will destroy the wooden and metal
statues
that are in the temple of your gods.
I will get your grave ready for you.
You are worthless."

15 Look at the mountains of Judah!
I see a messenger running to bring
good news!
He's telling us that peace has come!
People of Judah, celebrate your feasts.
Carry out your promises.
The evil Assyrians won't attack you
again.
They'll be completely destroyed.

The LORD Will Destroy Nineveh

2 Nineveh, armies are coming to attack
you.
Guard the forts!
Watch the roads!
Get ready!
Gather all your strength!

2 Assyria once took everything of value
from God's people.
Its army destroyed all their vines.
But the LORD will bring back
the glory of Jacob's people.
He'll make Israel glorious again.

3 The shields of the soldiers are red.
The warriors are dressed in bright
red uniforms.
The metal on their chariots flashes
when they are prepared for war.
Their spears made out of juniper are
ready to use.
4 The chariots race through the main
streets.
They rush back and forth through
them.
They look like flaming torches.
They dart around like lightning.

5 Nineveh sends for their special troops.
But they trip and fall on their way.
They run toward the city wall.
They keep their shield in front of
them.

6 The attackers open the gates that hold
back
the waters of the river.
And the palace falls down.
7 The attackers order that Nineveh's people
be taken away as prisoners.
The female slaves sound like doves as
they mourn.
They beat their chests.
8 Nineveh is like a pool
whose water is draining away.
"Stop running away!" someone cries out.
But no one turns back.
9 "Steal the silver!" the attackers shout.
"Grab the gold!"
The supply is endless.
There is plenty of wealth
among all the city's treasures.
10 Nineveh is destroyed, robbed and
stripped!
Hearts melt away in fear.
Knees give way.
Bodies tremble with fear.
Everyone's face turns pale.

11 Assyria is like a lion.
Where is the lions' den now?
Where did they feed their cubs?
Where did all the lions go?
In their den they had nothing to fear.
12 The lion killed enough for his cubs to
eat.
He choked what he caught for his
mate.
He filled his home with what he had
killed.
He brought to his dens what he had
caught.

13 "Nineveh, I am against you,"
announces the LORD who rules over
all.
"I will burn up your chariots with fire.
Your young lions will be killed by
swords.
I will leave you nothing on earth to
catch.
The voices of your messengers
will no longer be heard."

The LORD Will Judge Nineveh

3 How terrible it will be for Nineveh!
It is a city of murderers!
It is full of liars!
It is filled with stolen goods!
The killing never stops!

² Whips crack!
　　Wheels clack!
Horses charge!
　　Chariots rumble!
³ Horsemen attack!
　　Swords flash!
　　Spears gleam!
Many people die.
　　Dead bodies pile up.
They can't even be counted.
　　People trip over them.
⁴ All of that was caused by the evil
　　　　desires
　　of the prostitute Nineveh.
That woman who practiced evil magic
　　was very beautiful.
She used her sinful charms
　　to make slaves out of the nations.
She worshiped evil powers
　　in order to trap others.

⁵ "Nineveh, I am against you,"
　　announces the LORD who rules over
　　　　all.
"I will pull your skirts up over your
　　　　face.
　　I will show the nations your naked
　　　　body.
　　Kingdoms will make fun of your
　　　　shame.
⁶ I will throw garbage at you.
　　I will look down on you.
　　I will make an example out of you.
⁷ All those who see you will run away
　　　　from you.
　　They will say, 'Nineveh is destroyed.
　　Who will mourn over it?'
Where can I find someone
　　to comfort your people?"

⁸ Nineveh, are you better than Thebes
　　on the Nile River?
There was water all around that city.
　　The river helped to keep it safe.
　　The waters were like a wall around
　　　　it.
⁹ Cush and Egypt gave it all the strength
　　　　it needed.
　　Put and Libya also helped it.
¹⁰ But Thebes was captured anyway.
　　Its people were taken away as
　　　　prisoners.
Its babies were smashed to pieces
　　at every street corner.
The Assyrian soldiers cast lots
　　for all its nobles.

They put them in chains
　　and made slaves out of them.
¹¹ People of Nineveh, you too will get
　　　　drunk.
　　You will try to hide from your
　　　　enemies.
　　You will look for a place of safety.

¹² All your forts are like fig trees
　　that have their first ripe fruit on
　　　　them.
When the trees are shaken,
　　the figs fall into the mouths
　　of those who eat them.
¹³ Look at your troops.
　　All of them are weak.
The gates of your forts
　　are wide open to your enemies.
　　Fire has destroyed the bars that lock
　　　　your gates.

¹⁴ Prepare for the attack by storing up
　　　　water!
　　Make your walls as strong as you can!
Make some bricks out of clay!
　　Mix the mud to hold them together!
　　Use them to repair the walls!
¹⁵ In spite of all your hard work,
　　fire will burn you up inside your city.
Your enemies will cut you down with
　　　　their swords.
　　They will destroy you
　　just as a swarm of locusts eats up
　　　　crops.

Nah. 3:14 A moat that was 150 feet wide and 60 feet deep surrounded Nineveh. The city walls were 100 feet high and wide enough to accommodate three chariots riding side by side. The city certainly looked intimidating!

Multiply like grasshoppers!
Increase your numbers like locusts!
[16] You have more traders
than the number of stars in the sky.
But like locusts they strip the land.
Then they fly away.
[17] Your guards are like grasshoppers.
Your officials are like swarms of
locusts.
They settle in the walls on a cold
day.
But when the sun appears, they fly
away.
And no one knows where they go.

[18] King of Assyria, your leaders are asleep.
Your nobles lie down to rest.
Your people are scattered on the
mountains.
No one is left to gather them together.
[19] Nothing can heal your wounds.
You will die of them.
All those who hear the news about you
clap their hands.
That's because you have fallen from
power.
Is there anyone who has not suffered
because of how badly you treated
them?

Habakkuk

The prophet Habakkuk is unique from most of the other prophets because he doesn't present a specific message from God addressed to a particular nation. Instead, this short book is more akin to a conversation between the prophet and God.

Habakkuk had the same questions many people have today. First, he knew his own people were misbehaving terribly, and he wanted to know why God hadn't done anything to stop them (1:2–4). God replied that He was about to punish the people by allowing the Babylonians to (borrowing military phraseology) sweep in and defeat them (1:5–11).

Habakkuk then admits to being confused. He allows that his people are sinful, but they aren't as bad as the Babylonians. How could God let an even worse nation destroy His people, even if they had strayed away from Him for a while? (1:12–2:1) God assured Habakkuk that the Babylonians would certainly be punished for their hostility toward Judah. God would eventually restore His people and bring them back to Him, but Babylon's judgment would be far worse (2:2–20).

Habakkuk concludes his book with a prayer expressed in poetry (chapter 3). He decides that no matter what happens, he will trust God to do what is right (3:17–19). Which begs the question: Do we trust that God will always do what is right in our circumstances today? Why or why not?

WHAT'S IT MEAN, EUGENE?

New Covenant/Old Covenant—The old agreement, or covenant, between God and His people was based upon God's Law and the blood of animal sacrifices that were offered to atone for the people's sins. The new agreement is based upon God's grace and mercy extended to us through the blood of Jesus Christ that He shed for us on the cross. "How much cleaner will the blood of Christ make us!" says Hebrews 9:14. "It washes away our feelings of guilt for committing sin."

1

This is a prophecy that Habakkuk the prophet received from the Lord. Here is what Habakkuk said.

Habakkuk Complains to the Lord

2 Lord, how long do I have to call out for
help?
Why don't you listen to me?
How long must I keep telling you
that things are terrible?
Why don't you save us?
3 Why do you make me watch while
people treat others so unfairly?
Why do you put up with the wrong
things
they are doing?
I have to look at death.
People are harming others.
They are arguing and fighting all the
time.
4 The law can't do what it's supposed to
do.
Fairness never comes out on top.
Sinful people surround those
who do what is right.
So people are never treated fairly.

The Lord Replies to Habakkuk

5 The Lord replies,

"Look at the nations. Watch them.
Be totally amazed at what you see.
I am going to do something in your
days
that you would never believe.
You would not believe it
even if someone told you about it.
6 I am going to send the armies of
Babylon to attack you.
They are very mean. They move
quickly.
They sweep across the whole earth.
They take over homes
that do not belong to them.
7 They terrify others.
They do not recognize any laws but
their own.
That is how proud they are.
8 Their horses are faster than leopards.
They are meaner than wolves at
sunset.
Their horsemen charge straight into
battle.
They ride in from far away.
They come down like an eagle
diving for its food.

WOOTON'S FUN FACTS
Hab. 1

Habakkuk has three k's in it. Can you think of another word with three k's in it? Hmmm. How about knickknack, kickback, or knickerbocker? How about a word with two k's that is the same backward as forward? Yep, you guessed it! Kayak. How about my wife's middle name, which is spelled with a silent k? Actually, she doesn't like to tell people that one. Sorry.

9 All of them are ready and willing to
destroy others.
Their huge armies advance like a
wind out of the desert.
They gather prisoners like sand.
10 They mock kings
and make fun of rulers.
They laugh at all the cities
that have high walls around them.
They build dirt ramps against the walls
and capture the cities.
11 They sweep past like the wind.
Then they go on their way.
They are guilty.
They worship their own strength."

Habakkuk Complains to the Lord Again

12 Lord, haven't you existed forever?
You are my holy God.
You will never die.
Lord, you have appointed the
Babylonians
to punish your people.
My Rock, you have chosen them to
judge us.
13 Your eyes are too pure to look at what is
evil.
You can't put up with the wrong
things people do.

So why do you put up
    with those who can't be trusted?
The evil Babylonians swallow up
    those who are more godly than
      themselves.
    So why are you silent?
14 You have made people to be like the fish
    in the sea.
    They are like the sea creatures that
      don't have a ruler.
15 The evil Babylonians pull all of them up
    with hooks.
    They catch them in their nets.
They gather them up.
    So they celebrate.
    They are glad.
16 They offer sacrifices to their nets.
    They burn incense to them.
Their nets allow them to live in great
    comfort.
    They enjoy the finest food.
17 Are you going to let them
    keep on emptying their nets?
Will they go on destroying nations
    without showing them any mercy?

2 1 I will go up to the lookout tower.
    I'll station myself on the city wall.
I'll wait to see how the LORD will reply
    to me.
    Then I'll try to figure out how
      his reply answers what I've
      complained about.

The LORD Replies to Habakkuk

2 The LORD replies,

"Write down the message I am giving
    you.
    Write it clearly on the tablets you
      use.
Then a messenger can read it
    and run to announce it.
3 The message I give you
    waits for the time I have appointed.
It speaks about what is going to happen.
    And all of it will come true.
It might take a while.
    But wait for it.
You can be sure it will come.
    It will happen when I want it to.

4 "The Babylonians are very proud.
    What they want is not good.

"But the person who is godly
    will live by his faithfulness.

5 "Wine makes the Babylonians do
    foolish things.
    They are proud. They never rest.
Like the grave, they are always hungry
    for more.
    Like death, they are never satisfied.
They gather all the nations to
    themselves.
    They take all those people away as
      prisoners.

6 "Won't those people laugh at the Babylonians? Won't they make fun of them? They will say to them,

Jason's Jargon

HABAKKUK 2

Your next mission: Hunt for a *lookout tower* in this chapter. The lookout tower is the high post of a fortress where a person stands to keep watch for approaching enemies.

" 'How terrible it will be for you
    who pile up stolen goods!
You get rich by cheating others.
    How long will this go on?'
7 Those you owe money to will suddenly
    rise up.
They will wake up
    and make you tremble with fear.
Then they will take away
    everything you have.
8 You have robbed many nations.
    So the nations that are left will rob
      you.
You have spilled human blood.
    You have destroyed lands and cities
    and everyone in them.

9 "How terrible it will be for the
      Babylonians!
    They build their kingdom with
      money
    that they gained by cheating others.
They have tried to make the kingdom
    as secure as possible.
    After all, they did not want to be
      destroyed.

¹⁰ They have planned to wipe out many
    nations.
    But they have brought shame on
        their own kingdom.
    So they must pay with their own
        lives.
¹¹ The stones in the walls of their homes
        will cry out.
    And the wooden beams will echo
        that cry.

¹² "How terrible it will be for the
        Babylonians!
    They build cities by spilling the
        blood of others.
    They establish towns by doing what
        is wrong.
¹³ I am the LORD who rules over all.
    Human effort is no better than wood
        that feeds a fire.
    So the nations wear themselves out
        for nothing.
¹⁴ The oceans are full of water.
    In the same way, the earth will be
        filled
    with the knowledge of my glory.

¹⁵ "How terrible it will be for the
        Babylonians!
    They give drinks to their neighbors.
    They pour the drinks from wineskins
        until their neighbors are drunk.
    They want to look at their naked
        bodies.
¹⁶ But the Babylonians will be filled
        with shame instead of glory.
    So now it is their turn to drink
        and be stripped of their clothes.
    The cup of anger in my powerful right
        hand
        is going to punish them.
    They will be covered with shame
        instead of glory.
¹⁷ The harm they have done to Lebanon
        will bring them down.
    Because they have killed so many
        animals,
        animals will terrify them.
    They have spilled human blood.
    They have destroyed lands and
        cities
        and everyone in them.

The Babylonians were a fierce and proud people, with the power to destroy or capture their enemies and plunder their treasure. They had a strong army, but also one destructive weakness: They worshiped false gods.

Habakkuk 2:18 describes how pointless this idol worship is: "If someone carves a statue of a god, what is it worth? What value is there in a god that teaches lies? The one who trusts in this kind of god worships his own creation. He makes statues of gods that can't speak."

The ancient Babylonians were not so different from many modern-day people. Both then and now, people fall into the sin of idolatry—loving something else more than we love God. Idolatry can be sneaky. Some people don't even know they have idols in their lives.

You see, whoever or whatever consumes our time ultimately defines who we are. We could become like our friends, our entertainment . . . or our Savior. It's up to us to make the right choice regarding who or what receives our time, energy, and devotion.

During the average day, how much time do you find yourself thinking about what matters to God? If we begin each morning with prayer and Bible study, it can give us a more heavenly focus throughout the day. Will being more disciplined make God love us more than He already does? No. But healthy spiritual habits will deepen our love and appreciation for Him.

ADVENTURES IN ODYSSEY

Kids' Radio told the story of being addicted to computers and how they can be modern-day idols in "My Girl Hallie" (A#37).

¹⁸ "If someone carves a statue of a god,
what is it worth?
What value is there in a god
that teaches lies?
The one who trusts in this kind of god
worships his own creation.
He makes statues of gods that can't
speak.
¹⁹ How terrible it will be for the
Babylonians!
They say to a wooden god, 'Come
to life!'
They say to a stone god, 'Wake up!'
Can those gods give advice?
They are covered with gold and silver.
They can't even breathe."

²⁰ The LORD is in his holy temple.
Let the whole earth be silent in front
of him.

Habakkuk Prays to the LORD

3 *This is a prayer of Habakkuk the prophet.
It is on* shigionoth. *Here is what
he said.*

² LORD, I know how famous you are.
I have great respect for you
because of your mighty acts.
Do them again for us.
Make them known in our time.
When you are angry,
please have mercy on us.

³ God came from Teman.
The Holy One came from Mount
Paran.
His glory covered the heavens.
His praise filled the earth.
⁴ His glory was like the sunrise.
Rays of light flashed from his mighty
hand.
His power was hidden there.
⁵ He sent plagues ahead of him.
Sickness followed behind him.
⁶ When he stood up, the earth shook.
When he looked at the nations,

they trembled with fear.
The age-old mountains crumbled.
The ancient hills fell down.
But he marches on forever.
⁷ I saw the tents of Cushan in trouble.
The people of Midian were suffering
greatly.

⁸ LORD, were you angry with the rivers?
Were you angry with the streams?
Were you angry with the Red Sea?
You rode your horses and chariots
to overcome it.
⁹ You got your bow ready to use.
You asked for many arrows.
You broke up the surface
of the earth with rivers.
¹⁰ The mountains saw you and shook.
Floods of water swept by.
The sea roared.
It lifted its waves high.

Jason's Jargon

HABAKKUK 3

Search this chapter for the word *ancient*. Something is ancient when it is very old and has stood the test of time. When God appears and ancient hills fall down, it shows His mighty power.

¹¹ The sun and moon stood still in the sky.
They stopped because your flying
arrows flashed by.
Your gleaming spear shone like
lightning.
¹² When you were angry, you marched
across the earth.
Because of your anger you destroyed
the nations.
¹³ You came out to set your people free.
You saved your chosen ones.
You crushed Pharaoh, the leader of that
evil land of Egypt.
You stripped him from head to
foot.
¹⁴ His soldiers rushed out to scatter us.
They were laughing at us.
They thought they would easily
destroy us.

They saw us as weak people who were
    trying to hide.
So you wounded Pharaoh's head
    with his own spear.
¹⁵ Your horses charged into the Red Sea.
    They stirred up the great waters.

¹⁶ I listened and my heart pounded.
    My lips trembled at the sound.
My bones seemed to rot.
    And my legs shook.
But I will be patient.
    I'll wait for the day of trouble to
        come on Babylon.
    It's the nation that is attacking us.
¹⁷ The fig trees might not bud.
    The vines might not produce any
        grapes.
The olive crop might fail.

The fields might not produce any
    food.
There might not be any sheep in the
    pens.
There might not be any cattle in the
    barns.
¹⁸ But I will still be glad
    because of what the LORD has done.
    God my Savior fills me with joy.

¹⁹ The LORD and King gives me strength.
    He makes my feet like the feet of a
        deer.
    He helps me walk on the highest
        places.

*This prayer is for the director of music. It should
be sung while being accompanied by stringed
instruments.*

Zephaniah

We've nearly reached the end of our journey through Old Testament with only four books remaining. Zephaniah is next and from the very beginning—the very first sentence, in fact—he lets us know he is a person of some position . . . a relative of King Hezekiah. In addition, he seems more familiar than most prophets with politics and events connected to royalty, so it's likely that he spoke to crowds in the royal courts rather than the common people. This makes sense because God's message is for everyone—rich or poor, popular or not.

Neither does God discriminate in His judgment of sin. Zephaniah was declaring a judgment of the whole world (1:2–3), and Judah was not to be excluded. They had fallen away from God and would suffer the consequences (1:4; 2:1–2) unless they repented and began to worship Him faithfully (2:3).

Zephaniah addresses a number of the enemies of God's people: the Philistines, Moabites, Assyrians, and others. Their future is decidedly bleak. And even though Jerusalem is on the list (3:1–8), God will punish only the proud and wicked people. He will not only restore those who continue to trust Him, but will also give them a reason to sing (3:9–17). I don't know about you, but I'd rather be trusting God and singing His praises than be stubborn and experience His punishment.

What's it mean, Eugene?

Reconciliation—Ms. Kendall and I have had a few, shall we say, disagreements through the years. However, we eventually find a common ground and reconcile with one another. Reconciling is a word for the mending of broken relationships. Likewise, our relationship with God, which has been broken by sin, can be healed—or *reconciled*—through the sacrifice of Jesus Christ.

1 A message from the LORD came to Zephaniah, the son of Cushi. Cushi was the son of Gedaliah. Gedaliah was the son of Amariah. Amariah was the son of King Hezekiah. The LORD spoke to Zephaniah during the rule of Josiah. He was king of Judah and the son of Amon.

The LORD Will Judge the Whole World

² "I will sweep away everything
     from the face of the earth,"
     announces the LORD.
³ "I will destroy people and animals alike.
     I will wipe out the birds in the sky
     and the fish in the waters.
I will destroy the statues of gods that
     cause evil people to sin.
     That will happen when I destroy all
     human beings on the face of
     the earth,"
     announces the LORD.
⁴ "I will reach out my powerful hand
     against Judah.
     I will punish all those who live in
     Jerusalem.
I will destroy from this place
     what is left of Baal worship.
The priests who serve other gods
     will be removed.
⁵ I will destroy those who bow down on
     their roofs
     to worship all the stars.
I will destroy those who make promises
     not only in my name but also in the
     name of Molek.
⁶ I will destroy those who stop following
     the LORD.
     They no longer look to him or ask
     him for advice.
⁷ Be silent in front of him.
     He is the LORD and King.
     The day of the LORD is near.
The LORD has prepared a sacrifice.
     He has set apart for himself
     the people he has invited.
⁸ When the LORD's sacrifice is ready to be
     offered,
     I will punish the officials and the
     king's sons.
I will also judge all those who follow
     the practices of other nations.
⁹ At that time I will punish
     all those who worship other gods.
They fill the temples of their gods
     with lies and other harmful things.

Zeph. 1:1 Since Zephaniah is the great-great grandson of King Hezekiah, that makes him the only prophet who is a royal.

¹⁰ "At that time people at the Fish Gate in
     Jerusalem
     will cry out," announces the LORD.
"So will those at the New Quarter.
     The buildings on the hills will come
     crashing down
     with a loud noise.
¹¹ Cry out, you who live in the market
     places.
     All your merchants will be wiped
     out.
     Those who trade in silver will be
     destroyed.
¹² At that time I will search Jerusalem
     with lamps.
     I will punish those who are so
     contented.
     They are like wine that has not been
     shaken up.
They think, 'The LORD won't do
     anything.
     He won't do anything good or bad.'
¹³ Their wealth will be stolen.
     Their houses will be destroyed.
They will build houses.
     But they will not live in them.
They will plant vineyards.
     But they will not drink the wine they
     produce.
¹⁴ The great day of the LORD is near.
     In fact, it is coming quickly.
The cries on that day are bitter.
     The Mighty Warrior shouts his battle
     cry.
¹⁵ At that time I will pour out my anger.
     There will be great suffering and pain.

Jason's Jargon

ZEPHANIAH 1

Find a *market place* in this chapter. The market place was an open area where people sold their goods, food, and crafts. It was an important place in Jerusalem.

It will be a day of horrible trouble.
It will be a time of darkness and
gloom.
It will be filled with the blackest
clouds.
¹⁶ Trumpet blasts and battle cries will be
heard.
Soldiers will attack cities
that have forts and corner towers.
¹⁷ I will bring great trouble on all people.
So they will feel their way around
like blind people.
They have sinned against the LORD.
Their blood will be poured out like dust.
Their bodies will lie rotting on the
ground.
¹⁸ Their silver and gold
won't save them
on the day the LORD pours out his
anger.
The whole earth will be burned up
when his jealous anger blazes out.
Everyone who lives on earth
will come to a sudden end."

The LORD Will Judge Judah and Jerusalem Along With the Nations

God Calls Judah to Turn Away From Their Sins

2 Gather together,
you shameful nation of Judah!
Gather yourselves together!
² Come together before the LORD's
judgment arrives.
The day of the LORD's judgment will
sweep in
like straw blown by the wind.
Soon the LORD's great anger will come
against you.
The day of his wrath will come
against you.

³ So look to him, all you people in the
land
who worship him faithfully.
You always do what he commands
you to do.
Continue to do what is right.
Don't be proud.
Then perhaps the LORD will keep you
safe
on the day he pours out his anger on
the world.

A Message About Philistia

⁴ Gaza will be deserted.
Ashkelon will be destroyed.
Ashdod will be emptied out at noon.
Ekron will be pulled up by its roots.
⁵ How terrible it will be for you
Kerethites
who live by the Mediterranean Sea!
Philistia, the LORD has spoken against
you.
What happened to Canaan will
happen to you.

The LORD says, "I will destroy you.
No one will be left."

⁶ The land by the sea will become
grasslands.
It will have wells for shepherds and
pens for flocks.
⁷ That land will belong to those who are
still left alive
among the people of Judah.
They will find grasslands there.
They will take over
the houses in Ashkelon and live in
them.
The LORD their God will take care of
them.
He will bless them with great success
again.

A Message About Moab and Ammon

⁸ The LORD says,

"I have heard Moab make fun of my
people.
The Ammonites also laughed at
them.
They told them that bad things
would happen to their land.
⁹ So Moab will become like Sodom,"
announces the LORD who rules over
all.
"Ammon will be like Gomorrah.

Weeds and salt pits will cover those
  countries.
They will be dry and empty deserts
  forever.
Those who are still left alive among my
  people
  will take all their valuable things.
So they will receive those lands as
  their own.
And that is just as sure as I am alive."
The Lord is the God of Israel.

¹⁰ Moab and Ammon will be judged
  because they are so proud.
They made fun of the Lord's people.
  They laughed at them.
¹¹ The Lord who rules over all will terrify
  Moab and Ammon.
  He will destroy all the gods on earth.
Then distant nations will bow down to
  him.
  All of them will serve him in their
  own lands.

A Message About Cush
¹² The Lord says, "People of Cush,
  you too will die by my sword."

Jason's Jargon

ZEPHANIAH 2

Next task: Review
this chapter for the
word *carefree*. To feel
carefree is to be relaxed
and not worried about
the future. Apparently,
Nineveh was a
carefree place.

A Message About Assyria
¹³ The Lord will reach out his powerful
  hand against the north.
  He will destroy Assyria.
He'll leave Nineveh totally empty.
  It will be as dry as a desert.
¹⁴ Flocks and herds will lie down there.
  So will creatures of every kind.
Desert owls and screech owls
  will rest on its pillars.
The sound of their hooting will echo
  through the windows.
The doorways will be full of trash.

The cedar beams will be showing.
¹⁵ Nineveh was a carefree city.
  It lived in safety.
It said to itself,
  "I am the one!
  No one is greater than I am."
But it has been destroyed.
  Wild animals make their home
  there.
All those who pass by laugh
  and shake their fists at it.

A Message About Jerusalem
3 How terrible it will be for Jerusalem!
  Its people crush others.
They refuse to obey the Lord.
  They are "unclean."
² They don't obey anyone.
  They don't accept the Lord's
  warnings.
They don't trust in him.
  They don't ask their God for his help.
³ Jerusalem's officials are like roaring
  lions.
  Their rulers are like wolves that hunt
  in the evening.
They don't leave anything to eat in
  the morning.
⁴ Their prophets care about nothing.
  They can't be trusted.
Their priests make the temple
  "unclean."
  They break the law they teach others
  to obey.
⁵ In spite of that, the Lord is good to
  Jerusalem.
  He never does anything that is
  wrong.
Every morning he does what is fair.
  Each new day he does the right
  thing.
But those who do what is wrong
  aren't even ashamed of it.

Jerusalem Remains Unrepentant
⁶The Lord says to his people,

"I have destroyed other nations.
  I have wiped out their forts.
I have left their streets deserted.
  No one walks along them.
Their cities are destroyed.
  They are deserted and empty.
⁷ Here is what I thought about Jerusalem.
  'Surely you will have respect for me.
  Surely you will accept my warning.'

Then the city you think is safe would
not be destroyed.
And I would not have to punish you so
much.
But they still wanted to go on
sinning
in every way they could.
⁸ So wait for me to come as judge,"
announces the LORD.
"Wait for the day I will stand up
to witness against all sinners.
I have decided to gather the nations.
I will bring the kingdoms together.
And I will pour out all my burning
anger on them.
The fire of my jealous anger
will burn the whole world up.

Israel Will Trust in the LORD

⁹ "But then I will purify what all the
nations say.
And they will use their words to
worship me.
They will serve me together.
¹⁰ My scattered people will come to me
from beyond the rivers of Cush.
They will worship me.
They will bring me offerings.
¹¹ Jerusalem, you have done many wrong
things to me.
But at that time you will not be put
to shame anymore.
That's because I will remove from this
city
those who think so highly of
themselves.
You will never be proud again
on my holy mountain of Zion.
¹² But inside your city I will leave
those who are not proud at all.
Those who are still left alive will
trust in the LORD.
¹³ They will not do anything wrong.
They will not tell any lies.
They will not say anything to fool
other people.
They will eat and lie down in peace.
And no one will make them afraid."

¹⁴ People of Zion, sing!
Israel, shout loudly!
People of Jerusalem, be glad!
Let your hearts be full of joy.
¹⁵ The LORD has stopped punishing you.
He has made your enemies turn
away from you.

CANDID CONVERSATIONS

When I first started learning about
Jesus, I was still pretty stubborn.
I thought I had life all figured out.
Because I was stubborn, I was sometimes judgmental and critical toward
other people. I'd argue with Eugene
or complain about the silliest things.
Okay, maybe I still do that sometimes,
but God knew how I needed to grow
back then. He didn't wait for me to be
perfect before He started working
on me.

Through Whit and others, God showed
His care for me. As I recognized His
unconditional love for me, I fell in love
with Him. I'm so, so, so thankful God
doesn't ignore us when we're messed
up. He's still working on me today!

Skim through your Bible to find some
imperfect people God used. Over
and over He forgave His people
and assured them of His love (see
Zephaniah 3:17). Since there are no
perfect people, *imperfect* people are
the ones who need Him the most!
Interview your youth pastor, Sunday
school teacher, or senior pastor about
mistakes they've made. Ask how God
turned him or her around with His
unconditional love.

The LORD is the King of Israel.
He is with you.
You will never again be afraid
that others will harm you.
¹⁶ The time is coming when people will
say to Jerusalem,
"Zion, don't be afraid.
Don't give up.
¹⁷ The LORD your God is with you.
He is the Mighty Warrior who
saves.
He will take great delight in you.

In his love he will no longer punish
 you.
Instead, he will sing for joy because
 of you."

¹⁸The Lord says to his people,

"You used to celebrate my appointed
 feasts in Jerusalem.
You are sad because you can't do that
 anymore.
Other people make fun of you
 because of that.
That sadness was a heavy load for you
 to carry.
But I will remove that load from
 you.

¹⁹ At that time I will punish
 all those who crushed you.
I will save those among you who are
 disabled.
I will gather those who have been
 taken away.
I will give them praise and honor
 in every land where they have been
 put to shame.
²⁰ At that time I will gather you together.
 And I will bring you home.
I will give you honor and praise
 among all the nations on earth.
I will bless you with great success
 again,"
 says the Lord.

Haggai

Have you ever had an advanced trigonometry assignment that you kept postponing, and the longer you put it off, the more overwhelming the equations seemed? No? Well, perhaps you've had a similar occasion with another field of study, such as English, math, or history. The next book on our journey finds the people of God in a similar situation to those assignments. When these people were released from Babylon and allowed to go back to Judah, they needed to rebuild the walls and Temple of Jerusalem. Instead, they built nice homes for themselves and kept putting off their proverbial "homework assignment" from God (1:2–4). And though they hadn't noticed, God had not blessed them in abundance. They should have had exceptional crops, yet they had just enough to survive (1:5–11).

Haggai the prophet was sent to encourage and motivate the people. He got them started on the project. Later they noticed the new Temple wasn't as magnificent as Solomon's Temple had been, and they were disappointed. But Haggai assured them that God had promised to fill this temple with His glory, and it would become more beautiful than the previous one (2:1–9).

Haggai also reminds us that while evil is contagious, holiness requires personal and individual pursuit of God (2:11–14). To put it simply, we can't "catch" holiness merely by going to church. But, conversely, we *can* develop wicked habits through frequent dealings with the wrong friends. Haggai challenges us to keep that in mind and make wise choices.

WHaT'S IT MeaN, EUGeNE?

Redemption—Perhaps you've sold or given something away and later wanted it back. You would then *redeem* it, or buy it back (assuming of course the other party was willing to do so). As used by the New Testament writers (in particular, the apostle Paul), the word *redemption* suggests images of slavery, in which it is possible to set captives free by paying for their release. Likewise, when we were slaves to sin, Jesus bought us out of our slavery by dying for us. Revelation 5:9 says that the price He paid for our *redemption* was His blood.

Haggai Tells His People to Rebuild the Lord's Temple

1 A message from the Lord came to Haggai the prophet. Haggai gave it to Zerubbabel and Joshua. Zerubbabel was governor of Judah and the son of Shealtiel. Joshua was high priest and the son of Jozadak. The message came on the first day of the sixth month of the second year that Darius was king of Persia. Here is what Haggai said.

²Here is what the Lord who rules over all says. "The people of Judah say, 'It's not yet time to rebuild the Lord's temple.'"

³So the message from the Lord came to me. The Lord said, ⁴"My temple is still destroyed. But you are living in your houses that have beautiful wooden walls."

⁵The Lord who rules over all says, "Think carefully about how you are living. ⁶You have planted many seeds. But the crops you have gathered are small. So you eat. But you never have enough. You drink. But you are never full. You put on your clothes. But you are not warm. You earn your pay. But it will not buy everything you need."

⁷He continues, "Think carefully about how you are living. ⁸Go up into the mountains. Bring logs down. Use them to rebuild the temple, my house. Then I will enjoy it. And you will honor me," says the Lord. ⁹"You expected a lot. But you can see what a small amount it turned out to be. I blew away what you brought home. I'll tell you why," announces the Lord who rules over all. "Because my temple is still destroyed. In spite of that, each one of you is busy with your own house. ¹⁰So because of what you have done, the heavens have held back the dew. And the earth has not produced its crops. ¹¹I ordered the rain not to fall on the fields and mountains. Then the ground did not produce any grain. There were not enough grapes to make fresh wine. The trees did not bear enough olives to make oil. People and cattle suffered. All your hard work failed."

¹²Zerubbabel was the son of Shealtiel. Joshua the high priest was the son of Jozadak. They obeyed the Lord their God. So did all the Lord's people who were left alive. The Lord had given his message to them through me. He had sent me to speak to them. And the people had respect for him.

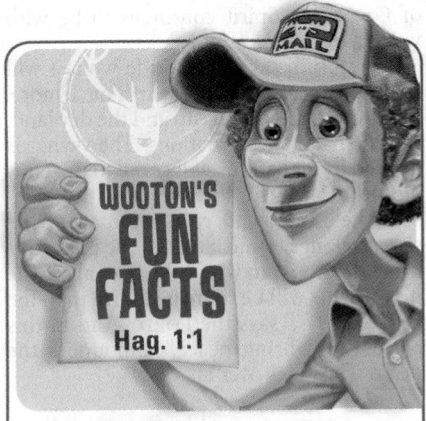

Haggai is a *minor* prophet, which means he wrote a shorter book than prophets like Isaiah and Jeremiah. That's different from a *miner* prophet who I guess digs up gold or silver while talking about God. There aren't any miner prophets in the Bible.

¹³Haggai was the Lord's messenger. So Haggai gave the Lord's message to the people. He told them, "The Lord announces, 'I am with you.'" ¹⁴So the Lord stirred up the spirits of Zerubbabel, the governor of Judah, and Joshua the high priest. The Lord also stirred up the rest of the people to help them. Then everyone began to work on the temple of the Lord who rules over all. He is their God. ¹⁵It was the 24th day of the sixth month.

The New Temple Will Be Beautiful

2 In the second year of King Darius, ¹a second message came from the Lord. It came to Haggai the prophet. The message came on the 21st day of the seventh month. The Lord said, ²"Speak to Zerubbabel, the governor of Judah and the son of Shealtiel. Also speak to Joshua the high priest, the son of Jozadak. And speak to all my people who are still left alive. Ask them, ³'Did any of you who are here see how beautiful this temple used to be? How does it look to you now? It doesn't look so good, does it? ⁴But be strong, Zerubbabel,' announces the Lord. 'Be strong, Joshua. Be strong, all of you people in the land,' announces the Lord. 'Start rebuilding. I am with you,' announces the Lord who rules over all. ⁵'That is what I promised you when you came out of Egypt. My Spirit continues to be with you. So do not be afraid.'"

[6] The LORD says, "In a little while I will shake the heavens and the earth once more. I will also shake the ocean and the dry land. [7] I will shake all the nations. Then what is desired by all nations will come to my temple. And I will fill the temple with glory," says the LORD who rules over all. [8] "The silver belongs to me. So does the gold," announces the LORD who rules over all. [9] "The new temple will be more beautiful than the first one was," says the LORD. "And in this place I will bring peace," announces the LORD who rules over all.

Jason's Jargon

HAGGAI 2

Your next job: Examine this chapter for *rot*. Rot is decay. When God strikes a farmer's land with rot, it wipes out a crop and the food it was supposed to produce.

The LORD Will Make His People Pure and "Clean"

[10] A third message from the LORD came to Haggai the prophet. The message came on the 24th day of the ninth month of the second year that Darius was king. [11] The LORD who rules over all speaks. He says, "Ask the priests what the law says. [12] Suppose someone carries holy meat in the clothes they are wearing. And the clothes touch some bread or stew. Or they touch some wine, olive oil or other food. Then do these things also become holy?"

The priests answered, "No."

[13] So Haggai said, "Suppose someone is made 'unclean' by touching a dead body. And then they touch one of these things. Does it become 'unclean' too?"

"Yes," the priests replied. "It does."

[14] Then here is what Haggai said. "The LORD announces, 'That is how I look at these people and this nation. Anything they do and anything they sacrifice on the altar is "unclean."

[15] "'Think carefully about this from now on. Think about how things were before the LORD's temple was built. This was before one stone was laid on top of another. [16] People went to get 20 measures of grain. But they could find only 10. They went to where the wine was stored to get 50 measures. But only 20 were there. [17] You worked very hard to produce all those things. But I struck them with rot, mold and hail. And you still did not return to me,' announces the LORD. [18] It is the 24th day of the ninth month. From this day on, here is what you should think carefully about. Think about the day when the foundation of my temple was laid. [19] Are any seeds still left in your barns? Until now, your vines and fig trees have not produced any fruit. Your pomegranate and olive trees have not produced any either.

"'But from this day on I will bless you.'"

The LORD Compares Zerubbabel to His Royal Ring

[20] A final message from the LORD came to Haggai. This message also came on the 24th day of the ninth month. The LORD said, [21] "Speak to Zerubbabel, the governor of Judah. Tell him I am going to shake the heavens and the earth. [22] I will throw down royal thrones. I will smash the power of other kingdoms. I will destroy chariots and their drivers. Horses and their riders will fall. They will be killed by the swords of their relatives.

[23] "'Zerubbabel, at that time I will pick you,' announces the LORD. 'You are my servant,' announces the LORD. 'You will be like a ring that has my royal mark on it. I have chosen you,' announces the LORD who rules over all."

Zechariah

It's appropriate that our trip continues from Haggai to Zechariah, because they were partners together when the Jewish people returned from Babylon to Jerusalem. Like Haggai, Zechariah scolded the people for being so slow to start rebuilding the Temple, and then he challenged them to get going!

God revealed to Zechariah a number of strange visions involving trees (1:7–17; 4:1–14), horns (1:18–21), a measuring line (chapter 2), the high priest dressed in filthy clothes (chapter 3), a flying scroll (5:1–4), a woman in a basket (5:5–11), chariots (6:1–8), and other items. Many times Zechariah had to ask the meaning of the visions, and God explained them to him. (Surprisingly, I've had a similar experience where people will ask my wife or Mr. Whittaker the meaning of what I just said. How peculiar.)

Zechariah was a priest in addition to being a prophet. And while we may think of prophets as being old men with gray hair—or bald heads, we are told that Zechariah was in fact a *young* man (2:4). He very likely had a long and faithful ministry of serving God's people. God has no age restrictions for people who are willing to take a stand for Him and make a difference in their world.

WHAT'S IT MEAN, EUGENE?

Angels/Demons—Far from the images of little cherubs flitting about with their delicate wings, *angels* are powerful spirit-beings created by God to function as His special messengers. Hebrews 1:14 says God sends them to "serve those who will receive salvation." *Demons*, on the other hand, are *fallen angels*—those who followed Satan when he rebelled against God and was thrown out of heaven.

The LORD Wants His People to Return to Him

1 A message from the LORD came to Zechariah the prophet. Zechariah was the son of Berekiah. Berekiah was the son of Iddo. It was the eighth month of the second year that Darius was king of Persia. Here is what Zechariah said.

[2] The LORD who rules over all was very angry with your people of long ago. [3] And now he says to us, "Return to me. Then I will return to you," announces the LORD. [4] "Do not be like your people of long ago. The earlier prophets gave them my message. I said, 'Stop doing what is evil. Turn away from your sinful practices.' But they would not listen to me. They would not pay any attention," announces the LORD. [5] "Where are those people now? And what about my prophets? Do they live forever? [6] I commanded my servants the prophets what to say. I told them what I planned to do. But your people refused to obey me. So I had to punish them.

"Then they had a change of heart. They said, 'The LORD who rules over all has punished us because of how we have lived. He was fair and right to do that. He has done to us just what he decided to do.'"

A Vision of a Horseman Among Some Myrtle Trees

[7] A message from the LORD came to Zechariah the prophet. Zechariah was the son of Berekiah. Berekiah was the son of Iddo. The message came during the second year that Darius was king. It was the 24th day of the 11th month. That's the month of Shebat.

[8] I had a vision at night. I saw a man sitting on a red horse. He was standing among the myrtle trees in a valley. Behind him were red, brown and white horses.

[9] An angel was talking with me. I asked him, "Sir, what are these?"

He answered, "I will show you what they are."

[10] Then the man standing among the myrtle trees spoke. He said, "They are the messengers the LORD has sent out. He told them to go all through the earth."

[11] They brought a report to the angel of the LORD. He was standing among the myrtle trees. They said to him, "We have gone all through the earth. We've found the whole world enjoying peace and rest."

[12] Then the angel of the LORD spoke up. He said, "LORD, you rule over all. How long will you keep from showing your tender love to Jerusalem? How long will you keep it from the towns of Judah? You have been angry with them for 70 years." [13] So the LORD replied with kind and comforting words. He spoke them to the angel who talked with me.

[14] Then the angel said, "Announce this message. Say, 'The LORD who rules over all says, "I am very jealous for my people in Jerusalem and Zion. [15] And I am very angry with the nations that feel secure. I was only a little angry with my people. But the nations went too far and tried to wipe them out."

[16] "So the LORD says, "I will return to Jerusalem. I will show its people my tender love. My temple will be rebuilt there. Workers will use a measuring line when they rebuild Jerusalem," announces the LORD.

[17] "He says, "My towns will be filled with good things once more. I will comfort Zion. And I will choose Jerusalem again."'"

A Vision of Four Horns and Four Skilled Workers

[18] Then I looked up and saw four animal horns. [19] I spoke to the angel who was talking with me. "What are these horns?" I asked.

He said, "They are the powerful nations that scattered Judah, Israel and Jerusalem."

[20] Then the LORD showed me four skilled workers. [21] I asked, "What are they coming to do?"

He answered, "The horns are the powerful nations that scattered the people of Judah. That made Judah helpless. But these four skilled workers have come to terrify the horns. The workers will destroy the power of those nations. Those nations had used their power to scatter Judah's people."

A Vision of a Man Holding a Measuring Line

2 Then I looked up and saw a man. He was holding a measuring line. [2] "Where are you going?" I asked.

"To measure Jerusalem," he answered. "I want to find out how wide and how long it is."

[3] The angel who was talking with me was leaving. At that time, another angel came

over to him. [4]He said to him, "Run! Tell that young man Zechariah, 'Jerusalem will be a city that does not have any walls around it. It will have huge numbers of people and animals in it. [5]And I myself will be like a wall of fire around it,' announces the LORD. 'I will be the city's glory.'

[6]"Israel, I have scattered you," announces the LORD. "I have used the power of the four winds of heaven to do it. Come quickly! Run away from the land of the north," announces the LORD.

[7]"Come, people of Zion! Escape, you who live in Babylon!" [8]The LORD rules over all. His angel says to Israel, "The Glorious One has sent me to punish the nations that have robbed you of everything. That's because anyone who hurts you hurts those the LORD loves and guards. [9]So I will raise my powerful hand to strike down your enemies. Their own slaves will rob them of everything. Then you will know that the LORD who rules over all has sent me.

[10]"'People of Zion, shout and be glad! I am coming to live among you,' announces the LORD. [11]At that time many nations will join themselves to me. And they will become my people. I will live among you,' says the LORD. Then you will know that the LORD who rules over all has sent me to you. [12]He will receive Judah as his share in the holy land. And he will choose Jerusalem again. [13]All you people of the world, be still because the LORD is coming. He is getting ready to come down from his holy temple in heaven."

A Vision of the High Priest Dressed in Fine Clothes

3 Then the LORD showed me Joshua the high priest. He was standing in front of the angel of the LORD. Satan was standing to the right of Joshua. He was there to bring charges against the high priest. [2]The LORD said to Satan, "May the LORD correct you! He has chosen Jerusalem. So may he correct you! Isn't this man Joshua like a burning stick pulled out of the fire?"

[3]Joshua stood in front of the angel. He was wearing clothes that were very dirty. [4]The angel spoke to those who were standing near him. He said, "Take his dirty clothes off."

He said to Joshua, "I have taken your sin away. I will put fine clothes on you."

[5]I added, "Put a clean turban on his head." So they did. And they dressed him while the angel of the LORD stood by.

[6]Then the angel spoke to Joshua. He said, [7]"The LORD who rules over all says, 'You must obey me. You must do what I have commanded. Then you will rule in my temple. You will be in charge of my courtyards. And I will give you a place among these who are standing here.

[8]"'High Priest Joshua, pay attention! I want you other priests who are sitting with Joshua to listen also. All you men are signs of things to come. I am going to bring to you my servant the Branch. [9]Look at the stone I have put in front of Joshua! There are seven eyes on that one stone. I will carve a message on it,' says the LORD who rules over all. 'And I will remove the sin of this land in one day.

[10]"'At that time each of you will invite your neighbors to visit you. They will sit under your vines and fig trees,' announces the LORD."

A Vision of the Gold Lampstand and Two Olive Trees

4 Then the angel who was talking with me returned. He woke me up. It was as if I had been asleep. [2]"What do you see?" he asked me.

"I see a solid gold lampstand," I answered. "It has a bowl on top of it. There are seven lamps on it. Seven tubes lead to the lamps. [3]There are two olive trees by the lampstand. One is on its right side. The other is on its left."

[4]I asked the angel who was talking with me, "Sir, what are these?"

[5]He answered, "Don't you know what they are?"

"No, sir," I replied.

[6]So he said to me, "A message from the LORD came to Zerubbabel. The LORD said, 'Your strength will not get my temple rebuilt. Your power will not do it either. Only the power of my Spirit will do it,' says the LORD who rules over all.

[7]"So nothing can stop Zerubbabel from completing the temple. Even a mountain of problems will be smoothed out by him. When the temple is finished, he will put its most important stone in place. Then the people will shout, 'God bless it! God bless it!'"

⁸Then a message from the LORD came to me. His angel said, ⁹"The hands of Zerubbabel have laid the foundation of this temple. His hands will also complete it. Then you will know that the LORD who rules over all has sent me to you.

¹⁰"Do not look down on the small amount of work done on the temple so far. The seven eyes of the LORD look over the whole earth. They will see Zerubbabel holding the most important stone. They will be filled with joy when they see it."

¹¹Then I said to the angel, "I see two olive trees. One is on the right side of the lampstand. The other is on the left. What are these trees?"

¹²I continued, "I also see two olive branches. They are next to the two gold pipes that pour out golden olive oil. What are these branches?"

¹³He answered, "Don't you know what they are?"

"No, sir," I said.

¹⁴So he told me, "They are Zerubbabel and Joshua. The Lord of the whole earth has anointed them to serve him."

A Vision of a Flying Scroll

5 I looked up again and saw a flying scroll.

²"What do you see?" the angel asked me.

"A scroll flying in the air," I replied. "It's 30 feet long and 15 feet wide."

³He said to me, "A curse sent by the LORD is written on it. It is going out over the whole land. Every thief will be driven out of the land. That is what it says on one side of the scroll. Everyone who lies when promising to tell the truth will also be driven out. That is what it says on the other side. ⁴The LORD who rules over all announces, 'I will send the curse out. It will enter the house of the thief. It will also enter the house of anyone who lies when making a promise in my name. It will remain in that house and destroy it completely. It will pull down its beams and stones.'"

A Vision of a Woman in a Basket

⁵Then the angel who was talking with me came forward. He said to me, "Look at what is coming."

⁶"What is it?" I asked.

"A basket," he replied. "The sins of the people all through the land are in it."

⁷Then the basket's cover was lifted up. It was made out of lead. A woman was sitting in the basket! ⁸The angel said, "She stands for everything that is evil." Then he pushed her down into the basket. He put the lead cover back over it.

⁹I looked up and saw two other women. They had wings like the wings of a stork. A wind sent by the LORD carried them along. They lifted the basket up between heaven and earth.

¹⁰"Where are they taking the basket?" I asked the angel.

¹¹He replied, "To the country of Babylon. A temple will be built for it. When the temple is ready, the basket will be set there in its place."

A Vision of Four Chariots

6 I looked up again and saw four chariots. They were coming out from between two mountains. The mountains were made out of bronze. ²The first chariot was pulled by red horses. The second one had black horses. ³The third had white horses. And the fourth had spotted horses. All the horses were powerful. ⁴I asked the angel who was talking with me, "Sir, what are these?"

⁵The angel answered, "The four spirits of heaven. They are going out to serve the Lord of the whole world. ⁶The chariot pulled by the black horses is going toward the north country. The one with the white horses is going toward the west. And the one with the spotted horses is going toward the south."

⁷The powerful horses went out. They were in a hurry to go all over the earth. The angel said, "Go all through the earth!" So they did.

⁸Then the LORD called out to me, "Look! The horses going toward the north have given my Spirit rest in the north country."

Jason's Jargon

ZECHARIAH 6

Search this chapter for the word *combine*. To combine means to join or merge. When his duties of a king and priest were combined, Joshua was made leader over both the government and the church.

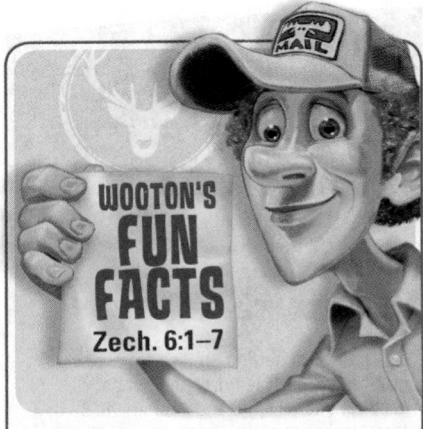

WOOTON'S FUN FACTS
Zech. 6:1–7

This isn't the only vision involving horses of differing colors. Turn to Revelation 6:1–8.

A Crown Is Given to Joshua

⁹A message from the LORD came to me. His angel said, ¹⁰"Get some silver and gold from Heldai, Tobijah and Jedaiah. They have just come back from Babylon. On that same day go to Josiah's house. He is the son of Zephaniah. ¹¹Use the silver and gold to make a crown. Set it on the head of Joshua the high priest. He is the son of Jozadak. ¹²Give Joshua a message from the LORD who rules over all. He says, 'Here is the man whose name is the Branch. He will branch out and build my temple. ¹³That is what he will do. He will be dressed in majesty as if it were his royal robe. He will sit as king on his throne. He will also be a priest there. So he will combine the positions of king and priest in himself.' ¹⁴The crown will be given to Heldai, Tobijah, Jedaiah and Zephaniah's son Hen. The crown will be kept in the LORD's temple. It will remind everyone that the LORD's promises will come true. ¹⁵Those who are far away will come to Jerusalem. They will help build the LORD's temple. Then his people will know that the LORD who rules over all has sent me to them. It will happen if they are careful to obey the LORD their God."

Have Justice and Mercy

7During the fourth year that Darius was king, a message from the LORD came to me. It was the fourth day of the ninth month. That's the month of Kislev. ²The people of Bethel wanted to ask the LORD for his blessing. So they sent Sharezer and Regem-Melek and their men. ³They went to the prophets and priests at the LORD's temple. They asked them, "Should we mourn and go without eating in the fifth month? That's what we've done for many years."

⁴Then the message came to me from the LORD who rules over all. He said, ⁵"Ask the priests and all the people in the land a question for me. Say to them, 'You mourned and fasted in the fifth and seventh months. You did it for the past 70 years. But did you really do it for me? ⁶And when you were eating and drinking, weren't you just enjoying good food for yourselves? ⁷Didn't I tell you the same thing through the earlier prophets? That was when Jerusalem and the towns around it were at rest and enjoyed success. People lived in the Negev Desert and the western hills at that time.'"

⁸Another message from the LORD came to me. ⁹Here is what the LORD who rules over all said to his people. "Treat everyone with justice. Show mercy and tender concern to one another. ¹⁰Do not take advantage of widows. Do not mistreat children whose fathers have died. Do not be mean to outsiders or poor people. Do not make evil plans against one another."

¹¹But they refused to pay attention to the LORD. They were stubborn. They turned their backs and covered their ears. ¹²They made their hearts as hard as the hardest stone. They wouldn't listen to the law. They wouldn't pay attention to the LORD's messages. So the LORD who rules over all was very angry. After all, his Spirit had spoken to his people through the earlier prophets.

¹³"When I called, they did not listen," says the LORD. "So when they called, I would not listen. ¹⁴I used a windstorm to scatter them among all the nations. They were strangers there. The land they left behind became dry and empty. No one could even travel through it. This is how they turned the pleasant land into a dry and empty desert."

The LORD Promises to Bless Jerusalem

8A message came to me from the LORD who rules over all.

He said, ²"I am very jealous for my people in Zion. In fact, I am burning with jealousy for them."

³He continued, "I will return to Zion. I will live among my people in Jerusalem. Then Jerusalem will be called the Faithful City. And my mountain will be called the Holy Mountain."

⁴He continued, "Once again old men and women will sit in the streets of Jerusalem. All of them will be using canes because they are old. ⁵The city streets will be filled with boys and girls. They will be playing there."

⁶He continued, "All of that might seem hard to believe to the people living then. But it will not be too hard for me."

⁷He continued, "I will save my people. I will gather them from the countries of the east and the west. ⁸I will bring them back to live in Jerusalem. They will be my people. I will be their faithful God. I will keep my promises to them."

⁹The LORD who rules over all says to his people, "Now listen to these words, 'Let your hands be strong so that you can rebuild the temple.' This also was said by the prophets Haggai and Zechariah. They spoke to you when the work on my temple began again. ¹⁰Before the work was started again, there was no pay for the people. And there was no money to rent animals. People could not go about their business safely because of their enemies. I had turned all of them against one another. ¹¹But now I will not punish you who are living at this time. I will not treat you as I treated your people before you," announces the LORD who rules over all.

¹²"Your seeds will grow well. Your vines will bear fruit. The ground will produce crops for you. And the heavens will drop their dew on your land. I will give all these things to those who are still left alive here. ¹³Judah and Israel, in the past you have been a curse among the nations. But now I will save you. You will be a blessing to others. Do not be afraid. Let your hands be strong so that you can do my work."

¹⁴The LORD who rules over all says, "Your people of long ago made me angry. So I decided to bring trouble on them. I did not show them any pity. ¹⁵But now I plan to do good things to Jerusalem and Judah again. So do not be afraid. ¹⁶Here is what you must do. Speak the truth to one another. Make true and wise decisions in your courts. ¹⁷Do not make evil plans against one another. When you promise to tell the truth, do not

Zech. 8:9 I'm getting an idea for a new graphic novel! It features the dynamic prophet duo: Haggai and Zechariah! By day, they worked together to encourage the Jews to rebuild the Temple (see Ezra 5:1). By night, they . . . uh . . . slept.

lie. Many people love to do that. But I hate all these things," announces the LORD.

¹⁸Another message came to me from the LORD who rules over all.

He said, ¹⁹"You have established special times to go without eating. They are your fasts in the fourth, fifth, seventh and tenth months. They will become days of joy. They will be happy times for Judah. It will happen if you take delight in telling the truth and bringing about peace."

²⁰He continued, "Many nations will still come to you. And those who live in many cities will also come. ²¹The people who live in one city will go to another city. They will say, 'Let's go right away to ask the LORD for his blessing. Let's look to him as our God. We ourselves are going.' ²²Large numbers of people and nations will come to Jerusalem. They will look to me. They will ask me to bless them."

²³He continued, "At that time many people of all nations and languages will take hold of one Jew. They will grab hold of the hem of his robe. And they will say, 'We want to go to Jerusalem with you. We've heard that God is with you.'"

The LORD Destroys Israel's Enemies

9 This is a prophecy.

It is the LORD's message
     against the land of Hadrak.
     He will judge Damascus.

That's because all the tribes of Israel
    look to him.
  So do all other people.
2 The Lord will judge Hamath too.
    It's next to Damascus.
  He will also punish Tyre and Sidon
    even though they are very clever.
3 Tyre's people have built a fort for
    themselves.
  They've piled up silver like dust.
  They have as much gold as the dirt
    in the streets.
4 But the Lord will take away everything
    they have.
  He'll destroy their power on the
    Mediterranean Sea.
  And Tyre will be completely burned
    up.
5 Ashkelon will see it and become afraid.
  Gaza will groan with pain.
  So will Ekron. Its hope will vanish.
  Gaza will no longer have a king.
  Ashkelon will be deserted.
6 A people who come from several
    nations will take over
    Ashdod.
  The Lord says, "I will put an end to
    the pride of the Philistines.
7 They will no longer drink the blood of
    their animal sacrifices.
  I will remove the 'unclean' food from
    between their teeth.
  The Philistines who are left will belong
    to our God.
  They will become a family group in
    Judah.
  And Ekron will be like the Jebusites.
  So the Philistines will become part
    of Israel.
8 But I will camp at my temple.
  I will guard it against enemy armies.
  No one will ever crush my people
    again.
  I will make sure it does not happen.

A King Comes to Zion

9 "City of Zion, be full of joy!
  People of Jerusalem, shout!
  See, your king comes to you.
  He always does what is right.
  He has won the victory.
  He is humble and riding on a donkey.
  He is sitting on a donkey's colt.
10 I will take the chariots away from
    Ephraim.

I will remove the war horses from
    Jerusalem.
  I will break the bows that are used
    in battle.
  Your king will announce peace to the
    nations.
  He will rule from ocean to ocean.
  His kingdom will reach from the
    Euphrates River
    to the ends of the earth.
11 I will set your prisoners free
    from where their enemies are
    keeping them.
  I will do it because of the blood
    that put into effect my covenant with
    you.
12 Return to your place of safety,
    you prisoners who still have hope.
  Even now I announce that I will give
    you back
    much more than you had before.
13 I will bend Judah as I bend my bow.
  I will make Ephraim's people my
    arrows.
  Zion, I will stir up your sons.
  Greece, they will attack your sons.
  My people, I will use you as my
    sword."

The Lord Will Appear

14 Then the Lord will appear over his
    people.
  His arrows will flash like lightning.
  The Lord and King will blow the
    trumpet of his thunder.
  He'll march out like a storm in the
    south.
15 The Lord who rules over all
    will be like a shield to his people.
  They will destroy their enemies.
  They'll use slings to throw stones at
    them.
  They'll drink the blood of their enemies
    as if it were wine.
  They'll be full like the bowl that is used
    for sprinkling the corners of the
    altar.
16 The Lord their God will save his
    people on that day.
  He will be like a shepherd who saves
    his flock.
  They will gleam in his land
    like jewels in a crown.
17 How very beautiful they will be!
  Grain and fresh wine

will make the young men and young
women strong.

The Lord Will Take Care of Judah

10 People of Judah, ask the Lord
to send rain in the spring.
He is the one who sends the
thunderstorms.
He sends down showers of rain on all
people.
He gives everyone the plants in the
fields.
² Other gods tell lies.
Those who practice magic
see visions that aren't true.
They tell dreams that fool people.
They give comfort that doesn't do
any good.
So the people wander around like sheep.
They are crushed because they don't
have a shepherd.

³ The Lord who rules over all says,

"I am very angry with the shepherds.
I will punish the leaders.
The Lord will take care of his flock.
They are the people of Judah.
He will make them like a proud
horse in battle.
⁴ The most important building stone
will come from the tribe of Judah.
The tent stake will also come from it.
And the bow that is used in battle will
come from it.
In fact, every ruler will come from it.
⁵ Together they will be like warriors in
battle.
They will stomp their enemies
into the mud of the streets.
The Lord will be with them.
So they will fight against the
horsemen
and put them to shame.

⁶ "I will make the family of Judah strong.
I will save the tribes of Joseph.
I will bring them back
because I have tender love for them.
It will be as if
I had not sent them away.
I am the Lord their God.
I will help them.
⁷ The people of Ephraim will become like
warriors.
Their hearts will be glad
as if they were drinking wine.

Their children will see it
and be filled with joy.
I will make their hearts glad.
⁸ I will signal for my people to come,
and I will gather them in.
I will set them free.
There will be as many of them as
before.
⁹ I have scattered them among the
nations.
But in lands far away they will
remember me.
They and their children will be kept
alive.
And they will return.
¹⁰ I will bring them back from Egypt.
I will gather them from Assyria.
I will bring them to Gilead and
Lebanon.
There will not be enough room for
them.
¹¹ They will pass through a sea of trouble.
The stormy sea will calm down.
All the deep places in the Nile River
will dry up.
Assyria's pride will be brought down.
Egypt's right to rule will disappear.
¹² I will make my people strong.
They will live in safety because of me,"
announces the Lord.

11 Lebanon, open your doors!
Then fire can burn up your cedar
trees.
² Juniper trees, cry out!
The cedar trees have fallen down.
The majestic trees are destroyed.
Cry out, you oak trees of Bashan!
The thick forest has been cut down.
³ Listen to the shepherds cry out!
Their rich grasslands are destroyed.

Jason's Jargon

ZECHARIAH 11

Review this chapter
for the word *potter*.
With the use of a turning
wheel, a potter is
able to turn a piece of
clay into decorative or
useful pots and bowls.

Listen to the lions roar!
The trees and bushes along the
Jordan River are gone.

The Two Shepherds

[4]The LORD my God says, "Take care of the sheep that are set apart to be sacrificed. [5]Those who buy them kill them. And they are not punished for it. Those who sell them say, 'Praise the LORD! We're rich!' And their own shepherds do not spare them. [6]I will no longer have pity on the people in the land," announces the LORD. "I will hand all of them over to their neighbors and their king. They will destroy the land. And I will not save anyone from their power."

[7]So I took care of the sheep set apart to be sacrificed. I took special care of those that had been treated badly. Then I got two shepherd's staffs. I called one of them Favor. I called the other one Union. And I took care of the flock. [8]In one month I got rid of three worthless shepherds.

The sheep hated me, and I got tired of them. [9]So I said, "I won't be your shepherd anymore. Let those of you who are dying die. Let those who are passing away pass away. Let those who are left eat one another up."

[10]Then I got my staff called Favor. I broke it. That meant the covenant the LORD had made with all the nations was broken. [11]It happened that day. The sheep that had been treated badly were watching me. They knew it was the LORD's message.

[12]I told them, "If you think it is best, give me my pay. But if you don't think so, keep it." So they paid me 30 silver coins.

[13]The LORD said to me, "Throw those coins to the potter." That amount shows how little they valued me! So I threw the 30 silver coins to the potter at the LORD's temple.

[14]Then I broke my second staff called Union. That broke the family connection between Judah and Israel.

[15]The LORD said to me, "Now pretend to be a foolish shepherd. Get the things you need. [16]I am going to raise up a shepherd over the land. He will not take care of those that are wounded. He will not look for the young ones. He will not heal those that are hurt. He will not feed the healthy ones. Instead, he will eat the best sheep. He will even tear their hooves off.

[17]"How terrible it will be for that
worthless shepherd!
He deserts the flock.
May a sword strike his arm and his
right eye!
May his powerful arm become weak!
May his right eye be totally blinded!"

The LORD Will Destroy Jerusalem's Enemies

12This is a prophecy. It is the LORD's message about Israel.

The LORD spreads out the heavens. He lays the foundation of the earth. He creates the human spirit within a person. He says, [2]"Jerusalem will be like a cup in my hand. It will make all the surrounding nations drunk from the wine of my anger. Judah will be attacked by its enemies. So will Jerusalem. [3]At that time all the nations on earth will gather together against Jerusalem. Then it will become like a rock that can't be moved. All the nations that try to move it will only hurt themselves. [4]On that day I will fill every horse with panic. I will make every rider crazy," announces the LORD. "I will watch over the people of Judah. But I will make all the horses of the nations blind. [5]Then the family groups of Judah will say in their hearts, 'The people of Jerusalem are strong. That's because the LORD who rules over all is their God.'

[6]"At that time Judah's family groups will be like a fire pot in a pile of wood. They will be like a burning torch among bundles of grain. They will destroy all the surrounding nations on every side. But Jerusalem will remain unharmed in its place.

[7]"I will save the houses in Judah first. The honor of David's family line is great. So is the honor of those who live in Jerusalem. But their honor will not be greater than the honor of the rest of Judah. [8]At that time I will be like a shield to those who live in Jerusalem. Then even the weakest among them will be great warriors like David. And David's family line will be like the angel of the LORD who leads them. [9]On that day I will begin to destroy all the nations that attack Jerusalem.

Israel's People Will Mourn Over the One They Pierced

[10]"I will pour out a spirit of grace and prayer on David's family line. I will also

send it on those who live in Jerusalem. They will look to me. I am the one they have pierced. They will mourn over me as someone mourns over an only child who has died. They will be full of sorrow over me. Their sorrow will be just like someone's sorrow over an oldest son. ¹¹At that time there will be a lot of weeping in Jerusalem. It will be as great as the weeping of the people at Hadad Rimmon. Hadad Rimmon is in the valley of Megiddo. They were weeping over Josiah's death. ¹²Everyone in the land will mourn. Each family will mourn by themselves and their wives by themselves. That will include the family lines of David, Nathan, ¹³Levi, Shimei and ¹⁴all the others.

The Lord Makes Israel Pure and "Clean"

13 "At that time a fountain will be opened for the benefit of David's family line. It will also bless the others who live in Jerusalem. It will wash away their sins. It will make them pure and 'clean.'

²"On that day I will remove the names of other gods from the land. They will not even be remembered anymore," announces the Lord who rules over all. "I will drive the evil prophets out of the land. I will get rid of the spirit that put lies in their mouths. ³Some people might still prophesy. But their own fathers and mothers will speak to them. They will tell them, 'You must die. You have told lies in the Lord's name.' When they prophesy, their own parents will stab them.

⁴"At that time every prophet will be ashamed of the vision they see. They will no longer pretend to be a true prophet. They will not put on clothes that are made out of hair in order to trick people. ⁵In fact, each one will say, 'I'm not really a prophet. I'm a farmer. I've farmed the land since I was young.' ⁶Suppose someone asks, 'What are these wounds on your body?' Then they will answer, 'I was given these wounds at the house of my friends.'

The Good Shepherd Is Killed and the Sheep Are Scattered

⁷ "My sword, wake up! Attack my
        shepherd!
    Attack the man who is close to me,"
    announces the Lord who rules over
        all.

"Strike down the shepherd.
    Then the sheep will be scattered.
    And I will turn my hand against
        their little ones.
⁸ Here is what will happen in the whole
        land,"
    announces the Lord.
"Two-thirds of the people will be struck
        down and die.
    But one-third will be left.
⁹ I will put this third in the fire.
    I will make them as pure as silver.
    I will test them like gold.
They will call out to me.
    And I will answer them.
I will say, 'They are my people.'
    And they will say, 'The Lord is our
        God.'"

The Lord Will Be King Over the Whole Earth

14 The day of the Lord is coming, Jerusalem. At that time your enemies will steal everything your people own. They will divide it up within your walls. ²The Lord will gather all the nations together. They will fight against Jerusalem. They'll capture the city. Its houses will be robbed. Its women will be raped. Half of the people will be taken away as prisoners. But the rest of them won't be taken. ³Then the Lord will march out and fight against those nations. He will fight as on a day of battle. ⁴On that day he will stand on the Mount of Olives. It's east of Jerusalem. It will be split in two from east to west. Half of the mountain will move north. The other half will move south. A large valley will be formed. ⁵The people will run away through that mountain valley. It will reach all the way to Azel. They'll run away just as they ran from the earthquake when Uzziah was king of Judah. Then the Lord my God will come. All the holy ones will come with him.

⁶There won't be any sunlight on that day. There will be no cold, frosty darkness either. ⁷It will be a day unlike any other. It will be a day known only to the Lord. It won't be separated into day and night. After that day is over, there will be light again.

⁸At that time water that gives life will flow out from Jerusalem. Half of it will run east into the Dead Sea. The other half will go west to the Mediterranean Sea. The water will flow in summer and winter.

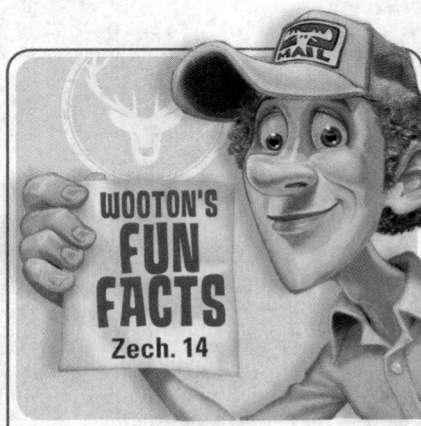

Good news: The Temple was rebuilt. Bad news: Zechariah's "blood was spilled," meaning he was murdered. Matthew 23:34–35 says he died near the Temple altar.

⁹The Lord will be king over the whole earth. On that day there will be one Lord. His name will be the only name.

¹⁰The whole land south of Jerusalem will be changed. From Geba to Rimmon it will become like the Arabah Valley. But Jerusalem will be raised up high. It will be raised from the Benjamin Gate to the First Gate to the Corner Gate. It will be raised from the Tower of Hananel to the royal winepresses. And it will remain in its place. ¹¹People will live in it. Jerusalem will never be destroyed again. It will be secure.

¹²The Lord will punish all the nations that fought against Jerusalem. He'll strike them with a plague. It will make their bodies rot while they are still standing on their feet. Their eyes will rot in their heads. Their tongues will rot in their mouths. ¹³On that day the Lord will fill people with great panic. They will grab one another by the hand. And they'll attack one another. ¹⁴Judah will also fight at Jerusalem. The wealth of all the surrounding nations will be collected. Huge amounts of gold, silver and clothes will be gathered up. ¹⁵The same kind of plague will strike the horses, mules, camels and donkeys. In fact, it will strike all the animals in the army camps.

¹⁶But some people from all the nations that have attacked Jerusalem will still be left alive. All of them will go up there to worship the King. He is the Lord who rules over all. Year after year these people will celebrate the Feast of Booths. ¹⁷Some nations might not go up to Jerusalem to worship the King. If they don't, they won't have any rain. ¹⁸The people of Egypt might not go up there to take part. Then they won't have any rain either. That's the plague the Lord will send on the nations that don't go to celebrate the Feast of Booths. ¹⁹Egypt will be punished. So will all the other nations that don't celebrate the feast.

²⁰On that day "Holy to the Lord" will be carved on the bells of the horses. The cooking pots in the Lord's temple will be just like the sacred bowls in front of the altar for burnt offerings. ²¹Every pot in Jerusalem and Judah will be set apart to the Lord. All those who come to offer sacrifices will get some of the pots and cook in them. At that time there won't be any Canaanites in the Lord's temple. He is the Lord who rules over all.

Malachi

Here we arrive not at the end of our journey, but certainly a milestone and a place to catch our proverbial breath. Malachi is the final book in the Old Testament. He ministered at a difficult time for God's people. They had been released from their exile in Babylon and they returned to Jerusalem (as we saw in our sojourn through the books of Ezra, Nehemiah, Haggai, and Zechariah). But it was no simple matter to start normal life again after the city had sat in ruins for decades. First the Temple and then the city walls were finally restored. Yet God's people still lacked enthusiasm for genuine worship. They were "going through the motions" of loving and serving God, but that was all there was to it. There wasn't a true heart behind it.

Malachi confronts the people about their less-than-ideal attitudes. The priests weren't attending to their responsibilities (2:1–9). The people were offering sick and blind animals to God—not the best of their flocks and herds as they were supposed to do (1:6–14). They were divorcing faithful spouses to marry others who worshiped false gods (2:11–16). They had stopped bringing their tithes, which was the same as "robbing God" (3:8–9).

Malachi wanted everyone to see the difference it would make to put God first in their lives once more. When they did, God's blessings would become very obvious to them (3:10–12). As you read Malachi, ponder how obedience to God removes the fear from life and replaces it with incredible joy. And also remember that God will remove fear in a different way when our journey continues in the New Testament!

WHAT'S IT MEAN, EUGENE?

Incarnation—This word comes from a Latin term that means "in the flesh." It presents a stunning and miraculous truth: *"God became human."* In the opening verses of his Gospel, the apostle John said: "In the beginning, the Word was already there. The Word was with God, and the Word was God . . . The Word became a human being. He made his home with us" (John 1:1, 14). This *incarnate* Word is Jesus Christ Himself.

This is a prophecy. It is the LORD's message to Israel through Malachi.

Israel Doubts God's Love

²"Israel, I have loved you," says the LORD.

"But you ask, 'How have you loved us?'

"Wasn't Esau Jacob's brother?" says the LORD. "But I chose Jacob ³instead of Esau. I have turned Esau's hill country into a dry and empty land. I left that land of Edom to the wild dogs in the desert.

⁴Edom might say, "We have been crushed. But we'll rebuild our cities."

The LORD who rules over all says, "They might rebuild their cities. But I will destroy them. They will be called the Evil Land. My anger will always remain on them. ⁵You will see it with your own eyes. You will say, 'The LORD is great! He rules even beyond the borders of Israel!'

Give Your Best to the LORD

⁶"A son honors his father. A slave honors his master. If I am a father, where is the honor I should have? If I am a master, where is the respect you should give me?" says the LORD who rules over all.

"You priests look down on me.

"But you ask, 'How have we looked down on you?'

⁷"You sacrifice 'unclean' food on my altar.

"But you ask, 'How have we made you "unclean"?'

"You do it by looking down on my altar. ⁸You sacrifice blind animals to me. Isn't that wrong? You sacrifice disabled or sick animals. Isn't that wrong? Try offering them to your governor! Would he be pleased with you? Would he accept you?" says the LORD who rules over all.

⁹"Now plead with God to be gracious to us! But as long as you give offerings like those, how can he accept you?" says the LORD.

¹⁰"You might as well shut the temple doors! Then you would not light useless fires on my altar. I am not pleased with you," says the LORD. "I will not accept any of the offerings you bring. ¹¹My name will be great among the nations. They will worship me from where the sun rises in the east to where it sets in the west. In every place, incense and pure offerings will be brought to me. That's because my name will be great among the nations," says the LORD.

Jason's Jargon

MALACHI 1

Inspect this chapter for the word *unclean*. Old Testament law defined unclean and clean animals in very specific ways. Unclean animals, such as bears, mice, and rabbits, were not to be eaten.

¹²"But you treat my name as if it were not holy. You say the LORD's altar is 'unclean.' And you look down on its food. ¹³You say, 'What a heavy load our work is!' And you turn up your nose. You act as if you hate working for me," says the LORD who rules over all.

"You bring animals that have been hurt. Or you bring disabled or sick animals. Then you dare to offer them to me as sacrifices! Should I accept them from you?" says the LORD. ¹⁴"Suppose you have a male sheep or goat that does not have any flaws. And you promise to offer it to me. But then you sacrifice an animal that has flaws. When you do that, you cheat me. And anyone who cheats me is under my curse. After all, I am a great king," says the LORD who rules over all. "The other nations have respect for my name. So why don't you respect it?

The LORD Warns the Priests

2 "Now I am giving this warning to you priests. ²Listen to it. Honor me with all your heart," says the LORD who rules over all. "If you do not, I will send a curse on you. I will turn your blessings into curses. In fact, I have already done that because you have not honored me with all your heart.

³"Because of what you have done, I will punish your children. I will smear the waste from your sacrifices on your faces. And you will be carried off to the dump along with it. ⁴You will know that I have given you this warning. I have warned you so that my covenant with Levi will continue," says the LORD who rules over all. ⁵"My covenant promised Levi life and peace. So I gave them to him. I required him to respect me. And he had great respect for my name. ⁶True teaching came from his

Connie and her mother felt the pain of divorce firsthand and were reminded why God hates divorce in "Father's Day" (A#14).

mouth. Nothing but the truth came from his lips. He walked with me in peace. He did what was right. He turned many people away from their sins.

[7]"The lips of a priest should guard knowledge. After all, he is the messenger of the LORD who rules over all. And people seek instruction from his mouth. [8]But you have turned away from the right path. Your teaching has caused many people to trip and fall. You have broken my covenant with Levi," says the LORD who rules over all. [9]"So I have caused all the people to hate you. They have lost respect for you. You have not done what I told you to do. Instead, you have favored one person over another in matters of the law."

Breaking the Covenant Through Divorce

[10]People of Judah, all of us have one Father. One God created us. So why do we break the covenant the LORD made with our people of long ago? We do this by being unfaithful to one another.

[11]And Judah has been unfaithful. A hateful thing has been done in Israel and Jerusalem. The LORD loves his temple. But Judah has made it impure. Their men have married women who worship other gods. [12]May the LORD punish the man who marries a woman like this. It doesn't matter who that man is. May the LORD who rules over all remove him from the tents of Jacob's people. May the LORD remove him even if he brings an offering to him.

[13]Here's something else you do. You flood the LORD's altar with your tears. You weep and cry because your offerings don't please him anymore. He doesn't accept them with pleasure from your hands. [14]You ask, "Why?" It's because the LORD is holding you responsible. He watches how you treat the wife you married when you were young. You have been unfaithful to her. You did it even though she's your partner.

You promised to stay married to her. And the LORD was a witness to it.

[15]Hasn't the one God made the two of you one also? Both of you belong to him in body and spirit. And why has the one God made you one? Because he wants his children to be like him. So be careful. Don't be unfaithful to the wife you married when you were young.

[16]"Suppose a man hates and divorces his wife," says the LORD God of Israel. "Then he is harming the one he should protect," says the LORD who rules over all.

So be careful. And don't be unfaithful.

Breaking the Covenant by Treating Others Unfairly

[17]You have worn out the LORD by what you keep saying.

"How have we worn him out?" you ask.

You have done it by saying, "All those who do evil things are good in the LORD's sight. And he is pleased with them." Or you ask, "Is God really fair?"

3 The LORD who rules over all says, "I will send my messenger. He will prepare my way for me. Then suddenly the Lord you are looking for will come to his temple. The messenger of the covenant will come. He is the one you long for."

[2]But who can live through the day when he comes? Who will be left standing when he appears? He will be like a fire that makes

Mal. 3:1 Malachi is talking about Jesus here. It will be 400 years before John the Baptist announces Jesus' arrival in John 1:29 and Matthew 3:3. Malachi also mentions Jesus' showing up at the Temple, which happens in Luke 2:41–52.

things pure. He will be like soap that makes things clean. ³He will act like one who makes silver pure. And he will purify the Levites, just as gold and silver are purified with fire. Then these men will bring proper offerings to the LORD. ⁴And the offerings of Judah and Jerusalem will be acceptable to him. It will be as it was in days and years gone by.

⁵"So I will come and put you on trial. I will be quick to bring charges against all of you," says the LORD who rules over all. "I will bring charges against you sinful people who do not have any respect for me. That includes those who practice evil magic. It includes those who commit adultery and those who tell lies in court. It includes those who cheat workers out of their pay. It includes those who treat widows badly. It also includes those who mistreat children whose fathers have died. And it includes those who take away the rights of outsiders in the courts.

Breaking the Covenant by Stealing From God

⁶"I am the LORD. I do not change. That is why I have not destroyed you members of Jacob's family. ⁷You have turned away from my rules. You have not obeyed them. You have lived that way ever since the days of your people of long ago. Return to me. Then I will return to you," says the LORD who rules over all.

"But you ask, 'How can we return?'

⁸"Will a mere human being dare to steal from God? But you rob me!

"You ask, 'How are we robbing you?'

"By holding back your offerings. You also steal from me when you do not bring me a tenth of everything you produce. ⁹So you are under my curse. In fact, your whole nation is under my curse. That is because you are robbing me. ¹⁰Bring the entire tenth to the storerooms in my temple. Then there will be plenty of food. Test me this way," says the LORD. "Then you will see that I will throw open the windows of heaven. I will pour out so many blessings that you will not have enough room to store them. ¹¹I will keep bugs from eating up your crops. And your grapes will not drop from the vines before they are ripe," says the LORD. ¹²"Then all the nations will call you blessed. Your land will be delightful," says the LORD who rules over all.

Israel Speaks With Pride Against the LORD

¹³"You have spoken with pride against me," says the LORD.

"But you ask, 'What have we spoken against you?'

¹⁴"You have said, 'It is useless to serve God. What do we gain by obeying his laws? And what do we get by pretending to be sad in front of the LORD? ¹⁵But now we call proud people blessed. Things go well with those who do what is evil. And God doesn't even punish those who test him.'"

Jason's Jargon

MALACHI 3

At last, it's time for your final assignment! Sift through this chapter for the word *tenth*. God asked His people to give a tenth of what they produced back to the church.

Those Who Respect the LORD

¹⁶Those who had respect for the LORD talked with one another. And the LORD heard them. A list of people and what they did was written in a book in front of him. It included the names of those who respected the LORD and honored him.

¹⁷"The day is coming when I will judge," says the LORD who rules over all. "On that day they will be my special treasure. I will spare them just as a father loves and spares his son who serves him. ¹⁸Then once again you will see the difference between godly people and sinful people. And you will see the difference between those who serve me and those who do not.

The Day of the LORD Is Coming

4 "You can be sure the day of the LORD is coming. My anger will burn like a furnace. All those who are proud will be like straw. So will all those who do what is evil. The day that is coming will set them on fire," says the LORD who rules over all. "Not even a root or a branch will be left to them. ²But here is what will happen for you who

Mal. 4:5 The prophet Elijah is another sign that Jesus is coming. Turn to Matthew 11:14 to see how this prophecy turned out!

have respect for me. The sun that brings life will rise. Its rays will bring healing to my people. You will go out and leap for joy like calves that have just been fed. ³Then you will stomp on sinful people. They will be like ashes under your feet. That will happen on the day I judge," says the Lord.

⁴"Remember the law my servant Moses gave you. Remember the rules and laws I gave him at Mount Horeb. They were for the whole nation of Israel.

⁵"I will send the prophet Elijah to you. He will come before the day of the Lord arrives. It will be a great and terrifying day. ⁶Elijah will bring peace between parents and their children. He will also bring peace between children and their parents. If that does not happen, I will come. And I will completely destroy the land."

The New Testament

Greetings and salutations! Eugene here. If you've joined in for our epic journey through the Holy Scriptures by starting in the New Testament, I heartily bid you welcome. If you're continuing on after perusing the Old Testament, then I must with equal joy thank you for continuing on this most wonderful of treks.

I sincerely hope that you are as exhilarated about this step of our journey as I am! Though significantly shorter than the Old Testament, the New Testament seems to be bursting at the seams with important and fascinating content (proverbially speaking). There are so many wonderful stops and excursions ahead that our agenda is simply overflowing!

It begins with the four gospel narratives of Jesus' life and ministry on earth (Matthew, Mark, Luke, and John). The word "gospel" means "good news," which is certainly appropriate for these books! We then continue to a book of history (Acts), proceed though nearly two dozen letters (Romans through Jude), and reach our glorious conclusion with a book of prophecy about the end of the world (Revelation).

Along the way, we'll see stories of incredible miracles, resurrections from the dead, stormy shipwrecks, and so much more. Perhaps more importantly, you'll learn the actual words of Jesus and find out how to apply them to your life.

I'm veritably shaking with excitement! Join me, won't you, as we continue our epic journey!

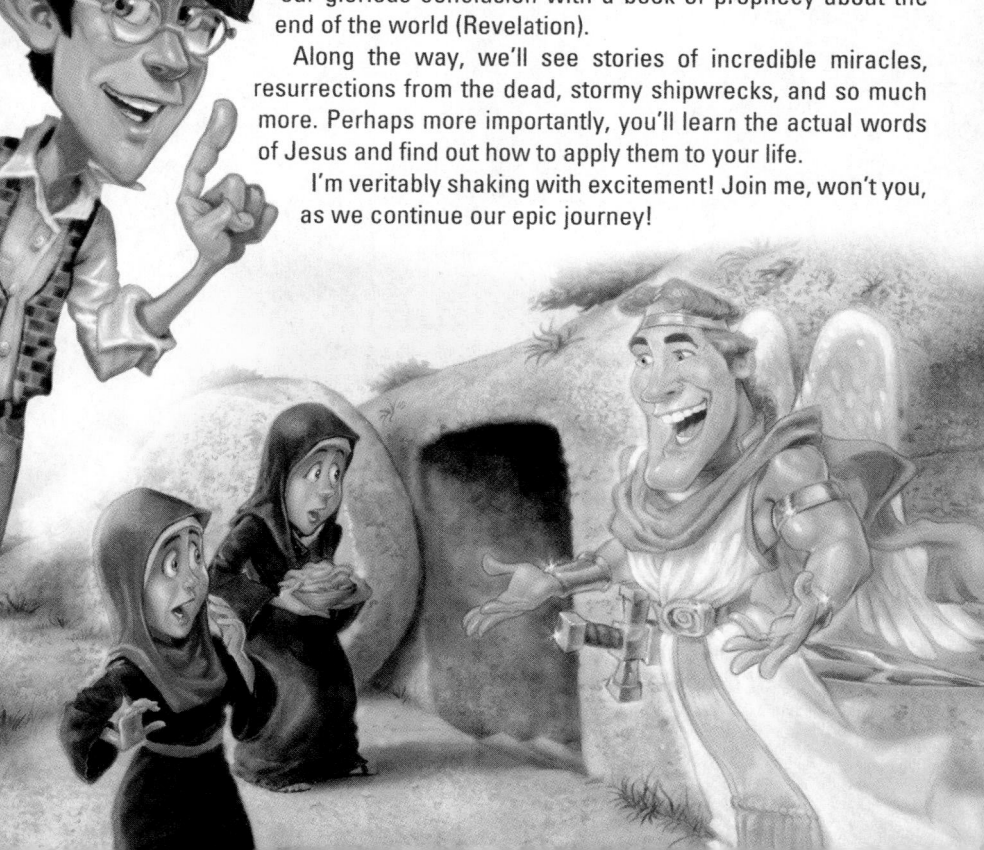

Matthew

Let's start with the name of this book: Matthew. To whom does it refer? Imagine this, if you will: On one occasion, when Jesus was teaching and healing, accompanied by some of His early disciples, they passed a tax booth. Jesus invited the man collecting taxes to follow Him, and Matthew immediately joined the other apostles (Matt. 9:9). That's how Matthew came to be a disciple and how now, centuries later, we have Matthew's eyewitness account of living and working with Jesus. Matthew provides the perspective of an "average" Jewish person in the first century. The Jews were under the rule of the Roman Empire, but they continued to look for the Messiah God had promised.

Matthew's narrative shares the wonderful news that the Messiah had indeed arrived. He tells the story from the birth of Jesus and visit of the wise men to Jesus' death and resurrection. He provides documentation of Jesus' Sermon on the Mount (chapters 5–7), which includes the Lord's Prayer (6:9–13). He also includes a notable assortment of Jesus' parables, teachings, and miracles.

If you've found the previous stops on our journey (such as the Minor Prophets) difficult to understand, you'll be pleased to dig in to the book of Matthew.

What's it Mean, Eugene?

Beatitudes—The Sermon on the Mount (Matthew chapters 5–7) is the longest continuous section of Jesus' teachings recorded in the New Testament. The Beatitudes are the beginning passages, or the "launching pad" to borrow the colloquialism, of that sermon. Here Jesus pronounces *blessings* on those who are poor in spirit, those who mourn, the meek, those who hunger and thirst for righteousness, the merciful, the pure in heart, peacemakers, and those who are persecuted for righteousness' sake. They are attributes to which we should all aspire.

The Family Line of Jesus the Messiah

1 This is the written story of the family line of Jesus the Messiah. He is the son of David. He is also the son of Abraham.

² Abraham was the father of Isaac.
Isaac was the father of Jacob.
Jacob was the father of Judah and his brothers.
³ Judah was the father of Perez and Zerah. Tamar was their mother.
Perez was the father of Hezron.
Hezron was the father of Ram.
⁴ Ram was the father of Amminadab.
Amminadab was the father of Nahshon.
Nahshon was the father of Salmon.
⁵ Salmon was the father of Boaz. Rahab was Boaz's mother.
Boaz was the father of Obed. Ruth was Obed's mother.
Obed was the father of Jesse.
⁶ And Jesse was the father of King David.

David was the father of Solomon. Solomon's mother had been Uriah's wife.
⁷ Solomon was the father of Rehoboam.
Rehoboam was the father of Abijah.
Abijah was the father of Asa.
⁸ Asa was the father of Jehoshaphat.
Jehoshaphat was the father of Jehoram.
Jehoram was the father of Uzziah.
⁹ Uzziah was the father of Jotham.
Jotham was the father of Ahaz.
Ahaz was the father of Hezekiah.
¹⁰ Hezekiah was the father of Manasseh.
Manasseh was the father of Amon.
Amon was the father of Josiah.
¹¹ And Josiah was the father of Jeconiah and his brothers. At that time, the Jewish people were forced to go away to Babylon.

¹² After this, the family line continued.
Jeconiah was the father of Shealtiel.
Shealtiel was the father of Zerubbabel.
¹³ Zerubbabel was the father of Abihud.
Abihud was the father of Eliakim.
Eliakim was the father of Azor.
¹⁴ Azor was the father of Zadok.
Zadok was the father of Akim.
Akim was the father of Elihud.

Matt. 1:20–25 Wow. Angel-sighting number one in the New Testament! A fulfilled prophecy from Isaiah 7:14! And a miracle baby—all in one passage!

¹⁵ Elihud was the father of Eleazar.
Eleazar was the father of Matthan.
Matthan was the father of Jacob.
¹⁶ Jacob was the father of Joseph. Joseph was the husband of Mary. And Mary was the mother of Jesus, who is called the Messiah.

¹⁷ So there were 14 generations from Abraham to David. There were 14 from David until the Jewish people were forced to go away to Babylon. And there were 14 from that time to the Messiah.

Joseph Accepts Jesus as His Son

¹⁸ This is how the birth of Jesus the Messiah came about. His mother Mary and Joseph had promised to get married. But before they started to live together, it became clear that she was going to have a baby. She became pregnant by the power of the Holy Spirit. ¹⁹ Her husband Joseph was faithful to the law. But he did not want to put her to shame in public. So he planned to divorce her quietly.

²⁰ But as Joseph was thinking about this, an angel of the Lord appeared to him in a dream. The angel said, "Joseph, son of David, don't be afraid to take Mary home as your wife. The baby inside her is from the Holy Spirit. ²¹ She is going to have a son. You must give him the name Jesus. That's because he will save his people from their sins."

²² All this took place to bring about what the Lord had said would happen. He had

said through the prophet, [23]"The virgin is going to have a baby. She will give birth to a son. And he will be called Immanuel." *(Isaiah 7:14)* The name Immanuel means "God with us."

[24]Joseph woke up. He did what the angel of the Lord commanded him to do. He took Mary home as his wife. [25]But he did not sleep with her until she gave birth to a son. And Joseph gave him the name Jesus.

The Wise Men Visit Jesus

2 Jesus was born in Bethlehem in Judea. This happened while Herod was king of Judea. After Jesus' birth, Wise Men from the east came to Jerusalem. [2]They asked, "Where is the child who has been born to be king of the Jews? We saw his star when it rose. Now we have come to worship him."

[3]When King Herod heard about it, he was very upset. Everyone in Jerusalem was troubled too. [4]So Herod called together all the chief priests of the people. He also called the teachers of the law. He asked them where the Messiah was going to be born. [5]"In Bethlehem in Judea," they replied. "This is what the prophet has written. He said,

[6] " 'But you, Bethlehem, in the land of Judah,
are certainly not the least important among the towns of Judah.
A ruler will come out of you.
He will rule my people Israel like a shepherd.' "   *(Micah 5:2)*

[7]Then Herod secretly called for the Wise Men. He found out from them exactly when the star had appeared. [8]He sent them to Bethlehem. He said, "Go and search carefully for the child. As soon as you find him, report it to me. Then I can go and worship him too."

[9]After the Wise Men had listened to the king, they went on their way. The star they had seen when it rose went ahead of them.

It finally stopped over the place where the child was. [10]When they saw the star, they were filled with joy. [11]The Wise Men went to the house. There they saw the child with his mother Mary. They bowed down and worshiped him. Then they opened their treasures. They gave him gold, frankincense and myrrh. [12]But God warned them in a dream not to go back to Herod. So they returned to their country on a different road.

Jesus' Family Escapes to Egypt

[13]When the Wise Men had left, Joseph had a dream. In the dream an angel of the Lord appeared to Joseph. "Get up!" the angel said. "Take the child and his mother and escape to Egypt. Stay there until I tell you to come back. Herod is going to search for the child. He wants to kill him."

[14]So Joseph got up. During the night, he left for Egypt with the child and his mother Mary. [15]They stayed there until King Herod died. So the words the Lord had spoken through the prophet came true. He had said, "I brought my son out of Egypt." *(Hosea 11:1)*

[16]Herod realized that the Wise Men had tricked him. So he became very angry. He gave orders about Bethlehem and the area around it. He ordered all the boys two years

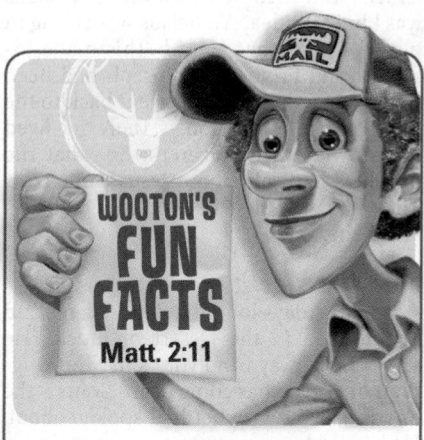

WOOTON'S FUN FACTS
Matt. 2:11

The wise men brought myrrh and frankincense to Jesus. Myrrh comes from a tree and could be used for medicine. Frankincense could be used to aid digestion and for skin care. Both of them have a strong scent. (Check out Exodus 30:34.)

BIBLE ADVENTURES

Eugene and Connie went on an Imagination Station adventure to see the visit of the Magi in "The Star" (A#12).

ADVENTURES IN ODYSSEY

Whit told the story of the Gift of the Magi (a famous tale by O. Henry) to show the true meaning of giving in "Gifts for Madge and Guy" (A#01).

old and under to be killed. This agreed with the time when the Wise Men had seen the star. [17]In this way, the words Jeremiah the prophet spoke came true. He had said,

[18] "A voice is heard in Ramah.
    It's the sound of crying and deep
        sadness.
Rachel is crying over her children.
    She refuses to be comforted,
    because they are gone."

(Jeremiah 31:15)

Jesus' Family Returns to Nazareth

[19]After Herod died, Joseph had a dream while he was still in Egypt. In the dream an angel of the Lord appeared to him. [20]The angel said, "Get up! Take the child and his mother. Go to the land of Israel. The people who were trying to kill the child are dead." [21]So Joseph got up. He took the child and his mother Mary back to the land of Israel. [22]But then he heard that Archelaus was king of Judea. Archelaus was ruling in place of his father Herod. This made Joseph afraid to go there. Joseph had been warned in a dream. So he went back to the land of Galilee instead. [23]There he lived in a town called Nazareth. So what the prophets had said about Jesus came true. They had said that he would be called a Nazarene.

John the Baptist Prepares the Way

3 In those days John the Baptist came and preached in the Desert of Judea. [2]He said, "Turn away from your sins! The kingdom of heaven has come near." [3]John is the one Isaiah the prophet had spoken about. He had said,

"A messenger is calling out in the
    desert,
'Prepare the way for the Lord.
    Make straight paths for him.'"

(Isaiah 40:3)

[4]John's clothes were made out of camel's hair. He had a leather belt around his waist. His food was locusts and wild honey. [5]People went out to him from Jerusalem and all Judea. They also came from the whole area around the Jordan River. [6]When they confessed their sins, John baptized them in the Jordan.

[7]John saw many Pharisees and Sadducees coming to where he was baptizing. He said to them, "You are like a nest of poisonous snakes! Who warned you to escape the coming of God's anger? [8]Live in a way that shows you have turned away from your sins. [9]Don't think you can say to yourselves, 'Abraham is our father.' I tell you, God can raise up children for Abraham even from these stones. [10]The ax is ready to cut the roots of the trees. All the trees that don't produce good fruit will be cut down. They will be thrown into the fire.

[11]"I baptize you with water, calling you to turn away from your sins. But after me, someone is coming who is more powerful than I am. I'm not worthy to carry his sandals. He will baptize you with the Holy Spirit and fire. [12]His pitchfork is in his hand to clear the straw from his threshing floor. He will gather his wheat into the storeroom. But he will burn up the husks with fire that can't be put out."

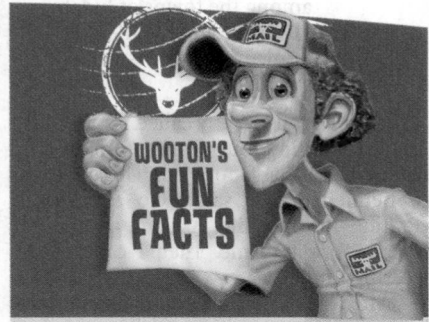

Matt. 3:4 Time for a recipe from Wooton's Gross Out Kitchen! Locusts are loaded with protein and could make a healthy dinner. Prepare them like french fries or boil them in soup. But be sure to snap off the heads or the dish may seem unappetizing. I mean, even more unappetizing than any meal made with locusts!

Jesus Is Baptized

[13]Jesus came from Galilee to the Jordan River. He wanted to be baptized by John. [14]But John tried to stop him. So he told Jesus, "I need to be baptized by you. So why do you come to me?"

[15]Jesus replied, "Let it be this way for now. It is right for us to do this. It carries out God's holy plan." Then John agreed.

[16]As soon as Jesus was baptized, he came up out of the water. At that moment heaven was opened. Jesus saw the Spirit of God coming down on him like a dove. [17]A voice from heaven said, "This is my Son, and I love him. I am very pleased with him."

Jesus Is Tempted in the Desert

The Holy Spirit led Jesus into the desert. There the devil tempted him. [2]After 40 days and 40 nights of going without eating, Jesus was hungry. [3]The tempter came to him. He said, "If you are the Son of God, tell these stones to become bread."

[4]Jesus answered, "It is written, 'Man must not live only on bread. He must also live on every word that comes from the mouth of God.'" *(Deuteronomy 8:3)*

[5]Then the devil took Jesus to the holy city. He had him stand on the highest point of the temple. [6]"If you are the Son of God," he said, "throw yourself down. It is written,

"'The Lord will command his angels to take good care of you.
They will lift you up in their hands.
Then you won't trip over a stone.'"

(Psalm 91:11,12)

[7]Jesus answered him, "It is also written, 'Do not test the Lord your God.'" *(Deuteronomy 6:16)*

[8]Finally, the devil took Jesus to a very high mountain. He showed him all the kingdoms of the world and their glory. [9]"If you bow down and worship me," he said, "I will give you all this."

[10]Jesus said to him, "Get away from me, Satan! It is written, 'Worship the Lord your God. He is the only one you should serve.'" *(Deuteronomy 6:13)*

[11]Then the devil left Jesus. Angels came and took care of him.

Jesus Begins to Preach

[12]John had been put in prison. When Jesus heard about this, he returned to Galilee. [13]Jesus left Nazareth and went to live in the city of Capernaum. It was by the lake in the area of Zebulun and Naphtali. [14]In that way, what the prophet Isaiah had said came true. He had said,

[15] "Land of Zebulun! Land of Naphtali!
Galilee, where Gentiles live!
Land along the Mediterranean Sea!
Territory east of the Jordan River!
[16] The people who are now living in darkness
have seen a great light.
They are now living in a very dark land.
But a light has shined on them."

(Isaiah 9:1, 2)

[17]From that time on Jesus began to preach. "Turn away from your sins!" he said. "The kingdom of heaven has come near."

Jesus Chooses His First Disciples

[18]One day Jesus was walking beside the Sea of Galilee. There he saw two brothers, Simon Peter and his brother Andrew. They were throwing a net into the lake, because they were fishermen. [19]"Come and follow me," Jesus said. "I will send you out to fish for people." [20]At once they left their nets and followed him.

[21]Going on from there, he saw two other brothers. They were James, son of Zebedee, and his brother John. They were in a boat with their father Zebedee. As they were preparing their nets, Jesus called out to them. [22]Right away they left the boat and their father and followed Jesus.

Jesus Heals Sick People

[23]Jesus went all over Galilee. There he taught in the synagogues. He preached the good news of God's kingdom. He healed every illness and sickness the people had. [24]News about him spread all over Syria. People brought to him all who were ill with different kinds of sicknesses. Some were suffering great pain. Others were controlled by demons. Some were shaking wildly. Others couldn't move at all. And Jesus healed all of them. [25]Large crowds followed him. People came from Galilee, from the area known as the Ten Cities, and from Jerusalem and Judea. Others came from the area across the Jordan River.

Jesus Teaches the Disciples and Crowds

5 Jesus saw the crowds. So he went up on a mountainside and sat down. His disciples came to him. ²Then he began to teach them.

Jesus Gives Blessings

He said,

³ "Blessed are those who are spiritually needy.
The kingdom of heaven belongs to them.
⁴ Blessed are those who are sad.
They will be comforted.
⁵ Blessed are those who are humble.
They will be given the earth.
⁶ Blessed are those who are hungry and thirsty for what is right.
They will be filled.
⁷ Blessed are those who show mercy.
They will be shown mercy.
⁸ Blessed are those whose hearts are pure.
They will see God.
⁹ Blessed are those who make peace.
They will be called children of God.
¹⁰ Blessed are those who suffer for doing what is right.
The kingdom of heaven belongs to them.

¹¹"Blessed are you when people make fun of you and hurt you because of me. You are also blessed when they tell all kinds of evil lies about you because of me. ¹²Be joyful and glad. Your reward in heaven is great. In the same way, people hurt the prophets who lived long ago.

Salt and Light

¹³"You are the salt of the earth. But suppose the salt loses its saltiness. How can it be made salty again? It is no longer good for anything. It will be thrown out. People will walk all over it.

¹⁴"You are the light of the world. A town built on a hill can't be hidden. ¹⁵Also, people do not light a lamp and put it under a bowl. Instead, they put it on its stand. Then it gives light to everyone in the house. ¹⁶In the same way, let your light shine so others can see it. Then they will see the good things you do. And they will bring glory to your Father who is in heaven.

Jesus Fulfills the Law

¹⁷"Do not think I have come to get rid of what is written in the Law or in the Prophets. I have not come to do this. Instead, I have come to fulfill what is written. ¹⁸What I'm about to tell you is true. Heaven and earth will disappear before the smallest

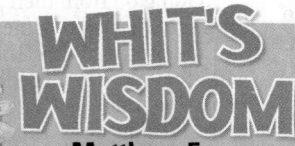

WHIT'S WISDOM

Matthew 5

Matthew was playing a portable video game at Whit's End, and apparently he was watching the screen and nothing else. When his sister Camilla asked if she could borrow some money for ice cream, Matthew just shrugged.

Camilla lightly tapped him on the shoulder, twice, and Matthew said, "Can't you see I'm busy? Don't bug me!"

Camilla took a deep breath and yelled so everyone could hear, "Matthew Parker, you've really got a beatitude!"

Matthew looked embarrassed, so he paused his game and got some money for Camilla. I had to smile. It wasn't right for Matthew to ignore Camilla or for Camilla to yell, but I had never heard the word "beatitude" used that way. After Camilla apologized and ordered a milkshake, I asked her what she meant. She said, "I heard about beatitudes at church and figured it was another way of saying 'bad attitude.' It saves you a few letters."

I explained that a beatitude is actually the *opposite* of a bad attitude. In Matthew 5:2–10, Jesus talks about the *good* attitudes (beatitudes) He wants us to have. Check out the list for yourself. Which ones apply to Matthew and Camilla's situation?

CANDID CONVERSATIONS

When Penny was my roommate, I got really mad at her for eating a piece of cake I'd left in the fridge. She didn't even ask me before having it for breakfast (and lunch)! I was so upset that I started thinking about creative ways to teach her a lesson. One idea involved baking a cake with lots of paprika. Then I realized that wouldn't help our friendship at all. It would only make her mad at me, and what good would that do? I decided that I had to let it go.

We can see in Matthew 5 that Jesus said harboring angry thoughts toward others is like committing murder! He taught it's not enough to make sure our actions are right. We need to make sure that our *thoughts* are right too. And we need to forgive each other.

Jesus didn't stop surprising us. He went on to talk about loving our *enemies*. It's not enough to just tolerate them or ignore them. God wants us to love them, no matter how hard that can be. Penny wasn't my enemy, but I still needed to love her—even though she took the cake!

Murder

²¹"You have heard what was said to people who lived long ago. They were told, 'Do not commit murder. *(Exodus 20:13)* Anyone who murders will be judged for it.' ²²But here is what I tell you. Do not be angry with a brother or sister. Anyone who is angry with them will be judged. Again, anyone who says to a brother or sister, 'Raca,' must stand trial in court. And anyone who says, 'You fool!' will be in danger of the fire in hell.

²³"Suppose you are offering your gift at the altar. And you remember that your brother or sister has something against you. ²⁴Leave your gift in front of the altar. First go and make peace with them. Then come back and offer your gift.

²⁵"Suppose someone has a claim against you and is taking you to court. Settle the matter quickly. Do this while you are still together on the way. If you don't, you may be handed over to the judge. The judge may hand you over to the officer to be thrown into prison. ²⁶What I'm about to tell you is true. You will not get out until you have paid the very last penny!

Adultery

²⁷"You have heard that it was said, 'Do not commit adultery.' *(Exodus 20:14)* ²⁸But here is what I tell you. Do not even look at a woman in the wrong way. Anyone who does has already committed adultery with her in his heart. ²⁹If your right eye causes you to sin, poke it out and throw it away. Your eye is only one part of your body. It is better to lose an eye than for your whole body to be thrown into hell. ³⁰If your right hand causes you to sin, cut it off and throw it away. Your hand is only one part of your body. It is better to lose a hand than for your whole body to go into hell.

letter disappears from the Law. Not even the smallest mark of a pen will disappear from the Law until everything is completed. ¹⁹Do not ignore even one of the least important commands. And do not teach others to ignore them. If you do, you will be called the least important person in the kingdom of heaven. Instead, practice and teach these commands. Then you will be called important in the kingdom of heaven. ²⁰Here is what I tell you. You must be more godly than the Pharisees and the teachers of the law. If you are not, you will certainly not enter the kingdom of heaven.

REMEMBER THIS

MATTHEW 5:16

"In the same way, let your light shine so others can see it. Then they will see the good things you do. And they will bring glory to your Father who is in heaven."

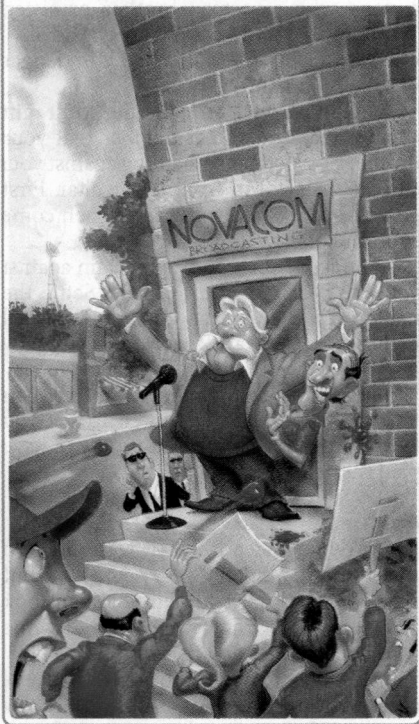

ADVENTURES IN ODYSSEY

Whit demonstrated loving his enemies when he tried to stop a riot at Novacom headquarters in "Green Eyes and Yellow Tulips" (A#36).

Divorce

³¹"It has been said, 'Suppose a man divorces his wife. If he does, he must give her a letter of divorce.' *(Deuteronomy 24:1)* ³²But here is what I tell you. Anyone who divorces his wife makes her a victim of adultery. And anyone who gets married to the divorced woman commits adultery. A man may divorce his wife only if she has not been faithful to him.

Promises

³³"Again, you have heard what was said to your people long ago. They were told, 'Do not break the promises you make to the Lord. Keep your promises to the Lord that you have made.' ³⁴But here is what I tell you. Do not make any promises like

that at all. Do not make them in the name of heaven. That is God's throne. ³⁵Do not make them in the name of the earth. That is the stool for God's feet. Do not make them in the name of Jerusalem. That is the city of the Great King. ³⁶And do not make a promise in your own name. You can't make even one hair of your head white or black. ³⁷All you need to say is simply 'Yes' or 'No.' Anything more than this comes from the evil one.

Be Kind to Others

³⁸"You have heard that it was said, 'An eye must be put out for an eye. A tooth must be knocked out for a tooth.' *(Exodus 21:24; Leviticus 24:20; Deuteronomy 19:21)* ³⁹But here is what I tell you. Do not fight against an evil person. Suppose someone slaps you on your right cheek. Turn your other cheek to them also. ⁴⁰Suppose someone takes you to court to get your shirt. Let them have your coat also. ⁴¹Suppose someone forces you to go one mile. Go two miles with them. ⁴²Give to the one who asks you for something. Don't turn away from the one who wants to borrow something from you.

Love Your Enemies

⁴³"You have heard that it was said, 'Love your neighbor. *(Leviticus 19:18)* Hate your enemy.' ⁴⁴But here is what I tell you. Love your enemies. Pray for those who hurt you. ⁴⁵Then you will be children of your Father who is in heaven. He causes his sun to shine on evil people and good people. He sends rain on those who do right and those who don't. ⁴⁶If you love those who love you, what reward will you get? Even the tax collectors do that. ⁴⁷If you greet only your own people, what more are you doing than others? Even people who are ungodly do that. ⁴⁸So be perfect, just as your Father in heaven is perfect.

Giving to Needy People

6 "Be careful not to do good deeds in front of other people. Don't do those deeds to be seen by others. If you do, your Father in heaven will not reward you.

²"When you give to needy people, do not announce it by having trumpets blown. Do not be like those who only pretend to be holy. They announce what they do in the synagogues and on the streets. They want to be honored by other people. What I'm

WHAT ABOUT YOU?

"Sure, Mason helped a little with the project, but I did most of the work."

"We only won because I caught that fly ball."

"Everyone else went outside to play, but I stayed to clear the table."

We like to get credit for our accomplishments, don't we? The work we do. The talents we display. The sacrifices we make.

God's Word warns us not to crave recognition from others. As we read in Matthew 6:1, Jesus Himself says: "Be careful not to do good deeds in front of other people. Don't do those deeds to be seen by others. If you do, your Father in heaven will not reward you."

Do you like doing positive things so that people see how smart, helpful, or talented you are? That attention might last for a little while, but it won't last as long as the kudos we'll receive from God for doing the right things for the right reason: honoring Him.

Write a note or leave a small gift for someone who needs encouragement, but don't sign your name. Give yourself a secret identity, such as "The Encourager." Then quietly enjoy the simple reward of making someone else's day special . . . and pleasing God.

---

about to tell you is true. They have received their complete reward. ³When you give to needy people, don't let your left hand know what your right hand is doing. ⁴Then your giving will be done secretly. Your Father will reward you, because he sees what you do secretly.

Prayer

⁵"When you pray, do not be like those who only pretend to be holy. They love to stand and pray in the synagogues and on the street corners. They want to be seen by other people. What I'm about to tell you is true. They have received their complete reward. ⁶When you pray, go into your room. Close the door and pray to your Father, who can't be seen. Your Father will reward you, because he sees what you do secretly. ⁷When you pray, do not keep talking on and on. That is what ungodly people do. They think they will be heard because they talk a lot. ⁸Do not be like them. Your Father knows what you need even before you ask him.

⁹"This is how you should pray.

"'Our Father in heaven,
    may your name be honored.
¹⁰ May your kingdom come.
    May what you want to happen be done
        on earth as it is done in heaven.
¹¹ Give us today our daily bread.
¹² And forgive us our sins,
    just as we also have forgiven those
        who sin against us.
¹³ Keep us from sinning when we are
        tempted.
    Save us from the evil one.'

¹⁴Forgive other people when they sin against you. If you do, your Father who is

REMEMBER THIS

MATTHEW 6:9-13

"Our Father in heaven, may your name be honored. May your kingdom come. May what you want to happen be done on earth as it is done in heaven. Give us today our daily bread. And forgive us our sins, just as we also have forgiven those who sin against us. Keep us from sinning when we are tempted. Save us from the evil one."

WOOTON'S FUN FACTS

Matt. 6:9–13 This whole prayer has fewer than seventy words and it would take less than a minute to say. Now I'm going to pray it every day whenever I have an extra minute. (But instead of daily bread, I'm going to ask for candy corn.)

in heaven will also forgive you. ¹⁵But if you do not forgive the sins of other people, your Father will not forgive your sins.

Fasting

¹⁶"When you go without eating, do not look gloomy like those who only pretend to be holy. They make their faces look very sad. They want to show people they are fasting. What I'm about to tell you is true. They have received their complete reward. ¹⁷But when you go without eating, put olive oil on your head. Wash your face. ¹⁸Then others will not know that you are fasting. Only your Father, who can't be seen, will know it. Your Father will reward you, because he sees what you do secretly.

Gather Riches in Heaven

¹⁹"Do not gather for yourselves riches on earth. Moths and rats can destroy them. Thieves can break in and steal them. ²⁰Instead, gather for yourselves riches in heaven. There, moths and rats do not destroy them. There, thieves do not break in and

steal them. ²¹Your heart will be where your riches are.

²²"The eye is like a lamp for the body. Suppose your eyes are healthy. Then your whole body will be full of light. ²³But suppose your eyes can't see well. Then your whole body will be full of darkness. If the light inside you is darkness, then it is very dark!

²⁴"No one can serve two masters at the same time. You will hate one of them and love the other. Or you will be faithful to one and dislike the other. You can't serve God and money at the same time.

Do Not Worry

²⁵"I tell you, do not worry. Don't worry about your life and what you will eat or drink. And don't worry about your body and what you will wear. Isn't there more to life than eating? Aren't there more important things for the body than clothes? ²⁶Look at the birds of the air. They don't plant or gather crops. They don't put away crops in storerooms. But your Father who is in heaven feeds them. Aren't you worth much more than they are? ²⁷Can you add even one hour to your life by worrying?

²⁸"And why do you worry about clothes? See how the wild flowers grow. They don't work or make clothing. ²⁹But here is what I tell you. Not even Solomon in all his royal robes was dressed like one of these flowers. ³⁰If that is how God dresses the wild grass, won't he dress you even better? Your faith is so small! After all, the grass is here only today. Tomorrow it is thrown into the fire. ³¹So don't worry. Don't say, 'What will we eat?' Or, 'What will we drink?' Or, 'What will we wear?' ³²People who are ungodly run after all those things. Your Father who is in heaven knows that you need them. ³³But put God's kingdom first. Do what he wants you to do. Then all those things will also be given to you. ³⁴So don't worry about tomorrow. Tomorrow will worry about itself. Each day has enough trouble of its own.

Be Fair When You Judge Other People

7 "Do not judge other people. Then you will not be judged. ²You will be judged in the same way you judge others. You will be measured in the same way you measure others.

³"You look at the bit of sawdust in your friend's eye. But you pay no attention to the

WHIT'S WISDOM

Matthew 7

The building that is now Whit's End is more than 100 years old. Originally built to be the mayor's house, today it's an ice cream and discovery emporium! The building has lasted a long time, but not every building lasts so long. Some fall down before they get as old as you are! Why do some stay and some fall? One big reason involves how and where they are built. It's something that the Bible talks about again and again: Whatever we're building, it's important to have a good foundation.

In Matthew 7:24, Jesus said that *people* are like buildings. Those who listened to His words were like builders who put a house on rock—a good foundation. They would last for a long time like the Whit's End building! Those who didn't follow His words were like builders who put houses on sand—a bad foundation. Their houses would fall like a sand castle. And the same would happen to Whit's End if it didn't have a solid foundation—it would fall apart!

Just like buildings, our faith needs to have a strong foundation. And Jesus explains that the right foundation begins with following His words.

piece of wood in your own eye. [4]How can you say to your friend, 'Let me take the bit of sawdust out of your eye'? How can you say this while there is a piece of wood in your own eye? [5]You pretender! First take the piece of wood out of your own eye. Then you will be able to see clearly to take the bit of sawdust out of your friend's eye.

[6]"Do not give holy things to dogs. Do not throw your pearls to pigs. If you do, they might walk all over them. They might turn around and tear you to pieces.

Ask, Search, Knock

[7]"Ask, and it will be given to you. Search, and you will find. Knock, and the door will be opened to you. [8]Everyone who asks will receive. The one who searches will find. The door will be opened to the one who knocks. [9]"Suppose your son asks for bread. Which of you will give him a stone? [10]Or suppose he asks for a fish. Which of you will give him a snake? [11]Even though you are evil, you know how to give good gifts to your children. How much more will your Father who is in heaven give good gifts to those who ask him! [12]In everything, do to others what you would want them to do to you. This is what is written in the Law and in the Prophets.

The Large and Small Gates

[13]"Enter God's kingdom through the narrow gate. The gate is large and the road

Last summer, Eugene and I had a sandcastle-building contest at Trickle Lake. He even sketched out blueprints! "It's a highly functional, Chicago School skyscraper," he explained.

As the day wore on, I crafted spiraling turrets, gravity-defying arches, and a waterslide that flowed into a free-form pool. Suddenly there was a crack of thunder. We both frowned as rain started falling. The storm passed, but the damage was done. Our castles had collapsed into sandy blobs.

We had to laugh. It reminded me of Matthew 7:26–27: "Everyone who hears my words and does not put them into practice is like a foolish man. He builds his house on sand. The rain comes down . . . And it falls with a loud crash."

If we don't build our lives on Jesus, it doesn't matter how great we look because we'll just end up like sandy blobs. It's a good reminder to focus on building our lives on the Rock of Jesus, not on the shifting sands of this world.

is wide that leads to ruin. Many people go that way. [14]But the gate is small and the road is narrow that leads to life. Only a few people find it.

True and False Prophets

[15]"Watch out for false prophets. They come to you pretending to be sheep. But on the inside they are hungry wolves. [16]You can tell each tree by its fruit. Do people pick grapes from bushes? Do they pick figs from thorns? [17]In the same way, every good tree bears good fruit. But a bad tree bears bad fruit. [18]A good tree can't bear bad fruit. And a bad tree can't bear good fruit. [19]Every tree that does not bear good fruit is cut down. It is thrown into the fire. [20]You can tell each tree by its fruit.

True and False Disciples

[21]"Not everyone who says to me, 'Lord, Lord,' will enter the kingdom of heaven. Only those who do what my Father in heaven wants will enter. [22]Many will say to me on that day, 'Lord! Lord! Didn't we prophesy in your name? Didn't we drive out demons in your name? Didn't we do many miracles in your name?' [23]Then I will tell them clearly, 'I never knew you. Get away from me, you who do evil!'

The Wise and Foolish Builders

[24]"So then, everyone who hears my words and puts them into practice is like a wise man. He builds his house on the rock. [25]The rain comes down. The water rises. The winds blow and beat against that house. But it does not fall. It is built on the rock. [26]But everyone who hears my words and does not put them into practice is like a foolish man. He builds his house on sand. [27]The rain comes down. The water rises. The winds blow and beat against that house. And it falls with a loud crash."

[28]Jesus finished saying all these things. The crowds were amazed at his teaching. [29]That's because he taught like one who had authority. He did not speak like their teachers of the law.

Jesus Heals a Man Who Had a Skin Disease

Jesus came down from the mountainside. Large crowds followed him. [2]A man who had a skin disease came and got down on his knees in front of Jesus. He said, "Lord, if you are willing to make me 'clean,' you can do it."

³Jesus reached out his hand and touched the man. "I am willing to do it," he said. "Be 'clean'!" Right away the man was healed of his skin disease. ⁴Then Jesus said to him, "Don't tell anyone. Go and show yourself to the priest, and offer the gift Moses commanded. It will be a witness to everyone."

A Roman Commander Has Faith

⁵When Jesus entered Capernaum, a Roman commander came to him. He asked Jesus for help. ⁶"Lord," he said, "my servant lies at home and can't move. He is suffering terribly."

⁷Jesus said, "Shall I come and heal him?"

⁸The commander replied, "Lord, I am not good enough to have you come into my house. But just say the word, and my servant will be healed. ⁹I myself am a man under authority. And I have soldiers who obey my orders. I tell this one, 'Go,' and he goes. I tell that one, 'Come,' and he comes. I say to my slave, 'Do this,' and he does it."

¹⁰When Jesus heard this, he was amazed. He said to those following him, "What I'm about to tell you is true. In Israel I have not found anyone whose faith is so strong. ¹¹I say to you that many will come from the east and the west. They will take their places at the feast in the kingdom of heaven. They will sit with Abraham, Isaac and Jacob. ¹²But those who think they belong in the kingdom will be thrown outside, into the darkness. There they will weep and grind their teeth."

¹³Then Jesus said to the Roman commander, "Go! It will be done just as you believed it would." And his servant was healed at that moment.

Jesus Heals Many People

¹⁴When Jesus came into Peter's house, he saw Peter's mother-in-law. She was lying in bed. She had a fever. ¹⁵Jesus touched her hand, and the fever left her. She got up and began to serve him.

¹⁶When evening came, many people controlled by demons were brought to Jesus. He drove out the spirits with a word. He healed all who were sick. ¹⁷This happened so that what Isaiah the prophet had said would come true. He had said,

"He suffered the things we should have suffered.
He took on himself the sicknesses that should have been ours."
(Isaiah 53:4)

The Cost of Following Jesus

¹⁸Jesus saw the crowd around him. So he gave his disciples orders to go to the other side of the Sea of Galilee. ¹⁹Then a teacher of the law came to him. He said, "Teacher, I will follow you no matter where you go."

²⁰Jesus replied, "Foxes have dens. Birds have nests. But the Son of Man has no place to lay his head."

²¹Another follower said to him, "Lord, first let me go and bury my father."

²²But Jesus told him, "Follow me. Let the dead bury their own dead."

Jesus Calms the Storm

²³Jesus got into a boat. His disciples followed him. ²⁴Suddenly a terrible storm came up on the lake. The waves crashed over the boat. But Jesus was sleeping. ²⁵The disciples went and woke him up. They said, "Lord! Save us! We're going to drown!"

²⁶He replied, "Your faith is so small! Why are you so afraid?" Then Jesus got up and ordered the winds and the waves to stop. It became completely calm.

²⁷The disciples were amazed. They asked, "What kind of man is this? Even the winds and the waves obey him!"

Jesus Heals Two Men Controlled by Demons

²⁸Jesus arrived at the other side of the lake in the area of the Gadarenes. Two men controlled by demons met him. They came from the tombs. The men were so wild that no one could pass that way. ²⁹"Son of God, what do you want with us?" they shouted. "Have you come here to punish us before the time for us to be judged?"

³⁰Not very far away, a large herd of pigs was feeding. ³¹The demons begged Jesus, "If you drive us out, send us into the herd of pigs."

³²Jesus said to them, "Go!" So the demons came out of the men and went into the pigs. The whole herd rushed down the steep bank. They ran into the lake and drowned in the water. ³³Those who were tending the pigs ran off. They went into the

town and reported all this. They told the people what had happened to the men who had been controlled by demons. [34]Then the whole town went out to meet Jesus. When they saw him, they begged him to leave their area.

Jesus Forgives and Heals a Man Who Could Not Walk

Jesus stepped into a boat. He went over to the other side of the lake and came to his own town. [2]Some men brought to him a man who could not walk. He was lying on a mat. Jesus saw that they had faith. So he said to the man, "Don't lose hope, son. Your sins are forgiven."

[3]Then some teachers of the law said to themselves, "This fellow is saying a very evil thing!"

[4]Jesus knew what they were thinking. So he said, "Why do you have evil thoughts in your hearts? [5]Is it easier to say, 'Your sins are forgiven'? Or to say, 'Get up and walk'? [6]But I want you to know that the Son of Man has authority on earth to forgive sins." So he spoke to the man who could not walk. "Get up," he said. "Take your mat and go home." [7]The man got up and went home. [8]When the crowd saw this, they were filled with wonder. They praised God for giving that kind of authority to a human being.

Jesus Chooses Matthew and Eats With Sinners

[9]As Jesus went on from there, he saw a man named Matthew. He was sitting at the tax collector's booth. "Follow me," Jesus told him. Matthew got up and followed him.

[10]Later Jesus was having dinner at Matthew's house. Many tax collectors and sinners came. They ate with Jesus and his disciples. [11]The Pharisees saw this. So they asked the disciples, "Why does your teacher eat with tax collectors and sinners?"

[12]Jesus heard this. So he said, "Those who are healthy don't need a doctor. Sick people do. [13]Go and learn what this means, 'I want mercy and not sacrifice.' (Hosea 6:6) I have not come to get those who think they are right with God to follow me. I have come to get sinners to follow me."

Jesus Is Asked About Fasting

[14]One day John's disciples came. They said to Jesus, "We and the Pharisees often go without eating. Why don't your disciples go without eating?"

[15]Jesus answered, "How can the guests of the groom be sad while he is with them? The time will come when the groom will be taken away from them. Then they will fast.

[16]"People don't sew a patch of new cloth on old clothes. The new piece will pull away from the old. That will make the tear worse. [17]People don't pour new wine into old wineskins. If they do, the skins will burst. The wine will run out, and the wineskins will be destroyed. No, people pour new wine into new wineskins. Then both are saved."

Jesus Heals a Dead Girl and a Suffering Woman

[18]While Jesus was saying this, a synagogue leader came. He got down on his knees in front of Jesus. He said, "My daughter has just died. But come and place your hand on her. Then she will live again." [19]Jesus got up and went with him. So did his disciples.

[20]Just then a woman came up behind Jesus. She had a sickness that made her bleed. It had lasted for 12 years. She touched the edge of his clothes. [21]She thought, "I only need to touch his clothes. Then I will be healed."

[22]Jesus turned and saw her. "Dear woman, don't give up hope," he said. "Your faith has healed you." The woman was healed at that moment.

[23]When Jesus entered the synagogue leader's house, he saw the noisy crowd and people playing flutes. [24]He said, "Go away. The girl is not dead. She is sleeping." But they laughed at him. [25]After the crowd had been sent outside, Jesus went in. He took the girl by the hand, and she got up. [26]News about what Jesus had done spread all over that area.

Jesus Heals Two Blind Men

[27]As Jesus went on from there, two blind men followed him. They called out, "Have mercy on us, Son of David!"

[28]When Jesus went indoors, the blind men came to him. He asked them, "Do you believe that I can do this?"

"Yes, Lord," they replied.

[29]Then he touched their eyes. He said, "It will happen to you just as you believed." [30]They could now see again. Jesus strongly

warned them, "Be sure that no one knows about this." [31]But they went out and spread the news. They talked about him all over that area.

[32]While they were going out, another man was brought to Jesus. A demon controlled him, and he could not speak. [33]When the demon was driven out, the man spoke. The crowd was amazed. They said, "Nothing like this has ever been seen in Israel."

[34]But the Pharisees said, "He drives out demons by the power of the prince of demons."

There Are Only a Few Workers

[35]Jesus went through all the towns and villages. He taught in their synagogues. He preached the good news of the kingdom. And he healed every illness and sickness. [36]When he saw the crowds, he felt deep concern for them. They were treated badly and were helpless, like sheep without a shepherd. [37]Then Jesus said to his disciples, "The harvest is huge. But there are only a few workers. [38]So ask the Lord of the harvest to send workers out into his harvest field."

Jesus Sends Out the Twelve Disciples

10 Jesus called for his 12 disciples to come to him. He gave them authority to drive out evil spirits and to heal every illness and sickness.

[2] Here are the names of the 12 apostles.

First there were Simon Peter and his brother Andrew.
Then came James, son of Zebedee, and his brother John.
[3] Next were Philip and Bartholomew, and also Thomas and Matthew the tax collector.
Two more were James, son of Alphaeus, and Thaddaeus.
[4] The last were Simon the Zealot and Judas Iscariot. Judas was the one who was later going to hand Jesus over to his enemies.

[5]Jesus sent these 12 out with the following orders. "Do not go among the Gentiles," he said. "Do not enter any town of the Samaritans. [6]Instead, go to the people of Israel. They are like sheep that have become lost. [7]As you go, preach this message, 'The kingdom of heaven has come near.' [8]Heal those who are sick. Bring those who are dead back to life. Make those who have skin diseases 'clean' again. Drive out demons. You have received freely, so give freely.

[9]"Do not get any gold, silver or copper to take with you in your belts. [10]Do not take a bag for the journey. Do not take extra clothes or sandals or walking sticks. A worker should be given what he needs. [11]When you enter a town or village, look for someone who is willing to welcome you. Stay at their house until you leave. [12]As you enter the home, greet those who live there. [13]If that home welcomes you, give it your blessing of peace. If it does not, don't bless it. [14]Some people may not welcome you or listen to your words. If they don't, leave that home or town, and shake the dust off your feet. [15]What I'm about to tell you is true. On judgment day it will be easier for Sodom and Gomorrah than for that town.

[16]"I am sending you out like sheep among wolves. So be as wise as snakes and as harmless as doves. [17]Watch out! You will be handed over to the local courts. You will be whipped in the synagogues. [18]You will be brought to governors and kings because of me. You will be witnesses to them and to the Gentiles. [19]But when they arrest you, don't worry about what you will say or how you will say it. At that time you will be given the right words to say. [20]It will not be you speaking. The Spirit of your Father will be speaking through you.

[21]"Brothers will hand over brothers to be killed. Fathers will hand over their children. Children will rise up against their parents and have them put to death. [22]You will be hated by everyone because of me. But anyone who remains strong in the faith will be saved. [23]When people attack you in one place, escape to another. What I'm about to tell you is true. You will not finish going through the towns of Israel before the Son of Man comes.

[24]"The student is not better than the teacher. A slave is not better than his master. [25]It is enough for students to be like their teachers. And it is enough for slaves to be like their masters. If the head of the house has been called Beelzebul, what can the others who live there expect?

[26]"So don't be afraid of your enemies. Everything that is secret will be brought

Camilla Parker learned about the sparrows and even adopted a bird in "For the Birds" (A#51). When the birds attacked Eugene, he decided to let Connie shave his head.

out into the open. Everything that is hidden will be uncovered. ²⁷What I tell you in the dark, speak in the daylight. What is whispered in your ear, shout from the rooftops. ²⁸Do not be afraid of those who kill the body but can't kill the soul. Instead, be afraid of the one who can destroy both soul and body in hell. ²⁹Aren't two sparrows sold for only a penny? But not one of them falls to the ground outside your Father's care. ³⁰He even counts every hair on your head! ³¹So don't be afraid. You are worth more than many sparrows.

³²"What if someone says in front of others that they know me? I will also say in front of my Father who is in heaven that I know them. ³³But what if someone says in front of others that they don't know me? I will say in front of my Father who is in heaven that I don't know them.

³⁴"Do not think that I came to bring peace to the earth. I didn't come to bring peace. I came to bring a sword. ³⁵I have come to turn

" 'sons against their fathers.
     Daughters will refuse to obey their
         mothers.
Daughters-in-law will be against their
         mothers-in-law.
³⁶   A man's enemies will be the
         members of his own family.'
                  (Micah 7:6)

³⁷"Anyone who loves their father or mother more than me is not worthy of me.

Anyone who loves their son or daughter more than me is not worthy of me. ³⁸Whoever does not pick up their cross and follow me is not worthy of me. ³⁹Whoever finds their life will lose it. Whoever loses their life because of me will find it.

⁴⁰"Anyone who welcomes you welcomes me. And anyone who welcomes me welcomes the one who sent me. ⁴¹Suppose someone welcomes a prophet as a prophet. They will receive a prophet's reward. And suppose someone welcomes a godly person as a godly person. They will receive a godly person's reward. ⁴²Suppose someone gives even a cup of cold water to a little one who follows me. What I'm about to tell you is true. That person will certainly be rewarded."

Jesus and John the Baptist

11 Jesus finished teaching his 12 disciples. Then he went on to teach and preach in the towns of Galilee.

²John the Baptist was in prison. When he heard about the actions of the Messiah, he sent his disciples to him. ³They asked Jesus, "Are you the one who is supposed to come? Or should we look for someone else?"

⁴Jesus replied, "Go back to John. Report to him what you hear and see. ⁵Blind people receive sight. Disabled people walk. Those who have skin diseases are made 'clean.' Deaf people hear. Those who are dead are raised to life. And the good news is preached to those who are poor. ⁶Blessed is anyone who does not give up their faith because of me."

⁷As John's disciples were leaving, Jesus began to speak to the crowd about John. He said, "What did you go out into the desert to see? Tall grass waving in the wind? ⁸If not, what did you go out to see? A man dressed in fine clothes? No. People who wear fine clothes are in kings' palaces. ⁹Then what did you go out to see? A prophet? Yes, I tell you, and more than a prophet. ¹⁰He is the one written about in Scripture. It says,

" 'I will send my messenger ahead of
     you.
     He will prepare your way for you.'
                  (Malachi 3:1)

¹¹What I'm about to tell you is true. No one more important than John the Baptist has ever been born. But the least important person in the kingdom of heaven is more

important than he is. ¹²Since the days of John the Baptist, the kingdom of heaven has been under attack. And violent people are taking hold of it. ¹³All the Prophets and the Law prophesied until John came. ¹⁴If you are willing to accept it, John is the Elijah who was supposed to come. ¹⁵Whoever has ears should listen.

¹⁶"What can I compare today's people to? They are like children sitting in the markets and calling out to others. They say,

¹⁷ " 'We played the flute for you.
   But you didn't dance.
We sang a funeral song.
   But you didn't become sad.'

¹⁸When John came, he didn't eat or drink as you do. And people say, 'He has a demon.' ¹⁹But when the Son of Man came, he ate and drank as you do. And people say, 'This fellow is always eating and drinking far too much. He's a friend of tax collectors and "sinners." ' By wise actions wisdom is shown to be right."

Towns That Do Not Turn Away From Sin

²⁰Jesus began to speak against the towns where he had done most of his miracles. The people there had not turned away from their sins. So he said, ²¹"How terrible it will be for you, Chorazin! How terrible for you, Bethsaida! Suppose the miracles done in you had been done in Tyre and Sidon. They would have turned away from their sins long ago. They would have put on clothes for mourning. They would have sat down in ashes. ²²But I tell you this. On judgment day it will be easier for Tyre and Sidon than for you. ²³And what about you, Capernaum? Will you be lifted to the heavens? No! You will go down to the place of the dead. Suppose the miracles done in you had been done in Sodom. It would still be here today. ²⁴But I tell you this. On judgment day it will be easier for Sodom than for you."

Rest for All Who Are Tired

²⁵At that time Jesus said, "I praise you, Father. You are Lord of heaven and earth. You have hidden these things from wise and educated people. But you have shown them to little children. ²⁶Yes, Father. This is what you wanted to do.

²⁷"My Father has given all things to me. The Father is the only one who knows the Son. And the only ones who know the Father are the Son and those to whom the Son chooses to make him known.

²⁸"Come to me, all you who are tired and are carrying heavy loads. I will give you rest. ²⁹Become my servants and learn from me. I am gentle and free of pride. You will find rest for your souls. ³⁰Serving me is easy, and my load is light."

Jesus Is Lord of the Sabbath Day

12 One Sabbath day Jesus walked through the grainfields. His disciples were hungry. So they began to break off some heads of grain and eat them. ²The Pharisees saw this. They said to Jesus, "Look! It is against the Law to do this on the Sabbath day. But your disciples are doing it anyway!"

³Jesus answered, "Haven't you read about what David did? He and his men were hungry. ⁴So he entered the house of God. He and his men ate the holy bread. Only priests were allowed to eat it. ⁵Haven't you read the Law? It tells how every Sabbath day the priests in the temple have to do their work on that day. But they are not considered guilty. ⁶I tell you that something more important than the temple is here. ⁷Scripture says, 'I want mercy and not sacrifice.' *(Hosea 6:6)* You don't know what those words mean. If you did, you would not bring charges against those who are not guilty. ⁸The Son of Man is Lord of the Sabbath day."

⁹Going on from that place, Jesus went into their synagogue. ¹⁰A man with a weak and twisted hand was there. The Pharisees were trying to accuse Jesus of a crime. So they asked him, "Does the Law allow us to heal on the Sabbath day?"

¹¹He said to them, "What if one of your sheep falls into a pit on the Sabbath day? Won't you take hold of it and lift it out? ¹²A person is worth more than sheep! So the Law allows us to do good on the Sabbath day."

¹³Then Jesus said to the man, "Stretch out your hand." So he stretched it out. It had been made as good as new. It was just as good as the other hand. ¹⁴But the Pharisees went out and planned how to kill Jesus.

God's Chosen Servant

¹⁵Jesus knew all about the Pharisees' plans. So he left that place. A large crowd followed him, and he healed all who were sick. ¹⁶But he warned them not to tell other people about him. ¹⁷This was to make what was spoken through the prophet Isaiah come true. It says,

¹⁸ "Here is my servant. I have chosen him.
He is the one I love. I am very
pleased with him.
I will put my Spirit on him.
He will announce to the nations that
everything will be made right.
¹⁹ He will not argue or cry out.
No one will hear his voice in the
streets.
²⁰ He will not break a bent twig.
He will not put out a dimly burning
flame.
He will make right win over wrong.
²¹   The nations will put their hope in
him."   *(Isaiah 42:1–4)*

Jesus and Beelzebul

²²A man controlled by demons was brought to Jesus. The man was blind and could not speak. Jesus healed him. Then the man could speak and see. ²³All the people were amazed. They said, "Could this be the Son of David?"

²⁴The Pharisees heard this. So they said, "This fellow drives out demons by the power of Beelzebul, the prince of demons."

²⁵Jesus knew what they were thinking. So he said to them, "Every kingdom that fights against itself will be destroyed. Every city or family that is divided against itself will not stand. ²⁶If Satan drives out Satan, he fights against himself. Then how can his kingdom stand? ²⁷You say I drive out demons by the power of Beelzebul. Then by whose power do your people drive them out? So then, they will be your judges. ²⁸But suppose I drive out demons by the Spirit of God. Then the kingdom of God has come to you.

²⁹"Or think about this. How can you enter a strong man's house and just take what the man owns? You must first tie him up. Then you can rob his house.

³⁰"Anyone who is not with me is against me. Anyone who does not gather sheep with me scatters them. ³¹So here is what I tell you. Every kind of sin and every evil word spoken against God will be forgiven. But speaking evil things against the Holy Spirit will not be forgiven. ³²Anyone who speaks a word against the Son of Man will be forgiven. But anyone who speaks against the Holy Spirit will not be forgiven. A person like that won't be forgiven either now or in days to come.

³³"If you make a tree good, its fruit will be good. If you make a tree bad, its fruit will be bad. You can tell a tree by its fruit. ³⁴You nest of poisonous snakes! How can you who are evil say anything good? Your mouths say everything that is in your hearts. ³⁵A good man says good things. These come from the good that is stored up inside him. An evil man says evil things. These come from the evil that is stored up inside him. ³⁶But here is what I tell you. On judgment day, everyone will have to account for every empty word they have spoken. ³⁷By your words you will be found guilty or not guilty."

The Sign of Jonah

³⁸Some of the Pharisees and the teachers of the law came to Jesus. They said, "Teacher, we want to see a sign from you."

³⁹He answered, "Evil and unfaithful people ask for a sign! But none will be given except the sign of the prophet Jonah. ⁴⁰Jonah was in the belly of a huge fish for three days and three nights. Something like that will happen to the Son of Man. He will spend three days and three nights in the grave. ⁴¹The men of Nineveh will stand up on judgment day with the people now living. And the Ninevites will prove that these people are guilty. The men of Nineveh turned away from their sins when Jonah preached to them. And now something more important than Jonah is here. ⁴²The Queen of the South will stand up on judgment day with the people now living. And she will prove that they are guilty. She came from very far away to listen to Solomon's wisdom. And now something more important than Solomon is here.

⁴³"What happens when an evil spirit comes out of a person? It goes through dry areas looking for a place to rest. But it doesn't find it. ⁴⁴Then it says, 'I will return to the house I left.' When it arrives there, it finds the house empty. The house has been swept clean and put in order. ⁴⁵Then the evil spirit goes and takes with it seven other spirits more evil than itself. They go

ADVENTURES IN ODYSSEY

The folks in Odyssey put on an Old West show to retell Jesus' story of the evil spirits from Matthew 12 in "Legacy" (A#62).

in and live there. That person is worse off than before. That is how it will be with the evil people of today."

Jesus' Mother and Brothers

⁴⁶While Jesus was still talking to the crowd, his mother and brothers stood outside. They wanted to speak to him. ⁴⁷Someone told him, "Your mother and brothers are standing outside. They want to speak to you."

⁴⁸Jesus replied to him, "Who is my mother? And who are my brothers?" ⁴⁹Jesus pointed to his disciples. He said, "Here is my mother! Here are my brothers! ⁵⁰Anyone who does what my Father in heaven wants is my brother or sister or mother."

The Story of the Farmer

13 That same day Jesus left the house and sat by the Sea of Galilee. ²Large crowds gathered around him. So he got into a boat and sat down. All the people stood on the shore. ³Then he told them many things using stories. He said, "A farmer went out to plant his seed. ⁴He scattered the seed on the ground. Some fell on a path. Birds came and ate it up. ⁵Some seed fell on rocky places, where there wasn't much soil. The plants came up quickly, because the soil wasn't deep. ⁶When the sun came up, it burned the plants. They dried up because they had no roots. ⁷Other seed fell among thorns. The thorns grew up and crowded out the plants. ⁸Still other seed fell on good soil. It produced a crop 100, 60 or 30 times more than what was planted. ⁹Whoever has ears should listen."

¹⁰The disciples came to him. They asked, "Why do you use stories when you speak to the people?"

¹¹He replied, "Because you have been given the knowledge of the secrets of the kingdom of heaven. It has not been given to outsiders. ¹²Everyone who has this kind of knowledge will be given more knowledge. In fact, they will have very much. If anyone

doesn't have this kind of knowledge, even what little they have will be taken away from them. ¹³Here is why I use stories when I speak to the people. I say,

"They look, but they don't really see.
    They listen, but they don't really hear
        or understand."

¹⁴In them the words of the prophet Isaiah come true. He said,

"'You will hear but never understand.
    You will see but never know what
        you are seeing.
¹⁵ The hearts of these people have become
        stubborn.
    They can barely hear with their ears.
    They have closed their eyes.
Otherwise they might see with their
        eyes.
    They might hear with their ears.
    They might understand with their
        hearts.
    They might turn to the Lord, and then
        he would heal them.'
                                    (Isaiah 6:9,10)

¹⁶But blessed are your eyes because they see. And blessed are your ears because they hear. ¹⁷What I'm about to tell you is true. Many prophets and godly people wanted to see what you see. But they didn't see it. They wanted to hear what you hear. But they didn't hear it.

¹⁸"Listen! Here is the meaning of the story of the farmer. ¹⁹People hear the message about the kingdom but do not understand it. Then the evil one comes. He steals what was planted in their hearts. Those people are like the seed planted on a path. ²⁰The seed that fell on rocky places is like other people. They hear the message and at once receive it with joy. ²¹But they have no roots. So they last only a short time. They quickly fall away from the faith when trouble or suffering comes because of the message. ²²The seed that fell among the thorns is like others who hear the message. But then the worries of this life and the false promises of

BIBLE ADVENTURES

Connie put on a play to illustrate the parable of the farmer in "Scattered Seeds" (A#07).

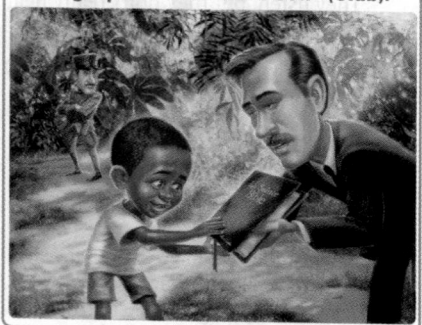

Dr. William Leslie spread the seeds of
the gospel in "The Good Soil" (Club).

wealth crowd it out. They keep the message
from producing fruit. [23]But the seed that
fell on good soil is like those who hear the
message and understand it. They produce
a crop 100, 60 or 30 times more than the
farmer planted."

The Story of the Weeds

[24]Jesus told the crowd another story.
"Here is what the kingdom of heaven is
like," he said. "A man planted good seed in
his field. [25]But while everyone was sleeping,
his enemy came. The enemy planted weeds
among the wheat and then went away.
[26]The wheat began to grow and form grain.
At the same time, weeds appeared.

[27]The owner's slaves came to him. They
said, 'Sir, didn't you plant good seed in your
field? Then where did the weeds come from?'

[28]'An enemy did this,' he replied.

"The slaves asked him, 'Do you want us
to go and pull up the weeds?'

[29]'No,' the owner answered. 'While you
are pulling up the weeds, you might pull up
the wheat with them. [30]Let both grow together until the harvest. At that time I will
tell the workers what to do. Here is what I
will say to them. First collect the weeds. Tie
them in bundles to be burned. Then gather
the wheat. Bring it into my storeroom.'"

The Stories of the Mustard Seed and the Yeast

[31]Jesus told the crowd another story.
He said, "The kingdom of heaven is like a
mustard seed. Someone took the seed and
planted it in a field. [32]It is the smallest of all
seeds. But when it grows, it is the largest of
all garden plants. It becomes a tree. Birds
come and rest in its branches."

[33]Jesus told them still another story.
"The kingdom of heaven is like yeast," he
said. "A woman mixed it into 60 pounds of
flour. The yeast worked its way all through
the dough."

[34]Jesus spoke all these things to the
crowd using stories. He did not say anything to them without telling a story. [35]So
the words spoken by the prophet came
true. He had said,

"I will open my mouth and tell stories.
I will speak about things that were
hidden since the world was
made."
(Psalm 78:2)

Jesus Explains the Story of the Weeds

[36]Then Jesus left the crowd and went
into the house. His disciples came to him.
They said, "Explain to us the story of the
weeds in the field."

[37]He answered, "The one who planted
the good seed is the Son of Man. [38]The field
is the world. The good seed stands for the
people who belong to the kingdom. The
weeds are the people who belong to the evil
one. [39]The enemy who plants them is the
devil. The harvest is judgment day. And the
workers are angels.

[40]"The weeds are pulled up and burned
in the fire. That is how it will be on judgment day. [41]The Son of Man will send out his
angels. They will weed out of his kingdom
everything that causes sin. They will also
get rid of all who do evil. [42]They will throw
them into the blazing furnace. There people
will weep and grind their teeth. [43]Then God's
people will shine like the sun in their Father's
kingdom. Whoever has ears should listen.

The Stories of the Hidden Treasure and the Pearl

[44]"The kingdom of heaven is like treasure that was hidden in a field. When a man
found it, he hid it again. He was very happy. So he went and sold everything he had.
And he bought that field.

[45]"Again, the kingdom of heaven is like
a trader who was looking for fine pearls.
[46]He found one that was very valuable. So

he went away and sold everything he had. And he bought that pearl.

The Story of the Net

⁴⁷"Again, the kingdom of heaven is like a net. It was let down into the lake. It caught all kinds of fish. ⁴⁸When it was full, the fishermen pulled it up on the shore. Then they sat down and gathered the good fish into baskets. But they threw the bad fish away. ⁴⁹This is how it will be on judgment day. The angels will come. They will separate the people who did what is wrong from those who did what is right. ⁵⁰They will throw the evil people into the blazing furnace. There the evil ones will weep and grind their teeth.

⁵¹"Do you understand all these things?" Jesus asked.

"Yes," they replied.

⁵²He said to them, "Every teacher of the law who has become a disciple in the kingdom of heaven is like the owner of a house. He brings new treasures out of his storeroom as well as old ones."

A Prophet Without Honor

⁵³Jesus finished telling these stories. Then he moved on from there. ⁵⁴He came to his hometown of Nazareth. There he began teaching the people in their synagogue. They were amazed. "Where did this man get this wisdom? Where did he get this power to do miracles?" they asked. ⁵⁵"Isn't this the carpenter's son? Isn't his mother's name Mary? Aren't his brothers James, Joseph, Simon and Judas? ⁵⁶Aren't all his sisters with us? Then where did this man get all these things?" ⁵⁷They were not pleased with him at all.

But Jesus said to them, "A prophet is honored everywhere except in his own town and in his own home."

⁵⁸He did only a few miracles in Nazareth because the people there had no faith.

John the Baptist's Head Is Cut Off

14 At that time Herod, the ruler of Galilee and Perea, heard reports about Jesus. ²He said to his attendants, "This is John the Baptist. He has risen from the dead! That is why he has the power to do miracles."

³Herod had arrested John. He had tied him up and put him in prison because of Herodias. She was the wife of Herod's brother Philip. ⁴John had been saying to Herod, "It is against the Law for you to have her as your wife." ⁵Herod wanted to kill John. But he was afraid of the people, because they thought John was a prophet.

⁶On Herod's birthday the daughter of Herodias danced for Herod and his guests. She pleased Herod very much. ⁷So he promised to give her anything she asked for. ⁸Her mother told her what to say. So the girl said to Herod, "Give me the head of John the Baptist on a big plate." ⁹The king was very upset. But he thought of his promise and his dinner guests. So he told one of his men to give her what she asked for. ¹⁰Herod had John's head cut off in the prison. ¹¹His head was brought in on a big plate and given to the girl. She then carried it to her mother. ¹²John's disciples came and took his body and buried it. Then they went and told Jesus.

Jesus Feeds Five Thousand

¹³Jesus heard what had happened to John. He wanted to be alone. So he went in a boat to a quiet place. The crowds heard about this. They followed him on foot from the towns. ¹⁴When Jesus came ashore, he saw a large crowd. He felt deep concern for them. He healed their sick people.

¹⁵When it was almost evening, the disciples came to him. "There is nothing here," they said. "It's already getting late. Send the crowds away. They can go and buy some food in the villages."

¹⁶Jesus replied, "They don't need to go away. You give them something to eat."

¹⁷"We have only five loaves of bread and two fish," they answered.

¹⁸"Bring them here to me," he said. ¹⁹Then Jesus directed the people to sit

down on the grass. He took the five loaves and the two fish. He looked up to heaven and gave thanks. He broke the loaves into pieces. Then he gave them to the disciples. And the disciples gave them to the people. ²⁰All of them ate and were satisfied. The disciples picked up 12 baskets of leftover pieces. ²¹The number of men who ate was about 5,000. Women and children also ate.

Jesus Walks on the Water

²²Right away Jesus made the disciples get into the boat. He had them go on ahead of him to the other side of the Sea of Galilee. Then he sent the crowd away. ²³After he had sent them away, he went up on a mountainside by himself to pray. Later that night, he was there alone. ²⁴The boat was already a long way from land. It was being pounded by the waves because the wind was blowing against it.

²⁵Shortly before dawn, Jesus went out to the disciples. He walked on the lake. ²⁶They saw him walking on the lake and were terrified. "It's a ghost!" they said. And they cried out in fear.

²⁷Right away Jesus called out to them, "Be brave! It is I. Don't be afraid."

²⁸"Lord, is it you?" Peter asked. "If it is, tell me to come to you on the water."

²⁹"Come," Jesus said.

So Peter got out of the boat. He walked on the water toward Jesus. ³⁰But when Peter saw the wind, he was afraid. He began to sink. He cried out, "Lord! Save me!"

³¹Right away Jesus reached out his hand and caught him. "Your faith is so small!" he said. "Why did you doubt me?"

³²When they climbed into the boat, the wind died down. ³³Then those in the boat worshiped Jesus. They said, "You really are the Son of God!"

³⁴They crossed over the lake and landed at Gennesaret. ³⁵The men who lived there recognized Jesus. So they sent a message all over the nearby countryside. People brought all those who were sick to Jesus. ³⁶They begged him to let those who were sick just touch the edge of his clothes. And all who touched his clothes were healed.

What Makes People "Unclean"?

15 Some Pharisees and some teachers of the law came from Jerusalem to see Jesus. They asked, ²"Why don't your disciples obey what the elders teach? Your disciples don't wash their hands before they eat!"

³Jesus replied, "And why don't you obey God's command? You would rather follow your own teachings! ⁴God said, 'Honor your father and mother.' *(Exodus 20:12; Deuteronomy 5:16)* He also said, 'Anyone who asks for bad things to happen to their father or mother must be put to death.' *(Exodus 21:17; Leviticus 20:9)* ⁵But suppose people have something that might be used to help their parents. You allow them to say it is instead 'a gift set apart for God.' ⁶So they do not need to honor their father or mother with their gift. You make the word of God useless in order to follow your own teachings. ⁷You pretenders! Isaiah was right when he prophesied about you. He said,

⁸ " 'These people honor me by what they say.
But their hearts are far away from me.
⁹ Their worship doesn't mean anything to me.
They teach nothing but human rules.' " *(Isaiah 29:13)*

¹⁰Jesus called the crowd to him. He said, "Listen and understand. ¹¹What goes into someone's mouth does not make them 'unclean.' It's what comes out of their mouth that makes them 'unclean.' "

¹²Then the disciples came to him. They asked, "Do you know that the Pharisees were angry when they heard this?"

¹³Jesus replied, "They are plants that my Father in heaven has not planted. They will be pulled up by the roots. ¹⁴Leave the Pharisees. They are blind guides. If one blind person leads another blind person, both of them will fall into a pit."

¹⁵Peter said, "Explain this to us."

¹⁶"Don't you understand yet?" Jesus asked them. ¹⁷"Don't you see? Everything that enters the mouth goes into the stomach. Then it goes out of the body. ¹⁸But the things that come out of a person's mouth come from the heart. Those are the things that make someone 'unclean.' ¹⁹Evil thoughts come out of a person's heart. So do murder, adultery, and other sexual sins. And so do stealing, false witness, and telling lies about others. ²⁰Those are the things that make you 'unclean.' But eating without washing your hands does not make you 'unclean.' "

WOOTON'S FUN FACTS

Matt. 15:17–18 It can take around twenty-four hours for food to get through your digestive system because your small intestines are four times longer than you are tall! But some food takes longer than others. Fruits and vegetables don't take as long as sugar.

The Faith of a Woman From Canaan

²¹Jesus left Galilee and went to the area of Tyre and Sidon. ²²A woman from Canaan lived near Tyre and Sidon. She came to him and cried out, "Lord! Son of David! Have mercy on me! A demon controls my daughter. She is suffering terribly."

²³Jesus did not say a word. So his disciples came to him. They begged him, "Send her away. She keeps crying out after us."

²⁴Jesus answered, "I was sent only to the people of Israel. They are like lost sheep."

²⁵Then the woman fell to her knees in front of him. "Lord! Help me!" she said.

²⁶He replied, "It is not right to take the children's bread and throw it to the dogs."

²⁷"Yes it is, Lord," she said. "Even the dogs eat the crumbs that fall from their owner's table."

²⁸Then Jesus said to her, "Woman, you have great faith! You will be given what you are asking for." And her daughter was healed at that moment.

Jesus Feeds Four Thousand

²⁹Jesus left there. He walked along the Sea of Galilee. Then he went up on a mountainside and sat down. ³⁰Large crowds came to him. They brought blind people and those who could not walk. They also brought disabled people, those who could not speak, and many others. They laid them at his feet, and he healed them. ³¹The

people were amazed. Those who could not speak were speaking. The disabled were made well. Those not able to walk were walking. Those who were blind could see. So the people praised the God of Israel.

³²Then Jesus called for his disciples to come to him. He said, "I feel deep concern for these people. They have already been with me three days. They don't have anything to eat. I don't want to send them away hungry. If I do, they will become too weak on their way home."

³³His disciples answered him. "There is nothing here," they said. "Where could we get enough bread to feed this large crowd?"

³⁴"How many loaves do you have?" Jesus asked.

"Seven," they replied, "and a few small fish."

³⁵Jesus told the crowd to sit down on the ground. ³⁶He took the seven loaves and the fish and gave thanks. Then he broke them and gave them to the disciples. And the disciples passed them out to the people. ³⁷All of them ate and were satisfied. After that, the disciples picked up seven baskets of leftover pieces. ³⁸The number of men who ate was 4,000. Women and children also ate. ³⁹After Jesus had sent the crowd away, he got into the boat. He went to the area near Magadan.

Jesus Is Asked for a Sign

16 The Pharisees and Sadducees came to test Jesus. They asked him to show them a sign from heaven.

²He replied, "In the evening you look at the sky. You say, 'It will be good weather. The sky is red.' ³And in the morning you say, 'Today it will be stormy. The sky is red and cloudy.' You know the meaning of what you see in the sky. But you can't understand the signs of what is happening right now. ⁴An evil and unfaithful people look for a sign. But none will be given to them except the sign of Jonah." Then Jesus left them and went away.

The Yeast of the Pharisees and Sadducees

⁵The disciples crossed over to the other side of the lake. They had forgotten to take bread. ⁶"Be careful," Jesus said to them. "Watch out for the yeast of the Pharisees and Sadducees."

[7]The disciples talked about this among themselves. They said, "He must be saying this because we didn't bring any bread."

[8]Jesus knew what they were saying. So he said, "Your faith is so small! Why are you talking to each other about having no bread? [9]Don't you understand yet? Don't you remember the five loaves for the 5,000? Don't you remember how many baskets of pieces you gathered? [10]Don't you remember the seven loaves for the 4,000? Don't you remember how many baskets of pieces you gathered? [11]How can you possibly not understand? I wasn't talking to you about bread. But watch out for the yeast of the Pharisees and Sadducees." [12]Then the disciples understood that Jesus was not telling them to watch out for the yeast used in bread. He was warning them against what the Pharisees and Sadducees taught.

Peter Says That Jesus Is the Messiah

[13]Jesus went to the area of Caesarea Philippi. There he asked his disciples, "Who do people say the Son of Man is?"

[14]They replied, "Some say John the Baptist. Others say Elijah. Still others say Jeremiah, or one of the prophets."

[15]"But what about you?" he asked. "Who do you say I am?"

[16]Simon Peter answered, "You are the Messiah. You are the Son of the living God."

[17]Jesus replied, "Blessed are you, Simon, son of Jonah! No mere human showed this to you. My Father in heaven showed it to you. [18]Here is what I tell you. You are Peter. On this rock I will build my church. The gates of hell will not be strong enough to destroy it. [19]I will give you the keys to the kingdom of heaven. What you lock on earth will be locked in heaven. What you unlock on earth will be unlocked in heaven." [20]Then Jesus ordered his disciples not to tell anyone that he was the Messiah.

Jesus Speaks About His Coming Death

[21]From that time on Jesus began to explain to his disciples what would happen to him. He told them he must go to Jerusalem. There he must suffer many things from the elders, the chief priests and the teachers of the law. He must be killed and on the third day rise to life again.

[22]Peter took Jesus to one side and began to scold him. "Never, Lord!" he said. "This will never happen to you!"

[23]Jesus turned and said to Peter, "Get behind me, Satan! You are standing in my way. You do not have in mind the things God cares about. Instead, you only have in mind the things humans care about."

[24]Then Jesus spoke to his disciples. He said, "Whoever wants to be my disciple must say no to themselves. They must pick up their cross and follow me. [25]Whoever wants to save their life will lose it. But whoever loses their life for me will find it. [26]What good is it if someone gains the whole world but loses their soul? Or what can anyone trade for their soul? [27]The Son of Man is going to come in his Father's glory. His angels will come with him. And he will reward everyone in keeping with what they have done.

[28]"What I'm about to tell you is true. Some who are standing here will not die before they see the Son of Man coming in his kingdom."

Jesus' Appearance Is Changed

17 After six days Jesus took Peter, James, and John the brother of James with him. He led them up a high mountain. They were all alone. [2]There in front of them his appearance was changed. His face shone like the sun. His clothes became as white as the light. [3]Just then Moses and Elijah appeared in front of them. Moses and Elijah were talking with Jesus.

[4]Peter said to Jesus, "Lord, it is good for us to be here. If you wish, I will put up three shelters. One will be for you, one for Moses, and one for Elijah."

[5]While Peter was still speaking, a bright cloud covered them. A voice from the cloud said, "This is my Son, and I love him. I am very pleased with him. Listen to him!"

[6]When the disciples heard this, they were terrified. They fell with their faces to the ground. [7]But Jesus came and touched them. "Get up," he said. "Don't be afraid." [8]When they looked up, they saw no one except Jesus.

[9]They came down the mountain. On the way down, Jesus told them what to do. "Don't tell anyone what you have seen," he said. "Wait until the Son of Man has been raised from the dead."

[10]The disciples asked him, "Why do the teachers of the law say that Elijah has to come first?"

[11]Jesus replied, "That's right. Elijah is supposed to come and make all things new again. [12]But I tell you, Elijah has already come. People didn't recognize him. They have done to him everything they wanted to do. In the same way, they are going to make the Son of Man suffer." [13]Then the disciples understood that Jesus was talking to them about John the Baptist.

Jesus Heals a Boy Who Is Controlled by a Demon

[14]When they came near the crowd, a man approached Jesus. He got on his knees in front of him. [15]"Lord," he said, "have mercy on my son. He shakes wildly and suffers a great deal. He often falls into the fire or into the water. [16]I brought him to your disciples. But they couldn't heal him."

[17]"You unbelieving and evil people!" Jesus replied. "How long do I have to stay with you? How long do I have to put up with you? Bring the boy here to me." [18]Jesus ordered the demon to leave the boy, and it came out of him. He was healed at that moment.

[19]Then the disciples came to Jesus in private. They asked, "Why couldn't we drive out the demon?"

[20-21]He replied, "Because your faith is much too small. What I'm about to tell you is true. If you have faith as small as a mustard seed, it is enough. You can say to this mountain, 'Move from here to there.' And it will move. Nothing will be impossible for you."

Jesus Speaks a Second Time About His Coming Death

[22]They came together in Galilee. Then Jesus said to them, "The Son of Man is going to be handed over to men. [23]They will kill him. On the third day he will rise from the dead." Then the disciples were filled with deep sadness.

Jesus Pays the Temple Tax

[24]Jesus and his disciples arrived in Capernaum. There the people who collect the temple tax came to Peter. They asked him, "Doesn't your teacher pay the temple tax?"

[25]"Yes, he does," he replied.

When Peter came into the house, Jesus spoke first. "What do you think, Simon?" he asked. "Who do the kings of the earth collect taxes and fees from? Do they collect them from their own children or from others?"

[26]"From others," Peter answered.

"Then the children don't have to pay," Jesus said to him. [27]"But we don't want to make them angry. So go to the lake and throw out your fishing line. Take the first fish you catch. Open its mouth. There you will find the exact coin you need. Take it and give it to them for my tax and yours."

Who Is the Most Important Person in the Kingdom?

18 At that time the disciples came to Jesus. They asked him, "Then who is the most important person in the kingdom of heaven?"

[2]Jesus called a little child over to him. He had the child stand among them. [3]Jesus said, "What I'm about to tell you is true. You need to change and become like little children. If you don't, you will never enter the kingdom of heaven. [4]Anyone who takes the humble position of this child is the most important in the kingdom of heaven. [5]Anyone who welcomes a little child like this one in my name welcomes me.

Do Not Cause People to Sin

[6]"What if someone causes one of these little ones who believe in me to sin? If they do, it would be better for them to have a large millstone hung around their neck and be drowned at the bottom of the sea. [7]How terrible it will be for the world because of the things that cause people to sin! Things like that must come. But how terrible for the person who causes them! [8]If your hand or foot causes you to sin, cut it off and throw it away. It would be better to enter the kingdom of heaven with only one hand than go into hell with two hands. It would be better to enter the kingdom of heaven with only one foot than go into hell with two feet. In hell the fire burns forever. [9]If your eye causes you to sin, poke it out and throw it away. It would be better to enter the kingdom of heaven with one eye than to have two eyes and be thrown into the fire of hell.

ADVENTURES IN ODYSSEY

Jimmy Barclay met an angel in an unexpected way in "Someone to Watch Over Me" (A#10).

The Story of the Wandering Sheep

¹⁰⁻¹¹"See that you don't look down on one of these little ones. Here is what I tell you. Their angels in heaven are always with my Father who is in heaven.

¹²"What do you think? Suppose a man owns 100 sheep and one of them wanders away. Won't he leave the 99 sheep on the hills? Won't he go and look for the one that wandered off? ¹³What I'm about to tell you is true. If he finds that sheep, he is happier about the one than about the 99 that didn't wander off. ¹⁴It is the same with your Father in heaven. He does not want any of these little ones to die.

When Someone Sins Against You

¹⁵"If your brother or sister sins against you, go to them. Tell them what they did wrong. Keep it between the two of you. If they listen to you, you have won them back. ¹⁶But what if they won't listen to you? Then take one or two others with you. Scripture says, 'Every matter must be proved by the words of two or three witnesses.' *(Deuteronomy 19:15)* ¹⁷But what if they also refuse to listen to the witnesses? Then tell it to the church. And what if they refuse to listen even to the church? Then don't treat them as a brother or sister. Treat them as you would treat an ungodly person or a tax collector.

¹⁸"What I'm about to tell you is true. What you lock on earth will be locked in heaven. What you unlock on earth will be unlocked in heaven.

¹⁹"Again, here is what I tell you. Suppose two of you on earth agree about anything you ask for. My Father in heaven will do it for you. ²⁰Where two or three people gather in my name, I am there with them."

The Servant Who Had No Mercy

²¹Peter came to Jesus. He asked, "Lord, how many times should I forgive my brother or sister who sins against me? Up to seven times?"

²²Jesus answered, "I tell you, not seven times, but 77 times.

²³"The kingdom of heaven is like a king who wanted to collect all the money his servants owed him. ²⁴As the king began to do it, a man who owed him 10,000 bags of gold was brought to him. ²⁵The man was not able to pay. So his master gave an order. The man, his wife, his children, and all he owned had to be sold to pay back what he owed.

²⁶"Then the servant fell on his knees in front of him. 'Give me time,' he begged. 'I'll pay everything back.' ²⁷His master felt sorry for him. He forgave him what he owed and let him go.

²⁸"But then that servant went out and found one of the other servants who owed him 100 silver coins. He grabbed him and

Your turn for an angel-sighting! Jesus says you have a guardian angel (see also Psalm 34:7 and Psalm 91:11). I'm not sure, but I think an angel saved me when I was trapped in a frog costume. Don't ask why I was in that costume.

BiBLe ADVentures

Israel's Most Wanted sought out
Bubba Servanti for a twist on the
parable of the unmerciful servant
in "B-TV: Forgiveness" (A#32).

began to choke him. 'Pay back what you owe me!' he said.

²⁹"The other servant fell on his knees. 'Give me time,' he begged him. 'I'll pay it back.'

³⁰"But the first servant refused. Instead, he went and had the man thrown into prison. The man would be held there until he could pay back what he owed. ³¹The other servants saw what had happened and were very angry. They went and told their master everything that had happened.

³²"Then the master called the first servant in. 'You evil servant,' he said. 'I forgave all that you owed me because you begged me to. ³³Shouldn't you have had mercy on the other servant just as I had mercy on you?' ³⁴In anger his master handed him over to the jailers. He would be punished until he paid back everything he owed.

³⁵"This is how my Father in heaven will treat each of you unless you forgive your brother or sister from your heart."

Jesus Teaches About Divorce

19 When Jesus finished saying these things, he left Galilee. He went into the area of Judea on the other side of the Jordan River. ²Large crowds followed him. He healed them there.

³Some Pharisees came to test Jesus. They asked, "Does the Law allow a man to divorce his wife for any reason at all?"

⁴Jesus replied, "Haven't you read that in the beginning the Creator 'made them male and female'? *(Genesis 1:27)* ⁵He said, 'That's why a man will leave his father and mother and be joined to his wife. The two

WHAT ABOUT YOU?

Pinky promise. Cross my heart. I do. So how important is keeping a promise? Can you let it slide if things get tough? Does it have a time limit? What about marriage vows?

Divorce has been a sensitive topic for a long time. Some Pharisees in Jesus' day were questioning the strength of a marriage vow. They asked Jesus, "Does the Law allow a man to divorce his wife for any reason at all?" Jesus knew they were looking for excuses for divorce, so He told them what God, His Father, had said when He first made Adam and Eve.

"Haven't you read that in the beginning the Creator 'made them male and female'? He said, 'That's why a man will leave his father and mother and be joined to his wife. The two will become one.' They are no longer two, but one. So no one should separate what God has joined together" (Matthew 19:4–6).

Some marriages do struggle and break apart. It's sad because that hurts everyone involved, not just the couple getting divorced. God knows best, and He designed marriage as more than just a promise between two people. It's a promise two people make to God—and a sacred symbol of His commitment to the church.

Can you find your parents' wedding video (if they have one)? Watch it with them, or ask them about their special day. What's something they mentioned in their wedding vows? If you've been touched by divorce, remember that God is there for you. He knows how much it hurts, which is why He designed marriage to last a lifetime.

Eugene and Connie prepared for Wooton and Penny's wedding in "A Very Bassett Wedding" (A#61).

will become one.' *(Genesis 2:24)* ⁶They are no longer two, but one. So no one should separate what God has joined together."

⁷They asked, "Then why did Moses command that a man can give his wife a letter of divorce and send her away?"

⁸Jesus replied, "Moses let you divorce your wives because you were stubborn. But it was not this way from the beginning. ⁹Here is what I tell you. Anyone who divorces his wife and marries another woman commits adultery. A man may divorce his wife only if she has not been faithful to him."

¹⁰Here is what the disciples said to him. "If that's the way it is between a husband and wife, it is better not to get married."

¹¹Jesus replied, "Not everyone can accept the idea of staying single. Only those who have been helped to live without getting married can accept it. ¹²Some men are not able to have children because they were born that way. Some have been made that way by other people. Others have chosen to live that way in order to serve the kingdom of heaven. The one who can accept this should accept it."

Little Children Are Brought to Jesus

¹³Some people brought little children to Jesus. They wanted him to place his hands on the children and pray for them. But the disciples told them not to do it.

¹⁴Jesus said, "Let the little children come to me. Don't keep them away. The kingdom of heaven belongs to people like them." ¹⁵Jesus placed his hands on them to bless them. Then he went on from there.

Rich People and the Kingdom of God

¹⁶Just then, a man came up to Jesus. He asked, "Teacher, what good thing must I do to receive eternal life?"

¹⁷"Why do you ask me about what is good?" Jesus replied. "There is only one who is good. If you want to enter the kingdom, obey the commandments."

¹⁸"Which ones?" the man asked.

Jesus said, "'Do not murder. Do not commit adultery. Do not steal. Do not be a false witness. ¹⁹Honor your father and mother.' *(Exodus 20:12–16; Deuteronomy 5:16–20)* And 'love your neighbor as you love yourself.'" *(Leviticus 19:18)*

²⁰"I have obeyed all those commandments," the young man said. "What else do I need to do?"

²¹Jesus answered, "If you want to be perfect, go and sell everything you have. Give the money to those who are poor. You will have treasure in heaven. Then come and follow me."

²²When the young man heard this, he went away sad. He was very rich.

²³Then Jesus said to his disciples, "What I'm about to tell you is true. It is hard for someone who is rich to enter the kingdom of heaven. ²⁴Again I tell you, it is hard for a camel to go through the eye of a needle. But it is even harder for someone who is rich to enter the kingdom of God."

²⁵When the disciples heard this, they were really amazed. They asked, "Then who can be saved?"

²⁶Jesus looked at them and said, "With people, this is impossible. But with God, all things are possible."

²⁷Peter answered him, "We have left everything to follow you! What reward will be given to us?"

²⁸"What I'm about to tell you is true," Jesus said to them. "When all things are made new, the Son of Man will sit on his glorious throne. Then you who have followed me will also sit on 12 thrones. You will judge the 12 tribes of Israel. ²⁹Suppose anyone has left houses, brothers or sisters, father or mother, husband or wife, children

or fields because of me. Anyone who has done that will receive 100 times as much. They will also receive eternal life. ³⁰But many who are first will be last. And many who are last will be first.

The Story of the Workers in the Vineyard

20 "The kingdom of heaven is like a man who owned land. He went out early in the morning to hire workers for his vineyard. ²He agreed to give them the usual pay for a day's work. Then he sent them into his vineyard.

³"About nine o'clock in the morning he went out again. He saw others standing in the market doing nothing. ⁴He told them, 'You also go and work in my vineyard. I'll pay you what is right.' ⁵So they went.

"He went out again about noon and at three o'clock and did the same thing. ⁶About five o'clock he went out and found still others standing around. He asked them, 'Why have you been standing here all day long doing nothing?'

⁷"'Because no one has hired us,' they answered.

"He said to them, 'You also go and work in my vineyard.'

⁸"When evening came, the owner of the vineyard spoke to the person who was in charge of the workers. He said, 'Call the workers and give them their pay. Begin with the last ones I hired. Then go on to the first ones.'

⁹"The workers who were hired about five o'clock came. Each received the usual day's pay. ¹⁰So when those who were hired first came, they expected to receive more. But each of them also received the usual day's pay. ¹¹When they received it, they began to complain about the owner. ¹²'These people who were hired last worked only one hour,' they said. 'You have paid them the same as us. We have done most of the work and have been in the hot sun all day.'

¹³"The owner answered one of them. 'Friend,' he said, 'I'm being fair to you. Didn't you agree to work for the usual day's pay? ¹⁴Take your money and go. I want to give the one I hired last the same pay I gave you. ¹⁵Don't I have the right to do what I want with my own money? Do you feel cheated because I gave so freely to the others?'

¹⁶"So those who are last will be first. And those who are first will be last."

Jesus Speaks a Third Time About His Coming Death

¹⁷Jesus was going up to Jerusalem. On the way, he took his 12 disciples to one side to talk to them. ¹⁸"We are going up to Jerusalem," he said. "The Son of Man will be handed over to the chief priests and the teachers of the law. They will sentence him to death. ¹⁹Then they will hand him over to the Gentiles. The people will make fun of him and whip him. They will nail him to a cross. On the third day, he will rise from the dead!"

A Mother Asks a Favor of Jesus

²⁰The mother of Zebedee's sons came to Jesus. Her sons came with her. Getting on her knees, she asked a favor of him.

²¹"What do you want?" Jesus asked.

She said, "Promise me that one of my two sons may sit at your right hand in your kingdom. Promise that the other one may sit at your left hand."

²²"You don't know what you're asking for," Jesus said to them. "Can you drink the cup of suffering I am going to drink?"

"We can," they answered.

²³Jesus said to them, "You will certainly drink from my cup. But it is not for me to say who will sit at my right or left hand. These places belong to those my Father has prepared them for."

²⁴The other ten disciples heard about this. They became angry at the two brothers. ²⁵Jesus called them together. He said, "You know about the rulers of the Gentiles. They hold power over their people. Their high officials order them around. ²⁶Don't be like that. Instead, anyone who wants to be important among you must be your servant. ²⁷And anyone who wants to be first must be your slave. ²⁸Be like the Son of Man. He did not come to be served. Instead, he came to serve others. He came to give his life as the price for setting many people free."

BIBLE ADVENTURES

Whit retold the parable of the workers through kids at Whit's End in "... The Last Shall Be First" (A#11).

Eugene and Trent both learned to have concern and compassion like Jesus in "The Invisible Dog" (A#44).

Two Blind Men Receive Their Sight

²⁹Jesus and his disciples were leaving Jericho. A large crowd followed him. ³⁰Two blind men were sitting by the side of the road. They heard that Jesus was going by. So they shouted, "Lord! Son of David! Have mercy on us!"

³¹The crowd commanded them to stop. They told them to be quiet. But the two men shouted even louder, "Lord! Son of David! Have mercy on us!"

³²Jesus stopped and called out to them. "What do you want me to do for you?" he asked.

³³"Lord," they answered, "we want to be able to see."

³⁴Jesus felt deep concern for them. He touched their eyes. Right away they could see. And they followed him.

Jesus Comes to Jerusalem as King

21 As they all approached Jerusalem, they came to Bethphage. It was on the Mount of Olives. Jesus sent out two disciples. ²He said to them, "Go to the village ahead of you. As soon as you get there, you will find a donkey tied up. Her colt will be with her. Untie them and bring them to me. ³If anyone says anything to you, say that the Lord needs them. The owner will send them right away."

⁴This took place so that what was spoken through the prophet would come true. It says,

⁵ "Say to the city of Zion,
    'See, your king comes to you.
He is gentle and riding on a donkey.
    He is riding on a donkey's colt.'"

(Zechariah 9:9)

⁶The disciples went and did what Jesus told them to do. ⁷They brought the donkey and the colt. They placed their coats on them for Jesus to sit on. ⁸A very large crowd spread their coats on the road. Others cut branches from the trees and spread them on the road. ⁹Some of the people went ahead of him, and some followed. They all shouted,

"Hosanna to the Son of David!"

"Blessed is the one who comes in the name of the Lord!"

(Psalm 118:26)

"Hosanna in the highest heaven!"

¹⁰When Jesus entered Jerusalem, the whole city was stirred up. The people asked, "Who is this?"

¹¹The crowds answered, "This is Jesus. He is the prophet from Nazareth in Galilee."

Jesus Clears Out the Temple

¹²Jesus entered the temple courtyard. He began to drive out all those who were buying and selling there. He turned over the tables of the people who were exchanging money. He also turned over the benches of those who were selling doves. ¹³He said to them, "It is written that the Lord said, 'My house will be called a house where people can pray.' *(Isaiah 56:7)* But you are making it 'a den for robbers.'" *(Jeremiah 7:11)*

¹⁴Blind people and those who were disabled came to Jesus at the temple. There he healed them. ¹⁵The chief priests and the teachers of the law saw the wonderful things he did. They also saw the children in the temple courtyard shouting, "Hosanna to the Son of David!" But when they saw all this, they became angry.

¹⁶"Do you hear what these children are saying?" they asked him.

"Yes," replied Jesus. "Haven't you ever read about it in Scripture? It says,

"'Lord, you have made sure that
    children and infants
    praise you.'" *(Psalm 8:2)*

¹⁷Then Jesus left the people and went out of the city to Bethany. He spent the night there.

Jesus Makes a Fig Tree Dry Up

¹⁸Early in the morning, Jesus was on his way back to Jerusalem. He was hungry. ¹⁹He saw a fig tree by the road. He went up to it but found nothing on it except leaves. Then he said to it, "May you never bear fruit again!" Right away the tree dried up.

²⁰When the disciples saw this, they were amazed. "How did the fig tree dry up so quickly?" they asked.

²¹Jesus replied, "What I'm about to tell you is true. You must have faith and not doubt. Then you can do what was done to the fig tree. And you can say to this mountain, 'Go and throw yourself into the sea.' It will be done. ²²If you believe, you will receive what you ask for when you pray."

The Authority of Jesus Is Questioned

²³Jesus entered the temple courtyard. While he was teaching there, the chief priests and the elders of the people came to him. "By what authority are you doing these things?" they asked. "Who gave you this authority?"

²⁴Jesus replied, "I will also ask you one question. If you answer me, I will tell you by what authority I am doing these things. ²⁵Where did John's baptism come from? Was it from heaven? Or did it come from human authority?"

They talked to one another about it. They said, "If we say, 'From heaven,' he will ask, 'Then why didn't you believe him?' ²⁶But what if we say, 'From human authority'? We are afraid of the people. Everyone believes that John was a prophet."

²⁷So they answered Jesus, "We don't know."

Jesus said, "Then I won't tell you by what authority I am doing these things either.

The Story of the Two Sons

²⁸"What do you think about this? A man had two sons. He went to the first and said, 'Son, go and work today in the vineyard.'

²⁹"'I will not,' the son answered. But later he changed his mind and went.

³⁰"Then the father went to the other son. He said the same thing. The son answered, 'I will, sir.' But he did not go.

³¹"Which of the two sons did what his father wanted?"

"The first," they answered.

Jesus said to them, "What I'm about to tell you is true. Tax collectors and prostitutes will enter the kingdom of God ahead of you. ³²John came to show you the right way to live. And you did not believe him. But the tax collectors and the prostitutes did. You saw this. But even then you did not turn away from your sins and believe him.

The Story of the Renters

³³"Listen to another story. A man who owned some land planted a vineyard. He put a wall around it. He dug a pit for a winepress in it. He also built a lookout tower. He rented the vineyard out to some farmers. Then he moved to another place. ³⁴When harvest time approached, he sent his slaves to the renters. He told the slaves to collect his share of the fruit.

³⁵"But the renters grabbed his slaves. They beat one of them. They killed another. They threw stones at the third to kill him. ³⁶Then the man sent other slaves to the renters. He sent more than he did the first time. The renters treated them the same way. ³⁷Last of all, he sent his son to them. 'They will respect my son,' he said.

³⁸"But the renters saw the son coming. They said to one another, 'This is the one who will receive all the owner's property someday. Come, let's kill him. Then everything will be ours.' ³⁹So they took him and threw him out of the vineyard. Then they killed him.

⁴⁰"When the owner of the vineyard comes back, what will he do to those renters?"

⁴¹"He will destroy those evil people," they replied. "Then he will rent the vineyard out to other renters. They will give him his share of the crop at harvest time."

⁴²Jesus said to them, "Haven't you ever read what the Scriptures say,

"'The stone the builders didn't accept
has become the most important
stone of all.
The Lord has done it.
It is wonderful in our eyes'?

(Psalm 118:22,23)

⁴³"So here is what I tell you. The kingdom of God will be taken away from you. It will be given to people who will produce its fruit. ⁴⁴Anyone who falls on that stone will be broken to pieces. But the stone will crush anyone it falls on."

⁴⁵The chief priests and the Pharisees heard Jesus' stories. They knew he was talking about them. ⁴⁶So they looked for a

BIBLE ADVENTURES

Jimmy and Donna Barclay lived
out the parable of the two sons
in "Over the Airwaves" (A#09).

way to arrest him. But they were afraid of the crowd. The people believed that Jesus was a prophet.

The Story of the Wedding Dinner

22 Jesus told them more stories. He said, [2]"Here is what the kingdom of heaven is like. A king prepared a wedding dinner for his son. [3]He sent his slaves to those who had been invited to the dinner. The slaves told them to come. But they refused.

[4]"Then he sent some more slaves. He said, 'Tell those who were invited that I have prepared my dinner. I have killed my oxen and my fattest cattle. Everything is ready. Come to the wedding dinner.'

[5]"But the people paid no attention. One went away to his field. Another went away to his business. [6]The rest grabbed his slaves. They treated them badly and then killed them. [7]The king became very angry. He sent his army to destroy them. They killed those murderers and burned their city.

[8]"Then the king said to his slaves, 'The wedding dinner is ready. But those I invited were not fit to come. [9]So go to the street corners. Invite to the dinner anyone you can find.' [10]So the slaves went out into the streets. They gathered all the people they could find, the bad as well as the good. Soon the wedding hall was filled with guests.

[11]"The king came in to see the guests. He noticed a man there who was not wearing wedding clothes. [12]'Friend,' he asked, 'how did you get in here without wedding clothes?' The man couldn't think of anything to say.

[13]"Then the king told his slaves, 'Tie up his hands and feet. Throw him outside into the darkness. Out there people will weep and grind their teeth.'

[14]"Many are invited, but few are chosen."

Is It Right to Pay the Royal Tax to Caesar?

[15]The Pharisees went out. They made plans to trap Jesus with his own words. [16]They sent their followers to him. They sent the Herodians with them. "Teacher," they said, "we know that you are a man of honor. You teach the way of God truthfully. You don't let others tell you what to do or say. You don't care how important they are. [17]Tell us then, what do you think? Is it right to pay the royal tax to Caesar or not?"

[18]But Jesus knew their evil plans. He said, "You pretenders! Why are you trying to trap me? [19]Show me the coin people use for paying the tax." They brought him a silver coin. [20]He asked them, "Whose picture is this? And whose words?"

[21]"Caesar's," they replied.

Then he said to them, "So give back to Caesar what belongs to Caesar. And give back to God what belongs to God."

[22]When they heard this, they were amazed. So they left him and went away.

Marriage When the Dead Rise

[23]That same day the Sadducees came to Jesus with a question. They do not believe that people rise from the dead. [24]"Teacher," they said, "here is what Moses told us. If a man dies without having children, his brother must get married to the widow. He must provide children to carry on his brother's name. [25]There were seven brothers among us. The first one got married and died. Since he had no children, he left his wife to his brother. [26]The same thing happened to the second and third brothers. It happened right on down to the seventh brother. [27]Finally, the woman died. [28]Now then, when the dead rise, whose wife will she be? All seven of them were married to her."

[29]Jesus replied, "You are mistaken, because you do not know the Scriptures. And you do not know the power of God. [30]When the dead rise, they won't get married. And their parents won't give them to be married. They will be like the angels in heaven. [31]What about the dead rising? Haven't you read what God said to you? [32]He said, 'I am the God of Abraham. I am the God of Isaac. And I am the God of Jacob.' (Exodus 3:6) He is not the God of the dead. He is the God of the living."

[33]When the crowds heard this, they were amazed by what he taught.

The Most Important Commandment

³⁴The Pharisees heard that the Sadducees weren't able to answer Jesus. So the Pharisees got together. ³⁵One of them was an authority on the law. So he tested Jesus with a question. ³⁶"Teacher," he asked, "which is the most important commandment in the Law?"

³⁷Jesus replied, "'Love the Lord your God with all your heart and with all your soul. Love him with all your mind.' *(Deuteronomy 6:5)* ³⁸This is the first and most important commandment. ³⁹And the second is like it. 'Love your neighbor as you love yourself.' *(Leviticus 19:18)* ⁴⁰Everything that is written in the Law and the Prophets is based on these two commandments."

Whose Son Is the Messiah?

⁴¹The Pharisees were gathered together. Jesus asked them, ⁴²"What do you think about the Messiah? Whose son is he?"

"The son of David," they replied.

⁴³He said to them, "Then why does David call him 'Lord'? The Holy Spirit spoke through David himself. David said,

⁴⁴ "'The Lord said to my Lord,
"Sit at my right hand
until I put your enemies
under your control."' *(Psalm 110:1)*

⁴⁵So if David calls him 'Lord,' how can he be David's son?" ⁴⁶No one could give any answer to him. From that day on, no one dared to ask him any more questions.

A Warning Against Doing Things for the Wrong Reasons

23 Jesus spoke to the crowds and to his disciples. ²"The teachers of the law and the Pharisees sit in Moses' seat," he said. ³"So you must be careful to do everything they say. But don't do what they do. They don't practice what they preach. ⁴They tie up heavy loads that are hard to carry. Then they put them on other people's shoulders. But they themselves aren't willing to lift a finger to move them.

⁵"Everything they do is done for others to see. On their foreheads and arms they wear little boxes that hold Scripture verses. They make the boxes very wide. And they make the tassels on their coats very long. ⁶They love to sit down in the place of honor at dinners. They also love to have the most important seats in the synagogues. ⁷They love to be greeted with respect in the markets. They love it when people call them 'Rabbi.'

⁸"But you shouldn't be called 'Rabbi.' You have only one Teacher, and you are all brothers. ⁹Do not call anyone on earth 'father.' You have one Father, and he is in heaven. ¹⁰You shouldn't be called 'teacher.' You have one Teacher, and he is the Messiah. ¹¹The most important person among you will be your servant. ¹²People who lift themselves up will be made humble. And people who make themselves humble will be lifted up.

How Terrible for the Teachers of the Law and the Pharisees

¹³⁻¹⁴"How terrible it will be for you, teachers of the law and Pharisees! You pretenders! You shut the door of the kingdom of heaven in people's faces. You yourselves do not enter. And you will not let those enter who are trying to.

¹⁵"How terrible for you, teachers of the law and Pharisees! You pretenders! You travel everywhere to win one person to your faith. Then you make them twice as much a child of hell as you are.

¹⁶"How terrible for you, blind guides! You say, 'If anyone makes a promise in the name of the temple, it means nothing. But anyone who makes a promise in the name of the gold of the temple must keep that promise.' ¹⁷You are blind and foolish! Which is more important? Is it the gold? Or is it the temple that makes the gold holy? ¹⁸You also say, 'If anyone makes a promise in the name of the altar, it means nothing. But anyone who makes a promise in the name of the gift on the altar must keep that promise.' ¹⁹You are blind! Which is more important? Is it the gift? Or is it the altar that makes the gift holy? ²⁰So anyone making a promise in the name of the altar makes a promise in the name of it and everything on it. ²¹And anyone making a promise in the name of the temple makes a promise in the name of it and the one who lives in it. ²²And anyone making a promise in the name of heaven makes a promise in the name of God's throne and the one who sits on it.

²³"How terrible for you, teachers of the law and Pharisees! You pretenders! You

give God a tenth of your spices, like mint, dill and cumin. But you have not practiced the more important things of the law, which are fairness, mercy and faithfulness. You should have practiced the last things without failing to do the first. ²⁴You blind guides! You remove the smallest insect from your food. But you swallow a whole camel!

²⁵"How terrible for you, teachers of the law and Pharisees! You pretenders! You clean the outside of a cup and dish. But on the inside you are full of greed. You only want to satisfy yourselves. ²⁶Blind Pharisee! First clean the inside of the cup and dish. Then the outside will also be clean.

²⁷"How terrible for you, teachers of the law and Pharisees! You pretenders! You are like tombs that are painted white. They look beautiful on the outside. But on the inside they are full of the bones of the dead. They are also full of other things that are not pure and 'clean.' ²⁸It is the same with you. On the outside you seem to be doing what is right. But on the inside you are full of what is wrong. You pretend to be what you are not.

²⁹"How terrible for you, teachers of the law and Pharisees! You pretenders! You build tombs for the prophets. You decorate the graves of the godly. ³⁰And you say, 'If we had lived in the days of those who lived before us, we wouldn't have done what they did. We wouldn't have helped to kill the prophets.' ³¹So you are witnesses against yourselves. You admit that you are the children of those who murdered the prophets. ³²So go ahead and finish the sins that those who lived before you started!

³³"You nest of poisonous snakes! How will you escape from being sentenced to hell? ³⁴So I am sending you prophets, wise people, and teachers. You will kill some of them. You will nail some to a cross. Others you will whip in your synagogues. You will chase them from town to town. ³⁵So you will pay for all the godly people's blood spilled on earth. I mean from the blood of godly Abel to the blood of Zechariah, the son of Berekiah. Zechariah was the one you murdered between the temple and the altar. ³⁶What I'm about to tell you is true. All this will happen to those who are now living.

³⁷"Jerusalem! Jerusalem! You kill the prophets and throw stones in order to kill those who are sent to you. Many times I have wanted to gather your people together. I have wanted to be like a hen who gathers her chicks under her wings. And you would not let me! ³⁸Look, your house is left empty. ³⁹I tell you, you will not see me again until you say, 'Blessed is the one who comes in the name of the Lord.'" *(Psalm 118:26)*

When the Temple Will Be Destroyed and the Signs of the End

24 Jesus left the temple. He was walking away when his disciples came up to him. They wanted to call his attention to the temple buildings. ²"Do you see all these things?" Jesus asked. "What I'm about to tell you is true. Not one stone here will be left on top of another. Every stone will be thrown down."

³Jesus was sitting on the Mount of Olives. There the disciples came to him in private. "Tell us," they said. "When will this happen? And what will be the sign of your coming? What will be the sign of the end?"

⁴Jesus answered, "Keep watch! Be careful that no one fools you. ⁵Many will come in my name. They will claim, 'I am the Messiah!' They will fool many people. ⁶You will hear about wars. You will also hear people talking about future wars. Don't be alarmed. Those things must happen. But the end still isn't here. ⁷Nation will fight against nation. Kingdom will fight against kingdom. People will go hungry. There will be earthquakes in many places. ⁸All these are the beginning of birth pains.

⁹"Then people will hand you over to be treated badly and killed. All nations will hate you because of me. ¹⁰At that time, many will turn away from their faith. They will hate each other. They will hand each other over to their enemies. ¹¹Many false prophets will appear. They will fool many people. ¹²Because evil will grow, most people's love will grow cold. ¹³But the one who remains strong in the faith will be saved. ¹⁴This good news of the kingdom will be preached in the whole world. It will be a witness to all nations. Then the end will come.

¹⁵"The prophet Daniel spoke about 'the hated thing that destroys.' *(Daniel 9:27; 11:31; 12:11)* Someday you will see it standing in the holy place. The reader should understand this. ¹⁶Then those who are in Judea should escape to the mountains. ¹⁷No one

on the housetop should go down into the house to take anything out. [18]No one in the field should go back to get their coat. [19]How awful it will be in those days for pregnant women! How awful for nursing mothers! [20]Pray that you will not have to escape in winter or on the Sabbath day. [21]There will be terrible suffering in those days. It will be worse than any other from the beginning of the world until now. And there will never be anything like it again.

[22]"If the time had not been cut short, no one would live. But because of God's chosen people, it will be shortened. [23]At that time someone may say to you, 'Look! Here is the Messiah!' Or, 'There he is!' Do not believe it. [24]False messiahs and false prophets will appear. They will do great signs and miracles. They will try to fool God's chosen people if possible. [25]See, I have told you ahead of time.

[26]"So if anyone tells you, 'He is a long way out in the desert,' do not go out there. Or if anyone says, 'He is deep inside the house,' do not believe it. [27]Lightning that comes from the east can be seen in the west. It will be the same when the Son of Man comes. [28]The vultures will gather wherever there is a dead body.

[29]"Right after the terrible suffering of those days,

" 'The sun will be darkened.
The moon will not shine.
The stars will fall from the sky.
The heavenly bodies will be shaken.'

(Isaiah 13:10; 34:4)

[30]"Then the sign of the Son of Man will appear in heaven. At that time, all the peoples of the earth will mourn. They will mourn when they see the Son of Man coming on the clouds of heaven. He will come with power and great glory. [31]He will send his angels with a loud trumpet call. They will gather his chosen people from all four directions. They will bring them from one end of the heavens to the other.

[32]"Learn a lesson from the fig tree. As soon as its twigs get tender and its leaves come out, you know that summer is near. [33]In the same way, when you see all these things happening, you know that the end is near. It is right at the door. [34]What I'm about to tell you is true. The people living now will certainly not pass away until all

these things have happened. [35]Heaven and earth will pass away. But my words will never pass away.

The Day and Hour Are Not Known

[36]"But no one knows about that day or hour. Not even the angels in heaven know. The Son does not know. Only the Father knows. [37]Remember how it was in the days of Noah. It will be the same when the Son of Man comes. [38]In the days before the flood, people were eating and drinking. They were getting married. They were giving their daughters to be married. They did all those things right up to the day Noah entered the ark. [39]They knew nothing about what would happen until the flood came and took them all away. That is how it will be when the Son of Man comes. [40]Two men will be in the field. One will be taken and the other left. [41]Two women will be grinding with a hand mill. One will be taken and the other left.

[42]"So keep watch. You do not know on what day your Lord will come. [43]You must understand something. Suppose the owner of the house knew what time of night the robber was coming. Then he would have kept watch. He would not have let his house be broken into. [44]So you also must be ready. The Son of Man will come at an hour when you don't expect him.

[45]"Suppose a master puts one of his slaves in charge of the other slaves in his house. The slave's job is to give them their food at the right time. The master wants a faithful and wise slave for this. [46]It will be good for the slave if the master finds him doing his job when the master returns. [47]What I'm about to tell you is true. The master will put that slave in charge of everything he owns. [48]But suppose that slave is evil. Suppose he says to himself, 'My master is staying away a long time.' [49]Suppose

he begins to beat the other slaves. And suppose he eats and drinks with those who drink too much. [50]The master of that slave will come back on a day the slave doesn't expect him. He will return at an hour the slave does not know. [51]Then the master will cut him to pieces. He will send him to the place where pretenders go. There people will weep and grind their teeth.

The Story of Ten Bridesmaids

25 "Here is what the kingdom of heaven will be like at that time. Ten bridesmaids took their lamps and went out to meet the groom. [2]Five of them were foolish. Five were wise. [3]The foolish ones took their lamps but didn't take any olive oil with them. [4]The wise ones took oil in jars along with their lamps. [5]The groom did not come for a long time. So the bridesmaids all grew tired and fell asleep.

[6]"At midnight someone cried out, 'Here's the groom! Come out to meet him!'

[7]"Then all the bridesmaids woke up and got their lamps ready. [8]The foolish ones said to the wise ones, 'Give us some of your oil. Our lamps are going out.'

[9]" 'No,' they replied. 'There may not be enough for all of us. Instead, go to those who sell oil. Buy some for yourselves.'

[10]"So they went to buy the oil. But while they were on their way, the groom arrived. The bridesmaids who were ready went in

Jesus' parable of the ten bridesmaids was about being watchful because we don't know the time when things will happen. Robyn Jacobs found out why being on time is important when a dog chased her in "Better Late than Never" (A#09).

with him to the wedding dinner. Then the door was shut.

[11]"Later, the other bridesmaids also came. 'Sir! Sir!' they said. 'Open the door for us!'

[12]"But he replied, 'What I'm about to tell you is true. I don't know you.'

[13]"So keep watch. You do not know the day or the hour that the groom will come.

The Story of Three Slaves

[14]"Again, here is what the kingdom of heaven will be like. A man was going on a journey. He sent for his slaves and put them in charge of his money. [15]He gave five bags of gold to one. He gave two bags to another. And he gave one bag to the third. The man gave each slave the amount of money he knew the slave could take care of. Then he went on his journey. [16]The slave who had received five bags of gold went at once and put his money to work. He earned five bags more. [17]The one with the two bags of gold earned two more. [18]But the man who had received one bag went and dug a hole in the ground. He hid his master's money in it.

[19]"After a long time the master of those slaves returned. He wanted to collect all the money they had earned. [20]The man who had received five bags of gold brought the other five. 'Master,' he said, 'you trusted me with five bags of gold. See, I have earned five more.'

[21]"His master replied, 'You have done well, good and faithful slave! You have been faithful with a few things. I will put you in charge of many things. Come and share your master's happiness!'

[22]"The man with two bags of gold also came. 'Master,' he said, 'you trusted me with two bags of gold. See, I have earned two more.'

[23]"His master replied, 'You have done well, good and faithful slave! You have been faithful with a few things. I will put you in charge of many things. Come and share your master's happiness!'

[24]"Then the man who had received one bag of gold came. 'Master,' he said, 'I knew that you are a hard man. You harvest where you have not planted. You gather crops where you have not scattered seed. [25]So I was afraid. I went out and hid your gold in the ground. See, here is what belongs to you.'

WHIT'S WISDOM

Matthew 25:14–29

One day, Donna Barclay told me about how her family had gotten into a big discussion about money and decided to go on a budget. Donna was concerned because she didn't know what would be part of the budget. Maybe she wouldn't be able to buy what she wanted. Maybe the family wouldn't be able to go on vacations anymore.

She was convinced the budget would be terrible!

I thought it could be a very good thing. It could help everyone in the family to be good stewards. A steward is a person who looks after someone else's business or money, like Jesus told in a parable in Matthew 25. We're all stewards of God. He's given us everything we have, and He expects us to take good care of what He has given us, and to use it wisely. It's very smart to learn responsibility with money early in life. It's easier to learn when you're young than when you're an adult.

²⁶"His master replied, 'You evil, lazy slave! So you knew that I harvest where I have not planted? You knew that I gather crops where I have not scattered seed? ²⁷Well then, you should have put my money in the bank. When I returned, I would have received it back with interest.'

²⁸"Then his master commanded the other slaves, 'Take the bag of gold from him. Give it to the one who has ten bags. ²⁹Everyone who has will be given more. They will have more than enough. And what about anyone who doesn't have? Even what they have will be taken away from them. ³⁰Throw that worthless slave outside. There in the darkness, people will weep and grind their teeth.'

The Sheep and the Goats

³¹"The Son of Man will come in all his glory. All the angels will come with him. Then he will sit in glory on his throne. ³²All the nations will be gathered in front of him. He will separate the people into two groups. He will be like a shepherd who separates the sheep from the goats. ³³He will put the sheep to his right and the goats to his left.

³⁴"Then the King will speak to those on his right. He will say, 'My Father has blessed you. Come and take what is yours. It is the kingdom prepared for you since the world was created. ³⁵I was hungry. And you gave me something to eat. I was thirsty. And you gave me something to drink. I was a stranger. And you invited me in. ³⁶I needed clothes. And you gave them to me. I was sick. And you took care of me. I was in prison. And you came to visit me.'

³⁷"Then the people who have done what is right will answer him. 'Lord,' they will ask, 'when did we see you hungry and feed you? When did we see you thirsty and give you something to drink? ³⁸When did we see you as a stranger and invite you in? When did we see you needing clothes and give them to you? ³⁹When did we see you sick or in prison and go to visit you?'

⁴⁰"The King will reply, 'What I'm about to tell you is true. Anything you did for one of the least important of these brothers and sisters of mine, you did for me.'

⁴¹"Then he will say to those on his left, 'You are cursed! Go away from me into the fire that burns forever. It has been prepared for the devil and his angels. ⁴²I was hungry. But you gave me nothing to eat. I was thirsty. But you gave me nothing to drink. ⁴³I was a stranger. But you did not invite me in. I needed clothes. But you did not give me any. I was sick and in prison. But you did not take care of me.'

⁴⁴"They also will answer, 'Lord, when did we see you hungry or thirsty and not help you? When did we see you as a stranger or needing clothes or sick or in prison and not help you?'

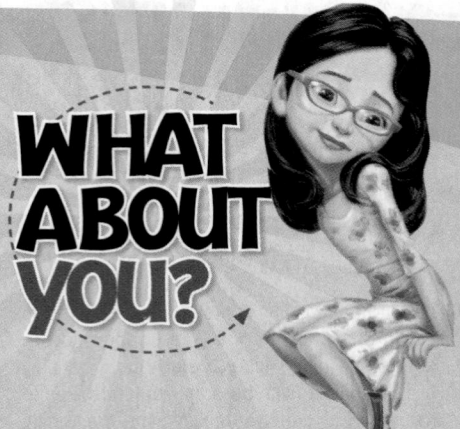

In the Adventures in Odyssey episode "Best Intentions," Connie and Eugene go overboard to help Whit recover from his hospital stay. But some peace and quiet would be even more helpful.

Does this example mean we should ignore our friends when they're sick or hurting? Of course not. It simply means that we need to invest enough in our friends' lives to know what they really need from us. Sometimes what a friend needs is exactly what you would have thought of yourself. But sometimes it's not. Ask questions. Dig deeper. That's a sign of compassion.

When we serve others, God treats it as if we're serving Him. (That's the point of Jesus' story in Matthew 25.) Serving is an act of worship that also blesses other people! With that in mind, remember Galatians 6:9: "Let us not become tired of doing good. At the right time we will gather a crop if we don't give up."

Visiting a sick friend may or may not be the best idea. But even if it's not (your friend might be weak, tired, or contagious), there are other ways to show that you care. Call or text on the phone. Write a nice note inside a get-well card. See if you can be of help by dropping off homework assignments, a favorite snack, or a movie. Take the time to see what your friend really needs right now. It might be your company. Or it could be something else.

---

⁴⁵"He will reply, 'What I'm about to tell you is true. Anything you didn't do for one of the least important of these, you didn't do for me.'

⁴⁶"Then they will go away to be punished forever. But those who have done what is right will receive eternal life."

The Plan to Kill Jesus

26 Jesus finished saying all these things. Then he said to his disciples, ²"As you know, the Passover Feast is two days away. The Son of Man will be handed over to be nailed to a cross."

³Then the chief priests met with the elders of the people. They met in the palace of Caiaphas, the high priest. ⁴They made plans to arrest Jesus secretly. They wanted to kill him. ⁵"But not during the feast," they said. "The people may stir up trouble."

A Woman Pours Perfume on Jesus

⁶Jesus was in Bethany. He was in the home of Simon, who had a skin disease. ⁷A woman came to Jesus with a special sealed jar of very expensive perfume. She poured the perfume on his head while he was at the table.

⁸When the disciples saw this, they became angry. "Why this waste?" they asked. ⁹"The perfume could have been sold at a high price. The money could have been given to poor people."

¹⁰Jesus was aware of this. So he said to them, "Why are you bothering this woman? She has done a beautiful thing to me. ¹¹You will always have poor people with you. But you will not always have me. ¹²She poured the perfume on my body to prepare me to be buried. ¹³What I'm about to tell you is true. What she has done will be told anywhere this good news is preached all over the world. It will be told in memory of her."

Judas Agrees to Hand Jesus Over

¹⁴One of the 12 disciples went to the chief priests. His name was Judas Iscariot. ¹⁵He asked, "What will you give me if I hand Jesus over to you?" So they counted

out 30 silver coins for him. [16]From then on, Judas watched for the right time to hand Jesus over to them.

The Lord's Supper

[17]It was the first day of the Feast of Unleavened Bread. The disciples came to Jesus. They asked, "Where do you want us to prepare for you to eat the Passover meal?"

[18]He replied, "Go into the city to a certain man. Tell him, 'The Teacher says, "My time is near. I am going to celebrate the Passover at your house with my disciples." ' " [19]So the disciples did what Jesus had told them to do. They prepared the Passover meal.

[20]When evening came, Jesus was at the table with his 12 disciples. [21]While they were eating, he said, "What I'm about to tell you is true. One of you will hand me over to my enemies."

[22]The disciples became very sad. One after the other, they began to say to him, "Surely you don't mean me, Lord, do you?"

[23]Jesus replied, "The one who has dipped his hand into the bowl with me will hand me over. [24]The Son of Man will go just as it is written about him. But how terrible it will be for the one who hands over the Son of Man! It would be better for him if he had not been born."

[25]Judas was the one who was going to hand him over. He said, "Surely you don't mean me, Teacher, do you?"

Jesus answered, "You have said so."

[26]While they were eating, Jesus took bread. He gave thanks and broke it. He handed it to his disciples and said, "Take this and eat it. This is my body."

[27]Then he took a cup. He gave thanks and handed it to them. He said, "All of you drink from it. [28]This is my blood of the covenant. It is poured out to forgive the sins of many people. [29]Here is what I tell you. From now on, I won't drink wine with you again until the day I drink it with you in my Father's kingdom."

[30]Then they sang a hymn and went out to the Mount of Olives.

Jesus Says That the Disciples Will Turn Away

[31]Jesus told them, "This very night you will all turn away because of me. It is written that the Lord said,

" 'I will strike the shepherd down.
  Then the sheep of the flock will be
    scattered.' " *(Zechariah 13:7)*

[32]But after I rise from the dead, I will go ahead of you into Galilee."

[33]Peter replied, "All the others may turn away because of you. But I never will."

[34]"What I'm about to tell you is true," Jesus answered. "It will happen tonight. Before the rooster crows, you will say three times that you don't know me."

[35]But Peter said, "I may have to die with you. But I will never say I don't know you." And all the other disciples said the same thing.

Jesus Prays in Gethsemane

[36]Then Jesus went with his disciples to a place called Gethsemane. He said to them, "Sit here while I go over there and pray." [37]He took Peter and the two sons of Zebedee along with him. He began to be sad and troubled. [38]Then he said to them, "My soul is very sad. I feel close to death. Stay here. Keep watch with me."

[39]He went a little farther. Then he fell with his face to the ground. He prayed, "My Father, if it is possible, take this cup of suffering away from me. But let what you want be done, not what I want."

[40]Then he returned to his disciples and found them sleeping. "Couldn't you men keep watch with me for one hour?" he asked Peter. [41]"Watch and pray. Then you won't fall into sin when you are tempted. The spirit is willing, but the body is weak."

[42]Jesus went away a second time. He prayed, "My Father, is it possible for this cup to be taken away? But if I must drink it, may what you want be done."

[43]Then he came back. Again he found them sleeping. They couldn't keep their eyes open. [44]So he left them and went away once more. For the third time he prayed the same thing.

[45]Then he returned to the disciples. He said to them, "Are you still sleeping and resting? Look! The hour has come. The Son of Man is about to be handed over to sinners. [46]Get up! Let us go! Here comes the one who is handing me over to them!"

Jesus Is Arrested

[47]While Jesus was still speaking, Judas arrived. He was one of the 12 disciples. A

large crowd was with him. They were carrying swords and clubs. The chief priests and the elders of the people had sent them. [48]Judas, who was going to hand Jesus over, had arranged a signal with them. "The one I kiss is the man," he said. "Arrest him." [49]So Judas went to Jesus at once. He said, "Greetings, Rabbi!" And he kissed him.

[50]Jesus replied, "Friend, do what you came to do."

Then the men stepped forward. They grabbed Jesus and arrested him. [51]At that moment, one of Jesus' companions reached for his sword. He pulled it out and struck the slave of the high priest with it. He cut off the slave's ear.

[52]"Put your sword back in its place," Jesus said to him. "All who use the sword will die by the sword. [53]Do you think I can't ask my Father for help? He would send an army of more than 70,000 angels right away. [54]But then how would the Scriptures come true? They say it must happen in this way."

[55]At that time Jesus spoke to the crowd. "Am I leading a band of armed men against you?" he asked. "Do you have to come out with swords and clubs to capture me? Every day I sat in the temple courtyard teaching. And you didn't arrest me. [56]But all this has happened so that the words of the prophets would come true." Then all the disciples left him and ran away.

Jesus Is Taken to the Sanhedrin

[57]Those who had arrested Jesus took him to Caiaphas, the high priest. The teachers of the law and the elders had come together there. [58]Not too far away, Peter followed Jesus. He went right up to the courtyard of the high priest. He entered and sat down with the guards to see what would happen.

[59]The chief priests and the whole Sanhedrin were looking for something to use against Jesus. They wanted to put him to death. [60]But they did not find any proof, even though many false witnesses came forward.

Finally, two other witnesses came forward. [61]They said, "This fellow claimed, 'I am able to destroy the temple of God. I can build it again in three days.'"

[62]Then the high priest stood up. He asked Jesus, "Aren't you going to answer? What are these charges that these men are bringing against you?" [63]But Jesus remained silent.

The high priest said to him, "I am commanding you in the name of the living God. May he judge you if you don't tell the truth. Tell us if you are the Messiah, the Son of God."

[64]"You have said so," Jesus replied. "But here is what I say to all of you. From now on, you will see the Son of Man sitting at the right hand of the Mighty One. You will see the Son of Man coming on the clouds of heaven."

[65]Then the high priest tore his clothes. He said, "He has spoken a very evil thing against God! Why do we need any more witnesses? You have heard him say this evil thing. [66]What do you think?"

"He must die!" they answered.

[67]Then they spit in his face. They hit him with their fists. Others slapped him. [68]They said, "Prophesy to us, Messiah! Who hit you?"

Peter Says He Does Not Know Jesus

[69]Peter was sitting out in the courtyard. A female servant came to him. "You also were with Jesus of Galilee," she said.

[70]But in front of all of them, Peter said he was not. "I don't know what you're talking about," he said.

[71]Then he went out to the gate leading into the courtyard. There another servant saw him. She said to the people, "This fellow was with Jesus of Nazareth."

[72]Again he said he was not. With a curse he said, "I don't know the man!"

[73]After a little while, those standing there went up to Peter. "You must be one of them," they said. "The way you talk gives you away."

[74]Then Peter began to curse and said to them, "I don't know the man!"

Right away a rooster crowed. [75]Then Peter remembered what Jesus had said. "The rooster will crow," Jesus had told him. "Before it does, you will say three times that you don't know me." Peter went outside. He broke down and cried.

Judas Hangs Himself

27 It was early in the morning. All the chief priests and the elders of the people planned how to put Jesus to death. [2]So they tied him up and led him away. Then they handed him over to Pilate, who was the governor.

³Judas, who had handed him over, saw that Jesus had been sentenced to die. He felt deep shame and sadness for what he had done. So he returned the 30 silver coins to the chief priests and the elders. ⁴"I have sinned," he said. "I handed over a man who is not guilty."

"What do we care?" they replied. "That's your problem."

⁵So Judas threw the money into the temple and left. Then he went away and hanged himself.

⁶The chief priests picked up the coins. They said, "It's against the law to put this money into the temple fund. It is blood money. It has paid for a man's death." ⁷So they decided to use the money to buy a potter's field. People from other countries would be buried there. ⁸That is why it has been called the Field of Blood to this day. ⁹Then the words spoken by Jeremiah the prophet came true. He had said, "They took the 30 silver coins. That price was set for him by the people of Israel. ¹⁰They used the coins to buy a potter's field, just as the Lord commanded me." *(Zechariah 11:12,13; Jeremiah 19:1–13; 32:6–9)*

Jesus Is Brought to Pilate

¹¹Jesus was standing in front of the governor. The governor asked him, "Are you the king of the Jews?"

"Yes. You have said so," Jesus replied.

¹²But when the chief priests and the elders brought charges against him, he did not answer. ¹³Then Pilate asked him, "Don't you hear the charges they are bringing against you?" ¹⁴But Jesus made no reply, not even to a single charge. The governor was really amazed.

¹⁵It was the governor's practice at the Passover Feast to let one prisoner go free. The people could choose the one they wanted. ¹⁶At that time they had a well-known prisoner named Jesus Barabbas. ¹⁷So when the crowd gathered, Pilate asked them, "Which one do you want me to set free? Jesus Barabbas? Or Jesus who is called the Messiah?" ¹⁸Pilate knew that the leaders wanted to get their own way. He knew this was why they had handed Jesus over to him.

¹⁹While Pilate was sitting on the judge's seat, his wife sent him a message. It said, "Don't have anything to do with that man. He is not guilty. I have suffered a great deal in a dream today because of him."

BiBLe ADVeNTURes

Harlowquin Doylecus, Private Roman Eye, interviewed Mrs. Dilberius, a fictional servant of Pilate's, in "B-TV: To Tell the Truth" (Club).

²⁰But the chief priests and the elders talked the crowd into asking for Barabbas and having Jesus put to death. ²¹"Which of the two do you want me to set free?" asked the governor.

"Barabbas," they answered.

²²"Then what should I do with Jesus who is called the Messiah?" Pilate asked.

They all answered, "Crucify him!"

²³"Why? What wrong has he done?" asked Pilate.

But they shouted even louder, "Crucify him!"

²⁴Pilate saw that he wasn't getting anywhere. Instead, the crowd was starting to get angry. So he took water and washed his hands in front of them. "I am not guilty of this man's death," he said. "You are accountable for that!"

²⁵All the people answered, "Put the blame for his death on us and our children!"

²⁶Pilate let Barabbas go free. But he had Jesus whipped. Then he handed him over to be nailed to a cross.

The Soldiers Make Fun of Jesus

²⁷The governor's soldiers took Jesus into the palace, which was called the Praetorium. All the rest of the soldiers gathered around him. ²⁸They took off his clothes and put a purple robe on him. ²⁹Then they twisted thorns together to make a crown. They placed it on his head. They put a stick in his right hand. Then they fell on their knees in front of him and made fun of him. "We honor you, king of the Jews!" they said. ³⁰They spit on him. They hit him on the head with the stick again and again. ³¹After they had made fun of him, they took off the robe. They put his own clothes back on him. Then they led him away to nail him to a cross.

Jesus Is Nailed to a Cross

³²On their way out of the city, they met a man from Cyrene. His name was Simon.

They forced him to carry the cross. ³³They came to a place called Golgotha. The word Golgotha means the Place of the Skull. ³⁴There they mixed wine with bitter spices and gave it to Jesus to drink. After tasting it, he refused to drink it. ³⁵When they had nailed him to the cross, they divided up his clothes by casting lots. ³⁶They sat down and kept watch over him there. ³⁷Above his head they placed the written charge against him. It read,

THIS IS JESUS, THE KING OF THE JEWS.

³⁸Two rebels against Rome were crucified with him. One was on his right and one was on his left. ³⁹Those who passed by shouted at Jesus and made fun of him. They shook their heads ⁴⁰and said, "So you are going to destroy the temple and build it again in three days? Then save yourself! Come down from the cross, if you are the Son of God!" ⁴¹In the same way the chief priests, the teachers of the law and the elders made fun of him. ⁴²"He saved others," they said. "But he can't save himself! He's the king of Israel! Let him come down now from the cross! Then we will believe in him. ⁴³He trusts in God. Let God rescue him now if he wants him. He's the one who said, 'I am the Son of God.' " ⁴⁴In the same way the rebels who were being crucified with Jesus also made fun of him.

Jesus Dies

⁴⁵From noon until three o'clock, the whole land was covered with darkness. ⁴⁶About three o'clock, Jesus cried out in a loud voice. He said, *"Eli, Eli, lema sabachthani?"* This means "My God, my God, why have you deserted me?" *(Psalm 22:1)* ⁴⁷Some of those standing there heard Jesus cry out. They said, "He's calling for Elijah."

⁴⁸Right away one of them ran and got a sponge. He filled it with wine vinegar and put it on a stick. He offered it to Jesus to drink. ⁴⁹The rest said, "Leave him alone. Let's see if Elijah comes to save him."

⁵⁰After Jesus cried out again in a loud voice, he died.

⁵¹At that moment the temple curtain was torn in two from top to bottom. The earth shook. The rocks split. ⁵²Tombs broke open. The bodies of many holy people who had died were raised to life. ⁵³They came out of the tombs. After Jesus was raised from the dead, they went into the holy city. There they appeared to many people.

⁵⁴The Roman commander and those guarding Jesus saw the earthquake and all that had happened. They were terrified. They exclaimed, "He was surely the Son of God!"

⁵⁵Not very far away, many women were watching. They had followed Jesus from Galilee to take care of his needs. ⁵⁶Mary Magdalene was among them. Mary, the mother of James and Joseph, was also there. So was the mother of Zebedee's sons.

Jesus Is Buried

⁵⁷As evening approached, a rich man came from the town of Arimathea. His name was Joseph. He had become a follower of Jesus. ⁵⁸He went to Pilate and asked for Jesus' body. Pilate ordered that it be given to him. ⁵⁹Joseph took the body and wrapped it in a clean linen cloth. ⁶⁰He placed it in his own new tomb that he had cut out of the rock. He rolled a big stone in front of the entrance to the tomb. Then he went away. ⁶¹Mary Magdalene and the other Mary were sitting there across from the tomb.

The Guards at the Tomb

⁶²The next day was the day after Preparation Day. The chief priests and the Pharisees went to Pilate. ⁶³"Sir," they said, "we remember something that liar said while he was still alive. He claimed, 'After three days I will rise again.' ⁶⁴So give the order to make the tomb secure until the third day. If you don't, his disciples might come and steal the body. Then they will tell the people that Jesus has been raised from the dead. This last lie will be worse than the first."

⁶⁵"Take some guards with you," Pilate answered. "Go. Make the tomb as secure as you can." ⁶⁶So they went and made the tomb secure. They put a royal seal on the stone and placed some guards on duty.

Jesus Rises From the Dead

28 The Sabbath day was now over. It was dawn on the first day of the week. Mary Magdalene and the other Mary went to look at the tomb.

²There was a powerful earthquake. An angel of the Lord came down from heaven. The angel went to the tomb. He rolled back

the stone and sat on it. ³His body shone like lightning. His clothes were as white as snow. ⁴The guards were so afraid of him that they shook and became like dead men.

⁵The angel said to the women, "Don't be afraid. I know that you are looking for Jesus, who was crucified. ⁶He is not here! He has risen, just as he said he would! Come and see the place where he was lying. ⁷Go quickly! Tell his disciples, 'He has risen from the dead. He is going ahead of you into Galilee. There you will see him.' Now I have told you."

⁸So the women hurried away from the tomb. They were afraid, but they were filled with joy. They ran to tell the disciples. ⁹Suddenly Jesus met them. "Greetings!" he said. They came to him, took hold of his feet and worshiped him. ¹⁰Then Jesus said to them, "Don't be afraid. Go and tell my brothers to go to Galilee. There they will see me."

The Guards Report to the Chief Priests

¹¹While the women were on their way, some of the guards went into the city. They reported to the chief priests all that had happened. ¹²When the chief priests met with the elders, they came up with a plan. They gave the soldiers a large amount of money. ¹³They told the soldiers, "We want

you to say, 'His disciples came during the night. They stole his body while we were sleeping.' ¹⁴If the governor hears this report, we will pay him off. That will keep you out of trouble." ¹⁵So the soldiers took the money and did as they were told. This story has spread all around among the Jews to this day.

Jesus' Final Orders to His Disciples

¹⁶Then the 11 disciples went to Galilee. They went to the mountain where Jesus had told them to go. ¹⁷When they saw him, they worshiped him. But some still had their doubts. ¹⁸Then Jesus came to them. He said, "All authority in heaven and on earth has been given to me. ¹⁹So you must go and make disciples of all nations. Baptize them in the name of the Father and of the Son and of the Holy Spirit. ²⁰Teach them to obey everything I have commanded you. And you can be sure that I am always with you, to the very end."

Mark

Intriguingly, we find out small details about John Mark, the writer of this second gospel, in other books of the New Testament. His mother housed a church in her home (Acts 12:12). His cousin was Barnabas (Col. 4:10), a prominent figure of the early church. And Mark himself traveled with Barnabas and Paul on a lengthy missionary journey (Acts 12:25). However, for reasons never revealed in the Bible, John Mark left before the trip was over, which eventually led to a sharp disagreement between Paul and Barnabas (Acts 15:36–38). Mark then ministered with Barnabas in Cyprus (Acts 15:39).

Clearly Mark was around a lot of knowledgeable people. Most scholars believe that he got his information about Jesus from Peter. A more reliable source about Jesus one would be hard-pressed to find!

For someone new to Christianity or unfamiliar with the life and teachings of Jesus, Mark is an excellent place to begin. It is the shortest of the four gospels, and probably the oldest. Mark didn't presume his readers would know a lot about Jewish customs. His goal was to recruit new disciples for Jesus by making their faith more relevant to real life. I pray that Mark's gospel will inspire you to a greater level of faithfulness in *your* life.

WHAT'S IT MEAN, EUGENE?

Evangelism—To *evangelize* is to spread the *evangelion*, which is the Greek word for "gospel" or "announcement of good tidings." Jesus commanded His followers to engage in the work of evangelism when He said, "Go into all the world. Preach the *evangelion* [good news] to everyone" (Mark 16:15).

John the Baptist Prepares the Way

1 This is the beginning of the good news about Jesus the Messiah, the Son of God. [2]Long ago Isaiah the prophet wrote,

"I will send my messenger ahead of you.
He will prepare your way."
(Malachi 3:1)

[3] "A messenger is calling out in the desert,
'Prepare the way for the Lord.
Make straight paths for him.'"
(Isaiah 40:3)

[4]And so John the Baptist appeared in the desert. He preached that people should be baptized and turn away from their sins. Then God would forgive them. [5]All the people from the countryside of Judea went out to him. All the people from Jerusalem went too. When they admitted they had sinned, John baptized them in the Jordan River. [6]John wore clothes made out of camel's hair. He had a leather belt around his waist. And he ate locusts and wild honey. [7]Here is what John was preaching. "After me, there is someone coming who is more powerful than I am. I'm not good enough to bend down and untie his sandals. [8]I baptize you with water. But he will baptize you with the Holy Spirit."

Jesus Is Baptized and Tempted

[9]At that time Jesus came from Nazareth in Galilee. John baptized Jesus in the Jordan River. [10]Jesus was coming up out of the water. Just then he saw heaven being torn open. Jesus saw the Holy Spirit coming down on him like a dove. [11]A voice spoke to him from heaven. It said, "You are my Son, and I love you. I am very pleased with you."

[12]At once the Holy Spirit sent Jesus out into the desert. [13]He was in the desert 40 days. There Satan tempted him. The wild animals didn't harm Jesus. Angels took care of him.

Jesus Preaches the Good News

[14]After John was put in prison, Jesus went into Galilee. He preached the good news of God. [15]"The time has come," he said. "The kingdom of God has come near. Turn away from your sins and believe the good news!"

Jesus Chooses His First Disciples

[16]One day Jesus was walking beside the Sea of Galilee. There he saw Simon and his brother Andrew. They were throwing a net into the lake. They were fishermen. [17]"Come and follow me," Jesus said. "I will send you out to fish for people." [18]At once they left their nets and followed him.

[19]Then Jesus walked a little farther. As he did, he saw James, the son of Zebedee, and his brother John. They were in a boat preparing their nets. [20]Right away he called out to them. They left their father Zebedee in the boat with the hired men. Then they followed Jesus.

Jesus Drives Out an Evil Spirit

[21]Jesus and those with him went to Capernaum. When the Sabbath day came, he went into the synagogue. There he began to teach. [22]The people were amazed at his teaching. That's because he taught them like one who had authority. He did not talk like the teachers of the law. [23]Just then a man in their synagogue cried out. He was controlled by an evil spirit. He said, [24]"What do you want with us, Jesus of Nazareth? Have you come to destroy us? I know who you are. You are the Holy One of God!"

[25]"Be quiet!" said Jesus firmly. "Come out of him!" [26]The evil spirit shook the man wildly. Then it came out of him with a scream.

[27]All the people were amazed. So they asked each other, "What is this? A new teaching! And with so much authority! He even gives orders to evil spirits, and they obey him." [28]News about Jesus spread quickly all over Galilee.

Jesus Heals Many People

[29]Jesus and those with him left the synagogue. Right away they went with James and John to the home of Simon and Andrew. [30]Simon's mother-in-law was lying in bed with a fever. They told Jesus about her right away. [31]So he went to her. He took her hand and helped her up. The fever left her. Then she began to serve them.

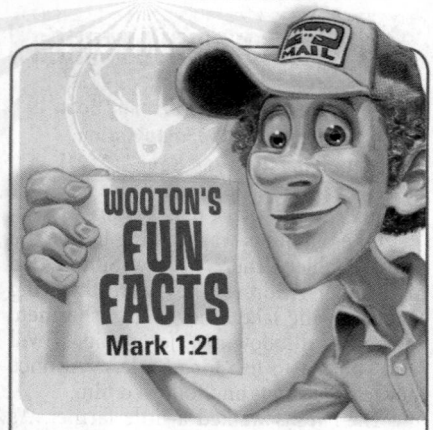

I once thought that *synagogue* just meant "temple"—and that it was a good word for the game Hangman! But in the Bible *Temple* refers to the ancient one in Jerusalem. A *synagogue* is a "place of assembly." There were a lot of synagogues but only one Temple.

³²That evening after sunset, the people brought to Jesus all who were sick. They also brought all who were controlled by demons. ³³All the people in town gathered at the door. ³⁴Jesus healed many of them. They had all kinds of sicknesses. He also drove out many demons. But he would not let the demons speak, because they knew who he was.

Jesus Prays in a Quiet Place

³⁵It was very early in the morning and still dark. Jesus got up and left the house. He went to a place where he could be alone. There he prayed. ³⁶Simon and his friends went to look for Jesus. ³⁷When they found him, they called out, "Everyone is looking for you!"

³⁸Jesus replied, "Let's go somewhere else. I want to go to the nearby towns. I must preach there also. That is why I have come." ³⁹So he traveled all around Galilee. He preached in their synagogues. He also drove out demons.

Jesus Heals a Man Who Had a Skin Disease

⁴⁰A man who had a skin disease came to Jesus. On his knees he begged Jesus. He said, "If you are willing to make me 'clean,' you can do it."

⁴¹Jesus became angry. He reached out his hand and touched the man. "I am willing to do it," Jesus said. "Be 'clean'!" ⁴²Right away the disease left the man, and he was "clean."

⁴³Jesus sent him away at once. He gave the man a strong warning. ⁴⁴"Don't tell this to anyone," he said. "Go and show yourself to the priest. Offer the sacrifices that Moses commanded. It will be a witness to the priest and the people that you are 'clean.'"

⁴⁵But the man went out and started talking right away. He spread the news to everyone. So Jesus could no longer enter a town openly. He stayed outside in lonely places. But people still came to him from everywhere.

Jesus Forgives and Heals a Man Who Could Not Walk

2 A few days later, Jesus entered Capernaum again. The people heard that he had come home. ²So many people gathered that there was no room left. There was not even room outside the door. And Jesus preached the word to them. ³Four of those who came were carrying a man who could not walk. ⁴But they could not get him close to Jesus because of the crowd. So they made a hole by digging through the roof above Jesus. Then they lowered the man through it on a mat. ⁵Jesus saw their faith. So he said to the man, "Son, your sins are forgiven."

⁶Some teachers of the law were sitting there. They were thinking, ⁷"Why is this fellow talking like that? He's saying a very evil thing! Only God can forgive sins!"

⁸Right away Jesus knew what they were thinking. So he said to them, "Why are you thinking these things? ⁹Is it easier to say to this man, 'Your sins are forgiven'? Or to say, 'Get up, take your mat and walk'? ¹⁰But I want you to know that the Son of Man has authority on earth to forgive sins." So Jesus spoke to the man who could not walk. ¹¹"I tell you," he said, "get up. Take your mat and go home." ¹²The man got up and took his mat. Then he walked away while everyone watched. All the people were amazed. They praised God and said, "We have never seen anything like this!"

Jesus Chooses Levi and Eats With Sinners

¹³Once again Jesus went out beside the Sea of Galilee. A large crowd came to him.

He began to teach them. [14]As he walked along he saw Levi, the son of Alphaeus. Levi was sitting at the tax collector's booth. "Follow me," Jesus told him. Levi got up and followed him.

[15]Later Jesus was having dinner at Levi's house. Many tax collectors and sinners were eating with him and his disciples. They were part of the large crowd following Jesus. [16]Some teachers of the law who were Pharisees were there. They saw Jesus eating with sinners and tax collectors. So they asked his disciples, "Why does he eat with tax collectors and sinners?"

[17]Jesus heard that. So he said to them, "Those who are healthy don't need a doctor. Sick people do. I have not come to get those who think they are right with God to follow me. I have come to get sinners to follow me."

Jesus Is Asked About Fasting

[18]John's disciples and the Pharisees were going without eating. Some people came to Jesus. They said to him, "John's disciples are fasting. The disciples of the Pharisees are also fasting. But your disciples are not. Why aren't they?"

[19]Jesus answered, "How can the guests of the groom go without eating while he is with them? They will not fast as long as he is with them. [20]But the time will come when the groom will be taken away from them. On that day they will go without eating.

[21]"No one sews a patch of new cloth on old clothes. Otherwise, the new piece will pull away from the old. That will make the tear worse. [22]No one pours new wine into old wineskins. Otherwise, the wine will burst the skins. Then the wine and the wineskins will both be destroyed. No, people pour new wine into new wineskins."

Jesus Is Lord of the Sabbath Day

[23]One Sabbath day Jesus was walking with his disciples through the grainfields. The disciples began to break off some heads of grain. [24]The Pharisees said to Jesus, "Look! It is against the Law to do this on the Sabbath day. Why are your disciples doing it?"

[25]He answered, "Haven't you ever read about what David did? He and his men were hungry. They needed food. [26]It was when Abiathar was high priest. David entered the house of God and ate the holy bread. Only priests were allowed to eat it. David also gave some to his men."

[27]Then Jesus said to them, "The Sabbath day was made for man. Man was not made for the Sabbath day. [28]So the Son of Man is Lord even of the Sabbath day."

Jesus Heals on the Sabbath Day

3 Another time Jesus went into the synagogue. A man with a weak and twisted hand was there. [2]Some Pharisees were trying to find fault with Jesus. They watched him closely. They wanted to see if he would heal the man on the Sabbath day. [3]Jesus spoke to the man with the weak and twisted hand. "Stand up in front of everyone," he said.

[4]Then Jesus asked them, "What does the Law say we should do on the Sabbath day? Should we do good? Or should we do evil? Should we save life? Or should we kill?" But no one answered.

[5]Jesus looked around at them in anger. He was very upset because their hearts were stubborn. Then he said to the man, "Stretch out your hand." He stretched it out, and his hand had become as good as new. [6]Then the Pharisees went out and began to make plans with the Herodians. They wanted to kill Jesus.

Crowds Follow Jesus

[7]Jesus went off to the Sea of Galilee with his disciples. A large crowd from Galilee followed. [8]People heard about all that Jesus was doing. And many came to him. They came from Judea, Jerusalem and Idumea. They came from the lands east of the Jordan River. And they came from the area around Tyre and Sidon. [9]Because of the crowd, Jesus told his disciples to get a small boat ready for him. This would keep the people from crowding him. [10]Jesus had healed many people. So those who were sick were pushing forward to touch him. [11]When people controlled by evil spirits saw him, they fell down in front of him. The spirits shouted, "You are the Son of God!" [12]But Jesus ordered them not to tell people about him.

Jesus Appoints the Twelve Disciples

[13]Jesus went up on a mountainside. He called for certain people to come to him,

ADVENTURES IN ODYSSEY

In the adventure "Follow Me" (Club), Whit presented a story from the Book of Speculations that imagined what Jesus' disciples might have been as children.

and they came. ¹⁴He appointed 12 of them so that they would be with him. He would also send them out to preach. ¹⁵And he gave them authority to drive out demons.

¹⁶ So Jesus appointed the 12 disciples.

Simon was one of them. Jesus gave him the name Peter.

¹⁷ There were James, son of Zebedee, and his brother John. Jesus gave them the name Boanerges. Boanerges means Sons of Thunder.

¹⁸ There were also Andrew,
Philip,
Bartholomew,
Matthew,
Thomas,
and James, son of Alphaeus.
And there were Thaddaeus
and Simon the Zealot.

¹⁹ Judas Iscariot was one of them too. He was the one who was later going to hand Jesus over to his enemies.

Jesus Is Accused by Teachers of the Law

²⁰Jesus entered a house. Again a crowd gathered. It was so large that Jesus and his disciples were not even able to eat. ²¹His family heard about this. So they went to take charge of him. They said, "He is out of his mind."

²²Some teachers of the law were there. They had come down from Jerusalem. They said, "He is controlled by Beelzebul! He is driving out demons by the power of the prince of demons."

²³So Jesus called them over to him. He began to speak to them using stories. He said, "How can Satan drive out Satan? ²⁴If a kingdom fights against itself, it can't stand. ²⁵If a family is divided, it can't stand. ²⁶And if Satan fights against himself, and his helpers are divided, he can't stand. That is the end of him. ²⁷In fact, none of you can enter a strong man's house unless you tie him up first. Then you can steal things from his house. ²⁸What I'm about to tell you is true. Everyone's sins and evil words against God will be forgiven. ²⁹But whoever speaks evil things against the Holy Spirit will never be forgiven. Their guilt will last forever."

³⁰Jesus said this because the teachers of the law were saying, "He has an evil spirit."

Jesus' Mother and Brothers

³¹Jesus' mother and brothers came and stood outside. They sent someone in to get him. ³²A crowd was sitting around Jesus. They told him, "Your mother and your brothers are outside. They are looking for you."

³³"Who is my mother? Who are my brothers?" he asked.

³⁴Then Jesus looked at the people sitting in a circle around him. He said, "Here is my mother! Here are my brothers! ³⁵Anyone who does what God wants is my brother or sister or mother."

The Story of the Farmer

4 Again Jesus began to teach by the Sea of Galilee. The crowd that gathered around him was very large. So he got into a boat. He sat down in it out on the lake. All the people were along the shore at the water's edge. ²He taught them many things using stories. In his teaching he said, ³"Listen! A farmer went out to plant his seed. ⁴He scattered the seed on the ground. Some fell on a path. Birds came and ate it up. ⁵Some seed fell on rocky places, where there wasn't much soil. The plants came up quickly, because the soil wasn't deep. ⁶When the sun came up, it burned the plants. They dried up because they had no roots. ⁷Other seed fell among thorns. The thorns grew up and crowded

CANDID CONVERSATIONS

With the sun shining and the flowers blooming, I suddenly felt the urge to plant a garden. Camilla volunteered to help. The first thing we did was to pull weeds. Before long, we were sweaty and sore—and had cleared only a few square feet of dirt. I rubbed my blistered hands, and we started digging.

Whit and Eugene brought us a picnic lunch. As we ate, I looked at the tiny square in the ground I called my garden. "Well, this is nice," Whit said.

"It's just dirt," I groaned.

"No, it's soil," Eugene said.

Before I could correct him on being a smarty-pants, Whit said, "He's right. Remember how the Bible talks about soil? You two worked hard to give your seeds a chance to grow. With water and sunshine—and a lot more work—those seeds will sprout into beautiful plants. You can't see it yet, but it's already started."

Of course, it made me think of Mark 4:8 and the seeds that fell on good soil—just like the seeds in my garden. Just then it started to rain. "I guess God's doing the watering for us today," Camilla said with a smile.

out the plants. So the plants did not bear grain. ⁸Still other seed fell on good soil. It grew up and produced a crop 30, 60, or even 100 times more than the farmer planted."

⁹Then Jesus said, "Whoever has ears should listen."

¹⁰Later Jesus was alone. The 12 disciples asked him about the stories. So did the others around him. ¹¹He told them, "The secret of God's kingdom has been given to you. But to outsiders everything is told using stories. ¹²In that way,

" 'They will see but never know what
        they are seeing.
    They will hear but never understand.
    Otherwise they might turn and be
        forgiven!' "   *(Isaiah 6:9,10)*

¹³Then Jesus said to them, "Don't you understand this story? Then how will you understand any stories of this kind? ¹⁴The seed the farmer plants is God's message. ¹⁵What is seed scattered on a path like? The message is planted. The people hear the message. Then Satan comes. He takes away the message that was planted in them. ¹⁶And what is seed scattered on rocky places like? The people hear the message. At once they receive it with joy. ¹⁷But they have no roots. So they last only a short time. They quickly fall away from the faith when trouble or suffering comes because of the message. ¹⁸And what is seed scattered among thorns like? The people hear the message. ¹⁹But then the worries of this life come to them. Wealth comes with its false promises. The people also long for other things. All of these are the kinds of things that crowd out the message. They keep it from producing fruit. ²⁰And what is seed scattered on good soil like? The people hear the message. They accept it. They produce a good crop 30, 60, or even 100 times more than the farmer planted."

A Lamp on a Stand

²¹Jesus said to them, "Do you bring in a lamp to put it under a large bowl or a bed? Don't you put it on its stand? ²²What is hidden is meant to be seen. And what is put out of sight is meant to be brought out into the open. ²³Whoever has ears should listen."

²⁴"Think carefully about what you hear," he said. "As you give, so you will receive. In

fact, you will receive even more. [25]Whoever has something will be given more. Whoever has nothing, even what they have will be taken away from them."

The Story of the Growing Seed

[26]Jesus also said, "Here is what God's kingdom is like. A farmer scatters seed on the ground. [27]Night and day the seed comes up and grows. It happens whether the farmer sleeps or gets up. He doesn't know how it happens. [28]All by itself the soil produces grain. First the stalk comes up. Then the head appears. Finally, the full grain appears in the head. [29]Before long the grain ripens. So the farmer cuts it down, because the harvest is ready."

The Story of the Mustard Seed

[30]Again Jesus said, "What can we say God's kingdom is like? What story can we use to explain it? [31]It is like a mustard seed, which is the smallest of all seeds on earth. [32]But when you plant the seed, it grows. It becomes the largest of all garden plants. Its branches are so big that birds can rest in its shade."

[33]Using many stories like these, Jesus spoke the word to them. He told them as much as they could understand. [34]He did not say anything to them without using a story. But when he was alone with his disciples, he explained everything.

Jesus Calms the Storm

[35]When evening came, Jesus said to his disciples, "Let's go over to the other side of the lake." [36]They left the crowd behind. And they took him along in a boat, just as he was. There were also other boats with him. [37]A wild storm came up. Waves crashed over the boat. It was about to sink. [38]Jesus was in the back, sleeping on a cushion. The disciples woke him up. They said, "Teacher! Don't you care if we drown?"

[39]He got up and ordered the wind to stop. He said to the waves, "Quiet! Be still!" Then the wind died down. And it was completely calm.

[40]He said to his disciples, "Why are you so afraid? Don't you have any faith at all yet?"

[41]They were terrified. They asked each other, "Who is this? Even the wind and the waves obey him!"

Jesus Heals a Man Controlled by Demons

5 They went across the Sea of Galilee to the area of the Gerasenes. [2]Jesus got out of the boat. A man controlled by an evil spirit came from the tombs to meet him. [3]The man lived in the tombs. No one could keep him tied up anymore. Not even a chain could hold him. [4]His hands and feet had often been chained. But he tore the chains apart. And he broke the iron cuffs on his ankles. No one was strong enough to control him. [5]Night and day he screamed among the tombs and in the hills. He cut himself with stones.

[6]When he saw Jesus a long way off, he ran to him. He fell on his knees in front of him. [7]He shouted at the top of his voice, "Jesus, Son of the Most High God, what do you want with me? Swear to God that you won't hurt me!" [8]This was because Jesus had said to him, "Come out of this man, you evil spirit!"

[9]Then Jesus asked the demon, "What is your name?"

"My name is Legion," he replied. "There are many of us." [10]And he begged Jesus again and again not to send them out of the area.

[11]A large herd of pigs was feeding on the nearby hillside. [12]The demons begged Jesus, "Send us among the pigs. Let us go into them." [13]Jesus allowed it. The evil spirits came out of the man and went into the pigs. There were about 2,000 pigs in the herd. The whole herd rushed down the steep bank. They ran into the lake and drowned.

[14]Those who were tending the pigs ran off. They told the people in the town and countryside what had happened. The people went out to see for themselves. [15]Then they came to Jesus. They saw the man who had been controlled by many demons. He was sitting there. He was now dressed and thinking clearly. All this made the people afraid. [16]Those who had seen it told them what had happened to the man. They told about the pigs as well. [17]Then the people began to beg Jesus to leave their area.

[18]Jesus was getting into the boat. The man who had been controlled by demons begged to go with him. [19]Jesus did not let him. He said, "Go home to your own people. Tell them how much the Lord has done for you. Tell them how kind he has been to you." [20]So the man went away. In

the area known as the Ten Cities, he began to tell how much Jesus had done for him. And all the people were amazed.

Jesus Heals a Dead Girl and a Suffering Woman

²¹Jesus went across the Sea of Galilee in a boat. It landed at the other side. There a large crowd gathered around him. ²²Then a man named Jairus came. He was a synagogue leader. When he saw Jesus, he fell at his feet. ²³He begged Jesus, "Please come. My little daughter is dying. Place your hands on her to heal her. Then she will live." ²⁴So Jesus went with him.

A large group of people followed. They crowded around him. ²⁵A woman was there who had a sickness that made her bleed. It had lasted for 12 years. ²⁶She had suffered a great deal, even though she had gone to many doctors. She had spent all the money she had. But she was getting worse, not better. ²⁷Then she heard about Jesus. She came up behind him in the crowd and touched his clothes. ²⁸She thought, "I just need to touch his clothes. Then I will be healed." ²⁹Right away her bleeding stopped. She felt in her body that her suffering was over.

³⁰At once Jesus knew that power had gone out from him. He turned around in the crowd. He asked, "Who touched my clothes?"

³¹"You see the people," his disciples answered. "They are crowding against you. And you still ask, 'Who touched me?'"

³²But Jesus kept looking around. He wanted to see who had touched him. ³³Then the woman came and fell at his feet. She knew what had happened to her. She was shaking with fear. But she told him the whole truth. ³⁴He said to her, "Dear woman, your faith has healed you. Go in peace. You are free from your suffering."

³⁵While Jesus was still speaking, some people came from the house of Jairus. He was the synagogue leader. "Your daughter is dead," they said. "Why bother the teacher anymore?"

³⁶Jesus heard what they were saying. He told the synagogue leader, "Don't be afraid. Just believe."

³⁷He let only Peter, James, and John, the brother of James, follow him. ³⁸They came to the home of the synagogue leader. There Jesus saw a lot of confusion. People

Mark 5:35–43 Resurrection alert! This girl is one of three people that Jesus brought to life (besides Himself). The disciple Peter was there watching. Okay, now read Acts 9:36–43. What parts are the same in each story?

were crying and sobbing loudly. ³⁹He went inside. Then he said to them, "Why all this confusion and sobbing? The child is not dead. She is only sleeping." ⁴⁰But they laughed at him.

He made them all go outside. He took only the child's father and mother and the disciples who were with him. And he went in where the child was. ⁴¹He took her by the hand. Then he said to her, "*Talitha koum!*" This means, "Little girl, I say to you, get up!" ⁴²The girl was 12 years old. Right away she stood up and began to walk around. They were totally amazed at this. ⁴³Jesus gave strict orders not to let anyone know what had happened. And he told them to give her something to eat.

A Prophet Without Honor

6 Jesus left there and went to his hometown of Nazareth. His disciples went with him. ²When the Sabbath day came, he began to teach in the synagogue. Many who heard him were amazed.

"Where did this man get these things?" they asked. "What's this wisdom that has been given to him? What are these remarkable miracles he is doing? ³Isn't this the carpenter? Isn't this Mary's son? Isn't this the brother of James, Joseph, Judas and Simon? Aren't his sisters here with us?" They were not pleased with him at all.

⁴Jesus said to them, "A prophet is honored everywhere except in his own town.

He doesn't receive any honor among his relatives or in his own home." [5]Jesus placed his hands on a few sick people and healed them. But he could not do any other miracles there. [6]He was amazed because they had no faith.

Jesus Sends Out the Twelve Disciples

Jesus went around teaching from village to village. [7]He called the 12 disciples to him. Then he began to send them out two by two. He gave them authority to drive out evil spirits.

[8]Here is what he told them to do. "Take only a walking stick for your trip. Do not take bread or a bag. Take no money in your belts. [9]Wear sandals. But do not take extra clothes. [10]When you are invited into a house, stay there until you leave town. [11]Some places may not welcome you or listen to you. If they don't, leave that place and shake the dust off your feet. That will be a witness against the people living there."

[12]They went out. And they preached that people should turn away from their sins. [13]They drove out many demons. They poured olive oil on many sick people and healed them.

John the Baptist's Head Is Cut Off

[14]King Herod heard about this. Jesus' name had become well known. Some were saying, "John the Baptist has been raised from the dead! That is why he has the power to do miracles."

[15]Others said, "He is Elijah."

Still others claimed, "He is a prophet. He is like one of the prophets of long ago."

[16]But when Herod heard this, he said, "I had John's head cut off. And now he has been raised from the dead!"

[17]In fact, it was Herod himself who had given orders to arrest John. He had him tied up and put in prison. He did this because of Herodias. She was the wife of Herod's brother Philip. But now Herod was married to her. [18]John had been saying to Herod, "It is against the Law for you to be married to your brother's wife." [19]Herodias couldn't forgive John for saying that. She wanted to kill him. But she could not, [20]because Herod was afraid of John. So he kept John safe. Herod knew John was a holy man who did what was right. When Herod

heard him, he was very puzzled. But he liked to listen to John.

[21]Finally the right time came. Herod gave a banquet on his birthday. He invited his high officials and military leaders. He also invited the most important men in Galilee. [22]Then the daughter of Herodias came in and danced. She pleased Herod and his dinner guests.

The king said to the girl, "Ask me for anything you want. I'll give it to you." [23]And he gave her his promise. He said to her, "Anything you ask for I will give you. I'll give you up to half my kingdom."

[24]She went out and said to her mother, "What should I ask for?"

"The head of John the Baptist," she answered.

[25]At once the girl hurried to ask the king. She said, "I want you to give me the head of John the Baptist on a big plate right now."

[26]The king was very upset. But he thought about his promise and his dinner guests. So he did not want to say no to the girl. [27]He sent a man right away to bring John's head. The man went to the prison and cut off John's head. [28]He brought it back on a big plate. He gave it to the girl, and she gave it to her mother. [29]John's disciples heard about this. So they came and took his body. Then they placed it in a tomb.

Jesus Feeds Five Thousand

[30]The apostles gathered around Jesus. They told him all they had done and taught. [31]But many people were coming and going. So they did not even have a chance to eat. Then Jesus said to his apostles, "Come with me by yourselves to a quiet place. You need to get some rest."

[32]So they went away by themselves in a boat to a quiet place. [33]But many people who saw them leaving recognized them. They ran from all the towns and got there ahead of them. [34]When Jesus came ashore, he saw a

large crowd. He felt deep concern for them. They were like sheep without a shepherd. So he began teaching them many things.

[35]By that time it was late in the day. His disciples came to him. "There is nothing here," they said. "It's already very late. [36]Send the people away. Then they can go to the nearby countryside and villages to buy something to eat."

[37]But Jesus answered, "You give them something to eat."

They said to him, "That would take more than half a year's pay! Should we go and spend that much on bread? Are we supposed to feed them?"

[38]"How many loaves do you have?" Jesus asked. "Go and see."

When they found out, they said, "Five loaves and two fish."

[39]Then Jesus directed them to have all the people sit down in groups on the green grass. [40]So they sat down in groups of 100s and 50s. [41]Jesus took the five loaves and the two fish. He looked up to heaven and gave thanks. He broke the loaves into pieces. Then he gave them to his disciples to pass around to the people. He also divided the two fish among them all. [42]All of them ate and were satisfied. [43]The disciples picked up 12 baskets of broken pieces of bread and fish. [44]The number of men who had eaten was 5,000.

Jesus Walks on the Water

[45]Right away Jesus made his disciples get into the boat. He had them go on ahead of him to Bethsaida. Then he sent the crowd away. [46]After leaving them, he went up on a mountainside to pray.

[47]Later that night, the boat was in the middle of the Sea of Galilee. Jesus was alone on land. [48]He saw the disciples pulling hard on the oars. The wind was blowing against them. Shortly before dawn, he went out to them. He walked on the lake. When he was about to pass by them, [49]they saw him walking on the lake. They thought he was a ghost, so they cried out. [50]They all saw him and were terrified.

Right away Jesus said to them, "Be brave! It is I. Don't be afraid." [51]Then he climbed into the boat with them. The wind died down. And they were completely amazed. [52]They had not understood about the loaves. They were stubborn.

[53]They went across the lake and landed at Gennesaret. There they tied up the boat. [54]As soon as Jesus and his disciples got out, people recognized him. [55]They ran through that whole area to bring to him those who were sick. They carried them on mats to where they heard he was. [56]He went into the villages, the towns and the countryside. Everywhere he went, the people brought the sick to the market areas. Those who were sick begged him to let them touch just the edge of his clothes. And all who touched his clothes were healed.

What Makes People "Unclean"?

7 The Pharisees gathered around Jesus. So did some of the teachers of the law. All of them had come from Jerusalem. [2]They saw some of his disciples eating food with "unclean" hands. That means they were not washed. [3]The Pharisees and all the Jews do not eat unless they wash their hands to make them "clean." That's what the elders teach. [4]When they come from the market, they do not eat unless they wash. And they follow many other teachings. For example, they wash cups, pitchers, and kettles in a special way.

[5]So the Pharisees and the teachers of the law questioned Jesus. "Why don't your disciples live by what the elders teach?" they asked. "Why do they eat their food with 'unclean' hands?"

[6]He replied, "Isaiah was right. He prophesied about you people who pretend to be good. He said,

" 'These people honor me by what they
say.
But their hearts are far away from me.
[7] Their worship doesn't mean anything to
me.
They teach nothing but human
rules.'   *(Isaiah 29:13)*

[8]You have let go of God's commands. And you are holding on to teachings that people have made up."

[9]Jesus continued speaking, "You have a fine way of setting aside God's commands! You do this so you can follow your own teachings. [10]Moses said, 'Honor your father and mother.' *(Exodus 20:12; Deuteronomy 5:16)* He also said, 'Anyone who asks for bad things to happen to their father or mother must be put to death.' *(Exodus 21:17; Leviticus*

20:9) ¹¹But you allow people to say that what might have been used to help their parents is Corban. Corban means A Gift Set Apart for God. ¹²So you no longer let them do anything for their parents. ¹³You make the word of God useless by putting your own teachings in its place. And you do many things like this."

¹⁴Again Jesus called the crowd to him. He said, "Listen to me, everyone. Understand this. ¹⁵⁻¹⁶Nothing outside of a person can make them 'unclean' by going into them. It is what comes out of them that makes them 'unclean.'"

¹⁷Then he left the crowd and entered the house. His disciples asked him about this teaching. ¹⁸"Don't you understand?" Jesus asked. "Don't you see? Nothing that enters a person from the outside can make them 'unclean.' ¹⁹It doesn't go into their heart. It goes into their stomach. Then it goes out of the body." In saying this, Jesus was calling all foods "clean."

²⁰He went on to say, "What comes out of a person is what makes them 'unclean.' ²¹Evil thoughts come from the inside, from a person's heart. So do sexual sins, stealing and murder. ²²Adultery, greed, hate and cheating come from a person's heart too. So do desires that are not pure, and wanting what belongs to others. And so do telling lies about others and being proud and being foolish. ²³All these evil things come from inside a person and make them 'unclean.'"

Jesus Honors a Greek Woman's Faith

²⁴Jesus went from there to a place near Tyre. He entered a house. He did not want anyone to know where he was. But he could not keep it a secret. ²⁵Soon a woman heard about him. An evil spirit controlled her little daughter. The woman came to Jesus and fell at his feet. ²⁶She was a Greek, born in Syrian Phoenicia. She begged Jesus to drive the demon out of her daughter.

²⁷"First let the children eat all they want," he told her. "It is not right to take the children's bread and throw it to the dogs."

²⁸"Lord," she replied, "even the dogs under the table eat the children's crumbs."

²⁹Then he told her, "That was a good reply. You may go. The demon has left your daughter."

³⁰So she went home and found her child lying on the bed. And the demon was gone.

Jesus Heals a Man Who Could Not Hear or Speak

³¹Then Jesus left the area of Tyre and went through Sidon. He went down to the Sea of Galilee and into the area known as the Ten Cities. ³²There some people brought a man to Jesus. The man was deaf and could hardly speak. They begged Jesus to place his hand on the man.

³³Jesus took the man to one side, away from the crowd. He put his fingers into the man's ears. Then he spit and touched the man's tongue. ³⁴Jesus looked up to heaven. With a deep sigh, he said to the man, "*Ephphatha!*" That means "Be opened!" ³⁵The man's ears were opened. His tongue was freed up, and he began to speak clearly.

³⁶Jesus ordered the people not to tell anyone. But the more he did so, the more they kept talking about it. ³⁷People were really amazed. "He has done everything well," they said. "He even makes deaf people able to hear. And he makes those who can't speak able to talk."

Jesus Feeds the Four Thousand

8 During those days another large crowd gathered. They had nothing to eat. So Jesus called for his disciples to come to him. He said, ²"I feel deep concern for these people. They have already been with me three days. They don't have anything to eat. ³If I send them away hungry, they will become too weak on their way home. Some of them have come from far away."

⁴His disciples answered him. "There is nothing here," they said. "Where can anyone get enough bread to feed them?"

⁵"How many loaves do you have?" Jesus asked.

"Seven," they replied.

⁶He told the crowd to sit down on the ground. He took the seven loaves and gave thanks to God. Then he broke them and gave them to his disciples. They passed the pieces of bread around to the people. ⁷The disciples also had a few small fish. Jesus gave thanks for them too. He told the disciples to pass them around. ⁸The people ate and were satisfied. After that, the disciples picked up seven baskets of leftover pieces. ⁹About 4,000 people were there. After Jesus sent them away, ¹⁰he got into a boat with his disciples. He went to the area of Dalmanutha.

[11]The Pharisees came and began to ask Jesus questions. They wanted to test him. So they asked him for a sign from heaven. [12]He sighed deeply. He said, "Why do you people ask for a sign? What I'm about to tell you is true. No sign will be given to you." [13]Then he left them. He got back into the boat and crossed to the other side of the lake.

The Yeast of the Pharisees and Herod

[14]The disciples had forgotten to bring bread. They had only one loaf with them in the boat. [15]"Be careful," Jesus warned them. "Watch out for the yeast of the Pharisees. And watch out for the yeast of Herod."

[16]They talked about this with each other. They said, "He must be saying this because we don't have any bread."

[17]Jesus knew what they were saying. So he asked them, "Why are you talking about having no bread? Why can't you see or understand? Are you stubborn? [18]Do you have eyes and still don't see? Do you have ears and still don't hear? And don't you remember? [19]Earlier I broke five loaves for the 5,000. How many baskets of pieces did you pick up?"

"Twelve," they replied.

[20]"Later I broke seven loaves for the 4,000. How many baskets of pieces did you pick up?"

"Seven," they answered.

[21]He said to them, "Can't you understand yet?"

Jesus Heals a Blind Man at Bethsaida

[22]Jesus and his disciples came to Bethsaida. Some people brought a blind man to him. They begged Jesus to touch him. [23]He took the blind man by the hand. Then he led him outside the village. He spit on the man's eyes and placed his hands on him. "Do you see anything?" Jesus asked.

[24]The man looked up. He said, "I see people. They look like trees walking around."

[25]Once more Jesus put his hands on the man's eyes. Then his eyes were opened so that he could see again. He saw everything clearly. [26]Jesus sent him home. He told him, "Don't even go into the village."

Peter Says That Jesus Is the Messiah

[27]Jesus and his disciples went on to the villages around Caesarea Philippi. On the way he asked them, "Who do people say I am?"

[28]They replied, "Some say John the Baptist. Others say Elijah. Still others say one of the prophets."

[29]"But what about you?" he asked. "Who do you say I am?"

Peter answered, "You are the Messiah."

[30]Jesus warned them not to tell anyone about him.

Jesus Tells About His Coming Death

[31]Jesus then began to teach his disciples. He taught them that the Son of Man must suffer many things. He taught them that the elders would not accept him. The chief priests and the teachers of the law would not accept him either. He must be killed and after three days rise again. [32]He spoke clearly about this. Peter took Jesus to one side and began to scold him.

[33]Jesus turned and looked at his disciples. He scolded Peter. "Get behind me, Satan!" he said. "You are not thinking about the things God cares about. Instead, you are thinking only about the things humans care about."

You Must Pick Up Your Cross

[34]Jesus called the crowd to him along with his disciples. He said, "Whoever wants to be my disciple must say no to themselves. They must pick up their cross and follow me. [35]Whoever wants to save their life will lose it. But whoever loses their life for me and for the good news will save it. [36]What good is it

if someone gains the whole world but loses their soul? [37]Or what can anyone trade for their soul? [38]Suppose anyone is ashamed of me and my words among these adulterous and sinful people. Then the Son of Man will be ashamed of them when he comes in his Father's glory with the holy angels."

9 Jesus said to them, "What I'm about to tell you is true. Some who are standing here will not die before they see that God's kingdom has come with power."

Jesus' Appearance Is Changed

[2]After six days Jesus took Peter, James and John with him. He led them up a high mountain. They were all alone. There in front of them his appearance was changed. [3]His clothes became so white they shone. They were whiter than anyone in the world could bleach them. [4]Elijah and Moses appeared in front of Jesus and his disciples. The two of them were talking with Jesus.

[5]Peter said to Jesus, "Rabbi, it is good for us to be here. Let us put up three shelters. One will be for you, one for Moses, and one for Elijah." [6]Peter didn't really know what to say, because they were so afraid.

[7]Then a cloud appeared and covered them. A voice came from the cloud. It said, "This is my Son, and I love him. Listen to him!"

[8]They looked around. Suddenly they no longer saw anyone with them except Jesus.

[9]They came down the mountain. On the way down, Jesus ordered them not to tell anyone what they had seen. He told them to wait until the Son of Man had risen from the dead. [10]So they kept the matter to themselves. But they asked each other what "rising from the dead" meant.

[11]Then they asked Jesus, "Why do the teachers of the law say that Elijah has to come first?"

[12]Jesus replied, "That's right. Elijah does come first. He makes all things new again. So why is it written that the Son of Man must suffer much and not be accepted? [13]I tell you, Elijah has come. They have done to him everything they wanted to do. They did it just as it is written about him."

Jesus Heals a Boy Who Is Controlled by an Evil Spirit

[14]When Jesus and those who were with him came to the other disciples, they saw a large crowd around them. The teachers of the law were arguing with them. [15]When all the people saw Jesus, they were filled with wonder. And they ran to greet him.

[16]"What are you arguing with them about?" Jesus asked.

[17]A man in the crowd answered. "Teacher," he said, "I brought you my son. He is controlled by an evil spirit. Because of this, my son can't speak anymore. [18]When the spirit takes hold of him, it throws him to the ground. He foams at the mouth. He grinds his teeth. And his body becomes stiff. I asked your disciples to drive out the spirit. But they couldn't do it."

[19]"You unbelieving people!" Jesus replied. "How long do I have to stay with you? How long do I have to put up with you? Bring the boy to me."

[20]So they brought him. As soon as the spirit saw Jesus, it threw the boy into a fit. He fell to the ground. He rolled around and foamed at the mouth.

[21]Jesus asked the boy's father, "How long has he been like this?"

"Since he was a child," he answered. [22]"The spirit has often thrown him into fire or water to kill him. But if you can do anything, take pity on us. Please help us."

[23]"'If you can'?" said Jesus. "Everything is possible for the one who believes."

[24]Right away the boy's father cried out, "I do believe! Help me overcome my unbelief!"

[25]Jesus saw that a crowd was running over to see what was happening. Then he ordered the evil spirit to leave the boy. "You spirit that makes him unable to hear and speak!" he said. "I command you, come out of him. Never enter him again."

[26]The spirit screamed. It shook the boy wildly. Then it came out of him. The boy looked so lifeless that many people said, "He's dead." [27]But Jesus took him by the hand. He lifted the boy to his feet, and the boy stood up.

[28]Jesus went indoors. Then his disciples asked him in private, "Why couldn't we drive out the evil spirit?"

[29]He replied, "This kind can come out only by prayer."

Jesus Speaks a Second Time About His Coming Death

[30]They left that place and passed through Galilee. Jesus did not want anyone to know

where they were. [31]That was because he was teaching his disciples. He said to them, "The Son of Man is going to be handed over to men. They will kill him. After three days he will rise from the dead." [32]But they didn't understand what he meant. And they were afraid to ask him about it.

Who Is the Most Important Person?

[33]Jesus and his disciples came to a house in Capernaum. There he asked them, "What were you arguing about on the road?" [34]But they kept quiet. On the way, they had argued about which one of them was the most important person.

[35]Jesus sat down and called for the 12 disciples to come to him. Then he said, "Anyone who wants to be first must be the very last. They must be the servant of everyone."

[36]Jesus took a little child and had the child stand among them. Then he took the child in his arms. He said to them, [37]"Anyone who welcomes one of these little children in my name welcomes me. And anyone who welcomes me also welcomes the one who sent me."

Anyone Who Is Not Against Us Is for Us

[38]"Teacher," said John, "we saw someone driving out demons in your name. We told him to stop, because he was not one of us."

[39]"Do not stop him," Jesus said. "For no one who does a miracle in my name can in the next moment say anything bad about me. [40]Anyone who is not against us is for us. [41]What I'm about to tell you is true. Suppose someone gives you a cup of water in my name because you belong to the Messiah. That person will certainly not go without a reward.

Leading People to Sin

[42]"What if someone leads one of these little ones who believe in me to sin? If they do, it would be better if a large millstone were hung around their neck and they were thrown into the sea. [43-44]If your hand causes you to sin, cut it off. It would be better for you to enter God's kingdom with only one hand than to go into hell with two hands. In hell the fire never goes out. [45-46]If your foot causes you to sin, cut it off. It would be better to enter God's kingdom with only one foot than to have two feet and be

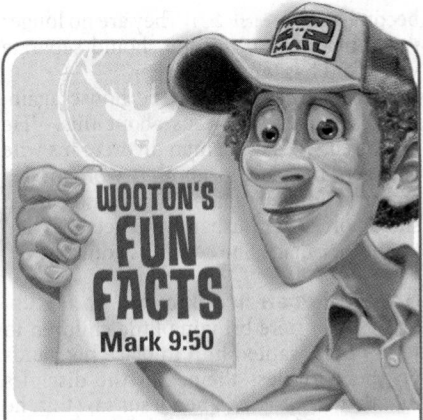

WOOTON'S FUN FACTS
Mark 9:50

Did you know that Roman soldiers were given a salt allowance or a *salarium*? (That word doesn't mean a room with lots of windows. That's a *solarium*!) Salt was valuable like money. This is where the word *salary* comes from.

thrown into hell. [47]If your eye causes you to sin, poke it out. It would be better for you to enter God's kingdom with only one eye than to have two eyes and be thrown into hell. [48]In hell,

"'The worms that eat them do not die.
    The fire is not put out.'   (Isaiah 66:24)

[49]Everyone will be salted with fire. [50]"Salt is good. But suppose it loses its saltiness. How can you make it salty again? Have salt among yourselves. And be at peace with each other."

Jesus Teaches About Divorce

10 Jesus left that place and went into the area of Judea and across the Jordan River. Again crowds of people came to him. As usual, he taught them.

[2]Some Pharisees came to test Jesus. They asked, "Does the Law allow a man to divorce his wife?"

[3]"What did Moses command you?" he replied.

[4]They said, "Moses allowed a man to write a letter of divorce and send her away."

[5]"You were stubborn. That's why Moses wrote you this law," Jesus replied. [6]"But at the beginning of creation, God 'made them male and female.' (Genesis 1:27) [7]'That's why a man will leave his father and mother and be joined to his wife. [8]The two of them will

become one.' *(Genesis 2:24)* They are no longer two, but one. ⁹So no one should separate what God has joined together."

¹⁰When they were in the house again, the disciples asked Jesus about this. ¹¹He answered, "What if a man divorces his wife and gets married to another woman? He commits adultery against her. ¹²And what if she divorces her husband and gets married to another man? She commits adultery."

Little Children Are Brought to Jesus

¹³People were bringing little children to Jesus. They wanted him to place his hands on them to bless them. But the disciples told them to stop. ¹⁴When Jesus saw this, he was angry. He said to his disciples, "Let the little children come to me. Don't keep them away. God's kingdom belongs to people like them. ¹⁵What I'm about to tell you is true. Anyone who will not receive God's kingdom like a little child will never enter it." ¹⁶Then he took the children in his arms. He placed his hands on them to bless them.

Rich People and the Kingdom of God

¹⁷As Jesus started on his way, a man ran up to him. He fell on his knees before Jesus. "Good teacher," he said, "what must I do to receive eternal life?"

¹⁸"Why do you call me good?" Jesus answered. "No one is good except God. ¹⁹You know what the commandments say. 'Do not murder. Do not commit adultery. Do not steal. Do not be a false witness. Do not cheat. Honor your father and mother.' " *(Exodus 20:12–16; Deuteronomy 5:16–20)*

²⁰"Teacher," he said, "I have obeyed all those commandments since I was a boy."

²¹Jesus looked at him and loved him. "You are missing one thing," he said. "Go and sell everything you have. Give the money to those who are poor. You will have treasure in heaven. Then come and follow me."

²²The man's face fell. He went away sad, because he was very rich.

²³Jesus looked around. He said to his disciples, "How hard it is for rich people to enter God's kingdom!"

²⁴The disciples were amazed at his words. But Jesus said again, "Children, how hard it is to enter God's kingdom! ²⁵Is it hard for a camel to go through the eye of a needle? It is even harder for someone who is rich to enter God's kingdom!"

²⁶The disciples were even more amazed. They said to each other, "Then who can be saved?"

²⁷Jesus looked at them and said, "With people, this is impossible. But not with God. All things are possible with God."

²⁸Then Peter spoke up, "We have left everything to follow you!"

²⁹"What I'm about to tell you is true," Jesus replied. "Has anyone left home or family or fields for me and the good news? ³⁰They will receive 100 times as much in this world. They will have homes and families

WHIT'S WISDOM

Mark 10:13

Do you remember your first day of kindergarten? Did you learn about letters or where to sit? What would have happened if the teacher were Eugene Meltsner? He might have said, "We're going to dispense with all of the remedial work and proceed straight to differential calculus! Please open your textbooks!"

You probably wouldn't have learned much that day, even if you were excited about kindergarten. Why? Because we have to start with the basics before we go on to harder things. Before we can do the harder things, we have to start out with a good foundation.

When you're thinking about the first day of kindergarten, look at Mark 10:13. Why was it good for parents to bring their children to the feet of Jesus? For one thing, children who learn from Jesus at an early age build a firm foundation for dealing with harder things later in life. It's a good idea to go to the feet of Jesus as a kid! If you learn the basics of faith from Him now, you'll be ready for the differential calculus later!

and fields. But they will also be treated badly by others. In the world to come they will live forever. [31]But many who are first will be last. And the last will be first."

Jesus Speaks a Third Time About His Coming Death

[32]They were on their way up to Jerusalem. Jesus was leading the way. The disciples were amazed. Those who followed were afraid. Again Jesus took the 12 disciples to one side. He told them what was going to happen to him. [33]"We are going up to Jerusalem," he said. "The Son of Man will be handed over to the chief priests and the teachers of the law. They will sentence him to death. Then they will hand him over to the Gentiles. [34]They will make fun of him and spit on him. They will whip him and kill him. Three days later he will rise from the dead!"

James and John Ask Jesus for a Favor

[35]James and John came to Jesus. They were the sons of Zebedee. "Teacher," they said, "we would like to ask you for a favor."

[36]"What do you want me to do for you?" he asked.

[37]They replied, "Let one of us sit at your right hand in your glorious kingdom. Let the other one sit at your left hand."

[38]"You don't know what you're asking for," Jesus said. "Can you drink the cup of suffering I drink? Or can you go through the baptism of suffering I must go through?"

[39]"We can," they answered.

Jesus said to them, "You will drink the cup I drink. And you will go through the baptism I go through. [40]But it is not for me to say who will sit at my right or left hand. These places belong to those they are prepared for."

[41]The other ten disciples heard about it. They became angry at James and John. [42]Jesus called them together. He said, "You know about those who are rulers of the Gentiles. They hold power over their people. Their high officials order them around. [43]Don't be like that. Instead, anyone who wants to be important among you must be your servant. [44]And anyone who wants to be first must be the slave of everyone. [45]Even the Son of Man did not come to be served. Instead, he came to serve others.

He came to give his life as the price for setting many people free."

Blind Bartimaeus Receives His Sight

[46]Jesus and his disciples came to Jericho. They were leaving the city. A large crowd was with them. A blind man was sitting by the side of the road begging. His name was Bartimaeus. Bartimaeus means Son of Timaeus. [47]He heard that Jesus of Nazareth was passing by. So he began to shout, "Jesus! Son of David! Have mercy on me!"

[48]Many people commanded him to stop. They told him to be quiet. But he shouted even louder, "Son of David! Have mercy on me!"

[49]Jesus stopped and said, "Call for him."

So they called out to the blind man, "Cheer up! Get up on your feet! Jesus is calling for you." [50]He threw his coat to one side. Then he jumped to his feet and came to Jesus.

[51]"What do you want me to do for you?" Jesus asked him.

The blind man said, "Rabbi, I want to be able to see."

[52]"Go," said Jesus. "Your faith has healed you." Right away he could see. And he followed Jesus along the road.

Jesus Comes to Jerusalem as King

11 As they all approached Jerusalem, they came to Bethphage and Bethany at the Mount of Olives. Jesus sent out two of his disciples. [2]He said to them, "Go to the village ahead of you. Just as you enter it, you will find a donkey's colt tied there. No one has ever ridden it. Untie it and bring it here. [3]Someone may ask you, 'Why are you doing this?' If so, say, 'The Lord needs it. But he will send it back here soon.'"

[4]So they left. They found a colt out in the street. It was tied at a doorway. They untied it. [5]Some people standing there asked, "What are you doing? Why are you untying that colt?" [6]They answered as Jesus had told them to. So the people let them go. [7]They

brought the colt to Jesus. They threw their coats over it. Then he sat on it. [8]Many people spread their coats on the road. Others spread branches they had cut in the fields. [9]Those in front and those in back shouted,

"Hosanna!"

"Blessed is the one who comes in the
    name of the Lord!"

(Psalm 118:25,26)

[10] "Blessed is the coming kingdom of our
    father David!"

"Hosanna in the highest heaven!"

[11]Jesus entered Jerusalem and went into the temple courtyard. He looked around at everything. But it was already late. So he went out to Bethany with the 12 disciples.

Jesus Curses a Fig Tree and Clears Out the Temple Courtyard

[12]The next day as Jesus and his disciples were leaving Bethany, they were hungry. [13]Not too far away, he saw a fig tree. It was covered with leaves. He went to find out if it had any fruit. When he reached it, he found nothing but leaves. It was not the season for figs. [14]Then Jesus said to the tree, "May no one ever eat fruit from you again!" And his disciples heard him say it.

[15]When Jesus reached Jerusalem, he entered the temple courtyard. He began to drive out those who were buying and selling there. He turned over the tables of the people who were exchanging money. He also turned over the benches of those who were selling doves. [16]He would not allow anyone to carry items for sale through the temple courtyard. [17]Then he taught them. He told them, "It is written that the Lord said, 'My house will be called a house where people from all nations can pray.' *(Isaiah 56:7)* But you have made it a 'den for robbers.'" *(Jeremiah 7:11)*

[18]The chief priests and the teachers of the law heard about this. They began looking for a way to kill Jesus. They were afraid of him, because the whole crowd was amazed at his teaching.

[19]When evening came, Jesus and his disciples left the city.

The Dried-Up Fig Tree

[20]In the morning as Jesus and his disciples walked along, they saw the fig tree. It was dried up all the way down to the roots. [21]Peter remembered. He said to Jesus, "Rabbi, look! The fig tree you put a curse on has dried up!"

[22]"Have faith in God," Jesus said. [23]"What I'm about to tell you is true. Suppose someone says to this mountain, 'Go and throw yourself into the sea.' They must not doubt in their heart. They must believe that what

WHIT'S WISDOM

Mark 11:24

Jimmy and Donna Barclay found me at Whit's End working on a new invention: a vending machine for prayers. You could choose a prayer, push a button, and the answer came out on the bottom. I had a button for just about everything: extra money, good grades, the latest fashions, the newest toys, popularity, and more.

Donna was convinced it was a joke and I had to admit that it was. You see, we often think of God like a giant vending machine giving us what we want if we just push the right buttons. But God isn't like that. Prayer is talking with God. It's a conversation. You don't have conversations with vending machines. God wants to hear what you're thinking and feeling. You can confess to Him when you sin. You can ask Him to help other people. And, yes, you can even ask Him for things for you. But we have to remember that God loves us like a parent. Good and loving parents don't always give their children what they want. It may not always be the answer we want, but He will answer, and at a time that's right for us. Isn't that better than a vending machine?

they say will happen. Then it will be done for them. [24]So I tell you, when you pray for something, believe that you have already received it. Then it will be yours. [25-26]And when you stand praying, forgive anyone you have anything against. Then your Father in heaven will forgive your sins."

The Authority of Jesus Is Questioned

[27]Jesus and his disciples arrived again in Jerusalem. He was walking in the temple courtyard. Then the chief priests came to him. The teachers of the law and the elders came too. [28]"By what authority are you doing these things?" they asked. "Who gave you authority to do this?"

[29]Jesus replied, "I will ask you one question. Answer me, and I will tell you by what authority I am doing these things. [30]Was John's baptism from heaven? Or did it come from human authority? Tell me!"

[31]They talked to each other about it. They said, "If we say, 'From heaven,' he will ask, 'Then why didn't you believe him?' [32]But what if we say, 'From human authority'?" They were afraid of the people. Everyone believed that John really was a prophet.

[33]So they answered Jesus, "We don't know."

Jesus said, "Then I won't tell you by what authority I am doing these things either."

The Story of the Renters

12 Jesus began to speak to the people using stories. He said, "A man planted a vineyard. He put a wall around it. He dug a pit for a winepress. He also built a lookout tower. He rented the vineyard out to some farmers. Then he went to another place. [2]At harvest time he sent a servant to the renters. He told the servant to collect from them some of the fruit of the vineyard. [3]But they grabbed the servant and beat him up. Then they sent him away with nothing. [4]So the man sent another servant to the renters. They hit this one on the head and treated

him badly. [5]The man sent still another servant. The renters killed him. The man sent many others. The renters beat up some of them. They killed the others.

[6]"The man had one person left to send. It was his son, and he loved him. He sent him last of all. He said, 'They will respect my son.'

[7]"But the renters said to each other, 'This is the one who will receive all the owner's property someday. Come, let's kill him. Then everything will be ours.' [8]So they took him and killed him. They threw him out of the vineyard.

[9]"What will the owner of the vineyard do then? He will come and kill those renters. He will give the vineyard to others. [10]Haven't you read what this part of Scripture says,

" 'The stone the builders didn't accept
    has become the most important
        stone of all.
[11] The Lord has done it.
    It is wonderful in our eyes'?"

(Psalm 118:22,23)

[12]Then the chief priests, the teachers of the law and the elders looked for a way to arrest Jesus. They knew he had told the story against them. But they were afraid of the crowd. So they left him and went away.

Is It Right to Pay the Royal Tax to Caesar?

[13]Later the religious leaders sent some of the Pharisees and Herodians to Jesus. They wanted to trap him with his own words. [14]They came to him and said, "Teacher, we know that you are a man of honor. You don't let other people tell you what to do or say. You don't care how important they are. But you teach the way of God truthfully. Is it right to pay the royal tax to Caesar or not? [15]Should we pay or shouldn't we?"

But Jesus knew what they were trying to do. So he asked, "Why are you trying to trap me? Bring me a silver coin. Let me look at it." [16]They brought the coin. He asked them, "Whose picture is this? And whose words?"

"Caesar's," they replied.

[17]Then Jesus said to them, "Give back to Caesar what belongs to Caesar. And give back to God what belongs to God."

They were amazed at him.

Marriage When the Dead Rise

¹⁸The Sadducees came to Jesus with a question. They do not believe that people rise from the dead. ¹⁹"Teacher," they said, "Moses wrote for us about a man who died and didn't have any children. But he did leave a wife behind. That man's brother must get married to the widow. He must provide children to carry on his dead brother's name. ²⁰There were seven brothers. The first one got married. He died without leaving any children. ²¹The second one got married to the widow. He also died and left no child. It was the same with the third one. ²²In fact, none of the seven left any children. Last of all, the woman died too. ²³When the dead rise, whose wife will she be? All seven of them were married to her."

²⁴Jesus replied, "You are mistaken because you do not know the Scriptures. And you do not know the power of God. ²⁵When the dead rise, they won't get married. And their parents won't give them to be married. They will be like the angels in heaven. ²⁶What about the dead rising? Haven't you read in the Book of Moses the story of the burning bush? God said to Moses, 'I am the God of Abraham. I am the God of Isaac. And I am the God of Jacob.' *(Exodus 3:6)* ²⁷He is not the God of the dead. He is the God of the living. You have made a big mistake!"

The Most Important Commandment

²⁸One of the teachers of the law came and heard the Sadducees arguing. He noticed that Jesus had given the Sadducees a good answer. So he asked him, "Which is the most important of all the commandments?"

²⁹Jesus answered, "Here is the most important one. Moses said, 'Israel, listen to me. The Lord is our God. The Lord is one. ³⁰Love the Lord your God with all your heart and with all your soul. Love him with all your mind and with all your strength.' *(Deuteronomy 6:4,5)* ³¹And here is the second one. 'Love your neighbor as you love yourself.' *(Leviticus 19:18)* There is no commandment more important than these."

³²"You have spoken well, teacher," the man replied. "You are right in saying that God is one. There is no other God but him. ³³To love God with all your heart and mind

Olivia tried to figure out how to live out the second greatest commandment in "Like a Good Neighbor" (Club).

and strength is very important. So is loving your neighbor as you love yourself. These things are more important than all burnt offerings and sacrifices."

³⁴Jesus saw that the man had answered wisely. He said to him, "You are not far from God's kingdom." From then on, no one dared to ask Jesus any more questions.

Whose Son Is the Messiah?

³⁵Jesus was teaching in the temple courtyard. He asked, "Why do the teachers of the law say that the Messiah is the son of David? ³⁶The Holy Spirit spoke through David himself. David said,

" 'The Lord said to my Lord,
   "Sit at my right hand
until I put your enemies
   under your control." '   *(Psalm 110:1)*

³⁷David himself calls him 'Lord.' So how can he be David's son?"

The large crowd listened to Jesus with delight.

Warning Against the Teachers of the Law

³⁸As he taught, he said, "Watch out for the teachers of the law. They like to walk around in long robes. They like to be greeted with respect in the market. ³⁹They love to have the most important seats in the synagogues. They also love to have the places of honor at dinners. ⁴⁰They take over the

houses of widows. They say long prayers to show off. God will punish these men very much."

The Widow's Offering

[41]Jesus sat down across from the place where people put their temple offerings. He watched the crowd putting their money into the offering boxes. Many rich people threw large amounts into them. [42]But a poor widow came and put in two very small copper coins. They were worth only a few pennies.

[43]Jesus asked his disciples to come to him. He said, "What I'm about to tell you is true. That poor widow has put more into the offering box than all the others. [44]They all gave a lot because they are rich. But she gave even though she is poor. She put in everything she had. That was all she had to live on."

When the Temple Will Be Destroyed and the Signs of the End

13 Jesus was leaving the temple. One of his disciples said to him, "Look, Teacher! What huge stones! What wonderful buildings!"

[2]"Do you see these huge buildings?" Jesus asked. "Not one stone here will be left on top of another. Every stone will be thrown down."

[3]Jesus was sitting on the Mount of Olives, across from the temple. Peter, James, John and Andrew asked him a question in private. [4]"Tell us," they said. "When will these things happen? And what will be the sign that they are all about to come true?"

[5]Jesus said to them, "Keep watch! Be careful that no one fools you. [6]Many will come in my name. They will claim, 'I am he.' They will fool many people. [7]You will hear about wars. You will also hear people talking about future wars. Don't be alarmed. These things must happen. But the end still isn't here. [8]Nation will fight against nation. Kingdom will fight against kingdom. There will be earthquakes in many places. People will go hungry. All these things are the beginning of birth pains.

[9]"Watch out! You will be handed over to the local courts. You will be whipped in the synagogues. You will stand in front of governors and kings because of me. In that way you will be witnesses to them. [10]The good news has to be preached to all nations before the end comes. [11]You will be arrested and brought to trial. But don't worry ahead of time about what you will say. Just say what God brings to your mind at the time. It is not you speaking, but the Holy Spirit.

[12]"Brothers will hand over brothers to be killed. Fathers will hand over their children. Children will rise up against their parents and have them put to death. [13]Everyone will hate you because of me. But the one who remains strong in the faith will be saved.

[14]"You will see 'the hated thing that destroys.' *(Daniel 9:27; 11:31; 12:11)* It will stand where it does not belong. The reader should understand this. Then those who are in Judea should escape to the mountains. [15]No one on the roof should go down into the house to take anything out. [16]No one in the field should go back to get their coat. [17]How awful it will be in those days for pregnant women! How awful for nursing mothers! [18]Pray that this will not happen in winter. [19]Those days will be worse than any others from the time God created the world until now. And there will never be any like them again.

[20]"If the Lord had not cut the time short, no one would live. But because of God's chosen people, he has shortened it. [21]At that time someone may say to you, 'Look! Here is the Messiah!' Or, 'Look! There he is!' Do not believe it. [22]False messiahs and false prophets will appear. They will do signs and miracles. They will try to fool God's chosen people if possible. [23]Keep watch! I have told you everything ahead of time.

[24]"So in those days there will be terrible suffering. After that, Scripture says,

" 'The sun will be darkened.
    The moon will not shine.
[25] The stars will fall from the sky.
    The heavenly bodies will be shaken.'
(Isaiah 13:10; 34:4)

[26]"At that time people will see the Son of Man coming in clouds. He will come with great power and glory. [27]He will send his angels. He will gather his chosen people from all four directions. He will bring them from the ends of the earth to the ends of the heavens.

[28]"Learn a lesson from the fig tree. As soon as its twigs get tender and its leaves

come out, you know that summer is near. [29]In the same way, when you see these things happening, you know that the end is near. It is right at the door. [30]What I'm about to tell you is true. The people living now will certainly not pass away until all those things have happened. [31]Heaven and earth will pass away. But my words will never pass away.

The Day and Hour Are Not Known

[32]"But no one knows about that day or hour. Not even the angels in heaven know. The Son does not know. Only the Father knows. [33]Keep watch! Stay awake! You do not know when that time will come. [34]It's like a man going away. He leaves his house and puts his servants in charge. Each one is given a task to do. He tells the one at the door to keep watch.

[35]"So keep watch! You do not know when the owner of the house will come back. It may be in the evening or at midnight. It may be when the rooster crows or at dawn. [36]He may come suddenly. So do not let him find you sleeping. [37]What I say to you, I say to everyone. 'Watch!' "

A Woman Pours Perfume on Jesus at Bethany

14 The Passover and the Feast of Unleavened Bread were only two days away. The chief priests and the teachers of the law were plotting to arrest Jesus secretly. They wanted to kill him. [2]"But not during the feast," they said. "The people may stir up trouble."

[3]Jesus was in Bethany. He was at the table in the home of Simon, who had a skin disease. A woman came with a special sealed jar. It contained very expensive perfume made out of pure nard. She broke the jar open and poured the perfume on Jesus' head.

[4]Some of the people there became angry. They said to one another, "Why waste this perfume? [5]It could have been sold for more than a year's pay. The money could have been given to poor people." So they found fault with the woman.

[6]"Leave her alone," Jesus said. "Why are you bothering her? She has done a beautiful thing to me. [7]You will always have poor people with you. You can help them any time you want to. But you will not always have me. [8]She did what she could. She poured perfume on my body to prepare me to be buried. [9]What I'm about to tell you is true. What she has done will be told anywhere the good news is preached all over the world. It will be told in memory of her."

[10]Judas Iscariot was one of the 12 disciples. He went to the chief priests to hand Jesus over to them. [11]They were delighted to hear that he would do this. They promised to give Judas money. So he watched for the right time to hand Jesus over to them.

The Last Supper

[12]It was the first day of the Feast of Unleavened Bread. That was the time to sacrifice the Passover lamb. Jesus' disciples asked him, "Where do you want us to go and prepare for you to eat the Passover meal?"

[13]So he sent out two of his disciples. He told them, "Go into the city. A man carrying a jar of water will meet you. Follow him. [14]He will enter a house. Say to its owner, 'The Teacher asks, "Where is my guest room? Where can I eat the Passover meal with my disciples?" ' [15]He will show you a large upstairs room. It will have furniture and will be ready. Prepare for us to eat there."

[16]The disciples left and went into the city. They found things just as Jesus had told them. So they prepared the Passover meal.

[17]When evening came, Jesus arrived with the 12 disciples. [18]While they were at the table eating, Jesus said, "What I'm about to tell you is true. One of you who is eating with me will hand me over to my enemies."

[19]The disciples became sad. One by one they said to him, "Surely you don't mean me?"

[20]"It is one of you," Jesus replied. "It is the one who dips bread into the bowl with me. [21]The Son of Man will go just as it is written about him. But how terrible it will be for the one who hands over the Son of Man! It would be better for him if he had not been born."

[22]While they were eating, Jesus took bread. He gave thanks and broke it. He handed it to his disciples and said, "Take it. This is my body."

[23]Then he took a cup. He gave thanks and handed it to them. All of them drank from it.

[24]"This is my blood of the covenant," he said to them. "It is poured out for many.

[25]What I'm about to tell you is true. I won't drink wine with you again until the day I drink it in God's kingdom."

[26]Then they sang a hymn and went out to the Mount of Olives.

Jesus Says That the Disciples Will Turn Away

[27]"You will all turn away," Jesus told the disciples. "It is written,

" 'I will strike the shepherd down.
    Then the sheep will be scattered.'
                              (Zechariah 13:7)

[28]But after I rise from the dead, I will go ahead of you into Galilee."

[29]Peter said, "All the others may turn away. But I will not."

[30]"What I'm about to tell you is true," Jesus answered. "It will happen today, in fact tonight. Before the rooster crows twice, you yourself will say three times that you don't know me."

[31]But Peter would not give in. He said, "I may have to die with you. But I will never say I don't know you." And all the others said the same thing.

Jesus Prays in Gethsemane

[32]Jesus and his disciples went to a place called Gethsemane. Jesus said to them, "Sit here while I pray." [33]He took Peter, James and John along with him. He began to be very upset and troubled. [34]"My soul is very sad. I feel close to death," he said to them. "Stay here. Keep watch."

[35]He went a little farther. Then he fell to the ground. He prayed that, if possible, the hour might pass by him. [36]"Abba, Father," he said, "everything is possible for you. Take this cup of suffering away from me. But let what you want be done, not what I want."

[37]Then he returned to his disciples and found them sleeping. "Simon," he said to Peter, "are you asleep? Couldn't you keep watch for one hour? [38]Watch and pray. Then you won't fall into sin when you are tempted. The spirit is willing, but the body is weak."

[39]Once more Jesus went away and prayed the same thing. [40]Then he came back. Again he found them sleeping. They couldn't keep their eyes open. They did not know what to say to him.

[41]Jesus returned the third time. He said to them, "Are you still sleeping and resting? Enough! The hour has come. Look! The Son of Man is about to be handed over to sinners. [42]Get up! Let us go! Here comes the one who is handing me over to them!"

Jesus Is Arrested

[43]Just as Jesus was speaking, Judas appeared. He was one of the 12 disciples. A crowd was with him. They were carrying swords and clubs. The chief priests, the teachers of the law, and the elders had sent them.

[44]Judas, who was going to hand Jesus over, had arranged a signal with them. "The one I kiss is the man," he said. "Arrest him and have the guards lead him away." [45]So Judas went to Jesus at once. Judas said, "Rabbi!" And he kissed Jesus. [46]The men grabbed Jesus and arrested him. [47]Then one of those standing nearby pulled his sword out. He struck the servant of the high priest and cut off his ear.

[48]"Am I leading a band of armed men against you?" asked Jesus. "Do you have to come out with swords and clubs to capture me? [49]Every day I was with you. I taught in the temple courtyard, and you didn't arrest me. But the Scriptures must come true." [50]Then everyone left him and ran away.

[51]A young man was following Jesus. The man was wearing nothing but a piece of linen cloth. When the crowd grabbed him, [52]he ran away naked. He left his clothing behind.

Jesus Is Taken to the Sanhedrin

[53]The crowd took Jesus to the high priest. All the chief priests, the elders, and the teachers of the law came together. [54]Not too far away, Peter followed Jesus. He went right into the courtyard of the high priest. There he sat with the guards. He warmed himself at the fire.

[55]The chief priests and the whole Sanhedrin were looking for something to use against Jesus. They wanted to put him to death. But they did not find any proof. [56]Many witnesses lied about him. But their stories did not agree.

[57]Then some of them stood up. Here is what those false witnesses said about him. [58]"We heard him say, 'I will destroy this temple made by human hands. In three days I will build another temple, not made by human hands.' " [59]But what they said did not agree.

⁶⁰Then the high priest stood up in front of them. He asked Jesus, "Aren't you going to answer? What are these charges these men are bringing against you?" ⁶¹But Jesus remained silent. He gave no answer.

Again the high priest asked him, "Are you the Messiah? Are you the Son of the Blessed One?"

⁶²"I am," said Jesus. "And you will see the Son of Man sitting at the right hand of the Mighty One. You will see the Son of Man coming on the clouds of heaven."

⁶³The high priest tore his clothes. "Why do we need any more witnesses?" he asked. ⁶⁴"You have heard him say a very evil thing against God. What do you think?"

They all found him guilty and said he must die. ⁶⁵Then some began to spit at him. They blindfolded him. They hit him with their fists. They said, "Prophesy!" And the guards took him and beat him.

Peter Says He Does Not Know Jesus

⁶⁶Peter was below in the courtyard. One of the high priest's female servants came by. ⁶⁷When she saw Peter warming himself, she looked closely at him.

"You also were with Jesus, that Nazarene," she said.

⁶⁸But Peter said he had not been with him. "I don't know or understand what you're talking about," he said. He went out to the entrance to the courtyard.

⁶⁹The servant saw him there. She said again to those standing around, "This fellow is one of them." ⁷⁰Again he said he was not.

After a little while, those standing nearby said to Peter, "You must be one of them. You are from Galilee."

⁷¹Then Peter began to curse. He said to them, "I don't know this man you're talking about!"

⁷²Right away the rooster crowed the second time. Then Peter remembered what Jesus had spoken to him. "The rooster will crow twice," he had said. "Before it does, you will say three times that you don't know me." Peter broke down and cried.

BIBLE ADVENTURES

The Slimey Awards showed Peter's denial of Jesus in "The Devil Made Me Do It" (A#32).

Jesus Is Brought to Pilate

15 It was very early in the morning. The chief priests, with the elders, the teachers of the law, and the whole Sanhedrin, made their plans. So they tied Jesus up and led him away. Then they handed him over to Pilate.

²"Are you the king of the Jews?" asked Pilate.

"You have said so," Jesus replied.

³The chief priests brought many charges against him. ⁴So Pilate asked him again, "Aren't you going to answer? See how many things they charge you with."

⁵But Jesus still did not reply. Pilate was amazed.

⁶It was the usual practice at the Passover Feast to let one prisoner go free. The people could choose the one they wanted. ⁷A man named Barabbas was in prison. He was there with some other people who had fought against the country's rulers. They had committed murder while they were fighting against the rulers. ⁸The crowd came up and asked Pilate to do for them what he usually did.

⁹"Do you want me to let the king of the Jews go free?" asked Pilate. ¹⁰He knew that the chief priests had handed Jesus over to him because they wanted to get their own way. ¹¹But the chief priests stirred up the crowd. So the crowd asked Pilate to let Barabbas go free instead.

¹²"Then what should I do with the one you call the king of the Jews?" Pilate asked them.

¹³"Crucify him!" the crowd shouted.

¹⁴"Why? What wrong has he done?" asked Pilate.

But they shouted even louder, "Crucify him!"

¹⁵Pilate wanted to satisfy the crowd. So he let Barabbas go free. He ordered that Jesus be whipped. Then he handed him over to be nailed to a cross.

The Soldiers Make Fun of Jesus

¹⁶The soldiers led Jesus away into the palace. It was called the Praetorium. They called together the whole company of soldiers. ¹⁷The soldiers put a purple robe on Jesus. Then they twisted thorns together to make a crown. They placed it on his head. ¹⁸They began to call out to him, "We honor you, king of the Jews!" ¹⁹Again and again

they hit him on the head with a stick. They spit on him. They fell on their knees and pretended to honor him. ²⁰After they had made fun of him, they took off the purple robe. They put his own clothes back on him. Then they led him out to nail him to a cross.

Jesus Is Nailed to a Cross

²¹A man named Simon was passing by. He was from Cyrene. He was the father of Alexander and Rufus. Simon was on his way in from the country. The soldiers forced him to carry the cross. ²²They brought Jesus to the place called Golgotha. The word Golgotha means the Place of the Skull. ²³Then they gave him wine mixed with spices. But he did not take it. ²⁴They nailed him to the cross. Then they divided up his clothes. They cast lots to see what each of them would get.

²⁵It was nine o'clock in the morning when they crucified him. ²⁶They wrote out the charge against him. It read,

THE KING OF THE JEWS.

²⁷⁻²⁸They crucified with him two rebels against Rome. One was on his right and one was on his left. ²⁹Those who passed by shouted at Jesus and made fun of him. They shook their heads and said, "So you are going to destroy the temple and build it again in three days? ³⁰Then come down from the cross! Save yourself!" ³¹In the same way the chief priests and the teachers of the law made fun of him among themselves. "He saved others," they said. "But he can't save himself! ³²Let this Messiah, this king of Israel, come down now from the cross! When we see that, we will believe." Those who were being crucified with Jesus also made fun of him.

Jesus Dies

³³At noon, darkness covered the whole land. It lasted three hours. ³⁴At three o'clock in the afternoon Jesus cried out in a loud voice, *"Eloi, Eloi, lema sabachthani?"* This means "My God, my God, why have you deserted me?" *(Psalm 22:1)*

³⁵Some of those standing nearby heard Jesus cry out. They said, "Listen! He's calling for Elijah."

³⁶Someone ran and filled a sponge with wine vinegar. He put it on a stick. He offered it to Jesus to drink. "Leave him alone," he said. "Let's see if Elijah comes to take him down."

³⁷With a loud cry, Jesus took his last breath.

³⁸The temple curtain was torn in two from top to bottom. ³⁹A Roman commander was standing there in front of Jesus. He saw how Jesus died. Then he said, "This man was surely the Son of God!"

⁴⁰Not very far away, some women were watching. Mary Magdalene was among them. Mary, the mother of the younger James and of Joseph, was also there. So was Salome. ⁴¹In Galilee these women had followed Jesus. They had taken care of his needs. Many other women were also there. They had come up with him to Jerusalem.

Jesus Is Buried

⁴²It was the day before the Sabbath. That day was called Preparation Day. As evening approached, ⁴³Joseph went boldly to Pilate and asked for Jesus' body. Joseph was from the town of Arimathea. He was a leading member of the Jewish Council. He was waiting for God's kingdom. ⁴⁴Pilate was surprised to hear that Jesus was already dead. So he called for the Roman commander. He asked him if Jesus had already died. ⁴⁵The commander said it was true. So Pilate gave the body to Joseph. ⁴⁶Then Joseph bought some linen cloth. He took down the body and wrapped it in the linen. He put it in a tomb cut out of rock. Then he rolled a stone against the entrance to the tomb. ⁴⁷Mary Magdalene and Mary the mother of Joseph saw where Jesus' body had been placed.

Jesus Rises From the Dead

16 The Sabbath day ended. Mary Magdalene, Mary the mother of James, and Salome bought spices. They were going to use them for Jesus' body. ²Very early on the first day of the week, they were on their way to the tomb. It was just after sunrise. ³They asked each other, "Who will roll the stone away from the entrance to the tomb?"

⁴Then they looked up and saw that the stone had been rolled away. The stone was very large. ⁵They entered the tomb. As they did, they saw a young man dressed in a white robe. He was sitting on the right side. They were alarmed.

[6]"Don't be alarmed," he said. "You are looking for Jesus the Nazarene, who was crucified. But he has risen! He is not here! See the place where they had put him. [7]Go! Tell his disciples and Peter, 'He is going ahead of you into Galilee. There you will see him. It will be just as he told you.'"

[8]The women were shaking and confused. They went out and ran away from the tomb. They said nothing to anyone, because they were afraid.

[9]Jesus rose from the dead early on the first day of the week. He appeared first to Mary Magdalene. He had driven seven demons out of her. [10]She went and told those who had been with him. She found them crying. They were very sad. [11]They heard that Jesus was alive and that she had seen him. But they did not believe it.

[12]After that, Jesus appeared in a different form to two of them. This happened while they were walking out in the country. [13]The two returned and told the others about it. But the others did not believe them either.

[14]Later Jesus appeared to the 11 disciples as they were eating. He spoke firmly to them because they had no faith. They would not believe those who had seen him after he rose from the dead.

[15]He said to them, "Go into all the world. Preach the good news to everyone. [16]Anyone who believes and is baptized will be saved. But anyone who does not believe will be punished. [17]Here are the miraculous signs that those who believe will do. In my name they will drive out demons. They will speak in languages they had not known before. [18]They will pick up snakes with their hands. And when they drink deadly poison, it will not hurt them at all. They will place their hands on sick people. And the people will get well."

[19]When the Lord Jesus finished speaking to them, he was taken up into heaven. He sat down at the right hand of God. [20]Then the disciples went out and preached everywhere. The Lord worked with them. And he backed up his word by the signs that went with it.

Luke

We now reach Luke, a gospel that is akin to a first-century news report. Luke was writing primarily for an individual named Theophilus to provide a written account about the life of Jesus (1:1–4). It's noteworthy that the book of Acts is the sequel! It is likewise written by Luke for the same person. (Wooton tells me that I should have issued a spoiler alert there. My apologies.)

Based on the name and the title that Luke used for him ("most excellent"), Theophilus was probably a prosperous Gentile. In the early church, many Gentiles were hearing about Jesus and showing an interest. However, they had little concept of Jewish history and few actual facts upon which to base their faith. Luke's purpose was to provide them with an accurate report from eyewitnesses.

It is in Luke's gospel where we finally come to the classic Christmas story with the angels and the shepherds (chapter 2). This account is unique to this book, and so are the parables of the Good Samaritan (10:25–37) and the Prodigal Son (15:11–32). And we can read of Jesus' encounter with Zacchaeus (19:1–10), the widow who gave God all she had (21:1–4), and other stories and teachings found nowhere else.

Theophilus may have been the first person to read Luke's report, but it's not an overstatement to say that *billions* of others have benefited from it since then.

WHAT'S IT MEAN, EUGENE?

Gospel—The word gospel springs from the Old English *god-spell,* which means "good news." And what good news it is! As we know, the gospels explain that God sent His only Son, Jesus Christ, to become the Savior of the world, so that we can all be forgiven for our sins and enter into an eternal relationship with Him through Jesus' sacrifice on the cross.

Luke Writes an Orderly Report

1 Many people have attempted to write about the things that have taken place among us. [2]Reports of these things were handed down to us. There were people who saw these things for themselves from the beginning. They saw them and then passed the word on. [3]With this in mind, I myself have carefully looked into everything from the beginning. So I also decided to write down an orderly report of exactly what happened. I am doing this for you, most excellent Theophilus. [4]I want you to know that the things you have been taught are true.

The Coming Birth of John the Baptist

[5]Herod was king of Judea. During the time he was ruling, there was a priest named Zechariah. He belonged to a group of priests named after Abijah. His wife Elizabeth also came from the family line of Aaron. [6]Both of them did what was right in the sight of God. They obeyed all the Lord's commands and rules faithfully. [7]But they had no children, because Elizabeth was not able to have any. And they were both very old.

[8]One day Zechariah's group was on duty. He was serving as a priest in God's temple. [9]He happened to be chosen, in the usual way, to go into the temple of the Lord. There he was supposed to burn incense. [10]The time came for this to be done. All who had gathered to worship were praying outside. [11]Then an angel of the Lord appeared to Zechariah. The angel was standing at the right side of the incense altar. [12]When Zechariah saw him, he was amazed and terrified. [13]But the angel said to him, "Do not be afraid, Zechariah. Your prayer has been heard. Your wife Elizabeth will have a child. It will be a boy, and you must call him John. [14]He will be a joy and delight to you. His birth will make many people very glad. [15]He will be important in the sight of the Lord. He must never drink wine or other such drinks. He will be filled with the Holy Spirit even before he is born. [16]He will bring back many of the people of Israel to the Lord their God. [17]And he will prepare the way for the Lord. He will have the same spirit and power that Elijah had. He will bring peace between parents and their children. He will teach people who don't obey to be wise and do what is right. In this way,

Luke 1:11–26

Angel return alert! The angel Gabriel was the same one who spoke to Daniel about the dream of the rams and goats (Daniel 8:16).

he will prepare a people who are ready for the Lord."

[18]Zechariah asked the angel, "How can I be sure of this? I am an old man, and my wife is old too."

[19]The angel said to him, "I am Gabriel. I serve God. I have been sent to speak to you and to tell you this good news. [20]And now you will have to be silent. You will not be able to speak until after John is born. That's because you did not believe my words. They will come true at the time God has chosen."

[21]During that time, the people were waiting for Zechariah to come out of the temple. They wondered why he stayed there so long. [22]When he came out, he could not speak to them. They realized he had seen a vision in the temple. They knew this because he kept gesturing to them. He still could not speak.

[23]When his time of service was over, he returned home. [24]After that, his wife Elizabeth became pregnant. She stayed at home for five months. [25]"The Lord has done this for me," she said. "In these days, he has been kind to me. He has taken away my shame among the people."

The Coming Birth of Jesus

[26]In the sixth month after Elizabeth had become pregnant, God sent the angel

Gabriel to Nazareth, a town in Galilee. [27]He was sent to a virgin. The girl was engaged to a man named Joseph. He came from the family line of David. The virgin's name was Mary. [28]The angel greeted her and said, "The Lord has blessed you in a special way. He is with you."

[29]Mary was very upset because of his words. She wondered what kind of greeting this could be. [30]But the angel said to her, "Do not be afraid, Mary. God is very pleased with you. [31]You will become pregnant and give birth to a son. You must call him Jesus. [32]He will be great and will be called the Son of the Most High God. The Lord God will make him a king like his father David of long ago. [33]The Son of the Most High God will rule forever over his people. They are from the family line of Jacob. That kingdom will never end."

[34]"How can this happen?" Mary asked the angel. "I am a virgin."

[35]The angel answered, "The Holy Spirit will come to you. The power of the Most High God will cover you. So the holy one that is born will be called the Son of God. [36]Your relative Elizabeth will have a child even though she is old. People thought she could not have children. But she has been pregnant for six months now. [37]That's because what God says will always come true."

[38]"I serve the Lord," Mary answered. "May it happen to me just as you said it would." Then the angel left her.

Mary Visits Elizabeth

[39]At that time Mary got ready and hurried to a town in Judea's hill country. [40]There she entered Zechariah's home and greeted Elizabeth. [41]When Elizabeth heard Mary's greeting, the baby inside her jumped. And Elizabeth was filled with the Holy Spirit. [42]In a loud voice she called out, "God has blessed you more than other women. And blessed is the child you will have! [43]But why is God so kind to me? Why has the mother of my Lord come to me? [44]As soon as I heard the sound of your voice, the baby inside me jumped for joy. [45]You are a woman God has blessed. You have believed that the Lord would keep his promises to you!"

Mary's Song

[46]Mary said,

"My soul gives glory to the Lord.
[47]   My spirit delights in God my Savior.
[48] He has taken note of me
     even though I am not considered
       important.
From now on all people will call me
       blessed.
[49]   The Mighty One has done great
       things for me.
     His name is holy.
[50] He shows his mercy to those who have
       respect for him,
     from parent to child down through
       the years.
[51] He has done mighty things with his
       powerful arm.
     He has scattered those who are proud
       in their deepest thoughts.
[52] He has brought down rulers from their
       thrones.
     But he has lifted up people who are
       not considered important.
[53] He has filled with good things those
       who are hungry.
     But he has sent away empty those
       who are rich.
[54] He has helped the people of Israel, who
       serve him.
     He has always remembered to be
       kind
[55] to Abraham and his children down
       through the years.
     He has done it just as he promised to
       our people of long ago."

[56]Mary stayed with Elizabeth about three months. Then she returned home.

John the Baptist Is Born

[57]The time came for Elizabeth to have her baby. She gave birth to a son. [58]Her neighbors and relatives heard that the Lord had been very kind to her. They shared her joy.

[59]On the eighth day, they came to have the child circumcised. They were going to name him Zechariah, like his father. [60]But his mother spoke up. "No!" she said. "He must be called John."

[61]They said to her, "No one among your relatives has that name."

[62]Then they motioned to his father. They wanted to find out what he would like to name the child. [63]He asked for something to write on. Then he wrote, "His name is John." Everyone was amazed. [64]Right away Zechariah could speak again. Right away he praised God. [65]All his neighbors were filled with fear and wonder. Throughout Judea's hill country, people were talking about all these things. [66]Everyone who heard this wondered about it. And because the Lord was with John, they asked, "What is this child going to be?"

Zechariah's Song

[67]John's father Zechariah was filled with the Holy Spirit. He prophesied,

[68] "Give praise to the Lord, the God of Israel!
He has come to his people and purchased their freedom.
[69] He has acted with great power and has saved us.
He did it for those who are from the family line of his servant David.
[70] Long ago holy prophets said he would do it.
[71] He has saved us from our enemies.
We are rescued from all who hate us.
[72] He has been kind to our people of long ago.
He has remembered his holy covenant.
[73] He made a promise to our father Abraham.
[74] He promised to save us from our enemies.
Then we could serve him without fear.
[75] He wants us to be holy and godly as long as we live.

[76] "And you, my child, will be called a prophet of the Most High God.
You will go ahead of the Lord to prepare the way for him.
[77] You will tell his people how they can be saved.
You will tell them that their sins can be forgiven.
[78] All of that will happen because our God is tender and caring.

His kindness will bring the rising sun to us from heaven.
[79] It will shine on those living in darkness and in the shadow of death.
It will guide our feet on the path of peace."

[80]The child grew up, and his spirit became strong. He lived in the desert until he appeared openly to Israel.

Jesus Is Born

2 In those days, Caesar Augustus made a law. It required that a list be made of everyone in the whole Roman world. [2]It was the first time a list was made of the people while Quirinius was governor of Syria. [3]Everyone went to their own town to be listed.

[4]So Joseph went also. He went from the town of Nazareth in Galilee to Judea. That is where Bethlehem, the town of David, was. Joseph went there because he belonged to the family line of David. [5]He went there with Mary to be listed. Mary was engaged to him. She was expecting a baby. [6]While Joseph and Mary were there, the time came for the child to be born. [7]She gave birth to her first baby. It was a boy. She wrapped him in large strips of cloth. Then she placed him in a manger. That's because there was no guest room where they could stay.

[8]There were shepherds living out in the fields nearby. It was night, and they were taking care of their sheep. [9]An angel of the Lord appeared to them. And the glory of the Lord shone around them. They were terrified. [10]But the angel said to them, "Do not be afraid. I bring you good news. It will bring great joy for all the people. [11]Today in the town of David a Savior has been born to you. He is the Messiah, the Lord. [12]Here is how you will know I am telling you the truth. You will find a baby wrapped in strips of cloth and lying in a manger."

[13]Suddenly a large group of angels from heaven also appeared. They were praising God. They said,

14 "May glory be given to God in the
   highest heaven!
   And may peace be given to those he
   is pleased with on earth!"

15The angels left and went into heaven. Then the shepherds said to one another, "Let's go to Bethlehem. Let's see this thing that has happened, which the Lord has told us about."
16So they hurried off and found Mary and Joseph and the baby. The baby was lying in the manger. 17After the shepherds had seen him, they told everyone. They reported what the angel had said about this child. 18All who heard it were amazed at what the shepherds said to them. 19But Mary kept all these things like a secret treasure in her heart. She thought about them over and over. 20The shepherds returned. They gave glory and praise to God. Everything they had seen and heard was just as they had been told.
21When the child was eight days old, he was circumcised. At the same time he was named Jesus. This was the name the angel had given him before his mother became pregnant.

Joseph and Mary Take Jesus to the Temple

22The time came for making Mary "clean" as required by the Law of Moses. So Joseph and Mary took Jesus to Jerusalem. There they presented him to the Lord. 23In the Law of the Lord it says, "The first boy born in every family must be set apart for the Lord." (Exodus 13:2,12) 24They also offered a sacrifice. They did it in keeping with the Law, which says, "a pair of doves or two young pigeons." (Leviticus 12:8)
25In Jerusalem there was a man named Simeon. He was a good and godly man. He was waiting for God's promise to Israel to come true. The Holy Spirit was with him. 26The Spirit had told Simeon that he would not die before he had seen the Lord's Messiah. 27The Spirit led him into the temple courtyard. Then Jesus' parents brought the child in. They came to do for him what the Law required. 28Simeon took Jesus in his arms and praised God. He said,

29 "Lord, you are the King over all.
   Now let me, your servant, go in peace.
   That is what you promised.

Around Christmastime in Odyssey, it seems like everyone gets busy. For the last few years, Eugene has been trying to perfect creating ornaments out of leftover pieces from science experiments. Penny and Wooton always go on a baking frenzy. In the evenings, Penny and I watch old Christmas movies. Well, actually *I* watch old Christmas movies. Penny gets distracted making snowmen out of popcorn. I don't think she knows the ending of *It's a Wonderful Life* even though we watch it every year

Then there's Whit. Unlike the rest of us, he slows down at Christmas. The other day, I found him in his office with his eyes closed, listening to carols on the radio. He'll spend hours writing letters to old friends. He says that Christmas is a time to rest and reflect on God's perfect Gift.

Sometimes a holiday is about activity, music, and parties. And sometimes it's about sitting by yourself, watching the snow fall outside your window. Both can be great! After all, Jesus came to Earth to bring us peace *and* joy. The angels sang in the heavens, while a star shone silently overhead. *How* you celebrate doesn't matter as much as *Who* you celebrate.

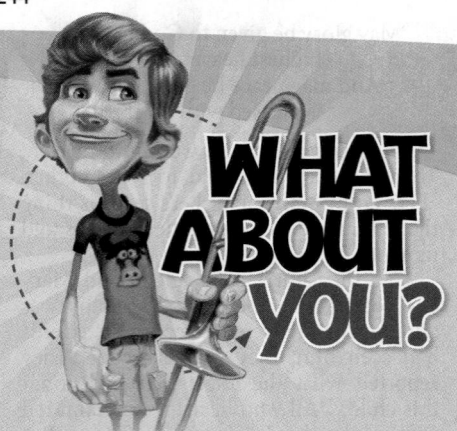

WHAT ABOUT YOU?

Schools are out, stores are packed, and the world is aglow with magic and wonder. What's the occasion? Christmas, of course! Even pets love this holiday. That's probably because (according to studies) 56 percent of dogs and 48 percent of cats receive Christmas presents from their owners. But beyond the glamor of tinsel and toys, Christians understand that there's more to the holiday than writing wish lists to a jolly guy in a red suit.

When the true Spirit of Christmas stirs, families and loved ones are drawn together. That Spirit is the Holy Spirit. It's God who works in the hearts of men. Christmas is all about love. It's about the greatest love of all: God's love for us before we knew how to love Him back. In 1 John 4:9 we read: "Here is how God showed his love among us. He sent his one and only Son into the world. He sent him so we could receive life through him."

First John 5:11 says: "God has given us eternal life. And this life is found in his Son."

All we have to do is believe. It's like opening a Christmas gift. You believe something good is inside, so you open it. It's the same with Jesus Christ. If you believe in Him, you open the gift of eternal life.

You can celebrate Christmas any time of year. Just think of ways you can show God's love to the people around you. Maybe you can rake leaves for your neighbor, donate toys to charity, or bake cookies for somebody special.

---

[30] My eyes have seen your salvation.
[31]   You have prepared it in the sight of all nations.
[32] It is a light to be given to the Gentiles.
    It will be the glory of your people Israel."

[33] The child's father and mother were amazed at what was said about him. [34] Then Simeon blessed them. He said to Mary, Jesus' mother, "This child is going to cause many people in Israel to fall and to rise. God has sent him. But many will speak against him. [35] The thoughts of many hearts will be known. A sword will wound your own soul too."

[36] There was also a prophet named Anna. She was the daughter of Penuel from the tribe of Asher. Anna was very old. After getting married, she lived with her husband seven years. [37] Then she was a widow until she was 84. She never left the temple. She worshiped night and day, praying and going without food. [38] Anna came up to Jesus'

family at that moment. She gave thanks to God. And she spoke about the child to all who were looking forward to the time when Jerusalem would be set free.

[39] Joseph and Mary did everything the Law of the Lord required. Then they returned to Galilee. They went to their own town of Nazareth. [40] And the child grew and became strong. He was very wise. He was blessed by God's grace.

The Boy Jesus at the Temple

[41] Every year Jesus' parents went to Jerusalem for the Passover Feast. [42] When Jesus was 12 years old, they went up to the feast as usual. [43] After the feast was over, his parents left to go back home. The boy Jesus stayed behind in Jerusalem. But they were not aware of it. [44] They thought he was somewhere in their group. So they traveled on for a day. Then they began to look for him among their relatives and friends. [45] They did not find him. So they went back to Jerusalem to look for him. [46] After three

days they found him in the temple court-yard. He was sitting with the teachers. He was listening to them and asking them questions. [47]Everyone who heard him was amazed at how much he understood. They also were amazed at his answers. [48]When his parents saw him, they were amazed. His mother said to him, "Son, why have you treated us like this? Your father and I have been worried about you. We have been looking for you everywhere."

[49]"Why were you looking for me?" he asked. "Didn't you know I had to be in my Father's house?" [50]But they did not understand what he meant by that.

[51]Then he went back to Nazareth with them, and he obeyed them. But his mother kept all these things like a secret treasure in her heart. [52]Jesus became wiser and stronger. He also became more and more pleasing to God and to people.

John the Baptist Prepares the Way

3 Tiberius Caesar had been ruling for 15 years. Pontius Pilate was governor of Judea. Herod was the ruler of Galilee. His brother Philip was the ruler of Iturea and Traconitis. Lysanias was ruler of Abilene. [2]Annas and Caiaphas were high priests. At that time God's word came to John, son of Zechariah, in the desert. [3]He went into all the countryside around the Jordan River. There he preached that people should be baptized and turn away from their sins. Then God would forgive them. [4]Here is what is written in the book of Isaiah the prophet. It says,

"A messenger is calling out in the
    desert,
'Prepare the way for the Lord.
  Make straight paths for him.
[5] Every valley will be filled in.
  Every mountain and hill will be
      made level.
The crooked roads will become straight.
The rough ways will become
      smooth.
[6] And all people will see God's
      salvation.'"   *(Isaiah 40:3–5)*

[7]John spoke to the crowds coming to be baptized by him. He said, "You are like a nest of poisonous snakes! Who warned you to escape the coming of God's anger? [8]Live in a way that shows you have turned away from your sins. And don't start saying to yourselves, 'Abraham is our father.' I tell you, God can raise up children for Abraham even from these stones. [9]The ax is already lying at the roots of the trees. All the trees that don't produce good fruit will be cut down. They will be thrown into the fire."

[10]"Then what should we do?" the crowd asked.

[11]John answered, "Anyone who has extra clothes should share with the one who has none. And anyone who has extra food should do the same."

[12]Even tax collectors came to be baptized. "Teacher," they asked, "what should we do?"

[13]"Don't collect any more than you are required to," John told them.

[14]Then some soldiers asked him, "And what should we do?"

John replied, "Don't force people to give you money. Don't bring false charges against people. Be happy with your pay."

[15]The people were waiting. They were expecting something. They were all wondering in their hearts if John might be the Messiah. [16]John answered them all, "I baptize you with water. But one who is more powerful than I am will come. I'm not good enough to untie the straps of his sandals. He will baptize you with the Holy Spirit and fire. [17]His pitchfork is in his hand to toss the straw away from his threshing floor. He will gather the wheat into his barn. But he will burn up the husks with fire that can't be put out." [18]John said many other things to warn the people. He also announced the good news to them.

[19]But John found fault with Herod, the ruler of Galilee, because of his marriage to Herodias. She was the wife of Herod's brother. John also spoke strongly to Herod about all the other evil things he had done. [20]So Herod locked John up in prison. Herod added this sin to all his others.

The Baptism and Family Line of Jesus

[21]When all the people were being baptized, Jesus was baptized too. And as he was praying, heaven was opened. [22]The Holy Spirit came to rest on him in the form of a dove. A voice came from heaven. It said, "You are my Son, and I love you. I am very pleased with you."

WHIT'S WISDOM

Luke 3:15–22

Eugene likes to ask questions. One day he asked Connie and me, "If you could be any Bible person for a single day, who would it be?"

Connie decided on the prophet Deborah. I said, "John the Baptist."

Connie gasped. "John the Baptist! He ate locusts—and he got his head cut off!"

I chuckled. "That's true, but John the Baptist had one of the best jobs I can imagine. He baptized people all day! And he had the honor of baptizing Jesus Himself! No one else in the Bible did that."

While different churches use different forms of baptism, water is a symbol used by all. In many churches, Christians are baptized to publicly proclaim that their old life—the time before they knew Jesus—is now gone, and their new life—with Jesus as their Savior—has begun. This is symbolized when they are dunked under the water, then brought back up, or when water is sprinkled on their heads. I know from experience that new life with Jesus is going to be an amazing, wonderful adventure.

Connie and Eugene had to agree that John the Baptist was a good choice.

²³Jesus was about 30 years old when he began his special work for God and others. It was thought that he was the son of Joseph.

Joseph was the son of Heli.
²⁴ Heli was the son of Matthat.
Matthat was the son of Levi.
Levi was the son of Melki.
Melki was the son of Jannai.
Jannai was the son of Joseph.
²⁵ Joseph was the son of Mattathias.
Mattathias was the son of Amos.
Amos was the son of Nahum.
Nahum was the son of Esli.
Esli was the son of Naggai.
²⁶ Naggai was the son of Maath.
Maath was the son of Mattathias.
Mattathias was the son of Semein.
Semein was the son of Josek.
Josek was the son of Joda.
²⁷ Joda was the son of Joanan.
Joanan was the son of Rhesa.
Rhesa was the son of Zerubbabel.
Zerubbabel was the son of Shealtiel.
Shealtiel was the son of Neri.
²⁸ Neri was the son of Melki.
Melki was the son of Addi.
Addi was the son of Cosam.
Cosam was the son of Elmadam.
Elmadam was the son of Er.
²⁹ Er was the son of Joshua.
Joshua was the son of Eliezer.
Eliezer was the son of Jorim.

Jorim was the son of Matthat.
Matthat was the son of Levi.
³⁰ Levi was the son of Simeon.
Simeon was the son of Judah.
Judah was the son of Joseph.
Joseph was the son of Jonam.
Jonam was the son of Eliakim.
³¹ Eliakim was the son of Melea.
Melea was the son of Menna.
Menna was the son of Mattatha.
Mattatha was the son of Nathan.
Nathan was the son of David.
³² David was the son of Jesse.
Jesse was the son of Obed.
Obed was the son of Boaz.
Boaz was the son of Salmon.
Salmon was the son of Nahshon.
³³ Nahshon was the son of Amminadab.
Amminadab was the son of Ram.
Ram was the son of Hezron.
Hezron was the son of Perez.
Perez was the son of Judah.
³⁴ Judah was the son of Jacob.
Jacob was the son of Isaac.
Isaac was the son of Abraham.
Abraham was the son of Terah.
Terah was the son of Nahor.
³⁵ Nahor was the son of Serug.
Serug was the son of Reu.
Reu was the son of Peleg.
Peleg was the son of Eber.
Eber was the son of Shelah.

³⁶ Shelah was the son of Cainan.
Cainan was the son of Arphaxad.
Arphaxad was the son of Shem.
Shem was the son of Noah.
Noah was the son of Lamech.
³⁷ Lamech was the son of Methuselah.
Methuselah was the son of Enoch.
Enoch was the son of Jared.
Jared was the son of Mahalalel.
Mahalalel was the son of Kenan.
³⁸ Kenan was the son of Enosh.
Enosh was the son of Seth.
Seth was the son of Adam.
Adam was the son of God.

Jesus Is Tempted in the Desert

Jesus, full of the Holy Spirit, left the Jordan River. The Spirit led him into the desert. ²There the devil tempted him for 40 days. Jesus ate nothing during that time. At the end of the 40 days, he was hungry.

³The devil said to him, "If you are the Son of God, tell this stone to become bread."

⁴Jesus answered, "It is written, 'Man must not live only on bread.'" *(Deuteronomy 8:3)*

⁵Then the devil led Jesus up to a high place. In an instant, he showed Jesus all the kingdoms of the world. ⁶He said to Jesus, "I will give you all their authority and glory. It has been given to me, and I can give it to anyone I want to. ⁷If you worship me, it will all be yours."

⁸Jesus answered, "It is written, 'Worship the Lord your God. He is the only one you should serve.'" *(Deuteronomy 6:13)*

⁹Then the devil led Jesus to Jerusalem. He had Jesus stand on the highest point of the temple. "If you are the Son of God," he said, "throw yourself down from here. ¹⁰It is written,

"'The Lord will command his angels to
take good care of you.
¹¹ They will lift you up in their hands.
Then you won't trip over a stone.'"
(Psalm 91:11,12)

---

¹²Jesus answered, "Scripture says, 'Do not test the Lord your God.'" *(Deuteronomy 6:16)*

¹³When the devil finished all this tempting, he left Jesus until a better time.

Jesus Is Not Accepted in Nazareth

¹⁴Jesus returned to Galilee in the power of the Holy Spirit. News about him spread through the whole countryside. ¹⁵He was teaching in their synagogues, and everyone praised him.

¹⁶Jesus went to Nazareth, where he had been brought up. On the Sabbath day he went into the synagogue as he usually did. He stood up to read. ¹⁷And the scroll of Isaiah the prophet was handed to him. Jesus unrolled it and found the right place. There it is written,

¹⁸ "The Spirit of the Lord is on me.
He has anointed me
to announce the good news to poor
people.
He has sent me to announce freedom
for prisoners.
He has sent me so that the blind will
see again.
He wants me to set free those who are
treated badly.
¹⁹ And he has sent me to announce
the year when he will set his
people free." *(Isaiah 61:1,2)*

²⁰Then Jesus rolled up the scroll. He gave it back to the attendant and sat down. The eyes of everyone in the synagogue were staring at him. ²¹He began by saying to them, "Today this passage of Scripture is coming true as you listen."

²²Everyone said good things about him. They were amazed at the gracious words they heard from his lips. "Isn't this Joseph's son?" they asked.

²³Jesus said, "Here is a saying you will certainly apply to me. 'Doctor, heal yourself!' And you will tell me this. 'Do the things here in your hometown that we heard you did in Capernaum.'"

²⁴"What I'm about to tell you is true," he continued. "A prophet is not accepted in his hometown. ²⁵I tell you for sure that there were many widows in Israel in the days of Elijah. And there had been no rain for three and a half years. There wasn't enough food to eat anywhere in the land. ²⁶But Elijah was not sent to any of those widows. Instead,

he was sent to a widow in Zarephath near Sidon. [27]And there were many in Israel who had skin diseases in the days of Elisha the prophet. But not one of them was healed except Naaman the Syrian."

[28]All the people in the synagogue were very angry when they heard that. [29]They got up and ran Jesus out of town. They took him to the edge of the hill on which the town was built. They planned to throw him off the cliff. [30]But Jesus walked right through the crowd and went on his way.

Jesus Drives Out an Evil Spirit

[31]Then Jesus went to Capernaum, a town in Galilee. On the Sabbath day he taught the people. [32]They were amazed at his teaching, because his words had authority.

[33]In the synagogue there was a man controlled by a demon, an evil spirit. He cried out at the top of his voice. [34]"Go away!" he said. "What do you want with us, Jesus of Nazareth? Have you come to destroy us? I know who you are. You are the Holy One of God!"

[35]"Be quiet!" Jesus said firmly. "Come out of him!" Then the demon threw the man down in front of everybody. And it came out without hurting him.

[36]All the people were amazed. They said to each other, "What he says is amazing! With authority and power he gives orders to evil spirits. And they come out!" [37]The news about Jesus spread throughout the whole area.

Jesus Heals Many People

[38]Jesus left the synagogue and went to the home of Simon. At that time, Simon's mother-in-law was suffering from a high fever. So they asked Jesus to help her. [39]He bent over her and commanded the fever to leave, and it left her. She got up right away and began to serve them.

[40]At sunset, people brought to Jesus all who were sick. He placed his hands on each one and healed them. [41]Also, demons came out of many people. The demons shouted, "You are the Son of God!" But he commanded them to be quiet. He would not allow them to speak, because they knew he was the Messiah.

[42]At dawn, Jesus went out to a place where he could be by himself. The people went to look for him. When they found him,

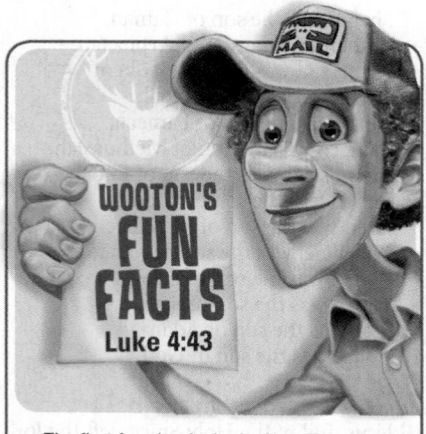

WOOTON'S FUN FACTS
Luke 4:43

The first four books in the New Testament are called the Gospels, meaning "good news." Jesus brings salvation to all people. That's even better news than a yearlong Comic Connellsville!

they tried to keep him from leaving them. [43]But he said, "I must announce the good news of God's kingdom to the other towns also. That is why I was sent." [44]And he kept on preaching in the synagogues of Judea.

Jesus Chooses His First Disciples

5 One day Jesus was standing by the Sea of Galilee. The people crowded around him and listened to the word of God. [2]Jesus saw two boats at the edge of the water. They had been left there by the fishermen, who were washing their nets. [3]He got into the boat that belonged to Simon. Jesus asked him to go out a little way from shore. Then he sat down in the boat and taught the people.

[4]When he finished speaking, he turned to Simon. Jesus said, "Go out into deep water. Let down the nets so you can catch some fish."

[5]Simon answered, "Master, we've worked hard all night and haven't caught anything. But because you say so, I will let down the nets."

[6]When they had done so, they caught a large number of fish. There were so many that their nets began to break. [7]So they motioned to their partners in the other boat to come and help them. They came and filled both boats so full that they began to sink.

[8]When Simon Peter saw this, he fell at Jesus' knees. "Go away from me, Lord!" he

said. "I am a sinful man!" [9]He and everyone with him were amazed at the number of fish they had caught. [10]So were James and John, the sons of Zebedee, who worked with Simon.

Then Jesus said to Simon, "Don't be afraid. From now on you will fish for people." [11]So they pulled their boats up on shore. Then they left everything and followed him.

Jesus Heals a Man Who Had a Skin Disease

[12]While Jesus was in one of the towns, a man came along. He had a skin disease all over his body. When he saw Jesus, the man fell with his face to the ground. He begged him, "Lord, if you are willing to make me 'clean,' you can do it."

[13]Jesus reached out his hand and touched the man. "I am willing to do it," he said. "Be 'clean'!" Right away the disease left him.

[14]Then Jesus ordered him, "Don't tell anyone. Go and show yourself to the priest. Offer the sacrifices that Moses commanded. It will be a witness to the priest and the people that you are 'clean.'"

[15]But the news about Jesus spread even more. So crowds of people came to hear him. They also came to be healed of their sicknesses. [16]But Jesus often went away to be by himself and pray.

Jesus Forgives and Heals a Man Who Could Not Walk

[17]One day Jesus was teaching. Pharisees and teachers of the law were sitting there. They had come from every village of Galilee and from Judea and Jerusalem. They heard that the Lord had given Jesus the power to heal the sick. [18]So some men came carrying a man who could not walk. He was lying on a mat. They tried to take him into the house to place him in front of Jesus. [19]They could not find a way to do this because of the crowd. So they went up on the roof. Then they lowered the man on his mat through the opening in the roof tiles. They lowered him into the middle of the crowd, right in front of Jesus.

[20]When Jesus saw that they had faith, he spoke to the man. He said, "Friend, your sins are forgiven."

[21]The Pharisees and the teachers of the law began to think, "Who is this fellow who says such an evil thing? Who can forgive sins but God alone?"

[22]Jesus knew what they were thinking. So he asked, "Why are you thinking these things in your hearts? [23]Is it easier to say, 'Your sins are forgiven'? Or to say, 'Get up and walk'? [24]But I want you to know that the Son of Man has authority on earth to forgive sins." So he spoke to the man who could not walk. "I tell you," he said, "get up. Take your mat and go home." [25]Right away, the man stood up in front of them. He took his mat and went home praising God. [26]Everyone was amazed and gave praise to God. They were filled with wonder. They said, "We have seen unusual things today."

Jesus Chooses Levi and Eats With Sinners

[27]After this, Jesus left the house. He saw a tax collector sitting at the tax booth. The man's name was Levi. "Follow me," Jesus said to him. [28]Levi got up, left everything and followed him.

[29]Then Levi gave a huge banquet for Jesus at his house. A large crowd of tax collectors and others were eating with them. [30]But the Pharisees and their teachers of the law complained to Jesus' disciples. They said, "Why do you eat and drink with tax collectors and sinners?"

[31]Jesus answered them, "Healthy people don't need a doctor. Sick people do. [32]I have not come to get those who think they are right with God to follow me. I have come to get sinners to turn away from their sins."

Jesus Is Asked About Fasting

[33]Some of the people who were there said to Jesus, "John's disciples often pray and go without eating. So do the disciples of the Pharisees. But yours go on eating and drinking."

[34]Jesus answered, "Can you make the friends of the groom fast while he is with them? [35]But the time will come when the groom will be taken away from them. In those days they will go without eating."

[36]Then Jesus gave them an example. He said, "No one tears a piece out of new clothes to patch old clothes. Otherwise, they will tear the new clothes. Also, the patch from the new clothes will not match the old clothes. [37]No one pours new wine into old wineskins. Otherwise, the new

wine will burst the skins. The wine will run out, and the wineskins will be destroyed. ³⁸No, new wine must be poured into new wineskins. ³⁹After drinking old wine, no one wants the new. They say, 'The old wine is better.'"

Jesus Is Lord of the Sabbath Day

6One Sabbath day Jesus was walking through the grainfields. His disciples began to break off some heads of grain. They rubbed them in their hands and ate them. ²Some of the Pharisees said, "It is against the Law to do this on the Sabbath day. Why are you doing it?"

³Jesus answered them, "Haven't you ever read about what David did? He and his men were hungry. ⁴He entered the house of God and took the holy bread. He ate the bread that only priests were allowed to eat. David also gave some to his men." ⁵Then Jesus said to them, "The Son of Man is Lord of the Sabbath day."

⁶On another Sabbath day, Jesus went into the synagogue and was teaching. A man whose right hand was weak and twisted was there. ⁷The Pharisees and the teachers of the law were trying to find fault with Jesus. So they watched him closely. They wanted to see if he would heal on the Sabbath day. ⁸But Jesus knew what they were thinking. He spoke to the man who had the weak and twisted hand. "Get up and stand in front of everyone," he said. So the man got up and stood there.

⁹Then Jesus said to them, "What does the Law say we should do on the Sabbath day? Should we do good? Or should we do evil? Should we save life? Or should we destroy it?"

¹⁰He looked around at all of them. Then he said to the man, "Stretch out your hand." He did, and his hand had been made as good as new. ¹¹But the Pharisees and the teachers of the law were very angry. They began to talk to one another about what they might do to Jesus.

Jesus Chooses the Twelve Apostles

¹²On one of those days, Jesus went out to a mountainside to pray. He spent the night praying to God. ¹³When morning came, he called for his disciples to come to him. He chose 12 of them and made them apostles. Here are their names.

¹⁴Simon, whom Jesus named Peter, and
    his brother Andrew
James
John
Philip
Bartholomew
¹⁵Matthew
Thomas
James, son of Alphaeus
Simon who was called the Zealot
¹⁶Judas, son of James
    and Judas Iscariot who would later
        hand Jesus over to his enemies

Jesus Gives Blessings and Warnings

¹⁷Jesus went down the mountain with them and stood on a level place. A large crowd of his disciples was there. A large number of other people were there too. They came from all over Judea, including Jerusalem. They also came from the coastland around Tyre and Sidon. ¹⁸They had all come to hear Jesus and to be healed of their sicknesses. People who were troubled by evil spirits were made well. ¹⁹Everyone tried to touch Jesus. Power was coming from him and healing them all.

²⁰Jesus looked at his disciples. He said to them,

"Blessed are you who are needy.
    God's kingdom belongs to you.
²¹ Blessed are you who are hungry now.
    You will be satisfied.
Blessed are you who are sad now.
    You will laugh.
²² Blessed are you when people hate you,
    when they have nothing to do with
        you
    and say bad things about you,
    and when they treat your name as
        something evil.
    They do all this because you are
        followers of the Son of Man.

REMEMBER THIS

LUKE 6:27-28

"Love your enemies. Do good to those who hate you. Bless those who call down curses on you. And pray for those who treat you badly."

²³"The prophets of long ago were treated the same way. When these things happen to you, be glad and jump for joy. You will receive many blessings in heaven.

²⁴ "But how terrible it will be for you who are rich!
> You have already had your easy life.
²⁵ How terrible for you who are well fed now!
> You will go hungry.
> How terrible for you who laugh now!
> You will cry and be sad.
²⁶ How terrible for you when everyone says good things about you!
> Their people treated the false prophets the same way long ago.

Love Your Enemies

²⁷"But here is what I tell you who are listening. Love your enemies. Do good to those who hate you. ²⁸Bless those who call down curses on you. And pray for those who treat you badly. ²⁹Suppose someone slaps you on one cheek. Let them slap you on the other cheek as well. Suppose someone takes your coat. Don't stop them from taking your shirt as well. ³⁰Give to everyone who asks you. And if anyone takes what belongs to you, don't ask to get it back. ³¹Do to others as you want them to do to you.

³²"Suppose you love those who love you. Should anyone praise you for that? Even sinners love those who love them. ³³And suppose you do good to those who are good to you. Should anyone praise you for that? Even sinners do that. ³⁴And suppose you lend money to those who can pay you back. Should anyone praise you for that? Even a sinner lends to sinners, expecting them to pay everything back. ³⁵But love your enemies. Do good to them. Lend to them without expecting to get anything back. Then you will receive a lot in return. And you will be children of the Most High God. He is kind to people who are evil and are not thankful. ³⁶So have mercy, just as your Father has mercy.

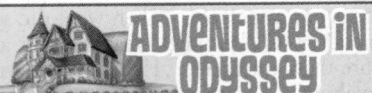

Mandy had to "do good" to her enemy and pray for someone who treated her badly in "Teacher's Pest" (A#41).

REMEMBER THIS

LUKE 6:31

"Do to others as you want them to do to you."

Be Fair When You Judge Other People

³⁷"If you do not judge other people, then you will not be judged. If you do not find others guilty, then you will not be found guilty. Forgive, and you will be forgiven. ³⁸Give, and it will be given to you. A good amount will be poured into your lap. It will be pressed down, shaken together, and running over. The same amount you give will be measured out to you."

³⁹Jesus also gave them another example. He asked, "Can a blind person lead another blind person? Won't they both fall into a pit? ⁴⁰The student is not better than the teacher. But everyone who is completely trained will be like their teacher.

⁴¹"You look at the bit of sawdust in your friend's eye. But you pay no attention to the piece of wood in your own eye. ⁴²How can you say to your friend, 'Let me take the bit of sawdust out of your eye'? How can you say this while there is a piece of wood in your own eye? You pretender! First take the piece of wood out of your own eye. Then you will be able to see clearly to take the bit of sawdust out of your friend's eye.

A Tree and Its Fruit

⁴³"A good tree doesn't bear bad fruit. And a bad tree doesn't bear good fruit. ⁴⁴You can tell each tree by the kind of fruit it bears. People do not pick figs from thorns. And they don't pick grapes from bushes. ⁴⁵A good man says good things. These come from the good that is stored up in his heart. An evil man says evil things. These come from the evil that is stored up in his heart. A person's mouth says everything that is in their heart.

The Wise and Foolish Builders

⁴⁶"Why do you call me, 'Lord, Lord,' and still don't do what I say? ⁴⁷Some people come and listen to me and do what I say. I will show you what they are like. ⁴⁸They are like a man who builds a house. He digs down deep and sets it on solid rock. When a flood comes,

the river rushes against the house. But the water can't shake it. The house is well built. ⁴⁹But here is what happens when people listen to my words and do not obey them. They are like a man who builds a house on soft ground instead of solid rock. The moment the river rushes against that house, it falls down. It is completely destroyed."

A Roman Commander Has Faith

7 Jesus finished saying all these things to the people who were listening. Then he entered Capernaum. ²There the servant of a Roman commander was sick and about to die. His master thought highly of him. ³The commander heard about Jesus. So he sent some elders of the Jews to him. He told them to ask Jesus to come and heal his servant. ⁴They came to Jesus and begged him, "This man deserves to have you do this. ⁵He loves our nation and has built our synagogue." ⁶So Jesus went with them.

When Jesus came near the house, the Roman commander sent friends to him. He told them to say, "Lord, don't trouble yourself. I am not good enough to have you come into my house. ⁷That is why I did not even think I was fit to come to you. But just say the word, and my servant will be healed. ⁸I myself am a man who is under authority. And I have soldiers who obey my orders. I tell this one, 'Go,' and he goes. I tell that one, 'Come,' and he comes. I say to my servant, 'Do this,' and he does it."

⁹When Jesus heard this, he was amazed at the commander. Jesus turned to the crowd that was following him. He said, "I tell you, even in Israel I have not found anyone whose faith is so strong." ¹⁰Then the men who had been sent to Jesus returned to the house. They found that the servant was healed.

Jesus Raises a Widow's Son From the Dead

¹¹Some time later, Jesus went to a town called Nain. His disciples and a large crowd went along with him. ¹²He approached the town gate. Just then, a dead person was being carried out. He was the only son of his mother. She was a widow. A large crowd from the town was with her. ¹³When the Lord saw her, he felt sorry for her. So he said, "Don't cry."

¹⁴Then he went up and touched the coffin. Those carrying it stood still. Jesus said, "Young man, I say to you, get up!" ¹⁵The dead man sat up and began to talk. Then Jesus gave him back to his mother.

¹⁶The people were all filled with wonder and praised God. "A great prophet has appeared among us," they said. "God has come to help his people." ¹⁷This news about Jesus spread all through Judea and the whole country.

Jesus and John the Baptist

¹⁸John's disciples told him about all these things. So he chose two of them. ¹⁹He sent them to the Lord. John told them to ask him, "Are you the one who is supposed to come? Or should we look for someone else?"

²⁰The men came to Jesus. They said, "John the Baptist sent us to ask you, 'Are you the one who is supposed to come? Or should we look for someone else?'"

²¹At that time Jesus healed many people. They had illnesses, sicknesses and evil spirits. He also gave sight to many who were blind. ²²So Jesus replied to the messengers, "Go back to John. Tell him what you have seen and heard. Blind people receive sight. Disabled people walk. Those who have skin diseases are made 'clean.' Deaf people hear. Those who are dead are raised to life. And the good news is announced to those who are poor. ²³Blessed is anyone who does not give up their faith because of me."

²⁴So John's messengers left. Then Jesus began to speak to the crowd about John. He said, "What did you go out into the desert to see? Tall grass waving in the wind? ²⁵If not, what did you go out to see? A man dressed in fine clothes? No. Those who wear fine clothes and have many expensive things are in palaces. ²⁶Then what did you go out to see? A prophet? Yes, I tell you, and more than a prophet. ²⁷He is the one written about in Scripture. It says,

" 'I will send my messenger ahead of you.
    He will prepare your way for you.'
                                    (Malachi 3:1)

BIBLE ADVENTURES

Grady saw the healing of the centurion's servant in the Imagination Station in "Run-of-the-Mill Miracle" (A#49).

²⁸I tell you, no one more important than John has ever been born. But the least important person in God's kingdom is more important than John is."

²⁹All the people who heard Jesus' words agreed that God's way was right. Even the tax collectors agreed. These people had all been baptized by John. ³⁰But the Pharisees and the authorities on the law did not accept for themselves God's purpose. So they had not been baptized by John.

³¹Jesus went on to say, "What can I compare today's people to? What are they like? ³²They are like children sitting in the market and calling out to each other. They say,

" 'We played the flute for you.
But you didn't dance.
We sang a funeral song.
But you didn't cry.'

³³That is how it has been with John the Baptist. When he came to you, he didn't eat bread or drink wine. And you say, 'He has a demon.' ³⁴But when the Son of Man came, he ate and drank as you do. And you say, 'This fellow is always eating and drinking far too much. He's a friend of tax collectors and sinners.' ³⁵All who follow wisdom prove that wisdom is right."

A Sinful Woman Pours Perfume on Jesus

³⁶One of the Pharisees invited Jesus to have dinner with him. So he went to the Pharisee's house. He took his place at the table. ³⁷There was a woman in that town who had lived a sinful life. She learned that Jesus was eating at the Pharisee's house. So she came there with a special jar of perfume. ³⁸She stood behind Jesus and cried at his feet. And she began to wet his feet with her tears. Then she wiped them with her hair. She kissed them and poured perfume on them.

³⁹The Pharisee who had invited Jesus saw this. He said to himself, "If this man were a prophet, he would know who is touching him. He would know what kind of woman she is. She is a sinner!"

⁴⁰Jesus answered him, "Simon, I have something to tell you."

"Tell me, teacher," he said.

⁴¹"Two people owed money to a certain lender. One owed him 500 silver coins. The other owed him 50 silver coins. ⁴²Neither of them had the money to pay him back. So he let them go without paying. Which of them will love him more?"

⁴³Simon replied, "I suppose the one who owed the most money."

"You are right," Jesus said.

⁴⁴Then he turned toward the woman. He said to Simon, "Do you see this woman? I came into your house. You did not give me any water to wash my feet. But she wet my feet with her tears and wiped them with her hair. ⁴⁵You did not give me a kiss. But this woman has not stopped kissing my feet since I came in. ⁴⁶You did not put any olive oil on my head. But she has poured this perfume on my feet. ⁴⁷So I tell you this. Her many sins have been forgiven. She has shown that she understands this by her great acts of love. But whoever has been forgiven only a little loves only a little."

⁴⁸Then Jesus said to her, "Your sins are forgiven."

⁴⁹The other guests began to talk about this among themselves. They said, "Who is this who even forgives sins?"

⁵⁰Jesus said to the woman, "Your faith has saved you. Go in peace."

The Story of the Farmer

8 After this, Jesus traveled around from one town and village to another. He announced the good news of God's kingdom. His 12 disciples were with him. ²So were some women who had been healed of evil spirits and sicknesses. One was Mary Magdalene. Seven demons had come out of her. ³Another was Joanna, the wife of Chuza. He was the manager of Herod's household. Susanna and many others were there also. These women were helping to support Jesus and the 12 disciples with their own money.

⁴A large crowd gathered together. People came to Jesus from town after town. As they did, he told a story. He said, ⁵"A farmer went out to plant his seed. He scattered the seed on the ground. Some fell on a path. People walked on it, and the birds ate it up. ⁶Some seed fell on rocky ground. When it grew, the plants dried up because they had no water. ⁷Other seed fell among thorns. The thorns grew up with it and crowded out the plants. ⁸Still other seed fell on good soil. It grew up and produced a crop 100 times more than the farmer planted."

When Jesus said this, he called out, "Whoever has ears should listen."

BiBLE ADVENTURES

Harlowquin Doylecus, Private Roman Eye, interviewed Mary Magdalene in "B-TV: To Tell the Truth" (Club).

[9]His disciples asked him what the story meant. [10]He said, "You have been given the chance to understand the secrets of God's kingdom. But to outsiders I speak by using stories. In that way,

" 'They see, but they will not know what
　　they are seeing.
　They hear, but they will not
　　understand what they are
　　hearing.'　　　　　　(Isaiah 6:9)

[11]"Here is what the story means. The seed is God's message. [12]The seed on the path stands for God's message in the hearts of those who hear. But then the devil comes. He takes away the message from their hearts. He does it so they won't believe. Then they can't be saved. [13]The seed on rocky ground stands for those who hear the message and receive it with joy. But they have no roots. They believe for a while. But when they are tested, they fall away from the faith. [14]The seed that fell among thorns stands for those who hear the message. But as they go on their way, they are choked by life's worries, riches and pleasures. So they do not reach full growth. [15]But the seed on good soil stands for those with an honest and good heart. Those people hear the message. They keep it in their hearts. They remain faithful and produce a good crop.

A Lamp on a Stand

[16]"No one lights a lamp and then hides it in a clay jar or puts it under a bed. Instead, they put it on a stand. Then those who come in can see its light. [17]What is hidden will be seen. And what is out of sight will be brought into the open and made known. [18]So be careful how you listen. Whoever has something will be given more. Whoever has nothing, even what they think they have will be taken away from them."

Jesus' Mother and Brothers

[19]Jesus' mother and brothers came to see him. But they could not get near him because of the crowd. [20]Someone told him,

"Your mother and brothers are standing outside. They want to see you." [21]He replied, "My mother and brothers are those who hear God's word and do what it says."

Jesus Calms the Storm

[22]One day Jesus said to his disciples, "Let's go over to the other side of the lake." So they got into a boat and left. [23]As they sailed, Jesus fell asleep. A storm came down on the lake. It was so bad that the boat was about to sink. They were in great danger. [24]The disciples went and woke Jesus up. They said, "Master! Master! We're going to drown!"

He got up and ordered the wind and the huge waves to stop. The storm quieted down. It was completely calm. [25]"Where is your faith?" he asked his disciples.

They were amazed and full of fear. They asked one another, "Who is this? He commands even the winds and the waves, and they obey him."

Jesus Heals a Man Controlled by Demons

[26]Jesus and his disciples sailed to the area of the Gerasenes across the lake from Galilee. [27]When Jesus stepped on shore, he was met by a man from the town. The man was controlled by demons. For a long time he had not worn clothes or lived in a house. He lived in the tombs. [28]When he saw Jesus, he cried out and fell at his feet. He shouted at the top of his voice, "Jesus, Son of the Most High God, what do you want with me? I beg you, don't hurt me!" [29]This was because Jesus had commanded the evil spirit to come out of the man. Many times the spirit had taken hold of him. The man's hands and feet were chained, and he was kept under guard. But he had broken his chains. And then the demon had forced him to go out into lonely places in the countryside.

[30]Jesus asked him, "What is your name?"

ADVENTURES IN ODYSSEY

After Whit discovered a hidden camera at his shop, he showed that what was once hidden would be seen in "Grand Opening" (A#37).

"Legion," he replied, because many demons had gone into him. [31]And they begged Jesus again and again not to order them to go into the Abyss.

[32]A large herd of pigs was feeding there on the hillside. The demons begged Jesus to let them go into the pigs. And he allowed it. [33]When the demons came out of the man, they went into the pigs. Then the herd rushed down the steep bank. They ran into the lake and drowned.

[34]Those who were tending the pigs saw what had happened. They ran off and reported it in the town and countryside. [35]The people went out to see what had happened. Then they came to Jesus. They found the man who was now free of the demons. He was sitting at Jesus' feet. He was dressed and thinking clearly. All this made the people afraid. [36]Those who had seen it told the others how the man who had been controlled by demons was now healed. [37]Then all the people who lived in the area of the Gerasenes asked Jesus to leave them. They were filled with fear. So he got into the boat and left.

[38]The man who was now free of the demons begged to go with him. But Jesus sent him away. He said to him, [39]"Return home and tell how much God has done for you." So the man went away. He told people all over town how much Jesus had done for him.

Jesus Heals a Dead Girl and a Suffering Woman

[40]When Jesus returned, a crowd welcomed him. They were all expecting him. [41]Then a man named Jairus came. He was a synagogue leader. He fell at Jesus' feet and begged Jesus to come to his house. [42]His only daughter was dying. She was about 12 years old. As Jesus was on his way, the crowds almost crushed him.

[43]A woman was there who had a sickness that made her bleed. Her sickness had lasted for 12 years. No one could heal her. [44]She came up behind Jesus and touched the edge of his clothes. Right away her bleeding stopped.

[45]"Who touched me?" Jesus asked.

Everyone said they didn't do it. Then Peter said, "Master, the people are crowding and pushing against you."

[46]But Jesus said, "Someone touched me. I know that power has gone out from me."

[47]The woman realized that people would notice her. Shaking with fear, she came and fell at his feet. In front of everyone, she told why she had touched him. She also told how she had been healed in an instant. [48]Then he said to her, "Dear woman, your faith has healed you. Go in peace."

[49]While Jesus was still speaking, someone came from the house of Jairus. Jairus was the synagogue leader. "Your daughter is dead," the messenger said. "Don't bother the teacher anymore."

[50]Hearing this, Jesus said to Jairus, "Don't be afraid. Just believe. She will be healed."

[51]When he arrived at the house of Jairus, he did not let everyone go in with him. He took only Peter, John and James, and the child's father and mother. [52]During this time, all the people were crying and sobbing loudly over the child. "Stop crying!" Jesus said. "She is not dead. She is sleeping."

[53]They laughed at him. They knew she was dead. [54]But he took her by the hand and said, "My child, get up!" [55]Her spirit returned, and right away she stood up. Then Jesus told them to give her something to eat. [56]Her parents were amazed. But Jesus ordered them not to tell anyone what had happened.

Jesus Sends Out the Twelve Disciples

9 Jesus called together the 12 disciples. He gave them power and authority to drive out all demons and to heal sicknesses. [2]Then he sent them out to announce God's kingdom and to heal those who were sick. [3]He told them, "Don't take anything for the journey. Do not take a walking stick or a bag. Do not take any bread, money or extra clothes. [4]When you are invited into a house, stay there until you leave town. [5]Some people may not welcome you. If they don't, leave their town and shake the dust off your feet. This will be a witness against the people living there." [6]So the 12 disciples left. They went from village to village. They announced the good news and healed people everywhere.

[7]Now Herod, the ruler of Galilee, heard about everything that was going on. He was bewildered, because some were saying that John the Baptist had been raised from the dead. [8]Others were saying that Elijah had

appeared. Still others were saying that a prophet of long ago had come back to life. ⁹But Herod said, "I had John's head cut off. So who is it that I hear such things about?" And he tried to see Jesus.

Jesus Feeds the Five Thousand

¹⁰The disciples returned. They told Jesus what they had done. Then he took them with him. They went off by themselves to a town called Bethsaida. ¹¹But the crowds learned about it and followed Jesus. He welcomed them and spoke to them about God's kingdom. He also healed those who needed to be healed.

¹²Late in the afternoon the 12 disciples came to him. They said, "Send the crowd away. They can go to the nearby villages and countryside. There they can find food and a place to stay. There is nothing here."

¹³Jesus replied, "You give them something to eat."

The disciples answered, "We have only five loaves of bread and two fish. We would have to go and buy food for all this crowd." ¹⁴About 5,000 men were there.

But Jesus said to his disciples, "Have them sit down in groups of about 50 each." ¹⁵The disciples did so, and everyone sat down. ¹⁶Jesus took the five loaves and the two fish. He looked up to heaven and gave thanks. He broke them into pieces. Then he gave them to the disciples to give to the people. ¹⁷All of them ate and were satisfied. The disciples picked up 12 baskets of leftover pieces.

Peter Says That Jesus Is the Messiah

¹⁸One day Jesus was praying alone. Only his disciples were with him. He asked them, "Who do the crowds say I am?"

¹⁹They replied, "Some say John the Baptist. Others say Elijah. Still others say that one of the prophets of long ago has come back to life."

²⁰"But what about you?" he asked. "Who do you say I am?"

Peter answered, "God's Messiah."

Jesus Speaks About His Coming Death

²¹Jesus strongly warned them not to tell this to anyone. ²²He said, "The Son of Man must suffer many things. The elders will not accept him. The chief priests and the teachers of the law will not accept him either. He must be killed and on the third day rise from the dead."

²³Then he said to all of them, "Whoever wants to follow me must say no to themselves. They must pick up their cross every day and follow me. ²⁴Whoever wants to save their life will lose it. But whoever loses their life for me will save it. ²⁵What good is it if someone gains the whole world but loses or gives up their very self? ²⁶Suppose someone is ashamed of me and my words. The Son of Man will come in his glory and in the glory of the Father and the holy angels. Then he will be ashamed of that person.

²⁷"What I'm about to tell you is true. Some who are standing here will not die before they see God's kingdom."

Jesus' Appearance Is Changed

²⁸About eight days after Jesus said this, he went up on a mountain to pray. He took Peter, John and James with him. ²⁹As he was praying, the appearance of his face changed. His clothes became as bright as a flash of lightning. ³⁰Two men, Moses and Elijah, appeared in shining glory. Jesus and the two of them talked together. ³¹They talked about how he would be leaving them soon. This was going to happen in Jerusalem. ³²Peter and his companions had been very sleepy. But then they became completely awake. They saw Jesus' glory and the two men standing with him. ³³As the men were leaving Jesus, Peter spoke up. "Master," he said to him, "it is good for us to be here. Let us put up three shelters. One will be for you, one for Moses, and one for Elijah." Peter didn't really know what he was saying.

³⁴While he was speaking, a cloud appeared and covered them. The disciples were afraid as they entered the cloud. ³⁵A voice came from the cloud. It said, "This is my Son, and I have chosen him. Listen to him." ³⁶When the voice had spoken, they found that Jesus was alone. The disciples kept quiet about this. They didn't tell anyone at that time what they had seen.

Jesus Heals a Boy Who Is Controlled by an Evil Spirit

³⁷The next day Jesus and those who were with him came down from the mountain. A large crowd met Jesus. ³⁸A man in the crowd

called out. "Teacher," he said, "I beg you to look at my son. He is my only child. [39]A spirit takes hold of him, and he suddenly screams. It throws him into fits so that he foams at the mouth. It hardly ever leaves him. It is destroying him. [40]I begged your disciples to drive it out. But they couldn't do it."

[41]"You unbelieving and evil people!" Jesus replied. "How long do I have to stay with you? How long do I have to put up with you?" Then he said to the man, "Bring your son here."

[42]Even while the boy was coming, the demon threw him into a fit. The boy fell to the ground. But Jesus ordered the evil spirit to leave the boy. Then Jesus healed him and gave him back to his father. [43]They were all amazed at God's greatness.

Jesus Speaks a Second Time About His Coming Death

Everyone was wondering about all that Jesus did. Then Jesus said to his disciples, [44]"Listen carefully to what I am about to tell you. The Son of Man is going to be handed over to men." [45]But they didn't understand what this meant. That was because it was hidden from them. And they were afraid to ask Jesus about it.

Who Is the Most Important Person?

[46]The disciples began to argue about which one of them would be the most important person. [47]Jesus knew what they were thinking. So he took a little child and had the child stand beside him. [48]Then he spoke to them. "Anyone who welcomes this little child in my name welcomes me," he said. "And anyone who welcomes me welcomes the one who sent me. The one considered least important among all of you is really the most important."

[49]"Master," said John, "we saw someone driving out demons in your name. We tried to stop him, because he is not one of us."

[50]"Do not stop him," Jesus said. "Anyone who is not against you is for you."

The Samaritans Do Not Welcome Jesus

[51]The time grew near for Jesus to be taken up to heaven. So he made up his mind to go to Jerusalem. [52]He sent messengers on ahead. They went into a Samaritan village to get things ready for him. [53]But the people there did not welcome Jesus. That was because he was heading for Jerusalem. [54]The disciples James and John saw this. They asked, "Lord, do you want us to call down fire from heaven to destroy them?" [55]But Jesus turned and commanded them not to do it. [56]Then Jesus and his disciples went on to another village.

The Cost of Following Jesus

[57]Once Jesus and those who were with him were walking along the road. A man said to Jesus, "I will follow you no matter where you go."

[58]Jesus replied, "Foxes have dens. Birds have nests. But the Son of Man has no place to lay his head."

[59]He said to another man, "Follow me."

But the man replied, "Lord, first let me go and bury my father."

[60]Jesus said to him, "Let dead people bury their own dead. You go and tell others about God's kingdom."

[61]Still another person said, "I will follow you, Lord. But first let me go back and say goodbye to my family."

[62]Jesus replied, "Suppose someone starts to plow and then looks back. That person is not fit for service in God's kingdom."

Jesus Sends Out the Seventy-Two

10 After this the Lord appointed 72 others. He sent them out two by two ahead of him. They went to every town and place where he was about to go. [2]He told them, "The harvest is huge, but the workers are few. So ask the Lord of the harvest to send out workers into his harvest field. [3]Go! I am sending you out like lambs among wolves. [4]Do not take a purse or bag or sandals. And don't greet anyone on the road.

[5]"When you enter a house, first say, 'May this house be blessed with peace.' [6]If someone there works to bring peace, your blessing of peace will rest on them. If not, it will return to you. [7]Stay there, and eat and drink anything they give you. Workers are worthy of their pay. Do not move around from house to house.

[8]"When you enter a town and are welcomed, eat what is given to you. [9]Heal the sick people who are there. Tell them, 'God's kingdom has come near to you.' [10]But what if you enter a town and are not welcomed? Then go into its streets and say, [11]"We wipe

from our feet even the dust of your town. We do it to warn you. But here is what you can be sure of. God's kingdom has come near.' ¹²I tell you this. On judgment day it will be easier for Sodom than for that town.

¹³"How terrible it will be for you, Chorazin! How terrible for you, Bethsaida! Suppose the miracles done in you had been done in Tyre and Sidon. They would have turned away from their sins long ago. They would have put on the rough clothing people wear when they're sad. They would have sat down in ashes. ¹⁴On judgment day it will be easier for Tyre and Sidon than for you. ¹⁵And what about you, Capernaum? Will you be lifted up to the heavens? No! You will go down to the place of the dead.

¹⁶"Whoever listens to you listens to me. Whoever does not accept you does not accept me. But whoever does not accept me does not accept the one who sent me."

¹⁷The 72 returned with joy. They said, "Lord, even the demons obey us when we speak in your name."

¹⁸Jesus replied, "I saw Satan fall like lightning from heaven. ¹⁹I have given you authority to walk all over snakes and scorpions. You will be able to destroy all the power of the enemy. Nothing will harm you. ²⁰But do not be glad when the evil spirits obey you. Instead, be glad that your names are written in heaven."

²¹At that time Jesus was full of joy through the Holy Spirit. He said, "I praise you, Father. You are Lord of heaven and earth. You have hidden these things from wise and educated people. But you have shown them to little children. Yes, Father. This is what you wanted to do.

²²"My Father has given all things to me. The Father is the only one who knows who the Son is. And the only ones who know the Father are the Son and those to whom the Son chooses to make the Father known."

²³Then Jesus turned to his disciples. He said to them in private, "Blessed are the eyes that see what you see. ²⁴I tell you, many prophets and kings wanted to see what you see. But they didn't see it. They wanted to hear what you hear. But they didn't hear it."

The Story of the Good Samaritan

²⁵One day an authority on the law stood up to test Jesus. "Teacher," he asked, "what must I do to receive eternal life?"

²⁶"What is written in the Law?" Jesus replied. "How do you understand it?"

²⁷He answered, " 'Love the Lord your God with all your heart and with all your soul. Love him with all your strength and with all your mind.' *(Deuteronomy 6:5)* And, 'Love your neighbor as you love yourself.' " *(Leviticus 19:18)*

²⁸"You have answered correctly," Jesus replied. "Do that, and you will live."

²⁹But the man wanted to make himself look good. So he asked Jesus, "And who is my neighbor?"

³⁰Jesus replied, "A man was going down from Jerusalem to Jericho. Robbers attacked him. They stripped off his clothes and beat him. Then they went away, leaving him almost dead. ³¹A priest happened to be going down that same road. When he saw the man, he passed by on the other side. ³²A Levite also came by. When he saw the man, he passed by on the other side too. ³³But a Samaritan came to the place where the man was. When he saw the man, he felt sorry for him. ³⁴He went to him, poured olive oil and wine on his wounds and bandaged them. Then he put the man on his own donkey. He brought him to an inn and took care of him. ³⁵The next day he took out two silver coins. He gave them to the owner of the inn. 'Take care of him,' he said. 'When I return, I will pay you back for any extra expense you may have.'

³⁶"Which of the three do you think was a neighbor to the man who was attacked by robbers?"

³⁷The authority on the law replied, "The one who felt sorry for him."

Jesus told him, "Go and do as he did."

Jesus at the Home of Martha and Mary

³⁸Jesus and his disciples went on their way. Jesus came to a village where a woman named Martha lived. She welcomed him into her home. ³⁹She had a sister named Mary. Mary sat at the Lord's feet listening to what he said. ⁴⁰But Martha was busy with

Charles put on a play of the story of the Good Samaritan with popsicle sticks in "The Pretty Good Samaritan" (A#26).

all the things that had to be done. She came to Jesus and said, "Lord, my sister has left me to do the work by myself. Don't you care? Tell her to help me!"

⁴¹"Martha, Martha," the Lord answered. "You are worried and upset about many things. ⁴²But few things are needed. Really, only one thing is needed. Mary has chosen what is better. And it will not be taken away from her."

Jesus Teaches About Prayer

11 One day Jesus was praying in a certain place. When he finished, one of his disciples spoke to him. "Lord," he said, "teach us to pray, just as John taught his disciples."

²Jesus said to them, "When you pray, this is what you should say.

" 'Father,
may your name be honored.
May your kingdom come.
³ Give us each day our daily bread.
⁴ Forgive us our sins,
    as we also forgive everyone who sins
        against us.
Keep us from falling into sin when we
    are tempted.' "

⁵Then Jesus said to them, "Suppose you have a friend. You go to him at midnight and say, 'Friend, lend me three loaves of bread. ⁶A friend of mine on a journey has come to stay with me. I have no food to give him.' ⁷And suppose the one inside answers, 'Don't bother me. The door is already locked. My children and I are in bed. I can't get up and give you anything.' ⁸I tell you, that person will not get up. And he won't give you bread just because he is your friend. But because you keep bothering him, he will surely get up. He will give you as much as you need.

⁹"So here is what I say to you. Ask, and it will be given to you. Search, and you will find. Knock, and the door will be opened to you. ¹⁰Everyone who asks will receive. The one who searches will find. And the door will be opened to the one who knocks.

¹¹"Fathers, suppose your son asks for a fish. Which of you will give him a snake instead? ¹²Or suppose he asks for an egg. Which of you will give him a scorpion? ¹³Even though you are evil, you know how to give good gifts to your children. How much more will your Father who is in heaven give the Holy Spirit to those who ask him!"

Jesus and Beelzebul

¹⁴Jesus was driving out a demon. The man who had the demon could not speak. When the demon left, the man began to speak. The crowd was amazed. ¹⁵But some of them said, "Jesus is driving out demons by the power of Beelzebul, the prince of demons." ¹⁶Others tested Jesus by asking for a sign from heaven.

¹⁷Jesus knew what they were thinking. So he said to them, "Any kingdom that fights against itself will be destroyed. A family that is divided against itself will fall. ¹⁸If Satan fights against himself, how can his kingdom stand? I say this because of what you claim. You say I drive out demons by the power of Beelzebul. ¹⁹Suppose I do drive out demons with Beelzebul's help. With whose help do your followers drive them out? So then, they will be your judges. ²⁰But suppose I drive out demons with the help of God's powerful finger. Then God's kingdom has come upon you.

²¹"When a strong man is completely armed and guards his house, what he owns is safe. ²²But when someone stronger attacks, he is overpowered. The attacker takes away the armor the man had trusted in. Then he divides up what he has stolen.

²³"Whoever is not with me is against me. And whoever does not gather with me scatters.

²⁴"What happens when an evil spirit comes out of a person? It goes through dry areas looking for a place to rest. But it doesn't find it. Then it says, 'I will return to the house I left.' ²⁵When it arrives there, it finds the house swept clean and put in order. ²⁶Then the evil spirit goes and takes seven other spirits more evil than itself. They go in and live there. That person is worse off than before."

CANDID CONVERSATIONS

When I first became a Christian, praying was kind of weird for me. I was talking out loud to someone I couldn't see, saying phrases I'd never said before like "Heavenly Father—" And I never knew when to quit. (Usually I stopped when I got hungry or fell asleep.)

The example Jesus gives the disciples in Luke 11:2–4 is called "The Lord's Prayer." Jesus wasn't saying that every time you pray, you should say *these* exact words, but He was giving a pattern of what prayer could look like. It included worshiping God, asking for things we want or need, and seeking forgiveness.

You can follow the same general idea when you pray, but you can add things that sound more like you. And that's really an important thing. Be yourself! God knows who you are and what you're like. After all, He created you. And don't forget to take a few minutes to simply listen to what God has to say to you.

²⁷As Jesus was saying these things, a woman in the crowd called out. She shouted, "Blessed is the mother who gave you birth and nursed you."

²⁸He replied, "Instead, blessed are those who hear God's word and obey it."

The Sign of Jonah

²⁹As the crowds grew larger, Jesus spoke to them. "The people of today are evil," he said. "They ask for a sign from God. But none will be given except the sign of Jonah. ³⁰He was a sign from God to the people of Nineveh. In the same way, the Son of Man will be a sign from God to the people of today. ³¹The Queen of the South will stand up on judgment day with the people now living. And she will prove that they are guilty. She came from very far away to listen to Solomon's wisdom. And now something more important than Solomon is here. ³²The men of Nineveh will stand up on judgment day with the people now living. And the Ninevites will prove that those people are guilty. The men of Nineveh turned away from their sins when Jonah preached to them. And now something more important than Jonah is here.

The Eye Is the Lamp of the Body

³³"No one lights a lamp and hides it. No one puts it under a bowl. Instead, they put a lamp on its stand. Then those who come in can see the light. ³⁴Your eye is like a lamp for your body. Suppose your eyes are healthy. Then your whole body also is full of light. But suppose your eyes can't see well. Then your body also is full of darkness. ³⁵So make sure that the light inside you is not darkness. ³⁶Suppose your whole body is full of light. And suppose no part of it is dark. Then your body will be full of light. It will be just as when a lamp shines its light on you."

Six Warnings

³⁷Jesus finished speaking. Then a Pharisee invited him to eat with him. So Jesus went in and took his place at the table. ³⁸But the Pharisee was surprised. He noticed that Jesus did not wash before the meal.

³⁹Then the Lord spoke to him. "You Pharisees clean the outside of the cup and dish," he said. "But inside you are full of greed and evil. ⁴⁰You foolish people! Didn't the one who made the outside make the inside also? ⁴¹Give freely to poor people to show what is inside you. Then everything will be clean for you.

⁴²"How terrible it will be for you Pharisees! You give God a tenth of your garden plants, such as mint and rue. But you have forgotten to be fair and to love God. You should have practiced the last things without failing to do the first.

⁴³"How terrible for you Pharisees! You love the most important seats in the synagogues. You love having people greet you with respect in the market.

⁴⁴"How terrible for you! You are like graves that are not marked. People walk over them without knowing it."

⁴⁵An authority on the law spoke to Jesus. He said, "Teacher, when you say things like that, you say bad things about us too."

⁴⁶Jesus replied, "How terrible for you authorities on the law! You put such heavy loads on people that they can hardly carry them. But you yourselves will not lift one finger to help them.

⁴⁷"How terrible for you! You build tombs for the prophets. It was your people of long ago who killed them. ⁴⁸So you show that you agree with what your people did long ago. They killed the prophets, and now you build the prophets' tombs. ⁴⁹So God in his wisdom said, 'I will send prophets and apostles to them. They will kill some. And they will try to hurt others.' ⁵⁰So the people of today will be punished. They will pay for all the prophets' blood spilled since the world began. ⁵¹I mean from the blood of Abel to the blood of Zechariah. He was killed between the altar and the temple. Yes, I tell you, the people of today will be punished for all these things.

⁵²"How terrible for you authorities on the law! You have taken away the key to the door of knowledge. You yourselves have not entered. And you have stood in the way of those who were entering."

⁵³When Jesus went outside, the Pharisees and the teachers of the law strongly opposed him. They threw a lot of questions at him. ⁵⁴They set traps for him. They wanted to catch him in something he might say.

Jesus Gives Words of Warning and Hope

12 During that time a crowd of many thousands had gathered. There were so many people that they were stepping on one another. Jesus spoke first to his disciples. "Be on your guard against the yeast of the Pharisees," he said. "They just pretend to be godly. ²Everything that is secret will be brought out into the open. Everything that is hidden will be uncovered. ³What you have said in the dark will be heard in the daylight. What you have whispered to someone behind closed doors will be shouted from the rooftops.

⁴"My friends, listen to me. Don't be afraid of those who kill the body but can't do any more than that. ⁵I will show you whom you should be afraid of. Be afraid of the one who has the authority to throw you into hell after you have been killed. Yes, I tell you, be afraid of him. ⁶Aren't five sparrows sold for two pennies? But God does not forget even one of them. ⁷In fact, he even counts every hair on your head! So don't be afraid. You are worth more than many sparrows.

⁸"What about someone who says in front of others that he knows me? I tell you, the Son of Man will say in front of God's angels that he knows that person. ⁹But what about someone who says in front of others that he doesn't know me? I, the Son of Man, will say in front of God's angels that I don't know him. ¹⁰Everyone who speaks a word against the Son of Man will be forgiven. But anyone who speaks evil things against the Holy Spirit will not be forgiven.

¹¹"You will be brought before synagogues, rulers and authorities. But do not worry about how to stand up for yourselves or what to say. ¹²The Holy Spirit will teach you at that time what you should say."

The Story of the Rich Fool

¹³Someone in the crowd spoke to Jesus. "Teacher," he said, "tell my brother to divide the family property with me."

¹⁴Jesus replied, "Friend, who made me a judge or umpire between you?" ¹⁵Then he said to them, "Watch out! Be on your guard against wanting to have more and more things. Life is not made up of how much a person has."

¹⁶Then Jesus told them a story. He said, "A certain rich man's land produced a very large crop. ¹⁷He thought to himself, 'What should I do? I don't have any place to store my crops.'

¹⁸"Then he said, 'This is what I'll do. I will tear down my barns and build bigger ones. I will store my extra grain in them. ¹⁹I'll say to myself, "You have plenty of grain stored away for many years. Take life easy. Eat, drink and have a good time."'

²⁰"But God said to him, 'You foolish man! Tonight I will take your life away

from you. Then who will get what you have prepared for yourself?'

²¹"That is how it will be for whoever stores things away for themselves but is not rich in the sight of God."

Do Not Worry

²²Then Jesus spoke to his disciples. He said, "I tell you, do not worry. Don't worry about your life and what you will eat. And don't worry about your body and what you will wear. ²³There is more to life than eating. There are more important things for the body than clothes. ²⁴Think about the ravens. They don't plant or gather crops. They don't have any barns at all. But God feeds them. You are worth much more than birds! ²⁵Can you add even one hour to your life by worrying? ²⁶You can't do that very little thing. So why worry about the rest?

²⁷"Think about how the wild flowers grow. They don't work or make clothing. But here is what I tell you. Not even Solomon in his royal robes was dressed like one of those flowers. ²⁸If that is how God dresses the wild grass, how much better will he dress you! After all, the grass is here only today. Tomorrow it is thrown into the fire. Your faith is so small! ²⁹Don't spend time thinking about what you will eat or drink. Don't worry about it. ³⁰People who are ungodly run after all those things. Your Father knows that you need them. ³¹But put God's kingdom first. Then those other things will also be given to you.

³²"Little flock, do not be afraid. Your Father has been pleased to give you the kingdom. ³³Sell what you own. Give to those who are poor. Provide purses for yourselves that will not wear out. Store up riches in heaven that will never be used up. There, no thief can come near it. There, no moth can destroy it. ³⁴Your heart will be where your riches are.

Be Ready

³⁵"Be dressed and ready to serve. Keep your lamps burning. ³⁶Be like servants waiting for their master to return from a wedding dinner. When he comes and knocks, they can open the door for him at once. ³⁷It will be good for those servants whose master finds them ready when he comes. What I'm about to tell you is true. The master will then dress himself so he can serve them.

He will have them take their places at the table. And he will come and wait on them. ³⁸It will be good for those servants whose master finds them ready. It will even be good if he comes in the middle of the night or toward morning. ³⁹But here is what you must understand. Suppose the owner of the house knew at what hour the robber was coming. He would not have let his house be broken into. ⁴⁰You also must be ready. The Son of Man will come at an hour when you don't expect him."

⁴¹Peter asked, "Lord, are you telling this story to us, or to everyone?"

⁴²The Lord answered, "Suppose a master puts one of his servants in charge of his other servants. The servant's job is to give them the food they are to receive at the right time. The master wants a faithful and wise manager for this. ⁴³It will be good for the servant if the master finds him doing his job when the master returns. ⁴⁴What I'm about to tell you is true. The master will put that servant in charge of everything he owns. ⁴⁵But suppose the servant says to himself, 'My master is taking a long time to come back.' Suppose that servant begins to beat the other servants, both men and women. Suppose he feeds himself. And suppose he drinks until he gets drunk. ⁴⁶The master of that servant will come back on a day the servant doesn't expect him. The master will return at an hour the servant doesn't know. Then the master will cut him to pieces. He will send the servant to the place where unbelievers go.

⁴⁷"Suppose a servant knows the master's wishes. But the servant doesn't get ready and doesn't do what the master wants. Then that servant will receive a heavy beating. ⁴⁸But suppose the servant does not know his master's wishes. And suppose the servant does things for which he should be punished. He will receive a lighter beating. Much will be required of everyone who has been given much. Even more will be asked of the person who is supposed to take care of much.

Jesus Will Separate People From One Another

⁴⁹"I have come to bring fire on the earth. How I wish the fire had already started! ⁵⁰But I have a baptism of suffering to go through. And I must go through it. ⁵¹Do you think I came to bring peace on earth?

No, I tell you. I have come to separate people. ⁵²From now on there will be five members in a family, each one against the other. There will be three against two and two against three. ⁵³They will be separated. Father will turn against son and son against father. Mother will turn against daughter and daughter against mother. Mother-in-law will turn against daughter-in-law and daughter-in-law against mother-in-law."

Understanding the Meaning of What Is Happening

⁵⁴Jesus spoke to the crowd. He said, "You see a cloud rising in the west. Right away you say, 'It's going to rain.' And it does. ⁵⁵The south wind blows. So you say, 'It's going to be hot.' And it is. ⁵⁶You pretenders! You know how to understand the appearance of the earth and the sky. Why can't you understand the meaning of what is happening right now?

⁵⁷"Why don't you judge for yourselves what is right? ⁵⁸Suppose someone has a claim against you, and you are on your way to court. Try hard to settle the matter on the way. If you don't, that person may drag you off to the judge. The judge may turn you over to the officer. And the officer may throw you into prison. ⁵⁹I tell you, you will not get out until you have paid the very last penny!"

Turn Away From Sin or Die

13 Some people who were there at that time told Jesus about certain Galileans. Pilate had mixed their blood with their sacrifices. ²Jesus said, "These people from Galilee suffered greatly. Do you think they were worse sinners than all the other Galileans? ³I tell you, no! But unless you turn away from your sins, you will all die too. ⁴Or what about the 18 people in Siloam? They died when the tower fell on them. Do you think they were more guilty than all the others living in Jerusalem? ⁵I tell you, no! But unless you turn away from your sins, you will all die too."

⁶Then Jesus told a story. "A man had a fig tree," he said. "It was growing in his vineyard. When he went to look for fruit on it, he didn't find any. ⁷So he went to the man who took care of the vineyard. He said, 'For three years now I've been coming to look for

Luke 13:20–21 In the Bible, *yeast* can mean something bad or "sin." But this time yeast represents something good: the spreading of the gospel. Penny and I use yeast a lot when we're baking, and Eugene tells me that a small, square packet of yeast has more than 20 billion yeast cells.

fruit on this fig tree. But I haven't found any. Cut it down! Why should it use up the soil?'

⁸"'Sir,' the man replied, 'leave it alone for one more year. I'll dig around it and feed it. ⁹If it bears fruit next year, fine! If not, then cut it down.'"

Jesus Heals a Disabled Woman on the Sabbath Day

¹⁰Jesus was teaching in one of the synagogues on a Sabbath day. ¹¹A woman there had been disabled by an evil spirit for 18 years. She was bent over and could not stand up straight. ¹²Jesus saw her. He asked her to come to him. He said to her, "Woman, you will no longer be disabled. I am about to set you free." ¹³Then he put his hands on her. Right away she stood up straight and praised God.

¹⁴Jesus had healed the woman on the Sabbath day. This made the synagogue leader angry. He told the people, "There are six days for work. So come and be healed on those days. But do not come on the Sabbath day."

¹⁵The Lord answered him, "You pretenders! Doesn't each of you go to the barn and untie your ox or donkey on the Sabbath day? Then don't you lead it out to give it water? ¹⁶This woman is a member of Abraham's family line. But Satan has kept her disabled for 18 long years. Shouldn't she be set free on the Sabbath day from what was keeping her disabled?"

[17]When Jesus said this, all those who opposed him were put to shame. But the people were delighted. They loved all the wonderful things he was doing.

The Stories of the Mustard Seed and the Yeast

[18]Then Jesus asked, "What is God's kingdom like? What can I compare it to? [19]It is like a mustard seed. Someone took the seed and planted it in a garden. It grew and became a tree. The birds sat in its branches."

[20]Again he asked, "What can I compare God's kingdom to? [21]It is like yeast that a woman used. She mixed it into 60 pounds of flour. The yeast worked its way all through the dough."

The Narrow Door

[22]Then Jesus went through the towns and villages, teaching the people. He was on his way to Jerusalem. [23]Someone asked him, "Lord, are only a few people going to be saved?"

He said to them, [24]"Try very hard to enter through the narrow door. I tell you, many will try to enter and will not be able to. [25]The owner of the house will get up and close the door. Then you will stand outside knocking and begging. You will say, 'Sir, open the door for us.'

"But he will answer, 'I don't know you. And I don't know where you come from.'

[26]"Then you will say, 'We ate and drank with you. You taught in our streets.'

[27]"But he will reply, 'I don't know you. And I don't know where you come from. Get away from me, all you who do evil!'

[28]"You will weep and grind your teeth together when you see those who are in God's kingdom. You will see Abraham, Isaac and Jacob and all the prophets there. But you yourselves will be thrown out. [29]People will come from east and west and north and south. They will take their places at the feast in God's kingdom. [30]Then the last will be first. And the first will be last."

Jesus' Sadness Over Jerusalem

[31]At that time some Pharisees came to Jesus. They said to him, "Leave this place. Go somewhere else. Herod wants to kill you."

[32]He replied, "Go and tell that fox, 'I will keep on driving out demons. I will keep on healing people today and tomorrow. And on the third day I will reach my goal.' [33]In any case, I must keep going today and tomorrow and the next day. Certainly no prophet can die outside Jerusalem!

[34]"Jerusalem! Jerusalem! You kill the prophets and throw stones in order to kill those who are sent to you. Many times I have wanted to gather your people together. I have wanted to be like a hen who gathers her chicks under her wings. And you would not let me. [35]Look, your house is left empty. I tell you, you will not see me again until you say, 'Blessed is the one who comes in the name of the Lord.' " *(Psalm 118:26)*

Jesus Eats at a Pharisee's House

14 One Sabbath day, Jesus went to eat in the house of a well-known Pharisee. While he was there, he was being carefully watched. [2]In front of him was a man whose body was badly swollen. [3]Jesus turned to the Pharisees and the authorities on the law. He asked them, "Is it breaking the Law to heal on the Sabbath day?" [4]But they remained silent. So Jesus took hold of the man and healed him. Then he sent him away.

[5]He asked them another question. He said, "Suppose one of you has a child or an ox that falls into a well on the Sabbath day. Wouldn't you pull it out right away?" [6]And they had nothing to say.

[7]Jesus noticed how the guests picked the places of honor at the table. So he told them a story. [8]He said, "Suppose someone invites you to a wedding feast. Do not take the place of honor. A person more important than you may have been invited. [9]If so, the host who invited both of you will come to you. He will say, 'Give this person your seat.' Then you will be filled with shame. You will have to take the least important place. [10]But when you are invited, take the lowest place. Then your host will come over to you. He will say, 'Friend, move up to a better place.' Then you will be honored in front of all the other guests. [11]All those who lift themselves up will be made humble. And those who make themselves humble will be lifted up."

[12]Then Jesus spoke to his host. "Suppose you give a lunch or a dinner," he said. "Do not invite your friends, your brothers or sisters, or your relatives, or your rich neighbors. If you do, they may invite you to eat with them. So you will be paid back. [13]But

when you give a banquet, invite those who are poor. Also invite those who can't see or walk. ¹⁴Then you will be blessed. Your guests can't pay you back. But you will be paid back when those who are right with God rise from the dead."

The Story of the Great Banquet

¹⁵One of the people at the table with Jesus heard him say those things. So he said to Jesus, "Blessed is the one who will eat at the feast in God's kingdom."

¹⁶Jesus replied, "A certain man was preparing a great banquet. He invited many guests. ¹⁷Then the day of the banquet arrived. He sent his servant to those who had been invited. The servant told them, 'Come. Everything is ready now.'

¹⁸"But they all had the same idea. They began to make excuses. The first one said, 'I have just bought a field. I have to go and see it. Please excuse me.'

¹⁹"Another said, 'I have just bought five pairs of oxen. I'm on my way to try them out. Please excuse me.'

²⁰"Still another said, 'I just got married, so I can't come.'

²¹"The servant came back and reported this to his master. Then the owner of the house became angry. He ordered his servant, 'Go out quickly into the streets and lanes of the town. Bring in those who are poor. Also bring those who can't see or walk.'

²²"'Sir,' the servant said, 'what you ordered has been done. But there is still room.'

²³"Then the master told his servant, 'Go out to the roads. Go out to the country lanes. Make the people come in. I want my house to be full. ²⁴I tell you, not one of those people who were invited will get a taste of my banquet.'"

The Cost of Being a Disciple

²⁵Large crowds were traveling with Jesus. He turned and spoke to them. He said, ²⁶"Anyone who comes to me must hate their father and mother. They must hate their wife and children. They must hate their brothers and sisters. And they must hate even their own life. Unless they do this, they can't be my disciple. ²⁷Whoever doesn't carry their cross and follow me can't be my disciple.

²⁸"Suppose one of you wants to build a tower. Won't you sit down first and figure out how much it will cost? Then you will see whether you have enough money to finish it. ²⁹Suppose you start building and are not able to finish. Then everyone who sees what you have done will laugh at you. ³⁰They will say, 'This person started to build but wasn't able to finish.'

³¹"Or suppose a king is about to go to war against another king. And suppose he has 10,000 men, while the other has 20,000 coming against him. Won't he first sit down and think about whether he can win? ³²And

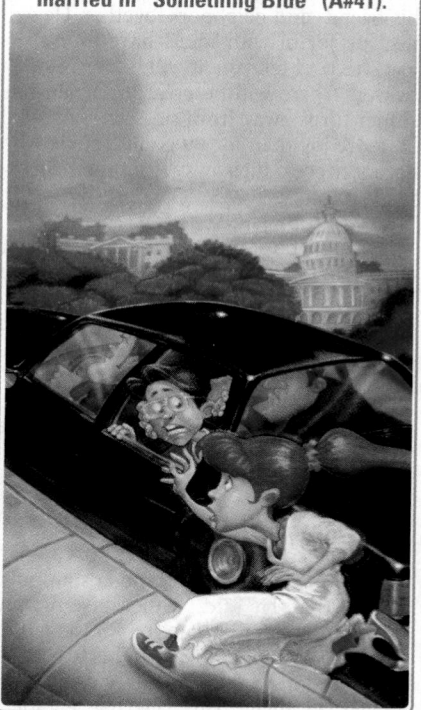

suppose he decides he can't win. Then he will send some men to ask how peace can be made. He will do this while the other king is still far away. ³³In the same way, you must give up everything you have. Those of you who don't cannot be my disciple.

³⁴"Salt is good. But suppose it loses its saltiness. How can it be made salty again? ³⁵It is not good for the soil. And it is not good for the trash pile. It will be thrown out.

"Whoever has ears should listen."

The Story of the Lost Sheep

15 The tax collectors and sinners were all gathering around to hear Jesus. ²But the Pharisees and the teachers of the law were whispering among themselves. They said, "This man welcomes sinners and eats with them."

³Then Jesus told them a story. ⁴He said, "Suppose one of you has 100 sheep and loses one of them. Won't he leave the 99 in the open country? Won't he go and look for the one lost sheep until he finds it? ⁵When he finds it, he will joyfully put it on his shoulders ⁶and go home. Then he will call his friends and neighbors together. He will say, 'Be joyful with me. I have found my lost sheep.' ⁷I tell you, it will be the same in heaven. There will be great joy when one sinner turns away from sin. Yes, there will be more joy than for 99 godly people who do not need to turn away from their sins.

The Story of the Lost Coin

⁸"Or suppose a woman has ten silver coins and loses one. Won't she light a lamp and sweep the house? Won't she search carefully until she finds the coin? ⁹And when she finds it, she will call her friends and neighbors together. She will say, 'Be joyful with me. I have found my lost coin.' ¹⁰I tell you, it is the same in heaven. There is joy in heaven over one sinner who turns away from sin."

The Story of the Lost Son

¹¹Jesus continued, "There was a man who had two sons. ¹²The younger son spoke to his father. He said, 'Father, give me my share of the family property.' So the father divided his property between his two sons.

¹³"Not long after that, the younger son packed up all he had. Then he left for a

ADVENTURES IN ODYSSEY

Jimmy Barclay felt like the Prodigal Son twice, in "The Prodigal Jimmy" (A#04) and in "Living in the Gray" (A#42).

country far away. There he wasted his money on wild living. ¹⁴He spent everything he had. Then the whole country ran low on food. So the son didn't have what he needed. ¹⁵He went to work for someone who lived in that country. That person sent the son to the fields to feed the pigs. ¹⁶The son wanted to fill his stomach with the food the pigs were eating. But no one gave him anything.

¹⁷"Then he began to think clearly again. He said, 'How many of my father's hired servants have more than enough food! But here I am dying from hunger! ¹⁸I will get up and go back to my father. I will say to him, "Father, I have sinned against heaven. And I have sinned against you. ¹⁹I am no longer fit to be called your son. Make me like one of your hired servants."' ²⁰So he got up and went to his father.

"While the son was still a long way off, his father saw him. He was filled with tender love for his son. He ran to him. He threw his arms around him and kissed him.

²¹"The son said to him, 'Father, I have sinned against heaven and against you. I am no longer fit to be called your son.'

²²"But the father said to his servants, 'Quick! Bring the best robe and put it on him. Put a ring on his finger and sandals on his feet. ²³Bring the fattest calf and kill it. Let's have a feast and celebrate. ²⁴This son of mine was dead. And now he is alive again. He was lost. And now he is found.' So they began to celebrate.

²⁵"The older son was in the field. When he came near the house, he heard music and dancing. ²⁶So he called one of the servants. He asked him what was going on. ²⁷'Your brother has come home,' the servant replied. 'Your father has killed the fattest calf. He has done this because your brother is back safe and sound.'

²⁸"The older brother became angry. He refused to go in. So his father went out and

begged him. ²⁹But he answered his father, 'Look! All these years I've worked like a slave for you. I have always obeyed your orders. You never gave me even a young goat so I could celebrate with my friends. ³⁰But this son of yours wasted your money with some prostitutes. Now he comes home. And for him you kill the fattest calf!'

³¹"'My son,' the father said, 'you are always with me. Everything I have is yours. ³²But we had to celebrate and be glad. This brother of yours was dead. And now he is alive again. He was lost. And now he is found.'"

The Story of the Clever Manager

16 Jesus told his disciples another story. He said, "There was a rich man who had a manager. Some said that the manager was wasting what the rich man owned. ²So the rich man told him to come in. He asked him, 'What is this I hear about you? Tell me exactly how you have handled what I own. You can't be my manager any longer.'

³"The manager said to himself, 'What will I do now? My master is taking away my job. I'm not strong enough to dig. And I'm too ashamed to beg. ⁴I know what I'm going to do. I'll do something so that when I lose my job here, people will welcome me into their houses.'

⁵"So he called in each person who owed his master something. He asked the first one, 'How much do you owe my master?'

⁶"'I owe 900 gallons of olive oil,' he replied.

"The manager told him, 'Take your bill. Sit down quickly and change it to 450 gallons.'

⁷"Then he asked the second one, 'And how much do you owe?'

"'I owe 1,000 bushels of wheat,' he replied.

"The manager told him, 'Take your bill and change it to 800 bushels.'

⁸"The manager had not been honest. But the master praised him for being clever. The people of this world are clever in dealing with those who are like themselves. They are more clever than God's people. ⁹I tell you, use the riches of this world to help others. In that way, you will make friends for yourselves. Then when your riches are gone, you will be welcomed into your eternal home in heaven.

¹⁰"Suppose you can be trusted with something very little. Then you can also be trusted with something very large. But suppose you are not honest with something very little. Then you will also not be honest with something very large. ¹¹Suppose you have not been worthy of trust in handling worldly wealth. Then who will trust you with true riches? ¹²Suppose you have not been worthy of trust in handling someone else's property. Then who will give you property of your own?

¹³"No one can serve two masters at the same time. Either you will hate one of them and love the other. Or you will be faithful to one and dislike the other. You can't serve God and money at the same time."

¹⁴The Pharisees loved money. They heard all that Jesus said and made fun of him. ¹⁵Jesus said to them, "You try to make yourselves look good in the eyes of other people. But God knows your hearts. What people think is worth a lot is hated by God.

More Teachings

¹⁶"The teachings of the Law and the Prophets were preached until John the Baptist came. Since then, the good news of God's kingdom is being preached. And everyone is trying very hard to enter it. ¹⁷It is easier for heaven and earth to disappear than for the smallest part of a letter to drop out of the Law.

¹⁸"Anyone who divorces his wife and marries another woman commits adultery. Also, the man who marries a divorced woman commits adultery.

The Rich Man and Lazarus

¹⁹"Once there was a rich man. He was dressed in purple cloth and fine linen. He lived an easy life every day. ²⁰A man named Lazarus was placed at his gate. Lazarus was

REMEMBER THIS

LUKE 16:13

"No one can serve two masters at the same time. Either you will hate one of them and love the other. Or you will be faithful to one and dislike the other. You can't serve God and money at the same time."

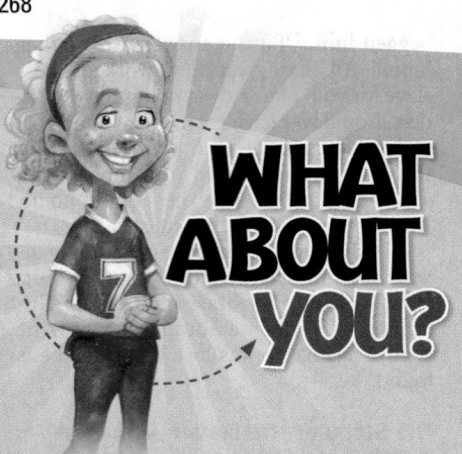

Are you familiar with the way credit cards work? They can be helpful tools if used correctly, or they can cause trouble—as Connie discovered in the Adventures in Odyssey episode "A Little Credit, Please."

That little piece of plastic whispers, *"Pssssst! You don't need to wait until you have real money to buy that. Just charge it. You deserve it!"* But when the bill comes due, the credit card company will expect real money. And if we don't have it, interest payments will drive the cost even higher. If we're not super careful, they can also drag us into financial ruin by tempting us to spend money we shouldn't spend—maybe even money we don't have. At least Connie's mother had the wisdom to set a low credit limit for Connie until she proved she could be responsible . . . or the consequences could have been a lot worse.

Similarly, God wants to see how responsible we can be with small things before He entrusts us with bigger things. It's a spiritual principle called "stewardship." Jesus explained it to His disciples in Luke 16:10–12. Indeed, once we show others that we can be responsible, we'll get more opportunities to do even bigger things.

Are you a good steward when it comes to money? How much do you earn each week? How much do you spend? If the second number is bigger than the first, you have some growing to do. Ask your parents to help you set a budget and stick to it.

a beggar. His body was covered with sores. [21]Even dogs came and licked his sores. All he wanted was to eat what fell from the rich man's table.

[22]"The time came when the beggar died. The angels carried him to Abraham's side. The rich man also died and was buried. [23]In the place of the dead, the rich man was suffering terribly. He looked up and saw Abraham far away. Lazarus was by his side. [24]So the rich man called out, 'Father Abraham! Have pity on me! Send Lazarus to dip the tip of his finger in water. Then he can cool my tongue with it. I am in terrible pain in this fire.'

[25]"But Abraham replied, 'Son, remember what happened in your lifetime. You received your good things. Lazarus received bad things. Now he is comforted here, and you are in terrible pain. [26]Besides, a wide space has been placed between us and you. So those who want to go from here to you can't go. And no one can cross over from there to us.'

[27]"The rich man answered, 'Then I beg you, father Abraham. Send Lazarus to my family. [28]I have five brothers. Let Lazarus warn them. Then they will not come to this place of terrible suffering.'

[29]"Abraham replied, 'They have the teachings of Moses and the Prophets. Let your brothers listen to them.'

[30]" 'No, father Abraham,' he said. 'But if someone from the dead goes to them, they will turn away from their sins.'

[31]"Abraham said to him, 'They do not listen to Moses and the Prophets. So they will not be convinced even if someone rises from the dead.' "

Sin, Faith and Duty

17 Jesus spoke to his disciples. "Things that make people sin are sure to come," he said. "But how terrible it will be for anyone who causes those things to come! [2]Suppose people lead one of these little ones to sin. It would be better for those people to be thrown into the sea with

ADVENTURES IN ODYSSEY

Jesse asked a detective to find her lost faith in "Harlow Doyle, Private Eye." (A#14).

a millstone tied around their neck. ³So watch what you do.

"If your brother or sister sins against you, tell them they are wrong. Then if they turn away from their sins, forgive them. ⁴Suppose they sin against you seven times in one day. And suppose they come back to you each time and say, 'I'm sorry.' You must forgive them."

⁵The apostles said to the Lord, "Give us more faith!"

⁶He replied, "Suppose you have faith as small as a mustard seed. Then you can say to this mulberry tree, 'Be pulled up. Be planted in the sea.' And it will obey you.

⁷"Suppose one of you has a servant plowing or looking after the sheep. And suppose the servant came in from the field. Will you say to him, 'Come along now and sit down to eat'? ⁸No. Instead, you will say, 'Prepare my supper. Get yourself ready. Wait on me while I eat and drink. Then after that you can eat and drink.' ⁹Will you thank the servant because he did what he was told to do? ¹⁰It's the same with you. Suppose you have done everything you were told to do. Then you should say, 'We are not worthy to serve you. We have only done our duty.'"

Jesus Heals Ten Men Who Have a Skin Disease

¹¹Jesus was on his way to Jerusalem. He traveled along the border between Samaria and Galilee. ¹²As he was going into a village, ten men met him. They had a skin disease. They were standing close by. ¹³And they called out in a loud voice, "Jesus! Master! Have pity on us!"

¹⁴Jesus saw them and said, "Go. Show yourselves to the priests." While they were on the way, they were healed.

¹⁵When one of them saw that he was healed, he came back. He praised God in a loud voice. ¹⁶He threw himself at Jesus' feet and thanked him. The man was a Samaritan.

¹⁷Jesus asked, "Weren't all ten healed? Where are the other nine? ¹⁸Didn't anyone else return and give praise to God except this outsider?" ¹⁹Then Jesus said to him, "Get up and go. Your faith has healed you."

The Coming of God's Kingdom

²⁰Once the Pharisees asked Jesus when God's kingdom would come. He replied, "The coming of God's kingdom is not something you can see. ²¹People will not say, 'Here it is.' Or, 'There it is.' That's because God's kingdom is among you."

²²Then Jesus spoke to his disciples. "The time is coming," he said, "when you will long to see one of the days of the Son of Man. But you won't see it. ²³People will tell you, 'There he is!' Or, 'Here he is!' Don't go running off after them. ²⁴When the Son of Man comes, he will be like the lightning. It flashes and lights up the sky from one end to the other. ²⁵But first the Son of Man must suffer many things. He will not be accepted by the people of today.

²⁶"Remember how it was in the days of Noah. It will be the same when the Son of Man comes. ²⁷People were eating and drinking. They were getting married. They were giving their daughters to be married. They did all those things right up to the day Noah entered the ark. Then the flood came and destroyed them all.

²⁸"It was the same in the days of Lot. People were eating and drinking. They were buying and selling. They were planting and building. ²⁹But on the day Lot left Sodom, fire and sulfur rained down from heaven. And all the people were destroyed.

³⁰"It will be just like that on the day the Son of Man is shown to the world. ³¹Suppose someone is on the housetop on that day. And suppose what they own is inside the house. They should not go down to get what they own. No one in the field should go back for anything either. ³²Remember Lot's wife! ³³Whoever tries to keep their life will lose it. Whoever loses their life will keep it. ³⁴I tell you, on that night two people

BIBLE ADVENTURES

Brenda Perry told the story of the ten lepers as a puppet show in "The Pretty Good Samaritan" (A#26).

will be in one bed. One person will be taken and the other left. ³⁵⁻³⁶Two women will be grinding grain together. One will be taken and the other left."

³⁷"Where, Lord?" his disciples asked.

He replied, "The vultures will gather where there is a dead body."

The Story of the Widow Who Would Not Give Up

18 Jesus told his disciples a story. He wanted to show them that they should always pray and not give up. ²He said, "In a certain town there was a judge. He didn't have any respect for God or care about what people thought. ³A widow lived in that town. She came to the judge again and again. She kept begging him, 'Make things right for me. Someone is treating me badly.'

⁴"For some time the judge refused. But finally he said to himself, 'I don't have any respect for God. I don't care about what people think. ⁵But this widow keeps bothering me. So I will see that things are made right for her. If I don't, she will someday come and attack me!'"

⁶The Lord said, "Listen to what the unfair judge says. ⁷God's chosen people cry out to him day and night. Won't he make things right for them? Will he keep putting them off? ⁸I tell you, God will see that things are made right for them. He will

make sure it happens quickly. But when the Son of Man comes, will he find people on earth who have faith?"

The Story of the Pharisee and the Tax Collector

⁹Jesus told a story to some people who were sure they were right with God. They looked down on everyone else. ¹⁰He said to them, "Two men went up to the temple to pray. One was a Pharisee. The other was a tax collector. ¹¹The Pharisee stood by himself and prayed. 'God, I thank you that I am not like other people,' he said. 'I am not like robbers or those who do other evil things. I am not like those who commit adultery. I am not even like this tax collector. ¹²I fast twice a week. And I give a tenth of all I get.'

¹³"But the tax collector stood farther away than the Pharisee. He would not even look up to heaven. He brought his hand to his heart and prayed. He said, 'God, have mercy on me. I am a sinner.'

¹⁴"I tell you, the tax collector went home accepted by God. But not the Pharisee. All those who lift themselves up will be made humble. And those who make themselves humble will be lifted up."

Little Children Are Brought to Jesus

¹⁵People were also bringing babies to Jesus. They wanted him to place his hands

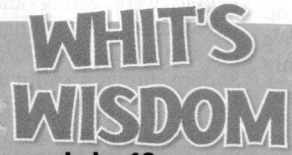

WHIT'S WISDOM

Luke 18

Today at Whit's End I heard an odd slurping sound at the end of the counter—and then a frustrated whimper. It was Jay Smouse, all red in the face, straining to suck a cherry through a soda straw. "Most kids use a spoon for that part, Jay," I suggested.

After reminding me that he is not "most kids," Jay asked sarcastically if the Bible had anything to say about his dilemma. I thought for a second. "Well," I said, "in Luke

18 a rich ruler turned his back on heavenly treasures because he wasn't willing to give up his wealth and follow Jesus." Naturally, Jay wanted to know what that had to do with his ice cream soda. I'll tell you what I told him.

Jesus explained that it's harder for someone who worships money to enter heaven than it is for a camel to go through the eye of a needle. Or, as Jay was discovering, for a whole cherry to pass through a soda straw. It's impossible. Indeed, to enter heaven, nothing can be more important to us than Jesus. Is there anything you wouldn't give up to follow Him?

on the babies. When the disciples saw this, they told the people to stop. [16]But Jesus asked the children to come to him. "Let the little children come to me," he said. "Don't keep them away. God's kingdom belongs to people like them. [17]What I'm about to tell you is true. Anyone who will not receive God's kingdom like a little child will never enter it."

Rich People and the Kingdom of God

[18]A certain ruler asked Jesus a question. "Good teacher," he said, "what must I do to receive eternal life?"

[19]"Why do you call me good?" Jesus answered. "No one is good except God. [20]You know what the commandments say. 'Do not commit adultery. Do not commit murder. Do not steal. Do not be a false witness. Honor your father and mother.'" *(Exodus 20:12–16; Deuteronomy 5:16–20)*

[21]"I have obeyed all those commandments since I was a boy," the ruler said.

[22]When Jesus heard this, he said to him, "You are still missing one thing. Sell everything you have. Give the money to those who are poor. You will have treasure in heaven. Then come and follow me."

[23]When the ruler heard this, he became very sad. He was very rich. [24]Jesus looked at him. Then he said, "How hard it is for rich people to enter God's kingdom! [25]Is it hard for a camel to go through the eye of a needle? It is even harder for someone who is rich to enter God's kingdom!"

[26]Those who heard this asked, "Then who can be saved?"

[27]Jesus replied, "Things that are impossible with people are possible with God."

[28]Peter said to him, "We have left everything we had in order to follow you!"

[29]"What I'm about to tell you is true," Jesus said to them. "Has anyone left home or wife or husband or brothers or sisters or parents or children for God's kingdom? [30]They will receive many times as much in this world. In the world to come they will receive eternal life."

Jesus Speaks a Third Time About His Coming Death

[31]Jesus took the 12 disciples to one side. He told them, "We are going up to Jerusalem. Everything that the prophets wrote about the Son of Man will come true. [32]He

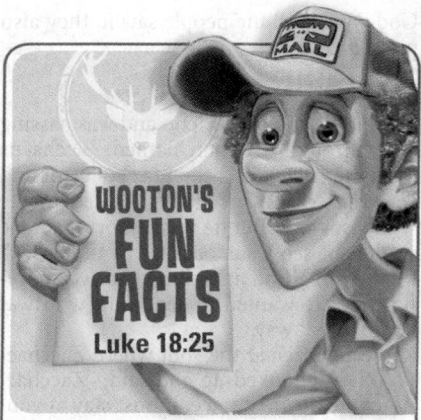

WOOTON'S FUN FACTS
Luke 18:25

The Babylonians had a similar saying, but instead of a camel they used an elephant. It doesn't really matter which animal you use. Even a mouse can't go through the eye of a needle. Jesus was trying to show something impossible that *is* possible with God!

will be handed over to the Gentiles. They will make fun of him. They will laugh at him and spit on him. [33]They will whip him and kill him. On the third day, he will rise from the dead!"

[34]The disciples did not understand any of this. Its meaning was hidden from them. So they didn't know what Jesus was talking about.

A Blind Beggar Receives His Sight

[35]Jesus was approaching Jericho. A blind man was sitting by the side of the road begging. [36]The blind man heard the crowd going by. He asked what was happening. [37]They told him, "Jesus of Nazareth is passing by."

[38]So the blind man called out, "Jesus! Son of David! Have mercy on me!"

[39]Those who led the way commanded him to stop. They told him to be quiet. But he shouted even louder, "Son of David! Have mercy on me!"

[40]Jesus stopped and ordered the man to be brought to him. When the man came near, Jesus spoke to him. [41]"What do you want me to do for you?" Jesus asked.

"Lord, I want to be able to see," the blind man replied.

[42]Jesus said to him, "Receive your sight. Your faith has healed you." [43]Right away he could see. He followed Jesus, praising

God. When all the people saw it, they also praised God.

Zacchaeus the Tax Collector

19 Jesus entered Jericho and was passing through. ²A man named Zacchaeus lived there. He was a chief tax collector and was very rich. ³Zacchaeus wanted to see who Jesus was. But he was a short man. He could not see Jesus because of the crowd. ⁴So he ran ahead and climbed a sycamore-fig tree. He wanted to see Jesus, who was coming that way.

⁵Jesus reached the spot where Zacchaeus was. He looked up and said, "Zacchaeus, come down at once. I must stay at your house today." ⁶So Zacchaeus came down at once and welcomed him gladly.

⁷All the people saw this. They began to whisper among themselves. They said, "Jesus has gone to be the guest of a sinner."

⁸But Zacchaeus stood up. He said, "Look, Lord! Here and now I give half of what I own to those who are poor. And if I have cheated anybody out of anything, I will pay it back. I will pay back four times the amount I took."

⁹Jesus said to Zacchaeus, "Today salvation has come to your house. You are a member of Abraham's family line. ¹⁰The Son of Man came to look for the lost and save them."

The Story of Three Slaves

¹¹While the people were listening to these things, Jesus told them a story. He was near Jerusalem. The people thought that God's kingdom was going to appear right away. ¹²Jesus said, "A man from an important family went to a country far away. He went there to be made king and then return home. ¹³So he sent for ten of his slaves. He gave them each about three months' pay. 'Put this money to work until I come back,' he said.

¹⁴"But those he ruled over hated him. They sent some messengers after him. They were sent to say, 'We don't want this man to be our king.'

¹⁵"But he was made king and returned home. Then he sent for the slaves he had given the money to. He wanted to find out what they had earned with it.

¹⁶"The first one came to him. He said, 'Sir, your money has earned ten times as much.'

¹⁷" 'You have done well, my good slave!' his master replied. 'You have been faithful in a very small matter. So I will put you in charge of ten towns.'

¹⁸"The second slave came to his master. He said, 'Sir, your money has earned five times as much.'

¹⁹"His master answered, 'I will put you in charge of five towns.'

²⁰"Then another slave came. He said, 'Sir, here is your money. I have kept it hidden in a piece of cloth. ²¹I was afraid of you. You are a hard man. You take out what you did not put in. You harvest what you did not plant.'

²²"His master replied, 'I will judge you by your own words, you evil slave! So you knew that I am a hard man? You knew that I take out what I did not put in? You knew that I harvest what I did not plant? ²³Then why didn't you put my money in the bank? When I came back, I could have collected it with interest.'

²⁴"Then he said to those standing by, 'Take his money away from him. Give it to the one who has ten times as much.'

²⁵" 'Sir,' they said, 'he already has ten times as much!'

²⁶"He replied, 'I tell you that everyone who has will be given more. But here is what will happen to anyone who has nothing. Even what they have will be taken away from them. ²⁷And what about my enemies who did not want me to be king over them? Bring them here! Kill them in front of me!' "

Jesus Comes to Jerusalem as King

²⁸After Jesus had said this, he went on ahead. He was going up to Jerusalem. ²⁹He approached Bethphage and Bethany. The hill there was called the Mount of Olives. Jesus sent out two of his disciples. He said to them, ³⁰"Go to the village ahead of you. As soon as you get there, you will find a

donkey's colt tied up. No one has ever ridden it. Untie it and bring it here. [31]Someone may ask you, 'Why are you untying it?' If so, say, 'The Lord needs it.' "

[32]Those who were sent ahead went and found the young donkey. It was there just as Jesus had told them. [33]They were untying the colt when its owners came. The owners asked them, "Why are you untying the colt?"

[34]They replied, "The Lord needs it."

[35]Then the disciples brought the colt to Jesus. They threw their coats on the young donkey and put Jesus on it. [36]As he went along, people spread their coats on the road. [37]Jesus came near the place where the road goes down the Mount of Olives. There the whole crowd of disciples began to praise God with joy. In loud voices they praised him for all the miracles they had seen. They shouted,

[38] "Blessed is the king who comes in the
    name of the Lord!"

(Psalm 118:26)

"May there be peace and glory in the
    highest heaven!"

[39]Some of the Pharisees in the crowd spoke to Jesus. "Teacher," they said, "tell your disciples to stop!"

[40]"I tell you," he replied, "if they keep quiet, the stones will cry out."

[41]He approached Jerusalem. When he saw the city, he began to weep. [42]He said, "I wish you had known today what would bring you peace! But now it is hidden from your eyes. [43]The days will come when your enemies will arrive. They will build a wall of dirt up against your city. They will surround you and close you in on every side. [44]You didn't recognize the time when God came to you. So your enemies will smash you to the ground. They will destroy you and all the people inside your walls. They will not leave one stone on top of another."

Jesus Clears Out the Temple

[45]Then Jesus entered the temple courtyard. He began to drive out those who were selling there. [46]He told them, "It is written that the Lord said, 'My house will be a house where people can pray.' *(Isaiah 56:7)* But you have made it a 'den for robbers.' "

(Jeremiah 7:11)

[47]Every day Jesus was teaching at the temple. But the chief priests and the teachers of the law were trying to kill him. So were the leaders among the people. [48]But they couldn't find any way to do it. All the people were paying close attention to his words.

The Authority of Jesus Is Questioned

20 One day Jesus was teaching the people in the temple courtyard. He was announcing the good news to them. The chief priests and the teachers of the law came up to him. The elders came with them. [2]"Tell us by what authority you are doing these things," they all said. "Who gave you this authority?"

[3]Jesus replied, "I will also ask you a question. Tell me, [4]was John's baptism from heaven? Or did it come from people?"

[5]They talked to one another about it. They said, "If we say, 'From heaven,' he will ask, 'Why didn't you believe him?' [6]But if we say, 'From people,' all the people will throw stones at us and kill us. They believe that John was a prophet."

[7]So they answered Jesus, "We don't know where John's baptism came from."

[8]Jesus said, "Then I won't tell you by what authority I am doing these things either."

The Story of the Renters

[9]Jesus went on to tell the people a story. "A man planted a vineyard," he said. "He rented it out to some farmers. Then he went away for a long time. [10]At harvest time he sent a slave to the renters. They were supposed to give him some of the fruit of the vineyard. But the renters beat the slave. Then they sent him away with nothing. [11]So the man sent another slave. They beat that one and treated him badly. They also sent him away with nothing. [12]The man sent a third slave. The renters wounded him and threw him out.

[13]"Then the owner of the vineyard said, 'What should I do? I have a son, and I love him. I will send him. Maybe they will respect him.'

[14]"But when the renters saw the son, they talked the matter over. 'This is the one who will receive all the owner's property someday,' they said. 'Let's kill him. Then everything will be ours.' [15]So they threw him out of the vineyard. And they killed him.

"What will the owner of the vineyard do to the renters? [16]He will come and kill them. He will give the vineyard to others."

BiBLE ADVENTURES

Kids' Radio told the parable of the renters as an Old West adventure in "Over the Airwaves" (A#09).

When the people heard this, they said, "We hope this never happens!"

[17]Jesus looked right at them and said, "Here is something I want you to explain the meaning of. It is written,

"'The stone the builders didn't accept
has become the most important
stone of all.' *(Psalm 118:22)*

[18]Everyone who falls on that stone will be broken to pieces. But the stone will crush anyone it falls on."

[19]The teachers of the law and the chief priests looked for a way to arrest Jesus at once. They knew he had told that story against them. But they were afraid of the people.

Is It Right to Pay the Royal Tax to Caesar?

[20]The religious leaders sent spies to keep a close watch on Jesus. The spies pretended to be sincere. They hoped they could trap Jesus with something he would say. Then they could hand him over to the power and authority of the governor. [21]So the spies questioned Jesus. "Teacher," they said, "we know that you speak and teach what is right. We know you don't favor one person over another. You teach the way of God truthfully. [22]Is it right for us to pay taxes to Caesar or not?"

[23]Jesus saw they were trying to trick him. So he said to them, [24]"Show me a silver coin. Whose picture and words are on it?"

"Caesar's," they replied.

[25]He said to them, "Then give back to Caesar what belongs to Caesar. And give back to God what belongs to God."

[26]They were not able to trap him with what he had said there in front of all the people. Amazed by his answer, they became silent.

Marriage When the Dead Rise

[27]The Sadducees do not believe that people rise from the dead. Some of them came to Jesus with a question. [28]"Teacher," they said, "Moses wrote for us about a man's brother who dies. Suppose the brother leaves a wife but has no children. Then the man must marry the widow. He must provide children to carry on his dead brother's name. [29]There were seven brothers. The first one married a woman. He died without leaving any children. [30]The second one married her. [31]And then the third one married her. One after another, the seven brothers married her. They all died. None left any children. [32]Finally, the woman died too. [33]Now then, when the dead rise, whose wife will she be? All seven brothers were married to her."

[34]Jesus replied, "People in this world get married. And their parents give them to be married. [35]But it will not be like that when the dead rise. Those who are considered worthy to take part in the world to come won't get married. And their parents won't give them to be married. [36]They can't die anymore. They are like the angels. They are God's children. They will be given a new form of life when the dead rise. [37]Remember the story of Moses and the burning bush. Even Moses showed that the dead rise. The Lord said to him, 'I am the God of Abraham. I am the God of Isaac. And I am the God of Jacob.' *(Exodus 3:6)* [38]He is not the God of the dead. He is the God of the living. In his eyes, everyone is alive."

[39]Some of the teachers of the law replied, "You have spoken well, teacher!" [40]And no one dared to ask him any more questions.

Whose Son Is the Messiah?

[41]Jesus said to them, "Why do people say that the Messiah is the son of David? [42]David himself says in the Book of Psalms,

"'The Lord said to my Lord,
"Sit at my right hand
[43] until I put your enemies
under your control."' *(Psalm 110:1)*

[44]David calls him 'Lord.' So how can he be David's son?"

Warning Against the Teachers of the Law

[45]All the people were listening. Jesus said to his disciples, [46]"Watch out for the teachers of the law. They like to walk around in long robes. They love to be greeted with respect in the market. They love to have the

most important seats in the synagogues. They also love to have the places of honor at banquets. [47]They take over the houses of widows. They say long prayers to show off. God will punish these men very much."

The Widow's Offering

21 As Jesus looked up, he saw rich people putting their gifts into the temple offering boxes. [2]He also saw a poor widow put in two very small copper coins. [3]"What I'm about to tell you is true," Jesus said. "That poor widow has put in more than all the others. [4]All these other people gave a lot because they are rich. But even though she is poor, she put in everything. She had nothing left to live on."

When the Temple Will Be Destroyed and the Signs of the End

[5]Some of Jesus' disciples were talking about the temple. They spoke about how it was decorated with beautiful stones and with gifts that honored God. But Jesus asked, [6]"Do you see all this? The time will come when not one stone will be left on top of another. Every stone will be thrown down."

[7]"Teacher," they asked, "when will these things happen? And what will be the sign that they are about to take place?"

[8]Jesus replied, "Keep watch! Be careful that you are not fooled. Many will come in my name. They will claim, 'I am he!' And they will say, 'The time is near!' Do not follow them. [9]Do not be afraid when you hear about wars and about fighting against rulers. Those things must happen first. But the end will not come right away."

[10]Then Jesus said to them, "Nation will fight against nation. Kingdom will fight against kingdom. [11]In many places there will be powerful earthquakes. People will go hungry. There will be terrible sicknesses. Things will happen that will make people afraid. There will be great and miraculous signs from heaven.

[12]"But before all this, people will arrest you and treat you badly. They will hand you over to synagogues and put you in prison. You will be brought to kings and governors. All this will happen to you because of my name. [13]And so you will be witnesses about me. [14]But make up your mind not to worry ahead of time about how to stand up for yourselves. [15]I will give you words of wisdom. None of your enemies will be able to withstand them or prove them wrong. [16]Even your parents, brothers, sisters, relatives and friends will hand you over to the authorities. The authorities will put some of you to death. [17]Everyone will hate you because of me. [18]But not a hair on your head will be harmed. [19]Remain strong in the faith, and you will receive eternal life.

[20]"A time is coming when you will see armies surround Jerusalem. Then you will know that it will soon be destroyed. [21]Those who are in Judea should then escape to the mountains. Those in the city should get out. Those in the country should not enter the city. [22]This is the time when God will punish Jerusalem. Everything will come true, just as it has been written. [23]How awful it will be in those days for pregnant women! How awful for nursing mothers! There will be terrible suffering in the land. There will be great anger against those people. [24]Some will be killed by the sword. Others will be taken as prisoners to all the nations. Jerusalem will be taken over by Gentiles until the times of the Gentiles come to an end.

[25]"There will be signs in the sun, moon and stars. The nations of the earth will be in terrible pain. They will be puzzled by the roaring and tossing of the sea. [26]Terror will make people faint. They will be worried about what is happening in the world. The sun, moon and stars will be shaken from their places. [27]At that time people will see the Son of Man coming in a cloud. He will come with power and great glory. [28]When these things begin to take place, stand up. Hold your head up with joy and hope. The time when you will be set free will be very close."

[29]Jesus told them a story. "Look at the fig tree and all the trees," he said. [30]"When you see leaves appear on the branches, you know that summer is near. [31]In the same way, when you see these things happening, you will know that God's kingdom is near.

[32]"What I'm about to tell you is true. The people living now will certainly not pass away until all these things have happened. [33]Heaven and earth will pass away. But my words will never pass away.

[34]"Be careful. If you aren't, your hearts will be loaded down with wasteful living, drunkenness and the worries of life. Then

the day the Son of Man returns will close on you like a trap. It will happen suddenly. ³⁵That day will come on every person who lives on the whole earth. ³⁶Always keep watching. Pray that you will be able to escape all that is about to happen. Also, pray that you will not be judged guilty when the Son of Man comes."

³⁷Each day Jesus taught at the temple. And each evening he went to spend the night on the hill called the Mount of Olives. ³⁸All the people came to the temple early in the morning. They wanted to hear Jesus speak.

Judas Agrees to Hand Jesus Over

22 The Feast of Unleavened Bread, called the Passover, was near. ²The chief priests and the teachers of the law were looking for a way to get rid of Jesus. They were afraid of the people. ³Then Satan entered Judas, who was called Iscariot. Judas was one of the 12 disciples. ⁴He went to the chief priests and the officers of the temple guard. He talked with them about how he could hand Jesus over to them. ⁵They were delighted and agreed to give him money. ⁶Judas accepted their offer. He watched for the right time to hand Jesus over to them. He wanted to do it when no crowd was around.

The Last Supper

⁷Then the day of Unleavened Bread came. That was the time the Passover lamb had to be sacrificed. ⁸Jesus sent Peter and John on ahead. "Go," he told them. "Prepare for us to eat the Passover meal."

⁹"Where do you want us to prepare for it?" they asked.

¹⁰Jesus replied, "When you enter the city, a man carrying a jar of water will meet you. Follow him to the house he enters. ¹¹Then say to the owner of the house, 'The Teacher asks, "Where is the guest room? Where can I eat the Passover meal with my disciples?"' ¹²He will show you a large upstairs room with furniture already in it. Prepare for us to eat there."

¹³Peter and John left. They found things just as Jesus had told them. So they prepared the Passover meal.

¹⁴When the hour came, Jesus and his apostles took their places at the table. ¹⁵He said to them, "I have really looked forward to eating this Passover meal with you. I wanted to do this before I suffer. ¹⁶I tell you, I will not eat the Passover meal again until it is celebrated in God's kingdom."

¹⁷After Jesus took the cup, he gave thanks. He said, "Take this cup and share it among yourselves. ¹⁸I tell you, I will not drink wine with you again until God's kingdom comes."

¹⁹Then Jesus took bread. He gave thanks and broke it. He handed it to them and said, "This is my body. It is given for you. Every time you eat it, do this in memory of me."

²⁰In the same way, after the supper he took the cup. He said, "This cup is the new covenant in my blood. It is poured out for you. ²¹But someone here is going to hand me over to my enemies. His hand is with mine on the table. ²²The Son of Man will go to his death, just as God has already decided. But how terrible it will be for the one who hands him over!" ²³The apostles began to ask one another about this. They wondered which one of them would do it.

²⁴They also started to argue. They disagreed about which of them was thought to be the most important person. ²⁵Jesus said to them, "The kings of the Gentiles hold power over their people. And those who order them around call themselves Protectors. ²⁶But you must not be like that. Instead, the most important among you should be like the youngest. The one who rules should be like the one who serves. ²⁷Who is more important? Is it the one at the table, or the one who serves? Isn't it the one who is at the table? But I am among you as one who serves. ²⁸You have stood by me during my troubles. ²⁹And I give you a kingdom, just as my Father gave me a kingdom. ³⁰Then you will eat and drink at my table in my kingdom. And you will sit on thrones, judging the 12 tribes of Israel.

³¹"Simon, Simon! Satan has asked to sift all of you disciples like wheat. ³²But I have prayed for you, Simon. I have prayed that your faith will not fail. When you have turned back, help your brothers to be strong."

³³But Simon replied, "Lord, I am ready to go with you to prison and to death."

³⁴Jesus answered, "I tell you, Peter, you will say three times that you don't know me. And you will do it before the rooster crows today."

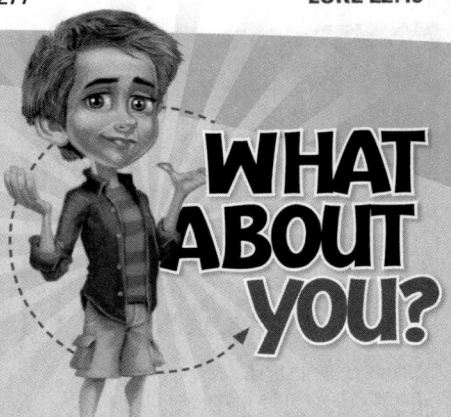

WHAT ABOUT YOU?

Have you ever wished to be a prince or princess? You could live in a castle, command servants to do whatever you want, eat terrific food, and wear a crown. You might even become king or queen one day! Sounds like the life.

But there's much more to being royalty. You have an entire kingdom looking to you for leadership. You have to protect your people, handle conflict, and create good laws. Hmmm. Maybe you don't want the job after all.

Jesus talked about being noble when His disciples were arguing about which of them was most important. He told them: "The kings of the Gentiles hold power over their people. And those who order them around call themselves Protectors. But you must not be like that. Instead, the most important among you should be like the youngest. The one who rules should be like the one who serves" (Luke 22:25–26).

People who are truly noble don't brag about their rank or use it to boss others around. They serve others and let others go first. Jesus was the ultimate example of this, humbling Himself enough to be put to death like a criminal. But He rose from the dead as the King of kings, and He wants to share His royalty with us.

Try acting like a prince or princess for a day. You could wear a crown or a medal. Or dress up like royalty. Practice having perfect manners. But most importantly, follow Jesus' instructions to be a servant to everyone.

---

³⁵Then Jesus asked the disciples, "Did you need anything when I sent you without a purse, bag or sandals?"

"Nothing," they answered.

³⁶He said to them, "But now if you have a purse, take it. And also take a bag. If you don't have a sword, sell your coat and buy one. ³⁷It is written, 'He was counted among those who had committed crimes.' *(Isaiah 53:12)* I tell you that what is written about me must come true. Yes, it is already coming true."

³⁸The disciples said, "See, Lord, here are two swords."

"Two swords are enough!" he replied.

Jesus Prays on the Mount of Olives

³⁹Jesus went out as usual to the Mount of Olives. His disciples followed him. ⁴⁰When they reached the place, Jesus spoke. "Pray that you won't fall into sin when you are tempted," he said to them. ⁴¹Then he went a short distance away from them. There he got down on his knees and prayed.

⁴²He said, "Father, if you are willing, take this cup of suffering away from me. But do what you want, not what I want." ⁴³An angel from heaven appeared to Jesus and gave him strength. ⁴⁴Because he was very sad and troubled, he prayed even harder. His sweat was like drops of blood falling to the ground.

⁴⁵After that, he got up from prayer and went back to the disciples. He found them sleeping. They were worn out because they were very sad. ⁴⁶"Why are you sleeping?" he asked them. "Get up! Pray that you won't fall into sin when you are tempted."

Jesus Is Arrested

⁴⁷While Jesus was still speaking, a crowd came up. The man named Judas was leading them. He was one of the 12 disciples. Judas approached Jesus to kiss him. ⁴⁸But Jesus asked him, "Judas, are you handing over the Son of Man with a kiss?"

⁴⁹Jesus' followers saw what was going to happen. So they said, "Lord, should we use

Luke 22:35 Did Jesus' disciples carry purses? It wasn't a purse like Connie or Penny might carry. It was actually a small basket strapped to the back for carrying food or other small objects. It's like the one David carried his five stones in while he was a shepherd.

our swords against them?" ⁵⁰One of them struck the slave of the high priest and cut off his right ear.

⁵¹But Jesus answered, "Stop this!" And he touched the man's ear and healed him.

⁵²Then Jesus spoke to the chief priests, the officers of the temple guard, and the elders. They had all come for him. "Am I leading a band of armed men against you?" he asked. "Do you have to come with swords and clubs? ⁵³Every day I was with you in the temple courtyard. And you didn't lay a hand on me. But this is your hour. This is when darkness rules."

Peter Says He Does Not Know Jesus

⁵⁴Then the men arrested Jesus and led him away. They took him into the high priest's house. Peter followed from far away. ⁵⁵Some people there started a fire in the middle of the courtyard. Then they sat down together. Peter sat down with them. ⁵⁶A female servant saw him sitting there in the firelight. She looked closely at him. Then she said, "This man was with Jesus."

⁵⁷But Peter said he had not been with him. "Woman, I don't know him," he said.

⁵⁸A little later someone else saw Peter. "You also are one of them," he said.

"No," Peter replied. "I'm not!"

⁵⁹About an hour later, another person spoke up. "This fellow must have been with Jesus," he said. "He is from Galilee."

⁶⁰Peter replied, "Man, I don't know what you're talking about!" Just as he was speaking, the rooster crowed. ⁶¹The Lord turned and looked right at Peter. Then Peter remembered what the Lord had spoken to him. "The rooster will crow today," Jesus had said. "Before it does, you will say three times that you don't know me." ⁶²Peter went outside. He broke down and cried.

The Guards Make Fun of Jesus

⁶³There were men guarding Jesus. They began laughing at him and beating him. ⁶⁴They blindfolded him. They said, "Prophesy! Who hit you?" ⁶⁵They also said many other things to make fun of him.

Jesus Is Brought to Pilate and Herod

⁶⁶At dawn the elders of the people met together. These included the chief priests and the teachers of the law. Jesus was led to them. ⁶⁷"If you are the Messiah," they said, "tell us."

Jesus answered, "If I tell you, you will not believe me. ⁶⁸And if I asked you, you would not answer. ⁶⁹But from now on, the Son of Man will be seated at the right hand of the mighty God."

⁷⁰They all asked, "Are you the Son of God then?"

He replied, "You say that I am."

⁷¹Then they said, "Why do we need any more witnesses? We have heard it from his own lips."

23 Then the whole group got up and led Jesus off to Pilate. ²They began to bring charges against Jesus. They said, "We have found this man misleading our people. He is against paying taxes to Caesar. And he claims to be Messiah, a king."

³So Pilate asked Jesus, "Are you the king of the Jews?"

"You have said so," Jesus replied.

⁴Then Pilate spoke to the chief priests and the crowd. He announced, "I find no basis for a charge against this man."

⁵But they kept it up. They said, "His teaching stirs up the people all over Judea. He started in Galilee and has come all the way here."

⁶When Pilate heard this, he asked if the man was from Galilee. ⁷He learned that Jesus was from Herod's area of authority. So Pilate sent Jesus to Herod. At that time Herod was also in Jerusalem.

[8]When Herod saw Jesus, he was very pleased. He had been wanting to see Jesus for a long time. He had heard much about him. He hoped to see Jesus perform a sign of some kind. [9]Herod asked him many questions, but Jesus gave him no answer. [10]The chief priests and the teachers of the law were standing there. With loud shouts they brought charges against him. [11]Herod and his soldiers laughed at him and made fun of him. They dressed him in a beautiful robe. Then they sent him back to Pilate. [12]That day Herod and Pilate became friends. Before this time they had been enemies.

[13]Pilate called together the chief priests, the rulers and the people. [14]He said to them, "You brought me this man. You said he was turning the people against the authorities. I have questioned him in front of you. I have found no basis for your charges against him. [15]Herod hasn't either. So he sent Jesus back to us. As you can see, Jesus has done nothing that is worthy of death. [16-17]So I will just have him whipped and let him go."

[18]But the whole crowd shouted, "Kill this man! But let Barabbas go!" [19]Barabbas had been thrown into prison. He had taken part in a struggle in the city against the authorities. He had also committed murder.

[20]Pilate wanted to let Jesus go. So he made an appeal to the crowd again. [21]But they kept shouting, "Crucify him! Crucify him!"

[22]Pilate spoke to them for the third time. "Why?" he asked. "What wrong has this man done? I have found no reason to have him put to death. So I will just have him whipped and let him go."

[23]But with loud shouts they kept calling for Jesus to be crucified. The people's shouts won out. [24]So Pilate decided to give them what they wanted. [25]He set free the man they asked for. The man had been thrown in prison for murder and for fighting against the authorities. Pilate handed Jesus over to them so they could carry out their plans.

Jesus Is Nailed to a Cross

[26]As the soldiers led Jesus away, they took hold of Simon. Simon was from Cyrene. He was on his way in from the country. They put a wooden cross on his shoulders. Then they made him carry it behind Jesus. [27]A large number of people followed Jesus. Some were women whose hearts were filled with sorrow. They cried loudly because of him. [28]Jesus turned and said to them, "Daughters of Jerusalem, do not weep for me. Weep for yourselves and for your children. [29]The time will come when you will say, 'Blessed are the women who can't have children! Blessed are those who never gave birth or nursed babies!' [30]It is written,

"'The people will say to the mountains,
        "Fall on us!"
    They'll say to the hills, "Cover us!"'

(Hosea 10:8)

[31]People do these things when trees are green. So what will happen when trees are dry?"

[32]Two other men were also led out with Jesus to be killed. Both of them had broken the law. [33]The soldiers brought them to the place called the Skull. There they nailed Jesus to the cross. He hung between the two criminals. One was on his right and one was on his left. [34]Jesus said, "Father, forgive them. They don't know what they are doing." The soldiers divided up his clothes by casting lots.

[35]The people stood there watching. The rulers even made fun of Jesus. They said, "He saved others. Let him save himself if he is God's Messiah, the Chosen One."

[36]The soldiers also came up and poked fun at him. They offered him wine vinegar. [37]They said, "If you are the king of the Jews, save yourself."

[38]A written sign had been placed above him. It read,

THIS IS THE KING OF THE JEWS.

[39]One of the criminals hanging there made fun of Jesus. He said, "Aren't you the Messiah? Save yourself! Save us!"

[40]But the other criminal scolded him. "Don't you have any respect for God?" he said. "Remember, you are under the same sentence of death. [41]We are being punished fairly. We are getting just what our actions call for. But this man hasn't done anything wrong."

[42]Then he said, "Jesus, remember me when you come into your kingdom."

[43]Jesus answered him, "What I'm about to tell you is true. Today you will be with me in paradise."

Jesus Dies

[44]It was now about noon. Then darkness covered the whole land until three o'clock. [45]The sun had stopped shining. The temple curtain was torn in two. [46]Jesus called out in a loud voice, "Father, into your hands I commit my life." After he said this, he took his last breath.

[47]The Roman commander saw what had happened. He praised God and said, "Jesus was surely a man who did what was right." [48]The people had gathered to watch this sight. When they saw what happened, they felt very sad. Then they went away. [49]But all those who knew Jesus stood not very far away, watching these things. They included the women who had followed him from Galilee.

Jesus Is Buried

[50]A man named Joseph was a member of the Jewish Council. He was a good and honest man. [51]Joseph had not agreed with what the leaders had decided and done. He was from Arimathea, a town in Judea. He himself was waiting for God's kingdom. [52]Joseph went to Pilate and asked for Jesus' body. [53]Joseph took it down and wrapped it in linen cloth. Then he placed it in a tomb cut in the rock. No one had ever been buried there. [54]It was Preparation Day. The Sabbath day was about to begin.

[55]The women who had come with Jesus from Galilee followed Joseph. They saw the tomb and how Jesus' body was placed in it. [56]Then they went home. There they prepared spices and perfumes. But they rested on the Sabbath day in order to obey the Law.

Jesus Rises From the Dead

24 It was very early in the morning on the first day of the week. The women took the spices they had prepared. Then they went to the tomb. [2]They found the stone rolled away from it. [3]When they entered the tomb, they did not find the body of the Lord Jesus. [4]They were wondering about this. Suddenly two men in clothes as bright as lightning stood beside them. [5]The women were terrified. They bowed down with their faces to the ground. Then the men said to them, "Why do you look for the living among the dead? [6]Jesus is not here! He has risen! Remember how he told

you he would rise. It was while he was still with you in Galilee. [7]He said, 'The Son of Man must be handed over to sinful people. He must be nailed to a cross. On the third day he will rise from the dead.'" [8]Then the women remembered Jesus' words.

[9]They came back from the tomb. They told all these things to the 11 apostles and to all the others. [10]Mary Magdalene, Joanna, Mary the mother of James, and the others with them were the ones who told the apostles. [11]But the apostles did not believe the women. Their words didn't make any sense to them. [12]But Peter got up and ran to the tomb. He bent over and saw the strips of linen lying by themselves. Then he went away, wondering what had happened.

On the Road to Emmaus

[13]That same day two of Jesus' followers were going to a village called Emmaus. It was about seven miles from Jerusalem. [14]They were talking with each other about everything that had happened. [15]As they talked about those things, Jesus himself came up and walked along with them. [16]But God kept them from recognizing him.

[17]Jesus asked them, "What are you talking about as you walk along?"

They stood still, and their faces were sad. [18]One of them was named Cleopas. He said to Jesus, "Are you the only person visiting Jerusalem who doesn't know? Don't you know about the things that have happened there in the last few days?"

[19]"What things?" Jesus asked.

"About Jesus of Nazareth," they replied. "He was a prophet. He was powerful in what he said and did in the sight of God and all the people. [20]The chief priests and our rulers handed Jesus over to be sentenced to death. They nailed him to a cross. [21]But we had hoped that he was the one who was going to set Israel free. Also, it is the third day since all this happened. [22]Some of our women amazed us too. Early this morning they went to the tomb. [23]But they didn't find his body. So they came and told us what they had seen. They saw angels, who said Jesus was alive. [24]Then some of our friends went to the tomb. They saw it was empty, just as the women had said. They didn't see Jesus' body there."

[25]Jesus said to them, "How foolish you are! How long it takes you to believe all

that the prophets said! ²⁶Didn't the Messiah have to suffer these things and then receive his glory?" ²⁷Jesus explained to them what was said about himself in all the Scriptures. He began with Moses and all the Prophets.

²⁸They approached the village where they were going. Jesus kept walking as if he were going farther. ²⁹But they tried hard to keep him from leaving. They said, "Stay with us. It is nearly evening. The day is almost over." So he went in to stay with them.

³⁰He joined them at the table. Then he took bread and gave thanks. He broke it and began to give it to them. ³¹Their eyes were opened, and they recognized him. But then he disappeared from their sight. ³²They said to each other, "He explained to us what the Scriptures meant. Weren't we excited as he talked with us on the road?"

³³They got up and returned at once to Jerusalem. There they found the 11 disciples and those with them. They were all gathered together. ³⁴They were saying, "It's true! The Lord has risen! He has appeared to Simon!" ³⁵Then the two of them told what had happened to them on the way. They told how they had recognized Jesus when he broke the bread.

Jesus Appears to the Disciples

³⁶The disciples were still talking about this when Jesus himself suddenly stood among them. He said, "May you have peace!"

³⁷They were surprised and terrified. They thought they were seeing a ghost. ³⁸Jesus said to them, "Why are you troubled? Why do you have doubts in your minds? ³⁹Look at my hands and my feet. It's really me! Touch me and see. A ghost does not have a body or bones. But you can see that I do."

⁴⁰After he said that, he showed them his hands and feet. ⁴¹But they still did not believe it. They were amazed and filled with joy. So Jesus asked them, "Do you have anything here to eat?" ⁴²They gave him a piece of cooked fish. ⁴³He took it and ate it in front of them.

⁴⁴Jesus said to them, "This is what I told you while I was still with you. Everything

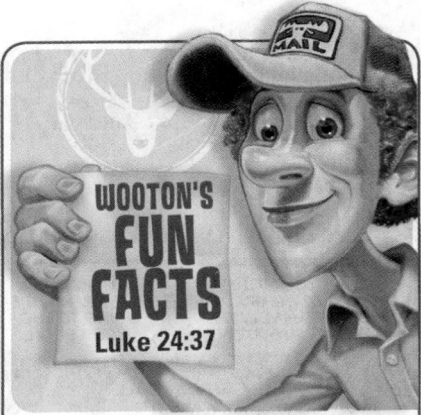

WOOTON'S FUN FACTS
Luke 24:37

This isn't the first time that Jesus' disciples thought He was a ghost. Check out Matthew 14:26 when Jesus was walking on the lake. Jesus is our Savior—with powers beyond what you can even imagine. That's *waaaay* better than a ghost!

written about me in the Law of Moses, the Prophets and the Psalms must come true."

⁴⁵Then he opened their minds so they could understand the Scriptures. ⁴⁶He told them, "This is what is written. The Messiah will suffer. He will rise from the dead on the third day. ⁴⁷His followers will preach in his name. They will tell others to turn away from their sins and be forgiven. People from every nation will hear it, beginning at Jerusalem. ⁴⁸You have seen these things with your own eyes. ⁴⁹I am going to send you what my Father has promised. But for now, stay in the city. Stay there until you have received power from heaven."

Jesus Is Taken Up Into Heaven

⁵⁰Jesus led his disciples out to the area near Bethany. Then he lifted up his hands and blessed them. ⁵¹While he was blessing them, he left them. He was taken up into heaven. ⁵²Then they worshiped him. With great joy, they returned to Jerusalem. ⁵³Every day they went to the temple, praising God.

IMAGINATION STATION ADVENTURES

MALCHUS'S EAR

Read Luke 22:47-53, John 18:25-27.

WHIT SENDS MATTHEW AND TORI TO THE GARDEN OF GETHSEMANE IN THE IMAGINATION STATION.

I THINK "THIS CUP" MEANS HE'S GOING TO THE CROSS SOON.

SHHH! YOU'LL WAKE THE DISCIPLES.

BUT—

FATHER, IF YOU'RE WILLING, REMOVE THIS CUP FROM ME.

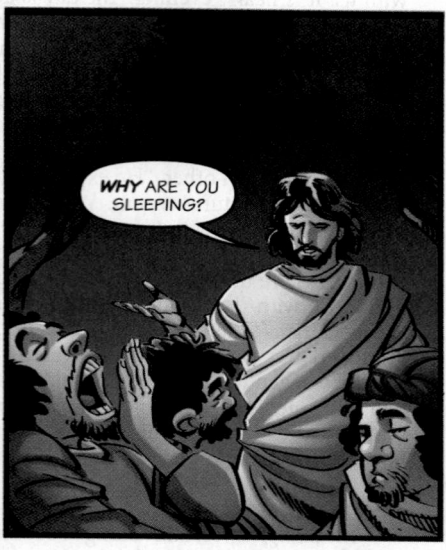

WHY ARE YOU SLEEPING?

JUDAS! WOULD YOU BETRAY ME WITH A KISS?

GRAB YOUR SWORDS!

LET MY FRIENDS GO THEIR WAY. DON'T HARM THEM.

1284

John

John is the last of the four gospels, but it is one of *five* Bible books that are traditionally credited to John, the apostle of Jesus. In addition to this gospel, John wrote three letters (1, 2, and 3 John) and the book of Revelation. Curiously, John rarely refers to himself by name. Instead he calls himself "the disciple Jesus loved." (See 13:23 and 19:26 for some examples.) But he must have started out with a rather boisterous personality, because Jesus nicknamed John and his brother James the "Sons of Thunder" (Mark 3:17).

Bible scholars are quick to point out that Matthew, Mark, and Luke are very similar in subject matter and presentation. John stands in contrast to the other three gospels. For example, Matthew and Luke begin with Jesus as a baby. Mark starts as Jesus begins His public ministry. But John starts "in the beginning," as in the very, very beginning. John is making a point that Jesus was already with God even before human time began. John also includes other information about Jesus exclusive to his gospel. Examples include Jesus' first miracle (2:1–11), His encounter with the woman at the well (4:1–42), and His raising of Lazarus (11:1–44). Everything in John's gospel was written so that his readers might believe in Jesus and discover the new life that only He can provide (20:31).

WHAT'S IT MEAN, EUGENE?

Communion—Also known as the Lord's Supper, Christians partake of bread and wine (or grape juice) in the same way the disciples did when Jesus shared the Passover meal with them. Christ said to "do this in memory of me." In so doing, we are "announcing the Lord's death until he comes again" (1 Corinthians 11:25, 26).

The Word Became a Human Being

In the beginning, the Word was already there. The Word was with God, and the Word was God. ²He was with God in the beginning. ³All things were made through him. Nothing that has been made was made without him. ⁴Life was in him, and that life was the light for all people. ⁵The light shines in the darkness. But the darkness has not overcome the light.

⁶There was a man sent from God. His name was John. ⁷He came to be a witness about that light. He was a witness so that all people might believe. ⁸John himself was not the light. He came only as a witness to the light.

⁹The true light that gives light to everyone was coming into the world. ¹⁰The Word was in the world. And the world was made through him. But the world did not recognize him. ¹¹He came to what was his own. But his own people did not accept him. ¹²Some people did accept him and did believe in his name. He gave them the right to become children of God. ¹³To be a child of God has nothing to do with human parents. Children of God are not born because of human choice or because a husband wants them to be born. They are born because of what God does.

¹⁴The Word became a human being. He made his home with us. We have seen his glory. It is the glory of the One and Only, who came from the Father. And the Word was full of grace and truth.

¹⁵John was a witness about the Word. John cried out and said, "This was the one I was talking about. I said, 'He who comes after me is more important than I am. He is more important because he existed before I was born.'" ¹⁶God is full of grace. From him we have all received grace in place of the grace already given. ¹⁷In the past, God gave us grace through the law of Moses. Now, grace and truth come to us through Jesus Christ. ¹⁸No one has ever seen God. But the One and Only is God and is at the Father's side. The one at the Father's side has shown us what God is like.

John the Baptist Says That He Is Not the Messiah

¹⁹The Jewish leaders in Jerusalem sent priests and Levites to ask John who he was. John spoke the truth to them. ²⁰He did not

John 1:15–37 Major confusion alert! This book is written by John and starts out talking about John the Baptist— but they are two different people. And now, spoiler alert! The writer is one of the disciples mentioned in verse 37.

try to hide the truth. He spoke to them openly. He said, "I am not the Messiah."

²¹They asked him, "Then who are you? Are you Elijah?"

He said, "I am not."

"Are you the Prophet we've been expecting?" they asked.

"No," he answered.

²²They asked one last time, "Who are you? Give us an answer to take back to those who sent us. What do you say about yourself?"

²³John replied, using the words of Isaiah the prophet. John said, "I'm the messenger who is calling out in the desert, 'Make the way for the Lord straight.'" *(Isaiah 40:3)*

²⁴The Pharisees who had been sent ²⁵asked him, "If you are not the Messiah, why are you baptizing people? Why are you doing that if you aren't Elijah or the Prophet we've been expecting?"

²⁶"I baptize people with water," John replied. "But someone is standing among you whom you do not know. ²⁷He is the one who comes after me. I am not good enough to untie his sandals."

²⁸This all happened at Bethany on the other side of the Jordan River. That was where John was baptizing.

What John Says About Jesus

²⁹The next day John saw Jesus coming toward him. John said, "Look! The Lamb of God! He takes away the sin of the world! ³⁰This is the one I was talking about. I said,

'A man who comes after me is more important than I am. That's because he existed before I was born.' ³¹I did not know him. But God wants to make it clear to Israel who this person is. That's the reason I came baptizing with water."

³²Then John told them, "I saw the Holy Spirit come down from heaven like a dove. The Spirit remained on Jesus. ³³I myself did not know him. But the one who sent me to baptize with water told me, 'You will see the Spirit come down and remain on someone. He is the one who will baptize with the Holy Spirit.' ³⁴I have seen it happen. I am a witness that this is God's Chosen One."

John's Disciples Follow Jesus

³⁵The next day John was there again with two of his disciples. ³⁶He saw Jesus walking by. John said, "Look! The Lamb of God!"

³⁷The two disciples heard him say this. So they followed Jesus. ³⁸Then Jesus turned around and saw them following. He asked, "What do you want?"

They said, "Rabbi, where are you staying?" Rabbi means Teacher.

³⁹"Come," he replied. "You will see."

So they went and saw where he was staying. They spent the rest of the day with him. It was about four o'clock in the afternoon.

⁴⁰Andrew was Simon Peter's brother. Andrew was one of the two disciples who heard what John had said. He had also followed Jesus. ⁴¹The first thing Andrew did was to find his brother Simon. He told him, "We have found the Messiah." Messiah means Christ. ⁴²And he brought Simon to Jesus.

Jesus looked at him and said, "You are Simon, son of John. You will be called Cephas." Cephas means Peter, or Rock.

Jesus Chooses Philip and Nathanael

⁴³The next day Jesus decided to leave for Galilee. He found Philip and said to him, "Follow me."

⁴⁴Philip was from the town of Bethsaida. So were Andrew and Peter. ⁴⁵Philip found Nathanael and told him, "We have found the one whom Moses wrote about in the Law. The prophets also wrote about him. He is Jesus of Nazareth, the son of Joseph."

⁴⁶"Nazareth! Can anything good come from there?" Nathanael asked.

"Come and see," said Philip.

⁴⁷Jesus saw Nathanael approaching. Here is what Jesus said about him. "He is a true Israelite. Nothing about him is false."

⁴⁸"How do you know me?" Nathanael asked.

Jesus answered, "I saw you while you were still under the fig tree. I saw you there before Philip called you."

⁴⁹Nathanael replied, "Rabbi, you are the Son of God. You are the king of Israel."

⁵⁰Jesus said, "You believe because I told you I saw you under the fig tree. You will see greater things than that." ⁵¹Then he said to the disciples, "What I'm about to tell you is true. You will see heaven open. You will see the angels of God going up and coming down on the Son of Man."

Jesus Changes Water Into Wine

2 On the third day there was a wedding. It took place at Cana in Galilee. Jesus' mother was there. ²Jesus and his disciples had also been invited to the wedding. ³When the wine was gone, Jesus' mother said to him, "They have no more wine."

⁴"Dear woman, why are you telling me about this?" Jesus replied. "The time for me to show who I really am isn't here yet."

⁵His mother said to the servants, "Do what he tells you."

⁶Six stone water jars stood nearby. The Jews used water from that kind of jar for special washings. They did that to make themselves pure and "clean." Each jar could hold 20 to 30 gallons.

⁷Jesus said to the servants, "Fill the jars with water." So they filled them to the top.

⁸Then he told them, "Now dip some out. Take it to the person in charge of the dinner."

They did what he said. ⁹The person in charge tasted the water that had been turned into wine. He didn't realize where it had come from. But the servants who had brought the water knew. Then the person in charge called the groom to one side. ¹⁰He said to him, "Everyone brings out the best wine first. They bring out the cheaper wine

BIBLE ADVENTURES

Kevin saw Jesus call Peter and Andrew in an Imagination Station adventure in "Hide and Seek" (A#31).

after the guests have had too much to drink. But you have saved the best until now."

[11]What Jesus did here in Cana in Galilee was the first of his signs. Jesus showed his glory by doing this sign. And his disciples believed in him.

[12]After this, Jesus went down to Capernaum. His mother and brothers and disciples went with him. They all stayed there for a few days.

Jesus Clears Out the Temple Courtyard

[13]It was almost time for the Jewish Passover Feast. So Jesus went up to Jerusalem. [14]In the temple courtyard he found people selling cattle, sheep and doves. Others were sitting at tables exchanging money. [15]So Jesus made a whip out of ropes. He chased all the sheep and cattle from the temple courtyard. He scattered the coins of the people exchanging money. And he turned over their tables. [16]He told those who were selling doves, "Get these out of here! Stop turning my Father's house into a market!" [17]His disciples remembered what had been written. It says, "My great love for your house will destroy me." *(Psalm 69:9)*

[18]Then the Jewish leaders asked him, "What sign can you show us to prove your authority to do this?"

[19]Jesus answered them, "When you destroy this temple, I will raise it up again in three days."

[20]They replied, "It has taken 46 years to build this temple. Are you going to raise it up in three days?" [21]But the temple Jesus had spoken about was his body. [22]His disciples later remembered what he had said. That was after he had been raised from the dead. Then they believed the Scripture. They also believed the words that Jesus had spoken.

[23]Meanwhile, he was in Jerusalem at the Passover Feast. Many people saw the signs he was doing. And they believed in his name. [24]But Jesus did not fully trust them. He knew what people are like. [25]He didn't need anyone to tell him what people are like. He already knew why people do what they do.

Jesus Teaches Nicodemus

3 There was a Pharisee named Nicodemus. He was one of the Jewish rulers. [2]He came to Jesus at night and said, "Rabbi,

WHIT'S WISDOM

John 3

Have you heard people talking about being "born again"? It's something that people talk about a lot, but do you know what it means?

The idea comes from John 3 when a man named Nicodemus visited Jesus. Jesus told Nicodemus, "No one can see God's kingdom unless they are born again." Does that sound confusing? Nicodemus was confused too. He didn't know how someone could be born a second time.

Jesus explained that we can't see God's Kingdom unless we are born again. He also said that we must be born with the Holy Spirit. God gives us our second birth.

Nicodemus still didn't understand. "How can this happen?" he asked.

Jesus told Nicodemus the way. You'll find it in a verse that you probably have heard before: John 3:16. Read it again, but try thinking "born again" when you read "have eternal life." Does it make sense to you now?

How can somebody be born again? Now you and Nicodemus both know. You can be born again by believing in Jesus! I remember the day that I was born again. I was a young boy and my stepmom Fionna walked me through it. I also remember the day that Connie became a Christian. It's always a special day when someone is born again. It's like celebrating a birthday, only much better!

we know that you are a teacher who has come from God. We know that God is with you. If he weren't, you couldn't do the signs you are doing."

³Jesus replied, "What I'm about to tell you is true. No one can see God's kingdom unless they are born again."

⁴"How can someone be born when they are old?" Nicodemus asked. "They can't go back inside their mother! They can't be born a second time!"

⁵Jesus answered, "What I'm about to tell you is true. No one can enter God's kingdom unless they are born with water and the Holy Spirit. ⁶People give birth to people. But the Spirit gives birth to spirit. ⁷You should not be surprised when I say, 'You must all be born again.' ⁸The wind blows where it wants to. You hear the sound it makes. But you can't tell where it comes from or where it is going. It is the same with everyone who is born with the Spirit."

⁹"How can this be?" Nicodemus asked.

¹⁰"You are Israel's teacher," said Jesus. "Don't you understand these things? ¹¹What I'm about to tell you is true. We speak about what we know. We are witnesses about what we have seen. But still you people do not accept what we say. ¹²I have spoken to you about earthly things, and you do not believe. So how will you believe if I speak about heavenly things? ¹³No one has ever gone into heaven except the one who came from heaven. He is the Son of Man. ¹⁴Moses lifted up the snake in the desert. In the same way, the Son of Man must also be lifted up. ¹⁵Then everyone who believes may have eternal life in him."

¹⁶God so loved the world that he gave his one and only Son. Anyone who believes in him will not die but will have eternal life. ¹⁷God did not send his Son into the world to judge the world. He sent his Son to save the world through him. ¹⁸Anyone who believes in him is not judged. But anyone who does not believe is judged already. They have not believed in the name of God's one

REMEMBER THIS

JOHN 3:16-17

"God so loved the world that he gave his one and only Son. Anyone who believes in him will not die but will have eternal life. God did not send his Son into the world to judge the world. He sent his Son to save the world through him."

and only Son. ¹⁹Here is the judgment. Light has come into the world, but people loved darkness instead of light. They loved darkness because what they did was evil. ²⁰Everyone who does evil deeds hates the light. They will not come into the light. They are afraid that what they do will be seen. ²¹But anyone who lives by the truth comes into the light. They live by the truth with God's help. They come into the light so that it will be easy to see their good deeds.

John the Baptist Is a Witness About Jesus

²²After this, Jesus and his disciples went out into the countryside of Judea. There he spent some time with them. And he baptized people there. ²³John was also baptizing. He was at Aenon near Salim, where there was plenty of water. People were coming and being baptized. ²⁴This was before John was put in prison. ²⁵Some of John's disciples and a certain Jew began to argue. They argued about special washings to make people "clean." ²⁶They came to John and here is what they said to him. "Rabbi, that man who was with you on the other side of the Jordan River is baptizing people. He is the one you told us about. Everyone is going to him."

²⁷John replied, "A person can receive only what God gives them from heaven. ²⁸You yourselves are witnesses that I said, 'I am not the Messiah. I was sent ahead of him.' ²⁹The bride belongs to the groom. The friend who helps the groom waits and listens for him. He is full of joy when he hears the groom's voice. That joy is mine, and it is now complete. ³⁰He must become more important. I must become less important. ³¹"The one who comes from above is above everything. The one who is from

BIBLE ADVENTURES

Harlowquin Doylecus, Private Roman Eye, interviewed Nicodemus about his talk with Jesus in "B-TV: To Tell the Truth" (Club).

the earth belongs to the earth and speaks like someone from the earth. The one who comes from heaven is above everything. [32]He is a witness to what he has seen and heard. But no one accepts what he says. [33]Anyone who has accepted it has said, 'Yes. God is truthful.' [34]The one whom God has sent speaks God's words. That's because God gives the Holy Spirit without limit. [35]The Father loves the Son and has put everything into his hands. [36]Anyone who believes in the Son has eternal life. Anyone who does not believe in the Son will not have life. God's anger remains on them."

Jesus Talks With a Woman From Samaria

4 Now Jesus learned that the Pharisees had heard about him. They had heard that he was gaining and baptizing more disciples than John. [2]But in fact Jesus was not baptizing. His disciples were. [3]So Jesus left Judea and went back again to Galilee.

[4]Jesus had to go through Samaria. [5]He came to a town in Samaria called Sychar. It was near the piece of land Jacob had given his son Joseph. [6]Jacob's well was there. Jesus was tired from the journey. So he sat down by the well. It was about noon.

[7]A woman from Samaria came to get some water. Jesus said to her, "Will you give me a drink?" [8]His disciples had gone into the town to buy food.

[9]The Samaritan woman said to him, "You are a Jew. I am a Samaritan woman. How can you ask me for a drink?" She said this because Jews don't have anything to do with Samaritans.

[10]Jesus answered her, "You do not know what God's gift is. And you do not know who is asking you for a drink. If you did, you would have asked him. He would have given you living water."

[11]"Sir," the woman said, "you don't have anything to get water with. The well is deep. Where can you get this living water? [12]Our father Jacob gave us the well. He drank from it himself. So did his sons and his livestock. Are you more important than he is?"

[13]Jesus answered, "Everyone who drinks this water will be thirsty again. [14]But anyone who drinks the water I give them will never be thirsty. In fact, the water I give them will become a spring of water in them. It will flow up into eternal life."

[15]The woman said to him, "Sir, give me this water. Then I will never be thirsty. And I won't have to keep coming here to get water."

[16]He told her, "Go. Get your husband and come back."

[17]"I have no husband," she replied.

Jesus said to her, "You are right when you say you have no husband. [18]The fact is, you have had five husbands. And the man you live with now is not your husband. What you have just said is very true."

[19]"Sir," the woman said, "I can see that you are a prophet. [20]Our people have always worshiped on this mountain. But you Jews claim that the place where we must worship is in Jerusalem."

[21]Jesus said, "Woman, believe me. A time is coming when you will not worship the Father on this mountain or in Jerusalem. [22]You Samaritans worship what you do not know. We worship what we do know. Salvation comes from the Jews. [23]But a new time is coming. In fact, it is already here. True worshipers will worship the Father in the Spirit and in truth. They are the kind of worshipers the Father is looking for. [24]God is spirit. His worshipers must worship him in the Spirit and in truth."

[25]The woman said, "I know that Messiah is coming." Messiah means Christ. "When he comes, he will explain everything to us."

[26]Then Jesus said, "The one you're talking about is the one speaking to you. I am he."

The Disciples Join Jesus Again

[27]Just then Jesus' disciples returned. They were surprised to find him talking with a woman. But no one asked, "What do you want from her?" No one asked, "Why are you talking with her?"

[28]The woman left her water jar and went back to the town. She said to the people, [29]"Come. See a man who told me everything I've ever done. Could this be the Messiah?" [30]The people came out of the town and made their way toward Jesus.

[31]His disciples were saying to him, "Rabbi, eat something!"

[32]But he said to them, "I have food to eat that you know nothing about."

[33]Then his disciples asked each other, "Did someone bring him food?"

[34]Jesus said, "My food is to do what my Father sent me to do. My food is to finish

his work. [35]Don't you have a saying? You say, 'It's still four months until harvest time.' But I tell you, open your eyes! Look at the fields! They are ripe for harvest right now. [36]Even now the one who gathers the crop is getting paid. They are already harvesting the crop for eternal life. So the one who plants and the one who gathers can now be glad together. [37]Here is a true saying. 'One plants and another gathers.' [38]I sent you to gather what you have not worked for. Others have done the hard work. You have gathered the benefits of their work."

Many Samaritans Believe in Jesus

[39]Many of the Samaritans from the town of Sychar believed in Jesus. They believed because of what the woman had said about him. She said, "He told me everything I've ever done." [40]Then the Samaritans came to him and tried to get him to stay with them. So he stayed two days. [41]Because of what he said, many more people became believers.

[42]They said to the woman, "We no longer believe just because of what you said. We have now heard for ourselves. We know that this man really is the Savior of the world."

Jesus Heals an Official's Son

[43]After the two days, Jesus left for Galilee. [44]He himself had pointed out that a prophet is not respected in his own country. [45]When he arrived in Galilee, the people living there welcomed him. They had seen everything he had done in Jerusalem at the Passover Feast. That was because they had also been there.

[46]Once more, Jesus visited Cana in Galilee. Cana is where he had turned the water into wine. A royal official was there. His son was sick in bed at Capernaum. [47]The official heard that Jesus had arrived in Galilee from Judea. So he went to Jesus and begged him to come and heal his son. The boy was close to death.

[48]Jesus told him, "You people will never believe unless you see signs and wonders."

[49]The royal official said, "Sir, come down before my child dies."

[50]"Go," Jesus replied. "Your son will live." The man believed what Jesus said, and so he left. [51]While he was still on his way home, his slaves met him. They gave him the news that his boy was living. [52]He asked what time his son got better. They said to

him, "Yesterday, at one o'clock in the afternoon, the fever left him."

[53]Then the father realized what had happened. That was the exact time Jesus had said to him, "Your son will live." So he and his whole family became believers.

[54]This was the second sign that Jesus did after coming from Judea to Galilee.

Jesus Heals a Man at the Pool

5 Some time later, Jesus went up to Jerusalem for one of the Jewish feasts. [2]In Jerusalem near the Sheep Gate is a pool. In the Aramaic language it is called Bethesda. It is surrounded by five rows of columns with a roof over them. [3-4]Here a great number of disabled people used to lie down. Among them were those who were blind, those who could not walk, and those who could hardly move. [5]One person was there who had not been able to walk for 38 years. [6]Jesus saw him lying there. He knew that the man had been in that condition for a long time. So he asked him, "Do you want to get well?"

[7]"Sir," the disabled man replied, "I have no one to help me into the pool when an angel stirs up the water. I try to get in, but someone else always goes down ahead of me."

[8]Then Jesus said to him, "Get up! Pick up your mat and walk." [9]The man was healed right away. He picked up his mat and walked.

This happened on a Sabbath day. [10]So the Jewish leaders said to the man who had been healed, "It is the Sabbath day. The law does not allow you to carry your mat."

[11]But he replied, "The one who made me well said to me, 'Pick up your mat and walk.'"

[12]They asked him, "Who is this fellow? Who told you to pick it up and walk?"

[13]The one who was healed had no idea who it was. Jesus had slipped away into the crowd that was there.

[14]Later Jesus found him at the temple. Jesus said to him, "See, you are well again. Stop sinning, or something worse may happen to you." [15]The man went away. He told the Jewish leaders it was Jesus who had made him well.

The Authority of the Son

[16]Jesus was doing these things on the Sabbath day. So the Jewish leaders began to oppose him. [17]Jesus defended himself. He said to them, "My Father is always doing

his work. He is working right up to this day. I am working too." [18]For this reason the Jewish leaders tried even harder to kill him. According to them, Jesus was not only breaking the law of the Sabbath day. He was even calling God his own Father. He was making himself equal with God.

[19]Jesus answered, "What I'm about to tell you is true. The Son can do nothing by himself. He can do only what he sees his Father doing. What the Father does, the Son also does. [20]This is because the Father loves the Son. The Father shows him everything he does. Yes, and the Father will show the Son even greater works than these. And you will be amazed. [21]The Father raises the dead and gives them life. In the same way, the Son gives life to anyone he wants to. [22]Also, the Father does not judge anyone. He has given the Son the task of judging. [23]Then all people will honor the Son just as they honor the Father. Whoever does not honor the Son does not honor the Father, who sent him.

[24]"What I'm about to tell you is true. Anyone who hears my word and believes him who sent me has eternal life. They will not be judged. They have crossed over from death to life. [25]What I'm about to tell you is true. A time is coming for me to give life. In fact, it has already begun. The dead will hear the voice of the Son of God. Those who hear it will live. [26]The Father has life in himself. He has allowed the Son also to have life in himself. [27]And the Father has given him the authority to judge. This is because he is the Son of Man.

[28]"Do not be amazed at this. A time is coming when all who are in their graves will hear his voice. [29]They will all come out of their graves. People who have done what is good will rise and live again. People who have done what is evil will rise and be found guilty. [30]I can do nothing by myself. I judge only as I hear. And my judging is fair. I do not try to please myself. I try to please the one who sent me.

Being a Witness About Jesus

[31]"If I am a witness about myself, what I say is not true. [32]There is someone else who is a witness in my favor. And I know that what he says about me is true.

[33]"You have sent people to John the Baptist. He has been a witness to the truth. [34]I do not accept what a person says. I only talk about what John says so that you can be saved. [35]John was like a lamp that burned and gave light. For a while you chose to enjoy his light.

[36]"What I say about myself is more important than what John says about me. I am doing the works the Father gave me to finish. These works are a witness that the Father has sent me. [37]The Father who sent me is himself a witness about me. You have never heard his voice. You have never seen what he really looks like. [38]And his word does not live in you. That's because you do not believe the one he sent. [39]You study the Scriptures carefully. You study them because you think they will give you eternal life. The Scriptures you study are a witness about me. [40]But you refuse to come to me and receive life.

[41]"I do not accept praise from human beings. [42]But I know you. I know that you do not have love for God in your hearts. [43]I have come in my Father's name, and you do not accept me. But if someone else comes in his own name, you will accept him. [44]You accept praise from one another. But you do not seek the praise that comes from the only God. So how can you believe?

[45]"Do not think I will bring charges against you in front of the Father. Moses is the one who does that. And he is the one you build your hopes on. [46]Do you believe Moses? Then you should believe me. He wrote about me. [47]But you do not believe what he wrote. So how are you going to believe what I say?"

Jesus Feeds the Five Thousand

6 Some time after this, Jesus crossed over to the other side of the Sea of Galilee. It is also called the Sea of Tiberias. [2]A large crowd of people followed him. They had seen the signs he had done by healing sick people. [3]Then Jesus went up on a mountainside. There he sat down with his disciples. [4]The Jewish Passover Feast was near.

[5]Jesus looked up and saw a large crowd coming toward him. So he said to Philip, "Where can we buy bread for these people to eat?" [6]He asked this only to test Philip. He already knew what he was going to do.

[7]Philip answered him, "Suppose we were able to buy enough bread for each person to have just a bite. That would take more than half a year's pay!"

[8]Another of his disciples spoke up. It was Andrew, Simon Peter's brother. He said, [9]"Here is a boy with five small loaves of barley bread. He also has two small fish. But how far will that go in such a large crowd?"

[10]Jesus said, "Have the people sit down." There was plenty of grass in that place, and they sat down. About 5,000 men were there. [11]Then Jesus took the loaves and gave thanks. He handed out the bread to those who were seated. He gave them as much as they wanted. And he did the same with the fish.

[12]When all of them had enough to eat, Jesus spoke to his disciples. "Gather the leftover pieces," he said. "Don't waste anything." [13]So they gathered what was left over from the five barley loaves. They filled 12 baskets with the pieces left by those who had eaten.

[14]The people saw the sign that Jesus did. Then they began to say, "This must be the Prophet who is supposed to come into the world." [15]But Jesus knew that they planned to come and force him to be their king. So he went away again to a mountain by himself.

Jesus Walks on the Water

[16]When evening came, Jesus' disciples went down to the Sea of Galilee. [17]There they got into a boat and headed across the lake toward Capernaum. By now it was dark. Jesus had not yet joined them. [18]A strong wind was blowing, and the water became rough. [19]They rowed about three or four miles. Then they saw Jesus coming toward the boat. He was walking on the water. They were frightened. [20]But he said to them, "It is I. Don't be afraid." [21]Then they agreed to take him into the boat. Right away the boat reached the shore where they were heading.

[22]The next day the crowd that had stayed on the other side of the lake realized something. They saw that only one boat had been there. They knew that Jesus had not gotten into it with his disciples. And they knew that the disciples had gone away alone. [23]Then some boats arrived from Tiberias. It was near the place where the people had eaten the bread after the Lord gave thanks. [24]The crowd realized that Jesus and his disciples were not there. So they got into boats and went to Capernaum to look for Jesus.

Jesus Is the Bread of Life

[25]They found him on the other side of the lake. They asked him, "Rabbi, when did you get here?"

[26]Jesus answered, "What I'm about to tell you is true. You are not looking for me because you saw the signs I did. You are looking for me because you ate the loaves until you were full. [27]Do not work for food that spoils. Work for food that lasts forever. That is the food the Son of Man will give you. For God the Father has put his seal of approval on him."

[28]Then they asked him, "What does God want from us? What works does he want us to do?"

[29]Jesus answered, "God's work is to believe in the one he has sent."

[30]So they asked him, "What sign will you give us? What will you do so we can see it and believe you? [31]Long ago our people ate the manna in the desert. It is written in Scripture, 'The Lord gave them bread from heaven to eat.'" (Exodus 16:4; Nehemiah 9:15; Psalm 78:24,25)

[32]Jesus said to them, "What I'm about to tell you is true. It is not Moses who has given you the bread from heaven. It is my Father who gives you the true bread from heaven. [33]The bread of God is the bread that comes down from heaven. He gives life to the world."

[34]"Sir," they said, "always give us this bread."

[35]Then Jesus said, "I am the bread of life. Whoever comes to me will never go hungry. And whoever believes in me will never be thirsty. [36]But it is just as I told you. You have seen me, and you still do not believe. [37]Everyone the Father gives me will come to me. I will never send away anyone who comes to me. [38]I have not come down from heaven to do what I want to do. I have come to do what the one who sent me wants me to do. [39]The one who sent me doesn't want me to lose anyone he has given me. He wants me to raise them up on the last day. [40]My Father wants all who look to the Son and believe in him to have eternal life. I will raise them up on the last day."

[41]Then the Jews there began to complain about Jesus. That was because he said, "I am the bread that came down from heaven." [42]They said, "Isn't this Jesus, the son of Joseph? Don't we know his father and

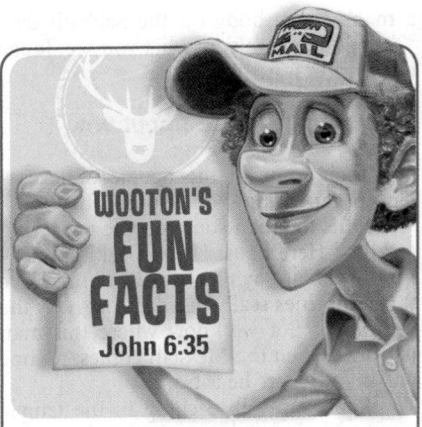

WOOTON'S FUN FACTS

John 6:35

Jesus makes seven "I am the" statements in this book: (1) Bread, (2) Light, (3) Door, (4) Good Shepherd, (5) Resurrection and the Life, (6) the Way, the Truth, and the Life, and (7) Vine. Seven is sometimes called "God's number." How many sevens can you find in the Bible?

mother? How can he now say, 'I came down from heaven'?"

⁴³"Stop complaining among yourselves," Jesus answered. ⁴⁴"No one can come to me unless the Father who sent me brings them. Then I will raise them up on the last day. ⁴⁵It is written in the Prophets, 'God will teach all of them.' *(Isaiah 54:13)* Everyone who has heard the Father and learned from him comes to me. ⁴⁶No one has seen the Father except the one who has come from God. Only he has seen the Father. ⁴⁷What I'm about to tell you is true. Everyone who believes has life forever. ⁴⁸I am the bread of life. ⁴⁹Long ago your people ate the manna in the desert, and they still died. ⁵⁰But here is the bread that comes down from heaven. A person can eat it and not die. ⁵¹I am the living bread that came down from heaven. Everyone who eats some of this bread will live forever. This bread is my body. I will give it for the life of the world."

⁵²Then the Jews began to argue sharply among themselves. They said, "How can this man give us his body to eat?"

⁵³Jesus said to them, "What I'm about to tell you is true. You must eat the Son of Man's body and drink his blood. If you don't, you have no life in you. ⁵⁴Anyone who eats my body and drinks my blood has eternal life. I will raise them up on the last day. ⁵⁵My

body is real food. My blood is real drink. ⁵⁶Anyone who eats my body and drinks my blood remains in me. And I remain in them. ⁵⁷The living Father sent me, and I live because of him. In the same way, those who feed on me will live because of me. ⁵⁸This is the bread that came down from heaven. Long ago your people ate manna and died. But whoever eats this bread will live forever." ⁵⁹He said this while he was teaching in the synagogue in Capernaum.

Many Disciples Leave Jesus

⁶⁰Jesus' disciples heard this. Many of them said, "This is a hard teaching. Who can accept it?"

⁶¹Jesus was aware that his disciples were complaining about his teaching. So he said to them, "Does this upset you? ⁶²Then what if you see the Son of Man go up to where he was before? ⁶³The Holy Spirit gives life. The body means nothing at all. The words I have spoken to you are full of the Spirit. They give life. ⁶⁴But there are some of you who do not believe." Jesus had known from the beginning which of them did not believe. And he had known who was going to hand him over to his enemies. ⁶⁵So he continued speaking. He said, "This is why I told you that no one can come to me unless the Father helps them."

⁶⁶From this time on, many of his disciples turned back. They no longer followed him.

⁶⁷"You don't want to leave also, do you?" Jesus asked the 12 disciples.

⁶⁸Simon Peter answered him, "Lord, who can we go to? You have the words of eternal life. ⁶⁹We have come to believe and to know that you are the Holy One of God."

⁷⁰Then Jesus replied, "Didn't I choose you, the 12 disciples? But one of you is a devil!" ⁷¹He meant Judas, the son of Simon Iscariot. Judas was one of the 12 disciples. But later he was going to hand Jesus over to his enemies.

Jesus Goes to the Feast of Booths

7 After this, Jesus went around in Galilee. He didn't want to travel around in Judea. That was because the Jewish leaders there were looking for a way to kill him. ²The Jewish Feast of Booths was near. ³Jesus' brothers said to him, "Leave Galilee and go to Judea. Then your disciples there will see the works that you do. ⁴No one who wants to be well known does things in secret. Since you are doing these things, show yourself to the world." ⁵Even Jesus' own brothers did not believe in him.

⁶So Jesus told them, "The time for me to show who I really am is not here yet. For you, any time would be the right time. ⁷The people of the world can't hate you. But they hate me. This is because I am a witness that their works are evil. ⁸You go to the feast. I am not going up to this feast. This is because my time has not yet fully come." ⁹After he said this, he stayed in Galilee.

¹⁰But when his brothers had left for the feast, he went also. But he went secretly, not openly. ¹¹At the feast the Jewish leaders were watching for Jesus. They were asking, "Where is he?"

¹²Many people in the crowd were whispering about him. Some said, "He is a good man."

Others replied, "No. He fools the people." ¹³But no one would say anything about him openly. They were afraid of the leaders.

Jesus Teaches at the Feast

¹⁴Jesus did nothing until halfway through the feast. Then he went up to the temple courtyard and began to teach. ¹⁵The Jews there were amazed. They asked, "How did this man learn so much without being taught?"

¹⁶Jesus answered, "What I teach is not my own. It comes from the one who sent me. ¹⁷Here is how someone can find out whether my teaching comes from God or from me. That person must choose to do what God wants them to do. ¹⁸Whoever speaks on their own does it to get personal honor. But someone who works for the honor of the one who sent him is truthful. Nothing about him is false. ¹⁹Didn't Moses give you the law? But not one of you obeys the law. Why are you trying to kill me?"

²⁰"You are controlled by demons," the crowd answered. "Who is trying to kill you?"

²¹Jesus said to them, "I did one miracle, and you are all amazed. ²²Moses gave you circumcision, and so you circumcise a child on the Sabbath day. But circumcision did not really come from Moses. It came from Abraham. ²³You circumcise a boy on the Sabbath day. You think that if you do, you won't break the law of Moses. Then why are you angry with me? I healed

a man's entire body on the Sabbath day! ²⁴Stop judging only by what you see. Judge in the right way."

People Don't Agree About Who Jesus Is

²⁵Then some of the people of Jerusalem began asking questions. They said, "Isn't this the man some people are trying to kill? ²⁶Here he is! He is speaking openly. They aren't saying a word to him. Have the authorities really decided that he is the Messiah? ²⁷But we know where this man is from. When the Messiah comes, no one will know where he is from."

²⁸Jesus was still teaching in the temple courtyard. He cried out, "Yes, you know me. And you know where I am from. I am not here on my own authority. The one who sent me is true. You do not know him. ²⁹But I know him. I am from him, and he sent me."

³⁰When he said this, they tried to arrest him. But no one laid a hand on him. The time for him to show who he really was had not yet come. ³¹Still, many people in the crowd believed in him. They said, "How will it be when the Messiah comes? Will he do more signs than this man?"

³²The Pharisees heard the crowd whispering things like this about him. Then the chief priests and the Pharisees sent temple guards to arrest him.

³³Jesus said, "I am with you for only a short time. Then I will go to the one who sent me. ³⁴You will look for me, but you won't find me. You can't come where I am going."

³⁵The Jews said to one another, "Where does this man plan to go? Does he think we can't find him? Will he go where our people live scattered among the Greeks? Will he go there to teach the Greeks? ³⁶What did he mean when he said, 'You will look for me, but you won't find me'? And what did he mean when he said, 'You can't come where I am going'?"

³⁷It was the last and most important day of the feast. Jesus stood up and spoke in a loud voice. He said, "Let anyone who is thirsty come to me and drink. ³⁸Does anyone believe in me? Then, just as Scripture says, rivers of living water will flow from inside them." ³⁹When he said this, he meant the Holy Spirit. Those who believed in Jesus would receive the Spirit later. Up to that

time, the Spirit had not been given. This was because Jesus had not yet received glory.

[40]The people heard his words. Some of them said, "This man must be the Prophet we've been expecting."

[41]Others said, "He is the Messiah."

Still others asked, "How can the Messiah come from Galilee? [42]Doesn't Scripture say that the Messiah will come from the family line of David? Doesn't it say that he will come from Bethlehem, the town where David lived?" [43]So the people did not agree about who Jesus was. [44]Some wanted to arrest him. But no one laid a hand on him.

The Jewish Leaders Do Not Believe

[45]Finally the temple guards went back to the chief priests and the Pharisees. They asked the guards, "Why didn't you bring him in?"

[46]"No one ever spoke the way this man does," the guards replied.

[47]"You mean he has fooled you also?" the Pharisees asked. [48]"Have any of the rulers or Pharisees believed in him? [49]No! But this mob knows nothing about the law. There is a curse on them."

[50]Then Nicodemus, a Pharisee, spoke. He was the one who had gone to Jesus earlier. He asked, [51]"Does our law find a man guilty without hearing him first? Doesn't it want to find out what he is doing?"

[52]They replied, "Are you from Galilee too? Look into it. You will find that a prophet does not come out of Galilee."

8 [53]Then they all went home. [1]But Jesus went to the Mount of Olives.

[2]At sunrise he arrived again in the temple courtyard. All the people gathered around him there. He sat down to teach them. [3]The teachers of the law and the Pharisees brought in a woman. She had been caught committing adultery. They made her stand in front of the group. [4]They said to Jesus, "Teacher, this woman was caught sleeping with a man who was not her husband. [5]In the Law, Moses commanded us to kill such women by throwing stones at them. Now what do you say?" [6]They were trying to trap Jesus with that question. They wanted to have a reason to bring charges against him.

But Jesus bent down and started to write on the ground with his finger. [7]They kept asking him questions. So he stood up and said to them, "Has any one of you not sinned? Then you be the first to throw a stone at her." [8]He bent down again and wrote on the ground.

[9]Those who heard what he had said began to go away. They left one at a time, the older ones first. Soon only Jesus was left. The woman was still standing there. [10]Jesus stood up and asked her, "Woman, where are they? Hasn't anyone found you guilty?"

[11]"No one, sir," she said.

"Then I don't find you guilty either," Jesus said. "Go now and leave your life of sin."

Challenge to What Jesus Says About Himself

[12]Jesus spoke to the people again. He said, "I am the light of the world. Anyone who follows me will never walk in darkness. They will have that light. They will have life."

[13]The Pharisees argued with him. "Here you are," they said, "appearing as your own witness. But your witness does not count."

[14]Jesus answered, "Even if I am a witness about myself, what I say does count. I know where I came from. And I know where I am going. But you have no idea where I come from or where I am going. [15]You judge by human standards. I don't judge anyone. [16]But if I do judge, what I decide is true. This is because I am not alone. I stand with the Father, who sent me. [17]Your own Law says that the witness of two people proves the truth about something. [18]I am a witness about myself. The other witness about me is the Father, who sent me."

[19]Then they asked him, "Where is your father?"

"You do not know me or my Father," Jesus replied. "If you knew me, you would know my Father also." [20]He spoke these words while he was teaching in the temple courtyard. He was near the place where the offerings were put. But no one arrested him. That's because the time for him to die had not yet come.

Challenge to Who Jesus Claims to Be

[21]Once more Jesus said to them, "I am going away. You will look for me, and you will die in your sin. You can't come where I am going."

[22]This made the Jews ask, "Will he kill himself? Is that why he says, 'You can't come where I am going'?"

²³But Jesus said, "You are from below. I am from heaven. You are from this world. I am not from this world. ²⁴I told you that you would die in your sins. This will happen if you don't believe that I am he. If you don't believe, you will certainly die in your sins."

²⁵"Who are you?" they asked.

"Just what I have been telling you from the beginning," Jesus replied. ²⁶"I have a lot to say that will judge you. But the one who sent me can be trusted. And I tell the world what I have heard from him."

²⁷They did not understand that Jesus was telling them about his Father. ²⁸So Jesus said, "You will lift up the Son of Man. Then you will know that I am he. You will also know that I do nothing on my own. I speak just what the Father has taught me. ²⁹The one who sent me is with me. He has not left me alone, because I always do what pleases him." ³⁰Even while Jesus was speaking, many people believed in him.

Challenge to the Claim to Be Children of Abraham

³¹Jesus spoke to the Jews who had believed him. "If you obey my teaching," he said, "you are really my disciples. ³²Then you will know the truth. And the truth will set you free."

³³They answered him, "We are Abraham's children. We have never been slaves of anyone. So how can you say that we will be set free?"

³⁴Jesus replied, "What I'm about to tell you is true. Everyone who sins is a slave of sin. ³⁵A slave has no lasting place in the family. But a son belongs to the family forever. ³⁶So if the Son of Man sets you free, you will really be free. ³⁷I know that you are Abraham's children. But you are looking for a way to kill me. You have no room for my word. ³⁸I am telling you what I saw when I was with my Father. You are doing what you have heard from your father."

³⁹"Abraham is our father," they answered.

Jesus said, "Are you really Abraham's children? If you are, you will do what Abraham did. ⁴⁰But you are looking for a way to kill me. I am a man who has told you the truth I heard from God. Abraham didn't do the things you want to do. ⁴¹You are doing what your own father does."

"We have the right to claim to be God's children," they objected. "The only Father we have is God himself."

Ugh. Homework. Or chores. Wouldn't it be more fun to go on an adventure like the ones in movies? Some people in Odyssey once thought the same thing when a film crew came to town. But they soon found out that while movies can be entertaining, there's something even bigger and better than made-up stories. It's called "real life"—taking part in God's story.

How can life be more exciting than your favorite film? It's not as if you get to fight killer robots or discover ancient ruins, mummies, and treasure. Besides, movie heroes don't have to feed the cat, clean their rooms, and take out the trash. They just go from one adventure to another. How could your life be more exciting than all of that?

In John 8:32, Jesus says, "The truth will set you free." The truth is that God has given you a very special purpose in life, something that you—and only you—can do for Him. Sometimes that special thing might look boring. It might seem unimportant. Especially when you compare it with the heroics in a blockbuster film. But here's the difference: The things you do have an eternal impact. You might be able to tell someone about Jesus. Maybe you can help a friend who is having a bad day. When we live for Jesus, no task is boring or insignificant.

So think of three "boring" things you can do today that will serve others and, in the end, give God glory.

ADVENTURES IN ODYSSEY

Knowing the truth is important, whether it's the truth about Jesus . . . or the truth behind a Hollywood movie version of Odyssey! Eugene and Connie found this out in "A Day in the Life" (A#11).

⁴²Jesus said to them, "If God were your Father, you would love me. I have come here from God. I have not come on my own. God sent me. ⁴³Why aren't my words clear to you? Because you can't really hear what I say. ⁴⁴You belong to your father, the devil. You want to obey your father's wishes. From the beginning, the devil was a murderer. He has never obeyed the truth. There is no truth in him. When he lies, he speaks his natural language. He does this because he is a liar. He is the father of lies. ⁴⁵But because I tell the truth, you don't believe me! ⁴⁶Can any of you prove I am guilty of sinning? Am I not telling the truth? Then why don't you believe me? ⁴⁷Whoever belongs to God hears what God says. The reason you don't hear is that you don't belong to God."

Jesus Makes Claims About Himself

⁴⁸The Jews answered Jesus, "Aren't we right when we say you are a Samaritan? Aren't you controlled by a demon?"

⁴⁹"I am not controlled by a demon," said Jesus. "I honor my Father. You do not honor me. ⁵⁰I am not seeking glory for myself. But there is one who brings glory to me. He is the judge. ⁵¹What I'm about to tell you is true. Whoever obeys my word will never die."

⁵²Then they cried out, "Now we know you are controlled by a demon! Abraham died. So did the prophets. But you say that whoever obeys your word will never die. ⁵³Are you greater than our father Abraham? He died. So did the prophets. Who do you think you are?"

⁵⁴Jesus replied, "If I bring glory to myself, my glory means nothing. You claim that my Father is your God. He is the one who brings glory to me. ⁵⁵You do not know him. But I know him. If I said I did not, I would be a liar like you. But I do know him. And I obey his word. ⁵⁶Your father Abraham was filled with joy at the thought of seeing my day. He saw it and was glad."

⁵⁷"You are not even 50 years old," they said to Jesus. "And you have seen Abraham?"

⁵⁸"What I'm about to tell you is true," Jesus answered. "Before Abraham was born, I am!" ⁵⁹When he said this, they picked up stones to kill him. But Jesus hid himself. He slipped away from the temple area.

Jesus Heals a Man Born Blind

9 As Jesus went along, he saw a man who was blind. He had been blind since he was born. ²Jesus' disciples asked him, "Rabbi, who sinned? Was this man born blind because he sinned? Or did his parents sin?"

³"It isn't because this man sinned," said Jesus. "It isn't because his parents sinned. He was born blind so that God's power could be shown by what's going to happen. ⁴While it is still day, we must do the works of the one who sent me. Night is coming. Then no one can work. ⁵While I am in the world, I am the light of the world."

⁶After he said this, he spit on the ground. He made some mud with the spit. Then he put the mud on the man's eyes. ⁷"Go," he told him. "Wash in the Pool of Siloam." Siloam means Sent. So the man went and washed. And he came home able to see.

⁸His neighbors and people who had seen him earlier begging asked questions. "Isn't this the same man who used to sit and beg?" they asked. ⁹Some claimed that he was.

Others said, "No. He only looks like him."

But the man who had been blind kept saying, "I am the man."

¹⁰"Then how were your eyes opened?" they asked.

¹¹He replied, "The man they call Jesus made some mud and put it on my eyes. He

John 9:6 I'm sure you've heard people say to "be like Jesus." But in this verse, Jesus spit on someone and it's a miracle. If you spit on someone, it's a reason for a time out. Take my advice and work on being like Jesus in other ways.

told me to go to Siloam and wash. So I went and washed. Then I could see."

[12]"Where is this man?" they asked him. "I don't know," he said.

The Pharisees Want to Know How the Blind Man Was Healed

[13]They brought to the Pharisees the man who had been blind. [14]The day Jesus made the mud and opened the man's eyes was a Sabbath day. [15]So the Pharisees also asked him how he was able to see. "He put mud on my eyes," the man replied. "Then I washed. And now I can see."

[16]Some of the Pharisees said, "Jesus has not come from God. He does not keep the Sabbath day."

But others asked, "How can a sinner do such signs?" So the Pharisees did not agree with one another.

[17]Then they turned again to the blind man. "What do you have to say about him?" they asked. "It was your eyes he opened."

The man replied, "He is a prophet."

[18]They still did not believe that the man had been blind and now could see. So they sent for his parents. [19]"Is this your son?" they asked. "Is this the one you say was born blind? How is it that now he can see?"

[20]"We know he is our son," the parents answered. "And we know he was born blind. [21]But we don't know how he can now see. And we don't know who opened his eyes. Ask him. He is an adult. He can speak

for himself." [22]His parents said this because they were afraid of the Jewish leaders. The leaders had already made this decision about Jesus. Anyone who said Jesus was the Messiah would be put out of the synagogue. [23]That was why the man's parents said, "He is an adult. Ask him."

[24]Again the Pharisees called the man who had been blind to come to them. "Give glory to God by telling the truth!" they said. "We know that the man who healed you is a sinner."

[25]He replied, "I don't know if he is a sinner or not. I do know one thing. I was blind, but now I can see!"

[26]Then they asked him, "What did he do to you? How did he open your eyes?"

[27]He answered, "I have already told you. But you didn't listen. Why do you want to hear it again? Do you want to become his disciples too?"

[28]Then they began to attack him with their words. "You are this fellow's disciple!" they said. "We are disciples of Moses! [29]We know that God spoke to Moses. But we don't even know where this fellow comes from."

[30]The man answered, "That is really surprising! You don't know where he comes from, and yet he opened my eyes. [31]We know that God does not listen to sinners. He listens to the godly person who does what he wants them to do. [32]Nobody has ever heard of anyone opening the eyes of a person born blind. [33]If this man had not come from God, he could do nothing."

[34]Then the Pharisees replied, "When you were born, you were already deep in sin. How dare you talk like that to us!" And they threw him out of the synagogue.

People Who Can't See the Truth

[35]Jesus heard that the Pharisees had thrown the man out of the synagogue. When Jesus found him, he said, "Do you believe in the Son of Man?"

[36]"Who is he, sir?" the man asked. "Tell me, so I can believe in him."

[37]Jesus said, "You have now seen him. In fact, he is the one speaking with you."

[38]Then the man said, "Lord, I believe." And he worshiped him.

[39]Jesus said, "I have come into this world to judge it. I have come so that people who are blind will see. I have come so that people who can see will become blind."

[40]Some Pharisees who were with him heard him say this. They asked, "What? Are we blind too?"

[41]Jesus said, "If you were blind, you would not be guilty of sin. But since you claim you can see, you remain guilty.

The Good Shepherd and His Sheep

10 "What I'm about to tell you Pharisees is true. What if someone does not enter the sheep pen through the gate but climbs in another way? That person is a thief and a robber. [2]The one who enters through the gate is the shepherd of the sheep. [3]The gatekeeper opens the gate for him. The sheep listen to his voice. He calls his own sheep by name and leads them out. [4]When he has brought out all his own sheep, he goes on ahead of them. His sheep follow him because they know his voice. [5]But they will never follow a stranger. In fact, they will run away from him. They don't recognize a stranger's voice." [6]Jesus told this story. But the Pharisees didn't understand what he was telling them.

[7]So Jesus said again, "What I'm about to tell you is true. I am like a gate for the sheep. [8]All who have come before me are thieves and robbers. But the sheep have not listened to them. [9]I'm like a gate. Anyone who enters through me will be saved. They will come in and go out. And they will find plenty of food. [10]A thief comes only to steal and kill and destroy. I have come so they may have life. I want them to have it in the fullest possible way.

[11]"I am the good shepherd. The good shepherd gives his life for the sheep. [12]The hired man is not the shepherd and does not own the sheep. So when the hired man sees the wolf coming, he leaves the sheep and runs away. Then the wolf attacks the flock and scatters it. [13]The man runs away because he is a hired man. He does not care about the sheep.

[14]"I am the good shepherd. I know my sheep, and my sheep know me. [15]They know me just as the Father knows me and I know the Father. And I give my life for the sheep. [16]I have other sheep that do not belong to this sheep pen. I must bring them in too. They also will listen to my voice. Then there will be one flock and one shepherd. [17]The reason my Father loves me is that I give up my life. But I will take it back again.

After a day of sled races, ice skating, and a snowball fight at McAlister Park with Wooton and Penny, I realized my Grandma Mildred's locket wasn't on my necklace anymore. It was missing! I knocked over our snowman and sifted through the snow. Tears filled my eyes and froze against my cheeks.

"We'll keep looking!" Penny insisted. We retraced our steps, kicking at snowdrifts. As darkness fell, I knew we had to quit looking. At home I flopped on the couch in despair. "Don't worry," Penny said. "Maybe it will turn up in the spring."

"No," said Wooton. "We can't give up!"

When he said that, he reminded me of my grandmother. She prayed for me for years. "The Good Shepherd wouldn't rest until He found His sheep," Grandma Mildred would say. "That's how much God loves us. He never gives up on us."

"Connie!" Penny shouted. "Look what I found in the sink!" My locket dangled from her fingers. It must have fallen off when I did the dishes that morning. I silently thanked God for the reminder of His love—and Grandma Mildred's too!

[18]No one takes it from me. I give it up myself. I have the authority to give it up. And I have the authority to take it back again. I received this command from my Father."

[19]The Jews who heard these words could not agree with one another. [20]Many of them said, "He is controlled by a demon. He has gone crazy! Why should we listen to him?"

[21]But others said, "A person controlled by a demon does not say things like this. Can a demon open the eyes of someone who is blind?"

Another Challenge to Jesus' Claims

²²Then came the Feast of Hanukkah at Jerusalem. It was winter. ²³Jesus was in the temple courtyard walking in Solomon's Porch. ²⁴The Jews who were gathered there around Jesus spoke to him. They said, "How long will you keep us waiting? If you are the Messiah, tell us plainly."

²⁵Jesus answered, "I did tell you. But you do not believe. The works that I do in my Father's name are a witness for me. ²⁶But you do not believe, because you are not my sheep. ²⁷My sheep listen to my voice. I know them, and they follow me. ²⁸I give them eternal life, and they will never die. No one will steal them out of my hand. ²⁹My Father, who has given them to me, is greater than anyone. No one can steal them out of my Father's hand. ³⁰I and the Father are one."

³¹Again the Jews who had challenged him picked up stones to kill him. ³²But Jesus said to them, "I have shown you many good works from the Father. Which good work are you throwing stones at me for?"

³³"We are not throwing stones at you for any good work," they replied. "We are stoning you for saying a very evil thing. You are only a man. But you claim to be God."

³⁴Jesus answered them, "Didn't God say in your Law, 'I have said you are "gods" '? *(Psalm 82:6)* ³⁵We know that Scripture is always true. God spoke to some people and called them 'gods.' ³⁶If that is true, what about the one the Father set apart as his very own? What about this one the Father sent into the world? Why do you charge me with saying a very evil thing? Is it because I said, 'I am God's Son'? ³⁷Don't believe me unless I do the works of my Father. ³⁸But what if I do them? Even if you don't believe me, believe these works. Then you will know and understand that the Father is in me and I am in the Father." ³⁹Again they tried to arrest him. But he escaped from them.

⁴⁰Then Jesus went back across the Jordan River. He went to the place where John had been baptizing in the early days. There he stayed. ⁴¹Many people came to him. They said, "John never performed a sign. But everything he said about this man was true." ⁴²And in that place many believed in Jesus.

Lazarus Dies

11 A man named Lazarus was sick. He was from Bethany, the village where Mary and her sister Martha lived. ²Mary would later pour perfume on the Lord. She would also wipe Jesus' feet with her hair. It was her brother Lazarus who was sick in bed. ³So the sisters sent a message to Jesus. "Lord," they told him, "the one you love is sick." ⁴When Jesus heard this, he said, "This sickness will not end in death. No, it is for God's glory. God's Son will receive glory because of it." ⁵Jesus loved Martha and her sister and Lazarus. ⁶So after he heard Lazarus was sick, he stayed where he was for two more days. ⁷And then he said to his disciples, "Let us go back to Judea."

⁸"But Rabbi," they said, "a short time ago the Jews there tried to kill you with stones. Are you still going back?"

⁹Jesus answered, "Aren't there 12 hours of daylight? Anyone who walks during the day won't trip and fall. They can see because of this world's light. ¹⁰But when they walk at night, they'll trip and fall. They have no light."

¹¹After he said this, Jesus went on speaking to them. "Our friend Lazarus has fallen asleep," he said. "But I am going there to wake him up."

¹²His disciples replied, "Lord, if he's sleeping, he will get better." ¹³Jesus had been speaking about the death of Lazarus. But his disciples thought he meant natural sleep.

¹⁴So then he told them plainly, "Lazarus is dead. ¹⁵For your benefit, I am glad I was not there. Now you will believe. But let us go to him."

¹⁶Then Thomas, who was also called Didymus, spoke to the rest of the disciples. "Let us go also," he said. "Then we can die with Jesus."

Jesus Comforts the Sisters of Lazarus

¹⁷When Jesus arrived, he found out that Lazarus had already been in the tomb for four days. ¹⁸Bethany was less than two miles from Jerusalem. ¹⁹Many Jews had come to Martha and Mary. They had come to comfort them because their brother was dead. ²⁰When Martha heard that Jesus was coming, she went out to meet him. But Mary stayed at home.

²¹"Lord," Martha said to Jesus, "I wish you had been here! Then my brother would not have died. ²²But I know that even now God will give you anything you ask for."

BiBLe ADVeNTUReS

Lucy went on an Imagination Station adventure to see Lazarus raised from the dead in "An Adventure in Bethany" (A#16).

²³Jesus said to her, "Your brother will rise again."

²⁴Martha answered, "I know he will rise again. This will happen when people are raised from the dead on the last day."

²⁵Jesus said to her, "I am the resurrection and the life. Anyone who believes in me will live, even if they die. ²⁶And whoever lives by believing in me will never die. Do you believe this?"

²⁷"Yes, Lord," she replied. "I believe that you are the Messiah, the Son of God. I believe that you are the one who is supposed to come into the world."

²⁸After she said this, she went back home. She called her sister Mary to one side to talk to her. "The Teacher is here," Martha said. "He is asking for you." ²⁹When Mary heard this, she got up quickly and went to him. ³⁰Jesus had not yet entered the village. He was still at the place where Martha had met him. ³¹Some Jews had been comforting Mary in the house. They noticed how quickly she got up and went out. So they followed her. They thought she was going to the tomb to mourn there.

³²Mary reached the place where Jesus was. When she saw him, she fell at his feet. She said, "Lord, I wish you had been here! Then my brother would not have died."

³³Jesus saw her crying. He saw that the Jews who had come along with her were crying also. His spirit became very sad, and he was troubled. ³⁴"Where have you put him?" he asked.

"Come and see, Lord," they replied.

³⁵Jesus wept.

³⁶Then the Jews said, "See how much he loved him!"

³⁷But some of them said, "He opened the eyes of the blind man. Couldn't he have kept this man from dying?"

Jesus Raises Lazarus From the Dead

³⁸Once more Jesus felt very sad. He came to the tomb. It was a cave with a stone in front of the entrance. ³⁹"Take away the stone," he said.

"But, Lord," said Martha, the sister of the dead man, "by this time there is a bad smell. Lazarus has been in the tomb for four days."

⁴⁰Then Jesus said, "Didn't I tell you that if you believe, you will see God's glory?"

⁴¹So they took away the stone. Then Jesus looked up. He said, "Father, I thank you for hearing me. ⁴²I know that you always hear me. But I said this for the benefit of the people standing here. I said it so they will believe that you sent me."

⁴³Then Jesus called in a loud voice. He said, "Lazarus, come out!" ⁴⁴The dead man came out. His hands and feet were wrapped with strips of linen. A cloth was around his face.

Jesus said to them, "Take off the clothes he was buried in and let him go."

The Plan to Kill Jesus

⁴⁵Many of the Jews who had come to visit Mary saw what Jesus did. So they believed in him. ⁴⁶But some of them went to the Pharisees. They told the Pharisees what Jesus had done. ⁴⁷Then the chief priests and the Pharisees called a meeting of the Sanhedrin.

"What can we do?" they asked. "This man is performing many signs. ⁴⁸If we let him keep on doing this, everyone will believe in him. Then the Romans will come. They will take away our temple and our nation."

⁴⁹One of the Jewish leaders spoke up. His name was Caiaphas. He was high priest at that time. He said, "You don't know anything at all! ⁵⁰You don't realize what is good for you. It is better if one man dies for the people than if the whole nation is destroyed."

⁵¹He did not say this on his own because he was high priest at that time. He prophesied that Jesus would die for the Jewish nation. ⁵²He also prophesied that Jesus would die for God's children scattered everywhere. He would die to bring them together and make them one. ⁵³So from that day on, the Jewish rulers planned to kill Jesus.

⁵⁴Jesus no longer moved around openly among the people of Judea. Instead, he went away to an area near the desert. He went to a village called Ephraim. There he stayed with his disciples.

⁵⁵It was almost time for the Jewish Passover Feast. Many people went up from the country to Jerusalem. They went there for the special washing that would make them pure before the Passover Feast. ⁵⁶They kept looking for Jesus as they stood in the temple courtyard. They asked one another, "What do you think? Isn't he coming to the feast at all?" ⁵⁷But the chief priests and the Pharisees had given orders. They had commanded anyone who found out where Jesus was staying to report it. Then they could arrest him.

Mary Pours Perfume on Jesus at Bethany

12 It was six days before the Passover Feast. Jesus came to Bethany, where Lazarus lived. Lazarus was the one Jesus had raised from the dead. ²A dinner was given at Bethany to honor Jesus. Martha served the food. Lazarus was among the people at the table with Jesus. ³Then Mary took about a pint of pure nard. It was an expensive perfume. She poured it on Jesus' feet and wiped them with her hair. The house was filled with the sweet smell of the perfume.

⁴But Judas Iscariot didn't like what Mary did. He was one of Jesus' disciples. Later he was going to hand Jesus over to his enemies. Judas said, ⁵"Why wasn't this perfume sold? Why wasn't the money given to poor people? It was worth a year's pay." ⁶He didn't say this because he cared about the poor. He said it because he was a thief. Judas was in charge of the money bag. He used to help himself to what was in it.

⁷"Leave her alone," Jesus replied. "The perfume was meant for the day I am buried. ⁸You will always have the poor among you. But you won't always have me."

⁹Meanwhile a large crowd of Jews found out that Jesus was there, so they came. But they did not come only because of Jesus. They also came to see Lazarus. After all, Jesus had raised him from the dead. ¹⁰So the chief priests made plans to kill Lazarus too. ¹¹Because of Lazarus, many of the Jews were starting to follow Jesus. They were believing in him.

Jesus Comes to Jerusalem as King

¹²The next day the large crowd that had come for the feast heard that Jesus was

WOOTON'S FUN FACTS

John 12: 10–11

Let's give the Wooton Award for Most Evil Villains to the chief priests. They wanted to kill someone who was just dead! And what's the point after Jesus already raised him to life?

on his way to Jerusalem. ¹³So they took branches from palm trees and went out to meet him. They shouted,

"Hosanna! "

"Blessed is the one who comes in the name of the Lord!"

(Psalm 118:25,26)

"Blessed is the king of Israel!"

¹⁴Jesus found a young donkey and sat on it. This is just as it is written in Scripture. It says,

¹⁵ "City of Zion, do not be afraid.
    See, your king is coming.
    He is sitting on a donkey's colt."

(Zechariah 9:9)

¹⁶At first, Jesus' disciples did not understand all this. They realized it only after he had received glory. Then they realized that these things had been written about him. They realized that these things had been done to him.

¹⁷A crowd had been with Jesus when he called Lazarus from the tomb and raised him from the dead. So they continued to tell everyone about what had happened. ¹⁸Many people went out to meet him. They had heard that he had done this sign. ¹⁹So the Pharisees said to one another, "This

isn't getting us anywhere. Look how the whole world is following him!"

Jesus Tells About His Coming Death

²⁰There were some Greeks among the people who went up to worship during the feast. ²¹They came to ask Philip for a favor. Philip was from Bethsaida in Galilee. "Sir," they said, "we would like to see Jesus." ²²Philip went to tell Andrew. Then Andrew and Philip told Jesus.

²³Jesus replied, "The time has come for the Son of Man to receive glory. ²⁴What I'm about to tell you is true. Unless a grain of wheat falls to the ground and dies, it remains only one seed. But if it dies, it produces many seeds. ²⁵Anyone who loves their life will lose it. But anyone who hates their life in this world will keep it and have eternal life. ²⁶Anyone who serves me must follow me. And where I am, my servant will also be. My Father will honor the one who serves me.

²⁷"My soul is troubled. What should I say? 'Father, keep me from having to go through with this'? No. This is the very reason I have come to this point in my life. ²⁸Father, bring glory to your name!"

Then a voice came from heaven. It said, "I have brought glory to my name. I will bring glory to it again." ²⁹The crowd there heard the voice. Some said it was thunder. Others said an angel had spoken to Jesus.

³⁰Jesus said, "This voice was for your benefit, not mine. ³¹Now it is time for the world to be judged. Now the prince of this world will be thrown out. ³²And I am going to be lifted up from the earth. When I am, I will bring all people to myself." ³³He said this to show them how he was going to die.

³⁴The crowd spoke up. "The Law tells us that the Messiah will remain forever," they said. "So how can you say, 'The Son of Man must be lifted up'? Who is this 'Son of Man'?"

³⁵Then Jesus told them, "You are going to have the light just a little while longer. Walk while you have the light. Do this before darkness catches up with you. Whoever walks in the dark does not know where they are going. ³⁶While you have the light, believe in it. Then you can become children of light." When Jesus had finished speaking, he left and hid from them.

Some Jews Believe and Some Don't

³⁷Jesus had performed so many signs in front of them. But they still would not believe in him. ³⁸This happened as Isaiah the prophet had said it would. He had said,

"Lord, who has believed what we've
        been saying?
    Who has seen the Lord's saving
        power?"   *(Isaiah 53:1)*

³⁹For this reason, they could not believe. As Isaiah says in another place,

⁴⁰ "The Lord has blinded their eyes.
    He has closed their minds.
So they can't see with their eyes.
    They can't understand with their
        minds.
    They can't turn to the Lord. If they
        could, he would heal them."
                          (Isaiah 6:10)

⁴¹Isaiah said this because he saw Jesus' glory and spoke about him.

⁴²At the same time that Jesus did those signs, many of the Jewish leaders believed in him. But because of the Pharisees, they would not openly admit they believed. They were afraid they would be thrown out of the synagogue. ⁴³They loved praise from people more than praise from God.

⁴⁴Then Jesus cried out, "Whoever believes in me does not believe in me only. They also believe in the one who sent me. ⁴⁵The one who looks at me sees the one who

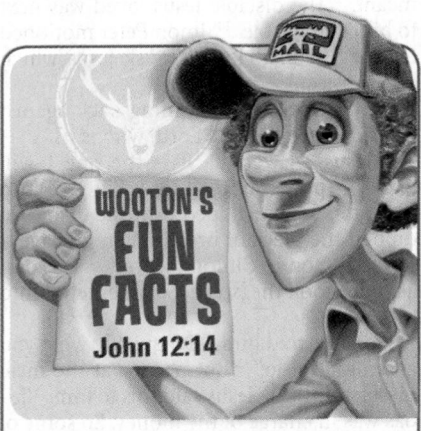

WOOTON'S FUN FACTS
John 12:14

This is the last donkey ride mentioned in the Bible. The first was Genesis 22:3 when Abraham was getting ready to sacrifice his son Isaac. Think of it! Two donkeys leading to two son sacrifices. Pretty cool parallel, if you ask me!

sent me. [46]I have come into the world to be its light. So no one who believes in me will stay in darkness.

[47]"I don't judge a person who hears my words but does not obey them. I didn't come to judge the world. I came to save the world. [48]But there is a judge for anyone who does not accept me and my words. These words I have spoken will judge them on the last day. [49]I did not speak on my own. The Father who sent me commanded me to say all that I have said. [50]I know that his command leads to eternal life. So everything I say is just what the Father has told me to say."

Jesus Washes His Disciples' Feet

13 It was just before the Passover Feast. Jesus knew that the time had come for him to leave this world. It was time for him to go to the Father. Jesus loved his disciples who were in the world. So he now loved them to the very end.

[2]They were having their evening meal. The devil had already tempted Judas, son of Simon Iscariot. He had urged Judas to hand Jesus over to his enemies. [3]Jesus knew that the Father had put everything under his power. He also knew he had come from God and was returning to God. [4]So he got up from the meal and took off his outer clothes. He wrapped a towel around his waist. [5]After that, he poured water into a large bowl. Then he began to wash his disciples' feet. He dried them with the towel that was wrapped around him.

[6]He came to Simon Peter. "Lord," Peter said to him, "are you going to wash my feet?"

[7]Jesus replied, "You don't realize now what I am doing. But later you will understand."

[8]"No," said Peter. "You will never wash my feet."

Jesus answered, "Unless I wash you, you can't share life with me."

[9]"Lord," Simon Peter replied, "not just my feet! Wash my hands and my head too!"

[10]Jesus answered, "People who have had a bath need to wash only their feet. The rest of their body is clean. And you are clean. But not all of you are." [11]Jesus knew who was going to hand him over to his enemies. That was why he said not every one was clean.

[12]When Jesus finished washing their feet, he put on his clothes. Then he returned to his place. "Do you understand what I have done for you?" he asked them. [13]"You call me 'Teacher' and 'Lord.' You are right. That is what I am. [14]I, your Lord and Teacher, have washed your feet. So you also should wash one another's feet. [15]I have given you an example. You should do as I have done for you. [16]What I'm about to tell you is true. A slave is not more important than his master. And a messenger is not more important than the one who sends him. [17]Now you know these things. So you will be blessed if you do them.

Jesus Tells What Judas Will Do

[18]"I am not talking about all of you. I know the ones I have chosen. But this will happen so that this passage of Scripture will come true. It says, 'The one who shared my bread has turned against me.' *(Psalm 41:9)* [19]"I am telling you now, before it happens. When it does happen, you will believe that I am who I am. [20]What I'm about to tell you is true. Anyone who accepts someone I send accepts me. And anyone who accepts me accepts the one who sent me."

[21]After he had said this, Jesus' spirit was troubled. He said, "What I'm about to tell you is true. One of you is going to hand me over to my enemies."

[22]His disciples stared at one another. They had no idea which one of them he meant. [23]The disciple Jesus loved was next to him at the table. [24]Simon Peter motioned to that disciple. He said, "Ask Jesus which one he means."

[25]The disciple was leaning back against Jesus. He asked him, "Lord, who is it?"

[26]Jesus answered, "It is the one I will give this piece of bread to. I will give it to him after I have dipped it in the dish." He dipped the piece of bread. Then he gave it to Judas, son of Simon Iscariot. [27]As soon as Judas took the bread, Satan entered into him.

So Jesus told him, "Do quickly what you are going to do." [28]But no one at the meal understood why Jesus said this to him. [29]Judas was in charge of the money. So some of the disciples thought Jesus was telling him to buy what was needed for the feast. Others thought Jesus was talking about giving something to poor people. [30]As soon as Judas had taken the bread, he went out. And it was night.

Adventures in Odyssey

Jesus told His disciples that everyone would know His disciples if they loved one another. Marvin Washington learned about loving others in "Unfair Game" (Club).

Peter Will Say He Does Not Know Jesus

³¹After Judas was gone, Jesus spoke. He said, "Now the Son of Man receives glory. And he brings glory to God. ³²If the Son brings glory to God, God himself will bring glory to the Son. God will do it at once.

³³"My children, I will be with you only a little longer. You will look for me. Just as I told the Jews, so I am telling you now. You can't come where I am going.

³⁴"I give you a new command. Love one another. You must love one another, just as I have loved you. ³⁵If you love one another, everyone will know you are my disciples."

³⁶Simon Peter asked him, "Lord, where are you going?"

Jesus replied, "Where I am going you can't follow now. But you will follow me later."

³⁷"Lord," Peter asked, "why can't I follow you now? I will give my life for you."

³⁸Then Jesus answered, "Will you really give your life for me? What I'm about to tell you is true. Before the rooster crows, you will say three times that you don't know me!

Jesus Comforts His Disciples

14 "Do not let your hearts be troubled. You believe in God. Believe in me also. ²There are many rooms in my Father's house. If this were not true, would I have told you that I am going there? Would I have told you that I would prepare a place for you there? ³If I go and do that, I will come back. And I will take you to be with me. Then you will also be where I am. ⁴You know the way to the place where I am going."

Jesus Is the Way to the Father

⁵Thomas said to him, "Lord, we don't know where you are going. So how can we know the way?"

⁶Jesus answered, "I am the way and the truth and the life. No one comes to the Father except through me. ⁷If you really know me, you will know my Father also. From now on, you do know him. And you have seen him."

⁸Philip said, "Lord, show us the Father. That will be enough for us."

⁹Jesus answered, "Don't you know me, Philip? I have been among you such a long time! Anyone who has seen me has seen the Father. So how can you say, 'Show us the Father'? ¹⁰Don't you believe that I am in the Father? Don't you believe that the Father is in me? The words I say to you I do not speak on my own authority. The Father lives in me. He is the one who is doing his work. ¹¹Believe me when I say I am in the Father. Also believe that the Father is in me. Or at least believe what the works I have been doing say about me. ¹²What I'm about to tell you is true. Anyone who believes in me will do the works I have been doing. In fact, they will do even greater things. That's because I am going to the Father. ¹³And I will do anything you ask in my name. Then the Father will receive glory from the Son. ¹⁴You may ask me for anything in my name. I will do it.

Jesus Promises That the Holy Spirit Will Come

¹⁵"If you love me, obey my commands. ¹⁶I will ask the Father. And he will give you another friend to help you and to be with you forever. ¹⁷That friend is the Spirit of truth. The world can't accept him. That's because the world does not see him or know him. But you know him. He lives with you, and he will be in you. ¹⁸I will not leave you like children who don't have parents. I will come to you. ¹⁹Before long, the world will not see me anymore. But you will see me. Because I live, you will live also. ²⁰On that day you will realize that I am in my Father. You will know that you are in me, and I am in you. ²¹Anyone who has my commands

REMEMBER THIS

JOHN 14:6

"Jesus answered, 'I am the way and the truth and the life. No one comes to the Father except through me.'"

and obeys them loves me. My Father will love the one who loves me. I too will love them. And I will show myself to them."

²²Then Judas spoke. "Lord," he said, "why do you plan to show yourself only to us? Why not also to the world?" The Judas who spoke those words was not Judas Iscariot.

²³Jesus replied, "Anyone who loves me will obey my teaching. My Father will love them. We will come to them and make our home with them. ²⁴Anyone who does not love me will not obey my teaching. The words you hear me say are not my own. They belong to the Father who sent me.

²⁵"I have spoken all these things while I am still with you. ²⁶But the Father will send the Friend in my name to help you. The Friend is the Holy Spirit. He will teach you all things. He will remind you of everything I have said to you. ²⁷I leave my peace with you. I give my peace to you. I do not give it to you as the world does. Do not let your hearts be troubled. And do not be afraid.

²⁸"You heard me say, 'I am going away. And I am coming back to you.' If you loved me, you would be glad I am going to the Father. The Father is greater than I am. ²⁹I have told you now before it happens. Then when it does happen, you will believe. ³⁰I will not say much more to you. The prince of this world is coming. He has no power over me. ³¹But he comes so that the world may learn that I love the Father. They must also learn that I do exactly what my Father has commanded me to do.

"Come now. Let us leave.

The Vine and the Branches

15 "I am the true vine. My Father is the gardener. ²He cuts off every branch joined to me that does not bear fruit. He trims every branch that does bear fruit. Then it will bear even more fruit. ³You are already clean because of the word I have spoken to you. ⁴Remain joined to me, just as I also remain joined to you. No branch can bear fruit by itself. It must remain joined

to the vine. In the same way, you can't bear fruit unless you remain joined to me.

⁵"I am the vine. You are the branches. If you remain joined to me, and I to you, you will bear a lot of fruit. You can't do anything without me. ⁶If you don't remain joined to me, you are like a branch that is thrown away and dries up. Branches like those are picked up. They are thrown into the fire and burned. ⁷If you remain joined to me and my words remain in you, ask for anything you wish. And it will be done for you. ⁸When you bear a lot of fruit, it brings glory to my Father. It shows that you are my disciples.

⁹"Just as the Father has loved me, I have loved you. Now remain in my love. ¹⁰If you obey my commands, you will remain in my love. In the same way, I have obeyed my Father's commands and remain in his love. ¹¹I have told you this so that you will have the same joy that I have. I also want your joy to be complete. ¹²Here is my command. Love one another, just as I have loved you. ¹³No one has greater love than the one who gives their life for their friends. ¹⁴You are my friends if you do what I command. ¹⁵I do not call you slaves anymore. Slaves do not know their master's business. Instead, I have called you friends. I have told you everything I learned from my Father. ¹⁶You did not choose me. Instead, I chose you. I appointed you so that you might go and

WHAT ABOUT YOU?

In John 15 Jesus said, "Love one another just as I have loved you." Whom do you love most in the world? Maybe it's your parents, siblings, grandparents, or friends. How do you show them you love them? Some of us write notes of encouragement, others give out hugs, buy presents, or spend time together. There are many ways to show you care!

For example, in the Adventures in Odyssey adventure "Greater Love," Timmy Riley shows his love for his friend P.D. in a few ways. First, he tells P.D. that he has a friend in Jesus who will never fail him and will always love him. Then, when P.D. falls into the water, Timmy jumps in after him. He is willing to sacrifice his own life for P.D.

When Jesus died on the Cross, He laid down His life for His friends—us. He took all of our sins upon Himself so that we would not have to face the punishment we deserve. His love has conquered all, and we can be thankful for it every day.

Try this: Fill a large bowl with water, then dip your finger into it and pull it out quickly. Look at the ripples your finger made, and think about how actions create ripples. In the story, because Timmy told P.D. about Jesus, P.D. received Jesus as his Savior and became a minister to inner-city kids. The things we do and say have an impact on the people around us, and these actions spread throughout the world, just like the ripples that fill the bowl.

bear fruit that will last. I also appointed you so that the Father will give you what you ask for. He will give you whatever you ask for in my name. [17]Here is my command. Love one another.

The World Hates the Disciples

[18]"My disciples, does the world hate you? Remember that it hated me first. [19]If you belonged to the world, it would love you like one of its own. But you do not belong to the world. I have chosen you out of the world. That is why the world hates you. [20]Remember what I told you. I said, 'A slave is not more important than his master.' *(John 13:16)* If people hated me and tried to hurt me, they will do the same to you. If they obeyed my teaching, they will obey yours also. [21]They will treat you like that because of my name. They do not know the one who sent me. [22]If I had not come and spoken to them, they would not be guilty of sin. But now they have no excuse for their sin. [23]Whoever hates me hates my Father also. [24]I did works among them that no one else did. If I hadn't,

they would not be guilty of sin. But now they have seen those works. And still they have hated both me and my Father. [25]This has happened so that what is written in their Law would come true. It says, 'They hated me without any reason.' *(Psalms 35:19; 69:4)*

The Work of the Holy Spirit

[26]"I will send the Friend to you from the Father. He is the Spirit of truth, who comes out from the Father. When the Friend comes to help you, he will be a witness about me. [27]You must also be witnesses about me. That's because you have been with me from the beginning.

16 "I have told you all this so that you will not turn away from the truth. [2]You will be thrown out of the synagogue. In fact, the time is coming when someone may kill you. And they will think they are doing God a favor. [3]They will do things like that because they do not know the Father or me. [4]Why have I told you this? So that when their time comes, you will remember that I warned you about them. I didn't tell you this

WOOTON'S FUN FACTS

John 16:7 Spoiler alert! The Friend that Jesus talks about is better than Penny or Connie or Eugene, or any person I know. This Friend is the Holy Spirit who goes with me *everywhere*. Since I've already spoiled the surprise, check out Acts 2 for the coming of the Holy Spirit.

from the beginning because I was with you. [5]But now I am going to the one who sent me. None of you asks me, 'Where are you going?' [6]Instead, you are filled with sadness because I have said these things. [7]But what I'm about to tell you is true. It is for your good that I am going away. Unless I go away, the Friend will not come to help you. But if I go, I will send him to you. [8]When he comes, he will prove that the world's people are guilty. He will prove their guilt concerning sin and godliness and judgment. [9]The world is guilty as far as sin is concerned. That's because people do not believe in me. [10]The world is guilty as far as godliness is concerned. That's because I am going to the Father, where you can't see me anymore. [11]The world is guilty as far as judgment is concerned. That's because the devil, the prince of this world, has already been judged.

[12]"I have much more to say to you. It is more than you can handle right now. [13]But when the Spirit of truth comes, he will guide you into all the truth. He will not speak on his own. He will speak only what he hears. And he will tell you what is still going to happen. [14]He will bring me glory. That's because what he receives from me he will show to you. [15]Everything that belongs to the Father is mine. That is why I said what the Holy Spirit receives from me he will show to you.

The Disciples' Sadness Will Turn Into Joy

[16]Jesus continued, "In a little while, you will no longer see me. Then after a little while, you will see me."

[17]After they heard this, some of his disciples spoke to one another. They said, "What does he mean by saying, 'In a little while, you will no longer see me. Then after a little while, you will see me'? And what does he mean by saying, 'I am going to the Father'?" [18]They kept asking, "What does he mean by 'a little while'? We don't understand what he is saying."

[19]Jesus saw that they wanted to ask him about these things. So he said to them, "Are you asking one another what I meant? Didn't you understand when I said, 'In a little while, you will no longer see me. Then after a little while, you will see me'? [20]What I'm about to tell you is true. You will weep and mourn while the world is full of joy. You will be sad, but your sadness will turn into joy. [21]A woman giving birth to a baby has pain. That's because her time to give birth has come. But when her baby is born, she forgets the pain. She forgets because she is so happy that a baby has been born into the world. [22]That's the way it is with you. Now it's your time to be sad. But I will see you again. Then you will be full of joy. And no one will take away your joy. [23]When that day comes, you will no longer ask me for anything. What I'm about to tell you is true. My Father will give you anything you ask for in my name. [24]Until now you have not asked for anything in my name. Ask, and you will receive what you ask for. Then your joy will be complete.

[25]"I have not been speaking to you plainly. But a time is coming when I will speak clearly. Then I will tell you plainly about my Father. [26]When that day comes, you will ask for things in my name. I am not saying I will ask the Father instead of you asking him. [27]No, the Father himself loves you because you have loved me. He also loves you because you have believed that I came from God. [28]I came from the Father and entered the world. Now I am leaving the world and going back to the Father."

[29]Then Jesus' disciples said, "Now you are speaking plainly. You are using examples that are clear. [30]Now we can see that

you know everything. You don't even need anyone to ask you questions. This makes us believe that you came from God."

³¹"Do you believe now?" Jesus replied. ³²"A time is coming when you will be scattered and go to your own homes. In fact, that time is already here. You will leave me all alone. But I am not really alone. My Father is with me.

³³"I have told you these things, so that you can have peace because of me. In this world you will have trouble. But be encouraged! I have won the battle over the world."

Jesus Prays for Himself

17 After Jesus said this, he looked toward heaven and prayed. He said,

"Father, the time has come. Bring glory to your Son. Then your Son will bring glory to you. ²You gave him authority over all people. He gives eternal life to all those you have given him. ³And what is eternal life? It is knowing you, the only true God, and Jesus Christ, whom you have sent. ⁴I have brought you glory on earth. I have finished the work you gave me to do. ⁵So now, Father, give glory to me in heaven where your throne is. Give me the glory I had with you before the world began.

Jesus Prays for His Disciples

⁶"I have shown you to the disciples you gave me out of the world. They were yours. You gave them to me. And they have obeyed your word. ⁷Now they know that everything you have given me comes from you. ⁸I gave them the words you gave me. And they accepted them. They knew for certain that I came from you. They believed that you sent me. ⁹I pray for them. I am not praying for the world. I am praying for those you have given me, because they are yours. ¹⁰All I have is yours, and all you have is mine. Glory has come to me because of my disciples. ¹¹I will not remain in the world any longer. But they are still in the world, and I am coming to you. Holy Father, keep them safe by the power of your name. It is the name you gave me. Keep them safe so they can be one, just as you and I are one. ¹²While I was with them, I guarded them. I kept them safe through the name you gave me. None of them has been lost, except the one who was headed for ruin. It happened so that Scripture would come true.

¹³"I am coming to you now. But I say these things while I am still in the world. I say them so that those you gave me can have the same joy that I have. ¹⁴I have given them your word. The world has hated them. That's because they are not part of the world any more than I am. ¹⁵I do not pray that you will take them out of the world. I pray that you will keep them safe from the evil one. ¹⁶They do not belong to the world, just as I do not belong to it. ¹⁷Use the truth to make them holy. Your word is truth. ¹⁸You sent me into the world. In the same way, I have sent them into the world. ¹⁹I make myself holy for them so that they too can be made holy by the truth.

Jesus Prays for All Believers

²⁰"I do not pray only for them. I pray also for everyone who will believe in me because of their message. ²¹Father, I pray they will be one, just as you

are in me and I am in you. I want them also to be in us. Then the world will believe that you have sent me. ²²I have given them the glory you gave me. I did this so they would be one, just as we are one. ²³I will be in them, just as you are in me. This is so that they may be brought together perfectly as one. Then the world will know that you sent me. It will also show the world that you have loved those you gave me, just as you have loved me.

²⁴"Father, I want those you have given me to be with me where I am. I want them to see my glory, the glory you have given me. You gave it to me because you loved me before the world was created.

²⁵"Father, you are holy. The world does not know you, but I know you. Those you have given me know you have sent me. ²⁶I have shown you to them. And I will continue to show you to them. Then the love you have for me will be in them. I myself will be in them."

Jesus Is Arrested

18 When Jesus had finished praying, he left with his disciples. They crossed the Kidron Valley. On the other side there was a garden. Jesus and his disciples went into it.

²Judas knew the place. He was going to hand Jesus over to his enemies. Jesus had often met in that place with his disciples. ³So Judas came to the garden. He was guiding a group of soldiers and some officials. The chief priests and the Pharisees had sent them. They were carrying torches, lanterns and weapons.

⁴Jesus knew everything that was going to happen to him. So he went out and asked them, "Who do you want?"

⁵"Jesus of Nazareth," they replied.

"I am he," Jesus said. Judas, who was going to hand Jesus over, was standing there with them. ⁶When Jesus said, "I am he," they moved back. Then they fell to the ground.

⁷He asked them again, "Who do you want?"

"Jesus of Nazareth," they said.

⁸Jesus answered, "I told you I am he. If you are looking for me, then let these men go." ⁹This happened so that the words Jesus

BIBLE ADVENTURES

Connie used the Bible Education Audio-Visual Research System to see Jesus' arrest in "Hallowed Be Thy Name" (A#17).

had spoken would come true. He had said, "I have not lost anyone God has given me." *(John 6:39)*

¹⁰Simon Peter had a sword and pulled it out. He struck the high priest's slave and cut off his right ear. The slave's name was Malchus.

¹¹Jesus commanded Peter, "Put your sword away! Shouldn't I drink the cup of suffering the Father has given me?"

¹²Then the group of soldiers, their commander and the Jewish officials arrested Jesus. They tied him up ¹³and brought him first to Annas. He was the father-in-law of Caiaphas, the high priest at that time. ¹⁴Caiaphas had advised the Jewish leaders that it would be good if one man died for the people.

Peter Says He Is Not Jesus' Disciple

¹⁵Simon Peter and another disciple were following Jesus. The high priest knew the other disciple. So that disciple went with Jesus into the high priest's courtyard. ¹⁶But Peter had to wait outside by the door. The other disciple came back. He was the one the high priest knew. He spoke to the servant woman who was on duty there. Then he brought Peter in.

¹⁷She asked Peter, "You aren't one of Jesus' disciples too, are you?"

"I am not," he replied.

¹⁸It was cold. The slaves and officials stood around a fire. They had made it to keep warm. Peter was also standing with them. He was warming himself.

The High Priest Questions Jesus

¹⁹Meanwhile, the high priest questioned Jesus. He asked him about his disciples and his teaching.

²⁰"I have spoken openly to the world," Jesus replied. "I always taught in synagogues or at the temple, where all the Jews come together. I didn't say anything in secret. ²¹Why question me? Ask the people who heard me. They certainly know what I said."

²²When Jesus said that, one of the officials nearby slapped him in the face. "Is this any way to answer the high priest?" he asked.

²³"Have I said something wrong?" Jesus replied. "If I have, then tell everyone what it was. But if I spoke the truth, why did you hit me?" ²⁴Annas sent him, tied up, to Caiaphas, the high priest.

Peter Again Says He Is Not Jesus' Disciple

²⁵Meanwhile, Simon Peter was still standing there warming himself by the fire. So they asked him, "You aren't one of Jesus' disciples too, are you?"

He said, "I am not."

²⁶One of the high priest's slaves was a relative of the man whose ear Peter had cut off. He said to Peter, "Didn't I see you with Jesus in the garden?" ²⁷Again Peter said no. At that exact moment a rooster began to crow.

Jesus Is Brought to Pilate

²⁸Then the Jewish leaders took Jesus from Caiaphas to the palace of the Roman governor. By now it was early morning. The Jewish leaders did not want to be made "unclean." They wanted to be able to eat the Passover meal. So they did not enter the palace. ²⁹Pilate came out to them. He asked, "What charges are you bringing against this man?"

³⁰"He has committed crimes," they replied. "If he hadn't, we would not have handed him over to you."

³¹Pilate said, "Take him yourselves. Judge him by your own law."

"But we don't have the right to put anyone to death," they complained. ³²This happened so that what Jesus said about how he was going to die would come true.

³³Then Pilate went back inside the palace. He ordered Jesus to be brought to him. Pilate asked him, "Are you the king of the Jews?"

³⁴"Is that your own idea?" Jesus asked. "Or did others talk to you about me?"

³⁵"Am I a Jew?" Pilate replied. "Your own people and chief priests handed you over to me. What have you done?"

³⁶Jesus said, "My kingdom is not from this world. If it were, those who serve me would fight. They would try to keep the Jewish leaders from arresting me. My kingdom is from another place."

³⁷"So you are a king, then!" said Pilate.

Jesus answered, "You say that I am a king. In fact, that's the reason I was born. I was born and came into the world to be a witness to the truth. Everyone who is on the side of truth listens to me."

³⁸"What is truth?" Pilate replied. Then Pilate went out again to the Jews gathered there. He said, "I find no basis for any charge against him. ³⁹But you have a practice at Passover time. At that time, you ask me to set one prisoner free for you. Do you want me to set 'the king of the Jews' free?"

⁴⁰They shouted back, "No! Not him! Give us Barabbas!" Barabbas had taken part in an armed struggle against the country's rulers.

Jesus Is Sentenced to Be Crucified

19 Then Pilate took Jesus and had him whipped. ²The soldiers twisted thorns together to make a crown. They put it on Jesus' head. Then they put a purple robe on him. ³They went up to him again and again. They kept saying, "We honor you, king of the Jews!" And they slapped him in the face.

⁴Once more Pilate came out. He said to the Jews gathered there, "Look, I am bringing Jesus out to you. I want to let you know that I find no basis for a charge against him." ⁵Jesus came out wearing the crown of thorns and the purple robe. Then Pilate said to them, "Here is the man!"

⁶As soon as the chief priests and their officials saw him, they shouted, "Crucify him! Crucify him!"

But Pilate answered, "You take him and crucify him. I myself find no basis for a charge against him."

⁷The Jewish leaders replied, "We have a law. That law says he must die. He claimed to be the Son of God."

⁸When Pilate heard that, he was even more afraid. ⁹He went back inside the palace. "Where do you come from?" he asked Jesus. But Jesus did not answer him. ¹⁰"Do you refuse to speak to me?" Pilate said. "Don't you understand? I have the power to set you free or to nail you to a cross."

¹¹Jesus answered, "You were given power from heaven. If you weren't, you would have no power over me. So the one who handed me over to you is guilty of a greater sin."

¹²From then on, Pilate tried to set Jesus free. But the Jewish leaders kept shouting,

"If you let this man go, you are not Caesar's friend! Anyone who claims to be a king is against Caesar!"

[13]When Pilate heard that, he brought Jesus out. Pilate sat down on the judge's seat. It was at a place called the Stone Walkway. In the Aramaic language it was called Gabbatha. [14]It was about noon on Preparation Day in Passover Week.

"Here is your king," Pilate said to the Jews.

[15]But they shouted, "Take him away! Take him away! Crucify him!"

"Should I crucify your king?" Pilate asked.

"We have no king but Caesar," the chief priests answered.

[16]Finally, Pilate handed Jesus over to them to be nailed to a cross.

Jesus Is Nailed to a Cross

So the soldiers took charge of Jesus. [17]He had to carry his own cross. He went out to a place called the Skull. In the Aramaic language it was called Golgotha. [18]There they nailed Jesus to the cross. Two other men were crucified with him. One was on each side of him. Jesus was in the middle.

[19]Pilate had a notice prepared. It was fastened to the cross. It read,

JESUS OF NAZARETH,
THE KING OF THE JEWS.

[20]Many of the Jews read the sign. That's because the place where Jesus was crucified was near the city. And the sign was written in the Aramaic, Latin and Greek languages. [21]The chief priests of the Jews argued with Pilate. They said, "Do not write 'The King of the Jews.' Write that this man claimed to be king of the Jews."

[22]Pilate answered, "I have written what I have written."

[23]When the soldiers crucified Jesus, they took his clothes. They divided them into four parts. Each soldier got one part. All that was left was Jesus' long, inner robe. It did not have any seams. It was made out of one piece of cloth from top to bottom.

[24]"Let's not tear it," they said to one another. "Let's cast lots to see who will get it."

This happened so that Scripture would come true. It says,

"They divided up my clothes among
    them.
They cast lots for what I was
    wearing." *(Psalm 22:18)*

So that is what the soldiers did.

[25]Jesus' mother stood near his cross. So did his mother's sister, Mary the wife of Clopas, and Mary Magdalene. [26]Jesus saw his mother there. He also saw the disciple he loved standing nearby. Jesus said to his mother, "Dear woman, here is your son." [27]He said to the disciple, "Here is your mother." From that time on, the disciple took her into his home.

Jesus Dies

[28]Later, Jesus knew that everything had now been finished. He also knew that what Scripture said must come true. So he said, "I am thirsty." [29]A jar of wine vinegar was there. So they soaked a sponge in it. They put the sponge on the stem of a hyssop plant. Then they lifted it up to Jesus' lips. [30]After Jesus drank he said, "It is finished." Then he bowed his head and died.

[31]It was Preparation Day. The next day would be a special Sabbath day. The Jewish leaders did not want the bodies left on the crosses during the Sabbath day. So they asked Pilate to have the legs broken and the bodies taken down. [32]The soldiers came and broke the legs of the first man who had been crucified with Jesus. Then they broke the legs of the other man. [33]But when they came to Jesus, they saw that he was already dead. So they did not break his legs. [34]Instead, one of the soldiers stuck his spear into Jesus' side. Right away, blood and water flowed out. [35]The man who saw it has been a witness about it. And what he has said is true. He knows that he tells the truth. He is a witness so that you also may believe. [36]These things happened in order that Scripture would come true. It says, "Not one of his bones will be broken." *(Exodus 12:46; Numbers 9:12; Psalm 34:20)* [37]Scripture also says, "They will look to the one they have pierced." *(Zechariah 12:10)*

Jesus Is Buried

[38]Later Joseph asked Pilate for Jesus' body. Joseph was from the town of Arimathea. He was a follower of Jesus. But he followed Jesus secretly because he was afraid of the Jewish leaders. After Pilate gave him permission, Joseph came and took the body away. [39]Nicodemus went with Joseph. He was the man who had earlier visited Jesus at night. Nicodemus brought

some mixed spices that weighed about 75 pounds. ⁴⁰The two men took Jesus' body. They wrapped it in strips of linen cloth, along with the spices. That was the way the Jews buried people. ⁴¹At the place where Jesus was crucified, there was a garden. A new tomb was there. No one had ever been put in it before. ⁴²That day was the Jewish Preparation Day, and the tomb was nearby. So they placed Jesus there.

The Tomb Is Empty

20 Early on the first day of the week, Mary Magdalene went to the tomb. It was still dark. She saw that the stone had been moved away from the entrance. ²So she ran to Simon Peter and another disciple, the one Jesus loved. She said, "They have taken the Lord out of the tomb! We don't know where they have put him!"

³So Peter and the other disciple started out for the tomb. ⁴Both of them were running. The other disciple ran faster than Peter. He reached the tomb first. ⁵He bent over and looked in at the strips of linen lying there. But he did not go in. ⁶Then Simon Peter came along behind him. He went straight into the tomb. He saw the strips of linen lying there. ⁷He also saw the funeral cloth that had been wrapped around Jesus' head. The cloth was still lying in its place. It was separate from the linen. ⁸The disciple who had reached the tomb first also went inside. He saw and believed. ⁹They still did not understand from Scripture that Jesus had to rise from the dead. ¹⁰Then the disciples went back to where they were staying.

Jesus Appears to Mary Magdalene

¹¹But Mary stood outside the tomb crying. As she cried, she bent over to look into the tomb. ¹²She saw two angels dressed in white. They were seated where Jesus' body had been. One of them was where Jesus' head had been laid. The other sat where his feet had been placed.

¹³They asked her, "Woman, why are you crying?"

"They have taken my Lord away," she said. "I don't know where they have put him." ¹⁴Then she turned around and saw Jesus standing there. But she didn't realize that it was Jesus.

¹⁵He asked her, "Woman, why are you crying? Who are you looking for?"

She thought he was the gardener. So she said, "Sir, did you carry him away? Tell me where you put him. Then I will go and get him."

¹⁶Jesus said to her, "Mary."

She turned toward him. Then she cried out in the Aramaic language, "*Rabboni!*" Rabboni means Teacher.

¹⁷Jesus said, "Do not hold on to me. I have not yet ascended to the Father. Instead, go to those who believe in me. Tell them, 'I am ascending to my Father and your Father, to my God and your God.'"

¹⁸Mary Magdalene went to the disciples with the news. She said, "I have seen the Lord!" And she told them that he had said these things to her.

Jesus Appears to His Disciples

¹⁹On the evening of that first day of the week, the disciples were together. They had locked the doors because they were afraid of the Jewish leaders. Jesus came in and stood among them. He said, "May peace be with you!" ²⁰Then he showed them his hands and his side. The disciples were very happy when they saw the Lord.

²¹Again Jesus said, "May peace be with you! The Father has sent me. So now I am sending you." ²²He then breathed on them. He said, "Receive the Holy Spirit. ²³If you forgive anyone's sins, their sins are forgiven. If you do not forgive them, they are not forgiven."

Jesus Appears to Thomas

²⁴Thomas was one of the 12 disciples. He was also called Didymus. He was not with the other disciples when Jesus came. ²⁵So they told him, "We have seen the Lord!"

But he said to them, "First I must see the nail marks in his hands. I must put my finger where the nails were. I must put my hand into his side. Only then will I believe."

²⁶A week later, Jesus' disciples were in the house again. Thomas was with them.

Even though the doors were locked, Jesus came in and stood among them. He said, "May peace be with you!" ²⁷Then he said to Thomas, "Put your finger here. See my hands. Reach out your hand and put it into my side. Stop doubting and believe."

²⁸Thomas said to him, "My Lord and my God!"

²⁹Then Jesus told him, "Because you have seen me, you have believed. Blessed are those who have not seen me but still have believed."

The Purpose of John's Gospel

³⁰Jesus performed many other signs in front of his disciples. They are not written down in this book. ³¹But these are written so that you may believe that Jesus is the Messiah, the Son of God. If you believe this, you will have life because you belong to him.

Jesus and the Miracle of Many Fish

21 After this, Jesus appeared to his disciples again. It was by the Sea of Galilee. Here is what happened. ²Simon Peter and Thomas, who was also called Didymus, were there together. Nathanael from Cana in Galilee and the sons of Zebedee were with them. So were two other disciples. ³"I'm going out to fish," Simon Peter told them. They said, "We'll go with you." So they went out and got into the boat. That night they didn't catch anything.

⁴Early in the morning, Jesus stood on the shore. But the disciples did not realize that it was Jesus.

⁵He called out to them, "Friends, don't you have any fish?"

"No," they answered.

⁶He said, "Throw your net on the right side of the boat. There you will find some fish." When they did, they could not pull the net into the boat. There were too many fish in it.

⁷Then the disciple Jesus loved said to Simon Peter, "It is the Lord!" As soon as Peter heard that, he put his coat on. He had taken it off earlier. Then he jumped into the water. ⁸The other disciples followed in the boat. They were towing the net full of fish. The shore was only about 100 yards away. ⁹When they landed, they saw a fire of burning coals. There were fish on it. There was also some bread.

¹⁰Jesus said to them, "Bring some of the fish you have just caught." ¹¹So Simon Peter climbed back into the boat. He dragged the net to shore. It was full of large fish. There were 153 of them. But even with that many fish the net was not torn. ¹²Jesus said to them, "Come and have breakfast." None of the disciples dared to ask him, "Who are you?" They knew it was the Lord. ¹³Jesus came, took the bread and gave it to them. He did the same thing with the fish. ¹⁴This was the third time Jesus appeared to his disciples after he was raised from the dead.

Jesus Gives Peter His Task

¹⁵When Jesus and the disciples had finished eating, Jesus spoke to Simon Peter. He asked, "Simon, son of John, do you love me more than these others do?"

"Yes, Lord," he answered. "You know that I love you."

Jesus said, "Feed my lambs."

¹⁶Again Jesus asked, "Simon, son of John, do you love me?"

He answered, "Yes, Lord. You know that I love you."

Jesus said, "Take care of my sheep."

¹⁷Jesus spoke to him a third time. He asked, "Simon, son of John, do you love me?"

Peter felt bad because Jesus asked him the third time, "Do you love me?" He answered, "Lord, you know all things. You know that I love you."

Jesus said, "Feed my sheep. ¹⁸What I'm about to tell you is true. When you were younger, you dressed yourself. You went wherever you wanted to go. But when you are old, you will stretch out your hands. Someone else will dress you. Someone else will lead you where you do not want to go." ¹⁹Jesus said this to point out how Peter would die. His death would bring glory to God. Then Jesus said to him, "Follow me!"

²⁰Peter turned around. He saw that the disciple Jesus loved was following them. He was the one who had leaned back against Jesus at the supper. He had said, "Lord, who is going to hand you over to your enemies?" ²¹When Peter saw that disciple, he asked, "Lord, what will happen to him?"

²²Jesus answered, "Suppose I want him to remain alive until I return. What does

that matter to you? You must follow me." [23]Because of what Jesus said, a false report spread among the believers. The story was told that the disciple Jesus loved wouldn't die. But Jesus did not say he would not die. He only said, "Suppose I want him to remain alive until I return. What does that matter to you?"

[24]This is the disciple who is a witness about these things. He also wrote them down. We know that what he says is true.

[25]Jesus also did many other things. What if every one of them were written down? I suppose that even the whole world would not have room for the books that would be written.

Acts

As our expedition heads farther into the New Testament and past the gospels, we first encounter a book that is often called "the Acts of the Apostles." However, many readers (myself included) would suggest that a better title would be "the Acts of the Holy Spirit." From the moment the Holy Spirit arrives as the followers of Jesus are gathered together (chapter 2), the apostles receive great power. From that point on the church begins to grow in spite of much resistance and persecution.

As we learned in the introduction to Luke, most scholars agree that *this* book is a continuation of that one. Not only does it begin promptly where the book of Luke concluded, but also both books are dedicated to the same person (a man named Theophilus). The first part of the book focuses on Peter and Jesus' other followers. A little less than halfway through, we meet a new believer, Saul of Tarsus, who has a dramatic conversion to Jesus (9:1–31). He soon becomes the dynamic apostle Paul and eventually goes on to write thirteen of the twenty-seven books of the New Testament.

In the writing of his gospel, Luke relied on other people's eyewitness reports to write about Jesus' life and ministry. But for this second book, he was personally involved and accompanied Paul in his ministry. If you read closely, you will notice sections describing Paul's travels where the perspective shifts from "he went from one place to another" to "*we* went from here to there." So pay close attention as you read through this action-packed book and put yourself into the stories as well! Your careful reading will be rewarded!

WHAT'S IT MEAN, EUGENE?

Pentecost—Pentecost was first an Old Testament festival that was celebrated fifty days (Greek *pentecosta* means "fifty") after Passover to give thanks for God's abundant provision. In the New Testament, it was on the Day of Pentecost that God poured out His Holy Spirit on the believers (see Acts 2:1–12), thus providing them with abundant *spiritual food* for the living of the Christian life.

Jesus Is Taken Up Into Heaven

Theophilus, I wrote about Jesus in my earlier book. I wrote about all he did and taught ²until the day he was taken up to heaven. Before Jesus left, he gave orders to the apostles he had chosen. He did this through the Holy Spirit. ³After his suffering and death, he appeared to them. In many ways he proved that he was alive. He appeared to them over a period of 40 days. During that time he spoke about God's kingdom. ⁴One day Jesus was eating with them. He gave them a command. "Do not leave Jerusalem," he said. "Wait for the gift my Father promised. You have heard me talk about it. ⁵John baptized with water. But in a few days you will be baptized with the Holy Spirit."

⁶Then the apostles gathered around Jesus and asked him a question. "Lord," they said, "are you going to give the kingdom back to Israel now?"

⁷He said to them, "You should not be concerned about times or dates. The Father has set them by his own authority. ⁸But you will receive power when the Holy Spirit comes on you. Then you will tell people about me in Jerusalem, and in all Judea and Samaria. And you will even tell other people about me from one end of the earth to the other."

⁹After Jesus said this, he was taken up to heaven. The apostles watched until a cloud hid him from their sight.

¹⁰While he was going up, they kept on looking at the sky. Suddenly two men dressed in white clothing stood beside them. ¹¹"Men of Galilee," they said, "why do you stand here looking at the sky? Jesus has been taken away from you into heaven. But he will come back in the same way you saw him go."

Matthias Is Chosen to Take the Place of Judas Iscariot

¹²The apostles returned to Jerusalem from the hill called the Mount of Olives. It is just over half a mile from the city. ¹³When they arrived, they went upstairs to the room where they were staying. Here is a list of those who were there.

Peter, John, James and Andrew.
Philip and Thomas
Bartholomew and Matthew,
James son of Alphaeus, Simon the
    Zealot and Judas son of James.

ADVENTURES IN ODYSSEY

Jason and Whit told people about Jesus across distant lands in "To the Ends of the Earth" (Club).

¹⁴They all came together regularly to pray. The women joined them too. So did Jesus' mother Mary and his brothers.

¹⁵In those days Peter stood up among the believers. About 120 of them were there. ¹⁶Peter said, "Brothers and sisters, a long time ago the Holy Spirit spoke through David. He spoke about Judas Iscariot. What the Scripture said would happen had to come true. Judas was the guide for the men who arrested Jesus. ¹⁷But Judas was one of us. He shared with us in our work for God."

¹⁸Judas bought a field with the payment he received for the evil thing he had done. He fell down headfirst in the field. His body burst open. All his insides spilled out. ¹⁹Everyone in Jerusalem heard about this. So they called that field Akeldama. In their language, Akeldama means the Field of Blood.

²⁰Peter said, "Here is what is written in the Book of Psalms. It says,

"'May his home be deserted.
    May no one live in it.'   *(Psalm 69:25)*

The Psalms also say,

"'Let someone else take his place as
            leader.'   *(Psalm 109:8)*

²¹So we need to choose someone to take his place. It will have to be a man who was with us the whole time the Lord Jesus was

living among us. ²²That time began when John was baptizing. It ended when Jesus was taken up from us. The one we choose must join us in telling people that Jesus rose from the dead."

²³So they suggested the names of two men. One was Joseph, who was called Barsabbas. He was also called Justus. The other man was Matthias. ²⁴Then the believers prayed. They said, "Lord, you know everyone's heart. Show us which of these two you have chosen. ²⁵Show us who should take the place of Judas as an apostle. He gave up being an apostle to go where he belongs." ²⁶Then they cast lots. Matthias was chosen. So he was added to the 11 apostles.

The Holy Spirit Comes at Pentecost

2 When the day of Pentecost came, all the believers gathered in one place. ²Suddenly a sound came from heaven. It was like a strong wind blowing. It filled the whole house where they were sitting. ³They saw something that looked like fire in the shape of tongues. The flames separated and came to rest on each of them. ⁴All of them were filled with the Holy Spirit. They began to speak in languages they had not known before. The Spirit gave them the ability to do this.

⁵Godly Jews from every country in the world were staying in Jerusalem. ⁶A crowd came together when they heard the sound. They were bewildered because each of them heard their own language being spoken. ⁷The crowd was really amazed. They asked, "Aren't all these people who are speaking Galileans? ⁸Then why do we each hear them speaking in our own native language? ⁹We are Parthians, Medes and Elamites. We live in Mesopotamia, Judea and Cappadocia. We are from Pontus, Asia, ¹⁰Phrygia and Pamphylia. Others of us are from Egypt and the parts of Libya near Cyrene. Still others are visitors from Rome. ¹¹Some of the visitors are Jews. Others have accepted the Jewish faith. Also, Cretans and Arabs are here. We hear all these people speaking about God's wonders in our own languages!" ¹²They were amazed and bewildered. They asked one another, "What does this mean?"

¹³But some people in the crowd made fun of the believers. "They've had too much wine!" they said.

Peter Speaks to the Crowd

¹⁴Then Peter stood up with the 11 apostles. In a loud voice he spoke to the crowd. "My fellow Jews," he said, "let me explain this to you. All of you who live in Jerusalem, listen carefully to what I say. ¹⁵You think these people are drunk. But they aren't. It's only nine o'clock in the morning! ¹⁶No, here is what the prophet Joel meant. ¹⁷He said,

" 'In the last days, God says,
      I will pour out my Holy Spirit on all
        people.
  Your sons and daughters will prophesy.
      Your young men will see visions.
      Your old men will have dreams.
¹⁸ In those days, I will pour out my Spirit
        on my servants.
  I will pour out my Spirit on both
        men and women.
      When I do, they will prophesy.
¹⁹ I will show wonders in the heavens
        above.
  I will show signs on the earth below.
      There will be blood and fire and
        clouds of smoke.
²⁰ The sun will become dark.
      The moon will turn red like blood.
      This will happen before the coming
        of the great and glorious day
        of the Lord.
²¹ Everyone who calls
      on the name of the Lord will be
        saved.'   (Joel 2:28–32)

²²"Fellow Israelites, listen to this! Jesus of Nazareth was a man who had God's approval. God did miracles, wonders and signs among you through Jesus. You yourselves know this. ²³Long ago God planned that Jesus would be handed over to you. With the help of evil people, you put Jesus to death. You nailed him to the cross. ²⁴But God raised him from the dead. He set him free from the suffering of death. It wasn't possible for death to keep its hold on Jesus. ²⁵David spoke about him. He said,

" 'I know that the Lord is always with
        me.
      Because he is at my right hand,
      I will always be secure.
²⁶ So my heart is glad and joy is on my
        tongue.
      My whole body will be full of hope.
²⁷ You will not leave me in the place of the
        dead.

You will not let your holy one rot
　　away.
[28] You always show me the path that leads
　　to life.
　You will fill me with joy when I am
　　with you.'　*(Psalm 16:8–11)*

[29]"Fellow Israelites, you can be sure that King David died. He was buried. His tomb is still here today. [30]But David was a prophet. He knew that God had made a promise to him. God had promised that he would make someone in David's family line king after him. [31]David saw what was coming. So he spoke about the Messiah rising from the dead. He said that the Messiah would not be left in the place of the dead. His body wouldn't rot in the ground. [32]God has raised this same Jesus back to life. We are all witnesses of this. [33]Jesus has been given a place of honor at the right hand of God. He has received the Holy Spirit from the Father. This is what God had promised. It is Jesus who has poured out what you now see and hear. [34]David did not go up to heaven. But he said,

" 'The Lord said to my Lord,
　　"Sit at my right hand.
[35] I will put your enemies
　　under your control." '　*(Psalm 110:1)*

[36]"So be sure of this, all you people of Israel. You nailed Jesus to the cross. But God has made him both Lord and Messiah."

[37]When the people heard this, it had a deep effect on them. They said to Peter and the other apostles, "Brothers, what should we do?"

[38]Peter replied, "All of you must turn away from your sins and be baptized in the name of Jesus Christ. Then your sins will be forgiven. You will receive the gift of the Holy Spirit. [39]The promise is for you and your children. It is also for all who are far away. It is for all whom the Lord our God will choose."

[40]Peter said many other things to warn them. He begged them, "Save yourselves from these evil people." [41]Those who accepted his message were baptized. About 3,000 people joined the believers that day.

The Believers Share Their Lives Together

[42]The believers studied what the apostles taught. They shared their lives together.

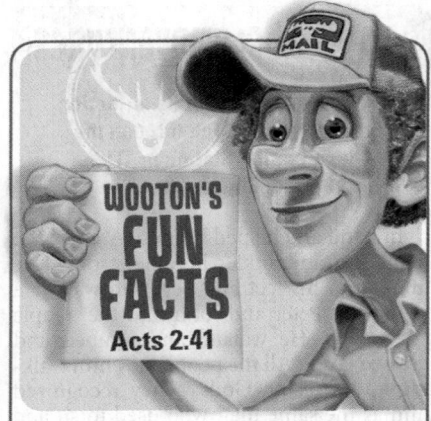

In Matthew 16:13–19, Jesus tells Peter he will be the rock of the church. Peter's first speech brings three thousand to join the church. I'd say that *does* rock!

They ate and prayed together. [43]Everyone was amazed at what God was doing. They were amazed when the apostles performed many wonders and signs. [44]All the believers were together. They shared everything they had. [45]They sold property and other things they owned. They gave to anyone who needed something. [46]Every day they met together in the temple courtyard. They ate meals together in their homes. Their hearts were glad and sincere. [47]They praised God. They were respected by all the people. Every day the Lord added to their group those who were being saved.

Peter Heals a Beggar Who Can't Walk

3 One day Peter and John were going up to the temple. It was three o'clock in the afternoon. It was the time for prayer. [2]A man unable to walk was being carried to the temple gate called Beautiful. He had been that way since he was born. Every day someone put him near the gate. There he would beg from people going into the temple courtyards. [3]He saw that Peter and John were about to enter. So he asked them for money. [4]Peter looked straight at him, and so did John. Then Peter said, "Look at us!" [5]So the man watched them closely. He expected to get something from them.

[6]Peter said, "I don't have any silver or gold. But I'll give you what I do have. In the name of Jesus Christ of Nazareth, get up and walk." [7]Then Peter took him by the

BiBLE ADVENTURES

Matthew witnessed the formation of the early church through the Imagination Station in "The Perfect Church" (A#56).

right hand and helped him up. At once the man's feet and ankles became strong. [8]He jumped to his feet and began to walk. He went with Peter and John into the temple courtyards. He walked and jumped and praised God. [9]All the people saw him walking and praising God. [10]They recognized him as the same man who used to sit and beg at the temple gate called Beautiful. They were filled with wonder. They were amazed at what had happened to him.

Peter Speaks to the People at the Temple

[11]The man was holding on to Peter and John. All the people were amazed. They came running to them at the place called Solomon's Porch. [12]When Peter saw this, he said, "Fellow Israelites, why does this surprise you? Why do you stare at us? It's not as if we've made this man walk by our own power or godliness. [13]The God of our fathers, Abraham, Isaac and Jacob, has done this. God has brought glory to Jesus, who serves him. But you handed Jesus over to be killed. Pilate had decided to let him go. But you spoke against Jesus when he was in Pilate's court. [14]You spoke against the Holy and Blameless One. You asked for a murderer to be set free instead. [15]You killed the one who gives life. But God raised him from the dead. We are witnesses of this. [16]This man whom you see and know was made strong because of faith in Jesus' name. Faith in Jesus has healed him completely. You can see it with your own eyes.

[17]"My fellow Israelites, I know you didn't realize what you were doing. Neither did your leaders. [18]But God had given a promise through all the prophets. And this is how he has made his promise come true. He said that his Messiah would suffer. [19]So turn away from your sins. Turn to God. Then your sins will be wiped away. The time will come when the Lord will make everything new. [20]He will send the Messiah. Jesus has been appointed as the

Messiah for you. [21]Heaven must receive him until the time when God makes everything new. He promised this long ago through his holy prophets. [22]Moses said, 'The Lord your God will raise up for you a prophet like me. He will be one of your own people. You must listen to everything he tells you. [23]Anyone who does not listen to him will be completely cut off from their people.' *(Deuteronomy 18:15,18,19)*

[24]"Beginning with Samuel, all the prophets spoke about this. They said these days would come. [25]What the prophets said was meant for you. The covenant God made with your people long ago is yours also. He said to Abraham, 'All nations on earth will be blessed through your children.' *(Genesis 22:18; 26:4)* [26]God raised up Jesus, who serves him. God sent him first to you. He did it to bless you. He wanted to turn each of you from your evil ways."

Peter and John Are Taken to the Sanhedrin

4 Peter and John were speaking to the people. The priests, the captain of the temple guard, and the Sadducees came up to the apostles. [2]They were very upset by what the apostles were teaching the people. The apostles were saying that people can be raised from the dead. They said this can happen because Jesus rose from the dead. [3]So the temple authorities arrested Peter and John. It was already evening, so they put them in prison until the next day. [4]But many who heard the message believed. The number of men who believed grew to about 5,000.

[5]The next day the rulers, the elders and the teachers of the law met in Jerusalem. [6]Annas, the high priest, was there. So were Caiaphas, John, Alexander and other people in the high priest's family. [7]They had Peter and John brought to them. They wanted to question them. "By what power did you do this?" they asked. "And through whose name?"

[8]Peter was filled with the Holy Spirit. He said to them, "Rulers and elders of the people! [9]Are you asking us to explain our actions today? Do you want to know why we were kind to a man who couldn't walk? Are you asking how he was healed? [10]Then listen to this, you and all the people of Israel! You nailed Jesus Christ of Nazareth

to the cross. But God raised him from the dead. It is through Jesus' name that this man stands healed in front of you. ¹¹Scripture says that Jesus is

> "'the stone you builders did not accept.
> But it has become the most
> important stone of all.'
> *(Psalm 118:22)*

¹²You can't be saved by believing in anyone else. God has given people no other name under heaven that will save them."

¹³The leaders saw how bold Peter and John were. They also realized that Peter and John were ordinary men with no training. This surprised the leaders. They realized that these men had been with Jesus. ¹⁴The leaders could see the man who had been healed. He was standing there with them. So there was nothing they could say. ¹⁵They ordered Peter and John to leave the Sanhedrin. Then they talked things over. ¹⁶"What can we do with these men?" they asked. "Everyone living in Jerusalem knows they have performed an unusual miracle. We can't say it didn't happen. ¹⁷We have to stop this thing. It must not spread any further among the people. We have to warn these men. They must never speak to anyone in Jesus' name again."

¹⁸Once again the leaders called in Peter and John. They commanded them not to speak or teach at all in Jesus' name. ¹⁹But Peter and John replied, "Which is right from God's point of view? Should we listen to you? Or should we listen to God? You be the judges! ²⁰There's nothing else we can do. We have to speak about the things we've seen and heard."

²¹The leaders warned them again. Then they let them go. They couldn't decide how to punish Peter and John. They knew that all the people were praising God for what had happened. ²²The man who had been healed by the miracle was over 40 years old.

The Believers Pray

²³Peter and John were allowed to leave. They went back to their own people. They reported everything the chief priests and the elders had said to them. ²⁴The believers heard this. Then they raised their voices together in prayer to God. "Lord and King," they said, "you made the heavens, the earth and the sea. You made everything in them.

²⁵Long ago you spoke by the Holy Spirit. You spoke through the mouth of our father David, who served you. You said,

> "'Why are the nations angry?
> Why do the people make useless
> plans?
> ²⁶ The kings of the earth rise up.
> The rulers of the earth gather together
> against the Lord
> and against his anointed king.'
> *(Psalm 2:1,2)*

²⁷In fact, Herod and Pontius Pilate met with the Gentiles in this city. They also met with the people of Israel. All of them made plans against your holy servant Jesus. He is the one you anointed. ²⁸They did what your power and purpose had already decided should happen. ²⁹Now, Lord, consider the bad things they say they are going to do. Help us to be very bold when we speak your word. ³⁰Stretch out your hand to heal. Do signs and wonders through the name of your holy servant Jesus."

³¹After they prayed, the place where they were meeting was shaken. They were all filled with the Holy Spirit. They were bold when they spoke God's word.

The Believers Share What They Own

³²All the believers were agreed in heart and mind. They didn't claim that anything they had was their own. Instead, they shared everything they owned. ³³With great power the apostles continued their teaching. They were telling people that the Lord Jesus had risen from the dead. And God's grace was working powerfully in all of them. ³⁴So there were no needy persons among them. From time to time, those who owned land or houses sold them. They brought the money from the sales. ³⁵They put it down at the apostles' feet. It was then given out to anyone who needed it.

³⁶Joseph was a Levite from Cyprus. The apostles called him Barnabas. The name Barnabas means Son of Help. ³⁷Barnabas

sold a field he owned. He brought the money from the sale. He put it down at the apostles' feet.

Ananias and Sapphira

5 A man named Ananias and his wife, Sapphira, also sold some land. [2]He kept part of the money for himself. Sapphira knew he had kept it. He brought the rest of it and put it down at the apostles' feet.

[3]Then Peter said, "Ananias, why did you let Satan fill your heart? He made you lie to the Holy Spirit. You have kept some of the money you received for the land. [4]Didn't the land belong to you before it was sold? After it was sold, you could have used the money as you wished. What made you think of doing such a thing? You haven't lied just to people. You've also lied to God."

[5]When Ananias heard this, he fell down and died. All who heard what had happened were filled with fear. [6]Some young men came and wrapped up his body. They carried him out and buried him.

[7]About three hours later, the wife of Ananias came in. She didn't know what had happened. [8]Peter asked her, "Tell me. Is this the price you and Ananias sold the land for?"

"Yes," she said. "That's the price."

[9]Peter asked her, "How could you agree to test the Spirit of the Lord? Listen! You can hear the steps of the men who buried your husband. They are at the door. They will carry you out also."

[10]At that moment she fell down at Peter's feet and died. Then the young men came in. They saw that Sapphira was dead. So they carried her out and buried her beside her husband. [11]The whole church and all who heard about these things were filled with fear.

The Apostles Heal Many People

[12]The apostles did many signs and wonders among the people. All the believers used to meet together at Solomon's Porch. [13]No outsider dared to join them. But the people thought highly of them. [14]More and more men and women believed in the Lord. They joined the other believers. [15]So people brought those who were sick into the streets. They placed them on beds and mats. They hoped that at least Peter's shadow might fall on some of them as he walked

by. [16]Crowds even gathered from the towns around Jerusalem. They brought their sick people. They also brought those who were suffering because of evil spirits. All of them were healed.

The Apostles Are Treated Badly

[17]The high priest and all his companions were Sadducees. They were very jealous of the apostles. [18]So they arrested them and put them in the public jail. [19]But during the night an angel of the Lord came. He opened the doors of the jail and brought the apostles out. [20]"Go! Stand in the temple courtyard," the angel said. "Tell the people all about this new life."

[21]Early the next day they did as they had been told. They entered the temple courtyard. There they began to teach the people.

The high priest and his companions arrived. They called the Sanhedrin together. The Sanhedrin was a gathering of all the elders of Israel. They sent for the apostles who were in jail. [22]The officers arrived at the jail. But they didn't find the apostles there. So they went back and reported it. [23]"We found the jail locked up tight," they said. "The guards were standing at the doors. But when we opened the doors, we didn't find anyone inside." [24]When the captain of the temple guard and the chief priests heard this report, they were bewildered. They wondered what would happen next.

[25]Then someone came and said, "Look! The men you put in jail are standing in the temple courtyard. They are teaching the people." [26]So the captain went with his officers and brought the apostles back. But they didn't use force. They were afraid the people would kill them by throwing stones at them.

[27]They brought the apostles to the Sanhedrin. The high priest questioned them. [28]"We gave you clear orders not to teach in Jesus' name," he said. "But you have filled Jerusalem with your teaching. You want to make us guilty of this man's death."

[29]Peter and the other apostles replied, "We must obey God instead of people!

BIBLE ADVENTURES

In "I Want My B-TV" (A#23), a trailer for a new movie called The Lion Thing told the story of Ananias and Sapphira.

[30]You had Jesus killed by nailing him to a cross. But the God of our people raised Jesus from the dead. [31]Now Jesus is Prince and Savior. God has proved this by giving Jesus a place of honor with him. He did it to turn Israel away from their sins and forgive them. [32]We are telling people about these things. And so is the Holy Spirit. God has given the Spirit to those who obey him."

[33]When the leaders heard this, they became very angry. They wanted to put the apostles to death. [34]But a Pharisee named Gamaliel stood up in the Sanhedrin. He was a teacher of the law. He was honored by all the people. He ordered the apostles to be taken outside for a little while. [35]Then Gamaliel spoke to the Sanhedrin. "Men of Israel," he said, "think carefully about what you plan to do to these men. [36]Some time ago Theudas appeared. He claimed he was really somebody. About 400 people followed him. But he was killed. All his followers were scattered. So they accomplished nothing. [37]After this, Judas from Galilee came along. This was in the days when the Romans made a list of all the people. Judas led a gang of men against the Romans. He too was killed. All his followers were scattered. [38]So let me give you some advice. Leave these men alone! Let them go! If their plans and actions only come from people, they will fail. [39]But if their plans come from God, you won't be able to stop these men. You will only find yourselves fighting against God."

[40]His speech won the leaders over. They called the apostles in and had them whipped. The leaders ordered them not to speak in Jesus' name. Then they let the apostles go.

[41]The apostles were full of joy as they left the Sanhedrin. They considered it an honor to suffer shame for the name of Jesus. [42]Every day they taught in the temple courtyards and from house to house. They never stopped telling people the good news that Jesus is the Messiah.

Seven Leaders Are Chosen

6 In those days the number of believers was growing. The Greek Jews complained about the non-Greek Jews. They said that the widows of the Greek Jews were not being taken care of. They weren't getting their fair share of food each day. [2]So the 12 apostles gathered all the believers together. They said, "It wouldn't be right for us to give up teaching God's word. And we'd have to stop teaching to wait on tables. [3]Brothers and sisters, choose seven of your men. They must be known as men who are wise and full of the Holy Spirit. We will turn this important work over to them. [4]Then we can give our attention to prayer and to teaching God's word."

[5]This plan pleased the whole group. They chose Stephen. He was full of faith and of the Holy Spirit. Philip, Procorus, Nicanor, Timon and Parmenas were chosen too. The group also chose Nicolas from Antioch. He had accepted the Jewish faith. [6]The group brought them to the apostles. Then the apostles prayed and placed their hands on them.

[7]So God's word spread. The number of believers in Jerusalem grew quickly. Also, a large number of priests began to obey Jesus' teachings.

Stephen Is Arrested

[8]Stephen was full of God's grace and power. He did great wonders and signs among the people. [9]But members of the group called the Synagogue of the Freedmen began to oppose him. Some of them were Jews from Cyrene and Alexandria. Others were Jews from Cilicia and Asia Minor. They all began to argue with Stephen. [10]But he was too wise for them. That's because the Holy Spirit gave Stephen wisdom whenever he spoke.

[11]Then in secret they talked some men into lying about Stephen. They said, "We heard Stephen speak evil things against Moses and against God." [12]So the people were stirred up. The elders and the teachers of the law were stirred up too. They arrested Stephen and brought him to the Sanhedrin. [13]They found witnesses who were willing to tell lies. These liars said, "This fellow never stops speaking against this holy place. He also speaks against the law. [14]We have heard him say that this Jesus of Nazareth will destroy this place. He says Jesus will change the practices that Moses handed down to us."

[15]All who were sitting in the Sanhedrin looked right at Stephen. They saw that his face was like the face of an angel.

Stephen Speaks to the Sanhedrin

7 Then the high priest questioned Stephen. "Is what these people are saying true?" he asked.

2"Brothers and fathers, listen to me!" Stephen replied. "The God of glory appeared to our father Abraham. At that time Abraham was still in Mesopotamia. He had not yet begun living in Harran. 3'Leave your country and your people,' God said. 'Go to the land I will show you.' *(Genesis 12:1)*

4"So Abraham left the land of Babylonia. He settled in Harran. After his father died, God sent Abraham to this land where you are now living. 5God didn't give him any property here. He didn't even give him enough land to set his foot on. But God made a promise to him and to all his family after him. He said they would possess the land. The promise was made even though at that time Abraham had no child. 6Here is what God said to him. 'For 400 years your family after you will be strangers in a country not their own. They will be slaves and will be treated badly. 7But I will punish the nation that makes them slaves,' God said. 'After that, they will leave that country and worship me here.' *(Genesis 15:13,14)* 8Then God made a covenant with Abraham. God told him that circumcision would show who the members of the covenant were. Abraham became Isaac's father. He circumcised Isaac eight days after he was born. Later, Isaac became Jacob's father. Jacob had 12 sons. They became the founders of the 12 tribes of Israel.

9"Jacob's sons were jealous of their brother Joseph. So they sold him as a slave. He was taken to Egypt. But God was with him. 10He saved Joseph from all his troubles. God made Joseph wise. He helped him to become the friend of Pharaoh, the king of Egypt. So Pharaoh made Joseph ruler over Egypt and his whole palace.

11"There was not enough food for all Egypt and Canaan. This brought great suffering. Jacob and his sons couldn't find food. 12But Jacob heard that there was grain in Egypt. So he sent his sons on their first visit. 13On their second visit, Joseph told

WHAT ABOUT YOU?

Nonbelievers often argue that churches should be full of perfect people. But is that true? Of course not. Christians will never be perfect because people aren't perfect. Jesus is the only exception. The rest of us continue to battle with sin. The Holy Spirit will help us make wise choices, but as long as we live in these fleshly bodies, we're going to struggle. It's part of being human.

The Adventures in Odyssey episode "The Perfect Church," helps us understand this by describing Stephen, an early Christian who would later die for his faith. Stephen says God works through flawed, fallen people. Fortunately, however, the church is full of *forgiven* people. When we put our faith in Jesus Christ, we are redeemed and become part of His body, the church. God forgives our sin and begins to transform us into the image of His Son.

So what do we need to do? It's our responsibility to put ourselves in a position to change. That means studying God's Word to learn about the Lord and the spiritual battles we'll face. It means talking with God in prayer. And it means going to church, where we can stay connected with other less-than-perfect people on this exciting spiritual journey.

What's your favorite part of going to church? You may have a friend whose family doesn't attend services. Invite that person to come with you sometime. Research shows that many people who don't go to church would go if someone just took the time to ask them. That person could be you!

his brothers who he was. Pharaoh learned about Joseph's family. [14]After this, Joseph sent for his father Jacob and his whole family. The total number of people was 75. [15]Then Jacob went down to Egypt. There he and his family died. [16]Some of their bodies were brought back to Shechem. They were placed in a tomb Abraham had bought. He had purchased it from Hamor's sons at Shechem. He had purchased it for a certain amount of money.

[17]"In Egypt the number of our people grew and grew. It was nearly time for God to make his promise to Abraham come true. [18]Then 'a new king came to power in Egypt. Joseph didn't mean anything to him.' (Exodus 1:8) [19]The king was very evil and dishonest with our people. He treated them badly. He forced them to throw out their newborn babies to die.

[20]"At that time Moses was born. He was not an ordinary child. For three months he was taken care of by his family. [21]Then he was placed outside. But Pharaoh's daughter took him home. She brought him up as her own son. [22]Moses was taught all the knowledge of the people of Egypt. He became a powerful speaker and a man of action.

[23]"When Moses was 40 years old, he decided to visit the people of Israel. They were his own people. [24]He saw one of them being treated badly by an Egyptian. So he went to help him. He got even by killing the man. [25]Moses thought his own people would realize that God was using him to save them. But they didn't. [26]The next day Moses saw two Israelites fighting. He tried to make peace between them. 'Men, you are both Israelites,' he said. 'Why do you want to hurt each other?'

[27]"But the man who was treating the other one badly pushed Moses to one side. He said, 'Who made you ruler and judge over us? [28]Are you thinking of killing me as you killed the Egyptian yesterday?' (Exodus 2:14) [29]When Moses heard this, he escaped to Midian. He lived there as an outsider. He became the father of two sons there.

[30]"Forty years passed. Then an angel appeared to Moses in the flames of a burning bush. This happened in the desert near Mount Sinai. [31]When Moses saw the bush, he was amazed. He went over for a closer look. There he heard the Lord say, [32]'I am the God of your fathers. I am the God of Abraham, Isaac and Jacob.' (Exodus 3:6) Moses shook with fear. He didn't dare to look.

[33]"Then the Lord said to him, 'Take off your sandals. You must do this because the place where you are standing is holy ground. [34]I have seen my people beaten down in Egypt. I have heard their groans. I have come down to set them free. Now come. I will send you back to Egypt.' (Exodus 3:5,7,8,10) [35]"This is the same Moses the two men of Israel would not accept. They had said, 'Who made you ruler and judge?' But God himself sent Moses to rule the people of Israel and set them free. He spoke to Moses through an angel. The angel had appeared to him in the bush. [36]So Moses led them out of Egypt. He did wonders and signs in Egypt, at the Red Sea, and for 40 years in the desert.

[37]"This is the same Moses who spoke to the Israelites. 'God will send you a prophet,' he said. 'He will be like me. He will come from your own people.' (Deuteronomy 18:15) [38]Moses was with the Israelites in the desert. He was with the angel who spoke to him on Mount Sinai. Moses was with our people of long ago. He received living words to pass on to us.

[39]"But our people refused to obey Moses. They would not accept him. In their hearts, they wished they were back in Egypt. [40]They told Aaron, 'Make us a god who will lead us. This fellow Moses brought us up out of Egypt. But we don't know what has happened to him!' (Exodus 32:1) [41]That was the time they made a statue to be their god. It was shaped like a calf. They brought sacrifices to it. They even enjoyed what they had made with their own hands. [42]But God turned away from them. He let them go on worshiping the sun, moon and stars. This agrees with what is written in the book of the prophets. There it says,

" 'People of Israel, did you bring me
        sacrifices and offerings
    for 40 years in the desert?
[43] You have taken with you the shrine of
        your false god Molek.
    You have taken with you the star of
        your false god Rephan.
    You made statues of those gods to
        worship.
So I will send you away from your
        country.'   (Amos 5:25–27)
    God sent them to Babylon and even
        farther.

[44]"Long ago our people were in the desert. They had with them the holy tent. The tent was where the tablets of the covenant law were kept. Moses had made the holy tent as God had commanded him. Moses made it like the pattern he had seen. [45]Our people received the tent from God. Then they brought it with them when they took the land of Canaan. God drove out the nations that were in their way. At that time Joshua was Israel's leader. The tent remained in the land until David's time. [46]David was blessed by God. So David asked if he could build a house for the God of Jacob. [47]But it was Solomon who built the temple for God.

[48]"But the Most High God does not live in houses made by human hands. As God says through the prophet,

[49] " 'Heaven is my throne.
　　The earth is under my control.
　What kind of house will you build for
　　　me?
　　　says the Lord.
　　Where will my resting place be?
[50] 　Didn't my hand make all these things?'
(Isaiah 66:1,2)

[51]"You stubborn people! You won't obey! You won't listen! You are just like your people of long ago! You always oppose the Holy Spirit! [52]Was there ever a prophet your people didn't try to hurt? They even killed those who told about the coming of the Blameless One. And now you have handed him over to his enemies. You have murdered him. [53]The law you received was given by angels. But you haven't obeyed it."

Stephen Is Killed

[54]When the members of the Sanhedrin heard this, they became very angry. They were so angry they ground their teeth at Stephen. [55]But he was full of the Holy Spirit. He looked up to heaven and saw God's glory. He saw Jesus standing at God's right hand. [56]"Look!" he said. "I see heaven open. The Son of Man is standing at God's right hand."

[57]When the Sanhedrin heard this, they covered their ears. They yelled at the top of their voices. They all rushed at him. [58]They dragged him out of the city. They began to throw stones at him to kill him. The people who had brought false charges against Stephen took off their coats. They placed them at the feet of a young man named Saul.

[59]While the members of the Sanhedrin were throwing stones at Stephen, he prayed. "Lord Jesus, receive my spirit," he said. [60]Then he fell on his knees. He cried out, "Lord! Don't hold this sin against them!" When he had said this, he died.

8 And Saul had agreed with the Sanhedrin that Stephen should die.

The Church Is Treated Badly and Scattered

On that day the church in Jerusalem began to be attacked and treated badly. All except the apostles were scattered throughout Judea and Samaria. [2]Godly Jews buried Stephen. They mourned deeply for him. [3]But Saul began to destroy the church. He went from house to house. He dragged away men and women and put them in prison.

Philip Goes to Samaria

[4]The believers who had been scattered preached the word everywhere they went. [5]Philip went down to a city in Samaria. There he preached about the Messiah. [6]The crowds listened to Philip and saw the signs he did. All of them paid close attention to what he said. [7]Evil spirits screamed and came out of many people. Many people who were disabled or who couldn't walk were healed. [8]So there was great joy in that city.

Acts 8:2 *To mourn* means "to be sad." The friends of Stephen had heavy hearts when he died. Since the heart of a blue whale weighs as much as a car, I figure whales must be very, very sad.

BiBLE ADVENTURES

Olivia met Simon the evil magician
in the Imagination Station in
"Hidden Gems" (Club).

Simon the Evil Magician

⁹A man named Simon lived in the city. For quite a while he had practiced evil magic there. He amazed all the people of Samaria. He claimed to be someone great. ¹⁰And all the people listened to him, from the least important of them to the most important. They exclaimed, "It is right to call this man the Great Power of God!" ¹¹He had amazed them for a long time with his evil magic. So they followed him. ¹²But Philip announced the good news of God's kingdom and the name of Jesus Christ. So men and women believed and were baptized. ¹³Simon himself believed and was baptized. He followed Philip everywhere. He was amazed by the great signs and miracles he saw.

¹⁴The apostles in Jerusalem heard that people in Samaria had accepted God's word. So they sent Peter and John to Samaria. ¹⁵When they arrived there, they prayed for the new believers. They prayed that they would receive the Holy Spirit. ¹⁶The Holy Spirit had not yet come on any of them. They had only been baptized in the name of the Lord Jesus. ¹⁷Then Peter and John placed their hands on them. And they received the Holy Spirit.

¹⁸Simon watched as the apostles placed their hands on them. He saw that the Spirit was given to them. So he offered money to Peter and John. ¹⁹He said, "Give me this power too. Then everyone I place my hands on will receive the Holy Spirit."

²⁰Peter answered, "May your money be destroyed with you! Do you think you can buy God's gift with money? ²¹You have no part or share in this holy work. Your heart is not right with God. ²²Turn away from this evil sin of yours. Pray to the Lord. Perhaps he will forgive you for having such a thought in your heart. ²³I see that you are very bitter. You are a prisoner of sin."

²⁴Then Simon answered, "Pray to the Lord for me. Pray that nothing you have said will happen to me."

²⁵Peter and John continued to preach the word of the Lord and tell people about Jesus. Then they returned to Jerusalem. On the way they preached the good news in many villages in Samaria.

Philip and the Man From Ethiopia

²⁶An angel of the Lord spoke to Philip. "Go south to the desert road," he said. "It's the road that goes down from Jerusalem to Gaza." ²⁷So Philip started out. On his way he met an Ethiopian official. The man had an important position in charge of all the wealth of the Kandake. Kandake means queen of Ethiopia. This official had gone to Jerusalem to worship. ²⁸On his way home he was sitting in his chariot. He was reading the Book of Isaiah the prophet. ²⁹The Holy Spirit told Philip, "Go to that chariot. Stay near it."

³⁰So Philip ran up to the chariot. He heard the man reading Isaiah the prophet. "Do you understand what you're reading?" Philip asked.

³¹"How can I?" he said. "I need someone to explain it to me." So he invited Philip to come up and sit with him.

³²Here is the part of Scripture the official was reading. It says,

"He was led like a sheep to be killed.
    Just as lambs are silent while their
        wool is being cut off,
    he did not open his mouth.
³³ When he was treated badly, he was
        refused a fair trial.
    Who can say anything about his
        children?
    His life was cut off from the earth."
                                    (Isaiah 53:7,8)

³⁴The official said to Philip, "Tell me, please. Who is the prophet talking about? Himself, or someone else?" ³⁵Then Philip began with that same part of Scripture. He told him the good news about Jesus.

³⁶⁻³⁷As they traveled along the road, they came to some water. The official said, "Look! Here is water! What can stop me from being baptized?" ³⁸He gave orders to stop the chariot. Then both Philip and the official went down into the water. Philip baptized him. ³⁹When they came up out of the water, the Spirit of the Lord suddenly took Philip away. The official did not see him again. He went on his way full of joy. ⁴⁰Philip was seen next at Azotus. From there he traveled all around. He preached the good news in all the towns. Finally he arrived in Caesarea.

Saul Becomes a Believer

9 Meanwhile, Saul continued to oppose the Lord's followers. He said they would be put to death. He went to the high priest. [2] He asked the priest for letters to the synagogues in Damascus. He wanted to find men and women who belonged to the Way of Jesus. The letters would allow him to take them as prisoners to Jerusalem. [3] On his journey, Saul approached Damascus. Suddenly a light from heaven flashed around him. [4] He fell to the ground. He heard a voice speak to him, "Saul! Saul! Why are you opposing me?"

[5] "Who are you, Lord?" Saul asked.

"I am Jesus," he replied. "I am the one you are opposing. [6] Now get up and go into the city. There you will be told what you must do."

[7] The men traveling with Saul stood there. They weren't able to speak. They had heard the sound. But they didn't see anyone. [8] Saul got up from the ground. He opened his eyes, but he couldn't see. So they led him by the hand into Damascus. [9] For three days he was blind. He didn't eat or drink anything.

[10] In Damascus there was a believer named Ananias. The Lord called out to him in a vision. "Ananias!" he said.

"Yes, Lord," he answered.

[11] The Lord told him, "Go to the house of Judas on Straight Street. Ask for a man from Tarsus named Saul. He is praying. [12] In a vision Saul has seen a man come and place his hands on him. That man's name is Ananias. In the vision, Ananias placed his hands on Saul so he could see again."

[13] "Lord," Ananias answered, "I've heard many reports about this man. They say he has done great harm to your holy people in Jerusalem. [14] Now he has come here to arrest all those who worship you. The chief priests have given him authority to do this."

[15] But the Lord said to Ananias, "Go! I have chosen this man to work for me. He will announce my name to the Gentiles and to their kings. He will also announce my name to the people of Israel. [16] I will show him how much he must suffer for me."

[17] Then Ananias went to the house and entered it. He placed his hands on Saul. "Brother Saul," he said, "you saw the Lord Jesus. He appeared to you on the road as you were coming here. He has sent me so

BIBLE ADVENTURES

Rodney and Sam saw Saul's conversion to Paul in the Imagination Station in "Saint Paul: The Man from Tarsus" and "Saint Paul: Set Apart by God" (A#23).

that you will be able to see again. You will be filled with the Holy Spirit." [18] Right away something like scales fell from Saul's eyes. And he could see again. He got up and was baptized. [19] After eating some food, he got his strength back.

Saul in Damascus and Jerusalem

Saul spent several days with the believers in Damascus. [20] Right away he began to preach in the synagogues. He taught that Jesus is the Son of God. [21] All who heard him were amazed. They asked, "Isn't he the man who caused great trouble in Jerusalem? Didn't he make trouble for those who worship Jesus? Hasn't he come here to take them as prisoners to the chief priests?" [22] But Saul grew more and more powerful. The Jews living in Damascus couldn't believe what was happening. Saul proved to them that Jesus is the Messiah.

[23] After many days, the Jews had a meeting. They planned to kill Saul. [24] But he learned about their plan. Day and night they watched the city gates closely in order to kill him. [25] But his followers helped him escape by night. They lowered him in a basket through an opening in the wall.

[26] When Saul came to Jerusalem, he tried to join the believers. But they were all afraid of him. They didn't believe he was really one of Jesus' followers. [27] But Barnabas took him to the apostles. He told them about Saul's journey. He said that Saul had seen the Lord. He told how the Lord had spoken to Saul. Barnabas also said that Saul had preached without fear in Jesus' name in Damascus. [28] So Saul stayed with the believers. He moved about freely in Jerusalem. He spoke boldly in the Lord's name. [29] He talked and argued with the Greek Jews. But they tried to kill him. [30] The other believers heard about this. They took Saul down to Caesarea. From there they sent him off to Tarsus.

[31] Then the church throughout Judea, Galilee and Samaria enjoyed a time of peace. The church was strengthened and

grew larger. That's because they worshiped the Lord and the Holy Spirit helped them.

Peter Heals Aeneas and Dorcas

³²Peter traveled around the country. He went to visit the Lord's people who lived in Lydda. ³³There he found a disabled man named Aeneas. For eight years the man had spent most of his time in bed. ³⁴"Aeneas," Peter said to him, "Jesus Christ heals you. Get up! Roll up your mat!" So Aeneas got up right away. ³⁵Everyone who lived in Lydda and Sharon saw him. They turned to the Lord.

³⁶In Joppa there was a believer named Tabitha. Her name in the Greek language is Dorcas. She was always doing good and helping poor people. ³⁷About that time she became sick and died. Her body was washed and placed in a room upstairs. ³⁸Lydda was near Joppa. The believers heard that Peter was in Lydda. So they sent two men to him. They begged him, "Please come at once!"

³⁹Peter went with them. When he arrived, he was taken upstairs to the room. All the widows stood around him crying. They showed him the robes and other clothes Dorcas had made before she died. ⁴⁰Peter sent them all out of the room. Then he got down on his knees and prayed. He turned toward the dead woman. He said, "Tabitha, get up." She opened her eyes. When she saw Peter, she sat up. ⁴¹He took her by the hand and helped her to her feet. Then he called the believers and especially the widows. He brought her to them. They saw that she was alive. ⁴²This became known all over Joppa. Many people believed in the Lord. ⁴³Peter stayed in Joppa for some time. He stayed with Simon, a man who worked with leather.

Cornelius Calls for Peter

10 A man named Cornelius lived in Caesarea. He was a Roman commander in the Italian Regiment. ²Cornelius and all his family were faithful and worshiped God. He gave freely to people who were in need. He prayed to God regularly. ³One day about three o'clock in the afternoon he had a vision. He saw clearly an angel of God. The angel came to him and said, "Cornelius!"

⁴Cornelius was afraid. He stared at the angel. "What is it, Lord?" he asked.

The angel answered, "Your prayers and gifts to poor people are like an offering to God. So he has remembered you. ⁵Now send men to Joppa. Have them bring back a man named Simon. He is also called Peter. ⁶He is staying with another Simon, a man who works with leather. His house is by the sea."

⁷The angel who spoke to him left. Then Cornelius called two of his servants. He also called a godly soldier who was one of his attendants. ⁸He told them everything that had happened. Then he sent them to Joppa.

Peter Has a Vision

⁹It was about noon the next day. The men were on their journey and were approaching the city. Peter went up on the roof to pray. ¹⁰He became hungry. He wanted something to eat. While the meal was being prepared, Peter had a vision. ¹¹He saw heaven open up. There he saw something that looked like a large sheet. It was being let down to earth by its four corners. ¹²It had all kinds of four-footed animals in it. It also had reptiles and birds in it. ¹³Then a voice told him, "Get up, Peter. Kill and eat."

¹⁴"No, Lord! I will not!" Peter replied. "I have never eaten anything that is not pure and 'clean.'"

¹⁵The voice spoke to him a second time. It said, "Do not say anything is not pure that God has made 'clean.'"

¹⁶This happened three times. Right away the sheet was taken back up to heaven.

¹⁷Peter was wondering what the vision meant. At that very moment the men sent by Cornelius found Simon's house. They stopped at the gate ¹⁸and called out. They asked if Simon Peter was staying there.

¹⁹Peter was still thinking about the vision. The Holy Spirit spoke to him. "Simon," he said, "three men are looking for you. ²⁰Get up and go downstairs. Don't let anything keep you from going with them. I have sent them."

²¹Peter went down and spoke to the men. "I'm the one you're looking for," he said. "Why have you come?"

²²The men replied, "We have come from Cornelius, the Roman commander. He is a good man who worships God. All the Jewish people respect him. A holy angel

told him to invite you to his house. Then Cornelius can hear what you have to say." ²³Then Peter invited the men into the house to be his guests.

Peter Goes to the House of Cornelius

The next day Peter went with the three men. Some of the believers from Joppa went along. ²⁴The following day he arrived in Caesarea. Cornelius was expecting them. He had called together his relatives and close friends. ²⁵When Peter entered the house, Cornelius met him. As a sign of respect, he fell at Peter's feet. ²⁶But Peter made him get up. "Stand up," he said. "I am only a man myself."

²⁷As he was talking with Cornelius, Peter went inside. There he found a large group of people. ²⁸He said to them, "You know that it is against our law for a Jew to enter a Gentile home. A Jew shouldn't have any close contact with a Gentile. But God has shown me that I should not say anyone is not pure and 'clean.' ²⁹So when you sent for me, I came without asking any questions. May I ask why you sent for me?"

³⁰Cornelius answered, "Three days ago at this very hour I was in my house praying. It was three o'clock in the afternoon. Suddenly a man in shining clothes stood in front of me. ³¹He said, 'Cornelius, God has heard your prayer. He has remembered your gifts to poor people. ³²Send someone to Joppa to get Simon Peter. He is a guest in the home of another Simon, who works with leather. He lives by the sea.' ³³So I sent for you right away. It was good of you to come. Now we are all here. And God is here with us. We are ready to listen to everything the Lord has commanded you to tell us."

³⁴Then Peter began to speak. "I now realize how true it is that God treats everyone the same," he said. ³⁵"He accepts people from every nation. He accepts anyone who has respect for him and does what is right. ³⁶You know the message God sent to the people of Israel. It is the good news of peace through Jesus Christ. He is Lord of all. ³⁷You know what has happened all through the area of Judea. It started in Galilee after John preached about baptism. ³⁸You know how God anointed Jesus of Nazareth with the Holy Spirit and with power. Jesus went around doing good. He healed all who were under the devil's power. God was with him.

³⁹"We are witnesses of everything he did in the land of the Jews and in Jerusalem. They killed him by nailing him to a cross. ⁴⁰But on the third day God raised him from the dead. God allowed Jesus to be seen. ⁴¹But he wasn't seen by all the people. He was seen only by us. We are witnesses whom God had already chosen. We ate and drank with him after he rose from the dead. ⁴²He commanded us to preach to the people. He told us to tell people that he is the one appointed by God to judge the living and the dead. ⁴³All the prophets tell about him. They say that all who believe in him have their sins forgiven through his name."

⁴⁴While Peter was still speaking, the Holy Spirit came on all who heard the message. ⁴⁵Some Jewish believers had come with Peter. They were amazed because the gift of the Holy Spirit had been poured out even on the Gentiles. ⁴⁶They heard them speaking in languages they had not known before. They also heard them praising God.

Then Peter said, ⁴⁷"Surely no one can keep these people from being baptized with water. They have received the Holy Spirit just as we have." ⁴⁸So he ordered that they be baptized in the name of Jesus Christ. Then they asked Peter to stay with them for a few days.

Peter Explains His Actions

11 The apostles and the believers all through Judea heard that Gentiles had also received God's word. ²Peter went up to Jerusalem. There the Jewish believers found fault with him. ³They said, "You went into the house of Gentiles. You ate with them."

⁴Starting from the beginning, Peter told them the whole story. ⁵"I was in the city of Joppa praying," he said. "There I had a vision. I saw something that looked like a large sheet. It was being let down from heaven by its four corners. It came down to where I was. ⁶I looked into it and saw four-footed animals of the earth. There were also wild animals, reptiles and birds. ⁷Then I heard a voice speaking to me. 'Get up, Peter,' the voice said. 'Kill and eat.'

⁸"I replied, 'No, Lord! I will not! Nothing that is not pure and "clean" has ever entered my mouth.'

⁹"A second time the voice spoke from heaven. The voice said, 'Do not say anything

is not pure that God has made "clean."' [10]This happened three times. Then the sheet was pulled up into heaven.

[11]"Just then three men stopped at the house where I was staying. They had been sent to me from Caesarea. [12]The Holy Spirit told me not to let anything keep me from going with them. These six brothers here went with me. We entered the man's house. [13]He told us how he had seen an angel appear in his house. The angel said, 'Send to Joppa for Simon Peter. [14]He has a message to bring to you. You and your whole family will be saved through it.'

[15]"As I began to speak, the Holy Spirit came on them. He came just as he had come on us at the beginning. [16]Then I remembered the Lord's words. 'John baptized with water,' he had said. 'But you will be baptized with the Holy Spirit.' [17]God gave them the same gift he gave those of us who believed in the Lord Jesus Christ. So who was I to think that I could stand in God's way?"

[18]When they heard this, they didn't object anymore. They praised God. They said, "So then, God has allowed even Gentiles to turn away from their sins. He did this so that they could live."

The Believers in Antioch

[19]Some believers had been scattered by the suffering that unbelievers had caused them. They were scattered after Stephen was killed. Those believers traveled as far as Phoenicia, Cyprus and Antioch. But they spread the word only among Jews. [20]Some believers from Cyprus and Cyrene went to Antioch. There they began to speak to Greeks also. They told them the good news about the Lord Jesus. [21]The Lord's power was with them. Large numbers of people believed and turned to the Lord.

[22]The church in Jerusalem heard about this. So they sent Barnabas to Antioch. [23]When he arrived and saw what the grace of God had done, he was glad. He told them all to remain true to the Lord with all their hearts. [24]Barnabas was a good man. He was full of the Holy Spirit and of faith. Large numbers of people came to know the Lord. [25]Then Barnabas went to Tarsus to look for Saul. [26]He found him there. Then he brought him to Antioch. For a whole year Barnabas and Saul met with the church.

They taught large numbers of people. At Antioch the believers were called Christians for the first time.

[27]In those days some prophets came down from Jerusalem to Antioch. [28]One of them was named Agabus. He stood up and spoke through the Spirit. He said there would not be nearly enough food anywhere in the Roman world. This happened while Claudius was the emperor. [29]The believers decided to provide help for the brothers and sisters living in Judea. All of them helped as much as they could. [30]They sent their gift to the elders through Barnabas and Saul.

An Angel Helps Peter Escape From Prison

12 About this time, King Herod arrested some people who belonged to the church. He planned to make them suffer greatly. [2]He had James killed with a sword. James was John's brother. [3]Herod saw that the death of James pleased some Jews. So he arrested Peter also. This happened during the Feast of Unleavened Bread. [4]After Herod arrested Peter, he put him in prison. Peter was placed under guard. He was watched by four groups of four soldiers each. Herod planned to put Peter on public trial. It would take place after the Passover Feast.

[5]So Peter was kept in prison. But the church prayed hard to God for him.

[6]It was the night before Herod was going to bring him to trial. Peter was sleeping between two soldiers. Two chains held him there. Lookouts stood guard at the entrance. [7]Suddenly an angel of the Lord appeared. A light shone in the prison cell. The angel struck Peter on his side. Peter woke up. "Quick!" the angel said. "Get up!" The chains fell off Peter's wrists.

[8]Then the angel said to him, "Put on your clothes and sandals." Peter did so. "Put on your coat," the angel told him. "Follow me." [9]Peter followed him out of the prison. But he had no idea that what the angel was doing was really happening. He thought he was seeing a vision. [10]They passed the first and second guards. Then they came to the iron gate leading to the city. It opened for them by itself. They went through it. They walked the length of one street. Suddenly the angel left Peter.

[11]Then Peter realized what had happened. He said, "Now I know for sure that the Lord has sent his angel. He set me free from Herod's power. He saved me from everything the Jewish people were hoping would happen."

[12]When Peter understood what had happened, he went to Mary's house. Mary was the mother of John Mark. Many people had gathered in her home. They were praying there. [13]Peter knocked at the outer entrance. A servant named Rhoda came to answer the door. [14]She recognized Peter's voice. She was so excited that she ran back without opening the door. "Peter is at the door!" she exclaimed.

[15]"You're out of your mind," they said to her. But she kept telling them it was true. So they said, "It must be his angel."

[16]Peter kept on knocking. When they opened the door and saw him, they were amazed. [17]Peter motioned with his hand for them to be quiet. He explained how the Lord had brought him out of prison. "Tell James and the other brothers and sisters about this," he said. Then he went to another place.

[18]In the morning the soldiers were bewildered. They couldn't figure out what had happened to Peter. [19]So Herod had them look everywhere for Peter. But they didn't find him. Then Herod questioned the guards closely. He ordered that they be put to death.

Herod Dies

Then Herod went from Judea to Caesarea and stayed there. [20]He had been quarreling with the people of Tyre and Sidon. So they got together and asked for a meeting with him. This was because they depended on the king's country to supply them with food. They gained the support of Blastus and then asked for peace. Blastus was a trusted personal servant of the king.

[21]The appointed day came. Herod was seated on his throne. He was wearing his royal robes. He made a speech to the people. [22]Then they shouted, "This is the voice of a god. It's not the voice of a man." [23]Right away an angel of the Lord struck Herod down. Herod had not given praise to God. So he was eaten by worms and died. [24]But God's word continued to spread and many people believed the message.

Barnabas and Saul Are Sent Off

[25]Barnabas and Saul finished their task. Then they returned from Jerusalem. They took John Mark with them. [1]In the church at Antioch there were prophets and teachers. Among them were Barnabas, Simeon, and Lucius from Cyrene. Simeon was also called Niger. Another was Manaen. He had been brought up with Herod, the ruler of Galilee. Saul was among them too. [2]While they were worshiping the Lord and fasting, the Holy Spirit spoke. "Set apart Barnabas and Saul for me," he said. "I have appointed them to do special work." [3]The prophets and teachers fasted and prayed. They placed their hands on Barnabas and Saul. Then they sent them off.

Events on Cyprus

[4]Barnabas and Saul were sent on their way by the Holy Spirit. They went down to Seleucia. From there they sailed to Cyprus. [5]They arrived at Salamis. There they preached God's word in the Jewish synagogues. John was with them as their helper.

[6]They traveled all across the island until they came to Paphos. There they met a Jew named Bar-Jesus. He was an evil magician and a false prophet. [7]He was an attendant of Sergius Paulus, the governor. Paulus was a man of understanding. He sent for Barnabas and Saul. He wanted to hear

WOOTON'S FUN FACTS

Acts 13:3

During Paul's trips to tell the world about Jesus, he traveled at least 10,282 miles. That's like going from Maine to Hawaii and back. And he did it before cars, planes, or bikes were invented. Talk about a world traveler!

God's word. [8]But the evil magician named Elymas opposed them. The name Elymas means Magician. He tried to keep the governor from becoming a believer. [9]Saul was also known as Paul. He was filled with the Holy Spirit. He looked straight at Elymas. He said to him, [10]"You are a child of the devil! You are an enemy of everything that is right! You cheat people. You use all kinds of tricks. Won't you ever stop twisting the right ways of the Lord? [11]Now the Lord's hand is against you. You are going to go blind. For a while you won't even be able to see the light of the sun."

Right away mist and darkness came over him. He tried to feel his way around. He wanted to find someone to lead him by the hand. [12]When the governor saw what had happened, he believed. He was amazed at what Paul was teaching about the Lord.

Paul Preaches in Pisidian Antioch

[13]From Paphos, Paul and his companions sailed to Perga in Pamphylia. There John Mark left them and returned to Jerusalem. [14]From Perga they went on to Pisidian Antioch. On the Sabbath day they entered the synagogue and sat down. [15]The Law and the Prophets were read aloud. Then the leaders of the synagogue sent word to Paul and his companions. They said, "Brothers, do you have any words of instruction for the people? If you do, please speak."

[16]Paul stood up and motioned with his hand. Then he said, "Fellow Israelites, and you Gentiles who worship God, listen to me! [17]The God of Israel chose our people who lived long ago. He blessed them greatly while they were in Egypt. With his mighty power he led them out of that country. [18]He put up with their behavior for about 40 years in the desert. [19]And he destroyed seven nations in Canaan. Then he gave the land to his people as their rightful share. [20]All this took about 450 years.

"After this, God gave them judges until the time of Samuel the prophet. [21]Then the people asked for a king. He gave them Saul, son of Kish. Saul was from the tribe of Benjamin. He ruled for 40 years. [22]God removed him and made David their king. Here is God's witness about him. 'David, son of Jesse, is a man dear to my heart,' he said. 'David will do everything I want him to do.'

[23]"From this man's family line God has brought to Israel the Savior Jesus. This is what he had promised. [24]Before Jesus came, John preached that we should turn away from our sins and be baptized. He preached this to all Israel. [25]John was coming to the end of his work. 'Who do you suppose I am?' he said. 'I am not the one you are looking for. But there is someone coming after me. I am not good enough to untie his sandals.'

[26]"Listen, fellow children of Abraham! Listen, you Gentiles who worship God! This message of salvation has been sent to us. [27]The people of Jerusalem and their rulers did not recognize Jesus. By finding him guilty, they made the prophets' words come true. These are read every Sabbath day. [28]The people and their rulers had no reason at all for sentencing Jesus to death. But they asked Pilate to have him killed. [29]They did everything that had been written about Jesus. Then they took him down from the cross. They laid him in a tomb. [30]But God raised him from the dead. [31]For many days he was seen by those who had traveled with him from Galilee to Jerusalem. Now they are telling our people about Jesus.

[32]"We are telling you the good news. What God promised our people long ago [33]he has done for us, their children. He has raised up Jesus. This is what is written in the second Psalm. It says,

"'You are my son.
    Today I have become your father.'
                              (Psalm 2:7)

[34]God raised Jesus from the dead. He will never rot in the grave. As God has said,

"'Holy and sure blessings were
        promised to David.
    I will give them to you.'   *(Isaiah 55:3)*

[35]In another place it also says,

"'You will not let your holy one rot
        away.'   *(Psalm 16:10)*

[36]"David carried out God's purpose while he lived. Then he died. He was buried with his people. His body rotted away. [37]But the one whom God raised from the dead did not rot away.

[38]"My friends, here is what I want you to know. I announce to you that your sins can be forgiven because of what Jesus has done.

[39]Through him everyone who believes is set free from every sin. Moses' law could not make you right in God's eyes. [40]Be careful! Don't let what the prophets spoke about happen to you. They said,

[41] " 'Look, you who make fun of the truth!
Wonder and die!
I am going to do something in your days
    that you would never believe.
You wouldn't believe it even if
    someone told you.' "

(Habakkuk 1:5)

[42]Paul and Barnabas started to leave the synagogue. The people invited them to say more about these things on the next Sabbath day. [43]The people were told they could leave the service. Many Jews followed Paul and Barnabas. Many Gentiles who faithfully worshiped the God of the Jews did the same. Paul and Barnabas talked with them. They tried to get them to keep living in God's grace.

[44]On the next Sabbath day, almost the whole city gathered. They gathered to hear the word of the Lord. [45]When the Jews saw the crowds, they became very jealous. They began to disagree with what Paul was saying. They said evil things against him.

[46]Then Paul and Barnabas answered them boldly. "We had to speak God's word to you first," they said. "But you don't accept it. You don't think you are good enough for eternal life. So now we are turning to the Gentiles. [47]This is what the Lord has commanded us to do. He said,

" 'I have made you a light for the
    Gentiles.
You will bring salvation to the whole
    earth.' "   *(Isaiah 49:6)*

[48]When the Gentiles heard this, they were glad. They honored the word of the Lord. All who were appointed for eternal life believed.

[49]The word of the Lord spread through the whole area. [50]But the Jewish leaders stirred up the important women who worshiped God. They also stirred up the men who were leaders in the city. The Jewish leaders tried to get the women and men to attack Paul and Barnabas. They threw Paul and Barnabas out of that area. [51]Paul and Barnabas shook the dust off their feet. This was a warning to the people who had opposed them. Then Paul and Barnabas went on to Iconium. [52]The believers were filled with joy and with the Holy Spirit.

Paul and Barnabas Preach in Iconium

14 At Iconium, Paul and Barnabas went into the Jewish synagogue as usual. They spoke there with great power. Large numbers of Jews and Greeks became believers. [2]But the Jews who refused to believe stirred up some of the Gentiles who were there. They turned them against the two men and the new believers. [3]So Paul and Barnabas spent a lot of time there. They spoke boldly for the Lord. He gave them the ability to do signs and wonders. In this way the Lord showed that they were telling the truth about his grace. [4]The people of the city did not agree with one another. Some were on the side of the Jews. Others were on the side of the apostles. [5]Jews and Gentiles alike planned to treat Paul and Barnabas badly. Their leaders agreed. They planned to kill them by throwing stones at them. [6]But Paul and Barnabas found out about the plan. They escaped to the Lycaonian cities of Lystra and Derbe and to the surrounding area. [7]There they continued to preach the good news.

Paul Preaches in Lystra

[8]In Lystra there sat a man who couldn't walk. He hadn't been able to use his feet since the day he was born. [9]He listened as Paul spoke. Paul looked right at him. He saw that the man had faith to be healed. [10]So he called out, "Stand up on your feet!" Then the man jumped up and began to walk.

[11]The crowd saw what Paul had done. They shouted in the Lycaonian language. "The gods have come down to us in human form!" they exclaimed. [12]They called Barnabas Zeus. Paul was the main speaker. So they called him Hermes. [13]Just outside the city was the temple of the god Zeus. The priest of Zeus brought bulls and wreaths to the city gates. He and the crowd wanted to offer sacrifices to Paul and Barnabas.

[14]But the apostles Barnabas and Paul heard about this. So they tore their clothes. They rushed out into the crowd. They shouted, [15]"Friends, why are you doing this? We are only human, just like you. We

are bringing you good news. Turn away
from these worthless things. Turn to the
living God. He is the one who made the
heavens and the earth and the sea. He
made everything in them. [16]In the past, he
let all nations go their own way. [17]But he
has given proof of what he is like. He has
shown kindness by giving you rain from
heaven. He gives you crops in their seasons. He provides you with plenty of food.
He fills your hearts with joy." [18]Paul and
Barnabas told them all these things. But
they had trouble keeping the crowd from
offering sacrifices to them.

[19]Then some Jews came from Antioch
and Iconium. They won the crowd over to
their side. They threw stones at Paul. They
thought he was dead, so they dragged him
out of the city. [20]The believers gathered
around Paul. Then he got up and went back
into the city. The next day he and Barnabas
left for Derbe.

Paul and Barnabas Return to Antioch

[21]Paul and Barnabas preached the good
news in the city of Derbe. They won large
numbers of followers. Then they returned
to Lystra, Iconium and Antioch. [22]There
they helped the believers gain strength.
They told them to remain faithful to what
they had been taught. "We must go through
many hard times to enter God's kingdom,"
they said. [23]Paul and Barnabas appointed
elders for them in each church. The elders
had trusted in the Lord. Paul and Barnabas
prayed and fasted. They placed the elders
in the Lord's care. [24]After going through
Pisidia, Paul and Barnabas came into Pamphylia. [25]They preached the good news in
Perga. Then they went down to Attalia.

[26]From Attalia they sailed back to Antioch. In Antioch they had been put in
God's care to preach the good news. They
had now completed the work God had
given them to do. [27]When they arrived
at Antioch, they gathered the church together. They reported all that God had
done through them. They told how he had
opened a way for the Gentiles to believe.

[28]And they stayed there a long time with
the believers.

Church Leaders Meet in Jerusalem

15 Certain people came down from Judea to Antioch. Here is what they
were teaching the believers. "Moses commanded you to be circumcised," they said.
"If you aren't, you can't be saved." [2]But
Paul and Barnabas didn't agree with this.
They argued strongly with them. So Paul
and Barnabas were appointed to go up
to Jerusalem. Some other believers were
chosen to go with them. They were told
to ask the apostles and elders about this
question. [3]The church sent them on their
way. They traveled through Phoenicia and
Samaria. There they told how the Gentiles
had turned to God. This news made all the
believers very glad. [4]When they arrived in
Jerusalem, the church welcomed them. The
apostles and elders welcomed them too.
Then Paul and Barnabas reported everything God had done through them.

[5]Some of the believers were Pharisees.
They stood up and said, "The Gentiles must
be circumcised. They must obey the law of
Moses."

[6]The apostles and elders met to consider
this question. [7]After they had talked it over,
Peter got up and spoke to them. "Brothers,"
he said, "you know that some time ago God
chose me. He appointed me to take the
good news to the Gentiles. He wanted them
to hear the good news and believe. [8]God
knows the human heart. By giving the Holy
Spirit to the Gentiles, he showed that he
accepted them. He did the same for them
as he had done for us. [9]God showed that
there is no difference between us and them.
That's because he made their hearts pure
because of their faith. [10]Now then, why are
you trying to test God? You test him when
you put a heavy load on the shoulders of
Gentiles. Our people of long ago couldn't
carry that load. We can't either. [11]No! We
believe we are saved through the grace of
our Lord Jesus. The Gentiles are saved in
the same way."

[12]Everyone became quiet as they listened
to Barnabas and Paul. They were telling
about the signs and wonders God had done
through them among the Gentiles. [13]When
they finished, James spoke up. "Brothers,"
he said, "listen to me. [14]Simon Peter has

explained to us what God has now done. He has chosen some of the Gentiles to be among his very own people. ¹⁵The prophets' words agree with that. They say,

¹⁶ "'After this I will return
　　and set up again David's fallen tent.
I will rebuild what was destroyed.
　　I will make it what it used to be.
¹⁷ Then everyone else can look to the
　　Lord.
This includes all the Gentiles who
　　belong to me, says the Lord.
The Lord is the one who does these
　　things.'　　　　　　*(Amos 9:11,12)*
¹⁸　The Lord does things that have been
　　known from long ago.

¹⁹"Now here is my decision. We should not make it hard for the Gentiles who are turning to God. ²⁰Here is what we should write to them. They must not eat food that has been made impure by being offered to statues of gods. They must not commit sexual sins. They must not eat the meat of animals that have been choked to death. And they must not drink blood. ²¹These laws of Moses have been preached in every city from the earliest times. They are read out loud in the synagogues every Sabbath day."

A Letter Is Written to Gentile Believers

²²Then the apostles, the elders and the whole church decided what to do. They would choose some of their own men who were leaders among the believers. They would send them to Antioch with Paul and Barnabas. So they chose Judas Barsabbas and Silas. They were leaders among the believers. ²³Here is the letter they sent with them.

The apostles and elders, your brothers, are writing this letter.

We are sending it to the Gentile believers in Antioch, Syria and Cilicia.

Greetings.

²⁴We have heard that some of our people came to you and caused trouble. You were upset by what they said. But we had given them no authority to go. ²⁵So we all agreed to send our dear friends Barnabas and Paul to you. We chose some other men

Acts 15:23 Paul wrote many letters. Thirteen of them are in the New Testament. They begin with Romans and end with Philemon. We know at least two are missing. See 1 Corinthians 5:9 and Colossians 4:16 for clues in the Case of the Long-lost Letters.

to go with them. ²⁶Barnabas and Paul have put their lives in danger. They did it for the name of our Lord Jesus Christ. ²⁷So we are sending Judas and Silas with them. What they say will agree with this letter. ²⁸Here is what seemed good to the Holy Spirit and to us. We will not give you a load that is too heavy. So here are a few basic rules. ²⁹Don't eat food that has been offered to statues of gods. Don't drink blood. Don't eat the meat of animals that have been choked to death. And don't commit sexual sins. You will do well to keep away from these things.

Farewell.

³⁰So the men were sent down to Antioch. There they gathered the church together. They gave the letter to them. ³¹The people read it. They were glad for its message of hope. ³²Judas and Silas were prophets. They said many things to give strength and hope to the believers. ³³⁻³⁴Judas and Silas stayed there for some time. Then the believers sent them away with the blessing of peace. They sent them back to those who had sent them out. ³⁵Paul and Barnabas remained in Antioch. There they and many others taught and preached the word of the Lord.

Paul and Barnabas Do Not Agree

³⁶Some time later Paul spoke to Barnabas. "Let's go back to all the towns where

we preached the word of the Lord," he said. "Let's visit the believers and see how they are doing." [37]Barnabas wanted to take John Mark with them. [38]But Paul didn't think it was wise to take him. Mark had deserted them in Pamphylia. He hadn't continued with them in their work. [39]Barnabas and Paul strongly disagreed with each other. So they went their separate ways. Barnabas took Mark and sailed for Cyprus. [40]But Paul chose Silas. The believers asked the Lord to give his grace to Paul and Silas as they went. [41]Paul traveled through Syria and Cilicia. He gave strength to the churches there.

Timothy Joins Paul and Silas

16 Paul came to Derbe. Then he went on to Lystra. A believer named Timothy lived there. His mother was Jewish and a believer. His father was a Greek. [2]The believers at Lystra and Iconium said good things about Timothy. [3]Paul wanted to take him along on the journey. So he circumcised Timothy because of the Jews who lived in that area. They all knew that Timothy's father was a Greek. [4]Paul and his companions traveled from town to town. They reported what the apostles and elders in Jerusalem had decided. The people were supposed to obey what was in the report. [5]So the churches were made strong in the faith. The number of believers grew every day.

Paul's Vision of the Man From Macedonia

[6]Paul and his companions traveled all through the area of Phrygia and Galatia. The Holy Spirit had kept them from preaching the word in Asia Minor. [7]They came to the border of Mysia. From there they tried to enter Bithynia. But the Spirit of Jesus would not let them. [8]So they passed by Mysia. Then they went down to Troas. [9]During the night Paul had a vision. He saw a man from Macedonia standing and begging him. "Come over to Macedonia!" the man said. "Help us!" [10]After Paul had seen the vision, we got ready at once to leave for Macedonia. We decided that God had called us to preach the good news there.

Lydia Becomes a Believer in Philippi

[11]At Troas we got into a boat. We sailed straight for Samothrace. The next day we went on to Neapolis. [12]From there we traveled to Philippi, a Roman colony. It is an important city in that part of Macedonia. We stayed there several days. [13]On the Sabbath day we went outside the city gate. We walked down to the river. There we expected to find a place of prayer. We sat down and began to speak to the women who had gathered together. [14]One of the women listening was from the city of Thyatira. Her name was Lydia, and her business was selling purple cloth. She was

WHIT'S WISDOM

Acts 16

One day, Olivia came in to Whit's End upset. I could tell by the way she threw her backpack on the counter, slammed her hand on the counter and said, "Mr. Whittaker, I'm upset."

She had been singing some praise songs at school when Jay Smouse started making fun of her. Then, she was singing on the way home and her brother Matthew told her that her voice was giving him a headache.

"Maybe I should just save singing praise songs for church," she said.

I reminded her that songs are a great way to let God know how you feel—and people in the Bible didn't just sing in church. I showed her Acts 16:25 where Paul and Silas were stuck in a prison cell. In the middle of the night they were singing and something amazing happened. An earthquake shook the prison from top to bottom, the doors flew open, and their chains came loose!

Olivia said, "Thanks, Mr. Whittaker. I'll show those verses to Jay and to Matthew tomorrow. And maybe I'll pick up some earplugs if they *really* don't want to hear. After all, I'm not singing for them. I'm singing for God!"

a worshiper of God. The Lord opened her heart to accept Paul's message. ¹⁵She and her family were baptized. Then she invited us to her home. "Do you consider me a believer in the Lord?" she asked. "If you do, come and stay at my house." She succeeded in getting us to go home with her.

Paul and Silas Are Thrown into Prison

¹⁶One day we were going to the place of prayer. On the way we were met by a female slave. She had a spirit that helped her tell people what was going to happen. She earned a lot of money for her owners by doing this. ¹⁷She followed Paul and the rest of us around. She shouted, "These men serve the Most High God. They are telling you how to be saved." ¹⁸She kept this up for many days. Finally Paul became upset. Turning around, he spoke to the spirit that was in her. "In the name of Jesus Christ," he said, "I command you to come out of her!" At that very moment the spirit left the woman.

¹⁹Her owners realized that their hope of making money was gone. So they grabbed Paul and Silas. They dragged them into the market place to face the authorities. ²⁰They brought them to the judges. "These men are Jews," her owners said. "They are making trouble in our city. ²¹They are suggesting practices that are against Roman law. These are practices we can't accept or take part in."

²²The crowd joined the attack against Paul and Silas. The judges ordered that Paul and Silas be stripped and beaten with rods. ²³They were whipped without mercy. Then they were thrown into prison. The jailer was commanded to guard them carefully. ²⁴When he received these orders, he put Paul and Silas deep inside the prison. He fastened their feet so they couldn't get away.

²⁵About midnight Paul and Silas were praying. They were also singing hymns to God. The other prisoners were listening to them. ²⁶Suddenly there was a powerful earthquake. It shook the prison from top to bottom. All at once the prison doors flew open. Everyone's chains came loose. ²⁷The jailer woke up. He saw that the prison doors were open. He pulled out his sword and was going to kill himself. He thought the prisoners had escaped. ²⁸"Don't harm yourself!" Paul shouted. "We are all here!"

²⁹The jailer called out for some lights. He rushed in, shaking with fear. He fell down in front of Paul and Silas. ³⁰Then he brought them out. He asked, "Sirs, what must I do to be saved?"

³¹They replied, "Believe in the Lord Jesus. Then you and everyone living in your house will be saved." ³²They spoke the word of the Lord to him. They also spoke to all the others in his house. ³³At that hour of the night, the jailer took Paul and Silas and washed their wounds. Right away he and everyone who lived with him were baptized. ³⁴The jailer brought them into his house. He set a meal in front of them. He and everyone who lived with him were filled with joy. They had become believers in God.

³⁵Early in the morning the judges sent their officers to the jailer. They ordered him, "Let those men go." ³⁶The jailer told Paul, "The judges have ordered me to set you and Silas free. You can leave now. Go in peace."

³⁷But Paul replied to the officers. "They beat us in public," he said. "We weren't given a trial. And we are Roman citizens! They threw us into prison. And now do they want to get rid of us quietly? No! Let them come themselves and personally lead us out."

³⁸The officers reported this to the judges. When the judges heard that Paul and Silas were Roman citizens, they became afraid. ³⁹So they came and said they were sorry. They led them out of the prison. Then they asked them to leave the city. ⁴⁰After Paul and Silas came out of the prison, they went to Lydia's house. There they met with the

brothers and sisters. They told them to be brave. Then they left.

Paul and Silas Arrive in Thessalonica

17 Paul and those traveling with him passed through Amphipolis and Apollonia. They came to Thessalonica. A Jewish synagogue was there. [2]Paul went into the synagogue as he usually did. For three Sabbath days in a row he talked with the Jews about the Scriptures. [3]He explained and proved that the Messiah had to suffer and rise from the dead. "This Jesus I am telling you about is the Messiah!" he said. [4]His words won over some of the Jews. They joined Paul and Silas. A large number of Greeks who worshiped God joined them too. So did quite a few important women.

[5]But other Jews were jealous. So they rounded up some evil people from the market place. Forming a crowd, they started all kinds of trouble in the city. The Jews rushed to Jason's house. They were looking for Paul and Silas. They wanted to bring them out to the crowd. [6]But they couldn't find them. So they dragged Jason and some other believers to the city officials. "These men have caused trouble all over the world," they shouted. "Now they have come here. [7]Jason has welcomed them into his house. They are all disobeying Caesar's commands. They say there is another king. He is called Jesus." [8]When the crowd and the city officials heard this, they became very upset. [9]They made Jason and the others give them money. The officials did this to make sure they would return to the court. Then they let Jason and the others go.

Paul and Silas Are Sent to Berea

[10]As soon as it was night, the believers sent Paul and Silas away to Berea. When they arrived, they went to the Jewish synagogue. [11]The Berean Jews were very glad to receive Paul's message. They studied the Scriptures carefully every day. They wanted to see if what Paul said was true. So they were more noble than the Thessalonian Jews. [12]Because of this, many of the Berean Jews believed. A number of important Greek women also became believers. And so did many Greek men.

[13]But the Jews in Thessalonica found out that Paul was preaching God's word in Berea. So some of them went there too. They stirred up the crowds and got them all worked up. [14]Right away the believers sent Paul to the coast. But Silas and Timothy stayed in Berea. [15]The believers who went with Paul took him to Athens. Then they returned with orders that Silas and Timothy were supposed to join him as soon as they could.

Paul Preaches in Athens

[16]Paul was waiting for Silas and Timothy in Athens. He was very upset to see that the city was full of statues of gods. [17]So he went to the synagogue. There he talked both with Jews and with Greeks who worshiped God. Each day he spoke with anyone who happened to be in the market place. [18]A group of Epicurean and Stoic thinkers began to argue with him. Some of them asked, "What is this fellow chattering about?" Others said, "He seems to be telling us about gods we've never heard of." They said this because Paul was preaching the good news about Jesus. He was telling them that Jesus had risen from the dead. [19]They took him to a meeting of the Areopagus. There they said to him, "What is this new teaching you're giving us? [20]You have some strange ideas we've never heard before. We would like to know what they mean." [21]All the people of Athens spent their time talking about and listening to the latest ideas. People from other lands who lived there did the same.

[22]Then Paul stood up in the meeting of the Areopagus. He said, "People of Athens! I see that you are very religious in every way. [23]As I walked around, I looked carefully at the things you worship. I even found an altar with

TO AN UNKNOWN GOD

written on it. So you don't know what you are worshiping. Now I am going to tell you about this 'unknown god.'

[24]"He is the God who made the world. He also made everything in it. He is the Lord of heaven and earth. He doesn't live in temples built by human hands. [25]He is not served by human hands. He doesn't need anything. Instead, he himself gives life and breath to all people. He also gives them everything else they have. [26]From one man he made all the people of the world. Now they live all over the earth. He decided exactly when they should live. And he decided

ADVENTURES IN ODYSSEY

Lucy and Connie saw bigotry in "Not One of Us" (A#08). Bigotry can happen when we forget that God made every person—like it says in Acts 17:24-27.

exactly where they should live. ²⁷God did this so that people would seek him. And perhaps they would reach out for him and find him. They would find him even though he is not far from any of us. ²⁸'In him we live and move and exist.' As some of your own poets have also said, 'We are his children.'

²⁹"Yes, we are God's children. So we shouldn't think that God is made out of gold or silver or stone. He isn't a statue planned and made by clever people. ³⁰In the past, God didn't judge people for what they didn't know. But now he commands all people everywhere to turn away from their sins. ³¹He has set a day when he will judge the world fairly. He has appointed a man to be its judge. God has proved this to everyone by raising that man from the dead."

³²They heard Paul talk about the dead being raised. Some of them made fun of this idea. But others said, "We want to hear you speak about this again." ³³So Paul left the meeting of the Areopagus. ³⁴Some of the people became followers of Paul and believed in Jesus. Dionysius was one of them. He was a member of the Areopagus. A woman named Damaris also became a believer. And so did some others.

Paul Goes to Corinth

18 After this, Paul left Athens and went to Corinth. ²There he met a Jew named Aquila, who was a native of Pontus. Aquila had recently come from Italy with his wife Priscilla. The emperor Claudius had ordered all Jews to leave Rome. Paul went to see Aquila and Priscilla. ³They were tentmakers, just as he was. So he stayed and worked with them. ⁴Every Sabbath day he went to the synagogue. He was trying to get both Jews and Greeks to believe in the Lord. ⁵Silas and Timothy came from Macedonia. Then Paul spent all his time preaching. He was a witness to the Jews that Jesus was the Messiah. ⁶But they opposed Paul.

They treated him badly. So he shook out his clothes in protest. Then he said to them, "God's judgment against you will be your own fault! Don't blame me for it! From now on I will go to the Gentiles."

⁷Then Paul left the synagogue and went to the house next door. It was the house of Titius Justus, a man who worshiped God. ⁸Crispus was the synagogue leader. He and everyone living in his house came to believe in the Lord. Many others who lived in Corinth heard Paul. They too believed and were baptized.

⁹One night the Lord spoke to Paul in a vision. "Don't be afraid," he said. "Keep on speaking. Don't be silent. ¹⁰I am with you. No one will attack you and harm you. I have many people in this city." ¹¹So Paul stayed in Corinth for a year and a half. He taught them God's word.

¹²At that time Gallio was governor of Achaia. The Jews of Corinth got together and attacked Paul. They brought him into court. ¹³They made a charge against Paul. They said, "This man is talking people into worshiping God in wrong ways. Those ways are against the law."

¹⁴Paul was about to give reasons for his actions. But just then Gallio spoke to them. He said, "You Jews don't claim that Paul has committed a great or small crime. If you did, it would make sense for me to listen to you. ¹⁵But this is about your own law. It is a question of words and names. Settle the matter yourselves. I will not be a judge of such things." ¹⁶So he made them leave. ¹⁷Then the crowd there turned against Sosthenes, the synagogue leader. They beat him up in front of the governor. But Gallio didn't care at all.

Priscilla and Aquila Teach Apollos

¹⁸Paul stayed in Corinth for some time. Then he left the brothers and sisters and sailed for Syria. Priscilla and Aquila went with him. Before he sailed, he had his hair cut off at Cenchreae. He did this because he had made a promise to God. ¹⁹They arrived at Ephesus. There Paul said goodbye to Priscilla and Aquila. He himself went into the synagogue and talked with the Jews. ²⁰The Jews asked him to spend more time with them. But he said no. ²¹As he left, he made them a promise. "If God wants me to," he said, "I will come back." Then he sailed from Ephesus. ²²When he landed at Caesarea, he

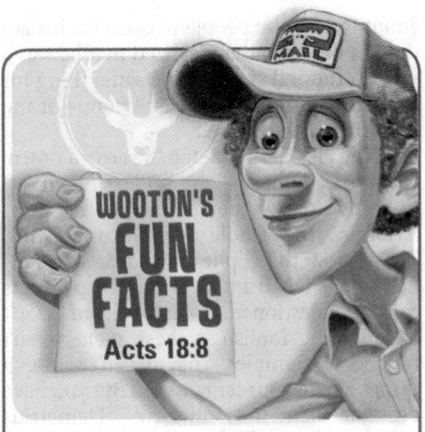

WOOTON'S FUN FACTS

Acts 18:8

The first person to die in the American Revolution was Crispus Attucks, who was shot during the Boston Massacre. His mother was raised as a Christian. It's possible that he was named after the Crispus in this verse.

went up to Jerusalem. There he greeted the church. He then went down to Antioch.

²³Paul spent some time in Antioch. Then he left and traveled all over Galatia and Phrygia. He gave strength to all the believers there.

²⁴At that time a Jew named Apollos came to Ephesus. He was an educated man from Alexandria. He knew the Scriptures very well. ²⁵Apollos had been taught the way of the Lord. He spoke with great power. He taught the truth about Jesus. But he only knew about John's baptism. ²⁶He began to speak boldly in the synagogue. Priscilla and Aquila heard him. So they invited him to their home. There they gave him a better understanding of the way of God.

²⁷Apollos wanted to go to Achaia. The brothers and sisters agreed with him. They wrote to the believers there. They asked them to welcome him. When he arrived, he was a great help to those who had become believers by God's grace. ²⁸In public meetings, he argued strongly against Jews who disagreed with him. He proved from the Scriptures that Jesus was the Messiah.

Paul Goes to Ephesus

19 While Apollos was at Corinth, Paul took the road to Ephesus. When he arrived, he found some believers there. ²He asked them, "Did you receive the Holy Spirit when you became believers?"

"No," they answered. "We haven't even heard that there is a Holy Spirit."

³So Paul asked, "Then what baptism did you receive?"

"John's baptism," they replied.

⁴Paul said, "John baptized people, calling them to turn away from their sins. He told them to believe in the one who was coming after him. Jesus is that one." ⁵After hearing this, they were baptized in the name of the Lord Jesus. ⁶Paul placed his hands on them. Then the Holy Spirit came on them. They spoke in languages they had not known before. They also prophesied. ⁷There were about 12 men in all.

⁸Paul entered the synagogue. There he spoke boldly for three months. He gave good reasons for believing the truth about God's kingdom. ⁹But some of them wouldn't listen. They refused to believe. In public they said evil things about the Way of Jesus. So Paul left them. He took the believers with him. Each day he talked with people in the lecture hall of Tyrannus. ¹⁰This went on for two years. So all the Jews and Greeks who lived in Asia Minor heard the word of the Lord.

¹¹God did amazing miracles through Paul. ¹²Even handkerchiefs and aprons that had touched him were taken to those who were sick. When this happened, their sicknesses were healed and evil spirits left them.

¹³Some Jews went around driving out evil spirits. They tried to use the name of the Lord Jesus to set free those who were controlled by demons. They said, "In Jesus' name I command you to come out. He is the Jesus that Paul is preaching about." ¹⁴Seven sons of Sceva were doing this. Sceva was a Jewish chief priest. ¹⁵One day the evil spirit answered them, "I know Jesus. And I know about Paul. But who are you?" ¹⁶Then the man who had the evil spirit jumped on Sceva's sons. He overpowered them all. He gave them a terrible beating. They ran out of the house naked and bleeding.

¹⁷The Jews and Greeks living in Ephesus heard about this. They were all overcome with fear. They held the name of the Lord Jesus in high honor. ¹⁸Many who believed now came and openly admitted what they had done. ¹⁹A number of those who had practiced evil magic brought their scrolls together. They set them on fire out in the open. They added up the value of the

scrolls. The scrolls were worth more than someone could earn in two lifetimes. ²⁰The word of the Lord spread everywhere. It became more and more powerful.

²¹After all this had happened, Paul decided to go to Jerusalem. He went through Macedonia and Achaia. "After I have been to Jerusalem," he said, "I must visit Rome also." ²²He sent Timothy and Erastus, two of his helpers, to Macedonia. But he stayed a little longer in Asia Minor.

Trouble in Ephesus

²³At that time many people became very upset about the Way of Jesus. ²⁴There was a man named Demetrius who made things out of silver. He made silver models of the temple of the goddess Artemis. He brought in a lot of business for the other skilled workers there. ²⁵One day he called them together. He also called others who were in the same kind of business. "My friends," he said, "you know that we make good money from our work. ²⁶You have seen and heard what this fellow Paul is doing. He has talked to large numbers of people here in Ephesus. Almost everywhere in Asia Minor he has led people away from our gods. He says that the gods made by human hands are not gods at all. ²⁷Our work is in danger of losing its good name. People's faith in the temple of the great goddess Artemis will be weakened. Now she is worshiped all over Asia Minor and the whole world. But soon she will be robbed of her greatness."

²⁸When they heard this, they became very angry. They began shouting, "Great is Artemis of the Ephesians!" ²⁹Soon people were making trouble in the whole city. They all rushed into the theater. They dragged Gaius and Aristarchus along with them. These two men had come with Paul from Macedonia. ³⁰Paul wanted to appear in front of the crowd. But the believers wouldn't let him. ³¹Some of the officials in Asia Minor were friends of Paul. They sent him a message, begging him not to go into the theater.

³²The crowd didn't know what was going on. Some were shouting one thing and some another. Most of the people didn't even know why they were there. ³³The Jews in the crowd pushed Alexander to the front. They tried to tell him what to say. But he motioned for them to be quiet. He was

about to give the people reasons for his actions. ³⁴But then they realized that he was a Jew. So they all shouted the same thing for about two hours. "Great is Artemis of the Ephesians!" they yelled.

³⁵The city clerk quieted the crowd down. "People of Ephesus!" he said. "The city of Ephesus guards the temple of the great Artemis. The whole world knows this. They know that Ephesus guards her statue, which fell from heaven. ³⁶These facts can't be questioned. So calm down. Don't do anything foolish. ³⁷These men haven't robbed any temples. They haven't said evil things against our female god. But you have brought them here anyhow. ³⁸Demetrius and the other skilled workers may feel they have been wronged by someone. Let them bring charges. The courts are open. We have our governors. ³⁹Is there anything else you want to bring up? Settle it in a court of law. ⁴⁰As it is, we are in danger of being charged with a crime. We could be charged with causing all this trouble today. There is no reason for it. So we wouldn't be able to explain what has happened." ⁴¹After he said this, he sent the people away.

Paul Travels Through Macedonia and Greece

20 All the trouble came to an end. Then Paul sent for the believers. After encouraging them, he said goodbye. He then left for Macedonia. ²He traveled through that area, speaking many words of hope to the people. Finally he arrived in Greece. ³There he stayed for three months. He was just about to sail for Syria. But some Jews were making plans against him. So he decided to go back through Macedonia. ⁴Sopater, son of Pyrrhus, from Berea went with him. Aristarchus and Secundus from Thessalonica, Gaius from Derbe, and Timothy went too. Tychicus and Trophimus from Asia Minor also went with him. ⁵These men went on ahead. They waited for us at Troas. ⁶But we sailed from Philippi after the Feast of Unleavened Bread. Five days later we joined the others at Troas. We stayed there for seven days.

Eutychus Is Raised From the Dead at Troas

⁷On the first day of the week we met to break bread and eat together. Paul spoke

to the people. He kept on talking until midnight because he planned to leave the next day. [8]There were many lamps in the room upstairs where we were meeting. [9]A young man named Eutychus was sitting in a window. He sank into a deep sleep as Paul talked on and on. Sound asleep, Eutychus fell from the third floor. When they picked him up from the ground, he was dead. [10]Paul went down and threw himself on the young man. He put his arms around him. "Don't be alarmed," he told them. "He's alive!" [11]Then Paul went upstairs again. He broke bread and ate with them. He kept on talking until daylight. Then he left. [12]The people took the young man home. They were greatly comforted because he was alive.

Paul Says Goodbye to the Ephesian Elders

[13]We went on ahead to the ship. We sailed for Assos. There we were going to take Paul on board. He had planned it this way because he wanted to go to Assos by land. [14]So he met us there. We took him on board and went on to Mitylene. [15]The next day we sailed from there. We arrived near Chios. The day after that we crossed over to Samos. We arrived at Miletus the next day. [16]Paul had decided to sail past Ephesus. He didn't want to spend time in Asia Minor. He was in a hurry to get to Jerusalem. If he could, he wanted to be there by the day of Pentecost.

[17]From Miletus, Paul sent for the elders of the church at Ephesus. [18]When they arrived, he spoke to them. "You know how I lived the whole time I was with you," he said. "From the first day I came into Asia Minor, [19]I served the Lord with tears and without pride. I served him when I was greatly tested. I was tested by the evil plans of the Jews who disagreed with me. [20]You know that nothing has kept me from preaching whatever would help you. I have taught you in public and from house to house. [21]I have told both Jews and Greeks that they must turn away from their sins to God. They must have faith in our Lord Jesus.

[22]"Now I am going to Jerusalem. The Holy Spirit compels me. I don't know what will happen to me there. [23]I only know that in every city the Spirit warns me. He tells

CANDID CONVERSATIONS

When the big freezer broke at Whit's End, Whit proclaimed it Free Ice Cream Day. You wouldn't believe how crowded this place was. People were driving all the way from Connellsville! Everyone was calling and texting their friends to tell them about the deal. It was nuts! I guess good news travels fast. But it made me wonder what would happen if we were that excited about sharing Jesus with other people. What would the world be like?

Just think about it: God has forgiven and saved you, given you a new heart, and promised you eternity in heaven with Him. Isn't that good news worth spreading, just like the crowds spread it in Jesus' day?

Think of someone you can share the good news of Jesus with. You don't have to recite a bunch of verses. Just share what Jesus has done in your life. That's a message even sweeter than a day with free ice cream!

me that I will face prison and suffering. [24]But my life means nothing to me. My only goal is to finish the race. I want to complete the work the Lord Jesus has given me. He wants me to tell others about the good news of God's grace.

[25]"I have spent time with you preaching about the kingdom. I know that none of you will ever see me again. [26]So I tell you today that I am not guilty if any of you don't believe. [27]I haven't let anyone keep me from telling you everything God wants you to do. [28]Keep watch over yourselves. Keep watch over all the believers. The Holy Spirit has made you leaders over them. Be shepherds of God's church. He bought it with his own blood. [29]I know that after I leave, wild wolves will come in among you.

WHIT'S WISDOM

Acts 20:35

I remember one Christmas at Whit's End. After we set up the Christmas tree in the main room, Tom, Connie, Officer Harley, and a couple of the kids gathered around while I told the story of a couple named Madge and Guy. I explained that the problem with gift giving these days is that most of us look forward to being the "givee," but not the giver. But Madge and Guy showed how it doesn't have to be that way.

Madge sold her long hair to buy her husband a watch chain. And Guy sold his watch to buy Madge some tortoiseshell combs for her hair. They were both willing to give up their most prized possession for each other. Neither of them expected a nice gift, or any present at all for that matter.

That's what real giving, true giving, is all about. It's like when God gave us the gift of Jesus, the best gift of all. Like it says in Acts 20:35, "It is more blessed to give than to receive."

They won't spare any of the sheep. ³⁰Even men from your own people will rise up and twist the truth. They want to get the believers to follow them. ³¹So be on your guard! Remember that for three years I never stopped warning you. Night and day I warned each of you with tears.

³²"Now I trust God to take care of you. I commit you to the message about his grace. It can build you up. Then you will share in what God plans to give all his people. ³³I haven't longed for anyone's silver or gold or clothing. ³⁴You yourselves know that I have used my own hands to meet my needs. I have also met the needs of my companions. ³⁵In everything I did, I showed you that we must work hard and help the weak. We must remember the words of the Lord Jesus. He said, 'It is more blessed to give than to receive.'"

³⁶Paul finished speaking. Then he got down on his knees with all of them and prayed. ³⁷They all wept as they hugged and kissed him. ³⁸Paul had said that they would never see him again. That's what hurt them the most. Then they went with him to the ship.

Paul Continues His Journey to Jerusalem

21 After we had torn ourselves away from the Ephesian elders, we headed out to sea. We sailed straight to Kos. The next day we went to Rhodes. From there we continued on to Patara. ²We found a ship crossing over to Phoenicia. So we went on board and headed out to sea. ³We came near Cyprus and passed to the south of it. Then we sailed on to Syria. We landed at Tyre. There our ship was supposed to unload. ⁴We looked for the believers there and stayed with them for seven days. The believers tried to keep Paul from going on to Jerusalem. They were led by the Holy Spirit to do this. ⁵When it was time to leave, we continued on our way. All the believers, including their whole families, went with us out of the city. There on the beach we got down on our knees to pray. ⁶We said goodbye to each other. Then we went on board the ship. And they returned home.

⁷Continuing on from Tyre, we landed at Ptolemais. There we greeted the brothers and sisters. We stayed with them for a day. ⁸The next day we left and arrived at

Caesarea. We stayed at the house of Philip the evangelist. He was one of the seven deacons. [9]He had four unmarried daughters who prophesied.

[10]We stayed there several days. Then a prophet named Agabus came down from Judea. [11]He came over to us. Then he took Paul's belt and tied his own hands and feet with it. He said, "The Holy Spirit says, 'This is how the Jewish leaders in Jerusalem will tie up the owner of this belt. They will hand him over to the Gentiles.'"

[12]When we heard this, we all begged Paul not to go up to Jerusalem. [13]He asked, "Why are you crying? Why are you breaking my heart? I'm ready to be put in prison. In fact, I'm ready to die in Jerusalem for the Lord Jesus." [14]We couldn't change his mind. So we gave up. We said, "May what the Lord wants to happen be done."

[15]After this, we started on our way to Jerusalem. [16]Some of the believers from Caesarea went with us. They brought us to Mnason's home. We were supposed to stay there. Mnason was from Cyprus. He was one of the first believers.

Paul Arrives in Jerusalem

[17]When we arrived in Jerusalem, the brothers and sisters gave us a warm welcome. [18]The next day Paul and the rest of us went to see James. All the elders were there. [19]Paul greeted them. Then he reported everything God had done among the Gentiles through his work.

[20]When they heard this, they praised God. Then they spoke to Paul. "Brother," they said, "you see that thousands of Jews have become believers. All of them try very hard to obey the law. [21]They have been told that you teach Jews to turn away from the Law of Moses. You teach this to the Jews who live among the Gentiles. They think that you teach those Jews not to circumcise their children. They think that you teach them to give up our Jewish ways. [22]What should we do? They will certainly hear that you have come. [23]So do what we tell you. There are four men with us who have made a promise to God. [24]Take them with you. Join them in the Jewish practice that makes people pure and 'clean.' Pay their expenses so they can have their heads shaved. Then everyone will know that these reports about you are not true in any way. They will

know that you yourself obey the law. [25]We have already given written directions to the believers who are not Jews. They must not eat food that has been offered to statues of gods. They must not drink blood. They must not eat the meat of animals that have been choked to death. And they must not commit sexual sins."

[26]The next day Paul took the men with him. They all made themselves pure and "clean" in the usual way. Then Paul went to the temple. There he reported the date when the days of cleansing would end. At that time the proper offering would be made for each of them.

Paul Is Arrested

[27]The seven days of cleansing were almost over. Some Jews from Asia Minor saw Paul at the temple. They stirred up the whole crowd and grabbed Paul. [28]"Fellow Israelites, help us!" they shouted. "This is the man who teaches everyone in all places against our people. He speaks against our law and against this holy place. Besides, he has brought Greeks into the temple. He has made this holy place 'unclean.'" [29]They said this because they had seen Trophimus the Ephesian in the city with Paul. They thought Paul had brought him into the temple.

[30]The whole city was stirred up. People came running from all directions. They grabbed Paul and dragged him out of the temple. Right away the temple gates were shut. [31]The people were trying to kill Paul. But news reached the commander of the Roman troops. He heard that people were making trouble in the whole city of Jerusalem. [32]Right away he took some officers and soldiers with him. They ran down to the crowd. The people causing the trouble saw the commander and his soldiers. So they stopped beating Paul.

[33]The commander came up and arrested Paul. He ordered him to be held with two chains. Then he asked who Paul was and what he had done. [34]Some in the crowd shouted one thing, some another. But the commander couldn't get the facts because of all the noise. So he ordered that Paul be taken into the fort. [35]Paul reached the steps. But then the mob became so wild that he had to be carried by the soldiers. [36]The crowd that followed kept shouting, "Get rid of him!"

Paul Speaks to the Crowd

³⁷The soldiers were about to take Paul into the fort. Then he asked the commander, "May I say something to you?"

"Do you speak Greek?" he replied. ³⁸"Aren't you the Egyptian who turned some of our people against their leaders? Didn't you lead 4,000 terrorists out into the desert some time ago?"

³⁹Paul answered, "I am a Jew from Tarsus in Cilicia. I am a citizen of an important city. Please let me speak to the people."

⁴⁰The commander told him he could. So Paul stood on the steps and motioned to the crowd. When all of them were quiet, he spoke to them in the Aramaic language.

22 ¹"Brothers and fathers," Paul began, "listen to me now. I want to give you reasons for my actions."

²When they heard that he was speaking to them in Aramaic, they became very quiet.

Then Paul said, ³"I am a Jew. I was born in Tarsus in Cilicia, but I grew up here in Jerusalem. I studied with Gamaliel. I was well trained by him in the law given to our people long ago. I wanted to serve God as much as any of you do today. ⁴I hurt the followers of the Way of Jesus. I sent many of them to their death. I arrested men and women. I threw them into prison. ⁵The high priest and the whole Council can be witnesses of this themselves. I even had some official letters they had written to their friends in Damascus. So I went there to bring these people as prisoners to Jerusalem to be punished.

⁶"I had almost reached Damascus. About noon a bright light from heaven suddenly flashed around me. ⁷I fell to the ground and heard a voice speak to me. 'Saul! Saul!' it said. 'Why are you opposing me?'

⁸"'Who are you, Lord?' I asked.

"'I am Jesus of Nazareth,' he replied. 'I am the one you are opposing.' ⁹The light was seen by my companions. But they didn't understand the voice of the one speaking to me.

¹⁰"'What should I do, Lord?' I asked.

"'Get up,' the Lord said. 'Go into Damascus. There you will be told everything

Have you ever seen a really strange-looking bug? Maybe you stopped to watch one crawling on the sidewalk. Perhaps you found a plastic cup, scooped up the bug, and carried it home so that the rest of your family could study it too. Why do we do things like that? Because we are curious.

It's natural to find ourselves studying things we don't understand. It's how we learn. For instance, kids from foreign countries (or distant parts of our own country) can command our attention. Have you ever been fascinated by someone who speaks with an accent? That's normal. Likewise, some people study Christians with particular scrutiny. They watch us, interested to see what makes us different and whether we act like God's children.

That's why it's so important to know your testimony. We share a testimony when we tell others about something we've witnessed or experienced. Testimonies are used in courtrooms all the time, but they're also part of our spiritual lives. In Acts 21–22,

the apostle Paul stood trial for preaching the truth about Jesus. He testified by telling people the good news about how the Lord had changed him (see Acts 22:3–16).

Our Christian behavior may be the closest thing to a Bible some people will ever read. So ask God to help you maintain a good testimony today by showing Christ's love to others. Christians aren't perfect, but with the help of the Holy Spirit, we should do our best to live like Jesus did, following His example.

you have been given to do.' [11]The brightness of the light had blinded me. So my companions led me by the hand into Damascus. [12]"A man named Ananias came to see me. He was a godly Jew who obeyed the law. All the Jews living there respected him very much. [13]He stood beside me and said, 'Brother Saul, receive your sight!' At that very moment I was able to see him.

[14]"Then he said, 'The God of our people has chosen you. He wanted to tell you his plans for you. You have seen the Blameless One. You have heard words from his mouth. [15]Now you will tell everyone about what you have seen and heard. [16]So what are you waiting for? Get up and call on his name. Be baptized. Have your sins washed away.'

[17]"I returned to Jerusalem and was praying at the temple. Then it seemed to me that I was dreaming. [18]I saw the Lord speaking to me. 'Quick!' he said. 'Leave Jerusalem at once. The people here will not accept what you tell them about me.'

[19]"'Lord,' I replied, 'these people know what I used to do. I went from one synagogue to another and put believers in prison. I also beat them. [20]Stephen was a man who told other people about you. I stood there when he was killed. I had agreed that he should die. I even guarded the coats of those who were killing him.'

[21]"Then the Lord said to me, 'Go. I will send you far away to people who are not Jews.'"

Paul the Roman Citizen

[22]The crowd listened to Paul until he said this. Then they shouted, "Kill him! He isn't fit to live!"

[23]They shouted and threw off their coats. They threw dust into the air. [24]So the commanding officer ordered that Paul be taken into the fort. He gave orders for Paul to be whipped and questioned. He wanted to find out why the people were shouting at him like this. [25]A commander was standing there as they stretched Paul out to be whipped. Paul said to him, "Does the law allow you to whip a Roman citizen who hasn't even been found guilty?"

[26]When the commander heard this, he went to the commanding officer and reported it. "What are you going to do?" the commander asked. "This man is a Roman citizen."

[27]So the commanding officer went to Paul. "Tell me," he asked. "Are you a Roman citizen?"

"Yes, I am," Paul answered.

[28]Then the officer said, "I had to pay a lot of money to become a citizen."

"But I was born a citizen," Paul replied.

[29]Right away those who were about to question him left. Even the officer was alarmed. He realized that he had put Paul, a Roman citizen, in chains.

Paul Is Taken to the Sanhedrin

[30]The commanding officer wanted to find out exactly what the Jews had against Paul. So the next day he let Paul out of prison. He ordered a meeting of the chief priests and all the members of the Sanhedrin. Then he brought Paul and had him stand in front of them.

23 Paul looked straight at the Sanhedrin. "My brothers," he said, "I have always done my duty to God. To this day I feel that I have done nothing wrong." [2]Ananias the high priest heard this. So he ordered the men standing near Paul to hit him on the mouth. [3]Then Paul said to him, "You pretender! God will hit you! You sit there and judge me by the law. But you yourself broke the law when you commanded them to hit me!"

[4]Those who were standing near Paul spoke to him. They said, "How dare you talk like that to God's high priest!"

[5]Paul replied, "Brothers, I didn't realize he was the high priest. It is written, 'Do not speak evil about the ruler of your people.'" (Exodus 22:28)

[6]Paul knew that some of them were Sadducees and the others were Pharisees. So he called out to the members of the Sanhedrin. "My brothers," he said, "I am a Pharisee. I come from a family of Pharisees. I believe that people will rise from the dead. That's why I am on trial." [7]When he said this, the Pharisees and the Sadducees started to argue. They began to take sides. [8]The Sadducees say that people will not rise from the dead. They don't believe there are angels or spirits either. But the Pharisees believe all these things.

[9]People were causing trouble and making a lot of noise. Some of the teachers of the law who were Pharisees stood up. They argued strongly. "We find nothing wrong

with this man," they said. "What if a spirit or an angel has spoken to him?" [10]The people arguing were getting out of control. The commanding officer was afraid that Paul would be torn to pieces by them. So he ordered the soldiers to go down and take him away from them by force. The officer had told them to bring Paul into the fort.

[11]The next night the Lord stood near Paul. He said, "Be brave! You have told people about me in Jerusalem. You must do the same in Rome."

The Plan to Kill Paul

[12]The next morning some Jews gathered secretly to make plans against Paul. They made a promise to themselves. They promised that they would not eat or drink anything until they killed him. [13]More than 40 men took part in this plan. [14]They went to the chief priests and the elders. They said, "We have made a special promise to God. We will not eat anything until we have killed Paul. [15]Now then, you and the Sanhedrin must make an appeal to the commanding officer. Ask him to bring Paul to you. Pretend you want more facts about his case. We are ready to kill him before he gets here."

[16]But Paul's nephew heard about this plan. So he went into the fort and told Paul.

[17]Then Paul called one of the commanders. He said to him, "Take this young man to the commanding officer. He has something to tell him." [18]So the commander took Paul's nephew to the officer.

The commander said, "Paul, the prisoner, sent for me. He asked me to bring this young man to you. The young man has something to tell you."

[19]The commanding officer took the young man by the hand. He spoke to him in private. "What do you want to tell me?" the officer asked.

[20]He said, "Some Jews have agreed to ask you to bring Paul to the Sanhedrin tomorrow. They will pretend they want more facts about him. [21]Don't give in to them. More than 40 of them are waiting in hiding to attack him. They have promised that they will not eat or drink anything until they have killed him. They are ready now. All they need is for you to bring Paul to the Sanhedrin."

[22]The commanding officer let the young man go. But he gave him a warning. "Don't tell anyone you have reported this to me," he said.

Paul Is Taken to Caesarea

[23]Then the commanding officer called for two of his commanders. He ordered them, "Gather a company of 200 soldiers, 70 horsemen and 200 men armed with spears. Get them ready to go to Caesarea at nine o'clock tonight. [24]Provide horses for Paul so that he may be taken safely to Governor Felix."

[25]Here is the letter the officer wrote.

[26]I, Claudius Lysias, am writing this letter.

I am sending it to His Excellency, Governor Felix.

Greetings.

[27]The Jews grabbed Paul. They were about to kill him. But I came with my soldiers and saved him. I had learned that he is a Roman citizen. [28]I wanted to know why they were bringing charges against him. So I brought him to their Sanhedrin. [29]I found out that the charge against him was based on questions about their law. But there was no charge against him worthy of death or prison. [30]Then I was told about a plan against the man. So I sent him to you at once. I also ordered those bringing charges against him to present their case to you.

[31]The soldiers followed their orders. During the night they took Paul with them. They brought him as far as Antipatris. [32]The next day they let the horsemen go on with him. The soldiers returned to the fort. [33]The horsemen arrived in Caesarea. They gave the letter to the governor. Then they handed Paul over to him. [34]The governor read the letter. He asked Paul where he was from. He learned that Paul was from Cilicia. [35]So he said, "I will hear your case when those bringing charges against you get here." Then he ordered that Paul be kept under guard in Herod's palace.

Paul's Trial in Front of Felix

24 Five days later Ananias the high priest went down to Caesarea. Some elders and a lawyer named Tertullus went with him. They brought their charges against Paul to the governor. ²So Paul was called in. Tertullus began to bring the charges against Paul. He said to Felix, "We have enjoyed a long time of peace while you have been ruling. You are a wise leader. You have made this a better nation. ³Most excellent Felix, we gladly admit this everywhere and in every way. And we are very thankful. ⁴I don't want to bother you. But would you be kind enough to listen to us for a short time?

⁵"We have found that Paul is a troublemaker. This man stirs up trouble among Jews all over the world. He is a leader of those who follow Jesus of Nazareth. ⁶⁻⁷He even tried to make our temple impure. So we arrested him. ⁸Question him yourself. Then you will learn the truth about all these charges we are bringing against him."

⁹The other Jews said the same thing. They agreed that the charges were true.

¹⁰The governor motioned for Paul to speak. Paul said, "I know that you have been a judge over this nation for quite a few years. So I am glad to explain my actions to you. ¹¹About 12 days ago I went up to Jerusalem to worship. You can easily check on this. ¹²Those bringing charges against me did not find me arguing with anyone at the temple. I wasn't stirring up a crowd in the synagogues or anywhere else in the city. ¹³They can't prove to you any of the charges they are making against me. ¹⁴It is true that I worship the God of our people. I am a follower of the Way of Jesus. Those bringing charges against me call it a cult. I believe everything that is in keeping with the Law. I believe everything that is in keeping with what is written in the Prophets. ¹⁵I have the same hope in God that these men themselves have. I believe that both the godly and the ungodly will rise from the dead. ¹⁶So I always try not to do anything wrong in the eyes of God or in the eyes of people.

¹⁷"I was away for several years. Then I came to Jerusalem to bring my people gifts for those who were poor. I also came to offer sacrifices. ¹⁸They found me doing this in the temple courtyard. I had already been made pure and 'clean' in the usual way. There was no crowd with me. I didn't stir up any trouble. ¹⁹But there are some other Jews who should be here in front of you. They are from Asia Minor. They should

bring charges if they have anything against me. ²⁰Let the Jews who are here tell you what crime I am guilty of. After all, I was put on trial by the Sanhedrin. ²¹Perhaps they blame me for what I said when I was on trial. I shouted, 'I believe that people will rise from the dead. That is why I am on trial here today.'"

²²Felix knew all about the Way of Jesus. So he put off the trial for the time being. "Lysias the commanding officer will come," he said. "Then I will decide your case." ²³He ordered the commander to keep Paul under guard. He told him to give Paul some freedom. He also told him to allow Paul's friends to take care of his needs.

²⁴Several days later Felix came with his wife Drusilla. She was a Jew. Felix sent for Paul and listened to him speak about faith in Christ Jesus. ²⁵Paul talked about how to live a godly life. He talked about how people should control themselves. He also talked about the time when God will judge everyone. Then Felix became afraid. "That's enough for now!" he said. "You may leave. When I find the time, I will send for you." ²⁶He was hoping that Paul would offer him some money to let him go. So he often sent for Paul and talked with him.

²⁷Two years passed. Porcius Festus took the place of Felix. But Felix wanted to do the Jews a favor. So he left Paul in prison.

Paul's Trial in Front of Festus

25 Three days after Festus arrived, he went up from Caesarea to Jerusalem. ²There the chief priests and the Jewish leaders came to Festus. They brought their charges against Paul. ³They tried very hard to get Festus to have Paul taken to Jerusalem. They asked for this as a favor. They were planning to hide and attack Paul along the way. They wanted to kill him. ⁴Festus answered, "Paul is being held at Caesarea. Soon I'll be going there myself. ⁵Let some of your leaders come with me. If the man has done anything wrong, they can bring charges against him there."

⁶Festus spent eight or ten days in Jerusalem with them. Then he went down to Caesarea. The next day he called the court together. He ordered Paul to be brought to him. ⁷When Paul arrived, the Jews who had come down from Jerusalem stood around him. They brought many strong charges

against him. But they couldn't prove that these charges were true.

⁸Then Paul spoke up for himself. He said, "I've done nothing wrong against the law of the Jews or against the temple. I've done nothing wrong against Caesar."

⁹But Festus wanted to do the Jews a favor. So he said to Paul, "Are you willing to go up to Jerusalem? Are you willing to go on trial there? Are you willing to face these charges in my court?"

¹⁰Paul answered, "I'm already standing in Caesar's court. This is where I should go on trial. I haven't done anything wrong to the Jews. You yourself know that very well. ¹¹If I am guilty of anything worthy of death, I'm willing to die. But the charges brought against me by these Jews are not true. No one has the right to hand me over to them. I make my appeal to Caesar!"

¹²Festus talked it over with the members of his court. Then he said, "You have made an appeal to Caesar. To Caesar you will go!"

Festus Talks With King Agrippa

¹³A few days later King Agrippa and Bernice arrived in Caesarea. They came to pay a visit to Festus. ¹⁴They were spending many days there. So Festus talked with the king about Paul's case. He said, "There's a man here that Felix left as a prisoner. ¹⁵When I went to Jerusalem, the Jewish chief priests and the elders brought charges against the man. They wanted him to be found guilty.

¹⁶"I told them that this is not the way Romans do things. We don't judge people before they have faced those bringing charges against them. They must have a chance to argue against the charges for themselves. ¹⁷When the Jewish leaders came back with me, I didn't waste any time. I called the court together the next day. I ordered the man to be brought in. ¹⁸Those bringing charges against him got up to speak. But they didn't charge him with any of the crimes I had expected. ¹⁹Instead, they argued with him about their own beliefs. They didn't agree about a man named Jesus. They said Jesus was dead, but Paul claimed Jesus was alive. ²⁰I had no idea how to look into such matters. So I asked Paul if he would be willing to go to Jerusalem. There he could be tried on these charges. ²¹But Paul made an appeal to have the Emperor

BiBLE ADVeNTUReS

Jack told the story of Paul's last journey and his imprisonment in Rome in "Saint Paul: Voyage to Rome" and "Saint Paul: An Appointment with Caesar" (A#27).

decide his case. So I ordered him to be held until I could send him to Caesar."

²²Then Agrippa said to Festus, "I would like to hear this man myself."

Festus replied, "Tomorrow you will hear him."

Paul in Front of Agrippa

²³The next day Agrippa and Bernice arrived. They were treated like very important people. They entered the courtroom. The most important military officers and the leading men of the city came with them. When Festus gave the command, Paul was brought in. ²⁴Festus said, "King Agrippa, and everyone else here, take a good look at this man! A large number of Jews have come to me about him. They came to me in Jerusalem and also here in Caesarea. They keep shouting that he shouldn't live any longer. ²⁵I have found that he hasn't done anything worthy of death. But he made his appeal to the Emperor. So I decided to send him to Rome. ²⁶I don't have anything certain to write about him to His Majesty. So I have brought him here today. Now all of you will be able to hear him. King Agrippa, it will also be very good for you to hear him. As a result of this hearing, I will have something to write. ²⁷It doesn't make sense to send a prisoner on to Rome without listing the charges against him."

26 Agrippa said to Paul, "You may now present your case."

So Paul motioned with his hand. Then he began to present his case. ²"King Agrippa," he said, "I am happy to be able to stand here today. I will answer all the charges brought against me by the Jews. ³I am very pleased that you are familiar with Jewish ways. You know the kinds of things they argue about. So I beg you to be patient as you listen to me.

⁴"The Jewish people all know how I have lived ever since I was a child. They know

all about me from the beginning of my life. They know how I lived in my own country and in Jerusalem. ⁵They have known me for a long time. So if they wanted to, they could tell you how I have lived. I have lived by the rules of the Pharisees. Those rules are harder to obey than those of any other Jewish group. ⁶Today I am on trial because of the hope I have. I believe in what God promised our people of long ago. ⁷It is the promise that our 12 tribes are hoping to see come true. Because of this hope they serve God with faithful and honest hearts day and night. King Agrippa, it is also because of this hope that these Jews are bringing charges against me. ⁸Why should any of you think it is impossible for God to raise the dead?

⁹"I believed that I should oppose the name of Jesus of Nazareth. So I did everything I could to oppose his name. ¹⁰That's just what I was doing in Jerusalem. On the authority of the chief priests, I put many of the Lord's people in prison. I agreed that they should die. ¹¹I often went from one synagogue to another to have them punished. I tried to force them to speak evil things against Jesus. All I wanted to do was hurt them. I even went looking for them in the cities of other lands.

¹²"On one of these journeys I was on my way to Damascus. I had the authority and commission of the chief priests. ¹³About noon, King Agrippa, I was on the road. I saw a light coming from heaven. It was brighter than the sun. It was shining around me and my companions. ¹⁴We all fell to the ground. I heard a voice speak to me in the Aramaic language. 'Saul! Saul!' it said. 'Why are you opposing me? It is hard for you to go against what you know is right.'

¹⁵"Then I asked, 'Who are you, Lord?'

" 'I am Jesus,' the Lord replied. 'I am the one you are opposing. ¹⁶Now get up. Stand on your feet. I have appeared to you to appoint you to serve me. And you must tell other people about me. You must tell others that you have seen me today. You must also tell them that I will show myself to you again. ¹⁷I will save you from your own people and from the Gentiles. I am sending you to them ¹⁸to open their eyes. I want you to turn them from darkness to light. I want you to turn them from Satan's power to God. I want their sins to be forgiven. They will be

forgiven when they believe in me. They will have their place among God's people.'

¹⁹"So then, King Agrippa, I obeyed the vision that appeared from heaven. ²⁰First I preached to people in Damascus. Then I preached in Jerusalem and in all Judea. And then I preached to the Gentiles. I told them to turn away from their sins to God. The way they live must show that they have turned away from their sins. ²¹That's why some Jews grabbed me in the temple courtyard and tried to kill me. ²²But God has helped me to this day. So I stand here and tell you what is true. I tell it to everyone, both small and great. I have been saying nothing different from what the prophets and Moses said would happen. ²³They said the Messiah would suffer. He would be the first to rise from the dead. He would bring the message of God's light. He would bring it to his own people and to the Gentiles."

²⁴While Paul was still presenting his case, Festus interrupted. "You are out of your mind, Paul!" he shouted. "Your great learning is driving you crazy!"

²⁵"I am not crazy, most excellent Festus," Paul replied. "What I am saying is true and reasonable. ²⁶The king is familiar with these things. So I can speak openly to him. I am certain he knows everything that has been going on. After all, it was not done in secret. ²⁷King Agrippa, do you believe the prophets? I know you do."

²⁸Then Agrippa spoke to Paul. "Are you trying to talk me into becoming a Christian?" he said. "Do you think you can do that in such a short time?"

²⁹Paul replied, "I don't care if it takes a short time or a long time. I pray to God for you and all who are listening to me today. I pray that you may become like me, except for these chains."

³⁰The king stood up. The governor and Bernice and those sitting with them stood up too. ³¹They left the room and began to talk with one another. "Why should this man die or be put in prison?" they said. "He has done nothing worthy of that!"

³²Agrippa said to Festus, "This man could have been set free. But he has made an appeal to Caesar."

Paul Sails for Rome

27 It was decided that we would sail for Italy. Paul and some other prisoners were handed over to a Roman commander named Julius. He belonged to the Imperial Guard. [2]We boarded a ship from Adramyttium. It was about to sail for ports along the coast of Asia Minor. We headed out to sea. Aristarchus was with us. He was a Macedonian from Thessalonica.

[3]The next day we landed at Sidon. There Julius was kind to Paul. He let Paul visit his friends so they could give him what he needed. [4]From there we headed out to sea again. We passed the calmer side of Cyprus because the winds were against us. [5]We sailed across the open sea off the coast of Cilicia and Pamphylia. Then we landed at Myra in Lycia. [6]There the commander found a ship from Alexandria sailing for Italy. He put us on board. [7]We moved along slowly for many days. We had trouble getting to Cnidus. The wind did not let us stay on course. So we passed the calmer side of Crete, opposite Salmone. [8]It was not easy to sail along the coast. Then we came to a place called Fair Havens. It was near the town of Lasea.

[9]A lot of time had passed. Sailing had already become dangerous. By now it was after the Day of Atonement, a day of fasting. So Paul gave them a warning. [10]"Men," he said, "I can see that our trip is going to be dangerous. The ship and everything in it will be lost. Our own lives will be in danger also." [11]But the commander didn't listen to what Paul said. Instead, he followed the advice of the pilot and the ship's owner. [12]The harbor wasn't a good place for ships to stay during winter. So most of the people decided we should sail on. They hoped we would reach Phoenix. They wanted to spend the winter there. Phoenix was a harbor in Crete. It faced both southwest and northwest.

The Storm

[13]A gentle south wind began to blow. The ship's crew thought they saw their chance to leave safely. So they pulled up the anchor and sailed along the shore of Crete. [14]Before very long, a wind blew down from the island. It had the force of a hurricane. It was called the Northeaster. [15]The ship was caught by the storm. We could not keep it sailing into the wind. So we gave up and were driven along by the wind. [16]We passed the calmer side of a small island called Cauda. We almost lost the lifeboat that was tied to the side of the ship. [17]So the men lifted the lifeboat on board. Then they tied ropes under the ship itself to hold it together. They were afraid it would get stuck on the sandbars of Syrtis. So they lowered the sea anchor and let the ship be driven along. [18]We took a very bad beating from the storm. The next day the crew began to throw the ship's contents overboard. [19]On the third day, they even threw the ship's tools and supplies overboard with their own hands. [20]The sun and stars didn't appear for many days. The storm was terrible. So we gave up all hope of being saved.

[21]The men had not eaten for a long time. Paul stood up in front of them. "Men," he said, "you should have taken my advice not to sail from Crete. Then you would have avoided this harm and loss. [22]Now I beg you to be brave. Not one of you will die. Only the ship will be destroyed. [23]I belong to God and serve him. Last night his angel stood beside me. [24]The angel said, 'Do not be afraid, Paul. You must go on trial in front of Caesar. God has shown his grace by sparing the lives of all those sailing with you.' [25]Men, continue to be brave. I have faith in God. It will happen just as he told me. [26]But we must run the ship onto the beach of some island."

The Ship Is Destroyed

[27]On the 14th night the wind was still pushing us across the Adriatic Sea. About midnight the sailors had a feeling that they were approaching land. [28]They measured how deep the water was. They found that it was 120 feet deep. A short time later they measured the water again. This time it was 90 feet deep. [29]They were afraid we would crash against the rocks. So they dropped four anchors from the back of the ship. They prayed that daylight would come. [30]The sailors wanted to escape from the ship. So they let the lifeboat down into the sea. They pretended they were going to lower some anchors from the front of the ship. [31]But Paul spoke to the commander and the soldiers. "These men must stay with the ship," he said. "If they don't, you can't be saved." [32]So the soldiers cut the ropes that held the lifeboat. They let it drift away.

[33]Just before dawn Paul tried to get them all to eat. "For the last 14 days," he said, "you

have wondered what would happen. You have gone without food. You haven't eaten anything. ³⁴Now I am asking you to eat some food. You need it to live. Not one of you will lose a single hair from your head." ³⁵After Paul said this, he took some bread and gave thanks to God. He did this where they all could see him. Then he broke it and began to eat. ³⁶All of them were filled with hope. So they ate some food. ³⁷There were 276 of us on board. ³⁸They ate as much as they wanted. They needed to make the ship lighter. So they threw the rest of the grain into the sea.

³⁹When daylight came, they saw a bay with a sandy beach. They didn't recognize the place. But they decided to run the ship onto the beach if they could. ⁴⁰So they cut the anchors loose and left them in the sea. At the same time, they untied the ropes that held the rudders. They lifted the sail at the front of the ship to the wind. Then they headed for the beach. ⁴¹But the ship hit a sandbar. So the front of it got stuck and wouldn't move. The back of the ship was broken to pieces by the pounding of the waves.

⁴²The soldiers planned to kill the prisoners. They wanted to keep them from swimming away and escaping. ⁴³But the commander wanted to save Paul's life. So he kept the soldiers from carrying out their plan. He ordered those who could swim to jump overboard first and swim to land. ⁴⁴The rest were supposed to get there on boards or other pieces of the ship. That is how everyone reached land safely.

On Shore at Malta

28 When we were safe on shore, we found out that the island was called Malta. ²The people of the island were unusually kind. It was raining and cold. So they built a fire and welcomed all of us. ³Paul gathered some sticks and put them on the fire. A poisonous snake was driven out by the heat. It fastened itself on Paul's hand. ⁴The people of the island saw the snake hanging from his hand. They said to one another, "This man must be a murderer. He escaped from the sea. But the female god Justice won't let him live." ⁵Paul shook the snake off into the fire. He was not harmed. ⁶The people expected him to swell up. They thought he would suddenly fall dead. They waited for a long

Acts 28:3 Some versions of the Bible say Paul was bitten by a viper. That snake is so poisonous that ancient warriors dipped their arrows into its venom to hasten the death of their enemies. No wonder the people of Malta thought that Paul was in trouble!

time. But they didn't see anything unusual happen to him. So they changed their minds. They said he was a god.

⁷Publius owned property nearby. He was the chief official on the island. He welcomed us to his home. For three days he took care of us. He treated us with kindness. ⁸His father was sick in bed. The man suffered from fever and dysentery. So Paul went in to see him. Paul prayed for him. He placed his hands on him and healed him. ⁹Then the rest of the sick people on the island came. They too were healed. ¹⁰The people of the island honored us in many ways. When we were ready to sail, they gave us the supplies we needed.

Paul Arrives in Rome

¹¹After three months we headed out to sea. We sailed in a ship from Alexandria that had stayed at the island during the winter. On the front of the ship the figures of twin gods were carved. Their names were Castor and Pollux. ¹²We landed at Syracuse and stayed there for three days. ¹³From there we sailed to Rhegium. The next day the south wind came up. The day after that, we reached Puteoli. ¹⁴There we found some believers. They invited us to spend a week with them. At last we came to Rome. ¹⁵The believers there had heard we were coming. They traveled as far as the Forum of Appius and the Three Taverns to meet us. When

Paul saw these people, he thanked God for them and was encouraged by them. [16]When we got to Rome, Paul was allowed to live by himself. But a soldier guarded him.

Paul Preaches in Rome

[17]Three days later Paul called a meeting of the local Jewish leaders. When they came, Paul spoke to them. He said, "My brothers, I have done nothing against our people. I have also done nothing against what our people of long ago practiced. But I was arrested in Jerusalem. I was handed over to the Romans. [18]They questioned me. And they wanted to let me go. They saw I wasn't guilty of any crime worthy of death. [19]But the Jews objected, so I had to make an appeal to Caesar. I certainly did not mean to bring any charge against my own people. [20]I share Israel's hope. That is why I am held with this chain. So I have asked to see you and talk with you."

[21]They replied, "We have not received any letters from Judea about you. None of our people here from Judea has reported or said anything bad about you. [22]But we want to hear what your ideas are. We know that people everywhere are talking against those who believe as you do."

[23]They decided to meet Paul on a certain day. At that time even more people came to the place where he was staying. From morning until evening, he told them about God's kingdom. Using the Law of Moses and the Prophets, he tried to get them to believe in Jesus. [24]Some believed what he said, and others did not. [25]They didn't agree with one another. They began to leave after Paul had made a final statement. He said, "The Holy Spirit was right when he spoke to your people long ago. Through Isaiah the prophet the Spirit said,

[26] "'Go to your people. Say to them,
  "You will hear but never understand.
    You will see but never know what
      you are seeing."
[27] These people's hearts have become
      stubborn.
    They can barely hear with their ears.
    They have closed their eyes.
  Otherwise they might see with their
      eyes.
    They might hear with their ears.
    They might understand with their
      hearts.
  They might turn, and then I would heal
      them.'   *(Isaiah 6:9,10)*

[28-29]"Here is what I want you to know. God has sent his salvation to the Gentiles. And they will listen!"

[30]For two whole years Paul stayed there in a house he rented. He welcomed all who came to see him. [31]He preached boldly about God's kingdom. He taught people about the Lord Jesus Christ. And no one could keep him from teaching and preaching about these things.

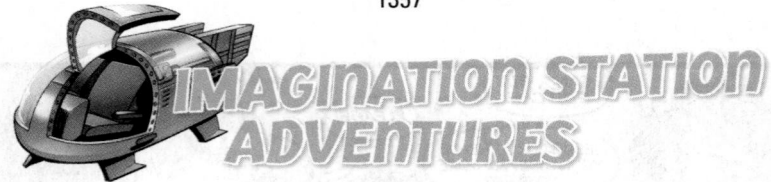

IMAGINATION STATION ADVENTURES

TABITHA'S GIFT Read Acts 9:36-43.

WILL YOU **PLEASE** HELP ME WITH THESE BASKETS?

SURE!

THIS FOOD SMELLS **REALLY GOOD.**

WHIT SENDS TAMIKA TO NEW TESTAMENT TIMES IN THE CITY OF JOPPA, NEAR THE MEDITERRANEAN COAST.

HERE'S SOME FOOD FOR YOU AND THE LITTLE ONES.

THANK YOU, TABITHA. THIS **HELPS** A LOT WHILE MY HORACE IS OUT TO SEA.

MAY THE **PEACE OF CHRIST** BE WITH YOU.

AT THE SHORE . . .

I MADE YOU A NEW TUNIC, MARCUS.

THANK YOU. **HOW DID YOU KNOW I NEEDED** A NEW ONE?

OH PLEASE, COVER THOSE KNOBBY KNEES!

MEANWHILE, MARVIN HAS BEEN SENT TO LYDDA, A NEARBY TOWN. HE'S ASSISTING THE APOSTLE PETER.

WHAT AILS YOU, SIR?

I HAVEN'T BEEN ABLE TO MOVE MY BODY FOR **EIGHT YEARS.**

CAN YOU **HELP** HIM?

"LET US NOT BECOME TIRED OF DOING GOOD."

GALATIANS 6:9

Romans

Take a moment to think of a hobby or interest you have. Mine would be studying patterns in the Periodic Table. Yours might be a sport, a craft, or something completely different. Now imagine how hard it would be to write a letter to a group of total strangers, telling them everything you know about the topic to get them as excited as you are. I've tried this with the Periodic Table, but had decidedly mixed success. This is the sort of task that was ahead of the apostle Paul as he sat down to write the book of Romans. He wanted everyone to understand Christianity and be as excited about it as he was!

A vision of Jesus had completely changed Paul's outlook on life (Acts 9:1–31). He spent the rest of his life telling others about the importance of believing in Jesus. The greatest city in the Roman Empire was, of course, Rome. However, a church had already started in Rome before Paul could visit personally, so he decided to begin with a letter. (Paul would later visit Rome, an account you can read in the latter parts of the previous book: Acts.)

Some Roman believers were Jews who based their worship habits on centuries of tradition. Others were Gentile (or non-Jewish) new believers who might have been worshiping Roman gods before putting their faith in Jesus. Now Jews and Gentiles were sitting together as a united church. It was a big challenge for Paul to provide clear instruction and guidelines, yet Paul wrote about essentially every doctrine of Christian faith. He earnestly desired to help Jews and Gentiles learn to relate to one another . . . and to God.

What's it Mean, Eugene?

Gifts, Spiritual—Various spiritual abilities given by the Holy Spirit to the members of Christ's church for use both in ministry to one another and in outreach to the nonbelieving world. Some of these gifts are outlined in Romans 12:3–8, 1 Corinthians 12:1–11, and Ephesians 4:7–12. I, for one, excel primarily in the gift of teaching. Miss Kendall suggests that I should ask for the gift of encouragement. In turn, I admonished her to pray for the gift of mercy.

1 I, Paul, am writing this letter. I serve Christ Jesus. I have been appointed to be an apostle. God set me apart to tell others his good news. [2]He promised the good news long ago. He announced it through his prophets in the Holy Scriptures. [3]The good news is about God's Son. He was born into the family line of King David. [4]By the Holy Spirit, he was appointed to be the mighty Son of God. God did this by raising him from the dead. He is Jesus Christ our Lord. [5]We received grace because of what Jesus did. He made us apostles to the Gentiles. We must invite all of them to obey God by trusting in Jesus. We do this to bring glory to him. [6]You also are among those Gentiles who are appointed to belong to Jesus Christ.

[7]I am sending this letter to all of you in Rome. You are loved by God and appointed to be his holy people.

May God our Father and the Lord Jesus Christ give you grace and peace.

Paul Longs to Visit Rome

[8]First, I thank my God through Jesus Christ for all of you. People all over the world are talking about your faith. [9]I serve God with my whole heart. I preach the good news about his Son. God knows that I always remember you [10]in my prayers. I pray that now at last it may be God's plan to open the way for me to visit you.

[11]I long to see you. I want to make you strong by giving you a gift from the Holy Spirit. [12]I want us to encourage one another in the faith we share. [13]Brothers and sisters, I want you to know that I planned many times to visit you. But until now I have been kept from coming. My work has produced results among the other Gentiles. In the same way, I want to see results among you.

[14]I have a duty both to Greeks and to non-Greeks. I have a duty both to wise people and to foolish people. [15]So I really want to preach the good news also to you who live in Rome.

[16]I want to preach it because I'm not ashamed of the good news. It is God's power to save everyone who believes. It is meant first for the Jews. It is meant also for the Gentiles. [17]The good news shows God's power to make people right with himself. God's power to be made right with him is given to the person who has faith. It happens by faith from beginning to end. It is written, "The one who is right with God will live by faith." *(Habakkuk 2:4)*

God's Anger Against Sinners

[18]God shows his anger from heaven. It is against all the godless and evil things people do. They are so evil that they say no to the truth. [19]The truth about God is plain to them. God has made it plain. [20]Ever since the world was created it has been possible to see the qualities of God that are not seen. I'm talking about his eternal power and about the fact that he is God. Those things can be seen in what he has made. So people have no excuse for what they do.

[21]They knew God. But they didn't honor him as God. They didn't thank him. Their thinking became worthless. Their foolish hearts became dark. [22]They claimed to be wise. But they made fools of themselves. [23]They would rather have statues of gods than the glorious God who lives forever. Their statues of gods are made to look like people, birds, animals and reptiles.

[24]So God let them go. He allowed them to do what their sinful hearts wanted to. He let them commit sexual sins. They made one another's bodies impure by what they did. [25]They chose a lie instead of the truth about God. They worshiped and served

WOOTON'S FUN FACTS
Rom. 1:1

You probably know from the book of Acts that Paul has another name—Saul. Saul is a typical name used in Jewish homes. Remember King Saul from 1 Samuel 9–15? Paul is a name more friendly to the Romans, who by and large weren't Jewish.

created things. They didn't worship the Creator. But he is praised forever. Amen. [26]So God let them continue to have their shameful desires. Their women committed sexual acts that were not natural. [27]In the same way, the men turned away from their natural love for women. They burned with sexual desire for each other. Men did shameful things with other men. They suffered in their bodies for all the wrong things they did.

[28]They didn't think it was important to know God. So God let them continue to have evil thoughts. They did things they shouldn't do. [29]They are full of every kind of sin, evil and ungodliness. They want more than they need. They commit murder. They want what belongs to other people. They fight and cheat. They hate others. They say mean things about other people. [30]They tell lies about them. They hate God. They are rude and proud. They brag. They think of new ways to do evil. They don't obey their parents. [31]They do not understand. They can't be trusted. They are not loving and kind. [32]They know that God's commands are right. They know that those who do evil things should die. But they continue to do those very things. They also approve of others who do them.

God Judges Fairly

2 If you judge someone else, you have no excuse for it. When you judge another person, you are judging yourself. You do the same things you blame others for doing. [2]We know that when God judges those who do evil things, he judges fairly. [3]Though you are only a human being, you judge others. But you yourself do the same things. So how do you think you will escape when God judges you? [4]Do you disrespect God's great kindness and favor? Do you disrespect God when he is patient with you? Don't you realize that God's kindness is meant to turn you away from your sins?

[5]But you are stubborn. In your heart you are not sorry for your sins. You are storing up anger against yourself. The day of God's anger is coming. Then his way of judging fairly will be shown. [6]God "will pay back each person in keeping with what they have done." *(Psalm 62:12; Proverbs 24:12)* [7]God will give eternal life to those who keep on doing good. They want glory, honor, and life that

never ends. [8]But there are others who only look out for themselves. They don't accept the truth. They go astray. God will pour out his great anger on them. [9]There will be trouble and suffering for everyone who does evil. That is meant first for the Jews. It is also meant for the Gentiles. [10]But there will be glory, honor and peace for everyone who does good. That is meant first for the Jews. It is also meant for the Gentiles. [11]God treats everyone the same.

[12]Some people do not know God's law when they sin. They will not be judged by the law when they die. Others do know God's law when they sin. They will be judged by the law. [13]Hearing the law does not make a person right with God. People are considered to be right with God only when they obey the law. [14]Gentiles do not have the law. Sometimes they just naturally do what the law requires. They are a law for themselves. This is true even though they don't have the law. [15]They show that what the law requires is written on their hearts. The way their minds judge them proves this fact. Sometimes their thoughts find them guilty. At other times their thoughts find them not guilty. [16]This will happen on the day God appoints Jesus Christ to judge people's secret thoughts. That's part of my good news.

The Jews and the Law

[17]Suppose you call yourself a Jew. You trust in the law. You brag that you know God. [18]You know what God wants. You agree with what is best because the law teaches you. [19]You think you know so much more than the people you teach. You think you're helping blind people. You think you are a light for those in the dark. [20]You think you can make foolish people wise. You act like you're teaching little children. You think that the law gives you all knowledge and truth. [21]You claim to teach others, but you don't even teach yourself! You preach against stealing. But you steal! [22]You say that people should not commit adultery. But you commit adultery! You hate statues of gods. But you rob temples! [23]You brag about the law. But when you break it, you rob God of his honor! [24]It is written, "The Gentiles say evil things against God's name because of you." *(Isaiah 52:5; Ezekiel 36:22)*

[25]Circumcision has value if you obey the law. But if you break the law, it is just as if

you hadn't been circumcised. ²⁶And sometimes those who aren't circumcised do what the law requires. Won't God accept them as if they had been circumcised? ²⁷Many are not circumcised physically, but they obey the law. They will prove that you are guilty. You are breaking the law, even though you have the written law and are circumcised.

²⁸A person is not a Jew if they are a Jew only on the outside. And circumcision is more than just something done to the outside of a man's body. ²⁹No, a person is a Jew only if they are a Jew on the inside. And true circumcision means that the heart has been circumcised by the Holy Spirit. The person whose heart has been circumcised does more than obey the written law. The praise that matters for that kind of person does not come from other people. It comes from God.

God Is Faithful

3 Is there any advantage in being a Jew? Is there any value in being circumcised? ²There is great value in every way! First of all, the Jews have been given the very words of God.

³What if some Jews were not faithful? Will the fact that they weren't faithful keep God from being faithful? ⁴Not at all! God is true, even if every human being is a liar. It is written,

"You are right when you sentence me.
  You are fair when you judge me."
(Psalm 51:4)

⁵Doesn't the fact that we are wrong prove more clearly that God is right? Then what can we say? Can we say that God is not fair when he brings his anger down on us? As you can tell, I am just using human ways of thinking. ⁶God is certainly fair! If he weren't, how could he judge the world? ⁷Someone might argue, "When I lie, it becomes clearer that God is truthful. It makes his glory shine more brightly. Why then does he find me guilty of sin?" ⁸Why not say, "Let's do evil things so that good things will happen"? Some people actually lie by reporting that this is what we say. They are the ones who will rightly be found guilty.

No One Is Right With God

⁹What should we say then? Do we Jews have any advantage? Not at all! We have already claimed that Jews and Gentiles are sinners. Everyone is under the power of sin. ¹⁰It is written,

"No one is right with God, no one at all.
¹¹ No one understands.
  No one trusts in God.
¹² All of them have turned away.
  They have all become worthless.
No one does anything good,
  no one at all."
(Psalms 14:1–3; 53:1–3; Ecclesiastes 7:20)
¹³ "Their throats are like open graves.
  With their tongues they tell lies."
(Psalm 5:9)
"The words from their lips are like the
  poison of a snake." *(Psalm 140:3)*
¹⁴ "Their mouths are full of curses and
  bitterness." *(Psalm 10:7)*
¹⁵ "They run quickly to commit murder.
¹⁶ They leave a trail of harmful actions.
¹⁷ They do not know how to live in peace."
(Isaiah 59:7,8)
¹⁸ "They don't have any respect for
  God." *(Psalm 36:1)*

¹⁹What the law says, it says to those who are ruled by the law. Its purpose is to shut every mouth and make the whole world accountable to God. ²⁰So no one will be considered right with God by obeying the law. Instead, the law makes us more aware of our sin.

Becoming Right With God by Faith

²¹But now God has shown us his saving power without the help of the law. But the Law and the Prophets tell us about this. ²²We are made right with God by putting our faith in Jesus Christ. This happens to all who believe. It is no different for the Jews than for the Gentiles. ²³Everyone has sinned. No one measures up to God's glory. ²⁴The free gift of God's grace makes us right with him. Christ Jesus paid the price to set us free. ²⁵God gave Christ as a sacrifice to pay for sins through the spilling of his blood. So God forgives the sins of those who have faith. God did all this to prove that

REMEMBER THIS

ROMANS 3:23

"Everyone has sinned.
No one measures up
to God's glory."

he does what is right. He is a God of mercy. So he did not punish for their sins the people who lived before Jesus lived. ²⁶God did all this to prove in our own time that he does what is right. He also makes right with himself those who believe in Jesus.

²⁷So who can brag? No one! Are people saved by the law that requires them to obey? Not at all! They are saved because of the law that requires faith. ²⁸We firmly believe that a person is made right with God because of their faith. They are not saved by obeying the law. ²⁹Or is God the God of Jews only? Isn't he also the God of Gentiles? Yes, he is their God too. ³⁰There is only one God. When those who are circumcised believe in him, he makes them right with himself. Suppose those who are not circumcised believe in him. Then God also will make them right with himself. ³¹Does faith make the law useless? Not at all! We agree with the law.

Abraham's Faith Made Him Right With God

4 What should we say about these things? What did Abraham, the father of our people, discover about being right with God? ²Did he become right with God because of something he did? If so, he could brag about it. But he couldn't brag to God. ³What do we find in Scripture? It says, "Abraham believed God. God accepted Abraham's faith, and so his faith made him right with God." *(Genesis 15:6)*

⁴When a person works, their pay is not considered a gift. It is owed to them. ⁵But things are different with God. He makes ungodly people right with himself. If people trust in him, their faith is accepted even though they do not work. Their faith makes them right with God. ⁶King David says the same thing. He tells us how blessed people are when God makes them right with himself. They are blessed because they don't have to do anything in return. David says,

⁷ "Blessed are those
    whose lawless acts are forgiven.
Blessed are those
    whose sins are taken away.
⁸ Blessed is the person
    whose sin the Lord never counts
        against them."   *(Psalm 32:1,2)*

⁹Is that blessing only for those who are circumcised? Or is it also for those who are not circumcised? We have been saying that God accepted Abraham's faith. So his faith made him right with God. ¹⁰When did it happen? Was it after Abraham was circumcised, or before? It was before he was circumcised, not after! ¹¹He was circumcised as a sign of the covenant God had made with him. It showed that his faith had made him right with God before he was circumcised. So Abraham is the father of all believers who have not been circumcised. God accepts their faith. So their faith makes them right with him. ¹²And Abraham is also the father of those who are circumcised and believe. So just being circumcised is not enough. Those who are circumcised must also follow the steps of our father Abraham. He had faith before he was circumcised.

¹³Abraham and his family received a promise. God promised that Abraham would receive the world. It would not come to him because he obeyed the law. It would come because of his faith, which made him right with God. ¹⁴Do those who depend on the law receive the promise? If they do, faith would mean nothing. God's promise would be worthless. ¹⁵The law brings God's anger. Where there is no law, the law can't be broken.

¹⁶The promise is based on God's grace. The promise comes by faith. All of Abraham's children will certainly receive the promise. And it is not only for those who are ruled by the law. Those who have the same faith that Abraham had are also included. He is the father of us all. ¹⁷It is written, "I have made you a father of many nations." *(Genesis 17:5)* God considers Abraham to be our father. The God that Abraham believed in gives life to the dead. Abraham's God also creates things that did not exist before.

¹⁸When there was no reason for hope, Abraham believed because he had hope. He became the father of many nations, exactly as God had promised. God said, "That is how many children you will have." *(Genesis*

15:5) ¹⁹Abraham did not become weak in his faith. He accepted the fact that he was past the time when he could have children. At that time Abraham was about 100 years old. He also realized that Sarah was too old to have children. ²⁰But Abraham kept believing in God's promise. He became strong in his faith. He gave glory to God. ²¹He was absolutely sure that God had the power to do what he had promised. ²²That's why "God accepted Abraham because he believed. So his faith made him right with God." *(Genesis 15:6)* ²³The words "God accepted Abraham's faith" were written not only for Abraham. ²⁴They were written also for us. We believe in the God who raised Jesus our Lord from the dead. So God will accept our faith and make us right with himself. ²⁵Jesus was handed over to die for our sins. He was raised to life in order to make us right with God.

Peace and Hope

5 We have been made right with God because of our faith. Now we have peace with him because of our Lord Jesus Christ. ²Through faith in Jesus we have received God's grace. In that grace we stand. We are full of joy because we expect to share in God's glory. ³And that's not all. We are full of joy even when we suffer. We know that our suffering gives us the strength to go on. ⁴The strength to go on produces character. Character produces hope. ⁵And hope will never bring us shame. That's because God's love has been poured into our hearts. This happened through the Holy Spirit, who has been given to us.

⁶At just the right time Christ died for ungodly people. He died for us when we had no power of our own. ⁷It is unusual for anyone to die for a godly person. Maybe someone would be willing to die for a good person. ⁸But here is how God has shown his love for us. While we were still sinners, Christ died for us.

⁹The blood of Christ has made us right with God. So we are even more sure that Jesus will save us from God's anger. ¹⁰Once we were God's enemies. But we have been brought back to him because his Son has died for us. Now that God has brought us back, we are even more secure. We know that we will be saved because Christ lives. ¹¹And that is not all. We are full of joy in

---

Last weekend, Penny and I went on a ski trip to Snow Mountain. Only one problem: I'd never skied since that time of the ski-slope disaster when I was twelve. I think the ski term for it is a "yard sale" where your skis, poles, hat, gloves, and everything else not attached goes flying when you crash. I told her, "If God wanted me to ski, He would have given me fifty-seven-inch feet so I'd be good at it."

"Huh." Penny slowly sipped her cocoa. "I guess God doesn't want me to vacuum, eat broccoli, or be patient. You know, since I'm not good at any of those things." With that, she went off to work on learning to knit.

Yes, I had to admit that I got her point: You don't give up on something just because it's difficult at first. In fact, Romans 5:3–4 encourages us to keep trying. I knew if I went back out on the mountain, eventually I'd get better. Not just at skiing, but at being the type of person who doesn't give up when things get hard. A person with character will be growing more and more like Jesus. We're going to try skiing *this* weekend. Oh boy. . . .

God because of our Lord Jesus Christ. Because of him, God has brought us back to himself.

Death Through Adam, Life Through Christ

[12]Sin entered the world because one man sinned. And death came because of sin. Everyone sinned, so death came to all people. [13]Before the law was given, sin was in the world. This is certainly true. But people are not judged for sin when there is no law. [14]Death ruled from the time of Adam to the time of Moses. Death ruled even over those who did not sin as Adam did. He broke God's command. But Adam also became a pattern of the Messiah. The Messiah was the one who was going to come.

[15]God's gift can't be compared with Adam's sin. Many people died because of the sin of that one man. But it was even more sure that God's grace would also come through one man. That man is Jesus Christ. God's gift of grace was more than enough for the whole world. [16]The result of God's gift is different from the result of Adam's sin. That one sin brought God's judgment. But after many sins, God's gift made people right with him. [17]One man sinned, and death ruled over all people because of his sin. What will happen is even more sure than this. Those who receive the rich supply of God's grace will rule with Christ. They will rule in his kingdom. They have received God's gift and have been made right with him. This will happen because of what the one man, Jesus Christ, has done.

[18]So one man's sin brought guilt to all people. In the same way, one right act made people right with God. That one right act gave life to all people. [19]Many people were made sinners because one man did not obey. But one man did obey. That is why many people will be made right with God.

[20]The law was given so that sin would increase. But where sin increased, God's grace increased even more. [21]Sin ruled and brought death. But grace rules in the lives of those who are right with God. The grace of God brings eternal life. That's because of what Jesus Christ our Lord has done.

Living a New Life in Christ

6 What should we say then? Should we keep on sinning so that God's grace can increase? [2]Not at all! As far as sin is concerned, we are dead. So how can we keep on sinning? [3]All of us were baptized into Christ Jesus. Don't you know that we were baptized into his death? [4]By being baptized, we were buried with Christ into his death. Christ has been raised from the dead by the Father's glory. And like Christ we also can live a new life.

[5]By being baptized, we have been joined with him in a death like his. So we will certainly also be joined with him in a resurrection like his. [6]We know that what we used to be was nailed to the cross with him. That happened so our bodies that were ruled by sin would lose their power. So we are no longer slaves of sin. [7]That's because those who have died have been set free from sin.

[8]We died with Christ. So we believe that we will also live with him. [9]We know that

Christ was raised from the dead and will never die again. Death doesn't control him anymore. ¹⁰When he died, he died once and for all time. He did this to break the power of sin. Now that he lives, he lives in the power of God.

¹¹In the same way, consider yourselves to be dead as far as sin is concerned. Now you believe in Christ Jesus. So consider yourselves to be alive as far as God is concerned. ¹²So don't let sin rule your body, which is going to die. Don't obey its evil desires. ¹³Don't give any part of yourself to serve sin. Don't let any part of yourself be used to do evil. Instead, give yourselves to God. You have been brought from death to life. So give every part of yourself to God to do what is right. ¹⁴Sin will no longer control you like a master. That's because the law does not rule you. God's grace has set you free.

Slaves to Right Living

¹⁵What should we say then? Should we sin because we are not ruled by the law but by God's grace? Not at all! ¹⁶Don't you know that when you give yourselves to obey someone you become that person's slave? If you are slaves of sin, then you will die. But if you are slaves who obey God, then you will live a godly life. ¹⁷You used to be slaves of sin. But thank God that with your whole heart you obeyed the teachings you were given! ¹⁸You have been set free from sin. You have become slaves to right living.

¹⁹Because you are human, you find this hard to understand. So I am using an everyday example to help you understand. You used to give yourselves to be slaves to unclean living. You were becoming more and more evil. Now give yourselves to be slaves to right living. Then you will become holy. ²⁰Once you were slaves of sin. At that time right living did not control you. ²¹What benefit did you gain from doing the things you are now ashamed of? Those things lead to death! ²²You have been set free from sin.

Connie, Donna, and Oscar saw a different side of fairness mentioned in Romans 6:23 in "That's Not Fair" (A#89).

REMEMBER THIS

ROMANS 6:23

"When you sin, the pay you get is death. But God gives you the gift of eternal life. That's because of what Christ Jesus our Lord has done."

God has made you his slaves. The benefit you gain leads to holy living. And the end result is eternal life. ²³When you sin, the pay you get is death. But God gives you the gift of eternal life. That's because of what Christ Jesus our Lord has done.

An Example From Marriage

7 Brothers and sisters, I am speaking to you who know the law. Don't you know that the law has authority over someone only as long as they live? ²For example, by law a married woman remains married as long as her husband lives. But suppose her husband dies. Then the law that joins her to him no longer applies. ³But suppose that married woman sleeps with another man while her husband is still alive. Then she is called a woman who commits adultery. But suppose her husband dies. Then she is free from that law. She is not guilty of adultery if she marries another man.

⁴My brothers and sisters, when Christ died you also died as far as the law is concerned. Then it became possible for you to belong to him. He was raised from the dead. Now our lives can be useful to God. ⁵The power of sin used to control us. The law stirred up sinful desires in us. So the things we did resulted in death. ⁶But now we have died to what used to control us. We have been set free from the law. Now we serve in the new way of the Holy Spirit. We no longer serve in the old way of the written law.

The Law and Sin

⁷What should we say then? That the law is sinful? Not at all! Yet I wouldn't have known what sin was unless the law had told me. The law says, "Do not want what belongs to other people." *(Exodus 20:17; Deuteronomy 5:21)* If the law hadn't said that, I would not have known what it was like to want

what belongs to others. ⁸But the commandment gave sin an opportunity. Sin caused me to want all kinds of things that belong to others. A person can't sin by breaking a law if that law doesn't exist. ⁹Before I knew about the law, I was alive. But then the commandment came. Sin came to life, and I died. ¹⁰I found that the commandment that was supposed to bring life actually brought death. ¹¹When the commandment gave sin the opportunity, sin tricked me. It used the commandment to put me to death. ¹²So the law is holy. The commandment also is holy and right and good.

¹³Did what is good cause me to die? Not at all! Sin had to be recognized for what it really is. So it used what is good to bring about my death. Because of the commandment, sin became totally sinful.

¹⁴We know that the law is holy. But I am not. I have been sold to be a slave of sin. ¹⁵I don't understand what I do. I don't do what I want to do. Instead, I do what I hate to do. ¹⁶I do what I don't want to do. So I agree that the law is good. ¹⁷As it is, I am no longer the one who does these things. It is sin living in me that does them. ¹⁸I know there is nothing good in my desires controlled by sin. I want to do what is good, but I can't. ¹⁹I don't do the good things I want to do. I keep on doing the evil things I don't want to do. ²⁰I do what I don't want to do. But I am not really the one who is doing it. It is sin living in me that does it.

²¹Here is the law I find working in me. When I want to do good, evil is right there with me. ²²Deep inside me I find joy in God's law. ²³But I see another law working in me. It fights against the law of my mind. It makes me a prisoner of the law of sin. That law controls me. ²⁴What a terrible failure I am! Who will save me from this sin that brings death to my body? ²⁵I give thanks to God who saves me. He saves me through Jesus Christ our Lord.

So in my mind I am a slave to God's law. But sin controls my desires. So I am a slave to the law of sin.

The Holy Spirit Gives Life

8 Those who belong to Christ Jesus are no longer under God's judgment. ²Because of what Christ Jesus has done, you are free. You are now controlled by the law of the Holy Spirit who gives you life. The law of the Spirit frees you from the law of sin that brings death. ³The written law was made weak by the power of sin. But God did what the written law could not do. He made his Son to be like those who live under the power of sin. God sent him to be an offering for sin. Jesus suffered God's judgment against our sin. ⁴Jesus does for us everything the holy law requires. The power of sin should no longer control the way we live. The Holy Spirit should control the way we live.

⁵So don't live under the control of sin. If you do, you will think about what sin

WHIT'S WISDOM
Romans 8:1–4

Can you think of some powerful three-word phrases? How about: "Never give up!" "This means war!" "Go for it!" How about: "Eugene, be quiet." (Just kidding.) I can think of one that's even more powerful: "I forgive you."

That phrase has ended wars and mended relationships. Telling people that you will no longer hold their sin against them changes lives! And when we ask God for forgiveness, He says, "I forgive you" every time. As Christians, guilt shouldn't weigh us down. Because of what Christ did for us on the Cross, we are free. Romans 8:4 says, "The power of sin should no longer control the way we live."

Think about it this way: the Bible tells us to confess our sins to God and ask for forgiveness. By asking for forgiveness, we are being obedient and honoring God! Ask God to forgive your sins so that *He* can be the One who controls the way you live.

wants. Live under the control of the Holy Spirit. If you do, you will think about what the Spirit wants. ⁶The thoughts of a person ruled by sin bring death. But the mind ruled by the Spirit brings life and peace. ⁷The mind ruled by the power of sin is at war with God. It does not obey God's law. It can't. ⁸Those who are under the power of sin can't please God.

⁹But you are not ruled by the power of sin. Instead, the Holy Spirit rules over you. This is true if the Spirit of God lives in you. Anyone who does not have the Spirit of Christ does not belong to Christ. ¹⁰If Christ lives in you, you will live. Though your body will die because of sin, the Spirit gives you life. The Spirit does this because you have been made right with God. ¹¹The Spirit of the God who raised Jesus from the dead is living in you. So the God who raised Christ from the dead will also give life to your bodies. He will do this because of his Spirit who lives in you.

¹²Brothers and sisters, we have a duty. Our duty is not to live under the power of sin. ¹³If you live under the power of sin, you will die. But by the Spirit's power you can put to death the sins you commit. Then you will live.

¹⁴Those who are led by the Spirit of God are children of God. ¹⁵The Spirit you received doesn't make you slaves. Otherwise you would live in fear again. Instead, the Holy Spirit you received made you God's adopted child. By the Spirit's power we call God *Abba*. Abba means Father. ¹⁶The Spirit himself joins with our spirits. Together they tell us that we are God's children. ¹⁷As his children, we will receive all that he has for us. We will share what Christ receives. But we must share in his sufferings if we want to share in his glory.

Suffering Now and Glory in the Future

¹⁸What we are suffering now is nothing compared with our future glory. ¹⁹Everything God created looks forward to the future. That will be the time when his children appear in their full and final glory. ²⁰The created world was held back from fulfilling its purpose. But this was not the result of its own choice. It was planned that way by the one who held it back. God planned ²¹to set the created world free. He

didn't want it to rot away. Instead, God wanted it to have the same freedom and glory that his children have.

²²We know that all that God created has been groaning. It is in pain as if it were giving birth to a child. The created world continues to groan even now. ²³And that's not all. We have the Holy Spirit as the promise of future blessing. But we also groan inside ourselves. We do this as we look forward to the time when God adopts us as full members of his family. Then he will give us everything he has for us. He will raise our bodies and give glory to them. ²⁴That's the hope we had when we were saved. But hope that can be seen is no hope at all. Who hopes for what they already have? ²⁵We hope for what we don't have yet. So we are patient as we wait for it.

²⁶In the same way, the Holy Spirit helps us when we are weak. We don't know what we should pray for. But the Spirit himself prays for us. He prays through groans too deep for words. ²⁷God, who looks into our hearts, knows the mind of the Spirit. And the Spirit prays for God's people just as God wants him to pray.

²⁸We know that in all things God works for the good of those who love him. He appointed them to be saved in keeping with his purpose. ²⁹God planned that those he had chosen would become like his Son. In

Rom. 8:28 Mr. Whittaker tells me that this is one of the most-quoted verses in the whole Bible. And you can see why. It certainly makes you feel good. If you ever make a mistake, like when you accidentally drop a pile of mail in the mud, then read verses 18 to 39 and you should feel better. They helped me last time!

WHIT'S WISDOM
Romans 8:28

I remember when a boy named Davey Holcomb came into Whit's End. He was frustrated because he felt like everything he did failed. I told him about an inventor by the name of Thomas Edison. Edison was what you'd call pretty successful. He invented the light bulb and the phonograph and the movie camera and a long list of other things. Well, when he was working on the lightbulb, he used more than 1,000 materials before he found one that would stay lit inside that little glass tube. And somewhere along the line, I'm guessing one of his assistants got frustrated and said, "Look, 500 failed experiments and we haven't learned a thing!" And I'm guessing Edison said, "Sure we have. We now know 500 things that won't work."

It takes time to find something that works. Sometimes what looks like today's flop turns into tomorrow's success. That's why we have to remember Romans 8:28. "We know that in all things God works for the good of those who love him." Now it doesn't say all things are good, does it? It says God works all things together for good. Sometimes, that process takes a little time. And sometimes, it takes a lot of time.

REMEMBER THIS
ROMANS 8:28
"We know that in all things God works for the good of those who love him. He appointed them to be saved in keeping with his purpose."

that way, Christ will be the first and most honored among many brothers and sisters. [30]And those God has planned for, he has also appointed to be saved. Those he has appointed, he has made right with himself. To those he has made right with himself, he has given his glory.

We Are More Than Winners
[31]What should we say then? Since God is on our side, who can be against us? [32]God did not spare his own Son. He gave him up for us all. Then won't he also freely give us everything else? [33]Who can bring any charge against God's chosen ones? God makes us right with himself. [34]Then who can sentence us to death? No one. Christ Jesus is at the right hand of God and is also praying for us. He died. More than that, he was raised to life. [35]Who can separate us from Christ's love? Can trouble or hard times or harm or hunger? Can nakedness or danger or war? [36]It is written,

> "Because of you, we face death all day long.
> We are considered as sheep to be killed." *(Psalm 44:22)*

[37]No! In all these things we are more than winners! We owe it all to Christ, who has

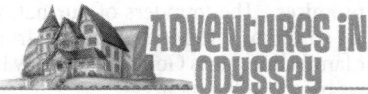

ADVENTURES IN ODYSSEY
Whit showed how God works all things together by turning a copier into a pizza oven in "Whit's Flop" (A#01).

REMEMBER THIS

ROMANS 8:39

"Nothing at all can ever separate us from God's love. That's because of what Christ Jesus our Lord has done."

loved us. ³⁸I am absolutely sure that not even death or life can separate us from God's love. Not even angels or demons, the present or the future, or any powers can separate us. ³⁹Not even the highest places or the lowest, or anything else in all creation can separate us from God's love. Nothing at all can ever separate us from God's love. That's because of what Christ Jesus our Lord has done.

Paul Mourns for Israel

9 I speak the truth in Christ. I am not lying. My mind tells me that what I say is true. It is guided by the Holy Spirit. ²My heart is full of sorrow. My sadness never ends. ³I am so concerned about my people, who are members of my own race. I am ready to be cursed, if that would help them. I am even willing to be separated from Christ. ⁴They are the people of Israel. They have been adopted as God's children. God's glory belongs to them. So do the covenants. They received the law. They were taught to worship in the temple. They were given the promises. ⁵The founders of our nation belong to them. The Messiah comes from their family line. He is God over all. May he always be praised! Amen.

God's Free Choice

⁶I do not mean that God's word has failed. Not everyone in the family line of Israel really belongs to Israel. ⁷Not everyone in Abraham's family line is really his child. Not at all! Scripture says, "Your family line will continue through Isaac." *(Genesis 21:12)* ⁸In other words, God's children are not just in the family line of Abraham. Instead, they are the children God promised to him. They are the ones considered to be Abraham's children. ⁹God promised, "I will return at the appointed time. Sarah will have a son." *(Genesis 18:10,14)* ¹⁰And that's not all. Rebekah's children were born at the same time by the same

father. He was our father Isaac. ¹¹Here is what happened. Rebekah's twins had not even been born. They hadn't done anything good or bad yet. So they show that God's purpose is based firmly on his free choice. ¹²It was not because of anything they did but because of God's choice. So Rebekah was told, "The older son will serve the younger one." *(Genesis 25:23)* ¹³It is written, "I chose Jacob instead of Esau." *(Malachi 1:2,3)*

¹⁴What should we say then? Is God unfair? Not at all! ¹⁵He said to Moses,

"I will have mercy on whom I have
    mercy.
I will show love to those I love."
                                (Exodus 33:19)

¹⁶So it doesn't depend on what people want or what they do. It depends on God's mercy. ¹⁷In Scripture, God says to Pharaoh, "I had a special reason for making you king. I decided to use you to show my power. I wanted my name to become known everywhere on earth." *(Exodus 9:16)* ¹⁸So God does what he wants to do. He shows mercy to one person and makes another stubborn.

¹⁹One of you will say to me, "Then why does God still blame us? Who can oppose what he wants to do?" ²⁰But you are a mere human being. So who are you to talk back to God? Scripture says, "Can what is made say to the one who made it, 'Why did you make me like this?'" *(Isaiah 29:16; 45:9)* ²¹Isn't the potter free to make different kinds of pots out of the same lump of clay? Some are for special purposes. Others are for ordinary use.

²²What if God chose to show his great anger? What if he chose to make his power known? But he put up with the people he was angry with. They were made to be destroyed. ²³What if he put up with them to show the riches of his glory to other people? Those other people are the ones he shows his mercy to. He made them to receive his glory. ²⁴We are those people. He has chosen us. We do not come only from the Jewish race. Many of us are not Jews. ²⁵God says in Hosea,

"I will call those who are not my people
    'my people.'
I will call the one who is not my
    loved one 'my loved one.'"
                                (Hosea 2:23)

[26]He also says,

"Once it was said to them,
'You are not my people.'
In that very place they will be called
'children of the living God.'"
(Hosea 1:10)

[27]Isaiah cries out concerning Israel. He says,

"The number of people from Israel
may be like the sand by the sea.
But only a few of them will be saved.
[28] The Lord will carry out his sentence.
He will be quick to carry it out on earth, once and for all."
(Isaiah 10:22,23)

[29]Earlier Isaiah had said,

"The Lord who rules over all
left us children and grandchildren.
If he hadn't, we would have become like Sodom.
We would have been like Gomorrah." *(Isaiah 1:9)*

Israel Does Not Believe

[30]What should we say then? Gentiles did not look for a way to be right with God. But they found it by having faith. [31]The people of Israel tried to obey the law to make themselves right with God. But they didn't reach their goal of being right with God. [32]Why not? Because they tried to do it without faith. They tried to be right with God by what they did. They tripped over the stone that causes people to trip and fall. [33]It is written,

"Look! In Zion I am laying a stone that
causes people to trip.
It is a rock that makes them fall.
The one who believes in him will
never be put to shame."
(Isaiah 8:14; 28:16)

10 Brothers and sisters, with all my heart I long for the people of Israel to be saved. I pray to God for them. [2]I can tell you for certain that they really want to serve God. But how they are trying to do it is not based on knowledge. [3]They didn't know that God's power makes people right with himself. They tried to get right with God in their own way. They didn't do it in God's way. [4]Christ has fulfilled everything the law was meant to do. So now everyone who believes can be right with God.

[5]Moses writes about how the law could help a person do what God requires. He writes, "The person who does these things will live by them." *(Leviticus 18:5)* [6]But the way to do what God requires must begin by having faith in him. Scripture says, "Do not say in your heart, 'Who will go up into heaven?'" *(Deuteronomy 30:12)* That means to go up into heaven and bring Christ down. [7]"And do not say, 'Who will go down into the grave?'" *(Deuteronomy 30:13)* That means to bring Christ up from the dead. [8]But what does it say? "The message is near you. It's in your mouth and in your heart." *(Deuteronomy 30:14)* This means the message about faith that we are preaching. [9]Say with your mouth, "Jesus is Lord." Believe in your heart that God raised him from the dead. Then you will be saved. [10]With your heart you believe and are made right with God. With your mouth you say what you believe. And so you are saved. [11]Scripture says, "The one who believes in him will never be put to shame." *(Isaiah 28:16)* [12]There is no difference between those who are Jews and those who are not. The same Lord is Lord of all. He richly blesses everyone who calls on him. [13]Scripture says, "Everyone who calls on the name of the Lord will be saved." *(Joel 2:32)*

[14]How can they call on him unless they believe in him? How can they believe in him unless they hear about him? How can they hear about him unless someone preaches to them? [15]And how can anyone preach without being sent? It is written, "How beautiful are the feet of those who bring good news!" *(Isaiah 52:7)*

[16]But not all the people of Israel accepted the good news. Isaiah says, "Lord, who has believed our message?" *(Isaiah 53:1)* [17]So faith comes from hearing the message. And the

message that is heard is the message about Christ. [18]But I ask, "Didn't the people of Israel hear?" Of course they did. It is written,

> "Their voice has gone out into the
>   whole earth.
> Their words have gone out from one
>   end of the world to the other."
>   *(Psalm 19:4)*

[19]Again I ask, "Didn't Israel understand?" First, Moses says,

> "I will use people who are not a nation
>   to make you jealous.
> I will use a nation that has no
>   understanding to make you
>   angry."   *(Deuteronomy 32:21)*

[20]Then Isaiah boldly speaks about what God says. God said,

> "I was found by those who were not
>   trying to find me.
> I made myself known to those who
>   were not asking for me."
>   *(Isaiah 65:1)*

[21]But Isaiah also speaks about what God says concerning Israel. God said,

> "All day long I have held out my hands.
> I have held them out to a stubborn
>   people who do not obey me."
>   *(Isaiah 65:2)*

The Israelites Who Are Faithful

11 So here is what I ask. Did God turn his back on his people? Not at all! I myself belong to Israel. I am one of Abraham's children. I am from the tribe of Benjamin. [2]God didn't turn his back on his people. After all, he chose them. Don't you know what Scripture says about Elijah? He complained to God about Israel. [3]He said, "Lord, they have killed your prophets. They have torn down your altars. I'm the only one left. And they are trying to kill me." *(1 Kings 19:10,14)* [4]How did God answer him? God said, "I have kept 7,000 people for myself. They have not bowed down to Baal." *(1 Kings 19:18)* [5]Some are also faithful today. They have been chosen by God's grace. [6]And if they are chosen by grace, then they can't work for it. If that were true, grace wouldn't be grace anymore.

[7]What should we say then? The people of Israel did not receive what they wanted

so badly. Those Israelites who were chosen did receive it. But the rest of the people were made stubborn. [8]It is written,

> "God made it hard for them to
>   understand.
> He gave them eyes that could not
>   see.
> He gave them ears that could not
>   hear.
> And they are still like that today."
>   *(Deuteronomy 29:4; Isaiah 29:10)*

[9]David says,

> "Let their feast be a trap and a snare.
> Let them trip and fall. Let them get
>   what's coming to them.
> [10] Let their eyes grow dark so they can't
>   see.
> Let their backs be bent forever."
>   *(Psalm 69:22,23)*

Two Kinds of Olive Branches

[11]Again, here is what I ask. The Israelites didn't trip and fall once and for all time, did they? Not at all! Because Israel sinned, the Gentiles can be saved. That will make Israel jealous of them. [12]Israel's sin brought riches to the world. Their loss brings riches to the Gentiles. So then what greater riches will come when all Israel turns to God!

[13]I am talking to you who are not Jews. I am the apostle to the Gentiles. So I take pride in the work I do for God and others. [14]I hope somehow to stir up my own people to want what you have. Perhaps I can save some of them. [15]When they were not accepted, it became possible for the whole world to be brought back to God. So what will happen when they are accepted? It will be like life from the dead. [16]The first handful of dough that is offered is holy. This makes all of the dough holy. If the root is holy, so are the branches.

[17]Some of the natural branches have been broken off. You are a wild olive branch. But you have been joined to the tree with the other branches. Now you enjoy the life-giving sap of the olive tree root. [18]So don't think you are better than the other branches. Remember, you don't give life to the root. The root gives life to you. [19]You will say, "Some branches were broken off so that I could be joined to the tree." [20]That's true. But they were broken off

because they didn't believe. You stand only because you do believe. So don't be proud, but tremble. ²¹God didn't spare the natural branches. He won't spare you either.

²²Think about how kind God is! Also think about how firm he is! He was hard on those who stopped following him. But he is kind to you. So you must continue to live in his kindness. If you don't, you also will be cut off. ²³If the people of Israel do not continue in their unbelief, they will again be joined to the tree. God is able to join them to the tree again. ²⁴After all, weren't you cut from a wild olive tree? Weren't you joined to an olive tree that was taken care of? And wasn't that the opposite of how things should be done? How much more easily will the natural branches be joined to their own olive tree!

All Israel Will Be Saved

²⁵Brothers and sisters, here is a mystery I want you to understand. It will keep you from being proud. Part of Israel has refused to obey God. That will continue until the full number of Gentiles has entered God's kingdom. ²⁶In this way all Israel will be saved. It is written,

"The God who saves will come from Mount Zion.

He will remove sin from Jacob's family.
²⁷ Here is my covenant with them.
I will take away their sins."

(Isaiah 59:20, 21; 27:9; Jeremiah 31:33, 34)

²⁸As far as the good news is concerned, the people of Israel are enemies. This is for your good. But as far as God's choice is concerned, the people of Israel are loved. This is because of God's promises to the founders of our nation. ²⁹God does not take back his gifts. He does not change his mind about those he has chosen. ³⁰At one time you did not obey God. But now you have received mercy because Israel did not obey. ³¹In the same way, Israel has not been obeying God. But now they receive mercy because of God's mercy to you. ³²God has found everyone guilty of not obeying him. So now he can have mercy on everyone.

Praise to God

³³ How very rich are God's wisdom and
    knowledge!
  How he judges is more than we can
    understand!
  The way he deals with people is
    more than we can know!

WHIT'S WISDOM

Romans 12:2

Shortly after Connie moved to Odyssey, she told me that everybody is good down deep inside. Naturally, she was surprised and offended when I told her that was one of the most ridiculous things I'd ever heard. You see, people's nature isn't good deep down. It's bad. I pointed out that you only have to look at the kids running around Whit's End. We don't have to tell any of them how to be bad—they already know that! But we do have to teach them how to be good.

Connie tried to prove me wrong by promising to be patient, but she couldn't handle that forever. The Bible says that all have sinned and fallen short of the glory of God. That's why I just kind of shake my head and laugh when someone tells me that they've made a promise to be a better person. The cause of our problems is our sinful nature. And we can't fix it on our own, no matter how good our intentions are.

We need Jesus to be our righteousness for us . . . to make it right in our souls. That's where the changing has to start. That's why the Bible says, "Don't live the way this world lives. Let your way of thinking be completely changed." Jesus has to change us on the inside before results start showing on the outside.

34 "Who can ever know what the Lord is
      thinking?
   Or who can ever give him advice?"

(Isaiah 40:13)

35 "Has anyone ever given anything to
      God,
   so that God has to pay them back?"

(Job 41:11)

36 All things come from him.
   All things are directed by him.
   All things are for his praise.
      May God be given the glory forever!
      Amen.

Living as a Holy Sacrifice to God

12 Brothers and sisters, God has shown
you his mercy. So I am asking you to
offer up your bodies to him while you are
still alive. Your bodies are a holy sacrifice
that is pleasing to God. When you offer
your bodies to God, you are worshiping
him in the right way. ²Don't live the way
this world lives. Let your way of thinking be completely changed. Then you will
be able to test what God wants for you.
And you will agree that what he wants is
right. His plan is good and pleasing and
perfect.

Serving One Another in the Body of Christ

³God's grace has been given to me. So
here is what I say to every one of you.
Don't think of yourself more highly than
you should. Be reasonable when you think
about yourself. Keep in mind the faith God
has given to each of you. ⁴Each of us has
one body with many parts. And the parts
do not all have the same purpose. ⁵So also
we are many persons. But in Christ we are
one body. And each part of the body belongs to all the other parts. ⁶We all have
gifts. They differ according to the grace
God has given to each of us. Do you have
the gift of prophecy? Then use it according to the faith you have. ⁷If your gift is
serving, then serve. If it is teaching, then
teach. ⁸Is it encouraging others? Then encourage them. Is it giving to others? Then
give freely. Is it being a leader? Then work
hard at it. Is it showing mercy? Then do it
cheerfully.

WHAT ABOUT YOU?

It's your first day at summer camp. Scoutmaster Steve points you to your cabin. You
walk through the door and chuck your lug-
gage on a lower bunk. A freckle-faced kid
lounging on the top bunk pokes his head
over the edge. "The name's Freddy," he tells
you. Then he hops off the top bunk, shoves
something into your hand, and leaves.

You look down and notice that you're
holding a can of green spray paint. Weird.
Just then, the scoutmaster walks into the
cabin and gasps. On the ceiling above your
bunk, green graffiti reads, "Scoutmaster
Steve has pickles for brains!" Uh oh.

Romans 12:18 says: "If possible, live in
peace with everyone. Do that as much as
you can." Living in harmony with others
should be our goal. But sometimes, despite
our best efforts, it's not possible to live at
peace with everyone—especially the Fred-
dys of the world.

Some people intentionally look for fights
or hold grudges. The Bible teaches that we
should forgive people for their offenses. But
that doesn't mean we're going to be best
friends with everyone we meet.

Think of someone you have a hard time
living at peace with. Write down as many
good qualities as you can about that person. If you have trouble, ask God to help you
identify those virtues. Then, as far as it depends on you, choose to live at peace with
that person.

Love in Action

[9] Love must be honest and true. Hate what is evil. Hold on to what is good. [10] Love one another deeply. Honor others more than yourselves. [11] Stay excited about your faith as you serve the Lord. [12] When you hope, be joyful. When you suffer, be patient. When you pray, be faithful. [13] Share with the Lord's people who are in need. Welcome others into your homes.

[14] Bless those who hurt you. Bless them, and do not curse them. [15] Be joyful with those who are joyful. Be sad with those who are sad. [16] Agree with one another. Don't be proud. Be willing to be a friend of people who aren't considered important. Don't think that you are better than others.

[17] Don't pay back evil with evil. Be careful to do what everyone thinks is right. [18] If possible, live in peace with everyone. Do that as much as you can. [19] My dear friends, don't try to get even. Leave room for God to show his anger. It is written, "I am the God who judges people. I will pay them back," *(Deuteronomy 32:35)* says the Lord. [20] Do just the opposite. Scripture says,

> "If your enemies are hungry, give them food to eat.
> If they are thirsty, give them something to drink.
> By doing those things, you will pile up burning coals on their heads."
> *(Proverbs 25:21,22)*

[21] Don't let evil overcome you. Overcome evil by doing good.

Obey Those in Authority

13 All of you must obey those who rule over you. There are no authorities except the ones God has chosen. Those who now rule have been chosen by God. [2] So whoever opposes the authorities opposes leaders whom God has appointed. Those who do that will be judged. [3] If you do what is right, you won't need to be afraid of your rulers. But watch out if you do what is wrong! You don't want to be afraid of those in authority, do you? Then do what is right, and you will be praised. [4] The one in authority serves God for your good. But if you do wrong, watch out! Rulers don't carry a sword for no reason at all. They serve God. And God is carrying out his anger

Both Lawrence and Maureen Hodges showed what it means to obey the authorities in "Subject Yourself" (A#24).

through them. The ruler punishes anyone who does wrong. [5] You must obey the authorities. Then you will not be punished. You must also obey them because you know it is right.

[6] That's also why you pay taxes. The authorities serve God. Ruling takes up all their time. [7] Give to everyone what you owe them. Do you owe taxes? Then pay them. Do you owe anything else to the government? Then pay it. Do you owe respect? Then give it. Do you owe honor? Then show it.

Love Fulfills the Law

[8] Pay everything you owe. But you can never pay back all the love you owe one another. Whoever loves other people has done everything the law requires. [9] Here are some commandments to think about. "Do not commit adultery." "Do not commit murder." "Do not steal." "Do not want what belongs to others." *(Exodus 20:13–15,17; Deuteronomy 5:17–19,21)* These and all other commands are included in one command. Here's what it is. "Love your neighbor as you love yourself." *(Leviticus 19:18)* [10] Love does not harm its neighbor. So love does everything the law requires.

The Day Is Near

[11] When you do these things, keep in mind the times we are living in. The hour has already come for you to wake up from your sleep. The full effects of our salvation are closer now than when we first believed in Christ. [12] The dark night of evil is nearly over. The day of Christ's return is almost here. So let us get rid of the works of darkness that harm us. Let us do the works of light that protect us. [13] Let us act as we should, like people living in the daytime. Have nothing to do with wild parties, and don't get drunk. Don't take part in sexual sins or evil conduct. Don't fight with each other or be jealous of anyone. [14] Instead, put on the Lord Jesus Christ as if he were your

clothing. Don't think about how to satisfy sinful desires.

The Weak and the Strong

14 Accept the person whose faith is weak. Don't argue with them where you have differences of opinion. [2]One person's faith allows them to eat anything. But another person eats only vegetables because their faith is weak. [3]The person who eats everything must not look down on the one who does not. And the one who doesn't eat everything must not judge the person who does. That's because God has accepted them. [4]Who are you to judge someone else's servant? Whether they are faithful or not is their own master's concern. And they will be faithful, because the Lord has the power to make them faithful.

[5]One person considers one day to be more holy than another. Another person thinks all days are the same. Each of them should be absolutely sure in their own mind. [6]Whoever thinks that one day is special does so to honor the Lord. Whoever eats meat does so to honor the Lord. They give thanks to God. And whoever doesn't eat meat does so to honor the Lord. They also give thanks to God. [7]We don't live for ourselves only. And we don't die for ourselves only. [8]If we live, we live to honor the Lord. If we die, we die to honor the Lord. So whether we live or die, we belong to the Lord. [9]Christ died and came back to life. He did this to become the Lord of both the dead and the living.

[10]Now then, who are you to judge your brother or sister? Why do you act like you're better than they are? We will all stand in God's courtroom to be judged. [11]It is written,

> "'You can be sure that I live,' says the
>   Lord.
> 'And you can be just as sure that
>   everyone will kneel down in
>   front of me.
> Every tongue will have to tell the
>   truth about God.'"   *(Isaiah 45:23)*

[12]So we will all have to explain to God the things we have done.

[13]Let us stop judging one another. Instead, decide not to put anything in the way of a brother or sister. Don't put anything in their way that would make them trip and fall. [14]I am absolutely sure that nothing is "unclean" in itself. The Lord Jesus has convinced me of this. But someone may consider a thing to be "unclean." If they do, it is "unclean" for them. [15]Your brother or sister may be upset by what you eat. If they are, you are no longer acting as though you love them. So don't destroy them by what you eat. Remember that Christ died for them. [16]So suppose you know something is good. Then don't let it be spoken of as if it were evil. [17]God's kingdom is not about eating or drinking. It is about doing what is right and having peace and joy. All this comes through the Holy Spirit. [18]Those who serve Christ in this way are pleasing to God. They are pleasing to people too.

[19]So let us do all we can to live in peace. And let us work hard to build up one another. [20]Don't destroy the work of God because of food. All food is "clean." But it's wrong to eat anything that might cause problems for someone else's faith. [21]Don't eat meat if it causes your brother or sister to sin. Don't drink wine or do anything else that will make them sin.

[22]Whatever you believe about these things, keep between yourself and God. Blessed is the person who doesn't feel guilty for what they do. [23]But whoever has doubts about what they eat is guilty if they eat. That's because their eating is not based on faith. Everything that is not based on faith is sin.

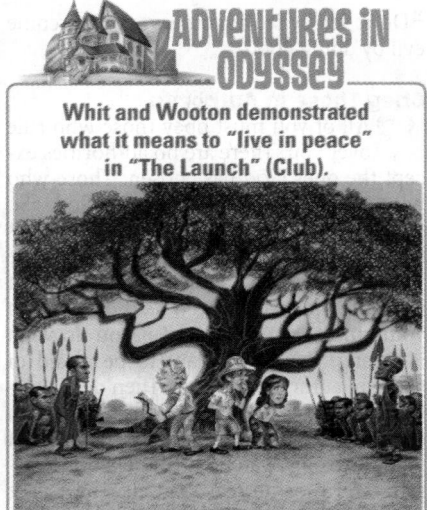

ADVENTURES iN ODYSSEY

Whit and Wooton demonstrated what it means to "live in peace" in "The Launch" (Club).

15 We who have strong faith should help the weak with their problems. We should not please only ourselves. ²Each of us should please our neighbors. Let us do what is good for them in order to build them up. ³Even Christ did not please himself. It is written, "The bad things people have said about you have been aimed at me also." *(Psalm 69:9)* ⁴Everything written in the past was written to teach us. The Scriptures give us strength to go on. They encourage us and give us hope.

⁵Our God is a God who strengthens and encourages you. May he give you the same attitude toward one another that Christ Jesus had. ⁶Then you can give glory to God with one mind and voice. He is the God and Father of our Lord Jesus Christ.

⁷Christ has accepted you. So accept one another in order to bring praise to God. ⁸I tell you that Christ has become a servant of the Jews. He teaches us that God is true. He shows us that God will keep the promises he made to the founders of our nation. ⁹Jesus became a servant of the Jews. He did this so that the Gentiles might give glory to God for his mercy. It is written,

"I will praise you among the Gentiles.
    I will sing the praises of your name."
                        (2 Samuel 22:50; Psalm 18:49)

¹⁰Again it says,

"You Gentiles, be full of joy.
    Be joyful together with God's
        people." *(Deuteronomy 32:43)*

¹¹And again it says,

"All you Gentiles, praise the Lord.
    Let all the nations sing praises to
        him." *(Psalm 117:1)*

¹²And Isaiah says,

"The Root of Jesse will grow up quickly.
He will rule over the nations.
The Gentiles will put their hope in
    him." *(Isaiah 11:10)*

Lucy tried to "please others"
and "build them up" in "The
Truth about Zachary" (A#23).

REMEMBER THIS

ROMANS 15:13

"May the God who gives hope fill you with great joy. May you have perfect peace as you trust in him. May the power of the Holy Spirit fill you with hope."

¹³May the God who gives hope fill you with great joy. May you have perfect peace as you trust in him. May the power of the Holy Spirit fill you with hope.

Paul Serves the Gentiles

¹⁴My brothers and sisters, I am sure that you are full of goodness. You are filled with knowledge and able to teach one another. ¹⁵But I have written to you very boldly about some things. I wanted to remind you of them again. The grace of God has allowed me ¹⁶to serve Christ Jesus among the Gentiles. I have the duty of a priest to preach God's good news. Then the Gentiles will become an offering that pleases God. The Holy Spirit will make the offering holy.

¹⁷Because I belong to Christ Jesus, I can take pride in my work for God. ¹⁸I will speak about what Christ has done through me. I won't try to speak about anything else. He has been leading the Gentiles to obey God. He has been doing this by what I have said and done. ¹⁹He has given me power to do signs and wonders. I can do these things by the power of the Spirit of God. From Jerusalem all the way around to Illyricum I have finished preaching. In those places, I preached the good news about Christ. ²⁰I have always wanted to preach the good news where Christ was not known. I don't want to build on what someone else has started. ²¹It is written,

"Those who were not told about him
    will understand.
Those who have not heard will know
    what it all means."

                            (Isaiah 52:15)

²²That's why I have often been kept from coming to you.

Paul Plans to Visit Rome

²³Now there is no more place for me to work in those areas. For many years I have wanted to visit you. ²⁴So I plan to see you when I go to Spain. I hope to visit you while I am passing through. And I hope you will help me on my journey there. But first I want to enjoy being with you for a while. ²⁵Now I am on my way to Jerusalem to serve the Lord's people there. ²⁶The believers in Macedonia and Achaia were pleased to take an offering. It was for those who were poor among the Lord's people in Jerusalem. ²⁷They were happy to do it. And of course they owe it to them. The Gentiles have shared in the Jews' spiritual blessings. So the Gentiles should share their earthly blessings with the Jews. ²⁸I want to finish my task. I want to make sure that the poor in Jerusalem have received this offering. Then I will go to Spain. On my way I will visit you. ²⁹I know that when I come to you, I will come with the full blessing of Christ.

³⁰Brothers and sisters, I ask you to join me in my struggle. Join me by praying to God for me. I ask this through the authority of our Lord Jesus Christ. Pray for me with the love the Holy Spirit provides. ³¹Pray that I will be kept safe from those in Judea who do not believe. I am taking the offering to Jerusalem. Pray that it will be welcomed by the Lord's people there. ³²Then I will come to you with joy just as God has planned. We will be renewed by being together. ³³May the God who gives peace be with you all. Amen.

Personal Greetings

16 I would like you to welcome our sister Phoebe. She is a deacon of the church in Cenchreae. ²I ask you to receive her as one who belongs to the Lord. Receive her in the way God's people should. Give her any help she may need from you. She has been a great help to many people, including me.

³Greet Priscilla and Aquila. They work together with me in serving Christ Jesus. ⁴They have put their lives in danger for me. I am thankful for them. So are all the Gentile churches.

⁵Greet also the church that meets in the house of Priscilla and Aquila.

Greet my dear friend Epenetus. He was the first person in Asia Minor to become a believer in Christ.

⁶Greet Mary. She worked very hard for you.

⁷Greet Andronicus and Junia, my fellow Jews. They have been in prison with me. They are leaders among the apostles. They became believers in Christ before I did.

⁸Greet Ampliatus, my dear friend in the Lord.

⁹Greet Urbanus. He works together with me in serving Christ. And greet my dear friend Stachys.

¹⁰Greet Apelles. He remained faithful to Christ even when he was tested.

Greet those who live in the house of Aristobulus.

¹¹Greet Herodion, my fellow Jew.

Greet the believers who live in the house of Narcissus.

¹²Greet Tryphena and Tryphosa. Those women work hard for the Lord.

Greet my dear friend Persis. She is another woman who has worked very hard for the Lord.

¹³Greet Rufus. He is a chosen believer in the Lord. And greet his mother. She has been like a mother to me too.

¹⁴Greet Asyncritus, Phlegon and Hermes. Greet Patrobas, Hermas and the other brothers and sisters with them.

Rom. 16:11 In Greek mythology, Narcissus was a young man who saw his reflection in a lake and thought he was beautiful. He couldn't stop looking at himself and he drowned. Paul must be writing about a different person named Narcissus here. The word *narcissist*, means "a person who is self-focused."

¹⁵Greet Philologus, Julia, Nereus and his sister. Greet Olympas and all of the Lord's people who are with them. ¹⁶Greet one another with a holy kiss.

All the churches of Christ send their greetings.

¹⁷I am warning you, brothers and sisters, to watch out for those who try to keep you from staying together. They want to trip you up. They teach you things opposite to what you have learned. Stay away from them. ¹⁸People like that are not serving Christ our Lord. They are serving only themselves. With smooth talk and with words they don't mean they fool people who don't know any better. ¹⁹Everyone has heard that you obey God. So you have filled me with joy. I want you to be wise about what is good. And I want you to have nothing to do with what is evil.

²⁰The God who gives peace will soon crush Satan under your feet.

May the grace of our Lord Jesus be with you.

²¹Timothy works together with me. He sends his greetings to you. So do Lucius, Jason and Sosipater, my fellow Jews.

²²I, Tertius, wrote down this letter. I greet you as a believer in the Lord.

²³⁻²⁴Gaius sends you his greetings. He has welcomed me and the whole church here into his house.

Erastus is the director of public works here in the city. He sends you his greetings. Our brother Quartus also greets you.

²⁵May God receive glory. He is able to strengthen your faith. He does this in keeping with the good news and the message I preach. It is the message about Jesus Christ. This message is in keeping with the mystery hidden for a very long time. ²⁶The mystery has now been made known through the writings of the prophets. The eternal God commanded that it be made known. God wanted all the Gentiles to obey him by trusting in him. ²⁷May the only wise God receive glory forever through Jesus Christ. Amen.

1 Corinthians

We now journey from Rome to Corinth, a distance of nearly 1,000 miles! And we begin with a familiar question: Does your church have any problems? Almost every church does and the church in Corinth was no exception. They would bicker about who was the best preacher (1:12). They weren't growing spiritually, forcing Paul to simplify things for them rather than challenging them (3:1–4). They were proud of their improper relationships, apparently believing (incorrectly) that God's grace allowed them to do anything they wanted to do (5:1–3).

What's more they couldn't work out their many disagreements and were suing one another in secular courts (6:1–8). They became intoxicated and greedy when observing the Lord's Supper, leaving many poor visitors to the church hungry (11:17–22). And they argued over whose spiritual gifts were "best" and tried to copy one another instead of using the gifts God had given them (12:12–31).

In attempting to help the Corinthians resolve their problems and arguments, Paul also provided guidelines that the church continues to follow today. These include matters such as marriage, lawsuits, taking communion, order in worship services, use of spiritual gifts, and more.

And while seeking to convince the Corinthians to work together, Paul wrote one of the most quoted passages in Scripture—1 Corinthians 13, best known as "the Love Chapter."

WHAT'S IT MEAN, EUGENE?

Body of Christ—The apostle Paul uses this phrase to name and describe the church. In 1 Corinthians 12:12–27 he says that the community of Christians is akin to a human body: though it is *one* body, it has *many* different parts. Christ, says Paul, is the Body's Head. Wooton, for example, may be a hand. Katrina would most definitely be a heart. I, of course, would be a brain. Under the lordship of Jesus Christ, we are intended to live and work together as one.

1 I, Paul, am writing this letter. I have been chosen to be an apostle of Christ Jesus just as God planned. Our brother Sosthenes joins me in writing.

²We are sending this letter to you, the members of God's church in Corinth. You have been made holy because you belong to Christ Jesus. God has chosen you to be his holy people. He has done the same for all people everywhere who pray to our Lord Jesus Christ. Jesus is their Lord and ours.

³May God our Father and the Lord Jesus Christ give you grace and peace.

Paul Gives Thanks

⁴I always thank my God for you. I thank him because of the grace he has given to you who belong to Christ Jesus. ⁵You have been blessed in every way because of him. You have been blessed in all your speech and knowledge. ⁶God has shown that what we have spoken to you about Christ is true. ⁷There is no gift of the Holy Spirit that you don't have. You are full of hope as you wait for our Lord Jesus Christ to come again. ⁸God will also keep you strong in faith to the very end. Then you will be without blame on the day our Lord Jesus Christ returns. ⁹God is faithful. He has chosen you to share life with his Son, Jesus Christ our Lord.

Taking Sides in the Church

¹⁰Brothers and sisters, I make my appeal to you. I do this in the name of our Lord Jesus Christ. I ask that all of you agree with one another in what you say. I ask that you don't take sides. I ask that you are in complete agreement in all that you think. ¹¹My brothers and sisters, I have been told you are arguing with one another. Some people from Chloe's house have told me this. ¹²Here is what I mean. One of you says, "I follow Paul." Another says, "I follow Apollos." Another says, "I follow Peter." And still another says, "I follow Christ."

¹³Does Christ take sides? Did Paul die on the cross for you? Were you baptized in the name of Paul? ¹⁴I thank God that I didn't baptize any of you except Crispus and Gaius. ¹⁵No one can say that you were baptized in my name. ¹⁶It's true that I also baptized those who live in the house of Stephanas. Besides that, I don't remember

if I baptized anyone else. ¹⁷Christ did not send me to baptize. He sent me to preach the good news. He commanded me not to preach with wisdom and fancy words. That would take all the power away from the cross of Christ.

Christ Is God's Power and Wisdom

¹⁸The message of the cross seems foolish to those who are lost and dying. But it is God's power to us who are being saved. ¹⁹It is written,

"I will destroy the wisdom of those who are wise.
I will do away with the cleverness of those who think they are so smart." *(Isaiah 29:14)*

²⁰Where is the wise person? Where is the teacher of the law? Where are the great thinkers of our time? Hasn't God made the wisdom of the world foolish? ²¹God wisely planned that the world would not know him through its own wisdom. It pleased God to use the foolish things we preach to save those who believe. ²²Jews require signs. Greeks look for wisdom. ²³But we preach about Christ and his death on the cross. That is very hard for Jews to accept. And everyone else thinks it's foolish. ²⁴But there are those God has chosen, both Jews and Greeks. To them Christ is God's power and God's wisdom. ²⁵The foolish things of God are wiser than human wisdom. The weakness of God is stronger than human strength.

²⁶Brothers and sisters, think of what you were when God chose you. Not many of you were considered wise by human standards. Not many of you were powerful. Not many of you belonged to important families. ²⁷But God chose the foolish things of the world to shame the wise. God chose the weak things of the world to shame the strong. ²⁸God chose the things of this world that are common and looked down on. God chose things considered unimportant to do away with things considered important. ²⁹So no one can boast to God. ³⁰Because of what God has done, you belong to Christ Jesus. He has become God's wisdom for us. He makes us right with God. He makes us holy and sets us free. ³¹It is written, "The one who boasts should boast about what the Lord has done." *(Jeremiah 9:24)*

2 And this was the way it was with me, brothers and sisters. When I came to you, I didn't come with fancy words or human wisdom. I preached to you the truth about God's love. ²My goal while I was with you was to talk about only one thing. And that was Jesus Christ and his death on the cross. ³When I came to you, I was weak and very afraid and trembling all over. ⁴I didn't preach my message with clever and compelling words. Instead, my preaching showed the Holy Spirit's power. ⁵This was so that your faith would be based on God's power. Your faith would not be based on human wisdom.

God's Wisdom Through the Holy Spirit

⁶The words we speak to those who have grown in the faith are wise. Our words are different from the wisdom of this world. Our words are different from those of the rulers of this world. These rulers are becoming less and less powerful. ⁷No, we announce God's wisdom. His wisdom is a mystery that has been hidden. But before time began, God planned that his wisdom would bring us heavenly glory. ⁸None of the rulers of this world understood God's wisdom. If they had, they would not have nailed the Lord of glory to the cross. ⁹It is written that

"no eye has seen,
no ear has heard,
and no human mind has known."
(Isaiah 64:4)
God has prepared these things for
those who love him.

¹⁰God has shown these things to us through his Spirit.

The Spirit understands all things. He understands even the deep things of God. ¹¹Who can know the thoughts of another person? Only a person's own spirit can know them. In the same way, only the Spirit of God knows God's thoughts. ¹²What we have received is not the spirit of the world. We have received the Spirit who is from God. The Spirit helps us understand what God has freely given us. ¹³That is what we speak about. We don't use words taught to us by people. We use words taught to us by the Holy Spirit. We use the words taught by the Spirit to explain spiritual truths. ¹⁴The person without the Spirit doesn't accept the things that come from the Spirit of God. These things are foolish to them. They can't understand them. In fact, such things can't be understood without the Spirit's help. ¹⁵The person who has the Spirit can judge all things. But no human being can judge those who have the Spirit. It is written,

¹⁶ "Who can ever know what is in the
Lord's mind?
Can anyone ever teach him?"
(Isaiah 40:13)

But we have the mind of Christ.

The Church and Its Leaders

3 Brothers and sisters, I couldn't speak to you as people who live by the Holy Spirit. I had to speak to you as people who were still following the ways of the world. You aren't growing as Christ wants you to. You are still like babies. ²The words I spoke to you were like milk, not like solid food. You weren't ready for solid food yet. And you still aren't ready for it. ³You are still following the ways of the world. Some of you are jealous. Some of you argue. So aren't you following the ways of the world? Aren't you acting like ordinary human beings? ⁴One of you says, "I follow Paul." Another says, "I follow Apollos." Aren't you acting like ordinary human beings?

⁵After all, what is Apollos? And what is Paul? We are only people who serve. We helped you to believe. The Lord has given each of us our own work to do. ⁶I planted the seed. Apollos watered it. But God has been making it grow. ⁷So the one who plants is not important. The one who waters is not important. It is God who makes things grow. He is the important one. ⁸The one who plants and the one who waters have the same purpose. The Lord will give

each of them a reward for their work. [9]We work together to serve God. You are like God's field. You are like his building.

[10]God has given me the grace to lay a foundation as a wise builder. Now someone else is building on it. But each one should build carefully. [11]No one can lay any other foundation than what has already been laid. That foundation is Jesus Christ. [12]A person may build on it using gold, silver, jewels, wood, hay or straw. [13]But each person's work will be shown for what it is. On judgment day it will be brought to light. It will be put through fire. The fire will test how good each person's work is. [14]If the building doesn't burn up, God will give the builder a reward for the work. [15]If the building burns up, the builder will lose everything. The builder will be saved, but only like one escaping through the flames.

[16]Don't you know that you yourselves are God's temple? Don't you know that God's Spirit lives among you? [17]If anyone destroys God's temple, God will destroy that person. God's temple is holy. And you all together are that temple.

[18]Don't fool yourselves. Suppose some of you think you are wise by the standards of the world. Then you should become "fools" so that you can become wise. [19]The wisdom of this world is foolish in God's eyes. It is written, "God catches wise people in their own evil plans." *(Job 5:13)* [20]It is also written, "The Lord knows that the thoughts of wise people don't amount to anything." *(Psalm 94:11)* [21]So no more bragging about human leaders! All things are yours. [22]That means Paul or Apollos or Peter or the world or life or death or the present or the future. All are yours. [23]You are joined to Christ and belong to him. And Christ is joined to God.

True Apostles of Christ

4 So here is how you should think of us. We serve Christ. We are trusted with the mysteries God has shown us. [2]Those who have been given a trust must prove that they are faithful. [3]I care very little if I am judged by you or by any human court. I don't even judge myself. [4]I don't feel I have done anything wrong. But that doesn't mean I'm not guilty. The Lord judges me. [5]So don't judge anything before the appointed time. Wait until the Lord returns. He will bring to light what is hidden in the dark. He will show

the real reasons why people do what they do. At that time each person will receive their praise from God.

[6]Brothers and sisters, I have used myself and Apollos as examples to help you. You can learn from us the meaning of the saying, "Don't go beyond what is written." Then you won't be proud that you follow one of us instead of the other. [7]Who makes you different from anyone else? What do you have that you did not receive? And if you did receive it, why do you brag as though you did not?

[8]You already have everything you want, don't you? Have you already become rich? Have you already begun to rule? And did you do that without us? I wish that you really had begun to rule. Then we could also rule with you! [9]It seems to me that God has put us apostles on display at the end of a parade. We are like people sentenced to die in front of a crowd. We have been made a show for the whole creation to see. Angels and people are staring at us. [10]We are fools for Christ. But you are so wise in Christ! We are weak. But you are so strong! You are honored. But we are looked down on! [11]Up to this very hour we are hungry and thirsty. We are dressed in rags. We are being treated badly. We have no homes. [12]We work hard with our own hands. When others

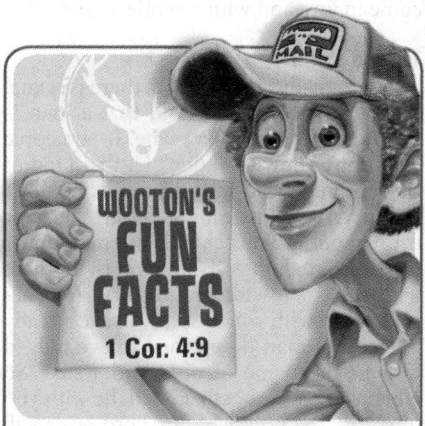

WOOTON'S **FUN FACTS**
1 Cor. 4:9

Penny and I love watching parades, but we wouldn't like the one in this verse. The "crowd" here is in a coliseum. It's talking about being a gladiator forced to fight and die in the arena. The games weren't outlawed until the fourth century, several hundred years after this letter was written.

curse us, we bless them. When we are attacked, we put up with it. [13]When others say bad things about us, we answer with kind words. We have become the world's garbage. We are everybody's trash, right up to this moment.

Paul Warns Against Pride

[14]I am not writing this to shame you. You are my dear children, and I want to warn you. [15]Suppose you had 10,000 believers in Christ watching over you. You still wouldn't have many fathers. I became your father by serving Christ Jesus and telling you the good news. [16]So I'm asking you to follow my example. [17]That's the reason I have sent Timothy to you. He is like a son to me, and I love him. He is faithful in serving the Lord. He will remind you of my way of life in serving Christ Jesus. And that agrees with what I teach everywhere in every church.

[18]Some of you have become proud. You act as if I weren't coming to you. [19]But I will come very soon, if that's what the Lord wants. Then I will find out how those proud people are talking. I will also find out what power they have. [20]The kingdom of God is not a matter of talk. It is a matter of power. [21]Which do you want? Should I come to you to correct and punish you? Or should I come in love and with a gentle spirit?

Throw Out the Evil Person!

5 It is actually reported that there is sexual sin among you. I'm told that a man is sleeping with his father's wife. Even people who don't know God don't let that kind of sin continue. [2]And you are proud! Shouldn't you be very sad instead? Shouldn't you have thrown out of your church the man doing this? [3]Even though I am not right there with you, I am with you in spirit. And because I am with you in spirit, I have already judged the man doing this. I have judged him in the name of our Lord Jesus. [4]So when you come together, I will be with you in spirit. The power of our Lord Jesus will also be with you. [5]When you come together like this, hand this man over to Satan. Then the power of sin in his life will be destroyed. His spirit will be saved on the day the Lord returns.

[6]Your bragging is not good. It is like yeast. Don't you know that just a little yeast makes the whole batch of dough rise? [7]Get rid of the old yeast. Then you can be like a new batch of dough without yeast. That is what you really are. That's because Christ, our Passover Lamb, has been offered up for us. [8]So let us keep the Feast, but not with the old bread made with yeast. The yeast I'm talking about is hatred and evil. Let us keep the Feast with bread made without yeast. Let us keep it with bread that is honesty and truth.

[9]I wrote a letter to you to tell you to stay away from people who commit sexual sins. [10]I didn't mean the people of this world who sin in this way. I didn't mean those who always want more and more. I didn't mean those who cheat or who worship statues of gods. In that case you would have to leave this world! [11]But here is what I am writing to you now. You must stay away from anyone who claims to be a believer but does evil things. Stay away from anyone who commits sexual sins. Stay away from anyone who always wants more and more things. Stay away from anyone who worships statues of gods. Stay away from anyone who tells lies about others. Stay away from anyone who gets drunk or who cheats. Don't even eat with people like these.

[12]Is it my business to judge those outside the church? Aren't you supposed to judge those inside the church? [13]God will judge those outside. Scripture says, "Get rid of that evil person!" *(Deuteronomy 17:7; 19:19; 21:21; 22:21,24; 24:7)*

Do Not Take Believers to Court

6 Suppose one of you wants to bring a charge against another believer. Should you take it to ungodly people to be judged? Why not take it to the Lord's people? [2]Or don't you know that the Lord's people will judge the world? Since this is true, aren't you able to judge small cases? [3]Don't you know that we will judge angels? Then we should be able to judge the things of this life even more! [4]So suppose you disagree with one another in matters like this. Who do you ask to decide which of you is right? Do you ask people who live in a way the church disapproves of? Of course not! [5]I say this to shame you. Is it possible that no one among you is wise enough to judge matters between believers? [6]Instead, one

believer goes to court against another. And this happens in front of unbelievers! ⁷When you take another believer to court, you have lost the battle already. Why not be treated wrongly? Why not be cheated? ⁸Instead, you yourselves cheat and do wrong. And you do it to your brothers and sisters. ⁹Don't you know that people who do wrong will not receive God's kingdom? Don't be fooled. Those who commit sexual sins will not receive the kingdom. Neither will those who worship statues of gods or commit adultery. Neither will men who sleep with other men. ¹⁰Neither will thieves or those who always want more and more. Neither will those who are often drunk or tell lies or cheat. People who live like that will not receive God's kingdom. ¹¹Some of you used to do those things. But your sins were washed away. You were made holy. You were made right with God. All of this was done in the name of the Lord Jesus Christ. It was also done by the Spirit of our God.

Sexual Sins

¹²Some of you say, "I have the right to do anything." But not everything is helpful. Again some of you say, "I have the right to do anything." But I will not be controlled by anything. ¹³Some of you say, "Food is for the stomach, and the stomach is for food. And God will destroy both of them." But the body is not meant for sexual sins. The body is meant for the Lord. And the Lord is meant for the body. ¹⁴By his power God raised the Lord from the dead. He will also raise us up. ¹⁵Don't you know that your bodies belong to the body of Christ? Should I take what belongs to Christ and join it to a prostitute? Never! ¹⁶When you join yourself to a prostitute, you become one with her in body. Don't you know this? Scripture says, "The two will become one." *(Genesis 2:24)* ¹⁷But whoever is joined to the Lord becomes one with him in spirit.

¹⁸Keep far away from sexual sins. All the other sins a person commits are outside the body. But sexual sins are sins against their own body. ¹⁹Don't you know that your bodies are temples of the Holy Spirit? The Spirit is in you, and you have received the Spirit from God. You do not belong to yourselves. ²⁰Christ has paid the price for you. So use your bodies in a way that honors God.

CANDID CONVERSATIONS

I have to admit, some days all I want to do is sit on the couch eating sour cream and onion potato chips. And popcorn. Maybe a donut or . . . four. Doing that every now and then isn't such a bad thing, but I know if I made it a habit, I would end up with what I like to call "Unconquerable Donut Belly."

The Bible tells us that our bodies "are temples of the Holy Spirit," and we are supposed to honor God with them. In other words, my donut binges are a little like spray-painting graffiti on the side of a cathedral. God gave you one body to use here on earth—so you can run, play, eat, talk, and do a million other things. But our bodies really aren't *ours*. They belong to God, and that means we should take really good care of them.

See if you can make an effort to strengthen your eating habits and get some exercise. I'm going to try jogging . . . brutal, huh? Then try to improve in those areas each day.

Advice for Those Who Are Married

7 Now I want to deal with the things you wrote me about. Some of you say, "It is good for a man not to sleep with a woman." ²But since sexual sin is happening, each man should sleep with his own wife. And each woman should sleep with her own husband. ³A husband should satisfy his wife's needs. And a wife should satisfy her husband's needs. ⁴The wife's body does not belong only to her. It also belongs to her husband. In the same way, the husband's body does not belong only to him. It also belongs to his wife. ⁵You shouldn't stop giving yourselves to each other. You might possibly do this when you both agree to it. And you should only agree to it to give yourselves time to pray. Then you should come together again. In that way, Satan will not tempt you when you can't control yourselves. [6]I say these things to you as my advice, not as a command. [7]I wish all of you were single like me. But you each have your own gift from God. One has this gift, and another has that one.

[8]I speak now to those who are not married. I also speak to widows. It is good for you to stay single like me. [9]But if you can't control yourselves, you should get married. It is better to get married than to burn with desire.

[10]I give a command to those who are married. It is a direct command from the Lord, not from me. A wife must not leave her husband. [11]But if she does, she must not get married again. Or she can go back to her husband. And a husband must not divorce his wife.

[12]I also have something to say to everyone else. It is from me, not a direct command from the Lord. Suppose a brother has a wife who is not a believer. If she is willing to live with him, he must not divorce her. [13]And suppose a woman has a husband who is not a believer. If he is willing to live with her, she must not divorce him. [14]The unbelieving husband has been made holy through his wife. The unbelieving wife has been made holy through her believing husband. If that were not the case, your children would not be pure and "clean." But as it is, they are holy.

[15]But if the unbeliever leaves, let that person go. In that case, the believer does not have to stay married to the unbeliever. God wants us to live in peace. [16]Wife, how do you know if you will save your husband? Husband, how do you know if you will save your wife?

Stay as You Were When God Chose You

[17]But each believer should live in whatever situation the Lord has given them. Stay as you were when God chose you. That's the rule all the churches must follow. [18]Was a man already circumcised when God chose him? Then he should not become uncircumcised. Was he uncircumcised when God chose him? Then he should not be circumcised. [19]Being circumcised means nothing. Being uncircumcised means nothing. Doing what God commands is what counts. [20]Each of you should stay as you were when God chose you.

[21]Were you a slave when God chose you? Don't let it trouble you. But if you can get your master to set you free, do it. [22]The person who was a slave when the Lord chose them is now the Lord's free person. The one who was free when God chose them is now a slave of Christ. [23]Christ has paid the price for you. Don't become slaves of human beings. [24]Brothers and sisters, each person is accountable to God. So each person should stay as they were when God chose them.

Advice for Those Who Are Not Married

[25]Now I want to say something about virgins. I have no direct command from the Lord. But I give my opinion. Because of the Lord's mercy, I give it as one who can be trusted. [26]Times are hard for you right now. So I think it's good for a man to stay as he is. [27]Are you engaged to a woman? Then don't try to get out of it. Are you free from such a promise? Then don't look for a wife. [28]But if you do marry someone, you have not sinned. And if a virgin marries someone, she has not sinned. But those who marry someone will have many troubles in this life. I want to save you from this.

[29]Brothers and sisters, what I mean is that the time is short. From now on, those who have a husband or wife should live as if they did not. [30]Those who mourn should live as if they did not. Those who are happy should live as if they were not. Those who buy something should live as if it were not theirs to keep. [31]Those who use the things of the world should not become all wrapped up in them. The world as it now exists is passing away.

[32]I don't want you to have anything to worry about. A single man is concerned about the Lord's matters. He wants to know how he can please the Lord. [33]But a married man is concerned about the matters of this world. He wants to know how he can please his wife. [34]His concerns pull him in two directions. A single woman or a virgin is concerned about the Lord's matters. She wants to serve the Lord with both body and spirit. But a married woman is concerned about the matters of this world. She wants

to know how she can please her husband. [35]I'm saying those things for your own good. I'm not trying to hold you back. I want you to be free to live in a way that is right. I want you to give yourselves completely to the Lord.

[36]Suppose someone is worried that he is not acting with honor toward the virgin he has promised to marry. Suppose his desires are too strong, and he feels that he should marry her. He should do as he wants. He is not sinning. They should get married. [37]But suppose the man has decided not to marry the virgin. And suppose he has no compelling need to get married and can control himself. If he has made up his mind not to get married, he also does the right thing. [38]So then, the man who marries the virgin does the right thing. But the man who doesn't marry her does a better thing.

[39]A woman has to stay married to her husband as long as he lives. If he dies, she is free to marry anyone she wants to. But the one she marries must belong to the Lord. [40]In my opinion, she is happier if she stays single. And I also think that I am led by the Spirit of God in saying this.

Food Sacrificed to Statues of Gods

Now I want to deal with food sacrificed to statues of gods. We know that "We all have knowledge." But knowledge makes people proud, while love builds them up. [2]Those who think they know something still don't know as they should. [3]But whoever loves God is known by God.

[4]So then, here is what I say about eating food sacrificed to statues of gods. We know that "a god made by human hands is really nothing at all in the world." We know that "there is only one God." [5]There may be so-called gods either in heaven or on earth. In fact, there are many "gods" and many "lords." [6]But for us there is only one God. He is the Father. All things came from him, and we live for him. And there is only one Lord. He is Jesus Christ. All things came because of him, and we live because of him.

[7]But not everyone knows this. Some people still think that statues of gods are real gods. They might eat food sacrificed to statues of gods. When they do, they think of it as food sacrificed to real gods. And because those people have a weak sense of what is right and wrong, they feel guilty.

[8]But food doesn't bring us close to God. We are no worse if we don't eat. We are no better if we do eat.

[9]But be careful how you use your rights. Be sure you don't cause someone weaker than you to fall into sin. [10]Suppose you, with all your knowledge, are eating in a temple of one of those gods. And suppose someone who has a weak sense of what is right and wrong sees you. Won't that person become bold and eat what is sacrificed to statues of gods? [11]If so, then your knowledge destroys that weak brother or sister for whom Christ died. [12]Suppose you sin against them in this way. Then you harm their weak sense of what is right and wrong. By doing this, you sin against Christ. [13]So suppose what I eat causes my brother or sister to fall into sin. Then what should I do? I will never eat meat again. In that way, I will not cause them to fall.

Paul's Rights as an Apostle

Am I not free? Am I not an apostle? Haven't I seen Jesus our Lord? Aren't you the result of my work for the Lord? [2]Others may not think of me as an apostle. But I am certainly one to you! You are the proof that I am the Lord's apostle.

[3]That is what I say to stand up for myself when people judge me. [4]Don't we have the right to eat and drink? [5]Don't we have the right to take a believing wife with us when we travel? The other apostles do. The Lord's brothers do. Peter does. [6]Or are Barnabas and I the only ones who have to do other work for a living? Are we the only ones who can't just do the work of apostles all the time?

[7]Who serves as a soldier but doesn't get paid? Who plants a vineyard but doesn't eat any of its grapes? Who takes care of a flock but doesn't drink any of the milk? [8]Do I say this only on human authority? The Law says the same thing. [9]Here is what is written in the Law of Moses. "Do not stop an ox from eating while it helps separate the grain from the straw." *(Deuteronomy 25:4)* Is it oxen that God is concerned about? [10]Doesn't he say that for us? Yes, it was written for us. Whoever plows and separates the grain hopes to share the harvest. And it is right for them to hope for this. [11]We have planted spiritual seed among you. Is it too much to ask that we receive from you some

One time at Camp What-a-Nut, Jason and I were partners in the canoe race. We practiced all week, so when the race started, we quickly took the lead. As we reached the finish line, I threw my paddle in the air to celebrate . . . at the same moment Jason leaned forward to give me a high five. My paddle smacked him right in the face. Hard.

One trip to the emergency room, two black eyes, and four stitches later, we returned to camp for pie . . . and to show everyone that he was (mostly) okay. As we told (and retold and retold!) the story, I started to feel bad for trying so hard to win. But then Whit reminded me that winning isn't a bad thing. The apostle Paul compares the Christian life to a race in 1 Corinthians 9—we're supposed to try our hardest to win! Whit explained that if you get too focused on winning, you'll lose sight of what's really important, and you might end up hurting the people close to you. I need to make sure that, win or lose, I'm racing for God's glory, not my own.

things we need? ¹²Others have the right to receive help from you. Don't we have even more right to do so?

But we didn't use that right. No, we have put up with everything. We didn't want to keep the good news of Christ from spreading.

¹³People who serve in the temple get their food from the temple. Don't you know this? People who serve at the altar eat from what is offered on the altar. Don't you know this? ¹⁴So those who preach the good news should also receive their living from their work. That is what the Lord has commanded.

¹⁵But I haven't used any of those rights. And I'm not writing because I hope you will do things like that for me. I would rather die than allow anyone to take away my pride in my work. ¹⁶But when I preach the good news, I can't brag. I have to preach it. How terrible it will be for me if I do not preach the good news! ¹⁷If I preach because I want to, I get a reward. If I preach because I have to, I'm only doing my duty. ¹⁸Then what reward do I get? Here is what it is. I am able to preach the good news free of charge. And I can do this without using all my rights as a person who preaches the good news.

Paul Uses His Freedom to Share the Good News

¹⁹I am free and don't belong to anyone. But I have made myself a slave to everyone. I do it to win as many as I can to Christ. ²⁰To the Jews I became like a Jew. That was to win the Jews. To those under the law I became like one who was under the law. I did this even though I myself am not under the law. That was to win those under the law. ²¹To those who don't have the law I became like one who doesn't have the law. I did this even though I am not free from God's law. I am under Christ's law. Now I can win those who don't have the law. ²²To those who are weak I became weak. That was to win the weak. I have become all things to all people. I have done this so that in all possible ways I might save some. ²³I do all this because of the good news. And I want to share in its blessings.

Training to Win the Prize

²⁴In a race all the runners run. But only one gets the prize. You know that, don't you? So run in a way that will get you the prize. ²⁵All who take part in the games train hard. They do it to get a crown that will not last. But we do it to get a crown that will last forever. ²⁶So I do not run like someone who doesn't run toward the finish line. I do not fight like a boxer who hits nothing but air. ²⁷No, I train my body and bring it

1 Cor. 9:25 Paul is talking about the discipline of famous Greek athletes, which his readers in Corinth would have known all about. By this time, the Olympics, a religious festival, had been going on for 800 years.

warn us. That's because we are living at the time when God's work is being completed. [12]So be careful. When you think you are standing firm, you might fall. [13]You are tempted in the same way all other human beings are. God is faithful. He will not let you be tempted any more than you can take. But when you are tempted, God will give you a way out. Then you will be able to deal with it.

Sharing in the Lord's Supper

[14]My dear friends, run away from statues of gods. Don't worship them. [15]I'm talking to people who are reasonable. Judge for yourselves what I say. [16]We give thanks for the cup at the Lord's Supper. When we do, aren't we sharing in the blood of Christ? When we break the bread, aren't we sharing in the body of Christ? [17]Just as there is one loaf, so we who are many are one body. We all share the one loaf.

[18]Think about the people of Israel. Don't those who eat the offerings share in the altar? [19]Do I mean that food sacrificed to a statue of a god is anything? Do I mean that a statue of a god is anything? [20]No! But what is sacrificed by those who worship statues of gods is really sacrificed to demons. It is not sacrificed to God. I don't want you to be sharing with demons. [21]You can't drink the cup of the Lord and the cup of demons too. You can't have a part in both the Lord's table and the table of demons. [22]Are we trying to make the Lord jealous? Are we stronger than he is?

The Believer's Freedom

[23]You say, "I have the right to do anything." But not everything is helpful. Again you say, "I have the right to do anything." But not everything builds us up. [24]No one should look out for their own interests. Instead, they should look out for the interests of others.

under control. Then after I have preached to others, I myself will not break the rules. If I did break them, I would fail to win the prize.

Warnings From Israel's History

10 Brothers and sisters, I want you to know something about our people who lived long ago. They were all led by the cloud. They all walked through the Red Sea. [2]They were all baptized into Moses in the cloud and in the sea. [3]They all ate the same spiritual food. [4]They all drank the same spiritual water. They drank from the spiritual rock that went with them. That rock was Christ. [5]But God was not pleased with most of them. Their bodies were scattered in the desert.

[6]Now those things happened as examples for us. They are supposed to keep us from wanting evil things. The people of Israel wanted these evil things. [7]So don't worship statues of gods, as some of them did. It is written, "The people sat down to eat and drink. Then they got up to dance wildly in front of their god." *(Exodus 32:6)* [8]We should not commit sexual sins, as some of them did. In one day 23,000 of them died. [9]We should not test the Messiah, as some of them did. They were killed by snakes. [10]Don't speak against God. That's what some of the people of Israel did. And they were killed by the destroying angel. [11]Those things happened to them as examples for us. They were written down to

REMEMBER THIS
1 CORINTHIANS 10:13
"God is faithful. He will not let you be tempted any more than you can take. But when you are tempted, God will give you a way out. Then you will be able to deal with it."

²⁵Eat anything sold in the meat market. Don't ask if it's right or wrong. ²⁶Scripture says, "The earth belongs to the Lord. And so does everything in it." *(Psalm 24:1)*

²⁷Suppose an unbeliever invites you to a meal and you want to go. Then eat anything that is put in front of you. Don't ask if it's right or wrong. ²⁸But suppose someone says to you, "This food has been sacrificed to a statue of a god." Then don't eat it. Keep in mind the good of the person who told you. And don't eat because of a sense of what is right and wrong. ²⁹I'm talking about the other person's sense of what is right and wrong, not yours. Why is my freedom being judged by what someone else thinks? ³⁰Suppose I give thanks when I eat. Then why should I be blamed for eating food I thank God for?

³¹So eat and drink and do everything else for the glory of God. ³²Don't do anything that causes another person to trip and fall. It doesn't matter if that person is a Jew or a Greek or a member of God's church. ³³Follow my example. I try to please everyone in every way. I'm not looking out for what is good for me. I'm looking out for the interests of others. I do it so that they might

11 be saved. ¹Follow my example, just as I follow the example of Christ.

Proper Worship

²I praise you for being faithful in remembering me. I also praise you for staying true to the teachings of the past. You have stayed true to them, just as I gave them to you. ³But I want you to know that the head of every man is Christ. The head of the woman is the man. And the head of Christ is God. ⁴Every man who prays or prophesies with his head covered brings shame on his head. ⁵But every woman who prays or prophesies with her head uncovered brings shame on her head. It is the same as having her head shaved. ⁶What if a woman does not cover her head? She might as well have

her hair cut off. But it is shameful for her to cut her hair or shave her head. So she should cover her head.

⁷A man should not cover his head. He is the likeness and glory of God. But woman is the glory of man. ⁸Man did not come from woman. Woman came from man. ⁹Also, man was not created for woman. Woman was created for man. ¹⁰That's why a woman should have authority over her own head. She should have this because of the angels. ¹¹But here is how things are for those who belong to the Lord. Woman is not independent of man. And man is not independent of woman. ¹²Woman came from man, and man is born from woman. But everything comes from God.

¹³You be the judge. Is it proper for a woman to pray to God without covering her head? ¹⁴Suppose a man has long hair. Doesn't the very nature of things teach you that it is shameful? ¹⁵And suppose a woman has long hair. Doesn't the very nature of things teach you that it is her glory? Long hair is given to her as a covering. ¹⁶If anyone wants to argue about this, we don't have any other practice. And God's churches don't either.

Celebrating the Lord's Supper in the Right Way

¹⁷In the following matters, I don't praise you. Your meetings do more harm than

good. ¹⁸First, here is what people are telling me. When you come together as a church, you take sides. And in some ways I believe it. ¹⁹Do you really think you need to take sides? You probably think God favors one side over the other! ²⁰So when you come together, it is not the Lord's Supper you eat. ²¹As you eat, some of you go ahead and eat your own private meals. Because of this, one person stays hungry and another gets drunk. ²²Don't you have homes to eat and drink in? You are shaming those in the church who have nothing. Do you think so little of God's church that you do this? What should I say to you? Should I praise you? Certainly not about the Lord's Supper!

²³I passed on to you what I received from the Lord. On the night the Lord Jesus was handed over to his enemies, he took bread. ²⁴When he had given thanks, he broke it. He said, "This is my body. It is given for you. Every time you eat it, do it in memory of me." ²⁵In the same way, after supper he took the cup. He said, "This cup is the new covenant in my blood. Every time you drink it, do it in memory of me." ²⁶You eat the bread and drink the cup. When you do this, you are announcing the Lord's death until he comes again.

²⁷Eat the bread or drink the cup of the Lord in the right way. Don't do it in a way that isn't worthy of him. If you do, you will be guilty. You'll be guilty of sinning against the body and blood of the Lord. ²⁸Everyone should take a careful look at themselves before they eat the bread and drink from the cup. ²⁹Whoever eats and drinks must recognize the body of Christ. If they don't, judgment will come upon them. ³⁰That is why many of you are weak and sick. That is why a number of you have died. ³¹We should think more carefully about what we are doing. Then we would not be found guilty for this. ³²When the Lord judges us in this way, he corrects us. Then in the end we will not be judged along with the rest of the world.

³³My brothers and sisters, when you come together to eat, you should all eat together. ³⁴Anyone who is hungry should eat something at home. Then when you come together, you will not be judged.

When I come, I will give you more directions.

Gifts of the Holy Spirit

12 Brothers and sisters, I want you to know about the gifts of the Holy Spirit. ²You know that at one time you were unbelievers. You were somehow drawn away to worship statues of gods that couldn't even speak. ³So I want you to know that no one who is speaking with the help of God's Spirit says, "May Jesus be cursed." And

WHIT'S WISDOM

1 Corinthians 12

Last week, Emily and Matthew were arguing over which jobs they wanted to volunteer for during the Kids' Carnival at church. They hoped to work together, but Emily really wanted to run a game booth, while Matthew wanted to volunteer to help out in the nursery. In desperation, Emily turned to me and said, "Mr. Whittaker! Why did God make Matthew *soooo* different?!"

I chuckled. "Are you really asking? You've heard about the parts of the body in 1 Corinthians 12, right?" I explained that the apostle Paul compared the Christian church to a body with many parts. All of the parts of the body are important and do different jobs. As Christians, we shouldn't think the jobs *other* Christians do are unimportant just because they aren't our jobs.

"So *that's* why God made Matthew different," I said. "It's why He made all of us different. He needs us to be different so we can do different things."

Emily sighed. "Well, it sounds like we'll have to do different things at the carnival, Matthew. I'll run the booth and you help out with the kids."

Matthew smiled. "Sounds good to me. If we split up, we'll be able to help twice as much."

WHIT'S WISDOM

1 Corinthians 12:12–31

A whole group of us put on a play at Whit's End about the "Brotherhood of Dutiful Youth" or the BODY. The BODY was dedicated to helping people and each person did his or her specific job. But when one of the BODY members—a young man named John LaFete—went off to do his own thing, the BODY had to disband.

After the play was over, Jack Davis, who played the part of John, was confused. He thought the play was too depressing and said that we shouldn't perform it at church. I told him that the play was about people at church. In the play, when one of the members stopped going to the meetings, the group couldn't do what it was supposed to do. And when people don't go to church, it can't do what it's supposed to do either.

First Corinthians 12:27 says that Christians are Christ's "body." And verse 18 says that God has placed each one of us in the body just where He wants us to be. Find out what part of the body God has made you into, and then do what that part is supposed to do. And when you do that—and do it cheerfully—going to church will be a whole new experience!

without the help of the Holy Spirit no one can say, "Jesus is Lord."

⁴There are different kinds of gifts. But they are all given to believers by the same Spirit. ⁵There are different ways to serve. But they all come from the same Lord. ⁶There are different ways the Spirit works. But the same God is working in all these ways and in all people.

⁷The Holy Spirit is given to each of us in a special way. That is for the good of all. ⁸To some people the Spirit gives a message of wisdom. To others the same Spirit gives a message of knowledge. ⁹To others the same Spirit gives faith. To others that one Spirit gives gifts of healing. ¹⁰To others he gives the power to do miracles. To others he gives the ability to prophesy. To others he gives the ability to tell the spirits apart. To others he gives the ability to speak in different kinds of languages they had not known before. And to still others he gives the ability to explain what was said in those languages. ¹¹All the gifts are produced by one and the same Spirit. He gives gifts to each person, just as he decides.

One Body but Many Parts

¹²There is one body, but it has many parts. But all its many parts make up one body. It is the same with Christ. ¹³We were all baptized by one Holy Spirit. And so we are formed into one body. It didn't matter whether we were Jews or Gentiles, slaves or free people. We were all given the same Spirit to drink. ¹⁴So the body is not made up of just one part. It has many parts.

¹⁵Suppose the foot says, "I am not a hand. So I don't belong to the body." By saying this, it cannot stop being part of the body. ¹⁶And suppose the ear says, "I am not an eye. So I don't belong to the body." By saying this, it cannot stop being part of the body. ¹⁷If the whole body were an eye, how could it hear? If the whole body were an ear, how could it smell? ¹⁸God has placed each part in the body just as he wanted it to be. ¹⁹If all the parts were the same, how could there be a body? ²⁰As it is, there are many parts. But there is only one body.

²¹The eye can't say to the hand, "I don't need you!" The head can't say to the feet, "I don't need you!" ²²In fact, it is just the opposite. The parts of the body that seem to be weaker are the ones we can't do without. ²³The parts that we think are less important we treat with special honor. The private parts aren't shown. But they are treated with special care. ²⁴The parts that can be shown don't need special care. But God has put together all the parts of the body. And he has given more honor to the parts

that didn't have any. [25]In that way, the parts of the body will not take sides. All of them will take care of one another. [26]If one part suffers, every part suffers with it. If one part is honored, every part shares in its joy.

[27]You are the body of Christ. Each one of you is a part of it. [28]First, God has placed apostles in the church. Second, he has placed prophets in the church. Third, he has placed teachers in the church. Then he has given to the church miracles and gifts of healing. He also has given the gift of helping others and the gift of guiding the church. God also has given the gift of speaking in different kinds of languages. [29]Is everyone an apostle? Is everyone a prophet? Is everyone a teacher? Do all work miracles? [30]Do all have gifts of healing? Do all speak in languages they had not known before? Do all explain what is said in those languages? [31]But above all, you should want the more important gifts.

Love Is Necessary

But now I will show you the best way of all.

13 Suppose I speak in the languages of human beings or of angels. If I don't have love, I am only a loud gong or a noisy cymbal. [2]Suppose I have the gift of prophecy. Suppose I can understand all the secret things of God and know everything about him. And suppose I have enough faith to move mountains. If I don't have love, I am nothing at all. [3]Suppose I give everything I have to poor people. And suppose I give myself over to a difficult life so I can brag. If I don't have love, I get nothing at all.

[4]Love is patient. Love is kind. It does not want what belongs to others. It does not brag. It is not proud. [5]It does not dishonor other people. It does not look out for its own interests. It does not easily become angry. It does not keep track of other people's wrongs. [6]Love is not happy with evil. But it is full of joy when the truth is spoken. [7]It always protects. It always trusts. It always hopes. It never gives up.

[8]Love never fails. But prophecy will pass away. Speaking in languages that had not been known before will end. And knowledge will pass away. [9]What we know now is not complete. What we prophesy now is not perfect. [10]But when what is complete comes, the things that are not complete will

ADVENTURES IN ODYSSEY

Jay, Priscilla, and Barrett learned how not to be clanging cymbals, and the meaning of God's love, in "Unbecoming Jay" (A#54).

pass away. [11]When I was a child, I talked like a child. I thought like a child. I had the understanding of a child. When I became a man, I put the ways of childhood behind me. [12]Now we see only a dim likeness of things. It is as if we were seeing them in a foggy mirror. But someday we will see clearly. We will see face to face. What I know now is not complete. But someday I will know completely, just as God knows me completely.

[13]The three most important things to have are faith, hope and love. But the greatest of them is love.

Worship in a Way That Helps People Understand

14 Follow the way of love. You should also want the gifts the Holy Spirit gives. Most of all, you should want the gift of prophecy. [2]Anyone who speaks in a language they had not known before doesn't speak to people. They speak only to God. In fact, no one understands them. What they say by the Spirit remains a mystery. [3]But the person who prophesies speaks to people. That person prophesies to make people stronger, to give them hope, and to comfort them. [4]Anyone who speaks in other languages builds up only themselves. But the person who prophesies builds up the church. [5]I would like all of you to speak in other languages. But I would rather have you prophesy. The person who prophesies is more helpful than those who speak in other languages. But that is not the case if someone explains what was said in the other languages. Then the whole church can be built up. ⁶Brothers and sisters, suppose I were to come to you and speak in other languages. What good would I be to you? None! I would need to come with new truth or knowledge. Or I would need to come with a prophecy or a teaching. ⁷Here are some examples. Certain objects make sounds. Take a flute or a harp. No one will know what the tune is unless different notes are played. ⁸Also, if the trumpet call isn't clear, who will get ready for battle? ⁹It's the same with you. You must speak words that people understand. If you don't, no one will know what you are saying. You will just be speaking into the air. ¹⁰It is true that there are all kinds of languages in the world. And they all have meaning. ¹¹But if I don't understand what someone is saying, I am a stranger to the person speaking. And that person is a stranger to me. ¹²It's the same with you. You want the gifts of the Spirit. So try to do your best in using gifts that build up the church.

¹³So here is what the person who speaks in languages they had not known before should do. They should pray that they can explain what they say. ¹⁴If I pray in another language, my spirit prays. But my mind does not pray. ¹⁵So what should I do? I will pray with my spirit. But I will also pray with my understanding. I will sing with my spirit. But I will also sing with my understanding. ¹⁶Suppose you are praising God in the Spirit. And suppose there are visitors among you who want to know what's going on. How can they say "Amen" when you give thanks? They don't know what you are saying. ¹⁷You are certainly giving thanks. But no one else is being built up.

¹⁸I thank God that I speak in other languages more than all of you do. ¹⁹In the church, I wouldn't want to speak 10,000 words in an unfamiliar language. I'd rather speak five words in a language people could understand. Then I would be teaching others.

²⁰Brothers and sisters, stop thinking like children. Be like babies as far as evil is concerned. But be grown up in your thinking. ²¹In the law it is written,

"With unfamiliar languages and through the lips of outsiders I will speak to these people. But even then they will not listen to me." *(Isaiah 28:11,12)*

That is what the Lord says.

²²So speaking in other languages is a sign for those who don't believe. It is not a sign for those who do believe. But prophecy is not for those who don't believe. It is for those who believe. ²³Suppose the whole church comes together and everyone speaks in other languages. And suppose visitors or unbelievers come in. Won't they say you are out of your minds? ²⁴But suppose unbelievers or visitors come in while everyone is prophesying. Then they will feel guilty about their sin. They will be judged by all. ²⁵The secrets of their hearts will be brought out into the open. They will fall down and worship God. They will exclaim, "God is really here among you!"

Proper Worship

²⁶Brothers and sisters, what should we say then? When you come together, each of you brings something. You bring a hymn or a teaching or a message from God. You bring a message in another language or explain what was said in that language. Everything must be done to build up the church. ²⁷No more than two or three people should speak in another language. And they should speak one at a time. Then someone must explain what was said. ²⁸If there is no one to explain, the person speaking should keep quiet in the church. They can speak to themselves and to God.

²⁹Only two or three prophets are supposed to speak. Others should decide if what is being said is true. ³⁰What if a message from God comes to someone else who is sitting there? Then the one who is speaking should stop. ³¹Those who prophesy can all take turns. In that way, everyone can be taught and be given hope. ³²Those who prophesy should control their speaking. ³³God is not a God of disorder. He is a God of peace, just as in all the churches of the Lord's people.

³⁴Women should remain silent in church meetings. They are not allowed to speak. They must follow the lead of those who are in authority, as the law says. ³⁵If they have a question about something, they should ask

their own husbands at home. It is shameful for women to speak in church meetings.

³⁶Or did the word of God begin with you? Or are you the only people it has reached? ³⁷Suppose anyone thinks they are a prophet. Or suppose they think they have other gifts given by the Holy Spirit. They should agree that what I am writing to you is the Lord's command. ³⁸But anyone who does not recognize this will not be recognized.

³⁹Brothers and sisters, you should want to prophesy. And don't stop people from speaking in languages they had not known before. ⁴⁰But everything should be done in a proper and orderly way.

Christ Rose From the Dead

15 Brothers and sisters, I want to remind you of the good news I preached to you. You received it and have put your faith in it. ²Because you believed the good news, you are saved. But you must hold firmly to the message I preached to you. If you don't, you have believed it for nothing.

³What I received I passed on to you. And it is the most important of all. Here is what it is. Christ died for our sins, just as Scripture said he would. ⁴He was buried. He was raised from the dead on the third day, just as Scripture said he would be. ⁵He appeared to Peter. Then he appeared to the 12 apostles. ⁶After that, he appeared to more than 500 brothers and sisters at the same time. Most of them are still living. But some have died. ⁷He appeared to James. Then he appeared to all the apostles. ⁸Last of all, he also appeared to me. I was like someone who wasn't born at the right time.

⁹I am the least important of the apostles. I'm not even fit to be called an apostle. I tried to destroy God's church. ¹⁰But because of God's grace I am what I am. And his grace was not wasted on me. No, I have worked harder than all the other apostles. But I didn't do the work. God's grace was with me. ¹¹So this is what we preach, whether I or the other apostles who preached to you. And that is what you believed.

Believers Will Rise From the Dead

¹²We have preached that Christ has been raised from the dead. So how can some of you say that no one rises from the dead? ¹³If no one rises from the dead, then not even

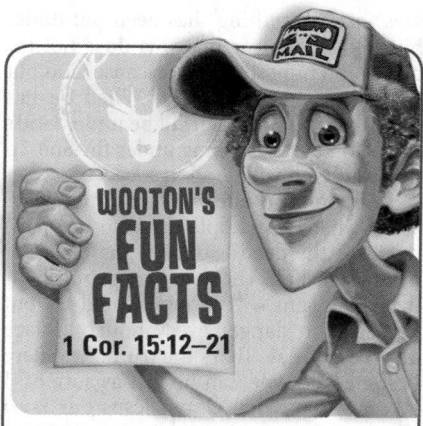

WOOTON'S FUN FACTS
1 Cor. 15:12–21

The Bible is jam-packed with miracles. Think of the parting of the Red Sea or a talking donkey. But the absolute most important miracle is that Jesus died and rose again.

Christ has been raised. ¹⁴And if Christ has not been raised, what we preach doesn't mean anything. Your faith doesn't mean anything either. ¹⁵More than that, we would be lying about God. We are witnesses that God raised Christ from the dead. But he did not raise him if the dead are not raised. ¹⁶If the dead are not raised, then Christ has not been raised either. ¹⁷And if Christ has not been raised, your faith doesn't mean anything. Your sins have not been forgiven. ¹⁸Those who have died believing in Christ are also lost. ¹⁹Do we have hope in Christ only for this life? Then people should pity us more than anyone else.

²⁰But Christ really has been raised from the dead. He is the first of all those who will rise from the dead. ²¹Death came because of what a man did. Rising from the dead also comes because of what a man did. ²²Because of Adam, all people die. So because of Christ, all will be made alive. ²³But here is the order of events. Christ is the first of those who rise from the dead. When he comes back, those who belong to him will be raised. ²⁴Then the end will come after Christ destroys all rule, authority and power. Then he will hand over the kingdom to God the Father. ²⁵Christ must rule until he has put all his enemies under his control. ²⁶The last enemy that will be destroyed is death. ²⁷Scripture says that God "has put everything under his control." *(Psalm 8:6)* It

says that "everything" has been put under him. But it is clear that this does not include God himself. That's because God put everything under Christ. [28]When he has done that, the Son also will be under God's rule. God put everything under the Son. In that way, God will be all in all.

[29]Suppose no one rises from the dead. Then what will people do who are baptized for the dead? Suppose the dead are not raised at all. Then why are people baptized for them? [30]And why would we put ourselves in danger every hour? [31]I face death every day. That's the truth. And here is something you can be just as sure of. I take pride in what Christ Jesus our Lord has done for you through my work. [32]Did I fight wild animals in Ephesus with nothing more than human hopes? Then what have I gotten for it? If the dead are not raised,

"Let us eat and drink,
   because tomorrow we will die."
                           (Isaiah 22:13)

[33]Don't let anyone fool you. "Bad companions make a good person bad." [34]You should come back to your senses and stop sinning. Some of you don't know anything about God. I say this to make you ashamed.

The Body That Rises From the Dead

[35]But someone will ask, "How are the dead raised? What kind of body will they have?" [36]How foolish! What you plant doesn't come to life unless it dies. [37]When you plant something, it isn't a completely grown plant that you put in the ground. You only plant a seed. Maybe it's wheat or something else. [38]But God gives the seed a body just as he has planned. And to each kind of seed he gives its own body. [39]Not all earthly creatures are the same. People have one kind of body. Animals have another. Birds have another kind. Fish have still another. [40]There are also heavenly bodies as well as earthly bodies. Heavenly bodies have one kind of glory. Earthly bodies have another. [41]The sun has one kind of glory. The moon has another kind. The stars have still another. And one star's glory is different from that of another star.

[42]It will be like that with bodies that are raised from the dead. The body that is planted does not last forever. The body that is raised from the dead lasts forever. [43]It is planted without honor. But it is raised in glory. It is planted in weakness. But it is raised in power. [44]It is planted as an earthly body. But it is raised as a spiritual body.

Just as there is an earthly body, there is also a spiritual body. [45]It is written, "The first man Adam became a living person." *(Genesis 2:7)* The last Adam became a spirit that gives life. [46]What is spiritual did not come first. What is earthly came first. What is spiritual came after that. [47]The first man came from the dust of the earth. The second man came from heaven. [48]Those who belong to the earth are like the one who came from the earth. And those who are spiritual are like the heavenly man. [49]We are like the earthly man. And we will be like the heavenly man.

[50]Brothers and sisters, here is what I'm telling you. Bodies made of flesh and blood can't share in the kingdom of God. And what dies can't share in what never dies. [51]Listen! I am telling you a mystery. We will not all die. But we will all be changed. [52]That will happen in a flash, as quickly as you can wink an eye. It will happen at the blast of the last trumpet. Then the dead will be raised to live forever. And we will be changed. [53]Our natural bodies don't last forever. They must be dressed with what does last forever. What dies must be dressed with what does not die. [54]In fact, that is going to happen. What does not last will be dressed with what lasts forever. What dies will be dressed with what does not die. Then what is written will come true. It says, "Death has been swallowed up. It has lost the battle." *(Isaiah 25:8)*

[55] "Death, where is the victory you
         thought you had?
   Death, where is your sting?"
                           (Hosea 13:14)

[56]The sting of death is sin. And the power of sin is the law. [57]But let us give thanks to God! He gives us the victory because of what our Lord Jesus Christ has done.

[58]My dear brothers and sisters, remain strong in the faith. Don't let anything move you. Always give yourselves completely to the work of the Lord. Because you belong to the Lord, you know that your work is not worthless.

You're all set to play tug-of-war when you notice that there are fifty people on your side—including all of the strongest people you know—and only ten on the other side. How do you feel about your chances? Before you even start, you're confident that you've already won.

We actually have a real-life enemy who has lost the battle. It's an enemy most people fear in spite of the advantage given to us by Jesus Christ. That enemy is death.

Death isn't something we like to talk about, is it? But Christians have no reason to fear death. We can trust God and know that we'll see our loved ones again in heaven.

It's not that Christians are happy when someone they love dies. It's very sad to lose a friend or family member. Death is still the enemy. But guess what? It is a *defeated* enemy! Jesus defeated death when He died on the Cross for us and came back to life, so we know He's telling the truth when He says

that death has no lasting power over us. That's why 1 Corinthians 15:57 sounds like a triumphant cheer: "But let us give thanks to God! He gives us the victory because of what our Lord Jesus Christ has done."

Earlier in the chapter, Paul says, "The last enemy that will be destroyed is death." What a wonderful promise—and words to hold onto when feeling the sting of sorrow when a fellow Christian passes away.

The Offering for the Lord's People

16 Now I want to deal with the offering of money for the Lord's people. Do what I told the churches in Galatia to do. [2]On the first day of every week, each of you should put some money away. The amount should be in keeping with how much money you make. Save the money so that you won't have to take up an offering when I come. [3]When I arrive, I will send some people with your gift to Jerusalem. They will be people you consider to be good. And I will give them letters that explain who they are. [4]If it seems good for me to go also, they will go with me.

What Paul Asks for Himself

[5]After I go through Macedonia, I will come to you. I will only be passing through Macedonia. [6]But I might stay with you for a while. I might even spend the winter. Then you can help me on my journey everywhere I go. [7]I don't want to see you now while I am just passing through. Instead, I hope to spend some time with you, if the Lord

allows it. [8]But I will stay at Ephesus until the day of Pentecost. [9]A door has opened wide for me to do some good work here. There are many people who oppose me.

[10]Timothy will visit you. Make sure he has nothing to worry about while he is with you. He is doing the work of the Lord, just as I am. [11]No one should treat him badly. Send him safely on his way so he can return to me. I'm expecting him to come back along with the others.

[12]I want to say something about our brother Apollos. I tried my best to get him to go to you with the others. But he didn't want to go right now. He will go when he can.

[13]Be on your guard. Remain strong in the faith. Be brave. [14]Be loving in everything you do.

[15]You know that the first believers in Achaia were from the family of Stephanas. They have spent all their time serving the Lord's people. Brothers and sisters, I am asking you [16]to follow the lead of people like them. Follow everyone who joins in

the task and works hard at it. ¹⁷I was glad when Stephanas, Fortunatus and Achaicus arrived. They have supplied me with what you couldn't give me. ¹⁸They renewed my spirit, and yours also. People like them are worthy of honor.

Final Greetings

¹⁹The churches in Asia Minor send you greetings.

Aquila and Priscilla greet you warmly because of the Lord's love. So does the church that meets in their house.

²⁰All the brothers and sisters here send you greetings.

Greet one another with a holy kiss.

²¹I, Paul, am writing this greeting with my own hand.

²²If anyone does not love the Lord, let a curse be on that person! Come, Lord!

²³May the grace of the Lord Jesus be with you.

²⁴I give my love to all of you who belong to Christ Jesus. Amen.

ADVENTURES IN ODYSSEY

First Corinthians 16:13 talks about remaining strong and being brave. Buddy had to do both of those things when he brought his Bible to school in "A Predicament of Biblical Proportions" (Club).

2 Corinthians

When Paul wrote 1 Corinthians, he was addressing various specific problems within the church. But then a new problem arose in Corinth. A group of smug and self-serving "super-apostles" (11:5) challenged Paul's authority. They were in Corinth and Paul wasn't, so Paul was forced to defend himself remotely using this letter.

As Miss Kendall and I will reluctantly attest, most disagreements start over a minor issue and grow from there. The disagreement in 2 Corinthians likewise had small beginnings. Paul had intended to make *two* short stops in Corinth on his missionary journey, but he had to cancel one of them (1:15–2:4). To use Miss Kendall's phrase, "No biggie," right? However, Paul's critics jumped on the opportunity to suggest that nothing Paul said could be trusted—including what he said about Jesus.

Paul's credentials were as good as anyone else's, but he allowed his sufferings to speak for his integrity. He was reluctant to talk about himself, so he first spoke in general terms (6:3–10). Later, he allowed his writing to become much more specific and personal (11:16–33). He even described a vision that he had of "the third heaven" where he had seen things he couldn't even describe (12:1–10).

Paul knew that Christians aren't supposed to brag about themselves or their accomplishments. However, there are times when we will come up against people who try to twist God's Word. In those circumstances, it is better to defend ourselves with the truth rather than let those individuals get away with spreading lies.

What's it Mean, Eugene?

Conversion—*Conversion* concerns "turning" or "change." Luke is thinking of *conversion* when, in Acts 15:3, he says, "the Gentiles [or non-Jews] had *turned to* God." To put your faith in Jesus means to become a *changed* individual. Paul concisely captures this thought in 2 Corinthians 5:17, where he says, "When anyone lives in Christ, the new creation has come." *That* is *conversion*.

1 I, Paul, am writing this letter. I am an apostle of Christ Jesus just as God planned. Timothy our brother joins me in writing.

We are sending this letter to you, the members of God's church in Corinth. It is also for all God's holy people everywhere in Achaia.

²May God our Father and the Lord Jesus Christ give you grace and peace.

Praise to the God Who Gives Comfort

³Give praise to the God and Father of our Lord Jesus Christ! He is the Father who gives tender love. All comfort comes from him. ⁴He comforts us in all our troubles. Now we can comfort others when they are in trouble. We ourselves receive comfort from God. ⁵We share very much in the sufferings of Christ. So we also share very much in his comfort. ⁶If we are having trouble, it is so that you will be comforted and renewed. If we are comforted, it is so that you will be comforted. Then you will be able to put up with the same suffering we have gone through. ⁷Our hope for you remains firm. We know that you suffer just as we do. In the same way, God comforts you just as he comforts us.

⁸Brothers and sisters, we want you to know about the hard times we had in Asia Minor. We were having a lot of trouble. It was far more than we could stand. We even thought we were going to die. ⁹In fact, we felt as if we were under the sentence of death. But that happened so that we would not depend on ourselves but on God. He raises the dead to life. ¹⁰God has saved us from deadly dangers. And he will continue to do it. We have put our hope in him. He will continue to save us. ¹¹You must help us by praying for us. Then many people will give thanks because of what will happen to us. They will thank God for his kindness to us in answer to the prayers of many.

Paul Changes His Plans

¹²Here is what we take pride in. Our sense of what is right and wrong tells us how we have acted. We have lived with honor and godly honesty. We have depended on God's grace and not on the world's wisdom. We lived that way most of all when we were dealing with you.

Tom, Alex, and Cal saw the importance of prayer in times of trouble and tragedy (2 Cor. 1:10–11) in "Expect the Worst" (A#38).

¹³We are writing only what you can read and understand. And here is what I hope. ¹⁴Up to this point you have understood some of the things we have said. But now here is what I hope for when the Lord Jesus returns. I hope that your pride in us will be the same as our pride in you. When this happens, you will understand us completely.

¹⁵Because I was sure of this, I wanted to visit you first. Here is how I thought you would be helped twice. ¹⁶I planned to visit you on my way to Macedonia. I would have come back to you from there. Then you would have sent me on my way to Judea. ¹⁷When I planned all this, was I ready to change my mind for no good reason? No. I don't make my plans the way the world makes theirs. In the same breath the world says both, "Yes! Yes!" and "No! No!"

[18]But just as sure as God is faithful, our message to you is not "Yes" and "No." [19]Silas, Timothy and I preached to you about the Son of God, Jesus Christ. Our message did not say "Yes" and "No" at the same time. The message of Christ has always been "Yes." [20]God has made a great many promises. They are all "Yes" because of what Christ has done. So through Christ we say "Amen." We want God to receive glory. [21]He makes both us and you remain strong in the faith because we belong to Christ. He anointed us. [22]He put his Spirit in our hearts and marked us as his own. We can now be sure that he will give us everything he promised us.

[23]I call God to be my witness. May he take my life if I'm lying. I wanted to spare you, so I didn't return to Corinth. [24]Your faith is not under our control. You remain strong in your own faith. But we work together with you for your joy. [1]So I made up my mind that I would not make another painful visit to you. [2]If I make you sad, who is going to make me glad? Only you, the people I made sad. [3]What I wrote to you I wrote for a special reason. When I came, I didn't want to be troubled by those who should make me glad. I was sure that all of you would share my joy. [4]I was very troubled when I wrote to you. My heart was sad. My eyes were full of tears. I didn't want to make you sad. I wanted to let you know that I love you very deeply.

Forgive Those Who Make You Sad

[5]Suppose someone has made us sad. In some ways, he hasn't made me sad so much as he has made all of you sad. But I don't want to put this too strongly. [6]He has been punished because most of you decided he should be. This punishment is enough. [7]Now you should forgive him and comfort him. Then he won't be sad more than he can stand. [8]So I'm asking you to tell him again that you still love him. [9]I wrote to you for another special reason. I wanted to see if you could stand the test. I wanted to see if you could obey everything asked of you. [10]Anyone you forgive I also forgive. Was there anything to forgive? If so, I have forgiven it for your benefit, knowing that Christ is watching. [11]We don't want Satan to outsmart us. We know how he does his evil work.

2 Cor. 2:14 What's a victory parade? Well, when a victorious Roman army came home, the people would watch the soldiers parade into Rome. The soldiers carried all the treasure they had captured and held it high above their heads. I think my arms would get tired doing that—just saying.

Serving Under the New Covenant

[12]I went to Troas to preach the good news about Christ. There I found that the Lord had opened a door of opportunity for me. [13]But I still had no peace of mind. I couldn't find my brother Titus there. So I said goodbye to the believers at Troas and went on to Macedonia.

[14]Give thanks to God! He always leads us as if we were prisoners in Christ's victory parade. Through us, God spreads the knowledge of Christ everywhere like perfume. [15]God considers us to be the pleasing smell that Christ is spreading. He is spreading it among people who are being saved and people who are dying. [16]To those who are dying, we are the smell of death. To those who are being saved, we are the perfume of life. Who is able to do this work? [17]Unlike many people, we aren't selling God's word to make money. In fact, it is just the opposite. Because of Christ we speak honestly before God. We speak like people God has sent.

[1]Are we beginning to praise ourselves again? Some people need letters that speak well of them. Do we need those kinds of letters, either to you or from you? [2]You yourselves are our letter. You are written on our hearts. Everyone knows you and reads you. [3]You make it clear that you are a letter from Christ. You are the result of our work for God. You are a letter written not with

ink but with the Spirit of the living God. You are a letter written not on tablets made out of stone but on human hearts.

[4]Through Christ, we can be sure of this before God. [5]In ourselves we are not able to claim anything for ourselves. The power to do what we do comes from God. [6]He has given us the power to serve under a new covenant. The covenant is not based on the written Law of Moses. It comes from the Holy Spirit. The written Law kills, but the Spirit gives life.

The Greater Glory of the New Covenant

[7]The Law was written in letters on stone. Even though it was a way of serving God, it led to death. But even that way of serving God came with glory. The glory lasted for only a short time. Even so, the people of Israel couldn't look at Moses' face very long. [8]Since all this is true, won't the work of the Holy Spirit be even more glorious? [9]The law that condemns people to death had glory. How much more glory does the work of the Spirit have! His work makes people right with God. [10]The glory of the old covenant is nothing compared with the far greater glory of the new. [11]The glory of the old lasts for only a short time. How much greater is the glory of the new! It will last forever.

[12]Since we have that kind of hope, we are very bold. [13]We are not like Moses. He used to cover his face with a veil. That was to keep the people of Israel from seeing the end of what was passing away. [14]But their minds were made stubborn. To this day, the same veil remains when the old covenant is read. The veil has not been removed. Only faith in Christ can take it away. [15]To this day, when the Law of Moses is read, a veil covers the minds of those who hear it. [16]But when anyone turns to the Lord, the veil is taken away. [17]Now the Lord is the Holy Spirit. And where the Spirit of the Lord is, freedom is also there. [18]None of our faces are covered with a veil. All of us can see the

Lord's glory and think deeply about it. So we are being changed to become more like him so that we have more and more glory. And this glory comes from the Lord, who is the Holy Spirit.

A Treasure in Clay Jars

4 So because of God's mercy, we have work to do. He has given it to us. And we don't give up. [2]Instead, we have given up doing secret and shameful things. We don't twist God's word. In fact, we do just the opposite. We present the truth plainly. In the sight of God, we make our appeal to everyone's sense of what is right and wrong. [3]Suppose our good news is covered with a veil. Then it is veiled to those who are dying. [4]The god of this world has blinded the minds of those who don't believe. They can't see the light of the good news that makes Christ's glory clear. Christ is the likeness of God. [5]The message we preach is not about ourselves. Our message is about Jesus Christ. We say that he is Lord. And we say that we serve you because of Jesus. [6]God said, "Let light shine out of darkness." *(Genesis 1:3)* He made his light shine in our hearts. His light gives us the light to know God's glory. His glory is shown in the face of Christ.

[7]Treasure is kept in clay jars. In the same way, we have the treasure of the good news in these earthly bodies of ours. That shows that the mighty power of the good news comes from God. It doesn't come from us. [8]We are pushed hard from all sides. But we are not beaten down. We are bewildered. But that doesn't make us lose hope. [9]Others make us suffer. But God does not desert us. We are knocked down. But we are not knocked out. [10]We always carry around the death of Jesus in our bodies. In that way, the life of Jesus can be shown in our bodies. [11]We who are alive are always in danger of death because we are serving Jesus. This happens so that his life can also be shown in our earthly bodies. [12]Death is at work in us. But life is at work in you.

[13]It is written, "I believed, and so I have spoken." *(Psalm 116:10)* We have that same spirit of faith. So we also believe and speak. [14]We know that God raised the Lord Jesus from the dead. And he will also raise us up with Jesus. And he will present both you and us to himself. [15]All this is for your benefit. God's grace is reaching more and more

Eugene was thinking deeply about God (2 Cor. 3:18) in "Thy Kingdom Come" (A#17).

CaNDiD CONVERSatiONS

Do you ever think about what you'll do on the day Jesus comes back to Earth? I think I'll hug Him. I'm not sure if I'll be able to speak in His presence, but I do plan on hugging Him. What a great day that will be . . . the day we get to see Jesus face-to-face and go to heaven to live with Him forever!

I think about how fulfilling my life will be at that moment, and how empty my life was before I knew Jesus. For a long time, I didn't want anything to do with Jesus. I thought a Christian life was silly. But Whit taught me so much about God's love for me and the truth that God sent His Son to die in my place. And suddenly it seemed silly to *not* invite Him into my heart.

If you've never given your life to Jesus, talk to someone, like a pastor or your parents, about it. It's *so* worth it.

were clothing. ³Then we will not be naked. ⁴While we live in this tent of ours, we groan under our heavy load. We don't want to be naked. Instead, we want to be fully dressed with our house in heaven. What must die will be swallowed up by life. ⁵God has formed us for that very purpose. He has given us the Holy Spirit as a down payment. The Spirit makes us sure of what is still to come.

⁶So here is what we can always be certain about. As long as we are at home in our bodies, we are away from the Lord. ⁷We live by believing, not by seeing. ⁸We are certain about that. We would rather be away from our bodies and at home with the Lord. ⁹So we try our best to please him. We want to please him whether we are at home in our bodies or away from them. ¹⁰We must all stand in front of Christ to be judged. Each one of us will be judged for what we do while in our bodies. We'll be judged for the good things and the bad things. Then each of us will receive what we are supposed to get.

Christ Brings Us Back to God

¹¹We know what it means to have respect for the Lord. So we try to help other people to understand it. What we are is plain to God. I hope it is also plain to your way of thinking. ¹²We are not trying to make an appeal to you again. But we are giving you a chance to take pride in us. Some people take pride in their looks rather than what's in their hearts. If you take pride in us, you will be able to answer them. ¹³Are we "out of our minds," as some people say? If so, it is because we want to serve God. Does what we say make sense? If so, it is because we want to serve you. ¹⁴Christ's love controls us. We are sure that one person died for everyone. And so everyone died. ¹⁵Christ died for everyone. He died so that those who live should not live for themselves anymore. They should live for Christ. He died for them and was raised again.

people. So they will become more and more thankful. They will give glory to God.

¹⁶We don't give up. Our bodies are becoming weaker and weaker. But our spirits are being renewed day by day. ¹⁷Our troubles are small. They last only for a short time. But they are earning for us a glory that will last forever. It is greater than all our troubles. ¹⁸So we don't spend all our time looking at what we can see. Instead, we look at what we can't see. That's because what can be seen lasts only a short time. But what can't be seen will last forever.

Waiting for Our New Bodies

5 We know that the earthly tent we live in will be destroyed. But we have a building made by God. It is a house in heaven that lasts forever. Human hands did not build it. ²During our time on earth we groan. We long to put on our house in heaven as if it

REMEMBER THIS

2 CORINTHIANS 5:17

"When anyone lives in Christ, the new creation has come. The old is gone! The new is here!"

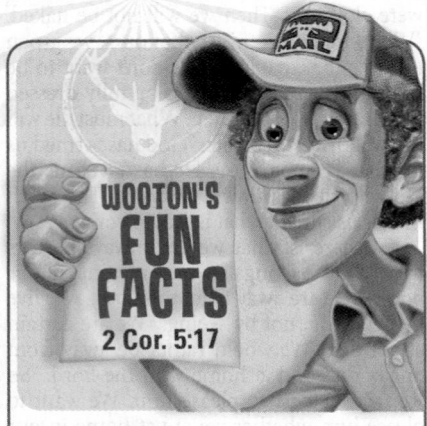

WOOTON'S FUN FACTS
2 Cor. 5:17

Have you ever seen a caterpillar transformed into a new creation when it comes out of its cocoon? The caterpillar spins its cocoon with silk. Do you know what other creature spins with silk? (Answer: a spider)

¹⁶So from now on we don't look at anyone the way the world does. At one time we looked at Christ in that way. But we don't anymore. ¹⁷When anyone lives in Christ, the new creation has come. The old is gone! The new is here! ¹⁸All this is from God. He brought us back to himself through Christ's death on the cross. And he has given us the task of bringing others back to him through Christ. ¹⁹God was bringing the world back to himself through Christ. He did not hold people's sins against them. God has trusted us with the message that people may be brought back to him. ²⁰So we are Christ's official messengers. It is as if God were making his appeal through us. Here is what Christ wants us to beg you to do. Come back to God! ²¹Christ didn't have any sin. But God made him become sin for us. So we can be made right with God because of what Christ has done for us.

6 We work together with God. So we are asking you not to receive God's grace and then do nothing with it. ²He says,

ADVENTURES IN ODYSSEY
Mandy became Christ's messenger (even though she didn't realize it) in "The Pact" (A#39).

"When I had mercy on you, I heard you.
    On the day I saved you, I helped
    you."   *(Isaiah 49:8)*

I tell you, now is the time God has mercy. Now is the day he saves.

Paul's Sufferings

³We don't put anything in anyone's way. So no one can find fault with our work for God. ⁴Instead, we make it clear that we serve God in every way. We serve him by standing firm in troubles, hard times and suffering. ⁵We don't give up when we are beaten or put in prison. When people stir up trouble in the streets, we continue to serve God. We work hard for him. We go without sleep and food. ⁶We remain pure. We understand completely what it means to serve God. We are patient and kind. We serve him in the power of the Holy Spirit. We serve him with true love. ⁷We speak the truth. We serve in the power of God. We hold the weapons of godliness in the right hand and in the left. ⁸We serve God in times of glory and shame. We serve him whether the news about us is bad or good. We are true to our calling. But people treat us as if we were pretenders. ⁹We are known, but people treat us as if we were unknown. We are dying, but we continue to live. We are beaten, but we are not killed. ¹⁰We are sad, but we are always full of joy. We are poor, but we make many people rich. We have nothing, but we own everything.

¹¹Believers at Corinth, we have spoken freely to you. We have opened our hearts wide to you. ¹²We are not holding back our love from you. But you are holding back your love from us. ¹³I speak to you as if you were my children. It is only fair that you open your hearts wide to us also.

Paul Warns Against Worshiping False Gods

¹⁴Do not be joined to unbelievers. What do right and wrong have in common? Can light and darkness be friends? ¹⁵How can Christ and Satan agree? Or what does a believer have in common with an unbeliever? ¹⁶How can the temple of the true God and the statues of other gods agree? We are the temple of the living God. God has said,

"I will live with them.
    I will walk among them.

Connie learned a difficult lesson
about being joined to an unbeliever
in "First Love" (A#08).

I will be their God.
And they will be my people."

*(Leviticus 26:12; Jeremiah 32:38;
Ezekiel 37:27)*

[17]So,

"Come out from among them
and be separate,
says the Lord.
Do not touch anything that is not pure
and 'clean.'
Then I will receive you."

(Isaiah 52:11; Ezekiel 20:34,41)

[18]And,

"I will be your Father.
You will be my sons and daughters,
says the Lord who rules over all."

(2 Samuel 7:14; 7:8)

7 Dear friends, we have these promises from God. So let us make ourselves pure from everything that makes our bodies and spirits impure. Let us be completely holy. We want to honor God.

Paul Has Joy When the Church Turns Away From Sin

[2]Make room for us in your hearts. We haven't done anything wrong to anyone. We haven't caused anyone to sin. We haven't taken advantage of anyone. [3]I don't say this to judge you. I have told you before that you have an important place in our hearts. We would live or die with you. [4]I have spoken to you very honestly. I am very proud of you. I am very happy. Even with all our troubles, my joy has no limit.

[5]When we came to Macedonia, we weren't able to rest. We were attacked no matter where we went. We had battles on the outside and fears on the inside. [6]But God comforts those who are sad. He comforted us when Titus came. [7]We were comforted not only when he came but also by the comfort you had given him. He told us how much you longed for me. He told us about your deep sadness and concern for me. That made my joy greater than ever.

[8]Even if my letter made you sad, I'm not sorry I sent it. At first I was sorry. I see that my letter hurt you, but only for a little while. [9]Now I am happy. I'm not happy because you were made sad. I'm happy because your sadness led you to turn away from your sins. You became sad just as God wanted you to. So you were not hurt in any way by us. [10]Godly sadness causes us to turn away from our sins and be saved. And we are certainly not sorry about that! But worldly sadness brings death. [11]Look at what that godly sadness has produced in you. You are working hard to clear yourselves. You are angry and alarmed. You are longing to see me. You are concerned. You are ready to make sure that the right thing is done. In every way you have proved that you are not guilty in that matter. [12]So even though I wrote to you, it wasn't because of the one who did the wrong. It wasn't because of the one who was hurt either. Instead, I wrote you so that in the sight of God you could see for yourselves how faithful you are to us. [13]All this encourages us.

We were also very glad to see how happy Titus was. You have all renewed his spirit. [14]I had bragged about you to him. And you have not let me down. Everything we said to you was true. In the same way, our bragging about you to Titus has also turned out to be true. [15]His love for you is even greater when he remembers that you all obeyed his teaching. You received him with fear and trembling. [16]I am glad I can have complete faith in you.

Giving Freely to the Lord's People

8 Brothers and sisters, we want you to know about the grace that God has given to the churches in Macedonia. [2]They have suffered a great deal. But in their suffering, their joy was more than full. Even though they were very poor, they gave very freely. [3]I tell you that they gave as much as they could. In fact, they gave even more than they could. Completely on their own, [4]they begged us for the chance to share in serving the Lord's people in that way. [5]They did more than we expected. First they gave themselves to the Lord. Then they gave themselves to us because that was what God wanted. [6]Titus had already started collecting money from you. So we asked him to help you finish making your kind gift. [7]You do well in everything else. You do well in faith and in speaking. You do well in knowledge and in complete commitment. And you do well in the love we have helped to start in you. So make sure that you also do well in the grace of giving to others.

[8]I am not commanding you to do it. But I want to test you. I want to find out if you really love God. I want to compare your love with that of others. [9]You know the grace shown by our Lord Jesus Christ. Even though he was rich, he became poor to help you. Because he became poor, you can become rich.

[10]Here is my opinion about what is best for you in that matter. Last year you were the first to give. You were also the first to want to give. [11]So finish the work. Then your desire to do it will be matched by your finishing it. Give on the basis of what you have. [12]Do you really want to give? Then the gift is measured by what someone has. It is not measured by what they don't have.

[13]We don't want others to have it easy at your expense. We want things to be equal. [14]Right now you have plenty in order to take care of what they need. Then they will have plenty to take care of what you need. The goal is to even things out. [15]It is written, "The one who gathered a lot didn't have too much. And the one who gathered a little had enough." *(Exodus 16:18)*

Paul Sends Titus to Corinth to Receive the Offering

[16]God put into the heart of Titus the same concern I have for you. Thanks should be given to God for this. [17]Titus welcomed our appeal. He is also excited about coming to you. It was his own idea. [18]Along with Titus, we are sending another brother. All the churches praise him for his service in telling the good news. [19]He was also chosen by the churches to go with us as we bring the offering. We are in charge of it. We want to honor the Lord himself. We want to show how ready we are to help. [20]We want to keep anyone from blaming us for how we take care of that large gift. [21]We are trying hard to do what both the Lord and people think is right.

[22]We are also sending another one of our brothers with them. He has often proved to us in many ways that he is very committed. He is now even more committed because he has great faith in you. [23]Titus is my helper. He and I work together among you. Our brothers are messengers from the churches. They honor Christ. [24]So show them that you really love them. Show them why we are proud of you. Then the churches can see it.

9 I don't need to write to you about giving to the Lord's people. [2]I know how much you want to help. I have been bragging about it to the people in Macedonia. I have been telling them that since last year you who live in Achaia were ready to give. You are so excited that it has stirred up most of them to take action. [3]But I am sending the brothers. Then our bragging about you in this matter will have a good reason. You will be ready, just as I said you would be. [4]Suppose people from Macedonia come with me and find out that you are not prepared. Then we, as well as you, would be ashamed of being so certain. [5]So I thought I should try to get the brothers to visit you ahead of time. They will finish the plans for the large gift you had promised. Then it will be ready as a gift freely given. It will not be given by force.

Paul's Advice to Give Freely

[6]Here is something to remember. The one who plants only a little will gather only a little. And the one who plants a lot will gather a lot. [7]Each of you should give what you have decided in your heart to give. You shouldn't give if you don't want to. You shouldn't give because you are forced to. God loves a cheerful giver. [8]And God is able to shower all kinds of blessings on you. So in all things and at all times you will have everything you need. You will do more and more good works. [9]It is written,

"They have spread their gifts around to
    poor people.
Their good works continue forever."
(Psalm 112:9)

[10]God supplies seed for the person who plants. He supplies bread for food. God will also supply and increase the amount of your seed. He will increase the results of your good works. [11]You will be made rich in every way. Then you can always give freely. We will take your many gifts to the people who need them. And they will give thanks to God.

¹²Your gifts meet the needs of the Lord's people. And that's not all. Your gifts also cause many people to thank God. ¹³You have shown yourselves to be worthy by what you have given. So other people will praise God because you obey him. That proves that you really believe the good news about Christ. They will also praise God because you share freely with them and with everyone else. ¹⁴Their hearts will be filled with love for you when they pray for you. God has given you grace that is better than anything. ¹⁵Let us give thanks to God for his gift. It is so great that no one can tell how wonderful it really is!

Paul Speaks Up for His Service to the Church

10 Christ is humble and free of pride. Because of this, I make my appeal to you. I, Paul, am the one you call "shy" when I am face to face with you. But when I am away from you, you think I am "bold" toward you. ²I am coming to see you. Please don't make me be as bold as I expect to be toward some people. They think that I live the way the people of this world live. ³I do

During an intense spiritual battle, Jack showed how the weapons to fight evil were not the ones the world used (2 Cor. 10:4) in "Darkness Before Dawn" (A#25).

live in the world. But I don't fight my battles the way the people of the world do. ⁴The weapons I fight with are not the weapons the world uses. In fact, it is just the opposite. My weapons have the power of God to destroy the camps of the enemy. ⁵I destroy

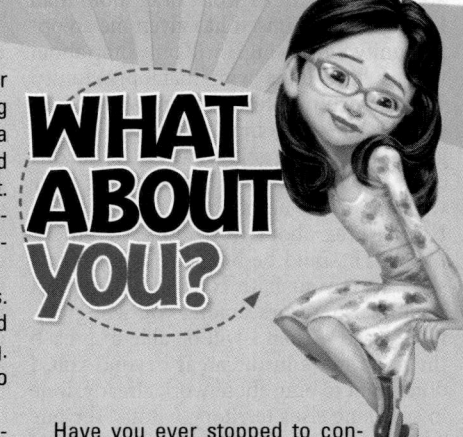

You may have noticed that you get better at the things you do over and over. Playing the piano. Dribbling a basketball. Beating a video game level. What may have been hard at first gets easier the more we practice it. That's because every time we repeat an activity, connections in our brains grow stronger and faster.

This ability benefits us in many ways. It's how you can do math in your head and memorize the words to your favorite song. That's all good. Unfortunately, this is also how we develop bad habits.

It has been said that thoughts lead to actions, actions lead to habits, and habits can shape our destiny. That's so true! As Jesus taught His disciples, sin begins with the way we think. But there's a way to fight back and reclaim our thoughts. In 2 Corinthians 10:5 the apostle Paul writes, "I keep every thought under control in order to make it obey Christ." Our goal should be to get rid of bad thoughts and keep only the ones that please God.

WHAT ABOUT YOU?

Have you ever stopped to consider where bad thoughts come from? See if you can name three places where a person's mind can become "infected." Then read Philippians 4:8 for God's list of healthy things to think about. It would be a good idea to memorize that verse. That way it will come to mind right away—like knowing how to ride a bike—whenever you face temptation.

every claim and every reason that keeps people from knowing God. I keep every thought under control in order to make it obey Christ. [6]Until you have obeyed completely, I will be ready to punish you every time you don't obey.

[7]You are judging only by how things look on the surface. Suppose someone is sure they belong to Christ. Then they should consider again that we belong to Christ just as much as they do. [8]Do I brag too much about the authority the Lord gave me? If I do, it's because I want to build you up, not tear you down. And I'm not ashamed of that kind of bragging. [9]Don't think that I'm trying to scare you with my letters. [10]Some say, "His letters sound important. They are powerful. But in person he doesn't seem like much. And what he says doesn't amount to anything." [11]People like that have a lot to learn. What I say in my letters when I'm away from you, I will do in my actions when I'm with you.

[12]I don't dare to compare myself with those who praise themselves. I'm not that kind of person. They measure themselves by themselves. They compare themselves with themselves. When they do that, they are not wise. [13]But I won't brag more than I should. God himself has given me an opportunity for serving. I will only brag about what I have done with that opportunity. This opportunity for serving also includes you. [14]I am not going too far in my bragging. I would be going too far if I hadn't come to where you live. But I did get there with the good news about Christ. [15]And I won't brag about work done by others. If I did, I would be bragging more than I should. As your faith continues to grow, I hope that my work among you will greatly increase. [16]Then I will be able to preach the good news in the areas beyond you. I don't want to brag about work already done in someone else's territory. [17]But, "The one who brags should brag about what the Lord has done." *(Jeremiah 9:24)* [18]Those who praise themselves are not accepted. Those the Lord praises are accepted.

Paul and Those Who Pretend to Be Apostles

11 I hope you will put up with me in a little foolish bragging. Yes, please put up with me! [2]My jealousy for you comes from God himself. I promised to give you to only one husband. That husband is Christ. I wanted to be able to give you to him as if you were a pure virgin. [3]But Eve's mind was tricked by the snake's clever lies. And here's what I'm afraid of. Your minds will also somehow be led astray. They will be led away from your true and pure love for Christ. [4]Suppose someone comes to you and preaches about a Jesus different from the Jesus we preached about. Or suppose you receive a spirit different from the Spirit you received before. Or suppose you receive a different message of good news. Suppose it was different from the one you accepted earlier. You put up with those kinds of things easily enough.

[5]I don't think I'm in any way less important than those "super-apostles." [6]It's true that I haven't been trained as a speaker. But I do have knowledge. I've made that very clear to you in every way. [7]I preached God's good news to you free of charge. When I did that, I was putting myself down in order to lift you up. Was this a sin? [8]I received help from other churches so I could serve you. This was almost like robbing them. [9]When I was with you and needed something, I didn't cause you any expense. The believers who came from Macedonia gave me what I needed. I haven't caused you any expense at all. And I won't ever do it. [10]I'm sure that the truth of Christ is in me. And I'm just as sure that nobody in Achaia will keep me from bragging. [11]Why? Because I don't love you? No! God knows I do!

[12]And I will keep on doing what I'm doing. That will stop those who claim they have things to brag about. They think they have a chance to be considered equal with us. [13]People like that are false apostles. They are workers who tell lies. They only pretend to be apostles of Christ. [14]That comes as no surprise. Even Satan himself pretends to be an angel of light. [15]So it doesn't surprise us that Satan's servants also pretend to be serving God. They will finally get exactly what they deserve.

Paul Brags About His Sufferings

[16]I will say it again. Don't let anyone think I'm a fool. But if you do, put up with me just as you would put up with a fool. Then I can do a little bragging. [17]When I brag about

WHIT'S WISDOM

2 Corinthians 11:24–28

What's the worst thing that happened to you in the last year? All of us have difficult things in our lives. Paul gives a list of the tough things in his life in 2 Corinthians 11:24–28. Read the list for yourself.

Paul had a rough life. Even Paul says, "It is a very heavy load." His life before he became a Christian was different. He had a good job, and lots of power and money. After he came to know Jesus, his life got really hard.

The Bible is full of people who made great sacrifices to follow God. Noah sacrificed his time (120 years!) and his reputation to build the ark. Matthew the tax collector gave up riches to follow Jesus. In every case, God honored those sacrifices. Is there anything in your life that you need to give up as a sacrifice to God? How have the difficult things you have gone through drawn you closer to Him?

myself like this, I'm not talking the way the Lord would. I'm talking like a fool. ¹⁸Many are bragging the way the people of the world do. So I will brag like that too. ¹⁹You are so wise! You gladly put up with fools! ²⁰In fact, you even put up with anyone who makes you a slave or uses you. You put up with those who take advantage of you. You put up with those who claim to be better than you. You put up with those who slap you in the face. ²¹I'm ashamed to have to say that I was too weak for that!

Whatever anyone else dares to brag about, I also dare to brag about. I'm speaking like a fool! ²²Are they Hebrews? So am I. Do they belong to the people of Israel? So do I. Are they Abraham's children? So am I. ²³Are they serving Christ? I am serving him even more. I'm out of my mind to talk like this! I have worked much harder. I have been in prison more often. I have suffered terrible beatings. Again and again I almost died. ²⁴Five times the Jews gave me 39 strokes with a whip. ²⁵Three times I was beaten with sticks. Once they tried to kill me by throwing stones at me. Three times I was shipwrecked. I spent a night and a day in the open sea. ²⁶I have had to keep on the move. I have been in danger from rivers. I have been in danger from robbers. I have been in danger from my fellow Jews and in danger from Gentiles. I have been in danger in the city, in the country, and at sea. I have been in danger from people who pretended they were believers. ²⁷I have worked very hard. Often I have gone without sleep. I have been hungry and thirsty. Often I have gone without food. I have been cold and naked. ²⁸Besides everything else, every day I am concerned about all the churches. It is a very heavy load. ²⁹If anyone is weak, I feel weak. If anyone is led into sin, I burn on the inside.

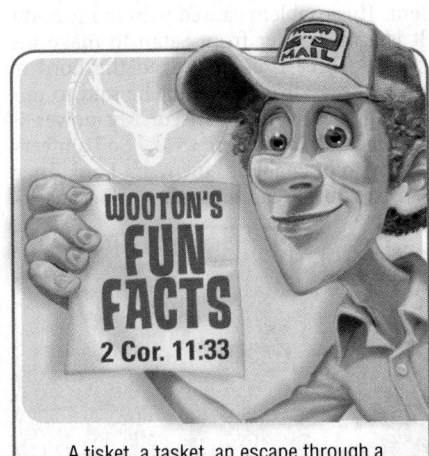

WOOTON'S FUN FACTS

2 Cor. 11:33

A tisket, a tasket, an escape through a basket . . . You should read this whole exciting story in Acts 9:22–25!

[30]If I have to brag, I will brag about the things that show how weak I am. [31]I am not lying. The God and Father of the Lord Jesus knows this. May God be praised forever. [32]In Damascus the governor who served under King Aretas had their city guarded. He wanted to arrest me. [33]But I was lowered in a basket from a window in the wall. So I escaped from the governor.

Paul's Vision and His Painful Problem

12 We can't gain anything by bragging. But I have to do it anyway. I am going to tell you what I've seen. I want to talk about what the Lord has shown me. [2]I know a believer in Christ who was taken up to the third heaven 14 years ago. I don't know if his body was taken up or not. Only God knows. [3]I don't know if that man was in his body or out of it. Only God knows. But I do know that [4]he was taken up to paradise. He heard things there that couldn't be put into words. They were things that no one is allowed to talk about. [5]I will brag about a man like that. But I won't brag about myself. I will brag only about how weak I am. [6]Suppose I decide to brag. That would not make me a fool, because I would be telling the truth. But I don't brag, so that no one will think more of me than they should. People should judge me by what I do and say. [7]God has shown me amazing and wonderful things. People should not think more of me because of it. So I wouldn't become proud of myself, I was given a problem. This problem caused pain in my body. It is a messenger from Satan to make me suffer. [8]Three times I begged the Lord to take it away from me. [9]But he said to me, "My grace is all you need. My power is strongest when you are weak." So I am very happy to brag about how weak I am. Then Christ's power can rest on me. [10]Because of

how I suffered for Christ, I'm glad that I am weak. I am glad in hard times. I am glad when people say mean things about me. I am glad when things are difficult. And I am glad when people make me suffer. When I am weak, I am strong.

Paul's Concern for the People of Corinth

[11]I have made a fool of myself. But you made me do it. You should have praised me. Even though I am nothing, I am in no way less important than the "super-apostles." [12]While I was with you, I kept on showing you the actions of a true apostle. These actions include signs, wonders and miracles. [13]How were you less important than the other churches? The only difference was that I didn't cause you any expense. Forgive me for that wrong!

[14]Now I am ready to visit you for the third time. I won't cause you any expense. I don't want what you have. What I really want is you. After all, children shouldn't have to save up for their parents. Parents should save up for their children. [15]So I will be very happy to spend everything I have for you. I will even spend myself. If I love you more, will you love me less? [16]In any case, I haven't caused you any expense. But I'm so tricky! I have caught you by tricking you! Or so you think! [17]Did I take advantage of you through any of the men I sent to you? [18]I asked Titus to go to you. And I sent our brother with him. Titus didn't take advantage of you, did he? Didn't we walk in the same footsteps by the same Spirit?

[19]All this time, have you been thinking that I've been speaking up for myself? No, I've been speaking with God as my witness. I've been speaking like a believer in Christ. Dear friends, everything I do is to help you become stronger. [20]I'm afraid that when I come I won't find you as I want you to be. I'm afraid that you won't find me as you want me to be. I'm afraid there will be arguing, jealousy and fits of anger. I'm afraid each of you will focus only on getting ahead. Then you will tell lies about each other. You will talk about each other. I'm afraid you will be proud and cause trouble. [21]I'm afraid that when I come again my God will put me to shame in front of you. Then I will be sad about many who sinned earlier and have not turned away from it.

REMEMBER THIS

2 CORINTHIANS 12:9

"He said to me, 'My grace is all you need. My power is strongest when you are weak.' So I am very happy to brag about how weak I am. Then Christ's power can rest on me."

They have not turned away from uncleanness, sexual sins and wild living. They have done all those things.

Final Warnings

13 This will be my third visit to you. Scripture says, "Every matter must be proved by the words of two or three witnesses." *(Deuteronomy 19:15)* [2] I already warned you during my second visit. I now say it again while I'm away. When I return, I won't spare those who sinned earlier. I won't spare any of the others either. [3] You are asking me to prove that Christ is speaking through me. He is not weak in dealing with you. He is powerful among you. [4] It is true that Christ was nailed to the cross because he was weak. But Christ lives by God's power. In the same way, we share his weakness. But by God's power we will live with Christ as we serve you.

[5] Take a good look at yourselves to see if you are really believers. Test yourselves. Don't you realize that Christ Jesus is in you? Unless, of course, you fail the test! [6] I hope you will discover that I haven't failed the test. [7] I pray to God that you won't do anything wrong. I don't pray so that people will see that I have passed the test. Instead, I pray this so that you will do what is right, even if it seems I have failed. [8] I can't do anything to stop the truth. I can only work for the truth. [9] I'm glad when I am weak but

REMEMBER THIS

2 CORINTHIANS 13:11

"Finally, brothers and sisters, be joyful! . . . Live in peace. And the God who gives love and peace will be with you."

you are strong. I pray that there will be no more problems among you. [10] That's why I write these things before I come to you. Then when I do come, I won't have to be hard on you when I use my authority. The Lord gave me the authority to build you up. He didn't give it to me to tear you down.

Final Greetings

[11] Finally, brothers and sisters, be joyful! Work to make things right with one another. Help one another and agree with one another. Live in peace. And the God who gives love and peace will be with you.

[12] Greet one another with a holy kiss.

[13] All God's people here send their greetings.

[14] May the grace shown by the Lord Jesus Christ be with you all. May the love that God has given us be with you. And may the sharing of life brought about by the Holy Spirit be with you all.

Galatians

Ah, Galatians! It is notable that while Rome and Corinth were cities in the ancient world, Galatia was an entire region, encompassing much of modern-day Turkey.

As the Christian church began to grow, it was soon infiltrated with various groups that didn't agree with the truth Paul was preaching. The Corinthian church had their "super-apostles" who opposed Paul. But the Galatian churches experienced trouble from a different group. They were known as the Judaizers, though they are not mentioned by name in the Bible.

Paul taught that belief in Jesus was all that was required for people to become Christians, but the Judaizers wanted to retain the old Jewish traditions as well. They wanted to continue to require a number of customs and rituals. By eliminating some of the old requirements, they felt that Paul was opening the door (to borrow the colloquialism) for people to ignore God's law in other areas. Paul compared their outlook to being freed from slavery and then choosing to continue wearing chains (4:8–11).

Paul realized that to require *anything* other than the belief that Jesus died for us is to distort the truth of the gospel message. This letter is now recognized as a masterpiece in explaining what "Christian freedom" is all about. It is a tremendous relief to realize that Jesus' sacrificial death has completely removed the problem of sin. All that is required to experience God's good gifts (5:22–23) is that we confess our sins and put our faith in Christ.

What's it Mean, Eugene?

Adoption—Theologically speaking, to be "adopted" is to be transplanted into God's family and given the position and privileges of sons and daughters. Galatians 4:5 says that God sent Jesus into the world because "he wanted us to be adopted as children with all the rights children have." What a unique privilege to be called children of God!

1 I, Paul, am writing this letter. I am an apostle. People have not sent me. No human authority has sent me. I have been sent by Jesus Christ and by God the Father. God raised Jesus from the dead. ²All the brothers and sisters who are with me join me in writing.

We are sending this letter to you, the members of the churches in Galatia.

³May God our Father and the Lord Jesus Christ give you grace and peace. ⁴Jesus gave his life for our sins. He set us free from this evil world. That was what our God and Father wanted. ⁵Give glory to God for ever and ever. Amen.

There Is No Other Good News

⁶I am amazed. You are so quickly deserting the one who chose you. He chose you to live in the grace that Christ has provided. You are turning to a different "good news." ⁷What you are accepting is really not the good news at all. It seems that some people have gotten you all mixed up. They are trying to twist the good news about Christ. ⁸But suppose even we should preach a different "good news." Suppose even an angel from heaven should preach it. Suppose it is different from the good news we gave you. Then let anyone who does that be cursed by God. ⁹I have already said it. Now I will say it again. Suppose someone preaches a "good news" that is different from what you accepted. That person should be cursed by God.

¹⁰Am I now trying to get people to think well of me? Or do I want God to think well of me? Am I trying to please people? If I were, I would not be serving Christ.

Paul Was Appointed by God

¹¹Brothers and sisters, here is what I want you to know. The good news I preached does not come from human beings. ¹²No one gave it to me. No one taught it to me. Instead, I received it from Jesus Christ. He showed it to me.

¹³You have heard how I lived earlier in my Jewish way of life. With all my strength

WHAT ABOUT YOU?

You've worked on a painting for weeks and it is breathtaking. But when you see it displayed at the art show, someone else is listed as the artist. You tell everyone that the masterpiece is yours, but no one will believe you.

Do you think God ever feels that way? After all, He created everything in the universe, but He doesn't always get credit for it. He also endows people with certain talents, but they don't always give Him the recognition He deserves.

For example, in the Adventures in Odyssey episode "And the Glory," the Odyssey Coyotes are virtually unstoppable because of Pete's incredible pitching talent. God has given him a gift, and Pete has worked hard to refine his skill. However, Pete forgets that his skills come from God, and he starts skipping church to get in extra practice. He leans entirely on his skill, not on God's strength, to get through every tough game.

It can be easy to forget that everything we have comes from God—even our talents. Whether you're skilled at painting, throwing a curveball, singing a solo, or encouraging others, that ability is a special gift. The Lord deserves the praise, recognition, and glory for everything He has created.

Galatians 1:5 says, "Give glory to God." To remember this, write down things you're grateful for on slips of paper. These could be clothes, toys, talents, food, shelter, and salvation. Then fold the papers and put them in a jar. Every day, pull one out and thank God for it.

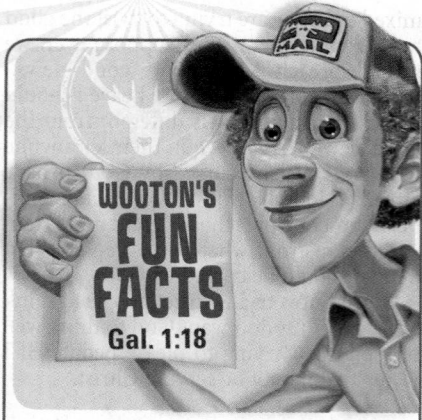

WOOTON'S FUN FACTS
Gal. 1:18

Chatwick Hill is always the hardest part of my mail route because of the "hill" part. Jerusalem is on a hill 2,500 feet above sea level. When a person was going there— whether from north or south—he or she would say, "I'm going up to Jerusalem."

I attacked the church of God. I tried to destroy it. [14]I was moving ahead in my Jewish way of life. I went beyond many of my people who were my own age. I held firmly to the teachings passed down by my people. [15]But God set me apart from before the time I was born. He showed me his grace by appointing me. He was pleased [16]to show his Son in my life. He wanted me to preach about Jesus among the Gentiles. When God appointed me, I decided right away not to ask anyone for advice. [17]I didn't go up to Jerusalem to see those who were apostles before I was. Instead, I went into Arabia. Later I returned to Damascus.

[18]Then after three years I went up to Jerusalem. I went there to get to know Peter. I stayed with him for 15 days. [19]I didn't see any of the other apostles. I only saw James, the Lord's brother. [20]Here is what you can be sure of. And God is even a witness to it. What I am writing you is not a lie.

[21]Then I went to Syria and Cilicia. [22]The members of Christ's churches in Judea did not know me in a personal way. [23]They only heard others say, "The man who used to attack us has changed. He is now preaching the faith he once tried to destroy." [24]And they praised God because of me.

Paul Is Accepted by the Apostles

2 Then after fourteen years, I went up again to Jerusalem. This time I went with Barnabas. I took Titus along also. [2]I went because God showed me what he wanted me to do. I spoke in private to those who are respected as leaders. I told them the good news that I preach among the Gentiles. I wanted to be sure I wasn't running my race for no purpose. And I wanted to know that I had not been running my race for no purpose. [3]Titus was with me. He was a Greek. But even he was not forced to be circumcised. [4]This matter came up because some people had slipped in among us. They had pretended to be believers. They wanted to find out about the freedom we have because we belong to Christ Jesus. They wanted to make us slaves again. [5]We didn't give in to them for a moment. We did this so that the truth of the good news would be kept safe for you.

[6]Some people in Jerusalem were thought to be important. But it makes no difference to me what they were. God does not treat people differently. Those people added nothing to my message. [7]In fact, it was just the opposite. They recognized the task I had been trusted with. It was the task of preaching the good news to the Gentiles. My task was like Peter's task. He had been trusted with the task of preaching to the Jews. [8]God was working in Peter as an apostle to the Jews. God was also working in me as an apostle to the Gentiles. [9]James, Peter and John are respected as pillars in the church. They recognized the special grace given to me. So they shook my hand and the hand of Barnabas. They wanted to show they accepted us. They agreed that we should go to the Gentiles. They would go to the Jews. [10]They asked only one thing. They wanted us to continue to remember poor people. That was what I had wanted to do all along.

Paul Opposes Peter

[11]When Peter came to Antioch, I told him to his face that I was against what he was doing. He was clearly wrong. [12]He used to eat with the Gentiles. But certain men came from a group sent by James. When they arrived, Peter began to draw back. He separated himself from the Gentiles. That's because he was afraid of the circumcision group sent by James. [13]Peter's actions were

not honest, and other Jews in Antioch joined him. Even Barnabas was led astray.

[14] I saw what they were doing. It was not in line with the truth of the good news. So I spoke to Peter in front of them all. "You are a Jew," I said. "But you live like one who is not. So why do you force Gentiles to follow Jewish ways?"

[15] We are Jews by birth. We are not sinful Gentiles. [16] Here is what we know. No one is made right with God by obeying the law. It is by believing in Jesus Christ. So we too have put our faith in Christ Jesus. This is so we can be made right with God by believing in Christ. We are not made right by obeying the law. That's because no one can be made right with God by obeying the law.

[17] We are seeking to be made right with God through Christ. As we do, what if we find that we who are Jews are also sinners? Does that mean that Christ causes us to sin? Certainly not! [18] Suppose I build again what I had destroyed. Then I would really be breaking the law.

[19] By the law, I died as far as the law is concerned. I died so that I might live for God. [20] I have been crucified with Christ. I don't live any longer, but Christ lives in me. Now I live my life in my body by faith in the Son of God. He loved me and gave himself for me. [21] I do not get rid of the grace of God. What if a person could become right with God by obeying the law? Then Christ died for nothing!

Faith or Obeying the Law

3 You foolish people of Galatia! Who has put you under an evil spell? When I preached, I clearly showed you that Jesus Christ had been nailed to the cross. [2] I would like to learn just one thing from you. Did you receive the Holy Spirit by obeying the law? Or did you receive the Spirit by believing what you heard? [3] Are you so foolish? You began by the Holy Spirit. Are you now trying to finish God's work in you by your own strength? [4] Have you experienced so much for nothing? And was it really for nothing? [5] So I ask you again, how does God give you his Spirit? How does he work miracles among you? Is it by doing what the law says? Or is it by believing what you have heard? [6] In the same way, Abraham "believed God. God

was pleased with Abraham because he believed. So his faith made him right with God." *(Genesis 15:6)*

[7] So you see, those who have faith are children of Abraham. [8] Long ago, Scripture knew that God would make the Gentiles right with himself. He would do this by their faith in him. He announced the good news ahead of time to Abraham. God said, "All nations will be blessed because of you." *(Genesis 12:3; 18:18; 22:18)* [9] So those who depend on faith are blessed along with Abraham. He was the man of faith.

[10] All who depend on obeying the law are under a curse. It is written, "May everyone who doesn't continue to do everything written in the Book of the Law be under God's curse." *(Deuteronomy 27:26)* [11] We know that no one who depends on the law is made right with God. This is because "the one who is right with God will live by faith." *(Habakkuk 2:4)* [12] The law is not based on faith. In fact, it is just the opposite. It teaches that "the person who does these things will live by them." *(Leviticus 18:5)* [13] Christ set us free from the curse of the law. He did it by becoming a curse for us. It is written, "Everyone who is hung on a pole is under God's curse." *(Deuteronomy 21:23)* [14] Christ Jesus set us free so that the blessing given to Abraham would come to the Gentiles through Christ. He did it so that we might receive the promise of the Holy Spirit. The promised Spirit comes by believing in Christ.

The Law and the Promise

[15] Brothers and sisters, let me give you an example from everyday life. No one can get rid of an official agreement between people. No one can add to it. It can't be changed after it has been made. It is the same with God's covenant agreement. [16] The promises were given to Abraham. They were also given to his seed. Scripture does not say, "and to seeds." That means many people. It says, "and to your seed." *(Genesis 12:7; 13:15; 24:7)* That means one person. And that one person is Christ. [17] Here is what I mean. The law came 430 years after the promise. But the law does not get rid of God's covenant and promise. The covenant had already been made by God. So the law does not do away with the promise. [18] The great gift that God has for us does not depend on the law. If it did, it would no longer depend on the

promise. But God gave it to Abraham as a free gift through a promise.

[19]Then why was the law given at all? It was added because of human sin. And it was supposed to control us until the promised Seed had come. The law was given through angels, and a go-between was put in charge of it. [20]A go-between means that there is more than one side to an agreement. But God didn't use a go-between when he made his promise to Abraham.

[21]So is the law opposed to God's promises? Certainly not! What if a law had been given that could give life? Then people could become right with God by obeying the law. [22]But Scripture has locked up everything under the control of sin. It does so in order that what was promised might be given to those who believe. The promise comes through faith in Jesus Christ.

Children of God

[23]Before faith in Christ came, we were guarded by the law. We were locked up until this faith was made known. [24]So the law was put in charge of us until Christ came. He came so that we might be made right with God by believing in Christ. [25]But now faith in Christ has come. So the law is no longer in charge of us.

[26]So in Christ Jesus you are all children of God by believing in Christ. [27]This is because all of you who were baptized into Christ have put on Christ. You have put him on as if he were your clothes. [28]There is no Jew or Gentile. There is no slave or free person. There is no male or female. That's because you are all one in Christ Jesus. [29]You who belong to Christ are Abraham's seed. So you will receive what God has promised.

4 Here is what I have been saying. As long as your own children are young, they are no different from slaves in your house. They are no different, even though they will own all the property. [2]People are in charge of the property. And other people are in charge of the children. The children remain under their care until they become adults. At that time their fathers give them the property. [3]It is the same with us. When we were children, we were slaves to the basic spiritual powers of the world. [4]But then the chosen time came. God sent his Son. A woman gave birth to him. He was born

under the authority of the law. [5]He came to set free those who were under the authority of the law. He wanted us to be adopted as children with all the rights children have. [6]Because you are his children, God sent the Spirit of his Son into our hearts. He is the Holy Spirit. By his power we call God *Abba*. Abba means Father. [7]So you aren't a slave any longer. You are God's child. Because you are his child, God gives you the rights of those who are his children.

Paul's Concern for the Believers in Galatia

[8]At one time you didn't know God. You were slaves to gods that are really not gods at all. [9]But now you know God. Even better, God knows you. So why are you turning back to those weak and worthless powers? Do you want to be slaves to them all over again? [10]You are observing special days and months and seasons and years! [11]I am afraid for you. I am afraid that somehow I have wasted my efforts on you.

[12]I make my appeal to you, brothers and sisters. I'm asking you to become like me. After all, I became like you. You didn't do anything wrong to me. [13]Remember when I first preached the good news to you? Remember I did that because I was sick. [14]And my sickness was hard on you. But you weren't mean to me. You didn't make fun of me. Instead, you welcomed me as if I were an angel of God. You welcomed me as if I were Christ Jesus himself. [15]So why aren't you treating me the same way now? Suppose you could have torn out your own eyes and given them to me. Then you would have done it. I am a witness to this. [16]Have I become your enemy now by telling you the truth?

[17]Those people are trying hard to win you over. But it is not for your good. They want to take you away from us. They want you to commit yourselves to them. [18]It is fine to be committed to something, if the purpose is good. And you shouldn't be committed only when I am with you. You should always be committed. [19]My dear children, I am in pain for you like I was when we first met. I have pain like a woman giving birth. And my pain will continue until Christ makes you like himself. [20]I wish I could be with you now. I wish I could change my tone of voice. As it is, I don't understand you.

Hagar and Sarah

²¹You who want to be under the authority of the law, tell me something. Don't you know what the law says? ²²It is written that Abraham had two sons. The slave woman gave birth to one of them. The free woman gave birth to the other one. ²³Abraham's son by the slave woman was born in the usual way. But his son by the free woman was born because of God's promise.

²⁴These things are examples. The two women stand for two covenants. One covenant comes from Mount Sinai. It gives birth to children who are going to be slaves. It is Hagar. ²⁵Hagar stands for Mount Sinai in Arabia. She stands for the present city of Jerusalem. That's because she and her children are slaves. ²⁶But the Jerusalem that is above is free. She is our mother. ²⁷It is written,

"Be glad, woman,
    you who have never had children.
Shout for joy and cry out loud,
    you who have never had labor pains.
The woman who is all alone has more
        children
    than the woman who has a
        husband."   *(Isaiah 54:1)*

²⁸Brothers and sisters, you are children because of God's promise just as Isaac was. ²⁹At that time, the son born in the usual way tried to hurt the other son. The other son was born by the power of the Holy Spirit. It is the same now. ³⁰But what does Scripture say? "Get rid of the slave woman. Get rid of her son. The slave woman's son will never have a share of the family's property. He'll never share it with the free woman's son." *(Genesis 21:10)* ³¹Brothers and sisters, we are not the slave woman's children. We are the free woman's children.

Christ Sets Us Free

5 Christ has set us free to enjoy our freedom. So remain strong in the faith. Don't let the chains of slavery hold you again.

²Here is what I, Paul, say to you. Don't let yourselves be circumcised. If you do, Christ won't be of any value to you. ³I say it again. Every man who lets himself be circumcised must obey the whole law. ⁴Some of you are trying to be made right with God by obeying the law. You have been separated from Christ. You have fallen away from God's grace. ⁵But we long to be made completely holy because of our faith in Christ. Through the Holy Spirit we wait for this in hope. ⁶Circumcision and uncircumcision aren't worth anything to those who believe in Christ Jesus. The only thing that really counts is faith that shows itself through love.

⁷You were running a good race. Who has kept you from obeying the truth? ⁸The God who chooses you does not keep you from obeying the truth. ⁹You should know that "just a little yeast works its way through the whole batch of dough." ¹⁰The Lord makes me certain that you will see the truth of this. The one who has gotten you all mixed up will have to pay the price. This will happen no matter who has done it. ¹¹Brothers and sisters, I no longer preach that people must be circumcised. If I did, why am I still being opposed? If I preached that, then the cross wouldn't upset anyone. ¹²So then, what about troublemakers who try to get others to be circumcised? I wish they would go the whole way! I wish they would cut off everything that marks them as men!

Living by the Holy Spirit's Power

¹³My brothers and sisters, you were chosen to be free. But don't use your freedom as an excuse to live under the power of sin. Instead, serve one another in love. ¹⁴The whole law is fulfilled by obeying this one command. "Love your neighbor as you love yourself." *(Leviticus 19:18)* ¹⁵If you say or do things that harm one another, watch out! You could end up destroying one another.

¹⁶So I say, live by the Holy Spirit's power. Then you will not do what your desires controlled by sin want you to do. ¹⁷The desires controlled by sin do not want what the Spirit delights in. And the Spirit does not want what the desires controlled by sin delight in. The two are at war with each other. That's why you are not supposed to do whatever you want. ¹⁸But if you are led by the Spirit, you are not under the authority of the law.

¹⁹The result of sin's control in our lives is clear. It includes sexual sins, impure acts and wild living. ²⁰It includes worshiping statues of gods and worshiping evil powers. It also includes hatred and fighting, jealousy and fits of anger. Sinful desire is interested only in getting ahead. It stirs up trouble. It separates people into their own little

WHIT'S WISDOM

Galatians 5:13

Imagine that a prisoner who has been in jail for ten years sits in front of our local judge, Simon Jones. The judge has just come across evidence that the prisoner was never guilty in the first place.

"You can go free!" Judge Jones says.

"No thanks," the prisoner says. "I'll stay in prison. I kind of like the food."

Can you believe it? Who would remain in jail if they have a chance to be free? That scene didn't really happen in Judge Jones' courtroom, but it does happen to people who are imprisoned by their sin. This is what the apostle Paul is talking about when he tells the Galatians, "You were chosen to be free."

It sounds like the Galatians were free in Christ, but they acted like slaves to sin. Before becoming Christians, we're all slaves to sin. We can get caught up in a cycle of bad habits and behaviors and the shame that follows them. That shame often leads to more sin. But when we become Christians, God gives us a way out. We can be free from the chains of sin by giving ourselves over to the holiness of God!

---

groups. [21]It wants what others have. It gets drunk and takes part in wild parties. It does many things of that kind. I warn you now as I did before. People who live like this will not receive God's kingdom.

[22]But the fruit the Holy Spirit produces is love, joy and peace. It is being patient, kind and good. It is being faithful [23]and gentle and having control of oneself. There is no law against things of that kind. [24]Those who belong to Christ Jesus have nailed their sinful desires to his cross. They don't want these things anymore. [25]Since we live by the Spirit, let us keep in step with the Spirit. [26]Let us not become proud. Let us not make each other angry. Let us not want what belongs to others.

ADVENTURES IN ODYSSEY

When Penny was considering Wooton's marriage proposal, both of them had to think about what it meant to be married and what the fruit of the Spirit really means in "Taking the Plunge" (A#59).

REMEMBER THIS

GALATIANS 5:22-23

"The fruit the Holy Spirit produces is love, joy and peace. It is being patient, kind and good. It is being faithful and gentle and having control of oneself."

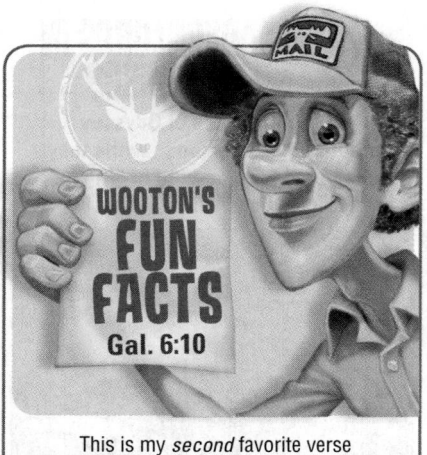

WOOTON'S **FUN FACTS** Gal. 6:10

This is my *second* favorite verse because I love doing good deeds! (Check out Micah 6:8 for my favorite.)

Do Good to Everyone

6 Brothers and sisters, what if someone is caught in a sin? Then you who live by the Spirit should correct that person. Do it in a gentle way. But be careful. You could be tempted too. ²Carry one another's heavy loads. If you do, you will fulfill the law of Christ. ³If anyone thinks they are somebody when they are nobody, they are fooling themselves. ⁴Each person should test their own actions. Then they can take pride in themselves. They won't be comparing themselves to someone else. ⁵Each person should carry their own load. ⁶But those who are taught the word should share all good things with their teacher.

⁷Don't be fooled. You can't outsmart God. A man gathers a crop from what he plants. ⁸Some people plant to please their desires controlled by sin. From these desires they will harvest death. Others plant to please the Holy Spirit. From the Spirit they will harvest eternal life. ⁹Let us not become tired of doing good. At the right time we will gather a crop if we don't give up. ¹⁰So when we can do good to everyone, let us do it. Let's try even harder to do good to the family of believers.

not Circumcision but the new Creation

¹¹Look at the big letters I'm using as I write to you with my own hand!

¹²Some people are worried about how things look on the outside. They are trying to force you to be circumcised. They do it for only one reason. They don't want to suffer by being connected with the cross of Christ. ¹³Even those who are circumcised don't obey the law. But they want you to be

WHIT'S WISDOM

Galatians 6:7

Craig Moorehead was always telling jokes and kids followed him around for a laugh. But one day, he came into Whit's End and sat down at the soda fountain without his usual crowd. I asked him what happened. He said that all the other kids wanted to do was laugh at his jokes. While Craig was sitting there, Tom Riley began eating an orange sherbet when he suddenly thought he found a raspberry seed. I said that it couldn't be: oranges give orange seeds and raspberries give raspberry seeds.

A lot of things work that way . . . like friends. Craig made a whole harvest of friends in Odyssey by being funny. There's nothing wrong with being funny. That was one seed he had planted. But the problem was that he hadn't planted any other seeds. It takes more to be a friend than just making someone laugh. There are all kinds of seeds in friendship. Like encouragement, sympathy, trust, listening to people when they talk, and the list goes on. I asked Craig if he could plant a few other seeds (besides jokes) the next time he was with his friends. Like it says in Galatians 6:7, "A man gathers a crop from what he plants."

CANDID CONVERSATIONS

"May I have your attention?" I shouted as I entered Whit's End. "I've made an important decision. I'm going to wake up earlier so I can read the Bible."

"You're not a morning person," Penny reminded me.

She was right. When my alarm went off at 5:30 a.m., my brain started making excuses about why I *had* to sleep longer. So I asked my friends for help and they all agreed. Penny gave me her super-loud alarm clock to put across the room, so I'd have to climb out of bed to turn it off. If I was still asleep when Wooton came by on his mail route, he'd spray a squirt gun through my window. Every day, when I got to Whit's End, Eugene asked me for a report.

I got soaked by the squirt gun more than a few times. But most days, I got up early and read the Bible. It helped to remember Galatians 6:9: "Let us not become tired of doing good. At the right time we will gather a crop if we don't give up."

ADVENTURES IN ODYSSEY

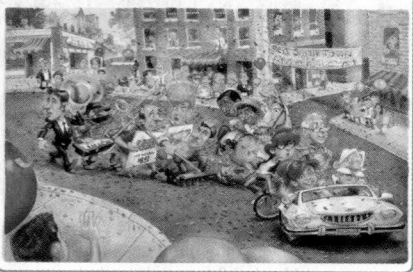

The whole town of Odyssey practiced "doing good" while they competed for an award in "Rights, Wrongs, and Winners" (A#50).

crucified as far as the ways of the world are concerned. [15]Circumcision and uncircumcision don't mean anything. What really counts is that the new creation has come. [16]May peace and mercy be given to all who follow this rule. May peace and mercy be given to the Israel that belongs to God.

[17]From now on, let no one cause trouble for me. My body has marks that show I belong to Jesus.

[18]Brothers and sisters, may the grace of our Lord Jesus Christ be with your spirit. Amen.

WOOTON'S FUN FACTS

Gal. 6:17 In Rome, slaves were marked with their owners' brands. Paul had "marks" that showed he belonged to Jesus; they were scars from whippings and beatings he endured. Turn over to 2 Corinthians 11:24–25 for a list of punishments Paul went through.

circumcised. Then they can brag about what has been done to your body. [14]I never want to brag about anything except the cross of our Lord Jesus Christ. Through that cross the ways of the world have been crucified as far as I am concerned. And I have been

Ephesians

Ephesus was an ancient city within the region of Galatia. We begin our stop there with a question asked by many people: "How much do I have to do in order for God to accept me?" Or as the Philippian jailer asked Paul, "What must I do to be saved?" (Acts 16:30) Some people ask this question in much the same way they might ask a teacher or professor how much work is required in order to get an A in a class or on a test.

We can work hard to make good grades and excel in school. In fact, academic responsibility compels me to remind you that working hard in school is vital for your future. But in Ephesians, the apostle Paul tells us that *our* work has *nothing* to do with God's acceptance. When we're discussing salvation, everything rests on the work Jesus has done for us. Of course, *after* we realize the great price that Jesus paid in order to provide our salvation, we should then want to thank Him with works of devotion and service and love for others.

But Paul is abundantly clear in Ephesians 2:8–10. Salvation is absolutely and completely a gift from God. This letter to the Ephesian church helps explain the depth of the relationships that people can have with God if they stop trying to earn His love and instead live in appreciation for what He has already done for us.

As a point of personal trivia, my wife Katrina counts this one of the most influential books upon her faith. Being uncompromising in her personality, she is fond of the truth contained within this book that encourages us to stand up for what we believe in and the reminder that said strength was given to us by God, our Father.

WHAT'S IT MEAN, EUGENE?

Grace—*Grace* is often defined as God's *unmerited favor*. Everything we have, everything we are, and everything we can ever hope to be comes to us as an unearned *gift* from God. Another way to explain it is that grace is *God giving us what we don't deserve*. As Paul says, "God's grace has saved you because of your faith in Christ. Your salvation doesn't come from anything you do. It is God's gift" (Ephesians 2:8).

1 I, Paul, am writing this letter. I am an apostle of Christ Jesus just as God planned.

I am sending this letter to you, God's holy people in Ephesus. Because you belong to Christ Jesus, you are faithful.

²May God our Father and the Lord Jesus Christ give you grace and peace.

Praise God for His Spiritual Blessings in Christ

³Give praise to the God and Father of our Lord Jesus Christ. He has blessed us with every spiritual blessing. Those blessings come from the heavenly world. They belong to us because we belong to Christ. ⁴God chose us to belong to Christ before the world was created. He chose us to be holy and without blame in his eyes. He loved us. ⁵So he decided long ago to adopt us. He adopted us as his children with all the rights children have. He did it because of what Jesus Christ has done. It pleased God to do it. ⁶All those things bring praise to his glorious grace. God freely gave us his grace because of the One he loves. ⁷We have been set free because of what Christ has done. Because he bled and died our sins have been forgiven. We have been set free because God's grace is so rich. ⁸He poured his grace on us. By giving us great wisdom and understanding, ⁹he showed us the mystery of his plan. It was in keeping with what he wanted to do. It was what he had planned through Christ. ¹⁰It will all come about when history has been completed. God will then bring together all things in heaven and on earth under Christ.

¹¹We were also chosen to belong to him. God decided to choose us long ago in keeping with his plan. He works out everything to fit his plan and purpose. ¹²We were the first to put our hope in Christ. We were chosen to bring praise to his glory. ¹³You also became believers in Christ. That happened when you heard the message of truth. It was the good news about how you could be saved. When you believed, he stamped you with an official mark. That official mark is the Holy Spirit that he promised. ¹⁴The Spirit marks us as God's own. We can now be sure that someday we will receive all that God has promised. That will happen after

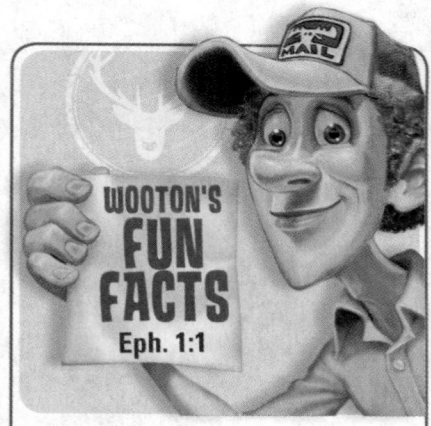

WOOTON'S **FUN FACTS** Eph. 1:1

What modern-day country is Ephesus in? Hint #1: You'll gobble up the answer. Hint #2: Think of the holiday with stuffing and cranberry sauce. Hint #3: Unscramble these letters to find out: RUTYEK.

God sets all his people completely free. All these things will bring praise to his glory.

Paul Prays and Gives Thanks

¹⁵I have heard about your faith in the Lord Jesus. I have also heard about your love for all God's people. That is why ¹⁶I have not stopped thanking God for you. I always remember you in my prayers. ¹⁷I pray to the God of our Lord Jesus Christ. God is the glorious Father. I keep asking him to give you the wisdom and understanding that come from the Holy Spirit. I want you to know God better. ¹⁸I pray that you may understand more clearly. Then you will know the hope God has chosen you to receive. You will know that what God will give his holy people is rich and glorious. ¹⁹And you will know God's great power. It can't be compared with anything else. His power works for us who believe. It is the same mighty strength ²⁰God showed. He showed this when he raised Christ from the dead. God seated him at his right hand in his heavenly kingdom. ²¹There Christ sits far above all who rule and have authority. He also sits far above all powers and kings. He is above every name that is appealed to in this world and in the world to come. ²²God placed all things under Christ's rule. He appointed him to be ruler over everything for the church. ²³The church is Christ's body and is filled by Christ. He fills everything in every way.

God Has Given Us new Life Through Christ

2 You were living in your sins and lawless ways. But in fact you were dead. [2]You used to live as sinners when you followed the ways of this world. You served the one who rules over the spiritual forces of evil. He is the spirit who is now at work in those who don't obey God. [3]At one time we all lived among them. Our desires were controlled by sin. We tried to satisfy what they wanted us to do. We followed our desires and thoughts. God was angry with us like he was with everyone else. That's because of the kind of people we all were. [4]But God loves us deeply. He is full of mercy. [5]So he gave us new life because of what Christ has done. He gave us life even when we were dead in sin. God's grace has saved you. [6]God raised us up with Christ. He has seated us with him in his heavenly kingdom. That's because we belong to Christ Jesus. [7]He has done it to show the riches of his grace for all time to come. His grace can't be compared with anything else. He has shown it by being kind to us. He was kind to us because of what Christ Jesus has done. [8]God's grace has saved you because of your faith in Christ. Your salvation doesn't come from anything you do. It is God's gift. [9]It is not based on anything you have done. No one can brag about earning it. [10]We are God's creation. He created us to belong to Christ Jesus. Now we can do good works. Long ago God prepared these works for us to do.

God's new Family of Jews and Gentiles

[11]You who are not Jews by birth, here is what I want you to remember. You are

CANDID CONVERSATIONS

My life changed a lot when I became Penny's roommate—back before she and Wooton got married. She tended to steal my coffee. She claimed she didn't do it on purpose, but that she wandered into the kitchen in her sleep. She was a "sleep stealer." I thought it would help to label my bags of coffee with pre-made stickers saying, "Property of Connie Kendall." It didn't. So I added exclamation points. That finally worked. I guess the extra exclamation points got through to her sleepy eyes. You might say I'm very possessive of my coffee.

Paul says that God "created us to belong to Christ Jesus." God is possessive of us too. He loves us and doesn't want Satan to have any part of us. He created us as special, unique people because we are important to Him. And when we allow Him to make us His own, Ephesians 2:10 says, "we can do good works."

Think of things in your life that you may be holding back from God. It's time to let Him possess you completely!

REMEMBER THIS

EPHESIANS 2:8-9

"God's grace has saved you because of your faith in Christ. Your salvation doesn't come from anything you do. It is God's gift. It is not based on anything you have done. No one can brag about earning it."

called "uncircumcised" by those who call themselves "circumcised." But they have only been circumcised in their bodies by human hands. [12]Before you believed in Christ, you were separated from him. You were not considered to be citizens of Israel. You were not included in what the covenants promised. You were without hope and without God in the world. [13]At one time you were far away from God. But now you belong to Christ Jesus. He spilled his blood for you. This has brought you near to God.

[14]Christ himself is our peace. He has made Jews and Gentiles into one group

of people. He has destroyed the hatred that was like a wall between us. [15]Through his body on the cross, Christ set aside the law with all its commands and rules. He planned to create one new people out of Jews and Gentiles. He wanted to make peace between them. [16]He planned to bring both Jews and Gentiles back to God as one body. He planned to do this through the cross. On that cross, Christ put to death their hatred toward one another. [17]He came and preached peace to you who were far away. He also preached peace to those who were near. [18]Through Christ we both come to the Father by the power of one Holy Spirit.

[19]So you are no longer outsiders and strangers. You are citizens together with God's people. You are also members of God's family. [20]You are a building that is built on the apostles and prophets. They are the foundation. Christ Jesus himself is the most important stone in the building. [21]The whole building is held together by him. It rises to become a holy temple because it belongs to the Lord. [22]And because you belong to him, you too are being built together. You are being made into a house where God lives through his Spirit.

God's Wonderful Plan for the Gentiles

3 I, Paul, am a prisoner because of Christ Jesus. I am in prison because of my work among you who are Gentiles.

[2]I am sure you have heard that God appointed me to share his grace with you. [3]I'm talking about the mystery God showed me. I have already written a little about it. [4]By reading about this mystery, you will be able to understand what I know. You will know about the mystery of Christ. [5]The mystery was not made known to people of other times. But now the Holy Spirit has made this mystery known to God's holy apostles and prophets. [6]Here is the mystery. Because of the good news, God's promises are for Gentiles as well as for Jews. Both groups are parts of one body. They share in the promise. It belongs to them because they belong to Christ Jesus.

[7]I now serve the good news because God gave me his grace. His power is at work in me. [8]I am by far the least important of all the Lord's holy people. But he

gave me the grace to preach to the Gentiles about the unlimited riches that Christ gives. [9]God told me to make clear to everyone how the mystery came about. In times past it was kept hidden in the mind of God, who created all things. [10]He wanted the rulers and authorities in the heavenly world to come to know his great wisdom. The church would make it known to them. [11]That was God's plan from the beginning. He has fulfilled his plan through Christ Jesus our Lord. [12]Through him and through faith in him we can approach God. We can come to him freely. We can come without fear. [13]So here is what I'm asking you to do. Don't lose hope because I am suffering for you. It will lead to the time when God will give you his glory.

Paul Prays for the Ephesians

[14]I bow in prayer to the Father because of my work among you. [15]From the Father every family in heaven and on earth gets its name. [16]I pray that he will use his glorious riches to make you strong. May his Holy Spirit give you his power deep down inside you. [17]Then Christ will live in your hearts because you believe in him. And I pray that your love will have deep roots. I pray that it will have a strong foundation. [18]May you have power together with all the Lord's holy people to understand Christ's love. May you know how wide and long and high and deep it is. [19]And may you know his love, even though it can't be known completely. Then you will be filled with everything God has for you.

[20]God is able to do far more than we could ever ask for or imagine. He does everything by his power that is working in us. [21]Give him glory in the church and in Christ Jesus. Give him glory through all time and for ever and ever. Amen.

Growing Up Together in the Body of Christ

4 I am a prisoner because of the Lord. So I am asking you to live a life worthy of what God chose you for. [2]Don't be proud at all. Be completely gentle. Be patient. Put up with one another in love. [3]The Holy Spirit makes you one in every way. So try your best to remain as one. Let peace keep you together. [4]There is one body and one Spirit. You were appointed to one hope when

Eph. 4:4–6 There are—count them—seven "ones" in this passage: one body, one Spirit, one hope, one Lord, one faith, one baptism, and one God. Remember how seven is God's number? He likes to use "one," too, especially when talking about Himself. Isn't that one-derful?

you were chosen. ⁵There is one Lord, one faith and one baptism. ⁶There is one God and Father of all. He is over everything. He is through everything. He is in everything.

⁷But each one of us has received a gift of grace. These gifts are given to us by Christ. ⁸That is why Scripture says,

"When he went up to his place on high,
    he took many prisoners.
He gave gifts to his people."

                 (Psalm 68:18)

⁹What does "he went up" mean? It can only mean that he also came down to the lower, earthly places. ¹⁰The one who came down is the same one who went up. He went up higher than all the heavens. He did it in order to fill all creation. ¹¹So Christ himself gave the gift of the apostles to the church. He gave the prophets and those who preach the good news. And he also gave the pastors and teachers as a gift to the church. ¹²He gave all these people so that they might prepare God's people to serve. Then the body of Christ will be built up. ¹³That will continue until we all become one in the faith. We will also become one in the knowledge of God's Son. Then we will be grown up in the faith. We will receive everything that Christ has for us.

¹⁴We will no longer be babies in the faith. We won't be like ships tossed around by the waves. We won't be blown here and there by every new teaching. We won't be blown around by cleverness and tricks. Certain people use them to hide their evil plans. ¹⁵Instead, we will speak the truth in love. So we will grow up in every way to become the body of Christ. Christ is the head of the body. ¹⁶He makes the whole body grow and build itself up in love. Under the control of Christ, each part of the body does its work. It supports the other parts. In that way, the body is joined and held together.

Teachings for Living as Christians

¹⁷Here is what I'm telling you. I am speaking for the Lord as I warn you. You must no longer live as the Gentiles do. Their thoughts don't have any purpose. ¹⁸They can't understand the truth. They are separated from the life of God. That's because they don't know him. And they don't know him because their hearts are stubborn. ¹⁹They have lost all feeling for what is right. So they have given themselves over to all kinds of evil pleasures. They take part in every kind of unclean act. And they are full of greed.

²⁰But that is not the way of life in Christ that you learned about. ²¹You heard about Christ and were taught about life in him. What you learned was the truth about Jesus. ²²You were taught not to live the way you used to. You must get rid of your old way of life. That's because it has been made impure by the desire for things that lead you astray. ²³You were taught to be made new in your thinking. ²⁴You were taught to start living a new life. It is created to be truly good and holy, just as God is.

²⁵So each of you must get rid of your lying. Speak the truth to your neighbor. We are all parts of one body. ²⁶Scripture says, "When you are angry, do not sin." *(Psalm 4:4)* Do not let the sun go down while you are still angry. ²⁷Don't give the devil a chance. ²⁸Anyone who has been stealing must never steal again. Instead, they must work. They must do something useful with their own

REMEMBER THIS

EPHESIANS 4:29

"Don't let any evil talk come out of your mouths. Say only what will help to build others up and meet their needs. Then what you say will help those who listen."

hands. Then they will have something to give to people in need.

²⁹Don't let any evil talk come out of your mouths. Say only what will help to build others up and meet their needs. Then what you say will help those who listen. ³⁰Do not make God's Holy Spirit mourn. The Holy Spirit is the proof that you belong to God. And the Spirit is the proof that God will set you completely free. ³¹Get rid of all hard feelings, anger and rage. Stop all fighting and lying. Don't have anything to do with any kind of hatred. ³²Be kind and tender to one another. Forgive one another, just as God forgave you because of what Christ has done. ¹You are the children that God dearly loves. So follow his example. ²Lead a life of love, just as Christ did. He loved us. He gave himself up for us. He was a sweet-smelling offering and sacrifice to God.

³There should not be even a hint of sexual sin among you. Don't do anything impure. And do not always want more and more. These are not the things God's holy people should do. ⁴There must not be any bad language or foolish talk or dirty jokes. They are out of place. Instead, you should give thanks. ⁵Here is what you can be sure of. Those who give themselves over to sexual sins are lost. So are people whose lives are impure. The same is true of those who always want more and more. People who do these things might as well worship statues of gods. No one who does them will receive a share in the kingdom of Christ and of God. ⁶Don't let anyone fool you with worthless words. People who say things like that aren't obeying God. He is angry with them. ⁷So don't go along with people like that.

⁸At one time you were in the dark. But now you are in the light because of what the Lord has done. Live like children of the light. ⁹The light produces what is completely good, right and true. ¹⁰Find out what pleases the Lord. ¹¹Have nothing to do with the acts of darkness. They don't produce anything good. Show what they are really like. ¹²It is shameful even to talk about what people who don't obey do in secret. ¹³But everything the light shines on can be seen. And everything that the light shines on becomes a light. ¹⁴That is why it is said,

WHIT'S WISDOM

Ephesians 5:8–11

The other day, Connie saw Detective Harlow Doyle on the street at night. She asked him, "What are you looking for?"

"I dropped a quarter over there," Harlow said, pointing down the street.

"If you dropped it over *there*, then why are you looking over *here*?" she asked.

"Because the light is better over here," Harlow said.

Yes, Harlow had it wrong, but when Connie told me the story, I started thinking about light and darkness. Harlow was looking for something in the light, even though what he really wanted was in the dark. Before we are Christians, it's the opposite: we're looking in the darkness even though what we really want is in the light.

Jesus tells us that those who follow Him will never walk in darkness because He is "the light of the world" (John 8:12). And Ephesians 5:9 says, "The light produces what is completely good, right and true." So why would we ever choose to look in darkness again? Think about the good, right, and true things in your life. And think about how you can live as a child of the light!

"Wake up, sleeper.
      Rise from the dead.
      Then Christ will shine on you."

[15]So be very careful how you live. Do not live like people who aren't wise. Live like people who are wise. [16]Make the most of every opportunity. The days are evil. [17]So don't be foolish. Instead, understand what the Lord wants. [18]Don't fill yourself up with wine. Getting drunk will lead to wild living. Instead, be filled with the Holy Spirit. [19]Speak to one another with psalms, hymns and songs from the Spirit. Sing and make music from your heart to the Lord. [20]Always give thanks to God the Father for everything. Give thanks to him in the name of our Lord Jesus Christ.

Teachings for Christian Families

[21]Follow the lead of one another because of your respect for Christ.

[22]Wives, follow the lead of your own husbands as you follow the Lord. [23]The husband is the head of the wife, just as Christ is the head of the church. The church is Christ's body. He is its Savior. [24]The church follows the lead of Christ. In the same way, wives should follow the lead of their husbands in everything.

[25]Husbands, love your wives. Love them just as Christ loved the church. He gave himself up for her. [26]He did it to make her holy. He made her clean by washing her with water and the word. [27]He did it to bring her to himself as a brightly shining church. He wants a church that has no stain or wrinkle or any other flaw. He wants a church that is holy and without blame. [28]In the same way, husbands should love their wives. They should love them as they love their own bodies. Any man who loves his wife loves himself. [29]After all, no one ever hated their own body. Instead, they feed and care for their body. And this is what Christ does for the church. [30]We are parts of his body. [31]Scripture says, "That's why a man will leave his father and mother and be joined to his wife. The two will become one." (Genesis 2:24) [32]That is a deep mystery. But I'm talking about Christ and the church. [33]A husband also must love his wife. He must love her just as he loves himself. And a wife must respect her husband.

6 Children, obey your parents as believers in the Lord. Obey them because it's the right thing to do. [2]Scripture says, "Honor your father and mother." That is the first commandment that has a promise. [3]"Then things will go well with you. You will live a long time on the earth." (Deuteronomy 5:16)

[4]Fathers, don't make your children angry. Instead, instruct them and teach them the ways of the Lord as you raise them.

[5]Slaves, obey your masters here on earth. Respect them and honor them with a heart that is true. Obey them just as you would obey Christ. [6]Don't obey them only to please them when they are watching. Do it because you are slaves of Christ. Be sure your heart does what God wants. [7]Serve your masters with all your heart. Work as serving the Lord and not as serving people. [8]You know that the Lord will give each person a reward. He will give it to them in keeping with the good they do. It doesn't matter whether they are a slave or not.

[9]Masters, treat your slaves in the same way. When you warn them, don't be too hard on them. You know that the God who is their Master and yours is in heaven. And he treats everyone the same.

God's Armor for Believers

[10]Finally, let the Lord make you strong. Depend on his mighty power. [11]Put on all of God's armor. Then you can remain strong against the devil's evil plans. [12]Our fight is not against human beings. It is against the rulers, the authorities and the powers of this dark world. It is against the spiritual forces of evil in the heavenly world. [13]So put on all of God's armor. Evil days will come. But you will be able to stand up to anything. And after you have done everything you can, you will still be standing. [14]So remain strong in the faith. Put the belt of truth around your waist. Put the armor of godliness on your chest. [15]Wear on your feet what will prepare you to tell the good news of peace. [16]Also, pick

REMEMBER THIS

EPHESIANS 6:12

"Our fight is not against human beings. It is against the rulers, the authorities and the powers of this dark world. It is against the spiritual forces of evil in the heavenly world."

to know how we are. And I want him to encourage you.

²³May God the Father and the Lord Jesus Christ give peace to the brothers and sisters. May they also give the believers love and faith.

²⁴May grace be given to everyone who loves our Lord Jesus Christ with a love that will never die.

up the shield of faith. With it you can put out all the flaming arrows of the evil one. ¹⁷Put on the helmet of salvation. And take the sword of the Holy Spirit. The sword is God's word.

¹⁸At all times, pray by the power of the Spirit. Pray all kinds of prayers. Be watchful, so that you can pray. Always keep on praying for all the Lord's people. ¹⁹Pray also for me. Pray that whenever I speak, the right words will be given to me. Then I can be bold as I tell the mystery of the good news. ²⁰Because of the good news, I am being held by chains as the Lord's messenger. So pray that I will be bold as I preach the good news. That's what I should do.

Final Greetings

²¹Tychicus is a dear brother. He is faithful in serving the Lord. He will tell you everything about me. Then you will know how I am and what I am doing. ²²That's why I am sending him to you. I want you

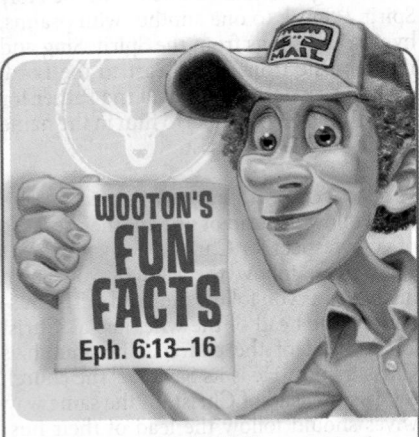

A Roman soldier's shield was made of two oval pieces of wood. They were glued together and then covered in leather. Finally, the shield was decorated. A typical shield weighed twenty-two pounds. This sounds like a craft project that Penny would love. I think I'll build a shield with her tonight.

Philippians

We now journey across the Aegean Sea! We move from two letters written to ancient regions of Turkey to one written to a place in ancient Greece: the city of Philippi. Paul's letter to this church is filled with encouragement, thanksgiving, appreciation for his friends, and all sorts of other positive themes. You might wonder about Paul's whereabouts as he wrote a letter filled with such joy. Was he on a Mediterranean cruise? Vacationing in the mountains? Celebrating with friends? To put it succinctly: No. Paul wrote this inspiring letter from prison (1:13–14).

Apart from what Paul actually *says* through the text of his letter, his spirit demonstrates that we need not let our circumstances determine how we feel. If we stay focused on our relationship with God and remain thankful for what He does for us, He can provide joy in any situation.

In addition, what Paul *does* say is inspiring. He reminds his readers that God is always working in us to make us better and stronger people (1:3–6). He reminds us that getting along with one another is not as difficult if we remember what Jesus has done for us and become humble in the same manner that He was (2:1–11). He likens the Christian life to a race with a prize at the finish for those who run faithfully (3:12–14). As we run, we should keep our minds focused on only positive things (4:8–9). Such an outlook results not only in joy, but in peace of mind as well (4:4–7).

WHAT'S IT MEAN, EUGENE?

Advent—A *coming.* The Bible states that Christ *comes to us*—in fact, we love Him only because He first loved us. There is, of course, also the season known as Advent, which precedes and leads up to Christmas. During *Advent* we celebrate Jesus *first coming* as the Baby in the manger. I grew up knowing about Advent but never truly understood the significance of the season until my first Advent in Odyssey.

1 We, Paul and Timothy, are writing this letter. We serve Christ Jesus.

We are sending this letter to you, all God's holy people in Philippi. You belong to Christ Jesus. We are also sending this letter to your leaders and deacons.

²May God our Father and the Lord Jesus Christ give you grace and peace.

Paul Prays and Gives Thanks

³I thank my God every time I remember you. ⁴In all my prayers for all of you, I always pray with joy. ⁵I am happy because you have joined me in spreading the good news. You have done so from the first day

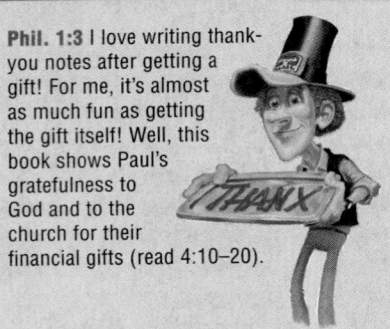

Phil. 1:3 I love writing thank-you notes after getting a gift! For me, it's almost as much fun as getting the gift itself! Well, this book shows Paul's gratefulness to God and to the church for their financial gifts (read 4:10–20).

CANDID CONVERSATIONS

I liked to surprise my mom on Mother's Day. One year, I planned a shopping spree at the mall. Another time, I signed us up for an all-day hike. But I was so determined to keep it a surprise that I forgot to tell my mom to wear hiking boots! She didn't get very far up the mountain in her work heels that time.

Then there was the boring Mother's Day when I forgot to make plans. Mom and I ended up eating lunch at Trickle Lake. We dipped our toes in the water and looked through old photos together. Later, I bought her a card and wrote down all the things I appreciate about her. My mom loved it and said it was the best Mother's Day ever!

In Philippians 1:3, the apostle Paul writes, "I thank my God every time I remember you." That's exactly how I felt about my mom. Now she's gone and I still think that way! Maybe you want to take time for no special reason today to thank your mom for all she does for you!

until now. ⁶God began a good work in you. And I am sure that he will carry it on until it is completed. That will be on the day Christ Jesus returns.

⁷It is right for me to feel this way about all of you. I love you with all my heart. I may be held by chains, or I may be standing up for the truth of the good news. Either way, all of you share in God's grace together with me. ⁸God is my witness that I long for all of you. I love you with the love that Christ Jesus gives.

⁹I pray that your love will grow more and more. And let it be based on knowledge and understanding. ¹⁰Then you will be able to know what is best. Then you will be pure and without blame for the day that Christ returns. ¹¹You will be filled with the fruit of right living produced by Jesus Christ. All these things bring glory and praise to God.

Paul Spreads the Good News While in Prison

¹²Brothers and sisters, here is what I want you to know. What has happened to me has actually helped to spread the good

ADVENTURES IN ODYSSEY

Philippians 1:6 says God gives us our talents, but that doesn't mean we will always be successful in using them. After losing continually at chess, Eugene was reminded of this in "Poor Loser" (A#30).

news. [13]One thing has become clear. I am being held by chains because I am a witness for Christ. All the palace guards and everyone else know it. [14]And because I am a prisoner, most of the believers have become bolder in the Lord. They now dare even more to preach the good news without fear.

[15]It's true that some preach about Christ because they are jealous. But others preach about Christ to help me in my work. [16]The last group acts out of love. They know I have been put here to be a witness for the good news. [17]But the others preach about Christ only to get ahead. They preach Christ for the wrong reasons. They think they can stir up trouble for me while I am being held by chains. [18]But what does it matter? Here is the important thing. Whether for right or wrong reasons, Christ is being preached about. That makes me very glad.

And I will continue to be glad. [19]I know that you are praying for me. I also know that God will give me the Spirit of Jesus Christ to help me. So no matter what happens, I'm sure I will still be set free. [20]I completely expect and hope that I won't be ashamed in any way. I'm sure I will be brave enough. Now as always Christ will receive glory because of what happens to me. He will receive glory whether I live or die. [21]For me, life finds all its meaning in Christ.

Death also has its benefits. [22]Suppose I go on living in my body. Then I will be able to carry on my work. It will bear a lot of fruit. But what should I choose? I don't know! [23]I can't decide between the two. I long to leave this world and be with Christ. That is better by far. [24]But it is more important for you that I stay alive. [25]I'm sure of this. So I know I will remain with you. And I will continue with all of you to help you grow in your faith. I will also continue to help you be joyful in what you have been taught. [26]I'm sure I will be with you again. Then you will be able to boast in Christ Jesus even more because of me.

Living to Honor the Good News

[27]No matter what happens, live in a way that brings honor to the good news about Christ. Then I will know that you remain strong together in the one Spirit. I will know this if I come and see you or only hear about you. I will know that you work together as one person. I will know that you work to spread the teachings about the good news. [28]So don't be afraid in any way of those who oppose you. This will show them that they will be destroyed and that you will be saved. That's what God will do. [29]Here is what he has given you to do for Christ. You must not only believe in him. You must also suffer for him. [30]You are going through the same struggle you saw me go through. As you have heard, I am still struggling.

Being Humble Like Christ

2 So does belonging to Christ help you in any way? Does his love comfort you at all? Do you share anything in common because of the Holy Spirit? Has Christ ever been gentle and loving toward you? [2]If any of these things has happened to you, then agree with one another. Have the same love. Be one in spirit and in the way you think and act. By doing this, you will make my joy complete. [3]Don't do anything only to get ahead. Don't do it because you are proud. Instead, be humble. Value others more than yourselves. [4]None of you should look out just for your own good. Each of you should also look out for the good of others.

[5]As you deal with one another, you should think and act as Jesus did.

Whit saw the importance of looking out for the good of others (Philippians 2:4) in "Silent Night" (A#45).

⁶ In his very nature he was God.
 Jesus was equal with God. But Jesus didn't take advantage of that fact.
⁷ Instead, he made himself nothing.
 He did this by taking on the nature of a servant.
 He was made just like human beings.
⁸ He appeared as a man.
 He was humble and obeyed God completely.
 He did this even though it led to his death.
 Even worse, he died on a cross!
⁹ So God lifted him up to the highest place.
 God gave him the name that is above every name.
¹⁰ When the name of Jesus is spoken, everyone will kneel down to worship him.
 Everyone in heaven and on earth and under the earth will kneel down to worship him.
¹¹ Everyone's mouth will say that Jesus Christ is Lord.
 And God the Father will receive the glory.

Live Without Complaining

¹²My dear friends, you have always obeyed God. You obeyed while I was with you. And you have obeyed even more while I am not with you. So continue to work out your own salvation. Do it with fear and trembling. ¹³God is working in you. He wants your plans and your acts to fulfill his good purpose.

¹⁴Do everything without complaining or arguing. ¹⁵Then you will be pure and without blame. You will be children of God without fault among sinful and evil people. Then you will shine among them like stars in the sky. ¹⁶You will shine as you hold on tight to the word of life. Then I will be able to boast about you on the day Christ returns. I can be happy that I didn't run or work for nothing. ¹⁷But my life might even be poured out like a drink offering on your sacrifices. I'm talking about the way you serve because you believe. Even so, I am glad. I am joyful with all of you. ¹⁸So you too should be glad and joyful with me.

Timothy and Epaphroditus

¹⁹I hope to send Timothy to you soon if the Lord Jesus allows it. Then I will be encouraged when I receive news about you. ²⁰I have no one else like Timothy. He will truly care about how you are doing. ²¹All the others are looking out for their own interests. They are not looking out for the interests of Jesus Christ. ²²But you know that Timothy has proved himself. He has served with me like a son with his father in spreading the good news. ²³So I hope to send him as soon as I see how things go with me. ²⁴And I'm sure I myself will come soon if the Lord allows it.

²⁵But I think it's necessary to send Epaphroditus back to you. He is my brother in the Lord. He is a worker and a soldier of Christ together with me. He is also your messenger. You sent him to take care of my needs. ²⁶He longs for all of you. He is troubled because you heard he was sick. ²⁷He was very sick. In fact, he almost died. But God had mercy on him. He also had mercy on me. God spared me sadness after sadness. ²⁸So I want even more to send him to you. Then when you see him again, you will be glad. And I won't worry so much. ²⁹So then, welcome him as a brother in the Lord with great joy. Honor people like him. ³⁰He almost died for the work of Christ. He put his life in danger to make up for the help you yourselves couldn't give me.

Do Not Trust in Who You Are or What You Can Do

3 Further, my brothers and sisters, be joyful because you belong to the Lord! It is no trouble for me to write about some important matters to you again. If you know about them, you will have a safe path to follow. ²Watch out for those dogs. They are people who do evil things. When they circumcise, it is nothing more than a useless cutting of the body. ³But we have been truly circumcised. We serve God by the power of his Spirit. We boast about what Christ Jesus has done. We don't put our trust in who we are or what we can do. ⁴I have many reasons to trust in who I am and what I have done. Someone else may think they have reasons to trust in these things. But I have even more.

⁵I was circumcised on the eighth day. I am part of the people of Israel. I am from the tribe of Benjamin. I am a pure Hebrew. As far as the law is concerned, I am a Pharisee. ⁶As far as being committed is concerned, I opposed and attacked the church. As far as keeping the law is concerned, I kept it perfectly.

⁷I thought things like that were really something great. But now I consider them to be nothing because of Christ. ⁸Even more, I consider everything to be nothing compared to knowing Christ Jesus my Lord. To know him is worth much more than anything else. Because of him I have lost everything. But I consider all of it to be garbage so I can know Christ better. ⁹I want to be joined to him. Being right with God does not come from my obeying the law. It comes because I believe in Christ. It comes from God because of faith. ¹⁰I want to know Christ better. Yes, I want to know the power that raised him from the dead. I want to join him in his sufferings. I want to become like him by sharing in his death. ¹¹Then by God's grace I will rise from the dead.

¹²I have not yet received all these things. I have not yet reached my goal. Christ Jesus took hold of me so that I could reach that goal. So I keep pushing myself forward to reach it. ¹³Brothers and sisters, I don't consider that I have taken hold of it yet. But here is the one thing I do. I forget what is behind me. I push hard toward what is ahead of me. ¹⁴I push myself forward toward the goal to win the prize. God has appointed me to win it. The heavenly prize is Christ Jesus himself.

Following Paul's Example

¹⁵So all of us who are grown up in the faith should see things this way. Maybe you think differently about something. But God will make it clear to you. ¹⁶Only let us live up to what we have already reached.

¹⁷Brothers and sisters, join together in following my example. You have us as a model. So pay close attention to those who live as we do. ¹⁸I have told you these things many times before. Now I tell you again with tears in my eyes. Many people live like enemies of the cross of Christ. ¹⁹The only thing they have coming to them is death. Their stomach is their god. They brag about what they should be ashamed of. They think only about earthly things. ²⁰But we are citizens of heaven. And we can hardly wait for a Savior from there. He is the Lord Jesus Christ. ²¹He has the power to bring everything under his control. By his power he will change our earthly bodies. They will become like his glorious body.

Remain Strong in the Lord

4 My brothers and sisters, in this way remain strong in the Lord. I love you and long for you. Dear friends, you are my joy and my crown.

²Here is what I'm asking Euodia and Syntyche to do. I'm asking them to work together in the Lord. That's because they both belong to the Lord. ³My true companion, here is what I ask you to do. Help these women, because they have served at my side. They have worked with me to spread the good news. So have Clement and the rest of those who have worked together

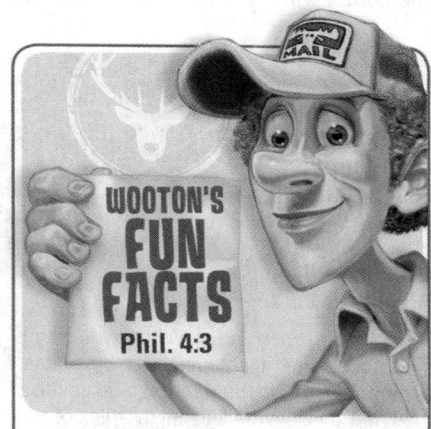

WOOTON'S
FUN
FACTS
Phil. 4:3

The Book of Life is mentioned here and in Daniel, Psalms, and Revelation. Even Moses knew about it. See Exodus 32:31–33. The Book lists the names of those who will live with God forever. I'm so glad that my name is in there!

aDveNtures iN ODYSSeY

Connie, Bernard, Tom, and Whit had to ask and pray for Eugene's health when he returned to Odyssey in "A Most Intriguing Question" (A#44).

with me. Their names are all written in the book of life.

Final Commands

[4]Always be joyful because you belong to the Lord. I will say it again. Be joyful! [5]Let

REMEMBER THIS

PHILIPPIANS 4:6-7

"Don't worry about anything. No matter what happens, tell God about everything. Ask and pray, and give thanks to him. Then God's peace will watch over your hearts and your minds. He will do this because you belong to Christ Jesus."

everyone know how gentle you are. The Lord is coming soon. [6]Don't worry about anything. No matter what happens, tell God about everything. Ask and pray, and give thanks to him. [7]Then God's peace will watch over your hearts and your minds. He will do this because you belong to Christ Jesus. God's peace can never be completely understood.

[8]Finally, my brothers and sisters, always think about what is true. Think about what is noble, right and pure. Think about what is lovely and worthy of respect. If anything is excellent or worthy of praise, think about those kinds of things. [9]Do what you have learned or received or heard from me. Follow my example. The God who gives peace will be with you.

WHIT'S WISDOM

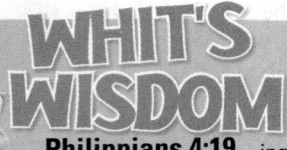

Philippians 4:19

Do you know anyone who is rich? When you think of riches, you might imagine a big house, a nice car, or money to take expensive trips. In Odyssey, the kids might think of the people who live on Chatwick Hill. But what makes someone rich?

Before the apostle Paul met Jesus, he was a powerful, wealthy Pharisee. Then he became a missionary for Jesus. He lost his position, power, and all of his old friends. He lived on the road, poor and in trouble more often than not. He even ended up in prison a few times. If you think being rich means having a big house or lots of money, Paul wasn't rich.

But listen to what Paul writes in Philippians 4:19: "My God will meet all your needs. He will meet them in keeping with his wonderful riches. These riches come to you because you belong to Christ Jesus." When Paul mentions "riches," he's not talking about cars, houses, and big screen TVs. He's talking about the richness of being children of God. We are "rich" when we have faith in a perfect, loving God who will supply all our needs.

Do you know anyone who is rich? If you follow Jesus, you do. *You* are rich!

REMEMBER THIS

PHILIPPIANS 4:8

"Finally, my brothers and sisters, always think about what is true. Think about what is noble, right and pure. Think about what is lovely and worthy of respect. If anything is excellent or worthy of praise, think about those kinds of things."

Paul Gives Thanks for the Philippians' Gifts

[10]At last you are concerned about me again. That makes me very happy. We belong to the Lord. I know that you were concerned. But you had no chance to show it. [11]I'm not saying this because I need anything. I have learned to be content no matter what happens to me. [12]I know what it's like not to have what I need. I also know what it's like to have more than I need. I have learned the secret of being content no matter what happens. I am content whether I am well fed or hungry. I am content whether I have more than enough or not enough. [13]I can do all this by the power of Christ. He gives me strength.

[14]But it was good of you to share in my troubles. [15]And you believers at Philippi know what happened when I left Macedonia. Not one church helped me in the matter of giving and receiving. You were the only one that did. That was in the early days when you first heard the good news. [16]Even when I was in Thessalonica, you sent me help when I needed it. And you did it more than once. [17]It is not that I want your gifts. What I really want is what is best for you. [18]I have received my full pay and have more than enough. I have everything I need. That's because Epaphroditus brought me the gifts you sent. They are a sweet-smelling offering. They are a gift that God accepts. He is pleased with it. [19]My God will meet all your needs. He will meet them in keeping with his wonderful riches. These riches come to you because you belong to Christ Jesus.

[20]Give glory to our God and Father for ever and ever. Amen.

Final Greetings

[21]Greet all God's people. They belong to Christ Jesus.

The brothers and sisters who are with me send greetings.

[22]All God's people here send you greetings. Most of all, those who live in the palace of Caesar send you greetings.

[23]May the grace of the Lord Jesus Christ be with your spirit. Amen.

Colossians

Now our journey takes us *back* across the sea to the city of Colossae. Evidence suggests that the apostle Paul never personally preached here (2:1). Most likely, the founder and pastor of the Colossian church was a local man named Epaphras (1:7; 4:12). But Paul was glad to hear that the church had spread to yet another city. He fully endorsed the ministry of Epaphras, who also appears in the book of Philemon.

However, all was not well in Colossae. Why? The church was being affected by false teachers (2:8). Paul never says exactly who they were, but he provides several clues as to their corrupted teachings. They were putting undue emphasis on feasts and special occasions. They were worshiping angels. And they practiced extreme self-denial and missed out on many of God's blessings (2:16–23).

Therefore, Paul thoroughly emphasized the importance of Jesus above everything and everyone else (1:15–23). He challenged his readers to get their priorities in proper order (3:1–17). And he laid out some basic rules to put those priorities into practice in daily life (3:18–4:1).

The church today is just as likely as the Colossian church to be influenced by false teachings. Colossians is a good book to read and help us challenge ourselves to always put Jesus first. When we do that, we automatically begin to treat one another with more love and respect (4:2–6).

WHAT'S IT MEAN, EUGENE?

Baptism—A *sacrament* of the church in which Christians *identify* with Jesus Christ in both His death and His resurrection. Different churches employ varying forms of baptism, but all of them use water in one way or another. Being immersed *under* the water symbolizes our *dying with Christ*. Likewise, emerging *up* out of the water symbolizes *being raised to new life in Him*.

1 I, Paul, am writing this letter. I am an apostle of Christ Jesus just as God planned. Our brother Timothy joins me in writing.

[2] We are sending this letter to you, our brothers and sisters in Colossae. You belong to Christ. You are holy and faithful.

May God our Father give you grace and peace.

Paul Prays and Gives Thanks

[3] We always thank God, the Father of our Lord Jesus Christ, when we pray for you. [4] We thank him because we have heard about your faith in Christ Jesus. We have also heard that you love all God's people. [5] Your faith and love are based on the hope you have. What you hope for is stored up for you in heaven. You have already heard about it. You were told about it when the true message was given to you. I'm talking about the good news [6] that has come to you. In the same way, the good news is bearing fruit. It is bearing fruit and growing all over the world. It has been doing that among you since the day you heard it. That is when you really understood God's grace. [7] You learned the good news from Epaphras. He is dear to us. He serves Christ together with us. He faithfully works for Christ and for us among you. [8] He also told us about your love that comes from the Holy Spirit.

[9] That's why we have not stopped praying for you. We have been praying for you since the day we heard about you. We keep asking God to fill you with the knowledge of what he wants. We pray he will give you the wisdom and understanding that the Spirit gives. [10] Then you will be able to lead a life that is worthy of the Lord. We pray that you will please him in every way. So we want you to bear fruit in every good thing you do. We pray that you will grow to know God better. [11] We want you to be very strong, in keeping with his glorious power. We want you to be patient. We pray that you will never give up. [12] We want you to give thanks with joy to the Father. He has made you fit to have what he will give to all his holy people. You will all receive a share in the kingdom of light. [13] He has saved us from the kingdom of darkness. He has brought us into the kingdom of the Son he loves. [14] Because of what the Son has done,

we have been set free. Because of him, all our sins have been forgiven.

The Son of God Is Better Than Everything Else

[15] The Son is the exact likeness of God, who can't be seen. The Son is first, and he is over all creation. [16] All things were created in him. He created everything in heaven and on earth. He created everything that can be seen and everything that can't be seen. He created kings, powers, rulers and authorities. All things have been created by him and for him. [17] Before anything was created, he was already there. He holds everything together. [18] And he is the head of the body, which is the church. He is the beginning. He is the first to be raised from the dead. That happened so that he would be far above everything. [19] God was pleased to have his whole nature living in Christ. [20] God was pleased to bring all things back to himself. That's because of what Christ has done. These things include everything on earth and in heaven. God made peace through Christ's blood, by his death on the cross.

[21] At one time you were separated from God. You were enemies in your minds because of your evil ways. [22] But because Christ died, God has brought you back to himself. Christ's death has made you holy in God's sight. So now you don't have any flaw. You are free from blame. [23] But you must keep your faith steady and firm. You must not move away from the hope the good news holds out to you. This is the good news that you heard. It has been preached to every creature under heaven. I, Paul, now serve the good news.

Paul's Work for the Church

[24] I am happy because of what I am suffering for you. My suffering joins with and continues the sufferings of Christ. I suffer for his body, which is the church. [25] I serve the church. God appointed me to bring the

complete word of God to you. ²⁶That word contains the mystery that has been hidden for many ages. But now it has been made known to the Lord's people. ²⁷God has chosen to make known to them the glorious riches of that mystery. He has made it known among the Gentiles. And here is what it is. Christ is in you. He is your hope of glory.

²⁸Christ is the one we preach about. With all the wisdom we have, we warn and teach everyone. When we bring them to God, we want them to be like Christ. We want them to be grown up as people who belong to Christ. ²⁹That's what I'm working for. I work hard with all the strength of Christ. His strength works powerfully in me.

2 I want you to know how hard I am working for you. I'm concerned for those who are in Laodicea. I'm also concerned for everyone who has not met me in person. ²My goal is that their hearts may be encouraged and strengthened. I want them to be joined together in love. Then their understanding will be rich and complete. They will know the mystery of God. That mystery is Christ. ³All the treasures of wisdom and knowledge are hidden in him. ⁴But I don't want anyone to fool you with words that only sound good. ⁵So even though I am away from you in body, I am with you in spirit. And I am glad to see that you are controlling yourselves. I am happy that your faith in Christ is so strong.

Having All Things in Christ

⁶You received Christ Jesus as Lord. So keep on living your lives in him. ⁷Have your roots in him. Build yourselves up in him. Grow strong in what you believe, just as you were taught. Be more thankful than ever before.

⁸Make sure no one controls you. They will try to control you by using false reasoning that has no meaning. Their ideas depend on human teachings. They also depend on the basic spiritual powers of this world. They don't depend on Christ.

⁹God's whole nature is living in Christ in human form. ¹⁰Because you belong to Christ, you have been made complete. He is the ruler over every power and authority. ¹¹When you received Christ, your circumcision was not done by human hands. Instead, your circumcision was done by Christ. He put away the person you used to be. At that time, sin's power ruled over you. ¹²When you were baptized, you were buried together with Christ. And you were raised to life together with him when you were baptized. You were raised to life by believing in God's work. God himself raised Jesus from the dead.

¹³At one time you were dead in your sins. Your desires controlled by sin were not circumcised. But God gave you new life together with Christ. He forgave us all our sins. ¹⁴He wiped out what the law said that we owed. The law stood against us. It judged us. But he has taken it away and

WHIT'S WISDOM
Colossians 2:6–7

The other day, it was what you might call a blustery day in Odyssey. Connie looked out the window at the trees in McAlister Park and said, "It's amazing that those trees don't fall over!"

Eugene immediately stepped forward to explain everything he knew about root systems . . . which took quite a while. He said, "In the case of those hickory trees, the root system under the ground is likely just as large as the branches above ground!"

Eugene went on, and it got me thinking about roots too. For something as large as those hickory trees to stand and grow, Eugene was right. They had to be firmly rooted.

In Colossians 2 the apostle Paul explains that we need to have our roots in Jesus. When we trust in Jesus, that's like being planted *in* Him. Growing strong in Him sounds a lot like those hickory trees, doesn't it?

When you see a beautiful tree standing strong against the wind, think about your roots. Being firmly planted in Jesus will help you stand up against anything that pushes against your faith.

nailed it to the cross. ¹⁵He took away the weapons of the powers and authorities. He made a public show of them. He won the battle over them by dying on the cross.

Freedom From Human Rules

¹⁶So don't let anyone judge you because of what you eat or drink. Don't let anyone judge you about holy days. I'm talking about special feasts and New Moons and Sabbath days. ¹⁷They are only a shadow of the things to come. But what is real is found in Christ. ¹⁸Some people enjoy pretending they aren't proud. They worship angels. But don't let people like that judge you. These people tell you every little thing about what they have seen. They are proud of their useless ideas. That's because their minds are not guided by the Holy Spirit. ¹⁹They aren't connected anymore to the head, who is Christ. But the whole body grows from the head. The muscles and tendons hold the body together. And God causes it to grow.

²⁰Some people still follow the basic spiritual powers of the world. But you died with Christ as far as these powers are concerned. So why do you act as if you still belong to the world? Here are the rules you follow. ²¹"Do not handle! Do not taste! Do not touch!" ²²Rules like these are about things that will pass away soon. They are based on merely human rules and teachings. ²³It is true that these rules seem wise. Because of them, people give themselves over to their own kind of worship. They pretend they are humble. They treat their bodies very badly. But rules like these don't help. They don't stop people from chasing after sinful pleasures.

Teachings About Holy Living

3 You have been raised up with Christ. So think about things that are in heaven. That is where Christ is. He is sitting at God's right hand. ²Think about things that are in heaven. Don't think about things that are only on earth. ³You died. Now your life is hidden with Christ in God. ⁴Christ is your life. When he appears again, you also will appear with him in heaven's glory.

⁵So put to death anything that comes from sinful desires. Get rid of sexual sins and impure acts. Don't let your feelings get out of control. Remove from your life all evil desires. Stop always wanting more

REMEMBER THIS

COLOSSIANS 3:2

"Think about things that are in heaven. Don't think about things that are only on earth."

and more. You might as well be worshiping statues of gods. ⁶God's anger is going to come because of these things. ⁷That's the way you lived at one time in your life. ⁸But now here are the kinds of things you must also get rid of. You must get rid of anger, rage, hate and lies. Let no dirty words come out of your mouths. ⁹Don't lie to one another. You have gotten rid of your old way of life and its habits. ¹⁰You have started living a new life. Your knowledge of how that life should have the Creator's likeness is being made new. ¹¹Here there is no Gentile or Jew. There is no difference between those who are circumcised and those who are not. There is no rude outsider, or even a Scythian. There is no slave or free person. But Christ is everything. And he is in everything.

¹²You are God's chosen people. You are holy and dearly loved. So put on tender mercy and kindness as if they were your

Col. 3:8 Old-fashioned words to show anger or surprise include "as I live and breathe," and "great Scott!" Penny likes to say "fiddlesticks," and sometimes I say, "Oh, balderdash!" It's good to have words to say that aren't dirty. Keep your mouth clean by brushing, flossing, and avoiding harsh language.

The town of Odyssey learned about "putting up with one another" (Colossians 3:13) in "The Ties that Bind" (A#58).

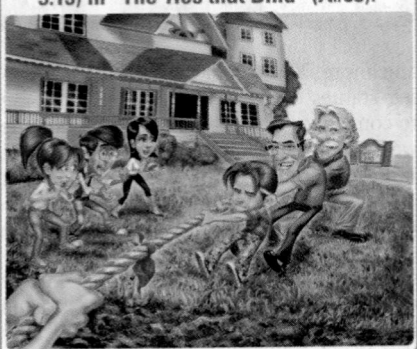

with all your heart. Work as if you were working for the Lord, not for human masters. ²⁴Work because you know that you will finally receive as a reward what the Lord wants you to have. You are slaves of the Lord Christ. ²⁵Anyone who does wrong will be paid back for what they do. God treats everyone the same.

Masters, give your slaves what is right and fair. Do it because you know that you also have a Master in heaven.

More Teachings

²Give a lot of time and effort to prayer. Always be watchful and thankful. ³Pray for us too. Pray that God will give us an opportunity to preach our message. Then we

clothes. Don't be proud. Be gentle and patient. ¹³Put up with one another. Forgive one another if you are holding something against someone. Forgive, just as the Lord forgave you. ¹⁴And over all these good things put on love. Love holds them all together perfectly as if they were one.

¹⁵Let the peace that Christ gives rule in your hearts. As parts of one body, you were appointed to live in peace. And be thankful. ¹⁶Let the message about Christ live among you like a rich treasure. Teach and correct one another wisely. Teach one another by singing psalms and hymns and songs from the Spirit. Sing to God with thanks in your hearts. ¹⁷Do everything you say or do in the name of the Lord Jesus. Always give thanks to God the Father through Christ.

Teachings About Christian Families

¹⁸Wives, follow the lead of your husbands. That's what the Lord wants you to do.

¹⁹Husbands, love your wives. Don't be mean to them.

²⁰Children, obey your parents in everything. That pleases the Lord.

²¹Fathers, don't make your children bitter. If you do, they will lose hope.

²²Slaves, obey your earthly masters in everything. Don't do it just to please them when they are watching you. Obey them with an honest heart. Do it out of respect for the Lord. ²³Work at everything you do

In honor of Jesus' resurrection, I made a resolution to do something to help someone every day until Easter. Wooton gave me the idea and said that I had to call it an "Easter-lution." He said that helping others makes him feel good and shows his thanks to God. It's kind of like what Paul wrote in Colossians 3:23.

When I got to work, I saw Whit carrying in a bunch of new ice cream bowls so I knew I had to help out. I tried to be extra helpful by carrying an extra-large stack of bowls . . . but then I dropped them. The rest of the day, I couldn't find any way to help anyone. I was just about to chalk the day up to a loss when Penny came home with bags of groceries. I helped put them away and even organized the soup cans by matching colors, since I know that makes her happy.

And you know, Wooton was right. It felt great to help my friend. What about you? Who could you help today?

can preach the mystery of Christ. Because I preached it, I am being held by chains. [4]Pray that I will preach it clearly, as I should. [5]Be wise in the way you act toward outsiders. Make the most of every opportunity. [6]Let the words you speak always be full of grace. Learn how to make your words what people want to hear. Then you will know how to answer everyone.

Final Greetings

[7]Tychicus will tell you all the news about me. He is a dear brother. He is a faithful worker. He serves the Lord together with us. [8]I am sending him to you for one reason. I want you to know what is happening here. I want him to encourage you and make your hearts strong. [9]He is coming with Onesimus, our faithful and dear brother. He is one of you. They will tell you everything that is happening here.

[10]Aristarchus is in prison with me. He sends you his greetings. So does Mark, the cousin of Barnabas. You have been given directions about him. If he comes to you, welcome him. [11]Jesus, who is called Justus, also sends greetings. They are the only Jews who have worked together with me for God's kingdom. They have been a comfort to me.

[12]Epaphras sends greetings. He is one of you. He serves Christ Jesus. He is always praying hard for you. He prays that you will hold on tightly to all that God has in mind for us. He prays that you will keep growing in your knowledge of what God wants. He also prays that you will be completely sure about it. [13]I am happy to tell you that he is working very hard for you. He is also working hard for everyone in Laodicea and Hierapolis. [14]Our dear friend Luke, the doctor, sends greetings. So does Demas.

[15]Give my greetings to the brothers and sisters in Laodicea. Also give my greetings to Nympha and the church that meets in her house.

[16]After this letter has been read to you, send it on. Be sure that it is also read to the church in Laodicea. And be sure that you read the letter from Laodicea.

[17]Tell Archippus, "Be sure that you complete the work the Lord gave you to do."

[18]I, Paul, am writing this greeting with my own hand. Remember that I am being held by chains. May grace be with you.

1 Thessalonians

If we were actually physically traveling through the New Testament, our ship captain would be exhausted. We now must travel across the Aegean Sea yet again to reach the city of Thessalonica. This book was probably the first of Paul's letters to be written. There has been some speculation that Galatians may be a little older, but no one is certain.

Paul visited Thessalonica in Acts 17. His visit was successful at first, but then he was promptly run out of town (Acts 17:10). People didn't like his message about Jesus. In fact, they were so tenacious in their dislike that they followed him to the next town and ran him out of that one as well (Acts 17:11–14). So with this letter Paul tried to do what he couldn't accomplish in person. He wanted to assist people who had recently become believers to grow in their faith. Many of them were non-Jewish people who had worshiped other gods, so it was of great importance for them to hear the truth.

The first half of the letter is both encouraging and affirming, as Paul tries to restore and build up the brief relationship he had formed with the Thessalonian church. He then expands on some of the things he had shared with them concerning the way Christians should live (3:6–12).

One of Paul's central points was the resurrection and the return of Jesus. Many people at the time thought of death as a terrifying and horrible end—a definitive conclusion of everything. But Paul assured them that, for Christians, death is like falling asleep and waking up with a loving and comforting Savior (4:13–5:11).

WHAT'S IT MEAN, EUGENE?

Second Coming—The Second Coming refers to the eventual return of Jesus Christ to earth at "the end of the age," as promised in 1 Thessalonians 4:13–18. Revelation chapter 20 indicates that at His return Jesus will establish His reign on earth as King of Kings, cast the Devil into the Lake of Fire, and pass judgment on those who died prior to His coming. A sobering event for some, but a glorious joy for those who trust in Jesus!

1 I, Paul, am writing this letter. Silas and Timothy join me in writing.

We are sending this letter to you, the members of the church in Thessalonica. You belong to God the Father and the Lord Jesus Christ.

May grace and peace be given to you.

Paul Gives Thanks for the Thessalonians' Faith

² We always thank God for all of you. We keep on praying for you. ³ We remember you when we pray to our God and Father. Your work is produced by your faith. Your service is the result of your love. Your strength to continue comes from your hope in our Lord Jesus Christ.

⁴ Brothers and sisters, you are loved by God. We know that he has chosen you. ⁵ Our good news didn't come to you only in words. It came with power. It came with the Holy Spirit's help. He gave us complete faith in what we were preaching. You know how we lived among you for your good. ⁶ We and the Lord were your examples. You followed us. You welcomed our message even when you were suffering terribly. You welcomed it with the joy the Holy Spirit gives. ⁷ So you became a model to all the believers in the lands of Macedonia and Achaia. ⁸ The Lord's message rang out from you. That was true not only in Macedonia and Achaia. Your faith in God has also become known everywhere. So we don't have to say anything about it. ⁹ The believers themselves report the kind of welcome you gave us. They tell about how you turned away from statues of gods. And you turned to serve the living and true God. ¹⁰ They tell about how you are waiting for his Son to come from heaven. God raised him from the dead. He is Jesus. He saves us from God's anger, and his anger is sure to come.

Paul's Work for God in Thessalonica

2 Brothers and sisters, you know that our visit to you produced results. ² You know what happened earlier in the city of Philippi. We suffered, and people treated us very badly there. But God gave us the boldness to tell you his good news. We preached to you even when people strongly opposed us. ³ The appeal we make is based on truth. It comes from a pure heart. We are not trying to trick you. ⁴ In fact, it is just the opposite. God has approved us to preach. He has trusted us with the good news. We aren't trying to please people. We want to please God. He tests our hearts. ⁵ As you know, we never praised you if we didn't mean it. We didn't put on a mask to cover up any sinful desire. God is our witness that this is true. ⁶ We were not expecting people to praise us. We were not looking for praise from you or anyone else. Yet as Christ's apostles, we could have used our authority over you. ⁷ Instead, we were like young children when we were with you.

As a mother feeds and cares for her little children, ⁸ we cared for you. We loved you so much. So we were happy to share with you God's good news. We were also happy to share our lives with you. ⁹ Brothers and sisters, I am sure you remember how hard we worked. We labored night and day while we preached to you God's good news. We didn't want to cause you any expense. ¹⁰ You are witnesses of how we lived among you believers. God is also a witness that we were holy and godly and without blame. ¹¹ You know that we treated each of you as a father treats his own children. ¹² We gave you hope and strength. We comforted you. We really wanted you to live in a way that is worthy of God. He chooses you to enter his glorious kingdom.

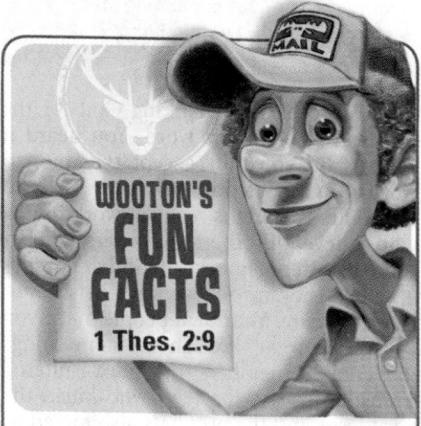

The Jews had a proverb that isn't in the Bible. It goes: "He who does not teach his son a trade, teaches him to be a thief." Paul's tent-making skills helped him support his preaching ministry.

CANDiD CONVERSATIONS

Imagine what the world would be like if nobody ever went out on a limb. History is full of people who stuck their necks out, did something against the grain, and the world became a better place for it. Think about what might have happened if Martin Luther King Jr., George Washington, or Harriet Tubman had just decided, "Eh, I'll just go along with the way things are." America would be a very different country today!

In order to make things happen, sometimes we have to simply stick our necks out and have faith. The same is true for our faith in God. When we believe with all of our hearts that God's Word is true and important, that's when He can change us and change the world. The Holy Spirit gives us power that we cannot imagine.

In what ways can you stick your neck out and stand for something, help someone, or tell a friend about Jesus?

[13] We never stop thanking God for the way you received his word. You heard it from us. But you didn't accept it as a human word. You accepted it for what it really is. It is God's word. It is really at work in you who believe. [14] Brothers and sisters, you became like the members of God's churches in Judea. They are believers in Christ Jesus, just as you are. Your own people made you suffer. You went through the same things the church members in Judea suffered from the Jews. [15] The Jews who killed the Lord Jesus and the prophets also forced us to leave. They do not please God. They are enemies of everyone. [16] They try to keep us from speaking to the Gentiles. These Jews don't want the Gentiles to be saved. In this way, these Jews always increase their sins

to the limit. God's anger has come on them at last.

Paul Wants to See the Believers in Thessalonica

[17] Brothers and sisters, we were separated from you for a short time. Apart from you, we were like children without parents. We were no longer with you in person. But we kept you in our thoughts. We really wanted to see you. So we tried very hard to do so. [18] We wanted to come to you. Again and again I, Paul, wanted to come. But Satan blocked our way. [19] What is our hope? What is our joy? When our Lord Jesus returns, what is the crown we will delight in? Isn't it you? [20] Yes, you are our glory and our joy.

3 We couldn't wait any longer. So we thought it was best to be left by ourselves in Athens. [2] We sent our brother Timothy to give you strength and hope in your faith. He works together with us in God's service to spread the good news about Christ. [3] We sent him so that no one would be upset by times of testing. You know very well that we have to go through times of testing. [4] In fact, when we were with you, here is what we kept telling you. We were telling you that our enemies would make us suffer. As you know very well, it has turned out that way. [5] That's the reason I sent someone to find out about your faith. I couldn't wait any longer. I was afraid that Satan had tempted you in some way. Then our work among you would have been useless.

Timothy Brings a Good Report

[6] But Timothy has come to us from you just now. He has brought good news about your faith and love. He has told us that you always have happy memories of us. He has also said that you desire to see us, just as we desire to see you. [7] Brothers and sisters, in all our trouble and suffering your faith encouraged us. [8] Now we really live, because you are standing firm in the Lord. [9] How can we thank God enough for you? We thank God because of all the joy we have in his presence. We have this joy because of you. [10] Night and day we pray very hard that we will see you again. We want to give you what is missing in your faith.

[11] Now may a way be opened up for us to come to you. May our God and Father

himself and our Lord Jesus do this. ¹²May the Lord make your love grow. May it be like a rising flood. May your love for one another increase. May it also increase for everyone else. May it be just like our love for you. ¹³May the Lord give you strength in your hearts. Then you will be holy and without blame in the sight of our God and Father. May that be true when our Lord Jesus comes with all his holy ones.

Living in a Way That Pleases God

4 Now I want to talk about some other matters, brothers and sisters. We taught you how to live in a way that pleases God. In fact, that is how you are living. In the name of the Lord Jesus we ask and beg you to do it more and more. ²You know the directions we gave you. They were given by the authority of the Lord Jesus.

³God wants you to be made holy. He wants you to stay away from sexual sins. ⁴He wants all of you to learn to control your own bodies. You must live in a way that is holy. You must live with honor. ⁵Don't desire to commit sexual sins like people who don't know God. ⁶None of you should sin against your brother or sister by doing that. You should not take advantage of your brother or sister. The Lord will punish everyone who commits these kinds of sins. We have already told you and warned you about this. ⁷That's because God chose us to live pure lives. He wants us to be holy. ⁸Suppose someone refuses to accept our teaching. They are not turning their back on us. They are turning their back on God. This same God gives you his Holy Spirit.

⁹We don't need to write to you about your love for one another. God himself has taught you to love one another. ¹⁰In fact, you do love all God's family all around Macedonia. Brothers and sisters, we are asking you to love one another more and more. ¹¹And do everything you can to live a quiet life. You should mind your own business. And work with your hands, just as we told you to. ¹²Then unbelievers will have respect for your everyday life. And you won't have to depend on anyone.

What Happens to Believers Who Have Died

¹³Brothers and sisters, we want you to know what happens to those who die. We don't want you to mourn, as other people do. They mourn because they don't have any hope. ¹⁴We believe that Jesus died and rose again. When he returns, many who believe in him will have died already. We believe that God will bring them back with

WHIT'S WISDOM

1 Thessalonians 4:9–10

Have you ever gotten a bad grade in school? I used to be a teacher at the middle school in Odyssey and I had to give out some bad grades from time to time. You know, report cards aren't the *only* things that can have bad grades. If you read through the letters written by the apostle Paul, you'll notice that the early churches either get passing grades or failing grades. No church wanted a failing grade from Paul! Paul was clearly upset with churches in Corinth and Galatia, and he gave them strict instructions to change their ways. But Paul was happy with the churches in Ephesus, Philippi, and Colossae.

Paul had good things to say about his friends in Thessalonica too. He said he didn't need to write to them about their love for one another. They were already taking care of everyone in their church and community. In fact, Paul said, "You do love all God's family all around Macedonia!"

We can follow Jesus' example and care for others by giving our time, belongings, and money to them. This week, think about a letter Paul could write to you or to your church. What would he say that you are doing well? What would he say that you need to fix?

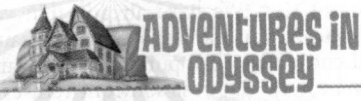

ADVENTURES IN ODYSSEY

Connie had hope in the midst of mourning the loss of her mother in "Life Expectancy" (A#57).

Jesus. [15]This agrees with what the Lord has said. When the Lord comes, many of us will still be alive. We tell you that we will certainly not go up before those who have died. [16]The Lord himself will come down from heaven. We will hear a loud command. We will hear the voice of the leader of the angels. We will hear a blast from God's trumpet. Many who believe in Christ will have died already. They will rise first. [17]After that, we who are still alive and are left will be caught up together with them. We will be taken up in the clouds. We will meet the Lord in the air. And we will be with him forever. [18]So encourage one another with these words of comfort.

The Day of the Lord Is Coming

5 Brothers and sisters, we don't have to write to you about times and dates. [2]You know very well how the day of the Lord will come. It will come like a thief in the night. [3]People will be saying that everything is peaceful and safe. Then suddenly they will be destroyed. It will happen like birth pains coming on a pregnant woman. None of the people will escape.

[4]Brothers and sisters, you are not in darkness. So that day should not surprise you as a thief would. [5]All of you are children of the light. You are children of the day. We don't belong to the night. We don't belong to the darkness. [6]So let us not be like the others. They are asleep. Instead, let us be wide awake and in full control of ourselves. [7]Those who sleep, sleep at night. Those who get drunk, get drunk at night. [8]But we belong to the day. So let us control ourselves. Let us put on our chest the armor of faith and love. Let us put on the hope of salvation like a helmet. [9]God didn't choose us to receive his anger. He chose us to receive salvation because of what our Lord Jesus Christ has done. [10]Jesus died for us. Some will be alive when he comes. Others will be dead. Either way, we will live together with him. [11]So encourage one another with the hope you have. Build each other up. In fact, that's what you are doing.

Final Teachings

[12]Brothers and sisters, we ask you to accept the godly leaders who work hard among you. They care for you in the Lord. They correct you. [13]Have a lot of respect for them. Love them because of what they do. Live in peace with one another. [14]Brothers and sisters, we are asking you to warn certain people. These people don't want to work. Instead, they make trouble. We are also asking you to encourage those who have lost hope. Help those who are weak. Be patient with everyone. [15]Make sure that no one pays back one wrong act with another. Instead, always try to do what is good for each other and for everyone else.

ADVENTURES IN ODYSSEY

Jimmy and Lawrence learned to "test prophecies" (1 Thes. 5:21) when they heard something fishy in "Terror from the Skies" (A#18).

[16] Always be joyful. [17] Never stop praying. [18] Give thanks no matter what happens. God wants you to thank him because you believe in Christ Jesus.

[19] Don't try to stop what the Holy Spirit is doing. [20] Don't treat prophecies as if they weren't important. [21] But test all prophecies. Hold on to what is good. [22] Say no to every kind of evil.

[23] God is the God who gives peace. May he make you holy through and through. May your whole spirit, soul and body be kept free from blame. May you be without blame from now until our Lord Jesus Christ comes. [24] The God who has chosen you is faithful. He will do all these things.

[25] Brothers and sisters, pray for us.

[26] Greet all God's people with a holy kiss.

[27] While the Lord is watching, here is what I command you. Have this letter read to all the brothers and sisters.

[28] May the grace of our Lord Jesus Christ be with you.

2 Thessalonians

We have arrived at Paul's second letter to the church of Thessalonica. Most biblical academics think this letter was written only a few months after his first one. After the first letter, apparently another arrived in short order. This dubious letter announced that Jesus had returned for His people but they had missed it! The suspicious letter had been signed with Paul's own name (2:2).

So Paul wrote this second letter posthaste to assure the Thessalonians that the return of Jesus would be a vital event that no one was going to miss! He said the world should first expect to see a wicked leader arise. He called this person "the man of sin" (2:3–4). By all indications, it is the same figure known as "the Beast" in Revelation. Both titles refer to the Antichrist.

Paul encouraged the church not to be fooled or to lose hope. They could know with confidence that Jesus would return one day. And when that day comes, nobody will miss it because "the Lord himself will come down from heaven . . . We will hear a blast from God's trumpet" (1 Thes. 4:16). In the interim, Paul strongly instructed everyone to do useful work and avoid making trouble for others (3:6–15). That's a good habit to establish when you're young to help you avoid many potential problems in life.

WHAT'S IT MEAN, EUGENE?

Church (the)—While most equate the word *church* with a building, the church is actually people—the followers of Jesus Christ. The church spans the globe and includes believers from every country and every era of time. When the apostle Peter declared that Jesus was the Messiah, Christ responded, "On this rock [Peter's confession] I will build my church" (Matthew 16:18).

1 I, Paul, am writing this letter. Silas and Timothy join me in writing.

We are sending this letter to you, the members of the church in Thessalonica. You belong to God our Father and the Lord Jesus Christ.

[2]May God the Father and the Lord Jesus Christ give you grace and peace.

Paul Prays and Gives Thanks

[3]Brothers and sisters, we should always thank God for you. That is only right, because your faith is growing more and more. We also thank God that the love you all have for one another is increasing. [4]So among God's churches we brag about the fact that you don't give up easily. We brag about your faith in all the suffering and testing you are going through.

[5]All of this proves that when God judges, he is fair. So you will be considered worthy to enter God's kingdom. You are suffering for his kingdom. [6]God is fair. He will pay back trouble to those who give you trouble. [7]He will help you who are troubled. And he will also help us. All these things will happen when the Lord Jesus appears from heaven. He will come in blazing fire. He will come with his powerful angels. [8]He will punish those who don't know God. He will punish those who don't obey the good news about our Lord Jesus. [9]They will be destroyed forever. They will be shut out of heaven. They will never see the glory of the Lord's strength. [10]All these things will happen when he comes. On that day his glory will be seen in his holy people. Everyone who has believed will be amazed when they see him. This includes you, because you believed the witness we gave you.

[11]Keeping this in mind, we never stop praying for you. Our God has chosen you. We pray that he will make you worthy of his choice. We pray he will make every good thing you want to do come true. We pray that he will do this by his power. We pray that he will make perfect all that you have done by faith. [12]We pray this so that the name of our Lord Jesus will receive glory through what you have done. We also pray that you will receive glory through what he has done. We pray all these things in keeping with the grace of our God and the Lord Jesus Christ.

The Man of Sin

2 Brothers and sisters, we want to ask you something. It has to do with the coming of our Lord Jesus Christ. It concerns the time when we will go to be with him. [2]What if you receive a message that is supposed to have come from us? What if it says that the day of the Lord has already come? If it does, we ask you not to become easily upset or alarmed. Don't be upset whether that message is spoken or written or prophesied. [3]Don't let anyone trick you in any way. That day will not come until people rise up against God. It will not come until the man of sin appears. He is a marked man. He is headed for ruin. [4]He will oppose everything that is called God. He will oppose everything that is worshiped. He will give himself power over everything. He will set himself up in God's temple. He will announce that he himself is God.

[5]Don't you remember? When I was with you, I used to tell you these things. [6]Now you know what is holding back the man of sin. He is held back so that he can make his appearance at the right time. [7]The secret power of sin is already at work. But the one who now holds back that power will keep doing it until he is taken out of the way. [8]Then the man of sin will appear. The Lord Jesus will overthrow him with the breath of his mouth. The glorious brightness of Jesus' coming will destroy the man of sin. [9]The coming of the man of sin will fit how Satan works. The man of sin will show his power through all kinds of signs and wonders. These signs and wonders will lead people astray. [10]So people who are dying will be fooled by this evil. These people are dying because they refuse to love the truth. The truth would save them. [11]So God will fool them completely. Then they will believe the lie. [12]Many will not believe the truth. They will take pleasure in evil. They will be judged.

Remain Strong in the Faith

[13]Brothers and sisters, we should always thank God for you. The Lord loves you. That's because God chose you as the first to be saved. Salvation comes through the Holy Spirit's work. He makes people holy. It also comes through believing the truth. [14]He chose you to be saved by accepting the good news that we preach. And you will share in the glory of our Lord Jesus Christ.

CANDID CONVERSATIONS

I've had a total of two massages in my whole life. Yesterday, my hairdresser said she gets one every week! These are serious massages—an hour and a half! I figured she had back problems, but she explained her life is filled with so much stress that she has to get away from it for at least 90 minutes a week or she would explode.

For me, I'm glad I have a God who promises us comfort and hope that will last forever. (See 2 Thessalonians 2:16–17.) My hairdresser's stress might leave her for a little while, but as soon as the massage is over, she has to go back and face her life. When my life gets difficult, I can go to God in prayer and He finds a way to comfort me, every time. Not only that, but I have the hope of a beautiful eternity with Him in heaven one day. And it doesn't cost me sixty dollars a pop!

If you're feeling sad or stressed, go to God in prayer.

---

¹⁵Brothers and sisters, remain strong in the faith. Hold on to what we taught you. We passed our teachings on to you by what we preached and wrote.

¹⁶Our Lord Jesus Christ and God our Father loved us. By his grace God gave us comfort that will last forever. The hope he gave us is good. May our Lord Jesus Christ and God our Father ¹⁷comfort your hearts. May they make you strong in every good thing you do and say.

Paul Asks for Prayer

3 Now I want to talk about some other matters. Brothers and sisters, pray for us. Pray that the Lord's message will spread quickly. Pray that others will honor it just as you did. ²And pray that we will be saved from sinful and evil people. Not everyone is a believer. ³But the Lord is faithful. He will strengthen you. He will guard you from the evil one. ⁴We trust in the Lord. So we are sure that you are doing the things we tell you to do. And we are sure that you will keep on doing them. ⁵May the Lord fill your hearts with God's love. May Christ give you the strength to go on.

Paul Warns Those Who Do Not Want to Work

⁶Brothers and sisters, here is a command we give you. We give it in the name of the Lord Jesus Christ. Keep away from every believer who doesn't want to work and makes trouble. Keep away from any believer who doesn't live up to the teaching you received from us. ⁷You know how you should follow our example. We worked when we were with you. ⁸We didn't eat anyone's food without paying for it. In fact, it was just the opposite. We worked night and day. We worked very hard so that we wouldn't cause any expense to any of you. ⁹We worked, even though we have the right to receive help from you. We did it in order to be a model for you to follow. ¹⁰Even when we were with you, we gave you a rule. We said, "Anyone who won't work shouldn't be allowed to eat."

¹¹We hear that some people among you don't want to work and are making trouble. They aren't really busy. Instead, they are

2 Thes. 3:13 Sometimes after I've helped people find lost cats, fix a lopsided curtain rod, or wash their dog named "Horse," I get a little tired. But I know that doing good is worth it.

WHIT'S WISDOM

2 Thessalonians 3:1–5

The apostle Paul tells the church at Thessalonica to "pray that we will be saved from sinful and evil people." What an important prayer request—and what an important statement from a man who used to be pretty "evil" himself. All of us are evil before Christ saves us from our sins, and Paul certainly showed that evil. He persecuted and killed people who preached about Jesus. Then he met Jesus and his eyes were opened—literally. Read Acts 9 for the whole story.

Eventually, Paul became perhaps the greatest Christian missionary who ever lived. He is a testimony to the life-changing power of God. And if you believe that God could change a life as wicked as Paul's, then you can believe God can do everything that Paul mentions in this chapter. God can spread His message quickly. He can save you from evil people. He can strengthen you and guard you from Satan.

Think of a mean person in your life who seems like he or she will never change. Start praying for that person. If God can change Paul, He can change anyone.

---

bothering others. ¹²We belong to the Lord Jesus Christ. So we strongly command people like that to settle down. They have to earn the food they eat. ¹³Brothers and sisters, don't ever get tired of doing what is good.

¹⁴Keep an eye on anyone who doesn't obey the teachings in our letter. Don't have anything to do with that person. Then they will feel ashamed. ¹⁵But don't think of them as an enemy. Instead, warn them as you would warn another believer.

Final Greetings

¹⁶May the Lord who gives peace give you peace at all times and in every way. May the Lord be with all of you.

¹⁷I, Paul, write this greeting in my own handwriting. That's how I prove that I am the author of all my letters. I always do it that way.

¹⁸May the grace of our Lord Jesus Christ be with you all.

1 Timothy

Our journey has led us to 1 Timothy. After the previous nine books named after places, you might guess that we are about to visit the town of Timothy. But, in fact, Timothy refers to a person. However, unlike many Bible books that are titled with the writer's name, this book is titled with the *receiver's* name. That's right. First Timothy is a letter *from* Paul *to* Timothy. (Paul's letters to Titus and Philemon will also bear the receiver's name.)

Timothy was a young person Paul had met on his travels. Timothy's mother was Jewish and his father was a Gentile (Acts 16:1–5). Since Paul was teaching both Jews and Gentiles the good news about Jesus, Timothy seemed like a good companion for him.

But Timothy soon became more than a mere companion. Paul began to love him like a son, and Timothy became a full participant in the ministry in spite of his young age (Phil. 2:19–24).

In fact, the purpose of this letter was to help Timothy to become a better spiritual leader. Paul's challenge applies to you just as much as it did Timothy: "Don't let anyone look down on you because you are young. Set an example for the believers in what you say and in how you live. Also set an example in how you love and in what you believe. Show the believers how to be pure" (4:12). That's a hefty responsibility, but with God's help, you can do it!

WHAT'S IT MEAN, EUGENE?

Cross—The cross is a brutal Roman instrument of torture and execution. The earliest cross was simply an upright wooden post. The cross on which Jesus suffered also had a transverse beam attached near the top. Victims of crucifixion were fastened to the cross with nails and left hanging there until they died. In the New Testament, the cross is the symbol of Christ's sacrifice for our sins (Galatians 6:14).

1 I, Paul, am writing this letter. I am an apostle of Christ Jesus, just as God our Savior commanded. Christ Jesus also commanded it. We have put our hope in him.

²Timothy, I am sending you this letter. You are my true son in the faith.

May God the Father and Christ Jesus our Lord give you grace, mercy and peace.

Paul Warns Timothy to Oppose False Teachers

³Timothy, stay there in Ephesus. That is what I told you to do when I went into Macedonia. I want you to command certain people not to teach things that aren't true. ⁴And command them not to spend their time on stories that are made up. They must not waste time on family histories that never end. These things only lead to fights about ideas. They don't help God's work move forward. His work is done by faith. ⁵Love is the purpose of my command. Love comes from a pure heart. It comes from a good sense of what is right and wrong. It comes from faith that is honest and true. ⁶Some have turned from these teachings. They would rather talk about things that have no meaning. ⁷They want to be teachers of the law. And they are very sure about that law. But they don't know what they are talking about.

⁸We know that the law is good if it is used properly. ⁹We also know that the law isn't made for godly people. It is made for those who break the law. It is for those who refuse to obey. It is for ungodly and sinful people. It is for those who aren't holy and who don't believe. It is for those who kill their fathers or mothers. It is for murderers. ¹⁰It is for those who commit sexual sins. It is for those who commit homosexual acts. It is for people who buy and sell slaves. It is for liars. It is for people who tell lies in court. It is for those who are a witness to things that aren't true. And it is for anything else that is the opposite of true teaching. ¹¹True teaching agrees with the good news about the glory of the blessed God. He trusted me with that good news.

The Lord Pours Out His Grace on Paul

¹²I am thankful to Christ Jesus our Lord. He has given me strength. I thank him that he considered me faithful. I thank him for appointing me to serve him. ¹³I used to speak evil things against Jesus. I tried to hurt his followers. I really pushed them around. But God showed me mercy anyway. I did those things without knowing any better. I wasn't a believer. ¹⁴Our Lord poured out more and more of his grace on me. Along with it came faith and love from Christ Jesus.

¹⁵Here is a saying that you can trust. It should be accepted completely. Christ Jesus came into the world to save sinners. And I am the worst sinner of all. ¹⁶But for that very reason, God showed me mercy. And I am the worst of sinners. He showed me mercy so that Christ Jesus could show that he is very patient. I was an example for those who would come to believe in him. Then they would receive eternal life. ¹⁷The eternal King will never die. He can't be seen. He is the only God. Give him honor and glory for ever and ever. Amen.

Paul Commands Timothy

¹⁸My son Timothy, I am giving you this command. It is in keeping with the prophecies once made about you. By remembering them, you can fight the battle well. ¹⁹Then you will hold on to faith. You will hold on to a good sense of what is right and wrong. Some have not accepted this knowledge of right and wrong. So they have destroyed their faith. They are like a ship that has sunk. ²⁰Hymenaeus and Alexander are among them. I have handed them over to

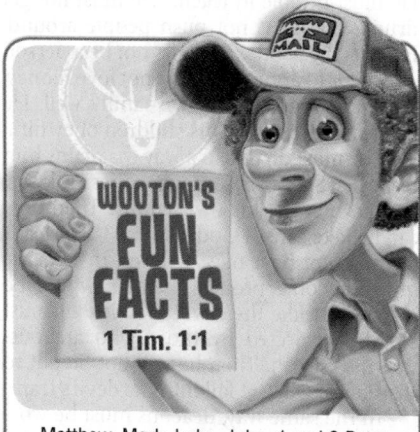

WOOTON'S FUN FACTS
1 Tim. 1:1

Matthew, Mark, Luke, John, 1 and 2 Peter, and 1, 2, and 3 John are named after the person they are written *by*. But 1 and 2 Timothy, Titus, and Philemon are named after the person they are written *to*.

WOOTON'S FUN FACTS

1 Tim. 1:19 You've probably heard of a shipwreck or two in history. But did you know that millions of ships lie at the bottom of the oceans and seas? The most famous one, the *RMS Titanic*, will one day disappear because metal-eating bacteria are eating away the hull. Doesn't sound very yummy to me!

ADVENTURES IN ODYSSEY

Donna Barclay had to be careful how she dressed in "Modesty Is the Best Policy" (A#13).

Satan. That will teach them not to speak evil things against God.

Teachings About Worship

2 First, I want you to pray for all people. Ask God to help and bless them. Give thanks for them. [2] Pray for kings. Pray for everyone who is in authority. Pray that we can live peaceful and quiet lives. And pray that we will be godly and holy. [3] This is good, and it pleases God our Savior. [4] He wants all people to be saved. He wants them to come to know the truth. [5] There is only one God. And there is only one go-between for God and human beings. He is the man Christ Jesus. [6] He gave himself to pay for the sins of all people. We have been told this message at just the right time. [7] I was appointed to be a messenger and an apostle to preach the good news. I am telling the truth. I'm not lying. God appointed me to be a true and faithful teacher of the Gentiles.

[8] So I want the men in every place to pray. I want them to lift up holy hands. I don't want them to be angry when they pray. I don't want them to argue. [9] In the same way, I want the women to be careful how they dress. They should wear clothes that are right and proper. They shouldn't wear their hair in very fancy styles. They shouldn't wear gold or pearls. They shouldn't wear clothes that cost a lot of money. [10] Instead, they should put on good works as if good works were their clothes. This is proper for women who claim to worship God.

[11] When a woman is learning, she should be quiet. She should follow her leaders in every way. [12] I do not let women teach or take authority over a man. They must be quiet. [13] That's because Adam was made first. Then Eve was made. [14] Adam was not the one who was tricked. The woman was tricked and became a sinner. [15] Will women be saved by having children? Only if they keep on believing, loving, and leading a holy life in a proper way.

Rules for Choosing Leaders and Deacons

3 Here is a saying you can trust. If anyone wants to be a leader in the church, they want to do a good work for God and people. [2] A leader must be free from blame. He must be faithful to his wife. In anything he does, he must not go too far. He must control himself. He must be worthy of respect. He must welcome people into his home. He must be able to teach. [3] He must not get drunk. He must not push people around. He must be gentle. He must not be a person who likes to argue. He must not love money. [4] He must manage his own family well. He must make sure that his children obey him. And he must do this in a way that gains him respect. [5] Suppose someone doesn't know how to manage his own family. Then how can he take care of God's church? [6] The leader must not be a new believer. If he is, he might become proud. Then he would be judged just like the devil. [7] The leader must also be respected by those who are outside the church. Then he will not be put to shame. He will not fall into the devil's trap.

[8] In the same way, deacons must be worthy of respect. They must be honest and true. They must not drink too much wine. They must not try to get money by cheating people. [9] They must hold on to the deep truths of the faith. Even their own minds

tell them to do that. [10]First they must be tested. Then let them serve as deacons if there is nothing against them.

[11]In the same way, the women must be worthy of respect. They must not say things that harm others. In anything they do, they must not go too far. They must be worthy of trust in everything.

[12]A deacon must be faithful to his wife. He must manage his children and family well. [13]Those who have served well earn the full respect of others. They also become more sure of their faith in Christ Jesus.

Paul's Reasons for Giving Instructions to Timothy

[14]I hope I can come to you soon. But now I am writing these instructions to you. [15]Then if I have to put off my visit, you will know how people should act in God's family. The family of God is the church of the living God. It is the pillar and foundation of the truth. [16]There is no doubt that true godliness comes from this great mystery.

Jesus came as a human being.
The Holy Spirit proved that he was
  the Son of God.
He was seen by angels.
He was preached among the nations.
People in the world believed in him.
He was taken up to heaven in glory.

4 The Holy Spirit clearly says that in the last days some people will leave the faith. They will follow spirits that will fool them. They will believe things that demons will teach them. [2]Teachings like those come from liars who pretend to be what they are not. Their sense of what is right and wrong has been destroyed. It's as though it has been burned with a hot iron. [3]They do not allow people to get married. They order them not to eat certain foods. But God created those foods. So people who believe and know the truth should receive them and give thanks for them. [4]Everything God created is good. You shouldn't turn anything down. Instead, you should thank God for it. [5]The word of God and prayer make it holy.

[6]Point out these things to the brothers and sisters. Then you will serve Christ Jesus well. You will show that you've grown in the truths of the faith. You will show that you've been trained by the good teaching you've obeyed. [7]Don't have anything to do with godless stories and silly tales. Instead, train yourself to be godly. [8]Training the body has some value. But being godly has value in every way. It promises help for the life you are now living and the life to come. [9]This is the truth you can trust and accept completely. [10]This is why we work and try so hard. It's because we have put our hope in the living God. He is the Savior of all people. Most of all, he is the Savior of those who believe.

[11]Command and teach these things. [12]Don't let anyone look down on you

WHIT'S WISDOM
1 Timothy 4:12

I remember when a girl named Erica Clark said, "I can't wait to be a grown-up!" Then she ordered a kid's size cone at the soda fountain.

"Why do you want to grow up? Don't you like being a kid?" I asked, serving the ice cream.

"Kinda," she said. "But grown-ups get to have all the fun."

"I don't know about that, but the Bible tells you the ways that you can *act* grown-up now." I showed her 1 Timothy 4:12. It shows that God doesn't think you're unimportant just because you're young. Plus, if you're old enough to believe in Jesus, you're already old enough to help other people believe in Him.

That's not how all grown-ups around you behave, but that's how you can act like a grown-up Christian. You can set an example in five ways: (1) "what you say" or your words, (2) "how you live" or your actions, (3) how you love, (4) "what you believe" or your faith, and (5) being "pure."

The next time you're dreaming about being a grown-up, think of this verse and how you can act more like a grown-up Christian by being an example to others.

CANDID CONVERSATIONS

Last month, I was directing the talent show at Whit's End when Emily Jones tried out. After attempting to sing a pop song, she flopped down in the chair next to me. "I was terrible," she said.

Next Olivia Parker took the stage to recite her poem "Ode to a Dead Hamster." "Olivia's so expressive," Emily said.

"You should tell her that," I said. So after Olivia finished, Emily whispered in her ear. Olivia grinned and gave Emily a hug.

For the rest of the auditions, Emily said something nice to everyone. As the performers filed out, she turned to me. "It'll be a great show this year. I wish I could be part of it."

"Are you kidding?" I said. "You're already part of it. We need your talent for seeing things other people miss. It makes you a great encourager. The Bible tells us over and over to use our gifts. You have the gift of encouragement, and it brings out the best in people. I'd choose you over a pop singer any day!"

because you are young. Set an example for the believers in what you say and in how you live. Also set an example in how you love and in what you believe. Show the believers how to be pure. [13]Until I come, spend your time reading Scripture out loud to one another. Spend your time preaching and teaching. [14]Don't fail to use the gift the Holy Spirit gave you. He gave it to you through a prophecy from God. It was given when the elders placed their hands on you.

[15]Keep on doing these things. Give them your complete attention. Then everyone will see how you are coming along. [16]Be careful of how you live and what you believe. Never give up. Then you will save yourself and those who hear you.

Instructions About Widows, Elders and Slaves

5 Correct an older man in a way that shows respect. Make an appeal to him as if he were your father. Treat younger men as if they were your brothers. [2]Treat older women as if they were your mothers. Treat younger women as if they were your sisters. Be completely pure in the way you treat them.

[3]Take care of the widows who really need help. [4]But suppose a widow has children or grandchildren. They should first learn to put their faith into practice. They should care for their own family. In that way they will pay back their parents and grandparents. That pleases God. [5]A widow who really needs help and is left all alone puts her hope in God. Night and day she keeps on praying. Night and day she asks God for help. [6]But a widow who lives for pleasure is dead even while she is still living. [7]Give these instructions to the people. Then no one can be blamed. [8]Everyone should provide for their own relatives. Most of all, everyone should take care of their own family. If they don't, they have left the faith. They are worse than someone who doesn't believe.

[9]No widow should be put on the list of widows unless she is more than 60 years old. She must also have been faithful to her husband. [10]She must be well known for the good things she does. That includes bringing up children. It includes inviting guests into her home. It includes washing the feet of the Lord's people. It includes helping those who are in trouble. A widow should

spend her time doing all kinds of good things.

[11]Don't put younger widows on that kind of list. They might want pleasure more than they want Christ. Then they would want to get married again. [12]If they do that, they will be judged. They have broken their first promise. [13]Besides, they get into the habit of having nothing to do. They go around from house to house. They waste their time. They also bother other people and say things that make no sense. They shouldn't say those things. [14]So here is the advice I give to younger widows. Get married. Have children. Take care of your own homes. Don't give the enemy the chance to tell lies about you. [15]In fact, some have already turned away to follow Satan.

[16]Suppose a woman is a believer and takes care of widows. She should continue to help them. She shouldn't let the church pay the expenses. Then the church can help the widows who really need it.

[17]The elders who do the church's work well are worth twice as much honor. That is true in a special way of elders who preach and teach. [18]Scripture says, "Do not stop an ox from eating while it helps separate the grain from the straw." *(Deuteronomy 25:4)* Scripture also says, "Workers are worthy of their pay." *(Luke 10:7)* [19]Don't believe a charge against an elder unless two or three witnesses bring it. [20]But those elders who are sinning should be corrected in front of everyone. This will be a warning to the others. [21]I command you to follow these instructions. I command you in the sight of God and Christ Jesus and the chosen angels. Treat everyone the same. Don't favor one person over another.

[22]Don't be too quick to place your hands on others to set them apart to serve God. Don't take part in the sins of others. Keep yourself pure.

[23]Stop drinking only water. If your stomach is upset, drink a little wine. It can also help the other sicknesses you often have.

[24]The sins of some people are easy to see. They are already being judged. Others will be judged later. [25]In the same way, good works are easy to see. But even good works that are hard to see can't stay hidden forever.

6 All who are forced to serve as slaves should consider their masters worthy of full respect. Then people will not speak evil things against God's name and against what we teach. [2]Some slaves have masters who are believers. They shouldn't show their masters disrespect just because they are also believers. Instead, they should serve them even better. That's because their masters are loved by them as believers. These masters are committed to caring for their slaves.

People Who Teach Lies or Love Money

These are the things you are to teach. Try hard to get the believers to do them. [3]Suppose someone teaches something different than I have taught. Suppose that person doesn't agree with the true teaching of our Lord Jesus Christ. Suppose they don't agree with godly teaching. [4]Then that person is proud and doesn't understand anything. They like to argue more than they should. They can't agree about what words mean. All of this results in wanting what others have. It causes fighting, harmful talk, and evil distrust. [5]It stirs up trouble all the time among people whose minds are twisted by sin. The truth they once had has been taken away from them. They think they can get rich by being godly.

[6]You gain a lot when you live a godly life. But you must be happy with what you have. [7]We didn't bring anything into the world. We can't take anything out of it. [8]If we have food and clothing, we will be happy with that. [9]People who want to get rich are tempted. They fall into a trap. They are tripped up by wanting many foolish and harmful things. Those who live like that are dragged down by what they do. They are destroyed and die. [10]Love for money causes all kinds of evil. Some people want to get rich. They have wandered away from the faith. They have wounded themselves with many sorrows.

Paul Gives a Final Command to Timothy

[11]But you are a man of God. Run away from all these things. Try hard to do what

is right and godly. Have faith, love and gentleness. Hold on to what you believe. [12]Fight the good fight along with all other believers. Take hold of eternal life. You were chosen for it when you openly told others what you believe. Many witnesses heard you. [13]God gives life to everything. Christ Jesus told the truth when he was a witness in front of Pontius Pilate. In the sight of God and Christ, I give you a command. [14]Obey it until our Lord Jesus Christ appears. Obey it completely. Then no one can find fault with it or you. [15]God will bring Jesus back at a time that pleases him. God is the blessed and only Ruler. He is the greatest King of all. He is the most powerful Lord of all. [16]God is the only one who can't die. He lives in light that no one can get close to. No one has seen him. No one can see him. Honor and power belong to him forever. Amen.

[17]Command people who are rich in this world not to be proud. Tell them not to put their hope in riches. Wealth is so uncertain. Command those who are rich to put their hope in God. He richly provides us with everything to enjoy. [18]Command the rich to do what is good. Tell them to be rich in doing good things. They must give freely. They must be willing to share. [19]In this way, they will store up true riches for themselves. It will provide a firm basis for the next life. Then they will take hold of the life that really is life.

[20]Timothy, guard what God has trusted you with. Turn away from godless chatter. Stay away from opposing ideas that are falsely called knowledge. [21]Some people believe them. By doing that they have turned away from the faith.

May God's grace be with you all.

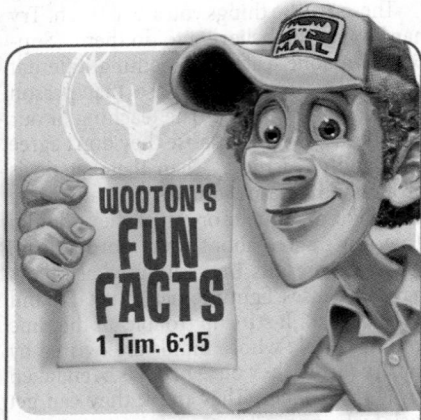

WOOTON'S FUN FACTS
1 Tim. 6:15

The *Second Coming* or the *return of Jesus* will be a great moment. Okay, that's an understatement. It will be an amazingly stupendously colossally awesome moment! And only God the Father knows when it will happen—as we learn in Matthew 24:36.

2 Timothy

In the time since his first letter to Timothy, Paul's situation had changed considerably. He and Timothy had worked together to spread the news about Jesus, and they had become very close. Paul wrote 1 Timothy to help his young friend overcome his shyness and encourage him to be a strong church leader. Paul later followed up with this letter to inform and encourage Timothy to an even greater degree.

There are hidden clues about Paul's situation throughout the text. If you read closely, you will note that Paul is not expecting to live much longer (4:6–8). Many of his friends had deserted him (1:15). Others were ministering in distant places (4:10–12). Paul was aged and lonely, and he valued the friendship of young Timothy (4:9, 13).

You may not realize how meaningful it can be for an older person to have a friendship with someone younger like you. Perhaps you can assist a grandparent with tasks he or she can't do alone. But more importantly, your company will often bring joy to another person's day. If you follow Timothy's example of service and devotion to a mentor, both of you will benefit from the time you spend.

WHAT'S IT MEAN, EUGENE?

Doctrine—A formal word for "teaching." Today, *doctrine* is most often used to refer to the official teachings of the church. In 2 Timothy 3:16, Paul says that all Scripture is inspired by God and that it is "useful for *teaching* us what is true." Thusly, Scripture is the basis for most of what we call doctrine. Knowing doctrine is essential in our walk with Christ.

1 I, Paul, am writing this letter. I am an apostle of Christ Jesus just as God planned. He sent me to tell about the promise of life found in Christ Jesus.

²Timothy, I am sending you this letter. You are my dear son.

May God the Father and Christ Jesus our Lord give you grace, mercy and peace.

Paul Gives Thanks

³I thank God, whom I serve as did our people of long ago. I serve God, knowing that what I have done is right. Night and day I thank God for you. Night and day I always remember you in my prayers. ⁴I remember your tears. I long to see you so that I can be filled with joy. ⁵I remember your honest and true faith. It was alive first in your grandmother Lois and in your mother Eunice. And I am certain that it is now alive in you also.

Paul Encourages Timothy to Be Faithful

⁶This is why I remind you to help God's gift grow, just as a small spark grows into a fire. God put his gift in you when I placed my hands on you. ⁷God gave us his Spirit. And the Spirit doesn't make us weak and fearful. Instead, the Spirit gives us power and love. He helps us control ourselves. ⁸So don't be ashamed of the message about our Lord. And don't be ashamed of me, his prisoner. Instead, join with me as I suffer for the good news. God's power will help us do that. ⁹God has saved us. He has chosen us to live a holy life. It wasn't because of anything we have done. It was because of his own purpose and grace. Through Christ Jesus, God gave us this grace even before time began. ¹⁰It has now been made known through the coming of our Savior, Christ Jesus. He has broken the power of death. Because of the good news, he has brought life out into the light. That life never dies. ¹¹I was appointed to announce the good news. I was appointed to be an apostle and a teacher. ¹²That's why I'm suffering the way I am. But this gives me no reason to be ashamed. That's because I know who I have believed in. I am sure he is able to take care of what I have given him. I can trust him with it until the day he returns as judge.

CANDID CONVERSATIONS

What is your biggest fear? Spiders? Darkness? Speaking in front of a crowd? I have this weird fear of staplers. Don't ask. Being afraid of certain things is natural, and there's nothing wrong with having fears. They become a problem only if we begin to make choices based on our fears. If we decide not to talk to the new kid in class because of our fear of rejection, then that's not an attitude that comes from God.

God didn't create us to have fear and be timid. He made us to have power, love, and self-discipline (see 2 Timothy 1:7).

You don't need to be afraid. God has given you His strength, showered you with His unconditional love, and gifted you with the ability to do great things! Whether it's talking to the new kid in class or picking up a stapler (yikes!), it's time to overcome your fears!

¹³Follow what you heard from me as the pattern of true teaching. Follow it with faith and love because you belong to Christ Jesus. ¹⁴Guard the truth of the good news that you were trusted with. Guard it with the help of the Holy Spirit who lives in us.

Examples of Faithful and Unfaithful People

¹⁵You know that all the believers in Asia Minor have deserted me. They include Phygelus and Hermogenes.

¹⁶May the Lord show mercy to all who live in the house of Onesiphorus. He often encouraged me. He was not ashamed that I was being held by chains. ¹⁷In fact, it was just the opposite. When he was in Rome, he looked everywhere for me. At last he found me. ¹⁸May Onesiphorus find mercy from the Lord on the day Jesus returns as judge! You know very well how many ways Onesiphorus helped me in Ephesus.

Paul Again Encourages Timothy to Be Faithful

2 My son, be strong in the grace that is yours in Christ Jesus. [2]You have heard me teach in front of many witnesses. Pass on to people you can trust the things you've heard me say. Then they will be able to teach others also. [3]Like a good soldier of Christ Jesus, join with me in suffering. [4]A soldier does not take part in things that don't have anything to do with the army. Instead, he tries to please his commanding officer. [5]It is the same for anyone who takes part in a sport. They don't receive the winner's crown unless they play by the rules. [6]The farmer who works hard should be the first to receive a share of the crops. [7]Think about what I'm saying. The Lord will help you understand what all of it means.

[8]Remember Jesus Christ. He came from David's family line. He was raised from the dead. That is my good news. [9]I am suffering for it. I have even been put in chains like someone who has committed a crime. But God's word is not held back by chains. [10]So I put up with everything for the good of God's chosen people. Then they also can be saved. Christ Jesus saves them. He gives them glory that will last forever.

[11]Here is a saying you can trust.

If we died with him,
 we will also live with him.

[12] If we don't give up,
 we will also rule with him.
If we say we don't know him,
 he will also say he doesn't know us.
[13] Even if we are not faithful,
 he remains faithful.
 He must be true to himself.

What to Do About False Teachers

[14]Keep reminding God's people of these things. While God is watching, warn them not to argue about words. That doesn't have any value. It only destroys those who listen. [15]Do your best to please God. Be a worker who doesn't need to be ashamed. Teach the message of truth correctly. [16]Stay away from godless chatter. Those who take part in it will become more and more ungodly. [17]Their teaching will spread like a deadly sickness. Hymenaeus and Philetus are two of those teachers. [18]They have turned away from the truth. They say that the time when people will rise from the dead has already come. They destroy the faith of some people. [19]But God's solid foundation stands firm. Here is the message written on it. "The Lord knows who his own people are." *(Numbers 16:5)* Also, "All who say they believe in the Lord must turn away from evil."

[20]In a large house there are things made out of gold and silver. But there are also things made out of wood and clay. Some

WHIT'S WISDOM

2 Timothy 2:15

One day Robyn Jacobs told me she didn't think she was cut out for studying the Bible. She had tried a few different methods that Connie and I used, but they didn't work for her. I reminded her how she liked to sing and had memorized 1 John 4:7 and 8 by singing it as a song. But she had to sing it many times before she memorized it. I said that's how she could study the Bible. She could take a short section of Scripture—say, five verses—and read them over and over again every day. She could even make up a song about them. Then, when she knew them by heart, she could move on to the next five and do the same thing.

This wasn't the way that I studied the Bible and it wasn't the way that Connie studied the Bible. But there's no "one best way" of studying. Each of us has to find the way that works best for us. The main thing is to keep reading the Scriptures every day. And if we do that, God will lead us to the right method, and help us understand His Word better. Then we can be what 2 Timothy 2:15 calls "a worker who doesn't need to be ashamed."

Connie learned about teaching the message of truth (2 Timothy 3:16) in "The Case of the Delinquent Disciples" (A#18).

have special purposes. Others have common purposes. ²¹Suppose someone stays away from what is common. Then the Master will be able to use them for special purposes. They will be made holy. They will be ready to do any good work.

²²Run away from the evil things that young people long for. Try hard to do what is right. Have faith, love and peace. Do these things together with those who call on the Lord from a pure heart. ²³Don't have anything to do with arguing. It is dumb and foolish. You know it only leads to fights. ²⁴Anyone who serves the Lord must not be hard to get along with. Instead, they must be kind to everyone. They must be able to teach. The one who serves must not hold anything against anyone. ²⁵They must gently teach those who are against them. Maybe God will give a change of heart to those who are against you. That will lead them to know the truth. ²⁶Maybe they will come to their senses. Maybe they will escape the devil's trap. He has taken them as prisoners to do what he wanted.

Here is what I want you to know. There will be terrible times in the last days. ²People will love themselves. They will love money. They will brag and be proud. They will tear others down. They will not obey their parents. They won't be thankful or holy. ³They won't love others. They won't forgive others. They will tell lies about people. They will be out of control. They will be wild. They will hate what is good. ⁴They will turn against their friends. They will act without thinking. They will think they are better than others. They will love what pleases them instead of loving God. ⁵They will act as if they were serving God. But what they do will show that they have turned their backs on God's power. Have nothing to do with these people.

⁶They are the kind who trick their way into the homes of some women. These women are ready to believe anything. And they take control over these women. These women are loaded down with sins. They give in to all kinds of evil desires. ⁷They are always learning. But they are never able to come to know the truth. ⁸Jannes and Jambres opposed Moses. In the same way, the teachers I'm talking about oppose the truth. Their minds are twisted. As far as the faith is concerned, God doesn't accept them. ⁹They won't get very far. Just like Jannes and Jambres, their foolish ways will be clear to everyone.

Paul Gives a Final Command to Timothy

¹⁰But you know all about my teaching. You know how I live and what I live for. You know about my faith and love. You know how patient I am. You know I haven't given up. ¹¹You know that I was treated badly. You know that I suffered greatly. You know what kinds of things happened to me in Antioch, Iconium and Lystra. You know how badly I have been treated. But the Lord saved me from all my troubles. ¹²In fact, everyone who wants to live a godly life in Christ Jesus will be treated badly. ¹³Evil people and pretenders will go from bad to worse. They will fool others, and others will fool them. ¹⁴But I want you to continue to follow what you have learned and are sure about. You know the people you learned it from. ¹⁵You have known the Holy Scriptures ever since you were a little child. They are able to teach you how to be saved by believing in Christ Jesus. ¹⁶God has breathed life into all Scripture. It is useful for teaching us what is true. It is useful for correcting our mistakes. It is useful for making our lives whole again. It is useful for training us to do what is right. ¹⁷By using Scripture, the servant of God can be completely prepared to do every good thing.

REMEMBER THIS

2 TIMOTHY 3:16

"God has breathed life into all Scripture. It is useful for teaching us what is true. It is useful for correcting our mistakes. It is useful for making our lives whole again. It is useful for training us to do what is right."

4 I give you a command in the sight of God and Christ Jesus. Christ will judge the living and the dead. Because he and his kingdom are coming, here is the command I give you. [2]Preach the word. Be ready to serve God in good times and bad. Correct people's mistakes. Warn them. Encourage them with words of hope. Be very patient as you do these things. Teach them carefully. [3]The time will come when people won't put up with true teaching. Instead, they will try to satisfy their own desires. They will gather a large number of teachers around them. The teachers will say what the people want to hear. [4]The people will turn their ears away from the truth. They will turn to stories that aren't true. [5]But I want you to keep your head no matter what happens. Don't give up when times are hard. Work to spread the good news. Do everything God has given you to do.

[6]I am already being poured out like a drink offering. The time when I will leave is near. [7]I have fought the good fight. I have finished the race. I have kept the faith. [8]Now there is a crown waiting for me. It is given to those who are right with God. The Lord, who judges fairly, will give it to me on the day he returns. He will not give it only to me. He will also give it to all those who are longing for him to return.

Personal Words

[9]Do your best to come to me quickly. [10]Demas has deserted me. He has gone to Thessalonica. He left me because he loved this world. Crescens has gone to Galatia.

Titus has gone to Dalmatia. [11]Only Luke is with me. Get Mark and bring him with you. He helps me in my work for the Lord. [12]I sent Tychicus to Ephesus. [13]When you come, bring my coat. I left it with Carpus at Troas. Also bring my books. Most of all, bring the ones made out of animal skins.

[14]Remember Alexander, the one who works with metal. He did me a great deal of harm. The Lord will pay him back for what he has done. [15]You too should watch out for him. He strongly opposed our message.

[16]The first time I was put on trial, no one came to help me. Everyone deserted me. I hope they will be forgiven for it. [17]The Lord stood at my side. He gave me the strength to preach the whole message. Then all the Gentiles heard it. I was saved from the lion's mouth. [18]The Lord will save me from every evil attack. He will bring me safely to his heavenly kingdom. Give him glory for ever and ever. Amen.

Final Greetings

[19]Greet Priscilla and Aquila. Greet those who live in the house of Onesiphorus.

[20]Erastus stayed in Corinth. I left Trophimus sick in Miletus. [21]Do your best to get here before winter.

Eubulus greets you. So do Pudens, Linus, Claudia and all the brothers and sisters.

[22]May the Lord be with your spirit. May God's grace be with you all.

Titus

Timothy wasn't the only promising church leader that Paul met on his travels. There was also Titus, and Paul's letter to him is our next stop. Titus demonstrated what Paul had been telling people about God's acceptance of everyone in the church. He had come from a Gentile (or non-Jewish) family. So when he put his faith in Jesus, a lot of people insisted he should go through the rites of the Jews as part of his conversion. But Paul refused, in no uncertain terms. Titus was proof that belief in Jesus provided freedom from the law. Thanks to the sacrifice of Jesus, nothing further needed to be added to a person's genuine faith in order to be accepted by both God and the church.

Titus went on to work with Paul in several locations. This letter, like Paul's letters to Timothy, was to help his young associate become a better pastor. Paul lists requirements for church leaders as well as topics that Titus should emphasize in his teaching.

Titus didn't appear to be as timid by nature as Timothy was, but both of these trainees under Paul turned out to be faithful and capable leaders. When it came to devotion to God, their youth was never seen as an excuse or hindrance.

What's it Mean, Eugene?

Regeneration—In the field of chemistry, regeneration refers mostly to polymer fibers. However, for the Christian, it is associated with spiritual *rebirth*. In John 3:3, Jesus tells a Pharisee named Nicodemus, "No one can see God's kingdom unless they are born again." We are spiritually reborn when Christ becomes our Savior and His Holy Spirit is given to us. As Jesus explains to Nicodemus: "No one can enter God's kingdom unless they are born with water and the Holy Spirit" (John 3:5).

1 I, Paul, am writing this letter. I serve God, and I am an apostle of Jesus Christ. God sent me to help his chosen people believe in Christ more and more. God sent me to help them understand even more the truth that leads to godly living. ²That belief and understanding lead to the hope of eternal life. Before time began, God promised to give that life. And he does not lie. ³Now, at just the right time, he has made his promise clear. He did this through the preaching that he trusted me with. God our Savior has commanded all these things.

⁴Titus, I am sending you this letter. You are my true son in the faith we share.

May God the Father and Christ Jesus our Savior give you grace and peace.

Choosing Elders Who Love What Is Good

⁵I left you on the island of Crete. I did this because there were some things that hadn't been finished. I wanted you to put them in order. I also wanted you to appoint elders in every town. I told you how to do it. ⁶An elder must be without blame. He must be faithful to his wife. His children must be believers. They must not give anyone a reason to say that they are wild and don't obey. ⁷A church leader takes care of God's family. That's why he must be without blame. He must not look after only his own interests. He must not get angry easily. He must not get drunk. He must not push people around. He must not try to get money by cheating people. ⁸Instead, a church leader must welcome people into his home. He must love what is good. He must control his mind and feelings. He must do what is right. He must be holy. He must control the desires of his body. ⁹The message as it has been taught can be trusted. He must hold firmly to it. Then he will be able to use true teaching to comfort others and build them up. He will be able to prove that people who oppose it are wrong.

Warning People Who Fail to Do Good

¹⁰Many people refuse to obey God. All they do is talk about things that mean nothing. They try to fool others. No one does these things more than the circumcision group. ¹¹They must be stopped. They are making trouble for entire families. They do this by teaching things they shouldn't. They do these things to cheat people. ¹²One of Crete's own prophets has a saying. He says, "People from Crete are always liars. They are evil beasts. They don't want to work. They live only to eat." ¹³This saying is true. So give a strong warning to people who refuse to obey God. Then they will understand the faith correctly. ¹⁴Then they will pay no attention to Jewish stories that aren't true. They won't listen to the mere human commands of people who turn away from the truth. ¹⁵To people who are pure, all things are pure. But to those who have twisted minds and don't believe, nothing is pure. In fact, their minds and their sense of what is right and wrong are twisted. ¹⁶They claim to know God. But their actions show they don't know him. They are hated by God. They refuse to obey him. They aren't fit to do anything good.

Doing Good Because of the Good News

2 But what you teach must agree with true teaching. ²Tell the older men that in anything they do, they must not go too far. They must be worthy of respect. They must control themselves. They must have true faith. They must love others. They must not give up.

³In the same way, teach the older women to lead a holy life. They must not tell lies about others. They must not let wine control them. Instead, they must teach what is good. ⁴Then they can advise the younger women to love their husbands and children. ⁵The younger women must control themselves and be pure. They must take good care of their homes. They must be kind. They must follow the lead of their husbands. Then no one will be able to speak evil things against God's word.

⁶In the same way, help the young men to control themselves. ⁷Do what is good. Set an example for them in everything. When you teach, be honest and serious. ⁸No one can question the truth. So teach what is true. Then those who oppose you will be ashamed. That's because they will have nothing bad to say about us.

⁹Teach slaves to obey their masters in everything they do. Tell them to try to please their masters. They must not talk back to

them. ¹⁰They must not steal from them. Instead, they must show that they can be trusted completely. Then they will make the teaching about God our Savior appealing in every way.

¹¹God's grace has now appeared. By his grace, God offers to save all people. ¹²His grace teaches us to say no to godless ways and sinful desires. We must control ourselves. We must do what is right. We must lead godly lives in today's world. ¹³That's how we should live as we wait for the blessed hope God has given us. We are waiting for Jesus Christ to appear in his glory. He is our great God and Savior. ¹⁴He gave himself for us. By doing that, he set us free from all evil. He wanted to make us pure. He wanted us to be his very own people. He wanted us to desire to do what is good.

¹⁵These are the things you should teach. Encourage people and give them hope. Correct them with full authority. Don't let anyone look down on you.

Do What Is Good Because You Are Saved

3 Remind God's people to obey rulers and authorities. Remind them to be ready to do what is good. ²Tell them not to speak evil things against anyone. Remind them to live in peace. They must consider the needs of others. They must always be gentle toward everyone.

³At one time we too acted like fools. We didn't obey God. We were tricked. We were controlled by all kinds of desires and pleasures. We were full of evil. We wanted what belongs to others. People hated us, and we hated one another. ⁴But the kindness and love of God our Savior appeared. ⁵He saved us. It wasn't because of the good things we had done. It was because of his mercy. He saved us by washing away our sins. We were born again. The Holy Spirit gave us new life. ⁶God poured out the Spirit on us freely. That's because of what Jesus Christ our Savior has done. ⁷His grace made us right with God. So now we have received the hope of eternal life as God's children. ⁸You can trust this saying. These things are important. Treat them that way. Then those who trust in God will be careful to commit themselves to doing good. These things are excellent. They are for the good of everyone.

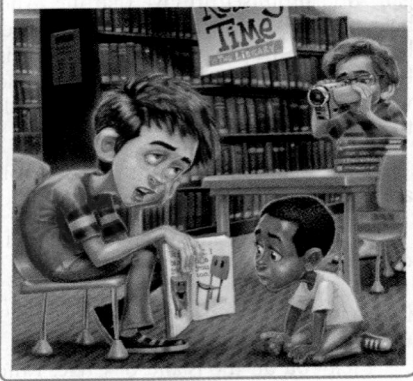

Jay learned that kindness is more than being nice to people in "30 Jays Hath September" (Club). God is shown to be the perfect example of kindness in Titus 3.

⁹But keep away from foolish disagreements. Don't argue about family histories. Don't make trouble. Don't fight about what the law teaches. Don't argue about things like that. It doesn't do any good. It doesn't help anyone. ¹⁰Warn anyone who tries to get believers to separate from one another. Warn that person more than once. After that, have nothing to do with them. ¹¹You can be sure that people like this are twisted and sinful. Their own actions judge them.

Final Words

¹²I will send Artemas or Tychicus to you. Then do your best to come to me at Nicopolis. I've decided to spend the winter there. ¹³Do everything you can to help Zenas the lawyer and Apollos. Send them on their way. See that they have everything they need.

¹⁴Our people must learn to commit themselves to doing what is good. Then they can provide for people when they are in great need. If they do that, their lives won't turn out to be useless.

¹⁵Everyone who is with me sends you greetings.

Greet those who love us in the faith.

May God's grace be with you all.

Philemon

In due course, we have arrived at the first of several books in the New Testament that consist of a single chapter. Though Philemon is a very short letter, it can still be challenging to understand what is happening. Like the previous twelve books, it is a letter from Paul, and this time he is addressing a man named Philemon. However, the main character in the story is not Philemon, but Onesimus.

Evidently, Onesimus had once been Philemon's slave, but he ran away (1:15–16). There is indication that he might have stolen something valuable when he left (1:18–19). But while Onesimus was out enjoying his undeserved freedom, he met Paul and became a Christian. This letter is Paul's attempt to reunite Onesimus and Philemon with a minimum of conflict or bad feelings.

By law, a runaway slave who had stolen property could be executed. So Paul's requests of Philemon were more than a simple favor. But Paul makes his request tactfully, with a nonthreatening and persuasive argument. As his previous letters have shown, he has what might be called today a "silver tongue."

There is another topic worthy of addressing at this point in our expedition. We have seen slavery mentioned and discussed several times. Just because Scripture passages like this talk about how to treat slaves doesn't mean the Bible endorses slavery. Slavery was a reality in first-century Roman culture, and people had to learn to deal with it. But if Philemon agreed to Paul's request to receive Onesimus as "a brother in the Lord" (1:16), it essentially made them equals in the eyes of the church. That was likely a good start for building mutual respect in other areas.

WHAT'S IT MEAN, EUGENE?

Justification—Justification is a long word with a simple meaning: being *made right* or *righteous* in God's sight—regardless of how badly we've sinned—through the atonement of Jesus Christ. When we come to faith in Jesus, He justifies us by taking our sins on Himself. Or in the vernacular of another theological term, our sins were *imputed* to Him. That means they were connected to Him, not you. That Jesus would offer to pay the price for our sins shows His immense love for us!

¹I, Paul, am writing this letter. I am a prisoner because of Christ Jesus. Our brother Timothy joins me in writing.

Philemon, we are sending you this letter. You are our dear friend. You work together with us. ²We are also sending it to our sister Apphia and to Archippus. He is a soldier of Christ together with us. And we are sending it to the church that meets in your home.

³May God our Father and the Lord Jesus Christ give you grace and peace.

Paul Prays and Gives Thanks

⁴I always thank my God when I remember you in my prayers. ⁵That's because I hear about your love for all God's people. I also hear about your faith in the Lord Jesus. ⁶I pray that what we share by believing will help you understand even more. Then you will completely understand every good thing we share by believing in Christ. ⁷Your love has given me great joy. It has encouraged me. My brother, you have renewed the hearts of the Lord's people.

Paul Makes an Appeal for Onesimus

⁸Because of the authority Christ has given me, I could be bold. I could order you to do what you should do anyway. ⁹But we love each other. And I would rather appeal to you on the basis of that love. I, Paul, am an old man. I am now also a prisoner because of Christ Jesus. ¹⁰I am an old man, and I'm in prison. This is how I make my appeal to you for my son Onesimus. He became a son to me while I was being held in chains. ¹¹Before that, he was useless to you. But now he has become useful to you and to me.

¹²I'm sending Onesimus back to you. All my love for him goes with him. ¹³I'm being held in chains because of the good news. So I would have liked to keep Onesimus with me. And he could take your place in helping me. ¹⁴But I didn't want to do anything unless you agreed. Any favor you do must be done because you want to do it, not because you have to. ¹⁵Onesimus was separated from you for a little while. Maybe that was so you could have him back forever. ¹⁶You could have him back not as a slave.

BIBLE ADVENTURES

Nicholas Adamsworth met Philemon in the Imagination Station in "A Prisoner for Christ" (A#06).

WHIT'S WISDOM

Philemon 4–6

The apostle Paul and my son Jason would have a lot in common. They're both very passionate about what they are working on and they both love to travel around the world. And they were both missionaries! Paul went to churches all over the place. He visited and started Christian churches in Rome, Corinth, Galatia, Ephesus, Philippi, Colossae, and more. He made friends with many people you've heard of in the New Testament: Timothy, Barnabas, Silas, Mark, the apostles, and one he called his "dear friend," Philemon. He traveled the world, teaching, baptizing, and even getting himself thrown into prison. He had a very busy schedule!

And yet, even though he was very busy, he found time to pray. He says to Philemon, "I always thank my God when I remember you in my prayers," and he says that over and over to the churches he visited. Paul believed in prayer and practiced it himself. Jason has told me that taking time to pray is the most important lesson he's learned when he's traveling.

Paul knew that prayer is a great gift from God. It's an honor to be able to talk to God at any time, for any reason. It's a time to show our appreciation for all He has done for us, to confess our sins to Him, and ask Him to help us and our friends and families. Find time to pray every day, no matter how busy you are.

Instead, he would be better than a slave. He would be a dear brother. He is very dear to me but even more dear to you. He is dear to you not only as another human being. He is also dear to you as a brother in the Lord.

[17]Do you think of me as a believer who works together with you? Then welcome Onesimus as you would welcome me. [18]Has he done anything wrong to you? Does he owe you anything? Then charge it to me. [19]I'll pay it back. I, Paul, am writing this with my own hand. I won't even mention that you owe me your life. [20]My brother, we both belong to the Lord. So I wish I could receive some benefit from you. Renew my heart. We know that Christ is the one who really renews it. [21]I'm sure you will obey. So I'm writing to you. I know you will do even more than I ask.

[22]There is one more thing. Have a guest room ready for me. I hope I can return to all of you in answer to your prayers.

[23]Epaphras sends you greetings. Together with me, he is a prisoner because of Christ Jesus.

[24]Mark, Aristarchus, Demas and Luke work together with me. They also send you greetings.

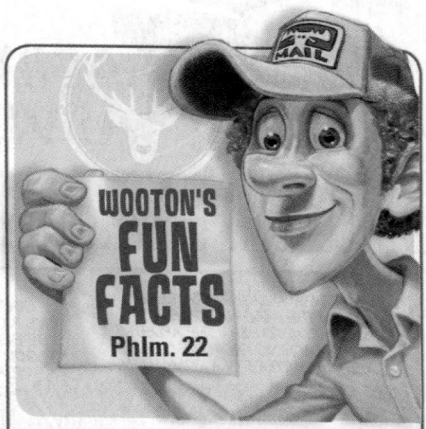

WOOTON'S FUN FACTS

Phlm. 22

Scholars believe Paul wrote at least thirteen books of the New Testament. It's believed he got out of house arrest and visited Philemon after this letter was written. Later Paul was arrested and put to death around AD 64 during Emperor Nero's reign. That makes me sad.

[25]May the grace of the Lord Jesus Christ be with your spirit.

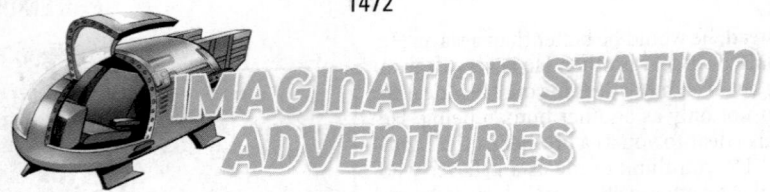

IMAGINATION STATION ADVENTURES

PHILEMON'S "BROTHER"   Read the Book of Philemon.

MATTHEW AND TORI TRAVEL TO ROME IN THE IMAGINATION STATION. THEY ARRIVE TO HEAR THE APOSTLE PAUL PREACHING FROM HIS "HOUSE ARREST" QUARTERS IN A ROMAN VILLA.

IF YOU ARE SLAVES WHO OBEY GOD, THEN YOU WILL LIVE A GODLY LIFE. YOU USED TO BE SLAVES OF SIN. *BUT THANK GOD* THAT YOU OBEYED THE TEACHINGS I GAVE YOU!

SO THEN IS *EVERY BELIEVER* FREE IN CHRIST?

YES. YOU HAVE BEEN SET FREE FROM SIN. YOU HAVE BECOME SLAVES TO RIGHT LIVING.

DON'T LEAVE YET, ONESIMUS. I NEED A WORD.

ONESIMUS IS A RECENT CONVERT TO CHRISTIANITY. HE HAS BEEN HELPING PAUL AND TIMOTHY WITH MINISTRY IN ROME. THEY KNOW HE IS A RUNAWAY SLAVE.

I THINK IT'S TIME FOR YOU TO RETURN TO YOUR OWNER IN COLOSSAE.

BUT I'M *FREE IN CHRIST*—YOU JUST SAID SO. WHY CAN'T I STAY *HERE*?

BECAUSE TO BE FREE IS TO LIVE RIGHTLY. YOU SHOULD GO BACK TO PHILEMON AND SERVE HIM.

BUT PHILEMON WILL BE ANGRY. HE HAS EVERY LEGAL RIGHT TO BEAT ME—*OR WORSE.*

YES. SLAVES CAN BE SENT TO THE COUNTRY TO WORK IN HARD LABOR. I COULD ALSO BE WHIPPED *TO DEATH.*

THE LETTER SAYS PAUL WILL REPAY YOUR DEBT TO PHILEMON. AND HERE'S WHAT'S LEFT OF OUR MONEY.

WHAT LETTER?

IT ASKS PHILEMON TO FORGIVE YOU AND TREAT YOU AS A BROTHER IN CHRIST, *NOT AS A SLAVE.*

PAUL IS SO *GENEROUS* —JUST LIKE GOD!

AT THE HOME OF PHILEMON...

PLEASE FORGIVE ME!

BACK AT WHIT'S END...

WHY DIDN'T PAUL ASK PHILEMON TO FREE ONESIMUS? *ISN'T SLAVERY WRONG?*

SLAVERY WAS COMMON IN ROME, BUT IT WAS STILL *WRONG.* PAUL WANTED PHILEMON TO SEE THAT FOR HIMSELF. PAUL SIMPLY ASKED HIM TO LOVE ONESIMUS.

AND LOVE SETS A PERSON FREE!

IF THE SON OF MAN SETS YOU FREE, YOU WILL *REALLY* BE FREE.

Hebrews

We have arrived at the first New Testament book with an anonymous writer. No one is certain who wrote Hebrews. Some have suggested that it could be another of Paul's letters, but as he clearly put his name on all his other letters, this one was probably written by someone else. Other potential authors include Barnabas (Acts 4:36) and Apollos (Acts 18:24).

Whoever wrote it was especially informed about Old Testament law and Jewish practices, explaining how Jesus fulfilled everything God had promised in the past. The Jewish people had always shown great reverence for angels and for Moses. So the writer of Hebrews showed how Jesus was superior to any angelic or human being (chapters 1–3).

For centuries the people had brought sacrifices to the priests, who would then offer them to God to cover their sins, albeit temporarily. In Hebrews we see that Jesus is now our Great High Priest. His death was the sacrifice that finally took care of our sins—whether past, present, or future (chapter 10). Like the Old Testament priests, Jesus stands between sinful human beings and a holy God. But now that our sins have been fully forgiven, we have no cause to be afraid of approaching God.

A favorite selection of Hebrews for many people is also my personal favorite: the "Hall of Fame" in chapter 11. It's a historical review of many of the faithful people throughout the Bible. It appears that the writer of Hebrews enjoys history as much as I do!

What's it Mean, Eugene?

Omnipotent/Omnipresent/Omniscient—The Latin element *omni*—which appears in each of these words—means "all." Therefore, to be *omnipotent* is to have *all power*. To be *omnipresent* is to be present in *all places* at the same time. To be *omniscient* is to possess *all knowledge*. These words describe God, who has complete control over *all* things. "Nothing God created is hidden from him. His eyes see everything. He will hold us responsible for everything we do" (Hebrews 4:13).

God Speaks His Final Word Through His Son

1 In the past, God spoke to our people through the prophets. He spoke at many times. He spoke in different ways. ²But in these last days, he has spoken to us through his Son. He is the one whom God appointed to receive all things. God also made everything through him. ³The Son is the shining brightness of God's glory. He is the exact likeness of God's being. He uses his powerful word to hold all things together. He provided the way for people to be made pure from sin. Then he sat down at the right hand of the King, the Majesty in heaven. ⁴So he became higher than the angels. The name he received is more excellent than theirs.

Heb. 1:1 Hebrews are Abraham's descendants through the line of Jacob. Joseph was the first person to use this word in the Bible. Read Genesis 40:15.

The Son Is Greater Than the Angels

⁵God never said to any of the angels,

"You are my Son.
Today I have become your Father."
(Psalm 2:7)

Or,

"I will be his Father.
And he will be my Son."
(2 Samuel 7:14; 1 Chronicles 17:13)

⁶God's first and only Son is over all things. When God brings him into the world, he says,

"Let all God's angels worship him."
(Deuteronomy 32:43)

⁷Here is something else God says about the angels.

"God makes his angels to be like spirits.
He makes those who serve him to be like flashes of lightning."
(Psalm 104:4)

⁸But here is what he says about the Son.

"You are God. Your throne will last for ever and ever.
Your kingdom will be ruled by justice.
⁹ You have loved what is right and hated what is evil.
So your God has placed you above your companions.
He has filled you with joy by pouring the sacred oil on your head."
(Psalm 45:6,7)

¹⁰He also says,

"Lord, in the beginning you made the earth secure. You placed it on its foundations.
The heavens are the work of your hands.
¹¹ They will pass away. But you remain.
They will all wear out like a piece of clothing.
¹² You will roll them up like a robe.
They will be changed as a person changes clothes.
But you remain the same.
Your years will never end."
(Psalm 102:25–27)

¹³God never said to an angel,

"Sit at my right hand
until I put your enemies
under your control." *(Psalm 110:1)*

¹⁴All angels are spirits who serve. God sends them to serve those who will receive salvation.

A Warning to Pay Attention

2 So we must pay the most careful attention to what we have heard. Then we will not drift away from it. ²Even the message God spoke through angels had to be obeyed. Every time people broke the Law, they were punished. Every time they didn't obey, they were punished. ³Then how will we escape if we don't pay attention to God's great salvation? The Lord first announced this salvation. Those who heard him gave us the message about it. [4]God showed that this message is true by signs and wonders. He showed that it's true by different kinds of miracles. God also showed that this message is true by the gifts of the Holy Spirit. God gave them out as it pleased him.

Jesus Was Made Fully Human

[5]God has not put angels in charge of the world that is going to come. We are talking about that world. [6]There is a place where someone has spoken about this. He said,

"What are human beings that you think
      about them?
   What is a son of man that you take
      care of him?
[7] You made them a little lower than the
      angels.
   You placed on them a crown of glory
      and honor.
[8]   You have put everything under their
      control."   *(Psalm 8:4–6)*

So God has put everything under his Son. Everything is under his control. We do not now see everything under his control. [9]But we do see Jesus already given a crown of glory and honor. He was made lower than the angels for a little while. He suffered death. By the grace of God, he tasted death for everyone. That is why he was given his crown. [10]God has made everything. He is now bringing his many sons and daughters to share in his glory. It is only right that Jesus

is the one to lead them into their salvation. That's because God made him perfect by his sufferings. [11]And Jesus, who makes people holy, and the people he makes holy belong to the same family. So Jesus is not ashamed to call them his brothers and sisters. [12]He says,

"I will announce your name to my
      brothers and sisters.
   I will sing your praises among those
      who worship you."   *(Psalm 22:22)*

[13]Again he says,

"I will put my trust in him."   *(Isaiah 8:17)*

And again he says,

"Here I am. Here are the children God
      has given me."   *(Isaiah 8:18)*

[14]Those children have bodies made out of flesh and blood. So Jesus became human like them in order to die for them. By doing this, he could break the power of the devil. The devil is the one who rules over the kingdom of death. [15]Jesus could set people free who were afraid of death. All their lives they were held as slaves by that fear. [16]It is certainly Abraham's children that he helps. He doesn't help angels. [17]So he had to be made like people, fully human in every way. Then he could serve God as a kind and faithful high priest. And then he could pay for the sins of the people by dying for them. [18]He himself suffered when he was tempted. Now he is able to help others who are being tempted.

WHIT'S WISDOM

Hebrews 2:8

I remember when I got a call at the shop that a young girl named Karen Crosby was back in the hospital. She had dealt with cancer in the past, but it seemed like she had been doing better. She had come out of the hospital and was doing fine. But then, the doctors became concerned that the cancer was back and was spreading. Connie couldn't understand how a girl as alive as Karen could get cancer. It didn't seem right.

I agreed. "I don't understand it either, Connie," I said. Some things are beyond understanding. People, even good people, get sick and die. All we can do is hang onto our faith that God is in control and He knows what He's doing, like it says in Hebrews 2:8.

Karen eventually died from her cancer and I hung onto this verse harder than ever. And soon after, Connie became a Christian too. God had everything in His control.

Jesus Is Greater Than Moses

3 Holy brothers and sisters, God chose you to be his people. So keep thinking about Jesus. We embrace him as our apostle and our high priest. [2]Moses was faithful in everything he did in the house of God. In the same way, Jesus was faithful to the God who appointed him. [3]The person who builds a house has greater honor than the house itself. In the same way, Jesus has been found worthy of greater honor than Moses. [4]Every house is built by someone. But God is the builder of everything. [5]"Moses was faithful as one who serves in the house of God." (Numbers 12:7) He was a witness to what God would say in days to come. [6]But Christ is faithful as the Son over the house of God. And we are his house if we hold tightly to what we are certain about. We must also hold tightly to the hope we boast in.

A Warning Against Unbelief

[7]The Holy Spirit says,

"Listen to his voice today.
[8]   If you hear it, don't be stubborn.
You were stubborn when you opposed
    me.
You did that when you were tested
    in the desert.
[9] There your people of long ago tested me.
Yet for 40 years they saw what I did.
[10] That is why I was angry with them.
I said, 'Their hearts are always going
    astray.
They have not known my ways.'
[11] So when I was angry, I made a promise.
I said, 'They will never enjoy the rest
    I planned for them.'"
                    (Psalm 95:7–11)

[12]Brothers and sisters, make sure that none of you has a sinful heart. Do not let an unbelieving heart turn you away from the living God. [13]But build one another up every day. Do it as long as there is still time. Then none of you will become stubborn. You won't be fooled by sin's tricks. [14]We belong to Christ if we hold tightly to the faith we had at first. But we must hold it tightly until the end. [15]It has just been said,

"Listen to his voice today.
If you hear it, don't be stubborn.
You were stubborn when you
    opposed me."   (Psalm 95:7,8)

[16]Who were those who heard and refused to obey? Weren't they all the people Moses led out of Egypt? [17]Who was God angry with for 40 years? Wasn't it with those who sinned? They died in the desert. [18]God promised that those people would never enjoy the rest he planned for them. God gave his word when he made that promise. Didn't he make that promise to those who didn't obey? [19]So we see that they weren't able to enter. That's because they didn't believe.

God's People Enter His Sabbath Rest

4 God's promise of enjoying his rest still stands. So be careful that none of you fails to receive it. [2]The good news was announced to our people of long ago. It has also been preached to us. The message they heard didn't have any value for them. That's because they didn't share the faith of those who obeyed. [3]Now we who have believed enjoy that rest. God said,

"When I was angry, I made a promise.
I said, 'They will never enjoy the rest
    I planned for them.'"
                    (Psalm 95:11)

Ever since God created the world, his works have been finished. [4]Somewhere he spoke about the seventh day. He said, "On the seventh day God rested from all his works." (Genesis 2:2) [5]In the part of Scripture I talked about earlier God spoke. He said, "They will never enjoy the rest I planned for them." (Psalm 95:11) [6]It is still true that some people will enjoy this rest. But those who had the good news announced to them earlier didn't go in. That's because they didn't obey. [7]So God again chose a certain day. He named it Today. He did this when he spoke through David a long time later. Here is what was written in the Scripture already given.

"Listen to his voice today.
If you hear it, don't be stubborn."
                    (Psalm 95:7,8)

[8]Suppose Joshua had given them rest. If he had, God would not have spoken later about another day. [9]So there is still a Sabbath rest for God's people. [10]God rested from his work. Those who enjoy God's rest also rest from their works. [11]So let us make every effort to enjoy that rest. Then no one will die by disobeying as they did.

Jesus Is the Great High Priest

¹⁴We have a great high priest. He has gone up into heaven. He is Jesus the Son of God. So let us hold firmly to what we say we believe. ¹⁵We have a high priest who can feel it when we are weak and hurting. We have a high priest who has been tempted in every way, just as we are. But he did not sin. ¹⁶So let us boldly approach God's throne of grace. Then we will receive mercy. We will find grace to help us when we need it.

5 Every high priest is chosen from among the people. He is appointed to act for the people. He acts for them in whatever has to do with God. He offers gifts and sacrifices for their sins. ²Some people have gone astray without knowing it. He is able to deal gently with them. He can do that because he himself is weak. ³That's why he has to offer sacrifices for his own sins. He must also do it for the sins of the people. ⁴And no one can take this honor for himself. Instead, he receives it when he is appointed by God. That is just how it was for Aaron.

⁵It was the same for Christ. He did not take for himself the glory of becoming a high priest. But God said to him,

"You are my Son.
Today I have become your Father."
(Psalm 2:7)

⁶In another place God said,

"You are a priest forever,
just like Melchizedek." *(Psalm 110:4)*

⁷Jesus prayed while he lived on earth. He made his appeal with sincere cries and tears. He prayed to the God who could save him from death. God answered Jesus because he truly honored God. ⁸Jesus was God's Son. But by suffering he learned what it means to obey. ⁹In this way he was made perfect. Eternal salvation comes from him. He saves all those who obey him. ¹⁰God appointed him to be the high priest, just like Melchizedek.

A Warning Against Falling Away

¹¹We have a lot to say about this. But it is hard to make it clear to you. That's because you are no longer trying to understand. ¹²By this time you should be teachers. But in fact, you need someone to teach you all over again. You need even the simple truths of God's word. You need milk, not

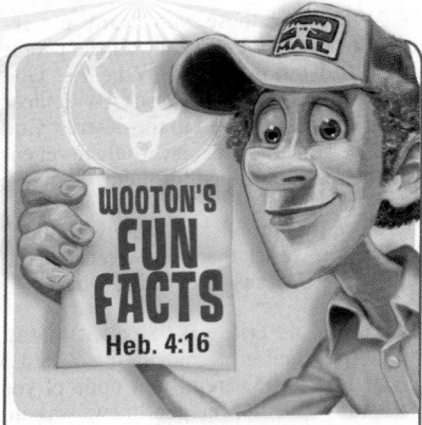

WOOTON'S FUN FACTS
Heb. 4:16

Jesus is a very gracious King to allow us to come close to Him. Many of the kings in Bible times were—what's the right word? Uppity? Snooty? Pretentious? If you came to their throne without an invitation, they might chop off your head—or worse. That's why Esther was so worried to see King Xerxes in Esther 4.

¹²The word of God is alive and active. It is sharper than any sword that has two edges. It cuts deep enough to separate soul from spirit. It can separate bones from joints. It judges the thoughts and purposes of the heart. ¹³Nothing God created is hidden from him. His eyes see everything. He will hold us responsible for everything we do.

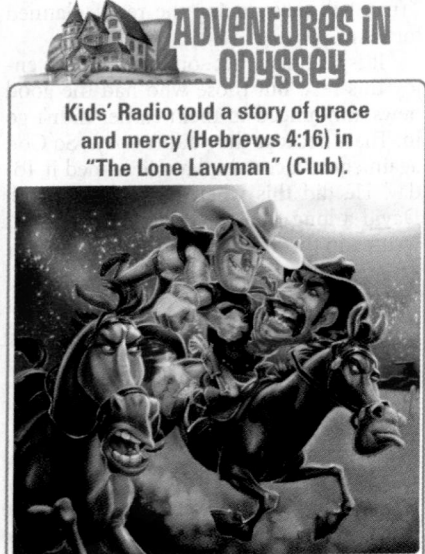

ADVENTURES IN ODYSSEY

Kids' Radio told a story of grace and mercy (Hebrews 4:16) in "The Lone Lawman" (Club).

solid food. [13]Anyone who lives on milk is still a baby. That person does not want to learn about living a godly life. [14]Solid food is for those who are grown up. They have trained themselves to tell the difference between good and evil. That shows they have grown up.

6 So let us move beyond the simple teachings about Christ. Let us grow up as believers. Let us not start all over again with the basic teachings. They taught us that we need to turn away from doing things that lead to death. They taught us that we must have faith in God. [2]These basic teachings taught us about different ways of becoming "clean." They taught us about placing hands of blessing on people. They taught us that people will rise from the dead. They taught us that God will judge everyone. And they taught us that what he decides will last forever. [3]If God permits, we will go beyond those teachings and grow up.

[4]What if some people fall away from the faith? It won't be possible to bring them back. It is true that they have seen the light. They have tasted the heavenly gift. They have shared in the Holy Spirit. [5]They have tasted the good things of God's word. They have tasted the powers of the age to come. [6]But they have fallen away from the faith. So it won't be possible to bring them back. They won't be able to turn away from their sins. They are losing everything. That's because they are nailing the Son of God to the cross all over again. They are bringing shame on him in front of everyone. [7]Some land drinks the rain that falls on it. It produces a crop that is useful to those who farm the land. That land receives God's blessing. [8]But other land produces only thorns and weeds. That land isn't worth anything. It is in danger of coming under God's curse. In the end, it will be burned.

[9]Dear friends, we have to say these things. But we are sure of better things in your case. We are talking about the things that have to do with being saved. [10]God is fair. He will not forget what you have done. He will remember the love you have shown him. You showed it when you helped his people. And you show it when you keep on helping them. [11]We want each of you to be faithful to the very end. If you are, then what you hope for will fully happen. [12]We don't want you to slow down. Instead, be

like those who have faith and are patient. They will receive what God promised.

God Keeps His Promise

[13]When God made his promise to Abraham, God gave his word. There was no one greater than himself to promise by. So he promised by making an appeal to himself. [14]He said, "I will certainly bless you. I will give you many children." *(Genesis 22:17)* [15]Abraham was patient while he waited. Then he received what God promised him.

[16]People promise things by someone greater than themselves. Giving your word makes a promise certain. It puts an end to all arguing. [17]So God gave his word when he made his promise. He wanted to make it very clear that his purpose does not change. He wanted those who would receive what was promised to know this. [18]When God made his promise, he gave his word. He did this so we would have good reason not to give up. Instead, we have run to take hold of the hope set before us. This hope is set before us in God's promise. So God made his promise and gave his word. These two things can't change. He couldn't lie about them. [19]Our hope is certain. It is something for the soul to hold on to. It is strong and secure. It goes all the way into the Most Holy Room behind the curtain. [20]That is where Jesus has gone. He went there to open the way ahead of us. He has become a high priest forever, just like Melchizedek.

Melchizedek the Priest

7 Melchizedek was the king of Salem. He was the priest of God Most High. He met Abraham, who was returning from winning a battle over some kings. Melchizedek blessed him. [2]Abraham gave him a tenth of everything. First, the name Melchizedek means "king of what is right." Also, "king of Salem" means "king of peace." [3]Melchizedek has no father or mother. He has no family line. His days have no beginning. His life has no end. He remains a priest forever. In this way, he is like the Son of God.

[4]Think how great Melchizedek was! Even our father Abraham gave him a tenth of what he had captured. [5]Now the law lays down a rule for the sons of Levi who become priests. They must collect a tenth from the people. They must collect it from the other Israelites. They must do this, even

though all of them belong to the family line of Abraham. ⁶Melchizedek did not trace his family line from Levi. But he collected a tenth from Abraham. Melchizedek blessed the one who had received the promises. ⁷Without a doubt, the more important person blesses the less important one. ⁸In the one case, the tenth is collected by people who die. But in the other case, it is collected by the one who is said to be living. ⁹Levi collects the tenth. But we might say that Levi paid the tenth through Abraham. ¹⁰That's because when Melchizedek met Abraham, Levi was still in Abraham's body.

Jesus Is Like Melchizedek

¹¹The law that was given to the people called for the priestly system. That system began with Levi. Suppose the priestly system could have made people perfect. Then why was there still a need for another priest to come? And why did he need to be like Melchizedek? Why wasn't he from Aaron's family line? ¹²A change of the priestly system requires a change of law. ¹³We are talking about a priest who is from a different tribe. No one from that tribe has ever served at the altar. ¹⁴It is clear that our Lord came from the family line of Judah. Moses said nothing about priests who were from the tribe of Judah. ¹⁵But suppose another priest like Melchizedek appears. Then what we have said is even more clear. ¹⁶He has not become a priest because of a rule about his family line. He has become a priest because of his powerful life. His life can never be destroyed. ¹⁷Scripture says,

"You are a priest forever,
    just like Melchizedek." *(Psalm 110:4)*

¹⁸The old rule is set aside. It was weak and useless. ¹⁹The law didn't make anything perfect. Now a better hope has been given to us. That hope brings us near to God.

²⁰The change of priestly system was made with a promise. Others became priests without any promise. ²¹But Jesus became a priest with a promise. God said to him,

"The Lord has given his word and made
    a promise.
He will not change his mind. He has
    said,
'You are a priest forever.'" *(Psalm 110:4)*

ADVENTURES IN ODYSSEY

In the adventure "Heroes" (A#03), Jimmy learned the importance of looking up to Jesus, who is holy, pure, and without blame, after one of his personal heroes let him down.

²²Because God gave his word, Jesus makes certain the promise of a better covenant. ²³There were many priests in Levi's family line. Death kept them from continuing in office. ²⁴But Jesus lives forever. So he always holds the office of priest. ²⁵People now come to God through him. And he is able to save them completely and for all time. Jesus lives forever. He prays for them.

²⁶A high priest like that really meets our need. He is holy, pure and without blame. He isn't like other people. He does not sin. He is lifted high above the heavens. ²⁷He isn't like the other high priests. They need to offer sacrifices day after day. First they bring offerings for their own sins. Then they do it for the sins of the people. But Jesus gave one sacrifice for the sins of the people. He gave it once and for all time. He did it by offering himself. ²⁸The law appoints as high priests men who are weak. But God's promise came after the law. By his promise the Son was appointed. The Son has been made perfect forever.

The High Priest of a New Covenant

8 Here is the main point of what we are saying. We have a high priest like that. He sat down at the right hand of the throne of the King, the Majesty in heaven. ²He serves in the sacred tent. The Lord set up the true holy tent. A mere human being did not set it up.

³Every high priest is appointed to offer gifts and sacrifices. So this priest also had to have something to offer. ⁴What if he were on earth? Then he would not be a priest. There are already priests who offer the gifts required by the law. ⁵They serve at a sacred tent. But it is only a copy and shadow of what is in heaven. That's why God warned Moses when he was about to build the holy tent. God said, "Be sure to make everything just like the pattern I showed you on the mountain." *(Exodus 25:40)* ⁶But Jesus has been

given a greater work to do for God. He is the go-between for the new covenant. This covenant is better than the old one. The new covenant is based on better promises.

⁷Suppose nothing had been wrong with that first covenant. Then no one would have looked for another covenant. ⁸But God found fault with the people. He said,

"The days are coming, announces the Lord.
I will make a new covenant
with the people of Israel.
I will also make it with the people of Judah.
⁹ It will not be like the covenant
I made with their people of long ago.
That was when I took them by the hand.
I led them out of Egypt.
My new covenant will be different
because they didn't remain faithful to my old covenant.
So I turned away from them,
announces the Lord.
¹⁰ This is the covenant I will establish with the people of Israel
after that time, says the Lord.
I will put my laws in their minds.
I will write them on their hearts.

I will be their God.
And they will be my people.
¹¹ People will not teach their neighbor anymore.
They will not say to one another,
'Know the Lord.'
That's because everyone will know me.
From the least important to the most important,
all of them will know me.
¹² I will forgive their evil ways.
I will not remember their sins anymore."   (Jeremiah 31:31–34)

¹³God called this covenant "new." So he has done away with the first one. And what is out of date and has been done away with will soon disappear.

Worship in the Holy Tent on Earth

9 The first covenant had rules for worship. It also had a sacred tent on earth. ²A holy tent was set up. The lampstand was in the first room. So was the table with its holy bread. That was called the Holy Room. ³Behind the second curtain was a room called the Most Holy Room. ⁴It had the golden altar for incense. It also had the wooden chest called the ark of the covenant. The ark was covered with gold. It held the gold jar

WHIT'S WISDOM
Hebrews 8:12

One day I found Jimmy Barclay playing with the trains at Whit's End. He said he couldn't go home because he had spent all his money on video games instead of staying home and studying. Now he was afraid that his dad would be angry with him.

I told him he reminded me of a young man from the Bible who took his father's inheritance and moved far away. After wasting his money, the man was starving. Finally, the young man went to his father and said, "I have sinned against heaven. And I have sinned against you. I'm no longer fit to be called your son. Make me like one of your hired servants." The son realized that what he'd been doing was wrong and he knew he had to make it right. That's called "repentance."

When the young man arrived home, the father was so happy he ran out to meet his son, threw his arms around his neck, and kissed him. That's the way God feels whenever we repent. He forgives us when we turn away from our wrongdoing and turn back to Him. And when we do, Hebrews 8:12 says that He won't remember our sins anymore. Jimmy still wasn't sure, but he decided to go home and face his dad.

of manna. It held Aaron's walking stick that had budded. It also held the stone tablets. The words of the covenant were written on them. [5]The cherubim were above the ark. God showed his glory there. The cherubim spread their wings over the place where sin was paid for. But we can't say everything about these things now.

[6]That's how everything was arranged in the holy tent. The priests entered it at regular times. They went into the outer room to do their work for God and others. [7]But only the high priest went into the inner room. He went in only once a year. He never entered without taking blood with him. He offered the blood for himself. He also offered it for the sins the people had committed because they didn't know any better. [8]Here is what the Holy Spirit was showing us. He was telling us that God had not yet clearly shown the way into the Most Holy Room. It would not be clearly shown as long as the first holy tent was still being used. [9]That's an example for the present time. It shows us that the gifts and sacrifices people offered were not enough. They were not able to remove the worshiper's feelings of guilt. [10]They deal only with food and drink and different kinds of special washings. They are rules people had to obey only until the new covenant came.

The Blood of Christ

[11]But Christ came to be the high priest of the good things already here now. When he came, he went through the greater and more perfect holy tent. This tent was not made with human hands. In other words, it is not a part of this creation. [12]He did not enter by spilling the blood of goats and calves. He entered the Most Holy Room by spilling his own blood. He did it once and for all time. In this way, he paid the price to set us free from sin forever. [13]The blood of goats and bulls is sprinkled on people. So are the ashes of a young cow. They are sprinkled on people the law called "unclean." The people are sprinkled to make them holy. That makes them "clean" on the outside. [14]But Christ offered himself to God without any flaw. He did this through the power of the eternal Holy Spirit. So how much cleaner will the blood of Christ make us! It washes away our feelings of guilt for committing sin. Sin always leads

to death. But now we can serve the living God.

[15]That's why Christ is the go-between of a new covenant. Now those God calls to himself will receive the eternal gift he promised. They will receive it now that Christ has died to save them. He died to set them free from the sins they committed under the first covenant.

[16]What happens when someone leaves a will? It is necessary to prove that the person who made the will has died. [17]A will is in effect only when somebody has died. It never takes effect while the one who made it is still living. [18]That's why even the first covenant was not put into effect without the spilling of blood. [19]Moses first announced every command of the law to all the people. Then he took the blood of calves. He also took water, bright red wool and branches of a hyssop plant. He sprinkled the Book of the Covenant. He also sprinkled all the people. [20]He said, "This is the blood of the covenant God has commanded you to keep." *(Exodus 24:8)* [21]In the same way, he sprinkled the holy tent with blood. He also sprinkled everything that was used in worship there. [22]In fact, the law requires that nearly everything be made "clean" with blood. Without the spilling of blood, no one can be forgiven.

[23]So the copies of the heavenly things had to be made pure with these sacrifices. But the heavenly things themselves had to be made pure with better sacrifices. [24]Christ did not enter a sacred tent made with human hands. That tent was only a copy of the true one. He entered heaven itself. He did it to stand in front of God for us. He is there right now. [25]The high priest enters the Most Holy Room every year. He enters with blood that is not his own. But Christ did not enter heaven to offer himself again and again. [26]If he had, he would have had to suffer many times since the world was created. But he has appeared once and for all time. He has come at the time when God's work is being completed. He has come to do away with sin by offering himself. [27]People have to die once. After that, God will judge them. [28]In the same way, Christ was offered up once. He took away the sins of many people. He will also come a second time. At that time he will not suffer for sin. Instead, he will come to bring salvation to those who are waiting for him.

Christ's Sacrifice Is Once and for All Time

10 The law is only a shadow of the good things that are coming. It is not the real things themselves. The same sacrifices have to be offered over and over again. They must be offered year after year. That's why the law can never make perfect those who come near to worship. ²If the law could, wouldn't the sacrifices have stopped being offered? The worshipers would have been made "clean" once and for all time. They would not have felt guilty for their sins anymore. ³But those offerings remind people of their sins every year. ⁴It isn't possible for the blood of bulls and goats to take away sins.

⁵So when Christ came into the world, he said,

"You didn't want sacrifices and
    offerings.
    Instead, you prepared a body for
      me.
⁶ You weren't pleased
    with burnt offerings and sin
      offerings.
⁷ Then I said, 'Here I am. It is written
    about me in the book.
I have come to do what you want,
    my God.'"   *(Psalm 40:6–8)*

⁸First Christ said, "You didn't want sacrifices and offerings. You didn't want burnt offerings and sin offerings. You weren't pleased with them." He said this even though they were offered in keeping with the law. ⁹Then he said, "Here I am. I have come to do what you want." He did away with the shadow of the good things that were coming. He did it to put in place the good things themselves. ¹⁰We have been made holy by what God wanted. We have been made holy because Jesus Christ offered his body once and for all time.

¹¹Day after day every priest stands and does his special duties. He offers the same sacrifices again and again. But they can never take away sins. ¹²Jesus our priest offered one sacrifice for sins for all time. Then he sat down at the right hand of God. ¹³And since that time, he waits for his enemies to be put under his control. ¹⁴By that one sacrifice he has made perfect forever those who are being made holy.

¹⁵The Holy Spirit also speaks to us about this. First he says,

¹⁶ "This is the covenant I will make with
    them
    after that time, says the Lord.
I will put my laws in their hearts.
    I will write my laws on their minds."
                (Jeremiah 31:33)

¹⁷Then he adds,

"I will not remember their sins
    anymore.
I will not remember the evil things
    they have done."   *(Jeremiah 31:34)*

¹⁸Where these sins have been forgiven, an offering for sin is no longer necessary.

An Appeal and Warning to Remain Faithful

¹⁹Brothers and sisters, we are not afraid to enter the Most Holy Room. We enter boldly because of the blood of Jesus. ²⁰His way is new because he lives. It has been opened for us through the curtain. I'm talking about his body. ²¹We also have a great priest over the house of God. ²²So let us come near to God with a sincere heart. Let us come near boldly because of our faith. Our hearts have been sprinkled. Our minds have been cleansed from a sense of guilt. Our bodies have been washed with pure water. ²³Let us hold firmly to the hope we claim to have. The God who promised is faithful. ²⁴Let us consider how we can stir up one another to love. Let us help one another to do good works. ²⁵And let us not give up meeting together. Some are in the habit of doing this. Instead, let us encourage one another with words of hope. Let us do this even more as you see Christ's return approaching.

²⁶What if we keep sinning on purpose? What if we do it even after we know the truth? Then there is no offering for our sins. ²⁷All we can do is to wait in fear for God to judge. His blazing fire will burn up his enemies. ²⁸Suppose someone did not obey

the law of Moses. And suppose two or three witnesses made charges against them. That person would die without mercy. [29]People who deserve even more punishment include those who have hated the Son of God. They include people who have said no to him. They include people who have treated as unholy the blood of the covenant that makes them holy. They also include people who have disrespected the Holy Spirit who brings God's grace. Don't you think people like this should be punished more than anyone else? [30]We know the God who said, "I am the God who judges people. I will pay them back." *(Deuteronomy 32:35)* Scripture also says, "The Lord will judge his people." *(Deuteronomy 32:36; Psalm 135:14)* [31]It is a terrible thing to fall into the hands of the living God.

[32]Remember those earlier days after you received the light. You remained strong in a great battle that was full of suffering. [33]Sometimes people spoke badly about you in front of others. Sometimes you were treated badly. At other times you stood side by side with people being treated like this. [34]You suffered along with people in prison. When your property was taken from you, you accepted it with joy. You knew that God had given you better and more lasting things. [35]So don't throw away your bold faith. It will bring you rich rewards.

[36]You need to be faithful. Then you will do what God wants. You will receive what he has promised.

[37] "In just a little while,
he who is coming will come.
He will not wait any longer."

[38]And,

"The one who is right with God will live by faith.
And I am not pleased with
the one who pulls back."

(Habakkuk 2:3,4)

[39]But we don't belong to the people who pull back and are destroyed. We belong to the people who believe and are saved.

Faith That Produces Action

11 Faith is being sure of what we hope for. It is being sure of what we do not see. [2]That is what the people of long ago were praised for.

[3]We have faith. So we understand that everything was made when God commanded it. That's why we believe that what we see was not made out of what could be seen.

[4]Abel had faith. So he brought to God a better offering than Cain did. Because of his faith Abel was praised as a godly man. God said good things about his offerings. Because of his faith Abel still speaks. He speaks even though he is dead.

WHIT'S WISDOM

Hebrews 11

Hebrews 11 is often called the "Hall of Faith." You might look at this list of incredible men and women and say, "Wow! Those were special people that God used! They're all so strong, talented, and powerful." But in some ways, this list shows just the opposite. It shows how God uses people that you might call "average." These people didn't have superpowers. In fact, many of them were less powerful or less strong than "average."

Hebrews 11:34 says: "Their weakness was turned to strength." How? Because of their *faith*. Faith in God can help us do far more than we could ever do in our own strength.

The kids at Whit's End often ask, "How do we have faith in a God we can't see?" But we can see evidence of God everywhere. Look at the wonders of His creation. Or see the way His love fills people around us. Or read through the Bible and see His great work throughout history . . . like right here in the Hall of Faith.

⁵Enoch had faith. So he was taken from this life. He didn't die. "He couldn't be found, because God had taken him away." *(Genesis 5:24)* Before God took him, Enoch was praised as one who pleased God. ⁶Without faith it is impossible to please God. Those who come to God must believe that he exists. And they must believe that he rewards those who look to him.

⁷Noah had faith. So he built an ark to save his family. He built it because of his great respect for God. God had warned him about things that could not yet be seen. Because of his faith Noah showed the world that it was guilty. Because of his faith he was considered right with God.

⁸Abraham had faith. So he obeyed God. God called him to go to a place he would later receive as his own. So he went. He did it even though he didn't know where he was going. ⁹Because of his faith he made his home in the land God had promised him. Abraham was like an outsider in a strange country. He lived there in tents. So did Isaac and Jacob. They received the same promise he did. ¹⁰Abraham was looking forward to the city that has foundations. He was waiting for the city that God planned and built. ¹¹And Sarah had faith. So God made it possible for her to become a mother. She became a mother even though she was too old to have children. But Sarah believed that the God who made the promise was faithful. ¹²Abraham was past the time when he could have children. But many children came from that one man. They were as many as the stars in the sky. They were as many as the grains of sand on the seashore. No one could count them.

¹³All these people were still living by faith when they died. They didn't receive the things God had promised. They only saw them and welcomed them from a long way off. They openly said that they were outsiders and strangers on earth. ¹⁴People who say things like that show that they are looking for a country of their own. ¹⁵What if they had been thinking of the country they had left? Then they could have returned to it. ¹⁶Instead, they longed for a better country. They wanted a heavenly one. So God is pleased when they call him their God. In fact, he has prepared a city for them.

¹⁷Abraham had faith. So when God tested him, Abraham offered Isaac as a sacrifice. Abraham had held on tightly to the promises. But he was about to offer his one and only son. ¹⁸God had said to him, "Your family line will continue through Isaac." *(Genesis 21:12)* Even so, Abraham was going to offer him up. ¹⁹Abraham did this, because he believed that God could even raise the dead. In a way, he did receive Isaac back from death.

²⁰Isaac had faith. So he blessed Jacob and Esau. He told them what was ahead for them.

²¹Jacob had faith. So he blessed each of Joseph's sons. He blessed them when he was dying. Because of his faith he worshiped God. Jacob worshiped as he leaned on the top of his walking stick.

²²Joseph had faith. So he spoke to the people of Israel about how they would leave Egypt someday. When his death was near, he spoke about where to bury his bones.

²³Moses' parents had faith. So they hid him for three months after he was born. They saw he was a special child. They were not afraid of the king's command.

²⁴Moses had faith. So he refused to be called the son of Pharaoh's daughter. That happened after he had grown up. ²⁵He chose to be treated badly together with the people of God. He chose not to enjoy sin's pleasures. They only last for a short time. ²⁶He suffered shame because of Christ. He thought it had great value. Moses considered it better than the riches of Egypt. He was looking ahead to his reward. ²⁷Because of his faith, Moses left Egypt. It wasn't because he was afraid of the king's anger. He didn't let anything stop him. That's because he saw the God who can't be seen. ²⁸Because of his faith, Moses was the first to keep the Passover Feast. He commanded the people of Israel to sprinkle blood on their doorways. He did it so that the destroying angel would not touch their oldest sons.

²⁹The people of Israel had faith. So they passed through the Red Sea. They went through it as if it were dry land. The Egyptians tried to do it also. But they drowned.

³⁰Israel's army had faith. So the walls of Jericho fell down. It happened after they had marched around the city for seven days.

³¹Rahab, the prostitute, had faith. So she welcomed the spies. That's why she wasn't killed with those who didn't obey God.

Heb. 11:17–31 Welcome to the Hall of Faith! On your left, you'll see the Patriarchs Abraham, Isaac, and Jacob. If you look to the right, you'll notice Joseph, Moses, and Rahab. Who is your favorite faithful Bible character in our gallery?

³²What more can I say? I don't have time to tell about all the others. I don't have time to talk about Gideon, Barak, Samson and Jephthah. I don't have time to tell about David and Samuel and the prophets. ³³Because of their faith they took over kingdoms. They ruled fairly. They received the blessings God had promised. They shut the mouths of lions. ³⁴They put out great fires. They escaped being killed by swords. Their weakness was turned to strength. They became powerful in battle. They beat back armies from other countries. ³⁵Women received back their dead. The dead were raised to life again. There were others who were made to suffer greatly. But they refused to be set free. They did this so that after death they would be raised to an even better life. ³⁶Some were made fun of and even whipped. Some were held by chains. Some were put in prison. ³⁷Some were killed with stones. Some were sawed in two. Some were killed by swords. They went around wearing the skins of sheep and goats. They were poor. They were attacked. They were treated badly. ³⁸The world was not worthy of them. They wandered in deserts and mountains. They lived in caves. They lived in holes in the ground.

³⁹All these people were praised because they had faith. But none of them received what God had promised. ⁴⁰That's because God had planned something better for us. So they would only be made perfect together with us.

12 A huge cloud of witnesses is all around us. So let us throw off everything that stands in our way. Let us throw off any sin that holds on to us so tightly. And let us keep on running the race marked out for us. ²Let us keep looking to Jesus. He is the one who started this journey of faith. And he is the one who completes the journey of faith. He paid no attention to the shame of the cross. He suffered there because of the joy he was looking forward to. Then he sat down at the right hand of the throne of God. ³He made it through these attacks by sinners. So think about him. Then you won't get tired. You won't lose hope.

God Trains His Children

⁴You struggle against sin. But you have not yet fought to the point of spilling your blood. ⁵Have you completely forgotten this word of hope? It speaks to you as a father to his children. It says,

> "My son, think of the Lord's training as important.
> Do not lose hope when he corrects you.
> ⁶ The Lord trains the one he loves.
> He corrects everyone he accepts as his son." *(Proverbs 3:11,12)*

⁷Put up with hard times. God uses them to train you. He is treating you as his children. What children are not trained by their parents? ⁸God trains all his children.

Renee learned the meaning of faith from Hebrews 11:1 in "Things Not Seen" (Club).

When I volunteered as a counselor at Camp What-A-Nut, I expected long hikes, sing-alongs, and a few pranks. But hanging from a rope twenty-five feet in the air?

Halfway up the climbing wall, I froze and felt like I couldn't go on. I just wanted to be back on solid ground again. Then I noticed a handhold not far above me. With everything I had in me, I pulled myself up. And I kept going. I asked God for strength as I focused on one move at a time. Finally I got to the very top. A wave of joy flooded over me. I did it!

Sometimes life as a Christian is like climbing a wall. You can reach a point where you don't know what to do next. You're tired and scared and want to give up. But God tells us to persevere—to keep going, no matter what (see Hebrews 12:1–2).

When I fix my eyes on Jesus, He shows me the next step and gives me strength to keep going—one day at a time, one decision at a time.

But what if he doesn't train you? Then you are not really his children. You are not God's true sons and daughters at all. ⁹Besides, we have all had human fathers who trained us. We respected them for it. How much more should we be trained by the Father of spirits and live! ¹⁰Our parents trained us for a little while. They did what they thought was best. But God trains us for our good. He does this so we may share in his holiness. ¹¹No training seems pleasant at the time. In fact, it seems painful. But later on it produces a harvest of godliness and peace. It does this for those who have been trained by it.

¹²So put your hands to work. Strengthen your legs for the journey. ¹³"Make level paths for your feet to walk on." *(Proverbs 4:26)* Then those who have trouble walking won't be disabled. Instead, they will be healed.

A Warning and an Appeal

¹⁴Try your best to live in peace with everyone. Try hard to be holy. Without holiness no one will see the Lord. ¹⁵Be sure that no one misses out on God's grace. See to it that a bitter plant doesn't grow up. If it does, it will cause trouble. And it will make many people impure. ¹⁶See to it that no one commits sexual sins. See to it that no one is godless like Esau. He sold the rights to what he would receive as the oldest son. He sold them for a single meal. ¹⁷As you know, after that he wanted to receive his father's blessing. But he was turned away. With tears he tried to get the blessing. But he couldn't change what he had done.

The Mountain of Fear and the Mountain of Joy

¹⁸You haven't come to a mountain that can be touched. You haven't come to a mountain burning with fire. You haven't come to darkness, gloom and storm. ¹⁹You haven't come to a blast from God's trumpet. You haven't come to a voice speaking to you. When people heard that voice long ago, they begged it not to say anything more to them. ²⁰What God commanded was too much for them. He said, "If even an animal touches the mountain, it must be killed with stones." *(Exodus 19:12,13)* ²¹The sight was terrifying. Moses said, "I am trembling with fear." *(Deuteronomy 9:19)*

²²But you have come to Mount Zion. You have come to the city of the living God. This is the heavenly Jerusalem. You have come to a joyful gathering of angels. There are thousands and thousands of them. ²³You have come to the church of God's people. God's first and only Son is over all

things. God's people share in what belongs to his Son. Their names are written in heaven. You have come to God, who is the Judge of all people. You have come to the spirits of godly people who have been made perfect. ²⁴You have come to Jesus. He is the go-between of a new covenant. You have come to the sprinkled blood. It promises better things than the blood of Abel.

²⁵Be sure that you don't say no to the one who speaks. People did not escape when they said no to the one who warned them on earth. And what if we turn away from the one who warns us from heaven? How much less will we escape! ²⁶At that time his voice shook the earth. But now he has promised, "Once more I will shake the earth. I will also shake the heavens." *(Haggai 2:6)* ²⁷The words "once more" point out that what can be shaken can be taken away. I'm talking about created things. Then what can't be shaken will remain.

²⁸We are receiving a kingdom that can't be shaken. So let us be thankful. Then we can worship God in a way that pleases him. Let us worship him with deep respect and wonder. ²⁹Our "God is like a fire that burns everything up." *(Deuteronomy 4:24)*

Final Appeals

13 Keep on loving one another as brothers and sisters. ²Don't forget to welcome outsiders. By doing that, some people have welcomed angels without knowing it. ³Keep on remembering those in prison. Do this as if you were together with them in prison. And remember those who are treated badly as if you yourselves were suffering.

⁴All of you should honor marriage. You should keep the marriage bed pure. God will judge the person who commits adultery. He will judge everyone who commits sexual sins. ⁵Don't be controlled by love for money. Be happy with what you have. God has said,

"I will never leave you.
    I will never desert you."

(Deuteronomy 31:6)

⁶So we can say boldly,

"The Lord helps me. I will not be afraid.
    What can mere human beings do to
    me?" *(Psalm 118:6,7)*

⁷Remember your leaders. They spoke God's word to you. Think about the results

ADVENTURES IN ODYSSEY

Donna Barclay hoped that a new dog would make her life more normal in the midst of changes in "Pet Peeves" (A#20). She saw that Jesus is the same in the midst of change.

of their way of life. Copy their faith. ⁸Jesus Christ is the same yesterday and today and forever.

⁹Don't let all kinds of strange teachings lead you astray. It is good that God's grace makes our hearts strong. Don't try to grow strong by eating foods that the law requires. They have no value for the people who eat them. ¹⁰The priests, who are Levites, worship at the holy tent. But we have an altar that they have no right to eat from.

¹¹The high priest carries the blood of animals into the Most Holy Room. He brings their blood as a sin offering. But the bodies are burned outside the camp. ¹²Jesus also suffered outside the city gate. He suffered to make the people holy by spilling his own blood. ¹³So let us go to him outside the camp. Let us be willing to suffer the shame he suffered. ¹⁴Here we do not have a city that lasts. But we are looking for the city that is going to come.

¹⁵So let us never stop offering to God our praise through Jesus. Let us talk openly about our faith in him. Then our words will be like an offering to God. ¹⁶Don't forget

REMEMBER THIS

HEBREWS 13:8

"Jesus Christ is the same yesterday and today and forever."

WHAT ABOUT YOU?

Have you ever met someone with a bad case of the "gimmies"? Symptoms are easy to spot. For instance, the face of an afflicted friend will turn red when you try to play with her new birthday gift or borrow something from her. She'll look miserable even when she has lots of stuff, because she always wants more.

Maybe this "sickness" sounds familiar. Perhaps you've suffered from it yourself. One reason for it might be that people are selfish by nature. It can be hard to think about others first. We want our stuff . . . for us. God knows that, which is why He reminds us in Hebrews 13:16: "Don't forget to do good. Don't forget to share with others. God is pleased with those kinds of offerings."

The good news? There's a cure for the gimmies. We can give our time, our stuff, and even offer kind words to others. When we're thinking of others first, we won't cling to our favorite toys, our time, or our talents. And, as we give it a try, we see that sharing with others makes us much happier than simply having a bunch of stuff.

What do you have to share? Maybe you have some stuffed animals you aren't really using that you could give to a children's shelter or day care center. Or maybe your parents can help you buy some canned food for a local pantry using money from your allowance. Think of one meaningful way you can share what you have with others.

---

to do good. Don't forget to share with others. God is pleased with those kinds of offerings.

[17]Trust in your leaders. Put yourselves under their authority. Do this, because they keep watch over you. They know they are accountable to God for everything they do. Do this, so that their work will be a joy. If you make their work a heavy load, it won't do you any good.

[18]Pray for us. We feel sure we have done what is right. We desire to live as we should in every way. [19]I beg you to pray that I may return to you soon.

Final Blessing and Greetings

[20]Our Lord Jesus is the great Shepherd of the sheep. The God who gives peace brought him back from the dead. He did it because of the blood of the eternal covenant. Now may God [21]supply you with everything good. Then you can do what he wants. May he do in us what is pleasing to him. We can do it only with the help of Jesus Christ. Give him glory for ever and ever. Amen.

[22]Brothers and sisters, I beg you to accept my word. It tells you to be faithful. Accept my word because I have written to you only a short letter.

[23]I want you to know that our brother Timothy has been set free. If he arrives soon, I will come with him to see you.

[24]Greet all your leaders. Greet all the Lord's people.

The believers from Italy send you their greetings.

[25]May grace be with you all.

James

Most scholars who study such things believe that the writer of James was the brother of Jesus. (Or more specifically, he was a *half*-brother because God was Jesus' Father.) Note that John 7:5 says that none of Jesus' brothers believed in Him at first. But over time James had come to believe and was even a leader in the first-century church (Acts 15:12–21).

The book of James is reasonably easy to understand, but challenging to put into practice. James challenges believers to not simply talk about what they believe, but to turn their words into deeds (1:22; 2:14–26). Among other sage council, he instructs readers to learn from difficulties and not give up on God when facing trouble (1:2–8). We are called to listen better and keep from being easily angered (1:19–21). We must be careful to treat everyone equally and not show favoritism (2:1–13). We should be humble instead of boastful, refrain from putting too much effort into having material things, and be more faithful in our prayers.

If you'll excuse me admitting a personal flaw, I can allow that one of my most difficult challenges is learning to control my words. Indeed, I have often been accused of being too loquacious (er, talkative) or of forcing others to engage in debate or of criticizing them too harshly. Just ask Connie . . . or Wooton . . . or, well, the list goes on. And so do I, on many occasions. However, I can take instruction from the words of James chapter 3 where we learn about "taming the tongue." I believe I shall read that passage again posthaste!

WHAT'S IT MEAN, EUGENE?

Faith—*Faith* is "belief" and a whole lot more. "Even the demons believe," writes James, "and they tremble!" (James 2:19) The Greek word for faith comes from a verb that means to be persuaded or convinced. It implies and includes all of the following: *confidence*, *trust*, *commitment*, *loyalty*, and *obedience*. Faith is what our relationship with Jesus is built upon.

1 I, James, am writing this letter. I serve God and the Lord Jesus Christ.

I am sending this letter to you, the 12 tribes scattered among the nations.

Greetings.

Facing All Kinds of Trouble

[2] My brothers and sisters, you will face all kinds of trouble. When you do, think of it as pure joy. [3] Your faith will be tested. You know that when this happens it will produce in you the strength to continue. [4] And you must allow this strength to finish its work. Then you will be all you should be. You will have everything you need. [5] If any of you needs wisdom, you should ask God for it. He will give it to you. God gives freely to everyone and doesn't find fault. [6] But when you ask, you must believe. You must not doubt. That's because a person who doubts is like a wave of the sea. The wind blows and tosses them around. [7] They shouldn't expect to receive anything from the Lord. [8] This kind of person can't make up their mind. They can never decide what to do.

[9] Here's what believers who are in low positions in life should be proud of. They should be proud that God has given them a high position in the kingdom. [10] But rich people should take pride in their low positions. That's because they will fade away like wild flowers. [11] The sun rises. Its burning heat dries up the plants. Their blossoms fall. Their beauty is destroyed. In the same way, rich people will fade away. They fade away even as they go about their business.

[12] Blessed is the person who keeps on going when times are hard. After they have come through hard times, this person will receive a crown. The crown is life itself. The Lord has promised it to those who love him.

[13] When a person is tempted, they shouldn't say, "God is tempting me." God can't be tempted by evil. And he doesn't tempt anyone. [14] But each person is tempted by their own evil desires. These desires lead them on and drag them away. [15] When these desires are allowed to remain, they lead to sin. And when sin is allowed to remain and grow, it leads to death.

[16] My dear brothers and sisters, don't let anyone fool you. [17] Every good and perfect gift is from God. This kind of gift comes down from the Father who created the

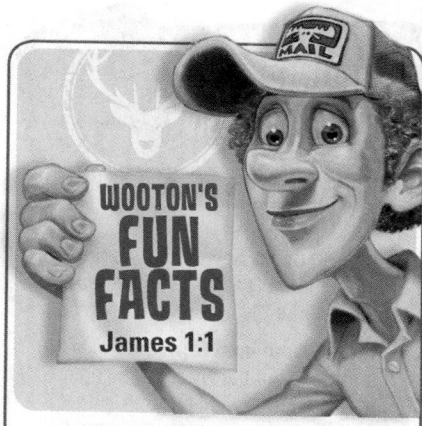

WOOTON'S FUN FACTS

James 1:1

Six US presidents were named James. Four were Johns. Two were Andrews. Which other presidents had biblical first names? Hint: Jefferson, Lincoln, and Harrison. (Barack Obama missed by one letter: c. So close!)

heavenly lights. These lights create shadows that move. But the Father does not change like these shadows. [18] God chose to give us new birth through the message of truth. He wanted us to be the first harvest of his new creation.

Listen to the Word and Do What It Says

[19] My dear brothers and sisters, pay attention to what I say. Everyone should be quick to listen. But they should be slow to

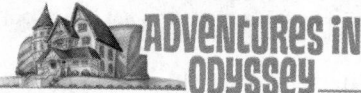

ADVENTURES IN ODYSSEY

While searching for Mr. Whittaker, Eugene and Jason encountered people trying to fool and deceive them—both in modern day and thousands of years ago—in "The Search for Whit" (A#27).

JAMES 1:22

"Don't just listen to the word. You fool yourselves if you do that. You must do what it says."

I figured that a new year was time for a new hairstyle, and Penny volunteered to be my personal hairdresser.

When I came in to work the next morning, Whit barely recognized me, Eugene tried to hide a laugh, and Wooton made a joke. By the time I got home after a long day, I was so frustrated that I said some really mean things about Penny's eye for style and her ability to follow directions. Penny started to cry and ran out of the room.

I felt awful and I remembered one of the first verses Whit had me memorize when I became a Christian. "Everyone should be quick to listen. But they should be slow to speak. They should be slow to get angry" (James 1:19). So I went after Penny. After a few minutes she let me in, and I apologized and asked for her forgiveness.

I wanted a fresh start this year, and I guess I got one. Penny immediately gave me another chance to be her friend. She was slow to get angry too!

speak. They should be slow to get angry. [20]Human anger doesn't produce the holy life God wants. [21]So get rid of everything that is sinful. Get rid of the evil that is all around us. Don't be too proud to accept the word that is planted in you. It can save you.

[22]Don't just listen to the word. You fool yourselves if you do that. You must do what it says. [23]Suppose someone listens to the word but doesn't do what it says. Then they are like a person who looks at their face in a mirror. [24]After looking at themselves, they leave. And right away they forget what they look like. [25]But suppose someone takes a good look at the perfect law that gives freedom. And they keep looking at it. Suppose they don't forget what they've heard, but they do what the law says. Then this person will be blessed in what they do.

[26]Suppose people think their beliefs and how they live are both right. But they don't control what they say. Then they are fooling themselves. Their beliefs and way of life are not worth anything at all. [27]Here are the beliefs and way of life that God our Father accepts as pure and without fault. When widows are in trouble, take care of them. Do the same for children who have no parents. And don't let the world make you impure.

Treat Everyone the Same

2 My brothers and sisters, you are believers in our glorious Lord Jesus Christ. So treat everyone the same. [2]Suppose a man comes into your meeting wearing a gold ring and fine clothes. And suppose a poor man in dirty old clothes also comes in. [3]Would you show special attention to the man wearing fine clothes? Would you say, "Here's a good seat for you"? Would you say to the poor man, "You stand there"? Or "Sit on the floor by my feet"? [4]If you would, aren't you treating some people better than others? Aren't you like judges who have evil thoughts?

[5]My dear brothers and sisters, listen to me. Hasn't God chosen those who are poor in the world's eyes to be rich in faith? Hasn't he chosen them to receive the kingdom? Hasn't he promised it to those who love him? [6]But you have disrespected poor people. Aren't rich people taking advantage of you? Aren't they dragging you into court? [7]Aren't they speaking evil things against the worthy name of Jesus? Remember, you belong to him.

[8]The royal law is found in Scripture. It says, "Love your neighbor as you love yourself." *(Leviticus 19:18)* If you really keep this law, you are doing what is right. [9]But you sin if you don't treat everyone the same. The law judges you because you have broken it.

[10]Suppose you keep the whole law but trip over just one part of it. Then you are guilty of breaking all of it. [11]God said, "Do not commit adultery." *(Exodus 20:14; Deuteronomy 5:18)* He also said, "Do not commit murder." *(Exodus 20:13; Deuteronomy 5:17)* Suppose you don't commit adultery but do commit murder. Then you have broken the law.

[12]Speak and act like people who are going to be judged by the law that gives freedom. [13]Those who have not shown mercy will not receive mercy when they are judged. To show mercy is better than to judge.

Show Your Faith by What You Do

[14]Suppose a person claims to have faith but doesn't act on their faith. My brothers and sisters, can this kind of faith save them? [15]Suppose a brother or a sister has no clothes or food. [16]Suppose one of you says to them, "Go. I hope everything turns out fine for you. Keep warm. Eat well." And suppose you do nothing about what they really need. Then what good have you done? [17]It is the same with faith. If it doesn't cause us to do something, it's dead.

[18]But someone will say, "You have faith. I do good deeds."

Show me your faith that doesn't cause you to do good deeds. And I will show you

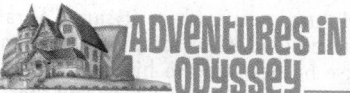

ADVENTURES IN ODYSSEY

Jason, Whit, and Eugene put their faith into action to stop a bad man in "The Top Floor" (A#48).

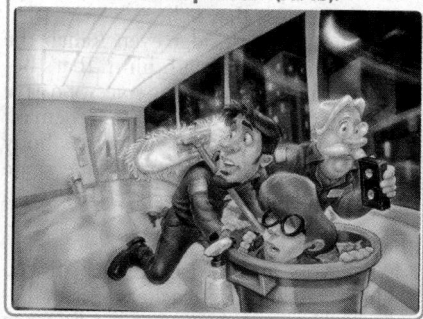

my faith by the goods deeds I do. [19]You believe there is one God. Good! Even the demons believe that. And they tremble!

[20]You foolish person! Do you want proof that faith without good deeds is useless? [21]Our father Abraham offered his son Isaac on the altar. Wasn't he considered to be right with God because of what he did? [22]So you see that what he believed and what he did were working together. What he did made his faith complete. [23]That is what

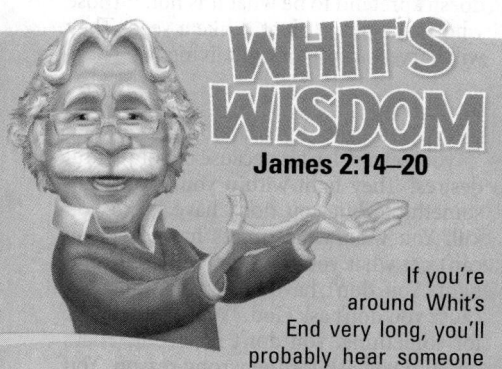

WHIT'S WISDOM

James 2:14–20

If you're around Whit's End very long, you'll probably hear someone talk about faith. Whether it's Connie, or Eugene, or Wooton, or the kids, someone will bring it up over an ice cream sundae or while they're checking out an invention. Why? Because faith is important to what we do every day.

All of us have faith in something whether we realize it or not. If you're sitting in a chair as you're reading this, you have faith that the chair will hold you. You didn't even have to think about it, but you put faith in the chair! And our faith in God should be even more important to us than our faith in our chairs.

James tells us that faith by itself isn't enough. Unless it produces good deeds, it is dead and useless (see v. 17). Does that sound harsh? Think about it. If we have faith that God is who He says He is, and we have a relationship with God, we'll want to please Him. For example, God has told us to take care of those in need. So, in helping others, our actions will please God. And they'll demonstrate to others that we really do have faith in Him. Our faith shouldn't be something that no one knows about. Our faith should be something we demonstrate through our actions.

Scripture means where it says, "Abraham believed God. God accepted Abraham because he believed. So his faith made him right with God." *(Genesis 15:6)* And that's not all. God called Abraham his friend. ²⁴So you see that a person is considered right with God by what they do. It doesn't happen only because they believe.

²⁵Didn't God consider even Rahab the prostitute to be right with him? That's because of what she did for the spies. She gave them a place to stay. Then she sent them off in a different direction. ²⁶A person's body without their spirit is dead. In the same way, faith without good deeds is dead.

Control What You Say

3 My brothers and sisters, most of you shouldn't become teachers. That's because you know that those of us who teach will be held more accountable. ²All of us get tripped up in many ways. Suppose someone is never wrong in what they say. Then they are perfect. They are able to keep their whole body under control.

³We put a small piece of metal in the mouth of a horse to make it obey us. We can control the whole animal with it. ⁴And how about ships? They are very big. They are driven along by strong winds. But they are steered by a very small rudder. It makes them go where the captain wants to go. ⁵In the same way, the tongue is a small part of a person's body. But it talks big. Think about how a small spark can set a big forest on fire. ⁶The tongue is also a fire. The tongue is the most evil part of the body. It makes the whole body impure. It sets a person's whole way of life on fire. And the tongue itself is set on fire by hell.

⁷People have tamed all kinds of wild animals, birds, reptiles and sea creatures. And they still tame them. ⁸But no one can tame the tongue. It is an evil thing that never rests. It is full of deadly poison.

⁹With our tongues we praise our Lord and Father. With our tongues we curse

people. We do it even though people have been created to be like God. ¹⁰Praise and cursing come out of the same mouth. My brothers and sisters, it shouldn't be this way. ¹¹Can fresh water and salt water flow out of the same spring? ¹²My brothers and sisters, can a fig tree produce olives? Can a grapevine produce figs? Of course not. And a saltwater spring can't produce fresh water either.

Two Kinds of Wisdom

¹³Is anyone among you wise and understanding? That person should show it by living a good life. A wise person isn't proud when they do good deeds. ¹⁴But suppose your hearts are jealous and bitter. Suppose you are concerned only about getting ahead. Then don't brag about it. And don't say no to the truth. ¹⁵Wisdom like this doesn't come down from heaven. It belongs to the earth. It doesn't come from the Holy Spirit. It comes from the devil. ¹⁶Are you jealous? Are you concerned only about getting ahead? Then your life will be a mess. You will be doing all kinds of evil things.

¹⁷But the wisdom that comes from heaven is pure. That's the most important thing about it. And that's not all. It also loves peace. It thinks about others. It obeys. It is full of mercy and good fruit. It is fair. It doesn't pretend to be what it is not. ¹⁸Those who make peace plant it like a seed. They will harvest a crop of right living.

Obey God

4 Why do you fight and argue among yourselves? Isn't it because of your sinful desires? They fight within you. ²You want something, but you don't have it. So you kill. You want what others have, but you can't get what you want. So you argue and fight. You don't have what you want, because you don't ask God. ³When you do ask for something, you don't receive it. That's because you ask for the wrong reason. You want to spend your money on your sinful pleasures.

⁴You are not faithful to God. Don't you know that to be a friend of the world is to hate God? So anyone who chooses to be the world's friend becomes God's enemy. ⁵Don't you know what Scripture says? God wants the spirit in us to belong only to him. God caused this spirit to live in us. Don't

ADVENTURES IN ODYSSEY

Jimmy Barclay saw firsthand
how words can be hurtful in
"A Tongue of Fire" (A#14).

you think Scripture has a reason for saying this? ⁶But God continues to give us more grace. That's why Scripture says,

"God opposes those who are proud.
But he gives grace to those who are humble." *(Proverbs 3:34)*

⁷So obey God. Stand up to the devil. He will run away from you. ⁸Come near to God, and he will come near to you. Wash your hands, you sinners. Make your hearts pure, you who can't make up your minds. ⁹Be full of sorrow. Cry and weep. Change your laughter to mourning. Change your joy to sadness. ¹⁰Be humble in front of the Lord. And he will lift you up.

¹¹My brothers and sisters, don't speak against one another. Anyone who speaks against a brother or sister speaks against the law. And anyone who judges another believer judges the law. When you judge the law, you are not keeping it. Instead, you are acting as if you were its judge. ¹²There is only one Lawgiver and Judge. He is the God who is able to save life or destroy it. But who are you to judge your neighbor?

Bragging About Tomorrow

¹³Now listen, you who say, "Today or tomorrow we will go to this or that city. We will spend a year there. We will buy and sell and make money." ¹⁴You don't even know what will happen tomorrow. What is your life? It is a mist that appears for a little while. Then it disappears. ¹⁵Instead, you should say, "If it pleases the Lord, we will live and do this or that." ¹⁶As it is, you brag. You brag about the evil plans your pride produces. This kind of bragging is evil. ¹⁷So suppose someone knows the good deeds they should do. But suppose they don't do them. By not doing these good deeds, they sin.

A Warning to Rich People

5 You rich people, listen to me. Cry and weep, because you will soon be suffering. ²Your riches have rotted. Moths have eaten your clothes. ³Your gold and silver have lost their brightness. Their dullness will be a witness against you. Your wanting more and more will eat your body like fire. You have stored up riches in these last days. ⁴You have even failed to pay the workers who mowed your fields. Their pay is crying

out against you. The cries of those who gathered the harvest have reached the ears of the Lord. He rules over all. ⁵You have lived an easy life on earth. You have given yourselves everything you wanted. You have made yourselves fat like cattle that will soon be butchered. ⁶You have judged and murdered people who aren't guilty. And they weren't even opposing you.

Be Patient When You Suffer

⁷Brothers and sisters, be patient until the Lord comes. See how the farmer waits for the land to produce its rich crop. See how patient the farmer is for the fall and spring rains. ⁸You too must be patient. You must remain strong. The Lord will soon come back. ⁹Brothers and sisters, don't find fault with one another. If you do, you will be judged. And the Judge is standing at the door!

¹⁰Brothers and sisters, think about the prophets who spoke in the name of the Lord. They are an example of how to be patient when you suffer. ¹¹As you know, we think that people who don't give up are blessed. You have heard that Job was patient. And you have seen what the Lord finally did for him. The Lord is full of tender mercy and loving concern.

¹²My brothers and sisters, here is what is most important. Don't make a promise by giving your word. Don't promise by heaven or earth. And don't promise by anything else to back up what you say. All you need to say is a simple "Yes" or "No." If you do more than this, you will be judged.

The Prayer of Faith

¹³Is anyone among you in trouble? Then that person should pray. Is anyone among you happy? Then that person should sing songs of praise. ¹⁴Is anyone among you sick? Then that person should send for the elders of the church to pray over them. They should ask the elders to anoint them with olive oil

in the name of the Lord. [15]The prayer offered by those who have faith will make the sick person well. The Lord will heal them. If they have sinned, they will be forgiven. [16]So confess your sins to one another. Pray for one another so that you might be healed. The prayer of a godly person is powerful. Things happen because of it.

[17]Elijah was a human being, just as we are. He prayed hard that it wouldn't rain. And it didn't rain on the land for three and a half years. [18]Then he prayed again. That time it rained. And the earth produced its crops.

[19]My brothers and sisters, suppose one of you wanders away from the truth. And

REMEMBER THIS

JAMES 5:16

"Confess your sins to one another. Pray for one another so that you might be healed. The prayer of a godly person is powerful. Things happen because of it."

suppose someone brings that person back. [20]Then here is what I want you to remember. Anyone who keeps a sinner from going astray will save them from death. God will erase many sins by forgiving them.

1 Peter

Only seven books remain on our journey: six rather short letters and one lengthier text (Revelation). As we pause at 1 Peter, we remember that the writer was one of Jesus' apostles. In point of fact, he was one of Jesus' so-called "inner circle" which also included James and John. This letter is addressed to "God's chosen people . . . who have had to wander in the world" (1:1). The primary reason that God's people were forced to wander was the worsening persecution of Christians in the Roman Empire. But Peter encouraged his readers, reminding them their troubles were like the intense heat applied to gold ore to provide pure gold (1:7). No matter what happens to us in this world, Peter said, God's Word lasts forever (1:24–25).

As we do our best to stay close to God, we may sometimes feel like "outsiders" in our world. But Peter reminds us that God sees us as royal priests . . . a holy nation . . . God's special people (2:9–11). We shouldn't be taken aback if nonbelievers mistreat us. After all, they did much worse to Jesus (2:21–24).

Peter encourages Christians to remain strong. Regular sufferings are difficult enough, but we also need to be watchful for evil spiritual forces that are always trying to trip us up (5:8–9). Our sufferings are only temporary, but life with God will last forever. As long as we remain on Earth, God promises to provide us with everything we need (5:10–11).

WHAT'S IT MEAN, EUGENE?

Apologetics—Far from suggesting that we should apologize for our faith, the word *apologetics* comes directly from 1 Peter 3:15, which states, "Always be ready to give an answer [*apologia*] to anyone who asks you about the hope you have." Therefore, apologetics is the part of Christianity that deals with logical defense of the Christian faith. A worthwhile, and important, pursuit for every Christian!

I, Peter, am writing this letter. I am an apostle of Jesus Christ.

I am sending this letter to you, God's chosen people. You are people who have had to wander in the world. You are scattered all over the areas of Pontus, Galatia, Cappadocia, Asia and Bithynia. [2] You have been chosen in keeping with what God the Father had planned. That happened through the Spirit's work to make you pure and holy. God chose you so that you might obey Jesus Christ. God wanted you to be in a covenant relationship with him. He established this relationship by the blood of Christ.

May more and more grace and peace be given to you.

Peter Praises God for a Living Hope

[3] Give praise to the God and Father of our Lord Jesus Christ. In his great mercy he has given us a new birth and a living hope. This hope is living because Jesus Christ rose from the dead. [4] He has given us new birth so that we might share in what belongs to him. This is a gift that can never be destroyed. It can never spoil or even fade away. It is kept in heaven for you. [5] Through faith you are kept safe by God's power. Your salvation is going to be completed. It is ready to be shown to you in the last days. [6] Because you know all this, you have great joy. You have joy even though you may have had to suffer for a little while. You may have had to suffer sadness in all kinds of trouble. [7] Your troubles have come in order to prove that your faith is real. Your faith is worth more than gold. That's because gold can pass away even when fire has made it pure. Your faith is meant to bring praise, honor and glory to God. This will happen when Jesus Christ returns. [8] Even though you have not seen him, you love him. Though you do not see him now, you believe in him. You are filled with a glorious joy that can't be put into words. [9] You are receiving the salvation of your souls. This salvation is the final result of your faith.

[10] The prophets searched very hard and with great care to find out about this salvation. They spoke about the grace that was going to come to you. [11] They wanted to find out when and how this salvation would come. The Spirit of Christ in them was telling them about the sufferings of the Messiah. These were his sufferings that were going to come. The Spirit of Christ was also telling them about the glory that would follow. [12] It was made known to the prophets that they were not serving themselves. Instead, they were serving you when they spoke about the things that you have now heard. Those who have preached the good news to you have told you these things. They have done it with the help of the Holy Spirit sent from heaven. Even angels long to look into these things.

Be Holy

[13] So be watchful, and control yourselves completely. In this way, put your hope in the grace that lies ahead. This grace will be brought to you when Jesus Christ returns. [14] You should obey your Father. You shouldn't give in to evil desires. They controlled your life when you didn't know any better. [15] The God who chose you is holy. So you should be holy in all that you do. [16] It is written, "Be holy, because I am holy." *(Leviticus 11:44,45; 19:2)*

[17] You call on a Father who judges each person's work without favoring one over another. So live as outsiders during your time here. Live with the highest respect for God. [18] You were set free from an empty way of life. This way of life was handed down to you by your own people of long ago. You know that you were not bought with things that can pass away, like silver or gold. [19] Instead, you were bought with the priceless blood of Christ. He is a perfect lamb. He doesn't have any flaws at all. [20] He was chosen before God created the world. But he came into the world for your sake in these last days. [21] Because of what Christ has done, you believe in God. It was God who raised him from the dead. And it was God who gave him glory. So your faith and hope are in God.

[22] You have made yourselves pure by obeying the truth. So you have an honest and true love for each other. So love one another deeply, from your hearts. [23] You have been born again by means of the living word of God. His word lasts forever. You were not born again from a seed that will die. You were born from a seed that can't die. [24] It is written,

"All people are like grass.
　　All their glory is like the flowers in
　　　　the field.
The grass dries up. The flowers fall to
　　　　the ground.
25　　But the word of the Lord lasts
　　　　forever."　　　　　*(Isaiah 40:6–8)*

And this is the word that was preached to you.

2 So get rid of every kind of evil, and stop telling lies. Don't pretend to be something you are not. Stop wanting what others have, and don't speak against one another. ²Like newborn babies, you should long for the pure milk of God's word. It will help you grow up as believers. ³You can do this now that you have tasted how good the Lord is.

The Living Stone and a Chosen People

⁴Christ is the living Stone. People did not accept him, but God chose him. God places the highest value on him. ⁵You also are like living stones. As you come to Christ, you are being built into a house for worship. There you will be holy priests. You will offer spiritual sacrifices. God will accept them because of what Jesus Christ has done. ⁶In Scripture it says,

"Look! I am placing a stone in Zion.
　　It is a chosen and very valuable
　　　　stone.
　　It is the most important stone in the
　　　　building.
The one who trusts in him
　　will never be put to shame."
　　　　　　　　　　　　　(Isaiah 28:16)

⁷This stone is very valuable to you who believe. But to people who do not believe,

"The stone the builders did not accept
　　has become the most important
　　　　stone of all."　　*(Psalm 118:22)*

⁸And,

"It is a stone that causes people to trip.
　　It is a rock that makes them fall."
　　　　　　　　　　　　　(Isaiah 8:14)

They trip and fall because they do not obey the message. That is also what God planned for them.

⁹But God chose you to be his people. You are royal priests. You are a holy nation. You are God's special treasure. You are all these

CANDID CONVERSATIONS

I remember when the Washington family adopted a girl named Kelly. At first, she wasn't sure how she felt about being adopted. But then Eugene talked to her. Did you know he was also adopted? Anyway, he told her that adoption is a privilege. Unlike being born to a mom and dad, you are "chosen." Someone looked at you, spent time with you, fell in love with you, and decided they wanted you to be a part of their family.

God chose us to be His people. That should make us feel great, but it should also change the way we make decisions. For instance, you might wonder if you should change who you are so a certain group of people will like you. But, no. God chose you the way He made you.

Knowing who you are in God's eyes can make it easier to value *yourself* the way He values you. Kelly certainly learned that when the Washington family chose her. How will you act when you know that God chose you?

things so that you can give him praise. God brought you out of darkness into his wonderful light. ¹⁰Once you were not a people. But now you are the people of God. Once you had not received mercy. But now you have received mercy.

Living Godly Lives Among People Who Don't Believe

¹¹Dear friends, you are outsiders and those who wander in this world. So I'm asking you not to give in to your sinful desires. They fight against your soul. ¹²People who don't believe might say you are doing wrong. But lead good lives among them. Then they will see your good deeds. And

Wooton's comic demonstrated that Christians are outsiders in the world (1 Peter 2:11–12) in "Drake the Cosmic Copper" (Club).

they will give glory to God on the day he comes to judge.

13Follow the lead of every human authority. Do this for the Lord's sake. Obey the emperor. He is the highest authority. 14Obey the governors. The emperor sends them to punish those who do wrong. He also sends them to praise those who do right. 15By doing good you will put a stop to the talk of foolish people. They don't know what they are saying. 16Live as free people. But don't use your freedom to cover up evil. Live as people who are God's slaves. 17Show proper respect to everyone. Love the family of believers. Have respect for God. Honor the emperor.

18Slaves, obey your masters out of deep respect for God. Obey not only those who are good and kind. Obey also those who are not kind. 19Suppose a person suffers pain unfairly because they want to obey God. This is worthy of praise. 20But suppose you receive a beating for doing wrong, and you put up with it. Will anyone honor you for this? Of course not. But suppose you suffer for doing good, and you put up with it. God will praise you for this. 21You were chosen to do good even if you suffer. That's because Christ suffered for you. He left you an example that he expects you to follow. 22Scripture says,

"He didn't commit any sin.
　　No lies ever came out of his mouth."
　　　　　　　　　　　　(Isaiah 53:9)

23People shouted at him and made fun of him. But he didn't do the same thing back to them. When he suffered, he didn't say he would make them suffer. Instead, he trusted in the God who judges fairly. 24"He himself carried our sins" in his body on the cross. (Isaiah 53:5) He did it so that we would die as far as sins are concerned. Then we would lead godly lives. "His wounds have healed you." (Isaiah 53:5) 25"You were like sheep wandering away." (Isaiah 53:6) But now you have returned to the Shepherd. He is the one who watches over your souls.

3 Wives, follow the lead of your own husbands. Suppose some of them don't believe God's word. Then let them be won to Christ without words by seeing how their wives behave. 2Let them see how pure you are. Let them see that your lives are full of respect for God. 3Fancy hairstyles don't make you beautiful. Wearing gold jewelry or fine clothes doesn't make you beautiful. 4Instead, your beauty comes from inside you. It is the beauty of a gentle and quiet spirit. Beauty like this doesn't fade away. God places great value on it. 5This is how the holy women of the past used to make themselves beautiful. They put their hope in God. And they followed the lead of their own husbands. 6Sarah was like that. She obeyed Abraham. She called him her master. Do you want to be like her? Then do what is right. And don't give in to fear.

7Husbands, consider the needs of your wives. They are weaker than you. So treat them with respect. Honor them as those who will share with you the gracious gift of life. Then nothing will stand in the way of your prayers.

Suffering for Doing Good

8Finally, I want all of you to agree with one another. Be understanding. Love one another. Be kind and tender. Be humble. 9Don't pay back evil with evil. Don't pay back unkind words with unkind words. Instead, pay back evil with kind words. This is what you have been chosen to do. You will receive a blessing by doing this. 10Scripture says,

"Suppose someone wants to love life
　　and see good days.

Then they must keep their tongues
    from speaking evil.
  They must keep their lips from
    telling lies.
¹¹ They must turn away from evil and do
    good.
  They must look for peace and go
    after it.
¹² The Lord's eyes look on godly people,
    and he blesses them.
  His ears are open to their prayers.
  But the Lord doesn't bless those who do
    evil." *(Psalm 34:12–16)*

¹³Who is going to hurt you if you really want to do good? ¹⁴But suppose you do suffer for doing what is right. Even then you will be blessed. Scripture says, "Don't fear what others say they will do to hurt you. Don't be afraid." *(Isaiah 8:12)* ¹⁵But make sure that in your hearts you honor Christ as Lord. Always be ready to give an answer to anyone who asks you about the hope you have. Be ready to give the reason for it. But do it gently and with respect. ¹⁶Live so that you don't have to feel you've done anything wrong. Some people may say evil things about your good conduct as believers in Christ. If they do, they will be put to shame for speaking like this about you. ¹⁷God may want you to suffer for doing good. That's better than suffering for doing evil. ¹⁸Christ also suffered once for sins. The one who did what is right suffered for those who don't do right. He suffered to bring you to God.

His body was put to death. But the Holy Spirit brought him back to life. ¹⁹After that, Christ went and made an announcement to the spirits in prison. ²⁰Long ago these spirits did not obey. That was when God was patient while Noah was building the ark. And only a few people went into the ark. In fact, there were only eight. Those eight people were saved through water. ²¹The water of the flood is a picture. It is a picture of the baptism that now saves you too. This baptism has nothing to do with removing dirt from your body. Instead, it promises God that you will keep a clear sense of right and wrong. This baptism saves you by the same power that raised Jesus Christ from the dead. ²²He has gone into heaven. He is at God's right hand. Angels, authorities and powers are under his control.

Living for God

4 Christ suffered in his body. So prepare yourselves to think in the same way Christ did. Do this because whoever suffers in their body is finished with sin. ²As a result, they don't live the rest of their earthly life for evil human desires. Instead, they live to do what God wants. ³You have spent enough time in the past doing what ungodly people choose to do. You lived a wild life. You longed for evil things. You got drunk. You went to wild parties. You worshiped statues of gods, which the Lord hates. ⁴Ungodly people are surprised that you no longer join them in

WHIT'S WISDOM
1 Peter 3:12–13

When you were younger, did you ever get scared during a thunderstorm and crawl into your parents' bed? When you think back, it didn't really make you safer to be in a different bed. The lightning outside the house couldn't get in, no matter what bedroom you were sleeping in! But it sure felt better to be with someone else, didn't it? You felt protected by your family, just because they were there.

This is a lot like what God does for us. He doesn't keep us from going through bad things in life. In fact, the Bible says that we will face troubles. You can probably think of troubles in your life. I think of the time my wife passed away or my son died in a war. But God tells us that He will go through the difficult times with us. His eyes will always be on us, and His ears will always be listening to our prayers and cries.

The next time you face a tough time (or a thunderstorm!), think about which is better: dealing with everything yourself or allowing God to help you through it.

what they do. They want you to join them in their wild and wasteful living. So they say bad things about you. [5]But they will have to explain their actions to God. He is ready to judge those who are alive and those who are dead. [6]That's why the good news was preached even to people who are now dead. It was preached to them for two reasons. It was preached so that their bodies might be judged. This judgment is made by human standards. But the good news was also preached so that their spirits might live. This life comes by means of God's power.

[7]The end of all things is near. So be watchful and control yourselves. Then you may pray. [8]Most of all, love one another deeply. Love erases many sins by forgiving them. [9]Welcome others into your homes without complaining. [10]God's gifts of grace come in many forms. Each of you has received a gift in order to serve others. You should use it faithfully. [11]If anyone speaks, they should do it as one speaking God's words. If anyone serves, they should do it with the strength God provides. Then in all things God will be praised through Jesus Christ. Glory and power belong to him for ever and ever. Amen.

Suffering for Being a Christian

[12]Dear friends, don't be surprised by the terrible things happening to you. The trouble you are having has come to test you. So don't feel as if something strange were happening to you. [13]Instead, be joyful that you are taking part in Christ's sufferings. Then you will have even more joy when Christ returns in glory. [14]Suppose people say bad things about you because you believe in Christ. Then you are blessed, because God's Spirit rests on you. He is the Spirit of glory. [15]If you suffer, it shouldn't be because you are a murderer. It shouldn't be because you are a thief or someone who does evil things. It shouldn't be because you interfere with other people's business. [16]But suppose you suffer for being a Christian. Then don't be ashamed. Instead, praise God because you are known by the name of Christ. [17]It is time for judgment to begin with the household of God. And since it begins with us, what will happen to people who don't obey God's good news? [18]Scripture says,

"Suppose it is hard for godly people to be saved.
Then what will happen to ungodly people and sinners?"
(Proverbs 11:31)

[19]Here is what people who suffer because of God's plan should do. They should commit themselves to their faithful Creator. And they should continue to do good.

To Older and Younger Believers

5 I'm speaking to the elders among you. I was a witness of Christ's sufferings. And I will also share in the glory that is going to come. I'm making my appeal to you as one who is an elder together with you. [2]Be shepherds of God's flock, the believers under your care. Watch over them, though not because you have to. Instead, do it because you want to. That's what God wants you to do. Don't do it because you want to get money in dishonest ways. Do it because you really want to serve. [3]Don't act as if you were a ruler over those under your care. Instead, be examples to the flock. [4]The Chief Shepherd will come again. Then you will receive the crown of glory. It is a crown that will never fade away.

[5]In the same way, I'm speaking to you who are younger. Follow the lead of those who are older. All of you, put on a spirit free of pride toward one another. Put it on as if it were your clothes. Do this because Scripture says,

"God opposes those who are proud.
But he gives grace to those who are humble." *(Proverbs 3:34)*

[6]So make yourselves humble. Put yourselves under God's mighty hand. Then he will honor you at the right time. [7]Turn all your worries over to him. He cares about you.

[8]Be watchful and control yourselves. Your enemy the devil is like a roaring lion. He prowls around looking for someone to swallow up. [9]Stand up to him. Remain strong in what you believe. You know that you are not alone in your suffering. The family of believers throughout the world is going through the same thing.

[10]God always gives you all the grace you need. So you will only have to suffer for a little while. Then God himself will build you up again. He will make you strong and steady. And he has chosen you to share in his eternal glory because you belong to Christ. [11]Give him the power for ever and ever. Amen.

Final Greetings

[12]I consider Silas to be a faithful brother. With his help I have written you this short letter. I have written it to encourage you. And I have written to speak the truth about the true grace of God. Remain strong in it.

[13]The members of the church in Babylon send you their greetings. They were chosen together with you. Mark, my son in the faith, also sends you his greetings.

[14]Greet each other with a kiss of friendship.

May God give peace to all of you who believe in Christ.

2 Peter

Peter's second letter was written from the perspective of someone who didn't expect to live much longer (1:13–15). So it makes logical sense that he writes about crucial topics that he wants the church to remember after he is gone.

The main emphasis of this short letter is the rise of a number of false teachers who were influencing the church (2:1–3). Peter trusted that God would in due course deal with those wicked people, but he didn't want to see good Christian people misled in the meantime.

God's judgment would be certain, said Peter. But before He puts a final end to evil, God is patiently waiting so more and more people will put their faith in Him. That means believers must learn to live in a sinful world without being caught up in the evil that is all around them.

It takes much effort to remain pure under such conditions (3:14–16). God gives us everything we need, but it's up to us to set the right priorities: faith, goodness, knowledge, self-control, spiritual strength, godliness, kindness, and love (1:3–8).

WHAT'S IT MEAN, EUGENE?

Heresy—In 1 Peter you learned about *apologetics,* which is about a well-thought-out defense for our faith. One reason we must be able to do that is because of *heresies*—false teachings or doctrines that don't line up with correct spiritual teachings. The ability to know and prove when beliefs are heretical is vitally important for every true Christian.

1

I, Simon Peter, am writing this letter. I serve Jesus Christ. I am his apostle.

I am sending this letter to you. You are those who have received a faith as valuable as ours. You received it because our God and Savior Jesus Christ does what is right.

[2]May more and more grace and peace be given to you. May they come to you as you learn more about God and about Jesus our Lord.

Showing That God Has Chosen You

[3]God's power has given us everything we need to lead a godly life. All of this has come to us because we know the God who chose us. He chose us because of his own glory and goodness. [4]He has also given us his very great and valuable promises. He did it so you could share in his nature. You can share in it because you've escaped from the evil in the world. This evil is caused by sinful desires.

[5]So you should try very hard to add goodness to your faith. To goodness, add knowledge. [6]To knowledge, add the ability to control yourselves. To the ability to control yourselves, add the strength to keep going. To the strength to keep going, add godliness. [7]To godliness, add kindness for one another. And to kindness for one another, add love. [8]All these things should describe you more and more. They will make you useful and fruitful as you know our Lord Jesus Christ better. [9]But what if these things don't describe someone at all? Then that person can't see very well. In fact, they are blind. They have forgotten that their past sins have been washed away.

[10]My brothers and sisters, try very hard to show that God has appointed you to be saved. Try hard to show that he has chosen you. If you do everything I have just said, you will never trip and fall. [11]You will receive a rich welcome into the kingdom that lasts forever. It is the kingdom of our Lord and Savior Jesus Christ.

Prophecy of Scripture Comes From God

[12]So I will always remind you of these things. I'll do it even though you know them. I'll do it even though you now have deep roots in the truth. [13]I think it is right for me to remind you. It is right as long as I live in this tent. I'm talking about my body. [14]I know my tent will soon be removed. Our Lord Jesus Christ has made that clear to me. [15]I hope that you will always be able to remember these things after I'm gone. I will try very hard to see that you do.

[16]We told you about the time our Lord Jesus Christ came with power. But we didn't make up clever stories when we told you about it. With our own eyes we saw him in all his majesty. [17]God the Father gave him honor and glory. The voice of the Majestic Glory came to him. It said, "This is my Son, and I love him. I am very pleased with him." *(Matthew 17:5; Mark 9:7; Luke 9:35)* [18]We ourselves heard this voice that came from heaven. We were with him on the sacred mountain.

[19]We also have the message of the prophets. This message can be trusted completely. You must pay attention to it. The message

Don't tell anyone, but sometimes I'm afraid of the dark. For a while, I slept in a truck that was converted to a bed. At night I left the headlights on so I didn't get scared. That's what Christians are supposed to be to the world—a light in a dark place. It's much better to be light in the dark than to be scared!

is like a light shining in a dark place. It will shine until the day Jesus comes. Then the Morning Star will rise in your hearts. [20]Above all, here is what you must understand. No prophecy in Scripture ever came from a prophet's own understanding of things. [21]Prophecy never came simply because a prophet wanted it to. Instead, the Holy Spirit guided the prophets as they spoke. So, although prophets are human, prophecy comes from God.

False Teachers Will Be Destroyed

2 But there were also false prophets among the people. In the same way there will be false teachers among you. In secret they will bring in teachings that will destroy you. They will even turn against the Lord and Master who died to pay for their sins. So they will quickly destroy themselves. [2]Many people will follow their lead. These people will do the same evil things the false teachers do. They will cause people to think badly about the way of truth. [3]These teachers are never satisfied. They want to get something out of you. So they make up stories to take advantage of you. They have been under a sentence of death for a long time. The God who will destroy them has not been sleeping.

[4]God did not spare angels when they sinned. Instead, he sent them to hell. He chained them up in dark prisons. He will keep them there until he judges them. [5]God did not spare the world's ungodly people long ago. He brought the flood on them. But Noah preached about the right way to live. God kept him safe. He also saved seven others. [6]God judged the cities of Sodom and Gomorrah. He burned them to ashes. He made them an example of what is going to happen to ungodly people. [7]God saved Lot, a man who did what was right. Lot was shocked by the evil conduct of people who didn't obey God's laws. [8]That good man lived among them day after day. He saw and heard the evil things they were doing. They were breaking God's laws. And the godly spirit of Lot was deeply troubled. [9]Since all this is true, then the Lord knows how to save godly people. He knows how to keep them safe in times of testing. The Lord also knows how to keep ungodly people under guard. He will do so until the day they will be judged and punished. [10]Most of all, this is true of people who follow desires that come from sin's power. These people hate to be under authority.

They are bold and proud. So they aren't even afraid to speak evil things against heavenly beings. [11]Now angels are stronger and more powerful than these people. But even angels don't speak evil things against heavenly beings. They don't do this when they bring judgment on them from the Lord. [12]These people speak evil about things they don't understand. They are like wild animals who can't think. Instead, they do what comes naturally to them. They are born only to be caught and destroyed. Just like animals, these people too will die.

[13]They will be paid back with harm for the harm they have done. Their idea of pleasure is to have wild parties in the middle of the day. They are like dirty spots and stains. They enjoy their sinful pleasures while they eat with you. [14]They stare at women who are not their wives. They want to sleep with them. They never stop sinning. They trap those who are not firm in their faith. They have mastered the art of getting what they want. God has placed them under his judgment. [15]They have left God's way. They have wandered off. They follow the way of Balaam, son of Beor. He loved to get paid for doing his evil work. [16]But a donkey corrected him for the wrong he did. Animals don't speak. But the donkey spoke with a human voice. It tried to stop the prophet from doing a very dumb thing.

[17]These people are like springs without water. They are like mists driven by a storm. The blackest darkness is reserved for them. [18]They speak empty, bragging words. They make their appeal to the evil desires that come from sin's power. They tempt new believers who are just escaping from the company of sinful people. [19]They promise to give freedom to these new believers. But they themselves are slaves to sinful living. That's because "people are slaves to anything that controls them." [20]They may have escaped the sin of the world. They may have come to know our Lord and Savior Jesus Christ. But what if they are once again caught up in sin? And what if it has become their master? Then they are worse off at the end than they were at the beginning. [21]Suppose they had not known the way of godliness. This would have been better

than to know godliness and then turn away from it. The way of godliness is the sacred command passed on to them. ²²What the proverbs say about them is true. "A dog returns to where it has thrown up." *(Proverbs 26:11)* And, "A pig that is washed goes back to rolling in the mud."

The Day of the Lord

3 Dear friends, this is now my second letter to you. I have written both of them as reminders. I want to encourage you to think in a way that is pure. ²I want you to remember the words the holy prophets spoke in the past. Remember the command our Lord and Savior gave through your apostles.

³Most of all, here is what you must understand. In the last days people will make fun of the truth. They will laugh at it. They will follow their own evil desires. ⁴They will say, "Where is this 'return' he promised? Everything goes on in the same way it has since our people of long ago died. In fact, it has continued this way since God first created everything." ⁵Long ago, God's word brought the heavens into being. His word separated the earth from the waters. And the waters surrounded it. But these people forget things like that on purpose. ⁶The waters also flooded the world of that time. And so they destroyed the world. ⁷By God's word the heavens and earth of today are being reserved for fire. They are being kept for the day when God will judge. Then ungodly people will be destroyed.

⁸Dear friends, here is one thing you must not forget. With the Lord a day is like a thousand years. And a thousand years are like a day. ⁹The Lord is not slow to keep his promise. He is not slow in the way some

CANDID CONVERSATIONS

When I was a brand-new Christian, I read 2 Peter 3:14, which talks about being "without blame," and decided I was going to go a day without sinning. I started my usual daily routine at Whit's End, and I kept repeating over and over "without blame, without blame."

Then one of the kids spilled an entire shake on the table—twice—and I got a little too mad and made him feel bad. I had to start over! I repeated, "without blame." Later, I found myself gossiping with a friend! *Wow! This is hard,* I thought.

When I told Whit about it, he said that being "without blame" was not about keeping myself from sinning. We're human, so that's not possible. It's about asking for God to forgive our sin and repenting—which means being sorry for and turning from our sin, then seeking to change for the better. It's God who makes us blameless by throwing our sin "as far as the east is from the west" (Psalm 103:12).

people understand it. Instead, he is patient with you. He doesn't want anyone to be destroyed. Instead, he wants all people to turn away from their sins.

¹⁰But the day of the Lord will come like a thief. The heavens will disappear with a roar. Fire will destroy everything in them. God will judge the earth and everything done in it.

¹¹So everything will be destroyed in this way. And what kind of people should you be? You should lead holy and godly lives. ¹²Live like this as you look forward to the day of God. Living like this will make the day come more quickly. On that day fire will destroy the heavens. Its heat will melt everything in them. ¹³But we are looking

REMEMBER THIS

2 PETER 3:9

"The Lord is not slow to keep his promise. He is not slow in the way some people understand it. Instead, he is patient with you. He doesn't want anyone to be destroyed. Instead, he wants all people to turn away from their sins."

forward to a new heaven and a new earth. Godliness will live there. All this is in keeping with God's promise.

¹⁴Dear friends, I know you are looking forward to this. So try your best to be found pure and without blame. Be at peace with God. ¹⁵Remember that while our Lord is waiting patiently to return, people are being saved. Our dear brother Paul also wrote to you about this. God made him wise to write as he did. ¹⁶Paul writes the same way in all his letters. He speaks about what I have just told you. His letters include some

things that are hard to understand. People who don't know better and aren't firm in the faith twist what he says. They twist the other Scriptures too. So they will be destroyed.

¹⁷Dear friends, you have already been warned about this. So be on your guard. Then you won't be led astray by people who don't obey the law. Instead, you will remain safe. ¹⁸Grow in the grace and knowledge of our Lord and Savior Jesus Christ.

Glory belongs to him both now and forever. Amen.

1 John

Unlike most of the letters in the New Testament, this one does not mention a writer. Nor does it say to whom the letter is addressed. But from the earliest scholars of the Christian church (men like Irenaeus, Tertullian, and Origen) to the present day, people have known that the author was John, the apostle of Jesus. Why? I'm pleased that you asked! It is because a close reading of this book shows a great number of similarities to John's gospel. Not only are there many similarities in vocabulary, but the writing style is highly comparable. In addition, this is believed to be a "circular letter." That means John intended it to be passed around to different churches, which is why it isn't addressed to one specific group.

Like a number of other letters in the New Testament, John's first warns of false teachers who had been making their way into the church and trying to make people believe things that weren't true about Jesus. John knew Jesus very well, and he was trying to help everyone see the truth. Yet mixed in with his warnings about avoiding such false prophets, he repeatedly challenges his readers to show love for one another. The love and power that God provides makes us strong enough to overcome the lies and influence of sinful people (4:4–6).

In conclusion, John says that it's easy to *say* we love God. But if we hope to prove it, we have to learn to love one another (4:19–21).

WHAT'S IT MEAN, EUGENE?

Repentance—The act of turning away from sin and deciding to follow Jesus. When Jesus began preaching, the first thing He said was, "The kingdom of God has come near. Turn away from your sins and believe the good news" (Mark 1:15). *Repentance* is a vital part of saving faith. It includes *confessing* our sins—that is, *admitting* to God that we have done wrong (see 1 John 1:9)—and actively choosing to live a holy life.

The Word of Life Became a Human Being

1 Here is what we announce to everyone about the Word of life. The Word was already here from the beginning. We have heard him. We have seen him with our eyes. We have looked at him. Our hands have touched him. ²This life has appeared. We have seen him. We are witnesses about him. And we announce to you this same eternal life. He was already with the Father. He has appeared to us. ³We announce to you what we have seen and heard. We do it so you can share life together with us. And we share life with the Father and with his Son, Jesus Christ. ⁴We are writing this to make our joy complete.

Walking in the Light

⁵Here is the message we have heard from him and announce to you. God is light. There is no darkness in him at all. ⁶Suppose we say that we share life with God but still walk in the darkness. Then we are lying. We are not living out the truth. ⁷But suppose we walk in the light, just as he is in the light. Then we share life with one another. And the blood of Jesus, his Son, makes us pure from all sin.

⁸Suppose we claim we are without sin. Then we are fooling ourselves. The truth is not in us. ⁹But God is faithful and fair. If we confess our sins, he will forgive our sins. He will forgive every wrong thing we have done. He will make us pure. ¹⁰If we claim we have not sinned, we are calling God a liar. His word is not in us.

2 My dear children, I'm writing this to you so that you will not sin. But suppose someone does sin. Then we have a friend who speaks to the Father for us. He is Jesus Christ, the Blameless One. ²He gave his life to pay for our sins. But he not only paid for our sins. He also paid for the sins of the whole world.

Instructions About Loving and Hating Other Believers

³We know that we have come to know God if we obey his commands. ⁴Suppose someone says, "I know him." But suppose this person does not do what God commands. Then this person is a liar and is not telling the truth. ⁵But if anyone obeys God's word, then that person truly loves God. Here is how we know we belong to him. ⁶Those who claim to belong to him must live just as Jesus did.

⁷Dear friends, I'm not writing you a new command. Instead, I'm writing one you have heard before. You have had it since the beginning. ⁸But I am writing what amounts to a new command. Its truth was shown in how Jesus lived. It is also shown in how you live. That's because the darkness is passing away. And the true light is already shining.

⁹Suppose someone claims to be in the light but hates a brother or sister. Then they are still in the darkness. ¹⁰Anyone who loves their brother and sister lives in the light. There is nothing in them to make them fall into sin. ¹¹But anyone who hates a brother or sister is in the darkness. They walk around in the darkness. They don't know where they are going. The darkness has made them blind.

Reasons for Writing

¹² Dear children, I'm writing to you
    because your sins have been
      forgiven.
    They have been forgiven because of
      what Jesus has done.
¹³ Fathers, I'm writing to you
    because you know the one who is
      from the beginning.
    Young men, I'm writing to you
    because you have won the battle over
      the evil one.

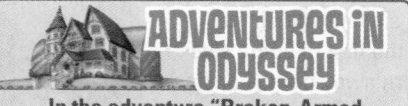

ADVENTURES IN ODYSSEY

In the adventure "Broken-Armed and Dangerous" (A#46), both Tamika and Eugene felt guilty because they were overlooking different parts of 1 John 1:9.

¹⁴ Dear children, I'm writing to you
    because you know the Father.
Fathers, I'm writing to you
    because you know the one who is
    from the beginning.
Young men, I'm writing to you
    because you are strong.
God's word lives in you.
You have won the battle over the evil
    one.

Do Not Love the World

¹⁵Do not love the world or anything in
it. If anyone loves the world, love for the
Father is not in them. ¹⁶Here is what people
who belong to this world do. They try to
satisfy what their sinful desires want to do.
They long for what their sinful eyes look at.
They take pride in what they have and what
they do. All of this comes from the world.
None of it comes from the Father. ¹⁷The
world and its evil desires are passing away.
But whoever does what God wants them to
do lives forever.

Warnings About Saying No to the Son

¹⁸Dear children, we are living in the
last days. You have heard that the great
enemy of Christ is coming. But even now
many enemies of Christ have already come.
That's how we know that these are the last
days. ¹⁹These enemies left our community
of believers. They didn't really belong to
us. If they had belonged to us, they would
have remained with us. But by leaving they
showed that none of them belonged to us.
²⁰You have received the Spirit from the
Holy One. And all of you know the truth.
²¹I'm not writing to you because you don't
know the truth. I'm writing because you
do know it. I'm writing to you because
no lie comes from the truth. ²²Who is the
liar? It is anyone who says that Jesus is not
the Christ. The person who says this is the
great enemy of Christ. They say no to the
Father and the Son. ²³The person who says
no to the Son doesn't belong to the Father.

But anyone who says yes to the Son belongs
to the Father also.

²⁴Make sure that you don't forget what
you have heard from the beginning. Then
you will remain joined to the Son and to the
Father. ²⁵And here is what God has promised us. He has promised us eternal life.

²⁶I'm writing these things to warn you.
I am warning you about people trying to
lead you astray. ²⁷But you have received the
Holy Spirit from God. He continues to live
in you. So you don't need anyone to teach
you. God's Spirit teaches you about everything. What he says is true. He doesn't lie.
Remain joined to Christ, just as you have
been taught by the Spirit.

God's Children and Sin

²⁸Dear children, remain joined to Christ.
Then when he comes, we can be bold. We
will not be ashamed to meet him when he
comes.

²⁹You know that God is right and always
does what is right. And you know that everyone who does what is right is God's child.

3 See what amazing love the Father has
given us! Because of it, we are called
children of God. And that's what we really
are! The world doesn't know us because it
didn't know him. ²Dear friends, now we
are children of God. He still hasn't let us
know what we will be. But we know that
when Christ appears, we will be like him.
That's because we will see him as he really
is. ³Christ is pure. All who hope to be like
him make themselves pure.

⁴Everyone who sins breaks the law. In fact,
breaking the law is sin. ⁵But you know that
Christ came to take our sins away. And there
is no sin in him. ⁶No one who remains joined
to him keeps on sinning. No one who keeps
on sinning has seen him or known him.

⁷Dear children, don't let anyone lead you
astray. The person who does what is right
is holy, just as Christ is holy. ⁸The person
who does what is sinful belongs to the devil. That's because the devil has been sinning
from the beginning. But the Son of God
came to destroy the devil's work. ⁹Those
who are God's children will not keep on
sinning. God's very nature remains in
them. They can't go on sinning. That's because they are God's children. ¹⁰Here is how
you can tell the difference between God's
children and the devil's children. Anyone

who doesn't do what is right isn't God's child. And anyone who doesn't love their brother or sister isn't God's child either.

More Instructions About Loving and Hating One Another

[11]From the beginning we have heard that we should love one another. [12]Don't be like Cain. He belonged to the evil one. He murdered his brother. And why did he murder him? Because the things Cain had done were wrong. But the things his brother had done were right. [13]My brothers and sisters, don't be surprised if the world hates you. [14]We know that we have left our old dead way of life. And we have entered into new life. We know this because we love one another. Anyone who doesn't love still lives in their old condition. [15]Anyone who hates their brother or sister is a murderer. And you know that no murderer has eternal life.

[16]We know what love is because Jesus Christ gave his life for us. So we should give our lives for our brothers and sisters. [17]Suppose someone sees a brother or sister in need and is able to help them. And suppose that person doesn't take pity on these needy people. Then how can the love of God be in that person? [18]Dear children, don't just talk about love. Put your love into action. Then it will truly be love.

[19]Here's how we know that we hold to the truth. And here's how we put our hearts at rest, knowing that God is watching. [20]If our hearts judge us, we know that God is greater than our hearts. And he knows everything. [21]Dear friends, if our hearts do not judge us, we can be bold with God. [22]And he will give us anything we ask. That's because we obey his commands. We do what pleases him. [23]God has commanded us to believe in the name of his Son, Jesus Christ. He has also commanded us to love one another. [24]The one who obeys God's commands remains joined to him. And he remains joined to them. Here is how we know that God lives in us. We know it because of the Holy Spirit he gave us.

Jesus Came as a Human Being

4 Dear friends, do not believe every spirit. Test the spirits to see if they belong to God. Many false prophets have gone out into the world. [2]Here is how you can recognize the Spirit of God. Every spirit agreeing that Jesus Christ came in a human body belongs to God. [3]But every spirit that doesn't agree with this does not belong to God. You have heard that the spirit of the great enemy of Christ is coming. Even now it is already in the world.

[4]Dear children, you belong to God. You have not accepted the teachings of the false prophets. That's because the one who is in you is powerful. He is more powerful than the one who is in the world. [5]False prophets belong to the world. So they speak from the world's point of view. And the world listens to them. [6]We belong to God. And those who know God listen to us. But those who don't belong to God don't listen to us. That's how we can tell the difference between the Spirit of truth and the spirit of lies.

We Love Because God Loved Us

[7]Dear friends, let us love one another, because love comes from God. Everyone who loves has become a child of God and knows God. [8]Anyone who does not love does not know God, because God is love. [9]Here is how God showed his love among us. He sent his one and only Son into the world. He sent him so we could receive life through him. [10]Here is what love is. It is not that we loved God. It is that he loved us and sent his Son to give his life to pay for our sins. [11]Dear friends, since God loved us this much, we should also love one another. [12]No one has ever seen God. But if we love one another, God lives in us. His love is made complete in us.

WHIT'S WISDOM

1 John 4:13–14

There's a room at Whit's End called the Gallery. It's filled with paintings like any other art gallery, but this one is different because the paintings actually talk! You can stand in front of people from history and the Bible. You can talk to Abraham Lincoln about the Gettysburg Address, swap baseball stories with Jackie Robinson, or perform a sonnet for William Shakespeare. So far, I haven't installed a portrait of Jesus in the Gallery.

Why? Because—if you think about it—Jesus is in the Gallery already. In fact, He's always with us.

Before Jesus left the disciples and went back to heaven, He told them He would never truly leave them. He said the Holy Spirit would be with us all the time, ready to communicate with us and be our conscience when we have to make a decision. The Holy Spirit gives us power to do and say things that we would never be able to do on our own. When we give our lives to Jesus, we are forever joined to Him through the Holy Spirit. Spend a few minutes praying and thanking Him that Jesus is with you at all times.

[13]Here's how we know that we are joined to him and he to us. He has given us his Holy Spirit. [14]The Father has sent his Son to be the Savior of the world. We have seen it and are witnesses to it. [15]God lives in anyone who agrees that Jesus is the Son of God. This kind of person remains joined to God. [16]So we know that God loves us. We depend on it.

God is love. Anyone who leads a life of love is joined to God. And God is joined to them. [17]Suppose love is fulfilled among us. Then we can be without fear on the day God judges the world. Love is fulfilled among us when in this world we are like Jesus. [18]There is no fear in love. Instead, perfect love drives away fear. That's because fear has to do with being punished. The one who fears does not have perfect love.

[19]We love because he loved us first. [20]Suppose someone claims to love God but hates a brother or sister. Then they are a liar. They don't love their brother or sister, whom they have seen. So they can't love God, whom they haven't seen. [21]Here is the command God has given us. Anyone who loves God must also love their brother and sister.

Faith in God's Son Who Became a Human Being

5 Everyone who believes that Jesus is the Christ is a child of God. And everyone who loves the Father loves his children as well. [2]Here is how we know that we love God's children. We know it when we love God and obey his commands. [3]In fact, here is what it means to love God. We love him by obeying his commands. And his commands are not hard to obey. [4]That's because everyone who is a child of God has won the battle over the world. Our faith has won the

WOOTON'S FUN FACTS

1 Jn. 4:21 The Bible uses "brother and sister" to mean other believers. But it can include your siblings too. My twin brother is much harder to love than Connie or Eugene. But I'm working on it.

ADVENTURES IN ODYSSEY

In the adventure "A Matter of Obedience" (Club), a young Tom Riley learned about obedience when he ran into trouble on a bridge while on a mission for his father.

battle for us. [5]Who is it that has won the battle over the world? Only the person who believes that Jesus is the Son of God.

[6]Jesus Christ was born as we are, and he died on the cross. He wasn't just born as we are. He also died on the cross. The Holy Spirit is a truthful witness about him. That's because the Spirit is the truth. [7]There are three that are witnesses about Jesus. [8]They are the Holy Spirit, the birth of Jesus, and the death of Jesus. And the three of them agree. [9]We accept what people say when they are witnesses. But it's more important when God is a witness. That's because it is what God says about his Son. [10]Whoever believes in the Son of God accepts what God says about him. Whoever does not believe God is calling him a liar. That's because they have not believed what God said about his Son. [11]Here is what God says about the Son. God has given us eternal life. And this life is found in his Son. [12]Whoever belongs to the Son has life. Whoever doesn't belong to the Son of God doesn't have life.

Final Words

[13]I'm writing these things to you who believe in the name of the Son of God. I'm writing so you will know that you have eternal life. [14]Here is what we can be sure of when we come to God in prayer. If we ask anything in keeping with what he wants, he hears us. [15]If we know that God hears what we ask for, we know that we have it. [16]Suppose you see any brother or sister commit a sin. But this sin is not the kind that leads to death. Then you should pray, and God will give them life. I'm talking about someone whose sin does not lead to death. But there is a sin that does lead to death. I'm not saying you should pray about that sin. [17]Every wrong thing we do is sin. But there are sins that do not lead to death.

[18]We know that those who are children of God do not keep on sinning. The Son of God keeps them safe. The evil one can't harm them. [19]We know that we are children of God. We know that the whole world is under the control of the evil one. [20]We also know that the Son of God has come. He has given us understanding. So we can know the God who is true. And we belong to the true God by belonging to his Son, Jesus Christ. He is the true God and eternal life.

[21]Dear children, keep away from statues of gods.

2 John

We have come to a book with two significant "seconds": Not only is it the second book of John, it is also the second shortest book in the Bible. (If you're curious about the shortest book, you needn't wait on our journey.) This *second* letter of John is addressed to "the lady chosen by God and to her children" (1). If John wrote it to an actual person, that woman has never been identified. Many scholars believe John used the image of a mother and children to symbolize the church and its many members.

Though much shorter than its immediate predecessor (1 John), this second letter continues to emphasize the importance of love. The basis for authentic Christian love is obedience to God's commands and genuine concern for one another (6). At the time the letter was written, it was common for Christian teachers to travel from place to place. They would be invited into people's homes where they were fed and given a place to sleep for the night before continuing to their next stop.

However, false teachers had started doing the same thing, receiving the people's hospitality while promoting lies. John warned believers to use good judgment in deciding whom to allow into their homes. By feeding and housing false teachers, they were inadvertently contributing to the spread of evil (9–11). The lesson here could be applied to us as well. While we should be kind to everyone, we must be wise in deciding whom we will support with our time, money, and possessions.

WHAT'S IT MEAN, EUGENE?

Holy Spirit/Ghost—The third Person of the Trinity. Like the Father and the Son, The Holy Spirit is fully God. He resides inside each believer (Romans 8:11), gives gifts to the church (1 Corinthians 12:11), and helps us to become like Christ (Galatians 5:22–26).

¹I, the elder, am writing this letter.

I am sending it to the lady chosen by God and to her children. I love all of you because of the truth. I'm not the only one who loves you. So does everyone who knows the truth. ²I love you because of the truth that is alive in us. This truth will be with us forever.

³God the Father and Jesus Christ his Son will give you grace, mercy and peace. These blessings will be with us because we love the truth.

⁴It has given me great joy to find some of your children living by the truth. That's just what the Father commanded us to do. ⁵Dear lady, I'm not writing you a new command. I'm writing a command we've had from the beginning. I'm asking that we love one another. ⁶The way we show our love is to obey God's commands. He commands you to lead a life of love. That's what you have heard from the beginning.

⁷I say this because many people have tried to fool others. These people have gone out into the world. They don't agree that Jesus Christ came in a human body. People like this try to trick others. These people are like the great enemy of Christ. ⁸Watch out that you don't lose what we have worked for. Make sure that you get your full reward. ⁹Suppose someone thinks they know more than we do. So they don't

CANDID CONVERSATIONS

Imagine someone walking up to you today and saying, "Two plus two equals seven." You'd say that person is nuts, right? I think Eugene would have a nervous breakdown about their mathematical profanity! He knows (and you know) that two plus two equals four, and you've known that for years, right? Not only did you learn that in school, but you can test the equation yourself very easily. If you have two coins on the table and add two more, there are clearly four. (Calm down, Eugene, it's just an example!)

Now imagine someone coming up to you and saying, "Jesus never lived on Earth." You might say that person is nuts, and you could point to the Bible to show that Jesus lived on the Earth and interacted with all sorts of people.

There will be people in your life who try to convince you of all sorts of wrong things about Jesus. The key is to already know the Bible, and to believe in your heart everything that God says in His Word. Read your Bible every day and be ready to answer all those questions!

2 Jn. 7 A false teaching about God is a *heresy*. One heresy in ancient times said that Jesus was only a spirit-like ghost, not flesh and bones. John said this wasn't true. Jesus was a man. If anyone tries to tell you that Jesus wasn't a person, show him or her this verse.

follow Christ's teaching. Then that person doesn't belong to God. But whoever follows Christ's teaching belongs to the Father and the Son. ¹⁰Suppose someone comes to you and doesn't teach these truths. Then don't take them into your house or welcome them. ¹¹Anyone who welcomes them shares in their evil work.

¹²I have a lot to write to you. But I don't want to use paper and ink. I hope I can visit you instead. Then I can talk with you face to face. That will make our joy complete.

¹³The children of your sister, who is chosen by God, send their greetings.

3 John

Our trek through the Scripture is nearly complete! We now arrive at a book notable for a number of reasons. Third John is the only "third" book in the Bible in addition to being the shortest. It contains only 13 verses and even fewer words than 2 John. But its brevity doesn't indicate its importance. The lessons in this little book resound as strongly today as they did for the early church: Wise people discover early in life that they can control only their *own* behavior. We have very little control over how *others* will respond to us.

In his previous letter, John referred to the practice of sending out people who would travel and tell others about Jesus. The letter of 3 John also involves that custom. Some of the people John had sent out were invited to the home of a man named Gaius, where they were welcomed and treated hospitably. Others had wanted to talk with a church member named Diotrephes. But for some reason (perhaps jealousy or resentment) Diotrephes didn't give them a warm reception.

John was planning to express his appreciation to Gaius in person, but he wrote this short letter first to thank him in advance. The fact that this letter is now a part of Scripture shows us the importance of remaining faithful to God even when others reject us and our message. And just as importantly, we need to always support other believers in their various ministries as we are able.

WHAT'S IT MEAN, EUGENE?

Parable—A brief fictional tale used to illustrate a truth about the kingdom of God or the spiritual life; i.e., "an earthly story with a heavenly meaning." In some of His parables, Jesus compared the Kingdom of God to a man planting seeds (Mark 4:3–8); a growing mustard plant (Mark 4:30–32); and a fishing net (Matthew 13:47–50). Perhaps the most well known biblical parable is that of the Lost Son (Luke 15:11–32).

¹I, the elder, am writing this letter.

I am sending it to you, my dear friend Gaius. I love you because of the truth.

²Dear friend, I know that your spiritual life is going well. I pray that you also may enjoy good health. And I pray that everything else may go well with you. ³Some believers came to me and told me that you are faithful to the truth. They told me that you continue to live by it. This news gave me great joy. ⁴I have no greater joy than to hear that my children are living by the truth.

⁵Dear friend, you are faithful in what you are doing for the brothers and sisters. You are faithful even though they are strangers to you. ⁶They have told the church about your love. Please help them by sending them on their way in a manner that honors God. ⁷They started on their journey to serve Jesus Christ. They didn't receive any help from those who aren't believers. ⁸So we should welcome people like them. We should work together with them for the truth.

⁹I wrote to the church. But Diotrephes will not welcome us. He loves to be the first in everything. ¹⁰So when I come, I will point out what he is doing. He is saying evil things that aren't true about us. Even this doesn't satisfy him. So he refuses to welcome other believers. He also keeps others

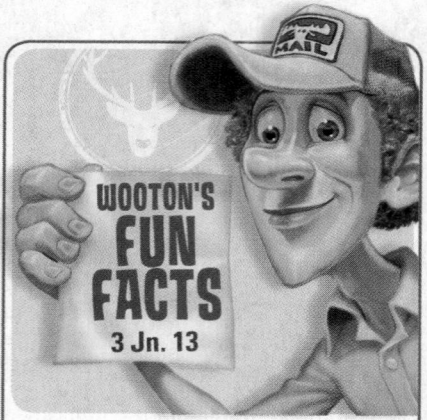

WOOTON'S **FUN FACTS**
3 Jn. 13

When Penny and I are painting together, we spend a lot of time refilling our paint containers because we keep changing our minds. John had to do something similar because the pen he used was likely made out of a reed with a hollowed-out stem. It held very little ink and had to be filled often.

from welcoming them. In fact, he throws them out of the church.

¹¹Dear friend, don't be like those who do evil. Be like those who do good. Anyone who does what is good belongs to God. Anyone who does what is evil hasn't really seen or known God. ¹²Everyone says good things about Demetrius. He lives in keeping with the truth. We also say good things about him. And you know that what we say is true.

¹³I have a lot to write to you. But I don't want to write with pen and ink. ¹⁴I hope I can see you soon. Then we can talk face to face.

May you have peace.

The friends here send their greetings. Greet each one of the friends there.

ADVENTURES IN ODYSSEY

Courtney showed how she could avoid being like those who do evil and learned some important truths in "The Election Deception" (A#21).

Jude

Jude is the penultimate book of the New Testament. Ah, how enjoyable! I've been anxious to use the word "penultimate" for some time as it's one of my personal favorite words and is not used often enough! (It means "second to last" if you're curious.) Anyway, returning to the topic at hand, the name *Jude* is a Hebrew version of the Greek name Judas. Since Judas Iscariot betrayed Jesus, the popularity of the name has greatly decreased! You probably don't know many children with the name "Judas." But prior to Iscariot's betrayal, Judas was actually a rather common name. Jesus had *another* apostle named Judas as well as a brother with that name (Luke 6:16; Matt. 13:55). In fact, it is generally believed that Jesus' brother is the "Jude" who wrote this letter.

The content is highly similar to that of 2 Peter, and one writer might have used the other as source material. Jude, like Peter, warns about false teachers who come into the church as "shepherds who feed only themselves" and "clouds without rain" (12). Jude urged his readers not to be deceived by such people.

What is the best way to keep from being misled by a silver-tongued false teacher? Jude instructs readers to keep building up their faith and listen to the Holy Spirit (20). Be merciful to others (22). And always give praise to God because He will always be there to strengthen you when you ask (24–25).

WHAT'S IT MEAN, EUGENE?

Resurrection—The hope of our salvation, *resurrection* means being raised to life from the dead. The New Testament word is *anastasis,* which means "standing up again." The *resurrection* of Jesus is the most important event in human history. The apostle Paul says that if we believe in Christ, "we will certainly also be joined with him in a resurrection like his" (Romans 6:5).

¹I, Jude, am writing this letter. I serve Jesus Christ. I am a brother of James.

I am sending this letter to you who have been chosen by God. You are loved by God the Father. You are kept safe for Jesus Christ.

²May more and more mercy, peace and love be given to you.

A Warning Against the Sin of Ungodly People

³Dear friends, I really wanted to write to you about the salvation we share. But now I feel I should write and ask you to stand up for the faith. God's holy people were trusted with it once and for all time. ⁴Certain people have secretly slipped in among you. Long ago it was written that they would be judged. They are ungodly people. They misuse the grace of our God as an excuse for sexual sins. They say no to Jesus Christ, our only Lord and King.

⁵I want to remind you about some things you already know. The Lord saved his people. At one time he brought them out of Egypt. But later he destroyed those who did not believe. ⁶Some of the angels didn't stay where they belonged. They didn't keep their positions of authority. The Lord has kept those angels in darkness. They are held by chains that last forever. On judgment day, God will judge them. ⁷The people of Sodom and Gomorrah and the towns around them also did evil things. They freely committed sexual sins. They committed sins of the worst possible kind. There is a fire that never goes out. Those people are an example of those who are punished with it.

⁸In the very same way, these ungodly people act on their evil dreams. So they make their own bodies impure. They don't accept authority. And they say evil things against heavenly beings. ⁹But even Michael, the leader of the angels, didn't dare to say these things. He didn't even say these things when he argued with the devil about the body of Moses. Michael didn't dare to judge the devil. He didn't say the devil was guilty of saying evil things. Instead, Michael said, "May the Lord judge you!" ¹⁰But these people say evil things against whatever they don't understand. And the very things they do understand will destroy them. That's because they are like wild animals that can't

Before Eugene became a Christian, he always wanted to pull me into a debate. One month, every day when he walked into Whit's End, he didn't even bother saying, "Hi, Connie." He would just launch into something like, "You know, Miss Kendall, French philosopher Pascal once said, 'Men never commit evil so fully—'" Don't tell Eugene, but I can't remember the rest of that quote. Anyway, it was just a way to get me all riled up so he could debate me.

I used to get mad, but then Whit told me how to deal with it. He said I shouldn't expect non-Christians to understand many of the things of God because non-Christians don't have the Holy Spirit to show them who God really is. He said to have mercy on Eugene, and to keep loving him like it says in Jude 22–23.

That's what Whit and I both did, and eventually the Holy Spirit penetrated Eugene's heart and he became a Christian. Now he *still* pulls me into debates, but it's more likely to be about parts of our shared faith. He doesn't try to prove that Christianity isn't true. Even while I can be annoyed by his constant bantering and bickering, I can be excited that we can argue as two Christians! Next time someone questions your beliefs, treat them with mercy and kindness. That could be one thing that eventually leads them to the truth.

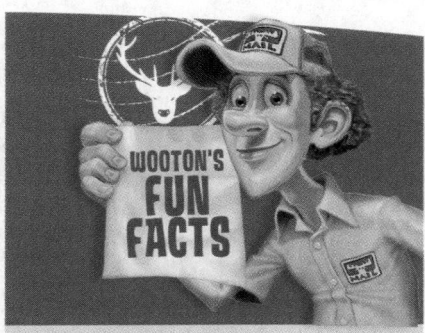

Jude 9 I wonder if fighting over Moses' body is the most bizarre task an angel ever performed. What do you think? This is the second-to-last appearance of the archangel Michael. He's also in Revelation 12:7.

think for themselves. Instead, they do what comes naturally to them.

[11]How terrible it will be for them! They have followed the way of Cain. They have rushed into the same mistake Balaam made. They did it because they loved money. They are like Korah. He turned against his leaders. These people will certainly be destroyed, just as Korah was.

[12]These ungodly people are like stains at the meals you share. They have no shame. They are shepherds who feed only themselves. They are like clouds without rain. They are blown along by the wind. They are like trees in the fall. Since they have no fruit, they are pulled out of the ground. So they die twice. [13]They are like wild waves of the sea. Their shame rises up like foam. They are like falling stars. God has reserved a place of very black darkness for them forever.

[14]Enoch was the seventh man in the family line of Adam. He gave a prophecy about these people. He said, "Look! The Lord is coming with thousands and thousands of his holy ones. [15]He is coming to judge everyone. He is coming to sentence all of them. He will judge them for all the ungodly acts they have done. They have done them in ungodly ways. He will sentence ungodly sinners for all the things they have said to oppose him." [16]These people complain and find fault with others. They follow their own evil desires. They brag about themselves. They praise others to get what they want.

Remain in God's Love

[17]Dear friends, remember what the apostles of our Lord Jesus Christ said would happen. [18]They told you, "In the last days, some people will make fun of the truth. They will follow their own ungodly desires." [19]They are the people who separate you from one another. They do only what comes naturally. They are not led by the Holy Spirit.

[20]But you, dear friends, build yourselves up in your most holy faith. Let the Holy Spirit guide and help you when you pray. [21]And by doing these things, remain in God's love as you wait. You are waiting for the mercy of our Lord Jesus Christ to bring you eternal life.

[22]Show mercy to those who doubt. [23]Save others by pulling them out of the fire. To others, show mercy mixed with fear of sin. Hate even the clothes that are stained by the sins of those who wear them.

Praise to God

[24]Give praise to the God who is able to keep you from falling into sin. He will bring you into his heavenly glory without any fault. He will bring you there with great joy. [25]Give praise to the only God our Savior. Glory, majesty, power and authority belong to him. Give praise to him through Jesus Christ our Lord. His praise was before all time, continues now, and will last forever. Amen.

Revelation

At last, we reach the final stop in our grand journey—our odyssey, if you will—through the Holy Scriptures. Revelation is a book like none other. Like several other books in the New Testament, it was written by Jesus' apostle John, but it is "worlds apart" from his gospel or letters (1, 2, and 3 John).

Perhaps of all the books in Scripture, Revelation generates the most curiosity. John describes events that are to occur in the future, but he does so by using numerous dreams, visions, and symbols.

On many occasions, we are told what the images mean. For example, John opens with a vision of stars and lampstands (1:9–16). He soon explains (1:20) that the lampstands represent churches. The stars are the "angels" of the churches (perhaps literal angels, or possibly the pastors of the churches).

Later John describes the rise of a "beast" (the Antichrist). In connection with this figure is brutal war, persecution of God's people, and death. The events described are most terrible and frightening.

Revelation will be a mysterious book no matter how you read it, but be sure to persevere all the way to its conclusion. God remains in control and emerges victorious, even as the world becomes increasingly (and irreversibly) horrible. God protects His people and provides a magnificent eternal home for them. As you reach the joyous conclusion in chapters 21 and 22, you'll realize this is not really the conclusion of our journey. Instead, it is a new beginning of an even greater story! To quote my dear friend Mr. Whittaker, "The best is yet to come."

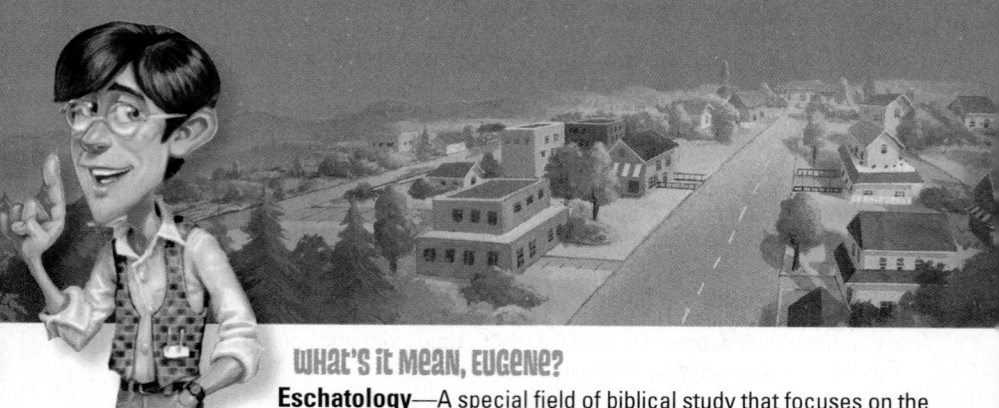

What's it Mean, Eugene?

Eschatology—A special field of biblical study that focuses on the events surrounding Jesus' Second Coming. The Greek word *eschatos* means "last," thus *eschatology* is the study of the "last things," or the things that will take place at the *end* of time. The biblical books that deal primarily with this robust field of study include the books of Daniel, Zechariah, and Revelation, in addition to the "apocalyptic" remarks of Jesus (Matthew 24, Mark 13, Luke 21).

The Revelation Is Given

1 This is the revelation from Jesus Christ. God gave it to him to show those who serve God what will happen soon. God made it known by sending his angel to his servant John. [2]John is a witness to everything he saw. What he saw is God's word and what Jesus Christ has said. [3]Blessed is the one who reads out loud the words of this prophecy. Blessed are those who hear it and think everything it says is important. The time when these things will come true is near.

Greetings and Praise to God

[4]I, John, am writing this letter.

I am sending it to the seven churches in Asia Minor.

May grace and peace come to you from God. He is the one who is, and who was, and who will come. May grace and peace come to you from the seven spirits. These spirits are in front of God's throne. [5]May grace and peace come to you from Jesus Christ. He is the faithful witness, so what he has shown can be trusted. He was the first to rise from the dead. He rules over the kings of the earth.

Glory and power belong to Jesus Christ who loves us! He has set us free from our sins by pouring out his blood for us. [6]He has made us members of his royal family.

He has made us priests who serve his God and Father. Glory and power belong to Jesus Christ for ever and ever! Amen.

[7] "Look! He is coming with the clouds!"
(Daniel 7:13)
"Every eye will see him.
Even those who pierced him will see him."
All the nations of the earth "will mourn because of him."
(Zechariah 12:10)
This will really happen! Amen.

[8]"I am the Alpha and the Omega, the Beginning and the End," says the Lord God. "I am the God who is, and who was, and who will come. I am the Mighty One."

John's Vision of Christ

[9]I, John, am a believer like you. I am a friend who suffers like you. As members of Jesus' royal family, we can put up with anything that happens to us. I was on the island of Patmos because I taught God's word and what Jesus said. [10]The Holy Spirit gave me a vision on the Lord's Day. I heard a loud voice behind me that sounded like a trumpet. [11]The voice said, "Write on a scroll what you see. Send it to the seven churches in Asia Minor. They are Ephesus, Smyrna, Pergamum, Thyatira, Sardis, Philadelphia and Laodicea."

[12]I turned around to see who was speaking to me. When I turned, I saw seven

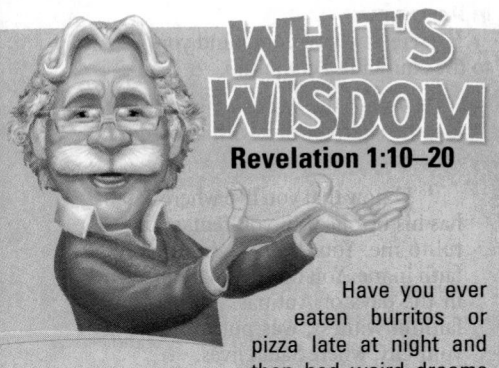

WHIT'S WISDOM
Revelation 1:10–20

Have you ever eaten burritos or pizza late at night and then had weird dreams afterward? Wooton told me about a time he dreamed his body was made of turkey and stuffing after eating Thanksgiving leftovers too many days in a row. But even that dream isn't as strange as the one that John had in Revelation 1:10–20.

In John's case, his dream is actually a vision coming directly from God. It symbolizes the wonderful moment when Jesus will come back to reign as King over the earth.

Jesus Himself talked about His return quite a few times. And there are many prophecies about it in the books of Daniel, Ezekiel, and Zechariah. Jesus wanted us to know He is coming back, because He knew that we might worry as we watch things in the world get worse and worse. But Jesus gives us hope when He says, "Do not be afraid. I am the First and the Last." He was with us from the beginning and will be with us until the end of the world. There is no need to fear. Jesus is returning one day!

golden lampstands. [13]In the middle of them was someone who looked "like a son of man." *(Daniel 7:13)* He was dressed in a long robe with a gold strip of cloth around his chest. [14]The hair on his head was white like wool, as white as snow. His eyes were like a blazing fire. [15]His feet were like bronze metal glowing in a furnace. His voice sounded like rushing waters. [16]He held seven stars in his right hand. Coming out of his mouth was a sharp sword with two edges. His face was like the sun shining in all its brightness.

[17]When I saw him, I fell at his feet as if I were dead. Then he put his right hand on me and said, "Do not be afraid. I am the First and the Last. [18]I am the Living One. I was dead. But now look! I am alive for ever and ever! And I hold the keys to Death and Hell.

[19]"So write down what you have seen. Write about what is happening now and what will happen later. [20]Here is the meaning of the mystery of the seven stars you saw in my right hand. They are the angels of the seven churches. And the seven golden lampstands you saw stand for the seven churches.

The Letter to the Church in Ephesus

2 "Here is what I command you to write to the church in Ephesus.

Here are the words of Jesus, who holds the seven stars in his right hand. He also walks among the seven golden lampstands. He says,

[2]"I know what you are doing. You work long and hard. I know you can't put up with evil people. You have tested those who claim to be apostles but are not. You have found out that they are liars. [3]You have been faithful and have put up with a lot of trouble because of me. You have not given up.

[4]"But here is something I hold against you. You have turned away from the love you had at first. [5]Think about how far you have fallen! Turn away from your sins. Do the things you did at first. If you don't, I will come to you and remove your lampstand from its place. [6]But you do have this in your favor. You hate the way the Nicolaitans act. I hate it too.

[7]"Whoever has ears should listen to what the Holy Spirit says to the churches. Here is what I will do for anyone who has victory over sin. I will let that person eat from the tree of life in God's paradise."

The Letter to the Church in Smyrna

[8]"Here is what I command you to write to the church in Smyrna.

Here are the words of Jesus, who is the First and the Last. He is the one who died and came to life again. He says,

[9]"I know that you suffer and are poor. But you are rich! Some people say they are Jews but are not. I know that their words are evil. Their worship comes from Satan. [10]Don't be afraid of what you are going to suffer. I tell you, the devil will put some of you in prison to test you. You will be treated badly for ten days. Be faithful, even if it means you must die. Then I will give you life as your crown of victory.

[11]"Whoever has ears should listen to what the Holy Spirit says to the churches. Here is what I will do for anyone who has victory over sin. I will not let that person be hurt at all by the second death."

The Letter to the Church in Pergamum

[12]"Here is what I command you to write to the church in Pergamum.

Here are the words of Jesus, who has the sharp sword with two edges. He says,

[13]"I know that you live where Satan has his throne. But you remain faithful to me. You did not give up your faith in me. You didn't give it up even in the days of Antipas. Antipas, my faithful witness, was put to death in your city, where Satan lives.

[14]"But I have a few things against you. Some of your people follow the teaching of Balaam. He taught Balak to lead the people of Israel into sin. So they ate food that had been offered to statues of gods. And they committed sexual sins. [15]You also have people

who follow the teaching of the Nicolaitans. [16]So turn away from your sins! If you don't, I will come to you soon. I will fight against those people with the sword that comes out of my mouth.

[17]"Whoever has ears should listen to what the Holy Spirit says to the churches. Here is what I will do for anyone who has victory over sin. I will give that person hidden manna to eat. I will also give each of them a white stone with a new name written on it. Only the one who receives this name will know what it is.'

The Letter to the Church in Thyatira

[18]"Here is what I command you to write to the church in Thyatira.

Here are the words of the Son of God. He is Jesus, whose eyes are like blazing fire. His feet are like polished bronze. He says,

[19]'I know what you are doing. I know your love and your faith. I know how well you have served. I know you don't give up easily. In fact, you are doing more now than you did at first.

[20]"But here is what I have against you. You put up with that woman Jezebel. She calls herself a prophet. With her teaching, she has led my servants into sexual sin. She has tricked them into eating food offered to statues of gods. [21]I've given her time to turn away from her sinful ways. But she doesn't want to. [22]She lay down to commit her sin so I will make her lie down in suffering. Those who commit adultery with her will suffer greatly too. Their only way out is to turn away from what she taught them to do. [23]I will strike her children dead. Then all the churches will know that I search hearts and minds. I will pay each of you back for what you have done.

[24]'I won't ask the rest of you in Thyatira to do anything else. You don't follow the teaching of Jezebel. You haven't learned what some people call Satan's deep secrets. [25]Just hold on to what you have until I come.

[26]'Here is what I will do for anyone who has victory over sin. I will do it for anyone who carries out my plans to the end. I will give that person authority over the nations. [27]It is written, "They will rule them with an iron scepter. They will break them to pieces like clay pots." *(Psalm 2:9)* Their authority is like the authority I've received from my Father. [28]I will also give the morning star to all who have victory. [29]Whoever has ears should listen to what the Holy Spirit says to the churches.'

The Letter to the Church in Sardis

3 "Here is what I command you to write to the church in Sardis.

Here are the words of Jesus, who holds the seven spirits of God. He has the seven stars in his hand. He says,

'I know what you are doing. People think you are alive, but you are dead. [2]Wake up! Strengthen what is left, or it will die. You have not done all that my God wants you to do. [3]So remember what you have been taught and have heard. Hold firmly to it. Turn away from your sins. If you don't wake up, I will come like a thief. You won't know when I will come to you.

[4]'But you have a few people in Sardis who are pure. They aren't covered with evil like dirty clothes. They will walk with me, dressed in white, because they are worthy. [5]Here is what I will do for anyone who has victory over sin. I will dress that person in white like those worthy people. I will never erase their names from the book of life. I will speak of them by name to my Father and his angels. [6]Whoever has ears should listen to what the Holy Spirit says to the churches.'

The Letter to the Church in Philadelphia

[7]"Here is what I command you to write to the church in Philadelphia.

Here are the words of Jesus, who is holy and true. He holds the key of David. No one can shut what he opens. And no one can open what he shuts. He says,

⁸"I know what you are doing. Look! I have put an open door in front of you. No one can shut it. I know that you don't have much strength. But you have obeyed my word. You have not said no to me. ⁹Some people claim they are Jews but are not. They are liars. Their worship comes from Satan. I will make them come and fall down at your feet. I will make them say in public that I have loved you. ¹⁰You have kept my command to remain strong in the faith no matter what happens. So I will keep you from the time of suffering.

That time is going to come to the whole world. It will test those who live on the earth.

¹¹"I am coming soon. Hold on to what you have. Then no one will take away your crown. ¹²Here is what I will do for anyone who has victory over sin. I will make that person a pillar in the temple of my God. They will never leave it again. I will write the name of my God on them. I will write the name of the city of my God on them. This is the new Jerusalem, which is coming down out of heaven from my God. I will also write my new name on them. ¹³Whoever has ears should listen to what the Holy Spirit says to the churches.'

The Letter to the Church in Laodicea

¹⁴"Here is what I command you to write to the church in Laodicea.

Here are the words of Jesus, who is the Amen. What he speaks is faithful and true. He rules over what God has created. He says,

They say there's treasure on Oak Island. Rumor has it, Blackbeard himself hid gold in a deep pit, and whoever dares intrude will be trapped and drowned. Of course, that hasn't stopped people from spending the past 200 years and millions of dollars looking for it. You'd think that after two centuries people would give up. But not true treasure hunters.

Do you know that you are God's treasure? Kevin learns that for himself in the Adventures in Odyssey episode "Hide and Seek." He slips into the Imagination Station, convinced Connie will never find him there. But he discovers that someone else is looking for him. Through the adventure, Kevin finds out that God sees him as a treasure worth hunting for. Adam, Moses, Jonah, and Saul (among others) show up to share how God patiently pursued them and showed them His love.

You are so valuable to God that He sent Jesus—His only Son—as the ransom for your sins. In Revelation 3:20, Jesus says

WHAT ABOUT YOU?

He's knocking at the door of your heart, patiently waiting for you to invite Him in. Have you done that yet? If not, talk to a parent or youth pastor about enjoying a share of the ultimate treasure (see Matthew 6:19–21).

Organize a game of hide-and-seek with friends. You may even get a chance to tell them about the greatest seeker of all: Jesus!

¹⁵'I know what you are doing. I know you aren't cold or hot. I wish you were either one or the other! ¹⁶But you are lukewarm. You aren't hot or cold. So I am going to spit you out of my mouth. ¹⁷You say, "I am rich. I've become wealthy and don't need anything." But you don't realize how pitiful and miserable you have become. You are poor, blind and naked. ¹⁸So here's my advice. Buy from me gold made pure by fire. Then you will become rich. Buy from me white clothes to wear. Then you will be able to cover the shame of your naked bodies. And buy from me healing lotion to put on your eyes. Then you will be able to see.

¹⁹'I warn and correct those I love. So be sincere, and turn away from your sins. ²⁰Here I am! I stand at the door and knock. If anyone hears my voice and opens the door, I will come in. I will eat with that person, and they will eat with me.

²¹'Here is what I will do for anyone who has victory over sin. I will give that person the right to sit with me on my throne. In the same way, I had victory. Then I sat down with my Father on his throne. ²²Whoever has ears should listen to what the Holy Spirit says to the churches.' "

The Throne in Heaven

4 After this I looked, and there in front of me was a door standing open in heaven. I heard the voice I had heard before. It sounded like a trumpet. The voice said, "Come up here. I will show you what must happen after this." ²At once the Holy Spirit gave me a vision. There in front of me was a throne in heaven with someone sitting on it. ³The one who sat there shone like jasper and ruby. Around the throne was a rainbow shining like an emerald. ⁴Twenty-four other thrones surrounded that throne. Twenty-four elders were sitting on them. The elders were dressed in white. They had gold crowns on their heads. ⁵From the throne came flashes of lightning, rumblings and thunder. Seven lamps were blazing in front of the throne. These stand for the seven spirits of God. ⁶There was something that looked like a

sea of glass in front of the throne. It was as clear as crystal.

In the inner circle, around the throne, were four living creatures. They were covered with eyes, in front and in back. ⁷The first creature looked like a lion. The second looked like an ox. The third had a man's face. The fourth looked like a flying eagle. ⁸Each of the four living creatures had six wings. Each creature was covered all over with eyes. It had eyes even under its wings. Day and night, they never stop saying,

" 'Holy, holy, holy
is the Lord God who rules over all.'
(Isaiah 6:3)
He was, and he is, and he will
come."

⁹The living creatures give glory, honor and thanks to the one who sits on the throne. He lives for ever and ever. ¹⁰At the same time, the 24 elders fall down and worship the one who sits on the throne. He lives for ever and ever. They lay their crowns in front of the throne. They say,

¹¹ "You are worthy, our Lord and God!
You are worthy to receive glory and
honor and power.
You are worthy because you created all
things.
They were created and they exist.
This is the way you planned it."

The Scroll and the Lamb

5 Then I saw a scroll in the right hand of the one sitting on the throne. The scroll had writing on both sides. It was sealed with seven seals. ²I saw a mighty angel calling out in a loud voice. He said, "Who is worthy to break the seals and open the scroll?" ³But no one in heaven or on earth or under the earth could open the scroll. No one could even look inside it. ⁴I cried and cried. That's because no one was found who was worthy to open the scroll or look inside. ⁵Then one of the elders said to me, "Do not cry! The Lion of the tribe of Judah has won the battle. He is the Root of David. He is able to break the seven seals and open the scroll."

⁶Then I saw a Lamb that looked as if he had been put to death. He stood at the center of the area around the throne. The Lamb was surrounded by the four living creatures

and the elders. He had seven horns and seven eyes. The eyes stand for the seven spirits of God, which are sent out into all the earth. [7]The Lamb went and took the scroll. He took it from the right hand of the one sitting on the throne. [8]Then the four living creatures and the 24 elders fell down in front of the Lamb. Each one had a harp. They were holding golden bowls full of incense. They stand for the prayers of God's people. [9]Here is the new song they sang.

"You are worthy to take the scroll
　and break open its seals.
You are worthy because you were put
　　to death.
With your blood you bought people
　　for God.
They come from every tribe, people
　　and nation,
　no matter what language they speak.
[10] You have made them members of a
　　royal family.
You have made them priests to serve
　　our God.
They will rule on the earth."

[11]Then I looked and heard the voice of millions and millions of angels. They surrounded the throne. They surrounded the living creatures and the elders. [12]In a loud voice they were saying,

"The Lamb, who was put to death, is
　　worthy!
He is worthy to receive power and
　　wealth and wisdom and
　　strength!
He is worthy to receive honor and
　　glory and praise!"

[13]All creatures in heaven, on earth, under the earth, and on the sea were speaking. The whole creation was speaking. I heard all of them say,

"Praise and honor belong
　to the one who sits on the throne
　　and to the Lamb!
Glory and power belong to God for
　　ever and ever!"

[14]The four living creatures said, "Amen." And the elders fell down and worshiped.

The Seals of the Scroll Are Broken

6 I watched as the Lamb broke open the first of the seven seals. Then I heard one of the four living creatures say in a voice that sounded like thunder, "Come!" [2]I looked, and there in front of me was a white horse! Its rider held a bow in his hands. He was given a crown. He rode out like a hero on his way to victory.

[3]The Lamb broke open the second seal. Then I heard the second living creature say, "Come!" [4]Another horse came out. It was red like fire. Its rider was given power to take peace from the earth. He was given power to make people kill each other. He was given a large sword.

[5]The Lamb broke open the third seal. Then I heard the third living creature say, "Come!" I looked, and there in front of me was a black horse! Its rider was holding a pair of scales in his hand. [6]Next, I heard what sounded like a voice coming from among the four living creatures. It said, "Two pounds of wheat for a day's pay. And six pounds of barley for a day's pay. And leave the olive oil and the wine alone!"

[7]The Lamb broke open the fourth seal. Then I heard the voice of the fourth living creature say, "Come!" [8]I looked, and there in front of me was a pale horse! Its rider's name was Death. Following close behind him was Hell. They were given power over a fourth of the earth. They were given power to kill people by swords. They could also use hunger, sickness and the earth's wild animals to kill.

[9]The Lamb broke open the fifth seal. I saw souls under the altar. They were the souls of people who had been killed. They had been killed because of God's word and their faithful witness. [10]They called out in a loud voice. "How long, Lord and King, holy and true?" they asked. "How long will you wait to judge those who live on the earth? How long will it be until you pay them back for killing us?" [11]Then each of them was given a white robe. "Wait a little longer," they were told. "There are still more of your believing brothers and sisters who will be killed. They will be killed just as you were."

[12]I watched as the Lamb broke open the sixth seal. There was a powerful earthquake. The sun turned black like the clothes people wear when they're sad. Those clothes are made out of goat's hair. The whole moon turned as red as blood. [13]The stars in the sky fell to earth. They dropped like figs from a tree shaken by a strong wind. [14]The

sky rolled back like a scroll. Every mountain and island was moved out of its place.

[15]Everyone hid in caves and among the rocks of the mountains. This included the kings of the earth, the princes and the generals. It included rich people and powerful people. It also included everyone else, both slaves and people who were free. [16]They called out to the mountains and rocks, "Fall on us! Hide us from the face of the one who sits on the throne! Hide us from the anger of the Lamb! [17]The great day of their anger has come. Who can live through it?"

144,000 People Are Marked With the Seal of the Living God

7 After this I saw four angels. They were standing at the four corners of the earth. They were holding back the four winds of the earth. This kept the winds from blowing on the land or the sea or on any tree. [2]Then I saw another angel coming up from the east. He brought the official seal of the living God. He called out in a loud voice to the four angels. They had been allowed to harm the land and the sea. [3]"Do not harm the land or the sea or the trees," he said. "Wait until we mark with this seal the foreheads of those who serve our God." [4]Then I heard how many people were marked with the seal. There were 144,000 from all the tribes of Israel.

[5] From the tribe of Judah, 12,000 were
  marked with the seal.
  From the tribe of Reuben, 12,000.
  From the tribe of Gad, 12,000.
[6] From the tribe of Asher, 12,000.
  From the tribe of Naphtali, 12,000.
  From the tribe of Manasseh, 12,000.
[7] From the tribe of Simeon, 12,000.
  From the tribe of Levi, 12,000.
  From the tribe of Issachar, 12,000.
[8] From the tribe of Zebulun, 12,000.
  From the tribe of Joseph, 12,000.
  From the tribe of Benjamin, 12,000.

The Huge Crowd Wearing White Robes

[9]After this I looked, and there in front of me was a huge crowd of people. They stood in front of the throne and in front of the Lamb. There were so many that no one could count them. They came from every nation, tribe and people. That's true no matter what language they spoke. They were wearing white robes. In their hands they were holding palm branches. [10]They cried out in a loud voice,

"Salvation belongs to our God,
  who sits on the throne.
Salvation also belongs to the Lamb."

[11]All the angels were standing around the throne. They were standing around the elders and the four living creatures. They fell down on their faces in front of the throne and worshiped God. [12]They said,

"Amen!
May praise and glory
and wisdom be given to our God for
      ever and ever.
Give him thanks and honor and power
      and strength.
Amen!"

[13]Then one of the elders spoke to me. "Who are these people dressed in white robes?" he asked. "Where did they come from?"

[14]I answered, "Sir, you know."

He said, "They are the ones who have come out of the time of terrible suffering. They have washed their robes and made them white in the blood of the Lamb. [15]So

"they are in front of the throne of God.
  They serve him day and night in his
      temple.
The one who sits on the throne
  will be with them to keep them safe.
[16] 'Never again will they be hungry.
  Never again will they be thirsty.
  The sun will not beat down on them.'
                    (Isaiah 49:10)
  The heat of the desert will not harm
      them.
[17] The Lamb, who is at the center of the
      area around the throne,
  will be their shepherd.
'He will lead them to springs of living
      water.'   (Isaiah 49:10)
'And God will wipe away every tear
      from their eyes.'"   (Isaiah 25:8)

The Seventh Seal and the Gold Cup

8 The Lamb opened the seventh seal. Then there was silence in heaven for about half an hour.

[2]I saw the seven angels who stand in front of God. Seven trumpets were given to them.

³Another angel came and stood at the altar. He had a shallow gold cup for burning incense. He was given a lot of incense to offer on the golden altar. The altar was in front of the throne. With the incense he offered the prayers of all God's people. ⁴The smoke of the incense rose up from the angel's hand. The prayers of God's people rose up together with it. The smoke and the prayers went up in front of God. ⁵Then the angel took the gold cup and filled it with fire from the altar. He threw it down on the earth. There were rumblings and thunder, flashes of lightning, and an earthquake.

The Trumpets

⁶Then the seven angels who had the seven trumpets got ready to blow them.

⁷The first angel blew his trumpet. Hail and fire mixed with blood were thrown down on the earth. A third of the earth was burned up. A third of the trees were burned up. All the green grass was burned up.

⁸The second angel blew his trumpet. Something that looked like a huge mountain on fire was thrown into the sea. A third of the sea turned into blood. ⁹A third of the living creatures in the sea died. A third of the ships were destroyed.

¹⁰The third angel blew his trumpet. Then a great star fell from the sky. It looked like a blazing torch. It fell on a third of the rivers and on the springs of water. ¹¹The name of the star is Wormwood. A third of the water turned bitter. Many people died from it.

¹²The fourth angel blew his trumpet. Then a third of the sun was struck. A third of the moon was struck. A third of the stars were struck. So a third of each of them turned dark. Then a third of the day had no light. The same thing happened to a third of the night.

¹³As I watched, I heard an eagle that was flying high in the air. It called out in a loud voice, "How terrible! How terrible it will be for those living on the earth! How terrible! They will suffer as soon as the next three angels blow their trumpets!"

9 The fifth angel blew his trumpet. Then I saw a star that had fallen from the sky to the earth. The star was given the key to the tunnel leading down into a bottomless pit. The pit was called the Abyss. ²The star opened the Abyss. Then smoke rose up from it like the smoke from a huge furnace. The sun and sky were darkened by the smoke from the Abyss. ³Out of the smoke came locusts. They came down on the earth. They were given power like the power of scorpions of the earth. ⁴They were told not to harm the grass of the earth or any plant or tree. They were supposed to harm only the people without God's official seal on their foreheads. ⁵The locusts were not allowed to kill these people. But the locusts could hurt them over and over for five months. The pain the people suffered was like the sting of a scorpion when it strikes. ⁶In those days, people will look for a way to die but won't find it. They will want to die, but death will escape them.

⁷The locusts looked like horses ready for battle. On their heads they wore something like crowns of gold. Their faces looked like human faces. ⁸Their hair was like women's hair. Their teeth were like lions' teeth. ⁹Their chests were covered with something that looked like armor made out of iron. The sound of their wings was like the thundering of many horses and chariots rushing into battle. ¹⁰They had tails that could sting people like scorpions do. And in their tails they had power to hurt people over and over for five months. ¹¹Their king was the angel of the Abyss. In the Hebrew language his name is Abaddon. In Greek it is Apollyon. His name means Destroyer.

¹²The first terrible judgment is past. Two others are still coming.

¹³The sixth angel blew his trumpet. Then I heard a voice coming from the four corners of the golden altar. The altar stands in front of God. ¹⁴The voice spoke to the sixth angel who had the trumpet. The voice said, "Set the four angels free who are held at the great river Euphrates." ¹⁵The four angels had been ready for this very hour and day and month and year. They were set free to kill a third of all people. ¹⁶The number of troops on horseback was 200,000,000. I heard how many there were.

¹⁷The horses and riders I saw in my vision had armor on their chests. It was red like fire, dark blue, and yellow like sulfur. The heads of the horses looked like lions' heads. Out of their mouths came fire, smoke and sulfur. ¹⁸A third of all people were killed by the three plagues of fire, smoke and sulfur that came out of the horses' mouths. ¹⁹The power of the horses was

in their mouths and in their tails. The tails were like snakes whose heads could bite.

20 There were people who were not killed by these plagues. But they still didn't turn away from what they had been doing. They did not stop worshiping demons. They kept worshiping statues of gods made out of gold, silver, bronze, stone and wood. These statues can't see or hear or walk. 21 The people also did not turn away from their murders, witchcraft, sexual sins and stealing.

The Angel and the Little Scroll

10 Then I saw another mighty angel coming down from heaven. He was wearing a cloud like a robe. There was a rainbow above his head. His face was like the sun. His legs were like pillars of fire. 2 He was holding a little scroll. It was lying open in his hand. The angel put his right foot on the sea and his left foot on the land. 3 Then he gave a loud shout like the roar of a lion. When he shouted, the voices of the seven thunders spoke. 4 When they had spoken, I was getting ready to write. But I heard a voice from heaven say, "Seal up what the seven thunders have said. Do not write it down."

5 I had seen an angel standing on the sea and on the land. This angel raised his right hand to heaven. 6 He made a promise in the name of the God who lives for ever and ever. This is the God who created the sky, earth and sea and all that is in them. The angel said, "There will be no more waiting! 7 God's plan will be carried out. This will happen when the seventh angel is ready to blow his trumpet. God told all this to the prophets who served him long ago."

8 Then the voice I had heard from heaven spoke to me again. It said, "The angel is standing on the sea and on the land. Go and take the scroll from him. It is lying open in his hand."

9 So I went to the angel and asked him to give me the little scroll. He said to me, "Take it and eat it. It will become sour in your stomach. But 'in your mouth it will taste as sweet as honey.'" (Ezekiel 3:3) 10 I took the little scroll from the angel's hand and ate it. In my mouth it tasted as sweet as honey. But when I had eaten it, it became sour in my stomach. 11 Then I was told, "You must prophesy again about many peoples, nations, languages and kings."

The Two Witnesses

11 I was given a long stick that looked like a measuring rod. I was told, "Go and measure the temple of God. And measure the altar where the people are worshiping. 2 But do not measure the outer courtyard. That's because it has been given to the Gentiles. They will take over the holy city for 42 months. 3 I will appoint my two witnesses. And they will prophesy for 1,260 days. They will be dressed in the rough clothes people wear when they're sad." 4 The witnesses are "the two olive trees" and the two lampstands. And "they stand in front of the Lord of the earth." (Zechariah 4:3,11,14) 5 If anyone tries to harm them, fire comes from their mouths and eats up their enemies. This is how anyone who wants to harm them must die. 6 These witnesses have power to close up the sky. Then it will not rain while they are prophesying. They also have power to turn the waters into blood. And they can strike the earth with every kind of plague. They can do this as often as they want to.

7 When they have finished speaking, the beast that comes up from the Abyss will attack them. He will overpower them and kill them. 8 Their bodies will lie in the main street of the great city. It is also the city where their Lord was nailed to a cross. The city is sometimes compared to Sodom or Egypt. 9 For three and a half days, people will stare at their bodies. These people will be from every tribe and nation, no matter what language they speak. They will refuse to bury them. 10 Those who live on the earth will be happy about this. That's because those two prophets had made them suffer. The people will celebrate by sending one another gifts.

11 But after the three and a half days, the breath of life from God entered the witnesses. They both stood up. Terror struck those who saw them. 12 Then the two witnesses heard a loud voice from heaven. It said to them, "Come up here." They went up to heaven in a cloud. Their enemies watched it happen.

13 At that same time there was a powerful earthquake. A tenth of the city crumbled and fell. In the earthquake, 7,000 people were killed. Those who lived through it were terrified. They gave glory to the God of heaven.

[14]The second terrible judgment has passed. The third is coming soon.

The Seventh Trumpet

[15]The seventh angel blew his trumpet. There were loud voices in heaven. They said,

> "The kingdom of the world has become
>> the kingdom of our Lord and of his Messiah.
> He will rule for ever and ever."

[16]The 24 elders were sitting on their thrones in front of God. They fell on their faces and worshiped God. [17]They said,

> "Lord God who rules over all, we give thanks to you.
> You are the God who is and who was.
> We give you thanks.
>> That's because you have begun to rule with your great power.
> [18] The nations were angry,
>> and the time for your anger has come.
> The time has come to judge the dead.
> It is time to reward your servants the prophets
>> and your people who honor you.
> There is a reward for all your people, both great and small.
> It is time to destroy those who destroy the earth."

[19]Then God's temple in heaven was opened. Inside it the wooden chest called the ark of his covenant could be seen. There were flashes of lightning, rumblings and thunder, an earthquake and a severe hailstorm.

The Woman and the Dragon

12 A great sign appeared in heaven. It was a woman wearing the sun like clothes. The moon was under her feet. On her head she wore a crown of 12 stars. [2]She was pregnant. She cried out in pain because she was about to have a baby. [3]Then another sign appeared in heaven. It was a huge red dragon. It had seven heads and ten horns. On its seven heads it wore seven crowns. [4]The dragon's tail swept a third of the stars out of the sky. It threw the stars down to earth. The dragon stood in front of the woman who was about to have a baby. The dragon wanted to eat her child the moment he was born. [5]She gave birth to a son. He "will rule all the nations with an iron scepter." *(Psalm 2:9)* And her child was taken up to God and to his throne. [6]The woman escaped into the desert where God had a place prepared for her. There she would be taken care of for 1,260 days.

[7]Then a war began in heaven. Michael and his angels fought against the dragon. And the dragon and his angels fought back. [8]But the dragon wasn't strong enough. Both he and his angels lost their place in heaven. [9]The great dragon was thrown down to the earth, and his angels with him. The dragon is that old serpent called the devil, or Satan. He leads the whole world astray.

[10]Then I heard a loud voice in heaven. It said,

> "Now the salvation and the power and
>> the kingdom of our God have come.
> The authority of his Messiah has come.
> Satan, who brings charges against our brothers and sisters,
>> has been thrown down.
> He brings charges against them in front of our God day and night.
> [11] They had victory over him
>> by the blood the Lamb spilled for them.
> They had victory over him
>> by speaking the truth about Jesus to others.

WOOTON'S FUN FACTS

Rev. 12 To leave my house, you have to go down a slide that looks like a dragon's tail. Did you know there's a dragon in the Bible? It's a doozy with seven heads and ten horns. Many scholars believe that Revelation 12 shows what was going on in heaven when Jesus was born. A little different from the usual Christmas story, isn't it?!

They were willing to risk their lives, even if it led to death.

12 So be joyful, you heavens!
Be glad, all you who live there!
But how terrible it will be for the earth and the sea!
The devil has come down to you.
He is very angry.
He knows his time is short."

13The dragon saw that he had been thrown down to the earth. So he chased the woman who had given birth to the boy. 14The woman was given the two wings of a great eagle. She was given these wings so that she could fly away. She could fly to the place prepared for her in the desert. There she would be taken care of for three and a half years. She would be out of the serpent's reach. 15Then out of his mouth the serpent spit water like a river. He wanted to catch the woman and sweep her away in the flood. 16But the earth helped the woman. It opened its mouth and swallowed the river that the dragon had spit out. 17The dragon was very angry with the woman. He went off to make war against the rest of her children. They obey God's commands. And they hold firmly to the truth they have said about Jesus.

The Beast Who Comes Out of the Sea

13 The dragon stood on the seashore. I saw a beast coming out of the sea. It had ten horns and seven heads. There were ten crowns on its horns. On each head was an evil name that brought shame to God. 2The beast I saw looked like a leopard. But it had feet like a bear and a mouth like a lion. The dragon gave the beast his power, his throne, and great authority. 3One of the beast's heads seemed to have had a deadly wound. But the wound had been healed. The whole world was amazed and followed the beast. 4People worshiped the dragon, because he had given authority to the beast. They also worshiped the beast. They asked, "Who is like the beast? Who can make war against it?"

5The beast was given a mouth to brag and speak evil things against God. The beast was allowed to use its authority for 42 months. 6The beast opened its mouth to speak evil things against God. It told lies about God and about the place where God lives. And it told lies about those who live in heaven with him. 7The beast was allowed to make war against God's holy people and to overcome them. It was given authority over every tribe, people and nation, no matter what language they spoke. 8Many people who live on the earth will worship the beast. They are the ones whose names are not written in the Lamb's book of life. The Lamb is the one whose death was planned before the world was created.

9Whoever has ears should listen.

10 "Everyone who is supposed to be captured
    will be captured.
Everyone who is supposed to be killed
    by a sword
    will be killed by a sword."
                                    (Jeremiah 15:2)

So God's people must be patient and faithful.

The Beast Who Comes Out of the Earth

[11]Then I saw a second beast. This one came out of the earth. It had two horns like a lamb. But it spoke like a dragon. [12]This beast had all the authority of the first beast. It did what the first beast wanted. It made the earth and all who live on it worship the first beast. The first beast was the one whose deadly wound had been healed. [13]The second beast performed great signs. It even made fire come from heaven to the earth. And the fire was seen by everyone. [14]The first beast had given the second beast the power to perform these signs. By these signs, the second beast tricked those who live on the earth. The second beast ordered people to set up a statue to honor the first beast. The first beast was the one who had been wounded by a sword and still lived. [15]The second beast was allowed to give breath to this statue so it could speak. The statue could kill all who refused to worship it. [16]It also forced everyone to receive a mark on their right hand or on their forehead. People great or small, rich or poor, free or slave had to receive the mark. [17]They could not buy or sell anything unless they had the mark. The mark is the name of the beast or the number of its name.

[18]This problem requires wisdom. Anyone who is wise should figure out what the beast's number means. It is the number of a man. And that number is 666.

The Lamb and the 144,000

14 I looked, and there in front of me was the Lamb. He was standing on Mount Zion. With him were 144,000 people. Written on their foreheads were his name and his Father's name. [2]I heard a sound from heaven. It was like the roar of rushing waters and loud thunder. The sound I heard was like the music of harps being played. [3]Then everyone sang a new song in front of the throne. They sang it in front of the four living creatures and the elders. No one could learn the song except the 144,000. They had been set free from the evil of the earth. [4]They had not committed sexual sins with women. They had kept themselves pure. They follow the Lamb wherever he goes. They were purchased from among human beings as a first offering to God and the Lamb. [5]They told no lies. They are without blame.

The Three Angels

[6]I saw another angel. He was flying high in the air. He came to tell everyone on earth the good news that will always be true. He told it to every nation, tribe and people, no matter what language they spoke. [7]In a loud voice he said, "Have respect for God. Give him glory. The hour has come for God to judge. Worship him who made the heavens and the earth. Worship him who made the sea and the springs of water."

[8]A second angel followed him. He said, " 'Fallen! Babylon the Great has fallen!' *(Isaiah 21:9)* The city of Babylon made all the nations drink the strong wine of her terrible sins."

[9]A third angel followed them. He said in a loud voice, "There will be trouble for anyone who worships the beast and its statue! There will be trouble for anyone who has its mark on their forehead or their hand! [10]They, too, will drink the wine of God's great anger. His wine has been poured full strength into the cup of his anger. They will be burned with flaming sulfur. The holy angels and the Lamb will see it happen. [11]The smoke of their terrible suffering will rise for ever and ever. Day and night, there will be no rest for anyone who worships the beast and its statue. There will be no rest for anyone who receives the mark of its name." [12]God's people need to be very patient. They are the ones who obey God's commands. And they remain faithful to Jesus.

[13]Then I heard a voice from heaven. "Write this," it said. "Blessed are the dead who die as believers in the Lord from now on."

"Yes," says the Holy Spirit. "They will rest from their labor. What they have done will not be forgotten."

The Harvest of the Earth

[14]I looked, and there in front of me was a white cloud. Sitting on the cloud was one who looked "like a son of man." *(Daniel 7:13)* He wore a gold crown on his head. In his hand was a sharp, curved blade for cutting grain. [15]Then another angel came out of the temple. He called in a loud voice to the one

sitting on the cloud. "Take your blade," he said. "Cut the grain. The time has come. The earth is ready to be harvested." [16]So the one sitting on the cloud swung his blade over the earth. And the earth was harvested.

[17]Another angel came out of the temple in heaven. He too had a sharp, curved blade. [18]Still another angel came from the altar. He was in charge of the fire on the altar. He called out in a loud voice to the angel who had the sharp blade. "Take your blade," he said, "and gather the bunches of grapes from the earth's vine. Its grapes are ripe." [19]So the angel swung his blade over the earth. He gathered its grapes. Then he threw them into a huge winepress. The winepress stands for God's anger. [20]In the winepress outside the city, the grapes were stomped on. Blood flowed out of the winepress. It spread over the land for about 180 miles. It rose as high as the horses' heads.

Seven Angels With Seven Plagues

15I saw in heaven another great and wonderful sign. Seven angels were about to bring the seven last plagues. The plagues would complete God's anger. [2]Then I saw something that looked like a sea of glass glowing with fire. Standing beside the sea were those who had won the battle over the beast. They had also overcome its statue and the number of its name. They held harps given to them by God. [3]They sang the song of God's servant Moses and of the Lamb. They sang,

"Lord God who rules over all,
    everything you do is great and
        wonderful.
King of the nations,
    your ways are true and fair.
[4] Lord, who will not have respect for
    you?
    Who will not bring glory to your
        name?
You alone are holy.
All nations will come
    and worship you.
They see that the things you do are
    right."

[5]After this I looked, and I saw the temple in heaven. And it was opened. The temple is the holy tent where the tablets of the covenant law were kept. [6]Out of the temple came the seven angels who were bringing

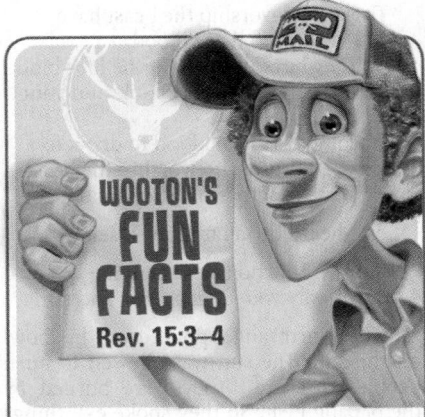

WOOTON'S FUN FACTS
Rev. 15:3–4

This is the first song recorded in the Bible. It's also the last. See, I told you! Check out Exodus 14–15.

the seven plagues. They were dressed in clean, shining linen. They wore gold strips of cloth around their chests. [7]Then one of the four living creatures gave seven golden bowls to the seven angels. The bowls were filled with the anger of God, who lives for ever and ever. [8]The temple was filled with smoke that came from the glory and power of God. No one could enter the temple at that time. They had to wait until the seven plagues of the seven angels were completed.

The Seven Bowls of God's Great Anger

16Then I heard a loud voice from the temple speaking to the seven angels. "Go," it said. "Pour out the seven bowls of God's great anger on the earth."

[2]The first angel went and poured out his bowl on the land. Ugly and painful sores broke out on people. Those people had the mark of the beast and worshiped its statue.

[3]The second angel poured out his bowl on the sea. It turned into blood like the blood of a dead person. Every living thing in the sea died.

[4]The third angel poured out his bowl on the rivers and springs of water. They became blood. [5]Then I heard the angel who was in charge of the waters. He said,

"Holy One, the way you judge is fair.
    You are the God who is and who
        was.

[6] Those who worship the beast have
poured out blood.
They have poured out the life's blood
of your holy people and your
prophets.
So you have given blood to drink to
those who worship the beast.
That's exactly what they should get."

[7] Then I heard the altar reply. It said,

"Lord God who rules over all,
the way you judge is true and fair."

[8] The fourth angel poured out his bowl
on the sun. The sun was allowed to burn
people with fire. [9] They were burned by
the blazing heat. So they spoke evil things
against the name of God, who controlled
these plagues. But they refused to turn
away from their sins. They did not give glory to God.

[10] The fifth angel poured out his bowl on
the throne of the beast. The kingdom of the
beast became very dark. People chewed on
their tongues because they were suffering
so much. [11] They spoke evil things against
the God of heaven. They did this because
of their pains and their sores. But they refused to turn away from the sins they had
committed.

[12] The sixth angel poured out his bowl
on the great river Euphrates. Its water dried
up to prepare the way for the kings from
the East. [13] Then I saw three evil spirits that
looked like frogs. They came out of the
mouths of the dragon, the beast and the
false prophet. [14] They are spirits of demons
that perform signs. They go out to gather
the kings of the whole world for battle. This
battle will take place on the great day of the
God who rules over all.

[15] "Look! I am coming like a thief!
Blessed is anyone who stays awake
and keeps their clothes on. Then they
will be ready. They will not be caught
naked and so be put to shame."

[16] Then the evil spirits gathered the kings
together. In the Hebrew language, the place
where the kings met is called Armageddon.

[17] The seventh angel poured out his bowl
into the air. Out of the temple came a loud
voice from the throne. It said, "It is done!"
[18] Then there came flashes of lightning,
rumblings, thunder and a powerful earthquake. There has never been an earthquake

as terrible as this. One like this hasn't happened while human beings have lived on
earth. [19] The great city split into three parts.
The cities of the nations crumbled and fell.
God remembered Babylon the Great. He
gave Babylon the cup filled with the wine of
his terrible anger. [20] Every island ran away.
The mountains could not be found. [21] Huge
hailstones weighing about 100 pounds each
fell from the sky. The hail crushed people.
And they spoke evil things against God
because of the plague. That's because the
plague of hail was so terrible.

Babylon the Great Prostitute Sits on the Beast

17 One of the seven angels who had the
seven bowls came to me. He said,
"Come. I will show you how the great prostitute will be punished. She is the one who
sits by many waters. [2] The kings of the earth
took part in her evil ways. The people living
on earth were drunk with the wine of her
terrible sins."

[3] Then in a vision the angel carried me
away to a desert. There the Holy Spirit
showed me a woman sitting on a bright red
beast. It was covered with names that say
evil things about God. It had seven heads
and ten horns. [4] The woman was dressed in
purple and bright red. She was gleaming
with gold, jewels and pearls. In her hand
she held a golden cup filled with things that
God hates. It was filled with her terrible,
dirty sins. [5] The name written on her forehead was a mystery. Here is what it said.

THE GREAT CITY OF BABYLON
THE MOTHER OF PROSTITUTES
THE MOTHER OF EVERYTHING ON EARTH
THAT GOD HATES

[6] I saw that the woman was drunk with the
blood of God's holy people. They are the
ones who are witnesses about Jesus.

When I saw her, I was very amazed.
[7] Then the angel said to me, "Why are you
amazed? I will explain to you the mystery
of the woman. And I will explain the mystery of the beast she rides on. The beast is
the one who has the seven heads and ten
horns. [8] The beast that you saw used to exist
and now does not. Yet it will come up out
of the Abyss and be destroyed. Some people on the earth will be amazed when they
see the beast. Their names have not been

written in the book of life from the time the world was created. They will be amazed at the beast. That's because it will come again even though it used to exist and now does not.

⁹"Here is a problem that you have to be wise to understand. The seven heads are seven hills that the woman sits on. ¹⁰They are also seven kings. Five have fallen, one is ruling, and the other has still not come. When he does come, he must remain for only a little while. ¹¹The beast who used to exist, and now does not, is an eighth king. He belongs to the other seven. He will be destroyed.

¹²"The ten horns you saw are ten kings. They have not yet received a kingdom. But for one hour they will receive authority to rule together with the beast. ¹³They have only one purpose. So they will give their power and authority to the beast. ¹⁴They will make war against the Lamb. But the Lamb will have victory over them. That's because he is the most powerful Lord of all and the greatest King of all. His appointed, chosen and faithful followers will be with him."

¹⁵Then the angel spoke to me. "You saw the waters the prostitute sits on," he said. "They stand for all the nations of the world, no matter what their race or language is. ¹⁶The beast and the ten horns you saw will hate the prostitute. They will destroy her and leave her naked. They will eat her flesh and burn her with fire. ¹⁷God has put it into their hearts to carry out his purpose. So they agreed to give the beast their royal authority. They will give him this authority until God's words come true. ¹⁸The woman you saw stands for the great city of Babylon. That city rules over the kings of the earth."

Weeping When Babylon Falls

18 After these things I saw another angel coming down from heaven. He had great authority. His glory filled the earth with light. ²With a mighty voice he shouted,

"'Fallen! Babylon the Great has fallen!'
(Isaiah 21:9)
She has become a place where
demons live.
She has become a den for every evil
spirit.
She has become a place where every
'unclean' bird is found.

She has become a place where every
'unclean' and hated animal is
found.
³ All the nations have drunk
the strong wine of her terrible sins.
The kings of the earth took part in her
evil ways.
The traders of the world grew rich
from her great wealth."

Warning to Run From Babylon's Judgment

⁴Then I heard another voice from heaven. It said,

"'Come out of her, my people.'
(Jeremiah 51:45)
Then you will not take part in her
sins.
You will not suffer from any of her
plagues.
⁵ Her sins are piled up to heaven.
God has remembered her crimes.
⁶ Do to her as she has done to others.
Pay her back double for what she has
done.
Pour her a double dose of what she
has poured for others.
⁷ Give her as much pain and suffering
as the glory and wealth she gave
herself.
She brags to herself,
'I rule on a throne like a queen.
I am not a widow.
I will never mourn.'　*(Isaiah 47:7,8)*
⁸ But she will be plagued by death,
sadness and hunger.
In a single day she will suffer all
these plagues.
She will be burned up by fire.
That's because the Lord God who
judges her is mighty.

How Terrible When Babylon Falls!

⁹"The kings of the earth who committed terrible sins with her will weep. They will mourn because they used to share her riches. They will see the smoke rising as she burns. ¹⁰They will be terrified by her suffering. They will stand far away from her. And they will cry out,

"'How terrible! How terrible it is for
you, great city!
How terrible for you, mighty city of
Babylon!

In just one hour you have been
destroyed!'

[11]"The traders of the world will weep
and mourn over her. No one buys what
they sell anymore. [12]Here is what they had
for sale.

Gold, silver, jewels, pearls.
Fine linen, purple, silk, bright red
cloth.
Every kind of citron wood.
All sorts of things made out of ivory, valuable wood, bronze, iron,
marble.
[13] Cinnamon, spice, incense, myrrh,
frankincense.
Wine, olive oil, fine flour, wheat.
Cattle, sheep, horses, carriages, and
human beings sold as slaves.

[14]"The merchants will say, 'The pleasure
you longed for has left you. All your riches
and glory have disappeared forever.' [15]The
traders who sold these things became rich
because of Babylon. When she suffers, they
will stand far away. Her suffering will terrify them. They will weep and mourn. [16]They
will cry out,

"'How terrible! How terrible it is for
you, great city,
dressed in fine linen, purple and
bright red!
How terrible for you, great city,
gleaming with gold, jewels and
pearls!
[17] In just one hour your great wealth has
been destroyed!'

"Every sea captain and all who travel by
ship will stand far away. So will the sailors
and all who earn their living from the sea.
[18]They will see the smoke rising as Babylon
burns. They will ask, 'Was there ever a city
like this great city?' [19]They will throw dust
on their heads. They will weep and mourn.
They will cry out,

"'How terrible! How terrible it is for
you, great city!
All who had ships on the sea
became rich because of her wealth!
In just one hour she has been
destroyed!'

[20] "You heavens, be glad for this!
You people of God, be glad!
You apostles and prophets, be glad!

God has judged her
with the judgment she gave to you.'"

Babylon's Judgment Is Final

[21]Then a mighty angel picked up a huge
rock. It was the size of a large millstone. He
threw it into the sea. Then he said,

"That is how
the great city of Babylon will be
thrown down.
Never again will it be found.
[22] The songs of musicians will never be
heard in you again.
Gone will be the music of harps,
flutes and trumpets.
No worker of any kind
will ever be found in you again.
The sound of a millstone
will never be heard in you again.
[23] The light of a lamp
will never shine in you again.
The voices of brides and grooms
will never be heard in you again.
Your traders were among the world's
most important people.
By your magic spell all the nations
were led astray.
[24] You were guilty of the murder of
prophets and God's holy people.
You were guilty of the blood of all
who have been killed on the
earth."

Three Hallelujahs for the Fall of Babylon!

19 After these things I heard a roar in
heaven. It sounded like a huge crowd
shouting,

"Hallelujah!
Salvation and glory and power belong
to our God.
[2]   The way he judges is true and fair.
He has judged the great prostitute.
She made the earth impure with her
terrible sins.
God has paid her back for killing those
who served him."

[3] Again they shouted,

"Hallelujah!
The smoke from her fire goes up for
ever and ever."

[4]The 24 elders and the four living creatures bowed down. They worshiped God,

who was sitting on the throne. They cried out,

"Amen! Hallelujah!"

[5]Then a voice came from the throne. It said,

"Praise our God,
    all you who serve him!
Praise God, all you who have respect
        for him,
    both great and small!"

[6]Then I heard the noise of a huge crowd. It sounded like the roar of rushing waters and like loud thunder. The people were shouting,

"Hallelujah!
    Our Lord God is the King who rules
        over all.
[7] Let us be joyful and glad!
    Let us give him glory!
It is time for the Lamb's wedding.
    His bride has made herself ready.
[8] Fine linen, bright and clean,
    was given to her to wear."

Fine linen stands for the right things that God's holy people do.

[9]Here is what the angel told me to write. "Blessed are those invited to the wedding supper of the Lamb!" Then he added, "These are the true words of God."

[10]When I heard this, I fell at his feet to worship him. But he said to me, "Don't do that! I serve God, just as you do. I am God's servant, just like believers who hold firmly to what Jesus has taught. Worship God! The Spirit of prophecy tells the truth about Jesus."

The Heavenly Warrior Has Victory Over the Beast

[11]I saw heaven standing open. There in front of me was a white horse. Its rider is called Faithful and True. When he judges or makes war, he is always fair. [12]His eyes are like blazing fire. On his head are many crowns. A name is written on him that only he knows. [13]He is dressed in a robe dipped in blood. His name is the Word of God. [14]The armies of heaven were following him, riding on white horses. They were dressed in fine linen, white and clean. [15]Coming out of the rider's mouth is a sharp sword. He will strike down the nations with the sword. Scripture says, "He will rule them with an iron scepter." *(Psalm 2:9)* He stomps on the grapes of God's winepress. The winepress stands for the terrible anger of the God who rules over all. [16]Here is the name that is written on the rider's robe and on his thigh.

THE GREATEST KING OF ALL AND THE
MOST POWERFUL LORD OF ALL

[17]I saw an angel standing in the sun. He shouted to all the birds flying high in the air, "Come! Gather together for the great supper of God. [18]Come and eat the dead bodies of kings, generals, and other mighty people. Eat the bodies of horses and their riders. Eat the bodies of all people, free and slave, great and small."

[19]Then I saw the beast and the kings of the earth with their armies. They had gathered together to make war against the rider on the horse and his army. [20]But the beast and the false prophet were captured. The false prophet had done signs for the beast. In this way the false prophet had tricked some people. Those people had received the mark of the beast and had worshiped its statue. The beast and the false prophet were thrown alive into the lake of fire. The lake of fire burns with sulfur. [21]The rest were killed by the sword that came out of the rider's mouth. All the birds stuffed themselves with the dead bodies.

The Thousand Years

20 I saw an angel coming down out of heaven. He had the key to the Abyss. In his hand he held a heavy chain. [2]He grabbed the dragon, that old serpent. The serpent is also called the devil, or Satan. The angel put him in chains for 1,000 years. [3]Then he threw him into the Abyss. He locked it and sealed him in. This was to keep Satan from causing the nations to believe his lies anymore. Satan will be locked away until the 1,000 years are ended. After that, he must be set free for a short time.

[4]I saw thrones. Those who had been given authority to judge were sitting on them. I also saw the souls of those whose heads had been cut off. They had been killed because they had spoken what was true about Jesus. They had also been killed because of the word of God. They had not worshiped the beast or its statue. They had not received

its mark on their foreheads or hands. They came to life and ruled with Christ for 1,000 years. [5]This is the first resurrection. The rest of the dead did not come to life until the 1,000 years were ended. [6]Blessed and holy are those who share in the first resurrection. The second death has no power over them. They will be priests of God and of Christ. They will rule with him for 1,000 years.

Satan Is Judged

[7]When the 1,000 years are over, Satan will be set free from his prison. [8]He will go out to cause the nations to believe lies. He will gather them from the four corners of the earth. He will bring Gog and Magog together for battle. Their troops are as many as the grains of sand on the seashore. [9]They marched across the whole earth. They surrounded the place where God's holy people were camped. It was the city he loves. But fire came down from heaven and burned them up. [10]The devil had caused them to believe lies. He was thrown into the lake of burning sulfur. That is where the beast and the false prophet had been thrown. They will all suffer day and night for ever and ever.

The Dead Are Judged

[11]I saw a great white throne. And I saw God sitting on it. When the earth and sky saw his face, they ran away. There was no place for them. [12]I saw the dead, great and small, standing in front of the throne. Books were opened. Then another book was opened. It was the book of life. The dead were judged by what they had done. The things they had done were written in the books. [13]The sea gave up the dead that were in it. And Death and Hell gave up their dead. Each person was judged by what they had done. [14]Then Death and Hell were thrown into the lake of fire. The lake of fire is the second death. [15]Anyone whose name was not written in the book of life was thrown into the lake of fire.

A New Heaven and a New Earth

21 I saw "a new heaven and a new earth." *(Isaiah 65:17)* The first heaven and the first earth were completely gone. There was no longer any sea. [2]I saw the Holy City, the new Jerusalem. It was coming down out of

CANDID CONVERSATIONS

The week my grandmother died was one of the worst weeks of my life. Then came the day my mother died, which was even worse. I loved them both so much, and it was really hard to say good-bye.

My grandmother used to sing hymns to me when I was a little girl. One of her favorites was "All Hail the Power of Jesus' Name." Now I imagine her singing those hymns in heaven, with Jesus sitting right next to her. I often read this passage in Revelation to remind me that my mom and grandma are both face-to-face with Him, and they're in a place with no tears, death, sadness, or pain. Everything is clean and bright, just as my mom liked my room to be. Angels on every street corner sing praises to God, and there's my mom and grandma, singing right along with them.

Think about (and maybe even draw) what you think heaven looks like. And thank God for creating such a beautiful place.

heaven from God. It was prepared like a bride beautifully dressed for her husband. [3]I heard a loud voice from the throne. It said, "Look! God now makes his home with the people. He will live with them. They will be his people. And God himself will be with them and be their God. [4]He will wipe away every tear from their eyes. There will be no more death.' *(Isaiah 25:8)* And there will be no more sadness. There will be no more crying or pain. Things are no longer the way they used to be."

[5]He who was sitting on the throne said, "I am making everything new!" Then he said, "Write this down. You can trust these words. They are true."

[6]He said to me, "It is done. I am the Alpha and the Omega, the Beginning and the End. I will give water to anyone who is thirsty. The water will come from the spring of the water of life. It doesn't cost anything! [7]Those who have victory will receive all this from me. I will be their God, and they will be my children. [8]But others will be thrown into the lake of fire that burns with sulfur. Those who are afraid and those who do not believe will be there. Murderers and those who make themselves impure will join them. Those who commit sexual sins and those who practice witchcraft will go there. Those who worship statues of gods and all who tell lies will be there too. The lake of fire is the second death."

The New Jerusalem Is the Bride of the Lamb

[9]One of the seven angels who had the seven bowls came and spoke to me. The bowls were filled with the seven last plagues. The angel said, "Come. I will show you the bride, the wife of the Lamb." [10]Then he carried me away in a vision. The Spirit took me to a huge, high mountain. He showed me Jerusalem, the Holy City. It was coming down out of heaven from God. [11]It shone with the glory of God. It gleamed like a very valuable jewel. It was like a jasper, as clear as crystal. [12]The city had a huge, high wall with 12 gates. Twelve angels were at the gates, one at each of them. On the gates were written the names of the 12 tribes of Israel. [13]There were three gates on the east and three on the north. There were three gates on the south and three on the west. [14]The wall of the city had 12 foundations.

Written on them were the names of the 12 apostles of the Lamb.

[15]The angel who talked with me had a gold measuring rod. He used it to measure the city, its gates and its walls. [16]The city was laid out like a square. It was as long as it was wide. The angel measured the city with the rod. It was 1,400 miles long. It was as wide and high as it was long. [17]The angel measured the wall as human beings measure things. It was 200 feet thick. [18]The wall was made out of jasper. The city was made out of pure gold, as pure as glass. [19]The foundations of the city walls were decorated with every kind of jewel. The first foundation was made out of jasper. The second was made out of sapphire. The third was made out of agate. The fourth was made out of emerald. [20]The fifth was made out of onyx. The sixth was made out of ruby. The seventh was made out of chrysolite. The eighth was made out of beryl. The ninth was made out of topaz. The tenth was made out of turquoise. The eleventh was made out of jacinth. The twelfth was made out of amethyst. [21]The 12 gates were made from 12 pearls. Each gate was made out of a single pearl. The main street of the city was made out of gold. It was gold as pure as glass that people can see through clearly.

[22]I didn't see a temple in the city. That's because the Lamb and the Lord God who rules over all are its temple. [23]The city does not need the sun or moon to shine on it. God's glory is its light, and the Lamb is its lamp. [24]The nations will walk by the light of the city. The kings of the world will bring their glory into it. [25]Its gates will never be shut, because there will be no night there. [26]The glory and honor of the nations will be brought into it. [27]Only what is pure will enter the city. No one who causes people to believe lies will enter it. No one who does shameful things will enter it either. Only those whose names are written in the Lamb's book of life will enter the city.

The Earth Is Made Like New Again

22 Then the angel showed me the river of the water of life. It was as clear as crystal. It flowed from the throne of God and of the Lamb. [2]It flowed down the middle of the city's main street. On each side of the river stood the tree of life, bearing 12 crops of fruit. Its fruit was ripe every month. The leaves of the tree bring healing to the nations. ³There will no longer be any curse. The throne of God and of the Lamb will be in the city. God's servants will serve him. ⁴They will see his face. His name will be on their foreheads. ⁵There will be no more night. They will not need the light of a lamp or the light of the sun. The Lord God will give them light. They will rule for ever and ever.

John and the Angel

⁶The angel said to me, "You can trust these words. They are true. The Lord is the God who gives messages to the prophets. He sent his angel to show his servants the things that must soon take place."

Rev. 22:8–9 Angels are cool—but they aren't to be worshiped. And this is the last angel-sighting in the Bible.

⁷"Look! I am coming soon! Words of prophecy are written in this book. Blessed is the person who obeys them."

⁸I, John, am the one who heard and saw these things. After that, I fell down to worship at the feet of the angel. He is the one who had been showing me these things. ⁹But he said to me, "Don't do that! I serve God, just as you do. I am God's servant, just like the other prophets. And I serve God along with all who obey the words of this book. Worship God!"

¹⁰Then he told me, "Do not seal up the words of the prophecy in this book. These things are about to happen. ¹¹Let the person who does wrong keep on doing wrong. Let the evil person continue to be evil. Let the person who does right keep on doing what is right. And let the holy person continue to be holy."

The Revelation Ends With Warnings and Blessings

¹²"Look! I am coming soon! I bring my rewards with me. I will reward each person for what they have done. ¹³I am the Alpha and the Omega. I am the First and the Last. I am the Beginning and the End.

¹⁴"Blessed are those who wash their robes. They will have the right to come to the tree of life. They will be allowed to go through the gates into the city. ¹⁵Outside the city are those who are impure. These people include those who practice witchcraft. Outside are also those who commit sexual sins and murder. Outside are those who worship statues of gods. And outside is everyone who loves and does what is false.

¹⁶"I, Jesus, have sent my angel to give you this witness for the churches. I am the Root and the Son of David. I am the bright Morning Star."

¹⁷The Holy Spirit and the bride say, "Come!" And the person who hears should say, "Come!" Anyone who is thirsty should come. Anyone who wants to take the free gift of the water of life should do so.

¹⁸I am warning everyone who hears the words of the prophecy of this book. Suppose someone adds anything to them. Then God will add to that person the plagues told about in this book. ¹⁹Suppose someone takes away any words from this book of prophecy. Then God will take away from that person the blessings told about in this book. God will take away their share in the tree of life. God will also take away their place in the Holy City.

²⁰Jesus is a witness about these things. He says, "Yes. I am coming soon." Amen. Come, Lord Jesus!

²¹May the grace of the Lord Jesus be with God's people. Amen.

Parables of Jesus

- ☐ Matthew 13:24-30, 36-43—The Wheat and the Weeds
- ☐ Matthew 13:33-36—The Yeast
- ☐ Matthew 13:44—The Hidden Treasure
- ☐ Matthew 13:45-46—The Pearl
- ☐ Matthew 13:47-50—The Net Full of Fish
- ☐ Matthew 18:12-14—The Lost Sheep
- ☐ Matthew 18:23-35—The Unmerciful Servant
- ☐ Matthew 20:1-16—The Workers in the Vineyard
- ☐ Matthew 22:1-14—The Wedding Feast
- ☐ Matthew 25:14-30—The Bags of Gold
- ☐ Mark 4:1-20—The Farmer Planting Seeds
- ☐ Mark 4:26-29—The Seeds Grow into Grain
- ☐ Mark 4:30-32—The Mustard Seed
- ☐ Mark 12:1-11—The Vineyard Renters
- ☐ Mark 13:28-32—The Budding Fig Tree
- ☐ Mark 13:33-37—The Faithful Servant
- ☐ Luke 6:43-35—The Tree and Its Fruit
- ☐ Luke 6:46-49—The Wise and Foolish Builders
- ☐ Luke 10:30-37—The Good Samaritan
- ☐ Luke 12:16-21—The Rich Fool
- ☐ Luke 15:8-10—The Lost Coin
- ☐ Luke 15:11-32—The Son Who Came Home
- ☐ Luke 16:1-8—The Dishonest Manager
- ☐ Luke 16:19-31—The Rich Man and Lazarus the Beggar

Miracles of Jesus

- ☐ John 2:1-11—Changing water to wine
- ☐ John 4:46-54—Healing the official's son
- ☐ Mark 1:21-28—Driving out an evil spirit in Capernaum
- ☐ Matthew 8:14-15—Healing Peter's mother-in-law
- ☐ Luke 4:40—Healing people at sunset
- ☐ Luke 5:3-10—Catching boatloads of fish
- ☐ Mark 1:40-45—Healing a man who had a skin disease
- ☐ Matthew 8:5-13—Healing a Roman commander's servant
- ☐ Luke 5:18-26—Healing a man who could not walk
- ☐ Mark 3:1-6—Healing a man with a twisted hand
- ☐ Luke 7:11-17—Raising a widow's son from the dead
- ☐ Matthew 8:23-27—Calming the storm
- ☐ Mark 5:1-13—Healing a man controlled by an evil spirit
- ☐ Luke 8:43-48—Healing a woman who was sick for twelve years
- ☐ Matthew 9:18-19, 23-25—Raising a dying daughter
- ☐ Matthew 9:27-31—Healing two blind men
- ☐ Matthew 9:32-33—Healing a demon-possessed man
- ☐ John 5:1-17—Healing a man in Bethesda
- ☐ John 6:5-14—Feeding 5,000 people
- ☐ John 6:16-21—Walking on the water
- ☐ Matthew 14:34-36—Healing sick people in Gennesaret
- ☐ Mark 7:24-30—Healing a demon-possessed daughter
- ☐ Mark 7:31-37—Healing a man who could not hear or speak
- ☐ Matthew 15:29-39—Feeding 4,000 people
- ☐ Mark 8:22-26—Healing a blind man in Bethsaida
- ☐ John 9:1-41—Healing a man born blind
- ☐ Luke 9:37-43—Healing a demon-possessed boy
- ☐ Matthew 17:24-27—Catching a fish with a coin in its mouth
- ☐ Luke 11:14—Healing a demon-possessed man who could not speak
- ☐ Luke 13:10-13—Healing a woman who suffered for eighteen years
- ☐ Luke 14:1-6—Healing a man on the Sabbath day
- ☐ Luke 17:11-19—Healing ten men from a skin disease
- ☐ John 11:1-44—Raising Lazarus from the dead
- ☐ Mark 10:46--52—Healing blind Bartimaeus
- ☐ Matthew 21:18-22—Drying up the fruitless fig tree
- ☐ Luke 22:45-54—Restoring an injured man's ear
- ☐ John 20—Rising from the dead
- ☐ Acts 1:1-11—Ascending into heaven

REMEMBER THIS

Here's the list of fifty-two verses to learn by heart. These passages are scattered through the Scriptures, and together they tell the story of God's great love for you. As you own God's Word in your heart and mind, you'll discover it's a gift for a lifetime.

1 "In the beginning, God created the heavens and the earth."— Genesis 1:1

2 "You are the God who sees me."— Genesis 16:13

3 "Honor your father and mother. Then you will live a long time in the land the Lord your God is giving you."— Exodus 20:12

4 "Do not try to get even. Do not hold anything against any of your people. Instead, love your neighbor as you love yourself."— Leviticus 19:18

5 "Love the Lord your God with all your heart and with all your soul. Love him with all your strength."— Deuteronomy 6:5

6 "Be strong and brave. Don't be afraid of them. Don't be terrified because of them. The Lord your God will go with you. He will never leave you. He'll never desert you."— Deuteronomy 31:6

7 "In peace I will lie down and sleep. Lord, you alone keep me safe."— Psalm 4:8

8 "The heavens tell about the glory of God. The skies show that his hands created them."— Psalm 19:1

9 "Lord, may these words of my mouth please you. And may these thoughts of my heart please you also. You are my Rock and my Redeemer."— Psalm 19:14

10 "The Lord is my light, and he saves me. Why should I fear anyone? The Lord is my place of safety. Why should I be afraid?"— Psalm 27:1

11 "How can a young person keep their life pure? By living according to your word." — Psalm 119:9

12 "I have hidden your word in my heart so that I won't sin against you." — Psalm 119:11

13 "Your word is like a lamp that shows me the way. It is like a light that guides me."— Psalm 119:105

14 "How you made me is amazing and wonderful. I praise you for that. What you have done is wonderful. I know that very well."— Psalm 139:14

15 "Trust in the Lord with all your heart. Do not depend on your own understanding. In all your ways obey him. Then he will make your paths smooth and straight."— Proverbs 3:5-6

16 "Everything has now been heard. And here's the final thing I want to say. Have respect for God and obey his commandments. This is what he expects of all human beings."— Ecclesiastes 12:13

17 "A child will be born to us. A son will be given to us. He will rule over us. And he will be called Wonderful Adviser and Mighty God."— Isaiah 9:6

18 "Don't you know who made everything? Haven't you heard about him? The Lord is the God who lives forever. He created everything on earth."— Isaiah 40:28

19 "Those who trust in the Lord will receive new strength. They will fly as high as eagles. They will run and not get tired. They will walk and not grow weak." — Isaiah 40:31

20 "So do not be afraid. I am with you. Do not be terrified. I am your God. I will make you strong and help you. I will hold you safe in my hands. I always do what is right."— Isaiah 41:10

21 "I know the plans I have for you," announces the Lord. "I want you to enjoy success. I do not plan to harm you. I will give you hope for the years to come."— Jeremiah 29:11

22 "The Lord has shown you what is good. He has told you what he requires of you. You must act with justice. You must love to show mercy. And you must be humble as you live in the sight of your God."— Micah 6:8

23 "In the same way, let your light shine so others can see it. Then they will see the good things you do. And they will bring glory to your Father who is in heaven."— Matthew 5:16

24 "Our Father in heaven, may your name be honored. May your kingdom come. May what you want to happen be done on earth as it is done in heaven. Give us today our daily bread. And forgive us our sins, just as we also have forgiven those who sin against us. Keep us from sinning when we are tempted. Save us from the evil one."— Matthew 6:9-13

25 "Love your enemies. Do good to those who hate you. Bless those who call down curses on you. And pray for those who treat you badly."— Luke 6:27-28

26 "Do to others as you want them to do to you."— Luke 6:31

27 "No one can serve two masters at the same time. Either you will hate one of them and love the other. Or you will be faithful to one and dislike the other. You can't serve God and money at the same time."— Luke 16:13

28 "God so loved the world that he gave his one and only Son. Anyone who believes in him will not die but will have eternal life. God did not send his Son into the world to judge the world. He sent his Son to save the world through him." — John 3:16-17

29 "Jesus answered, 'I am the way and the truth and the life. No one comes to the Father except through me.'"— John 14:6

30 "Everyone has sinned. No one measures up to God's glory." — Romans 3:23

31 "When you sin, the pay you get is death. But God gives you the gift of eternal life. That's because of what Christ Jesus our Lord has done."— Romans 6:23

32 "We know that in all things God works for the good of those who love him. He appointed them to be saved in keeping with his purpose."— Romans 8:28

33 "Nothing at all can ever separate us from God's love. That's because of what Christ Jesus our Lord has done." — Romans 8:39

34 "May the God who gives hope fill you with great joy. May you have perfect peace as you trust in him. May the power of the Holy Spirit fill you with hope." — Romans 15:13

35 "God is faithful. He will not let you be tempted any more than you can take. But when you are tempted, God will give you a way out. Then you will be able to deal with it."— 1 Corinthians 10:13

36 "When anyone lives in Christ, the new creation has come. The old is gone! The new is here!"— 2 Corinthians 5:17

37 "He said to me, 'My grace is all you need. My power is strongest when you are weak.' So I am very happy to brag about how weak I am. Then Christ's power can rest on me."— 2 Corinthians 12:9

38 "Finally, brothers and sisters, be joyful! . . . Live in peace. And the God who gives love and peace will be with you."—2 Corinthians 13:11

39 "The fruit the Holy Spirit produces is love, joy and peace. It is being patient, kind and good. It is being faithful and gentle and having control of oneself."— Galatians 5:22-23

40 "God's grace has saved you because of your faith in Christ. Your salvation doesn't come from anything you do. It is God's gift. It is not based on anything you have done. No one can brag about earning it."— Ephesians 2:8-9

41 "Don't let any evil talk come out of your mouths. Say only what will help to build others up and meet their needs. Then what you say will help those who listen."— Ephesians 4:29

42 "Our fight is not against human beings. It is against the rulers, the authorities and the powers of this dark world. It is against the spiritual forces of evil in the heavenly world."— Ephesians 6:12

43 "Don't worry about anything. No matter what happens, tell God about everything. Ask and pray, and give thanks to him. Then God's peace will watch over your hearts and your minds. He will do this because you belong to Christ Jesus." — Philippians 4:6-7

44 "Finally, my brothers and sisters, always think about what is true. Think about what is noble, right and pure. Think about what is lovely and worthy of respect. If anything is excellent or worthy of praise, think about those kinds of things."— Philippians 4:8

45 "Think about things that are in heaven. Don't think about things that are only on earth."— Colossians 3:2

46 "Don't let anyone look down on you because you are young. Set an example for the believers in what you say and in how you live. Also set an example in how you love and in what you believe. Show the believers how to be pure." — 1 Timothy 4:12

47 "God has breathed life into all Scripture. It is useful for teaching us what is true. It is useful for correcting our mistakes. It is useful for making our lives whole again. It is useful for training us to do what is right."— 2 Timothy 3:16

48 "Jesus Christ is the same yesterday and today and forever."— Hebrews 13:8

49 "Don't just listen to the word. You fool yourselves if you do that. You must do what it says."— James 1:22

50 "Confess your sins to one another. Pray for one another so that you might be healed. The prayer of a godly person is powerful. Things happen because of it."— James 5:16

51 "The Lord is not slow to keep his promise. He is not slow in the way some people understand it. Instead, he is patient with you. He doesn't want anyone to be destroyed. Instead, he wants all people to turn away from their sins." — 2 Peter 3:9

52 "God is faithful and fair. If we confess our sins, he will forgive our sins. He will forgive every wrong thing we have done. He will make us pure." — 1 John 1:9

Journey through the Bible

CREATION
Gen. 1:1-2:25

THE FALL
Gen. 3:1-24

THE FLOOD
Gen. 6:1-9:17

GOD CALLS ABRAM
Gen. 12

EXODUS
Ex. 3:1-15:21

TEN COMMANDMENTS
Ex. 19-20

PROMISED LAND
Josh. 1

DAVID & GOLIATH
1 Sam. 17

TEMPLE BUILT
1 Kings 6-8

TEMPLE DESTROYED
2 Kings 25:10-21

PROMISE OF JESUS' BIRTH
Isaiah 7:14

JESUS IS BORN
Luke 2

JESUS IS BAPTIZED
Matthew 3

JESUS HEALS & TEACHES
The Gospels

JESUS IS CRUCIFIED
Mark 15

JESUS RISES
John 20

GOSPEL SPREADS
Acts 9-28

PROMISE OF VICTORY
Revelation

Old Testament Events

Noah's ark
Mt. Ararat

Caspian Sea

ASSYRIA

TIGRIS RIVER

Nineveh •
Jonah warns
Ninevites

MESOPOTAMIA

EUPHRATES RIVER

ARABIAN
DESERT

The fiery furnace

Tower
of Babel

Babylon
Daniel in
the lions' den

BABYLONIA

Shushan
•
Esther saves
her people

Persian
Gulf

Location and order of Old Testament events.

1. Noah's ark, Gen. 8
2. Tower of Babel, Gen. 11
3. Abram's home, Gen. 12
4. Abraham offers Isaac, Gen. 22
5. Esau sells birthright, Gen. 25
6. Jacob wrestles with God, Gen. 32
7. Joseph sold into slavery, Gen. 37
8. Joseph becomes ruler, Gen. 41
9. Moses in Pharaoh's court, Exod. 2
10. Israelites escape, Exod. 13
11. Ten Commandments, Exod. 20
12. 12 spies sent out, Num. 13

13. Wilderness wanderings, Num. 14
14. Battle of Jericho, Josh. 6
15. Mighty Samson dies, Judg. 16:23-30
16. Ruth marries Boaz, Ruth 4
17. David defeats Goliath, 1 Sam. 17
18. Solomon builds Temple, 1 Kings 7
19. Elijah defeats bad prophets, 1 Kings 18
20. Jonah swallowed by fish, Jon. 1
21. Jonah warns Ninevites, Jon. 3
22. The fiery furnace, Dan. 3
23. Daniel in the lions' den, Dan. 6
24. Esther saves her people, Esther 8

MAP NOT TO SCALE.